@Frommer's
USA

POSTCARDS FROM

D0395967

No other monument so embodies the nation's ideals of political freedom and economic potential as the Statue of Liberty. See chapter 2. © Jon Ortner/Tony Stone Images.

Fall in New England is one of the nation's great spectacles, with the rolling hillsides blanketed in fiery shades of red and stunning oranges that reach their peak around mid-October. Along winding country roads, you'll find heaps of pumpkins for sale beneath blazing red sugar maples, and crisp apples available by the bushel. See chapter 3.
© Kindra Clineff Photography.

As the place where America's elected representatives formulate, debate, and pass into law the nation's policies and principles, the Capitol is perhaps the most important edifice in the United States. In addition to its superb design, the Capitol also contains more than 800 artworks, from grand canvases encased by gilded 19th-century frames to frescoes, ornamental bronze stair railings, and stained-glass windows. See chapter 4.

© Kelly/Mooney Photography.

There's nothing like Mardi Gras in New Orleans. It's a 2-week-long party throughout the city, and everybody's invited. See chapter 6. © Jackson Hill/Southern Lights Photography.

The Florida Keys offer some of the best snorkeling and scuba diving in Florida. See chapter 7. © Stephen Frink Photography.

At Chicago's beloved Wrigley Field, fans soak up the sun as the Cubs hit 'em out of the park. See chapter 8. © Robert Holmes Photography.

A magnificent view of the Grand Canyon from Cape Solitude on the South Rim. The canyon is the country's most popular national park. See chapter 11. © Chuck Lawsen/Adstock Photos.

The Las Vegas strip at night, lit up in all its neon glory, is one of the most spectacular sights in the world. See chapter 13. © *Richard Cummins Photography.*

Few sights are more breathtaking than a view of San Francisco from the Golden Gate Bridge, which you can cross on foot. See chapter 15. © Jose Fuste Ragal The Stock Market.

California's beaches range from the fabled surfing-and-bikini scenes of Los Angeles to the rocky, rugged coastlines of the north, where the scenery and seclusion compensate for icy waters. See chapters 14 and 15. © Dave G. Houser Photography.

Snow and glaciers notwithstanding, Washington state's Mount Rainier has a heart of fire. Steam vents at the mountain's summit are evidence that, though this volcanic peak has been dormant for more than 150 years, it will surely erupt again someday. In the meantime, visitors enjoy spring wildflowers in its alpine meadows and opportunities for hiking, horseback riding, cross-country skiing, and more. See chapter 16. © Greg Vaughn/Viewfinders.

A cow moose with calf in tow crosses Alaska's rolling Glenn Highway, with the Chugach Mountains rising majestically beyond. See chapter 18. © Ken Graham/Accent Alaska.

USA

8th Edition

Here's what the critics say about Frommer's:

"Amazingly easy to use. Very portable, very complete."
—*Booklist*

"Detailed, accurate, and easy-to-read information for all price ranges."
—*Glamour Magazine*

"Hotel information is close to encyclopedic."
—*Des Moines Sunday Register*

"Frommer's Guides have a way of giving you a real feel for a place."
—*Knight Ridder Newspapers*

Wiley Publishing, Inc.

Published by:

Wiley Publishing, Inc.

909 Third Ave.
New York, NY 10022

ISBN 0-7645-6733-0
ISSN 1094-0227

Editor: Naomi Kraus
With: Elizabeth Albertson, Leslie Shen, and Kathleen Warnock
Production Editor: Tammy Ahrens
Cartographer: Roberta Stockwell
Photo Editor: Richard Fox
Production by Wiley Indianapolis Composition Services
Front cover photo: A cowboy on a rearing horse in Arizona
Back cover photo: A boy among the giant sequoias in Humboldt Redwoods State Park, northern California

For information on our other products and services or to obtain technical support, please contact our Customer Care Department within the U.S. at 800-762-2974, outside the U.S. at 317-572-3993 or fax 317-572-4002.

Wiley also publishes its books in a variety of electronic formats. Some content that appears in print may not be available in electronic formats.

Manufactured in the United States of America

5 4 3 2 1

Contents

6 The South   246

7 Florida   356

8 Chicago   439

9 The Midwest   465

List of Maps

Acknowledgments

This book has been created from dozens of Frommer's guides covering the United States, and it simply couldn't exist without the tireless efforts of our many talented writers. They deserve special recognition for spending countless hours hitting the pavement, inspecting hotels, sampling restaurants, chasing down information, and visiting attractions so they can offer you the best logistical tips.

Thanks for a job well done year in and year out to: Lesley Abravanel, David Baird, Elizabeth Canning Blackwell, Wayne Curtis, Elise Ford, Jeanette Foster, Jocelyn Fujii, Jay Golan, Bill Goodwin, Mary Herczog, Lesley King, Don and Barbara Laine, Cheryl Farr Leas, Erika Lenkert, Herbert Bailey Livesey, Marie Morris, Matthew Poole, Darwin Porter and Danforth Prince, Laura Reckford, Linda Romine, Karl Samson and Jane Aukshunas, Mary K. Tilgman, Jim and Cynthia Tunstall, Charles Wohlforth, and Stephanie Avnet Yates.

Special thanks also go to another group of contributors, who covered destinations especially for this guide: **Annie Stoltie** (upstate New York), **Jay Golan** (Philadelphia, Pittsburgh, and the Jersey Shore), **Karen Hill** (Atlanta), **Darwin Porter** and **Danforth Prince** (Carolinas and Georgia), **Linda Romine** (Cleveland, Cincinnati, Kentucky, and Tennessee), **Amy Eckert** (Michigan, Wisconsin, Minneapolis, and St. Paul), **Beth Reiber** (St. Louis, Kansas City, and Branson), **David Baird** (Texas), **Don** and **Barbara Laine** (Colorado, Utah, Montana, and Wyoming), **Karl Samson** (Oregon), **Harry Basch** and **Shirley Slater** (South Dakota), and **Jan House** (Idaho).

This book also owes much to these on-staff contributors: **Stephen Bassman, John Decamillis, Brice Gosnell, Naomi Kraus, Elizabeth Puhl,** and **Nicholas Trotter.**

An Invitation to the Reader

In researching this book, we discovered many wonderful places—hotels, restaurants, shops, and more. We're sure you'll find others. Please tell us about them, so we can share the information with your fellow travelers in upcoming editions. If you were disappointed with a recommendation, we'd love to know that, too. Please write to:

Frommer's USA, 8th Edition
Wiley Publishing, Inc. • 909 Third Ave. • New York, NY 10022

An Additional Note

Please be advised that travel information is subject to change at any time—and this is especially true of prices. We therefore suggest that you write or call ahead for confirmation when making your travel plans. The authors, editors, and publisher cannot be held responsible for the experiences of readers while traveling. Your safety is important to us, however, so we encourage you to stay alert and be aware of your surroundings. Keep a close eye on cameras, purses, and wallets, all favorite targets of thieves and pickpockets.

The following abbreviations are used for credit cards:

AE American Express	DISC Discover	V Visa
DC Diners Club	MC MasterCard	

FROMMERS.COM

Now that you have the guidebook to a great trip, visit our website at **www.frommers.com** for travel information on nearly 2,500 destinations. With features updated regularly, we give you instant access to the most current trip-planning information available. At Frommers.com, you'll also find the best prices on airfares, accommodations, and car rentals—and you can even book travel online through our travel booking partners. At Frommers.com, you'll also find the following:

- Online updates to our most popular guidebooks
- Vacation sweepstakes and contest giveaways
- Newsletter highlighting the hottest travel trends
- Online travel message boards with featured travel discussions

Planning Your Trip to the USA

If the United States has one defining quality, it's variety. This vast area of some 3.6 million square miles—it's 2,500 miles from New York to Los Angeles, and that again to Hawaii—has something for everyone.

Although TV, suburban sprawl, strip malls, and chain restaurants have a homogenizing effect, America hasn't yet become a monolithic place. Each region still speaks with its own accent, enjoys its own favorite foods, and has its own political and social attitudes. Indeed, foreign travelers often go away with the impression that we aren't one nation but an amalgam of 50 little countries. Whatever you want to see, do, or eat, you're likely to find it within the vast and diverse confines of the United States of America.

WHAT'S HERE & WHAT'S NOT

It's not easy to boil down the essence of such a huge, varied, complicated country. No doubt, some of you will look at the table of contents and raise an eyebrow at what's missing. That's sure to be the case with any guide professing to cover the entire United States.

This book doesn't pretend to be comprehensive. It's simply not possible to cover every great destination in the country in one usable volume. So we concentrated on a select group of destinations that will appeal to a wide cross-section of road-trippers, foreign visitors, and business travelers. This way, rather than glossing over lots of destinations with coverage that's broad but an inch deep, we've been able to offer you in-depth, practical coverage you can really use on the road.

Take, for example, Martha's Vineyard and Nantucket: We'd love to cover both islands, but we chose to focus on Martha's Vineyard instead. Few travelers have time to visit both, so we used the space to include more detailed and useful information on the Vineyard, which is larger and easier to reach. We've applied the same sort of logic to our destination choices throughout.

In the end, we've come up with a list of destinations that's representative of the very best America has to offer—cities, national parks, beaches, resort areas, and more.

We hope you'll discover your own America as you hit the road and start exploring. If you'd like more coverage of the destinations covered here, or if any of them prompt you to want to explore further—if you want to see Nantucket, say, after the Vineyard has charmed you—chances are good that we have a more dedicated, in-depth guidebook for you; see the complete list of destinations covered by Frommer's guides at the end of this book. Happy trails!

1 Getting Started: What You Need to Know Before You Go

There's no central visitor information office for the entire country. Your best bet is to contact the state or local visitor information offices mentioned throughout this book and gathered in appendix B. If you live in another country, check with the **U.S. Information Agency (USIA)** office at an American embassy or consulate in your home country.

ENTRY REQUIREMENTS

Check at any U.S. embassy or consulate for current information and requirements. You can also obtain a visa application and other information online at the **U.S. State Department**'s website, at **www.travel.state.gov**.

VISAS The U.S. State Department has a **Visa Waiver Program** allowing citizens of certain countries to enter the United States without a visa for stays of up to 90 days. At press time these included Andorra, Australia, Austria, Belgium, Brunei, Denmark, Finland, France, Germany, Iceland, Ireland, Italy, Japan, Liechtenstein, Luxembourg, Monaco, the Netherlands, New Zealand, Norway, Portugal, San Marino, Singapore, Slovenia, Spain, Sweden, Switzerland, the United Kingdom, and Uruguay. Citizens of these countries need only a valid passport and a round-trip air or cruise ticket in your possession upon arrival. If you first enter the United States, you may also visit Mexico, Canada, Bermuda, and/or the Caribbean islands and return to the United States without a visa. Further information is available from any U.S. embassy or consulate. Canadian citizens may enter the United States without visas; you need only proof of residence.

Citizens of all other countries must have (1) a valid passport that expires at least 6 months later than the scheduled end of your visit to the United States, and (2) a tourist visa, which

may be obtained without charge from any U.S. consulate.

To obtain a visa, the traveler must submit a completed application form (either in person or by mail) with a 1½-inch-square photo, and must demonstrate binding ties to a residence abroad. Usually you can obtain a visa at once or within 24 hours, but it may take longer during the summer rush June through August. If you cannot go in person, contact the nearest U.S. embassy or consulate for directions on applying by mail. Your travel agent or airline office may also be able to provide you with visa applications and instructions. The U.S. consulate or embassy that issues your visa will determine whether you will be issued a multiple- or single-entry visa and any restrictions regarding the length of your stay.

British subjects can obtain up-to-date passport and visa information by calling the **U.S. Embassy Visa Information Line** (© 0891/200-290) or the **London Passport Office** (© 0990/210-410 for recorded information), or you can also find the visa information on the U.S. Embassy Great Britain website at **www.passport.gov.uk**.

Irish citizens can obtain up-to-date passport and visa information through the **Embassy of USA Dublin,** 42 Elgin Rd., Dublin 4, Ireland (© 353/1-668-8777), or by checking the visa website at **www.irigov.ie/iveagh/services/passports/passportforms.htm**.

Australian citizens can obtain up-to-date passport and visa information by calling the **U.S. Embassy Canberra,** Moonah Place, Yarralumla, ACT 2600 (© 02/6214-5600), or by checking the website's visa page (**www.usisaustralia.gov/consular/niv.html**).

Citizens of **New Zealand** can obtain up-to-date passport and visa information by calling the **U.S. Embassy New Zealand,** 29 Fitzherbert Terrace, Thorndon, Wellington, New Zealand, at ℂ **644/472-2068,** or get the information directly from the website (**http://usembassy.org. nz**).

CUSTOMS
WHAT YOU CAN BRING IN

Every visitor more than 21 years of age may bring in, free of duty, the following: (1) 1 liter of wine or hard liquor; (2) 200 cigarettes, 100 cigars (but not from Cuba), or 3 pounds of smoking tobacco; and (3) $100 worth of gifts. These exemptions are offered to travelers who spend at least 72 hours in the United States and who have not claimed them within the preceding 6 months. It is altogether forbidden to bring into the country foodstuffs (particularly fruit, cooked meats, and canned goods) and plants (vegetables, seeds, tropical plants, and the like). Foreign tourists may bring in or take out up to $10,000 in U.S. or foreign currency with no formalities; larger sums must be declared to U.S. Customs on entering or leaving, which includes filing form CM 4790. For more specific information regarding U.S. Customs, call your nearest U.S. embassy or consulate; or contact the **U.S. Customs** office at ℂ **202/927-1770** or **www.customs.ustreas.gov**.

WHAT YOU CAN TAKE HOME

For Customs information, **U.K. citizens returning from a non-EC country** should contact HM Customs & Excise, Passenger Enquiry Point, 2nd Floor Wayfarer House, Great South West Road, Feltham, Middlesex, TW14 8NP (ℂ **0181/910-3744,** or 44/181-910-3744 from outside the U.K.), or consult the website at **www. open.gov.uk**.

For a clear summary of **Canadian** Customs rules, write for the booklet *I Declare,* issued by **Revenue Canada,** 2265 St. Laurent Blvd., Ottawa, ON K1G 4K3 (ℂ **506/636-5064**).

A helpful brochure, available from **Australian** consulates or Customs offices, is *Know Before You Go.* For more information, contact **Australian Customs Services,** GPO Box 8, Sydney NSW 2001 (ℂ **02/6275-6666** in Australia, or 202/797-3189 in the U.S.), or check out **www.customs. gov.au**.

Most Customs questions are answered in a free pamphlet available at **New Zealand** consulates and Customs offices: *New Zealand Customs Guide for Travellers, Notice no. 4.* For more information, contact New Zealand Customs, 50 Anzac Ave., P.O. Box 29, Auckland (ℂ **09/359-6655**).

WHEN TO GO

Climate differences are dramatic across the United States. When it's shivering cold in New England, the upper central states, and Alaska, it's sunny and warm in Florida, California, and Hawaii. When it's raining cats and dogs along the Northwest coast, it's dry as a bone in the Southwest desert. It can be a pleasant 75°F (24°C) on the beaches of Southern California in summer yet 120°F (49°C) just a few miles inland.

And there isn't a nationwide high or low season. In summer, room rates are highest on the Northeast and Mid-Atlantic beaches but lowest on the sands of hot-and-humid Florida. Winter snows virtually close the great Rocky Mountain national parks, but they bring crowds to the nearby ski slopes.

The Northeast and Mid-Atlantic states have their summer beach season from June to Labor Day and their great fall foliage in September and October. Summer can be brutally hot and humid in the Southeast, but spring and fall last longer there, and winter is mild—with snow the exception rather than the rule. Southern

Major Interstate Highways

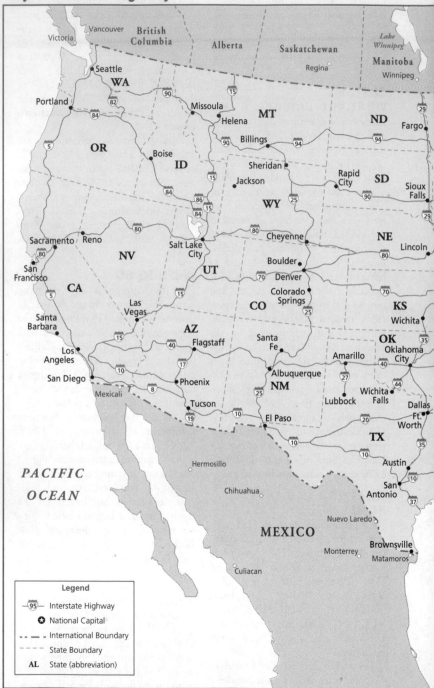

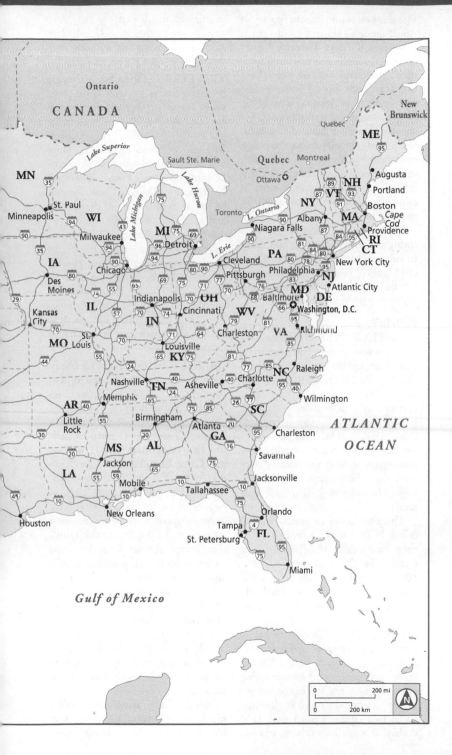

Florida's best season is from January to April, though cold snaps can turn it nippy for a few days. The central states see brutal winters and scorching summers. Southwest weather varies from east Texas's hot, humid summers and mild winters to Arizona's dry, 110°F (43°C) summers and pleasant, dry winters. The mountains of Colorado, Utah, and the Northwest have dry, moderately hot summers and cold, snowy winters. The California coast is fine all year but early spring, when it rains; the Northwest coast is wet all the time but July.

The long and short of it: Late spring and early fall are the best times to visit most of the country. See "Special Events & Festivals" in all the chapters that follow for more dates around which to plan your trip.

MONEY

CURRENCY The U.S. monetary system is very simple: The most common **bills** are the $1 (colloquially, a "buck"), $5, $10, and $20 denominations. There are also $2 bills (seldom encountered), $50 bills, and $100 bills (the last two are usually not welcome as payment for small purchases). All the paper money was recently redesigned, making the famous faces adorning them disproportionately large. The old-style bills are still legal tender.

There are seven denominations of coins: 1¢ (1 cent, or a penny); 5¢ (5 cents, or a nickel); 10¢ (10 cents, or a dime); 25¢ (25 cents, or a quarter); 50¢ (50 cents, or a half dollar); the new gold "Sacagawea" coin worth $1; and, prized by collectors, the rare, older silver dollar.

Note: The "foreign-exchange bureaus" so common in Europe are rare even at airports in the United States, and nonexistent outside major cities. It's best not to change foreign money (or traveler's checks denominated in a currency other than U.S. dollars) at a small-town bank, or even at a branch in a big city; in fact, leave any currency other than U.S. dollars at home—it may prove a greater nuisance to you than it's worth.

TRAVELER'S CHECKS Though traveler's checks are widely accepted, *make sure that they're denominated in U.S. dollars,* as foreign-currency checks are often difficult to exchange. The three traveler's checks most widely recognized—and least likely to be denied—are **Visa, American Express,** and **Thomas Cook.** Be sure to record the numbers of the checks, and keep that information in a separate place in case they get lost or stolen. Most businesses are pretty good about taking traveler's checks, but you're better off cashing them in at a bank (in small amounts, of course) and paying in cash. *Remember:* You'll need identification, such as a driver's license or passport, to change a traveler's check.

CREDIT CARDS & ATMS Credit cards are the most widely used form of payment in the United States: **Visa** (BarclayCard in Britain), **MasterCard** (EuroCard in Europe, Access in Britain, Chargex in Canada), **American Express, Diners Club, Discover,** and **Carte Blanche.** There are, however, a handful of stores and restaurants that do not take credit cards, so be sure to ask in advance. Most businesses display a sticker near their entrance to let you know which cards they accept. (*Note:* Businesses may require a minimum purchase, usually around $10, to use a credit card.)

It is strongly recommended that you bring at least one major credit card. You must have a credit or charge card to rent a car. Hotels and airlines usually require a credit-card imprint as a deposit against expenses, and in an emergency a credit card can be priceless.

You'll find **automated teller machines (ATMs)** on just about every block—at least in almost every town—across the country. **Cirrus** (*©* 800/424-7787; www.mastercard. com) and **PLUS** (*©* 800/843-7587; www.visa.com) are the two most popular networks in the U.S.; call or check online for ATM locations at your destination. Some ATMs will allow you to draw U.S. currency against your bank and credit cards. Check with your bank before leaving home, and remember that you will need your personal identification number (PIN) to do so.

Most ATMs accept Visa, Master-Card, and American Express, as well as ATM cards from other U.S. banks. Expect to be charged up to $3 per transaction, however, if you're not using your own bank's ATM. One way around these fees is to ask for cash back at grocery stores that accept ATM cards and don't charge usage fees. Of course, you'll have to purchase something first.

ATM cards with major credit card backing, known as "debit cards," are now a commonly acceptable form of payment in most stores and restaurants. Debit cards draw money directly from your checking account. Some stores enable you to receive "cash back" on your debit-card purchases as well.

HEALTH, INSURANCE & SAFETY
HEALTH
The United States doesn't present any unusual health hazards to domestic or foreign visitors. Tap water is safe to drink throughout the country. You aren't likely to catch any dangerous diseases, but AIDS (acquired immunodeficiency syndrome) is very present

here, so exercise the same safe-sex practices you would at home.

If you have a serious condition or an allergy, consider wearing a Medic Alert identification bracelet; contact the **Medic Alert Foundation,** 2323 Colorado Ave., Turlock, CA 95382 (*©* 800/432-5378; www.medicalert. com). Membership is $35, plus a $15 annual fee. If you have dental problems, a nationwide referral service known as **1-800-DENTIST** (*©* 800/ 336-8478) can give you the name of a nearby dentist or clinic.

If you plan to head into the great outdoors, keep in mind that injuries often occur when people fail to follow instructions. Believe the experts who tell you to stay on the established ski trails and hike only in designated areas. Follow the marine charts if you're piloting your own boat. If you're rafting, wear a life jacket. Mountain weather can be fickle at any time of the year, so carry rain gear and pack a few warm layers. Watch out for summer thunderstorms that can leave you drenched or send bolts of lightning your way. And if you plan to visit the country's sunnier spots, limit your exposure to the sun, especially during the first few days of your trip and, thereafter, from 11am to 2pm. Use a sunscreen with a high protection factor and apply it liberally. Remember that children need more protection than adults do.

Unless you're arriving from an area known to be suffering from an **epidemic** (particularly cholera or yellow fever), inoculations or vaccinations are not required for entry into the United States. If you have a medical condition that requires **syringe-administered**

Small Change

When you change money, ask for some small bills or loose change. Petty cash will come in handy for tipping and public transportation. Consider keeping the change separate from your larger bills, so it's readily accessible and you'll be less of a target for theft.

medications, carry a valid signed prescription from your physician—the Federal Aviation Administration (FAA) no longer allows airline passengers to pack syringes in their carry-on baggage without documented proof of medical need. In addition, a signed prescription from your physician will allay any suspicions that you may be smuggling narcotics (a serious offense that carries severe penalties in the U.S.).

For **HIV-positive visitors,** health requirements for entering the States are somewhat vague and change frequently. For up-to-the-minute information about HIV-positive travelers, contact the Centers for Disease Control's **National Center for HIV** (© **404/332-4559;** www.hivatis.org) or the **Gay Men's Health Crisis** (© **212/367-1000;** www.gmhc.org).

INSURANCE

Although it's not required of travelers, health insurance is highly recommended. Unlike many European countries and Canada, the United States does not usually offer free or low-cost medical care to its citizens or visitors. Doctors and hospitals are expensive, and in most cases will require advance payment or proof of coverage before they render their services. You might also consider trip-cancellation insurance if you're buying a package or otherwise paying a lot of your vacation costs up front. Good policies will also cover the costs of an accident, repatriation, or death. The coverage you choose should depend on how you're getting here and how much protection is already in your existing policies. Some credit- and charge-card companies insure you against travel accidents if you buy plane, train, or bus tickets with their cards. Lastly, you might also want to consider lost luggage insurance if it isn't covered by your homeowner's or renter's policy, or by your platinum or gold card.

And keep in mind that in the aftermath of the September 11, 2001, terrorist attacks, a number of airlines, cruise lines, and tour operators are no longer covered by insurers. *The bottom line:* Always, always check the fine print before you sign on; more and more policies have built-in exclusions and restrictions that may leave you out in the cold if something does go awry.

For information, contact one of the following popular insurers:

- **Access America** (© 800/284-8300; www.accessamerica.com)
- **Travel Guard International** (© 800/826-1300; www.travel guard.com)
- **Travel Insured International** (© 800/243-3174; www.travel insured.com)
- **Travelex Insurance Services** (© 800/228-9792; www.travelex-insurance.com)

Packages such as **Europ Assistance's "Worldwide Healthcare Plan"** are sold by European automobile clubs and travel agencies at attractive rates. **Worldwide Assistance Services, Inc.** (© **800/821-2828;** www.worldwideassistance.com) is the agent for Europ Assistance in the United States.

Note: Though lack of health insurance may prevent you from being admitted to a hospital in nonemergencies, don't worry about being left on a street corner to die: the American way is to fix you now and bill the living daylights out of you later.

INSURANCE FOR BRITISH TRAVELERS Most big travel agents offer their own insurance, and will probably try to sell you their package when you book a holiday. Think before you sign. **Britain's Consumers' Association** recommends that you insist on seeing the policy and reading the fine print before buying travel insurance. **The Association of British Insurers** (℡ 0171/600-3333; www.abi.org.uk) gives advice by phone and publishes *Holiday Insurance,* a free guide to policy provisions and prices. You might also shop around for better deals: Try **Columbus Direct** (℡ 0171/375-0011; www.columbusdirect.net) or, for students, **Campus Travel** (℡ 0171/730-2101; www.campustravel.co.uk).

INSURANCE FOR CANADIAN TRAVELERS Canadians should check with your provincial health plan offices or call **Health Canada** (℡ 613/957-2991; www.hc-sc.gc.ca) to find out the extent of your coverage and what documentation and receipts you must take home in case you are treated in the United States.

SAFETY
GENERAL SAFETY SUGGESTIONS Although tourist areas are generally safe, U.S. urban areas tend to be less safe than those in Europe or Japan. You should always stay alert. This is particularly true of large American cities. If you're in doubt about which neighborhoods are safe, don't hesitate to make inquiries with the hotel front desk staff or the local tourist office.

Avoid deserted areas, especially at night, and don't go into public parks after dark unless there's a concert or similar occasion that will attract a crowd.

Avoid carrying valuables with you on the street, and keep expensive cameras or electronic equipment bagged up or covered when not in use. If you're using a map, try to consult it inconspicuously—or better yet, study it before you leave your room. Hold onto your pocketbook, and place your billfold in an inside pocket. In theaters, restaurants, and other public places, keep your possessions in sight.

Always lock your room door—don't assume that once you're inside the hotel you are automatically safe and no longer need to be aware of your surroundings. Hotels are open to the public, and in a large hotel, security may not be able to screen everyone who enters.

DRIVING SAFETY Driving safety is important too, and carjacking is not unprecedented. Question your rental agency about personal safety and ask for a traveler-safety brochure when you pick up your car. Obtain written directions—or a map with the route clearly marked—from the agency showing how to get to your destination. And, if possible, arrive and depart during daylight hours.

If you drive off a highway and end up in a dodgy-looking neighborhood, leave the area as quickly as possible. If you have an accident, even on the highway, stay in your car with the doors locked until you assess the situation or until the police arrive. If you're bumped from behind on the street or are involved in a minor accident with no injuries, and the situation appears to be suspicious, motion to the other driver to follow you. Never get out of your car in such situations. Go directly to the nearest police precinct, well-lit service station, or 24-hour store. You may want to look into renting a cellphone on a short-term basis. One recommended wireless rental company is **InTouch USA** (℡ 800/872-7626; www.intouchusa.com).

Park in well-lit and well-traveled areas whenever possible. Always keep your car doors locked, whether the vehicle is attended or unattended. Never leave any packages or valuables in sight. If someone attempts to rob you or steal your car, don't try to resist the thief/carjacker. Report the incident to the police department immediately by calling ℡ **911.**

SIZE CONVERSION CHART

Women's Clothing

American	4	6	8	10	12	14	16
French	34	36	38	40	42	44	46
British	6	8	10	12	14	16	18

Women's Shoes

American	5	6	7	8	9	10
French	36	37	38	39	40	41
British	4	5	6	7	8	9

Men's Suits

American	34	36	38	40	42	44	46	48
French	44	46	48	50	52	54	56	58
British	34	36	38	40	42	44	46	48

Men's Shirts

American	14½	15	15½	16	16½	17	17½
French	37	38	39	41	42	43	44
British	14½	15	15½	16	16½	17	17½

Men's Shoes

American	7	8	9	10	11	12	13
French	39½	41	42	43	44½	46	47
British	6	7	8	9	10	11	12

RESOURCES FOR TRAVELERS WITH SPECIAL NEEDS

FOR TRAVELERS WITH DISABILITIES

The U.S. National Park Service offers a **Golden Access Passport** that gives free lifetime entrance to U.S. national parks for persons who are blind or permanently disabled, regardless of age. You may pick up a Golden Access Passport at any NPS entrance fee area by showing proof of medically determined disability and eligibility for receiving benefits under federal law. Besides free entry, the Golden Access Passport also offers a 50% discount on federal-use fees charged for such facilities as camping, swimming, parking, boat launching, and tours. For more information, go to www.nps.gov/fees_passes.htm or call © 888-GO-PARKS.

The **Society for Accessible Travel and Hospitality** (© 212/447-7284; fax 212/725-8253; www.sath.org) offers a wealth of travel resources for all types of disabilities and informed recommendations on destinations, access guides, travel agents, tour operators, vehicle rentals, and companion services. Annual membership costs $45 for adults; $30 for seniors and students. **The Moss Rehab Hospital** (© 215/456-9603; www.moss resourcenet.org) provides friendly, helpful phone assistance through its **Travel Information Service.**

Travelers with disabilities may also want to consider joining a tour that caters specifically to them. Agencies that offer a variety of itineraries for disabled travelers include **Flying Wheels Travel** (© 800/535-6790; www.flyingwheelstravel.com), with both private and escorted tours, as well as cruises; **Access Adventures** (© 716/889-9096), for sports-related vacations; and **Accessible Journeys** (© 800/TINGLES or 610/521-0339; www.disabilitytravel.com), which caters to slow walkers and wheelchair travelers.

In addition, both **Amtrak** (© 800/USA-RAIL; www.amtrak.com) and **Greyhound** (© 800/752-4841; www.greyhound.com) offer special fares and services for travelers with disabilities. Call at least a week in advance of your trip for details.

The American Foundation for the Blind (© 800/232-5463; www.afb.org) provides information on traveling with Seeing Eye dogs.

FOR SENIORS

Mention the fact that you're a senior when you first make your travel reservations. All major airlines and many hotels offer discounts for seniors. Major airlines also offer coupons for domestic travel for seniors over 60. Typically, a book of four coupons costs less than $700, which means you can fly anywhere in the continental U.S. for under $350 round-trip. In most cities, people over the age of 60 qualify for reduced admission to theaters, museums, and other attractions, as well as discounted fares on public transportation.

Members of **AARP**, 601 E St. NW, Washington, DC 20049 (© 800/424-3410 or 202/434-2277; www.aarp.org), get discounts on hotels, airfares, and car rentals. AARP offers members a wide range of benefits, including *Modern Maturity* magazine and a monthly newsletter. Anyone over 50 can join.

The Alliance for Retired Americans, 8403 Colesville Rd., Ste. 1200, Silver Spring, MD 20910 (© 301/578-8422; www.retiredamericans.org), offers a newsletter six times a year and discounts on hotel and auto

rentals; annual dues are $13 per person or couple. *Note:* Members of the former National Council of Senior Citizens receive automatic membership in the Alliance.

The **U.S. National Park Service** offers a **Golden Age Passport** that gives seniors 62 years or older lifetime entrance to U.S. national parks for a one-time processing fee of $10, which must be purchased in person at any NPS facility that charges an entrance fee. Besides free entry, a Golden Age Passport also offers a 50% discount on federal-use fees charged for such facilities as camping, swimming, parking, boat launching, and tours. For more information, visit www.nps.gov/fees_passes.htm or call © 888-GO-PARKS.

Grand Circle Travel (© 800/221-2610 or 617/350-7500; www.gct.com) is an agency that offers package deals for the 50-plus market, mostly of the tour-bus variety, with free trips thrown in for those who organize groups of 10 or more. The agency also puts out an informative publication, *101 Tips for the Mature Traveler.* Another option is **Elderhostel** (© 877/426-8056; www.elderhostel.org), which arranges study programs for those ages 55 and over (and a spouse or companion of any age) in the U.S. Most courses last 5 to 7 days, and many include airfare, accommodations in university dormitories or modest inns, meals, and tuition.

Another publication with good tips for senior travelers is *The Book of Deals,* a collection of more than 1,000 senior discounts on airlines, lodging, tours, and attractions around the country; it's available for $9.90 by calling © 800/460-6676.

FAMILY TRAVEL

The family vacation is a rite of passage for many households, one that in a split second can devolve into a *National Lampoon* farce. But as any veteran family vacationer will assure you, a family trip can be among the most pleasurable and rewarding times of your life.

Familyhostel (© **800/733-9753;** www.learn.unh.edu/familyhostel) takes the whole family on moderately priced domestic and international learning vacations. All trip details are handled by the program staff, and lectures, fields trips, and sightseeing are guided by a team of academics. It's for kids ages 8 to 15 accompanied by their parents and/or grandparents.

An excellent website that offers a "45-second newsletter" where experts weigh the best websites and resources for tips for traveling with children is **The Busy Person's Guide to Travel with Children** (http://wz.com/travel/TravelingWithChildren.html).

TRAVELING WITH PETS

These days, more and more lodgings and restaurants are going the pet-friendly route. Policies vary, however, so call ahead to find out the rules. A number of the hotels reviewed in this book allow pets, but many charge an extra fee for welcoming Fido or Fluffy. Ask when you book so you don't get a surprise when you check out.

An excellent resource is **www.pets welcome.com**, which dispenses medical tips, names of animal-friendly lodgings and campgrounds, and lists of kennels and veterinarians. Also check out *The Portable Petswelcome. com: The Complete Guide to Traveling with Your Pet* (Howell Book House), which features the best selection of pet travel information anywhere.

If you plan to fly with your pet, the FAA has compiled a list of all requirements for transporting live animals at **www.dot.gov/airconsumer/ animals.htm**. You may be able to carry your pet on board a plane if it's small enough to put inside a carrier that can slip under the seat. Pets usually count as one piece of carry-on luggage. Note that many airlines will not check pets as baggage in the hot summer months as a safety measure. And, speaking of safety, if you are driving on your vacation, note that in many states—Florida for one—it is illegal to leave an animal in a parked vehicle, even if you roll the windows down.

And keep in mind that dogs are prohibited on hiking trails and must be leashed at all times on federal lands administered by the National Park Service (national parks and monuments).

2 Getting to the United States

Many international carriers and several U.S. airlines offer service to the United States. The major gateway cities are Boston, New York, Washington, D.C. (and nearby Baltimore), Atlanta, Orlando, Miami, Houston, Dallas, Chicago, Los Angeles, San Francisco, Seattle, Anchorage, and Honolulu. You can also fly direct—though flights are less frequent—to many other cities.

NEW AIR TRAVEL SECURITY MEASURES

In the wake of the terrorist attacks of September 11, 2001, the airline industry began implementing sweeping

security measures in airports. Expect a lengthy check-in process and extensive delays. Although regulations vary from airline to airline, you can expedite the process by taking the following steps:

- **Arrive early.** Arrive at the airport at least 2 hours before your scheduled flight.
- **Try not to drive your car to the airport.** Parking and curbside access to the terminal may be limited. Call ahead and check.
- **Don't count on curbside check-in.** Some airlines and airports have stopped curbside check-in altogether, whereas others offer it on a

limited basis. For up-to-date information on specific regulations and implementations, check with the individual airline.

- **Be sure to carry plenty of documentation.** A government-issued photo ID (federal, state, or local) is now required. You may need to show this at various checkpoints. With an E-ticket, you may be required to have with you printed confirmation of purchase, and perhaps even the credit card with which you bought your ticket. This varies from airline to airline, so call ahead to make sure you have the proper documentation. And be sure that your ID is **up to date:** An expired driver's license, for example, may keep you from boarding the plane altogether.

- **Know what you can carry on—and what you can't.** Travelers in the United States are now limited to one carry-on bag, plus one personal bag (such as a purse or a briefcase). The Transportation Security Administration (TSA) has also issued a list of newly restricted carry-on items; see the box "What You Can Carry On—and What You Can't."

- **Prepare to be searched.** Expect spot-checks. Electronic items, such as a laptop or cellphone, should be readied for additional screening. Limit the metal items you wear on your person.

- **It's no joke.** When a check-in agent asks if someone other than you packed your bag, don't decide that this is the time to be funny. The agents will not hesitate to call an alarm.

- **No ticket, no gate access.** Only ticketed passengers will be allowed beyond the screener checkpoints, except for those people with specific medical or parental needs.

Ⓒ What You Can Carry On—and What You Can't

The Transportation Security Administration (TSA), the government agency that now handles all aspects of airport security, has devised new restrictions for carry-on baggage, not only to expedite the screening process but to prevent potential weapons from passing through airport security. Passengers are now limited to bringing just one carry-on bag and one personal item onto the aircraft (previous regulations allowed two carry-on bags and one personal item, like a briefcase or a purse). For more information, go to the TSA's website, **www.tsa.gov**. The agency has released an updated list of items passengers are not allowed to carry onto an aircraft:

Not permitted: knives and box cutters, corkscrews, straight razors, metal scissors, golf clubs, baseball bats, pool cues, hockey sticks, ski poles, ice picks.

Permitted: nail clippers, nail files, tweezers, eyelash curlers, safety razors (including disposable razors), syringes (with documented proof of medical need), walking canes, and umbrellas (must be inspected first).

The airline you fly may have **additional restrictions** on items you can and cannot carry on board. Call ahead to avoid problems.

FLY FOR LESS: TIPS FOR GETTING THE BEST AIRFARES

Passengers within the same airplane cabin are rarely paying the same fare. Business travelers who need to purchase tickets at the last minute, change their itinerary at a moment's notice, or get home for the weekend pay the premium rate. Passengers who can book their ticket long in advance, who can stay over Saturday night, or who are willing to travel on a Tuesday, Wednesday, or Thursday after 7pm, will pay a fraction of the full fare. On many flights, even the shortest hops, the full fare is close to $1,000 or more, while a 7- or 14-day advance purchase ticket may cost less than half that amount. Here are a few other easy ways to save.

- **Keep your eyes peeled for sales.** Check your newspaper for advertised discounts or call the airlines directly and ask if any promotional rates or special fares are available. You'll almost never see a sale during the peak summer vacation months of July and August or during the Thanksgiving or Christmas seasons, but in the off season, there have been astoundingly low fares between the United States and Europe in the past few years. If you already hold a ticket when a sale breaks, it may even pay to exchange your ticket, which usually incurs a $100 to $150 charge. *Note:* The lowest-priced fares are often nonrefundable, require advance purchase of 1 to 3 weeks and a certain length of stay, and carry penalties for changing dates of travel.

- **Ask the reservations agent lots of questions.** If your schedule is flexible, ask if you can secure a cheaper fare by staying an extra day, by staying over a Saturday night, or by flying midweek. Many airlines won't volunteer this information, so you've got to be persistent on the phone.

- **Consolidators,** also known as bucket shops, are a good place to find low fares. Consolidators buy seats in bulk from the airlines and then sell them back to the public at prices usually below even the airlines' discounted rates. Their small ads usually run in Sunday newspaper travel sections. And before you pay, request a confirmation number from the consolidator and then call the airline to confirm your seat. Be aware that bucket shop tickets are usually nonrefundable or rigged with stiff cancellation penalties, often as high as 50% to 75% of the ticket price. Protect yourself by paying with a credit card rather than cash. Keep in mind that if there's an airline sale going on, or if it's high season, you can often get the same or better rates by contacting the airlines directly, so do some comparison shopping before you buy. Also check out the name of the airline; you may not want to fly on some obscure Third World airline, even if you're saving $10. And check whether you're flying on a charter or a scheduled airline; the latter is more expensive but more reliable.

  Council Travel (© 800/226-8624; www.counciltravel.com) and **STA Travel** (© 800/781-4040; www.sta.travel.com) cater especially to young travelers, but their bargain-basement prices are available to people of all ages. **The TravelHub** (© 888/AIR-FARE; www.travelhub.com) represents nearly 1,000 travel agencies, many of whom offer consolidator and discount fares. Other reliable consolidators include **1-800-FLY-CHEAP** (www.1800flycheap.com); **TFI Tours International** (© 800/745-8000 or 212/736-1140; www.lowestprice.com), which serves as a clearinghouse for

Canceled Plans

If your flight is canceled, don't book a new fare at the ticket counter. Find the nearest phone and call the airline directly to reschedule. You'll be relaxing while other passengers are still standing in line.

---

unused seats; or "rebators" such as **Travel Avenue** (© 800/333-3335; www.travelavenue.com) and the **Smart Traveller** (© 800/448-3338 in the U.S., or 305/448-3338), which rebate part of their commissions to you.

- Search **the Internet** for cheap fares. Great last-minute deals are available through free weekly e-mail services provided directly by the airlines. See "Planning Your Trip Online," below, for more information.
- Join **frequent-flier clubs.** It's best to accrue miles on one program, so you can rack up free flights and achieve elite status faster. But it makes sense to open as many accounts as possible, no matter how seldom you fly a particular airline. It's free, and you'll get the best choice of seats, faster response to phone inquiries, and prompter service if your luggage is stolen, your flight is canceled or delayed, or if you want to change your seat.

IMMIGRATION & CUSTOMS CLEARANCE Visitors arriving by air, no matter what the port of entry, should cultivate patience and resignation before setting foot on U.S. soil. Getting through immigration control can take as long as 2 hours on some days, especially on summer weekends, so be sure to carry this guidebook or something else to read. This is especially true in the aftermath of the September 11, 2001, terrorist attacks, when security clearances have been considerably beefed up at U.S. airports.

People traveling by air from Canada, Bermuda, and certain countries in the Caribbean can sometimes clear Customs and Immigration at the point of departure, which is much quicker.

PACKAGE TOURS

Travel agents offer hundreds of package tour options to the United States. Quite often a package tour results in savings not just on airfares, but on hotels and other activities. Packages always cover airfare, transfers, and accommodations, and sometimes meals and activities. The specifics vary, so consult your travel agent to find out the best deals at the time you want to travel.

Package tours are not the same thing as escorted tours. With a package tour, you travel independently but pay a group rate. Packages usually include airfare, a choice of hotels, and car rentals, and packagers often offers several options at different prices. In many cases, a package that includes airfare, hotel, and transportation to and from the airport will cost you less than just the hotel alone would have, had you booked it yourself. That's because packages are sold in bulk to tour operators—who resell them to the public at a cost that drastically undercuts standard rates.

Packages, however, vary widely. Some offer a better class of hotels than others. Some offer the same hotels for lower prices. Some offer flights on scheduled airlines, while others book charters. In some packages, your choice of accommodations and travel days may be limited. Some packages let you choose between escorted vacations and independent vacations; others allow you to add on just a few excursions or escorted day trips (also at lower prices than you could find on your own) without booking an entirely escorted tour. Each destination often has one or two packagers that are usually cheaper than the rest because they buy in even greater bulk. Always ask about the type of accommodations offered in a given package and look for hidden expenses—airport departure fees and taxes, for example—that may not be included in the total cost. If you spend the time to shop around, you will save in the long run. Use the reviews in this book to help you evaluate the offerings; it always pays to be a well-informed consumer.

One good source of package deals is the airlines themselves. Most major airlines offer air/land packages, including **American Airlines Vacations** (② 800/321-2121; http://aav1.aavacations.com), **Delta Vacations** (② 800/221-6666; www.deltavacations.com), and **US Airways Vacations** (② 800/455-0123 or 800/422-3861; www.usairwaysvacations.com), **Continental Airlines Vacations** (② 800/301-3800; www.coolvacations.com), and **United Vacations** (② 888/854-3899; www.unitedvacations.com).

3 Getting Around the United States

BY PLANE

Some large airlines (for example, Northwest and Delta) offer travelers on their transatlantic or transpacific flights special discount tickets under the name **Visit USA,** allowing mostly one-way travel from one U.S. destination to another at very low prices. These discount tickets are not on sale in the United States and *must be purchased abroad in conjunction with your international ticket.* This system is the best, easiest, and fastest way to see the United States at low cost. You should obtain information well in advance from your travel agent or the office of the airline concerned, since the conditions attached to these discount tickets can be changed without advance notice.

See appendix A at the end of this book for a list of airlines, with their toll-free numbers and websites.

You might also look into booking various legs of your trip through so-called **no-frills airlines.** Ask your travel agent to look into these fares, which can sometimes dramatically undercut those on the major U.S. carriers. **Southwest Airlines** (② 800/435-9792; www.iflyswa.com), the oldest, biggest, and best of

the lot, has flights to and from many U.S. cities. Their success caused Delta to launch **Delta Express** (② 800/325-5205; www.delta-air.com), which at press time was flying from several East Coast cities. Others worth calling are **Air South** (② 866/861-3559), **Airtran** (② 800/247-8726), **American Trans Air** (② 800/225-2995), **Frontier** (② 800/432-1359), **Jet Blue** (② 800/538-2583), **Midwest Express** (② 800/452-2022), **Pan American** (② 800/359-7262), **Spirit** (② 800/772-7117), and **Sun Country** (② 800/752-1218).

BY CAR

The most cost-effective, convenient, and comfortable way to travel around the United States is by car. Many highlights of the country just can't be seen any other way.

The interstate highway system connects cities and towns all over the country; in addition to these high-speed, limited-access roadways, there's an extensive network of federal, state, and local highways and roads.

If you plan to rent a car in the United States, you probably won't need the services of an additional automobile organization. If you're planning to buy or borrow a car, automobile-association membership is recommended. **AAA, the American Automobile Association** (℡ **800/ 222-4357**), is the country's largest auto club and supplies its members with maps, insurance, and, most importantly, emergency road service. The cost of joining runs from $63 for singles to $87 for two members, but if you're a member of a foreign auto club with reciprocal arrangements, you can enjoy free AAA service in America.

See appendix A at the end of this book for a list of car-rental agencies, with their toll-free numbers and websites. These national companies have offices at most airports and in many cities. You must have a valid credit card to rent a vehicle. Most also require a minimum age, ranging from 19 to 25, and some also set maximum ages. Others deny cars to anyone with a bad driving record. Ask about rental requirements and restrictions when you book to avoid problems later.

Foreign visitors, please note: In the United States, we *drive on the right side of the road,* not on the left side as in the United Kingdom, Australia, and New Zealand.

Car-rental rates vary even more than airfares. The price you pay depends on the size of the car, where and when you pick it up and drop it off, the length of the rental period, where and how far you drive it, whether you purchase insurance, and a host of other factors. A few key questions could save you hundreds of dollars; you should comparison shop and be persistent because reservations agents don't often volunteer money-saving strategies.

- Is a weekly rate cheaper than the daily rate? If you need to keep the car for 4 days, it may be cheaper to keep it for 5, even if you don't need it that long.

- Does the agency assess a drop-off charge if you do not return the car to the same location where you picked it up? Is it cheaper to pick up the car at the airport instead of a downtown location?
- How much tax will be added to the rental bill? Local tax? State use tax?
- What is the cost of adding an additional driver's name to the contract?

Before you drive off in a rental car, be sure you're insured. Hasty assumptions about your personal auto insurance or a rental agency's additional coverage could end up costing you tens of thousands of dollars—even if you're involved in an accident that was clearly the fault of another driver.

If you are foreign and hold a policy outside the United States, be sure to find out whether you are covered outside your native country. If you are American and already hold a private auto insurance policy, you are most likely covered for loss of or damage to a rental car, and liability in case of injury to any other party involved in an accident. Be sure to ask whether your policy extends to all persons who will be driving the rental car, how much liability is covered in case an outside party is injured in an accident, and whether the type of vehicle you are renting is included under your contract.

The basic insurance coverage offered by most car-rental companies, known as the **Loss/Damage Waiver (LDW)** or **Collision Damage Waiver (CDW),** can cost as much as $20 per day. It usually covers the full value of the vehicle with no deductible if an outside party causes an accident or other damage to the rental car. In all states but California, you will probably be covered in case of theft as well. **Liability coverage** varies according to the company policy and state law, but the minimum is usually at least $15,000. If you are at fault in an accident, however, you will be covered for the full replacement value of the car but not for liability. Some states allow you to buy additional liability coverage for such cases. Most rental companies require a police report to process any claims you file, but your private insurer is not notified of the accident.

Most major credit cards offer some degree of coverage as well—if they were used to pay for the rental. Terms vary widely, however, so be sure to call your credit-card company directly before you rent.

If you're uninsured, your credit card provides primary coverage as long as you decline the rental agency's insurance. That means the credit card will cover damage or theft of a rental car for the full cost of the vehicle. (In a few states, however, theft is not covered; ask specifically about state law where you will be renting and driving.) If you already have insurance, your credit card will provide secondary coverage—which basically covers your deductible.

Credit cards will not cover liability, or the cost of injury to an outside party and/or damage to an outside party's vehicle. If you do not hold an insurance policy, you may seriously want to consider purchasing additional liability insurance from your rental company, even if you decline collision coverage. Be sure to check the terms, however: Some rental agencies cover liability only if the renter is not at fault; even then, the rental company's obligation varies from state to state.

Internet resources can make comparison shopping easier. **Microsoft Expedia** (www.expedia.com), **Travelocity** (www.travelocity.com or www.frommers.travelocity.com), and the rental-car specialty site, **BreezeNet** (www.bnm.com), can help you compare prices and find car-rental bargains from companies nationwide. They'll even make your reservation once you've found the best deal.

BY TRAIN

Long-distance trains in the United States are operated by **Amtrak** (© **800/USA-RAIL;** www.amtrak.com), the national rail passenger corporation. Be aware, however, that with a few notable exceptions (for instance, the Northeast Corridor line between Boston and Washington, D.C.), intercity service is not up to European standards. Delays are common, routes are limited and often infrequently served, and fares are seldom much lower than discount airfares. Therefore, approach cross-country train travel with caution.

International visitors (excluding Canada) can also buy a **USA Railpass,** good for 15 or 30 days of unlimited travel on Amtrak (© **800/USA-RAIL;** www.amtrak.com). The pass is available through many foreign travel agents. Prices in 2002 for a 15-day pass were $295 off-peak, $440 peak; a 30-day pass costs $385 off-peak, $550 peak. With a foreign passport, you can also buy passes at some Amtrak offices in the United States, including locations in San Francisco, Los Angeles, Chicago, New York, Miami, Boston, and Washington, D.C. Reservations are generally required and should be made for each part of your trip as early as possible. Regional rail passes are also available.

BY BUS

Although bus travel is often the most economical form of public transit for short hops between U.S. cities, it can also be slow and uncomfortable—certainly not an option for everyone (particularly when Amtrak, which is far more luxurious, offers similar rates). **Greyhound/Trailways** (© **800/231-2222**), the sole nationwide bus line, offers an **International Ameripass** that must be purchased before coming to the United States, or purchased by phone through the Greyhound International Office at the Port Authority Bus Terminal in New York City (© **212/971-0492**). The pass can be obtained from foreign travel agents and costs less than the domestic version. 2002 passes cost as follows: 4 days ($135), 7 days ($184), 10 days ($234), 15 days ($274), 21 days ($324), 30 days ($364), 45 days ($404), or 60 days ($494). You can get more info on the pass at **www. greyhound.com**, or by calling © **212/ 971-0492** (14:00–21:00 GMT) and © **402/330-8552** (all other times). In addition, special rates are available for seniors and students.

4 Planning Your Trip Online

Researching and booking your trip online can save time and money. Then again, it may not. It is simply not true that you always get the best deal online. Most booking engines do not include schedules and prices for budget airlines, and from time to time you'll get a better last-minute price by calling the airline directly, so it's best to call the airline to see if you can do better before booking online.

On the plus side, Internet users today can tap into the same travel-planning databases that were once accessible only to travel agents—and do it at the same speed. Sites such as **Frommers.com**, **Travelocity.com**, **Expedia.com**, and **Orbitz.com** allow consumers to comparison shop for airfares, access special bargains, book flights, and reserve hotel rooms and rental cars.

But don't fire your travel agent just yet. Although online booking sites offer tips and hard data to help you bargain shop, they cannot endow you with the hard-earned experience that makes a seasoned, reliable travel agent an invaluable resource, even in the Internet age. And for consumers with a complex itinerary, a trusty travel agent is still the best way to arrange the most direct flights to and from the best airports.

Still, there's no denying the Internet's emergence as a powerful tool in researching and plotting travel time. The benefits of researching your trip online can be well worth the effort.

TRAVEL PLANNING & BOOKING SITES

Keep in mind that because several airlines are no longer willing to pay commissions on tickets sold by online

---

Frommers.com: The Complete Travel Resource

For an excellent travel-planning resource, we highly recommend **Frommers. com** (www.frommers.com). We're a little biased, of course, but we guarantee that you'll find the travel tips, reviews, monthly vacation giveaways, and online-booking capabilities thoroughly indispensable. Among the special features are our popular **Message Boards,** where Frommer's readers post queries and share advice (sometimes even our authors show up to answer questions); **Frommers.com Newsletter,** for the latest travel bargains and inside travel secrets; and Frommer's **Destinations Section,** where you'll get expert travel tips, hotel and dining recommendations, and advice on the sights to see for more than 2,500 destinations around the globe. When your research is done, the **Online Reservation System** (www.frommers.com/booktravelnow) takes you to Frommer's favorite sites for booking your vacation at affordable prices.

travel agencies, these agencies may either add a $10 surcharge to your bill if you book on that carrier—or neglect to offer those carriers' schedules.

The list of sites below is selective, not comprehensive. Some sites will have evolved or disappeared by the time you read this.

- **Travelocity** (www.travelocity.com or www.frommers.travelocity.com) and **Expedia** (www.expedia.com) are among the most popular sites, each offering an excellent range of options. Travelers search by destination, dates, and cost.
- **Orbitz** (www.orbitz.com) is a popular site launched by United, Delta, Northwest, American, and Continental airlines. (Stay tuned: At press time, travel-agency associations were waging an antitrust battle against this site.)
- **Qixo** (www.qixo.com) is another powerful search engine that allows you to search for flights and accommodations from some 20 airline and travel-planning sites (such as Travelocity) at once. Qixo sorts results by price.
- **Priceline** (www.priceline.com) lets you "name your price" for airline tickets, hotel rooms, and rental cars. For airline tickets, you can't say what time you want to fly—you have to accept any flight between 6am and 10pm on the dates you've selected, and you may have to make one or more stopovers. Tickets are nonrefundable, and no frequent-flyer miles are awarded.

SMART E-SHOPPING

The savvy traveler is armed with insider information. Here are a few tips to help you navigate the Internet successfully and safely.

- **Know when sales start.** Last-minute deals may vanish in minutes. If you have a favorite booking site or airline, find out when last-minute deals are released to the public. (For example, Southwest's specials are posted every Tues at 12:01am central time.)
- **Shop around.** If you're looking for bargains, compare prices on different sites and airlines—and against a travel agent's best fare. Try a range of times and alternative airports before you make a purchase.
- **Stay secure.** Book only through secure sites (some airline sites are not secure). Look for a key icon (Netscape) or a padlock (Internet Explorer) at the bottom of your web browser before you enter credit card information or other personal data.
- **Avoid online auctions.** Sites that auction airline tickets and frequent-flier miles are the number-one perpetrators of Internet fraud, according to the National Consumers League.
- **Maintain a paper trail.** If you book an E-ticket, print out a confirmation, or write down your confirmation number, and keep it safe and accessible—or your trip could be a virtual one!

ONLINE TRAVELER'S TOOLBOX

Veteran travelers usually carry some essential items to make their trips easier. Following is a selection of online tools to bookmark and use.

- **Visa ATM Locator** (www.visa. com), for locations of PLUS ATMs worldwide, or **MasterCard ATM Locator** (www.mastercard. com), for locations of Cirrus ATMs worldwide.
- **Intellicast** (www.intellicast.com) and **Weather.com** (www.weather. com). Gives weather forecasts for all 50 states and for cities around the world.
- **Mapquest** (www.mapquest.com). This best of the mapping sites lets

Easy Internet Access Away from Home

There are a number of ways to get your e-mail on the Web, using any computer.

- Your **Internet Service Provider (ISP)** may have a Web-based interface that lets you access your e-mail on computers other than your own. Just find out how it works before you leave home. The major ISPs maintain local access numbers around the world so that you can go online by placing a local call. Check your ISP's website or call its toll-free number and ask how you can use your current account away from home, and how much it will cost. Also ask about the cost of the service before you leave home. If you're traveling outside the reach of your ISP, you may have to check the Yellow Pages in your destination to find a local ISP.
- You can open an account on a free, web-based **e-mail provider** before you leave home, such as Microsoft's **Hotmail** (hotmail.com) or **Yahoo! Mail** (mail.yahoo.com). Your home ISP may be able to forward your home e-mail to the Web-based account automatically.
- Check out **www.mail2web.com**. This amazing free service allows you to type in your regular e-mail address and password and retrieve your e-mail from any web browser, anywhere, so long as your home ISP hasn't blocked it with a firewall.
- Call your hotel in advance to see whether Internet connection is possible from your room.

you choose a specific address or destination, and in seconds, it will return a map and detailed directions.

- **Cybercafes.com** (www.cybercafes.com) or **Net Café Guide** (www.netcafeguide.com/mapindex.htm). Locate Internet cafes at hundreds of locations around the globe. Catch up on your e-mail and log onto the Web for a few dollars per hour.
- **Universal Currency Converter** (www.xe.net/currency). See what your euro or pound is worth in U.S. dollars.

5 A Special-Interest Vacation Planner

Here's a sampling of companies that offer escorted adventures and tours, and some suggestions on where to go to enjoy your favorite activities. For information on the individual states mentioned below, see the appropriate destination chapter in the book.

ADVENTURE-TRAVEL COMPANIES

Scores of "soft" and "hard" adventure-travel companies have sprung up in recent years. Most travel agents have catalogs that list upcoming trips. More than 500 different tour operators are represented in the **Specialty Travel Index Online** at www.specialtytravel.com. Another good source of up-to-date information is the monthly *Outside* magazine, available on newsstands throughout the country, or online at **http://outsidemag.com**.

Mountain Travel—Sobek (© 888/687-6235 or 510/527-8100; www.mtsobek.com) is perhaps the granddaddy of adventure-travel companies, guiding its own trips and acting as an agent for other outfitters. It began with river rafting, which is still its strong suit. **Backroads** (© **800/462-2848** or 510/527-1555; www.backroads.com) originally sold bicycle tours, but now has walking, hiking, cross-country skiing, trail running, and other trips. **Backcountry** (© **800/575-1540** or 406/655-4591; www.backcountry tours.com) is another firm that started with bikes, but now has hiking, skiing, and other packages. The venerable **Sierra Club** (© **415/977-5500**; www.sierraclub.com) offers a number of trips each year.

Alyson Adventures (© **800/825-9766;** www.alysonadventures.com) specializes in gay and lesbian adventure travel.

These and other operators plan their adventures at least a year ahead of time, so ask them or your travel agent for their schedules and catalogs as far in advance as possible.

WHERE SHOULD I GO FOR . . . ?

BEACHES Miami and Florida's west coast and Southern California have the best beaches in the continental United States, though they all pale in comparison to the spectacular sands on all the islands of Hawaii.

The entire **Atlantic** is lined with sand where you can sun and swim in the summer, and you'll find no shortage of resorts and beach motels. If you try hard enough, you can even find a little undeveloped solitude at the **Cape Cod National Seashore** in Massachusetts and at **Cape Hatteras National Seashore** on North Carolina's Outer Banks.

The **Maine coast** is gorgeous, but too cold for actual swimming. The same goes for the lovely, dramatic scenery in **Northern California** and along the **Oregon coast.**

BIKING Biking is a great way to see the country up close and personal. Except for the interstate highways, you can bike on most roads in the United States. Among the best are the **Maine coast, Cape Cod,** and the hills of **New England** (especially Vermont); Virginia's rolling **Shenandoah Valley;** the combined **Skyline Drive** and **Blue Ridge Parkway** in Virginia and North Carolina; the **Outer Banks** of North Carolina; the dramatic **California coast;** the **Oregon coast;** the **San Juan Islands** near Seattle; and the road circling the **Big Island** of Hawaii. Biking is an excellent way to see some of the national parks, especially **Shenandoah, Yosemite, Yellowstone, Grand Tetons,** and **Glacier.**

An ongoing nationwide program is converting some 50,000 miles of abandoned railroad beds into biking-and-walking paths. For a list, contact the **Rails to Trails Conservancy,** 1100 17th St. NW, 10th Floor, Washington, DC 20005 (© **202/331-9696**).

Several companies and organizations offer escorted bike excursions, including **Backroads** and **Backcountry** (see "Adventure-Travel Companies," above). **American Youth Hostels** (© **202/783-6161**) has trips for its members. **CROSSROADS Bike Tours** (© **800/971-2453**) offers nationwide excursions, including California to Massachusetts and Maine to Florida.

BIRDING The entire East Coast is on the Atlantic Flyway for migrating waterbirds and waterfowl. You can see them all the way from the Maine coast, particularly **Monhegan and Machias islands,** to the **Wellfleet Wildlife Sanctuary** on Cape Cod, and on south to Maryland's eastern shore, where **Chincoteague National Wildlife Refuge** on the Maryland–Virginia line is the best bet (© **757/336-6122**).

Shorebirds also migrate along the Pacific side of the country, with good viewing anywhere along the Washington and Oregon coasts but especially in **Malheur National Wildlife Refuge** in southeastern Oregon.

Once endangered, the **bald eagle** is now widespread across the country. Dozens make their winter home at **Lake Cachuma** near Santa Barbara in California. In January they flock to the **Skagit River** north of Seattle to feast on salmon, and you can even spot them while riding a Washington State ferry through the **San Juan Islands.** In September, look for them along **Alaska's southeastern coast,** especially in the **Chilkat River Valley.** Alaska also has many other birds not found in the lower 48 states.

In the Arizona desert, **Ramsey Canyon Preserve** is internationally known as home to 14 species of **hummingbird,** more than anywhere else in the United States. **San Pedro Riparian National Conservation Area** is another good spot in Arizona, with more than 300 species.

For tropical species, head to **Florida,** especially to **Everglades National Park.** The **J. N. "Ding" Darling National Wildlife Refuge** on Sanibel Island is another good spot, as is **Corkscrew Swamp Sanctuary** near Naples, home to countless wood storks. You can see rare white pelicans on wintertime cruises from Captiva Island.

Hawaii's tropical birds are found nowhere else on earth, including the rare **o'o,** whose yellow feathers Hawaiians once plucked to make royal capes. Large colonies of seabirds nest at **Kilauea National Wildlife Preserve** and along the **Na Pali coast** on Kauai, and **Molokai's Kamakou Preserve** is home to the Molokai thrust and Molokai creeper, found nowhere else.

For information about escorted bird-watching trips, contact **Field Guide** (✆ **512/263-7295;** fgileader@aol.com) or **Victor Emanual Nature Tours** (✆ **800/328-VENT** or 512/328-5221; www.ventbird.com). The **National Audubon Society** (✆ **212/979-3000;** www.audubon.com) runs superb bird-watching programs for both aspiring and experienced naturalists.

CANOEING & KAYAKING
There's a wide variety of rivers, streams, lakes, and sounds for canoeing and kayaking enthusiasts. In fact, most cities with rivers running through them now have a contingent of outfitters.

Out in the hinterlands, some of the best paddling takes place along **Maine's coast** or through its 92-mile **Allagash Wilderness Waterway,** a series of remote rivers, lakes, and ponds.

In summer, it's hot and humid in **Florida's Everglades National Park,** but winter offers great opportunities along a maze of well-marked trails. You can rent canoes at the main park center at **Flamingo.**

The peaceful lakes of Minnesota's **Boundary Waters Canoe Area** north of Minneapolis are another good choice.

Puget Sound's **San Juan Islands** near Seattle are enchanting when seen by canoe or kayak. **San Juan Kayak Expeditions** (✆ **360/378-4436**) and **Shearwater Adventures** (✆ **360/376-4699**) both have multiday trips to the islands, and biologists and naturalists lead educational expeditions sponsored by the nonprofit **Sea Quest Expedition/Zoetic Research** (✆ **360/378-5767**).

For a truly unique kayaking experience, you can paddle among the humpback whales taking their winter break in Hawaii. Contact **South Pacific Kayaks** (✆ **800/776-2326** or 808/661-8400).

For general information, contact the **American Canoe Association,** 7432 Alban Station Blvd., Ste. B226, Springfield, VA 22150 (© **703/451-0141**), the nation's largest organization, for lists of trips and local clubs.

CIVIL WAR BATTLEFIELDS The Civil War started in 1861 at **Fort Sumter** in Charleston, South Carolina. Battles raged all over the South during the next 4 years. Gen. Ulysses S. Grant took **Vicksburg, Mississippi,** after a long siege, and Gen. William Tecumseh Sherman burned **Atlanta,** but the most famous fighting took place within 100 miles of **Washington, D.C.** This area has more national battlefield parks than any other part of the country.

It won't be in chronological order, but you can tour them by starting at the battles of **Fredericksburg, Chancellorsville,** and **The Wilderness** in and near Fredericksburg, Virginia. Proceed north to the two **Battles of Manassas** (or Bull Run) southwest of Washington, then north across the Potomac River to the **Battle of Antietam** at Sharpsburg, Maryland. From there, go northwest through Harpers Ferry to the **Battle of Gettysburg,** the turning point of the war, in south central Pennsylvania. Gettysburg is perhaps the most moving and well-preserved of the battlegrounds. You'll also pass several battlefields driving through the **Shenandoah Valley.**

FALL FOLIAGE Fall in New England is one of the great natural spectacles on earth, with rolling hills blanketed in brilliant reds and stunning oranges. The colors start to peak in mid-September in the **Green and White Mountains** of Vermont and New Hampshire, and then bleed down into the **Berkshires** of Massachusetts. The colors move progressively south down the East Coast into October, when bumper-to-bumper traffic jams **Virginia's Skyline Drive** through Shenandoah National Park.

The precise dates for prime viewing vary from year to year, depending on temperatures and rainfall, but the local newspapers and TV stations closely track the coloration.

Fall is also quite spectacular in the Rockies, especially in **Colorado.**

Tauck World Discovery (© **800/788-7885;** www.tauck.com), **Maupintour** (© **800/255-4266** or 913/843-1211; www.maupintour.com), and several other escorted tour operators have foliage tours; see your travel agent.

FISHING The United States can boast of record-setting catches and has every type of fishing invented—from surf-casting off **Cape Cod** or **Cape Hatteras** to flicking a fly in **Maine** or **Montana.**

Fly-fishing camps are as prolific as fish in the Maine woods. **Grant's Kennebago Camps** in Oquossoc has 18 of them, built on Kennebago Lake in 1905. Over in Vermont, **Orvis** (© **800/548-9548**) runs one of the top fly-fishing schools in the country. See chapter 3 for more on New England fishing.

The nation's other great fly-fishing area is in the Montana and Wyoming mountains near **Yellowstone National Park,** made famous by *A River Runs Through It.* The top river out here is Montana's **Madison,** with headquarters starting in the park, but cutthroat trout make the **Snake River** over in Wyoming almost as good—and the resort of **Jackson Hole** offers luxury relief within casting distance (see chapter 17).

Most ports along the nation's seaboards have deep-sea charter-fishing fleets and less expensive party boats (all you have to do is show up for the latter). The best tropical strikes are in the **Florida Keys** and off the **Kona coast** of the **Big Island** in Hawaii. **Florida's southwest coast** is noted for fighting snook and tarpon. **Alaska** is famous for summertime salmon and halibut fishing, with the biggest in the **Kenai River** and on **Kodiak Island,** which has the state's best roadside salmon fishing.

FLOWERS & GARDENS Flower lovers have many opportunities to stop and smell the roses, especially in **Portland, Oregon,** which calls itself the City of Roses. Many other cities have gardens of note, including **Atlanta, Boston, Denver, New Orleans, New York, Seattle,** and **Tucson. Longwood Gardens** in the **Brandywine Valley** is noted for its greenhouses as well as its grounds. The **Biltmore Estate** in Asheville, North Carolina, has a walled English garden on its 25 acres. **Magnolia Plantation** near Charleston, South Carolina, is famed for its azaleas, camellias, and 60-acre cypress swamp. If you like gardens from the Elizabethan era, head for **Colonial Williamsburg,** Virginia.

It's also a spectacular sight to see the commercial flower farms of **Washington State's Skagit Valley.** In the spring, tulips and daffodils carpet the farmlands surrounding the town of **La Conner** with great swaths of red, yellow, and white. In March and April, the town hosts an annual Tulip Festival; the countryside erupts with color in a display that matches the legendary flower fields of the Netherlands.

You may also be interested in seeing wildflowers in bloom out West. Springtime brings glorious color to the **Texas Hill Country,** just north of San Antonio. The **deserts of New Mexico, Arizona, and Southern California** are also magical in the spring. Two of California's prettiest viewing areas are **Anza-Borrego Desert State Park,** near San Diego, and the **Antelope Valley Poppy Reserve,** in the high desert near L.A. There are also beautiful spring blooms in the Washington Cascades, especially in **Olympic National Park,** and throughout the **Rocky Mountains.**

A few travel companies have escorted tours of gardens, others include them on their general sightseeing excursions, and still others organize trips for local botanical gardens or gardening and horticultural groups. Check with those in your hometown for upcoming trips or try **Maupintour** (© **800/255-4266** or 913/843-1211; www.maupintour. com).

GOLF & TENNIS You can play golf and tennis almost anywhere in the country, although the southern tier of states, where the outdoor seasons are longest, offer the best opportunities. In the Southeast, top golfing destinations are the **North Carolina Sandhills; Hilton Head Island** and **Myrtle Beach,** South Carolina; and almost anywhere in **Florida,** with the highest concentration of courses on the southwest coast around Naples. You can get information about most Florida courses, including current greens fees, and reserve tee times through **Tee Times USA** (© **888/ 465-3356** or 904/439-0001; www.tee timesusa.com). This company also publishes a vacation guide that includes many stay-and-play golf packages.

In the Southwest, the twin desert cities of **Phoenix** and **Scottsdale,** Arizona, have some of the country's most luxurious golf resorts. The same can be said of **Palm Springs** and the **Monterey coast** in California.

And **Hawaii** has some of the most famous and most unique courses in the world.

Most of the nation's top golf resorts also have excellent **tennis** facilities. For the top 50 tennis resorts, see *Tennis* magazine's rankings each November. Perennial favorites include the **Colony Beach & Tennis Resort** on Longboat Key, Florida (© **800/4-COLONY** or 941/383-6464), and **Sea Pines Plantation** on Hilton

Head, South Carolina (© **800/ SEA-PINES** or 803/785-3333).

MOUNTAIN BIKING If mountain bikes are your thing, you'll find plenty of dirt roads and backcountry pathways to explore. Many national parks and forests have a good selection of trails—**Acadia National Park**'s carriage roads, for example, are unique. You can also take guided tours through 60 miles of connected trails in the **Sebago Lake area,** near the New Hampshire border, with **Back Country Excursions** (© 207/625-8189), which operates a mountain-biking playground called the "Palace" in Limerick, Maine.

Out in Colorado, ski areas often open their lifts to bikers in the summer. **Winter Park** is considered the state's mountain-bike capital (© **800/ 903-PARK** or 970/726-4118). The state's single best route, the 30-mile **Tipperary Creek Trail,** ends at Winter Park.

In **Deschutes National Forest,** outside the town of Bend in central Oregon, dry ponderosa pine forests are laced with trails past lakes, waterfalls, and great views of the surrounding mountains. Contact the **Bend/ Fort Rock Ranger Station** (© 541/388-5664). Another popular area is the **Bryce, Zion,** and **Canyonlands** regions of southern Utah. Contact **Rim Tours** (© **800/626-7335**) or **Kaibab Mountain Bike Tours** (© 800/451-1133), based in the town of Moab.

The companies mentioned under "Biking," above, also offer mountain-biking expeditions throughout the country and abroad.

NATURE & ECOLOGY TOURS Not just for bird-watchers, the **National Audubon Society** (© 212/979-3000; www.audubon.com) has its Ecology Camp on Hog Island off the Maine coast and another in the Grand Tetons of Wyoming, and it sponsors ecology excursions to such

places as California's Death Valley. The **Sierra Club** maintains base camps in the Rockies and sponsors a wide variety of nature- and conservation-oriented trips (© **415/ 977-5630;** www.sierraclub.com). The **National Wildlife Federation** has four annual "conservation summits" dedicated to preserving the great outdoors, including one on Hawaii's Big Island (© **800/245-5484** or 703/790-4265; www.nwf.com).

On a tour sponsored by a conservation association, you'll learn more about our national parks than you could just by driving through them. To find out what's available, contact the individual park you plan on visiting.

RIVER RAFTING The most famous place to run the rapids is the **Grand Canyon,** with steep walls that tower above you as you race down the **Colorado River.** It's also the most popular spot, with bumper-to-bumper rafts in summer.

You may have less unwanted company on the Colorado upstream in **Utah**—which also has good rafting on the **Green River.** Call the **Utah Travel Council** (© **800/200-1160** or 801/538-1030) and ask for a copy of *Raft Utah.* The **Snake River** south of Yellowstone National Park near Jackson Hole, Wyoming, is also a best bet. The **Snake River** flows into Idaho, where its wild Hells Canyon offers exciting rides—as do the Salmon and Middle Fork rivers.

Up in Alaska, you can see plenty of birds and an occasional moose on the **Kenai River.**

The **New River** cuts a dramatic, 2,000-foot-deep gorge through the Appalachian Mountains near the town of Beckley, West Virginia, making it the most scenic rapids route in the east. The **Southern West Virginia Convention & Visitors Bureau** has more general information (© **800/ VISIT-WV** or 304/252-2244).

SCENIC DRIVES There are so many wonderful driving tours that it's impossible to offer anything like a comprehensive list, but here are just a few favorites.

The dramatic **Kancamagus Highway** (N.H. 112) cuts through New Hampshire's White Mountains between Lincoln and Conway. Nearby is the privately owned **Mount Washington Auto Road,** to the top of one of the tallest peaks in the east. The loop road in Maine's **Acadia National Park** is another beauty.

In the Mid-Atlantic, you can't beat Virginia's **Skyline Drive** and the **Blue Ridge Parkway,** which continues south to North Carolina's Great Smoky Mountains near Asheville.

Out West, driving doesn't get any more dramatic than it is along the **California** and **Oregon coasts.** In the **Arizona desert,** the drive from Phoenix through Prescott and Sedona includes huge red rocks and the cool oasis of Oak Creek Canyon. The desert's most spectacular scenery is in **Monument Valley** on the Arizona–Utah border in Navajo and Hopi country and the nearby **Canyonlands.**

In Colorado, a driving tour of the Western Slope follows the **Million Dollar Highway** (U.S. 550) across 11,008-foot **Red Mountain Pass,** an unforgettable drive. The **San Juan Skyway,** a 236-mile circuit that crosses five mountain passes, takes in the magnificent scenery of the San Juan Mountains, including some wonderful Old West towns. In Montana, the driving tour of Glacier Country puts you on **Going-to-the-Sun Road** through Glacier National Park, one of the great summertime drives in the country. Over the border in Wyoming, the **Beartooth Scenic Byway** (U.S. 212) from the northern part of Yellowstone National Park east to Red Lodge climbs over 10,947-foot **Beartooth Pass,** from where you can see mile upon mile of Wyoming and Montana mountains.

Up in Alaska, one of the world's great drives begins in Anchorage and leads roughly 50 miles south on the **Seward Highway** to Portage Glacier; chipped from the rocky Chugach Mountains, the **Turnagain Arm** provides a platform for viewing an untouched landscape full of wildlife.

Out in Hawaii, the drive from Honolulu to Oahu's Windward coast on **Highway 61** offers an unparalleled view down from the near-vertical Pali cliff. The narrow, winding **Hana Road** on Maui will reward your driving skills with wonderful seascapes.

SKIING New England may have started downhill skiing in the United States, but for the best, forget about the East altogether and head for the deep powder out West.

Colorado is endowed with more than two dozen ski resorts, including world-renowned Aspen, Vail, Breckenridge, and Wolf Creek; **Utah** is home to Alta, Beaver Mountain, Snowbasin, Park City, and Deer Valley; and **Taos** in New Mexico has well-known slopes. In California's Sierras, **Lake Tahoe** is home to Alpine Meadows, Heavenly Resort, and the famous Squaw Valley USA. And there's **Jackson Hole** in Wyoming, plus the Big Mountain and Big Sky resorts nearby in Montana.

New England does have good cross-country skiing, especially at the **Trapp Family Lodge Cross-Country Ski Center** (© **800/826-7000** or 802/253-8511) in Stowe, Vermont, and the entire village of Jackson, New Hampshire, which is laced with a network of ski trails maintained by the **Jackson Ski Touring Foundation** (© **603/383-9355**). Out West, many of the downhill resorts mentioned above have cross-country trails as well. The best are in **Yosemite, Yellowstone,** and **Glacier** national parks.

The rims of the **Grand Canyon** and **Bryce Canyon** national parks also present some unusual skiing venues.

WHALE- & WILDLIFE WATCHING   The best whale- watching on the East Coast leaves from **Provincetown** on Cape Cod, where some boats sight humpbacks and finbacks with a 99% success rate from April to November.

On the West Coast, you can see Pacific gray whales during their spring and fall migrations from **Point Reyes National Seashore** north of San Francisco, **Depot Bay** and other points on the Oregon coast, and the **San Juan Islands** near Seattle, which also have orcas.

The ports of **Petersburg** and **Sitka** in southeastern Alaska and **Kenai Fjords National Park** and nearby **Seward** are great spots to watch humpbacks feeding in summer—plus a profusion of seals, otters, and other marine mammals.

For many humpbacks, the fall migration takes them south to sunny Hawaii, where they frolic in the warm waters from December to May. They are best seen here from **Maui's west coast.**

For wildlife watching, you can see moose in **Baxter State Park** in Maine, maybe a bear in the **Great Smoky Mountains,** or alligators and other critters in **Florida's Everglades.** But the best places to spot a variety of animals are undoubtedly the national parks out west and in **Alaska.** Without question, **Yellowstone** offers some of the top opportunities, with an abundance of elk and bison. Some of them will walk right up to your car. **Glacier** has this and more—mountain elk and the occasional grizzly bear. Alaska's **Denali** and **Katmai** national parks offer the best chance to see grizzlies and other types of bears. In particular, at the **Brooks Camp Lodge** in Katmai, they walk right by on their way to a salmon spawning area.

6 Tips on Accommodations

The United States has such a vast array of accommodations—from rock-bottom roadside motels and quaint bed-and-breakfasts to some of the world's finest resorts and the planet's largest hotels—that we can cover only the tip of the iceberg in this book. Whether you spend a pittance or a bundle depends on your budget and your tastes. But, to repeat a well-worn phrase, you can enjoy "champagne on a beer budget"—if you plan carefully.

UNDERSTANDING HOTEL ROOM RATES

The rates quoted in this book are "rack" or "published" rates; that is, the highest regular rates charged by a hotel or motel at the time we researched this edition. Not long ago, the rack rate was what you paid, unless you were part of a tour group or had purchased a vacation package. These days, however, most hotels give discounts to corporate travelers, government employees, seniors, automobile-club members, active-duty military personnel, and others. Most hotels don't advertise these discounted rates or even volunteer them at the front desk, so it's important to ask.

Computerized reservations systems also have permitted many larger properties to adjust their rates on an almost daily—if not hourly—basis, depending on how much business they anticipate having.

Most hotels also have free self-parking, but parking fees can run up the cost at some hotels, especially in major cities, such as Washington, D.C., New York City, Los Angeles, and Miami. We've indicated in the listings if a hotel or resort charges for parking; if no charge is given, parking is free.

TIPS FOR SAVING ON YOUR HOTEL ROOM

The **rack rate** is the maximum rate that a hotel charges for a room. It's the rate you get if you walk in off the street and ask for a room for the night. Hardly anybody pays these prices, however, and there are many ways around them.

- **Don't be afraid to bargain.** Most rack rates include commissions of 10% to 25% for travel agents, which some hotels may be willing to reduce if you make your own reservations and haggle a bit. Always ask whether a room less expensive than the first one quoted is available, or whether any special rates apply to you. You may qualify for corporate, student, military, senior, or other discounts. Be sure to mention membership in AAA, AARP, frequent-flier programs, or trade unions, which may entitle you to special deals as well. Find out the hotel policy on children—do kids stay free in the room or is there a special rate?

- **Rely on a qualified professional.** Certain hotels give travel agents discounts in exchange for steering business their way, so if you're shy about bargaining, an agent may be better equipped to negotiate discounts for you.

- **Dial direct.** When booking a room in a chain hotel, compare the rates offered by the hotel's local line with that of the toll-free number. Also check the hotel website, as many hotels offer special Internet-only discounts. A hotel makes nothing on a room that stays empty, so the local hotel reservation desk may be willing to offer a special rate unavailable elsewhere.

- **Remember the law of supply and demand.** Resort hotels are most crowded and therefore most expensive on weekends, so discounts are usually available for midweek stays. Business hotels in major cities such as New York, Atlanta, and Chicago are busiest during the week, so you can expect discounts over the weekend. Avoid high-season stays whenever you can: planning your vacation just a week before or after official peak season can mean big savings. Just keep in mind that destinations have an off season for a reason—it may be cheaper to visit the Southeast in the summer, for example, but the heat and humidity can reach almost unbearable levels for those not accustomed to it.

- **Look into group or long-stay discounts.** If you come as part of a large group, you should be able to negotiate a bargain rate, since the hotel can then guarantee occupancy in a number of rooms. Likewise, if you're planning a long stay (at least 5 days), you might qualify for a discount.

- **Avoid excess charges.** When you book a room, ask whether the hotel charges for parking. Many hotels charge a fee just for dialing out on the phone in your room. Find out whether your hotel imposes a surcharge on local and long-distance calls. A pay phone, however inconvenient, may save you money, although many calling cards charge a fee when you use them on pay phones. Some hotels charge extra if children stay in the same room as their parents (many of the major Las Vegas hotels do this), others don't—ask before you book. Those hotels that accept pets often charge you extra money for bringing Fido or Fluffy along. Many hotels—especially those on the West Coast—assess an outrageous energy surcharge on top of their rates. Another unfortunate practice at resort hotels, especially those in Florida, is to assess a "Resort Fee" that can add as much as $10 to $20 per day to your total room cost. Make sure to inquire about all of these potentially hidden costs. Finally, ask about local taxes and service charges, which can increase the cost of a room by 25% or more.

- Consider the pros and cons of **all-inclusive** resorts and hotels. The term "all-inclusive" means different things at different hotels. Many all-inclusive hotels will include three meals daily, sports equipment, spa entry, and other amenities; others may include all or most drinks. In general, you'll save money going the "all-inclusive" way—as long as you use the facilities provided. The down side is that your choices are limited and you're stuck eating and playing in one place for the duration of your vacation.
- **Watch for coupons and advertised discounts.** Scan ads in your local Sunday newspaper travel section, an excellent source for up-to-the-minute hotel deals.
- **Consider a suite.** If you are traveling with your family or another couple, you can pack more people into a suite (which usually comes with a sofa bed), and thereby reduce your per-person rate. Remember that some places charge for extra guests.
- **Try a hostel.** If you're on a strict budget, keep in mind that many hostels offer more than just stereotypical dorm-style rooms. "Family rooms" can be found in many hostels and offer beds that can accommodate families of up to five.
- **Book an efficiency.** A room with a kitchenette allows you to shop for groceries and cook your own meals. This is a big money-saver, especially for families on long stays.
- Join hotel **frequent-visitor clubs,** even if you don't use them much. You'll be more likely to get upgrades and other perks.
- Put in a bid on **Priceline** (www.priceline.com), which offers rooms in hotels throughout the United States. You can specify the class of hotel you want and the location, but you won't find out what hotel you're staying in until your bid has been accepted and your credit card charged. Rates do not include any taxes or extra charges assessed by individual properties. Note that you are guaranteed double occupancy, but not two beds; and if you're traveling with more than two people in your party, you might need to bid on more than one room. You'll need to do a little legwork in order to make a good bid, but we've gotten deluxe hotel rooms in many major U.S. cities for exceptionally low prices. If you do use Priceline, make sure to go to **www.biddingfortravel.com**, a bulletin board that lists hotels the site books in major U.S. cities and also posts the amounts of recent winning hotel bids.
- **Investigate reservations services.** These outfits usually work as consolidators, buying up or reserving rooms in bulk, and then dealing them out to customers at a profit. You can get 10% to 50% off; but remember, these discounts apply to inflated rack rates that savvy travelers rarely end up paying. You may get a decent rate, but always call the hotel as well to see if you can do better.

Among the more reputable reservations services, offering both telephone and online bookings, are: **Hotels.com** (℃ **800/2-HOTELS;** www.hotels.com); **Hotel Reservations Network** (℃ **800/715-7666;** www.hotel discounts.com or www.180096 HOTEL.com); and **Quikbook** (℃ **800/789-9887,** includes fax on demand service; www.quik book.com). Other online booking sites that feature affordable lodgings at many U.S. destinations include **All-Hotels** (www. allhotels.com), **Frommers.com** (www.frommers.com), **Expedia** (www.expedia.com), and **Travelocity** (www.travelocity.com).

LANDING THE BEST ROOM

Somebody has to get the best room in the house. It might as well be you.

Always ask about a corner room. They're often larger and quieter, with more windows and light, and they often cost the same as standard rooms.

When you make your reservation, ask if the hotel is renovating; if it is, request a room away from the construction. Ask about nonsmoking rooms, rooms with views, and rooms with twin, queen- or king-size beds. If you're a light sleeper, request a quiet room away from vending machines, elevators, restaurants, bars, and discos. Ask for one of the rooms that have been most recently renovated or redecorated. If you aren't happy with your room when you arrive, talk to the front desk. If they have another room, they may be willing to accommodate you. Join the hotel's frequent-visitor club; you may qualify for upgrades.

In resort areas, particularly in warm climates, there are some other questions to ask before you book a room:

- What's the view like? Cost-conscious travelers may be willing to pay less for a back room facing the parking lot, especially if they don't plan to spend much time in their room.
- Does the room have air-conditioning or just ceiling fans?
- Do the windows open?
- What is the noise level outside the room? If the climate is warm and nighttime entertainment takes place alfresco, you may want to find out when showtime is over. And if you plan on staying in the heart of a major city and like to sleep in, you might want to ask for an interior room to avoid the traffic sounds on the streets outside.
- What's included in the price? A so-called moderate hotel that charges for extras such as access to the fitness center, and so on, may cost a lot more than a so-called expensive hotel that includes extras in the price.
- If it's off season at some of the seasonal destinations, will any facilities be shut down while you're there?
- What programs are available for kids? Are kids allowed as guests? (Many B&Bs will not allow children to stay on premises.)
- What is the cancellation policy?

---

② **FAST FACTS: For the International Traveler**

Automobile Organizations Auto clubs will supply maps, suggested routes, guidebooks, accident and bail-bond insurance, and emergency road service. The **American Automobile Association (AAA)** is the major auto club in the United States. If you belong to an auto club in your home country, inquire about AAA reciprocity before you leave. You may be able to join AAA even if you're not a member of a reciprocal club; to inquire, call AAA ((€ **800/222-4357**). AAA is actually an organization of regional auto clubs; so look under "AAA Automobile Club" in the White Pages of the telephone directory. AAA has a nationwide emergency road service telephone number ((€ **800/AAA-HELP**).

Business Hours Offices are usually open weekdays from 9am to 5pm. Banks are open weekdays from 9am to 3pm or later and sometimes Saturday mornings. Stores typically open between 9 and 10am and close between 5 and 6pm Monday through Saturday. Stores in shopping complexes or malls tend to stay open late: until about 9pm on weekdays and weekends. Many malls and larger department stores are open on Sundays.

Currency & Currency Exchange See "Entry Requirements" and "Money" under "Getting Started: What You Need to Know Before You Go," above.

Drinking Laws The legal age for purchase and consumption of alcoholic beverages is 21; proof of age is required and often requested at bars, nightclubs, and restaurants, so it's always a good idea to bring ID when you go out. Beer and wine often can be purchased in supermarkets, but liquor laws vary from state to state.

Do not carry open containers of alcohol in your car or any public area that isn't zoned for alcohol consumption. The police can fine you on the spot. And nothing will ruin your trip faster than getting a citation for DUI ("driving under the influence"), so don't even think about driving while intoxicated.

Driver's Licenses Foreign driver's licenses are recognized in most states, but you may want to get an international driver's license written in English.

Electricity Like Canada, the United States uses 110 to 120 volts AC (60 cycles), compared to 220 to 240 volts AC (50 cycles) in most of Europe, Australia, and New Zealand. If your small appliances use 220 to 240 volts, you'll need a 110-volt transformer and a plug adapter with two flat parallel pins to operate them here. Downward converters that change 220 to 240 volts to 110 to 120 volts are difficult to find in the United States, so bring one with you.

Embassies & Consulates All embassies are located in the nation's capital, Washington, D.C. Some consulates are located in major U.S. cities, and most nations have a mission to the United Nations in New York City. If your country isn't listed below, call for directory information in Washington, D.C. ((€ **202/555-1212**), for the number of your national embassy.

The embassy of **Australia** is at 1601 Massachusetts Ave. NW, Washington, DC 20036 ((€ **202/797-3000;** www.austemb.org). There are consulates in New York, Honolulu, Houston, Los Angeles, and San Francisco.

The embassy of **Canada** is at 501 Pennsylvania Ave. NW, Washington, DC 20001 ((€ **202/682-1740;** www.cdnemb-washdc.org). Other Canadian consulates are in Buffalo (NY), Detroit, Los Angeles, New York, and Seattle.

The embassy of **Ireland** is at 2234 Massachusetts Ave. NW, Washington, DC 20008 ((€ **202/462-3939;** www.irelandmb.org/contact.html). Irish consulates are in Boston, Chicago, New York, and San Francisco.

The embassy of **Japan** is at 2520 Massachusetts Ave. NW, Washington, DC 20008 (✆ **202/238-6700;** www.embjapan.org). Japanese consulates are located in Atlanta, Kansas City, San Francisco, and Washington, D.C.

The embassy of **New Zealand** is at 37 Observatory Circle NW, Washington, DC 20008 (✆ 202/328-4800; www.emb.com/nzemb). New Zealand consulates are in Los Angeles, Salt Lake City, San Francisco, and Seattle.

The embassy of the **United Kingdom** is at 3100 Massachusetts Ave. NW, Washington, DC 20008 (✆ **202/462-1340;** www.britainusa.com/consular/embassy). Other British consulates are in Atlanta, Boston, Chicago, Cleveland, Houston, Los Angeles, New York, San Francisco, and Seattle.

Emergencies Call ✆ **911** to report a fire, call the police, or get an ambulance anywhere in the United States. This is a toll-free call. (No coins are required at public telephones.)

If you encounter serious problems, contact the **Traveler's Aid Society International** (✆ **202/546-1127;** www.travelersaid.org) for directions to a local branch. This nationwide, nonprofit, social-service organization geared to helping travelers in difficult straits offers services that might include reuniting families separated while traveling, providing food and/or shelter to people stranded without cash, or even emotional counseling. If you're in trouble, seek them out.

Gasoline (Petrol) Petrol is known as gasoline (or simply "gas") in the United States, and petrol stations are known as both gas stations and service stations. Gasoline costs about half as much here as it does in Europe (about $1.65 per gallon at press time), and taxes are already included in the printed price. One U.S. gallon equals 3.8 liters or .85 Imperial gallons.

Holidays Banks, government offices, post offices, and many stores, restaurants, and museums are closed on the following legal national holidays: January 1 (New Year's Day), the third Monday in January (Martin Luther King, Jr., Day), the third Monday in February (Presidents' Day, Washington's Birthday), the last Monday in May (Memorial Day), July 4 (Independence Day), the first Monday in September (Labor Day), the second Monday in October (Columbus Day), November 11 (Veterans' Day/Armistice Day), the fourth Thursday in November (Thanksgiving Day), and December 25 (Christmas). Also, the Tuesday following the first Monday in November is Election Day and is a federal government holiday in presidential-election years (held every 4 years, and next in 2004).

Legal Aid If you are "pulled over" for a minor infraction (such as speeding), never attempt to pay the fine directly to a police officer; this could be construed as attempted bribery, a much more serious crime. Pay fines by mail, or directly into the hands of the clerk of the court. If accused of a more serious offense, say and do nothing before consulting a lawyer. Here the burden is on the state to prove a person's guilt beyond a reasonable doubt, and everyone has the right to remain silent, whether you are suspected of a crime or actually arrested. If arrested, you can make one telephone call to a party of your choice. Call your embassy or consulate.

Liquor Laws The legal age for purchase and consumption of alcoholic beverages is 21; proof of age is required and often requested at bars, nightclubs, and restaurants, so it's always a good idea to bring ID when you go out. Beer and wine can often be purchased in supermarkets, but liquor laws vary from state to state. Many states don't allow the purchase of liquor on Sundays, or restrict Sunday purchase hours.

Do not carry open containers of alcohol in your car or any public area that isn't zoned for alcohol consumption. The police can, and probably will, fine you on the spot. And nothing will ruin your trip faster than getting a citation for DUI ("driving under the influence"), so don't even think about driving while intoxicated.

Mail If you aren't sure what your address will be in the United States, mail can be sent to you, in your name, c/o General Delivery at the main post office of the city or region where you expect to be. (Call © 800/ 275-8777 for information on the nearest post office.) The addressee must pick up mail in person and must produce proof of identity (driver's license, passport, for example). Most post offices will hold your mail for up to 1 month, and are open Monday through Friday from 8am to 6pm, Saturday from 9am to 3pm.

Generally found at intersections, mailboxes are blue with a red-and-white stripe and carry the inscription u.s. MAIL. If your mail is addressed to a U.S. destination, don't forget to add the five-digit postal code (or ZIP code), after the two-letter abbreviation of the state to which the mail is addressed. This is essential to prompt delivery.

At press time, domestic postage rates are 23¢ for a postcard and 37¢ for a letter. For international mail, a first-class letter of up to one-half ounce costs 80¢ (60¢ to Canada and Mexico); a first-class postcard costs 70¢ (50¢ to Canada and Mexico); and a preprinted postal aerogramme costs 70¢.

Measurements See the chart on the inside front cover of this book for details on converting metric measurements to U.S. equivalents.

Newspapers & Magazines Every American city has its own daily newspaper. *USA Today* and the *Wall Street Journal* are distributed nationally. In many areas you can also buy the *New York Times.* Newsstands are loaded with a plethora of magazines aimed at every special interest. The major weekly news magazines are *Time, Newsweek,* and *U.S. News & World Report.*

Shopping Many foreign visitors find the United States to be a bargain basement. The U.S. federal government charges very low duties on imports compared to the rest of the world, so you can get some excellent deals here on imported electronic goods, cameras, and clothing. Of course, it all depends on the value of your home currency versus the dollar, and how much duty you'll have to pay on your purchases when you get home. You'll pay a sales tax, which varies from state to state and is added to the price of items you buy, but the United States has no value-added tax (VAT).

Most computers and other electronic equipment sold here use only 110- to 120-volt, 60-cycle electricity. You will need a transformer to use them at home if your power is 220 to 240 volts, 50 cycles. Be sure to ask the salesperson if an item has a universal power adapter.

The major department store chains are Sears, Macy's, Saks Fifth Avenue, and JCPenney. You'll also find Burdines, Dillard's, and Nordstrom in many locales. You get real deals in department stores only during sales, when selected merchandise is marked down 25% or more. The Marshall's and TJ Maxx chains carry name-brand clothing at department-store sale prices, but their stock tends to vary greatly.

Another source is outlet malls in which manufacturers operate their own shops, selling directly to the consumer. Sometimes you can get very good buys at the outlets, especially when sales are going on. Most lingerie and china outlets have good prices when compared to department stores, but that's not necessarily the case with designer clothing. In addition, some manufacturers produce items of lesser quality so they can charge less at their outlets, so inspect all merchandise carefully. The main advantage to outlet malls is that if you are looking for a specific brand—Levi's jeans, for example—the company's outlet will have it.

You'll find national chain stores, department stores, and outlet malls throughout the United States. Look in the White Pages of the local telephone directory for their addresses and phone numbers.

Smoking The United States has more restrictions on smoking than any other country. Federal and state laws prohibit tobacco products from being sold to anyone under 18 years old, and tobacco vendors are required by federal law to request a photo identification of any customer who appears to be under the age of 27. Other rules vary from state to state and city to city, but smoking is absolutely prohibited on all airplanes, trains, and buses, and in most public and private buildings. Nonsmoking hotel rooms and seating sections in most restaurants and bars now far outnumber those in which you can light up. If you smoke, ask for a smoking room when you make your hotel reservations.

Taxes In the United States there is no value-added tax (VAT) or other indirect tax at the national level. Every state, county, and city has the right to levy its own local tax on all purchases, including hotel and restaurant bills, airline tickets, and so on.

Telephone, Telegraph & Fax The telephone system in the United States is run by private corporations, so rates, especially for long-distance service and operator-assisted calls, can vary widely. Generally, hotel surcharges on long-distance and local calls are astronomical, so you're almost always better off using a **public pay telephone,** which you'll find clearly marked in most public buildings and private establishments as well as on the street. Convenience grocery stores and gas stations always have them. Many convenience groceries and packing services sell **prepaid calling cards** in denominations up to $50; they can be the least expensive way to call home. Many public phones at airports now accept American Express, MasterCard, and Visa credit cards. **Local calls** made from public pay phones in most locales cost 25¢ or 35¢. Pay phones do not accept pennies, and few take anything larger than a quarter.

Most long-distance and international calls can be dialed directly from any phone. **For calls within the United States and to Canada,** dial 1 followed by the area code and the seven-digit number. **For other**

international calls, dial 011 followed by the country code, city code, and the telephone number of the person you are calling.

Calls to area codes **800, 888, 877,** and now **866** and **855** are toll free. However, calls to numbers in area codes **700** and **900** (chat lines, bulletin boards, "dating" services, and so on) can be very expensive—usually a charge of 95¢ to $3 or more per minute, and they sometimes have minimum charges that can run as high as $15 or more.

For **reversed-charge** or **collect calls,** and for **person-to-person** calls, dial 0 (zero, not the letter O) followed by the area code and number you want; an operator then comes on the line, and you should specify that you are calling collect, or person-to-person, or both. If your operator-assisted call is international, ask for the overseas operator.

For **local directory assistance** ("information"), dial 🌀 **411;** for long-distance information, dial 1, and then the appropriate area code and 555-1212.

Telegraph services are provided primarily by **Western Union.** You can bring your telegram into the nearest Western Union office (there are hundreds across the country) or dictate it over the phone (🌀 **800/325-6000**). You can also telegraph money, or have it telegraphed to you, very quickly over the Western Union system, but this service can cost as much as 15% to 20% of the amount sent.

Most hotels have **fax machines** available for guest use (be sure to ask about the charge to use one), and many hotel rooms are even wired for guests' fax machines. A less expensive way to send and receive faxes may be at stores such as **Mail Boxes Etc.,** a national chain of packing service shops (look in the Yellow Pages directory under "Packing Services").

There are two kinds of telephone directories in the United States. The so-called **White Pages** list private households and business subscribers in alphabetical order. The inside front cover of the directory lists emergency numbers for police, fire, ambulance, the Coast Guard, poison-control center, crime-victims' hot line, and so on. The first few pages tell you how to make long-distance and international calls, complete with country codes and area codes. Government numbers are usually printed on blue paper within the White Pages. Printed on yellow paper, the so-called **Yellow Pages** list all local services, businesses, industries, and houses of worship according to activity with an index at the front or back. (Drugstores/pharmacies and restaurants are also listed by geographic location.) The Yellow Pages also include city plans or detailed area maps, postal ZIP codes, and public transportation routes.

Time The continental United States is divided into four time zones: Eastern Standard Time (EST), Central Standard Time (CST), Mountain Standard Time (MST), and Pacific Standard Time (PST). Alaska and Hawaii have their own zones. For example, noon in New York City (EST) is 11am in Chicago (CST), 10am in Denver (MST), 9am in Los Angeles (PST), 8am in Anchorage (AST), and 7am in Honolulu (HST).

Daylight saving time is in effect from 1am on the first Sunday in April through 1am the last Sunday in October, except in Arizona, Hawaii, part of Indiana, and Puerto Rico. Daylight saving time moves the clock 1 hour ahead of standard time.

Tipping Tipping is so ingrained in the American way of life that the annual income tax of tip-earning service personnel is based on how much they should have received in light of their employers' gross revenues. Accordingly, they may have to pay tax on a tip you didn't actually give them.

Here are some rules of thumb:

In hotels, tip **bellhops** at least $1 per bag ($2–$3 per bag if you have a lot of luggage) and tip the **chamber staff** $1 to $2 per day (more if you've left a disaster area for him or her to clean up, or if you're traveling with kids and/or pets). Tip the **doorman** or **concierge** only if he or she has provided you with some specific service (for example, calling a cab for you or obtaining difficult-to-get theater tickets). Tip the **valet-parking attendant** $1 every time you get your car.

In restaurants, bars, and nightclubs, tip **service staff** 15% to 20% of the check, tip **bartenders** 10% to 15%, tip **checkroom attendants** $1 per garment, and tip **valet-parking attendants** $1 per vehicle. Tip the **doorman** only if he has provided you with some specific service (such as calling a cab for you). Tipping is not expected in cafeterias and fast-food restaurants.

Tip **cab drivers** 15% of the fare.

As for other service personnel, tip **skycaps** at airports at least $1 per bag ($2–$3 per bag if you have a lot of luggage) and tip **hairdressers** and **barbers** 15% to 20%.

Tipping ushers at movies and theaters, and gas-station attendants, is not expected.

Toilets You won't find public toilets or "restrooms" on the streets in most U.S. cities, but they can be found in hotel lobbies, bars, restaurants, museums, department stores, railway and bus stations, and service stations. Large hotels and fast-food restaurants are probably the best bet for good, clean facilities. If possible, avoid the toilets at parks and beaches, which tend to be dirty; some may be unsafe. Restaurants and bars in resorts or heavily visited areas may reserve their restrooms for patrons. Some establishments display a notice indicating this. You can ignore this sign or, better yet, avoid arguments by paying for a cup of coffee or a soft drink, which will qualify you as a patron.

New York City & Upstate New York

New York remains the nerve center of world finance and trade; the international hub of advertising, publishing, entertainment, and fashion; and the creative core for the arts. Just about every language and any dialect is spoken here, from Mandarin to Brooklynese, and no other dot on the map is quite so ethnically, culturally, socially, and economically diverse.

Despite its overwhelming diversity, the city's sense of community is strong. In fact, it's stronger than ever before. Yes—despite the devastating terrorist attack of September 11, 2001, New York is still a marvelous place to visit.

After the planes hit, we were devastated. The destruction of the World Trade Center left an empty hole in the skyline, and an irrevocable gash in the hearts of New Yorkers. But the city managed to start moving again within a week of the event—believing that we must forge ahead, even with tears in our eyes.

Now the city is back in full swing, and its spirit is robust. We have not forgotten; we will never forget, but we know we must move onward.

1 Essentials

GETTING THERE

BY PLANE   Three major airports serve New York City: **John F. Kennedy International Airport** (© 718/244-4444) in Queens, about 15 miles (1 hr. driving time) from Midtown Manhattan; **LaGuardia Airport** (© 718/533-3400), also in Queens, about 8 miles (30 min.) from Midtown; and **Newark International Airport** (© 973/961-6000) in nearby New Jersey, about 16 miles (45 min.) from Midtown. Information about all three is available online at www.panynj.gov; click on the "Airports" tab on the left.

Taxis are available at stands outside the terminals, with dispatchers on hand during peak hours at JFK and LaGuardia, around the clock at Newark. To Manhattan from JFK, you'll pay a flat rate of $30; expect to pay a metered rate of $20 to $25 from LaGuardia, $40 to $45 from Newark. Fares, whether fixed or metered, do not include bridge and tunnel tolls ($3.50–$4) or a tip for the cabbie (15%–20% is customary). Taxis have a limit of four passengers.

Buses and **shuttle services** provide a comfortable, less expensive (but usually more time-consuming) option for airport transfers than taxis and car services.

Gray Line Air Shuttle and **SuperShuttle** serve all three airports; **New York Airport Service** serves JFK and LaGuardia; **Olympia Trails** serves Newark. These services are our favorite option for getting to and from Newark during peak travel times because the drivers take local streets that end up getting you there faster than a taxi.

Gray Line Express Shuttle USA (© **800/451-0455** or 212/315-3006; www.graylinenewyork.com) vans depart JFK, LaGuardia, and Newark every 20 to 30 minutes between 7am and 11:30pm. No reservation is required; just go to the ground-transportation desk or dial **24** on the Gray Line courtesy phone in the baggage-claim area. Service from mid-Manhattan to all three airports operates daily from 5am to 9pm; you must call a day in advance to arrange a hotel pickup. The regular one-way fare to and from JFK is $19, to and from LaGuardia is $16, and to and from Newark is $19, but you can save a few bucks by prepaying your round-trip at the airport ($28 for JFK and Newark, $26 for LaGuardia).

The blue vans of **SuperShuttle** (② **800/BLUE-VAN** or 212/258-3826; www.supershuttle.com) serve all three area airports, providing door-to-door service to Manhattan and points on Long Island every 15 to 30 minutes around the clock. You don't need to reserve your airport-to-Manhattan ride; just go to the ground-transportation desk or use the courtesy phone in baggage claim and ask for SuperShuttle. Fares run from $13 to $22 per person, depending on the airport, with discounts available for additional persons in the same party.

New York Airport Service (② **718/875-8200;** www.nyairportservice.com) buses travel from JFK and LaGuardia to the Port Authority Bus Terminal (42nd St. and Eighth Ave.), Grand Central Terminal (Park Ave. between 41st and 42nd sts.), and to select Midtown hotels between 27th and 59th streets, plus the Jamaica LIRR Station in Queens, where you can pick up a train for Long Island. Buses depart the airport every 20 to 70 minutes between 6am and midnight. Buses to JFK and LaGuardia depart the Port Authority and Grand Central Terminal on the Park Avenue side every 15 to 30 minutes, depending on the time of day and the day of the week. One-way fare for JFK is $13, round-trip $23; one-way fare for LaGuardia is $10, round-trip $17.

BY TRAIN   Amtrak (② **800/USA-RAIL;** www.amtrak.com) runs frequent service to New York City's **Penn Station,** on Seventh Avenue between 31st and 33rd streets. If you're traveling along Amtrak's Northeast Corridor—to or from Boston, Philadelphia, Baltimore, or Washington, D.C.—Amtrak may be your best travel bet. The **Acela Express** trains cut travel time from D.C. down to 2½ hours, and travel time from Boston to a lightning-quick 3 hours.

BY BUS   Buses arrive at the **Port Authority Terminal** (② **212/564-8484;** www.ny.com/transportation/port_authority.html), on Eighth Avenue between 40th and 42nd streets. The fares up and down the East Coast are usually cheaper than the train, and if you get an express bus, they don't take much longer.

VISITOR INFORMATION

For information before you leave home, your best source is **NYC & Company,** the organization that fronts the New York Convention & Visitors Bureau (NYCVB), 810 Seventh Ave., New York, NY 10019. You can call ② **800/NYC-VISIT** or 212/397-8222 to order the **Official NYC Visitor Kit,** which contains the *Official NYC Guide* detailing hotels, restaurants, theaters, attractions, events, and more; a foldout map; a decent newsletter on the latest goings-on in the city; and brochures on attractions and services. It costs $5.95 to receive the packet (payable by credit card) in 7 to 10 days, $9.95 for rush delivery (3–4 business days) to U.S. addresses and international orders. (*Note:* We have received complaints that packages don't always strictly adhere to these time frames.)

You can also find a wealth of free information on the bureau's website, **www.nycvisit.com**. To speak with a travel counselor who can answer specific questions, call ② **212/484-1222,** staffed on weekdays from 8:30am to 6pm EST, weekends from 9am to 5pm EST.

GETTING AROUND

For the most part, you can get where you're going in Manhattan pretty quickly and easily using some combination of subways, buses, and cabs; this section will tell you how to do just that. But between traffic gridlock and subway delays, sometimes you just can't get there from here—unless you walk. During rush hours, you'll easily beat car traffic on foot. You'll also just see a whole lot more by walking than you will if you ride beneath the street in the subway or fly by in a cab. So pack your most comfortable shoes and hit the pavement—it's the best, cheapest, and most appealing way to experience the city.

BY SUBWAY   Run by the **Metropolitan Transit Authority (MTA),** the much-maligned subway system is actually the fastest way to travel around New York, especially during rush hours. The subway is quick, inexpensive, relatively safe, and pretty efficient, as well as being a genuine New York experience.

The subway runs 24 hours a day, 7 days a week. The rush-hour crushes are roughly from 8 to 9:30am and from 5 to 6:30pm on weekdays; the rest of the time the trains are relatively uncrowded.

By Bus   Less expensive than taxis and more pleasant than subways (they provide a mobile sightseeing window on Manhattan), MTA buses are a good transportation option. Their very big drawback: They can get stuck in traffic, sometimes making it quicker to walk. For long distances, the subway is your best bet; but for short distances or traveling crosstown, try the bus.

Paying Your Way   The subway fare is $1.50 (half price for seniors and those with disabilities), and children under 44 inches tall ride free (up to three per adult). *Note:* As of this writing, a fare increase was being discussed, so it's entirely possible that the fare will be higher by the time you visit.

While **tokens** still exist, most people pay with the **MetroCard,** a magnetically encoded card that debits the fare when swiped through the turnstile (or fare box). Once you're in the system, you can transfer freely to any subway line that you can reach without exiting your station. MetroCards—not tokens—also allow you **free transfers** between the bus and subway within a 2-hour period.

MetroCards can be purchased from each station's token booth, where you can only pay with cash; at the ATM-style vending machines now located in just about every subway station in the city, which accept cash, credit cards, and debit cards; from a MetroCard merchant, such as most Rite Aid drugstores or Hudson News at Penn Station and Grand Central Terminal; or at the MTA information desk at the Times Square Visitor Center, 1560 Broadway, between 46th and 47th streets.

MetroCards come in a few different configurations:

Pay-Per-Ride MetroCards can be used for up to four people by swiping up to four times (bring the whole family). You can put any amount from $3 (two rides) to $80 on your card. Every time you put $15 on your Pay-Per-Ride MetroCard, it's automatically credited 10%—that's one free ride for every $15. You can buy Pay-Per-Ride MetroCards in any denomination at any subway station; an increasing number of stations now have automated MetroCard vending machines, which allow you to buy MetroCards using your major credit card. MetroCards are also available from shops and newsstands around town in $15 and $30 values.

Unlimited-Ride MetroCards can't be used for more than one person at a time or more frequently than 18-minute intervals. They are available in four values: the **daily Fun Pass,** which allows you a day's worth of unlimited subway

> ### ✐ Subway Service Interruption Notes
>
> Due to ongoing work by the Metropolitan Transit Authority (MTA) on the Manhattan Bridge into 2004, and the World Trade Center disaster, subway service will experience numerous interruptions during the life of this book.
>
> Train interruptions resulting from the **World Trade Center disaster** had largely been rectified by this writing. Service interruptions are almost exclusively limited to the nos. 1 and 9 lines, which run local along the west side of Manhattan to the southern tip of the island. At press time, nos. 1 and 2 trains were running local to Chambers Street, where they veered to Brooklyn; no. 3 trains run express from 14th Street north; and no. 9 service was suspended.
>
> Contact the **Metropolitan Transit Authority (MTA)** for the latest details; call ✆ **718/330-1234,** or visit **www.mta.nyc.ny.us,** where you'll find system updates that are thorough, timely, and clear.

and bus rides for $4; the **7-Day MetroCard,** for $17; and the **30-Day Metro-Card,** for $63. Seven- and 30-day Unlimited-Ride MetroCards can be purchased at any subway station or a MetroCard merchant. Fun Passes, however, cannot be purchased at token booths—you can only buy them at a MetroCard vending machine; from a MetroCard merchant; at the MTA information desk at the Times Square Visitor Center; or from **www.metrocard.citysearch.com.** Unlimited-Ride MetroCards go into effect not at the time you buy them but the first time you use them—so if you buy a card on Monday and don't begin to use it until Wednesday, Wednesday is when the clock starts ticking on your Metro-Card. A Fun Pass is good from the first time you use it until 3am the next day, while 7- and 30-day MetroCards run out at midnight on the last day. These MetroCards cannot be refilled; throw them out once they've been used up and buy a new one.

For any MetroCard questions, call ✆ **800/METROCARD** or 212/METRO-CARD (212/638-7622) Monday through Friday from 7am to 11pm, weekends from 9am to 5pm. Or go online to **www.mta.nyc.ny.us/metrocard,** which can give you a full rundown of MetroCard merchants in the tristate area.

BY TAXI   If you don't want to deal with public transportation, then take a taxi. The biggest advantages are, of course, that cabs can be hailed on any street (providing you find an empty one—often simple, yet at other times nearly impossible) and will take you right to your destination. We find they're best used at night when there's little traffic to keep them from speeding you to your destination and when the subway may seem a little daunting.

Official New York City taxis, licensed by the Taxi and Limousine Commission (TLC), are yellow, with the rates printed on the door and a light with a medallion number on the roof. You can hail a taxi on any street. *Never* accept a ride from any other car except an official city yellow cab (private livery cars are not allowed to pick up fares on the street). The base fare on entering the cab is $2. The cost is 30¢ for every one-fifth mile or 20¢ per minute in stopped or slow-moving traffic (or for waiting time). You must pay bridge or tunnel tolls.

You'll also pay a 50¢ night surcharge after 8pm and before 6am. A 15% to 20% tip is customary.

Always make sure the meter is turned on at the start of the ride. You'll see the red LED readout register the initial $2 and start calculating the fare as you go. I've witnessed unscrupulous drivers buzzing unsuspecting visitors around the city with the meter off, and then overcharging them at drop-off time.

For driver complaints and lost property, call the 24-hour Consumer Hotline at ℂ **212/NYC-TAXI.** For further taxi information point your browser to www.ci.nyc.ny.us/taxi.

BY CAR   It's not worth the headache. Traffic is horrendous, and you don't know the rules of the road or the arcane alternate-side-of-the-street parking regulations. If you do arrive in New York City by car, park it in a garage (expect to pay at least $25–$45 per day) and leave it there for the duration of your stay.

FAST FACTS

Doctor referrals are available at ℂ **212/737-2333.** Walk-in service for non-emergency illnesses is available from **DOCS at New York Healthcare,** 55 E. 34th St., between Park and Madison avenues (ℂ **212/252-6001;** subway: 6 to 33rd St.). Hospitals with emergency rooms include **Beth Israel Medical Center,** First Avenue and 16th St. (ℂ **212/420-2000;** subway: L to First Ave.); **New York University Medical Center,** 560 First Ave., at 33rd Street (ℂ **212/ 263-7300;** subway: 6 to 33rd St.); and many others. There are several 24-hour pharmacies, including **Duane Reade** at Broadway and 57th Street (ℂ **212/ 541-9708;** subway: A, B, C, D, 1, 9 to 59th St./Columbus Circle).

Sales tax is 8.24% on meals, some services, and all goods except for clothing and footwear under $110. Hotel tax is 13.25% plus $2 per room per night (excluding sales tax). Parking garage tax is 18.25%.

SPECIAL EVENTS & FESTIVALS

For a complete New York City events schedule, point your browser to **www.nycvisit.com** and click on "Calendar of Events." Here are some favorites:

More than 150,000 marchers participate in the **St. Patrick's Day Parade** March 17, as Fifth Avenue from 44th to 86th streets rings with the sounds of bands and bagpipes. The parade usually starts at 11am, but go extra early if you want a good spot. The **Easter Parade** isn't a traditional parade, per se: It's more about flamboyant exhibitionism, with hats and costumes that get more outrageous every year—and anybody can join right in for free. The parade generally runs along Fifth Avenue on Easter Sunday from about 10am to 3 or 4pm.

The U.S. Open Tennis Championships are held at the Arthur Ashe Stadium at the USTA National Tennis Center, the largest public tennis center in the world, at **Flushing Meadows Park** in Queens around Labor Day.

The Greenwich Village Halloween Parade is Halloween at its most outrageous. It's on October 31, of course. The **New York City Marathon** features some 30,000 hopefuls from around the world; more than a million fans will cheer them on as they follow a route that touches on all five New York boroughs and finishes at Central Park.

Macy's Thanksgiving Day Parade that proceeds from Central Park West and 77th Street and down Broadway to Herald Square at 34th Street continues to be a national tradition. The night before, you can usually see the big blow-up on Central Park West at 79th Street. On **New Year's Eve,** the biggest party of them all happens in **Times Square,** where thousands of raucous revelers count down in unison the year's final seconds until the new lighted ball drops at midnight.

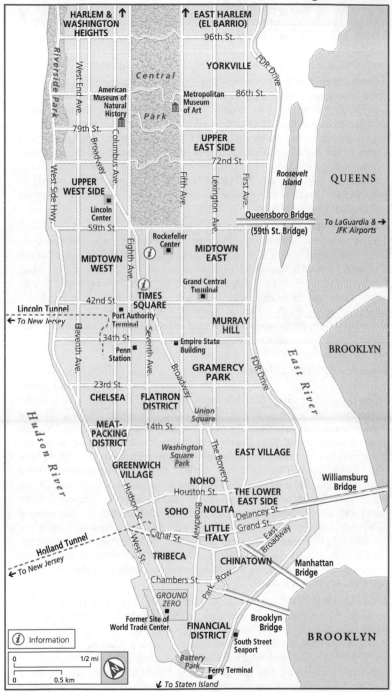

Manhattan Neighborhoods

HARLEM & WASHINGTON HEIGHTS

EAST HARLEM (EL BARRIO)

96th St.

YORKVILLE

Riverside Park

West End Ave.

Central Park

American Museum of Natural History

Metropolitan Museum of Art

86th St.

79th St.

Columbus Ave.

Broadway

UPPER EAST SIDE

72nd St.

West Side Hwy.

UPPER WEST SIDE

Lincoln Center

59th St.

Roosevelt Island

QUEENS

Fifth Ave.

Lexington Ave.

First Ave.

FDR Drive

Queensboro Bridge
(59th St. Bridge)

To LaGuardia & JFK Airports

Rockefeller Center

MIDTOWN EAST

Eighth Ave.

MIDTOWN WEST

TIMES SQUARE

Grand Central Terminal

42nd St.

Port Authority Terminal

MURRAY HILL

Lincoln Tunnel
← To New Jersey

Eleventh Ave.

34th St.

Penn Station

Empire State Building

Seventh Ave.

Broadway

GRAMERCY PARK

FDR Drive

East River

BROOKLYN

23rd St.

CHELSEA

FLATIRON DISTRICT

Union Square

MEAT-PACKING DISTRICT

14th St.

Washington Square Park

EAST VILLAGE

Hudson River

GREENWICH VILLAGE

The Bowery

NOHO

Houston St.

THE LOWER EAST SIDE

Williamsburg Bridge

Hudson St.

SOHO

Broadway

NOLITA

Delancey St.

Grand St.

Holland Tunnel
← To New Jersey

Canal St.

LITTLE ITALY

East Broadway

West St.

TRIBECA

CHINATOWN

Manhattan Bridge

Chambers St.

Park Row

GROUND ZERO

Former Site of World Trade Center

Brooklyn Bridge

FINANCIAL DISTRICT

South Street Seaport

BROOKLYN

(i) Information

Battery Park

Ferry Terminal

↓ To Staten Island

0   1/2 mi
0   0.5 km

N

2 What to See & Do

SOME TOP ATTRACTIONS

In addition to the choices below, don't forget about **Central Park,** the great green swath that is, just by virtue of its existence, New York City's greatest marvel.

American Folk Art Museum   New Yorkers can't stop raving about the brand-new home of the American Folk Art Museum. (The original home near Lincoln Center remains open, as well). The modified open-plan interior features an extraordinary collection of traditional works from the 18th century to the self-taught artists and craftspeople of the present, reflecting the breadth and vitality of the American folk-art tradition. A splendid variety of quilts, in particular, makes the textiles collection the museum's most popular. 45 W. 53rd St. (between Fifth and Sixth aves.). (C) 212/265-1040. www.folkartmuseum.org. Admission $9 adults, $5 seniors and students, free for children under 12, free to all Fri 6–8pm. Tues–Thurs and Sat–Sun 10am–6pm; Fri 10am–8pm.

American Museum of the Moving Image   Head here if you love movies. This is a thought-provoking museum examining how moving images—film, video, and digital—are made, marketed, and shown. It's housed in part of the Kaufman Astoria Studios, which once were host to W. C. Fields and the Marx Brothers, and more recently have been used by Martin Scorsese and *Sesame Street.* There are more than 1,000 artifacts on hand, as well as interactive exhibits. 35th Ave. at 36th St., Astoria, Queens. (C) 718/784-0077 or 718/784-4777. www. ammi.org. Admission $8.50 adults, $5.50 seniors and college students, $4.50 children 5–18. Tues–Fri noon–5pm; Sat–Sun 11am–6pm (evening screenings Sat–Sun at 6:30pm). Subway: R to Steinway St.; N to Broadway.

American Museum of Natural History   This is one of the hottest museum tickets in town, thanks to the $210-million **Rose Center for Earth and Space,** whose planetarium sphere hosts the Space Show, "Are We Alone?" The diversity of the museum's holdings is astounding: some 36 million specimens ranging from microscopic organisms to the world's largest cut gem, the Brazilian Princess Topaz (21,005 carats). Rose Center aside, it would take you all day to see the entire museum, and then you *still* wouldn't get to everything. If you don't have a lot of time, you can see the best of the best on free **highlights tours** offered daily every hour at 15 minutes after the hour from 10:15am to 3:15pm. If you only see one exhibit, see the **dinosaurs,** which take up the entire fourth floor. Central Park West (between 77th and 81st sts.). (C) 212/769-5100 for information, or 212/769-5200 for tickets (tickets can also be ordered online). www.amnh.org. Suggested admission $10 adults, $7.50 seniors and students, $6 children 2–12. Space Show and museum admission $19 adults, $14 seniors and students, $12 children under 12. Additional charges for IMAX movies and some special exhibitions. Daily 10am–5:45pm; Rose Center open Fri to 8:45pm. Subway: B, C to 81st St.; 1, 9 to 79th St.

Bronx Zoo Wildlife Conservation Park   Founded in 1899, the Bronx Zoo is the largest metropolitan animal park in the United States, with more than 4,000 animals living on 265 acres. The **Children's Zoo** (open Apr–Oct) allows young humans to learn about their wildlife counterparts. **Getting there:** Liberty Lines' BxM11 express bus, which makes various stops on Madison Avenue, will take you directly to the zoo; call (C) 718/652-8400. By subway, take the no. 2 train to Pelham Parkway and then walk west to the Bronxdale entrance. Fordham Rd. and Bronx River Pkwy., the Bronx. (C) 718/367-1010. www.wcs.org/zoos. Admission $9 adults, $5 seniors and children 2–12; discounted admission Nov–Mar; free Wed year-round. There

Money- & Time-Saving Tip

CityPass may be New York's best sightseeing deal. Pay one price ($38, or $31 for kids 12–17) for admission to seven Big Apple attractions: The American Museum of Natural History (does not include Space Show); the Guggenheim Museum; the Empire State Building; the *Intrepid* Sea-Air-Space Museum; the Whitney Museum of American Art; MoMA QNS; and a 2-hour Circle Line harbor cruise. If you purchased admission ticket by ticket, you'd spend more than twice as much.

More important, CityPass is not a coupon book. It contains actual admission tickets, so you can bypass lengthy ticket lines. This can literally save you hours of time wasting, because popular sights such as the Empire State Building often have ticket lines of an hour or more.

CityPass is good for 9 days from the first time you use it. It's sold at all participating attractions and online at **www.citypass.net**. For more information call CityPass at *C* **707/256-0490** (CityPass is not sold over the phone). Pricing and attractions are confirmed through March 2003; call or check the website if your visit falls later in the year.

may be nominal additional charges for some exhibits. Nov–Mar daily 10am–4:30pm (extended hours for Holiday Lights late Nov to early Jan); Apr–Oct Mon–Fri 10am–5pm, Sat–Sun 10am–5:30pm. Transportation: See "Getting There," earlier in this chapter.

Brooklyn Bridge Its Gothic-inspired stone pylons and intricate steel-cable webs have moved poets like Walt Whitman and Hart Crane to sing the praises of this great span, completed in 1883. Walking the Brooklyn Bridge is one of our all-time favorite New York activities, although there's no doubt that the Lower Manhattan views from the bridge now have a painful resonance as well as a joyous spirit. A wide wood-plank pedestrian walkway is elevated above the traffic, making it a relatively peaceful, and popular, walk.

For Manhattan skyline views, take an A or C train to High Street, one stop into Brooklyn. From there, you'll be on the bridge in no time: Come above-ground, then walk through the little park to Cadman Plaza East and head downslope (left) to the stairwell that will take you up to the footpath. (Following Prospect Place under the bridge, then turning right onto Cadman Plaza E., will also take you directly to the stairwell.) It's a 20- to 40-minute stroll over the bridge to Manhattan. Subway: A, C to High St.; 4, 5, 6 to Brooklyn Bridge–City Hall.

Cathedral of St. John the Divine The world's largest Gothic cathedral has been a work in progress since 1892. Its sheer size is amazing enough—a nave that stretches two football fields and a seating capacity of 5,000—but keep in mind that there is no steel structural support. The church is being built using traditional Gothic engineering; blocks of granite and limestone are carved out by master masons and their apprentices. You can explore the cathedral on your own, or on the **Public Tour,** offered 6 days a week. 1047 Amsterdam Ave. (at 112th St.). *C* **212/316-7540**, 212/932-7347 for tour information and reservations, 212/662-2133 for event information and tickets. www.stjohndivine.org. Suggested admission $2; tour $3; vertical tour $10. Mon–Sat 7am–6pm; Sun 7am–8pm. Tours offered Tues–Sat 11am; Sun 1pm. Worship services Mon–Sat 8 and 8:30am (morning prayer and Holy Eucharist), 12:15pm, and 5:30pm (1st Thurs service 7:15am); Sun 8, 9, and 11am and 6pm. AIDS memorial service 4th Sat of the month at 1pm. Subway: B, C, 1, 9 to Cathedral Pkwy.

Center for Jewish History This 125,000-square-foot complex is the largest repository of Jewish history, art, and literature in the Diaspora. The collection includes 100 million archival documents, 500,000 books, and tens of thousands of objects of art and ephemera, ranging from Thomas Jefferson's letter denouncing anti-Semitism to memorabilia of famous Jewish athletes. The main gallery space is the Yeshiva Museum, which comprises four galleries, an outdoor sculpture garden, and a children's workshop; a range of exhibits also showcase various holdings belonging to the other institutions as well. 15 W. 16th St. (between Fifth and Sixth aves.). ⓒ 212/294-8301. www.cjh.org. Admission to Yeshiva University Museum $6 adults, $4 seniors and students; free admission to all other facilities. Yeshiva University Museum Sun and Tues–Wed 11am–5pm; Thurs 11am–8pm. Reading Room and Genealogy Institute Mon–Thurs 9:30am–4:30pm; Fri by appt. All other exhibition galleries Mon–Thurs 9am–5pm; Fri 9am–4pm. Subway: L, N, R, 4, 5, 6 to 14th St./Union Sq.; F, V to 14th St.

Chrysler Building This is perhaps the 20th century's most romantic architectural achievement, especially at night, when the lights in its triangular openings play off its steely crown. As you admire its facade, be sure to note the gargoyles reaching out from the upper floors, looking for all the world like streamline Gothic hood ornaments. The lobby ceiling mural depicting airplanes and other early marvels of the first decades of the 20th century evince the promise of technology. The elevators are works of art, masterfully covered in exotic woods (especially note the lotus-shaped marquetry on the doors). 405 Lexington Ave. (at 42nd St.). Subway: S, 4, 5, 6, 7 to 42nd St./Grand Central.

The Cloisters This remote, lovely spot is devoted to the art and architecture of medieval Europe. Atop a cliff overlooking the Hudson River, you'll find a 12th-century chapter house, parts of five cloisters from medieval monasteries, a Romanesque chapel, and a 12th-century Spanish apse brought intact from Europe. Surrounded by peaceful gardens, this is the one place on the island that can even approximate the kind of solitude suitable to such a collection. Inside you'll find extraordinary works that include the famed unicorn tapestries, sculpture, illuminated manuscripts, stained glass, ivory, and precious metal work. At the north end of Fort Tryon Park. ⓒ 212/923-3700. www.metmuseum.org. Suggested admission (includes same-day entrance to the Metropolitan Museum of Art) $10 adults, $5 seniors and students, free for children under 12. Nov–Feb Tues–Sun 9:30am–4:45pm; Mar–Oct Tues–Sun 9:30am–5:15pm. Subway: A to 190th St., then a 10-min. walk north along Margaret Corbin Dr., or pick up the M4 bus at the station (1 stop to Cloisters). Bus: M4 Madison Ave. (Fort Tryon Park–The Cloisters).

Ellis Island Roughly 40% of Americans can trace their heritage back to an ancestor who came through Ellis Island. For the 62 years when it was America's main entry point for immigrants (1892–1954), Ellis Island processed some 12 million people. The **Immigration Museum** relates the story of immigration in America by placing the emphasis on personal experience. Outside, the **American Immigrant Wall of Honor** commemorates more than 500,000 immigrants and their families. *Touring tips:* Ferries run daily to Ellis Island and Liberty Island from Battery Park and Liberty State Park at frequent intervals; see the Statue of Liberty listing (p. 49) for details. In New York Harbor. ⓒ 212/363-3200 (general info), or 212/269-5755 (ticket/ferry info). www.nps.gov/elis or www.ellisisland.org. Free admission (ferry ticket charge). Daily 9:30am–5pm (last ferry departs around 3:30pm). For subway and ferry details, see the Statue of Liberty listing on p. 49 (ferry trip includes stops at both sights).

Empire State Building It took 60,000 tons of steel, 10 million bricks, 2½ million feet of electrical wire, 120 miles of pipe, and seven million man-hours to build. On September 11, 2001, it once again regained its status as New York City's tallest building. And through it all, the Empire State Building has remained one of the city's favorite landmarks, and its signature high-rise. Completed in 1931, the limestone-and-stainless-steel streamline Deco dazzler climbs 102 stories (1,454 ft.) and harbors the offices of fashion firms, and, in its upper reaches, a jumble of broadcast equipment. It glows every night, bathed in colored floodlights to commemorate events of significance—red, white, and blue for Independence Day; green for St. Patrick's Day; red, black, and green for Martin Luther King Day; blue and white for Hanukkah; lavender and white for Gay Pride Day. The familiar silver spire can be seen from all over the city. But the views that keep nearly three million visitors coming every year are the ones from the 86th- and 102nd-floor **observatories.** The lower one is best, the higher observation deck is glass-enclosed and cramped. 350 Fifth Ave. (at 34th St.). (C) **212/ 736-3100.** www.esbnyc.com. Observatory admission $10 adults, $9 seniors and children 12–17, $4 children 6–11, free for children under 5. Mon–Fri 10am–midnight; Sat–Sun 9:30am–midnight; tickets sold until 11:25pm. Subway: B, D, F, N, R, V, Q, W to 34th St.; 6 to 33rd St.

Grand Central Terminal   The 1913 landmark has been reborn as one of the most magnificent public spaces in the country. Its restoration is an utter triumph, putting the "grand" back into Grand Central. The greatest visual impact comes when you enter the vast **main concourse.** The high windows once again allow sunlight to penetrate the space, glinting off the half-acre Tennessee marble floor. The masterful **sky ceiling,** again a brilliant greenish blue, depicts the constellations of the winter sky above New York. They're lit with 59 stars, surrounded by 24-carat gold and emitting light fed through fiber-optic cables, their intensities roughly replicating the magnitude of the actual stars as seen from Earth. The **Municipal Art Society** (C) **212/935-3960;** www.mas.org) offers a free walking tour of Grand Central Terminal on Wednesday at 12:30pm, which meets at the information booth on the Grand Concourse. The **Grand Central Partnership** (C) **212/697-1245)** runs its own free tour every Friday at 12:30pm. Call to confirm before either tour. 42nd St. at Park Ave. (C) **212/340-2210** (events hot line). www.grandcentralterminal.com. Subway: S, 4, 5, 6, 7 to 42nd St./Grand Central.

Metropolitan Museum of Art   Home of blockbuster after blockbuster exhibition, the Metropolitan Museum of Art attracts some five million people a year, more than any other spot in New York City. This is the largest museum in the Western Hemisphere. Nearly all the world's cultures are on display through the ages—from Egyptian mummies to ancient Greek statuary to Islamic carvings to Renaissance paintings to Native American masks to 20th-century decorative arts—and masterpieces are the rule. Unless you plan on spending your entire vacation in the museum, you cannot see the entire collection. Our recommendation is to give it a good day—or better yet, 2 half days so you don't burn out. One good way to get an overview is to take advantage of the **Museum Highlights Tour,** offered every day at various times throughout the day (usually 10:15am–3:15pm). The least overwhelming way to see the Met on your own is to pick up a map at the round desk in the entry hall and choose to concentrate on what you like, whether it's 17th-century paintings, American furniture, or the art of the South Pacific. Don't forget the marvelous **special exhibitions,** which can range from "Orazio and Artemisia Gentileschi: Father and Daughter Painters in Baroque Italy" to "Earthly Bodies: Irving Penn's Nudes, 1949–50." Fifth Ave. at 82nd St. (C) **212/535-7710.** www.metmuseum.org. Admission (includes same-day entrance to the Cloisters) $10 adults, $5 seniors and students, free for children under 12 when accompanied by an adult. Sun and Tues–Thurs 9:30am–5:30pm; Fri–Sat 9:30am–9pm. No strollers allowed Sun (back carriers available at 81st St. entrance coat-check area). Subway: 4, 5, 6 to 86th St.

Museum of Modern Art/MoMA QNS   The Museum of Modern Art (or MoMA, as it's usually called) boasts the world's greatest collection of painting and sculpture from the late 19th century to the present, including everything from Monet's *Water Lilies* to masterworks by Frida Kahlo, Edward Hopper, Andy Warhol, Robert Rauschenberg, and others. Top that off with an extensive collection of drawings, photography, iconic design objects ranging from tableware to sports cars, and film and video, and you have quite a museum. If you're into modernism, this is the place to be. The museum is undergoing a monster $650 million renovation of its West 53rd Street home, which will be closed until 2005. The museum has opened temporary exhibit space called **MoMA QNS** in Long Island City, Queens. The 45,000-square-foot gallery will exhibit highlights of the museum's collection, including van Gogh's *Starry Night,* Picasso's early *Les Demoiselles d'Avignon,* and Warhol's *Gold Marilyn Monroe.* Getting there is quick and easy; in fact, from Midtown, you can be there quicker than you can get to the Village. 45–20 33rd St., Long Island City, Queens. ✆ 212/708-9400. www.moma.org. Admission $12 adults, $8.50 seniors and students, free for children under 16 accompanied by an adult; pay what you wish Fri 4:30–8:15pm. Sat–Tues and Thurs 10:30am–5:45pm; Fri 10:30am–8:15pm. Subway: 7 to 33rd St. (MoMA QNS is across the street).

Neue Gallerie New York   This new museum is dedicated to German and Austrian art and design. The collection features painting, works on paper, decorative arts, and other media from such artists as Klimt, Kokoschka, Kandinsky, Klee, and leaders of the Wiener Werkstätte decorative arts and Bauhaus applied arts movements such as Adolf Loos and Mies van der Rohe, respectively. Once occupied by Mrs. Cornelius Vanderbilt III, the impeccably restored, 1914 Carrèrre & Hastings building is worth a look itself. 1048 Fifth Ave. (at 86th St.). ✆ 212/ 628-6200. www.neuegalerie.org. Admission $10. Fri–Mon 11am–7pm. Subway: 4, 5, 6 to 86th St.

Rockefeller Center   A streamline modern masterpiece, Rockefeller Center is one of New York's central gathering spots for visitors and New Yorkers alike. A prime example of the city's skyscraper spirit and historic sense of optimism, it was erected mainly in the 1930s, when the city was deep in the Depression as well as its most passionate Art Deco phase. The **Rink at Rockefeller Center** (✆ 212/332-7654; www.rockefellercenter.com) is tiny but romantic, especially during the holidays, when the giant Christmas tree's multicolored lights twinkle from above. **Radio City Music Hall,** 1260 Sixth Ave., at 50th Street (✆ 212/247-4777; www.radiocity.com), is perhaps the most impressive architectural feat of the complex. Designed by Donald Deskey and opened in 1932, it's one of the largest indoor theaters, with 6,200 seats. But its true grandeur derives from its magnificent Art Deco appointments. The crowning touch is the stage's great proscenium arch, which evokes a faraway sun setting on the horizon of the sea. The men's and women's lounges are also splendid. The theater hosts the annual **Christmas Spectacular,** starring the Rockettes. The 1-hour **Stage Door Tour** is offered Monday through Saturday from 10am to 5pm, Sunday from 11am to 5pm; tickets are $16 for adults, $10 for children under 12. Between 48th and 50th sts., from Fifth to Sixth aves. ✆ 212/332-6868. www.rockefeller center.com. Subway: B, D, F, V to 47th–50th sts./Rockefeller Center.

Solomon R. Guggenheim Museum   It's been called a bun, a snail, a concrete tornado, and a giant wedding cake. Whatever description you choose to apply, Frank Lloyd Wright's only New York building, completed in 1959, is a brilliant work of architecture. Inside, a spiraling rotunda circles over a slowly inclined ramp that leads you past changing exhibits. Permanent exhibits of 19th- and 20th-century art, including strong holdings of Kandinsky, Klee, Picasso, and French Impressionists, occupy a stark annex called the **Tower Galleries.** 1071 Fifth Ave. (at 88th St.). ✆ 212/423-3500. www.guggenheim.org. Admission $12 adults, $8 seniors and students, free for children under 12; pay what you wish Fri 6–8pm. Sun–Wed 9am– 6pm; Fri–Sat 9am–8pm. Subway: 4, 5, 6 to 86th St.

South Street Seaport & Museum   Dating back to the 17th century, this landmark historic district on the East River encompasses 11 square blocks of historic buildings, a maritime museum, several piers, shops, and restaurants. The mainly 18th- and 19th-century buildings lining the cobbled streets and alleyways are impeccably restored but have a theme-park air about them. The Seaport's biggest tourist attraction is Pier 17, a barge converted into a mall. But there's a good amount of history to be discovered here, most of it around the **South Street Seaport Museum,** a fitting tribute to the sea commerce that once thrived here.

A variety of events take place year-round, ranging from street performers to concerts to fireworks; check the website or dial ✆ **212/SEA-PORT.** At Water and South sts.; museum visitor center is at 12 Fulton St. ✆ **212/748-8600** or 212/SEA-PORT. www.southstseaport.org or www.southstreetseaport.com. Museum admission $6 adults, $5 seniors, $4 students, $3 children. Museum: Apr–Sept Fri–Wed 10am–6pm, Thurs 10am–8pm; Oct–Mar Wed–Mon 10am–5pm. Subway: 2, 3, 4, 5 to Fulton St. (walk east, or downslope, on Fulton St. to Water St.).

Staten Island Ferry   Here's New York's best freebie—especially if you just want to glimpse the Statue of Liberty and not climb her steps. You get an enthralling hour-long excursion (round-trip) into the world's biggest harbor. The old orange-and-green boats usually have open decks along the sides or at the bow and stern. Grab a seat on the right side of the boat for the best view. On the way out of Manhattan, you'll pass the Statue of Liberty, Ellis Island, Governor's Island, and the Verrazano Narrows Bridge. Departs from the Whitehall Ferry Terminal at the southern tip of Manhattan. ✆ 718/815-BOAT. www.ci.nyc.ny.us/html/dot. Free admission ($3 for car transport on select ferries). 24 hr.; every 20–30 min. weekdays, less frequently during off-peak and weekend hr. Subway: N, R to Whitehall St.; 4, 5 to Bowling Green; 1, 9 to South Ferry (ride in the 1st 5 cars).

Statue of Liberty   For the millions who first came by ship to America in the last century, Lady Liberty, standing in the Upper Bay, was their first glimpse of America. The statue was designed by sculptor Frédéric-Auguste Bartholdi and unveiled on October 28, 1886. After nearly 100 years of wind, rain, and

---

Lady Liberty Touring Updates

At press time, **only the grounds of Liberty Island were open to the public,** pending additional security arrangements. Whether and when the pedestal, museum, and/or the body of the statue itself will reopen to the public was unknown at this writing, but the close-up view from the grounds alone is breathtaking enough to make the journey worthwhile.

All policies regarding access to the Statue of Liberty and Ellis Island are subject to change at any time. Call or check the official website (**www.nps.gov/stli**) for the latest access information.

---

exposure to the harsh sea air, Lady Liberty received a resoundingly successful $150-million face-lift in time for her centennial celebration on July 4, 1986.

Touring tips: Ferries leave daily every half hour to 45 minutes from 9am to about 3:30pm (their clock), with more frequent ferries in the morning and extended hours in summer. Try to go early on a weekday to avoid the crowds that swarm in the afternoon, on weekends, and on holidays. You can **buy ferry tickets in advance** via **www.statueoflibertyferry.com**, which will allow you to board the boat without standing in the sometimes-long ticket line; however, there is an additional service charge. On Liberty Island in New York Harbor. ✆ 212/363-3200 (general info), or 212/269-5755 (ticket/ferry info). www.nps.gov/stli or www.statueofliberty ferry.com. Free admission; ferry ticket to Statue of Liberty and Ellis Island $8 adults, $6 seniors, $3 children 3–17. Daily 9am–5pm (last ferry departs around 3:30pm); extended hours in summer. Subway: 4, 5 to Bowling Green; 1, 9 to South Ferry (note that 1, 9 had not resumed service to Lower Manhattan at press time). Walk south through Battery Park to Castle Clinton, the fort housing the ferry ticket booth.

United Nations   The U.N. headquarters occupies 18 acres of international territory—neither the city nor the United States has jurisdiction here—along the East River from 42nd to 48th streets. The complex along the East River weds the 39-story glass-slab Secretariat with the free-form General Assembly on beautifully landscaped grounds. **Guided tours** leave every half hour or so and last 45 minutes to an hour. Your guide will take you to the General Assembly Hall and the Security Council Chamber and introduce the history and activities of the United Nations and its related organizations. Along the tour you'll see donated objects and artwork, including charred artifacts that survived the atomic bombs at Hiroshima and Nagasaki, stained-glass windows by Chagall, a replica of the first *Sputnik,* and a colorful mosaic called *The Golden Rule,* based on a Norman Rockwell drawing, which was a gift from the United States in 1985. At First Ave. and 46th St. ✆ 212/963-8687. www.un.org/tours. Guided tours $8.50 adults, $7 seniors, $6 high school and college students, $5 children 5–14 (children under 5 not permitted). Daily tours every half hour 9:30am–4:45pm; closed weekends Jan–Feb. A limited schedule may be in effect during the general debate (late Sept to mid-Oct). Subway: S, 4, 5, 6, 7 to 42nd St./Grand Central.

World Trade Center Site (Ground Zero)   The World Trade Center dominated lower Manhattan. About 50,000 people worked in its precincts, and some 70,000 others (tourists and businesspeople) visited each day. The vast complex included two 110-story towers—one of which awarded visitors with breathtaking views from the Top of the World observation deck, more than 1,350 feet in the air. Then the first plane hit the north tower, Tower 1, at 8:45am on Tuesday, September 11, 2001. By 10:30am, it was all gone. The former Trade Center is now a vast crater. Clean-up was scheduled to be complete by the end of 2002, but no decisions had yet been finalized as to what would replace it. What will be left to see when you arrive is anybody's guess. At press time, a **temporary viewing platform** was in place at Broadway and Fulton streets, open daily from 9am to 8pm; it is scheduled to remain in place through summer 2002, but its fate thereafter is yet unknown. Bounded by Church, Barclay, Liberty, and West sts. ✆ 212/484-1222. www.nycvisit.com or www.southstseaport.org for viewing information; www.down townny.com for Lower Manhattan area information and rebuilding updates. Subway: C, E to World Trade Center; N, R to Cortlandt St.

ORGANIZED SIGHTSEEING TOURS

Double-decker bus tours are popular ways to get an overview of Manhattan. Among the operators who offer tours narrated by a guide are **Gray Line New**

York Tours (② 800/669-0051 or 212/445-0848; www.graylinenewyork.com), which has hop-on/hop-off privileges on tours day and night, uptown, downtown, and all around the town for about $30 adults, $20 children 5 to 11.

You can see New York Harbor aboard **Bateaux New York** (② 212/352-1366; www.bateauxnewyork.com). They offer evening dinner cruises complete with live music, departing from Pier 61, Chelsea Piers, West 23rd Street and Twelfth Avenue, with 2-hour lunch cruises $46; 3-hour dinner cruises $103 to $117.

The Circle Line (② 212/563-3200; www.circleline.com, www.ridethe beast.com, and www.seaportmusiccruises.com) circumnavigates the entire 35 miles around Manhattan. The panorama is riveting, and the commentary isn't bad. The big boats are basic, with lots of deck room. Snacks, soft drinks, coffee, and beer are available onboard. They depart from Pier 83, at West 42nd Street and Twelfth Avenue, and from Pier 16 at South Street Seaport. Sightseeing cruises range from $13 to $25 adults, $11 to $20 seniors, $7 to $12 children 12 and under.

WALKING TOURS

The **Municipal Art Society** (② 212/439-1049 or 212/935-3960; www.mas. org) offers historical and architectural walking tours aimed at individualistic travelers, not the mass market. Highly qualified guides give insights into the significance of buildings, neighborhoods, and history. Weekday walking tours are $12, weekend tours are $15.

Big Onion Walking Tours (② 212/439-1090; www.bigonion.com) provides informed, enthusiastic guides to peel back the layers of history. The 2-hour tours include the "The Bowery," "Irish New York," and the popular "Multiethnic Eating Tour," where you munch on everything from dim sum and dill pickles to fresh mozzarella. Tour prices range from $12 to $18 for adults, $10 to $16 for students and seniors. No reservations are necessary, but Big Onion *strongly recommends that you call to verify schedules.*

All tours from **Joyce Gold History Tours of New York** (② 212/242-5762; www.nyctours.com) are offered by Gold herself, an instructor of Manhattan history at New York University and the New School for Social Research, who has been conducting history walks around New York since 1975.

Harlem Spirituals (② 800/660-2166 or 212/391-0900; www.harlem spirituals.com) specializes in gospel and jazz tours of Harlem that can be combined with a traditional soul-food meal.

TOP SHOPPING STREETS & NEIGHBORHOODS

DOWNTOWN   Lower Manhattan continues to shine in the discount department. In spring 2002, the king of discount department stores, **Century 21,**

Take Me Out to the Ballgame

The world famous **Yankees** play at Yankee Stadium (subway: C, D, 4 to 161st St./Yankee Stadium). For tickets ($8–$65 in 2002), call **Ticketmaster** (② 212/307-1212 or 212/307-7171; www.ticketmaster.com) or **Yankee Stadium** (② 718/293-6000; www.yankees.com). Bleacher seats ($8) are sold only on the day of the game. The **Mets** play at **Shea Stadium** in Queens (subway: 7 to Willets Point/Shea Stadium). For tickets (which ran $12–$43 for regular-season games in the 2002 season) and information, call the **Mets Ticket Office** at ② 718/507-TIXX, or visit **www.mets.com**.

reopened its doors for the first time since the terrorist attack. In **Chinatown, Canal Street** and **Mott Street,** between Pell Street and Chatham Square, boast the most interesting shopping. The highlight is the **Pearl River** Chinese emporium. On **The Lower East Side,** there's the **Historic Orchard Street Shopping District** where prices on leather bags, shoes, luggage, and fabrics on the bolt are still quite good.

People love to complain about **SoHo**—it's become too trendy, too tony, too Mall of America. But it is still one of the best shopping 'hoods in the city—and few are more fun to browse. It's the epicenter of cutting-edge fashion and boasts plenty of unique boutiques.

Elizabeth Street is the star of the neighborhood known as **Nolita.** Its boutiques are largely the province of sophisticated shopkeepers specializing in high-quality, fashion-forward products and design.

The **East Village** personifies bohemian hip. **East 9th Street** between Second Avenue and Avenue A has become one of our favorite shopping strips. Up-and-coming designers sell excellent-quality and affordably priced original fashions for women here.

Lafayette Street has grown into a full-fledged Antiques Row, especially strong in mid-century furniture. Prices are high, but so is quality. The **West Village** is great for browsing and gift shopping. Specialty book- and record stores, antiques and crafts shops, and gourmet food markets dominate.

MIDTOWN   The **Chelsea** and the **Flatiron Districts** have superstores and off-pricers filling up the renovated spaces.

Herald Square—where 34th Street, Sixth Avenue, and Broadway converge— is dominated by **Macy's.** At Sixth Avenue and 33rd Street is the **Manhattan Mall** (℃ 212/465-0500; www.manhattanmallny.com).

Times Square and the **Theatre District** have become increasingly family oriented with a **Virgin Megastore; Toys "R" Us** has its own Ferris wheel. West 47th Street between Fifth and Sixth avenues is the city's **Diamond District.**

The heart of Manhattan retail is the corner of **Fifth Avenue and 57th Street. Tiffany & Co.** has long reigned supreme here, near **Niketown** and the **NBA Store.** In addition, a good number of mainstream retailers have flagships along Fifth. Still, you will find a number of big-name, big-ticket designers radiating from the crossroads, including **Versace, Chanel, Dior,** and **Cartier.** You'll also find big-name jewelers along here, as well as chi-chi department stores like **Bergdorf Goodman, Henri Bendel,** and **Saks Fifth Avenue.**

UPTOWN   **Madison Avenue** from 57th to 79th streets has usurped Fifth Avenue as *the* tony shopping street in the city. This strip is home to the most luxurious designer boutiques in the world—particularly in the high 60s—with **Barneys New York** as the anchor.

The **Upper West Side's** best shopping street is **Columbus Avenue.** Small shops catering to the neighborhood's mix of young hipsters and families line both sides of the pleasant avenue from 66th Street to about 86th Street. You won't lack for good browsing along here.

Boutiques also dot Amsterdam Avenue, but **Broadway** is most notable for its terrific gourmet edibles at **Zabar's,** 2445 Broadway, at 80th St. (℃ 212/ 496-1234) and **Fairway,** 2127 Broadway, at 74th St. (℃ 212/595-1888) markets.

3 Where to Stay

Below is a selection of hotels in various Manhattan neighborhoods, ranging in price from very expensive ($300 and way up a night), to expensive ($200 and up), to moderate ($125 and up), to inexpensive ($70 and up). We've given you a choice of chain hotels and independent properties, traditional and avant-garde, in neighborhoods from fast-paced to quiet (well, for New York).

The Algonquin   This 1902 hotel is one of the Theater District's best-known landmarks. The past isn't just a memory—a 1998 restoration returned this place to its Arts-and-Crafts splendor. The oak-paneled lobby is made for lingering over afternoon tea or an elegant cocktail. While posher than ever, the small rooms are comfortable but on the cramped side. Extras include stocked candy jars (a nice touch). The bathrooms boast short but deep tubs, terry robes, and an appealing period feel. Twins are the roomiest doubles. For the ultimate New York vibe, opt for one of the surprisingly affordable literary-themed suites. 59 W. 44th St. (between Fifth and Sixth aves.), New York, NY 10036. ℂ 800/555-8000 or 212/840-6800. Fax 212/944-1419. www.algonquinhotel.com. 165 units. $199–$369 double; from $299 suite. Inquire about discounted rates or package deals. AE, DC, DISC, MC, V. Parking $28 across street. Subway: B, D, F, V to 42nd St. **Amenities:** Restaurants (2); fitness room.

The Carlyle   Countless movie stars and heads of states have lain their heads on the pillows in this legendary hotel. With a staff-to-guest ratio of about two-to-one, the service is simply the best. The decor is luxurious but not excessive. Guest rooms range from singles to seven-room suites, some with terraces and dining rooms. All have marble bathrooms with whirlpool tubs and the amenities you'd expect. Some have kitchenettes or full kitchens. 35 E. 76th St. (at Madison Ave.), New York, NY 10021. ℂ 800/227-5737 or 212/744-1600. Fax 212/717-4682. 180 units. $495–$750 double; from $750 1- or 2-bedroom suite. AE, DC, MC, V. Parking $50. Subway: 6 to 77th St. **Amenities:** Restaurants (4); fitness room; pets accepted.

Comfort Inn–Central Park West   This newly renovated hotel is a great place if you can snag a good rate. It's in the Upper West Side's best residential territory, steps from Central Park. Everything is fresh, new, and professionally done. Rooms aren't huge or stylish, but there's no arguing with the quality. Layout is smart; bedding, fabrics, and window treatments are good; and blackout drapes let you sleep until noon if you so choose. Closets are on the small side, but you'll have a new tiled bathroom. Executive rooms are outfitted in a more modern, less chain-standard style, with mahogany built-ins and individual climate controls. An extended continental breakfast is served in the breakfast room (with free newspapers), which helps up the ante on the value. 31 W. 71st St. (between Columbus Ave. and Central Park West), New York, NY 10023. ℂ 800/228-5150 (worldwide reservations), 877/727-5236 (direct), or 212/721-4770. Fax 212/579-8544. www.comfortinn.com or www.best nyhotels.com. 96 units. $119–$209 standard double; $179–$299 executive double. Ask about senior, AAA, corporate, and promotional discounts; check www.hotelchoice.com for deals (as low as $80–$90). Extra person $15. Children 12 and under stay free in parents' room. Rates include continental breakfast. AE, DC, DISC, MC, V. Parking $25 nearby. Subway: B, C to 72nd St. **Amenities:** Fitness room.

Comfort Inn Midtown   Rates can climb in autumn or at Christmas, but low-season rates often make the rooms here one of Midtown's best bargains. The petite but comfortable guest rooms boast neo-Shaker furnishings, blackout drapes, and marble-and-tile bathrooms; a few have showers only, so request a tub if it matters. Rollaways aren't available, so families are better off elsewhere.

New York City Accommodations & Dining

ACCOMMODATIONS ■

The Algonquin **19**
The Carlyle **4**
Comfort Inn-Central Park West **2**
Comfort Inn Midtown **15**
Cosmopolitan Hotel-Tribeca **32**
Excelsior Hotel **2**
Four Seasons Hotel New York **9**
Helmsley Middletowne **14**
Hotel Chelsea **24**
Hotel Metro **21**
The Kimberly **12**
The Marcel **23**
New York City Howard Johnson
  Express Inn **32**
Plaza Hotel **7**
Thirty Thirty **22**
Trump International Hotel
  & Tower **6**
Waldorf-Astoria and the Waldorf
  Towers **13**
Washington Square Hotel **29**

DINING ◆

Alain Ducasse at the Essex House **11**
Aquagrill **27**
Aquavit **10**
Babbo **28**
Bubby's **25**
Chanterelle **25**
Churrascaria Plataforma **18**
Daniel **5**
Florent **25**
Il Cortile **25**
Joe's Shanghai **30**
Katz's Delicatessen **31**
Le Bernardin **16**
Lombardi's **30**
Oyster Bar & Restaurant **20**
Pisces **31**
Serendipity Three **8**
Sylvia's **1**
Siam Inn **17**
Tavern On The Green **3**
Tea & Sympathy **26**

Ⓜ Subway stop

Don't expect much in the way of service, but the location is excellent—steps from Times Square, Rockefeller Center, and Broadway theaters. As of August 2001, the Comfort Inn Midtown is a non-smoking hotel. 129 W. 46th St. (between Sixth Ave. and Broadway), New York, NY 10036. © 800/567-7720 or 212/221-2600. Fax 212/790-2760. www.applecorehotels.com or www.comfortinn.com. 79 units. $89–$329 double. Ask about senior, AAA, corporate, and promotional discounts; check www.comfortinn.com for online booking discounts. Extra person $10. Children under 14 stay free in parents' room. Rates include continental breakfast. AE, DC, DISC, MC, V. Parking $20 nearby. Subway: 1, 2, 3, 9 to 42nd St./Times Sq.; N, R to 49th St.; B, D, F, V to 47th–50th sts./Rockefeller Center. **Amenities:** Fitness room.

Cosmopolitan Hotel–Tribeca   This is one of the best hotel deals in Manhattan for budget travelers who insist on a private bathroom. Everything is strictly budget, but nice. Beds are comfy, and sheets and towels are of good quality. Rooms are small but make the most of the limited space, and the place is pristine. The two-level mini-lofts have lots of character, but expect to duck on the second level. Management does a great job of keeping everything fresh. Services are kept at a bare minimum to keep costs down, so you must be a low-maintenance guest to be happy here. 95 W. Broadway (at Chambers St.), New York, NY 10007. © 888/895-9400 or 212/566-1900. Fax 212/566-6909. www.cosmohotel.com. 113 units. $119–$159 double. AE, DC, MC, V. Parking $20, 1 block away. Subway: 1, 2, 3, 9 to Chambers St.

Excelsior Hotel   Now that renovations are complete, everything at the Excelsior is fresh from the wood-paneled lobby to the comfy guest rooms to the small state-of-the-art exercise room. The chic location is across from the Museum of Natural History and just steps from Central Park. Freshly done in a traditional style, the guest rooms boast high-quality furnishings, two-line phones, bathrobes, a work desk, free bottled water, and full-length mirrors. The two-bedded rooms are large enough to accommodate budget-minded families, and suites feature pullout sofas and pants presses. On the second floor is a library-style lounge with fireplace, books, games, desks, and a flat-screen TV with VCR and DVD player. 45 W. 81st St. (between Columbus Ave. and Central Park West), New York, NY 10024. © 800/368-4575 or 212/362-9200. Fax 212/721-2994. www.excelsiorhotelny.com. 198 units. $179–$279 double; $239–$359 1-bedroom suite, $459–$639 2-bedroom suite. Inquire about seasonal rates and specials (winter rates can go as low as $145; $209 for suites). Extra person $20. Children 12 and under stay free in parents' room. AE, DC, DISC, MC, V. Parking $27 nearby. Subway: B, C to 81st St./Museum of Natural History. **Amenities:** Fitness room.

Four Seasons Hotel New York   Hollywood meets Manhattan in the grand but frosty lobby of this ultraluxury hotel. Designed by I. M. Pei, the tower of honey-hued limestone rises 52 stories, providing hundreds of rooms with a view. The soundproofed guest rooms are among the city's largest, averaging 600 square feet. Each is furnished in an understated but plush style and has an foyer, a sitting area, an oval desk with two leather chairs, coffered ceilings, and massive windows (50% of which boast Central Park views). The marble bathrooms have soaking tubs that fill in 60 seconds, and separate showers with pressure controls. Other special touches include goose-down pillows, Frette-made linens, oversize bath towels, and cushy robes. 57 E. 57th St. (between Park and Madison aves.), New York, NY 10022. © 800/819-5053, 800/487-3769, or 212/758-5700. Fax 212/758-5711. www.fourseasons.com. 368 units. $585–$865 double; from $1,350 suite. Weekend rates from $435; also check for value-added packages and other deals. Extra person $50. AE, DC, DISC, MC, V. Parking $42. Subway: N, R, 4, 5, 6 to 60th St. **Amenities:** Restaurant; spa; fitness center.

Helmsley Middletowne   This value-laden member of the Helmsley chain boasts little in the way of style, services, or amenities, but rooms and suites are spacious, comfortable, and well priced, and the location is great. Room decor is generic and furnishings are older, but beds are firm and everything is well kept. Each room has a refrigerator, multiple-line phones, and a wealth of closet space. The one- and two-bedroom suites are well priced and big enough to accommodate families. They also boast walk-in kitchenettes (some lack dishware, so request it or bring plastic); some have fireplaces and/or balconies. 148 E. 48th St. (between Third and Lexington aves.), New York, NY 10017. ℂ 800/221-4982 or 212/755-3000. Fax 212/832-0261. www.helmsleyhotels.com. 192 units. $195–$205 double; from $235 1- or 2-bedroom suite. Ask about weekend packages. Children under 12 stay free in parents' room. Rates include continental breakfast. AE, DC, MC, V. Parking $30. Subway: 6 to 51st St. **Amenities:** Restaurant.

Hotel Chelsea   If it's Warhol's New York you're here to discover, the Hotel Chelsea is the only place to stay. Long-term residents of a creative bent inhabit most of the 400 rooms, so the bohemian spirit and sense of community are as strong as ever. The 1884 redbrick Victorian boasts cast-iron balconies and a lobby filled with museum-quality works by current and former residents. A recent renovation has taken the seediness out, but it's still quirky, and not for everybody: Accommodations tend to be sparsely furnished, but they're large and soundproof. The bellhops will deliver takeout meals to you or run your clothes to the cleaners. 222 W. 23rd St. (between Seventh and Eighth aves.), New York, NY 10011. ℂ 212/243 3700. Fax 212/675-5531. www.hotelchelsea.com. 400 units, about 100 available to travelers. $135–$250 single; $165–$300 double or junior suite; $300–$350 suite. Ask about long-stay discounts. AE, MC, V. Parking $20 nearby. Subway: C, E, 1, 9 to 23rd St. **Amenities:** Restaurant.

Hotel Metro   The Metro is the best choice in Midtown for those who don't want to sacrifice either style or comfort for affordability. This Art Deco–style jewel's rooms are outfitted with retro furnishings, refrigerators, and marble bathrooms. Only about half the bathrooms have tubs, but the others have shower stalls big enough for two (junior suites have whirlpool tubs). The "family room" is a two-room suite that has a second bedroom in lieu of a sitting area. The comfy library/lounge area off the lobby, where complimentary buffet breakfast is laid out and the coffeepot's on all day, is a popular hangout. The rooftop terrace boasts a breathtaking view of the Empire State Building. 45 W. 35th St. (between Fifth and Sixth aves.), New York, NY 10001. ℂ 800/356-3870 or 212/947-2500. Fax 212/279-1310. www.hotelmetronyc.com. 179 units. $150–$250 double; $165–$300 triple or quad; $200–$350 family room; $225–$400 suite. Ask about package deals. Extra person $25. 1 child under 14 stays free in parents' room. Rates include continental breakfast. AE, DC, MC, V. Parking $17 nearby. Subway: B, D, F, N, R, V to 34th St. **Amenities:** Restaurant; fitness room.

The Kimberly   Surprisingly good rates on suites mean that you could be standing on your private balcony overlooking Manhattan for less than you'd think. These are full apartments with dining areas, living rooms, kitchens, marble bathrooms, tons of closet space, and balconies (in all but eight suites). The two-bedroom suites each have two bathrooms. The 21 regular rooms are handsome and comfortable, with bathrooms with deep tubs. Additional amenities include refrigerators and robes. A unique perk is complimentary boarding of a 75-foot yacht for a sunset cruise (weekends May–Oct, always weather-dependent). 145 E. 50th St. (between Lexington and Third aves.), New York, NY 10022. ℂ 800/683-0400, 212/755-0400, or 212/702-1600. Fax 212/750-0113. www.kimberlyhotel.com. 186 units.

$259–$349 double; $299–$1,000 1-bedroom suite (including specialty suites), $459–$689 2-bed-room suite. Check on discounted off-season and weekend rates and package deals. Extra person $25. Children 17 and under stay free in parents' room. AE, DC, DISC, MC, V. Parking $30. Subway: 6 to 51st St.; E, F to Lexington Ave. **Amenities:** Restaurants (2); free access to New York Health & Racquet Club.

The Marcel   This Gramercy Park hotel offers style and a super-hip scene at low prices. The Marcel sits on the cutting edge style-wise. *Mod Squad*–era Scandinavian stylings in the lobby lead to rooms boasting blond-wood built-ins that make clever use of space. The designer furnishings and textiles look and feel expensive, even if the beds don't. Even if the service isn't fabulous or the little details aren't perfect, you should feel like you're getting a great deal here. 201 E. 24th St. (at Third Ave.), New York, NY 10011. ✆ **888/66-HOTEL** or 212/696-3800. Fax 212/696-0077. www.nychotels.com. 97 units. $125–$175 double. AE, DISC, MC, V. Parking: $24. Subway: 6 to 28th St. **Amenities:** Restaurant.

New York City Howard Johnson Express Inn   This brand-new construction is a boon to budget-minded travelers looking for quality comforts at a great price, a trendy location, or both. The East Village action is just across Houston (pronounced *how*-ston) Street, and SoHo is to the west. The neighborhood may be on the cutting edge, but this HoJo is wonderfully predictable. Rooms are small, but furnishings and textiles are of good quality: Mattresses are firm, work desks boast desk-level inputs and an ergonomic chair, and the granite bathrooms are nicer than those in some luxury hotels (some even have Jacuzzis). Those with room numbers ending in 01, 02, or 03 are the largest. 135 E. Houston St. (at Forsyth St.), New York, NY 10002. ✆ **800/406-1411** or 212/358-8844. Fax 212/473-3500. www.hojo.com. 54 units. $119–$149 double. Inquire about AAA, AARP, and other discounts. Rates include continental breakfast. AE, DC, DISC, MC, V. Parking $29, 4 blocks away. Subway: F to Second Ave.

Plaza Hotel   The 1907 landmark French Renaissance palace has been beautifully refurbished by the Fairmont chain, who recently renovated the guest rooms and lobby and added a honey of a spa. Halls and rooms have been redone in an opulent traditional style in soft, elegant colors, with nice touches such as pillow-top mattresses, CD players, and big leather-top desks. Even the smallest room is a reasonable size, and the building's U shape means that every room gets a measure of fresh air and sunlight. 768 Fifth Ave. (at 59th St.), New York, NY 10019. ✆ **800/441-1414** or 212/759-3000. Fax 212/546-5256. www.fairmont.com. 805 units. $250–$584 double; from $549 suite. Some rate plans include continental breakfast. AE, DC, DISC, MC, V. Subway: N, R to Fifth Ave. **Amenities:** Restaurants (4); spa; health club.

Thirty Thirty   This new-in-2001 hotel from the CityLife Hotel Group is on the Upper West Side, and just right for bargain-hunting travelers looking for a splash of style with an affordable price tag. Rooms are done in a natural palette with a creative edge. Configurations are split between twin/twins, queens, and queen/queens. Nice features include cushioned headboards, firm mattresses, two-line phones, built-in wardrobes, and nicely tiled bathrooms. A few larger units have kitchenettes. 30 E. 30th St. (between Madison and Park aves.), New York, NY 10016. ✆ **800/497-6028** or 212/689-1900. Fax 212/689-0023. www.thirtythirty-nyc.com. 240 units. $125–$185 double; $145–$195 double with kitchenette; $185–$245 quad. Call for last-minute deals, or check website for promotions (as low as $99 at press time). AE, DC, DISC, MC, V. Parking $35 1 block away. Subway: 6 to 28th St. **Amenities:** Pets accepted with advance approval.

Trump International Hotel & Tower   The hotel is on 14 lower floors of a 52-story mirrored monolith at the southwest corner of Central Park, with unobstructed views on all sides. Rooms are on the small side, but high ceilings and smart design make them feel uncluttered. They're done in a contemporary style, with clean-lined furniture, beautiful fabrics, and Tuscan tones. Floor-to-ceiling windows maximize the views, breathtaking on the park side. Each room boasts a Jacuzzi tub in the marble bathroom, bathrobes, umbrellas, DVD/CD players, and a telescope for taking in the views. Suites also have a European-style kitchen stocked with china and crystal. Each guest is assigned a Trump attaché who functions as your personal concierge. The 6,000-foot spa and fitness center features a lap pool, trainers, and a full treatment menu. 1 Central Park West (at 60th St.), New York, NY 10023. ℭ 888/44-TRUMP or 212/299-1000. Fax 212/299-1150. www.trump intl.com. 167 units. $525–$575 double; from $795 1- or 2-bedroom suite. Check website for special rates and package deals. Children under 18 stay free in parents' room. AE, DC, DISC, MC, V. Parking $42. Subway: A, B, C, D, 1, 9 to 59th St./Columbus Circle. **Amenities:** Restaurant; pool; spa; health club.

Waldorf-Astoria and the Waldorf Towers   Hilton Hotels spent a fortune renovating this Art Deco landmark. No two rooms are exactly alike. All boast traditional decor, quality linens, comfy beds, marble bathrooms, closets, refrigerators, and the luxury amenities. Renowned for its butler service and respect for privacy, the residential-style Waldorf Towers occupies floors 27 to 42 and has a separate entrance. Many of these gorgeous rooms and suites are outfitted with original art and antiques, plus full dining rooms, kitchens, and maid's quarters. The Presidential Suite is aptly named, having cosseted many world leaders. 301 Park Ave. (between 49th and 50th sts.), New York, NY 10022. ℭ 800/WALDORF, 800/774-1500, or 212/355-3000. Fax 212/872-7272 (Astoria), or 212/872-4799 (Towers). www.waldorfastoria. com or www.waldorf-towers.com. 1,242 units (159 in the Towers). Waldorf-Astoria: $259–$485 double; from $349 suite. Waldorf Towers: $429–$625 double; from $515 suite. Corporate, senior, seasonal, and weekend discounts may be available (as low as $189 at press time), as well as package deals. Extra person $40. Children under 18 stay free in parents' room. AE, DC, DISC, MC, V. Parking $45. Subway: 6 to 51st St. **Amenities:** Restaurants (4); fitness center.

Washington Square Hotel   Popular with a young international crowd, this affordable hotel sits facing Washington Square Park in the heart of Greenwich Village. A marble-and-brass lobby leads to tiny rooms that benefited from a pleasant freshening in 2000. Each comes with a firm bed, a private bathroom, and a small closet with a pint-size safe. It's worth paying a few extra dollars for a south-facing room on a high floor, because others can be a bit dark. The heart-of-campus location is ideal for youthful (or youth-minded) travelers who want to be near Village restaurants, bars, and jazz clubs. 103 Waverly Place (between Fifth and Sixth aves.), New York, NY 10011. ℭ 800/222-0418 or 212/777-9515. Fax 212/979-8373. www.wshotel.com. 170 units. $101–$131 single; $118–$151 double; $145–$188 quad. Inquire about special rates and jazz packages. Rollaway $20. Rates include continental breakfast. AE, MC, V. Parking $20 nearby. Subway: A, C, E, F, V to W. 4th St. (use 3rd St. exit). **Amenities:** Restaurant.

4 Where to Dine

New York is one of the finest, most diverse restaurant cities in the world. Below we've assembled descriptions of a range of eateries in many cuisine styles and price ranges all over town, from very expensive (count on spending over $100 with drinks), to expensive ($75 and up), to moderate ($20–$50), to inexpensive (eat well for $10 or less per person). To save money at the most expensive restaurants, consider going at lunch or ordering a prix-fixe or tasting menu.

In addition to the restaurants below, check out good-value/good food chains all over Manhattan like **Burritoville** (fresh, inexpensive Mexican), **Xando/Cosí** (gourmet sandwiches/takeout), and **Le Pain Quotidien** (French bakery/cafe).

Alain Ducasse at the Essex House CLASSIC FRENCH   When Europe's most famous Michelin three-star chef debuted his first New York restaurant in 2000, initial reviews said nothing to justify the price tags. In the subsequent year, however, Ducasse put his staff to the grindstone, and mellowed the restaurant into a winner. The intimate, antique-filled dining rooms are bold, colorful, and richly formal. Expect ultra-elegant haute French cuisine with the occasional Mediterranean flair. The standard $160 prix-fixe dinner features five courses, the $145 version only four. The wine list is phenomenally expensive but fabulous. Service is smooth and elegant, exactly as it should be. 158 W. 58th St. (between Sixth and Seventh aves.). *©* **212/265-7300.** www.alain-ducasse.com. Reservations required. Jacket and tie required for men. 3- to 4-course dinner $145–$160; tasting menus $160–$280. AE, DC, DISC, MC, V. Tues–Wed and Sat 6:30–9pm; Thurs–Fri noon–2pm and 6:30–9pm. Subway: B, D, F, V to 42nd St.

Aquagrill SEAFOOD   Attention, seafood lovers: This marvelous little restaurant serves up some of the city's best fish. The raw bar flies in a phenomenal selection of oysters from around the world. If you like sea urchin, don't pass on the fresh Maine version if it's available, served in the shell with citrus soy and shaved scallions. Among the entrees, you can keep it cheap and simple with preparations that let the fish's own fresh, clean flavors sing. Service is knowledgeable and efficient, the wine list boasts a number of affordable choices, and there's outdoor seating. 210 Spring St. (at Sixth Ave.). *©* **212/274-0505.** Reservations highly recommended. Main courses $15–$26; $17 3-course "Shucker's Special" lunch (a half dozen oysters, salad, soup). AE, MC, V. Tues–Thurs noon–3pm and 6–10:45pm; Fri noon–3pm and 6–11:45pm; Sat noon–3:45pm and 6–11:45pm; Sun noon–3:45pm and 6–10:30pm. Subway: C, E to Spring St.

Aquavit SCANDINAVIAN   The main dining room is soaring, with birch trees and an indoor waterfall; the more casual upstairs cafe is one of New York's best dining bargains. Both focus on good-value fixed-price meals. Some of our favorite selections are well-prepared Scandinavian standards, such as the smorgasbord plate, an assortment of delicacies including smoky herring and zesty hot-mustard glazed salmon, and the venison meatballs. The bar offers a wide selection of aquavits, distilled liquors flavored with fruit and herbs. Most fixed-price menus offer a beverage accompaniment option, which lets you enjoy the food, setting, and service without a worry. 13 W. 54th St. (between Fifth and Sixth aves.). *©* **212/307-7311.** www.aquavit.org. Reservations recommended. Cafe: Main courses $9–$20; 3-course fixed-price dinner $32. Main dining room: Fixed-price dinner $65 dinner ($39 for vegetarians); 3-course pre-theater dinner (5:30–6:15pm) $39. Tasting menus $85 dinner ($58 for vegetarians); supplement for paired wines $35. AE, DC, MC, V. Daily noon–2:30pm and 5:30–10:30pm. Subway: E, F to Fifth Ave.

Babbo NORTHERN ITALIAN   I consider Babbo the best Italian restaurant in the city. Tucked behind an inviting butter-yellow facade, the restaurant is warm and intimate, with well-spaced tables and a relaxed air. Chef Mario Batali has reinvented the notion of antipasti with such starters as fresh anchovies beautifully marinated in lobster oil, and Faicco soppressata accented with roasted beets, shaved fennel, and Macintosh vinegar. The chef has no equal when it comes to creative pastas. The *secondi* menu features such wonders as tender fennel-dusted sweetbreads; and smoky grilled quail in a heavenly fig and duck liver vinaigrette. The sommelier can help you choose from the excellent Italian wine list. 110 Waverly Place (just east of Sixth Ave.). ℭ 212/777-0303. Reservations highly recommended. Pastas $16–$24 (most under $21); meats and fish $23–$29; 7-course tasting menus $59–$85 ($45 supplement for accompanying wines, $90 for reserves). AE, MC, V. Mon–Sat 5:30–11:30pm; Sun 5–11pm. Subway: A, C, E, F, V to W. 4th St. (use 8th St. exit).

Bubby's AMERICAN   In the Village, we love Bubby's for the sublime macaroni and cheese, for the divine garlic burger and fries, for the homemade meatloaf with warm cider gravy and garlic mashies. We love Bubby's for the roasted rosemary chicken and chipotle-crusted Black Angus steak, and the classic cocktail the bartender will make when we're in the mood. We love Bubby's generous portions and fresh-from-the-field greens. We love the friendly waitstaff that doesn't neglect us. Best of all, we love Bubby's pies: the core of Bubby's business, baked fresh daily, a half dozen to choose from! 120 Hudson St. (at N. Moore St.). ℭ 212/219-0666. www.bubbys.com. Reservations recommended for dinner (not accepted for brunch). Main courses $10–$22. AE, DC, DISC, MC, V. Mon–Thurs 8am–11pm; Fri 8am–midnight; Sat 9am–4:30pm and 6pm–midnight; Sun 9am–10pm. Subway: 1, 9 to Franklin St.

Chanterelle CONTEMPORARY FRENCH   This West Village spot is our favorite special-occasion restaurant. The dining room is simple but beautiful, with a pressed-tin ceiling, widely spaced tables, and gorgeous floral displays. Your server will know the handwritten menu in depth and can describe preparations in detail and suggest complementary combinations. The artful cuisine is based on traditional French technique, but Pacific and Pan-European notes sneak into the culinary melodies, and lots of dishes are lighter than you'd expect. The seasonal menu changes every few weeks, but one signature dish appears on almost every menu: a marvelous if expensive grilled seafood sausage. 2 Harrison St. (at Hudson St.). ℭ 212/966-6960. www.chanterellenyc.com. Reservations recommended well in advance. 3-course fixed-price dinner $84; tasting menu $95 ($155 with wines). AE, DC, DISC, MC, V. Mon 5:30–11pm; Tues–Sat noon–2:30pm and 5:30–11pm. Subway: 1, 9 to Franklin St.

Churrascaria Plataforma BRAZILIAN   It's a carnival for carnivores at this colorful, upscale, all-you-can-eat Brazilian rotisserie. A large selection of teasers like paella, and carpaccio at the salad bar, may tempt you to fill up, but hold out for the parade of meat. Servers deliver beef, ham, chicken (the chicken hearts are great, trust me), lamb, and sausage—more than 15 delectable varieties—and traditional sides such as fried yucca, plantains, and rice until you cannot eat another bite. The ideal accompaniment to the meal is a pitcher of Brazil's signature cocktail, the *caipirinha,* a margaritalike blend of limes, sugar, crushed ice, and raw sugarcane liquor; Plataforma's are the best in town. 316 W. 49th St. (between Eighth and Ninth aves.). ℭ 212/245-0505. www.churrascariaplataforma.com. Reservations recommended. All-you-can-eat fixed-price $39 dinner; half-price for children 5–10. AE, DC, DISC, MC, V. Daily noon–midnight. Subway: C, E to 50th St.

Daniel FRENCH COUNTRY   Daniel Boulud's *New York Times* four-star has gorgeous neo-Renaissance features—rich mahogany doors, sensuous arches, elegant Corinthian columns, and soaring terra-cotta–tiled ceilings—that make an ideal setting for Boulud's classic-goes-country French cooking. The menu is heavy with game dishes, plus Daniel signatures like black sea bass in a crisp potato shell with tender leeks and a light Barolo sauce. But you really can't go wrong with anything—the kitchen doesn't take a false turn. The wine list is terrific and the desserts are uniformly excellent. The staff is more formal than we would like. Dining in the lounge is a great way to sample the marvelous cuisine.

60 E. 65th St. (between Madison and Park aves.). ℂ 212/288-0033. www.danielnyc.com. Reservations required. Jacket and tie required for men in main dining room. 3-course fixed-price dinner $82; tasting menus $110–$145. Main courses $34–$38 in bar and lounge. AE, MC, V. Mon–Sat 5:45–11pm (lounge until 11:30pm). Subway: 6 to 68th St.

Florent DINER/FRENCH BISTRO   In the Meat-Packing District, Florent, the nearly 24-hour French bistro dressed up as a '50s-style diner, is a perennial hot spot. But it's after the clubs close that the joint really jumps. Tables are packed, but it's all part of the festivities. This place has a sense of humor (check out the menu boards above the bar). The food's good, too: The grilled chicken with herbs and mustard sauce is a winner, as is the onion soup crowned with melted Gruyère. There are always faves like burgers and chili in addition to standards like moules frites, and the comfort food specialties such as chicken potpie make regular appearances. The fries are light, crispy, and addictive. 69 Gansevoort St. (2 blocks south of 14th St. and 1 block west of Ninth Ave., between Greenwich and Washington sts.). ℂ 212/989-5779. www.restaurantflorent.com. Reservations recommended for dinner. Main courses $8–$21 (most less than $15); 3-course fixed-price dinner $19 before 7:30pm, $21 7:30pm–midnight. No credit cards. Mon–Wed 9am–5am; Thurs–Sun 24 hr. Subway: A, C, E, L to 14th St.

Il Cortile CREATIVE ITALIAN   The best restaurant in Little Italy stands out thanks to its warm, sophisticated demeanor. There's an old-world elegance to the menu, which is folded and sealed with gold foil. Prepared under the guiding hand of executive chef Michael DeGeorgio, the northern Italian fare is well prepared and pleasing—the greens fresh and crisp, the sauces appropriately seasoned, the pastas perfectly al dente. A standout is the polenta with mushrooms in a savory white-wine sauce. The waitstaff is attentive and reserved. The wine cellar contains a number of reasonably priced selections. 125 Mulberry St. (between Canal and Hester sts.). ℂ 212/226-6060. www.ilcortile.com. Reservations recommended. Main courses $9.50–$32 (most $13–$25). AE, DC, DISC, MC, V. Daily noon–midnight. Subway: N, R, 6 to Canal St.

Joe's Shanghai SHANGHAI CHINESE   Just off the Bowery, this Chinatown institution serves up authentic cuisine to enthusiastic crowds. The stars of the menu are the signature soup dumplings, steamed pockets filled with hot broth and your choice of pork or crab, accompanied by a side of seasoned soy. Listed as "steamed buns" (item nos. 1 and 2), these culinary marvels never disappoint. The room is set mostly with round tables of 10 or so, and you'll be asked if you're willing to share. We encourage you to do so! 9 Pell St. (between Bowery and Mott sts.). ℂ 212/233-8888. Reservations recommended for 10 or more. Main courses $4.25–$17. No credit cards. Daily 11am–11pm. Subway: N, R, Q, W, 6 to Canal St.; F to Delancey St. Also at 24 W. 56th St., between Fifth and Sixth aves. (ℂ 212/333-3868; subway: B, Q to 57th St.).

Katz's Delicatessen JEWISH DELI   On the Lower East Side is the city's best deli. All of Katz's eats are first-rate: matzo ball and chicken noodle soups, potato knishes, cheese blintzes, and the beloved all-beef hot dogs. There's no faulting the pastrami—piled high on rye—or the dry-cured roast beef, either. All of the well-stuffed sandwiches are cheaper than you'll find at any other deli in town. What's more, Katz's is the only deli cool enough to let you split one without adding a $2 to $3 "sharing" charge. 205 E. Houston St. (at Ludlow St.). ℂ 212/254-2246. Reservations not accepted. Sandwiches $2.15–$10; main courses $5–$18. AE, MC, V ($20 minimum). Sun–Tues 8am–10pm; Wed–Thurs 8am–11pm; Fri–Sat 8am–2:30am. Subway: F to Second Ave.

Le Bernardin FRENCH/SEAFOOD   Le Bernardin is our favorite splurge restaurant in the city. Food doesn't get better than the flash-marinated black bass ceviche, the freshest fish awash in cilantro, mint, jalapeños, and diced tomatoes. Chef Eric Ripert's tuna tartare always exhilarates, its Asian seasoning a welcome touch. The formal service is impeccable, as is the outrageously pricey wine list. The fixed-price lunch is a bargain, given the master in the kitchen. The desserts—especially the chocolate dome with crème brûlée on a macaroon—end the meal with a flourish. 155 W. 51st St. (between Sixth and Seventh aves.). (£) 212/489-1515. www.le-bernardin.com. Reservations required. Jacket required/tie optional. Fixed-price dinner $79; tasting menus $95–$130. AE, DC, DISC, MC, V. Mon–Thurs noon–2:30pm and 5:30–10:30pm; Fri noon–2:30pm and 5:30–11pm; Sat 5:30–11pm. Subway: N, R to 49th St.; 1, 9 to 50th St.

Lombardi's PIZZA   Lombardi's makes the best pizza in Manhattan, hands down. First opened in 1905, "America's first licensed pizzeria" cooks its delectable pies in its original coal brick oven. The wonderfully smoky crust (a generations-old family recipe that Gennaro Lombardi hand-carried from Naples at the turn of the century) is topped with fresh mozzarella, basil, pecorino Romano, and San Marzano tomato sauce. Lombardi's specialty is the fresh clam pie, with hand-shucked clams, oregano, fresh garlic, Romano, extra-virgin olive oil, and fresh-ground pepper (no sauce). 32 Spring St. (between Mott and Mulberry sts.). (£) 212/941-7994. Reservations accepted for parties of 6 or more. Pies $12–$21; extra charge for additional toppings. No credit cards. Mon–Thurs 11:30am–11pm; Fri–Sat 11:30am–midnight; Sun 11:30am–10pm. Subway: 6 to Spring St., N, R to Prince St.

Oyster Bar & Restaurant SEAFOOD   The city's most famous seafood joint lies in the beautifully renovated Grand Central Terminal. The restaurant is spiffy, too, with a main dining room under an impressive curved and tiled ceiling, a more casual luncheonette-style section for walk-ins, and a wood-paneled saloon-style room for smokers. A new menu is prepared every day. The oysters are irresistible. The list of daily catches, which can range from Arctic char to mako shark to ono, is equally impressive. Most dinners cost between $20 and $25 (you'll pay $20 for a combo pan roast rich with oysters, clams, shrimp, lobster, and scallops); try pairing the New England clam chowder (at $5, an unbeatable lunch) with a smoked starter to make a great meal. In Grand Central Terminal (lower level), 23 Vanderbilt Ave. (at 42nd St.). (£) 212/490-6650. www.oysterbarny.com. Reservations recommended. Main courses $10–$35. AE, DC, MC, V. Mon–Fri 11:30am–9:30pm (last seating); Sat noon–9:30pm. Subway: 4, 5, 6, 7, S to 42nd St./Grand Central.

Pisces SEAFOOD   In the East Village, Pisces serves up the best inexpensive seafood in the city. All the fish is top quality and fresh daily. The mesquite-smoked whole trout in sherry oyster sauce is better than trout I've had for twice the price; start with the phyllo-fried shrimp or the tuna ceviche with curried potato chips and roasted pepper coulis. The wine list is appealing and very well priced, the decor suitably nautical without being kitschy, and the service friendly and attentive. For wallet-watchers, the early bird fixed-price meal makes an already terrific value even better. 95 Ave. A (at 6th St.). (£) 212/260-6660. Reservations recommended. Main courses $8–$20; 2-course fixed-price dinner (Mon–Thurs 5:30–7pm; Fri–Sun 5:30–6:30pm) $15. AE, DC, MC, V. Mon–Thurs 5:30–11:30pm; Fri 5:30pm–1am; Sat 11:30am–3:30pm and 5:30pm–1am; Sun 11:30am–3:30pm and 5:30–11:30pm. Subway: 6 to Astor Place; F to Second Ave.

Serendipity 3 AMERICAN   Tucked into a brownstone a few steps from Bloomingdale's, this delightful restaurant is where the quintessential American soda fountain still reigns supreme. Happy people gather at marble-topped ice-cream parlor tables for burgers and foot-long hot dogs. The food isn't great, but the main courses aren't the point—they're just an excuse to get to the desserts. The restaurant's signature is Frozen Hot Chocolate, a slushy version of every-body's cold-weather favorite, but other crowd pleasers include dark double devil mousse, lemon icebox pie, and anything with hot fudge. 225 E. 60th St. (between Second and Third aves.). ℂ 212/838-3531. www.serendipity3.com. Reservations accepted for lunch and dinner (not just dessert). Main courses $7–$18; sweets and sundaes $5–$17 (most under $10). AE, DC, DISC, MC, V. Sun–Thurs 11:30am–midnight; Fri 11:30am–1am; Sat 11:30am–2am. Subway: N, R to Lexington Ave.; 4, 5, 6 to 59th St.

Siam Inn THAI   Siam Inn is an attractive outpost of very good Thai food. All of your Thai favorites are here, well prepared and served by a brightly attired and courteous waitstaff. *Tom kah gai soup* (with chicken, mushrooms, and coconut milk), chicken satay with yummy peanut sauce, and light, flaky curry puffs all make good starters. Among noteworthy entrees are the masaman and red curries (the former rich and peanuty, the latter quite spicy), spicy sautéed squid with fresh basil and chiles, and perfect pad Thai. The decor is pretty and pleasing—black Deco tables and chairs, cushy rugs underfoot, and soft lighting. 854 Eighth Ave. (between 51st and 52nd sts.). ℂ 212/757-4006. www.siaminn.com. Reservations sug-gested. Main courses $8–$16. AE, DC, MC, V. Mon–Fri noon–11:30pm; Sat–Sun 4–11:30pm. Sub-way: C, E to 50th St.

Sylvia's SOUL FOOD   South Carolina–born Sylvia Woods is the last word in New York soul food. Since 1962, this Harlem institution has dished up authentic Southern-fried goods: turkey with stuffing; smothered chicken and pork chops; fried chicken and baked ham; collard greens and candied yams; and sweet tea. And then, of course there's "Sylvia's World Famous, Talked About, Bar-B-Que Ribs Special"—the sauce is sweet, with a potent afterburn. This Harlem landmark is still presided over by 74-year-old Sylvia, who's likely to greet you at the door herself. Sunday gospel brunch is a joyous time to go. 328 Lenox Ave. (between 126th and 127th sts.). ℂ 212/996-0660. www.sylviassoulfood.com. Reser-vations only accepted for parties of 10 or more. Main courses $8–$19; lunch special Mon–Fri 11am–3pm $3.75–$9.25; Sun gospel brunch $17 (includes a cocktail). AE, DISC, MC, V. Mon–Thurs 8am–10:30pm; Fri–Sat 7:30am–10:30pm; Sun 11am–8pm. Subway: 2, 3 to 125th St.

Tavern on the Green AMERICAN/CONTINENTAL   This legendary Cen-tral Park restaurant is one of a kind. Antiques and Tiffany glass fill the space, crystal chandeliers cast a romantic light, tiny twinkling lights glimmer on nearby trees, and the views over the park are wonderful. When it comes to the food, it's hard to be completely consistent in an operation this mammoth. Generally speaking, the seasonal menus are good, particularly if you stick with classic fare. The superb al dente pastas are house-made, and the grilled pork porterhouse is delicious and thick. Despite its reputation, the Tavern is known for its down-to-earth manner. It can be plagued by uneven service, especially during holiday periods. Book well ahead. In Central Park, Central Park West and W. 67th St. ℂ 212/873-3200. www.tavernonthegreen.com. Reservations highly recommended, necessary well in advance on holidays. Main courses $20–$40; 3-course lunch $20–$26; 3-course pre-theater fixed-price din-ner (Sun–Fri 5–6:30pm) $36–$42; children's complete meals $14–$19. AE, DC, DISC, MC, V. Mon–Thurs noon–3pm and 5–10:30pm; Fri noon–3pm and 5–11:30pm; Sat 10am–3:30pm and 5–11:30pm; Sun 10am–3:30pm and 5–10:30pm. Subway: 1, 9 to 66th St./Lincoln Center.

Tea & Sympathy AFTERNOON TEA/BRITISH   When Londoner Nicky Perry moved to New York, she opened her own British tearoom in the West

Village. Tea & Sympathy seems transplanted wholesale from Highgate, complete with an oddball collection of creamers and teapots, a snappy British waitstaff, and plenty of old-time charm. It's worth the squeeze for the full afternoon tea, which comes on a tiered tray with crustless finger sandwiches, scones with jam and Devonshire cream, and cakes and cookies for a sugary finish. The menu also features such traditional British comforts as shepherd's pie, bangers and mash, and a savory chicken and leek pie. 108 Greenwich Ave. (between 12th and 13th sts.). ℂ **212/807-8329** or 212/989-9735. www.teaandsympathynewyork.com. Reservations not accepted. Main courses $11–$17; full afternoon tea $19 ($35 for 2). MC, V. Daily 11:30am–10pm. Subway: A, C, E, 1, 2, 3, 9 to 14th St.

5 New York City After Dark

For the latest, most comprehensive nightlife listings, the magazine *Time Out New York* (www.timeoutny.com) is our favorite weekly source; it comes out every Thursday. The free weekly *Village Voice*'s (www.villagevoice.com) arts and entertainment coverage is extensive, and just about every live music venue advertises here. The *New York Times* (www.nytoday.com) features terrific entertainment coverage, particularly in the two-part Friday "Weekend" section.

THE THEATER SCENE

I can't tell you precisely what will be on while you're in town, so check the publications listed above for specifics. Another good source is the **Broadway Line** (ℂ **888/BROADWAY** or 212/302-4111; www.broadway.org), where you can obtain details and descriptions on current Broadway shows, and choose to be transferred to TeleCharge or Ticketmaster. There's also **NYC/Onstage** (ℂ **212/768-1818;** www.tdf.org), providing the same kind of service for Broadway and Off-Broadway productions.

Ticket prices vary dramatically. Expect to pay for good seats; the high end for any given show is likely to be between $60 and $100. Off-Broadway and Off-Off-Broadway shows tend to be cheaper, with tickets often as low as $10 or $15.

TICKET-BUYING TIPS   Phone ahead or go online for tickets to the most popular shows as far in advance as you can. You need only call such general numbers as **TeleCharge** (ℂ **212/239-6200;** www.telecharge.com) or **Ticketmaster** (ℂ **212/307-4100;** www.ticketmaster.com).

Theatre Direct International (TDI) is a ticket broker (meaning they sell you the tickets with an additional service charge), which might be an option if you want to see a sold-out show. Check to see if they have seats to the shows you're interested in by calling ℂ **800/BROADWAY** or 212/541-8457; you can also order tickets through TDI via their website, **www.broadway.com**.

Three commercial sites—**Broadway.com** (**www.broadway.com**), **Playbill Online** (**www.playbill.com** or www.playbillclub.com), and **TheaterMania** (**www.theatermania.com**)—offer information on Broadway and Off-Broadway shows, with links to the ticket-buying agencies. Each offers an **online theater club** that's free to join and can yield substantial savings—as much as 50%—on advance-purchase theater tickets for select Broadway and Off-Broadway shows.

When you arrive, try the **Broadway Ticket Center,** run by the League of American Theatres and Producers (the same people behind the Broadway Line, above) at the Times Square Visitors Center, 1560 Broadway, between 46th and 47th streets (open Mon–Sat 9am–7pm, Sun 10am–6pm). They often have tickets available for otherwise sold-out shows, both for advance and same-day purchase, and only charge about $5 extra per ticket.

Even if saving money isn't an issue for you, check the boards at the **TKTS Booth** in Times Square for same-day discounted tickets.

THE PERFORMING ARTS

In addition to the listings below, see what's happening at **Carnegie Hall,** 881 Seventh Ave. (© 212/247-7800; www.carnegiehall.org; subway: N, R, W to 57th St.); and at the **92nd Street Y,** 1395 Lexington Ave. at 92nd Street (© **212/415-5500;** www.92ndsty.org), which offers many excellent cultural events.

LINCOLN CENTER FOR THE PERFORMING ARTS   New York is the world's premier performing arts city, and Lincoln Center at Broadway and 64th Street (© **212/546-2656** or 212/875-5456; www.lincolncenter.org; subway: 1/9 6th St.) is its premier institution.

Resident companies include **The Chamber Music Society of Lincoln Center** (© **212/875-5788;** www.chambermusicsociety.org); **The Film Society of Lincoln Center** (© **212/875-5600;** www.filmlinc.com), which shows films at the Walter Reade Theater; **Jazz at Lincoln Center** (© **212/258-9800;** www.jazzatlincolncenter.org), led by Wynton Marsalis; and **Lincoln Center Theater** (© **212/362-7600;** www.lct.org), with the Vivian Beaumont Theater, a home to Broadway shows and the Mitzi E. Newhouse Theater, an Off-Broadway house.

Other major tenants are the **Metropolitan Opera** (© **212/362-6000;** www.metopera.org), **New York City Opera** (© **212/870-5570;** www.nycopera.com), **New York City Ballet** (© **212/870-5570;** www.nycballet.com), **New York Philharmonic** (© **212/875-5656;** www.newyorkphilharmonic.org), and **American Ballet Theatre** (© **212/581-1212;** www.abt.org).

Most of the companies' **major seasons** run from about September or October to April, May, or June. **Tickets** for all performances at Avery Fisher and Alice Tully halls can be purchased through **CenterCharge** (© **212/721-6500**) or online at www.lincolncenter.org (click on "Box Office & Schedule" in the upper-right corner). Tickets for all Lincoln Center Theater performances can be purchased thorough **TeleCharge** (© **212/239-6200;** www.telecharge.com). Tickets for New York State Theater productions (New York City Opera and Ballet companies) are available through **Ticketmaster** (© **212/307-4100;** www.ticketmaster.com), while tickets for films showing at the Walter Reade Theater can be bought up to 7 days in advance by calling © **212/496-3809.**

OTHER CONCERT HALLS & VENUES   Modern dance takes center stage at **City Center,** 131 W. 55th St. between Sixth and Seventh avenues (© **877/ 581-1212** or 212/581-1212; www.citycenter.org.; subway: F, N, Q, R, W to 57th St.; B, D, E to Seventh Ave.); and at the **Joyce Theater,** one of the world's greatest modern dance institutions, located at 175 Eighth Ave. at 19th Street (© **212/242-0800;** www.joyce.org.; subway: C, E to 23rd St.; 1, 9 to 18th St.).

The **Apollo Theatre** (© **212/749-5838;** subway: 1, 9 to 125th St.) at 253 W. 125th St. (between Adam Clayton Powell and Frederick Douglass boulevards) is internationally renowned for its African-American acts of all musical genres. The **Brooklyn Academy of Music** presents cutting-edge theater, opera, dance, and music at 30 Lafayette Ave. (off Flatbush Ave.), Brooklyn (© **718/636-4100;** www.bam.org.; subway: 2, 3, 4, 5, M, N, Q, R, W to Pacific St./Atlantic Ave.).

⊘ Park It! Shakespeare, Music & Other Free Fun

As the weather warms, New York culture comes outdoors to play.

Shakespeare in the Park, held at Central Park's Delacorte Theater, is by far the city's most famous alfresco arts event. The schedule consists of one or two summertime productions, usually of the Bard's plays. Productions often feature big names and range from traditional to avant-garde interpretations. The theater itself, next to Belvedere Castle near 79th Street and West Drive, is a dream—on a beautiful starry night, there's no better stage in town. Tickets are given out free on a first-come, first-served basis (two per person), at 1pm on the day of the performance at the theater. The Delacorte might have 1,881 seats, but each is a hot commodity, so people generally line up on the baseball field next to the theater about 2 to 3 hours in advance (even earlier if a big-box-office name is involved). You can also pick up same-day tickets between 1 and 3pm at the Public Theater, at 425 Lafayette St., where the Shakespeare Festival continues throughout the year. For more information, call the Public Theater at *©* **212/539-8750** or the Delacorte at *©* **212/861-7277,** or go online to **www.publictheater.org**.

With summer also comes the sound of music to Central Park, where the **New York Philharmonic** and the **Metropolitan Opera** regularly entertain beneath the stars, for the current schedule, call *©* **212/360-3444,** 212/875-5709, or 212/362-6000; or visit **www.lincolncenter.org**.

The most active music stage in the park is **SummerStage,** at Rumsey Playfield, midpark around 72nd Street. The season usually lasts from mid-June to early August. While some big-name shows charge admission, tickets aren't usually required; donations are warmly accepted, however. For the latest performance info, call the SummerStage hot line at *©* **212/360-2777** or visit **www.summerstage.org**.

LIVE POPULAR MUSIC

For rock, pop, and sometimes jazz and folk, a good smaller venue is **The Bottom Line,** 15 W. 4th St. at Mercer Street in Greenwich Village (*©* **212/228-7880;** www.bottomlinecabaret.com; subway: A, B, C, D, E, F to W. 4th St.). A midsize venue for national acts is **The Bowery Ballroom,** 6 Delancey St., at the Bowery (*©* **212/533-2111;** www.boweryballroom.com), an atmospheric general admission space that holds about 500. Its slightly bigger brother, **Irving Plaza,** is another old hall near Union Square at 17 Irving Place (*©* **212/777-1224;** www.irvingplaza.com; subway: L, N, R, 4, 5, 6 to 14th St.–Union Sq.).

B. B. King Blues Club & Grill anchors Times Square's "new" 42nd Street with pop, funk, and rock names, mainly from the past (*©* **212/997-4144,** or 212/307-7171 for tickets; www.bbkingblues.com; subway: A, C, E, Q, W, 1, 2, 3, 7, 9 to 42nd St.). **The Knitting Factory,** at 74 Leonard St. between Broadway and Church Street (*©* **212/219-3006;** www.knittingfactory.com; subway: 1, 9 to Franklin St.), is the city's premier avant-garde music venue. Folk rock's legendary **Bitter End,** 147 Bleecker St., between Thompson and LaGuardia streets (*©* **212/673-7030;** www.bitterend.com), is still going strong.

JAZZ   **Birdland** has an excellent sound system and a top-notch talent roster at 315 W. 44th St. between Eighth and Ninth avenues (© **212/581-3080;** www.birdlandjazz.com; subway: A, C, E to 42nd St.). **The Blue Note** attracts the biggest names in jazz to its intimate setting at 131 W. 3rd St. at Sixth Avenue (© **212/475-8592;** www.bluenote.net.; subway: A, C, E, F, V to W. 4th St.). **The Lenox Lounge** (© **212/427-0253;** subway: 2, 3 to 125th St.) is Harlem's best jazz club at 288 Malcolm X Blvd. (Lenox Ave.; between 124th and 125th sts.).

CABARET   **Cafe Carlyle** is where you'll find Bobby Short—and that's all those who know cabaret need to know. It's at the Carlyle hotel, 781 Madison Ave. at 76th Street (© **212/570-7189;** subway: 6 to 77th St.). Closed from July to August. **Joe's Pub** is a popular cabaret and supper club at the Joseph Papp Public Theater, 425 Lafayette St. between Astor Place and 4th Street (© **212/ 539-8777;** www.joespub.com; subway: 6 to Astor Place).

COMEDY   **Carolines on Broadway** presents today's headliners in its Theater District showroom at 1626 Broadway between 49th and 50th streets (© **212/ 757-4100;** www.carolines.com; subway: N, R to 49th St.; 1, 9 to 50th St.). The **Comedy Cellar** is an intimate club at 117 MacDougal St. between Bleecker and West 3rd streets (© **212/254-3480;** www.comedycellar.com; subway: A, C, E, F, V, S to W. 4th St., use 3rd St. exit).

BARS & COCKTAIL LOUNGES

DOWNTOWN   In TriBeCa, **Bubble Lounge** at 228 W. Broadway between Franklin and White streets (© **212/431-3443**) is dedicated to the bubbly with more than 300 champagnes and sparkling wines. No jeans, sneakers, or baseball caps. Chinatown's **Double Happiness** at 173 Mott St. between Grand and Broome streets (© **212/941-1282;** subway: 6 to Spring St.) is a speakeasy-ish lounge with artistic nods to the neighborhood throughout. Don't miss the green tea martini.

On the Lower East Side, **Barramundi** (© **212/569-6900;** subway: F to Second Ave.) is notable for its outdoor garden and friendly staff at 147 Ludlow St. between Stanton and Rivington streets. **Idlewild**'s (© **212/477-5005;** subway: F to Second Ave.) interior is a repro of a jet airplane, complete with reclining seats, tray tables, and too-small bathrooms. Drinks are downright affordable. It's at 145 E. Houston St. (between First and Second aves. on the south side of Houston).

In the East Village, **Burp Castle** (© **212/982-4576**) is a must for serious beer lovers. There are more than 500 bottled and on-tap beers to choose from at 41 E. 7th St. between Second and Third avenues (subway: 6 to Astor Place). In the West Village, **Chumley's** (© **212/675-4449**) dates back to Prohibition, at 86 Bedford St. at Barrow Street (subway: 1, 9 to Christopher St.). **Hogs & Heifers** (© **212/929-0655**), complete with "bra tree," is a good bit of fun with a bridge-and-tunnel crowd at 859 Washington St. at 13th Street (subway: A, C, E, L to 14th St.).

MIDTOWN   Near Gramercy Park, **Pete's Tavern** (© **212/473-7676**) opened while Lincoln was still president. There's Guinness on tap and a terrific happy hour at 129 E. 18th St. at Irving Place (subway: L, N, R, 4, 5, 6 to 14th St./Union Sq.). **Spread/Coal** (© **212/683-8888;** www.spreadnyc.com) is a sexy lounge/restaurant hybrid at the Marcel Hotel, 323 Third Ave. at 24th Street (subway: 6 to 23rd St.).

On the West Side, at the **Algonquin Bar** (℃ 212/840-6800), you can feel the spirit of Dorothy Parker and the legendary Algonquin Round Table at 59 W. 44th St. between Fifth and Sixth avenues (subway: B, D, F, V to 42nd St.). The **Russian Vodka Room** (℃ 212/307-5835) is a Theater District find, with more than 50 vodkas plus the RVR's own miraculous infusions, at 265 W. 52nd St. between Broadway and Eighth Avenue (subway: C, E, 1, 9 to 50th St.).

On the East Side, **The Campbell Apartment** in Grand Central Terminal, 15 Vanderbilt Ave. (℃ 212/953-0409; subway: S, 4, 5, 6, 7 to 42nd St./Grand Central), is a high-ceilinged room restored to its full Florentine glory, and serves wines and champagnes by the glass, single-malt Scotches, fine stogies, and haute noshies to a well-heeled commuting crowd. There's a dress code.

UPTOWN   On the Upper West Side, the **Hi-Life Bar & Grill** at 477 Amsterdam Ave. at 83rd Street (℃ 212/787-7199; subway: 1, 9 to 79th St.) is from the days when men wore gray flannel suits and everybody had a doozy of a before-dinner cocktail. **The Shark Bar,** at 307 Amsterdam Ave. between 74th and 75th streets (℃ 212/874-8500; subway: 1, 2, 3, 9 to 72nd St.), is a popular and classy spot, well known for its soul food and singles' scene. It's also a hangout for sports celebs.

On the Upper East Side, **Bemelmans Bar** at the Carlyle hotel, 35 E. 76th St. at Madison Avenue (℃ 212/744-1600; subway: 6 to 77th St.), is a luxurious spot for cocktails. There's live entertainment Monday through Saturday from 9:30am to 1am ($15 cover). **Elaine's,** at 1703 Second Ave. between 88th and 89th streets (℃ 212/534-8103; subway: 4, 5, 6 to 86th St.), is where the glittering literati still come for dinner and book parties.

DANCE/NIGHTCLUBS

Baktun at 418 W. 14th St. between Ninth Avenue and Washington Street (℃ 212/206-1590; www.baktun.com; subway: A, C, E, L to 14th St.) has been hot, hot, hot since the word go. The music tends toward electronica, with some live acts in the mix. If you're going to spend one night out on the town, go to **Nell's** at 246 W. 14th St. between Seventh and Eighth avenues (℃ 212/675-1567; www.nells.com; subway: A, C, E, 1, 2, 3, 9 to 14th St.), the self-proclaimed "Classic New York Nightclub" that attracts a grown-up crowd ranging from homeboys to Wall Streeters. Dress nicely—Nell's deserves respect.

Swing is a nightly affair at **Swing 46.** Music is live nightly except Monday and runs the gamut from big band to boogie-woogie to jump blues. Even first-timers can join in, as free swing lessons are offered Wednesday through Saturday at 9:15pm. No jeans or sneakers. It's at 349 W. 46th St. between Eighth and Ninth avenues (℃ 212/262-9554; www.swing46.com; subway: C, E to 50th St.).

THE GAY & LESBIAN SCENE

To get a thorough, up-to-date take on what's happening in gay and lesbian nightlife, pick up *HX* (www.hx.com), *New York Blade* (www.nyblade.com), *Next* (www.nextnyc.com), or *Gay City News* (www.lgny.com). They're available for free all around town or at **The Lesbian & Gay Community Services Center,** at 208 W. 13th St., between Seventh and Eighth avenues (℃ 212/620-7310; www.gaycenter.org).

These days, many bars, clubs, cabarets, and cocktail lounges are neither gay nor straight but a bit of both, either catering to a mixed crowd or to varying orientations on different nights of the week.

Highlights of the GLBT bar scene include Chelsea's **Barracuda** (*©* 212/ **645-8613;** subway: C, E, 1, 9 to 23rd St.), a trendy, loungey place that's regularly voted "Best Bar" by the readers of *HX*. Look for the regular drag shows at 275 W. 22nd St. (between Seventh and Eighth aves.). **The Stonewall Inn** (*©* **212/463-0950;** subway: 1, 9 to Christopher St.) is where it all started. A mixed gay and lesbian crowd—old and young, beautiful and great personalities—makes this an easy place to begin. At least pop in to relive a defining moment in queer history at 53 Christopher St. (east of Seventh Ave.). In the East Village, **The Boiler Room** (*©* 212/254-7536; subway: F to Second Ave.) is everybody's favorite gay dive. Despite the mixed guy-girl crowd, it's a serious cruising scene for beautiful boys and a fine hangout for those who'd rather play pool. It's at 86 E. 4th St. (between First and Second aves.).

Meow Mix (*©* **212/254-0689;** www.meowmixchix.com; subway: F to Second Ave.) is a funky, divey East Villager that's a great lesbian hangout. It draws a young, artsy riot grrrrl crowd with nightly diversions like DJs, live bands, and the world-famous Xena Night to 269 E. Houston St. (at Suffolk St.).

6 Upstate New York Highlights

THE ADIRONDACK PARK

The Adirondack State Park is a six-million-acre chunk of land in northern New York, larger than Yellowstone and Yosemite combined, and unique in the diversity of its terrain. The scenery—rugged peaks, pastoral countryside, wild backcountry, and quaint lakeside hamlets—is stunning in all corners of the park. Wildlife is plentiful, and attractions, from French and Indian War battle sites to lavish Great Camps built by wealthy industrialists, dot the landscape. The once-impenetrable wilderness is now easily accessible, although the extreme North Country weather can dump an average of 10 feet of snow in one season, closing roads but delighting winter sports enthusiasts. A range of accommodations and activities is available for all tastes and interests: Visitors can relax at a posh resort with full-service spa and 18-hole golf course or bushwhack through tangled forests and sleep beneath the stars.

ESSENTIALS

GETTING THERE   The Adirondack region is best appreciated by car. The New York State Thruway, I-87, a toll road from New York City to Albany, becomes the scenic, toll-free Adirondack Northway. It hugs the region's eastern border, with exits to Lake George (about 4 hr. from the Big Apple), Blue Mountain Lake, Ticonderoga, Lake Placid, and other areas of interest, eventually reaching Canada. The western side of the Adirondacks can be accessed from either I-81 North at Watertown to Route 3 or by following I-90 east through Utica to Routes 8 and 12. Inside the park, a sparse network of roads squeezes between mountain ranges and tunnel into dense forests. Route 73, which begins at Exit 30 of the Northway and ends in Lake Placid, provides a particularly picturesque tour through the High Peaks region. **Amtrak** (*©* **800/USA-RAIL;** www.amtrak.com) services the Adirondacks, with frequent trains connecting Penn Station, in New York City, with depots along Lake Champlain, all the way to Montreal. Trains from Utica to Old Forge, or Thendara, in the southwestern edge of the region, are also available. The **Adirondack Airport at Lake Clear** (*©* **518/891-2290**) is about 25 miles from Lake Placid. There are other airports nearby in Albany and Burlington, Vermont.

VISITOR INFORMATION   For more information about the Adirondacks, call the **Lake Placid Visitors' Bureau** at © 800/447-5224 or check out www.lakeplacid.com. Contact the **Warren County Tourism Department** at © 800/958-4748 or www.visitlakegeorge.com. Other good sources of information are www.adirondacks.com or www.adirondacklife.com.

FAST FACTS   If you need a doctor, call or visit **Adirondack Medical Center,** Lake Colby Drive, Saranac Lake (© 517/891-4141). **Rite Aid Pharmacy,** 85 Saranac Ave., Lake Placid (© 518/523-5303), is open Monday through Saturday from 9am to 9pm and Sunday from 9am to 5pm.

EXPLORING THE ADIRONDACKS

As an all-season destination, the Adirondack region has its highlights and its hazards. Icy roads and winter storms can make driving precarious, so call ahead to check road conditions. Visitors planning an outdoor excursion should anticipate unpredictable dips in temperature and unexpected precipitation year-round. For workshops on outdoor skills, like paddling or mountain climbing, call the **Adirondack Mountain Club** (© 518/668-4447; www.adk.org). And before hitting the trails, a visit to the **Adirondack Park Agency's Visitor Interpretive Centers** in Paul Smiths (© 518/327-3000) or Newcomb (© 518/582-2000) will provide a crash course on local flora and fauna.

THE HIGH PEAKS   After gaining fame as the host of the 1932 and 1980 Olympic winter games, the alpine village of Lake Placid has evolved into the hub of activity in this region. It's home to Mount Marcy, the state's highest peak, an Olympic training center and a bustling Main Street lined with boutiques, outlet stores, and restaurants. Events like the ESPN Great Outdoor Games, Lake Placid Film Forum, Lake Placid Horseshow, and USA Ironman triathlon draw summertime crowds, and nearby Whiteface Mountain Ski Center, in Wilmington, attracts skiers and snowboarders from all over the world. Just west of Lake Placid is Saranac Lake, a college town and cultural center. Charming Keene Valley and Keene are located to the southwest of Lake Placid. Jagged mountains flank these hamlets, and roadside trail heads lead to the mountain summits.

The spectacular **Whiteface Mountain Veterans Memorial Highway,** at the intersection of Routes 86 and 431 (© 518-946-2223; www.whiteface.com), snakes its way 8 miles up Whiteface Mountain, in Wilmington, for a panoramic view of the Adirondacks. When the sky's clear there's no better showcase of the region's topography—craggy mountains, scattered lakes, and crooked rivers carving their way through the valley below. Beyond the parking area on the shoulder of Whiteface, visitors have the option of riding an elevator inside the mountain or climbing an exposed rocky staircase to the summit. Allow 1 hour for the drive and ascent. The highway costs $8 for each car and driver, an additional $4 per passenger, and $5 for motorcyclists. The highway and summit are open from May 18 to June 28 daily from 9am to 4pm, from June 29 to September 2 daily from 8:30am to 5pm, from September 3 to October 14 daily from 9am to 4 pm.

The hottest attraction in the High Peaks is the **MacKenzie–Intervale Ski Jumping Complex,** 8 John Brown Rd. off Route 73 (© 518/523-2202; www.orda.org), adjacent to Kodak Sports Park and boasting five ski-jumping hills, including 300- and 400-foot jump towers. Although visitors can't use the ski jumps, they can still experience the thrill of standing 20 stories in the sky, with a view down the tower's sloping ramp from the starting gate. A chairlift brings visitors to the top of the landing hills—which are great tubing slopes in the winter—then glass elevators ascend to the tip of the highest tower. Ski jumpers and aerial freestyle skiers practice their jumps, flips, and twists and host dare-devil competitions. You can get tickets to all of these exciting events. Allow 1 hour for a tour, more for shows. Admission is $5 for adults, $2 in winter and $3 in summer for children ages 7 to 12. Chairlift and elevator admission for adults is $7 in winter, $8 in summer; for children ages 7 to 12, it's $4 in winter, $5 in summer. Children under 7 are admitted free. The complex is open daily from December 16 to March 19 and from May 20 to October 22 from 9am to 4pm. Free parking.

THE CHAMPLAIN VALLEY This picturesque corridor, between Lake Champlain and the resource-rich High Peaks, is steeped in Native American, French, British, and Revolutionary American history. Scenic Route 22 weaves between villages and hilly farmsteads in these foothills.

If you imagine away the necessities of the 21st century, like power lines and telephone poles, the historic town of **Essex,** on Route 22, is frozen in time. Unspoiled and meticulously preserved, there's no better example of pre–Civil War architecture—Federal, Greek Revival, Carpenter Gothic, Italianate and French Second Empire—in New York State. While these buildings are interesting, it's the integrity of Essex as a whole—the entire village is a historical landmark—that makes it worth a visit. If you arrive between 9am and 5pm, Monday through Friday, swing by the **Essex Community Heritage Organization** (located on the second floor of the brick Cyrus Stafford House, on the left, in front of the village's only flashing traffic light; ✆ **518/963-7088;** www. essexny.net) for a free walking-tour brochure.

Fort Ticonderoga (Rte. 74, Ticonderoga; ✆ **518/585-2821;** www.fort ticonderoga.org) was once a grimy, bloody stage for battle during the French and Indian War and the American Revolution. The fort has been impressively restored and is surrounded by 2,000 acres of carefully manicured grounds. The fort maintains one of the most extensive collections of colonial weapons in the country: Muskets, cannons, and arrowheads are displayed in the museum. A 20-minute narrated tour by staff historians offers background on the fort, and then visitors are on their own to explore the fort's historic corridors, barracks, and even a walk-in cooking oven used to feed the troops. Daily musket demonstrations staged by period-costume–clad staff are heaven for imaginative kids. And the King's Garden, an unexpected pleasure, is lovely; benches are scattered throughout for admiring the peonies, day lilies, and other flowers. Allow 2 to 4 hours. Admission is $12 for adults, $11 for seniors, $6 for children 7 to 12, free for children under 7. Open daily from May 10 to October 20 from 9am to 5pm. The King's Garden is open from June 15 to September 15 from 10am to 4pm. Free parking.

CENTRAL ADIRONDACKS The wilderness in the heart of this region drew the likes of J. P. Morgan, Andrew Carnegie, and the Vanderbilts, who built elaborate rustic retreats, some accessible only by rail, during the Gilded Age. The Vanderbilts' estate, Great Camp Sagamore, in Raquette Lake, is open to the public and is a spectacular achievement in rustic craftsmanship.

Just about everything there is to learn about the Adirondacks can be absorbed at **The Adirondack Museum** (Rte. 30, Blue Mountain Lake, off Rtes. 28 and 30; ✆ **518/352-7311;** www.adirondackmuseum.org). This indoor/outdoor museum is located on 32 acres of Blue Mountain, overlooking Blue Mountain Lake. It's an enlightening learning center, including exhibits about logging and mining in the North Country, a gallery displaying paintings of the region by artists like Rockwell Kent, a building devoted solely to boats and boating, and a lengthy roster of workshops and live demonstrations for kids and adults. In September, the museum hosts its annual rustic furniture fair, a popular event that features regional artisans. Allow 3 to 4 hours. Admission is $12 adults, $11 seniors (62 and up), $5 children 7 to 17, free for children under 7. It's open from Memorial Day weekend to mid-October from 9:30am to 5:30pm. Free parking.

THE SOUTHEASTERN REGION   James Fenimore Cooper had Lake George and environs in mind when he penned *Last of the Mohicans*. This area, once a battle zone, then a busy 18th-century port, and later a getaway for the elite, is now a lively, family-friendly vacation spot in summer and a sleepy, though lovely, destination in winter. There's historic Fort William Henry, kitschy arcades, mini-golf courses, a local rodeo, an amusement park, and accommodations galore. Lake George village hosts a range of events, such as Americade (a huge biker rally), the Adirondack Balloon Festival, and Jazz Fest.

For lake excursions, nothing beats **Lake George Steamboat Company,** Steel Pier, Lake George (€ 800/553-2628 or 518/668-5777; www.lakegeorgesteam boat.com). Its small fleet, a trio of handsome boats, includes the *Minne-Ha-Ha*, a paddle-wheel cruiser; the *Mohican*, one of the longest-running excursion vessels in the U.S.; and the *Lac du Saint Sacrement*. Trips include shoreline excursions, moonlight cruises, fireworks tours, and the popular dinner cruises in the elegant dining room of the *Lac du Saint Sacrament*, among others. Prices for adults range from $9.25 to $34. Prices for children range from $5.75 to $20. Various cruises are offered from May 2 to October 27. Call to find out which cruises will be going on when you're in town.

The Great Escape, Route 9 South, Lake George (€ 518/792-3500; www.thegreatescape.com), a fun park owned by industry giant Six Flags, is worth the hassle of large crowds and parking nightmares if you're into high-speed roller coasters and rides that boomerang, dive, swing, and spin. **Splashwater Kingdom Water Park** is also owned by Six Flags (contact information is the same as The Great Escape information). Monsoon-size artificial waves and flume and raft rides make playing in the sun a joy. At press-time, rates were adults $33; children under 48 inches $20; seniors (55 and up) $20, free for children 2 and under. The park is open Monday through Friday from 10am to 8pm and Saturday and Sunday from 10am to 10pm.

WHERE TO STAY

In addition to the numerous hotels, B&Bs, and motels in the Adirondacks, the Department of Environmental Conservation maintains roughly 40 state campgrounds in the park. For information on sleeping alfresco, call € 518/457-2500 or visit www.dec.state.ny.us.

Lake Placid Lodge   Travelers have been escaping to this quintessential Adirondack retreat for over a century. The Lodge is an upscale, exclusive Relais & Châteaux property that sits on the western bank of Lake Placid, isolated from Main Street crowds. The landscaped grounds and rustic-style architecture are extraordinary—every room houses a stone fireplace and unique furniture crafted by local artisans. The lodge boasts a restaurant famous for its organic cuisine and lofty prices. Though activities are plentiful—guests may snowshoe or ski here in winter or paddle around Lake Placid in summer—this resort caters to the quiet, private set, often celebrities and CEOs, and does not encourage small children. If there ever was a storybook backdrop for a romantic getaway, this is it. Whiteface Inn Rd., Lake Placid, NY 12946. ℂ 518/523-2700. Fax 518/523-1124. www.lakeplacidlodge. com. 34 units. Cabins $350–$950; rooms $350–$725. AE, MC, V. Free parking. Children under 12 not permitted. **Amenities:** 2 restaurants; 18-hole golf course; 6 tennis courts on adjacent property.

The Sagamore Hotel   The venerable Sagamore Hotel dominates the south-western shoreline of Lake George. Anyone looking for a little decadence will find it here, particularly at the resort's new spa. The hotel spans a 72-acre island, with just about every activity available—there's even a rock-climbing wall and mini-golf course—and nothing beats the dining choices here: There's a classy dining room, a casual pub, even tapas on the veranda, where guests in top hats and corseted gowns once mingled in the 19th century. Today the Sagamore draws all kinds, and offers upscale rooms in the historic hotel, a striking castle that can be rented by the month (the entire castle can be rented, and accom-modates 12 people), or relatively plain, modular lodges available for families looking to stay a while. This is an excellent choice for travelers with children. 110 Sagamore Rd., Bolton Landing. ℂ **518/644-9400** or 800/358-3585. Fax 518/743-6036. www.the sagamore.com. 350 units. $139–$339 double; $259–$519 suite. AE, DC, DISC, MC, V. Free parking. **Amenities:** 4 restaurants; indoor pool; 18-hole golf course; 6 tennis courts (1 indoor, 5 outdoor); spa; fitness center.

The Wawbeek Resort   The original Wawbeek was an Adirondack Great Camp and, remarkably, following renovations and rebuilding after it burned in 1980, the new structure is equally stunning and authentic in style. The resort offers guests a range of accommodations, from simple, rustic cabins to rooms and suites in an elegant lake house. Proprietors Nancy and Norman Howard strive to disconnect guests from the busy, hectic outside world: There are no tel-evisions or telephones in rooms (unless requested). Visitors have backyard access to Upper Saranac Lake, one of the region's most treasured waterways. There are also 7 miles of hiking, biking, and cross-country ski trails. Panther Mountain Rd. (Rte. 30), Tupper Lake, NY 12986. ℂ **800/953-2656** or 518/359-2656. Fax 518/359-2475. www. wawbeek.com. 31 units. $90–$290 double; $310–$400 suite. AE, MC, V. Free parking. **Amenities:** Restaurant; tennis court.

WHERE TO DINE

Friends Lake Inn NEW AMERICAN   This quaint inn wows foodies and wine connoisseurs alike. *Wine Spectator* magazine recognized Friends Lake Inn as one of the top 100 wine cellars in the world. Entrees like veal roulade with shiitake mushrooms, goat cheese, rosemary-scented polenta, and caramelized shallot essence make dining here an experience. The atmosphere is front-of-the-fireplace cozy, perfect for an intimate celebration. The inn's casual Bistro serves lighter fare, and is perfect after a long day of skiing or antiquing. 963 Friends Lake Rd., Chestertown, NY 12817. ℂ **518/494-4751**. www.friendslake.com. Reservations required for dining room. Main courses in restaurant $18–$30, Bistro $18–$30. AE, DC, MC, V. Restaurant Mon–Fri 5:30–9pm; Sat, Sun, and holidays 5:30–9:30pm. Bistro daily 4–10pm.

Lake Placid Pub & Brewery PUB STYLE   Brewmaster Christopher Eric-son's popular beer, Ubu Ale, made on-site, has flooded taps across the North Country, and visitors can't get enough of his High Peaks Hefeweizen, Barkeater Amber, and Moose Island Ale. At heart, this is a local watering hole, a fun hot spot off Main Street. Regulars drink downstairs in the smoky pub-style bar known as P. J. O'Neill's, or gather upstairs in the cozy dining room, where a fire blazes in winter and an outdoor deck is open in summer. Expect standard pub fare here: shepherd's pie, bangers and mash, and a selection of delicious burgers. You can't miss with the heaping plate of supreme nachos as a starter. There's often a lengthy waiting list for tables during busier seasons, but pool, darts, foosball, and a lively crowd keep things interesting. 14 Mirror Lake Dr., Lake Placid. ℂ 518/523-3813. www.ubuale.com. Reservations not accepted. Main courses $5–$15. MC, V. Restaurant open Mon–Thurs 11:30am–10pm; Fri–Sat 11:30am–11pm; Sun noon–10pm. Down stairs bar open daily 3pm–3am.

Richard's Freestyle Cuisine NEW AMERICAN   Richard's is a pleasant surprise. Meals are pricey, but the atmosphere is casual, service is excellent, the food—entrees are simply described on a succinct menu as "The Sea Bass," "The Quail," and "The Steak"—is exquisite, and there's a lengthy wine list. Chef Richard Brousseau is known for his classical culinary training and unique flair. The restaurant decor is muted and sophisticated, a change from most local dining rooms, which are crowded with Adirondackana. Guests may dine on the porch, overlooking picturesque Mirror Lake. 51 Main St., Lake Placid, NY 12946. ℂ 518/523-5900. www.freestylecuisine.com. Reservations recommended. Main courses $18–$30. AE, DC, MC, V. Wed–Mon 5:30–9:30pm.

ALEXANDRIA BAY & THE THOUSAND ISLANDS REGION

Nestled in the Thousand Islands region of New York State, Alexandria Bay is a lively, scenic port wedged between the United States and Canada on the St. Lawrence River. Despite prevalent tacky T-shirt shops and vendors peddling knickknacks, strolling around is fun, particularly by the docks where travelers park their motorboats and yachts. Alexandria Bay is best used as a jumping-off-point for sights and activities on the St. Lawrence River. Some 1,800 islands pepper this span of the river, and exploring quiet, pristine coves or popular water routes is an exciting summertime activity. Where else can you buy lunch at a floating hot dog stand? Alexandria Bay is a ghost town in winter, but vacationers should take advantage of the low rates to cross-country ski or snowmobile on the river.

ESSENTIALS

GETTING THERE   If you're approaching Alexandria Bay from the south— in other words, from anywhere other than Canada—drive north on Interstate 81 to Exit 50, where you'll practically bump into the Canadian border. Take Route 12 East and follow it for approximately 4 miles. Turn left onto Church Street, which will bring you directly into Alexandria Bay.

VISITOR INFORMATION   To learn more about Alexandria Bay and the Thousand Islands region, visit the **Alexandria Bay Chamber of Commerce** at 11 Market St., or contact the chamber at ℂ **800/541-2110,** 315/482-9531, or www.alexbay.org. You can also visit **www.visit1000islands.com.**

FAST FACTS   If you need a doctor, call or visit **E. J. Noble Hospital,** 19 Fuller St. (ℂ **315/482-2511**). **Kinney Drugs,** 81 Church St. (ℂ **315/482-6171**), is open Monday through Friday from 8am to 9pm, Saturday from 8am to 7pm, and Sunday from 8am to 6pm.

EXPLORING ALEXANDRIA BAY & THE THOUSAND ISLANDS

Boldt Castle, on Heart Island off Alexandria Bay (© **315/482-9724;** www.boldtcastle.com), is a breathtaking landmark in the Thousand Islands region. It was here that multi-millionaire George C. Boldt, proprietor of the Waldorf-Astoria in New York City—and the man responsible for the salad dressing we refer to as "Thousand Island"—commissioned the ultimate homage to his beloved wife, Louise, in 1900. Boldt Castle, a six-story, 120-room stone fortress, was nearly finished when Louise suddenly died. Construction ceased, and ever since, the island has remained uninhabited. Tour boats shuttle passengers back and forth to Heart Island; you can also rent a small paddleboat and portage yourself. Tours of Boldt are interesting, but wandering the grounds on your own and hunkering down for a picnic is even better. Allow 1½ hours for the entire experience. Admission is $4.75 adults, $3 kids ages 6 to 12. Open from mid-May to June 30 and from September 1 to mid-October daily from 10am to 6:30pm, from July to August daily from 10am to 7:30pm.

Uncle Sam's Boat Tours, 47 James St. (© **800/253-9229** or 315/482-2611; www.usboattours.com), is the best, most affordable way to explore the Thousand Islands. There are a number of packages available for land-weary visitors. Uncle Sam's fleet is well-maintained, clean, and comfortable. Scheduled tours take visitors back and forth to Boldt Castle, ply international waters for a "Two Nation Tour," float to historic French and Indian War battle sites during evening tours, and ferry people throughout the entire region on a comprehensive Thousand Islands exploration, a 3-hour trip. Lunch and dinner cruises are also available. Adult tickets range from $9 to $28; for kids ages 4 to 12, tickets range from $4.25 to $20. Cruises are offered from May 1 to October 31 from 10am to 7pm. Free parking. Take Route 12 East to the 1,000 Islands Alexandria Bay Archway. Turn left onto Church Street until it becomes James Street. Follow James Street to the marina.

10 miles south of Alexandria Bay, you'll find the **Antique Boat Museum,** 750 Mary St., Clayton (© **315/686-4104;** www.abm.org), a true sanctuary for boat enthusiasts. Hundreds of vessels, ranging from Native American dugouts to hydroplanes, are exhibited along with motors, boat hardware, building plans, and prints in a brand-new building on the banks of the St. Lawrence River. The library maintains an extensive collection of books and historic archives. Visitors can sign up for boat-building workshops and other demonstrations. Weather permitting, speed demons are invited to cruise the river in a 1929 Hacker Craft reproduction; tours leave every hour. Allow 1 hour to explore. Admission is $6 adults, $5 seniors (65 and up), $2 kids ages 6 to 17, free for kids under 5. Speedboat rides are $12. Open daily from 9am to 5pm. Free parking for boats and cars.

WHERE TO STAY

Bonnie Castle   A popular honeymoon haven in the 1980s, all rooms were recently updated with new furniture, wallpaper, and carpeting, and management is soon planning to tackle the grounds. There's no castle to speak of, but Bonnie Castle is an impressive, sprawling resort with a marina, miniature golf course, driving range, ice rink, cross-country ski trails, stable, and much more. This is a great family destination and is also appropriate for couples looking for a romantic getaway: Between the picturesque sunsets over nearby Boldt Castle, the 700-seat Vegas-style nightclub, the waterfront bar, and a new casino directly across the river (10 min. by boat) in Gananoque, Canada, there's plenty of evening entertainment. Holland St. (at the junction of Rtes. 12 and 81), Alexandria Bay, NY 13607-0218. ℭ **800/955-4511** or 315/482-4511. Fax 315/482-9600. www.bonniecastle.com. 128 units. $79–$250 double. AE, DC, MC, V. Free self-parking. **Amenities:** 2 restaurants; pools (1 outdoor, 1 indoor); tennis court.

The Riveredge Resort Hotel   The colonial-style brick facade of this classy, immaculately-maintained hotel, known for excellent service, is easy to spot from downtown Alexandria Bay—its proximity to village shops and the St. Lawrence River waterfront makes it one of the most popular and accessible hotels in the region. Accommodations range from comfortable standard rooms to deluxe, two-story or "loft" Jacuzzi suites; be sure to request a room with a balcony overlooking the Thousand Islands. The hotel's Jacques Cartier Room is touted as the most elegant restaurant around, with an extensive wine list recognized by the *Wine Spectator.* 17 Holland St., Alexandria Bay, NY 13607. ℭ **800/365-6987** or 315/482-9917. Fax 315/482-5010. www.riveredgeresort.com. 129 units. $89–$298 double; $141–$318 suite. AE, DC, MC, V. Free self- and valet parking. **Amenities:** 2 restaurants; pools (1 outdoor, 1 indoor); fitness room.

WHERE TO DINE

Admiral's Inn STEAK/SEAFOOD   The popularity of this family-owned restaurant owes more to the atmosphere than the food, although locals rave about the prime rib. Dine at the restaurant's sidewalk cafe for prime people-watching. Expect basic, no-nonsense American and Italian fare like fried seafood and pasta dishes in a kid-friendly, ultra-casual atmosphere. 20 James St ℭ **315/482-2781.** Reservations recommended. Main courses $4.50–$12 lunch, $9.95–$35 dinner. AE, DC, MC, V. Sun–Thurs 11am–10pm; Fri–Sat 11am–11pm.

Cavallario's Steak and Seafood House STEAK/SEAFOOD   Cavallario's is the granddaddy of restaurants here, a venerable business with excellent fare and service. The restaurant is austere and a bit dark, decorated with suits of armor, red velvet, and heavy furniture. The food is equally serious and heavy—grilled veal loin chops, Maine lobster, peppercorn sirloin. Dining is casual and families are welcome, though dinner may take some time here. 26 Church St. ℭ **315/482-2160.** Main courses $13–$25. AE, DC, MC, V. Daily 5–10pm.

CORNING

Corning is a charming destination in New York's southern tier, surrounded by the natural beauty of the Finger Lakes region. The town's claim to fame is its Glassworks Center, but its downtown, particularly Market Street, draws visitors to quaint brick storefronts housing funky boutiques, art studios, and eateries.

ESSENTIALS

GETTING THERE   Easily accessible by car from most points in the northeast, Corning is located at the intersection of Routes 17 and 414, and Routes 17 and 15, between New York City and Niagara Falls.

VISITOR INFORMATION   Call the Greater Corning Area Chamber of Commerce at ℭ **607/936-4686** or check out **www.corningny.org**. Once in town, stop by the Corning Information Center at 42 E. Market St. in the Baron Steuben Building at Centerway Square.

FAST FACTS   If you need a doctor, call or visit **Corning Hospital,** 176 Denison Pkwy. E. (ℭ **607/937-7200**). **Eckerd Drug Company,** 45 E. Market St. (ℭ **607/962-3111**), is open Monday through Friday from 9am to 8pm, Saturday from 9am to 6pm, and Sunday from 10am to 5pm.

EXPLORING CORNING

The dazzling **Corning Museum of Glass,** One Museum Way (℡ **800/732-6845** or 607/937-5371; www.cmog.org), is a shrine to all things glass—even the architecture showcases the beauty and versatility of the material. You'll find live entertainment during the popular Hot Glass Show, as glassblowers strut their stuff for an audience. In The Glass Innovation Center, you'll encounter some scientific uses of glass. The art gallery boasts 35,000 pieces of glass art, from 9th- and 10th-century vases and flasks to Tiffany lamps. Other highlights are a bird's-eye view of the inner workings of a functioning glass factory and opportunities to try your hand at glass-crafting in the workshop. Allow 2 to 3 hours. Admission is $11 adults, $10 seniors (60 and up), $6 kids ages 6 to 17, free for children under 6. Open September through June daily from 9am to 5pm, July through August daily from 9am to 8pm.

Recently renovated, the kid-friendly **Rockwell Museum of Western Art,** 111 Cedar St. (℡ **607/937-5386;** www.rockwellmuseum.org), boasts the largest collection of Western art east of the Mississippi. Visitors can view an impressive series of galleries displaying an eclectic range of American Western and Native American work, from beaded costumes and woven rugs to bronze sculpture. The collections showcase traditional Native American artisans as well as classic and contemporary artists, including Frederic Remington, C. M. Russell, and Andy Warhol. Take a look at the museum's Web page as you plan your visit because there's always something going on here—a salsa band, pottery lessons, fireworks. Allow 1 hour. Admission is $6.50 adults, $5.50 seniors (60 and up), $4.50 kids ages 6 to 10, free for children under 5. The museum is open Monday through Saturday from 9am to 5pm, Sunday from 11am to 5pm.

WHERE TO STAY

Fairfield Inn by Marriott   This three-story hotel is comfortable and predictable, with a reputation for quality service and the advantage of close proximity to area attractions. 3 S. Buffalo St., Corning, NY 14830. ℡ **607/937-9600.** Fax 607/937-3155. www.fairfieldinn.com. 63 units. $89 double. AE, DC, MC, V. Free self-parking. **Amenities:** Indoor pool.

Hillcrest Manor Bed and Breakfast   This lovely late-19th-century Classic Greek Revival bed-and-breakfast, just 4 blocks from downtown Corning, is the ultimate in Victorian lodging. Hosts Dick Bright and Kyle Goodman have meticulously decorated every room of the mansion with period antiques and glassware, creating an extraordinary backdrop. Hillcrest Manor is located in a residential neighborhood where guests are protected from noisy traffic. 227 Cedar St., Corning, NY 14830. ℡ **607/936-4548.** www.corninghillcrestmanor.com. 4 units. $125–double; $135–$225 suite. No credit cards. Free self-parking.

3

New England

One of the greatest challenges of traveling in New England is choosing from an abundance of superb restaurants, accommodations, and attractions. Do you want the mountains or the beach? Shining cities or quiet vistas? In this chapter, we give you an overview of one of the most historic regions of the United States, and still one of the most vital. We start in Massachusetts with Boston; go out to Cape Cod and Martha's Vineyard; swing by Connecticut's Mystic seaport and by glamorous Newport, Rhode Island; and return to Massachusetts to the Berkshires. We head inland to the natural glories of Southern Vermont and New Hampshire's White Mountains, then up the rocky, majestic Maine coast.

1 Boston & Cambridge

Boston embodies contrasts and contradictions—it's blue blood and blue collar, Yankee and Irish, home to budget-conscious graduate students and free-spending computer wizards (still!). Rich in colonial history and 21st-century technology, it's a living landmark whose unofficial mascot is the construction worker. A new highway, a dramatic new bridge, and new buildings of all sizes are altering the landscape of eastern Massachusetts.

Take a few days (or weeks) to get to know the Boston area, or use it as a gateway to the rest of New England. Here's hoping your experience is memorable and delightful.

ESSENTIALS

GETTING THERE By Plane Most major domestic carriers and many international carriers serve Boston's Logan International Airport (© 800/23-LOGAN; www.massport.com), across the harbor from downtown. Access to the city is by subway (the "T"), cab, and boat. The **subway** is fast and cheap—10 minutes to Government Center and $1 for a token (good for one ride). Free **shuttle buses** run from each terminal to the Airport Station on the Blue Line of the T from 5:30am to 1am. The Blue Line stops at State Street and Government Center, downtown points where you can exit or transfer (free) to the other lines. A **cab** from the airport to downtown or the Back Bay costs about $18 to $24. The ride into town takes 10 to 45 minutes, depending on traffic and the time of day.

The trip to the downtown waterfront (near cabstands and several hotels) in a **boat** takes 7 minutes. The free no. 66 shuttle bus connects all terminals to the Logan ferry dock. The **Airport Water Shuttle** (© 617/330-8680) runs to Rowes Wharf on Atlantic Avenue Monday through Friday from 6am to 8pm, Saturday and Sunday from 10am to 8pm. The one-way fare is $10 for adults, $5 for seniors, and free for children under 12. **Harbor Express** (© 617/376-8417; www.harbor express.com) runs from the airport to Long Wharf Monday through Friday from 6:30am to 9pm (to 11pm on Fri), less frequently on weekends. The one-way fare is $8 for adults, $4 for children 6 to 12, and $1 for children under 6.

Boston Accommodations & Dining

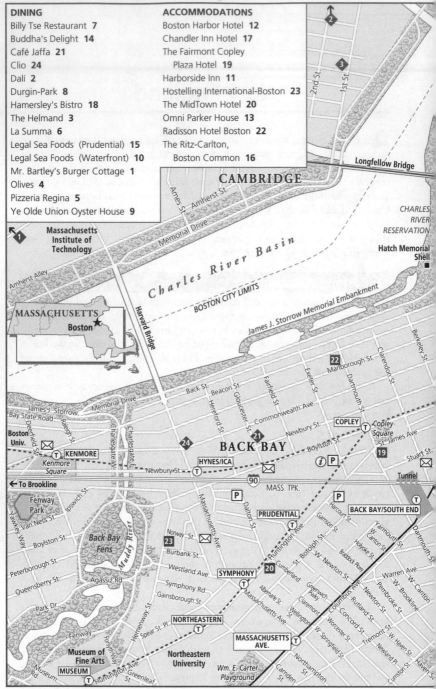

DINING
Billy Tse Restaurant **7**
Buddha's Delight **14**
Café Jaffa **21**
Clio **24**
Dalí **2**
Durgin-Park **8**
Hamersley's Bistro **18**
The Helmand **3**
La Summa **6**
Legal Sea Foods (Prudential) **15**
Legal Sea Foods (Waterfront) **10**
Mr. Bartley's Burger Cottage **1**
Olives **4**
Pizzeria Regina **5**
Ye Olde Union Oyster House **9**

ACCOMMODATIONS
Boston Harbor Hotel **12**
Chandler Inn Hotel **17**
The Fairmont Copley
 Plaza Hotel **19**
Harborside Inn **11**
Hostelling International-Boston **23**
The MidTown Hotel **20**
Omni Parker House **13**
Radisson Hotel Boston **22**
The Ritz-Carlton,
 Boston Common **16**

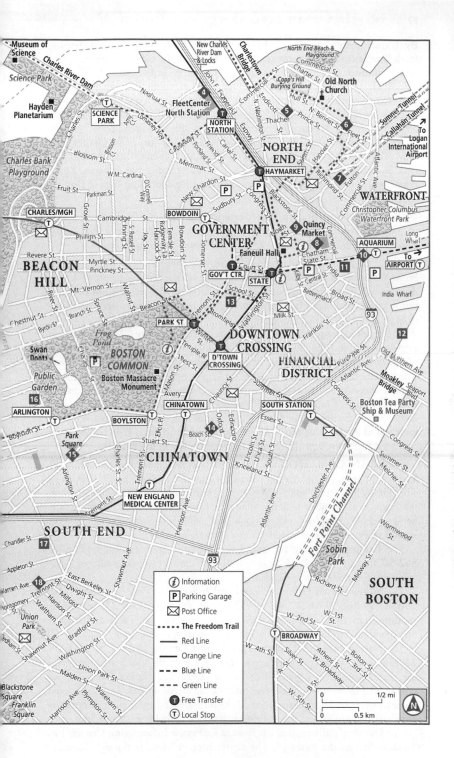

By Train   Boston has three rail centers: **South Station,** on Atlantic Avenue; **Back Bay Station,** on Dartmouth Street across from the Copley Place mall; and **North Station,** on Causeway Street near the FleetCenter. **Amtrak** (© **800/ USA-RAIL** or 617/482-3660; www.amtrak.com) serves all three. Each train station is also a rapid-transit station. South Station is a stop on the Red Line, which runs to Cambridge by way of Park Street, the hub of the **subway** (© **800/ 392-6100** outside Massachusetts, or 617/222-3200; www.mbta.com). At Park Street you can connect to the Green, Blue, and Orange lines. The Orange Line links Back Bay Station with Downtown Crossing (where there's a walkway to Park St. Station) and other points. The **commuter rail** serves Ipswich, Rockport, and Fitchburg from North Station, and points south and west of Boston, including Plymouth, from South Station.

By Bus   The **South Station Transportation Center,** on Atlantic Avenue next to the train station, is served by regional and national lines, including **Greyhound** (© **800/231-2222** or 617/526-1801; www.greyhound.com).

By Car   Boston is 218 miles from New York; driving time is about 4½ hours. From Washington, it takes about 8 hours to cover the 468 miles; the 992-mile drive from Chicago takes around 21 hours. Driving to Boston is not difficult, but if you're thinking of using the car to get around town, you won't need one to explore Boston and Cambridge.

The major highways are **I-90,** the Massachusetts Turnpike ("Mass. Pike"), an east-west toll road that leads to the New York State Thruway; **I-93/U.S. 1,** which extends north to Canada; and **I-93/Route 3,** the Southeast Expressway, which connects with the south, including Cape Cod. **I-95** (Mass. Rte. 128) is a beltway about 11 miles from downtown that connects to I-93 and to highways in Rhode Island, Connecticut, and New York to the south and New Hampshire and Maine to the north. The **Mass. Pike** extends into the city and connects with the **Central Artery** (the John F. Fitzgerald Expwy.). To avoid Big Dig construction, exit at Cambridge/Allston or Prudential Center in the Back Bay.

VISITOR INFORMATION   Contact the **Greater Boston Convention & Visitors Bureau,** 2 Copley Place, Ste. 105, Boston (© **888/SEE-BOSTON** or 617/536-4100; 0171/431-3434 in the U.K.; fax 617/424-7664; www. bostonusa.com). It offers a comprehensive information kit ($6.25) with a planner, guidebook, map, and coupon book; and a *Kids Love Boston* guide ($5). Free smaller planners for specific seasons or events are often available.

The **Cambridge Office for Tourism,** 18 Brattle St., Cambridge (© **800/ 862-5678** or 617/441-2884; fax 617/441-7736; www.cambridge-usa.org), distributes information about Cambridge.

The **Massachusetts Office of Travel and Tourism,** 10 Park Plaza, Ste. 4510, Boston (© **800/227-6277** or 617/973-8500; fax 617/973-8525; www.mass vacation.com), distributes the *Getaway Guide,* a free magazine with information on attractions and lodgings, a map, and a seasonal calendar.

The **Boston National Historic Park Visitor Center,** 15 State St. (© **617/ 242-5642;** www.nps.gov/bost), across the street from the Old State House and the State Street T, is a good place to start exploring. National Park Service rangers staff the center and lead free tours of the Freedom Trail. The audiovisual show provides basic information on 16 historic sites on the trail. The center is wheelchair accessible and has restrooms. It's open daily from 9am to 5pm.

The Freedom Trail begins at the **Boston Common Information Center,** 146 Tremont St., on the common. The center is open Monday through Saturday from 8:30am to 5pm, Sunday from 9am to 5pm. The **Prudential Information Center,** on the main level of the Prudential Center, is open Monday through Friday from 8:30am to 6pm, Saturday and Sunday from 10am to 6pm. The **Greater Boston Convention & Visitors Bureau** (© **888/SEE-BOSTON** or 617/536-4100) operates both centers.

GETTING AROUND   When you reach your hotel, leave your car in the garage and walk or use public transportation. Free maps of downtown Boston and the transit system are available at visitor centers around the city. *Where* and other tourism-oriented magazines, available free at most hotels, include maps of central Boston and the T. *Streetwise Boston* ($5.95) and *Artwise Boston* ($5.95) are sturdy, laminated maps available at most bookstores.

By Public Transportation   The **Massachusetts Bay Transportation Authority,** or MBTA (© **800/392-6100** outside Massachusetts, or 617/222-3200; www.mbta.com), is known as the "T," and its logo is the letter in a circle. It runs subways, trolleys, buses, and ferries in Boston and many suburbs, as well as the commuter rail. Its website includes maps, schedules, and other information.

Newer stations on the Red, Blue, and Orange lines are wheelchair accessible; the Green Line is being converted. All T buses have lifts or kneelers; call © 800/ LIFT-BUS for information. To learn more, call the **Office for Transportation Access** (© **617/222-5438** or TTY 617/222 5854).

The **Boston Visitor Pass** (© **877/927-7277** or 617/222-5218; www.mbta. com) includes unlimited travel on the subway and local buses, in commuter rail zones 1A and 1B, and on two ferries. The cost is $6 for 1 day (thus tokens are cheaper for fewer than six trips), $11 for 3 days, and $22 for 7 days. The $13 **weekly combo pass** covers subways and buses but not ferries, and is good only from Sunday through Saturday. You can buy a pass in advance by phone or online, or when you arrive at the Airport T station, South Station, Back Bay Station, or North Station. They're also for sale at the Government Center and Harvard T stations; the Boston Common, Prudential Center, and Faneuil Hall Marketplace information centers; and some hotels.

Red, Blue, and Orange line trains and Green Line trolleys make up the **subway** system, which runs partly aboveground. The local fare is $1—you'll need a token—and can be as much as $2.50 for some surface line extensions. Transfers are free. Route and fare information and timetables are available through the website and at centrally located stations. Service begins around 5:15am and ends around 12:30am. A sign on the token booth in every station gives the time of the last train in either direction.

T buses and **"trackless trolleys"** (buses with electric antennae) provide service around town and to and around the suburbs. The local bus fare is 75¢; express buses are $1.50 and up. Exact change is required. You can use a token, but you won't get change. Important local routes include **no. 1** (Mass. Ave. from Dudley Sq. in Roxbury through the Back Bay and Cambridge to Harvard Sq.); **nos. 92** and **93** (between Haymarket and Charlestown); and **no. 77** (Mass. Ave. from Harvard Sq. north to Porter Sq. and Arlington).

Two useful **ferry** routes (both included in the T visitor pass) run on the Inner Harbor. The first connects **Long Wharf** (near the New England Aquarium), the **Charlestown Navy Yard**—it's a good final leg of the Freedom Trail—and **Lovejoy Wharf,** off Causeway Street behind North Station. The other runs between **Lovejoy Wharf** and the **World Trade Center.** The fare is $1.25. Call © **617/ 227-4321** for information.

Taxis are expensive and not always easy to flag—find a cabstand or call a dispatcher. To call ahead, try the **Independent Taxi Operators Association** (© 617/426-8700), **Boston Cab** (© 617/536-5010 or 617/262-2227), **Metro Cab** (© 617/242-8000), or **Town Taxi** (© 617/536-5000). In Cambridge, call **Ambassador Brattle** (© 617/492-1100) or **Yellow Cab** (© 617/547-3000). Boston Cab can dispatch a wheelchair-accessible vehicle; advance notice is recommended.

FAST FACTS If you need medical attention, your hotel concierge should be able to help you. Hospital referral services include **Brigham and Women's** (© 800/294-9999), **Massachusetts General** (© 800/711-4MGH), and **Tufts New England Medical Center** (© 617/636-9700). An affiliate of Mass. General, **MGH Back Bay,** 388 Comm. Ave. (© 617/267-7171), offers walk-in service and honors most insurance plans.

Downtown Boston has no 24-hour **drugstore.** The **CVS** at 155–157 Charles St. (© 617/523-1028), next to the Charles/MGH Red Line T stop, is open until midnight. The **CVS** at the Porter Square Shopping Center, off Mass. Ave. in Cambridge (© 617/876-5519), is open 24 hours.

The visitor center at 15 State St. has **public restrooms,** as do most tourist attractions, hotels, department stores, shopping centers, coffee bars, and public buildings. Free-standing, self-cleaning pay toilets (25¢) occupy eight locations downtown, including City Hall Plaza and Commercial Street at Snowhill Street, off the Freedom Trail.

On the whole, Boston and Cambridge are safe cities for walking. As in any urban area, stay out of parks (including Boston Common, the Public Garden, and the Esplanade) at night unless you're in a crowd. Areas to avoid at night include Boylston Street between Tremont and Washington, and Tremont Street from Stuart to Boylston. Try not to walk alone late at night in the Theater District and around North Station. Public transportation is busy and safe, but service stops between 12:30 and 1am.

The 5% **sales tax** does not apply to food, prescription drugs, newspapers, or clothing that costs less than $175; the tax on meals and takeout food is 5%. The lodging tax in Boston and Cambridge is 12.45%.

SPECIAL EVENTS & FESTIVALS Every March 17, a 5-mile parade salutes both **St. Patrick's Day** and the day British troops left Boston in 1776 (© 800/888-5515). **Patriot's Day,** the third Monday in April, features re-enactments of the events of April 18 and 19, 1775, which signified the start of the Revolutionary War, as well as the running of the **Boston Marathon;** call the Boston Athletic Association (© 617/236-1652; www.bostonmarathon.org). The third week in June sees the *Boston Globe* Jazz & Blues Festival (© 617/267-4301; www.boston.com/jazzfest). Big names and rising stars of the jazz world appear at lunchtime, after-work, evening, and weekend events, some of which are free. The **Boston Pops Concert and Fireworks Display,** held at Hatch Memorial Shell on the Esplanade during Boston, Massachusetts Independence Week, culminates in the famous Boston Pops' **Fourth of July** concert. The program includes Tchaikovsky's *1812 Overture* with actual cannon fire that segues into the fireworks. Call © 617/727-5215.

WHAT TO SEE & DO IN BOSTON

If you'll be in town for more than a couple of days, consider purchasing a **BosTix** (© 617/262-8632; www.bostix.org) that offers discounts on admission to many area attractions. It's not worth the money ($9) for single travelers, but couples and families can take good advantage of it.

A **CityPass** offers great savings in money and time. It's a booklet of tickets to the Harvard Museum of Natural History, Kennedy Library, Museum of Fine Arts, Museum of Science, New England Aquarium, and Prudential Center Skywalk. The price (at press time, $30 for adults, $19 for children 3–17) represents a 50% savings for adults who visit all six attractions, and having a ticket means you can go straight to the entrance without waiting in line. The passes, good for 9 days from the date of purchase, are on sale at participating attractions, the Boston Common and Prudential Center visitor centers, through the **Greater Boston Convention & Visitors Bureau** (© **800/SEE-BOSTON;** www. bostonusa.com), and at www.citypass.com.

THE TOP ATTRACTIONS

Faneuil Hall Marketplace   Since Boston's most popular attraction opened in 1976, cities all over the country have imitated the "festival market" concept. The complex of shops, food counters, restaurants, bars, and public spaces is such a magnet for tourists and suburbanites that you could be forgiven for thinking that the only Bostonians in the crowd are employees. The five-structure complex sits on brick-and-stone plazas that teem with crowds shopping, eating, performing, watching performers, and people-watching. **Quincy Market** is the central Greek Revival–style building; its central corridor is an enormous food court. On either side, glass canopies cover full-service restaurants as well as pushcarts that hold everything from crafts created by New England artisans to hokey souvenirs. In the plaza between the **South Canopy** and the South Market building is an **information kiosk. Faneuil Hall** itself—nicknamed the "Cradle of Liberty"—sometimes gets overlooked, but it's worth a visit. National Park Service rangers give free 20-minute talks every half hour from 9am to 5pm in the auditorium. Between North, Congress, and State sts. and I-93. © **617/523-1300.** www. faneuilhallmarketplace.com. Marketplace Mon–Sat 10am–9pm; Sun noon–6pm. Food court opens earlier; some restaurants close later. T: Green or Blue Line to Government Center, Orange Line to Haymarket, or Blue Line to Aquarium.

Isabella Stewart Gardner Museum   Isabella Stewart Gardner (1840–1924) designed her exquisite home in the style of a 15th-century Venetian palace and filled it with European, American, and Asian painting and sculpture. You'll see works by Titian, Botticelli, Raphael, Rembrandt, Matisse, and Mrs. Gardner's friends James McNeill Whistler and John Singer Sargent. The building holds a hodgepodge of furniture and architectural details imported from European churches and palaces. The pièce de résistance is the magnificent courtyard, filled year-round with fresh flowers from the museum greenhouse. 280 The Fenway. © **617/566-1401.** www.gardnermuseum.org. Admission $11 adults Sat–Sun, $10 adults Mon–Fri; $7 seniors; $5 college students; free for children under 18. Tues–Sun and some Mon holidays 11am–5pm. T: Green Line E to Museum.

John F. Kennedy Library and Museum   The Kennedy era springs to life at this dramatic library, museum, and research complex overlooking Dorchester Bay. It captures the 35th president's accomplishments in sound and video recordings as well as fascinating displays of memorabilia and photos. A visit begins with a 17-minute film about Kennedy's early life. The exhibits start with the 1960 campaign and end with a tribute to Kennedy's legacy. There's a film about the Cuban Missile Crisis, along with displays on Attorney Gen. Robert F.

Kennedy, the civil-rights movement, the Peace Corps, the space program, First Lady Jacqueline Bouvier Kennedy, and the Kennedy family. Columbia Point. © 877/616-4599 or 617/929-4500. www.jfklibrary.org. Admission $8 adults, $6 seniors and college students, $4 youths 13–17, free for children under 13. Surcharges may apply for special exhibitions. Daily 9am–5pm (last film at 3:55pm). T: Red Line to JFK/UMass, then free shuttle bus, which runs every 20 min. By car, take Southeast Expwy. (I-93/Rte. 3) south to Exit 15 (Morrissey Blvd./JFK Library), turn left onto Columbia Rd., and follow signs to free parking lot.

Museum of Fine Arts   One of the world's great museums, the MFA works constantly to become even more accessible and interesting and is especially noted for its **Impressionist paintings** (including 43 Monets—the largest collection outside Paris), Asian and Old Kingdom Egyptian collections, classical art, Buddhist temple, and medieval sculpture and tapestries. The American and European paintings and sculpture are a remarkable assemblage of timeless works. Pick up a floor plan at the information desk, or take a free **guided tour** (weekdays except Mon holidays at 10:30am and 1:30pm; Wed at 6:15pm; and Sat at 10:30am and 1pm). Note that the MFA's admission fees are among the highest in the country. A Boston CityPass is a great deal if you plan to visit enough of the other included attractions. 465 Huntington Ave. © 617/267-9300. www.mfa.org. Admission $14 adults, $12 seniors and students (when entire museum is open; $12 and $10, respectively, when only West Wing is open), $5 children 7–17 on school days before 3pm (otherwise free). Admission good for 2 visits within 30 days. Voluntary contribution ($14 suggested) Wed 4–9:45pm. Surcharges may apply for special exhibitions. Free admission for museum shop, library, restaurants, and auditoriums. Entire museum Mon–Tues 10am–4:45pm; Wed 10am–9:45pm; Thurs–Fri 10am–5pm; Sat–Sun 10am–5:45pm. West Wing only Thurs–Fri 5–9:45pm. T: Green Line E to Museum or Orange Line to Ruggles.

Museum of Science   Among the 600-plus exhibits, you might meet an iguana or a dinosaur, find out how much you'd weigh on the moon, or climb into a space module. Activity centers focus on fields of interest—natural history (with live animals), light and optics, computers, and the human body—as well as interdisciplinary approaches. The separate-admission theaters are worth planning for, even if you're skipping the exhibits. Buy all your tickets at once, not only because it's cheaper but also because shows sometimes sell out. Tickets are for sale in person and, subject to a service charge, over the phone and online (www.tickets.mos.org). The **Mugar Omni Theater,** which shows IMAX movies on a five-story screen, is an intense experience. The **Charles Hayden Planetarium** takes you into space with daily star shows as well as shows on special topics that change several times a year. Science Park. © 617/723-2500. www.mos.org. Admission to exhibit halls $12 adults, $8 seniors and children 3–11. Mugar Omni Theater, Hayden Planetarium, or laser shows $7.50 adults, $5.50 seniors and children 3–11. Discounted tickets to 2 or 3 parts of complex available. July 5 to Labor Day Sat–Thurs 9am–7pm, Fri 9am–9pm; day after Labor Day to July 4 Sat–Thurs 9am–5pm, Fri 9am–9pm. T: Green Line to Science Park.

New England Aquarium   This entertaining complex is home to more than 7,000 fish and aquatic mammals. You'll want to spend at least half a day here, and afternoon crowds can make getting around painfully slow. A Boston City-Pass allows you to skip the ticket line, which can be uncomfortably long. The worthwhile **Simons IMAX Theatre,** which has its own hours and admission fees, shows 3D films that concentrate on the natural world. The focal point of the main building is the four-story, 200,000-gallon **Giant Ocean Tank.** Other exhibits focus on freshwater and tropical specimens, sea otters, the Aquarium

Medical Center, denizens of the Amazon, and the ecology of Boston Harbor. The hands-on **Edge of the Sea** exhibit contains a tide pool with resident sea stars, sea urchins, and horseshoe crabs. Central Wharf. © 617/973-5200. www.neaq.org. Admission summer weekends and holidays $15 adults, $13 seniors, $8 children 3–11; weekdays year-round and off-season weekends $13 adults, $11 seniors, $7 children. Harbor tours $13 adults, $10 seniors and college students, $9 youths 12–18, $8.50 children 3–11. Free admission for outdoor exhibits, cafe, and gift shop. July to Labor Day Mon–Tues and Fri 9am–6pm, Wed–Thurs 9am–8pm, Sat–Sun and holidays 9am–7pm; day after Labor Day to June Mon–Fri 9am–5pm, Sat–Sun and holidays 9am–6pm. Simons IMAX Theatre: © 866/815-4629. Tickets $7.50 adults, $5.50 seniors and children 3–11. Daily 10am–9pm. T: Blue Line to Aquarium.

THE FREEDOM TRAIL

A line of red paint or red brick on the sidewalk, the 3-mile Freedom Trail links 16 historic sights. Markers identify the stops, and plaques point the way from one to the next. The trail begins at **Boston Common,** where the Information Center, 146 Tremont St., distributes pamphlets that describe a self-guided tour. For a preview, visit the Freedom Trail Foundation's website at **www.thefreedom trail.org**.

You can also explore the **Black Heritage Trail.** Stops include stations on the Underground Railroad and homes of famous citizens as well as the African Meeting House, the oldest standing black church in the country. A 2-hour guided tour starts at the visitor center at 46 Joy St. (© 617/742-5415; www.nps.gov/boaf), daily in summer and by request at other times.

As you follow the Freedom Trail, you'll come to the **Boston National Historic Park Visitor Center,** 15 State St. (© 617/242-5642; www.nps.gov/bost). From here, rangers lead free tours of the heart of the trail. An audiovisual show provides basic information on the stops. The wheelchair-accessible center has restrooms and a bookstore. It's open daily from 9am to 5pm.

The hard-core history fiend who peers at every artifact and reads every plaque along the trail will wind up at Bunker Hill some 4 hours later. The family with restless children will appreciate the efficiency of the 90-minute ranger-led tour.

The highlights of the trail include **Boston Common;** the **Massachusetts State House** (© 617/727-3676), the **Old Granary Burying Ground,** which contains the graves of Samuel Adams, Paul Revere, and John Hancock; **the First Public School;** the **Old South Meeting House** (© 617/482-6439), the starting point of the Boston Tea Party; the **Boston Massacre Site;** the **Paul Revere House** (© 617/523-2338; www.paulreverehouse.org); **Old North Church** (© 617/523-6676; www.oldnorth.com), where Revere saw a signal in the steeple and set out on his "midnight ride"; the USS *Constitution* (© 617/242-5670), where active-duty sailors in 1812 dress uniforms give free tours of "Old Ironsides"; and the **Bunker Hill Monument** (© 617/242-5644), the 221-foot granite obelisk that honors the memory of the men who died in the Battle of Bunker Hill on June 17, 1775.

The best-known **park** in Boston is the **Public Garden,** bordered by Arlington, Boylston, Charles, and Beacon streets. Something lovely is in bloom at least half of the year. For 5 months, the lagoon is home to the celebrated **swan boats** (© 617/522-1966; www.swanboats.com). The pedal-powered vessels—the attendants pedal, not the passengers—come out of hibernation on the Saturday before Patriot's Day (the 3rd Mon of Apr). The 15-minute ride costs $2 for adults, $1.50 for seniors, and $1 for children under 16.

ORGANIZED TOURS

From May to October, the nonprofit **Boston by Foot,** 77 N. Washington St. (© **617/367-2345,** or 617/367-3766 for recorded info; www.bostonbyfoot.com), conducts historical and architectural walking tours that focus on neighborhoods or themes. Buy tickets ($9) from the guide; reservations are not required. The 90-minute tours take place rain or shine.

The **Boston Park Rangers** (© **617/635-7383;** www.ci.boston.ma.us/parks) offer free guided walking tours. The best-known focus is the Emerald Necklace, a loop of green spaces designed by pioneering landscape architect Frederick Law Olmsted. They include Boston Common, the Public Garden, the Commonwealth Avenue Mall, the Muddy River in the Fenway, Olmsted Park, Jamaica Pond, the Arnold Arboretum, and Franklin Park. Call for schedules.

The nonprofit **Boston History Collaborative** (© 617/350-0358; www.bostonhistorycollaborative.org) coordinates several heritage trails. Presented as guided and self-guided walking tours, longer excursions by bus and boat, and copiously documented websites, they focus on maritime history, immigration, literary history, and inventions.

The most unusual way to see Boston is with **Boston Duck Tours** (© 800/226-7442 or 617/723-DUCK; www.bostonducktours.com). From April to November, sightseers board a "duck," a reconditioned World War II amphibious landing craft, on the Boylston Street side of the Prudential Center (the Pru). The 80-minute narrated tour begins with a quick but comprehensive jaunt around the city. Then the duck lumbers down a ramp, splashes into the Charles River, and takes a spin around the basin. Tickets cost $23 for adults, $20 for seniors and students, $13 for children 4 to 12, and 25¢ for children under 4.

The **sightseeing cruise** season runs from April to October, with spring and fall offerings often restricted to weekends. **Boston Harbor Cruises,** 1 Long Wharf (© **617/227-4321;** www.bostonharborcruises.com), is the largest company. Ninety-minute historic sightseeing cruises, which tour the Inner and Outer harbors, depart daily at 11am, 1pm, 3pm, and 6 or 7pm (the sunset cruise), with extra excursions at busy times. Tickets are $17 for adults, $14 for seniors, and $12 for children under 12. Tours leave Long Wharf hourly from 10:30am to 4:30pm, and on the hour from the Navy Yard from 11am to 5pm. Tickets are $10 for adults, $9 for seniors, and $8 for children.

EXPLORING CAMBRIDGE

Harvard Square is a people-watching paradise of students, instructors, commuters, and sightseers. Restaurants and stores pack the three streets that radiate from the center of the square and the streets that intersect them.

Harvard University is the oldest college in the country. Free student-led tours of the main campus leave from the **Events & Information Center,** in Holyoke Center, 1350 Mass. Ave. (© **617/495-1573**), during the school year twice a day Monday through Friday and once on Saturday (except during vacations), and during the summer four times a day Monday through Saturday and twice on Sunday. The Events & Information Center has maps, illustrated booklets, and self-guided walking-tour directions.

The Harvard Museum of Natural History and **Peabody Museum of Archaeology & Ethnology**   These museums house the university's collections of items and artifacts related to the natural world. The **Botanical Museum** displays the **Glass Flowers,** 3,000 models of more than 840 plant species devised by Leopold and Rudolph Blaschka. Children love the **Museum of**

Comparative Zoology, where dinosaurs share space with preserved and stuffed insects and animals that range in size from butterflies to giraffes. Young visitors enjoy the dollhouselike "Worlds in Miniature" display at the **Peabody Museum,** which represents people from all over the world in scaled-down homes. The Peabody also boasts the **Hall of the North American Indian,** where 500 artifacts representing 10 cultures are on display. Museum of Natural History: 26 Oxford St. ℂ 617/495-3045. www.hmnh.harvard.edu. Peabody Museum: 11 Divinity Ave. ℂ 617/496-1027. www.peabody.harvard.edu. Admission to both $6.50 adults, $5 seniors and students, $4 children 3–13; free to all Sun until noon year-round and Wed 3–5pm Sept–May. Daily 9am–5pm. T: Red Line to Harvard. Cross Harvard Yard, keeping John Harvard statue on right, and turn right at Science Center. First left is Oxford St.

Harvard University Art Museums   The **Fogg Art Museum,** 32 Quincy St., near Broadway, offers a broad range of items—17th-century Dutch and Flemish landscapes, 19th-century British and American paintings and drawings, French paintings and drawings from the 18th century through the Impressionist period, contemporary sculpture, and changing exhibits. The **Busch–Reisinger Museum,** in Werner Otto Hall (enter through the Fogg), is the only museum in North America devoted to the art of northern and central Europe. The early-20th-century collections include works by Kandinsky and other Bauhaus artists. The **Arthur M. Sackler Museum,** 485 Broadway, at Quincy Street, houses the university's collections of Asian, ancient, and Islamic art. 32 Quincy St. and 485 Broadway. ℂ 617/495-9400. www.artmuseums.harvard.edu. Admission to all 3 museums $5 adults, $4 seniors, $3 students, free for children under 18; free to all Wed and until noon Sat. Mon–Sat 10am–5pm; Sun 1–5pm. T: Red Line to Harvard. Cross Harvard Yard diagonally from the T station and cross Quincy St.

Longfellow National Historic Site   By the time you visit, this ravishing yellow mansion, a unit of the National Park Service, should have reopened after 3 years of refurbishment. The books and furniture have remained intact since the poet Henry Wadsworth Longfellow died in 1882. During the siege of Boston in 1775 and 1776, the house served as the headquarters of Gen. George Washington. On the tour—the only way to see the house—you'll learn about the history of the building and its famous occupants. 105 Brattle St. ℂ 617/876-4491. www.nps.gov/long. Guided tours $2 adults, free for seniors and children under 17. Call ahead to confirm hours and tour times. Mid-Mar to mid-Dec Wed–Sun 10am–4:30pm. Tours 10:45am, 11:45am, 1pm, 2pm, 3pm, and 4pm. Closed mid-Dec to mid-Mar. T: Red Line to Harvard, then follow Brattle St. about 7 blocks; house is on the right.

SPECTATOR SPORTS

BASEBALL   No other experience in sports matches watching the **Boston Red Sox** play at **Fenway Park.** The Fenway Park **ticket office** (ℂ 617/267-1700 for tickets, 617/482-4SOX for touch-tone ticketing; www.redsox.com) is at 4 Yawkey Way, off Brookline Avenue. Tickets go on sale in January. Prices start at $18. **Tours** (ℂ 617/236-6666) are offered May through September, Monday through Friday at 9am, 11am, noon, and 1pm, plus 2pm when the team is away. There are no tours on holidays or before day games. The cost is $5 for adults, $4 for seniors, and $3 for children under 16.

THE MARATHON   Every year on Patriot's Day (the third Mon in Apr), the **Boston Marathon** rules the roads from Hopkinton to Copley Square in Boston. For information about qualifying, contact the **Boston Athletic Association** (ℂ 617/236-1652; www.bostonmarathon.org).

SHOPPING

The Back Bay is the area's premier shopping district. Dozens of galleries, shops, and boutiques make **Newbury Street** a world-famous destination. Nearby, a weatherproof walkway across Huntington Avenue links upscale **Copley Place** (© 617/375-4400) and the **Shops at Prudential Center** (© 800/SHOP-PRU). If you're passionate about art, set aside a couple of hours for a stroll along **Newbury Street.** Besides being a prime location for upscale boutiques, it boasts an infinite variety of styles and media in the dozens of art galleries at street level and on the higher floors. (Remember to look up.) Pick up a copy of the free monthly *Gallery Guide* at businesses along Newbury Street, or check with the **Newbury Street League** (© 617/267-7961; www.newbury-st.com).

Downtown, **Faneuil Hall Marketplace** (© 617/523-1300) is the busiest attraction in Boston not only for its smorgasbord of food outlets, but also for its shops, boutiques, and pushcarts. If the hubbub here is too much for you, stroll over to **Charles Street,** at the foot of Beacon Hill. A short but commercially dense (and picturesque) street, it's home to perhaps the best assortment of gift and antiques shops in the city. One of Boston's oldest shopping areas is **Downtown Crossing.** Now a traffic-free pedestrian mall along Washington, Winter, and Summer streets near Boston Common, it's home to two major department stores (**Filene's** and **Macy's**); tons of smaller clothing, shoe, and music stores; food and merchandise pushcarts; and **Barnes & Noble** and **Borders.**

In **Cambridge** the bookstores, boutiques, and T-shirt shops of **Harvard Square** lie about 15 minutes from downtown Boston by subway. You'll find a mix of national and regional outlets, and more than a few persistent independent retailers. For a less generic experience, walk along **Mass. Ave.** in either direction to the next T stop. The stroll takes about an hour.

Bookworms flock to Cambridge; Harvard Square in particular caters to general and specific audiences. Check out the basement of the **Harvard Book Store,** 1256 Mass. Ave. (© 800/542-READ outside 617, or 617/661-1515; www.harvard.com), for great deals on remainders and used books; and **WordsWorth Books,** 30 Brattle St. (© 800/899-2202 or 617/354-5201; www.wordsworth.com), for a huge discounted selection. Up the street, children's books have their own store at **Curious George Goes to WordsWorth,** 1 John F. Kennedy St. (© 617/498-0062; www.curiousg.com). Barnes & Noble runs the book operation at the **Harvard Coop,** 1400 Mass. Ave. (© 617/499-2000; www.thecoop.com), which stocks textbooks, academic works, and a large general selection.

WHERE TO STAY

Boston has one of the busiest hotel markets in the country, with some of the highest prices. Rates at most downtown hotels are lower on weekends than on weeknights; leisure hotels offer discounts during the week. It's always a good idea to make a reservation, especially during foliage season. The area is also busy during spring and fall conventions, July and August, and college graduations (May and early June).

The hotels below range from very expensive ($300 and up per night) to expensive ($150 and up) to moderate ($120 and up) to one supercheap sleep (Hostelling International Boston). The state **hotel tax** is 5.7%. Boston and Cambridge (like Worcester and Springfield) add a 2.75% convention-center tax to the 4% city tax, bringing the total tax to 12.45%.

The Convention & Visitors Bureau **Hotel Hot Line** (© 800/777-6001) can help make reservations even at the busiest times. It's staffed Monday through Friday until 8pm, Saturday and Sunday until 4pm.

Boston Harbor Hotel   The Boston Harbor Hotel is one of the finest in town, an excellent choice for both business and leisure travelers. The 16-story brick building is within walking distance of downtown and the waterfront attractions; the Airport Water Shuttle stops behind the hotel. Each guest room is a luxurious combination of bedroom and living room, with mahogany furnishings. Rooms with city views are less expensive than those that face the harbor. The best units are suites with private terraces and dazzling water vistas. Rowes Wharf (entrance on Atlantic Ave.), Boston, MA 02110. (C) 800/752-7077 or 617/439-7000. Fax 617/330-9450. www.bhh.com. 230 units. $365–$555 double; from $455 suite. Extra person $50. Children under 18 stay free in parents' room. Weekend packages available. AE, DC, DISC, MC, V. Self-parking $15–$26, valet parking $20–$28. T: Red Line to South Station or Blue Line to Aquarium. **Amenities:** Restaurants (2); indoor pool; spa; health club; pets accepted.

Chandler Inn Hotel   The Chandler Inn is a bargain for its location, 2 blocks from the Back Bay. It underwent $1 million in renovations in 2000, and even with the accompanying price hike, the comfortable, unpretentious hotel is a deal. Guest rooms have individual climate control and contemporary-style furniture. Each holds a queen or double bed or two twin beds. Bathrooms are tiny, and the one elevator in the eight-story inn can be slow, but the staff is welcoming and helpful. This is a gay-friendly hotel—**Fritz**, the bar next to the lobby, is a neighborhood hangout—that often books up early. 26 Chandler St. (at Berkeley St.), Boston, MA 02116. (C) 800/842-3450 or 617/482-3450. Fax 617/542-3428. www.chandlerinn.com. 56 units. Apr–Dec $139–$169 double; Jan–Mar $129–$139 double. Children under 12 stay free in parents' room. Rates include continental breakfast. AE, DC, DISC, MC, V. No parking. T: Orange Line to Back Bay. **Amenities:** Pets accepted with prior approval.

The Fairmont Copley Plaza Hotel   The "grande dame of Boston" is a true grand hotel, an old-fashioned lodging that recalls the days when an out-of-town trip (by train, of course) was an event, not an ordeal. Built in 1912, the six-story Renaissance Revival building faces Copley Square. Already known for superb service, the Copley Plaza has enjoyed a renaissance since becoming a Fairmont property in 1996. Extensive renovations included restoration of the spacious guest rooms, which contain reproduction Edwardian antiques and offer VCRs. The traditional furnishings reflect the elegance of the opulent public spaces. Rooms that face the lovely square afford better views than those that overlook busy Dartmouth Street. 138 St. James Ave., Boston, MA 02116. (C) 800/441-1414 or 617/267-5300. Fax 617/247-6681. www.fairmont.com/copleyplaza. 379 units. From $249 double; from $429 suite. Extra person $30. Weekend and other packages available. AE, DC, MC, V. Valet parking $32. T: Green Line to Copley, or Orange Line to Back Bay. **Amenities:** Restaurants (2); fitness room; access to nearby health club; pets up to 20 lb. accepted ($25 per day).

Harborside Inn   The Harborside Inn offers a good combination of location and (for this neighborhood) value. The renovated 1858 warehouse is near Faneuil Hall Marketplace, the harbor, the Financial District, and the Big Dig. The guest rooms have hardwood floors, Oriental rugs, and Victorian-style furniture. They surround a sky-lit atrium; city-view units are more expensive but can be noisier. Still, they're preferable to the interior rooms, whose windows open only to the atrium. Units on the top floors have lower ceilings but better views. 185 State St. (between I-93 and the Custom House Tower), Boston, MA 02109. (C) 617/723-7500. Fax 617/670-2010. www.hagopianhotels.com. 54 units. $120–$210 double; $235–$310 suite. Extra person $15. Rates may be higher during special events. AE, DC, DISC, MC, V. No parking. T: Blue Line to Aquarium or Orange Line to State. **Amenities:** Restaurant; access to nearby health club ($15 fee).

Hostelling International–Boston   This hostel near the Berklee College of Music and Symphony Hall caters to students, youth groups, and other travelers in search of comfortable, no-frills lodging. Accommodations are dorm-style, with six beds per room; there are also a couple of private units. The hostel has two kitchens, 19 bathrooms, and a large common room. It provides linens, or you can bring your own; sleeping bags are not permitted. The enthusiastic staff organizes free and inexpensive cultural, educational, and recreational programs. *Note:* To get a bed in summer, you must be a member of Hostelling International–American Youth Hostels. For information, contact HI–AYH (✆ 202/783-6161; www.hiayh.org). If you are not a U.S. citizen, apply to your home country's hostelling association. 12 Hemenway St., Boston, MA 02115. ✆ 888/HOST222, HI–AYH 800/909-4776, or 617/536-9455. Fax 617/424-6558. www.bostonhostel.org. 205 beds. Members $29 per bed; nonmembers $32 per bed. Members $81 per private room; nonmembers $84 per private room. MC, V. T: Green Line B, C, or D to Hynes/ICA.

The MidTown Hotel   Even without free parking and an outdoor pool, this centrally located hotel would be a good deal for families and budget-conscious businesspeople. It's on a busy street within walking distance of Symphony Hall and the Museum of Fine Arts. The well-maintained rooms are large, bright, and attractively outfitted, although bathrooms are on the small side. Some units have connecting doors that allow families to spread out. The best rooms are on the side of the building that faces away from Huntington Avenue. 220 Huntington Ave., Boston, MA 02115. ✆ 800/343-1177 or 617/262-1000. Fax 617/262-8739. www.midtownhotel. com. 159 units. Apr–Aug $139–$209 double; Sept to mid-Nov $159–$259; mid-Nov to Dec $109–$169; Jan–Mar $99–$159. Extra person $15. Children under 18 stay free in parents' room. AAA, AARP, and government discounts available, subject to availability. AE, DC, DISC, MC, V. Free parking. T: Green Line E to Prudential, or Orange Line to Mass. Ave. **Amenities:** Restaurant (breakfast only); heated outdoor pool (in season).

Omni Parker House   The Parker House offers a great combination of nearly 150 years of history and extensive renovations. It has been in continuous operation longer than any other hotel in America, since 1855. Since the Omni chain took over in the late 1990s, the hotel has been upgraded throughout. Guest rooms aren't huge, but they are thoughtfully laid out and nicely appointed. Business travelers can book a room with an expanded work area, while sightseers can economize by requesting a smaller, less expensive unit. 60 School St., Boston, MA 02108. ✆ 800/THE-OMNI or 617/227-8600. Fax 617/742-5729. www.omnihotels.com. 552 units (some with shower only). $189–$309 double; $249–$385 superior double; $279–$445 suite. Children under 18 stay free in parents' room. Weekend packages and AARP discount available. AE, DC, DISC, MC, V. Self-parking $20, valet parking $27. T: Green or Blue Line to Government Center, or Red Line to Park St. **Amenities:** Restaurant; fitness center; pets under 25 lb. accepted ($50).

Radisson Hotel Boston   The chain only recently started expanding in the Northeast and the location isn't the most attractive, so this hotel can be a pleasant surprise. It's convenient to both the Back Bay and downtown, and the guest rooms are among the largest in the city, each with a private balcony and sitting area. The well-maintained hotel has become as popular with business travelers as it already was with tour groups and families. The best units are the executive-level rooms on the top five floors of the 24-story building. The hotel hosts the **Stuart Street Playhouse** (✆ 617/426-4499), a small theater that often books one-person shows. 200 Stuart St. (at Charles St. S.), Boston, MA 02116. ✆ 800/333-3333 or 617/482-1800. Fax 617/451-2750. www.radisson.com/bostonma. 356 units (some with shower only). $159–$359 double. Extra person $20; cot $20; cribs free. Children under 18 stay free in parents' room. Weekend, theater, and other packages available. AE, DC, DISC, MC, V. Self-parking $19, valet parking $21. T: Green Line to Boylston, or Orange Line to New England Medical Center. **Amenities:** Restaurants (2); indoor pool; fitness room.

The Ritz-Carlton, Boston Common   This plush, ultramodern hotel is at the heart of a new complex of offices, condos, a 19-screen movie theater, and the state-of-the-art Sports Club/LA. Challenging the Four Seasons' claim to A-list celebrities, the "new Ritz" opened in September 2001. It boasts the cachet and service of the original Ritz in the Back Bay, without a ruffle in sight. Guest rooms occupy the top four floors of the 12-story building; you'll pay more for a room with a view of the common. The accommodations contain the latest in indulgent amenities, including luxury linens, feather duvets, and phones in the bathrooms. The neighborhood is the urban-planning equivalent of a self-fulfilling prophecy: It's not the greatest, but the presence of the hotel automatically improves it. 10 Avery St. (between Tremont and Washington sts.), Boston, MA 02111. (C) 800/ 241-3333 or 617/574-7100. Fax 617/574-7200. www.ritzcarlton.com. 193 units. From $495 double; from $595 Club Level; from $695 suite. Weekend and other packages available. AE, DC, DISC, MC, V. Self-parking $28, valet parking $32. T: Green Line to Boylston. **Amenities:** Restaurant; access to nearby health club; pets accepted.

WHERE TO DINE

Travelers from around the world relish the variety of skillfully prepared seafood available in the Boston area. Lunch is an excellent, economical way to check out a fancy restaurant without breaking the bank. For those who like to dine alfresco, the **food court** at Faneuil Hall Marketplace is a great place to pick up picnic fare.

Billy Tse Restaurant CHINESE/PAN-ASIAN/SUSHI   This casual spot on the edge of the Italian North End serves excellent renditions of the usual Chinese dishes and good fresh seafood. The Thai- and Vietnamese-influenced selections are just as enjoyable. 240 Commercial St. (C) 617/227-9990. Reservations recommended for dinner on weekends. Main courses $5–$20; lunch specials $5.50–$7.50. AE, DC, DISC, MC, V. Mon–Thurs 11:30am–11:30pm; Fri–Sat 11:30am–midnight; Sun 11:30am–11pm. T: Blue Line to Aquarium, or Green or Orange Line to Haymarket.

Buddha's Delight VEGETARIAN/VIETNAMESE   Fresh and healthful meet cheap and filling here. The menu lists "chicken," "pork," and even "lobster"—in quotes because the chefs substitute fried and barbecued tofu and gluten for meat, poultry, fish, or dairy (some beverages have condensed milk) to create more-than-reasonable facsimiles of traditional dishes. Try spring rolls—fresh (in paper-thin mung-bean wrappers) are better than fried—then "shrimp" or "pork" with rice noodles, or excellent chow fun. 5 Beach St., 2nd floor. (C) 617/ 451-2395. Main courses $6–$12. MC, V. Sun–Thurs 11am–9:30pm; Fri–Sat 11am–10:30pm. T: Orange Line to Chinatown.

Café Jaffa MIDDLE EASTERN   A narrow brick room with a glass front, Café Jaffa looks more like a snazzy pizza place than the excellent Middle Eastern restaurant it is. Reasonable prices, high quality, and large portions draw hordes of people for traditional dishes such as falafel, baba ghanoush, and hummus, as well as burgers and steak tips. For dessert, try the baklava if it's fresh. 48 Gloucester St. (C) 617/536-0230. Main courses $5–$13. AE, DC, DISC, MC, V. Mon–Thurs 11am–10:30pm; Fri–Sat 11am–11pm; Sun 1–10pm. T: Green Line B, C, or D to Hynes/ICA.

Clio ECLECTIC   Clio is a plush room with funky accents—check out the leopard-print rug—that match the mood of food. Chef Ken Oringer's lofty reputation rests on exotic ingredients and elaborate preparations. The menu changes daily—more than at any other restaurant in town. Rely on the good-natured servers' advice. A common complaint is that portions are too small for the price, but this chowhound disagrees. They're not so skimpy, and you would-n't want too much of food this rich and complicated, anyway. You'll be more than satisfied—and you'll have room for dessert. In the Eliot Hotel, 370A Comm. Ave. (C) 617/536-7200. www.cliorestaurant.com. Reservations recommended. Main courses $29–$45. AE, DC, DISC, MC, V. Sun and Tues–Thurs 5:30–10pm; Fri–Sat 5:30–10:30pm. Valet parking available. T: Green Line B, C, or D to Hynes/ICA.

Dalí SPANISH   The bar at this festive restaurant fills with people cheerfully waiting an hour or more for a table. The payoff is authentic Spanish food, notably tapas. Entrees include excellent paella, but most people come in a group and explore the three dozen or more tapas offerings. They include delectable garlic potatoes, salmon balls with not-too-salty caper sauce, pork tenderloin with blue goat cheese, and delicious sausages. The staff sometimes seems rushed, but never fails to supply bread for sopping up juices, and sangria for washing it all down. Finish with excellent flan, or try the rich *tarta de chocolates*. 415 Washington St., Somerville. (C) 617/661-3254. www.DaliRestaurant.com. Reservations not accepted. Tapas $4–$8; main courses $19–$24. AE, DC, MC, V. Daily summer 6–11pm; winter 5:30–11pm. T: Red Line to Harvard; follow Kirkland St. to intersection of Washington and Beacon sts. (20-min. walk).

Durgin-Park NEW ENGLAND   For huge portions of delicious food, a rowdy atmosphere where CEOs share tables with students, and famously cranky waitresses, Bostonians have flocked to Durgin-Park since 1827. They come for prime rib the size of a hubcap, piles of fried seafood, fish dinners broiled to order, and bounteous portions of roast turkey. Steaks and chops are broiled on an open fire over wood charcoal. Vegetables come a la carte—now is the time to try Boston baked beans. For dessert, the strawberry shortcake is justly celebrated. 340 Faneuil Hall Marketplace. (C) 617/227-2038. www.durgin-park.com. Reservations accepted for parties of 15 or more. Main courses $7–$25; specials $19–$40. AE, DC, DISC, MC, V. Daily 11:30am–10pm (Sun to 9pm). Validated parking available. T: Green or Blue Line to Government Center, or Orange Line to Haymarket.

Hamersley's Bistro ECLECTIC   This is the place that put the South End on Boston's culinary map, a pioneering restaurant that's both classic and contemporary. One of its many claims to fame is its status as a Julia Child favorite. The seasonal menu offers entrees noted for their emphasis on local ingredients and classic techniques. Cassoulet with pork, duck confit, and garlic sausage is a gorgeously executed combination of flavors and textures. The kitchen also has a way with fish—perhaps salmon au poivre with sorrel, leeks, and fingerling potatoes. The wine list is excellent. 553 Tremont St. (C) 617/423-2700. www.hamersleysbistro.com. Reservations recommended. Main courses $23–$38; tasting menu varies. AE, DISC, MC, V. Mon–Fri 6–10pm; Sat 5:30–10pm; Sun 5:30–9:30pm. Closed 1 week in Jan. Valet parking available. T: Orange Line to Back Bay.

The Helmand AFGHAN   The Helmand enjoyed a burst of publicity when the manager's brother took over the provisional government of Afghanistan, and it's hardly had a slow night since. Unusual cuisine, an elegant setting, and reasonable prices had already made this spot near the CambridgeSide Galleria mall a favorite. Afghan food is vegetarian friendly; many non-veggie dishes use meat as one element rather than the centerpiece. *Aushak*, pasta pockets filled with leeks or potatoes and topped with split-pea-and-carrot sauce, also comes with meat sauce. For dessert, don't miss the Afghan version of baklava. 143 First

St. ℂ **617/492-4646.** Reservations recommended. Main courses $10–$18. AE, MC, V. Sun–Thurs 5–10pm; Fri–Sat 5–11pm. T: Green Line to Lechmere.

La Summa SOUTHERN ITALIAN   La Summa maintains a neighborhood atmosphere in the North End. It's worth seeking out for homemade pasta and desserts; the more elaborate entrees are scrumptious, too. Try any seafood special, lobster ravioli, *pappardelle e melanzane* (eggplant strips tossed with ethereal fresh pasta), or the house special—veal, chicken, sausage, shrimp, artichokes, pepperoncini, olives, and mushrooms in white-wine sauce. Desserts are terrific. 30 Fleet St. ℂ **617/523-9503.** Reservations recommended. Main courses $11–$24. AE, DC, DISC, MC, V. Mon–Sat 4:30–10:30pm; Sun 2–10:30pm. T: Green or Orange Line to Haymarket.

Legal Sea Foods SEAFOOD   The food at Legal Sea Foods ("Legal's," to Bostonians) isn't the fanciest, cheapest, or trendiest. It's the freshest, and management's commitment to that policy has produced a thriving chain. The menu includes regular selections plus whatever looked good at the market that morning, prepared in every imaginable way. The clam chowder is famous, the fish chowder lighter but equally good. We suggest the Prudential Center branch because it takes reservations (at lunch only). Equally annoying but traditional is the policy of serving each dish when it's ready, instead of one table at a time. In the Prudential Center, 800 Boylston St. ℂ **617/266-6800.** www.legalseafoods.com. Reservations recommended at lunch, not accepted at dinner. Main courses $7–$15 lunch, $14–$35 dinner; lobster priced daily. AE, DC, DISC, MC, V. Mon–Thurs 11am–10:30pm; Fri–Sat 11am–11:30pm; Sun noon–10pm. T: Green Line B, C, or D to Hynes/ICA or E to Prudential. Also at: 255 State St. (ℂ 617/227-3115; T: Blue Line to Aquarium); 36 Park Sq. (between Columbus Ave. and Stuart St.; ℂ **617/426-4444;** T: Green Line to Arlington); Copley Place, 2nd level (ℂ **617/266-7775;** T: Orange Line to Back Bay or Green Line to Copley); 5 Cambridge Center, Cambridge (ℂ **617/ 864-3400;** T: Red Line to Kendall/MIT).

Mr. Bartley's Burger Cottage AMERICAN   Great burgers and the best onion rings in the world make Bartley's a perennial favorite with a cross section of Cambridge. The 40-year-old family business is a high-ceilinged, crowded room plastered with signs and posters. There are also some good dishes that don't involve meat, notably veggie burgers and creamy, garlicky hummus. 1246 Mass. Ave. ℂ **617/354-6559.** Most items under $9. No credit cards. Mon–Wed and Sat 11am–9pm; Thurs–Fri 11am–10pm. T: Red Line to Harvard.

Olives ECLECTIC   At this informal bistro, the flagship of celebrity chef Todd English's growing empire, a line often forms shortly after 5pm; if you don't arrive by 5:45pm, expect the front-desk staff to banish you for at least 2 hours. Once you're seated, you'll find the noise level high, the service uneven, and the customers festive. Happily, the food is worth the ordeal. Classics on the menu include the delicious Olives tart (olives, caramelized onions, and anchovies) and spit-roasted chicken flavored with herbs and garlic. Grilling is a popular technique—yellowfin tuna, atop parsley mashed potatoes and accented with perfect mussels, demonstrates why. When you order your entree, the server will ask if you want falling chocolate cake for dessert. Say yes. 10 City Sq. ℂ **617/242-1999.** Reservations accepted for parties of 6 or more. Main courses $18–$32. AE, DC, MC, V. Mon–Fri 5:30–10pm; Sat 5–10:30pm. Valet parking available. T: Orange or Green Line to North Station; 15-min. walk.

Pizzeria Regina PIZZA   Regina's looks like a movie set, but it's the real thing. Busy waitresses weave through the boisterous dining room, delivering peerless pizza hot from the brick oven. The list of toppings includes nouveau ingredients such as sun-dried tomatoes, but that's not authentic. House-made sausage, maybe some pepperoni, and a couple of beers—now, *that's* authentic. 11½ Thacher St. ℭ 617/227-0765. Reservations not accepted. Pizza $9–$16. No credit cards. Mon–Thurs 11am–11:30pm; Fri–Sat 11am–midnight; Sun noon–11pm. T: Green or Orange Line to Haymarket.

Ye Olde Union Oyster House NEW ENGLAND/SEAFOOD America's oldest restaurant in continuous service, the Union Oyster House opened in 1826. Its New England fare is popular with tourists on the Freedom Trail as well as savvy locals. They're not here for anything fancy; try oyster stew or a cold seafood sampler of oysters, clams, and shrimp. Follow with a broiled or grilled dish such as scrod or salmon, or fried seafood. A "shore dinner" (chowder, steamers, lobster, corn, and dessert) is an excellent introduction to local favorites. 41 Union St. (between North and Hanover sts.). ℭ 617/227-2750. www.union oysterhouse.com. Reservations recommended. Main courses $10–$21 lunch, $15–$31 dinner. Children's menu $5–$11. AE, DC, DISC, MC, V. Sun–Thurs 11am–9:30pm (lunch until 5pm); Fri–Sat 11am–10pm (lunch until 6pm). Union Bar daily 11am–midnight (lunch until 3pm, late supper until 11pm). Valet parking available. T: Green or Orange Line to Haymarket.

BOSTON & CAMBRIDGE AFTER DARK

For up-to-date entertainment listings, consult the "Calendar" section of the Thursday *Boston Globe,* the "Scene" section of the Friday *Boston Herald,* or the Sunday arts sections of both papers. Three free publications, available at newspaper boxes around town, publish nightlife listings: the *Boston Phoenix,* the *Stuff@Night* (a *Phoenix* offshoot), and the *Improper Bostonian.*

Gay & lesbian specific events and venues list what's happening in *Bay Windows* (www.baywindows.com), available at newsstands and at Glad Day Bookstore, 673 Boylston St., Back Bay (ℭ **617/267-3010;** T: Copley).

Visit a **BosTix** (ℭ **617/482-2849;** www.bostix.org) booth at Faneuil Hall Marketplace (on the south side of Faneuil Hall) or in Copley Square (at the corner of Boylston and Dartmouth sts.). Same-day tickets to musical and theatrical performances are half price, subject to availability. Credit cards are not accepted, and there are no refunds or exchanges. BosTix also sells coupon books ($9) with discounted and two-for-one admission to many area museums; full-price advance tickets; and tickets to museums, historic sites, and attractions in and around town. The booths, which are also Ticketmaster outlets, are open Tuesday through Saturday from 10am to 6pm (half-price tickets go on sale at 11am), Sunday from 11am to 4pm. The Copley Square location is open Monday from 10am to 6pm.

THE PERFORMING ARTS The **Boston Symphony Orchestra**, one of the world's greatest, performs at Symphony Hall, 301 Mass. Ave. (ℭ **617/266-1492;** www.bso.org; T: Green Line E to Symphony, or Orange Line to Mass. Ave.). The season runs from October to April. From May to July, members of the BSO lighten up. Tables and chairs replace the floor seats at Symphony Hall, and drinks and light refreshments are served. The **Boston Pops** (same contact info as the BSO) play a range of music from light classical to show tunes to popular music, sometimes with celebrity guest stars.

The **Boston Ballet**'s reputation seems to jump a notch every time someone says, "So it's not just *The Nutcracker.*" The country's fourth-largest dance company performs the holiday staple from Thanksgiving to New Year's. During the rest of the season (Oct–May), it presents an eclectic mix of classic ballets and contemporary work. Call ℭ **617/695-6955** or check out www.bostonballet. com. Performances are held at the Wang Theatre, 270 Tremont St. (T: Green Line to Boylston).

The excellent local theater scene boasts the **Huntington Theatre Company,** which performs at the Boston University Theatre, 264 Huntington Ave. (© 617/266-0800; www.huntington.org); and the **American Repertory Theatre,** which makes its home at Harvard University's Loeb Drama Center, 64 Brattle St., Cambridge (© 617/547-8300; www.amrep.org).

You'll find most of the shows headed to or coming from Broadway in the **Theater District.** The promoter often is **Broadway in Boston** (© 617/880-2400; www.broadwayinboston.com).

THE CLUB SCENE The Boston-area club scene changes constantly, and somewhere out there is a good time for everyone. Bars close at 1am, clubs at 2am. The subway shuts down between 12:30 and 1am; Night Owl bus service operates until 2:30am on Friday and Saturday. Be prepared to show ID.

For **dancing,** try **Avalon,** 15 Lansdowne St. (© 617/262-2424; T: Green Line B, C, or D to Kenmore), a cavernous space divided into several levels. When the stage isn't in use, DJs spin for the crowd of 20- and 30-somethings. The dress code calls for jackets and shirts with collars, and no jeans or athletic wear. Cover is $5 to $20. Avalon is open Thursday (international night) through Sunday (gay night) from 10pm to 2am. **The Roxy,** in the Tremont Boston hotel, 279 Tremont St. (© 617/338-7699; T: Green Line to Boylston), boasts excellent DJs and live music, a huge dance floor, a stage, and a balcony. Occasional concerts and boxing cards take good advantage of the sightlines. No jeans or athletic shoes. Cover is $10 to $15. The Roxy is open from 8pm to 2am Thursday through Saturday, plus some Wednesdays and Sundays.

FOLK & ECLECTIC Legendary coffeehouse **Club Passim** at 47 Palmer St., Cambridge (© 617/492-7679; www.clubpassim.org; T: Red Line to Harvard), is where Joan Baez, Suzanne Vega, and Tom Rush started out. The tradition continues with featured acts like Melissa Ferrick and Vance Gilbert. There's live music nightly, and coffee and food (no alcohol is served) until 10pm. Cover is $5 to $25; most shows $12 or less. Open Sunday through Thursday from 11am to 11pm, Friday and Saturday until 4am.

JAZZ & BLUES On summer Fridays the **Waterfront Jazz Series** (© 617/635-3911) brings amateurs and professionals to Christopher Columbus Park, for a refreshing interlude of free music and cool breezes. On summer Thursdays, the **Boston Harbor Hotel** (© 617/439-7000) stages performances on the "Blues Barge," in the water behind the hotel. The original **House of Blues** still packs 'em in. It attracts tourists, music buffs, and big names. The restaurant is open Monday through Saturday from 11:30am to 11pm, Sunday from 4:30 to 11pm; the music hall Sunday through Wednesday until 1am, Thursday through Saturday until 2am. Sunday gospel buffet brunch seatings are at 10am, noon, and 2pm; advance tickets ($26 adults, $13 children) are highly recommended. The House of Blues is at 96 Winthrop St., Cambridge (© 617/491-2583, or 617/497-2229 for tickets; www.hob.com; T: Red Line to Harvard). Dining reservations (© 617/491-2100) are accepted for parties of 25 or more. Cover for the music hall is $6 to $30; no cover for the Friday or Saturday matinee.

Wally's Café is a Boston institution in the South End, opened in 1947. It draws a diverse crowd—black, white, straight, gay, affluent, indigent—and features nightly live music by local ensembles, students and instructors from the Berklee College of Music, and (on occasion) renowned musicians at 427 Mass. Ave. (© 617/424-1408; www.wallyscafe.com; T: Orange Line to Mass. Ave.).

ROCK & ALTERNATIVE   Big-name acts play the **FleetCenter,** 150 Causeway St. ((C) **617/624-1000;** www.fleetcenter.com).

The **Middle East** books an impressive variety of progressive and alternative acts upstairs and downstairs every night at 472–480 Mass. Ave., Central Square, Cambridge ((C) **617/864-EAST;** www.mideastclub.com; T: Red Line to Central). Cover is $7 to $15. Other good venues are the **Paradise Rock Club** near Boston University, which draws enthusiastic crowds for top local and national performers at 967 Comm. Ave. ((C) **617/562-8800,** or 617/423-NEXT for ticket; www.dlclive.com; T: Green Line B to Pleasant St.); and **T. T. the Bear's,** a no-frills spot with bookings ranging from alternative rock to ska to up-and-coming pop acts. It's open Sunday and Monday from 7pm to midnight, Tuesday through Saturday from 6pm to 1am at 10 Brookline St., Cambridge ((C) **617/492-0082** or 617/492-BEAR [concert line]; www.ttthebears.com; T: Red Line to Central).

BARS & LOUNGES   If you want to go "where everybody knows your name," you have two choices: There's the **Bull & Finch Pub,** inspiration for the television show *Cheers.* It looks nothing like the bar on TV. It really is a neighborhood bar, but it's far better known for attracting legions of out-of-towners, who find good pub grub and plenty of souvenirs at 84 Beacon St. ((C) **617/227-9605;** www.cheersboston.com; T: Green Line to Arlington). Then there's **Cheers,** a bar that replicates the set of the TV show at Faneuil Hall Marketplace ((C) **617/ 227-0150;** www.cheersboston.com; T: Green or Blue Line to Government Center, or Orange Line to Haymarket).

At **The Black Rose,** purists might sneer at the touristy location, but performers don't. Sing along with the entertainment at this jam-packed pub and restaurant at the edge of Faneuil Hall Marketplace, 160 State St. ((C) **617/ 742-2286;** www.irishconnection.com; T: Orange or Blue Line to State). Cover is $3 to $5. At **Casablanca,** students and professors jam this legendary Harvard Square watering hole, especially on weekends. It offers an excellent jukebox, excellent food, and excellent eavesdropping at 40 Brattle St., Cambridge ((C) **617/876-0999;** T: Red Line to Harvard). At **Top of the Hub** the 52nd-story view of greater Boston from this appealing lounge is lovely at sunset. There's music and dancing nightly. Dress is casual but neat. It's atop the Prudential Center, 800 Boylston St. ((C) **617/536-1775;** T: Green Line E to Prudential).

A SIDE TRIP TO CONCORD

Concord revels in its legacy as a center of groundbreaking thought and its role in the country's political and intellectual history. For an excellent overview of town history, start your explorations at the Concord Museum.

After just a little time in this lovely town, you may find yourself adopting the local attitude toward two of its most famous residents: Ralph Waldo Emerson, who comes across as a well-respected uncle figure, and Henry David Thoreau, everyone's favorite eccentric cousin. The first official battle of the Revolutionary War took place at the North Bridge, now part of Minute Man National Historical Park. By the middle of the 19th century, Concord was the center of the Transcendentalist movement. Homes of Emerson, Thoreau, Nathaniel Hawthorne, and Louisa May Alcott are open to visitors.

GETTING THERE   From Boston by **car** (30–40 min.), take Route 2 into Lincoln and stay in the right lane. Where the main road makes a sharp left, go straight onto Cambridge Turnpike, and follow signs to HISTORIC CONCORD. To go directly to Walden Pond, use the left lane, take Route 2/2A another mile or so, and turn left onto Route 126. There's parking throughout town.

The **commuter rail** (© **800/392-6100** outside Massachusetts, or 617/222-3200; www.mbta.com) takes about 45 minutes from North Station in Boston, with a stop in Cambridge. The round-trip fare is $8.

VISITOR INFORMATION The **chamber of commerce,** 155 Everett St. (© **978/369-3120;** www.concordmachamber.org), maintains an information booth on Heywood Street, 1 block southeast of Monument Square. It's open from 9:30am to 4:30pm on weekends in April and daily May through October. Ninety-minute tours are available Friday through Sunday and on Monday holidays. Weekday and group tours are available by appointment. The community (**www.concordma.com**) and town (**www.concordnet.org**) websites include visitor information. You can also contact the **Greater Merrimack Valley Convention & Visitors Bureau** (© **800/443-3332** or 978/459-6150; www. merrimackvalley.org).

WHAT TO SEE & DO

Concord Museum   This is a great place to start your visit. The **History Galleries** explore the question "Why Concord?" Artifacts, murals, films, maps, documents, and other presentations illustrate the town's role as a Native American settlement, Revolutionary War battleground, 19th-century intellectual center, and focal point of the 20th-century historic preservation movement. You'll also see the contents of Ralph Waldo Emerson's study and a collection of Henry David Thoreau's belongings. Pick up a **family activity pack** as you enter and use the games and reproduction artifacts (including a quill pen and powder horn) to give the kids a hands-on feel for life in the past. 200 Lexington Rd. (at Cambridge Tpk.). © **978/369-9609** (recorded info) or 978/369-9763. www.concordmuseum.org. Admission $7 adults, $6 seniors and students, $3 children under 16; $16 per family. Apr–Dec Mon–Sat 9am–5pm, Sun noon–5pm; Jan–Mar Mon–Sat 11am–4pm, Sun 1–4pm. Parking allowed on road. Follow Lexington Rd. out of Concord Center and bear right at museum onto Cambridge Tpk.; entrance is on left.

The Old Manse   The history of this home touches on the military and the literary, but it's mostly the story of a family. The Rev. William Emerson built the Old Manse in 1770 and watched the Battle of Concord from his yard. For almost 170 years, the house was home to his descendants and to two famous friends. Nathaniel Hawthorne and his bride, Sophia Peabody, moved in in 1842 and stayed for 3 years. As a wedding present, Henry David Thoreau sowed the vegetable garden for them. This is also where William's grandson Ralph Waldo Emerson wrote the essay "Nature." Today, you'll see mementos and memorabilia of the Emerson and Ripley families and of the Hawthornes. 269 Monument St. (at North Bridge). © **978/369-3909.** www.thetrustees.org. Guided tours $6.50 adults, $5.50 seniors and students, $4.50 children 6–12; $20 per family. Mid-Apr to Oct Mon–Sat 10am–5pm, Sun and holidays noon–5pm (last tour at 4:30pm). Closed Nov to mid-Apr. From Concord Center, follow Monument St. to North Bridge parking lot (on right); Old Manse is on left.

Orchard House   *Little Women* (1868), Louisa May Alcott's most popular work, was written and set at Orchard House. Seeing the family home brings the Alcotts to life for legions of visitors. Fans won't want to miss the tour, illustrated with heirlooms. Check in advance for information on holiday programs and other special events. Louisa's father, Amos Bronson Alcott, created Orchard House by joining and restoring two homes. The family lived here from 1858 to 1877. Her mother, Abigail May Alcott, frequently assumed the role of breadwinner—Bronson, Louisa wrote in her journal, had "no gift for money making."

Note: Call before visiting; an extensive preservation project is underway. 399 Lexington Rd. © **978/369-4118.** www.louisamayalcott.org. Guided tours $7 adults, $6 seniors and students, $4 children 6–17; $16 per family. Apr–Oct Mon–Sat 10am–4:30pm, Sun 1–4:30pm; Nov–Mar Mon–Fri 11am–3pm, Sat 10am–4:30pm, Sun 1–4:30pm. Closed Jan 1–15, Easter, Thanksgiving, Dec 25. Follow Lexington Rd. out of Concord Center, bear left at Concord Museum; house is on left. Overflow parking across the street.

Ralph Waldo Emerson House   Emerson, also an essayist and poet, lived here from 1835 until his death in 1882. He moved here after marrying his second wife, Lydia Jackson, whom he called "Lydian"; she called him "Mr. Emerson," as the staff still does. The tour gives a good look at his personal side and at the fashionably ornate interior decoration of the time. You'll see original furnishings and some of Emerson's personal effects. 28 Cambridge Tpk. © **978/369-2236.** Guided tours $6 adults, $4 seniors and students. Call to arrange group tours (10 people or more). Mid-Apr to Oct Thurs–Sat 10am–4:30pm, Sun 2–4:30pm. Closed Nov to mid-Apr. Follow Cambridge Tpk. out of Concord Center; just before Concord Museum; house is on right.

Sleepy Hollow Cemetery   Follow the signs for AUTHOR'S RIDGE to the graves of some of the town's literary lights. Emerson's grave is marked by an uncarved quartz boulder. Thoreau's grave is nearby; at his funeral in 1862, Emerson concluded his eulogy with these words: ". . . wherever there is knowledge, wherever there is virtue, wherever there is beauty, he will find a home." Entrance on Rte. 62 W. © **978/318-3233.** Daily 7am to dusk. Call ahead for wheelchair access. No buses allowed.

The Wayside   The Wayside was Nathaniel Hawthorne's home from 1852 until his death in 1864. The Wayside is part of Minute Man National Historical Park, and the fascinating 45-minute ranger-led tour illuminates the occupants' lives and the house's crazy-quilt architecture. The exhibit in the barn (free admission) consists of audio presentations and figures of the authors. 455 Lexington Rd. © **978/369-6975.** www.nps.gov/mima/wayside. Guided tours $4 adults, free for under 17. May–Oct Thurs–Tues 10am–4:30pm. Closed Nov–Apr. Follow Lexington Rd. out of Concord Center past Concord Museum and Orchard House. Parking across the street.

MINUTE MAN NATIONAL HISTORICAL PARK

This 900-acre park preserves the scene of the first Revolutionary War battle, which took place on April 19, 1775. Encouraged by their victory at Lexington, the British continued to Concord in search of stockpiled arms (which the colonists had already moved). Warned of the advance, the Minutemen crossed the North Bridge, evading the "regulars" standing guard, and awaited reinforcements on a hilltop. The British searched nearby homes and burned any guns they found, and the Minutemen, seeing the smoke, mistakenly thought the soldiers were burning the town. The gunfire that ensued, the opening salvo of the Revolution, is remembered as "the shot heard round the world."

The park is open daily year-round. A visit can take as little as half an hour—for a jaunt to the North Bridge—or as long as half a day (or more), if you stop at both visitor centers and participate in a ranger-led program. To reach the bridge from Concord Center, follow Monument Street until you see the parking lot on the right. On one side of the bridge is a plaque commemorating the British soldiers who died in the Revolutionary War. On the other side is Daniel Chester French's ***Minute Man*** statue, engraved with a stanza of the poem Emerson wrote for the dedication ceremony in 1876.

You can also start at the **North Bridge Visitor Center,** 174 Liberty St., off Monument Street (© **978/369-6993;** www.nps.gov/mima), which overlooks the Concord River and the bridge. A diorama and video illustrate the Battle of Concord; exhibits include uniforms, weapons, and tools of colonial and British soldiers. Park rangers lead programs and answer questions. The center is open daily from 9am to 5:30pm (until 4pm in winter).

At the Lexington end of the park, the **Minute Man Visitor Center** (© 781/862-7753; www.nps.gov/mima), off Route 2A, about a half mile west of I-95, Exit 30B, is open daily from 9am to 5pm (until 4pm in winter). You'll see a multimedia program on the Revolution, displays, and a 40-foot mural illustrating the battle. On summer weekends, rangers lead tours—call ahead for times. The **Battle Road Trail,** a 5½-mile interpretive path, carries pedestrian, wheelchair, and bicycle traffic. Panels and granite markers display information about the area's history.

Also on the park grounds, on Old Bedford Road, is the **Hartwell Tavern.** Costumed interpreters demonstrate daily life on a farm and in a tavern in colonial days. It's open from 9:30am to 5pm, daily June through August and weekends only in April, May, September, and October. Admission is free.

WILDERNESS RETREATS

Henry David Thoreau's first published works can serve as starting points: *A Week on the Concord and Merrimack Rivers* (1849) and *Walden* (1854).

To see the area from water level, rent a **canoe** at the **South Bridge Boathouse,** 496 Main St. (© 978/369-9438; www.sbridge.qpg.com), about ⅔ mile west of the center of town, and paddle to the North Bridge and back. Rates are about $11 per hour on weekends, less on weekdays.

At the **Walden Pond State Reservation,** 915 Walden St., Route 126 (© 978/369-3254; www.state.ma.us/dem/parks/wldn.htm), a pile of stones marks the site of the cabin where Thoreau lived from 1845 to 1847. Today the picturesque reservation is a popular destination for walking, swimming, and fishing. Call for the schedule of interpretive programs. No dogs or bikes are allowed. From Memorial Day to Labor Day, a daily parking fee is charged and the lot fills early every day—call before setting out, as the rangers turn away visitors if the park has reached capacity (1,000). To get here from Concord Center, take Walden Street (Rte. 126) south, cross Route 2, and follow signs to the parking lot.

2 Cape Cod

Curling some 70 miles into the Atlantic, Cape Cod offers miles of beaches, freshwater ponds, and richly historic New England villages; it's a popular summer destination, with plenty of activities after the sun goes down as well.

ESSENTIALS

GETTING THERE   By Car   From Providence and New York, cross the Cape Cod Canal on the Bourne Bridge; from Boston, cross on the Sagamore Bridge. Head east on Route 6. Exits are marked for all major destinations. Traffic can be a nightmare on peak weekends, so plan accordingly.

By Plane   The Cape's major hub is **Barnstable Municipal Airport,** Hyannis (© 508/775-2020), served by several major carriers and smaller airlines from Boston's Logan Airport and New York's LaGuardia and Newark. **Provincetown Airport** (© 508/487-0241) is served by **Cape Air** (© 800/352-0714; www.fly capeair.com) from Boston.

Cape Cod

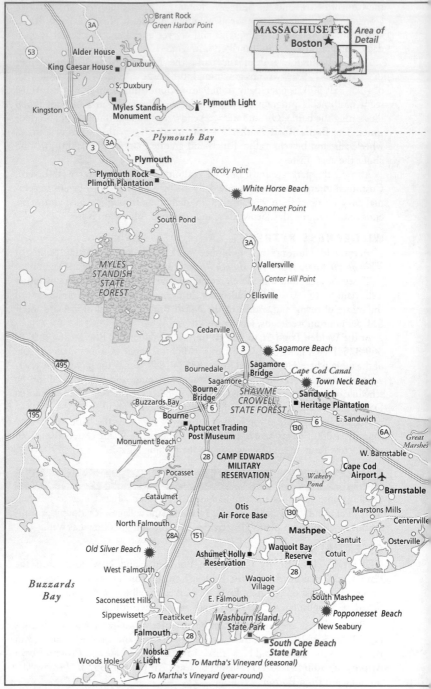

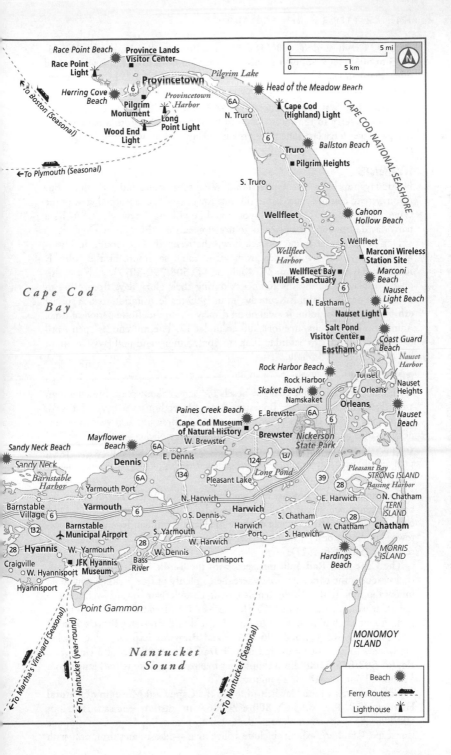

By Bus   Greyhound (© 800/231-2222) and **Bonanza Bus Lines** (© 800/556-3815 or 508/548-7588) offer service to Cape Cod from Boston, New York, and other destinations. **Plymouth & Brockton** (© 508/771-6191) offers service from Boston to Hyannis, with connections along the rest of the Cape.

By Boat   Bay State Cruises (© 617/748-1428; www.baystatecruisecompany. com) runs a ferry to Provincetown from Boston, in addition to a daily round-trip passenger ferry late June through Labor Day, and on weekends late May to late September.

HYANNIS

Hectic Hyannis has a diverse selection of restaurants, bars, and nightclubs. But if you were to confine your visit to this one town, you'd get a warped view of the Cape. Along Routes 132 and 28, you could be visiting Anywhere, USA. It's a rainy day destination, or a place to go if you need something from a mall.

Don't even bother trying to track down the Kennedy Compound in Hyannisport; it's effectively screened from view. You'll see more at the **John F. Kennedy Hyannis Museum,** 397 Main St. (© 508/790-3077), with a multimedia display capturing the Kennedys during their glory days from 1934 to 1963. The death of John F. Kennedy, Jr., in 1999 made visitation soar. A special exhibit of photos of John, Jr., will be on display for an indefinite period of time. Admission is $3 adults, free for children under 17. The museum is open April to October Monday to Saturday 10am to 4pm, Sunday and holidays 1 to 4pm; last admission is at 3:30pm.

BREWSTER

With miles of placid Cape Cod Bay beach and acres of state park, Brewster is an attractive place for families. Brewster's Main Street houses a bevy of B&Bs, restaurants, and the Cape's finest **antiques** shops. Brewster also welcomes tens of thousands of campers and day-trippers headed for Nickerson State Park.

VISITOR INFORMATION   The **visitor center** is behind Brewster Town Hall, 2198 Main St./Rte. 6A (© 508/896-3500; fax 508/896-1086; www. capecodtravel.com/brewster).

Brewster's eight bay **beaches** have minimal facilities. When the tide is out, the beach extends as much as 2 miles, leaving behind tidal pools to splash in. On a clear day, you can see the whole curve of the Cape, from Sandwich to Provincetown. Purchase a beach parking sticker ($8 per day, $25 per week) at the visitor center (© 508/896-4511).

The **Cape Cod Rail Trail** intersects with the 8-mile **Nickerson State Park** trail system at the park entrance, where there's plenty of free parking; you could follow the Rail Trail back to Dennis (about 12 miles) or toward Wellfleet (13 miles). In season, **Idle Times** (© 508/255-8281) provides rentals within the park. About a half mile south of Route 6A, you'll find **Brewster Bicycle Rental,** 442 Underpass Rd. (© 508/896-8149); and **Brewster Express,** which makes sandwiches to go. Just up the hill is **Rail Trail Bike & Blade,** 302 Underpass Rd. (© 508/896-8200). Both shops offer free parking. Bike rentals range from $12 for 4 hours to $18 for 24 hours.

Noted naturalist John Hay helped found the **Cape Cod Museum of Natural History,** 869 Rte. 6A (© 800/479-3867 in eastern Massachusetts, or 508/896-3867; www.ccmnh.org), dedicated to preserving Cape Cod's unique landscape. Children's exhibits include a "live hive"—like an ant farm, only with busy bees—and marine-room tanks. The bulk of the museum is outdoors. There's an on-site archaeology lab on Wing Island. Admission is $5 adults, $4.50 seniors, $2 children 5 to 12.

WHERE TO STAY & DINE

The Beechcroft Inn, 1360 Rte. 6A (② **877/233-2446** or 508/896-9534; fax 508/896-8812; www.beechcroftinn.com), is in an 1828 building that started as a meetinghouse. It's atop a hillock crowned with beeches. The innkeepers have spruced up the place with antiques. The **Brewster Tea Pot** serves lunch and an authentic afternoon tea. **The Bramble Inn,** 2019 Rte. 6A (② **508/896-7644;** www.brambleinn.com), is comprised of two rambling mid-19th-century homes, decorated in a breezy, country-casual manner. The main inn, built in 1861, houses one of the Cape's best restaurants. The 1849 Greek Revival house next door has cozy and quaint bedrooms, with antique touches like crocheted bedspreads.

One of the best restaurants on Cape Cod, the **Bramble Inn Restaurant,** 2019 Main St. (② **508/896-7544**), is also one of the most expensive—but worth it. To get the gist of the expression "chow down," just observe the early-evening crowd happily doing so at **Brewster Inn & Chowder House,** 1993 Rte. 6A (② **508/896-7771**), a century-old restaurant where the draw is hearty staples at prices geared to ordinary people.

CHATHAM

Chatham (say *Chatt*-um) is small-town America the way Norman Rockwell imagined it. Roses climb white picket fences in front of Cape cottages within a stone's throw of the ocean. Visit the **Chatham Chamber of Commerce,** 533 Main St. (② **800/715-5567** or 508/945-5199; www.chathamcapecod.org); or the **Chatham Chamber booth,** at the intersection of Routes 137 and 28.

BEACHES & OUTDOOR PURSUITS

Chatham has an unusual array of **beaches,** from the peaceful shores of Nantucket Sound to the shifting shoals along the Atlantic. For beach stickers ($8 per day, $35 per week), call the **Permit Department,** on George Ryder Road in West Chatham (② **508/945-5180**). Among the beaches are **Cockle Cove Beach, Ridgevale Beach,** and **Hardings Beach;** lined up along the sound, each at the end of its namesake road south of Route 28, these family-pleasing beaches offer gentle surf and full facilities. **Oyster Pond Beach,** off Route 28, is only a block from Chatham's Main Street. This sheltered saltwater pond (with restrooms) swarms with children. **North Beach** extends all the way south from Orleans. This 5-mile barrier beach is accessible from Chatham only by boat; you can take the **Beachcomber** (② **508/945-5265**), a water taxi, which leaves from the fish pier. The round-trip costs $12 for adults, $8 for children.

Though Chatham has no separate recreational paths per se, a demarcated **biking/skating** lane makes a scenic 8-mile circuit of town, heading south onto "The Neck," east to the Chatham Light, up Shore Road all the way to North Chatham, and back to the center of town. A brochure prepared by the **chamber of commerce** (② **800/715-5567** or 508/945-5199) shows the route. Rentals are available at **Bikes & Blades,** 195 Crowell Rd. (② **508/945-7600**).

Chatham has five ponds and lakes that permit **fishing.** For saltwater fishing sans boat, try the fishing bridge on Bridge Street at the south end of Mill Pond. First, get a license at **Town Hall,** 549 Main St. (② **508/945-5101**). If you hear the deep sea calling, sign on with the *Booby Hatch* (② **508/430-2312**) or the

Banshee (© 508/945-0403). Shellfishing licenses are available at the **Permit Department,** on George Ryder Road in West Chatham (© 508/945-5180).

Heading southeast from the Hardings Beach parking lot, the 2-mile round-trip **Seaside Trail** offers beautiful parallel panoramas of Nantucket Sound and Oyster Pond River. Access to 40-acre Morris Island, southwest of the Chatham Light, is easy: Walk or drive across and start right in on a marked ¾-mile trail.

The *Beachcomber* (© 508/945-5265) runs seal-watching cruises out of Stage Harbor. Parking is behind the former Main Street School just on the left before the rotary. The cruises cost $18 for adults, $12 for children 3 to 15.

Uninhabited **Monomoy Island,** 2,750 acres of brush-covered sand favored by some 285 species of migrating birds, is the perfect pit stop along the Atlantic flyway. Harbor and gray seals carpet the coastline from late November to May. Both the **Wellfleet Bay Wildlife Sanctuary,** operated by the Audubon Society (© 508/349-2615), and Brewster's **Cape Cod Museum of Natural History** (© 508/896-3867) offer guided trips.

Seaworthy vessels, from surfboards to Sunfish, can be rented from **Monomoy Sail and Cycle,** 275 Rte. 28, North Chatham (© 508/945-0811). Pleasant Bay is the best place to play for those with sufficient experience; if the winds don't seem to be going your way, try Forest Beach on the South Chatham shore. Kayaks and sailboards rent for $45 per day.

WHERE TO STAY

For those allergic to inns, Chatham has several decent motels. The basic **Hawthorne,** 196 Shore Rd. (© 508/945-0372; www.thehawthorne.com), is on the water, with views of Chatham Harbor, Pleasant Bay, and the Atlantic. The **Seafarer of Chatham,** 2079 Rte. 28, about a half mile east of Route 137 in West Chatham (© 800/786-2772 or 508/432-1739; www.chathamseafarer.com), lacks a pool, but is close to Ridgevale Beach.

Set above the beach in Chatham with commanding views, the grand old **Chatham Bars Inn,** Shore Road (© 800/527-4884 or 508/945-0096; www.chathambarsinn.com), is the premier hotel on Cape Cod. The colonnaded 1914 brick building is surrounded by 26 shingled cottages. Take in the sweeping views on the breezy veranda. Amenities include an outdoor heated pool; putting green; public 9-hole golf course next door; tennis courts; basic fitness room; summer children's programs; shuffleboard; croquet; volleyball; and a complimentary launch to Nauset Beach. Cottage rooms are cheery with painted furniture and Waverly fabrics. Guests can take meals in **The Main Dining Room,** the **Tavern,** or the seasonal **Beach House Grill** right on the private beach.

The Captain's House Inn, 369–377 Old Harbor Rd. (© 800/315-0728 or 508/945-0127; www.captainshouseinn.com), is an 1839 Greek Revival house, along with a cottage and carriage house, a shining example of 19th-century style. Bedrooms are richly furnished with canopied four-posters, beamed ceilings, and, in some cases, brick hearths and Jacuzzis. Rates include full breakfast and afternoon tea. There are bikes for the guests to use, and each room has a fridge and coffeemaker.

The Dolphin of Chatham, 352 Main St. (© 800/688-5900 or 508/945-0070; www.dolphininn.com), is made up of an 1805 main building, motel units, and cottages, for a wide range of lodging options. Even on exquisitely groomed Main Street, this property's colorful gardens stand out. The main inn has seven rooms with romantic touches like beamed ceilings and canopy beds. The inn has a terrific bar, where guests can enjoy light dinner fare from a screened porch. Lighthouse Beach is a stroll away. Rates include continental breakfast. There's an outdoor heated pool and Jacuzzi. Each room has a fridge and coffeemaker.

WHERE TO DINE

We highly recommend **The Main Dining Room** at the Chatham Bars Inn (see above for location). This is not delicate food, but it is delicious—and the chowder may be the best on Cape Cod.

The **Chatham Wayside Inn,** 512 Main St. (© **508/945-5550**), is a good spot for a reasonably priced meal in town. Specialties include crab cakes, rack of lamb, and pesto cod. For something a little different, try the Portuguese-style chowder, with double-smoked bacon, fresh quahogs, and red bliss potatoes.

CHATHAM AFTER DARK

Chatham's free **band concerts** attract crowds in the thousands. This is small-town America at its most nostalgic, as the band plays old standards that never go out of style. Held in Kate Gould Park (off Chatham Bars Ave.) from July to early September, they kick off at 8pm every Friday.

PROVINCETOWN

You've made it all the way to the end of the Cape, to one of the most interesting spots on the eastern seaboard. Charles Hawthorne, the painter who "discovered" this near-derelict fishing town in the late 1890s and introduced it to the Greenwich Village intelligentsia, was besotted by this "jumble of color in the intense sunlight accentuated by the brilliant blue of the harbor."

The whole town, in fact, is dedicated to creative expression, both visual and verbal. That same open-mindedness may account for Provincetown's ascendancy as a gay and lesbian resort. The street life also includes families, art lovers, and gourmands. In short, Provincetown has something for just about everyone.

Contact the **Provincetown Chamber of Commerce,** 307 Commercial St. (© **508/487-3424;** fax 508/487-8966; www.ptownchamber.com), or the gay-oriented **Provincetown Business Guild,** 115 Bradford St. (© **800/637-8696** or 508/487-2313; fax 508/487-1252; www.ptown.org).

BEACHES & OUTDOOR PURSUITS

BEACHES   With nine-tenths of its territory protected by the Cape Cod National Seashore, Provincetown has miles of beaches. The 3-mile bay beach that lines the harbor, though certainly swimmable, is not all that inviting compared to the ocean beaches overseen by the National Seashore. The two official access areas tend to be crowded; however, you can always find a less densely populated stretch if you're willing to hike down the beach a bit.

BICYCLING   North of town is one of the more spectacular bike paths in New England, the 7-mile **Province Lands Trail,** a heady swirl of steep dunes anchored by wind-stunted scrub pines. With its free parking, the **Province Lands Visitor Center** (© **508/487-1256**) is a good place to start. Rentals are offered in season by **Nelson's Bike Shop,** 43 Race Point Rd. (© **508/487-8849**). In town, rentals are available at **Ptown Bikes,** 42 Bradford St. (© **508/487-8735**); reserve several days in advance.

BOATING   **Flyer's Boat Rental,** 131 Commercial St., in the West End (© **508/487-0898**), offers all sorts of craft, from kayaks to sailboats; lessons and fishing-gear rentals are available. **Off the Coast Kayak Company,** 3 Freeman St., in the center of town (© **508/487-2692**), offers tours and rentals in season.

MUSEUMS   Anywhere you go in town, the **Pilgrim Monument & Province-town Museum** on High Pole Hill Road (℗ **508/487-1310;** www.pilgrim-monument.org) looms. Climb the 60 gradual ramps interspersed with 116 steps and you'll get a gargoyle's-eye view of the spiraling coast and Boston against a backdrop of New Hampshire's mountains. Admission is $6 adults, $3 children 4 to 12. It's Closed December to March. The **Provincetown Art Association & Museum,** 460 Commercial St. (℗ **508/487-1750;** www.paam.org), is an extraordinary cache of 20th-century American art begun by Charles Hawthorne. Founded in 1914, the museum was the site of innumerable "space wars," as classicists and modernists vied for square footage. Suggested donation is $5 adults, $1 seniors and children under 12.

TOURS   **Art's Dune Tours** is at the corner of Commercial and Standish streets (℗ **800/894-1951** or 508/487-1950; www.artsdunetours.com). In 1946, Art Costa started driving sightseers out to ogle the "dune shacks" where Eugene O'Neill, Jack Kerouac, and Jackson Pollock found their respective muses. The tours typically take 1 to 1½ hours. Tickets are $13 to $16 for adults, $8 to $10 for children 4 to 11. There's also a sunset clambake dune tour ($40) and Race Point Lighthouse tour ($18).

WHALE-WATCHING   Stellwagen Bank, 8 miles off Provincetown, is a feeding ground for whales. The *Dolphin* **Fleet** at MacMillan Wharf (℗ **800/ 826-9300** or 508/349-1900) was the first, and by most accounts is still the best, outfitter running whale-watching trips to Stellwagen. Tickets for the 3½-hour trips are $20 for adults, $18 for seniors, and $17 for children 7 to 12. Call to reserve. Closed November through March.

WHERE TO STAY

The Brass Key Guesthouse, 67 Bradford St. (℗ **800/842-9858** or 508/487-9005; www.brasskey.com), is the fanciest place in town. The innkeepers have thought of everything: down pillows, jetted showers, and iced tea and lemonade delivered poolside. Rooms in the 1828 Federal-style Captain's House and the Gatehouse are outfitted in a country style, while the Victorian-era building is elegant. Most deluxe rooms have gas fireplaces and whirlpool tubs. Rates include continental breakfast and afternoon wine and cheese. There's a heated outdoor pool, a Jacuzzi, and fridges and safes in the rooms. No children under 18.

The **Best Western Tides Beachfront,** 837 Commercial St (℗ **800/528-1234** or 508/487-1045; www.bwprovincetown.com), is set on 6 acres away from Provincetown's bustle. Every inch of this complex has been groomed to the max. The spotless guest rooms are decorated in a soothing pastel palette. There's a heated outdoor pool and a coin-op laundry; in each room there's a fridge and a coffeemaker, as well as a dataport.

Rainer and Jurgen run **Carpe Diem,** 12 Johnson St. (℗ **800/487-0132** or 508/ 487-4242; www.carpediemguesthouse.com), a stylish 1884 house on a quiet side street that suits most P-town habitués to a T. Guest rooms are outfitted with antiques, down comforters, and robes. Two deluxe garden suites boast private entrances, Jacuzzis, and fireplaces. The cottage has a two-person Jacuzzi and a wet bar. Breakfasts feature homemade German bread and muffins served at the family-size dining-room table. On clear days, sun worshippers prefer the patio. Rates include continental breakfast. The rooms have dataports.

Set back from the street in the quiet West End, **Captain Lysander Inn,** 96 Commercial St. (℗ **508/487-2253**), an 1840 Greek Revival, is fronted by a flower-lined path leading to a sunny patio. The conservatively furnished rooms are quite nice for the price, and some have partial water views. Tall windows make these rooms feel light and airy. The whole gang can fit in either the apartment or the cottage, both with TV/VCRs and kitchenettes. Continental breakfast is included. There are no phones in the rooms.

Look for the house with the bright yellow door in the East End; it's the very embodiment of Provincetown's Bohemian mystique: the **White Horse Inn,** 500 Commercial St. (© **508/487-1790**). Frank Schaefer has been tinkering with this late-18th-century house since 1963; a number of his fellow artists helped him out in cobbling together the studio apartments out of salvage. Some units have shared bathrooms; there are no televisions or phones in the room, adding to the serenity.

WHERE TO DINE

Spiritus, 190 Commercial St. (© **508/487-2808**), is an extravagant pizza parlor open until 2am. Peruse the scrumptious meat pies and pastries at the **Provincetown Portuguese Bakery,** 299 Commercial St. (© **508/487-1803**). Both establishments are closed November through March.

Martin House, 157 Commercial St. (© **508/487-1327**), is easily one of the most charming restaurants on the Cape. The chef favors local delicacies, such as the littlenecks that appear in a kafir-lime-tamarind broth with Asian noodles. Main courses might include grilled rack of pork with mango salsa and cactus-pear demi-glace on spicy masa.

Bubala's by the Bay, 183 Commercial St. (© **508/487-0773**), promises "serious food at sensible prices." And that's what it delivers: from buttermilk waffles to creative focaccia sandwiches to ostrich served with a grilled pepper crust and a caramelized onion and balsamic glaze. The huge patio facing Commercial Street is particularly popular in the morning. **Cafe Heaven,** 199 Commercial St. (© **508/487-9639**), is prized for its leisurely country breakfasts. The dinner choices have expanded to include local seafood, steaks, chops, and poultry; create-your-own pastas; and "heavenly" burgers.

The best gourmet takeout shop is **Angel Foods,** 467 Commercial St., in the East End (© **508/487-6666**), which offers Italian specialties and other prepared foods. The rollwiches—pita bread packed with a wide range of fillings—at **Box Lunch,** 353 Commercial St. (© **508/487-6026**), are ideal for a strolling lunch.

PROVINCETOWN AFTER DARK

There's so much going on in season that you might want to simplify your search by calling or stopping by the **Provincetown Reservations System office,** 293 Commercial St., in the center of town (© **508/487-6400**).

The hottest club in town is **Antro,** 258 Commercial St., 2nd floor (© **508/487-8800**). Perhaps the nation's premier gay bar, the **Atlantic House,** 6 Masonic Place, off Commercial Street (© **508/487-3821**), is open year-round. The "A-house" welcomes straight folks, except in the leather-oriented Macho Bar upstairs. Come late afternoon, it's a safe bet that the crowds are at the gay-lesbian tea dance held daily in season from 3:30 to 6:30pm on the pool deck at the **Boatslip Beach Club,** 161 Commercial St. (© **508/487-1669**). The action then shifts to the **Pied,** 193A Commercial St. (© **508/487-1527;** www.thepied.com), for its After Tea T-Dance from 5 to 10pm.

The women's bar **Vixen,** at the Pilgrim House, 336 Commercial St. (© **508/487-6424**), occupies the lower floors of a former hotel. On the roster are jazz, blues, and comedy. There are also pool tables.

3 Martha's Vineyard

With 100 square miles, Martha's Vineyard is New England's largest island, yet each of its six communities is blessed with endearing small-town charm. Admire the sea captains' homes in **Edgartown.** Stroll down Circuit Avenue in **Oak Bluffs,** then ride the Flying Horses Carousel, said to be the oldest working carousel in the nation. Check out the cheerful "gingerbread" cottages behind Circuit Avenue. Then journey "up-island" to marvel at the red-clay cliffs of **Aquinnah.** Or bike the country roads of **West Tisbury** and **Chilmark.** Buy a lobster roll in the fishing village of **Menemsha.**

ESSENTIALS

GETTING THERE   By Ferry   Most visitors take ferries from the mainland to the Vineyard. It's easy to get a passenger ticket on almost any of the ferries, but space for cars is limited. We advise you to leave your car on the mainland. It's easy to take the shuttle buses from town to town or bike around.

From **Falmouth, The Steamship Authority** (© 508/477-8600; www.island ferry.com) operates daily year-round, weather permitting. These ferries make the 45-minute trip to Vineyard Haven throughout the year; some boats go to Oak Bluffs from late May to late October. You can park your car in Woods Hole or Falmouth. Parking costs $10 per day. Free buses run regularly to the ferry terminal. If you're leaving your car on the mainland, plan to arrive at the parking lots in Falmouth at least 45 minutes before sailing time. The cost of a round-trip passenger ticket to Martha's Vineyard is $11 for adults and $5.50 for children 5 to 12. Bringing a bike costs an extra $6 round-trip. You do not need a ferry reservation if you're traveling without a car.

From **Falmouth Inner Harbor,** you can board the *Island Queen* (© 508/ 548-4800; www.islandqueen.com) for a 35-minute cruise to Oak Bluffs (passengers only). The **Falmouth–Edgartown Ferry Service,** 278 Scranton Ave. (© 508/548-9400; www.falmouthferry.com), operates a 1-hour passenger ferry, called the *Pied Piper,* from Falmouth Inner Harbor to Edgartown. The boat runs from late May to mid-October; reservations are required. From **Hyannis,** May through October, **Hy-Line** (© 508/778-2600; www.hy-linecruises.com) operates from the Ocean Street Dock to Oak Bluffs on Martha's Vineyard.

By Plane   You can fly into **Martha's Vineyard Airport** (© 508/693-7022), in West Tisbury, about 5 miles outside Edgartown.

Airlines serving the Vineyard include **Cape Air/Nantucket Airlines** (© 800/ 352-0714 or 508/771-6944) from Boston, Hyannis, and New Bedford; **Continental Express/Colgan Air** (© 800/525-0280), with seasonal nonstop flights from Newark; and **US Airways Express** (© 800/428-4322), which has seasonal weekend service from LaGuardia.

By Bus   Bonanza Bus Lines (© 800/556-3815; www.bonanzabus.com) connects the Woods Hole ferry port with Boston (from South Station), New York City, and Providence, Rhode Island. **Relax and Ride** is a bus service that leaves from the Route 128 MBTA/Amtrak station in Westwood, south of Boston, and goes to the Woods Hole ferry terminal. The service operates from late June to early September. Your fare includes the ferry from Woods Hole to the Vineyard.

GETTING AROUND   By Bicycle & Moped   The best way to explore the Vineyard is on two wheels. There's a little of everything for cyclists, from paved paths to hilly country roads. You need a driver's license to rent a moped.

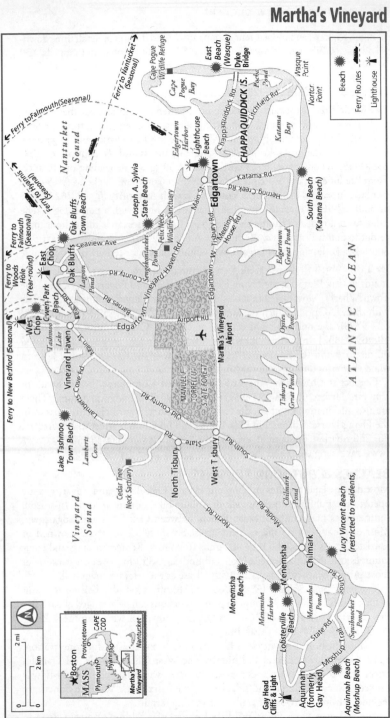

Bike-, scooter-, and moped-rental shops are clustered throughout all three down-island towns. Bike rentals cost about $15 to $30 a day; scooters and mopeds, $30 to $80. In Vineyard Haven, try **Strictly Bikes,** Union Street (© **508/ 693-0782**). In Edgartown, you'll find **Wheel Happy,** 204 Upper Main St. and 8 S. Water St. (© **508/627-5928**), which rents only bikes.

By Shuttle Bus   In season, shuttle buses run often enough to make them a practical means of getting around. Connecting Vineyard Haven (across from the ferry terminal), Oak Bluffs (near the Civil War statue in Ocean Park), and Edgartown (Church St., near the Old Whaling Church), the **Island Transport** (© **508/ 693-0058**) yellow school buses cost about $1.50 to $4, depending on distance. From late June to early September, they run from 6am to midnight every 15 or 30 minutes. In season, the **Martha's Vineyard Transit Authority** (© **508/627-7448** or 508/627-9663) operates several shuttles (white buses with a purple logo). The Edgartown downtown shuttle and the South Beach buses circle throughout town or out to South Beach every 20 minutes. A one-way trip in town is 50¢; a trip to South Beach (leaving from Edgartown's Church St. visitor center) is $1.50.

By Taxi   You'll find taxis at all ferry terminals and the airport, as well as taxi stands in Oak Bluffs (at the Flying Horses Carousel) and Edgartown (next to the Town Wharf). Most taxi companies operate vans for larger groups and travelers with bikes. Options include **Accurate Cab** (© **888/557-9798** or 508/ 627-9798), the only all-night service; and **Adam Cab** (© **800/281-4462** or 508/693-3332). In summer, rates from town to town are generally flat fees based on distance and the number of passengers. Late-night revelers should keep in mind that rates double from midnight until 7am.

Contact the **Martha's Vineyard Chamber of Commerce,** Beach Road, in Vineyard Haven (© **508/693-0085;** fax 508/693-7589; www.mvy.com). There are also information booths at the ferry terminal in Vineyard Haven, across from the Flying Horses Carousel in Oak Bluffs, and on Church Street in Edgartown. For information on current events, check the newspapers *Vineyard Gazette* (www.mvgazette.com) and the *Martha's Vineyard Times* (www.mvtimes.com).

BEACHES & OUTDOOR PURSUITS

Most down-island **beaches** in Vineyard Haven, Oak Bluffs, and Edgartown are open to the public and just a walk or a short bike ride from town. In season, shuttle buses make stops at **State Beach,** between Oak Buffs and Edgartown. Most of the Vineyard's magnificent up-island shoreline is privately owned or restricted to residents, and thus off-limits to visitors. Renters in up-island communities can obtain a beach sticker (around $35–$50 for a season sticker) for those private beaches by applying with a lease at the relevant town hall.

The party boat *Skipper* (© **508/693-1238**) offers half-day **fishing** trips out of Oak Bluffs Harbor in season. Deep-sea excursions can be arranged aboard **Big Eye Charters** (© **508/627-3649**) out of Edgartown, or with **Summer's Lease** (© **508/693-2880**) out of Oak Bluffs.

About a fifth of the Vineyard's landmass has been set aside for conservation, and it's accessible to **bikers** and **hikers.** The **West Chop Woods,** off Franklin Street in Vineyard Haven, comprise 85 acres with marked trails. Midway between Vineyard Haven and Edgartown, the **Felix Neck Wildlife Sanctuary** includes a 6-mile network of trails over varying terrain.

The 633-acre **Long Point Wildlife Refuge,** off Waldron's Bottom Road in West Tisbury (© **508/693-7392** for gatehouse), offers heath and dunes, freshwater ponds, a beach, and interpretive nature walks for children.

Some remarkable botanical surprises can be found at the 20-acre **Polly Hill Arboretum,** 809 State Rd., West Tisbury (② **508/693-9426**). Horticulturist Polly Hill has developed this property over the past 40 years and allows the public to wander the grounds Thursday through Tuesday from 7am until 7pm. There's a requested donation of $5 for adults and $3 for children under 12.

Wind's Up, 199 Beach Rd., Vineyard Haven (② **508/693-4252**), rents canoes, kayaks, and various sailing craft, including windsurfers, and offers instruction on a placid pond. Canoes and kayaks rent for $18 to $20 per hour.

WHERE TO STAY

The **Charlotte Inn,** 27 S. Summer St., Edgartown (② **508/627-4751**), is one of only two Relais & Châteaux properties on the Cape and Islands. Linked by formal gardens, each of the 18th- and 19th-century houses has a distinctive look and feel, though the predominant mode is English country. All but one of the rooms have TVs; some have VCRs. Some of the luxurious bathrooms are bigger than those of most standard hotel rooms. The inn's restaurant, **L'étoile,** is one of the island's finest. Rates include continental breakfast; full breakfast is offered for $15 extra. No children under 14. There are no phones in the rooms.

With its graceful wraparound colonnaded front porch, the **Jonathan Munroe House,** 100 Main St., Edgartown (② **877/468-6763** or 508/627-5536; www.jonathanmunroe.com), stands out from the other inns and captains' homes on this stretch of upper Main Street. Guest rooms are immaculate, antique-filled, and dotted with clever details. Many units have fireplaces. At breakfast (included in room rates), don't miss the homemade waffles and pancakes. No children under 12 are permitted.

Do you long to stay at a reasonably priced inn that's bigger than a B&B but smaller than a Marriott? **The Victorian Inn,** 24 S. Water St., Edgartown (② **508/627-4784;** www.thevic.com), is a freshened-up version of those old-style hotels that used to exist in every New England town. With three floors of long, graceful corridors, the Victorian could serve as a stage set for a 1930s romance. Several units have canopy beds and balconies. Rates include full breakfast and afternoon tea. Dogs are welcome. There are no phones in the rooms.

The Edgartown Inn, 56 N. Water St. (② **508/627-4794;** www.edgartowninn.com), offers perhaps the best value on the island. It's a lovely 1798 Federal manse. Rooms are no-frills but traditional; some have TVs and harbor views. Modernists may prefer the cathedral-ceilinged quarters in the annex. Service is excellent. The inn does not accept credit cards, and there are no phones in the rooms.

WHERE TO DINE

Outside Oak Bluffs and Edgartown, all of Martha's Vineyard (including Vineyard Haven) is "dry," so bring your own bottle; some restaurants charge a small fee for uncorking.

Alchemy is a spiffy restaurant that's a little slice of Paris on 71 Main St. (② **508/627-9999**). There's also a large selection of cocktails, liqueurs, and wines. In addition to lunch and dinner, a bar menu is served from 2:30 to 11pm.

Everything's appealing at **Among the Flowers Cafe** on Mayhew Lane (② **508/627-3233**) near the dock. The breakfasts are the best around, and the comfort-food dinners are among the most affordable options in this pricey town.

At **The Newes from America,** a subterranean tavern at 23 Kelly St. (② **508/627-4397**) built in 1742, beers are a specialty: Try a rack of five brews, or let your choice of food—from a wood-smoked oyster "Island Poor Boy" sandwich to a porterhouse steak—dictate your draft.

The **Black Dog Tavern,** at the Beach Street Extension on the harbor (© 508/693-9223), is a national icon (with cool T-shirts). Soon after Robert Douglas decided in 1971 that this port could use a good restaurant, vacationers waiting for the ferry began to wander into this saltbox to tide themselves over with a bit of "blackout cake" or peanut-butter pie. The food is still home-cooking good. Come early, when it first opens, and sit on the porch, where the views are perfect.

MARTHA'S VINEYARD AFTER DARK

BARS & CLUBS   All towns except for Oak Bluffs and Edgartown are dry, and last call at bars and clubs is at midnight. Hit Oak Bluffs for the rowdiest bar scene and best nighttime street life. In Edgartown, you may have to hop around before you find the evening's most happening spot.

Young and loud are the watchwords at **The Lampost** and the **Rare Duck,** 111 Circuit Ave., Oak Bluffs (© 508/696-9352), a pair of clubs in the center of town. The Lampost features live bands and a dance floor, the Rare Duck, acoustic acts. Entertainment includes such prospects as "'80s night" and "male hot-body contest." Cover is from $1 to $5.

4 Mystic

The spirit and texture of the maritime life and history of New England are captured in many ports along its indented coast, but nowhere more cogently than beside the Mystic River estuary and its harbor. The town is home to one of New England's most singular attractions, the Mystic Seaport museum village.

GETTING THERE   By **car** from New York or Boston, take I-95 to Exit 90 at Mystic. **Amtrak** (© 800/USA-RAIL) serves Mystic with three **trains** daily from New York (trip time 3¼ hr.) and Boston (1¾ hr.).

VISITOR INFORMATION   A **visitor center** is in Building 1D of the Olde Mistick Village shopping center, at Route 27 and Coogan Boulevard, near I-95 (© 860/536-1641).

EXPORING MYSTIC SEAPORT

The village of **Mystic Seaport,** 75 Greenmanville Ave., Route 27 (© **888/ 9SEAPORT** or 860/572-5315; www.mysticseaport.org), encompasses an entire waterfront settlement, more than 60 buildings on and near a 17-acre peninsula. A useful map guide is available at the ticket counter in the **visitor center** in the building opposite the museum stores (which stay open later than the village most of the year, so make them your last stop).

Exit the visitor center and bear right along the path between the Galley Restaurant and the village green. It bends to the left, intersecting with a street of shops, public buildings, and houses. At that corner is an 1870s hardware and dry-goods store. Turning right here, you'll pass a schoolhouse, a chapel, and an 1830s home. Stop at the **children's museum,** which invites youngsters to play games characteristic of the seafaring era. It faces a small square that is the starting point for **horse-drawn wagon tours.**

From here, the barque *Charles W. Morgan,* built in 1841, one of the proudest possessions of the Seaport fleet of over 400 craft, is a few steps away.

If you're a fan of scrimshaw and ship models, continue along the waterfront until you reach the **Stillman Building,** which contains fascinating exhibits of both. Otherwise, head left toward the lighthouse. Along the way, you'll encounter a tavern, an 1833 bank, a cooperage, and other shops and services that did business with the whalers and clipper ships that put in at ports such as this.

The docents in the village are highly competent at the crafts they demonstrate and always ready to impart information. The fact that they aren't dressed in period costumes enhances the village's feeling of authenticity by avoiding the contrived air of many such enterprises.

The next vessel is the iron-hulled square-rigger *Joseph Conrad,* which dates from 1881. Up ahead is a **lighthouse,** which looks out across the water toward the riverside houses that line the opposite shore. Round the horn, go past the boat sheds, the fishing shacks, and the ketches and sloops moored here in season until you come to the dock for the 1908 **SS** *Sabino.* This working ship gives half-hour river rides from mid-May to early October, daily from 11am to 4pm, and 1½-hour evening excursions. A few steps away is the 1921 fishing schooner *L. A. Dunton.*

A few steps south is the **Henry B. Du Pont Preservation Shipyard,** where the boats are painstakingly restored. One recent project was the re-creation of the schooner *Amistad,* which inspired an exhibit exploring the historical incident.

Also on the grounds are the **Galley Restaurant,** which serves fish and chips, fried clam strips, and lobster rolls; and **Sprouter's Tavern,** which offers snacks and sandwiches. When you exit for the day, ask the gatekeeper to validate your ticket so you can come back the next day for free.

Across the courtyard with the giant anchor is a building containing several **museum stores** as well as an art gallery. These superior shops stock books, kitchenware, fresh-baked goods, nautical prints and paintings, and ship models.

Admission to the shipyard is $17 adults, $9 for children 6 to 12 (second day included with validation). The ships and exhibits are open from April to October daily from 9am to 5pm, November to March daily from 10am to 4pm; the grounds are open 9am to 5pm.

While you're in town, check out the **Mystic Aquarium,** 55 Coogan Blvd. at Exit 90 off I-95 (✆ **860/572-5955;** www.mysticaquarium.org). The show illuminates as it entertains, and at 15 minutes in length, it doesn't test the attention spans of the very young. The adorable sea lions squawk, click, roll up onto the apron of their pool, tail walk, and joyously splash the nearer rows of spectators. And there are a host of other exhibits featuring marine mammals and other creatures of the deep.

The other exhibits are enough to occupy at least another hour. Near the entrance is a tank of fur seals, and out back are sea lions and African black-footed penguins. A $52-million expansion was completed in 1999 under the direction of the undersea explorer Robert Ballard. It includes a 1-acre outdoor habitat called the Alaskan Coast, which contains a pool for resident white beluga whales and harbor seals. Visitors are practically eye to eye with such creatures as sea horses, jellyfish, and the pugnacious yellow-head jaw fish, which spends its hours digging fortifications in the sand.

Admission is $16 adults, $15 seniors, $11 children 3 to 12.

WHERE TO STAY & DINE

Mystic's most appealing lodging is **The Steamboat Inn,** 73 Steamboat Wharf (✆ **860/536-8300**), a yellow-clapboard structure that has apartment-size downstairs bedrooms, with Jacuzzis and wet bars, while the upstairs units have woodburning fireplaces. Every room is decorated uniquely and all but one have water views. The inn commissioned the 97-foot yacht, *Valiant,* that is moored at its dock. The staterooms can be rented when the yacht isn't chartered. Rates include breakfast. Children over 9 are welcome. Each room has a dataport, a fridge, and a coffeemaker.

There are plenty of adequate area motels. Pick of the litter may be the **Best Western Sovereign,** north of Exit 90 (© 800/528-1234), with a pool and restaurant. Nearby competitors are the **Comfort Inn** (© 800/228-5150 or 860/572-8531), **Days Inn** (© 800/325-2525 or 860/572-0574), and **Residence Inn** (© 800/331-3131 or 860/536-5150).

For dining, **Abbott's Lobster in the Rough,** 117 Pearl St., Noank (© 860/536-7719), is a nitty-gritty lobster shack with plenty of picnic tables. The classic shore dinner rules. That means clam chowder, boiled shrimp, mussels, and a lobster, with coleslaw, chips, and drawn butter. Bring your own beer.

Similarly, **Kitchen Little** on Route 27, 1 mile south of I-95 (© 860/536-2122), is not much more than a shack by the water, but the menu offers 45 distinct breakfast choices and some of the coast's tastiest clam and scallop dishes. At lunch, you must have the definitive clear broth clam chowder, maybe the whole belly clam rolls, and absolutely the fried scallop sandwich.

5 Newport

Newport occupies the southern tip of Aquidneck Island in Narragansett Bay, and is connected to the mainland by three bridges and a ferry. Wealthy industrialists, railroad tycoons, coal magnates, financiers, and robber barons were drawn to the area in the 19th century. They bought up property at the ocean's rim to build what they called summer "cottages"—patterned after European palaces.

But despite Newport's prevailing image as a collection of ornate mansions and regattas, the city is, for the most part, middle class and moderately priced. Scores of inns and B&Bs assure lodging even during festival weeks, at rates and fixtures from budget to luxury level.

GETTING THERE From New York City, take I-95 to the third Newport exit, picking up Route 138 east (which joins briefly with Rte. 4) and crossing the Newport toll bridge slightly north of the downtown district. From Boston, take Route 24 through Fall River, picking up Route 114 into town.

T. F. Green/Providence Airport (© 401/737-8222) in Warwick, south of Providence (Exit 13, I-95), handles national flights into the state on several major carriers. A few of the larger Newport hotels provide shuttle service, as does **Cozy Cab** (© 401/846-2500).

VISITOR INFORMATION For information call (© 800/976-5122 outside Rhode Island, 800/556-2484 in Rhode Island). In town, stop by the **Newport Gateway Visitor Center,** 23 America's Cup Ave. (© 800/326-6030 or 401/849-8048; www.gonewport.com). Open daily from 9am to 5pm (until 6pm Fri–Sat), it has attendants, brochures, a lodging-availability service, a souvenir stand, restrooms, and photos of the mansions, parks, and other landmarks.

GETTING AROUND Most of Newport's attractions, except for the mansions, can be reached on foot. If you'd prefer not to hoof it, the **Rhode Island Public Transit Authority,** or **RIPTA** (© 401/781-9400), has a free shuttle bus that follows a roughly circular route through town, making stops at major sights.

SPECIAL EVENTS Arrive any day in summer and expect to find at least a half dozen festivals, competitions, or other events. In the off season, there's **Christmas in Newport** (© 401/849-6454; www.christmasinnewport.org) and the **February Winter Festival** (© 888/976-5122; www.newportevents.com), which focuses on food and winter sports. In June, there's **Great Chowder Cook-Off** (© 401/846-1600; www.newportfestivals.com). During 2 weeks in July, the **Newport Music Festival** (© 401/846-1133; www.newportmusic.org) offers classical concerts daily. August brings **Ben & Jerry's Folk Festival** (www.newportfolk.com) and the **JVC Jazz Festival** (© 401/847-3700 for both), both held at Fort Adams State Park.

THE COTTAGES

That's what wealthy summer people called the sumptuous mansions they built in Newport. We suggest you visit only one or two per day: The sheer opulence can soon become numbing. Each residence requires 45 minutes to an hour for its guided tour. If at all possible, go during the week to avoid crowds and traffic.

Six of the mansions are maintained by the **Preservation Society of Newport County,** 424 Bellevue Ave. (© 401/847-1000; www.newportmansions.org), which also operates the 1748 Hunter House, the 1860 Italianate Chepstow villa, the 1883 Isaac Bell House, and the Green Animals Topiary Gardens in Portsmouth. The Society sells a **combination ticket,** good for a year, to five of its properties; the cost is $29 for adults, $10 for children 6 to 17. Individual tickets for the Breakers are $15 for adults, $4 for children, while individual tickets for Kingscote, the Elms, Chateau-sur-mer, Marble House, Hunter House, and Rosecliff are $10 for adults, $4 for children. They can be purchased at any of the properties. Parking is free at all the Society properties.

Mansions that aren't operated by the Preservation Society but are open to the public are **Belcourt Castle, Beechwood,** and **Rough Point.**

The cottages include **Kingscote** on Bowery Street (west of Bellevue Ave.), built in 1839, considered one of the Newport Cottages because it was acquired in 1864 by the sea merchant William Henry King, who furnished it with porcelains and textiles accumulated in the China trade. Architect Richard Upjohn designed the mansion in the same Gothic Revival style he used for Trinity Church in New York. The firm of McKim, Mead & White was commissioned to design the 1881 dining room, notable for its Tiffany glass panels.

Architect Horace Trumbauer is said to have been inspired by the Château d'Asnieres outside Paris, and a first look at the dining room of **The Elms,** on Bellevue Avenue, buttresses that claim. So, too, do the sunken gardens, laid out and maintained in the formal French manner. Trumbauer completed the cottage in 1901 and filled it with genuine Louis XIV and XV furniture as well as paintings and accessories true to the late 18th century.

If you have time to see only one cottage, make it **The Breakers** on Ochre Point Avenue. Architect Richard Morris Hunt was commissioned to create this replica of a Florentine Renaissance palazzo. The high iron entrance gates alone weigh over 7 tons. The 50-by-50-foot great hall has 50-foot-high ceilings, forming a giant cube, and is sheathed in marble. Such mind-numbing extravagance shouldn't really be surprising—Hunt's patron was Cornelius Vanderbilt II, grandson of railroad tycoon Commodore Vanderbilt. The mansion's foundation is approximately the size of a football field, and the Breakers took nearly 3 years to build (1892–95). Platoons of artisans were imported from Europe to apply gold leaf, carve wood and marble, and provide mural-sized baroque paintings. The furnishings on view are original.

From the Breakers, return to Bellevue Avenue and turn left (south); **Rosecliff** is on the left. Stanford White thought the Grand Trianon of Louis XVI at Versailles a suitable model for this 1902 commission for heiress Tessie Fair Oelrichs. It has the largest ballroom of all the cottages, not to mention a storied heart-shaped grand staircase. It was used as a setting for some scenes in the Robert Redford movie of F. Scott Fitzgerald's *The Great Gatsby* (1974).

Mrs. William Backhouse Astor—*the* Mrs. Astor—was the arbiter of who constituted New York and Newport society. "The 400" list of socially acceptable folk was influenced or perhaps even drawn up by her. Being invited to **The Astors' Beechwood** at 580 Bellevue Ave. (© **401/846-3772;** www.astors-beechwood.com) was a coveted prize. Rebuilt in 1857 after a fire destroyed the original version, the mansion isn't as large or impressive as some of its neighbors. But it provides a little theatrical pizzazz with a corps of actors who pretend to be friends, children, and servants of Mrs. Astor. In set pieces, they share details about life in the late Victorian era. Admission is $10 for adults, $8.50 for seniors and children 6 to 12; $30 per family.

OUTDOOR PURSUITS: THE BEACH & BEYOND

Fort Adams State Park, Harrison Avenue (© **401/847-2400**), is on the thumb of land that partially encloses Newport Harbor. It can be seen from the downtown docks and reached by driving or biking south on Thames Street and west on Wellington Avenue (a section of Ocean Dr., which becomes Harrison Ave.). Boating, ocean swimming, fishing, and sailing are all possible in the park's 105 acres. The park is open from Memorial Day to Labor Day; admission is $4 per car ($2 for Rhode Islanders and seniors).

Farther along Ocean Drive is **Brenton Point State Park,** a scenic preserve that borders the Atlantic, with nothing to impede the waves rolling in and collapsing on the rock-strewn beach. Scuba divers are often seen surfacing offshore, anglers enjoy casting from the long breakwater, and on a windy day the sky is dotted with colorful kites.

On Ocean Drive, less than 2 miles from the south end of Bellevue Avenue, is **Gooseberry Beach,** which is privately owned but open to the public. Parking costs $8 Monday through Friday, $12 Saturday and Sunday.

Cliff Walk skirts the edge of the southern section of town where most of the cottages were built, and provides better views of many of them than can be seen from the street.

Biking is one of the best ways to get around town, especially out to the mansions and along **Ocean Drive.** Among several rental shops are **Firehouse Bicycle,** 25 Mill St. (© **401/847-5700**); **Ten Speed Spokes,** 18 Elm St. (© **401/847-5609**); and **Fun Rentals,** 1 Commercial Wharf (© **401/846-3474**). The last firm also rents mopeds.

Adventure Sports Rentals, at the Inn on Long Wharf, 142 Long Wharf (© **401/849-4820**), rents not only bikes and mopeds, but also outboard boats, kayaks, and sailboats; parasailing outings can be arranged.

ORGANIZED TOURS The **Newport Historical Society,** 82 Touro St. (© **401/846-0813**), offers two itineraries. Tours of Historic Hill leave on Thursday and Friday at 10am and tours of the Point on Saturday at 10am; each takes about 1½ hours. Tours of Cliff Walk leave on Saturday at 10am and take about 2 hours. Tickets cost $7 and can be purchased at the Society or at the Gateway Visitor Center. **Viking Tours,** based at the Gateway Visitor Center, 23 America's Cup Ave. (© **401/847-6921**), has bus tours of the mansions and harbor cruises on the excursion boat *Viking Queen.* Bus tours—daily in summer, Saturdays from November to March—are 1½ to 4 hours and cost $18 to $38 for adults, $10 to $17 for children 5 to 11. Boat tours, from late May to early October, are 1 hour and cost $10 for adults, $8 for seniors, and $5 for kids.

Booked seat 6A, open return.

Rented red 4-wheel drive.

Reserved cabin, no running water.

Discovered space.

With over 700 airlines, 50,000 hotels, 50 rental car companies and ,000 cruise and vacation packages, you can create the perfect get-way for you. Choose the car, the room, even the ground you walk on.

Travelocity.com
A Sabre Company
Go Virtually Anywhere.

The *Spirit of Newport*, 2 Bowen's Wharf (© 401/849-3575), offers 1½-hour cruises of the bay and harbor. The **Old Colony & Newport Railway**, 19 America's Cup Ave. (© 401/624-6951; www.ocnrr.com), features 80-minute round-trip excursions in vintage trains along the edge of the bay. Fares are $6 for adults, $5 for seniors, and $3.50 for children under 14.

For nautical shopping, try the shops along **Lower Thames Street**. For example, **J. T.'s Ship Chandlery** (no. 364) outfits recreational sailors with sea chests, ship lanterns, and foul-weather gear. **Aardvark Antiques** (no. 475) specializes in salvaged architectural components. **Spring Street** is noted for its antiques shops and purveyors of crafts, jewelry, and folk art. Antique boat models are displayed along with marine paintings and navigational instruments at **North Star Gallery** (no. 105). **The Drawing Room/The Zsolnay Store** (nos. 152–154) stocks estate furnishings and specializes in Hungarian Zsolnay ceramics. Folk art and furniture are the primary goods at **Liberty Tree** (no. 104).

WHERE TO STAY

The **Gateway Visitor Center** (© 800/976-5122 or 401/849-8040; www.gonewport.com) lists vacancies in motels, hotels, and inns.

Newport Reservations (© 800/842-0102 or 401/842-0102) is a free service representing a number of hotels, motels, inns, and B&Bs. **Anna's Victorian Connection** (© 401/849-2489) is similar, but charges a fee and doesn't represent hotels or motels. **Bed & Breakfast Newport, Ltd.** (© 800/800-8765 or 401/846-5408) claims to offer 350 choices of accommodation.

Many of the better motels are located in Middletown, about 2 miles north of downtown Newport. Possibilities include the **Courtyard by Marriott**, 9 Commerce Dr. (© 401/849-8000); **Newport Ramada Inn**, 936 W. Main Rd. (© 401/846-7600); **Newport Gateway Hotel**, 31 W. Main Rd. (© 401/847-2735); and **Howard Johnson**, 351 W. Main Rd. (© 401/849-2000). Newport itself has a **Marriott** at 25 America's Cup Ave. (© 401/849-1000).

At the **Francis Malbone House**, 392 Thames St. (© 800/846-0392 or 401/846-0392; www.malbone.com), several modern rooms were added in a wing attached to the original 1760 colonial house. They are nice, with king-size beds, reproductions of period furniture, and CD players. Given a choice, take a room in the old section, where antiques outnumber repros, Oriental rugs adorn buffed wide-board floors, and silks and linens are deployed unsparingly. Rates include breakfast and afternoon tea. No children under 12.

The **Admiral Fitzroy Inn**, 398 Thames St. (© 866/848-8780 or 401/848-8000; www.admiralfitzroy.com), attracts Europeans and Australians for yachting events and festivals held here. Many rooms have "peek" harbor views, but you'll get a better look from the roof deck. In addition to the breakfast buffet, the kitchen serves a choice of hot dishes. The staff is unfailingly pleasant. Children are accepted here, so lots of families make this home base. Each room has a fridge and a coffeemaker.

The **Jailhouse Inn**, 13 Marlborough St. (© 800/427-9444 or 401/847-4638; www.historicinnsofnewport.com), was supposedly once a colonial jail, although it doesn't look as if it's that old or served that purpose. In any case, what remains, including the caged reception desk, isn't as cute as someone thinks, but there are compensations—the prices, primarily. Rates include breakfast and afternoon tea. Guests have access to a nearby health club. The rooms have fridges.

WHERE TO DINE

There are far too many restaurants in Newport to give full treatment even to only the best among them. Equal in many ways to those recommended below are **Canfield House,** 5 Memorial Blvd. (© **401/847-0416**); **Yesterday's & the Place,** 28 Washington Sq. (© **401/847-0116**); and **The West Deck,** 1 Waites Wharf (© **401/847-3610**).

Asterix & Obelix, 599 Lower Thames St. (© **401/841-8833**), is a cheerful place that offers classic Gallic bistro dishes. Come and discover how delectable a near-perfect roast herbed chicken or sole meunière can be. Sunday dinners are served to live jazz from 7pm. Breads are provided by the chef/owner's **Boulangerie Obelix,** 382 Spring St. (© **401/846-3377**).

Still going strong after almost 330 years, the **White Horse Tavern,** 25 Marlborough St. (© **401/849-3600**), makes a credible claim of being the oldest tavern in America. On the ground floor are a bar and two dining rooms. The food is quite good, from the daily lunch specials to the spice-rubbed venison with pears poached with rosemary. About a third of the dishes involve seafood. Prices are significantly lower on the tavern menu available from 5pm Sunday through Thursday. At **Scales & Shells,** 527 Lower Thames St. (© **401/846-3474**), the graceless name reflects the uncompromising character of this clangorous fish house. Diners who insist on a modicum of elegance should head for the upstairs room, called **Upscales.** Myriad fish and shellfish, listed on the blackboard, are offered in guileless preparations that allow the natural flavors to prevail.

NEWPORT AFTER DARK

The most likely places to spend an evening lie along **Thames Street.** One of the most obvious possibilities, **The Red Parrot,** 348 Thames St., near Memorial Boulevard (© **401/847-3140**), has the look of an Irish saloon and features jazz combos Thursday through Sunday. **One Pelham East,** at Thames and Pelham streets (© **401/847-9460**), has a cafe, a small dance floor, a pool table, and another bar upstairs, with mostly college-age patrons attending to rockers on the stage at front. **Park Place Tavern,** at Thames and Church streets (© **401/ 847-1767**), makes room for jazz duos Thursday through Sunday.

A full schedule of live music is featured at the **Newport Blues Café,** 286 Thames St., at Green Street (© **401/841-5510**), plus a Sunday gospel brunch. With its fireplace, dark wood, and massive steel back door that used to guard the safe of this former bank, the cafe has a lot more class than most of the town's bars. Meals are available nightly in summer, Thursday through Sunday off season.

6 The Berkshires

More than hills but less than mountains, the Taconic and Hoosac ranges that define this region at the western end of the state go by the collective name "The Berkshires." Mohawks and Mohegans lived and hunted here. Farmers, drawn to fertile flood plains of the Housatonic, were supplanted in the 19th century by manufacturers. Artists and writers came for the mild summers and seclusion offered by these hills and lakes. Nathaniel Hawthorne, Herman Melville, and Edith Wharton were among those who put down temporary roots. By the 1930s, theater, dance, and music performances had established themselves as regular summer fixtures. Tanglewood, Jacob's Pillow, and the Berkshire and Williamstown Theatre festivals draw tens of thousands of visitors every summer.

The Berkshires

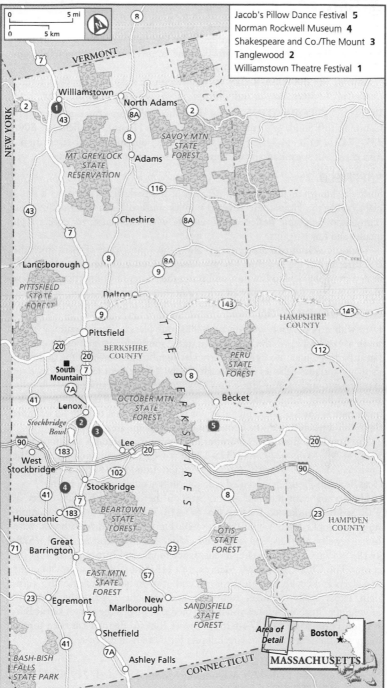

Jacob's Pillow Dance Festival **5**
Norman Rockwell Museum **4**
Shakespeare and Co./The Mount **3**
Tanglewood **2**
Williamstown Theatre Festival **1**

VERMONT

NEW YORK

Williamstown

North Adams

SAVOY MTN. STATE FOREST

MT. GREYLOCK STATE RESERVATION

Adams

Cheshire

Lanesborough

PITTSFIELD STATE FOREST

Dalton

Pittsfield

BERKSHIRE COUNTY

HAMPSHIRE COUNTY

PERU STATE FOREST

South Mountain

Lenox

OCTOBER MTN. STATE FOREST

Becket

Stockbridge Bowl

Lee

West Stockbridge

Stockbridge

Housatonic

BEARTOWN STATE FOREST

THE BERKSHIRES

Great Barrington

EAST MTN. STATE FOREST

Egremont

New Marlborough

OTIS STATE FOREST

SANDISFIELD STATE FOREST

HAMPDEN COUNTY

Sheffield

BASH-BISH FALLS STATE PARK

Ashley Falls

CONNECTICUT

Area of Detail

Boston

MASSACHUSETTS

ESSENTIALS

GETTING THERE   The Massachusetts Turnpike (**I-90**) runs east-west from Boston to the Berkshires, with an exit near Lee and Stockbridge. From New York City, the scenic Taconic State Parkway connects with I-90 not far from Pittsfield.

Amtrak (© 800/USA-RAIL; www.northeast.amtrak.com) operates several trains daily between Boston and Chicago, stopping in Pittsfield each way.

VISITOR INFORMATION   The **Berkshire Visitors Bureau,** Berkshire Common (off South St., near the entrance to the Hilton), Pittsfield (© 800/ 237-5747 or 413/443-9186), can assist with questions and lodging reservations. Also check out **www.berkshires.com** and **www.westernmassvisit.net**.

SHEFFIELD

Sheffield, known as the "Antiques Capital of the Berkshires," occupies a flood plain beside the Housatonic River, 11 miles south of Great Barrington. The canny, knowledgeable dealers know exactly what they have, so expect high quality and few bargains.

There are at least two dozen dealers along this route. Most of them stock the **free directory** of the Berkshire County Antiques Dealers Association, which lists dealers from Sheffield to Cheshire and across the border in Connecticut and New York. Look, too, for the pamphlet called *The Antique Hunter's Guide to Route 7.*

GREAT BARRINGTON

Even with a population well under 8,000, this pleasant retail center, 7 miles south of Stockbridge, is the largest town in the southernmost part of the county. Great Barrington has no sights of particular significance, leaving time to browse its many antiques galleries and specialty shops. Convenient as a home base for excursions to such nearby attractions as Monument Mountain, Bash-Bish Falls, Butternut Basin, Tanglewood concerts, and Stockbridge, it has a number of adequate motels north of the center along or near Route 7 that tend to fill up more slowly on weekends than the better-known inns in the area.

The **Southern Berkshire Chamber of Commerce** maintains an information booth at 362 Main St. (© 413/528-1510; www.greatbarrington.org), near the town hall. It's open Tuesday through Saturday from 9am to 5pm. *Note:* The local Board of Health has banned smoking in *any* public space in town.

Head straight for Railroad Street. Start on the corner with Main Street, at **T. P. Saddle Blanket & Trading Co.** (© 413/528-6500). An unlikely emporium that looks lifted whole from the Rockies, it's packed with boots, hats, Indian jewelry, blankets, and jars of salsa. **Mistral's,** 6 Railroad St. (© 413/528-1618), stocks Gallic tableware, linens, fancy foods, and furniture. Around the corner, **The Chef's Shop,** 290 Main St. (© 413/528-0135), features a bounty of gadgets and cookbooks. In the north end of town, just before Route 7 turns right across a short bridge, Route 41 goes straight, toward the village of Housatonic. In about 4 miles you'll see a shed that houses the kiln of **Great Barrington Pottery** (© 413/274-6259). Owner Richard Bennett has been throwing pots according to Japanese techniques for more than 30 years.

WHERE TO STAY & DINE

North of town on Route 7 is **Monument Mountain Motel,** 249 Stockbridge Rd. (© 413/528-3272; fax 413/528-3132), which has a pool, tennis courts, and a riverside location. The **chamber of commerce** operates a lodging hot line at © 800/269-4825 or 413/528-4006.

The Old Inn on the Green & Gedney Farm on Route 57, New Marlborough (© **800/286-3139** or 413/229-3131; www.oldinn.com), comprises a former 1760 tavern/general store and the 18th-century Thayer House, a pair of converted dairy barns; and 1906 Gedney Manor, with a spa and fitness center now under construction. Among the most desirable units are those in Thayer House, some with fireplaces and all with air-conditioning, and those in the barn, where contemporary furnishings are combined with Oriental rugs. All five intimate dining rooms have fireplaces; reservations are advised. Rates include breakfast, and there is a courtyard pool at Thayer House.

A roadside lodging built in the middle of the last century in Federal style, **The Windflower Inn**, 684 S. Egremont Rd. (© **800/992-1993** or 413/528-2720; www.windflowerinn.com), commands a large plot of land opposite the Egremont Country Club. Six rooms have fireplaces; four have canopy beds. Rates include breakfast and afternoon tea; children stay in parents' rooms for an additional $25. There's an outdoor pool, and a dataport in each room.

The Castle Street Cafe, 10 Castle St. (© **413/528-5244**), is a storefront bistro that has ruled the Great Barrington roost for some time now, and has expanded into the next building. While a Francophilic inclination is apparent in the main room, what with duck breast with potato galette and steak au poivre, it isn't overpowering. An award-winning wine list is another reason to stop in.

STOCKBRIDGE

Stockbridge's ready accessibility to Boston and New York (about 2½ hr. from each and reachable by rail since the mid–19th century) transformed the frontier settlement into a Gilded Age summer retreat for the rich. The town has long been popular with artists and writers.

Stockbridge lies 7 miles north of Great Barrington and 6 miles south of Lenox. The **Stockbridge Chamber of Commerce** (© **413/298-5200;** www.stockbridgechamber.org) maintains an information booth opposite the row of stores depicted by Rockwell. It's open May through October.

WHAT TO SEE & DO

From June to August, the **Berkshire Theatre Festival,** Main Street (© **413/298-5576;** www.berkshiretheatre.org), holds its season of classic and new plays, often with marquee names starring or directing. Dianne Wiest and Joanne Woodward have been participants. Its venue is a "casino" built in 1887 to plans by architect Stanford White.

The striking **Norman Rockwell Museum,** Route 183 (© **413/298-4100;** www.nrm.org), opened in 1993 to house the works of Stockbridge's favorite son. The illustrator used both his neighbors and the town to tell stories about an America now rapidly fading from memory. Most of Rockwell's paintings adorned covers of the *Saturday Evening Post:* warm and often humorous depictions of homecomings, first proms, and visits to the doctor. He addressed serious concerns, too, notably with his poignant portrait of a little African-American girl being escorted by U.S. marshals into a previously segregated school. The lovely 36-acre grounds also contain Rockwell's last studio (closed Nov–Apr). Admission is $9 adults, $2 children 6 to 18; $20 per family.

WHERE TO STAY

The Inn at Stockbridge, 30 East St. (© **888/466-7865** or 413/298-3337; www.stockbridgeinn.com), is a 1906 building with a grandly columned porch. It's set well back from the road on 12 acres. The innkeepers are eager to please, serving full breakfasts by candlelight and afternoon spreads of wine and cheese. Four new bedrooms have fireplaces and whirlpools. There's an outdoor pool. No children under 12.

So well known that it serves as a symbol of the Berkshires, **The Red Lion Inn,** Main Street (© 413/298-5545; www.redlioninn.com), had its origins as a stagecoach tavern in 1773. The rocking chairs on the porch are the perfect place to while away an hour. Six satellite buildings have been added, all within 3 miles of the inn. Jackets are required for men in the main dining room, but not in the casual **Widow Bingham Tavern** nor, in good weather, in the courtyard out back. The wine cellar has been recognized with important awards. **The Lion's Den** has nightly live entertainment, usually of the folk-rock variety. There's an outdoor pool, golf and tennis nearby, an exercise room, babysitting, and a laundry.

LEE & JACOB'S PILLOW

While Stockbridge and Lenox were developing into luxurious recreational centers, Lee was a thriving paper-mill town and thus remained essentially a town of workers and merchants. The town's contribution to the Berkshire cultural calendar is the Jacob's Pillow Dance Festival, which first thrived as "Denishawn," a fabled alliance between founders Ruth St. Denis and Ted Shawn.

Lee is 5 miles southeast of Lenox. In summer and early fall, the **Lee Chamber of Commerce** (© 413/243-0852; www.leechamber.org) operates an **information center** on the town common, Route 20 (© 413/243-4929).

The Jacob's Pillow Dance Festival, George Carter Road, Becket (© 413/243-0745; www.jacobspillow.org), began in 1933 when Ted Shawn decided to put on a show in the barn. Jacob's Pillow is now to dance what Tanglewood is to classical music. The theater has long welcomed troupes of international reputation, including the Mark Morris Dance Group, Twyla Tharp, and the Paul Taylor Dance Company. The season runs from mid-June to late August, and tickets go on sale April 1. The growing campus includes a store, pub, dining room, tent restaurant, and exhibition space. Picnic lunches can be pre-ordered 24 hours in advance.

WHERE TO STAY

On the road to Lenox, the **Best Western Black Swan,** 435 Laurel St./Rte. 20 (© 413/243-2700; www.travelweb.com), has a pool and restaurant; some rooms have fireplaces.

Applegate, 279 W. Park St. (© 800/691-9012 or 413/243-4451; www.apple gateinn.com), is in a gracious 1920s Georgian colonial manse. The top unit has a canopy bed, Queen Anne reproductions, a steam shower, and a fireplace (with real wood). Two suites have TVs, Jacuzzis, and gas fireplaces. Breakfast is by candlelight, and the innkeepers set out wine and cheese in the afternoon. There's a heated outdoor pool, a nine-hole golf course across the street, a tennis court, access to a nearby health club, and bikes. No children under 12.

The Chambéry Inn, 199 Main St. (© 413/243-2221; www.berkshireinns. com), was the Berkshires' first parochial school (1885), named for the French hometown of the nuns who ran it. The extra-large bedrooms were formerly classrooms. Six of them, with 13-foot ceilings and the original woodwork and blackboards, are equipped with whirlpool tubs and gas fireplaces. Some rooms have TV/VCRs, CD players, and fridges. A breakfast basket is delivered to your door each morning. No children under 18.

LENOX & TANGLEWOOD

Stately homes and fabulous mansions mushroomed in this former agricultural settlement, and Lenox remains a repository of extravagant domestic architecture surpassed only in such resorts as Newport and Palm Beach. And because many of the cottages have been converted into inns and hotels, it is possible to get inside some of these beautiful buildings, if only for a cocktail or a meal.

The reason for so many lodgings in a town with a population of barely 5,000 is Tanglewood, a nearby estate where a series of concerts by the Boston Symphony Orchestra is held every summer.

Lenox lies 7 miles south of Pittsfield. The **Lenox Chamber of Commerce** (© 413/637-3646; www.lenox.org) provides visitor information and lodging referrals.

TANGLEWOOD MUSIC FESTIVAL

Lenox is filled with music every summer, and the undisputed headliner is the **Boston Symphony Orchestra (BSO).** Concerts are given at Tanglewood estate, beginning in July, ending the weekend before Labor Day. The estate is on West Street (actually in Stockbridge township). From Lenox, take Route 183 1½ miles southwest of town.

The program features a menagerie of other performers and musical idioms. These run the gamut from popular artists (like James Taylor and Bonnie Raitt) and jazz musicians (including Dave Brubeck and Wynton Marsalis) to such guest soloists as Itzhak Perlman and Yo-Yo Ma.

The **Koussevitzky Music Shed** is an open auditorium that seats 5,000, surrounded by a lawn where an audience lounges on folding chairs and blankets. Chamber groups and soloists appear in the smaller **Ozawa Hall.** Major performances are on Friday and Saturday nights and Sunday afternoon.

Tentative programs are available after January 1; the schedule is usually locked in by March. Tickets can sell out quickly, so get yours as far in advance as possible. If you decide to go at the last minute, take a blanket or lawn chair and get tickets for lawn seating, which is almost always available. You can also attend open rehearsals during the week, as well as the rehearsal for the Sunday concert on Saturday morning.

The estate (© 413/637-5165 June–Aug), with over 500 acres of lawns and gardens, was put together starting in 1849 by William Aspinwall Tappan. Admission to the grounds is free when concerts aren't scheduled. In 1851, a structure on the property called the Little Red Shanty was rented to Nathaniel Hawthorne, who stayed here long enough to write a children's book, *Tanglewood Tales,* and meet Herman Melville, who lived in nearby Dalton. The existing Hawthorne Cottage is a replica (and isn't open to the public). On the grounds is the original Tappan mansion, with fine views.

For recorded information, call © 617/266-1492 from September to June 10 (information on Tanglewood concerts is not available until the program is announced in Mar or Apr). Children under 5 are not allowed in the Shed or Ozawa Hall. To order tickets by mail before June, write the Tanglewood Ticket Office at Symphony Hall, 301 Massachusetts Ave., Boston, MA 02115. After June 1, write the Tanglewood Ticket Office, 297 West St., Lenox, MA 01240. Tickets can be charged to a credit card through **Symphony Charge** (© 888/266-1200 outside Boston, or 617/266-1200; www.bso.org).

OTHER ATTRACTIONS

The Mount, 2 Plunkett St. (© 413/637-1899; www.edithwharton.org), was the home of Edith Wharton, who won a Pulitzer for her novel *The Age of Innocence,* and was singularly equipped to write that detailed examination of the upper classes of the Gilded Age. She traveled in the circles that made the Berkshires a regular stop between New York, Florida, Newport, and the Continent. Wharton had her villa built on this 130-acre property in 1902 and lived here for 10 years. She took an active hand in its creation—one of the few designated National Historic Landmarks designed by a woman. A $15-million restoration campaign is under way, with work so far completed on the terrace and greenhouse and continuing on the interior and gardens.

The repertory theater group **Shakespeare & Company,** 70 Kemble St. (© 413/637-1199; www.shakespeare.org), has long used buildings and amphitheaters on the grounds of the Mount to stage its May-to-October season of plays by the Bard, works by Edith Wharton and George Bernard Shaw, and works by new American playwrights. After conflict with the custodians of the Wharton property, company officials offered to purchase the National Music Foundation on Kemble Street. This purchase is expected to take place in a series of staggered moves up until 2003, when the lease at the Mount expires. In the meantime, performances take place Tuesday through Sunday (weekends only after Labor Day). Lunch and dinner picnic baskets can be purchased on-site.

WHERE TO STAY

The list of lodgings below is only partial, and most can accommodate only small numbers of guests. The Tanglewood concert season is a powerful draw, so prices are highest in summer as well as during the foliage season. Minimum 2- or 3-night stays are usually required during the Tanglewood weeks, foliage season, weekends, and holidays. Reserve well in advance for Tanglewood.

If all the area's inns are booked or if you want to be assured the full quota of 21st-century conveniences, Routes 7 and 20 north and south of town harbor a number of motels, including the **Mayflower Motor Inn** (© 413/443-4468), the **Susse Chalet** (© 413/637-3560), the **Lenox Motel** (© 413/499-0324), and the **Comfort Inn** (© 413/443-4714).

The Canyon Ranch in the Berkshires, 165 Kemble St. (© 800/726-9900 or 413/637-4100; www.canyonranch.com), is a one-of-a-kind spa/resort, with its core the 1897 mansion modeled after Le Petit Trianon at Versailles. Sweat away the pounds in the spa complex, with 40 exercise classes a day, weights, an indoor track, racquetball, squash, and all the equipment you might want. Canoeing and hiking are added possibilities. Guest rooms are in contemporary New England style, with every hotel convenience except minibars. After you're steamed, exhausted, pummeled, and showered, the real events of each day are mealtimes: "nutritionally balanced gourmet," naturally.

The Cliffwood Inn, 25 Cliffwood St. (© 800/789-3331 or 413/637-3330; www.cliffwood.com), is one of the relatively compact manses of the Vanderbilt era, with a long veranda in back overlooking the pool. Antiques and reproductions of many styles and periods fill the common and private spaces. Six guest rooms have working fireplaces (including one in a bathroom!). Three units have TVs. Rates include breakfast daily in high season, weekends in shoulder season. Children over 10 are welcome.

At **Whistler's Inn,** 5 Greenwood St. (© 413/637-0975; www.whistlersinn lenox.com), both innkeepers are travelers who bring things back from every trip, filling the rooms of their 1820 Tudor mansion with cut glass, painted screens, clocks, Persian rugs, and shelf after shelf of books. The result: rooms that are not so much decorated as gathered, without a single boring corner. Most units have TVs and air-conditioning; some have fireplaces as well. The carriage house has one room decked out in African style, the other suggesting Santa Fe. A bottle of sherry or port is kept in the library for guests to enjoy along with tea and cookies. Facilities for children are limited. Rates include breakfast.

WHERE TO DINE

See also "Where to Stay," above, as many inns have dining rooms. In high season, **Spigalina,** 80 Main St. (© **413/637-4455**), serves imaginative Mediterranean cooking. Note that three of the restaurants listed below serve lunch, in a region where most restaurants don't open until evening.

Café Lucia, 80 Church St. (© **413/637-2640**), is where the post-preppie crowd of regulars and weekend refugees from the city is attired in country-casual cashmere and tweed, a taste no doubt honed at campuses of the Ivy League and Seven Sisters. The waitresses display a professionalism rarely experienced in these hills, bringing satisfying starters—carpaccio, bruschetta, and the like—followed by superior renditions of *saltimbocca alla Romana* and eight pastas. Dine out on the broad deck in warmer months.

The Church Street Café, 65 Church St. (© **413/637-2745**), is the most popular place in town, delivering combinations that please the eye and pique the taste buds. Creative appearances on past menus have included seared salmon on a crisp noodle cake and a pizza topped with lobster and mascarpone with white truffle oil. Lunch is a busy time, with crab-cake sandwiches among the favorites.

The Roseborough Grill, 71 Church St. (© **413/637-2700**), is inside an old farmhouse with wooden tables that are unadorned at lunch but dressed with linen and candles at night. Jazz drifts out of the stereo, and often-surprising food issues from the kitchen. Past dishes have included pan-seared Chilean sea bass escabeche, lobster linguine, and shrimp and white bean stew, all of which demonstrate that the chefs gambol in many scented fields.

WILLIAMSTOWN

This community and its prestigious college were named for Col. Ephraim Williams, killed in 1755 in one of the French and Indian Wars. He bequeathed the land for creation of a school and a town. Over the town's long history, buildings have been erected in several styles of the times. That makes Main Street a virtual museum of institutional architecture, with representatives of the Georgian, Federal, Gothic Revival, Romanesque, and Victorian modes, as well as a few yet to be labeled.

A free weekly newspaper, the *Advocate* (© **413/664-7900**), produces useful guides to both the northern and southern Berkshires. For a copy, write to the *Advocate,* 87 Marshall St., North Adams, MA 01267. An unattended **information booth,** at North Street (Rte. 7) and Main Street (Rte. 2), has an abundance of pamphlets and brochures free for the taking.

WHAT TO SEE & DO

The Williamstown Theatre Festival (© **413/597-3400** for box office, 413/597-3399 for recorded information; www.wtfestival.org) is the town's premier summer attraction at the Adams Memorial Theatre. Staging classic and new plays from late June to August, the festival attracts top actors and directors, from Gwyneth Paltrow to Frank Langella, Ethan Hawke, and Bebe Neuwirth.

The Main Stage presents works by major playwrights, while the Nikos Stage often features more experimental productions. The schedule is usually announced by April. It's not too difficult to get tickets, but if a particular performance is said to be sold out, there are often cancellations in the 30 minutes before curtain.

The **Sterling and Francine Clark Art Institute,** 225 South St. (© 413/458-2303; www.clarkart.edu), is a gem with canvases by Renoir (34 of them), Degas, Gauguin, Toulouse-Lautrec, Pissarro, and Corot. Also on display is the Degas sculpture *Little Dancer.* While they are the stars, there are also works by 15th- and 16th-century Dutch portraitists, European genre and landscape painters, and Americans Sargent and Homer, as well as porcelain, silver, and antiques. Apart from the collection, the Clarks' farsighted endowment funded the modern wing added to the original building and has covered all acquisitions, upkeep, and renovations. Admission mid-June to October is $5 adults, free for students and children; free to all Tuesday and November to June. Open September to June Tuesday to Sunday 10am to 5pm; July to August daily 10am to 5pm.

The **Williams College Museum of Art,** 15 Lawrence Hall Dr. (© 413/597-2429; www.williams.edu/WCMA), is the second leg of Williamstown's two prominent art repositories. It exists in large part thanks to the college's collection of almost 400 paintings by the American modernists Maurice and Charles Prendergast. The museum also has works by Gris, Léger, Whistler, Picasso, Warhol, and Hopper. Admission is free. The museum is open Tuesday through Saturday (and some Mon holidays) from 10am to 5pm; Sunday from 1 to 5pm.

7 Southern Vermont

ARLINGTON & MANCHESTER

Southwestern Vermont is the turf of Ethan Allen, Robert Frost, Grandma Moses, and Norman Rockwell. The rolling Green Mountains are rarely out of view from this region. And in midsummer, the lush green hereabouts gives Ireland a good run for its money—verdant hues are found in the forests blanketing the hills, the valley meadows, and the mosses along the tumbling streams, making it obvious how these mountains earned their name.

These Vermont villages make an ideal destination for romantic getaways, antiquing, and outlet shopping. **Arlington** has a town center that borders on microscopic; with its auto-body shops and redemption center (remnants of a time when the main highway artery passed through town), it gleams a bit less than its sibling towns to the north.

To the north, **Manchester** and **Manchester Center** share a town line, but maintain distinct characters. The more southerly Manchester has an old-world elegance with a campuslike town centered around the Equinox Hotel. Just to the north, Manchester Center is a major mercantile center with dozens of national outlets offering discounts on brand-name clothing, accessories, and housewares.

ESSENTIALS

GETTING THERE   From I-91 at Brattleboro, take Route 9 west. Arlington, Manchester, and Manchester Center are north of Bennington on Historic Route 7A, which runs parallel to and west of Route 7. **Vermont Transit** (© 800/451-3292 or 802-362-1226) offers bus service to Manchester.

VISITOR INFORMATION   The **Manchester and the Mountains Chamber of Commerce,** 5046 Main St., Ste. 1, Manchester Center (© 802/362-2100; www.manchestervermont.net), maintains an information center. Hours are Monday through Saturday from 9:30am to 5pm. From Memorial Day to October, it's also open Sunday from 9:30am to 3pm.

For information on outdoor recreation, the **Green Mountain National Forest** maintains a ranger office (© **802/362-2307**) in Manchester on Routes 11 and 30 east of Route 7. It's open Monday through Friday from 8am to 4:30pm.

EXPLORING THE AREA

Arlington has long been associated with illustrator Norman Rockwell, who lived here from 1939 to 1953. Its residents were regularly featured in Rockwell covers for the *Saturday Evening Post.* "Moving to Arlington had given my work a terrific boost. I'd met one or two hundred people I wanted to paint . . . the sincere, honest, homespun types that I love to paint," Rockwell wrote. Visitors can catch a glimpse of this in the **Norman Rockwell Exhibition** (© **802/ 375-6423**). This small museum features a variety of displays, including many of those famous covers, along with photographs of the original models. Reproductions are available at the gift shop. Admission is $2 for adults, free for children under 12.

Manchester has long been one of Vermont's moneyed resorts, attracting prominent summer residents. This town is worth visiting to wander its quiet streets, bordered by distinguished homes dating from the early Federal period. Be sure to note the sidewalks made of irregular marble slabs. The town is said to have 17 miles of such sidewalks, composed of the castoffs from Vermont's marble quarries.

Hildene, Route 7A (© **802/362 1788;** www.hildene.org), was built by Robert Todd Lincoln, the only son of Abraham and Mary Todd Lincoln to survive to maturity. Lincoln summered in this 24-room Georgian Revival mansion between 1905 and 1926 and delighted in showing off its features, including a sweeping staircase and a 1908 Aeolian organ with 1,000 pipes. Lincoln had formal gardens designed after the patterns in a stained-glass window and planted on a gentle promontory with outstanding views of the flanking mountains. The home is viewed on group tours that start at the visitor center; allow time following the tour to explore the grounds. Admission is $8 adults, $4 children 6 to 14. Tours are given from mid-May to October daily from 9:30am to 4pm; grounds close at 5:30pm.

Skiers head to **Bromley Mountain Ski Resort** in Manchester Center (© **800/865-4786** for lodging, or 802/824-5522; www.bromley.com) to learn to ski. Gentle and forgiving, the mountain also features long, looping intermediate runs tremendously popular with families. **Stratton** (© **800/843-6867** for lodging, or 802/297-2200; www.stratton.com) is another popular resort, where new owners have added $25 million in improvements in recent years, mostly in snowmaking, with coverage now up over 80%. The slopes are especially popular for snowboarding, a sport invented here. Expert skiers should seek out Upper Middlebrook, a fine, twisting run off the summit.

WHERE TO STAY & DINE

The Arlington Inn, Route 7A (© **800/443-9442** or 802/375-6532; www.arlingtoninn.com), is an 1848 Greek Revival that would be at home in the Virginia countryside. But it anchors this village well, on a lawn bordered with sturdy maples. Inside, unique wooden ceilings adorn the first-floor rooms and a tavern that borrows its atmosphere from an English hunt club. If you prefer modern comforts, ask for a room in the 1830 parsonage next door, where you'll find phones and TVs. The quietest units are in the detached carriage house. There's a tennis court and babysitting. Rates include breakfast.

Southern Vermont

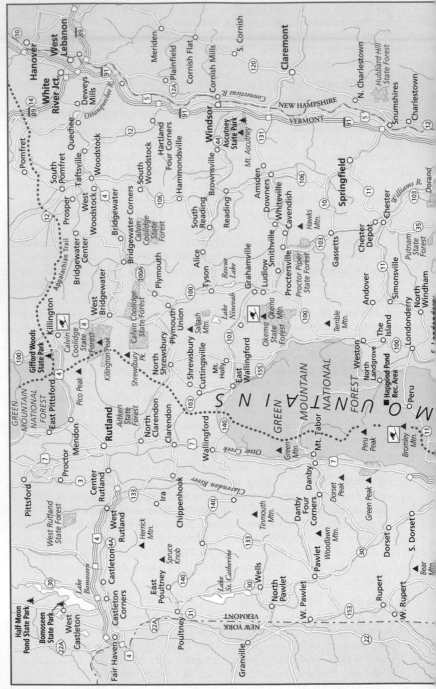

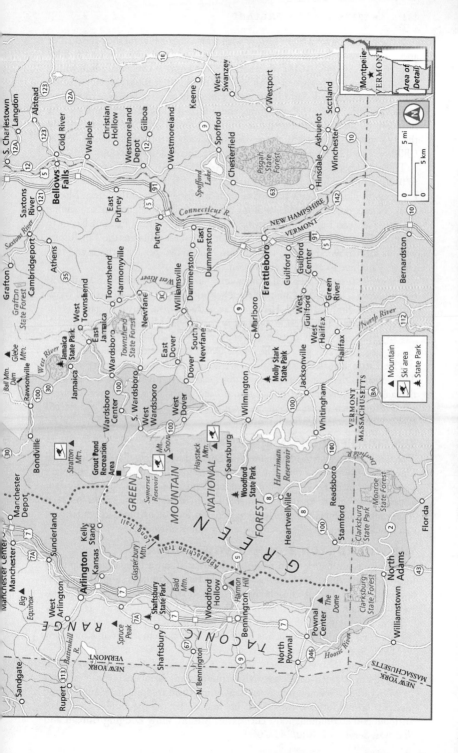

If you're looking for a bit of history with your lodging but are shell-shocked by area rates, consider the **Barnstead Inn,** Route 30, Manchester Center (© **800/ 331-1619** or 802/362-1619; www.barnsteadinn.com), a congenial place within walking distance of Manchester. All but two of the guest rooms are in an 1830s barn; many are decorated in a rustic style, some with exposed beams. Expect vinyl bathroom floors, industrial carpeting, and a mix of motel-modern and antique furniture. Among the more desirable units are room B, which is the largest, and the two rooms (12 and 13) above the office, each with original round beams. Children over 12 are welcome. In the summer, there's a heated pool.

The oldest part of the **Inn at Ormsby Hill,** Route 7A near Hildene (© **800/ 670-2841** or 802/362-1163; www.ormsbyhill.com), dates to 1764. Today, it's a harmonious medley of eras and styles, with inspiring views of the Green Mountains. Guests enjoy those views along with gourmet breakfasts in the dining room, which was built by prominent 19th-century attorney Edward Isham to resemble the interior of a steamship. Among the best units are the Taft Room, with its vaulted wood ceiling. Nine rooms feature two-person Jacuzzis and fireplaces. Children 14 and over are welcome.

If you like superbly prepared Continental fare but are put off by the stuffiness of highbrow restaurants, **Chantecleer** on Route 7A, 3½ miles north of Manchester Center (© **802/362-1616**), is the place for you. Rustic elegance is the best description for this century-old dairy barn. Chef Michel Baumann specializes in game and might feature veal with a roasted garlic, sage, and balsamic demi-glace. Especially good is the whole Dover sole, filleted tableside.

The Little Rooster Café, Route 7A South, Manchester Center (© **802/ 362-3496**), is the best choice in town for breakfast or lunch. Start the day with flapjacks, a Cajun omelet, or a luscious corned-beef hash. Lunches feature a creative sandwich selection, such as a commendable roast beef with pickled red cabbage and a horseradish dill sauce.

THE SOUTHERN GREEN MOUNTAINS

The southern Green Mountains are New England writ large. If you've developed a notion in your head of what New England looks like, this may be the place you've envisioned. This region is known for its pristine, historic villages. Stop for a spell in Brattleboro to stock up on supplies, then head for the southern Green Mountains and continue your explorations on foot or by bike. In winter, you can plumb the snowy hills by cross-country ski or snowshoe.

THE WILMINGTON/MOUNT SNOW REGION

Wilmington has managed to retain its charm as an attractive village despite its location on two busy roads. It has a nice selection of antiques shops, boutiques, and pizza joints. Except on holiday weekends, it still manages to feel like a gracious mountain village untroubled by the times.

From Wilmington, the ski resort of **Mount Snow/Haystack** is accessible to the north via Route 100, which is brisk, busy, and close to impassable on sunny weekends in early October.

The **Mount Snow/Haystack Region Chamber of Commerce** (© 877/ **887-6884** or 802/464-8092; www.visitvermont.com) maintains a visitor center at 21 W. Main St., Wilmington, open daily from 10am to 5pm. Its room-booking service is helpful for locating smaller inns and B&Bs; call the number above. For on-mountain accommodations, check with **Mount Snow Lodging Bureau and Vacation Service** (© 800/245-7669).

WHAT TO SEE & DO

The **Marlboro Music Festival** offers classical concerts by accomplished masters as well as talented younger musicians from mid-July to mid-August in Marlboro, east of Wilmington on Route 9. The retreat was founded in 1951 and has hosted countless musicians, including Pablo Casals, who participated between 1960 and 1973. Concerts are in the 700-seat auditorium at Marlboro College, and advance ticket purchases are recommended. Between September and June, contact the festival's winter office at Marlboro Music, 135 S. 18th St., Philadelphia, PA 19103 (© **215/569-4690**). In summer, write Marlboro Music, Marlboro, VT 05344; or call the box office (© **802/254-2394**; www.marlboromusic.org).

For **downhill skiing, Mount Snow** (© **800/245-7669** for lodging, or 802/464-3333; www.mountsnow.com) is noted for its widely cut runs on the front face, yet remains an excellent destination for intermediates and advanced intermediates. More advanced skiers migrate to the North Face, which is its own little world of bumps and glades. Mount Snow's village is arrayed along the base of the mountain. The most imposing structure is the balconied hotel overlooking a small pond. Mount Snow's post-skiing activities have mellowed somewhat and embraced the family market, although 20-somethings will still find a good selection of après-ski diversions.

For **cross-country skiing,** the Mount Snow area offers 9 miles of groomed trail at **Timber Creek Cross-Country Touring Center** (© **802/464-0999**), in West Dover, popular with beginners. The **Hermitage Ski Touring Center** (© **802/464-3511**) attracts more advanced skiers to its varied terrain and 30 miles of trails. The **White House Ski Touring Center,** at the inn by the same name on Route 100 (© **800/541-2135** or 802/464-2135), has easy access to the woods, a good range of terrain, and 25 miles of trails. A pass costs $12. The center also maintains snowshoe trails and offers rentals.

WHERE TO STAY & DINE

The Mount Snow area has a surfeit of lodging options, ranging from basic motels to luxury inns to slopeside condos. Rates drop quite a bit in summer. Call Mount Snow (© **800/245-7669**) to ask about packages and accommodations.

The **Inn at Quail Run,** 106 Smith Rd., Wilmington (© **800/343-7227** or 802/464-3362), is an intimate B&B that welcomes families (and even pets). Set on 13 acres in the hills east of Route 100, the converted ski lodge was renovated in 1997, with guest rooms done up in a contemporary country style. Family accommodations include king and bunk beds; four rooms have gas fireplaces. Rates include full breakfast. Pets are allowed in some rooms. There's a heated outdoor pool, Jacuzzi, sauna, and game room.

The **Inn at Sawmill Farm,** Crosstown Road and Route 100, West Dover (© **800/493-1133** or 802/464-8131; www.vermontdirect.com/sawmill), is a Relais & Châteaux property. Guest rooms in this old farmhouse, parts of which date back to 1797, are different, but all share contemporary country styling and colonial reproduction furniture. Among the best are Cider House No. 2, with its rustic beams and canopy bed. Some guests report that in recent years the inn has lost a bit of its burnish, and especially given the high room rates, service is no longer as crisp as it once was. There's an outdoor pool and tennis court.

Wilmington is proud of **Dot's,** West Main Street (© **802/464-7284**), offering good, cheap food in the face of creeping boutique-ification elsewhere in town. Dot's is a classic, with pine paneling, swivel counter stools, and checkerboard linoleum tile. It's famous for its chili and pancakes, but don't overlook the

Cajun skillet—a medley of sausage, peppers, onions, and home fries sautéed and served with eggs and melted Jack cheese.

NEWFANE & TOWNSHEND

These two villages, about 5 miles apart on Route 30, are the epitome of Vermont. Both are set within the serpentine West River Valley and built around open town greens. Both consist of impressive white-clapboard houses and public buildings that share the grace and scale of the surrounding homes. Both boast striking examples of Early American architecture, notably Greek Revival.

For visitors, inactivity is often the activity of choice. Guests find an inn or lodge that suits their temperament, then spend the days strolling, driving the back roads, soaking in a mountain stream, hunting for antiques, or striking off on foot for one of the rounded, wooded peaks that overlook villages and valleys.

ESSENTIALS

GETTING THERE   Newfane and Townshend are located on Route 30 northwest of Brattleboro. The nearest interstate access is off Exit 3 from I-91.

VISITOR INFORMATION   There's no formal information center serving these towns. Brochures are available at the **state visitor center** (© **802/254-4593**) on I-91 in Guilford, south of Brattleboro.

WHAT TO SEE & DO

Newfane was originally founded on a hill a few miles from the current village in 1774; in 1825, it was moved to its present location on a valley floor. Some of the original buildings were dismantled and rebuilt, but most date from the early to mid–19th century. The **National Historic District** comprises some 60 buildings around the green and on nearby side streets. You'll find styles ranging from Federal to Colonial Revival, although Greek Revival appears to carry the day. For more information on area buildings, get a copy of the free walking-tour brochure at the Moore Free Library on West Street or at the Historical Society.

Newfane's history is explored at the **Historical Society of Windham County,** on Route 30 across from the village common, in a 1930s Colonial Revival brick building. There's an assemblage of local artifacts (dolls, melodeons, rail ephemera), along with changing exhibits. It's open from late May to mid-October, Wednesday through Sunday from noon to 5pm; admission is by donation.

More than two dozen **antiques shops** are on or near Route 30 in the West River Valley. They provide good grazing and are a fine resource for collectors. At any of the shops, look for the brochure *Antiquing in the West River Valley.* Among the options: the **Riverdale Antiques Center** (© **802/365-4616**), with about 65 dealers selling some furniture but mostly smaller collectibles.

On Route 30 between Townshend and Jamaica, you'll pass the **Scott Covered Bridge** below the Townshend Dam (closed to car traffic). It dates from 1870 and is an example of a Towne lattice-style bridge, with an added arch. At 166 feet long, it is the longest single-span bridge in the state.

WHERE TO STAY & DINE

You can't help but notice the **Four Columns Inn,** West Street, Newfane (© **800/787-6633** or 802/365-7713; www.fourcolumnsinn.com). It's the regal white-clapboard building with four Ionic columns just off the green. Rooms in the Main House and Garden Wing are larger (and more expensive) than those above the restaurant. Four units have been made over as luxury suites. The best choice in the house is room 12, with a Jacuzzi, skylight, gas fireplace, and private deck with a view of a small pond. Low beams and white damask tablecloths characterize the inn's dining room, which features creative New American cooking. Rates include continental breakfast. There's an outdoor pool, babysitting, and hiking trails. Pets are accepted with prior permission.

The **Windham Hill Inn,** Windham Hill Road, West Townshend (© **800/944-4080** or 802/874 4080; www.windhamhill.com), is situated on 160 acres at the end of a dirt road in a high upland valley. It was built in 1823 as a farmhouse. The guest rooms are appointed in an elegant country style; six have Jacuzzis or soaking tubs, nine have balconies or decks, 13 have gas fireplaces, and all have views. The dining room features creative cooking with a strong emphasis on local ingredients. Rates include breakfast. There's a heated pool, tennis court, game alcove and, in winter, 6 miles of cross-country ski trails. Children over 12 are welcome.

WOODSTOCK

For more than a century, the resort community of Woodstock has been considered one of New England's most exquisite villages. The downtown is compact and neat, populated largely by galleries and boutiques. The village green is surrounded by handsome homes, creating what amounts to a comprehensive review of architectural styles of the 19th and early 20th centuries.

It was first settled in 1765, rose to some prominence as a publishing center in the mid–19th century, and began to attract wealthy families who summered here in the late 19th century. Much of the town is on the National Register of Historic Places, and the Rockefeller family has deeded 500 acres surrounding Mount Tom to the National Park Service.

ESSENTIALS

GETTING THERE   Woodstock is 13 miles west of White River Junction on Route 4 (take Exit 1 off I-89). From the west, Woodstock is 20 miles east of Killington on Route 4. **Vermont Transit** (© **800/451 3292**) offers bus service from Boston and Burlington.

VISITOR INFORMATION   The **Woodstock Area Chamber of Commerce,** 18 Central St. (© **888/496-6378** or 802/457-3555; www.woodstockvt.com), staffs an information booth on the green, open June to October daily from 9:30am to 5:30pm.

EXPLORING THE AREA

The heart of the town is the shady, elliptical green. To put local history in perspective, stop by the **Woodstock Historical Society,** 26 Elm St. (© **802/457-1822**). Housed in the beautiful 1807 Charles Dana House, it has rooms furnished in Federal, Empire, and Victorian styles. It's open from late May to October, plus weekends in December. Hours are Monday through Saturday from 10am to 5pm and Sunday from noon to 4pm. Admission is $2.

The **Billings Farm and Museum** on Elm Street, about a half mile north of town on Route 12 (© **802/457-2355;** www.billingsfarm.org), was the creation of Frederick Billings, who is credited with completing the Northern Pacific Railroad. The 19th-century dairy farm was once renowned for its scientific breeding of Jersey cows and its fine architecture, especially the gabled 1890 Victorian farmhouse. A tour includes hands-on demonstrations of farm activities, exhibits of farm life, a look at an heirloom kitchen garden, and a visit to active milking barns. Admission is $8 adults, $7 seniors, $6 children 13 to 17, $4 children 5 to 12, $1 children 3 to 4.

The Billings Farm and the National Park Service have teamed up to manage the new **Marsh–Billings–Rockefeller National Historic Park** (© 802/457-3368; www.nps.gov/mabi), focusing on the history of conservation. Visitors can tour the elaborate Victorian mansion, walk the carriage roads surrounding Mount Tom, and view one of the oldest professionally managed woodlands in the nation.

Admission to the grounds is free; mansion tours cost $6 adults, $3 children 16 and under. Advance reservations are recommended for mansion tours.

OUTDOOR PURSUITS

The terrain around Woodstock is ideal for exploring by **bike.** Few roads don't lead to great rides; just grab a map and go. Mountain bikes are available for rent ($20 per day) at **Woodstock Sports,** 30 Central St. (© **802/457-1568**).

Mount Tom is the prominent hill overlooking Woodstock, and its low summit has great views over the village and to the Green Mountains to the west. You can ascend the mountain right from the village: Start at Faulkner Park. To reach the trail head from the green, cross Middle Covered Bridge and continue straight on Mountain Avenue. The road soon arrives at the park at the base of Mount Tom.

The area's best **cross-country skiing** is at the **Woodstock Ski Touring Center** (© **800/448-7900** or 802/457-6674), at the Woodstock Country Club, just south of town on Route 106. The center maintains 36 miles of trails, including 12 miles of trails groomed for skate-skiing.

WHERE TO STAY & DINE

Jackson House Inn, 114–3 Senior Lane (© **800/448-1890** or 802/457-2065; www.jacksonhouse.com), was built in 1890 by a lumber baron who hoarded the best wood for himself; the cherry and maple floors are so beautiful you'll feel guilty for not taking off your shoes. The guest rooms are well appointed with antiques, although some of the older rooms are rather small. A well-executed addition (1997) created four suites with fireplaces and Jacuzzis. The inn welcomes guests with complimentary evening hors d'oeuvres and champagne and a 3-acre backyard with formal English gardens. There are no phones in the rooms except for suites. The dining room is well regarded. Rates include breakfast. There's a small fitness room and steam room. Children 14 and over are welcome.

The **Shire Motel,** 46 Pleasant St. (© **802/457-2211;** www.shiremotel.com), is within walking distance of the green and with its colonial decor is better appointed than your average motel. The rooms are bright, with most facing the river that runs behind the property. At the end of the second-floor porch is an outdoor kitchen where you can sit on rockers overlooking the river and enjoy a cup of coffee. The yellow-clapboard house next door has three modern suites, all with gas fireplaces and Jacuzzis.

The **Woodstock Inn,** 14 The Green (© **800/448-7900** or 802/457-1100; www.woodstockinn.com), is central Vermont's best resort. The inn appears to be a venerable and long-established institution at first glance. But it's not—it wasn't built until 1969. The inn adopted a dignified Colonial Revival look well suited for Woodstock. Guest rooms are decorated in either country pine or a Shaker-inspired style. The best units, in the wing built in 1991, feature plush carpeting, fridges, and fireplaces. There are two restaurants; indoor and outdoor pools; a Robert Trent Jones–designed golf course (at inn-owned Woodstock Country Club); tennis courts; a free shuttle to a fitness center (squash, racquetball, steam rooms); bike rental; and cross-country ski trails.

KILLINGTON

Killington is not the Vermont pictured on calendars and place mats. But the region around the mountain boasts Vermont's most active winter scene. Those most content here are skiers, singles in search of mingling, and travelers who want a wide selection of amenities.

ESSENTIALS

GETTING THERE Killington Road extends southward from Routes 4 and 100 (marked on some maps as Sherburne). It's about 12 miles east of Rutland on Route 4. Many inns offer shuttles to the Rutland airport. **Amtrak** (© 800/ USA-RAIL; www.amtrak.com) offers service from New York to Rutland, with connecting shuttles to the mountain and various resorts. The **Marble Valley Regional Transit District** (© 802/773-3244) operates the **Skibus,** offering service between Rutland and Killington ($1).

VISITOR INFORMATION The **Killington & Pico Areas Association** (© 802/773-4181) supplies information on lodging and packages. It also staffs an information booth on Route 4 at the base of the access road, open Monday through Friday from 9am to 5pm, Saturday and Sunday from 10am to 2pm. For information on accommodations and travel to Killington, contact the **Killington Lodging and Travel Service** (© 800/621-6867).

SKIING & MORE

Killington (© 800/621-6867 for lodging, or 802/422-3261; www.killington. com) is New England's largest ski area, offering greater vertical drop than any other New England mountain. You'll find the broadest selection of slopes, with trails ranging from long, narrow, old-fashioned runs to killer bumps high on its flanks. Thanks to this diversity, it has long been the destination of choice for serious skiers. That said, it's also a huge operation run with efficiency and not much of a personal touch. To avoid getting lost, ask about the free tours of the mountain, led by the ski ambassadors based at Snowshed. If you're looking for the big mountain experience, with lots of evening activities and plenty of challenging terrain, it's a good choice. If you're looking for a more local sense of place, head for a more intimate resort like Sugarbush.

Nearest to the downhill ski area (just east of Killington Rd. on Rte. 100/Rte. 4) is **Mountain Meadows Cross Country Ski Resort** (© 800/221-0598 or 802/775-7077), with 34 miles of trails groomed for both skating and classic skiing. The trails are largely divided into three pods, with beginner trails closest to the lodge, an intermediate area a bit further along, and an advanced 6-mile loop farthest away. Rentals and lessons are available. A 1-day pass is $14, a half-day pass (after 1pm) $11.

The intricate network of trails at the **Mountain Top Inn** (© 802/483-6089) activity center has a loyal local following. The 66-mile network runs through mixed terrain with pastoral views and is groomed for both traditional and skateskiing. The area is often deep with snow owing to its high ridge-top location in the hills east of Rutland, and snowmaking along key portions of the trail ensure that you won't have to walk across bare spots during snow droughts.

WHERE TO STAY

Skiers headed to Killington for a week or so should consider the condo option. A number of condo developments spill down the hillside and along the low ridges flanking the access road. These vary in elegance, convenience, and size. **Highridge** features units with saunas and Jacuzzis, along with access to a compact health club. **Sunrise Village** has a more remote setting, along with a health club and access to the Bear Mountain lifts. **The Woods at Killington** is farthest from the slopes (free shuttle) but offers access to the finest health club and the best restaurant. Rates fluctuate, depending on time of year, number of bedrooms, and length of stay. You can line up a vacation by contacting the **Killington Lodging and Travel Bureau** (© **800/621-6867;** www.killington.com), which also arranges stays at area inns and motels.

The **Blueberry Hill Inn,** Goshen–Ripton Road, Goshen (© **800/448-0707** or 802/247-6735; www.blueberryhillinn.com), is along a quiet road about 45 minutes northwest of Killington. It's an extraordinary destination for those inclined toward spending time outdoors. The inn dates to 1813; one graceful addition is the greenhouse walkway, which leads to the cozy guest rooms. Family-style meals are served in a rustic dining room, with a great stone fireplace and homegrown herbs drying from the wooden beams. Rates include breakfast and dinner. There's lake swimming nearby, a sauna, bike rental, and cross-country ski trails. There are no phones in the rooms.

WHERE TO DINE

It's our impression that *every* Killington restaurant serves up chicken wings, and plenty of them. If you love wings, especially free wings, you'll be in heaven. Most restaurants are okay spots to carbo-load for a day on the slopes, and if you're with a group of friends, you may not mind the middling quality—but for the most part, don't expect much of a dining adventure.

8 The White Mountains of New Hampshire

The White Mountains are northern New England's outdoor-recreation capital. This cluster of ancient mountains is a sprawling, rugged playground that attracts kayakers, mountaineers, rock climbers, skiers, mountain bikers, bird-watchers, and especially hikers.

The **White Mountain National Forest** encompasses some 773,000 acres of rocky, forested terrain, more than 100 waterfalls, dozens of remote backcountry lakes, and miles of clear brooks and cascading streams. The center of the White Mountains—in spirit if not in geography—is its highest point: 6,288-foot **Mount Washington,** an ominous, brooding peak that's often cloud-capped and mantled with snow both early and late in the season.

JACKSON & MOUNT WASHINGTON

Jackson is a village in a picturesque valley just off Route 16, about 15 minutes north of North Conway. The village center, approached on a single-lane covered bridge, is tiny, but touches of old-world elegance remain—vestiges of a time when Jackson was a favored destination for the East Coast upper middle class.

ESSENTIALS

GETTING THERE   Jackson is off Route 16 about 11 miles north of North Conway. Look for the covered bridge on the right when heading north.

VISITOR INFORMATION   The **Jackson Chamber of Commerce** (© **800/ 866-3334** or 603/383-9356; www.jacksonnh.com) can provide information and make lodging reservations.

WHAT TO SEE & DO

Mount Washington, just north of Jackson, is the highest mountain in the Northeast at 6,288 feet. It holds the world's record for the highest surface wind speed ever recorded—231 miles per hour, in 1934. Mount Washington may also be the mountain with the most options for getting to the top. Visitors can ascend by cog railroad, by car, by guide-driven van, or on foot.

The summit is home to a train platform, a parking lot, a snack bar, a gift shop, a museum, and a handful of outbuildings, some of which house the weather observatory. And there are the crowds, which can be thick on a clear day. Then again, on a clear day the views can't be beat, with vistas extending into four states and to the Atlantic Ocean.

The best place to learn about Mount Washington is rustic **Pinkham Notch Camp** (© 603/466-2721), operated by the Appalachian Mountain Club. At the crest of Route 16 between Jackson and Gorham, Pinkham Notch offers overnight accommodations and meals, maps, and advice from the helpful staff. A number of hiking trails depart from Pinkham Notch.

The **Mount Washington Auto Road** (© 603/466-3988; www.mt-washington. com) opened in 1861 as a carriage road, and has since remained one of the most popular White Mountain attractions. The steep, winding, 8-mile road (with an average grade of 12%) is partially paved and incredibly dramatic. The ascent will test your iron will; the descent will test your car's brakes. The trip's not worth doing if the summit is in the clouds.

Van tours also ascend throughout the day, allowing you to relax, enjoy the views, and learn about the mountain from informed guides. The Auto Road, which is on Route 16 north of Pinkham Notch, is open from mid-May to late October from 7:30am to 6pm (limited hours early and late in the season). The cost is $16 for car and driver, $6 for each additional adult ($4 for children). The fee includes audiocassette narration pointing out sights along the way. Management has imposed some curious restrictions on cars; for instance, Acuras and Jaguars with automatic transmissions must show a "1" on the shifter to be allowed on the road, and no Lincoln Continentals before 1969 are permitted.

WHERE TO STAY & DINE

The Covered Bridge Motor Lodge, Route 16 (© 800/634-2911 or 602/383-9151; www.jacksoncoveredbridge.com), is a pleasant motel on 5 acres between Route 16 and the river next to Jackson's covered bridge. Rooms are priced well for this area. The best units have balconies that overlook the river. Ask about the two-bedroom apartments with kitchen and fireplace. While pretty basic, the lodge features lovely gardens and other appealing touches that make it a good value. Rates include continental breakfast. There's an outdoor pool, a tennis court, and a Jacuzzi.

The **Inn at Thorn Hill,** Thorn Hill Road (© 603/383-4242; www.innat thornhill.com), is a great choice for a romantic getaway. Designed by Stanford White in 1895, the inn sits outside the village center surrounded by hills. Inside, there's a Victorian feel and luxuriously appointed guest rooms. Our favorites include Catherine's Suite, with a fireplace and two-person Jacuzzi. The hospitality is warm and top-notch, and the meals are among the best in the valley. There's a restaurant and an outdoor pool.

CRAWFORD NOTCH

Crawford Notch is a wild, rugged mountain valley that angles through the heart of the White Mountains. Route 302 (which is wide and speedy on the lower sections) runs through it, becoming steeper as it approaches the narrow defile of the notch itself. The views up the cliffs from the road can be spectacular on a clear day; on an overcast or drizzly day, the effect is nicely foreboding.

The **Twin Mountain Chamber of Commerce** (© **800/245-8946** or 603/ 846-5407; www.twinmountain.org) offers information and lodging referrals at its booth near the intersection of Routes 302 and 3.

WHAT TO SEE & DO

Much of the land flanking Route 302 falls under the jurisdiction of **Crawford Notch State Park,** established in 1911 to preserve land that elsewhere had been decimated by logging. The headwaters of the Saco River form in the notch, and what's generally regarded as the first permanent trail up Mount Washington also departs from here. The trail network on both sides of Crawford Notch is extensive; consult the *AMC White Mountain Guide* or *White Mountains Map Book* for detailed information.

The **Mount Washington Cog Railway,** Route 302, Bretton Woods (© **800/ 922-8825** or 603/846-5404; www.thecog.com), was a marvel of engineering when it opened in 1869. Part moving museum, part slow-motion roller-coaster ride, the cog railway steams to the summit at about 4 miles per hour. Passengers enjoy the expanding view on this 3-hour round-trip. (There are stops to add water to the steam engine, to check the track switches, and to allow other trains to ascend or descend.) There's also a 20-minute stop at the summit. Be aware that the ride is noisy and sulfurous. Dress warmly and expect to acquire a patina of cinder and soot.

WHERE TO STAY & DINE

The Mount Washington Hotel, Route 302, Bretton Woods (© **800/258-0330** or 603/278-1000; www.mtwashington.com), was built in 1902. In its heyday, it attracted luminaries like Babe Ruth, Thomas Edison, and Woodrow Wilson. Guest rooms vary in size and decor; many have grand views of the mountains and countryside. A 900-foot veranda makes for relaxing afternoons. Meals are enjoyed in an impressive octagonal dining room. This remains one of our favorite spots in the mountains, partly for the sheer improbability of it all, and partly for its direct link to a lost era. There are indoor and outdoor pools, two PGA golf courses, 12 clay tennis courts, a shuttle to a nearby health club, bike rental, and summer children's programs.

FRANCONIA NOTCH

Franconia Notch is rugged New Hampshire writ large. Most of the notch is included in a well-managed state park. Those seeking the sublime should plan on a leisurely trip through the notch, allowing enough time to get out of the car and explore forests and craggy peaks.

ESSENTIALS

GETTING THERE   I-93 runs through Franconia Notch, gearing down from four lanes to two (where it becomes the Franconia Notch Pkwy.) in the most scenic and sensitive areas of the park. Several roadside turnoffs dot the route.

VISITOR INFORMATION   Information on the park and surrounding area is available at the **Flume Information Center** (© **603/745-8391**), at Exit 1 off the parkway. It's open in summer daily from 9am to 4:30pm. North of the notch, head to the **Franconia Notch Chamber of Commerce,** on Main Street next to the town hall (© **800/237-9007** or 603/823-5661; www.franconianotch. org). It's open spring through fall, Tuesday through Sunday from 10am to 5pm (days and hours often vary).

EXPLORING FRANCONIA NOTCH STATE PARK

Franconia Notch State Park's 8,000 acres, nestled within the surrounding White Mountain National Forest, hosts an array of scenic attractions easily accessible from I-93 and the Franconia Notch Parkway. For information on any of the following, contact the park offices (© **603/823-8800**).

The most famous park landmark is the **Old Man of the Mountains,** near Cannon Mountain. From the right spot on the valley floor, this 48-foot rock formation bears an uncanny resemblance to the profile of a craggy old man—early settlers said it was Thomas Jefferson. **The Flume** is a rugged gorge through which the Flume Brook tumbles. The gorge, a popular attraction in the mid–19th century, is 800 feet long, 90 feet deep, and as narrow as 20 feet at the bottom; visitors explore it on a 2-mile walk through a network of boardwalks and bridges. Admission is $8 for adults, $5 for children 6 to 12.

Echo Lake is a picturesquely situated recreation area, with a 28-acre lake, a handsome swimming beach, and picnic tables scattered within view of Cannon Mountain on one side and Mount Lafayette on the other. A bike path runs alongside the lake and meanders up and down the notch for a total of 8 miles. Mountain bikes, canoes, and paddleboats can be rented for $10 per hour. Admission to the park is $3 for all visitors over 12.

Robert Frost lived in New Hampshire from the time he was 10 until he was 45. This humble farmhouse on Ridge Road (© **603/823-5510**) is where Frost lived with his family. Wandering the grounds, it's not hard to see how his granite-edged poetry evolved at the fringes of the White Mountains. First editions of Frost's works are on display; a nature trail in the woods nearby is posted with excerpts from his poems. Admission is $3 adults, $1.50 children 6 to 15.

WHERE TO STAY & DINE

The Franconia Inn, 1300 Easton Rd. (© **800/473-5299** or 603/823-5542; www.franconiainn.com), is in a bucolic valley 2 miles from the village of Franconia. The inn has an informal feel, with wingback chairs around the fireplace and jigsaw puzzles in the paneled library. Guest rooms are appointed in a relaxed country fashion; three feature gas fireplaces, while four have Jacuzzis. The inn is a haven for cross-country skiers—38 miles of groomed trails start right outside the front door. Rates include breakfast. There's a restaurant, a heated outdoor pool, tennis courts, free use of bikes, and bridle trails and horse rentals. There are no phones in the rooms.

9 The Maine Coast

Maine's southern coast runs from the state line at Kittery to about Portland. Thanks to quirks of geography, nearly all of Maine's sandy beaches are located in this 60-mile stretch of coastline. It's not wilderness here—most beaches have beach towns nearby, and these range from classic 19th-century villages to more honky-tonkish resorts. Swimming sessions tend to be brief and accompanied by shrieks, whoops, and agitated hand-waving. These beaches are more suited for early-morning walks than for swimming.

KITTERY & THE YORKS

Kittery is the first town you'll come to if you're driving to Maine from the south on I-95 or Route 1. Kittery was once famous for its naval yard, but regionally it's now better known for its dozens of factory outlets.

"The Yorks," to the north, are three towns that share a name but little else. In fact, it's rare to find three such well-defined and diverse New England archetypes in such a compact area. **York Village** is redolent with early American history and architecture. **York Harbor** reached its zenith during America's Victorian era, when wealthy urbanites built cottages at the ocean's edge. **York Beach** has an early-20th-century beach-town feel, with loud amusements, taffy shops, and summer homes in crowded enclaves near the beach.

The **Kittery Information Center** (© 207/439-1319) is located at a rest area on I-95. It's open daily from 8am to 6pm in summer, from 9am to 5:30pm the rest of the year. The **York Chamber of Commerce** (© 207/363-4422) operates an information center at 571 Rte. 1, near the turnpike. It's open in summer from 9am to 5pm (until 6pm Fri); limited hours the rest of the year.

FUN ON & OFF THE BEACH

Kittery's consumer mecca is 4 miles south of York on Route 1. Some 120 factory outlets flank the highway, including Calvin Klein, Coach, Crate & Barrel, Le Creuset, DKNY, Polo/Ralph Lauren, and Tommy Hilfiger.

In summer, navigating the area can be frustrating. (A free shuttle bus links the outlets and lessens some of the frustration.) The selection of outlets is more diverse than in Freeport an hour north, which is more clothing oriented. But Freeport's quaint village setting is more appealing. Information on current outlets is available from the **Kittery Outlet Association** (© 888/548-8379; www.thekitteryoutlets.com).

Learn about the area at the **Old York Historical Society,** 5 Lindsay Rd., York (© 207/363-4974). First settled in 1624, York Village has several early buildings open to the public. A good place to start is **Jefferds Tavern,** across from the handsome old burying ground. Changing exhibits here document various facets of early life. Next door is the **School House,** furnished as it might have been in the last century. A 10-minute walk along Lindsay Road will bring you to **Hancock Wharf,** which is next door to the **George Marshall Store.** Also nearby is the **Elizabeth Perkins House,** with its well-preserved Colonial Revival interiors. The one don't-miss structure is the intriguing **Old Gaol,** built in 1719 with musty dungeons for criminals. (The jail is the oldest surviving public building in the U.S.) Just down the knoll is the **Emerson-Wilcox House,** built in the mid-1700s. Added to periodically over the years, it's a virtual catalog of architectural styles and early decorative arts.

York Beach consists of two beaches—**Long Sands Beach** and **Short Sands Beach**—separated by a rocky headland and a small island capped by scenic **Nubble Light.** Both offer plenty of room when the tide is out. When the tide is in, they're both cramped. Short Sands fronts the town of York Beach, with its candlepin bowling and video arcades. It's the better bet for families with kids. Long Sands runs along Route 1A, across from a profusion of motels and convenience stores. Changing rooms, restrooms, and parking (50¢ per hr.) are available at both beaches.

WHERE TO STAY & DINE

York Beach has a proliferation of motels facing Long Sands Beach. Reserve ahead during prime season. Simple options on or near the beach include the **Anchorage Motor Inn** (© 207/363-5112); the **Long Beach Motor Inn** (© 207/363-5481); and the vintage but somewhat threadbare **Nevada Motel** (© 207/363-4504), which is still run by the same man who built it in 1953.

Southern Maine Coast

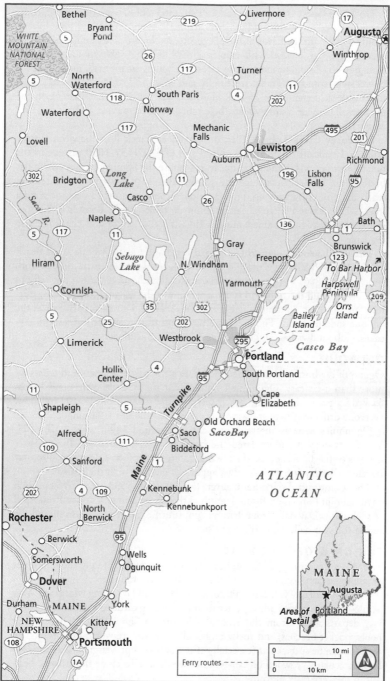

Ferry routes - - - -

0   10 mi
0   10 km

Dockside Guest Quarters in York (© 207/363-2868; www.docksidegq.com) was established by David and Harriet Lusty in 1954, and recent additions haven't changed the maritime flavor of the place. Situated on a 7-acre peninsula, the inn occupies grounds shaded with maples and white pines. Five rooms are in the main house (1885), but most of the accommodations are in small, modern, town house–style cottages. These are bright and airy, and all have private decks that overlook the entrance to York Harbor. There's a seafood restaurant on the premises. There are also rowboats, bike rental, laundry service, badminton, and croquet.

Chauncey Creek Lobster Pier, on Chauncey Creek Road between Kittery Point and York off Route 103, Kittery Point (© 207/439-1030), is one of the best lobster pounds in the state, not least because the Spinney family, which has been selling lobsters here since the 1950s, takes such pride in the place. You reach the pound by walking down a wooden ramp to a broad deck on a tidal inlet, where some 42 festively painted picnic tables await. Lobster is the specialty, of course, but steamed mussels (in wine and garlic) and clams are also available. It's BYOB.

The Goldenrod Restaurant, Railroad Road and Ocean Avenue, York Beach (© 207/363-2621; www.thegoldenrod.com), has been an institution in York Beach since 1896. Visitors gawk at the ancient machines churning out taffy in volumes. Behind the taffy and fudge operation is the restaurant, short on gourmet fare but long on atmosphere. Diners sit around a stone fireplace or at the antique soda fountain. The meals are basic and filling; expect waffles, griddlecakes, club sandwiches, and deviled egg and bacon sandwiches.

OGUNQUIT

Ogunquit is a bustling beachside town that's attracted vacationers and artists for more than a century. Ogunquit is famous for its 3½-mile white-sand beach, backed by grassy dunes. The beach serves as the town's front porch, and most everyone drifts over here at least once a day when the sun is shining.

Ogunquit's fame as an art colony dates to around 1890, when Charles H. Woodbury arrived and declared the place an "artist's paradise." In the latter decades of the 19th century, the town found quiet fame as a destination for gay travelers. Ogunquit has retained its appeal for gays through the years.

The **Ogunquit Welcome Center** (© 207/646-5533 or 207/646-2939; www.ogunquit.org) is on Route 1 south of the village center. It's open from April to Columbus Day daily from 9am to 5pm (until 8pm in peak season), and the rest of the year daily from 10am to 2pm.

FUN ON & OFF THE BEACH

The village center is good for an hour or two of browsing among the boutiques or sipping a cappuccino at one of the several coffee emporia.

From the village, you can walk to scenic Perkins Cove along **Marginal Way,** a mile-long oceanside pathway once used for herding cattle to pasture. The pathway departs across from the Seacastles Resort on Shore Road. It passes tide pools, pocket beaches, and rocky bluffs, all of which are worth exploring. The seascape can be spectacular (especially after a storm), but Marginal Way can also be spectacularly crowded on fair-weather weekends. To elude the crowds, head out in the very early morning.

Perkins Cove, accessible either from Marginal Way or by driving south on Shore Road and veering left at the Y intersection, is a small, well-protected harbor that seems custom-designed for a photo opportunity. As such, it attracts visitors by the busload and boatload, and is often heavily congested. A handful of touristy galleries, restaurants, and T-shirt shops occupy a cluster of quaint buildings between the harbor and the sea. An intriguing pedestrian drawbridge is operated by whoever happens to be handy, allowing sailboats to come and go.

Not far from the cove is the **Ogunquit Museum of American Art,** 183 Shore Rd. (© **207/646-4909**), one of the best small art museums in the nation. The engaging modern building is set in a glen overlooking the shore. The curators have a track record for staging superb shows and attracting national attention. It's open July to September, Monday through Saturday from 10:30am to 5pm and Sunday from 2 to 5pm. Admission is $4 for adults, $3 for seniors and students, and free for children under 12.

Ogunquit's **main beach** is 3½ miles long. The beach appeals to everyone— there's a more lively scene at the south end near the town itself, and it's more unpopulated as you head north, where it's backed with dunes and, beyond them, clusters of summer homes. The most popular access point is at the foot of Beach Street, which runs into Ogunquit Village. The beach ends at a sandy spit, where the Ogunquit River flows into the sea; here you'll find a handful of informal restaurants. It's also the most crowded part of the beach. Less congested options are **Footbridge Beach** (turn on Ocean Ave. off Rte. 1 north of the village center) and **Moody Beach** (turn on Eldridge Ave. in Wells). Restrooms and changing rooms are maintained at all access points.

WHERE TO STAY & DINE

Just a few steps from Ogunquit's main downtown intersection is the meticulously maintained **Studio East Motel,** 267 Main St. (© **207/646-7297**). It's open from April to mid-November, with rates running from $99 to $119 in high season.

The Beachmere Inn, 62 Beachmere Place (© **800/336-3983** or 207/646-2021; www.beachmereinn.com), sprawls across a grassy hillside, and nearly every room has a view of the beach, which is a 10-minute walk via footpath. The Beachmere Victorian dates to the 1890s and is all turrets and porches; next door is the mid-century-modern Beachmere South, a motel-like structure whose spacious rooms have balconies or patios. When the main buildings are full, guests are offered one of five rooms in the Bullfrog Cottage, a short drive away. Rates include continental breakfast.

For breakfast (served until 1pm), it's hard to beat **Amore,** 178 Shore Rd. (© **207/646-6661**). This isn't the place for waist-watchers, but . . . you're on vacation!

Arrows, Berwick Road (© **207/361-1100;** www.arrowsrestaurant.com), put Ogunquit on the national culinary map by serving up some of the most innovative cooking in New England. The emphasis is on local products, and the menu depends on what's in season or available from the fishing boats, but it tends to be informed by an Asian way of thinking. Recent entrees have included duck confit with caramelized ginger and lemon-grass sauce. Arrive a half hour or so before your reservation to stroll the gardens with a glass of wine.

THE KENNEBUNKS

"The Kennebunks" are the villages of **Kennebunk** and **Kennebunkport,** situated along the shores of small rivers, both claiming a portion of rocky coast. The region was settled in the mid-1600s and flourished after the American Revolution, when ship captains, boat builders, and merchants constructed imposing, solid homes.

The **Kennebunk–Kennebunkport Chamber of Commerce** (© 800/982-4421 or 207/967-0857; www.kkcc.maine.org) can answer questions by phone or at its office on Route 9. The **Kennebunkport Information Center** (© 207/967-8600), operated by an association of local businesses, is off Dock Square (next to Ben & Jerry's) and is open daily in summer and fall.

FUN ON & OFF THE BEACH

Kennebunkport is the summer home of Pres. George Bush the Elder, whose family has summered here for decades. As such, it's possessed of the tweedy, upper-crust feel that you might expect. The tiny downtown, whose streets were laid out during days of travel by boat and horse, is subject to traffic jams. If the municipal lot off the square is full, head north on North Street to the free long-term lot and catch the trolley back into town. Or go about on foot—it's a pleasant walk of about 10 to 15 minutes from the satellite lot to Dock Square.

Dock Square has an architecturally eclectic wharflike feel to it, with low buildings of mixed vintages and styles, but the flavor is mostly clapboard and shingles. Kennebunkport's deeper appeal is found in the surrounding blocks, where the side streets are lined with Federal-style homes.

The **Richard A. Nott House,** 8 Maine St. (© 207/967-2751), is an imposing Greek Revival structure built in 1853. It was donated to the local historical society with the stipulation that it remain unchanged. It still has the original wallpaper, carpeting, and furnishings. The house is open from mid-June to mid-October on Tuesday and Friday from 1 to 4pm, Saturday from 10am to 1pm. Admission is $5 for adults, $2 for children under 18.

A bit further afield, in the neighborhood around the Colony Hotel (about 1 mile east of Dock Sq. on Ocean Ave.), is a collection of homes of the uniquely American shingle style. Ocean Drive from Dock Square to **Walkers Point** and beyond is lined with summer homes overlooking surf and rocky shore. You'll likely recognize the former president's home at Walkers Point when you arrive (look for the shingle-style Secret Service booth). There's nothing to do here but park for a minute, take a picture of the house, then push on.

The Seashore Trolley Museum, 95 Log Cabin Rd. (© 207/967-2800; www.trolleymuseum.org), is a local marvel: a scrapyard-masquerading-as-a-museum. Founded in 1939 to preserve a disappearing way of life, today it contains one of the largest collections in the world—more than 200 trolleys, including specimens from Glasgow, Moscow, San Francisco, and Rome. (Naturally, there's a streetcar named "Desire.") About 40 cars still operate, and admission includes rides on a 2-mile track. Admission is $7.25 adults, $5.25 seniors, $4.75 children 6 to 16; $24 per family.

The area around Kennebunkport is home to several of the state's best **beaches.** Across the river are **Gooch's Beach** and **Kennebunk Beach. Goose Rocks Beach** is north of Kennebunkport off Route 9 (watch for signs), and is a good destination for those who like their crowds light. Offshore is a narrow barrier reef that has historically attracted flocks of geese. No restrooms are available here.

WHERE TO STAY & DINE

Housed in a Federal-style home that peers down a shady lawn toward the river, **Captain Lord,** Pleasant and Green streets (© 207/967-3141; www.captain lord.com), is one of the most architecturally distinguished inns in New England. You'll know this is the genuine article once you spot the grandfather clocks and Chippendale highboys in the front hall. Guest rooms are furnished with antiques; all feature gas fireplaces. There's not a single unappealing room.

Among our favorites: Excelsior, a corner unit with a massive four-poster and a two-person Jacuzzi; and Hesper, the best of the lower-priced rooms. Rooms feature dataports and minibars. Children 12 and over are welcome.

The Colony Hotel, 140 Ocean Ave. (© **800/552-2363** or 207/967-3331; www.thecolonyhotel.com/maine), is one of the handful of resorts that have preserved intact the classic New England vacation experience, complete with social director. This mammoth Georgian Revival (1914) lords over the ocean and the mouth of the Kennebunk River. All rooms in the main inn have been renovated but there is no air-conditioning or TV in most. Rooms in two of the three outbuildings carry over the rustic elegance of the main hotel; the exception is the East House, a 1950s-era hotel at the edge of the property with 20 motel-style rooms. A staff naturalist leads coastal ecology tours on Saturdays in July and August; on Fridays, there's a lobster buffet dinner. There's a restaurant, a lounge, a heated saltwater pool, a putting green, tennis courts, bike rental, and a shuffleboard court.

The Franciscan Guest House, Beach Street (© **207/967-2011**), on the grounds of St. Anthony's Monastery, is a unique budget choice. Rooms are all rather institutional (though they have TVs). On the other hand, all have private (if small) bathrooms, and guests can stroll the lovely riverside grounds or walk over to Dock Square, about 10 minutes away. A Lithuanian breakfast (cheese, oatmeal, salami, fruit, juice, and homemade bread) is served downstairs. Although this is one of the most spartan lodgings we've seen, the fact that reservations are often needed a year in advance tells the story.

Prices for lobster in the rough tend to be a bit more expensive around Kennebunkport than further up the coast. But if you can't wait, **Nunan's Lobster Hut,** on Route 9 north of Kennebunkport at Cape Porpoise (© **207/967-4362**), is a good choice.

Grissini, 27 Western Ave. (© **207/967-2211;** www.restaurantgrissini.com), is a handsome trattoria that offers good value. The mood is elegant but rustic. Italian advertising posters line the walls of the soaring, barnlike space, while the stone fireplace takes the chill off a cool evening. The menu includes a wide range of pastas and pizza, served with considerable flair. Expect an exceedingly pleasant experience.

The White Barn Inn, Beach Avenue (© **207/967-232**), attracts gourmands from New York and Boston. It's pricey, but worth it. It is housed in a rustic barn with a soaring interior and a collection of country antiques displayed in a hayloft. The setting is magical, the service is attentive, and the kitchen rarely produces a flawed dish. You might start with a lobster spring roll, then graduate to roasted pheasant breast with butternut squash. Anticipate a meal to remember.

ACADIA NATIONAL PARK

It's not hard to fathom why Acadia is one of the biggest draws in the U.S. national park system. The park, located on Mount Desert Island, offers a rich tapestry of rugged cliffs, restless ocean, and quiet woods.

The park's more recent roots can be traced back to the 1840s, when Hudson River School painter Thomas Cole packed his sketchbooks and easels for a trip to this remote island, then home to a small number of fishermen and boat builders.

By the early 1900s, the popularity and growing development of the island began to concern its most ardent supporters. Boston textile heir and conservationist George Dorr and Harvard president Charles Eliot, aided by the largesse of John D. Rockefeller, Jr., started acquiring large tracts for the public's enjoyment. These parcels were donated to the government, and in 1919 the land was designated Lafayette National Park. Renamed Acadia in 1929, the park has grown to encompass nearly half the island.

ESSENTIALS

GETTING THERE Acadia National Park is reached from the town of Ellsworth via Route 3. If you're driving from southern Maine, avoid the coastal congestion along Route 1 by taking the Maine Turnpike to Bangor, picking up I-395 to Route 1A, then continuing south on Route 1A to Ellsworth. It's the quickest route in summer.

Daily flights from Boston to the airport in Trenton, just across the causeway from Mount Desert Island, are offered year-round by US Airways affiliate **Colgan Air** (© **800/523-3273** or 207/667-7171). In summer, **Concord Trailways** (© **888/741-8686** or 207/942-8686) offers van service between Bangor (including an airport stop), Ellsworth, and Bar Harbor; reservations are required.

VISITOR INFORMATION The **Thompson Island Information Center,** on Route 3 (© **207/288-3411**), is maintained by the local chambers of commerce; park personnel are usually on hand to answer inquiries. It's the best stop for lodging and restaurant information. The center is open from mid-May to mid-October. For more detailed information, continue on Route 3 to the National Park Service's **Hulls Cove Visitor Center,** about 7½ miles beyond Thompson Island. This stone-walled center includes displays and a short film. You can request brochures on trails and carriage roads, or purchase guidebooks. The center is open from mid-April to October.

ENTRY POINTS & FEES A 1-week park pass, which includes unlimited trips on Park Loop Road, costs $10 per car; no additional charge per passenger. (No daily pass is available.) The main point of entry to Park Loop Road is the visitor center at **Hulls Cove.** Mount Desert Island consists of an interwoven network of park and town roads, allowing visitors to enter the park at numerous points. A glance at a park map (available free at the visitor center) will make these access points self-evident. The entry fee is collected at a toll booth on Park Loop Road a half mile north of Sand Beach.

OUTDOOR PURSUITS

CAMPING The national park offers no overnight accommodations other than two campgrounds. Both are extremely popular; in July and August, expect them to fill by early to mid-morning.

Blackwoods (© **207/288-3274**) tends to fill first. It has a better location—bikers and pedestrians are just off the Park Loop Road and the rocky shore via a short trail—and, more important, it's the only one of the two that accepts reservations (required from mid-May to mid-Sept). Blackwoods is open year-round; late fall through spring, sites are easy to come by. You can reserve up to 5 months in advance by calling © **800/365-2267.** (This is a national reservations service whose contract is reviewed from time to time by the park service; if the number doesn't work, call the campground directly to ask for the current toll-free reservation number.) Reservations may also be made online, between 10am and 10pm only, at **http://reservations.nps.gov.** Fees are $18 per night.

First-come, first-served **Seawall** (© **207/244-3600**) is on the quieter western half of the island, near the fishing village of Bass Harbor. This is a good base for road biking, and several short coastal hikes are within easy striking distance. Drive-in RV sites are available, but none have hookups. The campground is open from late May to September. In general, if you get here by 9 or 10am,

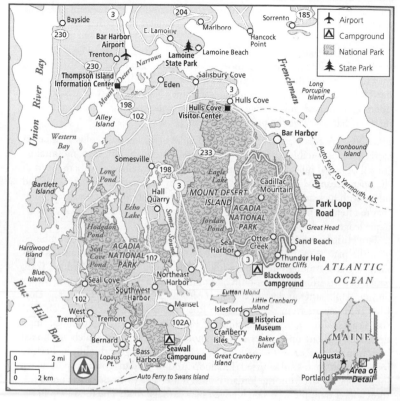

Mount Desert Island & Acadia National Park

you'll have little trouble securing a site, even in midsummer. No showers are on-site, but they're available nearby. Fees are $12 to $18 per night.

Private campgrounds handle the overflow. The region south of Ellsworth has 14 private campgrounds; the **Thompson Island Information Center** (℃ 207/ 288-3411) posts up-to-the-minute information on vacancies.

CANOEING Mount Desert's several ponds offer scenic if limited canoeing, and most have public boat access. Canoe rentals are available at the north end of Long Pond (the largest pond on the island at 3 miles long) in Somesville from **National Park Canoe Rentals** (℃ 207/244-5854).

CARRIAGE RIDES Carriage rides are offered by **Wildwood Stables** (℃ 207/ 276-3622; www.acadia.net/wildwood), a park concessionaire located a half mile south of Jordan Pond House. The 1-hour trip departs three times daily and takes in sweeping ocean views; it costs $14 for adults, $7 for children 6 to 12, and $4 for children 2 to 5. Longer tours are available, as is a special carriage designed to accommodate disabled passengers.

DRIVING THE PARK LOOP ROAD The 20-mile Park Loop Road is the park's premier attraction. This remarkable roadway starts near the Hulls Cove Visitor Center and follows the high ridges above Bar Harbor before dropping down along the rocky coast. Here, the spires of spruce and fir cap dark granite, and the earthy tones contrast sharply with the frothy white surf and the steely blue sea. After following the picturesque coast and touching on several coves, the road loops back inland along Jordan Pond and Eagle Lake, with a detour to the summit of the island's highest peak.

From about 10am to 4pm in July and August, anticipate large crowds along the Park Loop Road, at least on those days when the sun is shining. Parking lots may fill at some of the more popular destinations, including Sand Beach, Thunder Hole, and the Cadillac Mountain summit. Make the best of wet days by donning rain gear and letting the weather work to your advantage. You'll discover that you have the place to yourself.

HIKING   Acadia National Park has 120 miles of hiking trails, plus 57 miles of carriage roads suitable for walking. The park is studded with low "mountains" (they'd be called hills elsewhere), and almost all have trails with superb views of the open ocean. Many pathways were crafted by experienced stonemasons and others with high aesthetic intent, and thus the routes aren't the most direct—but they're often the most scenic, taking advantage of fractures in the rocks, picturesque ledges, and sudden vistas.

The **Hulls Cove Visitor Center** offers a brief chart of area hikes; combined with the park map, this is all you'll need to explore the well-maintained, well-marked trails. Among our favorite hikes is the **Dorr Mountain Ladder Trail,** which departs from near the south end of the Tarn, a pond near Sieur de Monts Spring. (Park either at the spring or just off Rte. 3 south at the Tarn.) The **Beehive Trail** departs from the Park Loop Road just across from Sand Beach. The trail begins with a fairly gentle climb of ¼ mile, then turns right and begins a demanding ascent up a series of vertiginous ledges, some of which are linked with iron ladders set in the rock. (The layers of ledges give the hill its beehive look—and its name, of course.) The loop around **Jordan Pond** is more like a long stroll. Depart from the Jordan Pond House. The east side of the pond features a level trail; the west side is edged by a carriage road. The total loop measures just over 3 miles. At the north end of the pond is a pair of oddly symmetrical mounds called **The Bubbles.** Detours to atop these peaks add about 20 minutes each to the loop; look for signs for these spur pathways off the Jordan Pond Shore Trail. Finish up your hike with tea and popovers at the Jordan Pond House (see "Dining," below).

On the island's west side, an ascent and descent of **Acadia Mountain** takes about 1½ hours, but hikers should allow plenty of time to enjoy the view of Somes Sound and the smaller islands off Mount Desert's southern shores.

MOUNTAIN BIKING   The 57 miles of **carriage roads** built by John D. Rockefeller, Jr., are among the park's most extraordinary treasures. These were maintained by Rockefeller until his death in 1960, after which they became shaggy and overgrown. A major restoration effort was launched in 1990, and the roads today are superbly restored and maintained. A map of the carriage roads is available free at the visitor centers; more detailed guides may be purchased at area bookshops, but they aren't necessary. Where the carriage roads cross private land (generally between Seal and Northeast harbors), they are closed to mountain bikes. Mountain bikes are also banned from hiking trails.

To get a taste of mountain biking without having to load rented bikes onto your car, ask the clerk at any of the Bar Harbor bike-rental shops about the route to **Witch Hole Pond** via West Street. The route is very steep (don't get discouraged!) but relatively traffic-free and relaxing; take your time, and look forward to coasting back into town once you're done.

Mountain bikes may be rented along Cottage Street in Bar Harbor, with rates around $15 to $17 for a day. Ask about closing times, because you may be able to get in a couple extra hours of pedaling with a later-closing shop. **Bar Harbor Bicycle Shop,** 141 Cottage St. (© **207/288-3886**), is the most convenient and friendliest; you might also try **Acadia Outfitters,** 106 Cottage St. (© **207/288-8118**), or **Acadia Bike & Coastal Kayak,** 48 Cottage St. (© **207/288-9605**).

SEA KAYAKING   Sea kayaking has boomed around Mount Desert Island over the past decade. Experienced kayakers arrive in droves with their own boats. Novices sign up for guided tours, which are offered by several outfitters. A variety of options can be found on the island, ranging from a 2½-hour harbor tour to a 7-hour excursion. Details are available from the following outfitters: **Acadia Outfitters,** 106 Cottage St. (© **207/288-8118**); **Coastal Kayaking Tours,** 48 Cottage St. (© **800/526-8615** or 207/288-9605); **Island Adventure Kayak Tours & Rentals,** 137 Cottage St. (© **207/288-3886**); and **National Park Sea Kayak Tours,** 39 Cottage St. (© **800/347-0940** or 207/288-0342). Sea-kayak rentals and delivery are available from **Loon Bay Kayaks,** located in summer at Barcadia Campground, at the junction of Routes 3 and 102 (© **888/786-0676** or 207/288-0099); and from **National Park Canoe Rental,** 1 West St., Bar Harbor (© **207/288-0007**).

DINING

Jordan Pond House on Park Loop Road near Seal Harbor (© **207/276-3316**) is the only full-service restaurant within park boundaries, on a grassy lawn looking northward up Jordan Pond. Afternoon tea with popovers is a hallowed tradition. Ladies who lunch sit next to bikers, and everyone feasts on tasty popovers and strawberry jam served with tea or lemonade. The lobster and crab rolls are abundant and filling; the lobster stew is expensive but good. Dinners include classic resort fare like prime rib, and baked scallops.

WHERE TO STAY IN BAR HARBOR

Bar Harbor provides most meals and beds to travelers coming to the island, as it has since the grand resort era of the late 19th century. After a period of quiet decay, Bar Harbor has been revived and rediscovered by both visitors and entrepreneurs. Its history, distinguished architecture, and beautiful location along Frenchman Bay make it a desirable base for exploring the rest of the island, and it offers the most varied selection of lodging, meals, supplies, and services.

The Bar Harbor Inn, Newport Drive (© **800/248-3351** or 207/288-3351; www.barharborinn.com), is a handsome combination of inn and motel, and has the best location of any lodging in Bar Harbor. On shady waterfront grounds just off downtown Agamont Park and at the start of the Shore Path, it offers convenience and charm. The rambling, shingled inn dates back to the turn of the 19th century. Guest rooms in the Oceanfront and Main Inn feature sweeping views of the bay, and many have private balconies; the less expensive Newport building lacks views but is comfortable and up-to-date. There's a formal dining room and outdoor grill, heated outdoor pool, and fitness room.

The Black Friar Inn, 10 Summer St. (© **207/288-5091;** www.blackfriar. com), is a shingled structure with quirky pediments and an eccentric air. A former owner "collected" interiors and installed them throughout the house. Among them are a replica of the namesake Black Friar Pub in London, complete with carved-wood paneling (it serves as a common room); and stamped tin walls in the breakfast room. Guest rooms, most of which are quite small, are furnished with a mix of antiques. Children 12 and over are welcome.

Reputable motels in or near town that offer at least some rooms under $100 include the conveniently located **Villager Motel,** 207 Main St. (© **207/288-3211**); the in-town, pet-friendly **Rockhurst Motel,** 68 Mount Desert St. (© **207/288-3140**); and the smoke-free **Highbrook Motel,** 94 Eden St. (© **800/338-9688** or 207/288-3591). About 4 miles west of Bar Harbor on Route 3 is **Hanscom's Motel and Cottages** (© **207/288-3744;** www.hanscomsmotel.com), an old-fashioned motor court with 12 well-maintained units (some two-bedroom).

WHERE TO DINE IN BAR HARBOR

For a tasty ice-cream cone, head to **Ben & Bill's Chocolate Emporium,** 66 Main St. (© **207/288-3281**). Visitors are often tempted to try the house novelty, lobster ice cream. Visitors often regret giving into that temptation.

Café This Way, 14½ Mount Desert St. (© **207/288-4483**), has the feel of a hip coffeehouse; bookshelves line one wall, and there's a bar tucked into a nook. The breakfasts are excellent and mildly sinful, with offerings like eggs Benedict with spinach, artichoke, and tomato. The robust coffee requires two creamers to lighten it. Dinners are equally appetizing, with tasty dishes like butternut-squash ravioli and filet mignon grilled with fresh basil.

Bar Harbor's only vegetarian restaurant, **Elaine's Starlight Oasis,** 78 West St. (© **207/288-3287;** www.starlightoasis.com), opened in 1998 and has been embraced by herbivorous visitors. Near the waterfront in a cozy, contemporary space, the menu includes the house specialty of "beef" burgundy (made with seitan). Other offerings include mushroom lasagna and tempeh Parmesan.

For more than 2 decades, **George's,** 7 Stephens Lane (© **207/288-4505;** www.georgesbarharbor.com), has been a Bar Harbor classic, offering fine dining in elegant yet informal surroundings. George's captures the joyous feel of summer. The service is upbeat, the meals wonderfully prepared. All entrees sell for one price, which includes salad, vegetable, and potato or rice. You won't go wrong with basic choices, but you're better off opting for more adventurous fare, like lobster strudel. The house specialty is lamb in its many incarnations.

Washington, D.C.

The nation's capital fully commands center stage. The terrorists who crashed a plane into the Pentagon on September 11, 2001, did nothing to diminish Washington's place in the world—quite the contrary. Their acts served only to rally the city itself, strengthen our federal government, and renew our country's commitment to democratic ideals, for all the world to see. Although security is tighter and additional safeguards have been put into place, Washington continues to offer its own special brand of excitement. You can still listen to Senate debates and hear the Supreme Court in session. Find inspiration in magnificent monuments to the greatest American presidents, and check out the palatial digs of the current chief executive. Wander the vast museums of the Smithsonian Institution. Learn how the FBI fights crime. In short, you can see firsthand just how the government of the United States works, as well as visit some of the most important museums in the country.

1 Essentials

GETTING THERE

BY PLANE Washington is served by three major airports. **Ronald Reagan Washington National Airport** (© 703/572-2700; www.metwashairports.com) is just across the Potomac River in Virginia and a 15-minute drive from downtown. This domestic-only facility is where you can catch the Delta and US Airways shuttle to and from New York's LaGuardia Airport. Covered walkways connect National Airport's modern new terminal to its own Metro station; the trip downtown takes about 20 minutes.

Washington Dulles International Airport (© 703/572-2700; www. metwashairports.com) is also in Virginia, about 45 minutes west of downtown. The Washington Flyer Express Bus runs between Dulles and the West Falls Church Metro station, where you can board a train for D.C. Buses run every 30 minutes. More convenient is the hourly Metrobus service that runs between Dulles and the L'Enfant Plaza Metro station, located near Capitol Hill and within walking distance of the National Mall.

Baltimore–Washington International (BWI) Airport (© 800/435-9294; www.bwiairport.com) is northeast of the city near Baltimore, about 45 minutes from downtown. BWI flights offer the most bargain fares, on discount airlines such as **Southwest** (© 800/435-9792). Both **Amtrak** (© 800/872-7245) and **Maryland Rural Commuter (MARC)** (© 800/325-7245) trains link BWI to Washington's Union Station.

SuperShuttle (© 800/258-3826; www.supershuttle.com) offers shared-ride, door-to-door van service between National, Dulles, and BWI airports and your destination downtown or in the Maryland or Virginia suburbs. Expect to pay anywhere from $9 to $26, depending on distance.

Washington, D.C.

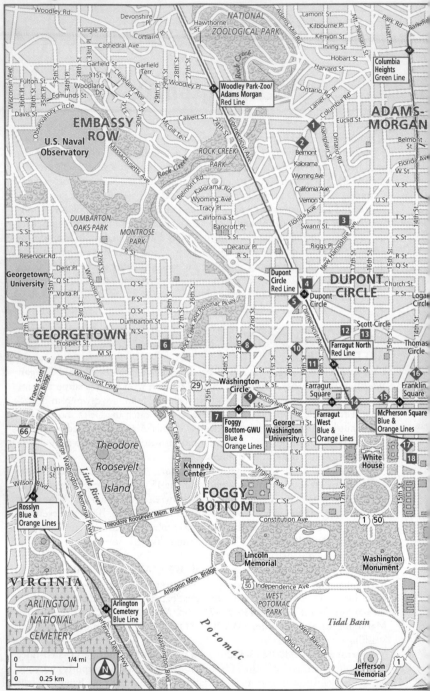

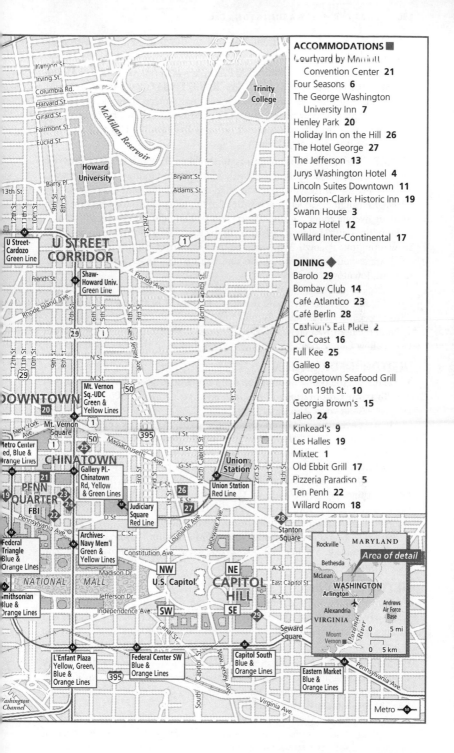

Taxi fares are $8 to $15 from National to downtown, $35 to $47 from Dulles, and $55 from BWI.

BY TRAIN   Amtrak (© 800/USA-RAIL; www.amtrak.com) serves **Union Station,** 50 Massachusetts Ave. NE (© 202/371-9441; www.unionstationdc. com), a turn-of-the-20th-century beaux arts masterpiece conveniently located near the Capitol; it now houses shops and restaurants. There's frequent service from New York (trip time: 2¾ to 3½ hr.) and Philadelphia (1¾ to 2 hr.), and daily service from Chicago (19 hr.).

BY CAR   From New York and points north, take I-95 south to I-495, the Capital Beltway, which loops around the city. Stay right and follow 495-West toward Silver Spring, until you see the sign for Connecticut Avenue/Chevy Chase–Kensington. Go left at the bottom of the ramp and travel south on Connecticut Avenue about 7 miles, which takes you straight into town.

From the south, follow I-95 North and pick up I-395 North as you get closer to Washington. Follow I-395 North to the 14th Street Bridge. Stay in the two left lanes as you cross the bridge, so that you can exit onto 14th Street, in the heart of downtown.

Coming from the west, pick up I-66 east, which will take you right into Rosslyn, VA, and over the Theodore Roosevelt Memorial Bridge, depositing you at 23rd Street and Constitution Avenue NW.

From the northwest on I-270, take I-495 east to the Connecticut Avenue south Exit. Follow Connecticut Avenue south about 7 miles to the center of town.

VISITOR INFORMATION

You can request advance information from the **Washington, D.C. Convention and Tourism Corporation,** 1212 New York Ave. NW (© 800/422-8644 or 202/789-7000; www.washington.org).

More convenient and accessible is the **D.C. Visitor Center** (© 202/ 328-4748; www.dcvisit.com), inside the Ronald Reagan Building and International Trade Center, at 1300 Pennsylvania Ave. NW. It's open Monday through Friday from 8am to 6pm and Saturday from 11am to 5pm.

Just down the street is the **White House Visitor Center,** in the Herbert Hoover Building, Department of Commerce, 1450 Pennsylvania Ave. NW, between 14th and 15th streets (© 202/208-1631, or 202/456-7041 for recorded information), open daily from 7:30am to 4pm.

You can also stop in at the **Smithsonian Information Center,** on the Mall at 1000 Jefferson Dr. SW (© 202/357-2700; www.si.edu), open daily from 9am to 5:30pm.

GETTING AROUND

If you're thinking about driving, bear in mind that traffic is thick during the week, parking spaces are sparse, and parking lots will cost you. Street signs and parking information are often confusing and illegible. Metrorail is definitely the easiest way to go.

BY METRO   Metrorail's 83 stations include locations at or near almost every sightseeing attraction and extend to suburban Maryland and northern Virginia. When entering a Metro station for the first time, go to the kiosk and ask for a free **"Metro System Pocket Guide."**

To enter or exit a Metro station, you need a computerized **farecard,** available at vending machines near the entrance. Charts posted near the farecard machines explain the fares, which start at $1.10. If you plan to take several

Metrorail trips during your stay, put more value on the farecard to avoid having to buy a new card each time you ride.

Metrorail opens at 5:30am Monday through Friday and 8am Saturday and Sunday, operating until midnight Sunday through Thursday and until 2am Friday and Saturday. Call ℭ **202/637-7000**, or visit **www.wmata.com**, for information.

BY TAXI   Taxis are plentiful, and you can hail them right off the street. Fares are based on a zone system rather than meters. The base fare in Zone 1 (extending from the U.S. Capitol through most of downtown) starts at $5 for one person, but there's a $1.50 charge for each additional passenger, plus surcharges for trips at rush hour, for large pieces of luggage, and for arranging a pickup by phone.

FAST FACTS

Emergency-room treatment is available at **Children's Hospital National Medical Center**, 111 Michigan Ave. NW (ℭ **202/884-5000**); and at **Georgetown University Medical Center**, 3800 Reservoir Rd. NW (ℭ **202/784-2000**). The **CVS** drugstore chain has two convenient locations—14th Street and Thomas Circle NW, at Vermont Avenue (ℭ **202/628-0720**), and Dupont Circle (ℭ **202/ 785-1466**)—both with round-the-clock pharmacies.

The sales tax on merchandise is 5.75% in the District, 5% in Maryland, and 4.5% in Virginia. The tax on restaurant meals is 10% in the District, 5% in Maryland, and 4.5% in Virginia. In the District, you pay 14.5% hotel tax. The hotel tax in Maryland averages 12%; in Virginia, about 9.75%.

SPECIAL EVENTS & FESTIVALS

For more information, go to **www.washington.org** or call ℭ **202/789-7000**.

In early April, the 3,700 Japanese cherry trees by the Tidal Basin in Potomac Park burst into spectacular bloom. The **Cherry Blossom Festival** features a major parade with floats, concerts, celebrity guests, and more. For specifics, call ℭ **202/547-1500**. Check out www.nps.gov/nacc/cherry to get the status of the buds.

The **White House Easter Egg Roll** takes place on Easter Monday. Entertainment on the White House South Lawn and the Ellipse might include clog dancers, clowns, puppet and magic shows, military drill teams, an egg-rolling contest, and a hunt for 1,000 or so wooden eggs, many of them signed by celebrities, astronauts, or the president. *Note:* Attendance is limited to children 3 to 6, who must be accompanied by an adult. Hourly timed tickets are issued at the National Park Service Ellipse Visitor Pavilion, just behind the White House at 15th and E streets NW, beginning at 7am. Call ℭ **202/208-1631** for details.

At 11am on **Memorial Day,** a wreath-laying ceremony takes place at the Tomb of the Unknowns in Arlington National Cemetery, followed by military band music, a service, and an address by a high-ranking government official (sometimes the president); call ℭ **202/685-2851** for details. There's also a ceremony at 1pm at the Vietnam Veterans Memorial, including a wreath-laying, speakers, and the playing of taps (ℭ **202/619-7222** for details), and activities at the U.S. Navy Memorial (ℭ **202/737-2300**). On the Sunday before Memorial Day, the National Symphony Orchestra performs a free concert at 8pm on the West Lawn of the Capitol; call ℭ **202/619-7222** for details.

Fourth of July festivities include a massive parade down Constitution Avenue. A morning program in front of the National Archives includes military demonstrations, period music, and a reading of the Declaration of Independence. In the evening, the National Symphony Orchestra plays on the west steps of the Capitol. Big-name entertainment precedes the fabulous fireworks display behind the Washington Monument. Check the *Washington Post* or call ☎ **202/ 789-7000** for details.

From late June to July 4th, crowds also flock to the National Mall for the **Smithsonian Festival of American Folklife** (☎ **202/357-2700;** www.si.edu) to enjoy traditional American music, crafts, food, games, concerts, and exhibits.

In October, Columbus Day weekend brings the **Taste of D.C. Festival.** Head to Pennsylvania Avenue between Ninth and 14th streets NW to sample food from dozens of D.C. restaurants. There's also live entertainment, dancing, storytellers, and games. Admission is free; but you need to buy tickets for tastings. Call ☎ **202/789-7000** for details.

The White House celebrates Christmas throughout December. On a select Wednesday or Thursday in the beginning of the month, the president or another family member lights the Christmas tree, inaugurating the 3-week **Pageant of Peace.** Festivities take place at the northern end of the Ellipse; call ☎ **202/ 208-1631** for details. On three evenings between Christmas and New Year's from 5 to 7pm, visitors can see the president's Christmas holiday decorations on the **White House Candlelight Tours.** Lines are long; arrive early. Call ☎ **202/ 208-1631** for details.

2 What to See & Do

Note: Many attractions are closed on federal holidays.

THE TOP SIGHTS

Arlington National Cemetery   Since the Civil War, these 612 wooded acres on a ridge overlooking the Potomac River and Washington have been a cherished shrine to members of the U.S. armed forces. Your first stop should be the **Women in Military Service for America Memorial** (☎ **800/222-2294** or 703/533-1155; www.womensmemorial.org), which was added to Arlington Cemetery to honor the more than 1.8 million women who have served in the armed forces from the American Revolution to the present. The impressive new memorial lies just beyond the gated entrance to the cemetery, a 3-minute walk from the visitor center. High atop a hill at the center of the cemetery is **Arlington House** (☎ **703/ 557-0613**), once the home of Robert E. Lee, who left here in 1861 to take command of the Confederate army (to spite him, the Union army buried its dead in his front yard). You can tour the house on your own. Below Arlington House is the **Gravesite of John Fitzgerald Kennedy.** Jacqueline Kennedy Onassis is buried next to her first husband, and Robert Kennedy is buried close by. America's most distinguished honor guard watches over the **Tomb of the Unknowns,** which contains the unidentified remains of service members from both world wars and the Korean War, and honors all Americans who gave their lives in war. Plan to see the changing of the guard, which takes place every half hour April to September, every hour on the hour October to March, and every hour at night. Across the Memorial Bridge from the base of the Lincoln Memorial. ☎ 703/607-8052. www.arlingtoncemetery.org or www.mdw.army.mil/cemetery.htm. Free admission. Apr–Sept daily 8am–7pm; Oct–Mar daily 8am–5pm. Metro: Arlington National Cemetery.

Bureau of Engraving & Printing   As many as 5,000 people line up each day to get a peek at some of the nearly $700 million of moolah being printed daily, around the clock. Get a VIP ticket from your senator or congressperson, or arrive early, especially in summer. Tickets for public tours are distributed at the ticket booth on Raoul Wallenberg Place from 8am to 2pm year-round, and in summer from 3:30 to 7pm as well. Allow time to explore the visitor center, where you can buy unique gifts ranging from bags of shredded money to copies of documents such as the Gettysburg Address. 14th and C sts. SW. (**©** **800/874-3188** or 202/874-2330. www.bep.treas.gov. Free admission. Mon–Fri 9am–2pm (last tour at 1:40pm); in summer, extended hours 5–6:40pm. Metro: Smithsonian (Independence Ave. exit).

The Capitol   The U.S. Congress has met here since 1800. The hub of the building is the **Rotunda,** under the soaring 180-foot-high Capitol dome. The adjoining **National Statuary Hall** was originally the House chamber. The Senate used to meet in the **Old Supreme Court Chamber,** now beautifully restored. You can obtain free tickets to the **House and Senate galleries** by contacting the office of your senator or representative. (Visitors who are not citizens can obtain a gallery pass by presenting a passport at the Senate or House appointments desk.) Check the weekday "Today in Congress" column in the *Washington Post* for details on times of the House and Senate sessions and committee hearings.

Important note: Since a new underground Capitol Visitor Center (to be completed in 2005) is being constructed directly beneath the plaza where people traditionally line up for tours on the east side of the Capitol, touring procedures have changed. Call ahead (**©** **202/225-6827**) to find out the new procedures and whether any parts of the building will be temporarily closed. At press time, self-guided tours and "VIP" tours (tours reserved in advance by individuals through their congressional offices) have been suspended, for the foreseeable future. The only way now to tour the Capitol Building is in groups of 40. Organized groups of no more than 40 can arrange tours in advance by contacting their congressional office. If you're on your own, get to the Capitol early, by 7:30am, to stand in line for one of only 540 timed tickets distributed daily, starting at 8:15am. At the east end of the Mall, entrance on E. Capitol St. and First St. NW. **©** **202/225-6827.** www.aoc.gov, www.house.gov, www.senate.gov. Free admission. Year-round Mon–Sat 9am–4:30pm, with 1st tour starting at 9:30am and last tour starting at 3:30pm. Metro: Union Station or Capitol South.

Corcoran Gallery of Art   The Corcoran occupies a beaux arts building just west of the White House. The collection spans American art from 18th-century portraiture to works by 20th-century moderns like Nevelson, Warhol, and Rothko. There's also an eclectic grouping of works by Dutch and Flemish masters and French Impressionists, plus Delft porcelains and a Louis XVI salon doré transported complete from Paris. 500 17th St. NW (between E St. and New York Ave.). **©** **202/639-1700.** www.corcoran.org. Admission $5 adults, $3 seniors, $1 students 13–18, $8 families, free for children under 12; free all day Mon, plus Thurs after 5pm. Wed–Mon 10am–5pm, plus Thurs until 9pm. Free walk-in tours daily (except Tues) at noon, as well as at 7:30pm Thurs and at 2:30pm Sat–Sun. Metro: Farragut West or Farragut North.

Federal Bureau of Investigation   Learn why crime doesn't pay by touring FBI headquarters. You'll see weapons used by big-time gangsters like Al Capone, John Dillinger, Bonnie and Clyde, and "Pretty Boy" Floyd; an exhibit on counter-intelligence operations; and photos of the 10 most wanted fugitives. The tour ends with a bang, when an agent gives a sharpshooting demonstration and discusses the FBI's firearm policy and gun safety. To beat the crowds, arrive for the tour before 8:45am or write to a senator or congressperson for a VIP tour. J. Edgar Hoover FBI Building, E St. NW (between Ninth and 10th sts.). **©** **202/324-3447.** www.fbi.gov. Free admission. Mon–Fri 8:45am–4:15pm. Metro: Metro Center or Federal Triangle.

Franklin Delano Roosevelt Memorial   The FDR Memorial has become the most popular of the presidential memorials since it opened in 1997. Set amid waterfalls and quiet pools, "outdoor rooms" are devoted to each of Roosevelt's four terms in office (1933–45). Ten bronze sculptures honor Franklin and wife Eleanor and memorialize the struggles of the Great Depression and America's rise to world leadership. In West Potomac Park, about midway between the Lincoln and Jefferson memorials, on the west shore of the Tidal Basin. ℂ 202/426-6841. Free admission. Ranger staff on duty daily 8am–11:45pm. Metro: Smithsonian, with a 30-min. walk.

Hirshhorn Museum & Sculpture Garden   Natural light from floor-to-ceiling windows makes the Hirshhorn's inner galleries the perfect venue for viewing sculpture—second only, perhaps, to the tree-shaded sunken Sculpture Garden across the street (don't miss it). The collection features sculpture and paintings from just about every well-known 20th-century artist and touches on most of the major trends in Western art since the late 19th century. Among the best-known pieces are Rodin's *The Burghers of Calais* (in the Sculpture Garden), Hopper's *First Row Orchestra*, de Kooning's *Two Women in the Country,* and Warhol's *Marilyn Monroe's Lips.* On the south side of the Mall (at Independence Ave. and Seventh St. SW). ℂ 202/357-2700. http://hirshhorn.si.edu. Free admission. Museum daily 10am–5:30pm; often Thurs until 8pm in summer. Sculpture Garden daily 7:30am–dusk. Metro: L'Enfant Plaza (Smithsonian Museums/Maryland Ave. exit).

Jefferson Memorial   The domed interior of this beautiful columned rotunda in the style of the Pantheon in Rome contains a 19-foot bronze statue of Thomas Jefferson, the third U.S. president, who also served as ambassador to France, secretary of state, and vice president—and still found time to pen the Declaration of Independence, create the University of Virginia, and pursue wide-ranging interests, including architecture, astronomy, anthropology, music, and farming. Rangers present 20- to 30-minute programs throughout the day as time permits. South of the Washington Monument on Ohio Dr. SW (at the south shore of the Tidal Basin). ℂ 202/426-6841. Free admission. Daily 8am–11:45pm. Metro: Smithsonian, with a 20- to 30-min. walk.

Lincoln Memorial   This beautiful neoclassical templelike structure, similar in design to the Parthenon in Greece, is a moving testament to the great Civil War president. Visitors are silently awed in the presence of Daniel Chester French's 19-foot-high seated statue of Lincoln in deep contemplation. Lincoln's enormously powerful Gettysburg Address is engraved on the interior walls. Especially at night, the view from the steps, across the Reflecting Pool to the Washington Monument and the Capitol beyond, is one of the city's most beautiful. Directly west of the Mall in Potomac Park (at 23rd St. NW, between Constitution and Independence aves.). ℂ 202/426-6842. Free admission. Daily 8am–11:45pm. Metro: Foggy Bottom, then a 30-min. walk.

National Air & Space Museum   A hit with kids of all ages, this museum chronicles the story of man's mastery of flight, from Kitty Hawk to outer space, including the Wright Brothers' first plane, Charles Lindbergh's *Spirit of St. Louis,* and the Apollo moon ships. Arrive before 10am to make a rush for the film-ticket line—the IMAX films are not to be missed. One highlight is the *How Things Fly* gallery, which includes wind and smoke tunnels, a boardable Cessna 150 airplane, and dozens of interactive exhibits that demonstrate principles of flight, aerodynamics, and propulsion. On the south side of the Mall (between Fourth and Seventh sts. SW), with entrances on Jefferson Dr. and Independence Ave. ℂ 202/357-2700, or 202/357-1686 for IMAX information. www.nasm.edu. Free admission. Daily 10am–5:30pm (often opens at 9am in summer, but call to confirm). Free tours daily at 10:15am and 1pm. Metro: L'Enfant Plaza (Smithsonian Museums/Maryland Ave. exit) or Smithsonian.

National Archives   The Rotunda of the National Archives closed for renovation in 2001, and will reopen in the summer or fall of 2003. Until then, you won't be able to look at the nation's three most important documents—the Declaration of Independence, the Constitution of the United States, and the Bill of Rights. You will, however, be able to use the National Archives center for genealogical research—this is where Alex Haley began his work on *Roots*. Nearby are changing exhibits of documents relating to American history, such as the Louisiana Purchase Treaty signed by Napoleon. The building itself is an impressive example of the beaux arts style, with 72 columns on each of the four facades. Constitution Ave. NW (between Seventh and Ninth sts.; enter on Pennsylvania Ave.). ℂ 202/ 501-5000 for general information, or 202/501-5400 for research information. www.nara.gov. Free admission. Call for research hours. Metro: Archives–Navy Memorial.

National Gallery of Art   Housing one of the world's foremost collections of Western painting, sculpture, and graphic arts from the Middle Ages through the 20th century, the National Gallery has a dual personality. You'll find the masters in the original West Building, a neoclassic marble masterpiece with a domed rotunda. This is your chance to see the only painting by Leonardo da Vinci housed outside Europe and one of the world's great Impressionist collections. The ultramodern East Building appropriately houses an important collection of 20th-century art, including a massive aluminum Calder mobile and masterpieces by Picasso, Miró, Matisse, Pollock, and Rothko. The National Gallery Sculpture Garden, just across from the West Wing, features open lawns, a central pool with a spouting fountain (the pool is converted into an ice rink in winter), and an exquisite, glassed-in pavilion housing a cafe and an impressive sculpture garden. *Note:* The best time to visit the National Gallery is Monday morning; the worst is Sunday afternoon. Fourth St. and Constitution Ave. NW, on the north side of the Mall (between Third and Seventh sts. NW). ℂ 202/737-4215. www.nga.gov. Free admission. Mon–Sat 10am–5pm; Sun 11am–6pm. Metro: Archives, Judiciary Square, or Smithsonian.

National Museum of American History   Dealing with "everyday life in the American past," the massive contents here run the gamut from George Washington's Revolutionary War tent to Archie Bunker's chair. Don't miss the huge flag that inspired Francis Scott Key to write the U.S. national anthem in 1814— it has just been painstakingly conserved by expert textile conservators. Other highlights include a display of First Ladies' gowns; exhibits on African-American migration between 1915 and 1940; and a new exhibit, *The American Presidency.* *Note:* By the time you read this, part, or even all, of the museum may be closed for renovations. For details, call ℂ **202/357-2700** or check www.american history.si.edu. On the north side of the Mall (between 12th and 14th sts. NW), with entrances on Constitution Ave. and Madison Dr. ℂ 202/357-2700. www.americanhistory.si.edu. Free admission. Daily 10am–5:30pm. Metro: Smithsonian or Federal Triangle.

National Museum of Natural History   Another hit with kids, this fascinating museum contains more than 120 million artifacts and specimens—everything from one of the largest African elephants to Marie Antoinette's diamond earrings. Before you enter the museum, stop on the Ninth Street side of the building to visit the new butterfly garden. Inside, dinosaurs loom large, including a life-size model of the pterosaur, which had a 40-foot wingspan. The Discovery Room is filled with creative hands-on exhibits for children; call ahead or inquire at the information desk about hours. The new Discovery Center, featuring an IMAX theater, is one of the most recent innovations. Purchase tickets as early as possible; the box office opens at 9:45am. On the north side of the Mall (at 10th St. and Constitution Ave. NW), with entrances on Madison Dr. and Constitution Ave. (© **202/357-2700,** or 202/633-7400 for IMAX information. www.mnh.si.edu. Free admission. Daily 10am–5:30pm (often until 8pm in summer, but call to confirm). Free tours Mon–Thurs 10:30am and 1:30pm; Fri 10:30am. Metro: Smithsonian or Federal Triangle.

Phillips Collection   In an elegant 1890s Georgian Revival mansion (plus an added wing) is the exquisite collection of Duncan and Marjorie Phillips, avid collectors and proselytizers of modernism. The original building was once the Phillipses' elegant abode, and it still has the warmth of a home. Among the highlights are some splendid small Vuillards, five van Goghs, Renoir's *Luncheon of the Boating Party,* seven Cézannes, and six works by Georgia O'Keeffe. It's a collection no art lover should miss. 1600 21st St. NW (at Q St.). (© **202/387-2151.** www.phillipscollection.org. Admission Sat–Sun $7.50 adults, $4 students and seniors, free for children 18 and under; contribution suggested Tues–Fri. Special exhibits may require an additional fee. Tues–Sat 10am–5pm (Thurs until 8:30pm); Sun noon–7pm. Free tours Wed and Sat at 2pm. Metro: Dupont Circle (Q St. exit).

The Supreme Court of the United States   The Supreme Court hears and decides its cases in this stately Corinthian marble temple Monday through Wednesday from 10am to noon and, on occasion, from 1 to 2pm, starting the first Monday in October through late April. From mid-May to late June, you can attend brief sessions (about 15 min.) at 10am on Monday, when the justices release orders and opinions. Find out what cases are on the docket by checking the *Washington Post's* "Supreme Court Calendar." Arrive at least an hour early— even earlier for a highly publicized case—to line up for the 150 seats allotted to the general public. If the court is not in session, you can attend a free lecture, given every hour on the half hour from 9:30am to 3:30pm. Consider contacting your senator or congressperson—at least 2 months in advance—to arrange for a guided tour of the building led by a Supreme Court staff member. (Or go on a less-detailed self-guided tour.) 1 First St. NE (between E. Capitol St. and Maryland Ave. NE). (© **202/479-3000.** www.supremecourtus.gov. Free admission. Mon–Fri 9am–4:30pm. Metro: Capitol South or Union Station.

United States Holocaust Memorial Museum   This extraordinarily powerful museum reminds us of what can happen when civilization goes awry. An outer wall is reminiscent of an extermination camp's exterior brickwork, and towers evoke the guard towers of Auschwitz. A reconstructed Auschwitz barracks, the yellow stars that Jews were forced to wear, instruments of genocide, and a gas-chamber door are among the artifacts on display. As you enter, you'll be given the identity card of a real person living in Europe in the 1930s; at the end of your visit, you'll learn that person's fate. A highlight is a 30-minute film called *Testimony,* in which Holocaust survivors tell their own stories. Do not bring children under 11 to this museum. Timed tickets are required; reserve them via Tickets.com (© **800/400-9373;** www.tickets.com) for a small service charge. You can also get them at the museum box office; get in line around 8am. 100 Raoul Wallenberg Place SW (formerly 15th St. SW; near Independence Ave., just off the Mall). (© **202/488-0400.** www.ushmm.org. Free admission. Daily 10am–5:30pm (until 8pm Tues and Thurs mid-Apr to mid-June). Metro: Smithsonian.

Vietnam Veterans Memorial   The Vietnam Veterans Memorial is possibly the most poignant sight in Washington. Even if no one close to you died in Vietnam, it's wrenching to watch visitors grimly studying the directories at either end of this 492-foot-long, sunken black granite wall inscribed with the names of the nearly 60,000 American men and women who gave their lives, or remain missing, in the longest war in our nation's history. The names are inscribed in chronological order, documenting an epoch in American history as a series of individual sacrifices from the date of the first casualty in 1959 to the last death in 1975. Across from the Lincoln Memorial (east of Henry Bacon Dr. between 21st and 22nd sts. NW). ☎ 202/426-6841. Free admission. Rangers on duty daily 8am–11:45pm. Ranger-led programs given throughout the day. Metro: Foggy Bottom.

Washington Monument   The 555-foot stark marble obelisk glowing under floodlights at night is the city's most visible landmark. You can't climb the 897 steps, but a large elevator whisks visitors to the top in just 70 seconds. The 360-degree views are spectacular. You can get free same-day tour tickets at 15th Street NW between Independence and Constitution avenues (arrive by 7:30 or 8am, especially in peak season). If you want to get them in advance, contact the National Park Reservation Service (☎ 800/967-2283; http://reservations.nps. gov); you'll pay $1.50 per ticket plus a 50¢ service charge. You can also call this number to reserve a spot on a "Walk Down" tour, given every Saturday at 10am and 2pm. Directly south of the White House (at 15th St. and Constitution Ave. NW). ☎ 202/ 426-6841. Free admission. Daily 9am–5pm. Last elevators depart 15 min. before closing (arrive earlier). Metro: Smithsonian, then a 10-min. walk.

Washington National Cathedral   The National Cathedral is the sixth-largest cathedral in the world. Officially, it's Episcopalian, but it seeks to serve the entire nation as a house of prayer for all people. It stands in the shape of a cross, complete with flying buttresses and gargoyles. Its 57-acre landscaped grounds have two lovely gardens (the lawn is ideal for picnicking). The best way to explore the cathedral and see its abundance of art, architectural carvings, and statuary is to take a guided tour; they leave continually, from the west end of the nave. Allow additional time to tour the grounds and to visit the Observation Gallery, where 70 windows provide panoramic views. Tuesday and Wednesday afternoon tours are followed by a high tea in the Observation Gallery for $18 per person; reservations are required (☎ 202/537-8993). Massachusetts and Wisconsin aves. NW (entrance on Wisconsin Ave.). ☎ 202/537-6200. www.cathedral.org/cathedral. Donation $3 adults, $2 seniors, $1 children. Cathedral daily 10am–4:30pm; May to Labor Day, nave level open Mon–Fri until 9pm. Gardens daily until dusk. Regular tours Mon–Sat 10–11:30am and 12:45–3:15pm; Sun 12:45–2:30pm. Worship services vary, but you can count on a weekday Evensong service at 4:30pm, a weekday noon service, and an 11am service Sun; call for other times. Metro: Tenleytown, with a 20-min. walk.

The White House   The White House is the only private residence of a head of state that has opened its doors to the public for free tours. It was Thomas Jefferson who started this practice, which is stopped only during wartime; the administration considers that we are currently fighting a war on terrorism, and, therefore, the White House, at this writing, remains closed for public tours (except to school groups and veterans' groups). For those who have arranged such tours, and in the hope that general public tours have resumed by the time you read this, we provide the following information. (To find out the latest White House tour information, call ☎ 202/456-7041.)

The White House is a repository of art and furnishings. Tours of the public areas include the gold-and-white East Room, scene of gala receptions and other dazzling events; the Green Room, used as a sitting room; the Oval Blue Room, where presidents and first ladies officially receive guests; the Red Room, used as a reception room and for afternoon teas; and the State Dining Room, a superb setting for state dinners and luncheons. White House tours take place mornings only, Tuesday through Saturday. There are no public restrooms or telephones, and picture-taking and videotaping are prohibited. 1600 Pennsylvania Ave. NW (visitor entrance gate at E St. and E. Executive Ave.). © 202/456-7041 or 202/208-1631. www. whitehouse.gov. Free admission. Tours only for school and veterans' groups, which must make arrangements through their congressional offices. Metro: McPherson Square.

ORGANIZED TOURS
TOURMOBILE & TROLLEY TOURS Tourmobile Sightseeing (© 888/ 868-7707 or 202/554-5100; www.tourmobile.com) provides open-air sightseeing trams that make more than 20 stops along the Mall, as well as stops at Arlington National Cemetery and Mount Vernon. Tickets are sold for a tour of Washington and Arlington Cemetery (or for the cemetery alone); you can get on and off as often as you like. You pay the driver when you first board the bus (you can also buy a ticket at the booth at the Washington Monument or inside the Arlington National Cemetery Visitor Center, or, for a small surcharge, order your ticket in advance from **Ticketmaster** at © 800/551-SEAT). The charge is $18 for adults, $8 for children 3 to 11. Tourmobile is the only narrated sightseeing shuttle tour authorized by the National Park Service.

Old Town Trolley Tours (© 202/832-9800; www.oldtowntrolley.com) stop at or near the same attractions visited by Tourmobile, as well as certain hotels, neighborhoods (like Georgetown), and attractions away from the Mall (like the National Geographic Society). You can purchase your ticket at the booth at Union Station, or board without a ticket and purchase it en route (except at the Lincoln Memorial stop). Buses operate daily from 9am to 5:30pm year-round. The cost is $24 for adults, $12 for children 4 to 12.

BOAT TOURS Spirit of Washington Cruises, Pier 4 at Sixth and Water streets SW (© 866/211-3811 or 202/554-8000; www.spiritcruises.com), offers a variety of lunch, dinner, and moonlight dance cruises daily, including a half-day excursion to Mount Vernon. Prices range from $30 to $44 for a lunch excursion and from $54 to $83 for a dinner cruise, drinks not included. Call to make reservations.

PARKS, GARDENS & THE NATIONAL ZOO
The **United States Botanic Garden,** 100 Maryland Ave., at First St. SW, at the east end of the Mall (© 202/225-8333; www.usbg.gov), has reopened at last, after undergoing a major renovation. The grand conservatory devotes half of its space to exhibits that focus on the importance of plants to people, and half to exhibits that focus on ecology and the evolutionary biology of plants. The new National Garden outside the conservatory includes a First Ladies Water Garden, formal rose garden, and lawn terrace. Admission is free; open daily from 10am to 5pm.

The **United States National Arboretum,** 3501 New York Ave. NE (© 202/ 245-2726; www.usna.usda.gov), is a must-see for the horticulturally inclined. Its 9½ miles of paved roads meander through 444 hilly acres of azaleas, magnolias, hollies, dwarf conifers, and boxwoods. One highlight is the **National Bonsai and Penjing Museum,** which includes 53 beautiful miniature trees, each one an exquisite work of art. Free admission. Open daily from 8am to 5pm.

West and East Potomac Parks, their 720 riverside acres divided by the Tidal Basin, are most famous for their spring display of cherry blossoms and all the hoopla that goes with it. West Potomac Park also encompasses Constitution Gardens; the Vietnam, Korean, Lincoln, Jefferson, and FDR memorials; a small island where ducks live; and the Reflecting Pool.

Rock Creek Park (www.nps/gov.rocr), a 1,750-acre valley within the District of Columbia, extends 12 miles from the Potomac River to the Maryland border. It's one of the biggest and finest city parks in the nation.

Adjacent to Rock Creek Park is the Smithsonian Institution's **National Zoological Park,** with its main entrance in the 3000 block of Connecticut Avenue NW (© **202/673-4800** or 202/673-4717; www.si.edu/natzoo). It's home to several thousand animals of some 500 species, many of them rare or endangered. The zoo animals live in large, open enclosures—simulations of their natural habitats—along two easy-to-follow numbered paths: Olmsted Walk and the Valley Trail. Free admission; open daily.

One of the great joys of Washington is the **C&O Canal** (© **301/739-4200;** www.nps.gov/choc) and its unspoiled 184½-mile towpath. Leave your urban cares behind while hiking, strolling, jogging, biking, or boating in this lush, natural setting of ancient oaks and red maples, giant sycamores, willows, and wildflowers.

SHOPPING HIGHLIGHTS

In **Adams-Morgan,** defined by 18th Street and Columbia Road NW, ethnic eateries are interspersed with the odd secondhand bookshop and eclectic collectibles stores. **Dupont Circle,** where young, mellow Washingtonians shop, is studded with art galleries, book and record shops, and gay and lesbian boutiques. Take the Metro to Farragut North at one end and Dupont Circle at the other. **Georgetown** is the city's perennial favorite shopping area, with stores lining Wisconsin Avenue and M Street NW at the heart of it, and fanning out along side streets from the central intersection. You'll find both chain and one-of-a-kind shops, chic as well as thrift. But you may come away with a headache from trying to make your way along its crowded streets, sidewalks, and shops. Visit Georgetown on a weekday morning, if you can. Consider taking a bus or taxi—the closest Metro stop is Foggy Bottom, a good 20- to 30-minute walk away.

One of the most popular tourist attractions in northern Virginia is **Potomac Mills Mall** (© **800/VA-MILLS** or 703/643-1770; www.potomacmills.com), a collection of 225-plus outlet and discount stores 25 miles south of Washington on I-95. Call © **703/551-1050** for information about shuttle service from the city.

D.C. isn't a serious shopper's town, but it does have outstanding museum shops. The **National Gallery of Art** shop sells printed reproductions, stationery, and jewelry whose designs are based on works in the gallery's collections. It also has one of the largest selections of books on art history and architecture in the country. The **National Museum of American History** store has a lot of junky trinkets, as well as an outstanding collection of books and recordings, such as CDs from the Ken Burns PBS special on jazz. The largest museum shop is at the **National Air and Space Museum** (three floors!), and the shop at the **Smithsonian's Arts and Industries Building,** 900 Jefferson Dr. SW, on the south side of the Mall, carries a selection of the most popular items from all of the other Smithsonian shops.

3 Where to Stay

For ease in booking a reservation, try contacting one of two well-established local reservation services: **Capitol Reservations** (© **800/VISIT-DC** or 202/452-1270; www.hotelsdc.com) or **Washington D.C. Accommodations** (© **800/554-2220** or 202/289-2220; www.dcaccommodations.com). Both services are free.

One of the best chain hotels in town, especially for families, is the **Holiday Inn on the Hill,** 415 New Jersey Ave. NW (② **800/638-1116** or 202/ 638-1616; www.basshotels.com/was-onthehill), which often has good-value packages. Children under 12 eat free when an adult orders a meal in the restaurant. A major renovation in 1999 added 25-inch TVs and Nintendo to each room. There's an outdoor pool and fitness room.

Courtyard by Marriott Convention Center   Downtown Washington needs more places like this—a conveniently situated, reasonably priced, medium-size property with a better-than-average restaurant. The FBI is a block away; the convention center is a 2½-block walk. The hotel opened in 1999, but the building, with its handsome stonework, is a historic 1891 landmark. Rooms have good-size bathrooms, firm mattresses, and views of downtown. The upscale brewery restaurant, Gordon Biersch, occupies the marble-floored, columned former bank lobby. 900 F St. NW (at Ninth St. NW), Washington, DC 20004. ② **800/321-2211** or 202/638-4600. Fax 202/638-4601. www.courtyard.com/wascn. 188 units. Weekdays $219 double, weekends $129–$189 double; from $265 suite. AE, DC, DISC, MC, V. Parking $22. Metro: Gallery Place or Metro Center. **Amenities:** Restaurant; pool; fitness center.

Four Seasons   Set just at the mouth of Georgetown, this hotel is where the rich and famous stay. Rooms, many overlooking Rock Creek Park or the C&O Canal, have an upscale, homey feel, with perks such as robes, down bedding, high-speed Internet access, and CD players. An adjoining building holds spacious rooms for clients who want state-of-the-art business amenities. Original avant-garde artwork hangs in every room. Afternoon tea is served in the lounge. Transmitters installed throughout the hotel allow you wireless Internet connection on your laptop. 2800 Pennsylvania Ave. NW (which becomes M St. a block farther along), Washington, DC 20007. ② **800/332-3442** or 202/342-0444. Fax 202/944-2076. www.four seasons.com. 260 units. Weekdays $455–$615 double, weekends from $295 double; weekdays $695–$5,150 suite, weekends from $550 suite. Extra person $40. Children under 16 stay free in parents' room. AE, DC, MC, V. Parking $26. Metro: Foggy Bottom. **Amenities:** Restaurant; fitness club and spa with lap pool; pets up to 15 lb. allowed.

George Washington University Inn   This eight-story, whitewashed brick inn, a former apartment building, is a great choice for families. Spacious rooms are equipped with fridges and microwaves; efficiencies and suites have kitchens. Try to mention prices quoted in the inn's *New York Times* ad, if you've seen it. This is a fairly safe and lovely neighborhood, within easy walking distance of Georgetown, the Kennedy Center, and downtown. 824 New Hampshire Ave. NW (between H and I sts.), Washington, DC 20037. ② **800/426-4455** or 202/337-6620. Fax 202/ 298-7499. www.gwuinn.com. 95 units. Weekdays $130–$175 double, weekends $99–$135 double; weekdays $140–$185 efficiency, weekends $110–$155 efficiency; weekdays $155–$220 1-bedroom suite, weekends $125–$170 1-bedroom suite. Children under 12 stay free in parents' room. AE, DC, MC, V. Limited parking $18. Metro: Foggy Bottom. **Amenities:** Restaurant; complimentary passes to nearby fitness center.

Henley Park   This intimate hotel is housed in a converted 1918 Tudor-style apartment house. Luxurious appointments make it a good choice for upscale romantic weekends, although these lodgings fill up with corporate travelers on weekdays. Rooms are decorated in the English-country-house mode. Afternoon tea is served daily from 4 to 6pm. There's complimentary weekday-morning sedan service to downtown and Capitol Hill. 926 Massachusetts Ave. NW (at 10th St.), Washington, DC 20001. ② **800/222-8474** or 202/638-5200. Fax 202/638-6740. www.henleypark. com. 96 units. Weekdays $185–$245 double, summer and weekends $99–$159 double; suites from

$325 weekdays, with lower rates on weekends. Extra person $20. Children under 14 stay free in parents' room. AE, DC, DISC, MC, V. Parking $16. Metro: Metro Center, Gallery Place, or Mt. Vernon Square. **Amenities:** Restaurant; access to fitness room in the Morrison–Clark Historic Inn (see below) across the street; very small pets allowed (call ahead).

Hotel George   The hip, modern Hotel George opened in 1998 in a building that dates back to 1928. The large, bright rooms sport a minimalist look, with marble bathrooms (with speakers that broadcast TV sounds from the other room), cordless phones, high-speed Internet access, umbrellas, and robes. Contributing to the hotel's hipness is the presence of its restaurant, **Bistro Bis,** which serves (duh) French bistro food to hungry lobbyists and those they are lobbying. (Capitol Hill is a block away.) 15 E St. NW (at N. Capitol St.), Washington, DC 20001. © 800/576-8331 or 202/347-4200. Fax 202/347-4213. www.hotelgeorge.com. 139 units. Weekdays $265–$350 double; weekends from $149 double; $950 suite. Extra person $25. Children under 16 stay free in parents' room. AE, DC, DISC, MC, V. Parking $24. Metro: Union Station. **Amenities:** Restaurant; fitness center.

The Jefferson, a Loews Hotel   Opened in 1923 just 4 blocks from the White House, the intimate Jefferson offers superb service, an acclaimed restaurant, sophisticated but comfortable accommodations, inviting public rooms (should you want to hang out), and proximity to attractions and restaurants (should you not want to hang out). A fine art collection, including original documents signed by Thomas Jefferson, graces the public areas. Guest rooms are decorated with antiques and lovely fabrics, evoking a European feel. In-room amenities include VCRs, CD players, and robes. A marvelous high tea is served in the paneled pub/lounge. 1200 16th St. NW (at M St.), Washington, DC 20036. © 800/235-6397 or 202/347-2200. Fax 202/331-7982. www.loewshotels.com. 100 units. Weekdays $319–$339 double, $350–$1,200 suite; weekends from $199 double, from $289 suite. Extra person $25. Children under 12 stay free in parents' room. AE, DC, DISC, MC, V. Parking $20. Metro: Farragut North. **Amenities:** Restaurant; access to nearby health club (with pool) at the University Club across the street ($20 per visit); pets welcomed and pampered.

Jurys Washington Hotel   Open since 2000, this hotel gets high marks for convenience (it's located right on Dupont Circle), service, and comfort. Despite its prime location in a sometimes raucous neighborhood, the Art Deco–ish guest rooms are insulated from the noise; all have high-speed Internet access, lots of light-wood furniture, and the usual array of hotel amenities. The hotel pub proudly features a bar imported from Ireland. 1500 New Hampshire Ave. NW (across from Dupont Circle), Washington, DC 20036. © 800/42-DOYLE or 202/483-6000. Fax 202/232-1130. www.jurysdoyle.com. 314 units. $145–$235 double; from $600 suite. Extra person $15. Children 17 and under stay free in parents' room. AE, DC, DISC, MC, V. Parking $17. Metro: Dupont Circle. **Amenities:** Restaurant; fitness room.

Lincoln Suites Downtown   This is a little hotel with a big heart. The all-suite, 10-story, nothing-fancy property is in the heart of downtown, just 5 blocks from the White House. About 28 suites offer full kitchens, while the rest have kitchenettes. The hotel is connected to an Irish pub, and Luigi's, an Italian restaurant around the corner, provides room service for lunch and dinner. 1823 L St. NW, Washington, DC 20036. © 800/424-2970 or 202/223-4320. Fax 202/223-8546. www.lincolnhotels.com. 99 units. Weekdays $129–$199, weekends $99–$139. Children under 16 stay free in parents' room. Rates include continental breakfast. AE, DC, DISC, MC, V. Parking $16. Metro: Farragut North or Farragut West. **Amenities:** Restaurant; free passes to the Bally's Holiday Spa nearby; pets under 25 lb. accepted ($15 a day).

Morrison–Clark Historic Inn   This magnificent property offers the homey ambience and personable service of an inn, coupled with hotel amenities such as a first-rate restaurant and a tiny fitness center. The inn, occupying twin 1865 Victorian town houses, is listed on the National Register of Historic Places. High-ceilinged rooms are individually decorated with original artwork and antique or reproduction 19th-century furnishings. Four have private porches; many others have plant-filled balconies. The adjoining Club boasts a marble fireplace and 13-foot windows flanking gilded mirrors. 1015 L St. NW (at 11th St. and Massachusetts Ave. NW), Washington, DC 20001. ℂ **800/332-7898** or 202/898-1200. Fax 202/ 289-8576. www.morrisonclark.com. 54 units. Weekdays $175–$245 double, weekends $99–$159 double. Extra person $20. Children under 16 stay free in parents' room. Rates include continental breakfast. AE, DC, DISC, MC, V. Parking $16. Metro: Metro Center or Mt. Vernon Square. **Amenities:** Restaurant; fitness center; very small pets allowed with advance notice.

Swann House   This stunning 1883 mansion, 4 blocks north of Dupont Circle, has exquisite rooms, two with private entrances and three with kitchens. The coolest is the Blue Sky Suite, which has its original rose-tiled (working) fireplace, a queen-size bed and sofa bed, a gabled ceiling, and its own roof deck. The most romantic is probably Il Duomo, with Gothic windows, cathedral ceiling, fireplace, and turreted bathroom with angel murals. The main floor has a turreted living room, columned sitting room, and sunroom (where breakfast is served) leading to the garden and pool. 1808 New Hampshire Ave. NW (between S and Swann sts.), Washington, DC 20009. ℂ **202/265-4414.** Fax 202/265-6755. www.swannhouse.com. 9 units, all with private bathroom (3 with shower only, 1 with tub only). $140–$295. 2-night minimum weekends, 3-night minimum holiday weekends. Extra person $35. Rates include expanded continental breakfast. Limited off-street parking $12. AE, MC, V. Metro: Dupont Circle. No children under 12. **Amenities:** Outdoor pool; access to nearby health club.

Topaz Hotel   The Topaz is an upscale boutique hotel for those who think young. Rooms are whimsically decorated with striped lime-green wallpaper, a polka-dot padded headboard, a bright-blue curved-back settee, and a round mirror set in a sunburst frame. The rooms are unusually large (in its former life as the Canterbury Hotel, these were "junior suites" and held kitchenettes). The Topaz pursues a sort of New Age wellness motif: Specialty rooms include a piece of exercise equipment and fitness magazines, while "yoga" rooms come with an exercise mat, instructional tape, and padded pillows. The hotel is set on a quiet residential street of picturesque town houses. 1733 N St. NW (between 17th and 18th sts.), Washington, DC 20036. ℂ **800/424-2950** or 202/393-3000. Fax 202/785-9581. www. topazhotel.com. 99 units. Weekdays $240–$275 double, $280 specialty room; weekends $145 double, $185 specialty room. Extra person $20. Children under 16 stay free in parents' room. Rates include complimentary morning energy potions. AE, DC, DISC, MC, V. Parking $20. Metro: Dupont Circle. **Amenities:** Restaurant; access to nearby health club ($5 per guest); pets welcome.

Willard Inter-Continental   The classy Willard is a stone's throw from the White House and the Smithsonian museums, down the block from the National Theater. Rooms in this National Historic Landmark are handsome, if staid, and furnished with Edwardian- and Federal-style reproductions. Those with the best views are the oval suites overlooking Pennsylvania Avenue to the Capitol. Weekend packages often include an upgrade to a suite or free valet parking. Stop in at the Round Robin Bar to hear bartender and manager Jim Hewes spin tales about the incredible history of the 1901 Willard and its predecessor, the City Hotel, built on this site in 1815. 1401 Pennsylvania Ave. NW (at 14th St.), Washington, DC 20004. ℂ **800/327-0200** or 202/628-9100. Fax 202/637-7326. www.washington.interconti.com.

341 units. Weekdays $480 double, weekends from $199; $850–$4,200 suite. Extra person $30. Children under 18 stay free in parents' room. AE, DC, DISC, MC, V. Parking $23. Metro: Metro Center. **Amenities:** Restaurants (2); fitness center; small pets allowed.

4 Where to Dine

Barolo PIEDMONTESE ITALIAN   This excellent, sophisticated Italian restaurant stands out among the pubs and eateries that line this stretch of Pennsylvania Avenue on Capitol Hill. The intimate main room has wooden floors, a working fireplace, and well-spaced tables. Although the menu changes daily, you can expect Piedmontese cuisine that may include saffron pappardelle with sautéed lobster, asparagus, roasted garlic, and fresh basil; or roasted red snapper over sweet potato, rosemary, black olives, and fresh basil. 223 Pennsylvania Ave. SE. (*) 202/547-5011. Reservations recommended. Main courses $15–$18 lunch, $15–$23 dinner. AE, DC, DISC, MC, V. Mon–Fri 11:30am–2:30pm; Mon–Thurs 5:30–10pm; Fri–Sat 5:30–10:30pm. Metro: Capitol South.

Bombay Club INDIAN   This used to be a favorite stop for the Clintons, but perhaps the menu is too exotic for the current president—no word yet of Bush sightings here. (The White House is just across Lafayette Park.) The menu ranges from fiery green-chile chicken ("not for the fainthearted," the menu warns) to the delicately prepared lobster malabar, a personal favorite. The wait staff seems straight out of *Jewel in the Crown,* attending to your every whim. 815 Connecticut Ave. NW. (*) 202/659-3727. Reservations recommended. Main courses $7.50–$19; Sun brunch $19. AE, DC, MC, V. Mon–Fri and Sun brunch 11:30am–2:30pm; Mon–Thurs 6–10:30pm; Fri–Sat 6–11pm; Sun 5:30–9pm. Metro: Farragut West.

Café Atlantico SOUTH AMERICAN   This place rocks on weekend nights, a favorite hot spot in Washington's still-burgeoning downtown. The colorful, three-tiered restaurant throbs with Latin, calypso, and reggae music. If the place is packed, try to snag a seat at the second-level bar, where you can sample a *caipirinha,* made of limes, sugar, and *cachacha* (sugarcane liqueur). Another treat is watching the waiter make fresh guacamole right before your eyes. As for the main dishes, you can't get a more elaborate meal for the price. The ceviche, Ecuadorean seared scallops, and Argentine rib eye are standouts. 405 Eighth St. NW. (*) 202/393-0812. Reservations recommended. Main courses $9–$13 lunch, $18–$24 dinner; pretheater menu $22 (5–6:30pm); Latino dim sum $20 (Sat 11:30am–1:30pm). AE, DC, DISC, MC, V. Mon–Fri 11:30am–2:30pm; Sun brunch 11:30am–3pm; Sun–Thurs 5–10pm; Fri–Sat 5–11pm. Bar closes later on weekends. Metro: Archives–Navy Memorial and Gallery Place/MCI Center.

Café Berlin GERMAN   You have to walk past the dessert display on your way to your table at Café Berlin, so forget your diet. These delicious homemade confections are the best reason to come here. Lunch is another—you can get a simple chicken-salad sandwich (laced with tasty bits of mandarin orange), soup of the day, and German potato salad, all for $6.75. The restaurant occupies two prettily decorated dining rooms on the bottom level of a Capitol Hill town house, whose front terrace serves as an outdoor cafe in warm weather. 322 Massachusetts Ave. NE. (*) 202/543-7656. Reservations recommended. Main courses $15–$19; lunch items $6.95–$11. AE, DC, DISC, MC, V. Mon–Thurs 11:30am–10pm; Fri–Sat 11:30am–11pm; Sun 4–10pm. Metro: Union Station.

Cashion's Eat Place AMERICAN   Owner/chef Ann Cashion continues to rack up culinary awards as easily as she pleases her patrons. Her menu features about eight entrees, split between seafood and meat: fritto misto of whole jumbo shrimp and black sea bass, or fried sweetbreads on a bed of sautéed spinach. Save room for chocolate cinnamon mousse or lime tartalette. In warm weather, the glass-fronted Cashion's opens invitingly to the sidewalk. 1819 Columbia Rd. NW (between 18th St. and Mintwood Place). © 202/797-1819. Reservations recommended. Brunch $7–$17; dinner main courses $17–$26. MC, V. Tues 5:30–10pm; Wed–Sat 5:30–11pm; Sun 11:30am–2:30pm and 5:30–10pm.

DC Coast AMERICAN   The dining room is sensational: two stories high, glass-walled balcony, immense oval mirrors, and a full-bodied stone mermaid poised to greet you at the entrance. Gather at the bar first to feel a part of the loud and trendy scene. This is one of the city's most popular restaurants, so call way ahead to book a reservation. Chef Jeff Tunks has returned from stints in Texas, California, and New Orleans, and some of the dishes Washingtonians remember from his years at the River Club have returned with him: Chinese-style smoked lobster with fried spinach is the most famous, and deservedly so. Seafood is a big part of the menu, but there are a handful of meat dishes, too. 1401 K St. NW. © 202/216-5988. Reservations recommended. Main courses $12–$18 lunch, $16–$29 dinner; light fare $6–$11. AE, DC, DISC, MC, V. Mon–Fri 11:30am–2:30pm; Mon–Thurs 5:30–10:30pm; Fri–Sat 5:30–11pm. (Light fare weekdays 2:30–5:30pm.) Metro: McPherson Square.

Full Kee CHINESE   Although it might not look like anything special, this is probably Chinatown's best restaurant. Chefs from some of Washington's best restaurants recommend ordering from the typed back page of the menu—specifically, the jumbo breaded oyster casserole with ginger and scallions, and the whole steamed fish. If you love dumplings, order the Hong Kong–style shrimp dumpling broth. BYOB. 509 H St. NW. © 202/371-2233. Reservations accepted. Lunch items $4.25–$9; dinner main courses $6.95–$17. No credit cards. Sun–Thurs 11am–1am; Fri–Sat 11am–3am. Metro: Gallery Place/Chinatown.

Galileo PIEDMONTESE ITALIAN   Galileo has been hailed as one of the best Italian restaurants in the country. It features the cuisine of the Piedmont region—think truffles, hazelnuts, porcini mushrooms, and veal. The atmosphere is relaxed; diners are dressed in jeans and suits alike. Typical entrees include a risotto with black truffles, whole roasted baby pig stuffed with sausage and porcini mushrooms, and a house-made saffron pasta with ragout of veal. The cellar boasts more than 900 vintages of Italian wine. 1110 21st St. NW. © 202/293-7191. Reservations recommended. Main courses $12–$19 lunch, $24–$35 dinner. AE, DC, DISC, MC, V. Mon–Fri 11:30am–2pm and 5:30–10pm; Sat 5:30–10:30pm; Sun 5:30–10pm. Metro: Foggy Bottom.

Georgetown Seafood Grill on 19th St. SEAFOOD   Two big tanks of lobsters greet you as you enter this downtown eatery, and the decor is nautical throughout. Although items like lobster Thermidor are on the menu, best bets are the "simply grilled" fish entrees and raw bar selections. Oysters arrive daily from Canada, Virginia, and Oregon, and may be the freshest in town. 1200 19th St. NW. © 202/530-4430. Reservations recommended. Main courses $15–$22 lunch, $15–$25 dinner; salads and sandwiches $8.95–$15. AE, DC, DISC, MC, V. Mon–Thurs 11:30am–10pm; Fri 11:30am–11pm; Sat 5:30–11pm; Sun 6–10pm. Metro: Dupont Circle.

Georgia Brown's SOUTHERN   In Washington restaurants, seldom do you find such a racially diverse crowd—but no one can resist such extraordinary food. Corn bread and biscuits come with a butter that's been whipped with diced peaches and honey. The menu is heavily Southern, with the emphasis on the Low Country cooking of South Carolina and Savannah: collards, grits, and lots of seafood, especially shrimp dishes. Georgia Brown's is famous for its Sunday brunch, lively with the sounds of jazz. 950 15th St. NW. © 202/393-4499.

Reservations recommended. Main courses $7–$20 lunch, $12–$23 dinner; Sun brunch $23. AE, DC, DISC, MC, V. Mon–Thurs 11:30am–10:30pm; Fri 11:30am–11:30pm; Sat 5:30–11:30pm; Sun 11:30am–4:30pm (brunch 10:30am–2:30pm) and 5:30–10:30pm. Metro: McPherson Square.

Jaleo SPANISH   Jaleo's attracts those going to see a performance at the Shakespeare Theater, right next door. Tapas choices include savory warm goat cheese served with toast points, a skewer of grilled chorizo atop garlic mashed potatoes, and a delicious mushroom tart served with roasted red-pepper sauce. Paella is among the few heartier entrees listed. The casual-chic interior focuses on a large mural of a flamenco dancer inspired by John Singer Sargent's painting *Jaleo*. On Wednesday evenings at 8 and 9pm, flamenco dancers perform. 480 Seventh St. NW (at E St.). ✆ 202/628-7949. Reservations accepted until 6:30pm. Main courses $7.50–$11 lunch, $11–$28 dinner; tapas $3.95–$7.95. AE, DC, DISC, MC, V. Sun–Mon 11:30am–10pm; Tues–Thurs 11:30am–11:30pm; Fri–Sat 11:30pm–midnight. Metro: Archives or Gallery Place.

Kinkead's AMERICAN/SEAFOOD   When a restaurant has been as roundly praised as Kinkead's, it's hard to live up to the hype—but Kinkead's is that good. Award-winning chef/owner Bob Kinkead is the star at this 220-seat restaurant, where booths and tables neatly fill the nooks and alcoves of the former town house. The signature dish, pepita-crusted salmon with shrimp, crab, and chiles, provides a nice hot crunch before melting in your mouth. If you're hungry but not ravenous in the late afternoon, stop in for some delicious light fare: fish and chips, lobster roll, soups, and salads. 2000 Pennsylvania Ave. NW. ✆ 202/296-7700. Reservations recommended. Main courses $13–$21 lunch, $21–$29 dinner; light fare (2:30–5:30pm) $5–$22. AE, DC, DISC, MC, V. Daily 11:30am–10:30pm. Metro: Foggy Bottom.

Les Halles FRENCH/STEAK   Everyone in this restaurant seems to be devouring the *onglet* (a boneless French-cut hangar steak), steak au poivre, steak tartare, New York sirloin, and other cuts, all of which come with *frites*, which are a must. The menu isn't all beef, but it is classic French. The banquettes, pressed-tin ceiling, mirrors, wooden floor, and side bar capture the feel of a brasserie. 1201 Pennsylvania Ave. NW. ✆ 202/347-6848. Reservations recommended. Main courses $12–$20 lunch, $13–$23 dinner. AE, DC, DISC, MC, V. Sun–Thurs 11:30am–midnight; Fri–Sat 11:30am–2am. Metro: Metro Center or Federal Triangle.

Mixtec REGIONAL MEXICAN   This cheerful Adams-Morgan spot serves delicious, authentic regional Mexican cuisine. Small dishes called *antojitos* ("little whims"), in the $2.50 to $4.95 range, are a bargain. *Tortas* are a kind of Mexican sub, layered with grilled pork, chiles, guacamole, and salsa. The freshly prepared guacamole is excellent. Choose from 30 kinds of tequila, tequila-mixed drinks, Mexican beers, and fresh fruit juices. 1792 Columbia Rd. (just off 18th St.). ✆ 202/332-1011. Main courses $3.95–$12. MC, V. Sun–Thurs 8:30am–10pm; Fri–Sat 8:30am–11pm.

Old Ebbitt Grill AMERICAN   You won't find this place listed among the city's best culinary establishments, but you can bet it's included in every tour book. It's an institution. Located 2 blocks from the White House, this is the city's oldest saloon, founded in 1856. The Old Ebbitt is an attractive place, with Persian rugs strewn on beautiful oak and marble floors. The menu changes daily, but always includes burgers, trout Parmesan, crab cakes, and oysters (there's an oyster bar). 675 15th St. NW (between F and G sts.). ✆ 202/347-4801. Reservations recommended. Breakfast $6.95–$9.95; brunch $5.95–$14; lunch items $6.95–$14; dinner main courses $14–$21 (up to $25 for crab cakes); burgers and sandwiches $6.95–$11. AE, DC, DISC, MC, V. Mon–Thurs 7:30am–2am; Fri 7:30am–3am; Sat 8:30am–3am; Sun 9:30am–2am (kitchen closes at 1am nightly). Raw bar open until midnight daily. Metro: McPherson Square or Metro Center.

Pizzeria Paradiso ITALIAN   Peter Pastan, master chef/owner of Obelisk (right next door), owns this classy, often crowded, 16-table pizzeria. An oak-burning oven at one end of the charming room produces exceptionally doughy but light pizza crusts. Pizzas range from the plain Paradiso, which offers chunks of tomatoes covered in melted mozzarella, to the robust Siciliano, a blend of nine ingredients, including eggplant and red onion. Also popular are the panini of homemade focaccia stuffed with marinated roasted lamb and vegetables and other fillings. 2029 P St. NW. © 202/223-1245. Reservations not accepted. Pizzas $7.95–$16; sandwiches and salads $3.95–$6.95. DC, MC, V. Mon–Thurs 11:30am–11pm; Fri–Sat 11:30am–midnight; Sun noon–10pm. Metro: Dupont Circle.

TenPenh ASIAN FUSION   What should bring you here is not just great service, but a warm atmosphere and stellar food. The dining room is inviting, with soft lighting, comfortable booths, and an open kitchen. In this, his second restaurant (DC Coast is his other), Jeff Tunks presents translations of dishes he's discovered in travels throughout Asia: halibut dusted with ground macadamia nuts and Japanese bread crumbs; whole deep-fried flounder; and wok-seared calamari. 1001 Pennsylvania Ave. NW (at 10th St.). © 202/393-4500. Reservations recommended. Main courses $12–$17 lunch, $14–$24 dinner. AE, DISC, MC, V. Mon–Fri 11:30am–2:30pm; Mon–Thurs 5:30–10:30pm; Fri–Sat 5:30–11pm. Metro: Archives–Navy Memorial.

The Willard Room AMERICAN/FRENCH   Like the rest of the hotel, the Willard Room has been restored to its original turn-of-the-20th-century splendor. Scattered among the statespeople and diplomats dining here are local couples seeking romance; the Willard has been the setting for more than one betrothal. The room has also been used in many movies. The chef changes the menu seasonally, and emphasizes lightness in cooking (sometimes too light). Dishes with a little more heft to them include beef tenderloin with red-wine and bone-marrow sauce. The wine list offers more than 250 fine selections. In the Willard Inter-Continental hotel, 1401 Pennsylvania Ave. NW. © 202/637-7440. Reservations recommended. Jacket and tie preferred for men. Breakfast $7–$15; lunch items $21–$35; dinner main courses $32–$42. AE, DC, DISC, MC, V. Mon–Fri 7:30–10am and 11:30am–2pm; Mon–Sat 6–10pm. Metro: Metro Center.

5 Washington After Dark

To find out who's playing when you're in town, check the Friday "Weekend" section of the *Washington Post.* The *City Paper,* available free at restaurants, bookstores, and other places around town, is another good source.

TICKETplace (© 202/TICKETS for information; www.ticketplace.org), Washington's discount, day-of-show ticket outlet, has one location: in the Old Post Office Pavilion, 1100 Pennsylvania Ave. NW. It's open Tuesday through Saturday from 11am to 6pm; half-price tickets for Sunday and Monday shows are sold on Saturday. Full-price tickets for most performances in town can be bought through **Ticketmaster** (© 202/432-SEAT; www.ticketmaster.com). You can buy tickets to Washington theatrical, musical, and other events before you leave home by calling © 800/551-SEAT. Another similar ticket outlet is **Tickets.com** (© 800/955-5566 or 703/218-6500; www.tickets.com).

THE KENNEDY CENTER   America's national performing-arts center, the hub of Washington's cultural and entertainment scene, is the **John F. Kennedy Center for the Performing Arts,** at the southern end of New Hampshire Avenue NW and Rock Creek Parkway (© 800/444-1324 or 202/467-4600; www.kennedy-center.org).

The center is actually made up of six different theaters: the Opera House, the Concert Hall, the Terrace Theater, the Eisenhower Theater, the Theater Lab, and the American Film Institute (AFI) theater. While the Opera House undergoes renovation throughout 2003, the **Washington Opera** (www.dc-opera.org) performs instead at the Daughters of the American Revolution's (DAR) Constitution Hall. The **National Symphony Orchestra** presents concerts in the Concert Hall from September to June. The Theater Lab continues by day as Washington's premier stage for children's theater and by night as a cabaret.

You should also know about the Kennedy Center's very popular free concert series: Known as "Millennium Stage," the series features daily performances by national and local musicians, each evening at 6pm in the center's Grand Foyer.

Discounted tickets are usually offered to students, seniors, people with permanent disabilities, enlisted military personnel, and people with fixed low incomes (call ☎ **202/416-8340** for details).

THE THEATER SCENE   D.C.'s theatrical productions are first-rate and varied. Almost anything on Broadway has been tried out here or will eventually come here. The city also has several nationally acclaimed repertory companies and a fine company specializing in Shakespearean productions. Check the *Washington Post* or the *City Paper* for specific listings of what's going on. Among the best are: **Arena Stage** (☎ **202/488-3300**; www.arenastage.org), **Ford's Theatre** (☎ **202/347-4833**; www.fordstheatre.org), the **National Theatre** (☎ **202/628-6161**, or 800/447-7400 to charge tickets by phone; www.nationaltheatre.org), and the **Shakespeare Theatre** (☎ **202/547-1122**; www.shakespearedc.org).

THE CLUB & MUSIC SCENE   The best nightlife districts are Adams-Morgan; the U Street Corridor, 12th to 15th streets NW, a still developing district that's in a somewhat dangerous part of town; the Seventh Street NW corridor near Chinatown and the MCI Center; and Georgetown.

Latin jazz is quite the thing in Washington, and one of the best places to salsa and merengue is **Habana Village**, 1834 Columbia Rd. NW (☎ **202/462-6310**), a fun three-story nightclub in Adams-Morgan. Another option is **Latin Jazz Alley**, also in Adams-Morgan at 1721 Columbia Rd. NW, on the second floor of **El Migueleno Cafe** (☎ **202/328-6190**).

Adams-Morgan, in general, is a convenient place to head if you're in a dancing mood. Stop in at **Chief Ike's Mambo Room,** 1725 Columbia Rd. NW (☎ **202/332-2211**), for a mix of DJ tunes, hip-hop to R&B; and at **Madam's Organ Restaurant and Bar,** 2461 18th St. NW (☎ **202/667-5370**; www.madamsorgan.com), if live jazz, blues, or R&B turns you on.

And if you like to mingle with an international crowd, stop by **Zanzibar on the Waterfront,** 700 Water St. SW (☎ **202/554-9100**; www.zanzibar-otw.com), where you can dine well, dance to live music, lounge, sip and listen, or sip and talk; the club features a different kind of music every night.

Blues Alley, 1073 Wisconsin Ave. NW, in an alley below M Street (☎ **202/337-4141**; www.bluesalley.com), in Georgetown, has been Washington's top jazz club since 1965.

Clubs hosting a combination of big names and up-and-coming bands for live rock include **Nation,** 1015 Half St. SE, at K Street (☎ **202/554-1500**; www.nationdc.com); **Black Cat,** 1811 14th St. NW, between S and T streets (☎ **202/667-7960**; www.blackcatdc.com); **Metro Café,** 1522 14th St. NW, between P and Q streets (☎ **202/588-9118**; www.metrocafe.net); and the **9:30 Club,** 815 V St. NW, at Vermont Avenue (☎ **202/265-0930**; www.930.com). Many of these clubs have DJs on nights when live acts aren't playing; another choice for

DJ-spun dance music is the swank **2:K:9,** 2009 Eighth St. NW (© **202/ 667-7750**), a Studio 54 for the millennium.

THE BAR SCENE   A spate of fun new bars has popped up in the triangle formed by the intersection of Connecticut Avenue, 18th Street, and M Street, in the Dupont Circle neighborhood. The **Big Hunt,** 1345 Connecticut Ave. NW (between N St. and Dupont Circle; © **202/785-2333**), is a casual and comfy hangout for the 20- to 30-something crowd, with a kind of *Raiders of the Lost Ark* jungle theme. If you like beer and you like choices, head for **Brickskeller,** 1523 22nd St. NW (© **202/293-1885**), which has been around for nearly 40 years and offers about 800 beers from all over the world. **The Rock,** 717 Sixth St. NW, across from the MCI Center (© **202/842-7625;** www.soccer-nation.com), will be sure to have the big game on. Capitol Hill staffers and their bosses, apparently at ease in dive surroundings, have been coming to the **Tune Inn,** 33½ Pennsylvania Ave. SE (© **202/543-2725**), since 1955. For a sophisticated setting, seek out a bar in one of the nicer hotels, like the **Willard,** the **Jefferson,** or the **Four Seasons** (see "Where to Stay," above).

THE GAY & LESBIAN SCENE   Gay nightlife centers around **Dupont Circle,** with at least 10 gay bars within easy walking distance of one another. Younger men pack **J. R.'s Bar and Grill,** 1519 17th St. NW (© **202/328-0090;** www.jrsdc.com). Women of all ages gather and dance at the **Hung Jury,** 1819 H St. NW (© **202/785-8181**), in Foggy Bottom.

6 Side Trips to Mount Vernon & Old Town Alexandria

MOUNT VERNON

Mount Vernon, George Washington's stunning Southern plantation, dates back to a 1674 land grant given to his great-grandfather. The restoration by the Mount Vernon Ladies' Association is an unmarred beauty; many of the furnishings are original pieces acquired by Washington, and the rooms have been repainted in the original colors favored by George and Martha. There are a number of family portraits, and the rooms are appointed as if actually in day-to-day use. After leaving the house, you can tour the kitchen, slave quarters, storeroom, smokehouse, overseer's quarters, coach house, stables, and a 4-acre exhibit area called "George Washington, Pioneer Farmer."

A museum on the property exhibits Washington memorabilia, and details of the restoration are explained in the museum's annex. Explore the grounds to see the wharf, the slave burial ground, the greenhouse and gardens, and the tomb containing George and Martha Washington's sarcophagi. There's no formal tour of the plantation, but attendants stationed throughout the house and grounds provide brief orientations and answer questions.

Admission is $9 for adults, $8.50 for seniors, and $4.50 for children 6 to 11. The house and grounds are open April to August, daily from 8am to 5pm; March, September, and October, daily from 9am to 5pm; and November to February, daily from 9am to 4pm. For more information, call © **703/780-2000** or go to www.mountvernon.org.

GETTING THERE   Mount Vernon is 16 miles south of Washington via the George Washington Memorial Parkway (Va. 400). **Tourmobile** (© **202/554-5100;** www.tourmobile.com) buses depart daily, mid-June through Labor Day only, from Arlington National Cemetery and the Washington Monument. You can also get here with the **Spirit of Washington Cruises** (© **202/554-8000;** www.spiritcruises.com).

OLD TOWN ALEXANDRIA

Founded by a group of Scottish tobacco merchants, the seaport town of Alexandria came into being in 1749. Today, the original 60 acres of lots in the hometown of George Washington and Robert E. Lee are the heart of Old Town, a multimillion-dollar urban-renewal historic district. An abundance of quaint shops, boutiques, art galleries, and restaurants cater to tourists who come in search of a taste of colonial times.

Your first stop should be the **Alexandria Convention and Visitors Association,** located at Ramsay House, 221 King St., at Fairfax Street (℃ **800/ 388-9119** or 703/838-4200; www.funside.com), open daily from 9am to 5pm. Here you can get a free 1-day parking permit. *Note:* Many Alexandria attractions are closed on Monday.

The top attractions include the **Lee-Fendall House Museum,** 614 Oronoco St., at Washington Street (℃ **703/548-1789;** www.leefendallhouse.org), a veritable Lee family museum of furniture, heirlooms, and documents. The **Carlyle House,** 121 N. Fairfax St., between Cameron and King streets (℃ **703/549- 2997;** www.carlylehouse.org), is one of Virginia's most architecturally impressive 18th-century homes. **Christ Church,** 118 N. Washington St., at Cameron Street (℃ **703/549-1450;** www.historicchristchurch.org), has been in continuous use since 1773. The **Torpedo Factory,** 105 N. Union St., between King and Cameron streets on the waterfront (℃ **703/838-4565),** is a block-long, three-story, former torpedo shell-case factory, which now accommodates some 160 professional artists and craftspeople who create and sell their own works on the premises.

For a fun time in a pubby setting, head to the **Union Street Public House,** 121 S. Union St. (℃ **703/548-1785),** where you can choose from burgers, po' boys, oysters, fried calamari, salads, and other simple fare. Or try authentic colonial grub at **Gadsby's Tavern,** 138 N. Royal St., at Cameron Street (℃ **703/548-1288).**

GETTING THERE   Old Town Alexandria is about 8 miles south of Washington. Take the George Washington Memorial Parkway south, which becomes Washington Street in Old Town Alexandria. Washington Street intersects with King Street, Alexandria's main thoroughfare. For an easier way to make the trip, take the **Metro** to King Street. From the King Street station, catch an eastbound AT2, AT5, or AT7 blue-and-gold **DASH bus** (℃ 703/370-DASH), marked either "Old Town" or "Braddock Metro," which will take you up King Street. Ask to be dropped at the corner of Fairfax and King streets, which will put you right across the street from Ramsay House, the visitor center.

5

The Mid-Atlantic

Part of the thrill of visiting the Mid-Atlantic states is following in the footsteps of George Washington, Thomas Jefferson, Abraham Lincoln, Robert E. Lee, and many others who cut wide paths through American history.

In Philadelphia, you can see where the Founding Fathers crafted the U.S. Constitution. In Baltimore, you can dine on Chesapeake Bay crabs near where Francis Scott Key wrote the words to "The Star-Spangled Banner." Williamsburg, Jamestown, and Yorktown recapture America's earliest beginnings, and the battlefields at Fredericksburg and Gettysburg vividly recall the Civil War.

Today Philadelphia, Baltimore, and Washington are part of the great East Coast megalopolis running south from Boston, but you can easily escape to broad bays, wide rivers, rolling piedmont, gentle mountains, and quaint small towns that make this region lovely and charming. Up in the mountains, the Shenandoah National Park is bisected by the Skyline Drive, one of America's most scenic routes, overlooking the lovely Shenandoah Valley.

See chapter 4 for complete coverage of Washington, D.C.

1 Philadelphia

It was in Philadelphia that the United States declared its independence on July 4, 1776, and where the Founding Fathers managed the Revolutionary War, wrote the U.S. Constitution, and governed the country until Washington, D.C., was built. Today, the Liberty Bell that proclaimed America's freedom from Great Britain, Independence Hall in which it all took place, and dozens of other historic treasures are preserved here in the largest colonial district in the country, with spanking-new interpretive centers coming in 2003.

But you'll find a lot more than history and old buildings in Philadelphia. Its smart Center City core is a stroller's paradise and a working urban environment, with restored Georgian and Federal structures integrated with sleek shops and fine restaurants. With Broad Street south of City Hall reconstituted as a first-class "Avenue of the Arts," and a waterfront and sports stadium complex in major development, it's a city filled with art, crafts, and music for every taste.

ESSENTIALS

GETTING THERE   By Plane   Philadelphia International Airport (© 215/ 937-6800; www.phl.org) is at the southwest corner of the city. For up-to-the-minute information on arrival and departure times and gate assignments, call © 800/PHL-GATE. Twelve new gates at Terminal A facilitate international flights. The areas with the most amenities are between Terminals B and C and between Terminals D and E. Go to Terminal B to catch taxis, buses, and hotel limousines.

A **taxi** from the airport to Center City takes about 25 minutes and costs a flat rate of $20 plus tip.

Airport limousine and shuttle service is provided by **Philadelphia Airport Shuttle** (© 215/333-1441); **Lady Liberty** (© 215/222-8888); or **Deluxe**

Limo (© 215/463-8787). All charge around $12 from the airport to Center City, $50 to Valley Forge, and $105 to Atlantic City.

A **high-speed rail link** (R1) with direct service between the airport and Center City runs daily every 30 minutes from 5:25am to 11:25pm. Trains follow the loop of a raised pedestrian bridge and stop in front of every terminal. Trains to the airport depart from Market East (and a Convention Center connection), Suburban Station at 16th Street, and 30th Street Station. The 30-minute trip costs $5.50 for adults; children's fares are $1.50 weekdays and $1 weekends; and the family fare is $16.

By Train   Amtrak (© 800/USA-RAIL; www.amtrak.com) serves Philadelphia's 30th Street Station, about 15 blocks from City Hall. There's frequent service from New York (trip time: 1½ hr.), Washington (1¾–2 hr.), and Boston (5½–7 hr.).

SEPTA commuter trains (© 215/580-7800; www.septa.org) connect 30th Street Station and several Center City stations to Trenton, New Jersey; Newark, Delaware; and airport terminals. **New Jersey Transit** (© 215/569-3752) operates commuter trains from New York and Newark to Trenton, where you can switch across the platform to the Philadelphia-bound SEPTA train.

By Car   Philadelphia is some 300 miles (6 or so hr.) from Boston, and 100 miles (2 hr.) from New York City. If you think of Center City as a rectangle, **I-95** whizzes by its bottom and right sides; **I-276,** the Pennsylvania Turnpike, is the top edge; and **I-76** splits off and snakes along the Schuylkill River along the left side into town. **I-676** traverses Center City under Vine Street, connecting I-76 to adjacent Camden, New Jersey, via the Ben Franklin Bridge ($3 inbound only) over the Delaware. The "Blue Route" of **I-476** forms a left edge for the suburbs, about 15 miles west of town, connecting I-276 and I-76 at its northern end with I-95 to the south.

VISITOR INFORMATION   The spanking-new **Independence Visitor Center,** 6th and Market streets, Philadelphia, PA 19106 (© 800/537-7676 or 215/965-7676; www.independencevisitorcenter.com), pulls together information on over 500 attractions in the city and region, sited at the heart of the historical Philadelphia. It also offers publications and wonderful orientation exhibitions, as well as a number of package tours combining special museum exhibitions, concerts, or sporting events with discount hotel prices, free city transit passes, and Amtrak discounts. Many bus tours, historic trolley rides, and walking tours begin here. The center is open from 8:30am to 5pm daily.

GETTING AROUND   Since Philadelphia is so pedestrian-friendly, we advise leaving your car in a garage while you explore. Many hotels offer free or reduced-rate parking to guests.

SEPTA (© 215/580-7800) operates a complicated and extensive network of trolleys, buses, commuter trains, and subways. Fares for any SEPTA route are $2 cash or $1.30 by token, plus 60¢ extra for a transfer; exact change or tokens are required. A five-pack costs $5.75; a 10-pack, $12. A $5.50 DayPass is good for buses, subways, and one ride on the Airport loop; a $19 weekly TransPass is good from Monday to the following Sunday.

Two **subway** lines crisscross the city, intersecting under City Hall. The Broad Street line connects directly to sporting events in the south. The Market–Frankford line stops at seven popular destinations and stretches to the west and northeast. In addition, the Subway–Surface line connects City Hall and 30th Street Station, stopping at 19th and 22nd streets along the way. West of the Amtrak station it branches out, moving aboveground to the north and south.

Purple **PHLASH** buses (℗ 215/474-5274; www.phillyphlash.com) designed for tourists link Independence Park sites, the Delaware River waterfront, the Convention Center, Rittenhouse Square shopping, the cultural institutions at Logan Circle, and now the Museum of Art and the zoo to the northwest. The total loop takes 50 minutes and makes 30 stops. A one-time pass is $2; the all-day unlimited-ride pass is $4 per person or $10 per family. The vans run every 10 to 15 minutes from 10am to midnight in summer (until 6pm off season).

The **PATCO** commuter rail line (℗ 215/922-4600; www.drpa.org) begins at Walnut and Locust streets around Broad Street, connects with rapid transit at 8th and Market, and crosses the Ben Franklin Bridge to Camden, where you can transfer to New Jersey Transit's Aqualink Shuttle to the aquarium.

The "Main Line," the posh suburbs north and west of the city, is served by one of the best **commuter rail** networks in America. From **Suburban Station,** at 16th Street and John F. Kennedy Boulevard, or **Reading Terminal,** at 12th and Market streets, you can reach Chestnut Hill, an enclave of fine shops; the Barnes Foundation art collection in Merion; and colleges in Bryn Mawr, Haverford, Swarthmore, and Villanova. One-way fares for all destinations are $3 to $7; you can buy tickets at station counters or vending machines.

Philadelphia has 1,400 licensed cabs; try **Olde City Taxi** (℗ 215/338-0838) or **Quaker City** (℗ 215/728-8000). Fares are $1.80 for the first ½ mile and 30¢ for each additional ½ mile or minute of the motor running.

FAST FACTS Call the **Philadelphia County Medical Society** (℗ 215/563-5343) for a doctor referral, or ℗ 215/925-6050 in a dental emergency. Major hospitals include **Children's Hospital,** 34th Street and Civic Center Boulevard and now doubling its size with a new building (℗ 215/590-1000); **University of Pennsylvania Hospital,** 3400 Spruce St. (℗ 215/662-4000); and **Thomas Jefferson,** 11th and Walnut streets (℗ 215/955-6000; SEPTA: 11th St.).

There are 24-hour pharmacies at the **CVS** at 1826 Chestnut St., at the corner of 19th Street (℗ 215/972-0909 or 215/972-1401; SEPTA: 19th St.) and at 10th and Reed streets (℗ 215/465-2130) in South Philadelphia.

Philadelphia is generally safe if you concentrate on major tourist destinations, but stay alert, be aware of your immediate surroundings, and keep a close eye on your possessions. Be especially careful at night and around college campuses in West Philadelphia.

There is a 7% **sales tax** on general sales and restaurant meals, but not on clothing. Lodging charges incur a 13% tax, 7% of which is state plus 6% city surcharge.

SPECIAL EVENTS & FESTIVALS The **Mummer's Parade** (℗ 215/336-3050), held on New Year's Day or the following Saturday in case of bad weather, attracts 15,000 spangled strutters marching with feathers and banjos. You can line up on Market Street between City Hall and Independence Hall on the day, or catch previews all December between 6pm and 7:45pm at various Center City squares.

The **Philadelphia Flower Show** is the largest and most prestigious indoor exhibition of its kind. Acres of gardens and rustic settings occupy the Convention Center in late February or early March. The Pennsylvania Horticultural Society, 100 N. 20th St. (℗ 215/988-8800; www.philaflowershow.com), sells tickets in advance.

The **Book and the Cook Festival** (℗ 215/683-2065), usually the third week in March, combines the love of reading and eating. Eminent food critics, cookbook authors, and restaurateurs plan dream meals with participating restaurants; food samplings and wine and beer tastings are held all over town. The list of participating restaurants is published in January, and many get booked quickly.

The 10 days before July 4th, the whole town turns out for the **Sunoco Welcome America!** festival (© **215/636-1666;** www.americasbirthday.com) to celebrate America's birthday. Among dozens of free events, there's fireworks on the Delaware River or the Phillies game the night of the 3rd, and the 4th brings special ceremonies to Independence Square, including a reading of the Declaration of Independence, and fireworks to conclude an evening parade up the Parkway.

WHAT TO SEE & DO

The city's top attraction is **Independence National Historical Park** (SEPTA: 5th St.), America's most historic square mile, centered around Independence Hall on Chestnut Street between 5th and 6th streets. The Declaration of Independence was conceived here in 1776, the U.S. Constitution was written here in 1787, and Philadelphia served as the nation's capital for 10 years during the construction of the new capital in Washington, D.C. The park is composed of 40 buildings on 45 acres of Center City real estate, including original sites such as **Independence Hall;** reconstructions such as **City Tavern** and **Declaration House;** and contemporary structures like the glass pavilion housing the **Liberty Bell** and **Franklin Court.** Hours for all buildings are from 9am to 5pm, but grounds are never closed. With security concerns, from 2002 all visitors will need free timed tickets to Independence Hall.

Make your first stop the **Independence Visitor Center,** 6th and Market streets (© **800/537-7676** or 215/965-7676), where you can pick up a map of the area; get tickets to tour Independence Hall; and reserve for the frequent ranger-led tours of the Second Bank of the United States, Bishop White House, and Todd House ($2).

Barnes Foundation   If you're an art buff, the magnificent Barnes Foundation will stun you. Albert Barnes crammed his French provincial mansion with more than 1,000 masterpieces—180 Renoirs, 69 Cézannes, innumerable Impressionists and post-Impressionists, and a generous sampling of European art from the Italian primitives onward. Local zoning restricts the museum to only 500 visitors per week, so reserve well in advance. 300 N. Latches Lane, Merion Station. © **610/667-0290.** www.barnesfoundation.org. Admission $5; audio tour $7. On-site parking $10. Reserve at least a month in advance by calling © 610/664-7917. Wed–Fri 9:30am–5pm July–Aug only; Fri–Sun 9:30am–5pm all other months. SEPTA: R5 (Paoli local train) to Merion; walk up Merion Ave. and turn left onto Latches Lane. Bus: 44 to Old Lancaster Rd. and Latches Lane. Car: I-76 (Schuylkill Expressway) west to City Line Ave., then south on City Line 1½ miles to Old Lancaster Rd. Turn right onto Old Lancaster, continue 4 blocks, and turn left onto Latches Lane.

Betsy Ross House   Elizabeth (Betsy) Ross was a Quaker needlewoman; nobody is sure if she did the original American flag of 13 stars set in a field of 13 stripes, but she was commissioned to sew ships' flags for the Revolutionary War fleet. The house takes only a minute or two to walk through; it's a great picture of average colonial life, from the low ceilings to the cellar kitchen and the model working areas for upholstering, making musket balls, and the like. 239 Arch St. © **215/627-5343.** Suggested contribution $2 adults, $1 children. Memorial Day to Labor Day daily 10am–5pm; closed Mon in off season. SEPTA: 2nd St. Bus: 5, 17, 33, 48, or PHLASH.

Christ Church   This is the most beautiful colonial building (1727–54) north of Market Street; its spire gleams white and can be seen from anywhere in the

Philadelphia

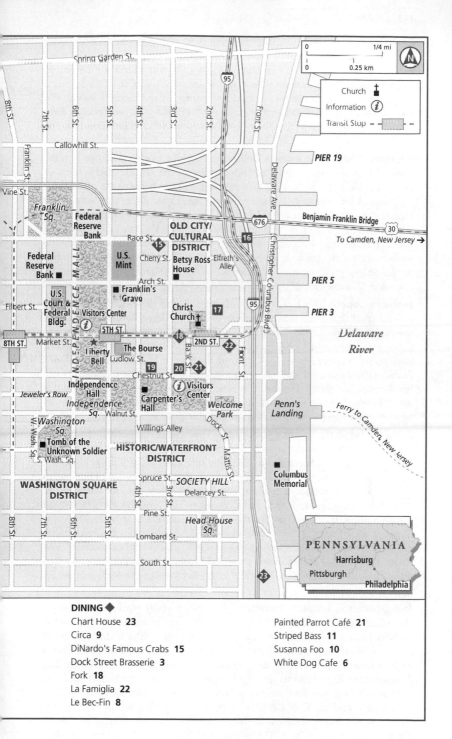

DINING ◆

Chart House **23**
Circa **9**
DiNardo's Famous Crabs **15**
Dock Street Brasserie **3**
Fork **18**
La Famiglia **22**
Le Bec-Fin **8**

Painted Parrot Café **21**
Striped Bass **11**
Susanna Foo **10**
White Dog Cafe **6**

neighborhood. The interior spans one large arch, with galleries above the sides as demanded by the Anglican church. Behind the altar, the massive Palladian window was the wonder of worshipers and probably the model for the one in Independence Hall. Seating is by pew—Washington's seat is marked with a plaque—and it's impossible to ignore the history in the church's stones and memorials. 2nd St., a half block north of Market St. ☎ 215/922-1695. Free admission; donations welcome. Mon–Sat 9am–5pm; Sun 1–5pm; Sun services at 9 and 11am. Closed Jan–Feb. SEPTA: 2nd St. Bus: 5, 17, 33, 48, or PHLASH.

Elfreth's Alley   The modern Benjamin Franklin Bridge shadows Elfreth's Alley, the oldest continuously inhabited street in the United States. Most of colonial Philadelphia looked like this: cobblestone lanes between the major thoroughfares, small two-story homes, and pent eaves over doors and windows, a local trademark. Jews, blacks, Welsh, and Germans made this a miniature melting pot in the 18th and 19th centuries. Number 126, the 1755 **Mantua Maker's House** (cape maker), now serves as a museum and is the only house open to the public. 2nd St., between Arch and Race sts. ☎ 215/574-0560. Street is public; Mantua Maker's House suggested admission $2 adults, $1 children, $5 families. Tues–Sat 10am–4pm; Sun noon–4pm. SEPTA: 2nd St. Bus: 5, 48, or PHLASH.

Franklin Court   This imaginative, informative, and downright fun museum was designed under and around the site of Ben Franklin's home and is run by the National Park Service. The exhibits reflect Franklin's wide interests as scientist, inventor, statesman, printer, politician, and diplomat. Enter through arched passages from either Market or Chestnut streets; the Market entrance adjoins Franklin's reconstructed and fully operational post office, where employees still hand-stamp the marks. Chestnut St., between 3rd and 4th sts., with another entrance at 316–318 Market St. Free admission, including the post office and postal museum. Daily, fall–winter 10am–5pm, summer 10am–6pm, spring 9am–5pm. SEPTA: 5th St.

Franklin Institute Science Museum   This science museum is thoroughly imaginative and shows the influence of science on our lives. The complex actually has four parts: a memorial to Ben Franklin; exhibitions such as a gigantic walk-through heart, ship models, and antique airplanes; a Futures Center with eight permanent interactive exhibits; and an imaginative outdoor science park. The texts throughout are witty and disarming. The museum also offers good dining options. It's a great spot for those traveling with kids. Logan Sq., 20th St. and Benjamin Franklin Pkwy. ☎ 215/448-1200. www.fi.edu. Basic admission to exhibitions and Mandell Center $12 adults, $9 children; with additional charge for admission to Planetarium and IMAX Theater $16 adults, $13 children. Science Center daily 9:30am–5pm; Mandell Center Sun–Thurs 9:30am–5pm, Fri–Sat 9:30am–9pm; First Union Science Park May–Oct daily 10am–3pm. Bus: 33, or PHLASH.

Independence Seaport Museum   This user-friendly maritime museum is the star of the city's waterfront. It's beautifully laid out, blending a first-class maritime collection with interactive exhibits for a trip through time that engages all ages. The **Workshop on the Water** lets you watch classes and amateurs undertake traditional wooden boat building and restoration throughout the year. The **Historic Ship Zone** includes the brig *Niagara*, built during the War of 1812; the USS *Becuna*, a guppy-sized submarine which served in Admiral Halsey's South Pacific fleet; and the USS *Olympia*, Admiral Dewey's flagship in the Spanish-American War. Across the river, the battleship *New Jersey* has recently berthed by the aquarium. Penn's Landing at 211 S. Columbus Blvd. ☎ 215/925-5439. Admission $8 adults, $6.50 seniors, $4 children. Combined admission to adjacent Historic Ship Zone, the RiverLink Ferry, and the New Jersey State Aquarium at Camden, $22 adults, $21 seniors, $16 children 3–11; this will take at least 5 hr. Daily 10am–5pm except major holidays. SEPTA. 2nd St. Bus: 17, 21, 33, or PHLASH.

Liberty Bell America's symbol of independence was commissioned in 1751 and hung in Independence Hall to "proclaim liberty throughout the land" as the Declaration of Independence was read aloud to the citizens. It last tolled to celebrate Washington's birthday in 1846. Since 1976, it has been housed in the glass Liberty Bell Pavilion. A new complex with more interpretation and background is scheduled to open in 2003 on the same block of the park mall. Chestnut St., between 5th and 6th sts. Free admission. Summer daily 9am–8pm; rest of year daily 9am–5pm. SEPTA: 5th St.

Penn's Landing Philadelphia started out as a major freshwater port of the Delaware River valley, and tourism is increasingly nudging it back to the water after 50 years of neglect. A pleasantly spacious waterfront park now includes the Independence Seaport Museum (see above), historic ships, performance and park areas, a skating rink, restaurants, cruise facilities, and a marina. A 740,000-square-foot family entertainment center will definitely include the fine Please Touch Museum and a Hyatt Regency Hotel, but other developments such as a bookstore, 18-screen megaplex, and aerial tram across the Delaware are still uncertain. Delaware River waterfront between Market and South sts. ℂ 215/629-3200. Open-air esplanade never restricted; several sites have separate admissions and hours. SEPTA: 2nd St. Bus: 17, 21, 33, or PHLASH. Car. From I-95 use the Columbus Blvd.–Washington St. Exit (16) and turn left onto Columbus Blvd; from I-76, take I-676 across Center City to I-95 south.

Philadelphia Museum of Art The third-largest art museum in the country is a resplendent Greco-Roman temple on a hill. It houses one of the finest groupings of art objects in the country, strong in American arts and crafts and in most aspects of classical European art. Upstairs is a chronological sweep in dozens of galleries of European arts from medieval times through about 1900. The 19th- and 20th century galleries highlight Cézanne's *Bathers* and Marcel Duchamp's *Nude Descending a Staircase*. There are also many works by Philadelphia's Thomas Eakins, which evoke the spirit of the city in watercolors and oil portraits. The museum has excellent dining facilities. 26th St. and Ben Franklin Pkwy. ℂ 215/763-8100, or 215/684-7500 for 24-hr. information. www.philamuseum.org. Admission $10 adults; $7 students, seniors, and children 13–18; free for children under 13; pay-what-you-wish Sun 10am–1pm. Tues–Sun 10am–5pm; Wed and Fri evening hours to 8:45pm with music, talks, movies, and socializing. Bus: 7, 32, 38, 43, 48, or PHLASH. Adjacent parking $5 for up to 6 hr.

Philadelphia Zoological Gardens The Philadelphia Zoo, opened in 1874, was the nation's first and remains a leader, with 1,500-plus animals (including rare white lions), a renovated Reptile House, a restored Primate House, a new Jungle Bird Walk, and a spectacular children's exhibit, the Treehouse ($1), which lets kids explore six larger-than-life habitats. 34th St. and Girard Ave. ℂ 215/243-1100. Admission $13 adults; $10 seniors and children 2–11; free for children under 2. Parking $6. Daily 9:30am–5pm Feb–Nov; 11am–4pm Dec–Jan. Bus: 76 or PHLASH.

ORGANIZED TOURS

American Trolley Tours (ℂ 215/333-2119) operates double-decker buses decked out like trolleys. Guided tours of historic areas ($15 adults and seniors, $5 kids 12 and under) leave from the Liberty Bell Pavilion at 5th and Market streets and stop at many hotels at 30-minute intervals.

From May to October, **Centipede Tours,** 1315 Walnut St. (ℂ 215/735-3123), leads Saturday-evening candlelit strolls of the historic area; costumed guides leave from Welcome Park at Second and Walnut streets at 6:30pm. Tours of Society Hill cost $5 per person. Call for reservations or customized tours.

To get the feel of Philadelphia as it was, try a narrated horse-drawn carriage ride. Operated daily by the **76 Carriage Co.** (© **215/923-8516**), tours begin at 5th and Chestnut streets in front of Independence Hall from 10am to 5pm, with later hours in summer at 2nd and South streets. Reservations aren't necessary.

SHOPPING

The best places to look for high fashion and international wares are the specialty shops around **Liberty Place** and **Rittenhouse Square.** The **Shops at Liberty Place,** 1625 Chestnut St., between 16th and 17th streets (© **215/851-9055**), offers more than 60 quality stores and stalls in a handsome, 60-story tower. The once-funky area on **South Street,** just south of Society Hill, has turned into big business. Because restaurants and nightlife now line South Street from Front to 8th streets, many of the 180 stores here are open well into the evening and offer goods ranging from the gentrified to the somewhat grotesque.

Certain neighborhoods are known for specific types of shopping. **Pine Street** from 9th to 12th Street is "Antiques Row," while **Sansom Street** from 7th to 9th Street is "Jeweler's Row." **Old City,** north of the historic park, and **Manayunk,** the northwestern corner of the city, are known for contemporary crafts. The latter is the city's hippest neighborhood.

Reading Terminal Market, 12th and Arch streets (© **215/922-2317**), is a 110-year-old landmark with a gastronomic bazaar of restaurants and greengrocers, snack shops, bakeries, butchers, fish markets, and more. You can still see the Amish in the big city on their market days (Wed and Sat), and you can buy sticky buns at **Beiler's Bakery,** soft pretzels at **Fisher's,** and individual egg custards and chicken potpies at **The Dutch Eating Place.** Closed Sunday.

While touring South Street or South Philadelphia, stop by the **Italian Market,** around 9th Street between Christian and Wharton streets. It feels straight out of another era, with pushcarts and open stalls selling fresh produce, cheese, pasta, and other culinary delights. Snack on fried dough or pastries as you browse.

WHERE TO STAY

Like many other cities, Philadelphia is struggling to absorb a boom in hotel rooms—beginning in January 1999, 5,200 new hotel beds were added to Center City to host the 2000 Republican National Convention and other large meetings. New construction has slowed, and occupancy rates for Center City's total of 12,700 rooms fell in 2001 and are still struggling to rebound—which means that competition is leading many hotels to offer weekend packages and discounts; be sure to inquire. Older hotels in the Rittenhouse Square area often have larger, more individualized spaces. Between City Hall and the Philadelphia Museum of Art, you'll find sleek 1980s hotels, and rehabbed and smaller properties sprouting near the Convention Center and historic Society Hill. Outside Center City, West Philadelphia and the airport area offer plenty of rooms at slightly cheaper rates. A state tax of 7% plus a city surcharge of 5% will be added to your lodging bill.

The **Independence Visitor Center,** 6th and Market streets (© **800/537-7676** or 215/965-7676) can help with any questions. For information on B&Bs, try **A Bed & Breakfast Connection/Bed & Breakfast of Philadelphia** (© **800/448-3619** or 610/687-3565; fax 610/995-9524; www.bnbphiladelphia.com).

Many of the city's more affordable options are chain hotels, including the **Best Western Independence Park Inn,** 235 Chestnut St. (© **800/528-1234** or

215/922-4443; www.bestwestern.com); the **Comfort Inn Downtown/Historic Area,** 100 N. Columbus Blvd. (© **800/220-5150** or 215/627-7900; www. comfortinn.com); and the **Clarion Suites Convention Center,** 1010 Race St. (© **800/252-7466** or 215/922-1730; www.comfortinn.com).

Hotel options near the airport include the **Sheraton Philadelphia Airport,** 4101 Island Ave. (© **800/325-3535** or 215/365-6600; www.sheraton.com); the **Radisson Hotel Philadelphia Airport,** 500 Stevens Dr. (© **800/333-3333** or 610/521-5900; www.radisson.com); and the **Comfort Inn Airport,** 53 Industrial Hwy., Essington (© **800/228-5150** or 610/521-9800; www.comfortinn.com).

Buttonwood Square Hotel   The amenities, the location, and the great views offered by this hotel—formerly the Korman Suites Hotel—make this an excellent value; the weekend packages make it an outstanding one. Look for the bright neon swoosh on the 28-story tower wall slightly to the northeast of the beaten track, connected by a marble-and-mahogany lobby and a glass-enclosed corridor to a restaurant and lush Japanese sculpture garden and pool. The standard rooms are unbelievably spacious, with a microwave and coffeemaker. The suites add a full kitchen with a dishwasher and stove. Each living area has a full dining table, TV, couch, and three closets, and bathrooms include a stacked washer/dryer. A complimentary shuttle runs hourly through Center City to Independence Park. 2001 Hamilton St. (just off the Pkwy.), Philadelphia, PA 19130. © 888/ 456-7626 or 215/569-7000. Fax 215/469 0130. www.korman i.com. 170 units. $179 efficiency; $199 2-bedroom plus kitchen; $239 1-bedroom suite with connecting den. Other options available for stays of 2 weeks or more. Children under 18 stay free in parents' room. AE, MC, V. Free covered parking. Bus: 33 or 76. **Amenities:** Restaurant; pool (indoor); spa; health club; 2 tennis courts, platform tennis court.

Embassy Suites Center City   This big 28-story cylinder of marble and glass, designed to house luxury apartments, looks dated, but the all-suite format actually works quite well. Fresh-air fans will enjoy the sliding doors that open up onto small balconies with great Parkway views. Kitchenettes come with microwave, fridge, and coffeemaker; dishes and silverware are provided on request. Patience is required—while the rooms are a treat, the elevators and lobby weren't built to handle hotel-style volume. Weekend packages make this hotel very affordable. 1776 Benjamin Franklin Pkwy. at Logan Sq., Philadelphia, PA 19103. © 800/362-2779 or 215/ 561-1776. Fax 215/561-5930. www.embassy-suites.com. 288 units. $174 suite. Children under 18 stay free in parents' room. Rates include full breakfast and lobby social hr. AE, DC, DISC, MC, V. Valet parking $20. Bus: 33. **Amenities:** Restaurant.

Four Seasons Hotel   This eight-story curlicue is one of the two best hotels in Philadelphia, with a refined but understated luxury that's perfect for business during the week or for romantic weekend getaways. The elegant rooms, mixing Federal-style furniture with rich Victorian colors, have windows that open or private verandas boasting marvelous views of Logan Circle or the interior courtyard. The Fountain, under newly promoted head chef Martin Hamann, is neck-and-neck with Le Bec Fin as Philadelphia's best restaurant, usually winning top honors for its unstuffy service and a fabulous Sunday brunch. Packages that offer tickets to ongoing museum exhibitions or Kimmel Center concerts, or discounted weekend rates can make it surprisingly affordable. One Logan Sq., Philadelphia, PA 19103. © 800/ 332-3442 or 215/963-1500. Fax 215/963-9506. www.fourseasons.com. 364 units. From $310 double; from $400 suite. Weekend rates from $220 available. Children under 18 stay free in parents' room. AE, DC, MC, V. Self-parking $20, valet parking $25. Bus: 33. **Amenities:** Restaurants (3); pool (indoor); spa; health club; pets permitted.

Hawthorn Suites Philadelphia at the Convention Center   Opened in summer 1998, the Hawthorn Suites is directly adjacent to the Convention Center, and weekend packages make it an excellent family choice. The second floor of the rehabbed factory building houses a fitness center and dining area, while the 14 floors above contain studio and one-bedroom suites, each with an efficiency or full kitchen, microwave, fridge, and coffeemaker. Another plus: free local phone calls. 1100 Vine St., Philadelphia, PA 19107. © 800/527-1133 or 215/829-8300. Fax 215/829-8104. www.hawthorn.com. 294 units. From $159 double. Children under 18 stay free in parents' room. Rates include full buffet breakfast and complimentary social hour Mon–Thurs. Weekend packages available. AE, DC, DISC, MC, V. Nearby self-parking $12, valet parking $19. SEPTA: Race-Vine or Chinatown. **Amenities:** Pets allowed for $40 additional charge.

Omni Hotel at Independence Park   This polished hotel has a terrific location in the middle of Independence National Historical Park. All units have been renovated since 2001 and have park views; watch horse-drawn carriages clip-clopping by. The classic lobby features current newspapers, huge vases of flowers, and a bar with piano or jazz trio nightly. Rooms are cheery, and equipped with opulent marble bathrooms and state-of-the-art conveniences; VCRs are available on request. The Azalea is one of Philadelphia's top restaurants. You can catch an after-dinner flick at the Ritz five-movie theater tucked into the hotel's back corner. 401 Chestnut St., Philadelphia, PA 19106. © 800/843-6664 or 215/925-0000. Fax 215/931-1263. www.omnihotels.com. 150 units. $179–$209 double; $375–$750 suite. Children under 10 stay free in parents' room. Weekend rates available. AE, DC, DISC, MC, V. Self-parking $15, valet parking $21. SEPTA: 5th St. **Amenities:** Restaurant; pool (indoor); spa; health club.

Penn's View Hotel   Tucked behind the Market Street ramp to I-95 in a renovated 1856 hardware store, this small, exquisite inn exudes a European flair. It was developed by the Sena family, who run La Famiglia—one of the city's best Italian restaurants (see "Where to Dine," below)—a couple of blocks away. The decor is floral and rich; the main concern is traffic noise, but rooms are well insulated. Ristorante Panorama is always bubbly, offering excellent contemporary Italian cuisine at moderate prices, and the connected world-class wine bar offers 120 different wines by the glass. Front and Market sts., Philadelphia, PA 19106. © 800/331-7634 or 215/922-7600. Fax 215/922-7642. www.pennsviewhotel.com. 52 units. $165 double. Rates include deluxe continental breakfast. Weekend rates available; a package at $275 includes 2 nights, champagne upon arrival, and Panorama restaurant voucher for $70. Reservations recommended. AE, MC, V. Parking $16 at adjacent lot. SEPTA: 2nd St. **Amenities:** Restaurant.

Philadelphia Marriott and Philadelphia Downtown Courtyard Marriott   The biggest hotel in Pennsylvania, linked by an elevated covered walkway to the Reading Terminal Shed of the Convention Center, got even bigger in 1999 when Marriott converted the historic City Hall Annex across 13th Street into a 498-room Courtyard by Marriott, and added an additional 210 oversize rooms in the renovated Headhouse Terminal across the skyway. Setbacks and terraces provide plenty of natural light and views from the rooms in floors 6 to 23, and the courtyard property has sensitively restored bronze and copper details throughout. Although tastefully outfitted, with spacious bathrooms, the rooms are slightly less elegant than those at the top hotels. Service is impeccable, thanks to the well-trained, knowledgeable staff. 1201 Market St. (at 12th St.) and 21 N. Juniper St., Philadelphia, PA 19107. © 800/228-9290 or 215/625-2900. Fax 215/625-6000. www.marriott.com/marriott/phldt. Marriott: 1,410 units. $245 double; $260–$275 concierge-level rooms. Courtyard by Marriott: 498 units. $155–$185 double. Weekend rates available. AE, DC, DISC, MC, V. Valet parking $23. SEPTA: Direct internal connection to 11th St.-Market E, or 13th St **Amenities:** Restaurants (4); pool (2; 1 in each hotel) spa (Marriott only); health club.

Rittenhouse Hotel Among Philadelphia's luxury hotels, the Rittenhouse has the fewest and largest rooms, the most satisfying views, and the most home-grown Philadelphia feel. Built in 1989, it's a jagged concrete-and-glass high-rise off the western edge of Philadelphia's most distinguished public square. The lobby is truly magnificent, with inlaid marble floors and frosted-glass chande-liers. Rooms have bay windows, reinforced walls, and VCRs. And everything you need for a wonderful vacation is on-premises: amenities include a world-class French restaurant, where Jean-Marie Lacroix jumped from the Four Seasons in 2001; an outpost of the renowned Smith & Wollensky steakhouses; and the Adolf Biecker spa and salon. 210 W. Rittenhouse Sq., Philadelphia, PA 19103. ℂ **800/635-1042** or 215/546-9000. Fax 215/732-3364. www.rittenhousehotel.com. 98 units. Doubles from $310. Special rates and packages from $200 including health club, dinners, and other extras usually available. AE, DC, MC, V. Valet parking $23. SEPTA: 19th St. **Amenities:** Restaurants (2); pool (indoor); spa; health club.

Wyndham Franklin Plaza Hotel The recently revamped Wyndham has been a convenient meeting center and urban resort since 1980; rooms were just renovated to cater more to individual travelers, and now offer full-length mir-rors, Bath & Body Works toiletries, and hair dryers. The complex's lobby, lounge, and two restaurants are beautifully integrated under a dramatic 70-foot glass roof. Request a west view above the 19th floor for an unobstructed peek at the Parkway, but be forewarned that the cathedral bells below ring at 7am daily. A fee of $10 gets you all-day access to racquetball, squash, outdoor handball, and tennis. 17th and Race sts., Philadelphia, PA 19103. ℂ **800/882-4200** or 215/448-2000. Fax 215/448-2864. www.wyndham.com. 758 units. $209 double. Children 18 and under stay free in parents' room. Excellent weekend rates available. AE, DC, MC, V. Self-parking $16, valet parking $19. SEPTA: Race-Vine. Bus: 33 or 76. **Amenities:** Restaurants (2); pool (indoor); spa; health club; tennis courts (2).

WHERE TO DINE

In addition to the choices below, you might want to head to South Philly for its numerous southern and central Italian restaurants. Try **The Saloon,** 750 S. 7th St. (ℂ **215/627-1811**), a dignified, elegant place; or the fourth-generation **Ralph's,** 760 S. 9th St. (ℂ **215/627-6011**).

Chart House STEAK/SEAFOOD The busiest restaurant in town has to be the Chart House, right on the Delaware River and back up after a rough patch in the late '90s. Expect a spirited crowd and frequent birthday celebrations, bal-anced out by reasonably priced dinners, with soup, fresh bread, and an unlim-ited salad bar included, and the signature mud pie dessert. All seats have spectacular views, and the service will make you wish you'd had camp counselors as enthusiastic. 555 S. Columbus Blvd. (formerly Delaware Ave.) at Penn's Landing. ℂ **215/625-8383.** Reservations recommended. Main courses $16–$36; Sun brunch $8.95–$14. AE, DC, MC, V. Mon–Thurs 5–10pm; Fri 5–11pm; Sat 4pm–midnight; Sun 11am–10pm. SEPTA: 2nd St. Bus: 17, 21, 33, 76, or PHLASH.

Circa AMERICAN/ECLECTIC This former beaux-arts bank building is now one of Philadelphia's hottest spots. Offering great food on a great restaurant block, it combines dinner with a sophisticated dance club. The strong, flavorful cuisine might include wood-grilled venison, duck breast with black cherries, or roast salmon osso buco. Friday and Saturday nights after 11pm (except in summer), the ground floor and mezzanine turn into a club with a jammed dance floor. 1518 Walnut St. © 215/545-6800. Reservations recommended. Main courses $17–$29. AE, DC, MC, V. Tues–Fri 11:30am–2:30pm; Mon–Thurs 5–10pm; Fri–Sat 5–11pm; Sun 4–9pm. SEPTA: Walnut–Locust.

DiNardo's Famous Crabs SEAFOOD   This is the best moderately priced spot in the area around the Betsy Ross House and Elfreth's Alley. DiNardo's is notable for both its site, which dates back to the Revolutionary War, and its reasonable prices. Prime catches from the Gulf of Mexico are flown in daily; experienced hands then season the crabs with the house blend of 24 spices and steam them to perfection. If you're not in a crabby mood, other seafood choices abound. 312 Race St. © 215/925-5115. Reservations required for 6 or more. Crabs $3 each; other main courses $14–$24. AE, DC, MC, V. Mon–Thurs 11am–10pm; Fri–Sat 5–11pm; Sun 3–9pm. SEPTA: 5th St.

Dock Street Brasserie FRENCH BISTRO   This relaxed, contemporary and popular restaurant has moved away from its original emphasis on an on-premises microbrewery, toward a more continental ambience and spacious banquettes. The French brasserie fare ranges from Alsatian choucroute to fisherman's cassoulet to codfish with caramelized onions and red butter sauce. Try the crab-cake sandwich for lunch. There's live jazz on Friday and Saturday nights in summer; no cover charge. 2 Logan Sq. (corner of 18th and Cherry sts.). © 215/496-0413. Reservations recommended. Main courses $15–$20; lunch $7–$20. AE, DC, DISC, MC, V. Mon–Sat 11:30am–midnight; Sun 11:30am–10pm. Bus: 33.

Fork CONTINENTAL   Fork is possibly the best example in Old City of an affordable, stylish bistro. Since it seats only 68 and has earned rave reviews, make sure to reserve a table in advance. The restaurant features a hip circular bar, open rear kitchen, and glorious lighting. Most of the ingredients come from organic farms and Amish purveyors; the menu changes daily. Signature dishes are the roasted sea bass with a dill pine nut crust and buttermilk mashed potatoes, and the marinated lamb chops and seared vegetables. 306 Market St. © 215/625-9425. Reservations recommended. Main courses $15–$25. AE, DC, DISC, MC, V. Mon–Thurs 11:30am–2:30pm and 5:30–10:30pm; Fri 11:30am–2:30pm and 5:30–11:30pm; Sat 5:30–11:30pm; Sun 11am–2:30pm and 5:30–10:30pm. Late bar menu Thurs 10:30–midnight, Fri–Sat 10:30pm–1am. SEPTA: 2nd St. or 5th St.

La Famiglia ITALIAN   *La Famiglia* refers to both the proprietors and the clientele of this refined spot. The Neapolitan Sena family aims for elegant dining, service, and presentation. The restaurant seats 60 in a private, warm setting of hand-hammered Venetian chandeliers and majolica tiles. Most of the pasta is homemade; you might try the *gnocchi al basilico*, which incorporates basil and sweet red-pepper sauce. The wine cellar here is legendary. For dessert, try a *mille foglie*, the Italian version of the napoleon, or profiteroles in chocolate sauce. People often stay here well after the closing hour, lingering over Sambuca while arias play in the background. 8 S. Front St. © 215/922-2803. Reservations recommended. Main courses $24–$50. AE, DC, MC, V. Tues–Fri noon–2:30pm and 5:30–9:30pm; Sat 5:30–10pm; Sun 5–9pm. SEPTA: 2nd St.

Le Bec-Fin FRENCH   Le Bec-Fin is unquestionably the best restaurant in Philadelphia and probably one of the top 10 in the country. Owner-chef Georges Perrier hails from Lyon, France's gastronomic capital, and commands the respect of restaurateurs on two continents. In the elegant but comfortable dining room, you'll enjoy a leisurely waltz through hors d'oeuvres, a fish course, a main course, a salad, cheese, a dessert, and coffee with petits fours. The dessert carts become grand opera as they zoom from guest to guest. The basement **Le Bar Lyonnais,** with just four tables and bar stools, has just joined its upstairs neighbor with a 29 Zagat's rating, and offers more affordable snacking and champagne toasts. Expect to spend about $10 a nibble and $7 for a glass of house wine. 1523 Walnut St. ℰ 215/567-1000. Reservations required a week ahead for weeknights, months ahead for Fri–Sat. Fixed-price lunch $38; fixed-price dinner $120. AE, DC, MC, V. Lunch seatings Mon–Fri at 11:30am and 1:30pm; dinner seatings Mon–Thurs at 6 and 9pm, Fri–Sat at 6 and 9:30pm. Bar Lyonnais downstairs serves food and drink until midnight, 1am on Sat. SEPTA: Walnut–Locust.

Painted Parrot Café AMERICAN   Beyond the Painted Parrot's signature desserts, this cafe offers innovative, affordable meals in a pretty space steps away from Independence Historical National Park. Lunch features such standards as a turkey burger or grilled salmon club. Dinner centers on imaginative pastas or simple roasted or grilled chicken or fish. The soup of the day is always superb. Wednesday nights, the delightful desserts are showcased in an all-you-can-savor $7.95 dessert buffet. Fudge torte, mousse torte—the list goes up to 17 most nights. 211 Chestnut St. ℰ 215/922-5971. Reservations recommended. Main courses $11–$16; lunch $5.95–$8.95; Tues fixed-price dinner $14. AE, MC, V. Tues–Fri 11:30am–2:30pm; Sat–Sun noon–3pm; Tues–Thurs 5–10pm; Fri–Sat 5–11pm; Sun 5–10pm; dessert menu until midnight. SEPTA: 2nd St.

Striped Bass SEAFOOD   This is one of the hottest seafood restaurants in the country. The setting and ambience are absolutely spectacular. The raw bar has over a dozen varieties of oysters, and the kitchen delivers simple, creative preparations of seafood, with an emphasis on fresh herbs and clean flavors. This is the type of place where you can feel comfortable asking the waitstaff for advice—or the owners, who are religious about stopping by tables. There's an extensive raw bar as well as extravagant desserts. 1500 Walnut St. ℰ 215/732-4444. Reservations almost always necessary. Main courses $18–42; lunch $14–$20. AE, DC, MC, V. Mon–Thurs 11:30am–2:30pm and 5–11pm; Fri 11:30am–2:30pm and 5–11:30pm; Sat 5–11:30pm; Sun 5–10pm; brunch Sun 11am–2:30pm. SEPTA: Walnut–Locust.

Susanna Foo CHINESE   Susanna Foo, winning raves for 20 years, is a national treasure for her blend of Asian and Western cuisines. Appetizers feature such delicacies as curried chicken ravioli with grilled eggplant, slightly crispy but not oily. Noodle dishes, salads, and main courses similarly combine East and West: water chestnuts and radicchio, savory quail with fresh litchi nuts, smoked duck and endive, and grilled chicken with Thai lemon-grass sauce. Desserts such as the ginger creme with strawberries and the hazelnut meringue are light and delicate. In the dim-sum cafe and bar upstairs, diners choose from up to 30 exquisite tidbit platters, including pork-stuffed jalapeños, lamb wontons, and tiny spring rolls. 1512 Walnut St. ℰ 215/545-2666. Reservations recommended for dinner. Main courses $18–$36; lunch $25 3-course prix fixe. AE, MC, V. Mon–Fri 11:30am–2:30pm and 5–10pm (Fri until 11pm); Sat 5–11pm; Sun 5–9pm. SEPTA: Walnut–Locust.

White Dog Café AMERICAN   The White Dog attracts everyone from Penn students to the mayor. Inside three funky row houses, sophisticated kitchen equipment and electronics are concealed behind an eclectic mélange of checkered tablecloths, antique furniture, and white dogs galore. There's a three-counter bar (specializing in all-American beers), several dining areas, and a new glassed-in porch. Local produce inspires the frequently changing menu as well as the theme dinners based on the season or a particular American region. The grilled yellowtail filet with sweet-and-sour eggplant relish is delicious, and the in-house pastry chef turns out signature rolls and cakes. 3420 Sansom St. (© 215/386-9224. Reservations recommended. Main courses $15–$23; lunch $8–$11. AE, DISC, MC, V. Mon–Fri 11:30am–2:30pm and 5:30–10pm (Fri until 11pm); Sat 5:30–11pm; Sun 5–10pm; brunch Sat–Sun 11am–2:30pm. Grill open until midnight. Frequent theme dinners and parties. SEPTA: 34th St.

PHILADELPHIA AFTER DARK

The best sources for what's going on are the "Weekend" supplement of the Friday *Philadelphia Inquirer*, and the free *City Paper* and *Philadelphia Weekly* (www.phillyweekly.com), which you can find throughout Center City. The visitor center is also an excellent information source. For monthly happenings, consult the back section of *Philadelphia* magazine. If you're online, **www.philly.com** gets you to the *Inquirer*'s listings.

Upstages (© 215/569-9700) is the city's premier nonprofit box-office service. Purchase by phone or stop by their location at the Prince Music Theater, 1412 Chestnut St. (SEPTA: City Hall). Hours are Monday through Friday from 10am to 6pm, Saturday from 10am to 5pm, and Sunday from noon to 5pm. For everything from theater to pop shows, call **Ticketmaster** (© 215/336-2000).

Lights of Liberty, Chestnut and 6th streets (© 215/542-3789; SEPTA: 5th St.), is a night-time high-tech dramatized American Revolution. A 3-D sound system accessible through wireless headsets and five-story images projected on a historic building in Independence Park are synchronized with a musical score and the voices of Walter Cronkite and Whoopi Goldberg among others, as you follow the path of the story. Admission is $18 adults, $16 students and seniors, $12 children 12 and under.

THE PERFORMING ARTS   Broad Street south of City Hall has been named "Avenue of the Arts" in acknowledgment of the number of stages it's home to. The **Philadelphia Orchestra,** one of the "Big Five" American orchestras, performs at brand-new Verizon Hall in the glass-enclosed **Kimmel Center,** Broad and Spruce streets (© 215/893-1999 for tickets, or 215/893-1900; SEPTA: Walnut–Locust). The regular season runs from September to May. In summer, the orchestra moves to **Mann Music Center,** in Fairmount Park near 52nd Street and Parkside Avenue (© 215/878-7707 box office), for 4 weeks of concerts. The **Curtis Institute,** 1726 Locust St. (© 215/893-5252, or 215/893-5261 for schedule; SEPTA: Walnut–Locust or 15th–16th sts.), a world-famous conservatory, presents mostly free concerts, operas, and recitals.

The **Opera Company Of Philadelphia,** 510 Walnut St., Ste. 1600 (© 215/928-2110), performs at the 1860s Academy of Music. It features younger opera stars such as Nathan Gunn and Lauren Flanigan.

The nationally renowned **Pennsylvania Ballet,** 1101 S. Broad St. (© 215/551-7014; www.paballet.org), performs at the Academy of Music and Kimmel Center, the Annenberg Center at U. Penn, and the Merriam Theater from September to June.

Philadelphia is an attentive theater town. The acclaimed **Wilma Theater** stages modern plays in a state-of-the-art space at Broad and Spruce streets (© 215/546-7824; SEPTA: Walnut–Locust). The popular **Arden Theatre Company,** 40 N. 2nd St. (© 215/922-8900, or UPSTAGES at 215/893-1145; SEPTA: 2nd St.), presents diverse productions in an intimate setting. **Philadelphia**

Theatre Company, 1714 Delancey Place (© **215/569-9700** for tickets, or 215/985-1400; SEPTA: Walnut–Locust or 15th–16th sts.), combines fine regional talent with Tony Award–winning actors and directors.

Founded in 1809, the **Walnut Street Theatre,** 9th and Walnut streets (© **215/574-3550;** SEPTA: 8th–Market or 9th–10th sts.), continues its distinctive role in the history of the American stage. The **Prince Music Theater** (© **215/567-0670** for tickets, or 215/893-1570; www.princemusictheater.org) presents opera, musical comedy, cabaret, and experimental theater at a dramatically renovated movie palace at 1412 Chestnut St. (SEPTA: City Hall or 15th St.).

THE CLUB & MUSIC SCENE The best nightlife areas are the **Delaware Avenue** piers; the neighborhoods next to the **waterfront,** west along either Spring Garden Street or into South Street; the **1500 block of Walnut,** between 15th and 16th streets, for sophisticated clubbing; the fringes of the **University of Pennsylvania,** west of the Schuylkill; and **South Philly,** for those craving cheesesteak or pasta.

Egypt, 520 N. Delaware Ave., at Spring Garden Street (© **215/922-6500;** SEPTA: Spring Garden), might be the city's foremost dance club, with a campy "oasis" setting and separate DJs and atmospheres in its bilevel areas.

Circa, 1518 Walnut St., in Center City (© **215/545-6800;** SEPTA: Walnut–Locust), reviewed above in the "Where to Dine" section, turns into a stylish club after the dinner hour, Thursday through Saturday. Music is DJ-spun house, pop, and '70s disco.

In the Old City area, try **Sugar Mom's Church Street Lounge,** 225 Church St., next door to Christ Church (© **215/925-8219;** SEPTA: 2nd St.), which draws a diverse, hip crowd.

Philadelphia is one of the great American hothouses for jazz. The Bynum brothers' elegant **Zanzibar Blue,** 200 S. Broad St. (© **215/732-4500;** SEPTA: Walnut–Locust), downstairs at the Park Hyatt at the Bellevue, features the best jazz bands, and singers such as Diane Schuur. The sophisticated **Warmdaddy's,** Front and Market streets in the historic district (© **215/627-2500;** SEPTA: 2nd St.), another Bynum brothers venture, features authentic live blues from Koko Taylor, Murali Coryell, and the like, accompanied by excellent traditional Southern cuisine.

Check out the **Khyber,** 56 S. 2nd St. (© **215/238-5888;** SEPTA: 2nd St.), a popular spot for jazz, funk, and rock nightly. The Khyber serves English ales and Irish stout and has a certain atticlike charm; $7 cover charge.

THE BAR SCENE The **Dock Street Brasserie,** 2 Logan Sq. (18th and Cherry sts.; © **215/496-0413;** Bus: 33) gets a sophisticated post-work crowd with live jazz and Latin music on Friday. Professionals also congregate at **Cutter's,** 2005 Market St. (© **215/85-6262;** Bus: 33), with its two-story wall of liquor. The best German beer bar in town is **Ludwig's Garten,** 1315 Sansom St. (© **215/985-1525;** SEPTA: Walnut–Locust).

One of the coolest spots of the moment is the **Continental Restaurant and Martini Bar,** 138 Market St. (© **215/923-6069;** SEPTA: 2nd St.), a vintage diner in Old City.

Serrano, 20 S. 2nd St., in the Historic District (© **215/928-0770;** SEPTA: 2nd St.), offers music upstairs and a wonderful collection of brews, along with eclectic world cuisine, in an intimate setting. The old wooden bar has antique stained glass behind it, and a spiced wood fire burns in the fireplace.

Many local professional athletes relax after a game at **Downey's,** Front and South streets (*©* **215/625-9500**), a terrific Irish pub with contemporary flair. A beautiful wraparound second-floor deck offers waterfront views for dining or cocktails.

The posh **Lounge at the Omni,** 4th and Chestnut streets (*©* **215/925-0000;** SEPTA: 5th St.), has dark woods and Oriental rugs, a crackling fireplace, a pianist, and large picture windows surveying Independence National Historical Park across the street.

THE GAY & LESBIAN SCENE To find out what's happening, check out the *Philadelphia Gay News* (www.epgn.com), available at **Giovanni's Room,** 345 S. 12th St. (*©* **215/923-2960;** www.giovannisroom.com; SEPTA: Walnut–Locust). The gay scene centers around 12th and 13th streets between Walnut and Pine. Perennially popular **Woody's,** 202 S. 13th St. (*©* **215/545-1893;** SEPTA: Walnut–Locust) has a downstairs video bar and upstairs disco. There's something for everyone at **12th Air Command,** 254 S. 12th St. (*©* **215/545-8088;** www.12thair.com; SEPTA: Walnut–Locust): a lounge, a game room, a disco, even an Italian restaurant. **Rodz,** 1418 Rodman St. (*©* **215/546-1900;** SEPTA: Lombard–South), is a cute piano bar/restaurant with excellent eclectic American cuisine. Women gather at **Sisters,** 1320 Chancellor St. (*©* **215/735-0735;** www. sistersnightclub.com; SEPTA: Walnut–Locust), a restaurant/bar/nightclub near City Hall.

2 Side Trips from Philadelphia: The Amish Country, the Brandywine Valley & More

THE AMISH COUNTRY

Fifty miles west of Philadelphia is a quietly beautiful region of rolling hills, winding creeks, neatly cultivated farms, covered bridges, and towns with picturesque names such as Paradise and Bird-in-Hand. The real attraction here is the Amish people themselves, who steadfastly retain a life of agrarian simplicity, centered on religious worship and family cohesiveness. The preservation of their world evokes feelings of curiosity, nostalgia, amazement, and respect.

The area is relatively small, with good roads for motorist and bicyclist alike. The attention on the Amish has spurred lots of interesting facsimiles and even some authentic pathways into Amish life, although you have to sift through them if you want to avoid overt religious messages. Tourism has promoted excellence in quilting, antiques, and farm-based crafts. There are historical sites, pretzel and chocolate factories, covered bridges, and wonderful farmers' markets, as well as modern diversions such as movie theaters, amusement parks, and great outlet-mall shopping. And, of course, the family-style, all-you-can-eat or gourmet Pennsylvania Dutch restaurants offer experiences as well as meals.

ESSENTIALS

GETTING THERE Lancaster County is 57 miles or a 90-minute drive west of Philadelphia, directly on Route 30. From the Northeast, take I-95 south from New York City onto the New Jersey Turnpike, then take Exit 6 onto the Pennsylvania Turnpike (I-76), turning south to Lancaster City via Exits 20 or 21 (trip time: 2¼ hr.). From the south, follow I-83 north for 90 minutes from Baltimore, then head east on Route 30 from York into the county. **Amtrak** provides frequent service from 30th Street Station in Philadelphia to the great old Lancaster station (trip time: 70 min.).

VISITOR INFORMATION   The **Pennsylvania Dutch Convention & Visitors Bureau**, 501 Greenfield Rd., Lancaster, PA 17601 (© **800/PA-DUTCH** or 717/299-8901, ext. 2405; www.padutchcountry.com), provides an excellent map and visitors' guide, along with answers to specific questions and interests. The office itself (off the Rte. 30 Bypass east of Lancaster) has direct telephone links to many local hotels and an overview slide show. Many towns such as Intercourse, Strasburg, and Lancaster have local information centers, and the **Exit 21 Tourist Information Center,** on Route 272 just south of I-76, is open daily from 10am to 2pm.

EXPLORING THE AREA

The suggestive name of **Intercourse** refers to the intersection of two old roads, the King's Highway (now Rte. 340 or Old Philadelphia Pike) and Newport Road (now Rte. 772). It's now "Ground Zero" for Amish life, in the midst of the wedge of country east of Lancaster; unfortunately, the number of commercial attractions, ranging from schlock to good quality, about equals places of genuine interest along Route 340. One not to miss is **The People's Place,** 3513 Old Philadelphia Pike (© **800/390-8436** or 717/768-7171), an interpretive center with a 30-minute documentary on the Amish as well as an excellent hands-on museum with antique quilts and a bookshop/gallery. Of the commercial developments, try **Kitchen Kettle Village** (© **800/732-3538** or 717/768-8261), where 32 stores selling crafts from decoys to fudge are grouped around the Burnleys' 1954 jam and relish kitchen.

Ephrata, near Exit 21 off I-76, combines a historic 18th-century Moravian religious site with some pleasant country and the area's largest farmers' market and auction center. **Ephrata Cloister,** 632 W. Main St. (© **717/733-6600**), near the junction of Routes 272 and 322, was one of America's earliest communal societies. The main street of Ephrata is pleasant for strolling, including an old rail car where the train line used to run. **Doneckers,** 318–324 N. State St. (© **800/377-2206** or 717/738-9502), has expanded from a single inn north of town into a hotel, shopping, farmers' market, and gourmet restaurant complex, open daily. Four miles north of town is the wonderful **Green Dragon Market** (© **717/738-1117**), open Friday from 9am to 9pm. You'll see goats and cows changing hands in the most elemental way, and kids are allowed total petting access in the process. Summer brings fresh corn, fruit, and melons.

Other charming towns in the region include **Lititz,** with its pretzel factory and a lovely park adjoining a purely 18th-century main street; **Strasburg,** with a preserved 9-mile track for iron steam locomotive and assorted rail-related attractions; and **Bird-in-Hand,** known for its farmers' market (Fri–Sat year-round, plus Wed and Thurs in summer) and homemade ice cream. For antiquing, the Sunday fairs in **Adamstown,** 2 miles east of Exit 21 off I-76, bring thousands of vendors to six or seven competing fairgrounds. The largest are **Stoudt's Black Angus Antique Mall,** with more than 350 permanent dealers, and **Renninger's Antique and Collectors Market,** with 370 dealers.

Lancaster itself is slightly down at the heels. In town, the one visitor highlight is **Central Market,** erected in 1889 just off Penn Square but operating since the 1730s as the nation's oldest farmers' market, with more than 80 stalls. You can savor regional produce and foods, from sweet bologna and scrapple to egg noodles and shoofly pie (Tues and Fri 6am–4:30pm; Sat 6am–2pm). To the city's east on Route 30, the outlet centers of **Rockvale Square** and **Tanger Outlets** offer dozens of top brands.

You're more apt to find solid, value-oriented quality than elegance in food and lodging in this family-oriented landscape. The **Best Western Eden Resorts Inn,** 222 Eden Rd., Routes 30 and 272 in Lancaster (© **800/528-1234** or 717/ 569-6444; eden@edenresorts.com), is a cut above, with pool, tropically landscaped atrium, and kitchenettes in some of the 275 rooms. **Country Inn of Lancaster,** 2133 Lincoln Hwy. E. (Rte. 30), Lancaster (© **717/393-3413**), lets you rock away on your back porch overlooking beautiful Amish farmland, with unusually charming decor and a heated pool. Dozens of bed-and-breakfasts and a scattering of working farms taking lodgers can be accessed through the Convention and Visitors Bureau.

Ben Franklin would be staggered at the size of a modern Pennsylvania Dutch meal or smorgasbord, but he'd recognize everything on it, from the German-style meats and potpies with boiled vegetables to the sweet desserts. Among the smorgasbords and family-style restaurants open Monday through Saturday, try **Good 'N' Plenty Restaurant,** Route 896 between Routes 30 and 340, Smoke-town (© **717/394-7111**); **Miller's Smorgasbord,** Route 30 at Ronks Road, 5 miles east of Lancaster (© **800/669-3568** or 717/687-6621), which has served millions since 1929; or **Plain & Fancy Farm & Dining Room,** Route 340, 7 miles east of Lancaster in Bird-in-Hand (© **800/669-3568** or 717/768-8281).

VALLEY FORGE

Only 30 minutes from central Philadelphia today, Valley Forge was hours of frozen trails away in the winter of 1777–78. The Revolutionary forces had just lost the battles of Brandywine and Germantown. While the British occupied Philadelphia, Washington's forces repaired to winter quarters near an iron forge where the Schuylkill met Valley Creek, 18 miles northwest. A sawmill and grist-mill were supposed to help provide basic requirements, but the British had destroyed them. Some 12,000 men and boys straggled into the encampment, setting up quarters and lines of defense.

Unfortunately, the winter turned bitter, with 6 inches of snow and iced-up rivers. Critical shortages of food and clothing, along with damp shelters, left nearly 4,000 men diseased and unfit for duty. Almost 2,000 perished, and many others deserted. Congress, which had left Philadelphia hurriedly, couldn't persuade the colonies to give money to alleviate the conditions. Nevertheless, the forces slowly gained strength and confidence, thanks in part to the Prussian army veteran Baron von Steuben, appointed by Washington to retrain the Continental Army under his revised and distinctly American "Manual of Arms." By springtime the Continentals were an army on which their new allies, the French, could rely. Replicas of their huts, some of the officers' lodgings, and later memorials dot the park today.

Admission to the park is free. Start your visit at the **National Historical Park Visitors Center** (© **610/783-1077**) at the junction of Pa. 23 and North Gulph Road. A 15-minute film depicting the encampment is shown at the visitor center every half hour. Also at the visitor center is a museum containing Washington's tent, an extensive collection of Revolutionary War artifacts, and a bookstore.

Highlights in the park include the **National Memorial Arch;** an 1865 covered bridge; the **Isaac Potts House** (1770), which Washington commandeered as his headquarters; and the 1993 Monument to Patriots of African Descent. Admission to Washington's headquarters is $3 for adults, $2 for children from April to November. A 1903 Gothic **Washington Memorial Chapel** is free, with Sunday carillon recitals in the bell tower at 2pm. A private-public partnership is working on an adjacent and extensive **National Center for the American Revolution**—don't look for completion before the mid-2000s, though.

The park is open daily from 9am to 5pm, later in summer.

GETTING THERE   From Philadelphia, access is from Exit 24 of the Pennsylvania Turnpike (I-76) or Exit 25 of the Schuylkill Expressway (I-76) to Route 363. Follow the signs.

TWO PREMIER ATTRACTIONS IN THE BRANDYWINE VALLEY

The Brandywine Valley, bridging Pennsylvania and Delaware, is beautiful rolling country filled with Americana from colonial days through the Gilded Age. Many of the farms that kept the Revolutionary troops fed have survived to this day. There are 15 covered bridges and 100 antiques stores in Chester County alone, with miles of country roads and horse trails between them.

Pierre S. Du Pont devoted his life to horticulture; he bought a 19th-century arboretum and created the ultimate estate garden on 1,050 acres. **Longwood Gardens,** one of the world's great garden displays, is on Route 1, 30 miles west of Philadelphia and just west of the junction with Pa. 52 (© **610/388-1000;** www.longwoodgardens.org).

Most people head to the left, toward the Main Fountain Garden, with special fluid fireworks shows on Tuesday, Thursday, and Saturday evenings from June to September, usually preceded by hour-long garden concerts. A topiary garden of closely pruned shrubs surrounds a 37-foot sundial. If you prefer indoors, 4 acres of massive bronze-and-glass conservatories are among the finest and largest in the United States. African violets, bonsai trees up to 400 years old, hibiscus, orchids, and tropical plants are among the specialties, but expect anything from Easter lilies to scarlet begonias. A parquet-floor ballroom was added later, along with a 10,000-pipe organ, a magnificent instrument played during the year and on Sunday afternoon in winter.

Admission is $12 for adults ($8 Tues), $6 for ages 16 to 20, $2 for ages 6 to 15, free for children under 6. It's open April through October daily from 9am to 6pm (conservatories 10am–6pm); November through March, daily from 9am to 5pm, though Christmastime brings special displays open until 9pm.

The later home of the Du Ponts now provides the setting for America's best native collection of decorative arts. **Winterthur Museum, Garden and Library** (© **800/448-3883** or 302/888-4600; www.winterthur.org) is 6 miles northwest of Wilmington, Delaware, on Route 52. Henry Francis Du Pont, a great-grandson of E. I. Du Pont, was a connoisseur of European antiques. But when he turned his attention to a simple Pennsylvania Dutch chest in 1923, he realized that no study had illustrated how American pieces are related to European ones or how the concepts of beauty and taste differed on the two continents. Du Pont collected furniture, then native decorative objects, then interior woodwork of entire homes built between 1640 and 1840. Finally, he added more than 200 rooms for the display of his collection. Because the museum started out as a private home, the rooms have a unique richness and intimacy.

The Main Museum, open for specific guided tours, displays the bulk of the collection and includes complete interiors from every eastern seaboard colony. Special landmarks include the famous Montmorenci Stair Hall, two Shaker Rooms, fine examples of Pennsylvania Dutch decorative arts, and the Du Pont dining room. The Campbell Soup Tureen collection, with 125 items currently on display, is housed in the Dorrance Gallery, between the museum and research building. In a new Touch-It Room, children can dress up in colonial costumes and take afternoon tea in the parlor.

In spring, the extensive Winterthur Gardens explode into an abundance of cherry and crabapple blossoms, rhododendrons, Virginia bluebells, and azaleas. The lush, carefully planned gardens are well worth viewing any season. Garden tram rides through the grounds are available when weather permits. There are two superb gift shops selling a selection of licensed reproductions, gifts, books, jewelry, and plants.

There are four admission options. The **General Admission ticket** ($10 adults, $8 seniors and students, $4 children 5–11) available year-round includes the Galleries, the Dorrance Gallery, the Touch-It Room, a self-guided garden walk, and the garden tram. The **Highlight Introduction to Winterthur** tour (an additional $5) adds a 1-hour guided tour of a selection of 175 period rooms. **Decorative Arts tours** (an additional $5 for each 45-min. segment) offer in-depth guided tours in small groups for ages 12 and up; reservations are required. In season, you can go on a **Guided Garden Walk** for $5 plus general admission. Winterthur is open Monday through Saturday from 9am to 5pm, Sunday from noon to 5pm; closed on major holidays.

Accommodations are few and on the precious side in Du Pont country. The **Brandywine River Hotel,** Routes 1 and 100 in Chadds Ford (© 610/388-1200) has adapted and expanded a historic inn. You can dine well at the **Chadds Ford Inn,** across the intersection (© 610/388-7361) with its Wyeth paintings, or sample the local specialty of white mushrooms on the menu at **Longwood Inn,** 815 E. Baltimore Pike (Rte. 1) in Kennett Square (© 610/444-3515).

GETTYSBURG

The battle that took place at this small university town in 1863 was the turning point of the Civil War. Over three broiling hot days in July, Gen. Robert E. Lee's 75,000-man Confederate Army of Northern Virginia clashed thrice with Gen. George Meade's 83,000-strong Union troops, each time failing to deliver the decisive blow that would convince President Lincoln to end the war. Over the 3 days, more than 51,000 men died and more than 40,000 others were wounded, making this the bloodiest battle in American history. The war didn't end until 2 years later, but after Gen. George E. Pickett's ill-fated charge up Cemetery Ridge on July 3, Lee realized he was beaten, and began his retreat south.

Lincoln traveled to Gettysburg 4 months after the battle to dedicate the cemetery that held 3,706 casualties, a third of them unknown. "Four score and seven years ago," Lincoln began his brief address—the most famous speech by any American president.

The battle and Lincoln's address are commemorated at **Gettysburg National Military Park Battlefield,** the country's premier battlefield shrine, with a monument to just about every company that served here (more than 1,000 in all) spread out along 40 scenic miles. Start your visit at the visitor center (© 717/334-1124), where you can sit in on the **Electric Map** presentation that provides a hokey but informative overview of the 3-day battle. Tour guides are available at the center for a fee, or pick up a copy of the highly recommended **Gettysburg Battlefield Tape Tour,** available at the gift shop, and do your own tour.

The battle is often reenacted, especially during **Gettysburg Civil War Heritage Days,** from July 1 to 7. Ken Burns's superb documentary "The Civil War" also provides a good background to the events at Gettysburg, as does Shelby Foote's book *Stars in Their Courses: The Gettysburg Campaign.*

For information about accommodations, restaurants, shopping, and other local attractions, contact the **Gettysburg Convention and Visitors Bureau,** 35 Carlisle St., Gettysburg, PA 17325 (✆ **717/334-6274;** www.gettysburg.com).

Gettysburg has outposts of most major motel chains. The ones within walking distance of the battlefield include **Holiday Inn Battlefield,** 516 Baltimore St. (✆ **717/334-6211**); **Quality Inn Gettysburg Motor Lodge,** 380 Steinwehr Ave. (✆ **800/228-5151** or 717/334-1103); and the historic 1797 **Best Western Gettysburg Hotel,** 1 Lincoln Sq. (✆ **800/528-1234** or 717/337-2000), which is right in the center of town. Bed-and-breakfast fanciers should try the **Brickhouse Inn,** 452 Baltimore St. (✆ **800/864-3464** or 717/338-9337; www. brickhouseinn.com); or the **Doubleday Inn,** 104 Doubleday Ave. (✆ **717/334-9119**), within the military park on Oak Ridge.

GETTING THERE   Gettysburg is about 125 miles west of Philadelphia, 180 miles east of Pittsburgh, and about 36 miles southwest of Harrisburg. Take I-76 (Pennsylvania Tpk.) west from Philadelphia or east from Pittsburgh to Harrisburg, then U.S. 15 south to Gettysburg. From Lancaster and Amish Country, take U.S. 30 west about 53 miles to Gettysburg.

3 Pittsburgh & Western Pennsylvania

PITTSBURGH

Gone are the days when Pittsburgh's steel mills belched so much carbon into the air that white-collar workers brought a second shirt to work and changed at noon. Since the last mills closed in the late 1980s, the Smoky City was scrubbed clean and has come to depend on high-tech industry. While it retains a steely, sober cast, Pittsburgh's natural beauty now shines through, with a whimsically hilly landscape hemmed in by the Allegheny mountains and trussed by the Ohio, Allegheny, and Monongahela rivers, which glint into view at every turn. The city gets high marks for friendliness; learning and culture, legacies of great magnates like Carnegie and Mellon; and neighborhood quirkiness and individuality.

ESSENTIALS

GETTING THERE   **By Plane**   **Pittsburgh International Airport** (✆ **412/472-3525;** www.pitairport.com) is 15 miles southwest of downtown. **US Airways** is the dominant carrier, with over 80% of total traffic. The public **28-X Airport Flyer bus** costs $1.95 to downtown, and **Airport Express** offers shuttle service to various neighborhoods for $12. A cab ride downtown costs $30. Car rentals are very inexpensive as well, and over 1,500 color-coded signs point the way to highways and attractions, making it easy to drive. The airport is a 20-minute drive (45 min. during rush hour) on Pa. 60 south, I-279 south, and the Fort Pitt Tunnel to downtown.

By Train   **Amtrak** (✆ **800/USA-RAIL** or 412/471-6172; www.amtrak.com) provides daily service from Philadelphia (trip time: 8 hr.), Washington, D.C. (7½ hr.), Cleveland (3½ hr.), and Chicago (10 hr.) to its station at 1100 Liberty Ave.

By Car   Major routes into the belt roads around Pittsburgh are I-76 from the northwest (Cleveland) and east (Philadelphia), I-70 from the west (Columbus) and southeast (Washington, D.C.), and I-79 from the north (Erie, PA) and south (Charleston, WV).

VISITOR INFORMATION   The **Greater Pittsburgh Convention & Visitors Bureau,** Four Gateway Center (✆ **800/359-0758** or 412/281-7711; www. VisitPittsburgh.com or www.pittsburgh-cvb.org), operates **Visitor Information**

Centers downtown, Liberty Avenue next to the Gateway Center, Monday through Friday from 9am to 5pm, Saturday from 9am to 3pm; at Mount Washington, 315 Grandview Ave., Tuesday, Wednesday, Friday, Saturday from 10am to 5pm, Thursday from 1 to 5pm; at Oakland, Forbes Avenue on the University of Pittsburgh campus, Monday from 9am to 4pm, Tuesday through Sunday from 10am to 4pm; and at the airport, daily from 8am to 8pm.

GETTING AROUND   The **Port Authority of Allegheny County** (© 412/ 442-2000; www.portauthority.org) operates subways and buses throughout the city as well as the "T" Light Rail downtown. The fare is free within the Golden Triangle downtown, and very cheap outside that.

FAST FACTS   For a **doctor** referral, call © **412/321-5030;** for a **dentist** referral, call © **800/917-6453.** A major local hospital is **UPMC Presbyterian,** 200 Lothrop St., Oakland (© **412/647-2345**).

WHAT TO SEE & DO

From the **Mount Washington Overlook** (Grandview Ave.), Pittsburgh still looks like a crucial junction of transportation and commerce, as it was in the 17th century as the first inlet to the Mississippi west of the Alleghenies: with 15 lovely bridges, many active railroads, and wooden houses marching uniformly up the mountains, the way their inhabitants over the years trudged uphill from the mills. On the **Duquesne,** 1220 Grandview Ave. (© **412/381-1665**), and **Monongahela Inclines,** 5 Grandview Ave. (© **412/442-2000**), 100-year-old cable cars ferry passengers up Mount Washington for a riveting view. The fare is $1.60 adults, 80¢ for children.

Pittsburgh's compact and easily walkable downtown is called the **Golden Triangle,** where the Allegheny and Monongahela rivers converge flowing west to form the Ohio. Here you'll find **Point State Park** (© **412/471-0235**), the historic site of Fort Pitt. Interesting architecture abounds, from the industrial boom a century ago and two post-industrial renaissances, including Philip Johnson and John Burgee's glittering **PPG Place** and H. H. Richardson's magnificent Romanesque Revival **Allegheny County Courthouse** on Grant Street.

Many of Pittsburgh's cultural institutions bear the names of American barons of industry who amassed their fortunes in railroads and steel manufacture here and gave back concert halls, museums, and libraries. In 1895, Andrew Carnegie endowed the Carnegie Museums (www.carnegiemuseums.org), which today include the **Carnegie Museum of Art,** 4400 Forbes Ave., Oakland (© **412/ 622-3131**), with contemporary exhibitions and Impressionist and post-Impressionist masterpieces; the **Carnegie Museum of Natural History,** 4400 Forbes Ave., Oakland (© **412/622-3361**), renowned for its Dinosaur Hall; and the **Carnegie Science Center,** 1 Allegheny Ave., North Side next to PNC Stadium and Heinz Field (© **412/237-3400**), where kids of all ages can experience an interactive planetarium, a World War II submarine, and 250 other hands-on exhibits. The **Andy Warhol Museum,** 117 Sandusky St., North Side (© **412/ 237-8300;** www.warhol.org), is a newer factory rehab devoted to the life and work of Pittsburgh's most fabulous native son. **Clayton,** the former home of Henry Clay Frick, shares a 6-acre site with the **Frick Art & Historical Center,** 7227 Reynolds St. (© **412/371-0600;** www.frickart.org). Many guests round out an afternoon of free chamber music with formal high tea on the grounds. One of the city's most dynamic institutions, the **Mattress Factory Museum,** 500 Sampsonia Way, North Side (© **412/231-3169;** www.mattress.org) is a serene refuge for site-specific art, with permanent installations by the likes of

James Turrell. Among the city's most unusual sights are the **Nationality Rooms** in the 42-story Cathedral of Learning, University of Pittsburgh's Oakland Campus (© **412/621-6150;** www.pitt.edu/~natnlyrm/countries/natrooms.html), 24 classrooms designed to reflect the customs and architectural styles of Pittsburgh immigrants.

The **Strip District,** a rare flat riverbank from 11th to 28th streets between Smallman Street and Liberty Avenue, is Pittsburgh's traditional waterfront market and popular plaza. Low-lying warehouse buildings and cobblestone streets house the city's best butchers, bakers, and vendors of Greek and Italian specialty foods. Here you'll also find the **Senator John Heinz Pittsburgh Regional History Center,** 1212 Smallman St. (© **412/454-6000;** www.hswp.org), housed in a massive renovated 1898 warehouse.

WHERE TO STAY & DINE

Business travelers might consider the downtown **Omni William Penn,** 530 William Penn Place (© **800/THE-OMNI** or 421/281-7100), a grande dame hotel in a historic landmark building, offering a 24-hour fitness center, luxurious rooms, a business center, and more. Those with more limited expense accounts can try the downtown **Doubletree Hotel Pittsburgh,** 1000 Penn Ave. (© **412/281-3700**). If you're on your own, consider the **Morning Glory Inn,** 2119 Sarah St., South Side (© **412/431-1707;** www.pittsburghbnb.com), in a traditional Victorian town house, with a piano and fireplace in the parlor, and antiques and computer hookups in each room. The **Hampton Inn–University Center,** 3315 Hamlet, Oakland (© **412/681-1000**), is convenient to museums and downtown, with free local calls and free shuttles to and from the airport. Both places are moderately priced.

Upscale restaurants are generally either traditional palaces, or newer bistros with great views from smaller neighborhoods. On the South Side, **Mallorca,** 2228 E. Carson St. (© **412/488-1818;** www.mallorcarestaurant.com), serves hearty roasted meats, from duck to suckling pig, prepared by a Galician chef. The service is impeccable and the decor suitably handsome. An elegant choice in a spectacular setting is the **Grand Concourse Restaurant,** 1 Station Sq. (© **412/261-1717**), where you dine in the landmark former Pittsburgh & Lake Erie rail terminal overlooking downtown and the Monongahela; fresh seafood is a specialty.

Pittsburgh's culinary glory is equally in fine "chowhound" eateries like **Primanti's,** a 60-year-old institution, famous for putting the fries in the chopped meat sandwiches along with coleslaw, cheese, and sliced tomato—quite a mess but delicious. It's in the Strip at 46 18th St. and at seven other locations (© **412/263-2142**). **Vincent's Pizza Park,** 998 Ardmore Blvd. in Forest Hills (© **412/271-9181**) looks like a truck stop and serves, simply, one of America's great pizza pies, on thick-crusted Italian dough.

PITTSBURGH AFTER DARK

PERFORMING ARTS Gilded and plush with red velvet, Italian marble, and Viennese crystal chandeliers, **Heinz Hall,** 600 Penn Ave., downtown (© **412/392-4900;** www.pittsburghsymphony.org), endowed by Henry John Heinz, is the elegantly opulent home of the renowned **Pittsburgh Symphony.** The nearby **Benedum Center,** 7th Street and Penn Avenue (© **412/456-6666**), is home to the **Pittsburgh Ballet Theatre** (© **412/281-0360;** www.pbt.org), **Pittsburgh Opera** (© **412/281-0912;** www.pghopera.org), and **Pittsburgh Civic Light Opera** (© **412/281-3973;** www.pittsburghclo.org), which produces a summer season of musicals. The professional **Playhouse of Point Park College,** 222 Craft Ave., Oakland (© **412/621-4445;** www.ppc.edu/playhouse), is known for its classics, and **Pittsburgh Public Theater,** 621 Penn Ave. (© **412/321-9800)** for premieres of new plays in state-of-the-art O'Reilly Theater.

THE BAR & CLUB SCENE   A good place to check out the nightlife is the **Strip District,** which becomes a club scene at night, with brewpubs and rock-concert halls like **Rosebud,** 1650 Smallman St. (© **412/261-2232).** Another area to check out is **Station Square** (© **800/859-8959;** www.stationsquare. com), across the Smithfield Street Bridge from downtown, south of the Monongahela River. Iron City beer is the local standard brew.

OUTSIDE PITTSBURGH

Laurel Highlands, 60 miles to the southeast, boasts a wealth of outdoor activities, including serious white-water rafting along the Youghiogheny River; hiking, biking, and fishing in Ohiopyle State Park; and touring Fort Necessity Battlefield, where George Washington had his first major test during the French and Indian War in 1754. **Idlewild Park** in Ligonier (© 724/238-3666) is one of America's great old amusement parks, with a fresh new Soak Zone water park and Storybook Forest for younger kids, inspired by Latrobe neighbor Mister Rogers. Contact the **Laurel Highlands Visitors Bureau** for details (© **800/ 925-7669;** www.laurelhighlands.org).

Fallingwater, Frank Lloyd Wright's 1936 masterpiece, is another premier draw. Not long ago, the American Institute of Architects deemed it "the best all-time work of American architecture." Three cantilevered levels extend from the side of a hill, allowing the namesake waterfall to run through the house's exterior. The effect is that the house appears to be carved out of the hillside, rather than appended to it. When Wright first designed the house for Pittsburgh department store magnate Edgar Kaufmann, most engineers said it wouldn't stand. And they were partly right; after more than 60 years only a major effort to reinforce the building's foundation and floors with steel girders has prevented Fallingwater from gradually rejoining the river that runs through it.

Tours of **Fallingwater,** on Pa. 381 near Ohiopyle (© **724/329-8501;** www.paconserve.org), are offered by the Western Pennsylvania Conservancy every day except Monday and major holidays from mid-March to November. Weather permitting, tours extend to December and the first two weekends in March. Advance reservations are strongly recommended. For the regular 45-minute-to-an-hour tour, admission is $10 weekdays and $15 weekends, and children under 6 are prohibited. The best and most popular tour is the 8:30am 2-hour version (admission $40 weekdays, $50 weekends; children under 9 prohibited), with many more interior rooms; photography is allowed. You'll see the furniture Wright designed specifically for the house, the teeny-tiny bedrooms he insisted on, the low ceilings that never bothered the 5-foot 5-inch architect, and the guesthouse and unheated dip pool added later by Wright. Children's tours and nature tours are also available by reservation only.

When I. N. Hagan saw the house Frank Lloyd Wright had built for his friend Edgar Kaufmann, he decided he too wanted a Wright home in the countryside. And the architect obliged him with **Kentuck Knob** (© **724/329-1901;** www.kentuckknob.com), a home that's smaller—one of Wright's "Usonian" models, in fact—and much less pivotal in architectural history. Fans should definitely make the side trip—it's a half an hour's drive from Fallingwater. The home is now owned by Lord Palumbo, whose penchant for self-promotion rivals

Wright's own ego. Fortunately, his impressive collection of decorative arts, furniture, and outdoor sculpture is a worthy match for the setting.

Kentuck Knob is on Kentuck Knob Road, just north of Chalk Hill. Guided tours are available Tuesday through Sunday from 10am to 4pm (tour times may vary Dec–Mar). No children under age 5. Admission is $10 weekdays, $15 weekends, and $50 daily for an in-depth tour only given at 8:30am. Advance reservations are suggested for all tours.

The closest places to stay near Fallingwater are in the tiny villages of Farmington and Chalk Hill. Farmington is home to two upscale resorts, the **Historic Summit Inn,** 101 Skyline Dr. (© **800/433-8594** or 724/438-8594; www.hhs. net/summit); and **Nemacolin Woodlands Resort and Spa,** 1001 Lafayette Dr. (© **800/422-2736** or 724/329-8555; www.nwlr.com), both of which offer a variety of upscale rooms and condos as well as restaurants, pools, tennis courts, golf courses, and a health club and spa. **The Lodge at Chalk Hill,** Route 40 East (© **800/833-4283** or 724/438-8880; www.dc1.net/~thelodge), offers more modest accommodations at more down-to-earth prices. In the slightly larger burg of Uniontown, 10 miles away, there's the **Hampton Inn Uniontown,** 698 W. Main St. (© **724/430-1000**); and the **Holiday Inn,** 700 W. Main St. (© **800/258-7238**).

GETTING THERE From Pittsburgh, take I-76 east to Exit 9. From there take Pa. 31 east, then Pa. 381 south to Fallingwater. To reach Farmington, Chalk Hill, and Uniontown, continue on Pa. 381, then take U.S. 40 west.

4 Highlights of the New Jersey Shore: Atlantic City & Cape May

ATLANTIC CITY

One of America's oldest seaside resorts, Atlantic City is most famous these days as a gambler's mecca. It's the East Coast's answer to Las Vegas, and home to many of the same names: Caesars, Bally's, Sands, the Tropicana. Tourists come by the millions to try their luck at the city's 12 casinos—10 of which line the world's first oceanfront boardwalk, opened in 1870.

Despite its historic pedigree, Atlantic City went to seed in the years following World War II, abandoned in the wake of cheap and easy air travel to Florida and the Caribbean. In the 1970s, in a last-ditch effort to reinvigorate this once-proud Victorian vacation resort, the state of New Jersey instituted casino gambling—and the unconventional urban-renewal plan has been a monster success.

If you haven't been here for a few years, you won't believe your eyes. The city is in the midst of a multibillion-dollar renewal plan that has already resulted in sparkling new convention and visitor centers, new bus and train terminals, and the "Grand Boulevard," a modern, streamlined approach to the city that's more welcoming and more easily navigable than the dilapidated city streets it replaced. The historic Boardwalk Convention Hall—where Miss America is crowned annually in September or October—has just undergone a $90-million face-lift. The bloom has faded slightly from the rose, with stalled plans for future casino growth; on the other hand, Atlantic City is a comfortable drive or trip for a third of all Americans, so its status as a vacation destination seems assured.

Still, this isn't Vegas—not by a long shot. First of all, there's not a lot to do beyond the casinos. If you aren't coming to gamble or catch a headliner's show, head to Cape May instead: It's cleaner and quieter, and the beaches are much nicer. Second, while some of the casinos are on par with their desert counterparts

Atlantic City

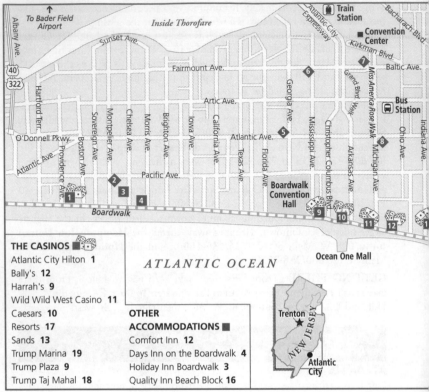

THE CASINOS

Atlantic City Hilton **1**
Bally's **12**
Harrah's **9**
Wild Wild West Casino **11**
Caesars **10**
Resorts **17**
Sands **13**
Trump Marina **19**
Trump Plaza **9**
Trump Taj Mahal **18**

OTHER ACCOMMODATIONS ■

Comfort Inn **12**
Days Inn on the Boardwalk **4**
Holiday Inn Boardwalk **3**
Quality Inn Beach Block **16**

in sophistication if not in scale (Trump's Taj Mahal and the newly expanded Caesars are of particular note), tacky souvenir shops give some stretches of the Boardwalk a worn, seedy air. And while many city blocks have been nicely gentrified, some still have a ways to go. Venture off the Boardwalk with care, only in recommended areas.

ESSENTIALS

GETTING THERE   By Plane   You can fly into Atlantic City International Airport (www.acairport.com), 10 miles from downtown, via US Airways Express (© **800/428-4322;** www.usairways.com), Delta Connection/American Eagle (© **800/221-1212;** www.delta.com), or Spirit Airlines (© **800/772-7117;** www.spiritair.com). PanAm Commuter service (© **800/359-7262**) serves New England, New York, and Baltimore. SuperShuttle (© **888/640-2222** or 609/340-0099) can whisk you to your hotel from the terminal; rental cars and taxis are also available.

By Train   NJ Transit's Atlantic City line (© **800/AC-TRAIN** or 215/569-3752; www.njtransit.state.nj.us) offers frequent service from Philadelphia (trip time: 1½ hr.). There's a shuttle bus from the station to the casinos.

By Bus   A car isn't necessary in Atlantic City, so if you prefer not to drive, bus service is available from Philadelphia and New York (trip time: about 2 hr.) via

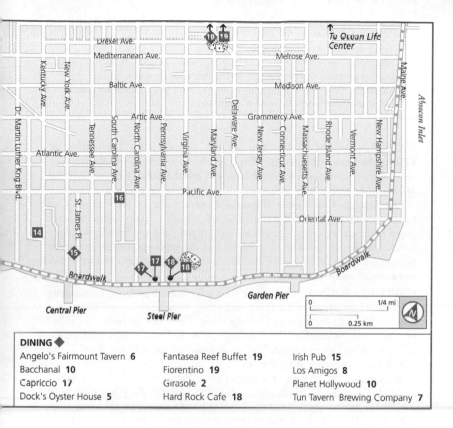

Greyhound (℡ 800/229-9424; www.greyhound.com) and **NJ Transit** (℡ 973/762-5100; www.njtransit.state.nj.us), whose buses arrive at the nice, new bus station adjacent to the Convention Center at Atlantic and Michigan avenues, 2 blocks from the Boardwalk. **Academy Bus Lines** (℡ 800/442-7272 or 800/992-0451; www.academybus.com) offers direct service from New York's Port Authority to a number of Boardwalk casinos.

Most Atlantic City casinos offer **bus packages,** which often include such value-added premiums as $20 in coins or free meals, from most major northeast cities—including New York, Philadelphia, Baltimore, Washington, D.C., and Pittsburgh, as well as secondary cities like Harrisburg, PA—aboard casino-direct charters. They generally cater to day visitors who want to come in to gamble for 12 hours or so without the expense of a hotel room. Call the casinos directly to learn about current offers (see "The Casinos," below).

By Car Atlantic City is on the southern New Jersey shoreline, 60 miles southeast of Philadelphia and 120 miles south of New York City. From Philadelphia, take I-76 to State Road 42, which connects to the Atlantic City Expressway. From New York, take the Lincoln or Holland tunnels or the George Washington Bridge to the New Jersey Turnpike (I-95) south; pick up the Garden State Parkway at Perth Amboy and follow it south to Exit 38, which connects to the Atlantic City Expressway.

Atlantic City Factoids
- The first-ever picture postcards were color views of Atlantic City.
- Monopoly® was created in 1933 by Pennsylvanian Charles Darrow, who used the streets of Atlantic City as the basis for his game board.
- Saltwater taffy was literally "discovered" on the Boardwalk in 1883—after an ocean storm flooded a candy store.

VISITOR INFORMATION   Contact the **Atlantic City Convention & Visitors Authority** (© **888/AC-VISIT** or 609/449-7130; www.atlanticcitynj. com). Online information is also available at **Virtual Atlantic City** (www.virtual AC.com).

The **Atlantic City Visitor Welcome Center,** right on the Atlantic City Expressway, makes an ideal first stop. You can't miss this state-of-the-art resource center at the city's gateway, open from 9am to 5pm daily and from 9am to 8pm summer weekends. In addition, a handful of **information kiosks** are located along the Boardwalk. The kiosk staff can give you a good map and brochures and answer specific questions.

GETTING AROUND   If you don't want to walk from casino to casino along the 1-mile-long stretch of the Boardwalk where most of the action is, you can catch a ride in an old-fashioned **rolling chair.** These shaded surreys are rolled up and down the length of the Boardwalk by experienced guides, who are out soliciting riders day and night. The fee is based on the distance traveled, but expect a minimum fare of $5 plus tip.

You can also travel between the casinos along Pacific Avenue, which runs parallel to the Boardwalk 1 block inland, aboard the **Atlantic City Jitney** (© **609/344-8642;** www.visitac.com/jitney), a fleet of minibuses that run 24 hours a day; the fare is $1.50. The baby-blue or green versions run to the Marina section of the city, where the Trump Marina and Harrah's casinos are located. If you need a taxi, call **Atlantic City Airport Taxi** (© **877/568-8294** or 609/383-1457).

THE CASINOS
The casino hotels are Atlantic City's big draw. First on the Boardwalk was **Resorts,** at Pennsylvania Avenue (© **888/336-6378** or 609/344-6000; www.resortsac.com), which boasts a sharp new look thanks to a stylish $50-million renovation. It's bright, casual, and colorful, with a beachy vibe and an active showroom with top-flight rock, country, and pop headliners. Next door is bad boy Donald Trump's **Trump Taj Mahal,** at Virginia Avenue (© **800/825-8888** or 609/449-1000; www.trumptaj.com). Done in a loose *Arabian Nights* theme, the Taj is the most glamorous and attractive of Atlantic City's casinos. (Nonsmokers, take note: It has the best ventilation, too.) The gaming tables sit off to the side so big bettors aren't interrupted by the ringing and clanging of the slots. There's a lovely white-sand beach at this end of the Boardwalk.

Clustered around the Boardwalk's midpoint are a number of notable casinos. Our favorite is **Caesars,** at Arkansas Avenue (© **800/443-0104** or 609/348-4411; www.caesars.com). A massive expansion has put it in league with its landmark Vegas counterpart. The marvelous Temple Lobby is home to the Temple Bar & Grill, the hippest lounge in town, and the Centurion Tower boasts AC's best guest rooms. The casino is glitzier and better ventilated than in the past, and the staff is still the best costumed in town. Expect first-class headliners ranging from Patti LaBelle to David Copperfield. The casino offers excellent packages and special promotions, too.

Next door is **Bally's,** at Michigan Avenue (© 888/537-0007 or 609/340-2000; www.ballys.com), a fun, festive casino with inviting gaming tables and lots of dollar slots. On the second floor is the sparkling new $25-million Gateway mall, connecting to the Claridge next door, and also to Bally's **Wild Wild West Casino,** Atlantic City's best themed casino. The casino is very well done in a Disneyesque style, with faux red rocks and talking animatronic figures that offer a fun change of pace from the standard glitz. The big, open sports book and 1800 slots are other attractions.

Nearby at Indiana Avenue is **Sands** (© 800/AC-SANDS or 609/441-4000; www.acsands.com), best known for its great package rates, best overall slot odds, and state-of-the-art spa. Rooms have been newly remodeled, so expect up-to-date comforts, too.

All that glitters isn't gold at **Trump Plaza,** at Mississippi Avenue (© 800/677-7378 or 609/441-6000; www.trumpplaza.com), but it sure is shiny. Behind the glitz, this is an everyman's casino; you can expect state-of-the-art slot action here. The showroom often showcases big-name stars (Ray Charles and Damon Wayans were on the bill when we last visited).

Farther down, at the cleanest and quietest end of the Boardwalk, is the **Atlantic City Hilton** (© 800/257-8677 or 609/347-7111; www.hiltonac.com). The Hilton does what AC's other casino hotels don't dare (lest you leave the casino, of course): Provide full beach services to their guests, including beach chairs, cabanas, kayaks, on-the-sand volleyball, and more. It also features the Boardwalk's only beachfront bar, plus a showroom that features Kenny Loggins, Trisha Yearwood, and the like. It's hands-down the best choice in town for those who'd like to play at the beach and/or bring the kids, before returning to high-quality rooms.

At Farley State Marina, a 10-minute drive from the Boardwalk via Brigantine Boulevard (Rte. 87), are two more casinos. With a Big '80s teal color scheme and oldies tunes playing over the sound system, **Harrah's** (© 800/HARRAHS or 609/441-5000; www.harrahs.com) draws a generally older crowd. High rollers seem to love it, as they choose it year in and year out as the city's top Overall Hotel Casino in *Casino Player's* annual readers' poll. **Trump Marina** (© 800/777-8477 or 609/441-2000; www.trumpmarina.com) targets a younger crowd with rock-and-roll Muzak and headliners, but it otherwise seems like just another glittery Trump property. These casinos are rather isolated, even from each other, so you may be better off basing yourself at one of the Boardwalk casino hotels.

IN THE SHOWROOMS   On any given night, Atlantic City's showrooms are peopled with acts ranging from Chris Rock to Tony Bennett to Tom Jones to the Spinners to Duran Duran—and the quality just keeps getting better. Check with the visitors bureau at © 888/AC-VISIT or www.atlanticcitynj.com, or contact the casinos directly for current schedules. You can also find out what's on and buy tickets through **Ticketmaster** (© 856/338-9000; www.ticketmaster.com).

MORE TO SEE & DO

Steel Pier, across from the Taj at Virginia Avenue (© 609/345-4893; www.steelpier.com), is Atlantic City's historic amusement pier, with carnival games and rides for the entire family; it's open daily Memorial Day to Labor Day, weekends only Palm Sunday to Memorial Day and again to October. At

Gardner's Basin, at the top end of New Hampshire Avenue, is the 1999 **Ocean Life Center** (© **609/348-2880;** www.oceanlifecenter.com), with eight giant aquariums (including a touch tank), shipwreck artifacts, and more marine-themed fun for the kids. Sightseeing cruises depart from Gardner's Basin from May to December; call **Atlantic City Cruises** (© **609/347-7600;** www.atlanticcitycruises.com).

WHERE TO STAY

There's no useful way to quote exact room rates at Atlantic City's casino hotels (see "The Casinos," above). Doubles vary from a low of about $89 to a high of $350, and the hotels stay generally competitive across the board. Rates are usually highest on summer weekends and lowest midweek in winter, but they can go through the roof during certain events—most notably the Miss America Pageant, in the fall—or if there's a major convention in town. Always ask about packages and special promotions, which may be able to save you big bucks.

If the big hotels are too expensive for you, you have some non-casino options. There are a few good motels right on or just off the Boardwalk—although these well-located options can be subject to similarly dramatic pricing, with rates fluctuating between $59 and $300 depending on the dates and property; again, always ask about packages. Near the very nice Hilton end of the Boardwalk is the **Holiday Inn Boardwalk,** at Chelsea Avenue (© **800/465-4329** or 609/348-2200; www.holiday-inn.com), and the **Days Inn on the Boardwalk,** 1 block over at Morris Avenue (© **800/325-2525** or 609/344-6101; www.daysinn.com), which even has rooms with ocean views. Just off the Boardwalk, near the Sands, is the **Comfort Inn,** 154 S. Kentucky Ave. (© **800/228-5150** or 609/348-4000; www.comfortinn.com), whose well-kept rooms feature Jacuzzi tubs.

Or you could choose to stay off the Boardwalk altogether in an area where rates tend to fluctuate less. A block inland at South Carolina and Pacific avenues is the **Quality Inn Beach Block** (© **800/228-5151** or 609/345-7070; www.qualityinn.com), the city's best chain motel, with nice decor, free parking, a game room, and a martini lounge.

WHERE TO DINE

On the Boardwalk at the Taj Mahal is the **Hard Rock Cafe** (© **609/441-0007**). **Planet Hollywood** is at Caesars (© **609/347-7827**).

If you're looking for something more sophisticated, take heart. At chic, Tuscan-inspired **Girasole,** in the Ocean Club Condos, 3108 Pacific Ave., at Montpelier Avenue (© **609/345-5554**), the creative kitchen has a welcoming light touch with wood oven–baked pizzas, excellent carpaccios, pastas, and seafood. Similarly moderately priced is century-old **Dock's Oyster House,** 2405 Atlantic Ave., at Georgia Avenue (© **609/345-0092**), still highly regarded for the quality of its seafood and service.

Atlantic City excels at old-world Italian, but none is better than **Angelo's Fairmount Tavern,** which has been going strong at the corner of Mississippi and Fairmount avenues (© **609/344-2439**) for just shy of 65 years; affordable, too.

Appreciably newer on the scene is **Tun Tavern Brewing Company,** across from the Atlantic City Convention Center at the corner of Baltic and Michigan avenues (© **609/347-7800;** www.tuntavern.com). Both quality pub grub and first-rate microbrews are served in a festive, modern setting. For contemporary Southwest-Mex fare served in Atlantic City's coolest building, visit **Los Amigos,** 1926 Atlantic Ave., at Michigan Avenue (© **609/344-2293**).

Among the casino restaurants, a few standouts are worth mentioning. The **Bacchanal,** at Caesars (© 609/348 4411), isn't just a restaurant—it's a complete theatrical event open Wednesday through Sunday. The multicourse feast is served by Ancient Roman gladiators, and wine goddesses pour without limit. It's good kitschy fun, and the gourmet fare is surprisingly well prepared. **Capriccio,** the Italian jewel at Resorts (© 609/344-6000), was rated among America's top 10 in 2002 by Zagat's, with an array of pastas, seafood, and specialties such as osso buco. Harrah's **Fiorentino** (© 609/441-5000) opened in 2001 to bravissimi, and its **Fantasea Reef Buffet** (© 609/441-5000) is the city's top all-you-can-eat fete, loved by locals and visitors alike for its high quality, good value, and stunning display.

The much-lauded **Irish Pub,** just off the Boardwalk at 164 St. James Place (© 609/344-9063; www.theirishpub.com), is appealingly old-fashioned, with friendly service and hearty, satisfying fare that's so cheap it's almost free (nothing over $6.95). Rooms above the pub start at $40, too.

CAPE MAY

At the southern tip of the Garden State is the jewel of the Jersey shore: Cape May, a beautifully preserved Victorian beach resort that's popular with romance-seeking couples drawn by the impeccably restored inns and quaint vibe, and families who like the town's easygoing nature and fine collection of affordable beachfront motels. Visiting Cape May is like taking a step back in time to the glory days of the Jersey shore, before frenetic amusement piers and summer-break college crowds overtook the scene. Even at the height of the summer season, the town stays relaxed and friendly; after a lazy day at the beach, most folks' big activity is to retire to a wide veranda, glass of iced tea in hand, to sit back and watch the world stroll by.

ESSENTIALS

GETTING THERE & GETTING AROUND   Cape May, a spit stretching 20 miles offshore between the Atlantic Ocean and Delaware Bay, is at the southern tip of New Jersey, about 40 miles south of the Atlantic City Toll Plaza at the end of the Garden State Parkway. **NJ Transit** buses (© 973/762-5100 or 215/569-3752; www.njtransit.state.nj.us) arrive from Philadelphia and Atlantic City year-round, and from New York City in summer. If you're arriving from points south, you can take the 70-minute **Cape May–Lewes Ferry** (© 800/64-FERRY; www.capemay-lewesferry.com), which carries passengers and vehicles between Lewes, DE, and Cape May daily year-round.

Cape May can become quite traffic-congested, particularly in summer, so most visitors park their cars for the length of their stay and walk or trolley around town. If you'd like to rent a bike or a four-wheeled surrey for two or for the entire family, stop into **Shields' Bike Rentals,** 11 Gurney St., just inland from Beach Drive (© 609/884-1818), or the **Village Bicycle Shop,** 605 Lafayette St. (© 609/884-8500). You can reserve in advance from **Cape Island Bicycles,** at Beach and Howard streets (© 609/889-8300; www.capeislandbikerentals.com).

VISITOR INFORMATION   For more information, contact the **Chamber of Commerce of Greater Cape May** (© 609/884-5508; www.capemaychamber.com), or the **Cape May County Chamber of Commerce** (© 609/465-5017; www.capemaycountychamber.com). Information is also available online at **www.capemay.com**. For events information, your best source is **www.capemaymac.org**. There's a staffed **information center** at the Ocean View

Plaza Rest Area, 1½ miles beyond the Garden State Parkway's Cape May Toll Plaza. The chamber of commerce runs an excellent **visitor center** a few minutes' drive south, at Exit 11 (on the right side of the road after the traffic light).

SPECIAL EVENTS & FESTIVALS   Highlights include the **Cape May Music Festival,** which draws distinguished classical performers from around the globe over 6 weeks in May and June; the **Cape May Food & Wine Festival,** where open-house food samplings at dozens of participating restaurants consume the better part of a week in late September; hugely popular **Victorian Week** in mid-October, celebrating the town's heritage with historic house tours and other nostalgic events; and **Christmas in Cape May,** a whole host of holiday-themed events that start in mid-November.

EXPLORING CAPE MAY

One of the best ways to explore Cape May is to take one of the many **trolley tours** offered by the Mid-Atlantic Center for the Arts (MAC), Cape May's premier preservation organization (© **800/275-4278** or 609/884-5404; www.capemaymac.org). You can buy tickets at the booth at the entrance to the Washington Street Mall, at Ocean Street; tours generally run a half hour to 45 minutes and concentrate on a specific area of town, so you may want to take more than one. MAC also offers **walking tours, train tours,** and **self-guided audio tours.**

Cape May's top attraction is the **Emlen Physick Estate,** a beautifully restored Victorian house museum. You can see the entire house on the wonderful 45-minute living history tour, which can be combined with a trolley tour. Housed in the carriage house on the estate is the **Twinings Tearoom,** serving lunch and elegant afternoon tea. Call MAC for reservations.

The **Cape May Carriage Co.** (© **609/884-4466**) offers half-hour guided tours in old-fashioned horse-drawn carriages that leave from Ocean Street and Washington Mall.

At the heart of town is the **Washington Street Mall,** a 3-block-long pedestrian mall lined with clothing and gift boutiques. A block over from the mall is **Caroline,** 400 Carpenters Lane (© **609/884-5055**), a first-rate clothing boutique for women. Another top shopping stop is **Cheeks,** at Ocean Street and Columbia Avenue (© **609/884-8484;** www.cheekscapemay.com), for casual wear (easy-care linen, cotton sweaters) and affordable gifts. For a list of local antiques dealers, go online to **www.capemay.com**, or stop by one of the visitor centers listed above and ask for the *Antique Shops of Cape May* map.

No visit to Cape May is complete without a sporting round of mini-golf. The best of the local courses is **Cape May Miniature Golf,** between Jackson and Perry streets (© **609/884-2222**).

BEACHES & NATURAL ATTRACTIONS   The big draws in summer are Cape May's calm waters and wide, white sandy beaches. The beach is accessible all along **Beach Drive,** with concessions and public restrooms available midbeach near Convention Hall (at Stockton Place) and at various points along the Promenade. In summer, **beach tags** are required on all Cape May beaches; virtually all inns and motels provide beach tags (currently $5/day, $10/week) to their guests for free or a deposit.

Locals usually head to **Sunset Beach** at Cape May Point (take West Perry St. to Sunset Blvd.; www.sunsetbeachnj.com), which has a nice swimming cove, easy parking, and a beach grill. It's worth visiting any time of year to see the *Atlantus,* one of 12 experimental concrete ships built during World War I.

Needless to say, this was not a good idea; the curious ship ran aground in 1926, and its remains poke through the waves just offshore.

The area's best beach is 2 miles south of town, at **Cape May Point State Park** (© **609/884-2159;** www.state.nj.us/dep/forestry/parks/capemay.htm), also accessible via Sunset Boulevard (turn left on Lighthouse Ave.). The quiet, noncommercial crescent of white sand has restrooms but no concessions, so pack a picnic. You can climb to the top of **Cape May Lighthouse** (© **609/884-5404;** www.capemay mac.org), the second-tallest operating lighthouse in the United States, for breathtaking coastline views. It's a grueling 199 steps (about 14½ stories), but exhibits give you an excuse to rest at various points along the way. The park also has 3 miles of **hiking trails** through wetlands, which are great for birders.

Avid birders will want to visit the **Cape May Migratory Bird Refuge,** just before the park turnoff on Sunset Boulevard. This 212-acre refuge is one of the East Coast's premier birding areas. Call the New Jersey Audubon Society's **Cape May Bird Observatory** (© **609/884-2736**) for more information.

WHERE TO STAY

Many of Cape May's historic homes have been wonderfully restored and converted into B&Bs. Rates tend to fluctuate dramatically, even for different rooms in the same inn, so it's worth calling around and asking questions. Rates are generally lowest in winter and highest over holiday and summer weekends. Many establishments require minimum stays in season.

The **Mainstay Inn,** 635 Columbia Ave. (© **609/884-8690;** www.mainstay inn.com), housed in an immaculate 1872 Italianate villa, is widely regarded as the town's finest inn. Nonguests can visit the main house by self-guided tour; call for details.

The **Humphrey Hughes House,** 29 Ocean St. (© **609/884-4428;** www. humphreyhugheshouse.com), is a grand museumlike home with intricate chestnut detailing, fabulous period antiques, and a somewhat formal air.

The **Fairthorne,** 111 Ocean St. (© **800/438-8742** or 609/884-8791; www.fairthorne.com), is our absolute favorite. This gorgeous Colonial Revival–style old sailing captain's home is impeccable without being too frilly or formal, and hosts Diane and Ed Hutchinson couldn't be more welcoming. Around the corner is the **John F. Craig House,** 609 Columbia Ave. (© **877/544-0314** or 609/884-0100; www.johnfcraig.com), a beautifully restored Carpenter Gothic inn with a cozy, homey vibe. (*Warning:* Some rooms have tiny bathrooms.)

If you like your lodgings to have a little personality but consider B&Bs too personal (or too expensive), consider one of these historic hotels: the small, elegant **Virginia Hotel,** a full-service hotel since 1879 at 25 Jackson St. (© **800/ 732-4236** or 609/884-5700; www.virginiahotel.com); or the attractive and well-outfitted 11-room **Queen's Hotel,** 601 Columbia Ave. (© **609/884-1613;** www.queenshotel.com), whose innkeepers have eliminated breakfast to emphasize privacy and keep rates low. Overlooking the ocean is the **Hotel Macomber,** 727 Beach Dr. (© **609/884-3020;** www.covesoft.com/Capemay/macomber), a charming old seashore hotel whose comfortable rooms are a steal and whose restaurant, **Union Park** (© **609/884-8811**), is a fine choice.

Beach Drive is lined with value-priced motels—all with pools—that are ideal for those who prefer to avoid the fussiness of historic properties. Our favorite of a very good bunch is the **Sandpiper Beach Inn,** 11 Beach Dr. (© **609/ 884-4256;** www.capemaysandpiper.com), a lovely gray-and-white clapboard across from an excellent stretch of beach at the quietest end of Beach Drive. The rooms are mostly spacious, like-new suites with nice furnishings and modern kitchenettes. Note that the Sandpiper mainly caters to adults—but not so the **Periwinkle Inn,** 1039 Beach Dr. (© **609/884-9200;** www.periwinkleinn.com), which has similarly nice efficiency apartment units, all situated around a lush lawn that makes a perfect playground for the kids. The pool is nicely set back from the street (rather than overlooking the parking lot, like most in the neighborhood), and there's a separate kiddie pool. Note, however, the Periwinkle's cash-only policy, and the fact that they don't issue beach tags.

Another good choice is **La Mer,** at 1317 Beach Dr. (© **609/884-9000;** www.lamermotorinn.com), whose new addition features very comfortable rooms that are big enough for budget-minded families. The rooms in the older building are cheaper but not nearly as spiffy.

WHERE TO DINE

Cape May boasts an excellent, if pricey, collection of restaurants. Very highly regarded is the **Water's Edge,** at Beach Drive and Pittsburgh Avenue (© **609/884-1717**), a romantic contemporary dining room with a consistently excellent creative chops-and-seafood menu and marvelous ocean views.

Cape May's finest is the elegant **Washington Inn,** 801 Washington St., at Jefferson Street (© **609/884-5697;** www.washingtoninn.com), whose winning New American takes on such classics as rack of lamb and filet mignon are complemented by faultless service and a super-romantic setting. Perfect for celebrating a special occasion. For similar quality with an ocean view and retro Miami feel, opt to dine at the Washington's brand-new sister restaurant, the **Pelican Club,** since 2000 atop the Marquis de Lafayette Hotel, 501 Beach Ave. (© **609/884-3500**).

For classics like clams casino, shrimp cocktail, and thick-cut steaks, head to the **Merion Inn,** 106 Decatur St., at Columbia Avenue (© **609/884-8363**), somewhat less expensive than the Washington Inn but no less romantic. This dimly lit, old-world restaurant also has an excellent mahogany bar and live soft jazz in summer.

For more affordable eats, the distinctive yellow striped awning signals the **Mad Batter,** 19 Jackson St., just off Carpenters Lane (© **609/884-5970;** www. madbatter.com), a comfortable, casual restaurant specializing in from-scratch-made breakfasts, fresh, leafy salads at lunch, and unfussy European-style entrees at dinner. Live music.

If you want a quick, inexpensive lunch, your best bet is the **Depot Market Cafe,** 409 Elmira St. (next to the Village Bike Shop on Ocean St.; © **609/ 884-8030**), an ultra-casual sandwich shop with homemade everything and a pleasing alfresco patio.

Overlooking the beach action is **McGlade's on the Pier,** on the Promenade at Convention Hall (© **609/884-2614**), where the stars of the otherwise-average burgers-and-seafood menu are the stellar crab cakes and omelets. Next door is **Henry's on the Beach** (© **609/884-8826**), serving a similar all-day menu.

5 Baltimore

A combination of interesting tourist attractions, historical sites, and friendly people in such picturesque old neighborhoods as Fells Point, Mount Vernon, Canton, and Federal Hill makes Baltimore an ever-more-popular tourist destination.

"Charm City" has welcomed visitors since 1729. It was founded as a shipping and ship-building town, so manufacturing has always been a big part of this city. General Motors and Bethlehem Steel have been a part of the east Baltimore landscape for decades. Domino Sugar's sign dominates the Inner Harbor. More

Baltimore

ACCOMMODATIONS ■
Days Inn Inner Harbor **5**
Harbor Court Hotel **10**
Holiday Inn Inner Harbor **4**
Hyatt Regency Baltimore **6**
Pier 5 Hotel **11**
Renaissance Harborplace
Hotel **8**

DINING ◆
Brass Elephant **1**
Charleston **12**
Hampton's **9**
Pisces **7**
Prime Rib **2**
Woman's Industrial
Exchange Restaurant **3**

recently, Baltimore has welcomed a new wave of service industries and nonprofits. And baseball fans flock to Camden Yards, Baltimore's beautiful ballpark, which has been instrumental in revitalizing the city's downtown area. Tourism plays an ever-increasing role in the city's economy, and a laid-back population welcomes its visitors with a friendly "Hello, hon!" in the unique Bawlamer accent.

ESSENTIALS

GETTING THERE   By Plane   Baltimore–Washington International Airport (© **800/I-FLY-BWI** or 410/859-7111) is 10 miles south of downtown Baltimore, off I-295 (the Baltimore–Washington Pkwy.). It's a major domestic and international hub. To drive to downtown Baltimore from the airport, take I-195 west to Route 295 north. **BWI Airport Shuttle** (known as SuperShuttle; © **800/258-3826** or 410/859-0800; www.supershuttle.com) operates vans between the airport and all major downtown hotels. Departures are scheduled every 30 minutes between 5:45am and 11:15pm, and the cost is $11 per person one-way or $18 round-trip. The **Light Rail** also connects the airport with downtown Baltimore and the Amtrak stations at BWI and at Penn Station.

By Car   I-95 provides the easiest routes to Baltimore from the north and south. Take I-95 south to I-395 (Exit 53), and follow signs to the Inner Harbor. If you're driving in from the north, you'll have to pass through the **Fort McHenry Tunnel** ($1 toll). From the west, take **I-70** east to Exit 91, I-695 south (the **Baltimore Beltway**) heading toward Glen Burnie. Take Exit 11A, I-95 to I-395, north to downtown.

Once you arrive, you'll find lots of parking garages, as well as metered on-street parking throughout the downtown district. Garages charge about $15 a day, or $5 to $8 for special events or evening visits. Parking meters must be fed $1 every hour.

By Train   Baltimore is a stop on Amtrak's (© **800/872-7245;** www.amtrak. com) Northeast Corridor, between Wilmington and Washington, D.C. Trains arrive at and depart from Pennsylvania Station, 1500 N. Charles St. (north of the Inner Harbor), and BWI Airport Rail station (© **410/672-6169**), off Route 170 about 1½ miles from the airport. In addition, the **Maryland Area Rail Commuter Service** (MARC; © **800/325-RAIL**) provides rail service on two routes from Washington, D.C., stopping at BWI en route. One ends at Camden Station, closest to the Inner Harbor, and the other ends at Penn Station about 20 blocks north.

VISITOR INFORMATION   Call the **Baltimore Area Convention and Visitors Association** at 100 Light St., Baltimore, MD 21202 (© **877/ BALTIMORE;** www.Baltimore.org). BACVA has all sorts of information to help you plan your trip, including maps, brochures, and water taxi schedules. In town, check out the visitor center at Harborplace. It is located in a gray trailer just beside the Light Street Pavilion. You can also pick up a copy of the *Baltimore Quick Guide,* a purse-sized guide to what's happening in and around the city.

GETTING AROUND   Because so many of Baltimore's major attractions are clustered around the Inner Harbor, walking is often the easiest way to get around.

Baltimore's **Mass Transit Administration (MTA)** operates **Light Rail,** a 27-mile trolley system that travels north-south from the northern suburb of Timonium to Glen Burnie in the south, with a spur to Penn Station. The key stop within the city is Camden Station, next to the Orioles' ballpark. The Light Rail is the ideal way to get to a game or to travel within the downtown area between

Camden Yards and the Inner Harbor to Lexington Market and the area around Mount Vernon Place. Tickets are $2.50 round trip and are dispensed at machines at each stop. Trains run every 15 to 30 minutes Monday through Friday between 6am and 11pm, Saturday between 8am and 11pm, and Sunday between 11am and 7pm.

Baltimore's MTA also operates **Metro,** a subway system that connects downtown with the northwest suburbs, and an extensive **bus** system. The fare is $1.35; you can also purchase a day pass that allows unlimited trips on the Light Rail, Metro, and city buses for $3. For information on both Light Rail and Metro service, call ℂ **800/543-9809** or 410/539-5000 or visit the MTA website at **www.mtamaryland.com**.

All taxis in the city are metered; two reputable companies are **Yellow Checker Cab** (ℂ **410/841-5573**) and **Arrow Cab** (ℂ **410/261-0000**).

A ride on a water taxi is a pleasant way to visit Baltimore's attractions, or even to go to dinner. Two companies operate water taxi service and both have different stops. But you can use either to get within walking distance of your waterfront destination. **Ed Kane's Water Taxi & Trolley** (ℂ **800/658-8947** or 410/563-3901) runs a continual service between about a dozen Inner Harbor locations including Harborplace, Fells Point, and Fort McHenry. The main stop at Harborplace is on the corner between the two pavilions. Tell the mate where you want to go, not all taxis stop at every destination. The cost is $5 for adults and $2 for children 10 and under for unlimited use of the water taxi and trolley for a full day. The **Seaport Taxi** (ℂ **410/675-2900**) goes to many of the same destinations as Ed Kane's, and their stops are usually next to each other. Adults can ride all day for $4 and children 10 and under for $2.

FAST FACTS   City hospitals include Johns Hopkins Hospital, 600 N. Wolfe St. (ℂ **410/955-5000**); University of Maryland Medical Center, 22 S. Greene St. (ℂ **410/328-8667**); and Mercy Medical Center, 301 St. Paul St. (ℂ **410/332-9000**).

There's a **Rite Aid** at 17 W. Baltimore St. (ℂ **410/539-0838**). **Walgreens** is at 19 E. Fayette St. (ℂ **410/625-1179**).

The state sales tax is 5%. The hotel tax is an additional 7.5%.

Baltimore has a nagging problem with property and violent crime. More police, along with the Downtown Partnership's safety guides, are doing a pretty good job of keeping the Inner Harbor and Mount Vernon areas fairly safe. But be alert and follow common-sense precautions. In some parts of the city, you're bound to be approached by a panhandler. Don't open your wallet or purse to give money. Offer only what's in your pocket. It's okay to say no, too.

SPECIAL EVENTS   The biggest and best-known event in Baltimore is the **Preakness Celebration** (www.preaknesscelebration.com), a weeklong, citywide party leading up to the Preakness Stakes in mid-May, the middle jewel of horse-racing's Triple Crown. Events include a 5K run, music festival, hot-air balloon races, a golf tournament, and much more. For tickets to the horse race, call ℂ **410/542-9400**.

WHAT TO SEE & DO

American Visionary Art Museum   Look for the "Whirligig," a 55-foot multicolored, wind-powered sculpture at the front of this curvaceous building housing some of the most interesting art you're bound to see. Visionary art is made by people who aren't trained as artists but feel compelled to draw, paint, or create something in an unusual medium. A 10-foot model of the *Lusitania* made from 193,000 matchsticks dominates a first-floor gallery. All the exhibits are fascinating, but some are disturbing and certainly too strong for children (alerts are posted). Other exhibits are a joy that children would love. There is also a sculpture barn and a sculpture garden filled with delights. 800 Key Hwy. ℂ 410/244-1900. Admission $6 adults, $4 seniors and children. Tues–Sun 10am–6pm. Closed Thanksgiving and Dec 25. Take Light St. south, turn left onto Key Hwy. (at the Maryland Science Center); museum is about 3 blocks on right.

Babe Ruth Birthplace and Museum/Baltimore Orioles Museum George Herman "Babe" Ruth was born in this row house. Two rooms are re-created as they would have looked when the Sultan of Swat was a boy. Other exhibits include a wall enumerating all his home runs, and memorabilia from his major league career as well as from his days at St. Mary's Industrial School in southwest Baltimore, where he learned to play the game. The Orioles and gone-but-not-forgotten Colts have their own exhibits here, as well. 216 Emory St. ℂ 410/727-1539. Fax 410/727-1652. www.baberuthmuseum.com. Admission $6 adults, $4 seniors, $3 ages 5–16. Apr–Oct daily 10am–5pm (until 7pm on Orioles home game days); Nov–Mar daily 10am–4pm. Closed Jan 1, Thanksgiving, and Dec 25. From Camden Yards walk 2 blocks west on Pratt and south on Emory. It's a tiny street.

Baltimore Museum of Art The largest museum in Maryland, the BMA boasts galleries dedicated to modern and contemporary art; European sculpture and painting; American painting and decorative arts; prints and photographs; arts of Africa, Asia, the Americas, and Oceania; and a 2.7-acre sculpture garden. The BMA is famous for the Matisse collection, now housed in the new $4-million Cone Wing, which also showcases other Impressionist paintings by Cézanne, Gauguin, van Gogh, and Renoir. Other highlights include the 35,000-square-foot West Wing for Contemporary Art, with works by Andy Warhol; a wonderful gallery of miniature rooms; and a new wing featuring a collection of Old Masters. 10 Art Museum Dr. (at N. Charles St. and 31st St.). ℂ 410/396-7100. www. artbma.org. Admission $7 adults, $5 seniors and students with ID, free for ages 18 and under, free admission on 1st Thurs of the month. Wed–Fri 11am–5pm; Sat–Sun 11am–6pm. Bus: 3 or 11. Take Howard St. north; bear right onto Art Museum Dr., about 3 miles north of the harbor.

Baltimore Zoo The third oldest zoo in the United States, this beloved attraction is in the midst of modernizing its facilities to the tune of $60 million. Some 2,000 animals live here, including a beloved polar bear, prairie dogs, and tigers. Several exhibits have already been renovated, including the Chimpanzee Forest, Leopard Lair, and African Watering Hole. The children's zoo is a must-see for kids with its lily pads, tree slide, farm animals, and Maryland wilderness exhibit. Plan to spend a few hours here. Druid Hill Park. ℂ 410/366-LION. www.baltimorezoo.org. Admission $10 adults, $6 seniors and ages 2–15. Daily 10am–4pm. Take Exit 7 (Druid Hill Lake Dr.) off I-83 and follow the signs for the zoo.

Basilica of the Assumption of the Blessed Virgin Mary This neoclassical gem has been a monument to religious freedom since 1806. As it nears its 200th birthday, this cathedral of the Catholic Archdiocese of Baltimore is undergoing a complete restoration. Designed by Benjamin Latrobe—who designed the U.S. Capitol at the same time—the neoclassical basilica is considered one of the most beautiful churches in the country. A national shrine and historic landmark, it was the first cathedral built in the United States. Do call ahead or check the website, as some parts of the renovation may require that the building be temporarily closed. 400 block of Cathedral St. ℂ 410/727-3564. Free admission. Masses daily; tours offered after the 10:45am Sun Mass and by appointment. Take Charles St. north; turn left on Franklin St. and left again onto Cathedral St. Parking garage located on Franklin and Cathedral is convenient

Edgar Allan Poe's Grave Site and Memorial Three modest memorials in this small old graveyard recall the poet who wrote "The Tell-Tale Heart" and "The Raven" (the only poem to inspire an NFL team's name). The main memorial features a bas-relief bust of Poe; a small gravestone adorned with a raven can be found at Poe's original burial lot; and there's also a plaque placed by the French, who, thanks to the poet Baudelaire, enjoy some of the best translations of Poe's works. The poet is remembered on his birthday every January when a mysterious visitor leaves half a bottle of cognac and roses at the grave. On the weekend closest to Poe's birthday, a party is held in his honor. Westminster Cemetery on the southeast corner of Fayette and Greene sts. ℂ 410/706-2072. Daily 8am–dusk. Closed major holidays.

Fort McHenry The flag that flies at Fort McHenry is 30 feet by 42 feet, big enough for Francis Scott Key to see by the dawn's early light and write "The Star-Spangled Banner." The star-shaped fort, now a national park, looks much as it did in 1814, the year of the British attack. Its buildings, repaired in the days following that attack, still stand. Exhibits recall Baltimore under siege during the War of 1812, the fort's Civil War service, and its use as an army hospital during World War I. Visitors are invited to take part in the daily changing of the flag, so stop by at 9:30am or 4:30pm (7:30pm June–Aug) to join in. A visit takes about 90 minutes. Fort McHenry National Monument and Historic Shrine, E. Fort Ave. ℂ 410/962-4290. Admission $5, free for under age 17. Sept–May daily 8am–5pm; June to Labor Day 8am–8pm. Free parking. Stop on water taxi and Seaport Taxi routes.

Maryland Science Center The Maryland Science Center doesn't shy away from anything scientific. Three floors of exhibits include the popular Outer Space Place, home of the Hubble Space Telescope National Visitor Center, and Space Link, which offers a live connection to NASA. Sometimes the exhibits are too crowded or have limited interest, but the IMAX theater and planetarium are always worth a visit. The IMAX theater presents shows as diverse as *Beauty and the Beast* and *Space Station 3D*. Lightspeed Laser Theater uses lasers to tell a scientific tale. The 3-D movies are breathtaking. IMAX is so popular, extra screenings are available Thursday and Sunday evenings. The stars are on display at the David Planetarium or The Crosby Ramsey Memorial Observatory (open Thurs nights free of charge). 601 Light St., Baltimore, MD 21230 (south side of the Inner Harbor). ℂ 410/685-5225. www.mdsci.org. Admission varies according to the special exhibits. A recent trip cost $18 for adults, $14 for children, and $15 for seniors. Mon–Fri 10am–5pm; Sat–Sun 11am–6pm with extended hours in summer. Call ahead, as hours change with some exhibits. Metered on-street parking and paid lots on Light St. and Key Hwy. Water taxi stop.

National Aquarium in Baltimore Visitors can walk into a room surrounded by patrolling sharks, wander among the coral reefs, follow the yearly migration of fish, and visit a rainforest on the roof at one of best aquariums in the country. In addition to the watery denizens, exhibits include a popular puffin display; *Maryland: Mountains to the Sea;* and a new Amazon River Forest filled with plants and animals as well as fish. The sharks are a main attraction, as is a dolphins exhibit/performance. New for 2001 was the small seahorse exhibit; these delicate, colorful little animals are a delight. **The Marine Mammal Pavilion** is where you'll find the dolphins: three generations from one family. Don't miss the presentations; reserve a seat when you get your tickets at no additional fee.

Insider tip: The aquarium draws huge crowds in summer. The best way to beat the crush is to buy timed tickets in advance and/or visit during non-peak times, especially weekday mornings, Friday evenings, or after 3pm. 501 E. Pratt St., on the harbor. (☎) 410/576-3800. www.aqua.org. Admission $16 adults, $13 seniors, $9.50 ages 3–11. July–Aug daily 9am–8pm; Mar–June and Sept–Oct Sat–Thurs 9am–5pm, Fri 9am–8pm; Nov–Feb Sat–Thurs 10am–5pm, Fri 10am–8pm. Hours and prices subject to change. Exhibits are open 2 hr. after last ticket is sold.

USS Constellation   You can't miss the *Constellation,* docked for years at the Inner Harbor (pre-dating Harborplace). A stunning triple-masted sloop-of-war originally launched in 1854, the *Constellation* is the last Civil War–era vessel afloat. Tour her gun decks, visit the wardrooms, see a cannon demonstration, and learn about the life of a sailor. Demonstrations begin with the raising of the colors at 10:30am and continue on the hour. Pier 1, 301 E. Pratt St. (☎) 410/539-1797. www.constellation.org. Admission $6.50 adults, $5 seniors, $3.50 ages 6–14. Admission includes audio tour. Daily May to mid-Oct 10am–6pm; mid-Oct to Apr 10am–4pm.

Walters Art Museum   The Walters, with its collections of ancient art, medieval armor, and French 19th-century painting, has always been one of Baltimore's great attractions. And a 3-year renovation, ended in late 2001, has only made it better. Walk through the galleries of sculpture, paintings, gold jewelry, mummies, and sarcophagi and see the progress of fine art through 50 centuries. The exhibits end with objects from the Middle Ages in the Knight's Hall, with tapestries, furnishings, and suits of armor. Free admission days make it easier for parents to bring their children to this wonderful place. 600 N. Charles St. (☎) 410/547-9000. www.thewalters.org. Admission $8 adults, $6 seniors, $5 students and young adults, free for 17 and under. No admission charged 1st Thurs or Sat of each month 10am–1pm. Tues–Sun 10am–5pm. Bus: 3, 11, or 22; Light Rail to Centre St.; or take Charles St. north to the Washington Monument.

WHERE TO STAY

It can be hard to find a double in Baltimore for under $100 during the week; but that also means that some hotels offer weekend rates and packages that represent savings of 35% to 50% off normal Sunday-through-Thursday tariffs. So don't be scared off by midweek rates—try to time your visit for a weekend.

Admiral Fell Inn   Updated and expanded over the years, this charming inn sits just a block from the harbor in the heart of Fells Point. It is composed of seven buildings, built between 1790 and 1920 and blending Victorian and Federal-style architecture. The inn features an antiques-filled lobby and library and guest rooms individually decorated with Federal period furnishings. Some have canopy beds, and one suite has a fireplace and Jacuzzi. Two rooms feature balconies. A more rustic loft room has sloping ceilings that tall guests might not like, but its three dormer windows offer some of the best views in the inn. There's a complimentary shuttle to downtown. 888 S. Broadway, Baltimore, MD 21231. (☎) 800/292-4667 or 410/522-7377. Fax 410/522-0707. www.AdmiralFell.com. 80 units. $215–$265 double. Rates include continental breakfast. AE, MC, V. Self-parking free, valet parking $7. **Amenities:** Restaurant; pets (crate-trained dogs) permitted with additional fee.

Celie's Waterfront Inn   This 18th-century town house is one of only a few bed-and-breakfasts in Baltimore and it's delightful. Each of the rooms has its own charms: two have a fireplace and whirlpool and harbor views. Two inside rooms are particularly quiet, as they overlook the courtyard filled with flowers in summer. Two rooms with city views as nice as the harbor view have private balconies and whirlpool tubs. One ground-floor room has its own courtyard. Furnishings were chosen with comfort in mind, with big beds, private bathrooms, and a homey parlor. Have breakfast in your room, on the deck, or in the garden. 1714 Thames St., Fells Point, Baltimore, MD 21231. © **800/432-0184** or 410/522-2323. Fax 410/522-2324. celies@aol.com. 7 units. $132–$242 double. Rate includes hearty continental breakfast. AE, DISC, MC, V. 2- or 3-night minimums may be required on weekends or holidays. Ask about parking arrangements. On water taxi route.

Days Inn Inner Harbor   If you're willing to give up proximity to the harbor (by 2 or 3 blocks), you can get a great deal at this modern nine-story hotel. It is located between the arena and convention center, and only 3 blocks from Camden Yards. "Work zone" rooms for business travelers offer large desks, a kitchenette, and plenty of room, but all rooms have the comfort you expect from this chain. Guest rooms offer standard chain-motel furnishings, plus hair dryers, irons, and Nintendo games. 100 Hopkins Place (between Lombard and Pratt sts.), Baltimore, MD 21202. © **800/DAYS-INN** or 410/576-1000. Fax 410/576-9437. www.daysinnerharbor.com. 250 units. $89–$174 double. Children under 17 stay free in parents' room. AE, DC, DISC, MC, V. Parking $11. **Amenities:** Restaurant; outdoor pool; complimentary access to nearby health club.

Harbor Court Hotel   The Harbor Court strives for quiet dignity, refinement, and graciousness. It's a treat to walk in the door, and if you spend the night, prepare to be pampered. Rooms are exquisitely furnished, from suites with hand-painted decorations, marble bathrooms, kitchenettes, and canopy beds to large standard rooms outfitted in fine furnishings. The hotel overlooks the harbor but only a few rooms have a clear harbor view. Dining options include two first-rate restaurants: **Hampton's** (see "Where to Dine" below) and **Brighton's,** which serves a rich afternoon tea; and the **Explorer's Lounge,** which offers music every night and is popular with locals as well as hotel guests. 550 Light St., Baltimore, MD 21202. © **800/824-0076** or 410/234-0550. Fax 410/659-5925. www.harborcourt. com. 195 units. $220–$250 double; $375–$2,000 suite. AE, DC, DISC, MC, V. Self-parking $14, valet parking $18. **Amenities:** Restaurants (3); indoor pool; fitness center with tennis.

Holiday Inn Inner Harbor   For value and location, it's hard to beat this oldtimer, the first major chain property in Baltimore. Located a block away from Oriole Park and 3 blocks from Harborplace, it has an executive tower with 175 rooms geared to business travelers and has been updated and renovated regularly. Guest rooms are decorated in bright colors with traditional furniture including a desk, brass fixtures, and wide windows offering views of the city skyline. 301 W. Lombard St., Baltimore, MD 21201. © **800/HOLIDAY** or 410/685-3500. Fax 410/727-6169. www.holiday-inn.com/bal-downtown. 375 units. $129–$189 double; $285 suite. Children under 18 stay free in parents' room. AE, DC, DISC, MC, V. Self-parking $8. **Amenities:** Restaurant; indoor pool.

Hyatt Regency Baltimore   The eye-catching all-glass Hyatt has the best location in town. It's a short walk across a skywalk to the Inner Harbor, across another skywalk to the convention center, and a few blocks to the stadiums. Rooms are standard hotel chain, but have breathtaking harbor views and terrific amenities. It's often busy but not too noisy. Staff here couldn't be nicer. Kids under 18 stay free here but if your family needs two rooms, the second one's half-price. 300 Light St., Baltimore, MD 21202. © **800/233-1234** or 410/528-1234. Fax 410/685-3362. 486 units. $125–$300 double. Ask for packages and discounts. AE, DC, DISC, MC, V. Self-parking $15, valet parking $20. **Amenities:** Restaurant; indoor pool; health club; putting green; 2 tennis courts.

Pier 5 Hotel   Painted in purple, yellow, and red, the lobby of the Pier 5 features furniture in a style combining Art Deco and Cartoon Network. It works, though. The rooms continue the color scheme, though at much quieter and more refined levels. Standard rooms are quite comfortable and have lots of conveniences—robes, bottled water, even room service from the Cheesecake Factory. Suites are luxurious with one, two, or even three tiny balconies overlooking the water or the National Aquarium next door. Just about every room has a water view. They offer lots of packages for both families and couples. 771 Eastern Ave. (at the end of Pier 5), Baltimore, MD 21202. ✆ 410/539-2000. Fax 410/783-1469. www. harbormagic.com. 65 units. $149–$269 double; $375 suite. AE, DC, DISC, MC, V. Self-parking $16, valet parking $20. Located on a water taxi stop. **Amenities:** Restaurants (4); pets welcome.

Renaissance Harborplace Hotel   The Renaissance is right in the middle of everything. It's part of The Gallery at Harborplace, five floors of shops and a food court topped by an office tower. Rooms are the biggest in Baltimore with comfortable furniture and wide windows that really open overlooking the Inner Harbor. (Its views are good; the Hyatt's are better.) There's a concierge level with a lounge where breakfast is served. 202 E. Pratt St., Baltimore, MD 21202. ✆ 800/ 468-3571 or 410/547-1200. Fax 410/783-9676. http://renaissancehotels.com. 622 units. $129–$309 double. Children under 17 stay free in parents' room. AE, DC, DISC, MC, V. Self-parking $16, valet parking $20. **Amenities:** Restaurant; indoor pool; fitness room.

WHERE TO DINE

Black Olive GREEK/SEAFOOD   This Greek *taverna*, just beyond the busier streets of Fells Point, is creating its own traffic. The combination of Greek fare and the freshest seafood have made this place a standout. Choose whatever the catch of the day is and trust the chef to make it wonderful. The restaurant has two small, intimate dining rooms, so small that reservations are a must. The service here is also top-notch and relaxed. 814 S. Bond St. ✆ 410/276-7141. www. blackolive.com. Reservations required. Main courses $22–$32. AE, MC, V. Mon–Thurs 5–10pm; Fri–Sat 5–10:30pm; Sun 5–9pm.

Brass Elephant AMERICAN   The Brass Elephant returned to its 1981 menu for its 20th anniversary, and the response was so enthusiastic, they've kept it. Lower prices and hearty American food have replaced the fancy entrees. So now you spend about $30 per person for some wine, some crab chowder, rockfish, or stuffed pork chops. And all of this comes in one of Baltimore's most elegant restaurant settings, an 1861 town house with fireplace, chandeliers, and gold-leaf trim. Valet parking is complimentary. 924 N. Charles St. ✆ 410/547-8480. Reservations required. Main courses $13–$24. AE, DC, DISC, MC, V. Sun–Thurs 5:30–9pm; Fri–Sat 5:30–11pm.

Charleston AMERICAN/SOUTHERN   With a beautiful setting and imaginative menu, the Charleston is a top choice for a special night out. The menu changes every day, but might include she-crab soup; a salad of kiwi, mango, baby arugula, and micro-greens dressed with lavender-honey and lemon vinaigrette; grilled yellowfin tuna with Andouille sausage; and fried green tomato and tomato-basil relish. Portions aren't so big you can't enjoy dessert, so splurge on homemade ice cream, napoleons, or crème brûlée. Can't decide? Charleston offers a five-course menu of the evening for about $60 a person or a seven-course tasting menu for about $70. There's a selection of 500 bottles of wine to choose from. All the dining rooms are warm and inviting—the main room gives diners an opportunity to see the open kitchen. 1000 Lancaster St., Inner Harbor E. ✆ 410/ 332-7373. Fax 410/332-8475. www.charlestonrestaurant.com. Reservations recommended. Main courses $20–$28. AE, DC, DISC, MC, V. Mon–Sat 5:30–10pm.

Hampton's NEW AMERICAN   Overlooking the Inner Harbor and the National Aquarium, this highly touted restaurant is the main dining room of the Harbor Court Hotel and worth a splurge for a special night out or sumptuous brunch. Dinner choices include Maine lobster *gratine;* pan-seared tenderloin *au poivre;* and a trio of lamb consisting of roast rack, seared loin, and braised osso buco with goat cheese polenta and zinfandel lamb jus. The brunch—appetizer, entree, dessert buffet, and flowing champagne—is quite popular, so be sure to make reservations. In the Harbor Court Hotel, 550 Light St. ℂ 410/234-0550. Reservations required. Jackets required for men. Main courses $28–$38; brunch $23–$33. AE, DC, DISC, MC, V. Sun and Tues–Thurs 5:30–10pm; Fri–Sat 5:30–11pm; brunch Sun 10:30am–2pm. Valet or self parking are complimentary for dinner and brunch guests.

Obrycki's SEAFOOD   Fells Point, the neighborhood where Baltimore began, is one of the city's best areas for seafood, and the benchmark of all the eateries here is Obrycki's. Foodies Craig Claiborne and George Lang rave about this place. The decor is charming, with stained-glass windows and brick archways. But the big attraction is the fresh seafood, especially crabs. There's crab soup, crab cocktail, crab balls, crab cakes, crab imperial, and soft-shell crabs. The rest of the menu is just as tempting—shrimp, lobster, scallops, haddock, flounder, and steaks. The service is extremely attentive. 1727 E. Pratt St., Upper Fells Point. ℂ 410/732-6399. Reservations accepted only until 7pm Mon–Fri and 6pm Sat–Sun. Main courses $15–$29; lunch/light fare $6.95–$14. AE, DC, DISC, MC, V Mon–Fri 11:30am–10pm; Sat 11:30am–11pm; Sun 11:30am–9pm. Closed late Nov to mid-Mar.

Pisces SEAFOOD   In a city where lots of restaurants have good views, this view tops them all. Overlooking the Inner Harbor, Camden Yards, and the downtown skyline, this two-tiered rooftop restaurant was voted "Baltimore's best view" by the readers of *Baltimore* magazine. The interior is sleek and modern, the menu small but intriguing. Soups can range from cream of crab to grilled seafood miso, while entrees are mostly seafood wrapped in creative sauces and seasonings. Though the dining area is not particularly large, the well-spaced tables offer a pleasantly intimate dining experience. The waitstaff is quite knowledgeable, and service is anything but hurried. This is a place to relax and enjoy a spectacular view and a well-prepared meal. In the Hyatt Regency Hotel, 300 Light St., 15th floor. ℂ 410/528-1234. Reservations recommended. Main courses $15–$29. AE, DC, DISC, MC, V. Daily 4:30pm–1am.

Prime Rib STEAK HOUSE   In the heart of Mount Vernon, this popular restaurant—a standout for fine beef since 1965—serves the best prime rib around. In fact, it could spoil you for all other steaks. The pork chops are huge; the Caesar salad is dressed to perfection; the lobster bisque is rich and creamy. If you want seafood, there are crab cakes, and a variety of fish dishes, such as blackened grouper. Tables are squeezed together and intimate conversation is impossible. But people come here for the food, not to talk. 1101 N. Calvert St. (between Biddle and Chase sts.). ℂ 410/539-1804. Reservations recommended. Main courses $17–$39. AE, DC, DISC, MC, V. Daily 5pm–midnight.

Sabatino's ITALIAN   Sabatino's still stands out for its exceptional Italian cuisine at reasonable prices. Everyone will tell you to get the house salad with the house dressing—it's thick and garlicky. Simple pasta dishes come in very large portions. The menu also has some seafood and meat dishes with pasta on the side. Dining rooms fill three floors of this narrow building. It's worth the wait to be seated upstairs where it's quieter. This is a particularly good late-night dining spot, a good place to people-watch after the bars have closed. 901 Fawn St.

(at the corner of High St.). (℃ **410/727-9414.** Fax 410/837-6540. www.sabatinos.com. Reservations recommended. Main courses $10–$17; lunch $8–$15. AE, DC, DISC, MC, V. Daily noon–3am.

Vaccaro's ITALIAN PASTRIES & DESSERTS   To top off a perfect day, stop at Vaccaro's, the always-busy restaurant for Italian desserts, coffee, and cappuccino. In addition to cannoli, rum cake, and tiramisu, it serves huge portions of decadently rich gelato. (Can't decide on a flavor? Ask the waitress for a sampler and you'll get three different flavors.) They don't take reservations, but the wait is never too long. There's also a location at the Light Street Pavilion in Harborplace. 222 Albemarle St. (℃ **410/685-4905.** Desserts $3.75–$7.50. AE, MC, V. Mon–Wed 7:30am–10pm; Thurs, Sun 7:30am–11pm; Fri–Sat 7:30am–1am.

Woman's Industrial Exchange Restaurant AMERICAN   Housed in an 1815 brick building, where you're greeted by a gracious doorman, this restaurant, along with the craft shop, has been helping women help themselves since post–Civil War days. The waitresses, wearing big white bows around their blue uniforms serve up delicious breakfasts and lunches. (In the movie *Sleepless in Seattle,* waitress Miss Marguerite made her acting debut at age 92.) The menu is simple, with homemade soups, salads, sandwiches, omelets, meat or fish platters, and luscious desserts (charlotte russe is a specialty). The chicken salad is terrific. Afterward, take time to browse in the shop. 333 N. Charles St. (℃ **410/685-4388.** Main courses $3.95–$6.95. MC, V. Mon–Fri 7am–3pm.

BALTIMORE AFTER DARK

Baltimore used to be very quiet after dark. Fells Point's bars always drew a crowd, and the streets were busy when a concert or play was scheduled. Now, however, the Inner Harbor, Federal Hill, Canton, Fells Point, and Mount Vernon have all developed lives after dark.

For major events, check the arts and entertainment sections of the *Baltimore Sun* and the *Washington Post.* The *City Paper,* a free Baltimore weekly, has very complete listings down to the smallest local bars and clubs.

Tickets for most major venues are available at the individual box offices, at **Ticketmaster** (℃ **410/481-SEAT;** www.ticketmaster.com), or at **Baltimore Tickets** (℃ **410/BALT-TIX**) at the visitor center at the Inner Harbor.

THE PERFORMING ARTS   The **Baltimore Symphony Orchestra** (℃ **410/ 783-8000;** www.baltimoresymphony.org) performs several concerts a week at the Joseph Meyerhoff Symphony Hall September through June. Each season brings classical and pops concerts. In the summertime, you'll find the BSO outside at Oregon Ridge Park, north of the city off I-83. Their Fourth of July concerts are terrific fun. Tickets range from $15 to $60.

Visiting Broadway shows often play at the **Morris A. Mechanic Theater** (℃ **410/625-4230**) at Baltimore and Charles streets, a block from the harbor; and there are several local professional theater companies.

Center Stage, 700 N. Calvert St. (℃ **410/332-0033;** www.centerstage.org), Maryland's state theater, has been presenting new and classic works since 1963. The theater has two spaces, one a traditional proscenium stage and the other offering directors more flexibility in set design and staging. Tickets cost $10 to $38.

For entertainment by local professional actors at affordable prices, check out these area theaters: the **Fells Point Corner Theater,** 251 S. Ann St. (℃ **410/276-7837;** www.fpct.org), presents eight productions a year. The **Vagabond Players,** 806 S. Broadway (℃ **410/563-9135**), presents a variety of classics, contemporary comedies, and dramas.

The city's prominent black theater company, **Arena Players** (801 McCulloh St., off Martin Luther King Blvd.; © 410/728-6500), presents contemporary plays and romantic comedies.

THE CLUB & MUSIC SCENE   National acts come to the **Baltimore Arena** near the Inner Harbor and to the **Pier Six Concert Pavilion** at the Inner Harbor. A number of smaller, local clubs welcome smaller touring acts and local performers, from rock to jazz to folk. **Bohager's,** 701 S. Eden St. (© 410/563-7220; www.bohagers.com), is the place to hear known-but-not-arena-touring rockers, along with local bands. Other music venues include **Buddies Pub & Jazz Club,** 313 N. Charles St. (© 410/332-4200), which has live jazz sessions on Friday and Saturday nights; the **Cat's Eye Pub,** 1730 Thames St. (© 410/276-9866; www.catseyepub.com), which features nightly live music ranging from traditional Irish music to bluegrass, zydeco, and jazz; and the **Eight by Ten,** 10 E. Cross St. (© 410/625-2000), where blues and rock groups play regularly.

Two top dance clubs are **Baja Beach Club,** 55 Market Place (at E. Lombard St.), Inner Harbor (© 410/727-0468), which is popular with locals and draws a crowd of energetic 20-somethings; and **The Depot,** 1728 N. Charles St. (© 410/528-0174), which draws a mostly young crowd with its house and retro music.

THE BAR SCENE   Baltimore locals like nothing better than to relax over a cold beer. The best drinking spots include the **Baltimore Brewing Company,** 104 Albemarle St., between Little Italy and the Inner Harbor (© 410/837-5000), a microbrewery that's part German restaurant, part beer hall; **John Steven, Ltd.,** 1800 Thames St. (© 410/327-5561), a great place to sit down and have a beer and some fresh shrimp; and **Wharf Rat,** 206 W. Pratt St., at Hanover Street across from the convention center (© 410/244-8900), a small brewpub with excellent stouts and ales.

THE GAY & LESBIAN SCENE   Along with the *Baltimore Gay Paper* and its website at **www.bgp.org**, you can find information and listings for events of interest to the LGBT community at the **Out in Baltimore** website (www. outinbaltimore.com); and from the **Gay, Lesbian, Bisexual & Transgender Community Center of Baltimore,** 241 W. Chase St. (© 410/837-5445; www.glccbaltimore.org). The gay scene centers around Charles Street in Mount Vernon. The popular disco **Hippo,** 1 W. Eager St. (© 410/547-0069), is a Baltimore mainstay. **Central Station,** 1001 N. Charles St. (© 410/752-7133; www.centralstationpub.com), offers jazz, drag, karaoke, and other theme nights. Women gather at the comfy and friendly **Coconuts Café,** 311 W. Madison St., at Linden Avenue (© 410/383-6064).

6 Charlottesville & Monticello

It was in Charlottesville that Thomas Jefferson built his famous mountaintop home, Monticello; selected the site for and helped plan James Monroe's Ash Lawn–Highland house near Monticello; designed his "academical village," the University of Virginia; and died at home. "All my wishes end where I hope my days will end," he wrote, "at Monticello." Charlottesville today is a growing cosmopolitan center, attracting an increasing number of rich and famous folks— author John Grisham, for one. But its prime attractions are still Thomas Jefferson and his magnificent creations.

ESSENTIALS

GETTING THERE   By Plane   US Airways, Delta, and United fly commuter planes to **Charlottesville–Albemarle Airport,** 201 Bowen Loop (✆ **434/973-8341;** www.gocho.com), north of town off U.S. 29.

By Train   The **Amtrak** station is at 810 W. Main St. (✆ **800/872-7245;** www. amtrak.com), about halfway between the town's commercial district and the University of Virginia.

By Car   Charlottesville is on I-64 from the east or west and U.S. 29 from the north or south. I-64 connects with I-81 at Staunton and with I-95 at Richmond.

VISITOR INFORMATION   For information, contact the **Monticello Visitor Center,** P.O. Box 178, Charlottesville, VA 22902 (✆ **877/386-1102** or 434/977-1783; fax 434/295-2176; www.charlottesvilletourism.org). The center is on Va. 20 at Exit 121 off I-64. The center sells block tickets to Monticello and other attractions. It also provides maps and literature about local and state attractions, and can make same-day, walk-in hotel/motel reservations for you. The center is open March through October, daily from 9am to 5:30pm; the rest of the year, daily until 5pm. Closed New Year's Day, Thanksgiving, and Christmas.

WHAT TO SEE & DO

The Monticello Visitor Center (see "Visitor Information," earlier) sells a **Presidents' Pass,** a discount block ticket combining admission to Monticello, Michie Tavern, and Ash Lawn–Highland. It costs $22 for adults but is not available for children. Those three attractions are within 2 miles of each other on the southeastern outskirts of town, near the Monticello Visitor Center. Allow at least a day to see them all.

Thomas Jefferson's architectural masterpiece, **Monticello** (✆ **434/984-9822** for tickets, 434/984-9844 on weekends, or 434/984-9800 daily for recorded information; www.monticello.org), is one of the highlights of any visit to Virginia. Jefferson designed it himself, combining the 16th-century Italian style of Andrea Palladio with features of the Parisian buildings that he knew and admired during his stint as U.S. minister (ambassador) to France.

Today the house has been restored as closely as possible to its appearance during Jefferson's retirement years. He or his family owned nearly all its furniture and other household objects. The garden has been extended to its original 1,000-foot length, and Mulberry Row—where slaves and free artisans lived and labored in light industrial shops such as a joinery, smokehouse-dairy, blacksmith shop-nailery, and carpenter's shop—has been excavated. Jefferson's grave is in the family burial ground, which is still in use. After visiting the graveyard, you can take a shuttle bus back to the visitor parking lot or walk through the woods via a delightful path.

Admission is $11 adults, $6 children 6 to 11, free for children under 6. You must take a 30-minute guided tour in order to go inside the house. These run March through October daily from 8am to 5pm, and November through February daily from 9am to 4:30pm. Expect long lines on spring and summer weekends and every day during the October "leaf season," so plan to get here when it opens in the morning. Timed passes are given out when the wait exceeds 30 to 40 minutes (these are given only to people standing in line, not at the ticket booth); you can spend the time exploring the gardens and outbuildings on your own (guided garden tours available Apr–Oct).

Ash Lawn–Highland, on C.R. 795, 2½ miles past Monticello on James Monroe Parkway (✆ **804/293-9539**), was the estate of America's fifth president,

James Monroe. Today Monroe's 535-acre estate is owned and maintained as a working farm by his alma mater, the College of William and Mary. Livestock, vegetable and herb gardens, and colonial crafts demonstrations recall daily life on the Monroes' plantation. Horses, sheep, and cattle graze in the fields, while peacocks roam the boxwood gardens. Five of the original rooms remain, along with the basement kitchen, the overseer's cottage, restored slave quarters, and the old smokehouse.

On the mandatory 30-minute house tour, you'll see some of the family's original furnishings and artifacts and learn a great deal about the fifth president. Admission is $8 adults, $7 seniors, $5 children 6 to 11, free for children under 6. The estate is open March through October daily from 9am to 6pm; November through February daily from 10am to 5pm. Many special events take place at Ash Lawn–Highland. The outdoor **Summer Festival** features opera and contemporary music performances; and a major colonial arts festival, **Plantation Days,** which takes place in July, showcases dozens of 18th-century crafts, historic reenactments, period music performances, and dressage.

Unless you're picnicking at Monticello, plan to have a colonial-style lunch at **Michie Tavern ca. 1784,** 683 Thomas Jefferson Pkwy. (© **804/977-1234**), which was built in 1784 and has been painstakingly reconstructed. Behind the tavern are reproductions of the "dependencies"—log kitchen, dairy, smokehouse, ice house, root cellar, and "necessary" (note the not-so-soft corncobs). The re-created general store houses an excellent crafts shop. Mandatory 30-minute tavern-museum tours depart as needed from April to October (self-guided tours with recorded narratives are available other months). Admission is $8 adults, $7 seniors, $3 children 6 to 11, free for children under 6. Meals cost $13 for adults, $6 for children. The museum is open daily from 9am to 5pm (last tour 4:20pm). The restaurant serves food daily from 11:30am to 3pm.

The **University of Virginia** (© **804/982-3200**), designed by Thomas Jefferson himself, is graced with spacious lawns, serpentine-walled gardens, colonnaded pavilions, and a classical rotunda inspired by the Pantheon in Rome. Jefferson was in every sense the university's father, since he conceived it, wrote its charter, raised money for its construction, drew the plans, selected the site, laid the cornerstone in 1817, supervised construction, served as the first rector, selected the faculty, and created the curriculum. His good friends Monroe and Madison sat with him on the first board. The focal point of the university is the **Rotunda** (at Rugby Rd.), today restored as Jefferson designed it. Some 600 feet of tree-dotted lawn extend from the south portico of the Rotunda to what is now Cabell Hall, designed at the turn of the 20th century by Stanford White. The room Edgar Allan Poe occupied when he was a student here is furnished as it would have been in 1826 and is open to visitors.

Students lead 45-minute campus tours daily at 10 and 11am and 2, 3, and 4pm, usually from the Rotunda. Self-guided walking tour brochures are available from the university's **Visitor Information Center** (© **804/924-7166**), located not on campus but in the University Police Headquarters, on Ivy Road (U.S. 250 Business) just east of the U.S. 29/U.S. 250 Bypass. The visitor center is open 24 hours a day. See "Essentials," above, for parking information. *Note:* The university is closed 3 weeks around Christmas.

WHERE TO STAY & DINE

The area around Charlottesville boasts several spectacular country inns and resorts. Leading the way is **Clifton, The Country Inn,** 1296 Clifton Inn Dr.,

ℯ Another Nearby Presidential Home

Twenty-five miles east of Charlottesville is **Montpelier,** 11407 Constitution Hwy. (Va. 20), Montpelier Station (ℭ **540/672-2728;** www.montpelier. org), a 2,700-acre estate facing the Blue Ridge Mountains that was home to President James Madison and his wife, Dolley. They are buried here in the family cemetery. Two structures remain from their time: the main house and the "Ice House Temple" (built over a well and used to store ice). William Du Pont, Sr., bought the estate in 1900; he enlarged the mansion and added barns, staff houses, a sawmill, a blacksmith shop, a train station, a dairy, and greenhouses, and his wife created a 21½-acre formal garden. In other words, the house has changed significantly since the Madisons' time, and their personal possessions have been widely dispersed, so don't expect the usual historical mansion tour. You'll start with a 14-minute video, which introduces James and Dolley Madison. A 45-minute audio cassette tape will then lead you through the "Discovering Madison" exhibit on the first floor of the mansion, and among key points on the grounds outside. Staffers are on hand in the house to answer questions.

Admission is $9 adults, $8 seniors, $4.50 children ages 6 to 11. Open April through October daily from 9:30am to 5:30pm (last tour at 4pm), November through March daily from 9:30am to 5:30pm (last tour at 3pm). Call ahead for a schedule of special events, such as birthday celebrations for James (Mar 16) and Dolley (May 20). To get there from Charlottesville, take U.S. 29 north to U.S. 33 east at Ruckersville; at Barboursville, turn left onto Va. 20 north.

about 5 miles east of Charlottesville (ℭ **888/971-1800** or 804/971-1800; www.cliftoninn.com). You'll think you've arrived at Tara from *Gone With the Wind* when you see this stately, 1790-vintage manse, a combination of Federal and Colonial Revival styles. You can relax in the main house's formal parlor, browse through hundreds of titles shelved in its cozy library, or partake of homemade cookies and pastries in its tearoom. Not only is staying here a delight, but the award-winning gourmet cuisine also makes this one of Virginia's finest places to dine. Wine comes from one of Virginia's finest cellars. Guests also enjoy a swimming pool (romantically lit at night), tennis and croquet, a 20-acre lake stocked for fishing, and hiking trails.

Also luxurious (and pricey) but slightly more formal is **Keswick Hall at Monticello,** 701 Country Club Dr., in nearby Keswick (ℭ **800/274-5391** or 804/979-3440; www.keswick.com). Many of its units have fireplaces, claw-foot tubs, and views over a golf course redesigned by Arnold Palmer. Dining here is gourmet all the way, and guests can also enjoy swimming pools, a fitness center, and tennis courts.

Not quite as expensive, although still plenty upscale, are **Silver Thatch Inn,** 3001 Hollymead Dr., Charlottesville (ℭ **800/261-0720** or 434/978-4686; www. silverthatch.com); and **The Inn at Monticello,** 1188 Scottsville Rd. (Va. 20), Charlottesville (ℭ **804/979-3593;** www.innatmonticello.com).

On the affordable end of the scale, one of Charlottesville's most reliable places is the **Hampton Inn & Suites,** 900 W. Main St. (at 10th St.; © **800/HAMP-TON** or 804/923-8600). You might also try the **English Inn of Charlottesville,** 2000 Morton Dr. (© **800/786-5400** or 804/971-9900; www.wytestone.com); or the **Holiday Inn Monticello,** 1200 5th St. (© **800/HOLIDAY** or 804/977-5100), which is convenient to Monticello, Ash Lawn-Highland, and Michie Tavern. The commercial strip along U.S. 29 north of the U.S. 250 Bypass has an abundance of chain motels.

Guesthouses Reservation Service, Inc., P.O. Box 5737, Charlottesville, VA 22905 (© **434/979-7264;** fax 434/293-7791; www.va-guesthouses.com), handles bed-and-breakfast accommodations in elegant homes and private cottages. You can write, fax, or visit the website for information on the properties, but reservations must be made by phone. Credit cards can be used for deposits. The office is open Monday through Friday from noon to 5pm.

Some of the area's finest dining is at the country inns, such as **Clifton, The Country Inn** and the **Silver Thatch Inn** (see above). Another favorite is the **C&O Restaurant,** 515 E. Water St. (© **804/971-7044**), whose excellent menu ranges across the globe—from France to Thailand, from New Mexico to Louisiana. One of Charlottesville's most popular dining spots is **Northern Exposure,** 1202 W. Main St. (at 12th St.; © **804/977-6002**), offering both traditional and inventive Italian-accented cuisine.

7 Richmond

Richmond supplanted the more militarily vulnerable Williamsburg as Virginia's capital in 1780, and it has been the scene of much of the state's history ever since. It was here in St. John's Church that Patrick Henry concluded his address to the second Virginia Convention with the stirring words, "Give me liberty, or give me death!" But Richmond really made its mark on American history during the Civil War. This is where Jefferson Davis presided over the Confederate Congress, and Robert E. Lee accepted command of Virginia's armed forces.

ESSENTIALS

GETTING THERE   By Plane   Richmond International Airport, Airport Drive off I-64, I-295, and Williamsburg Road (U.S. 60) (© **804/226-3052;** www.flyrichmond.com), known locally as Byrd Field, is about 15 minutes east of downtown. American, Continental, Delta, TWA, United, and US Airways fly there.

The major car-rental companies have desks at the airport.

By Train   Several daily **Amtrak** trains pull into the station at 7519 Staples Mill Rd., north of Exit 185 off I-64 (© **800/872-7245;** www.amtrak.com). Amtrak shuttle buses run to and from the Marriott and Omni hotels downtown.

By Car   Richmond is at the junction of **I-64,** traveling east-west, and **I-95,** traveling north-south. **I-295** bypasses the city on its east and north sides. **U.S. 60** (east-west) and **U.S. 1** and **U.S. 301** (north-south) are other major arteries.

VISITOR INFORMATION   The **Richmond Visitors Center,** 405 N. 3rd St. (at Clay St.), Richmond, VA 23219 (© **800/RICHMOND;** www.richmondva. org), provides information and operates a hotel reservation service. It's open Monday through Friday from 8:30am to 5pm. In addition, the **Richmond International Airport Visitors Center** (© **804/236-3260**) is open Monday through Friday from 9:30am to 4:30pm. It will make same-day hotel reservations.

EXPLORING RICHMOND

Richmond was probably the most important city in the South during the Civil War, and was therefore a prime military target. The key sites are preserved by the **Richmond National Battlefield Park** (© 804/226-1981; www.nps.gov/rich), whose visitor center is in the Tredegar Irons Works, Tredegar and 5th streets, at the western end of the city's new **Riverfront Canal Walk,** a promenade running along the tow path of the old James River & Kanawha Canal. Rangers can give information on and driving directions to the several Civil War battlefields that lie on the city's eastern suburbs. The **Museum and White House of the Confederacy,** 1201 E. Clay St. (© **804/649-1861;** www.moc.org), houses the largest collection of Confederate objects in the country, many of them contributed by veterans and their descendants.

But Richmond's history goes back even further than the Civil War. **St. John's Church,** 2401 E. Broad St. (© **804/648-5015**), dates to 1741 and was the site of the second Virginia Convention in 1775, with Thomas Jefferson, George Washington, and Richard Henry Lee in attendance. In support of a bill to assemble and train a militia to oppose Great Britain, Patrick Henry stood up and delivered his famous speech: "I know not what course others may take, but as for me, give me liberty or give me death!"

Designed by Thomas Jefferson, the **Virginia State Capitol,** 9th and Grace streets (© **804/698-1619;** www.virginia.org), has been in continuous use since 1788. Jefferson modeled it on the Maison Carrée, a Roman temple built in Nîmes during the 1st century A.D.

History buffs should also visit the **John Marshall House,** 818 E. Marshall St., at 9th Street (© **804/648-7998;** www.apva.org/apva/marshall.html), the restored home of the first chief justice of the United States.

In addition, Richmond is home to the **Virginia Museum of Fine Arts,** Boulevard and Grove Avenue (© **804/367-0844;** www.vmfa.state.va.us), noted for the largest public Fabergé collection outside Russia—more than 300 objets d'art created at the turn of the 20th century for czars Alexander III and Nicholas II. Other highlights include the Goya portrait *General Nicholas Guye,* a rare life-size marble statue of Roman emperor Caligula, and Monet's *Iris by the Pond.*

A great place to take the kids is **Paramount's Kings Dominion** (© **804/ 876-5000;** www.pkd4fun.com), north of the city in Doswell (take I-95 to Va. 30). This family-oriented theme park, one of the most popular in the east, offers a variety of rides and entertainment, mostly based on themes from Paramount movies and TV shows.

WHERE TO STAY

Top hotels in Richmond include the magnificent **Jefferson Hotel,** Franklin and Adams streets (© **800/484-8014** or 804/788-8000; www.jefferson-hotel.com), a stunning beaux arts sightseeing attraction in its own right, which has hosted countless presidents and celebrities over the years.

Other options include the intimate, upscale **The Berkeley Hotel,** 1200 E. Cary St. (© **888/780-4422** or 804/780-1300; www.berkeleyhotel.com), and the more moderately priced **Linden Row Inn,** 100 E. Franklin St. (© **800/348-7424** or 804/783-7000; www.lindenrowinn.com), which comprises a row of seven small, separate 140-year-old Greek Revival town houses and their garden dependencies.

If you're looking for a B&B, contact **Bensonhouse of Richmond** (© **804/ 353-6900;** fax 804/355-5050; www.bensonhouse.com). Administrator Lyn

A Side Trip to Petersburg

The nearby town of Petersburg, 23 miles south of Richmond on I-95, offers an excellent excursion for history buffs. Petersburg was the site of the siege that ended in the Civil War's last great battle, which resulted in Robert E. Lee's surrender. When you arrive, take Washington Street (Exit 52) west and follow the Petersburg Tour signs to the **visitor center**, 425 Cockade Alley (P.O. Box 2107), Petersburg, VA 23804 (© **800/368-3595** or 804/733-2400; www.petersburg-va.org), where you can get a complimentary parking permit (valid for 1 day), maps, and literature. The center is open daily from 9am to 5pm.

Petersburg's Old Town holds many interesting historic sights and museums, all within a short walk of the visitor center. Ringing the eastern and southern outskirts of town, the impressive **Petersburg National Battlefield** (© **804/732-3531**; www.nps.gov/pete) preserves the key sites of the protracted siege that ended the war. The battlefield's visitor center is 2½ miles east of downtown on East Washington Street (Va. 36).

Benson offers listings within 5 to 15 minutes of Richmond's major attractions, including her own lovingly restored **Emmanuel Hutzler House** (© **804/355-4885;** www.bensonhouse.com), an Italian Renaissance–style inn built in the early 1900s with mahogany paneling, leaded-glass windows, and a coffered-beam ceiling.

The pleasant, campuslike Executive Center area, on West Broad Street (U.S. 33/250) at I-64 (Exit 183), about 5 miles west of downtown, has a wide selection of chain hotels and restaurants. Best of the hotels is the redwood-and-brick **Sheraton Richmond** (© **800/325-3535** or 804/285-1234).

WHERE TO DINE

East Cary Street between 12th and 15th streets is Richmond's premier dining mecca, with a bevy of good-to-excellent restaurants. Consistently popular with young professionals as a watering hole, **Siné Irish Pub & Restaurant,** 1327 E. Cary St. (© **804/649-7767**), is anything but a typical Irish pub, offering a wide selection of seafood, steaks, and chicken in addition to the usual corned beef and cabbage. In warm weather you can dine and drink on the deck out back. In the city's hip Shockhoe Bottom dining and entertainment area, **Havana '59,** 16 N. 17th St. (© **804/649-2822**), presents an incongruous Cuban scene across the street from the covered stalls of Richmond's ancient Farmers' Market. Up on Church Hill, **Millie's Diner,** 2603 E. Main St. (© **804/643-5512**), looks like the diner it used to be but now serves as a noisy temple of creative cuisine.

For picnic fare, head to **Coppola's Delicatessen,** in the Carytown section at 2900 W. Cary St. (© **804/359-NYNY**), with its aromatic clutter of cheeses, sausages, olives, pickles, and things marinated.

8 Williamsburg & Colonial Virginia

The narrow peninsula between the James and York rivers saw the very beginnings of colonial America and the rebellion that eventually created the United States. Visitors today can get an extensive history lesson in the beautifully restored 18th-century town of Colonial Williamsburg, see the earliest permanent English settlement in North America at Jamestown, and walk the Yorktown ramparts where Washington decisively defeated Cornwallis, thus turning the colonists' dream of a new nation into a reality.

More than history, however, makes this one of America's family vacation meccas. There's also the Busch Gardens Williamsburg theme park with entertainment and rides, world-class shopping in the factory outlet stores near Williamsburg, and golf on some of Virginia's finest courses.

ESSENTIALS

GETTING THERE   By Plane   AirTran, United Express, and US Airways Express serve **Newport News/Williamsburg Airport** (© 757/877-0221; www. nnwairport.com), 14 miles east of Williamsburg. More flights (and certainly more jets) arrive at **Richmond International Airport** (see "Essentials" under "Richmond," above), about 45 miles west of town via I-64.

By Train   Amtrak trains (© 800-USA-RAIL; www.amtrak.com) serves the Transportation Center, 468 N. Boundary St. at Lafayette Street (© 757/229-8750), within walking distance of the historic area.

By Car   I-64 passes Williamsburg on its way between Richmond and Norfolk. For the historic area, take Exit 238 (Va. 143) off I-64 and follow the signs. The Colonial Parkway, one of Virginia's most scenic routes, connects Williamsburg to Jamestown and Yorktown (it runs through a tunnel under the Historic Area).

VISITOR INFORMATION   You and a few other million persons who come here every year will begin your visit at the **Colonial Williamsburg Visitor Center,** off U.S. 60 Bypass, just east of Va. 132 (© 800/HISTORY or 757/ 220-7645; www.colonialwilliamsburg.com). You can't miss it; bright green signs point the way from all access roads to Williamsburg. This is where you buy your tickets for the dozens of attractions that make up Colonial Williamsburg. It's open 365 days a year, from 8:30am to 7pm in summer, to 5pm the rest of the year. Parking is free for the first 2 hours and all day if you buy an attractions pass; otherwise you'll pay $20 if you stay more than 2 hours.

GETTING AROUND   Since few cars are allowed into the Historic Area from 8am to 10pm daily, you must park elsewhere. The visitor center has ample parking and operates a **shuttle bus** to and from the Historic Area. It's free for holders of tickets to the Historic Area attractions. There's also a footpath from the visitor center to the Historic Area.

The easiest way to get around outside the Historic Area is by air-conditioned **Williamsburg Visitors Shuttle** (© 757/259-4111), which runs every 30 minutes Memorial Day to Labor Day, daily from 9am to 10pm. The buses follow U.S. 60 from the Williamsburg Pottery Factory in the west to Busch Gardens Williamsburg in the east, with a detour to the Bypass Road hotels. It runs through the Historic Area on Henry and Lafayette streets. Fare is $1.

Bike rentals are available year-round from **Tazewell Club Fitness Center,** at the Williamsburg Lodge (© 757/220-7690), and from Easter to October from the **Williamsburg Woodlands hotel** (© 757/229-1000). **Yellow Cab** (© 757/ 722-1111) and **Williamsburg Taxi** (© 757/566-3009) are based at the Transportation Center.

TICKETS   It costs nothing to stroll the streets of the Historic Area, and perhaps debate revolutionary politics with the actors playing Thomas Jefferson or Patrick Henry. However, you will need a **ticket** to enter the key buildings and all the museums, see the 35-minute orientation film at the visitor center, use the Historic Area shuttle bus, and take a 30-minute Orientation Walk through the restored village (reservations required).

Adults pay $32 for a **Day Pass** to the museums, Historic Area exhibits, and Carter's Grove Plantation. It is good until 5pm. For only an additional $6, adults can get a **Freedom Pass,** which is good for 1 year and includes admission to the museums, Historic Area exhibits, Carter's Grove, and nighttime activities and performances. Children ages 6 to 17 are charged half price for all passes.

Note: The Colonial Williamsburg Foundation is notorious for frequently changing its system of tickets and passes, so the ticket structure above may be outdated by the time you arrive. Call the visitor center or check the Colonial Williamsburg website for the latest information.

Whatever the price structure, passes are available at the Colonial Williamsburg Visitor Center and at a **ticket booth** at the Merchants Square shops, on Henry Street at Duke of Gloucester Street.

WHAT TO SEE & DO

In addition to the sights below, look for the numerous 18th-century crafts demonstrations on view throughout the Historic Area. You can stroll the Historic Area streets anytime, but in general, its attractions are open from April to October daily from 9am to 5pm, to 6pm Memorial Day to Labor Day. Some places are closed on specific days, and hours can vary, so check the *Colonial Williamsburg Companion* for current information.

THE COLONIAL BUILDINGS

Brush-Everard House   The Brush-Everard House was occupied without interruption from 1717—when Public Armorer and master gunsmith John Brush built it as a residence-cum-shop—to 1946. Its most distinguished owner was Thomas Everard, clerk of York County from 1745 to 1771 and two-time mayor of Williamsburg. Today the home is restored and furnished to its Everard-era appearance. The smokehouse and kitchen out back are original. Special programs here focus on African-American life in the 18th century.

The Capitol   Virginia legislators met in the Capitol at the eastern end of Duke of Gloucester Street from 1704 to 1780. The House of Burgesses became a training ground for patriots and future governors such as George Washington, Thomas Jefferson, Richard Henry Lee, and Patrick Henry. The original Capitol burned down in 1747, was rebuilt in 1753, and succumbed to fire again in 1832. The reconstruction is of the 1704 building, complete with Queen Anne's coat of arms adorning the tower and the Great Union flag flying overhead. **Tours** (of about 25 min.) are given throughout the day.

The Courthouse   An intriguing window on the criminal justice system of colonial life is offered in the courthouse, which dominates Market Square. An original building, the courthouse was the scene of widely varying proceedings, ranging from dramatic criminal trials to the prosaic issuance of licenses. Visitors can participate in the administration of colonial justice at the courthouse by sitting on a jury or acting as a defendant.

George Wythe House   On the west side of the Palace Green is the elegant restored brick home of George Wythe (pronounced "With"), the first Virginia signer of the Declaration of Independence. On principle, Wythe did not sign the Constitution, however, because it did not contain a bill of rights or antislavery provisions. This house, in which he lived with his second wife, was Washington's headquarters before the siege of Yorktown and Rochambeau's after the surrender of Cornwallis. Open-hearth cooking is demonstrated in the outbuilding.

Governor's Palace   This building is a meticulous reconstruction of the Georgian mansion that was the residence and official headquarters of royal governors from 1714 until Lord Dunmore fled before dawn in the face of armed resistance in 1775, thus ending British rule in Virginia. The sumptuous surroundings, nobly proportioned halls and rooms, 10 acres of formal gardens and greens, and vast wine cellars all evoke splendor. **Tours,** given continuously throughout the day, wind up in the gardens, where you can explore at your leisure the elaborate geometric parterres, topiary work, bowling green, pleached allées, and a holly maze patterned after the one at Hampton Court. Plan at least 30 minutes to wander the stunning grounds and to visit the kitchen and stable yards.

James Geddy House & Silversmith Shop   This two-story L-shaped 1762 home (with attached shops) is an original building. Here visitors can see how a comfortably situated middle-class family lived in the 18th century. Unlike the fancier abodes you'll visit, the Geddy House has no wallpaper or oil paintings; a mirror and spinet from England, however, indicate relative affluence. At a foundry on the premises, craftsmen cast silver, pewter, bronze, and brass items at a forge.

The Magazine & Guardhouse   The magazine is a sturdy octagonal brick building constructed in 1715 to house ammunition and arms for the defense of the British colony. It has survived intact to the present day. Today, the building is stocked with 18th-century equipment—British-made flintlock muskets, cannons and cannonballs, barrels of powder, bayonets, and drums, the latter for communication purposes.

Peyton Randolph House   The Randolphs were one of the most prominent—and wealthy—families in colonial Virginia. This house (actually two connected homes) dates to 1715. Robertson's Windmill, in back of the house, is a post mill of a type popular in the early 18th century.

The Public Gaol   Imprisonment was not the usual punishment for crime in colonial times, but people awaiting trial (at the Capitol in Williamsburg) and runaway slaves sometimes spent months in the Public Gaol. Beds were rudimentary piles of straw; leg irons, shackles, and chains were used frequently; and the daily diet consisted of "salt beef damaged, and Indian meal." This thick-walled redbrick building served as the Williamsburg city jail until 1910. The building today is restored to its 1720s appearance.

The Public Hospital   Opened in 1773, the "Public Hospital for Persons of Insane and Disordered Minds" was America's first lunatic asylum. On a self-guided tour you'll see a 1773 cell—with a filthy straw-filled mattress on the floor, ragged blanket, and manacles—as well as rooms from later periods.

Raleigh Tavern   This most famous of Williamsburg taverns was named for Sir Walter Raleigh. After the Governor's Palace, it was the social and political hub of the town. Regular clients included George Washington and Thomas Jefferson, who met here in 1774 with Patrick Henry, Richard Henry Lee, and Francis Lightfoot Lee to plot revolution.

THE MUSEUMS

Abby Aldrich Rockefeller Folk Art Center   This delightful museum contains more than 2,600 folk-art paintings, sculptures, and art objects. The collection includes household ornaments and useful wares, mourning pictures, shop signs,

Williamsburg Historic Area

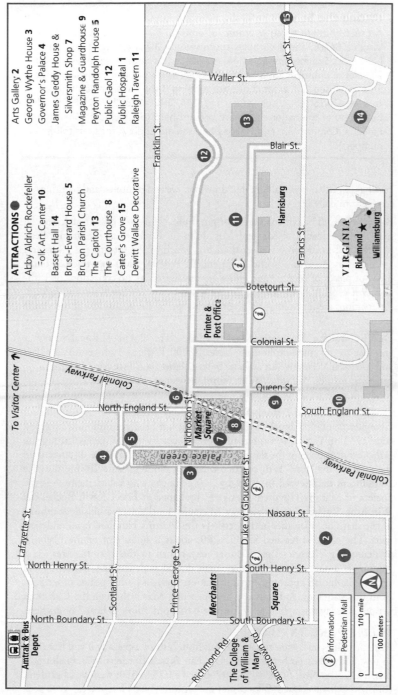

ATTRACTIONS ●

Arts Gallery **2**
George Wythe House **3**
Governor's Palace **4**
James Geddy House &
Silversmith Shop **7**
Magazine & Guardhouse **9**
Peyton Randolph House **5**
Public Gaol **12**
Public Hospital **1**
Raleigh Tavern **11**

Abby Aldrich Rockefeller
Folk Art Center **10**
Bassett Hall **14**
Brush-Everard House **5**
Bruton Parish Church
The Capitol **13**
The Courthouse **8**
Carter's Grove **15**
Dewitt Wallace Decorative

VIRGINIA
Richmond ★
● Williamsburg

ⓘ Information
Pedestrian Mall

0   1/10 mile
0   100 meters

Amtrak & Bus
Depot

Lafayette St.
North Henry St.
North Boundary St.
Scotland St.
Prince George St.
Richmond Rd.
The College
of William &
Mary
Jamestown Rd.
South Boundary St.
South Henry St.
Nassau St.
Merchants
Square
To Visitor Center
Colonial Parkway
North England St.
Palace Green
Nicholson St.
Market Square
Duke of Gloucester St.
Queen St.
Colonial St.
Botetourt St.
Printer &
Post Office
Franklin St.
Waller St.
York St.
Blair St.
Harrisburg
Francis St.
South England St.
Colonial Parkway

Hitting the Beach

A great antidote to an overdose of colonial history is to head over to **Virginia Beach,** about 60 miles southwest of Williamsburg (take I-64 to I-264 east). Summertime vacationers flock to this resort area to enjoy over 20 miles of unbroken sand and surf, as well as the popular Virginia Marine Science Museum. A great choice for lodging is the **Cavalier Hotel,** ocean-front at 42nd Street, Virginia Beach (© **888/SINCE-27** or 757/425-8555). All but a few of the major chains are present here too, including Sheraton, Ramada, Comfort Inn, and Holiday Inn (see appendix A for their toll-free numbers).

carvings, whittled toys, calligraphic drawings, weavings, quilts, and paintings of scenes from daily life.

Bassett Hall   Though colonial in origin (built 1753–66), Bassett Hall was the mid-1930s residence of Mr. and Mrs. John D. Rockefeller, Jr., and it's been restored and furnished to reflect their era. Much of the furniture is 18th- and 19th-century American in the Chippendale, Federal, and Empire styles. Hundreds of pieces of ceramic and china are on display, as are collections of 18th- and 19th-century American and English glass, Canton enamelware, and folk art. Reservations are required; make them at the Special Programs desk at the visitor center.

DeWitt Wallace Decorative Arts Gallery   The Public Hospital serves as entrance to this museum housing some 10,000 17th- to 19th-century English and American decorative art objects. In its galleries, you'll see period furnishings, ceramics, textiles, paintings, prints, silver, pewter, clocks, scientific instruments, mechanical devices, and weapons.

Carter's Grove & the Rockefeller Archeology Museum   The magnificent Georgian plantation home at **Carter's Grove** has been continuously occupied since 1755 on a site that was settled over 3½ centuries ago. One fascinating site is the reconstruction of the slave quarters. Archaeologists have also discovered on the grounds the "lost" 17th-century village of Wolstenholme Towne, site of a 20,000-acre tract settled in 1619 by 220 colonists who called themselves the Society of Martin's Hundred. Designed by famed architect Kevin Roche, the **Winthrop Rockefeller Archeology Museum,** nestled into a hillside southeast of the mansion, identifies and interprets the Martin's Hundred clues and artifacts. The estate is reached via U.S. 60, about 8 miles east of the Colonial Williamsburg Historic Area. Visitors may return to the Historic Area via a stunningly scenic one-way country road dotted with markers indicating old graveyards, Indian encampments, plantation sites, and other points of interest. Both the plantation and museum are open mid-March through the Christmas season, Tuesday through Sunday from 9am to 4 pm. Allow at least 3 hours here.

THEME PARK THRILLS

At some point you'll want to take a break from history, especially if you have kids in tow, and there's no better place here than **Busch Gardens Williamsburg,** 1 Busch Gardens Blvd. (© **800/343-9746** or 757/253-3350; www.buschgardens. com), on U.S. 60 about 3 miles east of the Historic Area. Here you can get a peek at European history, albeit fanciful, in authentically detailed 17th-century hamlets from England, Scotland, France, Germany, and Italy—but little mental effort is required to enjoy all the attractions you'll find here. Each village here has its own shops, crafts demonstrations, restaurants, rides, shows, and other entertainment. The sights are connected by trains pulled by reproductions of European steam locomotives, so you can easily skip around.

Admission and hours vary from year to year and season to season, so call ahead, check the website, or pick up a brochure at the visitor centers. Admission is at least $43 adults, $33 children 3 to 6, free for children under 3. Tickets include unlimited rides, shows, and attractions.

SHOPPING

Duke of Gloucester Street, in the historic area, is the center for 18th-century wares created by craftspeople plying the trades of American forefathers. You'll find hand-wrought silver jewelry, hats, handwoven linens, leather-bound books, gingerbread cakes, and much more.

Don't miss **Craft House,** also run by the Colonial Williamsburg Foundation. There are two locations, one in Merchants Square, the other near the Abby Aldrich Rockefeller Folk Art Center. Featured at Craft House are exquisite works by master craftspeople and authentic reproductions of colonial furnishings. There are also reproduction wallpapers, china, toys, games, maps, books, prints, and souvenirs aplenty.

Shopping in the Historic Area is fun, but the biggest merchandising draws are along **Richmond Road** (U.S. 60) between Williamsburg and Lightfoot, an area 5 to 7 miles west of the Historic Area. If you like outlet shopping, Richmond Road will seem like paradise.

WHERE TO STAY

The Colonial Williamsburg Foundation operates four hotels in all price categories, in the Historic Area. For advance reservations, call the **Visitor Center reservations service** (© **800/HISTORY;** www.colonialwilliamsburg.com). You also can make walk-in reservations at the Colonial Williamsburg Visitor Center. The **Williamsburg Hotel and Motel Association** (© **800/446-9244** or 757/220-3330; www.mywilliamsburgvacation.com) operates a very good free reservations service. Its clerks will help you to find the best rates at the scores of hotels and motels in the area. Their listings include most of the accommodations mentioned below.

Courtyard By Marriott This four-story member of the fine chain designed for business travelers (and very comfortable for the rest of us) enjoys an attractively landscaped setting of trees and shrubs on the eastern side of town near Busch Gardens. There's also a swimming pool. 470 McLaws Circle, Williamsburg, VA 23185. © 800/321-2211 or 757/221-0700. Fax 757/221-0741. www.courtyard.com. 151 units. $99–$139 double; $119–$199 suite. Weekend rates available. AE, DC, DISC, MC, V. Free parking. From Williamsburg, follow U.S. 60 east about 2 miles to Busch Corporate Center, turn right at light, and bear right on McLaws Circle. **Amenities:** Restaurant (breakfast only); outdoor pool.

The Fife & Drum Inn This relaxed and interesting charmer—opened in 2002—is the only privately-owned accommodation in the Historic Area. Guests can gather under the cathedral ceiling of the common room complete with fireplace and a small library of books about Williamsburg. A sky-lit hallway with faux brick floor and clapboard siding leads to the B&B's seven medium-size rooms and two suites, some of which have dormer windows. The Conservancy room is the most romantic, with a canopied double bed and a claw-foot bathtub.

Smokers need to look elsewhere. 441 Prince George St., Williamsburg, VA 23185. ✆ 888/
838-1783 or 757/345-1776. Fax 757/253-1676. www.fifeanddruminn.com. 9 units, all with bathroom. $145–$165 double. Rates include full breakfast. AE, DISC, MC, V. Free on-premises parking.

Governor's Inn   Least expensive of the foundation's hotels, the Governor's Inn
is a two- and three-story brick motel surrounded by parking lots. Natural wood
furniture brightens the standard motel-style rooms, which have been spiffed up
recently. There's a small outdoor pool for cooling off. It's near the visitor center
on the northwest edge of the Historic Area. Some rooms are "pet friendly." Note
that the Governor's Inn is near the Transportation Center, which means that
trains come by during the night. 506 Henry St. (Va. 132), at Lafayette St. (P.O. Box 1776),
Williamsburg, VA 23185. ✆ 800/HISTORY or 757/229-1000. Fax 757/220-7480. www.
colonialwilliamsburg.com. 200 units. $55–$99 double. Rates include continental breakfast. AE, DC,
DISC, MC, V. **Amenities:** Outdoor pool; access to nearby health club; pets accepted (no fee).

Heritage Inn   This pleasant, 1963-vintage motel is convenient to the Historic
Area. The spacious and comfortable rooms are in a two-story motel block. Some
have king beds and sofas, but most have two double beds. Your pets can stay free
with you in the ground floor rooms here. 1324 Richmond Rd. (at Mt. Vernon Ave.),
Williamsburg, VA 23185. ✆ 800/782-3800 or 757/229-6220. Fax 757/229-2774. www.heritage
innwmsb.com. 54 units. $42–$84. Rates include continental breakfast (except Jan–Feb). AE, DC,
DISC, MC, V. **Amenities:** Outdoor pool; pets accepted (no fee).

Williamsburg Hospitality House   Just 2 blocks from the Historic Area and
opposite William and Mary College, this four-story brick hotel is as convenient
to the major sights as any non-foundation hotel. Built around a central courtyard with flowering trees and plants, the spacious guest rooms and public areas
are appointed with a gracious blend of 18th-century reproductions, and The
Colony dining room adds to the ambience by specializing in colonial fare. 415
Richmond Rd., Williamsburg, VA 23185. ✆ 800/932-9191 or 757/229-4020. Fax 757/220-1560.
www.williamsburghosphouse.com. 308 units. $79–$169 double; $375–$475 suite. AE, DC, DISC,
MC, V. **Amenities:** Restaurants (2); outdoor pool.

Williamsburg Inn   Already one of the nation's most distinguished hotels, this
rambling white-brick Regency-style inn is looking even better thanks to a 2001
renovation. Upstairs, the renovation has cut the number of rooms and suites by
a third, enlarging all of them (suites now range up to 600 sq. ft.). They have
marble bathrooms and are exquisitely furnished with reproductions, books, and
photos of famous prior guests. The Regency Dining Room features classic
American cuisine (coats and ties required after 6pm) and a view of one of the
inn's three top-flight golf courses. The inn shares the Tazewell Club fitness center and spa with the Williamsburg Lodge, which is across the side street.

Rooms in a modern building called **Providence Hall,** adjacent to the inn, are
furnished in a contemporary blend of 18th-century and Asian style, with
balconies or patios overlooking tennis courts and a beautiful wooded area. The
inn provides the services. Rates range from $300 to $350. 136 Francis St. (P.O. Box
1776), Williamsburg, VA 23187. ✆ 800/HISTORY or 757/229-1000. Fax 757/220-7096. www.
colonialwilliamsburg.com. 63 units. $425–$575 double; $750 suite. AE, DC, DISC, MC, V.
Amenities: Restaurant; 2 outdoor pools; spa; health club; 3 golf courses; 8 tennis courts.

Williamsburg Lodge   Across the street from the Williamsburg Inn, the
foundation's second-best hotel offers the use of all of the inn's sports facilities
except golf. The flagstone-floored lobby is indeed lodgelike, with cypress paneling and a large working fireplace. Accommodations are contemporary but warm

and homey, with polished wood floors and handcrafted furniture. West Wing rooms have window walls overlooking duck ponds or a wooded landscape, and 12 have working fireplaces. Rooms in the Tazewell Wing have balconies facing landscaped courtyards; those in the West Wing do not have balconies. S. England St. (P.O. Box 1776), Williamsburg, VA 23187. © 800/HISTORY or 757/229-1000. Fax 757/ 220-7685. www.colonialwilliamsburg.com. 264 units. $179–$235 double. AE, DC, DISC, MC, V. Free parking. **Amenities:** Restaurants (2); 2 outdoor pools; spa; health club; 8 tennis courts.

Williamsburg Woodlands Hotel & Suites   The foundation's newest and third-best hotel, next to the visitor center, sports lodgelike public rooms, and guest rooms with colonial-style pine furniture and photos of the Historic Area on their walls. The more expensive suites have separate living and sleeping rooms, and a wet bar with fridge and microwave oven. The hotel has its own family restaurant, plus a Burger King. It shares two swimming pools and other facilities with the Cascades Motel, in which the foundation houses tour groups. There's plenty to keep kids occupied here, and when you couple that with the pullout sofa beds in the suites, it's a good choice for families of moderate means. 105 Visitors Center Dr. (P.O. Box 1776), Williamsburg, VA 23187. © 800/HISTORY or 757/ 229-1000. Fax 757/229 7079. www.colonialwilliamsburg.com. 300 units. $89–$189 double. Rates include continental breakfast. AE, DC, DISC, MC, V. **Amenities:** Restaurants (2); 3 outdoor pools; access to nearby health club.

WHERE TO DINE

The Colonial Williamsburg Foundation runs four popular reconstructed colonial taverns: **Christiana Campbell's Tavern,** on Waller Street; and **Josiah Chowning's Tavern, Kings Arms Tavern,** and **Shields Tavern,** all on Duke of Gloucester Street. While the food is good and interesting, it's also expensive, so dine at one of the taverns primarily for the experience. All are reconstructed 18th-century *ordinaries,* or taverns, and aim at authenticity in fare, ambience, and costuming of the staff. Advance reservations at the taverns are essential during the summer and on weekends during spring and fall. Except at Josiah Chowning's Tavern, which accepts reservations only up to 24 hours in advance and only at the door, you can reserve up to 60 days in advance by dropping by or calling the visitor center (© 800/TAVERNS or 757/229-2141).

There are benches throughout the restored area (lots of grass, too) if you feel like a picnic, and if you have a car you can drive to nearby scenic overlooks along Colonial Parkway (the parking areas along the James and York rivers are best, but they don't have picnic tables or other facilities). **The Cheese Shop,** 424 Prince George St. in Merchants Square, between North Boundary and North Henry streets (© 757/220-0298), is a good place to purchase takeout sandwiches and other fixings. Out on Richmond Road, a good choice is **Padow's Hams & Deli,** in the Williamsburg Shopping Center at Monticello Avenue (© 757/220-4267).

Berret's Restaurant & Raw Bar   SEAFOOD   The congenial, casual Berret's has a popular outdoor raw bar that seems to be busy all day in warm weather. The adjoining restaurant is bright and airy, with several dining rooms. Canvas sailcloth shades, blue-trimmed china, and marine artifacts on the walls make an appropriate backdrop for the excellent seafood. For your entree, try the pan-fried crab cakes served with a sweet bell pepper sauce and an apple and pear salad. 199 S. Boundary St. (at Francis St.). © 757/253-1847. Reservations recommended for dinner. Main courses $18–$25. AE, DISC, MC, V. Restaurant: Apr–Dec daily 11:30am–3:30pm and 5–10pm; Jan–Mar Tues–Sun 11:30am–5pm and 5:30–9pm. Outdoor raw bar: Apr–Oct Mon–Fri 5–11pm, Sat–Sun noon–11pm.

Giuseppe's Italian Cafe ITALIAN   This pleasant local favorite may be difficult to see from Richmond Highway (it's at the end of a strip mall with a Food Lion supermarket at its center), but it's a great place for a meal during or after a shopping expedition. The chef's lentil-and-andouille soup won justified raves from *Bon Appetit* magazine. Also on the menu: heaping plates of spaghetti, a page full of vegetarian pastas, and single-size pizzas with some unusual toppings such as smoked oysters. 5601 Richmond Rd. (U.S. 60 at Airport Rd.), in Ewell Station Shopping Center. ℂ 757/565-1977. Reservations not accepted. Main courses $4.50–$17. AE, DISC, MC, V. Mon–Thurs 11:30am–2pm and 5–9pm; Fri–Sat 11:30am–2pm and 5–9:30pm. Closed 1st 2 weeks in Jan. From Historic Area, go 4 miles west on U.S. 60 to shopping center on left.

Old Chickahominy House TRADITIONAL SOUTHERN   One of the great places to sample traditional, down-home Virginia cooking, the Old Chickahominy House is a reconstructed 18th-century house with mantels from old Gloucester homes and wainscoting from Carter's Grove. The entire effect is extremely cozy and charming, from the rocking chairs on the front porch to the blazing fireplaces within. This is the best place in town for hearty Southern plantation food. 1211 Jamestown Rd., at Va. 199. ℂ 757/229-4689. Reservations not accepted. Breakfast $3–$8; lunch $2.50–$8. MC, V. Daily 8:30–10:15am and 11:45am–2:15pm. Closed Easter, July 4, Thanksgiving, Christmas.

Trellis Cafe, Restaurant & Grill AMERICAN   Executive chef Marcel Desaulniers has brought national recognition to this restaurant, whose decor evokes delightful establishments in California's wine country. The imaginative menu of American regional fare changes seasonally to take advantage of local produce. If it's offered, try his exciting combination of grilled fish, thinly sliced Virginia country ham, pine nuts, and Zinfandel-soaked raisins. And don't skip the sinful Death by Chocolate for dessert. If the weather is fine, you might dine alfresco on the planter-bordered brick terrace. Duke of Gloucester St. (between Henry and Boundary sts.). ℂ 757/229-8610. Reservations suggested at dinner. Sandwiches $7–$10; main courses $18–$28; fixed-price dinners $26. AE, DC, DISC, MC, V. Daily 11am–9:30pm.

A SIDE TRIP TO JAMESTOWN

The first permanent English settlement in the New World was established miles of southwest of Williamsburg. Except for the partial remains of their brick church, little remains of the riverside settlement. But its story is documented here in museum exhibits and living-history interpretations. Archaeologists have excavated more than 100 building frames, evidence of manufacturing ventures (pottery, winemaking, brick making, and glass blowing), early wells, and old roads, as well as scores of artifacts of everyday life.

Allow a full day for your visit and consider packing a lunch. Other than a cafe at Jamestown Settlement, there are no restaurants, so you may want to take advantage of the picnic areas at the National Park Service site.

GETTING THERE   From Williamsburg, follow the Jamestown Road (Va. 31 south), or the Colonial Parkway.

JAMESTOWN ISLAND

The National Park Service's **Jamestown Island** (ℂ 757/898-2410 or 757/229-1773; www.nps.gov/colo), site of the actual colony, is separated by an isthmus from the mainland, at the western terminus of the Colonial Parkway. At the Ranger Station entrance gate, you'll pay $6 for each person over 15 years old; admission is good for 7 days. Or you can buy a Joint Jamestown–Yorktown

Passport for $9 per person over 15, which will admit you for 7 days both here and at the Yorktown National Battlefield (see "A Side Trip to Yorktown," below). The gate is open daily from 8:30am to 5pm in summer. You can stay on the grounds until dusk.

Begin your visit at the **visitor center** and then follow the footpaths to the actual site of **"James Cittie,"** where rubbly brick foundations of 17th-century homes, taverns, shops, and statehouses are enhanced by artists' renderings, text, and audio stations. A fascinating **5-mile loop drive** begins at the visitor center parking lot and winds through 1,500 wilderness acres of woodland and marsh that have been allowed to return to their natural state in order to approximate the landscape as 17th-century settlers found it. Illustrative markers interpret aspects of daily activities and industries of the colonists—tobacco growing, lumbering, silk and wine production, pottery making, farming, and so on.

JAMESTOWN SETTLEMENT

Operated by the state of Virginia, **Jamestown Settlement,** an indoor/outdoor museum, is open daily from 9am to 5pm (© **888/593-4682** or 757/253-4838; www.historyisfun.org). Admission is $11 adults, $5.25 children 6 to 12, free for children under 6; or you can buy a combination ticket with Yorktown Victory Center (see "A Side Trip to Yorktown," below) for $16 adults, $7.75 children 6 to 12, free for kids under 6.

After purchasing tickets, you can watch a 20-minute film that gives you an introduction to Jamestown. Beyond the theater, three large permanent galleries feature artifacts and dioramas relating to the Jamestown period. Leaving the museum complex, you'll come directly into the **Powhatan Indian Village,** representing the culture and technology of a highly organized chiefdom of 32 tribes that inhabited coastal Virginia in the early 17th century. There are several mat-covered lodges, or longhouses, which are furnished as dwellings, as well as a garden and a ceremonial dance circle. Historical interpreters tend gardens, tan animal hides, and make bone and stone tools and pottery. Triangular **James Fort** is a re-creation of the one constructed by the Jamestown colonists on their arrival in the spring of 1607. Interpreters are engaged in activities typical of early 17th-century life, such as agriculture, animal care, carpentry, blacksmithing, and meal preparation. A short walk from James Fort are reproductions of the three **ships,** the *Susan Constant, Godspeed,* and *Discovery,* which transported 104 colonists to Virginia in 1607.

A SIDE TRIP TO YORKTOWN

Yorktown, the setting for the last major battle of the American Revolution, is about 14 miles northeast of Williamsburg. Today, the battlefield is a national park, and the Commonwealth of Virginia has built an interpretive museum explaining the road to revolution, the war itself, and the building of a new nation afterwards. The old town of Yorktown itself is also worth seeing. For lunch, consider a picnic in a large tree-shaded area at the Victory Center or at a riverside picnic area with tables and grills on Water Street at the foot of Comte de Grasse Street.

GETTING THERE   From Williamsburg, drive to the eastern end of the Colonial Parkway. From Norfolk, take I-64 west to U.S. 17 north.

YORKTOWN NATIONAL BATTLEFIELD

The **National Park Service Visitor Center** (© **757/898-2410** or 757/898-3400) displays Washington's actual military headquarters tent, a replica (which you can board and explore) of the quarterdeck of H.M.S. *Charon,* additional objects recovered from the York River in the excavations, exhibits about Cornwallis's surrender and the events leading up to it, and dioramas detailing the siege. Upstairs, an "on-the-scene" account of the Battle of Yorktown is given by a 13-year-old soldier in the Revolutionary army, his taped narrative accompanied by a sound-and-light show. National Park Service rangers are on hand to answer questions; they also give free tours of the British inner defense line.

The park service visitor center is the starting point for the 7-mile Battlefield route and the 10.2-mile Encampment route **auto tours** of the battlefield. You'll be given a map indicating both routes and detailing major sites. At each stop there are explanatory historical markers (sometimes taped narratives as well), but for the most interesting experience, rent a cassette player and tape at the visitor center.

Self-guided or ranger-led walking tours of **Old Yorktown**—including some places of interest not related to the famed battle—are also available here.

The center is open daily from 9am to 5pm, with extended hours from spring to fall. Admission is $5 per person over 16, good for 7 days. Or you can buy a Joint Jamestown–Yorktown Passport for $9 per person over 15, which will admit you for 7 days here and at Jamestown Island. Audiotape tours cost $2.

YORKTOWN VICTORY CENTRE
Set on 21 acres overlooking part of the battlefield of 1781, the state-owned **Yorktown Victory Center** (© **888/593-4682** or 757/253-4838; www.historyis fun.org) offers an excellent orientation to Yorktown, including a film, a living-history program, and museum exhibits. In the outdoor Continental army encampment, costumed interpreters re-create the lives of men and women who took part in the American Revolution. Admission is $8.25 adults, $4 children 6 to 12, free for children under 6; or you can buy a **combination ticket** for this and Jamestown Settlement at $16 adults and $7.75 children 6 to 12, free for children under 6. Open daily from 9am to 5pm.

9 The Shenandoah Valley

Native Americans called the 200-mile-long valley in northwestern Virginia *Shenandoah,* meaning "Daughter of the Stars." Today the Shenandoah National Park offers spectacular landscapes and a plethora of hiking and riding trails, and protects the beauty and peace of the Blue Ridge Mountains along the eastern boundary of the valley. Along the Blue Ridge crest, the 105-mile-long Skyline Drive—one of America's great scenic drives—runs the full length of the park and connects directly with the Blue Ridge Parkway, which continues south into North Carolina. Pioneers moved west from the Tidewater in the early 1700s to found picturesque small towns on the rolling valley floor, which was later to play a major role in the Civil War.

SHENANDOAH NATIONAL PARK
Running for 105 miles down the spine of the Blue Ridge Mountains, Shenandoah National Park is a haven for plants and wildlife. Although long and skinny, the park encompasses some 300 square miles of mountains, forests, waterfalls, and rock formations. It has more than 60 mountain peaks higher than 2,000 feet, with Hawksbill and Stony Man exceeding 4,000 feet. From overlooks along the road through the park, called the Skyline Drive, you can see many of the park's wonders and enjoy panoramic views over the Piedmont to the east and the

Shenandoah Valley to the west. The drive gives you access to the park's visitor facilities and to more than 500 miles of glorious hiking and horse trails, including the Appalachian Trail. Animals such as deer, bear, bobcat, and turkey live here; the park also boasts more than 100 species of trees.

ESSENTIALS

ENTRANCES & ORIENTATION   The park and its Skyline Drive have four entrances. Northernmost is at **Front Royal** on U.S. 340 near the junction of I-81 and I-66, about 1 mile south of Front Royal and 90 miles west of Washington, D.C. The two middle entrances are at **Thornton Gap,** 33 miles south of Front Royal on U.S. 211 between Sperryville and Luray, and at **Swift Run Gap,** 68 miles south of Front Royal on U.S. 33 between Standardsville and Elkton. The southern gate is at **Rockfish Gap,** 105 miles south of Front Royal at I-64 and U.S. 250, some 21 miles west of Charlottesville and 18 miles east of Staunton.

The Skyline Drive is marked with **Mile Posts,** starting at zero at the Front Royal entrance and increasing as you go south, with Rockfish Gap on the southern end at Mile 105.

VISITOR INFORMATION   For free information, call or write Superintendent, **Shenandoah National Park,** 3655 U.S. Hwy., 211 East, Luray, VA 22835 (© **540/999-3500;** www.nps.gov/shen). The headquarters is 4 miles west of Thornton Gap and 5 miles east of Luray on U.S. 211.

FEES, REGULATIONS & BACKCOUNTRY PERMITS   Entrance permits good for 7 consecutive days are $10 per car, $5 for each pedestrian or bicyclist. A Shenandoah Passport ($20) is good for 1 year, as is the National Park Service's Golden Eagle Passport ($50). Park entrance is free to holders of Golden Access (for U.S. citizens with disabilities) and Golden Age (U.S. citizens 62 or older) passports. The former is free; the latter is available at the entrance gates for $10.

Speed limit on the Skyline Drive is 35 miles per hour, although given the number of camper vans and rubberneckers creeping along this two-lane road, you'll be lucky to go that fast.

Plants and animals are protected; so all hunting is prohibited. Pets must be kept on a leash at all times and are not allowed on some trails. Wood fires are permitted only in fireplaces in developed areas. The Skyline Drive is a great bike route, but neither bicycles nor motor vehicles of any sort are allowed on the trails.

Most of the park is open to backcountry camping. Permits, which are free, are required; get them at the entrance gates, at the visitor centers, or by mail from park headquarters (see "Visitor Information," above). Campers are required to leave no trace of their presence. No permits are necessary for backcountry hiking, but the same "no-trace" rule applies.

VISITOR CENTERS   There are two park visitor centers. The **Dickey Ridge Visitor Center,** at Mile 4.6, is usually open daily from 8:30am to 5pm April through November, and on an intermittent schedule in December. **Byrd Visitor Center,** at Mile 51 in Big Meadows, is open daily from 8:30am to 5pm from early April to October and on an intermittent schedule through December. Both provide information, maps of nearby hiking trails, interpretive exhibits, films, slide shows, and nature walks. There is a small information center at **Loft Mountain** (Mile 79.5), which is open daily from 9am to 5pm during the summer months. In addition, the privately run **Rockfish Gap Information Center,** on U.S. 211 outside the park's southern gate (© **540/949-8203;** www.augusta chamber.org), has information about the park and the surrounding area.

SEASONS   The park is most popular from mid- to late October, when the fall foliage peaks and weekend traffic on the Skyline Drive can be bumper to bumper. Days also tend to be clearer in fall than in summer, when lingering haze can obscure the views. In spring, the green of leafing trees moves up the ridge at the rate of about 100 feet a day. Wildflowers begin to bloom in April, and by late May the azaleas are brilliant and the dogwood is putting on a show. Nesting birds abound, and the normally modest waterfalls are at their highest during spring, when warm rains melt the highland snows. You'll find the clearest views across the distant mountains during winter, but many facilities are closed then, and snow and ice can shut down the Skyline Drive. Also, parts of the drive are closed at night during Virginia's hunting season from mid-November to early January.

SEEING THE HIGHLIGHTS

Unless you're caught in heavy traffic on fall foliage weekends, you can drive the entire length of the **Skyline Drive** in about 3 hours without stopping. But why rush? Give yourself at least a day for this drive and its 75 designated scenic overlooks. Better yet, get out of your car and take at least a short hike down one of the hollows to a waterfall.

If you have only a day, head directly to the **Central District** between Thornton Gap and Swift Run Gap, the most developed but also most interesting part of the park. It has the highest mountains, the best views, nearly half of the park's 500 miles of hiking trails, and the park's only stables and overnight accommodations. Most visitors make Big Meadows or Skyland their base of operations for stays of more than a day, but if you plan to do this, place your lodge reservations early (see "Where to Camp & Stay," below).

Among the more interesting of the 75 designated overlooks along the drive are the **Shenandoah Valley Overlook** (Mile 2.8), with views west to the Signal Knob of Massanutten Mountain across the south fork of the river; **Range View Overlook** (Mile 17.1; elevation 2,800 ft.), providing fine views of the central section of the park, looking south; **Stony Man Overlook** (Mile 38.6), offering panoramas of Stony Man Cliffs, the valley, and the Alleghenies; **Thoroughfare Mountain Overlook** (Mile 40.5; elevation 3,595 ft.), one of the highest, with views from Hogback Mountain south to cone-shaped Robertson Mountain and the rocky face of Old Rag Mountain; **Old Rag View Overlook** (Mile 46.5), dominated by Old Rag, sitting all by itself in an eastern extremity of the park; **Franklin Cliffs Overlook** (Mile 49), offering a view of the cliffs and the Shenandoah Valley and Massanutten Mountain beyond; and **Big Run Overlook** (Mile 81.2), which looks down on rocky peaks and the largest watershed in the park.

HIKING

The park's 112 hiking trails total more than 500 miles, varying in length from short walks to a 101-mile segment of the Appalachian Trail running the entire length of the park. Access to the trails is marked along the Skyline Drive. There are parking lots at the major trail heads, but they fill quickly on weekends.

Free maps of many trails are available at the visitor centers, which also sell topographic maps published by the Potomac Appalachian Trail Conference, as well as a one-sheet map of all of the park's walks published by Trails Illustrated. See "Visitor Information," above, for addresses and phone numbers.

Try to take at least one of the short hikes on trails at Dickey Ridge Visitor Center (Mile 4.6), Byrd Visitor Center/Big Meadows (Mile 51), and Loft

Mountain (Mile 79.5). There's an excellent 1.6-mile hike at Stony Man (Mile 41.7). The following are a few of the more popular trails.

Limberlost Accessible Trail   At Mile 43 south of Skyland, Limberlost is accessible to visitors in wheelchairs. The 1.3-mile loop runs through an old-growth forest of ancient hemlocks. The trail has a 5-foot-wide, hard-packed surface; crosses a 65-foot bridge; and includes a 150-foot boardwalk.

Dark Hollow Falls   One of the park's most popular hikes is the 1.4-mile walk to Dark Hollow Falls, the closest cascade to the Skyline Drive. The trail begins at Mile 50.7 near the Byrd Visitor Center. Allow 1¼ hours for the round-trip.

Camp Hoover/Mill Prong   Starting at the Milam Gap parking area (Mile 52.8), this 4-mile round-trip hike drops down the Mill Prong to the Rapidan River, where Pres. Herbert Hoover, an avid fisherman, had a camp during his administration (sort of the Camp David of his day). The total climb is 850 feet. Allow 4 hours.

South River Falls   Third-highest in the park, South River Falls drops a total of 83 feet in two stages. From the parking lot at South River Overlook (Mile 62.7), the trail is a moderately easy 2.6 miles round-trip, with a total climb of about 850 feet. Allow 2½ hours.

Doyles River Falls   Starting at a large parking lot at Mile 81.1, a trail drops to a small waterfall in a natural amphitheater surrounded by large trees. Continue another quarter of a mile to see an even taller falls (63 ft.). This hike is 2.7 miles round-trip, with a few steep sections in its 850-foot climb. Allow 3 hours.

Appalachian Trail   Access points to the Appalachian Trail are well marked at overlooks along the Skyline Drive. Along the trail, five backcountry shelters for day use each offer only a table, fireplace, pit toilet, and water. The **Potomac Appalachian Trail Club** (© **703/242-0693;** www.patc.net) maintains seven huts and six fully enclosed cabins that can accommodate up to 12 people. Use of the huts is free, but they are intended for long-distance hikers only. Cabins cost $10 to $20 on weekdays, $15 to $40 on weekends, and must be reserved in advance through the park or by contacting PATC Monday through Thursday between 7 and 9pm, Thursday and Friday from noon to 2pm Eastern time (*only* during these hours).

WHERE TO CAMP & STAY

The park has four campgrounds with tent and trailer sites (but no hookups anywhere): **Big Meadows** (Mile 51.2), **Mathews Arm** (Mile 22.2), **Lewis Mountain** (Mile 57.5), and **Loft Mountain** (Mile 79.5). The latter three are on a first-come, first-served basis at $14 per site per night. They are open from mid-May to late October.

Big Meadows Lodge and Skyland Lodge (see below) are the only hotels in the park. They are managed by the park concessionaire, **Aramark Virginia Sky-Line Co.,** P.O. Box 727, Luray, VA 22835 (© **800/999-4714** or 540/743-5108; www.visitshenandoah.com), which also operates food and other services for park visitors. Lodge reservations should be made well in advance—up to a year ahead for the peak fall season. In addition, cottages are available at Lewis Mountain.

Big Meadows Lodge   Accommodations at Big Meadows consist of rooms in the main lodge and in rustic cabins, and multi-unit lodges with suites. Many of them have great views. You'll have a private bathroom but no TV, phone, or any other modern amenities in your room. Some have fireplaces and balconies or terraces. Big Meadows is a major recreational center; many hiking trails start here, and it's also the site of the Byrd Visitor Center. The resort is built near a large grassy meadow where families of deer often come to graze at dawn and dusk. A grocery store is nearby. The dining room features traditional regional dishes such as fried chicken and mountain trout. Wine, beer, and cocktails are available. During the season, live entertainment keeps the Taproom busy. P.O. Box 727, Luray, VA 22835 (on Skyline Dr. at Mile 51.2). (𝄐 800/999-4714 or 540/999-2221. Fax 540/ 999-2011. www.visitshenandoah.com. 97 units. $67–$120 double main lodge; $79–$107 double motel; $107–$142 double suite; $75–$87 double cabin room. Highest rates charged in Oct. Packages available. AE, DISC, MC, V. Closed Nov to early May. **Amenities:** Restaurant.

Skyland Lodge   Skyland was built by naturalist George Freeman Pollock in 1894 as a summer retreat atop the highest point on the Skyline Drive. Encompassing 52 acres, the resort offers rustic wood-paneled cabins as well as motel-type accommodations with wonderful views (ask for a room with a view), but like at Big Meadows, you won't have TVs, phones, or other amenities. Some of the buildings are dark-brown clapboard, others fieldstone, and all nestle among the trees. The central building has a lobby with a huge stone fireplace, seating areas, and a TV. Complete breakfast, lunch, and dinner menus are offered at reasonable prices. There's a fully stocked taproom. P.O. Box 727, Luray, VA 22835 (on Skyline Dr. at Mile 41.8). (𝄐 800/999-4714 or 540/999-2211. Fax 540/999-2231. www.visitshenandoah.com. 177 units. $79–$122 double in lodge; $52–$105 double cabin rooms; $113–$177 suite. Highest rates charged in Oct. Packages available. Closed Nov to early May. AE, DISC, MC, V. **Amenities:** Restaurant.

LEXINGTON

A lively college atmosphere prevails in Lexington, which consistently ranks as one of America's best small towns. Fine old homes line tree-shaded streets, among them the house where Stonewall Jackson lived when he taught at Virginia Military Institute. A beautifully restored downtown looks much like it did in the 1800s. Besides VMI, the town is also home to Washington & Lee University, which has one of the oldest and most beautiful campuses in the country.

ESSENTIALS

GETTING THERE   Lexington lies about 60 miles south and west of the southern end of the Skyline Drive. From Washington, D.C., take I-66 west, than I-81 south. From Richmond, take I-64 west.

VISITOR INFORMATION   The **Lexington & Rockbridge Area Visitor Center,** 106 E. Washington St., Lexington, VA 24450 ((𝄐 877/453-9822 or 540/463-3777; www.lexingtonvirginia.com), is a block east of Main Street. It offers museumlike displays about the town's history and distributes free walking-tour brochures (you can park in the center's lot while touring the town). Be sure to see the engrossing slide show on Lexington's history. It's open daily from 8:30am to 6pm June through August, from 9am to 5pm the rest of the year.

WHAT TO SEE & DO

The **Lee Chapel and Museum,** near Letcher Avenue on the Washington and Lee University campus ((𝄐 540/463-8768), is a magnificent Victorian-Gothic chapel of brick and native limestone, built in 1867 at the request of General Lee. Lee's remains are in a crypt below the chapel. His office was in the lower level of the building, now part of the chapel museum and preserved just as he left it on September 28, 1870. His beloved horse, Traveller, is buried in a plot outside the office.

The fine **Virginia Military Institute Museum,** in the basement of Jackson Memorial Hall, VMI Campus (℗ 540/464-7232; www.vmi.edu/museum), displays uniforms, weapons, and memorabilia from cadets who attended the college and fought in numerous wars. Of special note is the bullet-pierced raincoat Stonewall Jackson was wearing when accidentally shot by his own men at Chancellorsville, and also, thanks to taxidermy, Jackson's unflappable war horse, Little Sorrel.

Also on the VMI campus is the **George C. Marshall Museum and Research Library** (℗ 540/463-7103; www.marshallfoundation.org), with the archives and research library of General of the Army George C. Marshall, a 1901 graduate of VMI who served as army chief of staff during World War II and as secretary of state and secretary of defense under President Truman. He is best remembered for the Marshall Plan, which fostered the economic recovery of Europe after the war. For his role in promoting peace, he became the first career soldier to be awarded the Nobel Peace Prize. In contrast to the many Civil War shrines here, this is an excellent World War II museum.

The **Stonewall Jackson House,** 8 E. Washington St. (between Main and Randolph sts.; ℗ 540/463-2552; www.stonewalljackson.org), is where the legendary Confederate general lived from early 1859 until he answered General Lee's summons to Richmond in 1861. Appropriate period furnishings duplicate the items on the inventory of Jackson's estate made shortly after he died near Chancellorsville in 1863.

An impressive attraction nearby is the **Natural Bridge** (℗ 800/533-1410 or 540/291-2121; www.naturalbridgeva.com), a limestone formation that Thomas Jefferson called "the most sublime of nature's works . . . so beautiful an arch, so elevated, so light and springing, as it were, up to heaven." This geological oddity rises 215 feet above Cedar Creek; its span is 90 feet long and spreads at its widest to 150 feet. The Monocan Indian tribes worshiped it as "the bridge of God." Today it is also the bridge of man, as U.S. 11 passes over it. The Natural Bridge is now a small tourist-industry enclave, with a cavern, department-store–size souvenir shop, restaurant, hotel, campground, wax museum, and zoo. The bridge is 12 miles south of Lexington on U.S. 11 (take Exit 175 off I-81). Admission to the bridge is $10 for adults, $5 for children 6 to 15.

Lexington's charming 19th-century downtown offers many interesting shops, most of them on Main and Washington streets. **Artists in Cahoots,** in the Alexander-Witherow House, at the corner of Main and Washington (℗ 540/464-1147), features an outstanding selection of arts and crafts. Antiques hunters will find fascinating browsing at the **Lexington Antique & Craft Mall** (℗ 540/463-9511), in which 250 dealers occupy 40,000 square feet of space in the Kroger Shopping Center on U.S. 11, about half a mile north of downtown.

The Maury River, which runs through Lexington, provides some of Virginia's best **white-water rafting** and **kayaking,** especially through the Goshen Pass, on Va. 39 northwest of town. The visitor center has information about several put-in spots, or you can rent equipment or go on expeditions on the Maury and James rivers with **James River Basin Canoe Livery** (℗ 540/261-7334; www.canoevirginia.com).

Two linear parks connect to offer hikers and joggers nearly 10 miles of gorgeous trail between Lexington and Buena Vista, a railroad town 7 miles to the southeast. The major link is the **Chessie Nature Trail,** which follows an old railroad bed along the Maury River between Lexington and Buena Vista. No vehicles (including bicycles) are allowed, but you can cross-country ski the trail

🖋 A Side Trip to Warm Springs & Hot Springs

A scenic drive 42 miles from Lexington will bring you to the towns of Warm Springs and Hot Springs, famous for their thermal springs. The most famous are the **Jefferson Pools** (📞 **540/839-5346**), which sit in a grove of trees at the intersection of U.S. 220 and Va. 39. Opened in 1761, they're still covered by the octagonal white clapboard bathhouses built in the 19th century, so the only luxuries you'll get are a clean towel and a rudimentary changing room. Use of the pools costs $12 an hour. Reservations aren't taken; just walk in. Hours are March through October, daily from 10am to 6pm; November through February, daily from 11am to 6pm, but call to confirm the winter hours.

In the tiny town of Hot Springs is the acclaimed and pricey **Homestead** (📞 **800/838-1766** or 540/839-1776; www.thehomestead.com.), a famous spa and golf resort that has hosted everyone from FDR to John D. Rockefeller. The Homestead's historic Dining Room is a lush palm court, in which an orchestra performs every evening during six-course dinners. The resort boasts three outstanding golf courses, indoor and outdoor pools, a spa with full health club facilities, 12 tennis courts, hiking trails, horseback and carriage rides, ice-skating on an Olympic-size rink, and much more. *Note:* Nonguests can pay to use all of the Homestead's facilities.

There are several B&B inns in the area as well as the **Roseloe Motel** (📞 **540/839-5373**), an inexpensive, family-run motel on U.S. 220 between Warm Springs and Hot Springs. It's near the **Garth Newel Music Center** (📞 540/839-5018; www.garthnewel.org), whose summer-long chamber music festival has been drawing critical acclaim since the early 1970s.

For more information, contact the **Bath County Chamber of Commerce**, P.O. Box 718, Hot Springs, VA 24445 (📞 **800/628-8092** or 540/839-5409; www.bathcountyva.org), whose visitor center is 2 miles south of Hot Springs on U.S. 220.

---

during winter. The Chessie trail connects with a walking path in **Woods Creek Park,** which starts at the Waddell School on Jordan Street and runs down to the banks of the Maury. Both trails are open from dawn to dusk. The visitor center has maps and brochures.

There are excellent hiking, mountain-biking, and horseback-riding trails in the **George Washington National Forest,** which encompasses much of the Blue Ridge Mountains east of Lexington. Small children might not be able to make it, but the rest of the family will enjoy the 3-mile trail up to **Crabtree Falls,** a series of cascades tumbling 1,200 feet down the mountain (the highest waterfall in Virginia). Crabtree Falls is on Va. 56 east of the Blue Ridge Parkway; from Lexington, go north on I-81 to Steeles Tavern (Exit 205), then east on Va. 56.

The National Forest Service has an **information office** at Natural Bridge (📞 **540/291-1806**), which offers free brochures and sells maps of trails and campgrounds. It's open from April to mid-November, daily from 9:30am to 5:30pm; the rest of the year, daily from 8:30am to 4pm.

WHERE TO STAY & DINE

In town and just outside are three lovely and historic country inns: **Alexander-Witherow House** and **McCampbell Inn,** both at 11 N. Main St., and the **Maple Inn,** which lies 7 miles north of town on U.S. 11. Make reservations for all three through **Historic Country Inns,** 11 N. Main St., Lexington, VA 24450 (© **877/463-2044** or 540/463-2044; www.innbook.com).

Another good lodging choice is the **Hampton Inn Col Alto,** 401 E. Nelson St. (© **800/HAMPTON** or 540/463-2223), an 1827 manor house built on a plantation that was then on the outskirts of town.

Lexington has several chain motels, especially at the intersection of U.S. 11 and I-64 (Exit 55), 1½ miles north of downtown. They include the **Best Western Inn at Hunt Ridge** (© **800/464-1501** or 540/464-1500), **Comfort Inn** (© **800/628-1956** or 540/463-7311), and **Country Inn & Suites** (© **800/ 456-4000** or 540/464-9000).

While you're walking around town, stop in at Lexington's famous **Sweet Things,** 106 W. Washington St., between Jefferson Street and Lee Avenue (© **540/463-6055**), for a cone or cup of "designer" ice cream or frozen yogurt. It's open Monday through Saturday from noon to 10:30pm, Sunday from 2 to 9:30pm. For more substantial fare, head to **Willson-Walker House Restaurant,** 30 N. Main St. (between Washington and Henry sts.; © **540/463-3020**), which offers some of the valley's finest cuisine.

6

The South

In the popular mind, the South is still the Old South, a land of magnolias and Spanish moss, of plantation manses and Scarlett and Rhett fleeing through Atlanta's burning streets. But the states of the Old Confederacy are much more modern—and a good deal more diverse—than this shopworn stereotype.

True, you can find many remnants of the genteel Old South in many places, especially in the charming seaports of Savannah and Charleston. But Dixie has long since made it into the mainstream, and many parts of the South (the so-called New South) are among the most prosperous and dynamic parts of the nation's economy.

Geographically, this is one of the most diverse parts of the country, from the gorgeous beaches of the Outer Banks to the misty peaks of the Great Smoky Mountains, from the Bluegrass Country of Kentucky to the bayous of Louisiana. We'll take you through the highlights in the pages that follow, making sure to stop off for the region's best music (from country to the blues to jazz) and dining (from down-home Carolina barbecue to the decadent Creole cuisine of New Orleans).

1 Atlanta

Atlanta is and always has been a city on the move. It is the city of Martin Luther King, Jr., father of one of the country's most important social revolutions, and of Ted Turner, who brought the world a revolution of another sort. The dramatic downtown skyline, with its gleaming skyscrapers, is testimony to Atlanta's inability to sit still—even for a minute.

Consistently ranked as one of the best cities in the world in which to do business, Atlanta is third in the nation for the number of Fortune 500 companies headquartered here—11, including Home Depot, United Parcel Service, and Coca-Cola. The metro area is vast and sprawling. With a population of 4.1 million and counting, the only limit to its growth appears to be interminable traffic congestion.

But commerce and development are not the only things that characterize this bustling metropolis. You'll still hear gentle Southern accents here, though at least half of Atlanta's citizens were born outside the South, with one of every 10 foreign-born. Those transplants, though, find themselves bending to the local customs, saying "please" and "ma'am" and holding doors open for each other.

ESSENTIALS
GETTING THERE   By Plane   Hartsfield Atlanta International Airport (www.atlanta-airport.com), 10 miles south of downtown, is the world's largest and now the nation's busiest passenger airport and transfer hub, accommodating 80.2 million passengers a year. The airport is undergoing a $5.4 billion expansion to relieve congestion, adding a fifth runway, upgrading the international concourse and terminal, and consolidating rental car terminals. Delta,

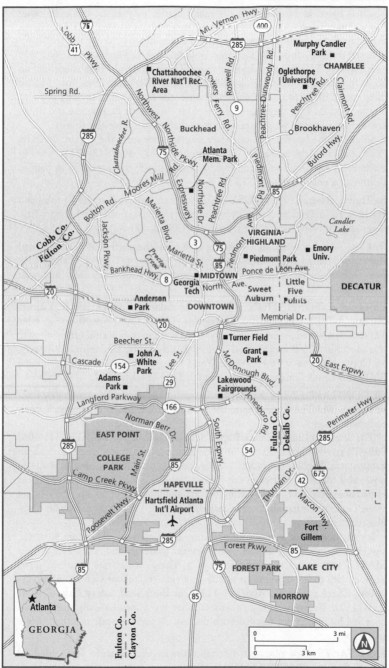

which is based at Hartsfield, is the major carrier to Atlanta, but most other major domestic and several international carriers have service, too. Despite its size, Hartsfield is well planned and easy to negotiate.

A taxi from the airport to a downtown hotel costs $25 for one passenger, $13 each for two, $10 each for three or more. The ride should take about half an hour. To midtown hotels, the fare is $28 for one passenger, $15 for two, $12 for three, and $10 for four. To Buckhead hotels, the fare is $35 for one passenger, $18 for two, $13 for three, and $11 for four. *Warning:* Be sure the taxi driver knows how to get to where you want to go before you leave the airport.

Several of the larger hotels offer free shuttle buses from the airport. **MARTA** (Metropolitan Atlanta Rapid Transit Authority; ✆ **404/848-4711;** www.its marta.com) rapid-rail trains run from a station inside the airport from 5am to 1am, with a one-way fare of $1.75.

By Train   Amtrak (✆ **800/USA-RAIL;** www.amtrak.com) serves **Brookwood Station,** 1688 Peachtree Rd., providing daily service from Washington (trip time: 14 hr.), New York (19 hr.), and New Orleans (11 hr.).

By Car   Major routes into Atlanta are I-75 from the northwest (Chattanooga) and south (Tampa and Miami), I-85 from the northeast (Charlotte) and southwest (Montgomery, AL), and I-20 from the east (Columbia, SC) and west (Birmingham, AL).

VISITOR INFORMATION   Contact the **Atlanta Convention & Visitors Bureau (ACVB),** 233 Peachtree St. NE, Ste. 100, Atlanta, GA 30303 (✆ **404/ 521-6600;** www.atlanta.net), weekdays from 8:30am to 5:30pm. Once in town, you can visit ACVB information centers at the airport; Underground Atlanta, 65 Upper Alabama St.; the Georgia World Congress Center, 285 International Blvd.; and Lenox Square Shopping Center, 3393 Peachtree Rd.

GETTING AROUND   It's possible to reach most major Atlanta sites by transit system (MARTA), but despite the growing problem of traffic jams, a car is preferable.

The **Metropolitan Atlanta Rapid Transit Authority (MARTA)** (✆ **404/ 848-4711;** www.itsmarta.com) operates subways and buses daily from about 5am to 1am. Regular fare is $1.75. There are token vending machines at all stations, and transfers are free. A convenient feature on MARTA's website is a list of popular attractions, followed by the rail stations and buses necessary to get there. Go to **www.itsmarta.com,** click on "Getting There," then click on "Popular Attractions."

It's not possible to step outside anywhere and hail a cab. There are, however, always cabs outside the airport, major hotels, Underground Atlanta, and most MARTA stations, except those downtown. There's a flat rate based on travel between city zones. If you need to call for a taxi, try **Yellow Cab** (✆ **404/521-0200**), **Checker Cab** (✆ **404/351-1111**), or **Buckhead Safety Cab** (✆ **404/ 233-1152**). *Warning:* Many Atlanta taxis are dirty, mechanically suspect, and operated by drivers not familiar with the city. Be sure the fare is settled before setting off.

FAST FACTS   For physician referrals, contact the **Georgia State Medical Association** (✆ **404/752-1564**). Major downtown hospitals are **Atlanta Medical Center** (the former Georgia Baptist Hospital), 303 Parkway Dr. NE (✆ **404/265-4000**); and **Grady Memorial Hospital,** 80 Butler St. SE (✆ **404/ 616-4307**).

A Note on Area Codes

In metro Atlanta, you must dial the area code (**404, 770, or 678**) and the seven-digit telephone number, even if you are calling a number within the same area code. It is not necessary to dial "1" before calling a different area code in metro Atlanta.

CVS Pharmacy has two centrally located pharmacies open 24 hours daily, at 1943 Peachtree Rd. (© **404/351-7153**) across from Piedmont Hospital between downtown and Buckhead; and at 2350 Cheshire Bridge Rd. NE (© **404/486-7289**), near Midtown, Buckhead, and Virginia-Highland.

In addition to the 7% city sales tax, there is a 7% hotel and motel tax.

SPECIAL EVENTS & FESTIVALS   The second week of January is King Week, honoring the late Rev. Martin Luther King, Jr., an Atlanta native. The week includes a variety of religious services, concerts, speeches, volunteer opportunities, and a parade. For details, contact the King Center (© **404/526-8900**; www.thekingcenter.com).

Mid-February brings the **Southeastern Flower Show** (© **404/888-5638**; www.flowershow.org), followed in mid-April by the **Atlanta Dogwood Festival** (© **404/329-0501**; www.dogwood.org). Also beginning in April and running for seven weekends is the **Georgia Renaissance Festival Spring Celebration** (© **770/964-8575**; www.garenfest.com), a re-creation of a 16th-century English country fair with a birds of prey show, jousting knights, jugglers, giant stiltwalkers, minstrels, and magicians. Mid-May brings big-name performers to **Music Midtown** (© **770/MIDTOWN**; www.musicmidtown.com).

WHAT TO SEE & DO

Atlanta Botanical Garden   This delightful garden, occupying 30 acres in Piedmont Park, includes a tranquil moon-gated Japanese garden, a rose garden, a fern glade, a camellia garden, a new children's garden featuring a three-story treehouse, gurgling streams, beautiful statuary, and more. The Fuqua Conservatory houses rare and endangered tropical and desert plants—and a fascinating exhibit of carnivorous plants and poison dart frogs. Allow 2 to 3 hours. 1345 Piedmont Ave. NE, in Piedmont Park at Piedmont Ave. and The Prado. © 404/876-5859. www.atlanta botanicalgarden.org. Admission $10 adults, $7 seniors, $5 ages 3 and up, including college students with ID; free for children under 3. Free every Thurs 3pm to closing. Tues–Sun 9am–6pm, until 7pm during daylight saving time.

Atlanta History Center   From the prehistory of the area that became Atlanta to the present, it's all here in vivid display in this vast museum. In addition to traveling exhibits, permanent exhibits focus on the Civil War, folk art, golf legend and Atlanta native Bobby Jones, and the Atlanta Braves baseball team. On the grounds is Swan House and Gardens, the finest residential design of architect Philip Trammel Schutze. This classical home—listed on the National Register of Historic Places—was constructed in 1928 by the Edward H. Inman family, heirs to a cotton fortune. Also on the grounds is a "plantation plain" home built around 1840, the Tullie Smith Farm. Here you can see how most Georgia farmers really lived. The grounds also include two children's playhouses and 33 acres of gardens and nature trails. Allow 2 to 3 hours. 130 W. Paces Ferry Rd., at Slaton Dr. © 404/814-4000. www.atlhist.org. Admission $12 adults, $10 seniors and students

18 or older, $7 children 3–17, free for children under 3. Mon–Sat 10am–5:30pm; Sun noon–5:30pm. Ticket sales stop at 4:30pm. MARTA: Lenox; then bus 23 to Peachtree St. and W. Paces Ferry Rd., then a 3-block walk.

Birth Home of Martin Luther King, Jr.   This Queen Anne–style house is where King was born on January 15, 1929. He was the eldest son of a Baptist minister and music teacher. The future civil rights leader lived at this modest house until he was 12. It has been restored to its appearance when young Martin lived here. A great deal of King memorabilia is displayed. *Note:* In summer, tickets to the house often run out because of the crowds. Plan to visit the nearby Ebenezer Baptist Church and Martin Luther King, Jr., Center for Nonviolent Social Change while you're here. For all, allow 2 to 3 hours. 501 Auburn Ave. ⓒ 404/331-6922. www.nps.gov/malu. Free admission (obtain tickets at 449 Auburn Ave.). Daily 9am–5pm. Closed major holidays. MARTA: Five Points, then bus 3.

Centennial Olympic Park   This is a living monument to the 1996 Olympic Games. A 21-acre swath of green space and bricks, the park was carved out of a blighted downtown area. It's an oasis of rolling lawns crisscrossed by brick pathways and punctuated by artwork, rock gardens, pools, and fountains, and it often hosts festivals, artists' markets, concerts, and other performances. The best part of the park is the fountain in the shape of five interlocking Olympic Rings. If you're here in summer, you and the kids can frolic in the fountain. Allow 1 hour. Andrew Young International Blvd. NW at Techwood Dr. ⓒ 404/222-PARK. www.centennialpark.com. Free admission. Daily 7am–11pm. MARTA: Philips Arena/Come/GWCC station, then walk 1 block (past CNN Center).

CNN Center   This building anchors the city's dynamic entertainment, news, sports, and business core and is adjacent to the Georgia Dome and the Georgia World Congress Center and across the street from Centennial Olympic Park. It houses the CNN, Headline News, and CNN International studios and offers guided, 50-minute tours of these facilities daily. *Note:* Reservations are highly recommended, and must be made at least 1 day in advance. Allow 2 hours. One CNN Center, Marietta St. at Techwood Dr. ⓒ 404/827-2300. www.cnn.com/studiotour. Admission $8 adults, $6 seniors, $5 children 6–12. **Note:** Children under 6 not permitted. Tours daily every 20 min. 9am–5pm. MARTA: Philips Arena/Dome/GWCC station.

Cyclorama   For a panorama of the Battle of Atlanta, go see this 42-foot-high, 356-foot-circumference, 1880s painting with a three-dimensional foreground and special lighting, music, and sound effects. When you see the monumental work, you'll know why Union Gen. William Sherman, who burned Atlanta to the ground, said, "War is hell." One of only three cycloramas in the United States, it recently was fully restored—an artistic and historical treasure that many visitors to Atlanta miss, erroneously thinking it's "strictly for kids." Allow 1 hour. 800 Cherokee Ave. in Grant Park. ⓒ 404/624-1071 or 404/658-7625. www.bcaatlanta.org. Admission $5 adults, $4 seniors, $3 children 6–12, free for children under 6. Daily June 1 to Labor Day 9:20am–5:30pm; after Labor Day, 9:20am–4:30pm. Closed major holidays. Shows begin every half hr., starting at 9:30am. MARTA: Five Points; then bus 31 (Cherokee Ave.). Zoo Atlanta is next door.

Ebenezer Baptist Church   From 1960 to 1968, this Gothic Revival–style church, founded in 1886 and completed in 1922, became a center of world attention. Martin Luther King, Jr., served as co-pastor of the church during the civil rights struggle. Martin Luther King, Sr., a civil rights leader before his son, was the pastor. A taped historical message and a 10-minute guided tour are available. Most church services are now conducted in a modern annex across the street. While here, visit the nearby Martin Luther King, Jr., Center for Nonviolent Social Change and the King Birth Home. Allow 2 to 3 hours total. 407 Auburn Ave. NE. ℰ 404/688-7263. www.nps/gov/malu/documents/ebcpage.htm. Free admission (donations appreciated). Mon–Fri 9am–5pm; Sat 9am–2pm; Sun only for services, 7:45am and 10:45am. MARTA: King Memorial Station, then a long, 8-block walk; or Five Points, then bus 3.

Fernbank Museum of Natural History This is the largest natural science museum in the Southeast, a $43-million complex opened in 1992 that abuts 65 acres of virgin forest near Emory University. One of its permanent exhibitions is "Giants of the Mesozoic," which includes skeletons of the world's largest meat- and plant-eating dinosaurs. In addition to other permanent and rotating exhibits, the museum has an IMAX Theater with a six-story screen. Allow 2 hours. 767 Clifton Rd. NE, off Ponce de Leon Ave. ℰ 404/929-6300. www.fernbank.edu. Admission museum only $12 adults, $11 students and seniors, $10 children 3–12, free under 2. Admission IMAX Theater only $10 adults, $9 students and seniors, $8 children, free under 2. Combined museum and theater admission $22 adults, $19 seniors and students, $16 children. Mon–Sat 10am–5pm; Sun noon–5pm. IMAX Theater last show on Fri begins at 10pm. MARTA: North Ave. station, then bus 2. Ask the driver to drop you at the corner of Clifton Rd. Walk down Clifton; Fernbank Museum is the 1st driveway on the right.

Fox Theatre This Moorish-Egyptian extravaganza began life as a Shriners' temple. It became a movie theater when movie mogul William Fox threw open its doors to the public. Its exotic lobby was decorated with lush carpeting; in the auditorium itself, a skyscape was transformed to sunrise, sunset, or starry night scene as the occasion demanded, and a striped Bedouin canopy overhung the balcony. By the 1970s, the Fox was slated for demolition, but Atlantans raised $1.8 million to save their treasured movie palace. Restored to its former glory, it now thrives as a venue for live entertainment. Allow 1 hour. 660 Peachtree St. NE, at Ponce de Leon Ave. ℰ 404/688-3353. www.foxtheatre.org. Tours $10 adults, $5 students and seniors. The Atlanta Preservation Center conducts walking tours of the Fox Theatre and surrounding area Mon, Wed, Thurs 10am; Sat 10 and 11am. Meet in theater arcade to buy tickets and begin tour. MARTA: North Ave., then walk 2 blocks east.

High Museum of Art This dazzling white porcelain-tiled building has an equally pristine white interior that houses four floors of galleries featuring more than 10,000 pieces. Among them is a significant group of 19th- and 20th-century American paintings that feature work of the Hudson River School. There's also an extensive sub-Saharan African art collection and the Virginia Carroll Crawford Collection of American Decorative Arts, covering changing tastes from 1825 to 1917. Allow 2 hours. 1280 Peachtree St. NE, at 16th St., part of the Woodruff Arts Center. ℰ 404/733-HIGH. www.high.org. Admission $8 adults, $6 seniors and students, $4 children 6–17, free for children under 6. Tues–Sat 10am–5pm; Sun noon–5pm. MARTA: Arts Center.

Jimmy Carter Library and Museum Set on 35 acres of gardens, lakes, and waterfalls 2 miles east of the center of downtown Atlanta, the library-museum is part of the Carter Presidential Center. The library-museum houses millions of documents, photographs, and videotapes from Jimmy Carter's White House years. You'll see an exact replica of the Oval Office during Carter's presidency, enhanced by a recording of Carter speaking about his experiences in that office. Nearby, in buildings open by appointment, a variety of scholars and public-policy experts, many of them shared with nearby Emory University, work on worldwide issues ranging from free elections to disease eradication. Allow 1 to 2 hours. 441 Freedom Pkwy. ℂ 404/331-3942. www.jimmycarterlibrary.org. Admission $5 adults, $4 seniors, free for children 16 and under. Mon–Sat 9am–4:45pm; Sun noon–4:45pm. MARTA: Five Points station, then bus 16 Noble.

Margaret Mitchell House and Museum (birthplace of *Gone With the Wind*) Restoration has saved the Tudor Revival apartment house where Margaret Mitchell, who called the place "The Dump," wrote most of her epic novel and lived from 1925 to 1932. Tours, which last about an hour, feature a 17-minute film, a visit to the apartment, and an exhibit that celebrates Mitchell's life and examines the impact of her book and the subsequent movie. Allow 1 to 2 hours. 999 Peachtree St. at 10th St. ℂ 404/249-7012. www.gwtw.org. Admission $12 adults, $9 seniors and students, $5 children 6–17, free for children under 6. Daily 9:30am–5pm. MARTA: Midtown station.

Martin Luther King, Jr., Center for Nonviolent Social Change The Nobel Prize winner's commitment to nonviolent social change lives on at this memorial and educational center. The self-guided tour includes the Freedom Hall complex, and several related sites nearby: Ebenezer Baptist Church, the King Birth Home, and the National Park Service Visitor's Center. The Freedom Hall portion includes memorabilia of King and the civil rights movement, including his Bible and clerical robe, a hand-written sermon, a photographic essay on his life and work, and, on a grim note, the suit he was wearing when a deranged woman stabbed him in New York City, as well as the key to his room at the Lorraine Motel in Memphis, Tennessee, where he was assassinated. In an alcove off the main exhibit area is a video display on King's life and work. There are other exhibits honoring Rosa Parks and Mahatma Gandhi. Outside in Freedom Plaza, Dr. King's white marble crypt rests surrounded by a five-tiered reflecting pool. An eternal flame burns in a small circular pavilion directly in front of the crypt. Allow 2 to 3 hours for all. 449 Auburn Ave. between Boulevard and Jackson St. ℂ 404/524-1956. www.thekingcenter.com. Free admission. Daily 9am–5pm. MARTA: Five Points, then bus 3; or King Memorial, then walk several blocks.

Michael C. Carlos Museum of Emory University Four human mummies and a wealth of funerary art from ancient Egypt, beautiful objects from the ancient Mediterranean, stunning art from Africa, and pre-Columbian art are among this museum's rich collections. There are also special shows mounted from the museum's vast holdings, including exquisite drawings—some from the 1600s. There's nothing in Georgia to equal this collection. The 1916 beaux arts building housing the museum is a National Historic Landmark. Allow 1 to 2 hours. 571 S. Kilgo St., near the intersection of Oxford and N. Decatur roads on the main quadrangle of campus. ℂ 404/727/4282. http://carlos.emory.edu. Admission $5. Tues, Wed, Fri, and Sat 10am–5pm; Thurs 10am–9pm; Sun noon–5pm. MARTA: Candler Park or Lindbergh station, then bus 6 Emory; or Avondale or Arts Center station, then bus 36 N. Decatur.

Oakland Cemetery Margaret Mitchell, author of *Gone With the Wind*, is buried here; perhaps she's swapping stories after dark with the 50,000 Union and Confederate soldiers who also share this 88-acre site. The cemetery opened 10 years before the Civil War and has become an outdoor museum of funerary architecture, including classic and Gothic Revival mausoleums. Many other notable Georgians are buried here, including golfing legend Bobby Jones. The cemetery, covered with a canopy of old oaks, is actually a beautiful city park. People often bring a picnic lunch and eat ham sandwiches among the dead.

Allow 1 to 2 hours. 248 Oakland Ave. SE; main entrance at Oakland Ave. and Martin Luther King, Jr., Dr. 🕐 404/688-2107. http://oaklandcemetery.com. Free admission, self-guided tour maps $1. Open daily dawn–dusk. Visitor center Mon–Sat 9am–5pm, Sun 1–5pm. Guided tours Mar–Nov weekends only, Sat 10am and 2pm, Sun 2pm: $5 adults, $3 children and seniors. MARTA: King Memorial station.

Stone Mountain Park   The world's largest granite outcropping, carved with a massive monument to the Confederacy, Stone Mountain is the focal point of a recreation area that covers 3,200 acres of lakes and beautiful wooded parkland. Over half a century in the making, Stone Mountain's neoclassic carving (90 ft. high and 190 ft. wide) depicts Confederate leaders Jefferson Davis, Robert E. Lee, and Stonewall Jackson galloping on horseback. Although the best view of the mountain is from below, the vistas from the top are spectacular. Visitors who are part mountain goat can take a walking trail up and down its moss-covered slopes, especially lovely in spring when they're blanketed in wildflowers. From the top, which you can also reach by cable car, you have an incredible view of Atlanta and the Appalachian Mountains. Other major park attractions include **Crossroads,** a re-creation of an 1870s Southern village plus a 3-D theater; the **Great Barn,** which offers four stories of children's activities such as rope nets to climb and the chance to play a character in a computer game; the **Stone Mountain Scenic Railroad,** which chugs around the 5-mile base of Stone Mountain and features a staged train robbery; the *Scarlett O'Hara,* a paddle-wheel riverboat that cruises the 363-acre Stone Mountain lake; the **Antique Car and Treasure Museum;** the **Antebellum Plantation and Farmyard;** a 36-hole golf course; miniature golf; 16 tennis courts built for the 1996 Summer Olympics; and a sandy lakefront beach with water slides, carillon concerts, boating, bicycle rental, fishing, hiking, picnicking, and more. Allow at least 4 hours. 6867 Memorial Dr., Stone Mountain, 16 miles east of downtown on U.S. 78. 🕐 800/317-2006 or 404/498-5690. www.stonemountainpark.com/newsite. $19 adults, $15 children 3–11, free for children under 3. Daily parking pass $7. Year-round, gates open 6am–midnight. Major attractions open 10am–5pm fall and winter; 10am–8pm spring and summer. MARTA: train to Avondale station, then bus 120 to Stone Mountain.

The World of Coca-Cola   A three-floor pavilion exhibits memorabilia of what's been called "the world's most popular product," including endorsements by fabled stars of yesterday, ranging from Clark Gable to the Supremes. The pavilion boasts what has to be one of the most innovative outdoor neon signs ever created: an 11-ton extravaganza hanging 18 feet above its entrance. In all, there are more than 1,000 exhibits, including a 1930s soda fountain, complete with a soda jerk. Allow 1 to 2 hours. 55 Martin Luther King, Jr., Dr. SW, at Central Ave., across from Underground Atlanta. 🕐 404/676-5151. www.woccatlanta.com. Admission $6 adults, $4 seniors, $3 children ages 6–11, free for children under 6. Mon–Sat 9am–5pm; Sun noon–6pm. June–Aug, stays open every day until 6pm; opens 1 hr. earlier Sun. MARTA: Five Points station.

GREAT SHOPPING AREAS

BUCKHEAD   The stomping ground of well-to-do Atlanta, Buckhead is the ultimate shopping area, with two major malls and lots of little boutiques, antiques shops, and galleries. Start at the corner of Peachtree and Lenox roads, where two major malls—**Phipps Plaza** (www.phippsplaza.com) and **Lenox Square** (www.lenox-square.com)—face off against each other. If you have more time and are interested in art, antiques, or decorative accessories, head straight to **Bennett Street** (**www.buckhead.org/bennettstreet**), where you'll find a healthy concentration of stores in a 2-block strip. There are also many shops in the **Buckhead West Village** (**www.buckhead.org/westvillage**), near the intersection of Peachtree and West Paces Ferry roads, but there are many more establishments up and down Peachtree and scattered along smaller side streets.

VIRGINIA-HIGHLAND   This charming area of town, centered on North Highland Avenue between University Drive and Ponce de Leon Avenue, boasts antiques shops, junk stores, trendy boutiques, and art galleries. There are three major concentrations: on North Highland just south of University Drive; at the intersection of North Highland and Virginia avenues; and just north of Ponce de Leon around St. Charles Place. From one end to the other, it's about a mile and a half, but it's a nice walk and there are cafes where you can stop and take a break. For more info, check out **www.virginiahighland.com**.

LITTLE FIVE POINTS   An area similar to Virginia-Highland, but a lot funkier and much rougher around the edges, Little Five Points (**www.l5p.com**) is as much a happening as an offbeat shopping area. There are still authentic hippies here and enough young people with wildly colored hair and pierced body parts to give you a '60s flashback. *Warning:* Though the area isn't especially known for racial tension, some locals have said they've noticed an increase in white supremacists in the area, and in spring 2002, two black visitors were badly beaten here by three white panhandlers. Also in this area, but not nearly as funky, is **Underground Atlanta,** on Alabama Street between Peachtree Street and Central Avenue (© **404/523-2311;** www.underatl.com). This 12-acre mix of shops, nightclubs, and restaurants is not as vibrant as it was a few years ago, but it still can be fun to browse. In addition to shops, there are vendors in Humbug Square selling merchandise off antique pushcarts. Of course, there's a food court and several good restaurants.

STONE MOUNTAIN   Stone Mountain Village (© **770/879-4971;** http://stonemountainvillage.com), just outside the West Gate of Stone Mountain Park, bounded by Second and Main streets to the north and south, and by Lucille Street and Memorial Drive to the east and west, is worth a visit. It has been developing since the 1800s, and many of the shops are housed in historic buildings. Merchants keep it to a high standard, and their wares are tasteful and of good quality. Many of the stores specialize in antiques, crafts, and collectibles. It's great fun to wander about this quaint village, and there's usually some festive event going on—perhaps an arts-and-crafts fair or live entertainment. During Christmas, the streets are candlelit and the village becomes a magical place populated by St. Nick, elves, carolers, and horse-drawn carriages.

WHERE TO STAY

Many of the hotels are quite full during the business week, but they're usually not sold out on the weekend. Most of the major hotels that cater to business travelers, especially those downtown, offer reduced weekend rates.

Bed & Breakfast Atlanta, 1001 St. Charles Ave., Atlanta, GA 30306 (© **800/967-3224** or 404/875-0525; www.bedandbreakfastatlanta.com), can book you into more than 80 carefully screened homes and inns.

Ansley Inn   This former stately home in the prestigious Ansley Park neighborhood mimics many of the trappings of an exclusive, small-scale European inn. In 1995, nine rooms were added to the back of the house in distinguished style. Those in the front of the house retain a semi-antique flair. Breakfast is served in a formal dining room. 253 15th St. NE (at Lafayette Dr., between Piedmont Ave. and Peachtree St.), Atlanta, GA 30309. ℂ 800/446-5416 or 404/872-9000. Fax 404/892-2318. www.ansleyinn.com. 22 units. $129–$189 double main house; $109–$149 double corporate wing. Extra person $50, although no extra charge for small children. Rates include full Southern breakfast. AE, DC, DISC, MC, V. Free parking. MARTA: Arts Center.

Beverly Hills Inn   Cozy and a bit eccentric, this English-style B&B is about 2 blocks from most of Buckhead's restaurants and shops. You'll find lots of English Victoriana, a small back garden with a fountain and sitting area, potted plants, and a vaguely bohemian atmosphere. Each unit has its own kitchen. 65 Sheridan Dr. NE (off Peachtree Rd.), Atlanta, GA 30305. ℂ 800/331-8520 or 404/233-8520. Fax 404/233-8659. www.beverlyhillsinn.com. 18 units. $110 double 1-bedroom suite; $130–$160 2-bedroom suite. Children stay free in parents' room. Rates include continental breakfast. AE, DC, DISC, MC, V. Free parking. MARTA: Lindbergh.

Four Seasons Hotel   Occupying 19 floors of a granite-sheathed tower that soars above midtown Atlanta, the Four Seasons has the most attentive and sophisticated staff and the most impressive and dramatic lobby of any hotel in Georgia. Accommodations are as plush as you'd expect from this top-notch chain, each with ultra-comfortable chaise longues, deep mattresses, and bathrobes. 75 14th St. (between Peachtree and W. Peachtree sts.), Atlanta, GA 30309. ℂ 800/332-3442 or 404/881/9898. Fax 404/873-4692. www.fourseasons.com/atlanta. 244 units. $260–$360 double; from $550 suites. Children stay free in parents' room. Weekend packages and other special offers often available. AE, DC, DISC, MC, V. Valet parking $24. MARTA: Arts Center. **Amenities:** Restaurant; pool (indoor); health club; pets accepted.

Gaslight Inn   This 1913 Craftsman-style house, whose decor has attracted international acclaim, is one of the most appealing B&Bs in Virginia-Highland. Accommodations, especially the suites, are exquisitely and individually decorated; some have four-poster beds, while others have whirlpool baths. Three of the seven units have full kitchens; the remainder have microwaves and refrigerators. A bountiful breakfast is served in the formal dining room or outside on the front porch. 1001 St. Charles Ave (between Frederica St. and N. Highland Ave.), Atlanta, GA 30306. ℂ 404/875-1001. Fax 404/876-1001. www.gaslightinn.com. 7 units. $95–$195 double. Children 5 and under stay free in parents' room; some suites reserved for families. Rates include breakfast. AE, DC, DISC, MC, V. Free parking. MARTA: North Ave. station, then bus 2 Ponce to Frederica St.

Ritz-Carlton Atlanta   Downtown Atlanta's finest hotel is a bastion of luxury whose public rooms are filled with antiques and fine art. The rooms are restful refuges decorated in traditional style, with bay windows, CD players, bathrobes, and fresh flowers. Bathrooms are as large and luxurious as you'd expect. And the service is impeccable—you'll be cosseted as never before. 181 Peachtree St. NE (at Ellis St.), Atlanta, GA 30303. ℂ 800/241-3333 or 404/659-1400. Fax 404/221-6578. www.ritzcarlton.com/hotels/atlanta_downtown. 444 units. $275–$325; $295–$375 club level; $450 and way up suites. Rates cover up to 4 people in room. Weekend packages available. AE, DC, DISC, MC, V. Valet parking $21. MARTA: Peachtree Center. **Amenities:** Restaurant; health club.

Ritz-Carlton Buckhead   A 22-story tower soaring above Buckhead, the elegant Ritz-Carlton has been likened to Claridges in London. The staff is polite, soft-spoken, and efficient. Located between Lenox Square and Phipps Plaza, it's a convenient way station for "shop-'til-you-drop" guests, with a lavish afternoon tea to revive their flagging energy. The recently upgraded guest rooms are large, yet manage to feel cozy; amenities include bay windows, bathrobes, CD players in some rooms, and large bathrooms. 3434 Peachtree Rd. NE (at Lenox Rd.), Atlanta, GA 30326. ⓒ 800/241-3333 or 404/237-2700. Fax 404/233-5168. www.ritzcarlton.com/hotels/ atlanta_buckhead. 553 units. $255–$335; $345–$435 club level; $425 and way up suites. Rates cover up to 4 people in room. Weekend packages available. AE, DC, DISC, MC, V. Self-parking $12, valet parking $22. MARTA: Buckhead or Lenox stations, then a short walk. **Amenities:** Restaurants (2); indoor pool; health club.

Shellmont Bed and Breakfast Lodge   The Shellmont is a stylish two-story Victorian mansion that's on the National Register of Historic Places. Elaborate restoration has filled it with discreetly concealed modern amenities as well as historically appropriate furnishings. All rooms have leaded-glass or bay windows and VCRs; the master suite has a full kitchen. Stand in the back garden, where there are verandas and three fishponds, and you'll swear you're in a small town in the Georgia countryside. 821 Piedmont Ave. NE (at 6th St.), Atlanta, GA 30308. ⓒ 404/ 872-9290. Fax 404/872-5379. www.shellmont.com. 5 units. $115–$175 double; $150–$250 suite. $25 charge per child in parents' room. Rates include full breakfast. AE, DC, DISC, MC, V. Free parking. MARTA: North Ave. or Midtown.

Swissôtel Atlanta   The Swissôtel is first class all the way and has a pronounced Euro-modern flavor that makes it popular with trendsetters. Public rooms are filled with contemporary artwork—the hotel has the second-largest private collection in the Southeast. The sleek guest rooms and suites are the largest in Buckhead, with Biedermeier-style furnishings. The King corner rooms are an especially good choice. Bathrooms in all rooms are luxurious and are stocked with bathrobes. The location is a good choice for those who plan to shop at Lenox Square and Phipps Plaza, both nearby. 3391 Peachtree Rd. NE (between Lenox and Piedmont roads), Atlanta, GA 30326. ⓒ 800/253-1397 or 404/365-0065. Fax 404/ 365-8787. www.swissotel.com. 365 units. $160–$320 double; $240–$370 club level; $285–$630 suite. Children 12 and under stay free in parents' room. AE, DC, DISC, MC, V. Self-parking $13, valet parking $18. MARTA: Buckhead or Lenox, then a short walk. Almost directly across from the Ritz-Carlton Buckhead. **Amenities:** Restaurant; indoor pool; spa; health club.

Westin Peachtree Plaza   Atlanta's most famous contemporary hotel is also the tallest, with 73 soaring floors. A bank of 18 elevators will carry you to the roof with its revolving restaurant, a grand spectacle for a special evening on the town. The hotel recently completed a $30-million renovation and is in tiptop shape. The elegant guest rooms are comfortably large, with all the expected luxuries and roomy marble bathrooms. Ask for a room on a higher floor for a more panoramic view. 210 Peachtree St. NW (at International Blvd.), Atlanta, GA 30303. ⓒ 800/ 228-3000 or 404/659-1400. Fax 404/589-7591. www.westin.com. 1,116 units. $169–$259 double; from $325 suite. Children 17 and under stay free in parents' room. AE, DISC, MC, V. No self-parking, valet parking $20. **Amenities:** Restaurants (2); indoor pool; fitness center.

WHERE TO DINE

Atlanta Fish Market   SEAFOOD   This place serves up a great mix of whimsy (there's a three-story copper fish outside the entrance) and really good food. The main dining area has been compared to an old Southern train station; the new Geechee Crab Lounge manages to be both upscale and comfortable. Some locals may be taken aback by the swordfish over creamy grits, but they're quickly won over. The Carolina mountain trout is the best, and crab cakes or deviled crab are highly recommended. The extensive menu changes daily.

265 Pharr Rd., between Peachtree Rd. and Piedmont Rd. © 404/262-3165. www.buckhead restaurants.com. Reservations recommended. Main courses $15–$20 lunch, $25–$35 dinner. AE, DC, DISC, MC, V. Mon–Fri 11am–3pm; Mon–Thurs 5–11pm; Fri 5pm–midnight; Sat 11:30am–midnight; Sun 4–10pm. MARTA: Buckhead.

Bacchanalia INTERNATIONAL   Posh and upscale, this establishment combines a stylish and sought-after restaurant with a boutique-style gourmet food shop. The setting is in a former 1920s meatpacking plant, on an unlikely-looking drab commercial stretch at the edge of midtown. At dinnertime, go for the butter-poached lobster. Unusual fruit-and-cheese pairings are hard to resist. Wines are offered by the half-bottle. 1198 Howell Mill Rd. © 404/365-0410. Reservations recommended. 3-course lunch $35; 4-course fixed-price dinner $58. AE, DISC, MC, V. Tues–Sat 11:30am–1:30pm and 6–10pm. MARTA: 10th St.

Bone's STEAK/SEAFOOD   In an atmosphere one food critic called "boardroom frat house," this is just the type of place to get that juicy rib-eye steak weighing in at 16 ounces. Fresh Maine lobster is flown in daily, and the corn-fed beef is cut into steaks on the premises. Locals favor cheese grits fritters. A cigar humidor can be brought to your table at your request after dinner, but one female CEO from New York found the service by the waiters "sexist." Piedmont Rd. NE, a half block past Peachtree Rd. © 404/237-2663. Reservations required. Main courses $10–$35 lunch, $19–$35 dinner, all extras a la carte. AE, DISC, MC, V. Mon–Fri 11:30am–2:30pm and 6–11pm; Sat 6–11pm; Sun 6–11pm. MARTA: Buckhead.

Buckhead Diner AMERICAN   Even though the place sounds like a hash house for truckers, it's one of the hottest spots in Atlanta, especially after a recent renovation. A highly theatrical venture, it has a gleaming stainless-steel exterior adorned with neon. Inside, the fare is roadhouse basic with a twist: braised lamb shank with yellow tomato baked beans, for example, or lemon icebox cake with lemon sorbet. A local favorite is homemade potato chips with blue cheese dressing. 3073 Piedmont Rd. at East Paces Ferry Rd. © 404/262-3336. www.buckheadrestaurants. com. Reservations not accepted, but you can call just before you go for "priority seating." Main courses $8–$18 lunch, $16–$20 dinner. AE, DC, DISC, MC, V. Mon–Sat 11am–midnight; Sun 10am–10pm. MARTA: Buckhead.

City Grill AMERICAN   One of Atlanta's most opulent restaurants, City Grill is a mecca for power-lunchers and couples seeking a special night out. The setting is the 1912 Hurt Building, with its rotunda lined in marble with a gold-leaf dome. The frequently changing menu incorporates many Southern standards such as shrimp and grits, or barbecued pork. A South Georgia dairy farm provides the choices for the nighttime cheese plates. The selection of French and California wines is about as good as Atlanta gets. 50 Hurt Plaza (at Edgewood Ave.) © 404/524-2489. www.greathospitalityrestaurants.com. Reservations recommended. Main courses $9–$19 lunch; fixed-price menu begins at $45 at dinner, rises according to number of courses. AE, DC, DISC, MC, V. Mon–Fri 11:30am–2pm and 6–10pm; Sat 6–10pm. MARTA: Peachtree Center.

The Colonnade SOUTHERN   An Atlanta favorite since 1927, this friendly joint offers great value, stiff drinks, and an authentic Southern-style meat-and-three. Inexpensively priced steaks, chops, seafood, and the inevitable Southern fried chicken round out the menu. Don't miss the yeast rolls. 1879 Cheshire Bridge Rd. NE, between Wellborne Dr. and Manchester St. © 404/874-5642. Reservations not accepted. Main courses $8–$15 lunch, slightly higher at dinner. No credit cards, but out-of-town personal checks accepted. Sun–Thurs 11am–9pm; Fri–Sat 11am–10pm.

Floataway Café COUNTRY FRENCH/ITALIAN   Mediterranean-inspired and innovative, this restaurant's menu features top-quality ingredients. Hand-cut pastas are wonderful; locals also rave about the steak with pommes frites, and a salad of beets and avocados topped with a citrus dressing. It's too far from Emory to walk and you really can't get here using MARTA; if the cab driver pulls up to an old warehouse, don't worry—you're in the right place. Get out and follow the crowd. If the inside is too noisy, move to one of the outdoor tables. 1123 Zonolite Rd. NE, between Briarcliff and Lenox roads, near Emory University. (𝒞 404/892-1414. Reservations recommended. Main courses $15–$24. AE, MC, V. Tues–Sat 5–10pm.

Horseradish Grill SOUTHERN   This restaurant began life as a country store, then a horse barn, and it retains much of that simple style. Organic vegetables and wildflowers are grown in a backyard garden, where guests are encouraged to pick and eat the strawberries growing against the back fence, and everything is made from scratch, including the ice cream. The menu is upscale Southern, simply prepared. Start with the North Carolina barbecue or fried chicken, and end with the Kentucky oatmeal cake topped with caramel ice cream. 4320 Powers Ferry Rd. at W. Wieuca Rd. (𝒞 404/255-7277. www.horseradishgrill. com. Reservations recommended. Main courses $6–$10 lunch; $15–$27 dinner. AE, DC, DISC, MC, V. Mon–Fri 11:30am–2:30pm; Mon–Thurs 5:30–9pm; Fri–Sat 5–11pm; Sun 5–9pm. MARTA: Buckhead.

Sotto Sotto TUSCAN   The best and most appealing restaurant in Inman Park occupies a former row of brick-fronted stores built around 1900. We recommend the excellent wood-roasted whole fish or the seafood risotto. A favorite pasta is *tortelli di Michelangelo*, stuffed with minced veal, pork, and chicken, served with brown butter and sage sauce. If the wait is too long (and it can be 45 min., even with a reservation), get a Neapolitan pizza at next-door sister restaurant Fritti Fritti. *Note:* The restaurant's name may mean "Hush Hush" in Italian, but the noise level here can climb to unbearable levels. If you're looking for an intimate, romantic meal, head elsewhere. 313 N. Highland Ave. (𝒞 404/523-6678. Reservations recommended. Main courses $12–$23. AE, DC, MC, V. Mon–Thurs 5:30–11pm; Fri–Sat 5:30pm–midnight.

The Varsity AMERICAN   Some 16,000 people dine daily at this Atlanta institution; 30,000 if there's a home football game at nearby Georgia Tech. This is the world's largest drive-in, opened in 1928. Service is fast both carside and inside, with seats and stand-up eating counters; prices are definitely low. Yes, the orange freezes are just like the ones you had after the senior prom. Ordering can be an adventure; counter workers drop all pretense of a slow-as-a-molasses drawl and greet you with a rapid-fire, "Whaddya have? Whaddya have?" Hot dogs are called "dawgs," and hamburgers are "steaks." If you order them plain, just say "nekkid dawg" or "nekkid steak," and so on. The french fries are fresh; if you can, leave room for the fried peach pie. *Tip:* If you want a cheeseburger, be sure to ask for pimento cheese. True, it's a mess, but you've never had anything like it.

For visitors staying closer to Buckhead or Virginia-Highland, there's a **Varsity Jr.** at 185 Lindbergh Dr., (𝒞 404-261-8843. 61 North Ave. at Spring St. (𝒞 404/881-1706. www.thevarsity.com. Under $5. No credit cards. Sun–Thurs 9am–11:30pm; Fri–Sat 9am–12:30am. MARTA: North Ave.

ATLANTA AFTER DARK

The biggest concentration of clubs and bars is in **Buckhead** (near the intersection of Peachtree and East Paces Ferry roads); in **Virginia-Highland** (at the intersection of Virginia and N. Highland aves., on **North Highland** just north of Ponce de Leon Ave.); In **Little Five Points** (near the intersection of Moreland and Euclid aves.); and downtown near Peachtree Center. The Buckhead scene, for the most part, is like a huge frat party, especially on weekends. (*Warning:* Serious crime, including hit-and-run fatalities and high-profile murders, has risen here in recent years as the club scene grows.) Virginia-Highland is full of professional 20- and 30-somethings. Little Five Points is an eclectic mix of wildly, weirdly dressed folks and neighborhood regulars. Downtown has a large proportion of out-of-town visitors and convention-goers.

To find out what's going on, consult the *Atlanta Journal-Constitution*'s Friday "Preview" section or Saturday "Leisure" section. Or pick up a free copy of *Creative Loafing,* available all over town.

THE PERFORMING ARTS   See "What to See & Do," earlier in this section, for details on the Fox Theatre, which hosts all kinds of performances.

The oldest continuously operating ballet company in the United States, the **Atlanta Ballet,** performs in the Fox Theatre (© **404/892-3303;** www.atlanta ballet.com).

The Atlanta Symphony Orchestra, Woodruff Arts, 1280 Peachtree St. NE, at 15th Street (© **404/733-4800;** www.atlantasymphony.org), is complemented by the 200-voice Atlanta Symphony Orchestra Chorus, enabling performances of large-scale symphonic/choral works. The season runs from September to May, plus summer concerts in Chastain Park Amphitheatre in Buckhead.

The Alliance Theatre Company, Woodruff Arts (© **404/733-5000;** www.alliancetheatre.org), is the largest regional theater in the Southeast, but there are many other excellent companies, with performances ranging from experimental to classic. Watch each summer for performances by the **Georgia Shakespeare Festival** (© **404/264-020;** www.gashakespeare.org).

THE CLUB & MUSIC SCENE   Atlanta's club scene is ephemeral; there's a good chance that the packed venue you visited on your last visit has since closed and reopened as something entirely different. Still, there are a few old reliables.

In Buckhead, **Johnny's Hideaway,** 3771 Roswell Rd. (2 blocks north of Piedmont Rd.; © **404/233-8026**), has been one of Atlanta's top nightspots for more than 2 decades. The music sweeps through the decades, from the big-band era to the '80s, attracting a crowd of all ages. Original owner Johnny Esposito, who retired for health reasons in 1999 and then un-retired due to boredom, opened a new club in June 2002 near his original. His new one, **Johnny's Side Door,** is part of the Landmark Diner, 3652 Roswell Rd. in Buckhead (© **404/844-0408**). An elegant cocktail lounge/dance club, **Tongue & Groove,** 3055 Peachtree Rd. (© **404/261-2325;** www.tongueandgrooveonline.com), attracts a chic crowd (there's a dress code). The DJ spins dance music with a different theme every night.

On the east side, closer to Emory, **Eddie's Attic,** 515-B N. McDonough St., Decatur (© **404/377-4976;** www.eddiesattic.com), is Atlanta's most popular venue for acoustic singer/songwriters. The Indigo Girls, Billy Pilgrim, and Shawn Mullins started their careers here.

In Virginia-Highland, the **Dark Horse Tavern,** 816 N. Highland Ave. (© **404/873-3607;** www.darkhorseatlanta.com), is known as the place for young professionals to meet. Those more interested in local bands than romance can visit 10 High in the Dark Horse basement.

East Atlanta Village, a newer, rougher version of Little Five Points but farther east at the intersection of Flat Shoals and Glenwood avenues, is home to several clubs featuring independent and underground acts: **The Earl,** 488 Flat Shoals Ave. SE (© **404/522-3950;** www.badearl.com); **Echo Lounge,** 551 Flat Shoals Ave. SE (© **404/681-3600;** http://echostatic.com); and the **Fountainhead Lounge,** 485 Flat Shoals Ave. (© **404/522-7841**), are among the better known.

Since so many nightclubs offering varying entertainment formats are grouped conveniently at **Underground Atlanta,** Kenny's Alley club-hopping is also popular.

THE BAR & CAFE SCENE   Downtown, **Champions,** at the Marriott Marquis, 265 Peachtree Center Ave. (© **404/586-6017;** MARTA: Peachtree Center), is the quintessential sports bar. **Mumbo Jumbo,** 89 Park Place NE, at Woodruff Park (© **404/523-0330;** www.mumbojumbo-atl.com; MARTA: Peachtree Center), is the place to see and be seen.

Fado', 3035 Peachtree Rd. NE, at the corner of Buckhead Avenue, just south of East Paces Ferry Road (© **404/841-0066;** www.fadoirishpub.com), is divided into five pub areas: a cottage pub with a peat-burning fireplace, a Victorian pub with dark wood and stained glass, and so on. There's often traditional Irish or Celtic music. It's a good place to watch televised soccer.

Not far from Virginia-Highland and Little Five Points is **Manuel's Tavern,** 602 N. Highland Ave. NE, at North Avenue (© **404/525-3447;** www.manuels tavern.com), a regular watering hole for journalists, politicos, cops, students, and writers. Jimmy Carter often drops by with the Secret Service when he's in town. It's lots of fun to watch a Braves game on TV here.

Gay visitors might head for the **Otherside,** 1924 Piedmont Rd. (© **404/875-5238**), a relaxed, slightly unhinged place to hang out and dance.

A classic San Francisco–style coffeehouse, the **Red Light Café,** 553 W. Amsterdam Ave., between Monroe Drive and Piedmont Park (© **404/874-7828;** www.redlightcafe.com), is a cybercafe with tables and comfy sofas, offering a mix of art, music, conversation, and beverages.

2 Savannah

Savannah's free spirit and hint of decadence gives it more kinship with Key West or New Orleans than with the Bible Belt down-home interior of Georgia. Savannah—pronounce it with a drawl—conjures up all the clichéd images of the Deep South: live oaks dripping with Spanish moss, stately antebellum mansions, and mint juleps sipped on the veranda. Old Savannah is beautifully restored, and is the largest urban National Historic Landmark District in the country. *Forrest Gump* first put Savannah on the tourist map, but nothing has changed the face of Savannah more than the 1994 publication of John Berendt's *Midnight in the Garden of Good and Evil.*

ESSENTIALS

GETTING THERE   By Plane   Savannah International Airport (www. savannahairport.com) is about 8 miles west of downtown just off I-16. It's served by American, Delta, United, and US Airways, and all major car-rental agencies have desks here. Limousine service to downtown locations (© **912/966-5364**) costs $16. The taxi fare should be about $22 for one person and $11 for each extra passenger.

Savannah

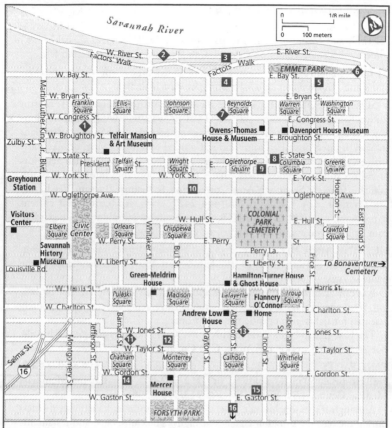

ACCOMMODATIONS ■

Ballastone Inn **10**

Bed and Breakfast Inn **14**

Courtyard by Marriott **16**

Fairfield Inn by Marriott **16**

Eliza Thompson House **12**

The Gastonian **15**

Hampton Inn **4**

The Kehoe House **8**

The Mulberry/Holiday Inn **5**

The Presidents' Quarters **9**

River Street Inn **3**

DINING ◆

Clary's Café **13**

45 South **6**

Huey's **2**

Lady and Sons **1**

Mrs. Wilkes' Boarding House **11**

The Olde Pink House Restaurant **7**

By Train Amtrak (© 800/USA-RAIL; www.amtrak.com) provides service from Charleston (trip time: 1¾ hr.), Washington, D.C. (11½ hr.), Jacksonville (2½ hr.), and Miami (11½ hr.) to its station at 2611 Seaboard Coastline Dr., some 4 miles southwest of downtown. Cab fare into the city is around $4.

By Car Major routes into Savannah are I-95 from the north (Richmond, VA) and south (Jacksonville), and I-16 from the west (Atlanta).

VISITOR INFORMATION The **Savannah Visitor Center,** 301 Martin Luther King Jr. Blvd., Savannah, GA 31401 (© 912/944-0455), is open Monday through Friday from 8:30am to 5pm and Saturday and Sunday from 9am to 5pm. It offers organized tours and self-guided walking, driving, or bike tours with excellent maps. (You'll also find a replica of Forrest Gump's bench here; lots of visitors still bring a box of chocolates for this photo op.) Information is also available from the **Savannah Area Convention & Visitors Bureau,** 101 E. Bay St., Savannah, GA 31402 (© 800/444-2427; www.savcvb.com). For current happenings, call © 912/233-ARTS. The website, www.midnightinthegarden. com, will tell you everything you want to know about The Book.

GETTING AROUND The grid-shaped Historic District is best seen on foot; the real point of your visit is to take leisurely strolls with frequent stops in the many squares.

You can reach many points of interest outside the Historic District by bus, but your own wheels will be much more convenient, and they're absolutely essential for sightseeing outside the city proper.

The base rate for taxis is 60¢, with a $1.20 additional charge for each mile. For 24-hour taxi service, call **Adam Cab Co.** at © 912/927-7466.

FAST FACTS There are 24-hour emergency-room services at **Candler General Hospital,** 5353 Reynolds St. (© 912/692-6637), and at the **Memorial Medical Center,** 4700 Waters Ave. (© 912/350-8390).

Although it's reasonably safe to explore the Historic and Victorian districts during the day, the situation changes at night. The clubs, bars, and restaurants along the riverfront have very little crime.

SPECIAL EVENTS & FESTIVALS In mid-September, there's the **Savannah Jazz Festival,** featuring national and local jazz and blues legends. Contact Host South at © 912/232-2222 for details. Late October brings the **Tom Turpin Ragtime Festival** (© 912/233-9989). December is especially festive, with the **Festival of Trees** at the Marriott Riverfront Hotel; **Christmas 1864,** a dramatic re-creation of the Civil War evacuation of Fort Jackson; and the **Annual Holiday Tour of Homes** (© 912/236-8362).

WHAT TO SEE & DO

Virtually every tour group in town offers tours of the *Midnight* sites, many of which are included on their regular agenda.

A delightful way to see Savannah is by horse-drawn carriage. An authentic antique carriage carries you over cobblestone streets as the coachman spins a tale of the town's history. The 1-hour tour ($17 adults, $8 children) covers 15 of the 20 squares. Reservations are required, so contact **Carriage Tours of Savannah** at © 912/236-6756.

Old Town Trolley Tours (© 912/233-0083) operates tours of the Historic District, with pickups at most downtown inns and hotels ($22 adults, $9 children 4–12), as well as a 1-hour **Haunted History** tour detailing Savannah's ghostly past (and present). Call to reserve for all tours.

Savannah Riverboat Cruises are offered aboard the *Savannah River Queen*, operated by the River Street Riverboat Co., 9 E. River St. (© **800/786-6404** or 912/232-6404). The fare for adults is $15; children $8.50. More expensive dinner cruises are available, too.

Andrew Low House   After her marriage, Juliette Low lived in this 1848 house, and it was here that she founded the Girl Scouts. She died on the premises in 1927. The classic mid-19th-century house facing Lafayette Square is of stucco over brick with elaborate ironwork, shuttered piazzas, carved woodwork, and crystal chandeliers. William Makepeace Thackeray visited here twice, and Robert E. Lee was entertained at a gala reception in the double parlors in 1870. Guided tours are offered every half hour. 329 Abercorn St. © **912/233-6854.** Admission $7 adults; $4.50 students, children 6–12, and Girl Scouts; free for children under 6. Mon–Sat 10am–4pm; Sun noon–4pm.

Davenport House Museum   This is where seven determined women started the whole Savannah restoration movement in 1954. They raised $22,500 and purchased the house, saving it from demolition. Constructed between 1815 and 1820 by master builder Isaiah Davenport, this is one of the truly great Federal-style houses in the United States, with delicate ironwork and a handsome elliptical stairway. Give yourself about an hour to explore. 324 E. State St. © **912/236-8097.** Admission $7 adults, $3.50 children 6–18, free for children under 6. Mon–Sat 10am–4pm; Sun 1–4pm.

Fort Jackson   Georgia's oldest standing fort, with a 9-foot-deep tidal moat around its brick walls, was begun in 1808 and manned during the War of 1812. It was enlarged and strengthened between 1845 and 1860 and saw its greatest use as headquarters for the Confederate river defenses during the Civil War. Its arched rooms, designed to support the weight of heavy cannons mounted above, hold 13 exhibit areas. Allow 1 hour. 1 Fort Jackson Rd., about 2½ miles east of Savannah via the Islands Expwy. © **912/232-3945.** Admission $3.50 adults, $2.50 seniors and children 6–18, free for children under 6. Daily 9am–5pm.

Fort McAllister   On the banks of the Great Ogeechee River stood this Confederate earthwork fortification. Constructed from 1861 to 1862, it withstood nearly 2 years of bombardments before it finally fell on December 13, 1864, in a bayonet charge that ended General Sherman's "March to the Sea." There's a visitor center with historic exhibits and also walking trails and campsites. A visit takes 45 minutes. Richmond Hill, 10 miles southwest on U.S. 17. © **912/727-2339.** Admission $2.50 adults, $1.50 children. Daily 8am–5pm.

Fort Pulaski   It cost $1 million and took 25 tons of brick and 18 years of toil to finish this fortress, which stands at the mouth of the Savannah River. Yet it was captured in just 30 hours by Union forces. Completed in 1847 with walls 7½ feet thick, it was taken by Georgia forces at the beginning of the war. However, on April 11, 1862, defense strategy changed worldwide when Union cannons, firing from more than a mile away on Tybee Island, overcame a masonry fortification. The effectiveness of rifled artillery (firing a bullet-shaped projectile with great accuracy at long range) was clearly demonstrated. The new Union weapon marked the end of the era of masonry fortifications. You can still find shells from 1862 imbedded in the walls. Visits average 45 minutes. 15 miles east of Savannah off U.S. 80 on Cockspur and McQueen islands. © **912/786-5787.** Admission $3 adults, under 16 free. Daily 9am–7pm.

Green-Meldrim Home   This impressive house was built on Madison Square for cotton merchant Charleston Green, but its moment in history came as the Savannah headquarters of Gen. William Tecumseh Sherman at the end of his 1864 "March to the Sea." It was from this Gothic-style house that the general sent a telegram to President Lincoln, offering him the city as a Christmas gift. Now the Parish House for St. John's Episcopal Church, the house is open to the public. A good look takes 30 minutes. 14 W. Macon St. ℭ 912/233-3845. Admission $5 adults, $3 children. Tues, Thurs,-Fri 10am–4pm; Sat 10am–1pm.

Owen-Thomas House & Museum   Famed as a place where Lafayette spent the night in 1825, this jewel box of a house evokes the heyday of Savannah's golden age. It was designed in 1816 by English architect William Jay, who instilled in it the grace of Georgian Bath in England and the splendor of Regency London. You can visit the bedchambers, kitchen, drawing and dining rooms, and garden in about 45 minutes. 124 Abercorn St. ℭ 912/233-9743. Admission $8 adults, $4 students, $2 children 6–12, free for children under 6. Mon noon–5pm; Tues–Sat 10am–5pm; Sun 1–5pm.

Savannah History Museum   Housed in the restored train shed of the old Central Georgia Railway station, this museum is a good introduction to the city. In the theater, *The Siege of Savannah* is replayed. In addition to theatrics, there's an exhibition hall displaying memorabilia from every era of Savannah's history. Allow 1 hour. 303 Martin Luther King Jr. Blvd. ℭ 912/238-1779. Admission $4 adults, $3.50 seniors and students. Daily 8:30am–5pm.

Telfair Mansion and Art Museum   The oldest public art museum in the South, housing both American and European paintings, was designed and built in 1818 by William Jay, a young English architect noted for introducing the Regency style to America. A sculpture gallery and rotunda were added in 1883, and Jefferson Davis attended the formal opening in 1886. William Jay's period rooms have been restored, and the Octagon Room and Dining Room are particularly outstanding. Visits last 45 minutes. 1212 Bernard St. ℭ 912/232-1177. www. telfair.org. Admission $8 adults, $2 students, $1 children 6–12, free for children under 6. Mon noon–5pm; Tues–Sat 10am–5pm; Sun 1–5pm.

LITERARY LANDMARKS

Long before John Berendt's *Midnight in the Garden of Good and Evil,* other writers were associated with Savannah.

Chief of them was **Flannery O'Connor** (1924–64), one of the South's greatest writers. Between October and May, an association dedicated to her offers readings, films, and lectures about her and other Southern writers. You can visit the **Flannery O'Connor Childhood Home** at 207 E. Charlton St. (ℭ 912/ 233-6014). From June to August, the house is open Saturday and Sunday from 1 to 4pm. Free admission.

Conrad Aiken (1889–1973), the American poet, critic, writer, and Pulitzer Prize winner, was also born in Savannah. He lived at 228 and later at 230 E. Oglethorpe Ave.

Mercer House, 429 Bull St., used in *Midnight in the Garden of Good and Evil,* is not open to the public. It's been called "the envy of Savannah," and thousands of visitors stop by to photograph it. It was here in May 1981 that wealthy antiques dealer Jim Williams fatally shot his lover/assistant, that blond "walking streak of sex," Danny Hansford, age 21. Mercer House is also where Williams gave his legendary Christmas parties each year. In January 1990, Jim Williams died of a heart attack at 59, in the same room where he'd killed Hansford. (And, no, Johnny Mercer never lived in this house, but it was built by his great-grand-father.)

All fans of The Book must pay a visit to **Bonaventure Cemetery,** filled with obelisks and columns and dense shrubbery and moss-draped trees. Bonaventure is open daily from 8am to 5pm. Take Wheaton Street east from downtown to Bonaventure Road. This cemetery lies on the grounds of what was once a great oak-shaded plantation. It was at the cemetery that John Berendt had martinis in silver goblets with Miss Harty, while they sat on the bench-gravestone of Conrad Aiken. Songwriter Johnny Mercer is buried in plot H-48.

SHOPPING

River Street is a shopper's delight, with some 9 blocks (including Riverfront Plaza) of interesting shops, offering everything from crafts to clothing to souvenirs. The **City Market,** between Ellis and Franklin squares on West St. Julian Street, boasts art galleries, boutiques, and sidewalk cafes along with horse-and-carriage rides. Bookstores, boutiques, and antiques shops are located between Wright Square and Forsyth Park.

J. D. Weed & Co., 102 W. Victory Dr. (② 912/234-8540), is one of our favorite antiques dealers. **Memory Lane,** 220 W. Bay St. (② 912/232-0975), offers more than 8,000 square feet of collectibles.

The leading galleries include **Gallery 209,** 209 E. River St. (② 912/236-4583); **John Tucker Gallery,** 5 W. Charlton St. (② 912/231-8161); **Morning Star Gallery,** 8 E. Liberty St. (② 912/233-4307); and the **Village Craftsmen,** 223 W. River St. (② 912/236-7280).

WHERE TO STAY

Because many of Savannah's historic inns are in former converted residences, price ranges can vary greatly. A very expensive hotel might also have some smaller and more moderately priced units—so it pays to ask.

Affordable chain hotel options include the **Courtyard by Marriott,** 6703 Abercorn St. (② 800/321-2211 or 912/354-7878), and the **Fairfield Inn by Marriott,** 2 Lee Blvd. at Abercorn Road (② 800/228-2800 or 912/353-7100).

Ballastone Inn This glamorous, award-winning B&B occupies a dignified 1838 building separated from the Juliette Gordon Low House by a well-tended formal garden; it's richly decorated with hardwoods, elaborate draperies, and antiques. There's an elevator, unusual for Savannah B&Bs, but no closets (they were taxed as extra rooms in the old days). A full-service bar is tucked into a corner of what was originally a double parlor. The four suites are in a clapboard town house that's a 5-minute walk away and staffed with its own live-in receptionists. A very good breakfast is served, as are afternoon tea and evening hors d'oeuvres. 14 E. Oglethorpe Ave., Savannah, GA 31401. ② 800/822-4553 or 912/236-1484. Fax 912/236-4626. www.ballastone.com. 17 units. $275–$375 double; $475 suite. Rates include full breakfast, afternoon tea, and evening hors d'oeuvres. AE, MC, V. Free parking. No children. **Amenities:** Access to nearby health club.

Bed and Breakfast Inn In the oldest part of historic Savannah, this is a dignified stone-fronted town house built in 1853. You climb a gracefully curved front stoop to reach the cool high-ceilinged interior, outfitted with a combination of antique and reproduction furniture. Some of the good-sized and tastefully furnished accommodations contain refrigerators and kitchenettes. 117 W. Gordon St., Savannah, GA 31401, at Chatham Sq. ② 912/238-0518. Fax 912/233-2537.

www.savannabbnb.com. 15 units. $89–$169 double. Children up to the age of 12 stay in their parents' room for $15. Rates include full breakfast. AE, DISC, MC, V. Free parking.

Eliza Thompson House The rooms of this stately home are equally divided between the original 1847 building and a converted carriage house. Steve and Carol Day have completely redecorated, using original Savannah colors, beautiful antiques, and Oriental carpets. You'll find comfortable cotton robes, fine linens, and well-kept bathrooms, which will be tasteful and elegant. The inn is also graced with one of the most beautiful courtyards in the city. Breakfast is a lavish affair, usually served outdoors. 5 W. Jones St., Savannah, GA 31401. © **800/348-9378** or 912/236-3620. Fax 912/238-1920. www.elizathompsonhouse.com. 25 units. $149–$269 double. Children under 14 stay free in parents' room. Rates include full breakfast. AE, DC, DISC, MC, V. Free parking.

The Gastonian One of the two or three most posh B&Bs in Savannah, the Gastonian incorporates a pair of Italianate Regency buildings constructed in 1868. Today everything is a testimonial to Victorian charm, except for a skillfully crafted serpentine bridge connecting the two buildings and curving above a verdant semitropical garden. Rooms are appropriately plush, comfortable, cozy, and beautifully furnished; all have tidily kept bathrooms, some of which feature whirlpool baths. Afternoon tea is served in a formal drawing room. 220 E. Gaston St., Savannah, GA 31401. © **800/322-6603** or 912/232-2869. Fax 912/232-0710. www.gastonian.com. 17 units. $250–$355 double; $395 suite. Rates include full breakfast. AE, DISC, MC, V. Free parking. No children under 10.

Hampton Inn Opened in 1997, it rises above busy Bay Street, across from Savannah's Riverwalk and some of the city's most hopping nightclubs. Its lobby was designed to mimic an 18th-century Savannah salon, thanks to heart-of-pine flooring and antique Savannah bricks. Rooms are simple and comfortable, with wall-to-wall carpeting and medium-size bathrooms. Some rooms are equipped with microwaves and a mini-fridge. 201 E. Bay St., Savannah, GA. © **800/426-7866** or 912/231-9700. Fax 912/231-0440. www.hotelsavannah.com. 144 units. Sun–Thurs $155 double; Fri–Sat $179 double. Children 18 and under stay free in parents' room. Rates include continental breakfast. AE, DC, MC, V. Parking $8. **Amenities:** Pool.

The Kehoe House This is a spectacularly opulent B&B, with a museum-quality collection of fabrics and furniture, although it might be too flawless and formal for some tastes. Tom Hanks stayed in room 301 during the filming of *Forrest Gump.* Rooms are spacious, with 12-foot ceilings, and each is tastefully furnished in English period antiques. All units have well-kept bathrooms with plush bathrobes. 123 Habersham St., Savannah, GA 31401. © **800/820-1020** or 912/232-1020. Fax 912/231-0208. www.williamkehoehouse.com. 15 units. $190–$230 double. Rates include full breakfast. AE, DC, DISC, MC, V. Free parking. No children under 12.

The Mulberry/Holiday Inn Built in 1868 as a stable and cotton warehouse, this place was transformed with a radical upgrade and a dash of decorator-inspired Chippendale glamour. Today, its lobby looks like that of a grand hotel in London, and its rooms have an English country-house look with a Southern accent. The newly renovated rooms are medium in size; the deluxe rooms come equipped with refrigerators, microwaves, and VCRs. The hotel's brick-covered patio, with its fountains, trailing ivy, and wrought-iron furniture, evokes New Orleans. 601 E. Bay St., Savannah, GA 31401. © **800/465-4329** or 912/238-1200. Fax 912/236-2184. www.savannahotel.com. 145 units. $229 double; $269 suite. Children under 18 stay free in parents' room. AE, DC, DISC, MC, V. Parking $8. **Amenities:** Restaurant; outdoor pool; fitness center.

The Presidents' Quarters This place manages to combine the charm of a B&B with the efficiency of a much larger place. There are many appealing aspects, including rooms—each named for a different American president—and bathrooms that are among the largest and most comfortable in Savannah. Some rooms feature four-poster beds; others have full-canopy beds. All rooms offer bathrobes. Continental breakfast and afternoon tea are served each day on the brick patio. 225 E. President St., Savannah, GA 31401. ℂ 800/233-1776 or 912/233-1600. Fax 912/238-0849. www.presidentsquarters.com. 19 units. $147–$167 double; $187–$235 suite. Children under 18 stay free in parents' room. Rates include continental breakfast. DC, DISC, MC, V. Free parking on premises.

River Street Inn This restored former cotton warehouse now has a dash of colonial pizzazz in its public areas, and the building's warren of brick-lined storerooms have been converted into some of the most comfortable and well-maintained rooms in town. All rooms offer a view of the Savannah River; some have four-poster beds. You'll be near tons of bars, restaurants, and nightclubs. Breakfast is served in Huey's (see "Where to Dine," below); a wine-and-cheese reception is held Monday through Saturday. 115 E. River St., Savannah, GA 31401. ℂ 800/253-4229 or 912/234-6400. Fax 912/234-1478. www.riverstreetinn.com. 86 units. $159–$229 double, $275 suite. Children under 12 stay free in parents' room. AE, DC, MC, V. Parking $4. **Amenities:** Restaurant.

WHERE TO DINE

Clary's Café AMERICAN Clary's has been a Savannah tradition since 1903, though the ambience today is decidedly 1950s. The place was famous long before it was featured in *Midnight in the Garden*. John Berendt is still a frequent patron, as is the fabled drag diva Lady Chablis. Begin your day with the classic Hoppel Poppel (scrambled eggs with chunks of kosher salami, potatoes, onions, and green peppers) or drop in for fresh salads, stir-fries, homemade chicken soup, or flame-broiled burgers. 404 Abercorn St., at Jones St. ℂ 912/233-0402. Breakfast $3.95–$7.95; main courses $5.95–$7.95. AE, DC, DISC, MC, V. Mon 7am–4pm; Tues–Sun 7am–7pm.

Elizabeth on 37th MODERN SOUTHERN This restaurant is the most glamorous and upscale in town. It's housed in a palatial neoclassical-style 1900 villa ringed with semitropical landscaping and cascades of Spanish moss. Menu items change with the season and manage to retain their gutsy originality despite an elegant presentation. They're likely to include roast quail with mustard-and-pepper sauce and apricot-pecan chutney, or broiled salmon with mustard-garlic glaze. The desserts are the best in Savannah. 105 E. 37th St. ℂ 912/236-5547. Reservations required. Main courses $23–$36. AE, DC, DISC, MC, V. Mon–Thurs and Sun 6–9:30pm; Fri–Sat 6–10:30pm.

45 South INTERNATIONAL Recommended by *Food & Wine, Southern Living*, and even *Playboy*, this ritzy restaurant has an ever-changing menu that might feature smoked North Carolina trout, rack of lamb flavored with crushed sesame seeds, or sliced breast of pheasant with foie gras. Appetizers might include everything from South Carolina quail to crab cakes. The food has been called "gourmet Southern." The setting is softly lit with elegantly set tables and a cozy bar; the service is impeccable. 20 E. Broad St. ℂ 912/233-1881. Reservations recommended. Jackets advised. Main courses $23–$32. AE, MC, V. Mon–Thurs 6–9pm; Fri–Sat 6–9:30pm.

Huey's CAJUN/CREOLE　This casual place overlooking the Savannah River even manages to please visitors from New Orleans—and that's saying a lot. It's usually packed with folks enjoying dishes such as an oyster po' boy, jambalaya with andouille sausage, crayfish étouffée, and crab-and-shrimp au gratin. The soups are homemade and the appetizers distinctive. In the River Street Inn, 115 E. River St. Ⓒ **912/234-7385.** Reservations recommended. Main courses $12–$22; sandwiches $6–$10. AE, DISC, MC, V. Mon–Fri 7am–10pm; Sat–Sun 8am–11pm.

Lady and Sons SOUTHERN　Paula Deen started this place in 1989 with $200; today she runs one of Savannah's most celebrated restaurants. Her cookbook is in its second printing. One taste of the food and you'll understand why. The wonderful crab cakes and amazing chicken potpie topped with puff pastry best exhibit her style. The locals love her buffets, which are very Southern—with fried chicken, meatloaf, collard greens, and macaroni and cheese. Lunches are busy with a loyal following; dinners are casual and inventive. 311 W. Congress St. Ⓒ **912/233-2600.** Reservations recommended for dinner. Main courses $6–$11 lunch, $12–$23 dinner; all-you-can-eat buffet $10 lunch, $15 dinner. AE, DISC, MC, V. Mon–Sat 11:30am–3pm; Mon–Thurs 5–9pm; Fri–Sat 5–10pm; Sun 11am–5pm.

Mrs. Wilkes' Boarding House SOUTHERN　Remember the days of the boardinghouse, when everybody sat together and belly-busting food was served in big dishes at the center of the table? Mrs. Selma Wilkes has been serving locals and travelers in just that manner since the 1940s. You won't find a sign, but you probably will find a long line of people patiently waiting for a seat. Mrs. Wilkes believes in freshness, and will fill you up with fried or barbecued chicken, red rice and sausage, black-eyed peas, corn on the cob, squash and yams, okra, corn bread, and collard greens. 107 W. Jones St., west of Bull St. Ⓒ **912/232-5997.** Reservations not accepted. Breakfast $6; lunch $12. No credit cards. Mon–Fri 8–9am and 11am–3pm.

The Olde Pink House Restaurant SEAFOOD/AMERICAN　Built in 1771 and glowing pink, this house has functioned as a private home, a bank, a tearoom, and headquarters for one of Sherman's generals. Today its interior is severe and dignified, with stiff-backed chairs, bare wooden floors, and a colonial ambience. The cuisine is richly steeped in the traditions of the Low Country, and includes black grouper stuffed with blue crab and drenched in Vidalia onion sauce, and grilled tenderloin of pork crusted with almonds and molasses. You can enjoy your meal in the candlelit dining rooms or in the basement-level piano bar. 23 Abercorn St. Ⓒ **912/232-4286.** Reservations recommended. Main courses $15–$25. AE, MC, V. Daily 5:30–10:30pm.

SAVANNAH AFTER DARK

River Street, along the Savannah River, is the heart of the action. Many night owls stroll the waterfront until they hear the sound of music they like, and then follow their ears inside.

The **Savannah Symphony Orchestra (www.savannahsymphony.org)** has city-sponsored concerts in addition to its regular ticketed events. There's nothing to equal spreading a blanket in Forsyth Park to listen to the symphony perform beneath the stars or being on River Street on the Fourth of July when the group sends rousing strains echoing across the river. The orchestra's regular season is presented in the Savannah Civic Center's **Johnny Mercer Theater,** Orleans Square (Ⓒ **800/537-7894** or 912/236-9536), which is also home to ballet, musicals, and Broadway shows.

In summer, concerts of jazz, Big Band, and Dixieland music fill downtown Johnson Square with lots of foot-tapping sounds. Some of Savannah's finest musicians perform regularly.

Hannah's East, at the Pirates' House, 20 E. Broad St. (© **912/233-2225**), is the most popular jazz club in Savannah, the former showcase for the late Emma Kelly, "The Lady of 6,000 Songs." **Planters Tavern,** in the Olde Pink House Restaurant, 23 Abercorn St. (© **912/232-4286**), is a beloved local spot, graced with a sprawling and convivial bar, a pair of fireplaces, and a decor of antique bricks and carefully polished hardwoods. You can listen to the melodies emanating from the sadder-but-wiser pianist, or perhaps you'll catch the endearingly elegant Gail Thurmond, one of Savannah's most legendary songstresses.

Head for elegant **Churchill's Pub,** 9 Drayton St., 1 block south of Bay Street (© **912/232-8501**), if you're in a martini mood. It's the oldest bar in Savannah, having originally been built in England in 1860, dismantled, and shipped to Savannah in the 1920s. More unpretentious is **Kevin Barry's Irish Pub,** 117 W. River St. (© **912/233-9626**), which is *the* place to be on St. Patrick's Day. **The Rail,** 405 W. Congress St. (© **912/238-1311**), is sophisticated but low-key.

Savannah's leading gay clubs are **Club One,** 1 Jefferson St. (© **912/232-0200**), where you can catch a drag show, sometimes Lady Chablis; and **Faces,** 17 Lincoln St. (© **912/233-3520**), which is the gay Cheers of Savannah.

3 Hilton Head

The largest sea island between New Jersey and Florida, Hilton Head offers broad, sandy beaches warmed by the Gulf Stream and fringed with palm trees and rolling dunes. The subtropical climate makes all this beauty the ideal setting for golf and saltwater fishing. Far more sophisticated and upscale than Myrtle Beach and the Grand Strand, Hilton Head feels like a luxurious planned community.

ESSENTIALS

GETTING THERE   It's easy to fly into Charleston, rent a car, and drive to Hilton Head (about 65 miles south). If you're driving from other points south or north, just exit off I-95 to reach the island (Exit 28 off I-95 South, Exit 5 off I-95 North). U.S. 278 leads over the bridge to the island. It's 52 miles northeast of Savannah and located directly on the Intracoastal Waterway.

VISITOR INFORMATION   The **Island Visitors Information Center,** on U.S. 278 at S.C. 46 (© **888/741-7666** or 843/785-4472; www.islandvisitor center.com), can be found just before you cross over from the mainland. It's open Monday through Saturday from 9am to 5:30pm.

Hilton Head Visitors and Convention Bureau, 1 Chamber Dr. (© **843/785-3673;** www.hiltonheadisland.org), offers a free vacation guide with golf and tennis tips and planning advice. It's open Monday through Friday from 8:30am to 5:30pm.

SPECIAL EVENTS & FESTIVALS   **Springfest,** a March festival, features seafood, live music, stage shows, and tennis and golf tournaments. In early or mid-April, top tennis players congregate for the **Family Circle Magazine Cup Tennis Tournament,** held at the Sea Pines Racquet Club. Outstanding PGA golfers also descend on the island in mid-April for the **MCI Heritage Classic** at the Harbour Town Golf Links. To herald fall, the **Hilton Head Celebrity Golf Tournament** is held on Labor Day weekend at Palmetto Dunes and Sea Pines Plantation.

BEACHES, GOLF & OTHER OUTDOOR PURSUITS

BEACHES   Hilton Head's beaches possess extremely firm sand, providing a sound surface for biking, hiking, jogging, and beach games. In summer, watch for the endangered loggerhead turtles that lumber ashore at night to bury their eggs.

All beaches on Hilton Head are public. Land bordering the beaches, however, is private property. Most beaches are safe, although there's sometimes an undertow at the northern end of the island. Lifeguards are posted only at major beaches, and concessions are available to rent beach chairs, umbrellas, and watersports equipment.

There are four public entrances to Hilton Head's beaches. The main parking and changing areas are found on Folly Field Road, off U.S. 278 (the main highway) and at Coligny Circle, close to the Holiday Inn. Other entrances (signposted) from U.S. 278 lead to Singleton and Bradley beaches.

Most frequently used is **North and South Forest Beach,** adjacent to Coligny Circle (enter from Pope Ave. across from Lagoon Rd.). You'll have to use the parking lot opposite the Holiday Inn, paying a $4 daily fee until after 4pm. The adjacent Beach Park has toilets and a changing area, as well as showers, vending machines, and phones. It's a family favorite.

Of the beaches on the island's north, we prefer **Folly Field Beach.** Toilets, changing facilities, and parking are available.

BIKING   Hilton Head has 25 miles of bicycle paths. Some beaches are firm enough to support wheels, and every year cyclists seem to delight in dodging the waves or racing the fast-swimming dolphins in the nearby water.

Most hotels and resorts rent bikes to guests. If yours doesn't, try **Hilton Head Bicycle Company,** off Sea Pines Circle at 112 Arrow Rd. (© **843/686-6888**); or **South Beach Cycles,** at the racquet club, just before South Beach Marina Village, Sea Pines (© **843/671-2453**).

CRUISES   To explore Hilton Head's waters, contact **Adventure Cruises, Inc.,** Shelter Cove Harbour, Suite G, Harbourside III (© **843/785-4558**). Outings include a nature cruise to Daufuskie Island, a dolphin watch, and a sunset dinner cruise.

FISHING   No license is needed for saltwater fishing, although freshwater licenses are required for the island's lakes and ponds. The season for fishing offshore is April through October. Inland fishing is good between September and December. Crabbing is also popular; these crustaceans are easy to catch in low water from docks, from boats, or right off a bank.

Off Hilton Head you can go deep-sea fishing for amberjack, barracuda, sharks, and king mackerel. **A Fishin' Mission,** P.O. 4941, Hilton Head, 29938 (© **843/785-9177**), and **Harbour Town Yacht Basin,** Harbour Town Marina (© **843/671-2704**), can set you up with personal service and a small boat. A cheaper way to go—for only $45 per adult, $35 per child—is aboard *The Drifter* (© **843/671-3060**), a party boat that departs from the South Beach Marina Village.

GOLF   With 22 challenging golf courses on the island, this area is a mecca for golfers.

Many of Hilton Head's championship courses are open to the public, including the **George Fazio Course** at Palmetto Dunes Resort (© **843/785-1130**), an 18-hole, 6,534-yard, par-70 course, named in the top 50 of *Golf Digest's* "75 Best American Resort Courses." Greens fees are $85.

Old South Golf Links, 50 Buckingham Plantation Dr., Bluffton (© **800/ 257-8997** or 843/785-5353), is an 18-hole, 6,772-yard, par-72 course, recognized by *Golf Digest* for its panoramic views and lovely setting. Greens fees are $62 to $75. The course lies on Hwy. 278, 1 mile before the bridge leading to Hilton Head.

Hilton Head National, Highway 278 (© **843/842-5900**), is a Gary Player Signature Golf Course, an 18-hole, 6,779-yard, par-72 course with gorgeous scenery that evokes Scotland. Greens fees are $50 to $85.

Island West Golf Club, Highway 278 (© **843/689-6660**), has a backdrop of oaks, elevated tees, and rolling fairways. It's a challenging but playable 18-hole, 6,803-yard, par-72 course. Greens fees are $40 to $56.

The **Robert Trent Jones Course** at the Palmetto Dunes Resort (© **843/ 785-1138**) is an 18-hole, 6,710-yard, par-72 course with a winding lagoon system that comes into play on 11 holes. Greens fees are $100 to $130.

HORSEBACK RIDING Riding through beautiful maritime forests and nature preserves is reason enough to visit Hilton Head. We like **Lawton Fields Stables,** 190 Greenwood Dr., Sea Pines (© **843/671-2586**), offering rides for both adults and kids (kids ride ponies) through the Sea Pines Forest Preserve. The cost is $40 per person for a ride lasting somewhat over an hour. Reservations are necessary.

NATURE PRESERVES The **Audubon-Newhall Preserve,** Palmetto Bay Road (© **843/689-2989**), is a 50-acre preserve on the south end of the island. Here you can walk along marked trails to observe wildlife in its native habitat. Guided tours are available when plants are blooming. Open from sunrise to sunset; free admission.

Sea Pines Forest Preserve, Sea Pines Plantation (© **843/671-6486**), is a 605-acre public wilderness with marked walking trails. Nearly all the birds and animals known to live on Hilton Head can be seen here (yes, there are alligators, but there are also less fearsome creatures, such as egrets, herons, osprey, and white-tailed deer). All trails lead to public picnic areas in the center of the forest. Open from sunrise to sunset year-round except during the Heritage Golf Classic in early April. Maps and toilets are available.

TENNIS *Tennis* magazine has rated Hilton Head one of its "50 Greatest U.S. Tennis Resorts." No other domestic destination can boast such a concentration of tennis facilities, with more than 300 courts ideal for beginning, intermediate, and advanced players. The island has 19 tennis clubs, 7 of which are open to the public. A wide variety of tennis clinics and daily lessons is also found here. The top tennis facility is the **Sea Pines Racquet Club,** along with the **Port Royal Racquet Club,** the **Hilton Head Island Beach and Tennis Resort,** and the **Palmetto Dunes Tennis Center;** see "Where to Stay," below, or ask your hotel to make arrangements.

WHERE TO STAY

Hilton Head Central Reservation Service (© **800/845-7018;** www.hilton headcentral.com) can book you into any hotel room or villa on the island at no charge.

Villa rentals are available from two secluded enclaves of privately owned condos. The **Palmetto Dunes Resort** (© **800/845-6130** or 843/785-1161; www.palmettodunesresort.com) has a wide variety of units available for rental and offers golf packages. It's ideal for families, with kitchens, washer/dryers, and balconies or patios. Facilities include a huge tennis center, five golf courses, 3 miles of beach, 20 restaurants, a 10-mile lagoon ideal for canoeing, and a 200-slip marina. **Sea Pines Plantation** (© **800/SEA-PINES** or 843/785-3333; www.seapines.com) is a huge development that's best for overnight stays; it attracts hordes of golfers since it's the home of the MCI Classic, a major stop on the PGA tour.

Moderately priced and affordable chain choices include the **Holiday Inn Oceanfront,** 1 S. Forest Beach Dr. (© **800/HOLIDAY** or 843/785-5126); **Fairfield Inn by Marriott,** 9 Marina Side Dr. (© **800/228-2800** or 843/842-4800); and **Hampton Inn,** 1 Dillon Rd. (© **800/HAMPTON** or 843/681-7900).

Disney Hilton Head Island Resort   This family-friendly resort is on a 15-acre island that rises above Hilton Head's widest estuary, Broad Creek. About 20 woodsy-looking buildings are arranged in a compound. Expect lots of pine trees and fallen pine needles, garlands of Spanish moss, and plenty of kids. All accommodations contain mini-kitchens, simple wooden furniture, and well-kept bathrooms. There are lots of summer camp–style activities (dolphin-watching cruises, eco-tours, canoeing lessons, marshmallow roasts), though the ambience is more low-key than what you'd expect from Disney. 22 Harbourside Lane, Hilton Head Island, SC 29928. © 800/453-4911 or 407/939-7540. Fax 843/341-4130. www.dvcresorts.com. 123 units. $105–$265 studio; $145–$340 larger villas. Children 17 and under stay free in parents' room. AE, DC, DISC, MC, V. Free parking. **Amenities:** Restaurant; 2 outdoor pools; spa; fitness center; 6 tennis courts.

Hilton Head Crowne Plaza Resort   On 800 landscaped acres, this five-story hotel gives the Westin (see below) stiff competition, because of the sheer beauty of its landscaping, with a golf course praised by the National Audubon Society for its respect for local wildlife. Bedrooms don't quite match the style and comfort level of its competitor's bedrooms, but they are neatly furnished with tidily kept bathrooms. The attentive service is just another reason that a stay here is memorable. 130 Shipyard Dr., Shipyard Plantation, Hilton Head Island, SC 29928. © 800/465-4329 or 843/842-2400. Fax 843/785-8463. www.crowneplaza.com. 340 units. $329–$406 double; $399–$525 suite. AE, DC, DISC, MC, V. Free parking. **Amenities:** 2 restaurants; 2 pools (1 indoor, 1 outdoor); health club.

Hilton Oceanfront Resort   We like the Hilton because of its hideaway position, tucked in at the end of the main road through Palmetto Dunes. Its low-rise design has hallways that open to sea breezes at either end. Rooms are some of the largest on the island, all with ocean views and well-kept bathrooms. The studio suites have full kitchens. 23 Ocean Lane (P.O. Box 6165), Hilton Head Island, SC 29938. © 800/345-8001 or 843/842-8000. Fax 843/341-8037. www.hiltonheadhilton.com. 323 units. $195–$285 double; $399–$499 suite. Children 18 and under stay free in parents' room. AE, DC, DISC, MC, V. Free parking. **Amenities:** Restaurants (3); 2 outdoor pools; health club.

South Beach Marina Inn   Of the dozens of available accommodations in Sea Pines Plantation, this complex of marina-front buildings is the only place offering traditional hotel-style rooms by the night. With lots of charm, it meanders over a labyrinth of catwalks and stairways above a complex of shops and restaurants. The one- and two-bedroom units each have a kitchenette and at least one bathroom, and are cozily outfitted with country-style braided rugs and pine floors. In the Sea Pines Plantation, 232 S. Sea Pines Dr., Hilton Head Island, SC 29938. © 843/671-6498. www.southbeachvillage.com. 17 units. $69–$159 1-bedroom apt; $186–$210 2-bedroom apt. Children under 18 stay free in parents' room. AE, DISC, MC, V. Free parking.

Westin Resort Set near the isolated northern end of Hilton Head Island on 24 landscaped acres, this is the most opulent European-style hotel in town and it's rather formal. Rooms, most with ocean views, are outfitted in Low Country Plantation style with touches of Asian art. Each room has a private balcony; refrigerators are available. The Barony Grill is an excellent restaurant; there's also poolside dining and a seafood buffet. 2 Grass Lawn Ave., Hilton Head Island, SC 29928. (C) **800/228-3000** or 843/681-4000. Fax 843/681-1087. www.westin.com. 412 units. $209–$459 double; $450–$1,900 suite. Children under 18 stay free in parents' room; children under 5 eat free. Packages often available. AE, DC, DISC, MC, V. Free parking. **Amenities:** Restaurants (3); pools (2 indoor, 1 outdoor); spa; health club; 18-hole golf courses (3); 16 tennis courts.

WHERE TO DINE

Café Europa CONTINENTAL/SEAFOOD This fine European restaurant is at the base of the Harbour Town Lighthouse, opening onto a panoramic view of Calibogue Sound and Daufuskie Island. In an informal, cheerful atmosphere, you can order poached, grilled, baked, or fried fish. Specialty dishes include a country-style chicken recipe from Charleston, with honey, fresh cream, and pecans. Fourteen omelets are perfectly prepared at breakfast, and the Bloody Mary is the island's best. Harbour Town, Sea Pines Plantation. (C) 843/671 3399. Reservations recommended for dinner. Main courses $8–$13 lunch, $18–$28 dinner. AE, MC, V. Daily 9am–2:30pm and 5–10pm.

Charlie's L'Etoile Verte INTERNATIONAL Outfitted like a Parisian bistro, our favorite restaurant on Hilton Head Island was also a favorite of former president Bill Clinton. The atmosphere is unpretentious but elegant, and it bursts with energy in an otherwise sleepy shopping center. Begin with shrimp-stuffed ravioli, and move on to grilled tuna with a jalapeño beurre blanc (white butter) sauce, grilled quail with shiitake mushrooms and a merlot sauce, or veal chops in peppercorn sauce. The wine list is impressive. 1000 Plantation Center. (C) **843/785-9277.** Reservations required. Main courses $21–$28. AE, DISC, MC, V. Tues–Sat 11:30am–2pm and 6–9pm.

Hudson's Seafood House on the Docks SEAFOOD Built as a seafood processing factory in 1912, this restaurant still processes fish, clams, and oysters for local distribution—so you know everything is fresh. We recommend the crab cakes, the steamed shrimp, or the especially appealing blackened catch of the day. Before dinner, stroll on the docks past shrimp boats and enjoy the sunset view of the mainland and nearby Parris Island. 1 Hudson Rd. (C) **843/681-2772.** Reservations not accepted. Main courses $14–$28. AE, DC, MC, V. Daily 11am–2:30pm and 5–10pm. Go to Skull Creek just off Square Pope Rd. (signposted from U.S. 278).

Santa Fe Café SOUTHWESTERN The decor is stylish Southwest all the way, and the cuisine infuses traditional recipes with a nouvelle flair. Dishes are often presented with colors as bright as the Painted Desert. Try the tequila shrimp or the herb-roasted chicken with jalapeño corn-bread stuffing and mashed potatoes laced with red chiles. The chiles rellenos are exceptional, stuffed with California goat cheese and sun-dried tomatoes. 700 Plantation Center. (C) **843/785-3838.** Reservations recommended. Main courses $8–$12 lunch, $20–$30 dinner. AE, MC, V. Mon–Fri noon–2pm; daily 6–10pm.

HILTON HEAD AFTER DARK

Nightlife starts with sunset cocktails and stays pretty mellow. There are lots of options in hotel bars and lounges. The **Quarterdeck,** Harbour Town, Sea Pines Plantation ((C) **843/671-2222**), is our favorite waterfront lounge, the best place on the island to watch sunsets. There's dancing every night to beach music and Top 40 hits. Soft guitar music or the strains of Jimmy Buffett records usually set the scene at the **Salty Dog Cafe,** South Beach Marina (℗ **843/671-2233**), where you can enjoy your beer outdoors under a sycamore.

4 Charleston

If the Old South still lives all through South Carolina's Low Country, it positively thrives in Charleston. In spite of earthquakes, hurricanes, fires, and Yankee bombardments, Charleston remains one of the best-preserved cities in America. It boasts 73 pre-Revolutionary buildings, 136 from the late 18th century, and more than 600 built before the 1840s. With its cobblestone streets and horse-drawn carriages, Charleston is a place of visual images and sensory pleasures. Tea, jasmine, and wisteria fragrances fill the air; the aroma of she-crab soup (the local favorite) wafts from sidewalk cafes; and antebellum architecture graces the historic cityscape.

ESSENTIALS

GETTING THERE   By Plane   Charleston International Airport is in North Charleston on I-26, about 12 miles west of the city. Taxi fare into the city runs about $25. If you're driving, follow the airport access road to I-26 into the heart of Charleston.

By Train   Amtrak (℗ **800/USA-RAIL;** www.amtrak.com) provides service from Savannah (trip time: 1¾ hr.) and Washington, D.C. (9½ hr.) to its station at 4565 Gaynor Ave., North Charleston.

By Car   The main routes into Charleston are I-26 from the northwest (Columbia, SC), and U.S. 17 from the north (Myrtle Beach) and south (Savannah).

VISITOR INFORMATION   The **Charleston Visitors Center,** 375 Meeting St., Charleston, SC 29402 (℗ **843/853-8000;** www.charlestncvb.com), provides maps and advice. Numerous tours depart hourly from here. It's open Monday through Friday from 8:30am to 5:30pm; also from April to October, Saturday and Sunday from 8am to 5pm.

GETTING AROUND   The **Downtown Area Shuttle (DASH)** (℗ **843/724-7420**) is the quickest way to get around the main downtown area daily. The fare is $1, and you'll need exact change. A pass good for the whole day costs $3. Leading taxi companies are **Yellow Cab** (℗ **843/577-6565**) and **Safety Cab** (℗ **843/722-4066**); within the city, fares seldom exceed $4 or $5. You must call for a taxi—there are no pickups on the street. Don't try to drive around downtown; park your car and save it for day trips to outlying areas.

FAST FACTS   For a physician referral or 24-hour emergency-room treatment, contact **Charleston Memorial Hospital,** 326 Calhoun St. (℗ **843/577-0600**). Call **Doctor's Care** (℗ **843/556-5585**) for the names of walk-in clinics.

SPECIAL EVENTS & FESTIVALS   Held from late May to early June, the **Spoleto Festival U.S.A.** (℗ **843/722-2764;** www.spoletousa.org) is the premier cultural event in the South. This famous international festival, the American counterpart to the equally celebrated one in Spoleto, Italy, showcases world-renowned performers in drama, dance, music, and art in various venues throughout the city.

Charleston

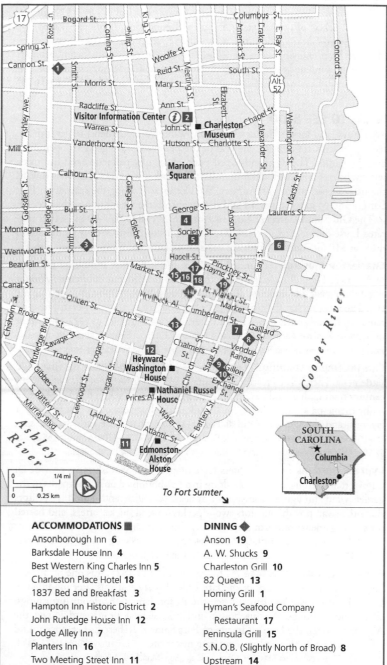

ACCOMMODATIONS ■

Ansonborough Inn **6**
Barksdale House Inn **4**
Best Western King Charles Inn **5**
Charleston Place Hotel **18**
1837 Bed and Breakfast **3**
Hampton Inn Historic District **2**
John Rutledge House Inn **12**
Lodge Alley Inn **7**
Planters Inn **16**
Two Meeting Street Inn **11**

DINING ◆

Anson **19**
A. W. Shucks **9**
Charleston Grill **10**
82 Queen **13**
Hominy Grill **1**
Hyman's Seafood Company
　Restaurant **17**
Peninsula Grill **15**
S.N.O.B. (Slightly North of Broad) **8**
Upstream **14**

During the mid-January **Low-Country Oyster Festival** (© 843/577-4030), steamed buckets of oysters greet visitors at Boone Hall Plantation. Enjoy live music, oyster-shucking contests, and children's events. For nearly 50 years, people have been enjoying some of Charleston's most prestigious neighborhoods and private gardens in the **Festival of Houses and Gardens,** from mid-March to mid-April. Contact the Historic Charleston Foundation (© **843/723-1623**) for details.

WHAT TO SEE & DO

We always head for the **Battery** (officially White Point Gardens) to get into the feel of this city. It's right on the end of the peninsula, facing the Cooper River and the harbor. There's a landscaped park, shaded by palmettos and live oaks, with walkways lined with old monuments and other war relics. The view toward the harbor goes out to Fort Sumter. We like to walk along the seawall on East Battery and Murray Boulevard and slowly absorb the Charleston ambience.

The **Old South Carriage Co.,** 14 Anson St. (© 843/577-0042), offers narrated horse-drawn carriage tours through the historic district daily from 9am to dusk, at $18 for adults, $16 for seniors and military, and $8 for children 6 to 12.

Charleston Museum   Founded in 1773, this is the first and oldest museum in America. The full-scale replica of the famed Confederate submarine *Hunley* standing outside the museum is one of the most photographed subjects in the city. The museum has the city's largest silver collection, plus early crafts, historic relics, and hands-on exhibits for children. 360 Meeting St. © 843/722-2996. www. charlestonmuseum.org. Admission $8 adults, $4 children 3–12; combination ticket to the museum, Joseph Manigault House, and Heyward-Washington House, $18. Mon–Sat 9am–5pm; Sun 1–5pm.

Charles Towne Landing   This 663-acre park is on the site of the first 1670 settlement. There's a re-creation of a small village, a full-scale replica of a 17th-century trading ship, and a tram tour for $1 (or you can rent a bike). There's no flashy theme-park atmosphere: You'll walk under huge old oaks, past freshwater lagoons, and through the Animal Forest, seeing what those early settlers saw. 1500 Old Towne Rd., S.C. 171, between U.S. 17 and I-126. © 843/852-4200. Admission $5 adults, $2.50 seniors and children 6–14, free for those with disabilities. Daily 8:30am–6pm.

Cypress Gardens   Giant cypress trees draped with Spanish moss provide an unforgettable setting as you glide along in a flat-bottomed boat. Footpaths in the garden wind through a profusion of azaleas, camellias, and daffodils. Visitors share the swamp with alligators, woodpeckers, wood ducks, otters, and barred owls. The gardens are worth a visit at any time of year, but they're at their most colorful in March and April. U.S. 52 (24 miles north of Charleston), Moncks Corner. © 843/553-0515. Admission $9 adults, $8 seniors, $3 children 6–12. Daily 9am–5pm.

Edmondston-Alston House   This house, built in 1825, was one of the earliest constructed in the city in the late Federalist style; it was later modified in Greek Revival style. You can still see the Alston family's heirloom furnishings, silver, and paintings. At this house in 1861 General Beauregard joined the Alstons to watch the bombardment of Fort Sumter. Robert E. Lee once found refuge here when his hotel uptown caught on fire. 21 E. Battery. © 843/722-7171. Admission $7. Guided tours Tues–Sat 10am–4:30pm; Sun–Mon 1:30–4:30pm.

Fort Sumter National Monument   It was here that the first shot of the Civil War was fired on April 12, 1861, as Confederate forces launched a 34-hour bombardment. Union forces eventually surrendered, and the Rebels' occupation became a symbol of Southern resistance. This action led to a declaration of war in Washington. Amazingly, Confederate troops held onto Sumter for nearly 4 years, although it was almost continually bombarded. When evacuation finally came, the fort was nothing but a heap of rubble. Park rangers today are on hand to answer your questions, and you can explore gun emplacements and visit a small museum filled with artifacts related to the siege. Expect to spend about 2 hours. We recommend the tour of the fort and harbor offered by **Fort Sumter Tours,** 205 King St., Ste. 204 (℃ **843/722-1691** or 843/881-7337). Sailing times change every month or so; call ahead. In Charleston Harbor. ℃ 843/883-3123. www.nps.gov/fosu. Free admission to fort; boat trip $11 adults, $6 children 6–11, free for children under 6. Daily 9am–5pm.

Heyward-Washington House   In a district called "Cabbage Row," this 1772 house was built by Daniel Heyward, "the rice king," and was also home to Thomas Heyward, Jr., a signer of the Declaration of Independence. President George Washington bedded down here in 1791. Many of the fine period pieces in the house are the work of Thomas Elfe, one of America's most famous cabinetmakers. The restored 18th-century kitchen is the only historic kitchen in the city open to the public. 87 Church St., between Tradd and Elliott sts ℃ 843/722-0354. Admission $8 adults, $4 children 3–12. Mon–Sat 10am–5pm; Sun 1–5pm. Tours leave every half hr until 4:30pm.

Magnolia Plantation   Ten generations of the Drayton family have lived here continuously since the 1670s. They haven't had much luck keeping a roof over their heads: The first mansion burned just after the Revolution and the second was set afire by General Sherman. But you can't call its replacement "modern." A simple, pre-Revolutionary house was barged down from Summerville and set on the foundations of its unfortunate predecessors. It's been furnished with museum-quality Early American furniture. The gardens of camellias and azaleas—among the most beautiful in America—reach their peak bloom in March and April but are colorful year-round. You can tour the house, the gardens, a petting zoo, and a waterfowl refuge, or walk or bike through wildlife trails. The **Audubon Swamp Garden,** also on the grounds, is an independently operated 60-acre cypress swamp offering a close look at wildlife, such as alligators, otters, turtles, and herons. S.C. 61 N. ℃ 800/367-3517 or 843/571-1266. www.magnoliaplantation. com. Admission to garden and grounds: $12 adults, $11 seniors, $9 children 13–19, $6 children 6–12. Tour of plantation house is an additional $7 for ages 6 and up; children under 6 not allowed to tour the house. Admission to Audubon Swamp Garden: $5 adults and seniors, $4 children 13–19, $3 children 6–12. Summer daily 8am–5:30pm; winter daily 9am–5pm.

Middleton Place   This was the home of Henry Middleton, president of the First Continental Congress. Today this National Historic Landmark includes America's oldest landscaped gardens, where ornamental lakes, terraces, and plantings of camellias, azaleas, magnolias, and crape myrtle accent the grand design. The Middleton Place House itself was built in 1755, but in 1865 all but the south flank was ransacked and burned by Union troops. It was restored in the 1870s as a family residence and today houses fine silver, furniture, rare first editions, and portraits. In the stableyards, craftspeople demonstrate life on a plantation of yesteryear. Ashley River Rd. (14 miles northwest of Charleston). ℃ 843/556-6020. www.middletonplace.org. Admission $20 adults, $15 children 6–12, free for children under 6. Tour of house, additional $10. Gardens and stableyards daily 9am–5pm; house Mon 1:30–4:30pm and Tues–Sat 10am–4:30pm.

Nathaniel Russell House   One of America's finest examples of Federal architecture, this 1808 house was completed by Nathaniel Russell, one of Charleston's richest merchants. It is celebrated for its "free-flying" staircase, spiraling unsupported for three floors. The interiors are ornate with period furnishings, especially the elegant music room with its golden harp and neoclassical-style sofa. 51 Meeting St. (C) **843/722-3405.** www.historicchalreston.org. Admission $6. Guided tours Mon–Sat 10am–4:30pm; Sun and holidays 2–4:30pm.

BEACHES & OUTDOOR PURSUITS

BEACHES   There are some great beaches within a 25-minute drive from Charleston. In the East Cooper area, both the **Isle of Palms** and **Sullivan's Island** offer miles of beaches, mostly bordered by beachfront homes. Windsurfing and jet-skiing are popular here. **Kiawah Island** has the area's most pristine beach at the **Beachwalker County Park,** on the southern end of the island.

GOLF   Charleston is said to be the home of golf in America. **Wild Dunes Resort,** Isle of Palms ((C) **843/886-6000**), offers two championship golf courses designed by Tom Fazio. **The Links** is a 6,722-yard, par-72 layout ending with a pair of oceanfront holes once called "the greatest east of Pebble Beach." The course has been ranked in the top 100 in the world by *Golf Magazine.* **The Harbor Course** offers 6,402 yards of Low Country marsh and Intracoastal Waterway views. This par-70 layout challenges players with two holes that play from one island to another across Morgan Creek. Greens fees at these courses can range from $60 to $165, depending on the season.

Your best deal if you'd like to play at any of the other Charleston-area golf courses is to contact **Charleston Golf Partners** ((C) **800/247-5786** or 843/216-7734). They represent 20 golf courses and offer packages that include greens fees and accommodations (they can also arrange rental cars and airfares).

SHOPPING

King Street is lined with many special shops and boutiques.

Two of the leading galleries are the **Waterfront Gallery,** 215 E. Bay St., across from the Custom House ((C) **843/722-1155**), and the **Wells Gallery,** 103 Broad St. ((C) **843/853-3233**), both specializing in the works of local artists.

Bookworms will love browsing through the thousands of used and rare volumes at **Atlantic Books,** 310 King St. ((C) **843/723-4751**), which specializes in titles on South Carolina and the Civil War and the works of Southern authors.

Charleston Crafts, 87 Hassell St. ((C) **843/723-2938**), offers locally made jewelry, basketry, leather, traditional crafts, and soaps. **Clown's Bazaar,** 56 Broad St. ((C) **843/723-9769**), features hand-carvings, silks, and pewter from exotic locales, with proceeds going to benefit developing nations. Also supporting a good cause, **Historic Charleston Reproductions,** 105 Broad St. ((C) **843/723-8292**), aids local restoration projects. Licensed replica products range from furniture to jewelry. The pride of the store is its home furnishings collection, with most in lovely mahogany. It operates shops in several historic houses and runs the Francis Edmunds Center Museum Shop at 108 Meeting St. ((C) **843/724-8484**).

WHERE TO STAY

For help with reservations, contact **Historic Charleston Bed and Breakfast** ((C) **800/743-3583** or 843/722-6606; www.historiccharlestonbedandbreakfast.com). During the major festivals, owners charge pretty much what the market will bear. Advance reservations are essential at those times.

Reliable moderately priced and affordable chain options include the **Hampton Inn Historic District,** 345 Meeting St. (© **800/HAMPTON** or 843/723-4000), across from the visitor center; and the **Best Western King Charles Inn,** 237 Meeting St. (© **800/528-1234** or 843/723-7451).

Ansonborough Inn Once past the not-very-promising exterior, most visitors really like the unusual configuration of rooms here. Set close to the waterfront, this former warehouse has a lobby that features exposed timbers and a soaring atrium filled with plants. Despite the building's height, there are only three floors, so rooms have ceilings of 14 to 16 feet and, in many cases, sleeping lofts. They're outfitted with copies of 18th-century furniture, and kitchenettes with microwaves and refrigerators. There's a panoramic terrace with a hot tub on the rooftop. 21 Hassell St., Charleston, SC 29401. © 800/522-2073 or 843/723-1655. Fax 843/577-6888. www.ansonboroughinn.com. 37 units. Mar–Nov $149–$209 double; off season $119–$159 double. Children under 12 stay free in parents' room. Rates include continental breakfast. AE, DISC, MC, V. Parking $8.

Barksdale House Inn This is a neat, well-proportioned Italianate building near the City Market, originally constructed as an inn back in 1778. Guests enjoy a flagstone-covered terrace where a fountain splashes. Most rooms contain four-poster beds and working fireplaces. About half a dozen of them have whirlpool tubs. Throughout, the furnishings, wallpaper, and fabrics evoke the late 19th century. Sherry and tea are served on the back porch in the evening. 27 George St., Charleston, SC 29401. © 843/577-4800. Fax 843/853-0482. www.barksdalehouse.com. 14 units. Summer $145–$205 double; off season $115–$155 double. Rates include continental breakfast. MC, V. Free parking. No children under 7.

Charleston Place Hotel Charleston's premier hotel is an eight-story landmark in the historic district that looks like a postmodern French château. It's big-time, glossy, and urban, with prices to match. Rooms are among the most spacious and handsomely furnished in town—stately, modern, and state-of-the-art. All units have well-maintained marble bathrooms with upscale amenities. Dine in the highly recommended upscale Charleston Grill (see "Where to Dine," below), then swim off the calories in the hotel's heated indoor pool. 130 Market St., Charleston, SC 29401; entrance at 205 Meeting St. © 800/611-5545 or 843/722-4900. Fax 843/724-72415. www.charlestonplacehotel.com. 420 units. $429–$519 double; $550–$1,500 suite. Children under 18 stay free in parents' room. Seasonal packages available. AE, DC, DISC, MC, V. Parking $10. **Amenities:** Restaurants (2); indoor pool; spa; fitness center; 2 tennis courts; pets accepted for $50 fee.

1837 Bed & Breakfast Built in 1837 by a cotton planter, this place was restored and decorated by two artists. It's only a single room wide—which makes for some interesting room arrangements. Our favorite is no. 2 in the Carriage House, which has authentic designs, exposed brick walls, and a beamed ceiling. All rooms have fridges, separate entrances, and canopied poster "rice beds." On one of the verandas you can sit under whirling ceiling fans and enjoy your breakfast or afternoon tea. 126 Wentworth St., Charleston, SC 29401. © 843/723-7166. www.1837bb.com. 9 units. $129–$159 double. Rates include full breakfast and afternoon tea. AE, DISC, MC, V. Free off-street parking. No children 7 or under accepted.

John Rutledge House Inn This fine 18th-century house is the premier inn in Charleston. Its original builder was one of the signers of the Declaration of Independence and later chief justice of the U.S. Supreme Court. Impeccably restored to its Federalist grandeur, the inn is enhanced with discreetly concealed electronic conveniences. Continental breakfast, tea, and afternoon sherry are served in a spacious upstairs sitting room, with antique firearms, elaborate moldings, and marble fireplaces. All of the beautifully decorated rooms have comfortable and modern furnishings. Some have canopy and four-poster beds, on which you'll find Godiva chocolates at evening turndown. 116 Broad St., Charleston, SC 29401. © 800/476-9741 or 843/723-7999. Fax 843/720-2615. www.charminginns.com. 19 units. $265–$295 double; $325–$375 suite. Children 12 and under stay free in parents' room. Rates include continental breakfast. AE, MC, V. Parking $10.

Lodge Alley Inn   This historic property sprawls from its entrance on the busiest commercial street of the Old Town to a quiet brick-floored courtyard in back. It was once a trio of 19th-century warehouses; today it evokes a miniature village in Louisiana, with a central square, a fountain, landscaped shrubs basking in the sunlight, and a Cajun restaurant. Throughout, the decor is American country, with pine floors and lots of colonial accents. Some rooms have fireplaces, and most have retained the massive timbers and brick walls of the original warehouses. All rooms also come equipped with microwaves and refrigerators. 195 E. Bay St., Charleston, SC 29401. © 800/845-1004 or 843/722-1611. Fax 843/722-1611, ext. 7777. www.lodgealleyinn.com. 87 units. $169 double; $189–$225 suite. Children 12 and under stay free in parents' room. Rates include continental breakfast. AE, DISC, MC, V. Parking $10.

Planters Inn   For many years this distinguished brick-sided inn next to the City Market was left to languish, but renovations have transformed it into a tasteful enclave of colonial charm. The spacious rooms have an award-winning 18th-century decor and a number of them overlook the hotel's garden courtyard. Some of the rooms have working fireplaces; others have whirlpool tubs. Afternoon tea is served in the lobby, and there's a well-recommended restaurant, the Peninsula Grill (see "Where to Dine," below). Market and Meeting sts., Charleston, SC 29401. © 800/845-7082 or 843/722-2345. Fax 843/577-2125. www.plantersinn.com. 62 units. $170–$350 double; $395–$650 suite. Children 12 and under stay free in parents' room. AE, DISC, MC, V. Parking $14. **Amenities:** Restaurant.

Two Meeting Street Inn   Set in an enviable position near the Battery, this house was built in 1892. Its proportions are as lavish and gracious as the Gilded Age could provide. Stained-glass windows, mementos, and paintings were either part of the original decorations or collected by the present owners, the Spell family. Most rooms contain four-poster beds, ceiling fans, and, in some cases, access to a network of balconies. None of the rooms contains a telephone, but there is one in the hallway of each floor. 2 Meeting St., Charleston, SC 29401. © 843/723-7322. 9 units. $170–$310 double. Rates include continental breakfast and afternoon tea. No credit cards. Free parking. No children under 12.

WHERE TO DINE

Foodies flock to Charleston for some of the finest dining in the South.

Anson LOW COUNTRY/MODERN AMERICAN   We think it's simply the best. Anson is a hip, stylish place with a dash of Low Country charm. The setting is a century-old brick-sided ice warehouse; the owners have added New Orleans–style iron balconies, Corinthian pilasters, and Victorian rococo. A well-trained staff offers sophisticated interpretations of traditional local dishes, including fried cornmeal oysters with potato cakes; and lobster, corn, and blackbean quesadillas. Our favorite is the crispy flounder. 12 Anson St. © 843/577-0551. Reservations recommended. Main courses $16–$29. AE, DC, DISC, MC, V. Sun–Thurs 5–10pm; Fri–Sat 5–11pm.

A. W. Shucks SEAFOOD   This is a hearty oyster bar where thousands of crustaceans have been cracked open over the years. The menu highlights oysters and clams on the half-shell, tasty seafood chowders, deviled crab, shrimp Creole, and a selection of international beers. Nobody cares how you dress—just dig in. 70 State St. ℂ **843/723-1151.** Reservations not necessary. Main courses $5–$11 lunch, $12–$18 dinner. AE, DC, DISC, MC, V. Sun–Thurs 11am–10pm; Fri–Sat 11am–11pm.

Charleston Grill LOW COUNTRY/FRENCH   Chef Bob Wagner has infused the menu here with French flair, drawing rave reviews. You'll be surprised at how well French and Low Country cuisine can meld. The decor makes no concessions to Southern folksiness, and the marble-floored, mahogany-sheathed dining room is one of the city's most luxurious. Try the absolutely delectable McClellanville lump crabmeat cakes with roasted pistachio and a chive sauce. In the Charleston Place Hotel, 224 King St. ℂ **843/577-4522.** Reservations recommended. Main courses $19–$32. AE, DC, DISC, MC, V. Sun–Thurs 6–10pm; Fri–Sat 6–11pm.

82 Queen LOW COUNTRY   Three 18th- and 19th-century houses are clustered around an ancient magnolia tree, with outdoor tables arranged in its shade. Menu items filled with flavor and flair include an award-winning version of she-crab soup laced with sherry; Carolina bouillabaisse; a down-home shrimp-and-chicken gumbo with andouille sausage and okra; and melt-in-the-mouth crab cakes with a sweet-pepper and basil rémoulade. 82 Queen St. ℂ **843/723-7591** Reservations recommended for dinner. Main courses $17–$23. AE, DC, MC, V. Daily 11:30am–2:30pm and 5:30–10pm.

Hominy Grill LOW COUNTRY   The Hominy Grill features beautifully prepared dishes. A devoted local following comes here to feast on barbecued chicken sandwiches; okra and shrimp beignets; and a brunch favorite—smothered or poached eggs on homemade biscuits with mushroom gravy. The catfish stew with corn bread at lunch is a temptation on a cold and rainy day, and the banana bread is worth writing home about. 207 Rutledge Ave. ℂ **843/937-0931.** Main courses $5.25–$8 lunch, $8.50–$17 dinner; brunch from $10. AE, MC, V. Mon–Fri 7:30–11am and 11:30am–2:30pm; Sat–Sun 9am–9:30pm; Wed–Fri 7–9:30pm.

Hyman's Seafood Company Restaurant SEAFOOD   Hyman's was established a century ago. It sprawls over most of a city block in the heart of Charleston's business district. Inside are at least six dining rooms and a take-away deli loaded with salmon, lox, and smoked herring. One sit-down section is devoted to deli-style sandwiches, chicken soup, and salads; another to a delectably messy choice of fish, shellfish, lobsters, and oysters. 215 Meeting St. ℂ **803/723-6000.** Seafood dinners and platters $9–$23. AE, DISC, MC, V. Daily 11am–11pm.

Peninsula Grill LOW COUNTRY/INTERNATIONAL   The Peninsula Grill has caused quite a stir, though it's quaint and quiet, full of 19th-century charm. The menu changes frequently. Start with the James Island clams with wild mushroom bruschetta, and follow with the chargrilled double pork chops with cheddar grits or the to-die-for pistachio crumb-crusted sea bass. The kitchen does a marvelous job of bringing new cuisine to an old city. In the Planters Inn, 112 N. Market St. ℂ **843/723-0700.** Reservations required. Main courses $21–$29. AE, DC, DISC, MC, V. Sun–Thurs 5:30–10pm; Fri–Sat 5:30–11pm.

S.N.O.B. (Slightly North of Broad) SOUTHERN   There's an exposed kitchen, a high ceiling crisscrossed with ventilation ducts, and a smattering of wrought iron in this snazzy, rehabbed warehouse. The place was one of the first in town to put a sophisticated modern spin on traditional Southern dishes.

Main courses can be ordered in medium and large sizes. Try the flounder stuffed with deviled crab or grilled tenderloin of beef with green-peppercorn sauce. For dessert, make it the chocolate pecan torte. 192 E. Bay St. © 843/723-3424. Reservations accepted only for parties of 6 or more. Main courses $14–$27. AE, DC, DISC, MC, V. Mon–Fri 11:30am–3pm; daily 5:30–11pm.

Upstream INTERNATIONAL/SEAFOOD   Veteran chef Gene Kato embraces his craft with great success. The decor is nautical in theme complete with wrought-iron ocean-life origami designed by local artist Jonathan Baxter. The tasty menu changes frequently, but we've enjoyed the macadamia-nut crusted mahi-mahi with crispy soft-shell crab rolls in an orange chili soy glaze and the grilled pork tenderloin with crispy Japanese noodles and garlic-infused clams. 200 Meeting St., in the Nations Bank Building. © 843-853-2550. Reservations required. Main courses $17–$26. AE, DC, DISC, MC, V. Sun–Thurs 5:30–10pm; Fri–Sun 11:30am–3pm and 5:30–11pm.

CHARLESTON AFTER DARK

THE PERFORMING ARTS   Charleston's major cultural venue is the **Dock Street Theater,** 133 Church St. (© **843/965-4032**), a 463-seat theater that hosts various companies throughout the year, especially during the annual Spoleto Festival USA in May and June. The **Robert Ivey Ballet,** 1910 Savannah Hwy. (© **843/556-1343**), offers both classical and contemporary dance as well as children's ballet programs. The **Charleston Ballet Theatre,** 477 King St. (© **843/723-7334;** www.charlestonballet.com), is one of the South's best professional ballet companies. The **Charleston Symphony Orchestra,** 14 George St. (© **843/723-7528;** www.charlestonsymphony.com), performs throughout the state, but its main venue is the Gaillard Auditorium and Charleston Southern University. The season runs from September to May.

THE CLUB & MUSIC SCENE   **Henry's,** 54 N. Market St. (© **843/723-4363**), also presents bands playing a wide range of music from Sunday to Thursday. There is a comedy club upstairs. In a restored warehouse in the City Market area, **Tommy Condon's Irish Pub,** 160 Church St. (© **843/577-3818**), features live Irish entertainment Wednesday through Sunday evenings. If your musical tastes run from the Delta blues to rock to reggae, head for **Cumberland's,** 26 Cumberland St. (© **843/577-9469**), where people of all ages lift a glass together; music is the common bond. The **Music Farm,** 32 Ann St. (© **843/722-8904**), covers nearly every taste in music from country to rock with a range of live acts.

THE BAR SCENE   Our favorite watering hole is the elegant and comfortable **First Shot Bar,** in the Mills House Hotel, 115 Meeting St. (© **843/577-2400**); if you get hungry, the kitchen will whip you up some shrimp and grits. **The Griffon,** 18 Vendue Range (© **843/723-1700**), is a popular place to share a pint. **Vicery's Bar & Grill,** 15 Beaufain (© **843/577-5300**), is one of the most frequented gathering places in Charleston for the younger crowd.

5 Myrtle Beach & the Grand Strand

One of the most popular destinations along the East Coast, the Grand Strand area stretches south from the South Carolina state line at Little River to Georgetown. It's 98 miles north of Charleston, but a world away in ambience. Development, mostly in the form of theme parks, kiddie attractions, mini-golf courses, and condos, has proceeded at a runaway pace.

The Grand Strand hosts more than twice as many visitors each year as Hawaii, mostly families and young singles from the Carolinas, who come year after year to enjoy the beach-party scene. It's become a rival to Branson and Nashville, with more than a dozen theaters offering "family-friendly" and country-music variety shows. The bustling resort city of Myrtle Beach is at the center of it all.

ESSENTIALS

GETTING THERE   The closest airport is **Myrtle Beach International Airport** (© 843/448-1589). If you're driving, major routes into Myrtle Beach are U.S. 17 from the north (Wilmington) and south (Charleston), and U.S. 501 from the west (I-95).

VISITOR INFORMATION   The **Myrtle Beach Area Chamber of Commerce** is at 1200 N. Oak St., Myrtle Beach, SC 29578 (© 800/356-3016, or 843/626-7444 to order literature only; www.mbchamber.com), open Monday through Friday from 8:30am to 5pm, and Saturday and Sunday from 9am to 5pm. Ask for their *Stay & Play* booklet.

THE BEACHES, THE LINKS & BEYOND

Everybody—and we mean that—heads for the **Myrtle Beach Pavilion Amusement Park,** Ninth Avenue North and Ocean Boulevard (© 843/448-6456), an entertainment complex with carnival rides (including a huge water flume), sidewalk cafes, and video games. An all-day pass costs $24 adults, $15 seniors 55 and up and children shorter than 42 inches tall. You can purchase individual tickets for $5 (allows seven rides). The park is open from March to October.

When you're ready to hit the beach, the main action is right around the pavilion, at Ocean Boulevard and Ninth Avenue North. For more seclusion, head north of 79th Avenue for several miles. The sands here are mostly hard-packed and the color of brown sugar. The beach has lifeguards and plenty of fast-food joints, but amazingly, no public toilets. However, South Carolina law obligates hotels to allow beach buffs to use their facilities.

At the southern tier of the beach, **Myrtle Beach State Park** (© 843/238-5325) offers 312 acres of pine woods and a sandy beach. Admission to the park is $2 per person. There are toilets, along with pavilions, picnic tables, and a swimming pool. It's possible to fish from the pier for $4.50. The park is full of nature trails, and offers 350 campsites, rented on a first-come, first-served basis at $20 per site.

Serious golfers will find plenty of places to play. Many golf packages are available, including accommodations and greens fees; call **Golf Holiday** (© 800/845-4653).

Legends, U.S. 501, Myrtle Beach (© 800/552-2660 or 843/236-9318), designed by Pete Dye and Tom Doak, is a 54-hole, par-72 course, charging greens fees of $49 to $106. We also like the following courses: **Arcadian Shores,** 701 Hilton Rd., Arcadian Shores (© 800/449-5217 or 843/449-5217), an 18-hole, par-72 course created by Rees Jones; **Azalea Sands,** 2100 U.S. 17, in North Myrtle Beach (© 800/253-2312 or 843/272-6191), an 18-hole course with white sand traps and blue lakes; and **Beachwood,** 1520 U.S. 17, Crescent Section, North Myrtle Beach (© 800/526-4889 or 843/272-6168), which annually hosts the Carolinas' PGA Seniors' Championship and Dupont World Amateur.

Anglers can go out after mackerel, amberjack, barracuda, sea bass, grouper, and red snapper. You'll get great fishing aboard any boat of **Captain Dick's,** Business Highway 17, at Myrtle Beach South Strand and Murrells Inlet (© **866/557-3474** or 843/651-3676), which provides half-day party boat outings. There are also sailings that are strictly for sightseeing, offering stunning views of the Grand Strand.

You can spend a day at the **Myrtle Waves Water Park,** 10th Avenue at U.S. 17N Bypass (© **843/448-1026**), enjoying the water slides, wave pool, children's play pool, video arcade, and tanning deck. Its Turbo-Twisters is the world's tallest water ride. Adults pay $22 and children are charged $13. The park is open daily from May to mid-September.

WHERE TO STAY

In addition to the listings below, other solid moderately priced and affordable choices include the **Holiday Inn Oceanfront,** 415 S. Ocean Blvd. (© **800/845-0313** or 843/448-4481); the **Landmark Resort,** 1501 S. Ocean Blvd. (© **843/448-9441**); the **Coral Beach Hotel,** 1105 S. Ocean Blvd. (© **800/843-2684** or 843/448-8421; and **St. John's Inn,** 6803 N. Ocean Blvd. (© **800/845-0624** or 843/449-5251).

The Breakers   This longtime family favorite is better than ever. With one of the best north beachfront locations, it occupies both a multistory complex and a 19-floor North Tower 7 blocks away. The accommodations range from tastefully furnished rooms to efficiencies with kitchenettes, and even one- to three-bedroom suites. Many rooms have balconies and refrigerators; some have microwaves. There's also a rooftop lounge with nightly entertainment. 2006 N. Ocean Blvd., Myrtle Beach, SC 29578. © 800/845-0688 or 843/626-5000. Fax 843/626-5001. www.breakers.com. 400 units. $39–$139 double; $55–$179 suite. Children 16 and under stay free in parents' room. AE, DC, DISC, MC, V. Free parking. **Amenities:** Restaurant; pools (1 indoor, 2 outdoor); fitness center.

Kingston Plantation & The Embassy Suites at Kingston Plantation This is the top choice along the strip, a 20-story main building along with two other high-rises opening onto its own 145 acres of oceanfront property. Suites with beach views have living/dining areas, kitchens, balconies, and tasteful furnishings. In addition, the hotel has two 18-story oceanfront condos and townhouse villas, all with fully equipped kitchens, beautiful bathrooms, living rooms, and balconies or decks; they're great for families. 9800 Lake Dr., Myrtle Beach, SC 29572. © 800/876-0010 or 843/449-0006. Fax 843/497-1110. www.kingstonplantation.com. 255 suites, 595 condos and villas. $129–$379 suite; $99–$429 condo or villa. Children 17 and under stay free in parents' room. AE, DC, DISC, MC, V. Free parking. **Amenities:** Restaurants (3); pools (1 indoor, 10 outdoor); fitness center; 9 tennis courts.

Ocean Creek Resort   One of the finest resorts along the beach, this first-class choice features studios and condos of varying sizes in half a dozen different complexes on almost 60 acres. Units vary in size; all contain kitchenettes with refrigerators, and well-kept bathrooms with shower-tub combinations. The Beach Club on the ocean operates in summer. 10600 N. Kings Hwy., Myrtle Beach, SC 29572. © 800/845-0353 or 843/272-7724. Fax 843/272-9627. www.oceancreek.com. 750 units. $51–$208 studio or condo. AE, DC, DISC, MC, V. **Amenities:** Restaurant; pools (2 indoor, 6 outdoor); putting green; tennis complex.

Ocean Reef Resort   North of the bustling beach center, this 16-floor oceanfront resort is newly renovated and better than most other moderately priced choices. All the rooms and efficiencies are well kept and tropically inspired. Most have two double beds and balconies; some offer refrigerators and microwaves. N. Ocean Blvd., at 71st Ave. N. © 800/542-0048 or 843/449-4441. Fax 843/497-3041. www.oceanreefmyrtlebeach.com. 291 units. $128–$157 double; $124–$365 suite. AE, DC, DISC, MC, V. Free parking. **Amenities:** Restaurant; pools (1 indoor, 1 outdoor); fitness center.

WHERE TO DINE

Murrells Inlet bills itself "The Seafood Capital of South Carolina." Just take U.S. 17 (Business) south 11 miles from Myrtle Beach, and prepare to dig in. Our favorite choices for a feast are the **Channel Marker** (© 843/651-6440), **Drunken Jacks** (© 843/651-2044), and **Oliver's Lodge** (© 843/651-2963). All of them are on U.S. 17 (Business), right along the water.

Nicks and 61st CONTINENTAL   Originally a French bakery, this place has expanded to become one of the finer restaurants along the Grand Strand. Appetizers might include snow-crab-and-lobster cocktail, or warm goat cheese baked in a pine-nut crust. For your main course, you may see an open ravioli of seared salmon, or grilled veal chops. Ingredients are exceptionally fresh and are deftly handled by the kitchen staff. Service is formal and polite. 503 61st Ave. at U.S. 17. © 843/449-1716. Reservations recommended. Main courses $8–$13 lunch, $17–$35 dinner. AE, MC, V. Mon–Sat 11am–2:30pm and 5:30–10pm.

Rosa Linda's Café MEXICAN   This is the leading south-of-the-border joint along the Grand Strand. Begin with baked stuffed mussels or Rosa's award-winning seafood stew. The chef's special is a paper seafood bag, with the catch of the day aromatically cooked in a bag with peppers, onions, mushrooms, and hot sauce. Paella, burritos, enchiladas, fajitas, and tacos are all here. 4635 U.S. 17 N., North Myrtle Beach. © 843/272-6823. Reservations accepted. Main courses $4.50–$8 lunch, $9–$15 dinner. AE, DISC, MC, V. Daily noon–10pm.

Sea Captain's House AMERICAN   In a 1930s beachfront home 1½ miles north of the center, this family-run restaurant is loved by locals. A glassed-in patio affords an ocean view. She-crab soup is a specialty. The seafood platter includes five different seafoods served with slaw, potatoes, and hush puppies; and there's a selection of succulent charcoal-broiled steaks, flavorful pork chops, and mama's Southern fried chicken. 3002 N. Ocean Blvd. © 843/448-8082. Reservations recommended in midsummer. Main courses $14–$26. AE, DISC, MC, V. Daily 7–10:30am, 11:30am–2:30pm, and 4:45–10pm.

THE GRAND STRAND AFTER DARK

Tickets for most of the following variety shows and revues begin at $30 for adults. You can catch Alabama and other top country stars, or a variety show, at the **Alabama Theatre,** Barefoot Landing, North Myrtle Beach (© 800/342-2262 or 843/272-1111), which is part of a waterside shopping complex. The **Carolina Opry,** North Kings Highway at U.S. 17 (© 800/843-6779 or 843/238-8888), might host country, bluegrass, big band, or patriotic music, plus comedy. The Christmas show is so popular that it's often sold out by June. The **Dixie Stampede Dinner and Show,** North Kings Highway at U.S. 17 (© 800/433-4401 or 843/497-9700), owned by Dolly Parton's Dollywood Productions, is so hokey that Dolly should be ashamed of herself. **Legends in Concert,** 301 U.S. 17, Surfside Beach (© 800/843-6779 or 843/238-8888), features an array of celebrity impersonators. **The Palace Theater at Myrtle Beach,** 1420 Celebrity Circle (© 800/905-4228 or 843/448-0588), hosts frequent headliner concerts and stand-up acts.

The **Fantasy Harbour Entertainment Complex,** U.S. 501 near Waccamaw Pottery (© **800/681-5209** or 843/236-8500), has several entertainment venues, including **Crook & Chase,** where shows are inspired by Broadway extravaganzas; **Medieval Times & Dinner Complex,** featuring falconry, sorcery, swordplay, and jousting, plus a four-course banquet (no utensils, of course); the **Ice Castle,** entirely devoted to skating spectacles; and **The Forum,** usually devoted to light comedies and drama.

Barefoot Landing, Highway 17 South, offers 14 restaurants, a variety and rock-music venue known as the Alabama Theater; an endlessly popular nightlife venue—the House of Blues—and a reptilian theme park known as Alligator Adventure. Everything about this place, frankly, is well-orchestrated except for parking, which can be very hard to come by. **Broadway at the Beach,** between 22nd and 29th boulevards, includes the Hard Rock Cafe, Ripley's Aquarium, and a collection of late-night bars and dance clubs that include everything from country-western line dancing to Latino salsa. The '50s live on at **Studebaker's,** 21st Avenue North and Highway 17 (© **843/448-9747**), site of the National Shag Dance Championship held annually in March.

6 Wilmington & the Outer Banks

WILMINGTON & CAPE FEAR

As the chief port of North Carolina, Wilmington is a major retail, trade, and manufacturing center, but tourism is looming larger than ever in its economy. Boasting one of the largest districts listed in the National Register of Historic Places, Wilmington is known for its preservation efforts, reflected in the restored grandeur of its antebellum, Victorian, Georgian, and Italianate homes.

ESSENTIALS

GETTING THERE   Wilmington International Airport, 1740 Airport Blvd. (© **910/341-4125**), is half a mile from the center of town. Taxis meet arriving planes. By car, Wilmington is reached via I-40 from the north (Raleigh), and U.S. 17 from the south (Charleston, SC).

VISITOR INFORMATION   Cape Fear Coast Convention and Visitors Bureau, 24 N. 3rd St., Wilmington, NC 28401 (© **800/222-4757** or 910/ 341-4030; www.cape-fear.nc.us), is open Monday through Friday from 8:30am to 5pm, Saturday from 9am to 4pm, and Sunday from 1 to 4pm.

WHAT TO SEE & DO

To get an overview of the historic Wilmington waterfront, hop aboard the *Capt. J. N. Maffitt* (© **910/343-1611**), which departs from the foot of Market Street for a 5-mile loop of the Cape Fear River. The 45-minute narrated cruise stops at the dock for passengers who want to tour the battleship USS *North Carolina* (see below).

The **Cotton Exchange** (© **910/343-9896**), an in-town shopping center, is in the old exchange building with its 2-foot-thick brick walls and hurricane rods. The small shops and restaurants are a delight, and the wrought-iron lanterns and benches add to the setting's charm. It's right on the riverfront, and there's ample parking deck next door.

In Historic Wilmington, the old residential area bounded roughly by Nun, Princess, Front, and 4th streets, the **Burgwin-Wright House,** 224 Market St. (© **910/762-0570**), was constructed in 1771 and used by British General

The North Carolina Coast

Airlie Gardens **8**
Cape Hatteras
  National Seashore **6**
Capt. J. N. Maffitt
  Riverboat **7**
Elizabethan Gardens **5**
Fort Fisher State
  Historic Sight **9**
Fort Raleigh National
  Historic Site **3**
Jockey's Ridge **2**
Pea Island Wildlife
  Refuge **4**
U.S.S. *North Carolina*
  Battleship Memorial **7**
Wright Brothers
  National Memorial **1**

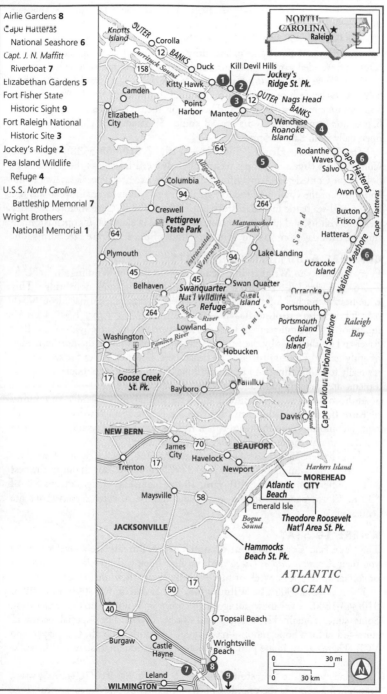

Cornwallis as his headquarters in 1781. You can tour the interior Tuesday through Saturday from 10am to 4pm; $6 adults, $3 children under 13.

Arlie Gardens, on U.S. 76 (© **910/793-7531**), grace the grounds of what was once the plantation home of a wealthy rice planter. These huge lawns, serene lakes, and wooded gardens hold just about every kind of azalea in existence.

The **USS *North Carolina* Battleship Memorial,** Eagle Island (© **910/251-5797;** www.battleshipnc.com), is a memorial to the state's World War II dead. You can tour most of the ship and an exhibit focusing on recollections of the battleship's former crew. Tours are $8 adults, $7 seniors, $4 children 6 to 11; open daily from 8am to 5pm.

Fort Fisher State Historic Site, Kure Beach (© **910/458-5538**), one of the Confederacy's largest and most technically advanced forts, was the last stronghold of the Confederate Army. After withstanding two of the heaviest naval bombardments of the Civil War, the fort finally fell to Union forces in what was the largest land-sea battle in U.S. history until World War II. Costumed tour guides welcome visitors, and living-history events are held in summer. It's open Monday through Saturday from 9am to 5pm and Sunday from 1 to 5pm. Free admission.

BEACHES & OUTDOOR PURSUITS

Everyone flocks to **Wrightsville Beach,** 6 miles east of Wilmington on U.S. 74/76. The island is separated from the mainland by a small drawbridge. This wide beach stretches for a mile, with beige sands set against a backdrop of sea oats. There's also **Carolina Beach State Park,** sprawling across 1,770 acres 10 miles north of Wilmington off U.S. 421. Flanked on one bank by the Cape Fear River and on the other by the Intracoastal Waterway, it lies at the northern edge of aptly named Pleasure Island. The beach here, however, is not for swimming; it's really for sunbathing and beachcombing. Facilities include toilets, a marina, a picnic area, hiking trails, and a family campground.

At the southern tip of Pleasure Island is the small, family-friendly community of **Kure Beach.** The white-sand beaches are generally uncrowded, the restaurants are informal, and the Kure Beach fishing pier is great for anglers. You can wander through the remains of Fort Fisher (see above).

The Belvedere **Plantation Golf & Country Club,** 2368 Country Club Dr., 14 miles from Wilmington in Hampstead (© **910/270-2703**), is one of the best courses, offering a par-71, 6,401-yard, 18-hole course. It charges greens fees of $20 to $35, depending on the season and the use of carts. Reservations are requested.

WHERE TO STAY

The **Cape Fear Coast Convention and Visitors Bureau** (see above) will send you their *Accommodations Guide* and can help hook you up with an apartment or cottage to rent for a week or more if you contact them well in advance.

The renovated 1906 **The Wilmington,** 101 S. 2nd St. (© **800/525-0909** or 910/343-1800; www.thewilmingtonian.com), is Wilmington's premier inn. Some suites contain kitchenettes and washer/dryers. The "special occasion" suite—ideal for a honeymoon—has a fireplace, whirlpool bath, CD player, and VCR. There's an intimate pub, and about a dozen restaurants are within walking distance.

In many ways, the **Graystone Inn,** 100 S. 3rd St. (© **910/763-2000;** www.graystoneinn.com), is the grandest of Wilmington's B&Bs. A neoclassical stone mansion from 1905, it offers 12- to 14-foot ceilings, Victorian period furnishings, and a grand staircase of hand-carved red oak. No children under 12.

Other choices include the moderately priced **Coast Line Inn,** 503 Nutt St. (℅ **910/763-2800;** www.coastline-inn.com), and **The Worth House Bed & Breakfast,** 412 S. 3rd St. (℅ **800/340-8559** or 910/762-8562; www.worth house.com). Nearby Wrightsville Beach has the expensive **Blockade Runner Resort Hotel & Conference Center,** 275 Waynick Blvd. (℅ **800/541-1161** or 910/256-2251; www.blockade-runner.com), a full-service resort with ocean views and a fine restaurant.

WHERE TO DINE

The tiny town of **Calabash,** 35 miles south of Wilmington on U.S. 17, is renowned for its seafood restaurants—about 20 of them, vying with one another to serve the biggest platter of seafood at the lowest price. In one recent year they served 1.5 million people some 668,000 pounds of flounder and 378,000 pounds of shrimp. Recommendations for specific restaurants? You won't need them—you can't miss, no matter which one you choose.

Moderately priced **Caffè Phoenix,** 9 S. Front St. (℅ **910/343-1395**), a block from the water in the center of town, is easily the best bistro in Wilmington. It has a light, open, and airy decor. Lunch choices include homemade soups, fresh salads, pasta, and sandwiches. Dinner becomes more elaborate, including spinach with prosciutto or chicken piccata. Many Wilmington artists dine here, and the place has a sizable gay following.

Elijah's, 2 Ann St., Chandler's Wharf (℅ **910/343-1448**), is installed in a renovated maritime museum offering outdoor dining and a view of the river. Lunches tend to emphasize sandwiches and simple platters that always include a fine version of crab cakes. Dinners are more elaborate, with classic and well-prepared dishes that include chicken piccata, soft-shell crabs, shrimp in a Dijon mustard and garlic sauce, and steaks.

On the Cape Fear River in the historic and restored Craig House, the **Pilot House,** 2 Ann St., Chandler's Wharf (℅ **910/343-0200**), is especially known for its Low Country specialties such as shrimp and grits or crunchy catfish. There are also prime cuts of beef, and it wouldn't be a Carolina restaurant if it didn't serve pork chops.

WILMINGTON AFTER DARK

The Water Street Bar & Restaurant, 5 S. Water St. (℅ **910/343-0042**), hosts folk bands, reggae, and the blues, though it's really a pub. **Mickey's,** 115 S. Front St. (℅ **910/251-1289**), is the top gay bar and dance club.

BEAUFORT

North Carolina's third-oldest town, Beaufort (pronounced *Bo*-fort) dates back to 1713. Along its narrow streets are two 200-year-old houses, and some hundred houses more than a century old. Access is on U.S. 70 just over the Grayden Paul Bridge from Morehead City. From New Bern, take U.S. 70 east. The **Beaufort Historical Association,** 138 Turner St. (℅ **252/728-5225**), is open Monday through Saturday from 9:30am to 5pm.

The **Beaufort Historic Site** in the 100 block of Turner Street includes the 1767 Joseph Bell House, the 1825 Josiah Bell House, the 1796 Carteret County Courthouse, the 1829 county jail, the 1859 apothecary shop and doctor's office, and the 1778 Samuel Leffers House, home of the town's first schoolmaster. Tours are given Monday through Saturday at 10am, 11:30am, 1pm, and 3pm. Adults pay $6 for the tour, and children over age 5 are charged $2.

Divers are attracted to this area because of the many wrecks off the coast. If you want to get into this action, contact **Discovery Diving Co.,** 414 Orange St. (✆ **252/728-2265**), whose staff knows the local waters best.

Our favorite local inns are the **Beaufort Inn,** 101 Ann St. (✆ **252/728-2600;** www.beaufort-inn.com); **Cedars By the Sea,** 305 Front St. (✆ **252/728-7036;** www.cedarsinn.com); the **Delamar Inn,** 217 Turner St. (✆ **800/349-5823** or 252/728-4300; www.bbonline.com/nc/delamarinn); and the **Pecan Tree Inn,** 116 Queen St. (✆ **252/728-6733;** www.pecantree.com).

CAPE HATTERAS NATIONAL SEASHORE

The Cape Hatteras National Seashore stretches 70 miles down the Outer Banks barrier islands. The drive along N.C. 12 (about 4½ hr.) takes you through a wildlife refuge and pleasant villages, past sandy beaches, and on to Buxton and the **Cape Hatteras Lighthouse,** the tallest on the coast and a symbol of North Carolina. The light has stood here since 1870 as a beacon for ships passing through these treacherous waters that have claimed more than 1,500 victims of foul weather, strong rip currents, and shifting shoals. Preservation efforts have attempted to save the lighthouse, which is constantly battered by erosion.

From the little village of **Hatteras,** with its colorful fishing fleet and popular fishing pier, a car ferry crosses to **Ocracoke Island,** where more than 5,000 acres, including 16 miles of beach, is preserved by the National Park Service. **Pea Island Wildlife Refuge** (✆ **252/473-1131**), on Hatteras Island (the northern part, south of Bonner Bridge), attracts birders from all over the country.

The National Seashore is best explored on an all-day trip, or on several half-day trips, from a Nags Head base (see "Nags Head & the Outer Banks," below, for lodging recommendations). Give yourself plenty of time for swimming, fishing, or just walking along the sand.

All along N.C. 12, you'll see places to pull off and park to reach the beaches, which are hidden from view by huge protective sand dunes. *Note: Don't* try to park anywhere else—the sand is very soft and it's easy to get stuck. Keep in mind that tides and currents along the Outer Banks are *very* strong, and ocean swimming can be dangerous at times.

NAGS HEAD & THE OUTER BANKS

Nags Head has been one of North Carolina's most popular beach resorts for more than a century. The town itself is a collection of nondescript beach houses and motels, but it has one of the finest beaches in the state. Toilets, showers, bathhouses, and picnic shelters line some 70 miles of beaches here. Ferocious tides, strong currents, and fickle, constantly changing winds alter the beach scene from day to day on the Outer Banks. These very conditions also make ocean swimming hazardous at certain periods. If you're with children, stick to the beaches along the northern banks that have lifeguard protection; they include Kitty Hawk, Kill Devil Hills, and Nags Head, all lying along Beach Road paralleling N.C. 12. Signs direct you to the parking lots.

From Virginia and points north, you can reach Nags Head via U.S. 158; from Raleigh, via U.S. 64; from Wilmington, via the Cedar Island ferry. N.C. 12 runs the length of the Outer Banks, from Ocracoke to Duck. The nearest airport is 80 miles northwest in Norfolk, Virginia.

Contact the **Outer Banks Visitors Bureau,** in Manteo (✆ **800/446-6262** or 252/441-8144; www.outerbanks.org), for information about accommodations

Learning to Fly

At Milepost 8 on U.S. 158 in Kill Devil Hills, you can visit the **Wright Brothers National Memorial** ((C) **252/441-7430**) for $3 per person or $5 a car; seniors and children 15 and under are admitted free. Both the hangar and Orville's and Wilbur's living quarters have been restored, and the visitor center holds a replica of that first airplane, as well as exhibits that tell the story of the two brothers who came here on vacation from their Dayton, Ohio, bicycle business to turn their dream into reality. The memorial is open daily from 9am to 6pm (to 5pm in winter). A park ranger gives a tour every hour from 10am to 4pm.

and outdoor activities. It's open Monday through Friday from 8am to 6pm, Saturday from 9am to 5pm, and Sunday from 10am to 4pm.

Jockey's Ridge, north of Nags Head, is the highest sand dune on the East Coast. Its smooth, sandy, 138-foot-high slopes are part of a state park. Also north of Nags Head at **Kill Devil Hills,** the Wright brothers made that historic first air flight back in 1903.

From Whalebone Junction, U.S. 64/264 leads to Roanoke Island and the village of Manteo. Four miles west, you'll reach **Fort Raleigh National Historic Site,** where the old fort has been excavated and reconstructed just as it stood in 1585. The **visitor center** ((C) **252/473-5772)** is a first stop, with a museum and an audiovisual program to acquaint visitors with the park's story. Most people visit Roanoke Island to see a performance of Paul Green's moving drama, *The Lost Colony,* presented from mid-June to late August, Sunday through Friday at 8:30pm. It's the country's oldest outdoor drama, running since 1937. All seats are reserved (contact the **Waterside Theater** at (C) **800/488-5012** or 252/473-3414 to charge tickets). The nearby **Elizabethan Gardens,** as well as the Tudor-style auxiliary buildings, remind us that this was the first connection between Elizabethan England and what was to become the United States of America. The gardens charge an admission price of $5 adults, $4.50 seniors, and $1 for children ages 6 to 18; free for under that.

One of the top local golf courses is **Nags Head Golf Links,** 5615 S. Seachase Dr., Nags Head ((C) **252/441-8073;** www.nagsheadgolflinks.com), which boasts an 18-hole, 6,130-yard, par-71 course. Greens fees range from $45 to $105. Reservations are required.

Kitty Hawk Water Sports Center, Bypass Highway, Milepost 16, Nags Head ((C) **252/441-2756**), offers watersports equipment, including windsurfers and kayaks.

Our favorite accommodations in the area include the **Sanderling Inn Resort and Spa,** 1461 Duck Rd., Duck ((C) **800/701-4111** or 252/261-4111; www.thesanderling.com), the premier inn of the Outer Banks, bordering the 3,400-acre Pine Island National Audubon Sanctuary, where wild horses run free. Edenton's top choice is **The Lords Proprietors',** 300 N. Broad St. ((C) **252/482-3641;** www.edentoninn.com). Manteo has the lovely **Tranquil House Inn,** Queen Elizabeth St. ((C) **800/458-7069** or 252/473-1404; www.tranquilinn.com). In Nags Head, we suggest the **First Colony,** 6720 S. Virginia Dare Trail ((C) **800/368-9390** or 252/441-2342; www.firstcolonyinn.com); or the **Nags Head Inn,** 4701 S. Virginia Dare Trail ((C) **800/327-8881** or 252/441-0454; www.nagsheadinn.com).

7 Pinehurst: Where Golf Is King

Midland Road (N.C. 2), a highway divided by a stately 6-mile row of pine trees and bordered by lavish homes and gardens, sets the tone for this golf mecca. About a third of the area's more than 35 golf courses are accessible via this road. (Also on Midland Rd. you'll pass a rambling white building, Midland Crafters, a virtual survey of American crafts.) In addition to golf, this area offers some of America's best tennis facilities and programs, and it's also known for its equestrian competitions. Most of these events are free to spectators. *Horse Days,* a monthly publication about events, with calendar listings, is available locally at information offices.

U.S. 1 runs north and south through Southern Pines; N.C. 211 runs east and west; U.S. 15/501 reaches Pinehurst from the north; there's direct area access to I-95, I-85, and I-40. Raleigh/Durham is the nearest commercial airport. We strongly recommend that you call ahead to the **Pinehurst Area Convention and Visitors Bureau,** P.O. Box 2270, Southern Pines, NC 28388 (© **800/346-5362** or 910/692-3330; www.homeofgolf.com).

The town of Pinehurst has retained its New England village air, with a village green and shaded residential streets. Moderate temperatures mean color through all seasons—camellias, azaleas, wisteria, and dogwoods.

With its more than 35 superb championship golf courses, some of which are among the highest rated in the world, Pinehurst represents golf's grandest era. Legends were born and nurtured here, and some of the finest golf architects of the 20th century designed courses in the area, including Donald Ross, Ellis Maples, Robert Trent Jones, Jack Nicklaus, and Rees Jones. The 1999 U.S. Open was held at the famed Pinehurst No. 2 Course.

There are too many courses here to list them all, but our favorites are **The Club at Longleaf** (© **800/889-5323** or 910/692-6100); the **Legacy Golf Links,** U.S. 15/501 South, Aberdeen (© **800/344-8825** or 910/944-8825), the only public course to receive *Golf Digest's* four-star rating; the **Pine Needles Resort,** Southern Pines (© **910/692-7111**), a Donald Ross masterpiece built in 1927; and the **Pinehurst Hotel & Country Club,** Carolina Vista (© **800/ITS-GOLF** or 910/295-6811), a resort with seven signature courses.

Tennis buffs will find nearly 100 public courts in the area (© **910/947-2504** for locations, hours, and fees), but most resorts have their own courts.

About an hour's drive to the northwest on U.S. 220 is the little town of **Seagrove,** which has been turning out pottery for more than 200 years. Many of the potters work in or behind their homes, with only a small sign outside to identify their trade; just stop and ask—everybody does, so don't be shy. While you're there, inquire about **Jugtown,** a group of rustic, log-hewn buildings in a grove of pines where potters demonstrate their art Monday through Saturday. **Friends of the North Carolina Pottery Center** (© **336/873-7887**) is at 250 East Ave., just off U.S. 220 and the intersection of N.C. 705 in Seagrove.

WHERE TO STAY

The **Pinehurst Hotel and Country Club,** Carolina Vista (© **800/487-4653** or 910/295-6811; www.Pinehurst.com), is one of the premier golf and tennis resorts in America. Set on 10,000 acres of landscaped grounds, it's a white, four-story clapboard landmark, with porches lined with comfortable rocking chairs. Here the art of gracious living is still practiced, and service is superb. The resort's Carolina Dining Room is the finest in the area. The major attractions, of course, are the seven 18-hole golf courses, especially the world-famous No. 2, and the 26 tennis courts. Guests also enjoy trap and skeet fields, croquet and bowling lawns, bicycles, a huge pool and deck area, and 200 acres of fishing, boating, and swimming at Lake Pinehurst.

Other hotels offer luxury and graciousness at more moderate prices. We like the intimate **Magnolia Inn,** 65 Magnolia Rd. (© **800/526-5562** or 910/295-6900; www.themagnoliainn.com), and the **Pine Crest Inn,** Dogwood Road (© **910/295-6121;** www.pinecrestinnpinehurst.com). In nearby Southern Pines, there's the lovely, old-fashioned, and affordable **Mid Pines Golf Club,** 1010 Midland Rd., Southern Pines (© **800/323-2114** or 910/692-2114; www.golfnc.com/midpines), as well as chain properties that include the **Hampton Inn,** 1675 U.S. 1 N (© **910/692-9266**), and the **Holiday Inn,** U.S. 1 at Morganton Road (© **800/HOLIDAY** or 910/692-8585).

If there's a hotel in the area that *doesn't* arrange golf times for its guests, we couldn't find it.

8 Charlotte

In the past decade or so, Charlotte has been sprouting skyscrapers. Suburban sprawl continues to grow, with landscaped housing developments and enormous strip malls springing up in every direction. This is the New South, built squarely on the foundation of the Old South. The city is booming, and business is just fine, thank you very much. The banking, insurance, and transportation industries keep feeding the economy. There's not much here for the casual tourist, but business travelers are certainly coming to town in droves.

ESSENTIALS

GETTING THERE   By Plane   Charlotte–Douglas International Airport is served by most major U.S. carriers (US Airways has the lion's share of flights), plus British Airways and Air Canada.

By Train   Amtrak (© **800/USA-RAIL;** www.amtrak.com) provides daily service from Atlanta (trip time: 5½ hr.) and Washington, D.C. (8 hr.) to its station at 1914 N. Tryon St.

By Car   Major routes into Charlotte are I-85 from the northeast (Greensboro, NC) and southwest (Atlanta), and I-77 from the north (Charleston, WV) and south (Columbia, SC).

VISITOR INFORMATION   Contact the **Charlotte Convention & Visitors Bureau,** 122 E. Stonewall St., Charlotte, NC 28202 (© **800/231-4636** or 704/334-2282; www.charlottecvb.org), open Monday through Friday from 8:30am to 5pm. For walk-in visits to pick up brochures once you're here, stop by **Info Charlotte,** at the same location.

SPECIAL EVENTS   In late April, **Springfest** brings the streets alive with music and other entertainment, and street vendors dispense a wide variety of foods. In late May, the **Coca-Cola 600** (© **704/455-3200**) packs 'em in at the Charlotte Motor Speedway. For 6 full days in mid-September, the **Festival in the Park** in Freedom Park celebrates regional arts and crafts.

WHAT TO SEE & DO

The stately **Mint Museum of Art,** 2730 Randolph Rd. (© **704/337-2000;** www.mintmuseum.org), displays a fine survey of European and American art, as well as the internationally recognized Delhom Collection of porcelain and pottery. New galleries exhibit studio glass and pottery from North Carolina studios. **Discovery Place,** 301 N. Tryon St. (© **800/935-0553** or 704/372-6261; www.discoveryplace.org), is one of the top hands-on science and technology museums in the region.

The **Wing Haven Gardens & Bird Sanctuary,** 248 Ridgewood Ave. (© **704/331-0664**), is a 3-acre enclosed area in the heart of a residential neighborhood. Some 142 winged species have been sighted in the walled garden. The gardens are at their most splendid in the spring, when birds are returning from their winter migration.

Charlotte is ringed by nature preserves and parks, including the nearly 1,000-acre **McDowell Park and Nature Preserve,** about 12 miles south of the center on N.C. 49, 15222 York Rd. (© **704/588-5224**). Even bigger is **Latta Plantation Nature Preserve,** 5226 Sample Rd., Huntersville (© **704/875-1391**), 12 miles northeast of the center. It's a favorite resting place for waterfowl. There are also stables where you can rent horses and ride along some 7 miles of trail. A nature center and picnic tables are available. Fishing is permitted, but there is no swimming.

WHERE TO STAY & DINE

The top business hotels include the **Adam's Mark Hotel,** 555 S. McDowell St. (© **800/444-2326** or 704/372-4100; www.adamsmark.com), only 4 blocks from the convention center; the **Hyatt Charlotte,** 5501 Carnegie Blvd. (opposite South Park Mall; © **800/233-1234** or 704/554-1234); the luxurious **Park Hotel,** 2200 Rexford Rd. (© **800/334-0331** or 704/364-8220; www.thepark hotel.com); and the more moderately priced **Residence Inn by Marriott,** 8503 N. Tryon Rd. (© **800/331-3131** or 704/547-1122).

The **Coffee Cup,** 914 S. Clarkson St. (© **704/375-8855**), is a roadside place where—as they say in the South—"all God's children got chicken grease on their fingers." The more formal **La Bibliothèque,** in the Morrison Office Building, 1901 Roxborough Rd. (© **704/365-5000**), serves the city's finest French cuisine. **Mangione's Italian Ristorante,** 1524 East Blvd. (© **704/334-4417**), prepares the city's best Italian cuisine.

CHARLOTTE AFTER DARK

The **Charlotte Symphony Orchestra** (© **704/972-2003;** www.charlotte symphony.org) plays from September to April; **Opera Carolina** (© **704/332-7177;** www.operacarolina.org) performs from September to April; and the **Charlotte Pops** (© **704/972-2003**) gives outdoor concerts in Freedom Park on Sunday evenings in the summer. Classic plays are often performed by **Theatre Charlotte,** 501 Queens Rd. (© **704/376-3777;** www.theatre charlotte.org).

Swing 1000, 1000 Central Ave. (© **704/334-4443**), is a nightclub/restaurant that's brought the neo-swing movement to town. The house band plays '30s and '40s big band, and the Continental cuisine is better than you'd expect. The same owners have another hot spot at 911 E. Morehead (© **704/347-4447**) called **The Big Chill** featuring live R&B several nights a week. The venerable **Double Door Inn,** 218 E. Independence Blvd. (© **704/376-1446**), is a legendary place to hear the blues. The popular lesbian and gay nightclub **Scorpio,** 2301 Freedom Dr. (© **704/373-9124**), has been going strong for years.

9 The Blue Ridge Parkway

One of America's most spectacular drives, the Blue Ridge Parkway takes up where Virginia's Skyline Drive leaves off, linking the southern end of Shenandoah National Park in Virginia with the eastern entrance of the Great Smoky Mountains National Park in North Carolina. It winds and twists along the mountain crests for 469 miles, offering panoramic views along the way. October brings incredible fall foliage that paints the valleys and slopes in vivid hues of scarlet, orange, and gold (expect big crowds and lots of traffic, though). At many overlooks you'll see a rifle-and-powderhorn symbol and the word TRAIL, which means there are marked walking trails through the woods.

There are frequent exits to nearby towns, plus 11 visitor centers, nine campgrounds (open May–Oct only; no reservations) with drinking water and comfort stations (but no shower or utility hookups), restaurants, and gas stations. Before you set out, get maps and detailed information from the Superintendent, Blue Ridge Parkway, 51 Ranger Dr., Asheville, NC 28805 (© 828/298-0358).

Don't plan to hurry down the Blue Ridge: If you don't have time to amble and drink in the beauty, you'll only be frustrated. If you want to drive the entire length of the parkway, allow at least 2 or 3 days. On the first day, drive the Virginia half, then stop for the night at Boone, North Carolina, not far from the state border. The final two legs of the trip (from Boone to Asheville and from there to Fontana Village) can easily be accomplished in another day's drive.

You can veer off the parkway to see a number of attractions, including **Linville Falls,** with parking at Milepost 316 on the parkway. The falls plunge into the 2,000-foot-deep Linville Gorge. A 1-mile round-trip hike leads to the upper falls; other trails lead to more views. Another stop, **Linville Caverns,** lies at Milepost 382 on the parkway, just off U.S. 221 between Linville and Marion (© 828/756-4171). The only caverns in North Carolina, these chilly tunnels go 2,000 feet underground.

TOWNS JUST OFF THE PARKWAY

BOONE   Boone has been called "the coolest spot in the South," with average temperatures around 68°F (20°C) in summer. It's a great place for golf, swimming, fishing, skiing, mountain biking, canoeing, and white-water rafting. It lies an hour from I-77, I-81, and I-40, and is accessible by three major highways, including U.S. 321, U.S. 421, and U.S. 221. N.C. 105 provides access from U.S. 221. The **Boone Area Convention and Visitors Bureau,** 208 Howard St., Boone, NC 28607 (© 800/852-9506 or 828/264-2225), is open Monday through Friday from 9am to 5pm.

Kermit Hunter's *Horn in the West* is presented in the Daniel Boone Theatre, 591 Horn in the West Dr. (© 828/264-2120), every night except Monday from late June to mid-August. It tells a vivid story of pioneer efforts to win freedom during the American Revolution. (Reserve tickets in advance.) Next door to the theater are the **Daniel Boone Native Gardens** (© 828/264-6390) and the **Hickory Ridge Homestead Museum** (© 828/264-2120), an 18th-century living-history museum in a re-created log cabin.

The **Tweetsie Railroad Theme Park,** Blowing Rock Road, halfway between Boone and Blowing Rock (© 800/526-5740 or 828/264-9061), is hokey but fun for kids.

The **Boone Golf Club,** U.S. 321/221 South, Blowing Rock Road (© **828/ 264-8760**), is the standard all High Country public courses are measured against. Greens fees are $22 to $45.

Wahoos, on U.S. 321 between Boone and the Tweetsie Railroad Theme Park (© **800/444-RAFT** or 828/262-5774), is the best all-around outfitter to get you out there white-water rafting, tubing, or fishing.

For overnight stays, we recommend the **Lovill House Inn,** 404 Old Bristol Rd. (© **800/849-9466** or 828/264-4204; www.lovillhouseinn.com). Families might prefer the **Holiday Inn Express,** 1943 Blowing Rock Rd. (© **800/ HOLIDAY** or 828/264-2451), the best motel in the area.

BANNER ELK & GRANDFATHER MOUNTAIN   The **Avery/Banner Elk Chamber of Commerce,** 4539 Tynecastle Hwy., no. 2 in the shops of Tynecastle (© **800/972-2183** or 828/898-5605; www.bannerelk.com), is open Monday through Friday from 9am to 5pm.

Kilt-clad revelers gather here early in July for the annual **Highland Games and Gathering of the Clans.** Bagpipe music, dancing, wrestling, and tossing the caber make this a spectacle not to miss.

Grandfather Mountain, on U.S. 221 near Linville (© **828/733-4337**), a mile off the Blue Ridge Parkway, is the highest peak in the Blue Ridge. You can see as far as 100 miles from the **Mile High Swinging Bridge,** and the **Environmental Habitat** is home to Mildred the Bear and her black bear friends. Grandfather Mountain is open daily except Thanksgiving and Christmas; admission is $12 adults, $6 children 4 to 12.

There's an excellent golf course at the **Hawksnest Golf & Ski Resort,** 2853 Skyland Dr., off N.C. 105, Seven Devils (© **800/822-4295** or 828/963-6561; www.hawksnest-resort.com); greens fees are $28 to $43, including cart.

Our favorite lodging in the area is the intimate **Banner Elk Inn Bed and Breakfast,** N.C. 407, Main Street East (© **828/898-6223**). Another recommended option is **Archer's Mountain Inn,** 2489 Beech Mountain Pkwy., Beech Mountain (© **888/827-6155** or 828/898-9004; www.archersinn.com), which has an excellent restaurant, the Jackalope's View.

BLOWING ROCK   Blowing Rock is filled with little B&Bs, inns, and galleries. To get there from Boone, take U.S. 321 South directly into Blowing Rock. The **Blowing Rock Chamber of Commerce,** 132 Park Ave. (© **800/295-7851** or 828/295-7851; www.blowingrock.com), is open Monday through Saturday from 9am to 5pm.

The area's biggest attraction is **Blowing Rock** (© **828/295-7111**), on U.S. 321, 2 miles south of town, rising 4,000 feet above John's River Gorge. Its strong updraft returns any light object (such as a handkerchief) thrown into the void. The observation tower, gazebos, and gardens offer panoramic views. Admission is $6 adults, $1 children 6 to 11, free for kids under 6.

Shoppers can check **Expressions Craft Guild & Gallery,** Main Street (© **828/295-7839**), a cooperative gallery featuring contemporary local crafts. The **Parkway Craft Center,** at Milepost 294 on the Bridge Ride Parkway in the Moses Cone Manor just off Route 221 (© **828/295-7938**), offers the finest quality mountain crafts.

For luxurious lodgings in a panoramic setting, there's the **Hound Ears Lodge,** off N.C. 105 South near Boone (© **828/963-4321;** www.houndears. com). We also like the time-worn charm of **Crippen's Country Inn,** 239 Sunset Dr. (© **828/295-3487**), a National Historic Landmark with a good restaurant.

The Blue Ridge Parkway

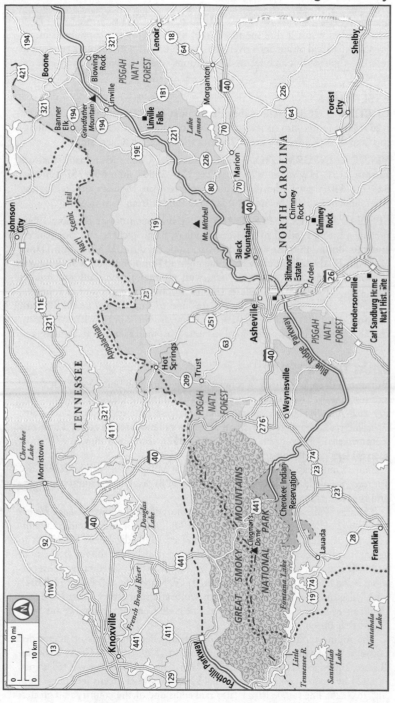

10 Asheville

Asheville, once just a tiny mountain trading village at the confluence of the French Broad and Swannanoa rivers, has grown up and turned into a year-round resort, complete with architectural gems from several eras and a lively cultural scene.

ESSENTIALS

GETTING THERE The **Asheville Airport** (© 828/687-9446) is just off I-26. Major routes into Asheville are I-40 from the east (Raleigh and Wilmington) and west (Knoxville), and I-26 from the southeast (Charleston).

VISITOR INFORMATION The **Asheville Convention and Visitors Bureau,** 151 Haywood St., Asheville, NC 28802 (© 800/257-1300 or 828/258-6101; www.ashevillechamber.org), is open Monday through Friday from 8:30am to 5:30pm and Saturday and Sunday from 9am to 5pm.

SPECIAL EVENTS & FESTIVALS Special happenings at Biltmore Estate include a spring **Festival of Flowers.** Fiddlers, banjo pickers, and clog dancers entertain during the first weekend of August at the **Annual Mountain Dance and Folk Festival.** Most every Saturday night in summer, there's a **Shindig-on-the-Green** at the City Country Plaza, with mountain musicians and dancers having an old-fashioned wingding. In Brevard, 27 miles southwest of Asheville, a major music festival is held from late June to mid-August at the **Brevard Music Center** (© 828/884-2019; www.brevardmusic.org), with symphony, chamber music, band, and choral concerts, as well as musical comedy and opera.

WHAT TO SEE & DO

Biltmore Village is a cluster of some 24 cottages housing boutiques, craft shops, and restaurants. The best of them is the **New Morning Gallery,** 7 Boston Way (© 828/274-2831), one of the South's largest galleries of arts and crafts. Asheville is also home to more than 50 other galleries around town. **The Kress Emporium,** 19 Patton Ave. (© 828/281-2252), serves as a showcase for more than 80 local artists and craftspeople.

Some 5 miles east of downtown Asheville, at Milepost 382 on the Blue Ridge Parkway, the **Folk Art Center** (© 828/298-7928) displays the finest handcrafts and runs a terrific crafts shop.

Thomas Wolfe, a native of Asheville, immortalized the town in *Look Homeward, Angel.* His mother's boardinghouse at 48 Spruce St. is maintained as a literary shrine. Unfortunately, in the summer of 1998, the house fell victim to arson; it will be closed until at least mid-2003. But before the fire, the city of Asheville had opened a vast exhibit on Wolfe's life, which saved many of his personal belongings in the **Visitors Center,** 52 N. Market St. (© 828/253-8304), which also runs a video biography. Both Wolfe and short-story writer **O. Henry** (William Sydney Porter) are buried in Riverside Cemetery (entrance on Birch St. off Pearson Dr.).

The rolling terrain around Asheville offers golfers hundreds of uncrowded fairways. Our favorite course, which opened in 1899, is at the **Grove Park Inn Resort,** 290 Macon Ave. (© 828/252-2711). The par-70 course was redesigned in 1924 by master golf architect Donald Ross. Seasonal greens fees range from $85 to $125. The Grove Park is also ranked as one of the country's 50 greatest tennis resorts by *Tennis* magazine. Courts can be booked by the hour.

Biltmore Estate This French Renaissance château, built by George W. Vanderbilt, has 250 rooms, and every inch of them is extraordinary. It's the largest private residence in the country, a National Historic Landmark now owned by Vanderbilt's grandson. The elder Vanderbilt journeyed through Europe and Asia purchasing paintings, porcelains, bronzes, carpets, and antiques, along with artwork by Renoir, Sargent, and Whistler, and furniture by Chippendale and Sheraton. Vanderbilt also hired Frederick Law Olmsted to create one of the most lavish formal gardens you'll ever see, ablaze with more than 200 varieties of azaleas. 1 N. Pack Sq., on U.S. 25, 2 blocks north of I-40. ℂ 800/543-2961 or 828/274-6333. www. biltmore.com. House and gardens $34 adults, $26 children 10–15. Daily 9am–6pm.

WHERE TO STAY

In the heart of downtown, the elegant all-suite **Haywood Park Hotel**, 1 Battery Park Ave. (ℂ **800/228-2522** or 828/252-2522; www.haywoodpark.com), is tops. Outstanding historic B&B choices include **Beaufort House Victorian Bed & Breakfast**, 61 N. Liberty St. (ℂ **800/261-2221** or 828/254-8334; www.beauforthouse.com); **The Lion and the Rose Bed & Breakfast**, 276 Montford Ave. (ℂ **800/546-6988** or 828/255-7673; www.lion-rose.com); and **The Old Reynolds Mansion Bed & Breakfast**, 100 Reynolds Heights (ℂ **828/254-0496**; www.oldreynoldsmansion.com). There's also the **Great Smokies Holiday Inn Sunspree Resort**, 1 Holiday Inn Dr. (ℂ **800/HOLIDAY** or 828/254-3211), lying directly off I-240, 3 miles from the center.

Cedar Crest Inn This Queen Anne mansion is one of the largest and most opulent residences surviving Asheville's 1890s boom. The mansion has a captain's walk, projecting turrets, and expansive verandas; inside it's a fantasy of leaded glass, ornately carved fireplaces, antiques, and a massive oak staircase. Rooms are romantic and whimsical, some sporting canopy beds. A few bathrooms have either claw-foot or whirlpool tubs. 674 Biltmore Ave., Asheville, NC 28803. ℂ 800/252-0310 or 828/252-1389. Fax 828/253-7667. www.cedarcrestvictorianinn.com. 12 units. $170–$200 double; $175–$240 suite. Rates include breakfast. AE, DISC, MC, V. Free parking. No children under 12 allowed.

The Greystone Inn Henry Ford and John D. Rockefeller once whiled away their summers here. Set on a wooded peninsula along the lake, this Swiss Revival mansion is a National Historic Landmark. For dedicated do-nothings, there are wicker rocking chairs on the glassed-in sun porch overlooking the lake. The midsize rooms are beautifully maintained; some offer Jacuzzis and working fireplaces. Complimentary midafternoon tea is served with cakes. Greystone Lane, Lake Toxaway, NC 28747. ℂ 800/824-5766 or 828/966-4700. Fax 828/862-5689. www.greystoneinn. com. 33 units. Nov–Apr Sun–Thurs $265 double, $435 suite; Fri–Sat $350 double, $550 suite. May–Oct $360 double, $595 suite. Children under 6 pay an additional $35, children 6–10 $70, and 10 years or older $95 per night. Rates include breakfast, dinner, champagne, afternoon tea, and sports activities except golf. MC, V. Free parking. **Amenities:** Restaurant; outdoor pool; health spa; 18-hole golf course; 6 tennis courts.

Grove Park Inn Resort With panoramic views and old-world charm, this resort, built in 1913, is one of the oldest and most famous in the South, and our favorite choice in all of western North Carolina. A National Historic Landmark, it's hosted F. Scott Fitzgerald, Thomas Edison, Henry Ford, and a couple of presidents. The large, recently refurbished guest rooms have microwaves, refrigerators, and CD players. Horizons Restaurant is the finest in the area; the Blue Ridge Dining Room has a legendary outdoor dining veranda. 290 Macon Ave.,

Asheville, NC 28804. ✆ 800/438-5800 or 828/252-2711. Fax 828/253-7053. www.groveparkinn. com. 510 units. High season $209–$429 double; $599 suite. Off season $139–$209 double; $379 suite. AE, DC, DISC, MC, V. Parking $12. **Amenities:** Restaurants (3); pools (1 indoor, 1 outdoor); spa; fitness center; 18-hole golf course; 6 tennis courts.

Richmond Hill Inn This inn is Asheville's premier remaining example of Queen Anne–style architecture. The interior is graced with family heirloom portraits and original oak paneling. Rooms are charming, with balconies, canopied beds, refrigerators, fireplaces, and bathrooms containing showers and claw-foot tubs. Nine cottages, containing rooms and suites, all with small porches and rockers, are across the way. The inn has an exceptional restaurant, Gabrielle, featuring American contemporary cuisine. 87 Richmond Hill Dr., Asheville, NC 28806. ✆ 828/252-7313. Fax 828/252-8726. www.richmondhillinn.com. 36 units. $155–$295 double; $325–$385 suite. Children under 18 stay free in parents' room. Rates include full breakfast. AE, MC, V. Free parking. **Amenities:** Restaurant; fitness center.

WHERE TO DINE

The **Richmond Hill Inn** and the **Grove Park Inn Resort** have outstanding restaurants; see above.

Charlotte St. Grill AMERICAN   Downstairs is an authentic-looking English pub, and upstairs is a restaurant with a Victorian decor offering more intimate dining. The pub keeps the longest hours, and is noted for serving one of the best-value lunches in Asheville, including freshly made pastas and house salads that are meals in themselves. The food is well prepared and based on fresh ingredients. 157 Charlotte St. ✆ 828/253-5348. Reservations recommended. Main courses $6–$14 lunch, $10–$21 dinner; pub lunches $7. Restaurant Mon–Fri 11:30am–2pm and 5–9pm, Sat 5–10pm; pub daily 11:30am–2am.

The Market Place CONTINENTAL   This upscale casual restaurant with candlelit tables offers impeccable service. The chef uses extra-fresh ingredients, and all herbs and vegetables are grown locally. Many dishes are nouvelle in style and preparation, and the staff is knowledgeable about the extensive wine list. 20 Wall St. ✆ 828/252-4162. Reservations recommended. Main courses $12–$27. AE, DC, MC, V. Mon–Sat 5:30–9:30pm.

11 Great Smoky Mountains National Park

The Great Smoky Mountains are the oldest mountains in the world, composed of peaks that range in elevation from 840 to 6,642 feet. The oval-shaped national park, bisected by the North Carolina–Tennessee border, encompasses more than 520,000 acres of forests, streams, rivers, waterfalls, and hiking trails. More than 200 kinds of birds and 70 species of mammals live in the park, including the lumbering black bear, the white-tailed deer, groundhogs, wild turkeys, and bobcats. Abundant wildflowers offer a kaleidoscope of colors in spring and early summer and a blanket of lush greenery in later summer.

See also section 12 of this chapter, "Eastern Tennessee," below, for information on Gatlinburg, a convenient gateway town on the western side of the park.

CHEROKEE: THE NORTH CAROLINA GATEWAY TO THE PARK

From the southern end of the Blue Ridge Parkway and points south, U.S. 441 leads to Cherokee; U.S. 19 runs east and west through the town. Asheville is 48 miles southwest. The **Cherokee Visitor Center,** U.S. 19 (✆ 800/438-1601 or 828/497-9195), is open daily from 8am to 5pm.

Oconaluftee Indian Village, U.S. 441 North (© **828/497-2111**), is a living museum of the mid-1750s Cherokee people. You'll see men and women shaping clay into pottery, chipping arrowheads, and firing blowguns. Lectures on all facets of Cherokee life are held at the Ceremonial Grounds and at the Council House. Admission is $12 adults, $5 children; it's open from mid-May to October daily from 9am to 5:30pm.

Unto These Hills, the most popular outdoor drama in America, is staged in Cherokee each summer, relating the story of the Cherokees from 1540 until the "Trail of Tears" exodus to Oklahoma in 1838, when thousands died. As you watch the first encounter with Hernando de Soto, you'll hear voices echoing off the surrounding mountainside, the very mountainside that became a hiding place for Cherokee determined to remain in their homeland instead of joining the long march to exile in Oklahoma. Performances are at the 2,800-seat **Mountainside Theater,** off U.S. 441 (© **828/497-2111**). Opening night is around June 15, and the curtain goes down for the last time at August's end. Tickets cost $16 for reserved seating or $14 for general admission; children are charged $6. No shows on Sunday.

The major outdoor pursuit on the reservation is fishing, with 30 miles of streams stocked with 400,000 trout annually. A tribal permit is required.

Cherokee has an abundance of motels, including the **Holiday Inn–Cherokee,** U.S. 19 South (© **800/HOLIDAY** or 828/497-9181); the **Hampton Inn,** U.S. 19 South (© **800/HAMPTON** or 828/497-3115); the **Newfound Lodge,** 34 U.S. 441, North Cherokee (© **828/497-2746**); and the **Riverside Motel,** U.S. 441 South at Old Route 441 (© **828/497-9311**).

PARK ESSENTIALS

ACCESS POINTS & ORIENTATION   Take I-40 from Asheville to U.S. 19, then U.S. 441 to the park's southern entrance near Cherokee, a distance of 50 miles west.

Although there are several side roads into the park, the best routes are through one of the three main entrances, two of which are on Newfound Gap Road, U.S. 441, a 33-mile road that stretches north-south through the park. The southern entrance is near Cherokee, North Carolina; the northern entrance is miles away near Gatlinburg, Tennessee (see "Eastern Tennessee," below). The third main entrance is on the western side of the park at Townsend, Tennessee. Other access points are from the campgrounds at the edge of the park. The park is open year-round, and admission is free.

VISITOR CENTERS   At each of the three main entrances are visitor centers for the park. Each center offers information on road, weather, camping, and backcountry conditions. You'll also find books, maps, and first-aid information.

The **Sugarlands Visitor Center and Park Headquarters** (© **865/436-1291** for park headquarters and all three visitor centers) is at the northern entrance, near Gatlinburg, Tennessee. The smaller **Oconaluftee Visitor Center** is at the southern entrance. Both of these offer useful exhibits to help you understand what you're seeing.

The **Cades Cove Visitor Center,** at the western end of the park, on Parson Branch Road about 12 miles southwest of Townsend, Tennessee, is set among a cluster of historic 19th-century farms and buildings (see "Seeing the Park's Highlights," below).

The visitor centers are open daily from April to October.

WHEN TO GO From late March to June, spring brings great bursts of color from the wildflowers, with mild daytime temperatures and cool evenings. As summer begins, the lush greenery comes into its full splendor and the weather gets warm and humid. Although the higher elevations offer milder temperatures, ranging from the low 50s to the mid-60s, the lower ones can bring on days that are in the 90s. Around the beginning of October, elevations above a mile have seen the end of fall, but lower elevations are just coming into their own with brilliant reds, yellows, oranges, purples, and browns. The best time to experience this change is from mid- to late October.

Throughout the year, weather can change rapidly. During the course of a day, you can witness several thunderstorms with breaks of clear, bright skies while temperatures change from cool and comfortable to hot and humid. The wettest months are generally March and July.

The height of the tourist season lasts from late May to late August. As autumn approaches, the park is swamped on weekends, but the crowds are much more manageable during weekdays. Early morning hours are always a good bet to avoid the hordes.

SEEING THE PARK'S HIGHLIGHTS

If you have only 2 days to see the park, start early in the morning to avoid the crowds. When crossing the park on the Newfound Gap Road (U.S. 441), you should allow, at the very least, 1 hour. The speed limit does not rise above 45 miles per hour anywhere in the park. When ascending the mountain slopes, you can rarely go over 25 to 30 miles per hour because of the winding roads. Pack a lunch—there are no restaurants in the park, but picnic sites abound.

Your best strategy is to visit the sights along the Newfound Gap Road. Begin at the Oconaluftee Visitor Center, where you can pick up park information and get a weather report. Today the Oconaluftee Mountain Farm Museum, a replica of a pioneer farmstead, operates here within a collection of original log buildings. Park staff, dressed in period costumes, make it a living-history farm from April to October. About half a mile north on the Newfound Gap Road is the Mingus Mill, constructed in 1886 and still grinding wheat and corn from mid-April to October.

As you travel north, you'll come to a turnoff for **Clingmans Dome,** the highest peak in the park, soaring 6,642 feet. Once you turn onto this road, you travel 7 miles southwest to a parking lot where you can walk a steep half-mile to a viewing platform featuring one of the park's best views. Next comes **Newfound Gap,** which, at 5,048 feet, is the center of the park. If the sky is clear, you can see for miles around; on other days you find yourself literally in the clouds.

The drive across the park leads you to the Sugarlands Visitor Center, where you can stroll through the nature exhibit, view a slide show, or browse through the gift shop. At this point, you can either head into Gatlinburg for the night or go west about 5 miles on Little River Road to Elkmont Campground. It's best to make reservations (accepted only mid-May to Oct).

On Day 2, continue your journey west on Little River Road to **Cades Cove,** where you'll find more pioneer structures than at any other location in the park. Plan to spend half a day exploring the many attractions along the 11-mile Cades Cove Loop. Stop at the visitor center for a pamphlet containing a key for the numbered sights. Founded in 1818, the cove was a thriving, self-supporting community for more than 100 years. Original homesites, smokehouses, and barns still stand today, giving visitors a glimpse into the lives of the original settlers. You'll also find cemeteries with such epitaphs as one from the Civil War that reads BAS SHAW—KILLED BY REBELS. Cades Cove offers several nature trails.

Once you've completed the Cades Cove Loop, head toward the Sugarlands Visitor Center to the Newfound Gap Road to recross the park, this time taking advantage of the numerous pull-off areas dotting the roadside, all offering good photo opportunities. At most of them you'll find "Quiet Walkways," short paths created for moments of solitude to experience nature. Don't be discouraged if a pull-off is full, because another one will appear within a mile.

OUTDOOR PURSUITS IN THE PARK

FISHING   The park contains more than 700 miles of streams suitable for fishing. Anglers must have a valid North Carolina or Tennessee state fishing license, which can be purchased in the gateway towns at sporting goods stores. The optimum seasons are spring and fall. Popular fishing areas include Abrams Creek, Big Creek, Fontana Lake, and Little River.

HIKING   With more than 800 miles of trails, the park offers folks of all fitness levels a chance to experience the great outdoors firsthand. (Before setting out, make sure to check the weather forecast; carry rain gear, because sudden storms are common.)

The **Laurel Falls Trail,** the most popular waterfall and dramatic trail in the park, is another easy, flat walk; it's 1¼ miles to the falls from the Laurel Falls parking area, a few miles from the Sugarlands Visitor Center. The **Abrams Falls Trail** has an elevation gain of 340 feet. You travel 2½ miles from the Abrams Falls parking lot at the west end of Cades Cove Loop Road to a 20-foot-high waterfall. The trail follows a clear stream and is relatively flat. The **Ramsay Cascades Trail** has a total elevation gain of 2,375 feet and is 8 miles long round-trip. This trail also leads to Ramsay Cascades, a 100-foot-high waterfall, the park's highest. From Greenbrier Cove, follow the signs to the trail head.

The famous **Appalachian Trail** stretches from Maine to Georgia and has 68 of its 2,100 miles situated in the park, following the Smokies' ridge line from east to west almost the entire length of the park. Access points are at Newfound Gap, Clingmans Dome, the end of Tenn. 32 just north of the Big Creek Campground, and the Fontana Dam. The most popular, if strenuous, section is from Newfound Gap to Charlies Bunion.

Self-guided nature trails offer even couch potatoes an opportunity to commune with nature. These trails are staked and keyed to pamphlets with descriptions of points of interest along the way. You can get a keyed pamphlet from one of the visitor centers or stands at the trail heads. There are about a dozen such trails ranging in length from ⅓ mile to 6 miles. All offer easy walks through peaceful surroundings.

HORSEBACK RIDING   The park offers some of the state's most beautiful scenery for equestrians. Off-trail and cross-country riding, as well as use of hiking trails, are prohibited. The following five drive-in horse camps offer easy access to designated horse trails: Anthony Creek, Big Creek, Cataloochee, Round Bottom, and Towstring. Reservations can be made 30 days in advance with the **Backcountry Reservations Office** by calling ✆ **865/436-1231.**

Horses can be rented for $15 an hour, from May to October. Ask for details at the individual concessions within the park at **Cades Cove** (✆ **865/448-6286**); **McCarter's Riding Stables,** Newfound Gap Road, near park headquarters (✆ **865/436-5354**); **Smokemont Campground** (✆ **828/497-2373**); and

Smoky Mountains Riding Stables, U.S. 321 (© **865/436-5634**). The park service requires that a guide accompany all rental treks.

WHITE-WATER RAFTING   Starting at the Waterville Power Plant, a 5-mile stretch of the Pigeon River has 10 rapids and offers some of the most challenging white-water rafting in the South. **Rafting in the Smokies** (© **865/436-5008**) rafts both the Pigeon and the Nantahala rivers. A trip on the Pigeon costs $39 per person, but only $30 on the Nantahala.

WHERE TO CAMP

The park contains 10 campgrounds with picnic tables, fire grills, cold running water, and flush toilets, but no showers or water and electrical hookups. There are three major campgrounds. **Cades Cove,** 161 sites, features a camp store, bike rentals, a disposal station, wood for sale, and naturalist programs held in the small amphitheater. **Elkmont,** 220 sites, offers a disposal station, firewood for sale, vending machines, and a telephone. **Smokemont,** 140 sites, has a disposal station and firewood for sale.

Reservations (© **800/365-CAMP**) can't be made more than 8 weeks in advance. The campgrounds are full on weekends beginning in April, and daily from July to October. The busiest months are July and October, and you should make reservations at least 4 weeks in advance. From mid-May to October, there's a 7-day maximum stay; from November to mid-May, with limited sites available, the maximum stay is 14 days. The charge is $17 per day. The seven smaller campgrounds, open from mid-May to October, are along the boundaries of the park and cost $13 per day.

WHERE TO STAY

See also "Cherokee: The North Carolina Gateway to the Park," above, and "Eastern Tennessee," just below, for information on Gatlinburg, Tennessee, which borders the other side of the park and also makes an excellent base.

The only accommodation in the park itself, **LeConte Lodge** (© **865/429-5704**), is on top of Mount LeConte, and it's very back-to-basics—no electricity, TV, phone, or indoor plumbing, although there are four flush toilets in outhouses. You have to hike in on a 4-mile one-way trip. Lodgings include private bedrooms in cabins with shared living rooms as well as private cabins. The rates include breakfast, dinner (served family style), and lunch for those staying more than 1 night. There are seven rooms to rent, costing $82 per adult. A two-bedroom lodge rents for $440 for up to eight people, plus $27 extra per person for meals. Reservations are difficult to come by if you don't make them in October for the following year. It's open from the last week in March to late November. No credit cards.

In Bryson City, there's the highly recommended and moderately priced **Fryemont Inn,** Fryemont Road (© **800/845-4879** or 828/488-2159; www.fryemontinn.com). In Maggie Valley, the **Cataloochee Ranch,** Fie Top Road, 119 Ranch Dr. (© **800/868-1401** or 828/926-1401; www.cataloocheeranch.com), is a 1,000-acre spread offering loads of activities.

12 Eastern Tennessee

There's much to see and do on the outskirts of majestic Smoky Mountain National Park, where strip malls and fast-food joints coexist peacefully alongside quaint historic towns. When you're snapping up bargains at outlets in Pigeon

Forge or riding Daredevil Falls at Dollywood, it's hard to imagine that a few towns over is genteel Rogersville, where the 20th century feels years away.

GATLINBURG

Just 7 miles south of Pigeon Forge on U.S. 321 is Gatlinburg, which borders the Great Smoky Mountains National Park. For more information, contact the **Department of Tourism** (© 800/267-7088 or 865/436-2392) at 234 Airport Rd.

Gatlinburg is a great place to base yourself if you're interested in being near Great Smoky Mountains National Park (see above), and want to enjoy a wide range of outdoor activities. As for the town itself, well, despite an aerial tramway/amusement park calling itself **Ober Gatlinburg** (© 865/436-5423; $9 adults, $6 ages 7–11) with admittedly superb views of the surrounding mountains, this is no little Switzerland. Though not as strip-malled as Pigeon Forge, Gatlinburg is still lined with hotels, restaurants, and other tourist traps.

Most of Gatlinburg's attractions line the Parkway (U.S. 441). In addition to the rides and views available at the Ober Gatlinburg amusement park, for $6 adults and $4 for seniors, and $2 ages 6 to 12, the **Space Needle Family Fun Center** (© 865/436-4629) offers a great overview of the town and a fun trip up; the **earthquake ride** (© 865/436-9765; 653 Pkwy.) can be a jolt of fun for $8 adults, $5 ages 5 to 11. Believe it or not, **Ripley's Aquarium of the Smokies** (© 888/240-1358) offers an up-close-and-personal look at our fishy friends. One day admission is $16 plus tax for ages 12 and up, $8 for children 6 to 11, and $4 for children ages 2 to 5. The museum is open 365 days a year.

Gatlinburg is packed with chain hotels and motels. All the big names, such as **Days Inn, Comfort Inn,** and **Holiday Inn,** have links here. Or try the **Greystone Lodge,** 559 Pkwy. at traffic light no. 5 (© 800/451-9202 or 865/436-5621), where the standard motel rooms come with balconies overlooking a stream.

For hearty, traditional dishes, such as moonshine chicken and barbecue ribs, try **The Park Grill Restaurant,** 1100 Pkwy. (© 865/436-2300).

PIGEON FORGE

Most of the action in Pigeon Forge lines U.S. 441 (Parkway), and attractions are measured by which traffic light they abut. As you enter the city on U.S. 441 driving south from Sevierville, you'll hit the first traffic light (no. 1A) at around .2 miles. Just outside the town limits of Gatlinburg, at .9 miles, you'll reach traffic light no. 10. The **visitor information center** (© 800/251-9100 or 865/453-8574) is between light nos. 2 and 3; there's another at light no. 5.

Pigeon Forge is honky-tonk development run amok. What it lacks in charm and beauty, though, it makes up for with its shopping bargains. There are more than 200 stores in Pigeon Forge's six outlet malls, and discounts of up to 75% can be had on almost everything you can imagine, from popular brand names like Levi's, Nike, and Black & Decker to Bibles, Christmas decorations, and cowboy boots.

For shopping that's more quaintly "Tennessee" in tone, check out The Old Mill at 160 Old Mill Ave. (© 865/453-4628). It may look out-of-place on Pigeon Forge's relentlessly overdeveloped strip, but it's a good place to pick up locally made gifts like jams and candy and stone-ground products for your own baking. Next door, the restaurant of the same name serves hearty Southern meals at breakfast, lunch, and dinner.

No trip to this part of Tennessee would be complete without a visit to **Dollywood,** 1020 Dollywood Lane, 1 mile off traffic light no. 8 (© 865/428-9488; www.dollywood.com), the amusement park owned by Pigeon Forge's beloved daughter, Dolly Parton. The park has been credited with putting Pigeon Forge on the map as a major tourist attraction and almost single-handedly turning around the city's economy. The park's souvenir stands, rides, and cheesy attractions are redeemed somewhat by Dollywood's tribute to Appalachia and the singer's own origins. Demonstrations showcase regional crafts such as basket making, pottery making, and glass blowing, and shops provide an outlet for these traditional skills that might otherwise be lost. A don't-miss attraction, even for non-Dolly fans (and for heaven's sake, don't let on if you're not), is the **"Dolly Parton Story" museum,** which depicts Dolly's rags-to-riches success through personal mementos. Admission, including tax, is $38 adults, seniors $33, and $28 ages 4 to 11. It includes all shows, craft demonstrations, rides, and attractions. Closed January through March.

Nightlife in Pigeon Forge focuses on musical theater. Hot tickets include Louise Mandrell's singing and dancing at the **Louise Mandrell Theater** (© 865/453-6263; 2046 Pkwy.). It's open from April to December and is located off light no. 1A.

There's no shortage of places to stay in Pigeon Forge. All the major chains are represented. If you want to be in the thick of it all, try the **Best Western Plaza Inn,** 3755 Pkwy. (© 800/232-5656 or 865/453-5538) at traffic light no. 8. If you prefer to be a little farther away from the crowds, **Mainstay Suites,** 410 Pine Mountain Rd. (© 888/428-8350 or 865/428-8350), is just off traffic light no. 6. Both hotels have indoor and outdoor pools, and rates include breakfast.

KNOXVILLE
ESSENTIALS
GETTING THERE   By Plane   You can fly directly into Knoxville's **McGhee Tyson Airport** (© 865/342-3333; www.tys.org).

By Car   Major routes into Knoxville are I-40 from the east (Winston-Salem, NC) and west (Nashville), I-75 from the north (Lexington, KY) and south (Chattanooga and Atlanta), I-81 from the northeast.

VISITOR INFORMATION   For information on the region, visit the new **Gateway Regional Visitor Center,** 900 Volunteer Landing Lane (© 800/727-8045). If you're interested in country music, pick up the "Cradle of Country Music" walking tour of downtown Knoxville; if you prefer your sights vintage, try the "Historic Homes" driving tour.

WHAT TO SEE & DO
Your one can't-miss attraction is the **Knoxville Zoo,** 3333 Woodbine Ave. (© 865/637-5331; www.knoxville-zoo.org), off I-40, near Rutledge Pike, Exit 392. In particular, watch for the sweet-looking (but apparently ill-tempered) red pandas, and the otter exhibit where you can see the otters swimming underwater. The zoo is justifiably popular, but unfortunately a little too close to the road; it's a little odd to watch a wrinkly baby rhino eating grass against a backdrop of whizzing cars. Admission is $7.95 adults, $5.95 seniors, and $4.95 children over 3. Parking is $3.

Fans of *Roots* will want to visit the larger-than-life-size **Alex Haley statue** at 1600 Dandridge Ave. in Morningside Park near downtown Knoxville. The writer was a native of Tennessee and adopted Knoxville as his home. The park is charming, and the seated figure provides a great photo op for those wanting to clamber into the storyteller's welcoming bronze lap.

In case of rain, head over to the **Knoxville Museum of Art,** 1050 World's Fair Park Dr. (© **865/525-6101;** www.knoxart.org). The museum features about 12 exhibitions a year, as well as a permanent collection that focuses on postmodern works. Admission is $3 adults and free for children under 12.

WHERE TO STAY & DINE

Try to stay downtown, where you'll be close to all major attractions. The **Marriott Knoxville,** 500 Hill Ave. (© **800/836-8031** or 865/637-1234), has an outdoor pool (necessary in summer), a restaurant, a lounge, and a small fitness center. The **Holiday Inn Select Downtown,** 525 Henley St. (© **800/ HOLIDAY** or 865/522-2800), has almost identical facilities, but its pool is indoors. Both are moderately priced.

CHATTANOOGA

Chattanooga is a great family destination, with historic districts, Civil War sites, and interactive museums, plus a whole range of outdoor activities.

ESSENTIALS

GETTING THERE   By Plane Major airlines serve the **Chattanooga Metropolitan Airport** (© **423/855-2200;** www.chattairport.com) from Atlanta, Cincinnati, Memphis, and Charlotte. To reach the city center, take Highway 153 south to I-75, and then go west on I-24. Exits 1A, 1B, and 1C all get you downtown.

By Car Major routes into Chattanooga are I-75 from the north (Knoxville) and south (Atlanta), I-24 from the northwest (Nashville), and I-59 from the southwest (Birmingham, AL).

VISITOR INFORMATION Start off your visit at the **Chattanooga Visitors Center,** 2 Broad St. (© **800/322-3344** or 423/756-8687; www.chattanooga fun.com), open daily from 8:30am to 5:30pm, where you can pick up some helpful brochures and maps. Here you can buy discount ticket packages, which get you into several of Chattanooga's most popular attractions. A free electric shuttle from the visitor center makes touring downtown attractions a snap.

WHAT TO SEE & DO

Adjacent to the visitor center is the **Tennessee Aquarium,** 1 Broad St. (© **800/ 262-0695** or 423/265-0698; www.tnaqua.org), the first major institution dedicated to freshwater ecosystems, with exhibits designed to take you on a journey from the Tennessee River's source in the Appalachian high country, down through the Mississippi Delta. Should you tire of watching the 9,000 critters here busily swimming, flying, and crawling, you can check out the IMAX theater on the premises. Open daily from 10am to 6pm, to 8pm some summer evenings. Admission is $13 adults, $6.95 ages 3 to 12, free for children under 12. Tickets to the IMAX theater are an additional $7.25 adults, $4.95 children.

The **Creative Discovery Museum,** 321 Chestnut St. (© **423/756-2738;** www.cdmfun.org), just 2 blocks from the aquarium, caters to toddlers as young as 18 months while also enthralling the older set with such interactive exhibits as the Artist's and Musician's Studios and the Inventor's Workshop. Hours are daily from 10am to 6pm Memorial Day to Labor Day; and Tuesday through Sunday from 10am to 5pm and Sunday from noon to 5pm otherwise. Admission is $7.95 adults, $4.95 children 2 to 12.

Culture lovers should be sure to visit the **Bluff View Art District** (© 423/265-5033), located just east of the Walnut Street Pedestrian Bridge. Check out the River Gallery or spend some time ambling through the free Sculpture Garden, perched scenically on a bluff overlooking the Tennessee River. The **Houston Museum of Decorative Arts,** 201 High St. (© 423/267-7176), houses an impressive glass collection. It's open Monday through Saturday from 9:30am to 4pm, summer Sundays from noon to 4pm. Admission is $6. You can see paintings, sculpture, decorative arts, and contemporary studio glass at the **Hunter Museum of American Art,** 10 Bluff View (© 865/267-0968; www.huntermuseum.org), open Tuesday through Saturday from 9:30am to 5pm, Sunday from noon to 5pm. Admission is $5 adults, $4 seniors, and $2.50 under 12.

Just across the Walnut Street bridge is Coolidge Park, with its beautiful hand-carved carousel; and Frasier Street, where you'll find some funky shops and cafes.

EXPLORING AROUND LOOKOUT MOUNTAIN

From downtown, Lookout Mountain attractions can be reached quickly and easily via Broad Street to Tenn. 58. Don't miss historic **Incline Railway,** 827 E. Brow Rd. (© 423/821-4224), the steepest passenger railway in the world with panoramic views of the city and the Great Smoky Mountains 100 miles away. Round-trips cost $9 adult and $4.50 ages 3 to 12. Open daily.

Civil War buffs should check out **The Battles for Chattanooga Museum,** 1110 E. Brow Rd. (© 423/821-2812; www.battlesforchattanooga.com). Just 3 blocks from the Incline Railroad's upper station at the entrance to **Point Park** (site of the "Battle above the Clouds" in 1863), this museum features a three-dimensional electronic battle map that presents details of major battles in Chattanooga's Civil War history. It's open daily; admission is $5.95 adults, $3.95 ages 3 to 12.

Also on Lookout Mountain is **Ruby Falls,** 1720 S. Scenic Hwy. (© 423/821-2544; www.rubyfalls.com), a 145-foot waterfall located 1,100 feet inside the mountain. If you're at all claustrophobic, or simply don't want to be herded through a cave with a large group of people, skip it. Open daily at 8am. Admission is $12 adults, $5.50 ages 3 to 12.

From **Rock City Gardens,** 1400 Patten Rd. (© 706/820-2531; www.see rockcity.com), you'll have a view of seven states on a clear day. Rock City's unique sandstone formations are striking, and younger kids will be fascinated by the displays based on classic fairy tales and nursery rhymes. Open daily year-round. Admission for adults is $12, for ages 3 to 12 $6.95.

WHERE TO STAY & DINE

If the name *Chattanooga* makes you yearn for the days of leisurely train travel, there's no better place to stay than the **Chattanooga Choo Choo/Holiday Inn,** 1400 Market St. (© 800/TRACK29 or 423/266-5000; www.choochoo.com), formerly Chattanooga's main railway terminal. Reserve the motel-issue rooms in the main building for all the comforts of a chain, or if you've got a sense of whimsy or are traveling with kids, try one of the converted train cars.

Alternatively, the **Read House Hotel and Suites,** MLK Boulevard and Broad Street (© 800/333-3333 or 423/266-4121; www.readhouse.com), is a lovely National Historic Landmark. The on-site restaurant, the **Green Room** (same phone), serves highly recommended though heavy meals. Both hotels are on the shuttle route downtown.

If you prefer a B&B atmosphere, head to the **Bluff View Inn,** 412 E. 2nd St. (© **423/265-5033**) in the Bluff View Arts District (see above). There are several dining options in the district, including **Tony's Pasta Shop and Trattoria** and **Rembrandt's Coffee House** (try the hand-dipped chocolates).

An all-in-one lunch/dinner/entertainment option is a ride on the Tennessee River in the **Southern Belle Riverboat,** 201 Riverfront Pkwy., Pier 2 (© **800/ 766-2784** or 423/266-4488; www.chattanoogariverboat.com). The food leaves something to be desired, but the gentle trip up and down the river is pleasant. Sightseeing, lunch, and dinner cruises are available; prices start at $11 adult for a 1½-hour sightseeing cruise, and climb to $40 for a weekend dinner cruise.

13 Highlights of Kentucky

LEXINGTON & THE BLUEGRASS REGION

Often called the Heart of Kentucky, the centrally located Bluegrass region offers much of what Kentucky is all about—thoroughbred horses, bourbon, basketball, natural beauty, history, and Southern hospitality.

Ringed by the stunning horse farms that give this area its reputation and personality is Lexington, the state's second largest city and a growing urban area that has just the right mix of big city excitement and small town charm.

ESSENTIALS

GETTING THERE   By Plane   Major airlines fly into **Blue Grass Airport** (© **859/425-3100;** www.bluegrassairport.com), 10 minutes from downtown. There's frequent service from most Midwest hubs.

By Car   The major routes into Lexington are I-75 from the north (Cincinnati) and south (Knoxville), and I-64 from the east (Charleston, WV) and west (Louisville).

VISITOR INFORMATION   Contact the **Lexington Convention and Visitors Bureau,** 301 E. Vine St., Lexington, KY 40507 (© **800/84-LEX-KY** or 859/233-1221; www.visitlex.com).

EXPLORING THE AREA

HORSE FARMS   Calumet Farms is the granddaddy of 'em all, breeder of nine Kentucky Derby champions, including Whirlaway (1941) and Citation (1948), as well as countless more winners of other legs of racing's Triple Crown. **Horse Farm Tours,** 3429 Montavesta Rd., Lexington (© **859/268-2906**), offers 2- to 3-hour tours daily at 9am and 1pm, visiting Calumet on Thursdays and other area farms on other days. Advance reservations, usually at least 10 days ahead, are essential.

Claiborne Farm, Winchester Road, Paris (© **859/233-4252**), is known in part for its association with Secretariat, the 1973 Triple Crown winner considered by many to be the greatest thoroughbred of all time. The horse once stood at stud at the farm. Tour schedules vary, so call in advance to arrange an appointment.

Another Triple Crown winner (in 1977), Seattle Slew, once stood at stud at **Three Chimneys Farm,** Old Frankfort Parkway, Versailles (© **859/873-7053**). The free tours fill up quickly, so call for schedule and reservations (a must). No tours are offered December through February.

Part museum, part equestrian arena, the state-run **Kentucky Horse Park,** 4089 Iron Works Pike, Lexington (© **800/568-8813** or 859/233-4303; www. kyhorsepark.com), is a virtual mecca for horse lovers, drawing more than

700,000 visitors yearly. A gravesite statue of Man o' War, who lost only one race in his career, welcomes visitors. Seasonal horse and pony rides please the kids. Open daily from 9am to 5pm (closed Mon and Tues, Nov–Mar). Admission is $12 for adults, $9 for students and seniors, and $6.50 for children ages 7 to 12. Rates are reduced during the winter but will be higher ($16 adults, $14 seniors, and $11 children) during "All the Queen's Horses: The Role of the Horse in British Society," from April 26 to September 27, 2003. One million visitors are expected to view the exclusive exhibition that will feature carriages, tack and harness, human and equine armor, and paintings associated with monarchs from Henry V to Elizabeth II.

Keeneland, 4201 Versailles Rd., Lexington (℅ **800/456-3412** or 606/254-3412; www.keeneland.com), a meticulously manicured racetrack, may not be as famous as its neighbor to the west, Churchill Downs, but most folks think it's one of the prettiest courses in America. Races are held here only 6 weeks a year: three in April, including the Blue Grass Stakes, a major Kentucky Derby tune-up, and three more in October. Post time is 1:10pm. Admission is $2.50. A reserved seat in the grandstand costs $5.50 weekdays, $7.50 weekends. Order tickets in advance for major stakes races.

BOURBON DISTILLERY TOURS   Bourbon, a whiskey made from at least 51% corn, is distilled in several Bluegrass region towns, but ironically, none are in Bourbon County, which is dry. (You can, however, buy bourbon in Christian County.) A number of the distilleries within easy driving distance of Lexington offer tours. For general information, contact the Kentucky Distillers Association (℅ **859/336-9612;** www.kybourbon.com).One of the oldest and largest is the **Wild Turkey Distillery,** 1525 Tyrone Rd., Lawrenceburg (℅ **502/839-4544;** www.wildturkeybourbon.com). It's the closest to Lexington. Free tours are conducted weekdays at 9am, 10:30am, 12:30pm, and 2:30pm. The distillery is closed the first week of January and the last 2 weeks of July.

The producers of Evan Williams bourbon, **Heaven Hill Distilleries,** 1064 Loretto Rd., Bardstown (℅ **502/348-3921;** www.heaven-hill.com), bill themselves as "America's largest family-owned distillery." Tours are free, and include a souvenir barrel stopper soaked in bourbon.

Family-owned **Maker's Mark Distillery,** 3350 Burks Spring Rd., Loretto (℅ **270/865-2099;** www.makersmark.com), a small-batch distillery (peak capacity is a mere 38 barrels), has attracted a devoted following. Its silky-smooth bourbon has garnered numerous awards. Free tours are offered on the half hour from 10:30am to 3:30pm Monday through Saturday; closed Saturdays in January and February.

The oldest operating distillery in Kentucky is **Labrot & Graham Distillery** (℅ **859-879-1812;** www.labrot-graham.com), 7855 McCracken Pike, Versailles, in Woodford County, a short drive from Lexington. This picturesque distillery is located among lush, rolling horse farms. Tours are held Tuesday through Saturday on the hour from 10am to 3pm, with a break at noon, and Sundays at 1, 2, and 3pm.

In nearby Frankfort, a 25-minute drive from Lexington, is **Buffalo Trace Distillery,** 1001 Wilkinson Blvd., Franklin County (℅ **800/654-8471** or 502/223-7641; www.buffalotrace.com). Bourbon-making on this 110-acre site dates back to 1787. In the last decade the distillery has won more international awards than any other in North America. Free tours are held every day except Sunday and holidays.

MORE ATTRACTIONS Downtown Lexington is home to several historic buildings, many of which are conveniently linked on the **Lexington Walk,** a walking tour of the city. Maps for this as well as a self-driving tour of the area and horse farms are available at the visitor center, 301 E. Vine (© **800/845-3959**). **Mary Todd Lincoln House,** 578 W. Main St. (© **859/233-9999**), was the first American historic site restored to honor a First Lady. Tours are offered from April to mid-December Tuesday through Saturday from 10am to 4pm. Admission is $7 for adults, $4 for ages 6 to 12. **Ashland,** 120 Sycamore Rd. (© **859/266-8581;** www.henryclay.org), is the beautiful 20-acre estate of famous 19th-century statesman and emancipationist Henry Clay. Open Tuesday through Saturday from 10am to 4:30pm, Sunday from 1 to 4:30pm. Closed during January. Admission is $6 for adults and $3 for ages 6 to 18.

A scenic, 25-mile drive southwest of Lexington takes you to **Shaker Village of Pleasant Hill,** 3501 Lexington Rd., Harrodsburg (© **800/734-5611** or 859/734-5441; www.shakervillageky.org), the largest historic community of its kind in America. The National Historic Landmark features 33 original 19th-century buildings and 28,000 acres of farmland. Self-guided tours, horseback riding, and riverboat excursions are offered. Dining, lodging, and two crafts shops are also on the premises. It's open daily year-round except December 24 and 25. Admission for village tours is $10.50 for adults, $6 for youth ages 12 to 17, $4 for children ages 6 to 11, and free for those 5 and under.

Opening in the spring of 2003 is the new **Kentucky Artisan Center at Berea.** Located off of I-75 in Berea, the state's folk–arts and crafts capital, the state-run center will combine cultural exhibits and tourist services along with options for shopping and dining. For more information, contact the Berea Tourism Center (201 N. Broadway; © **800/598-5263** or 859/986-2540).

WHERE TO STAY

Marriott's Griffin Gate Resort and Golf Club, 1800 Newtown Pike (at the intersection of I-64 and I-75), Lexington (© **800/228-9290** or 859/231-5100), is a favorite of golf fanatics. In addition to an acclaimed golf course, the resort boasts three lighted tennis courts, indoor and outdoor swimming pools, and a full-service health club. Four restaurants, three bars, and two lounges keep guests entertained any time of day or night. Pets are accepted, too, for a flat fee per visit.

Across the street, another popular property offering first-class service is the new **Embassy Suites,** 1801 Newtown Pike (© **800/362-2779** or 859/455-5000). The upscale, 230-suite hotel offers amenities including a business center, an executive fitness center, a lap pool, a jogging track, and a restaurant and lounge. Guests receive a complimentary breakfast and evening reception.

In downtown Lexington, you can't beat the luxurious **Gratz Park Inn,** 120 W. Second St. (© **800/752-4166;** www.gratzparkinn.com), for convenience or attentive service. Each room is individually decorated with antiques and other historic pieces. You'll get fresh flowers every morning, and there's limo service to downtown restaurants.

The wrought-iron furniture, live jazz performances on weekends, and Cajun restaurant in the lobby of the **Sheraton Suites,** 2601 Richmond Rd. (© **800/262-3774** or 859/268-0060), make you feel like you're in New Orleans, but you're right next door to the Lexington Mall. Every room is a suite with hot tubs, refrigerators, and coffeemakers. There's also an outdoor pool and a fitness center.

If you just want a comfortable, affordable chain hotel, the best options are the **Best Western Regency of Lexington,** 2241 Elkhorn Rd., Lexington (© **800/ 528-1234** or 859/293-2202); the **Courtyard by Marriott,** 775 Newtown Court, Lexington (© **606/253-4646**), located on a quiet, shady street but convenient enough to I-75 and downtown to suit business travelers; and **Holiday Inn South,** 5532 Athens-Boonesboro Rd., Lexington (© **800/HOLIDAY** or 859/263-5241), a family-style motel that's big on facilities and welcomes pets. All three have swimming pools.

Prohibition ended Silver Springs Farm's life as a bourbon distillery in 1919, but the old springhouse still stands, providing water for the horses and garden at **Bed & Breakfast at Silver Springs Farm,** 3710 Leestown Pike, Lexington (© **877/255-1784** or 859/255-1784), an affordable horse country B&B just 5 miles from downtown.

LOUISVILLE

Kentucky's largest city, Louisville (say it either "*Loo*-uh-vul" or "*Looey*-ville") sits on the southeast bank of the Ohio River across from Indiana. It's about 100 miles west of Lexington.

Louisville is best-known for hosting the Kentucky Derby, held on the first Saturday in May every year. It's all but impossible to get tickets to the Derby, but Churchill Downs is open other times of the year when it's not nearly as crowded.

ESSENTIALS

GETTING THERE   By Plane   Major airlines fly into **Louisville International Airport** (© **502/368-6524;** www.louintlairport.com), 10 minutes from downtown. There's frequent service from all major Midwest hubs. The flat rate for a taxi downtown is $15.40 (except during Derby week).

By Car   The major routes into Louisville are I-71 from the northeast (Cincinnati), I-65 from the north (Indianapolis) and south (Nashville), and I-64 from the east (Lexington) and west (St. Louis).

VISITOR INFORMATION   Contact the **Louisville and Jefferson County Convention and Visitors Bureau,** 400 S. First St., Louisville, KY 40202 (© **800/626-5646** or 502/584-2121; www.gotolouisville.com). There's also an **Information Booth** at the airport (© **502/367-4636**). To find out what's happening around town, go online to **The Louisville Scene** (www.louisvillescene. com).

WHAT TO SEE & DO

Louisville celebrates its lazily idyllic waterfront with a 7-mile **RiverWalk** along the shore. Among the varied area attractions under construction is the **Muhammad Ali Center** (www.alicenter.org), a $60-million museum and conflict-resolution center inspired by the life of boxing's "Greatest," Louisville native Ali. Nearby, the **Kentucky Center for African-American Heritage** (www.kcaah. com) promises to become the state's pre-eminent black-history and educational center. Both attractions are scheduled to open in 2004.

Churchill Downs, 700 Central Ave. (© **502/636-4400;** www.churchill downs.com), will remain open while undergoing a $127-million reconstruction beginning in late 2003. The venue has hosted the Kentucky Derby since it was first run in 1875 and is run the first Saturday in May. The season runs from late April to early July and from late October to November; post times vary. Admission is $2 for adults, $1 for seniors, and free for children 12 and under. Reserved seats start at $2 extra. Parking is free in certain areas, or $3 in a lot near Gate 17.

Within the same grounds is the **Kentucky Derby Museum** (© 502/637-1111; www.derbymuseum.org), with photos, films, and exhibits, and even a chance to sit on a saddle in a real starting gate. It's open year-round Monday through Saturday from 8am to 5pm, and Sunday from noon to 5 pm. Admission is $8 for adults, $7 for seniors, and $3 for children ages 5 to 12; guided tours are available every half hour.

The **Six Flags Kentucky Kingdom Amusement Park,** 937 Phillips Lane, Kentucky Fair and Exposition Center (© 800/SCREAMS or 502/366-2231; www.sixflags.com), boasts one of the largest wooden roller coasters in the world and a 750,000-gallon wave pool among its 60-plus rides and attractions. Different parts of the park are open at different times of year, so call before you arrange to spend the entire day. It's open from April to October. Admission is $35 for adults, $20 for seniors and children shorter than 48 inches; free for children under 3.

Don't miss the **Louisville Slugger Museum,** 800 W. Main St. (© 502/588-7228; www.sluggermuseum.org). Look for the giant bat (the world's tallest) standing outside the door. Inside, you can see a bat used by Babe Ruth as well as souvenir miniature bats, and feel what it's like to stare down the stitches of a 90-mile-per-hour fastball. Right next door is the Hillerich & Bradsby factory, where they turn out thousands of bats for major leaguers every year. It's open Monday through Saturday from 9am to 5pm, with 90-minute tours of the factory every 20 minutes from 9am to 3:30pm. Admission is $6 for adults, $5 for seniors, $3.50 for children ages 6 to 12, and free for children 5 and under.

The **Belle of Louisville,** moored at Fourth Street and River Road (© 502/574-2355; www.belleoflouisville.org), is the oldest operating steamboat on the Mississippi River system. The stern-wheeler was built in 1914, and is now a National Historic Landmark. There's even an old-fashioned calliope on board. The *Belle* and a larger, more modern paddle-wheeler, *Spirit of Jefferson,* carry passengers along the Ohio River. Admission for a 2-hour sightseeing cruise is $10 for adults, $9 for seniors, and $6 for ages 3 to 12.

WHERE TO STAY & DINE

The two grande dames of Louisville hotels are the **Camberley Brown,** Fourth Street and West Broadway (© 502/583-1234; www.thebrownhotel.com), and the **Seelbach Hilton,** 500 Fourth St. (© 502/585-3200). The Seelbach opened in 1905, the Camberley Brown in 1923; both are downtown (within boasting distance of each other). Both also have top-flight formal restaurants: The English Grill at the Camberley Brown and The Oakroom at the Seelbach Hilton.

The gigantic **Galt House,** Fourth Street and River Road (© 502/589-5200), is almost always hosting one convention or another, and often two or more at the same time.

Holiday Inn alone has 14 different properties in the Louisville area. Call © 800/HOLIDAY for locations. **Best Western** can be found at 4805 Brownsboro Rd. (© 502/893-2551) and at 1301 Kentucky Mills Dr. (© 502/267-8100).

Everybody's favorite restaurant is **Lilly's,** 1147 Bardstown Rd., east of downtown (© 502/451-0447; http://lillyslapeche.com). Owner-chef Kathy Cary, a frequent guest chef at New York's James Beard House, combines local meats and homegrown organic vegetables to create an innovative cuisine that changes with the seasons. **Lynn's Paradise Cafe,** 984 Barrett Ave. (© 502/583-3447; www.lynnsparadisecafe.com), is considerably more downscale. Folks go here for the melt-in-your-mouth buttermilk biscuits, the portobello mushroom wraps, and the famed breakfast burrito. Lunch and dinner are served Tuesday through Sunday.

NORTHERN KENTUCKY

One of the fastest growing areas of Kentucky is the northern tip, across the Ohio from Cincinnati. Its many riverfront restaurants and hotels provide spectacular views of the Ohio River and Cincinnati skyline.

ESSENTIALS

GETTING THERE   See "Cincinnati" in chapter 9.

VISITOR INFORMATION   Contact the **Northern Kentucky Convention and Visitors Bureau,** 50 E. River Center Blvd., Ste. 40, Covington, KY 41011 (© **800/STAYNKY;** www.nkycvb.com).

WHAT TO SEE & DO

One of the newest and most popular attractions is the **Newport Aquarium,** One Aquarium Way, Newport (© **859/491-FINS;** www.newportaquarium. com), located on the banks of the Ohio directly across from downtown Cincinnati. The aquarium displays 11,000 marine animals, including 50 sharks and 16 king penguins. It also offers 200 feet of clear, seamless tunnels that put visitors literally face-to-face with sharks and other creatures of the deep. The aquarium is open 365 days a year, from 10am to 7pm Memorial Day to Labor Day, from 10am to 6pm the rest of the year. Admission is $16 for adults, $10 for children ages 3 to 12, and $14 for seniors. Late afternoon and early evening are the best times to avoid crowds.

A block south of the aquarium at Fourth and York streets in Newport is the **World Peace Bell,** which at 62,000 pounds is the world's largest free-swinging bell.

Head west on Fourth Street, across the Licking River, and in about 2 miles you'll come to Main Street, Covington. A left turn takes you into **Main Strasse Village,** a neighborhood that recalls Northern Kentucky's German heritage. Main Strasse is centered around a town square that features the Goose Girl Fountain. Over several blocks visitors will find an inviting and interesting collection of shops, antiques stores, restaurants, art galleries, pubs, and neighborhood taverns. It's rarely overcrowded and great for a late afternoon stroll for some window-shopping followed by dinner in a local haunt.

BB Riverboats, 1 Madison Ave., Covington (© **800/261-8586** or 859/261-8500; www.bbriverboats.com), offers short afternoon and evening excursions up and down the Ohio River past the city's skyline, particularly beautiful from the water at night.

WHERE TO STAY

Northern Kentucky has become a popular alternative overnight destination for business and leisure travelers visiting Cincinnati. Most hotels offer shuttle buses to the city or other locations in Northern Kentucky. The traffic is not as bad as Cincinnati's, and guests are close to nightlife and restaurants on the south side of the Ohio River.

The **Cincinnati Marriott at RiverCenter** (© **859/261-2900**) is a new highrise hotel right on the river at the foot of Madison Avenue in Covington and directly across from the Northern Kentucky Convention Center. It's a favorite of business travelers; weekend packages are available for leisure visitors.

A local landmark known for its circular style, the Radisson Hotel **Riverview** ((*C*) 859/491-1206) sits hard against I-75—the major north-south route through Ohio and Kentucky—along Covington's Fifth Street. Kids love the revolving restaurant that turns slowly on the top floor for spectacular panoramic views of the Cincinnati skyline, Ohio River, and Kentucky hills.

Other riverfront hotels include **Comfort Suites Hotel** (*C* 859/291-6700) on Newport's Riverboat Row; **Embassy Suites** (*C* 888/EMBASSY or 859/261-8400) at Covington's RiverCenter; **Hampton Inn/Cincinnati Riverfront**, 200 Crescent Ave., Covington (*C* 800/HAMPTON or 859/581-7800); and **Holiday Inn/Riverfront**, 600 W. Third St., Covington (*C* 859/291-4300).

Northern Kentucky's historic riverfront neighborhoods also offer some quaint bed-and-breakfasts. Two of the best are the **Amos Shinkle Townhouse B&B**, 215 Garrard St., Covington (*C* 859/431-2118), which is just 2 blocks from the river near the Mike Fink restaurant; and **Christopher's Bed and Breakfast**, 604 Poplar St., Bellevue (*C* 888/585-7085; www.christophersbb.com), located in a restored turn-of-the-20th-century church that features the intriguing combination of whirlpool tubs and stained-glass windows in the guest rooms.

WHERE TO DINE

For great views of the Cincinnati skyline and the Ohio River, you can't beat the restaurants along the shorelines in Covington and Newport.

One of the best restaurants in Kentucky is found in Covington's Main Strasse. **Dee Felice Café,** Sixth and Main streets (*C* 859/261-2365), mixes live jazz and spicy New Orleans–style cuisine.

The Waterfront (*C* 859/581-1414; www.waterfrontinc.com) is a trendy restaurant and nightspot located off of Covington's Third Street. The place is fancy and the food is fabulous, but it's not for a family on a budget.

Just upriver on the east side of the Roebling Suspension Bridge—a Civil War–era span that connects Kentucky with downtown Cincinnati—is **Mike Fink's** (*C* 859/261-4212). Named for a legendary riverman, the restaurant is housed in a paddle-wheeler replica at the foot of Greenup Street. Known for its seafood and raw bar, this is a fun place with moderate to expensive prices.

Though it's not directly on the river, **Behle Street Café,** on the ground floor of the Embassy Suites Hotel just off the riverfront in Covington (*C* 859/291-4100), offers the rare combination of great food and low prices. This is a great place to hit for a quick meal or drink before a Reds game or other evening event.

Newport, just east of Covington across the Licking River, has a whole strip of restaurants along an area known as **Riverboat Row.** Most are family-friendly and offer outdoor docks and decks that provide wonderful views of the city and give the kids a chance to feed the ducks.

We recommend: **Barleycorn's** (*C* 859/442-3400), featuring relaxed and inexpensive casual dining; **Don Pablo's** (*C* 859/261-7100), a chain geared toward family Tex-Mex dining; and the **Chart House** (*C* 859/261-0300), an elegant seafood restaurant.

MAMMOTH CAVE NATIONAL PARK

This is the world's longest system of caves and one of America's most popular national parks, drawing almost two million visitors a year. They come not just for the miles and miles of underground exploring, but also for the 53,000 acres of pristine hardwood forest aboveground, where you can hike, ride horses, canoe, go boating, go birding, or camp.

The best way to see everything Mammoth Cave has to offer is by taking a cave tour and then hiking the surface afterward. The parks department runs several cave tours for all ability levels, including one that's open to visitors in wheelchairs. All tours sell out quickly, especially in summer, so reserve in advance.

ESSENTIALS

GETTING THERE   Mammoth Cave is in western Kentucky, about 100 miles south of Louisville. From Louisville, take I-65 south to Cave City; from Lexington, take the Bluegrass Parkway to I-65, then I-65 south to Cave City. From Cave City, take Ky. 70 west to the East Entrance Road. From Nashville, take I-65 north to Park City, then Ky. 255 north to the South Entrance Road.

VISITOR INFORMATION   Entrance to Mammoth Cave National Park (© 270/758-2328; www.nps.gov/maca) is free. All entrances converge at the visitor center in the southeastern corner of the park. It's open year-round, usually from 8am to 5pm (from 9am in Jan and Feb). Ranger-led tours of the caves leave from the visitor center at different times throughout the day.

CAVE TOURS

Rangers lead a host of different tours through the cave, varying in difficulty from a moderate walk to an all-day affair involving crawling on hands and knees. Call the park or check the website for a complete list. Reservations are strongly recommended for all cave tours. Tours range in price from $4 to $35.

> **Travel Tip**
> The temperature inside the cave is always approximately 54°F (12°C).

OTHER ACTIVITIES IN THE PARK

A variety of hiking trails are available throughout the park. Pick up a hiking map and a schedule of ranger-led walks and campfire and evening programs at the visitor center.

Mammoth Cave has more than 30 miles of canoeing along the Green and Nolin rivers. Pick up a map at the visitor center.

WHERE TO STAY

There are three campgrounds in the park, as well as a dozen backcountry campsites where you might not see another soul. Permits are required for both types of camping. Fees range from $5 to $20 for the campgrounds; backcountry permits are free. All campgrounds have toilets, grills, and drinking water.

The **Mammoth Cave Hotel** (© 270/758-2225) is the only lodging within the park boundaries.

Cave City is the primary gateway to the park. It has a **Best Western Kentucky Inn** (© 270/773-3161), a **Comfort Inn** (© 270/773-2030), and a **Super 8 Motel** (© 270/773-2500).

DANIEL BOONE NATIONAL FOREST

When the legendary explorer Daniel Boone first crossed into now what is Kentucky more than 200 years ago, he found a naturally beautiful yet rugged landscape, a place of deep forests, high mountains, steep cliffs, pristine lakes, lush valleys, and abundant wildlife. Today, more than five million people a year come to the eastern Kentucky mountains to see what Boone saw as he helped blaze a trail west.

The **Daniel Boone National Forest,** headquartered in Winchester, KY ((℉) **859/745-3100**), covers 693,043 acres and 21 Kentucky counties.

Hiking, camping, rock climbing, fishing, caving, horseback riding, boating, exploring, and hunting are among the activities available to visitors.

In addition to the 269-mile Sheltowee Trace National Recreation Trail, there are hundreds of shorter hiking trails to explore.

Several campgrounds are located throughout the park. Most are on a first-come, first-served basis, but reservations are available at some sites by calling ℉ **877/444-6777.** The forest does not offer lodges or cabins. However, several Kentucky state parks (℉ **800/225-8747**)—among the best in the country—are located within the forest, and most have lodges, cabins, and campsites. Fishing and boating are available at Cave Run and Laurel River lakes.

A favorite attraction within the forest is **Natural Bridge State Park** (℉ **800/ 325-1710** or 606/663-2214). More than 300,000 people a year visit the park's namesake, a huge sandstone arch over a deep gorge. A sky-lift takes passengers on a panoramic journey that features spectacular views of the park. Hiking is the most popular activity in the park. Maps are available at the park's main Activities Center.

BLUEGRASS MUSIC & BEYOND

The new $6-million **Kentucky Music Hall Of Fame and Museum** (℉ **859-351-2447;** www.kentuckymusicmuseum.com) in Renfro Valley honors the rich history of Kentucky performers. In the foothills of the Daniel Boone National Forest, the log cabin–like venue showcases everything from country to contemporary music and honors home-state natives from Loretta Lynn and The Judds to Lionel Hampton to Rosemary Clooney—and even two of the Backstreet Boys!

Bill Monroe (1911–96), the legendary Father of Bluegrass, was born in Rosine in Ohio County, where work is underway to restore his old homestead, located about 6 miles east of Beaver Dam along Highway 62. For more information, call ℉ **888/987-6444** or visit www.thebillmonroefoundation.com.

In Owensboro, the reopened, state-of-the-art **International Bluegrass Music Museum** (207 E. Second St.; ℉ **270/926-7891;** www.bluegrass-museum.org) is a must-see for both longtime fans of bluegrass as well as the legions of new listeners who have embraced the genre thanks to the smash soundtrack from *O Brother, Where Art Thou?* The museum is open from 10am to 5pm Tuesday through Friday and from 1 to 5pm Saturday and Sunday. Admission is $8 for adults, $5 for seniors, $4 for youth through age 16, and free to children 6 and under.

For more information, contact the Owensboro Tourist Commission, 215 E. Second St. (℉ **800/489-1131** or 270/926-1100; www.visitowensboro.com).

14 Nashville

Nashville may be the capital of Tennessee, but it's better known as Music City USA, the country music capital of the world. This is where the country music "thang" happens, where the deals are cut, where the stars are made, and where the Grand Ole Opry broadcasts. Country music's increased popularity has brought a newfound importance to the city, and a rejuvenation to its neighborhoods.

ESSENTIALS

GETTING THERE   By Plane   Nashville International Airport (℉ **615/ 275-1675;** www.nashintl.com) is about 8 miles east of downtown Nashville, a

Nashville

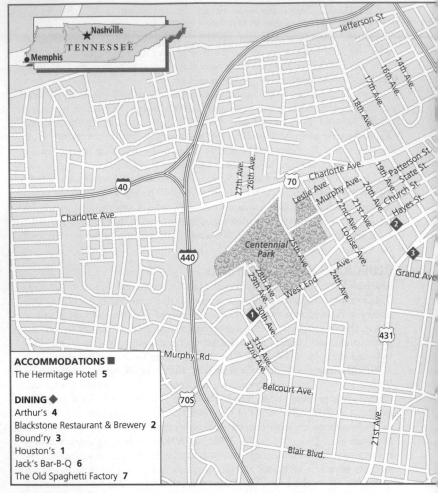

ACCOMMODATIONS ■
The Hermitage Hotel **5**

DINING ◆
Arthur's **4**
Blackstone Restaurant & Brewery **2**
Bound'ry **3**
Houston's **1**
Jack's Bar-B-Q **6**
The Old Spaghetti Factory **7**

15-minute drive away. Many hotels near the airport offer a complimentary shuttle service, while others slightly farther away have their own fee shuttles; check when you make your reservation. The **Gray Line Airport Express** (© **800/669-9463** or 615/275-1180) operates shuttles between the airport and downtown and West End hotels every 15 to 20 minutes daily between 6am and 11pm. Rates are $11 one-way and $17 round-trip. A taxi from the airport into downtown Nashville will cost you about $20.

By Car   Major routes into Nashville are I-40 from the east (Knoxville) and west (Memphis), I-65 from the north (Louisville) and south (Birmingham, AL), and I-24 from the northwest (St. Louis) and southeast (Chattanooga and Atlanta).

VISITOR INFORMATION   Contact the **Nashville Convention & Visitors Bureau,** 211 Commerce St., Nashville, TN 37201 (© **800/657-6910;** www. nashvillecvb.com). Their **Visitor Information Center** is in the Gaylord Entertainment Center, Fifth Avenue and Broadway (© **615/259-4747**), in downtown Nashville.

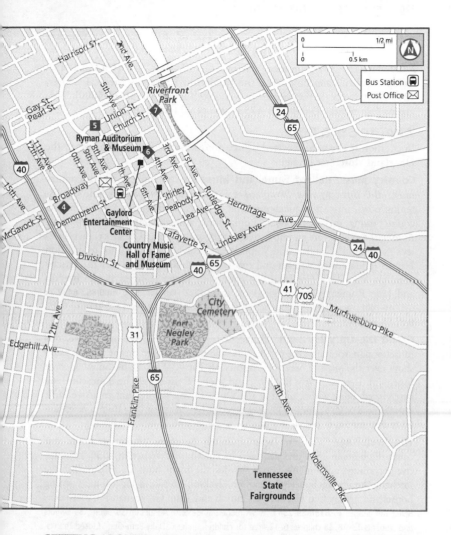

GETTING AROUND Because the city and its attractions are spread out, the best way to get around Nashville is by car.

Though it won't get you everywhere you need to go, Nashville is served by the **Metropolitan Transit Authority (MTA)** bus system (© 615/862-5950). The MTA information center and ticket booth is on Deaderick Street at Fifth Avenue. Fares are $1.45 ($1.75 for express buses) for adults, and 70¢ for seniors, students, and riders with disabilities; children under 4 ride free. You can ride for 25¢ on any MTA bus within the downtown area bordered by James Robertson Parkway, Franklin Street, the Cumberland River, and I-40; just ask the bus driver for a **RUSH card** and return it when you leave.

The **Nashville Trolley Company** (© 615/862-5950) operates three trolley routes around the city—Downtown, Music Row, and Music Valley. The fare is $1 or $3 for a day pass. Call for the hours of operation, which vary throughout the year.

For quick cab service, call **Music City Taxi** (© 615/262-0451), **Checker Cab** (© 615/256-7000), or **Allied Taxi** (© 615/244-7433).

FAST FACTS   For a medical referral, call **Medline** (© 615/342-1919). Among Nashville area hospitals is the **Vanderbilt University Medical Center**, 1211 22nd Ave. S., in the downtown/Vanderbilt area (© 615/322-5000). **Walgreens** pharmacies (© 800/925-4733) are open 24 hours a day.

WHAT TO SEE & DO

In addition to the sights covered below, don't miss the fantastic atriums at the **Opryland Hotel** (see below).

Country Music Hall of Fame and Museum   If you're a fan of country music, this stunning new showplace is it. Multimedia stations include CD listening posts, interactive jukeboxes, and displays on bluegrass, cowboy music, country swing, rockabilly, Cajun, honky-tonk, and contemporary country hits. Among the exhibits are an impressive history of the Grand Ole Opry, Elvis Presley's "solid-gold" Cadillac, and Webb Pierce's cowboy Cadillac, not to mention Naomi Judd's rusted wringer-and-tub style washing machine and the kitschy cornfield from TV's *Hee Haw*, complete with Junior Samples' denim overalls and Lulu Roman's plus-size gingham dress. 222 Fifth Ave. S. © 800/852-6437 or 615/416-2001. www.countrymusichalloffame.com. Admission $15 adults, $7.95 children 6–15. Daily 10am–6pm.

Grand Ole Opry Museum   Adjacent to the Grand Ole Opry House, this museum pays tribute to the performers who have appeared on the famous radio show over the years: There are exhibits on Patsy Cline, Hank Snow, George Jones, Jim Reeves, Marty Robbins, and more recent stars. These museums are best visited along with a night at the Opry, so you might want to arrive early. 2804 Opryland Dr. © 615/871-6779. www.opry.com. Free admission. Daily 10am to varied closing hours, depending on performance schedule. Closes for special events; call ahead.

The Hermitage   Andrew Jackson's stately Southern plantation house was originally built in 1821 and acquired its current appearance in 1836. Descriptive recordings accompany tours. Besides the main house, you can visit the kitchen, the smoke house, the garden, Jackson's tomb, a log cabin, a spring house, and nearby Old Hermitage Church and Tulip Grove mansion. Old Hickory Blvd., Hermitage. © 615/889-2941. www.thehermitage.com. Admission $9 adults, $9 seniors and students 13–18, $5 children 6–12, free for children under 6. Daily 9am–5pm. Closed Thanksgiving, Dec 25, 3rd week in Jan. Take I-40 east to Exit 221, then go 4 miles north.

The Parthenon   This full-size replica of Athens' Parthenon was built as the centerpiece of the Tennessee Centennial Exposition in 1897. Reconstructed in 1931, it houses a 421-foot statue of Athena Parthenos, the tallest indoor sculpture in the country, as well as plaster casts of the Elgin Marbles. Basement galleries house 19th- and 20th-century American art. Centennial Park, West End and 25th aves. © 615/862-8431. www.parthenon.org. Admission $3.50 adults, $2 seniors and children. Oct–Mar Tues–Sat 9am–4:30pm; Apr–Sept Tues–Sat 9am–4:30pm, Sun 12:30–4:30pm.

Ryman Auditorium & Museum   The site of the Grand Ole Opry from 1943 to 1974, the Ryman Auditorium is the most historic site in the world of country music. Its stage has seen the likes of Sarah Bernhardt, Enrico Caruso, Katharine Hepburn, Will Rogers, and Elvis Presley. In 1943, the Grand Ole Opry began broadcasting from here, and for the next 31 years, the Ryman Auditorium hosted the most famous country-music radio show in the country until it moved to a new theater in 1974. Today its stage is again home to country music and other performances, but with a renovation in 1994, the auditorium lost most of its historic character. Visitors can get the same feel and hear some music by attending a show instead of taking the self-guided tour. 116 Fifth Ave. N. ℂ 615/254-1445 or 615/889-3060. www.ryman.com. Admission $8 adults, $4 children 4–11. Daily 9am–4pm. Closed Thanksgiving, Dec 25, and Jan 1.

WHERE TO STAY

Hotel reservations can be made through the **Nashville CVB's Housing Bureau** (ℂ **800/657-6910**). Chain hotels in the Music Valley area include the **Doubletree Guest Suites,** 2424 Atrium Way (ℂ 615/889-8889); **Homewood Suites,** 2640 Elm Hill Pike (ℂ 615/884-8111); **Best Suites,** 2521 Elm Hill Pike (ℂ 615/391-3919); **La Quinta Inn Airport,** 2345 Atrium Way (ℂ 615/885-3000); and **SpringHill Suites by Marriott,** 1100 Airport Center Dr. (ℂ 615/884-6111). Other good budget bets include such old standbys as **Best Western Calumet Inn,** 701 Stewart's Ferry Pike (ℂ 615/889-9199); **Days Inn-Nashville East,** 3445 Percy Priest Dr. (ℂ 615/889-8881); and **Red Roof Inn-Nashville East,** 510 Claridge Dr. (ℂ 615/872-0735); **Super 8 Motel-Nashville/Airport/Music City,** 720 Royal Pkwy. (ℂ 615/889-8887); **Fairfield Inn,** 211 Music City Circle (ℂ 615/872-8939); and **Holiday Inn Express,** 2516 Music Valley Dr. (ℂ 615/889-0086).

Embassy Suites Nashville   This all-suite hotel is a great choice for both families and business travelers. Not only do you get a two-room suite with a wet bar and fridge, but breakfast and evening cocktails are included in the rates. The centerpiece of the hotel is its atrium, which is full of tropical plants, including palm trees. 10 Century Blvd., Nashville, TN 37214. ℂ 800/EMBASSY or 615/871-0033. Fax 615/883-9245. www.embassy-suites.com. 296 units. $99–$179 suite. Children 17 and under stay free in parents' room. Rates include full breakfast. AE, DC, DISC, MC, V. Free parking. **Amenities:** Restaurant; indoor pool; spa; health club.

The Hermitage Hotel   Closed while undergoing a $15-million renovation, this historic downtown property, built in 1910 in the classic beaux-arts style, is Nashville's grand hotel and the city's top choice if you crave both space and elegance. The lobby, with its marble columns, gilded plasterwork, and stained-glass ceiling, is the most elegant and luxurious in the city, and although the guest rooms (all are suites) aren't quite as spectacular, they are spacious and comfortable. Most feature large windows and marble-floored bathrooms. North-side rooms have good views of the capitol. It's set to reopen on Valentine's Day (Feb 14), 2003. 231 Sixth Ave. N., Nashville, TN 37219. ℂ 888/888-9414 or 615/244-3121. Fax 615/254-6909. www.thehermitagehotel.com. 120 units. $129–$209 suite. Children 17 and under stay free in parents' room. AE, DC, DISC, MC, V. Parking $15. **Amenities:** Restaurant; pet deposit $50 per stay.

Holiday Inn Express–Airport   From the minute you pull up to the hotel's grand entry portico, you'll see that this is a great value, far removed from the generic mainstream. There are moose-antler chandeliers hanging from exposed roof beams, a stone floor, and a river-rock fireplace. The guest rooms are all fairly spacious, with country-pine furniture and extra-large bathrooms. Many rooms have little balconies overlooking the courtyard gardens or the rolling hills of the surrounding office park. 1111 Airport Center Dr., Nashville, TN 37214. ℂ 800/HOLIDAY or 615/883-1366. Fax 615/889-6867. www.holiday-inn.com. 206 units. $69–$99 double. Children 17 and under stay free in parents' room. All rates include full breakfast. AE, DC, DISC, MC, V. Free parking. **Amenities:** Outdoor pool.

The Millennium (Maxwell House) Hotel   This modern 10-story hotel is convenient to both downtown and Music Valley. South-side rooms on the upper floors of the hotel have a commanding view of the Nashville skyline and are worth requesting. Furnishings feature traditional styling, and there are executive-level rooms with upgraded amenities. 2025 MetroCenter Blvd., Nashville, TN 37228-1505. (C) 800/457-4460 or 615/259-4343. Fax 615/242-4967. www.millennium-hotels. com. 289 units. $96–$158 double; $175–$400 suite. Children 17 and under stay free in parents' room. AE, DC, DISC, MC, V. Free self-parking. **Amenities:** Restaurant; outdoor pool; 2 lighted tennis courts.

Opryland Hotel   This Disneyesque hotel attracts thousands of visitors daily to its tropical atriums. The largest is The Delta, which covers 4½ acres and has a quarter-mile-long "river," a 110-foot-wide waterfall, an 85-foot-tall fountain, and an island modeled after the French Quarter in New Orleans. The Cascade Conservatory consists of two linked atriums with a 40-foot-tall waterfall, a fountain, bridges and meandering paths, palm trees, a revolving gazebo bar, and a patio restaurant. Guest rooms, while modern and comfortable, don't quite live up to the public areas. Some suites have kitchens or kitchenettes. Colonial American decor and tasteful floral wallpaper give them a touch of classic elegance, but they are neither large nor overly plush. 2800 Opryland Dr., Nashville, TN 37214-1297. (C) 615/883-2211 or 615/889-1000. Fax 615/871-5728. www.opryhotels.com. 2,883 units. $99–$279 double; suites and deluxe units $259 and up. Children 11 and under stay free in parents' room. AE, DC, DISC, MC, V. Self-parking $6, valet parking $12. **Amenities:** Restaurants (14); 2 heated outdoor pools; Springhouse Golf Club.

Sheraton Music City   Big, elegant, and set on 23 acres near the airport, this large convention hotel has a commanding vista of the surrounding area. Classic Georgian styling conjures up the feel of an antebellum mansion. The guest rooms are well designed, with three phones, large work desks, plenty of closet space, and comfortable chairs. 777 McGavock Pike, Nashville, TN 37214-3175. (C) 800/325-3535 or 615/885-2200. Fax 615/231-1134. www.sheratonmusiccity.com.com. 468 units. $120–$165 double; $150–$600 suite. Children 17 and under stay free in parents' room. AE, DC, DISC, MC, V. Self-parking free, valet parking $8. **Amenities:** Restaurant; outdoor pool; spa; health club; lighted tennis court.

WHERE TO DINE

If you're looking for barbecue, in addition to our favorite, **Whitt's** (reviewed below), try the baby-back ribs at **Bar-B-Cutie,** 501 Donelson Pike ((C) 615/872-0207) or 5221 Nolensville Rd. ((C) 615/834-6556); the slow-smoked pulled pork, ribs, brisket, and chicken at **Corky's Bar-B-Q,** 100 Franklin Rd., Brentwood ((C) 615/373-1020), Nashville's most upscale barbecue joint; or the pork shoulder, Texas beef brisket, and St. Louis ribs at **Jack's Bar-B-Que,** 416 Broadway ((C) 615/254-5715).

Arthur's CONTINENTAL   Arthur's is a contender for most elegant restaurant in the city. There are huge plantation-style shutters on the windows, gilded plasterwork and stained glass, lots of lace and walnut paneling, a stone fireplace, and comfortable banquettes. Set aside at least 2 or 3 hours for a meal—you'll want to savor every course. The menu changes daily but you can count on a plethora of meat dishes like rack of lamb, chateaubriand, and tournedos of beef. The flambéed desserts and coffees shouldn't be missed. In the Union Station hotel, 1001 Broadway. (C) 615/255-1494. Reservations highly recommended. Jacket and tie preferred for men. 7-course fixed-price dinner $60. AE, DC, DISC, MC, V. Mon–Thurs 5:30–10pm; Fri–Sat 5:30–11pm; Sun 5:30–9pm.

Blackstone Restaurant & Brewery BURGERS/AMERICAN   At this big, glitzy brewpub, brewing tanks crank out half a dozen beers ranging from a pale ale to a dark porter. Whether you're looking for pub grub (pizzas, soups, pub-style burgers) or a more formal dinner (a meaty pork loin well complemented by apple chutney and a smidgen of rosemary, garlic, and juniper berries), you'll be happy here, especially if you're into good microbrews. 1918 West End Ave. ℂ 615/327-9969. Sandwiches, pizza, and main courses $6–$16. AE, DC, MC, V. Mon–Thurs 11am–midnight; Fri–Sat 11am–1am; Sun noon–10pm.

Bound'ry NEW AMERICAN/NEW SOUTHERN   This fun yet sophisticated spot is popular with everyone from college students to families to businesspeople in suits. Add some jazz to the wild, Dr. Seuss–style interior design and you get a very energetic atmosphere. From the tapas to the large plates, everything is good, but should it still be on the menu, don't miss the stack of polenta, eggplant, portobello mushrooms, squash, roasted-red-pepper goat cheese, and smoked provolone with puttanesca sauce, pesto, and tapenade. 911 20th Ave. S. ℂ 615/321-3043. Reservations accepted for large parties. Tapas $5–$8; main courses $13–$23. AE, DC, DISC, MC, V. Daily 4pm–2:30am.

Cock of the Walk SOUTHERN   This big, barnlike restaurant near the Opryland Hotel is known for having the best catfish in town, an assertion backed up by the late, great food critic, Craig Claiborne, when he ate here. Start your meal with that most bizarre of Southern appetizers, the fried dill pickle, then move on to the fried catfish filets with a pot o' greens. 2624 Music Valley Dr. ℂ 615/889-1930. Reservations not accepted. Main courses $9–$12. AE, DISC, MC, V. Mon–Thurs 5–9pm; Fri–Sat 5–10pm; Sun 11am–9pm.

Houston's AMERICAN   You can be sure that popular Houston's will be packed when you visit. Despite the fact that this is a new building, interior brick arches and exposed beams give the restaurant the feel of a renovated warehouse. There's even a dark oak bar with lots of brass and pine. The salads and burgers are consistently voted the best in town, and they do a good job on prime rib and barbecue. 3000 West End Ave. ℂ 615/269-3481. Reservations not accepted; phone ahead for wait list. Main courses $12–$25. AE, MC, V. Sun–Mon 10:45am–9:30pm; Tues–Thurs 10:45am–10pm; Fri–Sat 10:45am–11pm.

Loveless Café SOUTHERN   This restaurant may be a little out of the way, but it's worth it if you like down-home cookin'. This old-fashioned roadhouse and popular Nashville institution is out Tenn. 100 about 7½ miles south of Belle Meade and the turnoff from U.S. 70 South. People rave about the country ham with red-eye gravy, Southern fried chicken, and homemade biscuits with home-made fruit jams. 8400 Tenn. 100. ℂ 615/646-9700. Reservations recommended. Breakfast $7–$9; main dinner courses $11–$15. AE, MC, V. Mon–Fri 8am–2pm and 5–9pm; Sat–Sun 8am–9pm.

The Old Spaghetti Factory ITALIAN   This is a great spot to bring the family to; a complete meal—including salad, bread, ice cream, and a beverage—costs you less than a cocktail in many restaurants. There's stained and beveled glass all around, antiques everywhere, and plush seating in the waiting area. The front of the restaurant is a large, very elegant bar. 160 Second Ave. N. ℂ 615/254-9010. Reservations not accepted. Main courses $5–$10. DC, DISC, MC, V. Mon–Fri 11:30am–2pm; Mon–Thurs 5–10pm; Fri–Sat 5–11pm; Sun noon–10pm.

Whitt's Barbecue BARBECUE   Walk in, drive up, or get it delivered. Whitt's serves some of the best barbecue in Nashville. There's no in-restaurant seating here, so plan to take it back to your hotel or plan a picnic. You can buy barbecued pork, beef, and even turkey by the pound, or order sandwiches and plates with the extra fixin's. The pork barbecue sandwiches, topped with a zesty coleslaw, get our vote for best in town. Other branches are at 2535 Lebanon Rd. (© 615/ 883-6907) and 114 Old Hickory Blvd. E. (© 615/868-1369). 5310 Harding Rd. © 615/356-3435. Sandwiches and platters $5–$6. AE, DISC, MC, V. Mon–Sat 10:30am–8pm.

NASHVILLE'S COUNTRY MUSIC SCENE

The Nashville nightlife scene is divided into two main entertainment districts— The District and Music Valley. The District, an area of renovated warehouses and old bars, is the livelier of the two areas, whereas Music Valley offers a more family-oriented, suburban nightlife scene.

The *Nashville Scene* is the city's arts-and-entertainment weekly. It comes out on Thursday and is available at restaurants, clubs, and convenience stores, as well as online at **www.nashvillescene.com**. Also on Thursday, the *Nashville Banner* newspaper publishes its "Weekender" section, which includes the Grand Ole Opry lineup for that weekend. Every Friday, *The Tennessean*, Nashville's morning daily, publishes the Opry lineup, and on Sunday it publishes "Show-case," a guide to the coming week's entertainment. Find it online at **www. tennessean.com**.

The show that made Nashville famous, the **Grand Ole Opry**, 2804 Opryland Dr. (© **615/889-6611**), is the country's longest continuously running radio show and airs every weekend from this theater next to the Opryland Hotel. Over the decades, the Opry has featured nearly all the greats of country music. There's no telling who you might see, but the show's membership roster includes Vince Gill, Martina McBride, Garth Brooks, Loretta Lynn, Porter Wagoner, Ricky Skaggs, and many others. Nearly all performances sell out, and though it's often possible to get last-minute tickets, you should try to order tickets as far in advance of your trip as possible. Tickets are $18 to $20.

Once the home of the Grand Ole Opry, **Ryman Auditorium**, 116 Fifth Ave. N. (© **615/254-1445** for information, 615/889-6611 for tickets), was reno-vated a few years back and is once again hosting performances with a country-music slant. The schedule at the Ryman also usually includes a weekly bluegrass night in the summer and occasional Sunday-night gospel/Christian contempo-rary shows. You can also catch pop, rock, and classical concerts.

The **Texas Troubadour Theatre**, Music Valley Village, 2416 Valley Dr. (© **615/885-0028**), is home to the Ernest Tubb Midnight Jamboree and the Sunday morning Cowboy Church.

The **Nashville Palace**, 2400 Music Valley Dr., across the street from the Opryland Hotel (© **615/885-1540**), is open nightly with live country-and-western music, a dance floor, and a full restaurant. This is where Randy Travis got his start.

The **Wildhorse Saloon**, 120 Second Ave. N. (© **615/251-1000**), is a mas-sive dance hall that's the hot spot for boot scooters, attracting everyone from country-music stars to line-dancing senior-citizen groups. Free dance lessons are available from 4 to 9pm.

The **Bluebird Café**, 4104 Hillsboro Rd. (© **615/383-1461**), is Nashville's premier venue for both up-and-coming and established songwriters. Between 6 and 7pm, there is frequently music in the round, during which four singer-song-writers play some of their latest works. After 9pm, when more established acts take the stage, there's a cover charge. Reservations are recommended. The Bluebird's main competition is the **Douglas Corner Café**, 2106A Eighth Ave. S. (© **615/298-1688**).

Four miles north of Opryland off Briley Parkway on Gallatin Road, **Denim & Diamonds,** 950 Madison Sq., Madison (℃ **615/868-1557**), boasts a massive 4,000-square-foot, horseshoe-shaped dance floor. There are free dance lessons Thursday and Sunday nights from 7 to 9pm.

If your tastes in country run to bluegrass straight from the hills, try the **Station Inn,** 402 12th Ave. S. (℃ **615/255-3307**), down in the warehouse district south of Broadway in downtown. **Tootsie's Orchid Lounge,** 422 Broadway (℃ **615/726-0463**), has been a Nashville tradition for decades, and still offers free live country music all day and all night.

SIDE TRIPS FROM NASHVILLE

To visit both the battlefield and the distillery, described below, head south from Nashville on I-24.

On New Year's Eve 1862, what would become the bloodiest Civil War battle west of the Appalachian Mountains began just north of Murfreesboro along the Stones River. By the end of the first day of fighting the Confederates thought they were assured a victory, but Union reinforcements turned the tide against the Rebels. By January 3, the Confederates were in retreat and 23,000 soldiers lay dead or injured on the battlefield. Today, 351 acres of the site of the conflict are preserved in the **Stones River National Battlefield,** 3501 Old Nashville Hwy., Murfreesboro (℃ **615/893-9501**). The site includes a national cemetery and the Hazen Brigade Monument, which was erected in 1863 and is the oldest Civil War memorial in the United States. In the visitor center, you'll find a museum full of artifacts and details of the battle. Free admission; open daily from 8am to 5pm.

Old Jack Daniel (or Mr. Jack, as he was known hereabouts) didn't waste any time setting up his whiskey distillery after the Civil War came to an end. Founded in 1866, the **Jack Daniel's Distillery,** Tenn. 55, Lynchburg (℃ **615/ 320-5477;** www.jackdaniels.com), is the oldest registered distillery in the United States and is on the National Register of Historic Places. After touring the distillery, you can glance into the office used by Mr. Jack and see the safe that did him in. Old Mr. Jack kicked that safe one day in a fit of anger and wound up getting gangrene for his troubles. If you want to take home a special bottle of Jack Daniel's, it can be purchased here at the distillery, but nowhere else in this county, which is another of Tennessee's dry counties. Free admission. It's open to the public daily except major holidays from 8am to 4pm, with tours at regular intervals throughout the day. No reservations.

15 Memphis

A trip to Memphis is a pilgrimage for Elvis fans and for music fans drawn to the birthplace of the most important musical styles of the 20th century—blues, soul, and rock-and-roll. Memphis is barbecue and Beale Street, the Mighty Mississippi and urban sprawl.

Located at the far western end of Tennessee, Memphis sits on a bluff overlooking the Mississippi River, Arkansas and, a few miles to the south, Mississippi. With a metropolitan area of one million, it is a sprawling city, with high-rises sprouting in suburban neighborhoods. The wealthy live, do business, and shop in East Memphis, but in recent years Midtown, with its old homes and tree-lined streets, has been rediscovered and now blossoms with hip restaurants, boutiques, and nightlife.

Memphis

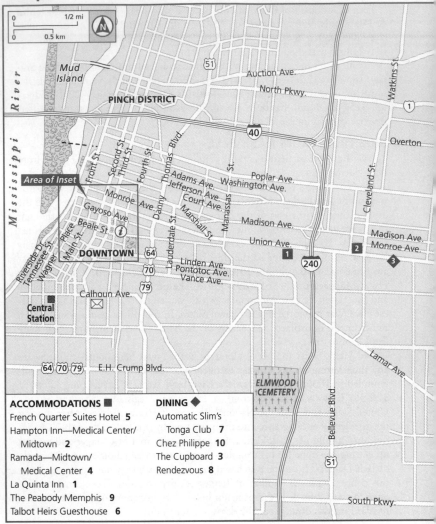

ACCOMMODATIONS ■
French Quarter Suites Hotel **5**
Hampton Inn—Medical Center/
　Midtown **2**
Ramada—Midtown/
　Medical Center **4**
La Quinta Inn **1**
The Peabody Memphis **9**
Talbot Heirs Guesthouse **6**

DINING ◆
Automatic Slim's
　Tonga Club **7**
Chez Philippe **10**
The Cupboard **3**
Rendezvous **8**

But it was the renovation of Beale Street that succeeded in bringing businesses and people back downtown in the '90s. Beale Street was home to W. C. Handy, B. B. King, Muddy Waters, and others who merged the gospel singing and cotton-field work songs of the Mississippi delta into a music called the blues.

ESSENTIALS
GETTING THERE By Plane Memphis International Airport (© 901/ 922-8000; www.mscaa.com) is about 11 miles from downtown Memphis and 9 miles from East Memphis, both via I-240. Generally, allow about 20 minutes to get downtown from the airport, 15 minutes to get to East Memphis—more during rush hour. Your best bet is the **Hotel Shuttle Service** (© 901/544-1550) operating between the airport and many area hotels throughout the day. Rates

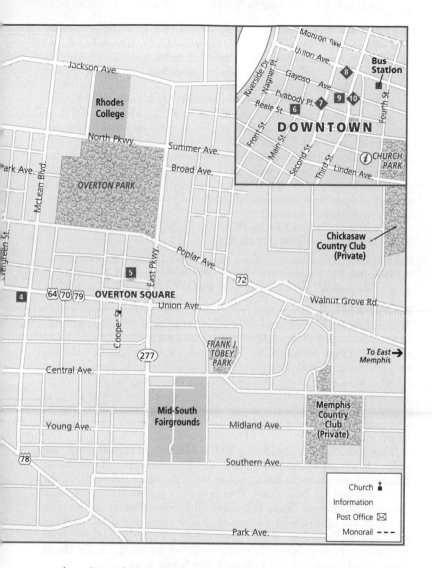

are about $10 to $20 per person one-way. A **taxi** to downtown Memphis is about $23, to East Memphis about $19.

By Train   **Amtrak** (© **800/USA-RAIL;** www.amtrak.com) provides daily service from Chicago (trip time: 10½ hr.) and New Orleans (8½ hr.) to its station at 545 S. Main St.

By Car   The main routes into Memphis include I-40 from the east (Nashville) and west (Little Rock), I-55 from the north (St. Louis) and south (New Orleans).

VISITOR INFORMATION   Contact the **Memphis Convention & Visitors Bureau,** 47 Union Ave., Memphis, TN 38103 (© **800/8-MEMPHIS** or 901/543-5300; www.memphistravel.com), open from 8am to 5pm daily.

GETTING AROUND   A car is nearly indispensable for traveling between downtown and East Memphis, yet traffic can make this trip take up to 45 minutes. East-west avenues and almost any road in East Memphis at rush hour are the most congested. When driving between downtown and East Memphis, you'll usually do better to take the interstate.

The **Memphis Area Transit Authority (MATA)** (© 901/274-MATA) operates citywide bus service. The standard fare is $1.10, and exact change is required. Transfers cost 10¢, and there's a 50% discount for travelers with disabilities and seniors with ID cards.

The **Main Street Trolley** (© 901/577-2640) operates on a circular route that includes Memphis's biggest attractions. The fare is 60¢ each way, with a special rate of 25¢ between 11am and 1:30pm. An all-day pass is $2; exact change is required, and passengers may board at any of the 20 stations along Main Street. Trolleys are wheelchair accessible.

Taxi companies include **Checker/Yellow Cab** (© 901/577-7777) and **City Wide Cab Company** (© 901/324-4202).

FAST FACTS   For a doctor, or if you need a hospital, contact **Baptist Memorial Hospital,** 899 Madison Ave. (© 901/362-8677). There's a 24-hour pharmacy at **Walgreens,** 1863 Union Ave. (© 901/272-1141 or 901/272-2006).

WHAT TO SEE & DO

To blues fans, **Beale Street** is the most important street in America. The musical form known as the blues—with roots that stretch back to the African musical heritage of slaves brought to the United States—was born here. W. C. Handy was performing on Beale Street when he penned "Memphis Blues," the first published blues song. Shortly after the Civil War, Beale Street became one of the most important streets in the South for African Americans. Many of the most famous musicians in the blues world got their starts here; besides W. C. Handy, other greats include B. B. King, Furry Lewis, Rufus Thomas, Isaac Hayes, and Alberta Hunter.

Today, Beale Street continues to draw fans of blues and popular music, and **nightclubs** line the blocks between Second and Fourth streets. The **Orpheum Theatre,** once a vaudeville palace, is now the performance hall for Broadway road shows, and the **New Daisy Theatre** features performances by up-and-coming bands and once-famous performers. **Historic markers** up and down the street relate the area's colorful past, and two statues commemorate the city's two most important musicians: W. C. Handy and Elvis Presley. In addition to the many clubs featuring nightly live music, check out the **W. C. Handy House Museum** and the museumlike **A. Schwab Dry Goods store.**

Dixon Gallery and Gardens   The South's finest collection of Impressionist and post-Impressionist art is the highlight of this exquisite little museum. The building and collection once belonged to avid art collectors Margaret and Hugo Dixon. You'll see paintings by Matisse, Renoir, Degas, Gauguin, Cassatt, Turner, and Constable. 4339 Park Ave., East Memphis. © 901/761-2409. www.dixon.org. Admission $5 adults, $4 seniors, $3 students, $1 children 5–11. Tues–Sat 10am–5pm; Sun 1–5pm. Gardens only Mon 10am–5pm, admission half-price.

Graceland   Graceland is the second most visited home in America (only the White House tops it). For decades, thousands of love-struck pilgrims have flocked here in search of the ghost of Elvis. Purchased in the late 1950s for $100,000, Graceland today is far more than the former home of the King: It's dripping with excess, resembling a small theme park or shopping mall in scope and design.

Visitors are given portable cassette players with recordings that describe each of the rooms open to the public. After touring the house, you can see Elvis's office; his racquetball building; a small exhibit of personal belongings, memorabilia, and awards; a display of his many gold records; and finally, his grave (in the Meditation Garden).

Other attractions include the **Elvis Presley Automobile Museum** with his famous 1955 pink Cadillac, a 1956 purple Cadillac convertible, and two Stutz Blackhawks from the early 1970s, as well as motorcycles and other vehicles; a re-creation of an airport terminal with Elvis's **private jets,** the *Lisa Marie* and *Hound Dog II;* and **Sincerely Elvis,** a collection of the King's personal belongings, everything from his personal record collection to a pair of his sneakers.

Throughout the year there are several special events at Graceland. Elvis's birthday (Jan 8, 1935) is celebrated each year with several days of festivities. However, mid-August's Elvis Week, commemorating his August 16, 1977, death, boasts the greatest Elvis celebrations both here at Graceland and throughout Memphis. Each year from Thanksgiving to January 8, Graceland is decorated with Elvis's original Christmas lights and lawn decorations.

Devoted fans who are early risers should be aware that most mornings it is possible to visit Elvis's grave before Graceland officially opens. This special free walk-up period lasts for 90 minutes and ends 30 minutes before the mansion opens. 3734 Elvis Presley Blvd. (C) 800/238-2000 or 901/332-3322. www.elvis-presley.com. Graceland Mansion Tour $16 adults, $14.40 seniors and students, $6 children 7–12. Elvis's jets $5.00 adults, $4.50 seniors, $3 children 7–12. Sincerely Elvis Museum $3.50 adults, $3.15 seniors, $2.50 children 7–12. The Platinum Tour (includes admittance to all Graceland attractions) $20 adults, $18 seniors, $11 children 7–12. Tour reservations can be made 24 hr. in advance and are recommended if you have a tight schedule. Memorial Day to Labor Day daily 8am–6pm; Rest of year daily 9am–5pm. No mansion tour Nov–Feb on Tues.

National Civil Rights Museum On April 4, 1968, Dr. Martin Luther King, Jr., stepped onto the balcony outside his room in the Lorraine Motel and was shot dead by James Earl Ray. Today, the Lorraine Motel serves as the nation's monument to the civil rights movement. In evocative displays, the museum chronicles the struggle of African Americans from the time of slavery to the present. Multimedia presentations and life-size, walk-through tableaux include a Montgomery, Alabama, public bus like the one on which Rosa Parks was riding when she refused to move to the back of the bus; a Greensboro, North Carolina, lunch counter; and the burned shell of a freedom-ride Greyhound bus. 450 Mulberry St. (C) 901/521-9699. www.civilrightsmuseum.org. Admission $8.50 adults, $7.50 students and seniors, $4 children 4–17, free for children under 4. Sept–May Mon, Wed, and Fri–Sat 9am–5pm, Thurs 9am–8pm, Sun 1–5pm; June–Aug Mon, Wed, and Fri–Sat 9am–6pm, Thurs 9am–8pm, Sun 1–6pm.

Sun Studio Here, in the early 1950s, such local artists as Elvis Presley, Jerry Lee Lewis, Roy Orbison, and Carl Perkins, created a sound that would become known as rock-and-roll. Over the years, owner and recording engineer Sam Phillips also helped start the recording careers of the blues greats B. B. King and Howlin' Wolf and country giant Johnny Cash. By night, Sun Studio is still an active recording studio and has been used by such artists as U2, Spin Doctors, The Tractors, and Bonnie Raitt. Next door is the Sun Studio Café, a 1950s-style diner that has long been a musicians' hangout. 706 Union Ave. (C) 901/521-0664.

www.sunstudio.com. Admission $8.50 adults, free for children under 12 accompanied by parents. Sept–May daily 10am–6pm; June–Aug daily 9am–7pm.

WHERE TO STAY

In addition to the hotels listed below, national and regional chain motels in the midtown area include **Hampton Inn–Medical Center/Midtown,** 1180 Union Ave. (© **901/276-1175**); and **La Quinta Inn,** 42 S. Camilla St. (© **901/526-1050**). In the airport/Graceland area, chains include the **Hampton Inn–Airport,** 2979 Millbranch Rd. (© **901/396-2200**); and **Graceland Airport Travelodge,** 1360 Springbrook Rd. (© **901/396-3620**).

Elvis Presley's Heartbreak Hotel   If your visit to Memphis is strictly a pilgrimage to Graceland, there should be no question as to where to stay. This hotel has a gate right into the Graceland parking lot, with Elvis's home right across Elvis Presley Boulevard. Rooms have small fridges and microwaves, not to mention 24-hour-airings of Elvis movies. 3677 Elvis Presley Blvd., Memphis, TN 38116. © **877/777-0606** or 901/332-1000. Fax 901/332-2107. www.elvis.com. 143 units. $90–$109 double. Children 17 and under stay free in parents' room. Rates include continental breakfast. AE, DC, DISC, MC, V. Free parking. **Amenities:** Outdoor pool.

Embassy Suites   With its many tropical plants and artificial stream, the lobby of this modern atrium hotel resembles a botanical conservatory. The spacious two-room suites have kitchenettes, two televisions, two phones, and sofa beds; they're good for both families and business travelers. Moderately priced Frank Gristani's Italian Restaurant is one of the best Italian restaurants in the city. 1022 S. Shady Grove Rd., Memphis, TN 38120. © **800/EMBASSY** or 901/684-1777. Fax 901/685-8185. www.embassy-suites.com. 220 units. $119–$169 double. Children 17 and under stay free in parents' room. Rates include full breakfast. AE, DC, DISC, MC, V. Free parking. **Amenities:** Restaurant; indoor pool.

French Quarter Suites Hotel   The French Quarter Suites Hotel draws on New Orleans for its architectural theme and is one of our favorite Memphis hotels. There are half-canopied king-size beds in some rooms, and all rooms have high ceilings and overhead fans. Double whirlpool tubs make the hotel popular with honeymooners. Many rooms have French doors opening onto private balconies. The atrium lobby features live jazz or Top-40 music on weekends; the Bourbon St. Café serves French and Cajun cuisine. 2144 Madison Ave., Memphis, TN 38104. © **800/843-0353** or 901/728-4000. Fax 901/278-1262. 105 units. $109–$119 double. Children 17 and under stay free in parents' room. AE, DC, DISC, MC, V. Free parking. **Amenities:** Restaurant; outdoor pool.

The Peabody Memphis   The Peabody is the most luxurious hotel in Memphis. The lobby's most prominent feature is its Romanesque fountain, where the famous Peabody ducks while away each day. The deluxe rooms have classic French styling, maple-burl armoires, and king-size beds. The hotel's Chez Philippe (see "Where to Dine," below) has long been one of the best restaurants in Memphis, and there are several other dining options. 149 Union Ave., Memphis, TN 38103. © **800/PEABODY** or 901/529-4000. Fax 901/529-3600. www.peabodymemphis.com. 418 units. $270–$345 double; suites and deluxe units $380 and up. Children 17 and under stay free in parents' room. AE, DC, DISC, MC, V. Self-parking $5, valet parking $13. **Amenities:** Restaurants (3); indoor pool; health club.

Ramada–Midtown/Medical Center   This midtown lodging is a good choice if you want to be close to both museums and nightclubs. Try to get a room on an upper floor so you can enjoy the views of the city at night. The king rooms are the best deal, with love seats and lots of space. The hotel's restaurant has lots of Elvis posters and is done in a combination of Art Deco and 1950s-diner styling. 1837 Union Ave., Memphis, TN 38104. ℭ 800/2RAMADA or 901/278-4100. Fax 901/272-3810. www.ramada.com. 179 units. $65–$76 double; $96–$160 suite. Children 17 and under stay free in parents' room. AE, DC, DISC, MC, V. Free parking. Amenities: Restaurant; outdoor pool.

Studio 6 Memphis A cheery, tiled lobby greets you as you step through the entrance of this all-suite hotel near the airport. Studios and one- and two-bedroom suites are available; all have kitchens with microwave ovens and coffeemakers. One-bedroom suites have large kitchens. 4300 American Way, Memphis, TN 38118. ℭ 888/897-0202 or 901/366-9333. Fax 901/366-7835. 120 units. $58 double. Children 17 and under stay free in parents' room. Rates include continental breakfast. AE, DC, DISC, MC, V. Free parking. Amenities: Outdoor pool.

Talbot Heirs Guesthouse Trendy, contemporary styling makes this upscale downtown B&B unique. Rooms vary in size from large to huge and are boldly decorated in a wide variety of styles. Most have interesting modern lamps, and many have kilim rugs; all have full kitchens. Children may stay free in parents' room. However, because each room has only one queen-size bed (cots may be requested from the front desk), the accommodations are practical for only younger children. 99 S. Second St., Memphis, TN 38103. ℭ 901/527-9772. Fax 901/527-3700. www.talbothouse.com. 9 units. $200–$250 double. Children stay free in parents' room. Rates include continental breakfast. AE, DISC, MC, V. Self-parking $10, nearby valet parking $13.

WHERE TO DINE
Automatic Slim's Tonga Club NEW AMERICAN   Artists from New York and Memphis created the decor with zebra-print upholstered banquettes, slag-glass wall sconces, and colorfully upholstered bar stools. The food and drinks are as inspired as the atmosphere—be sure to try a cocktail with fruit-soaked vodka. The coconut-mango shrimp with citrus pico de gallo makes for an interesting starter. Follow this with the Caribbean voodoo stew with mussels, shrimp, whitefish, and crab legs for a typical Tonga Club meal. 83 S. Second St. ℭ 901/525-7948. Reservations recommended. Main courses $13–$20. AE, DC, MC, V. Mon–Fri 11am–2:30pm; Mon–Thurs 5–10pm; Fri–Sat 5–11pm.

Buntyn Restaurant SOUTHERN   A trip to Buntyn is truly an old-fashioned Southern experience. Whether you order the calves' liver smothered in onions, fried chicken, homemade meatloaf, catfish steak, or maybe chicken and dumplings, you can be sure the portions will be large. Meats come with your choice of two vegetables from a long list that includes fried okra, turnip greens, purple-hull peas, and lime-cream salad. 4972 Park Ave. ℭ 901/458-8776. Main courses $4–$8. MC, V. Mon–Fri 11am–8pm.

Chez Philippe NEW SOUTHERN   In an elegant atmosphere you'll find an ever-changing mix of contemporary French and down-home New Southern dishes. To start, you might order an appetizer of hush puppies stuffed with shrimp Provençal or a crawfish bisque with crunchy hominy dumplings. For a main course, try the smoked pork tenderloin brushed with Jack Daniel's mustard on grits couscous. Prices are high, but expect to be pampered. Sunday brunch is a particularly elegant affair. In the Peabody Memphis hotel, 149 Union Ave. ℭ 901/529-4188. Reservations recommended. Main courses $21–$28. AE, DC, DISC, MC, V. Mon–Sat 6–10pm.

Corky's Bar-B-Q BARBECUE   Corky's is jolly and noisy, with a tempting aroma of barbecue permeating the air. Controversy rages over which is the best barbecue restaurant in Memphis, but we think this one pretty much leads the pack when it comes to pulled pork-shoulder barbecue. Photographs and letters from satisfied customers line the rough-paneled lobby, where you always have to wait for a table. There's also a drive-up window for immediate barbecue gratification. 5259 Poplar Ave. ℂ 901/685-9744. www.corkysbbq.com. Reservations not accepted. Dinners $3–$11. AE, DC, DISC, MC, V. Sun–Thurs 10:45am–10pm; Fri–Sat 10:45am–10:30pm.

The Cupboard SOUTHERN   This place is usually packed with locals having a filling home-cooked meal of Southern-style meat and vegetables. "Meat" includes such dishes as baked chicken, hamburger steak, or catfish filets, and the "vegetables" can be anything from turnip greens to fried green tomatoes to macaroni and cheese. We also like the pecan pie. 1495 Union Ave. ℂ 901/276-8015. Reservations not accepted. Meat and 2 vegetables $5.50; meat and 3 vegetables $7. AE, DC, DISC, MC, V. Mon–Fri 11am–8pm; Sat–Sun 11am–3pm.

Rendezvous BARBECUE   The Rendezvous has been a downtown Memphis institution since 1948, and it has a well-deserved reputation for serving top-notch barbecue and the best ribs in town. Your nose will immediately perk up as the fragrance of hickory-smoked pork wafts past. Get an order of ribs, and be sure to ask if they still have any of the red beans and rice that are served nightly until the pot is empty. 52 S. Second St. ℂ 901/523-2746. Main plates $8–$13. AE, DC, DISC, MC, V. Tues–Thurs 4:30–11pm; Fri 11:30am–midnight; Sat noon–midnight.

MEMPHIS AFTER DARK

To find out what's happening, pick up a copy of the *Memphis Flyer,* Memphis's arts-and-entertainment weekly, which comes out on Thursday. You'll find it in convenience, grocery, and music stores, some restaurants, and nightclubs. You could also pick up the Friday edition of the *Commercial Appeal,* Memphis's morning daily newspaper. The "Playbook" section has very thorough events listings.

BEALE STREET   This is the epicenter of Memphis's nightclub scene. Every Friday night is Big Ass Block Party night, and $10 will get you a wristband good for admission to all the clubs on the street.

The "King of the Blues" does play occasionally, though not regularly, at **B. B. King's Blues Club,** 147 Beale St. (ℂ 901/524-5464). However, any night of the week you can catch blazing blues played by one of the best house bands in town here. Across the street, the **Blues City Café,** 138–140 Beale St. (ℂ 901/526-3637), takes up two old storefronts, with live blues wailing in one room (called the Band Box) and a restaurant serving steaks in the other.

With a gospel Sunday brunch and live rock and blues several nights a week, **Elvis Presley's Memphis,** 126 Beale St. (ℂ 901/527-6900), is one of the most touristy clubs on Beale Street. Before the bands come on, there are Elvis video clips and great recorded music.

Dozens of autographed guitars, including ones signed by Carl Perkins, Stevie Ray Vaughan, Billie Gibbons of ZZ Top, Joe Walsh, George Thorogood, Albert Collins, and other rock and blues guitar wizards, hang from the ceiling at the **Rum Boogie Cafe & Mr. Handy's Blues Hall,** 182 Beale St. (ℂ 901/528-0150). There's live music nightly, with guest artists alternating with the house band, which plays everything from blues to country. Another good choice for live blues is **The Black Diamond,** 153 Beale St. (ℂ 901/521-0800).

Though actually 4 blocks south of Beale Street, **Earnestine & Hazel's,** 531 S. Main St. (© **901/523-9754**), is a downtown dive that has become one of Memphis's hottest nightspots. Things don't really get cookin' here until after midnight. The music is a mix of blues, R&B, and rock, and the clientele is equally mixed.

MORE MUSIC & DANCING **Hernando's Hideaway,** 3210 Old Hernando Rd. (© **901/398-7496**), a run-down old two-story brick building near Grace-land, is a legendary honky-tonk, where country and rock greats have been known to drop by just to listen to the live music or play a few songs.

Retro coffeehouse **Java Cabana,** 2170 Young St. (© **901/272-7210**), has poetry readings and live acoustic music on different nights of the week. Although you can't get alcohol here, you can order an espresso.

Together, **Denim & Diamonds** and **The Mine,** 5353 S. Mendenhall Rd. at Winchester Road (© **901/365-3633**), have more than 4,000 square feet of dance floor. Half the space is dedicated to a country dance club and the other half is devoted to rock.

GAMBLING ON THE MISSISSIPPI Just a few miles south of Memphis, across the Mississippi state line, casinos are sprouting like cotton plants in the spring. Near the town of Robinsonville, you'll find **Goldstrike Casino,** 1010 Casino Center Dr. (© **800/924-7287** or 662-357-1111), and **Sheraton Casino,** 1107 Casino Center. (© **800-/391-3777**). Driving south on U.S. 61 and then west on Miss. 304, you come to **Sam's Town Hotel and Gambling Hall,** 1477 Commerce Landing/Casino Strip (© **800/456-0711**); **Fitzgerald's Casino,** 711 Lucky Lane (© **800/766-LUCK** or 662/363-LUCK); the **Holly-wood Casino,** 1150 Commerce Landing (© **800/871-0711** or 662/357-7700); **Harrah's Tunica Mardi Gras Casino & Hotel,** 1100 Casino Strip Resorts Blvd. (© **800/HARRAHS** or 662/363-7777); and **Isle of Capri Casino,** 1600 Isle of Capri Dr. (© **662/357-6500**). Continuing south on U.S. 61 to Tunica and then heading west on either Mhoon Landing Road or Miss. 4, you'll come to **Bally's Saloon and Gambling Hall,** 1450 Bally's Blvd. (© **800/38-BALLY**).

16 New Orleans

It may sound clichéd to call New Orleans magical and seductive, but it's the truth. Every one of your senses is engaged from the moment you arrive. Visu-ally, the city is superb, from the lacy ironwork wrapped around the buildings of the French Quarter, to the stately, graceful old homes of the Garden District, to the giant oaks that drip with ghostly Spanish moss in City Park. Aurally, music pours out of every doorway or is played right in the street. Jazz, Cajun, blues, whatever—you'll find yourself moving to a rhythm, and the very streets seem to dance along with you. There are delicious smells in the air, which seems to carry a whiff of the Caribbean. The moist, honeyed air caresses your skin and almost seems alive.

And then there's the food. Don't get us started on the food.

This is a city that is fully, totally alive. It's sensual and joyous, decadent but not exploitative. Indulgences are many, but for the right reason—they are fun.

ESSENTIALS

GETTING THERE **By Plane** Among the airlines serving the city's newly renamed **Louis Armstrong New Orleans International Airport** are: **America West** (© 800/235-9292; www.americawest.com), **American** (© 800/433-7300; www.aa.com), **Continental** (© 800/525-0280 or 504/581-2965;

New Orleans

ACCOMMODATIONS ■
Chimes B&B **4**
Grand Victorian Bed & Breakfast **7**
Hotel Monaco **14**
The House on Bayou Road **18**

International House **14**
The McKendrick-Breaux House **9**
Melrose Mansion **16**
Pontchartrain Hotel **8**
Windsor Court **12**

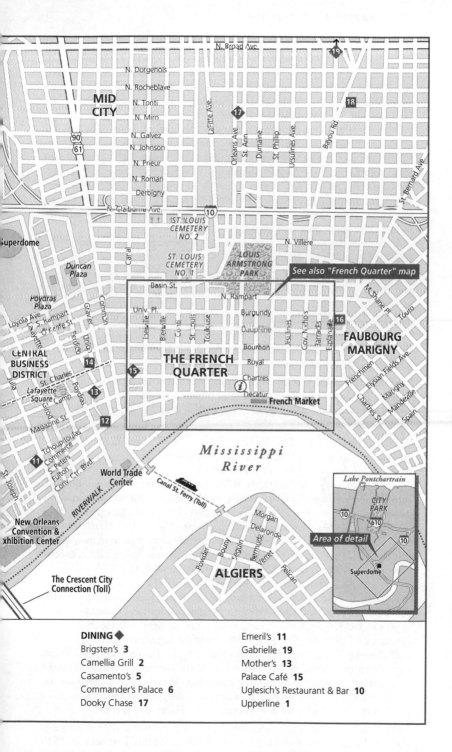

DINING ◆
Brigsten's **3**
Camellia Grill **2**
Casamento's **5**
Commander's Palace **6**
Dooky Chase **17**

Emeril's **11**
Gabrielle **19**
Mother's **13**
Palace Café **15**
Uglesich's Restaurant & Bar **10**
Upperline **1**

www.continental.com), **Delta** (© 800/221-1212; www.delta.com), **Northwest** (© 800/225-2525; www.nwa.com), **Southwest** (© 800/435-9792; www.south west.com), **US Airways** (© 800/428-4322; www.usairways.com), and **United** (© 800/241-6522; www.united.com). You'll find information booths scattered around the airport and in the baggage claim area. There's also a branch of the **Travelers Aid Society** (© 504/464-3522).

From the airport, you can reach the Central Business District by bus for $1.50 (exact change required). Buses run from 6am to 6:30pm. For more information, call the **Louisiana Transit Company** (© 504/818-1077). You can also get to your hotel on the **Airport Shuttle** (© 504/522-3500). For $10 per person (one-way), the van will take you directly to your hotel. There are Airport Shuttle information desks (staffed 24 hr.) in the airport. If you plan to take the Airport Shuttle *to* the airport when you depart, you must call a day in advance and let them know what time your flight is leaving.

A taxi from the airport will cost about $21; if there are three or more passengers, the fare is $8 per person.

By Train   **Amtrak** (© 800/USA-RAIL or 504/528-1610; www.amtrak.com) provides service to **Union Passenger Terminal,** 1001 Loyola Ave., from Washington, D.C. (trip time: 26 hr.), Atlanta (11½ hr.), Orlando (23½ hr.), Chicago (19½ hr.), Houston (9 hr.), San Antonio (14 hr.), and Los Angeles (43 hr.). Plenty of taxis wait outside the rail terminal.

By Car   You can drive to New Orleans via **I-10, I-55, U.S. 90, U.S. 61,** or across the Lake Pontchartrain Causeway on **La. 25.**

VISITOR INFORMATION   Contact the extremely friendly and helpful **New Orleans Metropolitan Convention and Visitors Bureau,** 1520 Sugar Bowl Dr., New Orleans, LA 70112 (© **800/672-6124** or 504/566-5055; www.neworleanscvb.com).

SPECIAL EVENTS & FESTIVALS   There is always something special going on, but we can cover only a few highlights. Details on Mardi Gras and Jazz Fest, the city's two premier events, are found below.

Late March brings the **Tennessee Williams New Orleans Literary Festival,** with theater, readings, discussion panels, musical events, and walking tours. For information, call or write 5500 Prytania St., Ste. 217, New Orleans, LA 70115 (© **504/581-1144;** www.tennesseewilliams.net). Also in late March to early April is **Spring Fiesta,** with tours of many of the city's private homes, courtyards, and plantations. For the schedule, call or write the Spring Fiesta Association, 826 St. Ann St., New Orleans, LA 70116 (© **504/581-1367**).

The mid-April **French Quarter Festival** kicks off with a parade down Bourbon Street. You can join people dancing in the streets, learn the history of jazz, visit historic homes, and take a ride on a riverboat. Many local restaurants set up booths in Jackson Square. For information, call or write 100 Conti St., New Orleans, LA 70130 (© **504/522-5730;** www.frenchquarterfestivals.org).

Halloween is celebrated with events including Boo-at-the-Zoo for children, costume parties (including a Monster Bash at the convention center), haunted houses (the best is in City Park), the Anne Rice Vampire Lestat Extravaganza, and the Moonlight Witches Run. You can catch the ghoulish action all over the city, but the French Quarter is the center of the Halloween universe.

FAST FACTS   Most major hotels have in-house doctors on call 24 hours a day. If not, call or go to the emergency room at **Ochsner Medical Institutions,** 1516 Jefferson Hwy. (© **504/842-3460**), or the **Tulane University Medical Center,**

1415 Tulane Ave. (© **504/588-5800**). The 24-hour pharmacy closest to the French Quarter is **Walgreens,** 3311 Canal St. at Jefferson Davis (© **504/822-8072**).

You're allowed to drink on the street, but not from a glass or bottle.

Don't walk alone at night, and don't go into the cemeteries alone at any time during the day or night. Ask around locally about safety before you go anywhere. People will tell you if you should take a cab instead of walking or using public transportation.

The **sales tax** in New Orleans is 9%. An additional 2% tax is added to hotel bills, for a total of 11%.

THE BIGGEST PARTIES OF 'EM ALL: MARDI GRAS & JAZZ FEST

MARDI GRAS   The granddaddy of all New Orleans celebrations is Mardi Gras (French for "Fat Tuesday," the day before Ash Wednesday, when Lent begins). Two or 3 weeks before Mardi Gras itself, parades begin chugging through the streets with increasing frequency. If you want to experience Mardi Gras but don't want to face the full force of craziness, consider coming for the weekend 10 days before Fat Tuesday (the season officially begins the Fri of this weekend). You can count on 10 to 15 parades during the weekend by lesser-known krewes (sort of a social club) like Cleopatra, Pontchartrain, Sparta, and Camelot.

Mardi Gras "krewe" Rex's King of Carnival arrives downtown from the Mississippi River on **Lundi Gras,** the Monday night before Fat Tuesday. Festivities at the riverfront begin in the afternoon, with lots of drink and live music leading up to the king's arrival around 6pm. Down the levee a few hundred feet, at Wolfenberg Park, the Zulu krewe has its own Lundi Gras celebration, with the king arriving around 5pm. That night, the Krewe of Orpheus holds their parade, with spectacular floats and a generous amount of trinkets and beads for parade-watchers.

The actual day of Mardi Gras starts with the two biggest parades, Zulu and Rex, which run back to back. Zulu starts near the Central Business District at 8:30am, Rex starts Uptown at 10am. It will be early afternoon when Rex spills into the Central Business District. Nearby, at about this time, you can find some of the most elusive New Orleans figures, the Mardi Gras Indians, small communities of African Americans, and Creoles (some of whom have Native American ancestors) mostly from the inner city, decked out in elaborate beaded and feathered costumes.

After the parades, the action picks up in the Quarter. The frat-party action is largely confined to Bourbon Street. The more interesting activity is in the lower Quarter and the Frenchmen section of the Faubourg Marigny, where the artists and gay community really know how to celebrate Mardi Gras. The costumes are elaborate works of art.

Tips: Accommodations in the city and the nearby suburbs are booked solid during Mardi Gras, *so make your plans well ahead and book a room as early as possible.* Many people plan a year or more in advance. Prices are *much* higher during Mardi Gras, and most hotels and guesthouses impose minimum-stay requirements. Many, many cops are out, making the walk from Uptown to Downtown safer than at other times of year, but, not surprisingly, the streets of New Orleans are a haven for pickpockets. Take precautions.

JAZZ FEST   The New Orleans Jazz & Heritage Festival, or simply Jazz Fest, is one of the best-attended, most-respected, and most musically comprehensive

Jazz Fest Planning in a Jiffy

If you want to go to Jazz Fest but would rather someone else did all the planning, contact **Festival Tours International** (ⓒ **310/454-4080**; Fest tours@aol.com). Packages include not just accommodations and tickets for Jazz Fest, but also a visit to Cajun country for unique personal encounters with some of the finest local musicians.

If you're flying to New Orleans specifically for the Jazz and Heritage Festival, consider calling **Continental Airlines** (ⓒ **800/525-0280** or 504/ 581-2965), the official airline of Jazz Fest, which offers special fares during the event. You'll need the Jazz Fest promotional code, available from the festival's information line (ⓒ **504/522-4786**).

festivals in the world. Stand in the right place and, depending on which way the wind's blowing, you can catch as many as 10 musical styles from several continents and smell the tantalizing aromas of a dozen different food offerings.

While such headliners as Van Morrison, Bob Dylan, and Jimmy Buffett have drawn record-setting crowds in recent years, serious Jazz Fest aficionados savor the lesser-known acts. They range from Mardi Gras Indians to old-time bluesmen who have never played outside the Delta, from Dixieland to avant-garde, from African artists making rare U.S. appearances to the top names in Cajun, zydeco, and, of course, jazz.

You must book hotels and flights months in advance, so you may have to schedule your visit around your own availability, not an appearance by a particular band. Just about every day at Jazz Fest is a good day, so this is not a hardship.

Try to purchase tickets as early as February. They're available by mail through **Ticketmaster** (ⓒ **504/522-5555;** www.ticketmaster.com). To order tickets by phone, or to get ticket information, call the **Heritage Festival** (ⓒ **800/488-5252** outside Louisiana, or 504/522-4786; fax 504/379-3291; www.nojazz fest.com). Admission for adults is $18 in advance and $25 at the gate; $2 for children. Evening events and concerts (order tickets in advance for these events as well) can be attended at an additional cost—usually between $20 and $30.

Parking at the Fair Grounds is next to impossible. Take public transportation or one of the available shuttles. The Regional Transit Authority operates bus routes from various pickup points to the Fair Grounds. For schedules and information, call ⓒ **504/248-3900.**

WHAT TO SEE & DO

Everyone starts out by strolling the **French Quarter,** one of the most visually interesting neighborhoods in America. Aside from Bourbon Street, you will find the most bustling activity at **Jackson Square,** where musicians, artists, fortune-tellers, and jugglers gather to sell their wares or entertain for change. Royal Street is home to numerous pricey antiques shops, with other interesting stores on Chartres and Decatur streets and the cross streets between. The closer you get to Esplanade Avenue and toward Rampart Street, the more residential the Quarter becomes. Walk through these areas, peeping in through any open gate; surprises wait behind them in the form of graceful brick and flagstone-lined courtyards filled with foliage and bubbling fountains.

You'll also want to stroll through the architecturally magnificent **Garden District,** located Uptown and bounded by St. Charles Avenue and Magazine Street

The French Quarter

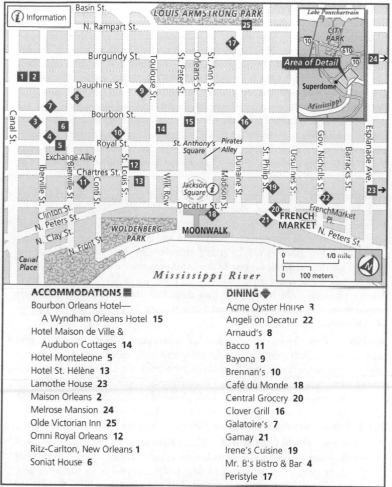

ACCOMMODATIONS ▬

Bourbon Orleans Hotel—
  A Wyndham Orleans Hotel **15**
Hotel Maison de Ville &
  Audubon Cottages **14**
Hotel Monteleone **5**
Hotel St. Hélène **13**
Lamothe House **23**
Maison Orleans **2**
Melrose Mansion **24**
Olde Victorian Inn **25**
Omni Royal Orleans **12**
Ritz-Carlton, New Orleans **1**
Soniat House **6**

DINING ◆

Acme Oyster House **3**
Angeli on Decatur **22**
Arnaud's **8**
Bacco **11**
Bayona **9**
Brennan's **10**
Café du Monde **18**
Central Grocery **20**
Clover Grill **16**
Galatoire's **7**
Gamay **21**
Irene's Cuisine **19**
Mr. B's Bistro & Bar **4**
Peristyle **17**

between Jackson and Louisiana avenues. It's simply beautiful. In some ways, even more so than the Quarter, this is New Orleans. Authors as diverse as Truman Capote and Anne Rice have been enchanted by its spell. Gorgeous homes of superb design stand quietly amid lush foliage, elegant but ever-so-slightly (or more) decayed.

The **Ogden Museum of Southern Art** (which will feature everything from acrylics to sculpture to mixed media) is due to open at the end of 2002 or early 2003 at 925 Camp St. A temporary exhibit can be found at 603 Julia St. (© **504/539-9600;** www.ogdenmuseum.org). The temporary collection is open Monday through Saturday from 10am to 5pm, or by appointment.

Aquarium of the Americas This is a world-class aquarium, highly entertaining and painlessly educational. It's on the banks of the Mississippi, along Woldenberg Park at the edge of the French Quarter. Five major exhibit areas and dozens of smaller aquariums hold a veritable ocean of aquatic life native to the region and to the Americas. You can walk through the underwater tunnel in the

Caribbean Reef exhibit, view a shark-filled re-creation of the Gulf of Mexico, or drop in to see the penguin exhibit. We particularly like the walk-through Waters of the Americas, where you wander in rainforests and see what goes on below the surface of swamps. The IMAX theater shows two or three films at regular intervals. The Audubon Institute also runs the city's zoo at Audubon Park uptown (see below). 1 Canal St., at Wells St. © **800/774-7394** or 504/581-4629. Fax 504/ 565-3010. www.auduboninstitute.org. Aquarium $14 adults, $10 seniors, $6.50 children 2–12. IMAX $7.75 adults, $6.75 seniors, $5 children. Combination tickets for Aquarium and IMAX $17 adults, $14 seniors, $11 children. Combination tickets for the Aquarium, the IMAX theater, the zoo, and a riverboat ride to the zoo are $27 adults, $13 children. You can also buy tickets for other combinations of the attractions. Aquarium opens daily at 9:30; closing hours vary by season. IMAX daily 10am–6pm. Shows every hr. on the hr.; advance tickets recommended. Closed Mardi Gras and Dec 25.

Audubon Park   Across from Loyola and Tulane universities, Audubon Park and the adjacent Audubon Zoo sprawl over 340 acres, extending from St. Charles Avenue all the way to the Mississippi River. There's a 1¾-mile paved traffic-free road that loops around the lagoon and golf course. Tennis courts and horseback-riding facilities can be found elsewhere in the park. Check out the pavilion on the riverbank for one of the most pleasant views of the Mississippi. The Audubon Zoo is toward the back of the park, across Magazine Street. *Note:* It's not advisable to be in the park after dark. 6500 Magazine St., between Broadway and Exposition. © **504/581-4629**. www.auduboninstitute.org. The park opens daily at 6am and officially closes at 10pm.

Audubon Zoo   Here, in a setting of subtropical plants, waterfalls, and lagoons, some 1,800 animals (including rare and endangered species) live in natural habitats rather than cages. Don't miss the replica of a Louisiana swamp (featuring a rare white alligator) or the "Butterflies in Flight" exhibit, where more than 1,000 butterflies live among lush, colorful vegetation. 6500 Magazine St. © **504/581-4629**. Admission $9 adults, $5 seniors (over 64), $4.75 children 2–12. Daily 9:30am– 5pm; 9:30am–6pm weekends in summer. Last ticket sold 1 hr. before closing. Closed holidays.

Blaine Kern's Mardi Gras World   Blaine Kern makes more than three-quarters of the floats used by the various krewes every Carnival season. Mardi Gras World offers tours of its collection of float sculptures and of its studios, where you can see floats being made year-round. The real attractions here, though, are the huge sculptures of cartoon and comic book characters, mythological figures, and imaginary creatures, and the opportunity to try on fabulous costumes for yourself. Bring your camera! 223 Newton St., Algiers Point. © **800/362-8213** or 504/368- 4628. www.mardigrasworld.com. Admission $14 adults, $10 seniors (over 62), $5.50 children 3–12. Daily 9:30am–4:30pm. Closed Mardi Gras, Easter, Thanksgiving, Dec 25. Cross the river on the Canal St. Ferry and take the free shuttle from the dock (it meets every ferry).

The Cabildo   Constructed from 1795 to 1799 as the Spanish government seat in New Orleans, the Cabildo was the site of the signing of the Louisiana Purchase transfer. It is now the center of the Louisiana State Museum's facilities in the French Quarter. A multiroom exhibition entertainingly and exhaustively traces the history of Louisiana from exploration through Reconstruction. Topics include antebellum music, mourning and burial customs, immigrants and how they fared here, and the changing roles of women in the South. Throughout are fabulous artifacts, including Napoléon's death mask. 701 Chartres St., on Jackson Sq. © **504/568-6968** or 504/568-6968. Fax 504/568-4995. Admission $5 adults; $4 students and seniors; free for children under 13. Tues–Sun 9am–5pm.

City Park   The extensive, beautifully landscaped grounds hold botanical gardens and a conservatory, four golf courses, picnic areas, a restaurant, lagoons for boating and fishing, tennis courts, horses for hire and lovely trails to ride them on, a bandstand, two miniature trains, and Children's Storyland, an amusement area with a carousel ride for children. At Christmastime, the mighty oaks, already dripping with Spanish moss, are strung with lights—quite a magical sight—and during Halloween, there is a fabulous haunted house. 1 Palm Dr. ℂ 504/482-4888. www.neworleanscitypark.com. Daily 6am–7pm.

Contemporary Arts Center   Redesigned in the early '90s to much critical applause, the Contemporary Arts Center (CAC) is a main anchor of the city's young arts district. The center consistently exhibits influential and ground-breaking work by artists in various mediums. Exhibitions hang for 6 to 8 weeks, and theater, dance, and music performances are weekly. 900 Camp St. ℂ 504/528-3805. Fax 504/528-3828. www.cacno.org. Gallery admission $5 adults, $3 seniors and students, free for members and kids 15 and under; free to all on Thurs. Performance and event tickets $3–$25. Tues–Sun 11am–5pm.

The Historic French Market   The 24-hour Farmers' Market makes a fun amble as you admire everything from fresh produce and fish to more tourist-ori-ented items like hot sauces and Cajun and Creole mixes. Snacks like gator on a stick (when was the last time you had that?) will amuse the kids. The Flea Market, a bit farther down from the Farmers' Market, is considered a must-shop place, but the reality is that the goods are kind of junky: T-shirts, jewelry, hats, crystals, toys, sunglasses. Still, some good deals can be had (even better if you are up for bargaining). The flea market is open daily. On Decatur St., toward Esplanade Ave. from Jackson Sq. Open daily roughly 9am–6pm.

Historic New Orleans Collection–Museum/Research Center   This museum of local and regional history is almost hidden away within a complex of historic French Quarter buildings. The oldest, constructed in the late 18th century, was one of the few structures to escape the disastrous fire of 1794. These buildings were owned by the collection's founders, Gen. and Mrs. L. Kemper Williams. Their former residence, behind the courtyard, is open to the public for tours. There are also excellent tours of the Louisiana history galleries, with expertly preserved and displayed art, maps, and original documents like the transfer papers for the Louisiana Purchase of 1803. 533 Royal St. (between St. Louis and Toulouse). ℂ 504/523-4662. Fax 504/598-7108. www.hnoc.org. Free admission; tours $4. Tues–Sat 10am–4:30pm; tours Tues–Sat 10am, 11am, 2pm, 3pm. Closed major holidays, Mardi Gras.

National D-Day Museum   Created by best-selling author (and *Saving Private Ryan* consultant) Stephen Ambrose, this unique museum tells the story of all 19 U.S. amphibious operations worldwide on that fateful day of June 6, 1944. A rich collection of artifacts (including some British Spitfire airplanes), plus top-of-the-line educational materials, make this museum one of the high-lights of New Orleans. 945 Magazine St. ℂ 504/527-6012. Admission $10 adults, $6 sen-iors, $5 children 5–17, free for children under 5. Daily 9am–5pm. Closed holidays.

New Orleans Historic Voodoo Museum   Here you'll find occult objects from all over the globe, plus some articles that allegedly belonged to the legendary voodoo-priestess Marie Laveau. It's touristy, but still, it's an adequate introduction—and who wouldn't want to bring home a voodoo doll from here? The people who run the museum are involved in voodoo, and there is generally a voodoo priestess on-site, giving readings and making personal gris-gris bags. The museum also offers a guided voodoo cemetery tour of St. Louis No. 1 to visit Marie Laveau's reputed grave. 217 N. Peters St. (contemporary voodoo exhibits). © 504/522-5223. Also 724 Dumaine St., at Bourbon St. (historic voodoo). © 504/523-7685. www.voodoomuseum.com. Admission $7 adults; $5.50 students, seniors and military; $4.50 high school students; $3.50 grade school students. Cemetery tour $22; tour of the Undead $22. Daily 10am–8pm.

New Orleans Museum of Art NOMA is in an idyllic section of City Park. The front portion is a large, imposing neoclassical building; the rear portion is a striking contrast of curves and contemporary styles. They house a collection that includes pre-Columbian and Native American ethnographic art; 16th- to 20th-century European paintings, drawings, sculptures, and prints; early American art; Asian art; and one of the largest decorative glass collections in the United States. Be sure to pick up a guide pamphlet from the information desk at the entrance. 1 Collins Diboll Circle, at City Park and Esplanade. © 504/488-2631. Fax 504/484-6662. www.noma.org. Admission $6 adults, $5 seniors (over 64), $3 children 3–17, free to Louisiana residents. Thurs 10am–noon; Tues–Sun 10am–5pm. Closed most major holidays.

The Presbytère The Presbytère, part of the Louisiana State Museum, has opened the smashing, and (so-far) definitive Mardi Gras Museum, full of detail-packed exhibits on every aspect of the social and cultural history of Mardi Gras. Five major themes (History, Masking, Parades, Balls, and the Courir du Mardi Gras) trace the history of this high-profile but frankly little-understood (outside of New Orleans) annual event. Interactive exhibits allow you to pretend you are riding a float, while elsewhere you can learn about the complicated traditions, admire lavish costumes, and even use bathrooms dressed up as the ubiquitous Port-a-Potty—just like on Mardi Gras Day! Plan on a couple of hours to take it all in. 751 Chartres St., Jackson Sq. © 504/568-6968. Admission $5 adults, $4 seniors and students, free for children under 13. Tues–Sun 9am–5pm.

ORGANIZED TOURS

Historic New Orleans Walking Tours (© 504/947-2120; www.tournew orleans.com) is the place to go for authenticity. Tour guides are carefully chosen for their knowledge and entertaining manner. They offer a "French Quarter Mystique" walking tour, a distinctive gumbo of legend and fact, daily at 10:30am. It leaves from C. C.'s Coffee Shop at 528 Peter St. on Jackson Square; the cost is $12 adults, $10 students and seniors. They also offer Garden District tours, plus a Cemetery and Voodoo Tour that goes through St. Louis Cemetery No. 1, Congo Square, and an active voodoo temple. It leaves Monday through Saturday at 10am and 1pm, Sunday at 10am only, from the courtyard at 334-B Royal St. Rates are $15 adults, $13 students and seniors, free for children under 12. The aboveground cities of the dead are part of New Orleans' indelible landscape. Their ghostly and inscrutable presence enthralls visitors, but it's often unsafe to enter the cemeteries alone, so going with a tour may be your best bet.

Half Pint's Swamp Adventures (© 318/280-5976 or 318/288-1544) offers private guided tours of the "beauty, serenity, and exotic wildlife" of the Atchafalaya Basin, the nation's largest swamp. Half Pint is more folk hero than man, and his tours come highly recommended.

The paddle-wheeler **Creole Queen,** Riverwalk Dock (© 800/445-4109 or 504/524-0814), departs from the Poydras Street Wharf adjacent to the Riverwalk at 10:30am and 2pm for 2½-hour narrated excursions to the port and to the historic site of the Battle of New Orleans. There is a 7pm jazz dinner cruise.

Daytime fares are $15 adults, $8 children; the jazz cruise is $45 adults, $22 children. Children under 3 ride free. They also offer swamp tours and harbor cruises.

SHOPPING

Among the hunting grounds you may want to explore is the **French Market,** which begins on Decatur Street across from Jackson Square. Offerings include candy, cookware, fashions, crafts, toys, New Orleans memorabilia, and candles.

Just across from Jackson Square at 600–620 Decatur St., the old **Jackson Brewery** building has been transformed into a jumble of shops (Cajun-Creole foodstuffs, souvenirs, fashion), cafes, and entertainment venues.

For the best gallery-hopping, head straight to **Julia Street.**

Magazine Street is the Garden District's premier shopping street. More than 140 shops (antiques, art galleries, boutiques, crafts, dolls) line the street in 19th-century brick storefronts and quaint cottagelike buildings.

At the foot of Canal Street (365 Canal St.), where the street reaches the Mississippi River, **Canal Place** shopping center holds more than 50 shops, many of them branches of some of this country's most elegant retailers.

If you need a Mardi Gras costume, head for the **Little Shop of Fantasy, 523** Dumaine St. (© **504/529-4243**), where the owners sell the work of a number of local artists and more than 20 mask makers. **Accent Annex Mardi Gras Headquarters,** Riverwalk (© **504/568-9000**), offers Mardi Gras beads, masks, and other accouterments.

The **Louisiana Music Factory,** 210 Decatur St. (© **504/586-1094;** www. louisianamusicfactory.com), carries a large selection of regional music. It also has frequent live music and beer bashes—shop while you bop!

WHERE TO STAY

If you want more guesthouse options, we highly recommend the **Bed and Breakfast, Inc. Reservation Service,** 1021 Moss St. (P.O. Box 52257), New Orleans, LA 70152 (© **800/729-4640** or 504/488-4640; www.historiclodging. com).

As a general rule, just to be on the safe side, always book ahead during spring, fall, and winter. And if your trip will coincide with Mardi Gras or Jazz Fest, book *way* ahead—up to a year in advance, if you want to be sure of a room. Rates frequently jump more than a notch or two for Mardi Gras and other festivals (sometimes they even double), and in some cases there's a 4- or 5-night minimum stay requirement.

Bourbon Orleans Hotel—A Wyndham Grand Heritage Hotel The Bourbon Orleans takes up an entire block of prime real estate at the intersection of—guess where—Bourbon and Orleans streets. Public areas are lavishly decorated but their elegant interest doesn't quite extend to the rooms. Bigger than average, they will give no cause for complaint about decor or comfort. There's an elegant lobby bar. 717 Orleans St., New Orleans, LA 70116. © **504/523-2222.** Fax 504/525-8166. 216 units. $125–$198 petite queen or twin; $145–$219 deluxe king or double; $188–$262 junior suite; $241–$398 town house suite; $272–$482 town house suite with balcony. Extra person $20. AE, DC, DISC, MC, V. Valet parking $25. **Amenities:** Restaurant; outdoor pool.

Chimes B&B   This is a real hidden gem, one that truly allows you to experience the city away from the typical tourist experience. The Chimes is in a less fashionable but more neighborhoodlike portion of the Garden District, just 2 blocks off St. Charles Avenue. Rooms vary in size from a two-story loft type (with a very small bathroom) to spaces that are downright cozy. All have antiques (including romantic old beds) but are so tastefully underdecorated that they are positively Zen. An ambitious continental breakfast is served in the hosts' house, and chatting with them can be so enjoyable you might get off to a late start. The hosts know and love their city. 1146 Constantinople St., New Orleans, LA 70115. ℂ 800/729-4640 (for reservations only) or 504/488-4640. Fax 504/899-9858. www. historiclodging.com/chimes.html. 5 units. $115–$155 double; off-season rates lower. Rates include breakfast. Look for rates and featured specials online. AE, MC, V. Limited off-street free parking. **Amenities:** Well-behaved pets accepted.

The Grand Victorian Bed & Breakfast   Owner Bonnie Rabe took a crumbling Queen Anne–style Victorian mansion right on the corner of Washington (2 blocks from Lafayette cemetery and Commander's Palace with a streetcar stop right in front) and resurrected it into a showcase B&B. The stunning rooms are full of antiques (each has a breathtaking four-poster or wood canopy bed), with the slightly fussy details demanded by big Victorian rooms. A generous continental breakfast is served. 2727 St. Charles Ave., New Orleans, LA 70130. ℂ 800/977-0008 or 504/895-1104. Fax 504/896-8688. www.gvbb.com. 8 units. $150–$350 double. Rates include breakfast. AE, DISC, MC, V.

Hotel Maison de Ville & Audubon Cottages   On the list of *Best Small Hotels in the World,* the Maison de Ville is a great splurge and a wonderful romantic getaway. Tennessee Williams was a regular guest in room 9. Most rooms surround an utterly charming courtyard (complete with fountain and banana trees), where it's hard to imagine you're in the thick of the Quarter. The hotel is elegant and antique-filled. Rooms vary dramatically in size, so ask about them when you reserve, as price is no indicator of size. The far more spacious Audubon Cottages (larger than many apartments, some with their own private courtyards), located a few blocks away and including a small, inviting pool, can go for less than the cramped queen rooms in the main hotel (and are farther from the hubbub of Bourbon). All accommodations are thoroughly lush, with nice touches like feather beds, and the service is helpful and courteous. Continental breakfast (the food is a bit disappointing) is served in your room, in the parlor, or on the patio. Le Bistro, the hotel's restaurant, is intimate and inviting. A concierge and room service (7am–10pm) are other perks. 727 Toulouse St., New Orleans, LA 70130. ℂ 800/634-1600 or 504/561-5858. Fax 504/528-9939. www.maison deville.com. $195–$225 double; $215–$235 queen; $235–$250 king; $325–$375 suite; $235–$345 1-bedroom cottage; $535–$675 2-bedroom cottage; $770–$930 3-bedroom cottage. Rates include continental breakfast. AE, DC, MC, V, DISC. Valet parking $18. **Amenities:** Restaurant; outdoor pool; access to nearby health club.

Hotel Monaco   There is much to like about this surprisingly whimsical boutique hotel. It's self-consciously quirky (check out the seashell fireplace in the lobby sitting area) but who cares when that translates to faux fur throws on the beds, leopard-patterned bathrobes, and, upon request, an in-room goldfish? Bathrooms are small but appointed richly enough so you don't mind. Public areas are most inviting (go ahead, canoodle in the jungle-frivolous lounge), even more so thanks to complimentary evening wine and foot massages. All in all, adult playful, but still good for families—especially during Papa Nöel season, when rooms go for something like $85 a night! 333 St. Charles Ave., New Orleans, LA 70130. ℂ 866/561-0010 or 504/561-0010. Fax 504/561-0036. www.Monaco-neworleans.com. 250 units. $135–$295 double. AE, DC, DISC, MC, V. Valet parking $25 (cheaper garages within walking distance). **Amenities:** Restaurant; fitness room; dog packages for canine guests.

Hotel Monteleone Opened in 1886, the Monteleone is the largest hotel in the French Quarter, and it seems to keep getting bigger without losing a trace of its trademark charm. Everyone who stays here loves it, probably because its staff is among the most helpful in town. All the rooms are being freshly renovated, with nice touches like four-poster beds and posh bathrooms (some with oval Jacuzzi tubs). If you want a river view, ask for a room on a higher floor. One of the city's best-kept secrets is the rooftop pool, with unencumbered views of the city. 214 Royal St., New Orleans, LA 70130. ☎ 800/535-9595 or 504/523-3341. Fax 504/561-5803. www.hotelmonteleone.com. 600 units. $169–$230 double; $360–$975 suite. Extra person $25. Children under 18 stay free in parents' room. Package rates available. AE, DC, DISC, MC, V. Valet parking $15 car, $17 van. **Amenities:** 3 restaurants; heated pool; fitness center.

Hotel Ste. Hélène This is what a slightly funky Quarter hotel should be. What it lacks in magnificence, it makes up for in character and location (less than 2 blocks from Jackson Sq.). Rooms vary in size and style; front rooms have balconies overlooking the street, others have beds set in alcoves with a sort of low-rent parlor sitting area. Suites, housed in a separate building, are spectacular. The property winds about several buildings, with surprises at every turn. Throughout are interior and exterior courtyards, some with flickering gas lamps. 508 Chartres St., New Orleans, LA 70130. ☎ 800/348-3888 or 504/522-5014. Fax 504/523-7140. www.stehelene.com. 26 units. $89–$325 double. Rates include continental breakfast and complimentary champagne. AE, DC, DISC, MC, V. Parking (about $10) in nearby lot. **Amenities:** Pool.

The House on Bayou Road If you want to stay in a rural plantation setting but still be near the French Quarter, try the House on Bayou Road, quite probably the most smashing guesthouse in town. This intimate Creole plantation home, built in the late 1700s, has been restored and the individually decorated rooms have a light, airy quality. Grounds are beautifully manicured, and there's an outdoor pool, Jacuzzi, patio, and screened-in porch. The House serves a plantation-style breakfast. 2275 Bayou Rd., New Orleans, LA 70119. ☎ 800/882-2968 or 504/945-0992. Fax 504/945-0993. www.houseonbayouroad.com. 8 units, 2 cottages. $150–$310 double. Rates include full breakfast. AE, MC, V. Free off-street parking. **Amenities:** Restaurant; outdoor pool.

International House Everyone's favorite new hotel, the International House, with creative design and meticulous attention to detail, has set a new standard. Rooms are simple, with muted (okay, beige) tones, tall ceilings, and ceiling fans, but also with black-and-white photos of local musicians and characters, books about the city, and other clever decorating touches, plus some cushy touches like fine towels and feather pillows. A branch of the popular local restaurant Lemongrass is here. The bar is a hip hangout—at night candles flicker and music plays. You'll find room service and dry cleaning. 221 Camp St., New Orleans, LA 70130. ☎ 800/633-5770 or 504/553-9550. Fax 504/553-9560. www.ihhotel.com. 119 units. $149–$379 double; $369–$1,799 suite. Rates include continental breakfast. AE, MC, V. Valet parking $22. **Amenities:** Restaurant; health club.

Lamothe House The Lamothe House has a slightly faded, somewhat threadbare elegance that's just right for New Orleans. The Creole-style plain facade of the 1840s town house hides a mossy, brick-lined courtyard with a fish-filled fountain and banana trees, and rooms filled with antiques that are worn in the right places, but not shabby. It's a short walk to the action in the Quarter and just a couple of blocks to the bustling Faubourg Marigny scene. 621 Esplanade Ave.,

New Orleans, LA 70116. ℭ 800/367-5858 or 504/947-1161. Fax 504/943-6536. www.new orleans.org. 20 units. $64–$275 double. Rates include breakfast. AE, DISC, MC, V. Free parking. **Amenities:** Pool.

Maison Orleans   This hotel is for those who say, "I'd stay at the Ritz-Carlton if only it was even nicer and had even better service." Voilà—this place is a boutique hotel, attached to the Ritz, with, get this, 24-hour butler service. Another fine touch: A phone call prior to your stay ensures that whatever you want or need will be in your room upon your arrival. You pay extra for most of this.

The rooms here are gorgeous, little classics of NOLA style: wood floors, paneling, and furniture; superb moldings; fireplace facades; and bathrooms containing about the deepest hotel tubs we've seen. Beds are lush. A continental breakfast is served downstairs, and from 5 to 8pm, there is an array of snacks. 904 Iberville St., New Orleans, LA 70112. ℭ 504/670-2900. Fax 504/670-2910. www.maison orleans.com. 75 units. $315–$495 double. AE, DC, DISC, MC, V. Valet parking $25. **Amenities:** 2 restaurants; spa; health club.

The McKendrick-Breaux House   Owner Eddie Breaux saved this 1865 building and turned it into one of the city's best B&Bs. The antique-filled rooms are spacious (some of the bathrooms are downright huge), quaint, and meticulously decorated, but not fussy. The public areas are simple, elegant, and comfortable. But the best part of the B&B is Breaux himself. You would be hard-pressed to find a better host and staff. The house is conveniently located right in the middle of the Lower Garden District. 1474 Magazine St., New Orleans, LA 70130. ℭ 888/570-1700 or 504/586-1700. Fax 504/522-7138. www.mckendrick-breaux.com. 9 units. $125–$195 double. Rates include tax and breakfast. AE, MC, V. Limited free off-street parking.

Olde Victorian Inn   This is an oasis of Victoriana and homey touches. Decor is cutesy, quaint, and cluttered—expect doilies and teddy bears—and the hearty breakfasts are legendary. The inn happily boasts that they can go 30 days without repeating a menu (on a recent visit, they stuffed us with goodies like Creole pancakes topped with peaches poached in homemade vanilla). The owners brim over with joy for their job, and you quickly feel like a welcome guest in their home. They also have three sweet, well-behaved dogs (not allowed in the rooms). 914 N. Rampart St., New Orleans, LA 70116. ℭ 800/725-2446 or 504/522-2446. Fax 504/522-8646. www.oldevictorianinn.com. 6 units. $120–$175 double. Rates include full breakfast. Senior discount and weekly rates available. AE, DC, DISC, MC, V. Parking available on street.

Omni Royal Orleans   Despite being part of a chain, this most elegant hotel doesn't feel sterile and generic. This is only proper given that it is on the former site of the venerable 1836 St. Louis Exchange Hotel, a center of New Orleans social life until the final years of the Civil War. Furnishings in the guest rooms are elegant, filled with muted tones and plush furniture, with windows that let you look dreamily out over the Quarter. Service is swift and conscientious. The classic Rib Room is a favorite dining spot; there's also a lounge, a bar, and the rooftop La Riviera bar and restaurant. A concierge, babysitting, 24-hour room service, beauty and barber shops, and a business center are among the other amenities. 621 St. Louis St., New Orleans, LA 70140. ℭ 800/THE-OMNI in the U.S. and Canada, or 504/529-5333. Fax 504/529-7089. www.omnihotels.com. 360 units. $199–$399 double; $399–$800 suite; $1,100 penthouse. Children under 18 stay free in parents' room. AE, DC, DISC, MC, V. Valet parking $21. **Amenities:** 3 restaurants; heated outdoor pool; health club.

Pontchartrain Hotel This dignified hotel has long been a local landmark. Its discreet ambience and pampering still make it a choice for celebrities and dignitaries. If you have a weakness for faded grandeur and evocative atmosphere (and we do), here's your spot. Some rooms have been renovated recently and these new rooms have mock French provincial furniture and newer baths (they are working on boosting the water pressure)—but regardless, it still looks like an old, formerly grand hotel, even with the newer fixtures. Beds are comfortable and rooms more spacious than many typical hotel rooms. Café Pontchartrain has a solid reputation. Stop for a drink in the Bayou Bar, which features live entertainment at night. Twenty-four-hour room service is on offer here. 2031 St. Charles Ave., New Orleans, LA 70140. (C) 800/777-6193 or 504/524-0581. Fax 504/529-1165. www.pontchartrainhotel.com. 112 units. $95–$380 double. Extra person $10, during special events $25. Seasonal packages and special promotional rates available. AE, DC, DISC, MC, V. Parking $16. **Amenities:** Restaurant; outdoor pool; access to nearby spa with health club.

Ritz-Carlton, New Orleans Being sentimentalists, we would rather find our luxury in a less—how shall we say it—*generic* way, but we cannot deny that with name-brand recognition comes a reliable standard. The staff falls all over themselves to be friendly and helpful, rooms have lovely beds (maybe not as nice as the W in the Central Business District), and the whole effect is very gracious and just a bit stuffy, an impression that deepens at night as cocktails are served in the lobby lounge where everything is very civil and jeans and other casual attire (even on guests) are frowned upon. The spa is by far the nicest in town, and though undeniably expensive, it's gorgeous and the treatments are utter perfection—it's so far ahead of the pack that it's probably not worth spending money at any other spa facility. There's also a Jacuzzi, a resistance pool, and personal trainers. 921 Canal St., New Orleans, LA 70112. (C) 800/241-3333 or 504/524-1331. Fax 504/524-7233. www.ritzcarlton.com. 452 units. $415 double; from $560 and way, way up for suites. AE, DC, MC, V. Valet parking $25. **Amenities:** Spa; health club; pets accepted.

Soniat House The highly acclaimed Soniat House lives up to the hype. Keeping a low profile behind a solid wood gate, it's classic Creole—the treasures are hidden off the street. The beyond-efficient staff will spoil you, and the sweet courtyards, candlelit at night, will soothe you. Rooms vary in distinction. All have antiques, but if you want, say, high ceilings and really grand furniture (room no. 23 has a 17th-century bed), you are better off in the main house or the suite-filled annex across the street. Many rooms feature Jacuzzi bathtubs. The "Southern Continental" breakfast costs extra, but it's worth it. You'll find a business center (additional charge) and concierge here. 1133 Chartres St., New Orleans, LA 70116. (C) 800/544-8808 or 504/522-0570. Fax 504/522-7208. www.soniathouse. com. 33 units. $195–$325 double; $350–$650 suite; $750 2-bedroom suite. AE, MC, V. Valet parking $19. Children over 12 welcome only in rooms that accommodate 3. **Amenities:** Access to nearby health club.

Windsor Court *Condé Nast Traveler* voted the Windsor Court the Best Hotel in North America. Everything is very, very chic, and the level of service is extraordinarily high. Accommodations are spacious, with classy decor. All feature large bay windows or a private balcony overlooking the river or the city, a private foyer, a large living room, a bedroom with French doors, a large marble bathroom with luxe amenities, two dressing rooms, and a "petite kitchen." The Polo Club Lounge has the ambience of a private English club; the exceptional Grill Room Restaurant serves breakfast, brunch, lunch, and dinner. The lobby lounge serves afternoon tea, cocktails, and sweets, and has chamber music and piano music during the day and evening. You'll find 24-hour suite service, a concierge, laundry, dry cleaning, and in-room massage. 300 Gravier St., New Orleans, LA 70130. ℂ 800/262-2662 or 504/523-6000. Fax 504/596-4749. www.windsorcourthotel.com. 324 units. $290–$400 standard double; $370–$505 junior suite; $400–$700 full suite; $700–$1,150 2-bedroom suite. Children under 12 stay free in parents' room. AE, DC, DISC, MC, V. Valet parking $20. **Amenities:** Restaurant; pool; health club.

WHERE TO DINE

We are going to take a stand and say to heck with New York and San Francisco: New Orleans has the best food in the United States. (There are natives who will gladly fight you if you say otherwise.) This is the city where the great chefs of the world come to eat—if they don't work here already.

Acme Oyster House SEAFOOD/SANDWICHES   This loud, crowded joint is the perfect place if you need an oyster fix or if you've never tried oyster shooting (taking a raw oyster, possibly doused in sauce, and letting it slide right down your throat). If you don't like them raw, try the oyster po' boy, with beer. 724 Iberville St. ℂ 504/522-5973. Oysters $4–$6.50 per half or whole dozen respectively; po' boys $5.50–$7.50; New Orleans specialties $6–$8; seafood $11–$14. AE, DC, DISC, MC, V.

Angeli On Decatur ITALIAN/MEDITERRANEAN   This is a highly welcome addition to the Quarter, featuring terrific (if not particularly New Orleans–specific) food with further praise for its nearly round-the-clock hours and local delivery service—all things hungry locals and tourists crave. It's perfect for a light, actually rather healthy meal (pizzas, salads, and the like are on the menu), a needed alternative to some of the extravaganzas offered by more formal restaurants in town. 1141 Decatur (at Gov. Nichols). ℂ 504/566-0077. Main courses $7–$18. AE, MC, V. Mon–Thurs 10am–4am; Fri–Sat 24 hr.

Arnaud's CREOLE   It's hard to maintain a reputation throughout a century. So it is a great relief to report that the food at Arnaud's is still solidly good and often excellent. The mosaic-tile floors, dark-wood paneling, ceiling medallions, and antique ceiling fans all make you feel as though you are dining in turn-of-the-19th-century New Orleans. Rave-producing fish dishes included snapper or trout Pontchartrain (topped with crabmeat). Any filet mignon entree is superb. Arnaud's also operates a less formal, less expensive brasserie, **Rémoulade,** right next door. 813 Bienville St. ℂ 504/523-5433. www.arnauds.com. Reservations recommended. Jackets required in main dining room at dinner. Main courses $19–$38. AE, DC, MC, V, DISC. Mon–Fri 11:30am–2:30pm; Sun Jazz brunch 10am–2:30pm; Sun–Thurs 6–10pm; Fri–Sat 6–10:30pm.

Bacco ITALIAN/CREOLE   Don't expect spaghetti and marinara sauce here. Instead, think arresting, rich, ecstasy-inducing creations such as *ravioli ripieni di formaggio,* featuring four creamy cheeses all melting into a sauce of olive oil, tomatoes, and browned garlic. Bacco is romantic and candlelit at night, more affordable and casual at lunchtime. Desserts include possibly the best tiramisu we've ever had. 310 Chartres St. ℂ 504/522-2426. Fax 504/521-8323. www.bacco.com. Reservations recommended. Main courses $18–$31. AE, DC, MC, V. Daily 11:30am–2pm and 6–10pm.

Bayona INTERNATIONAL   One of the city's top dining experiences, Bayona is beloved by savvy New Orleanians. Chef Susan Spicer offers elegant, eclectic contemporary cuisine with Asian and Mediterranean flavors in a quiet, romantic atmosphere. The wine selection is extensive, and the staff is extremely helpful in suggesting the right wine. Also, check out Spicer's new, fantastic

restaurant, **Cobalt,** at 333 St. Charles Ave. (ⓒ **504/565-5595**). 430 Dauphine St.
ⓒ **504/525-4455**. www.bayona.com. Reservations required at dinner; recommended at
lunch. Main courses $9–$13 lunch, $14–$23 dinner. AE, DC, DISC, MC, V. Mon–Fri 11:30am–2pm;
Mon–Thurs 6–10pm; Fri–Sat 6–11pm.

Brennan's FRENCH/HAUTE CREOLE   For more than 40 years, breakfast
at Brennan's has been a New Orleans tradition, an expensive multicourse extravaganza that is unabashedly sauce- and egg-intensive. You'll find yourself rubbing
elbows with loyal locals and tourists in search of a classic. Breakfast and lunch
are quite crowded; dinner is less so (head straight to the gas lamp-lined balcony
for dinner). 417 Royal St. ⓒ **504/525-9711**. Reservations recommended. Main courses
$16–$39; fixed-price lunch $35; fixed-price 4-course dinner $39. AE, DC, DISC, MC, V. Daily 8am–
2:30pm and 6–10pm. Closed Dec 25.

Brigtsen's CAJUN/CREOLE   Chef Frank Brigtsen serves some of the city's
best contemporary Creole cuisine. The individual dining rooms are romantic
and cozy, and the menu changes daily. Brigtsen has a special touch with rabbit;
one of his most mouthwatering dishes is an appetizer of rabbit tenderloin on a
tasso- (ham-) Parmesan grits cake, with sautéed spinach and a Creole mustard
sauce. The rabbit and andouille gumbo is delicious, intensely flavored, and well
balanced. Save room for dessert, including the signature banana bread pudding
with banana rum sauce. The "Early Evening" dinner special is an excellent bargain. 723 Dante St. ⓒ **504/861-7610**. Reservations required. Main courses $18–$26; 3-course
"Early Evening" dinner (Tues–Thurs 5:30–6:30pm) $17. AE, DC, MC, V. Tues–Sat 5:30–10pm.

Café du Monde COFFEE & SWEETS   Since 1862, Café du Monde has
been selling café au lait and beignets on the edge of Jackson Square. A New
Orleans landmark, it's *the* place for people-watching. What's a beignet? (Say ben-
yay.) A square French doughnut-type cake, hot and covered in powdered sugar.
You might be tempted to shake off some of the sugar. Don't. Trust us. Pour more
on, even. You'll be glad you did. At three for about $1, they're a hell of a deal.
Wash them down with chicory coffee. In the French Market, 813 Decatur St. ⓒ **504/581-
2914**. Beignets 3 for $1.25. No credit cards. Daily 24 hr. Closed Dec 25. Additional locations at
Riverwalk Mall and at New Orleans Centre at The Superdome.

Camellia Grill HAMBURGERS/SANDWICHES   Right off the St. Charles
Avenue streetcar, the Camellia Grill has been a fixture since 1946. As you sit on
a stool at counter, white-jacketed waiters pamper you. There's often a wait, but
it's always worth it. The Camellia is famous for its omelets—heavy and fluffy at
the same time, and almost as big as a rolled-up newspaper. Don't forget the pecan
waffle, a moan-inducing work of art. The burgers are big and sloppy—among the

---

Whole Lotta Muffaletta Goin' On

Muffalettas are almost mythological sandwiches, enormous concoctions
of round Italian bread, Italian cold cuts and cheeses, and olive salad. One
person cannot eat a whole one—at least not in one sitting. Instead,
share; a half makes a good meal. Judging from the line that forms at
lunchtime, many others agree with us that **Central Grocery**, 923 Decatur
St. (ⓒ **504/523-1620**), makes the best muffaletta there is. Take your sandwich across the street and eat it on the banks of the Mississippi for an
inexpensive, romantic meal (about $7 for a whole sandwich).

best in town. 626 S. Carrollton Ave. © **504/866-9573.** All items under $10. No credit cards. Mon–Thurs 9am–1am; Fri 9am–3am; Sat 8am–3am; Sun 8am–1am.

Casamento's SEAFOOD   This restaurant takes oysters so seriously that it closes down when they're not in season. It pays off—this is *the* oyster place. Casamento's also has terrific gumbo—perhaps the best in town. It's small (you have to walk through the kitchen to get to the restrooms), and the atmosphere is light, with the waitresses serving up jokes and poking good-natured fun. 4330 Magazine St. © **504/895-9761.** Main courses $4.95–$11. No credit cards. Tues–Sun 11:30am– 1:30pm and 5:30–9pm. Closed June to mid-Sept.

Clover Grill COFFEE SHOP   You'll find juicy, perfect burgers cooked under a hubcap (they say it seals in the juices, and it seems to work). So well, in fact, that we're going to break with tradition and declare them the best burgers in New Orleans. Breakfast is served around the clock. 900 Bourbon St. © **504/598- 1010.** All items under $7. AE, MC, V. Daily 24 hr.

Commander's Palace CREOLE   Voted the best restaurant in the United States—that's right, in the *whole country*—by the James Beard Foundation in 1996 (and recently given their Lifetime Outstanding Restaurant award), Commander's is one place that lives up to its reputation. In a beautiful 1880s Victorian house, it consists of a series of dining rooms, from large to intimate, each more appealing and romantic than the last. On balmy nights, you can eat in the lovely courtyard. The waitstaff is incredibly attentive and pampers you throughout your meal. The famous turtle soup with sherry is outstanding, so thick it's nearly a stew. Other marvelous appetizer choices include the shrimp and tasso with five-pepper jelly, and the hearty crawfish bisque with homemade biscuits. For a main course, you're best off sticking with Creole-type offerings, such as the frequently available dreamy boned Mississippi roasted quail stuffed with Creole crawfish sausage. Your serving team will tell you to try the famous bread pudding soufflé. Trust them, though all the desserts are exceptional. There's an excellent wine list. 1403 Washington Ave. © **504/899-8221.** Reservations required. Jackets required at night and Sun brunch; no shorts, T-shirts, tennis shoes. Main courses $29–$32; full brunch $20–$32. AE, DC, DISC, MC, V. Mon–Fri 11:30am–1:30pm; Sat 11:30am–12:30pm; Sun brunch 10:30am–1:30pm; daily 6–9:30pm.

Dooky Chase SOUL FOOD/CREOLE   In the elegant dining rooms of Dooky Chase, classic soul food interacts gloriously with the city's French, Sicilian, and Italian traditions. Chef Leah Chase dishes up one of New Orleans's best bowls of gumbo along with more esoteric dishes. The fried chicken is exquisite. 2301 Orleans Ave. © **504/821-0600** or 504/821-2294. Reservations recommended at dinner. Main courses $10–$25; fixed-price 4-course meal $25; Creole feast $38. AE, DC, MC, V. Sun–Thurs 11:30am–10pm; Fri–Sat 11:30am–11pm.

Emeril's CREOLE/NEW AMERICAN   Emeril Lagasse is one of the Crescent City's finest chefs. Emeril's specialty is what he calls *New* New Orleans Cuisine, based upon Creole classics but taking them in new and exciting directions. Each plate dances with color and texture, and side dishes are perfectly paired with entrees. The signature dessert, astonishingly rich banana cream pie with banana crust and caramel drizzle sauce, will leave you moaning and pounding on the table (we've seen it happen). 800 Tchoupitoulas St. © **504/528-9393.** Reservations required at dinner. Main courses $22–$36; tasting menu $75. AE, DC, DISC, MC, V. Mon–Fri 11:30am–2pm; Mon–Sat 6–11pm.

Gabrielle CREOLE   This rather small but casually elegant restaurant just outside the French Quarter is gaining a big reputation. For a main course, you can't go wrong with any fish on the menu, from the pompano cooked in paper with garlic and tomatoes to the pan-fried trout with shrimp and roasted pecan butter. A standout was the double-thick-cut pork chop with a tomato salsa, topped with stuffed Anaheim chile—it had some masterful flavors. Gabrielle offers an early evening special Tuesday through Thursday from 5:30 to 6:15pm for only $16. You'll get a choice of three appetizers, two entrees, and two desserts. 3201 Esplanade Ave. © **504/948-6233.** Reservations recommended. Main courses $16–$28; early evening special (Tues–Thurs 5:30–6:15pm) $16. AE, DC, DISC, MC, V. Oct–May Fri 11:30am–2pm; year-round Tues–Sat 5:30–10pm.

Galatoire's FRENCH   The venerated Galatoire's causes heated discussions these days among local foodies: still the best restaurant in New Orleans, or past its prime? It's worth the trip, though you may not have the same experience as a knowledgeable local, unless you get a waiter who can really guide you (ask for John). We love the lump crabmeat appetizer (think coleslaw, only with all crab instead of cabbage), the shrimp rémoulade, and the oysters Rockefeller. For an entree, get the red snapper or redfish topped with sautéed crabmeat meunière. Don't miss out on the terrific creamed spinach and the puffy potatoes with béarnaise sauce. 209 Bourbon St. © **504/525-2021.** Reservations accepted for upstairs. Jackets required after 5pm and all day Sun. Main courses $14–$27. AE, DC, DISC, MC, V. Sun noon–10pm; Tues–Sat 11:30am–10pm. Closed July 4, Memorial Day, Thanksgiving, and Dec 25.

Gamay CONTEMPORARY CREOLE   Another offering from the chef/owners of Gabrielle (see above). By comparison, Gamay is a little bit more starched and formal than its predecessor, but the food is so darn good we don't really care all that much. The menu changes often, but if you can, try appetizers like barbecue shrimp pie, and entrees such as almond-crusted soft-shell crab with garlic shrimp and saffron pasta, which may be too huge and rich to leave room for heavenly strawberry shortcake—though do try. In the Bienville House Hotel, 320 Decatur St. © **504/299-8800.** Reservations recommended. Main courses $18–$28. AE, DC, DISC, MC, V. Tues–Sat 6–10pm.

Irene's Cuisine FRENCH/ITALIAN   When you enter, after being lured in from a block away by the potent smell of garlic, you will find a cluttered, dark tavern, not unromantic, with ultra-friendly waiters and prompt service. On a recent visit, we were thrilled by soft-shell crab pasta, an entirely successful Italian/New Orleans hybrid consisting of a whole fried crustacean atop a bed of pasta with a cream sauce of garlic, crawfish, tomatoes, and wads of whole basil leaves. Expect a long wait. 539 St. Phillip St. © **504/529-8811.** Reservations accepted only for Christmas Eve, New Year's Eve, and Valentine's Day. Main courses $14–$18. AE, MC, V. Sun–Thurs 5:30–10:30pm; Fri–Sat 5:30–11pm. Closed New Year's Day, July 4, Labor Day, and Thanksgiving Day.

Mother's SANDWICHES/CREOLE   Perhaps the proudest of all restaurants when New Orleans was named Fattest City in the U.S. was Mother's, whose overstuffed, mountain-size po' boys absolutely helped contribute to the results. It has long lines and zero atmosphere, but who cares when faced with a Ferdi special—a giant roll filled with baked ham, roast beef, gravy, and debris (the bits of beef that fall off when the roast is carved). 401 Poydras St. © **504/523-9656.** Menu items $1.75–$20. AE, MC, V. Mon–Sat 6:30am–10pm; Sun 7am–10pm.

Mr. B's Bistro & Bar CONTEMPORARY CREOLE   Run by Cindy Brennan, this deceptively simple place only helps solidify the Brennan reputation. The food, mostly modern interpretations of Creole classics, is simple, but with spices that elevate the flavors. The crab cakes and the not-too-spicy andouille sausage are superb. 201 Royal St. ✆ **504/523-2078.** Reservations recommended. Main courses $17–$28. AE, DC, DISC, MC, V. Mon–Sat 11:30am–3pm; Sun brunch 10:30am– 3pm; Sun–Fri 5:30–10pm; Sat 5–10pm.

Palace Café CONTEMPORARY CREOLE   The Palace Café offers contemporary Creole food. There are meat dishes on the menu, but *definitely* go for the seafood: catfish pecan meunière or andouille-crusted fish of the day. Don't miss the near-ecstasy-inducing white chocolate bread pudding, a Palace Café original. 605 Canal St. ✆ **504/523-1661.** Reservations recommended. Main courses $11–$25. AE, DC, DISC, MC, V. Mon–Fri 11:30am–2:30pm; Sat–Sun brunch 10:30am–2:30pm; daily 5:30–10pm.

Peristyle FRENCH/AMERICAN/ITALIAN/BISTRO   If you miss eating here, you've really missed something special. From lovely salads and fun appetizers like the caramelized onion tart or the country paté of the day to the always generously sized entrees (we fought over which was more outstanding—farm-raised quail with roasted shallot-applewood bacon-pecan relish; sage-marinated pork chop with butternut squash gnocchi; or lemon-fennel tuna with crispy potato cake), it's all just a delight, innovative without being threatening, and a near-perfect melding of flavors. And desserts are wonderful. 1041 Dumaine St. ✆ **504/593-9535.** Reservations recommended. Main courses $24–$27. AE, DC, MC, V. Fri 11:30am–1:30pm; Tues–Sat 6–10pm.

Uglesich's Restaurant & Bar SEAFOOD   It's dangerous to call any one place "the best in New Orleans," but it's mighty tempting to make an exception for "Ugly's," a tiny, crowded, greasy neighborhood place that serves some of the most divine seafood in town. At lunch time, you might have a very long wait. But we swear it will be worth it. Among the musts are fried green tomatoes with shrimp rémoulade, shrimp in creamy sauce on a fried cake of grits, voodoo shrimp (in a peppery butter sauce), and trout all kinds of ways. 1238 Barrone St. ✆ **504/523-8571.** Menu items $7–$14. No credit cards. Mon–Fri 9am–4pm; open 1 Sat a month. Closed July–Aug.

Upperline ECLECTIC/CREOLE   In a small, charming house in a largely residential area, the Upperline is a great low-key place to try imaginative food at reasonable prices. Standout appetizers include the fried green tomatoes with shrimp rémoulade, spicy shrimp on jalapeño corn bread, duck confit, and fried sweetbreads. For entrees, there's moist, herb-crusted pork loin, roast duck with a sauce that tingles, and a fall-off-the-bone lamb shank. 1413 Upperline St. (St. Charles Streetcar to the Upperline stop). ✆ **504/891-9822.** Reservations required. Main courses: $17–$24. AE, DC, MC, V. Wed–Sun 5:30–9:30pm.

NEW ORLEANS AFTER DARK

This is a city of music and rhythm. It is impossible to imagine New Orleans without a soundtrack of jazz, Cajun, and zydeco. Every night, dozens of clubs all over town offer music that can range from average to extraordinary, but is never less than danceable. When the clubs get too full, no matter; the crowd spills into the street, talking, drinking, and still dancing right there on the sidewalk.

For up-to-date information on what's happening around town, look for current editions of *Gambit, Offbeat,* and *Where,* all distributed free in most hotels and all record stores. Other sources include the *Times-Picayune*'s daily entertainment calendar and Friday's "Lagniappe" section.

JAZZ & BLUES CLUBS   Donna's, 800 N. Rampart St. (© **504/596-6914**), a corner bar at the edge of the Quarter, has become one of the top spots for the revival of the brass band experience and for a variety of jazz and blues traditions.

No, the **Funky Butt,** 714 N. Rampart St. (© **504/558-0872**), isn't a strip bar. Upstairs is a pleasing and mature performance space. Bookings emphasize jazz but can also include anything from the Wild Magnolias (the most famous of the Mardi Gras Indians) to an amazing Billie Holiday tribute band to the New Orleans Klezmer All Stars. Although the club itself is safe, the neighborhood around it isn't. Take a cab (yes, it seems silly, but take one even from Bourbon St.).

It doesn't get any more authentic than the jazz at **Preservation Hall,** 726 St. Peter St. (© **504/522-2841,** or 504/523-8939 after 8pm). With no seats, terrible sightlines, and constant crowds, you won't be able to see much, but you won't care, because you will be having too much fun.

If your idea of jazz extends beyond Dixieland, and if you prefer a concert-type setting over a messy nightclub, head for **Snug Harbor,** 626 Frenchmen St. (© **504/949-0696**). On the fringes of the French Quarter (1 block beyond Esplanade Ave.), Snug Harbor is the city's premier showcase for contemporary jazz, with a few blues and R&B combos thrown in for good measure. Buy tickets in advance.

Storyville District, 125 Bourbon St. (© **504/410-1000**), aims to bring high-quality jazz back to Bourbon Street without the frat-party atmosphere. Music plays much of the day, starting in the red-walled parlor room in the afternoon, with bigger bands playing in a larger, more clublike space at night. Check out piano great Eddie Bo.

Swing has finally caught on in New Orleans with a vengeance, helped in part by **The Red Room,** 2040 St. Charles Ave. (© **504/528-9759**), a hot, fairly new, '40s-style jazz and supper club. There's live swing and jazz every night, perfect for dancing and romancing. Jackets recommended for men.

ZYDECO   It doesn't get any more authentic than a club in the middle of a bowling alley, in the middle of a strip mall. **Mid City Lanes Rock & Bowl,** 4133 S. Carrollton Ave. (© **504/482-3133**), is the best place for zydeco.

RHYTHM, ROCK & THE REST OF THE MUSIC SCENE   By day, **Cafe Brasil,** 2100 Chartres St. (© **504/949-0851**), is a great place to get a cup of coffee. By night, it's the center of the lively and popular Frenchmen section of the Faubourg Marigny. It features Latin or Caribbean music, R&B, or jazz almost every night, and chances are whatever is playing will be infectious.

The House of Blues, 225 Decatur St. (© **504/529-2583;** www.hob.com), is a little too Disney for New Orleans, but give them credit for adequate sight lines, good sound, and first-rate bookings, from local legends like the Neville Brothers to such ace out-of-towners as Los Lobos and Nanci Griffith.

The Howlin' Wolf, 828 S. Peters St. (© **504/522-WOLF;** www.howlin wolf.com), is arguably the premier club in town for top bookings. It draws some top touring rock acts, but it is not at all limited to rock—El Vez, the Mexican Elvis, is as likely to play as a country, indie or alternative band.

The **Maple Leaf Bar,** 8316 Oak St. (© **504/866-9359**), is what a New Orleans club is all about. More often than not, the crowd spills onto the sidewalk and into the street to dance and drink. If Beausoleil or the ReBirth Brass Band is playing, do not miss it; go and dance till you drop.

THE BAR SCENE   The **Apple Barrel,** 609 Frenchmen St. (℃ **504/949-9399**), is a small, dusty, wooden-floored watering hole, with jukebox and darts, where you can find refuge from the hectic Frenchmen scene—or gear up to join in.

The **Bombay Club,** 830 Conti St. (℃ **504/586-0972**), is a posh jazz piano bar that offers the best martinis in town. There's also piano music Tuesday through Saturday at the **Carousel Bar & Lounge,** in the Monteleone Hotel, 214 Royal St. (℃ **504/523-3341**), but the real attraction is the bar itself—it really is a carousel, and it really does revolve. **Feelings,** 2600 Chartres (℃ **504/945-2222**), is a low-key, funky neighborhood restaurant and hangout, set around a classic New Orleans courtyard, where you can hang out with the fabulous piano player.

Pat O'Brien's, 718 St. Peter St. (℃ **504/525-4823**), is world famous for its gigantic, rum-based hurricane drink, served in signature 29-ounce glasses.

Lafitte's Blacksmith Shop, 941 Bourbon St. (℃ **504/522-9377**), dating from the 1770s, is the oldest building in the Quarter. In other towns, this would be a tourist trap. Here, it feels authentic.

Outside the Quarter, **Circle Bar,** 1032 St. Charles Ave. (℃ **504/588-2616**), is the new happening place, with a quirky romantic mood.

THE GAY & LESBIAN SCENE   The gay community is quite strong and visible in New Orleans, and the gay bars are some of the most bustling places in town—full of action nearly 24 hours a day. For more information, check *Ambush,* 828-A Bourbon St. (℃ **504/522-8049;** www.ambushmag.com), a great source for the gay community in New Orleans and for visitors. Once you're in New Orleans, you can pick up a copy at Tower Records, 408 N. Peters St., in the French Quarter; or at Lenny's News, 5420 Magazine St., uptown.

The **Bourbon Pub–Parade Disco,** 801 Bourbon St. (℃ **504/529-2107**), is the most centrally located of the gay bars. The downstairs pub offers a video bar; Parade Disco upstairs features a high-tech dance floor complete with lasers and smoke. It consistently appears on lists of the top dance clubs in America.

Café Lafitte in Exile, 901 Bourbon St. (℃ **504/522-8397**), is one of the oldest gay bars in the United States. There's a bar downstairs, and upstairs you'll find a pool table and a balcony that overlooks Bourbon Street. The whole shebang is open 24 hours daily. Come Sunday evening for "Trash Disco" music.

The congenial **Good Friends Bar & Queens Head Pub,** 740 Dauphine St. (℃ **504/566-7191**), often wins the Gay Achievement Award for Best Neighborhood Gay Bar.

DANCE CLUBS   **Oz,** 800 Bourbon St. (℃ **504/593-9491**), is the place to see and be seen, with a primarily young crowd. *Details* magazine named it one of the top 50 clubs in the country. The music is great, there's an incredible laser light show, and from time to time there are go-go boys atop the bar.

SIDE TRIPS FROM NEW ORLEANS: PLANTATIONS

You can still capture some of the Old South in the form of restored plantation homes. In just an hour's jaunt from New Orleans, you can travel back over 100 years. Located on the same road (La. 18), you can visit both Laura Plantation and Oak Alley on the same trip.

Laura: A Creole Plantation   If you see only one plantation, make it this one. The hoop skirted tours found elsewhere are banished in favor of a comprehensive view of daily life on an 18th- and 19th-century plantation, a cultural history of Louisiana's Creole population, and a dramatic, entertaining look at one extended Creole family. Much is known about this classic Creole house and the family that lived here, thanks to the detailed memoirs of Laura Locoul (for whom the plantation is named). On display are more than 375 original artifacts that cover a 200-year period and include household items like clothes and jewelry. Basic tours of the main building and the property (the only way to see the plantation) last about 55 minutes and are organized around true (but spiced-up) stories from the history of the home and its residents. 2247 La. 18, Vacherie, LA 70090. ℂ 888/799-7690 or 225/265-7690. www.lauraplantation.com. Admission $10 adults, $5 students and children, free for children under 6. Tours depart every 20 min., beginning at 9:30am daily; last tour departs at 4pm. Closed major holidays.

Oak Alley Plantation   This is the most famous plantation home in Louisiana. A splendid white house, its porch lined with giant columns, approached by a magnificent drive lined with stately oak trees—yep, it's all here. It's also the slickest operation, with a large parking lot, expensive lunch buffet (bring your own picnic), hoop-skirted guides, and golf carts traversing the property. The furnishings are not original, but are strict to the time period and mostly correspond to the original inhabitant's actual inventory.

Overnight accommodations are available in five early-1900s Creole cottages (complete with sitting rooms, porches, and air-conditioning). Rates are $105 to $135, and include breakfast but not a tour. The restaurant is open for breakfast and lunch daily from 9am to 3pm. 3645 La. 18 (60 miles from New Orleans), Vacherie, LA 70009. ℂ 800/44-ALLEY or 225/265-2151. Admission $10 adults, $5 students, $3 children 6–12, free for children under 6. Mar–Oct daily 9am–5:30pm; Nov–Feb daily 9am–5pm. Closed Jan 1, Thanksgiving, Dec 25.

Florida

Every year millions of visitors escape bleak northern winters to bask in Florida's warmth, lured to the Sunshine State by the promise of clear skies and 800 miles of spectacular sandy beaches. A host of kid-pleasers, from Busch Gardens to Walt Disney World, make this the country's most popular year-round family vacation destination.

For general information, contact **Visit Florida,** P.O. Box 1100, Tallahassee, FL 32302-1100 (© **888/7-FLA-USA;** www.flausa.com). You can request a visitors' guide for the entire state in English, Spanish, German, or Portuguese.

1 Walt Disney World & Orlando

When Disney opened the Magic Kingdom in 1971, few imagined what Central Florida would be like 3 decades later. Today, it's bursting (and in some cases imploding) with newer, bigger, and better things for you to do. Walt Disney World (WDW) has four theme parks, dozens of smaller attractions, tens of thousands of hotel rooms, scores of restaurants, a ton of bars and clubs, and two cruise ships. When Universal Orlando, SeaWorld, and the marginal players add their share, well, it's safe to say that you won't have a problem finding something to do here.

PACKAGE DEALS

The number and diversity of package tours to Orlando is staggering, and, if you're willing to do the research, they will net you significant savings.

If you plan to spend all of your time in Mickeyville, contact the **Walt Disney World Travel Company** (© **800/828-0228;** www.disneyworld.com) for a wide assortment of packages available.

Universal Orlando packages can be booked at © **888/322-5537.** You can get online information at **www.universalorlando.com.** For **SeaWorld,** call © **800/423-8368** or go to **www.seaworld.com.**

Almost all of the major airlines offer packages, and **American Express Travel** (© **800/732-1991;** http://travel.americanexpress.com/travel) has special deals for card holders.

GETTING THERE **By Plane** More than 35 million people fly into **Orlando International Airport** each year. The airport, which just finished up a major expansion, is user-friendly, with centrally located information kiosks. The airport is 25 miles from Walt Disney World.

Mears Transportation (© **407/423-5566**) shuttles people to and from the airport. The vans run 24 hours a day, departing every 15 to 25 minutes. Round-trip fares are $23 to $27 for adults and $16 to $19 for children 4 to 11.

By Train **Amtrak** (© **800/USA-RAIL;** www.amtrak.com) provides daily service from Jacksonville (trip time: 3¾ hr.), Miami (5¼ hr.), and Washington, D.C. (18 hr.). Trains pull into stations in downtown Orlando (23 miles from Walt

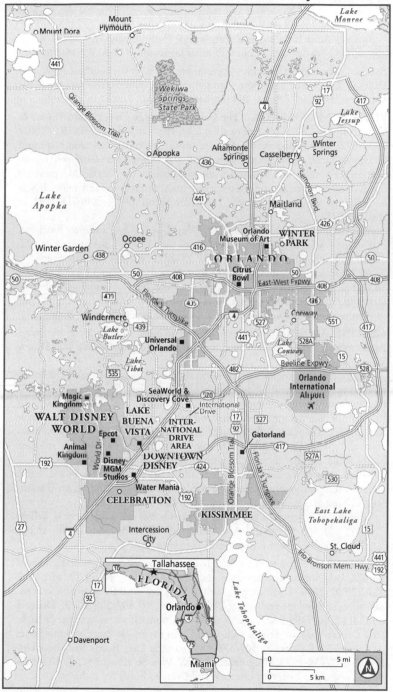

Orlando & Walt Disney World Area

Lake Monroe

Mount Plymouth

Mount Dora

441

Wekiwa Springs State Park

Orange Blossom Trail

Lake Jessup

17
92
417

Apopka

Altamonte Springs

Casselberry

436

Winter Springs

Lake Apopka

441

Maitland

426

Winter Garden

Ocoee

416

Orlando Museum of Art

WINTER PARK

ORLANDO

438

50

50

408

Citrus Bowl

East-West Expwy

50

408

408

Florida's Turnpike

435

136

429

4

Conway

551

417

Windermere

Lake Butler

439

527

441

Universal Orlando

Lake Tibet

528A

Lake Conway

Beeline Expwy

15

528

535

482

Orlando International Airport

Magic Kingdom

SeaWorld & Discovery Cove

International Drive

520

WALT DISNEY WORLD

LAKE BUENA VISTA

INTER-NATIONAL DRIVE AREA

17
92

527

Epcot

Gatorland

192

Animal Kingdom

World Dr.

Disney-MGM Studios

DOWNTOWN DISNEY

424

417

527A

530

27

Water Mania

CELEBRATION

192

KISSIMMEE

East Lake Tohopekaliga

15

4

Intercession City

St. Cloud

Irlo Bronson Mem. Hwy.

441
192

Tallahassee

FLORIDA

10

17

92

Orlando

4

95

Lake Tohopekaliga

Davenport

75

Miami

0   5 mi
0   5 km

N

357

Disney World) and Kissimmee (15 miles from Disney). There are also stops in Winter Park (10 miles north of downtown).

Amtrak's **Auto Train** provides daily service from Lorton, VA, outside Washington, D.C., to Sanford, FL, just 23 miles northeast of Orlando (16½ hr.).

By Car   The major routes into Orlando are I-4 from the northeast (I-95 and Daytona Beach) and southwest (Tampa), and the Florida Turnpike from the northwest (I-75 and Atlanta) and southeast (Miami).

VISITOR INFORMATION   The **Orlando/Orange County Convention & Visitors Bureau,** 8723 International Dr., Ste. 101, Orlando, FL 32819 (© **407/ 363-5872;** www.orlandoinfo.com), can answer questions and send maps and brochures, such as the *Official Visitors Guide* and *Official Accommodations Guide.* The packet should reach you in 3 weeks and include the "Magicard," good for up to $500 in discounts on rooms, car rentals, attractions, and more. If you don't require a human voice, you can order by calling © **800/643-9492** or 800/551-0181.

For information about **Walt Disney World**—including vacation brochures and videos—write or call Walt Disney World, Box 10000, Lake Buena Vista, FL 32830-1000 (© **407/934-7639** or 407/824-2222; www.disneyworld.com).

For information about **Universal Orlando,** call © **800/837-2273** or 407/ 363-8000, surf over to **www.universalorlando.com**, or write to **Universal Orlando,** 1000 Universal Studios Plaza, Orlando, FL 32819.

You can obtain SeaWorld information online at **www.seaworld.com**.

GETTING AROUND   Although you can manage without a car, it's always handy to have one, especially if you want to see attractions outside Walt Disney World.

A thorough, free transportation network runs throughout the WDW complex. Disney resorts and official hotels offer unlimited free transportation via bus, monorail, ferry, or water taxi to all WDW parks and properties 14 to 18 hours a day. You can get to Universal and other attractions, too, but you'll have to pay extra. *The pluses:* The system is free; you can save on a rental car, insurance, and gas; and you don't have to pay for theme-park parking. *The minuses:* You're at the mercy of the schedule, which is often slow and *very* indirect.

Mears Transportation operates vans and buses that go to all of the theme parks, as well as Cypress Gardens, Kennedy Space Center, and Busch Gardens (yes, in Tampa), among others. Call © **407/423-5566** for rates.

Taxis gather at resorts, and smaller properties will call a cab for you. **Yellow Cab** (© **407/699-9999**) and **Ace Metro** (© **407/855-0564**) usually charge $2.50 for the first mile, $1.50 per mile thereafter.

FAST FACTS   If you need medical assistance, you can get a reputable referral from **Ask-A-Nurse.** In Kissimmee, call © **407/870-1700;** in Orlando, call © **407/897-1700.** There are basic first-aid centers in all the major parks. **Disney** offers in-room medical service 24 hours a day (© **407/238-2000). Doctors on Call** (© **407/399-3627**) makes house and room calls in most of the Orlando area. **Centra-Care** lists several walk-in clinics in the Yellow Pages, including ones on International Drive, © **407/370-4881,** and at Lake Buena Vista near Disney, © **407/934-2273. Walgreens,** 1003 W. Vine St. (Hwy. 192; © **407/847- 5252**), operates a 24-hour pharmacy. It delivers to hotels for a charge.

Florida's 6% sales tax is charged on all goods except most grocery store items and medicines. Additionally, hotels add another 5% or 6% to your bill for a total of 11% or 12%.

A Note on Area Codes

When making a local call in Orlando, you must dial the area code and phone number for all numbers within the 407 area code covering Orlando. A rapidly growing population makes this 10-digit dialing necessary, even if you are calling somewhere just down the block.

TIPS FOR VISITING WALT DISNEY WORLD ATTRACTIONS

Walt Disney World is the umbrella above four theme parks: the Magic Kingdom, Epcot, Disney–MGM Studios, and Animal Kingdom, which drew almost 40 million guests despite an economic decline in 2001, according to *Amusement Business* magazine. All four ranked in the top five in attendance nationally (No. 2 was Disneyland in California).

Besides its theme parks, Disney has an assortment of other venues, including Downtown Disney (Cirque du Soleil & DisneyQuest, Pleasure Island, Blizzard Beach, Typhoon Lagoon, River Country, and more).

AVOIDING THE CROWDS There isn't a real off season, but crowds are usually thinner mid-January through March and mid-September until the week before Thanksgiving. The busiest days at all of the theme parks are generally Saturdays and Sundays, when the locals visit. Beyond that, Monday, Thursday, and Saturday are pretty frantic in the Magic Kingdom; Tuesday and Friday are hectic at Epcot; Sunday and Wednesday are crazy at Disney–MGM Studios; and Monday, Tuesday, and Wednesday are a zoo at Animal Kingdom. Major holidays attract throngs: Christmas through New Year's is a frenzied time.

Note: Summer is the worst time: Crowds + heat + humidity = theme-park hell.

ARRIVE EARLY Always arrive at the parks a good 30 to 45 minutes before opening time, thus avoiding a traffic jam entering the park and a long line at the gate. Early arrival also lets you experience one or two major attractions before big lines form.

PARKING Cars, light trucks, and vans currently pay $6 (though we expect Disney to follow Universal and SeaWorld and go to $7). Visitors with mobility impairments can park in special areas near the entrances; ask the parking-lot attendants or call © **407/824-4321.** *Don't forget* to write down where you parked (area and row number), because it's easy to get lost after a long day.

WHEN YOU ARRIVE Grab a park guide map! It not only tells you where the fun is but lists the daily entertainment schedule. If you want to see certain shows or parades, arrive early to get a good seat. Use this guide and the map to come up with a game plan on where to eat, what to ride, and what to see during your stay.

OPERATING HOURS Park hours vary and are influenced by special events and the economy. So call ahead or go to **www.disneyworld.com** to check. Generally, expect Animal Kingdom to be open from 8 or 9am to 5 or 6pm; Epcot to be open from 10am to 9pm; and Magic Kingdom and Disney–MGM to be open from 9am to 5 or 6pm. All may open or close earlier or later.

TICKETS There are several options, from 1-day to multiday tickets. The best choices are 4- and 5-day passes. Some don't save you money—they may even cost more—but they add the flexibility of moving from park to park and returning on the same or multiple days. The following *don't include 6% sales tax* unless noted. **Note:** Price hikes are frequent occurrences, so call © **407/824-4321** or visit WDW's website (**www.disneyworld.com**) for up-to-the-minute fees.

1-day/1-park tickets, for admission to the Magic Kingdom, Epcot, Animal Kingdom, or Disney–MGM, are $50 for adults, $40 for children 3 to 9. (Ouch!)

4-Day Park Hopper Passes provide unlimited admission to the Magic Kingdom, Epcot, Animal Kingdom, and Disney–MGM Studios. Adults pay $199; children 3 to 9 pay $159. **5-Day Park Hopper Plus Passes** also include your choice of two admissions to Typhoon Lagoon, River Country, Blizzard Beach, Pleasure Island, or Disney's Wide World of Sports. They sell for $259 for adults and $209 for children 3 to 9. Passes for 6 and 7 days are available, too.

A **1-day ticket to Typhoon Lagoon or Blizzard Beach** is $31 for adults, $25 for children 3 to 11. A **1-day ticket to Pleasure Island** is $21 including tax. Since this is primarily an 18 and over entertainment complex, there's no bargain price for children.

If you're staying at a WDW resort, you're eligible for a money-saving **Ultimate Park Hopper,** priced according to the length of your stay.

THE MAGIC KINGDOM

The Magic Kingdom offers 40 attractions, plus restaurants and shops, in a 107-acre package. Its symbol, Cinderella Castle, forms the hub of a wheel whose spokes reach to **seven "lands."**

MAIN STREET, USA   The gateway to the Kingdom, Main Street is designed to resemble a turn-of-the-20th-century American street. Don't dawdle here when you enter the park; leave it for the end of the day when you're heading back to your hotel. You can board an authentic 1928 steam-powered railroad for

FASTPASS

Don't want to stand in line as long as the other guests, yet not flush enough to hire a stand-in? Disney parks use a reservation system whereby you go to the primo rides, feed your theme-park ticket into a small ticket-taker machine, and get an assigned time to return. When you reappear at the appointed time, you get into a short line and climb aboard. Here's the drill:

Hang onto your ticket stub when you enter, and head to the hottest ride on your dance card. If it's a FASTPASS attraction (they're noted in the guide map you get when you enter) and there's a line, feed your stub into the waist-level ticket taker. Retrieve your stub and the FASTPASS stub that comes with it. Look at the two times stamped on the FASTPASS. Come back during that 1-hour window and you can enter the ride with almost no wait. In the interim, go to another attraction or show.

Note: Early in the day, your window may begin 40 minutes after you feed the FASTPASS machine, but later in the day it may be hours. Initially, Disney allowed you to do this on only one ride at a time, but now you can get a pass for a second attraction 2 hours after your first assigned time.

a 15-minute journey clockwise around the perimeter of the park, with stops in Frontierland and Mickey's Toontown Fair. At the end of Main Street, in the center of the park, you'll come to Cinderella Castle, 185 feet high, housing a restaurant and shops. Cinderella herself, dressed for the ball, often makes appearances in the lobby.

ADVENTURELAND   Cross a bridge to your left and stroll into an exotic jungle of lush tropical foliage, thatch-roofed huts, and carved totems.

The **Swiss Family Treehouse** is based on *The Swiss Family Robinson,* about a shipwrecked family who created an ingenious dwelling in the branches of a sprawling banyan tree. Visitors ascend the 50-foot tree for a close-up look into these rooms with their Rube Goldberg devices.

In the course of 10 minutes on the **Jungle Cruise,** your boat sails through an African veldt and an Amazon rainforest, and along the Mekong River in Southeast Asia and the Nile. Amid the cascading waterfalls and lush foliage are audio-animatronic zebras, lions, giraffes, crocodiles, tigers, even fluttering butterflies. Passengers are menaced by everything from water-spouting elephants to fierce warriors who attack with spears. It's Disney at its cheesy best.

Next up is **Pirates of the Caribbean.** You'll board a boat that sails into a pitch-black cave. There, amid fiery explosions and a redundant sea shanty, are a ragtag collection of yo-ho-hoing mates. It's a WDW classic, but loud explosions can make it scary for young children.

The **Enchanted Tiki Room**'s newly updated show features 250 tropical birds, chanting totem poles, and singing flowers that whistle, tweet, and warble. The kids will love it, and it's a cool place to perch on a hot afternoon.

The first major ride added to Adventureland since 1971, **The Magic Carpets of Aladdin** delights wee ones and some older kids. Its 16 four-passenger carpets circle a giant genie's bottle while camels spit water at riders. The fiberglass carpets spin and move up, down, forward, and back.

FRONTIERLAND   Themed after *Song of the South,* **Splash Mountain** takes you on a leisurely journey in a hollowed-out log craft. The audio-animatronics and theme song of the first portion of Splash Mountain are a bit too cute, but the ride culminates in a breathtaking five-story splashdown from mountaintop to pond at 40 miles per hour. You *will* get wet!

Big Thunder Mountain Railroad, a mining disaster-themed roller coaster, derives its thrills from hairpin turns and descents in the dark. You'll board a runaway train that careens through the ribs of a dinosaur, under a thundering waterfall, past spewing geysers and bubbling mud pots, and over a bottomless volcanic pool. The effects are even better at night.

The **Diamond Horseshoe Saloon Revue & Medicine Show** is an opportunity to sit down in air-conditioned comfort and enjoy a rousing Western revue. The **Country Bear Jamboree** is a 15-minute show featuring a troupe of fiddlin', banjo-strummin' audio-animatronic bears belting out country tunes.

LIBERTY SQUARE   Liberty Square evokes 18th-century America with Georgian architecture and Colonial Williamsburg–type shops.

In the redbrick colonial **Hall of Presidents,** all American presidents are represented by extremely realistic audio-animatronic figures. If you look closely, you'll see them fidget and whisper.

The **Haunted Mansion** is another WDW classic, replete with bizarre scenes and objects: a ghostly banquet and ball, luminous spiders, a talking head in a crystal ball, weird flying objects, and much more. It's more amusing than terrifying, so you can take small children.

FANTASYLAND **Legend of the Lion King** is a great stage show based on Disney's blockbuster motion picture; it combines animation, movie footage, sophisticated puppetry, and high-tech special effects. Don't miss it.

In the **Mad Tea Party,** riders sit in oversize pink teacups on saucers that careen around a circular platform. **The Many Adventures of Winnie the Pooh** features the cute-and-cuddly fellow, but empties into a gift shop.

Cinderella's Golden Carousel is a beauty, built by Italian wood-carvers in the Victorian tradition in 1917, and refurbished by Disney artists who added scenes from the Cinderella story. **Dumbo, the Flying Elephant** is a very tame kiddie ride, but exciting for wee ones.

Next up is **It's a Small World.** You know the song—and if you don't, you will. It plays continually as you sail "around the world" through vast rooms designed to represent different countries. It's sickeningly cute, but it's almost a required rite of passage.

Riding in Captain Hook's ship, passengers careen through dark tunnels and over nighttime London into Never-Never Land while experiencing **Peter Pan's Flight.** It's fun, but the lines can be endless. The same can be said for **Snow White's Scary Adventures,** which aren't all that frightening.

MICKEY'S TOONTOWN FAIR Head off those cries of "Where's Mickey?" by taking the kids to this 2-acre area where they can meet their favorite characters. Everything is brightly colored and kid-friendly in the best Disney tradition; there is even a kid-size roller coaster. There are also really long lines.

TOMORROWLAND Tomorrowland depicts the future as a galactic, science fiction–inspired community inhabited by humans, aliens, and robots. There's also a vast state-of-the-art video-game arcade.

Director George Lucas contributed his space-age vision to the **Extra "Terror"estrial Alien Encounter.** Dark and truly scary, it has lots of high-tech effects, from the alien's breath on your neck to a mist of alien slime. Young children should sit it out.

Space Mountain entertains visitors in its long lines with space-age music, exhibits, and celestial objects whizzing about overhead. These "illusioneering" effects, enhanced by appropriate audio, continue during the ride itself, which is a cosmic roller coaster making thrilling hairpin turns and rapid plunges in the inky starlit blackness of outer space.

In **Buzz Lightyear's Space Ranger Spin,** you'll pilot your own cruiser while shooting laser cannons at evil aliens as you spin through a world filled with gigantic toys. The **Tomorrowland Speedway** is a great thrill for kids who get to put the pedal to the metal, steer, and vroom down a speedway in an actual gas-powered sports car; adults and teens will be considerably less happy.

PARADES, FIREWORKS & MORE You'll get an *Entertainment Show Schedule* when you enter the park, which lists all kinds of special goings-on for the day.

SpectroMagic is a 20-minute production featuring fiber optics, holographic images, old-fashioned twinkling lights, and a soundtrack of classic Disney tunes. The parade runs on a *very limited basis.*

Fantasy in the Sky Fireworks is one of the most explosive displays in Orlando. Disney has pyrotechnics down to an art form, and this is clearly the best way to end your day in the Magic Kingdom. The fireworks go off nightly during peak periods, but only on selected nights the rest of the year. Suggested viewing areas are Liberty Square, Frontierland, and Mickey's Toontown Fair.

EPCOT

Epcot is an acronym for Experimental Prototype Community of Tomorrow, and it was Walt Disney's dream for a planned residential community. But, after his death, it opened in 1982 as Central Florida's second theme park.

The 260-acre park has two sections, **Future World** and **World Showcase.** It's so large that hiking World Showcase from tip to tip (1.3 miles) can be exhausting. That's why some folks say Epcot really stands for "Every Person Comes Out Tired." Depending on how long you intend to linger at each of the 11 countries in World Showcase, this park can be seen in 1 day, but it's better over 2.

FUTURE WORLD **Spaceship Earth,** a massive, silvery geosphere, symbolizes Epcot, but all that awaits inside is a 15-minute yawn of a show/ride that takes you through the history of communications. *Tip:* Skip it.

Innoventions showcases cutting-edge technologies and future products. You'll get a chance to preview virtual reality, experience interactive television, and try out new computer programs and games.

The Living Seas pavilion is a 5.7-million-gallon saltwater aquarium (complete with a coral reef) inhabited by thousands of sharks, barracudas, parrotfish, rays, and dolphins. After a film, visitors enter hydrolators for a rapid descent to the ocean floor, where they enjoy stunning close-up views of ocean denizens in a natural coral-reef habitat.

The Land, the largest of Future World's pavilions, highlights humankind's relation to food and nature. **Living with the Land** is a boat ride that takes you through a rainforest, an African desert, and windswept American plains. Combining spectacular live-action footage with animation, the excellent 15-minute motion picture called *Circle of Life* is a cautionary environmental tale featuring characters from *The Lion King.* There's also a crowd-pleasing animatronic lesson in nutrition at **Food Rocks.**

The recently-redone **Imagination** pavilion offers a new show that welcomes back an old park favorite—Figment the dinosaur. But the headliner here is **Honey, I Shrunk the Audience,** a 3-D attraction based on the Disney *Honey, I Shrunk the Kids* films. Dramatic 3-D action is enhanced by vibrating seats and creepy tactile effects.

Test Track puts guests in the driver's seat to experience the rigors of automobile testing. Six-passenger test cars travel upon what appears to be an actual roadway, accelerating on long straightaways, hugging hairpin turns, climbing steep hills, and braking abruptly. This ride's the best in the park and has the long lines to prove it.

Wonders of Life offers some of Future World's most engaging shows and attractions, including *The Making of Me,* a captivating movie starring Martin Short in a sweet introduction to the facts of life. In **Body Wars,** you're miniaturized to the size of a single cell to take part in a medical rescue mission inside the immune system of a human body. This motion-simulator ride takes you on a wild journey through gale-force winds (in the lungs) and pounding heart chambers. It's not for the faint of heart. **Cranium Command,** a hilarious multimedia attraction, features Buzzy, an audio-animatronic brain-pilot-in-training who's charged with the seemingly impossible task of controlling the brain of a typical 12-year-old boy. It's a definite must.

Universe of Energy, a 32-minute ride-through attraction with visitors seated in solar-powered "traveling theater" cars, aims to better our understanding of America's energy problems. **Ellen's Energy Adventure** features Ellen DeGeneres as an energy expert tutored to be a *Jeopardy!* contestant by Bill Nye, the Science Guy. The dinosaur section of this ride has been revamped and is better than ever.

WORLD SHOWCASE   Surrounding a 40-acre lagoon at the park's southern end is a permanent community of 11 miniaturized nations, all with indigenous landmark architecture, landscaping, background music, restaurants, and shops. A special new pavilion representing dozens more countries is being unveiled as part of Epcot's millennium celebration.

Canada features an Inuit village, Rocky Mountains scenery, and stunning floral displays inspired by the Butchart Gardens in Victoria. The pavilion's highlight is *O Canada!,* a dazzling 360° CircleVision film that reveals Canada's scenic splendor.

United Kingdom evokes Merry Olde England. Four centuries of architecture are represented along quaint cobblestoned streets; troubadours and minstrels entertain in front of a British pub; and there's a formal garden with a stereotypical red phone booth. A tea shop occupies a replica of Anne Hathaway's thatchroofed, 16th-century cottage in Stratford-upon-Avon.

In **France,** a one-tenth replica of the Eiffel Tower looms above the *grands boulevards* and a park inspired by Seurat. Shown in a palatial (and mercifully a sit-down) theater a la Fontainebleau, **Impressions de France** is an entertaining 18-minute film journey through France, projected on a vast wraparound screen. A marketplace revives the defunct Les Halles.

Exotic **Morocco** is heralded by a minaret. The Medina (old city), entered via a replica of an arched gateway in Fez, leads to Fez House (a traditional Moroccan home) and the narrow winding streets of the *souk,* a bustling marketplace where authentic handcrafts are on display.

Heralded by a flaming-red *torii* (gate of honor) and the graceful Goju No To pagoda, **Japan** features an exquisite Japanese garden. The Yakitori House is based on the renowned 16th-century Katsura Imperial Villa in Kyoto. Exhibits ranging from 18th-century bunraku puppets to samurai armor take place in the moated White Heron Castle. Be sure to include a demonstration of traditional Japanese music and dance in your schedule; it's one of the best shows in the World Showcase.

Housed in a vast Georgian-style structure, **U.S.A.–The American Adventure** is a 29-minute dramatization of U.S. history using a 72-foot rear-projection screen, rousing music, and a large cast of lifelike audio-animatronic figures. You view Jefferson writing the Declaration of Independence, the expansion of the frontier, the Civil War, the attack on Pearl Harbor, and the Eagle heading toward the moon.

One of the prettiest World Showcase pavilions, **Italy** lures visitors over an arched stone footbridge to a central piazza enclosing a version of Bernini's Neptune Fountain. Mediterranean citrus, olive, and cypress trees frame a formal garden. Gondolas are moored on the lagoon.

Enclosed by towered castle walls, festive **Germany** is centered on a cobblestoned *platz* (square). The pavilion's outdoor **Biergarten**—where it's Oktoberfest all year long—was inspired by medieval Rothenberg. Model-train enthusiasts shouldn't miss the detailed miniature German village.

Bounded by a serpentine wall, **China** is entered via a vast ceremonial gate inspired by the Temple of Heaven in Beijing. Gardens simulate those in Suzhou, with miniature waterfalls, fragrant lotus ponds, groves of bamboo, and weeping mulberry trees. The highlight is *Wonders of China,* a 360° CircleVision film that explores 6,000 years of history and the breathtaking diversity of the Chinese landscape. The **Yong Feng Shangdian Shopping Gallery** offers an array of merchandise.

In **Norway,** a replica of Oslo's 14th-century **Akershus Castle,** next to a cascading woodland waterfall, is the setting for the pavilion's featured restaurant. Other buildings simulate the red-roofed cottages of Bergen and the timber-sided farm buildings of the Nordic woodlands. **Maelstrom,** a boat ride in a dragon-headed Viking vessel, traverses Norway's fjords and mythical forests to the music of *Peer Gynt,* while you're menaced by polar bears and trolls. You'll disembark in a 10th-century Viking village to view the 70mm film *Norway,* which documents 1,000 years of history.

You'll hear the music of marimba and mariachi bands as you approach **Mexico,** fronted by a towering Mayan pyramid. Upon entering, you'll find yourself in a museum of pre-Columbian art and artifacts. **El Rio del Tiempo** (River of Time) is a pleasant, 8-minute cruise through Mexico's history and culture.

SHOWS & SPECTACULARS   The **World Showcase Pavilion Shows** make up an important part of the Epcot experience. There are Chinese lion dancers and acrobats, German oompah bands, Moroccan belly dancers, Scottish pipers, and much more. Don't miss the Voices of Liberty Singers at American Adventure and the traditional music and dance displays in Japan.

A backdrop of classical music, high-tech lighting effects, darting laser beams, fireworks, and rainbow-lit dancing fountains combine to create the awesome 16½-minute Epcot spectacular called **IllumiNations,** presented nightly. Don't miss it! The best places to see the show are at the Crossroads of the World shopping arcade, United Kingdom, and Canada. For a good seat around the lagoon, stake out a spot at least a half hour before show time.

DISNEY–MGM STUDIOS

You'll probably spy the Tower of Terror and the Earful Tower—a water tower outfitted with gigantic mouse ears—before you enter this park, which Disney bills as "the Hollywood that never was and always will be." Once inside, you'll find pulse-quickening rides such as the **Rock 'n' Roller Coaster** and movie- and TV-themed shows such as **Who Wants to Be a Millionaire—Play It!.** On Hollywood and Sunset boulevards, Art Deco movie sets remember the golden age of Hollywood. New York Street is lined with miniature renditions of Gotham's landmarks and typical characters, including peddlers hawking knock-off watches. This 110-acre park has some of the best street performing anywhere.

The **Rock 'n' Roller Coaster** is a fast-and-furious coaster that blasts you from 0 to 60 miles per hour in 2.8 seconds, and takes you on a wild ride through a make-believe California freeway system in semidarkness. The ride lasts 3 minutes, 12 seconds, about the running time of Aerosmith's hit "Sweet Emotion." It's the best thrill ride at Disney.

The **Twilight Zone Tower of Terror** is a thrilling and stomach-churning journey to another dimension. Rod Serling narrates as you become the star in a special episode of *The Twilight Zone* that climaxes with a terrifying 13-story free-fall plunge! Many believe that this one tops the Rock 'n' Roller Coaster in the thrills department.

In **The Magic of Disney Animation,** you'll see Disney characters come alive at the stroke of a pencil as you tour actual glass-walled animation studios and watch artists at work. The tour includes a grand finale of magical moments from Disney classics. Try to visit this popular attraction early in the morning to beat the inevitable long lines.

The 25-minute **Disney–MGM Studio Backlot Tour** takes you behind the scenes for a close-up look at props, costumes, sets, and special effects used in your favorite movies and TV shows. You'll also visit **Catastrophe Canyon,** where an earthquake causes canyon walls to rumble.

Voyage of *The Little Mermaid* is a charming musical spectacular based on the Disney feature film. The show combines live performers with more than 100 puppets, movie clips, and innovative special effects. A must for your little Ariel fan. Try to see it early in the day.

Beauty and the Beast Live On is a live Broadway-style production of the Disney film. The sets and costumes are lavish, and the production numbers spectacular. Arrive early to get a good seat. The **Hunchback of Notre Dame: A Musical Adventure** is another rollicking stage show that brings the animated feature's main characters to life, mainly in costumes but sometimes in puppets.

Jim Henson's MuppetVision 3D combines Jim Henson's puppets with Disney audio-animatronics and special-effects wizardry, 70mm film, and cutting-edge 3-D technology. The coming-at-you action includes flying Muppets, cream pies, cannonballs, fiber-optic fireworks, bubble showers, even an actual spray of water. Do not miss it!

Cutting edge when it first debuted, **Star Tours,** a galactic journey based on the original *Star Wars* trilogy (George Lucas collaborated on its conception), can't compete with the latest technology, but it's still plenty of fun. You'll board a 40-seat "spacecraft" for an otherworldly journey that includes sudden drops, violent crashes, and oncoming laser blasts.

Film footage and audio-animatronic replicas of movie stars take you on a nostalgic journey through some of the most famous scenes in Hollywood history in **The Great Movie Ride.** The setting for this attraction is a full-scale reproduction of Hollywood's famous Chinese Theatre, complete with hand- and footprints of the stars out front.

Sounds Dangerous, starring Drew Carey, is a fantastic attraction that allows you to experience sensational "3-D" sound effects that will have you squirming in your seat.

Younger audiences (2–5) love **Playhouse Disney—Live on Stage!,** a 20-minute show where they meet characters from Bear in the Big Blue House, The Book of Pooh, and others. It encourages preschoolers to dance, sing, and play along with the cast.

At the **Indiana Jones Epic Stunt Spectacular,** visitors get an inside look at the world of movie stunts in a dramatic 30-minute show, which re-creates major scenes from the Indiana Jones series.

With more than 50 performers, more than one million gallons of water, a 32,000-pound dragon, a 59-foot-high mountain, laser lights, and pyrotechnics, **Fantasmic!** is one of the best nighttime shows in Disney World. It mixes special effects with classic movie clips projected on huge water screens and features Sorcerer Mickey and a host of other Disney favorites. It is held in a 6,500-seat theater behind the Tower of Terror off Sunset Boulevard. There is also room for 2,500 standing guests, but you need to arrive at least 30 minutes early to get a seat.

ANIMAL KINGDOM

Disney's fourth major park combines animals, elaborate landscapes, and a handful of rides to create yet another reason that many guests don't venture outside this World. The bulk of the $800-million park opened in 1998; the most recent "land," Asia, was born in 1999.

THE OASIS   With its garden entrance and chirping birds, this painstakingly landscaped point of entry has streams, grottoes, and waterfalls that set the tone for the rest of the park. It's a good place to see animals, if you get here early or stay late. But it's mainly a pass-through zone.

SAFARI VILLAGE   The 14-story **Tree of Life** is the park's central landmark. It is an intricately carved free-form representation of animals hand-crafted by Disney artists. Inside, **It's Tough to Be a Bug!** is a 3-D attraction with creepy-crawly special effects and a special surprise ending that will send a real shiver up your spine. Tots may be frightened by the dark, cavelike atmosphere and the sometimes scary bugs. **The Discovery Island Trails** offer a leisurely stroll through the root system of The Tree of Life, where you might spot otters, flamingos, lemurs, tortoises, and colorful cockatoos.

DINOLAND U.S.A.   Enter by passing under "Olden Gate Bridge," a 40-foot tall brachiosaurus reassembled from excavated fossils.

Ride past an array of snarling dinosaurs in **Dinosaur**, as you travel back in time to retrieve one of the creatures. The combination of height restrictions and realistic reptiles will probably keep youngsters from riding this one.

The **Tarzan Rocks** show pulses with music and occasional aerial theatrics. The cast of 27 includes tumblers, dancers, and in-line skaters who really get the audience into the act. The costumes and music are pretty spectacular, second only to Festival of the Lion King in Camp Minnie-Mickey.

Kids love the chance to slip, slither, slide, and crawl through **The Boneyard,** a giant playground and dig site. Discover the remains of triceratops, T-rex, and other vanished giants.

CAMP MINNIE-MICKEY   Join your favorite Disney characters "on vacation" in Camp Minnie-Mickey, an entire land that re-creates a kid-friendly Adirondack resort.

Head immediately for the best show in the park, **Festival of the Lion King,** which regularly draws enough people to fill the 1,000-seat pavilion. Based loosely on the animated movie, this stage show combines the pageantry of a parade with a tribal celebration.

The **Character Greeting Pavilions** are a must for people traveling with children. The lines here can be considerable as hundreds of kids line up to meet their favorite characters.

AFRICA   Enter through the town of Harambe, a realistic representation of an African coastal village. Whitewashed structures built of coral stone and thatched with reed by craftspeople brought over from Africa surround a central marketplace rich with local wares and colors.

On the **Pangani Forest Exploration Trail,** there are no visible barriers between you and the animals as you watch a troop of African gorillas emerging from the reeds. Bathed in lush jungle foliage, this entire area is filled with exotic East African animals that range from toothy reptiles to brightly colored birds. Don't forget to visit the underwater hippo-viewing area and a savanna overlook.

You have to pay close attention to see the animals as they move amid this realistic landscape, and small children may have a hard time seeing above the crowd.

Animal Kingdom doesn't have many rides, so calling **Kilimanjaro Safaris** the best may sound like a qualified endorsement. But the animals make it a winner as long as your timing is right. They're scarce at midday most times of year (in cooler months you may get lucky), so *ride this one as close to the park's opening or closing as you can.* Your vehicle is a very large truck that takes you through a simulated African landscape. These days, you might see black rhinos, hippos, antelopes, crocodiles, wildebeests, zebras, and lions.

Board an open-sided train near Pangani Forest Exploration Trail for the trip to **Rafiki's Planet Watch,** which has three attractions. **Conservation Station** offers a behind-the-scenes look at how Disney cares for animals. **Habitat Habit!** is a trail with small animals such as cotton-top tamarins. The **Affection Section**'s petting zoo has goats and potbelly pigs.

ASIA Disney's Imagineers did a good job of creating the mythical kingdom of **Anandapur.** The intricately painted artwork out front helps make the lines seem to move a tad faster.

On the **Kali River Rapids,** 12-person rafts plunge through a churning, turning waterway. The ride starts out slow, with a gentle glide through a rainforest and temple ruins, but you'll soon find yourself spinning past a burning forest on the way to a watery drop. Birds of many feathers are the stars of **Flights of Wonder,** a comic look at the many kinds of flying creatures native to Asia. The rainforest environments of Nepal, India, Thailand, and Indonesia are all represented on the **Maharajah Jungle Trek,** along with the species that call these tropical locales home. This is a great spot for viewing and photographing tigers, deer, and giant fruit bats.

UNIVERSAL ORLANDO

Universal Orlando encompasses the original Universal Studios Florida park; its high-tech theme park, Islands of Adventure; the nighttime entertainment district, CityWalk; and three resort hotels.

Multiday tickets allow you to park-hop between Universal Studios Florida and Islands of Adventure. The cheapest way to see Universal, SeaWorld, *and* Wet 'n Wild is a FlexTicket, which allows you to pay one price to visit the participating parks during a 14-day period. A four-park pass to Universal Studios Florida, Islands of Adventure, Wet 'n Wild, and SeaWorld is $170 for adults and $135 for children 3 to 9. The **FlexTicket** can be ordered through Universal (© **407/363-8000;** www.universalorlando.com).

UNIVERSAL STUDIOS FLORIDA

Even with fast-paced, grown-up rides such as Twister, Terminator, and Men in Black Alien Attack, Universal Studios Florida (© **800/711-0080,** 800/837-2273, or 407/363-8000; www.universalorlando.com) is fun for kids. And as a plus, it's a working motion-picture and TV studio, so occasionally there's filming being done at Nickelodeon's sound stages or elsewhere in the park. And a talented group of actors portraying a wide range of characters, from Ricky and Lucy to the Men in Black, can usually be found roaming the park.

A **1-day ticket** costs $50 (plus 6% sales tax) for adults, $41 for children 3 to 9. A 2-day 2-park unlimited-access escape pass is $95 for adults, $82 for children 3 to 9; a 3-day 2-park pass is $110 for adults, $97 for children 3 to 9. **Parking** costs $8 for cars, light trucks, and vans.

The park is open 365 days a year, usually at least from 9am to 6pm, though it's open as late as 8 or 9pm in summer and around holidays. And sometimes the park also closes early for special events, so your best bet is to call before you go so that you're not caught by surprise.

The Major Attractions

A Day in the Park with Barney, set in a parklike theater-in-the-round, is a musical show starring the popular purple one. For young children, this could be the highlight of the day. For parents, our condolences.

Terminator 2: 3-D Battle Across Time is the *best* 3-D live-action show in Orlando. The $60 million production starts slow but finishes strong. Arnold and other original cast members (on film) mix with live actors to create some thrilling technical effects. Non-human stars include a custom-built Harley Davidson "Fat Boy" and six 8-foot-tall cyberbots.

Men in Black: Alien Attack is a new ride where you cruise the streets of New York and use your "alienator" to zap the baddies. Trouble is, you also have to battle environmental stimuli that can send you spinning out of control. Split-second decisions determine your fate, which ranges from a hero's welcome to being labeled bug bait.

You didn't *really* think it was safe to go back into the water, did you? As your boat heads out to the open seas, an ominous dorsal fin appears on the horizon. What follows is a series of terrifying attacks from **Jaws,** a 3-ton, 32-foot-long great white shark that tries to sink its teeth into passengers. And that's not all. The boat is surrounded by a 30-foot wall of flame from burning fuel that lets you truly feel the heat. The effects look better at night.

In the **E.T. Adventure,** you'll soar with E.T. on a mission to save his ailing planet, through the forest and into space, aboard a star-bound bicycle. This one's good for the more timid members of your party.

In **Back to the Future,** you'll blast through the space-time continuum, plummet into volcanic tunnels ablaze with molten lava, thunder through caves and canyons, and be swallowed by a dinosaur in this spectacular multisensory adventure.

In **Kongfrontation,** you'll stand in line in a replica of a grungy New York subway station before boarding a tram to Roosevelt Island to escape King Kong's rampage. Cars collide and hydrants explode below, police helicopters hover overhead, the tram malfunctions, and, of course, you encounter Kong—32 feet tall and 13,000 pounds.

For **Earthquake, the Big One,** you board a BART train in San Francisco for a peaceful subway ride, but just as you pull into the Embarcadero station there's an earthquake—the big one, 8.3 on the Richter scale! As you sit helplessly trapped, vast slabs of concrete collapse around you, a propane truck bursts into flames, a runaway train comes hurtling at you, and the station floods (60,000 gallons of water cascade down the steps).

Visitors from the twister-prone Midwest may find **Twister . . . Ride It Out** a little too close to the real thing. An ominous funnel cloud, five stories tall, is created by two million cubic feet of air per minute. And a sound like a freight train fills the theater, as cars, signs, and a cow fly about while the audience watches just 20 feet away. It packs quite a wallop.

The **Nickelodeon Studios Tour** allows you to tour the soundstages where Nick shows are produced, visit the kitchen where gak and green slime are made, play typical show games, and try out new Sega video games. There's lots of audience participation.

In the **Wild, Wild, Wild West Show,** stunt people demonstrate falls from three-story balconies, gun and whip fights, and dynamite explosions. This is a well-performed, lively show. Kids, do not try this at home.

Woody Woodpecker's Nuthouse Coaster is the top attraction in Woody Woodpecker's KidZone, an 8-acre concession Universal Studios made after being criticized for having too little for young visitors. This ride is a kiddie coaster that will thrill some moms and dads too. While only 30 feet at its peak, it offers quick, banked turns while you sit in a miniature steam train. The ride lasts only 50 seconds and waits can be 30 minutes, but few children will want to miss it. Kids have to be 48 inches or above to ride without an adult.

ISLANDS OF ADVENTURE
Universal's second theme park opened in 1999. At 110 acres, it's the same size as its big brother, Universal Studios Florida, but it seems larger. Roller coasters roar above pedestrian walkways and water rides slice through the park. It is, bar none, *the* Orlando theme park for thrill-ride junkies.

A few words of caution: *Nine of the park's 14 major rides have height restrictions.* Those with very young kids should think twice before coming here. And many of the same rides may not be suitable for those who are tall enough but are pregnant or have health problems, physical restrictions, or a tendency toward motion sickness.

A **1-day ticket** costs $50 (plus 6% sales tax) for adults, $41 for children 3 to 9. A 2-day 2-park unlimited-access escape pass is $95 for adults, $82 for children 3 to 9; a 3-day 2-park pass is $110 for adults, $97 for children 3 to 9. Multiday tickets allow you to park-hop between Universal Studios Florida and Islands of Adventure.

If you park in the multilevel garage, remember the theme and music on your floor to help you later identify your car. Or do it the old-fashioned way: Write it down. Parking costs $8 for cars, light trucks, and vans. *Note:* It's a long walk to the park from the garage and there is no tram service; parents of young children should bring strollers and those with mobility issues may want to rent a wheelchair or motor cart.

The park is open 365 days a year, generally from 9am to 6pm, though often later, especially in summer and around holidays, when it's sometimes open until 9pm.

Major Attractions
Seuss Landing, a 10-acre island, brings Dr. Seuss's world-famous characters and children's books to life. It's also the only "island" where a young child will feel totally at home. Six-passenger couches travel through 18 show scenes in **The Cat in the Hat.** The highlight is a revolving 24-foot tunnel that alters your perceptions and leaves your head spinning. In **One Fish, Two Fish, Red Fish, Blue Fish,** try to avoid getting sprayed as you guide your fish through the ride, taking directions from a Seussian rhyme. **If I Ran the Zoo** is an interactive playland for kids of all ages, with everything from flying water snakes to a chance to tickle the toes of a Seussian animal. It's a nice place to let the kids burn off some excited energy. And all ages will enjoy a ride on the whimsical **Caro-Seuss-El,** which sports Seussian characters instead of traditional horses.

Thrill junkies will love the twisting, turning, and stomach-churning rides on **Marvel Super Hero Island,** based on characters from Marvel Comics. **The Amazing Adventures of Spider-Man** combines a moving simulator ride with 3-D action and special effects, as guests find themselves in the midst of a battle between evil villains and Spider-Man. The high-tech ride, the favorite of many Universal employees and possibly the best in the park, includes a simulated 400 foot drop that feels an awful lot like the real thing. You'll blast from 0 to 40 miles per hour in 2 seconds, and spin upside down 100 feet from the ground on the **Incredible Hulk Coaster.** Coaster lovers love this 2-minute, 15-second ride that includes seven roll-overs and two deep drops. On **Dr. Doom's Fearfall,** you're in for a rush as you drop, with feet dangling, down one of two 200-foot steel towers. **Storm Force Accelatron** is a spinning attraction in which guests help comic-book hero Storm harness weather to fight her archenemy, Magneto. Special effects here include a swirling storm of light and sound.

More than 150 life-size sculpted cartoon images let you know you have entered the **Toon Lagoon,** dedicated to your favorites from the Sunday funnies. **Dudley Do-Right's Ripsaw Falls,** touted as the first flume ride to send riders plummeting below the water's surface, takes you around a 400,000-gallon lagoon, culminating in a 75-foot drop at 50 miles per hour. (You *will* get wet. Very wet.) **Popeye & Bluto's Bilge Rat Barges** are whirling 12-person rafts that bump and churn their way through a white-water ride encountering some scary creatures along the way, including the twirling octopus boat wash. *Note:* You will get either very wet or completely soaked.

All the basics, and some of the high-tech wizardry, from Steven Spielberg's wildly successful movies are incorporated in a lushly landscaped tropical locale in **Jurassic Park.** In the exceptional **Jurassic Park River Adventure,** you come face to face with the living, breathing inhabitants of Jurassic Park. Five-story dinosaurs come within inches of the ride where Tyrannosaurus Rex decides you look like a tasty morsel. To escape, you take an 85-foot plunge straight down the longest, fastest, steepest water descent ever built. It's another chance to get completely soaked. In the **Triceratops Encounter,** pet a "living" dinosaur and learn from the trainers about the care and feeding of the 24-foot long, 10-foot-high triceratops.

Although they've mixed their millennia here ancient Greek gods with medieval forests—Universal has done a great job creating a foreboding mood in the **Lost Continent** section of the park. **Poseidon's Fury** is a multimedia presentation that exposes you to torrents of waters, blasts of fire, and a 42-foot vortex of rushing water, as Poseidon battles Zeus for divine supremacy, but it's not really worth waiting in a long line for this one. **Dueling Dragons** is a coaster crazy's fantasy. The ride is staged on intertwined tracks that hold you suspended with your legs dangling freely beneath you, like you're sitting on a jet-propelled swing. Be warned—it's not for the faint of heart. At times, riders of the dueling coasters—that zip along at 60 miles per hour—are just 12 inches apart. **The 8th Voyage of Sinbad** is a stunt show that explores the next voyage of the mythical traveler and relies heavily on pyrotechnics for its thrill factor. It may be too intense for younger children, and parents may find it underwhelming. **The Flying Unicorn,** a small roller coaster designed for kids, travels through a mythical forest. It's located next to Dueling Dragons. If you are traveling with kids, make sure to give the **Mystic Fountain** a hearty greeting—it will usually respond in kind.

SEAWORLD

This 200-acre marine-life park at 7007 Sea World Dr. (© **800/327-2424** or 407/351-3600; www.seaworld.com) explores the mysteries of the deep by combining conservation awareness with entertainment. The stars of the park are

Shamu, a killer whale, and his ever-expanding family, which includes baby orcas. The pace is much more laid-back than either Universal or Disney, and is a good way to end a long week of trudging through the other parks. Be sure to budget some extra money to buy smelt to feed the animals—the close encounters offered at many wading and feeding pools are more than half the fun.

A **1-day ticket** costs $50 for ages 10 and over, $41 for children 3 to 9, plus 6% sales tax. See the Universal Studios Florida section earlier in this chapter for information on the Flex Ticket option. Parking is $8 for cars, light trucks, and vans.

The park is usually open from 9am to 6pm and sometimes later, 365 days a year.

MAJOR ATTRACTIONS

Wild Arctic combines a high-definition adventure film with flight-simulator technology to display breathtaking Arctic panoramas. After a hazardous flight over the frozen north, visitors enter an exhibit where you can see a playful polar bear or two, beautiful beluga whales, and walruses performing aquatic ballets.

Taking a cue from Disney imagineers, SeaWorld created a story to go with its $30 million water coaster, **Journey to Atlantis.** But what really matters is the drop—a wild plunge from 60 feet with lugelike curves. No hidden lessons here, just a splashy thrill.

SeaWorld's newest thrill ride, the **Kraken,** features floorless and open-sided 32-passenger trains that plant you on a pedestal high above the track. When the monster breaks loose, you'll climb 151 feet, fall 144 feet, hit speeds of 65 miles per hour, go underground three times (spraying bystanders with water), and make seven loops over a 4,177-foot track. It may be the longest 3 minutes, 39 seconds of your life.

Terrors of the Deep houses 220 specimens of venomous and otherwise scary sea creatures in a tropical-reef habitat. Immense acrylic tunnels provide close encounters with slithery eels, three dozen sharks, barracudas, lionfish, and poisonous pufferfish.

Today the Florida manatee is in danger of extinction, with as few as 2,000 remaining. Underwater viewing stations, innovative cinema techniques, and interactive displays in **Manatees: The Last Generation?** combine to teach visitors about the manatee and its fragile ecosystem.

Key West at SeaWorld, a 5-acre paved paradise dotted with palms, hibiscus, and bougainvillea, is set in a Caribbean village offering island cuisine, street vendors, and entertainers. The attraction comprises three naturalistic animal habitats: **Stingray Lagoon,** where visitors enjoy hands-on encounters with harmless southern diamond and cownose rays; **Dolphin Cove,** a massive habitat for bottlenose dolphins set up for visitor interaction; and **Sea Turtle Point,** home to threatened and endangered species such as green, loggerhead, and hawksbill sea turtles.

At **Key West Dolphin Fest,** Atlantic bottlenose dolphins perform flips and high jumps, twirl, swim on their backs, and give rides to trainers.

In **Clyde & Seamore Take Pirate Island,** a lovable sea lion-and-otter duo, with a supporting cast of walruses and harbor seals, appears in this fishy comedy with a swashbuckling conservation theme.

Top billing at SeaWorld goes to **The Shamu Adventure.** Everyone comes to SeaWorld to see the big guy and his friends—the stars of this well-choreographed show. When you hear the warning that Hurricane Shamu is approaching, it's time for those sitting in the first 14 rows to hightail it. Those who don't are drenched with *icy water* as the orcas race around the pool, creating a huge wave that rolls over the edge and into the audience.

Shamu: Close Up!, an adjoining exhibit, lets you get close to killer whales and talk to trainers; don't miss the underwater viewing area here and a chance to see a mother whale with her offspring. Talk about a big baby!

The **Penguin Encounter,** a rather superficial display of hundreds of penguins (including adorable babies), also serves as a living laboratory for protecting and preserving polar life.

And finally, parents can rest their weary feet while their offspring work off some energy at **Shamu's Happy Harbor,** a 3-acre play area that has a four-story net tower with a 35-foot-high crow's nest, water cannons, remote-controlled vehicles, nine slides, a submarine, and a water maze. Most kids love it.

DISCOVERY COVE

In the summer of 2000, SeaWorld opened its second theme park, **Discovery Cove** (© **800/423-8368** or 877/434-7268; www.discoverycove.com). About 1,000 guests are admitted daily to this unique attraction, but you'll pay for the privilege of avoiding the crowds. Visitors can choose from two options: a whopping $229 per person plus 6% sales tax—ages 6 and up—if you want to swim with a dolphin; $129 if you can skip that luxury. The gate price includes an arrival tour, all activities, gear, towels, a meal, and 7 days of unlimited admission to SeaWorld. Guests who choose the dolphin option will swim with, snorkel with, and feed dolphins; everyone can swim and snorkel with other aquatic life.

HITTING THE LINKS: ORLANDO AREA GOLF

Disney operates five 18-hole, par-72 golf courses and one 9-hole, par-36 walking course. The rates are $105 to $170 per 18-hole round for resort guests ($5 more if you're not staying at a WDW property). For tee times and information, call © **407/824-2270** up to 7 days in advance (up to 30 days for guests of the Disney resort and official properties). Call © **407/934-7639** about golf packages.

Beyond Mickey's shadow, **Golfpac** (© **800/327-0878** or 407/260-2288; www.golfpacinc.com) is an organization that packages golf with accommodations and arranges tee times at more than 40 Orlando-area courses. **Tee Times USA** (© **800/465-3356;** www.teetimesusa.com) and **Florida Golfing** (© **866/833-2663;** www.floridagolfing.com) are two others offering package information and course reservations.

Golf magazine recognized the 45 holes designed by Jack Nicklaus at the **Villas of Grand Cypress** resort as among the best in the nation. Tee times begin at 8am daily. Special rates are available for children under 18. For information call © **407/239-1909.** The course is generally restricted to guests or guests of guests (an average of $175), but there's limited play available to those not staying at the resort. Those fees begin at $225.

WHERE TO STAY

There are more than 111,000 rooms in the Orlando area with thousands added annually. While the economy softened the second half of 2001, occupancy is generally high—as much as 90% at Disney, so if you plan to stay in one of Mickey's resorts, book as far ahead as possible. The lowest rates are usually available from September to November and from January to April. High season occurs during holidays and the summer months.

The rates below represent "rack rates," basic prices that should be used as a basis for comparison shopping only. You should be able to get a better deal as part of a package (see above).

Important note: In addition to the accommodations described here, there are scores of chain hotels and motels. See Appendix A at the end of this book for toll-free numbers and websites.

WALT DISNEY WORLD CENTRAL RESERVATIONS OFFICE   In addition to their proximity to the parks, rooms at Disney's resorts, villas, campgrounds, and official hotels offer additional advantages: complimentary transportation to and from the Disney parks; character breakfasts and/or dinners; a guest-services desk; use of the five Disney-owned golf courses and preferred tee times; and much more. Some of our favorite Disney resorts are listed in this section, as are our favorite hotels in Orlando. Keep in mind that non-Disney hotels tend to be far more favorably priced.

To reserve a room at a Disney property, call the **Walt Disney World Travel Company** at © **800/828-0228;** or contact **Central Reservation Operations (CRO)**, P.O. Box 10000, Lake Buena Vista, FL 32830-1000 (© **407/934-7639;** www.disneyworld.com). Both can recommend accommodations suited to your price range and specific needs, such as proximity to your favorite park or those with supervised child-care centers. The clerks who answer the telephones can be very helpful but usually won't volunteer information about a better deal or a special *unless you ask.*

Disney's All-Star Movie Resort   Kids love the larger-than-life themes at the All-Star resorts, but adults usually cringe at the visual overload. Giant cartoon characters such as Buzz Lightyear adorn this one and help hide a 21st-century rendition of a 1950s Holiday Inn. The rooms are spartan and very small—the bathrooms are even worse. Like its two siblings, the adjacent and also recommended **Disney's All-Star Sports Resort** and **Disney's All-Star Movies,** the All-Star Movie Resort is buried in WDW's southwest corner to avoid frightening the higher-paying guests. Refrigerators are available for an extra $10 per day. 1991 W. Buena Vista Dr., Lake Buena Vista, FL 32830-1000. © **407/934-7639** or 407/939-7000. Fax 407/939-7111. www.disneyworld.com. 1,900 units. $77–$124 double. Extra person $10. Children 17 and under stay free in parents' room. AE, DC, DISC, MC, V. Free parking. **Amenities:** Restaurant; 2 heated outdoor pools; kids' pool; pets $9 a night.

Disney's Fort Wilderness Resort & Campground   Pines, cypress trees, and fish-filled lakes and streams surround this woodsy 780-acre camping resort. It's quite far from Epcot, Disney–MGM Studios, and Animal Kingdom, but it's close to the Magic Kingdom, and if you're a true outdoors type, you'll enjoy the break from some of the Mickey madness. There are 784 campsites for RVs, pull-behind campers, and tents (110/220-volt outlets, grills, and comfort stations with showers and restrooms). Some sites are open to pets—at a cost of $3 per site, not per pet—which is cheaper than using the WDW overnight kennel, where you pay $9 per pet. The 408 wilderness cabins (actually trailers) are large enough for six people once you pull down the Murphy beds, and they also have kitchens and hair dryers. 3520 N. Fort Wilderness Trail (P.O. Box 10000), Lake Buena Vista, FL 32830-1000. © **407/934-7639** or 407/824-2900. Fax 407/824-3508. www.disneyworld.com. 784 campsites, 408 wilderness cabins. Campsite $34–$80 double; wilderness cabin $224–$314 double. Extra person $2 for campsite, $5 for cabin. Children 17 and under stay free with parent. AE, DC, DISC, MC, V. Free parking. **Amenities:** Restaurants (3); 2 heated outdoor pools; kids' pool; 2 lighted tennis courts.

Disney's Grand Floridian Resort & Spa   From the moment you step into the opulent five-story domed lobby, you'll feel as if you've slipped back to an era when a guy named Gatsby was at the top of his game. High tea is served in the afternoon; later, a small band plays music from the 1940s. The Floridian has become the romantic choice for couples, especially honeymooners, who like luxuriating in the first-class spa and health club—the best in WDW. The Victorian-style rooms sleep at least four; virtually all overlook a garden, a pool, a courtyard, or the Seven Seas Lagoon. This, too, is on the monorail system and close to the Magic Kingdom. Refrigerators are available for an extra $10 per day. 4401 Floridian Way (P.O. Box 10000), Lake Buena Vista, FL 32830-1000. © 407/934-7639 or 407/824-3000. Fax 407/824-3186. www.disneyworld.com. 900 units. $329–$815 double; $810–$2,175 suite. Extra person $25. Children 17 and under stay free in parents' room. AE, DC, DISC, MC, V. Self-parking free, valet parking $6. **Amenities:** Restaurants (6); heated outdoor pool; kids' pool; 2 lighted tennis courts; spa; health club; pets $9 a night.

Disney's Port Orleans Resort   This resort, resembling turn-of-the-20th-century New Orleans, includes the old Dixie Landings property that was merged into it in 2000. It has the best location, best landscaping, and perhaps the coziest atmosphere of all resorts in this class. Its Doubloon Lagoon pool has a water slide that curves out of a dragon's mouth. Rooms are big enough for four, but are still a tight fit. Port Orleans is east of Epcot and Disney–MGM Studios. Refrigerators are available for an extra $10 per day. *Note:* Disney sometimes closes this resort during slow times of the year, so call and check its status before you set your heart on staying here. 2201 Orleans Dr. (off Bonnet Creek Pkwy.; P.O. Box 10000), Lake Buena Vista, FL 32830-1000. © 407/934-7639 or 407/934-5000. Fax 407/934-5353. www.disneyworld.com. 3,056 units. $133–$219 double. Extra person $15. Children 17 and under stay free in parents' room. AE, DC, DISC, MC, V. Free parking. **Amenities:** Restaurants (3); 6 heated outdoor pools; 2 kids' pools; pets $9 a night.

Disney's Wilderness Lodge   The geyser out back, the mammoth stone hearth in the lobby, and bunk beds for the kids are just a few reasons this resort is a favorite of couples and families. The resort is patterned after the national park lodge at Yellowstone. The geyser "blows" periodically throughout the day, and nightly electric water pageants can be seen from the shore. Standard rooms sleep four, and if a view is important to you, those with woods views are best. The nearest park is Magic Kingdom, but the resort is in a pretty remote area. Refrigerators are available for an extra $10 per day. 901 W. Timberline Dr. (on the southwest shore of Bay Lake just east of the Magic Kingdom; P.O. Box 10000), Lake Buena Vista, FL 32830-1000. © 407/934-7639 or 407/938-3200. Fax 407/824-3232. www.disneyworld.com. 909 units. $194–$500 lodge; $340–$460 concierge; $640–$1,090 suite; $269–$920 villa. Extra person $25. Children 17 and under stay free in parents' room. AE, DC, DISC, MC, V. Free parking. **Amenities:** Restaurants (2); heated outdoor pool; kids' pool; pets $9 a night.

Disney's Yacht Club Resort   The Yacht Club is geared more toward adults and families with older children, although young kids are catered to (this is Disney). It shares a 25-acre lake—Stormalong Bay—a first-class swimming pool, and magnificent landscaping with its sister property, the Beach Club. The theme is turn-of-the-20th-century New England. The comfortable rooms have space for up to five people, and most have balconies. Stay here and you can walk to Epcot, but you can save shoe leather by using the free buses. Refrigerators are available for an extra $10 per day. 1700 Epcot Resorts Blvd. (off Buena Vista Dr.; P.O. Box 10000), Lake Buena Vista, FL 32830-1000. © 407/934-7639 or 407/934-7000. Fax 407/924-3450. www.disneyworld.com. 630 units. $289–$495 double; $415–$640 concierge-level;

$510–$2,180 suite. Extra person $25. Children 17 and under stay free in parents' room. AE, DC, DISC, MC, V. Self-parking free, valet parking $6. **Amenities:** Restaurants (4); 2 heated outdoor pools; kids' pool; 2 lighted tennis courts; pets $9 a night.

Fairfield Inn International Drive   If you're looking for I-Drive's best value, it's hard to beat the Fairfield. This one combines a quiet location off the main drag, down-to-earth rates, and a clean, modern motel in one package. The rooms are very comfortable and there are a number of restaurants within walking distance of the hotel. 8342 Jamaican Court (off International Dr. between the Bee Line Expwy. and Sand Lake Rd.), Orlando, FL 32819. © **800/228-2800** or 407/363-1944. Fax 407/363-1944. www.fairfieldinn.com. 135 units. $69–$89 for up to 4. AE, DC, DISC, MC, V. Self-parking free. **Amenities:** Outdoor heated pool.

Hard Rock Hotel   You can't get any closer than this to CityWalk or Universal Studios Florida. Opened in January 2001, this California mission–style resort sports a rock 'n' roll theme and is a cut above some of Disney's comparable properties. The rooms are very comfortable, although the bathrooms aren't big. Unfortunately, though the rooms are fairly soundproof, a few notes seep through the walls, so ask for one that's away from the lobby area. *Note:* Guests get no-line access to most rides at Universal Studios Florida and Islands of Adventure. 5000 Universal Blvd., Orlando, FL 32819. © **800/232-7827** or 407/363-8000. Fax 407/224-7118. www.hardrock.com/locations/hotels/orlando. 650 units. $199–$359 double; $395–$1,575 suite. Extra person $20. Children 17 and under stay free in parents' room. AE, DC, DISC, MC, V. Self-parking $6, valet $10. **Amenities:** Restaurants (3); outdoor heated pool; kids' pool; fitness center.

Hawthorn Suites Lake Buena Vista   One of the features that appeals to us most about this property, which opened in summer 2000, is its floor plan. Standard rooms have a living room with pullout sofa, chair, and TV; full kitchen with dining-room table for four; bathroom with vanity; and bedroom with recliner and TV. Two-bedroom units are also available. The atmosphere is friendly, the service is good, and it's just 3 minutes from Hotel Plaza Boulevard. 8303 Palm Pkwy., Orlando, FL 32836. © **800/269-8303**, 800/527-1133, or 407/597-5000. Fax 407/597-6000. www.hawthornsuiteslbv.com. 120 units. $104–$159 for 4–6. AE, DC, DISC, MC, V. Self-parking free. From I-4, take the Hwy. 535/Apopka–Vineland Rd. exit east to Palm Pkwy., continue right ¼ mile to hotel. **Amenities:** Outdoor heated pool.

Holiday Inn Family Suites Resort   This all-suite property opened in July 1999 and does a fantastic job of catering to a diverse clientele. Families appreciate the two-bedroom Kid Suites that feature a second semiprivate bedroom equipped with bunk beds and changing themes (from Disney to Coke to the comics). In the Classic Suites, the semiprivate bedroom has a queen-size bed. Others cater to honeymooners and romantics (Sweet Heart Suites with a heart-shaped tub) and movie buffs (Cinema Suites with a 60-inch big-screen TV and DVD players). All suites have small kitchenettes. The resort, voted in 2001 best Holiday Inn property in North America, has themed activity nights (movies, magic, variety shows and more). *Note:* If you are child-free, ask to stay in the West Track Courtyard section, which is much quieter. 14500 Continental Gateway (off Hwy. 536), Lake Buena Vista, FL 328360. © **877/387-5437** or 407/387-5437. Fax 407/387-1489. www.hifamilysuites.com. 800 units. $109–$169 Kid Suite; $109–$169 Classic Suite; $129–$189 Cinema Suite; $129–$189 Sweet Heart Suite. AE, DC, DISC, MC, V. Free self-parking. From I-4, take the Hwy. 536/International Dr. exit east 1 mile to the resort. **Amenities:** Restaurant; 2 pools; fitness center; mini-golf course.

Hyatt Regency Grand Cypress   A favorite of honeymooners and those seeking a resort without Mickey doodads, this romantic getaway's lobby has lush foliage from which macaws wave to passersby. The 18-story atrium has inner and outer glass elevators (ride the outers to the roof for a panoramic rush). The rooms are beautifully decorated and sleep four. The Hyatt has a golf club and academy, racquet club, and equestrian center, and offers excellent packages aimed at the sports set. The Hyatt's half-acre, 800,000-gallon pool is one of the best in Orlando and features caves, grottoes, waterfalls, and a 45-foot water slide. 1 N. Jacaranda (off Hwy. 535), Orlando, FL 32836. ✆ 800/233-1234 or 407/239-1234. Fax 407/239-3800. www.grandcypress.com. 750 units. $229–$469 double; $479–$1,500 suite. Extra person $25. Children 17 and under stay free in parents' room. AE, DC, DISC, MC, V. Self-parking free, valet parking $12. **Amenities:** Restaurants (4); heated outdoor pool; 45 holes of golf; 12 tennis courts (5 lighted); spa; health club.

Marriott's Orlando World Center   Golf, tennis, and spa lovers find plenty to do at this 230-acre resort. The sports facilities are first-class and the largest of its five pools has water slides and waterfalls. The location, only 2 miles from the Disney parks, is another plus. The large comfortable rooms sleep four, and the higher poolside floors offer views of Mickeyville. 8701 World Center Dr. (on Hwy 536 between I-4 and Hwy. 535), Orlando, FL 32821. ✆ 800/621-0638 or 407/239-4200. Fax 407/238-8777. www.marriottHotels.com/MCOWC. 2,111 units. $189–$410 for up to 5; $425–$2,400 suite. Children 17 and under stay free in parents' room. AE, DC, DISC, MC, V. Self-parking free, valet parking $12. **Amenities:** Restaurants (4); heated pools (3 outdoor, 1 indoor); kids' pool; 18-hole golf course; 8 lighted tennis courts; spa; health club.

Peabody Orlando   The five mallards that march into a lobby fountain every morning at 11am and then back out at 5pm, accompanied by John Philip Sousa's *King Cotton March*, are just part of the appeal of Central Florida's friendliest hotel. The Peabody Orlando is primarily a business and convention destination, but it's one of our top picks in O-Town. It's classy without being stuffy, and if your budget allows the splurge, you won't be disappointed. Rooms sleep up to five, and those on the west side (sixth floor and higher) offer a distant view of Disney and its fireworks displays. 9801 International Dr. (between Bee Line Expwy. and Sand Lake Rd.), Orlando, FL 32819. ✆ 800/732-2639 or 407/352-4000. Fax 407/354-1424. www.peabody-orlando.com. 891 units. $380–$475 standard room for up to 3; $520–$1,600 suite. Extra person $20. Children 17 and under stay free in parents' room. AE, DC, DISC, MC, V. Self-parking free, valet parking $8. **Amenities:** Restaurants (4); outdoor heated pool; kids' pool; 4 lighted tennis courts; spa; fitness center.

Ramada Disney Eastgate   Remodeled in 1998, this Ramada is a cut cleaner than many of the chain's standard motels, but no fancier. Standard rooms sleep four but are somewhat cramped. One child eats free for each paying adult. The inn is 4 miles from Disney. 5150 W. Irlo Bronson Memorial Hwy. (U.S. 192), Kissimmee, FL 34746. ✆ 888/298-2054 or 407/396-1111. Fax 407/396-1607. www.ramada.com. 402 units. $59–$129 double. Extra person $10. Children 17 and under stay free in parents' room. AE, DC, DISC, MC, V. Free self-parking. **Amenities:** Restaurant; outdoor heated pool; kids' pool.

WHERE TO DINE

Artist Point SEAFOOD/STEAKS   Enjoy a grand view of Disney's Wilderness Lodge while you select from a menu that changes seasonally. You might discover roasted halibut with a basil crust, grilled veal tenderloin with mushrooms, pan-roasted shrimp with capers and tomatoes, or a mixed grill of elk, ostrich, and venison. Expect a reasonably extensive wine list. *Note:* Artist Point isn't

---

How to Arrange Priority Seating at Disney Restaurants

Priority seating *isn't* a reservation. It's a promise that you'll get the next available table once you arrive. There may be a wait, but if you don't use this system you may have a longer one. To get priority seating at any WDW restaurant, call ✆ **407/939-3463.** You can book as far as 60 days in advance of your arrival.

If you're staying on Disney property, you can arrange priority seating at your resort. At Epcot, you can do it at the WorldKey interactive terminals at Guest Relations near Innoventions East, the WorldKey Information Service on the main concourse to the World Showcase, and the restaurant of your choice.

---

as "discovered" as some other WDW resort restaurants (enjoy that while it lasts), which makes for a more relaxed atmosphere. 901 W. Timberline Dr., in Disney's Wilderness Lodge. ✆ **407/939-3463** or 407/824-1081. www.disneyworld.com. Priority seating is recommended. Main courses $18–$32. AE, DC, DISC, MC, V. Daily 5:30–10pm.

B-Line Diner AMERICAN   Come to have fun in a chrome-plated '50s-style diner where you can sink into upholstered booths or belly up to the counter. It gets noisy, partly due to an exuberant staff. The round-the-clock menu features comfort foods such as chicken potpie that's up to what mom made; a ham and cheese sandwich on a baguette; and roast pork with grilled apples, sun-dried cherry stuffing, and brandy-honey sauce. The portions are hearty, but so are the prices for diner fare. There's a full bar. 9801 International Dr., in the Peabody Orlando. ✆ **407/345-4460.** www.peabody-orlando.com. Reservations not accepted. Main courses $4–$14 breakfast, $7–$17 lunch, $9–$26 (most under $17) dinner. AE, DC, DISC, MC, V. Daily 24 hr.

Bubbaloo's Bodacious BBQ BARBECUE   This spot serves some of the best barbecue in Florida. Go for the full pork platter that comes with a heaping helping of pork and all the fixin's. The uninitiated should stay away from the "Killer" sauce, which produces a tongue buzz that's likely to last for hours; you might even taste-test the mild sauce before moving up to the hot. 1471 Lee Rd., Winter Park (about 5 min. from downtown Orlando). ✆ **407/628-1212.** Reservations not accepted. Main courses $5–$15. AE, MC, V. Mon–Thurs 10am–9pm; Fri–Sat 10am–10:30pm.

California Grill CALIFORNIA   Settle onto the 15th floor of the Contemporary Resort and enjoy views of the Magic Kingdom while you drool over menu options prepared in an exhibition kitchen. Headliners change often, but they sometimes include seared yellowfin tuna served rare, roasted striped bass, or grilled pork tenderloin. The Grill has a very nice sushi menu (crab, eel, tuna, and more). This is one of the few spots in WDW that isn't crawling with kids. The list of California wines helps complement the meal and views, but it can be tough to get a table, so make a reservation as far ahead as possible. 4600 N. World Dr., at Disney's Contemporary Resort. ✆ **407/939-3463** or 407/824-1576. www.disneyworld. com. Reservations recommended. Main courses $20–$30; sushi $10–$30. AE, DC, DISC, MC, V. Daily 5:30–10pm.

Dux INTERNATIONAL   The name is a tribute to the Peabody Orlando's resident ducks, who parade ceremoniously in and out of the lobby every day, while the food is a tribute to chefs who create a marvelous menu that changes often. It might include oven-roasted grouper with bok choy, mushrooms, and ginger sauce. Hope, too, for a veal chop roasted medium rare with an artichoke-basil fricassee and garlic au jus. Dux is best reserved for a very special night out or a meal on an expense account. It has impeccable service and one of the best wine lists in Orlando. 9801 International Dr., in the Peabody Orlando. © 407/345-4550. www. peabody-orlando.com. Reservations recommended. Main courses $26–$45. AE, DC, DISC, MC, V. Mon–Sat 6–10pm.

Emeril's NEW ORLEANS   It's next to impossible to get short-term reservations for dinner unless you're willing to take your chances with no-shows, but most who wait say the food is worth it. A good bet is the andouille-crusted redfish (a moist white fish with roasted pecan-vegetable relish and meunière sauce). If you want some *vino* with your meal, the back half of the building is a glass-walled 12,000-bottle above-ground cellar. Prices are high enough that Emeril can afford tons of legroom between tables. If you want a show, we recommend one of eight counter seats where you can watch chefs working their magic, but to get one, reservations are required *excruciatingly* early. 6000 Universal Studios Blvd., in CityWalk. © 407/224-2424. www.universalorlando.com or www.emerils.com/restaurants/ orlando. Reservations necessary. Main courses $17–$26 lunch, $18–$42 dinner. AE, DISC, MC, V. Daily 11:30am–2:30pm and 5:30–10pm (until 11pm Fri–Sat). AE, DISC, MC, V.

Little Saigon VIETNAMESE   Asian immigrants created the demand for this great little eatery that's yet to be discovered by tourists. Try the summer rolls— a soft wrap filled with rice, shrimp, and pork served with a delicious peanut sauce. Head next for the grilled pork and egg over rice and noodles or barbecued beef with fried egg and rice. The numbered menu isn't translated well, but your server or the manager can help. 1106 E. Colonial Dr./Hwy. 50 (near downtown Orlando). © 407/423-8539. Reservations not accepted. Main courses under $5 lunch, $5–$8 dinner. AE, DISC, MC, V. Daily 10am–9pm.

Pebbles CALIFORNIA   If you want to dine like a gourmet without the hefty price, here's your ticket. This restaurant is one of a local four-restaurant chain that has a reputation for great food, a sexy-if-small wine list, and creative appetizers. The chèvre-coated lamb chops, when available, are worth fighting for. The twin brie filet mignons are a good second. Like many entrees, they come with three-cheese mashed potatoes and zucchini wedges. 12551 Apopka-Vineland Rd., in the Crossroads Shopping Center. © 407/827-1111. www.pebblesworldwide.com. Reservations not accepted. Main courses $10–$21. AE, DC, DISC, MC, V. Sun–Thurs noon–11pm; Fri–Sat 11am–11pm.

Siam Orchid THAI   Tim and Krissnee Martsching grow the mint, chiles, cilantro, lemon grass, and wild lime that go into their entrees. The star attractions include *Pad Thai* (rice noodles tossed with ground pork, garlic, shrimp, crab claws, crabmeat, and crushed peanuts in a tongue-twanging sweet sauce) and Royal Thai (chicken chunks, potato, and onion in yellow curry sauce). Siam Orchid serves sake, plum wine, and Thai beers from a full bar. 7575 Universal Dr. (between Sand Lake Rd. and Carrier Dr.). © 407/351-0821. Reservations recommended. Main courses $11–$21. AE, DC, DISC, MC, V. Mon–Fri 11am–2pm; daily 5–11pm.

Victoria & Albert's INTERNATIONAL   It's not often we can describe dinner as "an event," but Disney's most elegant restaurant earns that distinction. Dinner is next-to-perfect—if the portions seem small, we dare you to make it through all seven courses—and the setting is exceptionally romantic. The fare changes nightly, but you might find main events such as Alaskan rockfish with couscous or filet mignon with Vidalia-onion mash. The dining room is crowned by a domed, chapel-style ceiling; 20 exquisitely appointed tables are lit softly by Victorian lamps; and your servers (always named Victoria and Albert) provide

The Chef's Table: Best Seat in the World

There's a special dining option at **Victoria & Albert's**. Reserve the **Chef's Table** (far, *far* in advance) and dine in a charming alcove at a candlelit table in the heart of the kitchen! Sip bubbly with the chef while discussing your preferences for a seven- to nine-course menu created for you. The Chef's Table can accommodate up to 12 people a night. It's a leisurely affair, lasting 3 or 4 hours. The price is $115 without wine, $160 per person including five wines. It's so popular that Disney takes reservations 180 days in advance, so reserve *early* (📞 **407/939-3463**).

service that will have you begging to take them home. There's an extensive wine list. We suggest splurging on the wine pairing. 4401 Floridian Way, in Disney's Grand Floridian Resort & Spa. 📞 **407/939-3463**. www.disneyworld.com. Reservations required. Jackets required for men. Not recommended for children. Prix fixe $85 per person, $35 additional for wine pairing; $115 Chef's Table, $160 with wine. AE, DC, DISC, MC, V. 2 dinner seatings daily, 5:45–6:30pm and 9–9:45pm. Chef's Table 6pm only.

Wolfgang Puck Café CALIFORNIA   The wait can be distressing and the sticker prices depressing, but the chefs turn out a mean menu of pizza, sushi, and fu-fu food. Possibilities include coriander-crusted tuna, fettuccine Wolf-fredo, Puck's pucks (crab cakes), and spicy tuna rolls. The eclectic eatery is often busy and noisy, making conversation difficult. But after enough sake, who cares? 1482 Buena Vista Dr., at Disney's West Side. 📞 **407/938-9653**. Reservations not accepted. Main courses $12–$28 (many under $20); pizza & sushi $5–$25. AE, DC, DISC, MC, V. Daily 11am–1am.

EPCOT

WORLD SHOWCASE   The World Showcase has the best dining options inside the WDW theme parks, thanks to the cultural cuisine of its 11 nation pavilions. There are many options beyond the ones we list below; these are only our favorites.

Le Cellier Steakhouse, in **Canada,** has a castlelike ambience accentuated by vaulted stone arches. Red-meat main events (all Midwest, corn-fed) include the usual range of cuts—filet, porterhouse, prime rib, sirloin, and so on. Wash down your meal with a Canadian wine or choose from a selection of Canadian beers.

The **United Kingdom's** Tudor-beamed **Rose & Crown** is a cozy pub suggestive of Victorian England. Visitors from the U.K. flock to this spot, where folk music and sometimes-saucy servers entertain you as you feast on a short but joyfully traditional menu including steak-and-mushroom pie and fish and chips. The outdoor dining area overlooks the lagoon and is a good place to see Illumi-Nations, but you'll need to reserve at least a month in advance.

Of all the Epcot restaurants, **Morocco's Marrakesh** exemplifies the spirit of the park, yet a lot of guests don't know it's there or ignore it because they're worried that the menu is too exotic. Expect belly dancers to entertain while you feast on such options as marinated beef shish kabob, braised chicken with green olives, and a medley of seafood, chicken, and lamb. The palatial restaurant—with handset mosaic tiles, latticed shutters, and a ceiling painted in elaborate Moorish motifs—represents 12 centuries of Arabic design.

If you've been to any of the Japanese steakhouse chains, you know the drill at **Japan's Teppanyaki:** Diners sit around grill tables while white-hatted chefs rapidly dice, slice, stir-fry, and sometimes launch the food onto your plate with amazing skill. Unfortunately, the culinary acrobatics here are better than the cuisine.

In **Italy,** and patterned after Alfredo De Lelio's celebrated ristorante in Rome, **L'Originale Alfredo di Roma** is Epcot's most popular restaurant. Nevertheless, critics say its pasta is overpriced and its servers are carefree. It's hard to take issue with the former when one meatless-pasta dish tops the $20 mark—the celebrated fettuccine.

When it comes to decor, **China's Nine Dragons** shines with carved rosewood furnishings and a dragon-motif ceiling. Some windows overlook the lagoon outside. Main courses feature Mandarin, Cantonese, and Szechwan cuisine, but portions are small and the food isn't quite as glorious as the surroundings.

Akershus is a re-created 14th-century castle in **Norway** where you can sample a 40-item smorgasbord of *smavarmt* (hot) and *koldtbord* (cold) dishes. Norwegian beer and aquavit complement a list of French and California wines.

It's always night at **Mexico's San Angel Inn,** where candlelit tables set the mood, and the menu delivers reasonably authentic food.

FUTURE WORLD   At the Living Seas pavilion, the mood is half the fun at the **Coral Reef,** where the tables circle a 5.6-million-gallon aquarium that has 4,000 denizens of the not-so-deep. Tiered seating ensures everyone a good view. Menu standards include garlic-roasted shrimp with seafood sausage and pan-seared salmon with garlic-pesto mashed potatoes. Lunch and dinner are $15 to $42.

IN THE MAGIC KINGDOM
In addition to these restaurants, there are plenty of fast-food outlets located throughout the park. But you may find that a quiet, sit-down meal is an essential though brief getaway from the forced-march madness. Don't forget to make priority-seating arrangements, and bear in mind that no alcohol is served in the Magic Kingdom.

Romantics may find it hard to beat the ambience of eating at **Cinderella's Royal Table** in Cinderella Castle, the Magic Kingdom's icon. Servers treat you like a lord or lady while fetching you headliners such as spice-crusted salmon, a New York strip, or roasted chicken.

The Liberty Tree Tavern's colonial decor and mood are fun, but the food (including the evening character buffet) is basic. Expect roast turkey, marinated flank steak, and honey mustard ham.

Lunch and dinner at **Tony's Town Square Restaurant** are nondescript (and in some cases cardboard-quality) Italian.

AT DISNEY–MGM STUDIOS
There are more than a dozen places to refuel in this Hollywood-style theme park. The ones listed below are the best of the bunch. Again, priority seating is a must.

Modeled after the Los Angeles celebrity haunt where Louella Parsons and Hedda Hopper held court, the **Hollywood Brown Derby** offers a good time and pricey meal. On the lighter side, try a Cobb salad, invented in the 1930s by Bob Cobb, who owned the restaurant in the other Hollywood. Dinner entrees at Disney's version include pan-seared black grouper and mustard-crusted rack of lamb. The Derby's signature dessert, grapefruit cake with cream-cheese icing, is a perfect meal-capper.

The concept behind the **50's Prime Time Cafe** is intriguing: Build a restaurant based on a 1950s time warp/sitcom psychodrama. The atmosphere delivers with black-and-white TV sets showing "My Little Margie" and servers threatening to withhold dessert if you don't eat all your food. But we won't blame you if you turn up your nose. Although the desserts are good, the meatloaf and pot roast don't deliver.

Take the above review for the 50's Prime Time Cafe, give it a science-fiction spin, and welcome to the **Sci-Fi Dine-In Theater Restaurant.** Diners sit in chrome-plated convertibles with the Hollywood hills as a backdrop and are treated to newsreels, cartoons, and "B" horror flicks. Forget food adjectives such as marinated, smoked, and pan-seared; it's still your basic beef, pork, poultry, tuna, and pasta.

IN THE ANIMAL KINGDOM

You'll find only a few dining options in Animal Kingdom and most of those are grab-and-go places. Nevertheless, there are two spots where you can park yourself.

Expect California fare with an island spin at the **Rainforest Cafe.** Menu offerings tend to be tasty and sometimes creative, but the cafe, like other Disney restaurants, charges more than it should. Dishes include a turkey pita with fried onions, romaine, and tomatoes. The mixed grill has ribs, steak on skewers, barbecued chicken, and peppered shrimp.

Taste at the **Tusker House** is there, even if quantity and quality aren't. The options are grilled chicken salad in a sourdough-bread bowl; rotisserie or fried chicken; and a chicken, ham, and Swiss cheese sandwich.

ONLY IN ORLANDO: DINING WITH DISNEY CHARACTERS

Dining with costumed characters is a treat for almost any Disney fan, but it's a special one for those under 10. Some of their favorite 'toons show up to greet them, sign autographs, pose for photos, and interact with the family. These meals aren't low-turnout events, so make priority-seating arrangements (© **407/ 939-3463**) as early as possible, and call for schedules. Prices vary, but generally expect breakfast (most serve it) to be $14 to $16 for adults, $8 to $10 for kids 3 to 11; those that serve dinner charge $19 to $22 for adults, $9 to $13 for kids. Character meals are offered at **Cape May Café** (in Disney's Beach Club Resort), **Chef Mickey's** (at Disney's Contemporary Resort), **Cinderella's Royal Table** (in Cinderella Castle, Magic Kingdom), **Crystal Palace Buffet** (at Crystal Palace, Magic Kingdom), **Donald's Prehistoric Breakfastosaurus** (in Dinoland U.S.A., Animal Kingdom), **Garden Grill** (in The Land Pavilion at Epcot), **Hollywood & Vine Character Dining** (at Hollywood & Vine, in Disney–MGM Studios), **Liberty Tree Tavern** (in Liberty Sq., in the Magic Kingdom), **'Ohana** (at Disney's Polynesian Resort), and **1900 Park Fare** (at Disney's Grand Floridian Resort & Spa).

ORLANDO AFTER DARK

The easiest way to find nighttime fun is to head for one of the massive entertainment complexes: Downtown Disney (Pleasure Island, Disney Village Marketplace, and Disney's West Side—separate entities but located near each other), and CityWalk.

Pleasure Island, in Walt Disney World, adjacent to Walt Disney World Village (© **407/934-7781**), is a 6-acre complex of nightclubs, restaurants, shops, and movie theaters; for a single admission price (free before 7pm, $21 including tax after), you can enjoy a night of club-hopping until the wee hours. The streets are festive with brightly colored lights and balloons. You'll be given a map and shown a schedule when you enter the park; take a look at it and plan your evening around shows that interest you. The on-premises clubs come and go, but expect to find a jazz club, a comedy club, an interactive entertainment club, a few dance clubs, live bands, a tropical bar, a video arcade, shops, restaurants, and more. And every night features a midnight New Year's Eve celebration with fireworks and confetti.

At **Disney Village Marketplace,** you'll find a collection of specialty shops and galleries highlighted by the LEGO Imagination Center. There is also the largest Disney gift shop on earth, plus a Rainforest Cafe.

Just down the block is **Disney's West Side.** It includes the 1,500-seat **House of Blues,** a three-story concert hall that books big-name acts, from rappers to blues legends. In addition to a number of specialty shops, there's a 24-screen movie complex; a **Wolfgang Puck Cafe;** and **Bongo's,** a restaurant created by Miami's favorite Home Girl, Gloria Estefan, featuring Latin American entertainment and delicious Cuban food.

Here you'll also find **Cirque du Soleil** (© **407/939-7600**). The international theater company known for combining acrobatics and elaborate avant-garde theatrics into a stage production has established its first permanent venue here. There are two shows a day, Wednesday through Sunday. The $40-million stage production, dubbed *La Nouba,* debuted in late 1998 in the circus tent-shaped building at Disney's West Side. Tickets to *La Nouba* cost $67 plus tax for adults and children 10 and older, $39 for children younger than 10.

Universal's answer to Pleasure Island and Disney's West Side, **CityWalk** opened in early 1999. A 12-acre entertainment complex, CityWalk is theme-restaurant heaven. Alcohol is prominently featured here, so an adult should accompany all teens, young children, and party-hearty peers. The nights can get pretty wild. Venues here include the Down Beat Jazz Hall of Fame located in **City Jazz,** a tribute to reggae mon Bob Marley, and a 5,000-seat Cineplex Odeon Megaplex. Those desiring to dance the night away can refine their moves at **the groove,** or try out their South American steps at **Latin Quarter.** NBA and NASCAR fans will find appropriately themed restaurants, and parrot-heads can make their way to **Jimmy Buffet's Margaritaville.** Music lovers will flock to **Hard Rock Live Orlando,** a 2,200-capacity venue featuring performances by top music stars.

There's no admission to walk through the two levels of clubs, restaurants, and shops, but because some charge a cover after 5 or 6pm, CityWalk also offers two **party passes.** A pass to all clubs costs $7.95 plus tax. For $12 plus tax, you can add a movie at Universal Cineplex (© **407/354-5998**) to the basic club access. Universal also offers free club access to those who buy 2- and 3-day theme-park tickets (see "Universal Orlando" earlier in this chapter). You can also opt to pay individual cover charges, usually under $6.

2 Highlights of Northeast Florida

COCOA BEACH, CAPE CANAVERAL & THE KENNEDY SPACE CENTER

The area around Cape Canaveral was once a sleepy place where city dwellers escaped the crowds from the exploding urban centers of Miami and Jacksonville. Then came the NASA space program. Today the region accommodates its own crowds, especially hordes of tourists who come to see where astronauts blast off into space.

ESSENTIALS

GETTING THERE   The nearest airport is **Melbourne International Airport** (© 321/723-6227; www.mlbair.com), 22 miles south of Cocoa Beach, but **Orlando International Airport,** about 35 miles to the west, is a much larger hub with more flight options and generally less expensive fares. **Comfort Travel** (© 800/567-6139 or 407/799-0442) or the **Cocoa Beach Shuttle** (© 407/ 784-3831) will take you from the Orlando airport to the beaches for about $20 per person. By car, major routes into Cocoa Beach are I-95 from the north (Daytona Beach and Jacksonville) and south (Miami), and Fla. 528 (Bee Line Expwy.) from the west (Orlando).

VISITOR INFORMATION   For information about the area, contact the **Florida Space Coast Office of Tourism,** 8810 Astronaut Blvd., Ste. 102, Cape Canaveral, FL 32920 (© **800/872-1969** or 321/868-1126; fax 321/868-1139; www.space-coast.com). The office is in the Sheldon Cove building, on Fla. A1A a block north of Central Boulevard, and is open Monday through Friday from 8am to 5pm.

EXPLORING THE AREA

The **Kennedy Space Center Visitor Complex,** on NASA Parkway (© **321/ 449-4444** for general information, 321/449-4444 for guided bus tours and launch reservations; www.KennedySpaceCenter.com), has exhibits, rockets, IMAX movies, and several dining venues. From there, bus tours go to the massive Vehicle Assembly Building, the International Space Station Center, and the impressive Apollo/Saturn V Center. The latter includes artifacts, photos, interactive exhibits, and the 363-foot-high Saturn V, the most powerful rocket ever launched by the United States.

Children will equally enjoy a playful visit to the **Astronaut Hall of Fame,** 6225 Vectorspace Blvd. (Fla. 405), Titusville (© **321/269-6100;** www.astronaut halloffame.com). In addition to honoring space voyagers, the hall has artifacts from the space program and several interactive exhibits.

NASA originally took over much more land than it needed to launch rockets. Rather than sell off the unused portions, it turned them over to the **Cape Canaveral National Seashore** (© **321/867-4077;** www.nps.gov/cana) and the **Merritt Island National Wildlife Refuge** (© **321/861-0667;** www.nbbd.com/ godo/minwr), both on Fla. 402. Together they protect tidal marshes, a bay known as Mosquito Lagoon, and 13 miles of barrier island beach. This is a great area for bird-watching, and giant sea turtles nest here May through August.

Appearing rustic and slapped-together, the **Cocoa Beach Pier,** on Meade Avenue east of Fla. A1A (© **321/783-7549**), was built in 1962 and shortly thereafter became the East Coast's surfing capital. It has 842 feet of fishing, shopping, and food and drinks overlooking a wide, sandy beach.

You can go sailing and take deep-sea fishing expeditions from the south bank of **Port Canaveral,** a man-made harbor that also is home port to cruise ships bound for the Bahamas and the Caribbean.

WHERE TO STAY

The six-story **DoubleTree Oceanfront Hotel,** 2080 N. Atlantic Ave. (© **800/ 552-3224** or 321/783-9222; www.cocoabeachdoubletree.com), is the pick of the beachfront properties here; all rooms have balconies with ocean views. **The Inn at Cocoa Beach,** 4300 Ocean Blvd. (© **800/343-5307** or 321/799-3460; www.theinnatcocoabeach.com), is the most romantic place in town and draws many couples with its well-furnished rooms, most with balconies.

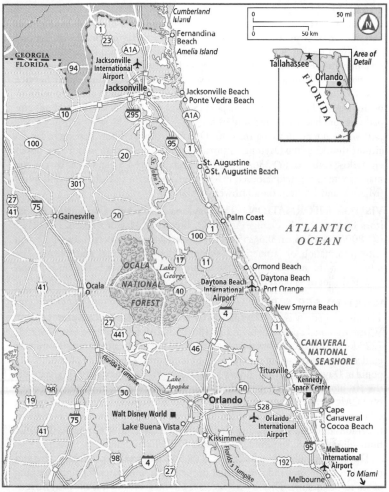

The family-friendly **Holiday Inn Cocoa Beach Oceanfront Resort,** 1300 N. Atlantic Ave. (© **800/206-2747** or 321/783-2271; www.holidayinnsofcentral florida.com), sprawls over 30 beachside acres and offers a wide variety of spacious hotel rooms, efficiencies, and apartments. A few suites even come equipped with bunk beds and Nintendo for the kids. The **Econo Lodge of Cocoa Beach,** 1275 N. Atlantic Ave. (© **800/553-2666** or 321/783-2252; www.choicehotels.com), is more charming than most members of this budget-priced chain (the seven original astronauts once owned it), and it accepts pets.

DAYTONA BEACH

Daytona Beach is the "World Center of Racing" and a mecca for spring breakers. Hundreds of thousands of race enthusiasts come here to see the Daytona 500, the Pepsi 400, and other races and to visit Daytona USA, a state-of-the-art motor-sports entertainment attraction worth a visit even by non-racing fans. But you don't have to be a car aficionado to enjoy Daytona, for here you'll find hard-packed sand along 24 miles of beaches.

ESSENTIALS

GETTING THERE   Fly into the small, pleasant, and calm **Daytona Beach International Airport** (© 904/248-8030; www.flydaytonafirst.com), 4 miles inland from the beach on International Speedway Boulevard (U.S. 92), or into **Orlando International Airport** (see "Walt Disney World & Orlando" earlier in this chapter), about an hour's drive away. **Daytona–Orlando Transit Service (DOTS)** (© 800/231-1965 or 904/257-5411) provides van transportation to or from Orlando International Airport ($26 for adults one-way, $46 round-trip; half fare for children 11 and under).

If you're intent on flying into the Daytona Airport, know that there are no airport shuttles at the Daytona Airport. The ride from here to most beach hotels via **Yellow Cab Co.** (© 386/255-5555) costs between $7 and $15. By car, the major route into Daytona Beach is I-95 from the north (Jacksonville) and south (Miami), and I-4 from the southwest (Orlando).

VISITOR INFORMATION   The **Daytona Beach Area Convention & Visitors Bureau,** 126 E. Orange Ave. (P.O. Box 910), Daytona Beach, FL 32115 (© 800/854-1234 or 386/255-0415; www.daytonabeach.com), can help you with information on attractions, accommodations, dining, and events. The office is on the mainland just west of the Memorial Bridge. The information area of the lobby is open daily from 9am to 5pm.

WHAT TO SEE & DO

The area's big draw is the **Daytona International Speedway complex,** at 1801 W. International Speedway Blvd. (© 386/253-RACE for race tickets, 386/253-7223 for information; www.daytonaintlspeedway.com). Entertaining 25-minute guided tram tours explain the track. The visitor center houses the phenomenally popular **Daytona USA** (© 386/947-6800; www.daytonausa.com), a state-of-the-art interactive attraction. Here you can participate in a pit stop on a NASCAR Winston Cup stock car, see the actual winning Daytona 500 car still covered in track dust, talk via video with favorite competitors, and play radio or television announcer by calling the finish of a race. An action-packed IMAX film will put you in the winner's seat of a Daytona 500 race.

The bustling hub of beach activity is the **Main Street Pier.** You can drive and park directly on the sand along most of the beach, but watch for signs warning of sea turtles nesting. There's a $5 access fee in most areas. Near the pier, **Adventure Landing,** 601 Earl St. (© 386/258-0071; www.adventurelanding.com), offers an assortment of indoor and outdoor activities to keep you and especially the kids entertained—and thoroughly wet.

WHERE TO STAY

A block from the Main Street Pier, **Adam's Mark Daytona Beach Resort,** 100 N. Atlantic Ave. (© 800/444-ADAM or 386/254-8200; www.adamsmark. com), is the town's largest beachfront hotel. Spacious rooms at the **Radisson Resort Daytona Beach,** 640 N. Atlantic Ave. (© 800/355-1721 or 386/239-9800; www.radisson.com), are among the best on the beach. The **Daytona Beach Hilton Oceanfront Resort,** 2637 S. Atlantic Ave. (© 800/525-7350 or 386/767-7350; www.hilton.com), is among the best choices in town, and far enough south to escape the maddening crowds at Main Street.

The most unusual beachside property here, and a good inexpensive choice, **Old Salty's Inn,** 1921 S. Atlantic Ave. (© 800/417-1466 or 386/252-8090; www.oldsaltys.com), carries out a *Gilligan's Island* theme. The refurbished **Shoreline All Suites Inn & Cabana Colony Cottages,** 2435 S. Atlantic Ave.

(℡ **800/293-0653** or 386/252-1692; www.daytonashoreline.com), has both spacious motel suites and small beachside cottages.

JACKSONVILLE

The sprawling metropolis of Jacksonville—residents call it "Jax," from its airport abbreviation—is one of the South's insurance and banking capitals. Development is rampant throughout Duval County, with hotels, restaurants, attractions, and clubs rapidly springing up, especially in suburban areas near the interstate highways.

ESSENTIALS

GETTING THERE **By Plane** Several airlines fly into **Jacksonville International Airport,** on the city's north side about 12 miles from downtown (℡ **904/741-2000;** www.jaxairports.org). The major car-rental firms have booths here. **Express Shuttle** (℡ **904/353-8880** or 904/355-2583) and **Gator City Taxi** (℡ **904/741-0008**) provide transportation to and from the airport.

By Train Amtrak (℡ **800/USA-RAIL;** www.amtrak.com) provides daily service from Orlando (trip time: 3¾ hr.), Tampa (4¾ hr.), and Miami (10 hr.) to its station at 3570 Clifford Lane.

By Car Major routes into Jacksonville are I-95 from the north (Savannah) and south (Miami), and I-10 from the west (Tallahassee).

VISITOR INFORMATION Contact the **Jacksonville and the Beaches Convention & Visitors Bureau,** 201 E. Adams St., Jacksonville, FL 32202 (℡ **800/733-2668** or 904/798-9111; fax 904/789-9103; www.jaxcvb.com), for maps, brochures, and advice. It's open Monday through Friday from 8am to 5pm.

WHAT TO SEE & DO

Spanning the broad, curving St. Johns River, downtown Jacksonville is a hub of activity during weekdays and on weekend afternoons and evenings, when many locals return to the restaurants and bars of **The Jacksonville Landing** and **Southbank Riverwalk,** two dining and entertainment complexes facing each other across the river. Like Baltimore's Inner Harbor, they have helped to revitalize downtown.

Also worth seeing here are the small but outstanding **Cummer Museum of Art & Gardens,** 829 Riverside Ave. (℡ **904/356-6857;** www.cummer.org), especially for its American Impressionist paintings; the **Jacksonville Zoo,** 8605 Zoo Rd. (℡ **904/757-4462** or 904/757-4463; www.jaxzoo.org), whose main exhibits center on an extensive and growing collection of African wildlife; and the **Fort Caroline National Memorial,** on Ft. Caroline Road (℡ **904/641-7155;** www.nps.gov/timu), a two-thirds replica of a 16th-century fort built by French Huguenots who attempted to settle here. The fort serves as the main visitor center for the **Timucuan Ecological and Historic Preserve,** a new breed of national park that includes natural preserves as well as historic sites.

You can fish, swim, snorkel, sail, sunbathe, or stroll on the sand dunes (at least Mar–Nov, since winter can get downright chilly here). They're all just a 20- to 30-minute drive east of downtown in **Atlantic Beach, Neptune Beach, Jacksonville Beach,** and the ritzy enclave of **Ponte Vedra Beach.** At the beach end of Atlantic Boulevard (Fla. 10), which straddles Atlantic and Neptune beaches, **Town Center** is a quaint community with a number of shops, restaurants, pubs, and hotels. You won't need your car to hit the beach, shop, dine, or imbibe here.

WHERE TO STAY

The 18-story **Adam's Mark Jacksonville,** 225 Coastline Dr. (© **800/444-ADAM** or 904/633-9095; www.adamsmark.com), is on a choice location a block east of Jacksonville Landing and caters mostly to corporate clients. Downtown on the Southbank Riverwalk, the 10-story **Jacksonville Hilton & Towers,** 1201 Riverplace Blvd. (© **800/HILTONS** or 904/393-8800; www.jacksonvillehilton.com), features the Elvis Presley Suite, where the King purportedly stayed half a dozen times (and, some say, still does).

A dozen modest chain hotels line Jacksonville Beach along the Atlantic Ocean, including the **Comfort Inn Oceanfront,** 1515 N. 1st St., 2 blocks east of Fla. A1A (© **800/654-8776** or 904/241-2311; www.comfortinnjaxbeach.com), which was completely renovated in 1998, and is one of the best-priced beachfront options. One of the anchors of quaint Town Center, the inexpensive **Sea Horse Oceanfront Inn,** 120 Atlantic Blvd. (© **800/881-2330** or 904/246-2175; www.seahorseresort.com), offers clean rooms with ocean views from balconies or patios. Also worth checking out in Town Center is the **Sea Turtle Inn,** 1 Ocean Blvd. (© **800/874-6000** or 904/249-7402; www.seaturtle.com), an older property that was completely gutted and restored in 2000.

In Ponte Vedra Beach, the upscale **Sawgrass Marriott Resort & Beach Club,** 1000 PGA Tour Blvd. (© **800/457-GOLF,** 800/228-9290, or 904/285-7777; www.sawgrassmarriott.com), and **Ponte Vedra Inn & Club,** 200 Ponte Vedra Blvd. (© **800/234-7842** or 904/285-1111; www.pvresorts.com), are both built around championship golf courses and offer a variety of accommodations, from hotel rooms to luxury condos. Smaller and more intimate, **The Lodge & Club at Ponte Vedra Beach,** 607 Ponte Vedra Blvd. (© **800/243-4304** or 904/273-9500; www.pvresorts.com), is one of Florida's more romantic hotels.

3 Fort Lauderdale & Palm Beach

FORT LAUDERDALE

Fort Lauderdale, once infamous for its annual spring break mayhem, began discouraging partying college kids and marketing its charms to a more affluent crowd in the mid-'90s. In addition to beautiful wide beaches, the city includes more than 300 miles of navigable waterways and innumerable canals that permit thousands of residents to anchor boats in their backyards. Boating is not just a hobby here; it's a lifestyle. Huge cruise ships also take advantage of Florida's deepest harbor, Port Everglades. It is the second-busiest cruise-ship base in Florida (after Miami) and one of the top five in the world.

ESSENTIALS

GETTING THERE   If you're driving from Miami, it's a straight shot north to Hollywood or Fort Lauderdale. Visitors on their way to or from Orlando should take the Florida Turnpike to Exit 53, 54, 58, or 62, depending on the location of your accommodations. The **Fort Lauderdale–Hollywood International Airport** is small, easy to negotiate, and located just 15 minutes from both of the downtown areas it services. **Amtrak** (© **800/USA-RAIL**) stations are at 200 SW 21st Terrace (Broward Blvd. and I-95), Fort Lauderdale (© **954/587-6692**), and at 3001 Hollywood Blvd., Hollywood (© **954/921-4517**).

VISITOR INFORMATION   The **Greater Fort Lauderdale Convention & Visitors Bureau,** 1850 Eller Dr., Ste. 303 (off I-95 and I-595 east), Fort Lauderdale, FL 33316 (© **954/765-4466;** fax 954/765-4467; www.sunny.org), is an excellent resource for area information in English, Spanish, and French. Once you are in town, you can call an **information line** ((Ⓒ **954/527-5600**) to get easy-to-follow directions, travel advice, and assistance from multilingual operators who staff a round-the-clock help line.

FUN ON & OFF THE BEACH

The **Fort Lauderdale Beach Promenade** recently underwent a $26-million renovation, and it looks fantastic. However, note that this beach is hardly pristine; it is across the street from an uninterrupted stretch of hotels, bars, and retail outlets. The unusually clear waters are under the careful watch of lifeguards. Freshen up afterward in any of the clean showers and restrooms conveniently located along the strip. Also nearby, on Fla. A1A, midway between Las Olas and Sunrise boulevards, **Beach Place** is a mega-retail and dining complex that underwent a $1.6-million renovation in 2001.

Fort Lauderdale provides ample opportunity for visitors to get on the water, either along the Intracoastal Waterway or out on the open ocean. **Bill's Sunrise Watersports,** 2025 E. Sunrise Blvd. (Ⓒ **954/462-8962**), can outfit you with a variety of watercraft.

The **IGFA World Fishing Center** at 300 Gulf Stream Way (Ⓒ **954/922-4212**) in Dania Beach is an angler's paradise. One of the highlights of this museum, library, and park is the virtual-reality fishing simulator, which allows visitors to actually reel in their own computer-generated catch. To get a list of local captains and guides, call IGFA headquarters and ask for the librarian (Ⓒ **954/927-2628**). Admission is $5 for adults, $4 for children between 3 and 12, and free for children under 3. On the grounds is also **Bass Pro Outdoor World Store,** a huge multifloor retail complex situated on a 3-acre lake.

More than 50 golf courses in all price ranges compete for players. Some of the best include **Emerald Hills** at 4100 N. Hills Dr., Hollywood, just west of I-95 between Sterling Road and Sheridan Street. This beauty consistently lands on "best of" lists of golf writers throughout the country. Greens fees start at $75. Call Ⓒ **954/961-4000** for tee times. For one of Broward's best municipal challenges, try the 18-holer at the **Orangebrook Golf Course,** 400 Entrada Dr., in Hollywood (Ⓒ **954/967-GOLF**), one of the area's best bargains. Morning and noon rates range from $21 to $33. After 2pm, you can play for less than $20, including a cart.

Plan to spend at least an afternoon or evening cruising Fort Lauderdale's 300 miles of waterways. The **Water Taxi of Fort Lauderdale** (Ⓒ **954/467-6677**) is a trusty fleet of old-port boats that serve the dual purpose of transporting and entertaining visitors. Taxis operate on demand and along a fairly regular route and carry up to 48 passengers. Choose a hotel on the route so that you can take advantage of this convenient and inexpensive system. You can be picked up at your hotel, usually within 15 minutes of calling, and then be shuttled to any of the dozens of restaurants, bars, and attractions on or near the waterfront. Your afternoon of cruising might start with a tour of **Millionaires' Row,** where Lauderdale's largest yachts are dwarfed only by the homes at which they are docked. Starting daily from 10am, boats usually run until midnight, and until 2am on weekends, depending on the weather. The cost is $7.50 per person per trip, $14 round-trip, and $16 for a full day. Children under 12 ride for half price and free on Sundays. Opt for the all-day pass; it's worth it.

If you are looking for unusual boutiques, especially art galleries, head to trendy **Las Olas Boulevard,** where there are literally hundreds of shops with alluring window decorations and intriguing merchandise. You may find kitchen utensils posing as modern art sculptures or mural-size oil paintings.

WHERE TO STAY

The **Lago Mar Resort and Club,** 1700 S. Ocean Lane, Fort Lauderdale (© 800/524-6627 or 954/523-6511; www.lagomar.com), is a casually elegant resort that occupies its own little island between Lake Mayan and the Atlantic. It's great for families, since most accommodations are suites with kitchenettes, and there are sports and facilities galore.

More moderately priced options include the **Banyan Marina Apartments,** 111 Isle of Venice, Fort Lauderdale (© 954/524-4430; www.banyanmarina. com). This hidden treasure is built around a dramatic 75-year-old banyan tree and is located directly on the active canals halfway between Fort Lauderdale's downtown and the beach. The one- and two-bedroom apartments are comfortable and spacious, with full kitchens and living rooms. Another magnificent find is the Spanish-Mediterranean **La Casa Del Mar,** 3003 Granada St. (© 954/467-2037; www.lacasadelmar.com), a small B&B situated right on the beach. Each of the property's 10 theme rooms has a private bathroom and is decorated in a motif inspired by an artist (such as Monet), regional style (such as Southwestern), or star (such as Judy Garland). The service is exceptional.

PALM BEACH & WEST PALM BEACH

Palm Beach has been the traditional winter home of America's aristocracy—the Kennedys, the Rockefellers, the Pulitzers, the Trumps, and plenty of CEOs. By contrast, West Palm Beach is a grittier workaday city. Recent renovations have made the metropolitan area a lively and affordable place to dine, shop, and hang out. In addition to good beaches, boating, and diving, you'll find great golf and tennis throughout the county.

ESSENTIALS

GETTING THERE   If you're driving up or down the Florida coast, you'll probably reach the Palm Beach area by I-95. Exit at Belvedere Road or Okeechobee Boulevard and head east to reach the most central part of Palm Beach. Visitors on their way to or from Orlando or Miami should take the Florida Turnpike, a toll road with a speed limit of 65 miles per hour. All major **airlines** fly to the Palm Beach International Airport, at Congress Avenue and Belvedere Road (© 561/471-7400).

VISITOR INFORMATION   The **Palm Beach County Convention and Visitors Bureau,** 1555 Palm Beach Lakes Blvd., Ste. 204, West Palm Beach, FL 33401 (© 800/554-PALM or 561/471-3995; www.palmbeachfl.com), distributes an informative brochure and will answer questions about visiting the Palm Beaches. Ask for a map as well as a copy of its "Arts and Attractions Calendar," a day-to-day guide to art, music, stage, and other events in the county.

FUN ON & OFF THE BEACH

Most of the island's best beaches are fronted by private estates and inaccessible to the general public. However, there are a few notable exceptions, including **Midtown Beach** on Ocean Boulevard, between Royal Palm Way and Gulfstream Road. There are no restrooms or concessions here, although a lifeguard is on duty until sundown. This newly widened sandy coast is now a centerpiece and a natural oasis in a town dominated by commercial glitz. To the south is a less popular but better equipped beach at **Phipps Ocean Park.** On **Ocean**

Boulevard, between the Southern Boulevard and Lake Avenue Causeways, is a large and lively public beach encompassing more than 1,300 feet of groomed and guarded oceanfront. With picnic and recreation areas, as well as plenty of parking, the area is especially good for families.

One of the state's best golf courses is **Emerald Dunes Golf Course,** 2100 Emerald Dunes Dr., in West Palm Beach (© **561/687-1700**). Designed by Tom Fazio, this dramatic 7,006-yard, par-72 course was voted "One of the Best 10 You Can Play" by *Golf* magazine. It is just off the Florida Turnpike at Okeechobee Boulevard. Bookings are taken up to 30 days ahead. Fees start at $130, including carts. The **Palm Beach Public Golf Course,** 2345 S. Ocean Blvd. (© **561/547-0598**), a popular public 18-hole course, is a par-54; the course is run on a first-come, first-served basis. Club rentals are available. Greens fees start at $20 per person.

The annual ritual of the ponies is played out each season at the posh **Palm Beach Polo and Country Club.** It is one of the world's premier polo grounds and hosts some of the sport's top-rated players. Matches are open to the public and are surprisingly affordable. Unless it is an opening game or some other special event, dress is casual. A navy or tweed blazer over jeans or khakis is a standard for men, while neat-looking jeans or a pantsuit is the norm for ladies. On warmer days, shorts and, of course, a polo shirt are fine, too. General admission is $6 to $10; box seats cost $10 to $36. Matches are held throughout the week. Schedules vary, but the big names usually compete on Sunday at 3:30pm January through April. The fields are at 11809 Polo Club Rd., Wellington, 10 miles west of the Forest Hill Boulevard Exit of I-95. Call © **561/793-1440** or surf over to **www.pbpolo.com/poloindex.html** for a detailed schedule of events.

The **Flagler Museum,** 1 Whitehall Way (at Coconut Row), Palm Beach (© **561/655-2833;** www.flagler.org), is a luxurious mansion commissioned by Henry Flagler, a cofounder of the Standard Oil Company. The must-see classically columned Edwardian-style mansion contains 55 rooms that include a Louis XIV music room and art gallery, a Louis XV ballroom, and 14 guest suites outfitted with original antique European furnishings.

A great spot for families, the **Lion Country Safari,** Southern Boulevard West at S.R. 80, West Palm Beach (© **561/793-1084;** www.lioncountrysafari.com), has more than 1,300 animals wandering on its 500-acre preserve. The animals—lions, elephants, buffalo, watusi, pink flamingos, and more—wander the grassy landscape while visitors remain in the safety of their cars. Also on the premises are an amusement park, a carousel, and an animal nursery. Picnics are encouraged. The best time to go is late afternoon, when they herd all the animals; plus, it's much cooler then, so the lions are more active.

Known as "the Rodeo Drive of the South," **Worth Avenue** is a window-shopper's dream. No matter what your budget, don't miss the Worth Avenue experience. The 4 blocks between South Ocean Boulevard and Cocoanut Row—a stretch of more than 200 boutiques, posh shops, art galleries, and upscale restaurants—are home to Armani, Louis Vuitton, Cartier, Polo Ralph Lauren, and Chanel, among others.

The heart of downtown West Palm Beach is **Clematis Street.** Artists' lofts, sidewalk cafes, bars, restaurants, consignment shops, and galleries dot the street from Flagler Drive to Rosemary Avenue, creating a hot spot for a night out.

WHERE TO STAY

The Breakers, 1 S. County Rd., Palm Beach (© **800/833-3141,** 888/ BREAKERS, or 561/655-6611; www.thebreakers.com), is a historic beauty that is the grandest of Palm Beach's luxury resorts. The lush 130-acre grounds also sport one of the island's only 18-hole golf courses. The Breakers is great for families, although the formality of the lobbies and restaurants may put some off.

For over-the-top pampering in a perfect location, the elegant **Four Seasons Resort Palm Beach,** 2800 S. Ocean Blvd., Palm Beach (© **800/432-2335** or 561/582-2800; www.fourseasons.com), is a favorite. The elegant marble lobby is replete with hand-carved European furnishings, grand oil paintings, tapestries, and dramatic flower arrangements. In addition to a host of services and sports facilities, there's a 6,000-square-foot spa and health club. For a more intimate experience, try **The Chesterfield,** 363 Cocoanut Row, Palm Beach (© **800/ 243-7871** or 561/659-5800; www.redcarnationhotels.com). Reminiscent of an English country manor, it is a magnificent, charming hotel with lovely rooms and exceptional service. It's located 3 blocks from the beach.

Looking for a bargain rather than a pricey resort? Try the **Beachcomber Apartment Motel,** 3024 S. Ocean Blvd., Palm Beach (© **800/833-7122** or 561/585-4646). A special find is **Hibiscus House,** 501 30th St., West Palm Beach (© **800/203-4927** or 561/863-5633; www.hibiscushouse.com), a 1920s-era B&B filled with handsome antiques. Every room here has its own private terrace or balcony.

4 Miami

There's much more to South Florida than the neon-hued nostalgia of *Miami Vice* and pink flamingos. Beyond the whole glitzy, *Access Hollywood*-meets-beach-blanket-bacchanalia-as-seen-on-TV, Miami has an endless number of sporting, cultural, and recreational activities to keep you entertained. Its sparkling beaches are beyond compare. Plus, there's excellent shopping and other nightlife activities that include ballet, theater, and opera.

ESSENTIALS

GETTING THERE   Miami International Airport (MIA) ranks tenth in the world for total passengers. Despite the heavy traffic, the airport is quite user-friendly and not as much of a hassle as you'd think. Visitor information is available 24 hours a day at the **Miami International Airport Main Visitor Counter,** Concourse E, second level (© **305/876-7000**). Information is also available at **www.miami-airport.com.** Miami International Airport is located about 6 miles west of downtown and about 10 miles from the beaches, so it's likely you can get from the plane to your hotel room in less than half an hour.

Note: Because MIA is the busiest airport in South Florida, travelers may want to consider flying into the less crowded **Fort Lauderdale–Hollywood International Airport (FLL)** (© **954/359-1200**), which is closer to north Miami than MIA, or into the **Palm Beach International Airport (PBI)** (© **561/471-7420**), which is about an hour and a half from Miami.

All the major car-rental firms operate off-site branches reached via shuttle from the terminals. (See appendix A for toll-free numbers and websites for all the major airlines and rental-car companies.) Signs at the airport's exit clearly point the way to various parts of the city.

We do not recommend taking public transportation to get from the airport to your hotel. **Taxis** line up in front of a dispatcher's desk outside the airport's arrivals terminals. Most cabs are metered, though some have flat rates to popular destinations. The fare should be about $20 to Coral Gables, $18 to downtown, and $24 to South Beach, plus tip, which should be at least 10% (add more for each bag the driver handles). One of the more reliable companies in the city is **Yellow Cab** (© **305/444-4444**).

Multipassenger vans circle the arrivals area looking for fares. Destinations are posted on the front of each van, and a flat rate is charged for door-to-door service to the area marked. **SuperShuttle** (© **305/871-2000;** www.supershuttle.com) is one of the largest airport operators, charging between $10 and $20 per person for a ride within the county. Its vans operate 24 hours a day and accept American Express, MasterCard, and Visa.

If you're driving to Miami, no matter where you start your journey, chances are you'll reach it by way of **I-95.** This north-south interstate is the city's lifeline, connecting all of Miami's different neighborhoods, the airport, and the beach, and it connects all of South Florida to the rest of America.

VISITOR INFORMATION   The most up-to-date information is provided by the **Greater Miami Convention and Visitor's Bureau,** 701 Brickell Ave., Ste. 700, Miami, FL 33131 (© **800/933-8448** or 305/539-3000; fax 305/530-3113; www.tropicoolmiami.com).

GETTING AROUND   If you're counting on exploring the city, even to a modest degree, a car is essential. You can manage to get by without one only if you are spending your entire vacation at a resort or if you are here for a short stay centered in one area of the city, such as South Beach.

Every major rental car agency is represented here, in the city and at the airport. A minimum age, generally 25, is usually required of renters, while some rental agencies have also set maximum ages! Many car-rental companies offer cellular phones or electronic map rentals. It might be wise to opt for these additional safety features (the phone will definitely come in handy if you get lost), although the cost can be exorbitant.

FAST FACTS   The Dade County Medical Association sponsors a **Physician Referral Service** (© **305/324-8717**), weekdays from 9am to 5pm. **Health South Doctors' Hospital,** 5000 University Dr., Coral Gables (© **305/666-2111**), is a 285-bed acute-care hospital with a 24-hour physician-staffed emergency department.

Walgreens has dozens of locations all over town. The branch at 5731 Bird Rd. at SW 40th Street (© **305/666-0757**) is open 24 hours, as is **Eckerd Drugs,** 1825 Miami Gardens Dr. NE, at 185th Street, North Miami Beach (© **305/932-5740**).

A 6% state **sales tax** (plus .5% local tax, for a total of 6.5% in Miami) is added on at the register for all goods and services purchased in Florida. In addition, most municipalities levy special taxes on restaurants and hotels. In Miami Beach (including South Beach), it's 11.5%; and in the rest of Dade County, it's a whopping 12.5%.

SPECIAL EVENTS   In January, **Art Deco Weekend** in South Beach features bands, food stands, antiques vendors, artists, tours, and other festivities. Call © **305/672-2014** for details.

March brings the **Calle Ocho Festival,** a salsa-filled blowout that marks the end of a 10-day extravaganza called Carnival Miami. It's one of the world's biggest block parties, held along 23 blocks of Little Havana's Southwest

8th Street between 4th and 27th avenues. Call © **305/644-8888** for more information.

June's **Coconut Grove Goombay Festival** is a Bahamian bacchanalia with dancing in the streets of Coconut Grove and music from the Royal Bahamian Police marching band. Call © **305/372-9966** for details.

New Year's Day is the date of the **Orange Bowl,** in which two of the year's top college football teams do battle at Pro Player Stadium. (Tickets to the game are available starting Mar 1 of the previous year through the Orange Bowl Committee at © **305/371-4600**).

HITTING THE BEACH

Perhaps Miami's most popular attraction is its incredible 35-mile stretch of beachfront, which runs from the tip of South Beach north to Sunny Isles and circles Key Biscayne and the numerous other pristine islands dotting the Atlantic. There are beaches for swimming, socializing, or serenity; for family, seniors, or gay singles; some to make you forget you're in the city, others darkened by huge condominiums. Whatever type of beach vacation you're looking for, you'll find it in one of Miami's two distinct beach areas: Miami Beach and Key Biscayne.

MIAMI BEACH'S BEACHES Collins Avenue fronts more than a dozen miles of white-sand beach and blue-green waters from 1st to 192nd streets. Although most of this stretch is lined with a solid wall of hotels and condos, beach access is plentiful. There are lots of public beaches here, wide and well maintained, complete with lifeguards, restroom facilities, concession stands, and metered parking (bring lots of quarters). Except for a thin strip close to the water, most of the sand is hard-packed—the result of a $10-million Army Corps of Engineers Beach Rebuilding Project meant to protect buildings from the effects of eroding sand.

In general, the beaches on this barrier island (all on the eastern, ocean side of the island) become less crowded the farther north you go. A wooden boardwalk runs along the hotel side of the beach from 21st to 46th streets—about 1½ miles—offering a terrific sun-and-surf experience without getting sand in your shoes. Miami's lifeguard-protected public beaches include 21st Street, at the beginning of the boardwalk; 35th Street, popular with an older crowd; 46th Street, next to the Fontainebleau Hilton; 53rd Street, a narrower, more sedate beach; 64th Street, one of the quietest strips around; and 72nd Street, a local old-timers' spot.

Lummus Park Beach, aka Glitter Beach, runs along Ocean Drive from about 6th to 14th streets on South Beach. It's the best place to go if you're seeking entertainment as well as a great tan. On any day of the week, you might spy models primping for a photo shoot, nearly naked sun-worshippers avoiding tan lines, and the best abs anywhere.

The **85th Street Beach,** along Collins Avenue, is the best place to swim away from the maddening crowds. It's one of Miami's only stretches of sand with no condos or hotels looming over sunbathers. Lifeguards patrol the area throughout the day and restrooms are available, though they are not exactly the benchmark of cleanliness.

KEY BISCAYNE'S BEACHES If Miami Beach doesn't provide the privacy you're looking for, try Virginia Key and Key Biscayne. Crossing the Rickenbacker Causeway ($1 toll), however, can be a lengthy process, especially on

Miami Beach & South Beach

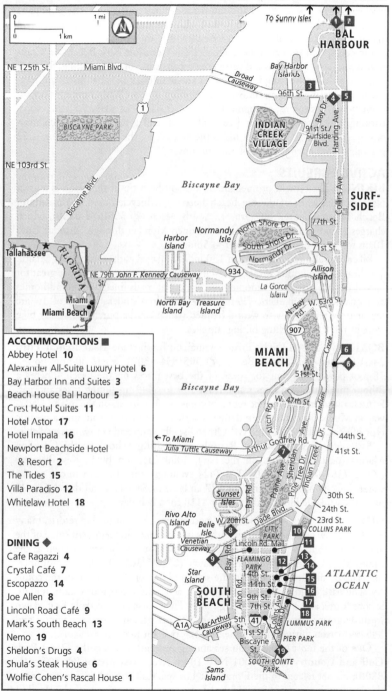

ACCOMMODATIONS ■
Abbey Hotel **10**
Alexander All-Suite Luxury Hotel **6**
Bay Harbor Inn and Suites **3**
Beach House Bal Harbour **5**
Crest Hotel Suites **11**
Hotel Astor **17**
Hotel Impala **16**
Newport Beachside Hotel
  & Resort **2**
The Tides **15**
Villa Paradiso **12**
Whitelaw Hotel **18**

DINING ◆
Cafe Ragazzi **4**
Crystal Café **7**
Escopazzo **14**
Joe Allen **8**
Lincoln Road Café **9**
Mark's South Beach **13**
Nemo **19**
Sheldon's Drugs **4**
Shula's Steak House **6**
Wolfie Cohen's Rascal House **1**

weekends, when beach bums and tan-o-rexics flock to the Key. The 5 miles of public beach there, however, are blessed with softer sand and are less developed and more laid-back than the hotel-laden strips to the north.

One exception to that is the party scene at **Crandon Park Beach,** on Crandon Boulevard, which has a diverse crowd consisting of dedicated beach bums and lots of leisure-seeking families, set to a soundtrack of salsa, disco, and reggae music blaring from a number of competing stereos. With 3 miles of oceanfront beach, restrooms, changing facilities, 493 acres of park, 75 grills, three parking lots, several soccer and softball fields, and a public 18-hole championship golf course, Crandon is like a theme park on the sand. Admission is $2 per vehicle. It's open daily from 8am to sunset.

ACTIVE PURSUITS

BIKING   The cement promenade on the southern tip of the island is a great place to ride. Most of the big beach hotels rent bicycles, as does the **Miami Beach Bicycle Center,** 601 5th St., South Beach (© **305/674-0150**), which charges $5 per hour or $14 per day. It's open Monday through Saturday from 10am to 7pm, Sunday from 10am to 5pm.

Bikers can also enjoy more than 130 miles of paved paths throughout Miami. The beautiful and quiet streets of Coral Gables and Coconut Grove are great for bicyclists. Old trees form canopies over wide, flat roads lined with grand homes and quaint street markers. *Biking note:* Children under the age of 16 are required by Florida law to wear a helmet, which can be purchased at any bike store or retail outlet selling biking supplies.

BOATING & SAILING   Private rental outfits include **Boat Rental Plus,** 2400 Collins Ave., Miami Beach (© **305/534-4307**), where 50-horsepower, 18-foot powerboats rent for some of the best prices on the beach. There's a 2-hour minimum and rates range from $99 to $449, including taxes and gas. Renters must be over 21. The rental office is at 23rd Street, on the inland waterway in Miami Beach. It's open daily from 10am to sunset. If you want a specific type of boat, call ahead to reserve. Otherwise, show up and take what's available.

Sailboats of Key Biscayne Rentals and Sailing School, in the Crandon Marina (next to Sundays on the Bay), 4000 Crandon Blvd., Key Biscayne (© **305/361-0328** days, 305/279-7424 evenings), can also get you out on the water. A 22-foot sailboat rents for $27 an hour or $81 for a half day. A Cat-25 or J24 is available for $35 an hour or $110 for a half day.

GOLF   Some of the area's best and most expensive are at the big resorts, many of which allow nonguests to play. Otherwise, the following represent some of the area's best public courses. **Crandon Park Golf Course,** formerly known as the Links, 6700 Crandon Blvd., Key Biscayne (© **305/361-9129**), is the number-one–ranked municipal course in the state and one of the top five in the country. The park is situated on 200 bay-front acres and offers a pro shop, rentals, lessons, carts, and a lighted driving range. The course is open daily from dawn to dusk; greens fees (including cart) are $86 per person during the winter and $45 per person during the summer. Special twilight rates are available.

One of the most popular courses among real enthusiasts is the **Doral Park Golf and Country Club,** 5001 NW 104th Ave., West Miami (© **305/591-8800**); it's not related to the Doral Hotel or spa. Call to book in advance, since this challenging, semiprivate 18-holer is extremely popular with locals. The course is open from 6:30am to 6pm during the winter and until 7pm during the summer. Cart and greens fees vary, so call © **305/594-0954** for information.

Known as one of the best in the city, the **Golf Club of Miami,** 6801 Miami Gardens Dr., at NW 68th Avenue, North Miami (© **305/829-8456**), has three 18-hole courses of varying degrees of difficulty. You'll encounter lush fairways, rolling greens, and some history to boot. The west course is where Jack Nicklaus played his first professional tournament and Lee Trevino won his first professional championship. The course is open daily from 6:30am to sunset. Cart and greens fees are $45 to $75 per person during the winter, and $20 to $34 per person during the summer. Special twilight rates are available.

SNORKELING & SCUBA DIVING   **Diver's Paradise** of Key Biscayne, 4000 Crandon Blvd. (© **305/361-3483**), offers two dive expeditions daily to the more than 30 wrecks and artificial reefs off the coast of Miami Beach and Key Biscayne. It's open Monday through Friday from 10am to 6pm and Saturday and Sunday from 8am to 6pm. Call ahead for times and locations of dives.

In addition, nearby **Biscayne National Park** offers a protected marine environment just 35 miles south of downtown (95% of the park is underwater). **Convoy Point,** the park's mainland entrance, with a visitor center, is 9 miles east of Homestead. The park's extensive reef system is extremely popular with divers and snorkelers. Beneath the surface, the aquatic universe pulses with multicolored life. Bright parrotfish and angelfish, gently rocking sea fans, and coral labyrinths abound. Snorkeling and scuba gear are rented and sold at Convoy Point, or bring your own. **Biscayne National Park Underwater Tours** (© **305/230-1100**) operates daily snorkeling trips that last about 4 hours and cost $30 per person. They also run two-tank dives for certified divers and offer instruction for beginners. The price is $45 per person.

WHAT TO SEE & DO

Located in South Beach, the **Art Deco District** is a whole community made up of outrageous and fanciful 1920s and 1930s architecture. The district is roughly bounded by the Atlantic Ocean on the east, Alton Road on the west, 6th Street to the south, and Dade Boulevard (along the Collins Canal) to the north.

Most of the finest examples of the whimsical Art Deco style are concentrated along three parallel streets—Ocean Drive, Collins Avenue, and Washington Avenue—from about 6th to 23rd streets. Hundreds of new hotels, restaurants, and nightclubs have been renovated or are in the process, and South Beach is on the cutting edge of Miami's cultural and nightlife scene.

If you're touring this unique neighborhood on your own, start at the **Art Deco Welcome Center,** 1001 Ocean Dr. (© **305/531-3484**), which is run by The Miami Design Preservation League. The only beachside building across from the Clevelander Hotel and bar, they give away lots of informational material including maps and pamphlets and run guided tours about the neighborhood. The center is open Monday through Saturday from 9am to 6pm, sometimes later.

Take a stroll along **Ocean Drive** for the best view of sidewalk cafes, bars, colorful hotels, and even more colorful people. Another great place for a walk is **Lincoln Road,** which is lined with boutiques, large chain stores, cafes, and funky art and antiques stores.

Bass Museum of Art   World-renowned Japanese architect Arata Isozaki designed the Bass Museum of Art's magnificent new facility, which has triple the former exhibition space, and added an outdoor sculpture terrace, a museum cafe and courtyard, and a museum shop. The museum's permanent collection includes European paintings from the 15th to the early 20th centuries with special emphasis on Northern European art of the Renaissance and baroque periods, including Dutch and Flemish masters such as Rubens and Jordaens. 2121 Park Ave. (1 block west of Collins Ave.), South Beach. ☎ 305/673-7530. www.bassmuseum.org. Admission $6 adults, $4 students and seniors, free for children 6 and under. Tues–Wed and Fri–Sat 10am–5pm; Thurs 10am–9pm; Sun 11am–5pm. Closed Mon.

Miami Art Museum at the Miami-Dade Cultural Center   The Miami Art Museum (MAM) features an eclectic mix of modern and contemporary works by such artists as Eric Fischl, Max Beckmann, Jim Dine, and Stuart Davis. Rotating exhibitions span the ages and styles, and often focus on Latin American or Caribbean artists. 101 W. Flagler St., Miami. ☎ 305/375-3000. Admission $5 adults, $2.50 seniors and students, free for children under 12. Tues–Fri 10am–5pm; 3rd Thurs of each month 10am–9pm; Sat–Sun noon–5pm. Closed major holidays. From I-95 S, exit at Orange Bowl–NW 8th St. and continue south to NW 2nd St.; turn left at NW 2nd St. and go 1½ blocks to NW 2nd Ave.; turn right.

Miami Metrozoo   This 290-acre complex is never really crowded and it's also completely cageless—animals are kept at bay by cleverly designed moats. This is a fantastic spot to take younger kids; there's a wonderful petting zoo and play area, and the zoo offers several daily programs designed to educate and entertain. Mufasa and Simba (of Disney fame) were modeled on a couple of Metrozoo's lions. Other highlights include two rare white Bengal tigers, a Komodo dragon, rare koala bears, a number of kangaroos, an African meerkat, a monorail tour, and an impressive aviary. *Note:* The distance between animal habitats can be great, so you'll be doing *a lot* of walking here. 12400 SW 152nd St., South Miami. ☎ 305/251-0400. www.zsf.org. Admission $8.95 adults, $4.75 children 3–12. Daily 9:30am–5:30pm (ticket booth closes at 4pm). Free parking. From U.S. 1 S., turn right on SW 152nd St. and follow signs about 3 miles to the entrance.

Miami Museum of Science and Space Transit Planetarium   The Museum of Science features more than 140 hands-on exhibits that explore the mysteries of the universe. Live demonstrations and collections of rare natural-history specimens make a visit here fun and informative for adults and kids alike. A Wildlife Center holds more than 175 live reptiles and birds of prey. The adjacent Space Transit Planetarium projects astronomy and laser shows as well as interactive demonstrations of computer technology and cyberspace features. Call, or visit their website, for a list of upcoming exhibits and laser shows. 3280 S. Miami Ave. (just south of the Rickenbacker Causeway), Coconut Grove. ☎ 305/646-4200 for general information or 305/854-2222 for planetarium show times. www.miamisci.org. $10 adults, $8 seniors and students, $6 children 3–12, free for children 2 and under; laser shows $6 adults, $3 seniors and children 3–12. After 4:30pm, ticket prices are half price. 25% discount for AAA members. Ticket prices include entrance to all museum galleries, planetarium shows, and the Wildlife Center. Museum of Science, daily 10am–6pm; call for planetarium show times (last show is at 4pm weekdays and 5pm on weekends). Closed Thanksgiving and Christmas Day.

Museum of Contemporary Art (MOCA)   MOCA boasts an impressive collection of internationally acclaimed art with a local flavor. A high-tech screening facility allows for film presentations to complement the exhibitions. You can see works by Jasper Johns, Roy Lichtenstein, Larry Rivers, Duane Michaels, and Claes Oldenberg, among others. Guided tours are offered in English, Spanish, French, Creole, Portuguese, German, and Italian. 770 NE 125th St., North Miami. ☎ 305/893-6211. Fax 305/891-1472. www.mocanomi.org. Admission $5 adults, $3 seniors and students with ID, free for children 12 and under. Tues by donation. Tues–Sat 11am–5pm; Sun noon–5pm. Closed major holidays and Mon.

Spanish Monastery Cloisters Did you know that the alleged oldest building in the Western Hemisphere dates from 1133 and is located in Miami? The Spanish Monastery Cloisters were first erected in Segovia, Spain. Centuries later, newspaper magnate William Randolph Hearst purchased and brought them to America in pieces. The carefully numbered stones were quarantined for years until they were finally reassembled on the present site in 1954. It has often been used as a backdrop for movies and commercials and is a very popular tourist attraction. 16711 W. Dixie Hwy. (at NE 167th St.), North Miami Beach. (C) 305/945-1461. monastery@earthlink.net. Admission $5 adults, $2.50 seniors, $2 children 3–12. Mon–Sat 9am–5pm; Sun 1–5pm.

Venetian Pool Miami's most beautiful and unusual swimming pool, dating from 1924, is hidden behind pastel stucco walls and is honored with a listing in the National Register of Historic Places. Underground artesian wells feed the free-form lagoon, which is shaded by three-story Spanish porticos and features both fountains and waterfalls. During summer, the pool's 800,000 gallons of water are drained and refilled nightly thanks to an underground aquifer, ensuring a cool, *clean* swim. Visitors are free to swim and sunbathe here, just as Esther Williams and Johnny Weissmuller did decades ago. For a modest fee, you or your children can learn to swim during special summer programs. 2701 DeSoto Blvd. (at Toledo St.), Coral Gables. (C) 305/460-5356. www.venetianpool.com. Admission and hours vary seasonally. Nov–Mar $5.50 ages 13 and older, $2.50 children under 13; Apr–Oct $8.50 ages 13 and older, $4.50 children under 13. Children must be 38 in. tall to enter or provide proof of 3 years of age with birth certificate. Hr. are at least 11am–4:30pm, but are often longer. Call for more information.

The Vizcaya Museum and Gardens Sometimes referred to as the "Hearst Castle of the East," this magnificent villa was built in 1916 as a winter retreat for James Deering, co-founder and former vice president of International Harvester. The industrialist was fascinated by 16th-century art and architecture; his ornate mansion, which took 1,000 artisans 5 years to build, became a celebration of that period. Most of the original furnishings, including dishes and paintings, are still intact. A free guided tour of the 34 furnished rooms on the first floor takes about 45 minutes. The second floor is open to tour on your own. Outside, lush formal gardens, accented with statuary, balustrades, and decorative urns, front an enormous swath of Biscayne Bay. Definitely take the villa tour, but immediately thereafter, you will want to wander and get lost in the resplendent gardens. 3251 S. Miami Ave. (just south of Rickenbacker Causeway), North Coconut Grove. (C) 305/250-9133. www.vizcayamuseum.com. Admission $10 adults, $5 children 6–12, free for children 5 and under. Villa daily 9:30am–5pm (ticket booth closes at 4:30pm); gardens daily 9:30am–5:30pm.

GREAT SHOPPING AREAS

Miami has earned a worldwide reputation as a shopping capital, especially among visitors from Latin America and the Caribbean. Take a quick glance around the airport, and you'll see more than a few departing passengers lugging refrigerator-size cardboard boxes and bulging suitcases. From exotic tropical fruits to high-tech electronics, fine art and Art Deco collectibles, Latin music and hand-rolled cigars, Miami has something for everyone.

AVENTURA On Biscayne Boulevard between Miami Gardens Drive and the county line at Hallandale Beach Boulevard is a 2-mile stretch of major retail stores including Best Buy, Borders, Circuit City, Linens N' Things, Marshall's, Sports Authority, and more. Also here is the mammoth **Aventura Mall,** housing a fabulous collection of shops and restaurants.

CALLE OCHO   For a taste of "Little Havana," take a walk down 8th Street between SW 27th Avenue and SW 12th Avenue, where you'll find some lively street life and many shops selling cigars, baked goods, shoes, and furniture, and record stores specializing in Latin music. For help, take your Spanish dictionary.

COCONUT GROVE   Downtown Coconut Grove, centered on Main Highway and Grand Avenue and branching onto the adjoining streets, is one of Miami's most pedestrian-friendly zones. The Grove's wide sidewalks, lined with cafes and boutiques, can provide hours of browsing pleasure. Coconut Grove is best known for its chain stores (Gap, Banana Republic, and others) and some funky holdovers from the days when the Grove was a bit more bohemian, plus excellent sidewalk cafes centered around CocoWalk and the Streets of Mayfair.

MIRACLE MILE (CORAL GABLES)   Actually only a half mile long, this central shopping street was an integral part of George Merrick's original city plan. Today, the strip still enjoys popularity, especially for its bridal stores, ladies' shops, haberdashers, and gift shops. Recently, newer chain stores, like Barnes & Noble, Old Navy, and Starbucks, have been appearing on the Mile. **Merrick Park,** a mammoth, 850,000-square-foot upscale outdoor shopping complex between Ponce de León Boulevard and Le Jeune Road, just off the Mile, opened in the fall of 2002 with Nordstrom, Neiman Marcus, Armani, and Yves St. Laurent on board, to name a few.

DOWNTOWN MIAMI   If you're looking for discounts on all types of goods—especially watches, fabric, buttons, lace, shoes, luggage, and leather—**Flagler Street,** just west of Biscayne Boulevard, is the best place to start. I wouldn't necessarily recommend buying expensive items here, as many stores seem to be on the shady side and do not understand the word *warranty.* However, you can still have fun here as long as you are a savvy shopper and don't mind haggling with people who may not have the firmest grasp on the English language. Most signs are printed in English, Spanish, and Portuguese; however, many shopkeepers may not be entirely fluent in English.

SOUTH BEACH   South Beach has come into its own as far as shopping is concerned. While the requisite stores—Gap, Banana Republic, and so on—have anchored here, several higher-end stores have also opened on the southern blocks of **Collins Avenue.** For the hippest clothing boutiques (including Armani, Ralph Lauren, Versace, Kenneth Cole, and Nicole Miller, among others), stroll along this pretty strip of the Deco District.

For those who are interested in a little more fun with their shopping, consider South Beach's legendary **Lincoln Road.** This pedestrian mall, originally designed in 1957 by Morris Lapidus, recently underwent a multimillion-dollar renovation restoring it to its former glory. Here, shoppers find an array of clothing, books, tchotchkes, and art as well as a menagerie of sidewalk cafes flanked on one end by a multiplex movie theater and at the other by the Atlantic Ocean.

WHERE TO STAY
Central Reservation Service (© **800/950-0232** or 305/274-6832; www. reservation-services.com) works with many of Miami's hotels and can often secure discounts of up to 40%. It also gives advice on specific locales, especially in Miami Beach and downtown. During holiday time, there may be a minimum

of a 3- to 5-day stay to use their services. Call for more information. For bed-and-breakfast information throughout the state, contact **Florida Bed and Breakfast Inns** (© 800/524-1880; www.florida-inns.com).

South Florida's tourist season is well defined, beginning in mid-November and lasting until Easter. Hotel prices escalate until about March, after which they begin to decline. During the off season, hotel rates are typically 30% to 50% lower than their winter highs. But timing isn't everything. In many cases, rates also depend on your hotel's proximity to the beach and how much ocean you can see from your window. Small motels a block or 2 from the water can be up to 40% cheaper than similar properties right on the sand.

Abbey Hotel   This charming, off-the-beaten-path '40s-revival boutique hotel is possibly the best deal on the entire beach. A haven for artists looking for quiet inspiration, the Abbey has recently undergone a $2.5-million renovation that restored its original Deco glory. Soft white-covered chairs and candles grace the lobby (which doubles as a chic Mediterranean-style restaurant), and the rooftop sun deck has been restored to its 1940s glamour as a bar and grill. Rooms are furnished with oversized earth-toned chairs and chrome beds that are surprisingly comfortable. It's extremely quiet at this hotel, as it is located in the midst of a sleepy residential neighborhood, but it's only 1 block from the beach. 300 21st St., Miami Beach, FL 33139. © 305/531-0031. Fax 305/672-1663. www.abbeyhotel.com. 50 units. Winter $150–$225 double; $225 studio. Off season $75–$150 double; $150 studio. AE, DC, DISC, MC, V. Off-site parking $17. **Amenities:** Restaurant; spa; fitness room; pets accepted with $500 deposit.

Alexander All-Suite Luxury Hotel   The luxurious Alexander is pricey, but worth it for the size of the suites and the doting attention. The hotel features spacious one- and two-bedroom mini-apartments with private balconies overlooking the Atlantic Ocean and Miami's Intracoastal Waterway. Each contains a living room, a fully equipped kitchen, *two* bathrooms (one with a shower and the other with a shower/tub combo), and a balcony. The rooms are elegant without being pretentious and have every convenience you could want. The hotel itself is well decorated, with sculptures, paintings, and antiques, most of which were garnered from the Cornelius Vanderbilt mansion. Two oceanfront pools are surrounded by lush vegetation; one of these "lagoons" is fed by a cascading waterfall. 5225 Collins Ave., Miami Beach, FL 33140. © 800/327-6121 or 305/865-6500. Fax 305/341-6553. www.alexanderhotel.com. 150 units. Winter $325 1-bedroom suite; $470 2-bedroom suite. Off season $250 1-bedroom suite; $370 2-bedroom suite. Additional person $35. Packages available. AE, MC, V. Valet parking $18. **Amenities:** Restaurants (2); 2 outdoor pools; fitness center; very small pets accepted for a $250 nonrefundable deposit for cleaning the suite

Bay Harbor Inn and Suites   Under the management of Johnson & Wales University, this thoroughly renovated inn is just moments from the beach and the Bal Harbour Shops. The inn comes in two parts: The more modern section overlooks a swampy river, a heated outdoor pool, and a yacht named *Celeste*, where guests eat a complimentary breakfast buffet. On the other side of the street, "townside," is the cozier, antiques-filled portion, where glass-covered bookshelves hold good beach reading. The rooms have a hodgepodge of wood furnishings (mostly Victorian replicas), while suites boast an extra half bathroom. 9660 E. Bay Harbor Dr., Bay Harbor Island, FL 33154. © 305/868-4141. Fax 305/867-9094. www.bayharborinn.com. 45 units. Winter $149–$239 double; $159–$279 suite. Off season $80–$159 double; $95–$179 suite. Additional person $35. Rates include continental breakfast. AE, MC, V. Free parking and dockage space. **Amenities:** Restaurant; fitness room.

Beach House Bal Harbour   The Beach House Bal Harbour is comfortable, unpretentious, and luxurious, yet decidedly low-key. In place of an elaborate hotel lobby, the public spaces are divided into a series of intimate homey environments, from the wicker-furnished screened-in porch to the Asian-inspired Bamboo Room. The 24-hour Pantry is packed with all the needs of the hotel's "unplugged" urban clientele. The ultraspacious rooms (those ending in 04 are the most spacious) are literally brimming with the comforts of home, including TV Web access, refrigerators, and stereo CD players. The 200-foot private beach, hammock grove, and topiary garden are incredibly lush. 9449 Collins Ave., Surfside, FL 33154. ℂ 877/RUBELLS or 305/535-8606. Fax 305/535-8602. www.rubellhotels.com. 170 units. Winter $215–$315 double; $245–$305 junior suite. Off season $180–$210 double; $230–$270 junior suite. Year-round $800 1-bedroom suite. AE, DC, DISC, MC, V. Valet parking $15. **Amenities:** Restaurant; heated pool; spa; health club.

Biltmore Hotel   A romantic sense of old-world glamour combined with a rich history permeate the Biltmore as much as the pricey perfume of the guests who stay here. Built in 1926, it's the oldest Coral Gables hotel and a National Historical Landmark. Rising above the Spanish-style estate is a majestic 300-foot copper-clad tower, modeled after the Giralda bell tower in Seville and visible throughout the city. The hotel is warm, welcoming, and extremely charming. It boasts large Moorish-style rooms decorated with tasteful period reproductions and some high-tech amenities. The enormous lobby, with its 45-foot vaulted ceilings, makes a bold statement of elegance. Always a popular destination for golfers, the Biltmore is situated on a lush, rolling 18-hole course that is as challenging as it is beautiful. The spa is fantastic and the enormous 21,000-square-foot winding pool (surrounded by arched walkways and classical sculptures) is legendary—it's where a pre-*Tarzan* Johnny Weismuller broke the world's swimming record. 1200 Anastasia Ave., Coral Gables, FL 33134. ℂ 800/727-1926 or 305/445-1926; Westin 800/228-3000. Fax 305/442-9496. www.biltmorehotel.com. 275 units. Winter $339–$509; off season $259–$479. Additional person $20. Special packages available. AE, DC, DISC, MC, V. Self-parking free, valet parking $14. **Amenities:** Restaurants (5); outdoor pool; 18-hole golf course; 10 lighted tennis courts; spa; health club.

Crest Hotel Suites   One of South Beach's best-kept secrets, the Crest Hotel features a quietly fashionable, contemporary, relaxed atmosphere with fantastic service. Built in 1939, the Crest was restored to preserve its Art Deco architecture, but the interior of the hotel is thoroughly modern, with rooms resembling cosmopolitan apartments. All suites have a living room/dining room area, kitchenette, and executive workspace. An indoor/outdoor cafe with terrace and poolside dining isn't besieged with trendy locals, but does attract a younger crowd. Crest Hotel Suites is conveniently located in the heart of the Art Deco Historic District, near all the major attractions. Around the corner from the hotel is Lincoln Road, with its sidewalk cafes, theaters, and galleries. 1670 James Ave., Miami Beach, FL 33139. ℂ 800/531-3880 or 305/531-0321. Fax 305/531-8180. www.cresthotel.com. 66 units. Winter $155–$235 double; off season $115–$175 double. Packages available and 10% discount offered if booked on website. AE, MC, V. **Amenities:** Restaurants (2); pool.

Hampton Inn   This very standard chain hotel, located in a quiet residential area, is a welcome reprieve in an city otherwise known for very pricey accommodations. The rooms are nothing exciting, but the freebies, such as local phone calls, parking, in-room movies, breakfast buffet, and hot drinks around the clock, make this a real steal. Although there is no restaurant or bar, it is close to lots of both—only about half a mile to the heart of the Grove's shopping and retail area and about as far from Coral Gables. Rooms are brand new, sparkling clean, and larger than that of a typical motel. If you'd rather save your money for dining and entertainment, this is a good bet. 2800 SW 28th Terrace (at U.S. 1 and SW 27th Ave.), Coconut Grove, FL 33133. © 888/287-3390 or 305/448-2800. Fax 305/442-8655. www.Hampton-inn.com. 137 units. Winter $134–$154 double. Off season $104–$124 double. Rates include continental breakfast buffet and local calls. AE, DC, DISC, MC, V. Free parking. **Amenities:** Outdoor pool; fitness room.

Hotel Astor Cozy-chic best describes this diminutive Deco hotel built in 1936. Though the hotel isn't as sceney (it has played host to Cameron Diaz and Madonna) as it once was, it's still a favorite spot for repeat visitors who wouldn't think of staying anywhere else. There is a small lap pool and a beautiful water-fall outside the bar area, but if you're looking to catch some sun, consider walking the 2 blocks to the beach because there are very few lounge chairs at the pool. The rooms are small but soothing, featuring plush and luxurious details—Belgian linens and towels, funky custom mood lighting with dimmer switches, and incredibly plush mattresses that are difficult to leave. The hotel staff is known for its extreme attentiveness—especially Arturo, the hotel's *Cheers*-y bartender who actually knows everybody's names and their drinks of choice. 956 Washington Ave., South Beach, FL 33139. © 800/270-4981 or 305/531-8081. Fax 305/531-3193. www.hotelastor.com. 40 units. Winter $155–$420 double; off season $110–$250 double. Additional person $30. AE, DC, MC, V. Valet parking $20. **Amenities:** Restaurant; outdoor pool; access to nearby health club.

Hotel Impala This renovated Mediterranean inn is one of the area's best, and it's just beautiful, from the Greco-Roman frescoes and friezes to an intimate garden that is perfumed with the scents from carefully hung lilies and gardenias. Rooms are extremely comfortable, with super-cushy sleigh beds, sisal floors, wrought-iron fixtures, imported Belgian cotton linens, wood furniture, stereo CD players, and fabulous roomy bathrooms done up in stainless steel and coral rock. Adjacent to the hotel is Spiga, an intimate, excellent Italian restaurant that is reasonably priced. Enclaves like this one are rare on South Beach. 1228 Collins Ave., South Beach, FL 33139. © 800/646-7252 or 305/673-2021. Fax 305/673-5984. hotel impala1@aol.com. 17 units. Winter $200–$400 double; off season $169–$279 double. AE, DC, MC, V. Valet parking $18. No children under 16 permitted. **Amenities:** Restaurant.

Hotel Place St. Michel This European-style hotel in the heart of Coral Gables is one of the city's most romantic options. The accommodations and hospitality are straight out of Old World Europe, complete with dark wood–paneled walls, cozy beds, beautiful antiques, and a quiet elegance that seems startlingly out of place in trendy Miami. One-of-a-kind furnishings make each room special. Bathrooms are on the smaller side but are hardly cramped. All have shower/tub combos except for two, which have either shower or tub. If you're picky, request your preference. Guests are treated to fresh fruit baskets upon arrival and enjoy perfect service throughout their stay. The exceptional Restaurant St. Michel is a very romantic dining choice. 162 Alcazar Ave., Coral Gables, FL 33134. © 800/848-HOTEL or 305/444-1666. Fax 305/529-0074. www.hotelplacest michel.com. 27 units. Winter $165 double; $200 suite. Off season $125 double; $160 suite. Additional person $10. Rates include continental breakfast and fruit basket upon arrival. AE, DC, MC, V. Self-parking $7. **Amenities:** Restaurant; access to nearby health club.

Newport Beachside Hotel & Resort This hotel is a great budget option, especially for young families who don't mind being away from the hustle and bustle of South Beach. The pool area is massive, which makes it great for kids. The hotel is situated directly on the beach, and for the aspiring angler, there is also a fishing pier out back. At night, by the poolside bar, a calypso band plays. Another plus is its location directly across the street from the R. K. Centres, a destination for both tourists and residents, with shopping and restaurants, from fine dining to fast food. Guest rooms are comfortable and spacious, and have microwaves and refrigerators. Most rooms have ocean views and balconies. 16701 Collins Ave., Sunny Isles, FL 33160. ℂ 800/327-5476 or 305/949-1300. Fax 305/947-5873. www. newportbeachsideresort.com. 300 units. Winter $129–$299 double; off season $95–$250 double. AE, DC, MC, V. Valet parking $5. **Amenities:** Restaurant; outdoor pool.

Ritz-Carlton Key Biscayne   Described by some as an oceanfront mansion, the luxurious Ritz-Carlton has 44 acres of tropical gardens, a 20,000-square-foot European-style spa, and a world-class tennis center. Decorated in British colonial style, the hotel looks as if it came straight out of Bermuda. The Ritz Kids programs provide children ages 5 to 12 with fantastic activities, and the 1,200-foot beachfront offers everything from pure relaxation to fishing, boating, or windsurfing. Spacious and luxuriously appointed rooms are elegantly Floridian, featuring large balconies overlooking the ocean or the lush gardens. The best spa in Miami is also here, with 20,000 square feet of space that overlooks the Atlantic Ocean and features a plethora of treatment options. 415 Grand Bay Dr., Key Biscayne, FL 33149. ℂ 800/241-3333 or 305/365-4500. Fax 305/365-4509. www.ritzcarlton.com. 402 units. Winter $440–$690 suite; off season $215–$405 suite. AE, DC, DISC, MC, V. Valet parking (call for fees). **Amenities:** Restaurants (2); 2 outdoor heated pools; tennis center; spa; health club.

The Tides   This 12-story Art Deco masterpiece is reminiscent of a gleaming ocean liner, with porthole windows and lots of stainless steel and frosted glass. Rooms are starkly white but are luxurious and comfortable; all are at least twice the size of a typical South Beach hotel room and have a view of the ocean. They feature king beds, spacious closets, large bathrooms, CD players, and even a telescope from which to view the vast ocean. Although small, the freshwater pool is a welcome plus, though it does lack ambience. The Tides is a place where celebrities such as Ben Affleck and Jennifer Lopez come to stay for some R&R, but you won't find gawkers or paparazzi lurking in the lobby, just an elegant clientele and staff who are respectful of people's privacy and desire for peace and quiet. 1220 Ocean Dr., South Beach, FL 33139. ℂ 800/OUTPOST or 305/604-5000. Fax 305/ 672-6288. www.islandoutpost.com. 45 units. Winter $525 suite; $3,000 penthouse. Off season $375 suite; $2,000 penthouse. Additional person $15. AE, DC, DISC, MC, V. Valet parking $18. **Amenities:** Restaurants (2); outdoor heated pool; small health club and discount at large nearby health club or yoga studio.

Turnberry Isle Resort & Club   One of Miami's classiest resorts, this gorgeous 300-acre compound has every possible facility for active guests, particularly golfers. The main attractions are two Trent Jones courses, available only to members and guests of the hotel. Treat yourself to a visit at the exceptional Turnberry Spa, which offers numerous classes, treatments, and a juice bar. Impeccable service from check-in to checkout consistently brings loyal fans back to this resort for more. The higher-priced resort rooms are your best bet. The well-proportioned rooms are gorgeously tiled to match the Mediterranean-style architecture and have numerous amenities, including CD players. The huge bathrooms even have a color TV mounted within reach of the whirlpool bathtubs and glass-walled showers. The resort's location in North Miami Beach's

Aventura section means you'll find excellent shopping and some of the best dining in Miami right in the neighborhood. The only drawback to this hotel is that you'll need to take a shuttle to the beach. 19999 W. Country Club Dr., Aventura, FL 33180. ℰ 800/327-7028 or 305/936-2929. Fax 305/933-6560. www.turnberryisle.com. 395 units. Winter $395–$495 double; $605–$1,200 suite; $3,000–$4,200 penthouse. Off season $175–$275 double; $375–$730 suite; $2,500–$3,500 penthouse. AE, DC, DISC, MC, V. Self-parking free, valet parking $12. **Amenities:** Restaurants (6); 2 outdoor pools; spa; 2 golf courses; 2 tennis complexes.

Villa Paradiso This guesthouse is more like a cozy apartment house than a hotel. There's no elegant lobby or restaurant, but the amicable hosts, Lisa and Pascal Nicolle, are happy to give you a room key and advice on what to do. The recently renovated spacious apartments are simple but elegant—hardwood floors, French doors, and stylish wrought-iron furniture—and are remarkably quiet considering their location, a few blocks from Lincoln Road and all of South Beach's best clubs. Most have full kitchens or at least a fridge, and Murphy beds or foldout couches for extra friends. Bathrooms have recently been renovated with marble tile. All rooms overlook the hotel's pretty courtyard garden. 1415 Collins Ave., Miami Beach, FL 33139. ℰ 305/532-0616. Fax 305/673-5874. www.villa paradisohotel.com. 17 units. Winter $100–$165 apt; off season $75–$129 apt. Weekly rates are 10% cheaper. Additional person $10. AE, DC, MC, V. Parking nearby $12. **Amenities:** Pets (including small "nonbarking" dogs) accepted for $10 with $100 deposit.

Whitelaw Hotel With a slogan that reads "clean sheets, hot water, and stiff drinks," the Whitelaw Hotel stands apart from the other boutique hotels with a fierce sense of humor, but never compromises on its fabulous amenities. Only half a block from Ocean Drive, this hotel, like its clientele, is full of distinct personalities. All-white rooms manage to be homey and plush and not at all antiseptic. All the rooms have luxurious Belgian sheets, refrigerators, and CD players. Bathrooms are large and well stocked with just about everything you may have forgotten at home. Complimentary cocktails in the lobby every night from 8 to 10pm contribute to a very social atmosphere. The hotel offers free airport pick-up from Miami International if you book a room through its website. 808 Collins Ave., Miami Beach, FL 33139. ℰ 305/398-7000. Fax 305/398-7010. www.whitelaw hotel.com. Winter $175 double; $195 suite. Off season $125 double; $145 suite. Rates include complimentary continental breakfast and free cocktails in the lobby 8–10pm every night. AE, MC, DC, V. Parking $18.

WHERE TO DINE

Don't be fooled by the plethora of superlean model types you're likely to see posing throughout Miami: Contrary to popular belief, dining in this city is as much a sport as the in-line skating on Ocean Drive. With over 6,000 restaurants to choose from, dining out in Miami has become a passionate pastime for locals and visitors alike. The biggest complaint when it comes to Miami dining isn't the haughtiness, but rather the dearth of truly moderately priced restaurants, especially in South Beach and Coral Gables. It's either really cheap or really expensive; the in-between somehow gets lost in the culinary shuffle. Quick-service diners don't really exist here as they do in other cosmopolitan areas. Budget accordingly.

Baleen SEAFOOD/MEDITERRANEAN While the prices aren't lean, the cuisine here is worth every pricey, precious penny. Oversize crab cakes, oak-smoked diver scallops, and steakhouse-quality meats are among Baleen's excellent offerings. The lobster bisque is the best on Biscayne Bay. Everything here is a la carte, so order wisely, as it tends to add up quicker than you can put your fork down. The restaurant's spectacular waterfront setting makes Baleen a true knockout. Brunch is particularly noteworthy as well. 4 Grove Isle Dr. (in the Grove Isle Hotel), Coconut Grove. ✆ 305/858-8300. Reservations recommended. Main courses $18–$34. AE, DC, MC, V. Sun–Wed 7am–10pm; Thurs–Sat 7am–11pm.

Cafe Ragazzi ITALIAN   This diminutive Italian cafe, with its rustic decor and a swift, knowledgeable waitstaff, enjoys great success for its tasty, simple pastas. The spicy puttanesca sauce with a subtle hint of fish is perfectly prepared. Also recommended is the salmon with radicchio. You can choose from many decent salads and carpaccio, too. Lunch specials are a real steal at $7, including soup, salad, and daily pasta. The restaurant is light on social scenery—people come here for the food only. Expect to wait on weekend nights. 9500 Harding Ave. (on the corner of 95th St.), Surfside. ✆ 305/866-4495. Reservations accepted for 4 or more. Main courses $9–$18. MC, V. Mon–Fri 11:30am–3pm; daily 5:30–11pm.

Chef Allen's NEW WORLD CUISINE   Chef Allen Susser, winner of the esteemed James Beard Award for Best American Chef in the Southeast, is royalty in this town. This restaurant is his province, and foodies are his disciples. It is under Chef Allen's magic that ordinary Key limes and mangos reappear in the form of succulent salsas and sauces. Whole yellowtail in coconut milk and curry sauce is a particularly spectacular entree. Unlike other restaurants where location is key, Chef Allen's, located in the rear of a strip mall, could be in the desert, and hordes of people would still make the trek. 19088 NE 29th Ave. (at Biscayne Blvd.), North Miami Beach. ✆ 305/935-2900. Reservations recommended. Main courses $22–$40. AE, DC, MC, V. Sun–Thurs 6–10pm; Fri–Sat 6–11pm.

Crystal Café CONTINENTAL/NEW WORLD   The setting is sparse, with a bottle of wine and Lucite salt and pepper grinders as the only centerpiece on each of the 15 or so tables. I promise you won't need the seasoning. Chef Klime has done it all with the help of his affable wife and a superb waitstaff. Enjoy his unique sparkle at this little-known hideaway, which attracts celebrities and in-the-know gourmands. The approximately 30 entrees, including a few nightly specials, are beautifully presented and perfectly prepared. The osso buco (veal shanks stewed in white wine with tomatoes, garlic, minced veggies, and more) is a masterpiece. 726 41st St., Miami Beach. ✆ 305/673-8266. Reservations recommended on weekends. Main courses $11–$25. AE, DC, DISC, MC, V. Tues–Thurs 5–10pm; Fri–Sat 5–11pm.

Escopazzo ITALIAN   *Escopazzo* means "crazy" in Italian, but the only sign of insanity in this primo Northern Italian eatery is the fact that it only seats 70. The wine bottles have it better—the restaurant's cellar holds 1,000 bottles of various vintages. Should you be so lucky to score a table at this romantic local favorite, you'll have trouble deciding between dishes that will have you swearing off the Olive Garden with your first bite. The hand-rolled pastas and risotto are near perfection. Eating here is like dining with a big Italian family—it's never boring (the menu changes five or six times a year), the service is excellent, and nobody's happy until you are blissfully full. 1311 Washington Ave., South Beach. ✆ 305/674-9450. Reservations required. Main courses $18–$28. AE, MC, V. Mon, Tues, and Thurs 6pm–midnight; Fri–Sat 6pm–1am; Sun 6–11pm.

Fishbone Grille SEAFOOD   Fish are flying in the open kitchen of this extremely popular, reasonably priced seafood joint. Whether you take yours grilled, blackened, or sautéed, the chefs here work wonders with super-fresh snapper, grouper, tuna, sea bass, and shrimp, to name just a few. For nonfish eaters, there are delicious pizzas and an excellent New York strip steak. All meals come with salad and a fantastic slab of jalapeño corn bread. The interior is plain and simple; the only thing elaborate is the long list of daily specials. 650 S. Miami Ave., Miami. (C) 305/530-1915. Reservations recommended for 6 or more. Main courses $9–$20. AE, DC, DISC, MC, V. Mon–Thurs 11:30am–10pm; Fri 11:30am–11pm; Sat 5–11pm; Sun 5:30–9pm.

Joe Allen AMERICAN   Located on the bay side of the beach, Joe Allen is nestled in an unassuming building in South Beach that is conspicuously devoid of neon lights, valet parkers, and fashionable pedestrians. Inside, however, you discover a hidden jewel: a stark yet elegant interior and no-nonsense, fairly priced, ample-portioned dishes such as meatloaf, pizza, fresh fish, and salads. The scene has a homey feel flavored by locals looking to escape the hype without compromising quality. 1787 Purdy Ave./Sunset Harbor Dr. (3 blocks west of Alton Rd.), South Beach. (C) 305/531-7007. Reservations recommended, especially on weekends. Main courses $15–$25. MC, V. Mon–Fri 11:30am–11:45pm; Sat–Sun noon–11:45pm.

Lincoln Road Café CUBAN   A local favorite, this down-to-earth Cuban-accented cafe is very popular for its cheap breakfasts. For $6, you can indulge in a hearty portion of eggs any style, with bacon, ham, sausage, Cuban toast, and coffee. Lunch and dinner specials are delicious and very cheap as well; try the ubiquitous black beans and rice. The few tables inside are usually passed up in favor of the several outdoors, but in the evenings the house is full inside and out, as talented Latin musicians perform out front. 941 Lincoln Rd., South Beach. (C) 305/538-8066. Items $6–$11. AE, DC, MC, V. Daily 8am–midnight.

Mark's South Beach NEW WORLD/MEDITERRANEAN   This cozy, contemporary restaurant—one of the best in Miami—is nestled in the basement of the quietly chic Hotel Nash. The New World and Mediterranean-influenced menu changes nightly. What doesn't change is the consistency and freshness of the restaurant's exquisite cuisine. The roasted rack of Colorado lamb with semolina gnocchi is exceptional and worth every bit of cholesterol it may have. Desserts here are outrageous, especially the pistachio cake with chocolate sorbet. In the Hotel Nash, 1120 Collins Ave., South Beach. (C) 305/604-9050. Reservations recommended. Main courses $16–$38. AE, DC, DISC, MC, V. Sun–Thurs 7–11pm; Fri–Sat 7pm–midnight.

Nemo PAN-ASIAN   Located on the quickly developing South Beach area known as SoFi (for "south of Fifth St."), Nemo is a funky, high-style eatery with an open kitchen and an outdoor courtyard canopied by trees and lined with an eclectic mix of model types and foodies. Chef Michael Schwartz serves up a masterful assortment of Pan Asian cuisine. Among the reasons to eat in this restaurant: grilled Indian-spiced pork chop; grilled local mahi with citrus and grilled sweet-onion salad, kimchi glaze, basil, and crispy potatoes; and an inspired dessert menu that's not for the faint of calories. Seating inside is comfy-cozy but borders on cramped. On Sunday mornings, the open kitchen is converted into a buffet counter for the restaurant's unparalleled brunch. Be prepared for a wait, which tends to spill out onto the street. 100 Collins Ave., South Beach. (C) 305/532-4550. Reservations recommended. Main courses $22–$36; Sun brunch $26. AE, MC, V. Mon–Fri noon–3pm and 7pm–midnight; Sun 11am–3pm and 6–11pm.

Nobu SUSHI   When Madonna ate here, no one really noticed because the real star at Nobu is the sushi. The raw facts: Nobu has been hailed as one of the best sushi restaurants in the world, with always-packed branches in New York, London, and Los Angeles. The Omakase, or Chef's Choice—a multicourse menu entirely up to the chef for $70 per person and up—gets consistent raves. And although you won't wait long for your food to be cooked, you will wait forever to score a table here. At the Shore Club Hotel, 1901 Collins Ave., South Beach. © **305/695-3100**. Reservations for parties of 6 or more. Main courses $10–$30. AE, MC, V. Sun–Thurs 6pm–12am; Fri–Sat 6pm–1am.

Norman's NEW WORLD CUISINE   *Gourmet* magazine named Norman's the best restaurant in South Florida and it is here that chef and cookbook author Norman van Aken takes New World Cuisine (which, along with chef Allen Susser, he helped create) to another plateau with dishes that have landed him on the wish lists of gourmands everywhere. The open kitchen invites you to marvel at the mastery that lands on your plate in the form of pan-roasted swordfish with black-bean *muneta;* or chargrilled New York strip steak with chimichurri sabayon, *pommes frites,* and Creole mustard–spiced caramelized red onions; just to name a few. The staff is adoring and professional and the atmosphere is tasteful without being too formal. The portions are realistic, but still, be careful not to overdo it. You'll want to try some of the funky, fantastic desserts. 21 Almeria Ave. (between Douglas and Ponce de León), Coral Gables. © **305/446-6767**. Reservations highly recommended. Main courses $22–$38. AE, DC, MC, V. Mon–Thurs 6–10:30pm; Fri–Sat 6–11pm. Bar opens at 5:30pm.

Sheldon's Drugs AMERICAN   This historic old-fashioned drugstore counter was a favorite breakfast spot of Isaac Bashevis Singer. Consider stopping by for a good piece of pie and a side of history. According to legend, the author was sitting at Sheldon's eating a bagel and eggs when his wife got the call in 1978 that he had won the Nobel Prize for Literature. The menu hasn't changed much since then. You can get eggs and oatmeal and a good tuna melt. A blue-plate special might be generic spaghetti and meatballs or grilled frankfurters. The food is pretty basic, but you can't beat the prices. 9501 Harding Ave., Surfside. © **305/866-6251**. Main courses $4–$8; soups and sandwiches $2–$5. AE, DISC, MC, V. Mon–Sat 7am–9pm; Sun 7am–4pm.

Shula's Steak House AMERICAN/STEAK   Climb a sweeping staircase in the Alexander All-Suite Luxury Hotel and go through the glass hallway and you'll find yourself in this magnificent restaurant that has been acclaimed as one of the greatest steakhouses in all of North America. If you're feeling adventurous, try the 48-ounce club (you can get your name engraved on a gold plaque if you can finish this absolutely *huge* piece of meat) or settle for the 20-ounce Kansas City strip or the 12-ounce filet mignon. Fresh seafood abounds when in season, and the oysters Rockefeller are a particularly good choice. The entertaining staff is very knowledgeable. In the Alexander Hotel, 5225 Collins Ave., Miami Beach. © **305/341-6565**. Reservations recommended. Main courses $18–$58. AE, DISC, MC, V. Daily 11am–3:30pm and 6–11pm.

Versailles CUBAN   Versailles is the meeting place of Miami's Cuban power brokers, who meet daily over *cafe con leche* to discuss the future of the exiles' fate. A glorified diner, the place sparkles with glass, chandeliers, murals, and mirrors meant to evoke the French palace. There's nothing fancy here—nothing French, either—just straightforward food from the home country. The menu is a veritable survey of Cuban cooking and includes specialties such as Moors and Christians (flavorful black beans with white rice), *ropa vieja* (shredded beef stew), and fried whole fish. Versailles is the place to come for *mucho* helpings of Cuban kitsch. With its late hours, it's also the perfect place to come after spending your night in Little Havana. 3555 SW 8th St., Little Havana. © **305/444-0240**. Soup and salad

$2–$10; main courses $5–$20. DC, DISC, MC, V. Mon–Thurs 8am–2am; Fri 8am–3:30am; Sat 8am–
4:30am; Sun 9am–1am.

Wolfie Cohen's Rascal House DELI Open since 1954 and still going
strong, this historic, nostalgic culinary extravaganza is one of Miami Beach's
greatest traditions. Scooch into one of the ancient vinyl booths—which have
hosted many a notorious bottom, from Frank Sinatra to mob boss Sam Gian-
cana—and review the huge menu that's loaded with authentic Jewish staples.
Consider the classic corned beef sandwich, stuffed cabbage, brisket, or potato
pancakes. If you're lucky, the waitress will give you a wax-paper doggy bag to
wrap up the leftover rolls and Danish from your breadbasket. 17190 Collins Ave. (at
163rd St.), Sunny Isles. © 305/947-4581. Main courses $8–$30. AE, MC, V. Daily 7am–1am. There
is another Wolfie Cohen's Rascal House in Boca Raton, at 2006 NW Executive Center Circle, Boca
Raton; © 561/982-8899.

MIAMI AFTER DARK

For up-to-date listing information, and to make sure time hasn't elapsed for the
club of the moment, check the *Miami Herald*'s "Weekend" section, which runs
on Friday, or the more comprehensive listings in *New Times,* Miami's free alternative weekly, available each Wednesday; or visit **www.miami.citysearch.com
online**.

THE PERFORMING ARTS One of the most important and longest-running
series is produced by the **Concert Association of Florida (CAF)**, 555 17th St.,
South Beach (© **305/532-3491**). Season after season, the schedules are punctuated by world-renowned dance companies and seasoned virtuosi like Itzhak
Perlman, Andre Watts, and Kathleen Battle. Since CAF does not have its own
space, performances are usually scheduled in either the Dade County Auditorium or the Jackie Gleason Theater of the Performing Arts. The season lasts from
October through April, and ticket prices range from $20 to $70.

The artistically acclaimed and innovative **Miami City Ballet** (© **305/532-
4880** or 305/532-7713) is directed by Edward Villella. Its season runs from September to April, with performances at its headquarters, the Ophelia and Juan Jr.
Roca Center on Collins Avenue and 22nd Street in Miami Beach.

For a taste of local Latin flavor, see the **Ballet Flamenco La Rosa** (© **305/
899-7729**) perform impressive flamenco and other styles of dance on various
Miami stages.

South Florida's premier symphony orchestra, under the direction of James
Judd, the **Florida Philharmonic Orchestra** (© **800/226-1812** or 305/476-
1234) presents a full season of classical and pops programs interspersed with several children's and contemporary popular-music dates. The Philharmonic performs Downtown in the Gusman Center for the Performing Arts and at the
Dade County Auditorium.

Nearing its 60th birthday, the **Florida Grand Opera** (© **800/741-1010;**
www.fgo.org) regularly features singers from top houses in both America and
Europe. All productions are sung in their original language and staged with projected English supertitles. Tickets become scarce when Placido Domingo or
Luciano Pavarotti (who made his American debut here in 1965) come to town.
The opera's season runs roughly from November to April, with five performances
each week. A new headquarters for the opera is scheduled to open in mid-2004.

LIVE MUSIC Tobacco Road, 626 S. Miami Ave. (over the Miami Ave.
Bridge near Brickell Ave., downtown; © **305/374-1198**), is an institution that's

been around since 1912. These days, you'll find a good bar menu along with the best live music anywhere—blues, zydeco, brass, jazz, and more.

Jazid, 1342 Washington Ave., South Beach (© **305/673-9372**), is warm, welcoming, and cheap, and even has a pool table. Music ranges from classic jazz to blues and often includes talented locals.

In Miami Beach, the elegant **Upstairs at the Van Dyke Cafe,** 846 Lincoln Rd. (© **305/534-3600**), has live jazz 7 nights a week until midnight.

DANCE CLUBS   Ask your hotel's concierge to get you on a club's guest list; you'll still have to wait to get in, but you won't need to fork over a ridiculous $20 to walk past the ropes. This is a fickle scene, but at press time, some of the hottest spots included **crobar,** 1445 Washington Ave., South Beach (© **305/531-8225**); **Liquid,** 1532 Washington Ave., South Beach (© **305/532-9154** for information, 305/532-8899 for table reservations); **Living Room Downtown,** 60 NE 11th St., downtown (© **305/342-7421**); **Rain,** 323 23rd St., South Beach (© **786/295-9540**); and Rumi, 330 Lincoln Rd., South Beach (© **305/672-4353**).

LATIN CLUBS   Casa Panza, 1620 SW 8th St. (Calle Ocho), Miami (© **305/643-5343**), is one of Little Havana's most happening nightspots. Make sure to catch the flamenco show here on Tuesday, Thursday, and Saturday nights.

If you want to dance to a funky, loud Brazilian beat till you drop, check out **Mango's,** 900 Ocean Dr., South Beach (© **305/673-4422**), which features nightly live Brazilian and other Latin music on a little patio bar. One of the most popular spots on Ocean Drive, this outdoor enclave of Latin liveliness shakes with the intensity of a Richter-busting earthquake. The hottest Latin joint in the city is **La Covacha,** 10730 NW 25th St. (at NW 107th Ave.), West Miami (© **305/594-3717**). It's a hut in the middle of nowhere, but this shack really jumps on weekend nights when the place is open until 5am.

THE BAR SCENE   On the beach, you'd do best to walk along Ocean Drive and Washington Avenue to see what's hot. In Coconut Grove, check out CocoWalk and Mayfair next door.

The Clevelander, 1020 Ocean Dr., South Beach (© **305/531-3485**), is an old standby that's always crowded. It attracts a lively, sporty, adults-only crowd who have no interest in being part of a scene, but are interested in the very revealing scenery. **The Delano,** 1685 Collins Ave., South Beach (© **305/672-2000**), is for amazing people-watching. In the lobby is the Rose Bar, one of the best spots in South Beach to see beautiful people decked out in trendy splendor. Lounge on a cushy sofa or in any of the plump beds casually arranged throughout the lobby and backyard, and grab an expensive drink.

The spirit of Frank Sinatra is alive and well at **Fox's Sherron Inn,** 6030 S. Dixie Hwy. (at 62nd Ave.), South Miami. © **305/661-9201**), a retro-fabulous dive bar. Cheap drinks, couples cozily huddling in booths, and a seasoned staff of bartenders and barflies make it the perfect anti-trendiness retreat. **Lola,** 247 23rd St., South Beach (© **305/695-8697**), located away from the South Beach mayhem, is a swank, sultry lounge where people are encouraged to come as they are, leaving the attitude at home. The upstairs deck at **Wet Willies,** 760 Ocean Dr., South Beach (© **305/532-5650**), is a prime spot for watching the hectic parade that defines South Beach craziness. Just watch out for the drinks; they taste like soda pop but bite like a mad dog.

THE GAY & LESBIAN SCENE   The gay scene in Miami is outrageous, especially on South Beach. Still, most of the gay clubs welcome hetero visitors, too.

And many of the normally "straight" clubs also have gay nights. Miami Beach is one of the major stops for circuit parties around the United States.

1771, 1771 West Ave., South Beach (© **305/673-6508**), is spacious but always filled to capacity with shirtless, sweaty circuit boys dancing themselves into oblivion. Major DJs spin here, and, at times, divas sing here, such as Bette Midler, who did a rare and ribald cabaret performance to an SRO audience. It's open only on Saturday nights. **Score,** 727 Lincoln Rd., South Beach (© **305/ 535-1111**), is a huge pick-up scene and offers a multitude of bars, dance floors, loungelike areas, and outdoor tables in case you need to come up for air. One of the most popular cruise bars on South Beach is **Twist,** 1057 Washington Ave. (© **305/53-TWIST**). South Florida's only 100% gay after-hours bar, **Pump,** 841 Washington Ave. (© **305/538-PUMP**), doesn't even open on weekends until 4am. The resident DJs spin techno music and keep the place packed to the pecs.

5 Everglades National Park

This vast and unusual ecosystem is actually a shallow, 40-mile-wide, slow-moving river. Rarely more than knee-deep, the water is the lifeblood of this wilderness, one of the few places where you can see dozens of endangered species in their natural habitat, including the swallowtail butterfly, American crocodile, leatherback turtle, southern bald eagle, West Indian manatee, and Florida panther. More than 350 species of birds make their homes in the Everglades. Tropical birds from the Caribbean and temperate species from North America can be found here, along with exotics that have blown in from more distant regions. The slow and subtle splendor of this exotic land may not be immediately appealing to kids, but they'll certainly remember the experience and no doubt thank you for it later. Meanwhile, you'll find plenty of dramatic fun around the park, like airboat rides, alligator wrestling, and biking, to keep the kids satisfied for at least a day.

Although the Everglades may seem overwhelmingly large and unapproachable, it's easy to get to the park's two main areas—the northern section, which is accessible via Shark Valley and Everglades City, or the southern section, accessible through the Ernest F. Coe Visitor Center, near Homestead and Florida City.

Shark Valley, a 13-mile paved road ending at an observation tower overlooking the pulsating heart of the Everglades, is the easiest and most scenic way to explore the Everglades. Shark Valley is best reached via the Tamiami Trail, South Florida's pre-Turnpike, two-lane road, which cuts across the southern part of the state along the park's northern border. Shark Valley is about an hour's drive from Miami. If you pick up State Road 29 and head south from the Tamiami Trail, you'll hit a modified version of civilization in the form of Everglades City (where the Everglades meets the Gulf of Mexico) and see another entrance to the park and the **Gulf Coast Visitor Center.** From Miami to Shark Valley: Go west on I-395 to State Road 821 south (the Florida Tpk.). Take the U.S. 41/SW 8th Street (Tamiami Trail) exit. The Shark Valley entrance is just 25 miles west. To get to Everglades City, continue west on the Tamiami Trail and head south on State Road 29.

If you're in a rush to hit the 'glades and don't care about the scenic route, the southern route is your best bet. Just southeast of Homestead and Florida City, off State Road 9336, the southern access to the park will bring you directly to the **Ernest F. Coe Visitor Center.** From Miami to the southern entrance: Go west on I-395 to State Road 821 south (Florida Tpk.). The Turnpike will end in Florida City. Take your first right turn through the center of town (you can't miss it) and follow the signs to the park entrance on State Road 9336. The Ernest F. Coe Visitor Center is about 1½ hours from Miami.

The **Royal Palm Visitor Center,** a small nature museum located 3 miles past the park's main entrance, is a smaller information center. The museum is not great (there are displays with recorded messages interpreting the park's ecosystem), but the center is the departure point for the popular Anhinga and Gumbo–Limbo trails (see below). Open daily from 8am to 4pm.

The **Flamingo Lodge, Marina and Outpost Resort,** 1 Flamingo Lodge Hwy., Flamingo (© **800/600-3813** or 941/695-3101; www.flamingolodge. com), is the one-stop clearinghouse—and the only option—for in-park accommodations, equipment rentals, and tours. Most people come on a day trip from Miami, but if you want to stay overnight, this is the number to call.

General inquiries and specific questions should be directed to **Everglades National Park Headquarters,** 40001 S.R. 9336, Homestead, FL 33034 (© **305/242-7700**). Ask for a copy of *Parks and Preserves,* a free newspaper filled with up-to-date information about goings-on in the Everglades. Headquarters is staffed by helpful phone operators daily from 8:30am to 4:30pm. You can also try **www.nps.gov/ever/visit/index.htm** or **www.florida-everglades.com**.

Permits and passes can be purchased at the main park entrance, the Chekika entrance, or the Shark Valley entrance stations only. Even if you are just visiting the park for an afternoon, you'll need to buy a 7-day permit, which costs $10 per vehicle. Pedestrians and cyclists are charged $5 each and $4 at Shark Valley.

There are two distinct seasons in the Everglades: high season and mosquito season. High season is also dry season and lasts from late November to May. Despite the bizarre cold and wet weather patterns that El Niño brought in 1998, most winters here are warm, sunny, and breezy—a good combination for keeping the bugs away. This is the best time to visit because low water levels attract the largest variety of wading birds and their predators. As the dry season wanes, wildlife follows the receding water; and by the end of May, the only living things you are sure to spot will cause you to itch. The worst, called "no-see-ums," are not even swattable. If you choose to visit during the buggy season, be vigilant in applying bug spray. Also, realize that many establishments and operators either close or curtail offerings in the summer, so always call ahead to check schedules.

SEEING THE HIGHLIGHTS

Shark Valley offers a fine introduction to the wonder of the Everglades, but don't plan on spending more than a few hours here. Bicycling or taking a guided tram tour can be a satisfying experience, but neither fully captures the wonders of the park.

Stop first along the **Anhinga and Gumbo–Limbo trails,** which start right next to one another, 3 miles from the park's main entrance. These trails provide a thorough introduction to Everglades flora and fauna and are highly recommended to first-time visitors. Alligators, turtles, river otters, herons, egrets, and other animals abound, making it one of the best trails for seeing wildlife. Take your time—at least an hour is recommended. If you treat the trails and modern boardwalk as pathways to get through quickly, rather than destinations to experience and savor slowly, you'll miss out on the still beauty and hidden treasures that await.

Also, it's worth climbing the observation tower at the end of the quarter-mile-long **Pa-hay-okee Trail**. The panoramic view of undulating grass and seemingly endless vistas gives the impression of a semiaquatic Serengeti. Flocks of tropical and semitropical birds traverse the landscape, alligators and fish stir the surface of the water, and small grottoes of trees thrust up from the sea of grass marking higher ground.

If you want to get closer to nature, a few hours in a **canoe** along any of the trails allows paddlers the chance to sense the park's fluid motion. Visitors who choose this option end up feeling more like explorers than merely observers. From a canoe, you'll get a closer look into the park's shallow estuaries where water birds, sea turtles, and endangered manatees make their homes. Everglades National Park's longest "trails" are designed for boat and canoe travel, and many are marked as clearly as walking trails. Park rangers can recommend trails that best suit your abilities, time limitations, and interests. You can rent a canoe at the Flamingo Lodge, Marina and Outpost Resort; the concessionaire will shuttle your party to the trail head of your choice and pick you up afterward.

Shark Valley offers South Florida's most scenic **bicycle trail.** You can ride the 17-mile loop with no other traffic in sight. Instead, you'll share the flat paved road only with other bikers and a menagerie of wildlife. Don't be surprised to see a 'gator lounging in the sun or a deer munching on some grass. Otters, turtles, alligators, and snakes are common companions in the Shark Valley area. You can rent bikes at the Flamingo Lodge, Marina and Outpost Resort or at **Shark Valley Tram Tours,** at the park's Shark Valley entrance (© **305/221-8455**).

6 The Keys & Key West

The islands of the Keys are strung out across the southern waters of Florida like cultured pearls, and each of the more than 400 islands that make up this 150-mile chain has a distinctive character. Some are crammed with strip malls and tacky shell shops, but most are filled with unusual species of tropical plants, birds, and reptiles. All are surrounded by calm blue waters, populated by stunning sea life, and graced by year-round warmth. This vibrant underwater habitat thrives on one of only two living tropical reefs in the entire North American continent (the other is off the coast of Belize). As a result, anglers, divers, snorkelers, and watersports enthusiasts of all kinds come to explore. The heavy traffic has taken its toll on this fragile ecoscape, but efforts are underway to protect it.

THE UPPER & MIDDLE KEYS: KEY LARGO TO MARATHON

This is the fishing and diving capital of America, and the swarms of outfitters and billboards never let you forget it. From Miami International Airport, take Le Jeune Road (NW 42nd Ave.) to Route 836 west. Follow signs to the Florida Turnpike south (about 7 miles). The turnpike extension connects with U.S. 1 in Florida City. Continue south on U.S. 1.

Make sure you get your information from official, not-for-profit centers. The **Key Largo Chamber of Commerce,** U.S. 1 at MM 106, Key Largo, FL 33037 (© **800/822-1088** or 305/451-1414; fax 305/451-4726; www.keylargo.org), runs an excellent facility, with free direct-dial phones and plenty of brochures. Headquartered in a handsome clapboard house, the chamber operates as an information clearinghouse for all of the Keys and is open daily from 9am to 6pm.

Key Largo is the largest Key and is more developed than its neighbors to the south. Dozens of chain hotels, restaurants, and tourist information centers service the many water enthusiasts who come to explore the nation's first underwater state park, **John Pennekamp Coral Reef State Park,** on U.S. 1 at MM 102.5 (© 305/451-1202). It's a sanctuary for part of the only living coral reef in the continental United States. Because the water is extremely shallow, the 40 species of corals and more than 650 species of fish here are particularly accessible to divers, snorkelers, and glass-bottomed-boat passengers. Your first stop should be the visitor center, which is full of educational fish tanks and a mammoth 30,000-gallon saltwater aquarium that re-creates a reef ecosystem. At the adjacent dive shop, you can rent snorkeling and diving equipment and join one of the boat trips that depart for the reef throughout the day. Visitors can also rent motorboats, sailboats, windsurfers, and canoes. The 2-hour glass-bottomed-boat tour ($18 for adults and $10 for children 11 and under) is the best way to see the coral reefs if you refuse to get wet. Park admission is $2.50 per vehicle for one occupant; for two or more, it is $4 per vehicle, plus 50¢ per passenger; $1.50 per pedestrian or bicyclist.

The **Florida Keys Dive Center,** on U.S. 1 at MM 90.5, Tavernier (© 305/852-4599), takes snorkelers and divers to the reefs of John Pennekamp Coral Reef State Park and environs every day. PADI (Professional Association of Diving Instructors) training courses are also available for the uninitiated. Tours leave at 8am and 12:30pm and cost $25 per person to snorkel (plus $8 rental fee for mask, snorkel, and fins) and $59 per person to dive (plus an extra $20 if you need to rent all the gear).

Islamorada, the unofficial capital of the Upper Keys, offers the area's best atmosphere, food, fishing, entertainment, and lodging. In these "purple isles," nature-lovers can enjoy nature trails, historic explorations, and big-purse fishing tournaments. At **Robbie's Pier,** U.S. 1 at MM 77.5, Islamorada (© 305/664-9814), the fierce steely tarpons have been gathering for the past 20 years. You may recognize these prehistoric-looking giants that grow up to 200 pounds; many are displayed as trophies and mounted on local restaurant walls. At Robbie's Pier, tens and sometimes hundreds of these behemoths circle the shallow waters waiting for you to feed them a bucket of fish. **Robbie's Partyboats & Charters,** on U.S. 1 at MM 84.5, Islamorada (© 305/664-8070 or 305/664-4196), located at the south end of the Holiday Isle Docks, offers day and night deep-sea and reef-fishing trips aboard a 65-foot party boat. Big-game fishing charters are also available, and "splits" are arranged for solo fishers. Phone for information and reservations. No trip is complete without a stop at the **Tiki Bar at the Holiday Isle Resort,** U.S. 1 at MM 84, Islamorada (© 305/664-2321). It claims to have invented the rum runner drink and we have no reason to doubt that. Hundreds of revelers visit this oceanside spot for drinks and dancing any time of day, but the live rock music starts at 8:30pm.

Marathon, smack in the middle of the chain of islands, is one of the most populated Keys. It is part fishing village, part tourist center, and part nature preserve. This area's highly developed infrastructure includes resort hotels, a commercial airport, and a highway that expands to four lanes. Thankfully, high-rises have yet to arrive. The best beach in the area is **Sombrero Beach,** in Marathon at the end of Sombrero Beach Road (near MM 50). More than 90 feet of sand is dotted with stands of palms, Australian pines, and royal poincianas. There are some barbecue grills and clean restrooms. A project is currently underway to add tiki huts, a pavilion, and a pier. Admission and parking at this little-known gem are free.

A stop at the **Seven-Mile Bridge,** between MM 40 and 47 on U.S. 1, is a rewarding and relaxing break from the drive south. Built alongside the ruins of oil magnate Henry Flagler's incredible Overseas Railroad, the "new" bridge (between MM 40 and 47) is still considered an architectural feat. The wide arched span, completed in 1982 at a cost of more than $45 million, is impressive, its apex being the highest point in the Keys. The new bridge and especially its now-defunct neighbor provide excellent vantage points from which to view the stunning waters of the Keys.

WHERE TO STAY

U.S. 1 is lined with chain hotels in all price ranges. In the Upper Keys, the best moderately priced option is the **Ramada Limited Resort & Casino** (© 800/ **THE-KEYS** or 305/451-3939) at MM 100, off U.S. 1 in Key Largo, which has three pools and a casino boat and is just 3 miles from John Pennekamp Coral Reef State Park. Another good option in the Upper Keys is **Islamorada Days Inn,** U.S. 1 at MM 82.5 (© **800/DAYS-INN** or 305/664-3681). In the Middle Keys, the **Wellesley Inn** at 13351 Overseas Hwy., MM 54 in Marathon (© **305/743-8550**), also offers reasonably priced oceanside rooms. If you want moderate prices but not a standard chain hotel, try **Conch Key Cottages,** near U.S. 1 at MM 62.3, Marathon (© **800/330-1577** or 305/289-1377; www. conchkeycottages.com); or the **Kona Kai Resort & Gallery,** U.S. 1 at MM 97.8, Key Largo (© **800/365-7829** or 305/852-7200; www.konakairesort. com).

More luxurious choices include the recently renovated **Hawk's Cay Resort,** U.S. 1 at MM 61, Duck Key (© **888/814-9104** or 305/743-7000; www.hawks cay.com), which is located on its own 60-acre island just outside Marathon; it's a sprawling, impressive resort encompassing a marina and a saltwater lagoon that's home to a half-dozen dolphins. **The Moorings,** 123 Beach Rd. near MM 81.5 on the ocean side, Islamorada (© **305/664-4708;** www.themoorings village.com), offers romantic whitewashed houses and a real sense that you've gotten away from it all, especially as you lounge on the 1,000-foot beach (one of the only real beaches around).

THE LOWER KEYS: BIG PINE KEY TO COPPITT KEY

The Lower Keys (farther south on U.S. 1, below the Seven-Mile Bridge) are less developed and more tranquil than the Upper Keys. If you're looking for haute cuisine and happening nightlife, look elsewhere. But if you want to commune with nature or adventure in solitude, you've come to the right place.

The **Big Pine and Lower Keys Chamber of Commerce,** ocean side of U.S. 1 at MM 31 (P.O. Box 430511), Big Pine Key, FL 33043 (© **800/872-3722** or 305/872-2411; fax 305/872-0752; www.lowerkeyschamber.com), is open Monday through Friday from 9am to 5pm and Saturday from 9am to 3pm. Call, write, or stop in for a comprehensive, detailed information packet.

Bahia Honda State Park, U.S. 1 at MM 37.5, Big Pine Key (© **305/872-2353**), has one of the most beautiful coastlines in South Florida. Bahia Honda (pronounced *Bah*-ya) is a great place for hiking, bird-watching, swimming, snorkeling, and fishing. The 524-acre park encompasses a wide variety of ecosystems, including coastal mangroves, beach dunes, and tropical hammocks. There are miles of trails packed with unusual plants and animals and a small white beach. Shaded seaside picnic areas are fitted with tables and grills. Although the beach is never wider than 5 feet even at low tide, this is the Lower Keys' best beach

Under the Sea

Snorkelers and divers should not miss the Keys' most dramatic reefs at the **Looe Key National Marine Sanctuary.** Here you'll see more than 150 varieties of hard and soft coral, some centuries old, as well as every type of tropical fish, including the gold and blue parrotfish, moray eels, barracudas, French angels, and tarpon. **Looe Key Dive Center,** U.S. 1 at MM 27.5, Ramrod Key (© 305/872-2215), offers a mind-blowing 2½-hour tour aboard a 45-foot catamaran with two shallow 1-hour dives for snorkelers and scuba divers. Snorkelers pay $23, and divers with their own equipment pay $35. Good-quality rentals are available.

area. The park has relatively deep waters close to shore that are perfect for snorkeling and diving, with beautiful vibrant fish and coral. Admission to the park is $4 per vehicle (plus 50¢ per person), $1.50 per pedestrian or bicyclist, free for children 5 and under. If you are alone in a car, you'll pay only $2.50. Open daily from 8am to sunset.

The most famous residents of the Lower Keys are the tiny Key deer. Of the estimated 300 existing in the world, two-thirds live on Big Pine Key's **National Key Deer Refuge.** To get your bearings, stop by the rangers' office at the Winn-Dixie Shopping Plaza near MM 30.5 off U.S. 1. They'll give you an informative brochure and map of the area. It is open Monday through Friday from 8am to 5pm.

A stopping point for migratory birds on the Eastern Flyway, the Lower Keys are populated with many West Indian bird species, especially during spring and fall. The small vegetated islands of the Keys are the only nesting sites in the United States for the great white heron and the white-crowned pigeon. They're also some of the very few breeding places for the reddish egret, the roseate spoonbill, the mangrove cuckoo, and the black-whiskered vireo. Look for them on Bahia Honda and the many uninhabited islands nearby.

The Overseas Highway (U.S. 1) touches on only a few dozen of the many hundreds of islands that make up the Keys. To really see the Lower Keys, rent a kayak or canoe—perfect for these shallow waters. **Reflections Kayak Nature Tours,** operating out of Parmer's Resort, on U.S. 1 at MM 28.5, Little Torch Key (© 305/872-2896), offers fully outfitted backcountry wildlife tours, either on your own or with an expert. The expert, Mike Wedeking, a former U.S. Forest Service guide, keeps up an engaging discussion describing the area's fish, sponges, coral, osprey, hawks, eagles, alligators, raccoons, and deer. The 3-hour tours cost $49 per person and include spring water, fresh fruit, granola bars, and use of binoculars. Bring a towel and sea sandals or sneakers.

WHERE TO STAY

Exclusive **Little Palm Island,** reached by launch at the ocean side of U.S. 1 at MM 28.5, Little Torch Key (© 800/343-8567 or 305/872-2524; www.little palmisland.com), offers pricey and posh thatch-roof bungalows on a private 5-acre island. Many villas have ocean views and private sun decks with rope hammocks. On the other end of the price scale is **Parmer's Resort,** near MM 28.5, Little Torch Key (© 305/872-2157; www.palmersresort.com), offering 41 modest but comfortable cottages. Some are waterfront, many have kitchenettes, and others are just a bedroom. Parmer's, a fixture here for more than 20 years, is well known for its charming hospitality and helpful staff.

KEY WEST

There are two schools of thought on Key West—one is that it has become way too commercial, and the other is that it's still a place where you can go and not worry about being prim, proper, or even well groomed. It's probably a bizarre fusion of both—a fascinating look at small-town America in which people truly live by the (off)beat of their own drum, albeit one with a Gap and Banana Republic thrown in to bring you back to some reality. The locals, or "conchs" (pronounced *conks*), and the developers here have been at odds for years. This once low-key island has been thoroughly commercialized—there's a Hard Rock Cafe smack in the middle of Duval Street, and thousands of cruise-ship passengers descend on Mallory Square each day. It's definitely not the seedy town Hemingway and his cronies once called their own. Or is it?

The heart of town offers party people a good time. Here you'll find good restaurants, fun bars, live music, rickshaw rides, and lots of shopping. Don't bother with a watch or tie—this is the home of the perennial vacation.

ESSENTIALS

GETTING THERE   If you're driving, continue south on U.S. 1. When entering Key West, stay in the far-right lane onto North Roosevelt Boulevard, which becomes Truman Avenue in Old Town. Continue for a few blocks, and you will find yourself on Duval Street, in the heart of the city.

American Eagle, Continental, Delta, and **US Airways Express** land at **Key West International Airport,** South Roosevelt Boulevard (© **305/296-5439**), on the southeastern corner of the island.

VISITOR INFORMATION   The **Florida Keys and Key West Visitors Bureau,** P.O. Box 1147, Key West, FL 33041 (© **800/FLA-KEYS;** www.key west.com), offers a free vacation kit packed with visitor information. The **Key West Visitor Center** is the area's best for information on accommodations, goings-on, and restaurants; the number is © **800/LAST-KEY.** It's open Monday through Friday from 8am to 5:30pm and Saturday and Sunday from 8:30am to 5pm.

GETTING AROUND   With limited parking, narrow streets, and congested traffic, driving in Old Town Key West is more of a pain than a convenience. Unless you're staying in one of the more remote accommodations, consider trading in the car for a bicycle. The island is small and as flat as a board, which makes it easy to negotiate, especially away from the crowded downtown. **The Bike Shop,** 1110 Truman Ave. (© **305/294-1073**), rents mountain bikes for $12 per day ($60 per week), with a $250 security deposit.

SPECIAL EVENTS   The last week of October brings **Fantasy Fest,** Florida's Halloween version of Mardi Gras. Crazy costumes, wild parades, and even wilder revelers gather for an opportunity to do things Mom said not to. Definitely leave the kids at home! Call © **305/296-1817.** Coinciding with Fantasy Fest is the **Goombay Festival,** in which you can sample Caribbean dishes and purchase art and ethnic clothing.

WHAT TO SEE & DO

The city's whole story is packed into a neat, 90-minute package on the **Conch Tour Train** (© **305/294-5161**), which covers the island and all its rich, raunchy history. Tours depart from both Mallory Square and the Welcome Center, near where U.S. 1 becomes North Roosevelt Boulevard, on the other side of the island. The cost is $18 for adults, $9 for children 4 to 12, and free for children 3 and under. Daily departures are every half hour from 9am to 4:30pm.

The **Old Town Trolley** (© 305/296-6688) is the choice in bad weather or if you are staying at one of the many hotels on its route. Humorous drivers maintain a running commentary as the enclosed tram loops around the island's streets past all the major sights. Trolleys depart from Mallory Square and other points around the island including many area hotels. Tours are $18 for adults, $9 for children 4 to 12, and free for children 3 and under. Departures are daily every half hour (though not always on the half hr.) from 9am to 4:45pm.

Dating from the early 19th century, the **Audubon House & Tropical Gardens,** 205 Whitehead St. (between Greene and Caroline sts.; © 305/294-2116), is a prime example of early Key West architecture. Named after the renowned painter and bird expert, John James Audubon, who was said to have visited the house in 1832, the graceful two-story home is a peaceful retreat from the bustle of Old Town. See rare Audubon prints, gorgeous antiques, historical photos, and lush tropical gardens. Admission is $8.50 for adults, $3.50 for children 6 to 12. Hours are daily from 9:30am to 5pm (last admission at 4:45pm).

Hemingway's particularly handsome stone Spanish Colonial house, now preserved as the **Ernest Hemingway Home and Museum,** 907 Whitehead St. (between Truman Ave. and Olivia St.; © 305/294-1136; www.hemingway home.com), was built in 1851. The author lived here from 1928 until 1940, along with about 50 six-toed cats, whose descendants still roam the premises. It was during those years that the Nobel Prize winner wrote *For Whom the Bell Tolls, A Farewell to Arms,* and *The Snows of Kilimanjaro.* Fans may want to take the optional half-hour tour. It's interesting and included in the price of admission, which is $9 for adults, $5 for children. It's open daily from 9am to 5pm.

Funky, picturesque **Key West Cemetery,** entrance at Margaret and Angela streets, perfectly captures the quintessential Key West attitude. Many tombs are stacked several high, condominium style—the rocky soil made digging 6 feet under nearly impossible for early settlers. "I Told You I Was Sick" is one of the more famous epitaphs, as is the tongue-in-cheek widow's inscription "At Least I Know Where He's Sleeping Tonight."

The **Mel Fisher Maritime Heritage Museum,** 200 Greene St. (© 305/294-2633), honors local hero Mel Fisher, who found a multimillion-dollar treasure trove in 1985 aboard the wreck of the Spanish galleon *Nuestra Señora de Atocha.* The admission price is somewhat steep, but if you're into diving, pirates, and the mystery of sunken treasures, check out this small informative museum, full of

---

Going, Going, Gone . . . Sunset in Key West

A daily tradition in Key West, the Sunset Celebration is the best example of local flavor and the Jimmy Buffett–inspired attitude that prevails throughout the Florida Keys. Every evening, locals and visitors alike gather at the docks behind Mallory Square (at the western end of Whitehead St.) to celebrate the day gone by. Secure a spot on the docks about an hour before sundown for the full effect, complete with portrait artists, acrobats, food vendors, and animal acts. If crowds aren't your thing, grab a seat at the Hilton's **Sunset Deck** (© 305/294-4000), at the intersection of Front and Greene streets. From the calm of the bar, you can relax with a drink and look down on the mayhem.

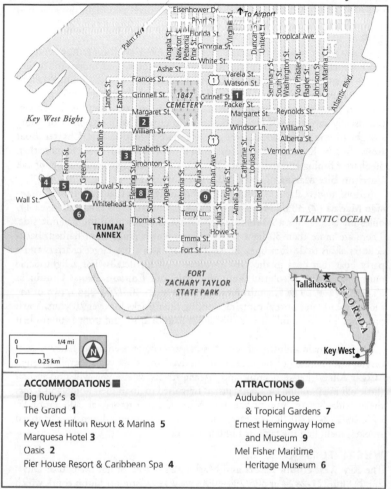

doubloons, pieces of eight, emeralds, and solid-gold bars. Admission is $7.50 for adults; $3.75 for children ages 6 to 12. Open daily from 9:30am to 5pm.

Unlike the rest of the Keys, Key West actually has a few small beaches, although they don't compare to the state's wide natural wonders up the coast. Here are your options: **Smathers Beach,** off South Roosevelt Boulevard west of the airport; **Higgs Beach,** along Atlantic Boulevard between White Street and Reynolds Road; and **Fort Zachary Beach,** off the western end of Southard Boulevard. Although there is an entrance fee ($3.75 per car, plus more for each passenger), we recommend Fort Zachary, since it includes a great historical fort, a Civil War museum, shade trees, and a large picnic area with tables, barbecue grills, restrooms, and showers.

One of the area's largest scuba schools, **Dive Key West Inc.,** 3128 N. Roosevelt Blvd. (© **800/426-0707** or 305/296-3823; fax 305/296-0609; www.dive keywest.com), offers instruction on all levels and its dive boats take participants to scuba and snorkel sites on nearby reefs. Wreck dives and night dives are two of the special offerings of **Lost Reef Adventures,** 261 Margaret St. (℗ **800/952-2749** or 305/296-9737).

As any angler will tell you, there's no fishing like Keys fishing. Key West has it all: bonefish, tarpon, dolphin, tuna, grouper, cobia, and more. You'll find plenty of competition among the charter fishing boats in and around Mallory Square. However, you should know that the bookers from the kiosks in town generally take 20% of a captain's fee in addition to an extra monthly fee. So you can usually save yourself money by booking directly with a captain or going straight to one of the docks. You can negotiate a good deal at **Charter Boat Row,** 1801 N. Roosevelt Ave. (across from the Shell station), home to more than 30 charter fishing and party boats. Just show up to arrange your outing, or call **Garrison Bite Marina** (℗ 305/292-8167) for details.

Serious anglers should consider the light-tackle boats that leave from **Ocean-side Marina** (℗ **305/294-4676**) on Stock Island, at 5950 Peninsula Ave., 1½ miles off U.S. 1. It's a 20-minute drive from Old Town on the Atlantic side. There are more than 30 light-tackle guides, which range from flatbed, back-country skiffs to 28-foot open boats. There are also a few larger charters and a party boat that goes to the Dry Tortugas. Call for details. For a light-tackle outing with a very colorful Key West flair, call **Captain Bruce Cronin** at ℗ **305/294-4929** or **Captain Kenny Harris** at ℗ **305/294-8843,** two of the more famous (and pricey) captains working these docks for over 20 years. You'll pay from $550 for a full day, usually about 8am to 4pm, and from $400 for half a day.

Once the main industry of Key West, cigar making is enjoying renewed success at the handful of factories that survived the slow years. Stroll through **"Cigar Alley,"** between Front and Greene streets, where you will find *viejitos* (little old men) rolling fat stogies just as they used to do in their homeland across the Florida Straits. Stop at the **Key West Cigar Factory,** at 308 Front St. (℗ **305/294-3470**), for an excellent selection of imported and locally rolled smokes, including the famous El Hemingway.

WHERE TO STAY

The **Key West Hilton Resort and Marina,** 245 Front St. (at the end of Duval St.; ℗ **800/221-2424** or 305/294-4000; www.keywestresort.hilton.com), which was lightly renovated in 2001, is Key West's only full-service resort, and it's situated in the middle of all of Old Town's action. The sparkling rooms are large and well appointed, and there's a full-service marina. Another upscale resort is the **Pier House Resort and Caribbean Spa,** 1 Duval St. (near Mallory Docks; ℗ **800/327-8340** or 305/296-4600; www.pierhouse.com), offering luxurious rooms, top-notch service, and even a full-service spa. Its excellent location—at the foot of Duval Street and just steps from Mallory Docks—is the envy of every hotel on the island. Set back from the busy street, on a short strip of beach, this hotel is a welcome oasis of calm.

One of our absolute favorites, the **Marquesa Hotel,** 600 Fleming St. (at Simonton St.; ℗ **800/869-4631** or 305/292-1919; www.marquesa.com), offers all the charm of a small historic hotel with the amenities of a large resort. It encompasses four different buildings, two adjacent swimming pools, and a three-stage waterfall that cascades into a lily pond. Rooms have stunning, plush decor. **The Grand,** 1116 Grinnell St. (between Virginia and Catherine sts.; ℗ **888/947-2630** or 305/294-0590), is an exceptionally run guesthouse with almost anything you could want, including a very moderate price tag. It's a well-kept secret and the best bargain in town.

If you're having trouble finding a room, contact **Vacation Key West** (© 800/ 595-5397 or 305/295-9500; www.vacationkw.com), a wholesaler that offers discounts of 20% to 30% and is skilled at finding last-minute deals. It represents mostly larger hotels and motels. The phones are answered weekdays from 9am to 6pm and Saturday from 11am to 2pm.

Gay travelers will want to call the **Key West Business Guild** (© 305/294- 4603), which represents more than 50 guesthouses and B&Bs in town, as well as many other gay-owned businesses. Be advised that most gay guesthouses have a clothing-optional policy. One of the most elegant and popular ones is **Big Ruby's** (© 800/477-7829 or 305/296-2323; rates start at $145 for a double during peak season and $85 during off season) at 409 Applerouth Lane (a little alley just off Duval St.). A low cluster of buildings surrounds a lushly landscaped courtyard where a hearty breakfast is served each morning and wine is poured at dusk. The mostly male guests hang out by a good-sized pool, tanning in the buff. Also popular is **Oasis** at 823 Fleming St. (© 305/296-2131; rates are $169–$229 in winter and $109–$169 in summer), which is super-clean and friendly, with a central location and a 14-seat hot tub.

KEY WEST AFTER DARK

Duval Street is the Bourbon Street of Florida. Amid the T-shirt shops and clothing boutiques, you'll find bar after bar serving neon-colored frozen drinks to revelers who bounce from one to the next from noon till dawn. Your best bet is to start at Truman Avenue and head up Duval to check them out for yourself. Cover charges are rare except in gay clubs, so stop into a dozen and see which you like.

Just around the corner from Duval's beaten path, **Captain Tony's Saloon,** 428 Greene St. (© 305/294-1838), is a smoky old wooden bar, about as authentic as you'll find. **Durty Harry's,** 208 Duval St. (© 305/296-4890), is a large entertainment complex that features live rock bands almost every night.

Epoch, 623 Duval St. (© 305/296-8521), with seven bars, a giant dance floor, a huge outside deck overlooking Duval Street, and a new state-of-the-art sound system, welcomes partiers of any sexual orientation. **Jimmy Buffett's Margaritaville Cafe,** 500 Duval St. (© 305/292-1435), named after another Key West legend, is a worthwhile stop. This kitschy restaurant/bar/gift shop features live bands every night—from rock to blues to reggae and everything in between. It's touristy, but fun. You'll have to stop into **Sloppy Joe's,** 201 Duval St. (© 305/294-5717), just to say you did. Scholars and drunks debate whether this is the same Sloppy Joe's that Hemingway wrote about, but there's no argument that this classic bar's turn-of-the-20th-century wooden ceiling and cracked tile floors are Key West originals. There's live music most days and nights.

The best music and dancing can be found at the predominantly gay clubs. None of the spots mentioned here discriminate—anyone open-minded and fun is welcome. Cover varies, but is rarely more than $10. Two adjacent popular late-night spots are the **801 Bourbon Bar/One Saloon** (801 Duval St. and 514 Petronia St.; © 305/294-9349 for both), featuring great drag and lots more disco. A mostly male clientele frequents this hot spot from 9pm until 4am. Another Duval Street favorite is **Diva's,** at 711 Duval St. (© 305/292-8500), where you might catch drag queens belting out torch songs or judges voting on the best package in the wet jockey shorts contest. Better known around town as La-Te-Da, **La Terraza de Martí,** the former Key West home of Cuban exile José

Martí, at 1125 Duval St. (© **305/296-6706**), is a great spot to gather poolside for the best martini in town—but don't bother with the food.

7 Highlights of Southwest Florida

Thanks to a citizenry intent on protecting the environment, Southwest Florida is one of the best parts of the state to enjoy the great outdoors. Bordered on the east by the wild, wonderful Everglades and on the west by an intriguing, island-studded coast, the region traces its nature-loving roots to inventor and amateur botanist Thomas A. Edison, who was so enamored of it that he spent his last 46 winters here. Some of the planet's best shelling and tarpon fishing have lured many other rich and famous folk. The unspoiled beauty of Sanibel and Captiva so entranced Pulitzer Prize–winning political cartoonist J. N. "Ding" Darling that he campaigned to preserve much of those islands in their natural states. And the millionaires who built Naples enacted tough zoning laws that to this day make their town one of the most alluring in Florida.

ESSENTIALS

GETTING THERE   By Plane   Most major airlines fly into Fort Myers's **Southwest Florida International Airport,** on Daniels Parkway east of I-75 (no phone; www.swfia.com). From here it's only 20 miles to Sanibel Island, 35 miles to Naples. A car is the best way to get around; major car-rental agencies have booths at the airport. Vans and taxis run from the airport to major hotels throughout the region.

American Eagle and US Airways Express fly commuter planes into **Naples Municipal Airport,** on North Road off Airport-Pulling Road (© **941/643-6875;** www.flynaples.com).

By Car   The major route into southwest Florida is I-75 from the north (Tampa) and east (Miami).

VISITOR INFORMATION   For advance information about Fort Myers, Fort Myers Beach, and Sanibel and Captiva islands, contact the **Lee Island Coast Visitor and Convention Bureau,** 2180 W. 1st St., Ste. 100, Fort Myers, FL 33901 (© **800/237-6444** or 239/338-3500; fax 239/334-1106; www.lee islandcoast.com). **The Sanibel–Captiva Islands Chamber of Commerce,** 1159 Causeway Rd., Sanibel Island, FL 33957 (© **239/472-1080;** fax 239/472-1070; www.sanibel-captiva.org), is open Monday through Saturday from 9am to 7pm, Sunday from 10am to 5pm. The **Naples Area Chamber of Commerce** maintains a visitor center at 895 5th Ave. S. (at U.S. 41), Naples, FL 34102 (© **239/262-6141;** fax 239/435-9910; www.napleschamber.org). It's open Monday through Saturday from 9am to 5pm.

SANIBEL & CAPTIVA ISLANDS

Sanibel and Captiva are unique in Florida. Here you will find none of the neon signs, amusement parks, and high-rise condos that clutter most beach resorts in the state. Indeed, Sanibel's main drag, Periwinkle Way, runs under a canopy of whispery pines and gnarled oaks so thick they almost obscure the small signs for chic shops and restaurants. This wooded ambience is the work of local voters, who have saved their trees and tropical foliage, limited the size and appearance of signs, and permit no building higher than the tallest palm and no WaveRun-ner or other noisy beach toy within 300 yards of their gorgeous, shell-strewn beaches.

Southwest Florida

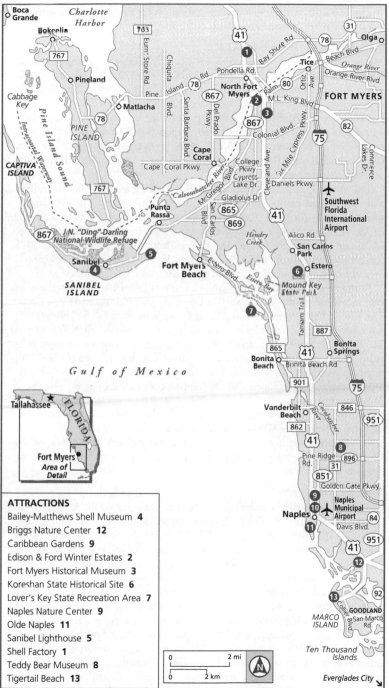

ATTRACTIONS

The islands have no public transportation, but a paved bike trail runs the length of Sanibel. Several firms rent bicycles and in-line skates.

FUN ON & OFF THE BEACH

About half of Sanibel is preserved in the **J. N. (Ding) Darling National Wildlife Refuge,** on Sanibel-Captiva Road (© 941/472-1100), home to alligators, raccoons, otters, and hundreds of species of birds. These 6,000-plus acres of mangrove swamps, winding waterways, and uplands have a 2-mile trail and a 5-mile, one-way **Wildlife Drive.** You'll get a lot more from your visit by taking a naturalist-narrated tram tour given by **Tarpon Bay Recreation,** at the north end of Tarpon Bay Road (© 239/472-8900; www.tarponbay.com). The tours last 2 hours and cost $10 for adults, $5 for children 12 and under. Schedules are seasonal, so call ahead.

The islands are equally as famous for their **shelling beaches.** Local residents and visitors alike can be seen in the "Sanibel stoop" or the "Captiva crouch" while searching for some 200 species of seashells from as far away as South Africa. February through April, or after any storm, are the best times to stoop. Make sure to visit the impressive **Bailey-Matthews Shell Museum,** 3075 Sanibel-Captiva Rd. (© 888/679-6450 or 239/395-2233; www.shellmuseum. org), the only museum in the United States devoted solely to shells.

With so many people scouring Sanibel, you may have better luck on the adjacent shoals and nearby islands, such as Upper (North) Captiva and Cayo Costa. The latter is home to the stunning **Cayo Costa State Park** (© 941/964-0375; www.floridastateparks.org/district4/cayocosta), a completely unspoiled barrier island with miles of white-sand beaches, pine forests, mangrove swamps, oak-palm hammocks, and grasslands. **Captiva Cruises** (© 941/472-5300; www.captivacruises.com) offers daily shelling trips and cruises to Cayo Costa. At least 15 charter-boat skippers also offer to take guests on shelling expeditions to these less-explored areas.

Another sight worth seeing back on Sanibel is the **Sanibel Lighthouse,** at the east end of Periwinkle Way, which has marked the entrance to San Carlos Bay since 1884. The lightkeepers used to live in the cottages at the base of the 94-foot tower. The now-automatic lighthouse isn't open to visitors, but the grounds and beach are.

WHERE TO STAY

Sanibel & Captiva Central Reservations, Inc. (© 800/325-1352 or 239/472-0457; fax 239/472-2178; www.sanibel-captivarent.com) and **1-800-SANIBEL** (© 800/726-4235 or 239/472-1800; fax 239/395-9690; www. 1-800-sanibel.com) are reservations services that will book you into most condominiums and cottages here. The islands also have several Old Florida–style cottages that offer charming and often less expensive alternatives to hotels and condominiums. Some of the best are members of the **Sanibel-Captiva Small Inns & Cottages Association.** You can contact the association (via its website only) at www.sanibelsmallinns.com for a complete listing of properties.

For a deluxe experience, head for Captiva's sprawling **South Seas Resort** (© 800/CAPTIVA or 239/472-5111; www.south-seas-resort.com), which offers golf, tennis, boating, and accommodations ranging from hotel rooms to luxurious private homes. Also on Captiva, you can still rent one of the old-Florida cottages where cartoonist J. N. "Ding" Darling and novelist Anne Morrow Lindbergh stayed at the **'Tween Waters Inn** (© 800/223-5865 or 941/472-5161; www.tween-waters.com). Bed-and-breakfast fans head to

Captiva Island Inn Bed & Breakfast (© 800/454-9898 or 941/395-0882; www.captivaislandinn.com), virtually surrounded by restaurants, art galleries, and boutiques along Andy Rosse Lane, Captiva's 1-block-long commercial street.

Sundial Beach Resort, 1451 Middle Gulf Dr. (© 800/237-4184 or 239/481-3636; www.sundialresort.com), is Sanibel's largest property, with 270 condo apartments, several dining options, and complete resort facilities. The condo-only **Casa Ybel Resort,** 2255 W. Gulf Dr. (© 800/276-4753 or 239/472-3145; www.casaybelresort.com), offers spacious one- and two-bedroom condominiums—all have screened porches facing the gulf. Also on Sanibel, two "reformed journalists" own **Brennen's Tarpon Tale Inn,** 367 Periwinkle Way (© 941/472-0939; www.tarpontale.com), a comfortable and moderately priced bed-and-breakfast near the island's eastern end.

WHAT TO SEE & DO IN FORT MYERS

The Victorian **Edison and Ford Winter Estates,** 2350 McGregor Blvd. (© 941/334-3614 for a recording, or 941/334-7419; www.edison-ford-estate.com), are furnished as they appeared in the 1920s. Costumed actors give "living history" accounts of how the wealthy lived in those days. A museum displays some of Edison's inventions, as well as his unique Model T, a gift from Ford. You must visit the homes via guided tours, which depart the visitor center every few minutes. A replica of Edison's electric boat *Reliance* takes guests on 30-minute scenic rides on the river on weekdays.

After visiting the homes, you can stop at the Georgian Revival **Burroughs Home,** 2505 1st St. (© 941/332-6125; www.cityftmyers.com/Attractions/burroughs.htm), which was built on the banks of the Caloosahatchee River in 1901. Nearby, the **Fort Myers Historical Museum,** 2300 Peck St. (© 941/332-5955; www.cityftmyers.com/attractions/historical.htm), features exhibits depicting the town's history from the ancient Calusa Indians to the present. About 15 miles south of downtown on U.S. 41, the **Koreshan State Historic Site** (© 941/992-0311; www.floridastateparks.org/district4/koreshan) is the site of an 1894 settlement of the Koreshan Unity Movement, a sect which believed that humans lived *inside* the earth. On U.S. 41 north of town, the kitschy **Shell Factory** (© 888/4-SHELLS or 941/995-2141; www.shell factory.com) carries one of the world's largest collections of shells, corals, sponges, and fossils.

Nature abounds in **Lover's Key State Recreation Area,** 8700 Estero Blvd. (© 239/463-4588; www.floridastateparks.org/district4/loverskey), where a tractor-pulled tram runs through a mangrove forest to one of Florida's best beaches. Lover's Key is just across the bridge from Fort Myers Beach.

NAPLES

Because its wealthy residents are accustomed to the very best, Naples is easily Southwest Florida's most sophisticated city. Indeed, its boutiques and galleries are at least on a par with those in Palm Beach or Beverly Hills. And yet Naples has an easygoing friendliness to everyone who comes to enjoy its long, magnificent beach. And you can find some surprisingly affordable places to stay within easy reach of the long, magnificent beach skirting **Olde Naples,** the town's historic district.

You can get around Olde Naples on foot or bicycle, or hop on and off the **Naples Trolley** (© 239/262-7300; www.naplestrolleytours.com); daily fares are

$16 for adults, $7 for children 5 to 12, free for children under 5, with free reboarding.

EXPLORING THE TOWN

Laid out on a grid, Olde Naples's tree-lined streets run between many century-old houses and along **Millionaires' Row,** literally a row of mansions virtually hidden in palms and casuarinas along the beach. The **Naples Pier,** at the gulf end of 12th Avenue South, is a focal point of the neighborhood. Local residents like strolling its length to catch both fish and fantastic gulf sunsets.

Near the Gordon River Bridge on Fifth Avenue South, the town's old corrugated waterfront warehouses are now a shopping-and-dining complex known as the **Marketplace at Tin City,** to which tourists throng—and which local residents assiduously avoid—during the busy winter season. But everyone hangs out on ritzy **Third Street South** and the only slightly less chic **Fifth Avenue South,** Olde Naples's shopping-and-dining venues.

Kids and adults both will enjoy the entertaining **Teddy Bear Museum,** 2511 Pine Ridge Rd. (© **800/365-2327** or 239/598-2711; www.teddymuseum.com), which cleverly displays 3,000-plus examples of stuffed teddy bears from around the world. The entire family also will enjoy **Caribbean Gardens,** 1590 Goodlette-Frank Rd. (© **239/262-5409;** www.caribbeangardens.com), an environmentally conscious zoo where a fascinating community of primates live free on their own island.

Naples abounds in parks and nature preserves. **The Conservancy's Naples Nature Center,** 14th Avenue North (© **239/262-0304;** www.conservancy.org), has nature trails, an aviary with bald eagles and other birds, guided boat rides, and canoe and kayak rentals.

FUN ON & OFF THE BEACH

In town, a free tram runs along a 3,000-foot boardwalk winding through mangrove swamps and across a back bay to a beach of fine white sand in **Clam Pass County Park** (© **239/353-0404**). It's a strange sight, what with high-rise condos standing beyond the mangrove-bordered backwaters of this mini-wilderness. At Vanderbilt Beach, about 4 miles north of Olde Naples, the **Delnor-Wiggins Pass State Recreation Area** (© **239/597-6196;** www.floridastateparks.org/district4/delnor-wiggins) has been listed among America's top 10 stretches of sand.

Cruise and fishing boats have ticket booths at the **Marketplace at Tin City,** on Fifth Avenue South at the Gordon River Bridge.

The area has some of America's best golf courses, including the **Lely Flamingo Island Club** (© **800/388-GOLF** or 239/793-2223), with hourglass fairways and fingerlike bunkers, and **Boyne South** (© **239/732-5108**), with lots of wildlife inhabiting its many lakes. Both are open to the public.

WHERE TO STAY

Naples has an extraordinarily broad range of accommodations. About 4 miles north of Olde Naples, **The Ritz-Carlton Naples,** 280 Vanderbilt Beach Rd. (© **888/856-4372** or 239/598-3300; www.ritzcarlton.com), is one of Florida's most luxurious beach resorts. Its main rival is the more sports-oriented **The Registry Resort,** 475 Seagate Dr. (© **239/597-3232** or 800/247-9810; www.registryhotels.com), bordering Clam Pass County Park (you'll have to ride the tram to reach the beach).

In the historic district, old-Florida charm prevails at the family-operated **Naples Beach Hotel & Golf Club,** 851 Gulf Shore Blvd. (© **800/237-7600** or 239/261-2222; www.naplesbeachotel.com), which has its own golf course, tennis center, full-service spa, and a prime beachside location (don't miss seeing a sunset from the "tiki" bar). Close by is the **Inn by the Sea,** 287 11th Ave. S. (© **941/649-4124**), which is listed on the National Register of Historic Places, and offers bed-and-breakfast accommodations in a home built of "tabby mortar" in 1937.

8 Tampa & St. Petersburg

Sitting on a large estuary midway down Florida's west coast, the city of Tampa boasts Busch Gardens Tampa Bay, one of the state's major theme parks. You can also see the sea life at the Florida Aquarium, stroll through the ornate, Moorish-style Henry B. Plant Museum, and experience exciting dining and nightlife in Ybor City, Tampa's historic Cuban enclave. Across the bay, St. Petersburg has one of the most picturesque and pleasant downtowns of any city in Florida, with a waterfront promenade, a famous pyramid-shaped pier, quality museums, interesting shops, and good restaurants. You'll find plenty of sun and sand on the 28 miles of slim barrier islands that skirt the gulf shore here. St. Pete Beach and Clearwater Beach are typical beach resort towns with towering hotels and condos, but this area also has protected some of the nation's finest beaches from development. From here, you can take a side trip south across the bay to affluent Sarasota, one of Florida's cultural centers.

Tampa, St. Petersburg, and the beaches are about 30- to 45-minute drives apart (longer in rush-hour traffic), so you should carefully plan your time here. Unless you're on business and need quick access to Tampa or downtown St. Petersburg, you may want to stay at the beaches.

ESSENTIALS

GETTING THERE   By Plane   Tampa International Airport (© **813/870-8770;** www.tampaairport.com), 5 miles northwest of downtown Tampa, is serviced by most major airlines. St. Petersburg–Clearwater International Airport, on the western side of the bay, offers limited service. **The Limo/SuperShuttle** (© **800/282-6817** or 727/527-1111; www.supershuttle.com) operates van services between the airport and hotels throughout the Tampa Bay area.

By Train   Amtrak trains arrive downtown at the **Tampa Amtrak Station,** 601 Nebraska Ave. N. (© **800/USA-RAIL;** www.amtrak.com).

By Car   Major routes into Tampa are I-75 from the north (Atlanta) and south (Fort Myers and Miami), and I-4 from the east (Orlando).

VISITOR INFORMATION   Contact the **Tampa Bay Convention and Visitors Bureau,** 400 N. Tampa St., Tampa, FL 33602-4706 (© **800/826-8358** or 813/342-4077; fax 813/229-6616; www.visittampabay.com), for advance information. The bureau's information center is at Ashley and Madison streets downtown (© **813/223-1111**); open Monday through Saturday from 9am to 5pm.

For advance information about both St. Petersburg and the beaches, contact the **St. Petersburg/Clearwater Area Convention & Visitors Bureau,** 14450 46th St. N., Clearwater, FL 34622 (© **800/345-6710,** or 727/464-7200 for advance hotel reservations; www.FloridasBeach.com for information specific to the beaches).

GETTING AROUND   You really need a car here. All major rental agencies have desks at the Tampa airport. If you need a taxi, call **Tampa Bay Cab**

Tampa & St. Petersburg

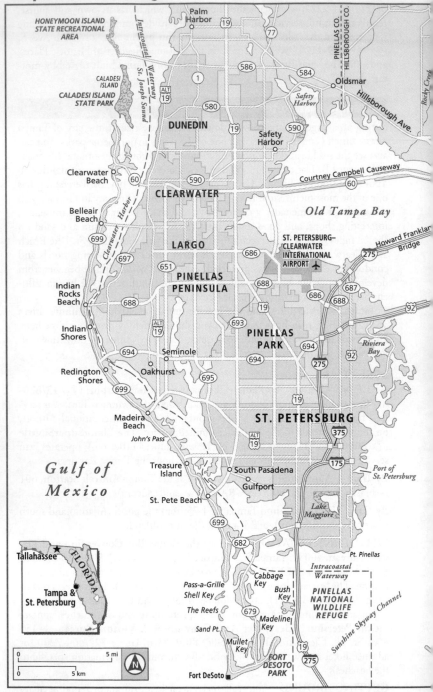

HONEYMOON ISLAND
STATE RECREATIONAL
AREA

CALADESI
ISLAND
CALADESI ISLAND
STATE PARK

Palm Harbor

19

77

586

584

Oldsmar

1

Safety
Harbor

580

DUNEDIN

19

Safety
Harbor

590

Courtney Campbell Causeway

Clearwater
Beach

60

590

CLEARWATER

Old Tampa Bay

Belleair
Beach

ST. PETERSBURG–
CLEARWATER
INTERNATIONAL
AIRPORT

Howard Franklar
Bridge

275

699

LARGO

686

697

651

PINELLAS
PENINSULA

688

686

687

Indian
Rocks
Beach

688

688

92

ALT
19

693

PINELLAS
PARK

Riviera
Bay

Indian
Shores

694

Seminole

694

92

694

275

Redington
Shores

Oakhurst

695

699

19

Madeira
Beach

ST. PETERSBURG

375

John's Pass

ALT
19

175

Gulf of
Mexico

Treasure
Island

South Pasadena

Port of
St. Petersburg

Gulfport

St. Pete Beach

Lake
Maggiore

699

682

Pt. Pinellas

Tallahassee

FLORIDA

Intracoastal
Waterway

Tampa &
St. Petersburg

Pass-a-Grille
Shell Key

Cabbage
Key

Bush
Key

PINELLAS
NATIONAL
WILDLIFE
REFUGE

The Reefs

679

Madeline
Key

Sand Pt.

Mullet
Key

FORT
DESOTO
PARK

19

275

Sunshine Skyway Channel

Fort DeSoto

0   5 mi
0   5 km

N

428

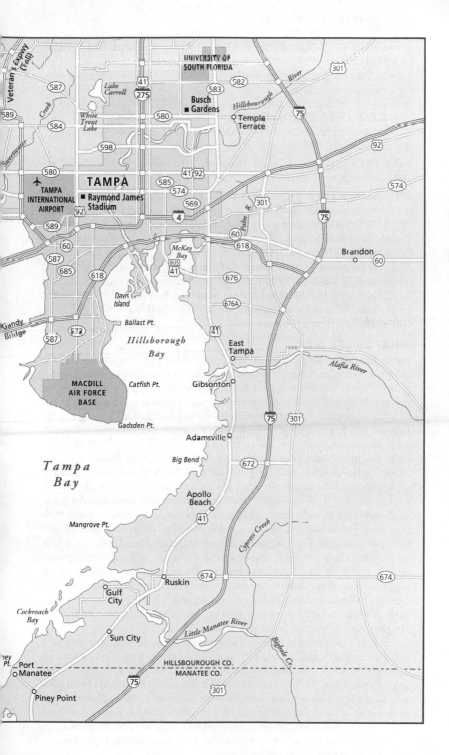

(℗ 813/251-5555), **Yellow Cab** (℗ 813/253-0121), or **United Cab** (℗ 813/253-2424).

In St. Petersburg, the **Downtown Trolley** (℗ 727/571-3440) runs past all of the attractions every 30 minutes from 11am to 5pm daily. Rides cost 50¢. For a cab in St. Petersburg, call **Yellow Cab** (℗ 727/821-7777) or **Independent Cab** (℗ 727/327-3444). **Pierside Rentals,** on The Pier (℗ 727/822-8697), rents bicycles and in-line skates. **BATS Taxi** (℗ 727/367-3702) is the major cab company along St. Pete Beach.

FAST FACTS   Tampa General Hospital, 2 Columbia Dr. (℗ 813/251-7000; www.tgh.org), offers 24-hour emergency service.

SPECIAL EVENTS & FESTIVALS   In early February, hundreds of boats and rowdy "pirates" invade downtown Tampa during the **Gasparilla Pirate Fest** (℗ 813/353-8108; www.gasparillapiratefest.com). In mid-February, the **Florida State Fair** in Tampa displays the best of the state's agriculture and crafts (℗ 800/345-FAIR; www.floridastatefair.com). During the first full week in April, St. Petersburg hosts the **Festival of States,** one of the South's largest civic celebrations (℗ 727/898-3654; festivalofstates@aol.com). On October 31, Ybor City's Latin-style Halloween celebration **Guavaween** begins with the "Mama Guava Stumble," a wacky costume parade (℗ 877/934-3782 or 813/248-3712; www.ybor.org).

WHAT TO SEE & DO

Busch Gardens Tampa Bay   Although its thrill rides (including some of the country's best roller coasters), live entertainment, shops, restaurants, and games get most of the ink, this venerable theme park ranks among the top zoos in the country. An overall African and Egyptian theme prevails in eight areas, all linked by a monorail train. Animals are scattered throughout, but the highlight is the **Edge of Africa,** where some 500 African beasts roam freely on a natural grassy veldt. **Morocco** has alligators and turtles to go along with crafts demonstrations, snake charmers, and an ice-skating show. **Egypt** juxtaposes Anheuser-Busch's fabled Clydesdale horses with King Tut's tomb. In **Nairobi** you'll see gorillas and chimpanzees, a baby animal nursery, a petting zoo, turtle and reptile displays, an elephant exhibit (sadly too small for these magnificent creatures), and a simu-lated environment with nocturnal animals. Re-creating an ancient desert trad-ing center, **Timbuktu** combines performing porpoises, otters, and sea lions with three roller coasters. **The Congo** has rare white Bengal tigers (again, sadly kept on an island that's too small), two more roller coasters, and a drenching water ride. A prototype African village, **Stanleyville** has orangutans living on an island, a show about children, and two more water rides. The park's original core, **Bird Gardens** offers rich foliage, lagoons, and a free-flight aviary for hun-dreds of exotic birds. If the young ones get bored, take them to **Land of the Dragons,** which is aimed exclusively at them.

Since the entertainment changes frequently, arrive early, pick up a park map and daily activity schedule, and plan your day carefully. And don't come if it's raining, since some rides don't operate in inclement weather, and you won't get a rain check. 3000 E. Busch Blvd. (at McKinley Dr./N. 40th St.). ℗ 888/800-5447 or 813/987-5283. www.buschgardens.com. **Note:** Admission and hr. vary so call ahead, check website, or get brochure at visitor centers. Admission at least $50 adults, $41 children 3–9, plus tax; free for chil-dren 2 and under. Annual pass $85 adults, $75 children 3–9, plus tax. Combination season pass with Adventure Island $115. Website sometimes offers discounts. Daily 10am–6pm (extended hr. to 7 and 8pm in summer and on holidays). Parking $7.

The Florida Aquarium   See more than 5,000 aquatic animals and plants that call Florida home at this entertaining and informative aquarium. Most impressive is a 43 foot-wide, 14-foot-tall panoramic window that lets you look out at schools of fish and lots of sharks and stingrays. Also worth visiting are the "Explore a Shore" playground to educate the kids, a deep-water exhibit, and a tank housing moray eels. 701 Channelside Dr. (✆ 813/273-4000. www.flaquarium.net. Admission $15 adults, $12 seniors, $10 children 5–13, free for children under 5. Dolphin Quest $18 adults, $17 seniors, $13 children 5–13, free for children under 5. Combination aquarium admission and Dolphin Quest $30 adults, $26 seniors, $20 children 5–13, free for children under 5. Website sometimes offers discounts. Parking $4. Daily 9:30am–5pm. Dolphin Quest Mon–Fri 2pm, Sat–Sun 1 and 3pm. Closed Thanksgiving, Christmas.

Henry B. Plant Museum   Built as a hotel in 1891 by railroad tycoon Henry B. Plant, this ornate structure with 13 silver minarets and distinctive Moorish architecture is a National Historic Landmark and worth a visit. It's filled with art and furnishings from Europe and Asia; and exhibits that explain the hotel's role as a staging point for Teddy Roosevelt's Rough Riders during the Spanish-American War. 401 W. Kennedy Blvd. (between Hyde Park and Magnolia aves.). (✆ 813/254-1891. www.plantmuseum.com. Admission free; suggested donation $5 adults, $2 children 12 and under Tues–Sat 10am 4pm; Sun noon–4pm. Closed Thanksgiving, Christmas Eve, and Christmas Day. Take Kennedy Blvd. (Fla. 60) across the Hillsborough River.

Museum of Fine Arts   Resembling a Mediterranean villa on the waterfront, this museum houses a permanent collection of European, American, pre-Columbian, and Far Eastern art, with works by such artists as Fragonard, Monet, Renoir, Cézanne, and Gauguin. Other highlights include period rooms with antiques and historical furnishings, plus a gallery of Steuben crystal, a decorative-arts gallery, and world-class rotating exhibits. 255 Beach Dr. NE (at 3rd Ave. N.). (✆ 727/896-2667. www.fine-arts.org. Admission Tues–Sat $6 adults, $5 seniors, $2 students, free for children under 6. Admission free on Sun (donation suggested). Admission includes guided tour. Tues Sat 10am 5pm; Sun 1–5pm. Winter, 3rd Thurs of each month 10am–9pm. Guided tours Tues–Sat 11am, 1, 2, and 3pm; Sun 1 and 2pm. Closed New Year's Day, Martin Luther King, Jr., Day, Thanksgiving, Christmas.

The Pier   The Pier is a festive waterfront dining-and-shopping complex overlooking Tampa Bay. Originally built as a railroad pier in 1889, today it's capped by a spaceshiplike inverted pyramid offering five levels of shops, three restaurants, a tourist information desk, an observation deck, catwalks for fishing, boat docks, miniature golf, boat and water-sports rentals, sightseeing boats, and a food court, plus an aquarium and **Great Explorations** (✆ 727/821-8992; www.greatexplorations.org), a hands-on children's museum offering a variety of exhibits—great for a rainy day or for kids who've overdosed on the sun and need to cool off indoors. 800 2nd Ave. NE. (✆ 727/821-6443. www.stpete-pier.com. Free admission to all the public areas and decks; donations welcome at the Pier Aquarium. Great Explorations $4, $2 seniors, free for children under 3. Valet parking $6; self-parking $3. Pier Mon–Thurs 10am–9pm; Fri–Sat 10am–10pm; Sun 11am–7pm. Aquarium Mon–Sat 10am–8pm; Sun 11am–6pm. Great Explorations Mon–Sat 10am–8pm; Sun 11am–6pm. Shop and restaurant hours vary.

Salvador Dalí Museum   This starkly modern museum houses the world's largest collection of works by the renowned Spanish surrealist, including 94 oil paintings, more than 100 watercolors and drawings, and 1,300 graphics, plus posters, photos, sculptures, objets d'art, and a 5,000-volume library on Dalí and

surrealism. 1000 3rd St. S. (near 11th Ave. S.). © 727/823-3767. www.salvadordalimuseum.
org. Admission $10 adults, $7 seniors, $5 students, free for children 10 and under. Thurs 5–8pm
50% discount. Mon–Wed and Fri–Sat 9:30am–5:30pm; Thurs 9:30am–8pm; Sun noon–5:30pm.
Closed Thanksgiving, Christmas.

Ybor City State Museum   Housed in the former Ferlita Bakery
(1896–1973), this small museum is a good starting point from which to explore
Ybor City, the city's historic Latin Quarter that now is its trendiest dining and
entertaining district. You can take a self-guided tour around the museum to see
a collection of cigar labels, cigar memorabilia, and works by local artisans.
Guides lead 30-minute guided tours of **La Casita,** a renovated cigar worker's
cottage adjacent to the museum; it's furnished as it was a century ago when Ybor
City produced more than 300,000 hand-rolled stogies a day. Check with the
museum about walking tours of the historic district. 1818 9th Ave. (between 18th and
19th sts.), Tampa. © 813/247-6323. www.ybormuseum.org. Admission $2. Daily 9am–5pm (La
Casita 10am–3pm).

FUN ON & OFF THE BEACH

This entire stretch of coast is one long beach, but since hotels, condos, and private homes line much of it, you may want to sun and swim at one of the area's
public parks. The best is **Caladesi Island State Park** (© 727/469-5942), which
boasts one of Florida's top beaches, a lovely, relatively secluded stretch with
fine soft sand edged in sea grass and palmettos. You can get here by ferry
(© 727/734-1501) from **Honeymoon Island State Recreation Area.**

At the very mouth of Tampa Bay, **Fort DeSoto Park** (© 727/582-2267;
www.fortdesoto.com) has a stunning white-sugar sand beach, a Spanish-
American War–era fort, great fishing from piers, large playgrounds for kids, and
4 miles of trails winding through the park for in-line skaters, bicyclists, and joggers. The park's 230 gorgeous, bay-side campsites usually are sold out, especially
on weekends.

You can indulge in parasailing, boating, cruises, deep-sea fishing, wave running, sightseeing, dolphin watching, water-skiing, and just about any other
waterborne diversion your heart could desire here. All you have to do is head to
one of two beach locations: **Hubbard's Marina,** at John's Pass Village and
Boardwalk (© 727/393-1947; www.hubbardsmarina.com), in Madeira Beach
on the southern tip of Sand Key; or **Clearwater Beach Marina,** at Coronado
Drive and Causeway Boulevard (© 800/772-4479 or 727/461-3133), at the
beach end of the causeway leading to downtown Clearwater. Agents in booths
there will give you the schedules and prices, answer any questions you have, and
make reservations if necessary.

The Tampa Bay area has a wide range of golf courses, with greens fees ranging from about $26 to more than $100. Contact the tourist information offices
for complete lists (see "Visitor Information," above). Call **Tee Times USA**
(© 800/374-8633; www.teetimesusa.com) to reserve times at all area courses.
The Westin Innisbrook Resort, 36750 U.S. 19 (P.O. Box 1088), Tarpon
Springs, FL 34688 (© 800/456-2000 or 727/942-2000; www.westin
innisbrook.com), is one of the country's best places to play (provided you stay
in one of the resort's 900 condo units). The JCPenney Classic, a major stop on
the PGA circuit, is played here the first weekend in December. St. Petersburg's
Mangrove Bay Golf Course, 875 62nd Ave. NE (© 727/893-7797), is one of
the nation's top 50 municipal courses. To learn or sharpen your game, the

Arnold Palmer Golf Academy World Headquarters is at Saddlebrook Resort (📞 800/729-8383 or 813/973 1111; www.saddlebrookresort.com); and TV "Golf Doctor" Joe Quinzi hosts his **Quinzi Golf Academy** (📞 727/725-1999) at the Safety Harbor Resort and Spa (see "Where to Stay," below).

SHOPPING

A terrific alternative to cookie-cutter suburban malls, Tampa's **Old Hyde Park Village** (📞 813/251-3500; www.oldhydeparkvillage.com), at Swann and South Dakota avenues in a picturesque Victorian neighborhood, is a cluster of 50 upscale shops and boutiques, including some of the mall regulars. Tampa's Ybor City no longer is a major producer of hand-rolled cigars, but you can watch artisans making stogies at the **Gonzales y Martinez Cigar Factory,** 2025 7th Ave. (📞 813/247-2469), in The Columbia restaurant building. You can stock up on fine domestic and imported cigars at several shops along East 7th Avenue, Ybor City's main drag.

In St. Petersburg, **Beach Drive** along the waterfront is the most fashionable downtown strolling and shopping venue. Be sure to check out the **Glass Canvas Gallery,** at 4th Avenue NE (📞 727/821-6767), featuring a dazzling array of glass sculpture and crafts items; the museum-grade **P. Buckley Moss** (📞 727/894-2899), carrying the works of the individualistic artist best known for her portrayal of the Amish and the Mennonites; and **Red Cloud** (📞 727/821-5824), an oasis for Native American crafts.

WHERE TO STAY

Most vacationers elect to stay at the beaches and drive into Tampa and St. Petersburg to see the sights. If you're going to Busch Gardens, the North Tampa area has several options. The 500-room **Embassy Suites Hotel and Conference Center,** 3705 Spectrum Blvd. (📞 800/EMBASSY or 813/977-7066), is the plushest and most expensive establishment near the park. Almost across the avenue stands **LaQuinta Inn & Suites,** 3701 E. Fowler Ave. (📞 800/NU-ROOMS or 813/910-7500). Side-by-side just south of Fowler Avenue are editions of **AmeriSuites,** 11408 N. 30th St. (📞 800/833-1516 or 813/979-1922), and **DoubleTree Guest Suites,** 11310 N. 30th St. (📞 800/222-TREE or 813/971-7690).

In downtown Tampa, the **Hyatt Regency Tampa,** 2 Tampa City Center (📞 800/233-1234 or 813/225-1234; www.hyatt.com), the **Radisson Riverwalk Hotel,** 200 N. Ashley St. (📞 800/333-3333 or 813/233-2222; www.radisson.com), and the **Tampa Marriott Waterside,** 710 N. Florida Ave. (📞 800/228-9290 or 813/221-4900), all cater primarily to the corporate crowd.

Across the bay is the **St. Petersburg Hilton,** 333 1st St. S. (📞 800/HILTONS or 727/894-5000; www.stpetehilton.com), a 15-story business and convention hotel within steps of the Salvador Dalí Museum.

St. Pete Beach and Clearwater Beach have national chain hotels and motels of every name and description. You can also use the St. Petersburg/Clearwater Convention & Visitors Bureau's free **reservations service** (📞 800/345-6710) to book rooms at most of them.

Best Western All Suites Hotel Enclosing a lush tropical courtyard with heated pool, hot tub, covered games area, and lively tiki bar offering inexpensive barbecues, this all-suite hotel is the most beachlike vacation venue close to Busch Gardens. Great for kids, 11 "family suites" have bunk beds in 1 bedroom. All rooms have refrigerators. The bar can get noisy before closing, and ground-level units are musty, so ask for an upstairs suite away from the action. Behind Busch Gardens, 3001 University Center Dr. (faces N. 30th St. between Busch Blvd. and Fowler Ave.), Tampa, FL 33612. ℭ **800/786-7446** or 813/971-8930. Fax 813/971-8935. www.thatparrotplace. com. 150 units. Winter $99–$159 suite for 2; off season $79–$99 suite for 2. Rates include hot and cold breakfast buffet. AE, DC, DISC, MC, V. **Amenities:** Restaurant; heated outdoor pool; access to nearby health club.

Best Western Beachfront Resort   Two long, gray buildings flank a court-yard with a heated swimming pool at this beachside property popular with young families. Furnished in dark woods and rich tones, most of the guest rooms have picture-window views of the courtyard. They open to wide exterior walkways, but each room has its own plastic chairs and drink table out there. About half of the units are efficiencies with kitchenettes (all rooms have refrig-erators). Jimmy B.'s beach bar is a fine place for a sunset cocktail and for evening entertainment, including beachside bonfires on Saturdays in winter. 6200 Gulf Blvd. (at 62nd Ave.), St. Pete Beach, FL 33706. ℭ **800/544-4222** or 727/367-1902. Fax 727/367-4422. www.bestwesternstpetebeach.com. 102 units. Winter $168–$228 double; off season $108–$168 double. Rates include continental breakfast. AE, DC, DISC, MC, V. **Amenities:** Restaurant; 2 heated outdoor pools; access to nearby health club.

Don CeSar Beach Resort & Spa   Dating from 1928, this romantic Moor-ish-style "Pink Palace"—listed on National Register of Historic Places—appeals to a wide range of clientele, from groups to families to honeymooning couples. Extensively renovated in 2000, some of the 275 rooms under the minarets of the original building may seem rather small by today's standards, but they have high windows and offer views of the gulf or Boca Ciega Bay. Some but not all of them have balconies. If you want more room but less charm, the resort has 70 spa-cious luxury condominiums in The Don CeSar Beach House, a mid-rise build-ing three-quarters of a mile to the north (there's 24-hr. complimentary transportation between the two). 3400 Gulf Blvd. (at 34th Ave./Pinellas Byway), St. Pete Beach, FL 33706. ℭ **800/282-1116,** 800/637-7200, or 727/360-1881. Fax 727/367-6952. www. doncesar.com. 347 units. Winter $288–$428 double; $304–$699 suite. Off-season $209–$329 double; $251–$505 suite. $10 per person per day resort fee. Packages available. AE, DC, DISC, MC, V. Self-parking free, valet parking $10. **Amenities:** Restaurants (4); 2 heated out-door pools; spa.

The Heritage Holiday Inn   The Heritage dates from the early 1920s and is the closest thing to a Southern mansion you'll find in the heart of St. Petersburg. A sweeping veranda, French doors, and a tropical courtyard help attract an eclec-tic clientele, from business travelers to seniors. The furnishings include period antiques. Some one-bedroom suites have sofa beds, two televisions, two phones, and two bathrooms. 234 3rd Ave. N. (between 2nd and 3rd sts.), St. Petersburg, FL 33701. ℭ **800/283-7829** or 727/822-4814. Fax 727/823-1644. www.sixcontinentshotels.com. 71 units. $100–$140 double. AE, DC, DISC, MC, V. **Amenities:** Restaurant; heated outdoor pool.

Hilton Garden Inn   This modern, four-story hotel stands just 2 blocks north of the heart of Ybor City's dining and entertainment district. A one-story brick structure in front houses the bright lobby, a comfy relaxation area with fireplace, and a small pantry selling beer, wine, soft drinks, and frozen dinners. You can heat up the dinners in your comfortable guest room's microwave oven or store them in your fridge. If you opt for a suite, you'll have a separate living room and a larger bathroom than in the regular units. 1700 E. 9th Ave. (between 17th and 18th sts.), Tampa, FL 33605. ℂ **800/HILTONS** or 813/769-9267. Fax 813/769-3299. 95 units. $99–$199 double. AE, DC, DISC, MC, V. Amenities: Restaurant; heated outdoor pool.

Island's End Resort A wonderful respite, and a great bargain to boot, this little all-cottage hideaway sits right on the southern tip of St. Pete Beach. You can step from the six contemporary cottages right onto the beach. And since the island curves sharply here, nothing blocks your view of the emerald bay. Linked by boardwalks, the comfortable one- or three-bedroom cottages have dining areas, living rooms, VCRs, and kitchens; the one three-bedroom unit has its own private beachside pool. 1 Pass-a-Grille Way (at 1st Ave.), St. Pete Beach, FL 33706. ℂ **727/ 360-5023.** Fax 727/367-7890. www.islandsend.com. 6 units. Winter $125–$235 cottage; off season $87–$235 cottage. Weekly rates available. Complimentary breakfast served Tues, Thurs, Sat. MC, V.

Renaissance Vinoy Resort and Golf Club Dominating the northern part of downtown, this elegant Spanish-style hotel overlooks Tampa Bay and is within walking distance of The Pier, Central Avenue, museums, and other attractions. Built as the Vinoy Park in 1925, it was reopened in 1992 after a total and meticulous $93-million restoration that made it more luxurious than ever. Rooms, many with lovely views of the bay, offer the utmost in comfort and equipment. Marchand's Grille serves the best steaks, seafood, and chops in town. The hotel has two swimming pools (connected by a roaring waterfall), a 14-court tennis complex, and an 18-hole private championship golf course on nearby Snell Isle. 501 5th Ave. NE (at Beach Dr.), St. Petersburg, FL 33701. ℂ **800/HOTELS-1** or 727/894-1000. Fax 727/822-2785. www.renaissancehotels.com. 360 units. Winter $239–$429 double; off season $139–$369 double. Packages available. AE, DC, DISC, MC, V. Self-parking $8, valet parking $12. **Amenities:** Restaurants (4); 2 heated outdoor pools; golf course; 12 tennis courts; spa; health club.

Saddlebrook Resort–Tampa Set on 480 acres, 30 minutes north of Tampa International Airport, this condominium development—renowned for its tennis and golf offerings—boasts two 18-hole championship golf courses and 45 tennis courts (hone your skills here at the Arnold Palmer Golf Academy or the Hopman Tennis Program), a 270-foot-long swimming pool, and a 7,000-square-foot luxury spa. Much more appealing than the standard rooms, the suites have kitchens and a patio or balcony overlooking lagoons and cypress and palm trees. 5700 Saddlebrook Way, Wesley Chapel, FL 33543. ℂ **800/729-8383** or 813/973-1111. Fax 813/973-4504. www.saddlebrookresort.com. 800 units. Winter $185–$197 per person; off season $120–$132 per person. Rates include breakfast and dinner. Packages available. AE, DC, DISC, MC, V. Self-parking free, valet parking $10. Take I-75 north to Fla. 54 (Exit 58); go 1 mile east to resort. **Amenities:** Restaurants (3); heated outdoor pool; spa; health club; 2 golf courses; 45 tennis courts.

Safety Harbor Resort and Spa You are in for some serious pampering at this venerable spa, a sprawling complex on 22 bay-front acres in Safety Harbor, a moss-draped town north of St. Petersburg. It has been in operation since 1926 and got a serious face-lift in 1998. Mineral springs enable the spa to offer acclaimed water-fitness programs. This is also a good place to work on your games at the Quinzi Golf Academy and the Phil Green Tennis Academy. Given the reasonable off-season room rates and special packages available, this is one of Florida's better spa values. 105 N. Bayshore Dr., Safety Harbor, FL 34695. ℂ **888/BEST-SPA** or 727/726-1161. Fax 727/724-7749. www.safetyharborspa.com. 193 units. Winter $209–$229 double; off season $139–$159 double. Packages available. AE, DC, DISC, MC, V. Self-parking free, valet parking $8. **Amenities:** Restaurants (2); heated indoor and outdoor pools; spa; golf course; 9 tennis courts; pets accepted ($35-per-night charge).

Sheraton Sand Key Resort Away from the honky-tonk of Clearwater, this nine-story Spanish-look hotel on 10 acres next to Sand Key Park is a big favorite with watersports enthusiasts and groups. It's only a 150-yard walk across the broad beach in front of the hotel to the water's edge. The moderately spacious guest rooms here all have traditional dark wood furniture and balconies or patios with views of the gulf or the bay. The fitness center here is on the top floor, rendering great workout views. 1160 Gulf Blvd., Clearwater Beach, FL 33767. © 800/325-3535 or 727/595-1611. Fax 727/596-8488. www.sheratonsandkey.com. 390 units. $135–$240 double. AE, DC, DISC, MC, V. **Amenities:** Restaurants (2); heated outdoor pool; fitness center; 3 tennis courts.

WHERE TO DINE

Don't overlook the food court at St. Petersburg's **The Pier,** where the inexpensive chow is accompanied by a rich, but quite free, view of the bay. You can take a shopping break at **Olde Hyde Park Village's** trendy sidewalk bistros (see "Shopping," above). You can pick up a latte and your e-mail at the **Internet Outpost Cafe,** 7400 Gulf Blvd. at Corey Avenue/75th Avenue, St. Pete Beach (© **727/360-7806**).

Bern's Steak House STEAKHOUSE This famous steak house has eight ornate dining rooms with themes such as Rhône, Burgundy, and Irish Rebellion. They set an appropriately dark atmosphere for huge charcoal-grilled steaks (beef or buffalo). The big surprise here is the dessert quarters upstairs, where 50 romantic booths can privately seat from 2 to 12 guests, who can select from a dessert menu offering almost 100 delicious selections, plus some 1,400 after-dinner drinks. 1208 S. Howard Ave. (at Marjory Ave.), Tampa. © **800/282-1547** within Florida or 813/251-2421. Reservations recommended. Main courses $17–$59; sandwiches $9. AE, DC, DISC, MC, V. Daily 5–11pm. Closed Christmas.

Cafe Creole and Oyster Bar CREOLE/CAJUN Resembling a turn-of-the-last-century railway station, this brick building dates from 1896 and was originally the home of the Cherokee Club, a gentlemen's hotel and private club with a casino and an opulent decor with stained-glass windows, wrought-iron balconies, Spanish murals, and marble bathrooms. Today it's home to Tampa's best Creole and Cajun restaurant. Specialties include exceptionally prepared Louisiana crab cakes, oysters, blackened grouper, and jambalaya. If you're new to bayou cuisine, try the Creole sampler. Dine inside or out. 1330 9th Ave. (at Avenida de Republica de Cuba/14th St.). © 813/247-6283. Reservations not accepted, but call for preferred seating. Main courses $11–$18. AE, DC, DISC, MC, V. Mon–Thurs 11:30am–10pm; Fri 11:30am–11:30pm; Sat 5–11:30pm.

Carmine's Restaurant & Bar CUBAN/ITALIAN/AMERICAN A great variety of loyal local patrons gather at this noisy corner cafe, one of Ybor's most popular hangouts, for genuine Cuban sandwiches—smoked ham, roast pork, Genoa salami, Swiss cheese, pickles, salad dressing, mustard, lettuce, and tomato on a crispy, submarine roll. There's a vegetarian version, too, and the combination half sandwich and a choice of black beans and rice or a bowl of Spanish soup makes a hearty meal. 1802 E. 7th Ave. (at 18th St.), Tampa. © 813/248-3834. Reservations not accepted. Main courses $7–$17; sandwiches $4–$8. No credit cards. Mon–Tues 11am–11pm; Wed–Thurs 11am–1am; Fri–Sat 11am–3am; Sun 11am–6pm.

Chateau France CLASSICAL FRENCH   Chef Antoine Louro provides St. Petersburg's finest cuisine and most romantic setting in this charming pink Victorian house built in 1910. He specializes in French classics such as homemade paté, Dover sole meunière, filet mignon au poivre, coq au vin, orange duck, and a rich seafood bouillabaisse. Fresh baby vegetables, Gruyère-cheese potatoes, and Antoine's special Eiffel Tower salad accompany all main courses. The wine list is excellent, as are the bananas flambé and crêpes Suzette. 136 4th Ave. N. (between Bayshore Dr. and 1st St. N.), St. Petersburg. ℂ 727/894-7163. Reservations recommended. Main courses $20–$30. AE, DC, DISC, MC, V. Daily 5–11pm.

Columbia SPANISH   Tourists flock to this famous hand-painted tile structure built in 1905. Here you can soak up Ybor City's Latin ambience and clap along during fire-belching Spanish flamenco floor shows Monday through Saturday at 7 and 9:30pm. Try the famous Spanish bean soup, the original "1905" salad, or Latin specialties such as the outstanding *paella à la valenciana*. Lighter appetites can choose from a limited menu of tapas. 2117 E. 7th Ave. (between 21st and 22nd sts.), Tampa. ℂ 813/248-4961. Reservations recommended. Main courses $14–$23. AE, DC, DISC, MC, V. Mon–Thurs 11am–10pm; Fri–Sat 11am–11pm.

Fourth Street Shrimp Store SEAFOOD   If you're anywhere in the area, don't miss at least driving by to see the colorful, cartoonlike mural on the outside of this eclectic establishment just north of downtown. Inside, you'll pass a seafood market counter when you enter, from which comes the fresh namesake shrimp, the star here. You can also pick from grouper, clam strips, catfish, or oysters fried, broiled, or steamed, all served in heaping portions. This is the best and certainly the most interesting bargain in town. 1006 4th St. N. (at 10th Ave. N.), St. Petersburg. ℂ 727/822-0325. Main courses $5–$14; sandwiches $2.50–$7. MC, V. Daily 11am–9pm.

Mise en Place ECLECTIC   This trendy bistro presents the freshest of ingredients, with a creative international menu that changes daily. Main courses often include fascinating choices such as Creole-style mahi mahi served with chili cheese grits and a ragout of black-eyed peas, andouille sausage, and rock shrimp. In Grand Central Place, 442 W. Kennedy Blvd. (at S. Magnolia Ave., opposite the University of Tampa), Tampa. ℂ 813/254-5373. Reservations recommended. Main courses $16–$27; tasting menu $35. AE, DC, DISC, MC, V. Tues–Thurs 11:30am–2:30pm and 5:30–10pm; Fri 11:30am–2:30pm and 5:30–11pm; Sat 5–11pm.

Ovo Cafe INTERNATIONAL   This cafe, popular with the business set by day and the club crowd on weekend nights, features a melange of sophisticated offerings. Pierogies and pasta pillows come with taste-tempting sauces and fillings, and there are several creative salads and unusual individual-size pizzas. Portions are substantial, but be careful of the strictly a la carte pricing here. The big black bar dispenses a wide variety of martinis, plus some unusual liqueur drinks. 1901 E. 7th Ave. (at 19th St.), Tampa. ℂ 813/248-6979. Reservations strongly recommended Fri–Sat. Main courses $10–$15; sandwiches $7–$8.50; pizza $8.50–$10. AE, DC, DISC, MC, V. Mon–Tues 11am–3pm; Wed–Thurs 11am–10pm; Fri–Sat 11am–1am.

The Salt Rock Grill SEAFOOD/STEAKS   Affluent professionals and other gorgeous folk make this high-powered waterfront restaurant *the* place to see and be seen on the beaches. In warm, fair weather you can dine out by the dock or slake your thirst at the lively tiki bar (bands play out here on Sun during the summer). Thick, aged steaks are the house specialties, as are crusted rack of lamb and Havana-style pork tenderloin. Pan-seared peppered tuna and salmon cooked on a cedar board lead the seafood selection. 19325 Gulf Blvd. (north of 193rd Ave.), Indian Shores. (𝒞 727/593-7625. Reservations strongly advised. Main courses $9–$36 (early-bird specials $8–$10). AE, DC, DISC, MC, V. Sun–Thurs 4–10pm; Fri–Sat 4–11pm (early-bird specials daily 4–5:30pm). Tiki bar open Sat–Sun 2pm.

TAMPA & ST. PETERSBURG AFTER DARK

The Tampa/Hillsborough Arts Council maintains an **Artsline** (𝒞 813/229-**ARTS**), a 24-hour information service providing the latest on current and upcoming cultural events. Racks in many restaurants and bars have copies of *Weekly Planet* (www.weeklyplanet.com), *Focus,* and *Accent on Tampa Bay,* three free publications detailing what's going on in the entire bay area. And you can also check the "Baylife" and "Friday Extra" sections of the *Tampa Tribune* (www.tampatrib.com) and the Thursday "Weekend" section of the *St. Petersburg Times* (www.sptimes.com).

THE PERFORMING ARTS   The four-theater **Tampa Bay Performing Arts Center,** 1010 N. MacInnes Place next to the Tampa Museum of Art (𝒞 800/**955-1045** or 813/229-STAR; www.tampacenter.com), is the focal point of Tampa's performing-arts scene, presenting a wide range of Broadway plays, classical and pop concerts, operas, cabarets, improv, and special events. A sightseeing attraction in its own right, the restored **Tampa Theatre,** 711 Franklin St. (𝒞 813/223-8981; www.tampatheatre.org), between Zack and Polk streets, dates from 1926 and is on the National Register of Historic Places. It presents a varied program of classic, foreign, and alternative films, as well as concerts and special events.

THE CLUB & BAR SCENE   **Ybor City** is Tampa's favorite nighttime venue by far. All you have to do is stroll along 7th Avenue East between 15th and 20th streets to find a club or bar to your liking. The avenue is packed with people, a majority of them high schoolers and early 20-somethings, on Friday and Saturday from 9pm to 3am, but you'll also find something going on from Tuesday to Thursday and even on Sundays. You don't need addresses or phone numbers; your ears will guide you along 7th Avenue East.

In St. Petersburg, the Moorish-style **Coliseum Ballroom,** 535 4th Ave. N. (𝒞 727/892-5202; www.stpete.org/coliseum.htm), has been hosting dancing, big bands, boxing, and other events since 1924 (it even made an appearance in the 1985 movie *Cocoon*).

At the beaches, the restored fishing community of **John's Pass Village and Boardwalk,** on Gulf Boulevard at John's Pass in Madeira Beach, has a handful of restaurants, bars, and shops to keep you occupied after the sun sets. Down south in Pass-a-Grille, there's the popular, always lively lounge in **Hurricane,** 807 Gulf Way at 9th Avenue opposite the public beach (𝒞 727/360-9558). In Clearwater Beach, the **Palm Pavilion Grill & Bar,** on the beach at 18 Bay Esplanade (𝒞 727/446-6777), has live music Tuesday through Sunday nights during winter, on weekends off season. Nearby, **Frenchy's Rockaway Grill,** at 7 Rockaway St. (𝒞 727/446-4844), is another popular hangout.

Chicago

With all due respect to the late Chairman of the Board, the city of Chicago is about as "toddlin'" as one of the Rat Pack's all-night blowouts. And don't call it the "Second City," either. It's certainly the first city of American architecture, not to mention its sizzling restaurant, music, and performing arts scenes. In fact, you could argue that Chicago is the quintessential American metropolis—not just the first great city carved from the young nation's western frontier, but an international capital of commerce and culture that somehow melds the urban swagger of New York with down-to-earth Midwestern charm. "Toddlin'?" More like "struttin'."

1 Essentials

GETTING THERE

BY PLANE O'Hare International Airport (© 773/686-2200; www.chicago airports.com) is one of the busiest airports in the country, served by most domestic carriers and many international airlines. It's northwest of the city proper, about a 30-minute to an hour's drive from downtown; a cab costs $30 to $35. From the airport, the "El" (elevated train) takes you to the Loop for $1.50 (30–40-min. ride).

On the southwest side of the city is Chicago's other major airport, **Midway** (© 773/838-0600; www.chicagoairports.com), smaller than O'Hare and served by fewer airlines. You may be able to get a cheaper fare to Midway; try **Airtran** (© 800/247-8726; www.airtran.com), **ATA** (© 800/435-9282; www.ata. com), **Frontier** (© 800/432-1359; www.frontierairlines.com), and **Southwest** (© 800/435-9792; www.southwest.com). The "El" can take you to the Loop in about half an hour.

Continental Air Transport (© 800/654-7871 or 312/454-7800; www. airportexpress.com) services most first-class hotels in Chicago; check with your bell captain. The cost is $20 one-way ($36 round-trip) from O'Hare and $15 one-way ($27 round-trip) from Midway.

BY TRAIN **Amtrak** (© 800/USA-RAIL; www.amtrak.com) pulls into **Union Station,** 210 S. Canal St., between Adams and Jackson streets (© 312/ 655-2385; Subway/El: Clinton or Quincy; bus: 1, 60, 151, or 156). There's frequent service from Milwaukee (trip time: 1½ hr.) and Cleveland (6½ hr.); daily service from Detroit (6 hr.), Indianapolis (5½ hr.) St. Louis (5½ hr.), Kansas City (8 hr.), New York (20 hr.), Washington, D.C. (19 hr.), New Orleans (19½ hr.), Los Angeles (30 hr.), San Francisco (53 hr.), and Seattle (37 hr.).

BY CAR The major routes into Chicago are I-80/I-90 from the east (Cleveland), I-80 and I-88 from the west (Des Moines), I-94 from the east (Detroit) and north (Milwaukee), I-65 from the southeast (Indianapolis), and I-55 from the southwest (Springfield, St. Louis). I-294 loops around the outer suburbs.

Approximate driving distances in miles to Chicago: from **Milwaukee,** 92; from **St. Louis,** 297; from **Detroit,** 286; from **Denver,** 1,011; from **Atlanta,** 716; from **Washington, D.C.,** 715; from **New York City,** 821; and from **Los Angeles,** 2,034.

VISITOR INFORMATION

The **Chicago Office of Tourism,** Chicago Cultural Center, 78 E. Washington St., Chicago, IL 60602 (© **312/744-2400** or TTY 312/744-2947; www.ci.chi. il.us/Tourism), will mail you a packet of materials with information on upcoming events and attractions. The **Illinois Bureau of Tourism** (© **800/ 2CONNECT** or TTY 800/406-6418; www.enjoyillinois.com) will also send you a packet of information about Chicago and other Illinois destinations.

GETTING AROUND

BY PUBLIC TRANSPORTATION   The **CTA (Chicago Transit Authority)** operates a useful information service (© **836-7000** or TTY 836-4949 from any area code in the city and suburbs; **www.transitchicago.com**) that functions daily from 5am to 1am. Excellent CTA maps are usually available at subway or El stations, or by calling the CTA.

Fares for the bus, subway, and El are $1.50, plus an additional 30¢ for a transfer that allows CTA riders to make two transfers on the bus or El within 2 hours of receipt. Children under 7 ride free, and those between the ages of 7 and 11 pay 75¢ (15¢ for transfers). Seniors can also receive the reduced fare if they have the appropriate reduced-fare permit (call © **312/836-7000** for details on how to obtain one). The CTA uses credit-card-size fare cards that automatically deduct the exact fare each time you take a ride. The reusable cards can be purchased with a preset value already stored ($14 for 10 rides, or $17 for 10 rides and 10 transfers), or riders can obtain cards at vending machines located at all CTA train stations and charge them with whatever amount they choose (a minimum of $3 and up to $100). Note if you don't have a fare card when boarding a bus, you'll need $1.50 in exact change in coins and/or dollar bills.

By "El"/Subway   The rapid transit system operates five major lines. The "El" (elevated train) runs partly above ground and partly below ground, so it's known as both the "El" and the subway. While most trains run every 5 to 20 minutes, decreasing in frequency in the off-peak and overnight hours, some stations close after work hours (as early as 8:30pm) and remain closed on Saturday, Sunday, and holidays.

By Bus   A few buses that are particularly handy for many visitors are the **no. 146 Marine/Michigan,** an express bus from Belmont Avenue on the North Side that cruises down North Lake Shore Drive (and through Lincoln Park during nonpeak times) to North Michigan Avenue, State Street, and the Grant Park museum campus; the **no. 151 Sheridan,** which passes through Lincoln Park en route to inner Lake Shore Drive and then travels along Michigan Avenue as far south as Adams Street, where it turns west into the Loop (and stops at Union Station); and the **no. 156 LaSalle,** which goes through Lincoln Park and then into the Loop's financial district on LaSalle Street.

By Metra   The **Metra** commuter railroad (© **312/322-6777** or TTY 312/ 322-6774 Mon–Fri 8am–5pm; www.metrarail.com) serves the six-county suburban area around Chicago with 12 train lines. Several terminals are located downtown, including **Union Station** at Adams and Canal streets, **LaSalle Street Station** at LaSalle and Van Buren streets, **North Western Station** at Madison

Chicago Neighborhoods

and Canal streets, and **Randolph Street Station** at Randolph Street and Michigan Avenue. Commuter trains have graduated fare schedules based on the distance you ride.

BY TAXI   The meter in Chicago cabs currently starts at $1.60 and increases $1.40 for each mile, with a 50¢ surcharge for each additional rider ages 12 to 65. Taxis are easy to hail, but if you can't find one, try calling **Flash Cab** (© 773/561-1444), **Yellow Cab** (© 312/TAXI-CAB or 312/829-4222), or **Checker Cab** (© 312/CHECKER or 312/243-2537).

FAST FACTS

The best hospital emergency room in Chicago is **Northwestern Memorial Hospital,** 251 E. Huron St. (© **312/926-2000;** www.nmh.org), with a state-of-the-art medical center right off North Michigan Avenue. The emergency department (© **312/926-5188** or 312/944-2358 for TDD access) is located at 240 E. Erie St. near Fairbanks Court. The hospital's **Physician Referral Service** can be reached at © **877/926-4664.**

The local **sales tax** is 8.75%. Restaurants in the central part of the city, roughly the 312 area code, are taxed an additional 1%, for a total of 9.75%. The **hotel room tax** is 3%.

SPECIAL EVENTS & FESTIVALS

The **Mayor's Office of Special Events** operates a recorded hot line (© **312/744-3370**) listing current special events, festivals, and parades occurring throughout the city. The city of Chicago also maintains a 24-hour information line for those with hearing impairments; call © **312/744-8599.**

During the first week of June, you can catch the **Chicago Blues Festival** at the Petrillo Music Shell, at Jackson Drive and Columbus Drive in Grant Park (© **312/744-3315**). Blues Fest is free, with dozens of acts performing over 4 days, but get there in the afternoon to get a good spot on the lawn for the evening show.

From the last week in June to July 6, **The Taste of Chicago** (© **312/744-3315**) brings 10 days of feasting in the streets, when scores of Chicago restaurants cart their fare to food stands set up throughout Grant Park. To avoid the heaviest crowds at this free event, try going weekdays earlier in the day.

The **Chicago Air & Water Show** (© **312/744-3315**) at North Avenue Beach is a hugely popular aquatic and aerial spectacular. It usually takes place on August 16 and 17.

On the Saturday before Thanksgiving, at the **Magnificent Mile Lights Festival** (© **312/642-3570**), a colorful parade of Disney characters makes its way south along Michigan Avenue, from Oak Street to the Chicago River, with lights being illuminated block by block as the procession passes.

2 What to See & Do

THE TOP ATTRACTIONS

Adler Planetarium and Astronomy Museum   The building—a zodiacal 12-sided structure at the end of ornamental Solidarity Drive—is historic, but some of the attractions here will captivate the most jaded video-game addict. The exhibit galleries feature a variety of displays and interactive activities designed to foster understanding of our solar system and more. The 60,000-square-foot **Sky Pavilion** features the must-do StarRider Theater, which takes you on a mind-blowing interactive virtual reality trip through the Milky Way and into deep space. On the first Friday evening of the month, visitors can view dramatic close-ups of the moon, the planets, and distant galaxies through a closed-circuit monitor connected to the planetarium's Doane Observatory telescope. Allow 2 hours, more if you want to see more than one show. 1300 S. Lake Shore Dr. ℂ **312/922-STAR**. Fax 312/922-2257. www.adlerplanetarium.org. Admission (including 1 show) $13 adults, $12 seniors, $11 children 4–17, free for children under 4. Free admission Mon and Tues Sept–Feb only. Mon–Fri 9am–5pm; 1st Fri of every month until 10pm. StarRider Theater and Sky Shows at numerous times throughout the day; call ℂ 312/922-STAR for current times. Bus: 12, 127, or 146.

Art Institute of Chicago   You can't (and shouldn't) miss the Art Institute, which features one of the world's major collections: Japanese *ukiyo-e* prints, ancient Egyptian bronzes and Greek vases, 19th-century British photography, masterpieces by most of the greatest names in 20th-century sculpture, and modern American textiles. Especially notable is the popular Impressionist collection, which boasts George Seurat's pointillist masterpiece *Sunday Afternoon on the Island of La Grande Jette*. Also worth seeing are the galleries of European and American contemporary art, ranging from paintings, sculptures, and mixed-media works by artists from Pablo Picasso and Salvador Dalí to Jackson Pollock and Andy Warhol. Don't miss Marc Chagall's stunning stained-glass windows. Allow 3 hours. 111 S. Michigan Ave. (at Adams St.). ℂ **312/443-3600**. www.artic.edu. Suggested admission $10 adults; $6 seniors, children, and students with ID. Additional cost for special exhibitions. Free admission Tues, Mon, Wed–Fri, and holidays 10:30am–4:30pm; Tues 10:30am–8pm; Sat–Sun 10am–5pm. Closed Thanksgiving and Dec 25. Bus: 3, 4, 60, 145, 147, or 151. Subway/El: Green, Brown, Purple, or Orange lines to Adams, or Red Line to Monroe or Jackson.

Auditorium Building and Theatre   A truly grand theater with historic landmark status, the auditorium is worth a visit to experience late 19th-century Chicago opulence. Designed and built in 1889 by Louis Sullivan and Dankmar Adler, the auditorium was a wonder of the world: the heaviest (110,000 tons) and most massive modern edifice on earth and the first large-scale building to be electrically lighted. The 4,000-seat theater is a marvel of visionary design and engineering with otherworldly acoustics and unobstructed sightlines. Don't miss the lobby fronting Michigan Avenue, with its faux ornamental marble columns, molded ceilings, mosaic floors, and Mexican onyx walls. 50 E. Congress Pkwy. ℂ **312/922-2110**. www.auditoriumtheatre.org. For ticket reservations or box-office information, call Ticketmaster at ℂ 312/902-1500. Call ℂ 312/431-2354 to arrange a 1-hr. theater tour. Admission $5 adults, $3 seniors and students. Bus: 145, 147, or 151. Subway/El: Brown, Green, Orange, or Purple lines to Library/Van Buren, or Red Line to Jackson.

Chicago Children's Museum   The popular museum has areas especially for preschoolers as well as for older children, and several permanent exhibits allow kids a maximum of hands-on fun. There are always creative temporary exhibitions on tap as well: Recent favorites included shows on Dr. Seuss and *Sesame Street*. Other exhibits explore such diverse topics as dinosaurs, water resources, prejudice, and more. Allow 2 to 3 hours. Navy Pier, 700 E. Grand Ave. ℂ **312/527-1000**. www.chichildrensmuseum.org. Admission $6.50 adults and children, $5.50 seniors. Free admission Thurs 5–8pm. Summer daily 10am–5pm (Thurs until 8pm); fall–spring Tues–Sun 10am–5pm (Thurs until 8pm). Bus: 29, 56, 65, or 66. Subway/El: Red Line to Grand/State; transfer to city bus or Navy Pier's free trolley bus.

Field Museum of Natural History   You may recognize the museum as the very suitable home turf of the intrepid archaeologist and adventurer hero of the

Indiana Jones movies. Spread over the museum's 9 acres of floor space are scores of permanent and temporary exhibitions—some interactive, but most requiring the old-fashioned skills of observation and imagination. Highlights include the largest, most complete *Tyrannosaurus rex* fossil ever unearthed—named **"Sue"** for the paleontologist who found it in 1990—an exhibit on Ancient Egypt, including 23 mummies; a kid-friendly Disneyesque insect exhibit; and a series of exhibits designed to re-create life in other cultures and areas of the world. Allow 3 hours. Roosevelt Rd. and Lake Shore Dr. ⓒ 312/922-9410 or 312/341-9299 TDD (for hearing-impaired callers). www.fmnh.org. Admission $8 adults; $4 seniors, children 3–11, and students with ID; free for teachers, armed-forces personnel in uniform, and children 2 and under. Free admission Mon–Tues Jan–Feb and late Sept to Dec 24. Daily 9am–5pm. Open Thurs to 8pm June 17–Aug 26. Closed Dec 25 and Jan 1. Bus: 6, 10, 12, 130, or 146.

John G. Shedd Aquarium   The Shedd is a city treasure and well deserving of its title as world's largest indoor aquarium. Its star attraction—and the first thing you'll see as you enter—is the **Caribbean Coral Reef** exhibit. This 90,000-gallon circular tank occupies the beaux arts–style central rotunda, entertaining spectators who press up against the glass to ogle divers feeding nurse sharks, barracudas, stingrays, and a hawksbill sea turtle. It's worth sticking around to catch one of the daily feedings, when a diver swims around the tank and (thanks to a microphone) talks about the species inside. The three-million-gallon saltwater **Oceanarium,** an indoor marine mammal pavilion that re-creates a Pacific Northwest coastal environment, is well worth the extra $3 admission charge. As you follow a winding nature trail, you'll encounter beluga whales, white-sided dolphins, Alaskan sea otters, and harbor seals along the way. Allow 2 to 3 hours. 1200 S. Lake Shore Dr. ⓒ 312/939-2438. www.sheddaquarium.org. Admission to both Aquarium and Oceanarium $15 adults, $11 seniors and children 3–11, free for children under 3. Aquarium only $8 adults, $6 children and seniors. Free admission to Aquarium Mon and Tues Sept–Feb. Summer Fri–Wed 9am–6pm, Thurs 9am–10pm; fall–spring Mon–Fri 9am–5pm, Sat–Sun 9am–6pm. Bus: 6, 10, 12, 130, or 146.

Museum of Contemporary Art   The MCA claims to be the largest contemporary art museum in the country, emphasizing experimentation in a variety of media—painting, sculpture, photography, video and film, dance, music, and performance. You can see the MCA's highlights in about an hour, although art lovers will want more time to wander (especially if a high-profile exhibit is in town). The permanent collection highlights works created since 1945 by such artists as Alexander Calder, Sol LeWitt, and Bruce Nauman. The museum's First Fridays program, featuring after-hours performances, live music, and food and drink, takes place the first Friday of every month. Allow 1 to 2 hours. 220 E. Chicago Ave. (1 block east of Michigan Ave.). ⓒ 312/280-2660. Fax 312/397-4095. www.mca chicago.org. Admission $10 adults, $6 seniors and students with ID, free for children under 12. Free admission on Tues. Wed–Sun 10am–5pm, Tues 10am–8pm. Bus: 3, 10, 11, 66, 125, 145, 146, or 151. Subway/El: Red Line to Chicago/State.

Museum of Science and Industry   The massive Museum of Science and Industry is the granddaddy of interactive museums, with some 2,000 exhibits spread over 14 acres in 75 exhibition halls. A headline attraction is the **Henry Crown Space Center,** where the story of space exploration is documented. A favorite is the dark descent into a full-scale replica of an Illinois **coal mine.** From historic railroad trains to submarines to space capsules, from special effects to the mysteries of the human immune system, you'll find the object of your curiosity somewhere in this amazing place. The five-story Omnimax Theater offers action-packed Friday and Saturday showings at 7 and 8pm. Recommended visiting time: 3 hours. 57th St, and Lake Shore Dr. ℰ 800/468-6674 outside the Chicago area, 773/684-1414, or TTY 773/684-3323. www.msichicago.org. Admission to museum only, $9 adults, $7.50 seniors, $5 children 3–11, free for children under 3. Free admission Mon and Tues Sept–Feb. Combination museum and Omnimax Theater $15 adults, $13 seniors, $10 children 3–11, free for children under 3 on an adult's lap. Omnimax Theater only, evening shows $10 adults, $8 seniors, $6 children, free for children under 3 on an adult's lap. Memorial Day to Labor Day daily 9:30am–5:30pm; rest of the year Mon–Fri 9:30am–4pm, Sat–Sun and holidays 9:30am–5:30pm. Closed Christmas. Bus: 6, 10, 55, 151, or 156.

Navy Pier   Built during World War I, this 3,000-foot-long pier has been transformed into Chicago's top attraction, with eight million visitors each year. A combination of carnival, food court, and boat dock, the pier makes a fun place to stroll (if you don't mind crowds), but you'll have to walk all the way to the end to get the best views back to the city. There's a winter garden, a 3-D IMAX theater, a concert stage, a space that holds an ice rink in winter and a merry-go-round in summer, and a giant 15-story Ferris wheel. Decorative arts fans shouldn't miss the free **Smith Museum of Stained Glass Windows** on the Pier's ground floor. The pier is also home to many bland shops and several restaurants (including a high-tech McDonald's replete with laser light shows). During the summer there are fireworks on Wednesday and Saturday. Allow 1 hour. 600 E. Grand Ave. (at Lake Michigan). ℰ 800/595-PIER (outside 312 area code), or 312/595-PIER. www.navypier.com. Free admission. Summer Sun–Thurs 10am–10pm, Fri–Sat 10am–midnight; fall–spring Mon–Sat 10am–10pm, Sun 10am–7pm. Bus: 29, 56, 65, 66, 120, or 121. Parking: Rates start at $10 for the 1st hr. and go up to $18 for up to 8 hr. However, the lots fill quickly. Valet parking is $7 with a restaurant validation. There are also surface lots west of the pier, and free trolley buses make stops on Grand Ave. and Illinois St. from State St. Subway/El: Red Line to Grand/State; transfer to city bus or board a free pier trolley bus.

Robie House   One of Frank Lloyd Wright's finest creations, Robie House is one of the great works of 20th-century American architecture. The open layout, linear geometry of form, and craftsmanship are typical of Wright's Prairie School design. Completed in 1909, the home is also notable for its exquisite leaded- and stained-glass doors and windows. The house is undergoing a massive, 10-year restoration and though it will be open throughout the process, your photos may include plenty of scaffolding. Recommended visiting time: 2 hours. 5757 S. Woodlawn Ave. (at 58th St.). ℰ 773/834-1847. Admission $9 adults, $7 seniors and children 7–18. Mon–Fri tours at 11am, 1pm, and 3pm; Sat–Sun tours every ½ hr. 11am–3:30pm. Bookshop open daily 10am–5pm. Bus: 55.

Sears Tower Skydeck   The view from the 103rd-floor Skydeck at the Sears Tower is everything you'd expect it to be—once you get there. Unfortunately, you're usually stuck in a very long, very noisy line, so by the time you make it to the top, your patience could be as thin as the atmosphere up there. On a clear day, visibility extends up to 50 miles, and you can catch glimpses of four surrounding states. The 70-second high-speed elevator trip will feel like a thrill ride for some, but it's a nightmare for anyone with even mild claustrophobia. Our recommendation: If your time is limited, skip it. Allow 1 to 2 hours, depending on the length of the line. 233 S. Wacker Dr. (enter on Jackson Blvd.). ℰ 312/875-9696. Admission $9.50 adults, $7.75 seniors, $6.75 children 3–12, free for children under 3 and military with active-duty ID. May–Sept daily 10am–10pm; Oct–April 10am–8pm. Bus: 1, 7, 126, 146, 151, or 156. Subway/El: Brown, Purple, or Orange lines to Quincy, or Red or Blue lines to Jackson; then walk a few blocks west.

Museums for Less
If you plan to visit lots of Chicago museums, you should invest in a City-Pass, a prepaid ticket that gets you into the biggest attractions (including the Art Institute, Field Museum of Natural History, Shedd Aquarium, Adler Planetarium, and Museum of Science and Industry). The cost at press time was $39 for adults, $29 for children, which is about 50% cheaper than paying all the museums' individual admission fees. You can buy a CityPass at any of the museums listed above, or purchase online before you get to town (**www.citypass.net**).

THE WRIGHT STUFF IN OAK PARK

The suburb of Oak Park has the highest concentration of houses or buildings anywhere designed and built by Frank Lloyd Wright, the dean of American architecture.

Oak Park is 10 miles west of downtown Chicago. By car, take the Eisenhower Expressway west (I-290) to Harlem Avenue (Ill. 43) and exit north. Continue on Harlem north to Lake Street. Take a right on Lake and continue to Forest Avenue. Turn left here and immediately on your right you'll see the **Oak Park Visitor Center,** 158 Forest Ave. (© **708/848-1500**), open daily from 10am to 5pm April through October and from 10am to 4pm November through March. Stop in for orientation, maps, and guidebooks. There's a parking lot next door. From here it's only a few blocks to the heart of the historic district and the Frank Lloyd Wright Home and Studio.

By public transportation, take the Green Line west to Harlem, roughly a 25-minute ride from downtown. Exit the station onto Harlem Avenue, and proceed north to Lake Street. Take a right on Lake to Forest Avenue, and then turn left.

Oak Park has, in all, 25 homes and buildings by Wright, constructed between the years 1892 and 1913, which constitute the core output of his Prairie School period. An extensive tour of the neighborhood leaves from the **Ginkgo Tree Bookshop,** 951 Chicago Ave., on weekends from 10:30am to 4pm. This tour lasts 1 hour and costs $9 for adults and $7 for seniors and children 7 to 18, and is free for children under 7. At other times, you can follow a self-guided map and audiocassette tour of the historic district (recorded in English, French, Spanish, German, Japanese, and Italian). Available at the Ginkgo Tree Bookshop from 10am to 3:30pm, the self-guided tour costs $9 for adults and $7 for seniors and children.

Frank Lloyd Wright Home and Studio   For the first 20 years of Wright's career, this remarkable complex served first and foremost as the sanctuary from which Wright was to design and execute more than 130 of an extraordinary output of 430 completed buildings. The home began as a simple shingled cottage that Wright built for his bride in 1889 at the age of 22, but it became a work in progress, as Wright remodeled it constantly until 1911 (he left there in 1909). The place has a certain whimsy even if it's not a masterpiece, and you should savor every room as an insight into the workings of a remarkable mind. Allow 2 hours. 951 Chicago Ave. © 708/848-1976. www.wrightplus.org. Admission $9 adults, $7 seniors and children 7–18, free for children under 7. Combined admission for home and studio tour and guided or self-guided historic district tour $15 adults, $11 seniors and children 7–18. Admission to home and studio is by guided tour only; tours depart from the Ginkgo Tree Bookshop

Mon–Fri 11am, 1pm, and 3pm; Sat–Sun every 20 min. 11am–3:30pm. Facilities for people with disabilities are limited; please call in advance.

Unity Temple   In 1871, a community of Unitarian/Universalists settled near here and built a timber-framed house of worship typical of their native New England. Fire destroyed it around the turn of the century. The congregation asked Frank Lloyd Wright, who was a member, to design an affordable replacement.

Using poured concrete with metal reinforcements—a necessity owing to the project's small budget of $40,000—Wright created a building that seems as forbidding as a mausoleum on the outside. But inside, its details capture the tenets of the Prairie School that has since made Wright's name immortal. His use of wood for trim and other decorative touches is exciting to behold; his sensitivity to grain and tone and placement was akin to that of an exceptionally gifted woodworker. Wright knew the materials he chose to use as intimately as the artisans who carried out his plans. And his stunning, almost minimalist use of form is what still sets him apart as a relevant and brilliant artist. Allow a half hour. 875 Lake St. 🕾 708/383-8873. Self-guided tours $6 adults; $3 seniors, children, and students with ID. 45-min. guided tours Sat–Sun on the hour 1–3pm at no extra charge. Mon–Fri 10:30am–4:30 pm; Sat–Sun 1–4pm. Church events can alter the schedule; call in advance.

ORGANIZED SIGHTSEEING TOURS

The **Chicago Trolley Company** (🕾 773/648-5000; www.chicagotrolley.com) offers guided tours on a fleet of rubber-wheeled "San Francisco–style" trolleys that stop at a number of popular spots around the city. An all-day hop-on, hop-off pass costs $15 adults, $12 seniors, and $8 children.

Windy, Navy Pier (🕾 312/595-5555), is a 148-foot-long, four-masted schooner that (along with its new sister ship, the *Windy II*) sets sail from the Navy Pier for 90-minute cruises two to five times a day, both day and evening. Call for sailing times and more information. Tickets cost $25 adults, $15 seniors and children under 12.

Chicago is the first city of architecture, and the **Chicago Architecture Foundation (CAF),** 224 S. Michigan Ave. (🕾 312/922-3432, or 312/922-TOUR for recorded information; www.architecture.org), offers first-rate guided programs, led by nearly 400 trained and enthusiastic docents. The foundation offers walking, bike, boat, and bus tours to more than 60 architectural sites and environments in and around Chicago.

We recommend CAF's popular 1½-hour **"Architecture River Cruise,"** which offers a unique perspective on some of Chicago's top buildings. The excellent docents generally do a good job of making the cruise enjoyable for visitors with all levels of architectural knowledge. Tickets are $21 per person weekdays, $23 on weekends and holidays, and are scheduled hourly every day May through October. The trips are extremely popular, so purchase tickets in advance through **Ticketmaster** (🕾 312/902-1500; www.ticketmaster.com/Illinois), or avoid the service charge and buy your tickets at one of the foundation's tour centers, 224 S. Michigan Ave. or the John Hancock Center, or from the boat launch on the southeast corner of Michigan Avenue and Wacker Drive.

ENJOYING THE LAKEFRONT

Public **beaches** line Lake Michigan all the way up north into the suburbs and Wisconsin and southeast through Indiana and into Michigan. The most well known is **Oak Street Beach,** at the northern tip of the Magnificent Mile. The most popular is **North Avenue Beach,** about 6 blocks farther north, which has

It's a Beautiful Day, So Let's Play Two

Forget about all these new old-style ballparks being built all over the country. **Wrigley Field** (© 773/404-CUBS; www.cubs.com), the home of the Cubs—with its ivy-covered outfield walls, its hand-operated score-board, and its "W" or "L" flag announcing the outcome of the game to the unfortunates who couldn't attend—is the real McCoy. To get here, simply take the Red Line to Addison. To order tickets in person, stop by the ticket windows Monday through Friday from 9am to 6pm, Saturday from 9am to 4pm, and game days. Or call © 312/831-CUBS for tickets through **Ticketmaster** (© 800/347-CUBS outside Illinois). Maybe Slammin' Sammy will hit one onto Waveland for you.

developed into a volleyball hot spot and recently rebuilt its landmark steamship-shaped beach house and added a Venice Beach–style gym. **Hollywood-Ardmore Beach** (officially Kathy Osterman Beach), at the northern end of Lake Shore Drive, is a lovely crescent that's less congested and has steadily become more popular with gays. For more seclusion, try **Ohio Street Beach,** an intimate sliver of sand in tiny Olive Park, just north of Navy Pier, which, incredibly enough, remains largely ignored despite its central location. (It also has the city's only designated area for open-water distance swimmers.) My personal favorite is **Montrose Beach,** a beautiful unsung treasure about midway between North Avenue Beach and Hollywood-Ardmore Beach. It has an expanse of beach mostly uninterrupted by piers or jetties, a huge adjacent park with soccer fields, and one big hill great for kite flying—even a small bait shop where you can get ready to head to a nearby long pier designated for fishing. Unlike at Oak Street and North Avenue beaches, there's also a ton of free parking available here.

Beaches are officially open with a full retinue of lifeguards on duty beginning about June 20, but swimmers can wade into the chilly water Memorial Day to Labor Day. Only the bravest souls venture into the water before July, when the temperature creeps up enough to make swimming an attractive proposition.

Biking or in-line skating are great ways to see the city, particularly the lake-front; a bike path extends along it for more than 18 miles. To rent bikes or in-line skates, try **Bike Chicago** (© 800/915-BIKE), at Navy Pier, open from 8am to 10pm May through October (weather permitting).

GREAT SHOPPING AREAS

THE MAGNIFICENT MILE   The nickname "Magnificent Mile" refers to the roughly mile-long stretch of North Michigan Avenue between Oak Street and the Chicago River. The density of first-rate shopping is unmatched any-where. Whether your passion is Tiffany diamonds, Chanel suits, or Gap jeans, you'll find it on this stretch of concrete. **Sony Gallery of Consumer Electronics,** 663 N. Michigan Ave. (© 312/943-3334), is a haven for reluctant male shoppers where the latest high-tech gadgets are displayed in a museumlike set-ting. At the intersection of Michigan Avenue and Erie Street is a Chicago retail institution, the appropriately barrel-shaped flagship store of **Crate & Barrel,** 646 N. Michigan Ave. (© 312/787-5900). Chicago's first—and still busiest—vertical mall is **Water Tower Place,** a block-size marble-sheathed building at 835 N. Michigan Ave. (© 312/440-3165), between East Pearson and East Chestnut streets.

If you're truly in the market for some designer duds, you'll have to venture off the Mag Mile and head over to **Oak Street.**

STATE STREET & THE LOOP   Marshall Field & Co., 111 N. State St., at Randolph ((C) **312/781-1000**), remains one of the world's largest department stores, occupying an entire city block and featuring the largest Tiffany glass mosaic dome in the United States. **Carson Pirie Scott & Co.,** 1 S. State St., at the corner of State and Madison ((C) **312/641-7000**), is a few blocks south. Both buildings are city landmarks and attractions in themselves. Although State Street has not recaptured the glamour of decades past, it manages to draw crowds of loyal customers from the Loop's office towers and Chicagoans turned off by Michigan Avenue's snob factor. There's no better example of the street's revival than the 2001 opening of a new **Sears** store ((C) **312/373-6000**) at the corner of State and Madison streets and a large **Old Navy** store at Washington and State streets ((C) **312/551-0522**).

RIVER NORTH   Along with becoming Chicago's primary art gallery district, River North—the area west of the Magnificent Mile and north of the Chicago River—has attracted many interesting shops, concentrated on Wells Street from Kinzie Street to Chicago Avenue. The neighborhood even has a mall of its own—**The Shops at the Mart** ((C) **312/527-7990**)—in the Merchandise Mart, at Wells and Kinzie streets, with stores geared to the middle bracket.

LINCOLN PARK   The North Side neighborhood of Lincoln Park has a variety of unique specialty shops that make it easy to browse your way through this leafy, picturesque community. Shops are located on the primary commercial arteries running through the area, including Armitage Avenue, Webster Avenue, Halsted Street, Clark Street, and Lincoln Avenue.

3 Where to Stay

You can check on the latest rates and availability, as well as book a room, by calling the **Illinois Reservation Service** ((C) **800/491-1800**). The 24-hour service is free. Another reservation service is **Hot Rooms** ((C) **800/468-3500** or 773/ 468-7666; www.hotrooms.com), which offers discounts at selected downtown hotels. The 24-hour service is free, but if you cancel a reservation, you're assessed a $25 fee. A centralized reservations service called **Bed & Breakfast/ Chicago Inc.,** P.O. Box 14088, Chicago, IL 60614 ((C) **800/375-7084** or 773/ 394-2000; www.chicago-bed-breakfast.com), lists more than 70 accommodations in Chicago.

Best Western River North Hotel   This hotel's rather cold exterior conceals a very attractive, sharply designed interior that hardly screams Best Western. It's within easy walking distance of theme restaurants, upscale dining, interesting shops on Wells Street, and lots of art galleries. Rooms are spacious and come with coffeemakers, hair dryers, and irons; the bathrooms are spotless (though no-frills). One-room suites have a sitting area, while other suites have a separate bedroom; all suites come with a sleeper sofa. The Best Western's reasonable rates and rooftop pool (with sweeping views) will appeal to families on a budget— and the almost unheard-of free parking can add up to significant savings for anyone planning to stay a week or more. 125 W. Ohio St. (at LaSalle St.), Chicago, IL 60610. (C) **800/528-1234** or 312/467-0800. Fax 312/467-1665. www.bestwestern.com. 150 units. $105– $149 double; $250 suite. AE, DC, DISC, MC, V. Free parking for guests (1 car per room). Subway/El: Red Line to Grand/State. **Amenities:** Restaurant; indoor pool; fitness room.

The Loop & Near North

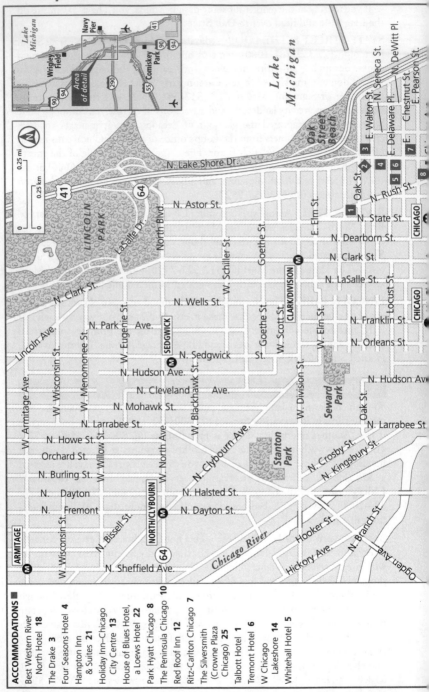

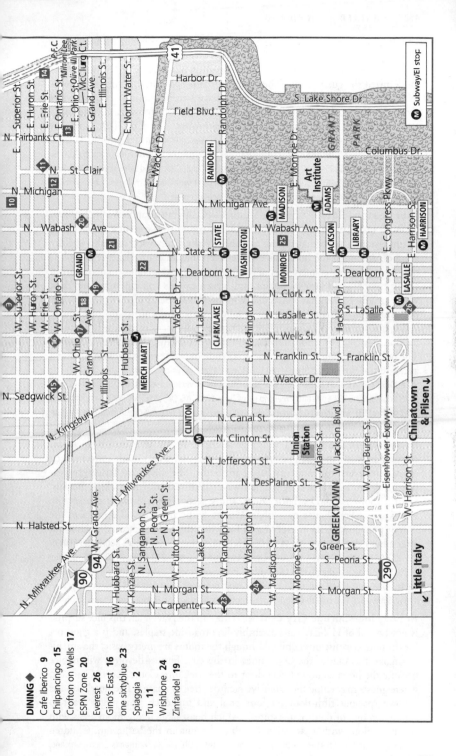

DINING ◆

Cafe Iberico 9
Chilpancingo 15
Crofton on Wells 17
ESPN Zone 20
Everest 26
Gino's East 16
one sixtyblue 23
Spiaggia 2
Tru 11
Wishbone 24
Zinfandel 19

The Drake   Fronting East Lake Shore Drive, this 1920 landmark building is Chicago's version of New York's Plaza or Paris's Ritz. This hotel is more old-time glamour than glitz, but a $100-million renovation has streamlined its design and modernized the guest rooms. The typical room is spacious and furnished comfortably with a separate sitting area; some have two bathrooms. The lake-view rooms are lovely, though you'll pay more for them. All rooms have coffeemakers, hair dryers, irons, refrigerators, and bathrobes. The Coq d'Or is one of Chicago's most atmospheric piano bars. 140 E. Walton Place (at Michigan Ave.), Chicago, IL 60611. (C) **800/55-DRAKE** or 312/787-2200. Fax 312/787-1431. www.hilton.com. 537 units. $255–$295 double; $335–$430 executive floor; from $600 suite. Weekend rates start at $289 with continental breakfast. AE, DC, DISC, MC, V. Valet parking $31 with in/out privileges. Subway/El: Red Line to Chicago/State. **Amenities:** Restaurants (3); fitness center.

Four Seasons Hotel   The Four Seasons—occupying a rarefied aerie between the 30th and 46th floors above the Mag Mile's most upscale vertical mall—offers an understated luxury that appeals to publicity-shy Hollywood stars and wealthy families. Although the hotel has every conceivable amenity, the overall look is that of an English country manor rather than a glitzy getaway. The beautiful rooms have English furnishings, custom-woven carpets and tapestries, and dark wood armoires. Each has VCRs and windows that open to let in the fresh air. Bathrooms boast such indulgences as a lighted makeup mirror, oversize towels and robes, scales, and Bulgari toiletries. Kid-friendly services include little robes, balloon animals, Nintendo, a special room-service menu, and milk and cookies. The hotel's elegant fitness center and spa exude the same upscale, old-money feel as the rest of the public areas. 120 E. Delaware Place (at Michigan Ave.), Chicago, IL 60611. (C) **800/332-3442** or 312/280-8800. Fax 312/280-1748. www.fourseasons.com. 343 units. $355–$575 double; $545–$3,500 suite. Weekend rates from $295. AE, DC, DISC, MC, V. Self-parking $23, valet parking $32 with in/out privileges. Subway/El: Red Line to Chicago/State. **Amenities:** Restaurants (2), indoor pool; spa; fitness center; pets accepted.

Hampton Inn & Suites   This is a great choice for travelers on a budget, and caters mostly to families. Rooms are residential and warm, with coffeemakers, irons, hair dryers, and modestly sized bathrooms. The apartment-style suites feature galley kitchens with fridges, microwaves, dishwashers, and cooking utensils. Off the lobby is the Dearborn Diner, and a second-floor skywalk connects to Ruth's Chris Steakhouse next door. Guests with children will appreciate the indoor pool and VCRs in every room for when the little ones need to chill out after a busy day. 33 W. Illinois St. (at Dearborn St.), Chicago, IL 60610. (C) **800/HAMPTON** or 312/832-0330. Fax 312/832-0333. www.hamptoninn-suites.com. 230 units. $139–$179 double; $189–$229 suite. Children under 18 stay free in parents' room. Rates include buffet breakfast. AE, DC, DISC, MC, V. Self-parking $13 with no in/out privileges, valet parking $28 with in/out privileges. Subway/El: Red Line to Grand/State. **Amenities:** Restaurant; indoor pool; fitness room.

Holiday Inn–Chicago City Centre   Close to the Navy Pier, this nice surprise is not typical of Holiday Inn's assembly-line roadside staples, and is a good bet for the budget-conscious family. Although the rooms are pretty basic, the amenities make this one of the best values in the city. Fitness devotees will rejoice because the hotel is located next door to the McClurg Court Sports Complex, where guests may enjoy the extensive facilities free of charge. The hotel also has its own spacious fifth-floor outdoor pool and sun deck. You might want to splurge on one of the "master suites," which boast large living-room areas with wet bars, along with a Jacuzzi-style tub and sauna in the bathroom. Children under 12 eat free in the hotel's restaurant. 300 E. Ohio St. (at Fairbanks Court), Chicago,

IL 60611. ℂ **800/HOLIDAY** or 312/787-6100. Fax 312/787-6259. www.chicc.com. 500 units. $128-$270 double. Weekend and promotional rates $99-$119. Children under 18 stay free in parents' room. AE, DC, DISC, MC, V. Valet parking $19. Subway/El: Red Line to Grand/State. **Amenities:** Restaurants (2); outdoor and indoor pools; access to nearby health club.

House of Blues Hotel, a Loews Hotel The funky vibe here makes this a great choice for teenagers and anyone who wants a hotel to be an experience— not just a place to sleep. Blending Gothic, Moroccan, East Indian, and New Orleans influences, the House of Blues lobby is a riot of crimsons and deep blues (stop by to check it out even if you're not staying here) and the casually dressed staff is friendly. Banquettes and couches heaped with pillows invite lounging— grab a drink at the Kaz Bar and soak it all in. You can catch your breath in the lighter, whimsical rooms, which feature CD players, VCRs, and some of the most exciting Southern folk art you'll ever come across. One of the hotel's biggest selling points is its location in the entertainment-packed Marina Towers complex. 333 N. Dearborn St. (at the river), Chicago, IL 60610. ℂ **877/569-3742** or 312/245-0333. Fax 312/923-2458. www.loewshotels.com. 367 units. $165-$349 double; $500-$750 suite. Weekend and promotional rates available. Children under 18 stay free in parents' room. AE, DC, DISC, MC, V. Valet parking $28 with in/out privileges. Subway/El: Brown Line to Clark/Lake, or Red Line to Grand/State. **Amenities:** Access to health and fitness center; pets accepted.

Majestic Hotel Located on a charming tree-lined street (but convenient to the many restaurants and shops of Lincoln Park), this is a good choice for anyone who wants a quiet, bed-and-breakfast type of hotel stay. Some of the larger suites—the most appealing are those with sun porches—offer butler's pantries with a fridge, microwave, and wet bar. Avoid the claustrophobic single rooms with alley views if you're traveling alone. 528 W. Brompton St. (at Lake Shore Dr.), Chicago, IL 60657. ℂ **800/727-5108** or 773/404-3499. Fax 773/404-3495. www.cityinns.com. 52 units. $139-$179. based on single occupancy. Rates include continental breakfast. AE, DC, DISC, MC, V. Self-parking $18 in nearby garage with no in/out privileges. Subway/El: Red Line to Addison; walk several blocks east to Lake Shore Dr. and then 1 block south. **Amenities:** Fitness room.

Park Hyatt Chicago For those in search of chic modern luxury, the Park Hyatt is the coolest hotel in town. The property's best rooms are those that face east, overlooking the bustle of the Mag Mile and the lake in the distance. Luxury might be the watchword here, but the look is anything but stuffy: The lobby feels like a sleek modern art gallery and rooms feature Eames and Mies van der Rohe reproduction furniture and window banquettes with stunning city views (the windows actually open). The comfortable beds are well appointed with several plush pillows. While most hotels might provide a TV and VCR, this is the kind of place where you get a DVD player and flat-screen TV. The bathrooms are especially wonderful: Slide back the cherrywood wall for views of the city while you soak in the tub. 800 N. Michigan Ave., Chicago, IL 60611. ℂ **800/233-1234** or 312/335-1234. Fax 312/239-4000. www.hyatt.com. 203 units. $375-$425 double; $695-$3,000 suite. AE, DC, DISC, MC, V. Valet parking $36 with in/out privileges. Subway/El: Red Line to Chicago/State. **Amenities:** Restaurant; indoor pool; spa; health club.

The Peninsula Chicago The luxury Peninsula hotel group's first Midwest location wowed us. Mixing an Art Deco sensibility with modern, top-of-the-line amenities, the Peninsula also features exceptional service. Rooms are average in size (and the "junior suites" are fairly small), but the hotel's in-room technology is cutting-edge: a "command station" by every bed allows guests to control all the lights, curtains, and room temperature without getting out from under the covers. The marble-filled bathrooms have separate shower stalls and tubs, vanities with plenty of room to sit, and another "command station" by the bathtub. Add in the flat-screen TVs and DVD players, and you have a classic hotel that's very much attuned to the present. Refrigerators are available upon request. The sultry hotel bar is already one of the city's top spots for romantic assignations. The bright, airy spa and fitness center fill the top two floors and make a lovely retreat (especially the outdoor deck). 730 N. Michigan Ave., Chicago, IL 60611. © 866/288-8889 or 312/337-2888. Fax 312/932-9529. www.peninsula.com. 339 units. $420–$495 double; $485–$4,500 suite. AE, DC, DISC, MC, V. Valet parking $32 with in/out privileges. Subway/El: Red Line to Chicago/State. Amenities: Restaurants (4), indoor pool; spa; fitness center; pets accepted.

Red Roof Inn   This is your best bet for the lowest-priced lodgings in downtown Chicago. The location is the main selling point: right off the Magnificent Mile. Previously a Motel 6, the building has been completely refurbished; the guest rooms are simple, but all have new linens and carpeting, along with hair dryers and irons. You're not going to find much in the way of amenities here, though free morning coffee is served in the small lobby. Room service is available through Coco Pazzo, an excellent Northern Italian restaurant around the corner from the hotel's front door. 162 E. Ontario St. (½ block east of Michigan Ave.), Chicago, IL 60611. © 800/RED-ROOF or 312/787-3580. Fax 312/787-1299. www.redroof.com. 195 units. $99–$121 double. AE, DC, DISC, MC, V. Self-parking $22, valet parking $24 with no in/out privileges. Subway/El: Red Line to Grand/State.

Ritz-Carlton Chicago   Top-notch service and an open, airy setting atop the Water Tower Palace make this one of Chicago's most welcoming hotels. The quality of the accommodations is of the highest caliber, although the standard rooms aren't very large. Doubles have space for a loveseat and desk but not much more; the bathrooms are elegant but not huge (for extra-large, lavish bathrooms, request a Premier Room on the 30th floor). Lake views cost more but are spectacular. The hotel also offers "allergy-sensitive" rooms that are cleaned with special nonirritating products and come stocked with hypoallergenic pillows and special bath products on request. Families will find this luxury crash pad quite welcoming. Every child receives a gift and can borrow toys and games from a stash kept by the concierge. 160 E. Pearson St., Chicago, IL 60611. © 800/621-6906 or 312/266-1000. Fax 312/266-1194. www.fourseasons.com. 430 units. $355–$475 double; $495–$3,500 suite. Weekend rates from $265. Self-parking $24 with no in/out privileges, valet parking $32 with in/out privileges. Subway/El: Red Line to Chicago/State. Amenities: Restaurants (4); indoor pool; spa; health club; pets accepted.

The Silversmith (Crowne Plaza Chicago)   This landmark building was built in 1897 to serve the jewelry and silver trade on Wabash Avenue, still known as Jeweler's Row. Rooms come in varying configurations, with 12-foot-high ceilings, 10-foot picture windows, Frank Lloyd Wright–inspired wrought-iron fixtures, armoires, and homey bedding; bathrooms are generously sized and some have whirlpool tubs. Because of the hotel's urban surroundings, natural light is limited in the rooms; those along the hotel's main corridor tend to be dark. And though windows are extra-thick to muffle the noise of nearby "El" trains, you'll want to avoid the lower-level floors if you like things quiet. For the best combination of natural light and views, request a Wabash Avenue room on the 9th or 10th floor. Word about The Silversmith has been slow getting out; rooms don't book up as quickly as other, hotter spots, so this is one place thrifty travelers can look for a good deal. 10 S. Wabash Ave. (at Madison St.), Chicago, IL 60603. ℭ 800/2CROWNE or 312/372-7696. Fax 312/372 7320. 143 units. $149–$249 double; from $289 suite. Weekend rates available. AE, DC, DISC, MC, V. Valet parking $25 with in/out privileges. Subway/El: Brown, Green, or Orange lines to Madison/Wabash, or Red Line to Washington/State. **Amenities:** Restaurant; tiny fitness room (with access to nearby health club at a charge).

Talbott Hotel The Talbott's cozy atmosphere and personal level of service appeal to visitors looking for the feeling of a small inn rather than a sprawling, corporate hotel. Constructed in the 1920s as an apartment building, the Talbott was converted to a hotel in 1989. The wood-paneled lobby, decorated with leather sofas and velvety armchairs, two working fireplaces, tapestries, and numerous French horns used for fox hunts, is intimate and inviting—all the better in which to enjoy your complimentary continental breakfast. Although comfortable, the rooms aren't quite as distinctive; they also vary in size, so ask when making reservations. Suites and the hotel's "executive king" rooms have Jacuzzi tubs; suites also have separate sitting areas with sofa beds and dining tables. 20 E. Delaware Place (between Rush and State sts.), Chicago, IL 60611. ℭ 800/TALBOTT or 312/944-4970. Fax 312/944-7241. www.talbotthotel.com. 149 units. $149–$289 double; $319–$449 suite. AE, DC, DISC, MC, V. Self-parking $21. Subway/El: Red Line to Chicago/State. **Amenities:** Access to nearby health club.

Tremont Hotel With its bright colors and solicitous service, the Tremont is one of the city's best picks for a romantic getaway. The building feels more like a secluded bed-and-breakfast than a hotel right off the busiest shopping street in the city. The cozy lobby with a fireplace sets the mood from the start. In the guest rooms, the tasteful furnishings, plush terrycloth robes, VCRs, CD players, vases of fresh flowers, and marble bathrooms invite lounging. Rooms in the Tremont House—a separate building next door—have kitchenettes. The steak-and-chops restaurant off the lobby, the memorabilia-filled Iron Mike's Grille, is co-owned by legendary former Chicago Bears football coach Mike Ditka. 100 E. Chestnut St. (1 block west of Michigan Ave.), Chicago, IL 60611. ℭ 800/621-8133 or 312/751-1900. Fax 312/751-8650. www.tremontchicago.com. 130 units. $149–$299 double; from $650 suite. AE, DC, DISC, MC, V. Valet parking $30. Subway/El: Red Line to Chicago/State. **Amenities:** Restaurant; small fitness room (and access to nearby health club).

W Chicago Lakeshore The only hotel in Chicago with a location on the lake, this property prides itself on being a hip boutique hotel—but sophisticated travelers may feel like it's trying way too hard. Reborn last year, this former Days Inn has been transformed: dance music plays in the lobby and the staff are clad in black. The compact rooms are decorated in deep red, black, and gray—a scheme that strikes some travelers as gloomy—and sport such high-tech amenities as VCRs and CD players. In W-speak, rooms and suites are designated "wonderful" (meaning standard, with a city view), which we prefer, or "spectacular" (meaning a lake view, for which you'll pay more). 644 N. Lake Shore Dr. (at Ontario St.), Chicago, IL 60611. ℭ 877/W-HOTELS or 312/943-9200. Fax 312/255-4411. www.whotels.com. 556 units. $229–$429 double; from $369 suite. AE, DC, DISC, MC, V. Valet parking $30 with in/out privileges. Subway/El: Red Line to Grand/State. **Amenities:** Restaurants (2), pool; fitness room; pets allowed.

Whitehall Hotel Staying here is like visiting a wealthy, sophisticated aunt's town house: elegant but understated, welcoming but not effusive. Before the Four Seasons and Ritz-Carlton entered the picture, the patrician Whitehall reigned as Chicago's most exclusive luxury hotel, with rock stars and Hollywood royalty dropping by when in town. Although those glory days have passed, the independently owned Whitehall still attracts a devoted, urbane clientele who relish its English manor ambience and highly personalized service. Rooms are furnished in 18th-century English style, with Asian accents. All rooms have hair dryers, terry bathrobes, and irons. Rooms on the Club Floors as well as all suites have four-poster beds and umbrellas, and guests receive complimentary breakfast. 105 E. Delaware Place (west of Michigan Ave.), Chicago, IL 60611. © **800/948-4295** or 312/944-6300. Fax 312/944-8552. www.slh.com/whitehall. 221 units. $249–$439 double; $525–$1,500 suite. Weekend packages from $229. AE, DC, DISC, MC, V. Valet parking $31 with in/out privileges. Subway/El: Red Line to Chicago/State. **Amenities:** Restaurant; fitness room (access to nearby health club for an extra charge).

4 Where to Dine

Ann Sather SWEDISH/AMERICAN   This is a real Chicago institution, where you can enjoy Swedish meatballs with buttered noodles and brown gravy, or the Swedish sampler of duck breast with lingonberry glaze, meatball, potato-sausage dumpling, sauerkraut, and brown beans. All meals are full dinners, including appetizer, main course, vegetable, potato, and dessert. It's the sticky cinnamon rolls, though, that make addicts out of diners. Weekend brunch here can get frenzied, but the people-watching is priceless: a cross section of gay and straight, young and old, from club kids to elderly couples. 929 W. Belmont Ave. (between Clark St. and Sheffield Ave.). © **773/348-2378.** Reservations accepted for parties of 6 or more. Main courses $7–$12. AE, DC, MC, V. Sun–Thurs 7am–10pm; Fri–Sat 7am–11pm. Free parking with validation. Subway/El: Red Line to Belmont.

Arun's THAI   It's been called the best Thai restaurant in the city—possibly the country. Chef/owner Arun Sampanthavivat prepares a refined traditional cuisine that's authentic and flavorful. The 12-course chef's menu is your only option here, and different tables receive different dishes on a given night. You might see courses of various delicate dumplings accented with edible, carved dough flowers; an alchemist's Thai salad of bitter greens and peanuts with green papaya, tomatoes, chiles and sticky rice; or a medley of clever curries, including a surprisingly delightful sea bass and cabbage sour curry. When classic dishes appear, such as pad Thai, they're always above the norm. The menu is paired with an award-winning wine list, and the restaurant is smoke-free. Arun's is definitely worth a trip to this out-of-the-way neighborhood. 4156 N. Kedzie (at Irving Park Rd.). © **773/539-1909.** Reservations required with credit card. 12-course chef's menu $85. AE, DC, DISC, MC, V. Tues–Thurs 5–9pm; Fri–Sat 5–10pm; Sun 5–9pm. Subway/El and bus: Blue Line to Irving Park, then transfer to eastbound no. 80 bus; or Brown Line to Irving Park, then transfer to westbound no. 80 bus.

Bistrot Margot FRENCH BISTRO   Bistrot Margot is not only one of the best restaurants in Old Town—it's also one of the city's better French bistros. It can get very busy and loud, and the tables are quite close together, but, for many, that only adds to its charm. Start with out-of-this-world mussels in white wine with fresh herbs, then try one of the specials for the main course. The usual suspects (roasted chicken with garlic, lemon, herbs, and pommes frites or a terrific steak frites) are proof that, when done right, it's hard to beat classic French cuisine. On warm summer nights, the restaurant sets about half a dozen tables on the sidewalk, which, on this colorful stretch of Wells Street, makes for a truly memorable meal. 1437 N. Wells St. © **312/587-3660.** Reservations recommended. Main courses $13–$20. AE, DC, MC, V. Sun–Mon 5–9pm; Tues–Thurs 5–10pm; Fri–Sat 5–11pm. Subway/El: Red Line to Clark/Division, or Brown Line to Sedgwick.

Cafe Iberico SPANISH/TAPAS This wildly popular tapas restaurant is spread over two levels with beautiful tile work and wine bottles forming a canopy overhead. After you've ordered a pitcher of fruity sangria, put a dent in your appetite with a plate of *queso de cabra* (baked goat cheese with fresh tomato-basil sauce). A few standout dishes are the vegetarian Spanish omelet and chicken brochette with caramelized onions and rice. Cafe Iberico gets very loud, especially on weekends, so it makes for a fun group destination, but is not the place for a romantic tête-à-tête. 739 N. LaSalle St. (between Chicago Ave. and Superior St.). (*C*) **312/573-1510.** Reservations accepted during the week for parties of 6 or more. Tapas $3.50–$4.95; main courses $7.95–$13. DC, DISC, MC, V. Mon–Thurs 11am–11pm; Fri 11am–1:30am; Sat noon–1:30am; Sun noon–11pm. Subway/El: Red Line to Chicago/State, or Brown Line to Chicago.

Charlie Trotter's NOUVELLE Foodies flock to the namesake restaurant of celebrity chef Charlie Trotter, and it is an appropriate shrine of creative fine dining. There is no a la carte menu, so this is not the place to come if you're a picky eater. Your choice of the vegetable ($90) or grand ($110) dégustation menu (the extensive non-meat choices make this an excellent spot for vegetarians with gourmet tastes) will feature an ever-changing lineup of exceptional dishes made with organic or free-range products (no guilt!). Recent menus featured ragout of leek confit, braised carrots, salsify, and cauliflower with Perigord black truffle emulsion; and black buck venison with Japanese kumai jasmine rice cake and red wine Kalamata olive emulsion. The dining room is relatively formal; the staff highly professional but not intimidating. The wine list is extensive, and a sommelier is on hand to help match wines with each course. The entire restaurant is nonsmoking. For a taste of Trotter's gourmet fare without the high price tag, check out **Trotter's To Go,** his new gourmet food store in Lincoln Park at 1337 W. Fullerton Ave. ((*C*) **773/868-6510**). 816 W. Armitage Ave. (at Halsted St.). (*C*) **773/248-6228.** www.charlietrotters.com. Reservations required. Jackets required, ties requested. Fixed-price menus $90 and $110. AE, DC, DISC, MC, V. Tues–Sat from 6pm. Subway/El: Brown Line to Armitage.

Chilpancingo MEXICAN This restaurant's loftlike interior is livened up with colorful Mexican folk art and masks, making this a very cheerful place to enjoy a meal. Chef Geno Bahena has built up a reputation with his mole sauces; the version to try here mixes 25 ingredients in a dark, complex sauce served over chicken. Salmon, rack of lamb, and tuna with squid also take adventurous diners far beyond enchiladas and tacos. The menu changes twice each month. Don't miss the Café Maya Xtabentun, coffee flavored with Kahlúa and a Mayan liquor, delivered by servers who light the Kahlúa before pouring it into your glass. For a mix of flavors, try the five-course tasting menu ($45). 358 W. Ontario St. (at Orleans St.) (*C*) **312/266-9525.** www.chilpancingo.citysearch.com. Reservations recommended. Main courses $7.50–$13 lunch, $15–$25 dinner. AE, DC, DISC, MC, V. Mon–Thurs 11:30am–2:30pm and 5–10pm; Fri–Sat 11:30am–2:30pm and 5–11pm; Sun 10:30am–3pm. Subway/El: Red Line to Grand.

Crofton on Wells CONTEMPORARY AMERICAN Chef-owner Suzy Crofton has devoted herself to this critically acclaimed restaurant, a 70-seat River North storefront with a loyal following. Crofton's food is simply sophisticated and decidedly American, and the relatively spare dining room fits in with her no-attitude, Midwestern aesthetic. The menu is based on seasonally available ingredients: You might start with a chilled cucumber and Vidalia onion soup with shrimp, melon, and avocado; then move on to grilled venison medallions, soaked in a red wine sauce with cabbage, huckleberries, and arugula pesto. Entree selections always include a vegan choice. Close with a Granny Smith apple tart or devil's food cake with toasted coconut, macadamia nuts, and chocolate glaze. 535 N. Wells St. (between Grand Ave. and Ohio St.). ℭ 312/755-1790. www. croftononwells.com. Reservations recommended. Main courses $7.75–$14 lunch, $18–$29 dinner. AE, DC, MC, V. Mon–Thurs 11:30am–2:30pm and 5–10pm; Fri 11:30am–2:30pm and 5–11pm; Sat 5–11pm. Subway/El: Brown Line to Merchandise Mart.

ESPN Zone AMERICAN   Sports fans, welcome to nirvana. This massive dining and entertainment complex features three components: the Studio Grill, designed with replicas of studio sets from the cable networks' shows (including SportsCenter); the Screening Room, a sports pub featuring a 16-foot screen and an armada of TV monitors and radio sets carrying live broadcasts of games; and the Sports Arena, a gaming area with interactive and competitive attractions. The food here is better-than-average tavern fare, including quite a few salads and upscale items. There's also a special kids' menu. 43 E. Ohio St. (at Wabash Ave.). ℭ 312/ 644-3776. Main courses $7.25–$20. Sun–Thurs 11:30 am–11:30pm; Fri–Sat 11:30am–midnight. Subway/El: Red Line to Grand.

Everest ALSATIAN/FRENCH   Forty stories above the Chicago Stock Exchange, the refined world of Everest is an oasis of four-star fine-dining civility. Its windows overlook the shimmering nightscape of downtown Chicago, and its culinary experience is one of the finest in town. Refined sensibilities, culinary imagination, and a focus on "noble" and "simple" ingredients inform chef Jean Joho's appreciation of the earthy cookery of his native Alsace. While the menu changes frequently, sample selections might include starters of salmon soufflé or cream of Alsace cabbage soup with smoked sturgeon and caviar, followed by entrees of roasted Maine lobster in Alsatian Gewürztraminer and ginger or poached tenderloin of beef cooked *pot au feu* style and served with horseradish cream. Desserts are suitably sumptuous and the wine list offers some wonderful American and Alsatian selections. 440 S. LaSalle St., 40th Floor (at Congress Pkwy.). ℭ 312/663-8920. www.leye.com. Reservations required. Main courses $27–$33; menu dégustation $79; 3-course pretheater dinner $44. AE, DC, DISC, MC, V. Tues–Thurs 5:30–9:30pm; Fri–Sat 5:30–10pm. Complimentary valet parking. Subway/El: Brown Line to LaSalle/Van Buren.

Gino's East PIZZA   Gino's East was once the only Chicago restaurant where patrons would wait outside nightly—even in the dead of winter—for pizza. Now that the restaurant has moved into vast new digs, there are no more lines out front, though diners still sit in dark-stained booths, surrounded by paneled walls covered with graffiti. True to its reputation, the pizza is heavy (a small cheese pizza is enough for two), so work up an appetite before chowing down. Specialty pizzas include the supreme, with layers of cheese, sausage, onions, green pepper, and mushrooms; and the vegetarian, with cheese, onions, peppers, asparagus, summer squash, zucchini, and eggplant. 633 N. Wells St. (at Ontario St.). ℭ 312/943-1124. Pizza $8.25–$17. AE, DC, DISC, MC, V. Mon–Thurs 11am–11pm; Fri–Sat 11am–midnight; Sun noon–10pm. Subway/El: Red Line to Chicago/State.

one sixtyblue CONTEMPORARY AMERICAN   Some Chicago foodies consider this the best contemporary American restaurant in town. Chef Martial Noguier's menu changes seasonally; dishes are artfully composed and perfectly satisfying. Appetizers run the gamut from ravioli with lobster-tarragon sauce to Thai lobster soup. Entrees include thinly sliced loin of lamb with a casserole of fresh vegetables, venison with dried plum bread pudding, and a rich honey-glazed salmon topped with an emulsion of chestnuts and walnuts. There is also a daily vegetarian entree selection. The setting is quietly sophisticated. Begin or end your meal with a drink in the stylish lounge. 1400 W. Randolph St. (at Ogden Ave.). ℂ 312/850-0303. Reservations recommended. Main courses $21–$30. AE, DC, MC, V. Mon–Thurs 5–10pm; Fri–Sat 5–11pm; Sun 5–9pm.

RoseAngelis NORTHERN ITALIAN   This is neighborhood dining at its best, a place with reliably good food and very reasonable prices. Tucked in a residential side street in Lincoln Park, the restaurant fills the ground floor of a former private home, with a charming series of cozy rooms and a garden patio. The menu emphasizes pasta (our favorites are the rich lasagna and the ravioli al Luigi, filled with ricotta and served with a sun-dried tomato cream sauce). RoseAngelis is vegetarian-friendly; there's no red meat on the menu, and many of the pastas are served with vegetables. Finish up with the deliciously decadent bread pudding with warm caramel sauce (it's big enough to share). Weeknights are your best bet here because you'll be fighting lots of locals on weekend nights (when you'll wait 2 hr. for a table). 1314 W. Wrightwood Ave. (at Lakewood Ave.). ℂ 773/296-0081. Reservations accepted for parties of 8 or more. Main courses $9.95–$15. DISC, MC, V. Tues–Thurs 5–10pm; Fri–Sat 5–11pm; Sun 4:30–9pm. Subway/El: Red Line to Fullerton.

Spiaggia ITALIAN   Spiaggia is widely acknowledged as the best fine-dining Italian restaurant in the city. Come here to linger over long European lunches, romantic interludes, and celebrations of that big merger. For your starter, consider carpaccio of smoked Sicilian swordfish. The pasta roster tempts with such dishes as pheasant-stuffed ravioli, pumpkin risotto, and gnocchi with wild mushrooms. Entrees include classic zuppa di pesce; duck breast with Ligurian black olives, tomatoes, fennel, and baby artichokes; and grilled squab over lentils with foie gras. For dessert, the chilled mascarpone cheese torte with rich chocolate gelato and espresso sauce is a high point. Adjacent to the restaurant in a narrow, window-lined space is the informal, lower-priced **Café Spiaggia** (ℂ 312/280-2764), which serves Sunday brunch. 980 N. Michigan Ave. (at Oak St.). ℂ 312/280-2750. www.levyrestaurants.com. Reservations required on weekends. Main courses $17–$25 lunch, $29–$38 dinner. Fixed-price 3-course lunch $35. AE, DC, DISC, MC, V. Tues–Thurs 11:30am–2pm and 5:30–9:30pm; Fri–Sat 11:30am–2pm and 5:30–10:30pm; Sun 5:30–9pm. Subway/El: Red Line to Chicago/State.

Tru PROGRESSIVE FRENCH   The sense of humor of chefs Rick Tramonto and Gale Gand shines through the menu (which recently included Insane Black Truffle Soup and "Nut 'n Honey" Foie Gras), making Tru an approachable fine-dining experience. The menu is divided into a series of prix-fixe options. Appetizers include a visually sensational caviar staircase (caviars and fixin's climbing a glass spiral staircase), and a black truffle risotto with rabbit confit and chanterelles. For entrees, "surf, turf and turf" combines roasted lobster with sweetbreads and foie gras; grilled beef tenderloin is paired with gratin of artichoke and marrow sauce. Sate your sweet tooth with roasted pineapple carpaccio or a duet of chocolate and blood orange soufflés. European-style team service is generally polished but not pompous; the expansive wine list is a treat for oenophiles. The restaurant is nonsmoking. 676 N. St. Clair St. (at Huron St.). ℂ 312/202-0001. www.trurestaurant.com. Reservations required. Dinner 3-course prix-fixe menu $75. AE, DC, DISC, MC, V. Mon–Thurs 5:30–10pm; Fri–Sat 5:30–11pm. Subway/El: Red Line to Chicago/State.

Wishbone SOUTHERN   Wishbone is a down-home, casual family spot that inspires intense loyalty (even if the food is only good rather than outstanding). Known for Southern food and big-appetite breakfasts, Wishbone's extensive, reasonably priced menu blends hearty, home-style choices with healthful and vegetarian items. Brunch is the 'Bone's claim to fame, when an eclectic crowd packs in for the plump and tasty salmon cakes, omelets, and red eggs (a lovely mess of tortillas, black beans, cheese, scallions, chile ancho sauce, salsa, and sour cream). Lunch and dinner offerings run from "yardbird" (charbroiled chicken with sweet red-pepper sauce) to hoppin' John or Jack (vegetarian variations on the black-eyed pea classic). There's a newer location at 3300 N. Lincoln Ave. (© 773/549-2663), but the original has more character. 1001 Washington St. (at Morgan St.). © 312/850-2663. Reservations accepted for parties of 6 or more (no reservations on Sun). Main courses $3.25–$8.75 breakfast and lunch, $5.75–$14 dinner. AE, DC, DISC, MC, V. Mon 7am–3pm; Tues–Fri 7am–3pm and 5–10pm; Sat–Sun 8am–3pm and 5–11pm.

Zinfandel ECLECTIC/AMERICAN   Chef Susan Goss and her husband Drew (the restaurant's wine buyer) put together menus that are both totally familiar and unique; each month the menu changes to reflect a specific region of the United States. Be sure to try Goss's signature buttermilk biscuits, cooked to order in a hot iron skillet. Recent monthly menus included "Florida, From Cuban to Cracker" (featuring Key West conch chowder) and California Mission (including stacked enchiladas of honey-glazed duck breast, with smoked mozzarella and olives). If you don't like that month's theme, you can order off the "Ethnic Favorites" menu, which includes a wide-ranging list of popular dishes from past menus. And, yes, as the name implies, you'll find an extensive and interesting list of American wines. 59 W. Grand Ave. (between Dearborn and Clark sts.). © 312/527-1818. www.zinfandelrestaurant.com. Main courses $16–$24. AE, DC, MC, V. Tues–Thurs 11:30am–2:30pm and 5:30–10pm; Fri 11:30am–2:30pm and 5:30–11pm; Sat 10:30am–2:30pm and 5:30–11pm. Subway/El: Red Line to Grand.

5 Chicago After Dark

For up-to-date entertainment listings, check the local newspapers and magazines, particularly the "Friday" and "Weekend Plus" sections of the two dailies, the *Chicago Tribune* and the *Chicago Sun-Times;* the *Chicago Reader* and *New City,* two free weekly tabloids with extensive listings; and the monthly *Chicago* magazine. The *Tribune's* entertainment-oriented website, **www.metromix.com**, and the *Reader's* website, **www.chireader.com**, are also excellent sources of information. For current listings of classical music concerts and opera, call the **Chicago Dance and Music Alliance** (© 312/987-1123).

THE PERFORMING ARTS

The world-class **Chicago Symphony Orchestra,** Orchestra Hall, Symphony Center, 220 S. Michigan Ave. (© 312/294-3000; www.chicagosymphony.org), is led by music director Daniel Barenboim, who has steadily introduced more modern works by 20th-century composers into the orchestra's traditional repertoire. Summertime visitors have an opportunity to hear a CSO performance at the delightful **Ravinia Festival** (© 847/266-5100) in suburban Highland Park, led by music director Christoph Eschenbach (many of the major hotels charter buses here during the season). It's also a tranquil setting for chamber music, world music, jazz and pop concerts, dance, and music study. Tickets are sold to both the covered pavilion, where you get a reserved seat and a view of the stage, and the lawn, which is the real joy of Ravinia: sitting under the stars and a canopy of leafy branches while listening to music and indulging in an elaborate picnic.

The **Lyric Opera of Chicago,** Civic Opera House, Madison Street and Wacker Drive (© 312/332-2244; www.lyricopera.org), attracts top-notch singers from all over the world and has a strong commitment to new American works. The season sells out far in advance, but last-minute cancellations often make tickets available just before a performance. The Lyric Opera performs in the handsome 3,563-seat 1929 Art Deco Civic Opera House, the second-largest opera house in the country.

If you're going to see just one dance performance while you're in town, make it **Hubbard Street Dance Chicago** (© 312/850-9744; www.hubbardstreet dance.com), which seamlessly combines elements of jazz, modern, ballet, and theater dance. The company operates out of a renovated dance center in Chicago's booming West Loop neighborhood, and recently became the flagship resident company of the new music and dance theater at Lakefront Millennium Park in Grant Park.

The **Joffrey Ballet of Chicago** (© 312/739-0120; www.joffrey.com), led by co-founder and artistic director Gerald Arpino, is committed to the classic works of the 20th century. It continues to draw crowds to its popular rock ballet, *Billboards,* set to the music of Prince, and tours internationally.

The Joffrey and other noted dance and musical performers and touring Broadway shows take the stage at the **Auditorium Theatre,** 50 E. Congress Pkwy., between Michigan and Wabash avenues (© 312/922-2110, 312/431-2354 to arrange a tour; www.auditoriumtheatre.org), which is reviewed earlier in this chapter.

THE THEATER SCENE

With more than 200 theaters, Chicago may have dozens of productions playing on any given weekend. It's one of the best theater cities in the country.

To order tickets for many plays and events, call **Ticketmaster Arts Line** (© 312/902-1500), a centralized phone-reservation system that allows you to charge full-price tickets (with an additional service charge) for productions at more than 50 Chicago theaters. For half-price tickets on the day of the show (on Fri, you can also purchase tickets for weekend performances), drop by one of the **Hot Tix** ticket centers (© 312/977-1755; www.hottix.org), located in the Loop at 78 W. Randolph St. (just east of Clark St.); at the Water Works Visitor Center, at 163 E. Pearson; in Lincoln Park at Tower Records, at 2301 N. Clark St.; and in several suburban locations.

The dean of legitimate theaters in Chicago is the **Goodman,** Dearborn Street, between Randolph and Lake streets (© 312/443-3800; www.goodman-theatre.org). The Goodman features both original productions and familiar standards, including Shakespeare, in its modern theater complex. You may not see anything revolutionary, but you'll get some of the best actors in the city and top-notch production values.

The **Steppenwolf Theater Company,** 1650 N. Halsted St., at North Avenue (© 312/335-1650; www.steppenwolf.org) is famous for launching the careers of luminaries such as John Malkovich, Gary Sinise, and John Mahoney (of *Frasier*). Unfortunately, it may be a victim of its own success. Though the acting is always high caliber, shows can be hit or miss, and unlike in the early days, you're certainly not guaranteed a thrilling theatrical experience.

The home of the **Shakespeare Theater on Navy Pier,** 800 E. Grand Ave. (© 312/595-5600; www.chicagoshakes.com), opened in October 1999, is a glittering glass-box complex that rises seven stories and cost $24 million. It features a 525-seat courtyard-style theater patterned loosely on the Swan Theater in Stratford-upon-Avon. But what keeps loyal subscribers coming back is the talented company of actors, including some of the finest Shakespearean performers in the country.

COMEDY & IMPROV

Chicago continues to nurture young comics, drawn to Chicago for the chance to hone their improvisational skills. The **ImprovOlympic,** 3541 N. Clark St. at Addison Street (© 773/880-0199; www.improvolymp.com), offers a nightclub setting for a variety of unscripted nightly performances, from free-form shows to shows loosely based on concepts such as *Star Trek* or dating. **Second City,** 1616 N. Wells St., in the Pipers Alley complex at North Avenue (© 312/337-3992; www.secondcity.com), remains the top comedy club in Chicago. You'll rarely see a weak or unfunny show—these actors are magicians at salvaging material that bombs with audiences.

LIVE MUSIC

Born in the Storyville section of New Orleans, **jazz** moved upriver to Chicago some 75 years ago, and it still has a home here. The **Green Mill,** 4802 N. Broadway and Lawrence (© 773/878-5552; Subway/El: Red Line to Lawrence), is a Chicago treasure; get there early to claim one of the plush velvet booths. Still retaining its speakeasy flavor, it was a popular watering hole during the '20s and '30s, when Al Capone was a regular and the headliners included Sophie Tucker and Al Jolson.

Jazz Showcase, 59 W. Grand St., at Clark Street (© 312/670-2473; Subway/El: Red Line to Grand), in River North, is a spacious and handsome room with two shows a night. Reservations are recommended when a big-name headliner is featured.

The Bucktown/Wicker Park neighborhood has been the center of the alternative rock movement. Scan the *Reader* or *New City* to see who's playing where. **Double Door,** 1572 N. Milwaukee Ave., at North Avenue (© 773/489-3160; www.doubledoor.com; Subway/El: Blue Line to Damen), has some of the better acoustics and sightlines in the city and attracts buzz bands and unknowns to its stage. **Metro,** 3730 N. Clark St., at Racine Avenue (© 773/549-0203; www. metrochicago.com; Subway/El: Red Line to Addison), in an old auditorium, is

---

I Got the Blues

With a few notable exceptions, Chicago's best and most popular blues showcases are located in the entertainment districts of the Near North Side. **B.L.U.E.S,** 2519 N. Halsted St., between Wrightwood and Fullerton avenues (© 773/528-1012; Subway/El: Red/Brown lines to Fullerton), is a small joint for the serious blues aficionado—you won't miss a single move of the musicians standing on stage only yards away. Nearby, at 2548 N. Halsted St. (between Wrightwood and Fullerton aves.) is **Kingston Mines** (© 773/477-4646; Subway/El: Red/Brown lines to Fullerton), one of Chicago's premier blues bars, which celebrates its 35th anniversary in 2003. Kingston Mines is where musicians congregate after their own gigs to jam together and to socialize. There's also a kitchen open late serving up burgers and ribs.

Chicago's premier venue for live alternative/rock acts on the verge of breaking into the big time. Everybody who is anybody has played here over the years, from REM to such local heroes as Smashing Pumpkins.

The **House of Blues**, 329 N. Dearborn St., at Kinzie Street (© **312/923-2000;** www.hob.com; Subway/El: Red Line to Grand), is a massive complex, extravagantly decorated with 600 pieces of Mississippi Delta folk art. It isn't really a blues club as much as a showcase for rock, R&B, zydeco, reggae, and more, consistently booking top national acts. The popular Sunday gospel brunch, offering a Southern-style buffet, brings a different Chicago gospel choir to the stage each week; get tickets in advance.

Country, folk, bluegrass, Latin & Celtic—the **Old Town School of Folk Music,** 4544 N. Lincoln Ave., between Wilson and Montrose avenues (© **773/728-6000;** http://oldtownschool.org; Subway/El: Brown Line to Montrose), has it. The school has hosted everyone from the legendary Pete Seeger to bluegrass phenom Alison Krauss. Its pristine 425-seat concert hall in a former 1930s library in Lincoln Square is the world's largest facility dedicated to presenting traditional and contemporary folk music.

THE CLUB SCENE

Chicago is the hallowed ground where house music was hatched in the 1980s, so it's no surprise to find a few big dance clubs pounding away the big beat. The **Funky Buddha Lounge,** 728 W. Grand Ave. (© **312/666-1695;** Subway/El: Blue Line to Grand), is one of the coolest temples of nightlife in the city, located west of the River North gallery district. The DJs flood the nice-size dance floor with a disco-tech mix infused with salsa, hip hop, and soul.

Harry's Velvet Room, 56 W. Illinois St. (© **312/527-5600;** Subway/El: Red Line to Grand), perhaps the coolest subterranean late-night scene in Chicago, is a champagne, dessert, and wine destination, with a dimly lit, romantic aura that has seduced scores of suave nightcrawlers. At **Le Passage,** One Oak Place, between Rush and State streets (© **312/255-0022;** Subway/El: Red Line to Chicago), the beautiful, the rich, and the designer-suited are attracted by the lush loungey aesthetic; cool blend of house, dance, R&B, soul, and acid jazz music; and a stellar French/international fusion menu.

Red Dog, 1958 W. North Ave., at Milwaukee Avenue (© **773/278-1009;** Subway/El: Blue Line to Damen), easily qualifies as one of the most underground nightspots in the city. The gay-themed Boom-Boom Room on Monday is hands-down the most exotic night on the social calendar, with club kids, drag queens, platform dancers, and everybody else bobbing to a house beat. **Transit,** 1431 W. Lake St. (©**312/491-8600;** Subway/El: Green Line to Ashland), is an excellent no-nonsense dance club that doesn't trick itself out under the auspices of any wacky theme.

THE BAR SCENE

The **Near North Side** has a few entertainment zones saturated with bright, upscale neighborhood bars. Around **Rush and Division streets** (Subway/El: Red Line to Clark/Division) are what a bygone era called singles bars—attracting primarily a college-aged contingent.

Near the Magnificent Mile, the **Billy Goat Tavern,** 430 N. Michigan Ave. (© **312/222-1525;** Subway/El: Red Line to Grand), has been a longtime hangout for newspaper reporters over the years, but it's the "cheezeburgers, cheezeburgers" served at the grill that gave inspiration to the famous *Saturday Night Live* sketch.

In the Old Town 'hood, the family-run **Corcoran's,** at 1615 N. Wells St. (© **312/440-0885;** Subway/El: Brown Line to Sedgwick), is a cozy local hangout.

At the top of any self-respecting Lincoln Park yuppie's list of meeting places is **Glascott's Groggery,** 2158 N. Halsted St., at Webster Avenue (© **773/281-1205;** Subway/El: Red/Brown lines to Fullerton), an Irish pub that's been in the same family since it opened in 1937. And another good Old Country choice is **Irish Oak,** at 3511 N. Clark St. (© **773/935-6669;** Subway/El: Red Line to Addison), which offers traditional Irish music sessions on Wednesdays.

Hundreds of travel books and guides line the shelves of **The Map Room,** 1949 N. Hoyne Ave., at Armitage Avenue (© **773/252-7636).** Peruse that to me on Fuji or Antarctica while sipping a pint of one of the 20-odd draft beers available.

Located in the historic Flat Iron Building, **The Note,** 1565 N. Milwaukee Ave., at North Avenue (© **773/489-0011;** Subway/El: Blue Line to Damen), is a great after-hours bar with pool tables and the right after-hours music: a jukebox exclusively devoted to blues and jazz and occasional live jazz.

THE GAY & LESBIAN SCENE

Most of Chicago's gay bars are conveniently clustered on a stretch of North Halsted Street in Lakeview, making it easy to sample many of them in a breezy walk. To find out what's happening, check out the weekly *Nightlines* and *Gab.*

Step into **Berlin,** 954 W. Belmont Ave., east of Sheffield Avenue (© **773/348-4975;** Subway/El: Red/Brown lines to Belmont), where the disco tunes pulse, the clubby crowd chatters, and the lighting bathes everyone in a cool reddish glow. **Sidetrack,** 3349 N. Halsted St., at Roscoe Street (© **773/477-9189),** is a sleek video bar where TV monitors are never out of your field of vision, nor are the preppy professional patrons.

The Midwest

The Midwestern states are America's heartland, where the ideal of small-town America and the values that go with it are epitomized. The area evokes images of neat farmlands, tree-lined small-town streets, and hardworking, industrialized cities.

This chapter concentrates on an area loosely composed of the states that originally made up the Northwest Territory: Illinois, Indiana, Michigan, Minnesota, Ohio, and Wisconsin, together with neighboring Missouri. America's richest farmland is found here as well as some of America's most important big cities, including the great metropolis of Chicago (see chapter 8)

The ideal small town still exists, and as you travel through the area you'll discover that people really do seem more open, friendly, and down-to-earth—even the cities have a sense of community. Sports are a way of life here, from rooting for your baseball or basketball team—national or local—to hiking, skiing, or biking in gently rolling landscape or rugged terrain. And history is everywhere, reflecting the Midwest's Native American legacy and its immigrant heritage, the pioneers of every nationality who first came to settle this land.

1 Cleveland

Those of you who tune into *The Drew Carey Show* have already heard the news: Cleveland rocks! Sprawling for 50 miles along the shores of Lake Erie, this industrial hub of the heartland has reinvented itself as a city for the new millennium. Once a microcosm of American industrial revolution—with steel mills, oil refineries, and auto and electronics plants as far as the eye could see—the city that served as the butt of many a joke has left behind its gritty, grimy past to become a model of urban reengineering.

Cleveland's rebirth is the result of luck, vision, and good old American-style fortitude. The city had a lot going for it from the start: George Washington himself said that a great city would stand in the blessed spot where the Cuyahoga River met Lake Erie. Industrial success infused money into the city early on, as its steel and oil barons drew upon their vast fortunes to build a monumental downtown and a rich cultural legacy that includes the well-regarded Cleveland Museum of Art, Case Western Reserve University, and the Cleveland Orchestra, America's most recorded symphony (and recently touted as its best by *The New Yorker* magazine). It was a solid foundation for the post-industrial urban vision, which took giant steps forward with the opening of Jacobs Field, the first of the nation's new wave of wonderfully retro-modern major league ballparks, at the gateway to downtown in 1994. A year later came I. M. Pei's splendid Rock & Roll Hall of Fame, which mirrors Pei's own grand Louvre expansion with its imposing yet playful pyramid-shaped design.

Despite its forward-thinking vitality, Cleveland's industrial foundation is very much in evidence. But the heavy industry has moved beyond the city limits;

today, downtown's steel warehouses and tool-and-die factories house trendy clubs and restaurants, and its many bridges lead to gentrified neighborhoods fueled by the optimism that comes with a measure of achievement. The city is still a work in progress, and plenty of areas are still rough around the edges. The message couldn't be clearer, however: Cleveland is striving for global recognition, and the droves of American and international visitors flocking to the reenergized city indicate that success is in the air.

ESSENTIALS

GETTING THERE   By Plane   Cleveland Hopkins International Airport (© 216/265-6030; www.clevelandairport.com) is 10 miles south of downtown. Major car-rental companies are housed at a central off-site lot; pick up the shared shuttle bus, which stops just outside baggage claim. It's an easy 20-minute drive into the city; take I-480 to I-71 north to I-90 into downtown.

If you're not renting, you can take the **RTA Red Line** into the city from the main airport terminal for $1.50 per person. The ride takes about 25 minutes to downtown's Tower City Center and about 40 minutes to the University Circle section of town. Trains generally leave every 15 minutes at peak times, but not all trains stop at University Circle. For more information, see "Getting Around," below. **Taxis** are available outside baggage claim exit 2; expect the fare to run about $22 to $25 (plus tip) to downtown. There's no shuttle, but for **limousine service** to downtown hotels, call **Hopkins Airport Limousine Service** (© 800/543-9912 or 216/267-8282); the per-person, one-way fare runs about $39.

By Train   Amtrak (© 800/USA-RAIL; www.amtrak.com) provides daily service from Chicago (trip time: 7 hr.), New York (12 hr.), and Washington, D.C. (11 hr.) to its downtown station, 200 Cleveland Memorial Shoreway, across from the Great Lakes Science Center (© 216/696-5115).

By Car   The principal highway routes into Cleveland are I-77 from the south (Akron); I-80 or I-76 from the east (Youngstown and Pittsburgh, both connecting with I-77 north near Akron); I-90 from the northeast (Buffalo); I-71 from the southwest (Columbus); and I-80/90 from the west (Toledo). Both I-77 and I-90 will take you right into downtown Cleveland.

VISITOR INFORMATION   Contact the **Convention and Visitors Bureau of Greater Cleveland,** 3100 Terminal Tower, 50 Public Sq., Cleveland, OH 44113-2290 (© 800/321-1004 or 216/621-5555; www.travelcleveland.com). Other useful sites—especially for the latest arts and entertainment coverage—are **Visit Cleveland!** (www.cleveland.com), **CitySearch** (www.cleveland.citysearch. com), and **Digital City** (www.digitalcities.com/cleveland).

The CVB's main **Visitor Information Center** is at Cleveland Hopkins International Airport, 5300 Riverside Dr. (© 216/265-3729). Other locations are Firstar Plaza/Ctix, 1280 Euclid Ave. (© 216/771-9118); Terminal Tower, 50 Public Sq. (© 216/621-7981); and, in the summertime only, on the east bank of the Flats at 1170 Old River Rd. (© 216/621-2218). The helpful staff will answer your questions and can sell you discounted tickets to the city's main attractions, so this makes a great first stop.

ORIENTATION   Cleveland's major attractions are concentrated in two areas: **Downtown,** where you'll find most hotels, government buildings and corporate headquarters, the major sports arenas, and attractions like the Rock & Roll Hall of Fame and Playhouse Square Center. **University Circle** is about 4½ miles east via Euclid Avenue; this leafy district is home to Case Western University (hence the name) and most of the city's major cultural institutions.

Cleveland

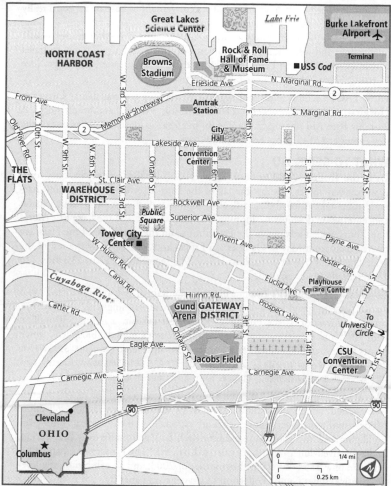

The Gateway and Warehouse districts are an easy walk from Public Square. You can also walk to North Coast Harbor and down to the east bank of the Flats (as long as you don't mind the steep slope), or take the RTA rail's Waterfront Line. You'll want to drive or take a taxi to the west bank of the Flats. Ohio City has its own RTA stop on the Red Line. (For RTA information, see directly below.)

GETTING AROUND The **Greater Cleveland Rapid Transit Authority (RTA) rail system** is not extensive. Visitors usually stick to the main Red Line, which travels between the airport and University Circle, with stops at downtown's Tower City Center and Ohio City; and the Waterfront Line, which connects Tower City with the Flats and North Coast Harbor. In addition, **RTA buses** cover five downtown loop routes from Public Square. For complete information, call the **RTA Answerline** at ℂ 216/621-9500.

For taxi service, call the **Yellow Cab Company of Cleveland** (ℂ 216/623-1500); **Ace Taxi Service** (ℂ 216/361-4700); **United Cab Company** (ℂ 216/398-9000); or **Americab** (ℂ 216/881-1111).

You don't need a car downtown, but it's convenient to have one if you'd really like to explore. The cost of taxis will negate what you save by not renting, however, and a 20- or 30-minute wait for a summoned cab is common, especially on evenings and weekends. Although you can use the RTA rail system to travel between downtown and University Circle, driving is the easiest way to go. (See "Getting There," above, for car-rental information.)

FAST FACTS   Emergency and urgent-care services are available at **Lutheran Hospital,** 1730 W. 25th St. (© **216/696-4300;** www.lutheranhospital.org). A 24-hour **Rite Aid** pharmacy (© **216/676-5561**) is located 8 miles out of the city center at 15149 Snow Rd., in Brookpark.

WHAT TO SEE & DO

Lolly the Trolley (© **800/848-0173** or 216/771-4484; www.lollytrolley.com) is a great way to get to know the lay of the land. Excellent 1- and 2-hour narrated tours take place aboard a fleet of replica trolley cars; the 1-hour version concentrates on downtown, skipping University Circle and the Lake Erie shoreline. Tours, which leave from the Powerhouse on the west bank of the Flats, are offered daily from May to October, on Friday and Saturday only the rest of the year. The fare is $10 or $15 adults, $9 or $14 seniors, and $7 or $10 kids 2 to 17; reservations are required.

Cleveland Metroparks Zoo   This well-maintained and well-organized zoo is a great place to spend half a day, especially if you're traveling with the kids. The standout attraction is the multilevel Rainforest exhibit, a recent $30-million addition. Don't miss the actual rainstorm inside this simulated biosphere, which boasts more than 600 animals and insects from all seven continents. 3900 Wildlife Way (off I-71, between W. 25th St. and Fulton Rd.). © 216/661-6500. www.clemetzoo.com. Admission $8 adults; $4 children 2–11. Daily 10am–5pm (Sat–Sun to 7pm in summer).

Cleveland Museum of Art   This museum is renowned for its consistently well-curated temporary exhibitions and its excellent permanent collection. Modern and postmodern movements are especially well chronicled. Among the highlights are Picasso's brilliant and little-seen *La Vie,* from his early Blue Period, and a massive Monet water lilies canvas. Look for "The History of Japanese Art Photography: 1854–2000" in the summer of 2003, and an exhibition of Cleveland native Agnes Gund's collection of drawing on paper by such 20th-century masters as Paul Klee, Roy Lichtenstein, and Jasper Johns (Oct 26, 2003–Jan 11, 2004). 11150 East Blvd., University Circle. © 216/421-7350, or 888/CMA-0033 for advance exhibition tickets. www.clevelandart.org. Free admission to museum (with fees for some special events and exhibitions). Tues, Thurs, Sat, Sun 10am–5pm; Wed and Fri 10am–9pm.

Cleveland Museum of Natural History   Here's another fine University Circle museum that, in early 2002, opened its new $6.9-million, sphere-shaped Shafran Planetarium. Among the museum's other draws are an excellent gem and jewels collection; a fascinating array of fossils and geological specimens, with a special emphasis on prehistoric Ohio; and a hands-on natural sciences Discovery Center for the little ones. 1 Wade Oval Dr., University Circle. © 800/317-9155 or 216/231-4600. www.cmnh.org. Admission $6.50 adults; $4.50 seniors, college students, and children 7–18; $3.50 children 3–6. Planetarium admission $3. Mon–Sat 10am–5pm, Sun noon–5pm; extended observatory hr. Sept–May, Wed to 10pm.

Great Lakes Science Center   Dramatically situated on the lakefront between the Rock & Roll Hall and the new football stadium, this exciting $55-million museum is a kid-pleaser extraordinaire. A stunning recent addition is the new 3,000-square-foot interactive Great Lakes Environment exhibition. Overall, the museum boasts more than 320 hands-on science experiments that explain through example: You'll learn about velocity by swinging a baseball bat, about momentum on a merry-go-round for one, and so on. An entire floor is dedicated to the latest technology and a state-of-the-art OMNIMAX theater that shows larger-than-life features. 601 Erieside Ave., downtown. ℂ 216/694-2000. www.greatscience.com. Museum only, $7.95 adults, $6.95 seniors, $5.95 children 3–17. Combination ticket (with OMNIMAX movie) $11 adults, $9.95 seniors, $7.95 children. Daily 9:30am–5:30pm; call for OMNIMAX showtimes.

Rock & Roll Hall of Fame & Museum   If any one thing is most responsible for Cleveland's rebirth, this controversial glass-and-porcelain pyramid is it. Designed by I. M. Pei, this temple to rock music is a venerable house of worship or an overblown house of cards, depending on whom you talk to. Ignore the nay-saying and come enjoy it for what it is: a high-concept, multimedia collection of exhibits, archives, and films that tell the story of rock through the ages from its earliest roots through the post-grunge days. There's just no arguing that this is the coolest collection of pop-culture memorabilia around. One of the grooviest recent additions is the Jimi Hendrix Surround Sound Theater and Exhibit, where fans can peruse the legend's guitars, costumes, handwritten lyrics and watercolor landscapes, not to mention revel in electrifying live video highlights of historic performances. 1 Key Plaza, downtown ℂ 888/764-ROCK or 216/781-7625. www.rockhall.org. Admission $17 adults, $13 seniors, $11 children 9–11; free to children 8 and under. Daily 10am–5:30pm (with extended evening hr. Memorial Day–Labor Day, Wed and Sat 10am–9pm).

WWII Submarine USS *Cod*   This World War II sub is credited with sinking nearly 30,000 tons of Japanese sea vessels. Completely intact and a designated National Historic Landmark, the *Cod* is particularly enlightening to tour because it has not been adapted for civilian access—visitors use the same vertical ladders and hatches that were used by the wartime crew. 1089 N. Marginal Dr. (just east of the Rock & Roll Hall of Fame). ℂ 216/566-8770. www.usscod.org. Admission $5 adults, seniors $4, $3 students 5–12. May–Sept daily 10am–5pm. Rapid: South Harbor.

MORE ATTRACTIONS

PARKS   In the University Circle section of the city is **Rockefeller Park,** a 296-acre oasis between Lake Erie and Case Western Reserve University. Take 105th Street, Martin Luther King Jr. Drive, or East Boulevard for easiest park access. In adjoining **Wade Park** are the Cleveland Museum of Art, the Museum of Natural History, and the **Cleveland Botanical Garden** (ℂ 216/721-1600), with 7 acres of gardens open to the public. Work is also underway on the Botanical Gardens' new $37-million expansion that will include an 18,000-square-foot conservatory showcasing the fragile ecosystems of Madagascar's deserts and Costa Rica's cloud forests. It's expected to open in 2003.

West of downtown is **Edgewater Park,** 6700 Memorial Shoreway, at West Boulevard (ℂ 216/881-8141), one of the city's best swimming beaches, with bathhouses, concessions, fishing piers, and more. Beach access is free.

CRUISES   The *Nautica Queen* (ℂ 800/837-0604 or 216/696-8888; www.nauticaqueen.com) offers lunch, brunch, and dinner cruises that also take in lake and river sights. Prices range from $22 to $45 adults, $12 to $21 kids. Cruises depart from the Nautica Entertainment Complex on the west bank of the Flats. Book ahead, as these hugely popular cruises regularly sell out in advance.

In the Grandstand

Cleveland is a monster sports town. Sentiments are heightened, no doubt, by the fact that all the city's pro teams play in first-rate venues within walking distance of one another in the heart of the city. When a game is on, downtown becomes electric with excitement (especially when the home team is winning, of course).

Popularly known as "the Tribe," the perennially contending Cleveland Indians play at state-of-the-art, 42,000-seat **Jacobs Field,** at Ontario Street and Carnegie Avenue (© **216/420-4636;** www.indians.com), a retro-modern ballpark that's the envy of many a major league owner. It's impossible to underestimate the effect that "The Jake" has had on the city's renaissance. Next door is **Gund Arena,** at Ontario Street and Huron Road (© **216/420-2200;** www.gundarena.com), home to the NBA's Cleveland Cavaliers (© **800/332-CAVS** or 216/420-CAVS; www.nba.com/cavs) and the WNBA's Cleveland Rockers (© **216/263-ROCK;** www.cleveland rockers.com). The NFL's Cleveland Browns play at **Cleveland Browns Stadium,** lakefront on Erieside Avenue (© **440/891-5050;** www.cleveland browns.com).

ATTRACTIONS NEAR CLEVELAND

Cedar Point Amusement Park   Regularly named the best amusement park in the world, lakefront Cedar Point boasts the world's biggest collection of rides (68) and more roller coasters (15) than any other park in the world. Thrill-seekers love the Magnum XL 200, considered the best steel coaster in the world, as well as the park's new Wicked Twister, touted as the world's first double-twisting impulse coaster featuring 450-degree corkscrews; and Millennium Force, which rises 310 feet and exceeds speeds of 92 miles per hour. Camp Snoopy is an all-ages playland with its own kid-friendly coaster. Also on-site are the 18-acre **Soak City** water park and **Challenge Park,** where you and the kids can race stock cars, play mini-golf, and ride RipCord, a "skycoaster" that combines free-fall skydiving and hang gliding. 1 Cedar Point Dr. (U.S. 250), Sandusky. © **419/ 627-2350.** www.cedarpoint.com. Admission $42 guests 48 in. tall and taller, $25 seniors 60 and over, $20 children shorter than 48-in. Additional admission charges for Soak City water park and Challenge Park. Check website for discount coupons. Open daily May–Labor Day; weekends Sept– Oct; call for exact operating schedule, which often changes. Cedar Point is 61 miles, or a 1¼-hr. drive, from Cleveland. Follow I-90 to I-71 south to I-480 west to I-80 west to Exit 118 (Sandusky); turn right onto U.S. 250.

Six Flags Worlds of Adventure   Formerly Geauga Lake Amusement Park, Six Flags recently completed an $80-million expansion and acquired adjacent Sea World Cleveland, making this park the only one of its kind in the world. Among the 10 powerhouse roller coasters are Batman Knight Flight, the world's longest "floorless" coaster (riders are secured solely by shoulder harnesses); Superman Ultimate Escape, the world's first vertical spiraling impulse coaster, with two vertical drops touted as genuine free-fall experiences; and the Villain, a white-knuckle, lightening-fast wooden coaster. New in 2002 is X-Flight, known as a "flying roller coaster," in which riders soar down a 115-foot hill through eight loops, spins, and spirals at 51 miles per hour. For tamer tastes, Looney Tunes characters and all-ages rides are also on hand. **Hurricane Harbor** water park is included in the price of admission. 1060 N. Aurora Rd., Aurora.

Ⓒ **330/562-8303**. www.sixflags.com. Admission $40 adults, $20 seniors and juniors (kids under 48 in. tall), free for ages 2 and under. Open daily Memorial Day to Labor Day, weekends only in May and Sept–Oct; call for exact operating schedule.

WHERE TO STAY

All of downtown's hotels also offer deeply discounted weekend rates, and some feature attractive packages that can include such additional premiums as admission to the Rock & Roll Hall of Fame or weekend brunch.

The Brownstone Inn   Built in 1874 and on the National Register of Historic Places, this quirky but charming inn is a good choice for independent, budget-minded travelers who like a little personality in their lodgings. The two attractively furnished front rooms are best. Facilities include a shared kitchenette with microwave and free snacks. Situated about halfway between Public Square and University Circle, the gentrified neighborhood is convenient to all major attractions. 3649 Prospect Ave. (at E. 36th St.), Cleveland, OH 44115. Ⓒ **216/426-1753**. www. brownstoneinndowntown.com. 5 units, 4 with shared bathroom and 1 with private bathroom. $75–$105 double. Rates include full breakfast. AE, DISC, MC, V. Free parking.

Cleveland Marriott Downtown at Key Center   This newish hotel is one of downtown's top moderately priced choices, with better decor and amenities than the often pricier Renaissance (see below). The bright, spacious rooms feature such extras as coffeemakers, irons, and hair dryers; request one with lake and Rock Hall views at no extra cost. 127 Public Sq., Cleveland, OH 44114. Ⓒ **800/228-9290** or 216/696-9200. Fax 216/696-0966. www.marriott.com. 400 units. $179–$199 double. Weekend rates as low as $119; ask about packages that include breakfast and parking. Children 17 and under stay free in parents' room. AE, DC, DISC, MC, V. Valet or self parking $15. **Amenities:** Restaurant; indoor pool.

Comfort Inn Downtown   On the eastern edge of downtown, this motel is just fine for travelers on a tight budget. Neatniks may have a few quibbles, but a VCR in every room, a free video lending library, and a complimentary continental breakfast fill the gaps. With such extras as a microwave, whirlpool tub, refrigerator and pullout sofa in the sitting room, the suites—which you can usually nab for $109 or less—are the best deal in the house. 1800 Euclid Ave. (at E. 18th St.), Cleveland, OH 44115. Ⓒ **800/228-5150** or 216/861-0001. www.comfortinn.com. 130 units. $69–$119 double; $109–$149 suite. Children 17 and under stay free in parents' room. Rates include continental breakfast. AE, DC, MC, V. Parking $6.50.

Glidden House   Cleveland's best bed-and-breakfast is housed in an elegant 1910 French Gothic mansion. The individually decorated guest rooms boast a pleasing blend of old-world style and modern conveniences. Situated in the leafy heart of University Circle, the location is tops for culture vultures. On-site is an English-style pub, and next door is Sergio's for fine Brazilian-accented dining (see "Where to Dine," below). 1901 Ford Dr., Cleveland, OH 44106. Ⓒ **800/759-8358** or 216/231-8900. Fax 216/231-2130. www.gliddenhouse.com. 60 units. $189–$229. Rates include European continental breakfast. AE, DC, DISC, MC, V. Free parking. **Amenities:** Restaurant.

Hampton Inn Cleveland–Downtown   Here's Cleveland's best budget hotel. Rooms have a fresh, new feel and come with the kinds of amenities that usually cost more: coffeemakers, hair dryers, and irons and boards, plus sofas in some king rooms. Same-day valet service is available. The location is excellent, on a nice downtown block within walking distance of all major attractions. 1460 E. 9th St. (at Superior Ave.), Cleveland, OH 44114. Ⓒ **800/HAMPTON** or 216/241-6600. Fax 216/241-8811. www.hampton-inn.com. 194 units. $79–$129 double. Children 17 and under stay free in parents' room. Rates include continental breakfast. AE, DC, DISC, MC, V. Parking $10. **Amenities:** Small fitness center; free access to nearby health club with Olympic-sized indoor pool.

Holiday Inn–City Center Lakeshore   The prime advantage of this basic hotel is its location, within walking distance of the Rock Hall, the Browns' stadium, and the convention center. The rest of downtown and the Flats are accessible via courtesy shuttle—a nice plus. Rooms are newly renovated, but don't expect more than a coffeemaker and a hair dryer in the bathroom in addition to the standard motel decor. 1111 Lakeside Ave. (at E. 9th St.), Cleveland, OH 44114. ℭ **888/ 425-3835** or 216/241-5100. Fax 216/241-7437. www.holiday-inn.com. 379 units. $109–$179 double. Children 17 and under stay free in parents' room. AE, DC, DISC, MC, V. Self-parking $10. **Amenities:** Restaurant; indoor pool.

Radisson Hotel at Gateway–Cleveland   This terrific, moderately priced hotel is perfect for sports fans, as both Jacobs Field and Gund Arena are just a block away (you may even see the visiting team in the halls). The plush, pretty Shaker-style rooms feature all the extras—coffeemakers, and so on—plus video games. Complimentary cookies are served in the lobby every evening. 651 Huron Rd. (across from Jacob's Field/Gund Arena), Cleveland, OH 44115. ℭ **800/333-3333** or 216/377-9000. Fax 216/377-9001. www.radisson.com. 142 units. $119–$175 double; from $175 suite. Extra person $15. Children 17 and under stay free in parents' room. AE, DC, DISC, MC, V. Valet parking $18. **Amenities:** Restaurant.

Renaissance Cleveland Hotel   Conveniently attached to Tower City Center, this somewhat formal hotel is an AAA four-diamond award winner and a member of Historic Hotels of America. The Americana-style rooms are smaller than most in town due to the building's age, which can also result in such quirks as sloping floors. Otherwise, they're perfectly comfortable (no coffeemakers, though). The interior ones tend to be dark. At Tower City Center, 24 Public Sq., Cleveland, OH 44113. ℭ **800/696-6898** or 216/696-5600. Fax 216/696-0432. www.renaissance hotels.com. 491 units. $159–$199 double; from $250 suite. Extra person $20. AE, DC, DISC, MC, V. Valet parking $16. **Amenities:** Restaurants (2); indoor pool.

The Ritz-Carlton, Cleveland   Adjoining the Avenue mall at Tower City Center, this AAA four-diamond winner is Cleveland's finest hotel. It offers the traditional Ritz-Carlton elegance and style, with expansive windows overlooking the waterfront. The extras include VCRs and plush terry robes in every room. At Tower City Center, 1515 W. 3rd St., Cleveland, OH 44113. ℭ **800/241-3333** or 216/623-1300. Fax 216/623-1491. www.ritz-carlton.com. 208 units. $185–$225 double; $225–$399 suite. Children 17 and under stay free in parents' room. AE, DC, DISC, MC, V. Valet parking $22. **Amenities:** Restaurant; indoor pool; spa; fitness center.

Wyndham Cleveland Hotel at Playhouse Square   This modern hotel, just a stone's throw from Jacobs Field and Playhouse Square, caters to both the business and leisure crowds. The location is great, and guests staying here are quick to commend the friendly service. The stylish public spaces lead to rooms that are large, comfortable, and outfitted with all the extras. 1260 Euclid Ave. (at Huron Rd.), Cleveland, OH 44115. ℭ **800/WYNDHAM** or 216/615-7500. Fax 216/615-3355. www.wyndham.com. 205 units. $139–$349 double (usually $139–$239). Inquire about packages. Children 17 and under stay free in parents' room. AE, DC, DISC, MC, V. Self-parking $12, valet parking $20. **Amenities:** Restaurant; indoor pool.

WHERE TO DINE

Cleveland's **Hard Rock Cafe** is at the Avenue mall at Tower City Center, 230 West Huron Rd. (ℭ **216/830-ROCK**).

Alice Coopers'town AMERICAN   Feed your inner Frankenstein at pioneering shock-rocker (and native son) Alice Cooper's new restaurant and sports bar. With a prime location across the street from Jacobs Field, the old brick warehouse is always packed on game days. The extensive menu ranges from hefty burgers to barbecued spare ribs, plus pizzas, pasta dishes, and salads. As with the Hard Rock Cafes, the place is filled with loud music, eye-popping memorabilia, plus souvenirs for purchase. 2217 E. 9th St. ℭ **216/566-8100.** Reservations accepted. Main courses $5.50–$17. AE, DC, MC, V. Daily 11am–1am.

Blue Point Grille SEAFOOD   This Warehouse District spot is Cleveland's hottest see-and-be-scene; don't be surprised if you spot a local sports hero or two among the stylish patrons. The kitchen excels at both creative and straightforward preparations of flown-in-daily fish, which can range from a masala-spiced sea bass to a simple seared sushi-grade ahi. The oysters are top-grade, natch, and steaks are on hand for non-fish eaters. 700 W. St. Clair Ave. (at W. 6th St.). ℭ **216/875-7827.** Reservations highly recommended. Main courses $19–$40. AE, DC, DISC, MC, V. Mon–Fri 11am–3pm and 5–10:30pm; Sat 4–11:30pm; Sun 4–9pm.

Frank Sterle's Slovenian Country House CENTRAL/EASTERN EUROPEAN   This authentic central European beer hall has a large, open dining room with hand-hewn beams, a hearty old-world menu (Wiener schnitzel a specialty), and late-night, weekend polka bands. At lunch, try the pierogi. 1401 E. 55th St. (off I-90). ℭ **216/881-4181.** Reservations recommended for 5 or more. Main courses $6–$8 lunch, $9–$12 dinner. AE, MC, V. Mon 11:30am–3pm; Tues–Sat 11:30am–9pm; Sun 4:30–7pm.

Great Lakes Brewing Company ECLECTIC PUB FOOD   When Drew Carey quaffs a beer on his Cleveland-based TV show, it's usually Burning River Pale Ale, a crisp, full-bodied amber that's just one of Great Lakes' excellent brews. The only American brewery ever to win the coveted "Microbrewery of the Year" award is just a comfortable Ohio City pub with a long mahogany bar, big booths, and pleasant garden seating. The simple pub grub is fine accompaniment for the brews; look for such locally accented fare as beer-battered cod and bratwurst as well as satisfying burgers. 2516 Market Ave. (1 block north of Lorain Ave. at W. 26th St.). ℭ **216/771-4404.** www.greatlakesbrewing.com. Reservations recommended. Main courses $8–$19. AE, DC, MC, V. Mon–Thurs 11:30am–midnight (kitchen closes at 10:30pm); Fri–Sat 11:30am–1am (kitchen to 11:30pm).

Greek Isles GREEK   Reminiscent of sunny Crete with its airy white-stucco interior, this eye-catching restaurant serves authentic, high-quality fare. Expect all your Greek favorites, including excellent moussaka and calamari, and savory stuffed grape leaves. The fish is always fresh, and the ample combo plates offer great value. 500 W. St. Clair Ave. (at W. 6th St.). ℭ **216/861-1919.** Reservations recommended. www.cleveland.com/sites/greekisles. Main courses and combination plates $10–$25. AE, MC, V. Sun–Thurs 11am–10pm; Fri–Sat 11am–midnight.

Lola NEW AMERICAN   Just minutes from downtown in the still-gentrifying Tremont district is Cleveland's hippest restaurant. Chef Michael Symon has been lauded in *Bon Appetit* for his winningly inventive urban comfort food. Highlights include moist and flavorful pan-roasted local walleye over a Midwestern potato risotto, and a crispy duck breast. Service is excellent. Call ahead for exact directions. 900 Literary Rd. ℭ **216/771-5652.** Reservations highly recommended. www.lolabistro.com. Main courses $17–$24. AE, DC, DISC, MC, V. Tues–Thurs 5pm–12am; Fri–Sat 5pm–2am; Sun 5–11pm.

Maxi's PIZZA   Close to University Circle's museums is this unassuming Little Italy bar and restaurant, which serves up excellent pizzas made from scratch with the freshest ingredients, including whole-clove garlic and garden-fresh mushrooms. The white pizzas are especially savory, and service is as friendly as can be. Down the street is **Mama Santa,** 12305 Mayfield Rd. (© 216/231-9567), another local favorite that bakes a top-notch pie. 12113 Mayfield Rd. © 216/421-1500. Reservations recommended. Pizzas $12–$16; pastas $11–$18. AE, DISC, MC, V. Mon–Sat 5pm–2am (pizza served until 11pm); Sun 5–10:30pm.

Sans Souci Mediterranean Cuisine FRENCH/MEDITERRANEAN Regularly touted as Cleveland's finest continental restaurant, this lovely French-country dining room is ideal for a special occasion. Expect such classics as osso buco and roasted veal chops as well as a selection of Mediterranean-style pastas for lighter tastes (and wallets). In the Renaissance Cleveland Hotel, 24 Public Sq. © 216/902-4095. Reservations recommended. Main courses $10–$18 lunch; $18–$32 dinner. AE, DC, DISC, MC, V. Mon–Fri 11:30am–2:30pm and 5:30–10pm; Sat 5:30–11pm; Sun 5:30–10pm.

Sergio's BRAZILIAN   This University Circle restaurant bursts with Mondrian-ish primary colors and festive South American flavors. Nothing is too adventurous, so even timid palates will be pleased with such choices as Brazilian-style beef tenderloin (marinated in garlic, black pepper, and port). There's a tropical-style patio for warm-weather dining and live Brazilian jazz on occasion. 1903 Ford Dr. (next to Glidden House). © 216/231-1234. Reservations recommended. Main courses $7–$13 lunch, $13–$25 dinner. AE, DISC, MC, V. Mon–Thurs 11:30am–2:30pm and 5:30–9:30pm; Fri 11:30am–2:30pm and 5:30–11pm; Sat 5:30–11pm; Sun 4–9pm during the summer.

Watermark Restaurant AMERICAN/SEAFOOD   This loftlike riverfront restaurant boasts stellar views and a reliably good menu, whose highlights include mustard-crusted Lake Erie walleye and a generous rib-eye in Cabernet sauce. The airy brick-walled main room has a lovely glassed-in veranda for year-round waterfront dining, plus an alfresco patio in summer. Ask about the summertime dessert cruises, which offer a dramatic view of the city's illuminated bridges. 1250 Old River Rd. © 216/241-1600. www.watermark-flats.com. Reservations recommended. Main courses $6.50–$10 lunch; $12–$26 dinner (most less than $30). AE, DC, DISC, MC, V. Mon–Thurs 11:30am–10pm; Fri–Sat 11:30am–11pm; Sun 10am–2:30pm and 5–10pm.

CLEVELAND AFTER DARK

Tickets for many events are sold through **Ticketmaster** (© 216/241-5555; www.ticketmaster.com). **Advantix** (© 800/766-6048 or 216/241-6000; www.tickets.com) sells tickets to events at Playhouse Square Center. For travelers on a budget, another great option is the **Ctix** outlet at Firstar Plaza, 1280 Euclid Ave. (© 216/771-9118), where culture vultures may purchase half-price, day-of-show theater tickets, as well as discounted movie tickets.

THE PERFORMING ARTS   Considered by many to be the finest symphony orchestra in the U.S., the world-renowned **Cleveland Orchestra** (© 800/686-1141 or 216/231-1111; www.clevelandorch.com) will be under the leadership of new music director Franz Welser-Most beginning in the 2002–2003 season. The orchestra performs at **Severance Hall,** 11001 Euclid Ave., at East Boulevard, in University Circle. The stately 1931 concert hall was greeted by rave reviews when it emerged from a massive renovation in early 2000. In summer, the orchestra takes up residence at the open-air **Blossom Music Center** in Cuyahoga Falls, 34 miles south of the city off I-77.

The nation's second-largest performing arts center (after New York City's Lincoln Center) is **Playhouse Square Center,** 1501 Euclid Ave. (℃ **216/771-4444;** www.playhousesquare.com), a prime symbol of Cleveland's cultural renaissance. Four beautifully restored theaters present theatrical and musical performances of all kinds, including touring productions of Broadway shows. It's also home to such resident companies as the **Ohio Ballet** (www.ohioballet.org) and **DanceCleveland** (www.dancecleveland.org), which presents such renowned modern companies as Alvin Ailey Trinity Irish Dance Company; and the 25-year-old **Cleveland Opera** (www.clevelandopera.org), among others.

THE BAR & CLUB SCENE   To find out what's happening, pick up one of the free weeklies, the *Cleveland Free Times* and the *Cleveland Scene,* which are available all over town.

The east bank of **the Flats** along Old River Road, between St. Clair Avenue and Front Street, is a former industrial area now chock-full of party-hearty bars and clubs.

Among the establishments are the **Odeon Concert Club,** 1295 Old River Rd. (℃ **888/633-6688** or 216/574-2525), a top-notch performance venue hosting national and up-and-coming rock acts.

On the west bank of the Flats is the waterfront **Nautica Entertainment Complex** (www.nauticaflats.com). Among its many after-dark attractions are **Shooters** (℃ **216/861-6900**), a hulking behemoth of a restaurant and dance club that caters to yuppies on the prowl and other revelers; the **Improv Comedy Club** (℃ **216/696-4677**), featuring up-and-coming stand-up talent; and romantic dinner cruises aboard the *Nautica Queen* (see "More Attractions," earlier in this chapter). Summer visitors should see what's on at the **Nautica Pavilion** (℃ **216/861-3229**), which has hosted everyone from Lynyrd Skynyrd to Britney Spears.

A somewhat more sophisticated crowd gathers in the **Warehouse District,** mainly along West 6th Street between Superior and Lakeside avenues. Highlights include **Spy Bar,** 1261 W. 6th St. (℃ **216/621-7907**), an upscale lounge with a well-dressed crowd and a stylish vibe; hometown boy Trent Reznor celebrated here after the opening show of Nine Inch Nails' 2000 U.S. tour. Young hipsters meet to relax in comfy chairs and play board games at lively **Liquid,** 1212 W. 6th St. (℃ **216/479-7717**). **Velvet Dog,** 1280 W. 6th St. (℃ **216/664-1116;** www.velvetdogcleveland.com) is a high-style dance club with an excellent martini bar and retro-hip DJs with a clue. Other trendy options for energetic bar-hoppers include the eclectic **Blind Pig Speakeasy,** 1228 W. 6th St. (℃ **216/621-0011;** www.theblindpig.com); and the upscale nightclub **Funky Buddha,** 1360 W. 9th St. (℃ **216/776-7777;** www.funkybuddhabar.com).

Meanwhile, jazz lovers flock to **Club Isabella,** 2025 University Hospital Dr. (℃ **216/229-1177**), or, for music mixed with comedy and avant-garde poetry, to **Robin's Nest,** 4059 St. Clair St. (℃ **216/881-5299**).

Chicago's famous **Second City** sketch-comedy theater has recently opened at 1422 Euclid Ave. (℃ **216/685-0100**), bringing to five the total of such clubs across the country.

Ohio City is great for those looking for an easygoing night on the town. The cozy, candlelit **Market Avenue Wine Bar,** 2526 Market Ave., at West 26th Street (℃ **216/696-9463**), boasts an extensive wine list and a pleasing light-bites menu. Next door is the celebrated **Great Lakes Brewing Company** (see "Where to Dine," above).

2 Cincinnati

Located along the winding banks of the Ohio River and tucked amid rolling hills that are home to its many historic and eclectic neighborhoods, Cincinnati is a major Midwestern hub of commerce, art, family attractions, and entertainment. When it became an important rail and river hub, Henry Wadsworth Longfellow pronounced it the "Queen City of the West." Settled primarily by Germans in the 19th century, Cincinnati today remains a clean, attractive, and dynamic urban center, where life proceeds at an unhurried pace.

ESSENTIALS

GETTING THERE   By Plane   Major airlines fly into **Cincinnati/Northern Kentucky International Airport** (© 859/767-3144; www.cvgairport.com), one of the fastest-growing airports in the world, which also serves as a gateway to northern Kentucky (see chapter 6). Look for the 14 Art Deco murals from Union Station before you leave the airport. **Airport Taxi Shuttle** (© 513/929-9999) provides regular service to downtown hotels for $25 one-way, $50 round-trip. Cab fare is about $22.

By Train   Amtrak (© 800/USA-RAIL; www.amtrak.com) serves Union Station, 1300 Western Ave. There's daily service from Chicago (trip time: 9 hr.), Indianapolis (3½ hr.), and Washington, D.C. (15½ hr.).

By Car   The major routes into Cincinnati are I-75 from the north (Dayton) and south (Lexington); I-71 from the northeast (Columbus) and southwest (Louisville); and I-74 from the northwest (Indianapolis).

VISITOR INFORMATION   Contact the **Greater Cincinnati Convention & Visitor Bureau,** 300 W. 6th St., Cincinnati, OH 45202 (© 800-543-2613 or 513/621-2142; www.cincyusa.com).

GETTING AROUND   The **Queen City Metro** provides inexpensive bus service (© 513/621-4455). Exact change or token is required. On weekdays before 3pm, the fare is 65¢; after 3pm it's 80¢. On weekends, the fare is 50¢. Transfers cost 10¢.

An odd city ordinance does not allow cabs to cruise downtown for fares. They must park at taxi stands and wait for passengers. Cabs can usually be found on the west end of Fifth Street, where the convention center and many hotels are located.

FAST FACTS   A major local hospital is **University Hospital,** 234 Goodman St., Clifton (© 513/584-1000). There's a 24-hour **CVS** pharmacy at 2520 Vine St. (© 513/569-4301).

SPECIAL EVENTS & FESTIVALS   Fans of choral music flock to Music Hall for the internationally renowned **May Festival** (© 513/381-3300; www.may festival.com), an annual event since 1875. Late July ushers in the **Coors Light Festival** (© 513/871-3900), bringing the sounds of soul and R&B to Cinergy Field. Summer officially kicks off downtown Memorial Day weekend with the **Taste of Cincinnati,** when dozens of area restaurants sell small but tasty portions of their best dishes. Summer closes with Labor Day weekend's **Riverfest,** featuring fireworks, entertainment, and food throughout the city's waterfront parks. In mid-September, Fountain Square becomes a German *biergarten* for **Oktoberfest–Zinzinnati,** complete with German music, dancing, food, and lots of beer.

WHAT TO SEE & DO

Cincinnati is built on hills overlooking the Ohio River. Take time to walk around the city's colorful and historic neighborhoods. The **Over-the-Rhine** district just north of downtown contains the largest collection of 19th-century civic, religious, and residential architecture in the U.S. It's home to Music Hall and historic **Findlay Market** (www.findlaymarket.org), a lively year-round open-air fresh foods market. The narrow, winding streets of **Mount Adams** reveal stunning views of downtown and the Ohio River. For attractions across the Ohio, see "Northern Kentucky" in chapter 6.

Cincinnati Art Museum (CAM)   Cincinnati's Art Museum houses a rich collection of paintings, sculptures, prints, photographs, costumes, tribal artifacts, and musical instruments. The Rookwood Pottery Gallery is especially worth seeing. 953 Eden Park Dr. ✆ 513/721-5204. www. cincinnatiartmuseum.org. Admission $5 adults, $4 seniors and students, children under 18 free; free Sat. Tues–Sat 10am–5pm; Sun noon–6pm. Closed Thanksgiving and Christmas Day.

Cincinnati Museum Center   The Cincinnati Museum Center is housed in Union Terminal, built in 1931 and recently restored to its original Art Deco grandeur. Inside you'll find three museums and the **Robert D. Lindner Family OMNIMAX Theater.** In the **Museum of Natural History and Science,** exhibits immerse you in different Ohio Valley environments. The **Cincinnati Historical Society Museum** has one of the largest regional collections in the

U.S. At the **Cinergy Children's Museum,** you'll find nine interactive exhibits, including Waterworks, Energy Zone, Little Sprouts Farm, and Kids at Work. 1300 Western Ave. (© 800/733-2077 or 513/287-7000. www.cincymuseum.org. "Best Buy" package (Omnimax and all museums): $16 adults, $11 children 3–12. Any 3 attractions: $13 adults, $8.75 children 3–12. Any 2 attractions: $9.75 adults, $6.75 children 3–12. Single attraction: $6.75 adults, $4.75 children 3–12. Seniors $1 off any individual or combination ticket. Mon–Sat 10am–5pm; Sun 11am–6pm. Parking $3.

Cincinnati Zoo & Botanical Garden   This 125-year-old zoo is America's second oldest and one of its best. Be sure to see the world's greatest collection of felines and new exhibits of elephants, manatees, and polar bears. There's also a Children's Zoo and a superb botanical garden. 3400 Vine St. (© **800/94-HIPPO** or 513/ 281-4700. www.cincyzoo.org. Admission $12 adults, $9 seniors, $6 children 2–12, free for children under 2. Memorial Day to Labor Day daily 9am–6pm (gates), till 8pm (grounds); other times daily 9am–5pm (gates), to dusk (grounds). Parking $6.50.

Taft Museum   The Taft is a gem housed in an 1820 Federal-style mansion filled with paintings by Rembrandt, Hals, Turner, and Gainsborough, and with Chinese and Limoges porcelain. At press time, the Taft was closed for an extensive renovation; it's expected to reopen by the summer of 2003. 316 Pike St. (© **513/ 241-0343.** www.taftmuseum.org. Admission $4 adults, $2 children under 18. Mon–Sat 10am–5pm; Sun 1–5pm.

MORE ATTRACTIONS

A favorite spring and summer pastime in Cincinnati since 1869 is professional baseball. The **Cincinnati Reds,** featuring future Hall of Famer Ken Griffey, Jr., will have a new place to play beginning in 2003. They'll take to the field of the **Great American Ballpark,** a nostalgic new facility that will anchor the eastern edge of Cincinnati's famed riverfront. Tickets range from $5 to $21. Call Ticketmaster at (© **513/421-REDS** or 800/829-5353.

Football fans were appeased in 2000 with the opening of the $400-million **Paul Brown Stadium,** another waterfront gem that has become a showcase for the NFL's **Cincinnati Bengals.** Single tickets range from $35 to $54. Call (© **513/621-8383.**

Paramount's Kings Island ((© **800/288-0808** or 513/754-5600; www.pki. com) is a roller coaster rider's dream. Located at Exits 24 and 25 on I-71 north of Cincinnati in Mason, Ohio, Kings Island boasts more than a dozen coasters, including the new Son of Beast, a wooden coaster that is among the longest, highest, and fastest in the world. New in 2002 were the multi-sensory Tomb Raider: The Ride, as well as two attractions for younger park visitors: Nickoledeon's Jimmy Neutron: Boy Genius, and Nick Jr.'s Dora the Explorer. All-day admission is $42 ages 7 to 59, $25 ages 4 to 6 and over 60, and $26 all ages after 5pm. Two-day, season, and family passes are available. Parking is $9. Kings Island is open daily from Memorial Day to late August at 9am; closing times vary from 8 to 11pm. Also open some weekends in April, May, September, and October.

Riverboat excursions on the Ohio, especially popular at night, leave from Covington, KY, just across the river from downtown Cincinnati (see "Northern Kentucky" in chapter 6).

Slated to open in the summer of 2004 along the Cincinnati waterfront is the **National Underground Railroad Freedom Center** (www.underground railroad.org). The $110-million complex will trace the heroic efforts of abolitionists as well as America's enduring legacy to free people everywhere from enslavement.

WHERE TO STAY

Ask about weekend packages that include Cincinnati Reds games or discount tickets to sights. For accommodations across the Ohio River, see "Northern Kentucky" in chapter 6.

Cincinnatian Hotel   The grande dame of the city's hotels is the elegant Cincinnatian. Built in 1882, and on the National Register of Historic Places, it offers award-winning, around-the-clock service. Rooms have oversize tubs, dual-head showers, and bathrobes, while some have even have whirlpools and fire-places. Laundry service is available. In addition to its excellent Palace restaurant, the Cricket Lounge offers lighter fare, including afternoon tea. 601 Vine St., Cincinnati, OH 45202. ✆ 800/942-9000 or 513/381-3000. www.cincinnatianhotel.com. 146 units. $195–$224 double. Children 17 and under stay free in parents' room. AE, DC, DISC, MC, V. Valet parking $25. **Amenities:** Restaurants (2); fitness center.

Hilton Cincinnati Netherland Plaza   Travelers looking for an older property in the heart of downtown need look no further than the Hilton Cincinnati Netherland Plaza, across from pretty Fountain Square. Listed on the National Register of Historic Places, the Art Deco property is connected to Tower Place, a four-story complex with shopping, restaurants, and entertainment. The rooms are Hilton standard and quite comfortable. The excellent Palm Court (see below) is a good place to dine. 35 W. 5th St., Cincinnati, OH 45202. ✆ 800/445-8667 or 513/421-9100. www.hilton.com. 624 units. $109–$154 double. Children 17 and under stay free in parents' room. AE, DC, DISC, MC, V. Valet parking $17. **Amenities:** 2 restaurants; health club.

Millennium Hotel   Business travelers favor The Millennium, located in the city's business district just west of Fountain Square and next to the convention center. The newly renovated rooms and suites have been modernized and feature all the usual amenities. Although the hotel has a popular ground-floor bistro, at press time, its revolving rooftop restaurant (Seafood 32) was closed. Plans are afoot to reopen the restaurant that offers spectacular views of downtown Cincinnati, the Ohio River Valley, and the rolling hills of northern Kentucky. 150 W. 5th St., Cincinnati, OH 45202. ✆ 800/876-2100 or 513/352-2100. www.millennium-hotels.com. 886 units. $79–$99 double. Children 17 and under stay free in parents' room. AE, DC, DISC, MC, V. Valet parking $18. **Amenities:** Restaurant; outdoor pool; fitness room.

Westin Cincinnati   Business and leisure travelers will also like the upscale Westin, a high-rise overlooking the Ohio River and Fountain Square at 5th and Vine streets. The hotel is a good choice for sports and culture fans, as the city's major performing arts center, as well as baseball and football fields, are all within a few blocks' walking distance. The comfortable guest rooms have all the amenities associated with a hotel of this class. 21 E. 5th St., Cincinnati, OH 45202. ✆ 513/621-7700. www.westin.com. 448 units. $265–$800 double. Children 17 and under stay free in parents' room. AE, MC, V. Valet parking $24. **Amenities:** Restaurants (2); indoor pool; fitness center; pets may be permitted so call the hotel.

WHERE TO DINE

For cheap eats, try **Skyline Chili,** with dozens of franchises all over the city. Be forewarned, this "chili" may look to novices more like spaghetti than soup. For dining with a view of the downtown skyline from across the Ohio River, see "Northern Kentucky" in chapter 6.

Barresi's ITALIAN   An elegant though moderately priced restaurant with a magnificent wine list, not to mention a mean cappuccino and espresso machine,

Barresi's offers a blend of northern and southern Italian specialties. Look for angel hair pasta mixed with huge shrimp; or jumbo scallops complemented with artichokes. 4111 Webster Ave., Deer Park. ℂ 513/793-2540. www.cincinnati.com/dining/barresis. Reservations recommended. Main courses $19–$31. AE, DC, DISC, MC, V. Mon–Sat 5–10pm.

La Normandie AMERICAN/CONTINENTAL   A 70-year-old Cincinnati institution, La Normandie, on 6th Street between Walnut and Main, is a pricey steakhouse, but with a casual atmosphere (think peanut shells strewn about the floor). The steaks and fresh fish are popular with regulars. One of our favorites is the broiled New Zealand rack of lamb. 118 E. 6th St. ℂ 513/721-2761. www.lanormandy.com. Reservations recommended. Main courses $13–$34. AE, DC, DISC, MC, V. Mon–Fri 11:30am–2:30pm and 5–10pm; Sat 5–11pm.

Maisonette FRENCH   For a special night out, try the five-star Maisonette, on 6th Street between Walnut and Main. Chef Bertrand Bouquin serves up classic French and Continental cuisine. One of the best entrees is the sautéed sea bass with light curry sauce served on a bed of spinach and portobello mushrooms with basmati rice. 114 E. 6th St. ℂ 513/721-2260. www.maisonette.com. Reservations strongly recommended. Jackets required for men at dinner; business casual fine at lunch. Main courses $35–$45. AE, DC, DISC, MC, V. Tues–Fri noon–2pm; Mon–Fri 6–10pm; Sat 5:30–11pm.

Palm Court AMERICAN/CONTINENTAL   The Palm Court is another good upscale choice, with fine American/continental cuisine, a dash of Art Deco style, and the smooth sounds of jazz. House favorites include grilled portobello mushrooms and duck breast; smoked salmon; herb-crusted grilled veal chop; and a wild mushroom meatloaf. Try the chocolate pear sensation for dessert. In the Hilton-Cincinnati Netherland Plaza. 35 W. 5th St. ℂ 513/421-9100. Reservations recommended. Main courses $13–$32. AE, DC, DISC, MC, V. Daily 6:30–10:30am and 5–10pm; Mon–Sat 11:30am–2pm; Sun brunch 11:30am–3pm.

CINCINNATI AFTER DARK

THE PERFORMING ARTS   Music Hall, 1241 Elm St. (ℂ 513/721-8222), is home of the fine Cincinnati Symphony Orchestra (ℂ **513/381-3300;** www.cincinnatisymphony.org) and the Cincinnati Opera (ℂ **513/241-2742;** www.cincyopera.com). The Cincinnati Ballet (ℂ **513/621-5219;** www.cincinnatiballet.com) performs at the Aronoff Center, 6th and Walnut (ℂ **513/621-2787**). Modern and classic plays and musicals are presented at Playhouse in the Park, Eden Park (ℂ **513/345-2242;** www.cincyplay.com).

THE BAR SCENE   **Arnold's Bar and Grill,** 210 E. 8th St., downtown between Main and Sycamore (ℂ **513/421-6234**), is Cincinnati's oldest tavern, with live Celtic, bluegrass, jazz, and swing music. In the **Over-the-Rhine** district, along Main Street beyond Central Parkway, you'll find many bars, cafes, and microbreweries that offer entertainment. Along narrow, cobblestone streets, with excellent city views, **Mount Adams** has many bars that also serve up entertainment. **Celestial,** 1071 Celestial St., Mount Adams (ℂ **513/241-4455**), features vocalists, cabaret, and jazz.

3 Indianapolis

Indianapolis is one serious sports town. The Indianapolis 500 and Brickyard 400 attract hundreds of thousands of visitors to the city in May and August. The

city also bills itself as the "Amateur Sports Capital of the World," and boasts world-class sports facilities. Indy natives rally behind the city's pro franchises— the NBA's Indiana Pacers, the NFL's Indianapolis Colts, and the Indianapolis Indians, whose beautiful, cozy downtown stadium has been voted one of the "best small ballparks in America." Hoosiers also fervently follow their local high school teams, especially the basketball team—the annual championship tournament gave rise to the term "Hoosier Hysteria."

In its passion for sports, however, the city does not neglect the arts. In addition to a few notable art museums, Indianapolis also has neighborhoods worth exploring: the Lockerbie Square district downtown with renovated Victorian homes on cobblestoned streets; Broad Ripple Village, a canal-side neighborhood with boutiques, restaurants, and nightlife; and the historic village of Zionsville, 20 minutes north of Indianapolis, with Victorian homes, antiques shops, and brick-paved streets.

ESSENTIALS

GETTING THERE   **By Plane**   Flights arrive at **Indianapolis International Airport** (www.indianapolisairport.com). Most major domestic airlines can get you there, although US Airways and Southwest have the most frequent service. There is no public transportation into town; taxis cost about $17 to downtown, but can go as high as $35 elsewhere. All major national car-rental agencies are represented at the airport.

By Train   Amtrak (© 800/USA-RAIL; www.amtrak.com) serves **Indianapolis Union Station,** 350 S. Illinois St. (© 317/263-0550), with service from Chicago (trip time: 5½ hr.), Cincinnati (3½ hr.), and Washington, D.C. (18½ hr.).

By Car   Major routes into Indianapolis are I-65 from the northwest (Chicago) and south (Louisville), I-70 from the west (St. Louis) and east (Columbus, OH), and I-74 from the southeast (Cincinnati).

VISITOR INFORMATION   The **Indianapolis Convention & Visitor Bureau** is at 200 S. Capitol Ave., Ste. 100, One RCA Dome, No. 100, Indianapolis, IN 46225 (© 317/639-4282; www.indy.org). The **Indiana Tourism Hotline** is © 800/958-INDY.

GETTING AROUND   Metro buses (© 317/635-3344) run on heavily traveled routes; fares are $1. But you can't rely on public transportation to get everywhere you want to go, so you'll really need a car. The city is easy to negotiate, because it's based on a grid system. Parking is relatively easy in downtown Indy, which has numerous parking garages and surface parking lots.

Cabs usually line up at downtown hotels, or you can call a radio-dispatched taxi. Try **Yellow Cab** (© 317/487-7777).

FAST FACTS   If you need a **doctor,** call **Methodist Hospital,** at I-65 and 21st Street (© 317/916-3525) for a referral. **Riley Children's Hospital,** 702 Barnhill Dr. (© 317/274-5000), is one of the nation's top children's hospitals.

Several CVS locations have **24-hour pharmacies,** including branches at 1744 N. Illinois St. (© 317/923-1491) and at 1315 W. 86th St. (© 317/253-6427).

Downtown Indianapolis nearly empties out after the retail shopping spots close; although Indianapolis is fairly safe, be careful walking alone to your car in large outdoor parking lots.

SPECIAL EVENTS   Both the **Indianapolis 500** (run the day before Memorial Day) and the **Brickyard 400** (the first Sat in Aug) sell out very early. Call the IMS Ticket Office at © 317/484-6700 10 to 12 months in advance.

WHAT TO SEE & DO

The center of downtown Indianapolis is **Monument Circle,** with the Soldiers' and Sailors' Monument at its core. The monument is crowned by a statue of Victory, known as *Miss Indiana.* An observation deck offers a panoramic view. Lights strung from the top of the monument during the holidays make it the "world's largest Christmas tree." In this area, you'll also find the **National Art Museum of Sport,** 111 Monument Circle (© 317/274-3627), which houses a collection of artworks illustrating sports through the ages. A Greek bronze from the 5th century B.C. depicts an Olympic athlete.

In addition to the listings below, you might want to check out the **Indiana Medical History Museum,** 3045 W. Vermont St. (© 317/635-7329), which houses some 15,000 medical artifacts (don't miss the "quack" devices used in the

19th and early 20th centuries). It's open Thursday to Saturday 10am to 4pm.The **Indiana State Museum,** 650 W. Washington St. (© 317/232-1637; www.indianamuseum.org), which moved into its new state-of-the-art $105 million headquarters in 2002, documents the history of Indiana since the pioneer era. Admission is $7.00 adults, $6.50 seniors, and $4.00 for children. ; it's open Monday through Saturday from 9am to 5pm and Sunday from 11am to 6pm.

The **Children's Museum of Indianapolis,** 3000 N. Meridian St. (© 317/334-3322), is one of the world's largest children's museums, with artifacts, interactive displays, and a planetarium. Admission is $9.50 adults, $4 children ages 3 to 17, free for children 2 and under; open daily from 10am to 5pm. If you have kids, this is the place to take them.

At the **NCAA Hall of Champions,** 700 W. Washington St., in White River State Park (© 800/735-NCAA; www.ncaahallofchampions.org), sports fanatics can see past collegiate sports highlights displayed on video monitors, as well as listen to university school songs on a push-and-play display. A 1920s gymnasium keeps the kids busy when not in use for educational programs. Admission is $7 adults, $6 seniors, $4 students (free for children 5 and under); it's open from 10am to 5pm Monday through Saturday, from noon to 5pm Sunday.

Eagle Creek Park, 7840 W. 56th St. (© 317/327-7110), is one of the largest municipal parks in the country, with 4,000 acres of wooded terrain for hiking, biking, and cross country skiing, and a 1,300-acre reservoir. The main attraction of the 128-acre **Garfield Park Conservatory,** 2505 Conservatory Dr. (© 317/327-7184), is a tropical greenhouse—complete with parrots and macaws, and waterfall-fed pools—planted with flora from around the world. Admission to the conservatory is $2 adults, $1.50 seniors, and $1 children; open daily from 10am to 6pm.

Conner Prairie Pioneer Settlement   Located 30 miles northeast of downtown, this restored 19th-century village faithfully reproduces pioneer life between 1820 and 1840 with the help of 36 carefully restored buildings, craft demonstrations, and reenactments of events on the frontier. 13400 Allisonville Rd., Fishers. © 317/776-6000. Admission $11 adults, $10 seniors, $7 children ages 5–12, free for children under 5. May–Oct Tues–Sat 9:30am–5pm; Sun 11am–5pm. Reduced hours off season.

Eiteljorg Museum of American Indian and Western Art   This impressive $14-million building houses one of the country's most notable collections of Native American and Western art. The "Art of the American West" collection includes works by Frederic Remington and Georgia O'Keeffe. The Native American artifacts include clothing, beadwork, and pottery from all over North America. 500 W. Washington St., White River State Park. © 317/636-9378. www.eiteljorg.org. Admission $5 adults, $4 seniors, $2 students and children 5–17. June–Aug Mon–Sat 10am–5pm; Sun noon–5pm. Reduced hr. off season.

Indianapolis Motor Speedway   Built in 1909, this is one of the most celebrated auto raceways in the world. Each May, more than 400,000 spectators throng to the 2.5-mile oval course to watch the Indianapolis 500, the largest single-day sporting event in the world, boasting the largest purse in motor racing. The Speedway also hosts the NASCAR Brickyard 400 in August and the Senior PGA Brickyard Crossing Tournament in September.

The **Indianapolis Motor Speedway Hall of Fame Museum** (open daily 9am–5pm; $3 adults, $1 children 6–15) is within the track's oval. The 433-acre speedway also features a PGA course (four holes inside the track and 14 outside).

4790 W. 16th St. © 317/481-8500, or 800/822-4639 or 317/484-6700 to charge tickets to events. www.brickyard.com. Daily 9am–5pm.

Indianapolis Museum of Art   This world-class museum has notable paintings by El Greco, Rubens, American Impressionists, and European neo-Impressionists. Other strengths include African art, Japanese Edo-period paintings, American furniture, textiles, costumes, and a superb collection of Turner works on paper. The sculpture garden includes Robert Indiana's famed *LOVE*. In summer, the museum hosts Summer on the Terrace, which is actually a swinging scene for singles. Outdoor movies are shown on the lawn during the summer; you can see one of your favorite camp classics while enjoying a picnic with friends. 1200 W. 38th St. © 317/923-1331. www.ima-art.org. Free admission. Tues–Wed and Fri–Sat 10am–5pm; Thurs 10am–8:30pm; Sun noon–5pm.

Indianapolis Raceway Park   Owned and operated by the National Hot Rod Association, the IRP's three courses host more than 60 events a year. Highlights include drag racing, car shows, and the NHRA U.S. Nationals (held during Labor Day weekend). 10267 E. U.S. 136. © 317/291-4090. Call for schedule, or call © 800/884-6472 to charge tickets to events. www.irponline.com. May–Oct.

Indianapolis Zoo   The Indianapolis Zoo is the only major new zoo in recent decades anywhere in the nation. This $64-million, 64-acre facility houses 2,000 animals roaming through simulated environments. Don't miss the world's largest enclosed Whale and Dolphin Pavilion. The zoo is in the 250-acre **White River State Park,** 801 W. Washington St. (© 317/634-4567; www.inwhite river.com).

The new **White River Botanical Gardens** are also located on the zoo grounds. Admission to the gardens is $6.50 adults, $5.50 seniors, $4.50 children in summer; reduced admission in winter. The gardens are open from 9am to 4pm. 1200 W. Washington St. © 317/630-2001. www.indyzoo.com. Admission $11 adults; $7.75 seniors; $6.75 children. Memorial Day to Labor Day daily 9am–6pm; late June to mid-Aug weekdays 9am–4pm, weekends 9am–5pm; Dec noon–9pm.

Morris-Butler House   Housed in an 1862 Victorian mansion, this museum focuses on Victorian decorative arts such as fine silver, tapestries, and Belter & Meeks furniture. 1204 N. Park Ave. © 317/636-5409. Suggested admission $5 adults, $4 seniors, $3 children 6–16. Tours every half hour Wed–Sat 10am–4pm; Sun 1–4pm, by reservation only.

SHOPPING

Downtown shopping was revitalized in 1995 with the opening of the **Circle Centre,** 49 W. Maryland St. (© 317/681-8000), with anchor stores Nordstrom and Parisian, 100 specialty shops, restaurants, nightclubs, and a cinema.

The **Fashion Mall, Keystone at the Crossing,** 86th Street and Keystone Avenue (© 317/574-4000), is the city's other leading mall, with anchor stores Saks Fifth Avenue (opening in 2003) and Parisian, a number of national chain stores, and numerous specialty and designer boutiques.

For something different, head to **Broad Ripple Village,** a charming neighborhood 15 minutes north of downtown. For unique and fun furnishings and home accessories, check out **Haus** at 6263 N. Carrollton Ave. **Turandot,** 912 E. Westfield Blvd., features funky jewelry and gifts.

The old **City Market,** 222 E. Market St. (© 317/634-9266), has been revitalized with many new food and produce stands opening. An outdoor farmers' market is open from 9:30am to 1:30pm on weekdays.

WHERE TO STAY

The more expensive hotels are downtown, but many moderate and budget hotels are in the surrounding area. Most downtown hotels offer weekend or theme packages.

Days Inn, 5860 Fortune Circle W., at the airport (© **800/DAYS-INN** or 317/248-0621), is your standard budget motel, with a restaurant, bar, small workout room, and outdoor pool. A special park-and-fly program is available. Another good airport choice is the **Holiday Inn,** 2501 S. High School Rd. (© **800/465-4329** or 317/244-6861), right on the airport grounds and 10 minutes from downtown. The noted Chanteclair restaurant is here, along with a health club and indoor pool; some units have small terraces or whirlpools.

Brickyard Crossing Golf Resort & Inn   This conventional motel with standard rooms is noteworthy because of its location—outside turn two on the Indianapolis Speedway. It's relatively quiet, except for race month in May. Refrigerators are available for $10. 4400 W. 16th St., Indianapolis, IN 46222. © 800/926-8276 or 317/241-2500. Fax 317/492-2715. 108 units. $65–$85 double. Extra person $10. Sunday buffet $9.95. AE, DC, DISC, MC, V. Free outdoor parking. **Amenities:** Restaurant; outdoor heated pool; 18-hole golf course; pets $25.

The Canterbury   This charming European-style hotel, with direct access into Circle Centre, sports "a bit of England." Rooms are large, with four-poster beds, armoires, bathroom telephones, and refrigerators. Tea is served daily. 123 S. Illinois St., Indianapolis, IN 46225; south end of Circle Centre Mall. © 800/538-8186 or 317/634 3000. Fax 317/685-2519. www.canterburyhotel.com. 99 units. $190–$220 double; $225–$1,100 suite. Extra person $25. All children stay free in parents' room. Free continental breakfast included. AE, DC, DISC, MC, V. Valet parking $14 per day. **Amenities:** Restaurant; health club.

Courtyard by Marriott   This downtown hotel is nicely situated on the edge of White River State Park and across the street from the Eiteljorg Museum. The unusually clean and well-maintained rooms are bright and cheerful, and some have terraces. 501 W. Washington St., Indianapolis, IN 46204. © 800/321-2211 or 317/635-4443. Fax 317/687 0029. www.marriott.com. 233 units. $119 double. Extra person $10. Children under 18 stay free in parents' room. AE, DC, DISC, MC, V. Free outdoor parking. **Amenities:** Restaurant; outdoor pool; exercise equipment.

Embassy Suites Downtown   Connected by a sky bridge to Circle Centre Mall and other downtown sites, this plush hotel offers suites with coffeemakers, wet bars, refrigerators, and microwaves. Some units have terraces, and you can enjoy complimentary beverages each evening. 110 W. Washington St., Indianapolis IN 46204. © 800/362-2779 or 317/236-1800. Fax 317/236-1816. www.embassysuites.com. 360 suites. $159–$209 suite. Extra person $10. Children under 12 stay free in parents' room. Buffet breakfast complimentary. AE, DC, DISC, MC, V. Self-parking $12, valet $16. **Amenities:** Restaurant; indoor pool; fitness center.

Embassy Suites North   This beautiful hotel, resembling a Moorish castle, is a standout amid a busy area. An eight-story atrium greets you as you enter. Rooms are large and well furnished, and include coffeemakers, irons, refrigerators, and microwaves. Complimentary cocktails are served each evening in the lobby. 3912 Vincennes Rd. (south of I-465 on Michigan Rd.), Indianapolis, IN 46268. © 800/ EMBASSY or 317/872-7700. www.embassysuites.com. 221 units. $129–$199 suite. Children under 17 stay free in parents' room. Buffet breakfast included. AE, DC, DISC, MC, V. Free outdoor parking. **Amenities:** Restaurant; indoor pool; fitness center; basketball court.

Hampton Inn Downtown at Circle Centre   Housed in a 1920s National Historic Landmark, this is one of downtown's newer hotels, and one of the few moderately priced choices in the area. It's convenient to all downtown attractions. There are two-room suites and king rooms with whirlpool tubs; all rooms feature coffeemakers, irons, and free local phone calls. 105 S. Meridian St., Indianapolis, IN 46225. ℂ 800/426-7866 or 317/261-1200. Fax 317/261-1030. www.hampton-inn.com. 180 units. $89–$139 double; $149–$179 suite. Children under 18 stay free in parents' room. Continental breakfast included. AE, DISC, MC, V. Valet parking $11 per night. **Amenities:** Fitness center.

Omni Indianapolis North Hotel   This high-rise hotel and conference center with an English ambience is the only full-service facility in the city's northeast corner, close to shopping and restaurants, Verizon Wireless Music Center, and Conner Prairie Pioneer Settlement. Guest rooms feature coffeemakers, irons, and hair dryers; the "Get Fit" rooms have portable treadmills. 8181 N. Shadeland Ave., Indianapolis, IN 46250; Exit 1 off I-69. ℂ 800/THE-OMNI or 317/849-6668. www.omni hotels.com. Fax 317/849-4936. 215 units. $99–$149 double; $199–$250 suite. Children under 18 stay free in parents' room. AE, DC, DISC, MC, V. Free outdoor parking. **Amenities:** Restaurant; indoor pool; fitness center.

Omni Severin Hotel   This classy, beautifully restored hotel is directly across from Union Station. The guest rooms were recently redone, and some have terraces. All rooms have coffeemakers, bathrobes, irons, hair dryers, and Nintendo game systems. 40 W. Jackson Place, Indianapolis, IN 46225. ℂ 800/THE-OMNI or 317/634-6664. www.omnihotels.com. Fax 317/687-3612. 423 units. $119–$209 double; $245–$800 suite. Extra person $20. Children under 18 stay free in parents' room. AE, DC, DISC, MC, V. Self-parking $8, valet parking $16. **Amenities:** Restaurants (2); indoor pool; fitness center.

Renaissance Tower Historic Inn   Located in the historic St. Joseph District on the north side of downtown, this hotel is a National Historic Landmark. Suites offer cherrywood furnishings, including four-poster beds and fully equipped kitchens with microwaves; local calls are free. 230 E. 9th St., Indianapolis, IN 46204; Exit 113 off I-65. ℂ 800/676-7786 or 317/261-1652. Fax 317/262-8648. 81 suites. $85 double. Children under 18 stay free in parents' room. Lower rates off season. AE, MC, V. Free outdoor parking. **Amenities:** Fitness center.

University Place Conference Center and Hotel   Located on the campus of Indiana University/Purdue University Indianapolis (IUPUI), this hotel offers well-furnished and functional rooms with refrigerators, coffeemakers, and hair dryers. Guests can use campus facilities, including a terrific indoor pool, fitness center, track-and-field stadium, and children's day-care center. 850 W. Michigan St., Indianapolis, IN 46202. ℂ 800/626-2700 or 317/269-9000. Fax 317/231-5168. 276 units. $89–$169 double; $150–$500 suite. Extra person $15. Children under 18 stay free in parents' room. AE, DISC, MC, V. Indoor parking $8. **Amenities:** Restaurants (2); indoor pool; fitness center; basketball court.

Westin Hotel Indianapolis   This luxury hotel with a sky bridge to Circle Centre Mall and Convention Center/RCA Dome is within walking distance of Union Station and downtown attractions, restaurants, and shops. Guest rooms feature the usual array of deluxe amenities, including bathrobes; refrigerators are available for an extra charge. 50 S. Capitol Ave., Indianapolis, IN 46204. ℂ 800/228-3000 or 317/262-8100. Fax 317/231-3928. 573 units. $224 double; $195–$1,000 suite. Extra person $30. Children under 18 stay free in parents' room. AE, DC, DISC, MC, V. Self-parking $16, valet indoor parking $20. **Amenities:** Restaurants (2); indoor pool; fitness center.

WHERE TO DINE

In addition to the places listed below, you'll find many new dining options in the Circle Centre Mall. Chains such as **Palomino Euro Bistro** and the **Alcatraz Brewing Co.** are consistent with most of what you'll find in the area. If you're heading to Broad Ripple Village for shopping or nightlife, you can't go wrong at longtime favorites **Bazbeaux Pizza,** 832 E. Westfield Blvd. (© 317/255-5711) and 334 Mass. Ave., downtown (© 317/636-7662), for gourmet pizza; or **Mama Carolla's,** 1031 E. 54th St. (© 317/259-9412), for neighborhood Italian in a renovated house.

Buca Di Beppo ITALIAN As chain restaurants go, this one isn't bad. Come here for authentic Italian food served family style. Loosely translated, the name means "Joe's Basement." You'll enjoy huge portions served by an almost overly eager staff, in surroundings that are almost kitschy. It's a wonderful experience that's worth a little wait (and frequently, you will have to wait). 35 N. Illinois St. © 317/632-2822. Reservations recommended. Main courses $14–$22. AE, DC, MC, V. Mon–Thurs 5–10pm; Fri 4–11pm; Sat noon–11pm; Sun noon–9pm.

Café Patachou NEW AMERICAN/FRENCH At this very popular lunch and breakfast cafe, diners enjoy a casual and contemporary atmosphere while paying New York prices ($1.50 for a cup of joe, anyone?). Although it can get pricey, the food is truly worth it. The omelets are some of the best in town and the turkey sandwich tastes like your Mom cooked a bird and made you a sandwich immediately afterward—you can't beat that kind of freshness anywhere else. There are two locations. This is the original (and the more funky of the two), but there is also another at Keystone at the Crossing (© 317/815-0765). If you come for Sunday brunch, be prepared to wait a long while. 4911 N. Pennsylvania. © 317/925-2823. Omelets and sandwiches $5–$8. AE, MC, V. Mon–Fri 7am–3pm; Sat–Sun 8am–2pm.

Lulu's SEAFOOD/CREOLE This trendy restaurant is loud, but it can get fun. Even if you're not in the mood for the Cajun-type food, just stopping in for a drink at the bar drops you into Indianapolis's trendy scene. And if you do decide to eat dinner, you won't be disappointed. 8487 Union Chapel Rd. (Keystone at the Crossing). © 317/251-5858. Main courses $15–$28. AE, DC, DISC, MC, V. Mon–Thurs 11am–2pm and 5–10pm; Fri–Sat 11am–2pm and 5–11pm.

Marco's AMERICAN It might not be fancy, but everyone loves this place. And when the servers call you "babe" and "hon," that will only endear it to you further. The food is not outstanding, but it is consistent. This is a great place for grabbing a bite with friends. 2380 E. 54th St. © 317/251-7000. Main courses $12–$18. AE, MC, V. Mon–Fri 11–3pm; Mon–Sat 5–10pm.

R. Bistro CONTEMPORARY AMERICAN This casual but chic new addition to the restaurant scene snuck in quietly but is gaining a local following. The dinner menu changes weekly and lunchtime menu changes seasonally. 888 Massachusetts Ave. © 317/423-0312. Main courses $14–$20. AE, DC, DISC, MC, V. Mon–Fri 11am–2:30pm; Wed–Sat 5–10pm.

Something Different INTERNATIONAL Something Different offers eclectic cuisine featuring wonderful new pairings. The menu changes seasonally (sometimes monthly) and you can call to find out the latest offerings. Appetizers can run up to $10, with main dishes going as high as $30—but the food is worth the primo price. For a less expensive but just as tasty meal, try **SNAX** at the same location. It stays open a half hour later and is a trendy tapas spot. Prices run from $6 to $10 a tapa, and the tab can run up quickly. Wear black. 4939 E. 82nd St., just west of Allisonville Rd. ℂ 317/570-7700. Reservations recommended. Main courses to $35. AE, DC, DISC, MC, V. Mon–Thurs 5–9:30pm; Fri–Sat 5–10:30pm.

St. Elmo Steak House AMERICAN/STEAK This National Historic Landmark has been the city's premier steak house for the last 100 years. The original bar and back bar are still in operation, and waiters wear tuxedos. With the capitol just blocks away, it's popular with legislators and lobbyists, but don't be surprised to see a Hollywood celebrity dining here in May when the town is full of Indy Race fans. 127 S. Illinois St., at the south edge of Circle Centre Mall. ℂ 317/637-1811. Reservations recommended. Main courses $23–$37. AE, DC, DISC, MC, V. Mon–Sat 4–10:30pm; Sun 4–9pm.

INDIANAPOLIS AFTER DARK

THE PERFORMING ARTS The **Indianapolis Symphony Orchestra** (ℂ **800/366-8457** or 317/639-4300) has its home in the Circle Theater, a vintage 1916 film palace on Monument Circle. **Clowes Memorial Hall,** 4600 Sunset Ave. (ℂ **800/732-0804,** 317/940-6444, or 317/940-9696), a performing arts center on the campus of Butler University, is home to the **Indianapolis Opera, the Butler Ballet,** and **Indianapolis Chamber Orchestra.** The professional **Indiana Repertory Theatre,** 140 W. Washington St. (ℂ **317/635-5277**), offers a September-to-May season.

The **Madame Walker Urban Life Center,** 617 Indiana Ave. (ℂ **317/236-2099** for information and tickets), is an ornate 1927 Art Deco theater offering jazz, gospel, drama, and dance performances. Every other Friday from 6 to 10pm, "Jazz on the Avenue" showcases local, regional, and national talent.

THE CLUB & BAR SCENE Indianapolis's nightlife is primarily located in the downtown area and in Broad Ripple Village, an artsy enclave of boutiques, bistros, and bungalows 15 minutes north of downtown.

For live jazz every night except Sunday, downtowners head to the cozy **Chatterbox Tavern,** 435 Massachusetts Ave. (ℂ **317/636-0584**), where big-name acts playing in town sometimes stop by. Another downtown top spot for live music is the **Slippery Noodle Inn,** 372 S. Meridian St. (ℂ **317/631-6974**), Indiana's oldest standing bar (established 1850) and *the* place in the city for blues. You can also check out the local scene at friendly **Old Point Tavern,** 401 Massachusetts Ave. (ℂ **317/634-8943**); in warm weather, the actions spills out onto an outside patio.

Gay travelers can check out **Our Place** (also known as OP's), 231 E. 16th St. (ℂ **317/638-8138**), for dancing and cruising, while lesbians can hop over to **Utopia,** 924 N. Pennsylvania (ℂ317/638-0215), to hang out in the casual bar up front or the more upbeat dance club in the back.

If you're not sure what you're in the mood for, check out **World Mardi Gras** on the top level of the Circle Centre Mall (ℂ **317/630-5483** or 317/488-ROCK), with four connected clubs, including a New Orleans–style bar with live music, a 1970s-ish dance club, and the obligatory sports pub. Expect a younger crowd. A more unusual offering is **Hollywood Bar & Filmworks,** 247 S. Meridian St. (ℂ **317/231-9255;** www.filmworksonline.com), a state-of-the-art cinema with cabaret-style seating where you can enjoy a movie while munching on pizza and sandwiches and sipping suds.

Broad Ripple Village, an easy drive north of downtown straight up Meridian Street, is where the local yuppies, college geeks, *and* high school cool kids go for weekend fun. Mature audiences head to the **Jazz Kitchen,** 5377 N. College Ave. (© 317/253-4900; www.thejazzkitchen.com), for live jazz Friday and Saturday. But everybody goes to **The Vogue,** 6259 N. College Ave. (© 317/259-7029), an Indianapolis institution where local bands and big names perform in a renovated movie theater. Other good bets are the casual **Broad Ripple Brew Pub,** 840 E. 65th St. (© 317/253-2739), and the cigar/martini bar on the second floor of the **Broad Ripple Steak House,** 929 E. Westfield Blvd. (© 317/253-8101).

4 Detroit & Highlights of Michigan

DETROIT

The American landscape was literally transformed by the ingenuity of Detroit, birthplace of the automobile and the Motown sound. The Motor City has been slower to rebound from the urban blight that plagued so many U.S. cities in the '70s and '80s, but there is no doubt that Detroit is in the throes of a rebirth. Vacant downtown buildings are quickly being replaced by new sports stadiums, posh hotels, casinos, and unique eateries. Add a renewed focus on the arts—such as the city's historic theater district—and you'll understand why Detroiters feel optimistic about their city's future. And why travelers are coming back.

ESSENTIALS

GETTING THERE   By Plane   The **Detroit Metropolitan Airport** (www.metroairport.com), 35 miles southwest of downtown, is a hub for **Northwest Airlines** (© 800/225-2525). Cab service to downtown costs $32.

By Train   Amtrak (© 800/USA-RAIL; www.amtrak.com) provides daily service from Chicago (trip time: 6 ½ hr.) and Ann Arbor (1 hr.) to its station at 11 W. Baltimore St. at Woodward Avenue. Trains also stop at Amtrak stations in Dearborn, 16121 Michigan Ave.; Royal Oak, 201 S. Sherman Dr.; Birmingham, 449 S. Eaton St.; and Pontiac, 1600 Wide Track Dr.

By Car   Major routes into Detroit are I-75 from the south (Toledo) and north (Flint), I-94 from the west (Chicago), and Route 401 from the east (Toronto).

VISITOR INFORMATION   Contact the **Detroit Metro Convention & Visitors Bureau,** 211 W. Fort St., Ste. 1000, Detroit, MI 48226 (© **800/ DETROIT;** www.visitdetroit.com).

GETTING AROUND   They don't call Detroit the Motor City for nothing. Residents are firmly attached to their cars, so there's not much in the way of public transportation. The elevated **People Mover** loops around downtown, and buses fan out across the city, but to reach attractions outside downtown and in the suburbs, it's best to rent a car.

FAST FACTS   To find a physician, contact the **Detroit Medical Center** (© **888/DMC-2500;** www.dmc.org). Medical assistance is available at **Detroit Receiving Hospital,** 4201 St. Antoine Blvd. (© 313/745-3000).

SPECIAL EVENTS & FESTIVALS   The Motor City displays her best and newest cars at the annual **North American International Auto Show** in mid-January. The weeklong Windsor-Detroit **International Freedom Festival** celebrates Canada Day (July 1) and American Independence Day, ending with fireworks over the Ambassador Bridge. The **African World Festival,** held the third week in August, features music, art, food, and cultural programs.

WHAT TO SEE & DO

The headquarters of Ford, Chrysler, and General Motors, the Motor City has always been synonymous with transportation. Visitors learn more of Detroit's history in the **Cultural Center,** an area flanking Woodward Avenue 3 blocks south of I-94. Here you'll find the Detroit Institute of Arts, the Detroit Historical Museum, the Charles H. Wright Museum of African American History, and the Detroit Science Center. The Detroit Public Library and Wayne State University also call the area home.

Greektown boasts great shopping and entertainment just east of downtown. **Pewabic Pottery,** 10125 E. Jefferson Ave., east of downtown (© **313/822-0954;** www.pewabic.com), manufactured much of the glazed tile decorating Detroit's buildings. A gallery and store are also on-site.

Several of Detroit's historic homes make enjoyable day trips. Nearby **Dearborn** is home to the Henry Ford Museum & Greenfield Village (see below) as well as the **Henry Ford Estate–Fair Lane,** 4901 Evergreen Rd. (© **313/593-5590;** www.umd.umich.edu/fairlane), the automaker's 1914 home. **Cranbrook,** 1221 N. Woodward Ave., in nearby Bloomfield Hills (© **877/GO-CRANBROOK;** www.cranbrook.edu), includes a stunning 1904 manor, exquisite formal gardens, and a superb museum of science and art. The **Edsel and Eleanor Ford House,** 1100 Lakeshore Rd., Grosse Pointe Shores (© **313/884-4222;** www.fordhouse.org), completed in 1929, was designed to resemble the stone buildings of the English Cotswolds.

Charles H. Wright Museum of African American History   In the mid-1800s, Detroit was a key stop on the Underground Railroad, through which thousands of slaves escaped to Canada. This and other aspects of African-American heritage, from African roots through slavery to civil rights struggles, are celebrated at the world's largest museum of African and African-American history and culture. Allow 1 hour. 315 E. Warren Ave. © 313/494-5800. www.maah detroit.org. Admission $5 adults, $3 children under 18. Tues–Sun 9:30am–5pm.

Detroit Historical Museum   Begin your exploration of Detroit with this repository of the city's history. You can walk a re-created cobblestone and brick street lined with 19th-century shops, and check out the two-story assembly line in the Motor City exhibit. Interactive displays entertain children of all ages. Allow 1 to 2 hours. 5401 Woodward Ave. © 313/833-1805. www.detroithistorical.org. Admission $4.50 adults, $2.25 seniors and children 12–18, free for children under 12; free to all on Wed. Tues–Fri 9:30am–5pm; Sat–Sun 10am–5pm.

Detroit Institute of Arts   America's sixth largest art museum features masterpieces by Rembrandt, Rubens, Brueghel the Elder, Botticelli, Caravaggio, van Gogh, Cézanne, Picasso, and Rothko. There are also ancient Egyptian, African, Asian, and Native American collections. Don't miss Diego Rivera's famous *Detroit Industry* murals in the central courtyard. First Fridays of every month feature free music, tours, artists' demonstrations, and workshops for all ages. Allow 2 to 3 hours. 5200 Woodward Ave. © 313/833-7900. www.dia.org. Admission $4 adults, $1 children and students. Wed–Fri 11am–4pm; Sat–Sun 11am–5pm. Open until 9pm 1st Fri of every month.

Detroit Zoo   The Detroit Zoo is one of the finest in the nation. Its newest addition, the **Arctic Ring of Life,** includes the world's largest polar bear exhibit. Visitors can watch frolicking polar bears and seals through a 70-foot-long underwater Polar Passage. Other highlights include the world's largest amphibian research and exhibition center, a butterfly and hummingbird garden, a free flight aviary, and a great apes exhibit. Allow 3 hours. Woodward Ave. and 10-Mile Rd., Royal Oak. ✆ 248/398-0900. www.detroitzoo.org. Admission $8 adults, $6 children 2–12 and seniors; free for children under 2. Daily 9am–5pm May–Aug; 10am–5pm Apr and Sept; 10am–4pm Nov–Mar.

Henry Ford Museum & Greenfield Village The **Henry Ford Museum,** a 12-acre repository of Americana, lies behind the doors of a replica of Philadelphia's Independence Hall. You'll see everything from telephones and refrigerators to steam engines, carriages, airplanes, and—of course—cars. The multimedia presentation "The Automobile in American Life" explores our nation's infatuation with cars. Look for Ford's 1901 Model-T, the Oscar Meyer Wienermobile, George Washington's camp bed, the Lincoln rocking chair, and a parade of presidential vehicles. Allow 3 hours.

Greenfield Village encapsulated Ford's ideal of small-town America. It's not quite like any real town you've ever seen, but it's fascinating nonetheless, with 100 genuine 17th-, 18th-, and 19th-century homes—including those of Edison and the Wright Brothers, among others. *Note:* The village is closed January through March. Allow 2 hours. 20900 Oakwood Blvd., Dearborn. ✆ 313/271-1620. www.hfmgv.org. Museum: $14 adults, $13 seniors, $8.50 children 5–12; Village: $16 adults, $15 seniors, $10 children 5–12; combination: $20 adults, $19 seniors, $14 children 5–12; free for children under 5. IMAX $10 adults, $8.50 seniors and children under 13. Mon–Sat 9am–5pm; Sun noon–5pm. Closed Thanksgiving and Dec 25. Village only closed Jan 2–Mar.

Motown Historical Museum The Motown sound was born in two simple houses under the sign HITSVILLE U.S.A. and American music has never been the same. See the original control room and studio (with linoleum worn through by tapping feet) where the Supremes, the Temptations, Stevie Wonder, the Jackson 5, and many others made gold records from 1959 to 1972. Also on display are costumes worn by the famous performers and Berry Gordy's apartment, left just the way it was in the 1960s when artists packed their records for shipment throughout the country. Allow 1 hour. 2648 W. Grand Blvd. ✆ 313/875-2264. Admission $6 adults, $3 children under 13. Tues–Sat 10am–5pm; Sun–Mon noon–5pm.

WHERE TO STAY

Atheneum Suite Hotel This all-suite hotel, housed in a converted 19th-century warehouse, is known for luxury and service. Befitting its Greektown location, murals of tales from Greek mythology decorate the lobby. Premium suites have whirlpools; all have minibars and complimentary shuttle service within a 5-mile radius. The hotel is adjacent to the Greektown Casino and connects to Fishbone's Rhythm Kitchen Café (see below). 1000 Brush St. (at Lafayette), Detroit, MI 48226. ✆ 800/772-2323 or 313/962-2323. Fax 313/962-2424. www.atheneumsuites. com. 174 units. Suites begin at $185. Children under 18 stay free in parents' room. Various packages available. AE, DC, DISC, MC, V. Self-parking $8, valet parking $15. "Greektown" People Mover station. **Amenities:** Restaurant; health club.

Detroit Marriott-Renaissance Center The Renaissance Center was built in the 1970s as General Motors headquarters, but a recent $100-million top-to-bottom refurbishing installed new carpeting, draperies, modern bathrooms, and a large atrium called the Wintergarden. Guests will appreciate the indoor pool, exercise room, proximity to downtown, and adjacent food and shopping court. Upper floors offer great views of the Detroit River and Windsor. Renaissance Center (Jefferson Ave. between Brush St. and Beaubien), Detroit, MI 48243. ✆ 888-228-9290 or

313/568-8000. Fax 313/568-8146. www.marriotthotels.com\DTWDT. 1,298 units. $99–179 double. Various packages available. AE, DC, DISC, MC, V. Self-parking $15, valet parking $15. Adjacent to "Renaissance Center" People Mover station. **Amenities:** Restaurant; indoor pool; health club.

Holiday Inn Fairlane   This typical example of the Holiday Inn chain features inexpensive, contemporary lodging that is very family friendly, including free meals for children under 13. Located near Dearborn, the hotel is convenient to the airport and near the Henry Ford Museum and Greenfield Village. 5801 Southfield Service Dr., Detroit, MI 48228. © **800/HOLIDAY** or 313/336-3340. Fax 313/336-7037. www. sixcontinentshotels.com. 347 units. $79–$124 double; $225 suite. Children under 20 stay free in parents' room. Children under 13 eat free in hotel restaurant. Greenfield Village packages available. AE, DC, DISC, MC, V. Free parking. **Amenities:** Restaurant; pools (1 indoor, 1 outdoor); fitness center.

The Inn on Ferry Street   The Inn on Ferry Street is actually a collection of four large 19th-century homes and their carriage houses. Once slated for demolition, the buildings were rescued and converted into a charming B&B complex, each with its own parlor with fireplace. The rooms have the usual array of modern amenities and updated, private bathrooms. The Inn is located in the heart of the Cultural Center, within easy walking distance of museums. Complimentary shuttle service is provided within a 5-mile radius. 84 E. Ferry St. (at Woodward Ave. in Cultural Center), Detroit, MI 48202. © **313/871-6000.** Fax 313/871-1473. www.theinnonferrystreet.com. 42 units. $149–$199 double midweek; $109–179 weekends. Rates include deluxe continental breakfast and midweek afternoon reception. Add $10 for Jacuzzi tub. Children under 18 stay free in parents' room. AE, DC, DISC, MC, V. Free parking.

The Townsend Hotel   The gorgeous Townsend is one of Michigan's finest hotels. You'll feel like a celebrity, and you just might see one—Hollywood's elite stay at the Townsend when they're in town. Rooms have Egyptian cotton linens, deep marble tubs, and terry robes. Suites sport full kitchens. The Rugby Grille serves award-winning (and expensive) Continental cuisine, and you can work off your meal in the hotel's state-of-the-art fitness center. 100 Townsend St., Birmingham, MI 48009. © **800/548-4172** or 248/642-7900. Fax 248/645-9061. www.townsendhotel.com. 150 units. $288–$320 double midweek, $189–$259 weekends; $350–2,000 suites. Children 18 and under stay free in parents' room. Weekend packages available. AE, DC, DISC, MC, V. Self-parking $8, valet parking $24. **Amenities:** Restaurant; health and fitness center; pets allowed for price of 1 night's room as deposit.

WHERE TO DINE

Cyprus Taverna GREEK   Widely considered Greektown's best Greek restaurant, Cyprus Taverna serves up all the requisite Greek dishes—moussaka, dolmathes (stuffed grape leaves), and gyros—as well as a number of Cypriot specialties and a selection of Greek beers and wines. Aegean fossils and Cypriot folk art decorate the walls. 579 Monroe St. © **313/961-1550.** Reservations accepted. Main courses $8–$20. AE, DC, DISC, MC, V. Mon–Thurs 11am–2:30pm; Fri–Sat 11am–4am; Sun 11am–2:30am.

Duet AMERICAN   Duet's red velvet curtains and vintage loge seating combine with urban chic to create an enjoyable and unique atmosphere, one that is almost as good as its food. For lunch try the almond-crusted chicken salad with apple slices, goat cheese, and warm honey mustard. For dinner, the crispy seared salmon with tomato shallot stew is good. Enjoy live jazz on the weekends. 3663 Woodward Ave. (adjacent to Orchestra Hall). © **313/831-3838.** Reservations required. Main courses $19–$32. AE, DC, DISC, MC, V. Tues–Fri 11am–2:30pm; Tues–Wed 5–9pm; Thurs 5–11pm; Fri–Sat 5pm–12am.

Fishbone's Rhythm Kitchen Café CAJUN Fishbone's is always buzzing, with lively conversation and with jazz music. It's a great place to visit with kids or a group. The food comes straight from Louisiana, including alligator voodoo (deep-fried alligator tail meat with rémoulade) and seafood gumbo. The restaurant's Sunday brunch is a veritable feast. 400 Monroe St. (in the Atheneum Suites hotel), downtown. © 313/965-4600. Main courses $11–$15. AE, DC, DISC, MC, V. Daily 6:30am–10pm. Sun brunch 10:30am–2pm.

Ja'da—A Barbecue Grill SOUL FOOD This friendly, hip embodiment of Motown serves upscale soul food, such as barbecued ribs and chicken with classic greens and black-eyed peas. Service is slow, but on the weekends you can enjoy live jazz while you wait. 546 E. Larned St. © 313/965-1700. Reservations accepted. Main courses $16–$20. AE, DC, DISC, MC, V. Mon–Thurs 11:30am–10pm; Fri 11:30am–1am; Sat 4pm–1am.

Tribute Restaurant AMERICAN The *New York Times* called Tribute "the best restaurant between New York and Chicago"; and *Food & Wine* named its chef, Takashi Yagihashi, one of the nation's 10 best in 2000. Tribute is quickly becoming known as *the* place to dine in Detroit. Try the grilled orange-anise glazed duck breast or the sautéed Pacific snapper "Thai" with oyster mushrooms and somen noodles. The elegant food and decor—which includes stained glass and orchids—create a memorable evening. Orchard Lake and 12-Mile Rd., Farmington Hills. © 248/848-9393. Reservations required. Main courses $18–$38. AE, DC, MC, V. Tues–Sat 5:30–9:30pm.

DETROIT AFTER DARK

PERFORMING ARTS The renowned **Detroit Symphony Orchestra** (© 313/576-5100; www.detroitsymphony.com) performs at Orchestra Hall, 3711 Woodward Ave. **Michigan Opera Theatre** (© 313/961-3500; www.mot opera.org) performs at the Detroit Opera House, 1526 Broadway. Touring Broadway shows come to the **Fox Theatre**, 2211 Woodward Ave. (© 313/471-3200), the **Fisher Theatre**, 3011 W. Grand Blvd. (© 313/872-1000), or the **Masonic Temple**, 500 Temple Ave. (© 313/832-2232).

Dance and theater fill **Music Hall**, 350 Madison Ave. (© 313/963-7622). For a little humor, visit **Second City Comedy Theatre**, 2301 Woodward Ave. (© 313/965-2222).

THE BAR & CLUB SCENE Centre Street Pub, 311 E. Grand River (© 313/965-3651) is near Comerica Park (home of the Detroit Tigers) and Ford Field (home of the Lions), and is popular for before- and after-game get-togethers (the food is a step above the average pub fare). **The Town Pump Tavern**, 100 W. Montcalm (© 313/961-1929), is located in the heart of the theater district. It's loud and smoky, but is always hopping. In Greektown, try **Marilyn's on Monroe**, 419 Monroe Ave. (© 313/963-1980). Nightly entertainment includes darts, dancing, and great music with rhythm and blues for your soul.

X/S, John R at Woodward Ave. (© 313/963-XSXS), is one of Detroit's newest nightclubs and features plenty of music, and a heaven and hell theme. Also new is the upscale **Envy**, 234 W. Larned near Cobo Hall, downtown (© 313/962-3689). Its decor has been described as a cross between '66 go-go and George Jetson with funky music.

THE GAY & LESBIAN SCENE Pronto!, 344 W. Nine Mile, Ferndale (© 248/414-7400), caters to a gay clientele at its Friday and Saturday night dance club. **Menjo's**, 938 W. McNichols Rd. (© 313/863-3934), is popular with gay men (Thurs is dance night), while women predominate at the **Rainbow Room,** 6640 E. 8-Mile Rd. (© **313/891-1020**).

CASINOS   In 1999, casino gambling came to Detroit with the opening of the **MGM Grand Detroit,** U.S. 10 and Abbott (© **877/888-2121;** detroit. mgmgrand.com); the **MotorCity Casino,** 2901 Grand River Ave., at U.S. 10 (© **877/777-0711;** www.motorcitycasino.com); and **Greektown Casino,** 555 E. Lafayette (© **888-771-4386;** www.greektowncasino.net). All casinos are open 24 hours daily, and have slots, table games, restaurants, entertainment, and secure parking. You must be 21 to enter.

WEST MICHIGAN BEACHES

Strung along the entire West Michigan shoreline, from Mackinaw City in the north to the Warren Dunes in the south, are hundreds of sandy white beaches, the finest in the Midwest. A quick glance at any Michigan map reveals lots of public beaches, perfect for sunning and swimming. **State parks** provide inexpensive access ($4/day, $20/year) and, oftentimes, great campgrounds. (They're also popular. Reserve your site *early*—a year in advance if possible.) Get more information at © **800/44-PARKS** or www.michigandnr.com.

TRAVERSE CITY

Traverse City, located near the "pinky" of Michigan's mitten-shaped Lower Peninsula, is known for unique shopping, wineries, and a vibrant arts scene as well as its watersports. **Traverse City State Park,** 1132 US 31 N.(© **231/922-5270**), and **Bayside Park,** US 31 N., 8 miles east in Acme, both offer great beaches, swimming, and picnicking. Twenty-five miles east, near Empire on M-22, **Sleeping Bear Dunes National Lakeshore** (© **231/326-5135;** www. nps.gov/slbe) boasts some of the best beaches and dunes in the state. Contact the **Traverse City Convention & Visitors Bureau** at © **800/TRAVERS** or www.mytraversecity.com.

WHERE TO STAY & DINE   There are many beachside hotels in Traverse City. The Victorian-style **Bayshore Resort,** 833 E. Front St. (© **800/634-4401** or 231/935-4400; www.bayshore-resort.com), has doubles beginning at $149. The **Grand Beach Resort Hotel,** 1683 U.S. 31 N. (© **800/968-1992** or 231/938-4455; www.grandbeach.com), is a great family choice, with doubles starting at $109. Both hotels include continental breakfast and are right off the beach. For deluxe pampering, visit **Grand Traverse Resort & Spa,** 100 Grand Traverse Blvd., Acme (just off U.S. 31 N.; © **800/748-0303** or 231/938-3781; www.grandtraverseresort.com), which features a trio of 18-hole golf courses, shopping, dining, and a spa. Doubles begin at $149.

For dining out, head to Traverse City's Front Street downtown, where you'll find a wide array of choices. For a special evening out, you can't beat **Windows,** 7677 W. Bay Shore Dr. (© **231/941-0100**), situated on Grand Traverse Bay. The finest restaurant in Traverse City, its menu is notable for its inclusion of locally grown cherries, in both entrees and desserts. Reservations are mandatory.

LUDINGTON

Even Michiganians (who are accustomed to great beaches) are wowed by **Ludington's** miles of pristine shoreline and wild dune vistas. Most of the lakeshore has free parking, both in the **Ludington City Park** (Lakeshore Dr.) and **Ludington State Park** (© **231/843-8671**), on M-116. The latter offers uncrowded beaches, dunes, and "Big Lake" boating in its western half; the eastern section borders Hamlin Lake, with calmer (and warmer) inland lake water. Contact the

Ludington Convention and Visitors Bureau at © 800/542-4600 or www.ludingtoncvb.com.

WHERE TO STAY & DINE   You'll find many chain hotels on U.S. 10 between U.S. 31 and the city of Ludington. If you want to be near the beach, your best bet is **Snyder's Shoreline Inn,** 903 W. Ludington Ave. (© 231/845-1261; www.snydersshoreinn.com), right across the street from the city beach. Doubles begin at $69. Two cozy B&B choices include **The Lamplighter,** 602 E. Ludington Ave. (© 800/301-9792 or 231/843-9792; www.ludington-michigan.com), with doubles for $100 to $155; and **The Inn at Ludington,** 701 E. Ludington Ave. (© 800/845-9170 or 231/845-7055; www.inn-ludington.com), with doubles for $90 to $110. Both include full breakfast and are within walking distance of Lake Michigan. **Ludington State Park** (see above) has three campgrounds.

Most restaurants are clustered along Ludington Avenue, but two good choices for dinner are **P. M. Steamers,** 502 W. Loomis St. (© 231/843-9555), which features casual American fare and a waterfront view; and **Scotty's,** 5910 W. U.S. 10 (© 231/843-4033), which is famous for its prime rib and seafood.

HOLLAND

Holland enjoys four great beach areas: **Holland State Park,** 2215 Ottawa Beach Rd. (© 616/399-9390); **Oval Beach,** Oval Drive just off Perryman Street, Saugatuck; **Saugatuck Dunes State Park,** western end of 138th Avenue, Saugatuck (© 616/637-2788); and **Tunnel Park,** Lakeshore Drive at Perry Street (© 616/738-4810), named for the dune tunnel that connects the playground area to the beach. All four have picnic and playground facilities, but it's the huge, white beaches that attract thousands every year. Contact the **Holland Convention and Visitors Bureau** at © 800/506-1299 or www.holland.org.

WHERE TO STAY & DINE   Holland's chain hotels cluster largely along U.S. 31. For a quieter, downtown location, try the **Haworth Inn,** 225 College Ave. (© 800/903-9142 or 616/395-7200; www.haworthinn.com), with doubles starting at $95, including continental breakfast. Want to stay near the beach? Your best bets are two cozy B&Bs. The **Inn at Old Orchard Road,** 1422 S. Shore Dr. (© 616/335-2525), provides rooms beginning at $90. **Shaded Oaks,** 444 Oak St. (© 616/399-4194; www.shadedoaks.com), offers lodging beginning at $125. Both B&Bs serve full breakfasts.

Several area restaurants are located in downtown Holland on 8th Street. Two favorites include **Till Midnight,** 208 College Ave. (© 616/392-6883), a spot for "eclectic fine dining," with unusual preparations of traditional dishes; and **Alpenrose,** 4 E. 8th St. (© 616/393-2111), which features hearty German and Austrian fare.

MACKINAC ISLAND

Set in the Straits of Mackinac, which separate Michigan's upper and lower peninsulas, Mackinac (pronounced *Mack*-i-naw) Island is one of the loveliest destinations in Michigan. **Mackinac Island State Park** (© 906/847-3328, summer only) constitutes 80% of the island, and cars are prohibited here. Visitors get around on foot, bicycles, and horse-drawn carriages (watch your step!). The lack of modern transportation helps cultivate the sense of 19th-century nostalgia pervading the island, a veritable repository of beautifully restored Victorian homes. For more information, contact the **Mackinac Island Chamber of Commerce** at © 800/454-5227, 906/847-3571, or www.mackinacisland.org.

The oldest structure in Michigan, **Fort Mackinac** (© 616/436-4100) looms high on a bluff overlooking the Straits of Mackinac. Originally a British outpost, Fort Mackinac was conquered by American soldiers 20 years after the Revolution. With stunning views over the water, the enormous ramparts have been faithfully restored along with the cannon, guardhouse, and barracks. Now they form the backdrop for a carnival of events: Victorian children's games; bagpipe, bugle, and drum corps music; hourly rifle and cannon firings; and military reenactments performed by costumed interpreters.

For another prime vantage on the spectacular straits, sit for a spell on the porch at the **Grand Hotel** (© 906/847-3331), which bills itself as "the world's longest veranda," built in 1887. For a $10 fee you can take in the view, drink cocktails, and tour this lovely—albeit pricey—landmark hotel (see below).

If you like to bike, take a spin around the island, following an 8-mile circuit on **Mich. 185 (Lake Shore Rd).** The view of the straits is spellbinding from here—and you can rubberneck without fear of oncoming trucks, given the prohibition on motorized vehicles. Bike rentals are available throughout downtown, at $5 per hour for 1-speeds, $6 to $8 per hour for tandems. Ask about day rates and children's seats.

In town, it's fun to get around by horse and buggy on **Mackinac Island Carriage Tours** (© 906/847-3325; $15 adults, $7.50 children 4–11). Trips begin near the boat docks in the center of the shopping district and last about 2 hours. Sites include the Governor's Mansion, the Grand Hotel, and Arch Rock—a boulder with a gaping 30- by 40-foot hole gouged in it by waves and glaciers.

Downtown, between Fort Mackinac and the Grand Hotel, a smattering of shops, galleries, and historic sites (all without street numbers) are worth an afternoon stroll. Don't leave the island without its famous fudge—many shops sell their share of this island specialty, unloading an estimated 10,000 pounds of it per day in the summer! At the **Benjamin Blacksmith Shop,** Market Street (© 906/847-3328), interpreters demonstrate forging techniques with 19th-century blacksmithing equipment. Built in 1838 as lodging for Chippewa and Ottawa tribes on their annual visit to the U.S. Indian Agency, the **Indian Dormitory,** Huron Street (© 906/847-3328), now houses a museum of Native American artifacts.

For fine dining on the island try the **Carriage House,** Main Street (© 906/847-3321), in the Hotel Iroquois. Specialties include broiled Lake Superior whitefish and pork tenderloin served with a chutney of Michigan apples and cherries. A nice family choice is **Dockside Inn,** near Star Line Ferry (© 906/847-3480), a casual restaurant serving local fish, chicken, ribs, burgers, and over 140 types of beer.

The **Grand Hotel** (© 800/33-GRAND or 906/847-3331; www.grandhotel.com) lives up to its name. Resort grounds include tennis courts, an 18-hole golf course, and formal gardens. Doubles start at $350, including breakfast and dinner daily. A great family resort is **Mission Point** (© 800/833-7711 or 906/847-3312; www.missionpoint.com), with 18 acres on the lakefront and a host of recreational facilities. Doubles begin at $189. One of the island's first summer hotels, the more affordable **Island House** (© 800/626-6304 or 906/847-3347; www.theislandhouse.com), is a Victorian mansion with an indoor pool, whirlpool/steam room, and tennis and golf privileges. Doubles begin at $169. Other moderately priced choices include **Iroquois on the Beach,** Main Street (© 906/847-3321), where doubles start at $160; and the **Lilac Tree,** Main Street (© 906/847-6575), whose suites start at $140.

GETTING THERE   The major route to Mackinac Island is I-75 from the south. From the lower peninsula, you can reach the island by ferry from **Mackinaw City**. From the upper peninsula, ferries depart from **St. Ignace. Shepler's Mackinac Island Ferry** (© **800/828-6157**), **Arnold Transit Company** (© **800/542-8528**), and **Star Line Ferry** (© **800/638-9892**) all service the island from both cities, and all charge the same rates: adults $16, children 5 to 12 $8, free for children under 5. Bike transport is $6.50. You can also travel by plane from St. Ignace on **Great Lakes Air** (© **906/643-7165**).

PICTURED ROCKS NATIONAL LAKESHORE

On the north coast of Michigan's upper peninsula, sandstone cliffs in a range of colors soar to a height of 200 feet along the shore of Lake Superior, from Munising to Grand Marais. Rain, wind, and waves have sculpted them into a natural wonder of caves, columns, overlooks, and arches that stretch along the coast for 17 miles.

Highway 58 is a rough gravel road that runs parallel to the lakeshore between Munising on Mich. 28 and Grand Marais on Mich. 77. You'll find accommodations, restaurants, information, and camping supplies in both these towns. For more information, call the **Grand Marais Chamber of Commerce** ((© **906/494-2766**) or the park superintendent at © **906/387-3700.**

Trails and roads such as the **North Country Hiking Trail** deliver you straight to the rocks for intimate views. Many visitors prefer to see the shore from a boat, which docks at the **Munising Municipal Pier,** Mich. 28 and Elm Avenue (© **906/387-2033**). Adults pay $24, children 6 to 12 $10; under 6 get in free.

In the summer, you can, hike, picnic, and swim (if you can brave Lake Superior's frigid waters) on the lakeshore. During winter months, you can snowshoe, snowmobile, or cross-country ski on 21 miles of trails.

Near **Grand Marais,** the cliffs ease into **giant sand dunes,** which lumberjacks used as chutes to send forested timber into the lake below. Inland, you'll find waterfalls, forests, abundant wildlife, and fish swarming in lakes, ponds, and streams. At the base of the cliffs, a sand beach stretches for 12 miles.

After a rigorous day in the outdoors, replenish your energy without depleting your funds at **Sydney's,** Mich. 28, Munising (© **906/387-4067**). Grilled steaks or fresh fish from Lake Superior are the specialties.

There are three drive-in campsites in the 40-mile Pictured Rocks National Lakeshore between Munising and Grand Marais. You can also hike into primitive campgrounds along the water. In Grand Marais, **North Shore Resort,** Canal Street, 1 mile east of Mich. 77 (© **906/494-2361**), offers affordable lodgings on a stretch of private beach.

GETTING THERE   To reach Pictured Rocks from the Mackinac Bridge (I-75), take U.S. 2 west immediately after the bridge, then Mich. 77 north to Grand Marais. For Munising, turn west on Mich. 28 at Seney.

ISLE ROYALE NATIONAL PARK

It's tough to get to Isle Royale National Park, which is precisely its appeal. The remote, craggy islands are lush with hardwood forests, rich wildlife, and lakes and streams teeming with trout, perch, and walleye. Cars are prohibited on this roadless oasis, accessible only by boat and floatplane, 50 miles from Michigan's northwest coast and surrounded by Lake Superior's icy waters. The main island is the largest (45 miles wide by 8 miles long) and most visited, but it is surrounded by 400 smaller islands. It's likely you'll have one all to yourself—provided you can paddle there.

A trip to Isle Royale takes careful planning. Ferries to the island return just a few hours after they dock—hardly worth the long voyage unless you plan to stay overnight. The one-way, 2½-hour cruise from Grand Portage, MN (on Hwy. 61 near Ontario) on *Voyager II* or *Wenonah* (© 715/392-2100) costs $49 adults, $32 children under 12. The 4½-hour, one-way trip from Copper Harbor, MI (on U.S. 41, on the Keweenaw Peninsula) on *The Isle Royale Queen* (© 906/289-4437) costs $42 adults, $21 children under 12. And the 6-hour trip from Houghton, MI (on U.S. 41, on the Keweenaw Peninsula) on *Ranger III* (© 906/482-0984) costs $49 adults, $24 children under 12. The *Ranger III* is the only ferry large enough to transport boats. Fees vary according to boat size. From Houghton you can also catch a **seaplane.** Contact the **Houghton Visitor Center** at © 906/482-0984 or ISRO_ParkInfo@nps.gov for current rates and schedules. Visitors also need to pay a daily use fee of $4 for individuals 12 and over.

You'll encounter Isle Royale's sole inhabitants—200 bird species, foxes, beavers, wolves, and about 700 moose—along the park's 165 miles of foot trails. **Greenstone Ridge Trail,** the main artery, is moderately strenuous, running east-west along the island—a 4- or 5-day trek even for fit hikers. Easier routes include the 2-mile **Washington Creek Trail,** on the island's west end, and the **Stoll Loop Trail** at Rock Harbor, a 4-mile hike through woods and along Lake Superior.

Isle Royale is generally thought of as a rugged backpacking destination—which it is. But you don't have to be a survivalist to enjoy this island's unspoiled environment. **Rock Harbor Lodge,** Rock Harbor (© 906/337-4993 summer, 270/773-2191 winter; open late May to mid-Sept), offers guest rooms and meals to those who need a little more in the way of amenities. The rate for a family of four is $260, including all meals. The lodge's dining room is open to all (even those who are staying elsewhere), or you can bring your own food and rent a cabin (with kitchenette) for $179 nightly. Rock Harbor Lodge also rents canoes and motorboats. Sightseeing cruises depart Rock Harbor for a variety of island destinations for $11 adults, $5.10 children under 12.

The campgrounds near Rock Harbor have three-sided wooden shelters, but they fill up fast because they are near the island's entry point. **Three Mile** and **Daisy Farm** are within a day's hike of Rock Harbor, west along the southern shore. **West Chickenbone** is a popular site, a 2- to 3-day hike from Rock Harbor, along the Greenstone Ridge Trail.

For more information, call **Park Headquarters** at © 906/482-0984. **Ranger stations** are at Windigo, Rock Harbor, Malone Bay, and Amygdaloid.

5 Milwaukee & Highlights of Wisconsin

MILWAUKEE

The Great Chicago Fire of 1871 put Milwaukee's breweries on the map—someone had to pick up the slack when the Windy City's brewhouses went up in smoke, and Milwaukee was happy to oblige. The beer capital of America is still home to breweries large and small, as well as Harley Davidson's international headquarters. But there's more to the city than industry. Visitors also enjoy great views of Lake Michigan, cultural opportunities, and some of the friendliest people in the Midwest.

ESSENTIALS

GETTING THERE **By Plane** The **General Mitchell International Airport** (© 414/747-5300; www.mitchellairport.com) is 10 miles south of downtown, a 15-minute drive on I-94 west to 794 east. One-way transportation to the downtown costs $10 via Airport Connection shuttle service (© **800/236-5150** or 414/769-2444; reservations recommended); $1.50 via the local Transit System (Rte. 80 serves the airport); and $20 via taxi.

By Train   Amtrak (© **800/USA-RAIL;** www.amtrak.com) provides service from Chicago (trip time: 1½ hr.) and St. Paul (6½ hr.) to its station at 433 W. St. Paul Ave.

By Car   Milwaukee is 93 miles from Chicago, a 1¾-hour drive; and 77 miles from Madison, a 1½-hour drive. Both cities are reached via I-94.

VISITOR INFORMATION   Contact the **Milwaukee Convention and Visitors Bureau,** 101 W. Wisconsin Ave., Ste. 425, Milwaukee, WI 53203 (© **800/554-1448;** www.officialmilwaukee.com).

GETTING AROUND   The **Milwaukee County Transit System** (© **414/344-6711;** www.ridemcts.com) offers service downtown and into the suburbs for $1.50. Downtown tourist attractions can be reached via the city's **Trolley** system, which costs 50¢.

SPECIAL EVENTS & FESTIVALS   There are dozens of festivals in Milwaukee—sometimes called "The City of Festivals"—ranging from the Asian Moon Festival to German Fest to African World Festival. The biggest and best include **Summerfest** (© **414/273-FEST;** www.summerfest.com), with entertainment on a dozen different stages throughout late June and early July; and **Irish Fest** (© **414/476-3378;** www.irishfest.com) in mid-August, referred to as the "Superbowl of Irish Music" by *Smithsonian Magazine.* In early August, there's the **Wisconsin State Fair** (© **414/266-7060;** www.wistatefair.com), with entertainment, auto races, exhibits, fireworks, and more.

WHAT TO SEE & DO

Stroll the **Port of Milwaukee,** on the west shore of Lake Michigan, where the Milwaukee, Menomonee, and Kinnickinnic rivers converge. **Iroquois Boat Line Tours** (© **414/384-8606**) offer a close-up view of the lakefront, harbor, lighthouse, and breakwater. Passengers board at the Clybourn Street Bridge.

Miller Brewing Company, 4251 W. State St. (© **414/931-BEER**), operates one of the world's largest breweries. After a free 1-hour tour, visitors sample the product outside in the city's last remaining *biergarten* during warm weather, or in the 19th-century Miller Inn the rest of the year. Another favorite factory tour is at the **Harley-Davidson Tour Center,** 11700 W. Capitol Dr., Wauwatosa (© **414/535-3666**). The free hour-long tour allows visitors to see Harley powertrains in production. No children under 12.

The lions lie down with the lambs at the **Milwaukee County Zoo,** 10001 W. Bluemound Rd. (© **414/771-5500;** www.milwaukeezoo.org). Prey-predator combos, such as cheetahs and gazelles, roam adjacent, cageless habitats, separated only by moats.

Mitchell Park Conservatory, better known as **"The Domes,"** 524 S. Layton Blvd. (© **414/649-9830**), is a botanical garden housed in three seven-story, aluminum and glass domes. The gardens include an Arid Dome, featuring desert plants; a Tropical Dome, with rainforest plants and orchids; and a Show Dome, featuring seasonal plantings.

Two museums share space on the corner of West Wells and James Lovell streets. **Milwaukee Public Museum** (© **414/278-2722;** www.mpm.edu) is home to a staggering array of re-created villages from around the world, a permanent live butterfly garden, dinosaur skeletons, and a simulated rainforest. In the same complex is **Discovery World** (© 414/765-9966; www.discovery world.org), where visitors enjoy hands-on science and technology exhibits.

Santiago Calatrava's redesign of the **Milwaukee Art Museum,** 700 N. Art Museum Dr. (© 414/224-3200; www.mam.org), renders the museum itself as stunning as any of the works on display inside. But go in anyway and see artwork from ancient Greece to modern American, Asian, and African art displayed in roughly chronological order.

WHERE TO STAY & DINE

The **Hilton City Center,** 509 W. Wisconsin Ave. (© 800/HILTONS or 414/271-7250; www.hiltonmilwaukee.com), is convenient to downtown and has a great restaurant and lounge. It's also home to the nation's first urban indoor waterpark, "Paradise Landing," with seven water slides. Doubles begin at $100. Milwaukee's most historic hotel, the 100-year-old **Pfister,** 424 E. Wisconsin Ave. (© 800/558-8222 or 414/273-8222; www.thepfisterhotel.com), is centrally located and offers an indoor pool, three restaurants, and lots of ambience. Doubles begin at $130 and go way up. **Four Points by Sheraton,** 4747 S. Howell Ave. (© 800/558-3862 or 414/481-8000; www.fourpointshotel.com), is the other leading upscale choice, with in-room modems, two pools, a superb restaurant, and a location near the airport. Doubles begin at $120.

Milwaukee Chop House, 509 W. Wisconsin Ave. (at the Hilton City Center; © 414/226-CHOP), specializes in mouthwatering steaks and offers an extensive wine list. **Crawdaddy's,** west of town at 6414 W. Greenfield Ave. (© 414/778-2228), is known for its Creole/Cajun seafood, although you'll find meat and pasta on the menu as well. **Water Street Brewery,** 1101 N. Water St. (© 414/272-1195), brews its own beers and serves pasta, ribs, seafood, and sandwiches in a fun atmosphere.

A SIDE TRIP TO KOHLER & THE AMERICAN CLUB

One hour north of Milwaukee is the planned garden community of Kohler; its centerpiece is the luxurious **American Club,** Highland Drive (© 800/344-2838; www.destinationkohler.com), the Midwest's top resort. Built in 1918 to house immigrants working in the Kohler factory, the grand Tudor-style American Club was converted into a hotel in 1981 and now offers 236 guest rooms. The resort is owned by the plumbing giant, who still has a factory here hidden behind a row of evergreens across from the hotel. Not surprisingly, the American Club is known for its bathrooms; each room has a whirlpool tub (some are intimate one- or two-person affairs; others are large enough for the whole gang). The resort's extensive facilities include four Pete Dye–designed golf courses; a 500-acre wilderness preserve with cross-country skiing, horseback riding, and 25 miles of trails; a salon and day spa; health and racquet facilities; upscale boutiques; and the Kohler Design Center. The golf is the star attraction, though, and guests are encouraged to reserve tee times when they book their room—greens fees begin at $148. Room rates begin at $265 during golf season, $170 in the winter.

MADISON

Wisconsin's state capital is a small city with lots of inexpensive entertainment. The "City of Four Lakes" is also a city of parks, and its streets are enlivened by bookstores, cafes, and student activity from the University of Wisconsin. Madison's most bustling thoroughfare, **State Street,** and the downtown area,

Capitol Square, are great places to browse eclectic shops and visit unique cafes and restaurants. In summer, Capitol Square hosts a vibrant, open-air **Dane County Farmer's Market** on Saturday and Wednesday mornings.

For more information, contact the **Greater Madison Convention and Visitors Bureau,** 615 E. Washington Ave. (© **800/373-6376;** www.visitmadison. com).

WHAT TO SEE & DO

Settled on an isthmus between Lake Mendota and Lake Monona, Madison is graced with over 150 public parks. One of the most popular is the **Henry Vilas Park Zoo,** 702 S. Randall Ave. (© **608/266-4732**), where many locals gather to picnic, feed ducks, and enjoy more than 600 animals in one of the nation's few free zoos. **Olbrich Park,** on Atwood Avenue, lies on the northeastern shore of Lake Monona, with picnic tables and a swimming area. Across the street is **Olbrich Gardens** (© **608/246-4550**), with 14 acres of outdoor flowering plants and a conservatory.

Madison's Roman Renaissance–style **State Capitol** (© **608/266-0382**) dominates the city center. Free tours offer a look at the white granite structure surmounted by Daniel Chester French's gilded bronze statue *Wisconsin.* Just a few blocks away is **Monona Terrace,** 1 John Nolen Dr., a free community and convention center designed by Frank Lloyd Wright, whose presence is richly felt in Madison and nearby Taliesin (see below). Its rooftop garden offers superb views of the adjoining lake and city, a perfect spot for a picnic lunch.

For more examples of Wright's legacy of Prairie School architecture, visit **First Unitarian Society,** 900 University Bay Rd. (© **608/233-9774**), which is open to the public, or drive past these private residences: **Airplane House** (1908), 120 Ely Place; **Dr. Arnold Jackson House** (1957), 3515 W. Beltline Hwy.; **Lamp House** (1899), 22 N. Butler St.; **J. C. Pew House** (1939), 3650 Lake Mendota Dr.; **Louis Sullivan Bradley's House,** 106 N. Prospect; and **"Jacobs I" House** (1937), 441 Toepfer Ave.

WHERE TO STAY & DINE

Canterbury Booksellers Café Inn, 315 W. Gorham at State St. (© **800/838-3850** or 608/258-8899; www.madisoncanterbury.com), is a combination bookstore, cafe, and B&B. Close to lively State Street, the inn is decorated with murals depicting Chaucer's *Canterbury Tales.* Doubles begin at $104 and include a hearty continental breakfast, wine and cheese, and a $10 gift certificate to the bookstore downstairs. Downtown, the **Edgewater,** 666 Wisconsin Ave. (© **800/922-5512** or 608/256-9071; www.theedgewater.com), on Lake Mendota, boasts beautiful lakeside sunsets and a fine restaurant. Doubles begin at $99, $139 lakefront, and $189 suites. The **Fairfield Inn by Marriott,** off I-90/94 Exit 135A at 4765 Hayes Rd. (© **800/228-2800** or 608/249-5300), offers comfortable lodgings about 5 miles from downtown near plenty of restaurants. Doubles begin at $49 and include continental breakfast.

A variety of casual ethnic restaurants line State Street. Forty homemade pasta dishes are served at **Tutto Pasta,** 305 State St. (© **608/294-1000**), most under $10. A popular university haunt is **State Street Brats,** 603 State St. (© **608/255-5544**), famous for tasty bratwurst on home-baked buns and microbrewed beers. For a fine dining experience, try **The Admiralty,** 666 Wisconsin Ave. (in the Edgewater Hotel; © **608/273-4900**), which serves steak and seafood in a romantic setting.

SPRING GREEN & TALIESIN

Frank Lloyd Wright's former home, which he built and perfected over the course of 40 years, **Taliesin** (Tally-ES-in), Highway 23 (© **608/588-7900;** www.taliesinpreservation.org), has been called the architect's "autobiography in wood and stone." Just north of the Wisconsin River on Route 23 in south-central Wisconsin, the 600-acre National Historic Landmark is now a studio, farm, and school for 40 undergraduates.

Welsh for "shining brow," Taliesin is built on the crest of a hill facing the Wisconsin River, on land where Wright's grandfather settled after immigrating from Wales. Wright built each of the grounds' five buildings during consecutive decades of his 50-year career. Visitors can purchase tickets to one of four Taliesin tours: the **Hillside Studio Tour** (1 hr., $10); the **Walking Tour** of the grounds (2 hr., $15); **Wright's House Tour** (2 hr., $35–$45); and the comprehensive **Estate Tour** (4 hr., $70). Tours operate daily May through October.

South of town on Route 23, the multilevel **House on the Rock,** Highway 23 (© **608/935-3639**), sits atop a 450-foot rock chimney. Built by Alexander Jordan, the stone house is an architectural curiosity, with massive fireplaces, trees, and pools of running water throughout the building. Views of the surrounding landscape are equally spectacular.

You can stay at **House on the Rock Resort,** 400 Springs Dr., just a few miles from its famous namesake. The all-suite resort features private patios and balconies as well as a fine restaurant. Doubles begin at $95. The **Silver Star Inn,** 3852 Limmex Hill Rd. (© **608/935-7297;** www.silverstarinn.com), is a huge log building on 350 acres of woods and farmland. Doubles begin at $95 and include a full breakfast. Another affordable choice is the **Round Barn Lodge,** on U.S. 14 and 23 (© **608/588-2568;** www.roundbarn.com), with an indoor pool and a good restaurant. Doubles start at $50; suites at $75.

For more information, contact the **Spring Green Chamber of Commerce,** E5028 Hwy. 14, Spring Green (© **800/588-2042;** www.springgreen.com).

THE WISCONSIN DELLS

Although Wisconsin Dells are the state's largest tourist attraction, its 15 miles of soaring, eroded sandstone cliffs and cool, fern-filled gullies remain relatively unspoiled. The Wisconsin River flowed through soft limestone for thousands of years to carve out the wild gorges here.

The Dells—both the town and the geologic wonder—are 55 miles north of Madison; Exits 85, 87, 89, and 92 off I-90/94 will deliver you here. For information, contact the **Wisconsin Dells Visitor and Convention Bureau,** 701 Superior St., P.O. Box 390, Wisconsin Dells, WI 53965 (© **800/223-3557;** www.wisdells.com).

April through October you can cruise the gorges on **Dells Boat Tours** (© **608/254-8555;** www.dellsboats.com), or aboard World War II amphibious "ducks" at **Original Wisconsin Ducks** (© **608/254-8751;** www.wisconsin ducktours.com). All offer 2-hour tours for roughly $17 adults, $9 children. During the warm months you can also explore the gorgeous landscape on horseback with a guide at the **Beaver Springs Fishing Park and Riding Stables,** 600 Trout Rd., off Highway 13 (© **608/254-2707**). Fifty-foot sandstone cliffs form the lakeshore of nearby **Mirror Lake State Park,** Fern Dell Road (off Hwy. 12; © **608/254-2333**). A popular boating spot, the lake is surrounded by pine and oak woods where visitors can picnic and camp.

Man-made attractions in the Dells greatly outnumber the natural ones. One of the most popular for families is **Noah's Ark Waterpark,** 1410 Wisconsin Dells Pkwy. (© **608/254-6351;** www.noahsarkwaterpark.com), the nation's largest, with 36 water slides, two wave pools, two endless rivers, mini-golf, and 12 restaurants and lounges. A day pass costs $27.

The popularity—and plethora—of indoor water parks in the Dells has made the area a year-round family destination. Parks combine water slides, wave pools, and squirty toys with resort-style accommodations under one roof, and at a very affordable price. **Great Wolf Lodge,** 1400 Great Wolf Dr. (off Hwy. 12/Gasser Rd.; © **800/559-WOLF;** www.greatwolflodge.com), has won "Best Family Resort" awards from several parenting magazines. Room rates begin at $149. **Treasure Island,** 1701 Wisconsin Dells Pkwy. (© **800/800-4997;** http:// wisdellstreasureisland.com), houses America's largest indoor water park. Room rates begin at $85. **Kalahari Resort,** 1305 Kalahari Dr. (off Hwy. 12/Gasser Rd.; © **877/253-5466;** www.kalahariresort.com), also has a day spa on-site. Room rates begin at $99. **Wilderness Lodge,** 511 E. Adams St. (© **800/867-WILD;** www.wildernessresort.com), has an 18-hole golf course in addition to water fun. Room rates begin at $89. *Note:* Rates for all of the hotels above are for double rooms with up to four people occupying them.

Wally's House of Embers, 935 Wisconsin Dells Pkwy. (© **608/253-6411**), is a friendly, family-owned restaurant specializing in ribs, but also serves fresh seafood, pasta, and steaks. For casual dining on fajitas, pasta, and stir-fry, try **Houlihan's,** 644 Dells Pkwy. (© **608/253-9109**).

DOOR COUNTY

Door County is often called the "Cape Cod of the Midwest," due to its low-key, rugged beauty and peninsular location. With Green Bay to the west and Lake Michigan to the east, Door County is a 75-mile-long limestone strip of cliffs and unsullied beaches, with 250 miles of scenic coastline. No matter where you are here, you're never more than 10 minutes from a water view.

Routes 57 and 42 circle the peninsula, passing through splendid natural scenery and inviting towns like the bayside villages of **Fish Creek, Sister Bay,** and **Ephraim,** each one charmingly different from the next. Tidy dairy farms and fruit orchards with ubiquitous red barns dot the landscape. Contact the **Door County Chamber of Commerce,** Box 406, Sturgeon Bay, WI 54235 (© **800/527-3529** or 920/743-4456; www.doorcountyvacations.com), for additional information.

Miles of hiking and biking trails, fishing, sailing, swimming, and championship golf have made **Peninsula State Park,** near Fish Creek (© **920/868-3258**) one of the state's most popular. Its campground is also popular—reserve a site early. Reached by ferry from the tip of the peninsula are tranquil **Washington Island,** another popular cycling spot and site of the oldest Icelandic settlement in the U.S., and remote **Rock Island** (no cars allowed). The less-populated Lake Michigan side of the peninsula has more rugged appeal. Ninety-foot dunes, jagged cliffs, and surf-carved caves lure visitors to **Whitefish Dunes State Park,** near Jacksonport (© **920/823-2400**). Scenic trails and great beaches and swimming can be found at **Ridges Sanctuary,** near Baileys Harbor (© **920/839-2802**).

Shopping is another popular pastime. Art galleries and craft boutiques are found in the towns and tucked down quiet country lanes. Two of the best are

Edgewood Orchard Gallery, located just outside Fish Creek on Peninsula Players Road (© **920/868-3579**), featuring works by nationally recognized artists; and **Blue Dolphin House,** on North Water Street, Ephraim (© **800/765-0141**).

French and Scandinavian fishermen settled the Door in the 17th century, and the surrounding waters are still a mother lode of walleye, northern pike, lake trout, and salmon. **Fish boils** are the stuff of ceremonial ritual here: Fresh whitefish are tossed into a cauldron to boil with onions and potatoes. Arrive at your chosen restaurant early—part of the fun is watching the concoction boil over the top. The fish chow is topped off with cherry pie, made from locally harvested fruit. The **White Gull Inn,** Main Street, Fish Creek (© **920/868-3517**), is famous for its fish boils, as is the **Viking,** Highway 42, Ellison Bay (© **920/854-2998**). For an authentic Swedish breakfast of pancakes with lingonberry sauce, everyone heads to **Al Johnson's Swedish Restaurant,** Sister Bay (© **920/854-2626**), where goats graze on the sod-covered roof. **Wilson's Restaurant and Ice Cream Parlor,** Route 42, Ephraim (© **920/854-2041**), has been serving sundaes, chocolate sodas, and burgers since 1906.

The all-suite, cedar-shingled **The Landing Resort,** 7741 Egg Harbor Rd., Egg Harbor (© **800/851-8919** or 920/868-3282; www.thelandingresort.com), is great for families, with beach access and two pools—one indoor and one out. Suites begin at $92. Another great family option is the **AmericInn,** 622 S. Ashland Ave., Sturgeon Bay (© **800/634-3444** or 920/743-5898; www.americinn. com), with its indoor pool and free continental breakfast. Doubles begin at $89. The luxurious **Ashbrooke,** 7942 Egg Harbor Rd., Egg Harbor (© **920/868-3113;** www.ashbrooke.net), has an indoor pool and health center on-site. Doubles begin at $95 and include continental breakfast. The area is also known for its numerous inns and B&Bs. **The Whistling Swan,** 4192 Main St., Fish Creek (© **888/277-4289** or 920/868-3442), is beautifully decorated with antiques. Doubles begin at $109 and include continental breakfast.

6 Minneapolis & St. Paul

Minnesota's twin cities—Minneapolis and St. Paul—lie on either side of the Mississippi River, and both cities are hubs for riverboat traffic all the way up from New Orleans. When the first explorers ventured up the mighty Mississippi, they found the river roaring over an 18-foot precipice here. Today the Falls of St. Anthony are tamed and bypassed by lock and dam.

Minneapolis was first settled by emigrants from New England in 1847, who were soon joined by waves of Scandinavians and Germans. Today the city is home to the University of Minnesota, the famous Guthrie Theater, and miles and miles of a climate-controlled skyway system that enables residents and visitors to do everything from park and shop to work and dine without stepping outdoors in the often-harsh winters.

Although St. Paul has its share of glass skyscrapers and 5 miles of skyways, it has preserved much of its Victorian architecture, and its downtown is a blend of the two styles. Somewhat smaller than Minneapolis, quieter and more conservative, it is also a cultural center with museums, universities, and theaters.

ESSENTIALS

GETTING THERE   By Plane   Minneapolis/St. Paul International Airport (www.mspairport.com), located between the cities, is 8 to 10 miles south

Downtown Minneapolis

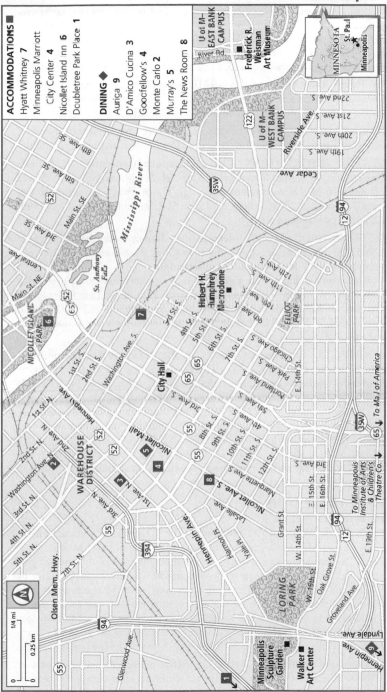

ACCOMMODATIONS ■
Hyatt Whitney **7**
Minneapolis Marriott
 City Center **4**
Nicollet Island nn **6**
Doubletree Park Place **1**

DINING ◆
Auriga **9**
D'Amico Cucina **3**
Goodfellow's **4**
Monte Carlo **2**
Murray's **5**
The News Room **8**

of both downtowns. The airport is a hub for Northwest Airlines. The **Metropolitan Transit Commission** runs buses to both cities (© 612/349-7000) for $1.75 off-peak hours and $2.25 during rush hour. **Airport Express** (© 612/827-7777) runs vans to many hotels for about $11 one-way. A taxi to downtown Minneapolis costs about $25; a taxi to downtown St. Paul costs about $14.

By Train   Amtrak (© 800/USA-RAIL; www.amtrak.com) provides service from Chicago (trip time: 8¼ hr.), Milwaukee (6½ hr.), and Seattle (36 hr.) to its station at 730 Transfer Rd., St. Paul (© 651/644-6012).

By Car   Major routes into the Twin Cities are I-94 from the east (Milwaukee) and west (Fargo), and I-35 from the south (Des Moines) and north (Duluth).

VISITOR INFORMATION   The **Minneapolis Convention & Visitors Bureau** is at 4000 Multifoods Tower, 33 S. 6th St., Minneapolis, MN 55402 (© 888/676-MPLS; www.minneapolis.org). The **St. Paul Convention & Visitors Bureau** is at 175 W. Kellogg Blvd., Ste. 502, St. Paul, MN 55102 (© 800/627-6101; www.stpaulcvb.org).

GETTING AROUND   The **Metropolitan Transit Commission** (© 612/373-3333) operates buses between the Twin Cities. Rush-hour fare is $2.25; off-peak fare is $1.75. A day pass is available for $6.

Minneapolis is laid out on a grid system, but many downtown streets that parallel the Mississippi River run on a diagonal. Each of the Twin Cities has an extensive skyway system (a godsend during below-zero winters) that makes it easy to explore downtown areas on foot. But you'll need a car to reach many attractions outside downtown and in the suburbs.

FAST FACTS   For physician referrals, try the Physician's Referral and Information Service (© 612-697-3333). There's an emergency room at the **Fairview University Medical Center,** 420 Delaware St. SE, Minneapolis (© 612/273-3000).

There is no **tax** on clothing in Minnesota. Sales tax is 7% in Minneapolis, 6.5% elsewhere in the state. Hotel tax is 13%; restaurant tax is 10%; alcohol tax is 9% (12% downtown).

Both Minneapolis and St. Paul are among the safest large cities in the country, and crime rates are extremely low; exercise the same caution you would in any other major city, and you should have no problems.

WHAT TO SEE & DO
IN MINNEAPOLIS

Frederick R. Weisman Art Museum   The Weisman Art Museum on the University of Minnesota campus sits on a bluff overlooking the Mississippi River. The spectacular Frank Gehry–designed building is probably the best part of the exhibit—the permanent collection inside is rather small. Canvases by Warhol and Lichtenstein share gallery space with other American artists from the early 20th century. Allow 30 minutes to an hour. 333 E. River Rd., Minneapolis. © 612/625-9494. http://hudson.acad.umn.edu. Free admission. Tues, Wed, and Fri 10am–5pm; Thurs 10am–8pm; Sat–Sun 11am–5pm. Head southeast on Washington Ave. and take the "Washington Ave. SE" ramp downhill and across the Mississippi. E. River Rd. is immediately to your right.

Minneapolis Institute of Arts   The MIA's permanent collection of over 100,000 objects of fine and decorative art represents more than 5,000 years of history. Highlights include a Paul Revere tea service and a 2,000-year-old mummy. There are re-created period rooms; African, Oceanic, and New World galleries; and paintings by European masters. If you're short on time, ask for the "Highlights" brochure. Allow 2 hours. 2400 3rd Ave. S., Minneapolis. ✆ 612/870-3131. www.artsmia.org. Free admission (excludes special exhibits). Tues, Wed, and Sat 10am–5pm; Thurs and Fri 10am–9pm; Sun noon–5pm.

University of Minnesota   One of the Midwest's oldest (1851) and most important universities, with 45,000 students, the campus offers three significant museums—the **James Ford Bell Museum of Natural History, the University Art Gallery,** and the **Frederick R. Weisman Art Museum** (see above). The 4,800-seat Northrop Auditorium has been a home for distinguished performances since 1929, and the University Theatre has four separate stages. Located between Mississippi and University aves. and 10th Ave. and Oak St. SE, Minneapolis. ✆ 800/752-1000 or 612/625-5000.

Walker Art Center/Minneapolis Sculpture Garden   The Walker Art Center is famous for its permanent collection of contemporary art, ranging from painting and sculpture to drawings, photographs, and multimedia installations. Across Vineland Place is the Minneapolis Sculpture Garden, the most extensive garden of its kind in the United States, with a wide variety of 20th-century sculpture, including the famous "Spoonbridge and Cherry." Allow 1 hour. 725 Vineland Place (at Lyndale Ave.), Minneapolis. ✆ 612/375-7622. www.walkerart.org. Admission $6 adults, $4 seniors and students, free for children under 12. Free every Thurs and first Sat of every month. Museum: Tues–Sat 10am–5pm, open until 9pm on Thurs; Sun 11am–5pm. Sculpture garden: daily 6am–midnight.

IN ST. PAUL

Cathedral of St. Paul   Built in 1915 on the highest point in the city, this cathedral is one of the largest in the country. A replica of St. Peter's in Rome, the building boasts a 175-foot-high dome, a massive rose window, and granite-and-travertine construction. Allow 30 minutes. 239 Selby Ave., St. Paul. ✆ 651/228-1766. www.cathedralsp.org. Free admission. Daily 8am–6pm. Guided tours Mon, Wed, and Fri 1pm.

Historic Fort Snelling   This living history museum commemorates the establishment of a fort here in the wilderness in 1819 by Col. Josiah Snelling and his troops, who opened the area for homesteaders. Costumed guides recreate the activities of everyday army life during the 1820s. Allow 1 to 2 hours. Highways 5 and 55, St. Paul, 1 mile east of airport. ✆ 612/726-1171. Admission $6 adults, $5 seniors, $4 children 6–12. Memorial Day to Labor Day Wed–Sat 10am–5pm; Sun noon–5pm. May, Sept, and Oct Sat and Sun only. Closed Nov–Apr.

James J. Hill House   Once the home of the Great Northern Railway builder James J. Hill, this 36,000-square-foot residence was completed in 1891. The red sandstone building has five floors, including 13 bathrooms, 16 crystal chandeliers, and a two-story sky-lit art gallery. Allow 30 minutes. 240 Summit Ave., St. Paul. ✆ 651/297-2555. Admission $6 adults, $5 seniors, $4 children 6–12. Wed–Sat 10am–3:30pm. Tours every half hour; call for reservations.

Minnesota History Center   An impressive array of artifacts are housed in this three-story museum, including photographs, music, and videos, much of it designed for hands-on learning, and all of it celebrating Minnesota history. Kids especially enjoy sitting in the re-created basement of a Minnesota farmhouse while a simulated tornado passes overhead. Avoid weekday mornings if you don't like to tour with school groups. Allow 1½ hours. 345 Kellogg Blvd. W., St. Paul. ✆ 800/657-3773. www.mnhs.org. Free admission. Tues 10am–8pm; Wed–Sat 10am–5pm; Sun noon–5pm.

Minnesota State Capitol   Built in 1905 on a hill overlooking downtown St. Paul, the capitol is crowned by the world's largest unsupported marble dome (modeled after the one Michelangelo created for St. Peter's Basilica in Rome). The interior is equally impressive, with its marble stairways, chambers, and halls, and its oil paintings. Allow 1 hour. 75 Constitution Ave., St. Paul. © **888/727-8386.** Free admission. Mon–Fri 9am–5pm; Sat 10am–4pm; Sun 1–4pm. Tours are offered every hr. on the hr.

Science Museum of Minnesota   Hands-on exhibits introduce visitors to natural history, science, and technology in this massive museum. Highlights include the Bloodstream Superhighway and navigating a virtual towboat down the Mississippi River, and the dinosaur lab in the Hall of Paleontology. There's also an Omnitheater. Allow 2 to 3 hours. 120 W. Kellogg Blvd., St. Paul. © **651/221-9444.** www.smm.org. Admission to exhibits $7 adults, $5 children and seniors; Omnitheater $7 adults, $5 children and seniors; laser show tickets and package deals also available. Mon–Wed 9:30am–5:30pm; Thurs–Sat 9:30am–9pm; Sun 10:30am–5:30pm. Extended hr. during the summer.

MORE TO SEE & DO

ARCHITECTURAL HIGHLIGHTS   Notable architecture in downtown Minneapolis includes the 57-story **Norwest Center,** 77 S. 7th St.; the flat-topped multifaceted **IDS Tower,** 80 S. 8th St.; and the city's oldest skyscraper, **Foshay Tower,** 821 Marquette Ave.; the observation deck has a great view of the city.

In St. Paul, don't miss a stroll down **Summit Avenue,** just west of St. Paul Cathedral, one of the finest collections of Victorian residential architecture in the nation. The area has been home to such authors as F. Scott Fitzgerald, Sinclair Lewis, and Garrison Keillor. Take a quiet stroll on your own, or join a guided walking tour. Tours depart from the James J. Hill House, 240 Summit Ave. (© **651/297-2555**), 11am and 2pm every Saturday, May through September.

PARKS   The **Eloise Butler Wildflower Garden and Bird Sanctuary,** inside Theodore Wirth Park at Glenwood Ave. (© **612/370-4903**), is the nation's oldest public wildflower garden, crisscrossed by hiking and bicycle trails. Guided tours are available. It's open April through October daily from 7:30am to sunset.

Minnehaha Park, Minnehaha Parkway at Hiawatha Avenue (© **612/661-4800**), on the Mississippi, is the site of the famed Minnehaha Falls, the "laughing water" Longfellow celebrated in his poem *Song of Hiawatha.* Other attractions include 15 miles of jogging and bicycle trails, picnic facilities, and a historic frame house that was the first built west of the Mississippi. The park is open daily from 6am to 10pm.

St. Paul's **Como Park,** 1250 Kaufman Dr. (© **651/487-2800**), is one of the busiest and most beautiful parks in the Twin Cities, best known for its free zoo and its flower conservatory, which includes a Japanese garden. There's also a golf course, ski trails, and footpaths, as well as paddleboats, canoes, bikes, and skates for rent. It's open daily from 10am to 6pm April through September; from 10am to 4pm off season.

BEST BETS FOR KIDS   The **Minnesota Zoo** (© **952-431-9500;** www.mnzoo.com), in Apple Valley, houses more than 2,300 animals in natural habitats, and has a monorail, a re-created farm, and an IMAX theatre. The **Children's Theater Company,** 2400 3rd Ave. S. (© **612/874-0400;** www.childrens theatre.org), presents a season of plays for all age groups. The Mall of America (see below) houses **Camp Snoopy** (© **952/883-8600**), an amusement park; **Underwater Adventures** (© **888/DIVE-TIME**), an aquarium; and **Cereal**

Downtown St. Paul

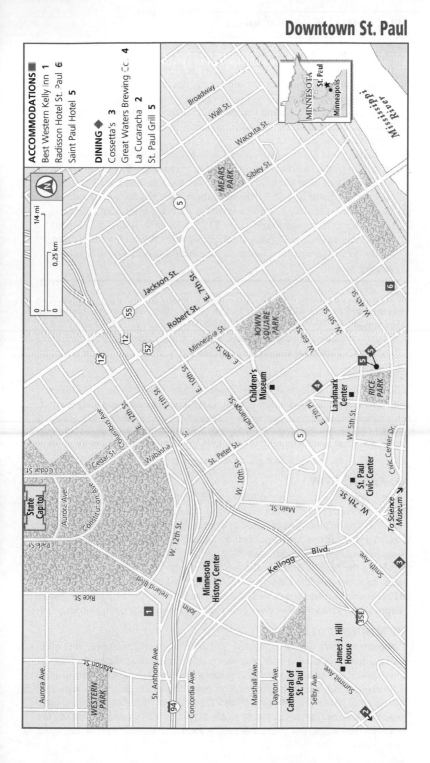

ACCOMMODATIONS ■
Best Western Kelly Inn **1**
Radisson Hotel St. Paul **6**
Saint Paul Hotel **5**

DINING ◆
Cossetta's **3**
Great Waters Brewing Co. **4**
La Cucaracha **2**
St. Paul Grill **5**

The Mother of All Malls

The **Mall of America** (© 952/883-8800; www.mallofamerica.com), the nation's largest shrine to consumerism, has everything—restaurants, major department stores like Bloomingdale's and Nordstrom, over 500 specialty stores and boutiques, movie theaters, nightclubs, and even bowling. The big draw for kids is Camp Snoopy, America's largest enclosed theme park.

The mall is in Bloomington, about a 20-minute drive from the city center during non-rush hours. Follow I-35W south to Minn. 62 East, go about 1 mile, and exit onto Minn. 77 South (Cedar Ave.). Follow the signs to the mall. To get there by public transportation, take bus 80, which stops at Nicollet Mall near South 7th Street at the rounded glass booth. The trip takes about 30 minutes and costs $1.75 non-peak hours, $2.25 peak hours. Mall hours are Monday through Saturday from 10am to 9:30pm, Sunday from 11am to 7pm. Restaurants, nightclubs, and movies may have varying hours.

Adventure (© 952/815-2900). In St. Paul: **The Minnesota Children's Museum,** 10 W. 7th St. (© 651/225-6000; www.mcm.org), offers popular features such as papermaking and a music studio. **Como Zoo,** 1250 Kaufman Dr. (© 651/487-2800), is Minnesota's only free zoo.

SHOPPING

Nicollet Mall, a pedestrian avenue in downtown Minneapolis, has Dayton's, Marshall Fields, and two malls, upscale **Gaviidae Common** and **City Center.** Hip galleries and antiques stores abound in the restored **Warehouse District,** north of Hennepin between North 1st and 7th streets. **Uptown,** near Hennepin and Lake streets, is the place to find trendy shops and boutiques. In St. Paul, good shopping can be found all along **Grand Avenue,** just west of the downtown.

WHERE TO STAY

In addition to the choices listed below, you'll find many chain hotels near shopping malls (especially the Mall of America) and along I-494 in the suburbs.

There are also a number of hotels at or near the airport. The **Minneapolis/St. Paul Airport Hilton,** 3800 E. 80th St. (© 800/774-1500 or 952/854-2100; www.hilton.com), offers extensive facilities and services, including free shuttle service to the Mall of America and other locations. Doubles begin at $89. Also near the airport are the **Courtyard Minneapolis Bloomington** (© 952/876-0100; www.courtyard.com), with doubles from $79; and the **Embassy Suites Airport** (© 952/854-1000; www.embassysuites.com), with doubles from $129.

IN MINNEAPOLIS

Doubletree Park Place   Located 3½ miles west of downtown, this hotel boasts a five-story pool atrium and reasonable rates outside the hubbub of the busy downtown area. The spacious guest rooms were designed with business travelers in mind, but are perfectly comfortable for leisure travelers as well. 1500 Park Place Blvd., Minneapolis, MN 55416. © 800/222-TREE or 952/542-8600. Fax 612/542-8063. www.doubletree.com. 297 units. $75–$156 double; $120–$225 suite. Children under 18 stay free in parents' room. AE, DC, DISC, MC, V. Free parking. **Amenities:** Restaurant; indoor pool; fitness center.

Hyatt Whitney Hotel   This 18th-century European-style hotel on the Mississippi River was once a 19th-century flour mill; it has been a hotel since 1987. The comfortable rooms are eclectically furnished and each room is shaped differently. South-facing rooms offer views of the river and outdoor patio and fountain. All rooms sport the usual amenities, plus bathrobes and refrigerators. 150 Portland Ave., Minneapolis, MN 55401. (C) **800/633-7313** or 612/375-1234. Fax 612/376-7512. www.whitney.hyatt.com. 97 units. $115–$280 king-bed room; $450 suite. Children under 18 stay free in parents' room. AE, DC, DISC, MC, V. Self-parking $7, valet parking $12. **Amenities:** Restaurant; fitness room.

Minneapolis Marriott City Center   Located in the heart of downtown, this facility adjoins the three-story City Center shopping mall and is within walking distance of Target Center and much of the city's nightlife. You can dine on-site at the Northern Shores Grille or the lounge. The hotel caters to the convention crowds and the rooms are standard business hotel issue. 30 S. 7th St., Minneapolis, MN 55402; between Hennepin and Nicollet. (C) **800/228-9290** or 612/349-4000. Fax 612/332-7165. www.marriott.com. 583 units. $99–$279 double; $169–$329 suite. Children under 18 stay free in parents' room. AE, DC, DISC, MC, V. Self-parking $15 Sun–Thurs, $4 Fri–Sat; valet parking $22. **Amenities:** Restaurant; health club; pets permitted with refundable $250 deposit.

Nicollet Island Inn   This lovely inn was once an 1893 window shade and blind company; it was converted into an inn in the 1970s. Rooms are furnished with offbeat originality; all rooms offer VCRs and freshly baked cookies, and some have Jacuzzis. The Nicollet Island Inn Restaurant is highly recommended (as are reservations), and serves an excellent Sunday brunch. 95 Merriam St., Minneapolis, MN 55401. (C) **866/636-2683** or 612/331-1800. Fax 612/331-6528. www.nicolletisland inn.com. 24 units. $135–$155 double; $170 double with Jacuzzi. Children stay free in parents' room; rollaway beds $25. Weekend bed-and-breakfast packages available. AE, DC, DISC, MC, V. Free parking. **Amenities:** Restaurant.

IN ST. PAUL

Best Western Kelly Inn   This older, plain facility still offers serviceable accommodations, and it is minutes from downtown. Some rooms offer scenic views and some units have whirlpools. 161 St. Anthony Ave., St. Paul, MN 55103. (C) **800/780-7234** or 651/227-8711. Fax 651/227-1698. www.bestwestern.com. 126 units. $89–$104 double; $125–$195 suite. Children under 15 stay free in parents' room. AE, DC, DISC, MC, V. Free parking. **Amenities:** Restaurant; indoor pool; pets permitted.

Radisson Riverfront St. Paul   Located downtown, overlooking the Mississippi River, the Radisson is topped by the Twin Cities' only revolving restaurant. The hotel's second-floor patio offers a nice river view, and the majority of the comfortable guest rooms have views as well. Make sure to request an upper or corner room—the others tend to be noisy. 11 E. Kellogg Blvd., St. Paul, MN 55101. (C) **800/333-3333** or 651/292-1900. Fax 651/224-8999. www.radisson.com. 475 units. $99–$209 double; $195–$350 suite. Children under 18 stay free in parents' room. AE, DC, DISC, MC, V. Self-parking $13. **Amenities:** Restaurant; heated indoor pool; health club.

Saint Paul Hotel   This beautiful, exquisitely decorated hotel, housed in a 1910 building, makes a great romantic getaway, but its modern amenities suit business travelers well, too. A number of rooms offer great views and all are done up in sophisticated European style. The hotel is also famous for its afternoon tea and the landmark St. Paul Grill (see "Where to Dine," below). A complimentary shuttle transports guests to local entertainment, shopping, and the Mall of

America. 350 Market St., St. Paul, MN 55102; at 5th St. ℂ **800/292-9292** or 651/292-9292. Fax 651/228-3810. www.stpaulhotel.com. 254 units. $179–$229 double; $242–$679 suite. AE, DC, DISC, MC, V. Parking $18. **Amenities:** Restaurants (2); fitness center.

WHERE TO DINE
IN MINNEAPOLIS

August Moon ASIAN FUSION   The unprepossessing facade of August Moon, set in a strip mall just off the highway, does not do justice to the amazing food inside. Despite the lava-lamp decor and quirky art on display, this is one of the best-kept secrets of Minneapolis foodies. The menu abounds with both simple and complex dishes; among the can't-miss items are goat cheese wontons and Murgh Aloo. The wine list is enjoyable and reasonably priced. 5340 Wayzata Blvd., Golden Valley, just off I-394. ℂ **952/544-7017.** Reservations accepted for large parties. Main courses $7–$17. AE, DISC, MC, V. Mon–Thurs 11am–9pm; Fri 11am–10pm; Sat 4–10pm; Sun 4–9pm.

Auriga AMERICAN   Opened by four young chefs who had previously worked in other fine restaurants in Minneapolis, Auriga has gained a reputation as the restaurants where the chefs go to eat. The emphasis is on fresh, quality ingredients and the menu varies according to seasonal availability. 1930 Hennepin Ave. S. ℂ **612/871-0777.** Reservations accepted. Main courses $25–$35. AE, DC, DISC, MC, V. Mon–Thurs 5:30–10pm; Fri–Sat 5:30–11pm; Sun 5–10pm.

Black Forest Inn GERMAN   The building's exterior resembles an old German house, while the interior is distinguished by dark wood, stained-glass windows, and a rustic bar area. Patio dining is popular in the warm weather months. Enjoy authentic sauerbraten, Wiener schnitzel, bratwurst, and other German specialties. 1 E. 26th St. ℂ **612/872-0812.** Reservations not accepted. Main courses $15–$25. AE, DC, DISC, MC, V. Mon–Sat 11am–1am; Sun noon–midnight.

Chino Latino SPICY FOOD   This trendy, late-night (and noisy) eatery is the hottest people-watching restaurant in Uptown—no pun intended. Specializing in foods from the "hot zones" of Mexico, Thailand, Polynesia, and Korea, Chino Latino serves up a menu that includes a five-spice duck that has become a popular favorite. 2916 Hennepin Ave. S. ℂ **612/824-7878.** Reservations recommended. Main courses $15–$25. AE, DC, DISC, MC, V. Sat–Thurs 4:30pm–1am; Sun 11am–1am.

D'Amico Cucina ITALIAN   This beautifully appointed restaurant with a distinctive atmosphere, enhanced by whitewashed wood beams and French doors, offers creative Italian dishes and over 150 Italian wines. In Butler Sq., 100 N. 6th St. ℂ **612/338-2401.** Reservations recommended. Main courses $25–$35. AE, DC, DISC, MC, V. Mon–Thurs 5:30–10pm; Fri–Sat 5:30–11pm; Sun 5–9pm.

Famous Dave's BBQ & Blues Club BARBECUE   Famous Dave's is modeled on a Chicago blues club, including Chicago street signs and an El train track. It's no surprise that the restaurant specializes in barbecue—you can't beat the ribs. Live blues bands entertain nearly every night. 3001 Hennepin Ave. S. at Lake St. ℂ **612/822-9900.** Reservations recommended. Main courses $15–$25. AE, DC, DISC, MC, V. Daily 11am–12am; bar 11am–1am.

Goodfellow's AMERICAN   This Art Deco–inspired restaurant serves an American menu amid a polished ambience with impressive table settings. The menu changes seasonally. All pastas, breads, stocks, and pastries are made from scratch, and the extensive wine list highlights American vintages. In the City Center, 40 S. 7th St. ℂ **612/332-4800.** Reservations recommended. Main courses $30–$45. AE, DC, DISC, MC, V. Mon–Fri 11:30am–2pm; Mon–Thurs 5:30–9pm; Fri–Sat 5:30–10pm.

Monte Carlo AMERICAN   This favorite old-timer has been around since 1906. Textured ceilings, low lighting, and booths provide a comfortable ambience and a touch of elegance. Offerings include a variety of specialty sandwiches (crab salad, turkey Reuben) and classic pasta dishes. 219 3rd Ave. N., Warehouse District. © 612/333-5900. Reservations recommended. Main courses $20–$30. AE, DC, DISC, MC, V. Mon–Sat 11am–1am; Sun 10am–1am.

Murray's AMERICAN   Since 1946 this family-owned establishment has delighted guests with steaks so tender they were awarded the "Silver Butter Knife" award. (You'll recognize it by the old neon sign out front.) The equally impressive wine list features over 500 wines. Located in the heart of downtown, Murray's is also known for its strolling violinist. 26 S. 6th St. © 612/339-0909. Reservations recommended. Main courses $20–$45. AE, DC, DISC, MC, V. Mon–Thurs 11am–10:30pm; Fri 11am–11pm; Sat–Sun 4–10:30pm.

The News Room AMERICAN   The News Room is a newspaper-themed restaurant, each room dedicated to a different section of the paper, such as Sports, Entertainment, and Travel. The dinner menu includes such entrees as coconut curry shrimp and chicken breast with wild mushrooms baked in puff pastry. There's a deli area for quick lunches, and a full bar for after-dinner or after-theater drinks. 990 Nicollet Mall at 10th St. © 612/343-0073. Reservations accepted. Main courses $10–$28. AE, DC, DISC, MC, V. Daily 11am–1am.

IN ST. PAUL

Cossetta ITALIAN   This enterprise began in 1911 as an Italian market; later it expanded to include this simple, fun, and charming restaurant. Food is served cafeteria style in a noisy atmosphere reminiscent of an Italian grandmother's house. The menu features great traditional dishes such as eggplant parmigiana and mostaccioli, but Cossetta is famous for its award-winning pizza. 211 W. 7th St., between Kellogg Blvd. and Chestnut. © 651/222-3476. Reservations not accepted. Main courses $5–$10. MC, V. Sun–Thurs 11am–9pm; Fri–Sat 11am–10pm.

Great Waters Brewing Co. AMERICAN   This restaurant is known for its beers, of course, and serves five selections daily of its homemade libations. Great Waters' menu goes beyond traditional pub fare. In addition to interesting sandwiches such as the bric green apple grilled chicken, you can enjoy a London broil, pasta, or seafood for dinner. 426 St. Peter St. © 651/224-2739. Reservations accepted. Main courses $10–$15. MC, V. Mon–Sat 11am–1am; Sun noon–1am.

La Cucaracha MEXICAN   Since 1961, the Flores family has served authentic Mexican fare at this St. Paul institution, which is well-hidden but worth the search. Don't let the name scare you off—the tasty menu includes mouthwatering favorites such as black-bean burritos and fajitas. 36 S. Dale St. © 651/221-9682. Reservations accepted. Main courses $10–$20. AE, DC, MC, V. Mon–Thurs 11am–10pm; Fri–Sat 11am–11pm; Sun 11am–10pm.

St. Paul Grill AMERICAN   Grilled meats and fish and excellent pastas are prepared here under the supervision of the St. Paul Hotel's executive chef. The elegant interior is enhanced by views of the hotel's lovely English garden and nearby Rice Park. The restaurant is popular for pre-theater dining. 350 Market St., in the Saint Paul Hotel. © 651/224-7455. Reservations recommended. Main courses $20–$40. MC, V. Mon 11:30am–10pm; Tues–Sat 11:30am–11pm; Sun 11am–10pm.

THE TWIN CITIES AFTER DARK

The best place to find out what's happening in the Twin Cities is the free newsweekly *City Pages*, which lists all events. Other good sources of information are the local papers (*Star Tribune* and *St. Paul Pioneer Press*), the calendar in *Minneapolis-St. Paul* magazine, and the monthly *Twin Cities Directory.* On the Web, check out **www.minneapolis.org** or **http://twincities.citysearch.com** for the most up-to-date information.

THE PERFORMING ARTS   There are more theater seats per capita in Minneapolis than anywhere outside New York City. The famous **Guthrie Theater,** 725 Vineland Place (✆ **877/44-STAGE** or 612/377-2224; www.guthrietheater. org), born in 1964, is one of the nation's premier classical repertory companies. **Théâtre de la Jeune Lune,** 105 1st St. N. (✆ **612/333-6200;** www.jeunelune. org), in the Warehouse District, is a strong and innovative acting company with a varied performance repertoire. Three historic, renovated theaters, **State** (805 Hennepin; ✆ **612/339-7007), Orpheum** (910 Hennepin; ✆ **612/339-7007),** and **Pantages** (700 Hennepin; ✆ **612/339-7007;** scheduled to open in Nov 2002), feature a variety of entertainment, from pop music to comedy to adult and children's theater. Information for all three can be found at **www.state orpheum.com**.

For more than 20 years, **Orchestra Hall,** 1111 Nicollet Mall (✆ **800/292-4141** or 612/371-5656; www.minnesotaorchestra.org), has been home to the internationally acclaimed **Minnesota Orchestra.** The annual **MusicFest** features 4 weeks of classical performances beginning in early July, drawing large audiences to a range of concerts, from light classics to orchestral masterworks.

In St. Paul, the **Schubert Club,** 302 Landmark Center (✆ **651/292-3268;** www.schubert.org), brings celebrated artists to perform, provides music lessons, and commissions new works. The **St. Paul Chamber Orchestra** (✆ **651/291-1144;** www.thespco.org) makes its home in the **Ordway Center for the Performing Arts,** 345 Washington St. (✆ **651/224-4222;** www.ordway.org). Opera, recitals, pop and classical concerts, and dance are also presented here.

Fitzgerald Theater, 10 E. Exchange St., St. Paul (✆ **651/290-1221**), is the home base of Garrison Keillor's wildly popular radio show, "A Prairie Home Companion." Touring companies also perform at this beautifully restored historic building.

THE CLUB & MUSIC SCENE   The **Warehouse District** is the heart of Minneapolis nightlife. **First Avenue,** 701 1st Ave. N. (✆ **612/338-8388**), is where Prince got his start. Connected to it is **7th Street Entry,** a small, loud venue for local music. A slightly older crowd frequents the upscale dance club **South Beach,** 325 1st Ave. N. (✆ **612/204-0790**). And **Fine Line Music Cafe,** 318 1st Ave. N. (✆ **612/338-8100**), caters to the 30-something crowd in an intimate music venue; musical groups vary from jazz trios to Alanis Morrisette.

The Loon Café, 500 1st Ave. N. (✆ **612/332-8342**), was one of the first bars in the Warehouse District. Its crowded, casual, sports-bar atmosphere is popular with the late 20s and early 30s business crowd, and the cafe is famous for its chili. **The Lounge,** 411 2nd Ave. N. (✆ **612/333-8800**), is a relaxed bar set up with couches and comfortable chairs in various rooms—a good place to chat with friends and people-watch. For late-night eats check out **Sapor,** 428 Washington Ave. N. (✆ **612/375-1971**). Their seasonally influenced world cuisine is dished up until 11pm on Fridays and Saturdays.

The Gay 90's, 408 Hennepin Ave. (✆ **612/333-7755**), caters (but not exclusively) to a gay clientele and features eight bars, two restaurants, a drag lounge, three dance floors, and some of the finest female impersonators in the Midwest. Another favorite gay bar is across the street, **Boom,** 401 Hennepin Ave. (✆ **612/ 378-3188**).

St. Paul has a big Irish neighborhood, and many Irish bars and clubs. **Chang O'Hara's Bistro,** 498 Selby Ave. (© **651/290-2330**), is a bar/restaurant featuring fondue cooking at your table. There's local music almost every night and Dixieland jazz on Sunday. Popular with the college crowd, **O'Gara's Bar & Grille,** 164 Snelling Ave. N. (© **651/644-3333**), is a dance club with live music. **Sweeney's,** 96 Dale St. N. (© **651/221-9157**), is a pub with a good beer selection where you can meet the locals.

For jazz, go to the **Artist's Quarter,** 366 Jackson St., St. Paul (© **651/292-1359**), which showcases national and local performers; or the **Dakota Bar and Grill,** 1021 Bandana Blvd. E., St. Paul (© **651/642-1442**), hailed as one of the best jazz bars in the Midwest.

7 Kansas City

Established as a trading post in 1821, Kansas City served as the starting point for wagon trains heading over the Santa Fe, California, and Oregon trails. Later, the area emerged as the nation's center for cattle stockyards and slaughterhouses. Today, greater Kansas City is a sprawling metropolis of 1.7 million straddling the Kansas-Missouri state line. Yet it retains something of a small-town atmosphere, with tree-lined boulevards and a large number of parks spread over gently rolling hills. Need further incentive to visit? Kansas City is famous for its steaks, barbecue, jazz, rich frontier history, and unique attractions.

ESSENTIALS

GETTING THERE   By Plane   Kansas City International Airport (© **816/243-3000;** www.kcairports.com) is 25 minutes northwest of downtown. **KCI Shuttle buses** (© **816/243-5000**) service more than 50 hotels for $13 to $17 one-way. Taxi fares are zoned; the fare to downtown is $28 to $34.

By Train   Amtrak (© **800/USA-RAIL;** www.amtrak.com) provides daily service from Chicago (trip time: 8 hr.) and St. Louis (less than 6 hr.) to Kansas City's station at 2200 Main St. (© **816/421-3622**) near Union Station (which houses the Science City museum). Take a taxi from the station to your hotel.

By Car   The major routes into Kansas City are I-70 from the east (St. Louis) and west (Denver); I-35 from the north (Des Moines) and southwest (Wichita); and I-29 from the northwest (Omaha).

VISITOR INFORMATION   The **Convention and Visitors Bureau of Greater Kansas City** is downtown at City Center Square, 1100 Main St., Ste. 2550, Kansas City, MO 64105 (© **800/767-7700** or 816/221-5242; www.visit kc.com), open Monday through Friday from 8:30am to 5pm. More convenient are the Visitor Information Centers at Country Club Plaza, 4709 Central, open Monday through Saturday from 10am to 6pm and Sunday from noon to 5pm, and at Union Station, Main and Pershing, open Monday through Saturday from 9am to 5:30pm and Sunday from noon to 5pm.

GETTING AROUND   A car is extremely useful in Kansas City; although the downtown is compact, attractions are located throughout the city. If you don't have access to a car, bus no. 111, the "Downtowner Shuttle," is the most convenient for visitors. This bus travels from City Market through downtown to Union Station and Crown Center every 10 minutes, Monday through Friday from 6:30am to 6pm. Fare is 25¢.

FAST FACTS   For walk-in Urgent Care facilities in Kansas City, call © **816/751-3751.** Major hospitals are **Trinity Lutheran Hospital,** 3030 Baltimore St.

Best Bets for Kids

Kansas City's newest and most popular attraction is **Science City**, in the restored 1914 Union Station, cater-cornered from Crown Center at 30 Pershing Rd. (© 816/460-2020; www.sciencecity.com). At this multi-level, interactive museum, kids can create a personal newspaper front page, anchor a TV news program, bicycle across a tightrope, train as an astronaut, solve a crime, play mini-golf, take a tour through the human body, drive a combine, dig for fossils, explore Kansas City's history, catch a movie in a domed or five-story-high theater, and much more. Science City is open daily. For outdoor fun, there's the 175-acre theme park **Worlds of Fun,** I-435 and Parvin Road (© 816/454-4545), open daily in summer and weekends in spring and fall, with thrill rides like the Mamba, one of the tallest, longest, and fastest steel roller coasters in the world; the tumble-and-spin Thunderhawk ride; and Snoopy Camp, featuring attractions based on Snoopy. Next door, you'll find Worlds of Fun's water-themed counterpart, the 60-acre **Oceans of Fun** (same contact information as Worlds of Fun, above), open June through August, featuring water rides, slides, and various pools (including a wave pool). The revitalized **Kansas City Zoo,** at I-435 and 63rd St. in Swope Park (© 816/513-5700), is open year-round (with reduced prices on Tues), and features animals of Australia, Africa, and more in their natural habitats. The zoo also houses the Sprint IMAX Theater.

(© 816/751-4600); and **Truman Medical Center,** 2301 Holmes (© 816/556-3000). **Walgreens** is a 24-hour pharmacy located at 39th St. and Broadway (© 816/561-6980).

SPECIAL EVENTS   The **Kansas City Blues and Jazz Festival** (© 800/530-KCMO; www.kcbluesjazz.org) takes place the third weekend in July. The **Spirit Festival** (© 816/221-4444; www.spiritfest.org) celebrates the city's musical and cultural heritage during Labor Day weekend with jazz, blues, rock, reggae, gospel, and other performances. Around since 1899, the **American Royal** celebration (© 816/221-7979; www.americanroyal.com) features a livestock show, parades, horse shows, a rodeo, big-name entertainment, and the world's largest barbecue competition in October or November. The **Kansas Speedway** (© 913/328-3300; www.kansasspeedway.com) attracts NASCAR fans with races several times a year.

WHAT TO SEE & DO

Downtown Kansas City is a blend of Art Deco buildings, brick warehouses dating from the 1880s, and modern skyscrapers. Main Street connects to many city attractions. Kansas City does not have a good public transportation system and the only bus useful for tourists is the Bus no. 111 Downtowner Shuttle, which runs every 10 minutes and costs 25¢. However, it runs only Monday through Friday from 6:30am to 6pm and travels between City Market and Union Station/Crown Center. We've listed stops at the attractions below that are on the shuttle routes. For the others, they're either easy to find or we've included brief locators.

Arabia Steamboat Museum   This cargo steamboat, laden with 220 tons of merchandise destined for settlers out west, sank in the Missouri River in 1856,

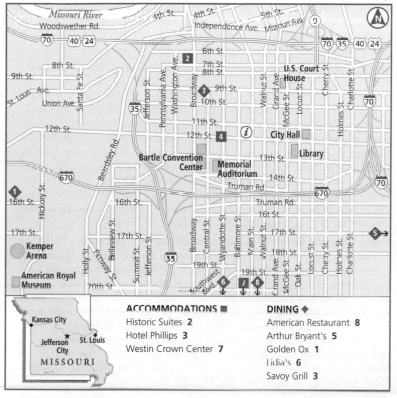

ACCOMMODATIONS ■
Historic Suites **2**
Hotel Phillips **3**
Westin Crown Center **7**

DINING ◆
American Restaurant **8**
Arthur Bryant's **5**
Golden Ox **1**
Lidia's **6**
Savoy Grill **3**

where it remained preserved in cold mud until it was excavated in the 1980s. A virtual time capsule of the 1850s and one of the best collections of pre–Civil War artifacts in the world, the museum provides a fascinating look at frontier life, with displays of the steamboat's cargo, from china and hardware to jewelry and leather boots (900 shoes and boots alone are on display; another 4,000 have yet to undergo the preservation process). Tours begin with a film of the excavation and restoration of parts of the boat (which are now on display); plan on 1½ hours here. 400 Grand Ave., City Market. ℂ 816/471-4030. Admission $9.75 adults, $9 seniors, $4.75 children 4–12. Mon–Sat 10am–4:30pm (last tour); Sun noon–3:30pm. Bus: 111 Downtowner Shuttle to 3rd and Grand.

City Market In operation since the 1850s, this outdoor market is busiest on Saturday, when 150 vendors offer everything from vegetables and flowers to live chickens and T-shirts. An arts and crafts market is featured Sundays, May through August. The outdoor market is surrounded by 37 permanent indoor specialty shops, international groceries, and restaurants occupying an Art Deco building and the Arabia Steamboat Museum. 5th and Main sts. ℂ 816/842-1271. Mon–Fri 8am–3pm; Sat 6am–5pm; Sun 10am–3pm. Bus: 111 Downtowner Shuttle to 3rd and Grand.

Country Club Plaza Built in 1922 to resemble a Spanish marketplace, the country's first suburban shopping center and Kansas City's premier shopping district consists of a tree-lined, 14-square-block area with more than 180 shops, dozens of restaurants and nightspots, 30-some statues and fountains, horse-drawn carriage rides, and, March through January, 40-minute Fiesta Cruises on Brush Creek (© **816/756-1331**). 47th St. and Ward Pkwy. © 816/753-0100. Most shops are open Mon–Wed and Fri–Sat 10am–7pm; Thurs 10am–9pm; Sun noon–5pm.

Crown Center   This 85-acre business and residential complex, owned by the world's largest greeting-card company, Hallmark, contains specialty shops, restaurants, hotels, theaters, and the free **Hallmark Visitor Center** (© **816/ 274-5672;** closed Sun), which chronicles 90 years of history with displays of Keepsake Ornaments and other Hallmark products and memorabilia, educational exhibits, and excerpts from Hallmark Hall of Fame television movies. For children, there's **Kaleidoscope,** a free, creative art workshop offered Monday through Saturday for ages 5 to 12 (© **816/274-8300**), and Crayola Cafe, which offers fun and casual dining for the whole family. 2450 Grand Ave. © 816/274-8444. Most shops open Mon–Wed and Sat 10am–6pm; Thurs–Fri 10am–9pm; Sun noon–5pm. Visitors Center open Mon–Fri 9am–5pm; Sat 9:30am–4:30pm. Call for hours at the Kaleidoscope, as they are erratic. Bus: 111 Downtowner Shuttle to Crown Center.

Negro Leagues Baseball Museum/American Jazz Museum   These two unique museums, housed under one roof, are in the historic jazz district. The Negro Leagues Baseball Museum tells the compelling story of segregated baseball, from the founding of the Negro National League just a few blocks away in 1920, until Jackie Robinson, who played for the Kansas City Monarchs, signed with the Brooklyn Dodgers in 1947. The Jazz Museum pays tribute to jazz greats ranging from Louis Armstrong and Duke Ellington to Ella Fitzgerald and Charlie Parker, with listening stations throughout. Be sure to see the film in the visitor center highlighting the golden days of the 1930s, when this very district boasted more than 60 jazz clubs and served as the commercial heart of Kansas City's African-American community. The Blue Room, attached to the complex, stages jazz concerts 4 nights a week. Plan on 2 hours here. 18th and Vine. © **816/ 221-1920** for Baseball Museum; © **816/474-8463** for Jazz Museum. Admission to either $6 adults, $2.50 children under 12; combination ticket to both $8 adults, $4 children. Both museums Tues–Sat 9am–6pm; Sun noon–6pm.

Nelson-Atkins Museum of Art   Kansas City's premier museum is especially noted for its Asian art, including T'ang dynasty bowls and Ming dynasty furniture; an outdoor sculpture garden with the largest U.S. collection of bronzes by Henry Moore; the largest public collection of works by Missouri native Thomas Hart Benton; a collection of 17th- and 18th-century European paintings; Impressionist and post-Impressionist pieces; and American art. The museum includes works by Caravaggio, Titian, Rembrandt, Renoir, Poussin, Degas, Monet, Gauguin, van Gogh, and Willem de Kooning. The airy Rozelle Court Restaurant has extended dinner hours on Friday, with live music. Plan on a minimum of 2 hours here. 4525 Oak St. (just east of Country Club Plaza). © **816/751-1278** or 816/561-4000. Free admission (special exhibitions cost extra). Tues–Thurs 10am–4pm; Fri 10am–9pm; Sat 10am–5pm; Sun noon–5pm.

Thomas Hart Benton Home   From 1939, until he died in his studio in 1975, this 1903, late-Victorian limestone house served as home and studio of Missouri's most renowned 20th-century artist. The house and studio are just as Benton left them, with many personal belongings like clothing, furniture, paints and brushes, and 13 original works, which you can see in about half an hour. 3616 Belleview. © **816/931-5722**. Admission $2.50 adults, $1.50 children 6–12. Mon–Sat 10am–4pm; Sun noon–5pm in summer, 11am–4pm in winter.

A Side Trip to Independence

For more about Kansas City area history, visit the town of **Independence**, a 20-minute drive east, with its **Harry S Truman Home National Historic Site**, at Truman and Main streets (℗ 816/254-9929); the **Harry S Truman Library & Museum**, U.S. 24 and Delaware (℗ 816/833-1400), with objects from Truman's presidency, including gifts from foreign heads of state and a reproduction of the Oval Office; the **National Frontier Trails Center**, 318 W. Pacific (℗ 816/325-7575), an excellent museum documenting the Santa Fe, Oregon, and California trails; and the **Bingham–Waggoner Estate**, 313 W. Pacific (℗ 816/461-3491), a 22-room, 1885 mansion and former home of Missouri artist George Caleb Bingham.

Toy and Miniature Museum   Occupying a 1911 mansion, this museum houses an extensive collection of antique dolls, more than 100 furnished dollhouses, marbles, and toys ranging from model trains to games, as well as perfect scale miniatures of houses, rooms, and furniture. The miniatures are fully functional—scissors cut, clocks run, and musical instruments can be played. You can easily spend a fascinating hour or more here. 5235 Oak St (southeast of Country Club Plaza). ℗ 816/333-2055. Admission $4 adults, $3.50 seniors and students, $2 children 3–12. Wed–Sat 10am–4pm; Sun 1–4pm. Closed 2 weeks after Labor Day in Sept.

WHERE TO STAY

The Elms Resort & Spa   The Kansas City area's only full-service resort and spa occupies a historic 1912 limestone hotel situated on 16 acres, about a 30-minute drive from downtown. Its holistic spa and wellness center offers body and beauty treatments, including Swiss and Vichy showers; mud, seaweed, and aloe body wraps; mineral baths; hydrotherapy; massage (including reflexology and couples massage); manicures and facials; and more. Recreational offerings include an indoor swim track (a donut-shaped lap pool), banked jogging track, hiking and biking trails, badminton, horseshoes, volleyball, and croquet. Rooms are basic, but the hotel's extensive recreational facilities, parklike setting, and rustic grandeur make this a top-choice restorative getaway. 401 Regent St., Excelsior Springs, MO 64024. ℗ 800/843-3567 or 816/630-5500. Fax 816/630-5380. www.elmsresort.com. 153 units. $119–$139 double; $169–$299 suite. Extra person $10. Children under 12 stay free in parents' room. Off-season and spa packages available. AE, DC, MC, V. Free outdoor parking. **Amenities:** Restaurants (2); pools (indoor and outdoor); spa; health club; pets $50.

Embassy Suites   Conveniently located between Westport and Country Club Plaza, this all-suite hotel imitates Country Club Plaza's Spanish architecture with a dramatic, 12-story courtyard atrium. All suites are two rooms, complete with kitchenette and video games, making this a good bet for both families and business travelers. Other pluses include free cooked-to-order breakfasts, nightly complimentary cocktail hour, small exercise room, hot and dry saunas, Jacuzzi, and business center. 220 W. 43rd St., Kansas City, MO 64111. ℗ 800/EMBASSY or 816/756-1720. Fax 816/756-3260. www.embassysuites.com. 266 suites. $139 suite for 2. Extra person $10. Children under 18 stay free in parents' room. Rates include breakfast. AE, DC, MC, V. Free indoor/outdoor parking. **Amenities:** Restaurant; indoor pool; access to nearby health club for $5.

Historic Suites   This downtown Kansas City historic hotel, occupying two turn-of-the-19th-century brick buildings, caters to long-term business travelers with studios and one- and two-bedroom suites featuring soaring, exposed-beam ceilings and stocked kitchens (there's even a weekday grocery shopping service). There are more than 30 floor plans; some rooms have skylights, loft bedrooms, and/or spiral staircases. Benefits include complimentary weekday shuttle service within a 5-mile radius, free week-night cocktail hour (with a light buffet on Wed), laundry facilities, and a fitness room. City Market, restaurants, and popular nightspots are within walking distance. 612 Central Ave., Kansas City, MO 64105. ✆ 800/733-0612 or 816/842-6544. Fax 816/842-0656. www.historicsuites.com. 83 suites. $180–$255 suite. Children stay free in parents' room. Weekend and long-term rates available. Rates include buffet breakfast. AE, DC, DISC, MC, V. Outdoor parking $3.50. **Amenities:** Outdoor pool.

Hotel Phillips   Built in 1931 and exalting the Art Deco style (it's listed on the National Register of Historic Places), this classic downtown boutique hotel was recently renovated but retains its original woodwork, marble, lighting, and fixtures—including an 11-foot-tall gilded goddess overlooking the lobby. Rooms rise above the ordinary with a mix of contemporary furnishings and vintage touches like plaster molding on the ceilings. If you opt for a standard room, request a brighter, corner room. Its restaurants, including an all-you-can-eat venue with a twist (the buffet is brought tableside), are popular with the local business crowd. There's a business center. A good choice for couples and business travelers. 106 W. 12th St., Kansas City, MO 64105. ✆ 800/433-1426 or 816/221-7000. Fax 816/221-3477. www.hotelphillips.com. 217 units. $169–$219 double. Children under 18 stay free in parents' room. AE, DC, DISC, MC, V. Valet parking $17. **Amenities:** Restaurants (2); fitness room.

The Quarterage Hotel Westport   Near Westport's nightlife but far enough away for a good night's sleep, this modest but well-kept locally-owned hotel, decorated with copies of Thomas Hart Benton's works, offers small, spotless, comfortable rooms with high-speed dataports, plus free extras like local phone calls, warm buffet breakfast, evening cocktail hour, Jacuzzi, and sauna. 560 Westport Rd., Kansas City, MO 64111. ✆ 800/942-4233 or 816/931-0001. Fax 816/931-8891. www.quarteragehotel.com. 123 units. $109–$119 double. Children under 17 stay free in parents' room. Rates include buffet breakfast. AE, DC, DISC, MC, V. Free outdoor parking. **Amenities:** Free access to nearby health club.

The Raphael   Overlooking Country Club Plaza, with its many shops and restaurants, this intimate, European-style hotel occupies a converted 1927 brick apartment house. Though not as grand as Kansas City's downtown historic hotels, it has a cozy ambience that attracts many repeat guests. Rooms are standard but vary in size; those facing the back are larger, but preferable are the smaller rooms with views of the plaza. 325 Ward Pkwy., Kansas City, MO 64112. ✆ 800/821-5343 or 816/756-3800. Fax 816/802-2131. www.raphaelkc.com. 123 units. $145 double; $170–$195 suite. Extra person $20. Children under 18 stay free in parents' room. Weekend packages available. AE, DC, DISC, MC, V. Free valet parking. **Amenities:** Restaurant.

Southmoreland on the Plaza   This is a gem of a bed-and-breakfast, located in a 1913 Colonial Revival mansion in a peaceful residential area near Country Club Plaza and the Nelson-Atkins Museum of Art. This nonsmoking B&B offers well-appointed, themed rooms named after famous Kansas Citians and equipped with one of three extras: a fireplace or Jacuzzi or an outdoor deck. They also boast a suite in a carriage house, which is equipped with all three. Rates include afternoon complimentary wine and appetizers and gourmet breakfast served in an enclosed veranda or on an outdoor deck. In addition to a small business center, TVs are available in rooms during the week but are removed on weekends; there are TVs in some of the common rooms along with videos—all with happy endings. 116 E. 46th St., Kansas City, MO 64112. ✆ 816/531-7979. Fax 816/531-2407. www.southmoreland.com. 13 units. $125–$235 double. Rates include breakfast. AE, MC, V. Free outdoor parking. No children under 13. **Amenities:** Free access to nearby fitness center.

Westin Crown Center   Connected to Crown Center, with its many shops and restaurants, and to Science City via walkway, the Westin incorporates a limestone bluff with a rock garden and 60-foot waterfall in its multi-level lobby. Rooms are endowed with all the comforts, including pullout desk space, the Westin's trademark Heavenly Beds (with 250-count sheets and down comforters), glass sliding doors to open-air balconies, and, on the north side, good views of downtown. The hotel's central location, facilities that include a jogging track and basketball court, and nearby attractions make this a popular choice for families—and conventions. One Pershing Rd., Kansas City, MO 64108. ✆ 800/WESTIN-1 or 816/474-4400. Fax 816/391-4438. www.westin.com. 729 units. $229 double; from $495 suite. Extra person $25. Children under 16 stay free in parents' room. Packages available. AE, DC, DISC, MC, V. Self-parking $9.50, valet parking $15. **Amenities:** Restaurants (2); outdoor heated pool; health club ($5 usage fee); 2 lighted, outdoor tennis courts; pets $25 a night.

WHERE TO DINE

Kansas City is known for steak and barbecue, but there are plenty of other cuisine possibilities downtown, in Country Club Plaza and Westport.

American Restaurant NEW AMERICAN   One of Kansas City's top fine-dining establishments for more than a quarter of a century, this elegant, high-ceilinged restaurant features the best in regional fare, offers one of the city's most extensive wine lists, and has good views of the downtown skyline. The changing menu may include grilled black angus filet with a three-onion ragout, or *foie gras* on toast with port wine sauce, as well as fresh seafood and a vegetarian entree. A great choice for a celebration. In Crown Center, 25th and Grand Blvd. ✆ 816/426-1133. Reservations recommended. Jackets preferred for men. Main courses $25–$36; fixed-price lunch $19. AE, DC, DISC, MC, V. Mon–Fri 11:15am–2pm; Mon–Thurs 6–10pm; Fri–Sat 6–11pm.

Arthur Bryant's BARBECUE   A few blocks east of 18th and Vine, this unpretentious self-serve restaurant, with origins stretching back to the Depression, is the most famous—and some swear the best—barbecue joint in town. White bread smothered with barbecued meat and barbecued ribs are the specialties, along with Bryant's signature gritty sauce. 1727 Brooklyn. ✆ 816/231-1123. Main courses $7–$15. AE, MC, V. Mon–Thurs 10am–9:30pm; Fri–Sat 10am–10pm; Sun 11am–8pm.

Cafe Allegro CONTEMPORARY CONTINENTAL   About a mile west of Westport, in a funky, eclectic neighborhood of ethnic restaurants, this upscale, hip restaurant in a turn-of-the-20th-century building features changing artwork on its brick walls and an intriguing menu with an emphasis on fresh seafood. Dining options may include crab cakes, grilled asparagus with Niçoise olive vinaigrette, and grilled salmon with sake and shitake mushrooms, complemented by an extensive wine list. 1815 W. 39th St. ✆ 816/561-3663. Reservations recommended. Main courses $21–$28. AE, DC, MC, V. Mon–Fri 11:30am–2pm; Mon–Sat 6–10pm.

Classic Cup Cafe CONTEMPORARY CONTINENTAL   Restaurants on the plaza seem to come and go with the swiftness of the changing of the seasons, but this decade-old, casual cafe has proven its staying power as a local favorite. Its glass facade and sidewalk seating make it a perfect spot for people-watching; there's also a backyard patio. Pizzas, sandwiches, pasta, steaks, and seafood are listed on a changing menu that may include such entrees as pan-seared salmon stuffed with Alaskan snow crab and served with rice and vegetables. Make reservations early for Sunday brunch, which features its own menu with breakfast and lunch items. 301 W. 47th St. ℂ **816/753-1840.** Reservations recommended. Main courses $9–$25. AE, DISC, MC, V. Mon–Thurs 7am–10pm; Fri 7am–11pm; Sat 8am–11pm; Sun 10am–10pm.

Golden Ox STEAKS   This popular steakhouse was established in 1949 by the founder of the Kansas City Stockyards Company to feed hungry ranchers. The stockyards are now history, but the Golden Ox retains its 1950-ish clubby atmosphere and is still the place for high-powered business lunches and some of the best, yet affordably-priced, steaks in town, aged and cut on the premises and broiled over a hickory-charcoal flame. Entrees come with a salad, vegetable, and garlic bread. 1600 Genessee. ℂ **816/842-2866.** Reservations recommended. Main courses $15–$34. AE, DC, MC, V. Mon–Fri 11:20–10pm; Sat 4–10:30pm; Sun 4–9pm.

Lidia's ITALIAN   Located in a renovated railway freight house behind Union Station, and sporting exposed ceiling beams, brick walls, and an outdoor patio, this very popular restaurant (owned by PBS culinary star Lidia Bastianich) specializes in excellent yet affordable Northern Italian cuisine. Try the three-pasta sampler, delivered to your plate straight from the kitchen via a frying pan (you can have as much as you wish) or the very popular veal shanks. There are two wine lists, one with about 60 choices of bottles all priced at $20. 101 W. 22nd St. ℂ **816/221-3722.** Reservations recommended. Main courses $13–$22. AE, DC, MC, V. Daily 11am–2pm; Mon–Thurs 5:30–9pm; Fri–Sat 5–10pm; Sun 5–9pm.

Savoy Grill AMERICAN   Located in downtown's historic Hotel Savoy and established in 1903, this well-known landmark exudes turn-of-the-20th-century Kansas City with stained-glass windows, dark wainscoting, murals depicting the Santa Fe Trail, and white-coated waiters with black bow ties. The menu is unabashedly straightforward American cuisine, primarily steaks and seafood, which sometimes falls short of the venue. You're dining here mainly for the old-fashioned ambience, so be sure to make reservations for a booth in the main dining room; it's in the smoking section, but few of the largely older clientele smoke. In the Hotel Savoy, 219 W. 9th St. ℂ **816/842-3890.** Reservations recommended. Main courses $17–$42. AE, DC, DISC, MC, V. Mon–Thurs 11am–11pm; Fri–Sat 11am–midnight; Sun 4–10pm.

Stroud's Oak Ridge Manor CHICKEN   In northeast Kansas City, not far from Worlds of Fun, this casual family restaurant is located in an expanded 1829 log cabin and farmhouse. It specializes in pan-fried chicken served with all the trimmings, but it also offers steaks, catfish, and sandwiches. There's a children's menu, a piano player obliges with old-time favorites, and portions are so hearty that few leave without doggie bags. There's a second location at 1015 E. 85th St. (ℂ **816/333-2132**). 5410 NE Oak Ridge Rd. (take the Brighton exit off I-35). Reservations not accepted. ℂ **816/454-9600.** Meals $11–$22. AE, DC, DISC, MC, V. Mon–Thurs 4–10pm; Fri 11am–11pm; Sat 2–11pm; Sun 11am–10pm.

Winstead's DINER   Just east of Country Club Plaza, this Art Deco–style diner has been going strong since 1940 and now has more than a dozen branches. Hamburgers made from steak (ground daily on the premises) are served in tissue paper, the jukebox plays golden oldies, and the milkshakes are the best in town. 101 Brush Creek. ℂ **816/753-2244.** Most items under $5. MC, V. Sun–Thurs 6:30am–midnight; Fri–Sat 6:30am–1am.

KANSAS CITY AFTER DARK

Much of the city's nightlife can be found downtown, in Westport, and at Country Club Plaza. For information about what's going on in jazz and blues clubs, pick up the free *Pitch Weekly* or the bi-monthly *Jam* published by the Kansas City Jazz Ambassadors; or call the **Jazz Hotline** (✆ 816/753-5277). For tickets to main events, call **Ticketmaster** (✆ 816/931-3330; www.ticketmaster. com).

THE PERFORMING ARTS   The Lyric Theater, 1029 Central, is the venue for both the **Lyric Opera of Kansas City** (✆ 816/471-4933), which presents four productions yearly in original language with projected translations, and the **Kansas City Symphony** (✆ 816/471-0400). The **Kansas City Ballet** (✆ 816/931-2232) performs at the Lyric Theater and the **Midland Theater**, 1228 Main St. (✆ 816/471-8600), a lavishly decorated 1927 theater that also stages musicals, concerts, and other performances. The turn-of-the-20th-century **Folly Theater**, 300 W. 12th St. (✆ 816/842-5500), is known for its Jazz and Children's series. In summer, open-air **Starlight Theatre** in Swope Park (✆ 816/363-7827) has presented Broadway musicals and concerts for more than 50 years.

THE CLUB & BAR SCENE   **Phoenix Piano Bar & Grill,** downtown at 302 W. 8th St. (✆ 816/472-0001), specializes in Kansas City–style jazz, seafood, and steaks, while the nearby **Majestic Steakhouse**, 931 Broadway (✆ 816/471-8484), offers jazz nightly. **Jardine's Restaurant**, 45436 Main St. (✆ 816/561-6480) near Country Club Plaza, offers live jazz and New American regional cuisine. **Club at Plaza III,** in Country Club Plaza at 4749 Pennsylvania (✆ 816/753-0000), features live jazz and a full menu, including steaks.

In the historic 18th and Vine district, venues offering live blues and jazz include the **Blue Room,** 1600 E. 18th St. (✆ 816/474-2929); and the **Mutual Musicians Foundation,** 1823 Highland Ave. (✆ 816/471-5212), which opens Saturday after midnight for jam sessions.

In Westport, **Blayney's,** 415 Westport Rd. (✆ 816/561-3747), offers blues, jazz, R&B, and rock in a pub setting, while the **Grand Emporium,** 3832 Main St. (✆ 816/531-7557), features primarily blues and barbecue, as well as reggae, jazz, zydeco, and alternative music.

RIVERBOAT GAMBLING   Riverboat gambling takes place on non-cruising boats along the banks of the Missouri River, including **Argosy,** Route 9 and I-635, Riverside (✆ 816/746-3144); **Harrah's Casino,** U.S. 210 and Chouteau Trafficway, North Kansas City (✆ 800-HARRAHS); **Ameristar Casino,** I-435 and Route 210 (✆ 816/414-7000); and the **Isle of Capri Casino,** off I-35 at 1800 E. Front St. (✆ 816/855-7777).

8 St. Louis

Established as a French trading post in 1764, St. Louis served as a gateway to the west after the Louisiana Purchase and as a major port for steamboats traveling the Mississippi. Today the city's landmark is the soaring, shining steel Gateway Arch, designed by Eero Saarinen in 1966 to commemorate western-bound pioneers. Though visitors often make it their first stop, there's plenty more beckoning, including the restored Union Station, first-rate museums, and numerous attractions geared toward children, many of them free, making St. Louis a prime family destination.

ESSENTIALS

GETTING THERE   By Plane   Flights arrive at **Lambert–St. Louis International Airport** (© 314/426-8000; www.lambert-stlouis.com), about 20 minutes northwest of downtown. The **MetroLink** light rail (© 314/231-2345) connects the airport with downtown for $3. **Taxis** cost about $25 to $30.

By Train   Amtrak (© 800/USA-RAIL; www.amtrak.com) provides daily service from Chicago and Kansas City (trip time for both: 5½ hr.) to its station at 550 S. 16th St. (© 314/331-3300), 2 blocks east of Union Station.

By Car   The major routes into St. Louis are I-70 from the east (Indianapolis) and west (Kansas City), I-55 from the north (Chicago) and south (Memphis), I-64 from the southeast (Louisville), and I-44 from the southwest (Springfield).

VISITOR INFORMATION   St. Louis Visitor Information Centers, both open Monday through Friday from 9am to 5pm and Saturday from 9am to 2pm, are located at America's Center, 7th Street and Washington Avenue (MetroLink: Convention Center), and at Kiener Plaza, 6th Street and Chestnut Street behind the Old Courthouse (closed Jan and Feb; MetroLink: 8th St. and Pine). There's also a **Visitor Information Center** at the airport, open daily from 10am to 8pm. **The Fun Phone** (© 314/421-2100) is a recording of special events. For more information, call © 800/916-0092 or check **www.explore stlouis.com.**

GETTING AROUND   The **MetroLink** (© 314/231-2345; www.bi-state.org) travels between the airport and East St. Louis, with stops at Forest Park, Central West End, Union Station, Busch Stadium, downtown (at 8th and Pine and Convention Center), Laclede's Landing, and other neighborhoods. A one-way ticket costs $1.25 for the entire zone minus the airport (tickets to and from the airport are $3) and a day pass $4. Travel is free on weekdays from 11:30am to 1:30pm between Union Station and Laclede's Landing.

You'll probably want to rent a car, but be aware that parking is costly. Most hotels and upper-end restaurants offer valet parking. Hotels almost always charge a fee for this service and restaurants sometimes charge, though sometimes only a tip is expected.

FAST FACTS   A major hospital is **Saint Louis University Hospital,** 3635 Vista Ave., at Grand Avenue (© 314/577-8000). **Walgreens** is open 24 hours at 4140 S. Broadway (© 314/832-4990) and in Clayton at 6733 Clayton Rd. (© 314/721-6013).

WHAT TO SEE & DO

Anheuser-Busch Brewery   Anheuser-Busch, one of the world's largest beer brewers, was established at this site in the 1860s, and many architectural gems remain. Tours of the brewing process take in the Clydesdale stable, the historic 1892 Brew House, and the packaging plant, ending with free drinks. Allow 2 hours. Tours begin at 12th and Lynch streets (I-55 at Arsenal). © 314/577-2626. Free admission. June–Aug Mon–Sat 9am–5pm, Sun 11:30am–5pm; Sept–May Mon–Sat 9am–4pm, Sun 11:30am–4pm. Tours are several times an hour on a first-come, first-served basis. Frequency depends on demand (as often as every 10 min. in summer and about every 30 min. in winter).

Cathedral Basilica of Saint Louis   Built after the turn of the 20th century and something of a curiosity, this cathedral combines a Romanesque exterior with a brilliant Byzantine interior and boasts the largest collection of mosaics in

St. Louis

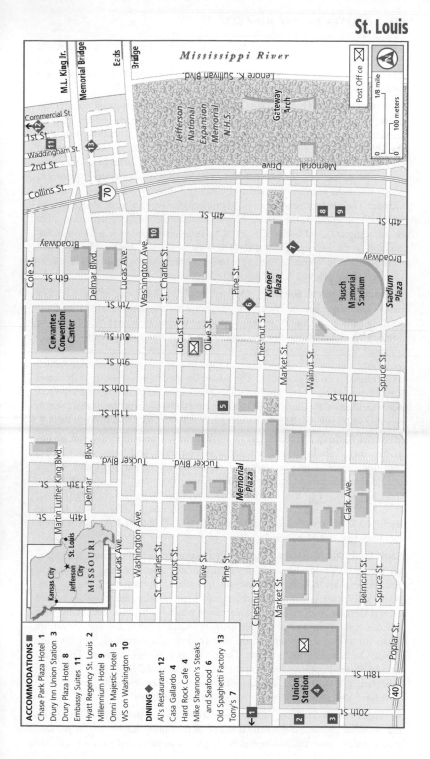

Mississippi River

Lenore K. Sullivan Blvd.

Post Office

1/8 mile
100 meters

M.L. King Jr.
Memorial Bridge
Eads
Bridge

Commercial St.
1st St.
Waddingham St.
2nd St.
Collins St.

70

Jefferson
National
Expansion
Memorial
N.H.S.

Gateway
Arch

Memorial Drive

4th St.
8
9
4th St.

Broadway
Cole St.
6th St.
Delmar Blvd.
Lucas Ave.
Washington Ave.
St. Charles St.
10
Pine St.
7
Kiener
Plaza
Busch
Memorial
Stadium
Broadway
Stadium
Plaza

7th St.
Locust St.
Olive St.
6
Chestnut St.
Market St.
Walnut St.
Spruce St.

Cervantes
Convention
Center

8th St.
9th St.
10th St.
11th St.
5
Tucker Blvd.
Market St.
10th St.

Blvd.
13th St.
Delmar
14th St.
Martin Luther King Blvd.
St.
St.

Tucker Blvd.
Memorial
Plaza

Clark Ave.

Lucas Ave.
Washington Ave.
St. Charles St.
Locust St.
Olive St.
Pine St.

Chestnut St.
Market St.

Belmont St.
Spruce St.

Poplar St.

Union
Station
4
18th St.
20th St.

40

Kansas City
St. Louis
Jefferson City
MISSOURI

ACCOMMODATIONS ■
Chase Park Plaza Hotel **1**
Drury Inn Union Station **3**
Drury Plaza Hotel **8**
Embassy Suites **11**
Hyatt Regency St. Louis **2**
Millennium Hotel **9**
Omni Majestic Hotel **5**
WS on Washington **10**

DINING ◆
Al's Restaurant **12**
Casa Gallardo **4**
Hard Rock Cafe **4**
Mike Shannon's Steaks
  and Seafood **6**
Old Spaghetti Factory **13**
Tony's **7**

1
2
3

the world—four million pieces of glass used in 83,000 square feet of mosaic art, created by 20 artists over a span of 75 years. Plan at least 15 minutes for this must-see. 4431 Lindell Blvd. (at Newstead Ave.) in Central West End. © 314/533-2824. Free admission. Daily 7am–7pm (in winter to dusk). MetroLink: Central West End.

Gateway Arch/Jefferson National Expansion Memorial America's tallest monument, this graceful rainbow of shining steel soars 630 feet above downtown and the Mississippi River, commemorating westward expansion in the 1800s. Tram rides to the top can involve lengthy waits in the summer and on weekends; come first thing in the morning to purchase tickets (or order tickets in advance online), then take in the free **Museum of Westward Expansion,** which traces the journey of Lewis and Clark and those who followed. The Arch Odyssey Theatre features changing, 45-minute movies on a giant IMAX screen, and the Monument to the Dream film documents the Arch's construction. Plan on spending at least 2 hours here. 707 N. 1st St. (between Memorial Dr. and Lenore K. Sullivan Blvd. on the riverfront). © 877/982-1410. www.gateway.com. Admission for tram and 1 movie $11 adults, $8 children 13–16, $5.50 children 3–12. Memorial Day to Labor Day daily 8am–10pm; rest of year daily 9am–6pm. MetroLink: Laclede's Landing.

Missouri Botanical Garden Opened in 1859, this is one of the country's best botanical gardens: a 79-acre delight featuring the nation's largest Japanese strolling garden, a Chinese garden, a geodesic-domed rainforest greenhouse, an 1882 brick conservatory housing camellias, a scented garden for the visually impaired, a sculpture garden with works by Carl Milles, a hedge maze, a home-gardening resource center, and themed gardens ranging from a Victorian garden to an English woodland garden. A must-see for gardeners, who can easily spend 2 or 3 hours of bliss here. 4344 Shaw Blvd. (Vandeventer exit off I-44). © 314/577-9400. Admission $7 adults, $5 seniors, free for children 12 and under. Memorial Day to Labor Day daily 9am–8pm; rest of year daily 9am–5pm. MetroLink: Central West End, then Garden Express 14.

Missouri History Museum St. Louis's history is presented through photographs, memorabilia, first-person narratives, portraits, and more, with displays featuring the city's role in westward expansion, the Dred Scott case (which upheld slavery), famous St. Louisans like Chuck Berry and Tennessee Williams, the 1904 World's Fair held at Forest Park, a replica of Charles Lindbergh's *Spirit of St. Louis* plane, and changing exhibits of the city's past. Allow 1 hour. Jefferson Memorial Building, Forest Park (at Lindell and DeBaliviere). © 314/746-4599. Free admission. Tues 10am–8pm; Wed–Mon 10am–6pm. MetroLink: Forest Park.

Saint Louis Art Museum Housed in a beaux arts–style building constructed for the 1904 World's Fair, this museum contains works ranging from ancient and medieval art to European old masters, French Impressionists, and contemporary art. Its pre-Columbian and German Expressionist collections are ranked among the best in the world (it owns more paintings by Max Beckmann than any museum in the world). Other galleries feature Islamic and ancient art, an Asian collection, an Egyptian collection (including a mummy), and art from Africa, Oceania, and the Americas. There are also displays of Chinese, European, and American decorative arts. You should spend at least 2 hours here. Fine Arts Dr., Forest Park. © 314/721-0072. Free admission; special exhibitions cost extra (but are free on Tues). Tues 1:30–8:30pm; Wed–Sun 10am–5pm. MetroLink: Forest Park.

St. Louis Union Station Once the nation's busiest passenger-rail terminal, this restored 100-year-old terminal is one of St. Louis's biggest attractions and now contains more than 80 specialty shops, restaurants, and even a small lake with paddleboats. Be sure to take a peak at the Grand Hall, now the lobby of the Hyatt Regency. 1820 Market St. (© 314/421 6655. Free admission. Shops open May Dec Mon–Thurs 10am–9pm, Fri–Sat 10am–10pm, Sun 11am–7pm; Jan–Apr Mon–Sat 10am–9pm, Sun 11am–6pm. MetroLink: Union Station.

MORE HIGHLIGHTS

HISTORIC HOMES The **Campbell House Museum,** 1508 Locust St. (© **314/421-0325**), is an elegant 1851 Victorian mansion with most of the original furnishings intact. The Romanesque Revival–style 1889 **Samuel Cupples House,** 3673 W. Pine Blvd. (© **314/977-3025**), is a gem of the Gilded Age on the campus of St. Louis University, containing 42 rooms, a glass collection, and other fine and decorative arts. The **DeMenil Mansion,** 3352 DeMenil Place (© **314/771-5828**), was a four-room farmhouse in 1845, later expanded to 14 rooms in the Greek Revival style. It contains period furnishings and two oil paintings by Missouri artist George Caleb Bingham.

The oldest standing residence in downtown St. Louis, built in 1845, was the home of children's poet Eugene Field, who wrote "Little Boy Blue." The **Eugene Field House and Toy Museum,** 634 S. Broadway (© **314/421-4689**), contains an antique toy and doll collection that spans more than 300 years.

From 1900 to 1903, the **Scott Joplin House State Historic Site,** 2658 Delmar Blvd. (© **314/340-5790**), was the modest four-family antebellum home of the musician and composer known as the "King of Ragtime." Now a National Historic Landmark, it offers 25-minute guided tours that include Joplin's second-floor apartment with furnishings representative of the times and a player-piano that rags out renditions of Joplin's best-known tunes, including "The Entertainer."

THE HOME RUN DERBY Watch the **St. Louis Cardinals** hit some homers at Busch Stadium, 7th Street downtown (© **314/421-2400;** www.stlcardinals. com).

BEST BETS FOR KIDS St. Louis is a children's town, with more than enough to keep them amused. The top-rated **St. Louis Zoo,** Forest Park (© **314/781-0900**), with its Big Cat Country, Jungle of the Apes, River's Edge with elephants and hippos, fascinating Insectarium with everything from giant cockroaches to a butterfly house, and animal-contact area called Children's Zoo is free (fees charged for Insectarium and Children's Zoo). Another freebie is the **St. Louis Science Center,** 5050 Oakland Ave. (© **800/456-7572** or 314/289-4444), with full-size, animated dinosaurs and many hands-on exhibits covering DNA and genetics, aviation, the environment, and more, as well as a space exploration exhibition, planetarium and OMNIMAX Theater (admission charged). And two more free attractions are **Grant's Farm,** 10501 Gravois (© **314/843-1700**), once farmed by Ulysses S. Grant and now part of the Busch family estate, open from mid-April to October and featuring a tram ride

---

Rollin' on the River

Gateway Riverboat Cruises (© **800/878-7411** or 314/621-4040), departing throughout the year from the levee below the Arch, offers 1-hour narrated sightseeing trips and dinner cruises aboard replica 19th-century paddle-wheelers called the *Tom Sawyer* and *Becky Thatcher.* One-hour cruises are $9 adults and $4 children.

through an exotic game preserve, a small zoo, animal shows, a Clydesdale stable, a carriage collection, and a free glass of Anheuser-Busch beer (alas, not for the kids); and **Purina Farms,** near Six Flags Over Mid-America at the Gray Summit exit off I-44 (© **314/982-3232**), open from mid-March to November with a hayloft play area, a petting area, dog shows, a barn full of animals, and educational displays.

Children up to age 12 will also love the whimsical, adventure-filled **City Museum,** 701 N. 15th St. (© **314/231-2489**), housed in a former shoe factory, and featuring a huge play area filled with imaginative caves, slides, and crawling tubes; a circus performance; train rides; art workshops; a collection of oddities; and an old-fashioned carnival display. At the more educational, hands-on **Magic House,** 516 S. Kirkwood Rd. (© **314/822-8900**), children can experiment with magnets, water, and tools, be a news anchor, test their fitness, play in a kid-size village, and climb the Fitness Safari jungle gym. The sections of the children's museum are geared to specific age ranges. In general, kids 12 and under will have a blast here.

The biggest attraction is the huge amusement park, **Six Flags Over Mid-America,** 30 miles west of St. Louis on I-44 (© **636/938-4800**), with thrill rides like the 5,000-foot-long Boss roller coaster, plus Looney Tunes Town and live entertainment. There is an adjoining water park with a wave pool, speed slides, and more.

WHERE TO STAY

Chase Park Plaza Hotel   Located across from Forest Park in the elegant Central West End, with its antiques shops, sidewalk cafes, and sophisticated restaurants, this recently restored, 1920s historic hotel is one of the city's poshest, offering luxuriously appointed rooms and one- and two-bedroom suites, the latter two featuring stocked kitchens. The hotel's many facilities, including a business center and five-screen movie complex, and the many attractions of Forest Park make this a winner for both business travelers and those on romantic getaways. 212–232 N. Kingshighway (at Lindell Blvd.), St. Louis, MO 63108. © 877/587-2427 or 314/633-3000. Fax 314/633-1144. www.chaseparkplaza.com. 251 units. $169 double; $189–$269 suites. No charge for additional room occupants. AE, DC, DISC, MC, V. Self-parking $5, valet parking $18. **Amenities:** Restaurants (3); outdoor heated pool; state-of-the-art health club.

Drury Inn Union Station   Part of a St. Louis–based chain, this beautifully restored former YMCA, built in 1907, is across from Union Station and offers rooms with refrigerators, microwaves, and free popcorn and Coke; free evening beverages and snacks (Mon–Thurs); free local calls; in-room coffeemakers; and many other perks (including an exercise room and laundry facilities), making this a great place for families. Note that some rooms face inward, meaning no views. Check-in is at 3pm. 201 S. 20th St., St. Louis, MO 63103. © 800/378-7946 or 314/231-3900. Fax 314/231-3900. www.druryinn.com. 176 units. $114–$124 double. Children under 18 stay free in parents' room. Rates include breakfast buffet. AE, DC, DISC, MC, V. Free parking. MetroLink: Union Station. **Amenities:** Restaurant; indoor pool; pets free.

Drury Plaza Hotel   More upscale than the other locally-owned Drury Inns, this downtown hotel, situated just minutes from the Arch, opened in 2000 in three renovated buildings, including the 1919 Fur Exchange Building, and boasts Italian marble, massive support columns, and Waterford crystal chandeliers in its lobby. Rooms, some with Arch and river views, have microwave ovens, refrigerators, coffeemakers, and free popcorn and soft drinks. Like all Drury properties, they offer free local calls and free evening cocktails, beverages, and snacks (Mon–Thurs). Good facilities, including a business center, laundry facilities, and an exercise room, make this a great location for both business and leisure travelers. 4th and Market sts., St. Louis, MO 63102. © 800/378-7946 or 314/231-3003. Fax 314/231-2952. www.druryinn.com. 367 units. $145–$155 double; from $165 suite. Children under 18 stay free in parents' room. Rates include breakfast buffet. AE, DC, DISC, MC, V. Parking $10. MetroLink: 8th and Pine. **Amenities:** Restaurants (2); indoor pool.

Embassy Suites   Located near the Arch and downtown, in the restored riverfront nightlife district (Laclede's Landing), this all-suite hotel features a sky-lit, eight-story atrium as its focal point and offers two-room suites equipped with refrigerators, coffeemakers, and microwaves. Ask for a room on a higher floor to get the best views of the Mississippi. Guests enjoy such extras as cooked-to-order breakfasts, free evening cocktails, billiards tables, and a game room, making this a good choice for couples and families alike. 901 N. 1st St., St. Louis, MO 63102. © 800/362-2779 or 314/241-4200. Fax 314/241-6513. www.embassysuites.com. 297 units. $169–$189 suite. Extra person $17. Children under 18 stay free in parents' room. Rates include free breakfast. Off-season rates available. AE, DC, DISC, MC, V. Parking $8. MetroLink: Laclede's Landing. **Amenities:** Restaurant; indoor pool; health club.

Hyatt Regency St. Louis   Located in restored Union Station, with its many shops and restaurants, this hotel boasts Missouri's most spectacular lobby—the station's former Grand Hall, with a six-story vaulted ceiling and gold-leaf frescoes. Most rooms are in a modern addition beneath the trusses of the former train shed and feature such luxuries as bathroom TVs and on-command pay movies. For more pampering, stay in the Regency Club in the historic part of the station, which has the added perks of its own lounge, concierge, and complimentary breakfast. Everyone from business travelers (there's a 24-hr. business center) to families stay here. One St. Louis Union Station, 18th and Market sts., St. Louis, MO 63103. © 800/233-1234 or 314/231-1234. Fax 314/923-3970. www.stlouis.hyatt.com. 539 units. $169–$189 double. Children under 18 stay free in parents' room. Packages available. AE, DC, DISC, MC, V. Self-parking $9, valet parking $15. MetroLink: Union Station. **Amenities:** Restaurants (2); outdoor pool; health club.

Millennium Hotel   This is the only downtown hotel to fully capitalize on its riverfront location with an airy, two-story lobby and rooms overlooking the Arch, as well as the city's only rooftop revolving restaurant (Top of the Riverfront on the 28th floor), plus a game room, business center, and laundry room. A convention hotel (and therefore crowded at times), it offers rooms in two round towers: a shorter, south tower with conventional rooms equipped with two double beds that appeals to families; and a taller, north tower sporting a more contemporary look with queen or king beds popular with couples and business travelers. Request a room facing the Arch. 200 S. 4th St., St. Louis, MO 63102. © 866/866-8086 or 314/241-9500. Fax 314/241-6171. www.millennium-hotels.com. 780 units. $209 double; from $350 suite. Extra person $20. Children under 18 stay free in parents' room. Seasonal packages available. AE, DC, DISC, MC, V. Parking $15. MetroLink: Busch Stadium. **Amenities:** Restaurants (3); indoor and outdoor pools; health club; deposit required for pets.

Omni Majestic Hotel   Built in 1914, this National Historic Landmark appeals to business travelers and celebrities alike with its old world charm, downtown location, complimentary downtown shuttle, excellent service, fitness room, and comfortable rooms equipped with mostly king-size beds, coffeemakers, and on-command pay movies. 1019 Pine St., St. Louis, MO 63101. © 800/THE-OMNI or 314/436-2355. Fax 314/436-0223. www.omnihotels.com. 91 units. $149–$159 double. Extra person $10. Children under 12 stay free in parents' room. AE, DC, DISC, MC, V. Parking $14. MetroLink: 8th and Pine. **Amenities:** Restaurant; deposit required for pets (up to 25 lb.).

WS on Washington   Occupying a late-19th-century Classical Revival building, this trendy downtown hotel is a leap above the ordinary with its unique contemporary furnishings, very popular bar, free laundry facilities, 24-hour business center, and rooms and suites—all with full-size kitchens, Jacuzzi tubs, huge closets, to-die-for beds, and drapes that block light—that are so spacious you can imagine moving in. 400 Washington Ave., St. Louis, MO 63102. © **866/216-8950** or 314/231-1100. Fax 314/231-1199. www.wshotels.com. 61 units. $169 double; $189–$299 suite. Up to four people stay for the flat rate in suites. Long-term rates available. AE, DC, DISC, MC, V. Parking $15. MetroLink: Convention Center. **Amenities:** Restaurant; spa; health club.

WHERE TO DINE

St. Louis is famous for its Italian restaurants, many in the Italian district known as The Hill, but you'll also find many other choices in Laclede's Landing, Union Station, and trendy Central West End. For children, good bets include **The Old Spaghetti Factory,** housed in an old warehouse in Laclede's Landing at 727 N. 1st St. (© **314/621-0276**), and **Hard Rock Cafe** in Union Station (© **314/ 621-7625**).

It's a St. Louis tradition to drop by **Ted Drewes Frozen Custard,** 6726 Chippewa (© **314/481-2652**), after a night on the town. Founded more than 75 years ago, this roadside parlor and Route 66 attraction specializes in frozen custards, including a thick dip called a Concrete, available in flavors ranging from chocolate chip to Heath Bar and so thick that it's served upside down. Open daily March through December. An additional location is open summers only at 4224 S. Grand (© **314/352-7376**).

Al's Restaurant SEAFOOD/STEAK   Located north of Laclede's Landing in a riverfront industrial area, Al's has been a St. Louis favorite for special occasions since 1925. There's no printed menu for the Italian-inspired cuisine; rather, the waiter displays a tray of steak, veal, rack of lamb, seafood, and other dishes of the day, carefully explaining each. Jackets are required for men, but the establishment is more comfortable than it is elegant. 1200 N. 1st St. © **314/421-6399.** Reservations recommended. Jackets required for men. Main courses $25–$48. AE, MC, V. Mon–Sat 5–11pm.

Blueberry Hill SANDWICHES/BURGERS   Located in the lively University City Loop district, this St. Louis institution is a treasure trove of pop-culture memorabilia, including vintage posters, lunch boxes, and more Chuck Berry memorabilia than you can shake a stick at. The CD jukebox, with 3,000 selections, is rated one of the best in the country, and its hamburgers are among the best in town. Live music is staged in the Elvis Room and Duck Room several nights a week (Chuck Berry still performs here), and outside on the sidewalk is the St. Louis Walk of Fame honoring famous St. Louisans, including Chuck Berry, Josephine Baker, Tennessee Williams, Ulysses S. Grant, and Tina Turner. 6504 Delmar, University City. © **314/727-0880.** Main courses $5–$7.50. AE, DC, DISC, MC, V. Mon–Sat 11am–1am; Sun 11am–midnight. MetroLink: Delmar, then bus 97.

Casa Gallardo MEXICAN   One of many restaurants in Union Station, this local chain is known for its colorful, festive atmosphere, happy hour, margaritas, and fresh food, including fajitas, chimichangas, and burritos. There's an outdoor patio, as well as a few non-Mexican dishes geared toward children. In Union Station, 1821 Market St. (C) 314/421-6766. Main courses $7.50–$13. AE, DC, DISC, MC, V. Mon–Thurs 11am–10pm, Fri–Sat 11am–11pm; Sun 11am–10pm. MetroLink: Union Station.

Meriwether's NEW AMERICAN   On the second floor of the Missouri History Museum, this light and airy casual restaurant overlooking Forest Park offers soups, salads (like a Mediterranean chicken salad with olives, artichoke hearts, feta, and red onion), sandwiches (like a crawfish and sweet corncake sandwich), quiche, and main dishes (like a grilled salmon puff pie), as well as a children's menu. This is a good place for lunch if you're visiting the many sights in Forest Park. Missouri History Museum, Forest Park. (C) 314/361-7313. Main courses $7–$10. AE, MC, V. Mon–Sat 11am–2pm; Sun 10am–2pm. MetroLink: Forest Park.

Mike Shannon's Steaks and Seafood STEAKS/SEAFOOD   Owned by a former Cardinals baseball player, this downtown fine-dining venue is formal yet relaxed, with white tablecloths in wood-paneled rooms and displays of sports memorabilia. It caters to a business crowd with a menu that concentrates on aged steaks and seafood. With Busch Stadium just a couple minutes' walk away, it's also popular for a meal before or after a Cardinals game. 100 N. 7th St. (C) 314/421-1540. Main courses $16–$42. AE, DC, MC, V. Mon–Fri 11am–11pm; Sat 5–11pm; Sun 5–10pm. MetroLink: 8th and Pine.

Saint Louis Brewery and Tap Room AMERICAN   A few blocks north of Union Station, in a 1904 brick building that used to house a printing company, this microbrewery brews 35 kinds of Schlafly brand beer on the premises (10 or so are usually on offer) and serves a variety of sandwiches and entrees, many of which include beer in their recipes, including beer-battered shrimp and beer-and-cheddar soup. Other offerings include meat pie, fish and fries, Wiener schnitzel, lamb sausage pasta, and lemon herb–roasted chicken. Save room for the toffee pudding. An upstairs bar offers live music on the weekends. 2100 Locust St. (C) 314/241-2337. Main courses $5.75–$13. AE, DC, MC, V. Mon–Thurs 11am–10pm; Fri–Sat 11am–midnight; Sun noon–9pm. MetroLink: Union Station.

Tony's ITALIAN   Agreement is near unanimous that Tony's is the finest restaurant in St. Louis. Open since 1949, it offers impeccable service, sublime cuisine, an extensive wine selection, one of the cleanest and quietest kitchens on earth, and sophisticated, elegant dining. Star dishes include the lobster Albanello (served in a heavy, white-wine cream sauce with mushrooms and shallots) and various veal dishes, but everything is fabulous. 410 Market St. (C) 314/231-7007. Reservations recommended. Jackets required for men. Main courses $20–$36; fixed-price meal $80. AE, DC, DISC, MC, V. Mon–Thurs 5–11pm; Fri–Sat 5–11:30pm. MetroLink: 8th and Pine.

Zoë Pan-Asian Café SOUTHEAST ASIAN/PAN-ASIAN   One of the hottest restaurants in the hip Central West End, this cool, sleek restaurant radiates a Zen-like simplicity with its black furnishings, white paper lanterns, flickering candles, and cast-iron tea kettles silhouetted on a ledge. A Thai chef turns out very tempting dishes, from grilled salmon with Asian barbecue sauce, Chinese mustard and potatoes, to vegetarian Pad Thai with rice noodles, cilantro, and peanuts. 4753 McPherson (at N. Euclid Ave). (C) 314/361-0013. Reservations recommended. Main courses $13–$20. AE, DC, MC, V. Mon–Fri 11:30am–3pm; Mon–Thurs 5:30–10pm; Fri 5:30–11pm; Sat 5–11pm; Sun 5–10pm. MetroLink: Central West End, then Forest Park Shuttle Bug.

ST. LOUIS AFTER DARK

To find out what's on when you're in town, pick up a copy of the free weekly *Riverfront Times* at restaurants, bars, and venues around town, or buy the Thursday edition of the *St. Louis Post-Dispatch* for its entertainment section. For tickets to major events, call **Ticketmaster** (© 314/421-4400; www.ticketmaster.com) or **Metrotix** (© 314/534-1111; www.mtix.com).

THE PERFORMING ARTS   Grand Center (MetroLink: Grand) is the premier performing arts district, with the 1920s-era **Powell Symphony Hall,** 718 N. Grand Blvd. (© 314/534-1700), home of the **St. Louis Symphony Orchestra** (www.slso.org), founded in 1880 and America's second-oldest symphony orchestra. The **Fox Theatre,** 527 N. Grand Blvd. (© 314/534-1111), is a lavish, 1929 Byzantine venue for musicals, dance, and concerts, and the **Grandel Theater,** 3610 Grandel Sq. (© 314/534-3810), is the home of the St. Louis Black Repertory Company which stages contemporary works by African-American playwrights. The **Riverport Amphitheatre,** 14141 Riverport Dr. (© 314/298-9944), presents big-name concerts, while **The Muny,** in Forest Park (© 314/361-1900; www.muny.com), features Broadway musicals and celebrates its 83rd season as the nation's oldest and largest outdoor musical theater.

THE CLUB & CASINO SCENE   St. Louis's nightlife is concentrated around Laclede's Landing and in Soulard, on the south edge of downtown. Good bets for live music most nights of the week include **BB's Jazz, Blues & Soups,** 700 S. Broadway (© 314/436-5222), and **Mississippi Nights,** which brings top-rated touring bands to Laclede's Landing at 914 S. 1st St. (© 314/421-3853). In Soulard, there's **Mike & Min's,** 925 Geyer (© 314/421-1655), St. Louis's oldest blues bar, and **1860 Hard Shell Cafe & Bar,** 1860 S. 9th St. (© 314/231-1860), with blues, R&B, zydeco, and rock. Among St. Louis's several gambling spots, the most convenient is the **President Casino,** docked at Laclede's Landing (© 800/772-3647 or 314/622-1111).

9 Branson & the Ozarks

With a population of 6,000 and a historic downtown, Branson attracts more than seven million visitors a year, primarily retirees, families, and RVers drawn by the irresistible lure—and improbable pairing—of outdoor recreation and big-time entertainment. Surrounded by three pristine lakes in the scenic, wooded, mountainous region of the Ozarks in southern Missouri, Branson offers fishing, swimming, golfing, and boating, and is also home to big-name entertainers who present everything from country music to comedy and magic acts in more than 80 live shows daily. If that's not enough, Branson also boasts theme parks such as Silver Dollar City.

ESSENTIALS

GETTING THERE & GETTING AROUND   The nearest airport is in Springfield, 40 miles to the north. **A1 Airport Shuttle** (© 417/335-6001) provides transportation from the airport to hotels beginning at $60 one-way for 1 or 2 people. Reservations are necessary. You'll really need a car here. The major highway into Branson, which is 3½ hours from Kansas City and 4 hours from St. Louis, is U.S. 65 from the north, where it intersects with I-44 at Springfield. Be forewarned that traffic on "The Strip" or "76 Country Boulevard" (West Hwy. 76) is notorious for traffic jams, but a number of relief roads help.

VISITOR INFORMATION   Contact the **Branson/Lakes Area Chamber of Commerce** (© 800/214 3661 or 417/334-4136, www.explorebranson.com) or stop by the Welcome Center at the junction of Highways 65 and 160 for brochures and maps; it's open Monday through Saturday from 8am to 5pm (to 6pm May–Dec) and Sunday from 10am to 4pm.

WHAT TO SEE & DO
THE SHOWS
It all started in 1959 with the **Baldknobbers Jamboree** (© 417/334-4528; www.baldknobbers.com), when four brothers began performing twice a week in a converted building by Lake Taneycomo. In 1968, the **Presleys' Country Jubilee** (© 417/334-4874; www.presleys.com) opened the first theater on West Highway 76. Both are still going strong, offering wholesome, family-oriented country music, dancing, and comedy. They're joined by more than 45 other theaters, many with morning, afternoon, and evening performances. Many performers sign autographs after the show.

Dixie Stampede Dinner & Show   Owned by Dolly Parton and billed as "Branson's Most Fun Place To Eat," this dinner show features roast chicken, potato wedges, corn on the cob, and other dishes served without silverware (you're supposed to eat with your fingers), along with horses, trick riders, races, singing, and dancing. Audience participation in friendly competition between Confederate and Yankee rivals may offend some. 1525 W. Hwy. 76. © 800/520-5544 or 417-336-3000. www.dixiestampede.com. Tickets $40 adults, $24 children. Mid-Mar to Dec daily at 5:30pm, sometimes also 8pm.

Jim Stafford Theater   High-energy comedian/musician Jim Stafford is a great hit with families, with a fun-filled, action-packed show full of music, spectacular special effects (including lasers and a 3-D virtual thrill ride made in-house), and hilarious comedy. 3440 W. Hwy. 76. © 417/335-8080. www.jimstafford.com. Tickets $28 adults, $8.50 children. Mid-Feb to Dec at 8pm, sometimes also 2pm.

Lawrence Welk Champagne Theatre   A tribute to musician Lawrence Welk, who developed light, sweet "champagne music," the first-rate Welk Show features the harmonies of the Lennon Sisters and the 20-piece Lawrence Welk Orchestra playing waltzes, polkas, and big band and Broadway tunes. Shows at 9:30am or 1:30pm feature the Lennon Brothers, performing classic swing music of the 1940s (you can buy tickets with lunch included). 1984 Mo. 165. © 800/505-WELK or 417/337-7469. www.welkresortbranson.com. Tickets to the Welk Show: $28.95–$32.50 adults, free for children under 18. Tickets to the Lennon Brothers $19.95–$27.90 adults, free for children up to 17. Welk Show: Apr–Dec Mon–Sat at 8pm, sometimes also at 2pm. Lennon Brothers show: Apr–Dec 9:30am or 1:30pm.

Mel Tillis Theater   Country songwriter and singer Tillis—who succeeded despite a stutter and good-naturedly capitalizes on it—is joined by a 16-piece band and often by a member of his family, including his talented daughter Pam. 2527 Mo. 248. © 417/335-8089. www.meltillis.com. Tickets $29 adults, $10 children. Apr to mid-Dec Tues–Sun at 8pm, often also at 2pm.

Shepherd of the Hills Homestead and Outdoor Theater   For more than 40 years, this outdoor amphitheater has presented reenactments of Harold Bell Wright's 1907 novel, *The Shepherd of the Hills*, which introduced the Ozarks to the world. The mystery/love drama unfolds on a football-field-size stage with 90 performers, 30 horses, a fire, a shootout, a hoedown, comedy, and, essentially, entertainment for the whole family. The Complete Pass includes the show, dinner, historical tours of the homestead (Wright wrote his novel here), and a trip up Inspiration Tower for fine views of the Ozarks. Daytime activities include homestead tours, rides on wagons pulled by Clydesdales, and horseback trail rides. 5586 W. Hwy. 76. ⓒ 800/OLD-MATT or 417/334-4191. www.theshepherdofthehills.com. Complete Pass $32 adults, $4.95 children, $86 families. Mid-Apr to Oct Mon–Sat, shows at 7:30 or 8pm, homestead park open 9am–4:30 or 5:30pm.

Shoji Tabuchi   This is one of the hottest shows in town, with elaborate production numbers, lasers and other stunning visual effects, an 18-piece orchestra, gorgeous costumes, and the violin/fiddling talent of Tabuchi, whose repertoire ranges from country and jazz to classical and Broadway. 3260 Shepherd of the Hills Expwy. ⓒ 417/334-7469. www.shoji.com. Tickets $32 adults, $21 children. Mid-Mar to mid-Dec Mon–Sat at 3 and/or 8pm.

Yakov Smirnoff Theatre   This Russian comedian gives a side-splitting, raucous commentary on life in America, making this Branson's best comedy show. 375TRv.com. Tickets $30 adults, $10 children. Mid-Apr to mid-Dec Tues or Wed–Sun at 3pm, sometimes at 9:30am.

THEME PARKS

Silver Dollar City   About 5 miles west of Branson, this is the biggest and best of the area's theme parks, featuring a half-dozen thrill rides, imaginative playgrounds, live entertainment at a dozen arenas (from gospel to swing and Dixieland jazz), restaurants featuring traditional cuisine, about 50 specialty shops, and nearly 100 resident craftspeople practicing their trades, all in a wooded, 1880s mountain-town setting. Marvel Cave, the site's original attraction, has 32 miles of passages, which you can explore with a guide on a 1-hour tour (included in the admission price to Silver Dollar City). Plan on arriving first thing in the morning to avoid traffic jams, and spend all day here. Kids of all ages love this place. W. Hwy 76. ⓒ 800/831-4FUN or 417/338-2611. www.silverdollarcity.com. Admission $37 adults; $25 children 4–11. Mid-May to mid-Aug daily 9:30am–7pm; mid-Apr to mid-May and mid-Aug to Oct Wed–Fri and Sun 9:30am–6pm, Sat 9:30am–7pm; Nov–Dec Wed–Sun 1–10pm.

White Water Park   This 12-acre water park features a dozen family rides, a lazy float down Paradise River, a wave pool, lots of water blasters, geysers, and shower shooters at Raintree Island. For the little ones, there's Splash Island with slides, tunnels, nozzles, and sprays. 3501 W. Hwy 76. ⓒ 800/532-7529 or 417/334-7487. Admission $28 adults, $22 children 4–11. May and Aug daily 10am–6pm; June–July daily 9am–8pm.

MORE HIGHLIGHTS

TRAIN & BOAT TRIPS   Departing from downtown Branson, the **Branson Scenic Railway,** 206 E. Main (ⓒ **417/334-6110**), revives the romance of classic rail travel with 40-mile trips through the wooded Ozark hills aboard restored 1940s and 1950s passenger cars. These trips appeal to a mostly older crowd. For a breakfast, lunch, or dinner cruise on Table Rock Lake, board the **Showboat Branson Belle,** 4800 Mo. 165 (ⓒ **800/775-2628** or 417/336-7171), a luxury paddle-wheeler boat offering 2-hour cruises with dining, music, and entertainment from April to December. For a land and water tour, **Ride the Ducks,** West Highway 76 (ⓒ **417/334-DUCK**), is a wacky 80-minute tour aboard World War II amphibious military assault vehicles. For younger kids, an absolute must is the **Sammy Lane Pirate Cruise,** 280 N. Lake Dr. (ⓒ **417/334-3015**), a Lake

Taneycomo attraction since 1913 that features a pirate attack and a chance to help pilot the boat.

OUTDOOR ACTIVITIES Fisherfolk favor Table Rock Lake for bass and Lake Taneycomo for trout. For swimming, go to one of the public swimming areas at Table Rock Lake. Hiking enthusiasts should head to **Henning State Forest** (© 417/334-3324) 1 mile west of Branson, where the Henning Home-steaders Trail takes about 3 hours to complete, or to **Dogwood Canyon Nature Park** (© 417/779-5983), a 10,000-acre private wilderness refuge for elk, bison, Texas longhorns, deer, and other wildlife, accessible by hiking and biking paths or open-air tram. Some of the Branson area's nine 18-hole golf courses, open to the public year-round, are described in the brochure "Branson Golf" available at the Welcome Center. A favorite is the nine-hole **Top of the Rock,** Big Cedar Lodge, 612 Devil's Pool Rd., Ridgedale, MO 65739 (© 417/335-2777). It's owned by Big Cedar Lodge (which does everything to perfection), was designed by Jack Nicklaus, has great views of Table Rock Lake and a good restaurant, and is one of only 11 courses in the nation to be recognized as an Audubon Signature Cooperative.

WHERE TO STAY

Branson offers resorts, countless motels and hotels, bed-and-breakfasts, and many camping facilities. For something unique, try a stay in a houseboat; contact **Table Rock Lake-Branson Houseboat Rentals** (© 800/255-5561 or 417/335-3042) or **Tri-Lakes Houseboat Rentals** (© 800/982-2628 or 417/739-2370).

All the hotels below offer free outdoor parking.

Big Cedar Lodge Spread over 250 beautifully cultivated acres on a hill over-looking Table Rock Lake and owned by Bass Pro Shop, Branson's most impres-sive and classiest resort is a lovely refuge from Branson's congested Strip and is great for families, reunions, and romantic getaways. It offers a wide range of accommodations, from rooms in a rustic and majestic Northwest-style lodge to luxurious log cabins with wood-burning fireplace, outdoor grill, kitchen, and Jacuzzi. Facilities are extensive and first class, including a spring-fed swimming pool, jogging and hiking trails, a children's center (ages 4–12), miniature golf, boat rentals, horse-back riding, a playground, and laundry facilities. 612 Devil's Pool Rd. (10 miles south of Branson at Table Rock Lake), Ridgedale, MO 65739. © 417/335-2777. Fax 417/335-2340. www.bigcedarlodge.com. 247 units, 61 cottages and cabins. $109–$299 dou-ble; $169–$619 cottage/cabin. Children under 12 stay free in parents' room. 2-night minimum stay weekends and 3-night minimum stay summer. Off-season rates and packages available. AE, DISC, MC, V. **Amenities:** Restaurants (3); 2 outdoor pools (and children's pool); health club; 9-hole golf course; 2 outdoor lighted tennis courts.

Branson Hotel Bed and Breakfast Established as an inn in 1903 and located just 2 blocks from historic downtown Branson, this nonsmoking B&B offers well-appointed, comfortable rooms, decorated in Victorian style with antique furniture and ceiling fans but also featuring cable TV and air-conditioning. Innkeepers Cynthia and Randy Parker, who live on the premises, serve breakfast in a bright, glass-enclosed room and, in the evenings, offer iced tea and coffee in the parlor. Guests can relax on the old-fashioned veranda, seated in Adirondack chairs. 214 W. Main St., Branson, MO 65615. © 800/933-0651 or 417/335-6104. www.bransonhotelbb.com. 7 units. $75–$105 double. A limited number of children accepted; young children stay free in parents' room (older children requiring rollaway bed $15). Rates include breakfast. AE, MC, V.

Branson Lodge   Dating from 1960, before Branson's surge in popularity, this motel is one of Branson's most unique—it's decorated in a corny country theme and offers rooms furnished with antique dressers, tables, beds, and other furniture. If you like what you see, you can buy it, as all furnishings in the motel are for sale. Quilts decorate all the beds, and suites have kitchens. Local calls are free. It's about a mile from Table Rock Lake. With a small playground and laundry facilities, it's a good value and offers more character than most motels. 2456 Mo. 165, Branson, MO 65616. *©* **800/334-3104** or 417/334-3105. Fax 417/335-3106. www. bransonlodge.com. 32 units. $50 double; $74–$105 suites. Extra person $5. Children under 12 stay free in parents' room. Rates include continental breakfast. Off-season rates available. AE, DC, DISC, MC, V. **Amenities:** Outdoor pool; small pets only, $10.

Indian Point Lodge   Situated on a wooded point on Table Rock Lake 2½ miles from Silver Dollar City and 6 miles from Branson, this casual, low-key lakefront resort appeals mainly to families with its recreational facilities (game room and marina with boat rentals) and comfortable if rather standard motel-like units, ranging from one-room efficiencies for two people to four-bedroom units that sleep 10, all equipped with stocked kitchens and barbecue grills. Slightly more upscale condos offer the additional luxuries of laundry facilities, dishwashers, fireplaces, and decks overlooking the lake. Nearby and under the same management is Trail's End Resort, with log cabins that sleep up to six. Indian Point Rd., Branson, MO 65616. *©* **800/888-1891** or 417/338-2250. Fax 417/338-3507. www.indianpoint.com. 50 units. $69–$92 double; $100–$145 condo double. Off-season rates and packages available. AE, DC, DISC, MC, V. **Amenities:** Outdoor pool.

WHERE TO DINE

Branson Café AMERICAN   This casual, busy, friendly diner in downtown Branson—a real regulars' hangout—is the place to go for down-home country cooking, including fried chicken and sandwiches. Leave room for one of the famous pies. 120 W. Main St. *©* **417/334-3021.** Reservations accepted. Main courses $5.50–$9.25. AE, DC, DISC, MC, V. Mon–Sat 5:30am–8pm.

BT Bones Steakhouse AMERICAN/STEAKS   Popular with a young crowd, but also welcoming to families, this dimly-lit restaurant/bar is one of the few places offering free live country music nightly. You can chow down on dinner as you listen, with choices ranging from sandwiches and buffalo burgers to steaks, prime rib, chicken, and barbecue ribs. There's also a children's menu. A soloist plays from 5pm, with bands starting at 8pm. 2280 Shepherd of the Hills Expwy. (at Roark Valley Rd.). *©* **417/335-2002.** Reservations not accepted. Main courses $6.50–$22. AE, DC, DISC, MC, V. Mon–Sat 11am–1am; Sun 11am–midnight (weekends only Jan–Feb; closed first 2 weeks in Jan).

Candlestick Inn STEAKS/SEAFOOD   On the other side of Lake Taneycomo, on a bluff with fine views over downtown Branson, this upscale restaurant with an outdoor deck specializes in fresh seafood like grilled lobster tail and aged Black Angus beef, but also has pasta and lighter fare. Lunch features sandwiches, salads, quiche, and daily specials. E. Hwy. 76. *©* **417/334-3633.** Reservations required. Main courses $15–$42. AE, DC, MC, V. Wed–Fri 11am–3pm; daily 5–9pm (closed Mon in winter).

Top of the Rock CALIFORNIAN   Perched atop a mountain with one of the Ozarks' best views, this casual, relaxed lodge overlooks a golf course and Table

Rock Lake. Sunsets are especially spectacular from the outdoor patio. Owned by Big Cedar Lodge and decorated in rustic woods and stone, it specializes in wood-fired pizzas, homemade pasta creations, and rotisserie half chicken, but also offers grilled salmon, Kansas City strip steak, hamburgers, sandwiches, and other fare. 150 Top of the Rock Rd. (at Mo. 65 and 86). © 417/339-5320. Reservations recommended (request a window seat). Main courses $7.50–$25. AE, DISC, MC, V. Summer daily 11am–9:30pm; off season Sun and Tues–Thurs 11am–8pm, Fri–Sat 11am–9:30pm.

A SIDE TRIP TO EUREKA SPRINGS

Eureka Springs was settled in the 1890s as a spa destination and survives as a charming Victorian hillside village with historic homes, winding roads, and antiques and crafts shops.

GETTING THERE   Eureka Springs is a scenic drive across the Missouri border to Arkansas. From Branson, take U.S. 65 south 30 miles to Bear Creek Springs, AR. Then take U.S. 62 west 37 miles to Route 23. Eureka Springs is just north on Route 23.

WHAT TO SEE & DO

Eureka Springs's biggest attraction is the **Great Passion Play,** U.S. 62 East (© 800/882-7529 or 501/253-9200; www.greatpassionplay.com), a religious extravaganza about the life of Jesus. It takes place in an outdoor theater with a cast of 250 people and live animals, and is watched over by the seven-story Christ of the Ozarks statue. Also on the grounds is the New Holy Land, with more than 40 reproductions of structures referred to in the Bible.

Other attractions worth seeking out are the **Abundant Memories Heritage Village,** 2½ miles north of Branson at 2434 Hwy. 23 N. (© 501/253-6764), with 25 village buildings packed with artifacts of yesteryear; and the **Eureka Springs and North Arkansas Railway,** 299 N. Main St. (© 501/253-9623), a restored 1906 steam passenger train that takes a scenic route through the Ozark Hills.

For more information, contact the **Eureka Springs Chamber of Commerce,** 137 W. Van Buren (U.S. 62 W.; © 501/253-8737; www.eurekasprings.org).

Texas

Texas has a strong identity and a mystique that no other state can match. It fought its own war for independence and was an independent country for several years. Its history is full of epic stories of wild characters and unlikely events: the Alamo with such courageous defenders as Davy Crockett and James Bowie; reckless and gritty Texas Rangers, such as John Coffee Hayes; empire-building ranchers such as Richard King; flamboyant wildcatters such as Glen McCarthy; and plenty of desperadoes such as Sam Bass or Bonnie and Clyde. Today, Texas is as much a land of modern cities and high-tech industries as of small towns and open prairies. But both places share a lot in common: pickup trucks and cowboy boots abound, the menu favorites are the same—steaks, chili con carne, fajitas, barbecue, and Tex-Mex enchiladas (beef being the common denominator)—and a good honky-tonk is thought to make for an agreeable way to pass the evening. And, of course, Texas is big. Driving through the state can be taxing; it's more than 800 miles from the Louisiana border in the east to El Paso in the west and roughly the same going north to south. But if you're not in a hurry, you can enjoy one more thing Texas is famous for—its hospitality.

1 Dallas

Dallas is situated in the northeast part of the state, where the Trinity River cuts through a gently sloping prairie. The city was born in the 1840s and became the commercial and financial center for the surrounding region. First cotton was king, and then oil. Now it's a mix of high-tech, financial, and service industries. Dallas is the ninth largest city in the United States. A modern, attractive city, it offers visitors fine restaurants, fashionable stores and boutiques, and a wide range of entertainment possibilities, including concerts, plays, club acts, golf, and spectator sports.

ESSENTIALS
GETTING THERE **By Plane** **Dallas–Fort Worth International Airport (DFW)** (© 972/574-8888; www.dfwairport.com) is a 40-minute drive from downtown Dallas. It is a hub for American Airlines, which offers the most frequent service. From DFW, a cheap and quick way to get to either downtown Dallas or Fort Worth is to catch the free shuttle to the Centreport station of the **Trinity Railway Express** (© 214/979-1111; www.dart.org). There is no ticket counter at the airport terminals; you must ask airport staff where to catch the shuttle. The trains are frequent but don't run after midnight or on Sundays; the fare is $2. **SuperShuttle** (© 800/258-3826; www.supershuttle.com) offers a 24-hour van service to anywhere in town ($20 for one person to downtown, $15 to a large hotel, and in both cases $7 for each additional person). A taxi into central Dallas will run you around $35. Southwest Airlines has its hub at **Love Field,** Cedar Springs (© 214/670-6073), which is a $19 taxi ride from downtown. A few other airlines offer limited service from Love Field.

SuperShuttle offers van service from Love Field at rates only slightly lower than from DFW.

By Train Amtrak (© **800/USA-RAIL** or 214/653-1101; www.amtrak.com) serves **Union Station,** 400 S. Houston St., with daily trains from Fort Worth (trip time: 1¼ hr.), Austin (6¼ hr.), San Antonio (9½ hr.), St. Louis (15 hr.), and Chicago (21 hr.). The Trinity Railway Express (see above) has several trains per day from Fort Worth.

By Car The principal routes into Dallas are I-35E from the north (Oklahoma City) and southwest (Austin and San Antonio); I-30 from the northeast (Little Rock) and west (Fort Worth); I-20 from the east (Shreveport) and west (Abilene); and I-45 from the southeast (Houston). The I-635 ring road (LBJ Fwy.) circles most of the city.

VISITOR INFORMATION Contact the **Dallas Convention and Visitors Bureau** at 1201 Elm St., Ste. 2000, Dallas, TX 75270 (© **800/232-5527;** www.visitdallas.com). When in town, go to the **Dallas Tourist Information Center** (© **214/571-1301**), in the Old Red Courthouse, 100 S. Houston St., in the West End Historic District. Here you'll find touch-screen computer kiosks, Internet access stations, and a helpful staff. It's open daily from 9am to 5pm. The *Dallas Morning News* website (**www.dallasnews.com**) is an additional source of local information.

GETTING AROUND Public transportation in Dallas is constantly improving, but having a car helps considerably. The **Dallas Area Regional Transit (DART)** (© **214/979-1111;** www.dart.org) operates citywide bus service, with stops indicated by yellow signs. A local day pass is $2, $1 for seniors and persons with disabilities. For getting around the center of town, trolley buses circle through the downtown area. These are easy to find and cost 50¢, but do not run on weekends. A **light-rail system** connects downtown with the northern and southern parts of town with stops at the Dallas Zoo, Union Station, the West End, and the Convention Center; the fare is $1. Tickets can be purchased at vending machines at each stop. Buses connect with light-rail stops. A restored **trolley** (© **214/855-0006**) runs 3.6 miles between uptown and the downtown Arts District. It's free. The trolley runs every 20 minutes during the day, with slightly reduced hours on the weekends.

It's almost impossible to hail a cab; call the dispatch or look for a hotel cabstand. Call **Yellow Checker Cab Co.** (© **817/534-5555** or 214/426-6262). The initial charge is $2 per passenger plus $1.60 per mile.

FAST FACTS **Baylor University Medical Center,** 3500 Gaston Ave. (© **214/820-0111**), provides world-class health care. Dallas has four area codes—214, 972, 817, and 469—with 10-digit dialing for all local numbers. The local hotel tax is 15%; the sales tax is 8.25%.

SPECIAL EVENTS The **State Fair of Texas** (© **214/565-9931;** www.bigtex.com), the largest state fair in the nation, takes place from late September to mid-October in Fair Park. The **SBC Cotton Bowl Classic Football Game** (Jan 1) **and Parade** (Dec 31) (© **888/792-BOWL** or 214/634-7525; www.sbccottonbowl.com) are important local events.

WHAT TO SEE & DO

Downtown Dallas is being revitalized and has several attractions worth visiting. These are located either in the West End Historic District or in the northern part of downtown, called the Arts District. In May of 2003, the much anticipated

Sports

Dallas is a sports town like no other. Golfers can contact **Alliance Golf Tours** (© 972/926-9700), which operates a daily scheduled shuttle service for golfers from local hotels to area courses. The cost and range of packages vary starting at $98, depending on equipment needs, location of hotel, and preferred course. Professional team sports include the NFL **Dallas Cowboys** football team (© 972/785-5000); the NBA **Mavericks** basketball team (© 214/747-6287); the American League **Texas Rangers** baseball team (© 817/273-5100); and the NHL **Stars** hockey team (© 214/ GO-STARS). Other spectator sports include horse racing at **Lone Star Park** (© 972/263-7223) and auto racing at **Texas Motor Speedway** (in Fort Worth, © 817/215-8500).

Nasher Sculpture Center will open in the Arts District. It will display pieces from Ray Nasher's vast collection of modern sculpture, perhaps the best private collection in the world. And the building itself promises to be an admirable setting for viewing the collection. A short distance east of downtown lies **Fair Park,** an enclosed area of several city blocks that holds nine museums, the Cotton Bowl, and a couple of concert halls amid landscaped grounds. This is the site for the annual Texas State Fair. Several of the museums occupy classic Art Deco buildings that date from the 1930s. Between downtown and Fair Park is Deep Ellum, the hip old warehouse district with restaurants and clubs. Just to the north of the Arts District, across the Woodall Rogers Freeway, begins uptown, or the McKinney Avenue District, with its antiques shops, clubs, and restaurants.

Dallas Arboretum   The arboretum contains 66 acres of beautiful gardens on the eastern shore of White Rock Lake, just minutes from downtown. The Camp Estate, designed by Texas's most famous residential architect, John Staub, and completed in 1938, serves as park headquarters. A stroll through the grounds brings you to historic DeGolyer House, a magnificent Spanish colonial–style mansion. More than 2,000 varieties of azaleas and 30 species of ferns are on display. Enjoy the wildflower trail and 11-mile path around the lake. Tours available. 8525 Garland Rd. (east Dallas). © 214/327-8263. www.dallasarboretum.org. Admission $6 adults, $5 seniors, $3 children 3–12. Parking $3. Daily 10am–5pm; additional evening hours Mon–Thurs during summer.

Dallas Museum of Art   The collection, from the ancient world to contemporary times, is housed in the critically acclaimed building with lovely and soothing exhibition spaces designed by Edward Larrabee Barnes. Look for pre-Columbian art, modern art (especially American), and decorative furnishings. There is also an attractive sculpture garden. 1717 N Harwood St. (Arts District). © 214/ 922-1200. www.dm-art.org. Admission $6 adults, $4 seniors and children under 12. Tues–Sun 11am–5pm.

Dallas Museum of Natural History   One of nine museums in the Fair Park grounds, this museum displays 60 dioramas of Texas flora and fauna in their natural habitats. For fossil fans, there's a fully reconstructed tenontosaurus, a 90-million-year-old giant sea turtle, and a mosasaurus. The museum also has a children's area that is especially fun. 3535 Grand Ave. (Fair Park). © 214/421-3466. www.dallasdino.org. Admission $6.50 adults, $5.50 seniors, $5 students, $4 children 3–12. Daily 10am–5pm.

Dallas World Aquarium and Zoological Garden This complex—one of the most modern and complete aquariums in the Southwest—contains both a rainforest ecosystem (from the Orinoco River region of South America) and a living coral reef ecosystem. These habitats are home to 350 species of fish, reptiles, and amphibians (not to mention a cool restaurant). 1801 N. Griffin St. (West End). (C) 214/720-2224. www.dwazoo.com. Admission $11 adults, $8 seniors and children 3–12. Daily 10am–5pm.

Science Place An especially good museum for children, this offers plenty of hands-on opportunities to explore in imaginative ways such matters as physics, electricity, space, and ecology. Another plus for all ages: the shows at its planetarium and IMAX theater. 1318 2nd Ave. (Fair Park). (C) 214/428-5555. www.scienceplace. org. Admission to exhibits $7.50 adults, $6.50 seniors, $4 children 3–12; IMAX theater admission $7 adults, $6 seniors and children 3–12; planetarium $3. Sun–Thurs 9:30am–5:30pm; Fri–Sat 9:30am–9pm.

Six Flags Over Texas In Arlington, halfway between Dallas and Fort Worth, is this large amusement park with lots of roller coasters and thrill rides. It is one of the largest parks in the country and draws more visitors than any other attraction in the state. Nearby is its sister park, **Hurricane Harbor,** 1800 E. Lamar Blvd. ((C) 817/265-3356; www.sixflags.com), a water park with pretty much the same thing in mind. In addition there are shows, theme rides, and other amusements. I-30 at Hwy. 360 (Arlington). (C) 817/640-8900. www.sixflags.com. $34 adults,

$15 children under 4 ft. and seniors. Daily mid May through Aug; weekends only in late spring and early fall. Parking $8.

Sixth Floor Museum   The museum is in a building whose former name—the Texas School Book Depository—might ring a bell. It was from here that Lee Harvey Oswald assassinated JFK (. . . or did he?). This and the many issues surrounding the Kennedy presidency and the events leading up to that fateful moment are effectively portrayed through the use of film, photographs, artifacts, and interpretive displays. The corner window from which Oswald fired the fatal shots is part of the exhibit. The museum does a good job of presenting the different findings on the assassination and lets visitors draw their own conclusions. As a counterpoint to this museum, you can visit the nearby **Conspiracy Museum** (② 214/741-3040), 110 S. Market St., across from the JFK Memorial (adults $7). This museum offers much fodder for conspiracy buffs and even has its own "assassinologist." 411 Elm St. (West End). ② 214/747-6660. www.jfk.org. Admission $10 adults, $9 seniors and kids 6–17; audio tour $3. Daily 9am–6pm.

Southfork Ranch   The Texas ranch that became internationally famous in the long-running CBS TV series *Dallas* is smaller than it looks on the tube, and its location isn't quite as rurally grand as you would expect. Yet the site, which operates today as both a tourist attraction and an event/conference facility, still packs 'em in. Guests can tour the Ewing Mansion and ranchland on a guided tram tour and view memorabilia in the *Dallas* museum. There's also a Westernwear store and a "Miss Ellie's Deli," where you can chew the fat about the show's global reach. It's a 40-minute drive from downtown Dallas. 3700 Hogge Rd. ② 972/442-7800. www.southforkranch.com. Admission $7.95 adults, $6.95 seniors, $5.95 children 4–12. Daily 9am–5pm. From central Dallas, go north on N. Central Expwy. (Hwy.75). Take Exit 430 Parker Rd.; turn right and go 5.5 miles to Murphy Rd.; turn right and look for signs.

SHOPPING

Shopping has been called Dallas's number-one indoor sport. Most of the city's shopping malls are north of downtown. **Highland Park Village** (② 214/559-2740), opened in 1931, was the first mall built in Dallas and is still one of *the* fashionable shopping centers, with many boutiques and small shops catering to its North Dallas clientele. **Northpark Center** (② 214/363-7441), anchored by a Neiman Marcus, is doubly notable because developer Raymond Nasher displays pieces from his famous modern art collection throughout the mall. You can get there by taking the light rail's red line to the Park Lane station, where you can catch a free shuttle to the mall. I must also mention **The Galleria,** LBJ Freeway and Dallas North Tollway (② 972/702-7100), one of Dallas's largest upscale malls, with more than 200 shops—including Nordstrom, Tiffany, and Saks Fifth Avenue. It has the advantage of activities to amuse those not interested in shopping, including a skating rink, race car simulators, and high-tech arcades.

Many shoppers frequent the **uptown** area, just north of downtown. On McKinney Avenue you'll find antiques stores and small shops, and in the Crescent development you'll find the upscale department store, **Stanley Korshak,** and several other shops. If you're **downtown** (or even if you're not) you might want to visit the original **Neiman Marcus,** a very popular destination for many visitors to Dallas.

WHERE TO STAY

Dallas's hotels get more business travelers than anything else, and often will offer weekend discounts.

Convenient to DFW Airport are the **Hyatt Regency DFW Airport,** International Parkway, at terminal C, inside the airport (© **800/233 1234** or 972/453 1234; fax 972/456-8668), a large hotel with 1,369 rooms and an array of restaurants, bars, exercise facilities, and shops. Easier on the budget are the pink **Embassy Guest Suites,** 4650 W. Airport Fwy., Irving (© **800/362-2779** or 972/790-0093), near the south entrance to DFW; and the **Holiday Inn Select South,** 4440 W. Airport Fwy., Irving (© **800/360-2242** or 972/399-1010), 2 miles outside the airport, about halfway between Dallas and Fort Worth.

If you are looking for a hotel in Arlington, close to the Six Flags and Hurricane Harbor amusement parks, you have 50 choices representing just about every chain of hotels and motels in America. Eighteen of these properties pay Arlington for trolley service to and from their hotel and the amusement parks and the ballpark. This will save you a little money on parking and is a real convenience; ask about it when making reservations. The nicest lodgings in the area are at the **Wyndham Arlington,** 1500 Convention Center Dr. (© **800/442-7275**), which is located close by both Six Flags and the ballpark. I also like the **Courtyard by Marriott,** 1500 Nolan Ryan Expwy. (© **800/321-2211**), for its location and rooms.

Amelia's Place Not your typical B&B, these lodgings occupy what was originally part of an old factory building. Rooms offer comfort with character, and the downtown location offers convenience. The owner, originally from Louisiana, adds to the enjoyment of staying here and cooks up a full breakfast. Smoking is allowed in the common rooms but not the bedrooms. Rooms vary from small to large, are named after famous Dallas women, and offer a variety of bedding choices. Two rooms share a bathroom. 1775 Young St., Dallas, TX 75201 (at St. Paul St., downtown). © **888/651-1775** or 214/651-1775. Fax 214/761-9475. www.amelias place.com. 7 units. $95 double with shared bathroom; $105–$125 double with private bathroom. Rates include full breakfast. AE, DC, DISC, MC, V. Limited free parking. No children.

Fairmont Hotel Combine elegance and comfort with a great location (between the Arts District and the West End), and the result is the Fairmont. The hotel occupies two towers with a terrace pool and patio in between. Rooms, thoughtfully furnished to make them equally suitable for business or pleasure, are large and attractive in a modern, uncluttered style, with a few flourishes such as granite tabletops. All the beds are extra long. Rates vary greatly depending on availability. 1717 N. Akard St., Dallas, TX 75201 (downtown). © **800/527-4727** or 214/720-2020. Fax 214/871-0673. www.fairmont.com. 550 units. $165–$350 double; $330–$509 suite. Special packages available. AE, DC, DISC, MC, V. Valet parking $18. **Amenities:** Restaurants (2); outdoor pool; health club.

Four Seasons Resort and Club Attention to detail and an amazing array of recreational facilities highlight this impressive resort. The main golf course is considered to be the best in the Dallas area and is the site of the Byron Nelson Classic, while the full European spa wins high praise from guests. In addition, the resort offers racquetball courts, 40 different exercise classes per week, and lovely settings for just relaxing. The grounds are expansive, with rooms occupying a nine-story tower (superior, deluxe, and suites) and separate villas distributed around the grounds. Rooms are large and well furnished with easy chairs and a writing table. Bathrooms are large, especially in the deluxe rooms and villas, which come with a large soaking tub (quite handy, if you've overdone it on the tennis court) and separate shower. 4150 N. McArthur Blvd., Irving, TX 75038 (west of

Dallas off Hwy. 114). © **800/332-3442** or 972/717-0700. Fax 972/717-2550. www.fourseasons. com. 357 units. $320–$360 double; $415 villa; $650–$2,000 suite. Children 17 and under stay free in parents' room. Golf packages available. AE, DC, DISC, MC, V. Self-parking free, valet parking $12. **Amenities:** Restaurants (3); pools (3 outdoor, 1 indoor); 18-hole golf courses (2); tennis courts (8 outdoor, 4 indoor); spa; health club; pets 15 lb. and under accepted.

Hotel Adolphus   The Adolphus is Dallas's original grand hotel, and it certainly exudes the most character. It occupies a classic skyscraper, built when American architecture was at its most exuberant. In contrast is the staid lobby, which holds a lovely collection of furniture, tapestries, and paintings plundered from Europe early in the century during an extended shopping trip by the wife of a former owner. It is the perfect setting for afternoon tea, which is one of the things this hotel is known for (reservations should be made when you reserve a room). Large rooms offer separate sitting areas, fresh flowers, and understated furnishings with large marble bathrooms. Rates vary by floor and size, with best values being the "superiors." The level of service could not be better. Close by is the original Neiman-Marcus. If you stay here, or even if you don't, try the hotel's restaurant, the French Room, perennially rated at the top of Dallas's restaurants. 1321 Commerce St., Dallas, TX 75202 (at Akard St., downtown). © **800/221-9083** or 214/742-8200. Fax 214/651-3561. www.hoteladolphus.com. 428 units. $175–$385 double; $215–$415 junior suite; $475–$3,000 suite. Children under 12 stay free in parents' room. Weekend packages available. AE, DC, DISC, MC, V. Valet parking $20. **Amenities:** 3 restaurants; health club; pets under 30 lb. accepted with $50 deposit.

Hotel Crescent Court   This seven-story hotel, owned by the same company as the Mansion on Turtle Creek, is part of an office and shopping center known as the Crescent. It offers the quintessential Dallas experience—pampering and shopping with lots of frills. In the complex is a shopping arcade anchored by the high-end Stanley Korshak department store. Guests can also take afternoon tea (make reservations when reserving a room as it is often booked up). But it's the Spa at the Crescent that is the standout and is strongly favored by Dallas high society, as attested to by the Rolls-Royces and Jaguars in the parkway. Guest rooms are large and comfortably furnished in a traditional style bordering on bland. They come with lots of extras, including CD players and well-stocked, spacious bathrooms. 400 Crescent Court, Dallas, TX 75201 (uptown). © **800/654-6541** or 214/871-3200. Fax 214/871-3272. www.rosewoodhotels.com. 218 units. $365–$465 double; $640–$2,500 suite. Extra person $30. Children under 12 stay free in parents' room. AE, DC, DISC, MC, V. Self-parking $9, valet parking $15. **Amenities:** 2 restaurants; small outdoor heated pool; spa.

Hyatt Regency Dallas at Reunion   One of the most photographed and recognizable hotels in the world, this complex—featured in the opening sequence of the TV show *Dallas*—is in the West End, near the convention center, and is connected by tunnel to Union Station. Standard rooms are large and comfortable but not lavishly decorated. All rooms have large windows; ask for a downtown view. The bathrooms are medium size and unremarkable. A noted feature of the hotel is the rotating **Antares** restaurant (© **214/651-1234**), sitting atop the glittering 50-story tower. You can enjoy the same view from a bar and an observation deck also on top of the tower. 300 Reunion Blvd., Dallas, TX 75207 (West End). © **800/233-1234** or 214/651-1234. Fax 214/742-8126. www.hyatt.com. 1,122 units. $209–$234 double; $750–$1,000 suite. Children under 18 stay free in parents' room. AE, DC, DISC, MC, V. Self-parking $7, valet parking $14. **Amenities:** Restaurants (3); outdoor pool; health club.

The Magnolia Hotel   A modern hotel nestled into a classic 1920s skyscraper (next to the Adolphus), the Magnolia has a casual feel about it and offers stylish rooms that are contemporary but have touches reminiscent of the '30s and '40s. Rooms are large and have more character than the those of the comparably priced Hyatt. All suites have full, well-stocked kitchens. Bathrooms vary quite a bit but are for the most part large and attractive. The hotel has a full kitchen but no restaurant. The kitchen turns out a breakfast buffet (always with one or two hot dishes) and fresh-baked cookies and milk in the evening, both of which are complimentary for guests (do try the cookies). 1401 Commerce, Dallas, TX 75201 (downtown). © **888/915-1110** or 214/915-6500. Fax 214/253-0053. www.themagnoliahotel. com. 330 units. $229 double; $289–$399 suite. Rates include breakfast buffet. Weekend packages available. AE, DC, DISC, MC, V. Valet parking $17. **Amenities:** Health club.

The Mansion on Turtle Creek   This flagship of the Rosewood group is the hotel of choice for a clientele of moguls, celebrities, and CEOs. Its flawless accommodations and world-class pampering get it regularly named as one of the top hotels in the country; it was recently singled out as the number one hotel for service in the world by *Travel and Leisure* magazine. The large, plush rooms exude comfort and coolness, and the bathrooms are very large, with double sinks and/or separate shower and tub. A large part of the hotel is in the original mansion (built by an old cotton baron in 1925), with lots of sculpted stone and polished marble. It is quite a sight. Many guests make a point of coming here just for the restaurant, which seems to be the consensus favorite for the best in town (see "Where to Dine," below). 2821 Turtle Creek Blvd., Dallas, TX 75219 (Oak Lawn). © **800/527-5432** or 214/559-2100. Fax 214/528-4187. www.mansiononturtlecreek.com. 141 units. $400–$530 double; $675–$2,400 suite. AE, DC, DISC, MC, V. Valet parking $15. **Amenities:** Restaurant; heated outdoor pool; health club; pets accepted.

Stoneleigh Hotel   This 1924 hotel in the McKinney Avenue area near downtown offers distinctive, well-furnished rooms at good prices. Most of the rooms have a king-size or two queen-size beds. Bathrooms are medium to large and attractively furnished. Some suites come with kitchens. The hotel gets a fair number of extended stays. Dallas never looks as good as it does from the hotel's penthouse bar at sunset. 2927 Maple Ave., Dallas, TX 75201, uptown. © **800/255-9299** or 214/871-7111. Fax 214/871-9379. www.stoneleighhotel.com. 153 units. $199 double; $269 suite. Extra person $15. Children under 18 stay free in parents' room. AE, DC, DISC, MC, V. Free valet parking. **Amenities:** Restaurants (2).

Westin Hotel Galleria Dallas   If you're the type to shop until you drop, you should drop into this hotel. The hotel is part of the Galleria complex, so you're only a short elevator ride from the mall. And the hotel has more to offer than just its location: Rooms are large and attractive, with big windows and little extra touches; the beds' thick, plush mattresses are certainly worth dropping on (they have their own registered trademark). 13340 Dallas Pkwy., Dallas, TX 75240. I-635 and N. Dallas Tollway. © **800/228-3000** or 972/934-9494. Fax 972/851-2869. www.westin.com. 431 units. $144–$192 double; $525–$1,275 suite. Children under 18 stay free in parents' room. AE, DC, DISC, MC, V. Free outdoor parking at connected Galleria shopping mall; valet parking $16. **Amenities:** Restaurant; outdoor pool; pets allowed.

WHERE TO DINE

Bob's Steak & Chop House   STEAK   Enjoy great steaks in a classic steakhouse dining room—lots of dark wood and crisp white tablecloths. Bob's is known for its perfectly aged, corn-fed, prime beef, and for his hearty side dishes.

Good salads, too. 4300 Lemmon Ave. (Oak Lawn). ⓒ **214/528-9446.** Reservations recommended. Steaks $20–$50. AE, DISC, MC, V. Mon–Thurs 5:30–10pm; Fri–Sat 5:30–11pm.

Gloria's LATIN AMERICAN   This little storefront eatery, with a strong reputation in Dallas for its excellent Latin American cuisine, draws an eclectic crowd. Salvadoran dishes such as fried yucca, pupusas, or tamales wrapped in banana leaves make for deliciously different lunch or dinner fare. Good margaritas, and several good meat dishes such as the carne asada, make for a satisfying dinner. There are additional locations at 4140 Lemmon Ave. (ⓒ **214/521-7576**) and 3715 Greenville, Ste. A (ⓒ **214/874-0088**). 600 W. Davis St., Oak Cliff, west of Zangs Blvd., near I-35. ⓒ **214/948-3672.** Reservations accepted. Main courses $7–$15. AE, DC, DISC, MC, V. Daily 11am–10pm.

The Green Room ECLECTIC   Deep Ellum is Dallas's vision of its anti-self, so restaurants in this part of town, even expensive ones such as this, look unpolished and askew of the mainstream. The Green Room hits the mark by mixing highbrow and lowbrow trappings in its cozy, softly lit dining room. The menu changes nightly, offering surprising combinations of Southwestern, Pacific Rim, and Mediterranean flavors. The chef also offers a four-course wine and dinner combination called "Feed me—Wine me" that is popular with the patrons. Have drinks on the roof, where you'll get a great view of downtown. 2715 Elm St., Deep Ellum. ⓒ **214/748-7666.** Reservations recommended. Main courses $18–$28. "Feed me" dinner with wine accompaniment $60, without $38. AE, DC, DISC, MC, V. Daily 5:30–11pm.

Jeroboam URBAN BRASSERIE   This restaurant is one of the bold and the few to open in Dallas's downtown area, which up until now has not been known for its nightlife. But success breeds change, and right now Jeroboam succeeds by offering a relatively simple menu of sophisticated dishes and a large selection of wines in a chic urban setting converted from the lobby of an old office building. The menu often changes, but representative dishes are roast chicken stuffed with black truffles and prosciutto or a veal chop with lemon-caper *beurre blanc*. 1501 Main St. (downtown). ⓒ **214/748-7226.** Reservations recommended. Main courses $19–$30. AE, DC, DISC, MC, V. Daily 11am–2:30pm and 5–10:30pm.

The Mansion on Turtle Creek NEW AMERICAN   If you really want to splurge while in Dallas, this restaurant, occupying the dining room of the original 1920s mansion, is the place to do it. It has captured a lot of national attention for its inventive menu of American and Southwestern dishes. Chef Dean Fearing still offers his signature dishes, such as the tortilla soup and the lobster tacos, but the specials always seem tantalizing. Consider the multicourse fixed-price menu for $85. The dining room is an opulent fantasy full of carved stone and marble from Italy and can be enjoyed for a lot less money by having lunch here instead of dinner. 2821 Turtle Creek Blvd. ⓒ **214/559-2100.** Reservations recommended. Jacket required for men. Main courses $26–$55. AE, DC, DISC, MC, V. Mon–Sat 11:30am–2pm; Sun–Thurs 6–9:45pm; Fri–Sat 6–10:30pm; brunch Sun 11am–2pm.

Monica's Aca Y Alla MEXICAN   The contemporary decor doesn't attempt to hide the warehouse origins of this restaurant's large dining room. In this way, it's very much in the Deep Ellum way of doing things. So is the menu. Alongside Mexican and Tex-Mex standards such as green enchiladas and chile con queso, you have unlikely hybrids such as the green pasta with chicken and black beans, pumpkin ravioli, and Mexican lasagna. This restaurant and bar is always popular and sometimes noisy. Thursdays and weekends you can dine to the sounds of live flamenco, and occasionally there will be some salsa and mambo, too. 2914 Main St. (Deep Ellum). ℭ **214/748-7140.** Reservations accepted for parties of 5 or more. Main courses $8–$17. AE, DISC, MC, V. Mon–Fri 11am–2pm; Tues–Thurs 5–10pm; Fri–Sat 5pm–midnight; Sun 11am–11pm. Sat–Sun brunch 11am–3pm.

Pomodoro ITALIAN This popular upscale restaurant, which just relocated into more spacious digs, fashions wonderful authentic regional Italian cuisine. A diverse clientele of young professionals and local celebrities flocks to this jewel, which offers Tuscan-influenced pastas and authentic Sardinian dishes. While the resulting throngs can generate a bit of noise, this spot is worth the trip. Try the swordfish carpaccio. 2708 Routh St. (near Cedar Springs). ℭ **214/871-1924.** Reservations recommended. Main courses $10–$25. AE, DC, MC, V. Mon–Fri 11:30am–2pm; Mon–Sat 6–10pm. Valet parking.

Sonny Bryan's Smokehouse BARBECUE This chain is the first place people think of for barbecue in Dallas. There are six locations in Dallas proper and several more in the greater metropolitan area. A lot of people consider the original site, at 2202 Inwood Rd. (ℭ **214/357-7120**), as special, but we can't tell the difference in the food between it and other locations such as this one in the West End. Sonny Bryan's is known for its brisket especially, but the ribs and sausage are also quite good, and, unlike many other barbecue joints, they do a great job with classic side dishes such as the potato salad and coleslaw. The surroundings are humble, and the service is friendly. 302 N. Market (West End). ℭ **214/744-1610.** Sandwiches $4–$5; plates $11–$15. AE, DC, MC, V. Sun–Thurs 11am–9pm; Fri–Sat 11am–10pm.

Star Canyon NEW TEXAS This friendly and fashionable upscale restaurant, founded by innovative chef Stephan Pyles, incorporates Southwestern, Southern, Texan, and Latin influences. The popular barbecued shrimp enchilada and bone-in cowboy rib-eye are excellent ways to sample the fare. Save room for the monstrous desserts, such as the sinful Heaven and Hell cake. Plan ahead: This eclectic restaurant packs them in, and reservations are hard to come by. In the Centrum, 3102 Oak Lawn (between Cedar Springs and Lennon, Oak Lawn). ℭ **214/520-7827.** Reservations recommended. Main courses $20–$32. AE, DC, DISC, MC, V. Mon–Fri 11:30am–2pm; Mon–Thurs 6–10pm; Fri–Sat 6–10:30pm; Sun 6–9:30pm. Valet parking.

Stoneleigh P. GRILL Across the street from the Stoneleigh Hotel, in the McKinney Avenue area, you'll find this bar and grill, which is the perfect place to relax over drinks and good food. The dining area, with its high, pressed-tin ceiling, whirring fans, and prominent bar, reminds us of favorite food joints from our past. It captures that homey feel. The burgers are made from all-natural beef from the B3R ranch and are top-notch, as are the daily specials such as the crab cakes. 2926 Maple. ℭ **214/871-2346.** Sandwiches $6–$7; main courses $9–$14. AE, MC, V. Daily 11am–midnight.

DALLAS AFTER DARK

THE PERFORMING ARTS The **Dallas Symphony Orchestra** (ℭ **214/692-0203;** www.dallassymphony.com) performs at the beautiful Meyerson Symphony Center, 2301 Flora St. (ℭ **214/670-3600**), designed by I. M. Pei. The **Fort Worth Dallas Ballet** (ℭ **214/369-5024;** www.fwdballet.org) performs at the Majestic Theatre and the Music Hall in Fair Park. The **Dallas Theater Center,** 3636 Turtle Creek Blvd. (ℭ **214/526-8857;** www.dallastheater center.com), designed by Frank Lloyd Wright, presents a 7-month season of productions ranging from Shakespeare to contemporary works.

THE CLUB & BAR SCENE **Deep Ellum** was once the city's blues and jazz center. It became popular again in the '80s and now has the best club scene in Dallas, with the widest variety of musical acts. Outside of a lunchtime infusion of downtown office workers, this area is sleepy for much of the day. But come nighttime, its restaurants, nightclubs, and shops spring to life. Representative of what you'll find is **Club Dada,** 2720 Elm St. (© **214/744-3232**), offering a variety of live acts from blues to hip-hop. **Club Clearview,** 2806 Elm St. (© **214/939-0077**), is loud and attracts a young crowd. Connected to this bar are a couple more that cater to a 30- and 40-something crowd: the **Art Bar & Cafe** (© **214/939-0077**) and **Red** (© **214/939-0077**). **Sambuca,** a Mediterranean restaurant, has live jazz on weekends at 2618 Elm St. (© **214/744-0820**). Close by is **Trees,** 2709 Elm St. (© **214/748-5009**), a cavernous club that hosts the larger alternative rock touring acts. For country, go to **Sons of Hermann Hall,** 3414 Elm St. (© **214/747-4422**), a dance hall (and real fraternal organization) that has live music on weekends—often Texas pickers—and attracts everyone from Grandpa to the kids, from straight-ahead country types to alternative club dabblers. **Blue Cat Blues,** 2617 Commerce St. (© **214/744-CATS**), is Deep Ellum's main blues spot.

A variety of clubs and bars can also be found along Greenville Avenue and McKinney Avenue (uptown). **Muddy Waters,** 1518 Greenville Ave. (© **214/823-1518**), is a good venue for hearing blues acts. **Poor David's Pub,** 1924 Greenville Ave. (© **214/821-9891**), is a dive, but it brings in good live folk/country and other interesting acts. **Red Jacket,** 3606 Lower Greenville Ave. (© **214/823-8333**), is a popular dance bar that goes to great lengths to get the crowd moving: swing dancing to live acts on Thursday; disco/funk on Friday and Saturday, and '80s retro on Sunday. **Velvet Elvis,** 1906 McKinney (© **214/969-5586**), has live blues, funk, and gospel.

2 Fort Worth

Fort Worth is a city of two tales. One is that of the cattle business, which drove herds from south Texas up to Fort Worth's stockyards to be shipped back East by rail. The cowboys who drove these herds were only too happy to celebrate the end of their trail ride, so a number of saloons and other establishments sprang up to cater to their wants. This made Fort Worth something of a rough-and-tumble place and earned it the nickname "cowtown." Today you can visit the historic stockyards district and see saloons, boardinghouses, Western-wear stores, a small cattle drive, and the biggest honky-tonk bar in the world.

The other tale is the story of rich philanthropists who have made their city a delightful place to visit, preserving many of the original Art Deco buildings downtown and funding some great museums (three of the finest in Texas) that belie the town's nickname. With all it has going for it, Fort Worth is a fun place to visit, possessing all the cosmopolitan pleasures of a bigger city with none of the drawbacks.

ESSENTIALS

GETTING THERE **By Plane** Flights to Fort Worth arrive at the **Dallas–Fort Worth International Airport (DFW);** see "Getting There" under "Dallas," above, for details. The **Trinity Railway Express** (© **817/215-8600**) can get you to the downtown area for $2, but it doesn't run on Sunday or late at night. **SuperShuttle** (© **800/258-3826**) offers 24-hour service to downtown for about $24, $16 if it's to a major hotel.

By Train   The Trinity Railway Express offers several trains to and from Dallas Monday through Saturday. **Amtrak** (© 800/USA-RAII, or 817/332-2931; www.amtrak.com) serves the old **Santa Fe Depot,** 1501 Jones St., with daily trains to and from Oklahoma City (4 hr.), Austin (4 hr.), San Antonio (7 hr.), St. Louis (16 hr.), and Chicago (22 hr.).

By Car   The principal routes into Fort Worth are I-35W from the north (Oklahoma City) and southwest (Austin and San Antonio); I-30 from the east (Dallas) and west (Abilene); and I-45 from the south (Houston). The city is circled by the I-820 loop.

VISITOR INFORMATION   The **Fort Worth Convention and Visitors Bureau** has its main office at 415 Throckmorton St., Fort Worth, TX 76102 (© 800/433-5747 or 817/336-8791; www.fortworth.com), open Monday through Friday from 8:30am to 5pm, Saturday from 10am to 4pm. There are also **visitor information centers** at the Stockyards National Historic District, 130 E. Exchange Ave. (© 817/624-4741), open Monday through Friday from 9am to 6pm, Saturday from 9am to 7pm, Sunday from noon to 5pm; and in the Cultural District/Zoo at 3401 W. Lancaster Ave. (© 817/882-8588), open Monday through Thursday from 9am to 5pm, Friday and Saturday from 9am to 6pm, Sunday from noon to 4pm.

GETTING AROUND   Many people find Fort Worth a much more manageable city to visit than Dallas because it's smaller and most of its attractions are located in three places (downtown, the stockyards historical district, and the cultural district), which are collectively known as the Western Triangle. **Taxi** service is by dispatch or hotel stand only (© 817/534-5555).

FAST FACTS   John Peter Smith Hospital (© 817/921-3431) provides 24-hour emergency services at 1500 S. Main St. The downtown area, especially around Sundance Square, has a lot of officers on bikes and is safe at all times. The local hotel tax is 15%; the local sales tax is 8.25%.

SPECIAL EVENTS & FESTIVALS   The **Southwestern Exposition Livestock Show and Rodeo** (© 817/877-2400; http://fwstockshowrodeo.com) takes place over a 2-week period from around mid-January to mid-February. During summer weekends, the Cowtown Coliseum holds **Pawnee Bill's Wild West Show,** a re-creation of the old Wild West shows that toured the country 90 years ago. The third weekend in June brings the **Chisholm Trail Roundup,** with a cowboy parade, barbecue, and square dancing. And in October, the Stockyards District holds the **Red Steagall Cowboy Gathering,** a cowboy music festival. Information on all of the events above can be found on the Ft. Worth CVB's comprehensive website at **www.fortworth.com**.

EXPLORING THE CITY

Fort Worth's **downtown** has great shopping, great dining, and a fun and relaxed nightlife. Most of the restaurants, shops, clubs, and the Bass Concert Hall are located in the **Sundance Square** section of downtown, which occupies 16 square blocks. It's a lively scene with crowds of pedestrians ambling along the streets.

The **Stockyards National Historic District** is 2 miles northwest of downtown, across the Trinity River. The old stockyards and surrounding buildings bring to mind the days of the Old West. Several stores sell Western wear. For high-quality boots, try **M. L. Leddy's Boot and Saddlery,** 2455 Main St.

(© 817/624-3149). In memory of the cattle drives of yore, each morning professional cowboys drive 12 longhorns from the stockyards to the nearby Trinity River to graze, and return them in the mid-afternoon to coincide with the arrival of an excursion train. The **Tarantula Excursion Train** (© 817/625-RAIL; www.tarantulatrain.com) offers train rides from the Stockyards Station to 8th Avenue and back Wednesday through Sunday. Fares are $10 adults, $9 seniors, and $6 children. The same company offers a longer train ride that goes round-trip from the town of Grapevine to the Stockyards Station, but to take this train, you must start and finish in Grapevine.

The **Cultural District** is home to the Amon Carter Museum, the Kimbell Art Museum, the Modern Art Museum of Fort Worth, and a few others. The district also holds the Fort Worth zoo and the botanical garden. Any of these are worth the short trip from downtown or the stockyards area. For attractions in nearby Dallas and Arlington, see the "Dallas" section, above.

Amon Carter Museum   With its large collection of American and Western art, this museum ranks among the premier museums of the state. Holdings include outstanding works of 19th- and early 20th-century American paintings, sculpture, and prints from artists such as Frederic Remington, Charles M. Russell, Georgia O'Keeffe, and Winslow Homer. There is also an impressive collection of American photographs from the likes of Ansel Adams and Eliot Porter. If you visit this museum you can skip the Sid Richardson Collection, downtown. 3501 Camp Bowie Blvd.(Museum District). © 817/738-1933. www.cartermuseum.org. Free admission. Audio tour $4 adults, $2 seniors and kids under 12. Free docent-guided tour daily at 2pm. Tues–Sat 10am–5pm; Sun noon–5pm.

Fort Worth Botanic Garden   The gardens showcase 150,000 plants representing 2,500 species, displayed in both formal and natural settings. A 10,000-square-foot glass conservatory houses more than 2,500 tropical plants native to Central and South America. Especially lovely is the Japanese Garden. Touring the entire grounds takes about 2 hours. 3220 Botanic Garden Blvd. (Cultural District). © 817/871-7686. Japanese Garden $2.50 adults, $1 children; conservatory $1 adults, 50¢ children. Japanese garden daily 10am–5pm. Conservatory Mon–Fri 10am–9pm; Sat 10am–6pm; Sun 1–6pm. Nov–Mar, gardens close 1–2 hr. earlier.

Fort Worth Museum of Science and History   Oriented towards kids, this museum presents hands-on exhibits dealing with the human body, rocks and fossils, medicine, dinosaurs, and computers. In addition, frequent programs are shown in the planetarium and the 80-foot domed Omni Theater. 1501 Montgomery St. (Cultural District). © 817/255-9300. www.fwmuseum.org. Museum $6 adults, $5 seniors, $4 children 3–12; Omni theater $6 adults, $5 seniors, $4 children 3–12; planetarium $3; combination tickets available. Mon–Thurs 9am–5:30pm; Fri–Sat 9am–8pm; Sun noon–5:30pm.

Kimbell Art Museum   A small but nationally acclaimed museum, the Kimbell thrills visitors with a collection of masterpieces ranging in scope from Fra Angelico and El Greco to Matisse and Mondrian. The collection includes some beautiful pieces from the ancient world as well. Another great thing about the Kimbell is that it attracts many of the finest traveling exhibitions in the country. Make a point of finding out what will be showing when you are in town. Allow 2 hours. 3333 Camp Bowie Blvd. (Cultural District). © 817/332-8451. www.kimbellart.org. Free admission. Tues–Thurs 10am–5pm; Fri noon–8pm; Sat 10am–5pm; Sun noon–5pm.

Modern Art Museum of Fort Worth   Texas's oldest museum has just moved into its new building, which increases gallery space fivefold. Now it can show

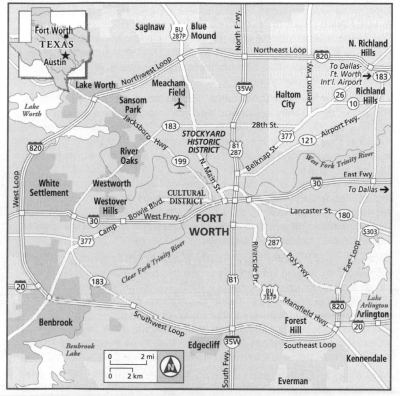

more of its permanent collection, including works by modern and contemporary masters such as Picasso and Rothko. The new building is the creation of Japanese architect Tadao Ando and is unabashedly modern in its use of stark lines and expansive surfaces. It creates a dramatic statement and an imaginative space. 3201 Camp Bowie Blvd. (Cultural District). © 817/738-9215. www.mamfw.org. Free admission. Tues–Fri 10am–5pm; Sat 11am–5pm; Sun noon–5pm.

Sid Richardson Collection of Western Art This one-room gallery located in the downtown area holds a collection of Western art assembled by the late oil tycoon Sid Richardson. Frederic Remington and Charles M. Russell are represented in about 60 paintings. If you plan to visit the Amon Carter, you can skip this museum. 309 Main St. (downtown). © 817/332-6554. www.sidrmuseum.org. Free admission. Tues–Wed 10am–5pm; Thurs–Fri 10am–8pm; Sat 11am–8pm; Sun 1–5pm.

WHERE TO STAY

See the "Dallas" section, above, for hotels near the DFW Airport. Most hotels offer weekend and promotional rates.

The Ashton Hotel A member of the Small Luxury Hotels of the World, the Ashton offers spacious, distinctive guest rooms with lots of comforts such as specially made Sealy mattresses, refrigerators, and large bathrooms. Aside from these features, rooms and suites vary quite a bit. Some come with Jacuzzis ("Romance Jacuzzi Kings" and "Signature Jacuzzi Suites"); others come with large sitting areas or larger bathrooms with separate shower and tub, such as the L-shaped "Signature Executive King" rooms, which are quite attractive. The service is excellent, and so is the location. 610 Main St., Fort Worth, TX 76102 (downtown). © 866/327-4866 or 817/332-0100. Fax 817/322-0110. www.theashtonhotel.com. 39 units. $230–$290 double; $320–$750 suite. Weekend rates available. AE, DC, DISC, MC, V. Valet parking $15. **Amenities:** Restaurant.

Courtyard by Marriott Downtown—Blackstone   Opened in 1929 as the Blackstone, this 20-story downtown hotel offers comfortable rooms for a reasonable price. The location couldn't be better, as it is next to the entertainment district and within easy walking distance of everything. Rooms are large (corner rooms are larger still and go for the same price) and the bathrooms are medium to large, with separate vanities. Four rooms on the 16th floor include balconies where guests can take in the view of downtown. Suites come with a microwave and a fridge. It is a popular hotel, so make reservations in advance. 601 Main St., Fort Worth, TX 76102 (downtown). © 800/321-2211 or 817/885-8700. Fax 817/885-8303. www.courtyard.com/dfwms. 203 units. $129–$159 double; $149–$179 suite. Weekend rates available. AE, DC, DISC, MC, V. Valet parking $10. **Amenities:** Restaurants (2).

Etta's Place   Named for Etta Place, the Sundance Kid's girlfriend, this B&B offers attractive lodging but don't expect the traditional Victorian look; it actually feels more like a small hotel than a B&B. The common areas are large and attractive and mostly modern in style. Guest rooms are large and comfortable and come with period furniture and one king- or one queen-size bed. Service is good and the people who run the show are quite helpful. 200 W. Third St., Fort Worth, TX 76102 (downtown). © 817/654-0267. Fax 817/878-2560. www.ettas-place.com. 10 units. $125–$145 double; $150 suite. Rates include full breakfast. AE, DC, DISC, MC, V.

Miss Molly's   Charming and different, Miss Molly's has preserved the floor plan of the original second-story boardinghouse/bordello built in 1910. Stairs lead from the street up to a large common room around which all the guest rooms are situated. All rooms come with ceiling fans (don't worry, there's A/C, too!) and are decorated in period furniture. Each depicts a different aspect of turn-of-the-19th-century Fort Worth society. All except one share the three bathrooms in back, and robes are provided for guests. This is a nonsmoking hotel. 109½ W. Exchange Ave., Fort Worth, TX 76106 (Stockyards District). © 800/99-MOLLY or 817/626-1522. Fax 817/625-2723. www.missmollys.com. 8 units. $125 with shared bathroom; $200 with private bathroom. Rates include breakfast. AE, DC, DISC, MC, V. Free parking.

Stockyards Hotel   A historic 1907 hotel, the Stockyards has spacious rooms decorated in several styles, all of which take their inspiration from the Old West. If cowhide chairs and mounted longhorn heads are your thing, this is the place for you. The hotel is just around the corner from the Billy Bob's honky-tonk, and 10 minutes from downtown. A saloon-style restaurant serves breakfast, lunch, and dinner. 109 E. Exchange Ave., Fort Worth, TX 76106 (1 block east of Main St., Stockyards District). © 800/423-8471 or 817/625-6427. Fax 817/624-2571. www.stockyards hotel.com. 52 units. $140–$160 double; $180–$360 suite. Extra person $10. Children under 17 stay free in parents' room. AE, DC, MC, V. Parking $10. **Amenities:** Restaurant.

WHERE TO DINE

Angelo's Barbecue BARBECUE   The emphasis at Angelo's is on the food, certainly not the decor. Step inside and you'll find a dimly lit large room with concrete floor, cheap tables, plastic chairs, and remarkably lazy ceiling fans. But the barbecue is cooked to perfection and the beer is as cold as it can be without turning to ice. The ribs and the brisket are especially noteworthy. 2533 White Settlement Rd. (between Henderson and University, near downtown). (C) 817/332-0357. Barbecue plates $7–$10; sandwiches $3–$5. No credit cards. Mon–Sat 11am–10pm.

Angeluna FUSION The food here is difficult to characterize but easy to enjoy. Sample dishes include the flash-fried calamari with a Thai-inspired sweet and hot chili sauce, the lobster dumplings, or perhaps the crab cakes with red chile mashed potatoes and tequila butter. Even the standard rib-eye isn't so standard here, but it will warm the hearts of the meat-and-potatoes crowd. The menu changes seasonally and always offers daily specials. Lunch will cost about half the price of dinner. The restaurant faces the dramatic facade of the Bass Performance Hall and attracts the concert-going crowd. The dining room is quite pleasant—not too large, softly lit, and decorated in a comfortable modernism. 215 E. 4th St. (downtown). (C) 817/334-0080. Reservations recommended. Main courses $14–$29. AE, DC, DISC, MC, V. Mon–Fri 11:30am–2pm; Sun–Thurs 5–9:30pm; Fri–Sat 5–11pm.

Cattlemen's Steak House STEAK This old-style steakhouse is a Fort Worth institution. Its character blends well with the rest of the establishments of the Stockyards District but seems less self-consciously cowboy. There's a lot of rough-cut wood paneling; plain, solid wood furniture; and some vivid cowboy murals for fun to brighten the place up. The steaks are great. Besides the rib-eyes and tenderloin, this place is known for the chicken-fried steak, the barbecued ribs, and the traditional side dishes—all of which are Texas food in its most classic form. 2458 N. Main St. (Stockyards District). (C) 817/624-3945. Reservations accepted. Main courses $12–$31. AE, DC, DISC, MC, V. Mon–Thurs 11am–10:30pm; Fri–Sat 11am–11pm; Sun 1–9pm.

Joe T. Garcia's MEXICAN Behind the small, nondescript entrance is a patio that seats 300 people amid fountains, a swimming pool, and a miniature park. Seating is also available indoors, but it's not quite the same. The friendly and casual service remains unaffected by celebrity patrons. Entrees include beef or chicken fajitas, or a family-style enchilada dinner. 2201 N. Commerce St. (Stockyards District). (C) 817/626-4356. Reservations accepted for groups of 20 or more. Main courses $11–$12. No credit cards. Mon–Thurs 11am–2:30pm and 5–10pm; Fri–Sat 11am–11pm; Sun 11am–10pm.

Kincaid's BURGERS It doesn't matter whether you're clad in Armani or overalls at this venerable burger shop. Recognized for serving some of the best burgers in beef-crazy Fort Worth, this well-known family-owned and -operated restaurant/grocery store has been serving quality food since 1946. Kincaid's half-pound burgers are bursting with sauce and flavor. Picnic seating in front is nice for lunch or an early dinner. The grocery shelves serve as tables for the large lunch crowd. 4901 Camp Bowie Blvd. (at Eldridge, near Hulen Blvd.). (C) 817/732-2881. Burgers $5–$6. No credit cards. Mon–Sat 11am–6pm.

Reata WESTERN Having recently settled in at its new location (where the jazz club Caravan of Dreams used to be), this restaurant has gotten right back into the business of serving hearty dishes with flair and the occasional twist thrown in. The plucky menu characterizes the food as Texas cowboy cuisine, which might be a tad misleading. Certainly the chicken-fried steak and the rib-eye topped with a pat of butter qualify, and perhaps even the smoked shrimp enchiladas, but what about the pecan-crusted chicken breast with a tomato and raspberry sauce? Or the angel hair pasta with Gulf shrimp? Regardless, the food is excellently prepared and is a good mix of innovation and tradition. The margaritas are outstanding. Leave room for dessert. Besides the large main dining room, there's a rooftop section and a quieter basement room decorated to look like the restaurant's original location atop the Bank One tower. 310 Houston St. (downtown). ℂ 817/336-1009. Reservations recommended. Main courses $14–$28. AE, MC, V. Daily 11am–2:30pm and 5–10:30pm.

FORT WORTH AFTER DARK

The **Sundance Square Downtown Entertainment District** is grabbing the lion's share of city nightlife these days. Dozens of dining and entertainment options abound. The most spectacular venue is the **Bass Performance Hall** (ℂ 817/212-4300), the 2,056-seat, acoustically amazing theater designed by David M. Schwartz, which serves as home for the **Fort Worth Symphony** (ℂ 817/665-6000; www.fwsymphony.org), **Fort Worth Dallas Ballet** (ℂ 817/763-0207; www.fwdballet.org), and **Fort Worth Opera** (ℂ 817/731-0200; www.fwopera.org).

Sundance Square's other options include the **Circle Theater** (ℂ 817/887-3040) and the **Jubilee Theatre** (ℂ 817/338-4411) as well as two multi-cinemas. For bars and clubs, you have quite a few to choose from and might do well just to walk through the area until you find one to your taste. For dancing, the main venue is **City Streets** (ℂ 817/335-5400), a collection of four clubs at 425 Commerce St. offering pop music and tunes from the '70s and '80s. **The Flying Saucer Beer Emporium** (ℂ 817/336-7468) offers a variety of music and libations. Also very popular is **The Fox & Hound** (ℂ 817/338-9200), a large, lively, publike bar at 604 Main St. Check out the **Grape Escape** (ℂ 818/336-9463) for its wine list and great desserts.

For cowboy entertainment, go to the **Stockyards District.** There you'll find one of Fort Worth's most popular attractions, **Billy Bob's Texas,** 2520 Rodeo Plaza (ℂ 817/624-7117), which bills itself as "the world's largest honky-tonk." But before going to Billy Bob's, try the **Cowtown Coliseum,** 121 E. Exchange Ave. (ℂ 817/625-1025), which has a small rodeo on Friday and Saturday nights, usually starting at 8pm.

3 Houston

Situated on a flat, nearly featureless Gulf Coast plain, Houston spreads out from its center in vast tracts of subdivisions, freeways, and shopping malls covering an area larger than half the state of Rhode Island. It is the largest, most cosmopolitan city in Texas, and like its terrain, Houston is wide open both economically and socially. This has made it the land of opportunity for many who have come here, which includes a large and varied immigrant population. Houston is also a seaport, the second busiest in the country thanks to a ship channel that cuts inland from Galveston Bay.

A few years back, residential construction shifted away from the suburbs and towards the downtown and inner-city areas as many Houstonians changed their minds about living in the suburbs. They preferred to live closer to many of Houston's main attractions, such as its excellent symphony orchestra, highly respected ballet and opera companies, a dynamic theater scene that few cities can equal, and some tip-top museums. Of less interest to them, but always the most popular attraction for visitors, is NASA's Johnson Space Center, which teamed up with Disney to create Space Center Houston. Aside from NASA, Houston is best known for its oil industry and for the Texas Medical Center, arguably the best in the country.

ESSENTIALS

GETTING THERE By Plane The George Bush Houston Intercontinental Airport (IAH) is an hour's ride north of downtown, with taxi fare around $40. The **W. P. Hobby Airport,** more convenient to downtown, is 40 minutes away; taxi fare is about $25. Fares to hotels in the Galleria shopping area run $42 from IAH and $37 from Hobby. Most major national and a few international carriers serve the area. **Southwest** (© 800/435-9792) has frequent service and usually offers bargain fares.

Weekday **city express bus service** (© 713/635-4000) from IAH (terminal C) to downtown costs $1.50. **Express Shuttles** (© 713/523-8888) go to several downtown locations serving both Hobby ($14) and IAH ($19), and run until 10:30pm.

By Train Amtrak (© 800/USA-RAIL; www.amtrak.com) serves the **Southern Pacific Station,** 902 Washington Ave. (© 713/224-1577), with trains from San Antonio (trip time: 4 hr.) and New Orleans (9 hr.).

By Car The principal routes into Houston are I-45 from the north (Dallas) and southeast (Galveston), and I-10 from the east (New Orleans) and west (San Antonio and El Paso). The outermost loop, known as Beltway 8 (Sam Houston Pkwy.), circles the outer city. Loop 610 circles the central city.

VISITOR INFORMATION The **Greater Houston Convention and Visitors Bureau** ((© 800/4-HOUSTON; www.houston-guide.com) runs a **Visitors Center** at City Hall, 901 Bagby St., Houston, TX 77002 (© 713/437-5200), open daily from 9am to 4pm. It's the most impressive visitor center we've seen, and while you're there make sure to see the Art Deco lobby of the city hall proper.

GETTING AROUND The **Metropolitan Transportation Authority (MTA)** (© 713/635-4000) operates citywide bus service with stops indicated by red, white, or blue signs. Exact change is required. Standard fare is $1; express fare is $1.50. Seniors and riders with disabilities pay 40¢; children under 4 ride free. On average, buses run about every 30 minutes. Free trolley-style buses operate at peak times in the downtown area.

Taxis are plentiful in the city, but trying to hail one on the street can be an exercise in frustration. Call ahead or use hotel taxi stands. The principal companies are **Yellow Cab** (© 713/236-1111), **Fiesta Cab** (© 713/225-2666), **Liberty Cab** (© 713/695-6700), and **United Cab** (© 713/699-0000).

FAST FACTS Ben Taub General Hospital, 1502 Taub Loop (© 713/793-2000), is a nationally recognized emergency center. The local hotel tax is 17%; the local sales tax is 8.25%. Houston has three area codes: **713, 281,** and **832.** Local calls require dialing the 10-digit number.

SPECIAL EVENTS & FESTIVALS The **Houston Livestock Show and Rodeo** (© 713/791-9000; www.rodeohouston.com) in mid-February is the largest event of its kind in the world. In April the city celebrates the **Houston International Festival,** which highlights a particular country each year. It takes place downtown for two weekends and gets more than a million celebrants. The festivities include Houston's famous **Art Car Parade,** which is not to be missed.

EXPLORING THE CITY
THE TOP ATTRACTIONS

Battleship _Texas_ & San Jacinto Monument and Museum The USS _Texas,_ built in 1914, is the world's last remaining dreadnought battleship. You can clamber up to its small-caliber guns or onto the navigation bridge, inspect the crew's quarters, or check out the engine room. It's on display on the grounds of the San Jacinto Historic State Park. It was on this land, in 1836, that Sam Houston and his Texas army carried out a surprise attack on the Mexican forces under Gen. López de Santa Anna, winning an overwhelming victory which led to Texas independence. The battle cry of the day was "Remember the Alamo!" The site is marked by an obelisk roughly the size of the Washington Monument but topped with a lone star, and you can elect to take the elevator up to the observation room, but the view is mostly of the Houston Ship Channel and is not inspiring. In the base of the obelisk is an interesting museum and a movie theater with shows describing the battle. This attraction is popular with kids, who especially enjoy the battleship and all the military regalia in the museum. It can take 3 hours to see both battleship and museum. 3527 Battleground Rd. (La Porte, off Hwy. 225). 🅒 281/479-2431. Admission to battleship $5 adults, $4 seniors, $3 kids 6–17. Monument and museum are free; observation room $3 adults, $2 children; movie $3.50 adults, $2.50 children. Daily 10am–5pm.

Bayou Bend Collection & Gardens   Twenty-eight rooms of the vast Renaissance-style home of Ima Hogg, daughter of a former governor of Texas and local philanthropist, house a beautiful collection of furniture and paintings from the 17th, 18th, and 19th centuries. These are seen by guided tour. Fourteen acres of gardens surrounding the estate can be viewed without a guide; children under 10 are not admitted except on rare occasions. Allow 2½ hours. 1 Westcott St. (off Memorial Dr.). 🅒 713/639-7750. www.mfah.org/Bayou. Admission $10 adults, $8.50 seniors, $5 ages 10–18. Tues–Fri 10am–5pm; Sat 10am–12:45pm. Reservations required.

George Ranch Historical Park   This "living museum" with costumed characters depicts pioneer life in the 19th century. It sits on 400 acres and is a working cattle ranch. Wander through a restored 1820s pioneer farm, an 1880s Victorian mansion, an 1890s cowboy encampment, and a 1930s ranch house. Savor Victorian-style tea on the porch of an 1890s mansion, or sit around the campfire with cowboys during a roundup and watch crafts demonstrations such as rope twisting. Picnic areas are provided. The whole experience is carried off with a good amount of verve, and the kids love it; allow 4 hours plus the 40-minute drive each way from central Houston. 10215 FM 762 (in Richmond). 🅒 281/343-0218. www.georgeranch.org. Admission $7.50 adults, $6.50 seniors 55 and over, $4 children 3–12. Daily 9am–5pm.

It's in the Air

Hot and humid Houston has earned the unofficial nickname of "Air Conditioning Capital of the World." If you are not accustomed to high humidity, allow a day to let your body adjust and drink plenty of water. Despite the heat, you might want to carry around a sweater for over-air-conditioned shops and restaurants.

Houston Museum of Natural Science   Yes, this museum is great for children, but it is also much more interesting for adults than your average natural history museum. The directors have had great success attracting important traveling exhibitions, and the permanent collection is one of the largest and most impressive for natural science museums in the country. Special highlights include the Burke Baker Planetarium, where visitors follow the paths of comets and planetary motions, and the Cockrell Butterfly Center, which houses 2,000 real butterflies flying

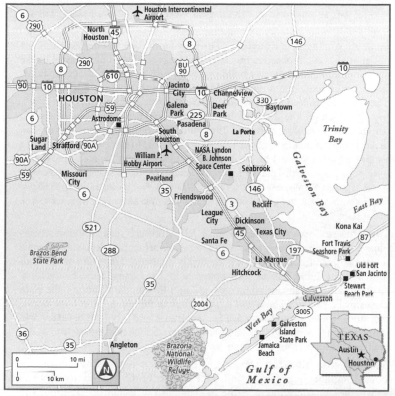

freely in a six-story glass cone. Be sure to check out the "bug zoo" with its live specimens of enormous insects from the world's tropical forests. A casual stroll through the permanent exhibition and the butterfly center can take 3 hours. 1 Hermann Circle Dr. (in Hermann Park). (C) **713/639-4629**. www.hmns.org. Admission $6 adults, $3.50 seniors and children 3–11; Planetarium and Butterfly Center each are $5 adults, $3.50 seniors and children; IMAX tickets $7 adults, $4.50 seniors and children. Multi-venue ticket packages available. General hours Mon–Sat 9am–6pm; Sun 11am–6pm; hours for Butterfly Center and IMAX can differ. Parking garage entrance on Caroline St., $3.

Menil Collection   The collections of this private museum, one of the world's most highly regarded, break down roughly into four sections: antiquity; Byzantine and medieval; tribal art; and the 20th century. This last section, with its large holdings of works by the modern masters, is what garners most of the attention, but the other sections provide many works that can make for striking exhibits. Besides the main building, there are satellite buildings worth visiting. Across the street is the new permanent installation of works by Cy Twombly. Down the block is the Rothko Chapel, with its 14 brooding paintings created specifically for the space by Mark Rothko in 1965 and 1966. Barnett Newman's *Broken Obelisk,* a sculpture dedicated to Martin Luther King, Jr., sits in a reflecting pool in front of the chapel. A block south of this is the Byzantine Fresco Chapel Museum. Because it's free and has easy access, it's perfect for a quick stop, but you might get hooked into staying a couple of hours. It's definitely a must-see.

1515 Sul Ross St. (Montrose). ✆ 713/525-9400. www.menil.org. Free admission. Wed–Sun 11am–7pm.

Museum of Fine Arts Houston   This is by far the best and biggest public art museum in Texas. It occupies two large buildings connected by a tunnel (make a point of seeing it): an earlier building largely designed by Mies van der Rohe, and a newer, more conservative building by Spanish architect Rafael Moneo. The museum's collection of over 40,000 pieces is wide and varied, but it is perhaps strongest in the areas of Impressionist and post-Impressionist works; baroque and Renaissance art; and 19th- and 20th-century American art. Also, make a point of inquiring about visiting exhibitions. In front of the museum, a sculpture garden, created by distinguished sculptor Isamu Noguchi, provides a setting for major 19th- and 20th-century sculpture. 1001 Bissonnet St. (at the intersection of S. Main and Montrose Blvd.). ✆ 713/639-7300. www.mfah.org. $5 adults, $2.50 seniors and children 6–18; free general admission Thurs. Tues–Wed 10am–5pm; Thurs 10am–9pm; Fri–Sat 10am–7pm; Sun 12:15–7pm.

The Orange Show   Former postman Jeff Mckissack spent 25 years assembling a collection of found objects and mundane artifacts to "encourage people to eat oranges, drink oranges, and be highly amused." The fruits of his labor form a unique urban folk-art park, preserved by The Orange Show Foundation. Great for kids and anyone who enjoys seeing a little outlandishness—the place can easily be seen in an hour and is on the way to the space center from central Houston. 2401 Munger St. (off the Gulf Fwy., exit Telephone Rd.). ✆ 713/926-6368. Admission $1 adults, free for children under 12. Memorial Day to Labor Day Wed–Fri 9am–1pm; Sat–Sun noon–5pm. Open only on weekends rest of the year.

Space Center Houston   Space Center Houston is the visitor center for NASA's Johnson Space Center, and is the product of the joint efforts of NASA and Disney Imagineering. It is the most popular attraction in Houston, and there's nothing quite like it anywhere else in the world. The center banks heavily on interactive displays and simulations on the one hand and actual access to the real thing on the other. For instance, the Feel of Space gallery simulates working in the frictionless environment of space by using an air-bearing floor (something like a giant air hockey table). Another simulator shows what it's like to land the lunar orbiter. For a direct experience of NASA, the 1½-hour tram tour takes you to the International Space Station Assembly Building and NASA control center, among other places. You get to see things as they happen, especially interesting if there's a shuttle mission in progress. You might also get to see astronauts in training. Of interest to both adults and children, a visit lasts an average of 4 hours. Johnson Space Center, 1601 NASA Rd. 1 (in Clear Lake, 20 miles south of downtown, off Gulf Fwy.). ✆ 281/244-2100. www.spacecenter.org. Admission (including tours and IMAX theater) $16 adults, $15 seniors, $12 children 4–11. Daily 9am–7pm in summer; otherwise Mon–Fri 10am–5pm, Sat–Sun 10am–7pm. Parking $4.

MORE TO SEE & DO

PARKS & ZOOS   The city's playground is **Hermann Park,** a 545-acre park minutes from downtown. It has an 18-hole golf course, picnic areas, the Garden Center, the Miller Outdoor Theater, and many other recreational facilities. It is also home to the **Houston Zoological Gardens,** 1513 N. MacGregor (✆ **713/ 523-5888**), open daily 10am to 6pm. This 50-acre zoo features a gorilla habitat, rare albino reptiles, a cat facility, a huge aquarium, and vampire bats that eat lunch every day at 2:30pm. The Brown Education Center, open daily from

10am to 6pm, allows visitors to interact with the animals. Admission is $3 adults, $2 seniors, 50¢ children 3 to 12.

ESPECIALLY FOR KIDS   The **Children's Museum of Houston,** 1500 Binz (© 713/522-1138; www.cmhouston.org), does a wonderful job of grabbing the attention and engaging the imaginations of children up to 12 years old. It blurs the distinction between museum and playhouse, and there always seems to be something special going on here.

Houston is also home to **Six Flags AstroWorld** and **Six Flags WaterWorld,** both at 9001 Kirby Dr. (© 713/799-1234; www.sixflags.com). AstroWorld is a 75-acre amusement park with high-tech roller coasters and other thrill rides, shows, and concerts. WaterWorld is a very popular aquatic amusement park in Texas. Day admission to both parks is $38 adults, $23 children. Hours vary seasonally; see the website for the parks' schedules.

SHOPPING

The main shopping area in Houston is called uptown, which includes the **Galleria,** home to 320 shops and a few other shopping centers nearby, along Post Oak Boulevard and Westheimer Road. Also worth visiting are the stores in the **River Oaks Shopping Center,** Houston's first shopping strip, at Shepherd Drive and Gray Street. And, in **The Village,** near Rice University, you'll find several blocks of mixed retail/restaurant space, including a number of boutiques and small shops. The **Parks Shops in Houston Center,** 1200 McKinney St., is the only downtown mall. The **Montrose** area, along Westheimer from Woodward to Mandell, is a jumble of dealers hawking antiques. Let the buyer beware.

WHERE TO STAY

A number of good hotels are at or near IAH, including the **Houston Airport Marriott,** 18700 John F. Kennedy Blvd. (© 800/228-9290 or 281/443-2310), between terminals B and C; and the **Wingate Inn,** 15615 JFK Blvd. (© 800/228-1000 or 281/987-8777). Near Hobby Airport there is a **Days Inn Hobby Airport,** 1505 College Ave. (© 800/DAYS-INN or 713/946-5900), which is also close to the Astrodome and the Texas Medical Center.

Allen Park Inn   The manicured, secluded Bayou Park surroundings offer a buffer from the bustle of downtown Houston at this pleasant, centrally located hotel/motel. The grounds are beautifully landscaped, the pool area rimmed by lovely palm trees. Some rooms offer terraces. Rooms could be better lit but are otherwise comfortable. 2121 Allen Pkwy., Houston, TX 77019 (along Buffalo Bayou between Taft and Montrose). © 800/231-6310 or 713/521-9321. Fax 713/521-9321. 242 units. $108–$120 double; $135–$250 suite. Extra person $10. Children under 10 stay free in parents' room. AE, DC, DISC, MC, V. Free outdoor parking. **Amenities:** Restaurants (2); outdoor pool.

Four Seasons Hotel Houston Center   Close by the city's theater and entertainment district, and even closer to the downtown ballpark, this hotel offers a convenient location. It has lots of space so that you can stretch out in the oversize guest rooms and large health club, but it also offers excellent service so you don't have to stretch too far. Rooms come with modern furnishings and good views to the west. The restaurant is highly regarded as the best fine dining in downtown. 1300 Lamar St., Houston, TX 77010 (downtown). © 800/332-3442 or 713/650-1300. Fax 713/276-4787. www.fourseasons.com. 406 units. $300–$320 double; $350–$2,400 suite. Children under 18 stay free in parents' room. Weekend rates available. AE, DC, MC, V. Valet parking $18. **Amenities:** Restaurants (2); outdoor heated pool; spa; health club.

Grant Palm Court Inn   This motel is a bargain offering attractive, immaculate rooms on well-kept grounds at low rates. Rooms are in a couple of two-story buildings separated by well-kept grounds that hold a pool, a Jacuzzi, and a wading pool. There is also a washer/dryer room, but no restaurant. The hotel is close to both the Texas Medical Center and the Astrodome/AstroWorld complex. As with all hotels in this part of Houston, you must reserve well in advance if you plan to arrive in February, when the rodeo comes to town. 8200 S. Main, Houston, TX 77025 (just south of intersection with Kirby). ℭ 800/255-8904 or 713/668-8000. Fax 713/668-7777. 64 units. $49 double. Rates include continental breakfast. AE, MC, V. Free off-street parking with spaces for RVs. **Amenities:** Outdoor pool.

La Colombe d'Or   If you enjoy the smallness of scale of a B&B and rooms that don't look like hotel rooms, but you want more space, more service, and more privacy, this is the hotel for you. The five suites are extremely large, with hardwood floors, area rugs, antiques, king-size beds, and large bathrooms built of marble tile. Some suites come with separate dining rooms, and the in-room dining is one of the things this hotel is known for. The original mansion that the hotel occupies was built in the 1920s for oilman Walter Fondren. 3410 Montrose Blvd., Houston, TX 77006. ℭ 713/524-7999. Fax 713/524-8923. www.lacolombedor.com. 6 units. $195–$275 suite; $575 penthouse. AE, DC, DISC, MC, V. Free valet parking. **Amenities:** Restaurant.

Lancaster Hotel   There is no better place to stay for those who enjoy the performing arts and nightlife in general. Within 1 block of this property you have the symphony, the ballet, the opera, and the theater, and, when reserving a room, you can have the concierge buy tickets for performances at any of these venues. The hotel occupies a small 12-story building that dates from the 1920s. Rooms are smaller than their counterparts at the Four Seasons, but they have character and a host of amenities. Service at the hotel is excellent and includes lots of personal touches. 701 Texas Ave., Houston, TX 77002 (downtown). ℭ 800/231-0336 or 713/228-9500. Fax 713/223-4528. www.lancaster.com. 93 units. $250–$350 double; $450–$1,000 suite. Children under 18 stay free in parents' room. Weekend rates available, from $130 double. AE, DC, DISC, MC, V. Parking $15. **Amenities:** Restaurant.

La Quinta Inn & Suites Galleria   You can tell at first glance that this sparkling inn, constructed in 1998, is a new breed of La Quinta. A gurgling fountain in the spacious lobby is yet another clue—but comfortable, efficient rooms, free local calls, a laundry room, and close proximity to Galleria shopping seal the deal here. 1625 West Loop S., Houston, TX 77027 (Galleria area at San Felipe). ℭ 800/687-6667 or 713/355-3440. Fax 713/355-2990. www.laquinta.com. 173 units. $99–$119 double; $147 suite. Children under 18 stay free in parents' room. Rates include continental breakfast. AE, DC, DISC, MC, V. Free parking. **Amenities:** Outdoor pool; fitness center.

Omni Houston Hotel   When you're lounging by the stunning swimming pools here, flanked by a lush green meadow, the city seems a long way off, but it's not. The soft, contemporary colors of the Omni's lobby contrast starkly with the guest rooms, which are pictures of traditionalism: 18th-century–style furniture, damask and brocade upholstery, wallpaper, and bedspreads with flounces in neoclassical patterns. The rooms are large and come with a view either of Memorial Park with downtown in the background or of the pools and the lawn. 4 Riverway, Houston, TX 77056 (Galleria area). ℭ 800/THE-OMNI or 713/871-8181. Fax 713/871-8116. 368 units. $229–$355 double; $259–$809 suite. Children under 18 stay free in parents' room. AE, DC, DISC, MC, V. Outdoor self-parking free, valet parking $15. **Amenities:** Restaurants (2); 2 outdoor pools; 2 lighted tennis courts; health club.

Sara's Bed and Breakfast Inn This is a traditional B&B with the full B&B experience, in a spotlessly maintained Victorian home. Located in the Houston Heights, one of Houston's oldest neighborhoods, it's perfect for that romantic getaway. Some of the individually decorated rooms and suites have private balconies, claw-foot tubs, or Jacuzzis. Be aware that some of the rooms' private bathrooms are actually across the hallway from the bedrooms. 941 Heights Blvd., Houston, TX 77008 (between 9th and 10th sts.). ℭ **800/593-1130** or 713/868-1130. Fax 713/868-3284. www.saras.com. 13 units, 11 with private bathrooms. $70–$125 standard; $110–$150 suite. AE, DC, DISC, MC, V. Free parking. No children under 12.

Warwick Hotel At one time the Warwick—opened in 1925—was *the* luxury hotel in Houston. Over the years, it has lost its premier ranking but not its charm or its enviable location on the most attractive part of South Main Street in the middle of the Museum District. Rooms distributed throughout its recently renovated 12 stories have lots of windows and offer good views in any direction. Most of the rooms are large; all come furnished in period-style, predominantly French pieces. The bathrooms are medium in size and offer Bath & Bodyworks toiletries. 5701 S. Main St., Houston, TX 77005 (at Montrose Blvd. in Museum District). ℭ **800/298-6199** or 713/526-1991. Fax 713/526-0359. www.warwickhotelhouston.com. 308 units. $159–$199 double; $189–$450 suite. Extra person $10. Children under 12 stay free in parents' room. Weekend rates available for standard rooms. AE, DC, DISC, MC, V. Self-parking $8, valet parking $15. **Amenities:** Restaurants (2); outdoor pool; fitness center.

Westin Oaks Connected to Houston's Galleria shopping center, this hotel is the right place to stay for dedicated shoppers. You can walk straight from your hotel room into the mall without ever leaving the great indoors. With its 24 stories, the hotel towers above the east side of the Galleria, and from the upper floors you get great views of the surrounding skyline, especially from the north side. All rooms have extra-comfortable beds and are well furnished. Bathrooms are medium size and feature bathrobes. The hotel offers a babysitting service should parents want a night out without the little ones. 5011 Westeimer Rd., Houston, TX 77056 (at the Galleria). ℭ **800/WESTIN-1** or 713/960-8100. Fax 713/960-6554. www.westin.com. 487 units. $249 double; $425 suite. AE, DC, DISC, MC, V. Self-parking free, valet parking $19. **Amenities:** Restaurant; outdoor pool.

WHERE TO DINE

Américas SOUTH AMERICAN While skeptics may grouse that the South American rainforest decor has become passé, Américas remains fun and imaginative with its cuisine. The Pan-American interpretations from the kitchen—be it quail taquitos or potato-crusted squid—feature an exquisite variety of seafood, poultry, and tasty sauces. 1800 Post Oak Blvd. (Galleria area). ℭ **713/961-1492.** Reservations recommended. Main courses $15–$30. AE, DC, DISC, MC, V. Mon–Thurs 11am–10pm; Fri 11am–11pm; Sat 5–11pm.

Brennan's SOUTHERN/CREOLE Fine dining New Orleans style, Brennan's is a perennial favorite spot for Houstonians. The various dining rooms are strikingly elegant and the service is superb. The selection of dishes varies daily but keeps a few classic Creole specialties such as a roux-less seafood gumbo or its well-known turtle soup. Brennan's is also known for is its chef's table, which is located in the restaurant's kitchen. The table must be reserved far in advance and can accommodate between 4 and 10 people at $75 per person. For that price, guests are treated to several of the chef's special creations right as they come off the stove. 3300 Smith St. (south of downtown, just before Southwest Fwy. entrance).

C **713/522-9711.** Reservations recommended. Main courses $27–$32. AE, DC, DISC, MC, V. Mon–Fri 11:30am–2pm and 5:45–10pm; Sat 11am–2pm and 5:45–10pm; Sun 10am–2pm and 5:45–10pm.

Churrascos SOUTH AMERICAN/STEAKS   The signature dish here is the beef tenderloin butterflied and served with *chimichurri* sauce, the Argentine condiment that always accompanies steak. Also very different for the Houston dining scene are the fried plantain chips served at every table, the Argentinean empanadas, the Cuban-style black bean soup, and the Peruvian-style ceviche. Grilled vegetables come "family style" with every entree. For dessert, the restaurant is justifiably famous for its *tres leches* cake. 2055 Westheimer. *C* **713/527-8300.** Reservations recommended. Main courses $16–$25; lunch $8–$10. AE, DC, DISC, MC, V. Mon–Thurs 11am–10pm; Fri 11am–11pm; Sat 5–11pm.

Goode Company Texas Barbecue BARBECUE   Buffalo trophies, snake skins, and stuffed armadillos adorn this very popular cowboy barbecue joint—a prime destination for those who love good, honest barbecue. Jim Goode's crew smokes delicious duck, chicken, links, and ribs. Try the brisket sandwich on jalapeño bread and see if you don't think you're onto something special. The pecan pie is a must for dessert. An additional location is at 8911 Katy Fwy. (*C* **713/464-1901**). 5109 Kirby Dr. (near the Village shopping center). *C* **713/522-2530.** Barbecue plates $7–$10. AE, DC, DISC, MC, V. Daily 11am–10pm.

Kim Son VIETNAMESE/CHINESE   The menu is the most imposing part of this casual, highly regarded Vietnamese restaurant. Don't worry, though, because there are no poor choices among the 100 or so options. Enjoy finely prepared delicacies as well as the expected fare, such as terrific spring rolls and lovely noodle dishes. (The pan-seared shrimp with jalapeños and onions proved a delightful combination.) The menu also features some vegetarian dishes. Look for the exotic fish pool at the entrance. 2001 Jefferson (at Chartres east of downtown). *C* **713/222-2461.** Reservations accepted for parties of 8 or more. Main courses $6–$15. AE, DC, DISC, MC, V. Daily 11am–midnight.

La Mexicana Restaurant MEXICAN   Once a little Mexican grocery store, La Mexicana started serving tacos and such before gradually turning exclusively to the restaurant business. It's well known for delicious Mexican breakfasts and classic enchilada plates (red or green are good choices). There is an extensive menu of tacos a la carte, and good fajitas as well. Service is good, and there's a choice of dining outside or inside. 1018 Fairview (in the Montrose area). *C* **713/521-0963.** Reservations not accepted. Main courses $7–$13. AE, DC, DISC, MC, V. Daily 7am–11pm.

Mark's NEW AMERICAN   Formerly chef at the renowned Tony's, Mark Cox now sets a formidable table inside a refurbished church. The ever-changing menu keeps regulars delighted; selections might include lamb in a basil sauce with white cheddar potatoes or bourbon-glazed pork with yams and an apple compote. Many dishes are elegant variations of American classics that can be satisfying while at the same time providing a sensation of newness. 1658 Westheimer (in the Montrose area). *C* **713/523-3800.** Reservations recommended. Main courses $15–$28. AE, DC, DISC, MC, V. Mon–Fri 11am–2pm; Mon–Thurs 6–11pm; Fri–Sat 5:30pm–midnight; Sun 5–10pm.

Treebeards SOUTHERN   A downtown tradition, this Cajun original dishes out red beans and rice and chicken and shrimp gumbo that'll fly with the best of them. Save room for the luscious strawberry shortcake. 315 Travis St. (downtown). *C* **713/228-2622.** Main courses $5.50–$8.50. AE, DC, MC, V. Mon–Fri 11am–2pm; Fri 5–9pm.

HOUSTON AFTER DARK

THE PERFORMING ARTS   Jesse H. Jones Hall for the Performing Arts, 615 Louisiana St. (© 713/227-3974), is the home of the noted **Houston Symphony Orchestra** (© 713/224-4240). The **Wortham Theater Center,** 550 Prairie St. (© 713/237-1439), opened in 1987, is home to the innovative **Houston Grand Opera** (© 800/227-ARTS or 713/227-ARTS; www.hgo.com), whose season runs September through March. The world-famous **Houston Ballet** (© 800/828-ARTS or 713/523-6300; www.houstonballet.org) also performs here.

The **Society for the Performing Arts (SPA),** 615 Louisiana St. (© 800/227-ARTS or 713/227-ARTS), sponsors distinguished artists and productions from all areas of the performing arts. Educational programs, master classes, and lectures are also included in its regular season schedule.

The **Alley Theatre,** 615 Texas Ave. (© 713/228-8421; www.alleytheatre.com), presents productions ranging from Shakespeare to contemporary plays in one of Houston's most innovative and futuristic structures, designed by Ulrich Fransen.

THE CLUB & MUSIC SCENE   There are many bars and clubs along Richmond Avenue. **Billy Blues Bar and Club,** 6025 Richmond (© 713/266-9294), features blues performers like Clarence "Gatemouth" Brown and Bo Diddley. For country-and-western and all kinds of music, try **City Streets,** 5078 Richmond (© 713/840-8555).

Downtown is now the hottest place to be. **Bayou Place,** 530 Texas Ave., is a large multivenue nightclub and restaurant complex in the heart of the Theater District, with live-music spots such as **Harlon's Bayou Blues** (© 713/230-0111). Close by, in the city's oldest commercial building, **La Carafe,** 813 Congress Ave. (© 713/229-9399), is one of the city's most interesting bars.

4 Galveston

Galveston is on the barrier island directly across from the mainland coast closest to Houston. It is older than Houston and was a prosperous port throughout most of the 19th century. One of its main attractions is the downtown historic district with its Victorian commercial buildings and houses. Another—the beaches—draw Houstonians and other Texans down in droves. Galveston was the site of the worst natural disaster ever to strike the United States—the 1900 Galveston Storm, which killed at least 6,000 people.

ESSENTIALS

GETTING THERE   Most visitors go through Houston (50 miles away). The Gulf Freeway (I-45) leads directly into Galveston. Houston's Hobby Airport, just off this freeway, is the most convenient airport for visitors flying in, though the island does have its own small airport called Scholes Field.

VISITOR INFORMATION   If you're planning a trip, contact the **Galveston Convention and Visitors Bureau** (© 888/GAL-ISLE; www.galveston.com). If you're in town already, check out their **Visitor Information Center,** 2428 Seawall Blvd. at 25th Street (© 409/763-4311), open daily from 8:30am to 6pm during the summer. Another office with reduced hours is at 2215 Strand in the historic part of the town.

GETTING AROUND   After leading into Galveston, I-45 becomes Broadway, Galveston's principal street. Instead of crossing straight to the water, it cuts across the island diagonally, heading eastward until it comes to the coastline at the level of Stewart Beach. Streets crossing Broadway are numbered; those parallel to Broadway have letters, and many have names as well. The East End Historic District and the historic Strand District are north of Broadway between 25th and 9th streets. Galveston has a restored **trolley line** that loops through the Strand District before heading down 25th Street to the beach and the sea wall. After the 1900 storm, Galveston built miles of sea wall along its seaward shore; here you'll find many of Galveston's hotels, motels, and restaurants. Starting this year, **electric shuttle bus** service will loop from the Strand and the harborside piers to the sea-wall hotels and then on to the Moody Gardens theme park. The fare will be $1. **Taxis** are not commonly seen; if you need one, call **Yellow Cab** (© **409/763-3333**).

FAST FACTS   Galveston's hospital is the **University of Texas Medical Branch** (© **409/772-1011**). The physician referral line is © **409/763-4111.** Sales tax is 8.25% and hotel tax is 13%.

SPECIAL EVENTS & FESTIVALS   In February/March, Galveston holds a 12-day **Mardi Gras** (© **888/425-4753;** www.mardigrasgalveston.com) with parades, masked balls, and a live entertainment district. Mardi Gras in Galveston has become immensely popular in the last few years. The first weekend in June is the annual **American Institute of Architects Sandcastle Competition** on East Beach. About 60 architectural firms take the building of sandcastles and sand sculptures to a new level; there are a lot of food and drink stalls, and everybody has a good time. During the first weekend in December, Galveston hosts **Dickens on The Strand** (© **409/765-7834;** www.dickensonthestrand.org), a street party in the historic district to celebrate the Victorian age (Galveston's heyday) and the upcoming Christmas holiday with parades, entertainers, lots of the locals in Victorian costume, and street vendors.

WHAT TO SEE & DO
Popular activities with many visitors and locals alike are to walk, skate, or ride a bike atop the **sea wall,** which extends 10 miles along the coast. The **beaches** are always Galveston's most popular attraction. They may not measure up to those of the most popular beach destinations; the sand is a light tan color instead of white (but it's pure sand without rocks), and the water isn't turquoise (but it's a wonderful temperature). **East Beach** and **Stewart Beach,** operated by the city, have pavilions with dressing rooms, showers, and restrooms, ideal for daytrippers. There's a $5-per-vehicle entrance fee. Most other beaches are free.

Many tours are offered on the island: **Galveston Harbour Tours** (© **409/ 765-1700**) offers a Saturday-morning dolphin watch tour and a frequent harbor tour; **Duck Tours** (© **409/621-4771**) offers bus tours of the island; **Ghost Tours** (© **409/949-2027**) offers a walking tour of the Strand District. On Broadway there are a few massive 19th-century mansions that offer tours: **Ashton Villa,** 2328 Broadway (© **409/762-3933**); the **Bishop's Palace,** 1402 Broadway (© **409/762-2475**); and the **Moody Mansion,** 2618 Broadway (© **409/762-7668**).

MUSEUMS   Except for Moody Gardens and its neighbor, the Lone Star Flight Museum (see below), all of Galveston's museums are in and around the Strand (the old commercial center). Highlights include **Pier 21 Theater** (© **409/763-8808**), which shows short films: one about the 1900 storm that devastated the town, and another about a one-time Galveston resident, the pirate Jean Laffite. On the same pier are the **Texas Seaport Museum** (© 409/ 763-1877; www.tsm-elissa.org) and the *Elissa*, a restored tall ship. Admission is $6 adults, $4 children.

Next door, at Pier 19, is a one-of-a-kind museum about offshore drilling rigs. These mammoth constructions often come to the Port of Galveston to be reconditioned. Since they spend most of their time far offshore, you don't see them often, but here in Galveston you have an opportunity to get up close to one, the **Ocean Star** (© 409/766-STAR), a rig converted into a museum. Through a short film, scale models, actual drilling equipment, and interactive displays, every aspect of the drilling process is explored, including the many rather daunting engineering challenges. Hours for this and the other museums around the Strand are roughly the same: from 10am to 4pm (5pm in summer).

The **Texas Aviation Hall of Fame and the Lone Star Flight Museum,** 2002 Terminal Dr. (© 409/740-7106; www.lsfm.org), just down the road from the Moody Gardens (see below), features restored historical aircraft. Admission is $6 adults, $5 students ages 13 to 17, $4 children ages 4 to 12.

Moody Gardens   This education/entertainment museum is easily recognizable for its three large glass pyramids. The first one built was the rainforest pyramid, which holds trees, plants, birds, fish, and butterflies from several different rainforest habitats. A stroll through the building is fascinating to anyone who has never been in a rainforest environment. The aquarium pyramid displays life from four of the world's oceans: penguins from Antarctica, harbor seals from the northern Pacific, and Caribbean and South Pacific reef dwellers. There is also a petting aquarium for the truly curious. The discovery pyramid focuses on space exploration but doesn't come close to the nearby Space Center Houston. Also of note are the two IMAX theaters: one is 3D and the other is a Ridefilm. On top of all this there are a pool and white-sand beach for children and parents, and an old paddle-wheel boat that journeys out into the bay. 1 Hope Blvd. © 800/582- 4673. www.moodygardens.com. Admission to aquarium $13 adults, $9.95 seniors, $6.95 children 4–12; admission to each of the following: rainforest pyramid, discovery pyramid, IMAX 3D, and IMAX Ridefilm $5.95–$8.95 adults, $5.95–$6.95 seniors, $5.95 children 4–12; day passes sometimes available. Daily 10am–9pm in summer; Sun–Thurs 10am–6pm, Fri–Sat 10am–9pm rest of the year.

WHERE TO STAY

All the economical hotel/motel chains have properties in Galveston, with higher prices for lodgings along the sea wall. Of the big chains, **La Quinta Galveston,** at 1402 Seawall Blvd. (© 800/531-5900), ranks highly; it was completely remodeled this year. Galveston also has a dozen B&Bs, most of which are in Victorian-era houses. The most unusual of these is actually a boat tied to a pier, **The Stacia Leigh B&B aboard the** *Chryseis* (© 409/750-8858; www.stacia- leigh.com). The owners renovated and modified a large yacht built in 1906 for the European industrialist Louis Renault.

Harbor House   A very different hotel for Galveston, the Harbor House is built on a pier looking out over the harbor instead of a beach. It's actually an excellent location, by the Strand District and next to a few restaurants and museums that have taken over some of the neighboring piers. The architecture and exterior design are quite different as well. Rooms are large and well appointed in the modern taste without a lot of clutter. Bleached wood floors, Berber carpets, and exposed wood and steel superstructure are design highlights. There's no restaurant, but there are many restaurants within 2 blocks of the hotel. No. 28, Pier 21, Galveston, TX 77550. (C) 800/874-3721 or 409/763-3321. Fax 409/765-6421. www.harbor housePier21.com. 42 units. Weekdays $99 double; weekends $135 double. Rates include continental breakfast. AE, DC, DISC, MC, V. Parking $8.

Hotel Galvez   Galveston's historic grand hotel located on the sea wall, the Galvez has been thoroughly renovated. The spacious, well-furnished, and conservatively decorated rooms come with marble bathrooms with bathrobes and lots of amenities. You have a choice of "gulf view" (about $30 extra) or "city view" rooms. Prices fluctuate a lot depending on the season. 2024 Seawall Blvd., Galveston, TX 77550. (C) 800/WYNDHAM or 409/765-7721. Fax 409/765-5780. www.wyndham. com. 231 units. $115–$245 double. Extra person $20. Packages available. AE, DC, DISC, MC, V. Self-parking free, valet parking $9. **Amenities:** Restaurant; outdoor pool.

WHERE TO DINE

Seafood is what people come to Galveston for, and there's quite a variety. There are local chain restaurants such as Landry's and Joe's Crab Shack, which do a credible job, but for the best of Galveston's seafood try one of the places listed below. If you hanker after steak, the best in town is **The Steakhouse** in the San Luis Resort, 5222 Seawall Blvd. ((C) **409/744-1500**).

Gaido's SEAFOOD   This is a Galveston tradition that has been owned and operated by the Gaido family now going on to its fourth generation. The Gaidos have maintained quality by staying personally involved in all the aspects of the restaurant; thus the seafood is fresh and the service attentive. The soups and side dishes are traditional recipes that have become comfort food for all the longtime customers. The seasonally changing menu includes a few chicken, pork, and beef items, but seafood rules for the most part. Fish and shellfish are prepared any number of ways: blackened, grilled, sautéed, and more. The dining room is large, with tables well spread out. There is a large bar area for people waiting to get a table. 3800 Seawall Blvd. (C) **409/762-9625.** Reservations not accepted. Main courses $15–$33; complete dinners $19–$29. AE, DISC, MC, V. Daily 11:45am–10:30pm. Closes 1–2 hr. earlier during low season.

Saltwater Grill SEAFOOD   The restaurant's seafood is quite fresh, and the preparation shows a light touch. The menu is printed up daily and generally includes some inventive seafood pasta dishes, perhaps a Gulf red snapper pan-sautéed and topped with lump crabmeat, a fish dish with an Asian bent, gumbo or bouillabaisse, and a few non-seafood options. Situated in an old building on Post Office Street (near the Strand), the dining room has a pleasant mix of past and present, formal and informal. 2017 Post Office St. (C) **409/762-FISH.** Reservations recommended. Main courses $14–$29. AE, DC, MC, V. Mon–Fri 11am–2pm; Mon–Thurs 5–10pm; Fri–Sat 5–11pm; Sun 5–9pm. Parking in rear.

GALVESTON AFTER DARK

This city isn't known for its nightlife. Your best bet is the so-called **Post Office St. Arts and Entertainment District,** which is the area around Post Office between 25th and 19th streets.

5 Austin

Austin, the state's capital, lies in an area of hills and lakes in the middle of Texas. It has a comfortable mix of cyberpunks and honky-tonkers, environmentalists and hedonists. With its leafy intellectual enclave and large university community,

Austin is often compared to Berkeley and Seattle, but its Texas flavor makes such comparisons a real stretch. The city has now passed the half-million population mark and is feeling its growing pains, but the society here retains a leisurely, small-town quality.

ESSENTIALS

GETTING THERE   By Plane   Austin–Bergstrom International Airport (© 512/530-ABIA; www.a-bia.com) is just off Highway 71, some 8 miles southwest of the center of town. Many hotels offer complimentary shuttle service from the airport. The 15-minute taxi ride between the airport and downtown generally costs $15 to $17. **SuperShuttle** (© 800/258-3826; www.supershuttle.com) charges $10 to downtown, $7 if you're going to a major hotel.

By Train   Amtrak (© 800/USA-RAIL; www.amtrak.com) provides daily service from Fort Worth (trip time: 4 hr.), Dallas (6 hr.), and San Antonio (2 hr.) to its station at 250 N. Lamar Blvd.

By Car   Major routes into Austin are I-35 from the southwest (San Antonio) and northeast (Dallas–Fort Worth), and Highway 71 (Ben White Blvd.) from the southeast (Houston).

VISITOR INFORMATION   Contact the **Austin Convention and Visitors Bureau,** 201 E. Second St., Austin, TX 78701, down the street from the convention center downtown, at © 800/926-2282 or 512/478-0098; www.austin texas.org; or stop by Monday through Friday from 8:30am to 6pm, Saturday and Sunday from 9am to 6pm. Or try the **Austin–Bergstrom International Airport Visitors Center,** baggage claim level (© 512/530-6810).

GETTING AROUND   There are two north-south freeways: I-35 on the east, and Mo-Pac on the west. The east-west freeways are Ben White Boulevard (Hwy. 71) in the south and Highway 183 in the north. The central city is bicycle-friendly—many streets have separate bicycle lanes.

Capital Metro (© 800/474-1200; www.capmetro.austin.tx.us) provides bus service throughout the Austin area. The fare is 50¢ for adults, 25¢ for kids. Free 'Dillo trolley buses circulate through downtown, the Capitol Complex, and the University of Texas campus; the orange 'Dillo is a good choice for those wishing to see the sights of central Austin.

Among the major cab companies are **Austin Cab** (© 512/478-2222) and **Roy's Taxi** (© 512/482-0000). It's $1.50 for the flag-drop fee, $1.75 for each additional mile.

FAST FACTS   The **Medical Exchange** (© 512/458-1121) has a physician referral service. **Brackenridge Hospital,** 601 E. 15th St. (© 512/324-7000), has emergency-care facilities. **Walgreens** at Capitol Plaza, I-35 and Cameron Road (© 512/452-9452), is open 24 hours. The tax on hotel rooms is 15%. Sales tax, added to restaurant bills as well as to other purchases, is 8.25%.

SPECIAL EVENTS & FESTIVALS   Around the third week of March, the Austin Music Awards kick off the acclaimed **South by Southwest (SXSW) Music & Media Conference** (© 512/467-7979; www.sxsw.com). The event schedules dozens of concerts at a variety of venues—all in a 5-day period.

Around June 19, Austin celebrates the **Juneteenth Freedom Festival** (© 512/933-0140), a celebration of African-American emancipation featuring parades, a jazz and blues festival, gospel singing, a rap competition, and a children's rodeo and carnival.

Mariachis and folk dancers, Tex-Mex *conjunto* and Tejano music, as well as fajitas, piñatas, and clowns, help celebrate **Mexican Independence Day** at the Fiesta Gardens (© 512/476-3868) on the 4 days around September 16.

WHAT TO SEE & DO

A lot of Austin life revolves around the local campus of the **University of Texas,** roughly bounded by Guadalupe and I-35, Martin Luther King Jr. Boulevard and 26th Street (© 512/471-3434). With 50,000 students, it is the largest university in the country. The special collections of the **Harry Ransom Center (HRC)** on 21st and Guadalupe streets (© 512/471-8944) contain approximately a million rare books, 36 million manuscripts, five million photographs, and more than 100,000 works of art, including a Gutenberg Bible, paintings by Diego Rivera and Frida Kahlo, and the original manuscript of *Death of a Salesman.* The gallery of the HRC is closed for remodeling and is due to open in March of 2003. Another great museum worth visiting is the **Jack S. Blanton Museum of Art** (© 512/471-7324) at the corner of San Jacinto and 23rd Street. It is one of the best university art museums in the United States, with an especially good Latin American collection. Another thing to do while on campus is take in the sights from atop the University of Texas Tower. The only way to do so is by guided tour, which costs $3. Hours for the tour are irregular; call © 877/475-6633 to book the tour in advance.

PBS's longest-running show, *Austin City Limits,* has showcased major country-and-western talent. It's taped live August through February at KLRU-TV (© 512/475-9077). Free tickets are distributed on a first-come, first-served basis, on the day of the taping.

Barton Springs Pool   The Native Americans who settled near here believed these waters had spiritual powers, and today's residents still place their faith in them. Each day approximately 32 million gallons of water from the underground Edwards Aquifer flow to the surface. Although the original limestone bottom remains, concrete was added to the banks to form uniform sides to what is now a swimming pool of about 1,000 feet by 125 feet. A large bathhouse offers changing facilities. Zilker Park, 2201 Barton Springs Rd. © 512/867-3080. Admission $2.50 adults Mon–Fri, $3 adults Sat–Sun; $1 students and children 12–17, 50¢ children 11 and under, free to all Nov to mid-Mar. Open daily 5am–10pm except during pool maintenance (Mon and Thurs from 7:30pm mid-Mar to Oct; Mon 10am–5pm Nov to mid-Mar). Lifeguard on duty Sept–May 9am–dusk; June–Aug 9am–10pm. Bus: 30 (Barton Creek Square).

Hanging Out at the Bat Bridge

In the evening hours between March and November, you're likely to see crowds of people standing on or under the Congress Avenue Bridge waiting for one of the city's star attractions to begin. At some point in the 1980s, a Mexican freetail bat discovered that the underside of the bridge made a good hideout during daylight hours. After only a short time, he and a million of his closest friends were hanging out under the bridge on a regular basis and—voilá!—an instant tourist attraction, as well as an easy way of keeping the local mosquito population under control, was born. The bats time their flights according to weather and feeding conditions; sometimes they leave early and you can get a good look; sometimes they leave later when there's less light. The best thing to do is call the **Bat Hotline** (© 512/416-5700) for their projected departure time.

Downtown Austin

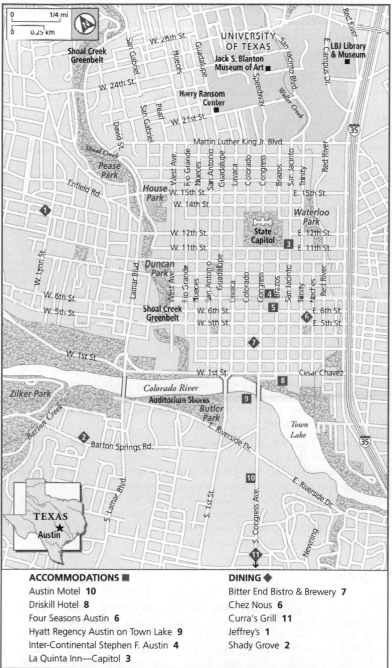

ACCOMMODATIONS ■
Austin Motel **10**
Driskill Hotel **8**
Four Seasons Austin **6**
Hyatt Regency Austin on Town Lake **9**
Inter-Continental Stephen F. Austin **4**
La Quinta Inn—Capitol **3**

DINING ◆
Bitter End Bistro & Brewery **7**
Chez Nous **6**
Curra's Grill **11**
Jeffrey's **1**
Shady Grove **2**

The Bob Bullock Texas State History Museum   To enjoy this museum you must make allowances for Texas chauvinism. Our first impression of it had us worried. The building looks grandiose for a history museum—with lots of polished granite, a mammoth lone star of bronze in front, and a dramatic domed entrance chamber. Yet another act of self-aggrandizement of the state? No. Actually, the collection (all three floors of it) is thoughtfully put together and focuses on social history rather than the spinning of myths and the worship of heroes. It is also state-of-the-art in its use of multimedia. Also in the museum are a 3-D IMAX theater and a special effects theater called Texas Spirit Theater, which is more along the lines suggested by the building's architecture. 1800 N. Congress Ave. ✆ 512/936-8746. www.thestoryoftexas.com. Admission to exhibits: $5 adults, $4.25 seniors, free for ages 18 and under. IMAX: $6.50 adults, $5.50 seniors, $4.50 youths 18 and under. Texas Spirit Theater: $5 adults, $4 seniors, $3.50 youths 18 and under. Mon–Sat 9am–6pm; Sun noon–6pm. Check website for IMAX showtimes.

Lady Bird Johnson Wildflower Center   Founded by Lady Bird Johnson in 1982, the center is dedicated to the study and preservation of native plants. The main attractions are naturally the display gardens—including one designed to attract butterflies—and the wildflower-filled meadow, but the native stone architecture of the visitor center and observation tower is attention-grabbing, too. 4801 La Crosse Ave. ✆ 512/292-4200. www.wildflower.org. Admission $5 adults, $4 students and seniors 60 and older, free for children 4 and under. Tues–Sun 9am–5:30pm. Take Loop 1 (Mo-Pac) south to Slaughter Lane; drive ⁴/₅ mile to La Crosse Ave.

LBJ Library and Museum   Set on a hilltop commanding an impressive campus view, the LBJ Library contains some 45 million documents relating to the colorful 36th president, along with gifts, memorabilia, and other historical objects. Johnson's large cartoon collection (even with him as the target) is one of the museum's most interesting rotating exhibits. Adults and kids alike are riveted by an animatronic version of LBJ, which looks eerily alive from afar. University of Texas, 2313 Red River. ✆ 512/916-5136. www.lbjlib.utexas.edu. Free admission. Daily 9am–5pm. Bus: Convention Center/U.T. Campus 'Dillo, U.T. Shuttle.

State Capitol   Constructed of pink granite in the usual Renaissance Revival style, this is the largest state capitol building in the country. It has an impressive dome that, though smaller than the U.S. Capitol's dome, is still a few feet taller. A striking new underground annex, which connects the capitol and four other state buildings by tunnels, was added in the mid-1990s. Take the tour, which is engaging for some of the oddities and tidbits you learn. 11th and Congress sts. ✆ 512/463-0063. Free admission. Mon–Fri 6am–10pm; Sat–Sun 9am–8pm. Free 45-min. guided tours every 15 min. Mon–Fri 8:30am–4:15pm; Sat–Sun 9:30am–4:15pm. Bus: All 3 'Dillo lines.

SHOPPING

Specialty shops and art galleries are slowly filtering back to the renovated 19th-century buildings along **Sixth Street** and **Congress Avenue.** Bargain hunters head out to the huge collections of factory outlet stores in **San Marcos** (26 miles south of Austin, Exit 200 on I-35) and **New Braunfels** (16 miles south of San Marcos). Little enclaves offering more intimate retail experiences can be found in the **West End** on Sixth Street west of Lamar and, nearby, north of 12th Street and West Lynn. Below Town Lake, **South Congress Avenue,** from Riverside south to Annie Street, has long been a fun place to seek vintage clothing and antiques.

WHERE TO STAY

Favorite affordable chain hotel deals include the **La Quinta Inn–Capitol**, 300 E. 11th St. ((*C*) **800/NU-ROOMS** or 512/476-1166), practically on the grounds of the state capitol; and the **Courtyard by Marriott**, 5660 N. I-35 ((*C*) **800/321-2211** or 512/458-2340), which stands out from many of the other drab chain motels along this stretch of the highway. If you need a room for the night, however, know that I-35 is a good hunting ground, lined with representatives of all the major national chains.

Austin Motel   A convenient (but not quiet) location in the hip new area just south of downtown, and reasonable rates are the reasons to stay at this motel, which has been run by the same family for more than 5 decades. Others are a classic kidney-shaped pool, a coin-op laundromat, free coffee in the lobby (donuts too, on Sun), and El Sol y La Luna, a good Mexican restaurant that's popular on weekend mornings. Ask to see the rooms—all are different and some are more recently renovated. 1220 S. Congress Ave., Austin, TX 78704. (*C*) and fax **512/441-1157.** www.austinmotel.com. 41 units. $65–$90 double; $107 suite. AE, DC, DISC, MC, V. Free parking. **Amenities:** Restaurant; outdoor pool.

Brook House   You get a great deal on sunny, appealing quarters at this immaculate but homey bed-and-breakfast, which is housed in a 1922 colonial revival–style home. The main house contains three lovely but simple rooms—two with their own screened porches and all with antique furnishings. A romantic private cottage has its own kitchen and sitting deck, as does the lower of the two bedrooms in the separate carriage house. On nice days, a full breakfast is served outside on the peaceful covered patio. 609 W. 33rd St., Austin, TX 78705. (*C*) **512/459-0534.** www.governorsinnaustin.com. 6 units. $85–$129 double. Rates include full breakfast. Lower weekday rates sometimes available Sun–Thurs. On-street parking. AE, DC, DISC, MC, V.

Driskill Hotel   Austin's original grand hotel, the Driskill has been renovated with a loving touch and is easily the most eye-catching hotel in town. It offers guests a choice between rooms in the original 1886 building (labeled "historic") or in the 1928 addition ("traditional"). Because the standard "traditionals" are both a little larger and cheaper, they are the better deal, especially those on the 12th floor, which have higher ceilings. Rooms are well lit, distinctively decorated, and furnished with period pieces. Bathrooms in both buildings are attractive and come with several amenities, including plush bathrobes. Note that some of the bathrooms in the king rooms are small. If you want to stay in the original building, consider the deluxe rooms called "senates," "premiers," or "balconies." Though they are quite comfortable, some of the rooms with balconies can be a little noisy since many are above Sixth Street. 604 Brazos St., Austin, TX 78701 (downtown, at Sixth St.). (*C*) **800/252-9367** or 512/474-5911. Fax 512/474-2214. www.driskillhotel. com. 188 units. $270–$290 double; $300–$340 deluxe; $450–$2,500 suite. Weekend rates available. AE, DC, DISC, MC, V. Valet parking $17. **Amenities:** Restaurants (2); health club.

Four Seasons Austin   Queen Elizabeth, Prince Charles, and King Philip of Spain have all bedded down in this, the most deluxe hotel on Town Lake. Polished sandstone floors, a cowhide sofa, horn lamps, and an elk head hanging over the fireplace in the lobby remind you you're in Texas, but airy, well-equipped rooms look European country elegant, with amenities such as CD players, terry bathrobes, and DVD players on request. Lake-view rooms cost more. You can gaze out at the lake over cocktails in the Lobby Lounge, which serves hors d'oeuvres from midday until the wee hours. Some of the best bat-watching in the city draws diners to vie for seating at dusk. Work off your meals at one of the best health clubs in town. 98 San Jacinto Blvd., Austin, TX 78701. ℂ 800/332-3442 or 512/478-4500. Fax 512/478-3117. www.fourseasons.com. 291 units. $240–$350 double; $395–$1,400 suite. Weekend rates sometimes available. Romance packages available. AE, DC, DISC, MC, V. Self-parking $10, valet parking $15. **Amenities:** Restaurant; outdoor pool; spa; health club; small pets welcome at no extra charge.

Hyatt Regency Austin on Town Lake   You'll enjoy lake views with stunning city backdrops at this choice on Town Lake's south shore, but it's the outdoor recreation that makes the hotel tick. Bat tours and other Town Lake excursions depart from a private dock, which also rents paddleboats and canoes; guests can rent mountain bikes for the hike-and-bike trail, right outside the door. Guest rooms are large and modern in decoration; the most sought-after are on the upper floors facing the lake. Bathrooms are medium in size. 208 Barton Springs Rd., Austin, TX 78704. ℂ 800/233-1234 or 512/477-1234. Fax 512/480-2069. www.hyatt.com. 447 units. $210–$230 double; $295–$600 suite. Weekend specials, corporate rates, and state-government rates available. AE, DC, DISC, MC, V. Self-parking $8, valet parking $12. **Amenities:** Restaurant; outdoor pool; health club.

Inter-Continental Stephen F. Austin   A convenient location, the character of an old hotel, and the comfort produced from a thorough renovation make this hotel a great choice for getting to know Austin. All the rooms are well equipped with amenities such as bathrobes, CD players, and down comforters. Standard rooms are medium to large; deluxe rooms are extra large and the most popular rooms in the hotel. Bathrooms are very attractive, roomy, and well lit. One of the delights of staying here is having a drink at the second-story bar overlooking Congress Avenue, but get there early because it has become very popular with the locals. 701 Congress Ave., Austin, TX 78701 (downtown). ℂ 512/457-8800. Fax 512/457-8896. www.austin.interconti.com. 189 units. $179–$239 standard; $199–$259 deluxe; $375–$2,000 suite. AE, DC, DISC, MC, V. Valet parking $17. **Amenities:** Restaurants (2); indoor pool; spa; health club .

WHERE TO DINE

Bitter End Bistro & Brewery NEW AMERICAN/MEDITERRANEAN The food is as good as the beer at this brewpub—and the beer is very good indeed, especially the smooth, light E-Z Wheat and the Imperial Stout. This renovated downtown warehouse is all tall windows, brick walls, and galvanized metal light fixtures. Pizzas, topped with such ingredients as jerked chicken, provolone, and goat cheese, are imaginative. So are the main courses, which fuse Mediterranean, American, and Asian ingredients and cooking styles. 311 Colorado St. ℂ 512/478-2337. Reservations accepted for 6 or more only. Pizzas $9–$11; main courses $13–$23; Sun and Mon fixed-price dinner $15 and $17. AE, DC, DISC, MC, V. Mon–Fri 11:30am–10:30pm; Sat 5–11pm; Sun 5–10:30pm.

Chez Nous FRENCH   Just around the corner from the Sixth Street action, this intimate little restaurant sports lace curtains, fresh flowers in anisette bottles, and Folies Bergère posters. The real bargain is the menu du jour, with a choice of soup, salad, or paté; one of three designated entrees; and crème caramel, chocolate mousse, or brie for dessert. Everything from the patés to the profiteroles is made on the premises. 510 Neches St. ℂ 512/473-2413. Reservations accepted only for 6 or more. Main courses $16–$27; menu du jour $21. AE, DC, MC, V. Tues–Fri 11:45am–2pm and 6–10:30pm; Sat–Sun 6–10:30pm.

Curra's Grill INTERIOR MEXICAN   This crowded restaurant serves up the best regional Mexican food in South Austin. A couple of breakfast tacos and a cup of special Mexican dark roast coffee are a great way to jump-start your day. The chiles rellenos topped with cream pecan sauce make a super dinner entree, but if you would like something lighter, try one of the fish dishes. The tamales are excellent here, and the margaritas are tops. 614 E. Oltorf. (512/444-0012. Reservations not accepted. Main courses $7–$15. AE, DC, DISC, MC, V. Sun–Thurs 7am–10pm; Fri–Sat 7am–11pm.

Fonda San Miguel MEXICAN   The beautifully lit dining room, with its carved wooden doors, colorful paintings, and live ficus tree, is a gorgeous backdrop to the food. The original chef, Miguel Ravago, is back and the food has improved tremendously. The menu offers up such interesting appetizers as Veracruz-style ceviche or quesadillas with *huitlacoche* (a corn fungus). *Conchinita pibil,* pork baked in banana leaves, is one of the Yucatán offerings—very good, as is the traditional mole poblano. The restaurant is famous for its mammoth Sunday brunches. 2330 W. North Loop. (512/459-4121. Reservations recommended. Main courses $15–$23. AE, DC, DISC, MC, V. Mon–Thurs 5–9:30pm; Fri–Sat 5–10:30pm. Sun brunch 11:30am–2pm.

Jeffrey's NEW AMERICAN   In a setting of soft tones and soft lighting, executive chef David Garrido designs dishes known for their creative combinations of flavors and textures. Among the appetizers are a wonderful goose liver paté served with mustard and blueberries, and oysters and crunchy yucca chips topped with honey garlic butter. The menu changes all the time, but on a recent trip, Jamaican beef and marinated scallops with mushrooms (yes, one dish) was among the tempting entrees. Desserts such as Chocolate Intemperance live up to their rich promise, and the wine list is outstanding. 1204 W. Lynn. (512/477-5584. Reservations advised. Main courses $22–$32. AE, DC, DISC, MC, V. Mon–Thurs 6–10pm; Fri–Sat 5:30–10:30pm; Sun 5–9:30pm.

The Salt Lick BARBECUE   Driftwood is a bit out of town, but the barbecue is worth it. From Austin, take Mo-Pac south, which becomes the Mo-Pac extension (45); this dead-ends at FM 1826. Turn left and go 7 miles to The Salt Lick, which will be on your right. Moist spare ribs, brisket, sausage, and chicken, as well as terrific homemade pickles, make for a glorious meal. Bring your own drinks. In warm weather, seating is outside at picnic tables under live oak trees; in winter, fireplaces blaze in a series of large, rustic rooms. The Salt Lick prides itself on its sauce, which has a sweet-and-sour tang. *Note:* Check out The Salt Lick's airport concession! 18300 FM 1826, Driftwood. (512/858-4959 or 888/SALT-LICK (mail order). Reservations not accepted. Main courses $14 for the all-you-can-eat "family style"; $10 for barbecue plates. No credit cards. Daily 11am–10pm.

Shady Grove TEX-AMERICAN   When you crave something spicy, Shady Grove's Airstream chili, cooked with 10 different peppers, might be just the thing. Try a Frito pie (chili in a corn-chip bowl), a burger, or the tortilla-fried queso catfish. Large salads—among them noodles with Asian vegetables—or the hippie sandwich (grilled eggplant, veggies, and cheese) will satisfy less hearty appetites. The inside dining area, with its Texas kitsch roadhouse decor and cushy booths, is plenty comfortable, but most people head for the large, tree-shaded patio when the weather permits. 1624 Barton Springs Rd. (512/474-9991. Reservations not accepted. Main courses $7–$12. AE, DC, DISC, MC, V. Sun–Thurs 11am–10:30pm; Fri–Sat 11am–11pm.

AUSTIN AFTER DARK

Live-music freaks in Austin enjoy a scene that rivals those of Seattle and Nashville, while culture vultures have local access to everything from classic lyric opera to high-tech modern dance. The best sources for what's on around town are the *Austin Chronicle* and *XLent,* the entertainment supplement of the *Austin-American Statesman;* both are free and available in hundreds of outlets every Thursday. If all you want to do is explore the nightlife, you should try two places: the well-known **Sixth Street,** which attracts patrons of all ages to bars and clubs with all kinds of music; and, across Congress and just a couple of blocks south, the **Warehouse District,** where you'll find large numbers of young professionals and an eclectic collection of bars.

The **Ticketmaster** number for the University of Texas, the locus for most of the city's performing-arts events, is (© **512/477-6060. The Box Office** (© **512/ 454-8497;** www.austix.com) handles phone charges for many of the smaller theaters in Austin as well as half-price ticket sales (© **512/454-4253**).

The **Continental Club,** 1315 S. Congress Ave. (© **512/441-2444**), is a not-to-be-missed Austin classic. Although Willie Nelson and crossover C&W bands such as the Austin Lounge Lizards have been known to turn up at **Antone's,** 213 W. Fifth St (© **512/474-5314**), the club owner's name has always been synonymous with the blues. The **Broken Spoke,** 3201 S. Lamar Blvd. (© **512/ 442-6189**), is the genuine item, a Western honky-tonk with a wood-plank floor and a cowboy-hatted, two-steppin' crowd.

A small, dark cavern with great acoustics, the **Cactus Cafe,** Texas Union, University of Texas campus, 24th and Guadalupe (© **512/475-6515**), is singer/songwriter heaven. The attentive listening vibes attract talented solo artists like Jimmy LaFave and nationally recognized Austin native Shawn Colvin. The adjacent **Texas Union Ballroom** (© **512/475-6645**) draws larger crowds with big names like Billy Bragg. Austin's last word in alternative music, **Emo's,** 603 Red River St. (© **512/477-EMOS**), draws acts of all sizes and flavors, from Johnny Cash to Green Day.

If swing's your thing, head for the **Caucus Club,** 912 Red River (© **512/472-8373**), or the **Speakeasy,** 412 Congress Ave. (© **512/476-8017**).

A terrific sound system and a casual country atmosphere make **The Backyard,** on Highway 71 West at R.R. 620, Bee Cave (© **512/263-4146** or 512/469-SHOW for tickets), a hot venue, attracting acts that range from the Allman Brothers to Bonnie Raitt to Jimmy Cliff. Come early and enjoy some barbecue. Another Austin classic, **La Zona Rosa,** 612 W. Fourth St. (© **512/263-4146**), mixes a Tex-Mex menu with high-quality music, from Latino and alternative country to punk rock.

Since 1866, when councilman August Scholz first opened his tavern near the state capitol, every Texas governor has visited Texas's oldest operating biergarten, **Scholz Garten,** 1607 San Jacinto Blvd. (© **512/474-1958**). Chow down on some barbecue while a state-of-the-art sound system cranks out the polka tunes; patio tables as well as a few strategically placed TV sets help Longhorn fans cheer on their team.

6 San Antonio

Remember the Alamo? Have you heard about the River Walk or the Mission Trail? Or SeaWorld? Or Six Flags Fiesta Texas? There's a lot to see and do in San Antonio. And even without the attractions, you would still be left with a city that is fascinating in its own right. To start with, it was settled in the early 1700s by Canary Islanders, of all people. It sits on the edge of South Texas, with Laredo and the Mexican border a scant 3 hours away, and has always been linked to the

Mexican world. But it is also on the edge of Texas Hill Country, which ties it to the frontier and to the culture of the German settlers who migrated here in large numbers in the mid-19th century. On top of this, San Antonio is Texas through and through, all of which makes it an intriguing multidimensional city that surprises and delights.

ESSENTIALS

GETTING THERE   By Plane   The two-terminal **San Antonio International Airport** (© 210/207-3411; www.ci.sat.tx.us/aviation) sits about 13 miles north of downtown. Among other carriers serving the city, **Southwest Airlines** (© 800/435-9792) offers direct flights from a number of cities.

If you're renting a car, it should take about 15 to 20 minutes to drive downtown via U.S. 281 South. VIA Metropolitan Transit's bus 2 is the cheapest (75¢) way to get downtown but also the slowest at 40 to 45 minutes. A taxi should cost about $25 to $30 to get downtown, including the 50¢ airport departure fee; 9pm to 5am there's an additional $1 after-hours charge.

By Train   Amtrak (© 800/USA-RAIL or 210/233-3226; www.amtrak.com) provides daily service to its station at 250 Hoefgen St. from Austin (trip time: 2 hr.), Fort Worth (7 hr.), Dallas (9 hr.), and Chicago (30 hr.); there is less frequent service from New Orleans (14 hr.) and Los Angeles (29 hr.).

By Car   Major routes into San Antonio are I-35 from the north (Austin) and south (Laredo), and I-10 from the east (Houston) and west (El Paso).

VISITOR INFORMATION   Contact the **San Antonio Convention and Visitors Bureau (SACVB),** P.O. Box 2277, San Antonio, TX 78298 (© 800/447-3372; www.sanantoniovisit.com), for an information packet. The **Texas Travel Information Center** has a toll-free number (© 800/452-9292). The **City of San Antonio Visitor Information Center,** 317 Alamo Plaza, across the street from the Alamo (© 210/207-6748), is open daily from 8:30am to 6pm. There are two unstaffed satellite offices at the airport.

GETTING AROUND   The **VIA Metropolitan Transit Service,** 112 N. Soledad (© 210/362-2020; www.viainfo.net), has bus routes that cost 75¢ for regular lines and $1.50 for express lines (5¢ for transfers). You'll need exact change. VIA also offers five convenient downtown streetcar routes that cover all the most popular tourist stops for 50¢ a ride (exact change only).

Taxis are next to impossible to hail on the street; call **Checker Cab** (© 210/222-2151) or **Yellow Cab** (© 210/226-4242). The base charge is $1.60; add $1.50 for each mile.

FAST FACTS   For a doctor referral, contact the **Bexar County Medical Society** at 202 W. French Place (© 210/734-6691). The main downtown hospital is **Baptist Medical Center,** 111 Dallas St. (© 210/297-7000). Sales tax is 7.75%; the city surcharge on hotel rooms is 16.25%.

SPECIAL EVENTS & FESTIVALS   The third week of April brings **Fiesta San Antonio** (© 210/227-5191; www.fiesta-sa.org), a huge celebration marking Texas independence with an elaborately costumed royal court presiding over 10 days of revelry: parades, balls, food fests, sporting events, concerts, and art shows all over town.

The **Tejano Conjunto Festival** (© 210/271-3151), at Rosedale Park and Guadalupe Theater, is an annual festival in mid-May that celebrates the lively and unique blend of Mexican and German music born in South Texas.

WHAT TO SEE & DO

It goes without saying that the River Walk (see below) is the place to take a stroll in San Antonio, but if you want to see a little more of town, stroll through **La Villita National Historic District,** which is bounded by Durango, Navarro, and Alamo streets and the River Walk. Boutiques, crafts shops, and restaurants occupy this historic district, which resembles a Spanish-Mexican village. Another good walking area is the **King William Historic District,** on the east bank of the river just south of downtown (within walking distance of the convention center). It has beautifully landscaped lawns and magnificent mansions.

Lone Star Trolley, 301 Alamo Plaza, in front of Ripley's Believe It or Not and Plaza Theater of Wax (© **210/224-9299**), runs 75-minute trolley tours that touch on all the downtown highlights. The river tours offered by **Yanaguana Cruises** (© **210/244-5700**) go more than 2 miles down the most built-up sections of the Paseo del Rio. There are several places along the River Walk where you can buy a ticket and catch a boat; just look for where the boats pull up to the bank. The cost is $5.25. Boats leave every half hour from 10am for the 40-minute cruise.

The Alamo   Inevitably, the first thing visitors think when they see the Alamo is "Hmmm, I thought it would be bigger." Such a reaction, of course, only underscores the heroic and desperate actions of the Alamo's defenders who in 1836 held off their attackers for 13 days against overwhelming odds. In fact, at the time of the battle, the Alamo was bigger than what you see today, but not so much as to make it a daunting fortification to the besieging army. More shrine than museum, the Alamo doesn't do the best job of explaining the battle. If you want to understand more, see the IMAX show "Alamo . . . The Price of Freedom," presented several times a day at the IMAX theater around the corner from the Alamo in the Rivercenter Mall (© **210/247-4629;** www.imax-sa.com). 300 Alamo Plaza. © 210/281-0710. http://thealamo.org. Free admission (donations welcome). Mon–Sat 9am–5:30pm; Sun 10am–5:30pm. Streetcar: Red, Brown, and Blue lines.

Market Square   Market Square will transport you south of the border. Stalls in El Mercado sell everything from onyx chess sets and cheap serapes to beautifully made crafts from the interior of Mexico. Every weekend food stalls hawk specialties such as *gorditas* (thick tortillas topped with a variety of goodies) and funnel cakes. Some of the buildings date back to the late 1800s. Between Dolorosa and Commerce sts. © 210/207-8600. Free admission. El Mercado and Farmer's Market Plaza open daily June–Aug 10am–8pm; Sept–May 10am–6pm; restaurants and some of the shops open later. Streetcar: Red and Yellow lines.

For Art Lovers

Art aficionados should check out the **Marion Koogler McNay Art Museum,** 6000 N. New Braunfels Ave. (© 210/824-5368; www.mcnay art.org), a gem of a small museum. It is particularly strong in French post-Impressionist and early 20th-century European painting, and the building and grounds are lovely. The **San Antonio Museum of Art,** 200 W. Jones Ave. (© 210/978-8100; www.sa-museum.org), has holdings that range from early Egyptian, Greek, and Asian to 19th- and 20th-century American works, but deserving special notice is its Rockefeller Center for Latin American Art. The center exhibits pre-Columbian, colonial, folk, and contemporary works from all over Latin America.

Downtown San Antonio

TEXAS
Austin
San Antonio

W. Cypress

E. Euclid Ave.
E. Elmira
Howard
Quincy St.
Brooklyn
Baltimore
Dallas
Lexington
Richmond
Augusta
St. Mary's

San Antonio
Museum of Art

Jones Ave.

N. St. Mary's

San Pedro

Main Ave.

Flores

Cameron

San Saba

Santa Rosa St.

N. Pecos

Southwest
Craft Center

Convent

Navarro

Municipal
Auditorium

W. Martin

E. Martin

Pecan St.

Travis Park

Travis

Soledad

St. Mary's

Jefferson

Lesoya

Riverwalk

La Mansión
del Rio

San Fernando
Cathedral

E. Houston

College

Alamo

City Hall

Market
Square

Dolorosa

Main
Plaza

Houston St.

Bonham

Rivercenter
Mall

W. Nueva

Villita

Villita Assembly Hall

Nueva

La Villita

Navarro

Presa

Commerce St.

Market

Convention
Center

Beethoven
Hall

HemisFair
Park

Tower of
the Americas

W. Durango

Dwyer

Main Ave.

San Antonio

S. St. Mary's

S. Presa

S. Alamo

Matagorda

Institute of
Texan Cultures

E. Durango Blvd.

Arsenal

Guadalupe

S. Laredo St.

W. Guenther

King William

Madison

Cedar

Pereida

Adams

KING WILLIAM
HISTORIC DISTRICT

Avenue B
Broadway
McCullough Ave.
N. Alamo St.
Ninth
Avenue E.
Fourth
Bowie
Elm St.
Austin
Chestnut St.
E. Crockett
Hoefgen

0   1/4 mi
0   0.25 km

N

ACCOMMODATIONS ■
Emily Morgan Hotel **5**
The Fairmont, a Wyndham Historic Hotel **9**
Havanna Riverwalk Inn **2**
La Mansión del Rio Hotel **3**
Menger Hotel **6**
Noble Inns **10**

DINING ◆
Boudro's **7**
County Line **4**
Mi Tierra **1**
Rosario's **11**
Schilo's **8**

The River Walk/Paseo Del Rio The quieter areas of these 2½ paved miles of winding riverbank, shaded by cypresses, oaks, and willows, exude a tropical, exotic aura; the Big Bend section, filled with sidewalk cafes, popular restaurants and bars, high-rise hotels, and even a huge shopping mall, has a festive, sometimes frenetic feel. Tour boats, water taxis, and floating picnic barges regularly ply the river, and local parades and festivals fill its banks with revelers. Downtown from the Municipal Auditorium on the north end to the King William Historic District on the south end. All streetcar lines.

San Antonio Missions National Historic Park The Alamo was originally just the first of five missions established by the Franciscans along the San Antonio River to Christianize the native population. The four missions that now fall under the aegis of the National Parks Department are still active parishes, run in cooperation with the Archdiocese of San Antonio. A visitor center just outside Mission San José offers a good introduction to the park. **Concepción,** 807 Mission Rd. at Felisa, is the oldest unrestored Texas mission, and looks much as it did 200 years ago. **San José,** 6707 Roosevelt Ave., established in 1720, was the largest, best known, and most beautiful of the Texas missions. It was reconstructed to give visitors a complete picture of life in a mission community. Moved from an earlier site in east Texas to its present location in 1731, **San Juan Capistrano,** 9102 Graf at Ashley, doesn't have the grandeur of the missions to the north. But a short (⅓ mile) interpretive trail winds through the woods to the banks of the old river channel. **San Francisco de la Espada,** 10040 Espada Rd., also has an ancient, isolated feel, although the beautifully kept-up church shows just how vital it still is to the local community. Getting a map and visiting these missions by rental car is a little complicated. It's easier to take a tour bus such as the one offered by Lone Star Trolley (see above). Headquarters: 2202 Roosevelt Ave. ℂ 210/534-8833. Visitor center: 6707 Roosevelt Ave. ℂ 210/932-1001. www.nps.gov/saan. Free admission; donations accepted. All the missions are open daily 9am–5pm. Bus: 40.

SeaWorld San Antonio Leave it to Texas to provide Shamu, the performing killer whale, with his most spacious digs: At 250 acres, this is the largest marine theme park in the world. The walk-through habitats where you can watch penguins, sea lions, sharks, tropical fish, and flamingos do their thing are endlessly fascinating, but the aquatic acrobatics at the stadium shows are even more fun. The Lost Lagoon has a huge wave pool and water slides aplenty, and the Texas Splashdown flume ride and the Rio Loco river-rapids ride also offer splashy fun. Stick around for the Summer Night Magic multimedia laser shows or one of the special high-season concerts. 10500 SeaWorld Dr. (16 miles northwest of downtown San Antonio at Ellison Dr. and Westover Hills Blvd.). ℂ 210/523-3611. www.seaworld.com. $37 adults, $30 seniors, $27 children ages 3–11, free for children under 3. Schedule varies with season; generally open weekends and some weekdays in spring and fall, daily during summer (through mid-Aug). Closed Nov to early Mar. Hours 10am–6pm, 8pm, or 10pm, depending on the season. Call ahead or check website. Parking $5. From Loop 410 or from Hwy. 90 West, exit Hwy. 151 West to the park.

Six Flags Fiesta Texas This $100-million theme park is a good way to get a taste—literally and figuratively—of the Lone Star State. A vast variety of food booths share the 200-acre amusement arena with rides, games, shops, and crafts demonstrations galore. The attractions are organized around four themes: Mexican fiesta, German village, country-and-western, and vintage rock 'n' roll (remember, Buddy Holly was from Texas). Loony Tunes cartoon characters are in evidence everywhere. There's also a million-gallon wave pool, a treehouse with

SAN ANTONIO **579**

75 gadgets for drenching your buddies, and a simulated seaside boardwalk with a Ferris wheel, roller-skating rink, and nine hole miniature golf course. The park hosts the Rattler, the highest and fastest wooden roller coaster in the world, and the Joker's Revenge, with a funhouse entryway and a reverse start. Newer and scarier is the Poltergeist, with incredibly tight twists and curves, and the Scream takes you on a 20-story space shot and turbo drop. There are laser games and virtual reality simulators, plus a series of big-name concerts in summer. 17000 I-10 West (corner of I-10 West and Loop 1604; about 15 min. from downtown). (© 210/697-5050. www.sixflags.com. Admission $37 adults, $25 seniors, $23 children under 48 in., free for children under 3. Prices do not include tax. The park is generally open daily late May to late Aug, Fri–Sun Mar–May and Sept–Nov, closed Nov–Feb. It opens at 8 or 10am, depending on the season, and closes at 10pm. Call ahead or check the website, since times often vary. Parking $7. Take Exit 555 on I-10 West.

Witte Museum The Witte focuses on Texas history, natural science, and anthropology, but often ranges as far afield as the Berlin Wall or the history of bridal gowns in the United States. An EcoLab is home to live Texas critters ranging from tarantulas to tortoises; the wonderful HEB Science Treehouse is a science center with hands-on activities for all ages. Outside are a butterfly and hummingbird garden and three restored historic homes. 3801 Broadway (at the edge of Brackenridge Park). (© 210/357-1900. www.wittemuseum.org. $5.95 adults, $4.95 seniors, $3.95 children 4–11, free for children 3 and under. Free on Tues 3–9pm. Mon and Wed–Sat 10am–5pm (until 6pm June–Aug); Tues 10am–9pm; Sun noon–5pm (until 6pm June–Aug). Bus: 9 or 14.

GOLF

Golf has become a big deal in San Antonio, with more and more visitors coming to town expressly to tee off. Of the city's six municipal golf courses, one of the most notable is **Brackenridge,** 2315 Ave. B (© 210/226-5612), the oldest public course in Texas, opened in 1916. Oaks and pecans shade its fairways, and greens fees are very reasonable. The $4.3-million **Cedar Creek,** 8250 Vista Colina (© 210/695-5050), in northwest San Antonio, offers three-tiered greens and scenic Hill Country views; it's repeatedly ranked as South Texas's best municipal course in golfing surveys. Getting rave reviews, too, is the high-end **Quarry,** 444 E. Basse Rd. (© 210/824-4500), one of San Antonio's newest 18-hole public golf courses, about 10 minutes from downtown. Another recent addition to the greens scene, **La Cantera,** 16401 La Cantera Pkwy. (© 800/446-3418 or 210/558-4653), also has a limestone quarry as its setting; designed by Jay Morish and Tom Weiskopf, it's both difficult and dramatic. The area's newest golf course, **Canyon Springs,** 24400 Canyon Golf Rd. (© 210/497-1770), sits at the north edge of town in the Texas Hill Country, lush with live oaks and dotted with historic rock formations. To get a copy of the free **San Antonio Golfing Guide,** call © 800/447-3372.

San Antonio Savings
The annual **SAVE (San Antonio Vacation Experience)** promotion, sponsored by local businesses, the San Antonio Convention and Visitors Bureau, and American Express, includes discounts on hotel rooms as well as on dining and entertainment; call © 800/447-3372 to request a packet.

SHOPPING

Most out-of-town shoppers will find all they need downtown, between the large **Rivercenter Mall;** the boutiques and crafts shops of **La Villita; Market Square,** with its colorful Mexican wares; and assorted souvenir retailers and galleries on and around **Alamo Plaza.**

In the Southtown section near King William, the **Blue Star Arts Complex,** 1400 S. Alamo (© **210/227-6960**), is the up-and-coming place to buy art. More and more galleries are opening downtown as well. You'll find a slew of **antiques shops** on Hildebrand between Blanco, and McCullough between Hildebrand and Basse.

Many of San Antonio's countless small *botánicas* specialize in articles used in the practice of *curandería,* a Latin American fusion of African and native American magical practices. **Papa Jim's,** 5630 S. Flores (© **210/922-6665**), is the best known of all the *botánicas.*

WHERE TO STAY

For information about bed-and-breakfasts around the city, contact the **San Antonio Bed & Breakfast Association** (© **800/210-8422;** www.sanantonio bb.org). One recommendable B&B is the **Bullis House Inn,** 621 Pierce St. (© **877/477-4100** or 210/223-9426), which is a good bargain if you don't mind sharing a bathroom. This graceful neoclassical mansion is just down the street from the Fort Sam Houston quadrangle, and has an outdoor pool.

Don't expect to find any bargains right on the River Walk. However, several moderate and affordable chain properties are near Market Square, on the west side of downtown, about 6 blocks from the river and easily accessible to it via the trolley line. The closest is **La Quinta Market Square,** 900 Dolorosa (© **800/687-6667** or 210/271-0001), offering a swimming pool. A little farther south, but equipped with restaurant, pool, exercise room, and room service, are the **Holiday Inn Market Square,** 318 W. Durango (© **800/HOLIDAY** or 210/225-3211), and **Courtyard by Marriott,** 600 S. Santa Rosa (© **800/648-4462** or 210/229-9449).

Emily Morgan Hotel   Centrally located right next to the Alamo, this hotel is set in a beautiful 1926 Gothic Revival skyscraper. Rooms are modern, bright, and immaculate. Corner rooms are called "plaza" rooms and come with a separate sitting area, a mini-fridge, CD players, and a large Jacuzzi. Executive rooms come with CD players and a normal Jacuzzi tub. Both have good views overlooking the Alamo. Many of the standard rooms also have normal Jacuzzis, and some offer views of the Alamo. 705 E. Houston St., San Antonio, TX 78205. © **800/824-6674** or 210/225-5100. Fax 210/225-7227. www.emilymorganhotel.com. 177 units. $199 standard; $229 executive room; $289 plaza room. Children 12 and under stay free in parents' room. Ask about special packages. AE, DC, DISC, MC, V. Valet parking $16. **Amenities:** Restaurant; outdoor pool.

The Fairmount, A Wyndham Historic Hotel   If you're looking for a small hotel with attentive service but without the intimacy of a B&B, this Victorian-era, downtown hotel is your place. Rooms are decorated in muted Southwestern tones, with rich wood furniture and original artwork; all have VCRs, deluxe toiletries, and balconies. The marble bathrooms have Bath and Body Works toiletries and plush bathrobes. From the graceful lobby, you can enter Polo's bar, plush and softly lit, or Polo's restaurant, which serves beautifully presented nouvelle cuisine. 401 S. Alamo St., San Antonio, TX 78205. © **800/642-3363,** 800/WYNDHAM, or

210/224-8800. Fax 210/224-2767. www.wyndham.com. 37 units. $215–$235 double; $269–$550 suite. AE, DC, MC, V. Valet parking $15. **Amenities:** Restaurant; fitness center.

Havana Riverwalk Inn   This small inn, built in 1914 in Mediterranean Revival style, avoids all the standard hotel room appointments. Lots of dark wood trim and window shutters provide a soft light, in sharp contrast to the harsh Texas sun outdoors. Worn wood floors, antique furnishings, and objects usually referred to as "conversation pieces" make staying here fun, and touches such as fresh flowers and bottled water add to the charm. All this character and charm come at a price, however, in that the medium-size rooms don't have closets. The inn is on a quiet section of the River Walk. 1015 Navarro, San Antonio, TX 78205. (C) **888/224-2008** or 210/222-2008. Fax 210/222-2717. 27 units. $145–$155 double; $185–$$195 deluxe; $275–$600 suites. Self-parking $10. **Amenities:** Restaurant.

La Mansión del Río Hotel   For many Texans who frequent San Antonio, staying at La Mansión is a requisite feature of any visit to the city. This stand-out hotel occupies a central yet relatively quiet section of the River Walk, and unlike the other big hotels that border the river, this one is not a skyscraper (it has six floors). From the river-view rooms, you can look out from the same level as the tops of the tall cypress trees outside and feel like you're in a treehouse. Rooms also have more character than at the Hilton or the Hyatt. They feature Mexican tile floors, beamed ceilings, and wrought-iron balconies that are pure San Antonio. Service is excellent, and the food at the featured restaurant, Las Canarias, is superb. 112 College St., San Antonio, TX 78205 (C) **800/292 7300** or 210/518-1000. Fax 210/226-0389. www.lamansion.com. 337 units. $199–$389 double; $549–$2,000 suite. Packages available. Children under 18 stay free in parents' room. AE, DC, DISC, MC, V. Valet parking $21. **Amenities:** Restaurants (2); outdoor pool.

Menger Hotel   Its location, between the Alamo and the Rivercenter Mall, a block from the River Walk, is perfect. Its history—it was built in 1859—is fascinating. A self-guided tour pamphlet will take you to halls, ballrooms, and gardens through which Ulysses S. Grant, Sarah Bernhardt, and Oscar Wilde walked. Its guest rooms are charming. Rooms range from ornate 19th-century style to modern but still full of character. The rooms that are not part of the orig-inal building go for significantly less. Some rooms offer kitchenettes and bal-conies. The Menger Bar is one of San Antonio's great historic taverns. 204 Alamo Plaza, San Antonio, TX 78205. (C) **800/345-9285** or 210/223-4361. Fax 210/228-0022. www. historicmenger.com. 318 units. $215 double; $250–$335 suite. Honeymoon packages available. AE, DC, DISC, MC, V. Self-parking $13, valet parking $17. **Amenities:** Restaurant; heated outdoor pool; spa.

Noble Inns   Donald and Liesl Noble provide gracious lodgings: the 1894 Jackson House, a traditional-style B&B; and, a few blocks away, the 1896 Pan-coast Carriage House, offering three suites with kitchens. Rooms, individually decorated with fine antiques, are ideal for both business and leisure travelers. All rooms have gas fireplaces, bathrobes, and nightly turndown service with Godiva chocolates; three in the Jackson House feature two-person Jacuzzi tubs. Guests at the Jackson House take a full breakfast in the dining room and enjoy a lovely conservatory with a 14-foot swimmable whirlpool; those at the Pancoast Car-riage House enjoy a continental breakfast and a swimming pool and a smaller whirlpool. A silver-gray classic Rolls-Royce is available for airport transportation or downtown drop-off by prior arrangement. 107 Madison St., San Antonio, TX 78204. (C) **800/221-4045** or 210/225-4045. Fax 210/227-0877. www.nobleinns.com. 9 units. $120–$225 double in the Jackson House; $175–$250 suite. Rates include breakfast. AE, DISC, MC, V. Free off-street parking. No children under 14. **Amenities:** Outdoor pool.

WHERE TO DINE

Boudro's NEW AMERICAN   Locals tend to look down their noses on River Walk restaurants, but Boudro's has always won their respect. And with good reason. The kitchen uses fresh local ingredients—Gulf Coast seafood, Texas beef, Hill Country produce—and the preparations and presentations do them justice. The setting is also out of the ordinary: If you've entered from the river, be sure to turn around and look inside the turn-of-the-19th-century limestone building to see its hardwood floors and handmade mesquite bar. 421 E. Commerce St./River Walk. (210/224-8484. Reservations strongly recommended. Main courses $15–$28. AE, DC, DISC, MC, V. Sun–Thurs 11am–11pm; Fri–Sat 11am–midnight.

County Line BARBECUE   The County Line has transplanted the menu and the signature 1940s Texas decor of this popular Austin-based restaurant to the River Walk, where it's thriving. Even locals come downtown to dig into the fall-off-the-bone beef ribs or the tender pork; all the meat has been smoked for more than 18 hours. Barbecued chicken, turkey, and even some salads are also available. Southbank complex, 111 W. Crockett St., Ste. 104. (210/229-1941. Reservations not accepted. Platters $8.95–$15. AE, DC, MC, V. Daily 11am–11pm.

La Calesa REGIONAL MEXICAN   Tucked away in a small house just off Broadway—look for Earl Abel's large sign across the street—this family-run restaurant features several dishes from the southern Yucatán, as well as those from the northern areas that influenced the Tex-Mex style. The difference is mainly in the sauces, and they're done to perfection. The mole, for example, strikes a fine balance between its rich chocolate base and the picante spices. The *conchinita pibil*, a classic Yucatecan pork dish, has a marvelous texture and taste. A separate margarita menu adds even more zest. 2103 E. Hildebrand (just off Broadway). (210/822-4475. Reservations not accepted. Main courses $6.95–$16. AE, DC, DISC, MC, V. Mon–Thurs 11am–9:30pm; Fri 11am–10:30pm; Sat 11:30am–10:30pm; Sun 11:30am–9pm.

Liberty Bar AMERICAN/SOUTHERN/MEXICAN   You'd be hard-pressed to guess from the outside that this ramshackle former brothel (opened in1890) near the Highway 281 underpass hosts one of the hippest haunts in San Antonio. But as every foodie in town can tell you, it's bright and inviting inside, and you'll find everything here from comfort food (pot roast, say, or a ham-and-Swiss sandwich) to regional Mexican cuisine (the *chiles rellenos en nogada* are super). 328 E. Josephine St. (210/227-1187. Reservations accepted. Main courses $7.95–$19. AE, MC, V. Sun–Thurs 11:30am–10:30pm; Fri–Sat 11:30am–midnight; Sun brunch 10:30am–2pm. Bar open until midnight Sun–Thurs, until 2am Fri–Sat.

Mi Tierra MEXICAN   This Market Square restaurant has been open since 1946. Much expanded and gussied up since then, it still draws a faithful clientele of Latino families and businesspeople along with busloads of tourists. Where else can you come at 2am and order anything from chorizo and eggs to an 8-ounce charbroiled rib-eye—and be serenaded by mariachis? Mi Tierra is justly renowned for its *panadería* (bakery). 218 Produce Row. (210/225-1262. Reservations accepted for large groups only. Main courses $6.95–$15. AE, MC, V. Open 24 hr.

Rosario's MEXICAN   Hip and colorful as ever, with lots of neon, glass blocks, and a concrete/metal bar that mixes killer margaritas, this restaurant remains popular. Consider ordering the large helpings of such entrees as pork carnitas in cascabel pepper sauce or the excellent mole enchiladas. The bargain weekday lunch specials—perhaps three chicken flautas with guacamole—draw a sizable local crowd, but it's on weekend nights, when a live tropical band plays, that the place really sizzles. 910 S. Alamo. ☎ 210/223-1806. Reservations not accepted. Main courses $5.95–$11. AE, DC, DISC, MC, V. Mon 11am–3pm; Tues–Thurs 11am–10pm; Fri–Sat 11am–11pm.

Schilo's GERMAN/DELI   You can't leave town without stopping at this San Antonio institution, if only for a hearty bowl of split-pea soup or a piece of the signature cherry cheesecake. The large, open room with its worn wooden booths gives a glimpse into the city's German past. An oompah band plays on Saturday from 5 to 8pm. It's a great place to come for refueling when you're sightseeing near Alamo Plaza; for under $5, a good Reuben sandwich or a bratwurst plate should keep you going for the rest of the day. 424 E. Commerce St. ☎ 210/223-6692. Sandwiches $3.85–$5.95; hot or cold plates $6.25–$7.95; main dishes (served after 5pm) $7.95–$11. AE, DC, DISC, MC, V. Mon–Sat 7am–8:30pm.

SAN ANTONIO AFTER DARK

A Latin flavor lends spice to some of the best local nightlife in San Antonio—this is America's capital for Tejano music, a unique blend of German polka and northern Mexico ranchero sounds, with a dose of pop for good measure. **Southtown,** with its many Hispanic-oriented shops and galleries, celebrates its art scene with the monthly First Friday, a kind of extended block party.

For the most complete listings of what's happening, pick up a free copy of the weekly alternative newspaper, the *Current,* or the Friday "Weekender" section of the *San Antonio Express-News.* You can also call the **San Antonio Arts Hotline** (☎ 800/894-3819 or 210/207-2166).

If you're visiting San Antonio in the summer, be sure to see something at the **Arneson River Theatre,** 418 La Villita, on the River Walk (☎ 210/207-8610), which stages shows on one side of the river while the audience watches from an amphitheater on the other. June to August the Fandango folkloric troupe performs every Wednesday; the Fiesta Rio del Noche performs Thursday through Saturday. Both offer lively music and dance with a south-of-the-border flair.

The closest San Antonio comes to having a club district is the stretch of North St. Mary's between Josephine and Magnolia—just north of downtown and south of Brackenridge Park—known as **the Strip.**

Boots, hats, and antique farm equipment hang from the ceiling of the typical Texas roadhouse known as **Floore Country Store,** 14664 Bandera Rd./Hwy. 16, Helotes, 2 miles north of Loop 1604 (☎ 210/695-8827), where there's always live music on weekends. **The Landing** at the Hyatt Regency Hotel, River Walk (☎ 210/223-7266), is one of the best traditional jazz clubs in the country.

The Laboratory, 7310 Jones-Maltsberger (☎ 210/824-1997), is one of the few microbreweries in San Antonio, and the only place in town that makes an "authentic" Bavarian *hefeweizen.* The history at the **Menger Bar** at the Menger Hotel, 204 Alamo Plaza (☎ 210/223-4361), dates back more than 100 years ago, when Teddy Roosevelt recruited men for his Rough Riders unit at this dark, wooded bar. It moved to its current location in 1956, but 90% of its historic furnishings remain intact. Just below the observation-deck level, the **Tower of the Americas Restaurant bar,** 600 HemisFair Park (☎ 210/223-3101), affords dazzling views of the city at night.

7 The Hill Country & the Mountains of West Texas

Directly west of Austin and north and west of San Antonio lies the Hill Country, one of Texas's prettiest parts, especially in early spring when wildflowers daub it with every pigment in nature's palette. It's dotted with old dance halls, country stores, and quaint Teutonic towns—more than 30,000 Germans emigrated to Texas during the great land-grant years of the Republic. If you travel I-10 West from San Antonio (you'll actually be heading northwest), you'll go through the heart of the Hill Country. After a little more than 100 miles, the hills begin to disappear and are gone by the time you reach the town of Sonora. From there the interstate runs west through 200 miles of emptiness before arriving at the Davis Mountains. These, together with the mountains of the **Big Bend** area to the south and the **Guadalupe Mountains** to the north, make up Texas's mountain region. The last two are large national parks that offer great hiking and camping in lovely mountain scenery.

BOERNE

From downtown San Antonio, it's a straight shot, 30 miles northwest on I-10, to Boerne (rhymes with "journey"). Boerne's biggest draw is its **antiques shops**—more than 20 of them line the "Hauptstrasse," or main street.

One of the most popular nearby attractions is **Cascade Caverns,** about 2 miles south of Boerne, Exit 543 on I-10 (© **830/755-8080**). This active cave boasts huge chambers, a 90-foot underground waterfall, and comfortable walking trails.

Victoria's on the Creek, in Ye Kendall Inn, 128 W. Blanco (© **830/249-7992**), serves Italian fare, seafood, and steaks in an elegant atmosphere. The more casual **Bear Moon Bakery,** 401 S. Main St. (© **830/816-BEAR**), is ideal for a hearty breakfast or light lunch.

CASTROVILLE

Even though Castroville is closer to San Antonio than Boerne—20 miles via U.S. 90 West—it has maintained more of a pristine, rural atmosphere. If you want to find everything open, come on Thursday, Friday, or Saturday. Almost 100 of the original settlers' unevenly slope-roofed houses remain in Castroville. The oldest standing structure, the **First St. Louis Catholic Church,** went up in 1846 on the corner of Angelo and Moy. A gristmill and wood-and-stone dam are among the interesting artifacts at the **Landmark Inn State Historical Park,** 402 Florence St. (© **830/931-2133**).

Get a delicious taste of the past at **Haby's Alsatian Bakery,** 207 U.S. 90 East (© **830/931-2118**), which offers apple fritters, strudels, breads, and coffee cakes. Among the specialties of the **Alsatian Restaurant,** 403 Angelo St. (© **830/931-3260**), set in an atmospheric 19th-century house, is the delicious boneless Strasbourg chicken seasoned with curry.

BANDERA

North of Castroville and west of Boerne, Bandera is a slice of life out of the Old West. Pick up a self-guided tour brochure and information about roping and rodeos at the **Bandera County Convention and Visitors Bureau,** 1808 Hwy. 16 S. (© **800/364-3833** or 830/796-3045). Most people take advantage of the town's living traditions by strolling along Main Street, where craftspeople work in the careful, hand-hewn styles of yesteryear.

You and your horse can canter through the **Hill Country State Natural Area,** 10 miles southwest of Bandera (© 830/796-4413), the largest state park in Texas allowing horseback riding. The nearest outfitter is the helpful and reliable **Running R Ranch,** Route 1 (© 830/796-3984).

If you want to stay overnight at a ranch, try the affordable **Dixie Dude Ranch** (© 800/375-Y'ALL or 830/796-4481; www.dixieduderanch.com), where you're likely to see white-tailed deer or wild turkeys as you trot on horseback through a 725 acre spread. Tubing on the Medina River and swimming in an Olympic-size pool are among the many things you might do during the day at the moderately priced **Mayan Ranch** (© 830/796-3312 or 830/460-3036; www.mayanranch. com). Rates at both ranches include three home-cooked meals, two trail rides, and other activities.

Main Street's **O.S.T.** (© 830/796-3836) serves down-home Texas and Tex-Mex fare. For a more upscale setting, but similarly down-home cooking, head to **Billy Gene's,** 1105 Main St. (© 830/460-3200). **Arkey Blue & The Silver Dollar Bar** (© 830/796-8826) is a genuine spit-and-sawdust cowboy honky-tonk on Main Street.

FREDERICKSBURG

Fredericksburg offers good shopping, lots of historic sites, and some of the most unusual accommodations around, all in a pretty rural setting. Many homes were built in the Hill Country version of the German *fachwerk* design, made out of limestone with diagonal wood supports. Fredericksburg became and remains the seat of Gillespie County, the largest peach-producing county in the state. The **Visitor Information Center** is on 106 N. Adams, Fredericksburg, TX 78624 (© 888-997-3600 or 830/997-6523).

More than 100 specialty shops, many of them in mid-19th-century houses, feature work by Hill Country artisans. The family-run **Fredericksburg Winery,** 247 W. Main St. (© 830/990-8747), sells its own hand-bottled, hand-corked, and hand-labeled wines. Becoming increasingly well known via its mail-order business is the **Fredericksburg Herb Farm,** 402 Whitney St. (© 800/259-HERB or 830/997-8615). There's an outlet on Main Street, but a short trip south of town will take you to the flower beds that produce salad dressings, teas, fragrances, and air fresheners.

Lots of well-known performers turn up in the dance hall of **Luckenbach** (11 miles southeast on R.R. 1376), immortalized in a song by Waylon Jennings and Willie Nelson. It's a great place to hang out on a weekend afternoon, when someone's almost always strumming the guitar.

Fredericksburg is known for its *gastehauses* (guest cottages). Many historic homes have been converted into romantic havens replete with robes, fire-places, and even spas. To get a booklet detailing some of the most interesting gastehauses, contact **Gastehaus Schmidt,** 231 W. Main St. (© 830/997-5612; www.ktc.com/GSchmidt).

The **Altdorf Biergarten,** 301 W. Main St. (© 830/997-7865), and **Fried-helm's Bavarian Inn,** 905 W. Main St. (© 830/997-6300), both feature hearty German schnitzels, dumplings, and sauerbraten, and large selections of beer.

LYNDON B. JOHNSON COUNTRY

Welcome to Johnson territory, where the forebears of the 36th president settled almost 150 years ago. Try to make a day out of a visit to LBJ's boyhood home and the sprawling ranch that became known as the Texas White House.

From Fredericksburg, take U.S. 290 east for 16 miles to the entrance of the **Lyndon B. Johnson State and National Historical Parks at LBJ Ranch** (© 830/868-7128 or 830/644-2252). Tour buses depart regularly from the visitor center to the still-operating Johnson Ranch. A reconstructed version of the former president's modest birthplace lies close to his final resting place, shared with five generations of Johnsons. On the side of the river sits the **Sauer–Beckmann Living History Farm,** which gives visitors a look at typical Texas-German farm life at the turn of the century. Farm animals roam freely or in large pens, while family members go about their chores. Nearby are nature trails, a swimming pool (open only in summer), and lots of picnic spots. Admission is $3 per person for bus tours; all other areas are free.

It's 14 miles farther east along U.S. 290 to **Johnson City,** a pleasant agricultural town named for founder James Polk Johnson, LBJ's first cousin once removed. The **Boyhood Home**—the house on Elm Street where Lyndon was raised after age 5—is the centerpiece of this unit of the National Historic Park. To get to the visitor center, take F Street to Lady Bird Lane and you'll see the signs.

TEXAS'S NATIONAL PARKS

If you travel on to West Texas, you'll mostly find the land empty of people. You don't see many cars except on the interstate. The towns are small and well scattered. Almost everyone who goes comments on this. And Big Bend and the Guadalupe Mountains are probably the least-visited national parks in the country, especially if you divide visitors by square miles. This is a hiker's best chance to get clear of the crowds and into some lovely mountain scenery.

To get to **Big Bend,** take Highway 385 south from Fort Stockton. You'll pass through the town of Marathon, where you'll find a great old hotel that is beautifully kept, called the **Gage Hotel** (© 800/884-4243). It's gorgeous, moderately priced, and one of a kind. From this town, it's still about 50 miles to the park. Once there, you can drive around on the paved roads that cross the park. The mountains are beautiful and the landscape is mostly desert. For information go to the visitor center at the end of Highway 385—you can't miss it. Entry fees are $10 per passenger vehicle and $5 per occupant. To go camping you must get a free permit. For advance information, contact the **Big Bend Travel Association** (© 915-477-2236; www.visitbigbend.com).

To get to the **Guadalupe Mountains,** stay on I-10 after Fort Stockton. After 40 miles, you will pass a turnoff for **Balmorhea State Park,** which has a desert spring–fed pool that makes a good swimming hole. Entrance to the park is $3. Fifty miles beyond the turnoff for Balmorhea is Highway 54, which heads straight north into the Guadalupe Mountains. From 50 miles away you can see the white cliffs of El Capitán, the most photographed mountain in the state. The road leads straight to the visitor center, which has a limited number of camping sites. If you want to spend the night in a hotel, it's best to cross through the park into New Mexico and stay at one of the hotels around Carlsbad Cavern, which is 35 miles north.

Arizona & New Mexico

From the rugged drama of the Grand Canyon to the manicured fairways of some of the country's best golf courses, from the galleries and chic restaurants of Santa Fe to the haunting ruins of centuries-old cliff dwellings, these two states form a land of extremes. The stunning landscapes of fanciful red-rock formations, the harsh and delicate beauty of the desert, and vestiges of the Wild West are irresistible to many travelers from overseas—to them, raised on a diet of classic Western double-features, this *is* America. And even for Americans, the attractions of this part of the country have become the stuff of the classic family road-trip vacation.

1 Phoenix & Scottsdale

Phoenix is one of the fastest-growing cities in the country today, and has become a sort of Los Angeles of the desert. The only thing missing is an ocean. The abundance of sunshine has made Phoenix a hot winter vacation spot, and adjacent Scottsdale has become one of the nation's top resort destinations, with dozens of challenging golf courses, rejuvenating health spas, and luxurious resorts, many of which boast sprawling pool complexes complete with waterfalls. Downtown Phoenix has become something of a sports and entertainment district, with several museums, the America West Arena, and the Arizona Diamondbacks' Bank One Ballpark, one of the country's only baseball stadiums with a retractable roof.

ESSENTIALS

GETTING THERE   By Plane   Major domestic and some international carriers fly into **Phoenix Sky Harbor International Airport** (© 602/273-3300; www.phxskyharbor.com), 3 miles from downtown Phoenix.

SuperShuttle (© 800/BLUE VAN or 602/244-9000) offers door-to-door van service to resorts, hotels, and homes throughout the valley. Fares average $7 to $10 to the downtown and Tempe area, and about $16 to $30 to Scottsdale and the northern area of the city. **Valley Metro** provides public bus service throughout the valley, with the Red Line operating between the airport and downtown Phoenix, Tempe, and Mesa.

By Car   The major routes into Phoenix are I-10 from the west (Los Angeles) and southeast (Tucson), and I-17 from the north (Flagstaff).

VISITOR INFORMATION   The **Greater Phoenix Convention & Visitors Bureau,** 50 N. Second St. (© 877/225-5749 or 602/254-6500; www.phoenix cvb.com), is on the corner of Adams Street in downtown Phoenix. If you're staying in Scottsdale, drop by the **Scottsdale Chamber of Commerce and Visitors Center,** 7343 Scottsdale Mall (© 800/877-1117 or 480/945-8481; www.scotts dalecvb.com).

Phoenix, Scottsdale & the Valley of the Sun

ACCOMMODATIONS ■

Arizona Biltmore Resort & Spa **8**
Best Western Airport Inn **33**
Best Western Inn Suites Hotel
   Phoenix **6**
The Buttes, A Wyndham Resort **31**
Days Inn–Scottsdale/Fashion
   Square Resort **23**
Doubletree Paradise Valley
   Resort **24**
The Fairmont Scottsdale
   Princess **12**
Fiesta Inn Resort **29**
Hermosa Inn **9**
Holiday Inn SunSpree Resort **17**
Hotel San Carlos **2**
Hyatt Regency Scottsdale **13**
Marriott's Camelback Inn **18**
The Phoenician **22**
Pointe Hilton Squaw Peak Resort **7**
Rodeway Inn–Airport East **28**
Royal Palms Hotel and Casitas **20**
Sanctuary on Camelback
   Mountain **19**
The Sunburst Resort **25**
Super8–Phoenix Metro/Central **1**

DINING ◆

Bloom **15**
Carlsbad Tavern **26**
El Guapo's Taco Shop &
   Salsa Bar **27**
Golden Swan **14**
Lon's **10**
MacAlpine's Nostalgic Soda
   Fountain & Coffee Shoppe **5**
Marquesa **11**
Mary Elaine's **21**
Pizzeria Bianco **3**
Roy's of Scottsdale **16**
Rustler's Rooste **32**
Sam's Café **4**
Top of the Rock **30**

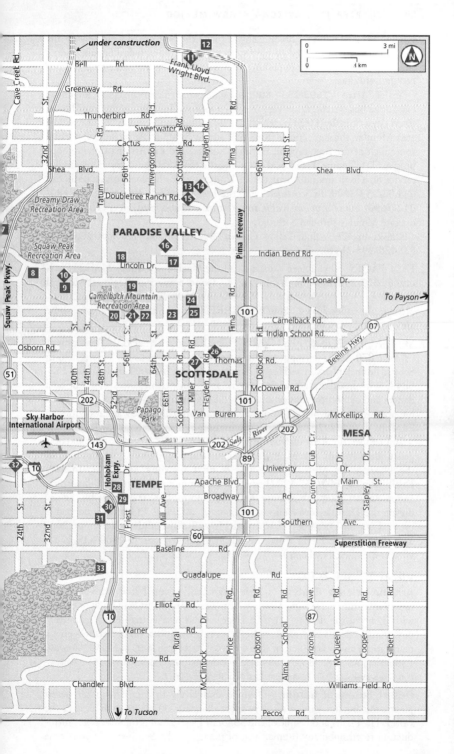

GETTING AROUND   If you want to make the best use of your time in this sprawling area, it's essential to have a car. Outside downtown Phoenix, there's almost always plenty of free parking wherever you go. Rental-car rates tend to be relatively cheap.

Valley Metro (℃ 602/253-5000; www.valleymetro.maricopa.gov), the Phoenix public bus system, is not very useful to tourists. Instead, try the free **Downtown Area Shuttle (DASH),** which provides bus service within the downtown area Monday through Friday from 6:30am to 5:30pm. Attractions along the route include the state capitol, Heritage Square, and the Arizona Center shopping mall. In Tempe, **Free Local Area Shuttle (FLASH)** buses provide a similar service on a loop around Arizona State University. For information on both, call ℃ 602/253-5000. In Scottsdale, ride the free **Scottsdale Round Up** (℃ 480/312-7696) buses between many area resorts and shopping areas. These buses operate Monday through Saturday.

Cab companies include **Yellow Cab** (℃ 602/252-5252) and **Scottsdale Cab** (℃ 480/994-1616).

FAST FACTS   If you need a doctor, call the **Maricopa County Medical Society** (℃ 602/252-2844) for a referral. The **Good Samaritan Regional Medical Center,** 1111 E. McDowell Rd. (℃ 602/239-2000), is one of the largest hospitals in the valley. Call ℃ **800/WALGREENS** for a pharmacy near you; some are open 24 hours.

SPECIAL EVENTS & FESTIVALS   The **Phoenix Open Golf Tournament** (℃ 602/870-4431; www.phoenixopen.com) is a prestigious PGA event held in Scottsdale in January. The **Heard Museum Guild Indian Fair** (℃ 602/252-8848; www.heard.org), held in March, includes performances of traditional dances and demonstrations of arts and crafts. **Cinco de Mayo** is celebrated in a big way, with food, music, and dancing (℃ 602/279-4669 for festivities in Phoenix, or 520/292-9326 for the celebration in Tucson's Kennedy Park).

In October, the **Arizona State Fair** (℃ 602/252-6771; www.azstatefair.com) gets underway, with rodeos, entertainment, and ethnic food. Also that month, the Phoenix Art Museum hosts the **Annual Cowboy Artists of America Exhibition** (℃ 602/257-1222), the most prestigious Western-art show in the region. In early November, more than 150 colorful hot-air balloons fill the sky during the **Thunderbird Balloon Classic** (℃ 602/978-7330). The old year is ushered out on December 31 with the **Fiesta Bowl Parade,** followed on New Year's Day by the **Fiesta Bowl,** a college football classic (℃ 800/635-5748; www.tostitosfiestabowl.com).

WHAT TO SEE & DO

Arizona Science Center   In this large facility you'll find state-of-the-art interactive exhibits covering a variety of topics, from the human body to coping with living in the desert. There's a huge ant farm, a virtual-reality game that puts you inside a video game, a flight simulator, and a cloud maker—plus a planetarium and a large-screen theater. 600 E. Washington St. ℃ 602/716-2000. www.azscience.org. Admission $8 adults, $6 seniors and children 3–12. Planetarium and film combination tickets available. Daily 10am–5pm. Bus: Red (R), Yellow (Y), 0.

Desert Botanical Garden   Devoted exclusively to cacti and other desert plants, this botanic garden displays more than 20,000 plants from all over the world. The Plants and People of the Sonoran Desert trail is the state's best introduction to ethnobotany (human use of plants) in the Southwest. If you come late in the day, you can stay after dark and see night-blooming flowers and dramatically lit cacti. A cafe on the grounds serves surprisingly good food. At Papago Park, 1201 N. Galvin Pkwy. © 480/941-1225. www.dbg.org. Admission $7.50 adults, $6.50 seniors, $4 students 13–18, $3.50 children 5–12. Oct–Apr daily 8am–8pm; May–Sept daily 7am–8pm. Bus: 3.

Heard Museum This is one of the nation's finest museums dealing exclusively with Native American cultures, and the *Native Peoples of the Southwest* exhibit examines the culture of each of the region's major tribes. The Crossroads Gallery offers a fascinating look at contemporary Native American art. On many weekends there are performances by Native American singers and dancers, and throughout the week artists demonstrate their work. 2301 N. Central Ave. © 602/252-8848. www.heard.org. Admission $7 adults, $6 seniors, $3 children 4–12. Daily 9:30am–5pm. Bus: Blue (B), Red (R), O.

Phoenix Art Museum This is the largest art museum in the Southwest, with a collection spanning the major artistic movements from the Renaissance to the present. The selection of modern and contemporary art is particularly good, with works by Diego Rivera, Frida Kahlo, Pablo Picasso, Mark Rothko, Alexander Calder, Henry Moore, Georgia O'Keeffe, Henri Rousseau, and Auguste Rodin. Other exhibits include decorative arts, historic fashions, Asian art, Spanish colonial furnishings and religious art, and works by members of the Cowboy Artists of America. 1625 N. Central Ave. (at McDowell Rd.). © 602/257-1222. www.phxart. org. Admission $7 adults, $5 seniors and students, $2 children 6–17; free on Thurs. Tues–Wed and Fri–Sun 10am–5pm; Thurs 10am–9pm. Bus: Blue (B), Red (R), O.

Scottsdale Museum of Contemporary Art Scottsdale may be obsessed with art featuring lonesome cowboys and solemn Indians, but this boldly designed museum makes it clear that patrons of contemporary art are also welcome here. Cutting-edge art, from the abstract to the absurd, fills the galleries. In addition to the main building, there are several galleries in the adjacent Scottsdale Center for the Arts, which also has a pair of Dale Chihuly art-glass installations. The museum shop is excellent. 7374 E. Second St., Scottsdale. © 480/994-ARTS. www.scottsdalearts.org. Admission $7 adults, $5 students, free for children under 15; free on Thurs. Tues–Wed and Fri–Sat 10am–5pm; Thurs 10am–8pm; Sun noon–5pm. Bus: 41, 50, 72. Also accessible via Scottsdale Round Up shuttle bus.

Taliesin West Frank Lloyd Wright fell in love with the Arizona desert and, in 1937, opened a winter camp here that served as his office and school. Today, Taliesin West is the headquarters of the Frank Lloyd Wright Foundation and School of Architecture. Tours explain the campus buildings and include a general introduction to Wright and his theories of architecture. Wright used local stone for the foundations and developed a number of innovative methods for dealing with the extremes of the desert climate. 12621 Frank Lloyd Wright Blvd. (at 114th St.), Scottsdale. © 480/860-2700, ext. 494 or 495. www.frank[l]loydwright.org. Basic tours: Nov–Apr $16 adults, $14 seniors and students, $3 children 4–12; June–Sept $13 adults, $10 students and seniors, $4.50 children 4–12. Oct–May daily 10am–4pm; June–Sept daily 9am–4pm. Closed Tues–Wed in July and Aug. From Scottsdale Rd., go east on Shea Blvd. to 114th St., then north 1 mile to the entrance road.

GOLF

With nearly 200 courses in the Valley of the Sun, golf is one of the main reasons people flock here during the winter months. Sunshine, spectacular views, and coyotes, quail, and doves for company make playing a round of golf in the valley a truly memorable experience. You can get more information on valley courses from the **Greater Phoenix Convention & Visitors Bureau,** 50 N. Second St. (© 877/225-5749 or 602/254-6500; www.phoenixcvb.com).

Despite the number of courses, it can still be difficult to get a tee time on any of the more famous and popular courses (especially Feb–Apr). If you're staying at a resort with a golf course, be sure to make your tee-time reservations at the same time you make your room reservations. If you aren't staying at a resort, you might still be able to play a round on a resort course if you can get a last-minute tee time. Try one of the tee-time reservation services below.

Greens fees at most public and resort courses range from $90 to $170, with the top courses often charging $200 or more. Municipal courses, on the other hand, charge under $40. You can save money on many courses by opting for twilight play, which usually begins between 1 and 3pm.

To ensure that you get to play those courses you've been dreaming about, make reservations well in advance. **Golf Xpress** (© 800/878-8580 or 602/404-GOLF; www.azgolfxpress.com) can make reservations farther in advance than you could if you called the golf course directly. This company also makes hotel reservations, rents clubs, and provides other assistance to golfers visiting the valley. For last-minute reservations, call **Stand-by Golf** (© 800/655-5345 or 480/874-3133).

For spectacular scenery, the two Jay Morrish–designed 18-hole courses at the **Boulders,** North Scottsdale Road and Carefree Highway, Carefree (© 800/553-1717 or 480/488-9009), just can't be beat. Given the option, play the South Course and watch out as you approach the tee box on the seventh hole—it's a real heart-stopper. Tee times for nonguests are very limited in the winter and spring, and you'll pay $220 for a round.

Jumping over to Litchfield Park, on the far west side of the valley, you'll find the **Wigwam Golf and Country Club,** 300 Wigwam Blvd. (© 623/935-3811), with three championship 18-hole courses. The Gold Course here is legendary, but even the Blue and Red courses are worth playing. These are traditional courses for purists who want vast expanses of green instead of cactus and boulders. In high season, greens fees are $120 for any of the three courses. Reservations for nonguests can be made no more than 7 days in advance.

Way over on the east side of the valley at the foot of the Superstition Mountains is the **Gold Canyon Golf Resort,** 6100 S. Kings Ranch Rd., Gold Canyon (© 800/827-5281), one of the best public courses in the state with three of the best holes—the second, third, and fourth holes on the Dinosaur Mountain course, a visually breathtaking desert-style course. Greens fees on this course range from $135 to $165 in winter. Reserve a week in advance. It's well worth the drive.

If you want to swing where the pros do, beg, borrow, or steal a tee time on the Tom Weiskopf– and Jay Morrish–designed Stadium Course at the **Tournament Players Club (TPC) of Scottsdale,** 17020 N. Hayden Rd. (© 480/585-4334), which hosts the Phoenix Open. The TPC's second 18, the Desert Course, is actually a municipal course. Stadium course fees are $214 in winter and spring. The Desert Course fees are down around $50.

If a traditional course that has challenged presidents and celebrities alike interests you, then try to get a tee time at one of the two 18-hole courses at the **Arizona Biltmore Country Club,** 24th Street and Missouri Avenue (© 602/955-9655). The two courses here are more relaxing than challenging, good to play if you're not yet up to par. Greens fees are $165 in winter and spring. Reservations can be made up to a month in advance

The two courses at the **Camelback Golf Club,** 7847 N. Mockingbird Lane (© **480/596-7050**), offer distinctly different experiences. The Resort Course underwent a $16-million redesign a few years ago and has new water features and bunkers. The Club Course is a links-style course with great mountain views and lots of water hazards. Greens fees are $90 to $145 in winter. Reservations can be made up to 30 days in advance.

Set at the base of Camelback Mountain, the **Phoenician Golf Club,** 6000 E. Camelback Rd. (© **800/888-8234** or 480/423-2449), at the valley's most glamorous resort, has 27 holes that mix traditional and desert styles. Greens fees for nonguests are $170 in winter and spring, and can be made a week in advance.

Of the valley's many daily-fee courses, the two 18-hole courses at **Troon North Golf Club,** 10320 E. Dynamite Blvd., Scottsdale (© **480/585-7700**), seemingly just barely carved out of raw desert, garner the most local accolades. Greens fees are $240 in winter and spring. Reservations are taken up to 30 days in advance.

The Pete Dye–designed **ASU–Karsten Golf Course,** 1125 E. Rio Salado Pkwy., Tempe (© **480/921-8070;** www.asukarsten.com), part of Arizona State University, is also highly praised and is a challenging training ground for top collegiate golfers. Greens fees are $69 to $93 in winter. Online reservations are taken up to 30 days in advance.

Another much-talked-about daily fee course is the **Kierland Golf Club,** 15636 Clubgate Dr., Scottsdale (© **480/922-9283**), which consists of three nine-hole courses that can be played in combination. Greens fees are $130 to $155 in winter. Book up to 60 days in advance.

Of the municipal courses in Phoenix, **Papago Golf Course,** 5595 E. Moreland St. (© **602/275-8428**), at the foot of the red-sandstone Papago Buttes, offers fine views and a killer 17th hole. **Encanto Golf Course,** 2745 N. 15th Ave. (© **602/253-3963**), is the third-oldest course in Arizona and, with its wide fairways and lack of hazards, is very forgiving. In winter, greens fees at either course are $26 to $35, plus cart.

OTHER OUTDOOR PURSUITS

HIKING The city's largest nature preserve, **Phoenix South Mountain Park,** said to be the largest city park in the world, contains miles of hiking, mountain-biking, and horseback-riding trails, and the views of Phoenix from the Buena Vista Overlook are spectacular, especially at sunset. To reach the park, simply drive south on Central Avenue or 48th Street.

Perhaps the most popular hiking trail in the city is the trail to the top of **Camelback Mountain,** in Echo Canyon Recreation Area, near the boundary between Phoenix and Scottsdale. This is the highest mountain in Phoenix, and the 1¼-mile trail to the summit is very steep. Don't attempt it in the heat of the day, and take at least a quart of water with you. The reward for your effort is the city's finest view. To reach the trail head, drive up 44th Street until it becomes McDonald Drive, then turn right on East Echo Canyon Drive and continue up the hill until the road ends at a large parking lot.

HORSEBACK RIDING Even in the urban confines of the Phoenix metro area, people like to play at being cowboys. On the south side of the city, try **Ponderosa Stables,** 10215 S. Central Ave. (© **602/268-1261**), or **South Mountain**

Stables, 10005 S. Central Ave. ((C) **602/276-8131**), both of which lead rides into South Mountain Park and charge $20 per hour. In the Scottsdale area, try **MacDonald's Ranch,** 26540 N. Scottsdale Rd. ((C) **480/585-0239**), which charges $24 for a 1-hour ride.

HOT-AIR BALLOONING   The still morning air of the Valley of the Sun is perfect for hot-air ballooning, and because of the stiff competition, prices are among the lowest in the country—between $125 and $150 per person for a 1- to 1½-hour ride. Companies to try include **Over the Rainbow** ((C) **602/225-5666;** www.letsgoballooning.com), **Zephyr Balloon/A Aerozona Adventure** ((C) **888/991-4260** or 480/991-4260; www.azballoon.com), and **Adventures Out West** ((C) **800/755-0935** or 602/996-6100; www.adventuresoutwest.com).

WATER PARKS   At **Waterworld Safari Water Park,** 4243 W. Pinnacle Peak Rd. ((C) **623/581-8446;** www.golfland-sunsplash.com/phoenix), you can free-fall down the Kilimanjaro speed slide. **Mesa Golfland-Sunsplash,** 155 W. Hampton Ave., Mesa ((C) **480/834-8318;** www.golfland-sunsplash.com/mesa), has a wave pool and a tunnel called the Black Hole. **Big Surf,** 1500 N. McClintock Rd. ((C) **480/947-2477;** www.golfland-sunsplash.com/tempe), has a wave pool and a speed slide. All three parks charge about $17 for adults and $14 for children. Waterworld Safari and Mesa Golfland-Sunsplash are open daily from around Memorial Day to Labor Day. Big Surf is open daily year-round.

WHITE-WATER RAFTING & TUBING   Up in the mountains to the northeast of Phoenix, the **Upper Salt River** still flows wild and free and offers some exciting rafting. Most years from late February to late May, snowmelt from the White Mountains turns the river into a Class III and IV river filled with exciting rapids. Companies operating full-day, overnight, and multi-day rafting trips include **Far Flung Adventures** ((C) **800/359-2627;** www.farflung.com), **Canyon Rio Rafting** ((C) **800/272-3353**), and **Mild to Wild Rafting** ((C) **800/567-6745;** wwwmild2wildrafting.com). Prices range from $100 to $114 for a day trip.

Tamer river trips can be had from **Salt River Recreation** ((C) **480/984-3305;** www.saltrivertubing.com), which has its headquarters 20 miles northeast of Phoenix on Power Road at Usery Pass Road in Tonto National Forest. For $12, the company will rent you a large inner tube and will shuttle you upriver for the float down. The season runs from May to September.

SHOPPING

Along the streets of Old Scottsdale you'll find dozens of **art galleries.** On Main Street, you'll find primarily cowboy art, while on North Marshall Way, you'll find much more imaginative and daring contemporary art.

For contemporary art, try **Art One,** 4120 N. Marshall Way, Scottsdale ((C) **480/946-5076**), specializing in work by art students and cutting-edge artists; or the **Lisa Sette Gallery,** 4142 N. Marshall Way, Scottsdale ((C) **480/990-7342**), which represents international and local artists working in a wide mix of media.

The **Heard Museum Gift Shop,** in the Heard Museum, 2301 N. Central Ave. ((C) **602/252-8344**), has an awesome collection of extremely well crafted and very expensive Native American jewelry, art, and crafts of all kinds. For one of the finest selections of Navajo rugs in the valley, visit **John C. Hill Antique Indian Art,** 6962 E. First Ave., Scottsdale ((C) **480/946-2910**).

WHERE TO STAY

During the winter, the Phoenix metro area has some of the highest room rates in the country. But keep in mind that most resorts offer a variety of weekend, golf, and tennis packages—it always pays to ask. Most places drop their rates in spring and fall, and prices really plummet for those who can take the summer heat.

Affordable chain motel options include the **Days Inn–Scottsdale/Fashion Square Resort,** 4710 N. Scottsdale Rd. (© 480/947-5411); the **Best Western Inn Suites Hotel Phoenix,** 1615 E. Northern Ave. at 16th Street, in north Phoenix (© 602/997-6285); and the **Super8–Phoenix Metro/Central,** 4021 N. 27th Ave., in north Phoenix (© 602/248-8880). Near the airport you'll find the **Best Western Airport Inn,** 2425 S. 24th St. (© 602/273-7251); and **Rodeway Inn–Airport East,** 1550 S. 52nd St. (© 480/967-3000).

Arizona Biltmore Resort & Spa   For timeless elegance, a prime location, and historic character, no other resort in the valley can touch the Biltmore, which was partly designed by Frank Lloyd Wright. While the golf courses and spa are the main draws, the children's center also makes this a popular choice for families. The "resort rooms" are comfortable and have balconies or patios; villa suites are the most spacious and luxurious of all. Afternoon tea, a Phoenix institution, is served in the lobby. 2400 E. Missouri Ave., Phoenix, AZ 85016. © 800/950-0086 or 602/955-6600. Fax 602/954-2571. www.arizonabiltmore.com. 730 units. Jan to early May $350–$550 double, from $675 suite; mid-May to late May and mid-Sept to Dec $310–$465 double, from $550 suite; June to early Sept $175–$260 double, from $340 suite (plus daily service fee of $12, year-round). AE, DC, DISC, MC, V. **Amenities:** Restaurants (3); 8 pools; spa; health club; 18-hole golf courses (2); 7 tennis courts; pets under 20 lb. accepted in cottage rooms ($250 deposit, $50 nonrefundable).

The Boulders   Set amid a jumble of giant boulders 45 minutes north of Scottsdale, this prestigious golf resort epitomizes the Southwest aesthetic. Adobe buildings blend unobtrusively into the desert, as do the two noted golf courses. Rooms continue the pueblo styling with stucco walls, beehive fireplaces, and beamed ceilings. Bathrooms are large and luxuriously appointed, with tubs for two and separate showers. If you can tear yourself away from the fairways, you can take advantage of the new Golden Door Spa or even try rock climbing. In addition to the on-site restaurants, there are several dining options at the adjacent El Pedregal Festival Marketplace. 34631 N. Tom Darlington Dr. (P.O. Box 2090), Carefree, AZ 85377. © 800/553-1717, 800/WYNDHAM, or 480/488-9009. Fax 480/488-4118. www.wyndham.com/luxury. 210 units. Late Dec to mid-May $495–$625 double, from $595 villa; late May to early Sept $205 double, from $245 villa; mid-Sept to early Dec $495 double, from $595 villa; mid-Dec $290 double, from $350 villa (plus nightly service charge of $27–$31, year-round). AE, DC, DISC, MC, V. **Amenities:** Restaurants (7); 4 pools; spa; fitness room; 18-hole golf courses (2); 8 tennis courts; pets accepted ($100).

The Buttes, A Wyndham Resort   This spectacular resort, 3 miles from Sky Harbor Airport, makes the most of its craggy hilltop location. Although some people complain that the freeway in the foreground ruins the view, the rocky setting and desert landscaping leave no doubt you're in the Southwest. Every inch of this resort is calculated to take your breath away. The pools and whirlpools (one of which is the most romantic in the valley) are the best reasons to stay here. Rooms are stylishly elegant. The Top of the Rock restaurant snags the best view around. 2000 Westcourt Way, Tempe, AZ 85282. © 800/WYNDHAM or 602/225-9000.

Fax 602/438-8622. www.wyndham.com. 353 units. Jan–Apr $239–$289 double, $475–$575 suite; May and mid-Sept to Dec $139–$189 double, from $475 suite; June to early Sept $109–$169 double, from $375 suite. AE, DC, DISC, MC, V. **Amenities:** Restaurants (2); 2 pools; spa services; fitness room; access to nearby health club; 4 tennis courts.

Doubletree Paradise Valley Resort   With its low-rise design, this resort gives a bow to the architectural style of Frank Lloyd Wright, and is built around several courtyards containing pools, fountains, and desert gardens. Mature palm trees lend a sort of Moorish feel to the grounds. Rooms have a contemporary feel, with lots of blond wood. With its distinctive styling and convenient location, this is an excellent close-in choice. 5401 N. Scottsdale Rd., Scottsdale, AZ 85250. (℃ **800/222-TREE** or 480/947-5400. Fax 480/481-0209. www.doubletreehotels.com. 387 units. Jan–Mar $179–$259 double, from $259 suite; Apr and Sept–Dec $99–$169 double, from $199 suite; May–Aug $65–$119 double, from $159 suite. AE, DC, DISC, MC, V. **Amenities:** Restaurants (2); 2 outdoor pools; fitness room; putting green; 2 tennis courts.

The Fairmont Scottsdale Princess   This modern rendition of a Moorish palace offers an exotic atmosphere unmatched by any other valley resort. It plays host to the Phoenix Open golf tournament and the city's top tennis tournament, and is also home to the Willow Stream spa and an impressive water playground. Located a 20-minute drive north of Old Town Scottsdale, this resort makes a good romantic hideaway as well as a family destination. Rooms have Southwestern decor and private balconies. 7575 E. Princess Dr., Scottsdale, AZ 85255. (℃ **800/ 344-4758** or 480/585-4848. Fax 480/585-0086. www.fairmont.com. 650 units. Jan to mid-Apr $359–$589 double, $569–$3,800 suite; late Apr to May and mid-Sept to Dec $249–$409 double, $439–$3,800 suite; June to early Sept $169–$319 double, $369–$3,800 suite. AE, DC, DISC, MC, V. **Amenities:** Restaurants (4); 4 pools; spa; fitness room; 18-hole golf courses (2); 7 tennis courts; pets accepted.

Fiesta Inn Resort   Reasonable rates, shady lawns, extensive recreational facilities (putting green, driving range, bike rentals, and more), and a location close to ASU and Tempe's Mill Avenue make this older, casual resort one of the best deals in the valley. Though rooms are a bit dark, they have an appealing retro mission styling and extras like fridges and coffeemakers. 2100 S. Priest Dr., Tempe, AZ 85282. (℃ **800/528-6481** or 480/967-1441. Fax 480/967-0224. www.fiestainnresort.com. 270 units. Jan to mid-Apr $175 double; late Apr to May $140 double; June–Sept $89 double; Oct–Dec $165 double. AE, DC, DISC, MC, V. **Amenities:** Restaurant; pool; fitness room; 3 tennis courts; pets accepted.

Hermosa Inn   If you don't like the crowds of big resorts but do enjoy the luxury, this is the spot for you. This boutique hotel in a quiet residential neighborhood is one of the few lodgings in the area to offer a bit of Old Arizona atmosphere. Rooms vary from cozy to spacious and are decorated in tastefully contemporary Western and Southwestern decor. The dining room, located in the original adobe home, serves excellent cuisine in a rustic, upscale setting. 5532 N. Palo Cristi Rd., Paradise Valley, AZ 85253. (℃ **800/241-1210** or 602/955-8614. Fax 602/955-8299. www.hermosainn.com. 35 units. Early Jan to Apr $285–$355 double, $475–$695 suite; early May to mid-May $220–$240 double, $360–$550 suite; late May to mid-Sept $95–$140 double, $300–$450 suite; late Sept to Dec $240–$290 double, $425–$625 suite. Rates include continental breakfast. AE, DC, DISC, MC, V. Take 32nd St. north from Camelback Rd., turn right on Stanford Rd., and turn left on N. Palo Cristi Rd. From Lincoln Dr., turn south on N. Palo Christi Rd. (east of 32nd St.). **Amenities:** Restaurant; outdoor pool; access to nearby health club; 3 tennis courts; pets under 20 lb. accepted ($250 deposit, $50 nonrefundable).

Holiday Inn SunSpree Resort   The SunSpree Resort is not as luxurious as most other area resorts, but it is a good choice for families (the adjacent McCormick-Stillman Railroad Park is a big hit with kids). Rooms have a plush feel that belies the reasonable rates, along with amenities such as fridges and safes; ask for a mountain-view unit or a lakeside room with a patio. 7601 E. Indian Bend Rd., Scottsdale, AZ 85250. (800/852-5205 or 480/991-2400. Fax 480/998-2261. www. arizonaguide.com/sunspree. 200 units. Jan to early Apr $139–$159 double; mid-Sept to Dec and mid-Apr to mid-May $115–$135 double; late May to early Sept $59–$79 double. AE, DC, DISC, MC, V. **Amenities:** Restaurant; 2 pools; fitness room; 18-hole golf course; 2 tennis courts.

Hotel San Carlos   If you don't mind staying in downtown Phoenix with the convention crowds, you'll get good value at this historic hotel. Listed on the National Register of Historic Places, the San Carlos provides that touch of elegance and charm missing from the other downtown choices. Unfortunately, rooms are rather small by today's standards, and the decor needs updating. 202 N. Central Ave., Phoenix, AZ 85004. (602/253-4121. Fax 602/253-4121. www.hotelsancarlos. com. 133 units. Jan–Apr $149 double, $210 suite; May–Sept $99 double, $149 suite; Oct–Dec $125 double, $199 suite. Rates include continental breakfast. AE, DC, DISC, MC, V. Valet and self-parking $15. **Amenities:** Restaurants (2); pool; pets allowed ($25).

Hyatt Regency Scottsdale   With its gardens full of stately palm trees and an extravagant water playground that encompasses 10 swimming pools, a water slide, a sand beach, a water-volleyball pool, waterfalls, and a huge whirlpool spa, this luxurious resort is designed to astonish. Guest rooms are luxurious and are designed to reflect the desert location. The top-end Golden Swan restaurant has an unusual sunken waterside terrace, while another restaurant provides afterdinner gondola rides. The resort's Hopi Learning Center provides a glimpse into Native American culture. 7500 E. Doubletree Ranch Rd., Scottsdale, AZ 85258. (800/55-HYATT or 480/991-3388. Fax 480/483-5550. www.scottsdale.hyatt.com. 493 units. Jan to mid-May $340–$545 double, from $830 suite and casita; late May to early Sept $190–$250 double, from $410 suite and casita; mid-Sept to Dec $300–$490 double, from $730 suite and casita. AE, DC, DISC, MC, V. **Amenities:** Restaurants (5); 10 pools; spa; health club; 27-hole golf course; 8 tennis courts.

Marriott's Camelback Inn   Set at the foot of Mummy Mountain and overlooking Camelback Mountain, the Camelback Inn is one of the grande dames of the Phoenix hotel scene and abounds in traditional Southwestern character. Although the two 18-hole golf courses are the main attraction, the spa is among the finest in the state. Rooms are decorated with Southwestern furnishings and art, and all have balconies or patios. The resort's top restaurant, the Chaparral, has long been a valley favorite. 5402 E. Lincoln Dr., Scottsdale, AZ 85253. (800/24-CAMEL or 480/948-1700. Fax 480/951-8469. www.camelbackinn.com. 453 units. Jan to early May $429–$460 double, $639–$2,075 suite; mid-May to early Sept $189–$360 double, $235–$1,550 suite; mid-Sept to Dec $360 double, $385–$1,550 suite. AE, DC, DISC, MC, V. **Amenities:** Restaurants (4); 3 pools; spa; fitness room; 18-hole golf courses (2); 6 tennis courts; small pets accepted.

The Phoenician   The palatial Phoenician consistently ranks among the finest resorts in the world. Service is second to none, the pool complex is one of the finest in the state, and there's a spa and 27 challenging holes of golf. Rooms have sunken bathtubs for two, large patios, and CD players. Mary Elaine's is Phoenix's ultimate special-occasion restaurant, while Windows on the Green is just a step behind. 6000 E. Camelback Rd., Scottsdale, AZ 85251. (800/888-8234 or 480/941-8200. Fax 480/947-4311. www.thephoenician.com. 654 units. Late Dec to early May $595 double, from $1,550 suite; mid-May to early June $495 double, from $1,420 suite; mid-June to mid-Sept $245 double, from $700 suite; late Sept to mid-Dec $495 double, from $1,425 suite. AE, DC, DISC, MC, V. Valet parking $22. **Amenities:** Restaurants (3); 9 pools; spa; health club; 27-hole golf course; 12 tennis courts; pets under 25 lb. accepted.

Pointe Hilton Squaw Peak Resort   Located at the foot of Squaw Peak, this lushly landscaped resort in north Phoenix makes a big splash with its 9-acre aquatic playground, featuring a tubing "river," water slide, waterfall, sports pool, and lagoon pool. An 18-hole putting course and game room also help make it a great family vacation spot. Rooms are outfitted with a mix of contemporary and Spanish colonial–style furnishings. The resort's Mexican restaurant is located in an 1880 adobe building. 7677 N. 16th St., Phoenix, AZ 85020-9832. ℂ **800/876-4683** or 602/997-2626. Fax 602/997-2391. www.pointehilton.com. 563 units. Jan to late Apr $199–$309 double, $950 grande suite; May and mid-Sept to Dec $109–$249 double, $659 grande suite; June to early Sept $109–$159 double, $659 grande suite (plus daily resort fee of $9, year-round). AE, DC, DISC, MC, V. **Amenities:** Restaurants (3); 7 pools; spa; health club; 18-hole golf course (4 miles away by shuttle); 4 tennis courts.

Royal Palms Hotel and Casitas   With its antique water fountains, lush walled gardens, and feel of a Mediterranean monastery cloister, this is one of the finest and most romantic resorts in the valley. The most memorable rooms are the deluxe casitas, each with a distinctive decor and two patios. T. Cook's is one of the city's most romantic restaurants. An adjacent lounge conjures up a Spanish villa setting. 5200 E. Camelback Rd., Phoenix, AZ 85018. ℂ **800/672-6011** or 602/840-3610. Fax 602/840-6927. www.royalpalmshotel.com. 116 units. Jan–May $365–$385 double, $405–$3,500 suite; June to early Sept $169–$179 double, $189–$2,500 suite; mid-Sept to Dec $345–$365 double, $375–$3,500 suite (plus daily service fee of $18, year-round). AE, DC, DISC, MC, V. **Amenities:** Restaurant; outdoor pool; fitness room; access to nearby health club; tennis court.

Sanctuary on Camelback Mountain   High on the northern flanks of Camelback Mountain is this lushly landscaped spa resort. Rooms are divided between the more conservative deluxe casitas and the contemporary spa casitas. These latter rooms are the only truly hip lodging option at any valley resort. With their cement floors, kidney-shaped daybeds, and streamline-moderne cabinetry, these units are absolutely stunning (but certainly not for everyone). Some bathrooms have private outdoor soaking tubs. The spa is one of the prettiest in the valley. 5700 E. McDonald Dr., Paradise Valley, AZ 85253. ℂ **800/245-2051** or 480/948-2100. Fax 480/483-3386. www.sanctuaryoncamelback.com. 98 units. Late Jan to early May, Oct to early Dec, and late Dec $360–$555 double, from $510 casita; mid-May to mid-June $280–$455 double, from $430 casita; late June to Sept and early to mid-Dec $135–$240 double, from $210 casita. AE, DC, DISC, MC, V. **Amenities:** Restaurants (2); 3 pools; spa; fitness center; 5 tennis courts; pets accepted.

The Sunburst Resort   Located in the heart of the Scottsdale shopping district, this resort features dramatic Southwestern design and a lushly planted courtyard with a small lagoon-style pool, complete with sand beach, short water slide, and flame-topped columnar waterfalls. Rooms are comfortable and decorated in new "Old West" styling, with French doors opening onto patios. 4925 N. Scottsdale Rd., Scottsdale, AZ 85251. ℂ **800/528-7867** or 480/945-7666. Fax 480/946-4056. www.sunburstresort.com. 210 units. Jan to mid-May $189–$259 double, $395–$750 suite; late May to early Sept $89–$119 double, $295–$500 suite; mid-Sept to Dec $189–$219 double, $350–$600 suite. AE, DC, DISC, MC, V. **Amenities:** Restaurant; 2 pools; fitness room; access to nearby health club.

GUEST RANCHES IN NEARBY WICKENBURG

Flying E Ranch This is the only real working cattle ranch still operating in Wickenburg, with 20,000 handsome acres for you and the cattle to roam. Family-owned since 1952, it's a particularly appealing down-home kind of place for those with kids. Rooms have Western-style furnishings and fridges. Three family-style meals are served in the wood-paneled dining room. Horseback riding costs an extra $30 to $40 per person per day; also on offer are guest rodeos, hayrides, and evening chuck-wagon dinners. 2801 W. Wickenburg Way, Wickenburg, AZ 85390-1087. (℃ 888/684-2650 or 928/684-2690. Fax 928/684-5304. www.flyingeranch.com. 17 units. $240–$305 double. Rates include all meals. 2- to 4-night minimum stay. No credit cards. Closed May–Oct. Drive 4 miles west of town on U.S. 60. **Amenities:** Restaurant; outdoor pool; fitness room; tennis court.

Kay El Bar Guest Ranch This is the smallest and oldest of the Wickenburg guest ranches, and its adobe buildings, built between 1914 and 1925, are listed on the National Register of Historic Places. The ranch is set on the bank of the Hassayampa River and the decor is quintessentially Wild West. While the cottage and the Casa Grande room are the most spacious, the smaller rooms in the adobe main lodge have original Monterey-style furnishings and other classic 1950s dude ranch decor (no phones or TVs in any rooms, though). The ranch has only 60 acres, but it abuts thousands of acres of public lands where guests can ride or hike. A tile floor and beehive fireplace in the dining room provide an authentic Southwestern feel. Horseback riding is included in the rates. Rincon Rd., off U.S. 93 (P.O. Box 2480), Wickenburg, AZ 85358. (℃ 800/684-7583 or 928/684-7593. Fax 928/ 684-4497. www.kayelbar.com. 11 units. $300–$330 double; $660 cottage for 4. Rates include all meals. Minimum stay may apply. MC, V. Closed May to mid-Oct. **Amenities:** Restaurant; outdoor pool.

WHERE TO DINE

Wild West–themed restaurants abound in the Phoenix area. These family restaurants generally provide big portions of grilled steaks and barbecued ribs, country music, and various sorts of entertainment, including stagecoach rides and shootouts in the street. For a fun, uniquely Phoenician experience, visit **Rawhide Western Town & Steakhouse,** 23023 N. Scottsdale Rd., Scottsdale (℃ 480/502-1880; www.rawhide.com), or order the enormous cowboy "stuff" platter at **Rustler's Rooste,** at the Pointe Hilton South Mountain, 7777 S. Pointe Hwy., Phoenix (℃ 602/431-6474), if you've got an appetite like a hungry cowpoke.

Bloom NEW AMERICAN Bloom is big and always full of energy. The minimalist decor emphasizes flowers, an elegant wine bar serves a wide range of flights (tasting assortments), and the bistro-style menu has lots of great dishes in a wide range of prices. Among the entrees, the roast duck with a crisp potato nest and drunken cherry sauce is excellent. Whatever you do, do not miss the bars of sin dessert! At Shops at Gainey Village, 8877 N. Scottsdale Rd., Scottsdale. (℃ 480/922-5666. www.tasteofbloom.com. Reservations recommended. Main courses $7–$12 lunch, $12–$24 dinner. AE, MC, V. Mon–Thurs 11am–2:30pm and 5–9:30pm; Fri–Sat 11am–2:30pm and 5–10:30pm.

Carlsbad Tavern NEW MEXICAN Carlsbad Tavern blends the fiery tastes of New Mexican cuisine with a hip and humorous bat-theme atmosphere (a reference to Carlsbad Caverns). The menu lists traditional New Mexican dishes such as *carne adovada,* pork simmered in a fiery red-chile sauce, as well as nouvelle Southwestern specialties like grilled chicken, andouille sausage, and pine nuts tossed with pasta in a spicy peppercorn-cream sauce. 3313 N. Hayden Rd. (south of Osborn), Scottsdale. ℂ **480/970-8164.** Reservations recommended for dinner. Main courses $6.25–$19. AE, DC, DISC, MC, V. Mon–Sat 11am–1am; Sun 1pm–1am (limited menu daily 10 or 11pm–1am).

El Guapo's Taco Shop & Salsa Bar MEXICAN   This nondescript hole-in-the-wall serves up mahi-mahi, carne asada, and marinated pork tacos, along with cheese crisps, burritos, and nachos. Try the armadillo eggs—jalapeño peppers stuffed with cheese and deep-fried. 3015 N. Scottsdale Rd. (in Plaza 777), Scottsdale. ℂ **480/423-8385.** Main dishes $2–$8. AE, MC, V. Mon–Sat 10am–8pm.

Golden Swan SOUTHWESTERN   If you're looking for bold Southwestern flavors in an unforgettable setting, this is the place. Entrees such as the grilled shrimp and scallops with *huitlacoche* quesadilla are always artistically arranged. Be sure to request a seat on the sunken patio, which really is below water level (a wall keeps back the waters). The open-air lounge is a romantic spot for a drink. At the Hyatt Regency Scottsdale, 7500 E. Doubletree Ranch Rd., Scottsdale. ℂ **480/991-3388.** Reservations recommended. Main courses $28–$36; Sun brunch $42. AE, DC, DISC, MC, V. Daily 6–10pm; Sun brunch 10am–2pm.

Lon's AMERICAN REGIONAL   This old adobe hacienda surrounded by colorful gardens is one of the most "Arizonan" places in the Phoenix area. Entrees are works of art, such as stuffed prawns on sun-dried tomato risotto with roasted corn and tomatillo sauce. The bar is cozy and romantic, and the patio affords beautiful views of Camelback Mountain. At the Hermosa Inn, 5532 N. Palo Cristi Rd. ℂ **602/955-7878.** www.lons.com. Reservations recommended. Main courses $9–$14 lunch, $18–$28 dinner. AE, DC, MC, V. Mon–Fri 11:30am–2pm and 6–10pm; Sat 6–10pm; Sun 10:30am–2pm (brunch) and 6–10pm.

MacAlpine's Nostalgic Soda Fountain & Coffee Shoppe AMERICAN   This is the oldest operating soda fountain in the Southwest, and it hasn't changed much since its opening in 1928. Wooden booths and worn countertops show the patina of time. Waffles are the breakfast specialty, while big burgers and sandwiches make up the lunch offerings. Wash it all down with a lemon phosphate, chocolate malted, or egg cream. 2303 N. Seventh St. ℂ **602/262-5545.** Sandwiches/specials $3.75–$6.50. AE, MC, V. Mon–Fri 7am–2pm; Sat 10am–3pm.

Marquesa MEDITERRANEAN   Thoroughly romantic, the Marquesa has an ambience reminiscent of an 18th-century Spanish villa. The offerings are ripe with exotic ingredients imported from around the world. *Paella Valenciana,* the signature dish, includes such ingredients as lobster, frogs' legs, mussels, shrimp, and cockles, and should not be missed. The Sunday brunch is one of the best in the valley. At the Fairmont Scottsdale Princess, 7575 E. Princess Dr. (about 12 miles north of downtown Scottsdale). ℂ **480/585-2735.** Reservations recommended. Main courses $35–$45; champagne brunch $49; tasting menus $80. AE, DC, DISC, MC, V. Wed–Sat 6–10pm; Sun 10am–2:30pm.

Mary Elaine's FRENCH   Mary Elaine's represents the pinnacle of Arizona dining for its haute cuisine, exemplary service, and superb table settings. The chef focuses on the seasonal flavors of the modern French-Mediterranean kitchen. You're almost certain to encounter the signature pan-seared John Dory with fennel, artichokes, and pearl onions. Wild game shows up regularly as well. The extensive wine list has won numerous awards. At the Phoenician, 6000 E. Camelback Rd., Scottsdale. ℂ **480/423-2530.** Reservations highly recommended. Jackets required for men. Main courses $41–$48; 6-course seasonal tasting menu $115 (matched wines are an additional $55). AE, DC, DISC, MC, V. Tues–Thurs 6–10pm; Fri–Sat 6–11pm

Pizzeria Bianco PIZZA Even though this historic brick building is smack-dab in the center of downtown Phoenix, the atmosphere is so cozy it feels like your neighborhood local. The wood-burning oven turns out deliciously rustic pizzas. Try one with red onion, Parmesan, rosemary, and crushed pistachios. Don't miss the fresh mozzarella, which can be ordered as an appetizer or on a pizza. At Heritage Sq., 623 E. Adams St. © 602/258-8300. Reservations accepted only for parties of 6 or more. Pizzas $8.50–$12. MC, V. Tues–Sat 5–10pm; Sun 5–9pm.

Roy's of Scottsdale EURO-ASIAN Even in Scottsdale you can now get Hawaiian chef Roy Yamaguchi's patented pan-Asian cuisine. Brilliant combinations and flamboyant presentations are the hallmarks, and despite the lively atmosphere, service usually runs like clockwork. The menu includes such signature dishes as blackened ahi tuna with a soy-mustard sauce. There's another Roy's at 2501 E. Camelback Rd., in the Camelback Esplanade (© **602/381-1155**). At the Scottsdale Seville shopping center, 7001 N. Scottsdale Rd. © **480/905-1155**. Reservations recommended. Main courses $17–$32; smaller plates $7.25–$12. AE, MC, V. Sun–Thurs 5–10pm; Fri–Sat 5–11pm.

Sam's Cafe SOUTHWESTERN Sam's Cafe, one of only a handful of decent downtown restaurants, offers food that's every bit as imaginative, but not nearly as expensive, as that served at other Southwestern restaurants in Phoenix. Breadsticks with picante-flavored cream cheese, grilled vegetable tacos, and angel-hair pasta in a spicy jalapeño sauce with shrimp and mushrooms all have a nice balance of flavors. The downtown Sam's has a large patio. Other Sam's are located in the Biltmore Fashion Park, 2566 E. Camelback Rd. (© **602/954-7100**), and in Scottsdale at 10010 N. Scottsdale Rd., at Shea Boulevard (© **480/368-2800**). At the Arizona Center, 455 N. Third St. © **602/252-3545**. Reservations recommended. Main courses $7–$18. AE, DISC, MC, V. Mon–Thurs 11am–10pm; Fri–Sat 11am–11pm; Sun 11am–9pm.

Top of the Rock NEW AMERICAN/SOUTHWESTERN For desert drama, no other view restaurant can compare with Top of the Rock, which, quite literally, is built into the top of a rocky hill looking north across the valley. Luckily, in addition to the setting, you can enjoy some very creative cuisine. Among the appetizers, don't miss the honey-glazed wild boar. Keep an eye out for the blue-corn–crusted halibut. The ambience is a little on the formal side, but you don't necessarily have to get dressed up. At the Buttes, A Wyndham Resort, 2000 Westcourt Way, Tempe. © **602/225-9000**. Reservations recommended. Main courses $24–$31; Sun brunch $36. AE, DC, DISC, MC, V. Sun–Thurs 5–10pm; Fri–Sat 5–11pm; Sun 10am–1:30pm and 5–10pm.

PHOENIX AFTER DARK

The best place to look for nightlife listings is in the *Phoenix New Times,* a weekly newspaper that tends to have the most comprehensive listings.

THE PERFORMING ARTS Phoenix's premier performance venue is **Symphony Hall,** 225 E. Adams St. (© **602/262-7272**), home to the **Phoenix Symphony** (www.phoenixsymphony.org) and the **Arizona Opera Company** (www.azopera.com) and host to other music performances and Broadway touring shows.

THE CLUB & MUSIC SCENE With a sports bar, several other bars and clubs, a multiplex theater, and several restaurants, downtown Phoenix's **Arizona**

Center is a veritable entertainment mecca. Another place to wander around until you hear your favorite type of music is **Mill Avenue** in Tempe. In **Scottsdale,** you'll find an eclectic array of clubs in the neighborhoods surrounding the corner of Camelback Road and Scottsdale Road. Clubs in this neighborhood tend to be the places to see and be seen.

At **Handlebar-J,** 7116 E. Becker Lane, Scottsdale (© **480/948-0110**), you'll hear live git-down two-steppin' music and can even get free dance lessons on Wednesday, Thursday, and Sunday. **Cajun House,** 7117 E. Third Ave., Scottsdale (© **480/945-5150**), a cavernous New Orleans–themed club, has bars, dining rooms, and lounges. **Axis/Radius,** 7340 E. Indian Plaza, Scottsdale (© **480/970-1112**), is currently Scottsdale's hottest club scene, the place where pro athletes and Hollywood celebs show up.

THE BAR SCENE   The **Hyatt Regency Scottsdale Lobby Bar,** 7500 E. Doubletree Ranch Rd., Scottsdale (© **480/991-3388**), is a romantic spot for nightly live music. The **Squaw Peak Bar,** in the Arizona Biltmore, 2400 E. Missouri Ave. (© **602/955-6600**), is a terrific spot for a cocktail at sunset. For the ultimate sports and rock bar, check out downtown Phoenix's **Alice Cooper's-town,** 101 E. Jackson St. (© **602/253-7337**), run by none other than Alice Cooper himself.

CASINOS   **Casino Arizona,** U.S. 101 and Indian Bend Road and U.S. 101 and McKellips Road (© **480/850-7777**), is a pair of casinos that together comprise the newest and most conveniently located casinos in the area. **Fort McDowell Casino,** on Fort McDowell Road off Ariz. 87, 2 miles northeast of Shea Boulevard, Fountain Hills (© **800/THE-FORT**), is the oldest in the state. **Harrah's Phoenix Ak-Chin Casino,** 15406 Maricopa Rd., Maricopa (© **800/427-7247**), 25 miles south of Phoenix and just south of the town of Maricopa, brings Vegas-caliber gambling to the Phoenix area.

2 Tucson

Melding Hispanic, Anglo, and Native American roots, Tucson is a city with a strong sense of identity—aware of its desert setting, confident in its style. Tucson supports an active cultural life, but it's the city's natural surroundings that set it apart. Four mountain ranges ring the city, and in those mountains and their foothills are giant saguaro cacti, a national park, an oasis, one of the finest zoos in the world, a ski area, and miles of hiking and horseback-riding trails.

ESSENTIALS

GETTING THERE   By Plane   Tucson International Airport (© **520/573-8000;** www.tucsonairport.org) is 6 miles south of downtown. Many resorts and hotels provide airport shuttle service. **Arizona Stagecoach** (© **520/889-1000**) operates 24-hour van service to downtown Tucson and the foothills resorts. Fares range from $15 to $26. A taxi to downtown costs around $19, to the resorts about $25 to $40.

Sun Tran (© **520/792-9222;** www.suntran.com), the local public transit, operates a bus service to and from the airport, though you'll have to make a transfer to reach downtown. The fare is $1.

By Train   Amtrak (© **800/USA-RAIL;** www.amtrak.com) provides service from Los Angeles (trip time: 10 hr.), San Antonio (18 hr.), and New Orleans (32 hr.) to its station at 400 E. Toole St.

By Car   The major routes into Tucson are I-10 from the northwest (Phoenix) and east (El Paso). I-19 connects Tucson with the Mexican border at Nogales. If you're headed downtown, take the Congress Street exit off I-10. If you're headed for one of the foothills resorts north of downtown, take the Ina Road exit.

VISITOR INFORMATION   The **Metropolitan Tucson Convention and Visitors Bureau (MTCVB),** 100 S. Church St. (at Broadway), Ste. 7199 (© **800/638-8350** or 520/624-1817; www.visitTucson.org), is an excellent source of information. Open Monday through Friday from 8am to 5pm, Saturday and Sunday from 9am to 4pm.

GETTING AROUND   Unless you plan to stay by the pool or on the golf course, you'll probably want to rent a car. Rates tend to be low. Downtown Tucson is still a relatively easy place to find a parking space, and parking fees are low. There are two huge parking lots on the south side of the Tucson Convention Center and plenty of metered parking on the smaller downtown streets. Almost all Tucson hotels and resorts provide free parking.

Sun Tran (© **520/792-9222;** www.suntran.com) public buses are $1 for adults, 40¢ for seniors, and free for children 5 and under. The bus system does not extend to all major tourist attractions and is of limited use to visitors.

Though they don't go very far, the restored electric streetcars of **Old Pueblo Trolley** (© **520/792-1802**) are a fun way to get from the Fourth Avenue shopping district to the University of Arizona. The trolleys operate Friday from 6 to 10pm, Saturday from noon to midnight, and Sunday from noon to 6pm. The fare is $1 for adults and 50¢ for children 6 to 12. All-day passes are $2.50 for adults and $1.25 for children.

For a taxi, phone **Yellow Cab** (© **520/624-6611**) or **Allstate Cab** (© **520/ 798-1111**).

FAST FACTS   For a doctor referral, call **University Health Connection** (© **520/694 8888**). The **University Medical Center** is at 1501 N. Campbell Ave. (© **520/694-0111**). Call © **800/WALGREENS** for the Walgreens pharmacy that's nearest you or that's open 24 hours.

WHAT TO SEE & DO

Arizona–Sonora Desert Museum   The full spectrum of Sonoran Desert life—from plants to insects to fish to reptiles to mammals—is on display in natural settings at this world-class zoo. Coyotes and javelinas (peccaries) seem very much at home in their compounds, which are surrounded by almost invisible wire mesh fences that make it seem as though there is nothing between you and the animals. These display areas are along the Desert Loop Trail, which is also where you'll find the museum's newest exhibits. There are black bears, mountain lions, beavers, otters, frogs, fish, tarantulas, scorpions, prairie dogs, and desert bighorn sheep. Our favorite exhibit is the walk-in hummingbird aviary. The museum has two dining options, which both serve good food. 2021 N. Kinney Rd. © 520/883-1380. www.desertmuseum.org. Admission $9.95 adults Nov–Apr, $8.95 May–Oct; $1.75 children 6–12. Oct–Feb daily 8:30am–5pm; Mar–Sept daily 7:30am–5pm. From downtown Tucson, go west on Speedway Blvd., which becomes Gates Pass Rd., and follow the signs.

Mission San Xavier del Bac   Called the White Dove of the Desert, Mission San Xavier del Bac, a blindingly white adobe building rising from a sere, brown landscape, is considered the finest example of mission architecture in the Southwest. The beautiful church, which was built between 1783 and 1797, incorporates Moorish, Byzantine, and Mexican Renaissance architectural styles. The

Tucson

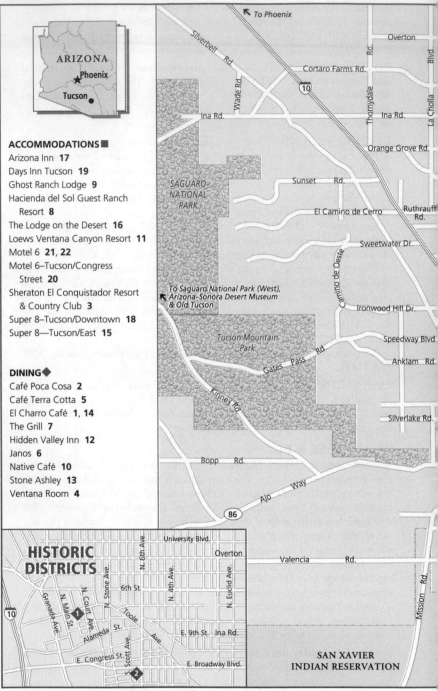

ARIZONA
Phoenix
Tucson

To Phoenix

Silverbelt Rd.
Cortaro Farms Rd.
Overton
Wade Rd.
Thornydale Rd.
Ina Rd.
La Cholla Blvd.
Ina Rd.
Orange Grove Rd.

SAGUARO NATIONAL PARK

Sunset Rd.
El Camino de Cero
Ruthrauff Rd.
Sweetwater Dr.
Camino de Oeste

To Saguaro National Park (West),
Arizona-Sonora Desert Museum
& Old Tucson

Ironwood Hill Dr.

Tucson Mountain Park

Gates Pass Rd.
Speedway Blvd
Anklam Rd.

Kinney Rd.

Silverlake Rd.

Bopp Rd.

Ajo Way

86

Valencia Rd.

Mission Rd.

HISTORIC DISTRICTS

10
Granada Ave.
N. Court Ave.
N. Main St.
N. Stone Ave.
Toole Ave.
Alameda St.
E. Congress St.
Scott Ave.

University Blvd.
Overton
N. 6th Ave.
N. 4th Ave.
N. Euclid Ave.
6th St.
E. 9th St.
Ina Rd.
E. Broadway Blvd.

**SAN XAVIER
INDIAN RESERVATION**

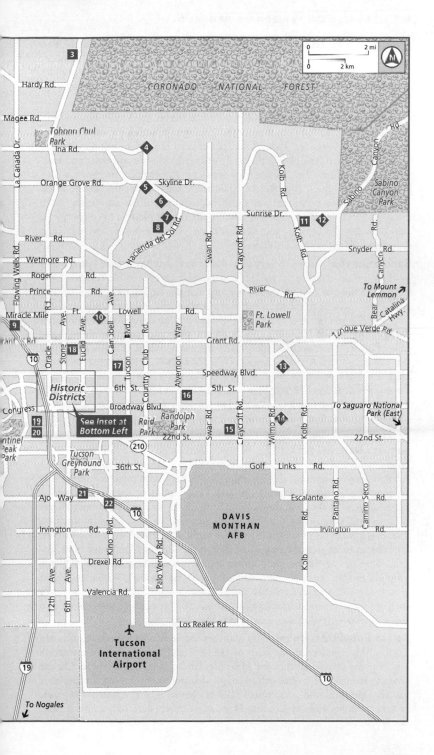

church was never actually completed, which becomes apparent when the two bell towers are compared. One is topped with a dome, while the other has none. Restored murals cover the walls, and behind the altar are colorful and elaborate decorations. 1950 W. San Xavier Rd. ⓒ **520/294-2624.** Free admission; donations accepted. Daily 7am–5pm. Take I-19 south 9 miles to Exit 92 and turn right.

Old Tucson Studios   Old Tucson was built as the set for the 1939 movie *Arizona* and since then has been used in the filming of countless movies, including *Tombstone* and *Geronimo*. Today, Old Tucson is far more than just a movie set; it's a Wild West theme park with family-oriented activities and entertainment. Throughout the day, there are staged shootouts in the streets, stunt shows, a can-can revue, and other performances. Train rides, stagecoach rides, kiddie rides, educational shows, restaurants, and gift shops round out the experience. 201 S. Kinney Rd. ⓒ **520/883-0100.** www.oldtucson.com. Admission $15 adults, $9.45 children 4–11. Daily 10am–6pm. Take Speedway Blvd. west, continuing in the same direction when it becomes Gates Pass Blvd., and turn left on S. Kinney Rd.

Sabino Canyon   Sabino Canyon is a desert oasis that has attracted people and animals for thousands of years. This spectacular and accessible corner of the desert contains not only impressive scenery, but also hiking trails and a stream. Many visitors come to splash in the canyon's waterfalls and pools, but for those who prefer just to gaze at the beauty of crystal-clear water flowing through a rocky canyon guarded by saguaro cacti, there are narrated tram rides through the lower canyon. There are also many trails and picnic tables. (Bring water if you want to hike.) 5900 N. Sabino Canyon Rd. ⓒ **520/749-2861,** or 520/749-2327 for shuttle information and moonlight reservations. www.fs.fed.us/r3/coronado/scrd. Parking $5. Sabino Canyon tram ride $6 adults, $2.50 children 3–12; Bear Canyon tram ride $3 adults, $1.25 children 3–12. Park daily dawn–dusk. Sabino Canyon tram rides daily 9am–4:30pm; Bear Canyon tram rides daily 9am–4pm (both trams more limited in summer). Take Grant Rd. east to Tanque Verde Rd., continuing east; at Sabino Canyon Rd., turn north and watch for the sign.

Saguaro National Park   The massive, treelike saguaro cactus is the quintessential symbol of the American desert. Since 1933, saguaros (and all the other inhabitants of this part of the Sonoran Desert) have been preserved in the two sections of what is now Saguaro National Park. The most impressive stands of saguaros are to be found in the western district, near the Arizona–Sonora Desert Museum and Old Tucson Studios. In the area near the Red Hills Information Center is a water hole that attracts wild animals. The eastern section of the park contains an older area of forest at the foot of the Rincon Mountains. Both sections have visitor centers, loop roads, nature trails, hiking trails, and picnic grounds. East district visitor center: 3693 S. Old Spanish Trail. ⓒ **520/733-5153.** West district visitor center: 2700 N. Kinney Rd. ⓒ **520/733-5158.** www.nps.gov/sagu. Entry fee $6 per car, $3 per hiker (charged in the east section only). East district daily 7am to sunset, west district 6am to sunset; visitor centers daily 8:30am–5pm; open to hikers 24 hr.

Tucson Botanical Gardens   Set amid residential neighborhoods in midtown Tucson, these gardens are an oasis of greenery and, though small, are worth a visit if you're interested in desert plant life, landscaping, or gardening. On the 5½-acre grounds are several small gardens that not only have visual appeal but are also historical and educational. 2150 N. Alvernon Way. ⓒ **520/326-9686.** www.tucsonbotanical.org. Admission $5 adults, $4 seniors, $1 children 6–11. Daily 8:30am–4:30pm. Bus: 11.

OUTDOOR PURSUITS

BICYCLING   Tucson is one of the best bicycling cities in the country, and the dirt roads and trails of the surrounding national forest and desert are perfect for mountain biking. Bikes can be rented for $25 a day at **Basement Bike,** 428 N. Fremont Ave., near the university (© **520/628-1015**). This store can also set you up with a bicycling map of the area.

If you'd rather confine your pedaling to paved surfaces, there are some great options around town. The number-one choice in town for cyclists in halfway decent shape is the road up **Sabino Canyon.** Keep in mind, however, that bicycles are allowed on this road only 5 days a week and then only before 9am and after 5pm (the road's closed to bikes all day on Wed and Sat). For a much easier ride, try the **Rillito River Park path,** a 4-mile trail that parallels River Road and the usually dry bed of the Rillito River between Campbell Avenue and La Cholla Boulevard. If you've got knobby tires, you can continue west on this trail after the pavement ends.

BIRD-WATCHING   Southern Arizona has some of the best bird-watching in the country, and though the best spots are south of Tucson, there are a few places around the city that birders will enjoy seeking out. **Roy P. Drachman Agua Caliente County Park,** 4002 N. Soldier Trail, at Roger Road in the northeast corner of the city, is just about the best place in Tucson to see birds. The year-round warm springs here are a magnet for dozens of species, including great blue herons, black phoebes, soras, and vermilion flycatchers. To find the park, follow Tanque Verde Road east 6 miles from the intersection with Sabino Canyon Road and turn left onto Soldier Trail. Watch for signs.

The best area birding is in **Madera Canyon National Forest Recreation Area** (© **520/281-2296**), about 40 miles south of the city, in the Coronado National Forest. Because of the year-round water to be found here, Madera Canyon attracts a surprising variety of bird life. Avid birders flock to this canyon in hopes of spotting more than a dozen species of hummingbirds, an equal number of flycatchers, warblers, tanagers, buntings, grosbeaks, and many rare birds not found in any other state. The shady picnic areas and trails still get a lot of use by those who don't carry binoculars. If you're heading out here for the day, arrive early—parking is very limited.

GOLF   Although there aren't quite as many golf courses in Tucson as in Phoenix, this is still a golfer's town. For last-minute tee-time reservations, contact **Standby Golf** (© **800/655-5345** or 520/882-2665).

In addition to the public and municipal links, there are numerous resort courses that allow nonguests to play. Perhaps the most famous of these are the two 18-hole courses at **Ventana Canyon Golf and Racquet Club,** 6200 N. Clubhouse Lane (© **520/577-1400**). These Tom Fazio–designed courses offer challenging desert target–style play that is nearly legendary. The third hole on the Mountain Course is one of the most photographed in the West. Greens fees are $169 to $179 in winter and $69 to $79 in summer.

As famous as Ventana Canyon courses are, it's the 27-hole **Omni Tucson National Golf Resort and Spa,** 2727 W. Club Dr. (© **520/575-7540**), a traditional course, that is perhaps more familiar to golfers as the site of the annual Tucson Open. Greens fees are $175 in winter, $65 in summer. **El Conquistador Country Club,** 10555 N. La Cañada Dr., Oro Valley (© **520/544-1800**), with two 18-hole courses and a nine-hole course, offers stunning views of the Santa Catalina Mountains. Greens fees are $99 in winter, $40 in summer.

La Paloma Resort and Country Club, 3660 E. Sunrise Dr. (© **520/299-1500**), features 27 holes designed by Jack Nicklaus. Fees are $185 to $205 in winter, $85 in summer. At **Starr Pass Golf Club,** 3645 W. Starr Pass Blvd. (© **520/670-0400**), players are seduced by the deceptively difficult 15th hole that plays right through the narrow Starr Pass, which was once a stagecoach route. Greens fees are $148 in winter, $50 in summer.

There are many public courses around town. The **Raven Golf Club at Sabino Springs,** 9777 E. Sabino Greens Dr. (© **520/749-3636**), incorporates stands of cactus and rocky outcroppings into the course layout. Greens fees are $140 to $170 in winter, $55 to $65 in summer. The **Golf Club at Vistoso,** 955 W. Vistoso Highlands Dr. (© **520/797-9900**), has a championship desert course, with fees of $150 in winter, $50 in summer. **Heritage Highlands Golf & Country Club,** 4949 W. Heritage Club Blvd., Marana (© **520/579-7000**), is a newer championship desert course at the foot of the Tortolita Mountains; fees are $125 in winter and $45 in summer.

Tucson Parks and Recreation operates five municipal golf courses, of which the **Randolph North** and **Dell Urich,** 600 S. Alvernon Way (© **520/791-4161**), are the premier courses. The former is the site of the LPGA Open. Greens fees for 18 holes at these two courses are $37 to $65 in winter and $16 in summer. Other municipal courses include **El Rio–Trini Alvarez,** 1400 W. Speedway Blvd. (© **520/791-4229**); **Silverbell,** 3600 N. Silverbell Rd. (© **520/791-5235**); and **Fred Enke,** 8251 E. Irvington Rd. (© **520/791-2539**). Greens fees at these three courses are $32 in winter and $14 in summer. Carts are available for $18. For information on all of the municipal courses, call © **520/791-4653;** to make tee-time reservations, call © **520/791-4336.** Online, check out **www.tucsoncity golf.com**.

HIKING Tucson is nearly surrounded by mountains, most of which are protected as city and state parks, national forest, or national park, and within these public areas are hundreds of miles of hiking trails. See the listings for Saguaro National Park and Sabino Canyon, above.

Tucson Mountain Park, at the end of Speedway Boulevard, is adjacent to Saguaro National Park and preserves a similar landscape. The parking area at Gates Pass, on Speedway, is a favorite sunset spot.

With Tucson's city limits pushing right out to the boundary of the Coronado National Forest, there are some excellent hiking options in Tucson's northern foothills. The **Ventana Canyon Trail** begins at a parking area adjacent to the Loews Ventana Canyon Resort (off Sunrise Dr. west of Sabino Canyon Rd.) and leads into the Ventana Canyon Wilderness. Over near the Westward Look Resort is the **Pima Canyon Trail,** which leads into the Ventana Canyon Wilderness and is reached off Ina Road just east of Oracle Road. Both of these trails provide classic desert canyon hikes of whatever length you feel like hiking (a dam at 3 miles on the latter trail makes a good turnaround point).

Catalina State Park, 11570 N. Oracle Rd. (© **520/628-5798**), is set on the rugged northwest face of the Santa Catalina Mountains, between 2,500 and 3,000 feet high. Hiking trails here lead into the Pusch Ridge Wilderness; however, the favorite park day hike is the 5½-mile round-trip to **Romero Pools,** a refreshing destination on a hot day. Admission to the park is $5. There are horseback-riding stables adjacent to the park, and within the park is an ancient Hohokam ruin.

One of the reasons Tucson is such a livable city is the presence of the cool (and, in winter, snow-covered) pine forests of 8,250-foot Mount Lemmon.

Within the **Mount Lemmon Recreation Area,** at the end of the Catalina High-way (also now called the Sky Island Scenic Byway), are many miles of trails, and the hearty hiker can even set out from down in the lowland desert and hike up into the Alpine forests. For a more leisurely excursion, drive to the top to start your hike. Keep in mind that in winter, when the weather is pleasant in Tucson, people may be skiing up here. There is a $5-per-vehicle charge to use any of the sites within this recreation area. Even if you only plan to pull off at a roadside parking spot and ogle the view, you'll need to stop at the roadside ticket kiosk at the base of the mountain and pay your fee.

HORSEBACK RIDING   In addition to renting horses and providing guided trail rides, some of the stables below offer sunset rides with cookouts. Reserva-tions are a good idea. You can also opt to stay at a guest ranch and do as much riding as your muscles can stand.

Pusch Ridge Stables, 13700 N. Oracle Rd. (© **520/825-1664**), is adjacent to Catalina State Park and Coronado National Forest. Rates are $20 for 1 hour, $35 for 2 hours, and $30 for a sunset ride.

Big Sky Rides (© **520/744-3789** or 520/299-RIDE; www.bigskyride.com) offers rides at several locations, including in the Tucson Mountains and Saguaro National Park West and at La Tierra Linda Guest Ranch Resort and Hacienda del Sol Guest Ranch Resort. Rates range from $25 for 1 hour to $95 for a full day.

HOT-AIR BALLOONING   Balloon Rides U.S.A. (© **520/299-7744;** www.balloonridesusa.com) offers breakfast flights over the desert or the foothills of the Santa Catalina Mountains, including a champagne toast. Flights cost $150 to $250 per person; the ballooning season runs October through June. **Fleur de Tucson Balloon Tours** (© **520/529-1025**) offers rides over the Tucson Moun-tains and Saguaro National Park. Rates are $155 per person, including brunch and a champagne toast.

WILDFLOWER VIEWING   Bloom time varies from year to year, but April and May are good times to view native wildflowers in the Tucson area. While the crowns of white blossoms worn by saguaro cacti are among the most visible blooms in the area, other cacti are far more colorful. Saguaro National Park and Sabino Canyon are among the best local spots to see saguaros, other cacti, and various wildflowers in bloom. If you feel like heading farther afield, the wild-flower displays at Picacho Peak State Park, between Tucson and Casa Grande, are considered the most impressive in the state.

SHOPPING

El Presidio Historic District around the Tucson Museum of Art is the city's center for crafts shops. This area is home to Old Town Artisans and the Tucson Museum of Art museum shop. The **"Lost Barrio"** on the corner of Southwest Park Avenue and 12th Street (a block off Broadway) is a good place to look for Mexican imports and Southwestern-style home furnishings.

Mark Sublette Medicine Man Gallery, Santa Fe Square, 7000 E. Tanque Verde Rd. (© **520/722-7798**), has the best and biggest selection of old Navajo rugs in the city, as well as Mexican and other Hispanic textiles, Acoma pottery, basketry, and artwork by cowboy artists. With its museum-quality goods (antique Navajo rugs, kachinas, furniture, and a huge selection of old Native American jewelry), **Morning Star Traders,** 2020 E. Speedway Blvd. (© **520/881-2112**), just may be the best store of its type in the entire state.

WHERE TO STAY

There are dozens of budget chain motels along I-10 as it passes through downtown Tucson. Among the better choices are **Days Inn Tucson,** 222 S. Fwy. (Exit 258; ☎ **520/791-7511**); **Motel 6–Tucson/Congress Street,** 960 S. Fwy. (Exit 258; ☎ **520/628-1339**); and **Super 8–Tucson/Downtown,** 1248 N. Stone St. (Exit 257; ☎ **520/622-6446**).

Near the airport, you have your choice of the **Motel 6** at 755 E. Benson Hwy. (Exit 262 off I-10; ☎ **520/622-4614**), or the one at 1031 E. Benson Hwy. (Exit 262; ☎ **520/628-1264**). **Super 8–Tucson/East** is at 1990 S. Craycroft Rd. (Exit 265 off I-10; ☎ **520/790-6021**).

Arizona Inn   With its pink-stucco buildings and immaculately tended gardens, the historic Arizona Inn is an absolute oasis. If you're searching for Old Arizona charm but also demand modern levels of comfort, then look no further. Most rooms have original or reproduction period furniture; some also have fireplaces. Most suites have private patios or enclosed sun porches. The main dining room is a casually elegant hall with plenty of outdoor seating as well. 2200 E. Elm St., Tucson, AZ 85719. ☎ **800/933-1093** or 520/325-1541. Fax 520/320-2182. www.arizona inn.com. 89 units. Late Jan to mid-Apr $225–$245 double, from $299 suite; late Apr to May $189 double, from $235 suite; June to mid-Sept $144 double, from $184 suite; late Sept to mid-Dec $140 double, from $193 suite; late Dec to mid-Jan $163 double, from $224 suite. AE, DC, MC, V. **Amenities:** Restaurants (2); outdoor pool; fitness room; 2 tennis courts.

Casa Tierra   If you've come to Tucson to be in the desert, this modern adobe B&B is worth considering. Built to look as though it has been here since Spanish colonial days, Casa Tierra is surrounded by 5 cactus-studded acres on the west side of Saguaro National Park. Sunsets are enough to take your breath away. Rooms open onto a landscaped courtyard, which is surrounded by a covered seating area. The outdoor whirlpool makes a perfect stargazing spot. 11155 W. Calle Pima, Tucson, AZ 85743. ☎ **866/254-0006** or 520/578-3058. Fax 520/578-8445. www.casa tierratucson.com. 4 units. Aug 15–June 15 $135–$195 double, $200–$300 suite. Rates include full breakfast. 2-night minimum stay. AE, DISC, MC, V. Closed June 16–Aug 14. **Amenities:** Fitness room.

Ghost Ranch Lodge   If you're looking for affordable Old Tucson, this is it. Situated on 8 acres, the lodge has a justly famous cactus garden, orange grove, and extensive lawns that together create an oasis atmosphere. Rooms, though modernized, retain a bit of Western flavor, with beamed ceilings, painted brick walls, and patios covered by red-tile roofs. The lodge's dining room has a poolside patio and a view of the Santa Catalina Mountains. The only drawback here is that this is a rather run-down stretch of road. 801 W. Miracle Mile, Tucson, AZ 85705. ☎ **800/456-7565** or 520/791-7565. Fax 520/791-3898. www.ghostranchlodge.com. 83 units. Mid-Jan to early Apr $86–$135 double; mid-Apr to early June $50–$80 double; mid-June to early Oct $44–$75 double; mid-Oct to early Jan $46–$90 double. Rates include continental breakfast. AE, DISC, MC, V. **Amenities:** Restaurant; outdoor pool; pets accepted.

Hacienda del Sol Guest Ranch Resort   With its colorful Southwest styling, historic character, desert gardens, and ridge-top setting, Hacienda del Sol is one of the most distinctive hotels in Tucson. Rooms have rustic and colorful Mexican character, with a decidedly artistic flair. If you prefer more modern accommodations, ask for a suite; if you want loads of space, ask for a casita. The Grill is one of Tucson's best restaurants. 5601 N. Hacienda del Sol Rd., Tucson, AZ 85718. ☎ **800/728-6514** or 520/299-1501. www.haciendadelsol.com. 30 units. Mid-Jan to May $155 double, $225 hacienda, $320 suite, $360–$440 casita; June–Sept $59–$70 double, $79–$99 hacienda, $125–$160 suite, $145–$230 casita; Oct to early Jan $135–$145 double, $205–$215 hacienda, $300–$310 suite, $340–$440 casita. 2-night minimum stay weekends and holidays. Rates include continental breakfast. AE, MC, V. **Amenities:** Restaurant; outdoor pool; tennis court.

The Lodge on the Desert Dating from 1936, the Lodge on the Desert is a restored romantic getaway in central Tucson. It offers a lush and relaxing retreat comparable in many ways to the Arizona Inn (though certainly not as deluxe). Numerous hacienda-style adobe buildings are tucked amid the cactus and orange trees. Inside the rooms, you'll find a mix of contemporary and South-western furnishings; many units have beamed ceilings or fireplaces, and some are carpeted while others have tile floors. 306 N. Alvernon Way, Tucson, AZ 85711. © 800/ 456-5634 or 520/325-3366. Fax 520/327-5834. www.lodgeonthedesert.com. 35 units. Mid-Jan to May $169–$289 double; June–Sept $79–$159 double; Oct to early Jan $119–$209 double. Rates include full breakfast. AE, DC, DISC, MC, V. **Amenities:** Restaurant; outdoor pool; pets accepted ($50 deposit plus $15 per day).

Loews Ventana Canyon Resort For breathtaking scenery and superb facil-ities (including two Tom Fazio golf courses and a full-service spa), no other Tuc-son accommodation can compare. The Santa Catalina Mountains rise behind the property, and despite its many amenities, the resort is firmly planted in the desert. Flagstone floors in the lobby give the public rooms a rugged but luxuri-ous appeal. Guest rooms have balconies overlooking city lights or mountains; some have fireplaces. Bathrooms include tubs built for two. The Ventana Room is one of Tucson's finest restaurants, while the Flying V has good food and good views. There are jogging and nature trails and a playground on the property. 7000 N. Resort Dr., Tucson, AZ 85750. © 800/23-LOEWS or 520/299-2020. Fax 520/299-6832. www. loewshotels.com. 398 units. Mid-Jan to mid-May $365 double, from $750 suite; late May to early Sept $150 double, from $295 suite; mid-Sept to early Jan $325 double, from $700 suite. AE, DC, DISC, MC, V. **Amenities:** Restaurants (4); 2 outdoor pools; spa; fitness room; 18-hole golf courses (2); 8 tennis courts.

Sheraton El Conquistador Resort & Country Club With the Santa Catalina Mountains as a backdrop, this resort in Tucson's northern foothills boasts a spectacular setting. Keep in mind that if you stay here, you'll be at least 30 minutes from downtown. Most rooms are built around a central courtyard with a large pool; because this area is often taken over by conventioneers, those seeking quiet may want a room in the separate casitas area. All units feature Southwestern-influenced furniture, marble bathrooms, and balconies or patios. In the Mexican restaurant, strolling mariachis entertain, while in the steakhouse, cancan dancers are the order of the day. 10000 N. Oracle Rd., Tucson, AZ 85737. © 800/ 325-7832 or 520/544-5000. Fax 520/544-1224. www.sheraton.com/elconquistador. 428 units. Jan to mid-May $259–$490 double, from $339 suite; late May to mid-Sept $119–$290 double, from $179 suite; late Sept to Dec $219–$420 double, from $299 suite (plus $8 service fee, year-round). AE, DC, DISC, MC, V. **Amenities:** Restaurants (5); 4 pools; spa; 2 fitness rooms; 45-hole golf course; 31 tennis courts; pets accepted.

Tanque Verde Ranch Tanque Verde, the most luxurious guest ranch in Tuc-son, borders both Saguaro National Park and the Coronado National Forest. The bird-watching here is excellent, and other activities include guided hikes, horseback rides, poolside luncheons, guided mountain-bike rides, and evening lectures and performances. Rooms are spacious and comfortable; many have fireplaces, patios, and fridges, but don't expect a TV. The casitas are absolutely huge and are among the most luxurious accommodations in the state. 14301 E. Speedway Blvd., Tucson, AZ 85748. © 800/234-DUDE or 520/296-6275. Fax 520/721-9426.

www.tanqueverderanch.com. 75 units. Mid-Dec to Apr $320–$500 double; May–Sept $260–$375 double; Oct to early Dec $280–$395 double. Rates include all meals and ranch activities. AE, DISC, MC, V. **Amenities:** Restaurant; indoor and outdoor pools; fitness room; 5 tennis courts.

WHERE TO DINE

If you're looking for a cowboy steakhouse and a great place for the whole family, try **Hidden Valley Inn,** 4825 N. Sabino Canyon Rd. (© **520/299-4941**), a brightly colored, false-fronted cow town serving cowpuncher-size steaks and barbecued ribs.

Café Poca Cosa NUEVO MEXICAN   The food here is not just *any* Mexican food; it's imaginative and different, and the flamboyant atmosphere of red and purple walls and Mexican and Southwestern artwork is equally unusual. The cuisine consists of creations such as chicken with a dark mole sauce made with Kahlúa, chocolate, almonds, and chiles. The staff is courteous and friendly. This lively restaurant is an excellent value, especially at lunch. At Clarion Hotel & Suites Santa Rita, 88 E. Broadway Blvd. © **520/622-6400.** Reservations highly recommended. Main courses $8.50–$10 lunch, $14–$18 dinner. MC, V. Mon–Thurs 11am–9pm; Fri–Sat 11am–10pm.

Café Terra Cotta SOUTHWESTERN   Café Terra Cotta is Arizona's original Southwestern restaurant, offering a combination of creative cooking, casual atmosphere, and local artwork. A brick oven is used to make pizzas, while salads, sandwiches, small plates, and main dishes flesh out the long menu. With so many choices, it's often difficult to decide, but the must-have signature dish is garlic custard, served with a warm salsa vinaigrette and herbed hazelnuts. 3500 Sunrise Dr. © **520/577-8100.** www.cafeterracotta.com. Reservations recommended. Main courses $8.25–$25. AE, DC, DISC, MC, V. Daily 11am–10pm.

El Charro Café SONORAN MEXICAN   Located in an old stone building in El Presidio Historic District, El Charro is Tucson's oldest family-operated Mexican restaurant. Its specialty is *carne seca,* an air-dried beef similar to jerky. The cafe can be packed at lunch, so arrive early or late. The adjacent ¡Toma!, a colorful bar/cantina, is under the same ownership. There's another El Charro at 6310 E. Broadway (© **520/745-1922**). 311 N. Court Ave. © **520/622-1922.** www.charrorestaurant.com. Reservations recommended for dinner. Main courses $6–$16. AE, DC, DISC, MC, V. Sun–Thurs 11am–9pm; Fri–Sat 11am–10pm.

The Grill REGIONAL   Located in a 1920s hacienda-style former dude ranch, the Grill is known for its classic Southwestern styling and great views of the city. For openers, consider the roasted tomato soup, which comes with garlic and goat-cheese croustade. The lamb chops are not to be missed; for greater creativity, opt for the applewood-smoked duckling with black currant and pomegranate vinaigrette. Sunday brunch here is a treat. At the Hacienda del Sol Guest Ranch Resort, 5601 N. Hacienda del Sol Rd. © **520/529-3500.** www.haciendadelsol.com. Reservations recommended. Main courses $23–$34; Sun brunch $30. AE, DC, DISC, MC, V. Mon–Sat 5:30–10pm; Sun 10am–2pm and 5:30–10pm.

Janos SOUTHWESTERN/REGIONAL   Janos Wilder is the city's most celebrated chef and in 2000 won the James Beard Award for Top Chef in the Southwest. His menu changes daily, with such offerings as lobster with papaya in champagne sauce, pistachio-crusted salmon with a rich mole sauce, and at least one sophisticated vegetarian entree. This is about as formal a restaurant as you'll find in this otherwise very casual city. Janos's adjacent J Bar dishes up equally memorable fare at much more moderate prices. At the Westin La Paloma, 3770

E. Sunrise Dr. ⓒ **520/615-6100**. Reservations highly recommended. Main courses $24–$45; 5-course tasting menu $75 ($110 with wines). AF, DC, MC, V. Mon–Thurs 5:30–9pm; Fri Sat 5:30–10pm.

Native Café NATURAL FOODS   With a mellow, arty atmosphere and a comfortable patio, the Native Café is a good place for a leisurely light meal or snack. Opulent salads and delicious sandwiches are the norm here. There are plenty of choices for everyone from vegans to meat eaters—and it's all healthful and impeccably fresh. 3073 N. Campbell Ave. ⓒ **520/881-8881**. Salads and sandwiches $5.50–$9. MC, V. Daily 9am–3pm.

Stone Ashley NEW AMERICAN   Housed in a historic home that looks as though it were shipped here from Tuscany, Tucson's most upscale restaurant will take your breath away. While the exterior has a classic old-world feel, the interior is thoroughly modern and very plush. Expect the likes of an artfully presented, slightly spicy yam soup, followed by pepper-crusted ahi with wasabi mashed potatoes. Fabulous! The chocolate espresso torte should not be missed. 6400 E. El Dorado Circle. ⓒ **520/886-9700**. Reservations highly recommended. Main courses $25–$36. AE, DC, DISC, MC, V. Tues–Sun 5:30–10:30pm.

Ventana Room NEW AMERICAN   *Ventana* means "window" in Spanish, and the views through the windows of this restaurant are every bit as memorable as the food that comes from the kitchen. Whether you're seated overlooking the resort's waterfall or the lights of Tucson far below, you'll likely have trouble concentrating on your food, but do try; you wouldn't want to miss any of the subtle nuances of such dishes as the velvety Dover sole or grilled buffalo tenderloin with seared foie gras. At Loews Ventana Canyon Resort, 7000 N. Resort Dr. ⓒ **520/299-2020**. www.ventanaroom.com. Reservations highly recommended. Jackets recommended for men. Main courses $32–$45; chef's 5-course tasting menu $55–$75 ($35 additional for wines). AE, DC, DISC, MC, V. Mon–Thurs 6–9pm; Fri–Sat 6–9:30pm.

TUCSON AFTER DARK

The best place to look for entertainment listings is in the free *Tucson Weekly.*

The **Downtown Arts District** is home to the Temple of Music and Art, the Tucson Convention Center Music Hall, and several nightclubs. The **University of Arizona campus,** only a mile away, is another hot spot for entertainment.

THE PERFORMING ARTS   Tucson's largest performance venue is the **Tucson Convention Center (TCC) Music Hall,** 260 S. Church Ave. (ⓒ **520/791-4266**). It's the home of the **Tucson Symphony Orchestra** (www.tucson symphony.org) and is where the Arizona Opera Company and Ballet Arizona usually perform. The **Temple of Music and Art,** 330 S. Scott Ave. (ⓒ **520/622-2823**), a restored theater dating from 1927, is the centerpiece of the Tucson theater scene.

THE CLUB & MUSIC SCENE   Tucson is the mariachi capital of the United States, and no one should visit without spending at least one evening listening to some of these strolling minstrels. **La Fuente,** 1749 N. Oracle Rd. (ⓒ **520/623-8659**), serves up good Mexican food, but what really draws the crowds is the live nightly mariachi music. If you just want to listen and not have dinner, you can hang out in the lounge.

Club Congress, 311 E. Congress St. (ⓒ **520/622-8848**), is Tucson's main alternative-music venue. There are usually a couple of nights of live music each week. With its tropical decor and overabundance of potted plants setting the mood, **El Parador** restaurant and dance club, 2744 E. Broadway (© **520/881-2808**), is Tucson's favorite spot for lively Latin jazz and salsa performances (salsa lessons on Sat nights).

THE BAR SCENE ¡Toma!, 311 N. Court Ave. (© **520/622-1922**), always has a festive atmosphere and serves good margaritas, which are also a good deal during the daily happy hour (3–6pm). If you can't afford the lap of luxury, you can at least pull up a chair at **Flying V Bar & Grill,** in the Loews Ventana Canyon Resort, 7000 N. Resort Dr. (© **520/299-2020**). Set next to a waterfall, this watering hole has a grand view over the golf course and Tucson.

THE GAY & LESBIAN SCENE To find out what's happening, check out the weekly *Observer* (www.tucsonobserver.com). Long the most popular gay dance bar, **IBT's,** 616 N. Fourth Ave. (© **520/882-3053**), always has an interesting crowd. **Ain't Nobody's Bizness,** 2900 E. Broadway Blvd. (© **520/318-4838**), is *the* lesbian gathering spot, with a dance floor, two pool tables, and a quiet, smoke-free room.

CASINOS **Casino of the Sun,** 7406 S. Camino de Oeste (© **800/344-9435** or 520/883-1700), is southern Arizona's largest casino and offers slot machines, keno, bingo, and a card room. **Desert Diamond Casino,** 7350 S. Nogales Hwy. (© **520/294-7777**), operated by the Tohono O'odham tribe and located 3 miles from Mission San Xavier del Bac, has similar offerings.

3 Central Arizona & Sedona

THE VERDE VALLEY

The Verde Valley has long been a magnet for both wildlife and people. With its headwaters in the Juniper Mountains of the Prescott National Forest, the Verde River flows down through a rugged canyon before meandering slowly across the Verde Valley, one of Arizona's richest agricultural and ranching regions. For information, contact the **Verde Valley Tourism Council,** 1010 S. Main St., Cottonwood (© **928/634-7593;** http://tourism.verdevalley.com).

The **Verde Canyon Railroad,** 300 N. Broadway, Clarkdale (© **800/293-7245** or 928/639-0010; www.verdecanyonrr.com), traverses unspoiled desert that's inaccessible by car. The views of the rocky canyon walls and green waters of the Verde River are quite dramatic, and if you look closely along the way, you'll see ancient Sinagua cliff dwellings. Tickets are $40 for adults, $36 for seniors, and $25 for children 2 to 12.

Consisting of two impressive stone pueblos, **Montezuma Castle National Monument,** Exit 289 off I-17 (© **928/567-3322**), is among the best preserved of Arizona's **cliff dwellings.** The more intriguing pueblo is set in a shallow cave 100 feet up in a cliff overlooking Beaver Creek. Construction on this five-story, 20-room village began sometime in the early 12th century.

Although most people staying at the **Lodge at Cliff Castle,** 333 Middle Verde Rd. (© **800/524-6343** or 928/567-6611; www.cliffcastle.com), are here to do a little gambling in the adjacent casino, the motel also makes a good base for exploring the Verde Valley. There is a pool in summer. **Cooks Market Café,** 1124 N. Main St., Cottonwood (© **928/649-9552**), has been luring people from far and wide since it first opened. You might try the delicious *pepita* (pumpkin seed) encrusted salmon or perhaps steak with three-mushroom sauce.

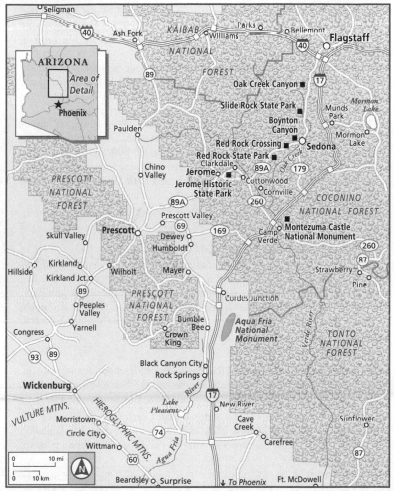

GETTING THERE Take I-17 north from Phoenix or south from Flagstaff to Camp Verde. Then take Ariz. 260 north through the Verde Valley for 12 miles to Cottonwood.

JEROME

Clinging to the slopes of Cleopatra Hill high on Mingus Mountain, Jerome looks much as it did when it was an active mining town, and has been designated a National Historic Landmark. For information, contact the **Jerome Chamber of Commerce** (© **928/634-2900;** www.jeromechamber.com).

Wandering the streets, soaking up the atmosphere, and shopping are the main pastimes in Jerome. However, you can also learn about the town's past at the **Jerome State Historic Park,** off U.S. 89A on Douglas Road in the lower section of town (© **928/634-5381**). Located in a 1916 mansion, the Jerome State Historic Park has exhibits on mining and a few of the mansion's original furnishings. Admission is $2.50 for adults, $1 for children 7 to 13.

For that classic mining-town tourist-trap experience, follow the signs up the hill from downtown Jerome to the **Gold King Mine** (© 928/634-0053), where you can see lots of old, rusting mining equipment and maybe even catch a demonstration.

If you can tear your eyes from the view of Sedona out the back of the **Raku Gallery,** 250 Hull Ave. (© 928/639-0239), you'll find lots of interesting art from around the country. **Sky Fire,** 140 Main St. (© 928/634-8081), has a fascinating collection of Southwestern and ethnic gifts and furnishings.

The moderately priced rooms at the **Inn at Jerome,** 309 Main St. (© 800/634-5094; www.innatjerome.com), are filled with antiques. More expensive, the three suites at the **Surgeon's House,** 101 Hill St. (© 800/639-1452 or 928/639-1452; www.surgeonshouse.com), have jaw-dropping views of the Verde Valley. The tiny **Flatiron Café,** at Main Street and Hull Avenue (© 928/634-2733), serves breakfast and light meals.

GETTING THERE   Follow directions to the Verde Valley, above. Jerome is 8 miles west of Cottonwood on Ariz. 89A.

SEDONA & OAK CREEK CANYON

The town of Sedona claims the most beautiful setting in the Southwest. Red-rock buttes, eroded canyon walls, and mesas rise into blue skies. Off in the distance, the Mogollon Rim looms, its forests of juniper and ponderosa pine dark against the red rocks. With this drop-dead scenery and a plethora of resorts and good restaurants, Sedona makes an excellent base for exploring central Arizona.

ESSENTIALS

GETTING THERE   Sedona is 116 miles north of Phoenix. Take I-17 north, then Ariz. 179 north to Sedona. From Jerome and the Verde Valley, take Ariz. 89A east to Sedona. From Flagstaff, take scenic Ariz. 89A south.

VISITOR INFORMATION   The **Sedona–Oak Creek Canyon Chamber of Commerce** (© 800/288-7336 or 928/282-7722; www.sedonachamber.com) operates a visitor center at the corner of Ariz. 89A and Forest Road near uptown Sedona.

SPECIAL EVENTS & FESTIVALS   The world-class **Sedona Chamber Music Festival** (© 928/204-2415; www.chambermusicsedona.org) is held in mid-May. September's **Jazz on the Rocks Benefit Festival** (© 928/282-1985; www.sedonajazz.com) is held outdoors with a superb view of the red rocks. In early October, Jackson Browne stages the **Verde Valley Music Festival** (© 928/284-2272), a benefit for the Native American Scholarship Project.

RED-ROCK COUNTRY

Just south of Sedona, on Ariz. 179, you'll see the aptly named **Bell Rock** on the east side of the road. From Bell Rock, you can see **Cathedral Rock** to the west. Adjacent to Bell Rock is **Courthouse Rock,** and not far from Bell Rock and visible from Chapel Road are **Eagle Head Rock,** the **Twin Nuns,** and **Mother and Child Rock** (to the left of the Twin Nuns).

If you head west through Sedona on Ariz. 89A and turn left onto Airport Road, you'll drive up onto **Airport Mesa.** The views from here are among the best in the region, and there are some easy hiking trails.

One of the most beautiful areas around Sedona is **Boynton Canyon.** Drive west out of Sedona on Ariz. 89A, turn right on Dry Creek Road, take a left at the T intersection, and at the next T intersection take a right. On the way to

Boynton Canyon, look north from Ariz. 89A and you'll see **Coffee Pot Rock,** rising 1,800 feet above Sedona. Three pinnacles, known as the **Three Golden Chiefs** by the Yavapai tribe, stand beside Coffee Pot Rock. As you drive up Dry Creek Road, on your right you'll see **Capitol Butte.** Just outside the gates of Enchantment Resort is a parking area for the **Boynton Canyon Trail.** From the parking area, the trail leads 3 miles up into the canyon.

In this same area, you can visit the Sinagua cliff dwellings at **Palatki Ruins.** To reach the ruins, follow the directions to Boynton Canyon, but instead of turning right at the second T intersection, turn left onto unpaved Boynton Pass Road (Forest Rd. 152). Follow this road to another T intersection and go right onto FR 125, then veer right onto FR 795. To visit the ruins, you'll need a Red Rock Pass, which costs $5 per car for a 1-day pass. Don't try this if the roads are at all muddy.

South of Ariz. 89A and a bit west of the turnoff for Boynton Canyon is Upper Red Rock Loop Road, which leads to **Crescent Moon Recreation Area** (formerly known as Red Rock Crossing), a National Forest Service recreation area that has become a must-see spot. Hiking trails beginning here lead up to Cathedral Rock. Park admission is $5 per vehicle.

If you continue on Upper Red Rock Loop Road, it turns into Lower Red Rock Loop Road and reaches **Red Rock State Park** (© **928/282-6907**), which flanks Oak Creek. The views here take in many of the rocks above, and you have the additional bonus of being right on the creek. Park admission is $5 per vehicle.

OAK CREEK CANYON

The **Mogollon Rim** is a 2,000-foot escarpment cutting diagonally across central Arizona and on into New Mexico. Of the many canyons cutting down from the rim, Oak Creek Canyon is the best known. Ariz. 89A runs through the canyon from Flagstaff to Sedona, winding its way down from the rim and paralleling Oak Creek. If you have a choice of how first to view Oak Creek Canyon, come at it from the north. Your first stop after traveling south from Flagstaff will be the **Oak Creek Canyon Vista,** which gives you a view far down the valley to Sedona and beyond.

The most popular spot in all of Oak Creek Canyon is **Slide Rock State Park** (© **928/282-3034**). Located 7 miles north of Sedona on the site of an old homestead, this park preserves a natural water slide. Admission is $7 per vehicle.

By far the most spectacular and popular hike in the canyon is the 6-mile round-trip up the **West Fork of Oak Creek.** Stop by the Sedona–Oak Creek Chamber of Commerce to pick up a free map.

WHAT TO SEE & DO AROUND TOWN

Sedona's most notable architectural landmark is the **Chapel of the Holy Cross** (© **928/282-4069**), located south of town just off Ariz. 179. The chapel sits high above the road and is built right into the red rock.

The **Sedona Arts Center,** Ariz. 89A at Art Barn Road (© **888/954-4442** or 928/282-3809), near the north end of town, serves both as a gallery for artwork by local and regional artists and as a theater for plays and music performances.

You'll find the greatest concentration of galleries and shops in the uptown area of Sedona (along Ariz. 89A just north of the Y) and at **Tlaquepaque** (© **928/ 282-4838;** www.tlaquepaque.net), the arts-and-crafts village on Ariz. 179 (at the bridge over Oak Creek on the south side of town).

With a large collection of contemporary and antique Navajo rugs, **Garland's Navajo Rugs,** 411 Hwy. 179 (© **928/282-4070**), is the premier Navajo rug shop in Sedona. **Hoel's Indian Shop,** 9440 N. Hwy. 89A, 10 miles north of Sedona (© **928/282-3925**), is one of the finest Native American arts-and-crafts galleries in the region. For those who love everything Southwestern, **Son Silver West,** 1476 Hwy. 179 (© **928/282-3580**), is a treasure trove, with everything from Native American crafts to rifles and garden art.

WHERE TO STAY & DINE

If you're searching for tranquillity or a romantic retreat amid the cool shade of Oak Creek Canyon, the **Briar Patch Inn,** 3190 N. Hwy. 89A (© **888/809-3030** or 928/282-2342; www.briarpatchinn.com), is the place. This inn's cottages are set amid beautiful shady grounds where bird songs and a babbling creek set the mood.

The pricey **Enchantment Resort,** 525 Boynton Canyon Rd. (© **800/826-4180** or 928/282-2900; www.enchantmentresort.com), more than lives up to its name. The setting is breathtaking, and the pueblo-style architecture of the hotel blends in with the canyon landscape. There are plenty of ways to keep busy—pools, tennis courts, a fitness center, hiking trails, and a putting green.

For a more moderate rate, **Saddle Rock Ranch,** 255 Rock Ridge Dr. (© **866/282-7640** or 928/282-7640; www.saddlerockranch.com), offers not only stunning views, but also classic Western ranch styling. **Sky Ranch Lodge,** Airport Road (© **888/708-6400** or 928/282-6400; www.skyranchlodge.com), a motel atop Airport Mesa, is another good, inexpensive place with fantastic views.

The **Cowboy Club,** 241 N. Hwy. 89A (© **928/282-4200**), may look like an ordinary steakhouse, but it's more than your average meat-and-potatoes joint. To start out, you can have fried cactus strips with black-bean caramel gravy, followed by grilled salmon with chipotle hollandaise. Because the view of Boynton Canyon is so much a part of the experience of dining at **Yavapai Dining Room,** at the Enchantment Resort, 525 Boynton Canyon Rd. (© **928/204-6000**), we recommend coming for lunch or a sunset dinner. The menu focuses on Southwestern flavors and changes regularly.

4 Flagstaff & the Grand Canyon

FLAGSTAFF: EN ROUTE TO THE GRAND CANYON

Perhaps best known as the jumping-off point for trips to the South Rim of the Grand Canyon, Flagstaff also has a wide variety of accommodations and restaurants, one of the state's finest museums, and a lively cultural community.

ESSENTIALS

GETTING THERE   By Plane   America West serves **Pulliam Airport,** 3 miles south of town off I-17.

By Train   Amtrak (© **800/USA-RAIL;** www.amtrak.com) provides daily service from Albuquerque (trip time: 5–6 hr.), Los Angeles (11 hr.), and Chicago (32 hr.) to its station at 1 E. Santa Fe Ave. There are direct bus connections to the Grand Canyon (see below).

By Car   The main routes into Flagstaff are I-40 from the east (Albuquerque) and west (Los Angeles), and I-17 from the south (Phoenix). Ariz. 89A connects Flagstaff to Sedona by way of Oak Creek Canyon, and U.S. 180 connects Flagstaff with the South Rim of the Grand Canyon.

Get Your Kicks on Route 66

The roadside establishments that survive on Route 66 are strange time capsules from another era, vestiges of this old highway's legendary past. Fans of retro architecture, design, and memorabilia shouldn't miss it. As you pass through Holbrook, look for the **Wigwam Motel** and the life-size concrete dinosaurs. West of Winslow, watch for the **Twin Arrows** truck stop. In Seligman, you'll find both the **Snow Cap Drive-In,** where fast food is served amid outrageous decor, and **Angel's Barber Shop,** something of a Route 66 information center and souvenir shop. In Kingman, check out the **Quality Inn,** on Andy Devine Avenue, with its lobby filled with Route 66 memorabilia; and **Mr. D'z Route 66 Diner,** a modern rendition of a 1950s diner (housed in an old gas station/cafe). Across the street is the restored powerhouse, which dates from 1907 and is home to the Kingman Area Chamber of Commerce Visitor Center, a 1950s-style malt shop, and the **Historic Route 66 Association of Arizona (© 928/753-5001).**

VISITOR INFORMATION   Contact the **Flagstaff Visitor Center,** 1 E. Rte. 66 (© **800/842-7293** or 928/774-9541; www.flagstaffarizona.org).

WHAT TO SEE & DO

Flagstaff is northern Arizona's center for outdoor activities. Chief among them is snow skiing at **Arizona Snowbowl** (© **928/779-1951;** www.arizonasnow bowl.com) on the slopes of Mount Agassiz, from which you can see all the way to the North Rim of the Grand Canyon. All-day lift tickets are $40 for adults, $22 for children 8 to 12, $20 for seniors, and free for children under 8 and seniors over 69. In summer, you can ride a chairlift almost to the summit and enjoy the expansive views across seemingly all of northern Arizona. The round-trip lift-ticket price is $9 for adults, $6.50 for seniors, and $5 for children 8 to 12.

When there's no snow on the ground, there are plenty of hiking trails throughout the San Francisco Peaks, and many national forest trails in the area are open to mountain bikes as well as to hikers. For information on the trails in the Coconino National Forest, contact the **Peaks Ranger District,** Coconino National Forest, 5075 N. Hwy. 89 (© **928/526-0866).**

Downtown Flagstaff along Route 66, San Francisco Street, Aspen Avenue, and Birch Avenue is the city's **historic district,** filled with interesting little shops. It's worth a walk even if you aren't shopping.

The small but surprisingly thorough **Museum of Northern Arizona,** 3101 N. Fort Valley Rd. (© **928/774-5213;** www.musnaz.org), is the ideal first stop on an exploration of northern Arizona. Here you'll learn about the archaeology, ethnology, geology, biology, and fine arts of the region. Admission is $5 adults, $4 seniors, $3 students, and $2 children 7 to 17.

Lowell Observatory, 1400 W. Mars Hill Rd. (© **520/774-2096;** www. lowell.edu), is one of the oldest astronomical observatories in the Southwest. The facility consists of several observatories, a large visitor center with numerous fun and educational exhibits, and outdoor displays. Admission is $3.50 for adults, $3 for seniors, and $1.50 for children 5 to 17.

WHERE TO STAY & DINE

The **Inn at 410,** 410 N. Leroux St. (© **800/774-2008** or 928/774-0088; www. inn410.com), is one of the best B&Bs in Arizona and provides convenience, pleasant surroundings, comfortable rooms, and delicious breakfasts. **Jeanette's Bed & Breakfast,** 3380 E. Lockett Rd. ((C) **800/752-1912** or 928/527-1912; www.jeanettesbb.com), is the place to stay if you've ever wanted to step back in time and live in the early 20th century. For outdoor-sports enthusiasts, *the* place to be is the **Sled Dog Inn,** 10155 Mountainaire Rd. ((C) **800/754-0664** or 928/ 525-6212; www.sleddoginn.com). The inn has more than a dozen Siberian huskies and offers dog-sled rides. Rooms are modern lodge rustic; don't be surprised if you wake up and see elk grazing right outside your window.

For great food in a casual atmosphere, try **Cottage Place Restaurant,** 126 W. Cottage Ave. ((C) **928/774-8431**), which most people in Flagstaff agree serves the best food in town. From a chair by the woodstove at **Beaver Street Brewery,** 11 S. Beaver St. ((C) **928/779-0079**), you can enjoy several good brews and great pizzas and burgers. People come to Flagstaff's counterculture hangout, **Macy's European Coffee House & Bakery,** 14 S. Beaver St. ((C) **928/774-2243**), for the espresso and baked goodies, but there are also decent vegetarian pasta dishes, soups, and salads.

The **Museum Club,** 3404 E. Rte. 66 ((C) **928/526-9434**), is a Flagstaff institution and one of America's classic roadhouses. There's live music, predominantly country and western, most nights.

THE GRAND CANYON SOUTH RIM

A mile deep, 277 miles long, and up to 18 miles wide, the Grand Canyon is truly one of the great natural wonders of the world. By raft, by mule, on foot, and in helicopters and small planes—more than four million people each year come to the canyon to gaze into this great chasm. You can expect parking problems and traffic congestion, but don't let these inconveniences dissuade you from visiting. Despite the crowds, the Grand Canyon more than lives up to its name and is one of the most amazing sights on earth.

ESSENTIALS

GETTING THERE   By Plane   Grand Canyon Airport, 6 miles south of Grand Canyon Village in Tusayan, primarily handles sightseeing tours and charters (see "Other Ways to See the Canyon," below).

By Train   Amtrak ((C) **800/USA-RAIL;** www.amtrak.com) provides daily service to Flagstaff (see above) and Williams. From Flagstaff, there's a bus directly to Grand Canyon Village; from Williams, the Grand Canyon Railway excursion train takes you to Grand Canyon Village.

By Bus   Bus service between Phoenix, Flagstaff, and Grand Canyon Village is provided by **Open Road Tours** ((C) **800/766-7117;** www.openroadtours.com). It charges $20 one-way between Flagstaff and the Grand Canyon. **Grand Canyon Coaches/Eco-Shuttle** ((C) **866/746-8439** or 928/638-0821; www. grandcanyoncoaches.com) provides a similar bus service.

By Car   If at all possible, travel into the park by some means *other* than car and avoid the traffic. From Flagstaff, 78 miles away, you can take U.S. 180 directly to the South Rim or U.S. 89 to Ariz. 64 and the east entrance to the park.

VISITOR INFORMATION   You can get advance information by contacting **Grand Canyon National Park,** P.O. Box 129, Grand Canyon, AZ 86023 ((C) **928/638-7888;** www.nps.gov/grca). When you arrive at the park, stop by the **Canyon View Visitor Center,** at Canyon View Information Plaza, 6 miles north of the south entrance. The center is open daily. Unfortunately, the information plaza has no adjacent parking, so you'll have to park where you can and

Grand Canyon Village

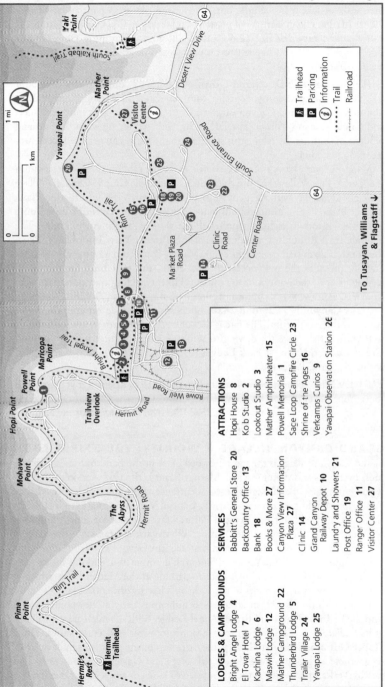

LEGEND

- 🥾 Trailhead
- 🅿 Parking
- ⓘ Information
- ········· Trail
- ┅┅┅┅ Railroad

LODGES & CAMPGROUNDS

Bright Angel Lodge **4**
El Tovar Hotel **7**
Kachina Lodge **6**
Maswik Lodge **12**
Mather Campground **22**
Thunderbird Lodge **5**
Trailer Village **24**
Yavapai Lodge **25**

SERVICES

Babbitt's General Store **20**
Backcountry Office **13**
Bank **18**
Books & More **27**
Canyon View Information Plaza **27**
Clinic **14**
Grand Canyon Railway Depot **10**
Laundry and Showers **21**
Post Office **19**
Ranger Office **11**
Visitor Center **27**

ATTRACTIONS

Hopi House **8**
Kolb Studio **2**
Lookout Studio **3**
Mather Amphitheater **15**
Powell Memorial **1**
Sage Loop Campfire Circle **23**
Shrine of the Ages **16**
Verkamps Curios **9**
Yavapai Observation Station **26**

then walk or take a free shuttle bus. The nearest places to park are at Mather Point, Market Plaza, park headquarters, and Yavapai Observation Station. If you're parked anywhere in Grand Canyon Village, you'll want to catch the Village Route bus. If you happen to be parked at Yaki Point, you can take the Kaibab Trail Route bus.

GETTING AROUND   Grand Canyon Coaches (© **866/746-8439** or 928/ 638-0821; www.grandcanyoncoaches.com) operates the Grand Canyon Eco-Shuttle between Grand Canyon Airport in Tusayan, at the park's south entrance, and Grand Canyon Village. The fare is $6, with service between 9:15am and 6:30pm in summer. By taking this shuttle into the park, you get a reduced entry fee of $4 per adult.

March through November, free shuttle buses operate on three routes within the park. The **Village Route** bus circles through Grand Canyon Village throughout the day with frequent stops at the Canyon View Information Plaza, Market Plaza, hotels, campgrounds, and restaurants. The **Hermit's Rest Route** bus takes visitors to eight canyon overlooks west of Bright Angel Lodge. The **Kaibab Trail Route** bus, which stops at the Canyon View Information Plaza, the South Kaibab trail head, Yaki Point, Mather Point, and Yavapai Observation Station, provides the only access to Yaki Point, the trail head for the South Kaibab Trail to the bottom of the canyon. Hikers needing transportation to or from Yaki Point when the bus is not running can use a taxi (© **928/638-2822**).

Trans Canyon (© **928/638-2820**) offers shuttle service between the South Rim and the North Rim. The fare is $65 one-way; reservations are required.

If you'd rather leave the driving to someone else, opt for a bus or van tour. **Grand Canyon National Park Lodges** (© **928/638-2631**) offers several tours within the park. Prices range from $12 to $33.

FAST FACTS   The **entry fee** is $20 per car (or $10 per person if you arrive on foot). Your ticket is good for 7 days. The **Grand Canyon Clinic** (© **928/638-2551**) is on Clinic Drive, off Center Road (the road that runs past the National Park Service ranger office).

GRAND CANYON VILLAGE & VICINITY: YOUR FIRST LOOK

Grand Canyon Village is the most crowded place in the park, but it also has the most overlooks and visitor services. **Mather Point** is the first overlook you reach if you enter the park through the south entrance, although just before Mather Point, you should now come to the new Canyon View Information Plaza. Continuing west, you'll come to **Yavapai Point,** a favorite spot for sunrise and sunset photos and the site of the **Yavapai Observation Station.** This historic building houses a small museum and has excellent views.

Continuing west from Yavapai Point, you'll come to a parking lot at park headquarters and a side road that leads to parking at the Market Plaza, which is one of the closest parking lots to the Canyon View Information Plaza.

In the historic district, in addition to numerous canyon viewpoints, you'll find the **El Tovar Hotel** and **Bright Angel Lodge,** both of which are worth brief visits. Adjacent to El Tovar are two historic souvenir and curio shops. **Hopi House Gift Store and Art Gallery,** the first shop in the park, was built in 1905 to resemble a Hopi pueblo and now sells Hopi and Navajo arts and crafts. The nearby **Verkamps Curios** is the main place to look for souvenirs and crafts.

To the west of Bright Angel Lodge, two buildings cling precariously to the rim of the canyon. These are the **Lookout** and **Kolb studios,** both of which are listed on the National Register of Historic Places.

HERMIT ROAD

Hermit Road leads 8 miles west from Grand Canyon Village to Hermit's Rest. Because it is closed to private vehicles March through November, it is also one of the most pleasant places to do a little canyon viewing or easy hiking during the busiest times of year. Free shuttle buses stop at most of the overlooks. From December to February, you can drive your own vehicle along this road, but keep in mind that winters usually mean a lot of snow.

The first two stops are **Trailview Overlook** and **Maricopa Point**. From both, you have a view of the Bright Angel Trail winding down into the canyon from Grand Canyon Village.

Powell Point, the third stop, is the site of a memorial to John Wesley Powell, the first person to navigate the Colorado River through the Grand Canyon.

Next along the drive is **Hopi Point,** from which you can see a long section of the Colorado River, and **Mohave Point,** where you can see Hermit Rapids.

The next stop is at the **Abyss,** the appropriately named 3,000-foot drop created by the Great Mojave Wall. This vertiginous view is one of the most awe-inspiring in the park. Layers of erosion-resistant sandstone have formed the free-standing pillars that are visible from here.

From **Pima Point,** it's possible to see the remains of Hermit Camp on the Tonto Plateau. At the end of Hermit Road stands **Hermit's Rest,** a log-and-stone building that is listed on the National Register of Historic Places.

DESERT VIEW DRIVE

Desert View Drive extends for 25 miles from Grand Canyon Village to Desert View. The first stop is **Yaki Point;** the spectacular view from here encompasses a wide section of the central canyon.

The next stop, **Grandview Point,** affords a view of Horseshoe Mesa, another interesting feature of the canyon landscape. Next along the drive is **Moran Point,** from which you can see a bright-red layer of shale in the canyon walls.

The **Tusayan Museum** (free admission) is the next stop. This small museum is dedicated to the Hopi tribe and ancient Anasazi people who inhabited this region 800 years ago.

At **Lipan Point,** you get one of the park's best views of the Colorado River. From here you can even see a couple of major rapids. From **Navajo Point,** the Colorado River and Escalante Butte are visible.

Desert View, with its trading post, general store, snack bar, service station, information center, bookstore, and watchtower, is the end of this scenic drive. The views are breathtaking from anywhere at Desert View, but the best lookout is from atop the Desert View Watchtower.

OTHER WAYS TO SEE THE CANYON

MULE RIDES   Mule rides into the canyon are one of the most popular activities at Grand Canyon Village. Trips of various lengths and to different destinations are offered. There are 1-day trips to Plateau Point and overnight trips to Phantom Ranch, the only lodge actually in the canyon. Make a reservation through **Grand Canyon National Park Lodges/Xanterra Parks & Resorts** (© **303/297-2757;** www.grandcanyonlodges.com). If at the last minute (5 days or fewer from the day you want to ride) you decide you want to go on a mule trip, contact Grand Canyon National Park Lodges at its Arizona phone number (© **928/638-2631**) for the remote possibility that there may be space available. If you arrive at the canyon without a reservation and decide that you'd like to go on a mule ride, stop by the Bright Angel Transportation Desk to get your name put on the next day's waiting list.

RIDING THE RAILS   The **Grand Canyon Railway** (© 800/843-8724 or 928/773-1976; www.thetrain.com), which runs from Williams to the South Rim of the Grand Canyon at Grand Canyon Village, uses early-20th-century steam engines (during the summer) and 1950s-vintage diesel engines (during other months) to pull 1920s passenger cars and a dome coach car. It's a fun trip that offers great scenery and a trip back in time, with the added bonus of allowing you to avoid the traffic in Grand Canyon Village.

A BIRD'S-EYE VIEW   Airplane and helicopter flights over the Grand Canyon remain one of the most popular ways to see these natural wonders. Companies offering tours by small plane include **Air Grand Canyon** (© 800/247-4726 or 928/638-2686; www.airgrandcanyon.com) and **Airstar Airlines** (© 800/962-3869 or 928/638-2139; www.airstar.com). Helicopter tours are available from **Airstar Helicopters** (© 800/962-3869 or 928/638-2622; www.airstar.com) and **Kenai Helicopters** (© 800/541-4537 or 928/638-2764; www.flykenai.com).

HIKING THE CANYON

No visit to the canyon is complete without journeying below the rim. While the views don't get any better than they are from the top, they do change considerably. This is some of the most rugged and strenuous hiking anywhere in the United States, and for this reason anyone attempting even a short walk should be well prepared. Wear sturdy footgear and carry at least 1 to 2 quarts of water for even a short hike. A long hike into or out of the canyon in the heat can require drinking more than a gallon of water. Remember while hiking that mules have the right of way. Don't attempt to hike from the rim to the Colorado River and back in a day; many people who have tried this have died.

DAY HIKES   Loop-trail day hikes are not possible in the Grand Canyon. The easiest day hikes are those along the **Rim Trail.** Head out early and get off at the Abyss shuttle stop. From here, it's a 4-mile hike to Hermit's Rest, which makes a great place to take a break. You can catch a shuttle bus back to the village.

Trails leading down into the canyon include the **Bright Angel Trail,** the **South Kaibab Trail, Grandview Trail,** and the **Hermit Trail.** If you plan to hike for more than 30 minutes, carry 2 quarts of water per person.

BACKPACKING   There are many miles of trails deep in the canyon and several established campgrounds for backpackers. The best times of year to backpack in the canyon are spring and autumn. Be sure to carry at least 2 quarts, and preferably 1 gallon, of water.

A **Backcountry Use Permit** is required of all hikers planning to overnight in the canyon unless you'll be staying at Phantom Ranch. Make reservations as soon as possible. Reservations are taken in person, by mail, by fax (but not by phone), and over the Internet. Contact the **Backcountry Office,** Grand Canyon National Park, P.O. Box 129, Grand Canyon, AZ 86023 (© **928/638-7875** 1–5pm for information; fax 928/638-2125; www.nps.gov/grca). The office begins accepting reservations on the first of every month for the following 5 months.

There are **campgrounds** at Indian Gardens, Bright Angel (near Phantom Ranch), and Cottonwood, but hikers are limited to 2 nights per trip at each of these campgrounds (except Nov 15–Feb 28, when 4 nights are allowed).

The *Backcountry Trip Planner* publication has information to help you plan your itinerary. It's available through the Backcountry Office. Maps are available through the **Grand Canyon Association,** P.O. Box 399, Grand Canyon, AZ 86023 (© **928/638-2481;** fax 928/638-2484; www.grandcanyon.org), and at bookstores and gift shops within the park.

WHERE TO STAY

Keep in mind that the Grand Canyon is one of the most popular national parks in the country; make reservations as far in advance as possible.

INSIDE THE PARK   Grand Canyon National Park Lodges/Xanterra Parks & Resorts, 14001 E. Iliff Ave., Ste. 600, Aurora, CO 80014 (© **303/ 297-2757;** www.xanterra.com), operates the hotels inside the park. Reservations are taken up to 23 months in advance. It is *sometimes* possible, due to cancellations and no-shows, to get a same-day reservation by calling © **928/638-2631.**

El Tovar Hotel is the park's premier lodge. Built of local rock and Oregon pine, it's a rustic yet luxurious mountain lodge that perches on the edge of the canyon, and has awe-inspiring views from some rooms. If you want modern amenities and a fairly large room, **Thunderbird & Kachina Lodges** should be your in-park choice. **Bright Angel Lodge & Cabins** is the most affordable lodge in the park, but you'll pay more for a private bathroom. The rim cabins are the most popular and are usually booked a year in advance. **Phantom Ranch** (© **928/638-2631** for reconfirmations) is the only lodge at the bottom of the Grand Canyon and is very popular. The accommodations are in rustic stone-walled cabins or gender-segregated dormitories. Prices include meals, which must also be reserved ahead.

IN TUSAYAN (OUTSIDE THE SOUTH ENTRANCE)   If you can't get a room in the park, this is the next closest place to stay. The **Seven Mile Lodge** (© **928/638-2291**) is the least expensive motel in town. However, it doesn't take reservations and is usually full by 2pm in the summer (it starts renting rooms at 9am). With its mountain-lodge styling, Native American cultural shows, modern guest rooms, and large restaurant, the **Grand Hotel** (© **888/63-GRAND** or 928/638-3333; www.canyon.com) is the best choice in Tusayan. For the most luxurious accommodations in the area, book one of the suites at the **Holiday Inn Express–Grand Canyon** (© **888/473-2269** or 928/638-3000; www.gcanyon.com/HI).

Fifty-four miles north of Flagstaff on U.S. 89 is the **Cameron Trading Post Motel** (© **800/338-7385** or 928/679-2231; www.camerontradingpost.com), offering some of the most attractive rooms anywhere in the vicinity of the Grand Canyon. Most have balconies and some have views of the Little Colorado River.

CAMPGROUNDS   Mather Campground, in Grand Canyon Village, has more than 313 campsites. Reservations can be made up to 5 months in advance and are required for stays between April and November (reservations not accepted for other months). Contact the National Park Reservation Service (© **800/365-2267** or 301/722-1257; http://reservations.nps.gov). **Desert View Campground,** with 50 sites, is 25 miles east of Grand Canyon Village and open from mid-May to mid-October only. No reservations are accepted. The **Trailer Village RV park,** with 80 RV sites, is in Grand Canyon Village. Reservations can be made up to 23 months in advance by contacting Xanterra Parks & Resorts (© **303/297-2757;** fax 303/297-3175).

In Tusayan, you'll find **Grand Canyon Camper Village** (© **928/638-2887**), open year-round. This is primarily an RV park, but it also has sites for tents. Two miles south of Tusayan is the U.S. Forest Service's **Ten-X Campground,** open May through September.

You can also camp just about anywhere within the **Kaibab National Forest,** which borders Grand Canyon National Park, as long as you are more than a quarter mile away from Ariz. 64/U.S. 180. Contact the **Tusayan Ranger District,** Kaibab National Forest, P.O. Box 3088, Grand Canyon, AZ 86023 (© **928/638-2443;** www.fs.fed.us/r3/kai).

WHERE TO DINE

You'll find several restaurants just outside the south entrance in Tusayan. The best of these is the **Canyon Star** at the Grand Hotel and the **Coronado Room** at the Best Western Grand Canyon Squire Inn. You'll also find a steakhouse and a pizza place, as well as familiar chains such as McDonald's, Taco Bell, Pizza Hut, and Wendy's.

For quick, inexpensive meals, there is Grand Canyon Village's **Bright Angel Fountain,** at the back of the Bright Angel Lodge, which serves hot dogs, sandwiches, and ice cream. **Hermit's Rest Snack Bar** is at the west end of Hermit Road. At Desert View (near the east entrance to the park), there's the **Desert View Trading Snack Bar.**

El Tovar Dining Room, in the El Tovar Hotel (© **928/638-2631,** ext. 6432), has one of the most awe-inspiring views in the world and serves up good, spicy, Southwestern food. Book early.

THE GRAND CANYON NORTH RIM

If Grand Canyon Village sounds like it's going to be more human zoo than the wilderness experience you had expected, the North Rim will probably be much more to your liking. The North Rim is on the Kaibab Plateau, more than 8,000 feet high on average. The higher elevation of the North Rim means you'll find dense forests of ponderosa pines, Douglas firs, and aspens interspersed with large meadows.

ESSENTIALS

GETTING THERE From Flagstaff, take U.S. 89 north to Bitter Springs, then U.S. 89A to Jacob Lake. From there take Ariz. 67 (the North Rim Pkwy.) to the end at the North Rim.

Trans Canyon (© **928/638-2820**) operates a shuttle between the North Rim and the South Rim. The trip takes 5 hours; the fare is $65 one-way (reservations required).

VISITOR INFORMATION For information before leaving home, contact **Grand Canyon National Park,** P.O. Box 129, Grand Canyon, AZ 86023 (© **928/638-7888;** www.nps.gov/grca). At the entrance gate, you'll be given a copy of *The Guide,* a small newspaper with information on park activities. There's also an **information desk** in the lobby of the Grand Canyon Lodge.

Note: Visitor facilities at the North Rim are open only from mid-May to mid-October. From late October to November (or until snow closes the road to the North Rim), the park is open for day use only. The campground may be open after mid-October, weather permitting.

For more information, see "Essentials" under "The Grand Canyon South Rim," earlier in this chapter.

EXPLORING THE AREA

The best spots for viewing the canyon are Bright Angel Point, Point Imperial, and Cape Royal. **Bright Angel Point** is the closest to Grand Canyon Lodge, and from here you can see and hear Roaring Springs, 3,600 feet below the rim and the North Rim's only water source. At 8,803 feet, **Point Imperial** is the highest point on the North Rim. A short section of the Colorado River can be seen far below, and off to the east the Painted Desert is visible.

Cape Royal, however, is the most spectacular setting on the North Rim, and along the 23-mile road to Cape Royal are several scenic overlooks. Across the road from the **Walhalla Overlook** are the ruins of an Anasazi structure, and just before reaching Cape Royal you'll come to the **Angel's Window Overlook,** which gives you a breathtaking view of the natural bridge that forms Angel's Window. Once at Cape Royal, you can follow a trail across this natural bridge to a towering promontory overlooking the valley.

After simply taking in the views, hiking along the rim is the most popular activity. Day hikes of varying lengths are possible here.

If you want to see the canyon from a saddle, contact **Grand Canyon Trail Rides** (© **435/679-8665**), which offers mule rides of 1 hour to a full day.

WHERE TO STAY & DINE

INSIDE THE PARK   Perched right on the canyon rim, **Grand Canyon Lodge,** c/o Xanterra Parks & Resorts, 14001 E. Iliff Ave., Aurora, CO 80014 (© **303/297-2757,** or 928/638-2611 for same-day reservations; fax 303/297-3175; www.grandcanyonnorthrim.com), is listed on the National Register of Historic Places and is one of the most impressive lodges in the national park system. A large dining hall serves straightforward American food. A saloon and a snack bar are outside the lodge's front entrance, and there's a tour desk in the lobby.

OUTSIDE THE PARK   You'll find numerous budget motels in Fredonia, Arizona (30 miles west of Jacob Lake), and Kanab, Utah (37 miles west of Jacob Lake). Located 5 miles north of the entrance to the North Rim, **Kaibab Lodge** (© **800/525-0924** or 928/526-0924; www.canyoneers.com) is on the edge of a large meadow where deer can often be seen grazing. The lodge's dining room serves all meals, and the kitchen also prepares box lunches.

CAMPGROUNDS   Located just north of Grand Canyon Lodge, the **North Rim Campground,** with 75 sites and no hookups for RVs, is the only campground at the North Rim. The campground opens in mid-May and may stay open past the mid-October closing of other North Rim visitor facilities. Reservations can be made up to 5 months in advance by contacting the National Park Reservation Service (© **800/365-2267** or 301/722-1257; http://reservations.nps.gov).

There are two nearby campgrounds outside the park in the Kaibab National Forest. **DeMotte Park Campground,** the closest to the park entrance, has 22 sites, while **Jacob Lake Campground,** 30 miles north of the park entrance, has 53 sites. Neither takes reservations. You can also camp anywhere in the Kaibab National Forest as long as you're more than a quarter mile from a paved road or water source.

5 Monument Valley & Canyon de Chelly

MONUMENT VALLEY NAVAJO TRIBAL PARK

You may not be aware of it, but you have almost certainly seen Monument Valley before. This otherworldly landscape has been an object of fascination for years and has served as a backdrop for countless commercials and movies.

Monument Valley is a vast flat plain punctuated by natural cathedrals of sandstone. These huge monoliths rise from the sagebrush with sheer walls that capture the light of the rising and setting sun and transform it into fiery hues. A 17-mile unpaved loop road winds among these 1,000-foot-tall buttes and mesas.

Human habitation has also left its mark. Within the park are more than 100 ancient Anasazi archaeological sites, ruins, and petroglyphs dating from before A.D. 1300. The Navajo have been living in the valley for generations, herding their sheep through the sagebrush scrublands, and some families continue to live here today.

ESSENTIALS

GETTING THERE   From Flagstaff, take U.S. 89 north, then U.S. 160 east, then U.S. 163 north. Monument Valley is 200 miles northeast of Flagstaff.

VISITOR INFORMATION & FEES   For information, contact **Monument Valley Navajo Tribal Park** (℗ 435/727-5870). The park is open May through September daily from 7am to 8pm; and October through April daily from 8am to 5pm. Admission to the park is $5 per person. *Note:* Because this is a tribal park and not a federal park, neither the National Park Service's National Park Pass nor its Golden Eagle Pass are valid here.

EXPLORING THE AREA

This is big country, and, like the Grand Canyon, primarily a point-and-shoot experience. Because this is reservation land and people still live in Monument Valley, backcountry or off-road travel is prohibited unless you have a licensed guide. So basically the only way to see the park is from the overlook at the visitor center; by driving the park's scenic (but very rough) dirt road; or by taking a four-wheel-drive, horseback, or guided hiking tour.

At the valley overlook parking area in Monument Valley Navajo Tribal Park, you'll find a small museum, gift shop, restaurant, snack bar, campground, and numerous local Navajo guides who offer tours of the park.

For four-wheel-drive adventures, try **Roland's Navajoland Tours** (℗ 800/368-2785 or 928/697-3524). Prices range from $25 for a 1½-hour tour to $80 for an all-day tour. **Totem Pole Tours** (℗ 800/345-8687 or 435/727-3313) offers similar options.

If you want to see the park on foot, arrange a guided hike through **Sacred Monument Tours** (℗ 435/727-3218), which charges from $25 for a 2½-hour hike to $77 for an 8-hour hike. Overnight hikes can be arranged. **Kéyah Hózhóní Tours** (℗ 928/309-7440; www.monumentvalley.com) also offers hiking tours.

If nothing but the cowboy thing will do for you in this quintessential Wild West landscape, contact **Ed Black's Monument Valley Trail Rides** (℗ 435/739-4285), located near the visitor center. A 1½-hour ride costs $30 and an all-day ride costs $100.

Another option is **Goulding's Tours** (℗ 435/727-3231), which has its office on the edge of the valley at Goulding's Lodge (see "Where to Stay & Dine," below), just a few miles from the park entrance. Goulding's offers 2½-hour tours ($26 for adults, $16 for children under 8), half-day tours ($31 for adults, $19 for children), and full-day tours ($61 for adults, $46 for children). In summer, full-moon tours are another option.

Before leaving the area, you might want to visit **Goulding's Museum and Trading Post,** at Goulding's Lodge. This old trading post was the home of the

Gouldings for many years and is set up as they had it back in the 1920s and 1930s. There are also displays about the many movies that have been shot here. The trading post is usually open April through October daily from 7:30am to 9pm, with shorter hours in other months; admission is by suggested $2 donation.

WHERE TO STAY & DINE

In addition to the lodgings listed here, you'll find numerous budget motels 22 miles north of Monument Valley in Mexican Hat, Utah.

Goulding's Lodge, Monument Valley, Utah (© **435/727-3231;** www. gouldings.com), is the only lodge actually in Monument Valley, and it offers superb views from the balconies of its rooms, which are furnished with Southwestern decor. A restaurant serves Navajo and American dishes.

Hampton Inn–Navajo Nation, U.S. 160, in Kayenta (© **800/HAMPTON** or 928/697-3170; www.hampton-inn.com), should be your second choice after Goulding's. The hotel was newly built in a modern Santa Fe style and has spacious rooms.

CANYON DE CHELLY NATIONAL MONUMENT

Canyon de Chelly National Monument consists of two major canyons— **Canyon de Chelly** (pronounced "canyon duh *shay*" and derived from the Navajo word *tséyi,* meaning "rock canyon") and **Canyon del Muerto** (Spanish for "Canyon of the Dead")—and several smaller canyons. The canyons extend for more than 100 miles through the rugged slick-rock landscape of northeastern Arizona, draining the seasonal runoff from the snowmelt of the Chuska Mountains.

Canyon de Chelly's smooth sandstone walls of rich reds and yellows contrast sharply with the deep greens of corn, pasture, and cottonwood on the canyon floor. Vast stone amphitheaters form the caves in which the ancient Anasazi built their homes, and today there are more than 100 prehistoric dwelling sites in the area. With its mysteriously abandoned cliff dwellings and breathtaking natural beauty, Canyon de Chelly is certainly as worthy of a visit as the Grand Canyon.

ESSENTIALS

GETTING THERE   Canyon de Chelly is 222 miles northeast of Flagstaff and 110 miles southeast of Monument Valley Navajo Tribal Park. From Flagstaff, the easiest route to Canyon de Chelly is to take I-40 east to Chambers, then U.S. 191 north to Chinle. If you're coming down from Monument Valley or Navajo National Monument, Indian Route 59, which connects U.S. 160 and U.S. 191, is an excellent road with plenty of beautiful scenery. Take U.S. 191 south to Chinle.

VISITOR INFORMATION   Before leaving home, you can contact **Canyon de Chelly National Monument** (© **928/674-5500;** www.nps.gov/cach) for information. The visitor center is open daily, May through September from 8am to 6pm (on daylight saving time) and October through April from 8am to 5pm. The monument itself is open daily from sunrise to sunset. Monument admission is free.

SEEING THE CANYON

Your first stop at Canyon de Chelly should be the **visitor center,** in front of which is an example of a traditional crib-style hogan, a hexagonal structure of logs and earth that Navajo use both as a home and as a ceremonial center. Inside, a small museum acquaints visitors with the history of Canyon de Chelly, and there's often a silversmith demonstrating Navajo jewelry-making techniques. From here most people tour the canyon by car.

The North and South Rim drives offer very different views of the canyon. The North Rim Drive overlooks Canyon del Muerto, and the South Rim Drive overlooks Canyon de Chelly. Each of the rim drives is around 20 miles in each direction, and with stops it can easily take 3 hours to visit each rim.

THE NORTH RIM DRIVE   The first stop on the North Rim is the **Ledge Ruin Overlook.** On the opposite wall, about 100 feet up from the canyon floor, you can see the Ledge Ruin. The Anasazi occupied this site between A.D. 1050 and 1275. Nearby, at the **Dekaa Kiva Viewpoint,** you can see a lone kiva (circular ceremonial building). This structure was reached by means of toeholds cut into the soft sandstone cliff wall.

The second stop is the **Antelope House Overlook.** The Antelope House ruin takes its name from the paintings of antelopes on a nearby cliff wall. It's believed that the paintings were done in the 1830s. Beneath the ruins, archaeologists have found the remains of an earlier pit house dating from A.D. 693. Though most of the Anasazi cliff dwellings were abandoned sometime after a drought began in 1276, Antelope House had already been abandoned by 1260, possibly because of flood damage. Across the wash from Antelope House, the Tomb of the Weaver was discovered in the 1920s by archaeologists. The ancient tomb contained the well-preserved body of an old man wrapped in a blanket of golden eagle feathers and accompanied by cornmeal, shelled and husked corn, piñon nuts, beans, salt, and thick skeins of cotton. Also visible from this overlook is **Navajo Fortress,** a red sandstone butte that the Navajo once used as a refuge from attackers. A steep trail leads to the top of Navajo Fortress, and through the use of log ladders that could be pulled up into the refuge, the Navajo were able to escape their attackers.

The third stop is at **Mummy Cave Overlook,** named for two mummies found in burial urns below the ruins. Archaeological evidence indicates that this giant amphitheater consisting of two caves was occupied from A.D. 300 to 1300. In the two caves and on the shelf between them there are 80 rooms, including three kivas. The central structure between the two caves is interesting because it includes a three-story building characteristic of the architecture in Mesa Verde, New Mexico. Archaeologists speculate that a group of Anasazi migrated here from New Mexico. Much of the original plasterwork of these buildings is still intact and indicates that the buildings were colorfully decorated.

The fourth and last stop on the North Rim is at the **Massacre Cave Overlook.** The cave got its name after an 1805 Spanish military expedition killed more than 115 Navajo at this site. The Navajo at the time had been raiding Spanish settlements that were encroaching on Navajo territory. Accounts of the battle at Massacre Cave differ. One claims that there were only women, children, and old men taking shelter in the cave, although the official Spanish records claim 90 warriors and 25 women and children were killed. Also visible from this overlook is Yucca Cave, which was occupied about 1,000 years ago.

THE SOUTH RIM DRIVE   The South Rim Drive climbs slowly but steadily, and at each stop you're a little bit higher above the canyon floor.

Near the mouth of the canyon, you'll find the **Tunnel Overlook** and, nearby, the **Tséyi Overlook.** *Tséyi* means "rock canyon" in Navajo, and that's just what you'll see when you gaze down from this viewpoint. A short narrow canyon feeds into Chinle Wash, formed by the streams cutting through the canyons of the national monument.

The next stop is **Junction Overlook,** so named because it overlooks the junction of Canyon del Muerto and Canyon de Chelly. Visible here is the Junction Ruin, with its 10 rooms and one kiva. The Anasazi occupied this ruin during the Great Pueblo Period, which lasted from around 1100 until the Anasazi disappeared shortly before 1300. Also visible is First Ruin, perched precariously on a long, narrow ledge. In this ruin are 22 rooms and two kivas.

The next stop, at **White House Overlook,** provides the only opportunity for descending into Canyon de Chelly without a guide or ranger. The **White House Ruins Trail** descends 600 feet to the canyon floor, crosses Chinle Wash, and approaches the White House Ruins. These buildings were constructed both on the canyon floor and 50 feet up the cliff wall in a small cave. You cannot enter the ruins, but you can get close enough to get a good look. You're not allowed to wander off this trail, and please respect the privacy of the Navajo living here. The 2½-mile round-trip hike takes about 2 hours. Be sure to carry water. If you aren't inclined to hike the trail, you can view the ruins from the overlook. This is one of the largest ruins in the canyon and contains 80 rooms. It was inhabited between 1040 and 1275. Notice the black streaks on the sandstone walls above the White House Ruins. These streaks were formed by seeping water that reacted with the iron in the sandstone. Iron gives the walls their reddish hue. Anasazi artists used to chip away at this black patina to create petroglyphs. Later the Navajo would use paints to create pictographs, painted images of animals, and records of historic events such as the Spanish military expedition that killed 115 Navajo at Massacre Cave. Many of these petroglyphs and pictographs can be seen if you take one of the guided tours into the canyon.

The next stop is at **Sliding House Overlook.** These ruins are built on a narrow shelf and appear to be sliding down into the canyon. Inhabited from about 900 until 1200, Sliding House contained between 30 and 50 rooms. This overlook is already more than 700 feet above the canyon floor, with sheer walls giving the narrow canyon a foreboding appearance.

The **Face Rock Overlook** provides yet another dizzying glimpse of the ever-deepening canyon. Here you gaze 1,000 feet down to the bottom of the canyon. The last stop on the South Rim is one of the most spectacular: **Spider Rock Overlook.** This viewpoint overlooks the junction of Canyon de Chelly and Monument Canyon, and at this wide spot in the canyon stands the monolithic pinnacle called Spider Rock. Rising 800 feet from the canyon floor, the freestanding twin towers of Spider Rock are a natural monument, a geologic wonder. Across the canyon from Spider Rock stands the similarly striking **Speaking Rock,** connected to the far canyon wall.

ALTERNATIVE WAYS OF SEEING THE CANYON   Access to the floor of Canyon de Chelly is restricted, so to enter the canyon *you must be accompanied by either a park ranger or an authorized guide* (unless you're on the White House Ruins Trail). **Navajo guides** charge $15 per hour with a 3-hour minimum and will lead you into the canyon on foot or in your own four-wheel-drive vehicle. **De Chelly Tours** (© **928/674-3772;** www.dechellytours.com) charges $20 per hour, with a 3-hour minimum, to go out in your four-wheel-drive vehicle; if it supplies the vehicle, the cost goes up to $125 for three people for 3 hours.

Another way to see Canyon de Chelly and Canyon del Muerto is on what locals call **shake-and-bake tours,** via six-wheel-drive truck. In summer, these excursions really live up to the name. (In winter, the truck is enclosed to keep out the elements.) The trucks operate out of **Thunderbird Lodge** (© **800/679-2473** or 928/674-5841) and are equipped with seats in the bed. Tours make frequent stops for photographs and to visit ruins, Navajo farms, and rock art. Half-day trips cost $39 per person ($30 for children 11 and under).

If you'd rather use a more traditional means of transportation, you can go on a guided horseback ride. Contact **Justin's Horse Rental** (© **928/674-5678**), which charges $10 per hour per person for a horse and $15 per hour per group for a guide, with a 2-hour minimum.

WHERE TO STAY & DINE

The **Holiday Inn–Canyon de Chelly,** Indian Route 7, Chinle (© **800/ HOLIDAY** or 928/674-5000), has rooms with patios or balconies, most facing the cottonwood-shaded pool courtyard. The restaurant serves the best food in town.

Thunderbird Lodge (© **800/679-BIRD** or 928/674-5841; www.tbird lodge.com), built on the site of an early trading post at the mouth of Canyon de Chelly, is the most appealing of the hotels in Chinle and the closest to the national monument. The red-adobe construction is reminiscent of ancient pueblos. American and Navajo meals are served.

Adjacent to the Thunderbird Lodge is the free **Cottonwood Campground,** which doesn't take reservations. In summer, the campground has water and restrooms, but in winter, you must bring your own water, and only portable toilets are available. On South Rim Drive 10 miles east of the Canyon de Chelly Visitor Center, you'll also find the private **Spider Rock Campground** (© **877/910-CAMP** or 928/674-8261), which charges about $10 per night for campsites. The next nearest campgrounds are at **Tsaile Lake** and **Wheatfields Lake,** both of which are south of the town of Tsaile on Indian Route 12. Tsaile is at the east end of the North Rim Drive.

6 The Petrified Forest & Painted Desert

Though petrified wood can be found in almost every state, the "forests" of downed logs here in northeastern Arizona are by far the most spectacular. A 27-mile scenic drive winds through the petrified forest and a small corner of the Painted Desert, providing a fascinating high desert experience.

It may be hard to believe when you drive across this arid landscape, but at one time this was a vast, humid swamp. That was 225 million years ago, when dinosaurs and huge amphibians ruled the earth and giant now-extinct trees grew on the high ground around the swamp. Fallen trees were washed downstream, gathered in piles in still backwaters, and were eventually covered over with silt, mud, and volcanic ash. As water seeped through this soil, it dissolved the silica in the volcanic ash and redeposited this silica inside the cells of the logs. Eventually the silica recrystallized into stone to form petrified wood.

This region was later inundated with water, and thick deposits of sediment buried the logs ever deeper. Eventually, the land was transformed yet again as a geologic upheaval thrust the lake bottom up above sea level. This upthrust of the land cracked the logs into the segments we see today. Wind and water gradually eroded the landscape, once again exposing the now-petrified logs and creating the Painted Desert and the many other colorful and fascinating landscape features of northern Arizona.

Throughout the region you'll see petrified wood in all sizes and colors, natural and polished, being sold in gift stores. This petrified wood comes from private land, *not* the national park. No piece of petrified wood, no matter how small, may be removed from Petrified Forest National Park.

ESSENTIALS

GETTING THERE   Take I-40 east from Flagstaff or west from Albuquerque. The north entrance to Petrified Forest National Park is 25 miles east of Holbrook on I-40. The south entrance is 20 miles east of Holbrook on U.S. 180.

VISITOR INFORMATION & FEES   For further information on the Petrified Forest or the Painted Desert, contact **Petrified Forest National Park** (© **928/524-6228;** www.nps.gov/pefo). For information on Holbrook and the surrounding region, contact the **Holbrook Chamber of Commerce,** 100 E. Arizona St. (© **800/524-2459** or 928/524-6558; www.ci.holbrook.az.us/ Chamber.htm). The park is open daily from 8am to 5pm, with longer hours in summer. The entry fee is $10 per car.

EXPLORING A UNIQUE LANDSCAPE

Petrified Forest National Park has both a north and a south entrance (and visitor centers at both entrances). Connecting the two park entrances is a 27-mile scenic road with more than 20 overlooks. For the most enjoyable visit, start at the southern entrance and work your way north. This way, you'll see the most impressive displays of petrified logs early in your visit.

At the south entrance, you'll find the **Rainbow Forest Museum,** which has exhibits on the geology and human history of the park. A snack bar here serves sandwiches and ice cream. Just outside the museum is the **Giant Logs self-guided trail,** which winds across a hillside strewn with logs. Almost directly across the parking lot from the museum is the entrance to the **Long Logs** and **Agate House** areas. On the Long Logs trail, you can see more big trees, while at Agate House you will see the ruins of a pueblo built from colorful agatized wood.

Heading north, you pass by the unusual formations known as the **Flattops.** These structures are caused by the erosion of softer soil deposits from beneath a harder and more erosion-resistant layer of sandstone. This is one of the park's wilderness areas (both of the park's visitor centers issue the free permits necessary to backpack into the park's wilderness areas). The **Crystal Forest** is the next stop to the north, named for the beautiful amethyst and quartz crystals that were once found in the cracks of petrified logs.

At the **Jasper Forest Overlook,** you can see logs that include petrified roots, and a little bit farther north, at the **Agate Bridge** stop, you can see a petrified log that forms a natural agate bridge. Continuing north, you'll reach **Blue Mesa,** where pieces of petrified wood form capstones over easily eroded clay soils. As wind and water wear away at the clay beneath a piece of stone, the balance of the stone becomes more and more precarious until it eventually comes toppling down. A 1-mile loop trail here leads into the park's badlands.

Erosion has played a major role in the formation of the Painted Desert, and to the north of Blue Mesa you'll see some of the most interesting erosional features of the area. It's quite evident why these hills of sandstone and clay are known as the **Teepees.** The layers of different color are due to different types of soils and stone and to minerals dissolved in the soil.

Human habitation of the area dates from more than 2,000 years ago, and at **Newspaper Rock,** you can see petroglyphs left by generations of Native Americans. At nearby **Puerco Pueblo,** which was probably constructed around 1400, you can see the remains of homes built by the people who created the park's petroglyphs.

North of Puerco Pueblo, the road crosses I-40. From here to the Painted Desert Visitor Center, there are eight overlooks onto the southernmost edge of the **Painted Desert.** Named for the vivid colors of the soil and stone that cover the land here, the Painted Desert is a dreamscape of pastel colors washed across a barren expanse of eroded hills. At Kachina Point, you'll find the historic **Painted Desert Inn,** open daily from 8am to 4pm. Just inside the park's northern entrance is the **Painted Desert Visitor Center,** which shows a short film explaining the process by which wood becomes fossilized. Adjacent to the visitor center are a cafeteria and a gas station.

WHERE TO STAY & DINE

Holbrook is the nearest town to Petrified Forest National Monument, and here you'll find lots of budget chain motels.

Although it's almost 50 miles from the park, **La Posada,** 303 E. Second St., Winslow (© **928/289-4366;** www.laposada.org), a restored historic railroad hotel, is this region's best and most memorable hotel. The hotel is a reproduction of a Spanish colonial hacienda. If you're willing to sleep on a saggy mattress for the sake of reliving a bit of Route 66 history, consider the concrete wigwams at the **Wigwam Motel,** 811 W. Hopi Dr., Holbrook (© **800/ 414-3021** or 928/524-3048; www.galerie-kokopelli.com/wigwam). This unique motel was built in the 1940s, when unusual architecture was springing up all along Route 66.

The **Butterfield Stage Co.,** 609 W. Hopi Dr. (© **928/524-3447**), serves well-prepared steak and seafood, plus a soup and salad bar that's usually fresh.

7 Albuquerque

Albuquerque may initially strike visitors as nothing more than one big strip mall. But look closely and you'll see ranchers, Native Americans, and Hispanic villagers stocking up on goods to take back to the New Mexico boot heel or the Texas panhandle. Climbing out of the valley is the legendary Route 66, a major route from the East to California before the interstates were built. It's well worth a drive, if only to see the rust time has left. Old court hotels still line the street, many with their funky 1950s signage. One enclave on this route is the University of New Mexico district, with a number of hippie-ish cafes and shops.

Farther downhill you'll come to downtown Albuquerque. During the day, this area is all suits and heels, but after dark it becomes a hip nightlife scene. People from all over the state come to Albuquerque to check out the live music and dance clubs, most within walking distance of one another. Old Town is also worth a visit; though touristy, it's a unique Southwestern village with a graceful, intact plaza.

ESSENTIALS

GETTING THERE   By Plane   Albuquerque International Sunport (© **505/842-4366**) is in the south-central part of the city, between I-25 on the west and Kirtland Air Force Base on the east, only about 4 miles from downtown. Most hotels have courtesy airport vans. In addition, **Checker Airport Express** (© **505/765-1234**) runs to and from city hotels. **Sun Tran** (© **505/ 843-9200**), Albuquerque's public bus system, also makes airport stops; it takes about 20 minutes. There is also efficient taxi service to and from the airport.

By Train   Amtrak (© **800/USA-RAIL;** www.amtrak.com) provides daily service from Chicago (trip time: 26 hr.), Flagstaff (5–6 hr.), and Los Angeles (26 hr.) to its station at 214 First St. SW.

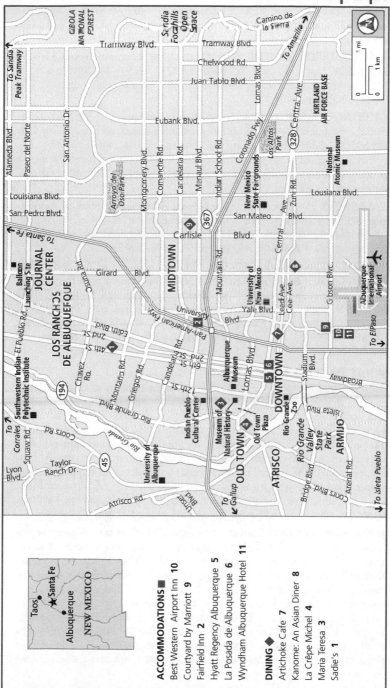

Central Albuquerque

ACCOMMODATIONS ■
Best Western Airport Inn **10**
Courtyard by Marriott **9**
Fairfield Inn **2**
Hyatt Regency Albuquerque **5**
La Posada de Albuquerque **6**
Wyndham Albuquerque Hotel **11**

DINING ◆
Artichoke Cafe **7**
Kanome: An Asian Diner **8**
La Crêpe Michel **4**
Maria Teresa **3**
Sadie's **1**

By Car   The major routes into Albuquerque are I-40 from the east (Amarillo) and west (Flagstaff), and I-25 from the north (Santa Fe and Denver) and south (El Paso).

VISITOR INFORMATION   The **Albuquerque Convention and Visitors Bureau,** 20 First Plaza NW (© **800/284-2282** or 505/842-9918), is open Monday through Friday from 8am to 5pm. There's another visitor center in Old Town at 303 Romero St. NW.

GETTING AROUND   Sun Tran of Albuquerque (© 505/843-9200) runs the city bus network. Call for information on routes and fares. **Yellow Cab** (© **505/247-8888**) serves the city and surrounding area 24 hours a day.

Parking is generally not difficult. Only the large downtown hotels charge for parking. Traffic is a problem only at rush hours. Avoid I-25 and I-40 at the center of town around 5pm.

FAST FACTS   For a doctor, call the **Greater Albuquerque Medical Association** (© 505/821-4583). **Presbyterian Hospital** is at 1100 Central Ave. SE (© **505/841-1234,** or 505/841-1111 for emergency services). **Walgreens,** 5001 Montgomery St. (© **505/881-5210**), runs a 24-hour pharmacy.

SPECIAL EVENTS & FESTIVALS   The last weekend in June brings the **New Mexico Arts and Crafts Fair** (© 505/884-9043) to the State Fairgrounds. The fairgrounds also host the **New Mexico State Fair and Rodeo** (© 505/ 265-1791), one of America's top state fairs, for 17 days in early September. In mid-October, there's the **Kodak Albuquerque International Balloon Fiesta** (© **800/733-9918**), the world's largest balloon rally, with races, contests, and special events.

WHAT TO SEE & DO

Albuquerque Museum   In this museum on the outskirts of Old Town, you can take an interesting journey into New Mexico's past. Drawing on the largest U.S. collection of Spanish colonial artifacts, displays here include Don Quixote–style helmets, swords, and horse armor. You can wander through an 18th-century house compound with adobe floor and walls, and see gear used by *vaqueros,* the original cowboys who came to the area in the 16th century. Kids can spin wool in the weaving exhibition and touch pelts in the trapping section. Upper floors house permanent art collections and a huge exhibit space where you'll find some extraordinary shows. 2000 Mountain Rd. NW, Albuquerque, NM 87104. © 505/243-7255. Admission $2 adults, $1 seniors and children 4–12. Tues–Sun 9am–5pm.

Indian Pueblo Cultural Center   Owned and operated as a nonprofit organization by the 19 pueblos of New Mexico, this is a fine place to begin an exploration of Native American culture. A permanent exhibit depicts the evolution from prehistory to present of the various pueblos, including displays of the distinctive crafts of each community. The Pueblo House Children's Museum, in a separate building, gives kids a hands-on opportunity to learn about Pueblo culture. On weekends, look for Native American dancers and artisans demonstrating their skills. A restaurant serves traditional Native American foods. 2401 12th St. NW, Albuquerque, NM 87104. © 800/766-4405 or 505/843-7270. Admission $4 adults, $3 seniors, $1 students, free for children 4 and under. AE, DISC, MC, V. Daily 9am–4:30pm; restaurant 8am–3pm.

National Atomic Museum   This is a good introduction to the nuclear age. The 51-minute film *Ten Seconds That Shook the World* is shown several times daily and is well worth seeing. There's a permanent Marie Curie exhibit, full-scale models of the "Fat Man" and "Little Boy" bombs, and displays on the peaceful application of nuclear technology. 1905 Mountain Rd. NW (P.O. Box 5800, MS1490), Albuquerque, NM 87185. ✆ 505/284-3243. www.atomicmuseum.com. Admission $4 adults, $3 seniors and children 7–18. Children under 12 not admitted without adult. Daily 9am–5pm.

New Mexico Museum of Natural History and Science A trip through this museum will take you through 12 billion years of natural history. Highlights include dinosaur skeletons; the Evolator (kids love this!), a simulated time-travel ride that moves and rumbles through 38 million years of history; a walk-in cave showing the inner workings of a volcano; FossilWorks, where paleontologists work behind glass excavating bones of a seismosaurus; and the LodeStar Astronomy Center, a sophisticated planetarium with Virtual Voyages, a simulation theater. 1801 Mountain Rd. NW. ✆ 505/841-2800. Admission $5 adults, $4 seniors, $2 children 3–12. DynaTheater, Planetarium, and Virtual Voyages cost extra. Daily 9am–5pm.

Sandia Peak Tramway This is a fun half-day or evening outing with incredible views of the Albuquerque landscape and wildlife. The Sandia Peak tram is a "jigback"; in other words, as one car approaches the top, the other nears the bottom. The two pass halfway through the trip, in the midst of a 1½-mile "clear span" of unsupported cable between the second tower and the upper terminal. There are several hiking trails; La Luz Trail travels to the top of the Sandias and is very steep and scenic. *Note:* The trails on Sandia may not be suitable for children. 10 Tramway Loop NE. ✆ 505/856-7325. Fax 505/856-6335. Admission $15 adults, $12 seniors, $10 children 5–12. Memorial Day to Labor Day daily 9am–9pm; spring and fall Sun–Thurs 9am–8pm, Wed 5–8pm, Fri–Sat 9am–9pm; ski season Thurs–Tues 9am–8pm, Wed noon–8pm. Parking $1. AE, DISC, MC, V. Take I-25 north to Tramway Rd. (Exit 234), then proceed east 5 miles on Tramway Rd. (N.M. 556); or take Tramway Blvd., Exit 167 (N.M. 556), north of I-40 approximately 8½ miles. Turn east the last half mile on Tramway Rd.

EXPLORING OLD TOWN

A maze of cobbled courtyard walkways leads to hidden patios and gardens, where many of Old Town's 150 galleries and shops are located. Adobe buildings, many refurbished in the Pueblo Revival style in the 1950s, are grouped around the tree-shaded **Plaza,** created in 1780. Pueblo and Navajo artisans often display their pottery, blankets, and jewelry on the sidewalks lining the Plaza. (Look especially for silver bracelets and strung turquoise. For something cheaper, buy a dyed corn necklace.)

When Albuquerque was established in 1706, the first building erected by the settlers was the cozy **Church of San Felipe de Neri,** with wonderful stained-glass windows and vivid *retablos* (religious paintings). Next door to the church is the **Rectory,** built about 1793. Also on the north plaza is **Loyola Hall,** the Sister Blandina Convent, built originally of adobe in 1881 as a residence for Sisters of Charity teachers who worked in the region. When the Jesuit fathers built **Our Lady of the Angels School,** 320 Romero St., in 1877, it was the only public school in Albuquerque.

The **Antonio Vigil House,** 413 Romero St., is an adobe-style residence with traditional viga ends sticking out over the entrance door. The **Florencio Zamora Store,** 301 Romero St., was built in the 1890s of "pugmill" adobe for a butcher and grocer. The **Jesus Romero House,** 205 Romero St., was constructed by another grocer in 1915. Just down the street, the **Jesus Romero Store,** built in 1893, has Territorial and Queen Anne structural features. On the south plaza, the **Manuel Springer House**'s hipped roof and bay windows are still visible under its present-day commercial facade. The adjacent **Cristobal Armijo House,** a banker's two-story adobe, combines Italianate and Queen Anne architectural styles.

Casa Armijo, in the 200 block of San Felipe Street, dates from before 1840; it was a headquarters for both Union and Confederate troops during the Civil War. The nearby **Ambrosio Armijo House and Store,** also on San Felipe, an 1882 adobe structure, once had the high false front of wooden boards so typical of Old West towns in movies. The **Herman Blueher House,** 302 San Felipe St., built by a businessman in 1898, is a three-story Italianate mansion with fancy porches on two levels, now obscured by storefronts.

An excellent Old Town historic walking tour starts at the Albuquerque Museum (see above) at 11am Tuesday through Sunday during spring, summer, and fall. The museum also publishes a brochure for a self-guided walking tour.

SHOPPING

The best buys in Albuquerque are Southwestern regional items, including arts and crafts of all kinds—traditional Native American and Hispanic as well as contemporary works. In local Native American art, look for silver and turquoise jewelry, pottery, weavings, baskets, sand paintings, and Hopi kachina dolls. Hispanic folk art (handcrafted furniture, tinwork, and religious paintings) is also worth seeking out. The best contemporary art is in paintings, sculpture, jewelry, ceramics, and fiber art, including weaving.

If you want a real bargain in Native American arts and crafts, **Skip Maisel's,** 510 Central Ave. SW (© **505/242-6526**), is the place to shop. You'll find a broad range of quality and price here in goods such as pottery, weavings, and kachinas. Fifty artisans show their talents at the lovely cooperative **Amapola Gallery,** 206 Romero St. (© **505/242-4311**), off a cobbled courtyard. You'll find pottery, paintings, textiles, carvings, baskets, jewelry, and other items.

WHERE TO STAY

The affordable Marriott-owned **Fairfield Inn,** 1760 Menaul Rd. NE (© **800/ 228-2800** or 505/889-4000), has exceptionally clean rooms and a location with easy access to freeways. Ask for an east-facing room to avoid highway noise. The **Best Western Airport Inn,** 2400 Yale Blvd. SE (© **800/528-1234** or 505/242-7022), is a good budget choice just blocks from the airport. Rooms are comfortable and have plenty of amenities. A courtesy van is available.

Courtyard by Marriott If you don't like high-rises, this is the best airport-area choice. Most of the hotel's clients are business travelers. All units are roomy and comfortable, with walnut furniture and firm beds. Ask for a balcony room on the courtyard. 1920 Yale Blvd. SE, Albuquerque, NM 87106. © 800/321-2211 or 505/843-6600. Fax 505/843-8740. www.marriott.com. 150 units. $71–$107 double. Weekend rates available. AE, DC, DISC, MC, V. **Amenities:** Restaurant; indoor pool; fitness room.

Hacienda Antigua Hacienda Antigua, a 200-year-old adobe home that's a 20-minute drive from the airport, was once the first stagecoach stop out of Old Town in Albuquerque. Now, it's one of Albuquerque's most elegant inns, with an artistically landscaped courtyard. Rooms are gracefully outfitted with antiques, fireplaces, and VCRs. Light sleepers, beware—the Santa Fe Railroad runs by this inn. 6708 Tierra Dr. NW, Albuquerque, NM 87107. © 800/201-2986 or 505/345-5399. Fax 505/345-3855. www.haciendantigua.com. 8 units. $109–$229 double. Extra person $25. Rates include breakfast. MC, V. **Amenities:** Outdoor pool; pets welcome ($30).

Hacienda Vargas This hotel is about 20 miles from Albuquerque, a good choice if you're visiting both Santa Fe and Albuquerque but don't want to stay in a downtown hotel in either. Unassuming in its elegance, Hacienda Vargas has a real Mexican feel, with brightly woven place mats in the breakfast room and Spanish suits of armor hanging in the common area. Each room has a private entrance, many opening onto a courtyard. All units have handmade kiva fireplaces and New Mexico antiques. The only drawback is the sometimes noisy train tracks near the back of the house. El Camino Real (P.O. Box 307), Algodones/Santa Fe, NM 87001. 𝒞 800/261-0006 or 505/867-9115. Fax 505/867-1902. www.haciendavargas. com. 7 units. $89–$179 double. Extra person $15. MC, V. **Amenities:** Some pets accepted with prior arrangement.

Hyatt Regency Albuquerque For a luxury stay right downtown, this is the place. The $60-million hotel is pure shiny gloss and Art Deco. The lobby features a palm-shaded fountain beneath a pyramidal skylight, and throughout the hotel's public areas is an extensive art collection, including original Frederic Remington sculptures. Rooms are spacious, with views of the mountains. The hotel is located right next door to the Galeria, a shopping area, and has a number of shops itself. 330 Tijeras Ave. NW, Albuquerque, NM 87102. 𝒞 800/233-1234 or 505/842-1234. Fax 505/766-6710. www.hyatt.com. 395 units. Weekdays $224 double, weekends $105 double; $335–$435 suite. AE, DC, DISC, MC, V. Self-parking $8, valet $11. **Amenities:** Restaurant; outdoor pool; health club.

La Posada de Albuquerque If you want a feel for downtown Albuquerque as well as easy access to Old Town, this hotel on the National Register of Historic Places will suit you well. With its elaborate Moorish fountain and old-fashioned tin chandeliers, it feels like Old Spain. Though the rooms here are fine, and many have city and mountain views, they do possess some of the quirks unique to an older hotel. Conrad's Downtown features Southwestern cuisine. 125 Second St. NW (at Copper Ave.), Albuquerque, NM 87102. 𝒞 800/777-5732 or 505/242-9090. Fax 505/242-8664. 114 units. $89–$115 double; $195–$275 suite. AE, DISC, MC, V. Valet parking $5. **Amenities:** Restaurant; access to nearby health club.

Wyndham Albuquerque Hotel This 15-story hotel right at the airport provides spacious rooms with a touch of elegance. The lobby, grill, and lounge areas employ sandstone, wood, copper, and tile to lend an Anasazi feel, which carries into the rooms, each with a broad view from a balcony. Air travelers enjoy this hotel's location, but because it has good access to freeways and excellent views, it could also be a wise choice for a few days of browsing around Albuquerque. 2910 Yale Blvd. SE, Albuquerque, NM 87106. 𝒞 800/227-1117 or 505/843-7000. Fax 505/843-6307. 276 units. $99–$179 double. AE, DC, DISC, MC, V. Free parking. **Amenities:** Restaurant; outdoor pool; access to golf club; 2 tennis courts; small pets welcome with prior approval.

WHERE TO DINE

Artichoke Cafe CONTINENTAL An art gallery as well as a restaurant, this popular spot has modern paintings and sculptures set against azure walls. Start with an artichoke steamed with three dipping sauces or roasted and stuffed with forest mushrooms and rock shrimp. For lunch, there are a number of salads and gourmet sandwiches, as well as entrees such as flash-fried sea scallops with ginger and lime sauce. At dinner, try wahoo on glass noodles with a miso broth, or the pumpkin ravioli with butternut squash, spinach, and ricotta filling. 424 Central Ave. SE. 𝒞 505/243-0200. Reservations recommended. Main courses $13–$24. AE, DC, DISC, MC, V. Mon–Fri 11am–2:30pm; Mon 5:30–9pm; Tues–Sat 5:30–10pm.

Kanome: An Asian Diner ECLECTIC ASIAN   Kanome has a contemporary atmosphere with burnished orange walls and wonderful collaged tables. It's not a cozy place, but service is friendly and efficient. The food is served with panache: Try the Balinese skewered pork and cashews or the Chinese duck with Tsing Tao peanut sauce. The chef uses free-range chicken and organic vegetables. Save room for the excellent homemade ice cream. During warm months, diners enjoy the patio. 3128 Central Ave. SE. (⌀ **505/265-7773**. Reservations recommended. Main courses $6–$14. AE, DISC, MC, V. Sun–Thurs 5–10pm; Fri–Sat 5–11pm.

La Crêpe Michel FRENCH   This small find has a cozy, informal European feel, with calm, friendly service. The *crêpe aux fruits de mer* (scallops and shrimp in a velouté sauce with mushrooms) is especially nice. Salmon is prepared with a green peppercorn brandy sauce. To accompany your meal, choose from a carefully planned beer and wine menu. For dessert, don't leave without having a strawberry crepe. 400 San Felipe C2. (⌀ **505/242-1251**. Reservations accepted. Main courses $5.95–$20. MC, V. Tues–Sun 11:30am–2pm; Thurs–Sat 6–9pm.

Maria Teresa AMERICAN/NEW MEXICAN   This 1840s Salvador Armijo House, a National Historic property, has 32-inch-thick adobe walls and is furnished with Victorian antiques and paintings. Tables are well spaced through seven rooms, a great place for an intimate meal; you can eat on an enchanting patio in summer. Dinner entrees may feature sautéed jumbo prawns or seared beef tenderloin topped with béarnaise sauce. Service is formal and professional, though occasionally slow. 618 Rio Grande Blvd. NW. (⌀ **505/242-3900**. Reservations recommended. Lunch $6.95–$14; dinner $13–$23. AE, DC, DISC, MC, V. Daily 5–9pm; Sat–Sun 11am–2:30pm.

Range Café NEW MEXICAN/AMERICAN   This cafe, about 15 minutes north of Albuquerque, is a perfect place to stop on your way out of town. However, the food's so good you may just want to make a special trip. Housed in what was once an old drugstore, the restaurant has a pressed-tin ceiling and is decorated with Western touches. The food ranges from enchiladas to chicken-fried steak to elegantly prepared meals. Try Tom's meatloaf, served with roasted garlic mashed potatoes, mushroom gravy, and sautéed vegetables. Seared Atlantic salmon is served over a fresh chipotle and white-corn ragout with roasted potatoes. Taos Cow ice cream is the order for dessert. 925 Camino del Pueblo, Bernalillo. (⌀ **505/867-1700**. Reservations accepted for parties of 8 or more. Breakfast/lunch $2.95–$8.95; dinner $6.50–$20. AE, DISC, MC, V. Daily 7:30am–9:30pm.

Sadie's NEW MEXICAN   Many New Mexicans lament the lost days when this restaurant was in a bowling alley. Though the current dining room is a little too big and the atmosphere a little too bright, the food is simply some of the best in New Mexico, with tasty sauces and large portions. Try the enchilada, either chicken or beef, or the stuffed sopaipilla dinner. There's a full bar, with excellent margaritas (and TV screens for you sports fans). 6230 Fourth St. NW. (⌀ **505/345-9440**. Main courses $7–$14. AE, DC, DISC, MC, V. Mon–Sat 11am–10pm; Sun 11am–9pm.

ALBUQUERQUE AFTER DARK

Current listings appear in the two daily newspapers; detailed weekend arts calendars can be found in the Thursday *Tribune* and the Friday *Journal.* The monthly *On the Scene* and the weekly *Alibi* also carry entertainment listings.

THE PERFORMING ARTS The **New Mexico Symphony Orchestra** (© **800/251-6676** or 505/881-9590) performs at Popejoy Hall, on the University of New Mexico campus; it also presents highly recommended outdoor concerts at the Rio Grande Zoo band shell. The **New Mexico Ballet Company** (© **505/292-4245**) has several performances a year at Popejoy Hall.

THE CLUB & MUSIC SCENE Top acts from each coast, including nationally televised comedians, are booked at **Laffs Comedy Cafe,** San Mateo Boulevard and Osuna Road (© **505/296-5653**).

If you prefer country to comedy, try **Midnight Rodeo,** 4901 McLeod Rd. NE, near San Mateo Boulevard (© **505/888-0100**), the Southwest's largest nightclub. A DJ spins records nightly; the dance floor is so big that it resembles an indoor horse track. A busy kitchen serves simple but hearty meals.

Brewsters Pub, 312 Central Ave. SW, downtown (© **505/247-2533**), offers live blues, jazz, folk, or light rock entertainment in a sports bar–type setting. **Burt's Tiki Lounge,** 313 Gold Ave. (© **505/243-BURT**), recently won the weekly paper *Alibi*'s award for the best variety of drinks. The club offers live music Thursday through Sunday.

OASIS IN THE DESERT: A SIDE TRIP TO BOSQUE DEL APACHE NATIONAL WILDLIFE REFUGE

Bosque del Apache National Wildlife Refuge is a haven for migratory waterfowl such as snow geese and cranes. Particularly if you're here November through March, the experience is thrilling, not only for the variety of birds—more than 300 species—but also for the sheer numbers of them. Huge clouds of snow geese and sandhill cranes take flight at dawn and dusk, the air filling with the sounds of their calls and their wings flapping. In early December, the refuge may harbor as many as 45,000 snow geese, 57,000 ducks of many different species, and 18,000 sandhill cranes. There are also plenty of raptors about, including numerous red-tailed hawks and northern harriers (sometimes called marsh hawks), Cooper's hawks and kestrels, and even bald and golden eagles. The refuge has a 15-mile auto tour loop, which you should drive very slowly. Dawn is the best time to be here.

GETTING THERE Bosque del Apache is about a 1½-hour drive from Albuquerque. Follow I-25 to the San Antonio exit. At the main intersection, turn south onto N.M. 1. In 3 miles you'll be on refuge lands, and another 4 miles will bring you to the excellent **visitor center** (© **505/835-1828**). The refuge is open daily year-round.

8 White Sands National Monument

Arguably the most memorable natural area in this part of the Southwest, White Sands National Monument preserves the best part of the world's largest gypsum dune field, an area of 275 square miles of pure white gypsum sand reaching out over the floor of the Tularosa Basin in wavelike dunes. Plants and animals have evolved in special ways to adapt to the bright white environment here. Some creatures have a bleached coloration to match the whiteness all around them, and some plants have evolved means for surviving the smothering pressures of the blowing sands.

The surrounding mountains—the Sacramentos to the east, with their forested slopes, and the serene San Andres to the west—are composed of sandstone, limestone, sedimentary rocks, and pockets of gypsum. Over millions of years, rains and melting snows dissolved the gypsum and carried it down into Lake Lucero. Here the hot sun and dry winds evaporate the water, leaving the pure white gypsum to crystallize. Then the persistent winds blow these crystals, in the form of minuscule bits of sand, in a northeastern direction, adding them to growing dunes. As each dune grows and moves farther from the lake, new ones form in what seems an endless procession.

The dunes are especially enchanting at sunrise and under the light of a full moon, but you'll have to camp to experience this extraordinary sight (see below). If you're not camping, you'll probably want to spend only a couple of hours here. Refreshments and snacks can be purchased at the visitor center, along with books, maps, posters, and other souvenirs; however, there are no dining or grocery facilities available.

ESSENTIALS

GETTING THERE   The visitor center is 15 miles southwest of Alamogordo on U.S. 70/82 (*Note:* Due to missile testing on the adjacent White Sands Missile Range, this road is sometimes closed for up to 2 hr. at a time.) The nearest major airport is El Paso International, 90 miles away. You can drive from there or take a commuter flight from Albuquerque to Alamogordo–White Sands Regional Airport. By car, take I-25 south from Albuquerque or north from El Paso to Las Cruces. From there take U.S. 70 east to White Sands.

VISITOR INFORMATION   Contact **White Sands National Monument,** P.O. Box 1086, Holloman AFB, NM 88330-1086 (☎ **505/479-6124**). When driving near or in the monument, tune your radio to 1610 AM for information on what's happening.

ADMISSION FEES & HOURS   Admission is $3 for adults age 17 and over. Memorial Day to Labor Day the visitor center is open from 8am to 7pm and Dunes Drive is open from 7am to 9pm. Ranger talks and sunset strolls are given nightly at 7 and 8:30pm during summer. During the rest of the year, the visitor center is open from 8am to 4:30pm and Dunes Drive is open from 7am to sunset.

SEEING THE HIGHLIGHTS

The 16-mile **Dunes Drive** loops through the "heart of sands" from the visitor center. Information available at the center tells you what to look for on your drive. Sometimes the winds blow the dunes over the road, which must then be rerouted. The dunes are, in fact, all moving slowly to the northeast, pushed by prevailing southwest winds, some at the rate of as much as 20 feet a year.

In the center of the monument, the road itself is made of hard-packed gypsum (it can be especially slick after an afternoon thunderstorm, so drive cautiously!). Visitors are invited to get out of their cars at established parking areas and explore a bit; some like to climb a dune for a better view of the endless sea of sand. If you'd rather experience the park by hiking instead of the long drive, a good option right near the entrance is the **Big Dune Trail.** It takes you on a 45-minute loop along the edges of the dunes and then into their whiteness, ending atop a 60-foot-tall one.

The National Park Service emphasizes that (1) tunneling in this sand can be dangerous, for it collapses easily and could suffocate a person; (2) sand-surfing down the dune slopes, although permitted, can also be hazardous, so it should be undertaken with care, and never near an auto road; and (3) hikers can get lost in a sudden sandstorm should they stray from marked trails or areas.

We strongly recommend camping here, especially to see the dunes at sunrise or under a full moon. If you don't camp, you'll miss both because the park closes at dusk and doesn't reopen until after dawn. There are no campgrounds and no facilities, however, so this is strictly a backcountry adventure. Only tent camping is allowed, and you must register and get clearance from monument headquarters before you pitch yours. Call ✆ **505/479-6124** for information.

9 Carlsbad Caverns National Park

One of the largest and most spectacular cave systems in the world, Carlsbad Caverns encompasses some 80 known caves that snake through the porous limestone reef of the Guadalupe Mountains. Fantastic and grotesque formations fascinate visitors, who find every shape imaginable sculpted in this underground world—frozen waterfalls, strands of pearls, soda straws, miniature castles, draperies, ice-cream cones, and everything in between.

ESSENTIALS

GETTING THERE   Take U.S. 62/180 from either Carlsbad, New Mexico, which is 23 miles to the northeast, or El Paso, Texas (150 miles west). The scenic entrance road to the park is 7 miles long and originates at the park gate at Whites City. Van service to Carlsbad Caverns National Park from Whites City, south of Carlsbad, is provided by **Sun Country Tours/Whites City Services** (✆ **505/785-2291**).

VISITOR INFORMATION   For more information about the park, contact **Carlsbad Caverns National Park,** 3225 National Parks Hwy., Carlsbad, NM 88220 (✆ **800/967-CAVE** for tour reservations, 505/785-2232, ext. 429, for information about guided tours, or 505/785-2107 for recorded information).

ADMISSION FEES & HOURS   General admission to the park is $6 for adults, $3 for children 6 to 15, free for children under 6. Admission is good for 3 days and includes entry to the two self-guided walking tours. Guided tours range in price from $7 to $20; reservations are required. The visitor center and park are open daily, except Christmas, from Memorial Day to mid-August from 8am to 7pm (last entrance at 5pm), and the rest of the year from 8am to 5pm (last entrance at 3:30pm).

WHAT TO SEE & DO

Two caves, Carlsbad Cavern and Slaughter Canyon, are open to the public. The National Park Service has provided facilities, including elevators, to make it easy for everyone to visit the cavern, and there is wheelchair access.

In addition to the options described below, ask at the visitor center about other ranger-guided tours, including climbing and crawling "wild" cave tours. Be sure to call in advance—some tours are offered only 1 day per week. Spelunkers who seek access to the park's undeveloped caves require special permission from the park superintendent.

CARLSBAD CAVERN TOURS   You can tour the caverns in one of three ways, depending on your time, interest, and level of ability. The first, and easiest, option is to take the elevator from the visitor center down 750 feet to the start of the self-guided tour of the Big Room. More difficult and time-consuming, but vastly more rewarding, is the 1-mile self-guided tour along the **Natural**

The Bat Cave!

Every sunset from May to October, a crowd gathers at the natural entrance of the cave to watch a quarter-of-a-million bats take flight for a night of insect feasting. (The bats winter in Mexico.) All day long the Mexican free-tailed bats sleep in the cavern; at night they all strike out on an insect hunt. A ranger program is offered around 7:30pm (verify the time at the visitor center) at the outdoor Bat Flight Amphitheater. On the second Thursday in August (usually; call to confirm), the park sponsors a **Bat Flight Breakfast** from 5 to 7am, during which visitors watch the bats return to the cavern.

Entrance route, which follows the traditional explorer's route, entering the cavern through the large historic natural entrance. The paved walkway winds into the depths of the cavern and leads through a series of underground rooms. This tour takes about an hour; parts of it are steep. At its lowest point, the trail reaches 750 feet below the surface, ending finally at an underground rest area.

Both those visitors who take the elevator and those who take the Natural Entrance route begin the self-guided tour of the spectacular **Big Room** near the rest area. The floor of this room covers 14 acres; the tour, over a relatively level path, is 1¼ miles and takes about an hour.

The third option is the 1½-hour ranger-guided **Kings Palace tour,** which also departs from the underground rest area. This tour descends 830 feet beneath the surface of the desert to the deepest portion of the cavern open to the public. Reservations are required and an additional fee is charged.

Tour tips: Wear flat shoes with rubber soles and heels because of the slippery paths. A light sweater or jacket feels good in the constant temperature of 56°F (13°C), especially when it's 100°F (38°C) outside in the sun. The cavern is well lit, but you might want to bring along a flashlight. Rangers are stationed in the cave to answer questions.

SLAUGHTER CANYON CAVE TOUR   Slaughter Canyon Cave consists of a corridor 1,140 feet long with many side passageways. The lowest point is 250 feet below the surface, and the passage traversed by the ranger-guided tours is 1¾ miles long but is more strenuous than hiking through the main cavern. There is also a demanding 500-foot-rise hike from the parking lot to the cave mouth. The tour lasts about 2½ hours. Reservations are required and there is a limit of 25 people. Everyone needs a flashlight, hiking boots or shoes, and a container of drinking water. Slaughter Canyon Cave is reached via U.S. 180, south 5 miles from Whites City, to a marked turnoff that leads 11 miles to a parking lot.

OTHER GUIDED TOURS   Be sure to ask about the Left Hand Tunnel, Lower Cave, Hall of the White Giant, and Spider Cave tours. They vary in degree of difficulty and adventure, from **Left Hand,** which is an easy half-mile lantern tour; to **Spider Cave,** where you can expect tight crawlways and canyon-like passages; to **Hall of the White Giant,** a strenuous tour in which you're required to crawl long distances, squeeze through tight crevices, and climb up slippery flow-stone–lined passages. Call in advance for times of each tour. All depart from the visitor center.

OTHER PARK ACTIVITIES   There's a 10-mile one-way scenic loop drive through the Chihuahuan Desert to view **Rattlesnake** and **Upper Walnut Canyons.** Picnickers can head for Rattlesnake Springs Picnic Area, on County

Road 418 near Slaughter Canyon Cave, a water source for hundreds of years for the Native Americans of the area. Backcountry hikers must register at the visitor center before going out on any of the trails.

10 Santa Fe

With a strong local flavor that's made rich by vibrant Native American and Hispanic communities, Santa Fe has become increasingly sophisticated in recent decades. Visitors flock here for cutting-edge cuisine, world-class opera, first-run art films, and some of the finest artwork in the world, seen easily while wandering on foot from gallery to gallery, museum to museum. They're also enchanted by the city's setting, backed by rolling hills and the blue peaks of the Sangre de Cristo Mountains.

Santa Fe was founded by Spanish governor Don Pedro de Peralta, who built the Palace of the Governors as his capitol on the north side of the central Plaza, where it stands today as an excellent museum of the city's 4 centuries of history. The Plaza, once the terminus of the Santa Fe Trail from Missouri and of the earlier Camino Real from Mexico, is the focus of numerous bustling art markets and Santa Fe's early September fiesta, celebrated annually since 1770. It's also one of the major attractions in the Southwest, and under its portico, Native Americans sit cross-legged, selling their crafts to eager tourists, as they have done for decades.

ESSENTIALS

GETTING THERE **By Plane** Although you can fly to **Santa Fe Municipal Airport** (© 505/955-2900), it's easier to fly to **Albuquerque International Sunport** (© 505/842-4366) and drive from there.

By Train **Amtrak** (© 800/USA-RAIL; www.amtrak.com) provides service from Albuquerque (trip time: 2 hr.), Chicago (24 hr.), and Los Angeles (19 hr.) to its station at nearby Lamy (approximately 20 miles from downtown Santa Fe). Amtrak's **Lamy Shuttle Service** (© 505/982-8829) will take you to and pick you up from your hotel in Santa Fe.

By Car The major route into Santa Fe is I-25 from the south (Albuquerque) and north (Denver and Colorado Springs). For those coming from the northwest, the most direct route is via Durango, Colorado, on U.S. 160 east, then U.S. 84 south to Santa Fe.

VISITOR INFORMATION The **Santa Fe Convention and Visitors Bureau** is at 201 W. Marcy St., in Sweeney Center at Grant Street downtown (© 800/777-CITY or 505/955-6200; www.santafe.org). You might also try www.visitsantafe.com and www.sol.com for more information.

GETTING AROUND The best way to see downtown Santa Fe is on foot. Street parking is difficult to find during summer months. You can pick up a wallet-size guide to parking areas at the visitor center. There's a parking lot near the federal courthouse, 2 blocks north of the Plaza; another one behind Santa Fe Village, a block south of the Plaza; and a third at Water and Sandoval streets.

The public bus system, **Santa Fe Trails** (© 505/955-2001), has seven routes. You can pick up a map from the visitor center. Buses operate Monday through Friday from 6am to 11pm and Saturday from 8am to 8pm. **Capital City Cab** (© 505/438-0000) is the main taxi company.

FAST FACTS **St. Vincent Hospital** is at 455 St. Michael's Dr. (© 505/983-3361, or 505/820-5250 for emergency services). **Del Norte Pharmacy,** 1691 Galisteo St. (© 505/988-9797), offers delivery and emergency service.

SPECIAL EVENTS & FESTIVALS   Santa Fe Plaza is often the site of special events. The last weekend in July brings the **Spanish Markets** (© 505/982-2226), when more than 300 Hispanic artists from New Mexico and southern Colorado exhibit and sell their work. In August, there's the **Annual Indian Market** (© 505/983-5220), with artisans' booths, musical entertainment, tribal dancing, and crafts demonstrations. Beginning Thursday night after Labor Day is **Fiesta de Santa Fe** (© 505/988-7575), the oldest community celebration in the United States. Events include masses, parades, mariachi concerts, and dances.

EXPLORING THE CITY

Four-day passes good at all branches of the Museum of New Mexico (the Palace of the Governors, the Museum of Fine Arts, the Museum of International Folk Art, and the Museum of Indian Arts and Culture) cost $15 for adults. The main office is at 113 Lincoln Ave. (© 505/476-5060).

El Rancho de las Golondrinas   This 200-acre ranch was once the last stopping place on the 1,000-mile El Camino Real from Mexico City to Santa Fe. Today, it's a living 18th- and 19th-century Spanish village, comprising a hacienda, a village store, a schoolhouse, and several chapels and kitchens. There's also a working molasses mill, wheelwright and blacksmith shops, shearing and weaving rooms, a threshing ground, a winery and vineyard, and four water mills, as well as dozens of farm animals. Costumed volunteers demonstrate traditional trades. The Spring Festival (in June) and the Harvest Festival (in Oct) are the year's highlights. 334 Los Pinos Rd. (15 miles south of the Santa Fe Plaza via I-25). © 505/ 471-2261. www.golondrinas.org. Admission $5 adults, $4 seniors and teens, $2 children 5–12. Festival weekends $7 adults, $5 seniors and teens, $3 children 5–12. June–Sept Wed–Sun 10am– 4pm; Apr–May and Oct open by advance arrangement. Closed Nov–Mar. I-25, Exit 276 will lead to N.M. 599 going north; turn left on W. Frontage Rd.; turn right on Los Pinos Rd.; continue 3 miles.

Georgia O'Keeffe Museum   This museum contains the largest collection of O'Keeffes in the world: 117 oil paintings, drawings, watercolors, pastels, and sculptures. It's the only museum in the United States dedicated solely to one woman's work. The rich and varied collection includes such works as *Jimson Weed* (1932) and *Evening Star No. VII* (1917). 217 Johnson St. © 505/946-1000. July–Oct daily 10am–5pm (Fri until 8pm); Nov–June Thurs–Tues 10am–5pm (Fri until 8pm). Admission $8 adults, free for students; Fri free 5–8pm.

Museum of Fine Arts   The museum's permanent collection of more than 20,000 works emphasizes regional art and includes landscapes and portraits by all the Taos masters, *los Cincos Pintores* (a 1920s organization of Santa Fe artists), and contemporary artists. The museum also has a collection of photographic works by such masters as Ansel Adams, Edward Weston, and Elliot Porter. 107 W. Palace (at Lincoln Ave.). © 505/476-5072. Admission $5 adults, free for seniors on Wed, free for youths 16 and under, free for all Fri 5–8pm. See above for information on 4-day passes good at all branches of the Museum of New Mexico ($15). Tues–Sun 10am–5pm (Fri until 8pm).

Museum of Indian Arts and Culture   A permanent interactive exhibit here makes this one of the most exciting Native American museum experiences in the Southwest. *Here, Now and Always* takes visitors through thousands of years of Native American history. More than 70,000 pieces of basketry, pottery, clothing, carpets, and jewelry—much of it quite old—are on continual rotating display. The rest of the museum houses a lovely pottery collection as well as changing exhibits. Call for information on demonstrations of traditional skills, lectures on native traditions and arts, and performances of Native American music and

Downtown Santa Fe

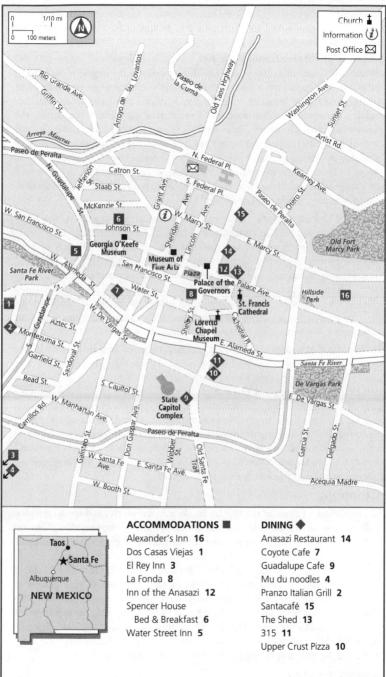

ACCOMMODATIONS ■
Alexander's Inn **16**
Dos Casas Viejas **1**
El Rey Inn **3**
La Fonda **8**
Inn of the Anasazi **12**
Spencer House
  Bed & Breakfast **6**
Water Street Inn **5**

DINING ◆
Anasazi Restaurant **14**
Coyote Cafe **7**
Guadalupe Cafe **9**
Mu du noodles **4**
Pranzo Italian Grill **2**
Santacafé **15**
The Shed **13**
315 **11**
Upper Crust Pizza **10**

dancing. 710 Camino Lejo. ℭ **505/476-1250.** Admission $5 adults, free for kids 16 and under. See above for information on 4-day passes good at all branches of the Museum of New Mexico ($15). Tues–Sun 10am–5pm.

Museum of International Folk Art   With a collection of some 130,000 objects from more than 100 countries, this museum is the largest of its kind in the world. The special collections include Spanish colonial silver, traditional and contemporary New Mexican religious art, Mexican tribal costumes, Mexican majolica ceramics, Brazilian folk art, European glass, African sculptures, the marvelous Morris Miniature Circus, and American weather vanes and quilts. 706 Camino Lejo. ℭ **505/476-1200.** Admission $7 adults, free for youths 16 and under. See above for information on 4-day passes good at all branches of the Museum of New Mexico ($15). Tues–Sun 10am–5pm. Located 2 miles southeast of the Plaza. Drive southeast on Old Santa Fe Trail (beware: Old Santa Fe Trail takes a left turn; if you find yourself on Old Pecos Trail, you've missed the turn). Look for signs pointing right onto Camino Lejo.

Palace of the Governors   Built in 1610 as the original capitol of New Mexico, the palace has been in continuous public use longer than any other structure in the United States. Today, this museum chronicles 400 years of New Mexico's history. Highlights include a world-class collection of pre-Columbian art objects, with ceramics, gold, and stone work; a stagecoach and tools used by early Hispanic residents; a replica of a mid-19th-century chapel; and restored Mexican and 19th-century U.S. Governors' offices. North Plaza. ℭ **505/476-5100.** Admission $5 adults, free for kids 16 and under. Free on Fri. See above for information on 4-day passes good at all branches of the Museum of New Mexico ($15). Tues–Sun 10am–5pm.

St. Francis Cathedral   Santa Fe's grandest religious structure, built in the style of the great cathedrals of Europe, is an architectural anomaly here. The small adobe Our Lady of the Rosary chapel on the northeast side is the only portion that remains from the original church, founded in 1610. Look for Our Lady of Peace, the oldest representation of the Madonna in the United States; and for the cathedral's front doors, featuring 16 carved panels and a plaque memorializing the 38 Franciscan friars who were martyred during New Mexico's early years. Cathedral Place at San Francisco St. ℭ **505/982-5619.** Donations appreciated. Open daily. Visitors may attend Mass Mon–Sat at 7am and 5:15pm; Sun at 8am, 10am, noon, and 5:15pm. Free parking in adjacent city lot to attend services.

SHOPPING

Some call Santa Fe one of the top art markets in the world, and it's no wonder. Galleries speckle the downtown area, and as an artists' thoroughfare, Canyon Road is preeminent. Still, the greatest concentration of Native American crafts is displayed beneath the portal of the Palace of the Governors.

LewAllen Contemporary, 129 W. Palace Ave. (ℭ **505/988-8997**), stocks bizarre and beautiful contemporary works in a range of media from granite to clay to twigs. **Joshua Baer & Company,** 116½ E. Palace Ave. (ℭ **505/988-8944**), is a great place to find 19th-century Navajo blankets, pottery, jewelry, and primitive art from around the world. **Gerald Peters Gallery,** 1011 Paseo de Peralta (ℭ **505/954-5700**), features the art of Georgia O'Keeffe, William Wegman, and the founders of the Santa Fe and Taos artists' colonies.

WHERE TO STAY

For help, call **Santa Fe Central Reservations,** 320 Artist Rd., Ste. 10 (ℭ **800/776-7669** or 505/983-8200; fax 505/984-8682).

Alexander's Inn   This 1903 Victorian/New England–style house, set just 6 blocks from the Plaza, is filled with delicious antiques, bedding, and draperies. The rooms have stenciling on the walls, muted colors such as apricot and lilac, and iron or four-poster beds. Cottages come complete with full kitchens and kiva fireplaces. Some have more Southwestern charm than others, so discuss your desires when making reservations. 529 E. Palace Ave., Santa Fe, NM 87501. ✆ **888/ 321-5123** or 505/986-1431. Fax 505/982 8572. www.alexanders-inn.com. 10 units, 8 with bathroom, 5 cottages. $85–$200 double. Rates include continental breakfast. AE, DISC, MC, V. Free parking. **Amenities:** Tennis club privileges; pets accepted ($20 deposit).

Bishop's Lodge   The 1,000-acre Bishop's Lodge is an active resort, and its many outdoor opportunities, including riding lessons, nature walks, and cookouts, make it an ideal place for families. Rooms, spread through many buildings, feature handcrafted furniture and regional artwork. Many have balconies; deluxe units have traditional kiva fireplaces and private decks or patios. Some new ones offer spectacular views of the Jemez Mountains. Bishop's Lodge Rd. (P.O. Box 2367), Santa Fe, NM 87504. ✆ **505/983-6377.** Fax 505/989-8739. 144 units. Midwinter $120–$270 double; fall and spring $175–$350 double; summer $240–$525 double. Extra person $15. Children 3 and under stay free in parents' room. AE, DC, DISC, MC, V. Free parking. **Amenities:** Restaurant; outdoor pool; spa; tennis courts.

Dos Casas Viejas   These two old houses, not far from the Plaza, offer the kind of luxury accommodations you'd expect from a fine hotel. Rooms are situated along a meandering brick lane behind an old wooden gate; each unit has a patio and private entrance. All have Mexican-tile floors, kiva fireplaces, Southwestern antiques, and fridges. Some have canopy beds, and one has a sleigh bed, all dressed with fine linens and down comforters. If you'd like a spa experience, Dos Casas now has in-room treatments, from massages to salt glows. 610 Agua Fría St., Santa Fe, NM 87501. ✆ **505/983-1636.** Fax 505/983-1749. www.doscasasviejas.com. 8 units. $195–$295 double. MC, V. Free parking. **Amenities:** Outdoor pool.

El Rey Inn   The two stories of suites around the Spanish colonial courtyard are a sweet deal. They feel like a Spanish inn, with carved furniture and cozy couches, and some have kitchenettes. Ten newer units offer more upscale amenities and gas log fireplaces. The oldest section feels a bit cramped, although the rooms have style, with Art Deco tile in the baths and vigas on the ceilings. Some have little patios. Be sure to request a room as far back as possible from Cerrillos Road. 1862 Cerrillos Rd. (P.O. Box 4759), Santa Fe, NM 87502. ✆ **800/521-1349** or 505/ 982-1931. Fax 505/989-9249. www.elreyinnsantafe.com. 86 units. $95–$155 double; $115– $199 suite. Rates include continental breakfast. AE, DC, DISC, MC, V. Free parking. **Amenities:** Outdoor pool.

Inn of the Anasazi   This fine luxury hotel, built in 1991 right off the Plaza, manages to suggest a feeling of grandness in a very limited space. Flagstone floors, oversize cacti, and Navajo rugs complete the look. The spacious rooms feature pearl-finished walls, cream-toned decor, iron sconces, four-poster beds, kiva gas fireplaces, and humidifiers. All rooms are quiet, though none have dramatic views. The Anasazi Restaurant serves creative Southwestern cuisine. 113 Washington Ave., Santa Fe, NM 87501. ✆ **800/688-8100** or 505/988-3030. Fax 505/988-3277. 59 units. Nov–Mar $209–$359 double; Apr–Oct $259–$429 double. AE, DC, DISC, MC, V. Valet parking $12. **Amenities:** Restaurant.

La Fonda   If you want a feel of the real Santa Fe, this is the place to stay—or at least stroll through. Once the inn at the end of the Santa Fe Trail, it saw trappers and traders, as well as notables like Ulysses S. Grant. Although the original inn was replaced in 1920, La Fonda still isn't the model of newness. Each room has its own funky touches, but some are more kitsch than quaint. Some have VCRs, fridges, fireplaces, and balconies. La Plazuela serves some of the best Southwestern cuisine in town on a sky-lit patio. The Bell Tower Bar is a great place for a cocktail and a view of the city. 100 E. San Francisco St. (P.O. Box 1209), Santa Fe, NM 87501. (℅ 800/523-5002 or 505/982-5511. Fax 505/988-2952. www.lafondasantafe.com. 167 units. $249 standard double, $269 deluxe double; $319–$529 suite. Extra person $15. Children under 12 stay free in parents' room. AE, DC, DISC, MC, V. Parking $9. **Amenities:** Restaurants (2); outdoor pool; spa; fitness room.

La Quinta Inn Though it's a good 15-minute drive from the Plaza, this is our pick among the economical Cerrillos Road chain hotels. Rooms in the three-story white-brick buildings have an unexpectedly elegant feel, with lots of deep colors and Art Deco tile in the bathrooms. The kidney-shaped pool has a nice lounging area. If you're a shopper or moviegoer, you'll enjoy the proximity to the Villa Linda Mall. 4298 Cerrillos Rd., Santa Fe, NM 87505. (℅ 800/531-5900 or 505/471-1142. Fax 505/438-7219. 130 units. June to mid-Oct $89–$110 double; late Oct to May $60–$66 double. Children 18 and under stay free in parents' room. Rates include continental breakfast. AE, DC, DISC, MC, V. Free parking. **Amenities:** Outdoor pool; maximum 2 pets stay free.

Spencer House Bed & Breakfast Inn The Spencer House is unique among Santa Fe B&Bs. Instead of Southwestern-style furnishings, you'll find beautiful antiques from England, Ireland, and colonial America. One room features an antique brass bed, another a pencil-post bed, yet another an English panel bed— all done up in Ralph Lauren linens and fluffy down comforters. A cottage out back contains two units, one with a full kitchen, fireplace, and patio. Some rooms have TVs and phones. 222 McKenzie St., Santa Fe, NM 87501. (℅ 800/647-0530 (7am–6pm) or 505/988-3024. Fax 505/984-9862. www.spencerhse-santafe.com. 6 units. $99–$175 double. Rates include full breakfast. AE, MC, V. Limited free parking.

Water Street Inn An award-winning adobe restoration 4 blocks from the Plaza, this friendly inn features beautiful Mexican-tile bathrooms, several kiva fireplaces and woodstoves, and antique furnishings. A happy hour, with quesadillas and margaritas, is offered in the living room or on the upstairs portal. Rooms are decorated in a Moroccan/Southwestern style and come with balconies or terraces, VCRs, and CD players. Four new suites have private patios with fountains. 427 Water St., Santa Fe, NM 87501. (℅ 800/646-6752 or 505/984-1193. Fax 505/984-6235. www.waterstreetinn.com. 12 units. $100–$250 double. Rates include continental breakfast. AE, DISC, MC, V. Free parking. **Amenities:** Pets welcome with prior approval.

WHERE TO DINE

Anasazi Restaurant CREATIVE SOUTHWESTERN/NATIVE AMERICAN This is one of Santa Fe's more interesting experiences. All the food is inventive, and organic meats and vegetables are used whenever available. A must with lunch or dinner is the grilled corn tortilla and lime soup. For an entree, try the grilled swordfish with a roasted corn puree. Desserts are thrilling—try the sour-cream chocolate cake, rich and moist. 113 Washington Ave. (℅ 505/988-3236. Reservations recommended. Main courses $7.50–$12 breakfast, $9.50–$15 lunch, $18–$33 dinner. AE, DC, DISC, MC, V. Daily 7–10:30am, 11:30am–2:30pm, 5:30–10pm.

Coyote Café CREATIVE SOUTHWESTERN/LATIN Chef Mark Miller's trendy restaurant offers cutting-edge cuisine in a fun atmosphere (but can be quite noisy on a busy night). An incredible lunch is the pork carnitas tamale, with chipotle-orange barbecue sauce and black bean–avocado relish. For dinner, you might try the slow-baked wild king salmon or prime New York strip steak. The Coyote Cafe has two adjunct establishments: the Rooftop Cantina, for summer cocktails, and the General Store, a gourmet Southwestern food market. 132 Water St. ✆ 505/983-1615. Reservations highly recommended. Main courses $5.95–$16 (Rooftop Cantina); $19–$36 (Coyote Café). AE, DC, DISC, MC, V. Cafe: daily 11:30am–9pm. Rooftop Cantina: daily 6–9:30pm (5:30–9pm during opera season).

Guadalupe Cafe NEW MEXICAN   This casually elegant cafe is in a white-stucco building that's warm and friendly, with a nice-size patio for dining in warmer months. For dinner, start with fresh roasted ancho chiles (filled with a combination of Montrachet and Monterey Jack cheese and piñon nuts) and move on to the sour-cream chicken enchilada or any of the other Southwestern dishes. There are also standards like salads, hamburgers, and chicken-fried steak. 422 Old Santa Fe Trail. ✆ 505/982-9762. Breakfast $4.50–$8.75; lunch $6–$12; dinner $6.95–$16. DISC, MC, V. Tues–Fri 7am–2pm; Sat–Sun 8am–2pm; Tues–Sat 5:30–9pm.

La Choza NEW MEXICAN   This warm, casual spot offers some of the best New Mexican food in town. The menu features enchiladas, tacos, and burritos on blue-corn tortillas, as well as green chile stew, chile con carne, and carne adovada. The portions are medium-size, so if you're hungry, start with gua-camole or nachos. The cheese or chicken enchiladas are reliable favorites, though you might check out the blue-corn burritos served with *posole*. Vegetarians and children get their own menus. 905 Alarid St. ✆ 505/982-0909. Lunch and dinner items $6.95–$8.75. AE, DISC, MC, V. Summer Mon–Sat 11am–9pm; winter Mon–Thurs 11am–8pm, Fri–Sat 11am–9pm.

mu du noodles PACIFIC RIM   If you're ready for a light, healthy meal with lots of flavor, head to this small restaurant, about an 8-minute drive from down-town. Of the two rooms, the back room is cozier, and the woodsy-feeling patio is worth requesting during warmer months. We recommend the Malaysian *laksa*, thick rice noodles in a blend of coconut milk, hazelnuts, onions, and red curry, stir-fried with chicken or tofu and julienned vegetables and sprouts. Wash it all down with the ginseng ginger ale. 1494 Cerrillos Rd. ✆ 505/983-1411. Reservations for parties of 5 or larger only. Main courses $9–$16. AE, DC, DISC, MC, V. Nightly 5:30–9pm (sometimes 10pm in summer); after 8:30pm, always call first.

Old Mexico Grill MEXICAN   This festive restaurant, very busy on weekends, will make you rethink Mexican food. Certainly you'll find tacos here, served the Mexican way on soft corn tortillas, with excellent salsas. But you'll also find tasty moles and pipians, with sauces of ground pumpkin seeds and the highest qual-ity chiles. Start with a shrimp and scallop ceviche, then move on to one of the beef or fish specials. There is a nice selection of soups and salads and a variety of homemade desserts. 2434 Cerrillos Rd., College Plaza South. ✆ 505/473-0338. Reservations recommended for large parties. Lunch $7.50–$12; dinner $10–$23. AE, DISC, MC, V. Mon–Sun 11:30am–2:30pm and 5:30–9pm.

Pranzo Italian Grill REGIONAL ITALIAN   Housed in a renovated ware-house decorated in warm Tuscan colors, this restaurant features steak, chicken, veal, and fresh seafood—heavy on the garlic—prepared on an open grill. Home-made soups, salads, creative thin-crust pizzas, and pastas are among the less expensive options. Favorites include black-and-white linguine with bay scallops in a seafood cream sauce. The rooftop terrace is lovely for seasonal moon-watch-ing over a glass of wine. 540 Montezuma St., Sanbusco Center. ✆ 505/984-2645. Reserva-tions recommended. Lunch $5.95–$9.95; dinner $5.95–$20. AE, DC, DISC, MC, V. Sun–Thurs 5–10pm; Fri–Sat 5–11pm.

Santacafé NEW AMERICAN/CREATIVE SOUTHWESTERN   Be prepared for spectacular bursts of flavor. The Southwestern food here has an Asian flair, and is served amid a minimalist decor that accentuates the graceful architecture of the 18th-century Padre Gallegos House. The dishes change to take advantage of seasonal specialties: Shiitake and cactus spring rolls are served with green chile salsa, while achiote-marinated halibut comes with orange salsa and green rice. Desserts are as elegant as the rest of the food. 231 Washington Ave. ℭ 505/984-1788. Reservations recommended. Main courses $5–$11 lunch, $19–$29 dinner. AE, MC, V. Mon–Sat 11:30am–2pm; daily 6–10pm. Sun brunch served in summer.

The Shed NEW MEXICAN   During lunch, lines often form outside the Shed, an institution since 1953. It occupies several rooms and the patio of a rambling hacienda built in 1692. Festive folk art adorns the doorways and walls. The food, like the cheese enchilada and the tacos and burritos, is some of the best in the state. All are served on blue-corn tortillas. The green chile soup is a local favorite. Vegetarian and low-fat dishes are available, as is full bar service. 113½ E. Palace Ave. ℭ 505/982-9030. Reservations accepted at dinner. Lunch $5.75–$9.50; dinner $7.25–$17. AE, DC, DISC, MC, V. Mon–Sat 11am–2:30pm and 5:30–9pm.

315 FRENCH   This simply excellent restaurant has an elegant atmosphere and, during warm months, a popular patio. The menu changes seasonally; you might start with a smooth and flavorful lobster bisque and move on to lamb chops served with a tart mustard sauce and mashed potatoes. The flourless chocolate cake is luscious, and not too sweet. 315 Old Santa Fe Trail. ℭ 505/986-9190. www.315santafe.com. Reservations highly recommended. Main courses $18–$25 dinner. AE, DISC, MC, V. Summer Mon–Sat 11:30am–2pm, Sun–Thurs 5:30–9pm, Fri–Sat 5:30–9:30pm; winter Tues–Sat 11:30am–2pm, Tues–Sun 5:30–9pm.

Upper Crust Pizza PIZZA/ITALIAN   Upper Crust serves Santa Fe's best pizzas, in an adobe house near the old San Miguel Mission. Try the Grecian gourmet (feta and olives) or the whole-wheat vegetarian pizza (topped with sesame seeds). You can either eat here or request free delivery to your downtown hotel. Beer and wine are available, as are salads, calzones, sandwiches, and stromboli. 329 Old Santa Fe Trail. ℭ 505/982-0000. Reservations not accepted. Pizzas $7.25–$16. DISC, MC, V. Summer daily 11am–midnight; winter Sun–Thurs 11am–11pm, Fri–Sat 11am–midnight.

SANTA FE AFTER DARK

Current listings on all major cultural events are published each Friday in the "Pasatiempo" section of the *New Mexican,* the city's daily newspaper, and in the *Santa Fe Reporter,* published every Wednesday.

Nicholas Potter, Bookseller, 211 E. Palace Ave. (ℭ 505/983-5434), carries tickets to select events. You can also order by phone from **Ticketmaster** (ℭ 505/883-7800).

THE PERFORMING ARTS   Many rank the **Santa Fe Opera** (ℭ 800/280-4654, or 505/986-5900 for tickets; www.santafeopera.org) second only to the Metropolitan Opera of New York as the finest company in the United States today. The company performs in an open-sided venue on a wooded hilltop 7 miles north of the city off U.S. 84/285. It consistently attracts famed conductors, directors, and singers, and is noted for its performances of the classics, little-known works by classical European composers, and American premieres of 20th-century works. The 8-week season runs from late June to late August.

The **Santa Fe Symphony Orchestra and Chorus** (ℭ 800/480-1319 or 505/983-1414) performs classical and popular works from October to May. An extraordinary group of international artists comes to Santa Fe every summer for the **Santa Fe Chamber Music Festival** (② 505/983-2075 or 505/982 1890).

The oldest extant theater group in New Mexico, **Santa Fe Playhouse,** 142 E. de Vargas St. (② **505/988-4262**), attracts thousands to its dramas, avant-garde theater, and musical comedy. The outstanding offerings at the **Santa Fe Stages,** 100 N. Guadalupe St. (② **505/982-6683;** www.santafestages.org), play to an intimate gathering.

You won't want to miss a performance of the **María Benitez Teatro Flamenco,** in the Maria Benitez Theater at the Radisson Hotel (② **888/435-2636** or 505/982-1237).

THE BAR, CLUB & MUSIC SCENE   El Farol, 808 Canyon Rd. (② **505/ 983-9912**), is the place to head for Santa Fe's largest and most unusual selection of tapas. Jazz, swing, folk, and ethnic musicians, some of national note, perform most nights.

There's live entertainment nightly at the **Cowgirl Hall of Fame,** 319 S. Guadalupe St. (② **505/982-2565**): folk, rock, blues guitar, comedy, and cowboy poetry. In the summer, this is a great place to sit under the stars and listen to music.

You'll find everyone from businesspeople to bikers at **Evangelo's,** 200 W. San Francisco St. (② **505/982-9014**), a raucous downtown hangout with tropical decor and a mahogany bar. More than 60 varieties of imported beer are available, and pool tables are an added attraction. You might catch live rock, jazz, or reggae.

Since its opening in 1998, the **Paramount Lounge and Night Club,** 331 Sandoval St. (② **505/982-8999**), has presented an ambitious array of entertainment, from live music to comedy to weekly DJ dance nights.

TOURING THE PUEBLOS & CLIFF DWELLINGS AROUND SANTA FE

The pueblos described in this section can easily be visited in a single day's round-trip from Santa Fe. Certain rules of etiquette should be observed in visiting the pueblos: These are personal dwellings and/or important historic sites, and must be respected as such. Don't climb on the buildings or peek into doors or windows. Don't enter sacred grounds, such as cemeteries and kivas. If you attend a dance or ceremony, remain silent while it's taking place and refrain from applause when it's over. Many pueblos prohibit photography or sketches; others require you to pay a fee for a permit.

San Ildefonso Pueblo   This pueblo has a broad, dusty plaza, with a kiva on one side, ancient dwellings on the other, and a church at the far end. It's nationally famous for its matte-finish black-on-black pottery, developed by tribeswoman María Martínez in the 1920s. A few shops surround the plaza, and the **San Ildefonso Pueblo Museum** is tucked away in the governor's office beyond the plaza. It's especially memorable to visit during ceremonial days. **San Ildefonso Feast Day,** on January 23, features the buffalo and Comanche dances in alternate years. **Corn Dances,** held in late August or early September, commemorate a basic element in pueblo life, the importance of fertility in all creatures—humans as well as animals—and plants. The pueblo has a ½-acre fishing lake surrounded by woodlands, open from April to October. Picnicking is encouraged, but camping is not allowed. Rte. 5. ② **505/455-3549.** Admission $3 per car. Still camera $10, video camera $20, sketching $25. Fishing $8 adults, free for seniors and children under 12. Summer daily 8am–5pm; call for weekend hours. Winter Mon–Fri 8am–4:30pm. Take U.S. 84/285 north, turn left on N.M. 502 at Pojoaque, and drive about 6 miles to the turnoff.

San Juan Pueblo   San Juan is the largest (pop. 1,950) and northernmost of the Tewa-speaking pueblos, as well as the headquarters of the **Eight Northern Indian Pueblos Council** (© 505/852-4265), a sort of chamber of commerce and social-service agency. San Juan is on the east side of the Rio Grande— opposite the 1598 site of San Gabriel, the first Spanish settlement west of the Mississippi River and the first capital of New Spain.

The past and present cohabit here. Though many of the tribe members are Catholics, most still practice traditional religious rituals. Thus, two rectangular kivas flank the church in the main plaza, and *caciques* (pueblo priests) share power with civil authorities. The annual **San Juan Fiesta** is held June 23 and 24, and the **turtle dance** is on December 26. The **matachine dance,** performed Christmas Day, vividly depicts the subjugation of the Native Americans by the Catholic Spaniards.

A crafts shop, **Oke Oweenge Arts and Crafts Cooperative** (© 505/852- 2372), specializes in local wares. This is a fine place to seek out San Juan's dis- tinctive red pottery. Also for sale are seed, turquoise, and silver jewelry; wood and stone carvings; indigenous clothing and weavings; embroidery; and paint- ings. **Sunrise Crafts** sells one-of-a-kind handcrafted pipes, beadwork, and burned and painted gourds. **Ohkay Casino** (© 505/747-1668) offers table games and slot machines, as well as live music Tuesday through Saturday nights. © 505/852-4400. Free admission. Photography or sketching with prior permission from the gov- ernor's office (call the pueblo number above). Fishing $8 adults, $5 children and seniors. Take U.S. 84/285 north, then N.M. 68 to N.M. 74, about 4 miles north of Española.

Santa Clara Pueblo   Close to Española, Santa Clara, with a population of about 1,800, is one of the largest pueblos. You'll see the village sprawling across the river basin near the beautiful Black Mesa, rows of tract homes surrounding an adobe central area. Though the setting is incredible, there's not much to see at the pueblo itself. It does, however, give a real feel for the contemporary lives of these people.

One stunning sight is the cemetery. Stop on the west side of the church and look over a 4-foot wall. It's a primitive site, with plain wooden crosses and some graves adorned with plastic flowers. Within the village are lots of little pottery and crafts shops. There are corn and harvest dances on **Santa Clara Feast Day** (Aug 12); information on other special days (including the corn or harvest dances) can be obtained from the pueblo office.

The famed **Puye Cliff Dwellings,** also on the Santa Clara reservation, are well worth visiting. They offer a view of centuries of culture so well preserved you can almost hear ancient life clamoring around you. First you encounter dwellings believed to have been built around 1450. Above, on a 200-foot cliff face, are dwellings dating from 1200. This series of rooms and caves is reached by sturdy ladders and steps, allowing visitors to clamber in and out of the homes. Petroglyphs are evident in many of the rocky cliff walls. On the 7,000-foot mesa top are ceremonial kivas as well as a labyrinth of dwellings.

About 6 miles farther west is the **Santa Clara Canyon Recreational Area,** a sylvan setting for camping that is open year-round for picnicking, hiking, and fishing in ponds and Santa Clara Creek. Española. © 505/753-7326. Pueblo: Free admission. Still cameras $5; video cameras and sketching not allowed. Daily during daylight hours. Visitor center Mon–Fri 8am–4:30pm. Cliff dwellings: Admission $5 adults, $4 children and seniors.

Summer daily 8am–8pm; winter daily 9am–4:30pm. Take U.S. 84/285 north to Española, then N.M. 30 south.

11 Taos

People either really like Taos or they really dislike it. Those who expect it to be neat and sophisticated like Santa Fe are generally disappointed. The best way to approach this town of 5,000 residents is as the renegade place it is. Its narrow streets tend to be dusty or muddy and are usually blocked by cars. Its residents are often funky, harking back to the hippie days, part of the town's 1960s history when communes set up camp in the hills outside the town. These are the impressions that often initially catch visitors.

But take a moment longer to look and you'll see the awe-inspiring adobe structures at Taos Pueblo, where some people still live as their ancestors did 1,000 years ago, without electricity or running water. These are set against giant blue mountains rising fast from irrigated meadows. You'll encounter a thriving art colony, not glitzy like Santa Fe, but very real and down to earth, often with artists selling work straight out of their studios. You'll wander through amazing galleries, many displaying the town's rich history in a variety of art forms. And you'll eat some of the most inventive food in the Southwest, at very affordable prices.

Taos is just 40 miles south of the Colorado border, about 70 miles north of Santa Fe, and 135 miles from Albuquerque. In addition to its collection of artists and writers, it's famous for the pueblo and for the nearby ski area, one of the most highly regarded in the Rockies.

ESSENTIALS

GETTING THERE   By Plane   The **Taos Municipal Airport** (✆ 505/758-4995) is about 8 miles northwest of town on U.S. 64. However, it's easier to fly into **Albuquerque International Sunport** (✆ 505/842-4366), rent a car, and drive from there (trip time: 2½ hr.). If you'd rather be picked up at the Albuquerque airport, call **Faust's Transportation** (✆ 505/758-3410), which offers daily service, as well as taxi service from Taos to Taos Ski Valley.

By Car   From Santa Fe, take U.S. 84/285 north, then N.M. 68 to Taos, about 79 miles. From Denver, take I-25 south to U.S. 64, then west about 95 miles to Taos.

VISITOR INFORMATION   The **Taos County Chamber of Commerce,** at the junction of N.M. 68 and N.M. 585 (✆ 800/732-TAOS or 505/758-3873; www.taosguide.com), is open year-round, daily from 9am to 5pm.

GETTING AROUND   Chile Line Town of Taos Transit (✆ 505/751-4459) operates local bus service Monday through Saturday from 7am to 7pm. There are two simultaneous routes running southbound from Taos Pueblo and northbound from the Ranchos de Taos Post Office on the half hour. Each route makes stops at the casino and various hotels in town, as well as Taos RV Park. Bus fares are 50¢ one-way, $1 round-trip, and $5 for a 7-day pass.

  Faust's Transportation (✆ 505/758-3410) has a taxi service linking town hotels and Taos Ski Valley; it runs three times a day for $10 round-trip.

  Parking can be difficult in summer. If you can't find a spot on the street or in the Plaza, check out some of the nearby roads. *Safety tips:* En route to many recreation sites, reliable paved roads can lead to poorer forest roads. Once you get off the main roads, you won't find gas stations or cafes. Four-wheel-drive vehicles are recommended on snow and much of the otherwise unpaved terrain of the region. If you're doing off-road adventuring, it's wise to go with a full gas tank, extra food and water, and warm clothing. Sudden summer snowstorms are not unheard of.

FAST FACTS   You can get information on road conditions from the **State Highway Department** (© 800/432-4269); if you have a highway emergency, contact the Taos area state police at © 505/758-8878. If you need a doctor, members of the **Taos Medical Group,** on Weimer Road (© 505/758-2224), are highly respected. **Holy Cross Hospital,** 1397 Weimer Rd., off Paseo del Canyon (© 505/758-8883), has 24-hour emergency service. **Raley's Pharmacy** (© 505/758-1203) and **Wal-Mart Pharmacy** (© 505/758-2743) are both located on Pueblo Sur and are easily seen from the road.

SPECIAL EVENTS & FESTIVALS   May brings the **Taos Spring Arts Festival,** with gallery openings, studio tours, performances by visiting theatrical and dance troupes, musical events, traditional ethnic entertainment, readings, and more. For dates and tickets, contact the **Taos County Chamber of Commerce** (© 800/732-TAOS or 505/758-3873). From mid-August to early September, there's **Music from Angel Fire** (© 505/377-3233; www.angelfirenm.com), an acclaimed program of chamber music.

WHAT TO SEE & DO

If you'd like to visit all seven museums that comprise the Museum Association of Taos—Blumenschein Home, Fechin Institute, Martinez Hacienda, Harwood Museum, Kit Carson Home and Museum, Millicent Rogers Museum, and Van Vechten Lineberry Taos Art Museum—you'll save money by purchasing a **combination ticket** for $20.

Given the town's historic associations with the arts, it isn't surprising that many visitors come to Taos to buy fine art. Some 50-odd galleries are within easy walking distance of the Plaza. The best-known modern artist in Taos is R. C. Gorman. His **Navajo Gallery,** 210 Ledoux St. (© 505/758-3250), is a showcase for his widely varied works. At the **Stables Fine Art Gallery,** 133 Paseo del Pueblo Norte (© 505/758-2036), a rotating group of exhibits features many of Taos's emerging and established artists.

Millicent Rogers Museum of Northern New Mexico   This museum is small enough to introduce some of the Southwest's finest arts and crafts without being overwhelming. Included are Navajo and Pueblo jewelry, Navajo textiles, Pueblo pottery, Hopi and Zuni kachina dolls, paintings from the Rio Grande Pueblo people, and basketry from a wide variety of Southwestern tribes. The permanent collection also includes Anglo arts and crafts and Hispanic religious and secular arts and crafts. Off N.M. 522, 4 miles north of Taos Plaza, on Millicent Rogers Rd. © 505/758-2462. Admission $6 adults, $5 students and seniors, $1 children 6–16. Daily 10am–5pm.

San Francisco de Asis Church   From N.M. 68, about 4 miles south of Taos, this famous church looks like a modern adobe sculpture with no doors or windows. Visitors must walk through the garden on the east side of this remarkable two-story church to enter and get a full perspective of its massive walls, authentic adobe plaster, and beauty. A video presentation is given in the church office every hour on the half hour. A few crafts shops surround the square. Ranchos de Taos. © 505/758-2754. Minimum $3 donation requested. Mon–Sat 9am–4pm. Visitors may attend Mass daily at 5:30pm; Sat at 6pm (Mass rotates from this church to the 3 mission chapels);

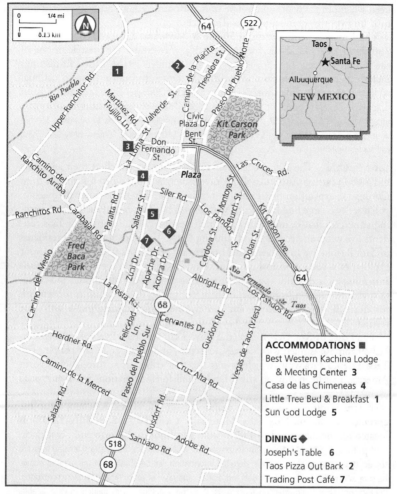

ACCOMMODATIONS ■
Best Western Kachina Lodge
 & Meeting Center **3**
Casa de las Chimeneas **4**
Little Tree Bed & Breakfast **1**
Sun God Lodge **5**

DINING ◆
Joseph's Table **6**
Taos Pizza Out Back **2**
Trading Post Café **7**

and Sun at 7am (Spanish), 9am, and 11:30am. Closed to the public the 1st 2 weeks in June, when repairs are done; however, services still take place.

Taos Historic Museums   These three historic homes afford visitors a glimpse of early Taos lifestyles.

The **Martinez Hacienda,** Lower Ranchitos Road, Highway 240, is remarkably beautiful, with thick, raw adobe walls and no exterior windows, to protect against raids by Plains tribes. The 21 rooms built around two interior courtyards give you a glimpse of the austerity of frontier lives. You'll see bedrooms, servants' quarters, stables, a kitchen, and a large fiesta room. The hacienda is also a living museum, with weavers, blacksmiths, and woodcarvers demonstrating their trades daily, more often during the **Taos Trade Fair** (in late Sept).

The **Kit Carson Home and Museum of the West,** East Kit Carson Road, a short block east of the Plaza intersection, is the town's only general museum of Taos history. The 12-room adobe home, with walls 2½ feet thick, was built in 1825. A living room, bedroom, and kitchen are furnished as they might have been when originally occupied. The Indian Room contains artifacts crafted and used by the original inhabitants of Taos Valley.

The **Ernest L. Blumenschein Home & Museum,** 222 Ledoux St. (✆ 505/758-0505), 1½ blocks southwest of the Plaza, re-creates the lifestyle of one of the founders of the Taos Society of Artists (founded 1915). Period furnishings include European antiques and handmade Taos furniture in Spanish colonial style. An extensive collection of works by early-20th-century Taos artists is on display in several rooms of the home. ✆ 505/758-0505 for information on all 3 museums. 3 museums $10 adults, $7 children 6–15, $20 per family. 2 museums $7.50 adults, $5 children, $15 per family. 1 museum $5 adults, $3 children, $10 per family. Summer daily 9am–5pm; call for winter hours.

Taos Pueblo The 200 residents of Taos Pueblo live much as their ancestors did 1,000 years ago, and the village looks much as it did when a regiment from Coronado's expedition first came upon it in 1540. When you enter the pueblo, you'll see two large buildings, each with rooms piled on top of each other, forming structures that mimic Taos Mountain nearby. Here, a portion of Taos residents live without electricity and running water. The remaining 2,000 residents of Taos Pueblo live in conventional homes on the pueblo's 95,000 acres. In your explorations, you can visit the residents' studios, look into the new **San Geronimo Chapel,** and wander past the fascinating ruins of the old church and cemetery. Ask permission from individuals before taking their photos; some will ask for a small payment. Kivas and other ceremonial underground areas are restricted.

The **Feast of San Geronimo** (the patron saint of Taos Pueblo), on September 29 and 30, is filled with dances, footraces, and artists and craftspeople. The **Taos Pueblo Powwow,** which brings together tribes from throughout North America, is held in July on tribal lands. Call for information on other special events.

To try traditional feast-day meals, stop at the **Tiwa Kitchen,** near the entrance to the pueblo. **Taos Mountain Casino** (✆ 888/WIN-TAOS) is located on the main road to Taos Pueblo and features slot machines, blackjack, and poker. ✆ 505/758-1028. Admission cost, as well as camera, video, and sketching fees, are subject to change on a yearly basis; detailed information can be obtained at the number above. Be sure to ask about telephoto lenses and digital cameras—at press time, they were prohibited. Photography is not permitted on feast days. Daily 8am–4:30pm, with guided tours available. Closed for 45 consecutive days every year in late winter or early spring (call for details). Also, since this is a living community, you can expect periodic closures.

Van Vechten Lineberry Taos Art Museum Taos's newest museum displays works of the Taos Society of Artists. The art is rich and varied, capturing

---

Hitting the Slopes

Taos Ski Valley (✆ 505/776-2291; www.skitaos.org) is the preeminent ski resort in the southern Rockies, internationally renowned for its light, dry powder (320 in. annually), its superb ski school, and its personal, friendly service. Experienced skiers will most appreciate Taos Ski Valley's steep, high-alpine, high-adventure skiing. The mountain is more intricate than it might seem at first glance, and it holds many surprises and challenges—even for the expert. *Note:* This is the only ski area in New Mexico that forbids snowboarders—for now, at least.

panoramas as well as the personalities of the Native American and Hispanic villagers in the late 19th and early 20th centuries. 501 Paseo del Pueblo Norte. ℭ 505/758-2690. Admission $5 adults, $3 for ages 6–16. Tues–Fri 11am–4pm; Sat–Sun 1:30–4pm.

WHERE TO STAY

Taos Central Reservations (ℭ 800/821-2437) can help book accommodations if the choices below are full.

Best Western Kachina Lodge & Meeting Center   This lodge on the north end of town, within walking distance of the Plaza, has a lot of charm despite the fact that it's really a motor hotel. The Southwest-style rooms surrounding a grassy courtyard are solidly built and quiet, and there's plenty of outdoor space for the kids. On summer nights, a family from Taos Pueblo builds a bonfire and performs, explaining the significance of the dances—a real treat for anyone baffled by the Pueblo rituals. 413 Paseo del Pueblo Norte (P.O. Box NN), Taos, NM 87571. ℭ 800/522-4462 or 505/758-2275. Fax 505/758-9207. www.kachinalodge.com. 118 units. $69–$179 double. Extra person $10. Children under 12 stay free in parents' room. AE, DC, DISC, MC, V. **Amenities:** Restaurants (2); pool.

Casa de las Chimeneas   This 82-year-old adobe home is a full-service luxury inn and a model of Southwestern elegance. The Río Grande and Territorial rooms have heated saltillo-tile floors and Jacuzzi tubs. If you prefer a more antique-feeling room, the older section is delightful, and renovation in the Library Suite has made it worth recommending. All have elegant bedding, private entrances, kiva fireplaces, VCRs, and fridges stocked with complimentary beverages. Most look out onto flower and herb gardens. 405 Cordoba Lane, at Los Pandos Rd. (5303 NDCBU), Taos, NM 87571. ℭ 877/758-4777 or 505/758-4777. Fax 505/758-3976. www.taos.com. 8 units. $165–$290 double; $325 suite (for 2). Rates include full breakfast and evening supper. AE, DC, DISC, MC, V. **Amenities:** Spa; fitness room.

Inn at Snakedance   This is our choice for on-slope accommodations just steps from the lift. Many of the comfortable rooms have wood-burning fireplaces. All come with modern furnishings, fridges, and humidifiers. Some rooms adjoin, connecting a standard hotel room with a fireplace room—perfect for families. The hotel also offers shuttle service to and from nearby shops and restaurants. 110 Sutton Place (P.O. Box 89), Taos Ski Valley, NM 87525. ℭ 800/322-9815 or 505/776-2277. Fax 505/776-1410. www.innsnakedance.com. 60 units. Value season $165 double; Christmas holiday $270 double; rest of ski season $225 double; summer $75 double. Closed mid-Apr to mid-June, mid-Oct to mid-Nov. AE, DISC, DC, MC, V. Children over 6 welcome. Free parking at Taos Ski Valley parking lot. **Amenities:** Restaurant; spa; fitness room.

Little Tree Bed & Breakfast   Little Tree is one of our favorite Taos B&Bs, partly because it has a beautiful, secluded setting (midway between Taos and the ski area), and partly because it's constructed with real adobe that's been left in its raw state, lending the place an authentic hacienda feel. The charming rooms have radiant heat under the floors, VCRs, and access to the portal and courtyard garden. Some units are equipped with fireplaces and private entrances. P.O. Drawer II, Taos, NM 87571. ℭ 505/776-8467. www.littletreebandb.com. 4 units. $105–$155 double. Rates include breakfast. MC, V.

Sun God Lodge   For an economical stay with a New Mexico ambience, this is our choice. This hotel, a 5-minute drive from the Plaza, has three distinct parts spread across 1½ acres of landscaped grounds. The oldest has some court-motel charm with a low ceiling and large windows. In a recently remodeled section, rooms are small but have little touches that make them feel cozy. The newest buildings have portal-style porches and balconies. Some rooms have kitchenettes; others have kiva fireplaces. 919 Paseo del Pueblo Sur (5513 NDCBU), Taos, NM 87571. ℂ 800/821-2437 or 505/758-3162. Fax 505/758-1716. www.sunlodge.com. 55 units. $69–$90 double; $65–$170 suite. AE, MC, DISC, V. **Amenities:** Pool; pets allowed ($10 per day).

WHERE TO DINE

Joseph's Table NEW AMERICAN/MEDITERRANEAN   Taos funk meets European flair at this intimate restaurant in Ranchos de Taos. At press time, the restaurant was slated to take on a new name and move to a larger space, so call before you head out. Chef/owner Joseph Wrede (once selected one of the 10 "Best New Chefs" in the U.S. by *Food & Wine*) serves up such delicacies as a lovely steak au poivre atop a layer of mashed potatoes and crowned with an exotic mushroom salad. An eclectic selection of beers and wines is available. 4167 Hwy. 68, Ranchos de Taos, a 10-min. drive from the Plaza (call to check on the new address and to find out about possible breakfast and lunch hours). ℂ 505/751-4512. Reservations recommended. Main courses $16–$35. AE, DISC, MC, V. Daily 6–10pm.

Taos Cow CAFE/BAKERY/ICE CREAM   Set in the charming village of Arroyo Seco en route to Taos Ski Valley, this cafe serves tasty sandwiches and some of the best ice cream around. The fun atmosphere hearkens back to Taos's hippie heritage. Kick back on the gravel patio with an egg sando—similar to an Egg McMuffin, but a thousand times better. 591 Hondo Seco Rd. (N.M. 150), about 10 min. north of the Plaza. ℂ 505/776-5640. Reservations not accepted. All menu items under $8. MC, V. Daily 7am–6pm.

Taos Pizza Out Back PASTA/GOURMET PIZZA   At this raucous old adobe restaurant, the level of informality is high, the food is great, and the portions are huge. What to order? One word: *Pizza*. All come with a delicious thin crust. The variations are broad: Thai chicken pizza (pineapple, peanuts, and a spicy sauce); the Killer (sun-dried tomatoes, Gorgonzola, green chile, and black olives); and our favorite, the Florentine (spinach, basil, sun-dried tomatoes, chicken, mushrooms, capers, and garlic sautéed in white wine). Don't leave without trying the Taos Yum (a "mongo" chocolate-chip cookie with ice cream, whipped cream, and chocolate sauce). 712 Paseo del Pueblo Norte (just north of Allsup's). ℂ 505/758-3112. Reservations recommended on weekends and holidays. Pizzas $11–$24, pastas and calzones $7–$12. AE, DISC, MC, V. Summer daily 11am–10pm; winter Sun–Thurs 11am–9pm, Fri–Sat 11am–10pm.

Trading Post Café NORTHERN ITALIAN/INTERNATIONAL   Ask anyone in town where they most like to eat, and they'll probably name the Trading Post. What draws the crowds is a gallery atmosphere, where rough plastered walls are set off by sculptures, paintings, and photographs from the Lumina Gallery. Be prepared to wait for a table, and don't expect quiet, unless you come at an off-time. Although the focus is on the fine food, diners can feel comfortable trying three appetizers and skipping the main course. You've probably never had a Caesar salad as good as the one here, and if you like pasta, you'll find a nice variety on the menu. There's also a fresh fish of the day and usually stews and soups. 4179 Paseo del Pueblo Sur, Ranchos de Taos. ℂ 505/758-5089. No reservations except for parties of 5 or more. Menu items $6–$28. DC, DISC, MC, V. Mon–Sat 11:30am–9:30pm; Sun 9–5pm.

TAOS AFTER DARK

You can get information on current events in the *Taos News*, published every Thursday.

For a small town, Taos has its share of top entertainment. Performers are attracted to Taos because of the resort atmosphere and the arts community, and the city enjoys annual programs in music and literary arts. State troupes, such as the New Mexico Repertory Theater and New Mexico Symphony Orchestra, make regular visits. Many events are scheduled by the **Taos Center for the Arts (TCA),** 133 Paseo del Pueblo Norte (© **505/758-2052**), at the **Taos Community Auditorium** (© **505/758-4677**). The TCA imports local, regional, and national performers in theater, dance, and concerts.

A favorite gathering place for locals and visitors, the **Adobe Bar,** in the Historic Taos Inn, 125 Paseo del Pueblo Norte (© **505/758-2233**), often hosts live music—classical, jazz, folk, Hispanic, and acoustic. The bar features a wide selection of international beers, wines by the glass, light New Mexican dining, desserts, and an espresso menu.

The **Alley Cantina,** 121 Teresina Lane (© **505/758-2121**), is a hot late-night spot with a kitchen open until 11pm and games such as pool, chess, and backgammon. The **Sagebrush Inn,** Paseo del Pueblo Sur (© **505/758-2254**), has pure Old West atmosphere, with a rustic wooden dance floor and plenty of smoke. Dancers generally two-step to country performers nightly. The **Thunderbird Lodge,** at the foot of the slopes in Taos Ski Valley (© **505/776-2280**), offers a variety of nightly entertainment in winter, from wine tastings to two-step dance lessons. The newest game in town, **Momentitos de la Vida,** 5 miles north of N.M. 150 and N.M. 522, Arroyo Seco (© **505/776-3333**), offers live jazz in a moody atmosphere.

A SCENIC DRIVE AROUND THE ENCHANTED CIRCLE

If you're in the mood to explore, take this 90-mile loop north of Taos through the old Hispanic villages of Arroyo Hondo and Questa, into a pass the Apaches, Kiowas, and Comanches once used to cross through the mountains to trade with the Taos Indians. Although you can drive the entire loop in 2 hours from Taos, most folks prefer to take a full day, and many take several days.

ARROYO HONDO   Traveling north from Taos via N.M. 522, it's a 9-mile drive to this village, the remains of an 1815 land grant along the Rio Hondo. Along the dirt roads that lead off N.M. 522, you may find a windowless *morada* or two, marked by plain crosses in front—places of worship for the still-active Penitentes, a religious order known for self flagellation. This is also the turnoff point for trips to the Rio Grande Box, an awesome 1-day, 17-mile white-water run for which you can book trips in Santa Fe, Taos, Red River, and Angel Fire. En route north, the highway passes near **San Cristobal,** where a side road turns off to the **D. H. Lawrence Ranch** and **Lama,** site of an isolated spiritual retreat.

Next, N.M. 522 passes through **Questa.** If you turn west onto N.M. 378 about 3 miles north of Questa, you'll drive 8 miles on a paved road to the edge of the Bureau of Land Management–administered **Wild Rivers Recreation Area** (© **505/770-1600**). Here, where the Red River enters the gorge, are over 20 miles of hiking and biking trails, some of which take you down to the Rio Grande. Information and hikers' trail maps can be obtained at the visitor center here.

The village of **Costilla,** near the Colorado border, is 20 miles north of Questa. This is the turnoff point for four-wheel-drive jaunts and hiking trips into **Valle Vidal,** a huge U.S. Forest Service–administered reserve with 42 miles of roads and many hiking trails. A day hike in this area can bring you sightings of hundreds of elk.

RED RIVER   To continue on the Enchanted Circle loop, turn east at Questa onto N.M. 38 for a 12-mile climb to Red River, a rough-and-ready 1890s gold-mining town that has parlayed its Wild West ambience into a pleasant resort village.

This community is a center for skiing, snowmobiling, fishing, hiking, off-road driving, horseback riding, mountain biking, river rafting, and other out-door pursuits. Frontier-style celebrations, honky-tonk entertainment, and even staged shootouts are held throughout the year.

Although it can be a charming, fun place, Red River's food and lodging are mediocre at best. If you do decide to stay, try the **Lodge at Red River** (© **800/ 91-LODGE** or 505/754-6280; www.redrivernm.com/lodgeatrr), in the center of town. If you're passing through and want a quick meal, the **Main Street Deli,** 316 E. Main St. (© **505/754-3400**), has tasty muffins and stuffed baked pota-toes, soups, and sub sandwiches.

For more information, contact the **Red River Chamber of Commerce,** P.O. Box 870, Red River, NM 87558 (© **800/348-6444** or 505/754-2366).

EAGLE NEST   About 16 miles east of Red River, on the other side of 9,850-foot Bobcat Pass, is the village of Eagle Nest, resting on the shore of Eagle Nest Lake in the Moreno Valley. Gold was mined in this area as early as 1866, start-ing in what is now the ghost town of **Elizabethtown,** about 5 miles north. The 4-square-mile lake is considered one of the top trout producers in the United States and attracts ice fishers in winter as well as summer anglers. Sailboats and windsurfers also use the lake, although swimming, water-skiing, and camping are not permitted.

If you're heading to Cimarron or Denver, proceed east on U.S. 64 from Eagle Nest. But if you're circling back to Taos, continue southwest on U.S. 38 and U.S. 64 to Agua Fría and Angel Fire.

Shortly before the Agua Fría junction, you'll see the **DAV Vietnam Veterans Memorial.** It's a stunning structure with curved white walls soaring high against the backdrop of the Sangre de Cristo Range.

ANGEL FIRE   If you like the clean efficiency of a resort complex, you may want to plan a night or two here. Opened in the late 1960s, this resort offers a hotel with spacious, comfortable rooms, as well as condos and cabins. This medium-size beginner and intermediate mountain is an excellent place for fam-ilies to ski and roam about. The views of the Moreno Valley are awe-inspiring. During spring, summer, and fall, the resort offers golf, tennis, hiking, mountain biking, fly-fishing, river rafting, and horseback riding.

The unofficial community center is the **Angel Fire Resort,** North Angel Fire Road (© **800/633-7463** or 505/377-6401; www.angelfireresort.com), a 155-unit hotel with spacious, comfortable rooms, some with fireplaces and balconies. Rates range from $85 to $199.

For more information on the Moreno Valley, contact the **Angel Fire Chamber of Commerce** (© **800/446-8117** or 505/377-6661; www.angelfirechamber. org). Visitors can also go horseback riding with **Roadrunner Tours** (© **505/ 377-6416;** www.rtours.com).

12

Colorado & Utah

These two states contain some of the most gorgeous scenery in the West, from the glorious peaks of the Rockies to the spectacular red-rock formations of Zion, Bryce Canyon, and Capitol Reef national parks. If you're interested in skiing, rafting, mountain biking, hiking, or wildlife viewing—or experiencing something with the flavor of the Old West—this area is for you. Read on.

1 Denver

Denver is the biggest city between the Great Plains and the Pacific, with about 500,000 residents in the city itself, and another 1.8 million in the metro area. Today, it's a sprawling city, extending from the Rocky Mountain foothills in the west, far into the plains to the south and east. It's also a major destination for both tourists and business travelers. Denver is noted for its dozens of tree-lined boulevards; 200 city parks comprising more than 20,000 acres; and its architecture, which ranges from Victorian to sleek contemporary.

ESSENTIALS

GETTING THERE   By Plane   Sprawling **Denver International Airport** (© 800/AIR2DEN or 303/342-2000; www.flydenver.com) is 23 miles northeast of downtown, usually a 35- to 45-minute drive. A city bus ride can take you downtown for $8. The **SuperShuttle** (© 800/525-3177 or 303/370-1300) has frequent scheduled service between the airport and downtown hotels for $18 one-way; door-to-door service is also available. Expect to spend anywhere from $30 to $50 if you take a taxi downtown, although you can share and split the fare.

By Train   Amtrak (© 800/USA-RAIL or 303/825-2583; www.amtrak.com) provides daily service to Union Station at 1701 Wynkoop St.

By Car   The principal routes into Denver are I-25 from the north (Fort Collins and Cheyenne) and south (Colorado Springs and Albuquerque); I-70 from the east (Kansas City) and west (Grand Junction); and I-76 from the northeast (Omaha). If you're driving into Denver from Boulder, take U.S. 36; from Salida and southwest, U.S. 285.

VISITOR INFORMATION   The **Denver Metro Convention and Visitors Bureau** (© 800/645-3446; www.denver.org) operates a visitor center at 1668 Larimer St. (© 303/892-1112), just off the 16th Street Mall, open Monday through Friday from 8am to 5pm and Saturday from 9am to 1pm. Information is also available in Tabor and Cherry Creek shopping centers and at the Colorado State Capitol and Denver International Airport. Two other good Internet resources are **www.denver.citysearch.com** and **www.denvergov.org**.

GETTING AROUND   The **Regional Transportation District (RTD)** (© 800/366-7433 or 303/299-6000 or TDD 303/299-6089; www.rtd-denver.com) runs buses and a light-rail system; and transfers are free. The local one-way fare is $1.10; seniors and passengers with disabilities pay only 50¢, and children ages 5 and under travel free. Exact change is required for buses, and train tickets can be purchased at vending machines beneath light-rail station awnings. Maps for all routes are available at any time at the **RTD Civic Center Station,** 16th Street and Broadway, and at the **Market Street Station,** at Market and 16th streets. All RTD buses and trains are completely wheelchair accessible.

Free buses run up and down the 16th Street Mall between the Civic Center and Market Street every 90 seconds during peak hours (less frequently at other times), daily from 6am to 1am.

The new light-rail **C-Line,** initiated in spring 2001, diverts from the main north-south light rail at Colfax Avenue, and stops at several popular tourist attractions before chugging into Union Station in Lower Downtown (aka LoDo). The fare is the same as other local routes, but the schedule is extended.

The main taxi companies are **Yellow Cab** (© 303/777-7777) and **Metro Taxi** (© 303/333-3333). Taxis can be hailed on the street, but it's preferable to call for a taxi or wait for one at a taxi stand outside a major hotel.

You don't need a car downtown; you can save on rental costs and parking fees by staying downtown your first few nights, and then renting a car when you leave the area.

FAST FACTS   Doctor and dentist referrals are available by calling © **800/ DOCTORS.** The **Walgreens** pharmacy at 2000 E. Colfax Ave. is open 24 hours a day (© **303/331-0917**). Among Denver-area hospitals is **St. Joseph's,** 1835 Franklin St. (© **303/837-7111**).

SPECIAL EVENTS & FESTIVALS   The second and third weeks of January bring the **National Western Stock Show and Rodeo** (© **303/297-1166;** www.nationalwestern.com), the world's largest livestock show and indoor rodeo. In mid-March, more than 1,500 American Indians, representing some 85 tribes, perform traditional music and dances in the **Pow Wow** (© **303/934-8045;** www.denvermarchpowwow.org). Early October brings the **Great American Beer Festival** (© **303/447-0816;** www.beertown.org), perhaps the largest and most prestigious beer event in the United States, with over 1,000 beers from 300 U.S. breweries to sample, plus seminars.

WHAT TO SEE & DO

Butterfly Pavilion & Insect Center   A walk through the butterfly conservatory introduces you to a world of grace and beauty. The constant mist creates a hazy habitat to support the lush green plants that are both food and home to the inhabitants. If you stand still for a few minutes, resident butterflies might land on you, but don't try to pick them up—the oils on your hands contaminate their senses, interfering with their ability to find food. In the insect room you'll discover that honeybees beat their wings some 200 times per second, and a fascinating "touch cart" allows you to get up close to a cockroach or tarantula—if you really want to. Allow 2 hours. 6252 W. 104th Ave., Westminster. © 303/469-5441. www.butterflies.org. Admission $6.95 adults, $4.95 seniors, $3.95 children 4–12, free for those under 4. Daily 9am–5pm. Take the Denver-Boulder Tpk. (U.S. 36) to W. 104th Ave. and go east for about a block. The Pavilion is on your right.

Colorado's Ocean Journey   Denver's state-of-the-art aquarium contains permanent exhibits that re-create ecosystems on opposite sides of the planet: the Colorado River in North America and the Kampar River in Indonesia. Both showcase the creatures of each river, from their mountainous origins to their oceanic destinations. The Colorado exhibit features the Colorado state fish—the greenback cutthroat trout—as well as river otters and innumerable other aquatic denizens, culminating in a flash flood simulation and the 187,000-gallon Sea of Cortez display, populated with angelfish, moray eels, and rays. The Kampar River display features endangered Sumatran tigers, as well as the 320,000-gallon Depths of the Pacific exhibit, replete with a variety of sharks among its 3,000 fish. There are also traveling exhibits on subjects such as sea otters, and several hands-on displays aimed at children. Allow 1 to 3 hours. 700 Water St, just east of I-25, Exit 211. © 303/561-4450. www.oceanjourney.org. $15 adults, $13 children 13–17 and seniors, $6.95 children 4–12, free for children under 4. Memorial Day to Labor Day daily 9am–6pm; rest of year daily 10am–5pm. Closed Dec 25.

Colorado State Capitol   The capitol was constructed in 1886 of granite from a Colorado quarry; its dome, rising 272 feet above the ground, is sheathed in gold. The first-floor rotunda offers a splendid view upward to the underside of the dome; the west lobby offers changing exhibits, and to the west of the main lobby is the governor's reception room. The second floor has main entrances to the House, Senate, and old Supreme Court chambers, and entrances to the public and visitor galleries for the House and Senate are on the third floor. The Colorado Hall of Fame is near the top of the dome; on clear days, the views from the dome are spectacular. Allow about an hour. (*Note:* At press time, the top of the dome was closed indefinitely for security and construction reasons. Call for up-to-date information.) Broadway and E. Colfax Ave. © 303/866-2604. Free admission. 40- to 45-min. tours offered year-round (more frequently in summer), Memorial Day to Labor Day Mon–Fri 9am–3:30pm, Sat 9:30am–2pm; rest of year Mon–Fri 9:15am–2:30pm.

Denver Art Museum   This seven-story museum, wrapped by a thin 28-sided wall faced with one million sparkling tiles, is the place to come to see art depicting the American West. Its expanding collection of Western and regional works includes Frederic Remington's bronze *The Cheyenne*, Charles Russell's painting *In the Enemy's Country*, plus 19th-century photography and historical pieces. The American Indian collection represents 150 tribes of North America, spanning nearly 2,000 years. Child-oriented and family programs are scheduled regularly. 2003 will see the start of a major construction project, which will double the size of the museum; the museum will remain open throughout the construction phase. Allow 1 to 3 hours. 100 W. 14th Ave. (at Civic Center Park). © 720/865-5000. www.denverartmuseum.org. Admission $6 adults, $4.50 students and seniors, free for children under 12; free for Colorado residents Sat. Tues–Sat 10am–5pm (until 9pm Wed); Sun noon–5pm.

Breathe Easier

Colorado's high elevation means there's less oxygen and lower humidity than elsewhere in the West. You can ease the transition to a higher elevation by changing altitude gradually. For instance, spend a couple of nights in Colorado Springs (elevation 6,012 ft.) before heading to the top of Pikes Peak (elevation 14,110 ft.). Help yourself adjust by getting sufficient rest, avoiding large meals, and drinking plenty of nonalcoholic fluids. Prescription drugs can help prevent altitude problems and relieve symptoms if they occur; consult your doctor.

Downtown Denver

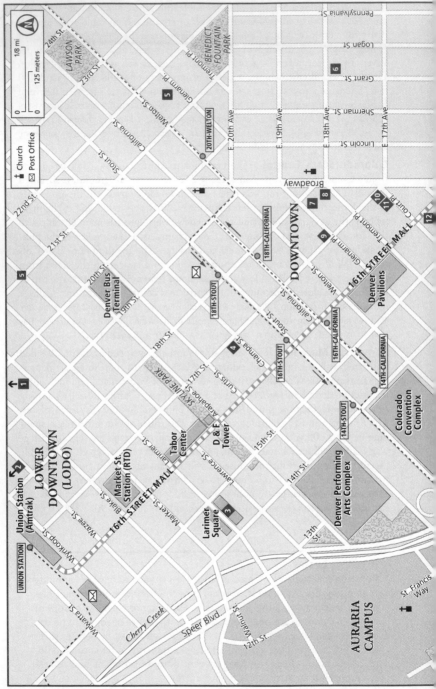

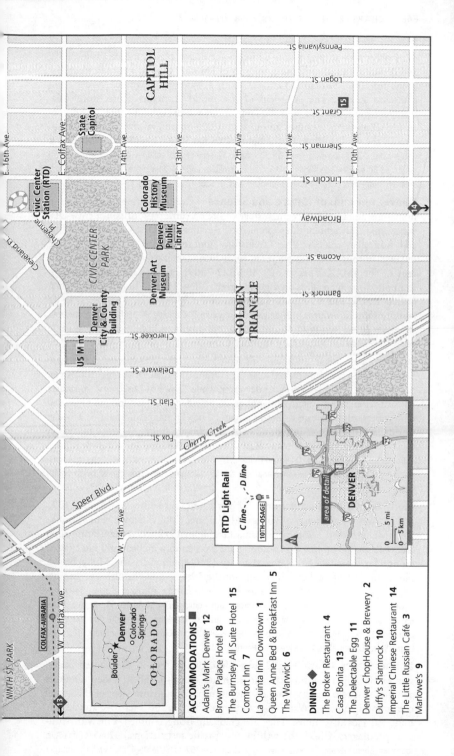

ACCOMMODATIONS ■
Adam's Mark Denver 12
Brown Palace Hotel 8
The Burnsley All Suite Hotel 15
Comfort Inn 7
La Quinta Inn Downtown 1
Queen Anne Bed & Breakfast Inn 5
The Warwick 6

DINING ◆
The Broker Restaurant 4
Casa Bonita 13
The Delectable Egg 11
Denver ChopHouse & Brewery 2
Duffy's Shamrock 10
Imperial Chinese Restaurant 14
The Little Russian Café 3
Marlowe's 9

RTD Light Rail
C line ----- D line
10TH-OSAGE

COLORADO
Boulder
Denver
Colorado
Springs

area of detail
DENVER

CAPITOL HILL

GOLDEN TRIANGLE

Denver Botanic Gardens   Twenty-three acres of outstanding indoor and outdoor gardens display plants native to the desert, plains, mountain foothills, and Alpine zones; there's also a traditional Japanese garden, a garden to attract songbirds, and "Romantic Gardens" with a waterway, fragrance garden, and courtyard garden. The "Gardens of the World" contains plants from Asia, Europe, Africa, Australia, and the Tropics. Even in the cold of winter, the dome-shaped conservatory houses more than 1,000 species of exotic plants from around the world. Allow 1 or 2 hours. 1005 York St. ⓒ 720/865-3500. www.botanic gardens.org. Admission May–Sept $6.50 adults, $4 seniors and children 4–15; Oct–Apr $5.50 adults, $3.50 seniors, $3 children 4–15; free for children under 4. May–Sept Sat–Tues 9am–8pm, Wed–Fri 9am–5pm; Oct–Apr daily 9am–5pm. Bus: 2, 6, or 10.

Denver Museum of Nature and Science   Exquisitely fashioned figures in numerous dioramas depict the history of life on earth on four continents. Displays explore ancient cultures, prehistoric American peoples, Colorado wildlife, and Australian ecology. The "Prehistoric Journey" traces the history of life on earth through 3.5 billion years, with fossils, interactive exhibits, and dioramas. The **IMAX Theater** (ⓒ 303/322-7009) presents science, nature, or technology-oriented films on a giant screen. Allow 1½ to 2 hours. City Park, 2001 Colorado Blvd. ⓒ 800/925-2250 outside Metro Denver, or 303/322-7009; 303/370-8257 for the hearing impaired. www.dmns.org. Admission to museum: $10 adults, $7 children 3–12, students, and seniors 60 and older. IMAX: $8 adults, $5.50 children, students, and seniors. Planetarium: $6 adults, $4 children and seniors. Daily 9am–5pm. Closed Dec 25. Bus: 24, 32, or 40.

Denver Zoo   Some 4,000 animals representing over 700 species call the zoo home. Feeding times are posted near the entrance. "Northern Shores" allows you to see polar bears and sea lions underwater, while "Tropical Discovery" re-creates an entire tropical ecosystem under glass, complete with crocodiles, piranhas, and king cobras, plus the rare Komodo dragon. The "Primate Panorama" is a 7-acre world-class primate exhibit with 29 species, ranging from a 6-ounce marmoset to a 581-pound gorilla. Allow at least 2 hours. City Park, 23rd Ave. and Steele St. (main entrance is between Colorado Blvd. and York St.). ⓒ 303/376-4800. www.denverzoo.org. Admission $7–$9 adults, $6–$7 seniors 62 and over, $4–$5 children 4–12 (accompanied by an adult), free for children under 4. Apr–Sept daily 9am–5pm; Oct–Mar daily 10am–4pm. Bus: 24 or 32.

Molly Brown House Museum   This is a neat, old house, which from 1894 to 1932 was the residence of James and Margaret (Molly) Brown. The "unsinkable" Molly Brown became a national heroine in 1912 when the *Titanic* sank: She took charge of a group of immigrant women in a lifeboat and later raised money for their benefit. Restored to its 1910 appearance, the Molly Brown House has a large collection of turn-of-the-19th-century furnishings and art objects, many of which belonged to the Brown family. Allow 1 hour. 1340 Pennsylvania St. ⓒ 303/832-4092. www.mollybrown.org. Admission $6.50 adults, $4.50 seniors over 65, $2.50 children 6–12, free for children under 7. Tues–Sat 10am–4pm; Sun noon–4pm; June–Aug also Mon 10am–4pm. Last tour of the day begins at 3:30pm. Closed major holidays. Bus: 2 on Logan St. to E. 13th, then 1 block east to Pennsylvania.

United States Mint   The Denver Mint, one of four in the United States, stamps 10 billion coins a year, and each has a small D on it. Video monitors along the visitors' gallery through the mint provide a close view of the actual coin-minting process. (*Note:* After the September 11, 2001, terrorist attacks, the mint was closed to tours. They are gradually being resumed, but with stringent parameters. Check the website for specific instructions.) 320 W. Colfax Ave. (between Cherokee and Delaware sts.). ⓒ 303/405-4757 or 303/405-4761. www.usmint.gov.

Free admission. Tickets available at the booth on Cherokee St. Mon–Fri 8am–2pm; tours every 15–20 min. Reservations not accepted; June to Labor Day expect a 60 min. wait. Closed 2 weeks in summer for audit.

SHOPPING

Prime hunting grounds include the **16th Street Mall** and adjacent areas, among them **Larimer Square,** a restored quarter of old Denver that includes galleries, boutiques, restaurants, and clubs, on the 1400 block of Larimer Street.

The huge **Cherry Creek Shopping Center**—a shopper's paradise—is south of downtown, between University Boulevard and Steele Street.

The gigantic **Tattered Cover Book Store,** 2955 E. First Ave. (opposite Cherry Creek Shopping Center; © **800/833-9327** or 303/322-7727; www. tatteredcover.com), is a book lover's dream-come-true—it's so huge you need (and they provide) a map to find your way around.

Model-train buffs will be in seventh heaven at **Caboose Hobbies,** 500 S. Broadway (© **303/777-6766;** www.caboosehobbies.com).

Sheplers, 8500 E. Orchard Rd. (at I-25 Exit 198), Englewood (© **303/773-3311;** www.sheplers.com), bills itself as the world's largest Western clothing store, with boots, cowboy hats, Western shirts, and more.

Denver also claims the world's largest sporting-goods store: **Gart Sports Castle,** on Broadway at 10th Avenue (© **303/861-1122;** www.gartsports.com). There are also a number of Gart outlets in the Denver area. Need to rent gear? Try **Sports Rent,** 8761 Wadsworth Blvd., Arvada (© **303/467-0200**), or **Grand West Outfitters,** 801 Broadway (© **303/825-0300**). A good source for maps and hiking guides is **Mapsco Map & Travel Center,** 800 Broadway (© **800/456-8703** or 303/623-4299).

WHERE TO STAY

Chains in the downtown area include the **Comfort Inn,** 401 17th St. (© **800/228-5150** or 303/296-0400), and **La Quinta Inn Downtown,** 3500 Park Ave. W. (at I-25 Exit 213; © **800/531-5900** or 303/458-1222). Outside downtown, the **Quality Inn Denver South,** 6300 E. Hampden Ave. (© **800/647-1986** or 303/758-2211), is a good choice for families. Choices near the airport include **Courtyard by Marriott at DIA,** 6900 Tower Rd. (© **800/321-2211** or 303/371-0300), and the **Fairfield Inn–DIA,** 6851 Tower Rd. (© **800/228-2800** or 303/576-9640).

Adam's Mark Denver   This striking complex is comprised of two buildings: the 22-floor Tower Building on the east side of Court Place, and the Plaza Building across the street (a pedestrian bridge on the second floor connects the two). From the upper floors of the Tower, west-facing rooms have marvelous views of the Front Range. The classic decor sports brass, marble, oak, and mahogany. Come here for real R&R—you can get room service, and each room has a coffeemaker and refrigerator. The executive level offers a concierge and business services, plus a full breakfast, and local and national newspapers. 1550 Court Place, Denver, CO 80202. © 800/444-2326 or 303/893-3333. Fax 303/626-2543. www.adamsmark. com. 1,225 units. $165–$249 double; $375–$1,200 suite. AE, DC, DISC, MC, V. Underground valet parking $15 per day or $22 overnight; self-parking $2 per half hour up to $12, or $15 overnight; 6 ft. 4 in. height limit. **Amenities:** Restaurants (4); heated outdoor pool; health club.

Brown Palace Hotel   For more than 100 years, this National Historic Landmark has been *the* place to stay in Denver. Designed in an odd triangular shape, it was built of Colorado red granite and Arizona sandstone. Elaborate cast-iron grillwork surrounds six tiers of balconies up to the stained-glass ceiling high above the lobby. Rooms are either Victorian or Art Deco style and have all the amenities of a modern luxury hotel, including complimentary high-speed Internet access. In-room massage is available for an extra charge. Excellent international cuisine is served in the elegant Palace Arms, and a full English tea served in the lobby. This is our choice for a special overnight stay in relaxed elegance. 321 17th St., Denver, CO 80202. © 800/228-2917 or 303/297-3111. Fax 303/312-5900. www. brownpalace.com. 241 units. $225–$325 double; $325–$1,275 suite. Weekend rates start at $169 double. AE, DC, DISC, MC, V. Valet parking $22 overnight. **Amenities:** Restaurants (3); fitness center; pets up to 20 lb. accepted.

The Burnsley All Suite Hotel   This small, elegant hotel (convenient to the Cherry Creek shopping areas, and only 5 blocks from downtown) offers handsomely furnished suites with private balconies, fully stocked kitchens, coffeemakers, and antique furnishings. There's a self-serve laundry, daily newspaper delivery, and free shuttle service to the local area. 1000 Grant St. (at E. 10th Ave.), Denver, CO 80203. © 800/231-3915 or 303/830-1000. Fax 303/830-7676. www.burnsley. com. 80 units. $109–$209 double. Weekend rates available. AE, DC, MC, V. Free covered parking. **Amenities:** Restaurant; outdoor heated pool; access to a nearby health club.

Cameron Motel   This small mom-and-pop motel about 10 minutes from downtown is a clean, quiet alternative to chain motels. Built in the 1940s, it has been completely renovated. Three units have kitchenettes. Note that 14 units have shower-only bathrooms. The owners live on-site and their personal touch shows. 4500 E. Evans Ave. (I-25 Exit 203), Denver, CO 80222. © 303/757-2100. Fax 303/757-0974. 35 units. $45–$58 double; $72 suite. AE, DISC, MC, V. Free off-street parking. **Amenities:** Pets accepted for $5 nightly fee each.

Queen Anne Bed & Breakfast Inn   The Queen Anne borders downtown and is within easy walking distance of just about everything. A favorite of both business travelers and couples seeking a romantic getaway, this impeccable B&B consists of two Victorian homes. Innkeeper Tom King provides piped-in chamber music and fresh flowers, but no televisions. Each of the 10 double rooms in the 1879 Pierce House is unique, decorated with period antiques (three of the rooms boast original murals). The entire property is nonsmoking. 2147–51 Tremont Place, Denver, CO 80205. © 800/432-4667 or 303/296-6666. Fax 303/296-2151. www.queen annebnb.com. 14 units. $85–$165 double; $165–$185 suite. Rates include hot breakfast and Colorado wine each evening. AE, DC, DISC, MC, V. Free off-street parking.

The Warwick   This handsome, recently renovated midsize choice has an almost Parisian feel. Rooms are outfitted with brass and mahogany furniture, and also have private balconies. Most rooms are equipped with a mini-fridge. There's also a lounge, a concierge, and courtesy limo service within a 5-mile radius. 1776 Grant St. (at E. 18th Ave.), Denver, CO 80203. © 800/525-2888 or 303/861-2000. Fax 303/839-8504. www.warwickhotels.com/denver. 220 units. $139–$210 double; $129–$650 suite. Weekend rates $79–$99 double; $129 and up suite. Children under 18 stay free in parents' room. AE, DC, DISC, MC, V. Self-parking $10 per day, valet parking $16 per day, both underground. **Amenities:** Restaurant; heated pool; access to nearby health club.

WHERE TO DINE

The Broker Restaurant STEAK/SEAFOOD   The historic Denver National Bank building is the site of the Broker, which is famous for its generous portions and is the place to go for beef and shrimp. House specialties include New York and porterhouse steaks, Rocky Mountain trout, rack of lamb, and blackened catfish. The Broker's trademark is a complimentary large bowl of steamed shrimp with a tangy sauce. Two additional locations are the **Airport Broker** (near DIA), 12100 E. 39th Ave., at Peoria just south of I-70 (© **303/371-6420**); and **DTC Broker,** 5111 DTC Parkway, east of I-25 in Greenwood Village (© **303/770-5111**). In Boulder, there's the **Broker Inn Restaurant,** 555 30th St., between the turnpike and Baseline Road (© **303/449-1752**). 821 17th St. © 303/292-5065. Reservations recommended. Main courses $12–$20 lunch, $26–$40 dinner. AE, DC, DISC, MC, V. Tues–Fri 11am–2:30pm; daily 5–10pm.

Casa Bonita MEXICAN/AMERICAN   A west Denver landmark, Casa Bonita is more theme park than restaurant. A pink Spanish cathedral-type bell tower greets visitors, and inside are divers plummeting into a pool beside a 30-foot waterfall, puppet shows, a video arcade, and strolling mariachi bands. Food is served cafeteria style: enchiladas, tacos, fajitas, country-fried steak, and fried chicken. Hot *sopaipillas* (deep-fried sweet dough), served with honey, are included with each meal. In the JCRS Shopping Center, 6715 W. Colfax Ave., Lakewood. © 303/232-5115. Reservations not accepted. Main courses $7–$13; children's meals around $3. DISC, MC, V. Mon–Thurs 11am–9:30pm; Fri–Sat 11am–10pm.

The Delectable Egg AMERICAN   Every city should have a cafe like this: There are more than two dozen egg dishes, pancakes, waffles, and French toast. Lunch includes a variety of salads and sandwiches. You can order eggs skillet-fried, baked in a frittata, scrambled into pita pockets, or smothered with chile or hollandaise. Another Delectable Egg can be found at 1625 Court Place (© **303/892-5720**). 1642 Market St. © 303/572-8146. Menu items $3.95–$7.25. AE, DC, DISC, MC, V. Mon–Fri 6:30am–2pm; Sat–Sun 7am–2pm.

Denver ChopHouse & Brewery STEAKS   A LoDo mainstay since it opened alongside Coors Field in 1995, this is one of the best places for carnivores in the Mile High City. Set in a restored early-19th-century train depot, the ChopHouse does classic red meat-and-potatoes fare (not to mention microbrews) as well as anyplace in town. Our picks are always the juicy steaks, from filet mignon to New York strip, and the white cheddar mashers are our side dish of choice. The restaurant also serves a nice selection of fresh seafood and some less expensive sandwiches and pizzas, but very little in the way of vegetarian fare. There is also a **Boulder ChopHouse,** 921 Walnut St. (© **303/443-1188**). 1735 19th St. © 303/296-0800. Reservations recommended for dinner. Main courses $10–$27. AE, DC, MC, V. Mon–Thurs 11am–2:30pm and 5–11pm; Sat–Sun 11am–2:30pm; Fri–Sat 4:30pm–midnight; Sun 4:30–10pm.

Duffy's Shamrock AMERICAN   This traditional Irish bar and restaurant with fast, cheerful service has been thriving since the late 1950s. It specializes in Irish coffees and imported Irish beers. Daily food specials may include prime rib, broiled mahi mahi, or grilled liver and onions. Sandwiches, on practically every kind of bread imaginable, include corned beef, Reuben, and Italian sausage. 1635 Court Place. © 303/534-4935. Main courses $2–$6 breakfast, $5–$8 lunch, $5–$12 dinner. AE, DC, DISC, MC, V. Mon–Fri 7am–2am; Sat 7:30am–2am; Sun 11am–2am.

The Fort ROCKY MOUNTAIN   There are several reasons to drive 18 miles southwest from downtown Denver to visit the Fort. First is the atmosphere: The building is a full-scale reproduction of Colorado's first fur-trading post. A second is the owner, Sam Arnold, a broadcast personality and master chef who just might open your champagne bottle with a tomahawk. The third (and best) reason to go is the food. The Fort built its reputation on high-quality, low-cholesterol buffalo. There's buffalo steak, buffalo tongue, broiled buffalo marrow bones, and even "buffalo eggs"—hard-boiled quail eggs wrapped in buffalo sausage. Our favorite is the game plate: elk chop, teriyaki-style quail, and a buffalo filet. 19192 Colo. 8 (just north of the intersection of Colo. 8 and W. Hampden Ave./U.S. 285), Morrison. ℂ 303/697-4771. www.thefort.com. Reservations recommended. Main courses $20–$45. AE, DC, DISC, MC, V. Mon–Fri 5:30–9:30pm; Sat 5–9:30pm; Sun 5–8:30pm. Call for special holiday hours.

Imperial Chinese Restaurant CHINESE   The best Chinese restaurant in Denver, the Imperial offers classic and innovative Szechwan, Hunan, Mandarin, and Cantonese dishes. Our favorites include the Nanking pork loin and sesame chicken. 431 S. Broadway. ℂ 303/698-2800. Reservations recommended. Main courses $9–$28; complete multicourse dinners $16–$30. AE, DC, MC, V. Mon–Thurs 11am–10pm; Fri 11am–10:30pm; Sat noon–10:30pm; Sun 4–10pm.

The Little Russian Cafe RUSSIAN   This quiet, charming cafe combines old-world atmosphere with authentic Russian cuisine. Choose the dimly lit dining room or the outdoor patio. In the Russian tradition, you can begin with a shot of ice-cold vodka and a bowl of borscht, before enjoying beef Stroganoff or goulash. Many dishes are meatless, and this is a popular spot with vegetarians. 1424H Larimer St. ℂ 303/595-8600. Main courses $10–$16. AE, DC, DISC, MC, V. Sun–Thurs 5:30–9:30pm; Fri–Sat 5–10pm.

Marlowe's STEAK/SEAFOOD   This popular spot occupies a corner of the 1891 Kittredge Building (a National Historic Landmark), with an antique cherrywood bar, granite pillars, and brass rails. It's a great place for cocktails and appetizers, especially in warm weather, when tables are set up outside. House specialties include a Texas T-bone, almond-crusted salmon, and live Maine lobster. 501 16th St. (at Glenarm St.). ℂ 303/595-3700. Reservations recommended. Main courses $7–$13 lunch, $9–$25 dinner. AE, DC, DISC, MC, V. Mon–Thurs 11am–midnight; Fri 11am–2am; Sat noon–2am; Sun noon–10pm.

DENVER AFTER DARK

Look for current entertainment listings in each Friday's *Denver Post* and *Rocky Mountain News. Westword,* a weekly newspaper distributed free throughout the city every Wednesday, has the best listings of all. Tickets for nearly all major events can be obtained from **Ticketman USA,** 51 W. 84th Ave., no. 110 (ℂ **303/430-1111**), with delivery to your hotel available. Also try **Ticketmaster** (ℂ **303/830-TIXS**), with several outlets in the Denver area.

THE PERFORMING ARTS   Denver's performing-arts scene is anchored by the 4-square-block **Denver Center for the Performing Arts,** located downtown just a few blocks from major hotels at 14th and Curtis streets (ℂ **800/641-1222** or 303/893-4100, or 303/893-DCPA for recorded information; www.denver center.org). The complex houses nine theaters, a concert hall, and what may be the nation's first symphony hall in the round. It is home to the **Colorado Symphony Orchestra** (ℂ **303/893-4100**), **Colorado Ballet** (ℂ **303/837-8888;** www.coloradoballet.org), **Opera Colorado** (ℂ **303/778-1500;** www.opera colorado.org), and more.

   Red Rocks Amphitheatre, I-70 Exit 259 South, 16351 County Rd. 93, Morrison (ℂ **303/295-4444**), is a venue for top-name outdoor summer concerts, set in the foothills of the Rocky Mountains, 15 miles west of the city. The 9,000-seat amphitheater is flanked by 400-foot-high red sandstone rocks, and at night, with the lights of Denver spread across the horizon, the atmosphere is magical.

THE BAR SCENE   The hip place for bar-hopping is **LoDo,** which attracts all manner of Gen-Xers and yuppies. Its trendy nightspots are often noisy and crowded, but if you're looking for action, this is where to find it, in spots like **The Falling Rock Tap House,** 1919 Blake St. (© **303/293-8338**), which has 69 beers on tap, darts and pool, and occasional live music.

Denver's first modern microbrewery, the **Wynkoop Brewing Co.,** 1634 18th St., at Wynkoop Street (© **303/297-2700**), offers tours Saturdays from 1 to 5pm. Housed in the renovated 1898 J. S. Brown Mercantile Building across from Union Station, the Wynkoop is also a popular restaurant. Ten beers are always on tap, and "tasters" provide a nice sampling. On the second floor is a top-notch pool hall with billiards, snooker, and darts.

You'll find an excellent selection of fine cigars, single malt Scotch, and after-dinner drinks at the refined **Churchill Bar,** 321 17th St., in the Brown Palace Hotel (© **303/297-3111**).

A bustling gay and lesbian bar, **60 South,** 60 S. Broadway (© **303/777-0193**), attracts all kinds to its dance floor, the thumping groove courtesy of some of Denver's best DJs.

THE CLUB & MUSIC SCENE   The historic **Bluebird Theater,** 3317 E. Colfax Ave. (at Adams St.; © **303/322-2308**), built in 1913 to show silent movies, has been restored and now offers a diverse selection of jazz, rock, alternative, and other live music, as well as films. One of the best spots in Denver to hear live local music is **The Cricket on the Hill,** 1209 E. 13th Ave. (© **303/830-9020**), which hosts musical acts of all kinds, from oddball punk to country. The **Mercury Café,** 2199 California St., at 22nd St. (© **303/294-9281**), has a wide array of live offerings, from avant-garde jazz to big band to progressive rock.

The **Grizzly Rose,** 5450 N. Valley Hwy., at I-25, Exit 215 (© **303/295-1330**), has a 5,000-square-foot dance floor and draws nationally known country performers offering live music every night.

A SIDE TRIP TO GOLDEN

Golden, 15 miles west of downtown Denver via U.S. 6 or Colo. 58 off I-70, is one of the fabled Gold Circle towns that boomed with the first strikes of the gold rush in 1859. For information, contact the **Greater Golden Area Chamber of Commerce,** 1010 Washington Ave. (© **800/590-3113** or 303/279-3113; www.goldencochamber.org).

Most folks head to Golden to see the **Coors Brewing Company,** at 13th and Ford streets (© **303/277-2337**), the world's largest single-site brewery, producing 1½ million gallons of beer each day. Free tours (offered Mon–Sat 10am–4pm) leave the central parking lot, where visitors board a bus for a short drive through historic Golden before arriving at the brewery. Yes, you'll get free samples.

Explore the history of mining in Colorado with a replica of a gold mine and other displays at the **Colorado School of Mines Geology Museum,** 13th and Maple streets (© **303/273-3815**). There are some 50,000 minerals, gems, fossils, and artifacts from around the world on exhibit, plus displays of geology, earth history, and paleontology.

Fans of steam trains won't want to miss the **Colorado Railroad Museum,** 17155 W. 44th Ave. (© **800/365-6263** or 303/279-4591; www.crrm.org), which has more than four dozen narrow- and standard-gauge locomotives and cars, plus other historic equipment, artifacts, photos, and documents, as well as model trains. Follow the signs from I-70 Exit 265 westbound, Exit 266 eastbound.

2 Boulder

Set at the foot of the Flatirons of the Rocky Mountains, just 30 miles northwest of downtown Denver, Boulder is a college town. With close to 27,000 students, the University of Colorado (C.U.) dominates the city. Sophisticated and artsy, Boulder is home to numerous high-tech companies; it has also attracted count-less outdoor enthusiasts, who have been drawn by the delightful climate, vast open spaces, and proximity to Rocky Mountain National Park. Boulder has 30,000 acres of open space within its city limits, 56 parks, and 200 miles of trails—on any given day, most of the population is outside making great use of this land, generally from the vantage point of a bicycle seat.

ESSENTIALS

GETTING THERE   By Plane   Air travelers must fly into **Denver Interna-tional Airport,** then make ground connections to Boulder.

By Bus   Buses operated by the **Regional Transportation District (RTD)** (© **800/366-7433** or 303/299-6000, TDD 303/299-6089; www.rtddenver. com) charge $10 for a one-way trip to or from the airport (exact change required). Buses leave from, and return to, the main terminal at 14th and Wal-nut streets daily every hour from 6am to 11pm.

By Car   The Boulder Turnpike (U.S. 36) branches off I-25 north of Denver and passes through Westminster, Broomfield, and Louisville before reaching Boulder some 25 minutes later.

VISITOR INFORMATION   The **Boulder Convention and Visitors Bureau,** 2440 Pearl St. (at Folsom St.), Boulder, CO 80302 (© **800/444-0447** or 303/442-2911; www.bouldercoloradousa.com), is open Monday through Thursday from 8:30am to 5pm, Friday from 8:30am to 4pm, and can provide excellent maps.

SPECIAL EVENTS & FESTIVALS   In the wacky, crowd-pleasing **Kinetic Conveyance Race** (© **303/444-5226**), held in early May at Boulder Reservoir, some 70 teams race over land and water in a variety of imaginative human-powered, handmade machines.

One of the best in the country, the annual **Colorado Shakespeare Festival** (© **303/492-0554;** www.coloradoshakes.org) takes place from late June to late August, with more than a dozen performances each of four Shakespeare plays. Tickets run $16 to $45 for single performances, with series packages available.

The **Colorado Music Festival** (© **303/449-1397;** www.coloradomusic fest.org) brings world-class musicians to the acoustically excellent Chautauqua Auditorium. The festival presents classical through modern works, and usually runs from mid-June to mid-August. Adult tickets are $10 to $37.

EXPLORING THE AREA

The tree-lined, pedestrian-only **Pearl Street Mall,** along Pearl Street from 11th to 15th streets, is the city's hub for dining, shopping, strolling, and people-watching. Musicians, mimes, jugglers, and other street entertainers hold court on the landscaped mall day and night, year-round.

Boulder maintains more than 200 miles of hiking trails and long stretches of bike paths. Several canyons lead down from the Rockies directly into Boulder, attracting mountaineers and rock climbers. Families enjoy picnicking and camping in the beautiful surroundings. Everywhere you look, people of all ages are running, walking, biking, skiing, or engaged in other active sports.

On some days, you can see more bikes than cars in Boulder. For rentals, maps, and tips on the best places to ride, check with **University Bicycles,** 839 Pearl St., about 2 blocks west of the Pearl Street Mall (© **303/444-4196;** www. ubikes.com).

The **Boulder Creek Path,** 55th Street and Pearl Parkway to the mouth of Boulder Canyon (© **303/413-7200**), provides a 16-mile-long oasis and recreation area through the city and west into the mountains. The C.U. campus and several city parks are linked by the path. Near the east end, watch for deer, prairie dog colonies, Canada geese, spotted sandpipers, owls, and woodpeckers.

I. M. Pei designed the striking pink-sandstone building that houses the **National Center for Atmospheric Research,** 1850 Table Mesa Dr. (© **303/497-1174;** www.ncar.ucar.edu), high atop Table Mesa in the southwestern foothills. Here, scientists study the greenhouse effect, wind shear, and ozone depletion. Among the technological tools on display are satellites, weather balloons, robots, and supercomputers that can simulate the world's climate. There are also hands-on, weather-oriented exhibits and the outdoor, interpretive Walter Orr Roberts Nature and Weather Trail (0.4 mile long and wheelchair accessible).

Celestial Seasonings, 4600 Sleepytime Dr. (off Spine Rd. at Colo. 119, Longmont Diagonal; © **303/581-1202;** www.celestialseasonings.com), the nation's leading producer of herbal teas, offers free tours on the hour every day.

WHERE TO STAY

The best chain hotel value is the **Days Inn Boulder,** 5397 S. Boulder Rd. (© **800/329-7466** or 303/499-4422), which offers large rooms, great views of the mountains, and an outdoor heated pool. We also recommend **The Alps,** a beautiful B&B housed in a historic log lodge, 38619 Boulder Canyon Dr. (© **800/414-2577** or 303/444-5445; http://alpsinn.com), and the series of pleasant log cabins near the east gate of Boulder Canyon at **Foot of the Mountain Motel,** 200 Arapahoe Ave. (© **303/442-5688;** www.footofthemountain motel.com).

Hotel Boulderado   This elegant, historic hotel boasts a colorful leaded-glass ceiling, a cantilevered, cherrywood staircase, and rich woodwork. The original five-story hotel, just a block off the Pearl Street Mall, has 42 bright and cozy rooms, all with a Victorian flavor. The newer North Wing rooms also capture the turn-of-the-19th-century feel with reproduction antiques. Some rooms have refrigerators and a few have jetted tubs. 2115 13th St. (at Spruce St.), Boulder, CO 80302. © **800/433-4344** or 303/442-4344. Fax 303/442-4378. www.boulderado.com. 160 units. $185–$215 double; $275–$325 suite. AE, DC, DISC, MC, V. **Amenities:** Restaurants (2); access to nearby health club.

WHERE TO DINE

An institution for almost 40 years, **Tom's Tavern,** 1047 Pearl St. (© **303/443-3893**), is Boulder's most popular place for a good burger.

Flagstaff House Restaurant   NEW AMERICAN/REGIONAL   Head here for excellent cuisine and a spectacular nighttime view of the lights of Boulder, spread out 1,000 feet below. This family-owned and -operated restaurant has an elegant, candlelit dining room with glass walls to maximize the view. The menu, which changes daily, offers an excellent selection of seafood and Rocky Mountain game prepared with a creative flair, plus the state's best wine cellar. 1138 Flagstaff Rd. (west up Baseline Rd.). (✆ 303/442-4640. www.flagstaffhouse.com. Reservations recommended. Main courses $28–$59. AE, DC, MC, V. Sun–Fri 6–10pm; Sat 5–10pm.

Turley's AMERICAN   A sunny family diner with a healthier menu than the norm, Turley's is a Boulder landmark. Its casual atmosphere and friendly staff provide a pleasant, homey backdrop for any meal, and breakfast is served all day. There are full espresso and juice bars. A menu featuring omelets, burgers, sandwiches, fresh fish, and dinner entrees ranging from buffalo meatloaf to tofu scramble ensures that everyone's tastes will be satisfied. 2350 Arapahoe Ave. (✆ 303/442-2800. Menu items $4–$14. AE, DC, DISC, MC, V. Mon–Sat 6:30am–9pm; Sun 7am–9pm.

BOULDER AFTER DARK

The Catacombs, in the basement of the Hotel Boulderado, 13th and Spruce streets (✆ 303/443-0486), offers live blues and jazz by local and regional performers. The **West End Tavern,** 926 Pearl St. (✆ 303/444-3535), is a great neighborhood bar with a wide-ranging selection of jazz, blues, and other live music.

Boulder's leading sports bar is **The Barrel House,** 2860 Arapahoe Rd. (✆ 303/444-9464), with 25 beers on tap and close to 40 TVs. Local brewpubs include the **Oasis Brewery,** 1061 Canyon Blvd. (✆ 303/449-0363), with an Egyptian motif and great beers; and the **Walnut Brewery,** 1123 Walnut St. (near Broadway; ✆ 303/447-1345), in a historic brick warehouse a block from the Pearl Street Mall. The spacey wall murals make **The Sink,** 1165 13th St. (✆ 303/444-SINK [7465]), one of Boulder's funniest nightspots. There's a full bar with over a dozen regional microbrews, live music, and light fare. A gay bar that attracts a diverse crowd, **The Yard,** 2690 28th St., Unit C (✆ 303/443-1987), features dancing (no cover) on Fridays and Saturdays, as well as pool.

3 Rocky Mountain National Park

ESTES PARK: THE GATEWAY

Estes Park is the eastern gateway to Rocky Mountain National Park, and Grand Lake is the closest town to the park's western entrance. Of the two, Estes Park is more developed, with more lodging and dining choices, plus lots of galleries and shopping. If you're driving to Rocky Mountain National Park via Boulder or Denver, you'll want to make the resort town of Estes Park your base camp. (The town of Grand Lake is more rustic, with plenty of spots to camp, a number of motels, and a few guest ranches. If you're coming from Steamboat Springs or Glenwood Springs, Grand Lake is a more convenient base.)

ESSENTIALS

GETTING THERE   The most direct route is U.S. 36 from Denver and Boulder. At Estes Park, U.S. 36 joins U.S. 34, which runs up the Big Thompson Canyon from I-25 and Loveland, and continues through Rocky Mountain National Park to Grand Lake and Granby.

VISITOR INFORMATION   The **Estes Park Chamber Resort Association,** 500 Big Thompson Ave., Estes Park, CO 80517 (✆ 800/44-ESTES or 970/586-4431; www.estesparkresort.com), has a visitor center on U.S. 34, just east of its junction with U.S. 36.

Rocky Mountain National Park

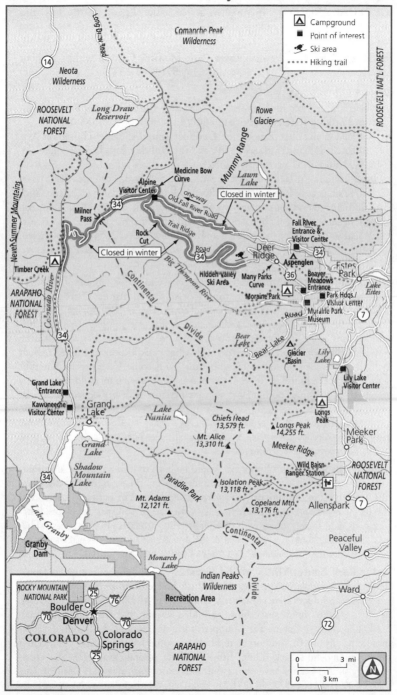

Legend:
- ▲ Campground
- ■ Point of interest
- 🎿 Ski area
- ···· Hiking trail

Comanche Peak Wilderness

Long Draw Road

(14)

Neota Wilderness

ROOSEVELT NATIONAL FOREST

Long Draw Reservoir

ROOSEVELT NAT'L FOREST

Rowe Glacier

Mummy Range

Lawn Lake

Medicine Bow Curve

Alpine Visitor Center

Closed in winter

one-way Old Fall River Road

Milner Pass

(34)

Never Summer Mountains

Trail Ridge

Rock Cut

Closed in winter

Fall River Entrance & Visitor Center

Trail Ridge Road (34)

Deer Ridge

(34)

Big Thompson River

Continental

Colorado River

Timber Creek

(34)

ARAPAHO NATIONAL FOREST

Hidden Valley Ski Area

Many Parks Curve

Moraine Park

Aspenglen

(36)

Beaver Meadows Entrance

Estes Park

Lake Estes

Park Hdqs./ Visitor Center

(7)

Moraine Park Museum

Divide

Bear Lake

Bear Lake Road

Glacier Basin

Lily Lake

Lily Lake Visitor Center

Grand Lake Entrance

Kawuneeche Visitor Center

Grand Lake

Lake Nanita

Chiefs Head 13,579 ft.

Longs Peak 14,255 ft.

Longs Peak

Meeker Park

(34)

Grand Lake

Shadow Mountain Lake

Mt. Alice 13,310 ft.

Meeker Ridge

ROOSEVELT NATIONAL FOREST

Paradise Park

Isolation Peak 13,118 ft.

Wild Basin Ranger Station

Lake Granby

Mt. Adams 12,121 ft.

Copeland Mtn. 13,176 ft.

Allenspark

(7)

Granby Dam

Continental

Peaceful Valley

Monarch Lake

Indian Peaks Wilderness

Divide

Ward

Recreation Area

ARAPAHO NATIONAL FOREST

(72)

| 0 | 3 mi |
| 0 | 3 km |

N

GETTING AROUND   In summer, a free national-park **shuttle bus** runs from the Glacier Basin parking area to Bear Lake, with departures every 10 to 20 minutes.

FAST FACTS   The hospital, **Estes Park Medical Center,** with a 24-hour emergency room, is at 555 Prospect Ave. (© **970/586-2317**).

WHERE TO STAY

For help finding accommodations, call the **Estes Park Chamber Resort Association Lodging Referral Service** (© **800/443-7837** or 970/586-4431).

National chains here include the **Comfort Inn,** 1450 Big Thompson Ave. (© **800/228-5150** or 970/586-2358); and the **Holiday Inn,** U.S. 36 and Colo. 7 (© **800/803-7837** or 970/586-2332).

In addition to the listings below, the pricey **Aspen Lodge at Estes Park,** 6120 Colo. 7, Longs Peak Route (© **970/586-8133;** or from outside Colorado, 800/ 332-6867 for reservations only; www.aspenlodge.com), is one of Colorado's top dude ranches, offering a host of activities and magnificent views.

Both tent and RV sites are available at **Estes Park KOA,** 2051 Big Thompson Ave. (© **800/562-1887** or 970/586-2888), and at the **National Park Resort,** 3501 Fall River Rd. (© **970/586-4563**).

Big Thompson Timberlane Lodge   A great choice for families, the lodge's wide range of units accommodate from 1 person to 10 people. There are motel suites, cabins, cottages, and log homes; all units have refrigerators and either a stove or microwave. Couples traveling alone will especially like the small, historic cabins, built in the early 1900s. Most of the units have a rustic feel, although the motel suites are pretty much what you'd expect in a motel. About half the units have showers only (no tubs), and some have private hot tubs and/or barbecue grills. There's a grassy playground, a separate children's wading pool, an "adults only" outdoor hot tub, picnic areas with barbecue grills, a self-serve laundry, and a stocked trout stream. 740 Moraine Ave. (P.O. Box 387), Estes Park, CO 80517. © 800/898-4373 or 970/586-3137. Fax 970/586-3719. www.bigthompsontimber lanelodge.com. 58 units. Summer $99–$335 per unit; off-season rates 20%–40% lower. AE, DISC, MC, V. **Amenities:** 2 outdoor heated pools.

Boulder Brook on Fall River   It would be hard to find a more beautiful setting than this all-suite property. Surrounded by tall pines, all of the suites face the Fall River, and feature private riverfront decks, full or partial kitchens, and VCRs. Spa suites are especially luxurious, with two-person spas, fireplaces, king-size beds, and sitting rooms with cathedral ceilings. 1900 Fall River Rd., Estes Park, CO 80517. © 800/238-0910 or 970/586-0910. Fax 970/586-8067. www.estes-park.com/boulder brook. 16 units. $89–$199 double; $129–$229 spa suite. AE, DISC, MC, V.

Estes Park Center/YMCA of the Rockies   This extremely popular family resort is an ideal place to get away from it all. Lodge units are basic but perfectly adequate, and many were completely renovated in 1998. Our choice, however, is the spacious mountain cabins, sprinkled among the trees in a national-park–like setting. Cabins are equipped with two to four bedrooms (accommodating up to 10) and complete kitchens; some have fireplaces. The center offers hiking, horseback riding, fishing, biking (rentals available), and cross-country skiing. Cabins have phones but lodge rooms do not. 2515 Tunnel Rd., Estes Park, CO 80511-2550. © 970/586-3341. 510 lodge units, 450 with bathroom, 205 cabins. Lodge rooms summer $52–$120 double, winter $41–$92 double; cabins year-round $60–$239. YMCA membership required (available at a nominal charge). No credit cards. **Amenities:** Pool (indoor heated); 3 tennis courts; pets permitted in cabins.

Romantic RiverSong Inn   Leave the kids at home when you head for a romantic escape at this delightful and elegant bed-and-breakfast inn on the banks of the Big Thompson River. Built in 1920, the mansion's rooms all have fireplaces and are decorated with a mix of antique and modern country furniture. Several have jetted tubs for two. Those so inclined can be married by innkeeper Gary Mansfield, a mail-order minister, at the inn or on a snowshoe trek into the national park. The property is entirely nonsmoking. 1765 Lower Broadview Rd. (P.O. Box 1910), Estes Park, CO 80517. ℂ 970/586-4666. www.romanticriversong.com. 9 units. $150–$275. Rates include full breakfast. MC, V. Not suitable for small children.

ROCKY MOUNTAIN NATIONAL PARK

One of the most beautiful spots in America, Rocky Mountain National Park should be at the top of your "must do" list for a trip to Colorado. The scenery is stupendous: snow-covered peaks—17 mountains above 13,000 feet—stand over lush valleys and shimmering Alpine lakes in the 415 square miles (265,727 acres) that comprise the park.

In relatively low areas, from about 7,500 to 9,000 feet, a lush forest of ponderosa pine and juniper cloaks the sunny southern slopes, with Douglas fir on the cooler northern slopes. Thirstier blue spruce and lodgepole pine cling to streamsides, with occasional groves of aspen. Elk and mule deer thrive. On higher slopes, a subalpine ecosystem exists, dominated by forests of Engelmann spruce and subalpine fir, but interspersed with wide meadows alive with wildflowers during spring and summer. This is also home to bighorn sheep, which have become unofficial symbols of the park. Above 11,500 feet, the trees become increasingly gnarled and stunted, until they disappear altogether and Alpine tundra predominates.

Trail Ridge Road, the park's primary east-west roadway, is one of America's great Alpine highways. It cuts west through the middle of the park from Estes Park, then south down its western boundary to Grand Lake. Climbing to 12,183 feet near Fall River Pass, it's the highest continuous paved highway in the United States. The road is usually open from sometime in May into October, depending on the snowfall. The 48-mile scenic drive from Estes Park to Grand Lake takes about 3 hours, allowing for stops at numerous scenic outlooks. Exhibits at the Alpine Visitor Center (open summer, daily 9–5pm) at Fall River Pass explain life on the Alpine tundra.

Fall River Road, the original park road, leads to Fall River Pass from Estes Park via Horseshoe Park Junction. West of the Endovalley picnic area, the road is one-way uphill, and closed to trailers and motor homes. As you negotiate its gravelly switchbacks, you get a clear idea of what early auto travel was like in the West. This road, too, is closed in winter.

One of the few paved roads in the Rockies that leads into a high mountain basin is **Bear Lake Road;** it is kept open year-round, with occasional half-day closings to clear snow. Numerous trails converge at Bear Lake, southwest of the park headquarters/visitor center, via Moraine Park.

PARK ESSENTIALS

ENTRY POINTS   Entry into the park is from either the east (through Estes Park) or the west (through Grand Lake). The two sides are connected by the

Trail Ridge Road. The **Beaver Meadows Entrance,** west of Estes Park via U.S. 36, leads to the Beaver Meadows Visitor Center and park headquarters, and is the most direct route to Trail Ridge Road. U.S. 34 west from Estes Park takes you to the Fall River Visitor Center (just outside the park) and the **Fall River Entrance,** which is north of the Beaver Meadows Entrance, and provides access to Old Fall River Road or Trail Ridge Road. Those entering the park from the west side should take U.S. 40 to Granby and then follow U.S. 34 north to the **Grand Lake Entrance.**

Park admission for up to 7 days is $15 per vehicle, $5 per person for bicyclists, motorcyclists, and pedestrians.

VISITOR CENTERS & INFORMATION   The **Beaver Meadows Visitor Center,** U.S. 36 on the park's east side (© **970/586-1206**), has interpretive exhibits including a relief model of the park, an audiovisual program, and a wide choice of books and maps for sale. In summer, this center is open daily from 8am to 9pm, in winter daily from 8am to 5pm. Just outside the park, on U.S. 34 on the park's east side, the **Fall River Visitor Center** (© **970/586-1206**) is staffed by park rangers and volunteers from the nonprofit Rocky Mountain Nature Association. It contains exhibits on park wildlife, a children's activity room, an information desk, and a bookstore, and is open daily from 9am to 6pm.

Near the park's west side entrance is the **Kawuneeche Visitor Center** (© **970/627-3471**), open in summer daily from 8am to 6pm, in winter daily from 8am to 5pm. Located high in the mountains (11,796 ft. above sea level) is the **Alpine Visitor Center,** at Fall River Pass, open in summer only, daily from 9am to 5pm; exhibits here explain life on the Alpine tundra. Visitor facilities are also available at the Moraine Park Museum on Bear Lake Road, open from mid-June to mid-September daily from 9am to 5pm.

For more information, contact **Rocky Mountain National Park,** 1000 U.S. 36, Estes Park, CO 80517-8397 (© **970/586-1206;** www.nps.gov/romo). You can also get information from the **Rocky Mountain Nature Association** (© **800/816-7662** or 970/586-0108; www.rmna.org), which sells a variety of maps, books, and videos.

WHEN TO GO   Because large portions of the park are closed half the year due to snowfall, practically everyone visits in spring and summer. The busiest period is from mid-June to mid-August (during school vacations). To avoid the largest crowds, try to visit just before or just after that period. For those who don't mind chilly evenings, late September and early October are less crowded and can be beautiful, although there's always the chance of an early winter storm. Regardless of when you visit, the absolute best way to avoid crowds is by putting on a backpack or climbing onto a horse. Rocky Mountain has almost 350 miles of trails leading into all corners of the park.

SPORTS & OUTDOOR PURSUITS IN & AROUND THE PARK

HIKING & BACKPACKING   Park bookstores sell topographic maps and guidebooks, and rangers can direct you to lesser-used trails.

One particularly easy park hike is the **Alberta Falls Trail** from the Glacier Gorge Parking Area (.6 mile one-way), which rises in elevation only 160 feet as it follows Glacier Creek to pretty Alberta Falls.

A slightly more difficult option is the **Bierstadt Lake Trail,** accessible from the north side of Bear Lake Road about 6.4 miles from Beaver Meadows. This

1.4-mile (one-way) trail climbs 566 feet through an aspen forest to Bierstadt Lake, where you'll find excellent views of Longs Peak.

Starting at Bear Lake, the trail up to **Emerald Lake** offers spectacular scenery en route, past Nymph and Dream lakes. The half-mile hike to Nymph Lake is easy, climbing 225 feet; from there the trail is rated moderate to Dream Lake (another .6 mile) and then on to Emerald Lake (another .7 mile), which is 605 feet higher than the starting point at Bear Lake. Another moderate hike is the relatively uncrowded **Ouzel Falls Trail,** which leaves from Wild Basin Ranger Station and climbs about 950 feet to a picture-perfect waterfall. The distance one-way is 2.7 miles.

Among our favorite moderate hikes here is the **Mills Lake Trail,** a 2½-mile (one-way) hike, with a rise in elevation of about 700 feet. Starting from Glacier Gorge Junction, the trail goes up to a picturesque mountain lake, nestled in a valley among towering mountain peaks. This lake is an excellent spot for photographing dramatic Longs Peak, especially in late afternoon or early evening, and it's the perfect place for a picnic.

HORSEBACK RIDING Many of the national park's trails are open to horseback riders, and a number of outfitters provide guided rides, both within and outside the park, ranging from 1 hour (about $20) to all day (about $80), plus breakfast and dinner rides and multi-day pack trips. Recommended companies include **Sombrero Ranch Stables,** opposite the Lake Estes dam at 1895 Big Thompson Hwy. (U.S. 34) (© **970/586-4577;** www.sombrero.com). **Hi Country Stables** operates two stables inside the park: **Glacier Creek Stables** (© **970/586-3244**) and **Moraine Park Stables** (© **970/586-2327**).

WILDLIFE VIEWING & BIRD-WATCHING Rocky Mountain National Park is a premier wildlife-viewing area; fall, winter, and spring are the best times, but summer's pretty good, too. Large herds of elk and bighorn sheep can often be seen in the meadows and on mountainsides. In addition, you might spot mule deer, beavers, coyotes, and river otters. Watch for moose among the willows on the west side of the park. In the forests are lots of songbirds and small mammals; particularly plentiful are gray and Steller's jays, Clark's nutcrackers, chipmunks, and golden-mantled ground squirrels. There's a good chance of seeing bighorn sheep, marmots, pikas, and ptarmigan along Trail Ridge Road.

WHERE TO CAMP

The park has five campgrounds with a total of almost 600 sites. About half are at **Moraine Park;** about 150 are at **Glacier Basin.** Moraine Park, **Timber Creek** (100 sites), and **Longs Peak** (26 tent sites) are open year-round; Glacier Basin and **Aspenglen** (54 sites) are seasonal. Camping is limited to 3 days at Longs Peak and 7 days at other campgrounds. Arrive early in summer if you hope to snare one of these first-come, first-served campsites. Moraine Park and Glacier Basin require reservations from Memorial Day to early September (© **800/365-2267**). Campsites cost $18 per night during the summer, $10 in the off season when water is shut off. No showers or RV hookups are available.

4 More Highlights of the Northern Colorado Rockies

The northern Rockies begin just outside Denver and extend on either side of the meandering Continental Divide down saw-toothed ridgelines, through precipitous river canyons, and across broad Alpine plains. Here, snowfall is measured in feet, not inches. And when spring's sun finally melts away the walls of white, a whole new world opens up amid the brilliantly colored Alpine wildflowers. Skis are replaced by mountain bikes, and summer festivals fill the mountains with music.

STEAMBOAT SPRINGS

In this resort town, ranchers still go about their business in cowboy boots and Stetsons, seemingly unaware of the fashion statement they're making to city-slicker visitors.

ESSENTIALS

GETTING THERE   By Plane   The **Yampa Valley Regional Airport,** 22 miles west of Steamboat Springs (© 970/276-3669), is served by several major airlines, with the most flights in winter. Car rentals are available at the airport from Avis and Hertz.

By Car   The most direct route to Steamboat Springs from Denver is via I-70 west 68 miles to Silverthorne, Colo. 9 north 38 miles to Kremmling, and U.S. 40 west 52 miles to Steamboat.

VISITOR INFORMATION   The **Steamboat Springs Chamber Resort Association,** 1255 S. Lincoln Ave. (P.O. Box 774408), Steamboat Springs, CO 80477 (© 970/879-0880; www.steamboatchamber.com), operates a visitor center.

SPECIAL EVENTS & FESTIVALS   The first full week in February brings the **Steamboat Springs Winter Carnival** (© 970/879-0880), with races, jumping, broomball, and skijoring street events. From mid-June through August, you'll hear top-notch classical, jazz, country, and pop musicians perform at the **Strings in the Mountains Festival of Music** (© 970/879-5056; www.stringsinthemountains.org).

SKIING & OTHER WINTER ACTIVITIES

When devoted skiers describe Steamboat, they practically invent adjectives to describe its incredibly light powder. Five peaks make up the ski area (Mounts Werner, Christie, Storm, Sunshine, and Thunderhead) and provide slopes for skiers of all ability levels. The 3,668-foot vertical drop here is among the highest in Colorado. There are 142 trails, served by 20 lifts, and it's also a great mountain for snowboarders. For further information, contact **Steamboat Ski & Resort Corporation** (© 800/922-2722 or 970/879-6111; www.steamboat-ski.com).

Seasoned cross-country skiers swear by the **Steamboat Ski Touring Center** at the Sheraton Steamboat Resort, Clubhouse Road (© 970/879-8180), with some 18½ miles of groomed cross-country trails near the foot of the mountain.

One of the best snowmobile trails in the Rockies, offering spectacular scenery, is the **Continental Divide Trail,** which runs over 50 miles from Buffalo Pass north of Steamboat to Gore Pass, west of Kremmling. You can choose from a variety of guided tours from **High Mountain Snowmobile Tours** (© 970/879-9073; www.steamboatsnowmobile.com).

WARM-WEATHER & YEAR-ROUND ACTIVITIES

Most outdoor recreation is enjoyed in 1.1-million-acre Routt National Forest, which virtually surrounds Steamboat Springs. For trail maps and information, contact **Medicine Bow–Routt National Forest,** Hahns Peak/Bears Ears Ranger District Office, 925 Weiss Dr. (© 970/879-1870; www.fs.fed.us/r2).

The Northern Colorado Rockies

Columbine

To Laramie

Cowdrey

ROUTT NATIONAL FOREST

Glendevey

Red Feather Lakes

Steamboat Lake

Clark

Mount Zirkel Wilderness Area

Walden

NORTH PARK

ROOSEVELT NATIONAL FOREST

Rustic

Beaver Creek

14

14

14

125

Steamboat Springs

Milner

Coalmont

Gould

Rand

Estes Park

34

Rocky Mountain National Park

Continental Divide

131

Rabbit Ears Pass

Oak Creek

ROUTT NAT'L FOREST

40

ARAPAHO NAT'L FOREST

Lake Granby

Grand Lake

Allens-park

Phippsburg

Yampa

ARAPAHO NAT'L FOREST

Granby

ROOSEVELT NATIONAL FOREST

Toponas

Flat Tops Wilderness Area

WHITE RIVER NAT'L FOREST

Kremmling

131

MIDDLE PARK

Arapaho Nat'l Recreation Area

ARAPAHO NAT'L FOREST

72

McCoy

Radium

9

Winter Park

Nederland

Burns

State Bridge

40

Blackhawk

131

Berthoud Pass

Central City

6   70

Wolcott

Eisenhower Memorial Tunnel

Georgetown

70

Idaho Springs

Eagle

Edwards

Vail

Silverthorne

Dillon

To Denver

Avon

Minturn

Vail Pass

Frisco

Dillon Res.

To Glenwood Springs

WHITE RIVER NAT'L FOREST

Red Cliff

Copper Mountain

Breckenridge

Basalt

Snowmass

Divide

24

Grant

Woody Creek

SAWATCH RANGE

91

9

Alma

PIKE NAT'L FOREST

Aspen

Continental

Turquoise Lake

Leadville

Fairplay

SOUTH PARK

82

Independence Pass

285

9

24

FRONT RANGE

GORE RANGE

Area of Detail

25   76

Boulder

70

Denver   70

COLORADO

Colorado Springs

25

0   20 mi
0   20 km

🎿 Ski area

⌇ Continental Divide

ⓒ Hitting Colorado's Slopes

For current ski conditions and general information, contact **Colorado Ski Country USA** (ⓒ **303/837-0793;** www.skicolorado.org). The useful **www.skinet.com** provides links to several skiing magazines.

The slopes are most crowded over Christmas and New Year's, and on the Martin Luther King and Presidents' Day holiday weekends, when lodging rates are at their highest. Those who can ski midweek will find more elbow room on the slopes, and the beginning and end of the season are the best times to avoid crowds—assuming snow conditions are good.

Expect to spend $50 to $60 a day for an adult lift ticket at a Colorado ski resort, but this can vary from less than $40 at the smaller ski areas to more than $60 at the glitzier resorts such as Aspen. Kids and seniors usually get hefty discounts, and seniors over 70 and very young kids often ski free. Always ask about multi-day passes, which can save you serious money, as well as multi-resort passes. Most skiers buy packages that often include lift tickets for a certain number of days, but might also include rental equipment, lessons, lodging and/or meals, transportation, and lift tickets for other nearby ski areas.

The Steamboat Springs Chamber Resort Association produces a **Trails Map,** available at the information center on Lincoln Avenue, showing which trails are open to what sport: biking, horseback riding, hiking, 4WDs, or ATVs. On the reverse side of the map are descriptions of several trails in the area.

BIKING & MOUNTAIN BIKING   The 5-mile, dual-surface **Yampa River Trail** connects downtown Steamboat Springs with Steamboat Village, and links area parks and national forest trails. The **Mount Werner Trail** links the river to the ski area, which has numerous slopes open to mountain bikers in summer. **Spring Creek Trail** climbs from Yampa River Park into Routt National Forest. Touring enthusiasts can try their road bikes on the 110-mile loop over Rabbit Ears and Gore passes, rated one of the 10 most scenic rides in America by *Bicycling* magazine.

Stop at **Sore Saddle Cyclery,** 1136 Yampa St. (ⓒ **970/879-1675;** www.sore saddle.com), for information on the best local trails (maps are on display), accessories, repairs, and rentals ($18 per day and up).

HOT SPRINGS   More than 150 mineral springs are located in and around the Steamboat Springs area. Heart Spring is part of the **Steamboat Springs Health & Recreation complex,** 136 Lincoln Ave. (ⓒ **970/879-1828**), in downtown Steamboat Springs. In addition to the man-made pools into which the spring's waters flow, there's a lap pool, water slide, spa, whirlpool, fitness center, and massage therapy.

The **Hot Springs at Strawberry Park,** 44200 County Rd. 36 (ⓒ **970/879-0342;** www.strawberryhotsprings.com), are 7 miles north of downtown (from Seventh St., follow the signs). It's a wonderful experience to spend a moonlit evening in a sandy-bottomed, rock-lined soaking pool, kept between 102° and 104°F (39° and 40°C).

MORE TO SEE & DO

You can learn about Steamboat's history at **Tread of Pioneers Museum,** 800 Oak St. (© **970/879-2214**), a beautifully restored Victorian home that features exhibits on pioneer ranch life, the Utes, and 100 years of skiing history.

Just 4 miles from downtown in Routt National Forest is **Fish Creek Falls** (© **970/879-1870**). A footpath leads to a historic bridge at the base of this breathtaking 283-foot waterfall. There's also a special overlook with a short ⅛-mile trail and ramp designed for those with disabilities, as well as a picnic area and hiking trails. Turn right off Lincoln Avenue onto Third Street, go 1 block, and turn right again onto Fish Creek Falls Road.

Lincoln Avenue, between Fifth and Ninth streets, is where most of the more interesting shops and galleries are located.

WHERE TO STAY

Steamboat Central Reservations (© **800/922-2722** or 970/879-0740; fax 970/879-4757) can book your lodging and make virtually all your travel arrangements. Be sure to ask about special packages and programs. **Steamboat Premier Properties** (© **866/634-9618** or 970/879-8811; fax 970/879-8485; www.steamboat-premier.com) and **Steamboat Resorts** (© **800/525-5502** or 970/879-8000; fax 970/879-8060; www.steamboatresorts.com) rent everything from ski-in/ski-out condos and town houses to lodge rooms.

Our favorite lodging choices include the impressive **Sheraton Steamboat Resort,** 2200 Village Inn Court (© **800/848-8878** or 970/879-2220; www. steamboat-sheraton.com), offering a host of facilities; **Steamboat Bed & Breakfast,** 442 Pine St. (© **877/335-4321** or 970/879-5724; www.steamboat b-b.com); and the relatively affordable **Rabbit Ears Motel,** 201 Lincoln Ave. (© **800/828-7702** or 970/879-1150; www.rabbitearsmotel.com).

BRECKENRIDGE & SUMMIT COUNTY

Summit County is a major recreational sports center, with skiing in winter and fishing, hiking, and mountain biking in summer. Breckenridge is a good place to base yourself, as the entire Victorian core of this 19th-century mining town has been carefully preserved, with colorfully painted shops and restaurants occupying the old buildings, most dating from the 1880s and 1890s.

ESSENTIALS

GETTING THERE   By Plane   You can fly into Denver International or Colorado Springs and continue to Breckenridge, Frisco, Keystone, and/or Copper Mountain via rental car or shuttle. **Resort Express** (© **800/334-7433** or 970/468-7600) offers shuttles.

By Car   I-70 runs through the middle of Summit County. For Keystone, exit on U.S. 6 at Dillon; the resort is 6 miles east of the interchange. For Breckenridge, exit on Colo. 9 at Frisco and head south 9 miles to the resort. Copper Mountain is right on I-70 at the Colo. 91 interchange.

VISITOR INFORMATION   The **Breckenridge Resort Chamber** has an information center at 309 N. Main St. and administrative offices at P.O. Box 1909, Breckenridge, CO 80424 (© **800/221-1091** or 970/453-6018; www. gobreck.com). For information about activities in Breckenridge, contact the **Activity Center,** 137 S. Main St., in Blue River Plaza (© **877/864-0868** or 970/453-5579).

SPECIAL EVENTS & FESTIVALS   The **Breckenridge Music Festival** (© **970/453-9142;** www.breckenridgemusicfestival.net) includes more than 50 classical and non-classical music performances, with concerts from mid-June through late August. The **Breckenridge Festival of Film** (© 970/453-6200; http://breckfilmfest.com), held in mid-September, attracts Hollywood directors and actors to town to discuss some two dozen films in all genres.

SKIING & OTHER WINTER ACTIVITIES

Arapahoe Basin, 28194 U.S. 6, between Keystone and Loveland Pass (© 888/ARAPAHOE or 970/468-0718; www.arapahoebasin.com), is one of Colorado's oldest ski areas. Most of its 490 acres are intermediate and expert terrain, and it's often the last Colorado ski area to close for the season—sometimes not until early July.

Spread across four large mountains on the west side of the town of Breckenridge, **Breckenridge** ranks third in size among Colorado's ski resorts. Once known for its wealth of open, groomed beginner and intermediate slopes, Breckenridge in recent years has expanded its acreage for expert skiers as well. All told, the resort has 139 trails served by 25 lifts. Contact **Breckenridge Ski Resort** (© 970/453-5000; www.breckenridge.snow.com).

Other notable ski areas in Summit County include **Copper Mountain** (© 800/458-8386 or 970/968-2882; www.ski-copper.com); **Keystone,** a superb mountain for intermediate skiers, but also one of the best spots for night skiing in America (© 877/625-1556 or 970/496-2316; www.keystone.snow. com); and **Loveland Ski Area** (© 800/736-3754 or 303/571-5580; www.ski loveland.com).

Frisco Nordic Center, on Colo. 9 south of Frisco (© 970/668-0866), sits on the shores of Dillon Reservoir. Its trail network includes 22 miles of set tracks and groomed skating lanes, and access to backcountry trails. From the Frisco Nordic Center you can ski to the **Breckenridge Nordic Ski Center,** on Willow Lane near the foot of Peak 8 (© 970/453-6855), with its own series of 17.4 miles of groomed trails. The **Gold Run Nordic Center** (© 970/547-7889), at Breckenridge Golf Club, offers 9 miles of groomed trails.

Snowboarding is permitted at all local resorts.

WARM-WEATHER & YEAR-ROUND ACTIVITIES

Two national forests—**Arapahoe** and **White River**—overlap the boundaries of Summit County. These recreational playgrounds offer opportunities not only for downhill and cross-country skiing and snowmobiling in winter, but also for hiking and backpacking, horseback riding, boating, fishing, hunting, and bicycling in summer.

The **U.S. Forest Service's Dillon Ranger District,** in the town of Silverthorne at 680 Blue River Pkwy., just north of I-70's Exit 205 (© 970/468-5400; www.fs.fed.us/r2), has unusually good information on outdoor recreation, including maps and guides. You can also get information on a wide variety of outdoor activities from the **Breckenridge Activity Center,** 137 S. Main St., in Blue River Plaza (© 970/453-5579).

BIKING   There are more than 40 miles of paved bicycle paths in the county, including a path from Breckenridge (with a spur from Keystone) to Frisco and Copper Mountain, continuing across Vail Pass to Vail. This spectacularly beautiful two-lane path is off-limits to motorized vehicles of any kind.

BOATING   Dillon Reservoir, a beautiful mountain lake along I-70 between Dillon and Frisco, is the place to go. At 9,017 feet in elevation, it claims to have America's highest altitude yacht club and holds colorful regattas most summer weekends. No swimming. The full-service **Dillon Marina,** 150 Marina Dr. ((C) **970/468-5100;** www.dillonmarina.com), is open the last weekend of May to the last weekend of October.

FISHING   Major fishing rivers within an hour of Breckenridge include the South Platte, Arkansas, Eagle, Colorado, and Blue rivers, and for lake fishing, try Dillon Reservoir and Spinney Mountain Reservoir. The Blue River, from Lake Dillon Dam to its confluence with the Colorado River at Kremmling, is rated a gold-medal fishing stream. For tips on where they're biting, as well as supplies, fishing licenses, and all the rest, stop at **Mountain Angler,** 311 S. Main St. in the Main Street Mall ((C) **800/453-4669** or 970/453-4665; www.mountain angler.com).

MOUNTAIN BIKING   Numerous trails beckon mountain bikers as they wind through the mountains, often following 19th-century mining roads and burro trails and ending at ghost towns. Energetic fat-tire fans can try the **Devil's Triangle,** a difficult 80-mile loop that begins and ends in Frisco after climbing four mountain passes (including 11,318-ft. Fremont Pass). Check with the U.S. Forest Service or Breckenridge Activity Center for directions and tips on other trails; for mountain bikers who prefer not to work so hard, check with the Breckenridge Activity Center on times and costs for taking your bike up the mountain on the Breckenridge chairlift.

WHERE TO STAY

Local reservation services include **Breckenridge Central Reservations** ((C) **877/ 593-5260**). Throughout the county, condominiums abound, including the excellent **East West Resorts at Breckenridge,** 505 S. Main St. ((C) **800/ 525-2258** or 970/453-2222; www.eastwestresorts.com). Our favorite B&B is **Allaire Timbers Inn Bed & Breakfast,** 9511 Colo. 9, Breckenridge ((C) **800/ 624-4904** or 970/453-7530; www.allairetimbers.com). There's also the **Holiday Inn–Summit County,** I-70 Exit 203 in Frisco ((C) **888/632-5465** or 970/668-5000).

VAIL

Vail is the big one. In fact, it's hard to imagine a more celebrated spot to schuss. Off the slopes, Vail is an incredibly compact Tyrolean village, frequented by almost as many Europeans as Americans, a situation which lends its restaurants, lodgings, and trendy shops a more cosmopolitan feel than other Colorado resorts. But the mountain's size and its exciting trails are still what draw the faithful.

ESSENTIALS

GETTING THERE   By Plane   Visitors can fly into **Denver International Airport** or directly into **Vail/Eagle County Regional Airport,** 35 miles west of Vail between I-70 Exits 140 and 147, on major national carriers. **Colorado Mountain Express** ((C) **800/525-6363** or 970/926-7230) offers shuttles from Denver ($62 one-way) and Vail/Eagle ($44 one-way).

By Car   Vail is right on the I-70 corridor, so it's easy to find. Just take Exit 176, whether you're coming from the east (Denver) or the west (Grand Junction). A more direct route from the south may be U.S. 24 through Leadville; this Tennessee Pass road joins I-70 5 miles west of Vail.

VISITOR INFORMATION   For information or reservations in the Vail Valley, contact the **Vail Valley Chamber and Tourism Bureau,** 100 E. Meadow Dr.,

Vail, CO 81657 (© **800/525-3875** or 970/476-1000; www.visitvailvalley.
com); or **Vail Resorts, Inc.,** P.O. Box 7, Vail, CO 81658 (© **800/525-2257** or
970/476-5601; www. snow.com). Information centers are at the parking structures in Vail and Lionshead on South Frontage Road.

GETTING AROUND   Vail is one of only a few Colorado communities where
you really don't need a car. The Town of Vail runs a free **shuttle-bus** service daily
from 7am to 2am.

SPECIAL EVENTS & FESTIVALS   The summer season's big cultural event
is the **Bravo! Vail Valley Music Festival** (© **970/827-5700;** www.vailmusic-
festival.org), from late June to early August, featuring everything from classical
orchestra and chamber music to vocal and pops, from baroque to modern jazz.

The **Vail International Dance Festival** features both classes and performances. The Bolshoi Ballet Academy at Vail is the satellite school of the famed
Bolshoi of Moscow, and presents a series of performances each summer. For
information, contact the **Vail Valley Foundation** (© **888/883-8245** or 970/
949-1999; www.vvf.com).

SKIING & OTHER WINTER ACTIVITIES

In *Skiing America,* Charles Leocha writes, "Vail comes closest of any resort in
America to epitomizing what many skiers would call perfection." You can arrive
at the base village, unload and park your car, and not have to drive again until
it's time to go. You'll find all the shops, restaurants, and nightlife you could want
within a short walk of your hotel or condominium.

Ski area boundaries stretch 7 miles from east to west along the ridgetop, from
Outer Mongolia to Game Creek Bowl, and the skiable terrain is measured at
5,289 acres. Virtually every lift on the front (north-facing) side of the mountain
has runs for every level of skier, with a predominance of novice and intermediate terrain. The world-famous Back Bowls are decidedly not for beginners, and
there are few options for intermediates. All told, there are 193 conventional
trails served by 33 lifts. Vail also has a highly respected children's program. For
further information, contact **Vail Resorts, Inc.** (© **800/404-3535** or 970/476-
5601; www.vail.snow.com).

Vail Resorts, Inc., also owns nearby **Beaver Creek Resort** (© **800/404-3535**
or 970/949-5750; www.beavercreek.snow.com), an outstanding resort in its own
right, with a more secluded atmosphere. Located in a valley 1½ miles off the
I-70 corridor, Beaver Creek combines European château-style elegance in its
base village with expansive slopes for novice and intermediate skiers. The Grouse
Mountain Express lift reaches expert terrain. Currently, 14 lifts serve 146 trails.
Snowboarding is permitted, and there is a snowboarding park with a half-pipe
located off the Moonshine Trail. There are seven mountain restaurants, including the highly praised **Beano's Cabin.**

Paragon Guides (© **877/926-5299** or 970/926-5299; www.paragonguides.
com) is one of the country's premier winter guide services, offering backcountry
ski trips on the Tenth Mountain Trail and Hut System between Vail and Aspen.
A variety of trips is available, lasting from 3 to 6 days and designed for all ability levels. Costs start at $990 per person for the 3-day trips and $1,860 for the
6-day trips.

Cross-country skiers won't feel left out here, with trails at both resorts as well
as a system of trails through the surrounding mountains. **Vail's Nordic Center**
(© **970/476-8366**) has 20 miles of trails, and offers guided tours, lessons, and

snowshoeing. The **Beaver Creek Nordic Center** (© 970/949-5750), on its golf course, has a 21 mile mountaintop track system with a skating lane in 9,840-foot McCoy Park. Most of the high-altitude terrain here is intermediate. For general information on backcountry trails, contact the **Holy Cross Ranger District Office** (© 970/827-5715; www.fs.fed.us/r2). Of particular note is the system of trails known as the **Tenth Mountain Division Hut System** (© 970/925-5775; www.huts.org). Generally following the World War II training network of the Camp Hale militia, the trails cover 300 miles and link Vail with Leadville and Aspen. There are a number of overnight cabins ($22–$35 per person per night), and hikers and mountain bikers also use this trail.

WARM-WEATHER & OTHER YEAR-ROUND ACTIVITIES

The **Piney River Ranch,** about 12 miles north of Vail on Piney Lake (© 970/477-1171), offers a variety of outdoor activities, including horseback rides, hayrides, a fishing lake, and a cattle roundup (see "Fishing," below).

Contact **Vail Recreation District** (© 970/479-2279) for information on various activities, including the town's children's programs. You'll find many of the companies listed below at **www.visitvailvalley.com**.

FISHING The streams and mountain lakes surrounding Vail are rich with trout. Gore Creek through the town of Vail is a popular anglers' venue, especially toward evening from its banks along the Vail Golf Course. Also good are the Eagle River, joined by Gore Creek 5 miles downstream near Minturn; the Black Lakes near the summit of Vail Pass; and 60-acre Piney Lake. The **Piney River Ranch** (see above) rents canoes ($20 per hr.) and fishing gear ($15 per day). For fishing supplies (sales and rentals) plus lessons and guided trips, contact **Gore Creek Fly Fisherman, Inc.,** 183 E. Gore Creek Dr., Vail (© 800/369-3044 or 970/476-3296; www.gorecreekflyfisherman.com).

HIKING & BACKPACKING The surrounding White River National Forest has a plethora of trails leading to pristine lakes and spectacular panoramic views. The Holy Cross Wilderness Area, southwest of Vail, encompasses 14,005-foot Mount of the Holy Cross and is an awesome region with over 100 miles of trails. Eagle's Nest Wilderness Area lies to the north, in the impressive Gore Range. For information for these and other hiking areas, consult the **Holy Cross Ranger District Office** (see "Skiing & Other Winter Activities," above).

MOUNTAIN BIKING Summer visitors can take the Lionshead Gondola to Eagle's Nest on Vail Mountain, rent mountain bikes (and helmets) there, and cruise downhill to return their bikes at the base of the gondola.

There are many choices for avid bikers, both on backcountry trails and road tours. A popular trip is the 12½-mile Lost Lake Trail along Red Sandstone Road to Piney Lake. The 30-mile Vail Pass Bikeway goes to Frisco, with a climb from 8,460 feet up to 10,600 feet. Pick up a trail list (with map) at an information center.

Mountain bike rentals are available at a number of shops, including **Christy Sports** (© 970/476-2244).

WHERE TO STAY

Like most of Colorado's ski resorts, Vail has an abundance of condominiums, and it seems that more are built every day. The **Vail Valley Tourism and Convention Bureau** (see above) can provide additional lodging information or make reservations for you.

Our favorite luxury resort in the area is the very posh **Park Hyatt Regency Beaver Creek Resort and Spa,** 50 W. Thomas Place, Avon (© **800/55-HYATT** or 970/949-1234; www.beavercreek.hyatt.com), an architecturally unique hotel at the foot of the Beaver Creek lifts. Other deluxe options include the **Vail Cascade Resort,** 1300 Westhaven Dr., Vail (© **800/420-2424** or 970/476-7111; www.vailcascade.com); **The Charter at Beaver Creek,** 120 Offerson Rd., Beaver Creek (© **800/525-6660** or 970/949-6660; www.thecharter.com); and **The Lodge & Spa at Cordillera,** 2205 Cordillera Way, Edwards (© **800/877-3529** or 970/926-2200).

More affordable options include the condominium-style **Park Meadows Lodge,** 1472 Matterhorn Circle, Vail (© **888/245-8086** or 970/476-5598; www.parkmeadowslodge.com); and our favorite, the **Black Bear Inn of Vail,** 2405 Elliott Rd. in West Vail (© **970/476-1304;** www.vail.net/blackbear), a large log cabin with 12 units where a delightful breakfast is included in the rate.

ASPEN

Aspen's glitzy, celebrity-studded reputation precedes it. But if you dig beneath the hype, you may be surprised by what you find. Aspen is a real town with a fascinating history, some great old buildings, and spectacular mountain scenery. If you're a serious skier, you owe yourself at least a few days' worth of hitting the slopes (as if you need us to tell you that). However, if you've never strapped on boards, and you're thinking of visiting in summer, you'll be doubly pleased: Prices are significantly lower, and the crowds thin out. The surrounding forests teem with great trails for hiking, biking, and horseback riding, and Aspen becomes one of the best destinations in the country for summer festivals.

ESSENTIALS

GETTING THERE   By Plane   Visitors who want to fly directly into Aspen can arrange to land at **Pitkin County Airport/Sardy Field,** 3 miles northwest of Aspen on Colo. 82. United Express and America West fly here year-round; other airlines sometimes operate during ski season. **Colorado Mountain Express** (© **800/525-6363** or 970/926-7230) offers shuttle service from both Denver International Airport and Eagle County Airport near Vail.

By Car   Aspen is on Colo. 82, halfway between I-70 at Glenwood Springs (42 miles northwest) and U.S. 24 south of Leadville (44 miles east). In summer, it's a scenic 3½-hour drive from Denver: Leave I-70 West at Exit 195 (Copper Mountain); follow Colo. 91 south to Leadville, where you pick up U.S. 24; turn west on Colo. 82 through Twin Lakes and over 12,095-foot Independence Pass. In winter, the Independence Pass road is closed, so you'll have to take I-70 to Glenwood Springs, and head east on Colo. 82. In optimal winter driving conditions, it takes about 4 hours from Denver.

VISITOR INFORMATION   Contact the **Aspen Chamber Resort Association,** 425 Rio Grande Place, Aspen, CO 81611 (© **970/925-1940;** www.aspen chamber.org), or drop by the **Aspen Visitor Centers** at the Wheeler Opera House, Hyman Avenue and Mill Street, or Rio Grande Place.

SPECIAL EVENTS & FESTIVALS   The **Aspen Music Festival and School** (© **970/925-9042;** www.aspenmusicfestival.com) originated in 1949. Lasting 9 weeks from mid-June to late August, it offers more than 150 events, including classical music, opera, jazz, choral, and children's programs.

Jazz Aspen at Snowmass (© 970/920-4996; www.jazzaspen.com), takes place at Snowmass Village in late June, and again on Labor Day weekend. Legendary performers such as Lou Rawls, the Neville Brothers, the Zion Harmonizers, B. B. King, Patti LaBelle, and Ray Charles have appeared.

SKIING & OTHER WINTER ACTIVITIES

Skiing Aspen really means skiing the four Aspen area resorts—Aspen Mountain, Aspen Highlands, Buttermilk, and Snowmass. All are managed by Aspen Skiing Company, and one ticket gives access to all. For further information, contact **Aspen Skiing Company** (© 800/525-6200 or 970/925-1220; www.aspen snowmass.com).

Aspen Mountain is not for the timid. It is the American West's original hardcore ski mountain, with no fewer than 23 of its named runs double diamond— for experts only. There are mountain-long runs for intermediate as well as advanced skiers, but beginners should look to one of the other Aspen areas.

Aspen Highlands has the most balanced skiable terrain—novice to expert, with lots of intermediate slopes—in the Aspen area. Freestyle Friday, a tradition at Highlands for 25 years, boasts some of the best freestyle bump and big air competitors in the state of Colorado every Friday from early January to mid-April.

Buttermilk is a premier beginners' mountain. In fact, *Ski* magazine has rated it the best place in North America to learn how to ski. But there's plenty of intermediate and ample advanced terrain as well. Special features include the ski and snowboard school's Powder Pandas program for 3- to 6-year-olds; and a snowboard park with a 23% grade.

A huge, intermediate mountain with something for everyone, **Snowmass** has 33% more skiable acreage than the other three Aspen areas combined! It's actually four distinct self-contained areas, each with its own lift system and restaurant, and its terrain varies from easy beginner runs to the pitches of the Cirque and the Hanging Valley Wall, the steepest in the Aspen area. The renowned Snowmass ski school has hundreds of instructors, as well as Snow Cubs and Big Burn Bears programs for children 18 months and older. The area also caters to snowboarders with two half-pipes and three terrain parks.

The **Aspen/Snowmass Nordic Council** operates a free Nordic trail system with nearly 50 miles of groomed double track extending throughout the Aspen–Snowmass area and incorporating summer bicycle paths. Instruction and rentals are offered along the trail at the **Aspen Cross-Country Center,** Colo. 82 between Aspen and Buttermilk (© 970/544-9246), and the **Snowmass Touring Center,** Snowmass Village (© 970/923-3148), both of which provide daily condition reports and information on the entire trail system.

WARM-WEATHER & YEAR-ROUND ACTIVITIES

Among the best one-stop outfitters is **Blazing Adventures,** Snowmass Village (© 800/282-7238 or 970/923-4544; www.blazingadventures.com), which offers river rafting, mountain biking, four-wheeling, and horseback riding.

Your best source for information on a wide variety of outdoor activities in the mountains around Aspen is the **White River National Forest,** 806 W. Hallam St. (© 970/925-3445; www.fs.fed.us/r2). Another good source of information and maps is **Ute Mountaineer,** 308 S. Mill St. (© 970/925-2849; www.ute mountaineer.com), which also sells and rents gear and clothing.

Photo Op

The two sheer, pyramidal peaks called **Maroon Bells,** on Maroon Creek Road 10 miles west of Aspen, are among the most photographed mountains in the Rockies. They're a beautiful scene any time, but especially in the fall, when their reflection in Maroon Lake is framed by the changing colors of the aspen leaves. For a small fee you can take a 30-minute narrated bus tour up Maroon Creek Valley (© **970/925-8484;** www.rfta.com).

FISHING   Perhaps the best trout fishing is in the Roaring Fork and Frying Pan rivers, both considered gold-medal streams. The Roaring Fork follows Colo. 82 through Aspen from Independence Pass; the Frying Pan starts near Tennessee Pass, northeast of Aspen, and joins the Roaring Fork at Basalt, 18 miles down the valley. Stop at **Aspen Sports,** with locations at 303 E. Durant Ave. (© **970/925-6332**) and Snowmass Center (© **970/923-3566**), for your fishing needs.

HORSEBACK RIDING   Several stables in the Aspen valley offer rides, and some outfitters even package gourmet meals and country-western serenades with their expeditions. Rates start at about $50 per hour, or $150 for a 4-hour trip. Inquire at **Blazing Adventures** (see above) or **T Lazy 7 Ranch,** 3129 Maroon Creek Rd. (© **888/875-6343** or 970/925-4614; www.tlazy7.com). The T Lazy 7 also offers lodging year-round (© **970/925-7254**), plus hayrides and fishing in summer, and snowmobiling, cross-country skiing, and sleigh rides in winter.

MOUNTAIN BIKING   There are hundreds of miles of trails through the White River National Forest that are perfect for mountain bikers, offering splendid views of the mountains, meadows, and valleys. Check with the forest service (see above) and local bike shops for tips on the best trails. Among full-service bicycle shops, with rentals, are **Hub of Aspen,** 315 E. Hyman Ave. (© **970/925-7970**), and **Aspen Velo Bike Shop,** 465 N. Mill St. (© **970/925-1495**).

RIVER RAFTING   **Colorado Riff Raft,** 520 E. Durant (© **800/759-3939** or 970/925-5405; www.riffraft.com), has been rafting the rapids since 1979. Trips are offered on the Roaring Fork, Arkansas, and Colorado rivers, with refreshments on half-day trips and lunch on full-day trips. Prices start at $69 for a half day and $82 for a full day.

WHERE TO STAY

It's essential to make reservations as early as possible. The easiest way to do so is to contact **Aspen Central Reservations** (© **888/649-5982;** www.aspen4u. com). Additional lodging is available in Snowmass, 12 miles west of Aspen; contact **Snowmass Central Reservations** (© **800/598-2004;** www.snowmass village.com).

Our favorite choice for luxury accommodations is the historic **Hotel Jerome,** 330 E. Main St. (© **800/331-7213** or 970/920-1000; www.hoteljerome.com), with its period antiques and lovingly preserved Eastlake Victorian architecture. Less expensive options include the **Snowflake Inn,** 221 E. Hyman Ave. (© **800/247-2069** or 970/925-3221; www.snowflakeinn.com); the **Limelite Lodge,** 228 E. Cooper Ave. (© **800/433-0832** or 970/925-3025; www. limelite.com); and the **Mountain Chalet,** 333 E. Durant Ave. (© **800/321-7813** or 970/925-7797).

5 Colorado Springs

Colorado Springs is a growing city of 358,000, with over half a million people in the metropolitan area. It's a conservative city, and in recent years, it has developed a reputation for right-wing political activism. To many visitors, however, it retains the feel and mood of a small Western town, and we're also pleased to report that Colorado Springs has some of the best lodging and dining in the state. Most tourists come to see the Air Force Academy, marvel at the scenery at Garden of the Gods and Pikes Peak, and explore the history of America's West.

ESSENTIALS

GETTING THERE   By Plane   Major airlines offer some 100 flights daily to **Colorado Springs Airport** (© 719/550-1972; www.flycos.com). Call © 719/550-1930 for information on ground transportation from the airport to local hotels and Denver.

By Car   The principal artery to and from the north (Denver: 70 miles) and south (Pueblo: 42 miles), I-25 bisects Colorado Springs. U.S. 24 is the principal east-west route through the city. Visitors arriving via I-70 from the east can take Exit 359 at Limon and follow U.S. 24 into the Springs. Arriving on I-70 from the west, the most direct route is Exit 201 at Frisco, then Colo. 9 through Breckenridge 53 miles to U.S. 24 (at Hartsel), and then east 66 miles to Colorado Springs. This route is mountainous, so check road conditions before setting out in winter.

VISITOR INFORMATION   The **Colorado Springs Convention and Visitors Bureau** is at 515 S. Cascade Ave., Colorado Springs, CO 80903 (© 800/888-4748 or 719/635-7506; www.coloradosprings-travel.com). The **Visitor Information Center,** in the same building, is open in summer daily from 8:30am to 5pm, in winter Monday through Friday from 8:30am to 5pm.

EXPLORING THE AREA

The **Colorado Springs Pioneers Museum,** 215 S. Tejon St. (© 719/385-5990), is an excellent place to begin your visit. Exhibits depict the community's rich history, including its beginning as a fashionable resort, the railroad and mining eras, and its growth and development into the 20th century.

One of the West's unique geological sites, the **Garden of the Gods,** 1805 N. 30th St. (I-25 Exit 146; © 719/634-6666), is a beautiful giant rock garden, composed of spectacular red sandstone formations sculpted by rain and wind over millions of years. Located where several life zones and ecosystems converge, the city-run park harbors a variety of plant and animal communities. Hiking maps for the 1,300-acre park are available at the visitor center.

Colorado Springs's pride and joy, the **United States Air Force Academy,** off I-25 Exit 156B (© 719/333-2025; www.usafa.af.mil), is open to the public daily. Soon after entering the grounds, you'll see an impressive outdoor B-52 bomber display. After another mile or so, look to your left to see the Parade Ground, where cadets can sometimes be spotted marching. Six miles from the entrance, signs mark the turnoff to the visitor center. Nearby is the Cadet Chapel, whose 17 gleaming aluminum spires soar 150 feet skyward. After leaving the visitor center, you will pass Falcon Stadium, and then Thunderbird Airmanship Overlook, where you might be lucky enough to see cadets parachuting, soaring, and practicing takeoffs and landings in U.S. Air Force Thunderbirds.

There is perhaps no view in Colorado to equal the 360-degree panorama from the 14,110-foot summit of Pikes Peak (but it's not for anyone with heart or breathing problems or a fear of heights). One way to get there is by taking a ride on the **Pikes Peak Cog Railway,** Manitou Springs (© **719/685-5401;** www.cograilway.com), after you've acclimated to Colorado's high elevations. The 9-mile route, with grades up to 25%, takes 75 minutes to reach the top of Pikes Peak, and the round-trip requires 3 hours and 10 minutes (including a 40-min. stopover at the top). Take a jacket or sweater—it can be cold and windy on top, even on warm summer days. The fare is $26 to $27 adults, $14 to $15 children under 12 (but those under 3 held on an adult's lap ride free). There are several departures daily, and reservations are required.

Another way to take in this spectacular view is to drive the **Pikes Peak Highway,** off U.S. 24 at Cascade. (Take I-25 Exit 141 west on U.S. 24 about 10 miles; © **800/318-9505** or 719/385-PEAK; www.pikespeakcolorado.com.) This 19-mile road (paved for 7 miles, graded gravel thereafter) starts at 7,400 feet, some 4 miles west of Manitou Springs, with numerous photo stops as you head up the mountain. There's a toll of $10 per person over age 16, or $35 per car.

The **United States Olympic Complex,** 1 Olympic Plaza, at the corner of Boulder Street (entrance) and Union Boulevard (© **888/659-8687** or 719/866-4618; www.usolympicteam.com), houses a sophisticated training center for numerous U.S. Olympic sports. Free guided tours, available daily, show off the center's state-of-the-art training facilities, where you may see the athletes sharpening their skills. There is also a gift shop that sells Olympic-logo merchandise.

The Welcome Center at the headquarters of **Focus on the Family,** 8685 Explorer Dr. (© **719/531-3328;** www.family.org), contains interactive displays describing the background and purpose of this Christian ministry, a theater that shows a 20-minute video, a Kids Korner with a play area, and a large bookstore. A free 45-minute guided tour of the campus describes the outreach of the ministry both in the United States and around the world.

WHERE TO STAY

In addition to the listings below, we recommend **The Cliff House at Pikes Peak,** 306 Cañon Ave., Manitou Springs (© **888/212-7000** or 719/685-3000; www.thecliffhouse.com), a beautifully restored historic hotel with an outstanding restaurant. Our favorite B&Bs are the **Old Town GuestHouse,** 115 S. 26th St. (© **888/375-4210** or 719/632-9194; www.oldtown-guesthouse.com); the **Holden House 1902 Bed & Breakfast Inn,** 1102 W. Pikes Peak Ave. (© **888/565-3980** or 719/471-3980; www.holdenhouse.com); and the **Two Sisters Inn,** 10 Otoe Place, Manitou Springs (© **800/2SISINN** or 719/685-9684). Bargain hunters should try the simple, well-maintained rooms at the **Travel Inn,** 512 S. Nevada Ave. (© **719/636-3986**).

The Broadmoor The best of the best, The Broadmoor is a sprawling, family-friendly resort complex of historic pink Italian Renaissance–style buildings, built in 1918 at the foot of Cheyenne Mountain. A $75-million renovation and restoration project was completed in early 2002, and the hotel's marble staircase, chandeliers, Italian tile, carved-marble fountain, and art collection are quite a spectacle. The spacious and luxurious rooms are beautifully decorated in European style, with Italian fabrics, rich wood, and original works of art. Service is impeccable. There's an array of bars and restaurants of every level of formality, including the outstanding Charles Court. Lake Circle, at Lake Ave. (P.O. Box 1439),

Colorado Springs, CO 80901. ℂ **800/634-7711** or 719/634-7711. Fax 719/577-5700. www. broadmoor.com. 700 units. Summer $355–$470 double, $450–$800 suite; winter $225–$345 double, $295–$635 suite. Winter packages available. AE, DC, DISC, MC, V. **Amenities:** Restaurants (8); pools (2 outdoor heated); golf courses (2 18-hole, 1 9-hole); tennis courts (9); spa; fitness center

Hearthstone Inn This comfortably elegant small downtown inn is actually two historic homes, built in 1885 and 1900, connected by a carriage house. There are no televisions, and only rooms on the first floor have phones. A National Historic Landmark, the inn is decorated with old photographs, many antiques, and reproductions. The inn's restaurant, which is open to nonguests, is wonderful. 506 N. Cascade Ave., Colorado Springs, CO 80903. ℂ **800/521-1885** or 719/473-4413. Fax 719/473-1322. www.hearthstoneinn.com. 25 units, 23 with bathroom. $99–$159 double with private bathroom, $69 with shared bathroom; $199 suite. Rates include full breakfast. AE, DISC, MC, V. **Amenities:** Restaurant; pets permitted in select rooms with prior arrangement.

WHERE TO DINE

In addition to the listings below, we recommend any of the restaurants at **The Broadmoor** plus the restaurants at the **Cliff House at Pikes Peak** and the **Hearthstone Inn** (see "Where to Stay," above).

Craftwood Inn COLORADO CUISINE Ensconced in an English Tudor building with beamed ceilings, stained-glass windows, and a copper-hooded fireplace, the Craftwood Inn specializes in regional game, including antelope and wild boar, plus seafood, steak, chicken, and vegetarian dishes. Save room for one of the superb desserts. 404 El Paso Blvd., Manitou Springs. ℂ **719/685-9000.** www. craftwood.com. Reservations recommended. Main courses $12–$32. AE, DC, DISC, MC, V. Daily 5:30–8:30pm. Turn north off Manitou Ave. onto Mayfair Ave., go uphill 1 block, and turn left onto El Paso Blvd.; the Craftwood is on your right.

The Margarita at PineCreek ECLECTIC This delightful restaurant, with a tree-shaded outdoor patio and simply decorated dining room, offers the perfect spot to sit and watch the sun setting over Pikes Peak. Six-course dinners offer three choices of entrees, often including a seafood selection, with an emphasis on fresh ingredients. The food is top rate. 7360 Pine Creek Rd. ℂ **719/598-8667.** Reservations recommended. Fixed-price dinner $27–$32. AE, DC, DISC, MC, V. Tues–Fri 11:30am–2pm; Tues–Sun 6–9pm.

Phantom Canyon Brewing Co. AMERICAN This popular brewpub is in the Cheyenne Building, home to the Chicago, Rock Island, & Pacific Railroad from 1902 to 1909. On any given day, ten of Phantom Canyon's specialty beers are on tap, including their homemade root beer. Selections here are typical brewpub at lunch, when you might get wood-fired pizzas, salads, burgers, and fish and chips. Dinner is more ambitious, with offerings such as charbroiled garlic chicken breast with three-grain rice and honey-beer mustard. 2 E. Pikes Peak Ave. ℂ **719/635-2800.** Main courses $5.75–$7.50 lunch, $9–$18 dinner. AE, DC, DISC, MC, V. Mon–Sat 11am–midnight; Sun 9am–10pm.

COLORADO SPRINGS AFTER DARK

Current weekly entertainment schedules can be found in the Friday *Gazette* . Also look at the listings in *Springs* magazine and *The Independent* (free entertainment tabloids); or call the city's weekly events line at ℂ **719/635-1723.** Tickets for nearly all major entertainment and sporting events can be obtained from **Ticketmaster** (ℂ **719/520-9090**).

THE PERFORMING ARTS Pikes Peak Center, the Colorado Springs Fine Arts Center, City Auditorium, Colorado College, and the various facilities at the U.S. Air Force Academy are all venues for the performing arts. The city's newest facility is the 8,000-seat Colorado Springs World Arena, at I-25 Exit 138 (© 719/477-2100), which hosts big-name country and rock concerts as well as a variety of sporting events.

THE BAR & CLUB SCENE Two-steppers and country-western music lovers flock to **Cowboys,** 3910 Palmer Park Blvd. (© 719/596-2152), which has the largest dance floor in the area and offers dance lessons. There's an eclectic offering of live music at **Poor Richard's Restaurant,** 324½ N. Tejon St. (© 719/632-7721). **Hide 'n' Seek,** 512 W. Colorado Ave. (© 719/634-9303), is one of the oldest and largest gay bars in the West. **MacKenzie's Chop House,** 128 S. Tejon St. (© 719/635-3536), a good steakhouse, specializes in martinis—shaken not stirred—with about 40 on the menu, plus a luxurious cigar lounge and an extensive wine list.

6 Southwestern Colorado

A land apart from the rest of the state, Southwestern Colorado is set off by the spectacular mountain wall of the San Juan Range. The Ancestral Puebloans (also called Anasazi) who once lived here created spectacular cliff dwellings, which you can see at Mesa Verde National Park.

This area is also John Wayne country, where the Duke slugged it out and shot it out as he tamed the West on movie screens from the late 1920s through the 1970s. It was also the location shoot for *Butch Cassidy and the Sundance Kid,* and for *City Slickers,* with Billy Crystal as a hapless city dweller on an Old West–style cattle drive.

DURANGO

Born as a railroad town more than a century ago, Durango remains a railroad town to this day, as thousands of visitors take a journey back in time aboard the Durango & Silverton Narrow Gauge Railroad.

ESSENTIALS

GETTING THERE Durango is at the crossroads of east-west U.S. 160 and north-south U.S. 550. By plane, there's frequent service from several major airlines to **Durango/La Plata County Airport** (© 970/247-8143), 14 miles southeast of Durango off Colo. 172.

VISITOR INFORMATION Contact the **Durango Area Chamber Resort Association,** 111 S. Camino del Rio (P.O. Box 2587), Durango, CO 81302 (© 800/525-8855 or 970/247-0312; www.durango.org). The chamber's visitor center is just south of downtown, on U.S. 160/550 opposite the intersection of East Eighth Avenue.

SPECIAL EVENTS & FESTIVALS From early June through the third week of August, the **Durango Pro Rodeo** series takes place every Tuesday and Wednesday at 7:30pm at the La Plata County Fairgrounds, Main Avenue and 25th Street (© 970/246-2790).

EXPLORING THE AREA

Colorado's most famous train, the **Durango & Silverton Narrow Gauge Railroad,** 479 Main Ave. (© 888/872-4607 or 970/247-2733; www.durangotrain.com), has been in continual operation since 1881. In all that time, its route has never varied: up the Rio de las Animas Perdidas (River of Lost Souls), through 45 miles of mountains and San Juan National Forest wilderness to the historic mining town of Silverton, and back. The coal-fired steam locomotives pull strings of gold-colored Victorian coaches on the 3,000-foot climb, past relics of mining and railroad activity from the last century. In summer, the spectacular trip takes 3¼ hours each way, with a 2-hour stopover in the picturesque town of Silverton before the return trip. Summer round-trip fare is $55 to $60 for adults, $27 to $30 for children ages 5 to 11. Winter trips are shorter and fares are less. Parking is $7 per day per car, $9 for RVs.

The **Durango & Silverton Narrow Gauge Railroad Museum,** 479 Main Ave. (© **970/247-2733**), contains exhibits on steam trains, historic photos, and railroad art. It also has restored railroad cars and a locomotive that can be entered. Hours correspond to the train depot hours and museum admission is included with train excursion tickets. Admission to the museum only is $5 adults, $2.50 children under 12.

Those interested in a close-up view of Durango's numerous historic buildings can pick up free copies of several Walking Tour brochures from the visitor center. There are particularly interesting banks, saloons, churches, and fine homes along Main Avenue and Third Avenue.

The varied terrain and myriad trails of **San Juan National Forest** have made Durango a nationally known mountain-biking center. The Colorado Trail, Hermosa Creek Trail (beginning 11 miles north of Durango off U.S. 550), and La Plata Canyon Road (beginning 11 miles west of Durango off U.S. 160) are favorite jaunts. You can get information, rent mountain bikes, and sign up for tours at **Southwest Adventures,** 12th Street and Camino del Rio (© **800/642-5389** or 970/259-0370).

The three stages of the Animas River provide excitement for rafters of all experience and ability levels. Most of the many outfitters in Durango offer a wide variety, such as half-day raft trips that cost $20 to $40 for adults and $15 to $30 for kids, and full-day river trips costing $65 to $135 for adults and $50 to $75 for kids. Local rafting companies include **Durango Rivertrippers** (© **800/292-2885** or 970/259-0289; www.durangorivertrippers.com) and **AAM's Mild to Wild Rafting** (© **800/567-6745** or 970/247-4789; www.mild2wildrafting.com).

Some 25 miles north of Durango on U.S. 550, **Durango Mountain Resort** (© **800/525-0892** or 970/247-9000; www.durangomountainresort.com) has a reputation of getting more sunshine than any other Colorado ski area, although the average annual snowfall is 240 inches. There are 75 trails for all levels, served by 11 lifts. Snowboarders are welcome on all lifts and trails, and a snowboard park offers jumps, slides, and a quarter-pipe. The Purgatory Cross-Country Ski Center offers 10 miles of trails for Nordic skiers.

WHERE TO STAY

An easy way to book accommodations is to contact the **Durango Area Chamber Resort Association** (© **800/525-8855** or 970/247-0312; www.durango.org).

Durango's most famous lodging is the 1887 **Strater Hotel,** 699 Main Ave. (© **800/247-4431** or 970/247-4431; www.strater.com), an exceptional example of American Victorian architecture, with one of the world's largest collections of American Victorian walnut antiques, and home to a superb restaurant plus the Diamond Belle Saloon, where prolific author Louis L'Amour gave life to his Western heroes. Service is superb.

A National Historic Landmark, the 1892 **Rochester Hotel,** 726 E. Second Ave. (© **800/664-1920** or 970/385-1920; www.rochesterhotel.com), also captures the feel of the Old West.

The **Wit's End Guest & Resort Ranch,** 254 County Rd. 500, Vallecito Lake (© **800/236-9483** or 970/884-4113; www.witsendranch.com), is a delightful if pricey dude ranch encompassing 550 acres on Vallecito Lake, surrounded by the peaks of the Weminuche Wilderness; it's a unique combination of rustic outdoors and sophisticated luxury. **Purgatory Village Condominium Hotel,** Durango Mountain Resort, 5 Skier Place (© **800/693-0175** or 970/385-2100; www.durangomountainresort.com), is a ski-in/ski-out hotel 25 miles north of Durango, at the base of the mountain.

THE SAN JUAN SKYWAY

The San Juan Skyway, a 236-mile circuit that crosses five mountain passes, takes in the magnificent San Juan Mountains, as well as the cities and towns of the region. It can be accomplished in a single all-day drive from Durango or divided into several days, incorporating stops in Cortez, Telluride, and Ouray. Check for closed passes in winter and early spring. The route can be driven either clockwise (heading west from Durango on U.S. 160) or counterclockwise (heading north from Durango on U.S. 550). We'll describe the clockwise route.

Leaving Durango, 11 miles west you'll pass through the village of Hesperus, from which a county road runs 10 miles north into **La Plata Canyon,** with its mining ruins and ghost towns.

Farther west, U.S. 160 passes the entrance road to **Mesa Verde National Park.** About 45 miles west of Durango, just before Cortez, turn north on Colo. 145, which traverses the historic town of Dolores, site of the **Anasazi Heritage Center and Museum,** then proceed up the Dolores River Valley, a favorite of trout fishermen.

Sixty miles from Cortez, the route crosses 10,222-foot **Lizard Head Pass,** named for a startling rock spire looming above the roadside Alpine meadows. It then descends 13 miles to the resort town of **Telluride,** set in a beautiful box canyon 4 miles off the main road.

Follow Colo. 145 west from Telluride down the San Miguel River valley to Placerville, then turn north on Colo. 62, across 8,970-foot Dallas Divide, to Ridgway, a historic railroad town and home of **Ridgway State Park** (© **970/ 626-5822**), with a sparkling mountain reservoir.

From Ridgway, turn south, and follow U.S. 550 to the scenic and historic town of Ouray. Here begins the remarkable **Million Dollar Highway,** so named for all the mineral wealth that passed over it.

The 23 miles from Ouray over 11,008-foot **Red Mountain Pass** to Silverton is an unforgettable drive. The drive shimmies up the sheer sides of the Uncompahgre Gorge, goes through tunnels and past cascading waterfalls, then follows a historic toll road built in the 19th century. Mining equipment and log cabins are in evidence on the slopes of the iron-colored mountains, many of them over 14,000 feet in elevation. Along this route you'll pass a monument to the snowplow operators who died trying to keep the road open during winter storms.

From Silverton, U.S. 550 climbs over the **Molas Divide** (elevation 10,910 ft.), then more or less parallels the track of the Durango & Silverton Narrow Gauge Railroad as it follows the Animas River south to Durango, passing en route the Durango Mountain Resort ski area (see above).

CORTEZ: GATEWAY TO THE ARCHAEOLOGICAL SITES OF THE FOUR CORNERS REGION

Cortez is surrounded by a vast complex of ancient villages that dominated the Four Corners region—where Colorado, New Mexico, Arizona, and Utah meet—1,000 years ago. The inhabitants of those ancient villages, called Ancestral Puebloans, have long been known as the Anasazi, but that Navajo word, considered offensive to some modern Pueblo peoples, is being phased out.

ESSENTIALS

GETTING THERE **By Plane** **Cortez Airport,** off U.S. 160 and 666, southwest of town, is served by Great Lakes Airlines, with daily flights from Denver.

By Car Cortez is at the junction of north-south U.S. 666 and east-west U.S. 160, 45 miles west of Durango. As it enters Cortez from the east, U.S. 160 crosses Dolores Road (Colo. 145, which goes north to Telluride and Grand Junction), then runs due west through town for about 2 miles as Main Street. The city's main thoroughfare, Main Street eventually intersects U.S. 666 (Broadway) at the west end of town.

VISITOR INFORMATION Stop at the **Colorado Welcome Center,** Cortez City Park, 928 E. Main St., or contact the **Mesa Verde Country Visitor Information Bureau,** P.O. Box HH, Cortez, CO 81321 ((C) **800/253-1616** or 970/565-3414; www.mesaverdecountry.com).

THE MAJOR ARCHAEOLOGICAL SITES

MESA VERDE NATIONAL PARK The largest archaeological preserve in the United States, Mesa Verde National Park, located about 10 miles east of Cortez, has some 4,000 known sites dating from A.D. 300 to 1300, including the most impressive cliff dwellings in the Southwest.

The earliest known inhabitants of Mesa Verde (Spanish for "green table") built subterranean pit houses on the mesatops. During the 13th century they moved into shallow caves and constructed complex cliff dwellings. Although a massive construction project, these homes were occupied for only about a century; their residents left around 1300 for unknown reasons.

The **Cliff Palace,** the park's largest and best-known site, is a four-story apartment complex with stepped-back roofs forming porches for the dwellings above. Accessible by guided tour only, it is reached by a quarter-mile downhill path. Its towers, walls, and kivas (large circular rooms used for ceremonies) are all set back beneath the rim of a cliff. Another ranger-led tour takes visitors up a 32-foot ladder to explore the interior of **Balcony House.** Each of these tours is given only in summer and into fall (call for exact dates).

Two more important sites—**Step House** and **Long House,** both on Wetherill Mesa—can be visited in summer only. Rangers lead tours to **Spruce Tree House,** another of the major cliff-dwelling complexes, only in winter, when other park facilities are closed. Visitors can also explore Spruce Tree House on their own at any time. Three-hour and 6-hour guided park tours are offered from Far View Lodge (see below) during the summer.

For those who want to avoid hiking and climbing, the 12-mile **Mesa Top Road** makes a number of pit houses and cliffside overlooks easily accessible by car.

Chapin Mesa, site of the park headquarters, museum, and a post office, is 21 miles from the park entrance on U.S. 160. **Morefield Village,** site of Mesa

Verde's 477-site campground, is 4 miles in from U.S. 160. The **Far View Visitor Center,** site of Far View Lodge (see below), has a restaurant, gift shop, and other facilities; it's 15 miles off U.S. 160. Open from mid-April to mid-October, **Morefield Campground** (© 800/449-2288 or 970/533-7731), 4 miles south of the park entrance, has over 400 sites, including 15 with water and electric hookups.

Admission to the park costs $10 per vehicle. Tours of Cliff Palace and Balcony House are $2.25. The **Far View Visitor Center** (© 970/529-5036; www.nps. gov/meve) is open early from April to mid-October; the **Chapin Mesa Museum** is open year-round. Located in the park, **Far View Lodge** (© 800/449-2288 or 970/529-4421; www.visitmesaverde.com) is open from late March to early November. Rooms aren't fancy, but the views are magnificent. The lodge serves three meals daily, with two restaurants and a bar.

UTE MOUNTAIN TRIBAL PARK   If you liked Mesa Verde but would have enjoyed it more without the crowds, you'll love the **Ute Mountain Tribal Park,** in Towaoc (© 800/847-5485 or 970/749-1452; www.utemountainute.com). Set aside by the Ute Mountain tribe to preserve its heritage, the 125,000-acre park—which abuts Mesa Verde National Park—includes hundreds of surface sites and cliff dwellings that compare in size and complexity with those in Mesa Verde, as well as wall paintings and ancient petroglyphs.

Accessibility to the park is strictly limited to guided tours, which are offered April through October. Full- and half-day tours begin at the **Ute Mountain Tribal Park Visitor Center** at the junction of U.S. 666 and U.S. 160, 20 miles south of Cortez. Mountain-biking and backpacking trips are also offered. No food, lodging, gasoline, or other services are available within the park. Some climbing is necessary. Charges for tours in your vehicle are $18 per person for a half day, $30 for a full day; there are extra charges for use of a tour guide's vehicle. Reservations are required.

WHERE TO STAY
Summer is the busy season and brings the highest rates. The **Travelodge,** 440 S. Broadway (© 800/578-7878 or 970/565-7778), is a good, economical choice in Cortez. Also providing comfortable, reasonably priced lodging are **Best Western Turquoise Inn & Suites,** 535 E. Main St. (© 800/547-3376 or 970/565-3778); and **Super 8,** 505 E. Main St. (© 800/800-8000 or 970/565-8888).

TELLURIDE
This was one seriously rowdy town a century ago—in fact, this is where Butch Cassidy robbed his first bank, in 1889. Telluride became a National Historic District in 1964, and in 1968 entrepreneur Joe Zoline set to work on a "winter recreation area second to none." Today, Telluride is a year-round outdoor recreation destination and hosts world-renowned film and music festivals.

ESSENTIALS
GETTING THERE   By Plane   Telluride Regional Airport (© 970/728-5313; www.tellurideairport.com) is served by American, America West, Continental, Great Lakes, and Continental airlines.

By Car   From Cortez, follow Colo. 145 northeast for 73 miles. From the north (Montrose), turn west off U.S. 550 at Ridgway, onto Colo. 62. Proceed 25 miles to Placerville, and turn left (southeast) onto Colo. 145. Thirteen miles ahead is a junction—a right turn will take you to Cortez, but for Telluride, continue straight ahead 4 miles to the end of a box canyon. From Durango, in summer take U.S. 550 north to Colo. 62 and follow the directions above; in winter it's best to take the route through Cortez and avoid Red Mountain Pass above Silverton.

VISITOR INFORMATION   Contact **Telluride & Mountain Village Visitor Services/Telluride Central Reservations,** 700 W. Colorado Ave. (P.O. Box 1009), Telluride, CO 81435 (© **888/783-0257;** www.visittelluride.com). The Telluride Visitor Information Center can be found with the visitor services and central reservations offices.

SPECIAL EVENTS & FESTIVALS   The **Telluride Film Festival** (© **603/ 643-1255;** www.telluridefilmfestival.com), an influential event that takes place over Labor Day weekend, has premiered award-winners such as *Crouching Tiger, Hidden Dragon* and *The Piano.* What truly sets it apart, however, is the casual interaction between stars and attendees. Open-air films and seminars are free. The **Telluride Bluegrass Festival** (© **800/624-2422;** www.bluegrass.com) is one of the most renowned bluegrass, folk, and country jam sessions in the United States. It's held over 4 days in late June.

WHAT TO SEE

To get a glimpse of Telluride's wild and wicked past, stop at the **Telluride Historical Museum,** 201 W. Gregory Ave. (© **970/728-3344;** www.telluride museum.com). It was built in 1888 as the community hospital; a $2-million restoration project was completed in 2000. The museum houses artifacts, historic photos, and exhibits that show what Telluride was like in its Wild West days, when the likes of Butch Cassidy stalked the streets. There are also exhibits on the area's Indian heritage, mining, and even Telluride's ski boom of the 1970s. The best way to see the Telluride National Historic District and get a feel for the West of the late 1800s is to take to the streets, following the excellent **walking tour** described in the *Telluride Visitor's Guide,* available at the Telluride Visitor Information Center (see "Visitor Information" above).

OUTDOOR PURSUITS

The elegant European-style Mountain Village offers a fascinating contrast to the laid-back community of artists, shopkeepers, and drop-outs in the 1870s Victorian mining town of Telluride below. Located mid-mountain at an elevation of 9,450 feet, the Mountain Village offers ski-in/ski-out accommodations; eight slopeside restaurants including Gorrono Ranch, a historic homestead; spectacular scenery; and, of course, great skiing for all ability levels. There are 81 trails served by 12 lifts and a three-stage gondola. For snow reports and additional information, contact **Telluride Ski and Golf Company** (© **800/801-4832** or 970/728-6900; www.tellurideskiresort.com).

The Mountain Village has 18.6 miles of **Nordic trails,** which connect with 12 miles of groomed trails at Town Park and River Corridor Trail, giving cross-country skiers a total of 31 miles. Telluride also has one of the top **snowboarding parks** in Colorado, offering more than 13 acres of terrain.

In addition to splendid skiing and snowboarding, there are numerous outdoor recreation opportunities year-round. The major outfitter and arranger of summertime outdoor activities here is the versatile and dependable **Telluride Outside** (© **800/831-6230** or 970/728-3895; www.tellurideoutside.com).

Town Park, at the east end of town (© **970/728-3071**), is home to the community's various festivals. It also has a public outdoor pool, open in summer, plus tennis courts, sand volleyball courts, a small outdoor basketball court, a skateboarding ramp, playing fields, a picnic area, and a fishing pond.

There's excellent **fishing** in the San Miguel River through Telluride, but it's even better in nearby Alpine lakes, including Silver Lake, reached by foot in Bridal Veil Basin, and Trout and Priest lakes, about 12 miles south via Colo. 145.

Telluride is a major **mountain-biking** center. The **San Juan Hut System** (© 970/626-3033) links Telluride with Moab, Utah, via a 206-mile-long network of backcountry dirt roads. Every 35 miles is a primitive cabin, with bunks, a woodstove, propane cooking stove, and cooking gear. The route is appropriate for intermediate-level riders in good physical condition. Cost for those making the whole trip is about $450, which includes use of the six huts, three meals daily, sleeping bags at each hut, and maps and trail descriptions. Shorter trips, guide services, and vehicle shuttles are also available.

WHERE TO STAY

One of the best ways to book lodging is with **Resort Quest** (© 800/463-0027; www.telluridelodging.com), which manages many lodging choices; or check out The **Telluride Visitor's Guide Online** (www.visittelluride.com), where you can research accommodations and make your own reservations. Be aware that rates vary considerably, from quite reasonable at slow times to outrageous at Christmas and during major festivals.

Among the top luxury choices is the **Camel's Garden Resort Hotel,** 250 W. San Juan Ave. (© 888/772-2635 or 970/728-9300; www.camelsgarden.com), which has a perfect location—it's ski-in/ski-out and only steps from the town gondola, and also within 2 short blocks of the main shopping and dining section of historic Telluride.

More moderately priced is the **New Sheridan Hotel,** 231 W. Colorado Ave. (© 800/200-1891 or 970/728-4351; www.newsheridan.com), a restored 1895 Victorian hotel. The **Victorian Inn,** 401 W. Pacific Ave. (© 800/611-9893 or 970/728-6601; www.tellurideinn.com), is an affordable B&B-style alternative to renting a condo.

7 Salt Lake City

Utah's capital is relatively small, with a population of less than 200,000. But travelers come from around the world to visit magnificent Temple Square, world headquarters of the Church of Jesus Christ of Latter-Day Saints (LDS), and to hear the inspired voices of the Mormon Tabernacle Choir.

Exhilarating outdoor recreation possibilities are only about an hour's drive from the city, including some of the country's best ski resorts, plus miles of terrific mountain trails for hiking, mountain biking, and horseback riding.

ESSENTIALS

GETTING THERE   By Plane   Salt Lake City International Airport is just north of I-80 at Exit 115, on the west side of the city. It's served by most major U.S. carriers.

By Train   Amtrak (© 800/USA-RAIL or 801/531-0188; www.amtrak.com) provides daily service from Chicago (trip time: 34 hr.), Denver (15½ hr.), and San Francisco (18 hr.) to Union Station at 310 S. Rio Grande St.

By Car   Major routes into Salt Lake City are I-80 from the east (Cheyenne) and west (Reno); I-15 from the north (Pocatello) and south Las Vegas); and

I-84 from the northwest (Boise). Motorists, however, should expect delays and detours during a massive construction project on I-15, which is expected to be completed before the 2002 Olympics. You can get the latest information by calling ℭ **888/463-6415.**

VISITOR INFORMATION   The **Salt Lake Convention and Visitors Bureau** information center downtown in the Salt Palace at 90 S. West Temple (ℭ **800/541-4955** or 801/521-2822; www.visitsaltlake.com) is open Monday through Friday from 8am to 5pm, and Saturday and Sunday from 9am to 5pm. The CVB also has an information center at the airport, terminal 2.

GETTING AROUND   Salt Lake is a fairly easy city in which to drive, with wide streets and ample parking. There are many public parking lots in the downtown area, costing from $1 to $6 per day. Parking on streets downtown is metered, costing 25¢ per half hour, and usually limited to 1 or 2 hours.

There's **bus service** throughout the city (schedules available at the information center—see above), including a free fare zone in the downtown area. The **Pioneer Trolley** (ℭ **801/240-6279**), operating June through August, provides free transportation in a short loop in the Temple Square area.

The main taxi companies are the **City Cab Co.** (ℭ **801/363-5550**), **Yellow Cab** (ℭ **801/521-2100**), and **Ute Cab** (ℭ **801/359-7788**).

FAST FACTS   For physician referrals, contact the **Utah Medical Association** (ℭ **801/355-7477**) during normal business hours. Hospitals include **LDS Hospital,** 8th Avenue and C Street (ℭ **801/321-1100**). Sales tax is 6.6%, and lodging taxes total 11.2%.

EXPLORING TEMPLE SQUARE

This is Mecca for members of the Church of Jesus Christ of Latter-Day Saints, also known as Mormons. The 10-acre square is enclosed by 15-foot walls, with a gate in the center of each. In addition to the church buildings, the square is home to the North and South Visitor Centers as well as lovely gardens and statuary. Even if you start at the **South Visitor Center,** you may want to stop into the **North Visitor Center** for a look at its murals and 11-foot replica of Thorvaldsen's *Christus.*

The **Temple** is used only for the Mormons' most sacred services and is not open to the public. Early church leader Brigham Young chose the site within 4 days of entering the valley, and work was begun on the six-spired granite structure in 1853. It took 40 years to complete.

The oval **Tabernacle** seats 6,500 people and has one of the West's largest unsupported domed roofs. Boasting unbelievable acoustics, it has served as the city's cultural center for over a century.

Thursday evenings at 8pm, you can listen to the **Mormon Tabernacle Choir** rehearse (except when they're on tour; call ℭ **801/240-3221** to check), and on Sunday mornings you can attend their broadcast from 9:30 to 10am (you must be seated by 9:15am). The choir, composed entirely of volunteers, was formed shortly after the first pioneers arrived; many husband-and-wife members and families participate, sometimes over several generations. The Tabernacle organ has been rebuilt several times over the years, and has grown from the original 1,600 pipes and two manuals to 10,857 pipes and five manuals. Half-hour organ recitals take place year-round Monday through Saturday at noon and Sunday at 2pm. In summer, an additional 2pm recital takes place Monday through Saturday. Admission to all these performances is free.

The Gothic-style **Assembly Hall** was constructed in 1880 from leftover granite from the Temple, and is often the site of concerts and lectures. Inquire at one of the visitor centers for schedules. Two monuments stand in front of the Assembly Hall: One depicts a pioneer family arriving with a handcart filled with their belongings, and the second commemorates the salvaging of the first crops from a plague of crickets (seagulls swooped down and ate the insects).

Guided tours of the square, lasting approximately 45 minutes, leave every 15 minutes or so from in front of the Tabernacle; personnel in the visitor center can direct you. (*Note:* The tour ends at the North Visitor Center with a short film on Mormon beliefs. You are then asked to fill out a card with your name and address, indicating whether you would like to receive a visit from Mormon missionaries.)

The square is bounded by Main Street on the east, and North, South, and West Temple streets. Tours are given daily from 9am to 8:10pm. Call ✆ 801/240-2534 for more information.

MORE ATTRACTIONS

Beehive House   Brigham Young built this house in 1854 as his family home, but he also kept an office and entertained church and government leaders here. Young, who loved New England architecture, used much of that style, even including a widow's walk for keeping an eye on the surrounding desert. The house has been restored and decorated with period furniture to resemble the way it appeared when Young lived here, and visitors see the home on escorted tours. Allow 1 hour. 67 E. South Temple. ✆ 801/240-2672. Free admission. Mon–Sat 9:30am–4:30pm (open until 6:30pm Mon–Fri in summer); Sun 10am–1pm; closes at 1pm on all holidays.

Capitol Building   Built between 1912 and 1915 of unpolished Utah granite and Georgia marble, the capitol rests on a hill in a beautifully landscaped 40-acre park. The state symbol, the beehive (representing industry and cooperation), is a recurring motif both inside and out. The Rotunda, which stretches upward 165 feet, is decorated with WPA murals and houses several busts of prominent historical figures, including Brigham Young and Philo T. Farnsworth, the man who brought us television. The chandelier is astounding—it weighs 6,000 pounds and hangs from a 7,000-pound chain. Allow 1 to 2 hours. Capitol Hill, at the north end of State St. ✆ 801/538-3000 or 801/538-1563 (tour information). Free admission. Tours every half hour, Mon–Fri 9am–4pm.

Family History Library   This incredible facility contains what is probably the world's largest collection of genealogical records under one roof. Most date from 1550 to 1920, and are from governments, churches, other organizations, and individuals. The collection is composed of a substantial number of records from around the United States, fairly comprehensive data from Scotland and England, and information from many other countries. When you enter the library, you'll find people ready to assist with your research. They'll offer forms you can fill out with any and all data you already know (so come prepared with copies of whatever you have), and can direct you from there. Allow at least 2 hours. 35 N. West Temple. ✆ 801/240-2331. www.familysearch.org. Free admission. Mon 7:30am–5pm; Tues–Sat 7:30am–10pm. Closed major holidays and July 24.

This Is the Place Heritage Park   Brigham Young and the first group of pioneers got their first glimpse of the Salt Lake Valley here. A tall granite and bronze sculpture was erected in 1947 to commemorate the centennial of their arrival. Old Deseret is a village made up of original pioneer buildings from across the

ACCOMMODATIONS ■
Brigham Street Inn **12**
Econo Lodge Downtown **1**
Hampton Inn Downtownn **2**
Hilton Salt Lake City Center **6**
Historic Peery Hotel **7**
Holiday Inn Airport **1**
Inn at Temple Square **4**
Little America
   Hotel & Towers **9**
Wyndham Hotel **3**
DINING ◆
Café Trang **10**
Crown Burgers **11**
Lamb's Restaurant **5**
New Yorker **8**

state. In the summer, it becomes a living history museum of the years 1847 to 1869, featuring people in period garb living and working the way their forefathers did. Pioneer events and demonstrations are offered throughout the year. The 1,600-acre park also offers hiking along part of the trail used by the pioneers, plus picnicking, bird-watching, and cross-country skiing. Allow 1 to 3 hours. 2601 Sunnyside Ave. ⓒ 801/582-1847. Admission $8 adults, $6 children 6–12 and seniors 62 and over. Daily 10am–5pm.

WHERE TO STAY

In addition to the properties discussed below, we recommend the **Hilton Salt Lake City Center,** 255 S. West Temple (ⓒ 800/HILTONS or 801/328-2000), a handsome modern lodging with spacious, well-appointed rooms, a good location just 2 blocks from Temple Square, and an excellent restaurant, Spencer's, that specializes in steaks and chops. The **Little America Hotel & Towers,** 500 S. Main St. (ⓒ 800/453-9450 or 801/363-6781), is among Salt Lake City's best hotels, offering a wide variety of rooms, all individually decorated, that range from standard courtside rooms in the two-story motel-like buildings to extra-large deluxe tower suites in the 17-story high-rise. The **Wyndham Hotel,** 215 W. South Temple (© **800/553-0075** or 801/531-7500), is a modern high-rise just a block from Temple Square.

More affordable is the comfortable, completely renovated **Holiday Inn Airport,** 1659 W. North Temple (© **800/HOLIDAY** or 801/533-9000); the **Econo Lodge Downtown,** 715 W. North Temple (© **877/233-2666** or 801/363-0062); and the **Hampton Inn Downtown,** 425 S. 300 West (© **800/ 426-7866** or 801/741-1110).

The huge Salt Lake City **KOA/VIP,** 1400 W. North Temple (© **800/562-9510** or 801/355-1214), is the closest camping and RV facility to downtown Salt Lake City. Sites are $20 to $35, cabins $39 to $44.

Brigham Street Inn Located in a handsome three-story historic mansion, the elegant but relaxed Brigham Street Inn is filled with antiques, reproductions, and original art, plus some modern touches. Most of the individually decorated rooms contain king-size beds, and more than half have fireplaces. Smoking is not permitted on the premises. 1135 E. South Temple, Salt Lake City, UT 84102. © 800/ 417-4461 or 801/364-4461. Fax 801/521-3201. www.brighamstreetinn.citysearch.com. 9 units. $125–$140 double; $185 suite. Rates include continental breakfast. AE, MC, V.

Historic Peery Hotel The 1910 Peery is one of the few truly historic hotels left in Salt Lake City. It has been meticulously restored and renovated, resulting in a European-style small luxury hotel that retains a classic feel while providing modern amenities. Each of the comfortable and tastefully decorated rooms is unique. In-room massage service is offered. 110 W. 300 South (Broadway), Salt Lake City, UT 84101. © 800/331-0073 or 801/521-4300. Fax 801/575-5014. www.peeryhotel.com. 73 units. $114–$184 double. Rates include full breakfast. AE, DC, DISC, MC, V. Self-parking $5, valet parking $10. **Amenities:** Restaurants (2); fitness room.

Inn at Temple Square Centrally located, the Inn at Temple Square is a gem. It feels like the grand hotels of old, but with a warm, homey touch. The lobby is like a living room, with fine artwork, couches, and chairs you can sink into. Rooms are spacious, with a comfortable, old-world feel. The property is nonsmoking. 71 W. South Temple, Salt Lake City, UT 84101. © 800/843-4668 or 801/531-1000. Fax 801/536-7272. www.theinn.com. 95 units. $135–$155 double; $170–$270 suite. Rates include full breakfast. AE, DC, DISC, MC, V. **Amenities:** Restaurant; free passes to nearby health club.

WHERE TO DINE

In-the-know locals say that **Crown Burgers,** 3190 S. Highland Dr. (© **801/ 467-6633**), serves the best fast-food burger in town. The upscale European hunting lodge decor sets it apart from your average hamburger joint. Additional locations include 377 E. 200 South (© **801/532-1155**) and 118 N. 300 West (© **801/532-5300**).

Café Trang VIETNAMESE/CHINESE   Serving the best Vietnamese food in the state, this family-run restaurant also serves Cantonese dishes with some Vietnamese influences. A popular vegetarian specialty is the fried bean curd with grilled onions and crushed peanuts, served with rice papers, a vegetable platter, and peanut sauce. The dining room is decorated with Vietnamese paintings, and two large aquariums give you something to watch while waiting for your food. 818 S. Main St. © 801/539-1638. Main courses $5–$12. AE, MC, V. Sun noon–10pm; Mon–Thurs 11am–10pm; Fri–Sat 11am–10:30pm.

Lamb's Restaurant AMERICAN/CONTINENTAL   Lamb's has been here since 1939, offering very good food at reasonable prices, with friendly, efficient service. Decorated with antiques and furnishings from the 1920s and '30s, Lamb's is comfortable and unpretentious. The extensive menu offers mostly basic American and continental fare, although the restaurant's Greek origins are also evident. Several lamb dishes appear on the menu, including broiled French-style lamb chops and barbecued lamb shank. Full liquor service is available. 169 S. Main St. (✆ 801/364-7166. Main courses $5–$21. AE, DC, DISC, MC, V. Mon–Fri 7am–9pm; Sat 8am–9pm.

The New Yorker AMERICAN   Among Salt Lake's finest restaurants, the elegant New Yorker is noted for quiet sophistication, excellent food, and impeccable service. As it's technically a private club (and thus able to offer complete liquor service even without a food purchase), you'll have to buy a membership to enter (a well-spent $5 for 2 weeks). Sit either in the dining room or in the less formal cafe, where you'll dine under the original stained-glass ceiling from the old Hotel Utah. From the dining-room dinner menu, you might choose the superb Dungeness crab cakes; or the roasted rack of American lamb with rosemary cream sauce. The cafe menu offers somewhat lighter choices. 60 Market St. (✆ 801/363 0166. www.gastronomyinc.com. Reservations recommended. Dining-room main courses $8–$19 lunch, $15–$33 dinner; cafe main courses $9–$26. AE, DISC, MC, V. Dining room Mon–Thurs 11:30am–2:30pm and 5:30–10pm; Fri 11:30–2:30pm and 5:30 11pm; Sat 5:30 11pm. Cafe Mon–Thurs 11:30am–11pm; Fri 11:30am–11:30pm; Sat 5:30–11:30pm.

SALT LAKE CITY AFTER DARK

THE PERFORMING ARTS   The historic **Capitol Theatre,** 50 W. 200 South (✆ 801/355-2787), is home to several local performing-arts companies, and the place to go for dance, theater, and musical productions.

The acclaimed **Utah Symphony** (✆ 801/533-6683; www.utahsymphony.org) performs year-round in **Abravanel Hall,** 123 W. South Temple, an elegant 2,800-seat venue known for its excellent acoustics. But the summer series in July is probably the best time to see the orchestra, when it performs Tchaikovsky's *1812 Overture,* using real cannons, at outdoor concerts at Snowbird and Park City.

THE CLUB & BAR SCENE   The **Dead Goat Saloon,** 165 S. West Temple, in Arrow Press Square (✆ 801/328-4628; www.deadgoat.com), is a fun, funky bar with live acoustic and blues bands most nights, plus satellite TV, darts, pool, and grill food. **New Sandy's Station,** 9132 S. 255 West, Sandy (✆ 801/255-2078; www.sandysstation.com), is a popular country-western swing bar, offering live music, dance lessons, karaoke, and televised sports. For jazz and blues, try the **Zephyr Club,** 301 S. West Temple (✆ 801/355-5646).

NEARBY SKIING

You say you want snow? Here it is, some 500 inches of it every year, just waiting for powder-hungry skiers to make that short drive from Salt Lake City. You'll find Brighton and Solitude ski resorts in Big Cottonwood Canyon, and Alta and Snowbird in its sister canyon, known as Little Cottonwood.

If you're skiing on a budget, you might want to stay in Salt Lake City, where lodging is much cheaper, rather than at the resorts themselves. The resorts are so close—less than an hour's drive—that city dwellers sometimes hit the slopes after a hard day at the office! Full-day adult lift ticket prices at these resorts range from the upper $30s to the upper $40s, with Alta and Brighton offering the best bargains.

But this area is more than just a winter playground. Big Cottonwood Canyon, cut by ancient rivers over centuries, is a spectacular setting for warm-weather picnicking, camping, mountain biking, and hiking. Rugged, glacier-carved Little Cottonwood Canyon is filled with lush fields of wildflowers in the summer; that rainbow of color later takes a back seat to the brilliant hues of autumn.

Brighton Ski Resort (© 800/873-5512 or 801/532-4731; www.ski brighton.com) is a low-key, family-friendly resort. The ski school is highly regarded, children 10 and under stay and ski free with their parents, and teens particularly enjoy the bumps of Lost Maid Trail as it winds through the woods. Brighton's slopes are graced with a full range of terrain, all the powder you can ski, and virtually no crowds. Brighton is also one of the best snowboarding destinations in the state.

Solitude Mountain Resort (© 800/748-4754 or 801/534-1400; www.ski solitude.com) is another friendly, family-oriented ski area that hasn't been discovered yet, so lift lines are virtually nonexistent. Solitude enjoys excellent powder. Its 1,200-plus acres of skiable terrain range from well-groomed, sunny beginner and intermediate trails to gently pitched bowls and glades. Intermediates also have several excellent forest runs and some great bumpy stretches on which to hone their mogul skills. Advanced skiers will also find plenty to keep them happy. Solitude boasts a world-class Nordic center out its back door, which connects to Brighton Ski Resort.

Alta Ski Area (© 801/359-1078; www.alta.com) is famous for its snow— over 500 inches annually of some of the lightest powder in the world. An added bonus is the fact that its lift tickets are one of the best skiing bargains in the country. This is an excellent choice for serious skiers of all levels. Intermediates will find plenty of open cruising ground, forested areas, and long arcing chutes to glide through; experts will find an abundance of the Cottonwood Canyons' famous powder and spectacular runs, like steep, long Alf's High Rustler. Alta has chosen to limit its uphill capacity by not installing high-speed quads, and people are turned away on those occasions when the ski gods determine there are already enough skiers on the mountain. There's a highly regarded ski school here, too, but less glitz than you'll find at big-name resorts like Vail. Snowboarding is not permitted.

Snowbird Ski & Summer Resort (© 800/453-3000 or 801/742-2222; www.snowbird.com) offers super skiing and super facilities. Consistently rated among America's top 10 ski resorts, Snowbird has been called Alta's "younger, slicker sister." You'll find the same wonderful snow here, but with a wider range of amenities, including Snowbird's extremely popular Cliff Spa and Salon— worth the trip even if you don't ski. Some, however, find its dense, modern village and resort atmosphere cold compared to Alta's historic, European-style lodges and ruggedly Western attitude. Snowbird gives over almost half of its skiable terrain to the expert skier. There's not a lot for beginners and intermediates, but enough to keep them happy—what is here is top-notch. The entire mountain is open to snowboarders.

GETTING THERE   From Salt Lake City, take I-215 south to Exit 7; follow Utah 210 south. Turn east onto Utah 190 to reach Solitude and Brighton in Big Cottonwood Canyon; continue on Utah 210 south and east to Snowbird and Alta in Little Cottonwood Canyon. From Salt Lake City International Airport, it'll take about an hour to reach any of the four ski areas.

8 Park City: Utah's Premier Resort Town

The cry of "Silver!" brought thousands to Park City in the 1870s, but today it's the thrill of skiing, biking, and other outdoor adventures that keeps the town bustling. Utah's most sophisticated resort community, Park City reminds us of Aspen, Colorado, and Taos, New Mexico, other historic Western towns that have made the most of excellent ski terrain while evolving into popular year-round vacation destinations. Like these towns, Park City offers a casual Western atmosphere—plus a touch of elegance for those willing to pay for it.

ESSENTIALS

GETTING THERE   Park City is 32 miles east of Salt Lake City via I-80. At Exit 145, take Utah 224 into Park City. Driving time from Salt Lake City International Airport is about 35 minutes.

VISITOR INFORMATION   The **Park City Chamber of Commerce/Convention and Visitors Bureau,** 1910 Prospector Ave. (P.O. Box 1630), Park City, UT 84060 (✆ **800/453-1360** or 435/649-6100; www.parkcityinfo.com), maintains an information center in the Park City Museum at 528 Main St. and at the **Visitor Information Center** at the junction of Routes 224 and 248 and Park Avenue as you enter town.

GETTING AROUND   Parking in Park City is tough, especially in the historic Main Street area. The best plan is to park your car once and ride the free city bus. Park City's efficient transit system connects Deer Valley, Main Street, The Canyons, the factory store area, and the Park City Mountain Resort. The Main Street Trolley traverses Main Street daily from 1 to 5pm in the summer and from 10am to 11pm in the winter, connecting to the bus loops at the bottom of Main.

SPECIAL EVENTS & FESTIVALS   Summer in Park City resounds with music and theater, offering free concerts, major festivals, and a variety of other events. For details on the following, as well as information about other performing arts events, contact the chamber of commerce (see above).

Throughout the summer, free concerts are presented each Wednesday evening from 6 to 8pm at City Park. One week you might hear bluegrass, the next, classical, and yet another it might be rock or jazz.

The **Utah Symphony Summer Series** (✆ 801/533-6683) takes place every Saturday night in July and August at the outdoor amphitheater at Snow Park Lodge in Deer Valley. The stage faces the mountainside, and listeners bring chairs or blankets and relax under the stars.

The **Park City International Music Festival** (✆ 435/649-5309) presents classical performances at locations throughout town, from chamber groups to full orchestras. The festival runs from early July to mid-August.

The annual **Fidelity Investments Park City International Jazz Festival** is one of the most popular events in the valley. Internationally known performers such as Ray Charles, Natalie Cole, and Al Jarreau perform at the 3-day event in mid-August.

In January, the **Sundance Film Festival** takes place, with numerous film showings in Park City (see "Sundance," below).

Golf fanatics can see the big names of their sport at the **United Fore Care Classic,** a Senior PGA Tournament, which attracts the likes of Lee Trevino and Arnold Palmer in mid-August.

SKIING THE PARK CITY AREA RESORTS

The three area ski resorts, all within a few minutes' drive of Park City, are vastly different. Lift tickets range from the mid-50s to the mid-60s, making this a pricier place to ski than the Cottonwood Canyon resorts.

Unquestionably Utah's most elegant and sophisticated ski area, **Deer Valley** (© 800/424-3337 or 435/649-1000; www.deervalley.com) offers perfectly manicured slopes, ski valet service, heated sidewalks, and some of the state's finest dining and lodging. Along with all this, you get great skiing—especially if you crave long, smooth, perfectly groomed cruising runs that let you enjoy the spectacular mountain scenery around you.

Park City Mountain Resort (© 800/222-7275 or 435/649-8111; www. parkcitymountain.com), among Utah's largest and liveliest resorts, is where the U.S. Olympic team comes to train. What brings them here? Plenty of good, dependable, powdery snow and a variety of terrain and runs that offer something for everyone, from novices to experts. Surveys continually rank Park City among the country's top resorts for both its terrain and its challenging runs. There's even a triple-chair access lift directly from the Old Town onto the mountain, as well as two runs that lead back into town, so those staying in Park City proper don't have to ride back and forth to the base resort every day. Snowboarding is allowed.

The **Canyons Resort** (© 888/CANYONS or 435/649-5400; www.the canyons.com) has undergone a number of changes since the American Skiing Company took over in 1997, investing millions of dollars to turn it into Utah's biggest ski resort, with skiing and snowboarding on eight peaks served by 16 lifts. The resort boasts 140 runs on more than 3,500 skiable acres. **White Pine** (© 435/649-8701), Park City's cross-country ski center, has 13 miles of groomed trails.

WARM-WEATHER ACTIVITIES IN & AROUND PARK CITY

Getting into the mountains above Park City in summer couldn't be easier for hikers and mountain bikers, thanks to the chairlifts at two resorts. **Deer Valley Resort** offers more than 55 miles of trails, and **Park City Mountain Resort's** chairlifts provide access to 32 miles of trails. As you might expect, the terrain is steep but beautiful.

FLY-FISHING There are numerous fishing opportunities in the mountains surrounding Park City. For tips on where they're biting, stop at **Jans Mountain Outfitters,** 1600 Park Ave. (© 800/745-1020 or 435/649-4949; www.jans. com), and at the **Park City Fly Shop,** 2065 Sidewinder Dr., Prospector Square (© 800/324-6778 or 435/645-8382; www.pcflyshop.com). Both companies offer guided trips and equipment rentals, and Park City Fly Shop has a sales outlet.

HIKING The mountains around Park City are great for hiking and backpacking. For maps and tips on the best trails, contact Jans Mountain Outfitters (see above). For a good description of several trails in the area, pick up a copy of the Park City *Hiking & Biking Trail Guide* at one of the visitor centers.

MOUNTAIN BIKING Among local companies offering guided mountain-bike tours are **Sport Touring Ventures,** 4719 Silver Meadows Dr. (© 435/649-1551; www.mtnbiketours.com), and **White Pine Touring,** 1685 Bonanza Dr. (© 435/649-8710; www.whitepinetouring.com). Rentals are available from these companies as well as **Cole Sport,** 1615 Park Ave. (© 435/649-4806;

www.colesport-usa.com), and Jans Mountain Outfitters (see above). Rates are about $22 for a half day and $34 for a full day.

The 30-mile **Historic Union Pacific Rail Trail State Park bike path** follows the old railroad bed from Park City to Echo Reservoir. The trail offers great views of meadows, the volcanic crags of Silver Creek Canyon, the Weber River, Echo Reservoir, and the steep walls of Echo Canyon. There's always the possibility of spotting deer, elk, moose, and bald eagles along the trail, too.

MORE TO SEE & DO IN & AROUND PARK CITY

The **Park City Museum of History & Territorial Jail,** 528 Main St. (© 435/649-6100), is a must-see—the dark, tiny cells were state-of-the-art in 1886! The upstairs is a bit more civilized, with an assay office, 19th-century mining equipment, historic photographs, early ski gear, and several beautifully tooled door-knobs and locks.

Historic **Main Street** is lined with galleries, boutiques, and a wide variety of shops, with transportation conveniently provided by the Main Street Trolley. Although you won't find many bargains here, prices aren't too far out of line for a tourist and ski town, and downright reasonable compared to places such as Aspen and Santa Fe.

Park City also makes a good base for exploring the area's state parks and other attractions. Jordanelle offers two recreation areas on **Jordanelle Reservoir** (© 435/649-9540) in the beautiful Wasatch Mountains. Both sites are great for boating, fishing, picnicking, and camping. The Rock Cliff area of the park offers great bird-watching, with more than 160 species either living here or passing through, including eagles and other raptors that often nest in the area.

Wasatch Mountain State Park (© 435/654-1791) is a year-round destination. It's terrific for camping, has trails for hikers and mountain bikers, and boasts two scenic golf courses. Tee times should be reserved the preceding Monday for weekends, and the preceding Saturday for Tuesday through Friday play. Call © 435/654-0532 for reservations. In the winter, a network of groomed cross-country skiing and snowmobiling trails leads from the park into the surrounding forest, and both cross-country ski and snowmobile rentals are available.

Nestled in Heber Valley, **Heber City** retains its small-town atmosphere, despite its proximity to Salt Lake City. Here you can ride the **Heber Valley Historic Railroad** (© 435/654-5601; www.hebervalleyrr.org). The diversity of the landscape along the route is unparalleled, especially in fall, when the mountain-sides are blanketed with colorful foliage. The round-trip fare is $16 to $24 adults, $10 to $14 children ages 3 to 12, and $13 to $21 seniors 60 and older. Trips of 1½ hours and 3½ hours are offered, with either steam or diesel power.

WHERE TO STAY

Rates are almost always higher—sometimes dramatically so—during ski season. Sales and lodging taxes in Park City total just over 10%.

Although it's possible to book your reservations directly with the individual lodges, many people find it's more convenient to call an agency, especially for a condo or private home. **Park City Reservations** (© 800/453-5789 or 435/649-9598; www.parkcityres.com) and **Deer Valley Lodging** (© 800/453-3833 or 435/649-4040; www.deervalleylodging.com) are both good bets.

Deer Valley Resort (© 800/424-3337 or 435/649-1000; www.deervalley.com) and **Park City Mountain Resort** (© 800/222-7275 or 435/649-0493;

www.pcski.com) both have central reservation offices that can reserve lodging for you at a nearby condo or lodge, and also make airline, car-rental, and lift-ticket reservations.

Among lodging chains in Park City are the **Best Western Landmark Inn,** 6560 N. Landmark Dr. (© **800/548-8824** or 435/649-7300); **Hampton Inn and Suites,** 6609 N. Landmark Dr. (© **800/426-7866** or 435-645-0900); **Radisson Inn,** 2121 Park Ave. (© **800/649-5012** or 435/649-5000); and **Park City Marriott,** 1895 Sidewinder Dr. (© **800/SKI-EASY** or 435/649-2900).

Goldener Hirsch Inn   This château-style inn combines warm hospitality with European charm. Austrian antiques dot the common areas and decorate the walls. The spacious rooms are elegantly furnished with hand-painted and hand-carved furniture from Austria and king-size beds with down comforters. Suites have wood-burning fireplaces and small private balconies. The restaurant features Continental cuisine, including Austrian specialties, wild game, and fresh fish. 7570 Royal St. E., Silver Lake Village, Deer Valley (P.O. Box 859), Park City, UT 84060. © 800/252-3373 or 435/649-7770. Fax 435/649-7901. www.goldenerhirsch.com. 20 units. Winter $230–$900 double; summer $100–$250 double. Winter rates include continental breakfast. AE, MC, V. Closed mid-Apr to mid-June and mid-Oct through Nov. **Amenities:** Restaurant.

Silver King Hotel   This five-story condominium hotel, located just 100 yards from the Park City Mountain Resort lifts, offers studio suites and one-, two-, and three-bedroom suites. Each unit is individually owned and decorated and comes with a fully equipped kitchen, a wood-burning fireplace, a whirlpool tub, and washer/dryer. All but the studio suites have pullout sofas. Some units have a Southwest look, some are done in country style, and others are furnished with antiques. A large locker area holds your skis and there's free heated underground parking. 1485 Empire Ave. (P.O. Box 2818), Park City, UT 84060. © 800/331-8652 or 435/649-5500. Fax 435/649-6647. www.silverkinghotel.com. 64 units. Winter $175–$765 double; mid-Apr to mid-Nov $115–$240 double. AE, DISC, MC, V. **Amenities:** Heated pools (1 indoor, 1 outdoor).

Stein Eriksen Lodge   This is a luxurious, full-service lodge with a warm, friendly atmosphere and Scandinavian decor and charm. The lobby is most impressive, with a magnificent three-story stone fireplace. There are 13 rooms in the main lodge, with the remaining units in nearby buildings. The connecting sidewalks are heated, and the grounds are beautifully landscaped with aspen trees, manicured lawns, and flowers cascading over rock gardens and retaining walls. The spacious deluxe rooms, each individually decorated, contain whirlpool tubs, vaulted ceilings, and tasteful, solid wood furniture. Deer Valley Resort (P.O. Box 3177), Park City, UT 84060. © 800/453-1302 or 435/649-3700. Fax 435/649-5825. www.steinlodge.com. 130 units. Winter $670–$910 double, from $1,200 suite; mid-Apr to late Nov $195–$230 double, suites starting at $270. Winter rates include buffet breakfast. AE, DC, DISC, MC, V. **Amenities:** Restaurants (2 year-round, 2 seasonal); outdoor heated pool; fitness center.

Washington School Inn   Housed in an 1889 limestone schoolhouse nestled against the Wasatch Mountains, this lovely country inn has preserved its original charm even though it's been completely modernized. Rooms are individually decorated, many in country style, with antiques and reproductions. Two suites have wood-burning fireplaces. Although there are no televisions or air-conditioning, there are ski lockers, a sauna, and a whirlpool area. The inn provides a full breakfast buffet each morning, afternoon tea in the summer, and some hearty après-ski refreshments in the winter. 543 Park Ave. (P.O. Box 536), Park City, UT 84060. © 800/824-1672 or 435/649-3800. Fax 435/649-3802. www.washingtonschoolinn.com.

15 units. Winter $145–$235 double, $225–$450 suite; summer $115–$175 double, $175–$215 suite. Rates include full breakfast and afternoon refreshments. AE, DC, DISC, MC, V.

WHERE TO DINE

The Eating Establishment AMERICAN   Boasting that it is the oldest continuously operating restaurant on Park City's historic Main Street—since 1972—The Eating Establishment is busy, casual, and comfortable, a great choice for families or anyone who wants a heaping serving of comfort food at reasonable prices. The dining room is brick and light-colored wood, with several fireplaces. Breakfast, served until 4pm, includes a variety of omelets, skillet dishes, and other egg dishes, plus Belgian waffles and fruit-filled crepes. Lunch selections include wonderful charbroiled half-pound burgers and a variety of sandwiches. Dinners offer a variety of salads, excellent barbecued baby back ribs, a certified black Angus Kansas City strip steak (charbroiled and served with sautéed whole mushrooms), and several pasta selections. There's full liquor service. 317 Main St. ✆ **435/649-8284.** www.theeatingestablishment.com. Main courses $4.50–$8.95 breakfast and lunch, $8.95–$16 dinner. AE, DISC, MC, V. Daily 8am–10pm.

Glitretind Restaurant CONTEMPORARY INTERNATIONAL   This elegant restaurant serves innovative, impeccably prepared cuisine and has full liquor service. The modern, airy dining room looks out on the spectacular Wasatch Mountains. Great breakfast offerings include the Glitretind omelet, filled with grilled onions, bacon, cheddar, and potatoes. At dinner, you might start with Russian caviar before enjoying grilled Atlantic swordfish or a wild game duo. In the Stein Eriksen Lodge, Deer Valley. ✆ **435/649-3700.** Reservations requested. Main courses $4–$15 breakfast, $7–$15 lunch, $21–$36 dinner. AE, DC, DISC, MC, V. Daily 7–10am, 11:30am–2:30pm, and 6–9pm.

Grappa Italian Restaurant ITALIAN   Grappa feels like a Tuscan farmhouse. The restaurant has three floors, with a small patio on the ground floor and a larger second-floor deck with a delightful view. Everything's made from scratch, using the freshest herbs and vegetables. Dishes include grilled chicken and spinach lasagna, and open-spit–roasted guinea fowl. The meats and fowl are seasoned, then grilled or rotisseried over a wood fire. There's full liquor service. 151 Main St. ✆ **435/645-0636.** www.grapparestaurant.com. Reservations required. Main courses $24–$34. AE, DISC, MC, V. Daily 5:30–10pm in winter; closed Tues in summer; may close several weeks in Nov and Apr.

Texas Red's Pit Barbecue & Chili Parlor BARBECUE/CHILE   This is about as Texan as you can get in Utah. The walls are decorated with moose, deer, and buffalo heads, Western music fills the air, and plenty of authentic Texas-style barbecue fills the paper plates. Barbecued beef is the specialty, but the barbecued pork ribs and homemade chili—made from a secret family recipe—are also popular. Beer, wine, and tequila drinks are offered. 440 Main St. ✆ **435/649-7337.** Reservations not accepted. Main courses $8–$19. AE, DISC, MC, V. Daily 11:30am–10pm.

PARK CITY AFTER DARK: THE CLUB SCENE

Park City is known as Utah's Party Town; it's got probably the best nightlife scene in the state. If you're looking for drinking and dancing, join a private club (2-week memberships cost $5 and entitle you to bring several guests).

Adolph's, 1500 Kearns Blvd. (✆ **435/649-7177**), is mainly a social bar with piano music on some nights. The **No Name Saloon,** 447 Main St. (✆ **435/649-6667**), offers live music and dancing most evenings, plus pool, darts, and pinball. **Cisero's,** downstairs at 306 Main St. (✆ **435/649-6800**), hosts good bands and has a large dance floor. Two fun bars are **The Spur,** 350½ Main St. (✆ **435/615-1618**), and **Renee's Bar & Cafe,** 136 Heber Ave. (✆ **435/615-8357**).

SUNDANCE

Situated in beautiful Provo Canyon at the base of 12,000-foot Mount Timpanogos, Sundance is a year-round resort that emphasizes its arts programs as much as its skiing and other outdoor activities. That should come as no surprise, though—it's owned by Robert Redford.

The goal for Sundance was to create a place where the outdoors and the arts could come together in a truly unique mountain community, and it seems to be a success. The rustic yet elegant, environmentally friendly retreat is a full-service ski resort in the winter. During the summer, you'll find great hiking trails and other outdoor activities.

For information, all reservations, and guest services, contact **Sundance,** R.R. 3 Box A-1, Sundance, UT 84604 (✆ **800/892-1600** or 801/225-4107, or 801/225-4100 for snow reports; fax 801/226-1937; www.sundanceresort.com).

OUTDOOR PURSUITS

Known for its quiet, intimate setting and lack of lift lines, Sundance offers **Alpine skiing** for all levels—some quite challenging—including several delightfully long cruising trails for novices. The area is also gaining a reputation as a good place to learn to ski and snowboard; and Sundance's excellent Nordic Center, 1½ miles north of the main Sundance entrance, has 10½ miles of Nordic trails groomed for both classic and skate skiing.

Its spectacular scenery makes Sundance just as popular in summer as in winter. The new quad ski lift operates in warm weather, carrying hikers and bikers to upper trails. Sundance has a terrific network of close to a dozen hiking trails, some of which connect to trails farther afield in the Uinta National Forest. The **Sundance Nature Trail,** a 1- to 1½-hour hike, winds through groves of spruce, oak, and maple and across Alpine meadows before reaching a cascading waterfall. The **Great Western Trail,** one of the Wasatch Front's most spectacular, is an all-day undertaking that climbs nearly 4,000 feet to some amazing scenic vistas.

The Provo River provides great **fly-fishing** just 10 minutes away. Sundance offers guided fishing trips starting at about $175 for a half day.

THE FESTIVAL, FILM & PERFORMING ARTS SCENE

The next Tarantino has to start somewhere—and that somewhere might just be the **Sundance Film Festival.** For more than a decade now, the hottest independent films have been discovered at this weeklong January event, hosted by Robert Redford's Sundance Institute. (The festival doesn't actually take place at Sundance, however; it's held 30 miles away, in Park City, covered above.)

Admission to the festival is nonexclusive, so you can rub shoulders with the rich and famous and the up-and-coming. To get a free guide or to reserve tickets, contact the **Sundance Institute,** P.O. Box 16450, Salt Lake City, UT 84116 (✆ **801/328-3456**).

The **Sundance Summer Theatre** showcases innovative productions in a beautiful outdoor setting, a natural amphitheater backed by firs. Generally, four productions are staged each season; call to find out what's planned during your visit. The institute's excellent screening room shows foreign films, movie classics, American independent films, and documentaries year-round. Screenings are free to Sundance guests.

WHERE TO STAY

Sundance offers studio units and suites, with a variety of bedroom combinations, with rates from $235 to $450 per night, as well as several luxury mountain homes. Each suite is outfitted with well-crafted handmade furnishings that suit the rustic luxury of the entire resort, as well as American Indian crafts, stone fireplaces, and outdoor decks; most have fully equipped kitchens. Summer theater packages and a complete range of ski packages are available.

9 Zion National Park

Early Mormon settler Isaac Behunin is credited with naming his homestead "Little Zion" because it seemed to be a bit of heaven on earth. Today, 150 years later, Zion National Park will cast a spell over you as you gaze upon its sheer multicolored walls of sandstone, explore its narrow canyons, hunt for hanging gardens of wildflowers, or listen to the roar of the churning, tumbling Virgin River.

Because of its extremes of elevation (3,666 ft.–8,726 ft.) and climate (with temperatures soaring over 100°F/38°C in the summer and a landscape carpeted in snow in the winter), Zion harbors a vast array of plants and animals. About 800 native species of plants have been found: cactus, yucca, and mesquite in the hot, dry desert areas; ponderosa pine trees on the high plateaus; and cottonwoods and box elders along the rivers and streams. And Zion is a veritable zoo, with mammals ranging from pocket gophers to mountain lions, hundreds of birds, and lizards of all shapes and sizes.

ESSENTIALS

Zion National Park has three sections: Zion Canyon, the main part of the park, where everyone goes, and the less-visited Kolob Terrace and Kolob Canyons. The main east-west road through Zion Canyon is the park-owned extension of Utah 9, from which you can access a 14-mile round-trip scenic drive/shuttle bus route that leads to most scenic overlooks and trail heads.

GETTING THERE/ACCESS POINTS   St. George and Cedar City are the closest towns with airports. From either, it's easy to rent a car and drive to Zion. The park is 46 miles northeast of St. George and 60 miles south of Cedar City. From I-15 on the park's western side, the drive into Zion Canyon, the main part of the park—following Utah 9, or Utah 17 and Utah 9 to the south entrance—is more direct but less scenic than the approach on the eastern side. It delivers you to Springdale, where most of the area's lodging and restaurants are located.

The Kolob Canyons section, in the park's northwest corner, can be reached via the short Kolob Canyons Road off I-15's Exit 40; and Kolob Terrace is accessed via the Kolob Terrace Road, which heads north off Utah 9 from the village of Virgin, about 15 miles west of the park's southern entrance. This road is closed in the winter.

From the east, it's a spectacularly scenic 24-mile drive from Mount Carmel on Utah 9, reached from either the north or south via U.S. 89. However, be aware that this route into the park drops over 2,500 feet in elevation, passes through the mile-long Zion–Mt. Carmel Tunnel, and winds down six steep switchbacks. The tunnel is too small for two-way traffic that includes vehicles larger than standard passenger cars, SUVs, and pickups. Buses, large trucks, and most RVs must be driven down the center of the tunnel, and therefore all oncoming traffic must be stopped (this incurs a $10 charge).

Zion National Park

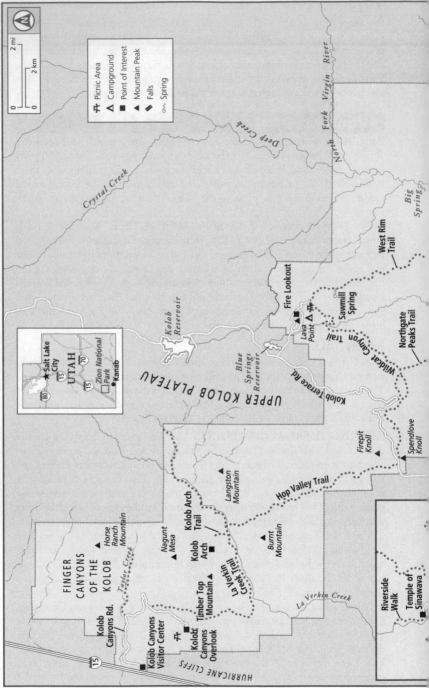

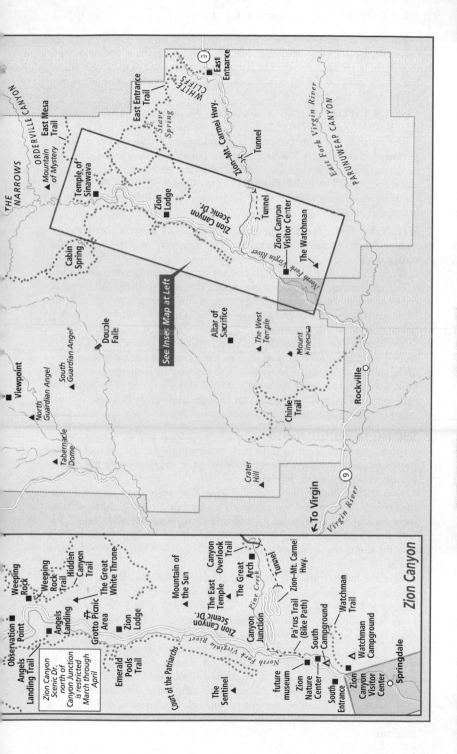

THE NARROWS

ORDERVILLE CANYON

East Mesa Trail

▲ Mountain of Mystery

East Mesa Trail

East Entrance Trail

Stave Spring

WHITE CLIFFS

East Entrance

13

Temple of Sinawava ■

Zion Lodge ■

Tunnel

Zion–Mt. Carmel Hwy.

Cabin Spring

Zion Canyon Scenic Dr.

Tunnel

Zion Canyon Visitor Center ■

The Watchman ▲

See Inset Map at Left

North Fork Virgin River

EAST FORK VIRGIN RIVER

PARUNUWEAP CANYON

East Fork Virgin River

■ Viewpoint

North Guardian Angel ▲

South Guardian Angel ▲

Double Falls

Tabernacle Dome ▲

Altar of Sacrifice ▲

▲ The West Temple

Mount Kinesava ▲

Chinle Trail

Rockville ○

Crater Hill ▲

9

←To Virgin

Virgin River

Zion Canyon

Observation Point ■

Angels Landing Trail

Zion Canyon Scenic Dr. north of Canyon Junction is restricted March through April

Weeping Rock ■

Weeping Rock Trail

Hidden Canyon Trail

Angels Landing ■

Grotto Picnic Area ⛏

The Great White Throne

Zion Lodge ■

Emerald Pools Trail

Court of the Patriarchs

The Sentinel ▲

Mountain of the Sun ▲

Zion Canyon Scenic Dr.

The East Temple ▲

Canyon Overlook Trail

The Great Arch

Pine Creek

Tunnel

Canyon Junction

Zion–Mt. Carmel Hwy.

Pa'rus Trail (Bike Path)

North Fork Virgin River

future museum

Zion Nature Center ■

South Campground △

South Entrance

Zion Canyon Visitor Center ■

Watchman Campground △

Watchman Trail ■

Springdale

Entry into the park (for up to 7 days) costs $20 per private vehicle or $10 per person on foot or bike (maximum $20 per family). The fee is the same year-round, although April through October it includes free use of the park's shuttle bus system, which is the only motorized method of exploring Zion Canyon permitted during that period.

VISITOR INFORMATION   Contact **Zion National Park,** Utah 9, Springdale, UT 84767-1099 (© **435/772-3256;** www.nps.gov/zion).

The park has two visitor centers. The **Zion Canyon Visitor Center & Transportation Hub** (© **435/772-3256**), near the south entrance to the park, has outdoor exhibits, an information desk where you can get brochures and permits, and a bookstore. The **Kolob Canyons Visitor Center** (© **435/586-9548**), in the northwest corner of the park off I-15, also provides information, permits, books, and maps.

WHEN TO GO   The park is open year-round, 24 hours a day, although weather conditions such as extreme heat or icy trails may limit some activities at certain times.

If possible, try to avoid June, July, and August, when Zion receives almost half of its annual visitors. The quietest months are December, January, and February, but of course it's cold and snowy then. A good compromise is to visit in April, May, September, or October, when the weather is usually good but the park is less crowded than in the summer.

The best way to avoid crowds is to simply walk away from them. It's sad but true—most visitors never venture far from their cars, and you can enjoy a wonderful solitary experience if you're willing to expend a little energy. You can also avoid hordes of tourists by spending time in Kolob Canyons, in the far northwest section of the park; it's spectacular and gets surprisingly little use. In summer, head to Kolob Terrace.

SEEING THE HIGHLIGHTS

If you have only a day or two at the park, we recommend making one of the visitor centers your first stop. Then, if your visit is during the shuttle bus operating season, we suggest the following:

Hop on the **shuttle bus** to explore Zion Canyon, getting off the bus at the major viewpoints and continuing on a later bus. At the **Temple of Sinawava** we suggest hiking the easy 2-mile round-trip Riverside Walk, which follows the Virgin River through a narrow canyon past hanging gardens. Then take the shuttle to Zion Lodge (total time: 2–4 hr.), where you might have lunch.

Near the lodge, you'll find the trail head for the **Emerald Pools.** Especially pleasant on hot days, this easy walk through a forest of oak, maple, fir, and cottonwood trees leads to a waterfall, a hanging garden, and the shimmering lower pool. This part of the walk should take about an hour round-trip, but those with a bit more ambition may want to add another hour and another mile to the loop by taking the moderately strenuous hike on a rocky, steeper trail to the upper pool. If time and energy remain, head back toward the south park entrance and stop at **Watchman Trail Head** (east of Watchman Campground) for the 2-mile, 2-hour round-trip, moderately strenuous hike to a plateau with beautiful views of several rock formations and the town of Springdale. That evening, try to take in the campground amphitheater program.

HIKING

Zion offers a wide variety of hiking trails, ranging from easy half-hour walks on paved paths to grueling overnight hikes over rocky terrain along steep drop-offs. Hikers with a fear of heights should be especially careful when choosing trails; many include steep, dizzying drop-offs. What follows are our hiking suggestions:

The **Weeping Rock Trail,** among the park's shortest and easiest rambles, is a half-mile round-trip walk to a rock alcove with a spring and hanging gardens of ferns and wildflowers. Although paved, the trail is steep and not suitable for wheelchairs.

Another short hike is the **Lower Emerald Pools Trail,** which can be an easy 1-hour walk or a moderately strenuous 2-hour hike, depending on how much of the loop you choose to do. A .6-mile paved path from the Emerald Pools Parking Area, through a forest of oak, maple, fir, and cottonwood, leads to a waterfall, a hanging garden, and the Lower Emerald Pool, and is suitable for those in wheelchairs, with assistance. From here, a steeper, rocky trail continues past cactus, yucca, and juniper another half mile to Upper Emerald Pool, with another waterfall. A third pool, just above Lower Emerald Pool, offers impressive reflections of the cliffs.

A moderately strenuous but relatively short hike is the **Watchman Trail,** which starts near the Zion Canyon Visitor Center. This 3-mile round-trip hike gets surprisingly light use, possibly because it can be very hot in the middle of the day. Climbing to a plateau near the base of the formation called The Watchman, it offers splendid views of lower Zion Canyon, the Towers of the Virgin, and West Temple formations.

Hiking the **Narrows** is not hiking a trail at all, but walking or wading along the bottom of the Virgin River, through a spectacular 1,000-foot-deep chasm that, at a mere 20 feet wide in spots, definitely lives up to its name. Passing fancifully sculptured sandstone arches, hanging gardens, and waterfalls, this moderately strenuous hike can be completed in 1 or several days. However, the Narrows are subject to flash flooding and can be very treacherous. Park service officials remind hikers that they are responsible for their own safety and should check on current water conditions and weather forecasts. This hike is *not* recommended when rain is forecast or threatening. Permits are required for full-day and overnight hikes in the Narrows, but are not required for easy, short day hikes, which you can access from just beyond the end of the Riverside Walk, a 2-mile trail that starts at the Temple of Sinawava parking area.

WHERE TO CAMP

There are two large and one small **national park campgrounds.** Both of the main campgrounds, just inside the park's south entrance, have paved roads, well-spaced sites, lots of trees, and that national park atmosphere you came here to enjoy. Facilities include restrooms with flush toilets but no showers, a dump station, and a public telephone. The fee is $14 per night for basic sites and $16 per night for sites with electricity. **South Campground** has 126 sites, first-come, first-served, and is usually open April through October; **Watchman Campground,** which accepts reservations from spring through fall (© 800/365-2267; http://reservations.nps.gov), has 231 sites, including about 50 with electric hookups, and is open year-round.

Lava Point, with only six sites, is on the Kolob Terrace. It has fire grates, tables, and toilets, but no water, and there is no fee. It is usually open from June to mid-October.

If you can't get a site in the park, or if you prefer hot showers or complete RV hookups, there are several campgrounds in the surrounding area. The closest, **Zion Canyon Campground,** on Zion Park Boulevard a half mile south of the park entrance (© **435/772-3237;** www.zioncanyoncampground.com), is open year-round and offers 205 sites, of which many are shaded. Although it's quite crowded in the summer, the campground is clean and well maintained, and in addition to the usual showers and RV hookups, you'll find a swimming pool; self-service laundry; dump station; store with groceries, souvenirs, and RV supplies; and restaurant. Tenters are welcome; rates are $16 to $22 for two people.

WHERE TO STAY

The only lodging actually in Zion National Park is at **Zion Lodge** (© **435/ 772-3213**). For information and reservations contact **Xanterra Parks & Resorts,** 14001 E. Iliff Ave., Ste. 600, Aurora, CO 80014 (© **303/338-6000;** www.xanterra.com). Situated in a forest, with spectacular views of the park's rock cliffs, the charming cabins each have a private porch, stone (gas-burning) fireplace, two double beds, pine-board walls, and log beams. The comfortable motel units are basically just that.

Springdale, a village of some 350 people at the park's south entrance, has literally become the park's bedroom. Comfortable, affordable motel rooms are available at the **Canyon Ranch Motel,** 668 Zion Park Blvd. (© **435/772-3357;** www.canyonranchmotel.com), where the rooms have spectacular views; and the budget-priced **El Rio Lodge in Zion Canyon,** 995 Zion Park Blvd. (© **888/ 772-3205** or 435/772-3205; www.elriolodge.com). More upscale are the moderately priced **Cliffrose Lodge & Gardens,** 281 Zion Park Blvd. (© **800/243- 8824** or 435/772-3234; www.cliffroselodge.com); **Desert Pearl Inn,** 707 Zion Park Blvd. (© **888/828-0898** or 435/772-8888; www.desertpearl.com); and **Best Western Zion Park Inn,** 1215 Zion Park Blvd. (© **800/934-7275** or 435/ 772-3200; www.zionparkinn.com).

We especially like **Flanigan's Inn,** 428 Zion Park Blvd., Springdale (© **800/ 765-7787** or 435/772-3244; www.flanigans.com), a very attractive complex just outside the park entrance. Parts of the inn date to 1947, but all rooms were completely renovated in the early 1990s, with Southwestern decor, wood furnishings, and local art. Flanigan's has a heated outdoor swimming pool and its own nature trail leading to a hilltop vista.

10 Bryce Canyon National Park

If you could visit only one national park in your lifetime, we'd send you to Bryce Canyon. Here you'll find magic, inspiration, and spectacular beauty among thousands of intricately shaped hoodoos: those silent sentinels gathered in these colorful cathedrals, in formations that let your imagination run wild.

Hoodoos, geologists tell us, are simply pinnacles of rock, often oddly shaped, left standing by the forces of millions of years of water and wind erosion. But perhaps the truth really lies in a Paiute legend. These American Indians, who lived in the area for several hundred years before being forced out by Anglo pioneers, told of a "Legend People" who lived here in the old days; because of their evil ways, they were turned to stone by the powerful Coyote, and even today they remain frozen in time.

Although the colorful hoodoos are the first things to grab your attention, it isn't long before you notice the deep amphitheaters that enfold them, with their cliffs, windows, and arches—all colored in shades of red, brown, orange, yellow, and white—that change and glow with the rising and setting sun. Beyond the rocks and light are the other faces of the park: three separate life zones, each with its own unique vegetation that changes with the elevation; and a kingdom of animals, from the busy chipmunks and ground squirrels to the stately mule deer and their archenemy, the mountain lion.

ESSENTIALS

GETTING THERE/ACCESS POINTS   **Bryce Canyon Airport** (© 435/834-5239) is several miles from the park entrance. There are no regularly scheduled direct flights to the airport, but charter service is available from **Bryce Canyon Airlines** (© 435/834-5050). Car rentals are available from **Bryce Canyon Car Rental** (© 800/432-5383 or 435/834-5200), which also has a desk in the lobby of Ruby's Inn.

You can also fly into St. George (126 miles southwest of the park on I-15) or Cedar City (also on I-15, about 80 miles west of the park), and rent a car at either of these airports from any of the major national agencies.

From St. George, travel north on I-15 10 miles to Exit 16, then head east on Utah 9 for 63 miles to U.S. 89, north 43 miles to Utah 12, and east 17 miles to the park entrance road. The entrance station and visitor center are just 3 miles south of Utah 12. From Cedar City (I-15 Exits 57, 59, and 62), take Utah 14 west 41 miles to its intersection with U.S. 89 and follow that north 21 miles to Utah 12, then east 17 miles to the park entrance road.

Situated in the mountains of southern Utah, the park is traversed east-west by Utah 12, with the bulk of the park, including the visitor center, accessible via Utah 63, which branches off from Utah 12 and goes south into the main portions of the park. Utah 89 runs north to south, west of the park, and Utah 12 heads east to Tropic and eventually Escalante.

Entry into the park (for up to 7 days) costs $20 per private vehicle or $15 for family groups that leave their vehicles outside the park and ride the shuttle into the park. Entry fees include unlimited use of the shuttle buses in season.

VISITOR INFORMATION   Contact **Bryce Canyon National Park,** P.O. Box 170001, Bryce Canyon, UT 84717-0001 (© 435/834-5322; www.nps.gov/brca).

The visitor center, at the north end as you enter the park, has exhibits and presents a short introductory slide show. Rangers can answer questions and provide backcountry permits. You can stock up on brochures, books, maps, videos, and postcards. The visitor center is open daily year-round except major holidays.

WHEN TO GO   Although Bryce Canyon National Park gets only two-thirds the number of annual visitors that pour into Zion, the park can still be crowded, especially from mid-June to mid-September. If you have to visit then, head for some of the lesser-used trails (ask rangers for recommendations), and start your hike as soon after sunrise as possible.

A better time to visit is spring or fall. If you don't mind a bit of cold and snow, the park is practically deserted in the winter—a typical January sees some 22,000 to 25,000 visitors, while August sees 10 times that number—and the sight of bright red hoodoos capped with fresh white snow is something you won't soon forget.

SEEING THE HIGHLIGHTS

Start at the visitor center, of course, and watch the short slide show that explains some of the area geology. Then drive the 18-mile (each way) dead-end park road, stopping at viewpoints to gaze down into the canyon. You can also take a guided tour (see below), or see the main section of the park on the shuttle bus, which operates from mid-May to September. The shuttles run every 10 to 15 minutes, and you can get on and off as frequently as you want.

Whichever way you choose to get around, be sure to spend at least a little time at **Inspiration Point,** which offers a splendid (and yes, inspirational) view into **Bryce Amphitheater** and its hundreds of statuesque pink, red, orange, and brown hoodoo stone sculptures. After seeing the canyon from the top down, it's time to get some exercise, so walk at least partway down the **Queen's Garden Trail.** If you can spare 3 hours, hike down the Navajo Loop and return to the rim via Queen's Garden Trail. Those not willing or able to hike into the canyon can enjoy a leisurely walk along the **Rim Trail,** which provides spectacular views down into the canyon, especially just after sunrise and about an hour before sunset.

Bryce Canyon Scenic Tours & Shuttles (© **800/432-5383** or 435/834-5200; www.brycetours.com) offers 2-hour tours year-round, leaving from Ruby's Inn just outside the park entrance several times daily. Cost is $26 for adults, $12 for children 5 to 15, and free for children under 5. Specialized sunrise and sunset tours are also offered.

HIKING

One of the things we like best about Bryce Canyon is that you don't have to be an advanced backpacker to really get to know the park. All trails below the rim have at least some steep grades, so you should wear hiking boots with a traction tread and good ankle support to avoid ankle injuries, the most common accidents in the park. During the hot summer months you'll want to hike either early or late in the day; it gets hotter the deeper you go into the canyon.

The **Rim Trail,** which does not drop into the canyon but offers splendid views from above, meanders along the rim for over 5 miles. An easy to moderate walk, it includes a half-mile section between two overlooks—Sunrise and Sunset—that is suitable for wheelchairs. Overlooking Bryce Amphitheater, the trail offers excellent views almost everywhere and is a good choice for an after-dinner walk, when you can watch the changing evening light on the rosy rocks below.

Your best bet for getting down into the canyon and seeing the most with the least amount of sweat is to combine two popular trails—**Navajo Loop** and **Queen's Garden.** The total distance is just under 3 miles, with a 521-foot elevation change, and it takes most hikers from 2 to 3 hours. It's best to start at the Navajo Loop trail head at Sunset Point and leave the canyon on the less-steep Queen's Garden Trail, returning to the rim at Sunrise Point, half a mile to the north. The Navajo Loop section is considered fairly strenuous, while Queen's Garden is rated moderate. Along the Navajo Loop section, you'll pass Thor's Hammer, wonder why it hasn't fallen, and ponder the towering skyscrapers of Wall Street. Turning onto the Queen's Garden Trail, you'll see some of the park's most fanciful formations, including majestic Queen Victoria herself, for whom the trail was named, plus the Queen's Castle and Gulliver's Castle.

WHERE TO CAMP

The two campgrounds in the park offer plenty of trees with a genuine "forest camping" experience, easy access to trails, and limited facilities. **North Campground** has 105 sites and **Sunset Campground** has 111 sites. A section of

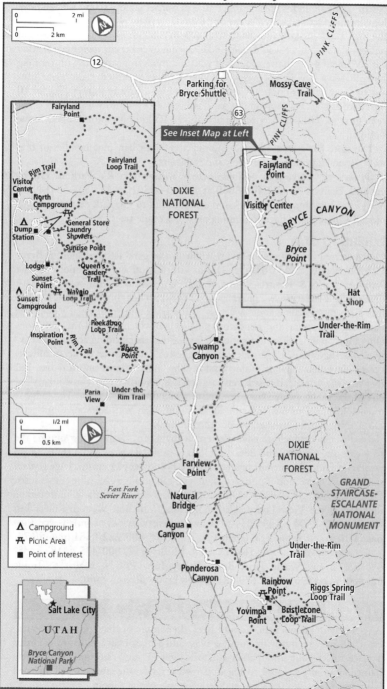

Bryce Canyon National Park

0 2 mi
0 2 km

(12)

Parking for
Bryce Shuttle

Mossy Cave
Trail

(63)

See Inset Map at Left

Fairland
Point

DIXIE
NATIONAL
FOREST

Visitor Center

BRYCE CANYON

Bryce
Point

PINK CLIFFS

Hat
Shop

Under-the-Rim
Trail

Swamp
Canyon

DIXIE
NATIONAL
FOREST

GRAND
STAIRCASE-
ESCALANTE
NATIONAL
MONUMENT

East Fork
Sevier River

Farview
Point

Natural
Bridge

Agua
Canyon

Under-the-Rim
Trail

Ponderosa
Canyon

Rainbow
Point

Riggs Spring
Loop Trail

Yovimpa
Point

Bristlecone
Loop Trail

Inset Map

Fairland
Point

Fairland
Loop Trail

Rim Trail

Visitor
Center

North
Campground

Dump
Station

General Store
Laundry
Showers

Sunrise Point

Lodge

Queen's
Garden
Trail

Sunset
Point

Navajo
Loop Trail

Sunset
Campground

Peekaboo
Loop Trail

Inspiration
Point

Rim Trail

Bryce
Point

Under the
Rim Trail

Paria
View

0 1/2 mi
0 0.5 km

△ Campground
⅌ Picnic Area
■ Point of Interest

Salt Lake City

UTAH

Bryce Canyon
National Park

North Campground is open year-round, but Sunset Campground is open from May to mid-October only. We prefer North Campground because it's closer to the Rim Trail—making it easier to rush over to catch those amazing sunrise and sunset colors—but we would gladly take any site in either campground. Neither has RV hookups or showers, but you will find modern restrooms with running water. Reservations are not accepted, so get to the park early to claim a site (usually by 2pm in the summer). Cost is $10 per night. Private showers ($2 for 10 min.) are at a general store in the park, although it's a healthy walk from either campground. The park service also operates an RV dump station ($2 fee) in the summer.

The store has a coin-operated laundry and snack bar, plus bundles of firewood, food and camping supplies, and souvenirs.

Outside the park, your options include **Ruby's Inn RV Park & Campground,** Utah 63 (© **800/468-8660** or 435/834-5301, or 435/834-5341 Nov–Mar; www.rubysinn.com), the closest campground to the park that offers complete RV hookups; it has a swimming pool and shade trees.

WHERE TO STAY

Our preferred lodging choice here is right in the park at the delightful **Bryce Canyon Lodge** (© **435/834-5361**). For information and reservations contact **Xanterra Parks & Resorts,** 14001 E. Iliff Ave., Ste. 600, Aurora, CO 80014 (© **303/338-6000;** www.xanterra.com). There's no denying that this is the perfect place to stay, allowing easy access to the trails and spectacular views. The handsome sandstone and ponderosa pine lodge, which opened in 1924, contains a busy lobby, with information desks for horseback riding and other activities. The luxurious lodge suites are wonderful, with white wicker furniture, ceiling fans, and separate sitting rooms. The motel rooms are just that, but they're pleasant and quite spacious. Our choice would be the "rustic luxury" of one of the cabins, which have been restored to their 1924 decor. The lodge is often sold out 4 to 6 months in advance, although you can sometimes get a room at the last minute because of cancellations.

Nearby choices include **Best Western Ruby's Inn,** Utah 63 just outside the park entrance (© **800/468-8660** or 435/834-5341; www.rubysinn.com), where you'll also find a liquor store, car rentals, a 1-hour film processor, a large general store, a post office, and tour desks where you can arrange excursions of all sorts. Outside are two gas stations. More basic (and less expensive) motel units can be found at **Bryce View Lodge,** Utah 63 across from Best Western Ruby's Inn (© **888/279-2304** or 435/834-5180; www.bryceviewlodge.com); **Bryce Pioneer Village,** 80 S. Main St. (Utah 12), Tropic (© **800/222-0381** or 435/679-8546; www.bpvillage.com); **Foster's,** Utah 12, Bryce (© **800/475-4318** or 435/834-5227); and **World Host Bryce Valley Inn,** 199 N. Main St., Tropic (© **800/442-1890** or 435/679-8811; www.brycevalleyinn.com).

11 Capitol Reef National Park

A relatively unknown gem, Capitol Reef offers more of that spectacular southern Utah scenery, but with a unique twist and a personality all its own. This is a place to let your imagination run wild, where you'll see the appropriately named Hamburger Rocks, sitting atop a white sandstone table; the tall, rust-red Chimney Rock; and the silent and eerie Temple of the Moon.

But Capitol Reef is more than just brilliant rocks and barren desert. Here the Fremont River has helped create a lush oasis in an otherwise unforgiving land, with cottonwoods and willows along its banks. In fact, 19th-century pioneers found the land so inviting and the soil so fertile that they established a community here, planting orchards that have been preserved by the park service.

ESSENTIALS

GETTING THERE   Capitol Reef National Park is about 225 miles south of Salt Lake City. It straddles Utah 24, which connects with I-70 both to the northeast and northwest. Entry into the park (for up to 7 days) costs $5 per vehicle or $2 per person on motorcycle, bicycle, or foot.

VISITOR INFORMATION   Contact **Capitol Reef National Park,** HCR 70 Box 15, Torrey, UT 84775-9602 (℮ **435/425-3791;** www.nps.gov/care). The visitor center is on the park access road at its intersection with Utah 24. A trail alongside the access road connects the visitor center and campground.

SEEING THE HIGHLIGHTS

Start at the visitor center, and watch the short slide show explaining the park's geology and early history. From the visitor center, a 25-mile round-trip scenic drive leads into the park, offering good views of its dramatic canyons, colorful cliffs, and commanding rock formations.

If the weather is dry, drive down the unpaved Capitol Gorge Road at the end of the paved scenic drive for a look at what many consider the best backcountry scenery in the park. It's a 6-mile round-trip drive. If you're up for a short walk, the relatively flat 2-mile (round-trip) **Capitol Gorge Trail,** which starts at the end of Capitol Gorge Road, takes you to the historic Pioneer Register, a rock wall where traveling pioneers "signed in."

FROM PETROGLYPHS TO A PIONEER SCHOOLHOUSE: CAPITOL REEF'S HISTORIC SITES

Throughout the park, you'll find evidence of man's presence through the centuries. The Fremont people lived along the river as early as A.D. 700, staying until about 1300. Primarily hunters and gatherers, the Fremont also grew corn, beans, and squash. They lived in pit houses dug into the ground, and the remains of one can be seen from the Hickman Bridge Trail. Many of the Fremont's **petroglyphs** (images carved into rock) and some **pictographs** (images painted on rock) are still visible on the canyon walls. If we could read them, they might even tell us why these early Americans left the area, a puzzle that continues to baffle archaeologists.

Prospectors and other travelers passed through the Capitol Gorge section of the park in the late 1800s, leaving their names on the **Pioneer Register.** You can reach the Pioneer Register via an easy 2-mile (round-trip) hike.

Mormon pioneers established the community of **Fruita** in 1880. A tiny **schoolhouse,** built in 1896, also served as a church, social hall, and community meeting hall. The school closed in 1941 but was restored by the National Park Service and is furnished with old wood and wrought-iron desks, a woodstove, a chalkboard, and textbooks. The orchards planted by the Mormon settlers continue to flourish, tended by park workers who invite you to sample the fruits of their labors.

SPORTS & ACTIVITIES

FOUR-WHEELING & MOUNTAIN BIKING   Capitol Reef has several so-called roads—actually little more than dirt trails—that provide exciting opportunities for those using 4×4s or pedal-power.

One recommended trip, the **Cathedral Valley Loop,** covers about 60 miles on a variety of road surfaces, including dirt, sand, and rock, and requires the fording of the Fremont River, where water is usually 1 to 1½ feet deep. But you'll be rewarded with beautiful, unspoiled scenery, including bizarre sandstone monoliths and majestic cliffs, in one of the park's most remote areas. Access to this loop is from Utah 24, just outside the park, 11.7 miles east of the visitor center, or 18.6 miles east of the visitor center on the Caineville Wash Road.

For information on guided backpacking, hiking, mountain biking, and four-wheel-drive excursions (many with an emphasis on photo opportunities), contact **Wild Hare Expeditions** (℃ **888/304-HARE** or 435/425-3999). Wild Hare also rents mountain bikes.

HIKING   Trails through Capitol Reef National Park offer sweeping panoramas of colorful cliffs and domes, eerie journeys through desolate steep-walled canyons, and cool oases along the tree-shaded Fremont River. Watch carefully for petroglyphs and other reminders of this area's first inhabitants. This is also the real Wild West, little changed from the way cowboys, bank robbers, settlers, and gold miners found it in the late 1800s.

Among our favorite short hikes here is the 2-mile round-trip **Capitol Gorge Trail.** It's easy, mostly level walking along the bottom of a narrow canyon, but looking up at the tall, smooth walls of rock conveys a strong sense of what the pioneers saw and felt 100 years ago. Starting at the end of the dirt Capitol Gorge Road, the hiking trail leads past the Pioneer Register, where early travelers carved their names.

Another short hike, but quite a bit more strenuous, is the 3½-mile round-trip **Cassidy Arch Trail.** This offers spectacular views as it climbs steeply from the floor of Grand Wash to high cliffs overlooking the park. From the trail, you'll also get several perspectives of Cassidy Arch, a natural stone arch named for outlaw Butch Cassidy, who is believed to have occasionally used the Grand Wash as a hideout. The trail is off the Grand Wash Road, which branches off the east side of the highway about halfway down the park's scenic drive.

WHERE TO CAMP

In the park, the 71-site **Fruita Campground,** open year-round, offers modern restrooms, drinking water, picnic tables, fire grills, and an RV dump station, but no showers or RV hookups. It's along the scenic drive, 1 mile south of the visitor center. Reservations are not accepted. Camping costs $10.

The park also has two primitive campgrounds, free and open year-round on a first-come, first-served basis. **Cedar Mesa Campground** has five sites and is in the southern part of the park, while **Cathedral Valley Campground,** with six sites, is in the northern part of the park. Each has pit toilets, fire grates, and picnic tables, but no water. Check on road conditions and get directions from park rangers.

Outside the park, there's the **Sandcreek RV Park & Hostel,** 540 Utah 24 (℃ **877/425-3578** or 435/425-3577), 5 miles west of the park entrance in Torrey; **Thousand Lakes RV Park & Campground,** on Utah 24, 6 miles west of the park in Torrey (℃ **800/355-8995** for reservations or 435/425-3500; www. thousandlakesrvpark.com); and the **Singletree Campground,** in the Dixie National Forest, on Utah 12 about 16 miles south of Torrey (℃ **435/425-3702;** reservations ℃ **877/444-6777;** www.reserveusa.com).

WHERE TO STAY

There are no lodging or dining facilities in the park itself, but the town of Torrey, just west of the park entrance, can take care of most needs.

The attractive **Days Inn,** 675 E. Utah 24 (at its intersection with Utah 12; ℂ **800/DAYSINN** or 435/425-3111), is a reliable option. Other affordable accommodations include **Austin's Chuck Wagon Lodge,** 12 W. Main St. (ℂ **800/863-3288** or 435/425-3335; www.austinschuckwagonmotel.com); **Best Western Capitol Reef Resort,** 2600 E. Utah 24 (ℂ **888/610-9600** or 435/425-3761; www.bwcapitolreef.com), which is only a mile from the park entrance; the **Capitol Reef Inn & Cafe,** 360 W. Main St. (Utah 24; ℂ **435/425-3270;** www.capitolreefinn.com); and the **Wonderland Inn,** at the junction of Utah 24 and 12 (ℂ **800/458-0216** or 435/425-3775). The **Skyridge Bed & Breakfast Inn,** on Utah 24, just east of its intersection with Utah 12 (ℂ **435/425-3222;** www.bbiu.org/skyridge), offers a delightful alternative to the standard motel.

Las Vegas

Las Vegas is a true original; there is nothing like it in America or arguably the world. In other cities, hotels are built near the major attractions. Here, the hotels *are* the major attractions. And if you tire of hotel-hopping, you can enjoy great works of art, five-star world-renowned chefs, and rock clubs and arenas that attract significant and still-current acts. With so many different options available, you don't have to gamble at all!

As if. Vegas is first and foremost a gambling destination. And though the hotels aren't undercharging for everything anymore in an effort to lure you into gambling round the clock, they still do their best to separate you from your cash. The cheap buffets and meal deals still exist, as do some cut-rate rooms, but both are likely to prove the old adage about getting what you pay for. Nevertheless, free drinks are handed to anyone lurking near a slot, and if show tickets aren't in the budget, you won't lack for entertainment. Free lounge shows abound, and the people-watching opportunities alone never pall.

In its own way, Vegas is every bit as amazing as the nearby Grand Canyon and every bit as much a must-see. It's one of the Seven Wonders of the Artificial World. And everyone should experience it at least once—you might find yourself coming back for more.

1 Essentials

GETTING THERE

BY PLANE Almost every major domestic airline, and some international airlines, fly into **McCarran International Airport** (© 702/261-5211; TDD 702/261-3111; www.mccarran.com), just a few minutes' drive from the southern end of the Strip. This big, modern airport—with a relatively new $500-million expansion—is rather unique in that it includes several casino areas with more than 1,000 slot machines.

Bell Trans (© 702/739-7990) runs 20-passenger minibuses daily between the airport and all major Las Vegas hotels and motels all day (7:30am–midnight). The cost is $4 per person each way to Strip and Convention Center area hotels, $5.25 to Downtown or other Off-Strip properties (any place north of the Sahara Hotel and west of I-15).

Even less expensive are **Citizen's Area Transit (CAT)** buses (© 702/CAT-RIDE). Bus no. 108 departs from the airport and will take you to the Stratosphere, where you can transfer to the no. 301, which stops close to most Strip and Convention Center area hotels. The no. 109 goes from the airport to the Downtown Transportation Center at Casino Center Boulevard and Stewart Avenue. The fare is $1.50, 50¢ for seniors and children.

Taxis are also plentiful, and a ride to the Strip costs around $12.

Las Vegas

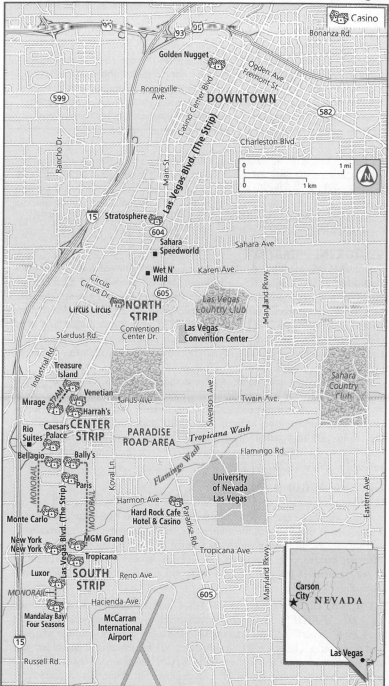

Adults Only!

Despite rumors to the contrary, Las Vegas is *not* a great place to take the kids. Many hotels actively discourage guests from bringing children and won't allow nonguests to bring strollers on the premises. Some casino hotels will not allow the children of nonguests on the premises after 6pm—and this policy is seriously enforced. And, of course, kids are not allowed in casinos. If you have to bring the kids along on a short trip, you'll survive; but if you're planning a major family excursion, look elsewhere.

BY CAR   The main highway connecting Las Vegas with the rest of the country is I-15 from the northeast (Salt Lake City) and southwest (Los Angeles and San Diego). Lots of folks drive up from Los Angeles, and thanks to the narrow two-lane highway, it can get very crowded on Friday and Sunday afternoons. Other major routes are U.S. 93 from the southeast (Phoenix) and U.S. 95 from the northwest (Reno).

VISITOR INFORMATION

For advance information, call or write the **Las Vegas Convention and Visitors Authority,** 3150 Paradise Rd., Las Vegas, NV 89109 (© 877/VISITLV or 702/892-7575; www.vegasfreedom.com). They can send you a comprehensive packet containing brochures, a map, a show guide, an events calendar, and an attractions list; help you find a hotel that meets your specifications (and even make reservations); and tell you if a major convention is scheduled during the time you would like to visit Las Vegas. Or stop by when you're in town. They're open daily from 8am to 5pm.

Another excellent information source is the **Las Vegas Chamber of Commerce,** 3720 Howard Hughes Pkwy., no. 100, Las Vegas, NV 89109 (© 702/735-1616; www.lvchamber.com). Ask them to send you their *Visitor's Guide,* which contains extensive information about accommodations, attractions, excursions, children's activities, and more. They can answer all your Las Vegas questions, including those about weddings and divorces. They're open Monday through Friday from 8am to 5pm.

GETTING AROUND

We highly recommend that visitors rent a car. The Strip is too spread out for walking (and Las Vegas is often too hot or too cold to make strolls pleasant), Downtown is too far away for a cheap cab ride, and public transportation is often ineffective in getting you from Point A to Point B. All the major hotels offer free parking, so finding a spot won't be an issue. However, if you plan to confine yourself to one part of the Strip or to Downtown, your feet will probably suffice.

BY BUS & TROLLEY   The no. 301 bus operated by **Citizens Area Transit** (© 702/CAT-RIDE) plies a route between the Downtown Transportation Center (at Casino Center Blvd. and Stewart Ave.) and a few miles beyond the southern end of the Strip. The fare is $1.50 for adults, 50¢ for seniors (62 and older) and children 5 to 17, and free for those under 5. CAT buses run 24 hours a day and are wheelchair-accessible. Exact change is required, but dollar bills are accepted.

Las Vegas Strip Trolley (© 702/382-1404) operates a classic streetcar replica that runs northward from Hacienda Avenue, stopping at all major hotels en route to the Sahara, and then looping back via the Las Vegas Hilton. They do not, however, go to the Stratosphere Tower or Downtown. Trolleys run about every 15 minutes daily between 9:30am and 2am. The fare is $1.30 (free for children under age 5), and exact change is required.

There are also a number of free transportation services, courtesy of the casinos. A free monorail connects Mandalay Bay with Luxor and Excalibur, another connects Bellagio with the Monte Carlo, still another runs between the MGM and Bally's, and a free tram shuttles between Mirage and Treasure Island.

BY TAXI   Since cabs line up in front of all major hotels, an easy way to get around town is by taxi. Cabs charge $2.30 at the meter drop and 20¢ for each additional ⅑ mile. A taxi from the airport to the Strip will run you $10 to $15, from the airport to Downtown $15 to $20, and between the Strip and Downtown about $10 to $12. You can often save money by sharing a cab with someone going to the same destination (up to five people can ride for the same fare).

If you want to call a taxi, any of the following companies can provide one: **Desert Cab Company** (© **702/386-9102**), **Whittlesea Blue Cab** (© **702/384-6111**), and **Yellow/Checker Cab/Star Company** (© **702/873-2000**).

FAST FACTS

For physician referrals, call the **Desert Springs Hospital** (© **800/842-5439** or **702/733-6875**). Hours are Monday through Friday from 8am to 5pm. Emergency services are available 24 hours a day at **University Medical Center,** 1800 W. Charleston Blvd., at Shadow Lane (© **702/383-2000**). **Sunrise Hospital and Medical Center,** 3186 Maryland Pkwy., between Desert Inn Road and Sahara Avenue (© **702/731-8080**), also has a 24-hour emergency room. There's a 24-hour **Walgreens** (which has a 1-hr. photo service) at 3765 Las Vegas Blvd. S. (© **702/895-6878**), almost directly across from the Monte Carlo.

The sales tax on meals, goods, and some services is 7%. Clark County hotel room tax is 9%, and in Henderson it's 10%.

2 What to See & Do

You can't sit at a slot machine forever. (Or maybe you can.) In any event, it shouldn't be too hard to find ways to fill your time between poker hands. The **hotels and casinos** are unquestionably the star attractions in Las Vegas (also see "Where to Stay" later in this chapter). Where else in the world can you sail the canals of Venice, take in a joust at a medieval castle, and explore King Tut's tomb, all in the space of 1 block? Just strolling down the Strip at night when everything is awash in neon is an experience like no other.

Many of the hotels offer free entertainment in the form of light shows, animal-filled parks, and strolling musical performers. Can't-miss shows include the **Bellagio's dancing fountains,** a musical ballet of water and light that is the best free show in town; **Treasure Island's nightly pirate battle,** where the bad guys always win; the **talking statues in Caesars' Forum Shops;** and the **Mirage's exploding "volcano."** Couch potatoes can watch the MGM Grand's 80-foot outdoor video screens, while adventurers head for a roller coaster celebrating that most daredevil of drivers—the New York cabbie. (This last one's not free, but that only heightens the reality of the experience.) And last but not least, the casinos offer one of the greatest free thrills of all—watching the high rollers win and lose big at the tables.

Nevertheless, when you finally tire of Strip-gazing (or your brain shuts down from the overload), there are plenty of other things to see and do in Las Vegas.

Auto Collections at the Imperial Palace   Even if you're not a car person, don't assume you won't be interested in this premier collection of antique, classic, and special-interest vehicles. Check out the graceful lines and handsome sculpture of one of the largest collection of Duesenbergs in the world. The vehicles on display change regularly, and some are occasionally sold, so there's no telling what you may see when you visit. Highlights include a 1964 Chaika that belonged to Soviet leader Nikita Krushchev; FDR's unrestored 1936 V-16 Cadillac; an ultra-rare 1934 Ford Coupe; and a 1965 Rolls-Royce Silver Cloud III once owned—at different times—by both Debbie Reynolds and Lucille Ball. In the Imperial Palace Hotel, 3535 Las Vegas Blvd. S. ⓒ 702/794-3174. www.autocollections.com. Admission $6.95 adults, $3 seniors and children under 12, free for children under 4 and AAA members. Check website for free admission coupon. Daily 9:30am–11:30pm.

Fremont Street Experience   The Fremont Street Experience in the heart of Downtown Vegas is a 5-block open-air pedestrian mall, a landscaped strip of outdoor cafes, vendor carts, and colorful kiosks purveying food and merchandise. Overhead is a 90-foot-high steel-mesh "celestial vault"; at night, it's the **Sky Parade,** a high-tech light-and-laser show enhanced by a concert hall–quality sound system, which takes place four times nightly. Not only does the canopy provide shade, it cools the area through a misting system in summer and warms you with radiant heaters in winter. It's a place where you can stroll, eat, or even dance to the music under the lights. The crowd it attracts is more upscale than in years past, and of course, it's a lot less crowded than the hectic Strip. Fremont St. (between Main St. and Las Vegas Blvd.), Downtown. www.vegasexperience.com. Free admission. Shows nightly.

King Tut's Tomb & Museum   This full-scale reproduction of King Tutankhamen's tomb was all handcrafted in Egypt by artisans using historically correct gold leaf and linens, pigments, tools, and ancient methods. It's hardly like seeing the real thing, but if you aren't going to Egypt any time soon, it's a surprisingly enjoyable Vegas fake. A 4-minute introductory film precedes a 15-minute audio tour (available in English, French, Spanish, and Japanese). In the Luxor Las Vegas, 3900 Las Vegas Blvd. S. ⓒ 702/262-4000. Admission $5. Sun–Thurs 9am–11pm; Fri–Sat 9am–11:30pm.

Liberace Museum   You can keep your Louvres and Vaticans and Smithsonians; *this* is a museum. Housed, like everything else in Vegas, in a strip mall, this is a shrine to the glory and excess that was the art project known as Liberace. You've got your costumes (bejeweled), your many cars (bejeweled), your many pianos (bejeweled), and many jewels (also bejeweled). It just shows what can be bought with lots of money and no taste. This is a one-of-a-kind place. Unless you have a severely underdeveloped appreciation for camp or take your museum-going very seriously, you shouldn't miss it. The museum is 2½ miles east of the Strip on your right. 1775 E. Tropicana Ave. (at Spencer St.). ⓒ 702/798-5595. www.liberace.org. Admission $12 adults, $8 seniors over 60 and students, free for children under 12. Mon–Sat 10am–5pm; Sun 1–5pm. Closed Thanksgiving, Christmas, and New Year's Day.

Madame Tussaud's Celebrity Encounter   Even if you aren't a fan of wax museums, this one is probably worth a stop—if you can stomach the ridiculous price. Figures here are state of the art, although some reproductions are considerably better than others. All the waxworks are free-standing, allowing—and indeed encouraging—guests to get up close and personal. Go ahead; lay your cheek next to Elvis's or Sinatra's and have your photo taken. The emphasis here is on film, television, music, and sports celebrities, plus some Vegas icons, who are housed in five themed rooms. There's also a behind-the-scenes look at the lengthy process involved in creating these figures. 3355 Las Vegas Blvd. S. ☎ 702/900 3530. Admission $15 adults, $9.95 children 3–12, $12 seniors and Nevada residents. Daily 11am–7pm.

MGM Grand Lion Habitat   Hit this attraction at the right time—when the crowds aren't here—and it's one of the best freebies in town. It's a large, multi-level glass enclosure, in which various lions frolic during various times of day. In addition to regular viewing spots, you can walk through a glass tunnel and get a worm's eye view of the underside of a lion (provided one is in position); note how very big Kitty's paws are. Multiple lions share show duties, so what you observe is definitely going to depend on who is in residence when you drop by. In the MGM Grand, 3799 Las Vegas Blvd. S. ☎ 702/891-7777. Free admission. Daily 11am–10pm.

Secret Garden of Siegfried and Roy & Mirage Dolphin Habitat   Get up close and personal with some of the famed duo's white tigers, lions, and plain old gray elephants, here at this mini-zoo; or better still, watch dolphins frolic in the neighboring Dolphin Habitat. There is nothing quite like the kick you get from seeing a baby dolphin play. If the knowledgeable staff isn't already, ask them to play ball with the dolphins; they toss large beach balls into the pools, and the dolphins hit them out with their noses, leaping out of the water cackling with dolphin glee. In the Mirage, 3400 Las Vegas Blvd. S. ☎ 702/791-7111. Admission $10, free for children under 10 if accompanied by an adult. On Wed, when only Dolphin Habitat is open, admission $5. Secret Garden open Mon–Tues and Thurs–Fri 11am–5pm, Sat–Sun 10am–5pm. Dolphin Habitat open Mon–Fri 11am–7pm, Sat–Sun 10am–7pm. Hours subject to change and vary by season.

Speedworld at Sahara   This popular stop has three attractions. The first is a remarkable 8-minute virtual-reality ride, **Cyber Speedway,** featuring a three-quarter-size replica of a NASCAR race car. In a separate **3-D motion theater,** you'll don goggles to view a film that puts you right inside another race car for yet another stomach-churning ride (even more dizzying than the virtual-reality portion). **Speed: The Ride** is a new roller coaster that blasts riders out through a hole in the wall by the new NASCAR Cafe, then through a loop, under the sidewalk, through the hotel's marquee, and finally straight up a 250-foot tower. At the peak, you feel a moment of weightlessness, and then you do the whole thing backwards! Not for the faint of heart. In the Sahara Hotel & Casino, 2535 Las Vegas Blvd. S. ☎ 702/737-2111. Stock car simulator $8 (you must be at least 48 in. tall to ride), 3-D simulator $3, Speed: The Ride (roller coaster) $6. Open daily at 10am; closing hours vary seasonally, but usually it's 10pm.

Stratosphere Thrill Rides   Atop the 1,149-foot Stratosphere Tower are two marvelous thrill rides. The **Let It Ride High Roller** (the world's highest roller coaster) was recently revamped to go at even faster speeds as it zooms around a hilly track that is seemingly suspended in midair. Even more fun is the **Big Shot,** a breathtaking free-fall ride that thrusts you 160 feet in the air along a 228-foot spire at the top of the tower, then plummets back down again. Sitting in an open car, you seem to be dangling in space over Las Vegas. We have one relative, a thrill-ride enthusiast, who said he never felt more scared than when he rode the Big Shot. After surviving, he promptly put his kids on it; they loved it. *Note:* The rides are shut down in inclement weather and high winds. Atop the Stratosphere Las Vegas, 2000 Las Vegas Blvd. S. ☎ 702/380-7777. Admission for Big Shot $8; for roller coaster $5; $5 per re-ride, plus $7 to ascend the Tower (if you dine in the buffet room or Top of the World, there's no charge to go up to the Tower). Multi-ride packages also available for varying costs. Sun–Thurs 10am–midnight; Fri–Sat 10am–1am. Hours vary seasonally. Minimum height requirement for both rides is 48 in.

WHERE TO ROLL THE DICE

What? You didn't come to Las Vegas for the Liberace Museum? We are shocked. *Shocked.*

Yes, there are gambling opportunities in Vegas. Let's not kid ourselves; gambling is what Vegas is about. The bright lights, the shows, the showgirls, the food—they are all there just to lure you in and make you open your wallet.

You should casino-hop at least once to marvel (or get dizzy) at the decor/spectacle and the sheer excess of it all. Beyond decoration, there isn't too much difference. All the casinos have slot and video poker machines and offer games such as blackjack, roulette, craps, poker, Pai Gow, keno, and baccarat. If you're a novice, many casinos offer free gambling lessons that include low stakes games, so you won't lose much while you learn.

Some notable places to gamble include the **MGM Grand,** the largest casino (you will get lost); **New York New York,** where the change carts look like yellow cabs; the light and airy **Mandalay Bay;** the tasteful **Venetian;** the **Las Vegas Hilton,** where the space-themed casino has light-beam–activated slots; **Harrah's,** where the "party pits" offer the most fun in town; **Paris–Las Vegas,** where you'll find a kitschy Disneyesque atmosphere; and **Binion's Horseshoe,** where all serious gamblers head, thanks to low minimum bets and the highest betting limits in town.

Remember that gambling is supposed to be entertainment. Pick a gaming table where the other players are laughing, slapping each other on the back, and generally enjoying themselves. Sometimes you can have a better time at one of the older places Downtown, where stakes are lower, pretensions are nonexistent, and the clientele are often friendlier. You don't have to be a high roller. You would not believe how much fun you can have with a nickel slot machine. You won't get rich, but neither will most of those guys playing the $5 slots, either.

3 Where to Stay

If there's one thing Vegas has in spades, it's hotels. Big hotels. You'll find the 10 largest hotels in the United States, if not in the world, right here. And you'll find a whole lot of rooms: 125,000 rooms, to be exact—or at least exact at this writing. Every 5 minutes, or so it seems, someone is putting up a new giant hotel, or adding another 1,000 rooms to an already existing one. The hotels here are the city's biggest tourist attraction, and they pack in the crowds accordingly. (Las Vegas usually has an occupancy rate of about 90%.) A last-minute Vegas vacation can turn into a housing nightmare. If possible, plan in advance so that you can have your choice: Ancient Egypt or Ancient Rome? New York or New Orleans? Strip or Downtown? Luxury or economy? Vegas has all that and way too much more.

First-time visitors will most likely stay on the Strip, although Downtown is a lot nicer than it used to be, and the rates there are cheaper. The **Las Vegas Convention and Visitors Authority** runs a room reservations hot line (© 877/VISITLV) that can be helpful. They can apprise you of room availability, quote rates, contact a hotel for you, and tell you when major conventions are in town. **Reservations Plus** (© 800/805-9528) is a free service that finds you a hotel in your price range that meets your specific requirements. Because they book rooms in volume, they are able to get discounted rates. They can also arrange packages (including meals, transportation, tours, show tickets, car rentals, and other features).

Vegas does have hotels that eschew the theme scheme. Unlike many of the casino hotels, they are far more likely to cater to kids, making them good choices for families. One of two great selections is the luxurious **Four Seasons** (© 877/632-5000 or 702/632-5000; www.fourseasons.com), inside the Mandalay Bay, although it has its own entrance and facilities. It offers a temporary respite from the Vegas hype since there's no casino, but guests who need a numbers fix can use Mandalay's with no problems. The **Residence Inn by Marriott**, 3225 Paradise Rd., Las Vegas, NV 89109, between Desert Inn Road and Convention Center Drive (© 800/331-3131 or 702/796-9300; www.marriott.com), offers clean apartmentlike accommodations with full kitchens and sitting rooms, making it popular with business travelers and families alike.

All the usual budget chains, including Motel 6, Days Inn, Howard Johnson, Fairfield by Marriott, and Econo Lodge are in Las Vegas. (See appendix A for their toll-free phone numbers and websites.)

Aladdin Resort & Casino   The new Aladdin is a handsome building and has a generic Middle East theme. Details that indicate that considerable thought went into the design are everywhere—what other casino has actual tile work throughout? But all that work came at a price, and the Aladdin has filed for bankruptcy (to the tune of $700 million), and will likely be sold to the highest bidder by the time you read this. Right now, the hotel teeters on the brink of glory; all it needs is a little TLC from the new owners and it could be precisely what a sexy, but distinctly Vegas, hotel ought to be: a little bit of kitsch, a little bit of class, all of it playful. The rooms are not distinctive, but they are pleasing, and the bathrooms have deep tubs and separate glass showers, plus little Aladdin's-lamp-shaped faucets and exotic spice-scented amenities. 3667 Las Vegas Blvd. S., Las Vegas, NV 89109. © **877/333-WISH (333-9474)** or 702/785-5555. Fax 702/785-5558. www.aladdincasino.com. 2,567 units. $99 and up double. Extra person $30. Children 11 and under stay free in parents' room. AE, DC, DISC, MC, V. Free self- and valet parking. **Amenities:** Restaurants (21); 2 outdoor pools; spa; health club.

Bellagio   This $1.6 billion luxury resort ushered in the new post-Vegas-is-for-families elegance epoch. Bellagio is not so much a romantic Italian village as its theme would suggest, but it's a big, grand, state-of-the-art Vegas hotel. Here you'll find fabulous fountains, classical gardens, an art gallery, and the best collection of restaurants in town. There is even an 8-acre Lake Como stand-in out front, complete with a dazzling choreographed water ballet extravaganza. Rooms are nicely decorated and the roomy bathrooms are even more luxurious. Service is surprisingly good given the size of the place. The pool area is exceptional and the spa is marvelous, if overpriced. This is not much like a getaway to a peaceful, romantic Italian village. But it is exactly like going to a big, grand, state-of-the-art Vegas hotel. 3600 Las Vegas Blvd. S. (at the corner of Flamingo Rd.), Las Vegas, NV 89109. © **888/987-6667** or 702/693-7111. Fax 702/693-8546. www.bellagio.com. 3,005 units. $139–$499 double. Extra person $35. No discount for children. AE, DC, DISC, MC, V. Free self- and valet parking. **Amenities:** Restaurants (16); 6 outdoor pools; spa; health club.

Caesars Palace   Caesars is the spectacle that every Vegas hotel should be. A combination of Vegas luxury and a good dose of camp, the hotel is graced by Roman colonnades, marble fountains, and staff members attired in gladiator outfits and togas. But the hotel has a confusing layout, and it takes forever to get anywhere—especially out to the Strip. Accommodations occupy four towers; art in the rooms keeps to the Greco-Roman theme (some have classical sculptures in niches). The newest rooms are handsome, if not as giggle-inducingly overwhelming as the classic ones, and have floor-to-ceiling windows that offer a hypnotizing panoramic view. You'll likely enjoy a lavish bathroom with marble floor, European fixtures, and oversize marble tubs (about half are whirlpools). The pool area, the $100 million **Garden of the Gods,** is a tasteful, undeniably "Caesar-esque" masterpiece. 3570 Las Vegas Blvd. S. (just north of Flamingo Rd.), Las Vegas, NV 89109. ℭ **800/634-6661** or 702/731-7110. Fax 702/731-6636. www.caesars.com. 2,471 units. From $99 standard double, $109–$500 "run of house deluxe" double; $549–$1,000 suite. Extra person $20. Children under 18 stay free in parents' room. AE, DC, DISC, MC, V. Free self- and valet parking. **Amenities:** Restaurants (24); 3 outdoor pools; spa; health club.

Circus Circus Hotel/Casino   Circus Circus, once the epitome of kitsch, is trying to be taken more seriously. The bright primary colors and garish trims have vanished in favor of subtle, muted tones and high-rent touches that appeal more to the Cirque du Soleil crowd. Nevertheless, the world's largest permanent circus and indoor theme park are still here, and kids will love it. Tower rooms have newish, just slightly better-than-average furnishings; the Manor section comprises five white three-story buildings out back, fronted by rows of cypresses. These rooms are usually among the least expensive in town, but we've said it before and we'll say it again: You get what you pay for. A recent renovation of these rooms added a coat of paint and some new photos on the wall, but not much else. The hotel also has its own RV park. 2880 Las Vegas Blvd. S. (between Circus Circus Dr. and Convention Center Dr.), Las Vegas, NV 89109. ℭ **800/444-CIRC** (444-2472), 800/634-3450, or 702/734-0410. Fax 702/734-5897. www.circuscircus.com. 3,744 units. Sun–Thurs $39 and up double, Fri–Sat $59 and up double. Extra person $12. Children under 18 stay free in parents' room. AE, DC, DISC, MC, V. Free self- and valet parking. **Amenities:** Restaurants (8); 2 outdoor pools.

The Flamingo Las Vegas   It may be the Strip's senior citizen, but a recent renovation has made Bugsy Siegel's "real class joint" better than ever. The Flamingo's exceptional pool area encompasses fishponds, two water slides, five swimming pools, two whirlpools, waterfalls, and a flamingo enclave—plus its spa and tennis courts are a big draw. The guest rooms occupy six towers and sport various styles of decor, most with pretty fabrics and the usual array of room amenities. 3555 Las Vegas Blvd. S. (between Sands Ave. and Flamingo Rd.), Las Vegas, NV 89109. ℭ **800/732-2111** or 702/733-3111. Fax 702/733-3353. www.flamingolv.com. 3,999 units. $69–$299 double; $250–$580 suite. Extra person $20. Children 17 and under stay free in parents' room. Inquire about packages and timeshare suites. AE, DC, DISC, MC, V. Free self- and valet parking. **Amenities:** Restaurants (11); 5 outdoor pools; 4 night-lit tennis courts; spa; health club.

Golden Nugget   The jewel in Downtown's crown, the Golden Nugget is a luxurious European-style resort featuring gleaming marble and brass and sunny interior spaces. Rooms are decorated in a gold color scheme and feature marble entryways, half-canopy beds, and vanity tables with magnifying makeup mirrors. Suites include a good-size parlor with a wet bar, and his-and-her bathrooms (the latter has whirlpool tubs and potpourri!). The presence of a pool, and general overall quality, make this the best hotel Downtown for families; the other Downtowners seem geared towards the much older set and/or the single-minded gambler set. 129 E. Fremont St. (at Casino Center Blvd.), Las Vegas, NV 89101. ℭ **800/ 634-3454** or 702/385-7111. Fax 702/386-8362. www.goldennugget.com. 1,907 units. $59 and up double; $275 and up suite. Extra person $20. AE, DC, DISC, MC, V. Free self- and valet parking. **Amenities:** Restaurants (4); outdoor pool; spa; health club.

Hard Rock Hotel & Casino   The hip flock to the Hard Rock, drawn by the cool 'n' rockin' ambience that pervades the place, from the piano-shaped roulette tables to the "backstage pass" room keys. The new and newly-updated rooms are still a bit too '60s-futuristic hip to come off as posh, but they're certainly less immediately drab than the older versions, and they're more comfortable. Bathrooms are a big step forward—bigger, brighter, shinier. On a high note, the beds have feather pillows, and mattresses are surprisingly comfortable. On warm days and nights the Hard Rock's beach-party pool is *the* hangout scene. 4455 Paradise Rd. (at Harmon Ave.), Las Vegas, NV 89109. ☎ **800/473-ROCK (473-7625)** or 702/693-5000. Fax 702/693-5588. www.hardrockhotel.com. 657 units. Sun–Thurs $79 and up double, Fri–Sat $145 and up double; from $250 suite. Extra person $35. Children 12 and under stay free in parents' room. AE, DC, MC, V. Free self- and valet parking. **Amenities:** Restaurants (6); 2 outdoor pools; spa; health club.

Harrah's Las Vegas   Harrah's sports an elegant European carnival theme, and overall, it's a comfortable and fun place to stay. Guest rooms are slowly being refurbished at press time—make sure to ask for a newly renovated room. All the rooms are larger than average; the points that emerge from both the old and the new tower wings translate inside into an extra triangle of space for a couch and table. The rooms also contain a kitchen. Spacious minisuites in this section, offering large sofas and comfortable armchairs, are especially desirable. The hotel's health club is one of the better ones on the Strip, but the pool is underwhelming. 3475 Las Vegas Blvd. S. (between Flamingo and Spring Mountain roads), Las Vegas, NV 89109. ☎ **800/HARRAHS** (427-7247) or 702/369-5000. Fax 702/369-6014. www.harrahs. com. 2,700 units. $65–$195 standard "deluxe" double, $85–$250 standard "superior" double; $195–$1,000 suite. Extra person $20. No discount for children. AE, DC, DISC, MC, V. Free self- and valet parking. **Amenities:** Restaurants (8); outdoor pool; spa; health club.

Las Vegas Hilton   This classy hotel is magnificent, from its lobby, glittering with massive chandeliers and gleaming marble, to its 8-acre recreation deck. The Hilton's location next to the convention center makes it the preferred choice of business travelers, and its Star Trek attraction—with its own space-themed casino—beams in the leisure crowd. The comfortable rooms, remodeled a few years ago, have bathrooms with large marble tubs; some rooms offer views of an adjacent golf course. *Note:* As we went to press, the Hilton was for sale. Be aware that by the time you read this, some of the information contained here may have changed. 3000 Paradise Rd. (at Riviera Blvd.), Las Vegas, NV 89109. ☎ **888/732-7117** or 702/732-5111. Fax 702/732-5805. www.lvhilton.com. 3,174 units. $49 and up double. Extra person $30. Children under 18 stay free in parents' room. AE, DC, DISC, MC, V. Free self- and valet parking. **Amenities:** Restaurants (13); outdoor pool; spa; health club; golf course adjacent; 6 tennis courts (4 night-lit).

Luxor Las Vegas   It would be hard to miss the Luxor's 30-story pyramid, even without the 315,000-watt light beam at the top. The hotel is, despite outward appearances, inviting, classy, and functional. The Egyptian Revival lobby has been redone in marble and cherrywood and is one of the nicest lobbies in town. Rooms, among the few that really stand out in Vegas, feature fine Art Deco and Egyptian furnishings and have excellent marble bathrooms, although the recently renovated Pyramid rooms have showers only. High-speed "inclinator" elevators run on a 39-degree angle, making the ride up to the Pyramid rooms a bit of a thrill. Regardless of which room you get, these are some of the few rooms in Las Vegas that stand out. 3900 Las Vegas Blvd. S. (between Reno and Hacienda aves.), Las Vegas, NV 81119. ☎ **800/288-1000** or 702/262-4000. Fax 702/262-4452. www.luxor.com. 4,400 units. Sun–Thurs $49–$259 double, Fri–Sat $99 and up double; $149 and up whirlpool suite; $249–$800 other suites. Extra person $25. Children under 12 stay free in parents' room. AE, DC, DISC, MC, V. Free self- and valet parking. **Amenities:** Restaurants (10); 5 outdoor pools; spa; health club.

Main Street Station   The Main Street Station, one of the best bargains in the city, is just 2 short blocks away from Fremont Street in Downtown, barely a 3-minute walk. The overall look is turn-of-the-20th-century San Francisco, and the details, from the ornate chandeliers to the wood-paneled lobby, are outstanding. The long and narrow rooms are possibly the largest in Downtown, decorated with French provincial furniture. The bathrooms are small but well appointed. If you're a light sleeper, request a room on the south side. 200 N. Main St. (between Fremont St. and I-95), Las Vegas, NV 89101. ✆ **800/465-0711** or 702/387-1896. Fax 702/386-4466. www.mainstreetcasino.com. 452 units. $45–$175 standard double. AE, DC, DISC, MC, V. Free self- and valet parking. **Amenities:** Restaurants (3); use of outdoor pool next door at California Hotel.

Mandalay Bay   It doesn't really evoke Southeast Asia, but the Mandalay Bay actually looks like a resort hotel rather than just a Vegas version of one. You don't have to walk through the casino to get to any of these public areas or the guest room elevators, the pool area is spiffy, and the whole complex is marginally less confusing and certainly less overwhelming than some of the neighboring behemoths. Rooms are perhaps the finest on the Strip, spacious and subdued in decor. The large bathrooms, stocked with a host of fabulous amenities, are certainly the best on the Strip and maybe the best in Vegas. The hotel's highly touted wave pool isn't very surf-friendly, but it does offer a nice afternoon's relaxation. 3950 Las Vegas Blvd. S. (at Hacienda Ave.), Las Vegas, NV 89119. ✆ **877/632-7000** or 702/632-7000. Fax 702/632-7228. www.mandalaybay.com. 3,309 units. From $99 standard double; from $149 suite; from $149 House of Blues Signature Rooms. Extra person $35. AE, DC, DISC, MC, V. Free self- and valet parking. **Amenities:** Restaurants (13); 4 pools; spa; health club.

MGM Grand Hotel/Casino   Set on 114 acres, the massive MGM Grand has a green exterior and a theme incorporating all MGM movies. The casino, of course, remains the size of four football fields, and almost all traces of a failed movement to turn this into a child-friendly venue—including the amusement park—have been summarily wiped out. That said, the lion habitat; the fabulous pool area; and the MGM Grand Youth Center (✆ **702/891-3200**), which offers an array of activities for children ages 3 to 16, make this place popular with families. The Grand Tower guest rooms are beautifully decorated in Hollywood, Casablanca, Oz, and Old South motifs. Avoid the older Emerald Tower rooms. 3799 Las Vegas Blvd. S. (at Tropicana Ave.), Las Vegas, NV 89109. ✆ **800/929-1111** or 702/ 891-7777. Fax 702/891-1030. www.mgmgrand.com. 5,034 units. $69–$329 standard double; $99–$2,500 suite. Extra person $20. Children under 13 stay free in parents' room. AE, DC, DISC, MC, V. Free self- and valet parking. **Amenities:** Restaurants (14); outdoor pool; spa; health club.

The Mirage   From the moment you walk into the Mirage and breathe the faintly tropically perfumed air, you'll just know you are on vacation. The hotel, fronted by waterfalls and tropical foliage, centers on a very "active" volcano that erupts every 15 minutes after dark. Inside, you'll find a verdant rainforest, complete with habitats for Siegfried and Roy's white tigers, and a bunch of Atlantic bottlenose dolphins. The rooms have recently been redone (from their dated and generic all-beige theme to a stronger palette) and while the results are not distinctive, they are handsome. Further up the price scale are super-deluxe rooms with whirlpool tubs. The staff is genuinely helpful; any problems that may arise are quickly smoothed out. The pool is one of the nicest in Vegas. 3400 Las Vegas Blvd. S. (between Flamingo Rd. and Sands Ave.), Las Vegas, NV 89109. ✆ **800/627-6667** or 702/791-7111. Fax 702/791-7446. www.mirage.com. 3,323 units. Sun–Thurs $79–$399 double; Fri–Sat and holidays $159–$399 double; $250–$3,000 suite. Extra person $30. No discount for children. AE, DC, DISC, MC, V. Free self- and valet parking. **Amenities:** Restaurants (14); outdoor pool; spa; health club.

Monte Carlo Resort & Casino   This European-styled hotel casino is not as theme-intensive as its Strip brethren—a nice change of pace from the usual Vegas kitsch. Especially noteworthy are its 20,000-acre pool area—including a miniature water park—and its well-stocked spa, which charges a relatively cheap access fee compared to others on the Strip. Spacious rooms exude a warmly traditional European feel with rich cherrywood furnishings and vivid floral-print fabrics and carpeting. The bathrooms are merely decent; bathtubs are somewhat smaller than at comparably priced hotels. 3770 Las Vegas Blvd. S. (between Flamingo Rd. and Tropicana Ave.), Las Vegas, NV 89109. © **800/311-8999** or 702/730-7777. Fax 702/ 730-7250. www.monte-carlo.com. 3,002 units. Sun–Thurs $59–$179 double, Fri–Sat $109–$269 double; $149–$339 suite. Extra person $25. No discounts for children. AE, DC, DISC, MC, V. Free self- and valet parking. **Amenities:** Restaurants (7); 2 pools (1 wave pool, 1 kiddie pool); 3 night-lit tennis courts; spa; health club.

New York–New York Hotel & Casino   A visit to this spectacular hotel, which looks like the New York City skyline (complete with a roller coaster running through it) is a must. Subtle it isn't. You can gamble in a casino done up as Central Park or play games in the Coney Island arcade. You'll experience a true taste of the Big Apple—including the noise and the crowds. Rooms come in 64 different styles; some are downright tiny and suffocating (just like New York), but the Art Deco–style decor is generally smashing. Light sleepers should request a room away from the roller coaster. If you're a pool person, go elsewhere—the one here is pretty mediocre. 3790 Las Vegas Blvd. S. (at Tropicana Ave.), Las Vegas, NV 89109. © **800/693-6763** or 702/740-6969. Fax 702/740-6920. www.nynyhotelcasino. com. 2,033 units. Sun–Thurs from $59 double, Fri–Sat from $109 double. Extra person $20. No discount for children. AE, DC, DISC, MC, V. Free self- and valet parking. **Amenities:** Restaurants (10); outdoor pool; spa; health club.

Paris–Las Vegas Casino Resort   *Sacre bleu!* The City of Light comes to Sin City in this Strip fantasy hotel. It's theme-run-amok time again, and we are so happy about it. You can stroll down a mini Rue de la Paix, ride an elevator to the top of the Eiffel Tower, stop at an over-priced bakery for a baguette, take your photo by several very nice fountains, and snicker at dubious French signage ("le car rental"). Rooms are nice enough but disappointingly uninteresting, with furniture that only hints at mock French Regency, and with small but pretty bathrooms that have deep tubs. Try to get a Strip-facing room so you can see the Bellagio's fountains across the street; note also that north-facing rooms give you nice Peeping Tom views right into neighboring Bally's. Overall, not a bad place to stay but a great place to visit—*quelle hoot!* 3655 Las Vegas Blvd. S., Las Vegas, NV 89109. © **888/BONJOUR (266-5687)** or 702/946-7000. Fax 702/967-3836. www.parislv.com. 2,916 units. $119–$269 double; $350 and up suites. Extra person $30. Children under 18 stay free in parents' room. AE, DC, DISC, MC. V. Free self- and valet parking. **Amenities:** Restaurants (11); outdoor pool; spa; health club.

Rio All Suite Hotel & Casino   Although it's not on the Strip, the Rio Suites has a carnival atmosphere that packs in the crowds—and the accompanying noise. In addition to its tropically themed resort, the Rio has an immensely popular 41-story tower and Masquerade Village that simulate a European village, complete with shops, restaurants, and a bizarre live-action show in the sky. The "suites" are actually one rather large room with a sofa and coffee table. Rooms feature extra amenities such as fridges, and floor-to-ceiling windows that offer panoramic views of the Strip. Note that the hotel actively discourages guests from bringing children. 3700 W. Flamingo Rd. (at I-15), Las Vegas, NV 89103. ✆ 888/752-9746 or 702/777-7777. Fax 702/777-7611. www.playrio.com. 2,582 units. Sun–Thurs $90 and up double-occupancy suite, Fri–Sat $140 and up double-occupancy suite. Extra person $30. No discount for children. Inquire about golf packages. AE, DC, MC, V. Free self- and valet parking. **Amenities:** Restaurants (13); 4 outdoor pools; 18-hole golf course; spa; health club.

Stratosphere Las Vegas   At 1,149 feet, the Stratosphere is the tallest building west of the Mississippi; it's also in the middle of nowhere on the Strip, which explains the lack of crowds. The panoramic views available from the top of the tower and some amazing thrill rides (see "What to See & Do," earlier in this chapter) are the big attractions here. A new owner has been pumping money into this joint, and it shows. Rooms are furnished in Biedermeier-style cherrywood pieces and suites have Jacuzzi tubs right by the windows for a romantic soaking experience unlike any other in town. Ask for a high floor when you reserve to optimize your view. Another good viewing spot—the fantastic new pool area on the 8th floor. Sure, you still have that location problem, but the rooms are the right price, so we say, nab 'em. 2000 Las Vegas Blvd. S. (between St. Louis St. and Baltimore Ave.), Las Vegas, NV 89104. ✆ 800/99-TOWER (998-6937) or 702/380-7777. Fax 702/383-5334. www.stratospherehotel.com. 2,500 units. Sun–Thurs $39 and up double, Fri–Sat $59 and up double; $69 and up suite. Extra person $15. Children 12 and under stay free in parents' room. AE, DC, DISC, MC, V. Free self- and valet parking. **Amenities:** Restaurants (11); outdoor pool.

Treasure Island at the Mirage   Treasure Island is a veritable pirate's lair, complete with plenty of skulls, crossbones, treasure chests, pirate ships' figureheads, animatronic skeletons, and pirate nautical paraphernalia. A $25-million face-lift added more marble and gilded the bones (literally in some cases), but it's still Disney's Pirates of the Caribbean, but with lots and lots of money thrown at it. The hotel's exterior is an entire 18th-century pirate village, with the front consisting of a wooden dock from which spectators can view the free live-action pirate stunt show that plays every 90 minutes. The well-sized rooms are decorated in modified French Regency and monochromatic colors; the good bathrooms feature large soaking tubs. Though MGM MIRAGE ranks it fourth among its Strip properties, we'd rank it tops in value for money. 3300 Las Vegas Blvd. S. (at Spring Mountain Rd.), Las Vegas, NV 89177-0711. ✆ 800/944-7444 or 702/894-7111. Fax 702/894-7446. www.treasureisland.com. 2,891 units. From $69 double; from $109 suite. Extra person $25. No discount for children. Inquire about packages. AE, DC, DISC, MC, V. Free self- and valet parking. **Amenities:** Restaurants (11); outdoor pool; spa; health club.

The Venetian   The Venetian falls squarely between an outright adult Disneyland experience and the luxury resort sensibility of other Vegas hotels. The hotel impressively re-creates the city of Venice, including the artwork, the marble pillars and arches, and—unfortunately—the outrageous prices. Rooms are the largest and probably the most handsome in town. They are all "suites," with a good-size bedroom giving way to steps down to a sunken living area, complete with pullout sofa bed. Other touches include half-canopied beds, two TVs, and crown moldings on ceilings. Bathrooms feature glassed-in showers, deep soaking tubs, double sinks, fluffy towels, and lots of space. A branch of the famous Canyon Ranch Spa is on the premises. If there's a weak point, it's the hotel's pool area, which is disappointing and bland. 3355 Las Vegas Blvd. S., Las Vegas, NV 89109. ✆ 888/2-VENICE (283-6423) or 702/414-1000. Fax 702/414-4805. www.venetian.com. 3,354 units. $125–$399 double. AE, DC, DISC, MC, V. Extra person $35. Kids under 13 stay free in parents' room. Free self- and valet parking. **Amenities:** Restaurants (17); 5 outdoor pools; spa; health club.

4 Where to Dine

The dining scene in Las Vegas is a melting pot of midnight steak specials, cheap buffets, and gourmet rooms that rival those found in New York or Los Angeles. One word of warning: You can eat well in Vegas, and you can eat cheaply in Vegas, but because the dining renaissance in Vegas seems to have hit only the high-end joints in town, it hard to do both at the same time. We list a few of the city's best bets in town, but the inexpensive ones can be hard to find.

Theme restaurant buffs can chow down at **House of Blues,** in Mandalay Bay, 3950 Las Vegas Blvd. S. (© **702/791-STAR**); the **Hard Rock Cafe** at 4475 Paradise Rd., at Harmon Avenue (© **702/733-7625**); **ESPN** at 3790 Las Vegas Blvd. S., in New York New York Hotel & Casino (© **702/933-3776**); the **Harley Davidson Cafe,** 3725 Las Vegas Blvd. S., at Harmon Avenue (© **702/ 740-4555**); or the **Rainforest Cafe** in the MGM Grand, 3799 Las Vegas Blvd. S. (© **702/891-8580**).

For those wanting to sample one of the many hotel buffets—and it's an essential part of the Las Vegas vacation—some of the better bets include **Luxor's Pharaoh's Pheast Buffet,** 3900 Las Vegas Blvd. S. (© 702/262-4000); **Mirage Buffet,** 3400 Las Vegas Blvd. S. (© 702/791-7111); **Rio's Carnival World Buffet,** 3700 W. Flamingo Rd. (© 702/252-7777); **Paris Le Village Buffet,** 3665 Las Vegas Blvd. S. (© 888/266-5687); **Golden Nugget Buffet,** 129 E. Fremont St. (© 702/385-7111); and **Main Street Station Garden Court,** 200 N. Main St. (© 702/387-1896). The best Sunday brunch buffet in Vegas is **Bally's Sterling Sunday Brunch,** 3645 Las Vegas Blvd. S. (© 702/739-4111), which costs $50 per person.

Gourmands will also find plenty of dining options. Wolfgang Puck owns several restaurants in town (**Spago** in Caesars Palace was one of the first gourmet choices in Vegas), and you'll also find Emeril Lagasse, of Food Network fame, dishing up seafood at his **New Orleans Fish House** in the MGM Grand and his **Delmonico's Steakhouse** in the Venetian. Other famous restaurants with branches here include Pinot, Le Cirque, Aqua, Aureole, Olives, Star Canyon, Lutèce, and Border Grill.

Border Grill MEXICAN   For our money, here's the best Mexican food in town. This big cheerful space—like a Romper Room for adults—houses a branch of the much lauded L.A. restaurant, conceived and run by the Food Network's "Two Hot Tamales," Mary Sue Milliken and Susan Feniger. This is truly authentic Mexican home cooking. Consequently, don't expect precisely the same food you would encounter in your favorite corner joint, but do expect fresh and fabulous food, arranged as brightly on the plates as the decor on the walls. Don't miss the dense but fluffy Mexican chocolate cream pie (with a meringue crust). In Mandalay Bay, 3950 Las Vegas Blvd. S. © 702/632-7403. Reservations recommended. Main courses $15–$20. AE, DC, DISC, MC, V. Sun–Thurs 11:30am–10pm; Fri–Sat 11:30am–11pm.

Canaletto ITALIAN   Come here for solid, true Italian fare—and that means less sauce-intensive than the red-checked-tablecloth establishments of our American youths. Here, the emphasis is on the pasta, not the accompaniments. This place is all the more enjoyable for being perched on the faux St. Mark's Square; in theory, you can pretend you are sitting on the edge of the real thing, a fantasy we don't mind admitting we briefly indulged in. A risotto of porcini, sausage, and white truffle oil was full of strong flavors, while the wood-fired roast chicken was perfectly moist. You know, a properly roasted chicken should be a much-celebrated thing and that alone may be a reason to come here. In The Venetian Grand

Canal Shoppes, 3377 Las Vegas Blvd. S. ℂ 702/733-0070. Reservations recommended for dinner. Main courses $12–$29. AE, DC, MC, V. Sun–Thurs 11:30am–11pm; Fri–Sat 11:30am–midnight.

Capriotti's SANDWICHES   It looks like a dump but there's a reason that Capriotti's is one of the fastest growing businesses in town. They roast their own beef and turkeys on the premises and stuff them (or Italian cold cuts, or whatever) into sandwiches mislabeled "small," "medium," and "large"—the latter clocks in at 20 inches, easily feeding two for under $10 total. And deliciously so; the "Slaw B Joe" (roast beef, coleslaw, and Russian dressing) is fabulous. They even have veggie varieties. We never leave town without a stop here, and you shouldn't, either. 324 W. Sahara Ave (at Las Vegas Blvd. S.). ℂ 702/474-0229. Most sandwiches under $10. No credit cards. Daily 10am–7pm.

Commander's Palace CREOLE   This is an offshoot of the famous New Orleans restaurant, so we did expect a lot, and they came through. Service is nearly as good as at the original; no group of waiters hovering to fulfill every whim and remove every crumb, but we hardly felt neglected. And the food was, if not yet as spectacular as that of their elder cousin's, just about the best we've had in Vegas yet, with not one thing, from appetizer to dessert, that disappointed our palates. Your best bet is probably the $39 three-course Creole favorite, featuring Commander's justly legendary turtle soup with sherry, Louisiana pecan-crusted fish, and signature bread pudding soufflé, three things they do very very well indeed. 3663 Las Vegas Blvd. S. (in the Desert Passage in the Aladdin Hotel). ℂ 702/892-8272. www.commanderspalace.com. Reservations suggested. Lunch $16–$28; dinner $25–$39. AE, DISC, MC, V. Daily 11:30am–4:30pm and 6–9:30pm.

Grand Wok and Sushi Bar PAN-ASIAN   A pan-Asian restaurant runs the risk of attempting to be a jack of all trades and master of none, but somehow, this MGM eatery pulls it off. We didn't try every cuisine offered (Japanese, Chinese, Korean, Vietnamese, and maybe more!), but a random sampling (including lovely fresh sushi, fat dumplings, and a huge Vietnamese combo soup full of noodles and different kinds of meat) produced really superb food, delicately prepared. Note that soup portions are most generous—four people could easily split one order and have a nice light (or even heavier) and very cheap lunch. In the MGM Grand, 3799 Las Vegas Blvd. S. ℂ 702/891-7777. Reservations not accepted. Main courses $8.95–$14; sushi $4.50–$9.50. AE, DC, DISC, MC, V. Restaurant open daily 11am–11pm. Sushi bar open daily 5–11pm.

Liberty Cafe at the White Cross Pharmacy DINER   The soda fountain/lunch counter at the White Cross Pharmacy was Las Vegas's first 24-hour restaurant, and it has been going strong for 60 years. The menu is basic comfort food: standard grill items (meatloaf, ground round steak, chops), fluffy cream pies, and classic breakfasts served "anytime"—try the biscuits and cream gravy at 3am. But the best bet is a one-third-pound burger and "thick creamy shake," both the way they were meant to be and about as good as they get. At around $5, this is half what you would pay for a comparable meal at the Hard Rock Cafe. Places like this are a vanishing species—the neighborhood may not be the best, but it's worth the short walk from the Stratosphere. 1700 Las Vegas Blvd. S. ℂ 702/383-0196. Reservations not accepted. Most items under $7. No credit cards. Daily 24 hr.

Lotus of Siam THAI   We don't feel guilty about dragging you out to a strip mall in the east end of Nowhere because here is what critic Jonathan Gold of *Gourmet* magazine called no less than the best Thai restaurant in North America. In addition to all the usual beloved Thai favorites, they have a separate menu featuring lesser-known dishes from Northern Thailand—they don't routinely hand this one out (since most of the customers are there for the more pedestrian, if still excellent, $6 lunch buffet) Standouts include the Issan sausage, a grilled sour pork number; and *Sua Rong Hai* ("weeping tiger"), a dish of soft sliced grilled marinated beef. If you insist on more conventional Thai, you certainly won't be disappointed. 953 E. Sahara Ave. no. A-5. ℂ **702/735-3033.** Reservations strongly suggested for dinner. Lunch buffet $6, other dishes $3.95–$14. AE, MC, V. Daily 11:30am–2:30pm and 5–9:30pm.

Monte Carlo Pub & Brewery PUB FARE   Lest you think we are big, fat foodie snobs who can't appreciate a meal unless it comes drenched in truffles and caviar, we hasten to direct you to this lively (and we mean lively) working micro-brewery and its hearty, not-so-high-falutin' food. There's no romantic atmosphere thanks to the 40 TV sets sprinkled around the room—but no fancy French frills and, best of all, no inflated prices. Earning recent raves were the short ribs, in a fine barbecue sauce, and cooked just right; the excellent chicken fingers and shrimp fried-in-beer appetizers; and the garlic pizza with mounds of our favorite aromatic herb. After 9pm, only pizza is served, and dueling pianos provide dance music and entertainment. In the Monte Carlo Resort & Casino, 3770 Las Vegas Blvd. S. (between Flamingo Rd. and Tropicana Ave.). ℂ **702/730-7777.** Reservations not accepted. Main courses $6–$8. AE, DC, DISC, MC, V. Sun–Thurs 11am–3am; Fri–Sat 11am–4am.

Picasso FRENCH   Madrid born chef Julian Serrano's cooking stands proudly next to the $30 million worth of Picassos that pepper the dining room's walls, making a meal here a truly memorable experience. This may well be the best restaurant in Vegas, and given the serious competition for such a title, that says a lot. The menu changes nightly and is always a choice between a four- or five-course fixed-price dinner or tasting menu. We were bowled over by roasted Maine lobster with a "trio" of corn—kernels, sauce, and flan. Hudson Valley foie gras was crusted in truffles and went down smoothly. And finally, the lamb rôti was an outstanding piece of lamb, crusted with truffles—just hope it's on the menu the night you're there. For dessert, a molten chocolate cake leaves any other you may have tried in the dust. In Bellagio, 3600 Las Vegas Blvd. S. ℂ **702/693-7111.** Reservations recommended. Fixed-price 4-course dinner $80; 5-course degustation $90. AE, DC, DISC, MC, V. Thurs–Tues 6–9:30pm.

Rosemary's Restaurant AMERICAN   A 15-minute (or so) drive down Sahara is all it takes to eat what the *Vegas-Review Journal* calls the best food in Las Vegas. The brain-child of Michael and Wendy Jordan, both veterans of the New Orleans food scene, Rosemary's cuisine covers most regions of the U.S., though Southern influences dominate. Interesting sides include ultra-rich bleu cheese slaw and perfect cornmeal jalapeño hush puppies, to say nothing of "Grandma's pickled cucumbers." A recent visit found the crispy striped bass fighting it out with the pan-seared honey glazed salmon for "best fish dish I've ever had." Desserts are most pleasant. The restaurant, unusually, will give beer suggestions to pair with courses, including some fruity Belgium numbers; this is such a rare treat that if you drink, you must try some of their suggestions. 8125 W. Sahara. ℂ **702/869-2251.** Reservations strongly suggested. Lunch $12–$16; dinner $18–$29. AE, MC, V. Mon–Fri 11:30am–2:30pm and 5:30–10:30pm; Sat–Sun 5:30–10:30pm.

Second Street Grill INTERNATIONAL/PACIFIC RIM   One of the better-kept secrets of Las Vegas, this Downtown jewel is a lovely bit of romantic, cozy class with excellent food to boot. There is hardly a misstep on the menu, from taste to beautiful presentation. To call this food Hawaiian-influenced would be accurate, but forget flaming whatevers, and sickly sweet-and-sour sauce. This is more like what you would find in a top-flight restaurant on the Big Island. For starters, try the unusual lemon-chicken pot stickers and the duck confit. Entrees include lobster, ahi tuna, and filet mignon, but the whole fish, served in a bowl with a giant tea-leaf lid, is the best bet. Don't skip the Chocolate Explosion: a piece of chocolate cake topped with chocolate mousse, covered with a rich chocolate shell. In the Fremont Hotel & Casino, 200 E. Fremont St. *C* **702/385-3232.** Main courses $17–$23. Reservations recommended. AE, DC, DISC, MC, V. Sun–Mon and Thurs 6–10pm; Fri–Sat 5–11pm.

5 Las Vegas After Dark

Las Vegas is a town that truly comes alive only at night, and you won't lack for things to do. In addition to the free street shows (see "What to See & Do," earlier in this chapter), the hotels all have lounges, usually featuring live music, and you haven't truly done Vegas if you don't hit at least one showroom.

For up-to-date listings, call the **Las Vegas Convention and Visitors Authority** (*C* **877/VISITLV**) and ask them to send you a free copy of *Showguide* or *What's On in Las Vegas* (one or both of which will probably be in your hotel room). You can also check out what's playing at **www.vegasfreedom.com**. It's best to plan well ahead if you have your heart set on seeing one of the most popular shows or catching a major headliner. Admission to shows runs the gamut, from about $19 for "An Evening at La Cage" (a female impersonator show at the Riviera) to $100 and more for top headliners or Siegfried and Roy. Prices may include drinks or, in rare instances, dinner.

THE SHOWS

There are shows all over town, ranging from traditional magic shows to cutting-edge acts like *Mystère*. The showgirls remain, topless and otherwise. Las Vegas revues are what happened to vaudeville, by the way, as chorus girls do their thing in between jugglers, comics, magicians, singers, and specialty acts of dubious category. Even the topless shows are tame.

You won't go wrong seeing one of **Cirque du Soleil**'s two productions—they're the best in town. *O,* at the Bellagio (*C* **888/488-7111**), is a breathtaking mix of artistry and acrobatics over a 1½-million-gallon pool; *Mystère,* at Treasure Island (*C* **800/288-7206**), is a sophisticated and surreal circus extravaganza. The **Blue Men Group** at the Luxor is performance art for the masses, but don't let that prevent you from going and laughing your head off (*C* **702/262-4000**). And if you want to see a classic Vegas topless revue—oh, why not?—check out *Jubilee!* at Bally's (*C* **800/237-7469** or 702/739-4567).

Magic fans will love **Lance Burton: Master Magician,** at the Monte Carlo (*C* **800/311-8999**), whose sleight-of-hand tricks are extraordinary; or you can head for the illusions of **Siegfried & Roy,** at The Mirage (*C* **800/963-9634**), a Vegas institution for 2 decades. (Get tickets as far in advance as possible!)

Nighttime Is the Right Time

For a great selection of nightlife on the Strip, head for Mandalay Bay; **Aureole, Red Square, rumjungle!,** and the **House of Blues** are all popular. You might also check out the incredible nighttime view at the bar atop the **Stratosphere**—nothing beats it.

THE CLUB & BAR SCENE

Most Las Vegas bars and clubs don't even get going until close to midnight. To find out what's going on where, consult the *Las Vegas Weekly* (great club and bar descriptions in its listings) and *City Life* (weekly, with comprehensive listings of what's playing where all over town). You can pick up both at local restaurants, bars, record and music stores, and hep retail stores.

The Beach, 365 S. Convention Center Dr., at Paradise Road ((C) 702/731-1925; www.beachlv.com), is an immense two-story club that caters to the young and pretty who are looking to party. **Club Rio,** in the Rio Suites, 3700 W. Flamingo Rd. ((C) 702/252-7777), is one of the hottest clubs in town; it takes itself seriously but comes off as a grown-up, not terribly drunken, frat and sorority mixer. **Light,** at the Bellagio, 3600 Las Vegas Blvd. S. ((C) 702/693-8300), is a grown-up nightclub that caters to the silver spoon crowd but has a party atmosphere that doesn't feel exclusive.

Country music fans might want to wander on over to the casual **Dylan's,** 4660 Boulder Hwy. ((C) 702/451-4006), which offers country music (live and otherwise) and line dancing, with free dance lessons.

The 24-hour gay bar **Angles/Lace,** 4633 Paradise Rd., at Naples Street ((C) 702/791-0100), although upscale, is a casual neighborhood hangout, while **Gipsy,** located right next door at 4605 Paradise Rd. ((C) 702/731-1919), is the gay dance club that draws the biggest crowds.

It's still an honor for a comedian to play Vegas, and a number of good comedy clubs are on the Strip. Some good choices are **Comedy Stop,** in the Tropicana, 3801 Las Vegas Blvd. S. ((C) 800/468-9494); **The Improv,** at Harrah's, 3475 Las Vegas Blvd. S. ((C) 800/392-9002); and **Catch a Rising Star,** at Excalibur, 3850 Las Vegas Blvd. S. ((C) 800/937-7777).

Southern California

Southern California is Disneyland and Hollywood, sun and surf, and a thousand images that are familiar the world over. This is the epicenter of American pop culture. It's a land of contrasts, too: Expect everything from lavish resorts to funky mom-and-pop motels on the beach, from stunning coastline to silent expanses of desert.

1 Los Angeles & Environs

Los Angeles is a real-life version of one of those souvenir postcard folders that spill out images accordion-style: tall palm trees sweeping an azure sky, the gleaming white HOLLYWOOD sign, freeways flowing like concrete rivers, a lone surfer riding the day's last wave. Here, in the city that everyone loves to hate—and to experience, at least once in a lifetime—everything seems larger than life. Drive down Sunset Boulevard, and you'll see: The billboards are just a little bit taller, the wacky folks just a touch wackier.

ESSENTIALS

GETTING THERE **By Plane** Most visitors fly into **Los Angeles International Airport (LAX)** (*©* 310/646-5252; www.lawa.org/lax). Situated oceanside just off I-405, LAX is minutes away from the city's beach communities, and about a half hour from Westside, Hollywood, or downtown. **Travelers Aid** (*©* 310/646-2270) kiosks are in all terminals. Expect to pay about $35 for a taxi to Hollywood and downtown, $25 to Beverly Hills, $20 to Santa Monica, and $45 to $60 to the Valley and Pasadena.

By Train Amtrak (*©* 800/USA-RAIL; www.amtrak.com) serves Union Station, 800 N. Alameda St., on downtown's northern edge. There's frequent service from San Diego (trip time: 3 hr.), as well as daily service from Santa Barbara (3 hr.), Oakland (12 hr.), and Chicago (30 hr.).

VISITOR INFORMATION The **Los Angeles Convention and Visitors Bureau** (*©* 800/366-6116, or 213/689-8822 for events hot line; www.lacvb.com) operates a visitor center downtown at 685 S. Figueroa St., between Wilshire Boulevard and Seventh Street, open Monday through Friday from 8am to 5pm, Saturday from 8:30am to 5pm.

Many Los Angeles–area communities also have their own visitor centers, including the **Beverly Hills Visitors Bureau** (*©* 800/345-2210 or 310/248-1015; www.bhvb.org), and the **Santa Monica Convention and Visitors Bureau** (*©* 310/393-7593; www.santamonica.com).

GETTING AROUND Despite its hassles, driving is the only way to go. L.A. is one of the cheapest places in the United States to rent a car. All the major national rental-car agencies have offices at LAX.

While it's difficult to travel around L.A. entirely without a car, public transportation is available. The city's buses, commuter trains, and limited subway system are operated by the **Metropolitan Transit Authority (MTA)** (© 213/922-2000; www.mta.net).

FAST FACTS   To find a doctor, contact the **Uni-Health Information and Referral Hotline** (© 800/922-0000).

The combined Los Angeles County and California state sales taxes amount to 8.25%; hotel taxes range from 12% to 17%, depending on the municipality you're in.

SPECIAL EVENTS & FESTIVALS   New Year's Day is greeted by the spectacular **Tournament of Roses** (© 626/449-4100; www.tournamentofroses.com) parade in Pasadena, with lavish floats, music, and extraordinary equestrian entries, followed by the Rose Bowl Game.

On weekends from late April to Memorial Day, there's the annual **Renaissance Pleasure Faire** (© 800/52-FAIRE; http://renaissance-faire.com) in San Bernardino. Performers dress in 16th-century costume and revel in this festive re-creation of a medieval English village.

In early May, **Cinco de Mayo** (© 213/485-6855) ushers in a weeklong celebration throughout the city. The fiesta's carnival-like atmosphere is created by large crowds, live music, dances, and food. The main festivities are held in El Pueblo de Los Angeles State Historic Park, downtown, with other events around the city.

The **Los Angeles County Fair** (© 909/623-3111; www.fairplex.com), held at the Los Angeles County Fair and Exposition Center in Pomona, usually runs throughout September, with horse racing, arts, agricultural displays, celebrity entertainment, and carnival rides. It's the largest county fair in the world.

WHAT TO SEE & DO

Autry Museum of Western Heritage   "Singing Cowboy" Gene Autry's eponymous museum is one of California's best, a collection of art and artifacts of the West that's remarkably comprehensive and intelligently displayed. Evocative exhibits illustrate the everyday lives of early pioneers, not only with antique firearms, tools, saddles, and the like, but also with hands-on displays that stir the imagination and the heart. There's footage from Buffalo Bill's Wild West Show, movie clips from the silent days, contemporary films, and plenty of memorabilia from Autry's own film and TV projects. The "Hall of Merchandising" displays Roy Rogers bedspreads, Hopalong Cassidy radios, and other items from the collective consciousness—and material collections—of baby boomers. 4700 Western Heritage Way (in Griffith Park). © 323/667-2000. www.autry-museum.org. Admission $7.50 adults, $5 students and seniors 60 and over, $3 children 2–12; free to all 2nd Tues of each month. Tues–Sun 10am–5pm (Thurs until 8pm).

California Science Center   Using high-tech sleight-of-hand, the center stimulates kids of all ages with lessons about the world. One of the museum's highlights is Tess, a 50-foot animatronic woman whose muscles, bones, organs, and blood vessels are revealed, demonstrating how the body reacts to a variety of conditions. For more thrilling action, try the high-wire bicycle ride or the zero-gravity Space Docking Simulator. The IMAX theater screens breathtaking surround-sound movies in 2-D and 3-D throughout the day until 9pm. 700 State Dr., Exposition Park. © 213/SCIENCE, or 213/744-7400; IMAX theater © 213/744-2014. www.casciencectr.org. Free admission to the museum; IMAX theater $7 adults, $5.25 seniors over 60 and children 13–17, $4.25 kids 4–12. Parking $6. Daily 10am–5pm.

Southern California

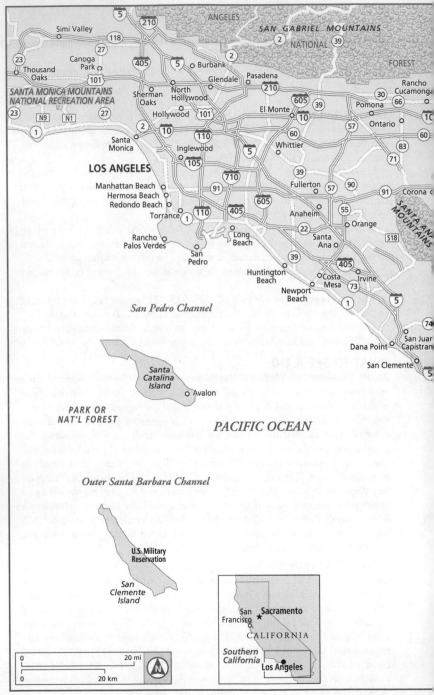

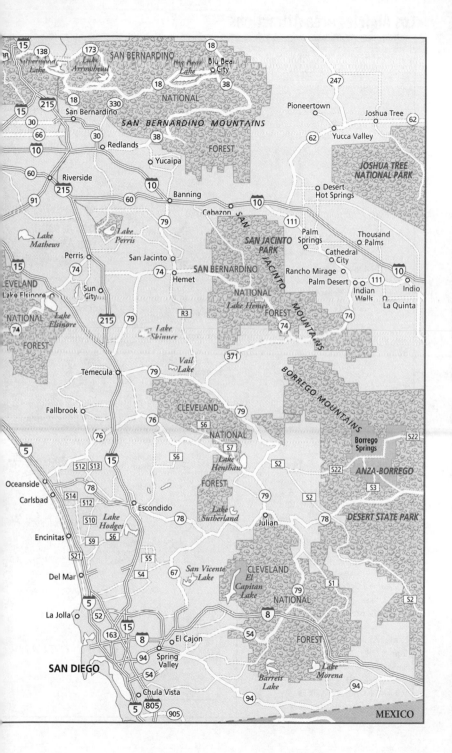

Los Angeles Area Attractions

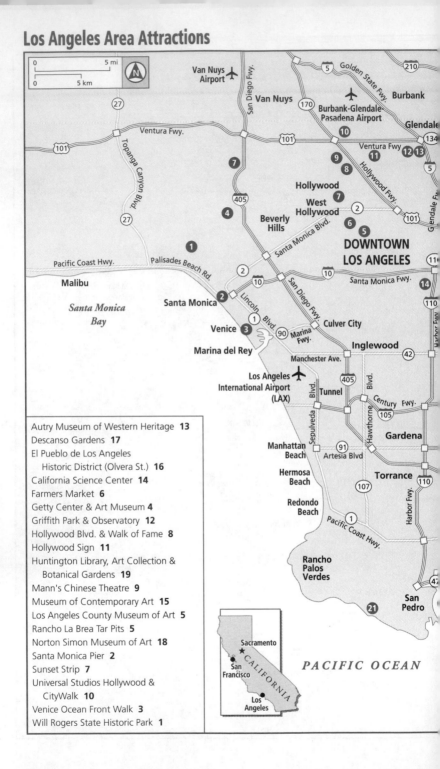

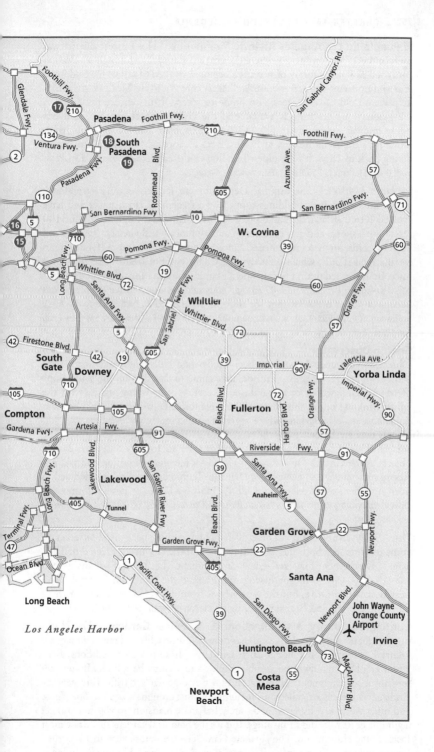

El Pueblo de Los Angeles Historic Monument   This historic district was built in the 1930s, on the site where the city was founded. Although it's a rather contrived nostalgic fantasy of the city's beginnings, L.A.'s Latinos have adopted it as an important cultural monument. At its core is a lively Mexican-style marketplace on old Olvera Street, also home to several 19th-century buildings. A self-guided tour brochure is available at the **visitor center,** in the Sepulveda house midway down Olvera (𝄐 **213/628-1274;** open Mon–Sat 10am–3pm). Don't miss the **Avila Adobe,** at E-10 Olvera St. (open Mon–Sat 10am–5pm); dating back to 1818, it's the oldest building in the city. Enter on Alameda St. across from Union Station. 𝄐 **213/628-3562.** www.cityofla.org/elp.

Farmers Market   The original Depression-era farmers' stands have slowly grown into permanent buildings topped by a trademark clock tower and have evolved into a sprawling marketplace with a carnival atmosphere. About 100 restaurants, shops, and grocers cater to a mix of locals and visitors. Retailers sell greeting cards, kitchen implements, candles, and souvenirs, but everyone comes for the food stands, which offer oysters, Cajun gumbo, fresh-squeezed orange juice, fresh-pressed peanut butter, and all kinds of international fast foods. Don't miss **Kokomo** (𝄐 **323/933-0773**), a "gourmet" outdoor coffee shop that has become a power breakfast spot for showbiz types. 6333 W. Third St. (at Fairfax Ave.), Hollywood. 𝄐 **323/933-9211.** www.farmersmarketla.com. Mon–Fri 9am–9pm; Sat 9am–8pm; Sun 10am–7pm.

Griffith Observatory   Made world-famous in *Rebel Without a Cause,* Griffith Observatory's bronze domes have been Hollywood Hills landmarks since 1935. Most visitors don't actually go inside; they come to this spot on the south slope of Mount Hollywood for unparalleled city views. On warm nights, with the lights twinkling below, this is one of the most romantic places in L.A. The main dome houses a planetarium, where narrated projection shows reveal the stars and planets that are hidden from the naked eye by the city's lights and smog. The adjacent Hall of Science holds exhibits on galaxies, meteorites, and other cosmic objects. *Note:* Griffith Observatory is closed for a major renovation and will not reopen until 2005. An "Observatory Satellite Temporary Facility" is scheduled to open near the Los Angeles Zoo. Call 𝄐 **323/664-1191** for more information. 2800 E. Observatory Rd. (in Griffith Park, at the end of Vermont Ave.). 𝄐 **323/664-1191.** www.griffithobservatory.org.

The "Hollywood" Sign   These 50-foot-high, white sheet-metal letters have come to symbolize both the movie industry and the city itself. Erected in 1923 as an advertisement for a real-estate development, the full text originally read HOLLYWOODLAND. A thorny hiking trail leads to the sign from Durand Drive near Beachwood Drive, but the best view is from down below, at the corner of Sunset Boulevard and Bronson Avenue. At the top of Beachwood Dr., Hollywood.

Huntington Library, Art Collections & Botanical Gardens   The Huntington Library is the jewel in Pasadena's crown. Industrialist and railroad magnate Henry E. Huntington collected such rarities as Shakespeare first editions, Benjamin Franklin's handwritten autobiography, and a Gutenberg Bible. If you prefer canvas to parchment, Huntington also put together a terrific 18th-century British and French art collection, including Gainsborough's *The Blue Boy.* These and other works are displayed in a stately Italianate mansion, so you can also get a glimpse of its splendid furnishings. But it's the botanical gardens that draw most locals to the Huntington. The Japanese Garden comes complete with a koi-filled stream and serene Zen garden. The cactus garden is exotic, the jungle garden is intriguing, the lily ponds are soothing—and there are many benches scattered about so you can sit and enjoy the surroundings. A popular English high tea (© 626/683-8131 for reservations) is served in the charming tearoom overlooking the Rose Garden. 1151 Oxford Rd., San Marino. © 626/405-2100. www.huntington.org. Admission $10 adults, $8.50 seniors 65 and over, $7 students and children 12 and over, free to children under 12; free to all 1st Thurs of each month. Sept–May Tues–Fri noon–4:30pm, Sat–Sun 10:30am–4.30pm, June–Aug Tues Sun 10:30am 4:30pm.

J. Paul Getty Museum at the Getty Center   Since opening in 1997, the Richard Meier–designed Getty Center has quickly assumed its place as a cultural cornerstone and international mecca. Museum galleries display J. Paul Getty's enormous art collection, which includes antiquities, Impressionist paintings, French decorative arts, illuminated manuscripts, contemporary photography, and graphic arts. One of the museum's finest holdings is van Gogh's *Irises*. Visitors park at the base of the hill and ascend via an electric tram. On clear days, the sensation is of being in the clouds, gazing across Los Angeles and the Pacific Ocean. Dining options include snack carts, a cafeteria, a cafe, and an elegant (though informal) restaurant. *Tip:* Avoid the crowds by visiting in the late afternoon or evening. 1200 Getty Center Dr. © 310/440-7300. www.getty.edu. Free admission. Tues–Thurs and Sun 10am–6pm; Fri–Sat 10am–9pm. Parking $5; reservations required Mon–Fri until 4pm.

Los Angeles County Museum of Art   This vast complex was designed by three very different architects and houses works by Degas, Rembrandt, Hockney, and Monet. The **Japanese Pavilion** contains a collection of Edo paintings rivaled only by the holdings of the emperor of Japan. The **Anderson Building** is home to 20th-century painting and sculpture by Matisse, Magritte, and a number of Dada artists. The **Ahmanson Building** houses the rest of the museum's permanent collections, everything from 2,000-year-old pre-Columbian Mexican ceramics to a unique glass collection spanning the centuries, plus one of the nation's largest holdings of costumes and textiles along with important Indian and Southeast Asian art. The **Hammer Building** is primarily used for major special-loan exhibitions. Film series are presented at the **Leo S. Bing Theater.** The museum recently took over the former May Company department store 1 block away, converting the historic Art Deco building into gallery space. 5905 Wilshire Blvd. © 323/857-6000. www.lacma.org. Admission $7 adults, $5 students and seniors 62 and over, $1 children 6–17; regular exhibitions free to all 2nd Tues of each month. Mon–Tues and Thurs noon–8pm; Fri noon–9pm; Sat–Sun 11am–8pm. Parking $5.

Mann's Chinese Theatre   One of the world's great movie palaces, the Chinese Theatre was opened in 1927 by entertainment impresario Sid Grauman, a brilliant promoter who's credited with originating the idea of the paparazzi-packed movie premiere. Original Chinese heavenly doves top the facade, and two of the theater's columns once propped up a Ming Dynasty temple. Visitors flock to the theater for its famous entry court, where stars like Elizabeth Taylor, Ginger Rogers, Humphrey Bogart, Frank Sinatra, Marilyn Monroe, and about 160 others set their signatures and hand- and footprints in concrete. 6925 Hollywood Blvd. (1 block west of Highland Ave.). © 323/464-MANN or 323/461-3331. www.mann theaters.com. Movie tickets $9. Call for showtimes.

Museum of Contemporary Art/Geffen Contemporary at MOCA MOCA is Los Angeles's only institution devoted to art from 1940 to the present. It's particularly strong in works by Cy Twombly, Jasper Johns, and Mark Rothko. MOCA is housed in three buildings: The main building at 250 S. Grand Ave. is a contemporary red-sandstone structure by renowned Japanese architect Arata Isozaki. The museum's second space, at 152 N. Central Ave. in Little Tokyo, houses a superior permanent collection in a warehouse-type space. Unless there's a visiting exhibit of great interest at the main museum, start at the Geffen building, where it's also easier to park. The third gallery, which opened in 2001, is next to the Pacific Design Center at 8687 Melrose Ave. in West Hollywood. Unlike the other two, admission to this gallery is only $3, and emphasis is on contemporary architecture and design, as well as new work by emerging and established artists. Main MOCA information line ☎ **213/626-6222**. www.moca-la.org. Admission $8 adults, $5 students and seniors 65 and over, free for children 11 and under. Tues–Wed and Fri–Sun 11am–5pm; Thurs 11am–8pm.

Norton Simon Museum of Art   Architect Frank Gehry recently helped remodel the galleries at what has become one of California's most important museums. Comprehensive collections of masterpieces by Degas, Picasso, Rembrandt, and Goya are augmented by sculptures by Henry Moore and Auguste Rodin. The "Blue Four" collection of works by Kandinsky, Jawlensky, Klee, and Feininger is impressive, as are the superb Southeast Asian sculptures. One of the most popular pieces is *The Flower Vendor/Girl with Lilies* by Diego Rivera. 411 W. Colorado Blvd., Pasadena. ☎ **626/449-6840**. www.nortonsimon.org. Admission $6 adults, $3 seniors, free for students and kids 12 and under. Wed–Mon noon–6pm (Fri until 9pm). Free parking.

Rancho La Brea Tar Pits   The La Brea Tar Pits are an awesome, primal sight right on Museum Row, where hot tar has been bubbling from the earth for more than 40,000 years. The glistening pools have enticed thirsty animals throughout history. Thousands of mammals, birds, amphibians, and insects mistakenly crawled into the sticky sludge and stayed forever. In 1906, scientists began a systematic removal and classification of entombed specimens, including ground sloths, giant vultures, mastodons, camels, and even prehistoric relatives of today's super-rats. The best finds are on display in the adjacent George C. Page Museum of La Brea Discoveries, which also shows an entertaining 15-minute film documenting the recoveries. 5801 Wilshire Blvd. (east of Fairfax Ave.). ☎ **323/934-PAGE**. www.tarpits.org. Admission $6 adults, $3.50 students and seniors 62 and over, $2 children 5–12; free to all 1st Tues of each month. Mon–Fri 9:30am–5pm; Sat–Sun 10am–5pm.

Universal Studios Hollywood   Universal is more than just one of the largest movie studios in the world—it's one of the biggest amusement parks. The main attraction is the **Studio Tour,** a 1-hour guided tram ride that gives you a peek at stars' dressing rooms, production offices, and back-lot sets that include the famous town square from the *Back to the Future* films. Along the way, the tram encounters several staged "disasters," which we won't divulge here lest we ruin the surprise. On **Back to the Future—The Ride,** you're seated in a mock time-traveling DeLorean and thrust into a fantastic multimedia roller-coasting extravaganza. The special-effects showcase **Jurassic Park—The Ride** is short in duration but long on dinosaur illusions and computer magic. The latest thrills are the **Mummy Returns Chamber of Doom** ride (scarrrrrrryyyy) and **Terminator 2 3-D,** a virtual adventure utilizing triple-screen technology to hit all the senses. The new **Animal Planet Live!** stars trained monkeys and other animals doing various tricks. It's all fun, but lines can be brutally long; skip weekends and school vacations if possible. Hollywood Fwy. (Universal Center Dr. or Lankershim Blvd. exits), Universal City. ☎ **818/662-3801**. www.universalstudios.com. Admission $45 adults, $35 children 3–9. Parking $7. Mon–Fri 10am–6pm; Sat–Sun 9am–7pm.

Venice Ocean Front Walk   No visit to Los Angeles would be complete without a stroll along Venice's famous beach path, an almost surreal assemblage of every L.A. stereotype—and then some. Among stalls and stands selling cheap sunglasses and Mexican blankets swirls a carnival of humanity that includes bikini-clad in-line skaters, tattooed bikers, muscle-bound pretty boys, panhandling vets, beautiful wannabes, and plenty of tourists and gawkers. On any given day, you're bound to come across all kinds of performers: mimes, buskers, chainsaw jugglers, talking parrots, and the occasional apocalyptic evangelist. On the beach, between Venice Blvd. and Rose Ave., Venice. www.venicebeach.com.

MORE HIGHLIGHTS
TV TAPINGS

Being part of the audience for the taping of a television show might be the quintessential L.A. experience. Timing is important here—remember that most series productions go on hiatus from March to July. Tickets to the top shows, like *Friends* and *Everybody Loves Raymond,* are in greater demand than others, so getting your hands on them usually takes advance planning—and possibly some time waiting in line.

Request tickets as far in advance as possible. In addition to the suppliers listed below, tickets are sometimes given away to the public outside popular tourist sites like Mann's Chinese Theatre in Hollywood and Universal Studios in the Valley; L.A.'s visitor centers in downtown and Hollywood often have tickets as well. But if you're determined to see a particular show, contact the following sources.

Audiences Unlimited, Inc. (℗ 818/753-3470; www.tvtickets.com) is a good place to start. It distributes tickets for most of the top sitcoms, including *Friends, That '70s Show, Will & Grace, The Drew Carey Show, Everybody Loves Raymond,* and many more. **Television Tickets** (℗ 323/467-4697) distributes tickets for talk and game shows, including *Jeopardy!,* as does **TVTIX.COM** (℗ 323/653-4105; www.tvtix.com). You can get tickets for *The Tonight Show with Jay Leno* in two ways: Pick them up at the NBC ticket counter on the day of the show, or, at least 6 weeks before your visit, send a self-addressed, stamped envelope with your ticket request to **NBC,** 3000 W. Alameda Ave., Burbank, CA 91523 (℗ 818/840-3537; www.nbc.com).

HITTING THE BEACH

Los Angeles County's 72-mile coastline sports over 30 miles of beaches, most of which are operated by the **Department of Beaches & Harbors,** 13837 Fiji Way, Marina del Rey (℗ 310/305-9503). County-run beaches usually charge for parking; alcohol, bonfires, and pets are prohibited. For recorded surf conditions (and coastal weather forecast), call ℗ 310/457-9701. The following are the county's best beaches, listed from north to south.

ZUMA BEACH COUNTY PARK   Jam-packed on warm weekends, L.A. County's largest beach park is located off the Pacific Coast Highway (Calif. 1), a mile past Kanan Dume Road. While it can't claim to be the loveliest beach in the Southland, Zuma has the most comprehensive facilities: plenty of restrooms, lifeguards, playgrounds, volleyball courts, and snack bars. The southern stretch, toward Point Dume, is Westward Beach, separated from the noisy highway by sandstone cliffs. A trail leads over the point's headlands to Pirate's Cove, once a popular nude beach.

MALIBU LAGOON STATE BEACH   Malibu Lagoon is not just a pretty white-sand beach, but an estuary and wetlands area as well. The entrance is on the Pacific Coast Highway (Calif. 1) south of Cross Creek Road, and there's a small admission charge. Marine life and shorebirds teem where the creek empties into the sea, and the waves are always mild. The historic Adamson House is here, a showplace of Malibu tile now operating as a museum.

SURFRIDER BEACH Without a doubt, L.A.'s best waves roll ashore here. One of the city's most popular surfing spots, this beach is located between the Malibu Pier and the lagoon. Few "locals-only" wave wars are ever fought here— surfing is not as territorial here as it can be in other areas, where out-of-towners can be made to feel unwelcome. Surfrider is surrounded by all of Malibu's hustle and bustle, so don't come here for peace and quiet.

WILL ROGERS STATE BEACH Three miles along the Pacific Coast Highway (Calif. 1), between Sunset Boulevard and the Santa Monica border, are named for the American humorist whose ranch-turned-state-historic-park is nestled above the palisades that provide the backdrop for this popular beach. Facilities include a pay parking lot, restrooms, lifeguards, and a snack hut in season. While the surfing is not the best, the waves are friendly for swimmers and there are always competitive volleyball games to be found.

SANTA MONICA STATE BEACH The beaches on either side of the Santa Monica Pier are popular for their white sands and easy accessibility. There are big parking lots, eateries, and lots of restrooms. A paved beach path runs along here, allowing you to walk, bike, or skate to Venice and points south. Colorado Boulevard leads to the pier; turn north on the Pacific Coast Highway (Calif. 1) below the coastline's bluffs, or south along Ocean Avenue; you can find parking in both directions.

VENICE BEACH Moving south from Santa Monica, the paved pedestrian Promenade becomes Ocean Front Walk and gets progressively weirder until it reaches an apex at Washington Boulevard and the Venice fishing pier. Although there are people who swim and sunbathe, Venice Beach's character is defined by the sea of humanity that gathers here, plus the bevy of boardwalk vendors and old-fashioned pedestrian streets a block away. Park on the side streets or in the plentiful lots west of Pacific Avenue.

HERMOSA CITY BEACH A very wide white-sand beach with tons to recommend it, Hermosa extends to either side of the pier and includes "The Strand," a pedestrian lane that runs its entire length. Main access is at the foot of Pier Avenue, which is lined with interesting shops. There's plenty of street parking, as well as restrooms, lifeguards, volleyball courts, a fishing pier, playgrounds, and good surfing.

ORGANIZED TOURS

STUDIO TOURS Paramount Pictures, 5555 Melrose Ave., Hollywood (© 323/956-5575; www.paramount.com), offers a 2-hour walking tour that's both a historical ode to filmmaking and a real-life look at a working studio. The $15 tour departs hourly from 9am to 2pm Monday through Friday. Cameras, recording equipment, and children under 10 are not allowed.

NBC Studios, 3000 W. Alameda Ave., Burbank (© 818/840-3537), offers guided 70-minute tours Monday through Friday from 9am to 3pm that feature a behind-the-scenes look at *The Tonight Show with Jay Leno* set, wardrobe, makeup, and set-building departments, and several sound studios. The tour includes some cool video demonstrations of high-tech special effects. Prices are $7.50 for adults, $$6.75 for seniors, and $4 for children.

Warner Brothers Studios, 4301 W. Olive Ave., Burbank (© **818/972-TOUR;** www.wbstudiotour.com), has the most comprehensive—and the least theme-park–like—of the studio tours. The 2-hour drive-and-walk jaunt goes around the studio's faux streets, including stops at active film and television sets. Whether it's an orchestra scoring a film or a TV show being taped or edited, you'll get a glimpse of how it's all done. Tours are $32 (kids under 8 not admitted), and are offered Monday through Friday from 9am to 4pm. Reservations are required.

SIGHTSEEING TOURS   L.A. Tours (© **323/993-0093;** www.la-tours.com) operates regularly scheduled tours of the city. Plush shuttle buses pick up riders from major hotels for morning or afternoon tours of Sunset Strip, movie studios, Farmers Market, Hollywood, homes of the stars, and other attractions. Tours vary in length from a half to a full day and cost $42 to $58 for adults. There are discounts for kids; book online for a $4 discount. Reservations are required.

GREAT SHOPPING AREAS

Serious shoppers often make Santa Monica their first stop; the seaside end of L.A. offers many diverse shopping neighborhoods, including **Third Street Promenade** (www.thirdst.com), a pedestrians-only outdoor mall boasting trendy chain stores and boutiques as well as dozens of restaurants and a large movie theater. The Promenade bustles on into the evening with a seemingly endless assortment of street performers and shoppers.

Main Street, between Pacific Street and Rose Avenue, is another good strip for strolling, boasting a healthy combination of mall standards as well as left-of-center boutiques and casually hip cafes; Main Street's relaxed, beach-community vibe sets it apart, straddling the fashion fence between upscale trendy and beach-bum edgy.

And there's **Montana Avenue,** between Seventh and 17th streets, a breezy, slow-traffic stretch where specialty shops still outnumber the chains. Look around and you'll see upscale moms with strollers shopping for designer fashions, country-home decor, and gourmet takeout.

Elsewhere in L.A., check out **West Third Street,** between Fairfax Avenue and Robertson Boulevard: You can shop till you drop on this trendy strip, anchored on the east end by the Farmers Market. "Fun" is more the catchword here than "funky," and the shops (including the vintage-clothing stores) tend a bit more to the refined. Nearby, **La Brea Avenue,** north of Wilshire Boulevard, is L.A.'s artsiest shopping strip. Anchored by the giant **American Rag, Cie.** alternacomplex (© **323/935-3157**), La Brea is home to lots of great urban antiques stores dealing in Deco, Arts and Crafts, 1950s modern, and the like. You'll also find vintage clothiers, furniture galleries, and other warehouse-size stores, as well as some of the city's hippest restaurants, such as Campanile.

Everyone knows about **Rodeo Drive,** the city's most famous shopping street. Couture shops from high fashion's old guard—like Gucci and Hermès—are here, along with plenty of newer high-end labels. The 16-square-block area surrounding Rodeo is known as Beverly Hills' **"Golden Triangle."** Shops off Rodeo are generally not as name-conscious as those on the strip, but they're nevertheless plenty upscale. **Niketown** (© **310/275-9998**) is a behemoth shrine to the reigning athletic-gear king.

Although stretches of **Melrose Avenue** are showing some wear, this is still one of the most exciting shopping streets in the country for cutting-edge fashions—and some eye-popping people-watching to boot. There are scores of shops selling the latest in clothes, gifts, jewelry, and accessories. Melrose is a playful stroll, dotted with plenty of hip restaurants and funky shops that are sure to shock. Where else could you find green patent-leather cowboy boots, a working 19th-century pocket watch, an inflatable girlfriend, and glow-in-the-dark condoms in the same shopping spree?

WHERE TO STAY

In sprawling Los Angeles, location is everything. Choosing the right neighborhood as a base can make or break your vacation; if you plan to while away a few days at the beach but base yourself downtown, for example, you're going to lose a lot of valuable relaxation time on the freeway. But wherever you stay, count on doing a good deal of driving—no hotel in Los Angeles is convenient to everything.

In general, **downtown** hotels are business-oriented; the top hotels here are very good, but cheaper ones can be downright nasty. **Hollywood,** centrally located between downtown and Beverly Hills and within easy reach of Santa Monica, makes a great base—but there are fewer hotels here than you'd expect, mostly moderately priced choices. Most visitors stay in the city's **Westside,** a short drive from the beach and close to many of L.A.'s most colorful sights. The city's most elegant—and expensive—accommodations are in Beverly Hills and Bel Air. You'll find the city's best hotel values in West Hollywood, an exciting and convenient place to settle in. Trendy, relatively smogless **Santa Monica** and its coastal neighbors are home to lots of hotels; book ahead because they fill up quickly in the summer. Santa Monica also enjoys convenient freeway access to the popular tourist sights inland. Malibu and the South Bay communities (Manhattan, Hermosa, and Redondo beaches) are more out of the way, and hence quieter. Families might want to head to the **San Fernando Valley** to be near Universal Studios.

Companies that can help you make bookings include **Accommodations Express** (© 800/950-4685; www.accommodationsexpress.com), **Hotel Reservations Network** (© 800/715-7666; www.hoteldiscounts.com), and **Quikbook** (© 800/789-9887, includes a fax-on-demand service; www.quikbook.com).

In addition to the listings below, other good bets near the beach include the **Cal Mar Hotel Suites,** 220 California Ave., Santa Monica (© **800/776-6007** or 310/395-5555), whose garden apartments are lovingly cared for and deliver a lot of bang for your vacation buck; and the **Best Western Marina Pacific Hotel & Suites,** 1697 Pacific Ave., Venice (© **800/780-7234** or 310/452-1111), a haven of smart value just off the newly renovated Venice Boardwalk.

The **Beverly Laurel Motor Hotel,** 8018 Beverly Blvd. (© **800/962-3824** or 323/651-2441), is a great choice for wallet-watching travelers who want a central location and a room with more style than your average motel.

If you need an airport hotel, two good, moderately priced choices are the **Sheraton Gateway Hotel,** 6101 W. Century Blvd., near Sepulveda Boulevard (© **800/325-3535** or 310/642-1111), and the **Marriott Los Angeles Airport,** 5855 Century Blvd. (© **800/228-9290** or 310/641-5700).

Avalon Hotel   Leading the pack of retro-stylish boutique hotels is this marvelous mid-century–inspired gem in the heart of Beverly Hills. The main building, the former Beverly-Carlton (seen on *I Love Lucy* and once home to Marilyn Monroe), is the hub of a chic but low-key scene; in the quieter Canon building, many of the units have kitchenettes and/or terraces. In-room fax machines, VCRs, CD players, terry robes, and top-of-the-line bedding are standard. Service is friendlier than you'll find in other style-minded hotels. 9400 W. Olympic Blvd. (at

Beverly Dr.), Beverly Hills, CA 90212. ⓒ 800/535-4715 or 310/277-5221. Fax 310/277-4928. www.avalon-hotel.com. 88 units. $100-$280 double; from $249 junior or 1-bedroom suite. Extra person $25. AE, DC, MC, V. Valet parking $17. **Amenities:** Restaurant; pool.

Beverly Hills Hotel & Bungalows   Behind the famous facade of the "Pink Palace" (pictured on the Eagles' *Hotel California*) lies this star-studded haven where legends were, and still are, made. The hotel's grand lobby and impeccably landscaped grounds retain their over-the-top glory, while the lavish rooms boast state-of-the-art luxuries such as marble bathrooms, CD players, VCRs, fax/copier/scanners, and butler service at the touch of a button. Many units feature private patios, Jacuzzis, and kitchens. Dining options include the iconic Polo Lounge, the famous Fountain Coffee Shop, and the alfresco Cabana Club Cafe. 9641 Sunset Blvd. (at Rodeo Dr.), Beverly Hills, CA 90210. ⓒ 800/283-8885 or 310/276-2251. Fax 310/281-2905. www.beverlyhillshotel.com. 203 units. $345–$375 double; from $745 suite or bungalow. AE, DC, MC, V. Parking $23. **Amenities:** Restaurants (3); outdoor pool; 2 lighted tennis courts; fitness center; pets accepted in bungalows only.

Casa del Mar   This Art Deco stunner is a dream of a resort hotel, radiating period glamour. The villalike building's shape awards ocean views to most of the guest rooms, whose abundant luxuries include sumptuously dressed beds, marble bathrooms with whirlpool tubs, CD players, VCRs, and playful treats like rubber duckies. The Oceanfront restaurant has earned justifiable kudos (and more than a few celebrity fans) for its lovely setting and seafood-heavy California cuisine. 1910 Ocean Way (next to the Santa Monica Pier), Santa Monica, CA 90405. ⓒ 800/898-6999 or 310/581-5533. Fax 310/581-5503. www.hotelcasadelmar.com. 129 units. $345–$625 double; from $875 suite. AE, DC, DISC, MC, V. Valet parking $21. **Amenities:** Restaurants (2); outdoor pool; health club.

Casa Malibu   Evoking the heyday of Malibu's Golden Age, this modest, low-rise inn on the beach is a refreshing alternative to sleek, impersonal resorts. Wrapped around a palm-studded inner courtyard, the rooms are comfortable, charming, and thoughtfully outfitted in a timeless "California beach cottage" look. Many have been upgraded with air-conditioning and VCRs, but even the older ones are in great shape and boast top-quality bedding, robes, and fridges. Some units have fireplaces, kitchenettes, and CD players. A handsome brick sun deck faces the blue Pacific, while wooden stairs lead to the hotel's private beach. 22752 Pacific Coast Hwy. (about ¼ mile south of Malibu Pier), Malibu, CA 90265. ⓒ 800/831-0858 or 310/456-2219. Fax 310/456-5418. www.casamalibu.com. 21 units. $99–$169 garden- or oceanview double; $199–$229 beachfront double; $229–$349 suite. Rates include continental breakfast. Extra person $15. AE, MC, V. Free parking. **Amenities:** Access to nearby private health club.

Georgian Hotel   This eight-story Art Deco beauty boasts luxury comforts, loads of historic charm, and a terrific location, just across the street from Santa Monica's beach and pier. The elegant Classical Revival architecture is beautifully accented with a well-chosen palette of bold pastels (à la Miami Beach's hotels of the same era). Every comfort is considered, from the cushy chaises on the veranda to the beautifully designed rooms, which contain down comforters, fax machines, and robes; suites have sleeper sofas and CD players as well. The hotel has an unobstructed coastal vista, so most rooms have at least a partial or full ocean view. 1415 Ocean Ave. (between Santa Monica Blvd. and Broadway), Santa Monica, CA 90401. ⓒ 800/538-8147 or 310/395-9945. Fax 310/656-0904. www.georgianhotel.com. 84 units. $235–$310 double; from $350 suite. AE, DC, DISC, MC, V. Valet parking $18. **Amenities:** Restaurant; fitness room.

Los Angeles Area Accommodations & Dining

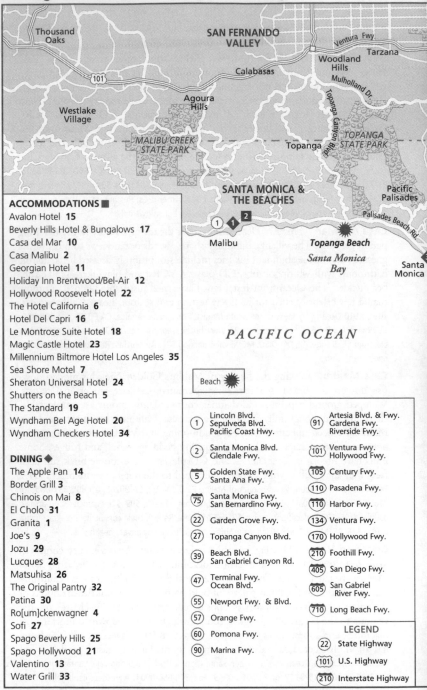

ACCOMMODATIONS ■
Avalon Hotel **15**
Beverly Hills Hotel & Bungalows **17**
Casa del Mar **10**
Casa Malibu **2**
Georgian Hotel **11**
Holiday Inn Brentwood/Bel-Air **12**
Hollywood Roosevelt Hotel **22**
The Hotel California **6**
Hotel Del Capri **16**
Le Montrose Suite Hotel **18**
Magic Castle Hotel **23**
Millennium Biltmore Hotel Los Angeles **35**
Sea Shore Motel **7**
Sheraton Universal Hotel **24**
Shutters on the Beach **5**
The Standard **19**
Wyndham Bel Age Hotel **20**
Wyndham Checkers Hotel **34**

DINING ◆
The Apple Pan **14**
Border Grill **3**
Chinois on Mai **8**
El Cholo **31**
Granita **1**
Joe's **9**
Jozu **29**
Lucques **28**
Matsuhisa **26**
The Original Pantry **32**
Patina **30**
Ro[um]ckenwagner **4**
Sofi **27**
Spago Beverly Hills **25**
Spago Hollywood **21**
Valentino **13**
Water Grill **33**

PACIFIC OCEAN

Beach 🌟

①	Lincoln Blvd. Sepulveda Blvd. Pacific Coast Hwy.	91	Artesia Blvd. & Fwy. Gardena Fwy. Riverside Fwy.
②	Santa Monica Blvd. Glendale Fwy.	101	Ventura Fwy. Hollywood Fwy.
5	Golden State Fwy. Santa Ana Fwy.	105	Century Fwy.
75	Santa Monica Fwy. San Bernardino Fwy.	110	Pasadena Fwy.
22	Garden Grove Fwy.	110	Harbor Fwy.
27	Topanga Canyon Blvd.	134	Ventura Fwy.
39	Beach Blvd. San Gabriel Canyon Rd.	170	Hollywood Fwy.
47	Terminal Fwy. Ocean Blvd.	210	Foothill Fwy.
55	Newport Fwy. & Blvd.	405	San Diego Fwy.
57	Orange Fwy.	605	San Gabriel River Fwy.
60	Pomona Fwy.	710	Long Beach Fwy.
90	Marina Fwy.		

LEGEND
22	State Highway
101	U.S. Highway
210	Interstate Highway

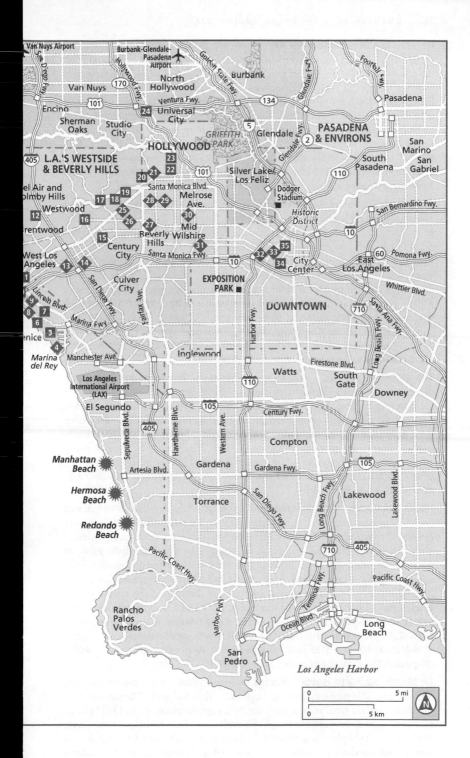

Holiday Inn Brentwood/Bel-Air   Popular with older travelers and museum groups, this L.A. landmark is the last of a vanishing breed of circular hotels from the 1960s and '70s. It's a short hop from the Getty Center (free shuttle service provided) and centrally located between the beaches, Beverly Hills, and the San Fernando Valley. Each pie-shaped room boasts a private balcony and little extras (like Nintendo games and great views) that add panache to otherwise unremarkable chain-style accommodations. The top-floor restaurant boasts a 360-degree view. 170 N. Church Lane (at Sunset Blvd. and I-405), Los Angeles, CA 90049. © 800/ HOLIDAY or 310/476-6411. Fax 310/472-1157. www.holiday-inn.com/brentwood-bel. 211 units. $149–$189 double; from $275 suite. AE, DC, DISC, MC, V. Self-parking $8, valet parking $10. **Amenities:** Restaurant; outdoor pool; fitness room; small pets accepted ($50).

Hollywood Roosevelt Hotel   This movie-city landmark, across from Mann's Chinese Theatre and down the street from the Walk of Fame, offers a prime location and buckets of Hollywood history (it played host to the first Academy Awards). Its stylish new Pan-Asian design is worlds better than the old, unappealing guest rooms. Those on the upper floors have unbeatable skyline views, while cabana rooms have a balcony or patio overlooking the pool, whose mural was painted by David Hockney. The Cinegrill supper club draws locals with live jazz and top-notch cabaret. A new spa should be completed by the time you read this. 7000 Hollywood Blvd., Hollywood, CA 90028. © 800/950-7667 or 323/466-7000. Fax 323/462-8056. www.hollywoodroosevelt.com. 330 units. $199–$269 double; from $289 suite. Children under 18 stay free in parents' room. AE, DC, DISC, MC, V. Valet parking $18. **Amenities:** Restaurant; outdoor pool; fitness room.

The Hotel California   This former backpackers' flophouse has been completely remade into a clean and welcoming beachfront motel. With an enviable location—right next door to the behemoth Loews—the inn offers small but comfortable rooms with down comforters, retiled bathrooms, fridges, and VCRs; some even have a (partially obstructed) ocean view. Five suites also have kitchenettes. There's direct access to the sand via a 5-minute walk along a pretty stepped path. 1670 Ocean Ave. (south of Colorado Ave.), Santa Monica, CA 90401. © 866/571-0000 or 310/393-2363. Fax 310/393-1063. www.hotelca.com. 26 units. $169–$279 double or suite. AE, DISC, MC, V. Self-parking $9.

Hotel Del Capri   This Westwood hotel is hugely popular, thanks to spacious rooms, a helpful staff, and retro pricing. There are two sections: a four-story tower and a charming two-story motel with white louver shutters and flowering vines. Rooms are clean and well cared for, though the decidedly discount decor won't be winning any style awards. The most notable feature is electrically adjustable beds, a novel touch. Many suites have kitchenettes, and some units have whirlpool tubs. Nothing is within walking distance of the ritzy high-rise neighborhood, but it's hard to be more centrally located, and there's free shuttle service to nearby attractions. 10587 Wilshire Blvd. (at Westholme Ave.), Los Angeles, CA 90024. © 800/44-HOTEL or 310/474-3511. Fax 310/470-9999. www.hoteldelcapri.com. 79 units. $110–$125 double; from $135 suite. Extra person $10. Rates include continental breakfast ($1 gratuity). AE, DC, MC, V. Free parking. **Amenities:** Pool.

Le Montrose Suite Hotel   Nestled on a quiet street just 2 blocks from the Sunset Strip, this property features large suites that feel more like upscale condos than standard hotel rooms. Each unit has a gas fireplace, VCR, DVD player, CD player, and fax/copier/scanner. Executive and one-bedroom suites have kitchenettes. This place is a favorite for long-term stays among the music and film crowd, so don't be surprised if you spot a famous face in the pleasant

Library restaurant. 900 Hammond St., West Hollywood, CA 90069. © **800/776-0666** or 310/855-1115. Fax 310/657-9192. www.lemontrose.com. 132 units. $295–$575 suite. AE, DC, DISC, MC, V. Valet and self-parking $18. **Amenities:** Restaurant; outdoor pool; lighted tennis court; fitness room; pets accepted ($100).

Magic Castle Hotel   Located a stone's throw from Hollywood Boulevard's attractions, this bargain offers newly refurbished units that are spacious and well kept. Named for the Magic Castle, the illusionist club just uphill, the former apartment building retains a sense of privacy. Situated around a pool courtyard, all units boast full kitchens with microwaves; several have balconies overlooking the large pool. Ideal for wallet-watching families or long-term stays. 7025 Franklin Ave. (between La Brea and Highland), Hollywood, CA 90028. © **800/741-4915** or 323/851-0800. Fax 323/851-4926. www.magiccastlehotel.com. 49 units. $79 double; $89–$169 suite. Extra person $10. AE, DC, DISC, MC, V. Free parking. **Amenities:** Outdoor pool.

Millennium Biltmore Hotel Los Angeles   Built in 1923, this landmark is the grande dame of L.A.'s hotels. You've seen the Biltmore in many movies, including *The Fabulous Baker Boys, Beverly Hills Cop,* and *A Star Is Born.* The former Regal Biltmore is now under the guiding hand of the Millennium group, and the sense of refinement and graciousness endures. The large guest rooms aren't quite as eye-popping, but they've recently undergone a sumptuous redecorating; bathrooms are on the small side, but peach marble and plush robes add luxurious touches. Off the lobby is the stunning Gallery Bar, named by *Los Angeles* magazine as one of the sexiest lounges in L.A. 506 S. Grand Ave. (between Fifth and Sixth sts.), Los Angeles, CA 90071, © **800/245-8673** or 213/624-1011. Fax 213/612-1545. www.millennium-hotels.com. 683 units. $174–$319 double; from $459 suite. Weekend discount packages available. AE, DC, DISC, MC, V. Parking $22. **Amenities:** Restaurants (3); pool; health club.

Sea Shore Motel   Most denizens of Santa Monica's stylish Main Street don't even know about this small, family-run motel in the heart of the dining and shopping action. A recent total upgrade of the property has made the entire place feel fresh. Rooms are small and unremarkable, but management has done a nice job with them, installing extras like dataports and fridges. A cute deli sells muffins, sandwiches, and soups. The beach is a couple of blocks away, making this a terrific bargain base for exploring the sandy side of the city. 2637 Main St. (south of Ocean Park Blvd.), Santa Monica, CA 90405. © **310/392-2787.** Fax 310/392-5167. www.seashoremotel.com. 20 units. $75–$95 double; $100–$120 suite. Extra person $5. Children under 12 stay free in parents' room. AE, DISC, MC, V. Free parking. **Amenities:** Pets accepted ($10 per night).

Sheraton Universal Hotel   Despite the addition of the sleekly modern Hilton just uphill, the 21-story Sheraton is still considered *the* Universal City hotel of choice for tourists, businesspeople, and industry folks visiting the studios. It has a spacious 1960s feel, with updated styling and amenities. Although the Sheraton does its share of convention business, the hotel feels more leisure-oriented than the Hilton next door. Choose a Lanai room for balconies that overlook the pool area, or a Tower room for stunning views and solitude. The hotel is very close to the Hollywood Bowl, and you can practically roll out of bed and into the theme park (via free shuttle). 333 Universal Dr., Universal City, CA 91608. © **800/325-3535** or 818/980-1212. Fax 818/985-4980. www.sheraton.com. 436 units. $149–$219 double; from $350 suite. Children stay free in parents' room. AE, DC, DISC, MC, V. Self-parking $11, valet parking $16. **Amenities:** Restaurant; outdoor pool; health club.

Shutters on the Beach   This Cape Cod–style luxury hotel is directly on the beach, a block from Santa Monica Pier. The beach-cottage rooms are more desirable than those in the towers. All units have balconies, VCRs, and CD players;

some have fireplaces and/or whirlpool tubs; and all have floor-to-ceiling windows that open. The elegant marble bathrooms come with waterproof radios and toy whales. Despite this welcome whimsy, there's a relaxed and elegant ambience throughout the contemporary art-filled hotel. The small pool and the sunny lobby lounge are two great celebrity-spotting perches. 1 Pico Blvd., Santa Monica, CA 90405. ℂ **800/334-9000** or 310/458-0030. Fax 310/458-4589. www.shutterson thebeach.com. 198 units. $380–$615 double; from $895 suite. AE, DC, DISC, MC, V. Valet parking $22. **Amenities:** Restaurants (2); outdoor pool; health club.

The Standard   Shag carpeting on the lobby *ceiling,* blue Astroturf around the pool—Andre Balazs's swank West Hollywood neo-motel is definitely left of center. Constructed from the bones of a vintage 1962 Sunset Strip property, it boasts comfortably sized rooms outfitted with silver beanbag chairs, orange bathroom tile, private balconies, VCRs, CD players, and minibars holding everything from sake to condoms to animal crackers. Look past the retro clutter and often-raucous party scene, and you'll find a level of service more often associated with hotels costing twice as much. 8300 Sunset Blvd. (at Sweetzer Ave.), West Hollywood, CA 90069. ℂ **323/650-9090.** Fax 323/650-2820. www.standardhotel.com. 139 units. $99–$225 double; from $450 suite. AE, DC, DISC, MC, V. Valet parking $18. **Amenities:** Restaurants (2); outdoor pool; access to nearby health club; pets under 30 lb. accepted ($100).

Wyndham Bel Age Hotel   This high-rise West Hollywood hotel has it all: huge suites, excellent service, terrific rooftop deck, and A-1 location just off the Sunset Strip. And thanks to an excellent art collection, the place has far more personality than your average chain hotel. The monster-size suites boast plush bedding, Herman Miller desk chairs, VCRs, Sony PlayStations, CD players, and robes. The best rooms face south; on a clear day, you can see all the way to the Pacific. 1020 N. San Vicente Blvd. (between Sunset and Santa Monica boulevards), West Hollywood, CA 90069. ℂ **800-WYNDHAM** or 310/854-1111. Fax 310/854-0926. www.wyndham.com. 200 units. $199–$339 suite. AE, DC, DISC, MC, V. Valet parking $18. **Amenities:** Restaurants (2); outdoor pool; fitness room.

Wyndham Checkers Hotel   The boutique Wyndham Checkers is as removed from "Hollywood" as a top L.A. hotel can get—like a European-styled hotel without a lot of flashy amenities, but first-class all the way. Built in 1927, the hotel's neutral, sand-colored decor accentuates the splendid architectural features that remain intact, despite a complete update over the past couple of years. Your room is a pristine temple, warmly radiant and immaculately outfitted. Public areas include a wood-paneled library, a classy bar, and a fine dining room with one of L.A.'s best weekend brunches. 535 S. Grand Ave. (between Fifth and Sixth sts.), Los Angeles, CA 90071. ℂ **800/423-5798** or 213/624-0000. Fax 213/626-9906. 188 units. $199–$289 double; from $500 suite. www.checkershotel.com. AE, DC, DISC, MC, V. Self-parking $20, valet parking $23. **Amenities:** Restaurant; pool; fitness room.

WHERE TO DINE

The Apple Pan SANDWICHES/AMERICAN   There are no tables, just a U-shaped counter, at this classic American burger shack and L.A. landmark. Open since 1947, the Apple Pan is a diner that looks—and acts—the part. It's famous for juicy burgers, speedy service, and authentic frills-free atmosphere. The hickory burger is best, though the tuna sandwich also has its share of fans. Definitely order fries and, if you're in the mood, the home-baked apple pie. 10801 Pico Blvd. (east of Westwood Blvd.), West Los Angeles. ℂ **310/475-3585.** Most menu items under $6. No credit cards. Tues–Thurs and Sun 11am–midnight; Fri–Sat 11am–1am. Free parking.

Border Grill MEXICAN   Before Mary Sue Milliken and Susan Feniger became cable TV's "Too Hot Tamales," they started this restaurant in West Hollywood. Now Border Grill has moved to a cavernous (read: loud) space in Santa Monica, and the gals aren't in the kitchen very much at all (though cookbooks and paraphernalia from their Food Network show are displayed prominently for sale). But their influence on the inspired menu is enough to maintain the cantina's popularity with folks who swear by the authentic flavor of Yucatán fish tacos, rock shrimp with ancho chiles, and *mulitas de hongos,* a layering of portobello mushrooms, poblano chiles, black beans, cheese, and guacamole. Save room for yummy coconut flan or Key lime pie. 1445 Fourth St. (between Broadway and Santa Monica Blvd.), Santa Monica. (310/451-1655. www.bordergrill.com. Reservations recommended. Main courses $10–$21. AE, DC, DISC, MC, V. Mon 5–10pm; Tues–Thurs 11:30am–10pm; Fri–Sat 11:30am–11pm; Sun 11:30am–10pm. Metered parking lots; valet parking $4.

El Cholo MEXICAN   El Cholo has been serving up south-of-the-border comfort food in this festive hacienda since 1927, even though the surrounding mid-Wilshire neighborhood has become Koreatown. The expertly blended margaritas and classic combination dinners don't break new culinary ground, but the kitchen has perfected these standards over 70 years. Specialties include rich enchilada sauce, seasonally available green-corn tamales, and creative sizzling vegetarian fajitas that go way beyond just eliminating the meat. Westsiders head to El Cholo's Santa Monica branch at 1025 Wilshire Blvd ((310/899-1106). 1121 S. Western Ave. (south of Olympic Blvd.). (323/734-2773. www.elcholo.com. Reservations suggested. Main courses $8–$14. AE, DC, DISC, MC, V. Mon–Thurs 11am–10pm; Fri–Sat 11am–11pm; Sun 11am–9pm. Free self-parking or valet parking $3.

Four Oaks CALIFORNIA   The country-cottage ambience of this canyon hideaway and chef Peter Roelant's superlative blend of fresh ingredients with Continental flourishes make a meal at the Four Oaks one of our favorite luxuries. Dinner is served beneath trees festooned with twinkling lights. Appetizers like lavender-smoked salmon with crisp potatoes and horseradish crème fraîche complement mouthwatering dishes like roasted chicken with sage, Oregon forest

---

The Wolfgang Puck Experience

Already a household word, Puck has a culinary empire that keeps growing. For perhaps the quintessential L.A. dining experience, be sure to try at least one of the master's L.A. restaurants. Of course, there's **Spago Beverly Hills,** 176 N. Canon Dr. ((**310/385-0880**). Puck also has two terrific restaurants near the beach. **Chinois on Main,** 2709 Main St., Santa Monica ((**310/392-9025**), serves terrifically quirky East-meets-West Franco-Chinese cuisine. At **Granita,** 23725 W. Malibu Rd. (in the Malibu Colony Plaza), Malibu ((**310/456-0488**), Puck applies his signature California style to seafood—very successfully, of course. If you're dining on a budget, try one of the several **Wolfgang Puck Cafe** branches around town, where Puck's cuisine is interpreted in an affordable style and served up in colorful surroundings. There's one in West Hollywood, at 8000 Sunset Blvd. ((**323/650-7300**); one in Santa Monica, at 1323 Montana Ave. ((**310/393-0290**); and one at Universal CityWalk ((**818/985-9653**). And cyber-gourmets can always get a foodie fix online at **www.wolfgangpuck.com.**

mushrooms, artichoke hearts, and port-balsamic sauce. 2181 N. Beverly Glen Blvd., Los Angeles. ℂ 310/470-2265. www.fouroaksrestaurant.com. Reservations required. Main courses $22–$29. AE, DISC, MC, V. Tues–Sat 11:30am–2pm and 6–10pm; Sun 10:30am–2pm and 6–10pm. Valet parking $4.

Joe's AMERICAN ECLECTIC   This is one of L.A.'s best dining bargains. Chef/owner Joeseph Miller excels in simple cuisine, particularly grilled fish and roasted meats accented with piquant herbs. Formerly a tiny, quirky storefront, the restaurant has been gutted and completely remodeled (the best tables are on the patio complete with waterfall). Entrees are sophisticated: fallow deer wrapped in bacon, served in a black currant sauce; monkfish in a saffron broth; wild striped bass with curried cauliflower coulis. Two four-course prix fixe menus are offered as well—a real bargain for under $40. 1023 Abbot Kinney Blvd., Venice. ℂ 310/399-5811. www.joesrestaurant.com. Reservations required. Main courses $8–$15 lunch, $18–$25 dinner. AE, MC, V. Tues–Fri 11:30am–2:30pm and 6–10pm; Sat–Sun 11am–2:30pm and 6–11pm. Free street parking.

Jozu PACIFIC RIM/CALIFORNIA   *Jozu* means "excellent" in Japanese, and the word perfectly describes everything about this tranquil restaurant. All meals begin with complimentary sake from Jozu's premium sake list. Chef Hisashi Yoshiara's menu presents Asian flavors interpreted with an international inventiveness. Outstanding dishes include delicately roasted sea bass on a bed of crunchy cabbage, accented with tangy *ponzu* sauce; and albacore tuna wrapped in a crispy potato nest and bathed in soy butter. The dessert of choice is Asian pear tart, lightly caramelized fruit laid in a buttery crust. The restaurant's interior is warmly comfortable and subtly lit; plenty of beautiful Hollywood types dine here, but it's quiet enough for real dinner conversation. 8360 Melrose Ave. (at Kings Rd.), West Hollywood. ℂ 323/655-5600. www.jozu.com. Reservations recommended. Main courses $16–$25. AE, MC, V. Mon–Fri 6–10:30pm; Sat–Sun 5:30–10:30pm. Valet parking $3.50.

Lucques FRENCH/MEDITERRANEAN   Pronounced "Luke," this quietly sophisticated restaurant has a clubby style and handsome enclosed patio. Chef Suzanne Goin cooks with bold flavors, fresh-from-the-farm produce, and an instinctive feel for the food of the Mediterranean. The short menu makes the most of unusual ingredients, such as salt cod and oxtail. Standout dishes include Tuscan bean soup with tangy greens and pistou, grilled chicken served alongside spinach sautéed with pancetta and shallots, and perfect vanilla pot de crème for dessert. Lucques's bar menu and tantalizing hors d'oeuvres are a godsend for late-night diners. 8474 Melrose Ave. (east of La Cienega), West Hollywood. ℂ 323/655-6277. Reservations recommended. Main courses $18–$30. AE, DC, MC, V. Tues–Sat noon–2:30pm and 6pm–1:30am; Sun 5:30pm–midnight. Closed the last 2 weeks of Aug. Metered street parking or valet ($3.50).

Matsuhisa JAPANESE/PERUVIAN   Chef/owner Nobuyuki Matsuhisa is true master of fish cookery, creating fantastic dishes by combining Japanese flavors with South American spices and salsas. Broiled sea bass with black truffles, sautéed squid with garlic and soy, and Dungeness crab tossed with chiles and cream are examples of the masterfully prepared delicacies that are available, in addition to nigiri and creative sushi rolls. Matsuhisa is popular with celebrities and foodies, so reserve early. If you dare, ask for *omakase,* and the chef will personally compose a selection of eccentric dishes. 129 N. La Cienega Blvd. (north of Wilshire Blvd.), Beverly Hills. ℂ 310/659-9639. Reservations recommended. Main courses $14–$26; sushi $4–$13 per order; full omakase dinner from $65. AE, DC, MC, V. Mon–Fri 11:45am–2:15pm; daily 5:45–10:15pm. Valet parking $3.50.

The Original Pantry AMERICAN/BREAKFAST   This L.A. institution has been serving huge portions around the clock for more than 60 years. It's especially popular with politicos and conferencegoers from the nearby Convention Center, as well as late-night clubbers. Famous for quantity rather than quality, the Pantry serves huge T-bone steaks, dense meatloaf, macaroni and cheese, and other American favorites. Breakfast is served all day. 877 S. Figueroa St. (at Ninth St.). © 213/972-9279. Main courses $6–$11. No credit cards. Daily 24 hr. Free parking with validation.

Patina CALIFORNIA/FRENCH   Joachim Splichal's Patina routinely wins high praise from demanding gourmands. The dining room is attractive, low-key, and professional, without a hint of stuffiness. The menu is equally disarming: "Mallard Duck with Portobello Mushrooms" gives little hint of the brilliant colors and flavors that appear on the plate. The seasonal menu features partridge, pheasant, venison, and other game in winter and spotlights exotic local vegetables in warmer months. Seafood is always available; if asparagus-wrapped John Dory is on the menu, order it. Patina is justifiably famous for its mashed potatoes and potato-truffle chips. 5955 Melrose Ave. (west of Cahuenga Blvd.). © 323/467-1108. www.patinagroup.com. Reservations required. Main courses $18–$30. AE, DC, DISC, MC, V. Mon–Thurs 6–10pm; Fri noon–2pm and 6–10pm; Sat 5:30–10:30pm. Valet parking $4.

Rockenwagner CALIFORNIA   Set in Frank Gehry's starkly modern Edgemar complex, chef Hans Röckenwagner's eponymous restaurant presents edible sculpture amid a gallerylike decor. Röckenwagner takes his food very seriously, once orchestrating an entire menu around the German white asparagus season. The unpretentious staff serves deliciously pretentious dishes fusing Pacific Rim ingredients with traditional European preparations; a good example is the langoustine ravioli with mango in port-wine reduction and curry oil. Desserts are to die for. Don't overlook the lunch bargains or the WunderBAR Wine and Snack Bar for a quick bite. 2435 Main St. (north of Ocean Park Blvd.), Santa Monica. © 310/399 6504. www.rockenwagner.com. Reservations recommended. Main courses $22–$31. AE, DC, MC, V. Mon–Fri 6–10pm; Sat 5:30–11pm; Sun 10am–2:30pm and 5:30–10pm. Valet parking $4.

Sofi GREEK   Look for the simple black awning that leads to this hidden Aegean treasure. Ask for a table on the romantic patio amid twinkling lights, and immediately order a plate of the thick, satisfying *tzatziki* (yogurt-cucumber-garlic spread) accompanied by a basket of warm pitas for dipping. Other specialties include herbed rack of lamb with rice, fried calamari salad, *saganaki* (kasseri cheese flamed with ouzo), and other hearty taverna favorites. 8030¾ W. Third St. (between Fairfax Ave. and Crescent Heights Blvd.). © 323/651-0346. Reservations recommended. Main courses $7–$14. AE, DC, MC, V. Mon–Sat noon–3pm; daily 5:30–11pm. Metered street parking or valet parking $3.

Valentino NORTHERN ITALIAN   Charming owner Piero Selvaggio's distinctive touch still pervades the 26-year-old Valentino, which former *New York Times* critic Ruth Reichl called the best Italian restaurant in the United States. Dinner here can be a lengthy affair; begin with *crespelle*, thin little pancakes with fresh porcini mushrooms and a rich melt of fontina cheese. A rich Barolo wine is the perfect accompaniment to rosemary-infused roasted rabbit; the fantastically fragrant risotto with white truffles is one of the most magnificent dishes we've ever had. 3115 Pico Blvd. (west of Bundy Dr.), Santa Monica. © 310/829-4313. www.welovewine.com. Reservations required. Main courses $22–$32. AE, DC, MC, V. Mon–Thurs 5:30–10:30pm; Fri 11:30am–2:30pm and 5:30–11pm; Sat 5:30–11pm. Valet parking $4.

Water Grill SEAFOOD   This restaurant is popular with the suit-and-tie crowd at lunch and with concertgoers en route to the Music Center at night.

The dining room is stylish and sophisticated, but gets a lighthearted lift from cavorting papier-mâché fish. Water Grill, considered by many to be L.A.'s best seafood house, is known for its shellfish. Imaginative main courses are influenced by the cuisines of Hawaii, the Pacific Northwest, New Orleans, and New England. Try the bluefin tuna tartare; Santa Barbara spot prawns paired with fingerling potato salad; or perfectly pan-roasted Alaskan halibut. 544 S. Grand Ave. (between Fifth and Sixth sts.). © 213/891-0900. Reservations recommended. Main courses $19–$31. AE, DC, DISC, MC, V. Mon–Tues 11:30am–9pm; Wed–Fri 11:30am–10pm; Sat 5–10pm; Sun 4:30–9pm. Valet parking $4.

LOS ANGELES AFTER DARK

The *L.A. Weekly* (www.laweekly.com), a free weekly paper available at sidewalk stands, shops, and restaurants, is the best place to find up-to-date news on what's happening in L.A.'s playhouses, cinemas, museums, and live-music venues. The "Calendar" section of the *Los Angeles Times* (www.calendarlive.com) is also a good resource.

Ticketmaster (© 213/480-3232; www.ticketmaster.com) is the major charge-by-phone ticket agency in the city, selling tickets to concerts, sporting events, plays, and special events.

THE PERFORMING ARTS   It's a little-known fact that on any given night, there's more live theater to choose from in Los Angeles than in New York. The all-purpose **Performing Arts Center of Los Angeles County,** 135 N. Grand Ave., downtown (formerly known as the Music Center), houses the **Ahmanson Theatre** and **Mark Taper Forum** (© 213/628-2772; www.taperahmanson. com), as well as the L.A. Philharmonic and L.A. Opera. The city is also home to nearly 200 small- and medium-size theaters and theater companies. Across town, the **Geffen Playhouse,** 10886 Le Conte Ave., Westwood (© 310/208-5454; www.geffenplayhouse.com), presents work by prominent and emerging writers. The venerable **Pasadena Playhouse,** 39 S. El Molino Ave., near Colorado Boulevard (© 626/356-7529; www.pasadenaplayhouse.org), has served as the training ground for many theatrical, film, and TV stars. The **Colony Studio Theatre,** 555 N. Third St., Burbank (© 818/558-7000; www. colonytheatre.org), has developed into a nationally recognized company. **Actors Circle Theater,** 7313 Santa Monica Blvd., West Hollywood (© 323/ 882-8043), is a 47-seater that's as acclaimed as it is tiny.

The world-class **Los Angeles Philharmonic** (© 323/850-2000; www.laphil. org), led by Finnish-born Esa-Pekka Salonen, performs at the **Dorothy Chandler Pavilion** in the all-purpose Performing Arts Center, 135 N. Grand Ave., with a summer season at the **Hollywood Bowl,** 2301 N. Highland Ave., Hollywood (© 323/850-2000; www.hollywoodbowl.org), an elegant Greek-style natural outdoor amphitheater. The Hollywood Bowl also hosts jazz, pop, and virtuoso performances in summer.

Slowly but surely, the **Los Angeles Opera** (© 213/972-8001; www.losangeles opera.com), which performs at the Dorothy Chandler Pavilion, is gaining respect and popularity with inventive stagings of classic and modern operas.

THE CLUB & MUSIC SCENE   Veteran record producer/executive Lou Adler opened the **Roxy,** 9009 Sunset Blvd., West Hollywood (© 323/276-2222), in the mid-1970s, and it's remained among the top showcase venues in Hollywood ever since.

There are plenty of reasons music fans and industry types keep coming back to the **House of Blues,** 8430 Sunset Blvd., West Hollywood (© 323/848-5100;

www.hob.com). Night after night, audiences are dazzled by hot acts of national acclaim, ranging from Soul Coughing to Eric Clapton.

Nearby is **The Troubadour,** 9081 Santa Monica Blvd. (© **310/276-6168;** www.troubadour.com), the infamous West Hollywood mainstay that radiates rock history. This beer- and sweat-soaked club likes it loud.

Louder still is the hip **Viper Room,** 8852 Sunset Blvd., West Hollywood (© **310/358-1880;** www.viperroom.com), owned by Johnny Depp. With an often star-filled scene, the club is known for late-night surprise performances from such powerhouses as Iggy Pop, Tom Petty, and Everclear.

B. B. King's Blues Club, CityWalk, Universal City (© **818/622-5464**), where the ribs alone are worth the trip, hosts plenty of great local and touring national blues acts.

The **Jazz Bakery,** 3233 Helms Ave., Culver City (© **310/271-9039;** www. jazzbakery.org), in the restored Helms Bakery factory, is renowned for attracting some of the most important names in jazz. It's a no-frills, all-about-the-music affair, and the place is pretty much BYO in the drinks department.

Dragonfly, 6510 Santa Monica Blvd., Hollywood (© **323/466-6111;** www.dragonfly.com), is soaring, with "surprise" shows by top-notch acts such as the Red Hot Chili Peppers and Alanis Morrissette. Overheated guests and smokers also enjoy its cool outdoor patio.

The Mint, 6010 W. Pico Blvd. (© **323/954-9630;** www.theminthollywood. com), is a gloriously loungey hangout with performances by such diverse artists as G. Love & Special Sauce, Gwen Stefani, and Duke Robillard.

Straight from New York, a West Coast branch of the famous **Knitting Factory,** 7021 Hollywood Blvd., Hollywood (© **323/463-0204;** www.theknitting factory.com/KFLA), has arrived in the Hollywood Boulevard district. It sees such diverse bookings as Kristin Hersh, Pere Ubu, and Jonathan Richman.

On the fringe of east Hollywood, **Spaceland,** 1717 Silver Lake Blvd., Silver Lake (© **323/661-4380**), has become one of the most important clubs on the L.A. circuit, with performances by Pavement, Mary Lou Lord, Elliott Smith, and the Eels.

When you've just gotta dance, head for **The Conga Room,** 5364 Wilshire Blvd. (© **323/938-1696;** www.congaroom.com), which attracts Latin-music luminaries and is *the* nightspot for live salsa and merengue. **El Floridita,** 1253 N. Vine St., Hollywood (© **323/871-8612**), is a Cuban restaurant-and-salsa-joint that's hot, hot, hot. **The Derby,** 4500 Los Feliz Blvd., Los Feliz (© **323/ 663-8979;** www.the-derby.com), attracts dancers who come dressed to the nines to swing the night away to such musical acts as Big Bad Voodoo Daddy and the Royal Crown Revue.

COMEDY CLUBS   You can't go wrong at the **Comedy Store,** 8433 Sunset Blvd., West Hollywood (© **323/650-6268;** www.comedystore.com). New comics develop their material, and established ones work out the kinks, at this landmark venue owned by Mitzi Shore (Pauly's mom). The talent here is always first rate and includes comics who regularly appear on *The Tonight Show.*

For more edgy fare, head to the **Groundling Theater,** 7307 Melrose Ave. (© **323/934-9700;** www.groundlings.com), the most innovative group in town. The Groundlings were the springboard to fame for Pee-Wee Herman, Elvira, and former *Saturday Night Live* stars Jon Lovitz, the late Phil Hartman, and Julia Sweeney.

The Improv, 8162 Melrose Ave., West Hollywood (© **323/651-2583;** www. improvclubs.com/hollywood), a showcase for top stand-ups since 1975, features the likes of Jay Leno and Billy Crystal more often than you'd expect. But even if the comedians on the bill are all unknowns, they won't be for long.

2 The Disneyland Resort

Opened in 1955, Disneyland is the original mega-theme park, and remains unsurpassed despite constant threats from pretenders to the crown. The Disney difference—and the one that keeps the park fresh and fantastic, whether you're 6 or 60—is *imagination.* Disneyland is about more than rides, shows, or carnival games . . . it's fantasy elevated to an art form. In 2001, Disney unveiled a brand-new theme park, Disney's California Adventure, and revamped its own name to "The Disneyland Resort," reflecting a greatly expanded array of entertainment options.

ESSENTIALS

GETTING THERE   Disneyland is about an hour's drive south of Los Angeles (about 30 min. from LAX), or 90 minutes north of San Diego. Follow I-5 till you see signs for Disneyland; off-ramps from both directions lead into parking lots and surrounding streets.

VISITOR INFORMATION   Point your Web browser to **www.disneyland. com**. The **Anaheim/Orange County Visitor and Convention Bureau,** 800 W. Katella Ave. (© **714/765-8888;** www.anaheimoc.org), can fill you in on other area activities.

ADMISSION & HOURS   Admission to *either* Disneyland or Disney's California Adventure is $43 for adults and children over 11, $41 for seniors, and $33 for children 3 to 11. Parking is $7. Multiday admission is available as well; 2- and 3-day passports offer substantial savings.

Disneyland and Disney's California Adventure are open every day of the year from morning until after nightfall, but operating hours vary (with extended summer and holiday hours), so we recommend that you call ahead (© **714/ 781-4565**). Hours, ride closures, and show schedules can also be found online at **www.disneyland.com**.

DISNEYLAND

Though many visitors tackle Disneyland systematically, beginning at the entrance and working their way clockwise around the park, the most effective method is to arrive early and run to the most popular rides first—the Indiana Jones Adventure, Star Tours, Space Mountain, Splash Mountain, the Haunted Mansion, and Pirates of the Caribbean—where midday lines can last an hour or more.

This time-honored plan of attack may eventually become obsolete, however, thanks to the new **FastPass** system. Here's how it works: Say you want to ride Space Mountain, but the line is long. Now you can head to the automated FastPass ticket dispensers, swipe the magnetic strip of your Disneyland entrance ticket, get a FastPass for later that day, and return to use the reduced-wait FastPass entrance. At press time, about a dozen rides were equipped with FastPass; several more will be added by the time you read this, including some at California Adventure (see below).

Only 1 day in the park? Then start by riding the most popular rides (see above) first—or obtaining a FastPass early—so you don't waste precious time in line. If you've got smaller children with you, concentrate on Fantasyland (behind Sleeping Beauty's Castle), a kids' paradise with fairy-tale–derived rides like **King Arthur Carousel, Dumbo the Flying Elephant, Mr. Toad's Wild Ride, Peter Pan's Flight, Alice in Wonderland, Pinocchio's Daring Journey,** and the

Disney signature ride, **it's a small world.** Elsewhere in the park, little ones will enjoy clambering through **Tarzan's Treehouse** and singing along with the audio-animatronic **Country Bear Jamboree.** Mickey's Toontown is a wacky, gag-filled world inspired by the *Roger Rabbit* films, featuring endless amusement for young imaginations.

If high-speed thrills are your style, then follow the **Indiana Jones Adventure** into the Temple of the Forbidden Eye, or jump on one of Disneyland's "mountain"-themed action roller coasters. There's perennial favorite **Space Mountain,** a pitch-black indoor roller coaster; **Splash Mountain,** a water flume ride (with a big, wet splash at the end) based on the Disney movie *Song of the South;* the **Matterhorn Bobsleds,** a zippy coaster through the landmark mountain's chilled caverns and drifting fog banks; and **Big Thunder Mountain Railroad,** where runaway railroad cars careen through a deserted 1870s gold mine. **Star Tours** is a *Star Wars*–inspired Tomorrowland simulation ride.

Disneyland highlights that have stood the test of time include the intriguingly spooky **Haunted Mansion,** which showcases the brilliance of Disney "imagineers"; and **Pirates of the Caribbean,** an enchanted world of swashbuckling, rum-running, and buried treasure.

If you've got more than 1 day, you'll have the luxury of enjoying some Disney extras not essential enough to pack into a single day. For example, avoid the midday crush by strolling along **Main Street U.S.A.,** shopping for Disney souvenirs, enjoying a sweet treat of ice cream or candy, and ducking into **Great Moments with Mr. Lincoln,** the patriotic look at America's 16th president that was Walt Disney's first foray into audio-animatronics.

The **parades and shows** within the park draw huge crowds. There's also a nighttime **fireworks** spectacular above Sleeping Beauty's Castle, and the after-dark pyrotechnic show **Fantasmic!**

DISNEY'S CALIFORNIA ADVENTURE

Disneyland's new "sister" theme park consists of three distinct themed areas. The **Golden State** represents California's history, heritage, and physical attributes. Sound boring? Actually, the park's splashiest attractions are here. The ride **Soarin' Over California** combines suspended seats with a spectacular IMAX-style movie (take advantage of FastPass for this one), while the **Grizzly River Run** is a wet gold-country ride through caverns and mine shafts. **Pacific Wharf,** inspired by Monterey's Cannery Row, features mouthwatering demonstration attractions by Boudin Sourdough Bakery and Mission Tortillas. Paying tribute to California's rich agriculture is the Robert Mondavi **Golden Vine Winery.** Using next-generation 3-D technology, the interactive film *It's Tough to Be a Bug* takes *A Bug's Life* characters on an underground romp with bees, termites, grasshoppers, spiders, and a few surprises that keep everyone laughing along.

At the fantasy boardwalk **Paradise Pier,** highlights include the **California Screamin'** roller coaster; the **Maliboomer,** a trio of towers that catapults riders to the tip-top bell, then lets them down bungee-style; the **Orange Stinger,** a whooshing swing ride inside an enormous orange; and all the familiar boardwalk games and guilty pleasure foods.

The **Hollywood Pictures Backlot** features the **Disney Animation** building, where visitors can learn how stories become animated features, and the **Hyperion Theater,** which presents a live-action tribute to classic Disney films. Across the way, step aboard the **Superstar Limo,** where you're cast as a hot new star being chauffered around Hollywood. **Who Wants To Be A Millionaire—Play It!** is an interactive, high-energy mock-up of the game show. **Jim Henson's**

MuppetVision 3D is a blast from the past featuring Kermit, Miss Piggy, Gonzo, and Fozzie Bear. Although it's not nearly as entertaining as *It's Tough to Be a Bug,* it has its moments and won't scare the bejeezus out of little kids.

WHERE TO STAY NEAR THE PARK

The **Disneyland Hotel,** 1150 Magic Way (© 714/956-MICKEY), is across the street and linked to the park by monorail. While the hotel's grounds are a theme park unto themselves, the 990 rooms are plainer, like those of a good-quality business hotel. Disney's new **Grand Californian Hotel,** 1600 S. Disneyland Dr. (© 714/956-MICKEY), is an Arts and Crafts–style high-rise hotel with 751 spacious rooms. Rates at both start at around $175 to $205, but you can almost always get a money-saving package that includes park admission.

A half block away is the **Anaheim Vagabond Hotel,** 1700 S. Harbor Blvd. (© 800/228-1357 or 714/772-5900), a 300-unit garden-style hotel consisting of two-story buildings arranged around an Olympic-size pool. It's pretty basic, with a low-tech charm and wallet-friendly prices. Other nearby hotels in the lower price range are the **Candy Cane Inn,** 1747 S. Harbor Blvd. (© 800/345-7057 or 714/774-5284), and **Best Western Anaheim Stardust,** 1057 W. Ball Rd. (© 800/222-3639 or 714/774-7600).

3 San Diego

San Diego is best known for its benign climate and fabulous beaches. On sunny days, the city is one big outdoor playground—you can choose from swimming, snorkeling, windsurfing, kayaking, bicycling, skating, and tons of other fun in or near the water. The city is also home to top-notch attractions, including three world-famous animal parks and splendid Balboa Park. Once dismissed as a conservative Navy town, San Diego now boasts an almost Los Angeles–like diversity of neighborhoods and residents. Several charming restored historic districts draw a stylish young crowd that's updating the face of San Diego dining, shopping, and entertainment. So pack a laid-back attitude along with your sandals and swimsuit; welcome to California's grown-up beach town.

ESSENTIALS

GETTING THERE   By Plane   San Diego International Airport, 3707 N. Harbor Dr. (© 619/231-2100), locally known as Lindbergh Field, is just 3 miles from downtown. If you're driving into the city from the airport, take Harbor Drive south to Broadway and turn left.

Metropolitan Transit System (MTS) bus no. 992 provides service between the airport and downtown San Diego. The one-way fare is $2.25. Several **shuttles** run regularly from the airport to downtown hotels, charging around $5 to $9 per person. **Taxis** line up outside both terminals and charge around $8 to take you to a downtown location.

By Train   Amtrak (© 800/USA-RAIL; www.amtrak.com) trains connect San Diego to Los Angeles (trip time: 3 hr.) and the rest of the country, arriving at **Santa Fe Station,** 1850 Kettner Blvd. (at Broadway), within walking distance of many downtown hotels and 1½ blocks from the Embarcadero.

VISITOR INFORMATION   The International Visitor Information Center (© 619/236-1212; www.sandiego.org) is on First Avenue at F Street, street level at Horton Plaza. The center is open Monday through Saturday from 8:30am to 5pm year-round and Sunday from 11am to 5pm June through August.

San Diego Area

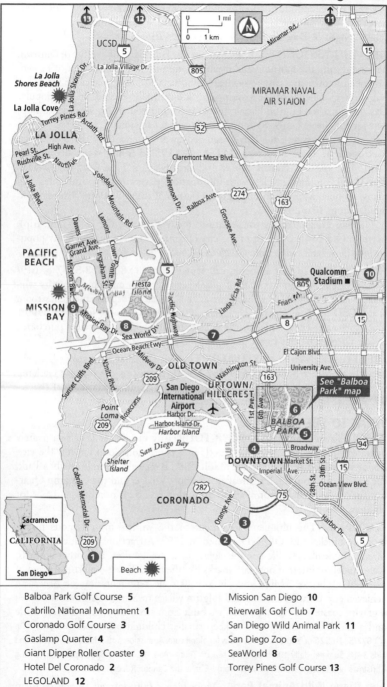

Balboa Park Golf Course **5**
Cabrillo National Monument **1**
Coronado Golf Course **3**
Gaslamp Quarter **4**
Giant Dipper Roller Coaster **9**
Hotel Del Coronado **2**
LEGOLAND **12**

Mission San Diego **10**
Riverwalk Golf Club **7**
San Diego Wild Animal Park **11**
San Diego Zoo **6**
SeaWorld **8**
Torrey Pines Golf Course **13**

Other sources of information include *San Diego Reader,* a free weekly news-paper available all over the city; and the Thursday entertainment supplement called **"Night & Day"** in the *San Diego Union-Tribune.*

GETTING AROUND   San Diego has its fair share of traffic downtown, heaviest during the morning and evening commute. Aside from that, it's a very car-friendly town, and easy to navigate. Finding a parking space can be tricky—but some reasonably priced parking lots are centrally located. In the popular Gaslamp Quarter, Horton Plaza's garage (G St. and Fourth Ave.) is free to shop-pers for the first 3 hours, $1 for every additional half hour.

Both city buses and the San Diego Trolley are operated by the **San Diego Metropolitan Transit System (MTS)** (© **619/233-3004;** www.sdcommute. com). The system's **Transit Store,** 102 Broadway, at First Avenue (© **619/ 234-1060**), supplies travelers with information, passes, tokens, timetables, and maps. It's open Monday through Friday from 8:30am to 5:30pm, Saturday and Sunday from 10am to 4pm.

The **San Diego Trolley** runs south to the Mexican border (a 40-min. trip), north to Old Town, and east to the city of Santee. Trolleys stop at many popu-lar locations; fares range from $1.25 to $2.50.

FAST FACTS   To find a doctor, call **Hotel Docs** (© **800/468-3537** or 619/ 275-2663), a 24-hour network of physicians, dentists, and chiropractors who make house/hotel calls. The most conveniently located hospital emergency room is at **UCSD Medical Center–Hillcrest,** 200 W. Arbor Dr. (© **619/543-6400**).

A 7.5% **sales tax** is added at the register for all goods and services purchased in San Diego. The **city hotel tax** is 10.5%.

SPECIAL EVENTS & FESTIVALS   The first weekend after Labor Day, the **San Diego Street Scene** (© **619/557-0505**) transforms the historic Gaslamp Quarter with a 3-day extravaganza featuring food, dance, international charac-ter, and live music on 12 separate stages.

WHAT TO SEE & DO

The **Old Town Trolley** (© **619/298-TOUR**) isn't a trolley at all; it's a privately operated open-air tour bus that travels in a continuous loop around the city. Major stops include Old Town, Presidio Park, Bazaar del Mundo, Balboa Park, the San Diego Zoo, the Embarcadero, Seaport Village, and the Gaslamp Quar-ter. Tours operate daily from 9am to 5pm; they cost $24 for adults and $12 for children 4 to 12.

LEGOLAND   The ultimate monument to the world's most famous plastic building blocks, LEGOLAND opened in 1999. Attractions include hands-on interactive displays; a life-size menagerie of tigers, giraffes, and other animals; scale models of international landmarks like the Eiffel Tower—all constructed of real LEGO bricks! "MiniLand" is a 1:20 scale representation of American achievement, from a New England Pilgrim village to Mount Rushmore. There's a gravity coaster ride (don't worry, it's built from steel) through a LEGO castle and a DUPLO building area to keep smaller children occupied. 1 Legoland Dr. © 877/534-6526 or 760/918-LEGO. www.legoland.com. Admission $40 adults, $34 seniors and kids 3–16. Summer daily 10am–8pm; off season Thurs–Mon 10am–5 or 6pm; open daily during Christmas and Easter vacation periods. From I-5 take the Cannon Rd. exit east.

San Diego Wild Animal Park   More than 3,000 animals, many of them endangered species, roam freely over 1,800 acres here—it's the humans who are enclosed. This living arrangement encourages breeding colonies, so it's not surprising that more than 75 white rhinoceroses have been born here. Several other species that had vanished from the wilds have been reintroduced to their natural habitats from stocks bred here. The best way to see the animals is by riding the 5-mile **monorail** (included in the price of admission), a 50-minute ride through areas resembling Africa and Asia. Photo caravan tours get you up-close-and-personal with the animals. 15500 San Pasqual Valley Rd., Escondido. ⟨ 760/747-8702. www.wildanimalpark.org. Admission $27 adults, $24 seniors, $20 children 3–11, free for military in uniform. Combination Zoo and Wild Animal Park package (includes deluxe zoo package) $47 adults, $28 children; valid for 5 days from date of purchase. Daily 9am–4pm (grounds close at 5pm); extended hours during summer and Festival of Lights in Dec. Take I-15 to Via Rancho Pkwy.; follow signs for about 3 miles.

San Diego Zoo   More than 4,000 animals reside at this world-famous zoo. Two giant pandas on loan from China—and their cub Hua Mei—are the big attention-getters, but there are also cuddly koalas from Australia, wild Przewalski's horses from Mongolia, lowland gorillas from Africa, and giant tortoises from the Galápagos. The usual lions, elephants, giraffes, and tigers are present, too, housed in barless, moated enclosures designed to resemble their natural habitats. There's a **Children's Zoo,** with a nursery for baby animals and a petting area where kids can cuddle up to sheep, goats, and the like. The zoo offers **bus tours,** which provide a narrated overview and show you about 75% of the park. You can get an aerial perspective via the **Skyfari.** 2920 Zoo Dr., Balboa Park. ⟨ 619/234-3153. www.sandiegozoo.org. Admission $20 adults, $12 children 3–11, free for military in uniform. Deluxe package (admission, bus tour, Skyfari aerial tram) $32 adults, $20 children. Combination Zoo and Wild Animal Park package (deluxe zoo package, Wild Animal Park admission) $47 adults, $28 children; valid for 5 days from date of purchase. Daily year round 9am–4pm (grounds close at 5pm). Bus: 7, 7A/B.

SeaWorld   This 165-acre, multimillion-dollar aquatic playground may be your main reason for visiting California. Several successive 4-ton black-and-white killer whales have functioned as the park's mascot, Shamu. At its heart, SeaWorld is a family entertainment center where the performers are dolphins, otters, sea lions, walruses, and seals. Shows run continuously throughout the day, while visitors can rotate through the various theaters.

The 2-acre hands-on area called **Shamu's Happy Harbor** encourages kids to handle things—and features everything from a pretend pirate ship to tube crawls, slides, and chances to get wet. The newest attraction is **Shipwreck Rapids,** a wet adventure ride on inner tubes through caverns, waterfalls, and rivers. Other draws include **Wild Arctic,** a virtual-reality trip to the frozen North, complete with polar bears, beluga whales, walruses, and harbor seals. 500 SeaWorld Dr., Mission Bay. ⟨ 619/226-3901. www.seaworld.com. Admission $39 adults, $35 seniors, $30 children 3–11. Guided tours $8 adults, $7 children. Memorial Day to Labor Day daily 9am–11pm or midnight; Sept–May daily 10am–5pm. Bus: 9. From I-5, take SeaWorld Dr. exit; from I-8, take W. Mission Bay Dr. exit.

EXPLORING BALBOA PARK

Balboa Park is one of the nation's largest and loveliest city parks, boasting walkways, gardens, historical buildings, a restaurant, an ornate pavilion with one of the world's largest outdoor organs, and the world-famous San Diego Zoo. Stroll along **El Prado,** the park's main street, and admire the distinctive Spanish/Mediterranean buildings, which house an amazing array of museums. El Prado is also popular with musicians and other performers whose busking provides an entertaining backdrop.

Entry to the park is free, but most of its museums have admission charges and varying open hours. A free tram transports you around the park. Get details from the **Balboa Park Visitor Center,** in the House of Hospitality (© **619/ 239-0512;** www.balboapark.org).

The **San Diego Aerospace Museum,** 2001 Pan American Plaza (© **619/ 234-8291;** www.aerospacemuseum.org), celebrates great achievers and achievements in the history of aviation and aerospace with a superb collection of aircraft and artifacts.

The impressive painting and sculpture collections at the **San Diego Museum of Art,** 1450 El Prado (© **619/232-7931;** www.sdmart.com), include outstanding Italian Renaissance and Dutch and Spanish baroque art, along with an impressive collection of works by Toulouse-Lautrec.

The **Museum of Photographic Arts,** 1649 El Prado (© **619/238-7559;** www.mopa.org), is one of few in the United States. If the names of Ansel Adams, Margaret Bourke-White, Imogen Cunningham, Edward Weston, and Henri Cartier-Bresson stimulate your interest, then don't miss this 3,600-plus image collection.

The best exhibits in the **San Diego Natural History Museum,** 1788 El Prado (© **619/232-3821;** www.sdnhm.org), focus on the plants, animals, and minerals of the Southwest. Kids enjoy exploring the Desert Lab, home to live snakes and tarantulas.

The **Reuben H. Fleet Science Center,** 1875 El Prado (© **619/238-1233;** www.rhfleet.org), features five galleries with hands-on exhibits as intriguing for grown-ups as for kids, plus SciTours, a simulator ride that voyages into space and the worlds of science and biology. Equally popular is the OMNIMAX movie theater, surrounding viewers with breathtaking adventure travelogues.

The graceful **Botanical Building** shelters more than a thousand varieties of tropical and flowering plants, and the lily pond out front attracts the occasional street performer.

The ornate **Spreckels Organ Pavilion** (© **619/226-0819**) houses a fantastic organ with more than 4,000 individual pipes. Free concerts are given Sundays at 2pm year-round and on summer evenings. In the nearby **Japanese Friendship Garden** (© **619/232-2721;** www.niwa.org), visitors can sample the tranquility of traditional elements like a koi-filled stream, pastoral meadow, and ancient *sekitei* (sand-and-stone garden). Visit the tearoom/snack bar for udon, sushi, or Pokémon candies.

OLD TOWN & BEYOND: A LOOK AT CALIFORNIA'S BEGINNINGS

The birthplace of San Diego is Old Town, the hillside where the Spanish Presidio and Father Junípero Serra's mission (the first in California) were built. By protecting the remaining adobes and historic buildings, **Old Town State Historic Park** brings to life Mexican California, which existed here until the mid-1800s. Much of the surrounding area, however, has become a mini-Mexican theme park. Free walking tours leave daily at 10:30am and 2pm from **Seeley Stables Visitor Center** (© **619/220-5422**).

In nearby Mission Valley lies **Mission Basilica San Diego de Alcala,** 10818 San Diego Mission Rd. (© **619/281-8449**). Established in 1769, Mission San Diego was the first link in the chain of 21 missions founded in California by Spanish missionary Junípero Serra. Mass is held regularly in this still-active Catholic parish. Admission is $3 for adults, $2 for seniors and students, and $1

Balboa Park

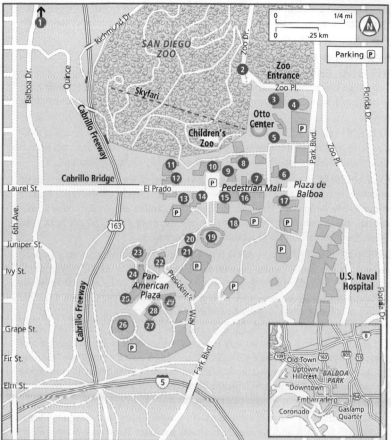

Alcazar Gardens **13**
Balboa Park Club **23**
Botanical Building **8**
Carousel **4**
Casa de Balboa **16**
  Hall of Champions Sports Museum
  Model Railroad Museum
  Museum of Photographic Arts
  San Diego Historical Society Museum
Casa del Prado **7**
Federal Building **29**
The Globe Theatres **11**
Hall of Nations **20**
House of Charm **14**
  Mingei International Museum
  San Diego Art Institute
House of Hospitality **15**
  Balboa Park Visitors Center
  Prado Restaurant
House of Pacific Relations
  International Cottages **22**

Japanese Friendship Garden **18**
Marston House Museum **1**
Municipal Museum **28**
Museum of Art **10**
Museum of Man **12**
Natural History Museum **6**
Palisades Building **24**
  Marie Hitchcock Puppet Theater
  Recital Hall
Reuben H. Fleet Science Center **17**
San Diego Aerospace Museum **26**
San Diego Automotive Museum **25**
San Diego Miniature Railroad **3**
San Diego Zoo **2**
Spanish Village Art Center **5**
Spreckels Organ Pavilion **19**
Starlight Bowl **27**
Timken Museum of Art **9**
United Nations Building **21**

for children 12 and under (free on Sun and for daily services). It's open daily from 9am to 5pm, with Mass daily at 7am and 5:30pm. To get here, take I-8 to Mission Gorge Road to Twain Avenue.

BEACHES & OUTDOOR PURSUITS
HITTING THE BEACH

San Diego County is blessed with 70 miles of sandy coastline. The following are some of our favorite San Diego beaches, arranged geographically from south to north.

CORONADO BEACH   Lovely, wide, and sparkling white, this beach is conducive to strolling and lingering, especially in the late afternoon. It fronts Ocean Boulevard and is especially pretty in front of the Hotel del Coronado.

OCEAN BEACH   The northern end is known as "Dog Beach," and is one of only two in San Diego where your pooch can roam freely on the sand. Surfers congregate around the Ocean Beach Pier. Rip currents are strong here and discourage most swimmers from venturing beyond waist depth. To get here, take West Point Loma Boulevard all the way to the end.

MISSION BAY PARK   In this 4,600-acre aquatic playground, you'll find 27 miles of bay front, 17 miles of oceanfront beaches, picnic areas, playgrounds, and paths for biking, roller skating, and jogging. The bay lends itself to windsurfing, sailing, water-skiing, and fishing. One of the most popular access points is off I-5 at Clairemont Drive, where there's a visitor center.

PACIFIC BEACH   Pacific Beach is the home of Tourmaline Surfing Park, where the sport's old guard gathers to surf waters where swimmers are prohibited; and there's always some action along Ocean Front Walk, a paved promenade featuring a human parade akin to that at L.A.'s Venice Beach boardwalk. It runs along Ocean Boulevard (just west of Mission Blvd.), north of Pacific Beach Drive.

LA JOLLA COVE   The protected, calm waters—praised as the clearest along the California coast—attract swimmers, snorkelers, divers, and families. There's a small sandy beach and, on the cliffs above, the Ellen Browning Scripps Park. The cove's "look but don't touch" policy protects the colorful marine life in this Underwater Park. La Jolla Cove can be accessed from Coast Boulevard.

LA JOLLA SHORES BEACH   The wide, flat mile of sand at La Jolla Shores is popular with joggers, swimmers, and beginning body- and board surfers, as well as with families. Weekend crowds can be enormous, though, quickly occupying both the sand and the metered parking spaces in the beach's lot.

MORE PLACES TO PLAY

Mission Bay and Coronado are especially good for leisurely biking. The boardwalks in Pacific Beach and Mission Beach can get very crowded, especially on weekends. Most major thoroughfares offer bike lanes. **Adventure Bike Tours,** in the San Diego Marriott (✆ **619/234-1500,** ext. 6514), offers bike and in-line skate rentals. Rent a pair of skates from **Hamel's Action Sports Center,** 704 Ventura Place (✆ **858/488-8889**).

San Diego's extensive waterways are popular for boating. You can rent a wide variety of boats, sailboats, kayaks, and other water toys from **Club Nautico,** at the San Diego Marriott Marina, 333 W. Harbor Dr. (✆ **619/233-9311**); **Seaforth Boat Rental,** 1641 Quivira Rd., Mission Bay (✆ **888/834-2628;** www.seaforth-boat-rental.com); and **Coronado Boat Rental,** 1715 Strand Way, Coronado (✆ **619/437-1514**).

San Diego County has nearly 80 golf courses, 50 of which are open to the public. Courses are diverse, some with vistas of the Pacific, others with views of country hillsides or of desert. **Balboa Park Municipal Golf Course** (© 619/239-1660) is nestled in the southeast corner of Balboa Park, and features old-growth trees and skyline views. Greens fees are $32 to $37 (excluding cart). **Coronado Municipal Golf Course** (© 619/435-3121) overlooks pretty Glorietta Bay; greens fees are $20 ($34 with cart). **Riverwalk Golf Club** (© 619/296-4653) is a Ted Robinson/Ted Robinson, Jr.–designed course meandering along the Mission Valley floor, with greens fees of $75 to $95 (including cart). In La Jolla, **Torrey Pines Golf Course** (© 800/985-4653 or 858/452-3226) comprises a pair of gorgeous championship clifftop courses overlooking the ocean; greens fees are $55 to $60 (excluding cart).

SHOPPING

Horton Plaza (© 619/238-1596; www.hortonplaza.shoppingtown.com) is the Disneyland of shopping malls, set in the heart of the revitalized city center. Within a rambling, colorful, and often confusing series of paths and bridges, the complex has tons of shops, including galleries, several fun shops for kids, a 14-screen cinema, three major department stores, and a variety of restaurants. Other downtown shopping opportunities include **Seaport Village,** on Harbor Drive (© 619/235-4014), a Cape Cod–style "village" of cutesy shops snuggled alongside San Diego Bay; it's worth a visit for the 1890 carousel imported from Coney Island, New York.

San Diego's self-proclaimed **Antique Row** is north of Balboa Park, along Park Boulevard (beginning at University Ave. in Hillcrest) and Adams Avenue (extending to around 40th St. in Normal Heights). For more information and an area brochure with map, contact the **Adams Avenue Business Association** (© 619/282-7329; www.gothere.com/adamsave).

Shopping in **La Jolla** tends toward the conservative and costly; women's fashion boutiques include Ann Taylor, Armani Exchange, Polo/Ralph Lauren, and Talbots; and Swiss watches, tennis bracelets, and pearl necklaces sparkle at you from windows along every street. No visit to La Jolla is complete without seeing **John Cole's Bookshop,** 780 Prospect St. (© 858/454-4766), an eclectic, family-run local favorite set in a charming old cottage.

WHERE TO STAY

For good prices in all accommodation categories, contact **San Diego Hotel Reservations** (© 800/SAVE-CASH or 619/627-9300; www.sandiegohotel-res.com). If you want a B&B, contact the **San Diego Bed & Breakfast Guild** (© 619/523-1300; www.bandbguildsandiego.org).

In addition to the listings below, other reliable choices include the historic and surprisingly affordable **Gaslamp Plaza Suites,** 520 E St., at Fifth Avenue (© 619/232-9500). Also downtown is the **Holiday Inn on the Bay,** 1355 N. Harbor Dr., at Ash Street (© 800/HOLIDAY or 619/232-3861), boasting magnificent views and popular with business travelers and families.

In Old Town there's the exquisite **Heritage Park Bed & Breakfast Inn,** 2470 Heritage Park Row, near Old Town (© 800/995-2470 or 619/299-6832; www.heritageparkinn.com); and **Vacation Inn,** 3900 Old Town Ave. (© 800/451-9846 or 619/299-7400). The **La Jolla Village Lodge,** 1141 Silverado St. (© 858/551-2001; www.lajollavillagelodge.com), is a basic motel that's a good value in tony La Jolla. Well-located and terrifically priced, the **Coronado Inn,**

266 Orange Ave. (at Third St.), Coronado (© **800/598-6624** or 935/435-4121; www.coronadoinn.com), is a charming renovated 1940s courtyard motel with a friendly ambience.

Catamaran Resort Hotel   Situated right on Mission Bay, the Catamaran has its own bay and ocean beaches. Built in the 1950s, the hotel has been fully renovated without losing its trademark Polynesian theme. Each guest room—in a 13-story building or one of the six two-story buildings—has a fridge and a balcony or patio; tower rooms have commanding views of the bay and San Diego skyline. Studios and suites have kitchenettes. The Catamaran is within walking distance of Pacific Beach's restaurant and nightlife, and steps away from the bay's exceptional jogging/biking path. 3999 Mission Blvd. (4 blocks south of Grand Ave.), San Diego, CA 92109. © **800/422-8386** or 858/488-1081. Fax 858/488-1619. www.catamaranresort.com. 313 units. $195–$265 double; from $400 suite. Children under 12 stay free in parents' room. AE, DC, DISC, MC, V. Self-parking $8, valet parking $10. Take Grand/Garnet exit off I-5 and go west on Grand Ave., then south on Mission Blvd. **Amenities:** Restaurant; outdoor pool; tennis courts; health club.

Crystal Pier Hotel   This historic, charming, and utterly unique cluster of cottages sits literally over the surf on the vintage Crystal Pier. Each self-contained hideaway has a living room, bedroom, full kitchen, and private patio with breathtaking ocean views. The sound of waves is soothing, but the boardwalk action is only a few steps away. Guests drive right out and park beside their cottages, a real boon on crowded weekends. Vending machines and movie rentals are available, as are boogie boards, fishing poles, beach chairs, and umbrellas. 4500 Ocean Blvd. (at Garnet Ave.), San Diego, CA 92109. © **800/748-5894** or 858/483-6983. Fax 858/483-6811. www.crystalpier.com. 26 units. Cottages for 2–6 people $135–$335 mid-June to mid-Sept; $105–$275 mid-Sept to mid-June. 3-night minimum in summer. DISC, MC, V. Free parking. Take I-5 to Grand/Garnet exit; follow Garnet to the pier.

Embassy Suites   What might seem like an impersonal business hotel is actually one of the better deals in town, providing modern accommodations with lots of space for families. Each suite has a city or bay view and contains a sofa bed in the living area and a kitchenette with microwave and fridge. A block from Seaport Village and 5 blocks from downtown, the Embassy Suites is the second choice of Convention Center groups (after the pricier Hyatt Regency) and as a result it can be fully booked at unexpected times. 601 Pacific Hwy. (at N. Harbor Dr.), San Diego, CA 92101. © **800/EMBASSY** or 619/239-2400. Fax 619/239-1520. 337 units. $189–$300 suite. Children under 18 stay free in parents' room. Rates include full breakfast. AE, DC, DISC, MC, V. Self-parking $11, valet parking $14. **Amenities:** Restaurants (2); indoor pool; tennis court; fitness room.

Horton Grand   A cross between an elegant hotel and a charming inn, the Horton Grand combines two historic 1880s hotels connected by an airy atrium lobby. Each room is utterly unique; all were renovated in 2000 with vintage furnishings, gas fireplaces, and business-savvy features. Rooms overlook either the city or the fig tree–filled courtyard. The Palace Bar serves afternoon tea Tuesday through Saturday. 311 Island Ave. (at Fourth Ave.), San Diego, CA 92101. © **800/542-1886** or 619/544-1886. Fax 619/544-0058. www.hortongrand.com. 132 units. $139–$199 double; $259 suite. Children under 18 stay free in parents' room. AE, DC, MC, V. Valet parking $15. **Amenities:** Restaurant.

Hotel del Coronado   Opened in 1888 and designated a National Historic Landmark, the "Hotel Del" is the last of California's grand old seaside hotels.

Legend has it that the Duke of Windsor met his duchess here, and Marilyn Monroe frolicked here in *Some Like It Hot*. This monument to Victorian grandeur boasts cupolas, turrets, and gingerbread trim, all spread out over 26 acres (including some contemporary tower additions). Rooms run the gamut from compact to extravagant, and all are packed with antique charm. The best have balconies fronting the ocean. Even if you don't stay here, take a stroll through the grand, wood-paneled lobby or along the pristine beach 1500 Orange Ave., Coronado, CA 92118. ℂ 800/468-3533 or 619/435-8000. Fax 619/522-8238. www. hoteldel.com. 700 units. $215–$340 double (garden or city view), $360–$640 double (oceanview); suites from $700. Children under 18 stay free in parents' room. AE, DC, DISC, MC, V. Self-parking $12, valet parking $16. From Coronado Bridge, turn left onto Orange Ave. **Amenities:** Restaurants (9); 2 outdoor pools; 3 tennis courts; spa; health club.

La Jolla Beach & Tennis Club   Pack your best tennis whites for a stay at La Jolla's private and historic "B&T." Rooms are unexpectedly plain, though equipped with all the basic amenities. Most have well-stocked kitchens ideal for families or longer stays. The beach is popular here; the staff sets up comfy chairs and umbrellas, racing to bring fluffy towels, beverages, and snacks. Kayaks and watersports equipment can be rented, and guests have full use of the club's championship tennis courts and nine-hole pitch-and-putt course. Although there's no room service, there are two on-site dining options and several nearby trattorias. 2000 Spindrift Dr., La Jolla, CA 92037. ℂ 800/624-CLUB or 858/454-7126. Fax 858/456-3805. www.ljbtc.com. 90 units. June–Sept $170–$349 double, from $275 suite; off season $139–$239 double, from $215 suite. Children under 12 stay free in parents' room. Extra person $20. AE, DC, MC, V. Take La Jolla Shores Dr., turn left on Paseo Dorado, and follow it to Spindrift Dr. **Amenities:** Restaurants (2); pool; 12 tennis courts; fitness room.

La Pensione Hotel   Offering modern amenities, remarkable value, a convenient location, and a friendly staff, the three-story La Pensione feels like a small European hotel. The decor throughout is modern and streamlined, with minimal furniture and plenty of sleek black and metallic surfaces. Rooms, while not overly large, make the most of their space. Each has a ceiling fan, microwave, and fridge; try for a bay or city view rather than the view of the concrete courtyard. La Pensione is in Little Italy, within walking distance of eateries and nightspots. 606 W. Date St. (at India St.), San Diego, CA 92101. ℂ 800/232-4683 or 619/236-8000. Fax 619/236-8088. www.lapensionehotel.com. 80 units. $60–$80 double. AE, DC, DISC, MC, V. Limited free underground parking. **Amenities:** Access to nearby health club.

La Valencia Hotel   Within bougainvillea-draped walls and wrought-iron gates is this gracious bastion of gentility. The clifftop hotel has been the centerpiece of La Jolla since opening in 1926; today, brides pose against a backdrop of La Jolla Cove and the Pacific, while well-coifed ladies lunch in the dappled shade of the garden patio. Rooms are comfortably and traditionally furnished, all with lavish appointments, VCRs, and signature toiletries. Because rates vary wildly according to view, we suggest getting the cheaper room and simply stepping outside to see the ocean. 1132 Prospect St. (at Herschel Ave.), La Jolla, CA 92037. ℂ 800/451-0772 or 858/454-0771. Fax 858/456-3921. www.lavalencia.com. 132 units. $250–$500 double; from $550 suite. Extra person $15. AE, DC, DISC, MC, V. Valet parking $14. Take Torrey Pines Rd. to Prospect Place and turn right. Prospect Place becomes Prospect St. **Amenities:** Restaurants (3); outdoor pool; fitness room with spa treatments.

Loews Coronado Bay Resort   This luxury resort opened in 1991 on a secluded 15-acre peninsula, slightly removed from downtown Coronado and San Diego. It's perfect for those who prefer a self-contained resort in a get-away-from-it-all location. All units offer terraces that look onto the private marina, the Coronado Bay Bridge, or San Diego Bay. A pedestrian underpass leads to nearby Silver Strand Beach. Rooms boast finely appointed marble bathrooms; VCRs are available free upon request. A highlight here is the Gondola Company (© **619/429-6317**), which offers gondola cruises through the canals of tony Coronado Cays. 4000 Coronado Bay Rd., Coronado, CA 92118. © **800/81-LOEWS** or 619/424-4000. Fax 619/424-4400. 438 units. $145–$265 double; from $450 suite. Children under 18 stay free in parents' room. AE, DC, DISC, MC, V. Self-parking $13, valet parking $16. From Coronado Bridge, go left onto Orange Ave. and continue 8 miles down Silver Strand Hwy. Turn left at Coronado Bay Rd. **Amenities:** Restaurants (3); 3 outdoor pools; tennis courts; spa; fitness center; pets under 25 lb. accepted.

Pacific Terrace Hotel   The best modern hotel on the boardwalk sports a soothing South Seas ambience and upscale atmosphere that make it stand apart from the casual beach pads in the area. Large guest rooms come with balconies or terraces; about half have kitchenettes. The lushly landscaped pool faces a relatively quiet stretch of beach. Several local restaurants allow meals to be billed to the hotel, but there's no restaurant on the premises. 610 Diamond St., San Diego, CA 92109. © **800/344-3370** or 858/581-3500. Fax 858/274-3341. www.pacificterrace.com. 75 units. $269 standard double; $369 oceanfront double; from $395 suite. Rates include continental breakfast. AE, DC, DISC, MC, V. Parking $5. Take I-5 to Grand/Garnet exit and follow Grand or Garnet west to Mission Blvd.; turn right (north), then left (west) onto Diamond; hotel is at the end of the street on the right. **Amenities:** Outdoor pool; access to nearby health club.

Paradise Point Resort & Spa   This Mission Bay hotel complex is as much a theme park as its closest neighbor, SeaWorld (a 3-min. drive). Single-story accommodations are spread across 44 acres of lagoons, gardens, and swim-friendly beaches; all have private patios and plenty of thoughtful conveniences like fridges and coffeemakers. Recently updated to keep its 1960s charm but lose tacky holdovers, the resort offers so much fun and recreation you may never want to leave! And despite daunting high-season rack rates, there's usually a deal to be had here. In 2001, the resort unveiled a stunning Indonesian-inspired spa that is a vacation in itself. 1404 W. Vacation Rd. (off Ingraham St.), San Diego, CA 92109. © **800/344-2626** or 858/274-4630. Fax 858/581-5977. www.paradisepoint.com. 462 units. Memorial Day to Labor Day $220–$350 double; from $325 suite. Off season $175–$325 double; from $300 suite. Extra person $20. Children 17 and under stay free in parents' room. AE, DC, DISC, MC, V. Free parking. Follow I-8 west to Mission Bay Dr. exit; take Ingraham St. north to Vacation Rd. **Amenities:** Restaurants (3); 6 outdoor pools; 18-hole putting course; tennis courts; spa; fitness center.

Red Lion Hanalei Hotel   At this comfort-conscious yet sophisticated Polynesian-themed hotel, rooms are split between two high-rise towers, set far away from the freeway. All have balconies that overlook the landscaped pool courtyard or the adjacent golf club. The hotel boasts an unmistakable 1960s vibe and Hawaiian ambience, but rooms sport contemporary furnishings and conveniences; some have microwaves and fridges. Services include a free shuttle to Old Town and other attractions. 2270 Hotel Circle N., San Diego, CA 92108. © **800/RED-LION** or 619/297-1101. Fax 619/297-6049. www.redlion.com. 416 units. $109–$159 double; $275–$375 suite. Extra person $10. AE, DISC, MC, V. Parking $8. From I-8, take Hotel Circle exit. **Amenities:** Restaurants (2); outdoor pool; adjacent golf course; fitness center; pets accepted ($25).

Sommerset Suites Hotel   This all-suite hotel on a busy street boasts unexpected amenities like huge closets, medicine cabinets, and fully equipped kitchens in all rooms. Extras include poolside barbecue facilities and a coin-op laundry. The hotel has a personal, welcoming feel, from the helpful staff to the snacks and drinks served each afternoon. Rooms are comfortably furnished, and each has a private balcony. Hillcrest's chic restaurants and shops (plus a movie multiplex) are within easy walking distance. There's courtesy van service to the airport and attractions within a 5-mile radius. 606 Washington St. (at Fifth Ave.), San Diego, CA 92103. ℂ 800/ 962-9665 or 619/692-5200. Fax 619/692-5299. www.sommersetsuites.com. 80 units. $109–$195 double. Children under 12 stay free in parents' room. Rates include continental breakfast. AE, DC, DISC, MC, V. Free covered parking. Take Washington St. exit off I-5. Bus: 16 or 25. **Amenities:** Outdoor pool.

U.S. Grant Hotel   In 1910, Ulysses S. Grant, Jr., opened this stately Italianate hotel in honor of his father. Its elegant style is more often found in East Coast manses: marble, crystal chandeliers, and decor that verges on the stuffy. All rooms are quite spacious, but extras in the suites make them worth the splurge; each has a fireplace and Jacuzzi, and suite rates include continental breakfast and afternoon cocktails. While the hotel has preserved a nostalgic formality, the surrounding neighborhood has become a hodgepodge of chic bistros, wandering panhandlers, and the visually loud Horton Plaza shopping center. 326 Broadway (between Third and Fourth aves.), San Diego, CA 92101. ℂ 800/237-5029 or 619/232-3121. Fax 619/232-3626. www.grandheritage.com. 340 units. $195–$215 double; from $275 suite. Children under 12 stay free in parents' room. AE, DC, MC, V. Parking $17. **Amenities:** Restaurant; fitness center; pets welcome.

WHERE TO DINE

If you're in the mood for a special-occasion meal that'll knock your socks off, consider **Azzura Point** (ℂ 935/424-4000), in Loews Coronado Bay Resort. With its plushly upholstered, gilded, and view-endowed setting, this dining room wins raves from deep-pocketed San Diego foodies willing to cross the bay for inventive California-Mediterranean creations.

Baleen SEAFOOD/CALIFORNIA   This fine waterfront eatery boasts a spectacular bay-front view and dining deck for pleasant weather. Start with chilled lobster in a martini glass, a warm salad of roasted mushrooms and asparagus, or fresh oysters shucked tableside. Then savor a selection of seafood simply grilled, wood-roasted, or sautéed, with hummus crust, honey wasabi glaze, or ginger sauce. Should you still have an appetite, indulge in an intricately rich dessert like chocolate fondue. In the Paradise Point Resort, 1404 Vacation Rd., Mission Bay. ℂ 858/ 490-6363. www.paradisepoint.com. Reservations recommended. Main courses $10–$21 lunch, $18–$30 dinner. AE, DC, DISC, MC, V. Daily 7am–11pm. Follow I-8 west to Mission Bay Dr. exit; take Ingraham St. north to Vacation Rd.

Brockton Villa BREAKFAST/CALIFORNIA   Located in a restored 1894 beach bungalow, this charming cafe has a varied, eclectic menu. The biggest buzz is at breakfast, which features inventive dishes such as soufflé-like "Coast Toast" (the house take on French toast) and Greek "steamers" (eggs scrambled with an espresso steamer, then mixed with feta, tomato, and basil). Lunch stars homemade soups and salads, plus unusual sandwiches like turkey meatloaf on sourdough bread with tomato-mint chutney. The dinner menu includes salmon *en croute* (wrapped in prosciutto, Gruyère, and sage), plus pastas, stews, and grilled meats. 1235 Coast Blvd. (across from La Jolla Cove). ℂ 858/454-7393. Reservations recommended (call by Thurs for Sun brunch). Breakfast $4–$8; dinner main courses $12–$21. AE, DISC, MC, V. Mon 8am–5pm; Tues–Sun 8am–9pm.

Cafe Pacifica CALIFORNIA   Inside this cozy Old Town casita, the decor is cleanly contemporary (but still romantic) and the food anything but Mexican. Cafe Pacifica serves upscale, imaginative seafood; among the temptations is crab-stuffed portobello mushroom topped with grilled asparagus. Signature items include Hawaiian ahi with shiitake mushrooms and ginger butter, griddled mustard catfish, and the "Pomerita," a pomegranate margarita. Patrons tend to dress up, though it's not required. 2414 San Diego Ave. ℂ 619/291-6666. www. cafepacifica.com. Reservations recommended. Main courses $12–$22. AE, DC, DISC, MC, V. Mon–Sat 5:30–10pm; Sun 5–9:30pm. Valet parking $4. Bus: 5/5A. Trolley: Old Town.

Chez Loma FRENCH   You'd be hard-pressed to find a more romantic dining spot than this intimate Victorian cottage filled with antiques and candlelight. Tables are scattered throughout the house and on the enclosed terrace; an upstairs wine salon is a cozy spot for coffee. Among the creative entrees are salmon with smoked-tomato vinaigrette and roast duckling with green-peppercorn sauce. Chez Loma's service is attentive, the herb rolls addictive, and early birds enjoy specially priced meals. 1132 Loma (off Orange Ave.). ℂ 619/435-0661. www.chezloma.com. Reservations recommended. Main courses $17–$25. AE, DC, MC, V. Daily 5–10pm. Bus: 901.

Croce's Restaurant & Bars AMERICAN/ECLECTIC   Ingrid Croce, widow of singer-songwriter Jim, was instrumental in the resurgence of the once-decayed Gaslamp Quarter, and her establishment has expanded to fill every corner of this 1890 Romanesque building. Croce's menu fuses Southern soul food and Southwestern spice with Asian flavors and Continental standards. Add the raucous Top Hat Bar & Grille and the intimate Jazz Bar, and the complex is the hottest ticket in town, with crowds lining up for dinner tables and nightclub shows. 802 Fifth Ave. (at F St.). ℂ 619/233-4355. www.croces.com. Reservations not accepted; call for same-day "priority seating" (before walk-ins). Main courses $14–$23. AE, DC, DISC, MC, V. Daily 5pm–midnight. Valet parking $7 with validation. Bus: 3, 5, 16, or 25. Trolley: Gaslamp Quarter.

Fio's NORTHERN ITALIAN   Fio's is the granddaddy of all the trendy Italian restaurants in the Gaslamp Quarter. Set in an 1881 Italianate Victorian, Fio's has a sophisticated ambience and is *always* crowded. The upscale trattoria menu is consistently superior, featuring jet-black linguini tossed with the freshest seafood, delicate angel-hair pasta perfectly balanced with basil and pine nuts, and gourmet pizzas served at your table or to diners seated at the special pizza bar. The impressive list of meat entrees includes mustard-rosemary rack of lamb, veal shank on saffron risotto, and delicately sweet hazelnut-crusted pork loin with Frangelico and peaches. 801 Fifth Ave. (at F St.). ℂ 619/234-3467. www.fioscucina. com. Reservations recommended. Main courses $11–$25. AE, DC, DISC, MC, V. Mon–Thurs 5–10:30pm; Fri–Sat 5–11pm; Sun 5–10pm. Valet parking $6 with validation. Bus: 3, 5, 16, or 25. Trolley: Gaslamp Quarter.

The Fish Market SEAFOOD   Ask any San Diegan where to go for the biggest selection of the freshest fish, and they'll send you to the bustling Fish Market on the end of the G Street Pier on the Embarcadero. Chalkboards announce the day's catches—be it Mississippi catfish, Maine lobster, Canadian salmon, or Mexican yellowtail—sold by the pound or available in a number of classic, simple preparations in the casual restaurant. Upstairs, the related Top of the Market offers similar fare at jacked-up prices; we recommend having a cocktail in Top's posh clubby atmosphere with stupendous bay views—then head downstairs for affordable fare and/or treats from the sushi and oyster bars. 750 N. Harbor Dr. ℂ 619/232-FISH. www.thefishmarket.com. Reservations not accepted. Main courses $9–$25. AE, DC, DISC, MC, V. Daily 11am–10pm. Valet parking $4. Bus: 7/7B. Trolley: Seaport Village.

George's at the Cove CALIFORNIA   A beloved La Jolla tradition, George's wins consistent praise for impeccable service, gorgeous views of the cove, and outstanding California cuisine. Dishes combine flavors with practiced artistry, ranging from the Asian-tinged grilled swordfish atop gingered vegetables to a Provençal-inspired rack of lamb in aromatic spices. George's signature smoked chicken, broccoli, and black-bean soup is still a mainstay. The tasting menu offers a seasonally composed five-course sampling for around $50 per person. The informal **Ocean Terrace Cafe** is upstairs. 1250 Prospect St. © 858/454-4244. www.georgesatthecove.com. Reservations recommended. Main courses $13–$17 lunch, $25–$35 dinner. AE, DC, DISC, MC, V. Mon–Fri 11:30am–2:30pm; Sat–Sun 11:30am–3pm; Mon–Thurs 5:30–10pm; Fri–Sat 5–10:30pm; Sun 5–10pm. Valet parking $5–$6.

The Green Flash AMERICAN   Known throughout Pacific Beach for its location and hip, local clientele, the Green Flash serves reasonably good (and typically beachy) food at decent prices. The menu includes plenty of grilled and deep-fried seafood, straightforward steaks, and giant main-course salads. Locals congregate on the patio to catch a glimpse of the sunset phenomenon for which this boardwalk hangout is named, and the decibel level rises with every round of drinks. 701 Thomas Ave. (at Mission Blvd.), Pacific Beach. © 858/270-7715. Reservations not accepted. Main courses $10–$20; sunset specials Sun–Thurs 4:30–7pm. AE, DC, DISC, MC, V. Daily 8am–10pm. Bus: 34/34A.

Laurel FRENCH/MEDITERRANEAN   Given its stylish decor, pedigreed chefs, prime Balboa Park location, and well-composed menu of country French dishes with a Mediterranean accent, it's no wonder this relatively new restaurant was an instant success. It's also popular with theatergoers, offering shuttle service to the Old Globe. Tantalizing choices include warm caramelized onion and Roquefort tart, crisp Muscovy duck confit, and venison in a rich shallot–port wine sauce. 505 Laurel St. (at Fifth Ave.). © 619/239-2222. www.laurelrestaurant.com. Reservations recommended. Main courses $15–$26. AE, DC, DISC, MC, V. Sun–Thurs 5–10pm; Fri–Sat 5–11pm. Valet parking $6. Bus: 1, 3, or 25.

Mixx CALIFORNIA/INTERNATIONAL   Aptly named for its subtle global fusion fare, Mixx embodies everything good about Hillcrest dining: a relaxing room, a sophisticated crowd, thoughtfully composed dinners, and polished service. Menu standouts include duck and wild mushroom ravioli and pepper filet mignon on truffle mashed potatoes. Even carnivores should check out the surprisingly inventive nightly vegetarian special. Prepared and presented with finesse, one meal here will quickly convince you that Mixx cares about style, substance, *and* value. 3671 Fifth Ave. (at Pennsylvania Ave.). © 619/299-6499. Reservations recommended, especially on weekends. Main courses $14–$24. AE, DC, DISC, MC, V. Sun–Thurs 5–10pm; Fri–Sat 5–11pm. Bus: 1, 3, or 25.

Nine-Ten CALIFORNIA/MEDITERRANEAN   Chef Michael Stebner delivers on a superbly crafted menu in a warmly stylish and understated space. Mouthwatering presentations might include chestnut agnolotti with fennel and sweet squash, rich veal tenderloin with rosemary and olives atop creamy polenta, and porcini risotto topped with lobster and aromatic white truffle oil. Leave room for desserts like persimmon panna cotta or honey-rosemary ice cream. This hotel eatery offers a classy experience with none of the fancy attitude. 910 Prospect St. (between Fay & Girard). © 858/964-5400. www.thegrandecolonial.com. Reservations recommended. Main courses $8–$12 lunch, $18–$32 dinner. AE, DC, DISC, MC, V. Daily 6:30–11am, 11:30am–2:30pm, and 6–10:30pm.

Old Town Mexican Café MEXICAN   This place is so popular that it's become an Old Town tourist attraction in its own right; the wait for a table is often 30 to 60 minutes. Pass the time gazing in from the sidewalk as tortillas are hand-patted the old-fashioned way, a hot-off-the-grill treat accompanying every meal. Once inside, order the best margarita in town, followed by one of the cafe's two specialties: *carnitas* (deep-fried pork served with tortillas, guacamole, sour cream, beans, and rice) or rotisserie chicken. It's loud and crowded and the *cerveza* flows like, well, beer. 2489 San Diego Ave. (© 619/297-4330. Reservations accepted only for parties of 10 or more. Main courses $7.50–$12. AE, DISC, MC, V. Sun–Thurs 7am–11pm; Fri–Sat 7am–midnight; bar service daily until 2am. Bus: 5/5A. Trolley: Old Town.

The Vegetarian Zone VEGETARIAN In Hillcrest, San Diego's only strictly vegetarian restaurant is a real treat—even if you're wary of tempeh and tofu, there are plenty of veggie ethnic options on the menu, ranging from Greek spinach-and-feta pie to savory Indian curry turnovers. If you're ordering salad, don't miss the tangy miso-ginger dressing. There's seating indoors and on a patio. In case you feel deserving of a treat after such a healthful meal, the heavenly Extraordinary Desserts is next door. 2949 Fifth Ave. (between Palm and Quince sts.). (© **619/ 298-7302**, or 619/298-9232 for deli and takeout. Reservations accepted only for parties of 6 or more. Main courses $5–$10. AE, DC, DISC, MC, V. Mon–Thurs 11:30am–9pm; Fri 11:30am–10pm; Sat 10:30am–10pm; Sun 10:30am–9pm. Free parking. Bus: 1, 3, or 25.

SAN DIEGO AFTER DARK

To find out what's on during your visit, pick up a copy of the *Reader,* a free weekly newspaper available all over the city. There's also the Thursday entertainment section in the *San Diego Union-Tribune.* Half-price tickets to theater, music, and dance events are available at the **ARTS TIX** booth, in Horton Plaza Park, at Broadway and Third Avenue, open Tuesday through Saturday from 10am to 7pm. For a daily listing of half-price offerings, call (© **619/497-5000.**

THE PERFORMING ARTS Near the entrance to Balboa Park, the Tony Award–winning **Old Globe Theatre** (© **619/239-2255** or 619/23-GLOBE; www.theglobetheatres.org) is fashioned after Shakespeare's, and has billed such notable performers as John Goodman, Marsha Mason, Jon Voight, and Christopher Walken. Another Tony winner, the **La Jolla Playhouse,** 2910 La Jolla Village Dr. (© **858/550-1010;** www.lajollaplayhouse.com), has staged such productions as *How to Succeed in Business Without Really Trying* (starring Matthew Broderick) before it went on to Broadway fame and fortune.

The **San Diego Repertory Theatre** offers professional, culturally diverse productions at the Lyceum Theatre in Horton Plaza (© **619/544-1000;** www.sandiegorep.com). In Coronado, **Lamb's Players Theatre,** at 1142 Orange Ave. (© **935/437-0600;** www.lambsplayers.org), is a professional repertory company that stages shows in the historic Spreckels Building, where no seat is more than seven rows from the stage.

THE CLUB & BAR SCENE The **Casbah,** 2501 Kettner Blvd., near the airport (© **619/232-4355;** www.casbahmusic.com), is a divey joint with a rep for breakthrough alternative and rock bands. **Croce's Bars,** 802 Fifth Ave., at F Street (© **619/233-4355;** www.croces.com), are attached to one of the Gaslamp Quarter's most popular restaurants, and feature jazz and rhythm and blues. Downtown, **4th & B,** 345 B St. (© **619/231-4343;** www.4thandb.com), is a quality venue with performances ranging from rock to chamber music. **Humphrey's,** 2241 Shelter Island Dr. (© **619/523-1010;** www.humphreysconcerts.com), is a 900-seat outdoor venue set on the water, and has a seasonal lineup that ranges from rock to folk to international.

The Gaslamp Quarter is the epicenter for the city's hottest dance clubs—the most popular at the moment are **Olé Madrid,** 751 Fifth Ave. (© **619/ 557-0146**), a loud, energetic club with tapas and sangria from the adjoining

Spanish restaurant; **Sevilla,** 555 Fourth Ave. (© **619/233-5979**), where you can salsa and merengue to Brazilian dance music; and **Harmony on Fifth,** 322 Fifth Ave. (© **619/235-4646**), where postmodern hipsters swing to 1940s tunes or recline with a martini.

Cannibal Bar, in the Catamaran Hotel, 3999 Mission Blvd., Mission Beach (© **858/539-8650**), features a tropical theme, Polynesian cocktails, DJ dancing, and occasional live bands. **The Bitter End,** 770 Fifth Ave., Gaslamp Quarter (© **619/338-9300;** www.thebitterend.com), has three levels for its martini bar, late-night dance club, and relaxing cocktail lounge. **Martini Ranch,** 528 F St., Gaslamp Quarter (© **619/235-6100**), is a split-level bar boasting 30 kinds of martinis. **Top O' The Cove,** 1216 Prospect Ave., La Jolla (© **858/454-7779**), offers an intimate setting for mellow piano music.

4 Santa Barbara

Nestled between palm-lined Pacific beaches and gently sloping foothills, this prosperous resort community presents a mosaic of red-tile roofs and a gracious, relaxed attitude.

ESSENTIALS

GETTING THERE By Plane The **Santa Barbara Municipal Airport** (© **805/967-7111**) is located in Goleta, 10 minutes from downtown Santa Barbara. Taxi fare is about $22 to downtown.

By Train Amtrak (© **800/USA-RAIL;** www.amtrak.com) trains arrive at the **Santa Barbara Rail Station,** 209 State St. (© **805/963-1015**), with service from Los Angeles (trip time: 3 hr.).

By Car U.S. 101 runs right through Santa Barbara; it's the fastest, most direct driving route from Los Angeles (2 hr.) or San Francisco (6 hr.).

VISITOR INFORMATION The **Santa Barbara Visitor Information Center,** 1 Santa Barbara St. (© **800/927-4688** or 805/965-3021; www.santabarbaraca. com), is on the ocean, at the corner of Cabrillo Street. Hours are Monday through Saturday from 9am to 4pm, Sunday from 10am to 4pm.

EXPLORING THE TOWN

State Street is the city's main thoroughfare and has the largest concentration of cafes, boutiques, antiques stores, and more. Electric shuttle buses (25¢) run up and down State Street. At the harbor end is the city's 1872-vintage Stearns Wharf, offering a small collection of souvenir shops, attractions, and restaurants, plus terrific inland views and fishing.

The town has an array of beaches. **Arroyo Burro Beach,** aka **Hendry's Beach,** at the end of Cliff Drive, is popular with families, boogie boarders, and sunset strollers. **East Beach** is a wide swath of clean white sand that hosts beach umbrellas, sand-castle builders, and spirited volleyball games.

A relatively flat, palm-lined, 2-mile coastal pathway runs along the beach and is perfect for biking and skating. More adventurous riders can pedal through town, up to the mission, or to Montecito, the next town over. For bike or skate rentals, head to **Beach Rentals,** 22 State St. (© **805/966-6733**).

Santa Barbara's most distinctive attraction is the 1786 **Santa Barbara Mission,** at Laguna and Los Olivos streets (© **805/682-4149;** www.sbmission.org), whose graceful Spanish-Moorish style earned the title "Queen of the Missions." It overlooks the town and the sea beyond. Admission is $4 for adults, free for children 11 and under; open daily from 9am to 5pm.

The **Red Tile Tour** of downtown (ask for details at the visitor center) passes many historic and architectural highlights, including the exquisite 1929 **County Courthouse,** 1100 Anacapa St. (© **805/962-6464**), the most flamboyant example of Spanish colonial revival architecture in the entire city. The observation deck atop the clock tower affords great views of the ocean, the mountains, and the courthouse's outstanding gardens.

WHERE TO STAY

The Convention and Visitors Bureau's free reservations service, **Hot Spots** (© **800/793-7666** or 805/564-1637), keeps an updated list of availability for the area's hotels, motels, inns, and B&Bs. Call Monday through Saturday from 9am to 9pm and Sunday from 9am to 4pm.

In addition to the listings below, there are moderately priced rooms at the **Casa del Mar Inn at the Beach,** 18 Bath St. (© **800/433-3097** or 805/963-4418; www.casadelmar.com), and the **Franciscan Inn,** 109 Bath St. (© **805/963-8845;** www.franciscaninn.com).

El Encanto Hotel & Garden Villas   This romantic hillside retreat was built in 1915 and is made up of charming Craftsman cottages and Spanish bungalows. El Encanto features a spectacular view, secluded nooks, peaceful gardens, and lush landscaping. The hotel's discreet service has made it a favorite among privacy-minded celebs. The spacious rooms are tastefully decorated in a European country style; many have fireplaces and patios. 1900 Lasuen Rd., Santa Barbara, CA 93103. © **800/346-7039** or 805/687-5000. Fax 805/687-3903. www.elencantohotel.com. 83 units. $229–$269 double; suites from $379. AE, DC, MC, V. Valet parking $10. **Amenities:** Restaurant; outdoor pool; tennis court; access to nearby health club;.

Four Seasons Biltmore   This grand Spanish-style hacienda, once patronized by Hollywood Golden Age celebs like Greta Garbo and Errol Flynn, manages to adhere to the most elegant standards of hospitality without making anyone feel unwelcome. Rooms have an airy feel, heightened by white plantation shutters and marble bathrooms with all the modern amenities. Guests can amuse themselves with a putting green, plus shuffleboard and croquet courts. In addition to two acclaimed dining rooms, the Biltmore offers a no-holds-barred Sunday brunch. 1260 Channel Dr. (at the end of Olive Mill Rd.), Santa Barbara, CA 93108. © **800/332-3442** or 805/969-2261. Fax 805/565-8323. 217 units. $295–$620 double; suites from $1,050. Extra person $35. Free for children 18 and under. AE, DC, MC, V. Self-parking free, valet parking $18. **Amenities:** Restaurants (2); 2 outdoor pools; 3 lighted tennis courts; spa; health club.

Hotel Oceana   New on the scene in 2002, this hotel has a beach-friendly feel but still offers a more upscale experience than the surrounding budget motels. The amalgam of four formerly independent motel properties combines vintage-era charm with contemporary comforts such as Frette linens and CD players. Cabrillo Boulevard and East Beach are just outside the front door. Oceanview rooms come at a premium, but we almost prefer the quieter garden- or poolside rooms. 202 W. Cabrillo Blvd., Santa Barbara, CA 93101. © **800/965-9776** or 805/965-4577. Fax 805/965-9937. www.hoteloceana.com. 122 units. $175–$350 double; $400 suite. AE, DISC, MC, V. Valet parking $8. **Amenities:** 2 outdoor pools; spa; fitness center.

Simpson House Inn Bed & Breakfast   Simpson House is truly something special. Rooms in the 1874 Historic Landmark house are decorated to Victorian perfection, with extras ranging from a claw-foot tub to French doors; cottages are nestled throughout the grounds. Accommodations have everything you could possibly need (including VCRs), but most impressive are the extras: the

Santa Barbara

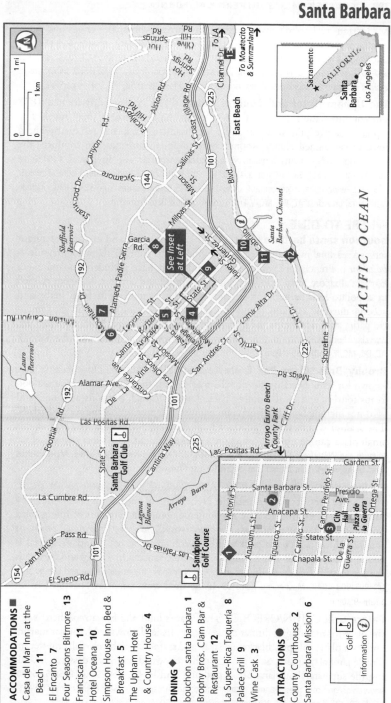

ACCOMMODATIONS ■

Casa del Mar Inn at the Beach **11**
El Encanto **7**
Four Seasons Biltmore **13**
Franciscan Inn **11**
Hotel Oceana **10**
Simpson House Inn Bed & Breakfast **5**
The Upham Hotel & Country House **4**

DINING ◆

bouchon santa barbara **1**
Brophy Bros. Clam Bar & Restaurant **12**
La Super-Rica Taqueria **8**
Palace Grill **9**
Wine Cask **3**

ATTRACTIONS ●

County Courthouse **2**
Santa Barbara Mission **6**

Golf ⛳
Information ⓘ

Mediterranean hors d'oeuvres and Santa Barbara wines, the enormous video library, and the heavenly gourmet breakfast. 121 E. Arrellaga St. (between Santa Barbara and Anacapa sts.), Santa Barbara, CA 93101. ✆ 800/676-1280 or 805/963-7067. Fax 805/ 564-4811. www.simpsonhouseinn.com. 14 units. $215–$435 double; $500–$550 suite/cottage. 2-night minimum on weekends. Rates include full breakfast. AE, DISC, MC, V. Free parking.

The Upham Hotel and Country House   This conveniently located 1871 inn combines the intimacy of a B&B with the service of a small hotel. The Upham has sweeping verandas and a Victorian cupola, a cozy restaurant, and a resident cat named Henry. Rooms come complete with modern comforts; the charming cottage units have private garden entrances and fireplaces. 1404 De La Vina St. (at Sola St.), Santa Barbara, CA 93101. ✆ 800/727-0876 or 805/962-0058. Fax 805/ 963-2825. www.uphamhotel.com. 50 units. $150–$275 double; suites from $290. Rates include continental breakfast. AE, DC, MC, V. Free parking. **Amenities:** Restaurant.

WHERE TO DINE

bouchon santa barbara CALIFORNIA   This warm and inviting restaurant serves a seasonal menu inspired by the wines of the Santa Barbara countryside— *bouchon* is French for "wine cork." Past delights have included smoked Santa Barbara albacore "carpaccio," luscious sweetbread and chanterelle ragout cradled in a potato-leek basket, and monkfish saddle fragrant with fresh herbs and accompanied by a creamy fennel-Gruyère gratin. Request a table on the romantic patio, and don't miss the chocolate soufflé. 9 W. Victoria St. ✆ 805/730-1160. www.bouchonsantabarbara.com. Reservations recommended. 2- or 3-course prix fixe $38/$45. AE, DC, MC, V. Daily 5:30–10pm.

Brophy Bros. Clam Bar & Restaurant SEAFOOD   This place is best known for its unbeatable view of the marina, but the dependable fresh seafood keeps tourists and locals coming back. Dress is casual, portions are huge, and favorites include New England clam chowder, cioppino, and the seafood salads. The scampi is consistently good, as is all the fresh fish. *Note:* The wait at this small place can be up to 2 hours on a weekend night. 119 Harbor Way (off Cabrillo Blvd. in the Waterfront Center). ✆ 805/966-4418. Reservations not accepted. Main courses $9–$18. AE, MC, V. Sun–Thurs 11am–10pm; Fri–Sat 11am–11pm.

La Super-Rica Taqueria MEXICAN   Looking at this street-corner shack, you'd never guess it's blessed with the Nobel Prize of cuisine: an endorsement by Julia Child. The tacos here are no-nonsense, generous portions of filling piled onto fresh, grainy corn tortillas. Try *bistec* (steak), *adobado* (marinated pork), or *gorditas* (thick corn *masa* pockets filled with spicy beans). Sunday's special is *pozole*, a stew of pork and hominy in red chile sauce. On Friday and Saturday, the specialty is freshly made tamales. 622 N. Milpas St. (between Cota and Ortega sts.). ✆ 805/963-4940. Most menu items $3–$6. No credit cards. Sun–Thurs 11am–9pm; Fri–Sat 11am–9:30pm.

Palace Grill CAJUN/CREOLE   The Palace's loud and fun atmosphere is not the place for meaningful dinner conversation. Instead, down a Mason-jar martini and try a platter of spicy blackened steak and seafood, a rich crawfish étouffée, or Creole jambalaya pasta. Save room for the renowned Southern desserts, including the superstar Louisiana bread pudding soufflé. 8 E. Cota St. ✆ 805/963-5000. www.palacegrill.com. Reservations recommended; not accepted Fri–Sat. Main courses $5–$13 lunch, $9–$25 dinner. AE, MC, V. Daily 11am–3pm and 5:30–10pm (until 11pm Fri–Sat).

Wine Cask CALIFORNIA/ITALIAN   Take an 18-year-old wine shop, a 1920s landmark dining room, outstanding Italian fare, and an attractive clientele, and you've got the Wine Cask. Heavenly creations include lamb sirloin with twice-baked au gratin potatoes, or perhaps potato- and prosciutto-wrapped halibut in cioppino sauce. The wine list reads like a novel, and has deservedly received the *Wine Spectator* award for excellence. In El Paseo Center, 813 Anacapa St. © 805/966-9463. Reservations recommended. Main courses lunch $8–$12; dinner $18–$29. AE, DC, MC, V. Mon–Thurs 11:30am–9pm; Fri 11:30am–10pm; Sat 5:30–10pm; Sun 5:30–9pm.

5 Palm Springs

Palm Springs, once known for polyester-clad golfing retirees and college-age spring breakers, has been quietly changing its image and attracting a whole new crowd. These days, the city fancies itself a European-style resort with a dash of good ol' American small town thrown in for good measure, and Hollywood's young glitterati are returning to "the Springs." One thing hasn't changed: Swimming, sunbathing, golfing, and playing tennis are still the primary pastimes in this convenient little oasis.

ESSENTIALS

GETTING THERE   By Plane   You can fly into **Palm Springs Regional Airport,** 3400 E. Tahquitz Canyon Way (© 760/323-8161). Flights from LAX take about 40 minutes.

By Car   Most visitors drive to Palm Springs, a trip that takes about 2 hours from either Los Angeles (via I-10 East and Calif. 111) or San Diego (via I-15 North to connect with I-10 East).

VISITOR INFORMATION   Be sure to pick up *Palm Springs Life* magazine's free monthly *Desert Guide,* which contains tons of information and a calendar of events. Copies are distributed in hotels and newsstands and by the **Palm Springs Desert Resorts Convention & Visitors Bureau,** in the Atrium Design Centre, 69930 Calif. 111, Ste. 201, Rancho Mirage (© **800/41-RELAX** or 760/770-9000; www.palmspringsusa.com), open Monday through Friday from 8:30am to 5pm. The bureau also operates a 24-hour information line (© **760/770-1992**).

The **Palm Springs Visitors Information Center,** 2781 N. Palm Canyon Dr. (© **800/34-SPRINGS;** www.palm-springs.org), offers maps, brochures, advice, souvenirs, and a free reservations service; open Monday through Saturday from 9am to 5pm, Sunday from 8am to 4pm.

SPECIAL EVENTS & FESTIVALS   Golf takes center stage in the desert at two high-profile events each year: January's **Bob Hope Chrysler Classic** (© **888/MR-BHOPE**), which features a celebrity-studded Pro-Am, and March's **Kraft Nabisco Championship** (© 760/324-4546), an LPGA event that coincides with a legendary lesbian convention in the desert. Other only-in-the-desert happenings include the 2-week **National Date Festival** (© 800/811-3247; www.datefest.org) in February, an Arabian Nights–esque pageant and fair celebrating the area's most abundant fruit.

WHAT TO SEE & DO

GOLF   The Palm Springs area is a world-famous mecca for golfers, with more than 90 courses. If you're planning a golf vacation, you're best off staying at one of the valley's many golf resorts (most are outside Palm Springs), where you can enjoy the proximity of your hotel's facilities as well as smart package deals that can give you a taste of country club membership. See "Where to Stay," below.

Tee times at many resort courses cannot be booked more than a few days in advance for nonguests, but several companies are able to make arrangements several months earlier and even construct a custom package for you with accommodations, golf, meals, and other extras. Among them is **Golf à la Carte** (© 877/ **887-6900** or 760-320-8713; www.palmspringsgolf.com).

The **Westin Mission Hills Resort Course,** Dinah Shore and Bob Hope drives, Rancho Mirage (© **760/328-3198**), is somewhat more forgiving than most of legendary architect Pete Dye's courses, but don't play the back tees unless you've got a consistent 220-yard drive and won't be fazed by the Dye-trademark giant sand bunkers and elevated greens. Water comes into play on only four holes, and the scenery is an exquisite reward for low-handicappers. Nonguest greens fees are $150 to $175, including cart.

One of our favorite desert courses is the **PGA West TPC Stadium Course,** La Quinta Resort & Club, 49499 Eisenhower Dr., La Quinta (© **760/ 564-4111**), which received *Golf* magazine's 1994 Gold Medal Award for the total golf-resort experience. The par-3 17th has a picturesque island green where Lee Trevino made Skins Game history with a spectacular hole-in-one. The rest of Pete Dye's 7,261-yard design is flat, with huge bunkers, lots of water, and severe mounding throughout. Also open for semiprivate play is the **Mountain Course at La Quinta,** another Dye design that regularly appears on U.S. top-100 lists. It's set dramatically against the rocky mountains, which thrust into fairways to create tricky doglegs, and its small Bermuda greens are well guarded by boulders and deep bunkers. Greens fees for nonguests vary seasonally, from $85 to $225, at both La Quinta courses.

Recommended public courses include **Tommy Jacobs' Bel-Air Greens,** 1001 El Cielo, Palm Springs (© **760/322-6062**), a scenic 9-hole, par-32 executive course well-suited for beginners and high-handicappers; greens fees range from $17 to $19.

Slightly more advanced amateurs will like **Tahquitz Creek Golf Resort,** 1885 Golf Club Dr., Palm Springs (© **760/328-1005**), whose two diverse courses both appeal to mid-handicappers; greens fees range from $55 to $100.

The **Palm Springs Country Club,** 2500 Whitewater Club Dr. (© **760/ 323-8625**), is the oldest public-access golf course within the city of Palm Springs, and is especially popular with budget-conscious golfers; greens fees are only $35 to $60, including cart.

OTHER OUTDOOR PURSUITS   Within an hour's drive of Palm Springs is **Joshua Tree National Park,** named for the curious shaggy succulent found only in California's Mojave Desert. A mecca for hikers, campers, and rock-climbers, the park's intriguing geology and abundant spring wildflowers can also be easily appreciated by car and makes for a wonderful day's outing. For more information, contact the park's visitor center (© **760/367-5500;** www.nps.gov/jotr).

Desert Adventures (© **888/440-JEEP** or 760/324-JEEP; www.red-jeep. com) offers four-wheel-drive off-road ecotours led by experienced naturalist guides; destinations include ancient Cahuilla grounds, San Andreas Fault ravines, and more. Tours range from 2 to 4 hours and cost $79 to $129, including hotel pickup and return. Reservations are required.

Cool family fun is found at **Palm Springs Oasis Waterpark,** off I-10 south on Gene Autry Trail between Ramon Road and East Palm Canyon Drive (© **760/ 325-7873;** www.oasiswaterresort.com), a water playground with slides, body- and boardsurfing, an inner-tube ride, and more. Admission is $12 to $19;

toddlers get in free. Open mid-March through Labor Day, daily from 11am to 6pm, plus weekends through all of October.

OTHER ATTRACTIONS   The **Living Desert Wildlife and Botanical Park,** 47900 Portola Ave., Palm Desert (© **760/346-5694;** www.livingdesert.org), is a 1,200-acre desert reserve designed to acquaint visitors with the unique habitats of California deserts. You can walk or take a tram, learning about bighorn sheep, mountain lions, rattlesnakes, lizards, owls, golden eagles, and the ubiquitous roadrunner. Admission is $8.50 for adults, $7.50 for seniors, and $4.25 for children 3 to 12. Open in summer daily from 8am to 1pm; the rest of the year, daily from 9am to 5pm.

To gain a bird's-eye perspective on the Coachella Valley, try the **Palm Springs Aerial Tramway,** off Calif. 111 (© **888/515-TRAM** or 760/325-1391; www. pstramway.com), a 14-minute, 2½-mile ascent to the top of Mount San Jacinto. At the top you'll find Alpine scenery, a ski-lodge–style restaurant and gift shop, and temperatures typically 40° cooler than the desert floor. Guided mule rides and cross-country ski equipment are available. Tickets are $21 for adults, $19 for seniors, and $14 for children 3 to 12; a Ride 'n' Dine combination is available. It runs Monday through Friday from 10am to 8pm, Saturday and Sunday from 8am to 8pm.

Unlikely though it may sound, the well-endowed **Palm Springs Desert Museum,** 101 Museum Dr. (© **760/325-7186;** www.psmuseum.org), is a must-see. Exhibits include world-class Western and Native American art, plus extensive artifacts of the local Cahuilla tribe. Plays, lectures, and other events are presented in the museum's Annenberg Theater. Admission is $7.50 for adults, $6.50 for seniors, and $3.50 for children 6 to 17. Open Tuesday through Saturday from 10am to 5pm, Sunday from noon to 5pm.

SHOPPING   Downtown Palm Springs revolves around **North Palm Canyon Drive;** many art galleries, souvenir shops, and restaurants are here, along with a couple of large-scale hotels and shopping centers. This wide, one-way boulevard is designed for pedestrians, with many businesses set back from the street itself—don't be shy about poking around the little courtyards you'll encounter. The

---

Gay Life in Palm Springs

The Palm Springs area is a major destination for gay travelers, who will want to check out *The Bottom Line,* the desert's free biweekly magazine of articles, events, and community guides for the gay reader; it's available at hotels and newsstands and from select merchants.

Be sure to visit **Village Pride,** 214 E. Arenas Rd. (© **760/323-9120**), a coffeehouse and local gathering place. This short block of Arenas is home to a score of gay establishments, including **Streetbar** (© **760/320-1266**), a neighborhood hangout for tourists and locals alike.

For accommodations, the Warm Sands area is home to the nicest "private resorts"—mostly discreet and gated B&B-style inns. Try the co-ed **El Mirasol,** 525 Warm Sands Dr. (© **800/327-2985** or 760/326-5913), a charming historic resort, or **Sago Palms,** 595 Thornhill Rd. (© **800/626-7246** or 760/323-0224), which is small, quiet, and affordable. The **Bee Charmer,** 1600 E. Palm Canyon Dr. (© **888/321-5699;** www.beecharmer.com), is one of the few all-women resorts in town.

northern section of Palm Canyon is becoming known for vintage collectibles and is being touted as the **Antique and Heritage Gallery District.**

Down in Palm Desert lies the delicious excess of **El Paseo,** a glitzy cornucopia of high-rent boutiques, salons, and upscale restaurants reminiscent of Rodeo Drive in Beverly Hills, along with a dozen or more major shopping malls just like back home.

WHERE TO STAY

Some of the best golf resorts in the country are in the resort towns just beyond Palm Springs. We've listed La Quinta below, but other equally fabulous choices, all with great golf, tennis, and complete resort services, include the **Marriott's Desert Springs Spa & Resort** in Palm Desert (ⓒ 760/341-2211), **Marriott's Rancho Las Palmas Resort & Spa** in Rancho Mirage (ⓒ 760/568-2727), the **Hyatt Grand Champions** in Indian Wells (ⓒ 760/341-1000), and the **Westin Mission Hills Resort** in Rancho Mirage (ⓒ 800/WESTIN-1 or 760/328-5955).

Casa Cody   Once owned by "Wild" Bill Cody's niece, this 1920s casa with a double courtyard has been restored to fine condition. It now sports a vaguely Southwestern decor and peaceful grounds marked by large lawns and mature fruit trees. You'll feel more like a houseguest than a hotel client here, in a residential area a couple of blocks from Palm Canyon Drive. All units have fridges; many have fireplaces and kitchens. Breakfast is served poolside. 175 S. Cahuilla Rd. (between Tahquitz Way and Arenas Rd.), Palm Springs, CA 92262. ⓒ 760/320-9346. Fax 760/ 325-8610. www.palmsprings.com/hotels/casacody. 23 units. $79–$99 double; $99–$159 studio; $149–$259 suite; 2-bedroom adobe $299–$359. Rates include expanded continental breakfast. AE, DC, DISC, MC, V. **Amenities:** 2 outdoor pools; pets accepted ($10 per night).

La Quinta Resort & Club   A luxury resort set amid citrus trees, towering palms, and cacti at the base of the rocky Santa Rosa Mountains, La Quinta is *the* place to be if you're serious about your golf or tennis game. Rooms are in single-story, Spanish-style buildings; each unit has a VCR, patio, and access to one of several dozen small pools, enhancing the feeling of privacy. Some rooms have fireplaces or Jacuzzis. The tranquil lounge in the original hacienda hearkens back to the early days of the resort, when Clark Gable, Greta Garbo, and other luminaries chose La Quinta as their hideaway. The resort is renowned for its five championship golf courses. Spa La Quinta has 35 treatment rooms for every pampering luxury. 49499 Eisenhower Dr., La Quinta, CA 92253. ⓒ 800/598-3828 or 760/ 564-4111. Fax 760/564-7656. www.laquintaresort.com. 919 units. High season $340–$460 double; mid-June to Sept $170–$290 double. Extra person $15. Children under 18 stay free in parents' room. AE, MC, V. Self-parking free, valet parking $3 ($12 overnight). **Amenities:** Restaurants (5); 42 outdoor pools; 23 tennis courts (10 lighted); spa; pets allowed with $250 refundable deposit.

Spa Resort Casino   One of the more unusual choices in town, this resort is on Indian-owned land above the city's eponymous mineral springs, believed by the Cahuilla to have healing properties. Today's travelers still come here to pamper both body and soul by "taking the waters" in this sleekly modern facility. There are three pools—one a conventional outdoor swimming pool, the other two filled from the underground natural springs. Inside the extensive spa are private marble swirlpools and many pampering treatments. Despite the addition of an adjoining Vegas-style casino, the Cahuilla have truly managed to integrate modern hotel comforts with the ancient healing and Indian spirit this land represents. 100 N. Indian Canyon Dr., Palm Springs, CA 92263. ⓒ 800/854-1279 or 760/325-1461. Fax 760/325-3344. www.sparesortcasino.com. 230 units. $159–$239 double; $219–$279 suite. AE, DC, MC, V. Free parking. **Amenities:** Restaurants (2); 3 outdoor pools; spa; fitness center.

Villa Royale   This charming inn, 5 minutes from downtown Palm Springs, evokes a European cluster of villas, complete with climbing bougainvillea and antique-filled rooms. Uniform luxuries (down comforters and other pampering touches) appear throughout. Rooms vary widely in size and ambience; larger isn't always better, as some of the most appealing rooms are in the more affordable range. Many rooms have fireplaces, patios with Jacuzzis, or kitchens. 1620 Indian Trail (off E. Palm Canyon), Palm Springs, CA 92264. © 800/245-2314 or 760/327-2314. Fax 760/322-3794. www.villaroyale.com. 31 units. High season (Oct–May) $139–$199 double, $249–$299 suite; summer $119–$179 double, $229–$279 suite. Rates include full breakfast. Extra person $25. AE, DC, DISC, MC, V. Free parking. **Amenities:** Restaurant; 2 outdoor pools.

WHERE TO DINE

Edgardo's Café Veracruz MEXICAN   The pleasant but humble ambience at Edgardo's is a welcome change from touristy Palm Springs. The expert menu features authentic Mayan, Huasteco, and Aztec cuisine. The postage-stamp–size patio with a trickling fountain is the best place to sample tangy quesadillas, desert-cactus salad, and traditional poblano chiles rellenos. 494 N. Palm Canyon (at W. Alejo Rd.). © 760/320-3558. Reservations recommended for weekend dinner. Main courses $3.50–$15. AE, DC, DISC, MC, V. Mon–Fri 11am–3pm and 5:30–9:30pm; Sat–Sun 8am–10pm (sometimes later).

Europa Restaurant CALIFORNIA/CONTINENTAL   Long advertised as the "most romantic dining in the desert," Europa is a sentimental favorite of many regulars among an equally gay and straight clientele. Whether you sit on the garden patio or in subdued candlelight indoors, you'll savor dinner prepared by one of Palm Springs' most dedicated kitchens. Standouts include deviled crab fritters on mango-papaya chutney, filet mignon on a bed of crispy onions with garlic butter, and a show-stopping salmon baked in parchment with crème fraîche and dill. For dessert, don't miss the signature chocolate mousse. 1620 Indian Trail (at the Villa Royale). © 760/327-2314. Reservations recommended. Main courses $18–$32. AE, DC, DISC, MC, V. Tues–Sat 5:30–10pm; Sun 11:30am–2pm and 5:30–10pm.

La Provence COUNTRY FRENCH   The casually elegant La Provence eschews heavy traditional French cream sauces in favor of carefully combined herbs and spices. The menu offers some expected items (escargots in mushroom caps, bouillabaisse, steak au poivre) as well as inventive pastas, like wild mushroom ravioli in a sun-dried tomato and sweet-onion sauce. 254 N. Palm Canyon Dr. (upstairs). © 760/416-4418. Reservations recommended. Main courses $12–$24. AE, DC, DISC, MC, V. Daily 5–10:30pm.

Las Casuelas Terraza CLASSIC MEXICAN   The original Las Casuelas, a tiny storefront several blocks away, is still open, but the bougainvillea-draped front patio here is a much better place to people-watch. You can order Mexican standards like quesadillas, enchiladas, and mountainous nachos, as well as equally super-size margaritas. Inside, the action heats up with live music and raucous happy-hour crowds. During hot weather, the patio and even sidewalk passersby are cooled by the restaurant's well-placed misters. 222 S. Palm Canyon Dr. © 760/325-2794. Reservations recommended on weekends. Main courses $7–$13. AE, DC, DISC, MC, V. Mon–Thurs 11am–10pm; Fri–Sat 11am–11pm; Sun 10am–10pm.

PALM SPRINGS AFTER DARK

Good sources for nightlife information are *The Desert Guide* (the official visitor publication) and *The Bottom Line* (a biweekly gay magazine). On Thursday nights, **VillageFest** turns Palm Canyon Drive into an outdoor party with vendors and colorful entertainment.

The **Fabulous Palm Springs Follies,** at the historic Plaza Theatre, 128 S. Palm Canyon Dr., Palm Springs (© **760/327-0225;** www.psfollies.com), is a vaudeville-style show filled with lively production numbers.

6 Death Valley National Park

Park? Death Valley National Park? The Forty-niners, whose suffering gave the valley its name, would have howled at the notion. To them, other four-letter words would have been more appropriate: gold, mine, heat, lost, dead. And the four-letter words shouted by teamsters who drove the 20-mule-team borax wagons need not be repeated.

Americans looking for gold in California's mountains in 1849 were forced to cross the burning sands to avoid severe snowstorms in the nearby Sierra Nevada. Some perished along the way, and the land became known as Death Valley.

Mountains stand naked, unadorned. The bitter waters of saline lakes evaporate into bizarre, razor-sharp crystal formations. Jagged canyons jab deep into the earth. Ovenlike heat, frigid cold, and the driest air imaginable combine to make this one of the most inhospitable locations in the world.

Human nature being what it is, however, it's not surprising that people have long been drawn to challenge the power of Mother Nature. Man's first foray into tourism began in 1925, a scant 76 years after the Forty-niners' harrowing experiences (which would discourage most sane folks from ever returning!). It probably would have begun sooner, but the valley had been consumed with lucrative borax mining since the late 1880s.

Today's visitor drives in air-conditioned comfort, stays in comfortable hotel rooms or at well-maintained campgrounds, orders meals and provisions at park concessions, even quaffs a cold beer at the local saloon. You can take a swim in the Olympic-size pool, tour a Moorish castle, shop for souvenirs, and enjoy the desert landscape while hiking along a nature trail with a park ranger.

ESSENTIALS

ACCESS POINTS   There are several routes into the park, all of which involve crossing one of the steep mountain ranges that isolate Death Valley from, well, everything. Perhaps the most scenic entry to the park is via Calif. 190, east of Calif. 178 from Ridgecrest. Another scenic drive to the park is by way of Calif. 127 and Calif. 190 from Baker. You'll be required to pay a $10-per-car entrance fee, valid for 7 days.

VISITOR CENTER & INFORMATION   The **Furnace Creek Visitor Center & Museum,** 15 miles inside the eastern park boundary on Calif. 190 (© **760/ 786-2331**), offers interpretive exhibits and an hourly slide program. Ask at the information desk for ranger-led nature walks and evening naturalist programs. The center is open daily from 8am to 6pm in winter (to 5pm in summer).

SEEING THE HIGHLIGHTS

A good first stop after checking in at the main park visitor center in Furnace Creek is the **Harmony Borax Works**—a rock-salt landscape as tortured as you'll ever find. Death Valley prospectors called borax "white gold"; this profitable—though unglamorous—substance was mined here until 1928. The famous 20-mule teams hauled huge loaded wagons 165 miles to the rail station at Mojave. To learn more about this colorful era, visit the Borax Museum at Furnace Creek Ranch and the park visitor center, also located in Furnace Creek.

Badwater—at 282 feet below sea level, the lowest point in the Western Hemisphere—is also one of the hottest places in the world, with regularly recorded summer temperatures of 120°F (38°C).

Salt Creek is the home of the **Salt Creek pupfish,** found nowhere else on earth. This little fish, which has made some amazing adaptations to survive in this arid land, can be glimpsed from a wooden-boardwalk nature trail.

Before sunrise, photographers set up their tripods at **Zabriskie Point** and aim their cameras down at the magnificent panoramic view of Golden Canyon's pale mudstone hills and the great valley beyond. For another grand vista, check out **Dante's View,** a 5,475-foot viewpoint looking out over the shimmering Death Valley floor, backed by the high Panamint Mountains.

Just south of Furnace Creek is the 9-mile loop of **Artists Drive,** an easy must-see for visitors (except those in RVs, which can't negotiate the sharp, rock-bordered curves in the road). From the highway, you can't see the splendid palette of colors splashed on the rocks behind the foothills; once inside, continue through to aptly named **Artists Palette,** where an interpretive sign explains the source of nature's rainbow.

Scotty's Castle & the Gas House Museum (© 760/786-2392), the 1930s Mediterranean hacienda in the northern part of the park, is Death Valley's premier tourist attraction. Visitors are wowed by the elaborate Spanish tiles, well-crafted furnishings, and innovative construction that included solar water heating. Even more compelling is the colorful history of this villa in remote Grapevine Canyon, brought to life by park rangers dressed in period clothing.

The 1-hour walking tour of Scotty's Castle is excellent, both for its inside look at the mansion and for what it reveals about the eccentricities of the millionaire who built the "castle"—and his unlikely cohort, prospector/cowboy/spinner-of-tall-tales Walter "Scotty" Scott. Tours fill up quickly; arrive early for the first available spots (there's an $8 fee). A snack bar and gift shop make the wait more comfortable.

Near Scotty's Castle is **Ubehebe Crater.** It's known as an explosion crater one look and you'll know why. When hot magma rose from the depths of the earth to meet the groundwater, the resultant steam blasted out a crater and scattered cinders.

WHERE TO CAMP & STAY

The park's nine campgrounds are at elevations ranging from below sea level to 8,000 feet. Camping reservations may be made online at http://reservations. nps.gov or by calling © **800/365-2267.**

The **Furnace Creek Inn** (© 800/236-7916 or 760/786-2345; www.furnace creekresort.com) is an elegant 66-room oasis with historic charm, pampering service, a spring-fed swimming pool, and a formal dining room. The **Furnace Creek Ranch** (© 760/786-2345) has 224 no-frills cottage units with air-conditioning, showers, and access to a pool, coffee shop, saloon, steakhouse, and general store. **Stove Pipe Wells Village** (© 760/786-2387) has 74 modest rooms with air-conditioning and showers, plus a casual dining room.

The only lodging in the park not operated by the official concessionaire is the **Panamint Springs Resort** (© 702/482-7680; www.deathvalley.com), a truly charming rustic motel, cafe, and snack shop about an hour east of Furnace Creek.

Tip: Meals and groceries are exceptionally costly due to the remoteness of the park. If possible, bring a cooler with snacks, sandwiches, and beverages to last the duration of your visit. Ice is easily obtainable, and you'll also be able to keep water chilled.

15

Northern California

Northern California is one of the most spectacular, and spectacularly diverse, regions of the country. We'll start in San Francisco, everyone's favorite tourist town, and explore the highlights from there. Easily reached from the city, the lush Napa and Sonoma valleys form one of the world's great wine regions; we'll show you the best wineries and take you to the best inns, restaurants, and spas. Then we'll head off to see some of California's most scenic wonders: crystal-clear Lake Tahoe; towering redwoods; majestic Yosemite; misty, mysterious Big Sur; and much more.

1 San Francisco

Consistently rated one of the top tourist destinations in the world, San Francisco abounds in multiple dimensions. Its famous, thrilling streets go up, and they go down; its multifarious citizens—and their adopted cultures, architectures, and cuisines—hail from San Antonio to Singapore; and its politics range from hyper-liberalism to an ever-encroaching wave of conservatism. Even something as mundane as fog takes on a new dimension as it creeps from the ocean and slowly envelops San Francisco in a resplendent blanket of mist.

In a city so multifaceted, so enamored with itself, it's hard not to find what you're looking for. Feel the cool blast of salt air as you stroll across the Golden Gate. Stuff yourself on dim sum in Chinatown. Browse the Haight for incense and crystals. Walk along the beach, pierce your nose, see a play, rent a Harley— the list is endless. It's all happening in San Francisco, and everyone's invited.

ESSENTIALS

GETTING THERE   By Plane   San Francisco International Airport (SFO) (© **650/877-0118;** www.flysfo.com), 14 miles south of downtown directly on U.S. 101, is served by almost four dozen major scheduled carriers. Travel time to downtown during commuter rush hours is about 50 minutes; at other times, it's about 20 to 25 minutes.

The airport offers a toll-free hot line available Monday through Friday from 7:30am to 5pm for information on ground transportation (© **800/736-2008**). Each of the three main terminals also has a desk where you can get the same information.

A cab from the airport to downtown costs $28 to $32, plus tip. **SFO Airporter** (© **415/495-8404**) buses depart from outside the baggage-claim area to downtown San Francisco every 30 minutes from 6:15am to 9:15pm. They stop at several Union Square–area hotels. No reservations are needed. The cost is $12 each way. **SuperShuttle** (© **415/558-8500;** www.supershuttle.com) will take you anywhere in the city, charging $17 to a residence or business, plus $8 for each additional person.

Oakland International Airport (© **510/577-4000;** www.oaklandairport.com), about 5 miles south of downtown Oakland, at the Hegenberger Road exit off Calif.

17 (U.S. 880), is used primarily by passengers with East Bay destinations. Some San Franciscans, however, prefer this less-crowded, accessible airport when flying during busy periods.

Taxis from the Oakland airport to downtown San Francisco cost approximately $45, plus tip. **Bayporter Express** (© 415/467-1800) shuttle service charges $23 for the first person, $10 for each additional person to downtown San Francisco (more to outer areas).

The cheapest way to downtown San Francisco involves taking the shuttle bus from the airport to **BART,** or Bay Area Rapid Transit (© 510/464-6000; www.bart.gov). The **AirBART** shuttle bus runs about every 15 minutes Monday through Saturday from 6am to 11:30pm and Sunday from 8:30am to 11:30pm. The cost is $2 for the 10-minute ride to BART's Coliseum terminal. The fare to downtown San Francisco is $2.75. The entire excursion takes around 45 minutes.

By Train Amtrak (© 800/USA-RAIL; www.amtrak.com) trains from Sacramento, Los Angeles, Chicago, Portland, and Seattle arrive at the Emeryville or Oakland stations in the East Bay. Shuttle buses take you to the Ferry Terminal or Caltrain station at Fourth and King streets in downtown San Francisco.

Caltrain (© 800/660-4287 or 415/546-4461; http://caltrain.com) operates train services between San Francisco and the towns of the peninsula. The city depot is at 700 Fourth St., at Townsend Street.

By Car Major routes into San Francisco are U.S. 101 from the north (Sonoma and the Napa Valley) and south (San Jose), I-80 from the northeast (Sacramento), and I-280 from the south (San Jose).

VISITOR INFORMATION The **San Francisco Visitor Information Center,** Hallidie Plaza, 900 Market St., at Powell Street (© 415/391-2000; www.sfvisitor. org), is the best source of information.

GETTING AROUND The San Francisco Municipal Railway, better known as **Muni** (© 415/673-6864), operates the city's cable cars, buses, and Metro streetcars. Bus and streetcar fares are $1 for adults, 35¢ for seniors and children 5 to 17; cable cars are $3.

BART, an acronym for **Bay Area Rapid Transit** (© 650/992-2278), is a high-speed rail network that connects San Francisco with the East Bay. Fares range from $1.10 to $4.30. Trains run Monday through Friday from 4am to midnight, Saturday from 6am to midnight, and Sunday from 8am to midnight.

FAST FACTS **Saint Francis Memorial Hospital,** 900 Hyde St., between Bush and Pine streets, Nob Hill (© 415/353-6000), provides 24-hour emergency-care service. The hospital also operates a physician-referral service (© 800/ 333-1355). The **Walgreens** on Divisadero Street at Lombard (© 415/931- 6415) has a 24-hour pharmacy.

San Francisco, like any large city, has its fair share of crime. Exercise extra caution, particularly at night, in the Tenderloin, the Mission District (especially around 16th and Mission sts.), the lower Fillmore area, around lower Haight Street, and around the Civic Center.

An 8.5% sales tax is added for all goods and services purchased in San Francisco. The city hotel tax is a whopping 14%.

EXPLORING THE CITY

Alcatraz Island The sheer cliffs, treacherous tides and currents, and frigid temperatures of the surrounding water supposedly made "the Rock" a totally escape-proof prison. Among the famous gangsters who did time here were

San Francisco

ACCOMMODATIONS ◾

Campton Place Hotel **27**
The Commodore Hotel **24**
Four Seasons Hotel San Francisco **32**
Golden Gate Hotel **25**
The Hotel Bohème **16**
The Hotel Majestic **5**
Huntington Hotel **23**
King George Hotel **29**
The Mandarin Oriental **21**
The Marina Inn **3**
The Parker Guest House **8**
Prescott Hotel **28**
Ritz-Carlton **22**
The Tuscan Inn **14**
Westin St. Francis **30**
The Wharf Inn **13**
W San Francisco Hotel **33**

DINING ◆

Andalé Taqueria **2**
Aqua **20**
Boulevard **19**
Cha Cha Cha **34**
Fifth Floor Restaurant **31**
Foreign Cinema **9**
Greens Restaurant **1**
House of Nanking **17**
Kokkari **18**
La Folie **11**
L'Osteria del Forno **15**
Masa's **26**
Mecca **7**
Restaurant Gary Danko **12**
Swan Oyster Depot **10**
Ton Kiang **4**
Zuni Café **6**

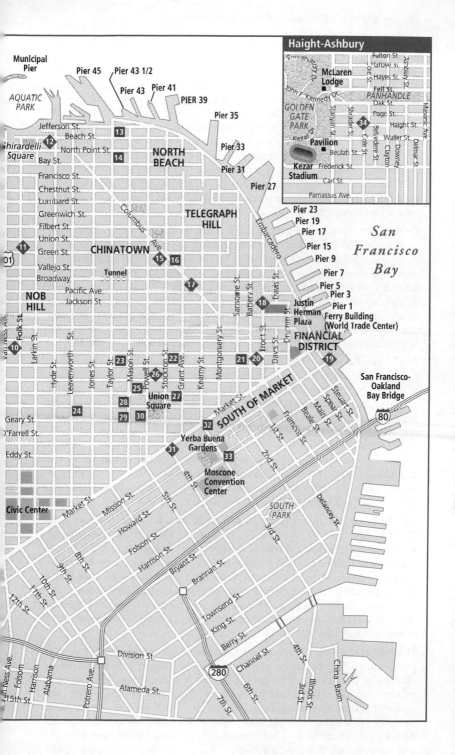

Al Capone, Robert Stroud (the Birdman of Alcatraz), and Machine Gun Kelly. In 1963, after an apparent escape in which no bodies were recovered, the government closed the prison, and in 1972 it became part of the Golden Gate National Recreation Area. Tours of Alcatraz include the ferry ride, an audio tour of the prison block, and a slide show. It's a popular excursion and space is limited, so purchase tickets as far in advance as possible. The tour is operated by Blue & Gold Fleet (© **415/705-5555;** www.blueandgoldfleet.com). Wear comfortable shoes (there are a lot of steps) and take a jacket; allow about 3 hours for the whole outing. Pier 41, near Fisherman's Wharf. © **415/773-1188** (info only). Admission (includes ferry trip and audio tour) $13 adults with headset, $9.25 without; $12 seniors with headset, $7.50 without; $8 children 5–11 with headset, $6 without. Winter daily 9:30am–2:15pm; summer daily 9:15am–4:15pm. Advance purchase advised. Ferries depart 15 and 45 min. after the hr. Arrive at least 20 min. before sailing time.

Cable Cars   Designated official historic landmarks by the National Park Service, the city's beloved cable cars clank across the hills like mobile museum pieces. Each weighs about 6 tons and is hauled along by a steel cable, enclosed under the street. They move at a constant 9½ miles per hour—never more, never less. This may strike you as slow, but it doesn't feel that way when you're cresting an almost perpendicular hill and looking down at what seems like a bobsled dive straight into the ocean. But in spite of the thrills, they're perfectly safe. © **415/673-6864.** www.sfcablecar.com. Fare $3. Powell-Hyde and Powell-Mason lines begin at Powell and Market sts.; California St. line begins at the foot of Market St. Fare $3.

California Palace of the Legion of Honor   Designed as a memorial to California's World War I casualties, the neoclassical structure is an exact replica of the Legion of Honor Palace in Paris, right down to the inscription HONNEUR ET PATRIE above the portal. Reopened after a 2-year, $29-million renovation and seismic upgrading project that was stalled by the discovery of almost 700 coffins underneath the building, the museum's collection contains paintings, sculpture, and decorative arts. The display of more than 800 years of European art includes a fine collection of Rodin sculpture. In Lincoln Park (34th Ave. and Clement St.). © **415/ 750-3600** or 415/863-3330 (recorded information). www.thinker.org. Admission $8 adults, $6 seniors, $5 youths 12–17, free for children under 12. Fees may be higher for special exhibitions. Free to all 2nd Tues of each month. Tues–Sun 9:30am–5pm. Bus: 18 or 38.

Coit Tower   In a city known for its panoramic views and vantage points, Coit Tower is "The Peak." If it's a clear day, it's wonderful to get here by walking up the Filbert Steps. Inside the base of the tower are the impressive WPA murals titled *Life in California, 1934,* which were completed during the New Deal by more than 25 artists, many of whom had studied under master muralist Diego Rivera. You can see the murals for free, so we recommend not paying the admission to go to the top; the view is just as good from the parking area. Atop Telegraph Hill. © **415/362-0808.** Admission (to the top of the tower) $3.75 adults, $2.50 seniors, $1.50 children 6–12. Daily 10am–6pm. Bus: 39.

The Exploratorium   This fun, hands-on science fair contains more than 650 permanent exhibits that explore everything from color theory to Einstein's theory of relativity. Every exhibit is designed to be used. You can whisper into a concave reflector and have a friend hear you 60 feet away, or you can design your own animated abstract art—using sound. 3601 Lyon St., in the Palace of Fine Arts (at Marina Blvd.). © **415/563-7337** or 415/561-0360 (recorded information). www.exploratorium.edu. Admission $10 adults, $7.50 seniors and college students, $6 children 5–17. Free to all 1st Wed of each month. AE, MC, V. Summer and holidays, Mon–Tues and Thurs–Sun 10am–6pm; Wed

10am–9pm. Rest of the year, Tues and Thurs–Sun 10am–5pm; Wed 10am–9pm. Bus: 30 from Stockton St. to the Marina stop.

Golden Gate Bridge With its spidery bracing cables and sky-high twin towers, the bridge looks more like a work of abstract art than one of the greatest engineering feats of the 20th century. The mile-long steel link reaches a height of 746 feet above the water, and is an awesome bridge to cross. Millions of pedestrians brave the cold, wind, and vibrations each year; it's one of the best ways to experience the bridge's immense scale. You can walk out onto the span from either end. From Marin's Vista Point, you can look back on one of the most famous cityscapes in the world. Hwy. 101 N. www.goldengatebridge.org. $3 toll collected when driving south. Bridge-bound Golden Gate Transit buses (© 415/923-2000) depart every 30–60 min. during the day for Marin County, starting from the Transbay Terminal (Mission and First sts.) and stopping at Market and Seventh sts., at the Civic Center, and along Van Ness Ave. and Lombard St.

Golden Gate Park Everybody loves Golden Gate Park: people, dogs, birds, frogs, turtles, bison, trees, bushes, and flowers. Literally everything feels unified here in San Francisco's enormous (1,017 acres) arboreal front yard. While many sites worth seeing are clearly visible, the park has infinite hidden treasures, so make your first stop the McClaren Lodge and Park Headquarters if you want detailed information on the park.

Within the park's confines, the **California Academy of Sciences** ((© 415/750-7145) is a collection of three noteworthy museums and exhibitions guaranteed to entertain the whole family. The **Steinhart Aquarium** is the most diverse aquarium in the world, housing some 14,000 specimens, and the **Natural History Museum** includes several halls displaying classic dioramas of fauna in their habitats and a multitude of interactive exhibits. The **Morrison Planetarium** presents light shows and exhibits, with titles such as "Stargazer's Guide to the Galaxy."

Other park highlights include **Stow Lake/Strawberry Hill** (© 415/752-0347), where you can rent a paddleboat, rowboat, or motorboat and cruise around the lake while joggers pass along the grassy shoreline and turtles bathe on rocks and logs. Strawberry Hill, the artificial island at the center of Stow Lake, is a perfect picnic spot. Finally, there are the dozens of special gardens in the park, including the **Rhododendron Dell,** the **Rose Garden,** and the **Strybing Arboretum,** where some 6,000 plant species grow in and around a grove of California redwoods. Between Fulton St. and Lincoln Way; main entrance at Fell and Stanyan sts. (© 415/831-2700. Bus: 16AX, BX, 5, 6, 7, 66, or 71.

Lombard Street Known (erroneously) as the "crookedest street in the world," the whimsically winding block of Lombard Street puts smiles on the faces of thousands of visitors each year. The elevation is so steep that the road has to snake back and forth to make a descent possible. This short stretch is one-way, downhill, and fun to drive. You can also take staircases up or down on either side of the street. Between Hyde and Leavenworth sts.

Mission Dolores This is the oldest structure in the city, built on order of Franciscan Father Junípero Serra by Father Francisco Palou. It was constructed of 36,000 sunbaked bricks and dedicated in 1776 at the northern terminus of El Camino Real, the Spanish road from Mexico to California. It's a moving place to visit, with its cool, serene buildings and especially the cemetery and gardens where the early settlers were buried. 16th St. (at Dolores St.). (© 415/621-8203. Donations appreciated. May–Oct daily 9am–4:30pm; Nov–Apr daily 9am–4pm; Good Friday 9am–noon. Muni Metro: J. Bus: 14, 26, or 33 to the corner of Church and 16th sts.

San Francisco Museum of Modern Art (MOMA)   MOMA's collection consists of more than 15,000 works, including close to 5,000 paintings and sculptures by artists such as Henri Matisse, Jackson Pollock, and Willem de Kooning. Other artists represented include Diego Rivera, Georgia O'Keeffe, Paul Klee, the Fauvists, and exceptional holdings of Richard Diebenkorn. MOMA was also one of the first to recognize photography as a major art form; its extensive collection includes more than 9,000 photographs by such notables as Ansel Adams, Alfred Stieglitz, Edward Weston, and Henri Cartier-Bresson. Whatever you do, check out the fabulous MuseumStore and cafe. 151 Third St. (2 blocks south of Market St., across from Yerba Buena Gardens). ℭ 415/357-4000. www. sfmoma.org. Admission $10 adults, $7 seniors, $6 students, free for children 12 and under. Half-price for all Thurs 6–8:45pm; free to all 1st Tues of each month. Thurs 11am–8:45pm; Fri–Tues 11am–5:45pm. Muni Metro: J, K, L, or M to Montgomery Station. Bus: 15, 30, or 45.

Yerba Buena Center for the Arts & Yerba Buena Gardens   This urban interactive wonderland could keep you busy all day. The **Center for the Arts** presents music, theater, dance, and visual arts. **Zeum** (ℭ 415/777-2800; www.zeum.org) is the children's addition, with a cafe, interactive cultural center, ice-skating rink, fabulous 1906 carousel, and interactive play and learning garden. Sony's **Metreon Entertainment Center** (ℭ 415/537-3400) is a 350,000-square-foot complex housing movie theaters, an **IMAX** theater, small restaurants, interactive shops and attractions (including one that features Maurice Sendak's *Where the Wild Things Are*), a bowling alley, and a child-care center. 701 Mission St. ℭ 415/978-ARTS (box office). www.yerbabuenaarts.org. Admission $6 adults, $3 seniors and students. Free to all 1st Thurs of each month 5–8pm. Tues–Wed and Fri–Sun 11am–6pm; Thurs 11am–8pm. Muni Metro: Powell or Montgomery. Bus: 30, 45, or 9X.

GOLDEN GATE NATIONAL RECREATION AREA & THE PRESIDIO

The largest urban park in the world, the Golden Gate National Recreation Area makes New York's Central Park look like a putting green. Run by the National Park Service, the recreation area covers three counties along 28 miles of stunning, condo-free shoreline. Much of it wraps around the northern and western edges of the city itself, and just about all of it is open to the public (with no access fees) for jogging, biking, hiking, windsurfing, golfing, fishing, sunbathing, and just about any outdoor activity you can name. Muni buses provide transportation to the more popular sites, including the Cliff House and Ocean Beach. For more information, contact the **National Park Service** (ℭ 415/556-0560).

At the northern end of Fillmore Street, **Marina Green** is a favorite spot for flying kites or watching the sailboats on the bay. Just west of here begins the 3½-mile paved **Golden Gate Promenade,** a favorite biking and hiking path, which leads ultimately to **Fort Point** (ℭ 415/556-1693), a National Historic Site under the Golden Gate Bridge. (You might recognize it from Alfred Hitchcock's *Vertigo*.)

Lincoln Boulevard sweeps around the western edge of the bay to two of the most popular beaches in San Francisco. **Baker Beach,** a small and beautiful strand just outside the Golden Gate, is a fine spot for sunbathing (nudists flock here), walking, or fishing. It's usually packed on sunny days, but if the cold water doesn't deter you from swimming here, the roaring currents will. If you want to get more than your toes wet, go instead to **China Beach,** a small cove where changing rooms, showers, a sun deck, and restrooms signify that swimming is permitted.

The western edge of the recreation area is home to the **Cliff House** (ℭ 415/556-8642), which has been serving refreshments to visitors since 1863.

Here you can view the **Seal Rocks,** home to a colony of sea lions and many marine birds. A little farther inland at the western end of California Street is **Lincoln Park,** which contains the Palace of the Legion of Honor as well as San Francisco's prettiest municipal golf course: **Lincoln Park Golf Course,** 34th Avenue and Clement Street (© 415/221-9911).

The Presidio, a 1,480-acre former military base, is now an urban park that combines historical, architectural, and natural aspects. It's adjacent to the Golden Gate National Recreation Area, but you could wander from one area to the other without knowing it. The Presidio is especially popular with hikers, bikers, bird-watchers, golfers, and joggers. On the 2-mile **Ecology Loop Trail,** walkers can see more than 30 different species of trees, including redwood, spruce, cypress, and acacias. Hikers can follow the 2½-mile **Coastal Trail** from Fort Point along this part of the coastline all the way to Land's End. The waters off **Crissy Field** have in recent years become known as a major challenge for expert windsurfers.

The Presidio is currently undergoing major changes so that it may pay for its upkeep. For the latest information on the Presidio, the best source is the **Golden Gate National Recreation Area Headquarters** (© 415/556-0560).

SHOPPING

UNION SQUARE   San Francisco's most congested and popular shopping mecca is home to the big department stores and many high-end specialty shops. Be sure to venture to Grant Avenue, Post and Sutter streets, and Maiden Lane.

If you're into art, pick up the *San Francisco Gallery Guide,* a comprehensive, bimonthly publication listing the city's current shows. One of our favorite galleries is the **Catharine Clark Gallery,** 49 Geary St.(© 415/399-1439). It exhibits up-and-coming contemporary artists, mainly from California, and nurtures beginning collectors by offering an unusual interest-free purchasing plan.

CHINATOWN   When you pass under the gate to Chinatown on Grant Avenue, say goodbye to the world of fashion and hello to a swarm of cheap tourist shops selling everything from linen and jade to plastic toys and $2 slippers. Grant Avenue is the main thoroughfare, but the real gems are found on the side streets between Bush Street and Columbus Avenue, in small, one-person shops selling Chinese herbs, original art, and jewelry. **Ten Ren Tea Company,** 949 Grant Ave. (© 415/362-0656), stocks more than 50 traditional and herbal teas and related paraphernalia.

SOMA   Though this area isn't suitable for strolling, you'll find almost all the discount shopping in warehouse spaces south of Market. You can pick up a discount-shopping guide at most major hotels. At the **SFMOMA MuseumStore,** 151 Third St. (© 415/357-4035), the array of cards, books, jewelry, housewares, and knickknacks makes it one of the locals' favorite shops. It also offers far more tasteful mementos than most Fisherman's Wharf options. Fashionable bargain hunters head to **Jeremys,** 2 South Park, at Second Street (© 415/882-4929), where top designer fashions from shoes to suits come at rock-bottom prices.

THE CASTRO   You could easily spend all day wandering through the home and men's-clothing shops of the Castro. We also come here to visit our favorite chocolate shop, **Joseph Schmidt Confections,** 3489 16th St. (© 415/861-8682), where you'll be hesitant to bite the head off your adorable chocolate panda bear.

FISHERMAN'S WHARF & ENVIRONS   The tourist-oriented malls— Ghirardelli Square, Pier 39, the Cannery, and the Anchorage—run along Jefferson

Street and include hundreds of shops, restaurants, and attractions. Standing out from the usual T-shirt shops and fudge emporiums is **Cost Plus Imports,** 2552 Taylor St. (© 415/928-6200), a vast warehouse crammed to the rafters with Chinese baskets, Indian camel bells, Malaysian batik scarves, and innumerable other items from Algeria to Zanzibar.

FILLMORE STREET   Some of the best shopping in town is packed into 5 blocks of Fillmore Street in Pacific Heights. **Zinc Details,** 1905 Fillmore St., between Bush and Pine streets (© 415/776-2100), has an amazing collection of locally handcrafted glass vases, pendant lights, ceramics, and furniture.

HAIGHT STREET   The shopping in the 6 blocks of upper Haight Street, between Central Avenue and Stanyan Street, reflects its green-haired, spiked-haired, and no-haired clientele, offering everything from incense and European and American street styles to furniture and antique clothing. **Recycled Records,** 1377 Haight St. (© 415/626-4075), easily one of the best used-record stores in the city, has a good selection of promotional CDs and cases of used classic rock LPs.

NORTH BEACH   Along with a great cup of coffee, Grant and Columbus avenues cater to their hip clientele with a small but worthy selection of boutiques and specialty shops. For a dose of local color, join the brooding literary types who browse **City Lights Booksellers & Publishers,** 261 Columbus Ave., at Broadway (© 415/362-8193), the famous bookstore owned by renowned Beat-generation poet Lawrence Ferlinghetti. The shelves here are stocked with a comprehensive collection of art, poetry, and political paperbacks, as well as more mainstream books.

You can pick up a great gift at **Biordi Art Imports,** 412 Columbus Ave. (© 415/392-8096). Its Italian majolica pottery is both exquisite and unique. Fun mementos are for sale at **Quantity Postcards,** 1441 Grant St., at Green Street (© 415/986-8866), where you'll find the perfect postcard for literally everyone you know.

WHERE TO STAY

Most of the hotels listed below are within easy walking distance of Union Square, the city's premier shopping and tourist district. Prices listed below do not include state and city taxes, which total 14%.

Bed-and-Breakfast Inns Online (www.bbonline.com/ca) offers a small selection of accommodations in San Francisco. **San Francisco Reservations** (© 800/677-1500 or 510/628-4450; www.hotelres.com) books rooms at more than 300 hotels.

Campton Place Hotel   This fabulous Union Square boutique hotel offers some of the best accommodations in town—not to mention the most expensive. Management recently replaced the furnishings with limestone, pear wood, and more Italian-modern and Asian-influenced decor. Guests will still find superlative service, robes, slippers, fax machines, and every necessity and whim that's made Campton Place a favored address. Chef Laurent Manrique delights diners at the excellent Campton Place Restaurant. 340 Stockton St. (between Post and Sutter sts.), San Francisco, CA 94108. © 800/235-4300 or 415/781-5555. Fax 415/955-5536. www. camptonplace.com. 110 units. $345–$475 double; $550–$2,000 suite. American breakfast $19. AE, DC, MC, V. Valet parking $32. **Amenities:** Restaurant; access to nearby health club.

The Commodore Hotel   This trendy budget hotel's "Neo-Deco" rooms feature bright colors and whimsical furnishings. (One unrenovated room is generic motel style and has twin beds with hard mattresses.) Stealing the show is the Red Room, a swank bar and lounge that's ruby red through and through. Adjoining is the Titanic Café, a cute little diner serving buckwheat griddlecakes and Vietnamese tofu sandwiches. 825 Sutter St (at Jones St.), San Francisco, CA 94109. ℭ **800/338-6848** or 415/923-6800. Fax 415/923-6804. www.thecommodorehotel.com. 110 units. $125–$169 double. AE, DC, DISC, MC, V. Parking $22. **Amenities:** Restaurant; access to nearby health club ($15 per day).

Four Seasons Hotel San Francisco Four Seasons does everything right. Go up to the lobby and you're instantly surrounded by calm, cool hotel perfection and a sexy cocktail lounge. Not too trendy, not too traditional, rooms are just right with custom-made mattresses, beautiful art, and huge marble bathrooms with deep tubs and Bulgari toiletries. Many of the oversized rooms overlook Yerba Buena Gardens. Adding to the perks are free access to the building's huge Sports Club L.A., round-the-clock business services, in-room fax machines, a 2-block walk to Union Square, and a vibe that combines sophistication and hipness. 757 Market St., between Third and Fourth sts., San Francisco, CA 94103. ℭ **800/332-3442** or 415/633-3000. Fax 415/633-3009. www.fourseasons.com. 277 units. $469–$600 double; $800 executive suite. AE, DC, DISC, MC, V. Parking $35. **Amenities:** Restaurant; spa; fitness center.

Golden Gate Hotel The Golden Gate Hotel, occupying a historic building, is a real gem, just 2 blocks north of Union Square. The hospitable innkeepers take obvious pleasure in making their guests comfortable. Each individually decorated room has handsome antiques (plenty of wicker), quilted bedspreads, and fresh flowers; some have claw-foot tubs. Guests are welcome to use the house fax and computer free of charge. 775 Bush St. (between Powell and Mason sts.), San Francisco, CA 94108. ℭ **800/835-1118** or 415/392-3702. Fax 415/392-6202. www.goldengatehotel.com. 23 units, 14 with bathroom. $85 double without bathroom, $130 double with bathroom. Rates include continental breakfast. AE, DC, MC, V. Self-parking $15. **Amenities:** Access to health club 1 block away.

The Hotel Bohème Although located in the center of North Beach, this hotel sports a style and demeanor more reminiscent of a prestigious home in upscale Nob Hill. The decor evokes the Beat generation; rooms are small but hopelessly romantic, with gauze-draped canopies. While the bathrooms are sweet, they're also absolutely tiny (no tubs). Request a room off the street side; they're quieter. The staff is ultra-hospitable. 444 Columbus Ave. (between Vallejo and Green sts.), San Francisco, CA 94133. ℭ **415/433-9111.** Fax 415/362-6292. www.hotelboheme. com. 16 units. $164–$184 double. AE, DISC, DC, MC, V. Parking $28 at nearby garage.

The Hotel Majestic This 1902 Japantown lodging meets every professional need while retaining the ambience of a luxurious old-world hotel. Rooms are furnished with French and English antiques, the centerpiece of each being a four-poster canopy bed. Some units also have fireplaces and fridges, along with easy access to a fantastic bar and elegant restaurant, Perlot. 1500 Sutter St. (between Octavia and Gough sts.), San Francisco, CA 94109. ℭ **800/869-8966** or 415/441-1100. Fax 415/673-7331. www.thehotelmajestic.com. 58 units. $175–$285 double; from $350 suite. Continental breakfast $8.50. AE, DC, DISC, MC, V. Valet parking $23. **Amenities:** Restaurant; access to nearby health club ($10 per day).

Huntington Hotel The stately Huntington has long been a favorite Nob Hill retreat for Hollywood stars and political VIPs who desire privacy and security. This family-owned hotel eschews pomp and circumstance; unobtrusive service is its mainstay. The apartmentlike guest rooms feature Brunschwig and Fils fabrics, French antiques, fax machines, fridges and kitchenettes in some units, and city views. 1075 California St. (between Mason and Taylor sts.), San Francisco, CA 94108. ℭ **800/227-4683** or 415/474-5400. Fax 415/474-6227. www.huntingtonhotel.com. 140 units. $310–$445 double; $485–$1,110 suite. Continental breakfast $13. AE, DC, DISC, MC, V. Valet parking $20. **Amenities:** Restaurant; indoor pool; spa; health club.

King George Hotel This utterly delightful hotel has fared well over the years, continuing to draw a mostly European clientele. The location—surrounded by cable-car lines, the Theater District, and Union Square—is superb, and the small guest rooms are surprisingly quiet for such a busy area. Afternoon tea, served Thursday through Sunday from 3 to 6:30pm, is a big hit. 334 Mason St. (between Geary and O'Farrell sts.), San Francisco, CA 94102. ℂ 800/288-6005 or 415/781-5050. Fax 415/835-5991. www.kinggeorge.com. 152 units. $155 double; $240 suite. Breakfast $6.50–$8. AE, DC, DISC, MC, V. Self-parking $18, valet parking $20. **Amenities:** Access to nearby health club.

The Mandarin Oriental The common areas at this Financial District hotel are a bit cold and impersonal, but the rooms are superfluously appointed and the views divine. Not every unit has tub-side views, but all have marble bathrooms with such luxuries as robes and silk slippers. The less opulent rooms are done in a reserved contemporary decor with Asian accents, plus amenities like CD players and fax machines. Don't miss out on the Asian teatime, complete with a bento box of uncommonly delicious goodies. 222 Sansome St. (between Pine and California sts.), San Francisco, CA 94104. ℂ 800/622-0404 or 415/276-9888. Fax 415/433-0289. www.mandarinoriental.com. 158 units. $515–$540 double; $675–$725 signature rooms; from $1,400 suite. Continental breakfast $21, American breakfast $32. AE, DC, DISC, MC, V. Valet parking $34. **Amenities:** Restaurant; fitness center.

The Marina Inn How this 1924 four-story Victorian offers so much for so little is mystifying. Each room looks as though it's been culled from a country-furnishings catalog, complete with four-poster bed topped by a silk-soft comforter. Extra perks include new TVs discreetly hidden in pine cabinetry, nightly turndown service, afternoon sherry, friendly service, and an armada of nearby shops and restaurants. Be sure to request one of the quieter rooms away from busy Lombard Street. 3110 Octavia St. (at Lombard St.), San Francisco, CA 94123. ℂ 800/274-1420 or 415/928-1000. Fax 415/928-5909. www.marinainn.com. 40 units. Nov–Feb $65–$105 double; Mar–May $75–$125 double; June–Oct $85–$135 double. Rates include continental breakfast. AE, DC, MC, V.

The Parker Guest House This is the best B&B option in the Castro, and one of the best in the entire city. The Edwardian home is a few blocks from the heart of the action. The spacious rooms are appointed with smart furnishings and spotless private bathrooms en suite or across the hall. Guests make themselves at home in the wood-paneled library (with fireplace and piano), sunny breakfast room, and spacious garden. 520 Church St. (between 17th and 18th sts.), San Francisco, CA 94114. ℂ 888/520-7275 or 415/621-3222. Fax 415/621-4139. www.parkerguesthouse.com. 20 units. $100–$180 double; $200 junior suite. Rates include extended continental breakfast. AE, DISC, MC, V. Self-parking $15. **Amenities:** Access to nearby health club.

Prescott Hotel It may be small, but boutique Prescott has some big things going for it. The staff treats you like royalty, rooms are attractively unfrilly and masculine, the location (a block from Union Square) is perfect, and limited room service is provided by one of the most popular restaurants in the city, Postrio. The view, alas, isn't so pleasant. The very small bathrooms contain terry robes and hair dryers. 545 Post St. (between Mason and Taylor sts.), San Francisco, CA 94102. ℂ 800/283-7322 or 415/563-0303. Fax 415/563-6831. www.kimptongroup.com. 164 units. $270–$325 double; $300 concierge-level double (including breakfast and evening cocktails); from $365 suite. AE, DC, DISC, MC, V. Valet parking $35. **Amenities:** Restaurant; fitness room.

Ritz-Carlton   Ranked among the top hotels in the world by readers of *Condé Nast Traveler*, the Ritz-Carlton has been the benchmark of Nob Hill's luxury hotels since it opened in 1991. It's outfitted with the finest furnishings, fabrics, and artwork, and the rooms offer every possible amenity, from Italian-marble bathrooms to plush terry robes. Services include a courtesy car, business center, and in-room massage. 600 Stockton St. (between Pine and California sts.), San Francisco, CA 94108. (℃ 800/241-3333 or 415/296-7465. Fax 415/986-1268. www.ritzcarlton.com. 336 units. $475–$575 double; $595–$695 club-level double; from $700 suite. Buffet breakfast $18; Sun brunch $55. Weekend discounts and packages available. AE, DC, DISC, MC, V. Parking $45. **Amenities:** Restaurants (2); indoor pool; health club.

The Tuscan Inn   The Tuscan is the best hotel at Fisherman's Wharf. Like an island of respectability in a sea of touristy schlock, it offers a level of style and comfort far beyond those of its neighbors. Splurge on parking—it's cheaper than the wharf's outrageously priced garages. The lack of views is a small price to pay for a good hotel in a great location. Cafe Pescatore serves standard Italian fare in an airy setting. 425 North Point St. (at Mason St.), San Francisco, CA 94133. (℃ 800/648-4626 or 415/561-1100. Fax 415/561-1199. www.tuscaninn.com. 221 units. $189–$269 double; $279–$339 suite. AE, DC, DISC, MC, V. Parking $22. **Amenities:** Access to nearby health club; pets welcome ($50).

Westin St. Francis   Although the St. Francis is too massive to offer the personal service found at smaller Nob Hill accommodations, few hotels can match its majestic aura. Stroll through the ornate lobby and you can feel 100 years of history oozing from its hand-carved redwood paneling. Rooms in the Tower, which was built in the 1970s and renovated in 2001, evoke a contemporary design in the vein of W Hotel style. The main building accentuates its history with traditional, more elegant ambience. High tea at the Compass Rose is one of San Francisco's most enduring traditions. 335 Powell St. (between Geary and Post sts.), San Francisco, CA 94102. (℃ 800/WESTIN-1 or 415/397-7000. Fax 415/774-0124. www.westin.com. 1,195 units. Main building: $199–$499 double; Tower (Grand View): $219–$549 double; from $550 suite. Extra person $30. Continental breakfast $15–$18. AE, DC, DISC, MC, V. Valet parking $39. **Amenities:** Restaurants (2); spa; health club; pets under 35 lb. accepted ($30).

The Wharf Inn   Our top choice for good-value lodging at Fisherman's Wharf, the Wharf Inn boasts newly refurbished rooms, free parking, and no charge for an extra kid in the room. Its main attribute, however, is its location—smack-dab in the middle of the wharf and within walking distance of North Beach. 2601 Mason St. (at Beach St.), San Francisco, CA 94133. (℃ 800/548-9918 or 415/673-7411. Fax 415/776-2181. www.wharfinn.com. 51 units. $99–$199 double; $270–$399 penthouse. AE, DC, DISC, MC, V. Free parking. **Amenities:** Access to nearby health club ($10 per day).

W San Francisco Hotel   This 31-story property adjacent to the San Francisco Museum of Modern Art is the hippest hotel in town. Sleek and stylish, its octagonal, three-story glass entrance and lobby give way to a great lounge and two bars. Rooms have a residential feel, with such accoutrements as "luxury" beds with down comforters, upholstered chaise lounges, VCRs, CD players, fax machines, Internet access, Aveda toiletries, and louvered blinds opening to usually great city views. 181 Third St. (between Mission and Howard sts.), San Francisco, CA 94103. (℃ 800/877-WHOTEL or 415/777-5300. Fax 415/817-7800. www.whotels.com. 423 units. From $469 double; from $1,800 suite. AE, DC, DISC, MC, V. Valet parking $38. **Amenities:** Restaurant; pool; fitness center.

WHERE TO DINE

San Francisco's dining scene is one of the best in the world. Since our space is limited, we had to make tough choices, but the end result is a cross section of the best in every cuisine and price range. Remember, for top restaurants, make your reservation weeks in advance.

Andalé Taqueria MEXICAN   Andalé (Spanish for "hurry up") offers incredible high-end fast food for the health-conscious. Salad dressings are made with double virgin olive oil, while salsas are composed of fresh fruits and veggies. Add the location (on a sunny shopping stretch), sophisticated decor, full bar, and check-me-out patio seating, and it's no wonder the Marina District considers this place home. Cafeteria-style service keeps prices low. 2150 Chestnut St. (between Steiner and Pierce sts.). (℃ 415/749-0506. Reservations not accepted. Most dishes $5.25–$9.50. AE, MC, V. Mon–Thurs and Sun 11am–10pm; Fri–Sat 11am–10:30pm. Bus: 22, 28, 30, 30X, 43, 76, or 82X.

Aqua SEAFOOD   Without question, this Financial District restaurant remains San Francisco's finest seafood spot. Chef Michael Mina dazzles with a bewildering juxtaposition of earth and sea in his seasonally changing menus. The ahi tartare, for example, is mixed tableside with pears, pine nuts, quail egg, and mint—truly divine. Desserts are equally impressive, particularly the soufflé of the day. Our only complaint: The dining room is rather stark and noisy. 252 California St. (near Battery). (℃ 415/956-9662. Reservations required. Main courses $29–$39; tasting menu $85 or $125; vegetarian tasting menu $55. AE, DC, MC, V. Mon–Fri 11:30am–2pm; Mon–Sat 5:30–10:30pm. Bus: All Market St. buses.

Boulevard AMERICAN   This SoMa spot is already an all-time favorite. What's the winning combination? The dramatic Belle Epoque interior combined with well-sculpted, mouthwatering dishes. Creative main courses might include pan-roasted miso-glazed sea bass with asparagus salad, Japanese rice, and shiitake-mushroom broth, or wild mushroom risotto with fresh chanterelles and Parmesan. Three levels of formality—bar, open kitchen, and main dining room—keep things from getting too snobby. 1 Mission St. (between Embarcadero and Steuart sts.). (℃ 415/543-6084. Reservations recommended. Main courses $14–$25 lunch, $24–$30 dinner. AE, DC, DISC, MC, V. Mon–Fri 11:30am–2pm; Sun–Wed 5:30–10pm; Thurs–Sat 5:30–10:30pm. Valet parking $10. Bus: 15, 30, 32, or 45.

Cha Cha Cha CARIBBEAN   Put your name on the list, crowd into the minuscule bar, and drink sangria while you wait. When you finally get seated (generally at least an hour later), you'll dine in a *loud* dining room with Santería altars, banana trees, and plastic tropical tablecloths. Come with friends and share a selection of tapas, such as the city's best calamari, fried new potatoes, and mussels in saffron broth. A second, larger location is open in the Mission at 2327 Mission St., between 19th and 20th streets ((℃ **415/648-0504**). 1801 Haight St. (at Shrader St.). (℃ **415/386-7670**. Reservations not accepted. Tapas $4.50–$8.75; main courses $9–$15. MC, V. Daily 11am–4pm; Sun–Thurs 5–11pm; Fri–Sat 5–11:30pm. Muni Metro: N. Bus: 6, 7, 66, 71, or 73.

Fifth Floor Restaurant MODERN FRENCH   Chef Laurent Gras's arrival in SoMa in 2001 was the best thing that's happened to San Francisco dining in a long time. Hailing from Restaurant Alain Ducasse and the Waldorf-Astoria's Peacock Alley, Gras's cuisine is as luxurious as the decor of rich fabrics, leather and velvet banquettes, Frette linens, and zebra-striped carpeting. You'd be a fool to pass on the avocado dome hiding a mound of crabmeat brought to life with jalapeño and basil. "Lobster cappuccino" is a genius combination of lobster broth emulsified with chestnuts, prawns, and sautéed lobster. Whatever you do, don't skip the butterscotch pudding, which defies description. In the Hotel Palomar, 12 Fourth St. (at Market St.). © 415/348-1555. Reservations recommended. Main courses $33–$39; tasting menu $85. AE, DC, DISC, MC, V. Mon–Thurs 5:30–10pm; Fri–Sat 5:30–11pm. Valet parking $10. Bus: All Market St. buses.

Foreign Cinema CALIFORNIA   This Mission spot is so chic that it's hard to believe it's a San Francisco restaurant. An indoor seat is a lovely place to watch the city's most fashionable; outdoors (heated, but still chilly), the enormous foreign film showing on the side of an adjoining building steals the show. Opt for roasted chicken with golden chanterelle and red mustard green risotto, or perhaps grilled Meyer Ranch natural tri-tip with Tuscan-style beans and rosemary-fried peppercorn sauce. The food's fine, but truth be told we'd come here even if the food sucked—it's just that cool. 2534 Mission St. (between 21st and 22nd sts.). © 415/648-7600. www.foreigncinema.com. Reservations recommended. Main courses $14–$20. AE, MC, V. Sun–Wed 6–10pm; Thurs–Sat 6–11pm. Valet parking $8. Bus: 14, 14L, or 49.

Greens Restaurant VEGETARIAN   Knowledgeable locals swear by Greens, where executive chef Annie Somerville cooks with the seasons, using produce from local organic farms. Located in an old warehouse, with enormous windows overlooking the bridge and the bay, the restaurant is both a pioneer and a legend. Entrees run the gamut from pizza with wilted escarole, red onions, lemon, and Parmesan to Vietnamese yellow curry. A special four-course dinner is served on Saturday. The adjacent Greens To Go bakery sells breads, sandwiches, soups, salads, and pastries. Building A, Fort Mason Center (enter Fort Mason opposite the Safeway at Buchanan and Marina sts.). © 415/771-6222. Reservations recommended. Main courses $9.50–$12 lunch, $15–$20 dinner; fixed-priced dinner $48; brunch $8–$12. DISC, MC, V. Tues–Fri 11:30am–2pm; Sat 11:30am–2:30pm; Sun 10am–2pm; Mon–Fri 5:30–9:30pm; Sat 5:30–9pm. Greens To Go Mon–Fri 8am–9:30pm; Sat 8am–4:30pm; Sun 9am–3:30pm. Free parking. Bus: 28 or 30.

House of Nanking CHINESE   To its legion of fans, the wait at this dive—sometimes up to an hour—is worth what's on the plate. When the line is reasonable, we drop by for pot stickers and chef/owner Peter Fang's signature shrimp-and-scallion pancake served with peanut sauce. Trust the waiters when they recommend a special. 919 Kearny St. (at Columbus Ave.). © 415/421-1429. Reservations not accepted. Main courses $6–$12. MC, V. Mon–Fri 11am–10pm; Sat noon–10pm; Sun 4–10pm. Bus: 9, 12, 15, or 30.

Kokkari GREEK   One of the best Financial District restaurants combines a beautifully rustic dining area (with fireplace) and stellar traditional Aegean dishes. Hearty eaters should opt for the to-die-for moussaka. Another boon: quail stuffed with winter greens served on oven-roasted leeks, orzo, and wild rice *pilaf*. *Kalithopita* is the most velvety chocolate cake you'll ever experience. 200 Jackson St. (at Front St.). © 415/981-0983. www.kokkari.com. Reservations recommended. Main courses $15–$21 lunch, $17–$33 dinner. AE, DC, DISC, MC, V. Lunch Mon–Fri 11:30am–2:30pm; bar menu 2:30–5:30pm; dinner Mon–Thurs 5:30–10pm, Fri 5:30–11pm, Sat 5–11pm. Closed Sun. Valet parking (dinner only) $8. Bus: 12, 15, 41, or 83.

La Folie FRENCH   This Pacific Heights favorite offers melt-in-your-mouth starters such as roast quail and foie gras with salad, wild mushrooms, and roasted garlic, and very generous main courses such as roast venison with vegetables, quince, and huckleberry sauce. The country-French decor is tasteful but not too serious, with whimsical chandeliers and a cloudy sky painted overhead. Finish off with any of the delectable desserts. 2316 Polk St. (between Green and Union sts.). *C* **415/776-5577.** Reservations recommended. Main courses $32–$45; 4-course tasting menu $75; 5-course chef's tasting menu $85; vegetarian tasting menu $55. AE, DC, DISC, MC, V. Mon–Sat 5:30–10pm. Bus: 19, 41, 45, 47, 49, or 76.

L'Osteria del Forno ITALIAN   L'Osteria del Forno is one of the top three authentic Italian restaurants in North Beach. Peer in the window, and you'll probably see two Italian women sweating from the heat of the brick-lined oven, which cranks out the best focaccia in the city. There's no pomp or circumstance: Locals come here strictly to eat. The menu features a variety of pizzas, salads, soups, and pastas, plus daily specials (pray for the roast pork braised in milk). Good news for folks on the go: You can get pizza by the slice. 519 Columbus Ave. (between Green and Union sts.). *C* **415/982-1124.** Reservations not accepted. Sandwiches $5.50–$6.50; pizzas $10–$17; main courses $6–$11. No credit cards. Sun–Mon and Wed–Thurs 11:30am–10pm; Fri–Sat 11:30am–10:30pm. Bus: 15 or 41.

Masa's FRENCH   One of the city's veteran contenders for best French restaurant underwent major changes in 2001. New chef Ron Siegel deftly designs tasting menus within an almost startlingly trendy room. Fortunately, one thing has remained the same: a dedication to culinary excellence. Anticipate delicate seared scallops elevated both literally and figuratively by microgreens and a dab of decadent uni. Desserts are too precious, but the candy cart, which is wheeled by so you can select lollipops, chocolates, and mini-cookies, almost makes up for it. In the Hotel Vintage Court, 648 Bush St. (at Stockton St.). *C* **415/989-7154.** Reservations required; accepted up to 3 months in advance. Fixed-price dinner $65–$109. AE, DC, DISC, MC, V. Tues–Sat 5:30–9:30pm. Closed 1st 2 weeks in Jan, 1st week in July. Valet parking $9. Cable car: Powell-Mason and Powell-Hyde lines. Bus: 2, 3, 4, 30, or 45.

Mecca AMERICAN   Mecca entered the Castro scene in 1996, unveiling the kind of industrial-chic supper club that makes you want to order a martini just so you'll match the ambience. A night here promises a live DJ spinning hot grooves and a fine American meal served at tables tucked into several dining nooks. Menu options include sake and miso glazed black cod, cilantro lemon chicken, and grilled prime rib. The food is very good, but it's that only-in-San-Francisco vibe that makes this place a smokin' hot spot. 2029 Market St. (by 14th and Church sts.). *C* **415/621-7000.** www.sfmecca.com. Reservations recommended. Main courses $16–$32. AE, DC, MC, V. Mon–Thurs 5–11pm; Fri–Sat 5pm–midnight; Sun 4–10pm; bar remains open later. Valet parking $8. Muni Metro: F, K, L, or M. Bus: 8, 22, 24, or 37.

Restaurant Gary Danko MODERN CLASSIC   Gary Danko, who received the James Beard Foundation award for Best Chef in California, presides over this romantic yet unfussy dining room. The three- to five-course menu is freestyle, so whether you want a sampling of appetizers or a flight of meat courses, you need only ask. Top picks? Glazed oysters, which are as creamy as the light accompanying sauce graced with leeks and intricately carved "zucchini pearls"; seared foie gras with peaches, caramelized onions, and verjus sauce; and adventurous Moroccan spiced squab with chermoula and orange-cumin carrots. Diners at the bar have the option of ordering a la carte. 800 North Point St. (at Hyde St.). *C* **415/749-2060.** www.garydanko.com. Reservations required. 3- to 5-course fixed-price menu $55–$74. AE, DC, MC, V. Sun–Wed 5:30–9:30pm; Thurs–Sat 5:30–10pm. Valet parking $10. Bus: 42. Cable car: Hyde.

Swan Oyster Depot SEAFOOD   Opened in 1912, this Russian Hill hole-in-the-wall boasts only 20 or so seats, jammed cheek-by-jowl along a long marble bar.

The menu is limited to fresh crab, shrimp, oyster, clam cocktails, Maine lobster, and Boston-style clam chowder, all of which are exceedingly fresh. Don't let the lunchtime line dissuade you—it moves fast. 1517 Polk St. (between California and Sacramento sts.). (© 415/673-1101. Reservations not accepted. Seafood cocktails $7–$15; clams and oysters on the half shell $7–$7.25 per half dozen. No credit cards. Mon–Sat 8am–5:30pm. Bus: 27.

Ton Kiang CHINESE/DIM SUM   Ton Kiang is the number-one place in the city to do dim sum. From stuffed crab claws, roast Peking duck, and a gazillion dumpling selections to the delicious and hard-to-find *doa miu* (snow-pea sprouts, flash-sautéed with garlic and peanut oil) and a mesmerizing mango pudding, every tray of morsels coming from the kitchen is an absolute delight. The full menu of Hakka cuisine is worth investigation as well. 5821 Geary Blvd. (between 22nd and 23rd aves.). (© 415/387-8273. Reservations accepted for parties of 8 or more. Dim sum $2–$5.50. AE, MC, V. Mon–Sat 10:30am–10pm; Sun 9am–10pm. Bus: 38.

Zuni Café MEDITERRANEAN   Trend-setting Zuni Café is, and probably always will be, a local favorite. Its expanse of windows and prime lower Castro location guarantee good people-watching, but even better is the incredibly satisfying menu. Stand at the bustling bar, order a glass of wine and a few oysters, and then take a seat amidst the exposed-brick maze of little dining rooms. The proven winners are the brick-oven-roasted chicken for two with Tuscan-style bread salad, the polenta with mascarpone, and the hamburger on grilled rosemary focaccia bread. 1658 Market St. (at Franklin St.). (© 415/552-2522. Reservations recommended. Main courses $10–$19 lunch, $15–$26 dinner. AE, MC, V. Tues–Sat 11:30am–midnight; Sun 11am–11pm. Valet parking $7. Muni Metro: All Market St. lines. Bus: 6, 7, 71, or 75.

SAN FRANCISCO AFTER DARK

For up-to-date nightlife information, turn to the *San Francisco Weekly* and the *San Francisco Bay Guardian,* available free at bars and restaurants, and from street-corner boxes all around the city. *Where,* a free tourist monthly, also has information on programs and performance times. The Sunday editions of the *San Francisco Examiner* and *Chronicle* feature a "Datebook" section with information and listings.

Half-price tickets to theater, dance, and music performances are available from **Tix Bay Area,** inside the Union Square Garage, at Geary and Powell streets (© 415/433-7827), on the day of the show only. Tix also sells advance, full-price tickets, as does **City Box Office,** 180 Redwood St., Ste. 100, between Golden Gate and McAllister streets off Van Ness Avenue (© 415/392-4400; www.cityboxoffice.com).

THE PERFORMING ARTS   The **American Conservatory Theatre** (© 415/749-2ACT; www.act-sfbay.org), one of the nation's premier theater ensembles, performs at the Geary Theater, 415 Geary St., at Mason Street, and features both classical and experimental works. The highly acclaimed **Magic Theatre** (© 415/441-8822; www.magictheatre.org) has nurtured the talents of such modern playwrights as Sam Shepard and Jon Robin Baitz. Performances are held at Building D, Fort Mason Center, Marina Boulevard, at Buchanan Street.

The well-regarded **San Francisco Symphony** (© 415/864-6000; www. sfsymphony.org) performs at Davies Symphony Hall, 201 Van Ness Ave., at Grove Street.

The War Memorial Opera House, 301 Van Ness Ave. (at Grove St.), is home to performances of both the **San Francisco Ballet** (© 415/865-2000; www.sfballet.org), the oldest professional ballet company in the nation, and the

San Francisco Opera (© 415/864-3330; www.sfopera.org), the first municipal opera in the United States.

COMEDY & CABARET   A San Francisco tradition for more than 2 decades, *Beach Blanket Babylon,* Club Fugazi, 678 Green St. (© 415/421-4222), is best known for its outrageous costumes and oversize headdresses. Almost every performance sells out, so get tickets at least 3 weeks in advance. **Cobb's Comedy Club,** 2801 Leavenworth St., at Beach Street (© 415/928-4320), features national headliners like George Wallace and Emo Philips.

JAZZ & BLUES CLUBS   Biscuits & Blues, 401 Mason St. (© 415/292-2583), boasts a blow-your-eardrums-out sound system in a New Orleans–style basement speakeasy. The **Blue Bar,** 501 Broadway (© 415/981-2233), is cozy-chic, with cushy couches, a laid-back atmosphere, and jazz and blues loud enough to be heard over late-night diners. **Lou's Pier 47 Club,** 300 Jefferson St. (© 415/771-5687), attracts few locals, but hosts decent jazz, blues, rock, and country bands near the Wharf. **Slim's,** 333 11th St. (© 415/522-0333; www.slims-sf.com), is co-owned by musician Boz Scaggs, who sometimes takes the stage under the name "Presidio Slim." California cuisine and American music—homegrown rock, jazz, blues, and alternative—star nearly nightly.

Jazz at Pearl's, 256 Columbus Ave. (© 415/291-8255), is one of the best venues for jazz in the city. Ribs and chicken are served with the sounds, too. **Cafe du Nord,** 2170 Market St. (© 415/861-5016), has been around since 1907, but only recently convinced a younger generation to appreciate it as a respectable jazz venue.

Made famous by promoter Bill Graham in the 1960s, **The Fillmore,** 1805 Geary Blvd. (© 415/346-6000; www.thefillmore.com), has reopened after years of neglect and is once again attracting big names.

SUPPER CLUBS   If you can eat dinner, listen to live music, and dance in the same room, we call it a supper club. And **Harry Denton's Starlight Room,** at the Sir Francis Drake Hotel, 450 Powell St., 21st floor (© 415/395-8595), is one of the best. Tourists and locals come to this 1930s-era lounge-turned-nightclub to sip drinks at sunset and boogie down to live swing and big-band tunes after dark. **Julie's Supper Club,** 1123 Folsom St. (© 415/861-0707), is a long-time standby for cocktails and late dining, especially for good-looking singles on the prowl.

DANCE CLUBS   Each night is different at **Club Ten 15,** 1015 Folsom St. (© 415/431-1200), an enormous warehouse with music ranging from yuppie to hip-hop, disco to acid jazz. Don't show up looking for dinner at **Nickie's BBQ,** 460 Haight St. (© 415/621-6508; www.nickies.com). The only hot thing you'll find is the small, crowded dance floor (don't expect a full bar either; it's beer and wine only). The labyrinthine **Paradise Lounge,** 1501 Folsom St. (© 415/861-6906), features three dance floors simultaneously vibrating to different beats.

THE BAR SCENE   Backflip, 601 Eddy St. (© 415/771-FLIP), a shimmering aqua-blue lounge, adjoins the rock-and-roll Phoenix Hotel and serves "cocktail fare" to mostly young, fashionable types. The **Bubble Lounge,** 714 Montgomery St. (© 415/434-4204), serves 300 kinds of champagne (30 of them by the glass).

Over in North Beach, **Vesuvio,** 255 Columbus Ave. (© **415/362-3370**), has been catering to local writers, artists, and musicians since Beatnik days (it's no coincidence that City Lights Bookstore is just across Jack Kerouac Alley).

The **Gordon-Biersch Brewery,** 2 Harrison St. (© **415/243-8246**), is a popular brewpub with the young Republican crowd. The **San Francisco Brewing Company,** 155 Columbus Ave. (© **415/434-3344**), is one of the city's few remaining old saloons, aglow with stained glass windows, tile floors, skylights, and a mahogany bar.

For cocktails with a view, try the **Carnelian Room,** 555 California St., in the Bank of America Building (© **415/433-7500**). Jacket and tie are required for men. **Top of the Mark,** in the Mark Hopkins Intercontinental, 1 Nob Hill (© **415/616-6916**), is the most famous cocktail lounge in the city. During World War II, thousands of Pacific-bound servicemen toasted their farewells to the States here.

THE GAY & LESBIAN SCENE **Twin Peaks Tavern,** 401 Castro St. (© **415/864-9470**), is considered the first gay bar in America. Because of its notoriety and its small size, the place becomes fairly crowded and convivial by 8pm. **The Stud,** 399 Ninth St. (© **415/863-6623**), around for over 30 years and one of the most successful gay establishments in town, is mellow enough for straights as well as gays. Music varies from cabaret nights and oldies to disco. **The Café,** 2367 Market St. (© **415/861-3846**), started out as a lesbian dance club on Saturday nights. But once the guys found out how much fun the girls were having, they joined the party. **The EndUp,** 401 Sixth St. (© **415/357-0827**), is a different club every night, but the place is always jumping with the DJs blasting tunes.

2 The Wine Country

California's Napa and Sonoma valleys are two of the most famous wine-growing regions in the world. Hundreds of wineries are nestled among the vines, and most are open to visitors. But even if you don't want to wine-taste, the fresh country air, beautiful rolling countryside, and world-class restaurants and spas are reason enough to come. If you can, plan on spending more than a day here; you'll need a couple of days just to get to know one of the valleys (don't try to do both unless you've got several days free).

NAPA VALLEY

Napa Valley dwarfs Sonoma Valley both in population and number of wineries. It also has more spas (some at far cheaper rates), a far superior selection of fine restaurants and hotels, and, of course, more traffic jams. But if your goal is to really learn about the wonderful world of winemaking, world-class wineries such as Sterling and Robert Mondavi offer the most edifying wine tours in North America, if not the world.

Napa Valley is just 25 miles long; you can venture from one end to the other in less than a half hour (traffic permitting). Conveniently, most of the large wineries—as well as most of the hotels, shops, and restaurants—are located along a single road, Calif. 29. The beauty of the valley is striking any time of the year, but it's most memorable in September and October when the grapes are being pressed and the wineries are in full production.

You can get Wine Country maps and brochures from the **Wine Institute,** 425 Market St., Ste. 1000, San Francisco (© **415/512-0151**). The **Napa Conference & Visitors Bureau,** 1310 Town Center Mall, Napa (© **707/226-7459;**

www.napavalley.com), publishes the slick *Napa Valley Guide*, both in print and online.

TOURING THE TOP WINERIES

No place in the valley brings together art and wine better than the **Hess Collection,** 4411 Redwood Rd., Napa (© 707/255-1144; www.hesscollection. com). After acquiring the old Christian Brothers winery in 1978, Swiss art collector Donald Hess also funded a huge restoration and expansion project to honor wine and the fine arts. The result is a working winery interspersed with gloriously lit rooms that exhibit his truly stunning art collection. The self-guided tour is free, but samples cost $3.

Domaine Chandon, 1 California Dr. (at Calif. 29), Yountville (© 707/ 944-2280; www.chandon.com), is the valley's most renowned sparkling winery. It was founded in 1973 by French champagne house Moët et Chandon. Stroll the manicured gardens, sip sparkling wine on the patio, then glide into the dining room for lunch. Bubbly is sold by the glass ($8–$12); the comprehensive tour of the facilities is worth the time.

At the magnificent mission-style **Robert Mondavi Winery,** 7801 St. Helena Hwy. (Calif. 29), Oakville (© 800/MONDAVI; www.robertmondaviwinery.com), almost every variable in the winemaking process is controlled by computer (fascinating to watch!). After the tour, you can sample the results in selected current wines, free of charge. If you don't tour, you have to pay to taste. Reserve at least a week in advance in summer.

PlumpJack Winery, 620 Oakville Cross Rd. in Oakville (© 707/945-1220; www.plumpjack.com), stands out as the Todd Oldham of wine tasting—chic, colorful, a little wild, and popular with a young and old crowd. This playfully medieval winery is a welcome diversion from the same old, same old. For $5 you can sample the impressive cabernet, chardonnay, and sangiovese. There are no tours or picnic spots, but this refreshingly friendly facility will make you want to linger nonetheless.

Hollywood meets Napa Valley at **Niebaum–Coppola,** 1991 St. Helena Hwy. (Calif. 29), Rutherford (© 707/968-1161; www.niebaum-coppola.com), owned by director Francis Ford Coppola. Amid the Oscars and other Tinseltown glitz, you'll find some decent wine, produced on spectacular grounds. The steep $7.50 tasting fee might make you wonder whether a movie is included— it's not—but you get to keep the souvenir glass, and you can picnic on the unforgettable grounds for free.

At **V. Sattui Winery,** 1111 White Lane (at Calif. 29), St. Helena (© 707/ 963-7774; www.vsattui.com), a combination winery and enormous gourmet deli, you can fill up on wine and cheese without ever reaching for your pocketbook. The gourmet store also stocks sandwich meats, breads, and exotic salads, while the wine bar in the back offers everything from chardonnay to a tasty Madeira. The expansive, lively picnic facilities make this a favorite for families.

Joseph Phelps Vineyards, 200 Taplin Rd., St. Helena (© 800/707-5789; www.jpvwines.com), is a favorite stop for serious wine lovers. The winery was founded in 1973 and has since become a major player in both the region and the worldwide wine market. The intimate tour and knockout tasting are available only by reservation, and the location—a quick and unmarked turn off the Silverado Trail in Spring Valley—makes it impossible to find unless you're looking for it.

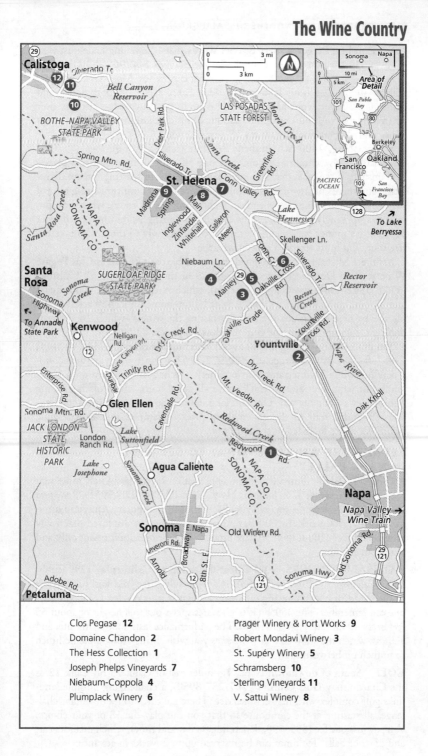

The Wine Country

Clos Pegase **12**

Domaine Chandon **2**

The Hess Collection **1**

Joseph Phelps Vineyards **7**

Niebaum-Coppola **4**

PlumpJack Winery **6**

Prager Winery & Port Works **9**

Robert Mondavi Winery **3**

St. Supéry Winery **5**

Schramsberg **10**

Sterling Vineyards **11**

V. Sattui Winery **8**

You can't beat **Prager Winery & Port Works,** 1281 Lewelling Lane (just west of Calif. 29, behind Sutter Home), St. Helena (© **800/969-PORT;** www. pragerport.com), for a real off-the-beaten-track experience. Most days, your host will be Jim Prager himself, a modern-day Santa Claus in both looks and demeanor. But you won't have to sit on his lap to get your wish—just fork over $5 (refundable with purchase) for a sample of his delicious Sweet Claire dessert wine, a late-harvest Riesling, or his 10-year-old port.

Schramsberg, 1400 Schramsberg Rd. (off Calif. 29), Calistoga (© **707/ 942-2414;** www.schramsberg.com), is one of our all-time favorite places. Schramsberg is the label that U.S. presidents serve when toasting foreign dignitaries, and there's plenty of memorabilia to prove it. The unintimidating tour of the 2½-mile champagne caves ends in a charming tasting room, where you can sample surprisingly varied selections of bubbly. Tasting prices are a bit dear at $10, but it's money well spent. Tastings are offered only to those who take the free tour; you must reserve a spot in advance.

Architect Michael Graves designed the incredible oasis known as **Clos Pegase Winery,** 1060 Dunaweal Lane (off Calif. 29 or the Silverado Trail), Calistoga (© **707/942-4981;** www.clospegase.com), which integrates art, 20,000 square feet of aging caves, and a luxurious private hilltop home on its 450 acres. Viewing the art here is as much the point as tasting the wines—which, by the way, don't come cheap. Tasting the current releases will cost $2.50.

You don't need climbing shoes to reach **Sterling Vineyards,** 1111 Dunaweal Lane (off Calif. 29), Calistoga (© **800/977-3242;** www.sterlingvineyards.com), a dazzling white Mediterranean-style winery, perched 300 feet up on a rocky knoll. Just hand over $6 and you'll arrive via aerial tram, which offers dazzling bucolic views along the way. Once on land, follow the valley's most comprehensive self-guided tour of the winemaking process. Samples at the panoramic tasting room are included in the tram fare.

BEYOND THE WINERIES: WHAT TO SEE & DO IN NAPA VALLEY

ART GALLERIES   Anyone with an appreciation for art absolutely must visit the **di Rosa Preserve,** 5200 Sonoma Hwy., Napa (© **707/226-5991**). Rene and Veronica di Rosa's world-renowned collection of contemporary American art—more than 1,500 works by 600 Bay Area artists alone—is displayed practically everywhere throughout their 53-acre estate. Visits are by appointment only and last about 2 hours.

NATURAL WONDERS   Old Faithful Geyser of California, 1299 Tubbs Lane, Calistoga (© **707/942-6463**), is one of only three "old faithful" geysers in the world. It's been blowing off steam at regular intervals for as long as anyone can remember. The 350°F (176°C) water spews out to a height of about 60 feet every 40 minutes, day and night. The performance lasts about a minute, and you can watch the show as many times as you wish. Bring along a picnic lunch to munch on between spews.

GOLF   South of downtown Napa, 1.3 miles east of Calif. 29 on Calif. 12, is the **Chardonnay Golf Club** (© **707/257-8950**), a challenging 36-hole landlinks golf complex with first-class service. There are three nines of similar challenge, all starting at the clubhouse so that you can play the 18 of your choice. You pay just one fee ($35–$90, depending on day and time), which includes cart and practice balls. Tee times can be reserved up to 2 weeks in advance.

SHOPPING Vanderbilt and Company, 1429 Main St., in St. Helena (℃ 707/963-1010), purveyor of gorgeous cookware and fine housewares, is a must for gourmands. So is **Napa Valley Olive Oil Manufacturing Company,** 835 Charter Oak Rd., at the end of the road behind Tra Vigne restaurant (℃ 707/963-4173). This tiny market presses and bottles its own oils and sells them at a fraction of the price you'll pay elsewhere.

SPAS & MUD BATHS The one thing you should do while you're in Calistoga is what people have been doing here for the past 150 years: Take a mud bath. The natural baths are composed of local volcanic ash, imported peat, and naturally boiling mineral hot-springs water, all mulled together to produce a thick mud that simmers at a temperature of about 104°F (40°C). Follow your soak in the mud with a warm mineral-water shower, a whirlpool bath, a visit to the steam room, and a relaxing blanket-wrap. The outcome: a rejuvenated, revitalized, squeaky-clean new you.

Indulge yourself at any of these Calistoga spas: **Dr. Wilkinson's Hot Springs,** 1507 Lincoln Ave. (℃ 707/942-4102); **Golden Haven Hot Springs Spa,** 1713 Lake St. (℃ 707/942-6793); **Calistoga Spa Hot Springs,** 1006 Washington St. (℃ 707/942-6269); and the **Calistoga Village Inn & Spa,** 1880 Lincoln Ave. (℃ 707/942-0991).

WHERE TO STAY

While we recommend shacking up in the more romantically pastoral areas such as St. Helena, there's no question you're going to find better deals in the towns of Napa or laid-back Calistoga.

The pricey, spectacular **Auberge du Soleil,** 180 Rutherford Hill Rd., Rutherford (℃ 800/348-5406; www.aubergedusoleil.com), is a Relais & Châteaux member, with bathrooms large enough to get lost in. The tub alone—an enormous hot tub with a skylight overhead—will entice you to grab a glass of California red and settle in for a while. The wood-burning fireplace, private deck, CD player, VCR, fresh flowers, original art, and terra-cotta floors round out the perfect romantic retreat. Dining here is another ethereal experience. All the deluxe amenities (and then some) are available, as well as massage rooms.

Meadowood Napa Valley, 900 Meadowood Lane, St. Helena (℃ 800/458-8080; www.meadowood.com), is summer camp for wealthy grown-ups. Rooms, furnished with American country classics, have beamed ceilings, patios, stone fireplaces, and wilderness views. Many are individual suite-lodges so far removed from the common areas that you must drive to get to them. With golf, tennis, croquet, pools, hiking trails, and a spa on-site, you might never leave the property.

The 1892 **Cedar Gables Inn,** 486 Coombs St., Napa (℃ 800/309-7969; www.cedargablesinn.com), is a cozy, romantic, moderately priced B&B in Old Town Napa. Rooms contain rich tapestries and stunning gilded antiques; five units have fireplaces.

The **Cottage Grove Inn,** 1711 Lincoln Ave., Calistoga (℃ 800/799-2284; www.cottagegrove.com), is our top pick for couples looking to do the Calistoga spa scene in comfort and style. This complex of cottages is well removed from the action once you step across the threshold. Each compact guesthouse comes complete with a wood-burning fireplace, cozy quilts, CD player, VCR, fridge, and an enormous bathroom with a skylight and a deep, two-person Jacuzzi tub. **Maison Fleurie,** 6529 Yount St., Yountville (℃ 800/788-0369; www.foursisters.com), is one of the prettiest hotels in the Wine Country, a trio of 1873 brick-and-fieldstone buildings overlaid with ivy. Some rooms feature private balconies, patios, Jacuzzis, and fireplaces. A full breakfast is served in the quaint dining room; afterwards, feel free to borrow a mountain bike or soak in the pool or outdoor spa.

If your idea of the ultimate vacation is a cozy cabin set among 330 acres of creeks, waterfalls, hot springs, hiking trails, and redwood trees, paradise is a short drive away from St. Helena. Established in 1852, **White Sulphur Springs Retreat & Spa,** 3100 White Sulphur Springs Rd., St. Helena (© **800/ 593-8873** or 707/963-8588; www.whitesulphursprings.com), claims to be the oldest resort in California. The large creek-side cabins are decorated with simple but homey furnishings; some have fireplaces and/or kitchenettes. If the solitude alone isn't relaxing enough, you can schedule a day of aromatherapy, massage, and other spa treatments.

The Art Deco **El Bonita Motel,** 195 Main St., St. Helena (© **800/ 541-3284;** www.elbonita.com), was built a bit too close to Calif. 29 for comfort, but the 2½ acres of beautifully landscaped gardens help even the score. The affordable rooms, while small, are spotlessly clean and decorated with comfy furnishings; some have kitchens or whirlpool tubs. Families like the larger bungalows with kitchenettes, but everybody loves the heated pool, Jacuzzi, and spa facility.

WHERE TO DINE

To best enjoy Napa's restaurant scene, keep one thing in mind: *Reserve*—especially for seats in a more renowned room.

If your restaurant has the chutzpah to post neither a sign nor an address, it had better be good. Fortunately, **The French Laundry,** 6640 Washington St., at Creek Street, Yountville (© **707/944-2380**), *is* that good. Chef/owner Thomas Keller has caught the attention of the judges of the James Beard awards, who dubbed him 1997's Chef of the Nation. Dinner here is an all-night affair; when it's finally over, you'll be ready to sit down and do it all over again—it's truly that wonderful. Reserve a month in advance.

Ultra-fresh food, gorgeous patio seating, all-day service, and "reasonable" prices make **Tra Vigne,** 1050 Charter Oak Ave., St. Helena (© **707/963-4444**), a long-standing favorite. Try irresistible oven-roasted polenta with cheese, mushrooms, and balsamic reduction, and then move on to the outstanding whole roasted fish. The adjoining **Cantinetta** offers sandwiches, pizzas, and lighter meals.

The most exciting opening of 2002 wasn't a big fancy dining room, but rather the tiny **ZuZu,** 829 Main St., Napa (© **707/224-8555**), serving delicious affordable tapas ($2–$11!). The kitchen cranks out fantastic paella, sizzling prawns, and Moroccan barbecued lamb chops guaranteed to make you swoon.

SONOMA VALLEY

Sonoma is often thought of as the "other" Wine Country, forever in the shadow of Napa Valley. Truth is, it's a very different experience. Sonoma still manages to maintain a backcountry ambience thanks to its much lower density of wineries, restaurants, and hotels; because it's far less traveled than its neighbor to the east, it offers a more genuine "escape from it all" experience. Small, family-owned wineries are its mainstay, and tastings and tours are usually free and low-key, and come with plenty of friendly banter between the winemakers and their guests.

While you're in Sonoma, stop by the **Sonoma Valley Visitors Bureau,** 453 First St. E. (© **707/996-1090;** www.sonomavalley.com), and pick up the $2

Sonoma Valley Visitors Guide, which lists most every lodging, winery, and restaurant in the valley.

TOURING THE VALLEY & WINERIES

Sonoma Valley is currently home to about 35 wineries. They tend to be a little more spread out than those in Napa, so decide where you're going before you get on the road.

A visit to the **Benziger Family Winery,** 1883 London Ranch Rd., off Arnold Drive, Glen Ellen (© **800/989-8890;** www.benziger.com), confirms that this is indeed a "family" winery. At any given time, three generations of Benzigers may be running around tending to chores. The pastoral, user-friendly property features an exceptional self-guided tour. Tastings of the standard-release wines are free, as are several scenic picnic spots.

Buena Vista Winery, 18000 Old Winery Rd., Sonoma (© **800/926-1266;** www.buenavistawinery.com), is the granddaddy of all California wineries, founded in 1857 by Count Agoston Haraszthy, the Hungarian émigré who returned from Europe in 1861 with 100,000 of the finest vine cuttings. The winery still maintains a complimentary tasting room (the really good stuff costs $3) inside the restored 1862 Press House—a beautiful stone-crafted room brimming with wines, wine-related gifts, and accessories.

When you've had it with chardonnays and pinots, visit **Gloria Ferrer Champagne Caves,** 23555 Carneros Hwy. (Calif. 121), Sonoma (© **707/996-7256;** www.gloriaferrer.com), home of Freixenet, the largest producer of sparkling wine in the world. If you're unfamiliar with the term *méthode champenoise,* take the free tour of the fermenting tanks, bottling line, and caves brimming with yeast-laden bottles. Afterwards, retire to the elegant tasting room for a flute of Brut or Cuvée ($3.50–$6 a glass).

Viansa Winery and Italian Marketplace, 25200 Arnold Dr. (Calif. 121), Sonoma (© **800/995-4740;** www.viansa.com), is the brainchild of Sam and Vicki Sebastiani, who left the family dynasty to create their own temple to food and wine. The marketplace is crammed with a cornucopia of high-quality gourmet foods; the winery has quickly established a favorable reputation for its cabernet, sauvignon blanc, and chardonnay.

WHERE TO STAY

If you're having trouble finding a vacancy, call the **Bed & Breakfast Association of Sonoma Valley** (© **800/969-4667**), which can refer you to a member B&B and make reservations for you as well.

The **El Dorado Hotel,** 405 First St. W., Sonoma (© **800/289-3031;** www.hoteleldorado.com), may look like a 19th-century Wild West relic from the outside, but inside it's all 20th-century deluxe. Each modern room—designed by the same folks who put together the ultra-exclusive Auberge du Soleil resort in Rutherford (p. 819)—has French windows and tiny terraces.

The **Gaige House Inn,** 13540 Arnold Dr., Glen Ellen (© **800/935-0237;** www.gaige.com), is the best B&B we've ever stayed in. The service, amenities, and decor are what you'd expect from an outrageously expensive resort, but without the snobbery. All 15 rooms have firm mattresses graced with wondrously silk-soft linens and premium down comforters. There's even a pool and outdoor hot tub on the manicured lawn out back.

Located well off the main highway on an oak-studded hillside, **Glenelly Inn,** 5131 Warm Springs Rd., off Arnold Drive, Glen Ellen (© **707/996-6720;** www.glenelly.com), comes with everything you would expect from a country retreat: eight bright, immaculate rooms, authentic antiques, down comforters, firm mattresses, a hot tub ensconced in a grape arbor, and long verandas with stunning views of the verdant Sonoma hillsides.

The honey-colored Italian-style buildings and pastoral views of vineyard-covered hills at the **Kenwood Inn & Spa,** 10400 Sonoma Hwy., Kenwood (© **800/353-6966;** www.kenwoodinn.com), are enough to make any Italian homesick for Tuscany. Each of the 12 spacious rooms is exquisitely decorated with imported tapestries and antiques, and boasts a fireplace, balcony, and down comforter.

The **Sonoma Hotel,** 110 W. Spain St., Sonoma (© **800/468-6016**), is a cute little historic hotel with 16 rooms on Sonoma's tree-lined Town Square. The adjoining Heirloom's restaurant serves very good California cuisine.

Set on 12 meticulously groomed acres, the **Sonoma Mission Inn, Spa & Country Club,** 18140 Sonoma Hwy. (Calif. 12), Sonoma (© **800/862-4945;** www.sonomamissioninn.com), is a popular retreat for the wealthy. The spa and the slew of attendant luxury amenities—massages, facials, tennis courts, hot tub, and two pools—are the main event.

WHERE TO DINE

Though Sonoma Valley has far fewer visitors than Napa Valley, its restaurants are often equally as crowded, so be sure to make reservations in advance.

the girl & the fig, 110 W. Spain St. (© **707/938-3634**), draws crowds nightly to its new downtown Sonoma digs. Figs are sure to be on the menu in one form or another, as in the wonderful winter fig salad made with arugula, pecans, dried figs, goat cheese, and a fig-and-port vinaigrette.

Kenwood Restaurant & Bar, 9900 Sonoma Hwy., Kenwood (© **707/ 833-6326**), is what Wine Country dining should be (but what it often, disappointingly, is not). The first-rate cuisine is perfectly balanced between tradition and innovation: Main dishes might include poached salmon in a creamy caper sauce, prawns with saffron Pernod sauce, or braised Sonoma rabbit with grilled polenta.

If you just can't take another expensive, chichi meal, follow the locals to **Della Santina's,** 133 E. Napa St., just east of the square, Sonoma (© **707/935-0576**). Every classic Tuscan dish is well flavored—without overbearing sauces or one *hint* of California pretentiousness. Don't worry about breaking the bank on a bottle of wine, as most of the choices here go for under $25.

Eclectic food, friendly owners, soothing atmosphere, and moderate prices make **Cafe La Haye,** 140 E. Napa St., Sonoma (© **707/935-5994**), a favorite. The small, straightforward menu offers just enough options, such as a risotto special; creative salads; and pan-roasted chicken breast with caramelized shallot jus and fennel mashed potatoes.

Cucina Viansa, 400 First St. E., Sonoma (© **707/935-5656**), is the sexiest thing going in Sonoma, a suave deli and wine bar owned by Sam and Vicki Sebastiani, who also run Viansa Winery (p. 821). Choose among the armada of cured meats, cheeses, pastas, salads, and breads; on your way out, treat yourself to some intense gelato.

3 The Northern Coast

North of San Francisco, you can forget about California's fabled surf-and-bikini scene; instead, you'll find miles and miles of rugged coastline with broad beaches and tiny bays harboring dramatic rock formations carved by the ocean waves. The best time to visit is in the spring or fall. In spring, the headlands are carpeted with wildflowers—golden poppy, iris, and sea foam—and in fall, the sun shines clear and bright. Summers are typically cool and windy, with the ubiquitous fog burning off by the afternoon. The water's too cold for much swimming this far north, but that doesn't mean you can't enjoy the beaches, whether by strolling along the water or taking in the panoramic views of towering cliffs and seascapes.

POINT REYES NATIONAL SEASHORE

This preserve is a 71,000-acre hammer-shaped peninsula jutting 10 miles into the Pacific and backed by Tomales Bay. It encompasses several surf-pounded beaches, bird estuaries, open swaths of land with roaming elk, and the Point Reyes Lighthouse, which offers spectacular views.

The infamous San Andreas Fault separates Point Reyes—the northernmost landmass on the Pacific Plate—from the rest of California, which rests on the North American Plate. In 1906, Point Reyes jumped north almost 20 feet in an instant, leveling San Francisco and jolting the rest of the state. The half-mile **Earthquake Trail,** near the Bear Valley Visitor Center, illustrates this geological drama with a loop through an area torn by the slipping fault. Shattered fences, rifts in the ground, and a barn knocked off its foundation by the quake illustrate how alive the earth is here.

Point Reyes is only 35 miles northwest of San Francisco, but it takes at least 90 minutes to reach by car (it's all the small towns, not the topography, that slow you down). The easiest route is via Sir Francis Drake Boulevard from U.S. 101 south of San Rafael. For a much longer but more scenic route, take the Stinson Beach/Calif. 1 exit off U.S. 101 just south of Sausalito and follow Calif. 1 north.

As soon as you arrive at Point Reyes, stop at the **Bear Valley Visitor Center** (© 415/464-5100; www.nps.gov/pore) on Bear Valley Road (look for the small sign posted just north of Olema on Calif. 1) and pick up a free Point Reyes trail map. The rangers here are extremely friendly and helpful. Be sure to check out the great natural-history and cultural displays as well. It's open Monday through Friday from 9am to 5pm, Saturday and Sunday from 8am to 5pm.

Entrance to the park is free. Camping is $10 per site per night, and permits are required; reservations can be made up to 3 months in advance by calling © 415/663-8054, Monday through Friday from 9am to 2pm.

WHAT TO SEE & DO

By far the most popular—and crowded—attraction at Point Reyes National Seashore is the venerable **Point Reyes Lighthouse,** located at the westernmost tip of Point Reyes. Even if you plan to forego the 308 steps down to the lighthouse, it's still worth the visit to marvel at the dramatic scenery, which includes thousands of common murres and prides of sea lions that bask on the rocks far below (binoculars come in handy). The lighthouse visitor center (© 415/669-1534) is open Thursday through Monday from 10am to 4:30pm, weather permitting.

The lighthouse is also the top spot on the California coast to observe **gray whales** as they make their southward and northward migration along the coast January through April. The whales head south in December and January, and return north in March. *Note:* If you plan to drive out to the lighthouse to whale-watch, arrive early as parking is limited. If possible, come on a weekday. On weekends and holidays from December to April (weather permitting), it's wise to park at the Drake's Beach Visitor Center and take the shuttle bus to the lighthouse; the bus costs $3.50 for adults, free for kids 12 and under. Dress warmly—it's often quite cold and windy—and bring binoculars.

North and South **Point Reyes Beach** face the Pacific and withstand the full brunt of ocean tides and winds—the water is far too rough for even wading, though the occasional deranged surfer will try to shred the waves. Along the southern coast, the waters of **Drake's Beach** can be as tranquil and serene as Point Reyes's are turbulent.

Some of the park's best—and least crowded—highlights can only be approached on foot, such as **Alamere Falls,** a freshwater stream that cascades down a 40-foot bluff onto Wildcat Beach, or **Tomales Point Trail,** which passes through the Tule Elk Reserve, a protected haven for roaming herds of tule elk that once numbered in the thousands.

One of our favorite things to do in Point Reyes is paddle through placid **Tomales Bay,** a haven for migrating birds and marine mammals. Kayak trips, including sunset outings, full-moon paddles, and day trips, are organized by **Tomales Bay Sea Kayaking** (© 415/663-1743; www.tamalsaka.com). Instruction, clinics, and boat delivery are available, and all ages and levels are welcome. Prices start at $60 for tours. Half-day rentals begin at $35 for one, $50 for two. Don't worry, the kayaks are very stable and there are no waves to contend with. The launching point is on Calif. 1 at the Marshall Boatworks in Marshall, 8 miles north of Point Reyes Station. Open daily from 9am to 6pm.

WHERE TO STAY & DINE

If you're having trouble finding a vacancy, **Inns of Marin** (© 800/887-2880 or 415/663-2000) and **West Marin Network** (© 415/663-9543) are two reputable services that will help you find accommodations, ranging from one-room cottages to inns and complete vacation homes. Keep in mind that many places here have a 2-night minimum, although in slow season they may make an exception.

An English Oak Bed & Breakfast, 88 Bear Valley Rd., Olema (© 415/663-1777; www.anenglishoak.com), a venerable 1899 Victorian, has survived everything from a major earthquake to a forest fire, which is lucky for you because you'll be hard-pressed to find a better B&B for the price in Point Reyes. Loaded with charm, it's in a great location, too, with two good restaurants within walking distance.

The **Point Reyes Country Inn & Stables,** 12050 Calif. 1, Point Reyes Station (© 415/663-9696; www.ptreyescountryinn.com), is a ranch-style home on 4 acres that offers pastoral accommodations for two- and four-legged guests (horses only), plus access to plenty of trails. Each room has either a balcony or a garden. Also available are two studios (with kitchens) above the stables, plus two Tomales Bay cottages with decks, kitchens, fireplaces, and a shared dock.

The **Station House Café,** Main Street, Point Reyes Station (© 415/663-1515), has been a low-key favorite for more than 2 decades, thanks to its open kitchen, garden seating, and live music on weekends. Breakfast dishes range from a hangtown fry with local Johnson's oysters to mashed-potato pancakes. Dinner specials might include fettuccine with fresh local mussels or two-cheese polenta served with fresh spinach sauté—all made from local produce and seafood.

Fresh, fast, good, and cheap: What more could you ask for in a restaurant? **Taqueria La Quinta,** 11285 Calif. 1, at Third and Main streets (© 415/663-8868), has been one of our favorite lunch stops in downtown Point Reyes for years and years. Try the spicy tomatillo sauce with a side of handmade corn tortillas.

BODEGA BAY

Beyond the tip of the Point Reyes peninsula, the road curves around toward the coastal village of Bodega Bay, which supports a fishing fleet of around 300 boats. It's a good place to stop for lunch or a stroll around town. **Bodega Head State Park** is a great vantage point for whale-watching during the annual migration season from January to April. At **Doran Beach,** there's a large bird sanctuary—remember that Bodega Bay was the setting for Hitchcock's scary *The Birds.*

The **Bodega Harbour Golf Links,** at 21301 Heron Dr. (© **707/875-3538**), enjoys a panoramic oceanside setting. It's an 18-hole Scottish-style course designed by Robert Trent Jones, Jr. A warm-up center and practice facility are free of charge to registered golfers. Rates are $60 to $90. If golfing isn't your thing, you can go horseback riding through some spectacular coastal scenery by contacting **Chanslor Horse Stables** (© **707/875-3333;** www.chanslor.com), which also has pony rides for the kids. Open daily from 9am to 5pm.

One of the bay's major events is the **Fisherman's Festival,** in April. Local fishing boats, decorated with ribbons and banners, sail out for a Blessing of the Fleet, while up to 25,000 landlubbers enjoy music, a lamb-and-oyster barbecue, and an arts-and-crafts fair.

For more information about these festivals and other goings on in Bodega Bay, call or stop in at the **Bodega Bay Area Visitors Center,** 850 Calif. 1, Bodega Bay (© **707/875-3866;** www.bodegabay.com), which has lots of information about the area, including maps of the beaches and the best local fishing spots.

If you'd like to stay over, the upscale **Bodega Bay Lodge and Spa,** 103 Calif. 1 (© **800/368-2468;** www.bodegabaylodge.com), is easily the best choice. Each room has a fireplace and a balcony with sweeping views. Guests have access to a beautiful fieldstone spa and heated pool perched above the bay. The lodge's Duck Club Restaurant also enjoys a reputation as Bodega Bay's finest.

The larger **Inn at the Tides,** 800 Coast Hwy. 1 (© **800/541-7788;** www. innatthetides.com), consists of a cluster of condolike complexes perched on the side of a gently sloping hill. The selling point here is the view; each unit is staggered just enough to guarantee a view of the bay across the highway.

In summer, as many as 1,000 diners a day pass through the **Tides Wharf Restaurant,** 835 Calif. 1 (© **707/875-3652**). Back in the 1960s, it served as one of the settings for Hitchcock's *The Birds,* but renovation has enlarged and redecorated the place beyond recognition. The best tables offer views overlooking the ocean, and the bill of fare includes oysters on the half shell, clam chowder, and fish fresh from the cold blue waters offshore.

THE SONOMA COAST STATE BEACHES, JENNER & FORT ROSS STATE HISTORIC PARK

Along 13 winding miles of Calif. 1—from Bodega Bay to Goat Rock Beach in Jenner—stretch the Sonoma Coast State Beaches, ideal for walking, tide-pooling, abalone picking, fishing, and bird-watching. Each beach is clearly marked from the road, and numerous pullouts are available for parking. Even if you don't stop at any of the beaches, the drive alone is spectacular.

At **Jenner,** the Russian River empties into the ocean. **Penny Island,** in the river's estuary, is home to otters and many species of birds; a colony of harbor seals lives out on the ocean rocks. **Goat Rock Beach** is a popular breeding ground for the seals; pupping season is March through June.

From Jenner, a 12-mile drive along some very dramatic coastline will bring you to **Fort Ross State Historic Park** (© 707/847-3286; www.parks.sonoma. net/fortross.html), a reconstruction of the fort that was established here in 1812 by the Russians as a base for seal and otter hunting. At the visitor center, you can view the silver samovars and elaborate table services that the Russians used. The fenced compound contains several buildings, including the first Russian Orthodox church ever built in North America outside Alaska. The park offers beach trails and picnic grounds on more than 1,000 acres. Admission to the park costs $2 per car.

North from Fort Ross, the road continues to **Salt Point State Park** (© 707/ 847-3221). This 3,500-acre expanse contains 30 campsites, 14 miles of trails, tide pools, a pygmy forest, and old Pomo village sites. Your best bet is to pull off the highway any place that catches your eye and start exploring on foot. At the north end of the park, head inland on Kruse Ranch Road to the **Kruse Rhododendron Reserve** (© 707/847-3221), where the wild purple and pink *Rhododendron californicum* grow up to a height of 18 feet under the redwood-and-fir canopy. Admission to the park costs $2 per car.

MENDOCINO

Mendocino is, to our minds, *the* premier destination on California's north coast. Despite (or because of) its relative isolation, it emerged as one of Northern California's major centers for the arts in the 1950s. It's easy to see why artists were—and still are—attracted to this idyllic community, a cluster of New England–style sea captains' homes and small stores set on headlands overlooking the ocean.

At the height of the logging boom, Mendocino became an important port. Its population was about 3,500, and eight hotels were built, along with 17 saloons and more than a dozen bordellos. Today, it has only about 1,000 residents, most of whom reside at the north end of town. On summer weekends, the population seems more like 10,000, as hordes of tourists drive up from the Bay Area— but despite the crowds, Mendocino manages to retain its small-town charm.

ESSENTIALS

GETTING THERE   The fastest route from San Francisco is via U.S. 101 north to Cloverdale, then Calif. 128 west to Calif. 1, then north along the coast. It's about a 4-hour drive. The most scenic route from the Bay Area, if you have the time and your stomach doesn't mind the twists and turns, is to take Calif. 1 north along the coast the entire way; it's at least a 5- to 6-hour drive.

VISITOR INFORMATION   Stock up on brochures and maps at the **Fort Bragg/Mendocino Coast Chamber of Commerce,** 332 N. Main St., Fort Bragg (© 800/726-2780 or 707/961-6300; www.mendocinocoast.com). Pick up a copy of the center's monthly magazine, *Arts and Entertainment,* which lists upcoming events. It's available at numerous stores and cafes.

EXPLORING THE TOWN

Stroll through town, enjoy the architecture, and browse through the dozens of galleries and shops. Our favorites include the **Highlight Gallery,** 45052 Main St. (© 707/937-3132), for its handmade furniture, pottery, and other crafts; and the **Gallery Bookshop & Bookwinkle's Children's Books,** at Main and Kasten streets (© 707/937-2665), one of the best independent bookstores in Northern California. Another popular stop is **Mendocino Jams & Preserves,** 440 Main St. (© 707/937-1037), which offers free tastings of its locally made gourmet wares.

After exploring the town, walk out on the headlands that wrap around the town and constitute **Mendocino Headlands State Park.** (The visitor center is in Ford House on Main St.; ✆ 707/937-5397.) Three miles of trails wind through the park, giving visitors panoramic views of sea arches and hidden grottoes. If you're here at the right time of year, the area will be blanketed with wildflowers. The headlands are home to many unique species of birds, including black oystercatchers. Behind the Mendocino Presbyterian Church on Main Street is a trail leading to stairs that take you down to the beach, a small but picturesque stretch of sand where driftwood formations have washed ashore.

In town, stop by the **Mendocino Art Center,** 45200 Little Lake St. (✆ **707/ 937-5818;** www.mendocinoartcenter.org), the town's unofficial cultural headquarters. It's also known for its gardens, galleries, and shops that sell local crafts. Open daily from 10am to 5pm.

For a special treat, go to **Sweetwater Spa & Inn,** 955 Ukiah St. (✆ **800/ 300-4140** or 707/937-4140; www.sweetwaterspa.com), which offers group and private saunas and hot-tub soaks by the hour, along with massages. Reservations are recommended. Private tub prices are $10 per person per half hour; group prices are $8.50 per person with no time limit. Open Monday through Thursday from 1 to 10pm, Friday and Sunday from noon to 10pm, Saturday and holidays from noon to 11pm.

OUTDOOR PURSUITS

Explore the Big River by renting a canoe, kayak, or outrigger from **Catch a Canoe & Bicycles Too** (✆ 707/937-0273), located on the grounds of the Stanford Inn by the Sea (see "Where to Stay," below). If you're lucky, you'll see osprey, blue herons, harbor seals, deer, and wood ducks. These same folks will also rent you a mountain bike so you can head up Calif. 1 and explore the nearby state parks on two wheels.

Horseback riding on the beach and into the redwoods is offered by **Ricochet Ridge Ranch,** 24201 N. Calif. 1, Fort Bragg (✆ **888/873-5777** or 707/964-PONY; www.horse-vacation.com). Prices range from $40 for a 2-hour beach ride to $200 for an all-day trail ride.

In addition to Mendocino Headlands State Park (see "Exploring the Town," above), there are several other nearby state parks; all are within an easy drive or bike ride and make for a good day's outing. Information on all the parks' features, including maps, is found in a brochure called *Mendocino Coast State Parks,* available from the visitor center in Fort Bragg. These areas include **Manchester State Park,** located where the San Andreas Fault sweeps to the sea; **Jughandle State Reserve;** and **Van Damme State Park,** with an easily accessible beach.

Our favorite of these parks, located directly on Calif. 1 just north of Mendocino, is **Russian Gulch State Park** (✆ 707/937-5804). It's one of the region's most spectacular parks, where roaring waves crash against the cliffs that protect the coastal redwoods. The most popular attraction is the **Punch Bowl,** a collapsed sea cave that forms a tunnel through which waves crash, creating throaty echoes. Inland, there's a scenic paved bike path, and visitors can also hike along miles of trails. Admission is $2; camping costs $12. Call ✆ **800/444-7275** for reservations; for general state park information, call ✆ **707/937-5804** or visit www.cal-parks.ca.gov.

Deep-sea fishing charters are available from Fort Bragg's harbor, just a short distance up the coast.

WHERE TO STAY

Just south of town, the rustic but ever-so-sumptuous **Stanford Inn by the Sea,** N. Calif. 1 and Comptche Ukiah Road (© **800/331-8884** or 707/937-5615; www.stanfordinn.com), has captivating grounds, with tiers of elaborate gardens, a pond for ducks and geese, and fenced pastures containing horses, llamas, and gnarled old apple trees. There's a gorgeous solarium-style indoor hot tub and pool. Rooms offer down comforters, fresh flowers, fireplaces or stoves, stereos and VCRs, and private decks from which you can look out onto the Pacific. The inn has the only totally vegetarian restaurant on the Mendocino coast, a big hit with both guests and locals.

Less expensive is the small **Agate Cove Inn,** 11201 N. Lansing St. (© **800/ 527-3111** or 707/937-0551; www.agatecove.com), with a sweeping vista of the waves crashing onto the dramatic bluffs. All but one of the 10 spacious units have views of the ocean, down comforters, CD players, VCRs, fireplaces, and private decks.

Right in the heart of town, the **Mendocino Hotel & Garden Suites,** 45080 Main St. (© **800/548-0513** or 707/937-0511; www.mendocinohotel.com), was built in 1878 and evokes California's gold-rush days. Rooms feature hand-painted French porcelain sinks with floral designs, quaint wallpaper, old-fashioned beds and armoires, and photographs of historic Mendocino. About half are located in four handsome small buildings behind the main house. Many of the deluxe rooms have fireplaces.

The moderately priced **Joshua Grindle Inn,** 44800 Little Lake Rd. (© **800/ GRINDLE** or 707/937-4143; www.joshgrin.com), is housed in a stately 1879 Victorian with a wraparound porch and large emerald lawns. Another affordable Victorian B&B choice is the **Mendocino Village Inn,** 44860 Main St. (© **800/ 882-7029** or 707/937-0246; www.mendocinoinn.com). A garden of flowers, plants, and frog ponds fronts the large blue-and-white guesthouse, built in 1882 and later occupied by famed local artist Emmy Lou Packard.

In the nearby town of Albion is the modern, upscale **Albion River Inn and Restaurant,** N. Calif. 1 (© **800/479-7944** or 707/937-1919; www.albionriver inn.com), perched on a bluff some 90 feet above the Pacific. Most rooms have decks; all have ocean views, fireplaces, down comforters, fridges, and CD players. The restaurant serves up stellar cuisine and stellar views.

WHERE TO DINE

Café Beaujolais, 961 Ukiah St. (© **707/937-5614;** www.cafebeaujolais.com), is one of Mendocino's—if not Northern California's—top dining choices. The venerable French country-style tavern is set in a century-old house; rose-colored chandeliers add a burnish to the wood floors and the heavy oak tables adorned with flowers. On warm nights, request a table at the enclosed deck overlooking the gardens. The menu usually lists about five main courses, such as roast free-range duck with wild-huckleberry sauce.

Large but surprisingly cozy, the **955 Ukiah Street Restaurant,** 955 Ukiah St. (© **707/937-1955;** www.955restaurant.com), is accented with massive railway ties and vaulted ceilings. Ask for a window table overlooking the gardens. The cuisine is creative and reasonably priced, a worthy alternative to the perpetually booked Café Beaujolais next door.

The moderately priced **Bay View Café,** 45040 Main St. (© **707/937-4197**), is one of the most popular in town and serves a good breakfast. From the second-floor dining area, there's a sweeping view of the Pacific and faraway headlands.

You'll find a menu with Southwestern selections, a good array of sandwiches, and the fresh catch of the day.

Tote Fete Bakery (℗ 707/937-3140) has a wonderful little takeout booth at the corner of Albion and Lansing streets. We like the foil-wrapped barbecue chicken sandwiches, but the pizza, focaccia, and twice-baked potatoes are also good choices. Regardless of preference—beef, chicken, turkey, or veggie—burger lovers won't be let down at **Mendo Burgers** (℗ 707/937-1111), arguably the best burger joint on the north coast. Hidden behind the Mendocino Bakery and Café at 10483 Lansing St., it's a little hard to find, but well worth searching out.

THE AVENUE OF THE GIANTS & FERNDALE

From Fort Bragg, Calif. 1 continues north along the shoreline for about 30 miles before turning inland to Leggett and the Redwood Highway (U.S. 101), which runs north to Garberville. Six miles beyond Garberville, the **Avenue of the Giants** (Calif. 254) begins around Phillipsville. It's an alternate route that roughly parallels U.S. 101, and there are about a half dozen interchanges between the two roads if you don't want to drive the whole thing. This stretch of Calif. 254 is one of the most spectacular scenic routes in the West, cutting along the Eel River through the 51,000-acre **Humboldt Redwoods State Park** (℗ 707/946-2409; www.humboldtredwoods.org). The Avenue ends just south of Scotia; from here, it's only about 10 miles to the turnoff to Ferndale, about 5 miles west of U.S. 101. Since Redwoods National Park is so remote, we recommend this outing as a more convenient way to see California's majestic giants.

For more information or a detailed map of the area, go to the **Humboldt Redwoods State Park Visitor Center** in Weott (℗ 707/946-2263; www. humboldtredwoods.org), in the center of the Avenue of the Giants.

Thirty-three miles long, the Avenue of the Giants was left intact for sightseers when the freeway was built. The giants, of course, are the majestic coast redwoods (*Sequoia sempervirens*); more than 50,000 acres of them make up the most outstanding display in the redwood belt. Their rough-bark columns climb 100 feet or more without a branch and soar to a total height of more than 340 feet. With their immunity to insects and fire-resistant bark, they have survived for thousands of years.

The state park has three **campgrounds** with 248 campsites: Hidden Springs, half a mile south of Myers Flat; Burlington, 2 miles south of Weott, near park headquarters; and Albee Creek State Campground, 5 miles west of U.S. 101 on the Mattole Road north of Weott. You'll also come across picnic and swimming facilities, motels, resorts, restaurants, and numerous rest and parking areas.

A few miles north of Weott is **Founders Grove,** named in honor of those who established the Save the Redwoods League in 1918. Farther north, close to the end of the Avenue, stands the 950-year-old **Immortal Tree,** just north of Redcrest. Near Pepperwood at the end of the Avenue, the **Drury Trail** and the **Percy French Trail** are two good short hikes. The park itself is also good for mountain biking. Ask the rangers for details.

Near the southern entrance to the Avenue of the Giants is the **Benbow Inn,** 445 Lake Benbow Dr., Garberville (℗ 800/355-3301 or 707/923-2124; www. benbowinn.com), a National Historic Landmark overlooking the Eel River and surrounded by marvelous gardens. The sumptuous lobby has a huge fireplace surrounded by cushy sofas, grandfather clocks, and Oriental carpets. Rooms are tastefully decorated with period antiques; the deluxe units have fireplaces,

Jacuzzis, private entrances and patios, and VCRs. Bicycles are available, and beautiful Benbow Lake State Park is right out the front door. Complimentary afternoon tea and scones are served in the lobby at 4pm, hors d'oeuvres in the lounge at 5pm, and port wine at 9pm—all very proper, of course. The dramatic high-ceilinged dining room opens onto a spacious terrace.

The landmark village of **Ferndale,** beyond the Avenue of the Giants and west of U.S. 101, has many Victorian homes and storefronts (which include a smithy and a saddlery). Despite its unbearably cute shops, it is nonetheless a vital part of the northern coastal tourist circuit.

The small town has a number of artists in residence and is also home to one of California's oddest events, the **World Championship Great Arcata to Ferndale Cross-Country Kinetic Sculpture Race,** a bizarre 3-day event held every Memorial Day weekend. The race, which draws more than 10,000 spectators, is run over land and water in whimsically designed human-powered vehicles. Stop in at the museum at 780 Main St. if you want to see some race entries.

If you'd like to stay over in Ferndale, try the **Gingerbread Mansion,** 400 Berding St. (© **800/952-4136** or 707/786-4000; www.gingerbread-mansion. com), a beautiful antiques-filled Victorian built in 1899. Some of the large rooms have claw-foot tubs for two; others offer fireplaces.

4 The Monterey Peninsula & the Big Sur Coast

MONTEREY

Monterey was one of the West Coast's first European settlements, and the capital of California under the Spanish, Mexican, and American flags. A major whaling center in the 1800s, Monterey eventually became the sardine capital of the Western Hemisphere. By 1913, the boats were bringing in 25 tons of sardines a night to the 18 canneries. The gritty lives of the mostly working-class residents were captured by local hero John Steinbeck in his 1945 novel *Cannery Row.*

After the sardines disappeared, Monterey was forced to fish for tourist dollars, hence the array of boutiques, knickknack stores, and theme restaurants that now reside along the bay. The city's saving grace is its historic architecture, world-class aquarium, and beautiful Monterey Bay, where sea lions and otters still frolic in abundance. More important, Monterey is only a short drive from Pacific Grove, Carmel, Pebble Beach, and Big Sur, and the lodgings here are far less expensive, which makes it a great place to set up base while exploring the coast.

ESSENTIALS

GETTING THERE   By Plane   Monterey Peninsula Airport (© **831/648-7000**) is 3 miles east of Monterey on Calif. 68. Many area hotels offer free airport shuttle service. If you take a taxi, it will cost about $10 to $15 to get to a peninsula hotel.

By Car   The major routes into Monterey are Calif. 1 from the north (Santa Cruz) and south (Carmel and Big Sur), and Calif. 68 from the east, which connects with U.S. 101 (San Francisco).

VISITOR INFORMATION   The **Monterey Peninsula Visitors and Convention Bureau** (© **888/221-1010** or 831/649-1770; www.monterey.com) has two visitor centers: one in Maritime Museum at Custom House Plaza near Fisherman's Wharf, and the other at Lake El Estero on Camino El Estero. Both locations, open daily, offer good maps and free publications, including the magazine *Coast Weekly.*

GETTING AROUND   The free **Waterfront Area Visitor Express (WAVE)** operates from Memorial Day weekend to Labor Day and takes passengers to and from the aquarium and other waterfront attractions. Stops are located at many hotels and motels in Monterey and Pacific Grove. For further information call **Monterey Salinas Transit (℃ 831/899-2555).**

WHAT TO SEE & DO

The enormous **Monterey Bay Aquarium,** 886 Cannery Row (℃ 800/756-3737 or 831/648-4888; www.montereybayaquarium.org), is home to more than 350,000 marine animals and plants. One of the main exhibits is a three-story, 335,000-gallon tank with clear acrylic walls; inside, hundreds of leopard sharks, sardines, anchovies, and other fish play hide-and-seek in a towering kelp forest. The outstanding Outer Bay exhibit features yellowfin tuna, large green sea turtles, barracuda, sharks, very cool giant ocean sunfish, and schools of bonito. The Outer Bay's jellyfish exhibit is guaranteed to amaze, and kids will love Flippers, Flukes, and Fun, a learning area for families. Mysteries of the Deep is the largest collection of live deep-sea species in the world. Everyone falls in love with the playful sea otters, and there's a petting pool where you can touch living bat rays and handle sea stars. Admission is $18 for adults, $15 for students and seniors, and $7.95 for children 3 to 12. Avoid lines by calling the above numbers and ordering tickets in advance. Open daily from 10am to 6pm.

Fisherman's Wharf, at 99 Pacific St., is a wooden pier jam packed with gift shops, fish markets, and seafood restaurants. The natural surroundings are so beautiful that if you cast your view toward the bobbing boats and surfacing sea lions, you might not even notice the hordes of tourists around you. Grab some clam chowder in a sourdough bread bowl and find a perch along the pier. **Sam's Fishing Fleet,** 84 Fisherman's Wharf (℃ 800/427-2675 or 831/372-0577; www.samsfishingfleet.com), offers fishing excursions for cod, salmon, and whatever else is running, as well as seasonal whale-watching tours.

Kayaks can be rented from several outfitters for a spin around the bay. Contact **Monterey Bay Kayaks,** 693 Del Monte Ave. (℃ 800/649-5357 or 831/373-5357; www.montereykayaks.com), north of Fisherman's Wharf, which offers instruction as well as natural-history tours. Prices start at $55 for tours, $30 for rentals. For bikes and in-line skates as well as kayak tours and rentals, contact **Adventures by the Sea,** 299 Cannery Row (℃ 831/372-1807; www.adventuresbythesea.com). Bikes cost $6 per hour or $24 a day; kayaks are $30 per person; and skates are $12 for 2 hours. Adventures by the Sea has another location at 201 Alvarado Mall (℃ 831/648-7235), at the Doubletree Hotel.

Once the center for an industrial sardine-packing operation immortalized by John Steinbeck, **Cannery Row,** between David and Drake avenues (℃ 831/373-1902), is now a congested strip of tacky gift shops, overpriced seafood restaurants, and an overall parking nightmare. Curious tourists continue to visit Steinbeck's fabled area, and where there are tourists, there are capitalists.

The dozen or so historic buildings clustered around Fisherman's Wharf and the adjacent town collectively form the "Path of History," a tour that examines 1800s architecture and lifestyle (pick up a brochure detailing the route at the visitor center). Many of the buildings are a part of the **Monterey State Historic Park,** 20 Custom House Plaza (℃ 831/649-7118).

The Monterey area has become an increasingly important and acclaimed winemaking region. Stop by **A Taste of Monterey,** 700 Cannery Row (℃ 831/646-5446; www.tastemonterey.com), daily between 11am and 6pm, to learn

The Monterey Peninsula

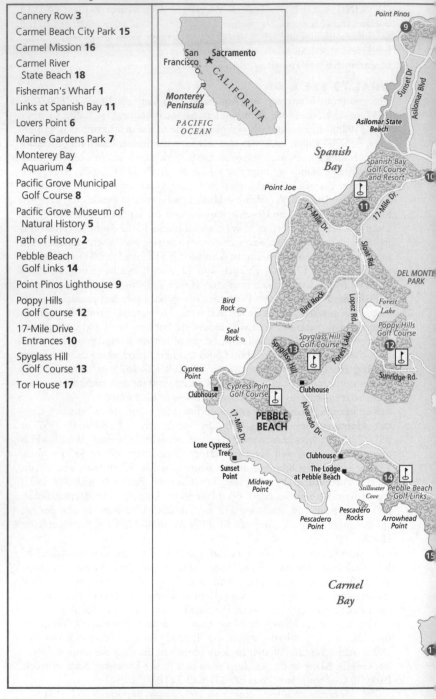

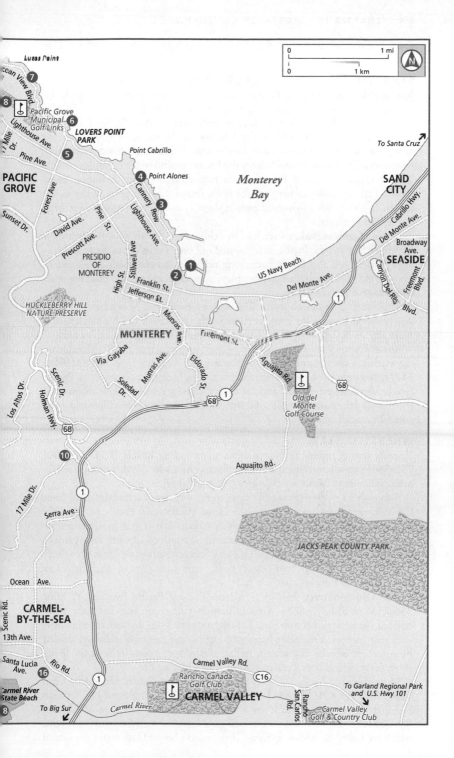

Lucas Point

Ocean View Blvd. ⑦

⑧ 🚏 Pacific Grove
Municipal
Golf Links ⑥

Lighthouse Ave.

LOVERS POINT
PARK

Pine Ave. ⑤

Point Cabrillo

17 Mile Dr.

Sunset Dr.

**PACIFIC
GROVE**

Forest Ave.

David Ave.

Prescott Ave.

Pine St.

Stillwell Ave.

④ Point Alones

③

Cannery Row

Lighthouse Ave.

**Monterey
Bay**

**SAND
CITY**

To Santa Cruz

Cabrillo Hwy.

Del Monte Ave.

Broadway
Ave.

SEASIDE

High St.

Franklin St.

Jefferson St.

② ①

US Navy Beach

Del Monte Ave.

Canyon Del Rey

Freemont Blvd.

Blvd.

PRESIDIO
OF
MONTEREY

HUCKLEBERRY HILL
NATURE PRESERVE

MONTEREY

Munras Ave.

Via Gayuba

Soledad Dr.

Munras Ave.

Eldorado St.

Freemont St.

Aguajito Rd.

🚏

Old del
Monte
Golf Course

⑥⑧

Los Altos Dr.

Scenic Dr.

Holman Hwy.

⑥⑧

⑩

Aguajito Rd.

JACKS PEAK COUNTY PARK

17 Mile Dr.

① 1

Serra Ave.

Ocean Ave.

**CARMEL-
BY-THE-SEA**

Scenic Rd.

13th Ave.

Santa Lucia
Ave.

⑯

Rio Rd.

① 1

Carmel River
State Beach

⑧

To Big Sur

Carmel Valley Rd.

Rancho Cañada
Golf Club

🚏

CARMEL VALLEY

Carmel River

C16

Rancho
San Carlos
Rd.

To Garland Regional Park
and U.S. Hwy 101

Carmel Valley
Golf & Country Club

0 ——————————— 1 mi
0 ——————————— 1 km

about and taste locally produced wines in front of huge bay-front windows. This is also the place to get a map and winery touring information.

STROLLING THROUGH NEARBY PACIFIC GROVE

Just next door to Monterey, Pacific Grove is a town to be strolled, so park the car, put on your walking shoes, and make an afternoon of it.

An excellent shorter alternative, or complement, to the 17-Mile Drive (see "Pebble Beach & the 17-Mile Drive," below) is the scenic drive or bike ride along Pacific Grove's **Ocean View Boulevard.** This coastal stretch starts near Monterey's Cannery Row and follows the Pacific around to the lighthouse point. Here it turns into Sunset Drive, which runs along secluded **Asilomar State Beach.** Park on Sunset and explore the trails, dunes, and tide pools of this sandy stretch of shore. You might find purple shore crabs, green anemone, sea bats, starfish, and limpets.

Marine Gardens Park, a stretch of shoreline along Ocean View Boulevard on Monterey Bay and the Pacific, is renowned not only for its ocean views and colorful flowers, but also for its fascinating tide-pool seaweed beds. Walk out to Lover's Point and watch the sea otters playing in the kelp beds and cracking open an occasional abalone for lunch.

Thousands of **monarch butterflies** migrate here from November to February, traveling from as far away as Alaska. Many settle in the Monarch Grove sanctuary, a eucalyptus stand on Grove Acre Avenue off Lighthouse Avenue.

Just as Ocean View Boulevard serves as an alternative to the 17-Mile Drive, the **Pacific Grove Municipal Golf Course,** 77 Asilomar Ave. (© **831/648-3177**), is a reasonably priced alternative to the high-priced courses at Pebble Beach. Views are panoramic, and the fairways and greens are better maintained than most semiprivate courses. Greens fees are $32 to $38. Optional carts cost $26.

WHERE TO STAY

If you're having trouble finding a vacancy, try calling **Resort II Me** (© **800/757-5646;** www.resort2me.com), a local reservations service that offers free recommendations of Monterey Bay–area hotels in all price ranges.

Although it's not waterfront (it's close to the wharf and across the street from the Monterey Conference Center), the **Hotel Pacific,** 300 Pacific St. (© **800/554-5542** or 831/373-5700; www.hotelpacific.com), is our favorite upscale choice in Monterey. Rooms are clustered around courtyards and gardens complete with spas and fountains. The cozy Southwestern-style suites have fluffy down comforters atop four-poster beds, terra-cotta floors, and fireplaces surrounded by cushy couches.

The **Old Monterey Inn,** 500 Martin St., off Pacific Avenue (© **800/350-2344** or 831/375-8284; www.oldmontereyinn.com), is an intimate, vine-covered, Tudor-style country inn. Though it's away from the surf, it's romantic, with rose gardens, a bubbling brook, and brick-and-flagstone walkways shaded by a panoply of oaks. Breakfast is stellar, and at 5pm guests retire to the living room for wine and hors d'oeuvres in front of a blazing fire.

In neighboring Pacific Grove is the opulent **Seven Gables Inn,** 555 Ocean View Blvd. (© **831/372-4341;** www.pginns.com), a compound of Victorian buildings constructed in 1886 by the Chase family (as in Chase Manhattan Bank). Everything here is luxurious and gilded, including the oceanview rooms, which are linked by verdant gardens. If the hotel's booked, ask about the Grand

View Inn, a slightly less ornate but comparable B&B next door that's run by the same owners.

Also in Pacific Grove is the affordable **Wilkies Inn,** 1038 Lighthouse Ave. (© 866/372-5960 or 831/372-5960), a motel offering great value and service.

For affordable choices in Monterey itself, you might opt for a motel. Some reliable options are **Motel 6** (© 800/4-MOTEL6), **Super 8** (© 800/800-8000), or **Best Western** (© 800/528-1234). **The Cypress Tree Inn,** 2227 N. Fremont St. (© 800/446-8303 or 831/372-7586; www.cypresstreeinn.com), is 2 miles from downtown, but the large rooms are spotless and there's a hot tub and coin-op laundry.

WHERE TO DINE

A historic 1833 adobe house has been converted into **Stokes Restaurant and Bar,** 500 Hartnell St., at Madison Street (© 831/373-1110; www.stokesadobe. com). The rustic yet stylish interior is the perfect showcase for chef Brandon Miller's carefully crafted California-Mediterranean fare.

The enormous dining room at **Montrio,** 414 Calle Principal, at Franklin (© 831/648-8880; www.montrio.com), is definitely the sharpest in town, awash with the buzz of well-dressed diners. Enjoy crispy Dungeness crab cakes with spicy rémoulade, or succulent grilled pork chops with apple, pear, and currant compôte.

On sunny afternoons, patrons at **Tarpy's Roadhouse,** 2999 Monterey-Salinas Hwy., at Calif. 68 and Canyon del Rey near the airport (© 831/647-1444; www.tarpys.com), relax under umbrellas on the huge outdoor patio, sipping margaritas and munching on Tarpy's legendary Caesar salad. Come nightfall, the place fills quickly with tourists and locals who pile in for the hefty plate of bourbon-molasses pork chops or Dijon-crusted lamb loin, all moderately priced.

If you want to take in the views at Fisherman's Wharf, avoid the many tourist traps overcharging for mediocre food. Stick with **Cafe Fina,** 47 Fisherman's Wharf (© 831/372-5200; www.cafefina.com), and the **Wharfside Restaurant & Lounge,** 60 Fisherman's Wharf (© 831/375-3956).

In nearby Pacific Grove, **Joe Rombi's,** 208 17th St. (© 831/373-2416; www. joerombis.com), offers an intimate dining room and very fresh Italian cuisine (pastas are made that day). At **Fandango,** 223 17th St. (© 831/372-3456; www.fandangorestaurant.com), provincial Mediterranean specialties from Spain to Greece to North Africa spice up the menu. The five upstairs and downstairs dining rooms have roaring fires, wood tables, and antiqued walls. There's an award-winning international wine list. The **Fishwife at Asilomar Beach,** 1996½ Sunset Dr. (© 831/375-7107; www.fishwife.com), is a casual, affordable, family-friendly spot offering terrific seafood.

PEBBLE BEACH & THE 17-MILE DRIVE

Pebble Beach is a world unto itself, a pricey, elite golfers' paradise where endless grassy fairways are interrupted only by a few luxury resorts and cliffs where the ocean meets the land.

But even if you can't afford to stay here, come and check out the beautiful **17-Mile Drive** (which is also a great bike ride). You'll have to fork over $8 to enter the drive, but you'll get to see some of the most exclusive coastal real estate in California. The drive can be entered from any of five gates: two from Pacific Grove to the north, one from Carmel to the south, or two from Monterey to the east. The most convenient entrance from Calif. 1 is just off the main road at the

Holman Highway exit. You may beat traffic by entering at the Carmel Gate and doing the tour backward.

Admission to the drive includes an informative map that lists 26 points of interest along the way. Aside from homes of the ultra-rich, highlights include **Seal and Bird Rocks,** where you can see countless gulls, cormorants, and other offshore birds as well as seals and sea lions; and **Cypress Point Lookout,** which gives you a 20-mile view all the way to the Big Sur Lighthouse on a clear day. Also visible is the famous **Lone Cypress** tree, inspiration to so many artists and photographers, which you can admire from afar but to which you can no longer walk. The drive also traverses the **Del Monte Forest,** thick with tame blacktail deer and often described as a "billionaire's private game preserve."

Pebble Beach is synonymous with golf; guests of the posh resorts get first crack at preferred tee times. The most famous of all is the **Pebble Beach Golf Links** (© 800/654-9300), at the Lodge at Pebble Beach (see below). It's home in winter to the AT&T Pebble Beach National Pro-Am. Jack Nicklaus has claimed, "If I could play only one course for the rest of my life, this would be it." Built in 1919, this 18-hole course is 6,799 yards and par 72; it's precariously perched over a rugged ocean. Greens fees are a staggering $350, plus cart fee.

Also frequented by celebrities is the **Spyglass Hill Golf Course,** at Stevenson Drive and Spyglass Hill Road (© 800/654-9300), one of the toughest courses in California. It's a justifiably famous links: 6,859 yards and par 72 with five oceanfront holes. Greens fees are $260, plus cart. Reservations for nonguests should be made a month in advance.

Poppy Hills (© 831/625-2035), an 18-hole, 6,219-yard course designed by Robert Trent Jones, Jr., on the 17-Mile Drive, was named one of the world's top 20 by *Golf Digest.* Greens fees are $125 to $150, plus $30 cart rental. You can make reservations 30 days in advance.

Lying on the north end of 17-Mile Drive at the Pebble Beach Resort and Inn at Spanish Bay, the **Links at Spanish Bay** (© 800/654-9300) is the most easily booked course and perhaps the most challenging. Robert Trent Jones, Jr., Tom Watson, and Frank Tatum designed it to duplicate a Scottish links course. Greens fees are $215. Cart rental is an additional $25. Reservations can be made 60 days in advance.

The **Del Monte Golf Course,** 1300 Sylvan Rd. (© 831/373-2700), is the oldest course west of the Mississippi, charging some of the most "reasonable" greens fees: $95 per player, plus a cart rental of $20. The course, often cited in magazines for its "grace and charm," is relatively short—only 6,339 yards. This seldom-advertised course, which is at the Hyatt east of Monterey, is part of the Pebble Beach complex, but is not along 17-Mile Drive.

WHERE TO STAY & DINE

The **Inn at Spanish Bay,** 2700 17-Mile Dr. (© 800/654-9300 or 831/647-7500; www.pebblebeach.com), surrounded by its world-renowned golf course, is a plush, super-expensive low-rise set on 236 manicured acres. Half the rooms face the ocean and are more expensive than their counterparts, which overlook the forest. Each spacious unit has a fireplace, four-poster bed with down comforter, and deck or patio. Roy Yamaguchi, Hawaii's celebrity chef, offers a Eurasian menu at Roy's, the best restaurant in Pebble Beach. A bagpiper strolls the terrace at dusk. Guests enjoy eight tennis courts, pro shops, a superb fitness center, an equestrian center, and a heated pool.

For the combined cost of greens fees and a room at the **Lodge at Pebble Beach,** 1700 17-Mile Dr. (© 800/654-9300 or 831/624-3811; www.pebblebeach.com), you could easily create a professional putting green in your own backyard. But if you're a dedicated hacker, you've got to play here at least once. Your ultra-plush room will have every conceivable amenity, including a wood-burning fireplace. Amenities include 12 tennis courts, a fitness room, horseback riding, a pool, and hiking trails.

CARMEL-BY-THE-SEA

Once a bohemian artists' village, Carmel is today an adorable (albeit touristy) town that knows how to celebrate its surroundings. Vibrant wildflower gardens flourish along each residential street, and gnarled cypress trees reach up from white sandy beaches. It's still intimate enough that there's no need for street numbers. But a few hints such as Saks Fifth Avenue, intolerable traffic, and lofty B&B rates indicate we're not in Kansas anymore, but rather a well-preserved upscale tourist haven. If the prices here are too high, you can easily stay in nearby Monterey or Pacific Grove.

The **Carmel Business Association** (© 831/624-2522) is on Scan Carlos Street between Fifth and Sixth aves. Pick up a copy of the *Guide to Carmel* and a schedule of local events. Hours are Monday through Friday from 9am to 5pm. On weekends, an information booth is set up from 11am to 3pm at Carmel Plaza, on Ocean Avenue between Junipero and San Carlos.

EXPLORING THE TOWN

A wonderful stretch of white sand backed by cypress trees, **Carmel Beach City Park** is a wee bit o' heaven (although the jammed parking lot can feel more like a visit to a car rally). There's plenty of room for families, surfers, and dogs with their owners (pooches are allowed to run off-leash here). If the parking lot is full, there are some spaces on Ocean Avenue, but take heed: They're generally good for 90-minute parking only. Farther south around the promontory, **Carmel River State Beach** is a less crowded option, with white sand and dunes, plus a bird sanctuary.

If the tourists aren't lying on the beach, then they're probably shopping. This small town packs in more than 500 boutiques and a veritable cornucopia of art galleries. Most of the commercial action is along the small stretch of Ocean Avenue between Junipero and San Antonio.

The **Mission San Carlos Borromeo del Rio Carmelo,** on Basilica Rio Road at Lasuen Drive, off Calif. 1 (© 831/624-3600; www.carmelmission.org), is the burial ground of Father Junípero Serra and the second oldest of the 21 Spanish missions he established. The stone church, with its gracefully curving walls and Moorish bell tower, was begun in 1793. The old mission kitchen, the first library in California, the high altar, and the flower gardens are all worth visiting. More than 3,000 Native Americans are buried in the adjacent cemetery; their graves are decorated with seashells. The mission is open June through August, Monday through Saturday from 9:30am to 7:30pm, Sunday from 10:30am to 7:30pm; in other months, Monday through Saturday from 9:30am to 4:30pm, Sunday from 10:30am to 4:30pm. A $2 donation is requested.

WHERE TO STAY

The pricey, intimate **Carriage House Inn,** Junipero Street, between Seventh and Eighth avenues (© 800/433-4732 or 831/625-2585; www.ibts-carriage house.com), offers a luxurious atmosphere and lots of pampering in the heart of "downtown." Each room comes with a VCR, fireplace, fridge, and king-size bed with down comforter. While most other choices in town are of the frill-and-lace variety, the Carriage House has a more mature, formal, yet cozy ambience.

If you want to stay a bit off the beaten track, consider **Mission Ranch,** 26270 Dolores St. (© **800/538-8221** or 831/624-6436), a converted 1850s dairy farm that was purchased and restored by Clint Eastwood. The accommodations are scattered amid different structures, both old and new, and surrounded by wetlands and grazing sheep. As befits a ranch, rooms are decorated in a provincial style, with carved wooden beds bedecked with handmade quilts. Most are equipped with whirlpool baths, fireplaces, and decks or patios. The restaurant is terrific (see below).

Inland from Carmel, in sunny Carmel Valley, is the super-plush, super-expensive **Quail Lodge Resort and Golf Club,** 8205 Valley Greens Dr. (© **888/828-8787** or 831/624-2888; www.quaillodge.com). Lying in the foothills of the Santa Lucia Range, Quail Lodge is set on 850 acres of sparkling lakes, secluded woodlands, and rolling meadows. Rooms have balconies or terraces; some have fireplaces and wet bars. Guests enjoy an excellent 18-hole golf course, four tennis courts, a full-service spa, and hiking and jogging trails.

Back in Carmel itself, more moderately priced choices (for Carmel, anyway) include the **Normandy Inn,** Ocean Avenue, between Monte Verde and Casanova streets (© **800/343-3825** or 831/624-3825; www.normandyinncarmel.com), 3 blocks from the beach. Rooms show their age a little, but are well appointed with French country decor and down comforters. The tiny heated pool is banked by a sweet flower garden. The three large family-style units are an especially good deal.

The **Cobblestone Inn,** on Junipero Street, between Seventh and Eighth avenues, 1½ blocks from Ocean Avenue (© **800/833-8836** or 831/625-5222; www.foursisters.com), is flowery, well kept, and cute, with hand-stenciled wall decorations and an abundance of teddy bears. Rooms vary in size; some can be small, and most have showers only, but the largest units include a wet bar, sofa, and separate bedroom.

A flower garden welcomes visitors to the **Sandpiper Inn by the Sea,** 2408 Bay View Ave. (© **800/633-6433** or 831/624-6433; www.sandpiper-inn.com), a quiet, midscale standby that's been in business for more than 60 years. Rooms are decorated with handsome country antiques and fresh flowers, and Carmel's white-sand beaches are a mere 100 yards away.

The **Carmel Sands Lodge,** San Carlos and Fifth streets (© **800/252-1255** or 831/624-1255; www.carmelsandslodge.com), and the **Carmel Village Inn,** Ocean Avenue and Junipero Street (© **800/346-3864** or 831/624-3864; www.carmelvillageinn.com), are both well-maintained motor lodges with excellent locations. If you're traveling with Fido, your best bet is the **Cypress Inn,** Lincoln and Seventh (© **800/443-7443** or 831/624-3871; www.cypress-inn.com), a moderately priced option run by actress Doris Day.

WHERE TO DINE

Though you may not spot owner Clint Eastwood, the **Restaurant at Mission Ranch,** 26270 Dolores St. (© **831/625-9040**), delivers quality food and a merry atmosphere. Large windows accentuate the view of the marshlands and bay beyond. At happy hour, you'll find some of the cheapest drinks around (and Clint often stops by when he's in town). Prime rib with twice-baked potato and vegetables is the favored dish. At the piano bar, locals and tourists croon their favorites. The Sunday buffet brunch with live jazz piano is hugely popular.

Dark and romantic, the moderately priced **Flying Fish Grill,** in Carmel Plaza, Mission Street between Ocean and Seventh avenues (© **831/625-1962**), features fresh seafood with exquisite Japanese accents. Prepare for seriously sensational main courses, like a savory fare peppered ahi, blackened and served with mustard-and-sesame-soy vinaigrette and angel hair pasta.

Il Fornaio, Ocean Avenue at Monte Verde (© **831/622-5100**), offers a great selection of salads, pastas, pizzas, and rotisserie chicken, duck, and rabbit fresh from the brick oven. Start with the decadent grilled polenta with sautéed wild mushrooms, provolone, and Italian truffle oil. The airy dining room and sunny terrace offer charming atmosphere.

The food and the festive atmosphere at the **Rio Grill,** in the Crossroads Shopping Center, 101 Crossroads Blvd. (© **831/625-5436;** www.riogrill.com), have won over even the locals. The whimsical Santa Fe–style dining room belies the kitchen's serious preparations, which include homemade soups; a rich quesadilla with almonds, cheeses, and smoked-tomato salsa; and barbecued baby back ribs from a wood-burning oven.

BIG SUR

Though there is an actual Big Sur Village approximately 25 miles south of Carmel, "Big Sur" refers to the entire 90-mile stretch of coastline between Carmel and San Simeon, blessed on one side by the majestic Santa Lucia Range and on the other by the rocky Pacific coastline. It's one of the most romantic and relaxing places on earth, often misty and mysterious, and if you need respite from the rat race, we can recommend no better place.

Contact the **Big Sur Chamber of Commerce** (© **831/667-2100;** www.bigsurcalifornia.org) for specialized information on places and events in Big Sur.

Most of this stretch is state park, and Calif. 1 runs its entire length, hugging the ocean the whole way. Restaurants, hotels, and sights are easy to spot—most are situated directly on the highway—but without major towns as reference points, their addresses can be obscure. For the purposes of orientation, we'll use the River Inn as our mileage guide. Located 29 miles south of Monterey on Calif. 1, the inn is generally considered to mark the northern end of Big Sur.

EXPLORING THE BIG SUR COAST

Big Sur offers visitors tranquility and natural beauty—ideal for hiking, picnicking, camping, fishing, and beachcombing. The inland **Ventana Wilderness,** maintained by the U.S. Forest Service, contains 167,323 acres straddling the Santa Lucia mountains and is characterized by steep-sided ridges separated by V-shaped valleys. The streams that cascade through the area are marked by waterfalls, deep pools, and thermal springs. The wilderness offers 237 miles of hiking trails that lead to 55 designated trail camps—a backpacker's paradise. One of the easiest trails to access is the **Pine Ridge Trail** at Big Sur station (© **831/667-2315**).

From Carmel, the first stop along Calif. 1 is **Point Lobos State Reserve** (© **831/624-4909;** www.pt-lobos.parks.state.ca.us), 3 miles south of Carmel. Sea lions, harbor seals, sea otters, and thousands of seabirds reside in this 1,276-acre reserve. Between December and May, you can also spot migrating California gray whales just offshore. Trails follow the shoreline and lead to hidden coves. Parking is limited; on weekends especially, arrive early.

From here, cross the Soberanes Creek, passing **Garrapata State Park** (© **831/624-4909**), a 2,879-acre preserve with 4 miles of coastline. It's unmarked and undeveloped, though the trails are maintained. To explore them, you'll need to park at one of the turnouts on Calif. 1 near Soberanes Point and hike in.

Ten miles south of Carmel, you'll arrive at North Abalone Cove. From here, Palo Colorado Road leads back into the wilderness to the first of the Forest

Service camping areas at **Bottchers Gap** (℅ 805/434-9199). It costs $12 to camp, $5 to park overnight.

Continuing south, about 13 miles from Carmel, you'll cross the **Bixby Bridge** and see the **Point Sur Lighthouse** off in the distance. The Bixby Bridge, one of the world's highest single-span concrete bridges, towers nearly 270 feet above Bixby Creek Canyon, and offers gorgeous canyon and ocean views from several observation alcoves at regular intervals along the bridge. The lighthouse, which sits 361 feet above the surf on a volcanic rock promontory, was built in 1889, when only a horse trail provided access to this part of the world. Lighthouse tours, which take 2 to 3 hours and involve a steep half-mile hike, are scheduled on most weekends. For information call ℅ 831/625-4419 or go to www.lighthouse-pointsur-ca.org. Admission is $5 for adults, $3 for youths 13 to 18, and $2 for children 5 to 12.

About 3 miles south of the lighthouse is **Andrew Molera State Park** (℅ 831/667-2315), which is much less crowded than Pfeiffer–Big Sur (see below). Miles of trails meander through meadows and along beaches and bluffs. **Molera Big Sur Trail Rides** (℅ 800/942-5486 or 831/625-5486; www.molerahorseback tours.com) offers coastal trail rides for riders of all levels of experience. The 2½-mile-long beach is accessible via a mile-long path flanked in spring by wildflowers and offers excellent tide-pooling. The park also has campgrounds.

Back on Calif. 1, you'll soon reach the village of Big Sur, where commercial services are available.

About 26 miles south of Carmel you'll come to **Big Sur Station** (℅ 831/667-2315), where you can pick up maps and other information about the region. It's located a quarter mile past the entrance to **Pfeiffer–Big Sur State Park** (℅ 831/667-2315), an 810-acre park that offers 218 camping sites along the Big Sur River (℅ 800/444-7275 for camping reservations), picnicking, fishing, and hiking. It's a scenic park of redwoods, conifers, oaks, and open meadows, but often gets crowded. Admission to the park is $5 per car, and it's open daily from dawn to dusk.

A mile south of the entrance to Pfeiffer–Big Sur State Park is the turnoff to Sycamore Canyon Road (unmarked), which will take you 2 winding miles down to beautiful **Pfeiffer Beach,** a great place to soak in the sun on the wide expanse of golden sand. It's open for day use only, there's no fee, and it's the only beach accessible by car (but not motor homes).

Back on Calif. 1, the road travels 11 miles past Sea Lion Cove to Julia Pfeiffer Burns State Park. High above the ocean is the famous **Nepenthe** restaurant (see "Where to Dine," below), the retreat bought by Orson Welles for Rita Hayworth in 1944. A few miles farther south is the **Coast Gallery** (℅ 831/667-2301), which shows lithographs of works by Henry Miller. The gallery's casual Coast Cafe offers simple serve-yourself lunches of soup, sandwiches, baked goods, and coffee drinks. Miller fans will also want to stop at the **Henry Miller Memorial Library** (℅ 831/667-2574; www.henrymiller.org) on Calif. 1, 30 miles south of Carmel and a quarter mile south of Nepenthe restaurant. The library displays and sells books and artwork by Miller and houses a permanent collection of first editions. Admission is free; hours are Wednesday through Monday from 11am to 6pm.

Julia Pfeiffer Burns State Park (℅ 831/667-2315) encompasses some of Big Sur's most spectacular coastline. To get a closer look, take the trail from the parking area at McWay Canyon, which leads under the highway to a bluff overlooking 80-foot-high McWay Waterfall dropping directly into the ocean. It's less crowded here than at Pfeiffer–Big Sur, and there are miles of trails to explore in the 3,580-acre park.

From here, the road skirts the Ventana Wilderness, passing Anderson and Marble Peaks and the Esalen Institute, before crossing the Big Creek Bridge to Lucia and several campgrounds farther south. **Kirk Creek Campground,** about 3 miles north of Pacific Valley, offers camping with ocean views and beach access. Beyond Pacific Valley, the **Sand Dollar Beach** picnic area is a good place to stop and enjoy the coastal view and take a stroll. Two miles south of Sand Dollar is **Jade Cove,** a popular spot for rockhounds. From here, it's about another 27 miles past the Piedras Blancas Light Station to San Simeon.

WHERE TO CAMP

Big Sur is one of the most spectacular places in the state for camping. One of the most glorious settings can be found at **Pfeiffer–Big Sur State Park,** on Calif. 1, 26 miles south of Carmel (© 831/667-2315), with hundreds of secluded sites in the redwood forest. Hiking trails, streams, and the river are steps away from your sleeping bag, and the most modern amenities are the 25¢ showers. Water faucets are located between sites, and each spot has its own picnic table and fire pit. There are, however, no RV hookups or electricity. At the entrance are a store, gift shop, restaurant, and cafe. Fees are $12 for regular sites, $26 for group sites. Dogs are permitted ($1 per night extra). Call 800/444-7275 or go to www.reserveamerica.com for reservations.

The entrance to **Ventana Campground,** Calif. 1, 28 miles south of Carmel, 4 miles south of the River Inn (© 831/667-2712; www.ventanabigsur.com), is adjacent to the entrance of the resort of the same name, but the comparison stops there. This is pure rusticity. The 75 campsites, on 40 acres of a redwood canyon, are set along a hillside and spaced well apart for privacy. Each is shaded by towering trees and has a picnic table and fire ring, but offers no electricity, RV hookups, or river access. There are, however, three bathhouses with hot showers (25¢). Rates are $25 for a site for two with one vehicle, $35 on weekends. It'll cost $5 to bring Fido. Open April through October. Call ahead to reserve a space.

The sites at the **Big Sur Campground and Cabins,** Calif. 1, 26 miles south of Carmel, half a mile south of the River Inn (© 831/667-2322), are cramped, so the feel is more like a camping village than an intimate retreat. However, it's well maintained and perfect for families, who love the playground, river swimming, and inner-tube rentals. Each campsite has its own fire pit, picnic table, and freshwater faucet within 25 feet of the pitching area. RV water and electric hookups are available. Facilities include bathhouses with showers, laundry, an aged volleyball/basketball court, and a grocery store. There are 81 tent sites (30 RV-ready with electricity and water hookups), plus 13 cabins (all with showers). The cabins are absolutely adorable, with country furnishings, wood-burning ovens, patios, and full kitchens. Rates are $26 for a tent site for two or an RV hookup (plus $3 extra for electricity and water), $48 for a tent cabin (bed, but no heat or plumbing), or $93 to $187 for a cabin for two. Pets cost $4 for campsites and $12 for tent cabins; pets are not allowed in the other cabins.

WHERE TO STAY

Only a handful of Big Sur's accommodations offer the kind of pampering and luxury you'd expect in a fine urban hotel; even direct-dial phones and TVs (often considered gauche in these parts) are rare. Big Sur hotels are especially busy in summer, when advance reservations are required. If you're having trouble securing a room or a site, contact the **Chamber of Commerce** (© 831/667-2100; www.bigsurcalifornia.org) for other options.

In a class by itself is the incredibly expensive **Post Ranch Inn,** on Calif. 1 (© **800/527-2200** or 831/667-2200; www.postranchinn.com), one of our very favorite places to stay on the planet. Perched on 98 acres of pristine seaside ridges 1,200 feet above the Pacific, the wood-and-glass cottages are built around existing trees—some are elevated on stilts to avoid damaging native redwood root structures—and the ultra-private Ocean and Coast cottages are so close to the edge of the earth that you get the impression you've joined the clouds. Each room has a fireplace, terrace, massage table, CD player, and wet bar filled with complimentary goodies. There's also a small workout room, the best Jacuzzi we've ever encountered (it's on a cliff and seems to join the sky), a mediocre pool, spa services, and sun decks. The only drawback is that the vibe can be stuffy, which is due more to the clientele than the staff. The Sierra Mar restaurant is open to the public nightly for dinner. It's one of the best (and most expensive) dining choices in the area.

Equally as expensive, but perhaps not delivering quite as much for your money, is the luxuriously rustic **Ventana Inn and Spa,** Calif. 1 (© **800/ 628-6500** or 831/667-2331; www.ventanainn.com). Located on 243 mountainous oceanfront acres, Ventana has an elegance that's atypical of the region, and continually attracts famous guests. The accommodations, in one- and two-story, natural-wood buildings along winding, wildflower-flanked paths, blend in with the magical Big Sur countryside. Rooms are divinely decorated in warm, cozy luxury, with such amenities as VCRs, fridges, and terraces or balconies overlooking the ocean or forest. Most offer fireplaces, and some have hot tubs and cathedral ceilings. A small fitness center offers the basics—but you'll be more inspired to hike the grounds, where you'll not only find plenty of pastoral respite, but also a pool, a rustic library, and clothing-optional tanning decks and spa tubs.

Affordable choices include the family-friendly **Big Sur Lodge,** in Pfeiffer–Big Sur State Park, Calif. 1, 26 miles south of Carmel (© **800/424-4787** or 831/ 667-3100; www.bigsurlodge.com). The rustic motel-style cabins are huge, clean, and heated. Some have fireplaces or kitchenettes. All offer porches or decks with views of the redwoods or the Santa Lucia Range. In addition, the lodge has its own pool, grocery store, and laundry facilities.

Deetjen's Big Sur Inn, Calif. 1 (© **831/667-2377;** www.deetjens.com), is affordable and very cute. Folks either love or hate the accommodations, which are set in a redwood canyon. They're rustic and adorable with their old-fashioned furnishings and down-home feel. But those who want extensive creature comforts should go elsewhere. Rooms are far from soundproof, so children under 12 are allowed only if families reserve both rooms of a two-room building; and not all of the units have private bathrooms. There's no insulation, so prepare to crank up the fire or wood-burning stove. The cabins near the river offer the most privacy. The restaurant is a local favorite (see below).

WHERE TO DINE
Cielo Restaurant, at the Ventana Inn and Spa (© 831/667-4242), is woodsy but extravagant. The airy cedar interior is divided into two spaces: the lounge, where a wooden bar and cocktail tables look onto a roaring fire and through

picturesque windows; and the dining room, which overlooks the mountains and ocean. But in summer it's the patio, with its views of the Big Sur coast, that's the coveted spot. Lunch offers sandwiches, burgers, and an array of gourmet salads; dinner includes stellar starters and main courses such as seared ahi tuna or roasted duck breast with hazelnut risotto.

Stop by **Nepenthe,** on Calif. 1, 28 miles south of Carmel, 5 miles south of the River Inn (© **831/667-2345;** www.nepenthebigsur.com), for the outrageous views. Sitting 808 feet above sea level along the cliffs overlooking the ocean, Nepenthe is naturally celestial. On a warm day, join the crowds on the terrace. On colder days, go the indoor route—the redwood-and-adobe structure offers an equally magical view, and with its fireplace, redwood ceilings, and bayfront windows, the atmosphere is something you can't find anywhere else. Unfortunately, that's not been our experience with the overpriced fare, so just come for lunch and spend big dinner bucks elsewhere.

One level below Nepenthe, **Café Kevah** (© **831/667-2344**) offers the same celestial view (at a fraction of the price), a more casual environment, and better food. Seating is entirely outdoors—a downside when the biting fog rolls in (bring a jacket), but perfect on a clear day. Fare here is more eclectic than Nepenthe's, with such choices as homemade granola, baby greens with broiled salmon and papaya, chicken brochettes, and new-potato hash.

The **Big Sur River Inn,** on Calif 1, 2 miles north of Pfeiffer–Big Sur State Park (© **831/667-2700;** www.bigsurriverinn.com), is an unpretentious, rustic, down-home restaurant that's got something for all tastes. In winter, the wooden dining room is the prime spot; on summer days, some folks grab their patio chair and a cocktail and hang out literally midstream. Along with the local color, attractions include a full bar and good ol' American fare.

With the feel of an English farmhouse, **Deetjen's Big Sur Inn Restaurant,** on Calif. 1 (© **831/667-2378**), is the perfect venue for delicious comfort food and friendly service, including great breakfasts.

The **Big Sur Bakery and Restaurant,** on Calif. 1, just past the post office and a mile south of Pfeiffer–Big Sur State Park (© **831/667-0520**), offers healthy fare, ranging from wood-fired pizzas and portobello burgers at lunch to salmon, tuna, and chicken selections at dinner. Pastries are baked on the premises. It's open daily from 8am to 10pm, but closes early on Mondays.

5 San Simeon: Hearst Castle

Few places on earth compare to Hearst Castle. The 165-room estate of publishing magnate William Randolph Hearst, situated high above the coastal village of San Simeon, is an ego trip par excellence. One of the last great estates of America's Gilded Age, it's an astounding, completely over-the-top monument to wealth—and to the power that money brings.

Hearst Castle is a sprawling compound, constructed over 28 years in a Mediterranean Revival architectural style, set in undeniably magical surroundings. The focal point of the estate is the you-have-to-see-it-to-believe-it Casa Grande, a 100-plus-room mansion brimming with priceless art and antiques. Hearst acquired most of his vast European collection via New York auction houses, where he bought entire rooms (including walls, ceilings, and floors) and shipped them here. Each week, railroad cars carrying fragments of Roman temples, lavish doors and carved ceilings from Italian monasteries, Flemish tapestries, ancient Persian rugs, and antique French furniture arrived—5 tons at a time—in San Simeon. The result is an old-world castle done in a priceless mix-and-match style.

Three opulent "guesthouses" also contain magnificent works of art. A lavish private movie theater was used to screen first-run films twice nightly—once for employees, and again for the guests and host. The ranch soon became a playground for the Hollywood crowd as well as dignitaries like Winston Churchill and George Bernard Shaw, who is said to have wryly remarked of the estate, "This is the way God would have done it if He had the money."

And then there are the swimming pools. The Roman-inspired indoor pool has intricate mosaic work, Carrara-marble replicas of Greek gods and goddesses, and alabaster globe lamps that create the illusion of moonlight. The breathtaking outdoor Greco-Roman Neptune pool, flanked by marble colonnades that frame the distant sea, is one of the mansion's most memorable features.

TOURING THE ESTATE

Hearst Castle can be visited only by guided tours, which are conducted daily beginning at 8:20am, except on New Year's Day, Thanksgiving, and Christmas. Two to six tours leave every hour, depending on the season. Allow 2 hours between starting times if you plan on taking more than one tour. Reservations are recommended and can be made up to 8 weeks in advance. Tickets can be purchased by phone through **California Reservations** (© **800/444-4445**). Daytime tours are $10 for adults, $5 for children 6 to 12. Evening tours are $20 for adults, $10 for children 6 to 12. Four distinct daytime tours are offered on a daily basis, each lasting almost 2 hours.

Tour 1 is recommended for first-time visitors and is the first to get booked up. In addition to the swimming pools, this tour visits several rooms on the ground floor of Casa Grande, including Hearst's private theater, where you'll see some home movies taken during the castle's heyday. You'll get to see the sculpture and flowers in the gardens and the formal esplanade, as well as the largest guesthouse, Casa del Sol.

Tour 2 focuses on Casa Grande's upper floors, including Hearst's opulent library, private suite of rooms, and lots of fabulous bathrooms. Ongoing efforts are made to lend a lived-in look to the house. Though Tour 1 is commonly recommended for first-timers, Tour 2 is a perfectly fine choice if your interest lies more in the home's private areas.

Tour 3 delves into the complex construction and subsequent alterations of Hearst Castle. You'll visit Casa del Monte, a guesthouse unaltered from its original design, then head to the North Wing of Casa Grande, the last portion of the property to be completed, to see the contrast in styles. Tour 3 is best for architecture buffs and detail hounds, not for first-timers.

Tour 4 is dedicated to the estate's gardens, terraces, and walkways, and is offered from April to October only. You'll tour the Casa del Mar guesthouse, the wine cellar of Casa Grande, and the colorful dressing rooms at the Neptune Pool. Like Tour 3, this one is best taken after you've seen some of the more essential areas of the estate.

Evening tours are held most Friday and Saturday nights during spring and fall. They last about 30 minutes longer than the daytime tours and visit highlights of the main house, the largest and most elaborate guesthouse, and the estate's pools and gardens, illuminated by hundreds of restored light fixtures. The pools in particular are most breathtaking when seen this way.

Tip: Because these are walking tours, be sure to wear comfortable shoes—you'll be walking about a half mile per tour, which includes between 150 and

400 steps to climb or descend. (Wheelchair tours are available by calling
© 805/927-2020 at least 10 days in advance.)

The latest addition to the estate is the giant-screen **Hearst Castle National
Geographic Theatre,** which you can visit regardless of whether you take a tour.
Films include *Hearst Castle: Building the Dream.* For information, call © 805/
927-6811 or see www.ngtheater.com. Tickets cost $7.50 for adults and $5.50
for children 12 and under.

GETTING THERE   Hearst Castle is directly on Calif. 1, about 42 miles
north of San Luis Obispo and 94 miles south of Monterey. From San Francisco
or Monterey, take U.S. 101 south to Paso Robles, then Calif. 46 west to Calif.
1, and Calif. 1 north to the castle. The total trip is 205 miles south of San Francisco. From Los Angeles, take U.S. 101 north to San Luis Obispo, then Calif. 1
north to the castle; the total trip is 254 miles. Park by the visitor center; a bus
will take you the 5 miles up the hill to the estate. The movie theater and visitor
center adjoin the parking lot and are easily accessible without heading up to the
actual estate.

WHERE TO STAY   A reliable lodging choice is the **Best Western Cavalier
Oceanfront Resort,** 9415 Hearst Dr. (Calif. 1), San Simeon (© **800/826-8168**
or 805/927-4688; www.cavalierresort.com), a family-friendly place that is
indeed the only true oceanfront resort in the area; and the **Ragged Point Inn,**
19010 Calif. 1. 15 miles north of Hearst Castle (© **805/927 4502**), with
sweeping ocean views from each basic motel-style room.

6 Lake Tahoe

Lake Tahoe has long been California's most popular recreational playground. In
summer, you can enjoy boating and watersports, in-line skating, camping, ballooning, horseback riding, hiking, parasailing—the list is endless. In winter,
Lake Tahoe becomes one of the nation's premier ski destinations.

And then there's the lake. It's disputable whether Lake Tahoe is the most beautiful lake in the world, but it's certainly near the top of the list. It's famous for
its pure water (a white dinner plate at a depth of 75 ft. would be clearly visible
from the surface) and its size: It's the second-deepest lake in the United States
(after Crater Lake, Oregon) and the eighth-deepest in the world.

The north and south shores have about as much in common as snow cones
and sand castles. The scenery is absolutely stunning on the less developed north
shore, although the lake isn't quite as accessible on this side. South Lake Tahoe
is brimming with developments: high-rise casinos, condos, and mini-malls.
Which side you choose to stay on is important, as driving from one end of the
lake to the other is a 1- to 2-hour affair on summer weekends and downright
treacherous during snowstorms. The selection of casinos is better and the
lodging more abundant in the south, which is is also the place for families
watching their wallets, as this is where you'll find the greatest concentration of
affordable motels. The north shore offers a better selection of upscale lodgings
and restaurants, and the scenery is more pristine.

ESSENTIALS
GETTING THERE   By Plane   Reno–Tahoe International Airport, 45
minutes from the north shore and 90 minutes from the south shore, is served by
major airlines. Rent a car or take a shuttle up to the lake: **No Stress Express**
(© **888/4-SHUTTLE**) serves the north and west shores; **Tahoe Casino Express**
(© **800/446-6128**) serves the south shore.

By Train   Amtrak (© 800/USA-RAIL; www.amtrak.com) stops in Truckee, 10 miles north of the lake. Public transportation (TART or Truce Trolley) is available from the train depot, or take a taxi to the north shore.

By Car   From San Francisco, take I-80 east to Sacramento, then U.S. 50 to the south shore, or I-80 east to Calif. 89 or Calif. 267 to the north shore. Be prepared for snow in the winter. During heavy storms, you won't be permitted to pass the checkpoints without four-wheel drive or chains. From Los Angeles, take I-5 through the Central Valley to Sacramento and then follow the directions above.

VISITOR INFORMATION   If you're in Tahoe City, stop by the **Visitor Service Center,** 245 N. Lake Blvd. (© **888/434-1262** or 530/583-3494; www.tahoefun.org). In Incline Village, go to the **Incline Village/Crystal Bay Visitors Center,** 969 Tahoe Blvd. (© **800/468-2463** or 775/832-1606; www.gotahoe.com). In South Lake Tahoe, go to the **Lake Tahoe Visitors Authority,** 1156 Ski Run Blvd. (© **800/288-2463** or 530/544-5050; www. virtualtahoe.com), or to the **South Lake Tahoe Chamber of Commerce,** 3066 Lake Tahoe Blvd. (© **530/541-5255;** www.tahoeinfo.com). Online, check out www.skilaketahoe.com, www.laketahoeconcierge.com, or www.tahoevacation guide.com.

LAKE CRUISES

Hornblower's *Tahoe Queen* (© **800/238-2463** or 530/541-3364; www. hornblower.com), departing from the Marina Village at Ski Run Boulevard in South Lake Tahoe, is an authentic paddle-wheeler with a capacity of 500. It offers Emerald Bay sightseeing tours ($22 adults, $11 children) and dinner cruises ($40), as well as full-service charters. Live music, a buffet breakfast, dinner, and appetizers are all available on board.

The *Tahoe Gal* (© **800/218-2464** or 530/583-0141; www.tahoegal.com), departing from the Lighthouse Marina (behind Safeway) in Tahoe City, is the only cruise boat on the north shore. Cruises include Scenic Shoreline ($19 adults, $8 children), Emerald Bay ($24 adults, $12 children), Happy Hour ($20 for 2 adults, $7 children), and Dinner ($20 adults, $10 children, not including food and beverages).

Woodwind Sailing Cruises (© **888/867-6394;** www.sailwoodwind.com) specializes in sightseeing cruises ($24 adults, $10 children), sunset champagne cruises ($28), weddings, and charters. The Woodwind fleet sails from Zephyr Cove Marina.

A DRIVE AROUND THE LAKE

We'll start at the California–Nevada border in South Lake Tahoe and loop around the western shore on Calif. 89 to Tahoe City and beyond. U.S. 50, which runs along the south shore, is an overdeveloped strip that obliterates any view of the lake, but keep heading west.

First stop is the **Tallac Historic Site,** a cluster of rustic 100-year-old mansions that provide a glimpse into Tahoe's past. Throughout the summer, the **Valhalla Festival of Arts and Music** (© **888/632-5859** or 530/541-4975; www.valhalla-tallac.com) showcases jazz, bluegrass, rock, mariachi, and classical music.

From here, Calif. 89 climbs northward. Soon you'll be peering down into beautiful **Emerald Bay,** a 3-mile-long inlet containing tiny Fanette Island, which has an old stone teahouse clearly situated at its peak. Across Calif. 89

from Emerald Bay, there's another parking area. From here, it's a short, steep, quarter-mile hike to a footbridge above **Eagle Falls,** then about a mile to **Eagle Lake.**

It's not surprising that someone chose to build a mansion right here over-looking the bay—**Vikingsholm** (© 530/541-3030; www.vikingsholm.com), a 38-room replica of a medieval Viking castle. Tours ($3) of this unique structure are available from mid June to Labor Day between 10am and 4pm.

From here, it's only about 2 miles to **D. L. Bliss State Park** (© 530/525-7982), where you'll find one of the lake's best beaches, though it's crowded in summer. The park also contains 168 campsites and several trails, including one along the shoreline.

About 7 miles farther on, **Sugar Pine State Park** (© 530/525-7232) is the largest of the lake's parks and also the only one that has year-round camping. In summer, you can visit the beaches in the park plus a nature trail; in winter, there's cross-country skiing on well-maintained trails.

It's a clear drive through the small town of Homewood (site of the ski resort of the same name) to Tahoe City, which is smaller and more appealing than South Lake Tahoe, although it, too, has its share of strip development.

At Tahoe City, Calif. 89 turns off to Truckee and to Alpine Meadows and Squaw Valley ski resorts. Squaw Valley is only 5 miles out, and a ride on the **Squaw Valley cable car** (© 530/583-6985) will reward you with incredible vis-tas from 2,000 feet above the valley floor. It operates year-round and costs $17 for adults, $5 for children under 13.

If you continue around the lake on Calif. 28, you'll reach Carnelian Bay, Tahoe Vista, and Kings Beach before crossing the state line into Nevada to Crys-tal Bay, Incline Village, the Ponderosa Ranch, and Sand Harbor Beach. **Kings Beach State Recreation Area** (© 530/546-7248), 12 miles east of Tahoe City, is a long, wide beach and picnic area, jammed in summer with sunbathers and swimmers.

The **Ponderosa Ranch,** off Nev. 28 at the east end of Incline Village (© 775/831-0691; www.ponderosaranch.com), is a theme park inspired by the popular 1960s TV show *Bonanza.* You can visit the original 1959 Cartwright Ranch House along with an Old West town complete with working blacksmiths, a saloon, a hay-wagon breakfast, and even live gunfights. It's open daily from April to October between 9:30am and 6pm; admission is $9.50 for adults, $4.50 for children 5 to 11.

The east shore of the lake is largely undeveloped and very scenic. Drive about 4 miles south of Incline Village to **Sand Harbor** (© 775/831-0494), one of the lake's best-loved beaches, home to the very popular **Lake Tahoe Shakespeare Festival** (© 800/747-4697; www.tahoebard.com) every mid-July to August. In addition to turquoise water dotted with big boulders and a wide sandy beach, you'll find nature trails, picnic areas, and boating.

South of Sand Harbor, if you wish, you can turn inland to Spooner Lake and Carson City, or continue south along Calif. 28 to an outcropping called **Cave Rock,** where the highway passes through 25 yards of solid stone. Farther along is **Zephyr Cove,** from which the tour boats depart. You'll then return to State-line and South Lake Tahoe, your original starting point.

SUMMER ACTIVITIES
MOUNTAIN BIKING   Biking is big at Lake Tahoe. For serious mountain bikers, there is a dizzying choice of trails. At both **Northstar** (© 530/562-1010)

and **Squaw Valley** (© 530/583-6985) you can take the cable car (Squaw) or chairlift (Northstar) up with your bike and ride the trails all the way down. For other trails, check with bike-rental shops for maps and information. In North Tahoe, try **The Back Country,** 255 N. Lake Blvd., Tahoe City (© 530/581-5861); **Olympic Bike Shop,** 620 N. Lake Blvd., Tahoe City (© 530/581-2500); **Tahoe Bike & Ski,** 8499 N. Lake Blvd., Kings Beach (© 530/546-7437); or **Porter's Sports Shop,** 885 Tahoe Blvd., Incline Village (© 775/831-3500). In South Tahoe, try **Anderson's Bike Rental,** 645 Emerald Bay Rd. (© 530/541-0500); or **Lakeview Sports,** 3131 Hwy. 50 at El Dorado Beach (© 530/544-0183).

Another great option is **Cyclepaths Mountain Bike Adventures,** 1785 West Lake Blvd. in Tahoe Park, a few miles south of Tahoe City (© **800/780-BIKE;** www.cyclepaths.com), where you can arrange a guided off-road tour. The expert guides offer day tours ($29 and up), weekenders ($199), and 3- and 5-day adventure camps (rates vary).

BOAT RENTALS, WATERSPORTS & PARASAILING Nothing beats actually getting out on the water. Take a guided tour, go off on your own, or just paddle around. Here are a few reliable choices: **Zephyr Cove Marina** (© 775/588-3833; www.tahoedixie2.com) is the lake's largest marina. Here you can parasail (© 775/588-3530), charter sportfishing trips (© 775/586-9338), or take guided tours. You can also rent motorized boats, pontoon boats, kayaks, canoes, and more. **Tahoe City Marina,** 700 N. Lake Blvd., Tahoe City (© 530/583-1039), rents motorized boats, sailboats, and fishing boats. Sailboat cruises are available. This is also the location for **Lake Tahoe Parasailing** (© 530/583-7245). **Camp Richardson Marina,** 1900 Jameson Beach Rd., off Calif. 89 on the south shore (© 530/542-6570), rents power and ski boats, kayaks, and paddleboats. It also offers fishing charters, cruises, and raft and kayak tours to Emerald Bay.

FISHING The cold, clear waters of Lake Tahoe are home to kokanee salmon and rainbow, brown, and Mackinaw trout. With lots of hiding places in the deep water, fishing here is a challenge, and many anglers opt to use a guide or charter boat. There are dozens of charter companies offering daily excursions. Rates run about $65 for a half day to $95 for a whole day. On the north shore, try **Mickey's Big Mack Charters,** at the Sierra Boat Company in Carnelian Bay (© 530/546-4444; www.mickeysbigmack.com); or **Reel Deal Sportfishing,** Tahoe City (© 530/581-0924). On the south shore, try **Avid Fisherman,** Zephyr Cove (© 775/588-7675); **Blue Ribbon Fishing Charters,** Tahoe Keys Marina (© 530/541-8801); or **Tahoe Sportfishing,** 900 Ski Run Blvd. (© 800/696-7797 or 530/541-5448).

GOLF With its world-class golf courses, mild summer weather, and magnificent scenery, Lake Tahoe is a golfer's paradise. All of these courses are very busy in the summer so call far in advance for tee times. Starting at the north end of the lake, there are four highly rated courses: **Incline Village Championship Course,** 955 Fairway Blvd., and the smaller **Incline Village Mountain (Executive) Course,** 690 Wilson Way (© 775/832-1144 for both); **Northstar** (© 530/562-2490); and **Squaw Creek** (© 800/327-3353).

In the south, there's **Edgewood,** U.S. 50 at Lake Parkway, Stateline, NV (© 775/588-3566), home of the Celebrity Golf Championship; and **Lake Tahoe Golf Course,** 2500 Emerald Bay Rd., South Lake Tahoe (© 530/577-0788). In addition, there are some good nine-hole municipal courses: **Old**

Brockway Golf Course, 7900 N. Lake Blvd., Kings Beach (© 530/546-9909); **Tahoe City Golf Course,** 251 N. Lake Blvd., Tahoe City (© 530/583-1516); and **Bijou Municipal Golf Course,** 3436 Fairway Ave., South Lake Tahoe ((© 530/542-6097).

HORSEBACK RIDING   Most stables offer a variety of guided trail rides and lessons. Choose the one that appeals to your sense of adventure: 1- to 2-hour trail rides; breakfast, lunch, or dinner rides; or half-day, day, overnight, and extended pack trips. Expect to pay $20 to $25 for a 1-hour ride. Try **Alpine Meadows Stables,** Alpine Meadows Road, Tahoe City (© 530/583-3905); **Northstar Stables,** Highway 267, 6 miles north of Kings Beach (© 530/ 562-2480); **Squaw Valley Stables,** 1525 Squaw Valley Rd., north of Tahoe City (© 530/583-7433); **Camp Richardson Corral,** Calif. 89, South Lake Tahoe (© 530/541-3113); or **Zephyr Cove Stables,** Zephyr Cove Resort, U.S. 50 at Zephyr Cove (© 775/588-5664).

RIVER RAFTING   For a swift but gentle ride down the Truckee River (the lake's only outlet), try **Truckee River Raft Rental,** 185 River Rd., Tahoe City (© **530/583-0123**). Only available in the summer, the rates are $25 for adults and $20 for children 5 and up.

SKIING

With the largest concentration of ski resorts in North America, Lake Tahoe offers California's best skiing. The ski season typically lasts from November to May and frequently extends into the summer. Lift tickets currently range from $35 to $60 per day for adults and from free to $29 for children. Most resorts and many motels/hotels offer ski packages. Contact the visitor centers or visit the websites listed above or for each resort to look for these great values. Most have free shuttles. The following are some of Tahoe's most popular resorts, though this list is not complete.

Six miles from Tahoe City, midsize **Alpine Meadows** (© 800/441-4423 or 530/583-4232; www.skialpine.com) is a great all-around performer, with something for everyone: unique kids' programs and a family ski zone, as well as its "wild side," for the double black diamond crowd.

Site of the 1960 Olympic Winter Games, **Squaw Valley USA** (© 800/ 545-4350 or 530/583-6985; www.squaw.com) offers the most challenging array of runs. Squaw's terrain is 70% for beginners and intermediates, 30% for the advanced, expert, and/or insane. There are 30 chairlifts, including a cable car and high-speed Funitel, the first of its kind in North America. The Cross-Country Ski Center at the Resort at Squaw Creek (© **530/583-6300**) has 400 acres of groomed trails.

Heavenly Resort (© 775/586-7000; www.skiheavenly.com), which straddles the California–Nevada border, has the highest elevation (10,000 ft.) of any ski area at the lake. Skiers of all levels will find something here to challenge them, and 100% of the mountain is available to snowboarders. The Heavenly Gondola takes passengers from the South Shore downtown area up to an observation deck at 9,200 feet.

Great choices for families include **Diamond Peak** (© 775/832-1177 or 775/831-3249; www.diamondpeak.com), which is smaller, less crowded, and less expensive than many of the other choices. It's primarily a mountain for intermediates; kids love the snowboard park and sledding area. There's also cross-country skiing and snowshoeing, as well as dining and lodging in nearby Incline Village. Another good family option is **Homewood Mountain Resort**

(© 530/525-2992; www.skihomewood.com), a homey little resort with gorgeous views of the lake. There's child care for 2- to 6-year-olds and ski schools for kids 4 to 12. It's 6 miles south of Tahoe City and 19 miles north of South Lake Tahoe. **Northstar-at-Tahoe** (© 800/466-6784 or 530/562-1010; www.northstarattahoe.com) also has a highly touted full-time kids' program. It offers 2,400 acres of downhill skiing with 63 runs, plus sleigh rides, snowmobiling, and various snow toys.

The only real drawback of **Kirkwood,** off Calif. 88 (© 209/258-6000; www.kirkwood.com), is that it's 30 miles from South Lake Tahoe. Otherwise, this is one of the top ski areas in Tahoe, with lots of snow and excellent spring skiing on its 2,300 acres.

WHERE TO STAY & DINE

ON THE SOUTH SHORE   Caesar's Tahoe, 55 U.S. 50 (© 800/648-3353 or 775/588-3515; www.caesars.com/tahoe), has the same glitter, glitz, and campiness of its Las Vegas counterpart. Many rooms offer views of the lake and sport extra-large Roman-style tubs. There is a 24-hour casino and showroom that hosts big-name entertainment. Guests also enjoy an indoor lagoon-style pool, tennis courts, and spa.

In hot competition with Caesar's is **Harrah's Casino Hotel,** U.S. 50 at Stateline Ave. (© 800/427-7247 or 775/586-6607; www.harrahstahoe.com), a glitzy, modern, Vegas-style palace. Rooms are among the largest in Tahoe, and most have bay windows overlooking the lake or the mountains. With families in mind, the casino has an enormous fun center with the latest in video and arcade games, virtual reality, and an indoor "playscape" for young children. Big names in showbiz headline at the casino's South Shore Room.

Harvey's Casino Resort, Lake Tahoe, U.S. 50 at Stateline Avenue, Stateline, NV (© 800/HARVEYS or 775/588-2411), is the largest (and possibly the ugliest) hotel in Tahoe, boasting an enormous casino, and a cabaret with glittering entertainment. Harvey's is like a city unto itself, with a pool, spa, salon, children's day camp, even a wedding chapel.

Perched near the state line, **Embassy Suites Resort,** 4130 Lake Tahoe Blvd., South Lake Tahoe (© 800/362-2779 or 530/544-5400; www.embassy-suites. com), competes for the upscale gambling crowd and the convention business with Nevada's glittering casino hotels across the way. A château-style hotel of character, it offers an indoor pool and a basic gym. Accommodations are typical Embassy Suites, with microwaves and VCRs. In summer, guests have access to a private beach.

Big, modern, and loaded with luxuries, the all-suites **Tahoe Seasons Resort,** 3901 Saddle Rd., off Ski Run Boulevard, South Lake Tahoe (© 800/540-4874 or 530/541-6700; www.tahoeseasons.com), lies in a relatively uncongested residential neighborhood at the base of the Heavenly Valley Ski Resort, 2 miles from Tahoe's casinos. Most suites have gas fireplaces, and all have huge whirlpools, VCRs, and fridges. Play a round of tennis on the roof or hop aboard the free casino shuttles.

More moderately priced choices include the **Best Western Station House Inn,** 901 Park Ave., South Lake Tahoe (© 800/822-5953 or 530/542-1101; www.stationhouseinn.com), one of the few hotels in town that has its own private "gated" beach on the lake. It offers free shuttle service to the casinos and most ski resorts. There's also an array of condo options at the **Lakeland Village**

Beach & Mountain Resort, 3535 Lake Tahoe Blvd., South Lake Tahoe (© 800/822-5969 or 530/544-1685; www.lakeland-village.com).

ON THE NORTH SHORE   Part ski chalet, part boutique hotel, the Plump-Jack Squaw Valley Inn, 1920 Squaw Valley Rd., off Calif. 89, Olympic Valley (© 800/323-7666 or 530/583-1576), is easily Tahoe's most refined hotel and restaurant. Swirling sconces and sculpted metal accents are candy for the eyes, while the rest of your body parts are soothingly enveloped in thick hooded robes, slippers, and down comforters atop expensive mattresses. Rooms have mountain views. The sleek and sexy PlumpJack Cafe has a wonderful wine list and terrific food. Guests also enjoy ski rentals and storage, a pool, and two Jacuzzis.

The most deluxe resort on the lake, the Resort at Squaw Creek, 400 Squaw Creek Rd., Olympic Valley (© 800/403-4434 or 530/583-6300; www.squawcreek.com), boasts ski-in/ski-out access to Squaw Valley skiing (in fact, a chairlift lands just outside the door). Rooms are not particularly spacious, but they're well equipped. Perks include children's activities, an 18-hole golf course, three pools, eight tennis courts, a fitness center, 20 miles of groomed cross-country skiing trails (marked for hiking and biking in the summer), an ice-skating rink, and an equestrian center with riding stables.

If you're looking for a romantic little B&B right on Lake Tahoe's shoreline, the Shore House, 7170 N. Lake Blvd., Tahoe Vista (© 800/207-5160 or 530/546-7270; www.shorehouselaketahoe.com), is a real charmer. Each room has its own entrance, handmade log furniture, fridge, gas-log fireplace, and blissfully comfortable feather bed. All guests have access to a private beach and landscaped lawn, as well as a common hot tub.

Situated alongside the Truckee River, the rustic River Ranch Lodge & Restaurant, on Calif. 89, at Alpine Meadows Road, Tahoe City (© 800/535-9900 or 530/583-4264; www.riverranchlodge.com), is a terrific bargain. It's minutes away from the Alpine Meadows and Squaw Valley ski resorts. All rooms have a handsome mountain-home decor; the best feature private balconies overlooking the river. In summer, guests relax on the patio, downing burgers while watching rafters float by. During ski season, the circular lounge and dining area, which cantilevers over the river, is a popular après-ski hangout.

Built as a private home in 1908, the moderately priced Sunnyside Lodge, 1850 W. Lake Blvd., off Calif. 89, Tahoe City (© 800/822-2754 or 530/583-7200; www.sunnysideresort.com), is one of the few grand old lodges still left on the lake, and has a popular restaurant. It looks very much like a giant wooden cabin, complete with dormers and steep pitched roofs; a large deck fronts a tiny marina. The place is rustic but fairly sophisticated.

The 14 reasonably priced cabins at the Tahoma Meadows Bed & Breakfast, 6821 W. Lake Blvd., on Calif. 89, 8½ miles from Tahoe City in Homewood (© 800/355-1596 or 530/525-1553; www.tahomameadows.com), are perched on a gentle forest slope. The largest cabin, Treehouse, sleeps six and is ideal for families. In the main lodge is the highly recommended Stoneyridge Cafe, serving breakfast, lunch, and dinner. Nearby activities include skiing at Ski Homewood (including shuttle service), fly-fishing at a private trout-stocked lake, and sunbathing at the lakeshore just across the street.

An inexpensive option is the Lake of the Sky Motor Inn, 955 N. Lake Blvd., Tahoe City (© 530/583-3305), which is not much more than a 1960s-style A-frame motel, but offers clean rooms in a central location, only steps away from shops and restaurants. There's a heated pool as well as a barbecue area.

TAHOE AFTER DARK

Tahoe is not particularly known for its nightlife, although there's always something going on in the showrooms of the major casino hotels on the south shore. Call **Harrah's** (© 775/588-6611), **Harvey's** (© 775/588-2411), **Caesar's** (© 775/588-3515), and the **Horizon** (© 775/588-6211) for current show schedules. Most cocktail shows cost $15 to $40. On the north shore, there's usually live music nightly in **Bullwhackers Pub,** at the Resort at Squaw Creek (© 530/583-6300). The **Pierce Street Annex,** 850 N. Lake Blvd. (© 530/583-5800), behind the Safeway in Tahoe City, has pool tables, shuffleboard, and DJ dancing every night. It's one of the livelier places around. If it's just a casual cocktail you're after, our favorite spot is the fireside lounge at **River Ranch Lodge,** on Calif. 89 at Alpine Meadows Road (© 530/583-4264), which cantilevers over a turbulent stretch of the Truckee River.

7 Yosemite National Park

It was in Yosemite that naturalist John Muir found "the most songful streams in the world . . . the noblest forests, the loftiest granite domes, the deepest ice sculpted canyons." Even today, despite the impact that hordes of people and cars have made, few visitors would disagree with Muir's early impressions as they explore this land of towering cliffs, Alpine lakes, river beaches, and fields of snow in winter.

YOSEMITE'S GATEWAYS

Towns on each gateway's periphery are virtually built around the tourism industry. They offer plenty of places to stay and eat and have natural wonders of their own. The bad news: If you stay here, reaching any point within the park requires at least a half-hour drive (usually closer to an hour), which is especially frustrating during high season, when motor homes and overall congestion cause traffic to move at a snail's pace.

But there's no shortage of options to encourage you to help the environment by leaving your car at your lodging or a parking area and entering the park on convenient, inexpensive buses (and then moving around the valley floor on free, readily available shuttles). The **Yosemite Area Regional Transit System (YARTS)** (© 877/989-2787; www.yarts.com) provides round-trip transit service from communities within Mariposa, Merced, and Mono counties to Yosemite. Fares vary, but generally range from $7 to $15 round-trip for adults, including entrance to the park.

BIG OAK FLAT ENTRANCE

Among the string of small communities along the way is charming **Groveland** (24 miles from the park's entrance), a throwback to gold-mining days complete with the oldest saloon in the state. It'll take about an hour to reach the park entrance from Groveland, but at least there's some extracurricular activity should you choose to hang around. (Big Oak Flat has a few hotels as well, but no town.) If you're driving from San Francisco, take I-580 (which turns into I-205) to Manteca, then Calif. 120 east. For information, contact the **Highway 120 Chamber of Commerce** (© 800/449-9120; www.groveland.org) for a list of hotels, motels, cabins, RV parks, and camping in the area.

Our favorite accommodations here are the affordable, rustic cabins at **Evergreen Lodge,** 33160 Evergreen Rd. (at Calif. 120), Groveland (© 800/935-6343 or 209/379-2606; www.evergreenlodge.com). It's only 8 miles from

Yosemite National Park

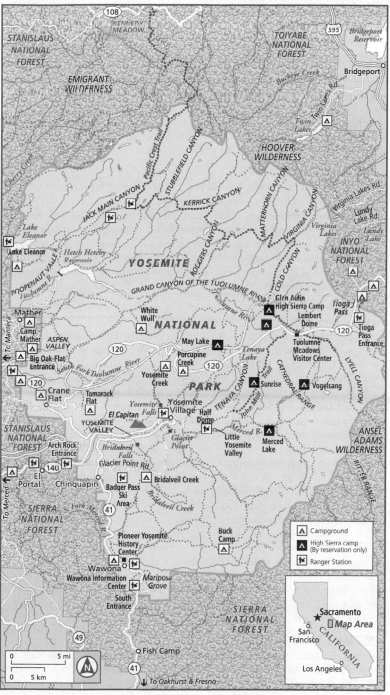

Yosemite's entrance. There are endless hiking trails and, in summer, access to Camp Mather's tennis courts, pool, and horseback riding. Though officially in Groveland, the lodge is 40 minutes east of downtown.

The moderately priced **Groveland Hotel,** 18767 Main St., Groveland (© **800/273-3314** or 209/962-4000; www.groveland.com), is a historic choice that complements the surroundings of the Wild West–like town. Rooms are sweetly appointed with antiques as well as modern amenities; the suite has a spa tub and fireplace. The staff is accommodating, and the restaurant (the best and most expensive in town) is surprisingly sophisticated for its remote location. Another place to eat well is the cool **Iron Door Saloon,** 18761 Main St. (© **209/962-8904**), right across the street from the hotel.

ARCH ROCK ENTRANCE

Arch Rock is 75 miles northeast of Merced. If you're driving from central California, take I-5 to Calif. 99 to Merced, then Calif. 140 east.

The **Yosemite View Lodge,** 11136 Calif. 140, El Portal (© **888/742-4371** or 209/379-2681; www.yosemite-motels.com), is a gargantuan compound set amid the otherwise awesome natural surroundings. This mega-motel is scheduled to offer around 500 rooms within the coming year. The motel-style units include fridges and microwaves; some offer river views, balconies, and fireplaces. There's also a general store, two restaurants, two pools, four hot tubs, and more public areas in the works.

SOUTH ENTRANCE

The South Entrance is 332 miles north of Los Angeles, 190 miles east of San Francisco, 59 miles north of Fresno, and 33 miles south of Yosemite Valley. Fish Camp and Oakhurst are the closest towns to the south entrance at Wawona. If you're driving from Los Angeles, take I-5 to Calif. 99 north, then Calif. 41 north. For more options, contact the **Yosemite Sierra Visitors Bureau,** 40637 Calif. 41, Oakhurst (© **559/683-4636;** www.yosemite-sierra.org). Ask for the helpful brochure on the area, and be sure to check out the excellent online guide.

Folks looking for moderately priced accommodations might check out the **Narrow Gauge Inn,** 48571 Calif. 41, Fish Camp (© **888/644-9050** or 559/683-7720; www.narrowgaugeinn.com), just 4 miles south of the park entrance. All of the super-clean motel-style units have a rustic cabin feel, complete with little balconies or decks, antiques, quilts, and lace curtains. On the property are a pool, a hot tub, and hiking trails, as well as a wonderfully old-fashioned, lodge-style restaurant.

The **Tenaya Lodge,** 1122 Calif. 41, Fish Camp (© **800/635-5807** or 559/683-6555; www.tenayalodge.com), is the best resort outside the southern entrance to Yosemite; it's idyllic for families, as it's set on 35 acres of forest a few miles outside of the national park. The decor is a cross between an Adirondack hunting lodge and a Southwestern pueblo, with a lobby dominated by a massive river-rock fireplace rising three stories; rooms are ultra-modern. Extras include restaurants, two pools, and a spa.

YOSEMITE NATIONAL PARK

Yosemite is a place of record-setting statistics: the highest waterfall in North America and three of the world's 10 tallest (Upper Yosemite Fall, Ribbon Fall, and Sentinel Falls); the tallest and largest single granite monolith in the world (El Capitan); the most recognizable mountain (Half Dome); one of the world's largest trees (the Grizzly Giant in the Mariposa Grove); and literally thousands of rare plant and animal species. But trying to explain its majesty is impossible: This is a place you simply must experience firsthand. Even after extensive world travel, it's still one of the most awe-inspiring places we've ever been every single time we visit.

Bears, too, are at home in the valley. Grizzlies are gone from the park now, but black bears are plentiful—and hungry for your food. They don't actually come begging by daylight, but they make their presence known through late-night ransacking of ice chests and have been known to rip into cars that have even the smallest treats inside.

Right in the middle of the valley's thickest urban cluster is the **Yosemite Valley Visitor Center** (© 209/372-0200; www.nps.gov/yose), with exhibits that will teach you about glacial geology, history, and the park's flora and fauna. Check out the **Yosemite Museum** next door for insight into what life in the park was once like. Excellent exhibits highlight the Miwok and Paiute cultures that thrived here. The **Ansel Adams Gallery** (© 209/372-4413; www. adamsgallery.com) displays the famous photographer's prints as well as other artists' works. You'll also find much history and memorabilia from the career of nature writer John Muir, one of the founders of the conservation movement.

Tenaya Lake and Tuolumne Meadows are two of the most popular high-country destinations, as well as starting points for many great trails to the backcountry. Since this area of the park is under snow November through June, summer is really more like spring. From snowmelt to the first snowfall, the high country explodes with wildflowers and long-dormant wildlife trying to make the most of the short season.

ESSENTIALS

ENTRY POINTS   There are four main entrances to the park. Most valley visitors enter through the Arch Rock Entrance on Calif. 140. The best entrance for Wawona is the South Entrance on Calif. 41 from Oakhurst. If you're going to the high country, you'll save a lot of time by coming in through the Big Oak Flat Entrance, which puts you straight onto Tioga Road without forcing you to deal with the congested valley. The Tioga Pass Entrance is only open in summer and is only really relevant if you're coming from the east side of the Sierra (in which case it's your only choice). A fifth, little-used entrance is the Hetch Hetchy Entrance, in the euphonious Poopenaut Valley, on a dead-end road.

FEES   It costs $20 per car per week to enter the park or $10 per person per week. Annual Yosemite Passes are a steal at only $40. Wilderness permits are free, but reserving them requires a $5 fee per person.

GAS   There are no gas stations in Yosemite Valley, so be sure to fill up your tank before entering the park.

VISITOR CENTERS & INFORMATION   There's a central, 24-hour recorded information line for the park (© 209/372-0200; www.nps.gov/yose). All visitor-related service lines, including hotels and information, can be accessed by calling © 209/372-1000 or going to www.yosemitepark.com.

By far the biggest visitor center is the **Valley Visitor Center** (© 209/ 372-0200). The **Wawona Information Station** (© 209/375-9501) gives general park information. For interesting biological and geological displays about the High Sierra, as well as trail advice, the **Tuolumne Meadows Visitor Center** (© 209/372-0263) is great. All can provide you with maps, newspapers, books, and leaflets.

REGULATIONS   Rangers in the Yosemite Valley spend more time being cops than being rangers. They even have their own jail, so don't do anything here you wouldn't do in your hometown. Despite the pressure, park regulations are pretty simple. Wilderness permits are required for all overnight backpacking trips. Fishing licenses are required. Use proper food-storage methods in bear country. Don't collect firewood in the valley. No off-road bicycle riding. Dogs are allowed in the park but must be leashed and are forbidden from trails. Don't feed the animals.

WHEN TO GO   Winter is one of the nicest times to visit the valley. It isn't crowded, as it is during summer, and a dusting of snow provides a stark contrast to all that granite. To see the waterfalls at their best, come in spring when snowmelt is at its peak. Fall can be cool, but it's beautiful and much less crowded than summer. Sunshine seekers will love summer—if they can tolerate the crowds.

The high country is under about 20 feet of snow November through May, so unless you're snow camping, summer is pretty much the only season to pitch a tent. Even in summer, thundershowers are a frequent occurrence, sometimes with a magnificent lightning show. Mosquitoes can be a plague during the peak of summer but get better after the first freeze.

RANGER PROGRAMS   Even though they're overworked just trying to keep the peace, Yosemite's wonderful rangers also take time to lead a number of educational and interpretive programs ranging from backcountry hikes to fireside talks to snow-country survival clinics. Call the main park-information number with specific requests for the season and park area you'll be visiting.

AVOIDING THE CROWDS   Unfortunately, popularity isn't always the greatest thing for wild places. Over the last 20 years, tourist-magnet Yosemite Valley has set records for the worst crowding, noise, crime, and traffic in any California national park.

The park covers more than 1,000 square miles, but most visitors flock to the floor of Yosemite Valley, a 1-mile-wide, 7-mile-long freak of glacial scouring that tore a deep and steep valley from the solid granite of the Sierra Nevada. It becomes a total zoo from Memorial Day to Labor Day. Cars line up bumper to bumper on almost any busy weekend.

Our best advice is to try to come before Memorial Day or after Labor Day. If you must go in summer, do your part to help out. It's not so much the numbers of people that are ruining the valley, but their insistence on driving from attraction to attraction within the valley. Once you're here, park your car, then bike, hike, or ride the shuttle buses. Curry Village (© **209/372-8319**) and Yosemite Lodge (© **209/372-1208**) both offer bicycle rentals in summer. It may take longer to get from point A to point B, but you're in one of the most gorgeous places on earth—so why hurry?

SEEING THE HIGHLIGHTS
The Valley

First-time visitors are often completely dumbstruck as they enter the valley from the west. The first two things you'll see are the delicate and beautiful **Bridalveil Fall** and the immense face of **El Capitan,** a stunning and anything-but-delicate 3,593-foot-tall solid-granite rock. A short trail leads to the base of Bridalveil, which at 620 feet tall is only a medium-size fall by park standards, but one of the prettiest.

It's a good idea to buy the excellent *Map and Guide to Yosemite Valley* for $2.50; it describes many hikes and short nature walks. Then go take a look. Walking and biking are the best ways to get around. To cover longer distances, the park shuttles run frequently around the east end of the valley.

The **Valley Floor Tour** is a 2-hour narrated bus or open-air-tram tour (depending on the season) that provides an introduction to the valley's natural history, geology, and human culture for $21 for adults. Purchase tickets at valley hotels or call © **209/372-1240** for advance reservations.

The best single view in the valley is from **Sentinel Bridge** over the Merced River. At sunset, Half Dome's face functions as a projection screen for all the sinking sun's hues from yellow to pink to dark purple, and the river reflects it all. Ansel Adams took one of his most famous photographs from this very spot.

VALLEY WALKS & HIKES   Yosemite Falls is within a short stroll of the visitor center. You can actually see it better elsewhere in the valley, but it's really impressive to stand at the base of all that falling water. The wind, noise, and blowing spray generated when millions of gallons catapult 2,425 feet through space onto the rocks below are sometimes so overwhelming you can barely stand on the bridge.

If you want more, the **Upper Yosemite Fall Trail** zigzags 3½ miles from Sunnyside Campground to the top of Upper Yosemite Fall. This trail gives you an inkling of the weird, vertically oriented world climbers enter when they head up Yosemite's sheer walls. As you climb this narrow switchback trail, the valley floor drops away until people below look like ants, but the top doesn't appear any closer. It's a little unnerving at first, but braving it promises indescribable rewards. Plan on spending all day on this 7-mile round-trip because of the incredibly steep climb.

A mile-long trail leads from the Valley Stables (take the shuttle; no car parking) to **Mirror Lake.** The already-tiny lake is gradually becoming a meadow as it fills with silt, but the reflections of the valley walls and sky on its surface remain one of the park's most memorable sights.

Also accessible from the Valley Stables or nearby Happy Isles is the best valley hike of all—the **John Muir Trail** to Vernal and Nevada falls. It follows the Sierra crest 200 miles south to Mount Whitney, but you only need go 1½ miles round-trip to get a great view of 317-foot **Vernal Fall.** Add another 1½ miles and 1,000 vertical feet for the climb to the top of Vernal Fall on the **Mist Trail,** where you'll get wet as you climb directly alongside the falls. On top of Vernal and before the base of Nevada Fall is a beautiful little valley and deep pool. For a truly outrageous view of the valley and one heck of a workout, continue on up the Mist Trail to the top of Nevada Fall. From 2,000 feet above Happy Isles where you began, it's a dizzying view straight down the face of the fall. To the east is an interesting profile perspective of Half Dome. Return either by the Mist Trail or the slightly easier John Muir Trail for a 7-mile round-trip hike.

Half Dome may look insurmountable to anyone but an expert rock climber, but thousands every year take the popular cable route up the backside. It's almost 17 miles round-trip and a 4,900-foot elevation gain from Happy Isles on the John Muir Trail. Many do it in a day, starting at first light and rushing home to beat nightfall. A more relaxed strategy is to camp in the backpacking campground in Little Yosemite Valley just past Nevada Fall. From here the summit is within easy striking distance of the base of Half Dome. If you plan to spend the night, you must have a Wilderness Pass (see "Where to Camp," below). You must climb up a very steep granite face using steel cables installed by the park service. In summer, boards are installed as crossbeams, but they're still far apart. Wear shoes with lots of traction and bring your own leather gloves for the cables (your hands will thank you). The view from the top is an unbeatable vista of the high country, Tenaya Canyon, Glacier Point, and the awe-inspiring abyss of the valley below. When you shuffle up to the overhanging lip for a look down the face, be extremely careful not to kick rocks or anything else onto the climbers below, who are earning this view the hard way.

The Southwest Corner

This corner of the park is densely forested and gently sculpted in comparison to the stark granite that makes up so much of Yosemite. Coming from the valley, Calif. 41 passes through a long tunnel. Just prior to the entrance is **Tunnel View,** site of another famous Ansel Adams photograph, and the best scenic outlook of the valley accessible by car. Virtually the whole valley is laid out below: Half Dome and Yosemite Falls straight ahead in the distance, Bridalveil to the right, and El Capitan to the left.

A few miles past the tunnel, Glacier Point Road turns off to the east. Closed in winter, this winding road leads to a picnic area at **Glacier Point,** site of another fabulous view of the valley, this time 3,000 feet below. Schedule at least an hour to drive here from the valley and an hour or two to absorb the view. This is a good place to study the glacial scouring of the valley below; the Glacier Point perspective makes it easy to picture the valley filled with sheets of ice.

Some 30 miles south of the valley on Calif. 41 are the **Wawona Hotel** and the **Pioneer Yosemite History Center.** The Wawona was built in 1879 and is the oldest hotel in the park. Its Victorian architecture evokes a time when travelers spent several days in horse-drawn wagons to get here. The Pioneer Center is a collection of early homesteading log buildings across the river from the Wawona.

One of the primary reasons Yosemite was first set aside as a park was the **Mariposa Grove** of giant sequoias. (Many good trails lead through the grove.) These huge trees have personalities that match their gargantuan size. Single limbs on the biggest tree in the grove, the Grizzly Giant, are 10 feet thick. The tree itself is 209 feet tall, 32 feet in diameter, and more than 2,700 years old. Totally out of proportion with the size of the trees are the tiny cones of the sequoia. Smaller than a baseball and tightly closed, the cones won't release their cargo of seeds until opened by fire.

The High Country

The high country of Yosemite is stunning: Dome after dome of beautiful crystalline granite reflects the sunlight above deep-green meadows and ice-blue rivers.

Tioga Pass is the gateway to the high country. At times it clings to the side of steep rock faces; in other places it weaves through canyon bottoms. Several good campgrounds make it a pleasing overnight alternative to fighting summertime crowds in the valley, although use is increasing here, too.

Near the top of Tioga Pass is beautiful **Tuolumne Meadows.** This enormous meadow covering several square miles is bordered by the Tuolumne River on one side and spectacular granite peaks on the other. The meadow is cut by many stream channels full of trout, and herds of mule deer are almost always present. The **Tuolumne Meadows Lodge** and store is a welcome counterpoint to the overdeveloped valley. In winter, the canvas roofs are removed and the buildings fill with snow. You can buy last-minute backpacking supplies here, and there's a basic burgers-and-fries cafe

TUOLUMNE MEADOWS HIKES & WALKS So many hikes lead from here into the backcountry that it's impossible to do them justice. A good trail passes an icy-cold spring and traverses several meadows.

On the far bank of the Tuolumne from the meadow, a trail leads downriver, eventually passing through the grand canyon of the Tuolumne and exiting at Hetch Hetchy. Shorter hikes will take you downriver past rapids and cascades.

An interesting geological quirk is the **Soda Springs** on the far side of Tuolumne Meadow from the road. This bubbling spring gushes carbonated water from a hole in the ground; a small log cabin marks its site.

For a great selection of Yosemite high-country hikes and backpacking trips, consult some of the specialized guidebooks to the area. Two of the best are published by Wilderness Press: *Tuolumne Meadows,* a hiking guide by Jeffrey B. Shaffer and Thomas Winnett; and *Yosemite National Park,* by Thomas Winnett and Jason Winnett.

SPORTS & OUTDOOR PURSUITS

BICYCLING With 10 miles of bike paths in addition to the valley roads, biking is the perfect way to go. You can rent bicycles at the **Yosemite Lodge** (© 209/372-1208) or **Curry Village** (© 209/372-8319) for $5.25 per hour or $20 per day. You can also rent bike trailers for little kids. All trails in the park are closed to mountain bikes.

FISHING The Merced River is catch-and-release only for native rainbow trout, and barbless hooks are required. Brown trout limits are five fish per day and 10 in possession. Trout season begins on the last Saturday in April and continues to November 15. A California license is required and is obtainable in the park at the **Yosemite Village Sport Shop** (© 209/372-1286).

HORSEBACK RIDING Three stables offer scenic day rides and multiday pack excursions. **Yosemite Valley Stables** (© 209/372-8348) is open spring through fall. The other two—**Wawona** (© 209/375-6502) and **Tuolumne Stables** (© 209/372-8427)—operate only in summer. Day rides run $40 to $80, depending on length. Multiday backcountry trips cost roughly $100 per day and must be booked almost a year in advance. The park wranglers can also be hired to make resupply drops at any of the backcountry High Sierra Camps if you want to arrange for a food drop while on an extended trip. See www.yosemiteparktours.com for more information.

ICE-SKATING In winter, the outdoor **Curry Village Ice Rink** (© 209/372-8341) is a lot of fun. Rates are $6.50 for adults and $5 for children. Skate rentals are available for $3.25.

ROCK CLIMBING Much of the most important technical advancement in climbing came out of the competitive Yosemite Valley climbing scene of the 1970s and 1980s. Yosemite is still one of the most desirable climbing destinations in the world. The **Yosemite Mountaineering School** (© 209/372-8344 or 209/372-8444; www.yosemitemountaineering.com) runs classes for beginners through advanced climbers. Considered one of the best climbing schools in the world, it offers private lessons for $170 per person per day, $90 for two people per day. Classes run from early spring to early October in the valley, during summer in Tuolumne Meadows.

SKIING & SNOWSHOEING Opened in 1935, **Badger Pass** (© 209/372-8430; www.yosemitepark.com) is the oldest operating ski area in California. It's nice for families. Four chairs and one rope tow cover a compact mountain of beginner and intermediate runs. At $31 for adults and $16 for children, it's a great place to learn how to ski or snowboard. There are naturalist-led winter children's programs and even babysitting.

Both the Badger Pass ski school and the mountaineering school run cross-country and snowshoeing trips and lessons. There are two ski huts available on guided cross-country tours; for information, call © **209/372-8444.**

WHERE TO CAMP

Campgrounds in Yosemite can be reserved up to 5 months in advance through the **National Park Reservation Service** (© **800/436-7275;** http://reservations. nps.gov). During the busy season, all valley campsites sell out within hours of becoming available on the service.

Backpacking into the wilderness and camping is always the least crowded option and takes less planning than reserving a campground. If you plan to backpack and camp in the wilderness, you must get a free **Wilderness Pass** (and still pay the park entrance fee). At least 40% of each trail head's quota is allocated up to 24 hours in advance; the rest is available by mail. Write to the Wilderness Center, P.O. Box 545, Yosemite, CA 95389, and specify the dates and trail heads of entry and exit, principal destination, number of people, and any accompanying animals; include a $5-per-person advance-registration fee. You may also secure a pass by calling © **209/372-0740.**

VALLEY CAMPGROUNDS

Until 1997, the park had five car campgrounds that were always full except in the dead of winter. Now the park has half the number of campsites available, and getting a reservation on short notice takes a minor miracle. (Yosemite Valley lost almost half of its 900 camping spaces in a freak winter storm that washed several campsites downstream and buried hundreds more beneath a foot of silt.)

The campgrounds that remain—**North Pines, Upper Pines,** and half of **Lower Pines**—charge $18 per night. All have water, flush toilets, pay phones, fire pits, and a heavy ranger presence. Showers are available for a fee at Curry Village. Upper Pines, North Pines, and Lower Pines allow small RVs (under 40 ft. long). If you're expecting a real nature experience, skip camping in the valley unless you like doing so with 4,000 strangers.

Camp 4 (previously named Sunnyside) is a year-round, walk-in campground in the valley and fills up with climbers since it's only $5 per night. Hard-core climbers used to live here for months at a time, but the park service has cracked down on that. It still has a much more bohemian atmosphere than any of the other campgrounds.

CAMPGROUNDS ELSEWHERE IN THE PARK

Outside the valley, things start looking up for campers. Two car campgrounds near the south entrance of the park, **Wawona** and **Bridalveil Creek,** offer a total of 210 sites with all the amenities. Wawona is open year-round, and reservations are required May through September; otherwise, it's first-come, first-served. Family sites at Wawona are $18 per night. Because it sits well above snow line at more than 7,000 feet, Bridalveil is open in summer only. Its rates are $12 per night for first-come, first-served sites.

Crane Flat, Hodgdon Meadow, and Tamarack Flat are all in the western corner of the park near the Big Oak Flat Entrance. **Crane Flat** is the nearest to the valley, about a half-hour drive, with 166 sites, water, flush toilets, and fire pits. Rates are $18 per night; it's open June through September. **Hodgdon Meadow** is directly adjacent to the Big Oak Flat Entrance at 4,800 feet elevation. It's open year-round, charges $18 per night, and requires reservations May through September through the National Park Reservation Service. Facilities include flush toilets, running water, a ranger station, and pay phones. It's one of the least crowded low-elevation car campgrounds, but there's not a lot to do here. **Tamarack Flat** is a waterless, 52-site campground with pit toilets. Open June through October, it's a bargain at $8 per night.

Tuolumne Meadows, White Wolf, Yosemite Creek, and Porcupine Flat are all above 8,000 feet and open in summer only. **Tuolumne Meadows** is the largest campground in the park, with more than 300 spaces, but it absorbs the crowd well and has all the amenities, including campfire programs and slide shows in the outdoor amphitheater. You will, however, feel sardine-packed between hundreds of other visitors. Half of the sites are reserved in advance; the rest are set aside on a first-come, first-served basis. Rates are $15.

White Wolf, west of Tuolumne Meadows, is the other full-service campground in the high country, with 87 sites available for $18 per night. It offers a drier climate than the meadow and doesn't fill up as quickly. Sites are available on a first-come, first-served basis.

Two primitive camps, **Porcupine Flat** and **Yosemite Creek,** are the last to fill up in the park. Both have pit toilets but no running water, and charge $8 per night on a first-come, first-served basis.

WHERE TO STAY IN THE PARK

Yosemite Concessions Services (✆ 559/252-4848; www.yosemitepark.com) operates all accommodations within the park and accepts all major credit cards. The reservations office is open Monday through Friday from 7am to 6pm, Saturday and Sunday from 8am to 5pm.

An intriguing option bridging the gap between backpacking and staying in a hotel is Yosemite's five backcountry **High Sierra Camps** (✆ 559/253-5674). The five camps—Glen Aulin, May Lake, Sunrise, Merced Lake, and Vogelsang—make for good individual destinations. Or you can link several together, since they're arranged in a loose loop about a 10-mile hike from one another. Due to the popularity of these camps, reservations are booked by lottery. Applications are accepted from October 15 to November 30. The lottery is then held in December and the winning applicants are notified by the end of March.

The grandest (and most expensive) accommodations in the park are found at the **Ahwahnee Hotel** (✆ 559/252-4848; www.yosemitepark.com), one of the most romantic and beautiful hotels in California. It's a special-occasion (doubles go for $366–$665) sort of affair.

Curry Village   Accommodations here range from a few motel-type rooms or heated wood cabins with private bathrooms to canvas tent cabins with central bathrooms; none have phones or TVs. Ironically, the older wood cabins are the nicest. The tent cabins have wood floors and canvas walls; without a real wall to stop noise, they lack any sort of privacy, but they're fun in that summer-camp sort of way. You'll have to sustain yourself with the fast-food court and buffet-style dining, as no cooking is allowed in the rooms. ✆ 559/252-4848. Fax 559/456-0542.

www.yosemitepark.com. 628 units. $54–$112 double. Children 12 and under stay free in parents' room. Extra person $8–$10, tent cabins $4. AE, DC, DISC, MC, V. **Amenities:** Heated outdoor pool; nearby golf course.

Wawona Hotel   If the Ahwahnee doesn't fit your plans or your pocketbook, the Wawona is the next best thing. Also a National Historic Landmark, the Wawona is a romantic throwback to another century. However, old-world charm has its ups and downs. Private bathrooms were not a big hit in the 19th century, rooms were small to hold in heat, there were no TVs or phones, and walls were thin—and all of the above still applies today. Still, the Wawona is less commercial than other accommodations on the valley floor. © **559/252-4848.** www.yosemitepark.com. 104 units. $101 double without private bathroom; $161 double with private bathroom. Children 12 and under stay free in parents' room. Extra person $17. AE, DC, DISC, MC, V. **Amenities:** Restaurant; outdoor pool; golf course; tennis court.

Yosemite Lodge   The next step down in valley accommodations, Yosemite Lodge is not actually a lodge but a large, more modern complex with two types of accommodations. The larger "Lodge" rooms with balconies have striking views of Yosemite Falls. Indeed, the largest bonus—and curse—is that every room's front yard is the valley floor, which means you're near glorious larger-than-life natural attractions and equally gargantuan crowds. © **559/252-4848.** www.yosemitepark.com. 245 units. $112–$136 double. Children 12 and under stay free in parents' room. Extra person $10–$12. AE, DC, DISC, MC, V. **Amenities:** Restaurants (2); heated outdoor pool; nearby golf course.

The Pacific Northwest

Washington and Oregon, the upper left-hand corner of the nation, are an amalgam of American life and landscapes; within their boundaries, these two states reflect a part of almost every region of the country. Take a bit of New England's rural beauty: covered bridges, steepled churches, and familiar place names such as Portland and Springfield. Temper the climate to that of the upper South to avoid harsh winters. Now bring in some low rolling mountains similar to the Appalachians; rugged, glaciated mountains like those in the Rockies; and even volcanoes, as in Hawaii. Add a river as large and important as the Mississippi. Toss in a coastline as rugged as California's, and an island-filled inland sea that offers as many sailing and kayaking opportunities as the coast of Maine. Even the deserts of the Southwest and wheat fields of the Midwest could be added. The wine country of California would be a nice touch, and so would some long sandy beaches. On top of all this, there should be a beautiful city, one with hills and a waterfront like those in San Francisco. Mix all these things together, and you have a portrait of the Northwest.

1 Seattle

Imagine yourself seated at a table on the Seattle waterfront, a double tall latte and an almond croissant close at hand. The snowy peaks of the Olympic Mountains shimmer on the far side of Puget Sound, and the ferryboats come and go across Elliott Bay. It just doesn't get much better than this, unless of course you swap the latte for a microbrew and catch a 9:30 summer sunset. No wonder people love this town so much.

GETTING THERE **By Plane** Seattle–Tacoma International Airport (© 800/544-1965 or 206/431-4444; www.seatac.org/seatac), most commonly referred to simply as Sea-Tac, is located about 14 miles south of Seattle.

Inside the arrivals terminal, you'll find a **Visitor Information Desk** (© 206/433-5218) in the baggage-claim area across from carousel no. 8. It's open daily from 9am to 6pm.

Also at the airport, you'll find a Thomas Cook currency exchange desk (© 206/248-0401) and branches of all the major car-rental companies (for further details see "Getting Around," below).

A **taxi** into downtown Seattle will cost you about $32. There are usually plenty of taxis around, but if not, call **Yellow Cab/Graytop** (© 206/622-6500) or **Farwest Taxi** (© 206/622-1717). The flag-drop charge is $1.80; after that, it's $1.80 per mile.

Gray Line Airport Express (© 800/426-7505 or 206/626-6088; www.graylineofseattle.com) provides service between the airport and downtown Seattle daily from about 5am to 11pm and is your best bet for getting to downtown. Fares are $8.50 one way and $14 round-trip. **Shuttle Express** (© 800/487-7433 in Washington, or 425/981-7000; www.shuttleexpress.com) provides

24-hour service between Sea-Tac and the Seattle and Bellevue areas. The rate to downtown Seattle is about $21 plus $3 for an additional person.

Metro Transit (© 800/542-7876 in Washington, or 206/553-3000; http://transit.metrokc.gov) operates two buses between the airport and downtown. Bus trips take 30 to 40 minutes. The fare is $1.25 during off-peak hours and $2 during peak hours. Call Metro Transit for current schedules.

By Train Amtrak (© 206/382-4125; www.amtrak.com) trains stop at King Street Station, which is located at Third Avenue South and Jackson Street, within a few blocks of the historic Pioneer Square neighborhood and adjacent to the south entrance of the downtown bus tunnel. Any bus running north through the tunnel will take you to within a few blocks of most downtown hotels.

By Car The major routes into Seattle are I-5 from the north (Vancouver) and south (Portland), and I-90 from the east (Spokane). I-405, Seattle's east-side bypass, leads to the cities of Bellevue, Redmond, and Kirkland on the east side of Lake Washington; Wash. 520 connects I-405 with Seattle just north of downtown; and Wash. 99, the Alaskan Way Viaduct, is another major north–south highway through downtown and the waterfront.

VISITOR INFORMATION Visitor information on Seattle and the surrounding area is available by contacting the **Seattle-King County Convention & Visitors Bureau Visitor Information Center,** Washington State Convention & Trade Center, 800 Convention Place, Galleria Level, at the corner of Eighth Avenue and Pike Street (© 206/461-5840; www.seeseattle.org). To find it, walk uphill on Union Street until it goes into a tunnel under the Convention Center. You'll see the information center on your left.

GETTING AROUND Seattle's **Metro** buses (© 800/542-7876 in Washington, or 206/553-3000; http://transit.metrokc.gov) are free if you ride only in the downtown area between 6am and 7pm. The Ride Free Area is between Alaskan Way (the waterfront) in the west, Sixth Avenue and I-5 in the east, Battery Street in the north, and South Jackson Street in the south. Within this area are Pioneer Square, the waterfront attractions, Pike Place Market, the Seattle Art Museum, and almost all of the city's major hotels. The Ride Free Area also encompasses the Metro Tunnel, which extends from the International District in the south to the Convention Center in the north and allows buses to drive underneath downtown Seattle.

Outside the Ride Free Area, fares range from $1.25 to $2, depending on the distance and time of day. (The higher fares are incurred during commuter hour.) Keep in mind when traveling out of the Ride Free Area that you pay when you get off the bus. When traveling into the Ride Free Area, you pay when you get on the bus. Exact change is required; dollar bills are accepted.

In addition to the bus system, **Metro** (© 800/542-7876 in Washington, or 206/553-3000; http://transit.metrokc.gov) also operates old-fashioned streetcars that follow a route along the waterfront from Pier 70 to Pioneer Square and then east to the corner of Fifth Avenue South and South Jackson Street, which is on the edge of the International District. In summer, streetcars operate Monday through Friday from 6:46am to 11:28pm; on Saturday, Sunday, and holidays from 8:46am to 11:58pm (shorter hr. in other months). One-way fare is $1 in off-peak hours and $1.25 in peak hours (75¢ for children ages 5–17); exact change is required. If you plan to transfer to a Metro bus, you can get a transfer good for 90 minutes. Streetcars are wheelchair accessible.

The **Seattle Monorail** (© 206/905-2600; www.seattlemonorail.com) connects Seattle Center with the Westlake Center shopping mall (Fifth Ave. and

Discount Passes

On Saturday, Sunday, and holidays, you can purchase an All Day Pass for $2; it's available on any Metro bus or the Waterfront Streetcar, and it's good for anywhere outside the Ride Free Area.

Pine St.). The elevated trains cover the 1.2 miles in 2 minutes and pass right through the middle of the Experience Music Project. The monorail operates Monday through Friday from 7:30am to 11pm, Saturday and Sunday from 9am to 11pm. Departures are every 10 minutes. The one-way fare is $1.25 for adults and 50¢ for seniors and children ages 5 to 11.

During the past few summers a **water taxi** has operated between the downtown Seattle waterfront (Pier 54) and West Seattle, providing access to West Seattle's popular Alki Beach and adjacent paved path. For a schedule of service, check with Metro (© **206/553-3000;** www.metrokc.gov/kcdot/tp). The one-way fare is $2 (free for children under age 5). Also free with a valid bus transfer or all-day pass.

FAST FACTS To find a physician, check at your hotel for a referral, or call the **Medical Dental Building,** 509 Olive Way, Ste. 1052 (© **206/448-CARE**).

Hospitals convenient to downtown include **Harborview Medical Center,** 325 Ninth Ave. (© **206/731-3000**), and **Virginia Mason Hospital and Clinic,** 925 Seneca St. (© **206/583-6433** for emergencies, or 206/624-1144 for information).

For 24-hour service, try **Bartell Drug Store,** 600 First Ave. N. (© **206/284-1353**), which is located upstairs from Larry's Market.

Although Seattle is a relatively safe city, it has its share of crime. The most questionable neighborhood you're likely to visit is the Pioneer Square area, which is home to more than a dozen bars and nightclubs. By day, this area is quite safe, but late at night, when the bars are closing, keep your wits about you. And keep an eye on your wallet or purse when you're in the crush of people at Pike Place Market. Whenever possible, try to park your car in a garage, instead of on the street, at night.

In Seattle you'll pay an 8.8% sales tax, and in restaurants you'll pay an additional 0.5% food-and-beverage tax on top of the sales tax. The hotel-room tax in the Seattle metro area ranges from 11.6% to 15.8%. On rental cars, you'll pay not only an 18.5% car-rental tax, but also, if you rent at the airport, an additional 10% airport concession fee, for a whopping total of 28.5%!

SPECIAL EVENTS & FESTIVALS Memorial Day weekend brings the **Northwest Folklife Festival** (© **206/684-7300;** www.nwfolklife.org), with dozens of national and regional folk musicians, crafts, and plenty of good food and dancing. All performances take place at Seattle Center.

By far the biggest event of the year is **Seafair** (© **206/728-0123;** www.seafair.org), with festivities occurring daily from early July to early August: parades, hydroplane boat races, the navy's Blue Angels, a Torchlight Parade, ethnic festivals, sporting events, and open house on naval ships.

The city's second most popular festival is **Bumbershoot** (© **206/281-8111;** www.bumbershoot.org), the Seattle Arts Festival. Rock, folk, jazz, rap, and world music performances draw crowds into Seattle Center and other venues over Labor Day weekend. You'll also find arts and crafts, film, theater, and more.

Downtown Seattle

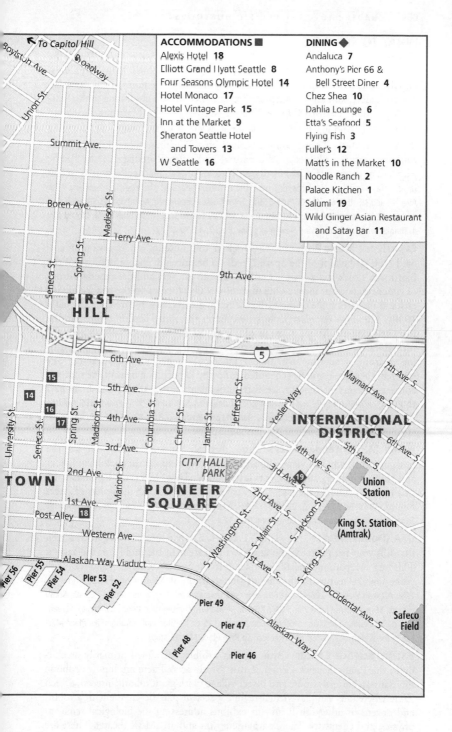

ACCOMMODATIONS ■
Alexis Hotel **18**
Elliott Grand Hyatt Seattle **8**
Four Seasons Olympic Hotel **14**
Hotel Monaco **17**
Hotel Vintage Park **15**
Inn at the Market **9**
Sheraton Seattle Hotel
   and Towers **13**
W Seattle **16**

DINING ◆
Andaluca **7**
Anthony's Pier 66 &
   Bell Street Diner **4**
Chez Shea **10**
Dahlia Lounge **6**
Etta's Seafood **5**
Flying Fish **3**
Fuller's **12**
Matt's in the Market **10**
Noodle Ranch **2**
Palace Kitchen **1**
Salumi **19**
Wild Ginger Asian Restaurant
   and Satay Bar **11**

WHAT TO SEE & DO

The Seattle waterfront, which lies along Alaskan Way between Yesler Way in the south and Bay Street and Myrtle Edwards Park in the north, is the city's most popular attraction. Yes, it's very touristy, with tacky gift shops, saltwater taffy, T-shirts galore, and lots of overpriced restaurants, but it's also home to the Seattle Aquarium, the IMAXDome Theater, Odyssey—The Maritime Discovery Center, and Ye Olde Curiosity Shop (king of the tacky gift shops).

Burke Museum   Located on the University of Washington campus, the Burke Museum features exhibits on the natural and cultural heritage of the Pacific Rim. It's noteworthy for its Northwest Native American art collection as well as its displays (with lots of fossils) on 500 million years of the region's history. 17th Ave. NE and NE 45th St. ℂ 206/543-5590. www.burkemuseum.org. Admission $5.50 adults, $4 seniors, $2.50 students, free for children under 6. Daily 10am–5pm (Thurs until 8pm). Closed July 4, Thanksgiving, Christmas, and New Year's Day. Bus: 7, 43, 70, 71, 72, or 73.

Experience Music Project   This rock 'n' roll museum is a massive multicolored blob at the foot of the Space Needle. The museum encompasses all of the Northwest's rock scene (from "Louie Louie" to grunge) and the general history of American popular music. One museum exhibit focuses on the history of guitars and includes some of the earliest electric guitars, which date from the early 1930s. The most popular exhibits here (after the Jimi Hendrix room) are the interactive rooms. In one you can play a guitar, drums, keyboards, or even DJ turntables. In another, you can experience what it's like to be onstage performing in front of adoring fans. In the museum's main hall, known as the Sky Church, there are regularly scheduled concerts. Expect long lines in the summer and leave plenty of time to see this unusual museum. 325 Fifth Ave. N. ℂ 877/ EMPLIVE or 206/EMPLIVE. www.emplive.com. Admission $20 adults, $16 seniors, $15 children 7–12, free for children 6 and under. Daily 9am–11pm. Bus: 1, 2, 3, 4, 13, 15, 16, 18, 24, or 33. Monorail: From Westlake Center at Pine St. and Fourth Ave.

Hiram M. Chittenden Locks   June through September (July–Aug are the peak months), you can view salmon both as they leap up the locks' fish ladder and through underwater observation windows. These locks, used primarily by small boats, connect Lake Union and Lake Washington with the waters of Puget Sound. 3015 NW 54th St. ℂ 206/783-7059. Free admission. Locks and surrounding park daily 7am–9pm. Visitor center daily 10am–6pm. Bus: 17.

IMAXDome Theater   The IMAXDome is a movie theater with a 180° screen that fills your peripheral vision and puts you right in the middle of the action. This huge wraparound theater is adjacent to the Seattle Aquarium, and for many years now has featured a film about the eruption of Mount St. Helens. Pier 59, 1483 Alaskan Way. ℂ 206/622-1868. www.seattleimaxdome.com. Admission $7 adults, $6.50 seniors, $6 youth, free for under 5 (IMAXDome–Aquarium combination tickets available). Screenings daily beginning at 10am. Closed Christmas. Bus: 15 or 18, then walk through Pike Place Market to the waterfront. Waterfront Streetcar: To Pike Place Market stop.

Pacific Science Center   Although its exhibits are aimed primarily at children, the Pacific Science Center is fun for all ages. There are life-size robotic dinosaurs, a butterfly house and insect village (with giant robotic insects), a Tech Zone where kids can play virtual-reality soccer or play tic-tac-toe with a robot, and dozens of other fun hands-on exhibits addressing the biological sciences, physics, and chemistry. There's a planetarium and an IMAX theater. There are always special exhibits, so be sure to check the schedule when you're in town. 200 Second Ave. N., Seattle Center. ℂ 206/443-2880. www.pacsci.org. Admission $8 adults,

Saving Money on Sightseeing

If you're a see-it-all, do-it-all kind of person, you'll definitely want to buy a **CityPass** ((C) 707/256-0490; www.citypass.com), which gets you into the Space Needle, Pacific Science Center, Seattle Aquarium, Woodland Park Zoo, and Museum of Flight at a savings of 50% if you visit all six attractions. The pass also includes a harbor cruise with Argosy Cruises. The passes, good for 9 days from date of first use, cost $34 for adults, $29 for seniors, and $22 for children. Purchase your CityPass at any of the participating attractions.

$5.50 seniors and children 3–13, free for children under 2. IMAX $6.75–$7.50 adults, $5.75–$6.50 seniors and children 3–13, free for children under 2. Laser show $5–$7.50. Various discounted combination tickets available. Mid-June to Labor Day daily 10am–6pm; the rest of the year Mon–Fri 10am–5pm, Sat–Sun and holidays 10am–6pm. Closed Thanksgiving and Christmas. Bus: 1, 2, 3, 4, 13, 15, 16, 18, 24, or 33. Monorail: To Seattle Center.

Pike Place Market   This 9-acre National Historic District is a bustling market with farmers and fishmongers, craftspeople and artists, restaurants and shops, and entertaining street performers. Pick up a free market map at the information booth almost directly below the large Pike Place Market sign. Watch for Rachel, the giant piggy bank, and the flying fish at the Pike Place Fish stall. For a glimpse behind the scenes at the market and to learn all about its history, you can take a 1-hour guided **Market Heritage Tour** ((C) 206/682-7453, ext. 653, for information and reservations). Tours are offered Wednesday through Saturday at 11am and 2pm and Sunday at noon and 2pm. One-hour tours are also offered by the **Pike Place Market Merchants Association** ((C) 206/587-0351; www.seattlepublicmarket.com). You'll get to meet some market merchants and hear their stories. Between Pike and Pine sts. at First Ave. (C) 206/682-PIKE. www.pikeplacemarket.org. Mon–Sat 10am–6pm; Sun 11am–5pm. Closed New Year's Day, Easter, Thanksgiving, Christmas. Bus: 15 or 18. Waterfront Streetcar: To Pike Place Market stop.

The Seattle Aquarium   The Seattle Aquarium's star attractions are the playful river otters and the sea otters, as well as the giant octopus. There's also an underwater viewing dome, and each September, you can watch salmon return up a fish ladder to spawn. There's also a beautiful large coral-reef tank, as well as many smaller tanks that exhibit fish from distant waters. Pier 59, 1483 Alaskan Way. (C) 206/386-4300. www.seattleaquarium.org. Admission $9 adults, $8 seniors, $6.25 children 6–18, $4.25 children 3–5 (joint Aquarium–IMAXDome tickets also available). Labor Day to Memorial Day daily 10am–5pm; the rest of the year daily 9:30am–7pm. Bus: 15 or 18, then walk through Pike Place Market to the waterfront. Waterfront Streetcar: To Pike Place Market stop.

Seattle Art Museum   The city's premier museum is a repository for everything from old masters to works by Andy Warhol, but is especially noteworthy for its Northwest Coast Indian art and artifacts, African collection, and Northwest contemporary art. Outside stands Jonathon Borofsky's *Hammering Man*, an animated three-story steel sculpture that hammers unceasingly. 100 University St. (C) 206/625-8900. www.seattleartmuseum.org. Admission $7 adults, $5 seniors and students, free for children 12 and under. Free 1st Thurs of each month (free for seniors 1st Fri of each month). Admission ticket also valid at Seattle Asian Art Museum if used within 1 week. Tues–Sun 10am–5pm (Thurs until 9pm). Also open Martin Luther King, Jr., Day, Presidents' Day, Memorial Day, and Labor Day. Closed Thanksgiving, Christmas, and New Year's Day (open holiday Mon). Bus: 10, 15, 18, or any bus using the bus tunnel.

Seattle Asian Art Museum   Housed in the renovated Art Deco building that once served as the city's main art museum, the Asian art collection emphasizes Chinese and Japanese art but also includes objects from Korea, Southeast Asia, South Asia, and the Himalayas. Collections of Chinese terra-cotta funerary art, snuff bottles, and Japanese *netsukes* (belt decorations) are among the museum's most notable. There are frequent lectures and concerts. 1400 E. Prospect St., Volunteer Park (14th Ave. E. and E. Prospect St.). ℂ 206/654-3100. www.seattleartmuseum. org. Admission $3 adults, free for children 12 and under. Free to all 1st Thurs and 1st Sat of each month (free for seniors 1st Fri of each month). Admission ticket plus $4 will get you into the Seattle Art Museum if used within 1 week. Tues–Sun 10am–5pm (Thurs until 9pm). Closed Thanksgiving, Christmas, and New Year's Day (open holiday Mon). Bus: 7, 9, or 10.

The Space Needle   From a distance it resembles a flying saucer on top of a tripod, and when it was built for the 1962 World's Fair, the 605-foot-tall Space Needle was meant to suggest future architectural trends. Today the Space Needle is the quintessential symbol of Seattle, and at 520 feet above ground level, the observation deck provides superb views of the city and its surroundings. Seattle Center, Fourth Ave. N. at Broad St. ℂ 800/937-9582 or 206/905-2100. www.spaceneedle.com. Admission $11 adults, $9 seniors, $5 children 5–12, free for children under 5. Free if dining in either restaurant. Summer daily 8am–midnight; other months Sun–Thurs 9am–11pm, Fri–Sat 9am–midnight. Valet parking $10 for 4 hr. Bus: 1, 2, 3, 4, 13, 15, 16, 18, 24, or 33. Monorail: From Westlake Center at Pine St. and Fourth Ave.

Woodland Park Zoo   Located in north Seattle, this sprawling zoo has outstanding exhibits focusing on Alaska, tropical Asia, the African savanna, and the tropical rainforest. The brown bear enclosure, one of the zoo's best exhibits, is a very realistic reproduction of an Alaskan stream and hillside. Don't miss the giant Komodo lizards from Indonesia. A farm animal area and petting zoo are big hits with the little ones. 5500 Phinney Ave. N. ℂ 206/684-4800. www.zoo.org. Admission $9 adults, $8.25 seniors and college students, $6.50 travelers with disabilities and children 6–17, $4.25 children 3–5, free for children 2 and under. Mar 15–Apr 30 daily 9:30am–5pm; May 1–Sept 14 daily 9:30am–6pm; Sept 15–Oct 14 daily 9:30am–5pm; Oct 15–Mar 14 daily 9:30am–4pm. Parking $3.50. Bus: 5.

PARKS & PUBLIC GARDENS

For serious communing with nature, nothing will do but **Discovery Park,** 3801 W. Government Way (ℂ **206/386-4236**). Occupying a high bluff and sandy point jutting into Puget Sound, this is Seattle's largest and wildest park. You can easily spend a day wandering the trails and beaches here. The park's visitor center is open daily from 8:30am to 5pm. To reach the park, follow the waterfront north from downtown Seattle toward the Magnolia neighborhood and watch for signs to the park.

Up on Capitol Hill, at East Prospect Street and 14th Avenue East, you'll find **Volunteer Park,** 1247 15th Ave. E. (ℂ **206/684-4075**), which is surrounded by the elegant mansions of Capitol Hill. It's a popular spot for sunning and playing Frisbee, and it's home to the Seattle Asian Art Museum (above), an amphitheater, a water tower with a superb view of the city, and a conservatory filled with tropical and desert plants.

Any avid gardener should be sure to make a trip across one of Seattle's two floating bridges to the city of Bellevue and the **Bellevue Botanical Garden,** Wilburton Hill Park, 12001 Main St., Bellevue (ℂ **425/452-2750;** www.bellevuebotanical. org). This 36-acre garden has become one of the Northwest's most talked-about perennial gardens. The summertime displays of flowers, in expansive mixed borders, are absolutely gorgeous. Free admission. Open daily from 7:30am to dusk; visitor center daily from 9am to 4pm. Take the NE Fourth Street exit off I-405.

Situated on 3½ acres of land, the **Japanese Garden** Washington Park Arboretum, Lake Washington Boulevard East, north of East Madison Street (© **206/ 684-4725;** Bus: 11), is a perfect little world unto itself, with babbling brooks, a lake rimmed with Japanese irises and filled with colorful koi (Japanese carp), and a cherry orchard (for spring color). A special Tea Garden encloses a Tea House, where, between April and October, on the third Saturday of each month at 1:30pm, you can attend a traditional tea ceremony. Unfortunately, noise from a nearby road can be distracting at times. Admission is $2.50 adults; $1.50 seniors, persons with disabilities, and children 6–18; free for children under 6. Hours are March daily from 10am to 6pm; April through May daily from 10am to 7pm; June through August daily from 10am to 8pm; September through October daily from 10am to 6pm; November daily from 10am to 4pm. Closed December through February. Acres of trees and shrubs stretch from the far side of Capitol Hill all the way to the Montlake Cut, a canal connecting Lake Washington to Lake Union. Within the 230-acre **Washington Park Arboretum,** 2300 Arboretum Dr. E. (© **206/543-8800;** Bus: 11, 43, or 48), there are 5,000 varieties of plants and quiet trails that are pleasant throughout the year but are most beautiful in spring, when the azaleas, cherry trees, rhododendrons, and dogwoods are all in flower. The north end of the arboretum, a marshland that is home to ducks and herons, is popular with kayakers, canoeists (see "Outdoor Pursuits," below, for places to rent a canoe or kayak), and bird-watchers. Free tours are offered Saturday and Sunday at 1pm. Admission is free. The arboretum is open daily 7am to dusk; Graham Visitors Center is open daily from 10am to 4pm. Enter on Lake Washington Boulevard off East Madison Street; or follow Wash. 520 off I-5 north of downtown, take the Montlake Boulevard exit, and go straight through the first intersection.

ORGANIZED TOURS

Seattle's most popular guided walking excursion is the **Underground Tour,** 608 First Ave. (© **888/608-6337** or 206/682-4646; www.undergroundtour.com), offering a seamier side of city history and off-color humor. The tours lead down below street level in the Pioneer Square area, where you can still see vestiges of businesses built before the great fire of 1889.

For an insider's glimpse of life in the International District, call **Chinatown Discovery Tours** (© **425/885-3085;** www.seattlechamber.com/chinatowntour). You'll learn the history of this colorful and historic neighborhood; some tours include a six-course lunch or eight-course banquet.

Seattle is a city surrounded by water; if you'd like to see it from this perspective, contact **Argosy Cruises** (© **206/623-4252;** www.argosycruises.com), which offers everything from a 1-hour harbor jaunt to a cruise around Lake Washington that will take you past the fabled Xanadu built by Bill Gates.

Tillicum Village Tours, Piers 55/56 (© **800/426-1205** or 206/443-1244), takes you across Puget Sound to Blake Island State Marine Park, where you'll enjoy a salmon dinner and Northwest Coast Indian masked dances in a "village" built in conjunction with the 1962 Seattle World's Fair.

OUTDOOR PURSUITS

See "Parks & Public Gardens," above, for a rundown of great places to play.

Money-Saving Tip

The **Ticket/Ticket** booth under the big clock at Pike Place Market sometimes has boat tour tickets available at discounted prices. If your schedule is flexible, be sure to check here first.

On the waterfront, bike rentals are available from **Blazing Saddles,** 1230 Western Ave. (© **206/341-9994**). Along with your bike you get detailed route descriptions for popular and fun rides originating on the waterfront, including a route on Bainbridge Island and mountain bike trails on Vashon Island. With its lush, green back roads, and variety of eateries at the end of a loop ride, Bainbridge Island is our favorite bike excursion from downtown Seattle. Blazing Saddles also rents bikes at Seattle Center. Rental rates range from $7 to $11 per hour and from $28 to $48 per day.

Gregg's Green Lake Cycle, 7007 Woodlawn Ave. NE (© **206/523-1822**); and the **Bicycle Center,** 4529 Sand Point Way NE (© **206/523-8300**), both rent bikes by the hour, day, or week. Rates range from $3 to $7 per hour and $15 to $30 per day. These shops are both convenient to the **Burke-Gilman/ Sammamish River Trail,** a 27-mile paved pathway created mostly from an old railway bed. This path is immensely popular and is a great place for a family bike ride or to get in a long, vigorous ride without having to deal with traffic. The Burke-Gilman portion of this trail starts in the Ballard neighborhood of north Seattle, but the most convenient place to start a ride is at **Gasworks Park** on the north shore of Lake Union. From here you can ride north and east to **Kenmore Logboom Park** at the north end of Lake Washington. Serious riders can then continue on from Kenmore Logboom Park on the Sammamish River portion of the trail, which leads to the north end of Lake Sammamish and Marymoor Park, the site of a velodrome (bicycle racetrack). This latter half of the trail is actually our favorite portion of a ride along this trail. This section of the path follows the Sammamish River and passes through several pretty parks. There are lots of great picnicking spots along both trails. The West Seattle bike path along **Alki Beach** is another good place to ride and offers great views of the sound and the Olympics.

Throughout the city, there are dozens of miles of paved paths perfect for skating. You can rent in-line skates at **Gregg's Green Lake Cycle,** 7007 Woodlawn Ave. NE (© **206/523-1822**), for $20 per day or $7 per hour. The trail around **Green Lake** in north Seattle and the **Burke-Gilman/Sammamish River Trail** (see the description above) are both good places for skating and are convenient to Gregg's. Other favorite skating spots to try include the paved path in **Myrtle Edwards Park** just north of the Seattle waterfront, the paved path along **Lake Washington Boulevard** north of Seward Park, and the **Alki Beach** pathway in West Seattle.

If you'd like to try your hand at **sea kayaking,** check out the **Northwest Outdoor Center,** 2100 Westlake Ave. N. (© **800/683-0637** or 206/281-9694), which is located on the west side of Lake Union. Here you can rent a sea kayak for between $10 and $15 per hour. You can also opt for guided tours lasting from a few hours to several days, and there are plenty of classes available for those who are interested.

SHOPPING

The heart of Seattle's shopping district is the corner of **Pine Street** and Fifth Avenue. Within 2 blocks of this intersection are two major department stores,

Nordstrom and the Bon Marché, and two upscale urban shopping malls—Pacific Place and Westlake Center. The most famous shopping area is **Pike Place Market** (see "What to See & Do," above). **Pioneer Square,** Seattle's historic district, is filled with art galleries and antiques stores. **Capitol Hill** is the center of both the gay community and the city's youth culture, and has the most eclectic selection of shops in the city. Even funkier is the **Fremont** neighborhood just north of Lake Union, filled with retro stores selling vintage clothing, collectibles, and curious crafts.

A couple of miles east of Fremont there's the **Wallingford** neighborhood, which is anchored by an old schoolhouse that has been converted into a shopping arcade with interesting crafts, fashions, and gifts. The **University District,** also in north Seattle, has everything necessary to support a student population and also goes upscale at the University Village shopping center.

If antiques are your passion, you won't want to miss the opportunity to spend a day browsing the many antiques stores in the historic farm town of **Snohomish,** located roughly 30 miles north of Seattle off I-5. The town has more than 400 antiques dealers and is without a doubt the antiques capital of the Northwest.

The Legacy Ltd., 1003 First Ave (© **800/729-1562** or 206/624-6350; www.thelegacyltd.com), is Seattle's oldest and finest gallery of contemporary and historic Northwest Coast Indian and Alaskan Eskimo art and artifacts.

Book lovers flock to **Elliott Bay Book Company,** 101 S. Main St. (© **206/624-6600**), a maze of rooms with battered wooden floors, a basement cafe, frequent author readings, and an excellent selection of books on the region.

Uwajimaya, 519 Sixth Ave. S., in the heart of the International District (© **206/624-6248**), is like your local supermarket—except that it sells nothing but Asian foods, housewares, produce, and toys.

REI (Recreational Equipment, Inc.), 222 Yale Ave. N. (© **206/223-1944**), was founded in Seattle back in 1938 and today is the nation's largest co-op selling outdoor gear. Its awesome flagship store, just off I-5, is a cross between a high-tech warehouse and a mountain lodge, with a 65-foot climbing pinnacle, a rain room for testing rain gear, a trail for test-riding mountain bikes, even a play area for kids.

WHERE TO STAY

Seattle is close on the heels of San Francisco as a West Coast summer-in-the-city destination, so its hotels stay pretty much booked solid for July and August, even with the recent proliferation of high-end hotels downtown. You may be faced with sticker shock at what the downtown hotels are charging. But if you're willing to head out a bit from downtown, you'll find prices a little easier to swallow.

In the following listings, price categories are based on rates for a double room in high season. Keep in mind that the rates listed do not include taxes, which add up to 15.8% in Seattle. Room rates are almost always considerably lower October through April (the rainy season), and downtown hotels often offer substantially reduced prices on weekends throughout the year (while budget hotels often charge more on weekends).

If you're having a hard time finding a room in your price range, consider using the services of **Pacific Northwest Journeys** (© **800/935-9730** or 206/935-9730; www.pnwjourneys.com). This company specializes in itinerary planning, but also offers a reservation service. The charge is $45 per reservation; however, you can usually make that up in savings on just a 2-night stay.

Every year November through March, more than two dozen Seattle hotels offer deep-cut discounts on their rooms through the **Seattle Hotel Hotline**'s (© 800/535-7071 or 206/461-5882) Seattle Super Saver Package. Room rates under this plan are generally 50% of what they would be in the summer months. Any time of year, you can call this hot line for help with making hotel reservations.

Often less expensive than downtown hotels, Seattle's many fine B&Bs provide an opportunity to see what life in Seattle is like for the locals. We've listed some of our favorites in the pages that follow, but to find out about other good B&Bs in Seattle, contact the **Seattle Bed and Breakfast Association** (© 800/ 348-5630 or 206/547-1020; www.seattlebandbs.com). Alternatively, you can contact **A Pacific Reservation Service** (© 800/684-2932 or 206/439-7677; www.seattlebedandbreakfast.com), which represents dozens of accommodations, mostly bed-and-breakfast homes, in the Seattle area.

Alexis Hotel   Listed in the National Register of Historic Places, this century-old building is a sparkling gem in an enviable location halfway between Pike Place Market and Pioneer Square and only 3 blocks from the waterfront, the Seattle Art Museum, and Benaroya Hall. Classic styling with a European flavor prevails in the guest rooms, each of which is unique. Almost half of the rooms here are suites, including very comfortable fireplace suites with whirlpool tubs. However, the spa suites are the real winners, offering lots of special amenities, plus whirlpool tubs in exceedingly luxurious bathrooms. The hotel's highly recommended restaurant, The Painted Table, serves creative Northwest cuisine. 1007 First Ave. (at Madison St.), Seattle, WA 98104. © 800/426-7033 or 206/624-4844. Fax 206/ 621-9009. www.alexishotel.com. 109 units. $295 double; $525–$825 suite. AE, DC, DISC, MC, V. Valet parking $23. **Amenities:** Restaurant; spa; fitness room; access to nearby health club; pets accepted with $25 fee.

Elliott Grand Hyatt Seattle   Luxury and technology merge at this, Seattle's newest downtown luxury hotel, which opened in summer 2000 and immediately raised the bar for all of Seattle's business hotels. If you are accustomed to staying in the finest hotels, book your room here. However, unless you spring for something pricier than the basic "deluxe guest room," you're going to be a bit cramped. The least expensive rooms at this hotel are definitely designed for solo business travelers. Although the health club is well outfitted and stylishly designed, there is no swimming pool. 721 Pine St., Seattle, WA 98101. © 800/233-1234 or 206/262-0700. Fax 206/625-1221. www.elliotthotel.com. 425 units. $370–420 double; $445–$3,000 suite. AE, DC, DISC, MC, V. Valet parking $28. **Amenities:** Restaurant; health club.

Four Seasons Olympic Hotel   If nothing but classically elegant surroundings will do, then head straight for the Four Seasons Olympic Hotel, an Italian Renaissance palace. Although many of the guest rooms tend to be rather small (with either two twin beds or one king), all have been recently renovated and are now very elegant. For plush surroundings, excellent service, and great amenities, this hotel can't be beat. In keeping with the overall character of the hotel, **The Georgian** is the most elegant restaurant in Seattle (with prices to match); its menu combines creative Northwest and Continental cuisines. 411 University St., Seattle, WA 98101. © 800/223-8772, 800/821-8106 in Washington, 800/268-6282 in Canada, or 206/621-1700. Fax 206/682-9633. www.fourseasons.com/seattle. 450 units. $315–$385 double; $365–$1,850 suite. AE, DC, MC, V. Valet parking $26. **Amenities:** 3 restaurants; indoor pool; spa; health club; pets accepted.

The Gaslight Inn   Anyone enamored of Craftsman bungalows and the Arts and Crafts movement of the early 20th century should enjoy a stay in this 1906 home. An annex next door has a studio and six suites with kitchens, dining areas, and separate bedrooms and living rooms. The innkeepers here can provide a wealth of information about the surrounding Capitol Hill neighborhood, which is the center of Seattle's gay scene. 1727 15th Ave., Seattle, WA 98122. © 206/ 325-3654. Fax 206/328-4803. www.gaslight-inn.com. 16 units, 2 with shared bathroom. $88–$148 double; $128 studio; $148–$198 suite. Rates include continental breakfast. AE, MC, V. Off-street parking for suites. **Amenities:** Outdoor pool; access to nearby health club.

Hotel Monaco   Downtown's hippest business hotel attracts a young and affluent clientele. Miss your pet? Call the front desk and they'll send up a pet goldfish for the night. Rooms, done in wild color schemes and bold patterns, come with fax machines, CD players, and all the standard extras. Other perks include the Sazerac restaurant (upscale Southern cuisine), a bar, 24-hour room service, and complimentary evening wine receptions. 1101 Fourth Ave., Seattle, WA 98101. © 800/945-2240 or 206/621-1770. Fax 206/624-0060. www.monaco-seattle.com. 189 units. $275–$295 double; $355–$960 suite. AE, DC, DISC, MC, V. Valet parking $24. **Amenities:** Restaurant; fitness room and access to nearby health club; pets accepted.

Hotel Vintage Park   Classically elegant, the Vintage Park is a must for wine lovers. Guests stay in rooms named for Washington wineries and enjoy complimentary wine tastings each evening. Deluxe rooms have the best views. Standard rooms, though smaller, are still very comfortable. Room service is available. 1100 Fifth Ave., Seattle, WA 98101. © 800/624-4433 or 206/624-0000. Fax 206/623-0568. www.hotelvintagepark.com. 126 units. $255–$300 double; $525 suite. AE, DC, DISC, MC, V. Valet parking $24. **Amenities:** Restaurant; access to nearby health club ($10 per day); pets accepted.

Inn at the Market   For romance and convenience, it's hard to beat this place. The small, European-style hotel is located right in Pike Place Market. Rooms have been recently renovated. Ask for one overlooking Puget Sound. Campagne serves excellent southern French cuisine, while Café Campagne offers casual country-style French fare. A cafe/juice bar serves fresh juices and simple breakfasts and lunches. 86 Pine St., Seattle, WA 98101. © 800/446-4484 or 206/443-3600. www.innatthemarket.com. 70 units. $180–$310 double; $285–$380 suite. AE, DISC, MC, V. Parking $17. **Amenities:** 3 restaurants; access to nearby health club.

Seattle Marriott Sea-Tac Airport   This is your best bet in the airport area. It's always sunny and warm inside this resortlike hotel, built around a steamy atrium garden with a pool, two whirlpool tubs, waterfalls, and totem poles. Rooms are comfortable and come with the standard extras. Ask for one with a view of Mount Rainier. You'll find a sauna, game room, room service, concierge, free airport shuttle, and car-rental desk. 3201 S. 176th St., Seattle, WA 98188. © 800/228-9290 or 206/241-2000. Fax 206/248-0789. www.marriott.com. 459 units. $129–$189 double ($79–$134 weekends); $225–$650 suite. AE, DC, DISC, MC, V. Parking $12. **Amenities:** Restaurant; indoor pool; fitness room; pets accepted.

Sheraton Seattle Hotel and Towers   At 35 stories, this is the largest hotel in Seattle. You'll almost always find the building buzzing with activity, but don't let the crowds put you off. From the collection of art glass in the lobby to the 35th-floor health club and pool, the Sheraton has figured out what travelers want. Rooms, although lacking in character, offer plenty of space and some decent views from the higher floors. 1400 Sixth Ave., Seattle, WA 98101. © 800/ 325-3535 or 206/621-9000. Fax 206/621-8441. www.sheraton.com/seattle. 840 units. $140–$405 double; $220–$750 suite. AE, DC, DISC, MC, V. Self-parking $22, valet parking $24. **Amenities:** 4 restaurants; indoor pool; fitness room.

Silver Cloud Inns Seattle–Lake Union   Located across the street from Lake Union, this moderately priced hotel offers good views from many of its spacious rooms, which come with microwaves, fridges, coffeemakers, hair dryers, and irons and boards. Plenty of waterfront restaurants are within walking distance, and floatplane tours leave from right across the street. 1150 Fairview Ave. N., Seattle, WA 98109. ℂ 800/330-5812 or 206/447-9500. Fax 206/812-4900. www.silvercloud.com. 184 units. June–Sept $160–$240 double; Oct–May $140–$215 double. Rates include continental breakfast. AE, DC, DISC, MC, V. Free parking. **Amenities:** Indoor pool and outdoor pool; fitness room and access to nearby health club.

W Seattle   The W hotel chain has won plenty of national attention and devoted fans for its oh-so-hip accommodations, and here in the land of dot.coms and espresso, the W is a natural. Sleek guest rooms are full of the usual amenities, as well as great perks such as Aveda bath products, goose-down comforters, and CD players (a CD library is available). 1112 Fourth Ave., Seattle, WA 98101. ℂ 877/W-HOTELS or 206/264-6000. Fax 206/264-6100. www.whotels.com. 419 units. $229–$390 double; from $500 suite. AE, DC, DISC, MC, V. Valet parking $22. **Amenities:** Restaurants (2); fitness room and access to nearby health club; pets accepted.

WHERE TO DINE

Andaluca NORTHWEST/MEDITERRANEAN   The sumptuous Andaluca mixes traditional and contemporary like no other restaurant in town. The menu changes frequently, but you'll usually find a traditional Spanish *zarzuela* (shellfish stew), cabrales-crusted beef tenderloin (made with blue cheese, grilled pears, and Marsala glaze), and the artful Dungeness crab tower, made with avocado, palm hearts, and gazpacho salsa. In the Mayflower Park Hotel, 407 Olive Way. ℂ 206/382-6999. www.andaluca.com. Reservations recommended. Main courses $19–$31; small plates $3–$9.25. AE, DC, DISC, MC, V. Mon–Thurs 6:30–11am, 11:30am–2:30pm, and 5–10pm; Fri–Sat 6:30–11am, 11:30am–2:30pm, and 5–11pm; Sun 7am–noon and 5–9pm.

Anthony's Pier 66 & Bell Street Diner SEAFOOD   There are lots of mediocre restaurants on the waterfront, but if you head up to the north end you'll find not only excellent food but also a stylish decor featuring lots of art glass. The upstairs dining room serves the likes of applewood-grilled salmon; downstairs, the Bell Street Diner offers meals easier on the wallet. There's also a walk-up window out front. In summer, the decks are the place to be. 2201 Alaskan Way. ℂ 206/448-6688. www.anthonys.com. Reservations recommended. Pier 66 main courses $15–$35. Bell Street Diner main courses $7.50–$30. AE, MC, V. Pier 66 Sun–Thurs 4:30–10:30pm; Fri–Sat 5–11:30pm. Bell Street Diner Sun–Thurs 11:30am–10:30pm; Fri–Sat 11:30am–11:30pm.

Canlis NORTHWEST   A local tradition since 1950, Canlis offers Northwest cuisine with Asian and Continental influences, keeping both traditionalists and adventurous diners content. This is the perfect place to close a big deal or celebrate a special occasion over filet mignon or Dungeness crab cakes with orange butter. To finish, go for the Grand Marnier soufflé. If wines hold your interest, Canlis has one of the best wine lists in Seattle. 2576 Aurora Ave. N. ℂ 206/283-3313. www.canlis.com. Reservations highly recommended. Main courses $22–$50; chef's tasting menu $95 with wines. AE, DC, DISC, MC, V. Mon–Sat 5:30pm–midnight. Valet parking $5.

Chez Shea NORTHWEST   Dark, romantic and intimate, this is one of Seattle's finest restaurants. Candlelit tables and views across Puget Sound to the Olympic Mountains provide the setting for the seasonally changing menu, prepared with ingredients fresh from the market below. On a recent summer evening, dinner started with savory basil panna cotta and then moved on to potato-leek bisque. There are usually five choices of entree. Though dessert is a la carte, you'll find it impossible to let it pass you by. For a more casual and economical meal, try **Shea's Lounge,** which serves dishes from the main restaurant as well as gourmet pizzas, soups, salads and nightly specials. Pike Place Market, Corner Market Building, 94 Pike St., Ste. 34. $\mathcal{C}$ 206/467-9990. www.chezshea.com. Reservations highly recommended. 4-course prix fixe dinner $43. AE, MC, V. Tues–Sun 5:30–10:30pm.

Dahlia Lounge PAN-ASIAN/NORTHWEST   One bite of any dish here will convince you that this is one of Seattle's finest restaurants. Mouthwatering and succulent Dungeness crab cakes are the house specialty and should not be missed. The menu, influenced by the far side of the Pacific Rim, changes regularly, with the lunch menu featuring many of the same offerings at slightly lower prices. For dessert, try the crème caramel. 2001 Fourth Ave. $\mathcal{C}$ 206/682-4142. www.tomdouglas.com. Reservations highly recommended. Main courses $18–$26. AE, DC, DISC, MC, V. Mon–Fri 11:30am–2:30pm; Mon–Thurs 5:30–10pm; Fri–Sat 5:30–11pm; Sun 5–10pm.

Etta's Seafood SEAFOOD   Located smack in the middle of the Pike Place Market area, this stylish, contemporary restaurant serves signature crab cakes (crunchy on the outside, creamy on the inside), which are not to be missed (if they're not on the menu, just ask), plus other great seafood dishes. 2020 Western Ave. $\mathcal{C}$ 206/443-6000. www.tomdouglas.com. Reservations recommended. Main courses $10–$28. AE, DC, DISC, MC, V. Mon–Thurs 11:30am–10pm; Fri 11:30am–11pm; Sat 9am–11pm; Sun 9am–10pm.

Flying Fish LATE-NIGHT/NORTHWEST/SEAFOOD   This hip Belltown restaurant offers bold combinations of vibrant, Asian-influenced flavors—and serves past midnight every night, keeping late-night partyers from going hungry. Diners can choose from small plates, large plates, and platters for sharing. The menu changes almost daily and every dish here is a work of art. Don't miss the smoked rock-shrimp spring rolls. 2234 First Ave. $\mathcal{C}$ 206/728-8595. www.flyingfishseattle. com. Reservations recommended. Main courses $15–$23. DC, MC, V. Daily 5pm–1am.

Fuller's NORTHWEST   Each dish here is as beautifully presented as it is superbly prepared, and surrounding you in this very elegant dining room are works of art by some of the Northwest's best artists. Fuller's menu changes seasonally, but Northwest flavors with Asian and Mediterranean accents predominate. A recent spring menu included ahi tuna carpaccio with a coconut emulsion. In the Sheraton Seattle Hotel and Towers, 1400 Sixth Ave. $\mathcal{C}$ 206/447-5544. Reservations recommended. Main courses $24–$34; tasting menus $55–$95. AE, DISC, MC, V. Tues–Sat 5:30–10pm.

Matt's in the Market AMERICAN REGIONAL/INTERNATIONAL Quite possibly the smallest gourmet restaurant in Seattle, Matt's is a tiny cubbyhole of a place in the Corner Market Building, which is directly across the street from the market information booth at First and Pike. The menu changes regularly, with an emphasis on fresh ingredients from the market stalls only steps away, and there's a good selection of reasonably priced wines. The menu pulls in whatever influences and styles happen to appeal to the chef at that moment. This is a real Pike Place Market experience. 94 Pike St. $\mathcal{C}$ 206/467-7909. Reservations not accepted. Main courses $8–$9 lunch, $15–$18 dinner. MC, V. Tues–Sat 11:30am–2:30pm and 5:30–9:30pm.

Noodle Ranch PAN-ASIAN   This Belltown hole-in-the-wall serves panAsian for the hip-but-financially-challenged crowd. It's a lively, boisterous scene, and the food is packed with intense, and often unfamiliar, flavors. Don't miss the fish grilled in grape leaves; nice presentation and knock-out dipping sauce. The Mekong grill is another dish not to be missed. Although the place is frequently packed, you can usually get a seat. Lots of vegetarian options. 2228 Second Ave. ℂ 206/728-0463. Main courses $7–$11. AE, MC, V. Mon–Thurs 11am–10pm; Fri 11am–11pm; Sat noon–11pm.

Palace Kitchen AMERICAN REGIONAL/LATE-NIGHT/MEDITERRANEAN Chef Tom Douglas's Palace Kitchen has an urban chic atmosphere, with cement pillars, simple wood booths, a few tables in the window, and a popular bar. The short menu features a nightly selection of unusual cheeses and different preparations from the applewood grill. Entrees often draw on Southern cooking influences: grilled prawns with grits and greens, catfish with greens and yam succotash. For dessert, the coconut cream pie is an absolute must. 2030 Fifth Ave. ℂ 206/448-2001. www.tomdouglas.com. Reservations not accepted. Main courses $11–$25. AE, DC, DISC, MC, V. Mon–Fri 11:30am–2:30pm; daily 5pm–1am.

Palisade NORTHWEST With a panorama that sweeps from downtown to West Seattle and across the sound to the Olympic Mountains, Palisade has one of the best views of any Seattle waterfront restaurant. It also happens to have great food and an inventive interior (a saltwater pond sits in the middle of the dining room). The extensive menu features dishes prepared on a grill, in a wood-fired oven, on a wood-fired rotisserie, and in an applewood broiler—adding up to numerous choices of flavorful seafoods and meats. Elliott Bay Marina, 2601 W. Marina Place. ℂ 206/285-1000. Reservations recommended. Main courses $17–$48. AE, DC, DISC, MC, V. Mon–Fri 11:30am–2pm and 5–10pm; Sat noon–2pm and 4:30–10pm; Sun 10am–2pm and 4:30–9pm.

Rover's NORTHWEST Tucked away in a quaint clapboard house behind a chic little shopping plaza is one of Seattle's most acclaimed restaurants. Chef Thierry Rautureau received classic French training before falling in love with the Northwest and the wonderful ingredients available here. The menu changes frequently, but may include smoked salmon and fennel-cucumber salad, spice-infused red wine sorbet, and venison with caramelized turnips and Armagnac sauce. You won't often find a vegetarian feast that can compare with the ones served here. 2808 E. Madison St. ℂ 206/325-7442. www.rovers-seattle.com. Reservations required. 5-course menu degustation $70 (vegetarian) and $80; chef's 8-course menu $115. AE, DC, MC, V. Tues–Sat 5:30 to about 9:30pm.

Salumi ITALIAN Salami, salami, and more salami. That's what you'll find at this Pioneer Square restaurant, which cures its own salami (as well as traditional Italian cured beef tongue). Order up a meat plate with a side of cheese and some roasted red bell peppers, pour yourself a glass of wine, and you have a perfect lunchtime repast in the classic Italian style. By the way, there's only one large table here, so expect to dine with strangers. 309 Third Ave. S. ℂ 206/621-8772. Reservations not accepted. Main courses $4.50–$9.50. AE, DC, DISC, MC, V. Tues–Fri 11am–4pm.

Serafina RUSTIC ITALIAN Off the beaten tourist track, Serafina is one of our favorite Seattle dining spots. It has a nice touch of sophistication but overall, it's a relaxed, rustic, romantic, neighborhood sort of place serving earthy, country-style dishes. The antipasti Serafina is always a good choice for a starter. Also try the bruschetta appetizers, which come with any of three different toppings. If you've brought a big appetite, the mixed grill is a great choice. There's live music (mostly jazz and Latin) several nights each week. 2043 Eastlake Ave. E. ℂ 206/323-0807. www.serafinaseattle.com. Reservations recommended. Pastas $8–$16; entrees $14–$22. MC, V. Mon–Fri 11:30am–2pm; Sun–Thurs 5:30–10pm; Fri–Sat 5:30–11pm.

Wild Ginger Asian Restaurant and Satay Bar PAN-ASIAN   This Pan-Asian restaurant has long been a Seattle favorite and is now located across the street from Benaroya Hall. Pull up a comfortable stool around the large satay grill and watch the cooks grill little skewers of anything from chicken to scallops to pork to prawns to lamb. Order three or four satay sticks and you have a meal. If you prefer to sit at a table and have a more traditional dinner, try the Panang beef curry (rib-eye steak in pungent curry sauce of cardamom, coconut milk, Thai basil, and peanuts). The lunch menu contains many of the dinner entrees at lower prices. 1401 Third Ave. ✆ 206/623-4450. Reservations recommended. Satay $2.75–$5.50; main courses $8.75–$23. AE, DC, DISC, MC, V. Mon–Thurs 11:30am–3pm and 5–11pm; Fri 11:30am–3pm and 5pm–midnight; Sat 11:30am–3pm and 4:30pm–midnight; Sun 4:30–11pm. Satay bar until 1am nightly.

SEATTLE AFTER DARK

To find out what's going on when you're in town, pick up a free copy of *Seattle Weekly* (www.seattleweekly.com), Seattle's arts-and-entertainment newspaper. You'll find it in bookstores, convenience stores, grocery stores, newsstands, and newspaper boxes around downtown and other neighborhoods. On Friday, the *Seattle Times* includes a section called "Ticket," which is a guide to the week's arts and entertainment offerings.

Ticketmaster (✆ 206/292-ARTS; www.ticketmaster.com) sells tickets to a wide variety of performances and events in the Seattle area. Half-price, day-of-show tickets to musical and theatrical performances are available at **Ticket/Ticket** (✆ 206/324-2744), with sales booths at Pike Place Market's information booth, in Capitol Hill's Broadway Market, 401 Broadway E., 2nd floor; and in Bellevue at Meydenbauer Center, NE Sixth Street and 112th Avenue.

THE PERFORMING ARTS   The **Seattle Opera** (✆ 206/389-7676; www.seattleopera.org), which performs at the Seattle Center Opera House, is considered one of the finest opera companies in the country, and *the* Wagnerian opera company. In addition to classical operas such as *The Magic Flute* and *The Barber of Seville,* the season usually includes a more contemporary production.

The 90-musician **Seattle Symphony** (✆ 206/215-4747; www.seattle symphony.org), which performs in the acoustically superb Benaroya Hall, offers an amazingly diverse musical season that runs September through July.

The **Northwest Chamber Orchestra** (✆ 206/343-0445; www.nwco.org), a perennial favorite with Seattle classical music fans, is a showcase for Northwest performers. The season runs September through May, and performances are held primarily in Benaroya Hall in downtown Seattle, although there are also concert series at the Seattle Asian Art Museum.

The **Seattle Repertory Theater** (✆ 877/900-9285 or 206/443-2222; www. seattlerep.org), which performs at the Bagley Wright and Leo K. theaters, Seattle Center, 155 Mercer St., is Seattle's top professional theater. The Rep's season runs September through June and productions range from classics to world premieres.

With a season that runs March through December, the **Intiman Theatre Company** (✆ 206/269-1900; www.intiman.org), which performs at the Inti-man Playhouse, Seattle Center, 201 Mercer St., fills in the gap left by those months when the Seattle Rep's lights are dark. Performing in the historic Eagles Building theater adjacent to the Washington State Convention and Trade Center, **A Contemporary Theater (ACT),** 700 Union St. (✆ 206/292-7676; www.acttheatre.org), offers slightly more adventurous productions than the other major theater companies in Seattle, though it's not nearly as avant-garde as some of the smaller companies. The season runs from the end of May to December.

Seattle's interest in fringe theater finds its greatest expression each September, when the **Seattle Fringe Theater Festival** (© 206/342-9172; www.seattlefringe. org), a showcase for small, self-producing theater companies, takes over various venues. There are usually performances by more than 70 theater groups from around the country.

The **Pacific Northwest Ballet,** Seattle Center Opera House, 301 Mercer St. (© 206/441-2424; www.pnb.org), is Seattle's premier dance company. During the season, which runs September through June, the company presents a wide range of classics, new works, and (the company's specialty) pieces choreographed by George Balanchine. This company's performance of *The Nutcracker,* with outstanding dancing and sets and costumes by children's book author Maurice Sendak, is the highlight of every season. **On the Boards,** Behnke Center for Contemporary Performance, 100 W. Roy St. (© 206/217-9888; www.ontheboards. com), is the area's best modern-dance venue.

THE CLUB & MUSIC SCENE   The Pioneer Square area is Seattle's main live music neighborhood, and the clubs have banded together to make things easy on music fans. The **"Joint Cover"** plan lets you pay one admission to get into nine different clubs. Participating clubs currently include Larry's Greenfront Cafe, Doc Maynard's, The Central Saloon, The Bohemian Café, Old Timer's Cafe, Zasu, and New Orleans.

For alternative rock, head **to Belltown's Crocodile Cafe,** 2200 Second Ave. (© 206/441-5611), a combination bar/club/restaurant that played a big role in Seattle's grunge movement. The **Showbox,** 1426 First Ave. (© 206/628-3151), books a variety of rock acts, many with a national following. **Ballard Firehouse,** 5429 Russell St. NW (© 206/784-3516), features an eclectic musical mix, from up-and-comers to revival bands. Cool and sophisticated, **Dimitriou's Jazz Alley,** 2033 Sixth Ave. (© 206/441-9729; www.jazzalley.org), has been Seattle's premier jazz club for more than 20 years, featuring only the best performers. The classic **Century Ballroom,** 915 E. Pine St. (© 206/324-7263), plays host to some of the best touring acts to come to town. This is Seattle's top spot for swing and salsa dancing. Established in 1892, **The Central Saloon,** 207 First Ave. S. (© 206/622-0209), is a Seattle institution. It's a must-stop during a night out in Pioneer Square. You might catch sounds ranging from funk to reggae.

THE BAR SCENE   Belltown's **The Virginia Inn,** 1937 First Ave. (© 206/ 728-1937), has a decidedly Old Seattle feel, due in large part to the fact that this place has been around since 1903. Best of all, this is a nonsmoking bar and it serves French food! **Oliver's,** located in the Mayflower Park Hotel, 405 Olive Way (© 206/623-8700), is martini central for Seattle.

You might see members of the Seahawks or Mariners at Pioneer Square's **FX McRory's,** 419 Occidental Ave. S. (© 206/623-4800), an upscale sports bar with an oyster bar and a large selection of bourbons and microbrews. For good stout and strong ales at a local brewpub, try **Capitol Hill's Elysian Brewing Company,** 1221 E. Pike St. (© 206/860-1920). South of Pioneer Square and popular before or after sports events is **Pyramid Ale House,** 1201 First Ave. S. (© 206/682-3377), part of the brewery that makes Thomas Kemper lagers and Pyramid ales.

THE GAY & LESBIAN SCENE   Capitol Hill is Seattle's main gay neighborhood, where you'll find the greatest concentration of gay and lesbian bars and dance clubs. Look for the readily available *Seattle Gay News* (© 206/ 324-4297), where you'll find ads for many of the city's gay bars and nightclubs. **Thumpers,** 1500 Madison St. (© 206/328-3800), is a classy restaurant/bar with a fireplace and two decks with great views. For dancing, head to **Neighbors,** 1509 Broadway Ave. (© 206/324-5358). For drinks and conversation, go to **C. C. Attle's,** 1501 E. Madison St. (© 206/726-0565), a cocktail bar with a 1940s look. A longtime favorite of the lesbian community is **Wildrose,** 1021 E. Pike St. (© 206/324-9210), a friendly restaurant/bar.

2 Whidbey Island & the San Juan Islands

WHIDBEY ISLAND

Whidbey Island, a mix of farms, forests, bluffs, and beaches just 30 miles north of Seattle, is a popular weekend getaway. Two historic towns, Langley and Coupeville, offer good restaurants, unique shops, art galleries, and charming inns.

ESSENTIALS

GETTING THERE   By Boat   From the south or west, Whidbey Island is accessible only by ferry. **Washington State Ferries** (© 800/84-FERRY or 206/ 464-6400) operate between Mukilteo and Clinton at the south end of the island and from Port Townsend to Keystone near Coupeville.

By Car   From the north, take I-5 to Wash. 20 west at Burlington. The highway turns south before you reach Anacortes and crosses the Deception Pass Bridge to reach the north end of Whidbey Island.

By Plane   The **Airporter Shuttle** (© 866/235-5247 or 360/380-8800) offers daily service from Sea-Tac International Airport to Oak Harbor.

VISITOR INFORMATION   Contact **Island County Tourism,** P.O. Box 1641, Coupeville, WA 98239 (© 888/747-7777; www.islandweb.org); **Central Whidbey Chamber of Commerce,** 107 S. Main St., Coupeville, WA 98239 (© 360/678-5434; www.whidbey.net/coup); or the **Langley South Whidbey Chamber of Commerce,** 208 Anthes St., Langley, WA 98260 (© 360/ 221-6765; www.whidbey.com/langley).

GETTING AROUND   Car rentals are available from **Budget** and **Enterprise** in Oak Harbor. **Island Transit** (© 360/678-7771) offers free public bus service on Whidbey Island.

EXPLORING THE ISLAND

If you're coming from the south via the ferry from Mukilteo, take Langley Road off Wash. 525 to the historic fishing village of **Langley.** First Street Park, right in downtown, provides access to a rocky beach and offers views of Saratoga Passage and the distant Cascades. There are several art galleries worth checking out here. The **Whidbey Island Center for the Arts,** 565 Camano Ave. (© 800/ 638-7631 or 360/221-8268), stages a wide range of performances year-round.

  Coupeville, in Central Whidbey just north of the turnoff for the ferry to Port Townsend, was founded in 1852. Several of the town's Victorian homes have been restored and turned into B&Bs and antiques stores. The quiet charm of yesteryear is Coupeville's greatest appeal. Learn about Whidbey's seafaring, farming, and military history at the **Island County Historical Society Museum,** 908 NW Alexander St. (© 360/678-3310).

  Three miles south of Coupeville is **Fort Casey State Park** (© 360/678-4519), a former military base built in the 1890s to guard Puget Sound. The park includes the 1897 Admiralty Head lighthouse, beaches, hiking trails, a campground, and an underwater reserve for scuba divers.

Deception Pass State Park (℃ 360/675-2417), at the northern tip of the island, is the most popular state park in Washington, with miles of beaches, quiet coves, freshwater lakes, forests, hiking trails, camping, and views of Deception Pass, the churning channel between Whidbey and Fidalgo islands.

If you'd like to explore the waters around Whidbey, the *Cutty Sark* (℃ 800/366-4097) offers day-sail cruises. The easiest way to explore the waters off Whidbey Island is to rent a sea kayak at Coupeville's **Harbor Store on the Wharf** (℃ 260/678-3625), which rents boats from the Coupeville Wharf. The country roads of Whidbey Island are perfect for exploring by bicycle. If you don't have your own bike, you can rent one from **Velocity Bikes,** 1832 Scott Rd., Freeland (℃ 360/331-2453; www.velocitybikes.com). Bikes rent for $25 per day.

WHERE TO STAY & DINE

The Inn at Langley, 400 First St., Langley (℃ 360/221-3033; www.innatlangley. com), is one of the most luxurious and romantic inns in the Northwest, with weathered cedar shingles, exposed beams, contemporary artwork, and rooms that boast 180-degree views and whirlpool tubs. The dining room serves an excellent fixed-price dinner focusing on Northwest flavors every Friday and Saturday.

Located right on Langley's little marina and designed to look like an old cannery building, the **Boatyard Inn,** 200 Wharf St. (P.O. Box 866), Langley (℃ 360/221-5120), is clad in a combination of wood, cedar shingles, and corrugated metal. Guest rooms are all huge and have full kitchens, water views, gas fireplaces, and small balconies. There are also four two-bedroom loft suites.

The Captain Whidbey Inn, 2072 W. Captain Whidbey Inn Rd., Coupeville (℃ 800/366-4097 or 360/678-4097; www.captainwhidbey.com), is a historic 1907 madrona-log structure, surrounded by shady, tranquil grounds. Rooms in the main building are small and lack private bathrooms, but they capture the feel of the island's seafaring past. Suites, cottages, and a few houses offer more space.

Built in 1855, **The Colonel Crockett Farm,** 1012 S. Fort Casey Rd., Coupeville (℃ 360/678-3711), is surrounded by rolling meadows and looks out over Crockett Lake to Admiralty Bay. The views are some of the best on the island, and no other inn on Whidbey better captures the island's idyllic rural feel.

In Langley, the intimate, romantic **Café Langley,** 113 First St. (℃ 360/221-3090), serves flavorful Middle Eastern dishes with a Northwest flair. The boisterous **Star Bistro,** 201½ First St. (℃ 360/221-2627), offers Mediterranean and Northwest-influenced pastas, salads, sandwiches, and seafood. On sunny days, head out to the rooftop patio.

In Coupeville, **Captain's Galley,** 10 Front St. (℃ 360/678-0241), serves straightforward fare at a waterfront location with fabulous views. Penn Cove mussels, crab cakes, and oysters are specialties here.

THE SAN JUAN ISLANDS

The idyllic San Juans have become a favorite getaway of urban Washingtonians, and in summer, there can be waits of several hours to get on a ferry with your car. One solution is to come over on foot or with a bicycle. You can then get around by renting a car or bike, hopping on the island shuttle buses, or calling taxis.

The San Juans consist of at least 175 named islands, or up to 786 if you include all the rocks and reefs that poke above the water at low tide. Only three (San Juan, Orcas, and Lopez) have anything in the way of tourist accommodations.

ESSENTIALS

GETTING THERE By Boat Washington State Ferries (© 800/84-FERRY or 206/464-6400; www.wsdot.wa.gov/ferries) operates car ferries between Anacortes and four of the San Juan Islands—Lopez, Shaw, Orcas, and San Juan—and Sidney, B.C. (on Vancouver Island near Victoria). Foot passengers are welcome to ride as well. **Victoria Clipper** (© 800/888-2535 or 206/448-5000; www.victoriaclipper.com) operates passenger ferries between Seattle and both Friday Harbor on San Juan Island and Rosario Resort on Orcas Island; it also stops in Victoria.

By Plane Kenmore Air, 950 Westlake Ave. N. (© 800/543-9595 or 425/486-1257), offers flights in floatplanes that take off from Lake Union (and also from the north end of Lake Washington). **West Isle Air** (© 800/874-4434 or 360/293-4691) flies from Bellingham and Anacortes to San Juan, Orcas, Lopez, and several of the outer islands. You can get from Sea-Tac Airport to the San Juan Islands ferry terminal in Anacortes on the **Airporter Shuttle** (© 866/235-5247 or 360/380-8800).

GETTING AROUND Car rentals are available on San Juan Island from **Susie's Mopeds** (© 800/532-0087 or 360/378-5244; www.susiesmopeds.com), the **Inn at Friday Harbor** (© 800/752-5752 or 360/378-3031; www.theinns. com), and **M&W Auto Sales** (© 360/378-2886). On Orcas Island, contact **Rosario Resort** (© 800/562-8820 or 360/376-2222). Expect to pay $45 to $96 per day.

San Juan Transit (© 800/887-8387, or 360/378-8887 on San Juan Island; www.sanjuantransit.com) operates a shuttle bus on San Juan during the summer.

SAN JUAN ISLAND

San Juan Island is the most populous and touristy of the islands. **Friday Harbor,** where the ferry docks, is the county seat for San Juan County and the only real town on all the islands. Friday Harbor's simple wood-frame buildings date back to the turn-of-the-20th-century and now house numerous shops, restaurants, motels, and inns.

Whale-watching is one of the most popular summer activities in the San Juans. At the **Whale Museum,** 62 First St. N. (© 800/946-7227 or 360/378-4710; www.whale-museum.org), you can see whale skeletons and models and learn all about the area's pods of orca whales. Here in Friday Harbor, you'll also find the headquarters of the **San Juan National Historic Park** (© 360/378-2240), at the corner of Spring and First streets. If you're interested in island history, stop by the **San Juan Historical Museum,** 405 Price St. (© 360/378-3949; www.sjmuseum.org)

Friday Harbor is also home to quite a few good art galleries and other interesting shops. At **Waterworks Gallery,** Argyle and Spring streets (© 360/378-3060), you'll find fine art and contemporary crafts by local and regional artists. At **Arctic Raven Gallery,** 1 Front St. (© 360/378-3433), you'll find contemporary Native American arts and crafts. At **The Garuda & I,** 60 First St. (© 360/378-3733), you'll find fascinating imported items from throughout the world, with an emphasis on Asian imports.

If you need some wine for your vacation or want to take some home with you, be sure to stop by the tasting room at **Island Wine Company,** Cannery Landing (© **360/378-3229**), which is the only place you can buy San Juan Cellars wines (made with grapes from eastern Washington). You'll find the wine shop on the immediate left as you leave the ferry.

At the north end of the island is **Roche Harbor Resort,** once the site of large limestone quarries. Amid the abandoned machinery stands the historic Hotel de Haro. Stop and admire the old-fashioned marina and colorful gardens, and then linger over a drink on the deck of the hotel's lounge.

South of Roche Harbor, on West Valley Road, you'll find the shady trees and spacious lawns of **English Camp.** Look inside the reconstructed buildings, imagine the days when this was one of the far-flung corners of the British Empire, and hike up 650-foot **Mount Young** for a panorama of the island.

South of English Camp, the Bay Road turnoff connects to Westside Road, which leads down the island's west coast. **Lime Kiln State Park,** the country's first whale-watching park, has a short trail leading down to a rocky coastline from which whales, porpoises, and sea lions can sometimes be spotted.

Whale-watching cruises lasting from 4 to 6 hours are offered in the summer by **San Juan Excursions** (© **800/80-WHALE** or 360/378-6636). Two- to 4-hour **sea-kayak tours** ($39–$49) are offered by **San Juan Safaris** (© **800/450-6858** or 360/378-1323; www.sanjuansafaris.com) at Roche Harbor Village and Friday Harbor; **Leisure Kayak Adventures** (© **800/836-1402** or 360/378-5992; www.leisurekayak.com); and **Crystal Seas Kayaking** (© **877/SEAS-877** or 360/378-7899; www.crystalseas.com). Most of these companies also offer full-day and overnight trips. Three- and 4-day trips are offered by **San Juan Kayak Expeditions** (© **360/378-4436;** www.sanjuankayak.com), which charges $325 and $420, respectively, for its outings.

Bicycling is another favorite sport of island visitors. If you didn't bring your own bike, you can rent one from **Island Bicycles,** 380 Argyle St., in Friday Harbor (© **360/378-4941**), which charges $6 per hour and $25 per day. Here on San Juan Island you can also rent scooters and mopeds. They're available in Friday Harbor by the hour or by the day from **Island Scooter Rental,** 85 Front St. (© **360/378-8811**), or from **Susie's Mopeds** (© **800/532-0087** or 360/378-5244; www.susiesmopeds.com), which is located at the top of the ferry lanes.

WHERE TO STAY & DINE

Friday Harbor House, 130 West St., Friday Harbor (© **360/378-8455;** www.fridayharborhouse.com), is a luxurious contemporary hotel. The bluff-top location ensures excellent views, and rooms contain fireplaces, whirlpool tubs, and balconies. The dining room is one of the best on the island, offering a seasonal menu with an emphasis on Northwest cuisine.

Olympic Lights Bed and Breakfast, 146 Starlight Way, Friday Harbor (© **888/211-6195** or 360/378-3186; www.olympiclightsbnb.com), on San Juan's dry southwestern tip, is a Victorian farmhouse surrounded by windswept meadows. The Ra Room has a bay window with a glorious view.

The Place Next to the San Juan Ferry, 1 Spring St. (© **360/378-8707**), is the island's finest waterfront restaurant. It aims to attract the upscale Seattle market with its regularly changing seafood menu. Located in the luxurious Friday Harbor House boutique hotel, **Friday Harbor House Dining Room,** 130 West St. (© **360/378-8455**), is the most sophisticated restaurant on San Juan

Island, boasting a great harbor view. The menu is short and relies heavily on local ingredients, including island-grown greens and Westcott Bay oysters.

ORCAS ISLAND

Orcas Island is a particular favorite of nature lovers, who come to enjoy the views of green rolling pastures, forested mountains, and fjordlike bays. **Eastsound** is the largest town on the island, with several interesting shops and good restaurants. To learn about local history, drop by the **Orcas Island Historical Museum,** 181 N. Beach Rd. (℃ **360/376-4849**).

A few miles west of Eastsound off Enchanted Forest Road is **Orcas Island Pottery** (℃ **360/376-2813**), the oldest pottery studio in the Northwest; at the end of this road, across from the West Beach Resort, you'll find **The Right Place Pottery Shop** (℃ **360/376-4023**). Between Eastsound and Orcas on Horseshoe Highway is **Crow Valley Pottery** (℃ **360/376-4260**), housed in an 1866 log cabin. On the east side of the island in the community of Olga, you'll find **Orcas Island Artworks** (℃ **360/376-4408**), which is full of beautiful work by more than 70 island artists.

Covering 5,000 acres, **Moran State Park** (℃ **360/376-2326**) is the largest in the San Juans and the main destination of most visitors to Orcas Island. On clear days, the summit of **Mount Constitution** (2,409 ft.) affords great views. Fishing, hiking, boating, mountain biking, and camping are all popular activities. The park is off Horseshoe Highway, about 12½ miles from the ferry landing.

Although Orcas is considered the most challenging of the San Juans for bicycling, plenty of visitors still pedal the island's roads. **Dolphin Bay Bicycles,** to the right as you get off the ferry (℃ **360/376-4157**), rents bikes and offers guided rides.

If you want to head out on the water in a 33-foot sailboat, call Capt. Don Palmer at **Amante Sail Tours** (℃ **360/376-4231**). Whale-watching excursions are offered by **Deer Harbor Charters** (℃ **800/544-5758** or 360/376-5989) and **Orcas Island Eclipse Charters** (℃ **800/376-6566** or 360/376-6556).

WHERE TO STAY & DINE

The **Spring Bay Inn,** Olga (℃ **360/376-5531;** www.springbayinn.com), is one of the only waterfront B&Bs in the San Juans. Innkeepers Sandy Playa and Carl Burger, both retired park rangers, make a stay here both fun and educational. You can soak in the hot tub on the beach, spot bald eagles, hike on the nature trails, and go for a guided sea-kayak tour. Four rooms have fireplaces, two have views from their tubs, and two have balconies. The **Turtleback Farm Inn,** 1981 Crow Valley Rd., Eastsound (℃ **800/376-4914** or 360/376-4914; www. turtlebackinn.com), is a restored farmhouse overlooking 80 idyllic acres of farmland at the foot of Turtleback Mountain. Simply furnished with antiques, the rooms range from cozy to spacious. The four rooms in the orchard house, with fireplaces and balconies, are among the most luxurious on Orcas.

Café Olga, Horseshoe Highway, Olga (℃ **360/376-5098**), is the best place for breakfast or lunch. Everything here is homemade, using fresh local produce whenever possible. Try the blackberry pie with Lopez Island Creamery ice cream. This building also houses Orcas Island Artworks, a gallery representing more than 70 local artists. **Christina's,** Main Street and North Beach Road., Eastsound (℃ **360/376-4904**), has a beautiful view down the sound. The deck is the place on the island for sunset dinners. The short menu changes regularly and features innovative cuisine prepared with an emphasis on local ingredients. Desserts can be heavenly.

3 The Olympic Peninsula & Olympic National Park

Olympic National Park is unique in the contiguous United States for its temperate rainforests, which are found in the valleys of the Hoh, Queets, Bogachiel, Clearwater, and Quinault rivers. Rainfall here can exceed 140 inches per year, trees grow more than 200 feet tall, and mosses hang from every limb. Trails lead from these valleys (and other points around the peninsula) into the interior of the park, providing access to hundreds of miles of hiking trails. In fact, trails are the only access to most of the park, which has fewer than a dozen roads, none of which lead more than a few miles into the park.

Within a few short miles of the park's rainforests, the jagged, snowcapped Olympic Mountains rise to the 7,965-foot peak of Mount Olympus and produce an Alpine zone where no trees can grow. Together, elevation and heavy rainfall combine to form 60 glaciers within the park. It is these glaciers that have carved the Olympic Mountains into the jagged peaks that mesmerize visitors and beckon to hikers and climbers. Rugged and spectacular sections of the coast have also been preserved as part of the national park, and offshore waters have been designated the Olympic Coast National Marine Sanctuary. June through September are much less wet than the other months. In winter, the road to Hurricane Ridge can be iffy, as it's plowed only Saturday through Monday.

ESSENTIALS

GETTING THERE **By Plane** **Fairchild International Airport** in Port Angeles is served by **Horizon Airlines.** There is bus service from Sea-Tac Airport to Port Angeles on **Olympic Bus Lines** (© **800/457-4492** or 360/417-0700).

By Bus There is service to Quinault Lake from Olympia and Aberdeen on **Grays Harbor Transit** (© **800/562-9730** or 360/532-2770).

By Boat Two ferries, one for pedestrians only and the other for both vehicles and pedestrians, connect Port Angeles and Victoria, B.C. The ferry terminal for both is at the corner of Laurel and Railroad streets. **Victoria Express** (© **800/633-1589**) is the faster of the two ferries (trip time: 1 hr.) and carries pedestrians only. It operates Memorial Day to September. The **Black Ball Transport** ferry (© **360/457-4491** or 250/386-2202) operates year-round, except for 2 weeks in late January and early February, and carries both cars and walk-on passengers (trip time: 1½ hr.).

By Car U.S. 101 circles Olympic National Park with main park entrances south of Port Angeles, at Lake Crescent, at Sol Duc, and at the Hoh River. The Port Angeles park entrance is 48 miles west of Port Townsend and 55 miles east of Forks.

VISITOR INFORMATION Contact **Olympic National Park,** 600 E. Park Ave., Port Angeles, WA 98362 (© **360/565-3130;** www.nps.gov/olym). For the Port Angeles area, contact the **Port Angeles Visitor Center,** 121 E. Railroad Ave., Port Angeles, WA 98362 (© **877/456-8372** or 360/452-2363; www.cityofpa.com). For the rest of the north Olympic Peninsula, contact the **North Olympic Peninsula Visitor and Convention Bureau,** 338 W. First St. (P.O. Box 670), Port Angeles, WA 98362 (© **800/942-4042** or 360/452-8552; www.olympicpeninsula.org). The **Olympic National Park Visitor Center,** 3002 Mt. Angeles Rd., on the south edge of Port Angeles on the road leading to Hurricane Ridge (© **360/565-3130**), has maps, books, and exhibits and is open daily year-round.

SEEING THE HIGHLIGHTS

From the **Olympic Park National Visitor Center,** continue 17 miles up to Hurricane Ridge, which offers breathtaking views of the park. Several hiking trails lead into the park; in winter, Hurricane Ridge is a popular cross-country skiing and snowshoeing area. The **Hurricane Ridge Visitor Center** has exhibits on Alpine plants and wildlife.

West of Port Angeles on U.S. 101 lies **Lake Crescent,** a glacier-carved lake. Near the east end of the lake, you'll find an information center and the 1-mile trail to 90-foot-tall **Marymere Falls.** At the west end, you'll find **Fairholm General Store** (© 360/928-3020), which has rowboats, canoes, and motorboats for rent.

Continuing west from Lake Crescent, watch for the turnoff to **Sol Duc Hot Springs** (© 360/327-3583). It's open daily from mid-May to September, weekends October through April. For 14 miles the road follows the Soleduck River, passing the Salmon Cascades along the way. In addition to the hot swimming pools and soaking tubs, you'll find cabins, a campground, a restaurant, and a snack bar. A 6-mile loop trail leads from the hot springs to **Sol Duc Falls** (from the end of the road, this is a 1½-mile hike).

Continuing west on U.S. 101 from the junction with the road to Sol Duc Hot Springs, you'll come to the crossroads of Sappho. Heading north at Sappho brings you to Wash. 112, an alternate route from Port Angeles. About 40 miles west, Wash. 112 reaches the community of **Neah Bay** on the Makah Indian Reservation. The reservation land includes **Cape Flattery,** the northwesternmost point of land in the contiguous United States. At the cape, there is a short trail to great viewpoints, and just offshore is **Tatoosh Island,** site of one of the oldest lighthouses in Washington. Neah Bay is a busy commercial and sportfishing port, and is also home to the impressive **Makah Cultural Center** (© 360/645-2711). Here is the most perfectly preserved collection of Native American artifacts in the Northwest. In late August, Makah Days are celebrated with canoe races, Indian dances, a salmon bake, and other events.

A turnoff 16 miles east of Neah Bay leads south to **Ozette Lake,** where there are boat ramps, a campground and, stretching north and south, miles of beaches accessible only on foot. A 3.3-mile trail on a raised boardwalk leads from the Ozette Lake trail head to **Cape Alava,** which, along with Cape Blanco in Oregon, claims to be the westernmost point in the contiguous United States.

Returning to U.S. 101, you soon reach the lumber town of **Forks.** At the heart of the controversy over protecting the northern spotted owl, Forks has long suffered high unemployment. The **Forks Timber Museum,** south of town on U.S. 101 (© 360/374-9663), chronicles the history of logging in this region, and has displays on Native American culture and pioneer days (open mid-Apr to Oct, daily 10am–4pm).

Just west of Forks is the first place you can drive to the Pacific Ocean. At the end of a spur road you come to the **Quileute Indian Reservation** and the community of La Push. In town is a beach at the mouth of the Quileute River; however, before you reach La Push, you'll see signs for Third Beach and Second Beach, two of the prettiest beaches on the peninsula. **Third Beach** is a 1.6-mile walk and **Second Beach** is just over a half mile from the trail head. **Rialto Beach** is just north of La Push and can be reached from a turnoff east of La Push.

This region's most notable feature is its rain, which has produced forests with some of the largest trees on earth. The rainiest spots are in westward-facing Bogachiel, Hoh, Queets, and Quinault river valleys. However, only the Hoh and

The Olympic Peninsula

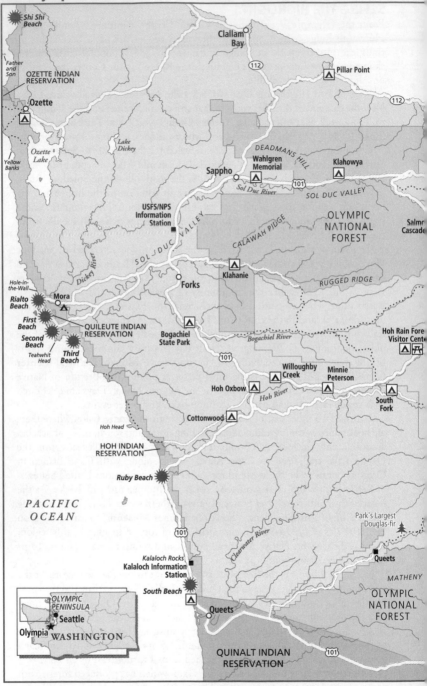

Shi Shi Beach

Clallam Bay

112

Pillar Point

Father and Son

OZETTE INDIAN RESERVATION

112

Ozette

Lake Dickey

DEADMANS HILL

Wahlgren Memorial

Klahowya

Sappho

Ozette Lake

Sol Duc River

SOL DUC VALLEY

Yellow Banks

USFS/NPS Information Station

OLYMPIC NATIONAL FOREST

Salmo Cascade

CALAWAH RIDGE

SOL DUC VALLEY

Dickey River

RUGGED RIDGE

Forks

Klahanie

Hole-in-the-Wall

Mora

Rialto Beach

Hoh Rain Fore Visitor Cent

First Beach

QUILEUTE INDIAN RESERVATION

Bogachiel State Park

Bogachiel River

Second Beach

101

Willoughby Creek

Minnie Peterson

Teahwhit Head

Third Beach

Hoh Oxbow

Hoh River

South Fork

Cottonwood

Hoh Head

HOH INDIAN RESERVATION

Ruby Beach

PACIFIC OCEAN

Park's Largest Douglas-fir

101

Clearwater River

Queets

Kalaloch Rocks

Kalaloch Information Station

MATHENY

South Beach

OLYMPIC PENINSULA

OLYMPIC NATIONAL FOREST

Seattle

Queets

Olympia

WASHINGTON

QUINALT INDIAN RESERVATION

101

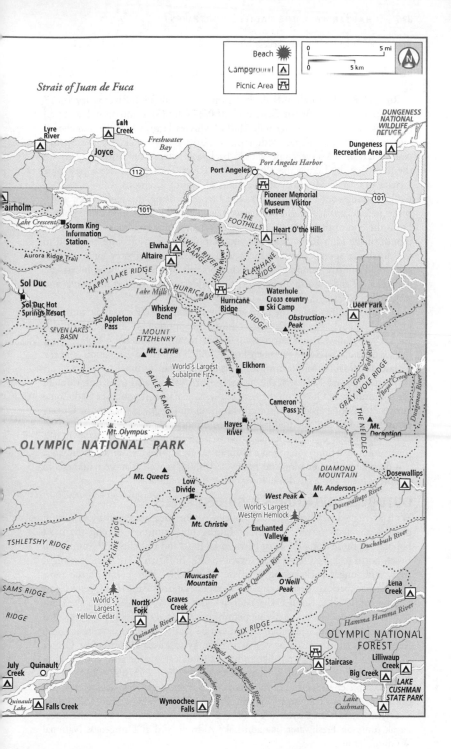

Strait of Juan de Fuca

Beach
Campground
Picnic Area

0   5 mi
0   5 km

N

Lyre River

Salt Creek

Joyce

Freshwater Bay

Port Angeles Harbor

Port Angeles

DUNGENESS NATIONAL WILDLIFE REFUGE

Dungeness Recreation Area

112

101

101

Fairholm

Lake Crescent

Storm King Information Station

Aurora Ridge Trail

Pioneer Memorial Museum Visitor Center

THE FOOTHILLS

Heart O'the Hills

Elwha Altaire

ELWHA RANGE

Elwha River Trail

Little River Trail

KLAHHANE RIDGE

HAPPY LAKE RIDGE

Sol Duc

Lake Mills

HURRICANE

Sol Duc Hot Springs Resort

Appleton Pass

SEVEN LAKES BASIN

Whiskey Bend

Hurricane Ridge

Waterhole Cross country Ski Camp

RIDGE

Deer Park

Obstruction Peak

MOUNT FITZHENRY

Mt. Carrie

World's Largest Subalpine Fir

Elwha River

Elkhorn

BAILEY RANGE

Cameron Pass

Gray Wolf River

GRAY WOLF RIDGE

Royal Creek

Dungeness River

Mt. Olympus

Hayes River

THE NEEDLES

Mt. Deception

OLYMPIC NATIONAL PARK

Mt. Queets

Low Divide

DIAMOND MOUNTAIN

West Peak

Mt. Anderson

Dosewallips River

Dosewallips

TSHLETSHY RIDGE

SKYLINE RIDGE

Mt. Christie

World's Largest Western Hemlock

Enchanted Valley

Duckabush River

SAMS RIDGE

RIDGE

World's Largest Yellow Cedar

North Fork

Muncaster Mountain

Graves Creek

East Fork Quinault River

O'Neill Peak

SIX RIDGE

OLYMPIC NATIONAL FOREST

Lena Creek

Hamma Hamma River

Quinault River

July Creek

Quinault

South Fork Skokomish River

Staircase

Lilliwaup Creek

Big Creek

LAKE CUSHMAN STATE PARK

Quinault Lake

Falls Creek

Wynoochee River

Wynoochee Falls

Lake Cushman

Bogachiel valleys are easily accessible. Several short trails along the coast lead through groves of old-growth trees. Among these are trails in the Hoh Valley (see below), the **Ancient Groves Trail** at Soleduck, and a short trail near the Lake Quinault Lodge.

Roughly 8 miles south of Forks is the turnoff for the Hoh River valley. It's 17 miles up to the **Hoh Visitor Center** (© 360/374-6925), campground, and trail heads. Walk the three-quarter-mile **Hall of Mosses Trail,** where the branches of big-leaf maples are draped with mosses. For a longer walk, try the **Spruce Nature Trail.** If you've come with a backpack, there's no better way to see the park than by hiking the 17-mile **Hoh River Trail,** which leads past Blue Glacier to Glacier Meadows on the flanks of Mount Olympus.

Continuing south on U.S. 101, but before crossing the Hoh River, you'll come to a secondary road heading west from the Hoh Oxbow campground. From the end of the road, it's a hike of less than a mile to a rocky beach at the mouth of the Hoh River. Sea lions and harbor seals feed offshore here, and to the north are several haystack rocks that serve as nesting sites for numerous seabirds. Primitive camping is permitted on this beach; from here, hikers can backpack 17 miles north along a pristine wilderness of rugged headlands and secluded beaches.

U.S. 101 finally reaches the coast at **Ruby Beach,** noted for its pink sand. The highway parallels the wave-swept coastline for another 17 miles. Along this stretch are pull-offs and short trails down to six numbered beaches. Near the south end, you'll find Kalaloch Lodge, which also has a gas station, and the **Kalaloch Information Station,** which is open only in summer.

Shortly beyond Kalaloch, the highway turns inland again, passing through the community of Queets on the river of the same name. If you'd like to do some rainy valley hiking away from the crowds, head up the gravel road to the **Queets campground** to find the trail leading up the valley.

A long stretch of clear-cuts and tree farms, mostly on the Quinault Indian Reservation, will bring you to **Lake Quinault.** Surrounded by forested mountains, this deep lake offers boating and freshwater fishing as well as more rainforests to explore. This is also a good area for spotting Roosevelt elk.

OUTDOOR ADVENTURES & GUIDED TOURS

With its rugged beaches, rainforest valleys, Alpine meadows, and mountaintop glaciers, the park offers a variety of **hiking** opportunities. Among the most popular are those along the coast between La Push and Oil City and from Rialto Beach north to Lake Ozette and onward to Shi Shi Beach. Day hikes, overnight trips, and longer backpacking trips are all possible. For several of the most popular backpacking destinations in Olympic National Park (the Ozette Coast Loop, Grand Valley, Royal Basin, Badger Valley, Flapjack Lakes, and Lake Constance), advance-reservation hiking permits are required or highly recommended between May 1 and September 30 and can be made up to 30 days in advance. Reservations can be made by contacting the **Wilderness Information Center** (© 360/565-3100). If you'd like to have a llama carry your gear, contact **Kit's Llamas,** P.O. Box 116, Olalla, WA 98359 (© 253/857-5274; www.northolympic.com/llamas). If you want to do a one-way backpacking trip, you can arrange a shuttle through **Olympic Tours and Charters** (© 360/452-3500).

Olympic Raft & Kayak (© 888/452-1443 or 360/452-1443) offers sea-kayak tours on Freshwater Bay and Lake Aldwell, and at Dungeness National Wildlife Refuge.

The town of Sekiu, on Clallam Bay, is a popular spot for both sportfishing and scuba diving. For salmon or deep-sea fishing, contact **Puffin Adventure** (© 888/305-2437 or 360/963-2744) or **Olson's Charters** (© 360/963-2311). Divers will want to stop in at the **Curley's Resort & Dive Center** (© 360/963-2281), on the main road through town.

WHERE TO STAY
IN & AROUND PORT ANGELES

As the peninsula's biggest town and a base for families exploring the national park, Port Angeles abounds in budget hotels. You'll find dozens along U.S. 101 east of downtown. Beyond town, accommodations are scarce, and those places worth recommending tend to be popular. It's wise to reserve before heading west from Port Angeles.

Red Lion Hotel, 221 N. Lincoln St., Port Angeles (© 800/RED-LION or 360/452-9215), is on the waterfront only steps from the ferry terminal, making it convenient when traveling to or from Victoria. Most rooms have balconies and large bathrooms; the more expensive units overlook the Strait of Juan de Fuca. There's an adjacent seafood restaurant, an outdoor pool, and a hot tub.

The 1910 **Tudor Inn,** 1108 S. Oak St., Port Angeles (© 360/452-3138; www.tudorinn.com), in a residential neighborhood 13 blocks from the waterfront, is surrounded by a large yard and lovely gardens. Furnished with European antiques, the inn offers a lounge and library, both with fireplaces. Several rooms have good views of the Olympic Mountains

Domaine Madeleine, 146 Wildflower Lane, 7 miles east of Port Angeles (© 360/457-4174; www.domainemadeleine.com), is a secluded B&B with a waterfront setting. Rooms are in several different buildings surrounded by colorful gardens, and all have views of the Strait of Juan de Fuca and the mountains beyond. All units have fireplaces and VCRs; four have whirlpool tubs.

The historic **Lake Crescent Lodge,** 416 Lake Crescent Rd. (© 360/928-3211; www.lakecrescentlodge.com), 20 miles west of Port Angeles on picturesque Lake Crescent, contains rustic wood paneling, a stone fireplace, and a sunroom. Rooms in the main lodge are the oldest, with shared bathrooms. More modern motel-style rooms and cottages are available, some with fireplaces and all with a lake or mountain view. The lodge features a dining room, a lobby lounge, and rowboat rentals.

Long a popular family vacation spot, the **Sol Duc Hot Springs Resort,** Sol Duc Road (© 360/327-3583; www.northolympic.com/solduc), 40 miles west of Port Angeles, attracts campers, day-trippers, and resort guests to its three hot spring–fed swimming pools. The grounds are grassy and open, but the forest is at arm's reach. The modern cabins are comfortable if not spacious. There's an excellent restaurant, a poolside deli, an espresso bar, a grocery store, and massage service. Closed November through March.

ON THE WEST SIDE OF THE PARK

The town of Forks has several inexpensive motels and is a good place to look if you happen to be out this way without a reservation. One option is the **Forks Motel,** 351 S. Forks Ave. (© 800/544-3416 or 360/374-6243).

Perched on a bluff above the thundering Pacific Ocean, the **Kalaloch Lodge,** 157151 U.S. 101 (© 360/962-2271), 35 miles south of Forks, has a breathtaking setting. Rooms in the old cedar-shingled lodge are the least expensive, but the oceanview bluff cabins are the most in demand. The Sea Crest House motel-style rooms are great for comfort. You'll find a coffee shop, dining room, general store, and gas station. Book at least 4 months ahead.

Set on Lake Quinault in the southwest corner of the park, **Lake Quinault Lodge,** 345 South Shore Rd., Quinault (© **800/562-6672** in Washington and Oregon, or 360/288-2900; www.visitlakequinault.com), is the grande dame of the Olympic Peninsula. It possesses an ageless tranquility, with towering firs and cedars shading the rustic lodge and deck. Some rooms have balconies or fireplaces, but none have TVs or phones. There's a dining room, an indoor pool, a sauna, lawn games, boat rentals, and massages.

WHERE TO CAMP

For information on the 16 campgrounds within the national park, contact the Olympic National Park (see above, for address and phone number). Campground fees are $10 to$12 per night. The **Deer Park campground,** in the high country south of Port Angeles, is one of the most spectacular, and **Sol Duc Hot Springs campground** is one of the most popular. There are national park and national forest campgrounds along the shores of Lake Quinault. North of the park, on the Strait of Juan de Fuca, are two county parks with campgrounds. **Salt Creek County Park** is 13 miles west of Port Angeles on Wash. 112; Pillar Point County Park is another 22 miles farther west.

The beaches offer some of the best camping, but do not have established campgrounds. Several beaches are within 3 miles or so of the nearest road, but others require several days of walking.

WHERE TO DINE

The casual **Bella Italia,** 118 E. First St. (© **360/457-5442**), is located in the basement of a natural foods store in downtown Port Angeles and serves reliable Italian food. Local seafood makes it onto the menu in a few places, including smoked salmon ravioli, smoked salmon fettuccine, and steamed mussels and clams.

On the west side of Port Angeles, **Toga's International Cuisine,** 122 W. Lauridsen Blvd. (© **360/452-1952**), is an unexpected and unusual treat. Chef Toga Hertzog apprenticed in the Black Forest, home of the traditional *Jagerstein* style of cooking in which diners cook their own meat or prawns on a hot rock. With 24 hours notice, you can also have Swiss cheese fondue or a lighter seafood fondue.

You can't miss the strikingly painted **C'est Si Bon,** 23 Cedar Park Rd. (© **360/ 452-8888**), 4 miles south of Port Angeles off U.S. 101. Inside, you'll find classic decor, European artwork, chandeliers, and a limited menu of flavorful French dishes.

4 Mount Rainier National Park

At 14,410 feet, Mount Rainier is the highest point in Washington, and to the sun-starved residents of Seattle, the dormant volcano is a giant weather gauge. Either "the Mountain" is out and the weather is good, or it isn't (out or good). And when the Mountain is out, all eyes turn to admire its broad slopes, which remain snow-covered year-round. The region's infamous moisture-laden air has made Mount Rainier one of the snowiest spots in the country; record snowfalls have created numerous glaciers on the mountain's flanks, and one of these, the Carbon Glacier, is the lowest-elevation glacier in the continental United States.

Snow and glaciers notwithstanding, Rainier has a heart of fire. Steam vents at the mountain's summit are evidence that, although this volcanic peak has been dormant for more than 150 years, it could erupt again at any time. However, scientists believe that Rainier's volcanic activity occurs in 3,000-year cycles—and luckily we have another 500 years to go before there's another big eruption.

ESSENTIALS

For advance information, contact **Mount Rainier National Park,** Tahoma Woods, Star Route, Ashford, WA 98304 (© **206/569-2211;** www.nps.gov/mora). We recommend visiting the park as early in the day as possible, especially on summer weekends, when traffic and crowds can be daunting. Keep in mind that in winter you must use the main entrance (Nisqually), at the southwest corner of the park. The entry fee is $10 per motor vehicle or $5 per person for pedestrians, motorcyclists, and bicyclists.

EXPLORING THE PARK

Just past the main entrance, you'll come to **Longmire,** site of the National Park Inn, the Longmire Museum (with exhibits on the park's natural and human history), a hiker information center that issues backcountry permits, and a ski-touring center where you can rent cross-country skis and snowshoes in winter.

The road then climbs to **Paradise** (elevation 5,400 ft.), the aptly named mountainside aerie that affords a breathtaking close-up view of the mountain. Paradise, 110 miles southeast of Seattle and 150 miles northeast of Portland, is the park's most popular destination, so expect crowds. In July and August, the meadows here are ablaze with wildflowers. The circular **Henry M. Jackson Memorial Visitor Center** (© **360/569-2211,** ext. 2328) provides 360-degree panoramic views, and includes exhibits on the flora, fauna, and geology of the park, as well as a display on mountain climbing. The visitor center is open daily from early May to mid-October, and on weekends and holidays the rest of the year.

A 1.2-mile walk from the visitor center leads to a spot from which you can look down on the **Nisqually Glacier.** Many miles of other trails lead out from Paradise, looping through meadows and up onto snowfields above timberline. It's not unusual to find plenty of snow here as late as July.

In summer, you can continue beyond Paradise to the **Ohanapecosh Visitor Center** (© **360/569-2211,** ext. 2352), which is open weekends from late May to mid-June and daily from mid-June to early October. Nearby, you can walk through the Grove of the Patriarchs, a forest of old-growth trees, some of which are more than 1,000 years old.

Continuing around the mountain, you'll come to the turnoff for Sunrise, at 6,400 feet the highest spot accessible by car. A beautiful old log lodge serves as the **Sunrise Visitor Center** (© **360/569-2211,** ext. 2357). From here you can see not only Mount Rainier, seemingly at arm's length, but also Mounts Baker and Adams, plus Emmons Glacier, the nation's largest glacier outside Alaska. Some of the park's most scenic trails begin at Sunrise.

If you want to avoid the crowds and see a bit of dense old-growth forest, head for the park's **Carbon River entrance** in the northwest corner. This is the least visited region of the park because it offers views only to those willing to hike several miles uphill. At 3 miles, there's a glacier plowing through the middle of the rainforest, and at about 5 miles, you reach meadows and in-your-face views of the northwest flank of Mount Rainier. The road into this area is in bad shape and has washed out twice in recent years. Currently, high-clearance vehicles are recommended, but regular passenger vehicles have been getting through by driving very slowly.

SPORTS & ADVENTURES

Hikers have more than 240 miles of trails to explore within the park. The 5-mile **Skyline Trail** is the highest trail at Paradise and climbs above the tree line, with views of Mount Adams, Mount St. Helens, and the Nisqually Glacier. The **Lakes Trail,** of similar length, heads downhill to the Reflection Lakes, which have picture-perfect views of the mountain reflected in their waters. The park's single most memorable low-elevation hike is the **Grove of the Patriarchs Trail.** This 1½-mile round-trip trail is fairly flat (good for kids) and leads through a forest of huge old trees to a grove of 1,000-year-old red cedars on an island in the Ohanapecosh River. The trail head for this hike is near the Steven Canyon park entrance (southeast entrance).

If you'd like to do some horseback riding, contact **EZ Times Outfitters,** 18703 Wash. 706, in Elbe (© 360/569-2449), or **Indian Creek Corral** (© 509/672-2400), east of White Pass on U.S. 12 near the shore of Rimrock Lake.

In winter, miles of trails are open for snowshoeing and cross-country skiing, but there is limited access because of road closures. At Longmire, you'll find a rental shop (© 360/569-2411) with skis and snowshoes. There are also guided snowshoe walks at Paradise. Just outside the northeast corner of the park, off Wash. 410, **Crystal Mountain Resort** (© 206/663-2265 for information, or 888/SKI-6199 for snow conditions; www.skicrystal.com) is the state's best all-around downhill ski area. Experienced backcountry skiers will also find some challenging cross-country skiing here at Crystal Mountain.

WHERE TO STAY & CAMP

Accommodations are available inside the park at two rustic lodges. The 25-room **National Park Inn** (© 360/569-2275) is in Longmire, at the southwest corner of the park. Because the setting here is not as spectacular as that of Paradise Inn (see below), reservations are easier to come by. The inn's front veranda does have a view of the mountain, and guests often gather here at sunset on clear days. Because this lodge stays open year-round, it's popular with cross-country skiers. A lounge with a river-rock fireplace is perfect for winter-night relaxing. Facilities include a restaurant, a gift shop, and a cross-country ski and snowshoe rental shop.

Up at Paradise, the **Paradise Inn** (© 360/569-2275), built in 1917, offers breathtaking views of the mountain. Miles of trails and flower-filled meadows make this the perfect spot for some relatively easy Alpine exploring. Cedar-shake siding, huge exposed beams, cathedral ceilings, and a gigantic stone fireplace all add up to a quintessential mountain retreat. The Sunday brunch at the inn's large dining room is legendary. There's also a snack bar and lounge.

Nearby lodging is available in the towns of Greenwater, Ashford, Elbe, and Packwood.

There are several campgrounds within the park. Two of these—Cougar Rock and Ohanapecosh—require reservations, which should be made several months in advance for summer weekends by contacting the **National Park Reservation Service** (© 800/365-CAMP; http://reservations.nps.gov). The others are available on a first-come, first-served basis. They stay full throughout the summer, so arrive early. No electrical or water hookups are available. Only the Sunshine Point Campground is open year-round. There are also numerous National Forest Service campgrounds along Wash. 410 east of the park.

5 Mount St. Helens National Volcanic Monument

Mount St. Helens was once considered the most perfect of the Cascade peaks, a snow-covered cone rising above lush forests. Then on May 18, 1980, a violent eruption blew out the side of the volcano and removed the top 1,300 feet of the peak, causing the largest landslide in history. More than 540 million tons of ash traveled nearly 16 miles into the atmosphere, raining down as far away as Denver.

ESSENTIALS

Today, the area surrounding the volcano is preserved as Mount St. Helens National Volcanic Monument. Admission to one monument visitor center (or Ape Cave) is $3 ($1 children 5–15), and to two or more visitor centers (and Ape Cave) is $6 ($2 children 5–15). If you just want to park at one of the monument's trail heads and go for a hike, all you need is a valid Northwest Forest Pass, which costs $5 per day. If it's winter, you'll need a SnoPark Permit ($8 per day). For more information, contact **Mount St. Helens National Volcanic Monument** (© 360/247-3900; www.fs.fed.us/gpnf/mshnvm).

EXPLORING THE PARK

The best place to begin is the **Mount St. Helens Visitor Center** at Silver Lake, 5 miles east of Castle Rock on Wash. 504 (© **360/274-2100**), which houses extensive exhibits on the eruption and its effects on the region. Before reaching this center, you can stop and watch a 25-minute, 70mm film about the eruption at the **Mount St. Helens Cinedome Theater** (© **877/ERUPTION** or 360/ 274-9844), at Exit 49 off I-5.

Continuing east, you'll come to the **Hoffstadt Bluffs Visitor Center** (© **360/274-7750**) at milepost 27, which has a snack bar and is home to the take-off site for 20-minute helicopter flights over Mount St. Helens. Just past milepost 33, you'll reach the **Forest Learning Center** (© **360/414-3439**), open from mid-May to October. The center shows fascinating video about the eruption in a theater designed to resemble an ash-covered landscape. There are also displays on how forests destroyed by the blast have been replanted. Outside either of these centers you can usually see numerous elk on the floor of the Toutle River valley far below.

The **Coldwater Ridge Visitor Center** (© **360/274-2131**), at milepost 47 on Wash. 504, only 8 miles from the crater, features interpretive displays on the events leading up to the eruption and the subsequent slow regeneration of life around the volcano. You'll also find a picnic area, interpretive trail, restaurant, and boat launch at Coldwater Lake.

The newest visitor center, the **Johnston Ridge Observatory** (© **360/ 274-2140**), is 10 miles past the Coldwater Ridge Visitor Center. This observatory houses the equipment currently used to monitor activity within Mount St. Helens. The view from here is stupendous. The observatory is open May through October. The best trail on this side of the monument is the **Boundary Ridge Trail,** which heads east from the Johnson Ridge Observatory.

Drive around to the monument's east side for a close-up view of how the eruption affected the surrounding lands. For the best views, take U.S. 12 east from Exit 68 off I-5. In Randle, head south on Local Route 25 and then take Local Route 26. The **Woods Creek Information Station,** on Route 25 just before the junction with Route 26, has information on this part of the monument. At Meta Lake, Route 26 joins Route 99, which continues to the **Windy**

Ridge Viewpoint, where visitors get their closest look at the crater. Below Windy Ridge lies Spirit Lake, which was once one of the most popular summer vacation spots in the Washington Cascades. Today the lake is desolate and lifeless.

On the south side of the monument, you can explore the Ape Cave, a 2-mile lava tube formed 1,900 years ago when lava poured from the volcano. At the cave's headquarters (open late May to early Sept), you can join a ranger-led excursion or rent a lantern and explore on your own.

If you'd like a bird's-eye view, take a helicopter flight from the Hoffstadt Bluffs Visitor Center (© 800/752-8439 in Washington or 360/274-7750). Mount St. Helens Tours (© 360/274-6542; www.mt-st-helens-tours.com) offers van tours and a tent-and-breakfast tour, and also rents out six log cabins.

WHERE TO STAY & CAMP

You'll find nearly a dozen campgrounds near the monument. Sequest State Park, on Wash. 504, is the closest public campground to Coldwater Ridge (call Reservations Northwest at © 800/452-5687). Iron Creek Campground is the closest to Windy Ridge. For information on national forest campgrounds in the area, contact the Cowlitz Valley Ranger District, 10024 U.S. 12 (P.O. Box 670), Randle (© 360/497-1100). For national forest campground reservations, contact the National Recreation Reservation Service (© 800/280-CAMP; www.reserveusa.com).

Blue Heron Inn Bed & Breakfast, 2846 Spirit Lake Hwy., Castle Rock (© 800/959-4049 or 360/274-9595; www.blueheroninn.com), is a modern B&B on the road to the Coldwater and Johnston Ridge visitor centers. It has an excellent view of Mount St. Helens and makes a very good choice if you're looking for comfortable accommodations.

6 Portland

Situated at the confluence of the Willamette and Columbia rivers, Portland is a laid-back city of discreet charms. Strolling through the tranquil Japanese Garden on a misty May morning; people-watching at Pioneer Courthouse Square; perusing the acres of books at Powell's; shopping for arts and crafts at the Saturday Market; beer sampling at one of the many brewpubs; kayaking around Ross Island; or leaving the city for a quick trip to the beach or Oregon wine country—these are the quintessential Portland experiences to seek out and savor.

ESSENTIALS

GETTING THERE   By Plane   Portland International Airport (PDX) (© 877/739-4636; www.portlandairportpdx.com) is 10 miles northeast of downtown, adjacent to the Columbia River. The airport recently completed a major expansion. Many hotels near the airport provide courtesy shuttle service; be sure to ask when you make a reservation.

If you're driving to central Portland from the airport, follow signs for downtown, which will take you first onto I-205 and then I-84 west. Take the Morrison Bridge exit to cross the Willamette River. The trip into town takes about 20 minutes.

If you haven't rented a car at the airport, the best way to get into town is to take the new Airport MAX (Red Line) light-rail system, which operates daily every 15 minutes between 4:30am and 11:30pm and takes about 40 minutes to make the trip from the airport to downtown Portland. The fare is $1.55. For information on this new service, contact **Tri-Met** (© **503/238-7433;** www. tri-met.org).

Taxis are around all the time and the trip downtown generally costs between $20 and $25.

By Train   Amtrak (© **800/872-7245;** www.amtrak.com) serves **Union Station,** 800 NW Sixth Ave. (© **503/273-4866**), about 10 blocks from the heart of downtown, with daily service from Seattle (trip time: 3½ hr.), Spokane (8 hr.), Chicago (37 hr.), Oakland (19¼ hr.), and Los Angeles (31 hr.).

By Car   The major routes into Portland are I-5 from the north (Seattle) and south (Sacramento), and I-84 from the east (Boise). I-405 arcs around the west and south of downtown; I-205 bypasses the city to the east; and U.S. 26 runs west to the coast.

VISITOR INFORMATION   The **Portland Oregon Visitors Association (POVA) Information Center,** 701 SW Sixth Ave., Portland, OR 97205 (© **877/678-5263** or 503/275-8355; www.travelportland.com), is underneath Pioneer Courthouse Square near Starbucks. Hours are Monday through Friday from 8:30am to 5pm, Saturday from 10am to 4pm, Sunday from 10am to 2pm. There's also an information booth by the baggage claim area at Portland Airport.

GETTING AROUND   City blocks in Portland are about half the size of average blocks elsewhere, and since the entire downtown area covers only about 13 by 26 blocks, it's easy to explore on foot. Because the city is committed to keeping this area uncongested, it has invested heavily in its public transportation system. **Tri-Met public buses,** the **MAX (Metropolitan Area Express) light-rail system,** and the **Portland Streetcar** are all free within Fareless Square, the area between I-405 on the south and west, Hoyt Street on the north, and the Willamette River on the east. There is also a Fareless Square extension that allows free rides across the Willamette River (on buses and the MAX) to the Lloyd Center area, which is the site of a large shopping mall, the Portland Convention Center, and the Rose Garden arena.

Outside Fareless Square, adult fares on both Tri-Met buses and MAX are $1.25 or $1.55, depending on distance. A $4 all-day ticket, available from any bus driver, is good for travel to all zones and is valid on both buses and MAX. Transfers between the bus and MAX are free. Pick up bus routes and schedules at the **Tri-Met Customer Assistance Office** (© **503/238-7433;** www.tri-met. org), behind the waterfall fountain at Pioneer Courthouse Square, open Monday through Friday from 8:30am to 5:30pm. The Portland Streetcar operates between downtown Portland and the Northwest shopping and restaurant district and passes through the trendy Pearl District. It costs $1.25 outside of Fareless Square.

Because Portland is fairly compact, getting around by taxi is not prohibitively expensive. Wait at a taxi stand at one of the major hotels, or call **Broadway Cab** (© **503/227-1234**) or **Radio Cab** (© **503/227-1212**). Fares are $2.50 for the first mile, $1.80 for each additional mile, and $1 for additional passengers.

FAST FACTS   Three conveniently located area hospitals are Legacy Good Samaritan, 1015 NW 22nd Ave. (© **503/413-7711**); Providence Portland Medical Center, 4805 NE Glisan St. (© **503/215-1111**); and the Oregon Health Sciences University Hospital, 3181 SW Sam Jackson Park Rd. (© **503/494-8311**), just southwest of the city center. If you need a physician referral, call the Medical Society of Metropolitan Portland (© **503/222-0156**).

A pharmacy convenient to most downtown hotels is **Central Drug,** 538 SW Fourth Ave. (© **503/226-2222**), open Monday through Friday from 9am to 6pm, Saturday from 10am to 4pm.

Portland is a relatively safe city. Take extra precautions, however, if you venture into the entertainment district along West Burnside Street or into Chinatown at night. Northeast Portland is one of the centers of gang activity in the city; before visiting any place in this area, be sure to get very detailed directions so you don't get lost. If you plan to go hiking in Forest Park, don't leave anything valuable in your car. This holds true in the Skidmore Historic District (Old Town) as well.

Portland is a shopper's paradise—there's no sales tax. However, there is an 11.5% tax on hotel rooms in the city. (Outside the city limits, the room tax varies.) On car rentals, there is a 12.5% tax and if you pick your car up at the airport, there is an additional airport concession fee of around 11%. You can avoid all of these taxes by renting your car over on the west side of the metro area in Beaverton, Tigard, or Hillsboro.

SPECIAL EVENTS & FESTIVALS Celebrated annually since 1888, the **Portland Rose Festival** (© **503/227-2681;** www.rosefestival.org) has blossomed into the city's biggest celebration. The festivities now span 3½ weeks and include a rose show, two parades, a Rose Queen contest, a music festival, art shows, car races, dragon boat races, and an air show. Most events take place during the middle 2 weeks of June. Contact **Ticketmaster** (© **503/224-4400**) for tickets to specific events.

The last full weekend in July brings the **Oregon Brewers Festival** (© **503/ 778-5917;** www.oregonbrewfest.com) at Tom McCall Waterfront Park. The country's largest festival of independent craft brewers features plenty of local and international microbrews and music.

WHAT TO SEE & DO

Pioneer Courthouse Square, at the corner of Southwest Broadway and Yamhill Street, is the heart of downtown Portland and acts as an outdoor stage for everything from flower displays to protest rallies. The square, with its tumbling waterfall fountain and free-standing columns, is the city's favorite gathering spot, especially at noon when the Weather Machine, a mechanical sculpture, forecasts the weather for the upcoming 24 hours. Keep your eyes on the square's brick pavement for some surprising names.

A few blocks away, at 1120 SW Fifth Ave., stands *Portlandia,* the symbol of the city and the second-largest hammered bronze statue in the country, second only to the Statue of Liberty.

International Rose Test Garden Covering 4½ acres of hillside in the West Hills above downtown Portland, the gardens were established in 1917 by the American Rose Society and are used as a testing ground for new varieties of roses. These are among the largest and oldest rose test gardens in the United States. Though you will likely see some familiar roses in the Gold Medal Garden, most of the 400 varieties on display here are new hybrids being tested before marketing. These acres of roses give Portland its nickname: "City of Roses." Allow 1 hour. 400 SW Kingston Ave., Washington Park. © **503/823-3636.** Free admission (donations accepted). Daily dawn–dusk. Bus: 63.

Japanese Garden Considered the finest example of a Japanese garden in North America, Portland's Japanese Garden is one of the city's most popular attractions. Don't miss it. There are five different styles of Japanese gardens scattered over 5½ acres, and a view of volcanic Mount Hood, which has a strong resemblance to Mount Fuji. This is a very tranquil spot and is even more peaceful on rainy days when the crowds stay away, so don't pass up a visit just because it's raining. Many special events, exhibits, and demonstrations are held here throughout the year (ikebana flower arranging, bonsai, Japanese-inspired art). Allow 2 hours. 611 Kingston Ave. (in Washington Park). ℂ 503/223-1321. www.japanese garden.com. Admission $6 adults, $5 seniors, $4 students, free for children under 6. Apr 1–Sept 30 Mon noon–7pm, Tues–Sun 10am–7pm; Oct 1–Mar 31 Mon noon 4pm, Tues Sun 10am–4pm Closed Thanksgiving, Christmas, and New Year's Day. Bus: 63. MAX: Washington Park Station (in summer months, take the shuttle bus or the Zoo Train).

Oregon Historical Society   Oregon history, from before the arrival of the first Europeans to well into the 20th century, is chronicled in fascinating educational exhibits. The displays incorporate Native American artifacts, a covered wagon, nautical and surveying instruments, and contemporary objects such as snow skis, dolls, and bicycles. Museum docents are often on hand to answer questions. Note that the galleries here will be closed through July 2003 for renovation. Allow 2 hours. 1200 SW Park Ave. ℂ 503/222-1741. www.ohs.org. Admission $6 adults and seniors, $3 students, $1.50 children 6–12, free for children under 6, seniors free on Thurs. Tues–Sat 10am–5pm (Thurs until 8pm); Sun noon–5pm. Bus: 15. MAX: Library Station. Portland Streetcar: Art Museum (northbound); 11th Ave. and Jefferson St. (southbound).

Oregon Museum of Science and Industry (OMSI)   Located on the east bank of the Willamette River, this modern science museum has six huge halls. This is a hands-on museum, and the simulated earthquakes and tornadoes are perennial favorites. The museum also has an OMNIMAX theater and the Murdock Sky Theater, which features laser-light shows and astronomy presentations. The USS *Blueback* submarine is docked here, and tours are given daily. 1945 SE Water Ave. ℂ 800/955-6674 or 503/797-6674. www.omsi.edu. Museum or OMNIMAX $7 adults, $5 seniors and children 4–13; $4 submarine tours; $4 planetarium shows; laser light shows $4 matinee, $7 evening; discounted combination tickets available. Thurs 2pm until closing most tickets are 2-for-1. Mid-June to Labor Day daily 9:30am–7pm; the rest of the year Tues–Sun 9:30am–5:30pm (open holiday Mon). Closed Dec 25. Bus: 14 or 83.

Oregon Zoo   The Oregon Zoo is best known for its large breeding herd of elephants. It also has an excellent Africa exhibit, which includes a rainforest and a savanna. The Cascade Crest exhibit includes mountain goats, and the Steller Cove exhibit has sea lions and sea otters. The Amazon Flooded Forest is the newest exhibit, displaying everything from poison dart frogs to two-toed sloths. In the summer, there are outdoor concerts. A miniature train connects the zoo with the International Rose Test and Japanese gardens. 4001 SW Canyon Rd., Washington Park. ℂ 503/226-1561. www.oregonzoo.org. Admission $7.50 adults, $6 seniors, $4.50 children ages 3–11, free for children under 2; free 2nd Tues of each month 1pm to closing. Apr 1–Sept 30 daily 9am–6pm; Oct 1–Mar 31 daily 9am–4pm. Bus: 63. MAX: Washington Park Station.

Portland Art Museum   While this relatively small art museum has a respectable collection of European, Asian, and American art, it has been positioning itself as the Northwest stop for touring blockbuster exhibits in recent years. An expansion a couple of years ago added several new galleries and a small sculpture court to the museum. The galleries of Native American art and Northwest art are the museum's most impressive displays. 1219 SW Park Ave. ℂ 503/226-2811. www.portlandartmuseum.org. Admission $13 adults, $11 seniors and students, $6 ages 5–18, free for children under 5. Tues–Sat 10am–5pm (Oct–May Wed 10am–8pm), Sun noon–5pm; 1st Thurs of each month until 8pm. Bus: 6. MAX: Library Station. Portland Streetcar: Art Museum (northbound); 11th Ave. and Jefferson St. (southbound).

Portland

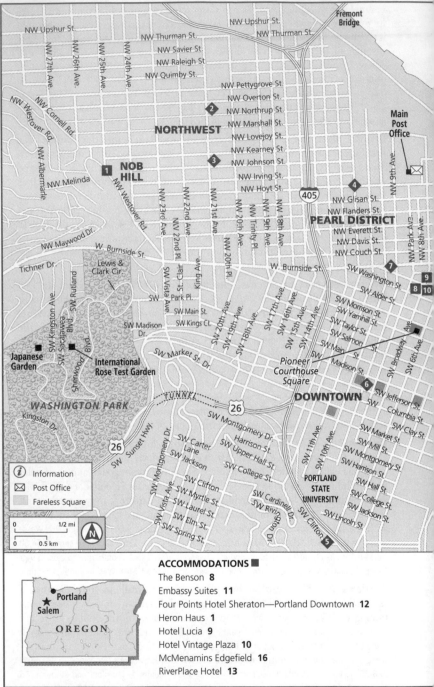

ACCOMMODATIONS ■

The Benson **8**
Embassy Suites **11**
Four Points Hotel Sheraton—Portland Downtown **12**
Heron Haus **1**
Hotel Lucia **9**
Hotel Vintage Plaza **10**
McMenamins Edgefield **16**
RiverPlace Hotel **13**

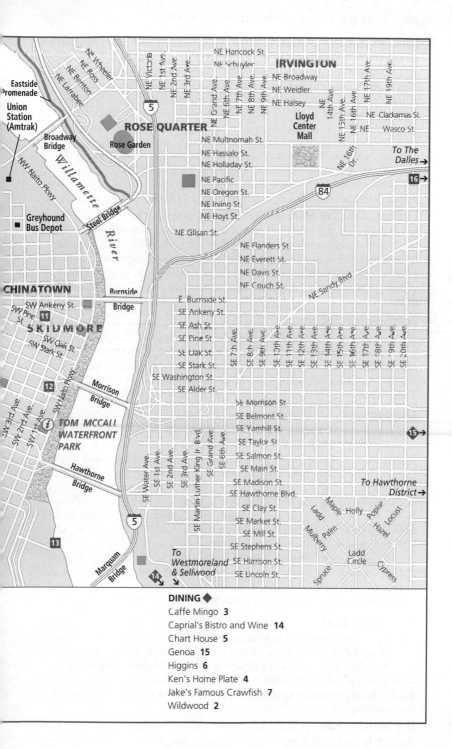

DINING ◆

Caffé Mingo **3**

Caprial's Bistro and Wine **14**

Chart House **5**

Genoa **15**

Higgins **6**

Ken's Home Plate **4**

Jake's Famous Crawfish **7**

Wildwood **2**

Portland Classical Chinese Garden   This classically styled Chinese garden takes up an entire city block and is the largest of its type outside of China. The garden, located in Portland's Chinatown, is surrounded by walls that separate the tranquil, timeless Chinese oasis from the buzz of 21st-century urban life that surrounds it. The garden is designed to evoke the wild mountains of China. With its many paved paths and small viewing pavilions, this garden has a completely different feel than the Japanese Garden. Try to visit as soon as the gardens open in the morning, before the crowds descend and the guided tours start circulating. Be sure to stop and have a cup of tea and maybe a snack in the garden's tearoom. Allow 2 hours. W. Everett St. and NW Third Ave. ℂ 503/228-8131. Admission $6 adults, $5 seniors and students, free for children 5 and under. Apr 1–Oct 31 daily 9am–6pm; Nov 1–Mar 31 daily 10am–5pm. Bus: 1, 4, 5, 8, 10, 16, 33, 40, or 77. MAX: Skidmore Fountain.

Portland Saturday Market   For years, the Northwest has attracted artists and craftspeople, and on Saturdays and Sundays throughout most of the year, nearly 300 of them can be found selling their creations at this outdoor market. 108 W. Burnside St. (underneath the west end of the Burnside Bridge between SW First Ave. and SW Naito Pkwy). ℂ 503/222-6072. www.portlandsaturdaymarket.com. Free admission. 1st weekend in Mar to Christmas Eve, Sat 10am–5pm and Sun 11am–4:30pm. Bus: 12, 19, 20. MAX: Skidmore Fountain.

OUTDOOR PURSUITS

If you want to check out the Portland skyline from water level, arrange for a sea-kayak tour through the **Portland River Company,** 0315 SW Montgomery St. (ℂ **503/229-0551;** www.portlandrivercompany.com). A 2½-hour tour circles nearby Ross Island; all-day trips on the lower Columbia River are also offered. The company also rents sea kayaks for independent use and offers raft trips.

SHOPPING

The blocks around **Pioneer Courthouse Square** are Portland's main upscale shopping streets. Here you'll find Nordstrom, Saks Fifth Avenue, the upscale Pioneer Place shopping mall, and numerous boutiques. The city's most stylish shopping area is the **Nob Hill/Northwest** neighborhood along NW 23rd Avenue beginning at West Burnside Street. Here you'll find block after block of interesting boutiques that are, unfortunately, being rapidly replaced by chains. For funkier shops, head out to the **Hawthorne District,** the city's counterculture shopping area. The **Pearl District,** centered around NW Glisan Street and NW 10th Avenue, has the greatest concentration of art galleries.

Well worth a visit is **Powell's City of Books,** 1005 W. Burnside St. (ℂ **503/ 228-4651;** www.powells.com), the bookstore to end all bookstores. Covering an entire city block three floors deep, Powell's is unusual in that it shelves new and used books together. You can easily spend hours browsing here.

WHERE TO STAY

The largest concentrations of hotels are downtown, which is the most convenient for visitors, and near the airport. Be sure to reserve as far in advance as possible.

If you're having trouble booking a room, contact the **Portland Oregon Visitors Association** (ℂ **877/678-5263** or 503/275-8355; www.travelportland.com), which offers a reservations service for the Portland metro area as well as information on B&Bs.

The Benson   Built in 1912, The Benson exudes old-world sophistication and elegance. In the French baroque lobby, walnut paneling frames a marble fireplace,

Austrian crystal chandeliers hang from the ornate plasterwork ceiling, and a marble staircase provides the perfect setting for grand entrances. The rooms vary considerably in size, but all are lavishly furnished in a plush Euro-luxe style. The deluxe king rooms are particularly roomy, but the corner junior suites are the hotel's best deal. Business travelers and the affluent are often found at this hotel. 309 SW Broadway, Portland, OR 97205. © **888/523-6766** or 503/228-2000, Fax 503/471-3920. www.bensonhotel.com 287 units. $230–$255 double; $350 junior suite; $600–$900 suite. AE, DC, DISC, MC, V. Valet parking $22. **Amenities:** Restaurant; pets accepted ($50 fee).

Embassy Suites   Located in the restored 1912 Multnomah Hotel, the Embassy Suites rivals the Benson hotel for the plushness of its lobby. This is a historic hotel in the grand style, with gilded plasterwork and potted palms in the lobby. Units are primarily two-room suites with classically styled furnishings and lots of space, a rarity in downtown hotels. The location is only a couple of blocks from the waterfront and the Portland Saturday Market. You'll find everyone from couples to families to business travelers here. 319 SW Pine St., Portland, OR 97204-2726. © **800/EMBASSY** or 503/279-9000. Fax 503/497-9051. www.embassyportland.com. 276 units. $129–$209 double. Rates include full breakfast. AE, DISC, MC, V. **Amenities:** Restaurant; indoor pool; spa.

Four Points Hotel Sheraton—Portland Downtown   Overlooking Waterfront Park and located on the MAX light-rail line, this 1960s vintage hotel looks nondescript from the outside, but interior renovations have made it one of the most stylish choices in town. You're only steps from the Willamette River and close to fine restaurants and shopping. Rooms are boldly contemporary in design. This is a favorite for young, cost-conscious travelers and business travelers. 50 SW Morrison Ave., Portland, OR 97204-3390. © **800/899-0247** or 503/221-0711. Fax 503/487-1417. www.fourpointsportland.com. 140 units. $99–$140 double. AE, DC, DISC, MC, V. Parking $11. **Amenities:** Restaurant; complimentary passes to Gold's Gym; pets accepted.

Heron Haus   A short walk from the bustling Nob Hill shopping and dining district of northwest Portland, the upscale, sedate Heron Haus B&B offers outstanding accommodations, spectacular views, and tranquil surroundings. Some rooms still have the original luxury plumbing fixtures (a plus, not a liability), including a shower with seven shower heads. There's also a room with a modern whirlpool spa that affords excellent views of the city. All rooms have fireplaces. 2545 NW Westover Rd., Portland, OR 97210. © **503/274-1846.** Fax 503/243-1075. www.heronhaus.com. 6 units. $135–$350 double. Rates include continental breakfast. MC, V. Free parking.

Hotel Lucia   Formerly the Hotel Imperial, this is downtown Portland's first truly hip hotel. Luckily the rates are surprisingly low, attracting stylish young visitors and business travelers. The location, across from the prestigious Benson Hotel, puts you within walking distance of most of the city's top attractions. Guest rooms boast dreamy beds with luxurious down comforters and bathrooms with gorgeous modern sinks. Try to get one of the corner rooms, which have lots of big windows and a bit more space than other rooms. 400 SW Broadway, Portland, OR 97205. © **877/225-1717** or 503/225-1717. Fax 503/225-1919. www.hotellucia.com. 128 units. $155–$185 double. **Amenities:** Restaurant.

Hotel Vintage Plaza   This 1894 National Historic Landmark hotel is the place to stay in Portland if you're a wine lover. A wine theme predominates in the decor, and there are complimentary evening tastings of Northwest wines. Although the standard rooms have much to recommend them, the starlight rooms and bilevel suites are the real scene-stealers. The starlight rooms, though small, have greenhouse-style windows that provide romantic views at night and let in tons of light during the day. The bilevel suites, some with Japanese soaking tubs, are equally impressive. The hotel's Pazzo Ristorante is one of Portland's best Italian restaurants. 422 SW Broadway, Portland, OR 97205. ✆ **800/263-2305** or 503/228-1212. Fax 503/228-3598. www.vintageplaza.com. 125 units. $139–$189 double; $189–$259 suite. AE, DC, DISC, MC, V. Valet parking $22. **Amenities:** Restaurant; pets accepted.

McMenamins Edgefield B&Bs don't usually have more than 100 rooms, but this is no ordinary inn. Located 30 minutes east of downtown and ideally situated for exploring the Columbia Gorge and Mount Hood, this is the flagship of the McMenamins' microbrewery empire. The property includes tastefully decorated rooms with antique furnishings, plus brewpub, beer garden, restaurant, movie theater, wine-tasting room, golf course, gardens, and hostel. The beautiful grounds give this inn the feel of a remote retreat. This is another favorite of young cost-conscious travelers. 2126 SW Halsey St., Troutdale, OR 97060. ✆ **800/669-8610** or 503/669-8610. www.mcmenamins.com. 114 units, 101 with shared bathroom, 24 hostel beds. $85–$105 double with shared bathroom; $115–$130 double with private bathroom; $20 per person for a bed in the hostel. Rates include full breakfast (not included with hostel). AE, DISC, MC, V. **Amenities:** 3 restaurants; 9-hole golf course.

RiverPlace Hotel With the Willamette River at its back doorstep and the sloping lawns of Waterfront Park to one side, the RiverPlace is one of Portland's only waterfront hotels, offering a quiet boutique-hotel atmosphere that seems to attract affluent couples and business travelers. There are standard river-view rooms, as well as slightly more expensive junior suites that provide a bit more space. Some rooms come with wood-burning fireplaces and whirlpool baths. 1510 SW Harbor Way, Portland, OR 97201. ✆ **800/227-1333** or 503/228-3233. Fax 503/295-6161. www.riverplacehotel.com. 84 units. $239–$379 double; $279–$389 junior suites; $309–$979 suite. All rates include continental breakfast. AE, DC, DISC, MC, V. Valet parking $18. **Amenities:** Restaurant; free access to nearby athletic club; pets accepted ($45 nonrefundable cleaning fee).

WHERE TO DINE

Caffé Mingo ITALIAN The menu here is short and focuses on scrupulously prepared Italian comfort food. From the antipasti platter with roasted fennel, fresh mozzarella, and roasted red pepper, to the unusual penne pasta with beef braised in Chianti and espresso, just about all of the items on the menu are winners. Arrive early or you'll have to wait for a table. 807 NW 21st Ave. ✆ **503/226-4646.** Reservations accepted only for parties of 6 or more. Main courses $8.50–$20. AE, DISC, MC, V. Sun–Thurs 5–10pm; Fri–Sat 5–11pm.

Caprial's Bistro and Wine NORTHWEST If you're a foodie, you're probably already familiar with celebrity chef Caprial Pence, who has written several cookbooks and hosted TV and radio food shows. That her eponymous restaurant is tucked away in a quiet residential neighborhood in southeast Portland may come as a surprise. Entrees combine perfectly cooked meats and seafoods with vibrant sauces such as cherry-barbecue. Pork loin is always a good bet here, as are the seasonal seafood dishes. 7015 SE Milwaukie Ave. ✆ **503/236-6457.** Dinner reservations highly recommended. Main courses $7–$12 lunch, $19–$28 dinner. MC, V. Tues–Thurs 11:30am–2:30pm and 5–9pm; Fri 11:30am–2:30pm and 5–9:30pm; Sat 11:30am–2:30pm and 5–9:30pm.

Chart House SEAFOOD Although this place is part of a national restaurant chain, it also happens to boast the best view of any restaurant in Portland. While you savor the best New England clam chowder in Portland, you can marvel at the views of the Willamette River, Mount Hood, Mount St. Helens, and nearly all of Portland's east side. Fresh fish (grilled, baked, or blackened) is the house specialty. 5700 SW Terwilliger Blvd. (C) 503/246-6963. Reservations recommended. Main courses $10–$16 lunch, $15–$40 dinner. AE, DC, DISC, MC, V. Mon–Fri 11:30am–2pm; daily 5–10pm.

Genoa REGIONAL ITALIAN   This has long been the best Italian restaurant in Portland, and with fewer than a dozen tables, it's also one of the smallest. Everything, from the breads to the luscious desserts, is made fresh in the kitchen with the best of locally available seasonal ingredients. This is an ideal setting for a romantic dinner. Service is attentive. The menu (fixed-price only) changes every couple of weeks. 2832 SE Belmont St. (C) **503/238-1464**. www.genoarestaurant.com. Reservations required. Fixed-price 4-course dinner $56, 7-course dinner $68. AE, DC, DISC, MC, V. Mon–Sat 5.30–9:30pm (4-course dinner limited to 5:30 and 6pm seatings only).

Higgins NORTHWEST/MEDITERRANEAN   Higgins, just up Broadway from the Heathman Hotel, strikes a balance between contemporary and classic in both its decor and its cuisine. The menu, which changes frequently, explores the contemporary culinary landscape, with the flavors of Asia and the Mediterranean emphasized. Dishes here are inventive, yet homey and satisfying. Be sure to leave room for dessert. Although the main dining room is quite formal, the bar in the back is a casual spot with its own less expensive menu (you can also order off the main menu in the bar). 1239 SW Broadway. (C) 503/222-9070. Reservations recommended. Main courses $7.75–$15 lunch, $16–$27 dinner. AE, DC, DISC, MC, V. Mon–Fri 11:30am–midnight; Sat 4pm–2:30am; Sun 4pm–midnight.

Jake's Famous Crawfish SEAFOOD   This place is a Portland institution and has been serving up crawfish since 1909 at an address that has housed a restaurant or bar since 1892. The noise level after work, when the bar is packed, can be high, and the wait for a table can be long if you don't have a reservation. However, don't let these obstacles dissuade you from visiting. A daily menu lists a dozen or more specials, but there's really no question about what to eat here: crawfish, which are served a variety of ways. 401 SW 12th Ave. (C) **503/226-1419**. Reservations recommended. Main courses $5–$13 lunch, $10–$24 dinner. AE, DISC, MC, V. Mon–Thurs 11:30am–11pm; Fri 11:30am–midnight; Sat 4pm–midnight; Sun 4–11pm.

Ken's Home Plate AMERICAN REGIONAL   Gourmet takeout food is the specialty of this small restaurant in the Pearl District. You'll find more than a dozen entrees, such as salmon-mushroom strudel, Tuscan meatloaf, and chicken Marsala. This a great place to grab some food to take back to your hotel room or out on a picnic (Forest Park and Washington Arboretum are both close), but there are a few tables here as well. 1208 NW Glisan St. (C) **503/517-8935**. Main courses $5–$8. MC, V. Tues–Sat 11am–8pm.

Wildwood AMERICAN REGIONAL   With a menu that changes daily and an elegant and spare interior decor straight out of *Architectural Digest,* Wildwood has for many years now been one of the best, most talked-about restaurants in Portland. Fresh seasonal ingredients are the basis for chef Cory Schreiber's simple yet imaginative dishes; often no more than four ingredients are used in order to let the flavors shine through. While entrees are always quite good, salads and sorbets are exceptional. 1221 NW 21st Ave. (C) **503/248-WOOD**. Reservations highly recommended. Main courses $10–$16 lunch, $19–$26 dinner. AE, MC, V. Mon–Sat 11:30am–2:30pm; Mon–Thurs 5:30–10pm, Fri–Sat 5:30–11pm; Sun 10am–2pm (brunch) and 5–9:30pm (family-style dinner).

PORTLAND AFTER DARK

To find out what's going on, pick up a copy of *Willamette Week* or the "A&E" section of Friday's *Oregonian*.

Tickets for many events can be purchased through **Ticketmaster** (© 503/224-4400; www.ticketmaster.com) or **Fastixx** (© 800/992-TIXX or 503/224-TIXX). The **Ticket Central** desk at the Portland Oregon Visitors Association's visitor center, 701 SW Sixth Ave., Ste. 1 (in Pioneer Courthouse Sq.), sells tickets to events and performances at almost all Portland venues.

THE PERFORMING ARTS   For the most part, the Portland performing arts scene revolves around the **Portland Center for the Performing Arts,** 1111 SW Broadway (© 503/248-4335; www.pcpa.com), which is comprised of four theaters in three different buildings.

Founded in 1896, the **Oregon Symphony** (© 800/228-7343 or 503/228-1353; www.orsymphony.org) is the oldest symphony orchestra on the West Coast. The diverse season runs September through June. Performances are held at the Arlene Schnitzer Concert Hall, 1111 SW Broadway at Main Street, an immaculately restored 1920s movie palace.

The **Oregon Ballet Theatre** (© 888/922-5538 or 503/222-5538; www.obt.org), which performs at the Portland Civic Auditorium, is best loved for its December performances of *The Nutcracker.*

Portland Center Stage (© 503/274-6588; www.pcs.org), which performs at the Portland Center for the Performing Arts, is the city's largest professional theater company. The season runs September through April.

THE CLUB & MUSIC SCENE   The **Crystal Ballroom,** 1332 W. Burnside St. (© 503/225-0047; www.danceonair.com), has over the years seen everyone from James Brown to the Grateful Dead. The theater is noted for its "floating" dance floor (set on rollers so that it bounces). The **Aladdin Theater,** 3017 SE Milwaukie Ave. (© 503/233-1994; www.aladdin-theater.com), is one of the city's main venues for touring performers such as Richard Thompson and Brian Wilson. A diverse performance calendar usually includes blues, rock, country, folk, and jazz, with regular singer-songwriter programs.

THE BAR SCENE   The cavernous **McMenamins Ringlers Pub,** 1332 W. Burnside St. (© 503/225-0047), with its mosaic pillars, Indonesian antiques, and big old signs, is about as eclectic a brewpub as you'll ever find. **Bridgeport Brewery and Brew Pub,** 1313 NW Marshall St. (© 503/241-7179), in the trendy Pearl District, is Portland's oldest microbrewery. The ivy-draped brick building has loads of character, just right for enjoying craft ales and great pizza.

Also in the Pearl District is ¡Oba!, 555 NW 12th Ave. (© 503/228-6161), one of the trendiest bars in Portland. This nuevo Latino restaurant has a tropical feel; after work, the bar is always packed with the stylish and upwardly mobile. **The Brazen Bean,** 2075 NW Glisan St. (© 503/294-0636), is a cocktail-and-cigar bar with a European elegance and a hip martini-drinking clientele.

7 The Oregon Coast

One of the most beautiful coastlines in the United States, the spectacular Oregon coast is this state's top tourist destination. Beginning less than 2 hours from Portland, you'll find everything from rugged coves to long sandy beaches, artists' communities to classic family beach towns.

The quickest route from Portland to the coast is via U.S. 26, also called the Sunset Highway. Just before reaching the coast and the junction with U.S. 101,

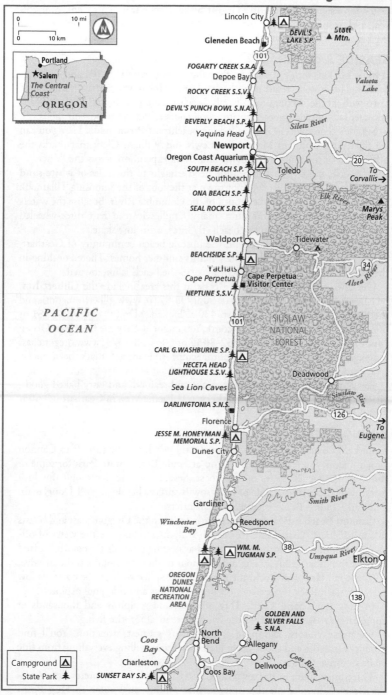

The Central Oregon Coast

0   10 mi
0   10 km

Portland
★Salem
The Central
Coast
OREGON

Lincoln City
Gleneden Beach
DEVIL'S
LAKE S.P.
Stott
▲ Mtn.

101

FOGARTY CREEK S.R.A.
Depoe Bay
ROCKY CREEK S.S.V.
DEVIL'S PUNCH BOWL S.N.A.
BEVERLY BEACH S.P.
Yaquina Head
Newport
Oregon Coast Aquarium
SOUTH BEACH S.P.
Southbeach
ONA BEACH S.P.
SEAL ROCK S.R.S.

Valseta
Lake

Siletz River

Toledo

20
To
Corvallis →

Elk River

Marys
▲ Peak

Waldport
BEACHSIDE S.P.
Yachats
Cape Perpetua
NEPTUNE S.S.V.

Cape Perpetua
Visitor Center

Tidewater

34

Alsea River

PACIFIC
OCEAN

101

SIUSLAW
NATIONAL
FOREST

CARL G.WASHBURNE S.P.
HECETA HEAD
LIGHTHOUSE S.S.V.
Sea Lion Caves
DARLINGTONIA S.N.S.
Florence
JESSE M. HONEYMAN
MEMORIAL S.P.
Dunes City

Deadwood

Siuslaw River

126
To
Eugene

Gardiner
Winchester
Bay
Reedsport

Smith River

WM. M.
TUGMAN S.P.

38

Umpqua River

Elkton

OREGON
DUNES
NATIONAL
RECREATION
AREA

GOLDEN AND
SILVER FALLS
S.N.A.

138

Coos
Bay
Charleston
SUNSET BAY S.P.

North
Bend

Coos Bay

Allegany

Dellwood

Coos River

Campground ▲
State Park ♠

watch for a sign for the **world's largest Sitka spruce tree.** This giant, over 750 years old, is in a small park just off the highway. The fight to preserve remaining big trees is a bitter one that troubles many citizens of Oregon.

SEASIDE & GEARHART

If you've got kids with you, turn north at the junction with U.S. 101 and head into Seaside. This historic resort dates back to 1899. Today it is a densely developed town with all the makings for a family beach vacation, including bumper boats, saltwater taffy, arcade games, miniature golf courses, and tacky souvenir shops.

Seaside's centerpiece is its 2-mile-long beachfront **Promenade.** Here you can see the bronze statue of Meriwether Lewis and William Clark that marks the official end of the trail for the Lewis and Clark expedition across the West.

Of course, most visitors to Seaside head straight to the miles of **white-sand beaches,** which begin just south of town at the foot of the imposing Tillamook Head and stretch north to the mouth of the Columbia River. Because the waters here are quite cold for swimming, many families instead rent three-wheeled "Funcycles" for pedaling on the beach, fly kites, or in-line skate.

Just north of Seaside, you'll find the upscale beach community of Gearhart, which is where Portland's old money has its summer homes. There's nothing in the way of commercial development here, so the beach is uncrowded.

Our favorite moderately priced B&Bs in this area include the **Gilbert Inn,** 341 Beach Dr. (© **800/410-9770** or 503/738-9770; www.gilbertinn.com), and the **Riverside Inn Bed & Breakfast,** 430 S. Holladay Dr. (© **800/826-6151** or 503/738-8254; www.riversideinn.com). You might also try the **Gearhart Ocean Inn,** 67 N. Cottage St. (© **800/352-8034** or 503/738-7373; www.oregoncoast lodgings.com/gearhart), an old motor court–style motel that's been nicely renovated.

For vintage Oregon style, decent steaks and seafood, and tasty baked goods, check out **Pacific Way Cafe and Bakery,** 601 Pacific Way, in Gearhart (© **503/ 738-0245**).

CANNON BEACH

From U.S. 26 and U.S. 101, head south and watch for the turnoff to Cannon Beach. Before you reach the town, stop at **Ecola Beach State Park** for some of the most spectacular views on the coast. Several trails lead through this lush forest, which contains stands of old-growth spruce, hemlock, and Douglas fir. The park's Indian Beach is popular with surfers.

Cannon Beach itself is the artsiest little town on the Oregon coast and boasts lots of galleries. What makes this beach truly memorable are the views of off-shore rocks, most of which are protected as nesting grounds for colorful **tufted puffins** and other seabirds. The most famous of these monoliths is the massive, 235-foot-tall **Haystack Rock,** the most photographed rock on the coast. At low tide, Haystack Rock is popular with beachcombers and tide-pool explorers.

In early June, **Sand Castle Day** attracts sand sculptors and thousands of appreciative viewers You'll find the winds here ideal for kite flying.

For many visitors, **shopping** is the town's greatest attraction. You'll find dozens of galleries and shops along Hemlock Street, selling everything from fine crafts to casual fashions.

Three miles south of the town on U.S. 101, watch for the pretty little **Arcadia Beach Wayside.** Another mile farther south, you'll come to **Hug Point State Recreation Site,** which has picnic tables and a sheltered beach. Rugged and remote **Oswald West State Park,** 10 miles south of Cannon Beach, is one of our favorites. A short trail takes you through dense forest to a driftwood-strewn beach on a small cove. Hiking trails lead to headlands on either side of the cove. The waves here are popular with surfers, and there are plenty of picnic tables and a walk-in campground.

The **Stephanie Inn,** 2740 S. Pacific St. (© **800/633-3466** or 503/436-2221; www.stephanie-inn.com), is one of the most classically romantic inns on the Oregon coast. **Cannon Beach Hotel Lodgings,** 1116 S. Hemlock St. (© **800/238-4107** or 503/436-1392; www.cannonbeachhotel.com), has a wide variety of rooms that fit a broad range of budgets.

TILLAMOOK COUNTY

U.S. 101 continues south from Oswald West State Park and climbs over **Neahkahnie Mountain.** Legend has it that the survivors of a wrecked Spanish galleon buried a fortune in gold at the base of this oceanside mountain. Keep your eyes open for elk, which frequently graze in the meadows here.

Just below this windswept mountain is the quiet resort village of **Manzanita.** Tucked under the fir, spruce, and hemlock trees are attractive summer homes. There's not much to do here except walk along the sandy beach, which is pre-cisely the appeal of the place.

Tillamook Bay is one of the largest bays on the Oregon coast; at its north end is the small town of **Garibaldi,** a popular sportfishing spot. If you aren't an angler, you can go on a whale-watching trip or take a quick cruise around the bay.

Just before reaching the busy town of **Tillamook,** which lies inland from the Pacific at the south end of Tillamook Bay, you'll come to the **Tillamook Cheese Factory** (© **503/842-4481**). Since 1851, this cheese factory has turned out a substantial portion of the cheese consumed in the Northwest. Each year, hun-dreds of thousands of visitors watch the cheese-making process through large windows. The store sells an assortment of tasty cheeses and ice creams.

From Tillamook, the **Three Capes Scenic Route** leads to Cape Meares, Cape Lookout, and Cape Kiwanda, all of which provide stunning vistas of rocky cliffs, misty mountains, and booming surf.

Cape Meares State Park is the site of the Cape Meares Lighthouse, built in 1890 and open to the public. Continuing around the cape, you'll come to the village of Oceanside. If you walk north along the beach, you'll find a pedestrian tunnel through the headland that protects this hillside community. Through the tunnel is another beautiful stretch of beach.

A few miles south of Oceanside is **Cape Lookout State Park.** A breathtaking trail leads to the end of Cape Lookout, which is an excellent spot for whale-watching in the spring and fall. **Cape Kiwanda,** which lies just outside the town of Pacific City, is the last of the three capes on this scenic loop. This sandstone headland, backed by a huge sand dune, is popular with hang-gliders. At the base of the cape is the staging area for Pacific City's beach-launched dory fishing fleet. The **Pelican Pub & Brewery,** right on the beach and boasting a terrific view (© **503/965-7007**), is a good spot to grab a burger and a beer.

With its artfully designed modern cabins, **Coast Cabins,** 635 Laneda Ave. (© **503/368-7113;** www.coastcabins.com), is our favorite lodging in Man-zanita. There's also the romantic **Inn at Manzanita,** 67 Laneda St. (© **503/368-6754;** www.neahkahnie.net), where double whirlpool tubs sit between the fireplace and the bed in every room, and balconies look out through shady pines to the ocean. In Pacific City, the **Inn at Cape Kiwanda,** 33105 Cape Kiwanda

Dr. (© **888/965-7001** or 503/965-7001; www.InnAtCapeKiwanda.com), a cedar-shingled modern (and romantic) hotel, has rooms with great views of Pacific City's Haystack Rock.

LINCOLN CITY

Lincoln City, 44 miles south of Tillamook, is not really a city, but a collection of five small towns that stretch for miles along the coast. Over the years, these towns all grew together as this area became a popular beach destination.

Family vacationers will love Lincoln City's 7½-mile-long sandy beach. The water may be too cold for swimming, but the steady winds here offer the best **kite flying** on the Oregon coast. The Spring Kite Festival takes place in early May, while the Fall International Kite Festival is held in early October.

Adding to the appeal of the Lincoln City beach area is **Devil's Lake,** which drains across the beach by way of the D River, the world's shortest river. Boating, sailing, water-skiing, boardsailing, swimming, fishing, and camping are all popular activities here.

Lincoln City is also home to some of Oregon's best art galleries and some interesting artists' studios. **Alder House III**, 611 Immonen Rd. (© **541/996-2483;** www.alderhouse.com), is the state's oldest glass-blowing studio, open daily from March 15 to November 30. Also on Immonen Road is **Mossy Creek Pottery** (© **541/996-2415**), with an imaginative selection of porcelain and stoneware by Oregon potters. The impressive **Freed Gallery,** 6119 SW U.S. 101 (© **541/994-5600;** www.freedgallery.com), offers an excellent selection of art glass and ceramic work. The latter two are open year-round.

Nearby Gleneden Beach is home to the largest full-service resort on the coast, the **Westin Salishan Lodge,** 7760 U.S. 101 (© **888/725-4742** or 541/764-2371; www.salishan.com), which has a fine dining room and golf course. For oceanfront rooms, try **The Inn at Spanish Head,** 4009 SW U.S. 101 (© **800/452-8127** or 541/996-2161; www.spanishhead.com), which is 10 stories high.

Prices are moderate for the inventive seafood dishes at **Kyllo's Seafood Grill,** 1110 NW First Court (© **541/994-3179**), where the decor has a touch of urban chic. On the drive down from Portland, don't miss the perfect pies and other terrific diner staples at the **Otis Cafe,** on Ore. 18, in Otis (© **541/994-2813**).

DEPOE BAY

Depoe Bay, 13 miles south of Lincoln City, calls itself the smallest harbor in the world, and although the tiny harbor covers only 6 acres, it's home to more than 100 fishing boats. Storm waves cause the impressive fountains of Depoe Bay's famous spouting tubes. These geyserlike fountains are produced when waves break in the narrow fissures of the area's rocky coastline, sending plumes of water into the air.

On U.S. 101, you'll find a row of garish souvenir shops, plus several family restaurants as well as charter-fishing and whale-watching outfitters.

The road south from Depoe Bay winds its way through grand, rugged scenery and passes through small, picturesque coves. Several miles south of town, watch for signs to the **Otter Crest State Scenic Viewpoint,** atop Cape Foulweather. Keep an eye out for sea lions sunning themselves on offshore rocks.

Just south of Cape Foulweather, you'll find **Devil's Punchbowl State Natural Area.** The site of a collapsed sea cave becomes a cauldron of churning foam during high tides or stormy seas. A short path here leads to the Marine Gardens, where you can explore numerous tide pools containing various sea creatures.

The **Inn at Otter Crest,** Otter Crest Loop Road, in Otter Rock (© **800/452-2101** or 541-765-2111; www.innatottercrest.com), is one of the premier resorts on the coast, located on a secluded cove and surrounded by 35 acres of forest and beautifully landscaped gardens. It's the perfect place to get away from it all. The **Channel House,** 35 Ellingson St., Depoe Bay (© **800/447-2140** or 541/765-2140; www.channelhouse.com), is a luxurious small inn built above the narrow channel into Depoe Bay.

NEWPORT

As coastal towns go, Newport has a split personality. Dockworkers unloading fresh fish mingle with vacationers licking ice-cream cones as freeloading sea lions wait for their next meal from the processing plants along the waterfront. Many of the town's old cottages and late-19th-century buildings still stand, and despite downtown's souvenir shops, galleries, and restaurants, Newport is still home to the largest commercial fishing fleet on the Oregon coast.

Newport is home to the **Oregon Coast Aquarium,** 2820 SE Ferry Slip Rd. (© **541/867-3474;** www.aquarium.org), the Oregon coast's top attraction. More than 190 animal species are represented, including seals, otters, sea lions, tufted puffins, and a giant octopus. Admission is $10.25 adults, $9.25 seniors, and $6.25 children 4 to 13. It's open Memorial Day to Labor Day daily from 9am to 6pm; the rest of the year daily from 10am to 5pm.

Beaches in the Newport area range from tiny, rocky coves where you can search for agate stones to long, wide stretches of sand perfect for kite flying. Right in town, north and west of the Yaquina Bay Bridge, you'll find the **Yaquina Bay State Park,** which borders both the ocean and the bay. North of Newport is **Agate Beach,** which has a stunning view of Yaquina Head. Two miles south of Newport, you'll find **South Beach State Park,** a wide, sandy beach with picnic areas and a large campground that rents yurts for shelter if you haven't brought your own tent.

Six miles south of Newport, you'll find **Ona Beach State Park,** a sandy beach with a picnic area under the trees. Beaver Creek, a fairly large stream, flows through the park and across the beach to the ocean. **Seal Rock State Recreation Site** is another 2 miles south. Here, a long wall of rock rises from the waves and sand, creating numerous tide pools and fascinating nooks and crannies to explore.

Located north of town in a grove of fir trees on the edge of a cliff, the condos at **Starfish Point,** 140 NW 48th St. (© **541/265-3751;** www.newportnet.com/starfishpoint), are our favorite rooms in the area. The bathrooms here are extravagant affairs with double whirlpool tubs and skylights or big windows. For unique accommodations, book a stateroom on the *Newport Belle,* Newport Marina (© **800/348-1922** or 541/867-6290; www.NewportBelle.com), a reproduction paddle-wheeler moored near the Oregon Coast Aquarium. The **Sylvia Beach Hotel,** 267 NW Cliff St. (© **541/265-5428;** www.sylviabeachhotel.com), has rooms named for different authors, and in each you'll find memorabilia, books, and decor that reflects these writers' lives, times, and works. The hotel's restaurant is a local favorite.

YACHATS

Located 26 miles south of Newport, the village of Yachats (pronounced *Yah*-hots) is known as something of an artists' community—small but sophisticated, with a great little cove and adjoining rocky beaches. The tiny Yachats River flows into the surf, while to the east, steep, forested mountains appear.

Barking Up a Storm with the Sea Lions

Approximately 10 miles south of Yachats, you'll find **Sea Lion Caves**, 91560 U.S. 101 N. (© **541/547-3111;** www.sealioncaves.com), the only year-round mainland home for Steller's sea lions, hundreds of which reside here. Admission is $7 adults, $4.50 children 6 to 15, free for children under 6. The cave is open daily from 9am (8am July–Aug) to 1 hour before dark.

Looming over the town is the impressive bulk of **Cape Perpetua,** which, at 800 feet, is the highest spot on the Oregon coast. The **Cape Perpetua Interpretive Center** (© 541/547-3289), located up a steep road off U.S. 101, houses displays on the cape's natural history and the Native Americans who harvested its bountiful seafood for hundreds of years. Within the Cape Perpetua Scenic Area are 18 miles of hiking trails, tide pools, ancient forests, scenic overlooks, and a campground.

If you're looking for wide, sandy **beaches,** continue south to the Stonefield Beach State Recreation Site, Muriel O. Ponsler Memorial State Scenic Viewpoint, or Carl G. Washburne Memorial State Park. Washburne offers 2 miles of beach, plus hiking trails and a campground.

The **Shamrock Lodgettes,** 105 U.S. 101 S. (© 800/845-5028 or 541/547-3312), classic log cabins set amid spacious lawns and old fir trees at the mouth of the Yachats River, are just bewitching. We also recommend the romantic **Overleaf Lodge,** 2055 U.S. 101 N. (© 800/338-0507 or 541/547-4880; www.overleaflodge.com). South of Yachats, there's the **Heceta Head Lightstation,** 92072 U.S. 101 S. (© **541/547-3696;** www.hecetalighthouse.com), a B&B housed in a historic lighthouse keeper's home in a state park.

One of the joys of driving the Oregon coast is discovering unexpected pleasant surprises. **La Serre,** 2nd Avenue and Beach Street (© **541/547-3420),** is one of these surprise discoveries. Its attractive greenhouse setting, hanging plants, and old Japanese glass fishing floats provide the backdrop for the best food in the area: everything from filet mignon to cioppino. Don't miss the fabulous desserts.

FLORENCE

Florence, 50 miles south of Newport, has long been a popular vacation spot for families. With few roads providing access to the ocean's shore, this area is known more for its lakes than for its beaches. Sand dunes, the Siuslaw River, and 17 freshwater lakes offer an abundance of recreational opportunities. Many area lakes are ringed with summer homes and public campgrounds. Popular activities include water-skiing, four-wheeling through the sand dunes, and fishing.

Florence's **Old Town,** on the north bank of the Siuslaw River, has quite a bit of charm, with many restored wood and brick buildings, interesting boutiques and galleries, and waterfront seafood restaurants.

In the middle part of the 19th century, paddle-wheelers plied many of Oregon's rivers. The *Westward Ho!* (© 541/997-9691) is a half-scale replica of an 1850s stern-wheeler and offers a variety of river cruises. Call for schedule and prices.

THE OREGON DUNES NATIONAL RECREATION AREA

The Oregon Dunes National Recreation Area, more than 14,000 acres of sand dunes, stretches for more than 40 miles along the coast between Florence and Coos Bay. Within this vast area of shifting sands are dunes more than 500 feet tall, numerous lakes both large and small, living forests, and skeletal forests of trees that were long ago "drowned" beneath drifting sands. It is here that you'll find the longest unbroken, publicly owned stretches of Oregon's coast.

Jessie M. Honeyman Memorial State Park, 3 miles south of Florence, is a unique spot with a beautiful forest-bordered lake and towering sand dunes. The park offers camping, picnicking, hiking trails, and access to Cleawox and Woahink lakes. Cleawox Lake has a swimming area and boat rentals, and adjacent dunes are open to off-road vehicles.

On the **Taylor Dunes Trail,** which begins at the Carter Lake Campground, 7½ miles south of Florence, a platform overlooks the dunes. It's an easy half-mile walk to the platform. If you want to get your shoes full of sand but have time for only a quick walk, you can continue on to the beach, which is less than a mile beyond the viewing platform; roughly half this distance is through dunes.

At the **Dunes Overlook,** 10 miles south of Florence, you'll find viewing platforms high atop a forested sand dune overlooking a vast expanse of bare sand. A 3½-mile loop trail leads from this overlook out to the beach by way of Tahkenitch Creek, a meandering stream that flows through the dunes. Another mile south of the Dunes Overlook, you'll find the **Tahkenitch Trail Head,** which gives you access to an 8-mile network of little-used trails that wander through dunes, forest, marshes, and meadows.

For truly impressive dunes, the best route is the **Umpqua Dunes Trail;** its trail head is half a mile south of **Eel Creek Campground,** which is 10½ miles south of Reedsport (32 miles south of Florence). This 2½-mile round-trip trail leads through an area of dunes 2 miles wide by 4 miles long. Don't get lost!

BANDON

Once known primarily as the cranberry capital of Oregon, Bandon is a quaint seaside village set on one of the most spectacular pieces of coastline in the Northwest. The beach here is littered with boulders, monoliths, and haystack rocks that seem to have been strewn by some giant hand. About 20 miles north of town, there are three state parks that together preserve more breathtaking shoreline. The Coquille River empties into the Pacific here at Bandon, and at the river's mouth stands a picturesque lighthouse.

Coquille Point, at the end of 11th Street, is one of the best places to view Bandon's famous rocks. Here you'll find a short, paved interpretive trail atop a bluff overlooking the beach, rock monoliths, and the river's mouth. From the nearby **Face Rock Viewpoint** you can see the area's most famous rock, which resembles a face gazing skyward.

At **Sunset Bay State Park,** 20 miles north of Bandon, you'll find a small bay almost completely surrounded by sandstone cliffs. The entrance to the bay is narrow, which means the waters here stay fairly calm. This is one of the few beaches in Oregon where the water gets warm enough for swimming. Picnicking and camping are available in the park, and there are lots of tide pools to explore.

Another 3 miles southwest brings you to **Shore Acres State Park,** once the estate of a local shipping tycoon who spent years developing his gardens. The park includes formal English and Japanese gardens. The gardens are atop sandstone cliffs overlooking the Pacific and a tiny cove. Here, rock walls rise from the water and have been sculpted by the waves into unusual shapes.

Continue a little farther along the same road and you'll come to **Cape Arago State Park.** Just offshore from the rugged cape are the rocks and small islands of

Simpson Reef, which offers sunbathing spots for hundreds of seals (including elephant seals) and sea lions. Their barking can be heard from hundreds of yards away. The best viewing point is the **Simpson Reef Viewpoint.**

The **Bandon Dunes Golf Resort,** 57744 Round Lake Dr. (℗ **888/345-6008** or 541/347-4380; www.bandondunesgolf.com), is one of the most tasteful and luxurious accommodations on the Oregon coast. However, the emphasis is so entirely on the golf course that anyone not interested in the game will most certainly feel like an interloper. Dozens of Bandon's famous monoliths rise from the sand and waves in front of the **Sunset Motel,** 1865 Beach Loop Dr. (℗ **800/842-2407** or 541/347-2453; www.sunsetmotel.com), making sunsets from the Sunset truly memorable.

8 The Columbia River Gorge & Mount Hood

Formed when 1,000-foot-high ice-age floodwaters raged down the Columbia River, the Columbia River Gorge is a landscape of rare beauty that has been preserved as the nation's first, and only, National Scenic Area. Within this flood-carved landscape, sheer basalt cliffs rise from the river and diaphanous waterfalls cascade down dark, forested heights. The Gorge is the only sea-level gap along the entire length of the Cascade Range, which stretches from California to Canada, and consequently, this massive opening in the mountains serves as a sort of natural wind tunnel that funnels air between the cool, moist coastal regions and the hot, dry interior.

Although I-84 runs beside the river on the Oregon side, and Wash. 14 follows the Washington shore, a leisurely drive along U.S. 30, the **Historic Columbia River Highway,** is the preferred way to see the Gorge. This winding highway parallels I-84 for 22 miles at the west end of the Gorge and for 15 miles at the east end. Along the way there are close-up views of numerous waterfalls, unequaled scenic vistas, and opportunities for hiking.

Rising to the south of the Gorge is 11,235-foot **Mount Hood,** Oregon's highest peak and a popular destination in both summer and winter. A drive up the Gorge can easily be combined with a loop around the mountain, and from Timberline, on the southern flanks of the mountain, you can get close-up views of Mount Hood, do a bit of hiking, and visit the historic Timberline Lodge.

From Portland, head east on I-84. At Troutdale, take the exit marked HISTORIC COLUMBIA RIVER HIGHWAY. This winding highway is an engineering marvel, but it's dwarfed by the spectacular vistas that present themselves at every turn. To learn more about the road and how it was built, stop at **Vista House,** 733 feet above the river on Crown Point, for displays and a spectacular view of the gorge, including Beacon Rock, an 800-foot-tall monolith on the far side of the river.

Of some 77 waterfalls in the Columbia Gorge, **Multnomah Falls** is by far the most impressive and best known. At 620 feet from the lip to the pool, it's also the tallest waterfall in Oregon and the fourth tallest in the United States. A paved trail leads to the top of the falls and a dizzying view from an observation platform.

Near **Ainsworth State Park,** the western segment of the Historic Columbia River Highway comes to an end. Five miles east of here on I-84, you'll come to **Bonneville Lock and Dam.** In operation since 1938, this is the oldest dam on the river. Thousands of visitors come each year to see its fish ladder, which allows salmon and other fish to migrate upstream. June and September are the best months to observe salmon.

Just east of the dam is the **Bridge of the Gods,** which connects Oregon and Washington at the site where an old Indian legend says a natural bridge once stood. Geologists believe that the legend may have some basis in fact. There is evidence that 500 years ago a massive rock slide blocked the river at this point.

On the Washington side of the Columbia, east of the Bridge of the Gods, is the **Columbia Gorge Interpretive Center,** 990 SW Rock Creek Dr., Stevenson (© 800/991-2338; www.columbiagorge.org). This modern and architecturally striking museum is the single best introduction to the natural and human history of the Columbia Gorge; it also boasts an awesome view. Admission is $6 adults, $5 seniors and students, and $4 children 6 to 12. Hours are daily from 10am to 5pm.

Just beyond Bridge of the Gods on the Oregon side is **Cascade Locks,** where, in 1896, navigational locks were built so that river traffic could avoid the treacherous passage through the cascades that once existed at this spot. There are two small museums here, one of which also holds the ticket office for the stern-wheeler *Columbia Gorge* (© 800/643-1354 or 541/374-8427; www.sternwheeler.com), which makes regular trips on the river all summer.

Anyone who boardsails (windsurfs) has likely heard of the town of Hood River. Because of the strong winds that blow through the gorge in summer, this section of the Columbia River is one of the most popular boardsailing spots in the world. If you want to try this thrilling sport, stop by one of the many sailboard shops downtown for rental and instruction information.

The **Mount Hood Railroad** excursion train, 110 Railroad Ave., Hood River (© 800/872-4661; www.mthoodrr.com), runs from late March to late December, carrying passengers in vintage cars up the Hood River Valley from the town of Hood River to Parkdale and back. Fares for the 4-hour excursion are $23 to $26 adults, $21 to $24 seniors, and $15 to $18 children 2 to 12. In July and August, the train runs daily except Monday. From late March through June and September through October, it runs Wednesday through Sunday; in November and December, it runs on weekends only.

If you continue heading east on I-84 from Hood River, you'll come to **The Dalles,** which was an important stop on the Oregon Trail. Here in The Dalles, you can learn more about the Columbia Gorge at the **Columbia Gorge Discovery Center,** 5000 Discovery Dr. (© 541/296-8600; www.gorgediscovery.org). Among the displays here are reproduced historic storefronts, Native American artifacts, and even a sailboarding simulator. Several films are screened throughout the day. Outside, during the warmer months, there are usually living history interpreters. Admission is $6.50 adults, $5.50 seniors, and $3.50 children ages 6 to 16. Hours are daily from 10am to 6pm (Jan to mid-Mar Tues–Sun 10am–4pm).

If you turn south on Ore. 35 from Hood River, you'll pass through thousands of acres of apple, pear, and cherry orchards. Just after Ore. 35 merges into U.S. 26, turn right onto the road to **Timberline Lodge.** As the name implies, this lodge is at the timberline, and a July or August walk on one of the trails in the vicinity will lead you through wildflower-filled meadows. Because of the glacier and snowfields above the lodge, you can ski and snowboard here all summer long.

WHERE TO STAY & DINE

The **Columbia Gorge Hotel,** 4000 Westcliff Dr., just west of Hood River (© 800/345-1921 or 541/386-5566; www.columbiagorgehotel.com), opened in 1915, and despite the attractive furnishings and gardens, it's almost impossible to notice anything but the view from the windows of the hotel, which is perched 200 feet above the river on a steep cliff. The dining room serves a mix of Northwest and Continental fare at dinner, but is best known for its five-course breakfast.

Constructed during the Depression as a WPA project, the classic Alpine-style **Timberline Lodge,** Timberline (© **800/547-1406** or 503/622-7979; www.timberlinelodge.com), boasts a grand stone fireplace, exposed beams, wide plank floors, wood carvings, wrought-iron fixtures, hand-hooked rugs, and handmade furniture. Rooms vary in size considerably, with the smallest lacking private bathrooms. The Cascade Dining Room enjoys a near-legendary reputation for its superb, if a bit pricey, Northwest cuisine. There are ski lifts, a ski school and ski rentals, an outdoor pool, hiking trails, and a coin-op laundry.

On the Washington side, **Dolce Skamania Lodge,** 1131 SW Skamania Lodge Way (© **800/221-7117** or 509/427-7700; www.skamania.com), in Stevenson, has the most spectacular vistas of any hotel in the Gorge, plus the only golf course. The interior features a cathedral-ceilinged lobby, stone fireplace, and Native American artwork and artifacts. The dining room serves good Northwest cuisine amid stupendous views of the Gorge. Facilities include tennis courts, indoor pool, whirlpools, sauna, exercise facility, nature trails, and bike rentals.

9 Crater Lake National Park

At 1,932 feet deep, Crater Lake is the deepest lake in the United States and the seventh deepest in the world. But depth alone is not what makes this one of the most visited spots in the Northwest—it's the startling sapphire-blue waters.

The caldera (crater) that today holds the serene lake was born in an explosive volcanic eruption 7,700 years ago. When the volcano now known as Mount Mazama erupted, its summit (thought to have been around 12,000 ft. high) collapsed, leaving a crater 4,000 feet deep. Thousands of years of rain and melting snow created cold, clear Crater Lake, which today is surrounded by walls nearly 2,000 feet high.

The drive into the park winds through forests that don't provide a single glimpse of the spectacular lake. With no warning except the signs leading to Rim Village, you'll suddenly find yourself gazing down into a vast bowl full of blue water. Toward one end of the lake rises the cone of Wizard Island, the tip of a volcano that has been slowly building since the last eruption of Mount Mazama.

Crater Lake is 57 miles north of Klamath Falls via U.S. 97 and Ore. 62, and 71 miles northeast of Medford via Ore. 62. In winter, only the south entrance is open. Due to deep snowpack, the north entrance usually doesn't open until sometime in late July.

Park admission is $10 per vehicle. For information, contact **Crater Lake National Park,** P.O. Box 7, Crater Lake, OR 97604 (© **541/594-3100;** www.nps.gov/crla).

After your first breathtaking view of the lake, you may want to stop by one of the park's two visitor centers—**Steel Information Center** and **Rim Village Visitor Center.** The park is open year-round, but in winter, when deep snows blanket the region, only the road to **Rim Village** is kept clear. In summer (roughly late June), the 39-mile Rim Drive provides stunning views.

Boat trips around the lake are the park's most popular activity. These tours last 2 hours and begin at Cleetwood Cove, at the bottom of a very steep 1-mile trail that descends 700 feet from the rim to the lakeshore. Be sure you're in good enough physical condition to make the steep climb back up to the rim. Bring warm clothes, as it can be quite a bit cooler on the lake than on the rim. A naturalist on each boat provides a narrative on the ecology and history of the lake; all tours include a stop on Wizard Island. Tours are offered late from June to mid-September.

Two World-Class Festivals in Southern Oregon

Each year, more than 300,000 people flock to the town of Ashland for the internationally acclaimed **Oregon Shakespeare Festival** (© 541/482-4331; www.orshakes.org). The season runs February through November, and typically includes four works by Shakespeare plus another seven classic or contemporary plays. In addition to theater, Ashland has galleries, interesting shops, fine restaurants, and dozens of B&Bs.

Nearby Jacksonville is home to the **Britt Festivals** (© 800/882-7488 or 541/773-6077; www.brittfest.org), which run June through September. Jacksonville, a gold boomtown in the mid-1800s, became a forgotten backwater after the Depression, inadvertently preserving its many historic buildings. In 1966, the entire town was declared a National Historic Landmark and more than 80 structures were restored. A ponderosa pine–shaded amphitheater on the grounds of 19th-century photographer, Peter Britt's estate is now home to folk, pop, country, jazz, and classical music concerts and modern dance performances. Past performers have included Natalie MacMaster, Jewel, Jethro Tull, the Beach Boys, Huey Lewis, and The Chieftains. If you opt for lawn seating, bring a blanket and a picnic.

Many miles of **hiking trails** can be found in the park, but the Cleetwood Trail is the only one that leads down to the lakeshore. The trail to the top of Mount Scott, although a rigorous 2½ miles, is the park's most rewarding hike. Shorter trails with good views include the 0.8-mile trail to the top of the Watchman, which overlooks Wizard Island, and the 1.7-mile trail up Garfield Peak. The short Castle Crest Wildflower Trail is best hiked in late July and early August when the wildflowers are at the height of their glory. Backpackers can hike the length of the park on the Pacific Crest Trail.

In winter, **cross-country skiing** is popular on the park's snow-covered roads. Skiers in good condition can usually make the entire circuit of the lake in 2 days, but must be prepared to camp in the snow. Spring, when the weather is warmer and there are fewer severe storms, is actually the best time to ski around the lake.

WHERE TO STAY & CAMP

The park contains two lodging options. Overlooking the lake from the rim, **Crater Lake Lodge** (© 541/830-8700; www.craterlakelodges.com) has the look and feel of a historic mountain lodge, but boasts modern conveniences. About half the rooms overlook the lake. The dining room serves creative Northwest cuisine and provides a view of both Crater Lake and the Klamath River basin. A short drive away, **Mazama Village Motor Inn** (© 541/830-8700; www.craterlakelodges.com) has modern motel-style rooms in 10 buildings that look much like traditional mountain cabins. These lodges are closed from mid-October to mid-May.

Tent camping and RV spaces are available on the south side of the park at the **Mazama Village Campground.** There are also tent sites at **Lost Creek Campground** on the park's east side. Reservations are not accepted at either campground, and both are closed November through May.

The Northern Rockies & Great Plains

Montana, Wyoming, and South Dakota proudly stand with one cocksure foot rooted in their Wild West past and the other firmly fixed in a setting of unparalleled splendor and majesty. Whether you come to this region to play cowboy on a guest ranch or to stay in one of the classic lodges in the national parks, you'll experience firsthand nature's magnanimity: Yellowstone's wild abundance, the less-traveled vastness of Glacier National Park, the towering peaks of the Grand Tetons, the eerie desolation of the Badlands.

But that's not all. People come here to experience the area's back-to-basics way of life, an attitude that makes these states so endearing to visitors and enduring to residents. The residents of these states are self-reliant, hardy folks. They like to fish with flies, hike with bears, and ride horses that buck. They've tried mining, logging, farming, and ranching and still believe that no matter what they have to do to live here, the mountains make it all worthwhile.

1 The Flathead & Montana's Northwest Corner

If it's mountains, lakes, and streams you've come for, you'll find them in northwestern Montana. The area, almost empty in the spring and fall, encompasses Flathead Lake, majestic Glacier National Park (see section 2 of this chapter), and Missoula.

AREA ESSENTIALS
GETTING THERE   By Plane   Several major airlines fly into the **Missoula County International Airport** (© **406/728-4381**) at Johnson Bell Field 9, northwest of downtown Missoula on U.S. 93.

By Car   From Idaho, I-90 heads east through Missoula and on to Wyoming. Two major roads will get you around this area: **U.S. 93** runs north to south (from the Bitterroot Valley south of Missoula to the state's nether regions), and **U.S. 2** runs east to west. **Mont. 200** follows the Clark Fork, Blackfoot, and Flathead rivers and is one of the state's most scenic highways.

VISITOR INFORMATION   The **Missoula Convention and Visitors Bureau** is located at 825 E. Front St. (© **800/526-3465** or 406/543-6623; www.exploremissoula.com). The **Bitterroot Valley Chamber of Commerce** has offices at 105 Main St., Hamilton, MT 59840 (© **406/363-2400**; www.bv chamber.com).

MISSOULA
The biggest city in the state's northwest corner, Missoula is also the most progressive city in the region. Home to the University of Montana, Missoula has an ever-increasing literary community of established and emerging writers. A

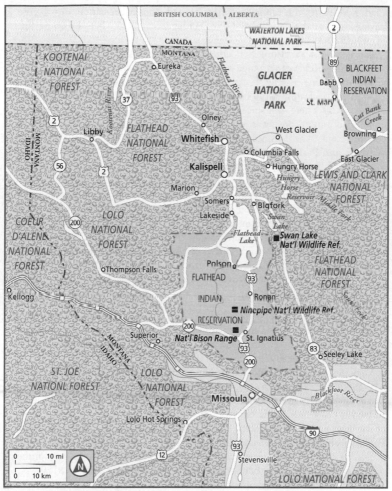

distinctly younger, very hip crowd populates this place, where Birkenstocks outnumber cowboy boots, and cars are likely to be equipped with sports racks.

The diverse transient collegiate community is reflected in several downtown shops. **Global Village World Crafts,** 519 S. Higgins, sells jewelry, clothing, and musical items from around the world. **Butterfly Herbs,** 232 N. Higgins Ave., features an eclectic collection, including fresh herbs, jewelry, coffee mugs, teapots, and handmade paper and candles. The largest newsstand is **The Garden City News,** 329 N. Higgins Ave., and not far away is a wonderful bookstore, **Fact and Fiction,** at 220 N. Higgins Ave.

You will probably recognize the artistry, if not the name, of **Monte Dolack,** whose gallery at 139 W. Front St. also features the art and culture of other prominent Montanans. Definitely worth a stop.

Although Missoula is full of progressive bookworms, the community does not live on text alone. A pleasant, easy downtown hike is the **Kim Williams Trail,** named for a deceased, much-beloved newspaper columnist, which follows the

Clark Fork River. You can get information and maps of recreation areas before leaving town at the **Bureau of Land Management,** 3255 Fort Missoula Rd. (*©* **406/329-3914**).

Venture West Vacations (*©* **406/825-6200**) and **Adventure Connections** (*©* **406/549-5034**) can arrange a variety of Missoula-area adventures for you, including hunting, fishing, backpacking, and dude ranch visits.

Norman Maclean grew up here, "haunted by waters"; his novel *A River Runs Through It* is set here. But since the **Blackfoot River** just isn't the same pristine, unpolluted water it once was, the **Bitterroot River** and **Rock Creek** are better bets for trout. The Missoula office of the **Montana Department of Fish, Wildlife, and Parks,** 3201 Spurgin Rd. (*©* **406/542-5500**), can direct you to some great fishing spots, including **Siria,** a more remote site 30 miles up Rock Creek Road.

Lewis & Clark Trail Adventures (*©* **800/366-6246**) offers white-water rafting on the Salmon River through the heart of the Frank Church No Return Wilderness. The main trip is on a 120-mile stretch of Idaho white water.

The best place to bike is at **Rattlesnake National Recreation Area.** Be sure to consult one of the free trail maps available at bike shops before setting out; straying into the wilderness portion of the recreation area is strictly forbidden. To rent bikes, contact **Open Road Bicycles and Nordic Equipment,** 517 S. Orange St. (*©* **406/549-2453**).

WHERE TO STAY & DINE

Information on renting old-fashioned **miners' cabins** at the ghost town of Garnet is available by contacting the **Garnet Preservation Association,** Box 20029, Missoula, MT 59801-0029 (*©* **406/329-1031**). Get information on camping at Missoula's **Bureau of Land Management,** 3255 Fort Missoula Rd., Missoula, MT 59804 (*©* **406/329-3914**).

The moderately priced **Holiday Inn Missoula** at 200 S. Pattee St. (*©* **406/721-8550**) isn't much different from any other Holiday Inn, except that none of the others overlook the Clark Fork River. Farther afield from Missoula, **The Fort at Lolo Trail Center and Lolo Hot Springs** (*©* **406/273-2201;** www. trailcenter.com), 25 miles west of Lolo, provides a stunning resort setting for the rejuvenating powers of the hot springs. Doubles range from $109 to $129.

The **Red Bird,** 120 W. Front St. (*©* **406/549-2906**), is the top restaurant in Missoula. **Bernice's Bakery,** 190 S. 3rd St. W. (*©* **406/728-1358**), is a popular spot to pick up a quick bite to eat in the mornings. **The Bridge,** 515 S. Higgins (*©* **406/542-0639** or 406/542-0002 for deliveries), shares space with the Crystal Theater and serves some of the best Italian food in Missoula.

SIDE TRIPS FROM MISSOULA

Founded in the early 1850s by Jesuit priests, the town of **St. Ignatius** (32 miles north of Missoula on U.S. 93), nestled in the heart of the Mission Valley, has one of Montana's most prized architectural treasures, the **St. Ignatius Mission.** Established in 1854, the mission contains 58 unique murals by Brother Joseph Carignano on its walls and ceilings.

The **Ninepipe National Wildlife Refuge,** just off U.S. 93 about 10 miles north of St. Ignatius, is home to a huge waterfowl population. Southwest off U.S. 93 on County Road 212 is the **National Bison Range,** a protected open range for buffalo, deer, bighorn sheep, and pronghorn located on reservation land.

FLATHEAD LAKE

This is one of the most beautiful areas in Montana. Glacier's towering peaks rise from the valley floor on the east, and the mountains of the Flathead National Forest define the edge of the valley to the west. You'll see a land of forest, cattle, and alfalfa—a velvet green valley floor, green and granite mountains, and, on a sunny day, a dramatic deep-blue ceiling.

This part of Montana offers something for everyone, whether your interests lie indoors or out, from an array of sports to a surprising cache of interesting shops and galleries in Bigfork. With much of this area lying within the tribal lands of the Salish-Kootenai, there is also a long-standing native heritage, especially evident in the summer when you may hear drums beating well into the night. **Bigfork** is just over a 30-minute drive from Glacier International Airport; **Polson** is roughly midway between Glacier and Missoula.

On the south end of the lake is the **Port Polson Chamber of Commerce,** P.O. Box 667, Polson, MT 59860 (© 406/883-5969; www.polsonchamber. com). For goings-on north of the lake, contact the **Bigfork Chamber,** 8155 Hwy. 3S (© 406/837-5888; www.bigfork.org).

Boat rentals are available at the **Bigfork Marina and Boat Center** (© 406/ 837-5556) and **Bayview Resort and Marina** (© 406/837-5861). One of the finest charter boats on the lake, *Lucky Too,* is based at Marina Cay (© 406/ 257-5214).

Excursion cruises are an excellent way for visitors to check out the beauty of Flathead Lake. The 65-foot *Far West* (© 406/857-3203) is one of the area's oldest, with daily dinner cruises and Sunday brunches.

The brochure "Fishing the Flathead" is available from the **Flathead Convention and Visitor Association** (© 800/543-3105). It provides information on 14 different fishing opportunities, as well as an outline of the licensing and catch-and-release regulations. To increase your odds of snagging something, contact **Glacier Fishing Charters** (© 406/892-2377).

Eagle Bend Golf Club (© 406/837-7300), a challenging Nicklaus-designed course with views of Flathead Lake and the surrounding mountains, is in Bigfork just off the highway on Holt Drive.

Besides strolling by the lake at one of the marinas or state parks, the best bet for trekking is in the **Jewel Basin,** a designated hiking area north of Bigfork that boasts over 30 miles of trails. Take Mont. 83 from either Bigfork or Somers, turn north onto Echo Lake Road, and follow the signs.

The **Flathead Raft Company** (© 800/654-4359) runs tours of the South Fork of the Flathead River, including a swing through the Buffalo Rapids and Kerr Dam.

WHERE TO STAY & DINE

There are five campgrounds in **Flathead Lake State Park,** each located at a different point around the lake. Call © 406/755-5255 for specific information.

Averill's Flathead Lake Lodge, P.O. Box 248, Bigfork, MT 59911 (© 406/ 837-4391; www.averills.com), provides the best (and most expensive) all-around vacation experience on the lake, encouraging families to stay for 1-week minimums. A beautiful log lodge surrounded by thousands of acres of forest is your home base for horseback riding, boating, fishing, sing-alongs, campfires, and barn dances. Twenty two- and three-bedroom cabins are scattered across the property and feature simple yet tasteful Western-style furnishings. Meals are served family-style in the main lodge.

Kwa Taq Nuk Resort at Flathead Bay, 303 U.S. 93 (© **800/882-6363** or 406/883-3636; www.kwataqnuk.com), is the nicest property on the Polson end of the lake, and it delivers a lot for your money, offering a restaurant, marina, and art gallery. Lakeside rooms have commanding views, enhanced by decks furnished with chairs and cocktail tables.

La Provence Restaurant, 408 Bridge St., Bigfork (© **406/837-2923**), is one of the best restaurants in the area, serving French-Mediterranean cuisine. In Somers, the locals like **Tiebuckers Pub and Eatery,** 75 Somers Rd. (© **406/ 857-3335**) for the fresh fish and steamed clams, but they also offer beef, pasta, chicken, and ribs. For burgers and pizza stop at **The Village Well** in Bigfork, 260 River St. (© **406/837-5251**).

WHITEFISH: A GATEWAY TO GLACIER

Whitefish is an excellent spot to stop: The scenery is spectacular, good restaurants and watering holes abound, and numerous shops sell interesting artwork. The town appeals as a jumping-off point to outdoor types of all strains mountaineers who hike and bike in the summer, and snowboarders and skiers during the winter.

Whitefish is extremely accessible. It's easier to get here than to virtually any other Montana town. It's a quick and easy drive up U.S. 93 from Kalispell. Call © **800/226-7623** for statewide road reports and 406/751-2037 for road information in the Whitefish area. **Glacier Park International Airport** (© **406/ 257-5994**) is 10 minutes away between Columbia Falls and Kalispell, with several airlines serving it daily. The **Amtrak** (© **800/USA-RAIL**) station is at the edge of downtown, with one eastbound and one westbound train daily.

The **Whitefish Chamber of Commerce** is in the Mountain Mall on U.S. 93 on the south edge of town. Here you'll find just about everything you need in the way of brochures, area maps, and travel information (© **406/862-3501;** www.whitefishchamber.com).

Just 12 miles north of Whitefish is one of the best ski resorts in the country, **The Big Mountain Ski and Summer Resort** (© **800/858-5439** or 406/862-1900; www.bigmtn.com). Geared for the intermediate skier (terrain difficulty is 25% beginner, 55% intermediate, and 20% advanced), it's the town's pride and joy come winter. Although prices have increased in recent years, skiers still love the quality of the runs and the dearth of crowds.

In summertime, mountain bikes are as prevalent as cars in the north part of the Flathead Valley. With old logging roads abandoned throughout the forestlands of northwest Montana, virtually any side road can become an excellent route for cyclists. **Glacier Cyclery,** 336 E. Second St. (© **406/862-6446**), provides excellent service and maintenance as well as rentals, area maps, and up-to-date information for the serious mountain biker.

It's not the Madison Valley, but Whitefish does have some hot spots for anglers wanting to try their hand. **Tally Lake** is a deep hole north of Whitefish off U.S. 93. Five miles north of town, turn left onto the Tally Lake Road (signs will direct you). You can expect cutthroat, rainbow, kokanee, brook trout, and whitefish. In town, across the viaduct toward the Big Mountain lies **Whitefish Lake.** If you can handle all the recreationists hovering about like flies, the lake offers some pretty good lake trout. Northern pike can be found here, and rainbow and cutthroat can be nabbed on dry flies in the evening. The **Lakestream Flyshop,** 15 Central Ave. (© **406/862-1298**), is the best resource in town for information about fly-fishing the Flathead River and local streams.

The **Whitefish Lake Golf Club,** U.S. 93 N. (© **406/862-4000**), is the only 36-hole course in the state and offers a wide variety of shots requiring the use of every club in your bag (and maybe some you forgot).

The main shopping area of Whitefish is on **Central Avenue** and stretches for approximately 5 blocks. As you'd expect in a tourist town, myriad stores act like magnets for a visitor's credit card.

WHERE TO STAY & DINE

Grouse Mountain Lodge, 2 Fairway Dr. (© **800/321-8822** or 406/862-3000; www.montanasfinest.com), is Montana's premier vacation lodge property, with a variety of rooms from standard hotel-style to loft rooms with kitchens—two even have sauna tubs. Also on-site is the popular Logan's Bar and Grill, plus a golf course and indoor pool. The moderately priced **Best Western Rocky Mountain Lodge,** 6510 U.S. 93 S. (© **800/862-2569** or 406/862-2569), offers good value, and the higher-priced rooms have jetted tubs.

Nestled in the pines along the highway between Whitefish and Columbia Falls, the **North Forty Resort,** 3765 Mont. 40 W. (© **800/775-1740** or 406/ 862-7740; www.northforty.com), offers rustic and private cabins that are great for families. All have living rooms with fireplaces, dining areas, complete kitchens (with china), and private bathrooms.

Lodging options are diverse on the Big Mountain. With an extensive rental pool of single-family homes, duplexes, and condominiums, in addition to several hotels, the Big Mountain is sure to fit any budget. When calling central reservations (© **800/858-5439**), ask about discounted lift and lodging packages.

The **Whitefish Lake Restaurant,** U.S. 93 N. (at the Whitefish Golf Course; © 406/862-5285), is the nicest place in town for dinner. Tables are covered with traditional Scottish tablecloths, and a large stone fireplace provides warmth on chilly evenings while guests enjoy straightforward Continental fare. **The Buffalo Cafe,** 514 3rd St. (© **406/862-2833**), is one of those great-for-breakfast, good-for-lunch, but don't-expect-much-in-the-way-of-atmosphere places, with a wide selection of Mexican entrees. The **Bulldog Saloon,** on Central Avenue (© **406/862-5601**), is a fun watering hole that turns out a pretty good burger, too.

2 Glacier National Park

Glacier National Park got its name from the 48 slow-moving glaciers that carved awe-inspiring valleys through this expanse, which stretches nearly one million acres. If your time is limited, drive along the **Going-to-the-Sun Road,** for a glimpse of the dramatic mountain scenery. Glacier's lakes, streams, ponds, and waterfalls are equally engaging. It's easy to while away your time fishing, rowing, and kayaking. Moose and elk still roam the land, as do grizzly bears.

ESSENTIALS

GETTING THERE The closest cities to the park with airline service are Kalispell, 29 miles southwest of the park, and Great Falls, 143 miles southeast of the park. If you're driving, you can reach the park from U.S. highways 2 and 89. **Amtrak** (© **800/USA-RAIL;** www.amtrak.com) makes daily stops at West Glacier and Essex year-round, and at East Glacier seasonally.

ACCESS/ENTRY POINTS Access is primarily at **West Glacier** on the southwest side and **St. Mary** on the east, at either end of Going-to-the-Sun Road, which cuts across the park. Visitor entrance passes are sold only at these two entrances. There are four other entrances: Camas Creek and Polebridge on the west and Many Glacier and Two Medicine on the east.

VISITOR INFORMATION   For advance information, contact **Glacier National Park,** West Glacier, MT 59936 (℗ **406/888-7800;** www.nps.gov/ glac). For up-to-date information when you arrive, check with the visitor centers at **St. Mary** (open mid-May to mid-Oct), **Apgar** (open daily May–Oct, weekends in winter), and **Logan Pass** (open mid-June to mid-Oct). You can also get information from the Many Glacier Ranger Station.

FEES   Entrance permits for up to 7 days are $10 per vehicle or $5 for an individual on foot or bike. An annual pass costs $20. A separate entrance fee is charged for visitors to adjacent Waterton Lakes National Park in Canada.

SEASONS   In winter, Glacier shuts itself off from the motorized world: even snowmobiles are forbidden. All unplowed roads—and very little is plowed— become trails for snowshoers and cross-country skiers, who rave about the vast powdered wonderland that exists here. Guided trips into the backcountry are a great way to experience the park in winter.

GUIDED TOURS   From mid-June to mid-September, Glacier Park Boat Co. (℗ **406/257-2426**) offers **narrated boat tours,** which often include hikes or picnics, daily from Lake McDonald, St. Mary, Two Medicine, and Many Glacier.

GOING-TO-THE-SUN ROAD

This 50-mile road lets you experience the full gamut of the park's beauty in a short period of time. The road bisects the park, going from West Glacier in the southwest portion of the park to St. Mary in the northeast. Pick up the park's brochure-map at a visitor center before setting out. *Note:* Mileage amounts below are from West Glacier.

Just a short drive from West Glacier is **Lake McDonald** (11 miles), the largest body of water in the park. **Sacred Dancing Cascade** and **Johns Lake** (13 miles) are visible after a half-mile hike from the roadside through a red cedar/hemlock forest, with occasional glimpses of waterfowl and even moose. Two good hiking trails (see below) are along here: the **Trail of the Cedars** (16 miles) and **The Loop** (25 miles). Just 2 miles farther is the **Bird Woman Falls Overlook** (27 miles), a place to gaze across the valley to the cascading falls of the same name. The **Weeping Wall** (29 miles), a wall of rock that does, in fact, weep profusely in the summer, is a popular photo stop.

At 32 miles from West Glacier is **Logan Pass,** one of the park's most highly trafficked areas and the starting point for one of its most popular hikes, **Hidden Lake.** Perched atop the Continental Divide is the **Logan Pass Visitor Center.**

Jackson Glacier (36 miles) is perhaps the most easily recognizable glacier in the entire park; turnouts at the overlook provide you with excellent vantage points for picture taking. **Sunrift Gorge** (39 miles) and **Sun Point** (40 miles) are two short trails with spectacular views and opportunities for wildlife viewing. **St. Mary** (50 miles) is the terminus for this road, with extensive visitor services, including restaurants, places to stay, gas stations, and gift shops.

OUTDOOR PURSUITS

FISHING   The crystal-clear mountain streams and lakes of Glacier are home to many native species of fish. Anglers looking to hook a big one should try the

North Fork of the Flathead for cutthroat and bull trout, and Bowman Lake, St. Mary Lake, and Lake McDonald for rainbow and brook trout, and whitefish. For equipment, advice, or a guided expedition, contact **Lakestream Flyshop,** in Whitefish ((C) **406/862-1298**).

HIKING   Glacier is a park that is best seen on foot and offers 151 trails, totaling 753 miles. **Trail maps** are available at outdoor stores in Whitefish and Kalispell as well as at the major visitor centers and ranger stations in the park. Before striking off into the wilderness, however, check with the nearest ranger station to determine the accessibility of your destination, trail conditions, and recent bear sightings.

Among the park's shorter and easier trails is the **Trail of the Cedars Nature Trail,** a level .25-mile wheelchair-accessible boardwalk through a lovely cedar/hemlock forest. Access is across from the Avalanche Campground Ranger Station. The 3-mile **Hidden Lake Nature Trail** (at the Logan Pass Visitor Center) is an easy-to-moderate interpretive trail. About halfway between Avalanche Campground and Logan Pass Visitor Center along Going-to-the-Sun Road is **The Loop,** a 7-mile moderate hike that climbs to Granite Park Chalet, and provides an excellent vantage point for views of **Heaven's Peak.**

One of our favorite hikes (because of its beautiful scenery) is the moderate **Iceberg Lake Trail** (9.5 miles round-trip; look for the trail head in a cabin area east of the Swiftcurrent Coffee Shop and Campstore).

The very easy **Running Eagle Falls Trail** (1 mile) west of the Two Medicine entrance winds .75 mile through a thick forest to a large, noisy waterfall. The popular **Twin Falls Trail** (from Two Medicine Campground) is an easy 7.5-mile hike to the scenic falls. You can walk the entire distance on a clearly identified trail, or boat across Two Medicine Lake and hike the last mile. The **St. Mary Falls Trail** is a fairly easy walk (1.75 miles) from Jackson Glacier Overlook.

HORSEBACK RIDING   Riding at East Glacier is made available by **Two Medicine River Outfitters** ((C) **406/226-9220**), a stone's throw from the front door of the lodge, and **Mule Shoe Outfitters** ((C) **406/888-5121**).

RAFTING   Montana Raft Company ((C) **800/521-7238** for reservations, or 406/387-5555) offers rafting trips in Glacier and the surrounding area. Trips range from ½ to 3 days.

WHERE TO CAMP & STAY

Glacier offers the RV and tent camper seven campgrounds accessible by paved road: **Apgar,** near the West Glacier entrance; **Avalanche Creek,** just up from the head of Lake McDonald; **Fish Creek,** on the west side of Lake McDonald; **Many Glacier,** in the northeast part of the park; **Rising Sun,** on the north side of St. Mary Lake; **St. Mary,** on the east side of the park; and **Two Medicine,** at the southeast part of the park near East Glacier. Although RV hookups are not supplied at these sites, fireplaces, picnic tables, washrooms, and cold running water are available. The nightly fee is $12 to $14, and campsites are obtained on a first-come, first-served basis only. Stop at any ranger station for information on closures and availability.

Glacier Campground, 12070 U.S. 2, West Glacier ((C) **406/387-5689**), 1 mile west of West Glacier, is the closest campground outside the park.

With only one exception, **Glacier Park, Inc. (GPI),** 106 Cooperative Way, Ste. 104, Kalispell, MT 59901 ((C) **406/756-2444** for reservations at any of the places listed here), operates the hostelries in Glacier National Park. **Lake**

McDonald Lodge, Glacier Park Lodge (in East Glacier), and Many Glacier Hotel are first-tier properties; Swiftcurrent Motor Inn (in Many Glacier), Village Inn (in Apgar Village), and Rising Sun Motor Inn (in St. Mary) are typical of the casual motel-style properties at the other end of the spectrum. Reserve well in advance.

Outside the park, the Mountain Pine Hotel, Mont. 49, East Glacier (© 406/ 226-4403), is a 1950s-type motel with inexpensive, clean, well-furnished rooms. Originally housing for railway workers, the historic, moderately priced Izaak Walton Inn, Essex (© 406/888-5700; www.izaakwaltoninn.com), maintains a railroad ambience. From Mother's Day to early October, the St. Mary Lodge, U.S. 89 and Going-to-the-Sun Road, St. Mary (© 800/368-3689 or 406/732-9265; www.glcpark.com), offers affordable rooms and cabins with tasteful Western lodgepole furniture. The Vista Motel (© 406/888-5311) in West Glacier boasts tremendous views of the mountains, but is open only March through October.

3 Bozeman & Southcentral Montana

Relatively unspoiled, yet one of the most heavily touristed areas in the state, south-central Montana is a world-class playground for the outdoor recreational enthusiast. Its biggest draws are the surrounding mountains that are a haven for hikers and campers, and, without a doubt, the fly-fishing waters of the four major rivers that flow through its valleys (the Madison, Jefferson, Gallatin, and Yellowstone), all of which double as recreation areas for rafting, kayaking, and canoeing.

Bozeman, home of Montana State University, provides the hip, intellectual charm and culture of a college town—good bookstores and restaurants, charming shops, even a brewpub—as well as cultural events that appeal to both the cosmopolitan and cowboy cultures.

BOZEMAN

In Bozeman, you'll find sandal-shod college kids, professors, businesspeople, and ranchers coexisting in harmony in a semi-hip Western society. This unlikely mixture of lifestyles meshes so well because Bozeman's residents share a common affection for the outdoor life found in surrounding mountains and waterways.

Bozeman's airport, Gallatin Field (© 406/388-8321), is served daily by several major airlines. Bozeman is easily reached if you're driving, as it's right on I-90.

The Bozeman Area Chamber of Commerce is at 200 Commerce Way (© 800/228-4224 or 406/586-5421; www.bozemanchamber.com). There's a downtown visitor center (© 406/586-4008) at 224 E. Main St., plus a visitor information kiosk at 1001 N. 7th Ave., open Memorial Day to Labor Day.

GETTING OUTSIDE

Many outdoor activities here take place in the Gallatin National Forest. For general information, maps, and current road and trail conditions, contact the Bozeman Ranger District, 3710 Fallon St., Ste. C (© 406/522-2520; www.fs. fed.ux/r1/gallatin).

There are several shops offering a variety of equipment and supplies. Panda Rentals, 621 Bridger Dr. (© 406/587-6280), rents bikes, rafts, canoes, skis, and snowboards; Chalet Sports, on Main and Willson streets (© 406/587-4595), is a full-line sporting goods store that sells skis as well as rents bikes,

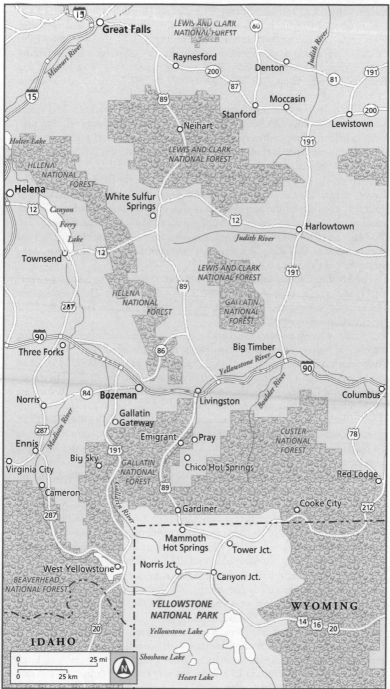

in-line skates, skis, and snowboards; **The Round House Ski and Sports Center,** 1422 W. Main St. (© **406/587-1258**), specializes in sales and rentals of bikes, rafts, and skis; **Northern Lights Trading Co.,** 1716 W. Babcock St. (© **406/586-2225**), is a full-service, high-end store selling gear for everything from kayaking to telemark skiing, and renting canoes, rafts, and kayaks; and **Bangtail Bicycle Shop,** 508 W. Main St. (© **406/587-4905**), offers rentals, expertise, and maps.

Just 16 miles north of Bozeman on Mont. 86, **Bridger Bowl** (15795 Bridger Canyon Rd.; © **800/223-9609** or 406/587-2111; www.bridgerbowl.com) provides excellent skiing with very short lift lines. It's a great hill for good skiers; there's plenty of expert terrain and a good bit of beginner terrain, but the intermediate ski zone is a little squeezed between the two.

Two outfitters will provide memorable if expensive **fly-fishing** outings. **The River's Edge,** 2012 N. 7th Ave. (© **406/586-5373**), offers instruction and guided trips to any of the area streams, as well as fly-fishing schools and equipment rentals and sales. The experienced guides at **Montana Troutfitters,** 1716 W. Main St. (© **406/587-4707**), offer guided float, walk-and-wade, and tube trips as well as fly-fishing schools; they are particularly good at instructing youngsters in the basics of the sport.

The **Hyalite Canyon and Reservoir** is a wonderful place to hike, scale small peaks, and take in some of the Bozeman area's scenic wealth. The reservoir is in the national forest south of Bozeman on South 19th Avenue; from there, it's 7 miles to the Canyon Road.

As well as being a center for outdoor activities, Bozeman offers a surprising number of indoor educational experiences for people of all ages. The unique **American Computer Museum,** 234 E. Babcock St. (© **406/587-7545**), traces the history of computing technologies from the abacus to the Apple. The **Emerson Cultural Center,** 111 S. Grand Ave. (© **406/587-9797**), is the home base for Bozeman's art scene, with gallery space and studios for more than 80 artists. The **Gallatin County Pioneer Museum,** 317 W. Main St. (© **406/522-8122**), gives an excellent perspective on early pioneer life in Montana, from its home in an old jail building—a murderer was hanged here in 1924—to the authentic homestead cabin on the premises.

The **Museum of the Rockies,** 600 W. Kagy Blvd. (© **406/994-2251**), on the campus of Montana State University, provides an interesting look into the past and continues to be an important center for studying the many fossils in the area. Kids will like the Berger Dinosaur Hall, with its interpretive history from prehistoric times to the present. Other exhibits explore Native American history, state history, and local art. Also on the premises is the **Taylor Planetarium,** a state-of-the-art, 40-foot domed multimedia theater.

Bozeman's historic district on **Main Street** runs east through the city center from the intersection at 7th Avenue to I-90. It's an eclectic mix of specialty shops, restaurants, galleries, and retail stores. We like **Vargo's Jazz City and Books,** 6 W. Main St. (© **406/587-5383**), for an enormous selection of new, used, and out-of-print books. Need a souvenir of your trip to Big Sky country? Check out the offerings at the **Montana Gift Corral,** 237 E. Main St., for regional crafts. If you like woodcarvings—from a variety of animals to all kinds of furniture—head west about 15 miles to the tiny town of Manhattan, and stop at **Big Sky Carvers Outlet Gallery,** 324 Main St. (© **406/284-6067;** www.bigskycarvers.com). They also have bronzes and castings.

WHERE TO STAY & DINE

You'll likely be more interested in staying in a guest ranch outside town (see "The Madison River Valley," below), but moderately priced hotel choices in town include the **Best Western Gran Tree Inn,** 1325 N. 7th Ave. (© **800/624-5865** or 406/587-5261), and the **Hampton Inn,** 75 Baxter Lane (© **800/HAMPTON** or 406/522-8000). The **Bozeman KOA** (© **406/587-3030**) is the city's largest campground, with sites for 50 tents and 100 RVs. It's 8 miles south of Belgrade on Mont. 85.

The folks at the **Mackenzie River Pizza Co.,** 232 E. Main St. (© **406/587-0055**), do pizza with a decidedly new twist. The **Baxter Grille,** 105 W. Main St. (© **406/586-1314**), is an upscale restaurant serving superb steaks and seafood. A popular choice is **John Bozeman's Bistro,** 125 W. Main St. (© **406/587-4100**), with buffalo, beef, and chicken plus vegetarian dishes. We love the Mexican food—and the prices—at **Casa Sanchez,** 719 S. 9th Ave. (© **406/586-4516**). Another inexpensive choice is **Main Street Overeasy,** 9 E. Main St. (© **406/587-3205**), which turns out great breakfasts and large gourmet sandwiches and salads at lunch.

THE MADISON RIVER VALLEY

The Madison Valley is an almost mythical place where anglers from the four points of the compass gather to fish in a valley surrounded by spectacular mountain scenery. The main attraction is the Madison River, which flows through the valley at the base of the Madison Range, a stretch of peaks that runs toward Yellowstone Park. Besides the phenomenal fishing, the area's historical significance makes a visit worthwhile.

The Bozeman airport, **Gallatin Field** (see above), is the closest airport to the valley. Three Forks, the largest town in the area, is on I-90 just 30 miles west of Bozeman, 170 miles west of Billings, and 173 miles east of Missoula.

For information contact the **Three Forks Chamber of Commerce** at PO Box 1103, Three Forks, MT 59752 (© **406/285-4880**).

WORLD-CLASS FISHING

Blissful stretches of fishing waters on both sides of the road lead from Three Forks to Quake and Hebgen lakes along U.S. 287. Farther south, you can walk beside stretches of the river that don't cut through private land, or stuff your legs into neoprene waders and waddle out to brave the cold waters of the Madison. The first such fishing access is Cobblestone, just a few miles south of Three Forks on the right side of U.S. 287. Between Ennis and Quake Lake, access becomes more frequent. McAtee Bridge, Wolf Creek, West Fork, and Reynolds Pass are all accessible from the roadside. Hebgen Lake, just south of the dam and Quake Lake, is a great fishing spot, but it's also used for other watersports.

The **Madison River Fishing Company,** 109 Main St., Ennis (© **800/227-7127** or 406/682-4293; www.mrfc.com), stocks fishing supplies and offers half- and full-day guided trips on the Madison River, which generally sends you home with a smile on your face rather than an empty creel. Also in Ennis, **Eaton Outfitters** (© **800/755-FISH** or 406/682-4514) offers guides to teach the basics of fly-fishing and take the seasoned angler to where the fish are biting. They also organize women-only fishing trips.

WHAT TO SEE & DO

The **Lewis & Clark Caverns** are midway between Butte and Bozeman on U.S. 2 (© **406/287-3541**; www.fwp.state.mt.us) about 19 miles west of Three Forks.

Over time, the interaction of water and limestone has created magnificent burled knobs, spear-shaped stalactites, and subterranean columns of copper-colored dripstone. Camping, picnic facilities, and rental cabins are available nearby.

To get to **Missouri Headwaters State Park** (© **406/994-4042;** www.fwp. state.mt.us/parks), go 3 miles east of Three Forks on I-90, then east on County Road 205, and finally 3 miles north on County Road 286 (follow the signs). You can easily spend an hour just exploring the interpretive signage at this historic state park. From the headwaters, drive back toward Three Forks, where, on the opposite side of the road, you'll see a parking area with interpretive markers. Allow plenty of time to read about Lewis and Clark and Sacajawea, the young Shoshone guide, as well as early American Indians, trappers, traders, and settlers. Camping and RV units are available as well as access to hiking, boating, and fishing.

WHERE TO STAY & DINE
Bud Lilly's Anglers Retreat, 16 W. Birch St., Three Forks (© **406/285-6690**), is small, but having him mastermind your fishing itinerary is reason enough to stay at his cozy place.

The best **guest ranch** in the area is the 200-acre **Diamond J Ranch,** 12 miles east of Ennis (© **406/682-4867;** www.diamondjranch.com). Among the first established dude ranches in Montana in the 1930s, the Diamond J may lack the stylishness of some of its competitors but it provides a great variety of outdoor activities, particularly riding and fishing. More affordable is **El Western Resort,** 1 mile south of Ennis on U.S. 287 (© **800/831-2773** or 406/682-4217; www. elwestern.com), with a choice in accommodations from simple duplex-style cabins to large three-bedroom lodges.

The **Willow Creek Cafe and Saloon,** 1st and Main streets, Willow Creek (© **406/285-3698**), is a find—if you can find it, that is. This restaurant, the best in the area, is 7 miles southwest of Three Forks on the Old Yellowstone Trail (don't let the bullet holes in the ceiling scare you off).

THE GALLATIN VALLEY
Nestled into this lush valley, on U.S. 191 almost exactly midway between Bozeman and Yellowstone, is Big Sky, Montana's premier resort. The skiing is world-class, and the summer brings superb fly-fishing, horseback riding, and white-water rafting.

Big Sky Ski & Summer Resort (© **800/548-4486** or 406/995-5900; www. bigskyresort.com) is one of the best undiscovered ski areas in the entire country. It's a huge hill, with more than 3,600 acres of terrain and 85 miles of trails. You can ski for nearly a vertical mile from the top of the tram at 11,150 feet elevation to the bottom of the Thunderwolf lift, at 6,970 feet. Terrain is rated 43% advanced, 47% intermediate, and 10% beginner. Big Sky gets 400 inches of snowfall annually, offering plenty of powder days, and its season runs from Thanksgiving through April. There's an ambitious children's program, offering lessons for kids as young as 3, and day care for kids who don't want to ski. Summer finds visitors to Big Sky just as busy golfing, hiking, mountain biking, rafting, or riding horses. The Arnold Palmer–designed **Big Sky Golf Course** (© **406/995-5780**) is a magnificent 18-hole, par-72 course suitable for play by scratch golfers and weekend duffers. Lodging choices include modest hotel rooms, luxury condominiums, and Western-style ranch cabins, and there are a good many dining choices on and near the mountain.

Nearby **Lone Mountain Ranch** (© **800/514-4644** or 406/995-4644; www. lmranch.com) differs from most guest ranch counterparts by nurturing the mind as well as the body. A dude ranch in summer and a premier cross-country skiing center in winter, Lone Mountain may well be the finest four-season guest ranch in all of Montana and Wyoming—pricey, but worth it for features such as naturalist programs, bird walks, and excursions into nearby Yellowstone, not to mention its incredible food. Lone Mountain prides itself on a family atmosphere, with educational activities for children of all ages, including flower pressing and animal tracking. Guests stay for 1 week (Sun–Sat) in cabins scattered around the property.

4 Little Bighorn Battlefield National Monument

It was on this battlefield, on the dry sloping prairies of southeastern Montana, that George Armstrong Custer met his end. Although the details of the actual battle that took place on June 25, 1876, are sketchy at best, much remains for the visitor to explore and ponder in this mysterious place. The **Little Bighorn Battlefield National Monument** chronicles the history of this world-famous engagement, offering a coherent look at how the battle developed, where the members of Custer's contingent died, and how it might have looked from the perspective of the American Indian warriors.

Stop at the **visitor center,** just inside the park entrance, to view actual uniforms worn by Custer, read about his life, and see an eerie reenactment of the battles on a small-scale replica of the battlefield. Then drive 4.5 miles to the **Reno-Benteen Monument Entrenchment Trail,** at the end of the monument road, and double back. Interpretive signs at the top of this bluff show the route followed by the companies under Custer, Capt. Frederick Benteen, and Maj. Marcus Reno as they approached the area from the south, and the positions from which they defended themselves from their Indian attackers.

Custer's Lookout is the spot from which the general first viewed the Indian village. Capt. Thomas Weir led his troops to **Weir Point** in hopes of assisting Custer, but was forced to retreat to the spot held by Reno. The **Medicine Trail Ford,** on the ridge, overlooks a spot where hundreds of warriors pushed across the river in pursuit of Custer and his army. Further north, a Cheyenne warrior led an attack up **Calhoun Ridge** against a company of the Seventh Cavalry, who retreated back up the hill and were slaughtered there.

Continuing to the north, you will find more descriptions of events, as well as white markers indicating where army troops fell in battle. The bodies of Custer, his brothers Tom and Boston, and nephew Autie Reed, all were found on Custer Hill. The survivors of the Reno-Benteen armies buried the bodies of Custer and his slain army where they fell. In 1881, many were re-interred at the base of a memorial shaft found overlooking the battlefield, and Custer's remains were reburied at the U.S. Military Academy at West Point in 1877.

Indian casualties during the rout are estimated at 60 to 100 warriors, and a monument commemorating the American Indians who fought to defend their homeland was recently constructed.

There are three **walking trails** within the monument for visitors wishing to explore the battle in greater depth.

The national monument is open daily from 8am to 9pm Memorial Day to Labor Day. Spring and fall hours are from 8am to 6pm, and winter hours are from 8am to 4:30pm. There is a $10 admission fee per vehicle, $4 for those on foot. For information call (C) **406/638-2621;** or check online at **www.nps.gov/libi**.

The nearest airport is **Logan International,** in Billings. From there, head east on I-90 about 60 miles to Exit 510.

The **Hardin Area Chamber of Commerce** (I-90 Exits 497 and 503) sponsors **Little Big Horn Days** around June 25 each year, but not at the monument. The events include a reenactment, parade, symposiums, and, of course, food. For information call (C) **406/665-1672.**

In nearby Hardin, there are two lodgings at I-90 Exit 495: **American Inn of Hardin** ((C) **406/665-1870**) and the **Western Motel** ((C) **406/666-2233**).

5 Jackson Hole & Grand Teton National Park

Grand Teton National Park may be smaller than Yellowstone, but in many ways it's no less spectacular—and it's far less crowded. The park encompasses towering mountain spires reaching almost 14,000 feet and the picturesque, glacier-fed waters of Jackson Lake and the Snake River. Jackson Hole, close to the end of Grand Teton National Park and within an easy drive of Yellowstone, is one of the nation's premier ski resorts and offers many other kinds of outdoor recreation year-round.

JACKSON HOLE

First of all: *Jackson Hole* is the name of the valley that runs the length of the Tetons on the east side; the main town nearby is named *Jackson.* But no matter what you call it, there's no arguing that the area draws tourists like honey draws bears. Summer days bring temperate weather perfect for playing golf at world-class courses, chasing trout in streams filled with fish, drifting down a river atop a raft, or riding horses on one of the area's dude ranches. And oh, yes—one of the most famous national parks in the country is just up the road. When the temperatures drop, skiers flock here for some of the best skiing in the country.

The town of Jackson has become more and more popular and trendy. Its streets are filled with upscale retail outlets: art galleries, antiques shops, clothing stores, and boutiques, plus fabulous places to stay and a nationally recognized art museum.

ESSENTIALS

GETTING THERE   The **Jackson Airport** is north of town at the southern end of Grand Teton National Park, and is served by American Airlines, Delta, and United Express. Alamo, Avis, and Budget have rental-car desks here. If you're driving, U.S. 189/191 leads here from the north or south before intersecting with U.S. 89, which runs the length of the national park and right through Jackson.

VISITOR INFORMATION   The **Jackson Hole Chamber of Commerce,** P.O. Box 550, Jackson, WY 83001 ((C) **307/733-3316;** www.jackson holechamber.com), has an excellent visitor center about 3 blocks north of the Town Square at 532 N. Cache St. Both the National Forest and National Park services have representatives at the center to help plan your visit.

WHAT TO SEE & DO

Beyond its role as a staging area for explorations of Grand Teton and Yellowstone national parks, Jackson is a place to relax, shop, golf, or simply check out the sights.

Jackson Hole & Grand Teton National Park

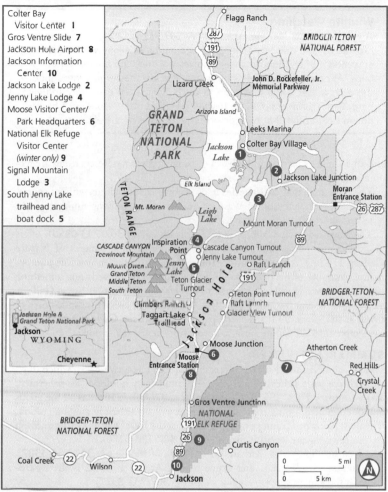

Colter Bay
Visitor Center **1**
Gros Ventre Slide **7**
Jackson Hole Airport **8**
Jackson Information
Center **10**
Jackson Lake Lodge **2**
Jenny Lake Lodge **4**
Moose Visitor Center/
Park Headquarters **6**
National Elk Refuge
Visitor Center
(winter only) **9**
Signal Mountain
Lodge **3**
South Jenny Lake
trailhead and
boat dock **5**

Flagg Ranch
287
191
89
BRIDGER-TETON
NATIONAL FOREST
Lizard Creek
John D. Rockefeller, Jr.
Memorial Parkway
GRAND
TETON
NATIONAL
PARK
Arizona Island
Leeks Marina
Colter Bay Village **1**
Jackson
Lake
2
Jackson Lake Junction
Moran
Entrance Station
26 287
Elk Island
3
TETON RANGE
Mt. Moran
Leigh
Lake
Mount Moran Turnout
89
CASCADE CANYON
Teewinot Mountain
Inspiration
Point **4**
Cascade Canyon Turnout
Jenny Lake Turnout
Mount Owen
Grand Teton
Middle Teton
South Teton
Jenny
Lake
5
Raft Launch
191
Teton Glacier
Turnout
Teton Point Turnout
Raft Launch
BRIDGER-TETON
NATIONAL FOREST
Climbers Ranch
Taggart Lake
Trailhead
Glacier View Turnout
Jackson Hole
Jackson Hole &
Grand Teton National Park
Jackson
WYOMING
Cheyenne ★
Moose Junction
Atherton Creek
Moose
Entrance Station
6
7
Red Hills
Crystal
Creek
8
Gros Ventre Junction
NATIONAL
ELK REFUGE
191
26
89 **9**
Curtis Canyon
BRIDGER-TETON
NATIONAL FOREST
Coal Creek 22
Wilson
22
10
Jackson
0   5 mi
0   5 km
N

Jackson Hole Aerial Tram Rides, at Jackson Hole Ski Resort, 7658 Teewinot, Teton Village (© **307/739-2753**), take you above 10,000 feet for a tremendous view of the Tetons. **The National Museum of Wildlife Art,** 2820 Rungius Rd. (3 miles north of town on U.S. 89, across from the National Elk Refuge; © **307/ 733-5771;** www.wildlifeart.org), is a 50,000-square-foot castle that houses some of the best wildlife art in the country.

If you don't have the time, money, or inclination for the full guest ranch experience, a fun alternative is to make a beeline for the nearest guest ranch around mealtime to enjoy Western cuisine served up to the strains of yodelin' cowpokes. The **Bar-J Ranch** (© **307/733-3370**), Teton Village Road, 1 mile north of Wyo. 22, is a big operation, with room for more than 700 people beneath its awnings. They serve a big meal of barbecued beef, beans, biscuits, and more, and there is cowboy humor and music. The **Bar-T-5,** 790 E. Cache Creek Dr., Jackson (© **800/772-5386** or 307/733-5386), offers a covered-wagon ride through Cache Creek Canyon to the "dining room" for an evening of Western victuals

Wildlife Watching

The **National Elk Refuge,** U.S. 26 ((**©** 307/733-9212), is a spectacular expanse of land that hosts the largest gathering of elk in North America, as well as moose, bighorn sheep, wolves, coyotes, and a wide variety of birds. Although wildlife viewing is excellent on the refuge throughout the year, winter is the best time to catch glimpses of the migrating elk herd. Each winter the Fish and Wildlife Service offers wonderful **horse-drawn sleigh rides** that provide up-close glimpses of the elk.

and after-dinner songs from the Bar-T-5's singing cowboys. Reservations are recommended for both.

There are more than 20 **galleries** in downtown Jackson alone, with, of course, an excellent representation of Western art, although a growing number of galleries are showing a variety of styles.

The **Martin-Harris Gallery,** at 60 E. Broadway (**©** 307/733-0350), offers original contemporary art, mainly with Western themes. **Images of Nature Gallery,** 170 N. Cache St., exhibits Tom Mangelson's excellent wildlife photography; a number of his photographs are signed and numbered (not something you'll find browsing through his mail-order catalog). The **Center Street Gallery,** 110 Center St., has the lock on abstract Western art in Jackson. A mile north of town, at 1975 U.S. 89 (toward the park), is the **Wilcox Gallery,** which showcases more than 20 painters and sculptors from across the nation.

SUMMER ACTIVITIES

Grand Teton National Park has incredible fishing. The Snake River, which flows through the park, is beat to a froth every summer by hordes of fly-fishermen. **High Country Flies,** 185 N. Center St. (**©** 307/733-7210), has all the goods and offers guided fishing trips and schools as well as the best in angling fashion. The most renowned fishing experts assemble at the **Jack Dennis Outdoor Shop** on the Town Square, at 50 E. Broadway (**©** 307/733-3270).

Adventure Sports, at Dornan's in the town of Moose (**©** 307/733-3307), has mountain-bike, kayak, and canoe rentals. At 245 Pearl St. is the **Boardroom,** a snowboard shop to end all shops (**©** 307/733-8327).

Trail rides are a staple of the Western vacation experience, and several companies in the area can put you in the saddle. Contact **Jackson Hole Trail Rides** (**©** 307/733-6992), **Snow King Stables** (**©** 307/733-5781), **Spring Creek Ranch Riding Stables** (**©** 800/443-6139), or the **Mill Iron Ranch** (**©** 307/733-6390).

The **Jackson Hole Golf and Tennis Club** (**©** 307/733-3111), north of Jackson off U.S. 89, has an 18-hole course that's one of the best in the country. The **Teton Pines Resort,** 3450 N. Clubhouse Dr. (**©** 800/238-2223 or 307/733-1005), designed by Arnold Palmer and Ed Seay, is a challenging course; and it's a cross-country ski center in winter. Both are open to the public.

There are two parts to the Snake River—the smooth water, north of Jackson, and the white water of the canyon, to the southwest. A **raft trip** on the north section is about wildlife rather than wild water; and white-water rafting—wet, wild, white-knuckle tours—is for the more adventurous. Contact **Lewis and Clark Expeditions,** at Snow King Ski Resort (**©** 800/824-5375 or 307/733-4022; www.lewisandclarkexpeds.com); or **Barker-Ewing** (**©** 800/365-1800) for either kind of river trip. Those companies specializing in white-water trips include **Dave Hansen Whitewater** ((℃) 307/733-6295); **Jackson Hole Whitewater** (℃ 800/648-2602 or 307/733-1007); and **Mad River Boat Trips** (℃ 800/458-7238 or 307/733-6203). Costs vary depending on the type and length of trip.

SKIING & OTHER WINTER SPORTS

This is one of the premier destinations for skiers in the entire country. **Jackson Hole Ski Resort,** 7658 Teewinot, Teton Village (℃ 307/733-2292 or 307/733-4005, 307/733-2291 for snow conditions, 800/443-6931 for central reservations; www.jacksonhole.com), has one of the best hills in North America and is constantly upgrading its facilities. Here's the trade-off: Prices are approaching those of Colorado resorts, although aficionados of the sport, who rate it one of the top ski areas in the country, just keep coming back for more. The novice skier will find solace on 8,481-foot Après Vous Mountain, which is a network of beginner and intermediate slopes. Aggressive skiers head for the more challenging slopes of 10,450-foot Rendezvous Mountain, designated with black-diamond and double-black-diamond runs that head straight for the bottom of the mountain. Cross-country skiers should contact the attached **Jackson Hole Nordic Center** (℃ 307/733-2629) or **Teton Pines Resort** (℃ 307/733-1005).

A newer (and less expensive) kid on the block, **Grand Targhee Resort,** Ski Hill Road, Alta (℃ 800/827-4433 or 307/353-2300; www.grandtarghee.com), gives Jackson Hole a run for its money, with great powder and plenty of opportunities to ski as much as your legs will allow. This may also be a better place for less-aggressive skiers: There's a beginner's powder area and hundreds of acres of wide-open powder slopes for intermediates and other cruisers. It's also 40 miles from Jackson, and when Teton Pass gets snowed on heavily, it can be pretty tough to get here. Still, many skiers break up a Jackson ski trip by making the trip over the pass for a couple of days on these slopes. There's also 7.5 miles of groomed cross-country ski trails.

For a change from skiing, you might want to try dog sledding. **Jackson Hole Iditarod** (℃ 800/554-7388 or 307/733-7388; www.jhsleddog.com) offers both half- and full-day trips—and you'll even get a chance to drive. The half-day ride gives the dogs an 11-mile workout and includes a lunch of hot soup and cocoa before heading back to the kennels. The full-day excursion takes you out to Granite Hot Springs, a 22-mile trip total. You get the hot lunch, plus your choice of freshly barbecued trout or steak for dinner. These trips book up pretty quickly, so call 3 to 4 days in advance to reserve.

WHERE TO STAY IN & AROUND JACKSON

There's a wide variety of lodging options in Jackson Hole, and most of the less expensive chain properties are clustered together west of town near the junction where Wyo. 22 leaves U.S. 26/89 and heads north toward Teton Village: **Motel 6** (600 S. Wyo. 22; ℃ 307/733-1620) and the not-just-numerically superior **Super 8** (750 S. Wyo. 22; ℃ 800/800-8000 or 307/733-6833). In the vicinity are the more upscale and expensive **Days Inn,** at 350 S. Wyo. 22 (℃ 800/329-7466 or 307/733-0033), with private hot tubs and fireplaces; and the **Red Lion Inn,** at 930 W. Broadway (℃ 800/844-0035 or 307/734-0035).

Amangani Cut into the side of East Gros Ventre Butte, Amangani's rough rock exterior blends incredibly well, so that the lights from its windows and pool appear at night to glow from within the mountain. The style is understated and rustic, but every detail is executed with taste. You'll find a high level of personal service, luxury, and all the little touches. The latter include CD players in every bedroom, cashmere throws on the day beds, and stunning slate and redwood interiors. You can get massages and facials at the health center, or dine at the Grill at Amangani. Some Jackson competitors seem jealous: One suggested that the resort operates on the theory that if you set your prices sky-high, a certain clientele feels it has to stay there. 1535 NE Butte Rd., Jackson, WY 83002 (on top of East Gros Ventre Butte). (*C*) **877/734-7333** or 307/734-7333. www.amangani.com. 40 units. $625–$900 double. AE, DC, DISC, MC, V. **Amenities:** Restaurant; outdoor pool; spa.

Jackson Hole Lodge   Though situated near one of the busiest intersections in town, and packed into a small space, this lodge is quiet and well designed, so that its location in the heart of town becomes a plus. You can relax in one of the whirlpools, take a sauna, or sit out on your own sun deck. Rooms are very comfortable, blending Western ambience with scads of in-room options. Best of all are the affordable condos, which are more spacious than the standard rooms and have kitchens that can help you cut your food costs. 420 W. Broadway, Jackson, WY 83001. (*C*) **800/604-9404** or 307/733-2992. www.jacksonholelodge.com. 59 units. $109–$134 double; $184–$304 condo. AE, DC, DISC, MC, V. **Amenities:** Outdoor pool.

Red Rock Ranch   This working cattle ranch is great for families looking for a fun experience amidst the peaceful wilderness. With excellent catch-and-release fly-fishing on a private stretch of Crystal Creek, horseback riding in the mountains, and activities that include overnighters for the kids, cookouts with live music, trips to the rodeo in Jackson, and weekly country dances, this guest ranch northeast of Jackson is a great spot to bring the whole bunch. All nine cabins (one or two bedrooms) are comfortable 1950s log structures decorated with Western trappings and a charming woodstove, and best of all—no telephone. P.O. Box 38, Kelly, WY 83011 (30 miles northeast of Jackson on U.S. 26/287). (*C*) **307/733-6288.** www.theredrockranch.com. 9 cabins. $1,350 per cabin per week. Rate includes all meals and horseback riding. Minimum 6-day stay (Sun–Sat). No credit cards. Closed Sept–May. **Amenities:** Outdoor pool.

Rusty Parrot Lodge and Spa   The name sounds like an out-of-tune jungle bird, but since 1990, the Rusty Parrot has shown excellent pitch, combining a country lodge with a full-service spa right in the heart of busy Jackson. Located across from Miller Park, the Parrot is an impressive rough-hewn log building, with an interior appointed with elegant furnishings and river rock fireplaces. Rooms are huge and several have private balconies. 175 N. Jackson, Jackson, WY 83001. (*C*) **800/458-2004** or 307/733-2000. www.rustyparrot.com. 31 units. $108–$275 double; $500 suite. Rates include full breakfast. AE, DC, DISC, MC, V. **Amenities:** Restaurant; spa.

Spring Creek Ranch   Perched atop East Gros Ventre Butte, 1,000 feet above the Snake River and minutes from both the airport and downtown Jackson, this resort commands a panoramic view of 1,500 acres of land populated by deer, moose, and the horses at its riding facility in the valley below. A little less exclusive now that Amangani has opened next door, Spring Creek still has much going for it: The guest rooms all have fireplaces, Native American floor and wall coverings, and balconies with views of the Tetons. Studio units boast kitchenettes. In addition to its own rooms, the resort arranges accommodations in the privately owned condominiums that dot the butte—large, lavishly furnished, and featuring fully equipped kitchens. 1800 Spirit Dance Rd. (on top of the East Gros Ventre Butte), P.O. Box 4780, Jackson, WY 83001. (*C*) **800/443-6139** or 307/733-8833. 125 units. $210 double; $375–$1,200 condo. AE, MC, V. **Amenities:** Restaurant; outdoor pool; tennis court; spa.

Trapper Inn   The employees here are some of the most helpful you'll find in Jackson, and they'll tip you off on the best deals in the valley. Just 2 short blocks north of the town square, the Trapper is hard to miss—there's that crazy Trapper guy on the sign on the left. You can walk anywhere downtown within minutes. The rooms are spacious, with cozy quilts, stately lodgepole pine furnishings, plus a microwave and refrigerator. 235 N. Cache, Jackson, WY 83001. (C) 800/341-8000 or 307/733-2648 (reservations). www.trapperinn.com. 54 units. $98–$178 double; $170–224 suite. AE, DC, DISC, MC, V.

Virginian Lodge   It's not brand-new, and the highway is right outside the door, but since its overhaul in 1995, the Virginian is a cheerful place to stay, with a location on Jackson's busy Broadway strip. You can get a room with a private Jacuzzi or a kitchenette, and many have "dry" bars and sofa sleepers. Beyond the rooms, kids can romp in the arcade, families can eat in the Howling Coyote, and parents can relax in the Virginian Saloon. 750 W. Broadway, Jackson, WY 83001. (C) 800/262-4999 or 307/733-2792. Fax 307/733-4063. www.virginianlodge.com. 181 units. $95–$109 double; $125–$185 suite. AE, DC, DISC, MC, V. **Amenities:** Restaurant; outdoor pool.

Wort Hotel   Located on Broadway just off the town square—an area constantly in flux with new buildings and new shops—the Wort stands like an old tree, though its Tudor-style two-story building was largely rebuilt after a 1980 fire. Opened in the early 1940s by the sons of Charles Wort, an early-20th century homesteader, it has an old-fashioned style to it, both in the noisy and relaxed bar and the quiet, formal dining room (there's also a Starbucks Coffee outlet on-site). In the manner of an old cattle-baron hotel, the lobby is graced by a warm, romantic fireplace; another fireplace and a huge, hand-carved mural accent a mezzanine sitting area, providing a second hideaway. The rooms aren't Tudor at all—the Wort labels them "New West"—but all of them were totally renovated in 2000. 50 N. Glenwood, Jackson, WY 83001. (C) 307/733-2190. www.wort hotel.com. 60 units. $140–$245 double; $275–$485 suite. AE, DISC, MC, V. **Amenities:** Restaurant.

WHERE TO DINE

The Blue Lion ECLECTIC   In the fast-moving, high-rent world of Jackson dining, the Blue Lion stays in the forefront by staying the same. The simple two-story blue clapboard building houses intimate rooms accented with soft lighting, where diners enjoy slow-paced, elegant meals. The menu features rack of lamb and the usual (in Jackson) wild game specialties, such as grilled elk loin in a peppercorn sauce. Fresh fish is flown in daily for such dishes as wine-basted rainbow trout stuffed with snow crab. Summer diners can eat outside on the patio deck just north of the entrance. 160 N. Millward St. (C) 307/733-3912. Reservations recommended. Main courses $15–$28. AE, DC, MC, V. Wed–Mon 5:30–10pm.

The Bunnery BREAKFAST/SANDWICHES/SOUPS   A Jackson mainstay, this bakery/restaurant is a great place for breakfast—perhaps a big soft spinach omelet with sour cream and Swiss, or a Bunnery Benedict, served on a healthful OSM (oats, sunflower, and millet) bun. These are cramped quarters, though, and you'll often find yourself waiting in a line that stretches down the boardwalk of the Hole-In-The-Wall Mall just off the square—not bad in summer, but tough on cold winter mornings. Sandwiches are reasonably priced, and portions are large. If you're in a hurry, there's also the Bunnery Express: muffins, baked goods, and drinks with a rapidly moving line. 130 N. Cache St. (C) 307/733-5474. Main courses $6–$8. MC, V. Summer daily 7am–3pm and 5–9pm; winter daily 7am–2pm.

The Granary at Spring Creek AMERICAN   Perched atop Gros Ventre Butte, 15 minutes from downtown Jackson, this restaurant at Spring Creek Ranch has one of the best views of the Teton Range, especially enjoyable over a plate of fresh snapper wrapped in prosciutto and potato. Breakfast (our favorite: rainbow trout and eggs) and lunch are particularly pleasant when weather allows dining outside on a wood deck. The menu changes seasonally, but you may find elk-flank fajitas and gourmet sandwiches at lunch or grilled elk tenderloin with blackberry barbecue sauce at dinner. On top of the East Gros Ventre Butte. ② **800/443-6139** or 307/733-8833. Reservations recommended. Breakfast $9–$13; lunch $8–$15; dinner $15–$28. AE, DC, MC, V. Daily 7:30–10am, noon–2pm, and 6–9pm.

Jedediah's House of Sourdough AMERICAN   You'll think you've wandered into the kitchen of some sodbuster's log home when you enter Jedediah's— the structure was built in 1910 and is on the National Register of Historic Places. (The sourdough starter is even older, 100 years and going strong.) Bring a big appetite for breakfast, plus a little patience—you may have to wait for a table, and then for your food, while gazing at the fascinating old photos on the wall and listening to the families packed closely around you. But it's worth it, especially for the rich flavor of the sourjacks, a stack of sourdough pancakes. During summer months, Jedediah's also serves dinners: steaks, barbecued chicken, rainbow trout, and the like. 135 E. Broadway. ② **307/733-5671.** Reservations not accepted. Breakfast $4–$8; lunch $5–$9; dinner $8–$18. AE, DC, DISC, MC, V. Year-round daily 7am–2pm; summer 5:30–9pm.

Nani's Genuine Pasta House ITALIAN   The setting is simple but the food is extraordinary at Nani's, where you are handed two menus: *a carta classico* featuring pasta favorites such as *amitriciana* (tomato, onion, pancetta, and freshly ground black pepper) and a bowl of mussels in wine broth; or a list of specialties from a different featured region of Italy, which might include swordfish stuffed with bread crumbs, Parmigiano Reggiano cheese, capers, and garlic. Your only problem with this restaurant might be finding it—it's tucked away behind a rather run-down motel, and rarely does it fill to the rafters. 240 N. Glenwood. ② **307/733-3888.** www.nanis.com. Reservations recommended. Main courses $10–$17. MC, V. Tues–Sat 5–10pm. ITALIAN.

Snake River Brewing Company PIZZA/PASTA   Microbreweries are sprouting (and spouting) all over the country, but this one is a cut above many others, judging from the prizes it has won for its pale ale and Zonker Stout. In this roomy, high-ceilinged new building, the brewery also serves excellent pizza cooked in a wood-fired oven—try the prosciutto and roasted red pepper or the barbecue chicken. There are also pastas, calzones, and various sandwiches. The 15 brewing vats are all around and above, sometimes humming a bit too loudly, and you can play foosball and pool on the mezzanine. Beer lovers enjoy happy hour (4–6pm), and occasionally there's live music—jazz or traditional Celtic. 265 S. Millward St. ② **307/739-2337.** Main courses $8–$12. AE, MC, V. Daily 11:30am–11pm.

JACKSON AFTER DARK

Head down to the **Silver Dollar Bar,** 50 N. Glenwood (② **307/733-2190**), in the Wort Hotel, for a drink with one of the real or imagined cowpokes bellied up to the bar. And, yes, those 1921 silver dollars are authentic. Stop at the famous **Million Dollar Cowboy Bar,** on the west side of the square at 25 N. Cache St. (② **307/733-2207**), to dance the two-step to live bands. For some high-octane dancing fun led by talented local hoofers, head out to Wilson (west of Jackson 5 miles on Wyo. 22) and the **Stagecoach Bar** (© 307/733-4407) on a Sunday night. It's the only night they have live music in this scruffy bar and hamburger joint, and the place is jammed wall-to-wall.

GRAND TETON NATIONAL PARK

Yellowstone may have its geysers, but only this park can boast the bare, towering spires of the Cathedral Group, "Les Trois Tetons" (or "the three breasts," as cheeky French trappers named them). The Grand Teton, the largest of the three (known as "The Grand" by locals), is a mountaineer's dream, and hiking throughout the park draws hundreds of thousands each year. In addition to unparalleled mountain views, wildlife watching is also immensely popular; elk, bison, bald eagles, moose, and beavers are just some of the critters with whom you'll be sharing park land.

ESSENTIALS

ACCESS/ENTRY POINTS   There are really only three ways to enter the park. From the **north,** you're coming from Yellowstone National Park on the John D. Rockefeller Memorial Parkway (U.S. 89/191/287). December through March, this entrance is open only to snowmobiles and snow coaches (though a potential snowmobile ban is pending for 2003). From the **east,** enter via U.S. 26/287 and the Moran entrance station. This route comes from Dubois, 55 miles east of the park on the other side of the Absaroka and Wind River Mountains, and takes you over Togwotee Pass, from which you get a breathtaking view of the Tetons soaring above the valley. From the **south,** you'll drive about 12 miles north of Jackson on the John D. Rockefeller Memorial Parkway (U.S. 26/89/191) to the Moose turnoff and the south entrance. Here can be found the park headquarters.

VISITOR INFORMATION   Contact **Grand Teton National Park,** P.O. Drawer 170, Moose, WY 83012 (© 307/739-3600; www.nps.gov/grte).

There are three visitor centers in Grand Teton National Park. The **Moose Visitor Center** (© 307/739-3399) is a half mile west of Moose Junction on the Teton Park Road, at the southern end of the park; it's open daily from 8am to 7pm June to Labor Day, and from 8am to 5pm the rest of the year. The **Colter Bay Visitor Center** (© 307/739-3594), the northernmost of the park's visitor centers, is open daily from 8am to 8pm from early June to Labor Day, and from 8am to 5pm from after Labor Day to early October. There is also **Jenny Lake Visitor Center** (© 307/739-3392), which is open daily from 8am to 7pm from early June to Labor Day, and from 8am to 5pm from after Labor Day to early October.

FEES   Travelers just passing through on U.S. 26/89/191 do not pay a fee. But to explore the park for a 7-day period, each vehicle pays $20, a snowmobile or motorcycle pays $15, and those on bicycle, skis, or foot pay $10; the entrance permit is valid at both Grand Teton and Yellowstone national parks. If you enter the park from the north, there's no entrance station as the park assumes you've paid at Yellowstone.

Free **backcountry permits** are required for overnight use of backcountry campsites. Permits can be reserved (for a $15 fee) only from January 1 to June 1; thereafter, all backcountry permits are issued on a first-come, first-served basis. Permits are issued at the Moose and Colter Bay visitor centers and the Jenny Lake ranger station. Reservations may be made by writing the **Permits**

Office, Grand Teton National Park, P.O. Drawer 170, Moose, WY 83012, or by sending a fax to **307/739-3438.** Phone reservations are not accepted.

SEASONS Spring is an excellent time to visit the park (remembering that spring comes a little later here than in many parts of the country); wildflowers are in bloom, and on a clear day the snow-covered Tetons stand out boldly against a crisp blue sky. Even better, trails are virtually devoid of hikers—although at higher elevations, snow might still block the paths. In May and June, mild days and cool nights intersperse with occasional rain and snow. The snow level usually remains above valley elevation until mid-June. Summer, of course, is the busiest time. In September, sunny days and cooler nights alternate with rain and occasional snowstorms, and by the middle of the month, fall colors begin to make their way across the landscape. The first big snow usually arrives by the beginning of November.

SEEING THE HIGHLIGHTS

Just viewing the spectacularly beautiful peaks is one of the main reasons to visit the park. The Cathedral Group is composed of **Grand Teton** (elevation 13,770 ft.), **Teewinot** (elevation 12,325 ft.), and **Mount Owen** (elevation 12,928 ft.). Nearby are **Middle Teton** (elevation 12,804 ft.) and **South Teton** (elevation 12,514 ft.). The best views of the Cathedral Group are found on the trails and roads that ring **Jenny Lake. Signal Mountain,** southeast of Jackson Lake, may not rank up there with the other Tetons, but it's got the best lookout in the park. Navigating the twisty, way-too-narrow road pays off in spades at the summit, where you can gaze out over Cascade Canyon, Jackson Lake, and the Tetons. Slightly north of Jenny Lake is the underrated, yet still awesome, **Mount Moran** (elevation 12,605 ft.), the fourth largest peak in the range.

MENOR'S FERRY   One of the most interesting historic sites in the park is Menor's Historic Ferry Site, just behind the Moose Visitor Center. In the late 1800s, Bill Menor had a country store and operated a ferry to get across the Snake River, and both have been reconstructed. Nearby is a historic cabin where, in 1923, the seed for the protection of the area was planted and eventually led to the creation of the national park.

JENNY LAKE   Perhaps the most popular of the glacial lakes, Jenny Lake nestles at the base of the tallest Teton peaks, a short walk from a turnout. A 6-mile hiking trail that encircles the lake is very popular, and parking is limited, so your best plan is to arrive early or late in the day; a midday arrival may be frustrating.

COLTER BAY   Located near the north entrance, Colter Bay is the place to stock up on groceries, postcards and stamps, T-shirts, and the like. Other services in the vicinity include a general store and do-it-yourself laundry, two restaurants, and boat rentals and tours. Accommodations for the weary traveler are in cabins; the campground provides campers and RVs a roost in a quiet, sheltered area away from the activity center.

JACKSON LAKE   Vast Jackson Lake dominates the northern section of the park and is a natural lake that has been enhanced by a dam for irrigation. The **Signal Mountain** recreational area, on the lake's southeast shore, offers camping, excellent accommodations in cabins and multiplex units, two restaurants, and a lounge with one of the few live televisions in the park. This is also the place to fill up on gasoline and provisions from the small convenience store. Boat rentals and scenic cruises of the lake also originate here.

KELLY & GROS VENTRE   Although situated outside the park boundaries near the town of Kelly, the Gros Ventre Slide area is both an interesting hiking area and historical site. It was at this spot in June 1925 that the side of Sheep Mountain broke loose and nearly 50 million cubic yards of rock fell into the Gros Ventre River, forming a natural dam. Two years later, the dam broke, and a cascade of water rushed down the canyon and through Kelly, taking several lives.

SPORTS & OUTDOOR ACTIVITIES

BIKING   The roads in Grand Teton were not built with bicyclists in mind, and the problem is safety—traffic is often heavy, with RVs careening about, and some roads have only narrow shoulders. Bikers should try **Antelope Flats Road,** beginning at a trail head 1 mile north of Moose Junction and going east. Sometimes called **Mormon Row,** this paved, 13-mile, mostly level route passes old ranch homesteads and the small town of Kelly. Leaving the paved road about 4 miles from Moose Junction, turn north onto unpaved **Shadow Mountain Road,** which goes into the national forest, climbing through the trees to the summit. Total distance is 7 miles, elevation gain is 1,370 feet, and views are of Mount Moran and the Tetons across the valley. A map that shows bicycle routes is available at park visitor centers or at **Adventure Sports** (© 307/733-3307) in Moose.

BOATING   There are more—and better—options on Grand Teton's lakes and the Snake River than in Yellowstone. Motorboats are permitted on Jenny, Jackson, and Phelps lakes. Rafts, canoes, dories, and kayaks are allowed on the Snake River within the park. No boats are allowed on Pacific Creek or the Gros Ventre River. Avid water lovers flock to Jackson Lake, where powerboats pull skiers, sailboats move noiselessly in summer breezes, and anglers ply the waters in search of trout. Scenic cruises (daily) of Jackson Lake, as well as twice-a-week floating steak-fry cruises, are available at the **Colter Bay** marina from May through September. Boat and canoe rentals, tackle, and fishing licenses are available at Colter and **Signal Mountain.** Shuttles to the west side of Jenny Lake, as well as cruises, are conducted by **Teton Boating Company** (© 307/733-2703).

CROSS-COUNTRY SKIING   Both flat and steep skiing are available here. The best approach may be to check with local guides to match up trails with your desires and ability. The two things to watch out for are hypothermia and avalanches. The relatively easy **Jenny Lake Trail** starts at the Taggart Lake Parking area, and follows Cottonwood Creek for about 8 flat, scenic miles. *Caution:* High winter winds can double the time necessary to take the trip. More difficult is the 5-mile **Taggart Lake-Beaver Creek Loop,** a 3-mile trek with some steep, icy patches on the return.

FISHING   One of the most popular fishing streams in the West, the **Snake River** flows through Teton for 27 miles. Although it's filled with cutthroat trout, some anglers insist it's overfished, and its banks may be crowded. Therefore, the best method of attacking the stream is in a drift float, preferably with a guide who knows where the fish are and understands river conditions. Check with **Jack Dennis Fishing Trips** (© 307/733-3270; www.jackdennis.com), **Triangle X-Osprey Float Trips** (© 307/733-5500), or **Fort Jackson Float Trips** (© 800/735-8430). As an alternative, take a boat into **Jackson Lake,** or stake out a position on the banks below the dam.

RAFTING & FLOAT TRIPS   One of the most effective, and environmentally sound, methods of viewing wildlife in Teton is aboard a floating watercraft that silently moves downstream without disturbing the critters. Several park concessionaires operate Snake River float trips, most of which run from mid-May to mid-September (depending on weather and river flow conditions). These companies offer 5- to 10-mile scenic floats, some with early-morning and evening wildlife trips. Try **Barker-Ewing Float Trips** (© 800/365-1800), **Fort Jackson Float Trips** (© 800/735-8430), or **Grand Teton Lodge Company** (© 307/543-2811).

THE TOP TWO HIKING TRAILS

THE JENNY LAKE–INSPIRATION POINT TRAIL   South Jenny Lake is a jumping-off point for serious mountaineers; hiking permits are available at the visitor center. The trail heads to Hidden Falls, Inspiration Point, and Cascade Canyon are at the south end of the lake, so here's where you have to make a choice. From the boat dock, the trip across the lake to the west side shortens the hike to Hidden Falls by two-thirds. The alternative is a 2-mile hike around the south end of the lake. Either choice is a good one, but given time and energy, we'd take the long route. With the jagged peaks of the Tetons immediately overhead, this trail offers better photo ops than those in Yellowstone or Glacier.

Knowledgeable hikers describe the **Cascade Canyon Trail** as the most popular in the park. However, it may be physically taxing. It's possible to reach the entrance to the canyon by taking a boat across Jenny Lake to the West Shore Boat Dock, then hiking .9 mile to **Inspiration Point.** From there, it's a steep climb to the entrance of the canyon, followed by a gentle ascent through a glacially sculpted canyon. Wildflowers carpet the area, ducks nest along Cascade Creek, and moose and bear may be spotted. The 4.5-mile hike, however, is quite difficult, because of the changes in elevation and length.

The full trail to Inspiration Point is level enough to be manageable by most children. The hike winds through a forest populated by marmots and squirrels, where you'll get filtered views of the lake. You'll hear **Hidden Falls** pouring through a narrow gap in the rocks long before you see it. After crossing a small bridge over the creek and traveling uphill another .2 mile, you'll arrive at Inspiration Point.

Two tips: Whichever route you take to Inspiration Point, start early in the day to avoid the crowds. Then pace yourself. The last .6 mile to Hidden Falls, and the path beyond that to Inspiration Point, are steeper and require more strenuous activity than lower sections. But they are well worth the effort; take time to relax along the way so you'll have the energy to make it to the top. The reward is a commanding view of Jenny Lake, the surrounding mountains, and the Jackson Hole Valley. It's an excellent vantage point from which to catch your breath.

THE SIGNAL SUMMIT MOUNTAIN TRAIL   Just footsteps from the entrance to the Signal Mountain Lodge is a sign marking the trail head for the 3-mile Signal Summit Mountain Trail. Although it's well marked, it's not well traveled, since most visitors drive their automobiles in this area. After negotiating the trail's steep beginning, you'll discover that it opens onto a broad plateau covered with lodgepole pines, grassy areas, and wildflowers. Cross the paved road and arrive at a large, lily-covered pond at the opening of a meadow; listen for the sounds of frogs, and spend some time watching wildlife and waterfowl. The trail then winds along the south and east perimeters of the pond before turning east and heading toward the summit, which can take up to 2 hours. Shortly after passing the pond, you'll come to a fork in the road that converts the trip into a loop trail. Take the northern route and you'll travel the rim of the mountain, meandering to the summit through a forest of sagebrush and pine trees.

On the return, a southern trail skirts large alpine ponds where you'll find waterfowl, moose, and, perhaps, black bear. Take one route up and the other down; you'll get the variety, and it has no effect on the total distance.

WHERE TO CAMP & STAY

The five National Park Service **campgrounds** in Grand Teton are relatively close together, so selecting one is more a matter of availability than geography. All have modern comfort stations and charge $12 per night. Campgrounds operate on a first-come, first-served basis, although reservations are available to groups of 10 or more. Write to **Campground Reservations,** Grand Teton National Park, Moose, WY 83012. Reservations for **trailer sites** at Colter Bay campground may be made by contacting the **Grand Teton Lodge Co.,** P.O. Box 240, Moran, WY 83013 (© **307/543-3100**). Additionally, **Grand Teton Campground** is a concessionaire-operated campground in the **Flagg Ranch** complex on the John D. Rockefeller, Jr., Memorial Parkway. The area has 121 sites, showers, and launderette. For reservations, contact Flagg Ranch, P.O. Box 187, Moran, WY 83013 (© **800/443-2311**).

For those who don't want to camp, the premier destination is the pricey **Jenny Lake Lodge** (© **800/628-9988** or 307/543-3300; www.gtlc.com), offering seclusion, award-winning food, and the individual attentions that come with a cabin resort kept intentionally small. The name is a misnomer, however, as the lodge is not near the lake but rather sits away from the highway among forested glades. Moreover, the lodge functions primarily as an upscale restaurant. Accommodations are in beautiful log cabins—rustic on the outside but luxurious within. Each has a traditional pitched shingle roof and a long, pillared porch.

Another top choice is **Jackson Lake Lodge** (© **800/628-9988** or 307/543-3100; www.gtlc.com), which is to Grand Teton what Old Faithful is to Yellowstone. It's situated on a bluff overlooking Willow Flats, 1 mile from Jackson Lake, and offers good accommodations, fine dining, and commanding views of Grand Teton and Mount Moran. The lobby has 60-foot-tall windows; and the cocktail lounge offers live entertainment. Guest rooms are in the three-story main lodge and in cottages scattered about the property, some of which have large balconies and mountain views.

The moderately priced **Signal Mountain Lodge** (© **307/543-2831;** www.signalmtnlodge.com) is the only resort on the shores of Jackson Lake inside the park. In addition to offering spectacular views across the lake to the Tetons, it's centrally located on the main route from Moran Junction to Jenny Lake and close to several hiking trails, including one to Signal Summit that begins across the road. Most accommodations are in free-standing cabins (motel-style rooms in four-unit buildings set amid the trees) and family bungalows, some of which enjoy beach frontage.

6 Yellowstone National Park

What other national park boasts such an assortment of thermal geysers and hot springs that their total exceeds the number found on the rest of the planet? On top of that, there's a waterfall that's twice as tall as Niagara Falls. Not to mention a canyon deep and colorful enough to fall into the "grand" category.

Wildlife? Ever focus your telephoto lens on a wild, untamed grizzly bear? Or a bald eagle? What about a wolf? Thousands of visitors have these experiences here every year.

ESSENTIALS

GETTING THERE   The most convenient airports to the park are in Bozeman, Montana, or in West Yellowstone. Bozeman's airport, **Gallatin Field** (© 406/388-8321), has daily service via Delta, Northwest, and United, as well as Horizon and Skywest commuter flights. From Bozeman, it's 91 miles via U.S. 191 south to U.S. 287, which takes you directly to the park's West Entrance. The **West Yellowstone Airport** (© 406/646-7359), U.S. 191, 1 mile north of West Yellowstone, provides commercial air service June through September only, on Skywest. In West Yellowstone, Avis is open May through September, and Budget is open year-round.

Billings, Montana, is 95 miles from Yellowstone's Northeast Entrance (closed from Oct 15 to Memorial Day). It's a 65-mile drive south on U.S. 212 to Red Lodge, then 30 miles on the Beartooth Highway to the park. The airport in Billings, **Logan International,** is the busiest in Montana.

Cody, Wyoming, is 52 miles from Yellowstone's East Entrance (closed Nov 1–Apr 30), via U.S. 14/16/20. Cody's **Yellowstone Regional Airport** (© 307/587-5096) serves the Northeast Entrance of Yellowstone National Park with year-round commercial flights via Skywest and United Express. To Yellowstone's Northeast Entrance, it's 53 miles via Wyo. 120/296 to the Beartooth Highway (closed Oct 15 to Memorial Day) intersection, and 14 miles beyond that to the entrance.

VISITOR CENTERS & INFORMATION   Contact Superintendent, P.O. Box 168, Yellowstone National Park, WY 82190 (© **307/344-7381;** www.nps.gov/yell).

There are five visitor centers in the park, open daily from 8am to 7pm. The **Albright Visitor Center** (© 307/344-2263), at Mammoth Hot Springs, is the largest of all the visitor centers. Next largest is the **Old Faithful Visitor Center** (© 307/545-2751), where projected geyser eruption times are posted. The **Canyon Visitor Center** (© 307/242-2550), in Canyon Village, offers extensive information on bison. The **Fishing Bridge Visitor Center** (© 307/242-2450), near Fishing Bridge on the north shore of Yellowstone Lake, has an excellent wildlife display. The **Grant Village Visitor Center** (© 307/242-2650) is just south of West Thumb on the west side of Yellowstone Lake. Other sources for information are the Madison and West Thumb information stations; and, in Norris, the Museum of the National Park Ranger and the Norris Geyser Basin Museum.

FEES   A 7-day **entrance permit** costs $20 per vehicle, and is valid at both Yellowstone and Grand Teton national parks. A snowmobile or motorcycle pays $15, and those on bicycle, skis, or foot pay $10. Free **backcountry permits** are required for any overnight trip, with camping allowed only in designated campsites. As these are often full, it's best to reserve your spot in advance, although it costs $20. Contact **Yellowstone Backcountry Office** (© 307/344-2160) at the above park address for their "Backcountry Trip Planner"; reservations can be made after April 1 for the following summer.

SEASONS   Traveling Yellowstone's roads during spring months can be a roll of the dice, since weather can delay openings for days (sometimes weeks) at a time, especially at higher altitudes. The only road open through the winter is Mammoth Hot Springs Cooke City Road. Everything's open in the summer, but expect to battle crowds.

EXPLORING THE PARK

WEST YELLOWSTONE TO NORRIS   Most visitors enter at the West Yellowstone Entrance. As you travel the 14 miles from the gate to Madison Junction, you will find the Two Ribbons Trail, which offers an opportunity to walk through and inspect the effects of the 1988 fire.

Madison Junction is where you'll enter the northern loop toward Norris Junction, along a windy 14-mile section of road that parallels the **Gibbon River.** At **Gibbon Falls,** which is 84 feet tall, you'll see water bursting out of the edge of a caldera in a rocky canyon. There's a delightful **picnic area** just below the falls, on an open plateau overlooking the Gibbon River. Before arriving at Norris Junction, you'll discover the **Artist Paint Pot Trail** in Gibbon Meadows 4.5 miles south of the Norris Junction, an interesting, worthwhile, and easy half-mile stroll.

NORRIS GEYSER BASIN   Here is one of the park's highest concentrations of thermal features, including the most active geysers. There are two loop trails, both mostly level with wheelchair access, to the Porcelain Basin and the Back Basin. If you take both of them, you'll see most of the area's interesting thermal features. If you're pressed for time, walk the shorter, **Porcelain Basin Trail,** a boardwalk that takes only 45 minutes. The 1.5-mile **Back Basin Loop** is easily negotiable in 1 hour and passes by **Steamboat Geyser,** which has been known to produce the world's highest and most memorable eruptions. However, these 400-foot waterspouts occur infrequently, so it will take some luck to see one. Check out the **Norris Geyser Basin Museum** and the **Museum of the National Park Ranger** while you're here.

NORRIS TO MAMMOTH HOT SPRINGS   From Norris Geyser Basin, it's a 21-mile drive north to Mammoth Hot Springs, past the Twin Lakes—beautiful, watery jewels surrounded by trees. Six miles up the road, you'll come to the Beaver Lake Picnic Area, an excellent little snack spot right on Beaver Lake. It's also a good place to keep an eye out for moose. Traveling the final few miles to Mammoth Hot Springs, you're in an area that is especially interesting because of its geologic diversity.

MAMMOTH HOT SPRINGS   Get out of your car! Two of Yellowstone's most unique, beautiful, and fascinating areas are the Upper and Lower Terraces. Contours are constantly undergoing change in the hot springs, as formations are shaped by large quantities of flowing water, the slope of the ground, and trees and rocks that determine the direction of the flow. The Lower Terrace Interpretive Trail is one of the best ways to see this area. After passing **Palette Spring,** where bacteria create a collage of browns, greens, and oranges, you're on your way to **Cleopatra** and **Minerva terraces.** Minerva is a favorite of visitors because of its bright colors and travertine formations, the product of limestone deposits.

The hike up the last 150 feet to the Upper Terrace Loop Drive is slightly steeper, although there are benches at frequent intervals. From here you can see all the terraces and several springs—**Canary Spring** and **New Blue Spring** being the most distinctive.

MAMMOTH HOT SPRINGS TO TOWER JUNCTION   About 8 miles in as you head east from Mammoth on the Tower Road is the **Blacktail Plateau**

Yellowstone National Park

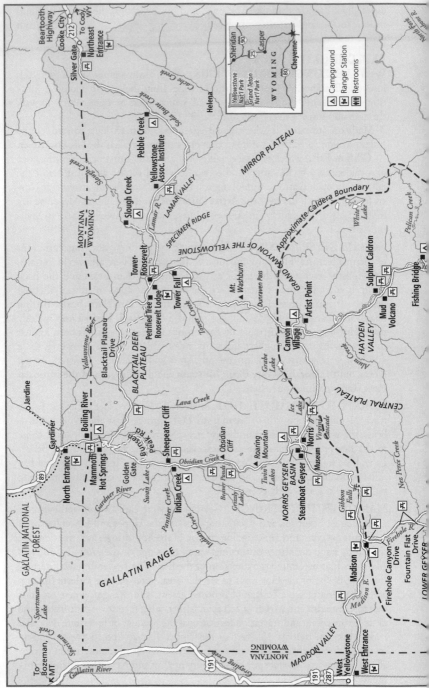

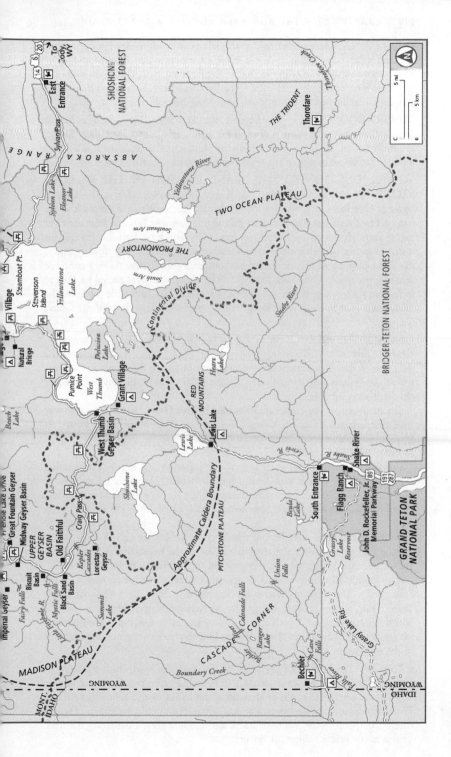

Drive, a 7-mile, one-way dirt road that offers great wildlife-viewing opportunities and a bit more solitude. You'll emerge back onto the Mammoth–Tower Road, about a mile west of the turnoff to the Petrified Tree. Turn right onto this half-mile-long road that dead-ends at the **Petrified Tree,** a redwood that, while standing, was burned by volcanic ash more than 50 million years ago.

TOWER–ROOSEVELT Just beyond the Petrified Tree, you'll come to **Tower–Roosevelt,** the most relaxed of the park's villages. At **Specimen Ridge,** 2.5 miles east of the Tower Junction on the Northeast Entrance road, you'll find a ridge that entombs one of the world's most extensive fossil forests.

TOWER JUNCTION TO THE GRAND CANYON OF THE YELLOW-STONE A few minutes' drive south from the Tower area is the **Calcite Springs Overlook.** A short loop along a boardwalk leads to the overlook at the rim of **The Narrows,** the narrowest part of the canyon. You can hear the river raging through the canyon some 500 feet below, and look across at the canyon walls composed of rock spires and bands of columnar basalt. Just downstream is the most prominent feature in the canyon, **Bumpus Butte.** As you continue south, approaching **Dunraven Pass** (8,859 ft.), keep your eyes peeled for the shy mountain sheep, since this is one of their prime habitats. One mile further is the **Washburn Hot Springs Overlook,** which offers sweeping views of the Grand Canyon.

CANYON VILLAGE You're in for yet another eyeful when you reach the **Grand Canyon** of Yellowstone National Park. It's impressive because of the steepness of the cliffs, which descend hundreds of feet to the bottom of a gorge where the Yellowstone River flows. It's also colorful, with displays of oranges, reds, yellows, and golds.

An auto tour of the canyon follows **North Rim Drive,** a two-lane, one-way road that begins in Canyon Village, to your first stop, **Inspiration Point.** At Inspiration Point, a moderately strenuous descent down 57 steps takes you to an overlook with views of the Lower Falls and canyon.

For the adventurous, an alternative to driving from one overlook to another is to negotiate the **North Rim Trail,** which is slightly more than 2.3 miles long, beginning at Inspiration Point. Unfortunately, the North Rim Trail is not a loop, so if you take the hike, you'll have to backtrack to get your car at Inspiration Point.

Whether you drive or walk, you should go to the **Upper Falls View,** where a .3-mile trail leads down from the parking lot to the brink of the **Upper Falls** and an overlook within splashing distance of the rushing river and the waterfall.

The **South Rim Drive** leads to several overlooks and better views of the Lower Falls. The most impressive vantage point is from the bottom of **Uncle Tom's Trail,** a steep, 500-foot route to the river's edge that begins at the first South Rim parking lot. South Rim Road continues to a second, lower parking lot and a trail that leads to **Artist Point.** The view here is astounding and best in the early morning.

CANYON VILLAGE TO FISHING BRIDGE The road winds through the Hayden Valley, which is a vast expanse of beautiful green meadows accented by brown cuts where the soil is eroded along the banks of the Yellowstone River. The valley is now a wide, sprawling area where bison and pronghorn play and where trumpeter swans, white pelicans, and Canada geese float along the river. This is also a prime habitat for the grizzly.

Nature is working at her acidic best at the **Sulphur Caldron** and **Mud Volcano** areas, 12 miles south of the Canyon Junction, which were described by the frontier minister Edwin Stanley as "unsightly, unsavory, and villainous." At **Dragon's Mouth Spring,** turbid water from an underground cavern is propelled by escaping steam and sulfurous gases to an earthside exit where it colors the earth with shades of orange and green. The belching of steam from the cavern, and the attendant sound, which is due to the splash of 180°F (82°C) water against the wall in a subterranean cavern, create a medieval quality; hence, the name of the spring.

The road across the Yellowstone River at **Fishing Bridge** was once the only eastern exit in the park, the route leading over Sylvan Pass to Cody, Wyoming. The bridge, which was built in 1902, spans the Yellowstone River as it exits Yellowstone Lake, and is another prime spawning area for native trout.

YELLOWSTONE LAKE AREA   At 7,773 feet, **Yellowstone Lake** (20 miles long and 14 miles wide) is North America's largest high-altitude lake. Because the lake has the largest population of native cutthroat trout in North America, it makes an ideal fishing spot during the summer. **Lake Village,** on the northwest shore of the lake, offers a wide range of amenities, the most prominent of which is the majestic 100-year-old **Lake Yellowstone Hotel,** perhaps the most beautiful structure in the park.

Just south of Lake Village is the **Bridge Bay Marina,** the center of the park's water activities. The marina is usually open from mid-June to mid-September.

Although the **Natural Bridge,** near Bridge Bay, is well marked on park maps, it's one of the park's best-kept secrets, and you may end up enjoying it by yourself. The mile-long path down to the bridge, a geologic masterpiece consisting of a massive rock arch 51 feet overhead, spanning Bridge Creek, is an excellent bike route.

The **West Thumb** area along the western shoreline is the *deepest* part of Yellowstone Lake. Because of its suspiciously craterlike contours, many scientists speculate that this 4-mile-wide, 6-mile-long, water-filled crater was created during volcanic eruptions approximately 125,000 years ago. The **West Thumb Geyser Basin** is notable for a unique series of geysers. Some are situated right on the shores, some overlook the lake, and some can be seen *beneath* the lake surface. The area is surrounded by half a mile of boardwalks, so it's easy to negotiate.

WEST THUMB TO OLD FAITHFUL   The most interesting phenomenon on the Old Faithful route is **Isa Lake** at Craig Pass. Unlike most lakes and streams in the park, it has both eastern and western drainages and ends up in the Pacific Ocean and the Gulf of Mexico.

Two-and-one-half miles southeast of Old Faithful, there's an overlook at the spectacular **Kepler Cascades,** a 150-foot, stair-step waterfall on the Firehole River only steps from the parking lot.

OLD FAITHFUL   Though **Old Faithful** is not the largest or most regular geyser in the park, its image has been seen on everything from postage stamps to whiskey bottles. The average interval between eruptions is 79 minutes, although it may vary 20 minutes in either direction. A typical eruption lasts 1½ to 5 minutes, during which 3,700 to 8,400 gallons of water are thrust upward to heights of 180 feet. For the best views and photo opportunities of the eruption in the boardwalk area, plan on arriving at least 15 minutes before the scheduled show to ensure a first-row view.

An alternative to a seat on the crowded boardwalk is a stroll from the Old Faithful Geyser up the **Observation Point Trail** to an observation area that provides better views of the entire geyser basin. The path up to the observation point is approximately half a mile, and the elevation gain is only 200 feet, so it's an easy 15-minute walk. The view of the eruption of the geyser is more spectacular from here and the crowds less obtrusive.

OLD FAITHFUL GEYSER AREA   Accessible by walkways from Old Faithful Village, the **Upper Geyser Basin Loop** is referred to as Geyser Hill on some maps. The 1.5-mile loop trail winds among several thermal attractions. **Anemone Geyser** may offer the best display of the various stages of a typical eruption as the pool fills and overflows, after which bubbles rising to the surface begin throwing water in 10-foot eruptions, a cycle that is repeated every 7 to 10 minutes.

The **Riverside Geyser** is situated on the bank of the Firehole River, near **Morning Glory Pool.** One of the most picturesque geysers in the park, its 75-foot column of water creates an arch over the river. The **Black Sand Basin** is a cluster of especially colorful hot springs and geysers a mile north of Old Faithful. It is interesting primarily because of its black sand, a derivative of obsidian. **Biscuit Basin,** 2 miles further up the road, was named for biscuitlike deposits that surrounded colorful **Sapphire Pool** until a 1959 earthquake caused the pool to erupt, sending them skyward. Both the Black Sand Basin and the Biscuit Basin can be viewed from flat, interpretive boardwalks.

The **Midway Geyser Basin** extends for about a mile along the Firehole River. The major attractions here are the **Excelsior Geyser,** the third-largest geyser in the world and once the park's most powerful geyser, and the well-known **Grand Prismatic Spring,** the largest hot spring in Yellowstone and the second largest in the world.

OLD FAITHFUL TO MADISON JUNCTION   Believe it or not, there are other superb geysers and hot springs on Firehole Lake Drive, all viewable without leaving your vehicle, along a 3-mile, one-way road. The turnoff for Firehole Lake Drive is about 8 miles north of the Old Faithful area. The largest is Great Fountain Geyser, which erupts every 8 to 12 hours, typically spouting water some 100 feet high for periods of 45 to 60 minutes. However, the lucky visitor may see the occasional "superburst" that reaches heights of 200 feet or more. About a half mile north of where Firehole Lake Drive rejoins the Grand Loop Road is the Fountain Paint Pots area. All types of thermal activity are on display here, so as you stroll along the half-mile boardwalk you'll be in an area that may have six geysers popping their lids at the same time.

HIKING TRAILS

If you have time for only one hike, hit the **Mount Washburn Trail** (trail heads are at the end of Old Chittenden Rd. and at Dunraven Pass). The rises are fairly gradual, and they're interspersed with long, fairly level stretches. The views are of the Absaroka Mountains, Yellowstone Lake to the south, and the Gallatin Mountains to the west. You might even see mountain sheep. The hike to the summit is an easy 90-minute walk at a steady pace, or 2 hours with breaks. Bring several layers of clothing—it can get cold at the top.

The **Lonestar Geyser Trail** (start at the parking lot opposite Kepler Cascades) is another great walk; it's an easy 5-mile outing, and its popularity is its only disadvantage. From the trail head you'll wend your way through a forested area along a trail that parallels the Firehole River. The payoff for your effort is the arrival at the geyser—a vanilla-chocolate ice-cream cone near the middle of a vast meadow partially covered by grass and trees, exposed rock, gravel, and volcanic debris. Surrounding it are small, bubbling geysers and steam vents.

OTHER SUMMER SPORTS & ACTIVITIES

BOATING   The best place to enjoy boating in Yellowstone is on Yellowstone Lake, with easy access and panoramic views, and one of the few areas where powerboats are allowed. Rowboats and outboard motorboats can be rented at **Bridge Bay Marina** (© 307/344-7381).

FISHING   Pick up a copy of the park's fishing regulations at a ranger station. With 136 square miles of surface, **Yellowstone Lake** is the most popular fishing hole, with boats available for rent at Bridge Bay Marina (see above). The lake is most accessible from Bridge Bay, Fishing Bridge, Mary Bay, West Thumb, and Lake Lodge.

HORSEBACK RIDING   **Yellowstone Park Lodges** (© 307/344-7311) offers riding tours from stables situated next to popular visitor centers in Canyon Village, Roosevelt Lodge, and Mammoth Hot Springs. Roosevelt Lodge also offers evening rides from June into September. If you're looking for a more serious riding experience, contact the parks and request a list of approved concessionaires that lead backcountry expeditions.

WINTER SPORTS & ACTIVITIES

In winter, Yellowstone is transformed into a surreal wonderland of snow and ice. The geyser basins take on a more dominant role, with the air's temperature in stark contrast to their steaming waters. Nearby trees are transformed into "snow ghosts" by frozen thermal vapors.

Transportation into the park is mainly by snowmobiles and tracked vehicles called snow coaches. Only two of the park's hostelries, **Mammoth Hot Springs Hotel** and the **Old Faithful Snow Lodge** (© 307/344-7311 for central reservations; www.travelyellowstone.com), are open December through March. The only road that's open for cars is the **Mammoth Hot Springs–Cooke City Road.**

For additional information on all the following winter activities, contact **Yellowstone Park Lodges** (© 307/344-7311). There are also many activities, outfitters, and rental shops in the park's gateway towns.

CROSS-COUNTRY SKIING   The best cross-country ski trails in Yellowstone may be the **Fern Cascades Trail,** which winds for 3 miles through a rolling woodland landscape on a loop close to the Old Faithful area; and the **Lonestar Geyser Trail,** a fairly level 5-mile round-trip through a remote setting which takes off from the Old Faithful Snow Lodge.

Equipment rentals, ski instruction, ski shuttles to various locations, and guided ski tours are all available at the park's two winter lodging options (see above). Discounts are available for multi-day rentals of skis or snowshoes. Ski rentals are available in West Yellowstone at **Bud Lilly's,** 39 Madison Ave. (© 406/646-7801).

ICE-SKATING   The **Mammoth Hot Springs ice rink** is behind the old Mammoth Hot Springs Recreation Center. On a crisp winter's night you can rent a pair of skates and glide across the ice while seasonal melodies are broadcast over the PA system. There's a warming fire at the rink's edge.

SNOW COACH TOURS   Imagine an Econoline van with tank treads for tires and water skis extending from its front—it may not be the fastest, smoothest, or most comfortable form of transportation, but it does allow large groups to travel together, and it's cheaper and warmer than a snowmobile. They're also available for rent at many snowmobile locations. Check also with **Yellowstone Alpen Guides** (© 800/858-3502).

SNOWMOBILING   An excellent way to winter sightsee at your own pace is by snowmobile. There are roads groomed specifically for snowmobile travel throughout the park. A driver's license is required for rental (check at Mammoth Hot Springs Hotel or Old Faithful Snow Lodge), and a quick lesson will put even a first-timer at ease. There are several warming huts offering snacks in the parks. Advance reservations are recommended. However, be aware that a ban on snowmobiling by 2003 is possible, so check with park officials before making your plans.

WHERE TO CAMP & STAY IN THE PARK

Of the 12 campgrounds in Yellowstone, seven are operated by the **National Park Service** and are available on a first-come, first-served basis. They are at Indian Creek, Lewis Lake, Mammoth, Norris, Pebble Creek, Slough Creek, and Tower Fall. The remaining five campgrounds are operated by **Yellowstone Park Lodges** (Bridge Bay, Canyon, Grant Village, Madison, and Fishing Bridge), and accept advance reservations.

Same-day and **advance reservations** can be made by calling © 307/344-7311 or by writing to **Yellowstone Park Lodges,** P.O. Box 165, Yellowstone National Park, WY 82190. Sites are not pre-assigned: you're reserving a space, not a *particular* site.

The only campground equipped with RV hookups is at **Fishing Bridge,** and it accepts hard-sided vehicles only (no tents or tent trailers); however, though there are no hookups at the other campgrounds, RVers can be accommodated at any of them. Campgrounds begin opening early in May and some remain open until November 1, although this varies, depending on the weather. Call the park's main telephone number (© 307/344-7381) for specifics.

To book a room within any Yellowstone lodging, you also need to contact **Yellowstone Park Lodges** (see above). Yellowstone accommodations are normally open from May to mid-October. The winter season begins in mid-December and runs through mid-March, when accommodations and meals are available at either Mammoth Hot Springs or Old Faithful Snow Lodge and Cabins. During the summer season, *make reservations at least 6 months in advance.*

The crown jewel of the park's hotels, the **Old Faithful Inn** is 30 miles from West Yellowstone and 39 miles from the South Entrance. The lazy geyser-watcher can avoid the crowds by watching the show from a comfortable second-floor terrace with excellent views of eruptions. The original rooms are well appointed but may not have private bathrooms, but the newer wing rooms offer better facilities and more privacy.

A "new" **Old Faithful Snow Lodge and Cabins** near the original location recently reopened. The modern rooms are spacious and comfortable, and there's also the usual selection of cabins. This is only one of two facilities in the park open during winter months.

In the Mammoth Hot Springs area, on the site of old Fort Yellowstone, 5 miles from the North Entrance, is the old-fashioned **Mammoth Hot Springs Hotel and Cabins** (at Mammoth Hot Springs). This is the only hotel that is open during both summer and winter seasons in the northern part of the park. Suites measure up to those of Old Faithful Inn and Lake Yellowstone Hotel.

Standard rooms and cabins offer minimal but adequate appointments. If you need a tub, make your request when you reserve. The cottage-style cabins are a viable alternative, some having private hot tubs and sun decks. There's also a formal dining room and a fast-food restaurant.

In the Canyon Village area, the newish **Canyon Lodge and Cabins** is a half mile from the Grand Canyon of the Yellowstone and Inspiration Point, one of the busiest spots in the park. The lodge offers tastefully appointed but ordinary motel-style accommodations in the three-story lodge building and in cabins.

The **Roosevelt Lodge Cabins** were built in the wake of one of Teddy Roosevelt's legendary treks west, although he didn't sleep here (he opted instead for a tent in the woods). It is a rugged but charming stone edifice with a building-long porch. Services here include horseback riding, Western trail cookouts, and stagecoach rides. The bare-bone cabins, called **Roughriders,** are aptly named, with showers nearby. More attractive **Frontier** cabins have showers.

At the affordable **Lake Lodge Cabins** (on Lake Yellowstone), the cabins are most suitable for outdoor types. The lodge is an old Western longhouse fronted by a porch and rockers that invite visitors to sit and gaze out across the waters. On the other hand, **Lake Yellowstone Hotel and Cabins** (Grand Loop Rd., on the north side of the lake) is one of the most attractive hotels in the park, although still pretty moderately priced. Accommodations are in the hotel, in a motel-style annex, and in cabins. Opt for one of the free-standing cabins decorated with knotty-pine panelling. Request a single cabin, rather than a duplex, because the walls are paper-thin.

WHERE TO STAY & DINE IN THE GATEWAY TOWNS

WEST YELLOWSTONE   Best Western (© 800/528-1234) owns a large portion of the lodging market in West Yellowstone, including two moderately priced choices: **Desert Inn,** 133 Canyon St. (© 406/646-7376), and **Executive Inn,** 236 Dunraven St. (© 406/646-7681).

All things considered, there is no finer hotel in the area than the moderately priced **West Yellowstone Conference Hotel Holiday Inn SunSpree Resort,** 315 Yellowstone Ave. (© 800/HOLIDAY or 406/646-7365; www.Yellowstone-conf-hotel.com). From its rooms to its restaurant to its conference facilities, this resort is first-rate. A heated indoor pool, exercise room, sauna, children's program, and activities desk round out the amenities.

Firehole Ranch, 11500 Hebgen Lake Rd. (© 406/646-7294; www.fire holeranch.com), is a perennial favorite among serious fly-fishers. The resort is surrounded by thousands of acres of national forest, where guests can hike, canoe, ride horses, or bike. Cocktails are served in a cozy nook before the serving of exquisite meals prepared by a French chef. Lodging is in 10 cabins, perfect for two, although several have sofa beds. Rates are high, but include meals and activities (except guided fishing). A 4-day minimum stay is required; no credit cards.

Bullwinkle's Saloon, Gambling and Eatery, 19 Madison Ave. (© 406/646-7974), has a traditional menu full of burgers, salads, steaks, and ribs. The saloon also features video poker machines. The delightful **Canyon Street Grill,** 22 Canyon St. (© 406/646-7548), is a '50s-style cafe that serves great food all day long. You can grill your own meat at **Eino's Tavern,** 8955 Gallatin Rd. (© 406/646-9344).

GARDINER   The **Absaroka Lodge,** U.S. 89 at the Yellowstone River Bridge (© 800/755-7414 or 406/848-7414; www.yellowstonemotel.com), offers well-appointed rooms with private balconies offering views into Yellowstone Park. The **Best Western by Mammoth Hot Springs,** U.S. 89 (© **800/828-9080** or 406/848-7311), also has nicely furnished rooms with spectacular views. Both choices are moderately priced.

The **Sawtooth Deli,** 270 W. Park St. (© **406/848-7600**), makes great sandwiches, plus pasta, steaks, and salads. A good wine list rounds out the offerings. On summer evenings, the breezy garden patio is delightful.

COOKE CITY   If you want to get totally away from anything even remotely resembling a crowd, head out the park's northeast entrance to Cooke City—less than 100 people call it home year-round. Rooms here are clean and comfortable, but that's about it. The 32-room **Soda Butte Lodge** on Main Street (© **406/838-2251**) is Cooke City's largest, with a restaurant, lounge, and heated pool. The somewhat smaller **Alpine Motel,** also on Main Street (© 406/838-2262), is well kept and reasonably priced.

CODY   The **Buffalo Bill Village Resort** is an oddly matched cluster of lodgings: Comfort Inn, Holiday Inn, and Buffalo Bill Village on 17th Street and Sheridan Avenue (© **800/527-5544**). Although the term *resort* is hardly appropriate, the central location is certainly convenient. The complex houses four restaurants, a swimming pool, and shops at the Ol' West Boardwalk, where you can even sign up for a tour or river trip.

Named for Buffalo Bill's daughter, **The Irma Hotel,** 1192 Sheridan Ave. (at 12th St.; © **800/745-4762** or 307/587-4221; www.irmahotel.com), is a tourist attraction in its own right because Buffalo Bill himself built it. The 15 affordable suites from the original hotel have been refurbished with a mixture of Victorian elegance and Wild West flamboyance.

If you're looking for locals, **Mack Bros. Brew Co.,** 1313 Sheridan Ave. (© **307/587-3554**), is where you'll find them. This down-and-dirty eating and drinking establishment is a Cody institution. The menu is equal parts gourmet burgers and Southern-style barbecue. **Stefan's Restaurant,** 1367 Sheridan Ave. (© **307/587-8511**), is one of the best restaurants in town, with a frequently changing menu of gourmet fare bearing little resemblance to usual Wyoming cuisine.

7 The Black Hills & the Badlands of South Dakota

The **Black Hills** area, with its wooded mountains, waterfalls, and rushing streams, is a natural delight. This is where you'll find Wind Cave, one of the country's most beautiful natural caverns; Custer State Park, with its herds of bison, elk, and deer; and the imposing visages carved on Mount Rushmore, as well as the dramatic and still-developing **Crazy Horse Memorial.**

To the east of the Black Hills lie the **Badlands,** a strange and mysterious place. From the ragged ridges and saw-toothed spires to the wind-ravaged desolation of Sage Creek Wilderness Area, Badlands National Park is an awe-inspiring sight and an unsettling experience. Few leave here unaffected by the vastness of this geologic anomaly, spread across 381 square miles of moonscape in western South Dakota. Steep canyons, towering spires, and flat-topped tables are all found among Badlands buttes.

AREA ESSENTIALS

GETTING THERE   The gateway to this area is the **Rapid City Regional Airport** (© 605/393-9924), 10 miles southeast of Rapid City on U.S. 44.

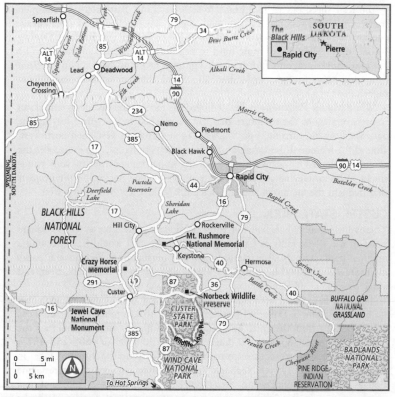

Northwest Airlines from Minneapolis, MN; Delta Skywest from Salt Lake City, UT; and United Express from Denver, CO, serve the airport with daily flights that connect to every major U. S. city. Rental cars from the major chains are available at the airport.

VISITOR INFORMATION For information about the area, call or write **South Dakota Tourism,** 711 E. Wells Ave., Pierre, SD 57501-3369 (© **800/ SDAKOTA,** 800/HELLOSD, or 605/773-3301; www.state.sd.us).

MOUNT RUSHMORE NATIONAL MEMORIAL

Widely regarded as one of the man-made wonders of the world, Mount Rushmore is as much a work of art as it is an engineering marvel. The faces of Washington, Jefferson, Lincoln, and Theodore Roosevelt carved into granite make up one of America's most enduring icons.

To get to Mount Rushmore, take I-90 to Exit 57 at Rapid City, and then take U.S. 16 (Mount Rushmore Rd.) for about 23 miles to the entrance. For information before you go, contact **Mount Rushmore National Memorial,** P.O. Box 268, Keystone, SD 57751-0268 (© **605/574-2523;** www.nps.gpve/moru). The **visitor center,** just inside the entrance to the memorial, is open every day of the year (except Dec 25) from 8am to 5pm in winter and 8am to 10pm in summer. Mount Rushmore has no admission charge, but there's a $5 fee for parking. Limited free parking is available across from the main parking lot as you arrive at Rushmore from Keystone.

You really need only 2 to 3 hours to see everything. Particularly in summer, try to come at the very beginning or end of your day. Excellent light at daybreak, coupled with its scenic setting and great breakfasts in the **Buffalo Dining Room,** make Mount Rushmore hard to beat for the first stop of the day. The patriotic ranger program and dramatic lighting ceremony, held nightly at 9pm from mid-May through September, also make the memorial memorable at night.

While Mount Rushmore is best enjoyed on foot, many visitors overlook an impressive view of the sculpture that can be reached by car. After leaving the park's parking lot, turn right on S. Dak. 244 and proceed west, then northwest, around the memorial. Less than a mile from the parking lot, you'll discover the proud profile of George Washington in the upper-right corner of your windshield. While surveying the scene, keep an eye out for Rocky Mountain goats that frequent the memorial and the Black Elk Wilderness Area to the west.

CUSTER STATE PARK

There's little doubt that, had not thoughtful state leaders preserved 83 square miles of the Black Hills as Custer State Park, the area would have become a national park. Its natural attractions are that outstanding. Perhaps the park's main draw is its 1,500-head herd of bison, along with its many elk, deer, and antelope.

The park is right between Mount Rushmore and Wind Cave. It's accessible via S. Dak. 79 and S. Dak. 36 from the east, U.S. 16A from the north and west, and S. Dak. 87 from the north and south. For advance information, contact the park directly at HC83, Box 70, Custer, SD 57730-9705 (© **605/255-4515;** www.state.sd.us/state/executive/tourism/sdparks/custer/custer.htm). Once in the park, head to the **Peter Norbeck Visitor Center,** between the State Game Lodge and the Coolidge Inn Store on U.S. 16A; it offers informational brochures, interpretive exhibits, and a variety of educational displays. Also, the **Wildlife Station Visitor Center,** on the southeast part of the Wildlife Loop, offers shade, information, and exhibits. An annual park pass is $20; a temporary license (valid for 7 days) is $5 per person or $12 per vehicle; an off-season temporary license is $2 per person or $5 per vehicle; and a motor coach license is $1.50 per person per visit.

For memorable sightseeing, pick any of the park's three scenic drives: the Needles Highway, the Wildlife Loop Road, or the Iron Mountain Road. Each of these winding drives is enjoyed at a slower pace—generally 25 miles per hour or slower.

The **Needles Highway** is a mesmerizing 14-mile journey through pine and spruce forests, meadows surrounded by birch and quaking aspen, and giant granite spires that reach to the sky. Visitors pass the picturesque waters of Sylvan Lake, through tunnels, and near a unique rock formation called the "Needle's Eye."

The **Wildlife Loop Road** is an 18-mile drive through open grasslands and pine-clad hills—an area that is home to most of the park's wildlife. Count pronghorn, bison, white-tailed deer and mule deer, elk, coyote, begging burros, prairie dogs, eagles, hawks, and other birds. The best wildlife viewing time is early morning and evening, when animals are most active. Stop by the Wildlife Station Visitor Center on the southeast part of the loop for information and interesting exhibits.

Although only a portion of the scenic **Iron Mountain Road** rests in Custer State Park, it ranks as a must-see on any South Dakota visit. The winding road runs between Mount Rushmore and the junction of U.S. 16A and S. Dak. 36. Along the route are wildfire exhibits, wooden pig-tail bridges, pullouts with wonderful views, and tunnels that frame the four presidents at Mount Rushmore. Some of the tunnels have vehicle height and width limits, so RV drivers should check restrictions ahead of time.

Custer State Park is home to a wide variety of **hiking** experiences, ranging from short nature walks to backcountry treks through some of the grandest scenery anywhere. A 22-mile segment of the South Dakota Centennial Trail, the **Harney Peak Summit Trail,** extends through Custer State Park. The **Cathedral Spires Trail** is also a popular choice. Most trails are open to mountain bikers, too.

CRAZY HORSE MEMORIAL

The world's largest mountain carving is so big that all four heads on Mount Rushmore would fit inside the chief's head. Begun in 1947 by the late Polish-American sculptor Korczak Ziolkowski in response to a request from Lakota chief Henry Standing Bear, the monument is being carried on by Korczak's large family with donations and private funding. The finished sculpture will be 641 feet long and 563 feet high. The carving is in Crazy Horse, north of Custer on U.S. 385. It's open year-round from 8am to 8pm and admission is $9 adults and children or $19 per carload. For more information, call © 605/673-4681 or go online to **www.crazyhorse.org**.

WIND CAVE NATIONAL PARK

The rolling prairies of western South Dakota run smack into the ponderosa pine forests of the Black Hills in Wind Cave National Park. The park is home to prairie dog towns, large herds of elk and pronghorn antelope, and over 300 bison—and that's just aboveground. Below lies the eighth longest cave in the world.

Wind Cave is about an hour's drive south of Mount Rushmore on Route 87. From points south or west, you can also take U.S. 385. For advance information, contact **Wind Cave National Park,** RR1, P.O. Box 190, Hot Springs, SD 57747-9430 (© **605/745-4600;** www.nps.gov/wica). The **visitor center** (right off U.S. 385) is open year-round from 8am to 4:30pm (except Thanksgiving and Christmas) and has books, brochures, exhibits, and slide programs about the cave and other park resources. It also has tickets for cave tours and a posted schedule of activities, including talks and nature walks. Wind Cave National Park has no entrance fee, but it does charge for cave tours, ranging from $6 adults, $3 ages 6 to 16 (half price with a Golden Age Passport) for a simple guided tour to $20 for a 4-hour introduction to basic caving techniques. The park's highways and backcountry roads provide the scenic backdrop for some of the best **wildlife viewing** opportunities in the region. Wildlife abounds in this rugged preserve, and you may be able to see some of them as you drive down through Custer State Park on S. Dak. 87 to Wind Cave.

No visitor should leave the park without taking a **cave tour.** Five are offered in the summer (fewer in the off season); call ahead for departure times, as they vary. They range from the easy 1-hour **The Garden of Eden Tour** to the adventuresome 4-hour **Caving Tour,** where participants must be 16 or older and wear long pants and boots. The **Candlelight Tour** is one of the most popular. Participants trek through a less-developed, unlighted part of the cave to experience the cave by candlelight. This strenuous tour covers 1 mile of rugged trail and lasts 2 hours. Reservations, available up to 1 month beforehand, are strongly advised. Most tours, even the easiest, involve climbing lots of steps, but all give you an excellent perspective on a unique underground world.

Visitors with more time should get out on the trail. The park hosts a 6-mile stretch of the **Centennial Trail,** which goes through the heart of the Black Hills and offers a taste of everything the area has to offer. There's also usually a ranger-led **prairie hike** in the morning.

WHERE TO STAY IN RAPID CITY & THE BLACK HILLS

Hotels in Rapid City include the **Alex Johnson Hotel,** 523 Sixth St. (© **800/ 888-2539** or 605/342-1210), a restored hotel with moderate prices listed on the National Historic Register; and the new **Econo Lodge,** on I-90 at Exit 59 (© **800/214-1971** or 605/342-6400; www.akershospitality.com), with an indoor water slide, cable TV, Jacuzzi, suites, and guest laundry facilities.

Custer State Park has four mountain resorts and seven campgrounds. **The State Game Lodge,** on U.S. 16A near the park's main visitor center, features historic decor and pine-shaded cabins. The **Sylvan Lake Lodge,** on S. Dak. 87 in the northeast corner of Custer State Park, overlooking scenic Sylvan Lake and the Harney Range, provides cozy lodge rooms and rustic family cabins. The **Blue Bell Lodge & Resort,** on S. Dak. 87, just before the turnoff for the Wildlife Loop Road (if you're traveling south), offers handcrafted log cabins as well as lodge rooms, the Buffalo Willow Lounge, and hayrides and chuck wagon cookouts. The **Legion Lake Resort,** near the junction of the Needles Highway (S. Dak. 87) and U.S. 16A, dates from 1913 and features cottages nestled in the pines on the lakeshore. Rates at these lodges range from around $85 for a sleeping cabin at Legion Lake, to $378 for a four-bedroom cabin at the State Game Resort. All are near outdoor activities such as fishing, hiking, and animal watching; some offer excursions into the backcountry. For more information or to make reservations at any of Custer State Park's resorts, call © **605/255-4521** or surf over to **www.custerresorts.com.**

WHERE TO DINE IN RAPID CITY & THE BLACK HILLS

Dining in the Black Hills tends to be a casual affair, but the selection can be wide, ranging from homemade pies and ranch-raised buffalo to hearty steaks and local pheasant.

The **Buffalo Dining Room,** at Mount Rushmore National Memorial (© **605/574-2515**), open 8am to 4:30pm, offers cafeteria breakfasts named for the presidents carved into the mountain: Washington is continental, Jefferson is French toast, Lincoln is scrambled eggs, and Roosevelt is biscuits and gravy. Lunch is also served. Near Mount Rushmore, in Keystone, you'll find **The Ruby House Restaurant,** Main Street (© **605/666-4404**), which offers steaks, seafood, and other specialties in a richly appointed Victorian dining room. It's closed in winter.

There's no dining at Wind Cave National Park; in Custer State Park, the **Pleasant Pheasant Dining Room** in the State Game Lodge serves great breakfasts, such as buffalo sausages with hot biscuits.

In Rapid City, try the **1915 Firehouse Brewing Co.,** 610 Main St. (© **605/ 348-1915**), where brats, burgers, buffalo, and chicken wings accompany the hearty microbrews on tap. The **Fireside Inn,** 7 miles west of Rapid City on U.S. 44 (© **605/342-3900**), with prime rib and an intimate fireside setting, makes a romantic choice for dinner.

BADLANDS NATIONAL PARK

The Badlands offers not only an unforgettably eerie landscape, but also a wealth of plant and animal life. You'll find 56 different types of grasses here—and almost no trees. Wildflowers abound in a good year. As for animals, you're likely to see bison and Rocky Mountain bighorn sheep (the native Audubon's bighorn is now extinct), as well as pronghorns and mule deer, if you travel at dawn and dusk. You can also see desert and eastern cottontail rabbits darting in and out of the grass. And prairie dogs thrive in the area; there's a prairie dog town just beyond the end of the Badlands Loop Road.

ESSENTIALS

GETTING THERE   Badlands National Park is easily accessed by car either on U.S. 44 east of Rapid City, or off Interstate 90 at Wall or Cactus Flat. Westbound I-90 travelers take Exit 131 south (Cactus Flat) onto S. Dak. 240, which leads to the park boundary and the Ben Reifel Visitor Center at Cedar Pass. This roadway becomes Badlands Loop Road, the park's primary scenic roadway. After passing through the park, S. Dak. 240 rejoins I-90 at Exit 110 at Wall.

VISITOR INFORMATION   For information in advance, check out the park's website at www.nps.gov/badl or call © **605/433-5361.** Once you're in the park, head to the visitor centers at Cedar Pass or White River. The **Ben Reifel Visitor Center** at Cedar Pass is open year-round (7am–8pm June 10–Aug 15, and 8am–4:30pm the rest of the year) and features exhibits on the park's natural and cultural history. The nearby Cedar Pass Lodge has cabins, a gift shop, and a restaurant; there's a campground here as well. The **White River Visitor Center** is open during the summer season only (late May through Aug) and houses exhibits about Oglala Sioux history.

ENTRANCE FEES   There is an entrance fee of $10 per passenger vehicle, which allows admission for up to 7 days. The single-person entry fee is $5 per motorcycle, bicycle, or person on foot, plus $5 for each additional passenger.

SEEING THE HIGHLIGHTS

It's relatively easy to see the highlights of the North Unit of Badlands National Park in a day. A few miles south of the park's northeast entrance (the closest entrance to I-90) is the **park headquarters,** open year-round, which includes the Ben Reifel Visitor Center, Cedar Pass Lodge, and a campground, amphitheater, and dump station. After stopping at the visitor center exhibits, bookstore, information desk, and restrooms, and watching an orientation video (which we recommend), it's time to hit the trail.

The visitor center is within 5 miles of several trail heads, scenic overlooks, and three self-guided nature trails. Each of the seven trails in the area offers an opportunity to view some of the formations for which the Badlands is famous. The **Fossil Exhibit Trail** is wheelchair accessible. The **Cliff Shelf Nature Trail** and the **Door Trail** are moderately strenuous and provide impressive glimpses of Badlands formations. But none is longer than a mile, and any one of them can be hiked comfortably in less than an hour.

Leading directly from the visitor center is the 30-mile-long **Badlands Loop Road,** the park's most popular scenic roadway. Angling northwest toward the town of Wall, this road passes numerous overlooks and trail heads, each of which commands inspiring views of the Badlands and the prairies of the Buffalo Gap National Grassland that forms its backdrop. Binoculars will increase your chances of spotting bison, pronghorn, bighorn sheep, or coyote.

Warnings in the Badlands

Water in the Badlands is too full of silt for humans to drink and will quickly clog a water filter. When hiking or traveling in the park, always carry an adequate supply of water. Drinking water is only available at the Cedar Pass area, the White River Visitor Center, and the Pinnacles Ranger Station.

Climbing Badlands buttes and rock formations is allowed, but can be extremely dangerous due to loose, crumbly rock. Watch for rattlesnakes and cacti hidden in the prairie grass.

Finally, Badlands **weather** is often unpredictable. Heavy rain, hail, and high, often damaging winds are possible, particularly during spring and summer. Lightning strikes are also common. And winters are simply brutal. But what were you expecting from a place called the Badlands?

The paved portion of the Loop Road ends at the turnoff for the **Pinnacles Entrance.** Beyond this point the pavement ends and the road becomes the Sage Creek Rim Road, a 30-mile gravel road, at the end of which is the **Sage Creek Campground,** although this one is primitive and does not offer drinking water. Five miles west of the end of the pavement, a visit to the **Roberts Prairie Dog Town** gives you a chance to watch black-tailed prairie dogs "barking" their warnings and protecting their "town." The Sage Creek Basin is the best spot to see bison and bighorn sheep.

Highway 27 leads from the town of Scenic south to the **White River Visitor Center** (© 605/455-2878), open from late May to August. The visitor center has drinking water, restrooms, information, Lakota exhibits, and a video program.

WHERE TO STAY & DINE IN THE BADLANDS

The night sky in the Badlands is an unforgettable sight, so we recommend staying overnight if you have time. **Camping** is available inside Badlands National Park at either the Cedar Pass Campground or the Sage Creek Primitive Campground (no reservations). Camping in pullouts, parking areas, or picnic grounds is not permitted. The park also provides free permits for backcountry camping.

The only other accommodation in the park is adjacent to the Ben Reifel Visitor Center at **Cedar Pass Lodge Cabins,** P.O. Box 5, Interior, SD 57750 (© 605/433-5460; fax 605/433-5560). The lodge also has an inexpensive restaurant, whose menu includes buffalo burgers, Indian tacos, and trout, as well as ice-cold soft drinks, beer, and wine.

You'll find a few more restaurants and two motels a few miles north of the park in the small town of Wall, home of the world-famous **Wall Drug Store,** 510 Main St.(© 605/278-2175; www.walldrug.com). The **Super 8 Motel,** 711 Glenn St. (2 blocks north of I-90 at Exit 110; © 800/800-8000 or 605/279-2688), has clean rooms at reasonable rates and is open year-round. The **Best Western Plains Motel,** 712 Glenn St. (2 blocks north of I-90 at Exit 110; © 605/279-2145; www.bestwesternplains.com), is another reliable choice.

A SIDE TRIP TO DEADWOOD

Deadwood was once known as the wildest, wickedest, woolliest town in the West, where Wild Bill Hickok was gunned down and where Calamity Jane Canary claimed she could out-drink, out-swear, and out-spit any man. At the same time, the city's merchants, bankers, and saloonkeepers invested their money in beautiful Victorian buildings and residences that still stand as solid testaments to civic pride.

Today, legalized gambling has revitalized the old town, with more than 80 casinos. Plan to park in one of the edge-of-town lots and take a trolley shuttle into town.

Deadwood is northwest of Rapid City off I-90 and U.S. 14. For more information on accommodations, walking tours, museums, attractions, special events, and gaming packages, contact the **Deadwood Chamber of Commerce & Visitor Bureau** (✆ 800/344-8826; www.deadwood.org), or stop by the **History and Information Center** in the classic train depot at 3 Siever St.

The **Adams Museum,** 54 Sherman St. (✆ 605/578-1714), is a treasure trove of local history and memorabilia including a stuffed two-headed calf. The **Broken Boot Gold Mine** (✆ 605/578-1876) has guided tours of a gold mine and offers gold-panning. Wild Bill Hickok, Calamity Jane, and other notorious residents are buried in **Mount Moriah Cemetery.**

Deadwood restaurants are more upscale than what you'll generally find in the rest of the area. **Jakes,** upstairs from the Midnight Star, 677 Main St. (✆ 800/999-6482 or 605/578-1555), owned by Kevin Costner and his brother Dan, offers a menu ranging from pheasant quesadillas to buffalo carpaccio. Locals consider it the best dining in the region. If you're not hungry, drop in anyhow to peruse the displays of movie costumes and props from *Dances with Wolves* at Diamond Lil's bar, adjacent to Jake's

In nearby Lead (pronounced Leed), **Homestake** is the oldest gold mine in continuous operation in the Western Hemisphere, with a visitor center open year-round at 160 W. Main St. (✆ 888/701-0164 or 605/584-3110; www.homestaketour.com).

8 Idaho

Think Idaho and imagine a state bursting with natural beauty. Within its borders you will find vast stretches of sage-covered high desert, white-water rivers rolling and roaring through rock canyons, eerie volcanic landscape, jagged snowy mountain peaks, glacier lakes, and green pine woods. Most of all, Idaho is home to welcoming and friendly people who will help make your visit a memorable one.

BOISE

Boise is one of the nation's fastest growing metropolitan areas. A remarkably sophisticated and culturally active city for its size, Boise offers a variety of scenery, indoor and outdoor activity, and great restaurants. The modern cityscape is nestled up against mainly undeveloped foothills and offers a moderate four-season climate with easy access to year-round activities.

ESSENTIALS
GETTING THERE   By Plane   Boise Airport (✆ 208/383-3110; www.boise-airport.com/transportation/airport), located about 3 miles south of the city center, serves much of southern Idaho with frequent service from most Western and some Midwestern hubs

By Car   The major route into Boise is I-84 from the southeast (Salt Lake City) and northwest (Portland and Seattle). Twenty-four-hour road conditions can be determined by calling ✆ 208/336-6600.

VISITOR INFORMATION   Visitor information can be found at several sites in Boise. The **Boise Convention and Visitors Bureau,** P.O. Box 2106, Boise, ID 83701 (© **800/635-5240** or 208/344-7777; www.boise.org), is open weekdays. **Visitor Information Centers** are located in the Boise Centre on the Grove, between Front and Main streets on the 8th Street pedestrian walkway (© **208/ 344-5338**), and near the airport at 2739 Airport Way, near I-84 at the Vista Avenue exit (© **208/385-0362**).

OUTDOOR PURSUITS

Boise offers a huge variety of outside activities. Whether you ski, bike, swim, jog, or just like to enjoy the out-of-doors from your favorite sidewalk cafe table, you will find something year-round here.

Twenty-five miles of Greenbelt, mostly paved, has been established along the Boise River and provide recreation for Boiseans and visitors of all ages. It connects most of the city's large downtown parks as well. You can access the Greenbelt from anywhere downtown—just head for the river.

For slightly more strenuous hiking or biking activity, check out the **Ridge to Rivers Trail System** (**www.ridgetorivers.org**) in the foothills above Boise. This system has been established by connecting public land and right-of-ways through private property to provide several multi-use non-motorized trails around the foothills.

While not a big spot for watersports, a Boise tradition is floating the Boise River. You can float on almost anything but tubes, and rafts can be rented at **Barber Park** (© **208/343-6564**). A guided river tour can be booked from **Boise River Tours** (© **208/333-0003;** www.boiserivertours.com). The Boise River is also a great place to fish. For fishing information pick up the **Idaho Department of Fish & Game**'s *Official Guide to Fishing in Idaho* and *General Fishing Seasons and Rules* in local shops, or contact the department at 600 S. Walnut, P.O. Box 25, Boise, ID 83707 (© **800/ASK-FISH** or 208/334-3700; www2.state.id.us/fishgame).

While not quite having the reputation of other ski areas in the state, **Bogus Basin** (© **800/367-4397** or 208/332-5100; www.bogusbasin.com) is located about a 45-minute drive (16 miles north) from Boise. With 2,600 acres of ski-able terrain, 51 runs, and 20 miles of Nordic trails, Bogus offers deep powder, short lift lines, and great night skiing. Open on average 140 days beginning Thanksgiving Day.

WHAT TO SEE & DO

Boise is home to more people of Basque ancestry than anywhere outside the Basque Country in Europe. You can learn more by visiting the **Basque Museum and Cultural Center,** 607 Grove St. (© **208/343-2671;** www.basquemuseum. com). Just a few blocks away you can wander Julia Davis Park, which houses the **Idaho Historical Museum** (© **208/334-2120;** www2.state.id.us/ishs/ Museum.html), the **Boise Art Museum** (© **208/345-8330;** www.boiseart museum.org), **Zoo Boise** (© **208/384-4260;** www.animalpark.org/zoo), and the **Discovery Center of Idaho** (© **208/343-9895;** www.scidaho.org).

Head up to the **Idaho State Capitol** (© **208/334-5174**), the nation's only state capitol building heated with geothermal water. Travel east of town and take a tour of the **Old Idaho Penitentiary** (© **208/368-6080**), built in territorial times and holding prisoners until 1973. Also part of the Old Pen complex are the History of Electricity in Idaho Museum, the Idaho Transportation Museum, and the Museum of Mining & Geology.

Further out of town don't miss the **World Center for Birds of Prey** (© 208/
362-8687; www.peregrinefund.org) for an introduction to the 500,000-acre
Snake River Birds of Prey National Conservation Area (© 208/384-3300;
www.id.blm.gov/bopnca), home to one of the densest concentrations of nesting
birds of prey along with over 250 other wildlife species.

WHERE TO STAY

For the best digs in town try the **Grove Hotel** (© 800/325-4000 or 208/333-
8000; www.westcoasthotels.com), with all the amenities and connected to the
Bank of America Centre, a sports and entertainment arena. Other downtown
hotels include the **Owyhee Plaza** (© 800/233-4611 or 208/343-4611; www.
owyheeplaza.com) and the **Statehouse Inn** (© 800/243-4622 or 208/342-
4622; www.statehouse-inn.com). Nearby is the **Courtyard by Marriott**
(© 800/321-2211 or 208/331-2700). The airport area, only 3 miles from downtown, offers some more moderately priced hotels, including the **Inn America**
(© 800/469-4667 or 208/389-9800; www.innamerica.com), the **Holiday Inn
Express** (© 800/465-4329 or 208/388-0800), and **Extended Stay America**
(© 800/398-7829 or 208/363-9040; www.extstay.com).

WHERE TO DINE

Boise has over 700 restaurants to choose from. One word of warning—call and
check to see if the one you want is still in business—even some of the best ones
don't last. For a unique dining experience try the **Cottonwood Grille** (© 208/
333-9800), **Milfords Fish House** (© 208/342-8382), or **Mosaic Wine Gallery**
(© 208/338-5006). For old-fashioned elegance and fine service try the **Game-
keeper** (© 208/343-4611). For local and regional brews check out **Tablerock**
(© 208/342-0944), **Bittercreek Ale House** (© 208/345-1813), **Bolos Downtown** (© 208/387-3838), or **Ha'Penny Bridge Pub** (© 208/343-5568). For a
truly unique experience try **Bardenay** (© 208/426-0538), the first "distillery-
pub" in the United States, featuring their own rum, vodka, and gin. Other good
local picks are **Richards Across the Street** (© 208/331 9855), **Angell's** (© 208/
342-4900), **Bar Gernika** (© 208/344-2175), and **Piper Pub & Grill** (© 208/
343-2444). Don't miss **Goldy's** downtown (© 208/345-4100) or Hyde Park
(© 208/368-0027) for breakfast.

SUN VALLEY

The nation's first destination ski resort, Sun Valley was developed near the small
town of Ketchum in 1936 by Averell Harriman and immediately attracted the
Hollywood set. Still a hangout for the stars, it has been named no. 1 ski resort
by *Condé Nast Traveler, Ski Magazine,* and *Gourmet Magazine.* It has received
numerous other honors as one of the top resorts in the nation.

ESSENTIALS

GETTING THERE   By Plane   The closest airport to Sun Valley is **Fried-
man Memorial Airport** (© 208/788-4956), 12 miles south in Hailey. There
are direct flights from Salt Lake City and Seattle. You can also fly into Boise and
take a **Sun Valley Express** bus (© 877-622-8267; www.sunvalleyexpress.com).
Be sure to check availability ahead of time and save by booking your bus ticket
in advance. There are also charter services from Twin Falls, Idaho Falls, and
Pocatello through **Sun Valley Stages** (© 800-574-8661; www.sunvalley
stages.cc).

By Car   The major route into Sun Valley is Highway 75 from the north (Missoula, MT) and south (Twin Falls).

VISITOR INFORMATION   You can get a vacation planner from the **Sun Valley–Ketchum Chamber of Commerce,** P.O. Box 2420, Sun Valley, ID 83353 (© **800/634-3347;** www.visitsunvalley.com). A **Visitor Information Center** for the area is located on the corner of 4th and Main in Ketchum. You can also check out the seasonally updated **Official Sun Valley Guide** at **www.svguide.com.**

OUTDOOR PURSUITS

Sun Valley's claim to fame is undoubtedly its world-class ski resort (© **800/786-8259** or 208/622-2151; www.sunvalley.com). You can choose from two mountains with over 2,000 skiable acres with 78 ski runs (the longest 3 miles), 149 miles of cross-country trails, and 17 chairlifts. For even more adventure try **Sun Valley Heli-ski** (© **800/872-3108;** www.svheli-ski.com). For backcountry skiing, try **Sun Valley Trekking Company** (© **208/788-1966;** www.svtrek.com) or **Venture Outdoors** (© **800/528-5262;** www.venout.com). For sleigh rides, try the **Sun Valley Horsemen's Center** (© **208/622-2387**). You can enjoy ice-skating year-round at the Sun Valley Resort Lodge with two rinks available. Saturday nights during the summer Olympic skaters perform on the outdoor ice rink adjoining the lodge (© **208/622-2135** for reservations).

Don't just visit Sun Valley in the winter. There is plenty to do in good weather. Almost anything you could ask for is available—from paragliding to skeet shooting. Trail systems around Ketchum offer miles of paved and unpaved trails for biking, hiking, skating, or walking. Information is available from the **Blaine County Recreation District** (© **208/788-2117;** www.bcrecdistrict. com) or at the Ketchum Visitor Center. If you want to really get away, try a llama trek with Venture Outdoors in Hailey (see above for phone). The **Sun Valley Resort Golf Course** (© **208/622-2251**) offers an 18-hole Robert Trent Jones, Jr., designed course, rated the no. 1 course in Idaho by *Golf Digest.* There are also two nine-hole courses in the area: **Warm Springs Golf Course** (© 208/726-3715) and **Bigwood Golf Course** (© 208/726-4024; www.bigwoodgolf. com). Other activities include tennis at the **Sun Valley Resort Tennis Club** (© 208/622-2156) and **Warm Springs Tennis Club** (© 208/726-4040), horseback riding at **Sun Valley Resort Horsemen's Center** (© 208/622-2387), trail rides with **Super Outfitter Adventures** (© 208/788-7731; www.sunvalleyout fitter.com), and fishing. A guide to area fishing is available at the Ketchum visitor center.

WHAT TO SEE & DO

The sights of Sun Valley are all around in the beauty of the countryside. Take a drive north of Ketchum to the **Sawtooth National Recreation Area** (© **208/727-5013;** www.fs.fed.us/r4/sawtooth) to view spectacular jagged peaks. The headquarters is located 8 miles north of Ketchum on Highway 75.

Southeast of Ketchum you will find the **Craters of the Moon National Monument,** a relatively recent (only 2,000 years old) lava bed. This eerie landscape will make you feel as if you've landed on the moon. There is a **visitor center** (© **208/527-3257**) off Highway 20/26/93 with maps of the area available.

Closer to Ketchum you can visit **Ernest Hemingway's grave** in the Ketchum Cemetery on Route 75 North at 10th Street East, or the **Ernest Hemingway Memorial** along side Trail Creek just north of Sun Valley Lodge. Check out the

Heritage and Ski Museum in Ketchum to see artifacts from Idaho's ski history (© 208/726-8118). For a history of Sun Valley and its famous visitors, check out the Sun Valley Lodge lobby to see dozens of photos dating back to the 1930s picturing visitors from the shah of Iran to Lucille Ball.

WHERE TO STAY

The **Sun Valley Resort** (© **800/786-8259** or 208/622-2151; www.sunvalley. com) has a number of different accommodation choices from the original lodge and inn and more than 100 separate apartments and condominiums. Check out the off-season rates (spring and fall) for some lower room rates. There are not many bargain rates in the Sun Valley area, but a couple of lower-priced hotels are **The Bald Mountain Lodge** (© **800/892-7407** or 208/726-9963) and the **Tamarack Lodge** (© **800/521-5379** or 208/726-3344).

WHERE TO DINE

Sun Valley and Ketchum offer a huge variety of restaurants for a community its size. Top of the line are the **Lodge Dining Room** at the Sun Valley Lodge (© 208/622-2150), **Michel's Christiania Restaurant** (© 208/726-3388), **Chandler's** (© 208/726-1776), and the **Sawtooth Club** (© 208/726-5233). Other more casual possibilities are **The Burger Grill** (© 208/726-7733), **KB's/ Ketchum Burritos** (© 208/726-2232), and the **Kneadery** (© 208/726-9462) for breakfast. For a funky Old West bar check out the **Casino** (© 208/726-9901).

COEUR D'ALENE

Idaho's northern resort town, Coeur d'Alene, sits amid sparkling lakes and green pines and offers year-round recreation and one of the world's top resort hotels and golf course.

ESSENTIALS

GETTING THERE   The closest major airport is **Spokane International Airport** (© **509/455-6455;** www.spokaneairports.net) in Spokane, Washington, 40 miles west. Major highways into Coeur d'Alene are I-90 from the west (Spokane) and east (Butte, MT), and Highway 95 from the south (Boise).

VISITOR INFORMATION   Contact the **Coeur d'Alene Visitor and Convention Services,** P.O. Box 850, Coeur d'Alene, ID 83816 (© **877/782-9232;** www.coeurdalene.org).

OUTDOOR PUTSUITS

Coeur d'Alene is a virtual outdoor playground. Twenty-five miles long, **Lake Coeur d'Alene** is the center of activities. Boating, sailing, jet-skiing, water-skiing, fishing, and anything else you can do on water are available. In fact, the world's first water skis were used on Lake Coeur d'Alene in the 1920s. Today you can also jet ski, take a seaplane tour with **Brooks Seaplane Service** (© **208/ 664-2842**), or parasail with **Coeur d'Alene Parasail** (© **208/765-5367**) on the lake. Try a **Lake Cruise** with dinner buffet for you and a friend or a whole group (© **800/688-5253**).

A summer visit means you can golf the **Coeur d'Alene Golf Course** (© **800/ 688-5253;** www.cdaresort.com/golf.asp), named one of only 16 golf resorts in America to receive the "five star" designation by *Golf Digest* and one of 20 with the *Golf Magazine* Gold Medal. The course is unique for its famous Floating Green, anchored to the lake bottom and reachable only by boat.

Winter in northern Idaho means skiing. A short drive east of Coeur d'Alene brings you to **Silver Mountain Ski Resort** (© **800/204-6428** or 208/783-1111; www.silvermt.com), with the world's longest gondola operating year-round. Summer concerts are also held at Silver Mountain. **Schweitzer Mountain Resort** (© **800/831-8810;** www.schweitzer.com) in Sandpoint offers stunning views of Lake Pend Oreille. Schweitzer also offers golf packages in summer.

WHAT TO SEE & DO

Coeur d'Alene has a variety of historic and natural sites for the visitor. The **Museum of North Idaho** (© **208/664-3448;** www.museumni.org) covers the long history of the area with exhibits and photos. Part of that history goes back to the **Cataldo Mission** (© **208/682-3814**) originally built in 1842 and the oldest standing building in Idaho. Climb **Tubbs Hill** in town for a great view of the area. For family fun check out what is becoming a major destination spot, **Silverwood Theme Park** (© **208/683-3400;** www.silverwood4fun.com) or **Wild Waters** (© **208/667-6491**).

WHERE TO STAY

Dominating the shoreline in Coeur d'Alene is the **Coeur d'Alene Resort** (© **800/688-5253;** www.cdaresort.com), named by the readers of *Condé Nast Traveler Magazine* as America's number one mainland resort. Other local accommodations include the **La Quinta Inn & Suites** (© **800/531-5900** or 208/667-6777), the **Coeur d'Alene Inn** (© **800/251-7829**), and the **Shilo Inn** (© **800/222-2244** or 208/664-2300).

WHERE TO DINE

Ask a local where to eat in Coeur d'Alene and you'll probably hear the names of several popular places over and over. These are **Jimmy D's Café** (© **208/664-9774**), the **Wine Cellar** (© **208/664-9463**), **Coeur d'Alene Brewing** (© **208/664-2739**), **Capone's** (© **208/667-4843**), and **Wolf Lodge Steakhouse** (© **208/664-6665**). For elegant dining, dress up and make reservations at **Beverly's** (© **208/765-4000**), recently named by the *Nation's Restaurant News* as one of the top 10 fine-dining restaurants in the country.

Alaska

Once you've driven across the continental United States and know how big that is, seeing a map of Alaska placed on top of the area you crossed, just about spanning it, provides some notion of the state's size. But for all that land, Alaska has only about 600,000 residents. If you placed each of them an equal distance apart, no one would be closer than a mile to anyone else. Of course, that couldn't happen, since no one has ever been to some parts of Alaska.

Yet facts fail to expresses what makes Alaska exceptional. It's not a matter of size or population. It's not an intellectual concept at all. None of that crosses your mind when you see a chunk of ice the size of a building fall from a glacier, sending a huge wave surging outward. Or when, at the end of a long summer day driving an Interior Alaska highway, the sun still high in what should be night, you crest the top of yet another mountain range and see more mountaintops, layered off as far as the horizon, in glorious, seemingly infinite multiplicity.

1 Alaska Essentials

Because of Alaska's size, you should count on seeing only a portion of the state in one visit. For travelers with limited time, **Southeast Alaska**—that thin, temperate portion of the state jutting down toward the rest of the United States and accessible by cruise ship or ferry—offers rainforest and glacier scenery, abundant wildlife, and a wonderful experience of Alaska Native culture. Adventurers can travel to Alaska on the **Alaska Highway,** which brings you through Canada's British Columbia and Yukon Territory to **Fairbanks.** From there, head south to **Denali National Park** and then to **Anchorage** and the **Kenai Peninsula,** in Southcentral Alaska. If you have more limited time, you can fly into Anchorage or Fairbanks and visit the Interior and Southcentral by rental car.

Planning a trip to Alaska can be a bit more complicated than traveling in the rest of the United States. Aside from the vast distances and range of climatic conditions, the best places book up for the high summer season. This section covers when and how to plan a trip to Alaska.

VISITOR INFORMATION

The **Alaska Travel Industry Association,** P.O. Box 143361, Anchorage, AK 99514-3361 (© **800/862-5275** or 907/929-2242; www.travelalaska.com), is the state's official visitor information agency.

For outdoor recreation, the **Alaska Public Lands Information Centers** are centralized sources of information on all government lands, which include more than 85% of the state. The centers, in Anchorage, Fairbanks, Ketchikan, and Tok, are operated cooperatively by many land agencies, including the National Park Service and U.S. Forest Service. The Anchorage center is at 605 W. Fourth Ave., Ste. 105, Anchorage, AK 99501 (© **907/271-2737,** TTY 907/271-2738; www.nps.gov/aplic).

Alaska

MILEAGE CHART
Approximate driving distances in miles between cities.

	Anchorage	Circle	Dawson City	Eagle	Fairbanks	Haines	Homer	Prudhoe Bay	Seattle	Seward	Skagway	Tok	Valdez
Anchorage		520	494	501	358	775	226	847	2234	126	832	328	304
Circle	520		530	541	162	815	746	1972	2271	646	872	368	526
Dawson City	494	530		131	379	548	713	868	1843	619	430	189	428
Eagle	501	541	131		379	620	727	868	1974	627	579	173	427
Fairbanks	358	162	379	379		653	584	489	2121	484	710	206	364
Haines	775	815	548	620	653		1001	1142	1774	901	359	447	701
Homer	226	746	713	727	584	1001		1073	2455	173	1058	554	530
Prudhoe Bay	847	1972	868	868	489	1142	1073		2610	973	1199	695	853
Seattle	2243	2271	1843	1974	2121	1774	2455	2610		2493	1577	1931	2169
Seward	126	646	619	627	484	901	173	973	2493		958	454	430
Skagway	832	872	430	579	710	359	1058	1199	1577	958		504	758
Tok	328	368	189	173	206	447	554	695	1931	454	504		254
Valdez	304	526	428	427	364	701	530	853	2169	430	758	254	

Chukchi Sea

Little Diòmede Island

Nome

Norton Sound

Yukon Delta National Wildlife Refuge

Bethel

Yukon Delta National Wildlife Refuge

Bering Sea

Nunivak Island

Bristol Bay

Alaska Peninsula

Attu Island

Pribilof Islands

Cape St. Stephen

Rat Islands

Unimak Island   Cold Bay

Dutch Harbor

Adak

Atka Island

Adak Island   Atka

Unalaska

Aleutian Islands

PACIFIC

ARCTIC OCEAN

Barrow

Prudhoe
Bay
Deadhorse

Beaufort Sea

Cape Krusenstern
National Monument
Noatak National
Preserve
Brooks Range
Anaktuvuk
Pass
Kobuk Valley
National Park
Kotzebue
Bettles

Dalton Hwy.
Brooks Range
Arctic National
Wildlife Refuge
United States
Canada

Bering Land Bridge
National Preserve

Gates of the Arctic
National Park
and Preserve

Fort Yukon
Yukon Flats
National Wildlife
Refuge

Arctic Circle

⑧

Dempster Hwy.

CANADA

YUKON

Galena

Unalakleet

Chena
Hot Springs ⑥
Circle
Yukon-Charley Rivers
National Preserve

⑤

Manley
Hot Springs
Nenana
② Fairbanks
North Pole
Eagle

⑤
Dawson City,
Yukon

Yukon River

McGrath

Denali
National Park
Mt. McKinley
Alaska Range
③ ⑧
④ ①
Talkeetna

Delta
Junction
⑨
Tok

United States
Canada

⑥

④
②

Willow
Wasilla Palmer
ANCHORAGE
Kenai
Soldotna
① Glennallen
Valdez ⑩ McCarthy
Wrangell Mts.
Wrangell–St. Elias
National Park and Preserve
①

Whitehorse,
Yukon

④

①

Kuskokwim River

Nenana

Lake Clark National
Park and Preserve

Dillingham

King
Salmon
Katmai National
Park and Preserve

Cook Inlet
Homer
Halibut Cove
Seldovia
① Seward
Whittier
Cordova
Prince
William
Sound
Yakutat
Glacier Bay National
Park and Preserve
Gustavus
Haines

⑦

Skagway

Juneau

BRITISH
COLUMBIA

Alaska
Marine
Highway
Gulf of Alaska

Kodiak

Kodiak Island

Aniakchak National
Monument and Preserve

Chichagof Island
Admiralty Island
Baranof Island
Sitka
Prince of Wales Island

Admiralty Island
National Monument

Petersburg
Wrangell

Craig
Ketchikan
Misty Fjords
National Monument
Prince Rupert,
B.C.

OCEAN

To Seattle

Dirt Road	———
Ferry	– – –
Paved Road	———
State or Provincial Route	―①―

On the Web, the **State of Alaska website** (www.state.ak.us) is the easiest starting point for navigating to some extremely useful sites, including the Alaska Department of Fish and Game, the Alaska Marine Highway System (in the Department of Transportation), and Alaska State Parks (in the Department of Natural Resources). Among the better commercial trip-planning sites are **Alaska Internet Travel Guide** (www.AlaskaOne.com/travel), **Alaska Wilderness and Tourism Association** (www.awrta.org), and **Alaskan.com**.

WHEN TO GO

The weather in Alaska can be extreme and unpredictable. The extremes of recorded temperatures are a high of 100°F (38°C) and low of −80°F (−62°C). At any time of year your vacation could be enlivened by weeks of unbroken sunny weather or weighed down by weeks of unbroken rain. All you can do is play the averages, hope for the best, and, if you do get bad weather, get out and have fun anyway—that's what Alaskans do.

JUNE, JULY & AUGUST   Summer in Alaska is a miraculous time, when the sun refuses to set, the salmon run upriver, and people are energized by limitless daylight. The sun dips below the horizon in Anchorage for only about 4 hours on June 21, the longest day of the year, and the sky is light all night. The state fills with people coming to visit and to work in the seasonal fishing, timber, and construction industries. Weather gets warmer, although how warm depends on where you go. June is the driest of the three summer months, July the warmest, and August generally the rainiest, but warmer than June. In most respects, June is the best summer month to make a visit, but it does have some drawbacks to consider: In the Arctic, snow doesn't melt completely till mid-June; in South-central Alaska, trails at high elevation or in the shade may be too muddy or snowy; and not all activities or facilities at Denali National Park remain open until late June. It's also the worst time for mosquitoes.

Summer also is the season of high prices. July is the absolute peak of the tourist season, when you must book well ahead and crowds are most prevalent. Before June 15 and after August 15, the season begins to decline, providing occasional bargains and more elbow room. But the length and intensity of the visitor season vary widely in different areas, and in some places it stays quite busy Memorial Day to Labor Day.

MAY & SEPTEMBER   More and more visitors are coming to Alaska during these shoulder months to take advantage of the lower prices, absence of crowds, and special beauty.

May is the drier of the two months and can be as warm as summer, if you're lucky, but as you go farther north and earlier in the month, your chances increase of finding cold, mud, and even snow. In Alaska, we don't have spring— the melt of snow and resultant seas of mud are called **break up.** Flowers show up with the start of summer. Many outdoor activities aren't possible during break up, which can extend well into May. Before May 15, most tourist-oriented activities and facilities are still closed, and a few don't open until Memorial Day or June 1. Where visitor facilities are open, they often have lower prices. Also, the first visitors of the year always receive an especially warm welcome. The very earliest salmon runs start in May, but for a fishing-oriented trip it's better to come later.

Sometime from late August to mid-September, weather patterns change, bringing clouds, frequent rainstorms, and cooling weather, and signaling the trees and tundra to turn bright, vivid colors. For a week or two (what week it is depends on your latitude), the bright yellow birches of the boreal forest and rich red of the heathery tundra make September the most lovely time of year. But the rain and the nip in the air, similar to late October or November in New England, mean you'll likely have to bundle up; and September is among the wettest months of the year. Most tourist-oriented businesses stay open, with lower prices, until September 15, except in the Arctic. After then, it's potluck. Some areas close up tight, but the silver salmon fishing hits prime time on the Kenai Peninsula, and the season stays active until the end of the month. A lucky visitor can come in September and hit a month of crisp, sunny, perfect weather, and have the state relatively to him- or herself. Or it can be cold and rainy all month. Cruise ships continue to ply the Inside Passage well into October, while the sky dumps torrential rains.

WINTER One of the most spectacular trips I ever took was a train ride from Fairbanks to Anchorage in January. Outside the windows, Mount McKinley stood clear and so vivid in a vast, smooth landscape of pale blue and rich orange that I felt as if I could reach out and touch it. A young woman from South Africa was on the train. When I asked her why she came to Alaska in January, she only had to point out the window.

She was right, but visitors and the people who serve them generally haven't figured that out yet. Some towns—such as Skagway and Dawson City—close down almost completely. In others—most places on the ocean, for example—nearly all activities and attractions are closed for the season, but services remain open for business travelers. Where facilities are open, hotel prices are often less than half of what you'd pay in the high season. Quite luxurious rooms sometimes go for the cost of budget motel rooms. Visitors who seek out places of interest can have an exceptional and memorable time, enjoying some of the best Alpine, Nordic, and backcountry skiing; outdoor ice-skating; dog mushing; snowmobiling; and aurora and wildlife watching available anywhere, at any time. The best time to come is late winter, from February to mid-March, when the sun is up longer and winter carnivals and competitive dog mushing hit their peak.

GETTING THERE
BY PLANE
Anchorage is the main entry hub for Alaska. It's also possible to fly into Fairbanks or Southeast Alaska. Most passengers come into Anchorage through Seattle, but for a bit more you can fly nonstop to Anchorage from many major cities. There are far more choices in summer than in winter. **Alaska Airlines** (© **800/ 252-7522;** www.alaskaair.com) has more flights than all other airlines combined, with 20 a day to Seattle in summer, and with nonstops to other cities including L.A., San Francisco, Chicago, Detroit, Minneapolis, and Dallas.

BY FERRY
The state-run **Alaska Marine Highway System,** 6858 Glacier Hwy., Juneau, AK 99801-7909 (© **800/642-0066** or 907/465-3941, TDD 800/764-3779; www.ak.gov/ferry), is a fun, inexpensive way to get to Southeast Alaska. The system is a subsidized fleet of big, blue-hulled ferries whose mission is to connect the roadless coastal towns of Alaska for roughly the same cost you'd pay if there were roads and you were driving. Call for a free schedule or download it from the website.

ROUTES   The system mostly serves Southeast, though it does cover most of coastal Alaska, with one sailing a month (the *Kennicott*) connecting Southeast Alaska with the Southcentral region nearer Anchorage, and two smaller ferries in the Southcentral region that link communities all the way out the Aleutian Chain.

In Southeast, five large, main-line ferries serve the Inside Passage. Two call on Prince Rupert, British Columbia, and run about 30 hours north to Haines and Skagway. Two more start in Bellingham, Washington, travel 37 hours nonstop to Ketchikan, then continue up to Skagway and Haines. Each of these four towns is connected to the rest of the world by roads, but none of the towns in between are. In the summer, the large ships stop at least daily (although sometimes in the middle of the night) in Ketchikan, Wrangell, Petersburg, Juneau, Haines, and Skagway. Some make a side trip to Sitka on the way. Juneau is the hub, with many extra sailings north on the Lynn Canal to Haines and Skagway; the *Malaspina* makes that round-trip daily.

The two smaller, feeder ferries, the *LeConte* and *Aurora*, connect the larger towns to tiny villages up and down the coast. They mostly take local residents back and forth to their villages, so they're rarely crowded. Those routes are definitely off the beaten track, offering the cheapest and easiest way to the real wilderness of the Alaska Bush. The feeder ferries have restaurants but no cabins.

CONNECTIONS From the South   The appeal of taking the ferry to Alaska from Bellingham, Washington, is obvious, but it does not save money over flying and it takes 2 days just to get to Ketchikan. The popular alternative is to board in Prince Rupert, B.C., which you can reach by rail, by car (you can leave your vehicle at a secured lot operated by **Park Avenue Corner Store,** ℭ **888/437-1373;** they have a shuttle to the dock), or by **B.C. Ferries (**ℭ **250/ 386-3431;** fax 250/381-5452; www.bcferries.bc.ca).

From the North   Two bus lines connect Skagway to the rest of the state, and rental cars are available in Skagway and Haines.

By Air   By flying to your starting point, you can save time and reduce the chance of staying the night in a chair on board while spending no more than if traveling over land. After arriving by air, explore by ferry.

WALK-ON FARES   The adult walk-on fare from Prince Rupert to Skagway is $145. Bellingham to Ketchikan is $184, Bellingham to Skagway $282, Juneau to Sitka $30. Fares for children 11 and under are half price, rounded up to the next dollar, and children 2 and under ride free. Off season, October through April, fares go down; during that time only, the driver of a vehicle does not need a separate walk-on ticket, and kids 4 and under ride free.

BRINGING VEHICLES   In the summer, you need a reservation for any real chance of taking a vehicle on the ferry, and you often need it several months ahead. Fares vary according to the size of the car as well as your destination; a passage from Prince Rupert to Haines for a typical 15-foot car is $303, or $617 from Bellingham. You also have to buy a ticket for each person, including, in summer, the driver. Renting a car at your destination will probably save money and enhance your trip by allowing you more flexibility in your stopovers.

CABIN RESERVATIONS   Sometimes you can snag a cabin from the standby list (approach the purser quickly upon boarding), but generally you must reserve ahead for the summer season. Cabins from Bellingham book far ahead. An overnight, two-berth outside cabin (one with a window) with a bathroom is around $60 on most sailings, or $136 from Prince Rupert to Haines, $305 from Bellingham to Haines, plus the cost of your ticket.

BY CRUISE SHIP

Most visitors to Southeast Alaska (and many visitors headed to Anchorage) arrive by cruise ship, stopping at the port towns by day and allowing the ship to do the traveling for them by night. It's by far the easiest and most comfortable way of seeing the state, though what you save in convenience you obviously give back in lack of control and spontaneity. Where the ship goes, you go, and on shore you're rarely out of a crowd.

Cruise ship **itineraries** can basically be broken down into Inside Passage cruises and Gulf of Alaska cruises. **Inside Passage cruises** generally run round-trip from Vancouver, visiting several ports along the way and usually turning around after visits to glacier areas like Glacier Bay and ports such as Skagway, Juneau, and Ketchikan. **Gulf of Alaska cruises** also visit ports along the Inside Passage (as well as areas in the Gulf), but travel only one-way, either northbound or southbound between Vancouver and Seward, the port for Anchorage.

The Alaska fleet is varied, but can be broken down into two types: small, expedition-type ships; and large, entertainment filled cruise ships. The **small ships** are the way to go if you want to really get a feel for the state, but you won't get many of the luxurious frills. On the **large ships,** on the other hand, you'll feel pampered as a pasha, and have innumerable activities and entertainment to keep you busy, but they may distract you from really seeing and experiencing Alaska.

Whether you travel by large or small ship, you'll be offered the opportunity to go beyond the shoreline on **shore excursions.** Ranging from simple bus and walking tours to river rafting, mountain biking, and airplane or helicopter flightseeing, these excursions are almost never included in the basic price you pay for your cruise, but they expand your experience of the state exponentially. If you want to see even more, all the cruise lines offer **pre- and post-cruise land tours** that can take you to Anchorage, Denali, and Fairbanks, and even to such remote destinations as Dawson City, Nome, and Prudhoe Bay. These trips are booked as a package with your cruise and are known as **cruisetours.** Or rent a car and discover the state on your own after the cruise.

THE CRUISE LINES   Almost all the major cruise lines have ships in Alaska during the summer, including **Holland America Line** (© 800/426-0327; www.hollandamerica.com), **Princess** (© 800/LOVE-BOAT; www.princess cruises.com), **Celebrity** (© 800/327-6700; www.celebrity-cruises.com), **Royal Caribbean** (© 800/ALL-HERE; www.royalcaribbean.com), **Carnival** (© 800/ CARNIVAL; www.carnival.com), and **Norwegian** (© 800/327-7030; www. ncl.com). They all offer a comparable experience, with large ships (carrying approximately 1,200–2,000 passengers) that give you the opportunity to relax, visit the spa, eat great food, and even swim in a heated pool while alongside a glacier. Among them, Holland America and Princess are by far the leaders in offering cruisetours, with HAL offering a classic shipboard experience geared primarily toward older guests, while Princess has a somewhat younger vibe. Celebrity has the most stylish, comfortable ships of the bunch, and the best food and service.

Crystal Cruises (© 800/446-6620; www.crystalcruises.com) and **Radisson Seven Seas** (© 800/285-1835; www.rssc.com) offer luxury cruises. Crystal's midsize, 940-passenger ship caters to the dress-up crowd, while Radisson's smaller, 700-passenger ship offers a more casually luxurious experience (all rooms are suites with balconies). For miniaturized luxury, **American Safari Cruises** (℃ 888/862-8881; www.amsafari.com) carries just 12 and 22 passengers aboard its two small, yachtlike vessels. Full charters are available.

Small-ship operators in Alaska include **Glacier Bay Cruiseline** (℃ 800/451-5952; www.glacierbaycruiseline.com), **Clipper Cruise Line** (℃ 800/325-0010; www.clippercruise.com), **Cruise West** (℃ 800/426-7702; www.cruisewest.com), and **Lindblad Expeditions** (℃ 800/397-3348; www.expeditions.com). Their ships generally carry 60 to 120 passengers, and they all cater to self-reliant people who want to really see some of Alaska. All offer itineraries that visit popular and lesser-known ports of call and include time for glacier and wildlife watching. Of the four, Glacier Bay Cruiseline offers the most individual experience, with three of its four ships sailing itineraries that focus on Southeast's outdoors, largely eschewing ports in favor of cruising wilderness areas and getting off the vessels for kayaking and hiking.

Somewhere between the small ship and big ship experiences is **World Explorer Cruises** (℃ 800/854-3835; www.wecruise.com), offering education-oriented cruising aboard its 731-passenger ship. The line's 14-day itinerary is the most comprehensive in the market.

BOOKING A CRUISE   Almost all cruise bookings are done through travel agents, but some small ship lines take direct bookings. If you're interested in a particular line and your agent doesn't handle it (or if you don't have an agent), call the line and ask them to refer you to one in your area. The Cruise Lines International Association's website (www.cruising.org) lists agents by region.

And remember: **Never pay retail.** Because of fierce competition, most of the cruise lines (excepting the small-ship lines) are constantly discounting their rates to fill their ships. This is one of the main reasons to use an agent, as they're the ones clued into the latest deals. In many cases you can get your cruise for up to 40% less than the published rate. Other great deals are often found at online travel sites like Orbitz (www.orbitz.com), Expedia (www.expedia.com), and even name-your-own-price services like Priceline (www.priceline.com).

For a much more in-depth examination of the cruise option, with detailed reviews of all the ships in the market and information on shore excursions in port, pick up a copy of *Frommer's Alaska Cruises & Ports of Call.*

BY CAR OR RV

Driving to Alaska is a great adventure, but it requires thousands of miles on the road, and you have to be ready to spend plenty of time. Anchorage is 2,250 miles from Seattle by car, 3,400 miles from Los Angeles, and 4,500 miles from New York City. Some of the 1,400-mile **Alaska Highway** is dull, but there are spectacular sections, too, and few experiences give you a better feel for the size and personality of Alaska. Putting your car on the ferry cuts the length of the trip considerably but raises the cost; you could rent a car for 2 weeks for the same price you'd pay to carry an economy car on the ferry one-way from Bellingham to Haines. *The Milepost* (Morris Communications; $25), contains mile-by-mile logs of all Alaska highways and approaches, and is sold widely.

BY RENTED CAR   This is the easiest way to see the Interior and Southcentral parts of the state. All major car-rental companies are represented in Anchorage, with base rates in the range of $50 a day for an economy car. One-way rentals between Alaska towns are an attractive way to travel, but you generally pay steep drop-off charges, so a more popular plan is to fly into and out of Anchorage and use it as a base to pick up and return the car. There are two popular circular routes from Anchorage: to Denali and Fairbanks on the Parks Highway and back on the Richardson and Glenn highways, or to Valdez by ferry from Whittier and back on another part of the Richardson Highway and the Glenn Highway.

BY RV   Many retirees come to Alaska in their motor homes, park the RV by a salmon stream, and spend the summer. Sounds nice, but for most of the rest of us, with limited time, it makes more sense to rent an RV after flying to Alaska. An RV rental saves nothing over traveling with a rental car, staying in hotels, and eating in restaurants (RVs rent for around $1,400 a week, plus gas and possibly mileage charges), but you gain freedom and spontaneity. **ABC Motorhome Rentals,** 3875 W. International Airport Rd., Anchorage, AK 99502 (© **800/ 421-7456** or 907/279-2000; www.abcmotorhome.com), charges no mileage fee and, if you want to drive to Alaska, you might be able to get a special rate by bringing up one of their new units. **Cruise America,** 8850 Runamuck Place (© **800/327-7799** or 907/349-0499; www.cruiseamerica.com), charges comparable prices, but you pay a mileage fee over a certain limit. Or, if you've got your own RV, you can drive it one-way only, then ship it back from Anchorage to Tacoma and fly or take a cruise to meet it. **Totem Ocean Trailer Express** (© **800/234-8683** in Anchorage, 800/426 0074 in Seattle; www.totemocean. com) offers this service.

2 Southeast Alaska

The Southeast Panhandle is the relatively narrow strip of mountains and islands between Canada and the Gulf of Alaska. It's a land of huge rainforest trees, glacier-garbed mountains, and countless islands, all of it reachable by the ferry system or cruise ships along the waterway known as the **Inside Passage.** This land of ice and forest may not look as large on the map as other parts of Alaska, but the better you know it, the bigger it becomes, until you have to surrender to its immensity. Nearly all of Southeast Alaska, stretching 500 miles from Ketchikan to Yakutat, is in **Tongass National Forest.** The towns sit in small pockets of private land surrounded by 17 million acres of land controlled by the U.S. Forest Service—an area nearly as large as the state of Maine, and considerably larger than any other national forest or any national park in the United States. Southeast contains **Juneau,** Alaska's capital and third-largest city, and **Ketchikan,** next in size to Juneau. Southeast's towns are as quaint and historic as any in Alaska, especially **Sitka,** which preserves the story of Russian America and its conflict with the indigenous Native people. Alaska **Native culture**—Tlingit and Haida—is rich and close at hand, as is the history of the region's **gold rush,** which towns like **Skagway** have turned into perpetual performance art. No other region is richer in opportunities for boating or seeing marine wildlife. The weather is wet and temperate.

ESSENTIALS

GETTING THERE   By Plane   Since most of Southeast Alaska's towns are not linked by road, anyone traveling to or around the region does so by plane or boat. Major towns without road access have jet service, provided by **Alaska Airlines** (© **800/252-7522;** www.alaskaair.com), the region's only major airline. **Juneau International Airport** (www.juneau.org/airport) is Southeast Alaska's

Fishing in Southeast

There is great fishing in Southeast Alaska. The best fishing is away from the roads. The Forest Service's lake cabins and the wilderness lodges around Ketchikan provide some of the best opportunities for remote fly-fishing. The Ketchikan Visitors Bureau can put you in contact with an operator for salmon and halibut fishing. Sea charters for salmon or halibut are great all over, but you can combine them with whale-watching in Gustavus, Sitka, Petersburg, and Juneau. The **Alaska Department of Fish and Game,** 802 Third St. (P.O. Box 240020), Douglas, AK 99824 (© **907/465-4270;** www.ak.gov/adfg, click "Sport Fish" then on "Region 1"), produces a fishing guide to Ketchikan with details on where to find fish in both fresh and salt water and a list of 17 spots accessible from the roads. You can pick up a copy at the Southeast Alaska Discovery Center. For licenses and other help, the local **Fish and Game** office is at 2030 Sea Level Dr., Ste. 205, Ketchikan, AK 99901 (© **907/225-2859**).

---

travel hub. Ketchikan and Sitka each have a few flights a day, while Wrangell, Petersburg, and Yakutat each have a flight going each direction daily.

By Ferry   For information on the **Alaska Marine Highway System,** see "By Ferry" under "Getting There," earlier in this chapter.

By Car   Three Southeast Alaska communities are accessible by road: Haines, Skagway, and the village of Hyder, which lies on the British Columbia border east of Ketchikan and is accessible from the gravel Cassiar Highway through Canada. If you're driving the Alaska Highway, passing through Haines and Skagway adds 250 miles of very scenic driving to the trip. Take the ferry the 15 miles between the two towns (they're separated by 362 road miles). This ferry route is not as heavily booked as the routes heading between either town and Juneau, but it's a good idea to reserve ahead anyway.

VISITOR INFORMATION   The **Southeast Alaska Discovery Center,** 50 Main St., Ketchikan, AK 99901 (© **907/228-6220** or 907/288-6237 TDD; fax 907/228-6234; www.fs.fed.us/r10/tongass), is a great resource for planning your trip. The center is open May through September daily from 8am to 5pm, October through April Tuesday through Saturday from 10am to 4:30pm.

The **Southeast Alaska Tourism Council,** P.O. Box 20710, Juneau, AK 99802-0710 (© **800/423-0568** or 907/586-4777; fax 907/463-4961; www.alaskainfo.org), covers all the communities, and has a very useful website.

GETTING AROUND   Planes and boats are your two options. See "By Ferry" under "Getting There," earlier in this chapter, for information on the ferry. Commuter lines operating prop-driven planes between Southeast towns include **L.A.B. Flying Service** (© **907/789-9160;** www.labflying.com) and **Wings of Alaska** (© **907/789-0790;** www.wingsofalaska.com).

KETCHIKAN

The rough waterfront streets and boardwalk red-light district of rainy Ketchikan have been prettified and packaged for the tourists, who cram streets of gift shops when the cruise ships dock. But when the ships leave, history's ghosts still lurk in the twisting, mountainside streets, and the totem poles look on with their forbidding magic. Tlingit and Haida culture are close at hand, as well as the watery attractions of the outdoors.

WHAT TO SEE & DO

Stop first at **The Southeast Alaska Discovery Center,** 50 Main St. (© 907/ **228-6220,** 907/288-6237 TDD; www.fs.fed.us/r10/tongass). This exceptional museum of the region's natural and cultural history and contemporary society costs $5. You can get free guidance for planning your time in the outdoors here.

Creek Street was Ketchikan's red-light district; now it's a quaint tourist mall. **Dolly's House** (© **907/225-6329**), a museum dedicated to a prostitute who had a long career here, is amusing, mildly racy, and a little sad. Admission is $4. The attractively situated **Tongass Historical Museum** (© **907/225-5600**) presents the history and Native heritage of Ketchikan.

Following the creek upstream, take a look at the **fish ladder** at the Park Avenue bridge, then continue to the **Deer Mountain Tribal Hatchery,** 1158 Salmon Rd. (© **800/252-5158** or 907/225-6760), a small king and silver salmon hatchery where you can see fry swimming in large tubs and even feed them. The hatchery is combined with the educational **Eagle Center,** which exhibits captive bald eagles and other raptors in indoor cages and a large outdoor eagle enclosure.

Beyond the hatchery is **City Park,** where Ketchikan Creek splits into a maze of ornamental pools and streams once used as a hatchery. You'll find the **Totem Heritage Center** (© **907/225-5900**) here. Admission is $4 in summer to see the largest collection of original 19th-century totem poles in existence. The poles are displayed indoors, mostly unpainted.

Two other major totem pole sites will require you to have transportation or join a tour. The excellent **Totem Bight State Historical Park,** 10 miles out of town on North Tongass Highway (© **907/247-8574**), presents poles and a clan house carved since 1938 by elders working with traditional tools to copy fragments of historic poles that had mostly rotted away. The setting, the site of a traditional fish camp, is a peaceful spot on the edge of Tongass Narrows, at the end of a short walk through the woods, so the experience is both aesthetic and educational. The **Saxman Native Village Totem Pole Park,** 2½ miles south of Ketchikan on the South Tongass Highway (© **907/225-4421**), has artifacts similar to those at Totem Bight Park, but with an added resource: You can watch carvers work in the building to the right of the park. The park offers 2-hour tours, which includes entry to the clan house, a short performance of a Tlingit legend, and traditional dance and song by the Cape Fox Dancers.

Southeast Exposure, 515 Water St. (© **907/225-8829;** www.southeast exposure.com), rents kayaks and guides day trips and overnights.

WHERE TO STAY & DINE

The **Westcoast Cape Fox Lodge,** 800 Venetia Way (© **866/225-8001;** www. westvcoasthotels.com), is the most beautiful hotel in Southeast Alaska. A sheer drop-off and tall rainforest trees create the lofty feeling of a treehouse in the rooms and restaurant. The hotel has an understated but inspired design; masterpieces of Tlingit art lend a sense of the peace and spirit of the rainforest.

Salmon Falls Resort, 16707 N. Tongass Hwy. (© **800/247-9059;** www. salmonfallsresort.net), a huge fishing lodge, has its own waterfall where salmon spawn in August, plus a dock on Clover Passage with boats for guests.

The gracious 1917 **Blueberry Hill B&B,** 500 Upper Front St. (© **877/449-2583;** www.blueberryhillbb.com), once a residence for nuns, stands atop the rocky cliff that bounds the north side of the downtown waterfront, above the tunnel. Rooms are large and light, with high ceilings and just-right country decor.

The large, quiet rooms at **Captain's Quarters Bed & Breakfast,** 325 Lund St. (© 907/225-4912; www.ptialaska.net/~captbnb), have a sweeping view of the city and ocean, and rival the best hotel rooms in Ketchikan but cost half as much.

The **New York Hotel,** 207 Stedman St. (© 907/225-0246), has a perfect central location just off Creek Street. The quirky building dates from 1924 and its charming, antiques-furnished rooms look out on a small boat harbor. The hotel's **New York Cafe** is an evening scene, with music, poetry, and even yoga and quilting meetings. They serve three healthy and hearty meals a day as well as salads, sandwiches, and pastries baked in-house, with most items under $10.

Ocean View Restaurante, 1831 Tongass Ave. (© 907/225-7566), is a lively local favorite, with a long menu featuring reasonably priced, tasty dishes. The restaurant offers Mexican and Italian cuisine (and an occasional Greek item), seafood and sautéed entrees, chicken, veal, steak, pasta, and pizza. Service is friendly and efficient. The pizza, delivered free, is the best in town.

Annabelle's Famous Keg and Chowder House, 326 Front St. (© 907/225-9423), serves steak and seafood in a formal dining room. A more limited selection, including the tasty chowder, is served in the spacious bar.

SITKA

Once the capital of Russian America—and the site of a historic battle between the Russian colonists and the proud Tlingit tribe—Sitka retains much of the influence of both of its formative cultures. Besides its historic significance, Sitka is fun to visit, with a friendly, authentic feel.

WHAT TO SEE & DO

A kiosk in the city-operated **Harrigan Centennial Hall visitor center,** 330 Harbor Dr., next to the Crescent Boat Harbor (© 907/747-3225), is staffed by volunteers who distribute information only when cruise ships are in town, although you may be able to ask questions of hall staff other times. The hall is open Monday through Friday from 8am to 10pm, Saturday and Sunday from 8am to 5pm. The **Sitka National Historic Park Visitor Center,** 106 Metlakatla St., Sitka, AK 99835 (© 907/747-6281; www.nps.gov/sitk), run by the National Park Service, maintains the key historic sites in Sitka, and is an essential stop where you can get information and learn about what happened here.

The **Sitka Tribal Tours Community House** is a good starting point, where you can join walking or bus tours, kayaking, and other outdoor activities, including trail hikes. **Sitka Tribe Dance Performances** presents traditional dances, put on by members of the tribe. The house is at 200 Katlian St. (© 888/270-8687 or 907/747-7290; www.sitkatribal.com).

Within walking distance are most of Alaska's most historic buildings. Up the road to your left, at Lincoln and Cathedral streets, **St. Michael's Cathedral** (© 907/747-8120) is the first Russian Orthodox cathedral built in the New World—or at least a facsimile of the 1848 building, which burned in 1966. The icons, saved from the fire, date to the 16th century. A $2 donation is requested. Continue on Lincoln Street to **Castle Hill,** where the American flag first rose over Alaska in 1867.

In the opposite direction on Lincoln Street, at Monastery Street, **The Bishop's House** is Alaska's most interesting historic site. Downstairs is a self-guided museum; upstairs, the bishop's quarters are furnished with original and period pieces. It's an extraordinary window into an alternate stream of American history, from a time before the founding of Seattle or San Francisco when Sitka was the most important city on North America's Pacific Coast. The tour concludes with a visit to a beautiful little chapel with many original icons from Russia. Admission is $3.

Farther on, at Lincoln Street and College Drive, the **Sheldon Jackson Museum** (© 907/747-8981; www.museums.state.ak.us) houses among the best collections of Alaska Native art to be found anywhere. Admission is $4. A few more blocks down Lincoln Street and you reach the **Sitka National Historical Park** (© 907/747-6281; www.nps.gov/sitk), the site of the 1804 battle in which the Russians won Southeast Alaska from its Tlingit owners. The visitor center contains a museum explaining the history and the art of totem carving and a series of workshops in which to see Native artisans at work. Outside, explore the rainforest battlefield on trails lined with an extraordinary collection of totem poles.

At 1101 Sawmill Creek Blvd., not far from the park, the **Alaska Raptor Rehabilitation Center** (© 907/747-8662) heals and displays bald eagles, owls, and other injured birds of prey. You'll have the opportunity to see the birds up close in large enclosures. Admission is $10 for adults, $5 for kids 12 and under.

The **Sitka Wildlife Quest,** operated by Allen Marine Tours (© 888/747-8101 or 907/747-8100; www.allenmarinetours.com), does terrific wildlife boat tours, guided by well-trained naturalist hosts. Sitka's waters and intricate shorelines are perfect for sea kayaking. Various companies offer guided paddles. Beginners will do well with **Sitka Sound Ocean Adventures** (© 907/747-6375).

WHERE TO STAY & DINE
Ebullient Carol and Bill Denkinger have a passion for making the **Alaska Ocean View Bed and Breakfast,** 1101 Edgecumbe Dr. (© 907/747-8310; www.sitka-alaska-lodging.com), a place you'll remember. They've thought of everything, from the covered outdoor Jacuzzi where you can watch eagles to games for the kids. The inn has a view of the Gulf of Alaska and is about a mile from the historic district.

The **Westmark Shee Atika,** 330 Seward St. (© 800/544-0970 or 907/747-5486; www.westmarkhotels.com), overlooks Crescent Harbor in the heart of the historic district. It's the community's main upscale hotel.

The **Bayview Restaurant,** 407 Lincoln St. (© 907/747-5440), though sometimes noisy and a bit cramped, offers a great view of the boat harbor, reasonable prices, and good food (especially the burgers and chowder). The **Channel Club,** 2906 Halibut Point Rd. (© 907/747-9916), serves amazing steak; the salad bar, which comes with every meal, is legendary. **Van Winkle and Daigler,** 228 Harbor Dr. (© 907/747-7652), concentrates on Sitka-caught seafood, prepared with a well-informed simplicity.

JUNEAU
Impossibly tucked into the mountains along the Gastineau Channel, Juneau is the nation's most remote state capital and surely its most beautiful. Eagles wheel over downtown streets and land on mountainside rainforest roosts just blocks from the capitol building. Yet the town also bustles like no other Alaska city, the downtown streets echoing with the mad shopping sprees of cruise ship passengers in the summer tourist season and the whispered intrigues of the politicians during the winter legislative session. The many government workers make it the

most cosmopolitan town between Vancouver and Anchorage, a place where you can get a great meal at the end of a day's mountain hike or kayak paddle.

WHAT TO SEE & DO

The **Visitor Information Center** is in the Centennial Hall at 101 Egan Dr., near the State Museum (© **888/581-2201** or 907/586-2201; fax 907/586-6304; www.traveljuneau.com). The center is open Monday through Friday from 8:30am to 5pm, Saturday and Sunday from 9am to 5pm in summer; Monday through Friday from 9am to 4pm in winter. Volunteers also staff a **visitor information desk** at the airport, near the door in the baggage-claim area, during the summer.

You can see a good many of Juneau's sights, and some of its nature, within walking distance of the downtown cruise ship dock. The bronze statue of **Patsy Ann** on the dock represents a beady-eyed bull terrier famous in the 1930s for greeting all arriving boats. To the right, as you face the mountains, the **Mount Roberts Tramway,** 490 S. Franklin St. (© **888/461-8726;** www.goldbelttours. com), whisks passengers from tourist-clogged Franklin Street to clear air, expansive trails, and overwhelming views at the tree line. It costs $22 adults, $13 children 12 and under. Closed October through April.

The intersection of Fourth and Main streets is the center of the city, where you'll find the state capitol, courthouse, state office building and the **Juneau–Douglas City Museum** (© **907/586-3572;** www.juneau.lib.ak.us/parksrec/museum). The small museum is worth a visit to learn about Tlingit culture and the city's pioneer and mining history. Admission is $3 adults. Even more significant and interesting, the **Alaska State Museum,** below the state office building at 395 Whittier St. (© **907/465-2901;** www.museums.state.ak. us), puts the whole state in context with its thoughtful display of a huge collection of Alaskan art and historic Alaska Native artifacts. Summer admission is $5 adults, ages 18 and under free.

The **Macaulay Salmon Hatchery,** 2697 Channel Dr., 3 miles from downtown (© **877/463-2486**), was ingeniously designed to allow visitors to watch from outdoor decks the entire process of harvesting and fertilizing eggs. From mid-June to October, salmon swim up a 450-foot fish ladder, visible through a window. Inside, large saltwater aquariums show off the area's marine life as it looks in the natural environment.

Juneau's most popular attraction is the **Mendenhall Glacier,** at the head of Glacier Spur Road (from Egan Dr., turn right on Mendenhall Loop Rd. to Glacier Spur; visitor center © **907/789-0097**). Simply standing in front of the blue ice and feeling its cool breath is worth the stop, but also check out the visitor center, a sort of glacier museum with excellent explanatory models, computerized displays and ranger talks. Excellent hiking trails start from here, too, ranging from a half-mile nature trail loop to two fairly steep, 3½-mile hikes approaching each side of the glacier. Those with experience and the proper equipment can hike on the glacier.

WHERE TO STAY & DINE

The **Baranof Hotel,** 127 N. Franklin St. (© **800/544-0970;** www.westmark hotels.com), has the feel of a grand hotel, although some rooms are on the small side. The upper-floor rooms have great views on the water side. The upscale **Goldbelt Hotel Juneau,** 51 W. Egan Dr. (© **888/478-6909;** www.goldbelt tours.com), is decorated with masterpieces of Tlingit art, including a new totem pole out front and a huge yellow cedar bas-relief by Nathan Jackson in the lobby-restaurant area. The large rooms are noticeably silent and immaculate. **Pearson's Pond Luxury B&B Inn and Adventure Spa,** 4541 Sawa Circle (© 888/658-6328; www.pearsonspond.com), has every amenity imaginable, including VCRs, CD players, bicycles, fishing rods, massage, yoga, a Jacuzzi and a separate hot tub in the garden (and maybe one in your room, too), a business center, modem ports, e-mail accounts and laptops, free laundry, and kitchenettes stocked with food, wine, and the owner's homebaked bread.

At the **Glacier Trail Bed & Breakfast,** 1081 Arctic Circle (© 907/789-5646; www.juneaulodging.com), you wake up to an expansive view of the Mendenhall Glacier filling a picture window in a big, quiet, tastefully decorated room. The hosts here are fascinating. The **Prospector Hotel,** 375 Whittier St. (© 800/331-2711; www.prospectorhotel.com), is a comfortable waterfront hotel with large standard rooms. The **Blueberry Lodge,** 9436 N. Douglas Hwy. (© 907/463-5886; www.blueberrylodge.com), feels like a first-class wilderness lodge, except it's only 6 miles from downtown Juneau.

The **Summit Restaurant,** 455 S. Franklin St. (© **907/586-2050**), has wonderfully formal service and an air of easy, world-weary elegance that can't be faked. It's the place in town for a romantic meal. The **Douglas Cafe,** 916 Third St. (© **907/364-3307**), turns out creative seafood, meat, and vegetarian dinners, drawing on world cuisines. To get there, turn left after crossing the bridge from Juneau, and continue till you see the cafe on the left. At **DiSopra/Fiddlehead Restaurant and Bakery,** 429 W. Willoughby Ave. (© **907/586-3150**), classically trained chefs turn out Northern Italian cuisine in the formal upstairs dining room with a great view, and offer sophisticated ethnically influenced dishes in an inexpensive downstairs area. **The Hangar,** handy to the docks at 2 Marine Way (© **907/586-5018**), is a fun bar and grill with great sea views.

SKAGWAY

It's hard to say Skagway was spoiled by tourism, because tourism is all Skagway has ever been about. Founded by a flood of gold rush stampeders who passed through quickly for a couple years starting in 1898, Skagway briefly was the last and among the wildest of the Wild West's lawless boomtowns. When that dried up, boosters quickly turned to selling the romantic history to visitors. A century later, the phony schlock and the gold rush history meld into a single stew whose flavors are difficult to distinguish. Is there a hidden basis of reality, or is the whole thing an ongoing gold rush phenomenon in which you yourself are a character? Today as many visitors can arrive on cruise ships in a few days as came through town in the whole of the gold rush, and certainly people are making more money than they ever did in 1898. I wouldn't miss it, but you need the right frame of mind.

WHAT TO SEE & DO

Broadway runs up the center of town and most of the historic buildings are there. Start with a visit to the museum at the **National Park Service Visitor Center,** Second Avenue and Broadway (© **907/983-2921;** www.nps.gov/klgo). It helps put everything else in context. Of greatest interest is a collection of food and gear similar to the ton of supplies each gold rush prospector was required to carry over the pass to gain entry into Canada. You'll also find rangers who answer questions about the town and surrounding area, give lectures and show films, and five times a day lead an excellent walking tour. The center is open

May through September daily from 8am to 6pm, the rest of the year Monday through Friday from 8am to 5pm.

Stop at the **Skagway Convention and Visitors Bureau,** 245 Broadway (P.O. Box 1025), Skagway, AK 99840 (© **907/983-2854;** www.skagway.org), in the driftwood-fronted **Arctic Brotherhood Hall** between Second and Third avenues, for information on the area's attractions, lodging, and restaurants, and for a historical **walking-tour map** that fills you in on every historic spot in town.

Skagway Museum and Archives, Seventh and Spring streets (© **907/983-2420**), contains a fine collection of gold rush artifacts. The building is Skagway's most impressive, and one of the state's most dignified architectural landmarks, a crisp granite block standing among tall shade trees on the edge of town. Admission is $2 adults, $1 students, free for children.

The National Park Service offers free tours of the 1897 **Moore House,** near Fifth Avenue and Spring Street, from 10am to 5pm during the summer. Ten years before the gold rush happened, Capt. William Moore brilliantly predicted it and homesteaded the land that would become Skagway, knowing that this would be a key staging area. He built a cabin in 1887, which stands nearby. But when the rush hit, the stampeders simply ignored his property claims and built the city on his land.

The town's most popular attraction is **The White Pass and Yukon Route** railway (Second Ave. depot; © **800/343-7373;** www.whitepassrailroad.com), a narrow-gauge railroad line that originally ran to Whitehorse. It's an engineering marvel and a fun way to see spectacular, historic scenery. A steam-engine locomotive pulls the train a couple of miles, then diesels take the cars, some of them originals more than 100 years old, up steep tracks that were chipped out of the side of the mountains. The summit excursion takes about 3 hours and costs $82. Children are charged half price. Don't bother with the trip if the day is really overcast, as the view is the real attraction here.

WHERE TO STAY & DINE

The **Gold Rush Lodge,** Sixth Avenue and Alaska Street (© **877/983-3509;** www.goldrushlodge.com), is a clean, comfortable motel, located just 3 blocks from the historic district, with a grassy picnic area out back. Rooms are on the small side but modern, and there's a cookie jar in the lobby. The **Golden North Hotel,** Third Avenue and Broadway (© **888/222-1898;** www.goldennorthhotel.com), is a big yellow landmark built in 1898. It's Alaska's oldest operating hotel and a fun, quirky place that makes you feel like you're sleeping in your own museum. Room 24 has a lovelorn gold rush ghost.

Built in 1897, the **Historic Skagway Inn Bed and Breakfast,** Seventh Avenue and Broadway (© **800/SKAGWAY;** www.skagwayinn.com), has frilly rooms ranging from small singles to a large front room with a porch above the street. **At The White House,** on the corner of Eighth and Main streets (© **907/983-9000;** www.atthewhitehouse.com), is a gable-roofed inn with comfortable rooms decorated in the style of the original owner, the most successful saloon owner of the gold rush years.

Restaurants go out of business and open up fast in Skagway. **The Stowaway Cafe,** at the end of Second Street near the small boat harbor (© **907/983-3463**), offers grilled and blackened salmon and halibut, plus beef, pasta, and all the usual waterfront restaurant items. **Sweet Tooth Cafe,** 315 Broadway (© **907/983-2405**), is one of Skagway's few year-round restaurants, making it through the winter with good, simple food, quick service, reasonable prices, and

The Streetcars of Skagway

No tour operator in Skagway goes to greater lengths for a unique experience than Steve Hites, whose **Skagway Street Car Company,** 270 Second Ave. ((C) 907/983-2908; www.skagwaystreetcar.com), uses antique touring vehicles with costumed guides who consider their work "theater without walls." The very personal and amusing 2-hour streetcar tour is $36 for adults. Like Skagway itself, the tours are hokey as they can be, but fun anyway.

hearty portions. The dining room is light and keeps with the town's quaint theme.

Incredibly, the fun, campy *Days of '98 Show* has been playing since 1927 in the Fraternal Order of Eagles Hall No. 25, at Sixth Avenue and Broadway ((C) 907/983-2545). The performance includes singing, cancan dancing, a Robert Service reading, and storytelling. Matinees are $14 and evening shows are $16. Children 15 and under are charged half price. The **Red Onion Saloon,** at Second Avenue and Broadway, is an authentic-feeling old bar that often has terrific live jazz and other live music. It was a brothel originally—what wasn't?

SOUTHEAST ALASKA'S NATURAL WONDERS

What you can see in Glacier Bay you can see few other places. Humpback whales often frequent the waters right in front of the visitor center and lodge, jumping out of the water as if putting on performances for sea kayakers. Glaciers of bright blue drop immense hunks of ice into the ocean at the head of the bay. And there's the land itself. Crushed under a mile-thick wall of ice less than 2 centuries ago, it today is an impossibly rugged fjord 65 miles long—brand new country, barely starting to be reclaimed by vegetation from the grip of the ice age. Mankind has left no mark on this new land; there are no roads or buildings beyond the edge of the park.

Most of the cruise ships on Inside Passage itineraries visit Glacier Bay, although the park service limits their number to protect the whales, so some lines skip it. Independent travelers can visit by day boat or fly over in a small plane, or join a sea kayaking adventure. The park headquarters and accommodations are at **Glacier Bay Lodge,** in Bartlett Cove ((C) 800/451-5952; www.glacierbaytours.com), far distant from the glaciers. The *Spirit of Adventure* tour boat leaves from there and takes visitors up the bay to the glaciers. The tour boat is operated by the same park concessionaire that operates the lodge: **Glacier Bay Cruiseline,** based at 107 W. Denny Way, Ste. 303, Seattle, WA 98119 ((C) 800/451-5952 or 206/623-2417; fax 206/623-7809; www.glacier baycruiseline.com), or, locally, in the summer only, at P.O. Box 199, Gustavus, AK 99826 ((C) 907/697-2226; fax 907/697-2408). The daily boat tour, led by a park naturalist, lasts 9 hours and costs $159 adults, $88 children. It's possible to do the trip in a single day from Juneau, Haines, or Skagway, but that's a very long day and leaves no time for anything but the tour boat ride. The package fare from Juneau is $347, more from Haines or Skagway. A better choice is to take their 2-day package, riding from Juneau to Gustavus on the *Auk Nu* passenger ferry, including a whale-watching trip in Icy Strait, then overnighting at Bartlett Cove, seeing Glacier Bay the second day, and flying back to Juneau, Haines, or Skagway. That package costs $481 from Juneau.

TRACY ARM & ENDICOTT ARM

About 50 miles due south of Juneau, these long, deep, and almost claustrophobically narrow fjords reach back into the coastal mountains to active glaciers—the **Sawyer Glacier** in Tracy Arm and **Dawes Glacier** in Endicott. Both calve ice constantly, sometimes discarding blocks of such size that they clog the narrow fjord passages, making navigation difficult. A passage up either fjord offers stunning views of high, cascading waterfalls; tree- and snow-covered mountain valleys; and wildlife that might include Sitka black-tailed deer, bald eagles, sea lions, harbor seals, and possibly even the odd black bear or whale.

The scenery and wildlife viewing in Tracy Arm easily rival the more widely known Glacier Bay, and for those not riding a cruise ship, Tracy Arm has a significant advantage: It's much easier and less expensive to visit. The largest operator is the Native-owned **Auk Nu Tours,** 76 Egan Dr., Juneau (© **800/820-2628;** www.goldbelttours.com), offering a day-long trip each morning in the summer, leaving at 9am, for $109 per person. The family-operated **Adventure Bound Alaska,** at 215 Ferry Way, Juneau (© **800/228-3875;** www.adventure boundalaska.com), prides itself on slower tours that allow more time to soak up the sights.

MISTY FJORDS NATIONAL MONUMENT

President Jimmy Carter set aside these 2.3 million acres of inviolate wilderness as a national monument in 1978, and they're still waiting to be discovered. The monument's **Rudyerd Bay** is like a place where the earth shattered open: The cliffs in its Punchbowl Cove rise vertically 3,150 feet from the surface of water that's 900 feet deep—topography in a league with the Grand Canyon. Waterfalls pound down out of the bay's granite. The glaciers of the northern part of the monument are also impressive, although they require a plane to visit.

Boat charters are available from Ketchikan, but it's 50 miles to Rudyerd Bay: an expensive ride. A better choice is to go on one of the tour boat excursions offered by **Alaska Cruises,** 220 Front St., Ketchikan (© **800/228-1905;** www.goldbelttours.com). They run a high-speed, 92-passenger catamaran on day-long trips out and back. Most passengers take a 4-hour version, riding the boat one-way and then flying back to Ketchikan on a floatplane to see the same amazing scenery from the air. The fare is $150 for adults, $125 for children.

3 Driving Alaska's Highways

Interior Alaska is so large—it basically includes everything that's not on the coasts or in the Arctic—that you could spend a week of hard driving and not explore it all. The **Alaska Highway** runs nearly 1,400 miles from Dawson Creek, British Columbia, to Delta Junction, Alaska, a couple of hours east of Fairbanks. From Delta, the Richardson Highway leads south to Valdez and Prince William Sound. From Fairbanks, the Parks Highway leads to Denali National Park and Anchorage, and the Dalton Highway leads north to the Arctic Ocean. You're at the center of Alaska with a car and the freedom to explore, an enviable position.

The region invites a footloose traveler. Long highways pass through mind-boggling mountain scenery—the Richardson and Denali highways particularly—where human settlements are rare and tiny. When you do find people, they're tough and independent, making a life in the harsh climate of the true middle of nowhere. Great glacial rivers span the region. Moose, caribou, and grizzly bears inhabit its scrubby forests and broad tundra hills.

Introductory information sources for these drives are based in Tok, the first town you hit after you cross the border from Canada. Although the town lacks its own attractions, it acts as a threshold for the entire state. Stop in to plan the journey ahead. The website **www.alcanseek.com**, with many links, specializes in advice for Alaska Highway travelers.

Crossing the U.S.–Canadian border is a bit more complicated than it was before the September 11, 2001, terrorist attacks. U.S. and Canadian citizens don't need visas going either way, but should carry **proof of citizenship** and **proof of residence.** (Citizens of other countries may need visas.) Canadian authorities now require American citizens to produce a piece of photo identification such as a driver's license combined with either a birth certificate or a passport. **Children** with their parents may need a birth certificate; children or teens under 18 unaccompanied by parents may need a letter from a parent or guardian, and children with a single parent should carry a letter from the other parent. Products you buy in Alaska made of **ivory, fur, or other wildlife** will probably require special permits to be taken out of the United States, and it's easiest to have the store where you bought the item take care of it. U.S. authorities no longer let noncitizens into the country with firearms except for permanent resident aliens or foreigners holding both a permit from the Bureau of Alcohol, Tobacco, and Firearms and a nonresident hunting license. Going into Canada, **firearms** other than hunting rifles or shotguns generally are not allowed, and you need to fill out a form and pay a $50 fee for guns that are allowed; contact the Canadian Firearms Center (© **800/731-4000;** www.cfc.gc.ca) before you go. If in doubt, call before you go, as the border is a long way from anywhere: **Canadian Customs** in Whitehorse (© **867/667-3943**) or **U.S. Customs** in Anchorage (© **907/271-2675**).

TOK

Originally called Tokyo Camp, a construction station on the highway, the name was shortened to Tok when "Tokyo" became politically incorrect after Pearl Harbor. Since then, Tok's role in the world hasn't expanded much beyond being a stop on the road. With its location at the intersection of the Alaska Highway and the Glenn Highway to Glennallen—the short way to Anchorage and Prince William Sound—the town has built an economy of gas stations, gift stores, cafes, and hotels to serve highway travelers.

Local boosters and public land agencies have combined to operate a large, informative visitor center to introduce highway travelers to Alaska. The government's part, the **Alaska Public Lands Information Center** (© **907/883-5667;** www.nps.gov/aplic), is open daily from 8am to 7pm in summer and from 8am to 4:30pm in winter. Besides answering questions, rangers offer talks and nature walks in the summer. The commercial portion, the **Main Street Visitor Center,** operated by the Tok Chamber of Commerce (© **907/883-5775;** www.Tok AlaskaInfo.com), provides information on Tok and anywhere else you may be bound on the highway. They're open from May 1 to September 15 daily from 8am to 7pm.

WHERE TO STAY & DINE

The 10 newer nonsmoking rooms are a bargain at **Snowshoe Motel & Fine Arts and Gifts,** across the highway from the information center (© **800/478-4511** in Alaska, Yukon, and part of B.C., or 907/883-4511). Each immaculate unit is divided into two sections by the bathroom, providing two separate

The Glenn Highway

The Glenn Highway (Rte. 1) is the road you'd take if you were coming from the Alaska Highway and wanted to skip Fairbanks and go straight from Tok 330 miles down to Southcentral Alaska for Prince William Sound, Anchorage, and the Kenai Peninsula. The northern section, from Tok to Glennallen, borders Wrangell–St. Elias National Park, with broad tundra and taiga broken by high, craggy peaks.

rooms—great for families. The **Westmark Tok,** at the intersection of the Alaska and Glenn highways (✆ **800/544-0970;** www.westmarkhotels.com), is made up of several buildings connected by boardwalks. Older rooms are narrow; the new section has larger, higher-priced rooms. Ask for the "highway rate," $99 for a double. **Young's Motel,** behind Fast Eddy's Restaurant on the Alaska Highway (✆ **907/883-4411**), has good standard motel rooms.

Restaurants in Tok are generally of the roadside diner variety, all located close together on the right as you come into town from the east on the Alaska Highway. Two noteworthy exceptions: the restaurant at the Westmark Tok hotel, and **Fast Eddy's** (✆ **907/883-4411**), which began as a roadside cafe but developed into a place where a wine list and fine-dining entrees don't seem out of place.

DELTA JUNCTION

This intersection with the Richardson Highway, which runs from Valdez to Fairbanks, is the official end of the Alaska Highway. It's an earnest little roadside town set in a broad plain between the Delta and Tanana rivers. Its two historic sites commemorate this crossroads. In town, next door to the visitor center, the 1905 **Sullivan Roadhouse** (✆ **907/895-4415**) has been relocated and set up as a museum, re-creating its look from the time it was abandoned as a stop on the horseback or dog-sled journey from Valdez to Fairbanks in 1922. Many of the Sullivan's original belongings have been set back in their original places, giving a strong feel for frontier life, but the heart of the restoration is the authentic hospitality of the local volunteers who show off the place with great pride.

The next stop on the old horseback and sled-dog trail was 16 miles toward Fairbanks. **Rika's Roadhouse and Landing,** 10 miles northwest of Delta on the Richardson Highway (✆ **907/895-4201;** http://rikas.com), still makes a pleasant stop on your drive. A state historical park preserves the 1917 log roadhouse and its lovely grounds. The grassy compound completes a fascinating picture of Alaska pioneer life with surviving outbuildings, including a telegraph office and museum, a gorgeous vegetable garden, and a pen of domestic fowl. A restaurant serves soups, salads, and sandwiches daily from 9am to 5pm; the grounds and museum are open from 8am to 8pm from May 15 to September 15. An impressive suspension bridge carries the trans-Alaska pipeline over the Tanana River, and boaters use the shoreline, at the confluence of the Tanana and Delta rivers, as a landing.

The cute, funny, and hospitable **Kelly's Country Inn,** at the intersection of Richardson and Alaska highways (✆ **907/895-4667;** www.kellysalaskacountry inn.com), has rooms for $89 to $109 (double) right in the middle of town. You'll find basic rooms with refrigerators and satellite TV for $70 (double) at **Alaska 7 Motel,** 3548 Richardson Hwy. (✆ **907/895-4848;** www.alaskan.com/ ak7motel). Check at the visitor center for a referral to one of the many B&Bs.

The **Buffalo Center Diner,** 1680 Richardson Hwy. (© **907/895-5089**), is where the locals eat, and for good reason. The dining room is light and clean and the menu covers everything you would hope for in a simple family restaurant—plus a seasonal list of buffalo dinners in honor of the Delta herd.

FAIRBANKS

The **Richardson Highway** (Rte. 2) takes you the 98 miles from Delta Junction to Fairbanks, Alaska's second-largest city, with a population of about 32,000 within the city and 84,000 in the greater area. They're still prospecting and mining for gold around here, fighting off environmental regulation and maintaining a traditional Alaskan attitude that it's them against the world. Fairbanks is the birthplace of strange political movements, including the secessionist Alaskan Independence Party. It's an adamant, loopy, affable place. Relax and take Fairbanks on its own terms, a fun, unpretentious town that never lost its sense of being on the frontier, and is full of activities and surprises.

The **Fairbanks Log Cabin Visitor Information Center,** in a large log building at 550 First Ave. and Cushman Street, on the Chena River at the center of town (© **800/327-5774** or 907/456-5774; www.explorefairbanks.com), provides maps (including a road map and detailed walking and driving-tour maps), books activities, and will help you find a room with a daily vacancy listing. The website has many useful links. The center is open daily in summer, Monday through Friday in winter. (At press time, hours were set to change but have not been finalized.)

The **Alaska Public Lands Information Center,** 250 Cushman St., at Third Avenue (© **907/456-0527;** www.nps.gov/aplic), is an indispensable stop for anyone planning to spend time in the outdoors, and an interesting one even if you're not. Open daily from 9am to 6pm in summer, Tuesday through Saturday from 10am to 6pm in winter.

WHAT TO SEE & DO

The University of Alaska contains Fairbanks's most interesting sights, including the superb **University of Alaska Museum** (© 907/474-7505; www.uaf.alaska. edu/museum), the **Georgeson Botanical Garden** (© 907/474-1944), and the **Large Animal Research Station** (© 907/474-7207). The excellent museum covers both culture and science—it's a trove of university researchers' output—but the natural history exhibits make it unique, helping sharpen visitors' understanding of the spectacular places they will see. Some of the objects have a real wow factor, such as Blue Babe, the mummified steppe bison; a 5,400-pound copper nugget, and the state's largest collection of gold. You'll find a mix of science and contemplation at the relaxed working botanical garden. Plots are laid out to compare seeds and cultivation techniques, usually well posted with explanatory information on the experiment, and the flowers and vegetables are spectacular. There are peaceful places to picnic. The animal research station, on Yankovich Road, offers a chance to see musk oxen and caribou close up.

Fairbanks has a variety of commercial tourist attractions as well, many of them focusing on gold mining. At the **El Dorado Gold Mine,** off the Elliot Highway, 9 miles north of town (© **866/479-6673;** www.eldoradogoldmine. com), visitors gather around a sluice to hear the amusing and authentic Dexter and Lynette (aka Yukon Yonda) Clark and watch a swoosh of water and gold-bearing gravel rush by. You pan the resulting pay dirt, and everyone goes home with enough gold dust to fill a plastic locket. The cost is $28 adults, $20 ages 3 to 12.

Gold Dredge Number 8, 1755 Old Steese Hwy. (© **907/457-6058**), the area's best gold-mining historic site, is a bit more serious. The centerpiece is a 1928 gold dredge that stands five decks tall on a barge floating in a pond it created. Relocated gold camp buildings, right next to the dredge, show the drab life lived by the miners and the tools they worked with. Tours are offered daily from mid-May to mid-September hourly from 9:30am to 3:30pm. Admission is $17 adults, $13 children; add $4 for gold panning; add another $8.50 for a cafeteria lunch. To get there, go north on the Steese Expressway, turn left on Goldstream Road, and left again on the Old Steese Highway.

The riverboat *Discovery,* 1975 Discovery Dr. (© **866/479-6673**), is a real stern-wheeler, cruising down the Chena and up the Tanana past demonstrations on shore—among others, a bush plane taking off and landing, fish cutting at a Native fish camp, and a musher's dog yard. The vessel pulls up at a bank for an hour-long tour of a mock Athabascan village. Tours are $40 adults, $30 ages 3 to 12.

The **Fort Knox Gold Mine** (© **907/488-GOLD**) is a new, unique attraction: a real, operating mine that takes visitors. It's a heavy industry site, and the attraction is immense equipment and machinery. It's 25 miles north of town on Steese Highway. Admission is $21 adults, $17 children. Call a day or two ahead for reservations. The tour is not a good choice for people with mobility problems.

Back in town, **Alaskaland,** at the intersection of Airport Way and Peger Road (© **907/459-1087**), is the boiled-down essence of Fairbanks. Alaskaland is a city park with a theme. Admission is free, and tours and activities are generally inexpensive. The park is open year-round, but the attractions operate only Memorial Day to Labor Day, daily from 11am to 9pm. The stern-wheeler **SS Nenana** (© **907/456-8848**), which plied the Yukon and Tanana rivers until 1952, is the park's centerpiece. A guided tour is $5 for adults, $3 children. For $2 adults, $1 children, you can see the ground-floor cargo deck with its engaging set of dioramas showing all the riverside towns and villages where the boat called, modeled as they looked in its heyday. **Judge Wickersham's house,** built around 1904, is now a museum, decorated according to the period of the town's founding. **President Warren Harding's fancy rail car,** from which he stepped to drive the golden spike into the Alaskan Railroad tracks, sits near the park entrance. The **Pioneer Air Museum** (© **907/451-0037**) is housed in a geodesic dome toward the back of the park. Besides the aircraft are displays and artifacts of the crashes of Alaska's aviation pioneers. The **Crooked Creek and Whiskey Island Railroad** circles the park twice, with a tour guide pointing out the sights. Rides cost $2 adults, $1 children; kids under age 4 ride free. Other attractions here include a gold rush museum, an illustrated gold rush show, kayak and bike rentals, a dance hall, and an art gallery. Tour groups generally come to Alaskaland in the evening from mid-May to mid-September for the **Alaska Salmon Bake,** at the mining valley area (© **907/452-7274**); and for the **Golden Heart Revue,** at the Palace Theatre (© **907/456-5960;** www.akvisit.com).

WHERE TO STAY & DINE

The **Westmark Fairbanks,** 813 Noble St. (© **800/544-0970;** www.westmark hotels.com), fulfills the role of Fairbanks's main central hotel. This remains an old-fashioned property. The rooms, although well kept, show signs of age. **Wedgewood Resort,** 212 Wedgewood Dr. (© **800/528-4916**), sprawls across a grassy, 23-acre complex in eight large buildings. Seven of them are converted three-story apartment buildings, without elevators but with large living rooms, separate dining areas, fully equipped kitchens, and balconies.

River's Edge Resort Cottages, 4200 Boat St. (© **800/770-3343;** www. riversedge.net), is a group of trim little cottages, all quite new, in a grassy compound along the gentle Chena River, where guests can fish for grayling, watch the river go by, and socialize with one another. Inside, each cottage is an excellent standard hotel room, with high ceilings and two queen beds. The **Aurora Express Bed and Breakfast,** 1540 Chena Ridge Rd. (© **800/221-0073;** www. aurora-express.com), set high in the hills south of Fairbanks, is made up of a still-growing collection of old train cars. Some are close to their original form; others were elaborately remodeled into small rooms on themes related to Fairbanks history. A full breakfast is served in the dining car.

Phil and Connie Horton built **Crestmont Manor Bed and Breakfast,** 510 Crestmont Dr. (© **888/456-3831**), a masterpiece of pale custom woodwork, to be their home and inn (Phil is a builder). They filled it with handmade quilts (Connie is a quilter), splashes of bright color, warm decorative themes, and huge impressionistic oil paintings (their son is an artist). The feel is crisp and airy. Just across the river from the downtown center, near the rail depot, at **Minnie Street Bed & Breakfast Inn,** 345 Minnie St. (© **888/456-1849**), two buildings around a garden courtyard contain clean, large, brightly decorated rooms with many amenities, custom-designed carpeting, handmade quilts, and stylish furniture. There's an air of perfection to the place.

Gambardella's Italian Cafe, 706 Second Ave. (© **907/456-3417;** www. gambardellas.com), is one of Alaska's best restaurants. Try the halibut or lasagna, and on a sunny day eat on the patio among the flowers. **Thai House,** 526 Fifth Ave. (© **907/452-6123**), is a simple restaurant with authentic cuisine.

HEADING SOUTH FROM FAIRBANKS

The **George Parks Highway** (Rte. 3), opened in 1972, is a straight line from Fairbanks to Anchorage, 358 miles south, and provides access to Denali National Park. There are some vistas of Mount McKinley from south of the park, but the Parks Highway is mostly just a transportation route, less scenic than the Richardson or Glenn highways. From the northern (Fairbanks) end, the highway passes Nenana, then Denali and Talkeetna, and finally the towns of the Matanuska and Susitna valleys, outside Anchorage.

4 Denali National Park

Denali (Den-*al*-ee) National Park gives regular people easy access to real wilderness. It's got sweeping tundra vistas, abundant wildlife, and North America's tallest mountain, Mount McKinley, all in a pristine natural environment where truly wild animals live in a complete ecosystem pretty much without human interference. A single National Park Service decision makes this possible: The only road through the park is closed to the public. This means that to get into the park, you must ride a crowded bus over a dusty gravel road hour after hour, but it also means that the animals are still there to watch, and their behavior remains essentially normal. From the window of the bus, you're likely to see grizzly bears doing what they would be doing even if you weren't there. It may be the only $20 safari in the world.

What's even more unique is that you can get off the bus whenever you want to and walk away across the tundra, out of sight of the road, to be alone in this primeval wilderness. Unfortunately, many Denali visitors never take the opportunity, which normally would cost a lot of money or require a lot of muscle and outdoor skill. Uniquely at Denali, you can be one more mammal on the tundra under the broad sky; and then, when you're ready to return to civilization, you can just walk to the road and catch the next bus—they come every half hour.

GETTING INTO THE PARK

ARAMARK/Denali Park Resorts, 241 W. Ship Creek Ave., Anchorage, AK 99501 (© **800/622-7275** or 907/272-7275, after May 15 907/683-8200; www. denalinationalpark.com), is the park concessionaire, operating the reservation system for the campgrounds and shuttle buses, plus three hotels, bus tours, a rafting operation, and a dinner theater. They have a desk in the Denali National Park Visitor Center. The easiest place to make in-person contact with the concessionaire or the park service itself is the **Denali National Park Visitor Center,** also known as the Visitor Access Center, on Denali Park Road, a half mile from the park entrance (P.O. Box 9), Denali National Park, AK 99755 (© **907/ 683-2294;** fax 907/683-9612; www.nps.gov/dena). Here you will find the ARAMARK/Denali Park Resorts reservation and ticketing desks and the park backcountry desk: basically, everything is covered in one room. Since there's no park entrance station, this center is also the stop for the park map, a copy of the *Alpenglow* park newspaper, and other handouts. A small bookstore offers a limited selection on the area, and films and programs take place in an auditorium. The visitor center is open from June to mid-September daily from 7am to 8pm; May and late September daily from 10am to 4pm. Closed October through April.

Sixty-five percent of shuttle-bus seats and all campground sites (except Morino, Sanctuary, and Igloo) are offered for booking by telephone, fax, or mail; the balance are held back for walk-ins. Reservations by mail or fax open for the entire summer on December 1 of the preceding year. Reservations by phone open in mid-February. After that date, lines are answered daily from 7am to 5pm Alaska time (remember, that's 4 hr. earlier than Eastern Standard Time). By faxing, you can get in before the phone lines open. Reservation forms to fax or mail are available on the park's website (www.nps.gov/dena). Include the dates, times, and campgrounds you want, plus alternate dates; the names and ages of the people in your party; and entrance and reservation fees (see park entrance fee below) along with a Visa, MasterCard, American Express, or Discover Card number with expiration date and signature. You can also pay by check if you're reserving by mail. But don't use the mail unless you write several months ahead, as you could miss getting a reservation at all. Mail to Alaska takes about 5 days from the East Coast.

A **confirmation** should be sent out by mail or fax within 2 days of receipt. Take the confirmation to the "will call" desk at the visitor center when you arrive to exchange it for a camping permit and bus ticket. If you'll be arriving after the center closes at 8pm, you must call © **907/683-1266** in advance to avoid losing your site or shuttle seat.

Phone, mail, and fax orders shut down the day before the visit starts, but walk-in reservations begin 2 days out, offering the remaining 35% of the shuttle bus seats, any leftover car-camping sites, and all sites in two primitive backcountry campgrounds, Igloo and Sanctuary. If it's a busy time of year, desirable shuttle reservations are snapped up early in the day. That means you may not get a good reservation for the day of your arrival or even the day after, only the next day after that. That's why it's so critical to reserve in advance. On the other hand, don't despair if you arrive without reservations, as the flow of visitors rises and falls unpredictably. It's perfectly possible that you'll walk into the visitor center and get a shuttle seat on the same day.

The **park entrance fee** is $10 per family or $5 per person, good for 7 days (an increase to $10 per person is under consideration at this writing). There is no entrance station to collect the fee; it's automatically added to your bill when you make shuttle or campground reservations. If you have a National Parks Pass or a Golden Age or Golden Access pass, mention it when you call to get your discount.

SEEING THE HIGHLIGHTS

There are no reserved seats on the park buses, but if you arrive early, choose a place on the left side, which has the best views on the way out. Most buses will see grizzly bears, caribou, Dall sheep, and moose, and occasionally wolves.

Here are some of the highlights along the road (check the visitor center or the park service information handouts to confirm times of the guided walks):

Mile 9: In clear weather, this is the closest spot to the park entrance with a view of Mount McKinley. This section also is a likely place to see moose, especially in the fall rutting season.

Mile 14: This is the end of the paved road at the Savage River Bridge. From the parking lot by the bridge, a simple climb over dry tundra leads to Primrose Ridge, also known as Mount Wright.

Mile 29: An hour and 10 minutes into the drive, a large rest stop overlooks the Teklanika River. The Teklanika, like many other rivers on Alaska's glacier-carved terrain, is a braided river—a stream wandering in a massive gravel streambed that's much too big for it.

Mile 34: Craggy Igloo Mountain is a likely place to see Dall sheep. Without binoculars, they'll just look like white dots. Manageable climbs on Igloo, Cathedral, and Sable mountains take off along the road in the section from Igloo Creek to Sable Pass.

Mile 38–43: Sable Pass, a critical habitat area for bears, is closed to people. A half-eaten sign helps explain why. Bears show up here mostly in the fall. This is the start of the road's broad Alpine vistas.

Mile 46: The top of 5-mile-wide Polychrome Pass, the most scenic point on the ride, and a toilet break, is 2 hours and 25 minutes into the trip. Caribou look like specks when they pass in the great valley below you. Note how the mountains of colored rock on either side of the plain match up—they were once connected before glacial ice carved this valley. Huge rocks on its floor are glacial erratics, plucked from the bedrock by moving ice and left behind when it melted.

Mile 53: The Toklat River, another braided river, is a flat plain of gravel with easy walking. The glaciers that feed the river are 10 miles upstream. The river bottom is habitat for bears, caribou, and wolves, and a good place for picnics.

Mile 58: Highway Pass is the highest point on the road. In good weather, dramatic views of Mount McKinley start here. The Alpine tundra from here to the Eielson Visitor Center is inviting for walking, but beware: Tundra is soft underfoot and can conceal holes and declivities that can twist an ankle.

Mile 64: Thorofare Pass, where the road becomes narrow and winding, is a good area to look for bears and caribou.

Mile 66: The Eielson Visitor Center, the end of most bus trips, has flush toilets, a covered picnic area, and a small area of displays where rangers answer

---

McKinley Flightseeing

Getting a good, close look at Mount McKinley itself is best accomplished by air. Small planes and helicopters fly from the park airstrip; from private heliports and airstrips along the Parks Highway; from the Healy airstrip; and from Talkeetna. **Denali Air** (𝒞 **907/683-2261;** www.denaliair.com) has an office in the Nenana Canyon area, and flight operations at Mile 229.5 of the Parks Highway. An hour-long flight going within a mile of the mountain costs $205 for adults, $105 for children age 12 and under. **Era Helicopters** (𝒞 **800/843-1947;** www.eraaviation.com) has 50-minute flights for $229, including pickup from hotels. Their heli-hikes land for a 4-hour hike on the mountain ridgeline, and they offer 75-minute glacier-landing flights. Both cost $315. Or fly from Talkeetna and land on McKinley. **Talkeetna Air Taxi** (𝒞 **800/533-2219;** www.talkeetnaair.com) is one of several operators offering these unforgettable flights.

---

questions. Among the exhibits is one explaining why you probably can't see the mountain from this best of vantage points, just 33 miles from its summit. There's a seismograph on display, registering the frequent small earthquakes that accompany McKinley's prodigious growth—about an inch every 3 years. Starting late in June, a ranger-guided tundra walk occurs daily at 1:30pm, lasting no more than an hour. If you leave the bus here for a hike, you can get a ride back later by signing up on the standby list kept by a ranger.

Mile 68.5: The incredibly rugged terrain to the north is the earth and vegetation covering Muldrow Glacier. The ice extends to McKinley's peak, and was the early and arduous route for climbers. McKinley's glaciers, falling 15,000 vertical feet and extending up to 45 miles in length, are among the world's greatest. The Ruth Glacier has carved the Great Gorge on the south side, which is almost 6,000 feet deep above the ice and another 4,000 below—almost twice the depth of the Grand Canyon. The park road comes within a mile of the Muldrow's face, then continues through wet, rolling terrain past beaver ponds, and finally descends into a small spruce patch near Mile 82.

Mile 86: Wonder Lake campground is the closest road point to Mount McKinley, 27 miles away. The fact that McKinley looks so massive from this considerable distance, dominating the sky, is a testament to its stupendous size. You'll likely never see a larger object on this planet. From its base (elevation here is only 2,000 ft.) to its top is an elevation gain greater than any other mountain on earth. Other mountains are taller overall, but they stand on higher ground.

WHERE TO CAMP, STAY & DINE

There are a number of campgrounds in and around Denali, bookable through ARAMARK (see "Getting into the Park," above). **Riley Creek campground,** near the visitor center, is best for those who want to be in the middle of things, near the store, showers, a bus stop for the free front-country shuttle, and a pay phone. **Savage River,** on Denali Park Road, 13 miles from the entrance, is a wonderful campground with unforgettable views.

Several campgrounds are beyond the checkpoint that limits car access to the park. The **Teklanika River campground,** on Denali Park Road, 29 miles from the entrance, is the only car campground beyond the checkpoint. You can drive in only if you don't move your vehicle for 3 days; otherwise, take the camper bus. **Wonder Lake campground,** on Denali Park Road, 85 miles from the entrance, sits near placid Wonder Lake, at the foot of Mount McKinley, in the most beautiful and coveted area of the park. **Igloo Creek and Sanctuary River campground,** on Denali Park Road, 23 miles and 34 miles from the park entrance, respectively, are primitive campgrounds, each with seven tent sites, that offer a backcountry experience away from cars. You can't reserve them in advance, only in person at the visitor center when you arrive. To use any of the campgrounds mentioned in this paragraph, you need a camper ticket on the shuttle bus, which costs $19 adults, $9.25 ages 15 to 17, free for ages 14 and under.

The **Denali Bluffs Hotel,** at Mile 238.4 on the Parks Highway (© **907/683-7000;** www.denalibluffs.com), looks down on the Nenana Canyon area from above the highway. Rooms are light and tastefully decorated. **Denali Crow's Nest Log Cabins,** at Mile 238.5 on the Parks Highway (© **888/917-8130** or 907/683-2723; www.denalicrowsnest.com), is a series of roomy and comfortable cabins perched in five tiers on the side of a mountain above the Nenana Canyon area. The **Grande Denali Hotel** (© **877/683-0803** or 907/683-5100; www.grandedenali.com) perches impossibly high above the Nenana Canyon; use caution and observe the mirrors at the switchbacks on the gravel road up from the highway. Views are great, but prices high: $199 for a double in high season.

You can't miss the tacky highway frontage of the **McKinley Denali Salmon Bake** in the Nenana Canyon area. It can be a fun place to eat in a picnic setting, and the food is fine. **The Overlook Bar and Grill,** at Mile 238.5 on the Parks Highway (© **907/683-2641**), is a fun, noisy place with the feeling of a classic bar and grill. A huge variety of craft beers is available, with several on tap. **The Perch,** at Mile 224 on the Parks Highway (© **907/683-2523**), is a friendly place serving a simple steak and seafood menu. The home-baked bread is noteworthy.

5 Talkeetna

Talkeetna, a funky little historic town with a sense of humor, but not much happening, slept soundly from its decline around World War I until just a few years ago. Now there are paved streets (both of them), a new National Park Service building, a new railroad depot, and two new luxury lodges. It seems that while Talkeetna slumbered, an explosion of visitors were showing up at Denali National Park. Now Talkeetna finds itself enveloped in that boom.

As a threshold to the park, Talkeetna has significant pros and cons that you should take into account. On the positive side, it's closer to Anchorage if you're coming from that direction; the development is much more interesting and authentic than at the park entrance; there's lots to do in the outdoors and great views of the mountain. On the negative side, a big minus: You can't get into the park from here, other than by plane. That means you miss the dramatic scenery, easy backcountry access, and unique wildlife viewing on the park road.

The town itself dates from the gold rush, and there are many charming log and clapboard buildings. With 15 sites of historic note, the entire downtown area has been listed on the National Register of Historic Places. You can spend several hours looking in the museums and meeting people in the 2-block main street, then go out on the Talkeetna or Susitna rivers for rafting, a jet boat ride, or fishing, or take a flightseeing trip to Denali.

WHAT TO SEE & DO

Along Main Street, artists and craftspeople have shops where you can often find them at work. The **Talkeetna Historical Society Museum,** on the Village Airstrip a half block south of Main Street (© **907/733-2487**), is well worth a stop. The first building contains artifacts and displays on local mining history. The second re-creates the old railroad depot. The third holds climbing displays and a huge scale model of Mount McKinley and the nearby mountains (don't miss it if you will fly over the mountain). The fourth is a 1916 trapper's cabin. The museum is a handy information stop. It's open daily in summer from 9:30am to 5:30pm; weekends only in winter. Admission is $2.50, free for children 12 and under.

Talkeetna is at the confluence of the wild Talkeetna and Susitna rivers. **Mahay's Riverboat Service** (© **800/736-2210** or 907/733-2223; www.mahays riverboat.com) is a guide service, offering 2-hour tours on a unique jet boat for $50 per person, leaving several times a day from a dock near the public boat launch on the Talkeetna River. Mahay's also operates fishing charters.

WHERE TO STAY & DINE

The **Talkeetna Alaskan Lodge,** at Mile 12.5 on the Talkeetna Spur Road (© **888/959-9590;** www.talkeetnalodge.com), is a luxurious place 2 miles from the town center that feels like it's out in the wilderness. The view from a high river bluff is a broad-canvas masterpiece of the Alaska Range, with McKinley towering in the center. The **Mt. McKinley Princess Lodge,** at Mile 133.1 on the Parks Highway (© **800/426-0500** or 907/733-2900; www.princesslodges. com), has a striking view of the mountain, and offers a full set of activities, including a short network of trails.

The **Swiss–Alaska Inn,** F Street, near the boat launch (© **907/733-2424**), is a friendly family business with a small restaurant serving good, familiar American meals, plus a few German dishes. **Café Michele** is a classy little bistro in a quaint house at the corner of Talkeetna Spur Road and Second Street (© **907/ 733-5300**). It serves homemade bread for lunch, and dinner entrees are under $25.

6 Anchorage

The state's largest city, Anchorage—where 40% of Alaska's population resides—is accused crushingly of being just like any other American city. It's true that the closer you get to Anchorage, the more the human development reminds you of the outskirts of any town in the United States. But Anchorage has one unique quality that no other large city can claim: it's surrounded by spectacular, pristine wild lands. Anyone in Anchorage with a few hundred dollars for a floatplane can be on a lake or river with bears and salmon in a matter of minutes, in wilderness deeper than any you could find in the Lower 48. **Chugach State Park** is largely within city limits—it's the size of Rocky Mountain National Park, and has similar Alpine terrain, with the critical difference that most of it is virtually never visited. From a downtown hotel, you can be climbing those mountains in half an hour. **Chugach National Forest,** the nation's second largest, is less than an hour down the road. In downtown's **Ship Creek,** people catch 40-pound salmon from under a freeway bridge. Even within the city, you can bike dozens of miles along the coast or through wooded greenbelts, or ski in one of the nation's best Nordic skiing parks.

ESSENTIALS

GETTING THERE   Major national and international airlines fly into **Ted Stevens Anchorage International Airport** (© 907/266-2525; www.anchorage airport.com). Bus, shuttle, and taxi services are available, and many hotels provide courtesy vans. For information on the **Alaska Marine Highway System,** see "By Ferry" under "Getting There," earlier in this chapter.

VISITOR INFORMATION   The **Anchorage Convention and Visitor Bureau,** 524 W. Fourth Ave. (© 907/276-4118; www.anchorage.net), operates several visitor information centers, distributing brochures and providing guidance for the whole state. The main location is the **Log Cabin Visitor Information Center,** downtown at Fourth Avenue and F Street (© 907/274-3531). It's open June through August daily from 7:30am to 7pm, May and September daily from 8am to 6pm, October through April daily from 9am to 4pm. If it's crowded, go to the storefront office right behind it. You'll also find visitor information desks at the airport—one in the baggage-claim area in the domestic terminal and two in the international terminal: in the lobby and in the transit area.

FAST FACTS   **Alaska Regional Hospital** is at 2801 DeBarr Rd. (© 907/ 276-1131), and **Providence Alaska Medical Center** is at 3200 Providence Dr. (© 907/562-2211).

WHAT TO SEE & DO

At the **Anchorage Museum of History and Art,** 121 W. Seventh Ave. (© 907/ 343-4326; www.anchoragemuseum.org), the Alaska Gallery offers an informative and enjoyable walk through the state's history and anthropology. In the art galleries, you can see what's happening in art in Alaska today; Alaska art isn't all scenery and walrus ivory, but the grandeur of the place does influence almost every work. Admission is $6.50 for adults, $6 for seniors 65 and older, free for children 17 and under.

   Alaska Native Heritage Center, near the intersection of the Glenn Highway and Muldoon Road (© 800/315-6608; www.alaskanative.net), is Alaska's best cultural site. Unable to bring visitors to small Alaska villages, Alaska Natives built this extraordinary center to bring their cultures to the visitors. What makes it so memorable is not the graceful building or the professional and informative displays, but the Native people themselves, real village people, who make a personal connection with visitors and don't come across as practiced or distant. The center takes most of a day to absorb. There is a hall where storytellers and dancers perform. There are also a 10-minute film, a gallery of educational displays, and a series of workshops where artisans practice traditional crafts. Finally, there's a pond surrounded by five traditional Native dwellings representing each cultural group, each hosted by a member of that group. Admission is $20 adults, $15 children ages 5 to 12. Open daily from 9am to 6pm in summer.

   At the **Alaska Zoo,** 4731 O'Malley Rd. (© 907/346-3242), gravel paths wander through the woods past large enclosures with natural flora for bears, seals, otters, musk oxen, mountain goats, moose, caribou, and waterfowl. Admission is $8 adults, $7 seniors, $5 children 12 to 17, $4 children 3 to 12. Drive out the New Seward Highway to O'Malley Road, then turn left and go 2 miles; it's 25 minutes from downtown, without traffic.

   Earthquake Park, on the west end of Northern Lights Boulevard, offers a sculpture and excellent interpretive signs commemorating and explaining the 1964 Good Friday earthquake (North America's largest earthquake ever) and pointing out its few remaining marks on the land. It is also a good access point to the **Coastal Trail,** which leads 10 miles from the western end of Second Avenue along the shore to **Kincaid Park.** It's a unique pathway to a natural environment from the heart of downtown. You can join the wide, paved trail at various points; downtown, **Elderberry Park,** at the western end of Fifth Avenue, is the most popular. From there, you might see beluga whales swimming along the trail at high tide. Moose are sometimes spotted toward the Kincaid Park end of the trail.

The **Eklutna Historical Park,** about 25 miles out the Glenn Highway (© 907/688-6026), has a fascinating old cemetery, still in use, in which each grave is enclosed by a decorated spirit house the size of a large dollhouse. The unique practice evolved in the melding of Athabascan and Russian Orthodox beliefs. There are two Russian Orthodox churches on the site, including the **St. Nicholas Orthodox Church.** Built north of here sometime prior to 1870, it is among the oldest buildings in the Southcentral region. Walk through the park by yourself or take an informative 30-minute tour for the same price: $6 adults, $3 children ages 6 to 12. Take the Glenn Highway to the Eklutna exit, then go left over the overpass.

For information on outdoors options from Anchorage, stop by the **Alaska Public Lands Information Center,** located at 605 W. Fourth Ave. (in the 1930s concrete federal building across the intersection from the log cabin at Fourth Ave. and F St.), Ste. 105, Anchorage (© **907/271-2737;** www.nps.gov/aplic), where staff can offer guidance for anyone planning to spend time in the outdoors anywhere in Alaska. You can buy ferry tickets from the Alaska Marine Highway System, there's an excellent selection of trail and field guides, and the rangers behind the desk know what they're talking about.

WHERE TO STAY

The **Hotel Captain Cook,** Fourth Avenue and K Street (© **800/843-1950;** www.captaincook.com), is Alaska's great, grand hotel, where royalty and rock stars stay. Inside, the decor has a fully realized (maybe a little excessive) nautical theme, with art memorializing Cook's voyages and enough teak to build a square-rigger. The standard rooms are large, with great views from all sides.

Rooms at the massive **Aurora Winds Inn B&B Resort,** 7501 Upper O'Malley Rd. (© **907/346-2533;** www.aurorawinds.com), are so grand and theatrically decorated you'll feel as if you're in a James Bond movie. Besides the outdoor hot tub set in luxurious gardens, they've installed a gym with a tiny swimming pool.

The **Oscar Gill House Bed and Breakfast,** 1344 W. 10th Ave. (© and fax **907/279-1344;** www.oscargill.com), is the oldest house in Anchorage—it was built in 1913, in Knik, before Anchorage was founded, and was moved here on a barge a few years later. The house is full of appropriate antiques, and manages to be both homey and immaculate.

About 40 miles south of Anchorage along the Seward Highway, the **Alyeska Prince Hotel,** 1000 Arlberg Ave., Girdwood (© **800/880-3880;** www.alyeska resort.com), is a large, first-class hotel in a nearly pristine mountain valley. The accommodations and service are as close to perfect as you're likely to find in Alaska. The standard rooms are not large but have extraordinary views and lovely cherrywood furniture. The swimming pool, with a cathedral ceiling and windows on the mountain, has no peer in Alaska. Two of the hotel's four restaurants—a cafeteria and the gourmet Seven Glaciers Restaurant (so named because that's how many are visible from its windows)—are 2,300 feet above the lobby on Mount Alyeska, at the end of a tram ride.

WHERE TO DINE

The **Marx Brothers Cafe,** 627 W. Third Ave. (© **907/278-2133;** www.marx cafe.com), has set a standard of excellence in the state. Dinner takes all night, but you can spend the time watching the chef pick herbs and vegetables for your meal from the garden behind the historic little building. The cuisine is varied and creative, ranging from Asian to Italian, and every dish is an adventure.

Simon and Seafort's Saloon and Grill, 420 L St. (© **907/274-3502**), is a jolly beef and seafood grill where voices boom off the high ceilings. On sunny summer evenings the rooms fill with light off Cook Inlet; views are magnificent.

The **Glacier Brewhouse,** 737 W. Fifth Ave. (© **907/274-BREW;** www.glacier brewhouse.com), features a tasty, eclectic, and ever-changing menu, served in a large dining room with lodge decor, where the pleasant scent of the wood-fired grill hangs in the air. They brew five hearty beers behind a glass wall.

19

Hawaii

There's no place quite like this handful of sun-drenched mid-Pacific islands, so remote from any continent yet visited by nearly seven million guests a year. The possibilities for adventure—and relaxation—are endless.

HAWAII ESSENTIALS

GETTING THERE   All major American and many international carriers fly to **Honolulu International Airport;** some also fly direct to the Big Island, Oahu, Maui, and Kauai. **Interisland service** is provided by **Aloha Airlines** (© **800/367-5250;** www.alohaairlines.com), **Island Air** (© **800/323-3345**), and **Hawaiian Air** (© **800/367-5320;** www.hawaiianair.com). If you're planning to island-hop, ask about multi-island passes.

Often the most cost-effective way to visit Hawaii is by booking a package deal that includes some combination of airfare, accommodations, and rental car; this need not be an escorted group tour—just a way to save money by booking everything in bulk. **Pleasant Hawaiian Holidays** (© **800/2-HAWAII** or 800/ 242-9244; www.pleasantholidays.com) is the biggest and most comprehensive packager, offering quality lodgings in every price range. Other reliable packagers include the airlines themselves, which often offer airfare/accommodations deals. On the Web, **www.vacationpackager.com** can link you up with many different package-tour operators, and **www.travelzoo.com** usually lists many Hawaiian packages on its site.

VISITOR INFORMATION   Contact the **Hawaii Visitors and Convention Bureau (HVCB),** Ste. 801, 2270 Kalakaua Ave., Honolulu, HI 96815 (© **800/ GO-HAWAII** or 808/923-1811; www.gohawaii.com). You can request the helpful *Accommodations and Car Rental Guide,* brochures, maps, and the *Islands of Aloha* magazine.

WHEN TO GO   Most visitors don't come when the weather's best in Hawaii; they come when it's at its worst everywhere else. The high season is generally from mid-December to March or mid-April, peaking during the last 2 weeks of December. The off seasons are spring (mid-Apr to mid-June) and fall (Sept to mid-Dec)—a paradox, since these times offer the most reliably great weather and money-saving deals. Due to the large number of families traveling in summer (June–Aug), you won't find fantastic bargains, but it's still a cheaper time to travel than winter. *Note:* If you're coming between the last week in April and mid-May, book all reservations far in advance; Japan's Golden Week holidays fall at this time, sending crowds of visitors to Hawaii.

1 Honolulu & Oahu

It's astounding to spend hours flying across the barren blue of the Pacific and then suddenly see below you the 26-mile-long metropolis of Honolulu, with its bright city lights, five-star restaurants, world-class shopping, and grand old hotels. Most visitors end up along the canyonlike streets of Waikiki, Honolulu's well-known hotel district and its most densely populated neighborhood. Some days, it seems like the entire world is sunning itself on Waikiki's famous beach.

Out in the country, the island of Oahu can be as down-home as a slack-key guitar. Here's where you'll find a big blue sky, perfect waves, empty beaches, rainbows and waterfalls, sweet tropical flowers, and fiery Pacific sunsets

ESSENTIALS

GETTING THERE   Honolulu International Airport sits on the south shore of Oahu, west of downtown Honolulu and Waikiki near Pearl Harbor. Shuttle vans operate 24 hours a day to all hotels and condos in Waikiki. **Trans-Hawaiian Services** (© 800/533-8765 or 808/566-7000; www.transhawaiian.com) operates the **Airport Waikiki Express Shuttles,** which leave every 20 to 30 minutes and charge $8 one-way to Waikiki. **TheBus** nos. 19 and 20 (Waikiki Beach and Hotels) take about an hour from the airport to downtown Honolulu and Waikiki. The one-way fare is $1, exact change only. You can bring a small suitcase, as long as it fits under your seat. **Taxi** fare is about $16 to downtown Honolulu, $23 to Waikiki.

VISITOR INFORMATION   The **Oahu Visitors Bureau,** 735 Bishop St., Ste. 1872, Honolulu (© **877/525-OAHU,** or 808/524-0722; www.visitoahu.com), distributes a free visitors' travel planner and map.

GETTING AROUND   Traffic can be extremely heavy on Oahu's mostly two-lane roads. You can avoid gridlock by driving between 9am and 3pm or after 6pm.

Taking **TheBus** (© 808/848-5555, or 808/296-1818 for recorded information; www.thebus.org) is often easier than parking your car. One of the best deals anywhere, TheBus goes around the whole island for $1.50. The most popular route is no. 8, which shuttles between Waikiki and Ala Moana Center every 10 minutes (trip time: 15–20 min.). Visitors' passes, good for 4 days of unlimited rides, are $10 at ABC convenience stores in Waikiki.

The fun, open-air, motorized **Waikiki Trolley** (© **800/824-8804** or 808/596-2199; www.enoa.com) loops around Waikiki and downtown Honolulu, stopping every 40 minutes at 12 key places, with commentary along the way. A 1-day pass ($20 for adults, $14 for kids ages 12–18, or $10 for kids under 12) allows you to jump on and off all day long.

The major cab companies offer islandwide service; vehicles with wheelchair lifts are available. **Star Taxi** (© 800/671-2999) offers a discount taxi service at the fixed price of $15 to Waikiki for up to five passengers, and no charge for baggage. **Handicabs of the Pacific** (© 808/524-3866; fax 808/523-6056) offers wheelchair taxi services and tours in specially equipped vehicles.

FAST FACTS   Hospitals with 24-hour emergency care include **Queens Medical Center,** 1301 Punchbowl St. (© 808/538-9011); **Kuakini Medical Center,** 347 Kuakini St. (© 808/536-2236); and **Moanalua Medical Center,** 3288 Moanalua Rd. (© 808/834-5333). **Straub Doctors on Call** (© 808/971-6000) can dispatch a van if you need help getting to any of its numerous clinics.

Although Oahu is generally safe, stay alert. The most common crime against tourists is rental-car break-in. Never leave any valuables in your car, not even in

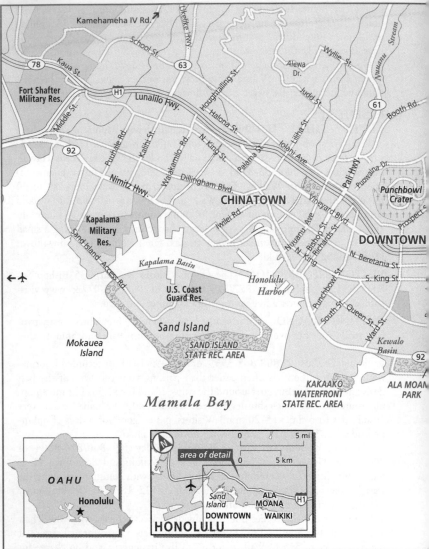

your trunk. Be especially leery of high-risk areas, such as beaches and resorts. And don't carry valuables or large amounts of cash in Waikiki and other tourist zones, including the USS *Arizona,* a high-theft area.

The sales tax is 4%. Hotel and room taxes total about 11.42%.

SPECIAL EVENTS & FESTIVALS   The world's top professional surfers come to Oahu's North Shore for the **Triple Crown of Surfing** (© 808/638-7266), from mid-November to mid-December. In February or March, you can watch **Buffalo's Big Board Classic,** Makaha Beach (© 808/951-7877), a traditional Hawaiian surfing, longboarding, and canoe-surfing contest.

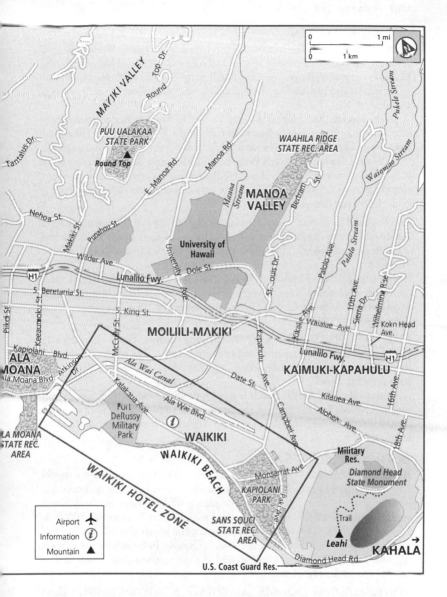

May Day (May 1) is **Lei Day** (℘ **808/924-8934** or 808/524-0722) in Hawaii, celebrated with lei-making contests, pageantry, arts and crafts, and a Brothers Cazimero concert at the Waikiki Shell. In mid-May, the Polynesian Cultural Center hosts the **World Fire-Knife Dance Championships and Samoan Festival** (℘ **808/293-3333**), with the most amazing performances you'll ever see, accompanied by authentic Samoan cuisine.

King Kamehameha Day (June 11) is a state holiday, celebrated the first weekend in June with a massive floral parade, *hoolaulea* (party), and much more (℘ **808/586-0333**).

HITTING THE BEACH

THE WAIKIKI COAST   No beach anywhere is as famous as **Waikiki Beach,** a narrow, 1½-mile-long crescent of sand at the foot of a string of high-rise hotels. Home to the world's longest-running beach party, Waikiki is fabulous for swimming, board- and bodysurfing, diving, sailing, and snorkeling. Go early—it gets crowded.

Of the beaches that make up Waikiki, we like **Kuhio Beach,** next to the Sheraton Moana Surfrider; **Gray's Beach,** in front of the Royal Hawaiian Hotel; and **Sans Souci,** the popular strip in front of the New Otani Kaimana Beach Hotel.

Gold-sand **Ala Moana Beach Park,** on sunny Mamala Bay, stretches for more than a mile between downtown and Waikiki. This 76-acre midtown park has spreading lawns, a lagoon, a yacht harbor, tennis courts, and more. The water is calm almost year-round.

EAST OAHU   Oahu's most popular snorkeling spot is **Hanauma Bay,** a marine-life conservation district with a small, gold-sand beach that's packed with people year-round. TheBus runs frequent shuttles from Waikiki. Closed Tuesdays.

Beautiful gold-sand **Makapuu Beach Park,** cupped in the stark black cliffs on Oahu's easternmost point, is worth a visit just for the scenery. In summer, the water's perfect for swimming and diving (in winter, the pounding waves are too dangerous).

THE WINDWARD COAST   Two-mile-long **Kailua Beach** is a 35-acre golden strand with dunes, palms, and panoramic views. The waters are great for swimming, windsurfing, bodysurfing, and kayaking. Best of all, the crowds haven't found it yet.

Postcard-perfect **Lanikai Beach** is good for sailing, windsurfing, and kayaking, and perfect for swimming in the crystal-clear lagoon. Because it's in a residential neighborhood, Lanikai has fewer crowds. There are no facilities or lifeguards.

OUTDOOR PURSUITS

BOATING   *Navatek I* (© 877/649-6990 or 808/973-1311; www.navatek-cruises.com) guarantees a "seasick-free" ride, whether on its sunset dinner cruise, lunch cruise (the best deal), or whale-watching trip. If you're not here during whale season, go dolphin watching instead with **Dream Cruises** (© 800/400-7300 or 808/592-5200; www.dream-cruises.com), which also offers a snorkel/splash tour and a Pearl Harbor coastal cruise. **Captain Bob's Adventure Cruises** (© 808/942-5077) can take you around the majestic windward coast and to snorkel spots full of tropical fish.

BODYBOARDING (BOOGIE BOARDING) & BODYSURFING   Good places to learn bodyboarding are in the small waves of **Waikiki Beach** and **Kailua Beach.** In Waikiki, you can rent boards and fins at **Aloha Beach Service,** Sheraton Moana Surfrider Hotel, 2365 Kalakaua Ave. (© 808/922-3111, ext. 2341); or at **Blue Sky Rentals,** Inn on the Park, 1920 Ala Moana Blvd. (© 808/947-0101).

GOLF   For same-day or next-day golfing and discount (10% to 40%) tee times, call **Stand-by Golf** (© 888/645-BOOK), from 7am to 11pm, for a guaranteed tee time.

The **Makaha Resort Golf Club,** 84–626 Makaha Valley Rd., Waianae, 45 miles west of Honolulu (© 800/695-7111 or 808/695-5239), is "The Best

Into the Deep: Submarine Rides

Here's your chance to play Jules Verne and experience the underwater world from the comfort of a submarine. Shuttle boats to the sub leave from Hilton Hawaiian Village Pier. The cost is $90 to $100 for adults, $40 for children 12 and under (kids must be at least 36 in. tall); call **Atlantis Submarines** (📞 **800/548-6262** or 808/973-9811; www.goatlantis.com) to reserve. To save money, ask about advance purchases for the shorter "Discovery Adventure" ($60 adults, $34 kids) and try to book your ride on the website, which often features discounts. *Warning:* Though the ride is safe for everyone, skip it if you suffer from claustrophobia.

Golf Course on Oahu," according to *Honolulu* magazine. Designed by William Bell, the challenging par-72, 7,091-yard course meanders toward the ocean before turning and heading into the valley; sheer volcanic walls tower above. For guests of Waikiki's Sheraton resorts, greens fees are $90 ($80 after noon); for nonguests, $100 ($90 after noon). There are also $35 twilight rates available.

Golf Digest once named the 6,867-yard, par-72 course at **Ko Olina Golf Club,** 92–1220 Alii Dr., West Beach (📞 **808/676-5309**), one of "America's Top 75 Resort Courses." The Ted Robinson–designed course has rolling fairways and elevated tee and water features. The signature hole— the 12th, a par-3—has an elevated tee that sits on a rock garden with a cascading waterfall. Greens fees are $145 for nonguests, $115 for resort guests, and $70 to $75 after 2:30pm.

The North Shore's **Turtle Bay Resort** (📞 **808/293-8574**) is home to two of Hawaii's top courses. The challenging 18-hole **Arnold Palmer Course** was designed by Arnold Palmer and Ed Seay. The front nine holes play like a British Isles course, with rolling terrain and lots of wind. The back nine have narrower, tree-lined fairways and water. The course circles Punahoolapa Marsh, a protected wetland for endangered Hawaiian waterfowl. Greens fees are $140 (twilight fees are $60–$83). The budget option—and more forgiving choice than the challenging Links course—is the **George Fazio–designed nine-hole course,** which can be played twice for a regulation par-71, 6,200-yard course. The course has two sets of tees, one designed for men and one for women, so you can get a slightly different play if you decide to tackle 18 holes. Greens fees are $55 for nine holes and $90 for 18 holes.

HIKING TO DIAMOND HEAD CRATER   A moderate but steep, 1½-hour, 1.4-mile walk leads to the summit of Hawaii's most famous landmark: a 760-foot volcanic cone that affords 360-degree views of Oahu. The hike, which costs $1 per person, starts at Monsarrat and 18th avenues on the crater's inland side. Take TheBus 58 from the Ala Moana Shopping Center or drive to the intersection of Diamond Head Road and 18th Avenue. Follow the road through the tunnel and park in the lot. The trail head proceeds along a paved walkway as it climbs the slope. You'll pass old World War I and II pillboxes, gun emplacements, and tunnels built as part of the Pacific defense network. Several steps take you up to the top observation post on Point Leahi. The views are indescribable.

Wear decent shoes (sneakers are fine) and bring a flashlight (for the tunnels you'll walk through), water, a hat, and binoculars. Try to head out just after the 6:30am opening, before the noonday sun starts beating down.

OCEAN KAYAKING   For a wonderful adventure, rent a kayak, arrive at Lanikai Beach just as the sun rises, and paddle across the emerald lagoon to the offshore island called Mokulua—it's an experience you won't forget. Equipment rentals are available in Waikiki at **Prime Time Sports,** Fort DeRussy Beach (© 808/949-8952); on the windward side, check out **Kailua Sailboards & Kayaks,** 130 Kailua Rd. (© 808/262-2555).

SCUBA DIVING One of the more famous wrecks is the *Mahi,* a 185-foot former minesweeper just south of Waianae. Abundant marine life makes this a great place to shoot photos. For nonwreck diving, a great spot in summer is **Kahuna Canyon,** near Mokuleia. Walls rising from the ocean floor create a massive amphitheater; inside, crabs, octopi, slippers, and spiny lobsters abound.

Since Oahu's best dives are offshore, your best bet is to book a two-tank dive from a dive boat. In Waikiki, try **South Sea Aquatics** (© 808/922-0852), which provides free transportation to and from Waikiki hotels. **Aaron's Dive Shop** (© 808/262-2333; www.aloha.com/~aarons), Hawaii's oldest and largest dive shop, offers boat-dive excursions as well.

SNORKELING Some of the best snorkeling is at the underwater park at Hanauma Bay. It's crowded, and sometimes it seems there are more people than fish, but Hanauma has clear, warm, protected waters and an abundance of friendly fish. The bay has two reefs, an inner and an outer—the first for novices, the other for experts. Closed on Tuesdays.

The uninitiated can take a lesson and a 2-hour snorkel tour with **Surf-N-Sea** (© 808/637-9887). Snorkel rentals are available at most dive shops and beach activity centers, including **Blue Sky Rentals,** Inn on the Park, 1920 Ala Moana Blvd., Waikiki (© 808/947-0101); and **Snorkel Bob's,** 700 Kapahulu Ave., Honolulu (© 808/735-7944; www.snorkelbob.com).

SPORTFISHING Kewalo Basin, located between the airport and Waikiki, is the main location for charter fishing boats. We recommend going through a booking agent; **Sportfish Hawaii** (© 877/388-1376 or 808/396-2607; www.sportfishhawaii.com) can arrange the type of fishing charter that you want at a reasonable price.

SURFING In summer, when the water's warm and there's a soft breeze in the air, the south swell comes up. It's surf season in Waikiki, the best place on Oahu to learn how to surf. For lessons, go early to **Aloha Beach Service,** next to the Sheraton Moana Surfrider (© 808/922-3111). Surfboards are available for rent at **Local Motion,** 1958 Kalakaua Ave., Honolulu (© 808/979-7873); and at **Surf-N-Sea,** 62–595 Kamehameha Hwy., Haleiwa (© 808/637-9887), which also offers lessons.

More experienced surfers should drop by any surf shop or call the **Surf News Network Surfline** (© 808/596-SURF) to get the latest conditions. A good spot for advanced surfers is **The Cliffs,** at the base of Diamond Head.

In winter, you can watch the serious surfers at the beach near **Kalalua Point.** Take the H-1 toward the North Shore, veering off at H-2, which becomes Kamehameha Highway (Hwy. 83). Keep going to the funky surf town of Haleiwa and Waimea Bay; the big waves will be on your left, just past Pupukea Beach Park.

WINDSURFING The oldest and most established windsurfing company is **Naish Hawaii/Naish Windsurfing Hawaii,** 115-A Hamakua Dr., Kailua (© 800/767-6068), which offers sales, rentals, instructions and free advice on where to go. **Surf-N-Sea,** 62–595 Kamehameha Hwy., Haleiwa (© 808/637-9887), on the North Shore, offers rentals and lessons

THE TOP ATTRACTIONS

Bishop Museum This forbidding, four-story Romanesque lava-rock structure holds a vast collection of natural and cultural artifacts from Hawaii and the Pacific. The Bishop is jam-packed with acquisitions, from insect specimens and ceremonial spears to pre-industrial Polynesian art. A visit here will give you a good basis for understanding Hawaiian life and culture. Hula performances take place daily, at 11am and 2 pm, and various Hawaiian crafts are demonstrated during the day. 1525 Bernice St., off Kalihi St. (also called Likelike Hwy.). (C) 808/847-3511. www.bishopmuseum.org. Admission $15 adults, $12 children 4–12 and seniors. Daily 9am–5pm. Bus: 2.

Bishop Museum at Kalia Now in Waikiki, this "mini" version of the Bishop Museum is just right for visitors who want to get an insider's view of Hawaiian culture but are pressed for time (an hour and a half will do). You can participate in a variety of interactive, hands-on activities like lei making, weaving cordage from coconut fibers, pounding kapa into cloth, learning the basic motions of the hula, or playing a Hawaiian instrument. Not to be missed! 2005 Kalia Rd. (C) 808/847-3511. www.bishopmusem.org. Admission $12 adults, $9.95 children 4–12 years. Daily 9am–9pm. Bus: 19 or 20.

Polynesian Cultural Center Experience the natural beauty and culture of the vast Pacific at this living museum of seven islands. You "travel" through the 42-acre park by foot or canoe on a man-made freshwater lagoon. Each re-created village is "inhabited" by native students from Polynesia, who attend Hawaii's Brigham Young University. The park, which is operated by the Mormon Church, also features a variety of stage shows celebrating the music, dance, history, and culture of Polynesia; there's a luau every evening. Since a visit can take up to 8 hours, it's a good idea to arrive before 2pm.

Just beyond the center is the Hawaii Temple of the Church of Jesus Christ of Latter-Day Saints, which is built of volcanic rock and concrete in the form of a Greek cross and includes reflecting pools, formal gardens, and royal palms. Completed in 1919, it was the first Mormon temple built outside the continental United States. 55–370 Kamehameha Hwy., Laie. (C) 800/367-7060, 808/293-3333, or 808/923-2911. www.polynesia.com. Admission only $27 adults, $16 children 5–11. Admission, buffet, and nightly show $47 adults, $30 children. Admission, IMAX, luau, and nightly show $64 adults, $43 children. Ambassador VIP (deluxe) tour $95 adults, $63 children. Mon–Sat 12:30–9:30pm. Take H-1 to Pali Hwy. (Hwy. 61) and turn left on Kamehameha Hwy. (Hwy. 83). Bus: 55. Polynesian Cultural Center coaches $15 round-trip.

USS *Arizona* Memorial at Pearl Harbor On December 7, 1941, the USS *Arizona*, while moored here in Pearl Harbor, was bombed in a Japanese air raid. The 608-foot battleship sank in 9 minutes without firing a shot, taking 1,177 sailors and Marines to their deaths. The deck of the ship lies 6 feet below the surface of the sea. The memorial, a stark white 184-foot rectangle that spans the sunken hull of the ship, contains the ship's bell, recovered from the wreckage, and a shrine room with the names of the dead carved in stone. Free U.S. Navy launches take visitors to the *Arizona*. Arrive early at the visitor center to avoid the huge crowds; waits of 1 to 3 hours are common. While you're waiting, explore the interesting museum, with personal mementos, photographs, and historic documents. A moving 20-minute film precedes your trip to the ship. *Warning:* Unfortunately, this is a high-theft area—leave valuables in your hotel. (C) 808/422-0561 (recorded info) or 808/422-2771. www.nps.gov/usar. Daily 7:30am–5pm (programs run 8am–3pm). Allow at least 4 hr. to visit the memorial. Free admission. Children under 12 should be accompanied by an adult. All babies must be carried; strollers, baby carriages, and baby backpacks are not allowed. Shirts and shoes required; no swimsuits or flip-flops allowed (shorts are okay). Wheelchairs gladly accommodated. Drive west on H-1 past the airport; take the USS Arizona Memorial exit and follow the green-and-white signs. Ample free parking. Bus: 20 and 47; or Arizona Memorial Shuttle Bus (© 808/839-0911), which picks up at Waikiki hotels 6:50am–1pm ($6 round-trip).

SHOPPING

Major shopping centers in the Waikiki area include the upscale **Royal Hawaiian Shopping Center,** 2201 Kalakaua Ave. (© **808/922-0588**), and the **Ala Moana Center,** 1450 Ala Moana Blvd. (© **808/955-9517**). Both are home to luxury stores like Chanel as well as local favorites such as **Little Hawaiian Craft Shop,** at the former.

Downtown at the **Ward Centre,** 1200 Ala Moana Blvd. (© **808/591-8411**), the **Vagabond House** displays attractive home accessories, one-of-a-kind crafts, and multicultural treasures. **Native Books & Beautiful Things,** located at the Ward Warehouse, 1050 Ala Moana Blvd. (© **808/591-8411**) as well as at the Bishop Museum, 1525 Bernice St. (© **808/847-5288**), and downtown at 222 Merchant St. (© **808/599-5511**), sells Hawaiian artists' creations, from musical instruments to jewelry, contemporary Hawaiian clothing to lauhala handbags, hand-painted fabrics, and other high-quality gifts.

Our top recommendations for Hawaiiana and gift items are the **Academy Shop,** Honolulu Academy of Arts, 900 S. Beretania St. (© **808/523-8703**), which offers jewelry, basketry, ethnic fabrics, and native crafts; and the **Contemporary Museum Gift Shop,** 2411 Makiki Heights Rd. (© **808/523-3447**), which focuses on avant-garde jewelry, stationery, and gift items made by Hawaiian artists.

WHERE TO STAY

The largest moderately priced hotel chain in Waikiki is **Ohana Hotels** (© **800/462-6262;** www.ohanahotels.com), which offers excellent accommodations and often features sales and package deals. All of its 15 properties feature dependable, well-appointed rooms, ranging from one-bedroom kitchenette units to no-thrills budget units, in three price ranges: from $109 (Waikiki Surf, Waikiki Royal Islander, Waikiki Edgewater, Maile Sky Court, Waikiki Hobron, and Waikiki Coral Seas), from $129 (Waikiki West, Waikiki Reef Towers, Waikiki Malia, Ohana Surf, Ala Moana Towers, and Waikiki Surf East), and from $139 (Waikiki Reef Lanai, Waikiki Tower, and Waikiki Village). Ohana Hotels also offer plenty of deals, including rooms from $99, a free night's stay after your fifth night, room-and-car packages, and bed-and-breakfast packages.

Consider using the top reservations service in the state: **Hawaii's Best Bed & Breakfasts** (© **800/262-9912** or 808/885-4550; fax 808/885-0559; www.best bnb.com). Barbara and Susan Campbell personally select traditional homestays, cottages, and inns, based on each one's hospitality, distinctive charm, and attention to detail. They also book vacation rentals, hotels, and resorts. They charge $15 to book the first two locations and $5 for each additional location.

Aston Coconut Plaza   This small hotel is an island of integrity in a sea of tourist schlock. Calling itself a "studio-apartment boutique hotel," it offers personalized service and a tropical-plantation feel, with airy, island-style rooms, terra-cotta tile, and lots of greenery. Rooms have private lanais; most have kitchenettes and views of the Ala Wai Canal and the mountains. Ala Wai Golf Course is just across the canal, and the beach is 4 blocks away. An outdoor pool, a sun deck, exercise equipment, and an activity desk are other perks. 450 Lewers St. (at Ala Wai Blvd.), Honolulu, HI 96815. © **800/92-ASTON** or 808/923-8828. Fax 808/922-8785. www.aston-hotels.com. 80 units. $85–$95 double; $100–$190 suites with kitchenette. Extra person $12. Rates include continental breakfast. AE, DC, MC, V. Parking $9. Bus: 19 or 20. **Amenities:** Outdoor pool; fitness equipment.

DoubleTree Alana Waikiki   This elegant boutique hotel is a welcome oasis of beauty and comfort, with service that's attentive enough to satisfy business travelers. Waikiki Beach is just a walk away. The unusually homey and inviting rooms have two-line phones, voice mail, computer-fax outlets, flashlights (great for that hike up Diamond Head), and coffee/teamakers. Bathrooms are compact but well-equipped. Room service, massage, and a business center will make your stay here comfortable and convenient. 1956 Ala Moana Blvd. (on the Ewa side, between Ena Rd. and Kalakaua Ave.), Honolulu, HI 96815. © **800/222-TREE** or 808/941-7275. Fax 808/949-0996. www.alana-doubletree.com. 313 units. $199–$219 double; from $250 suite. Extra person $30; children 18 or younger stay free in parents' room. AE, DC, DISC, MC, V. Valet parking $10. Bus: 19 or 20. **Amenities:** Restaurant; outdoor heated pool; fitness center.

The Halekulani   For the ultimate heavenly Hawaii vacation, this luxury resort is the place. Spread over 5 acres of prime Waikiki beachfront are five buildings, interconnected by courtyards and lush, tropical gardens. Rooms, 90% of which face the ocean, are spacious, with separate sitting areas, furnished lanais, fridges, and safes. Bathrooms have deep soaking tubs, separate showers, and luxurious robes. The superb dining facilities include the award-winning neoclassic French La Mer (see "Where to Dine," below); the hotel also has the lovely House Without a Key, an open-air bar on the ocean where there's live entertainment and hula most nights. Business services, massage, and easy access to a superb stretch of Waikiki Beach are the icing on this luxurious cake. 2199 Kalia Rd. (at ocean end of Lewers St.), Honolulu, HI 96815. © **800/367-2343** or 808/923-2311. Fax 808/926-8004. www.halekulani.com. 456 units. $325–$520 double; from $750 suite. Extra person $125; 1 child under 17 stays free using existing bedding; maximum 3 people per room. AE, DC, MC, V. Parking $10. Bus: 19 or 20. **Amenities:** 4 restaurants; outdoor pool; small fitness room.

Hawaiiana Hotel   At this intimate low-rise hotel, you'll find lush tropical flowers and carved tikis at the entrance, a pineapple waiting for you at check-in, complimentary Kona coffee and tropical juice served poolside each morning, and flower leis at checkout. Each concrete hollow-tiled room contains a kitchenette, two beds (a double and a single), a fridge, a coffeemaker, and a view of the gardens and pools. The hotel is about a block from the beach and within walking distance of Waikiki shopping and nightlife. Extras include weekly Hawaiian entertainment and free use of washer/dryers. 260 Beach Walk (near Kalakaua Ave.), Honolulu, HI 96815. © **800/367-5122** or 808/923-3811. Fax 808/926-5728. www.hawaiianahotelatwaikiki.com. 95 units (some with shower only). $85–$95 double; $165–$190 studio with kitchenette; $135 1 bedroom with kitchenette for 4. Extra person $10. AE, DC, DISC, MC, V. Parking $8. Bus: 19 or 20. **Amenities:** 2 outdoor pools.

Hawaii Prince Hotel Waikiki   The first hotel at the entrance to Waikiki is this striking 33-story modern structure: high tech with a view. A grand piano sits in the midst of the lobby's raised seating area, where high tea is served every afternoon. All rooms face the Ala Wai Yacht Harbor, with floor-to-ceiling sliding-glass windows that let you enjoy the view; sorry, no lanais. The rooms are comfortably appointed—but the higher the floor, the higher the price. 100 Holo-moana St. (just across Ala Wai Canal Bridge, on the ocean side of Ala Moana Blvd.), Honolulu, HI 96815. ℂ **800/321-OAHU** or 808/965-1111. Fax 808/946-0811. www.princeresortshawaii.com. 521 units. $310–$450 double; from $550 suite. Extra person $40; children 17 or under stay free using existing bedding in parents' room. AE, DC, MC, V. Self-parking $10, valet parking $14. Bus: 19 or 20. **Amenities:** 2 restaurants; outdoor pool; 27-hole golf course reached by hotel shuttle; fitness room.

Hilton Hawaiian Village Beach Resort & Spa

A great place to stay with the kids, this is Waikiki's biggest resort, with nearly 3,000 rooms spread over 20 acres. You'll find tropical gardens dotted with exotic birds, award-winning restaurants, a secluded lagoon, and a gorgeous stretch of Waikiki Beach. Accommodations in the four towers range from simply lovely to ultradeluxe; rooms are large and beautifully furnished. We love the Alii Tower, right on the ocean; it has its own exclusive health club and pool, and its rooms and suites come equipped with amenities galore. Other amenities found throughout the hotel complex are bars, room service, massage, Hawaiiana instruction, walking tours, a children's program, and a business center. 2005 Kalia Rd. (at Ala Moana Blvd.), Honolulu, HI 96815. ℂ **800/HILTONS** or 808/949-4321. Fax 808/947-7898. www.hawaiianvillage.hilton.com. 2,998 units. $365–$465 double; $390–$495 Alii Tower double; from $455 suite. Extra person $45; children 18 and under stay free in parents' room. AE, DISC,MC, V. Self-parking $10, valet parking $14. Bus: 19 or 20. **Amenities:** 18 restaurants; 3 outdoor pools; spa; fitness center; 2 minigolf courses.

Ilima Hotel

The 17-story, pale-pink Ilima offers good value. This small, condo-style hotel has huge rooms, a great location (near the International Marketplace and the Royal Hawaiian Shopping Center, 2 blocks to Waikiki Beach), and affordable rates. You won't get an ocean view, but all units do come with full kitchens and sofa beds, making this a particularly good deal for families. Sun decks, free local phone calls, and an incredibly friendly staff make this a real winner. 445 Nohonani St. (near Ala Wai Blvd.), Honolulu, HI 96815. ℂ **800/801-9366** or 808/923-1877. Fax 888/864-5462. www.ilima.com. 99 units. $129–$175 double; $159–$209 1-bedroom for 4; $230–$270 2-bedroom rate for 4, sleeps 6; $355–$375 3-bedroom rate for 6, sleeps 8. Extra person $10. Discounts available for seniors and business travelers. AE, DC, DISC, MC, V. Limited free parking, $8 parking across the street. Bus: 19 or 20. **Amenities:** Outdoor pool; fitness room.

Royal Garden at Waikiki

Deals, deals, deals—that's what you'll find at this elegant 25-story boutique hotel, tucked away on a quiet, tree-lined side street. Each plush room contains a kitchenette (fridge, wet bar, coffeemaker), lots of closet space, a lanai, voice mail, and computer/fax hookups. The beach is a few blocks away, but at these prices, it's worth the hike. The hotel offers a free shuttle to shopping areas. 440 Olohana St. (between Kuhio Ave. and Ala Wai Blvd.), Honolulu, HI 96815 ℂ **800/367-5666** or 808/943-0202. Fax 808/946-8777. www.royalgardens.com. 220 units. $150–$250 double; $325–$425 1-bedroom double; $500–$1,000 2-bedroom (sleeps up to 4). Extra person $25; children under 12 stay free in parents' room. AE, DC, DISC, MV, V. Parking $8. Bus: 19 or 20. **Amenities:** 2 restaurants; 2 outdoor pools; fitness room.

Royal Kuhio

Families, take note: This high-rise condo is one of the best deals in Waikiki. Several companies handle apartments here, but we recommend Paradise Management. Its units have full kitchens, separate bedrooms, living areas, and lanais. Since the units are individually owned, each is uniquely decorated and furnished. Ask for a corner unit, and if you plan to go in February (the busiest month), try to book a year in advance. It's 2 blocks from Waikiki Beach, and within walking distance of everything else of interest. If you want to hang out on the property, you can keep yourself amused with the sun deck, volleyball court, billiards, basketball court, and putting green. 2240 Kuhio Ave. (between Royal Hawaiian and Seaside aves.), c/o Paradise Mgmt., 50 S. Beretania St., Ste. C207, Honolulu, HI 96813. (©) 800/367-5205 or 808/538-7145. Fax 808/533-4621. 389 units. $105 $140 apt for 4. Extra person $15. AF, MC, V. Free parking. Bus: 19 or 20. **Amenities:** Fitness room; putting green.

Sheraton Moana Surfrider Step back in time at Waikiki's first hotel, a National Historic Landmark which dates back to 1901. The aloha spirit pervades this classy and charming place. You'll even see female employees wearing traditional Victorian-era muumuus. Most rooms have ocean views; all come with fridges, irons, hair dryers, plush robes, safes, and voice mail. We especially like the Banyan Wing rooms; they're on the smallish side and lack lanais, but make up for it in style. The hotel sits on a prime stretch of beach, with lifeguards, beach chairs, towels, and service. Daily activities include Hawaiian arts and crafts. Room service and a seasonal children's program are offered. 2365 Kalakaua Ave. (ocean side of the street, across from Kaiulani St.), Honolulu, HI 96815. (©) 800/ 325-3535 or 808/922-3111. Fax 808/923-0308. www.moana-surfrider.com. 793 units. $265–$545 double; suites from $975. Extra person and rollaway bed $45; children under 18 stay free in parents' room, using existing bedding. Ask about Sure Saver rates, which could mean as much as 32% in savings. AE, DC, MC, V. Self-parking at sister property $10, valet parking $15. Bus: 19 or 20. **Amenities:** 5 restaurants; outdoor pool, fitness center.

Waikiki Joy This hidden jewel offers not only outstanding personal service but also a Bose entertainment system and a Jacuzzi in every room! The marble-accented open-air lobby and the tropical veranda—with pool, sauna, and fur nished deck—set the tone for the beautifully decorated rooms. All come with voice mail, modem hookups, fridge, and lanai. A downside: The beach is a 10- to 15-minute walk away. 320 Lewers St. (between Kuhio and Kalakaua aves.), Honolulu, HI 96815. (©) 800/92-ASTON or 808/923-2300. Fax 808/924-4010. www.aston-hotels.com. 94 units. $129–$185 double; $180–$205 club suite; $220 $240 junior suite with kitchen (sleeps up to 4); $280–$300 1-bedroom executive suite with kitchen (up to 4). Extra person $20. Rates include continental breakfast. Ask about Island Hopper rates (25% off if you stay 7 or more consecutive nights with Aston). AE, DC, DISC, MC, V. Parking $10. Bus: 19 or 20. **Amenities:** Restaurant; outdoor pool.

WHERE TO DINE

Akasaka JAPANESE/SUSHI BAR Cozy, busy, casual, and occasionally smoky, with a tiny tatami room for small groups, Akasaka wins high marks for sushi, sizzling tofu and scallops, miso-clam soup, and the overall quality of its cuisine. Highlights include the zesty, spicy tuna hand-roll (temaki); scallop roll with flying-fish roe; and hamachi. During soft-shell crab season, you can order these spiny delicacies in sushi—a novel, tasty treat. Ordering specials, noodles or other less-expensive a la carte items help ease the bite of the bill. 1646B Kona St. (©) 808/942-4466. Reservations recommended. Main courses $10–$25. AE, DC, DISC, MC, V. Mon–Sat 11am–2:30pm and 5pm–2am; Sun 5pm–midnight.

Alan Wong's Restaurant HAWAII REGIONAL CUISINE This 90-seat room, with a glassed-in terrace and open kitchen, is accented with stylish and imposing floral arrangements and avant-garde lighting. Vertical cuisine is the trend here: high-rise towers such as the famous ahi cake with layers of grilled eggplant, Maui onion, seared ahi, and Big Island goat cheese with lemon grass sauce. The menu changes daily, but always sizzles with Asian flavors deftly melded with fresh seafood and island produce. The California roll is a triumph, made with salmon roe, wasabi, and Kona lobster instead of rice, and served warm. We love the opihi shooters, day-boat scallops, and fresh-fish preparations. 1857 S. King St., 3rd floor. ☏ **808/949-2526.** Reservations recommended. Main courses $26–$38; chef's tasting menu $65. AE, DC, MC, V. Daily 5–10pm.

Chef Mavro Restaurant PROVENÇAL/HAWAII REGIONAL   Chef/ owner George Mavrothalassitis, a native of Provence, runs this warm and elegant place in an accessible, nontouristy neighborhood in McCully. To his list of signature items (ahi tartare with caviar, award-winning onaga baked in Hawaiian-salt crust), he's added new taste sensations: Keahole lobster in an Asian broth; a Hawaiian/Marseilles bouillabaisse; and you-can-cut-it-with-a-fork filet of beef tenderloin crusted with red wine-onion confit. Hints of Tahitian vanilla, lemon grass, ogo, rosemary, and Madras curry add exotic flavors to the French-inspired cooking and fresh island ingredients. 1969 S. King St. ☏ **808/944-4714.** Reservations recommended. Main courses $27–$38; prix-fixe $48–$85. AE, DC, DISC, MC, V. Daily 6–9:30pm.

Duke's Canoe Club STEAK/SEAFOOD   Named after fabled surfer Duke Kahanamoku, this casual, all-day, upbeat, oceanfront hot spot buzzes with diners and Hawaiian-music lovers throughout the day. Open-air dining gives a front-row view of the sunset. Dinner fare is steak and seafood, with high marks for the prime rib, macadamia-crab wontons, and several preparations of the daily catch. Duke's is also loved for its barefoot bar with top-notch island entertainment and its island-style ambience. There's live entertainment nightly from 4pm to midnight, with no cover. Outrigger Waikiki Hotel, 2335 Kalakaua Ave. ☏ **808/ 922-2268.** Reservations recommended for dinner. Main courses $10–$20; breakfast buffet $9.95. AE, DC, MC, V. Daily 7am–midnight.

La Mer NEOCLASSIC FRENCH   Honolulu's most sumptuous and expensive dining takes place at La Mer, the only AAA Five-Diamond restaurant in the state. Classical French influences meld with fresh island ingredients in this second-floor, open-sided oceanside room with views of Diamond Head and the sunset. Samplings from the rarefied world of Michelin-award–winning chef Yves Garnier include mussel soup with saffron, chanterelles, and delicate goatfish filets; kumu (goatfish) in a rosemary salt crust, a Halekulani signature; and the masterful onaga (ruby snapper) filets, skin crisped, with truffle juice and fried basil. The wine list, desserts, and service are formal without being stiff. Halekulani, 2199 Kalia Rd. ☏ **808/923-2311.** Reservations recommended. Long-sleeve collared dress shirts for men; jackets provided if necessary. Main courses $36–$45; 9-course prix-fixe $105, with wine pairings $145. AE, DC, MC, V. Daily 6–10pm.

Orchids INTERNATIONAL SEAFOOD   Orchids highlights fresh local produce and seafood in elegant presentations, in a dream setting with consummate service. Seafood lovers applaud Orchids' new seafood appetizer bar, only $10.50 when ordered with an entree. Winning entrees include tandoori-roasted island chicken; mustard-herb rack of lamb; paella for two; opakapaka with wasabi cream and wasabi mashed potatoes; sautéed broadbill swordfish; and a stunning appetizer of fresh oysters in a muscadet wine sauce, lightly fried. Halekulani, 2199 Kalia Rd. ☏ **808/923-2311.** Reservations recommended. Dinner main courses $25–$35. AE, DC, MC, V. Daily 7:30–11am and 6–10pm; Mon–Sat 11:30am–2pm; Sun brunch 9:30am–2:30pm.

Roy's Restaurant EUROPEAN/ASIAN   Roy Yamaguchi's flagship restaurant was the first of what now number more than a dozen throughout Hawaii, Asia, and the Pacific. A prolific winner of culinary awards, Yamaguchi devised a winning formula: open kitchen, fresh ingredients, ethnic touches, and a good dose of nostalgia mingled with European techniques. The menu changes nightly, but you can generally count on individual pizzas, a varied appetizer menu (summer rolls, blackened ahi), a small pasta selection, and entrees such as lemongrass-roasted chicken, hibachi-style salmon in ponzu sauce, and several types of fresh catch. 6600 Kalanianaole Hwy. © 808/396-7697. Reservations recommended. Main courses $14–$29. AE, DC, DISC, MC, V. Mon–Thurs 5:30–9pm; Fri 5:30–9:30pm; Sat 5–9:30pm; Sun 5–9pm.

Sam Choy's Breakfast, Lunch, Crab & Big Aloha Brewery ISLAND CUISINE/SEAFOOD   Sam Choy's crab house is a happy, carefree eatery—elegance and cholesterol be damned. The menu assures delightfully messy dining—if not on beef stew, omelets, and fried rice at breakfast or the Hawaiian plate and fresh fish at lunch, then decidedly at dinner, when all thoughts turn to the featured attraction: crab. A 2,000-gallon live-crab tank lines the open kitchen, serving as temporary shelter for the assortment of crabs in season. Clam chowder, seafood gumbos, oysters, and assorted poke are also offered at dinner. Children's menus are an additional family feature. The eight varieties of "Big Aloha Beer," brewed on-site, go well with the crab and poke, Wednesday nights bring live local entertainment. 580 Nimitz Hwy., Iwilei. © 808/545-7979. Reservations recommended for lunch and dinner. Main courses $5–$10 breakfast, $6–$27 lunch, $19–$35 dinner. AE, DC, DISC, MC, V. Daily 6:30am–4pm (breakfast until 10:30am Mon–Fri; 11:30am Sat–Sun) and 5–10pm. Located in the Iwilei industrial area near Honolulu Harbor, across the street from Gentry Pacific Center.

Sushi Sasabune SUSHI   The Sasabune way is otherwise known as "trust-me" sushi: Obey the chef, eat what's served, and may God help you if you drop a grain of rice or dip something in wasabi without permission. There is no California roll, no avocado, nothing that's not authentically Japanese. Don't miss the chirashi/fish bowl, a neat rectangular box with warm rice, several types of tuna and white fish, marinated octopus, and other slices of sashimi. If you wish to order from the menu, grab a table; if you're brave enough to sit at the sushi bar, you'll receive what the chef serves. Whether it's salmon from Nova Scotia, sea urchin from Japan, halibut from Boston, Louisiana blue crab, or farmed oyster from Washington, it comes with a strict protocol: Dip only with permission, and then with restraint. This is an extraordinary experience for sushi aficionados—a journey into new tastes, textures, and sensations, expensive but well worth it. 1419 S. King St. © 808/947-3800. Reservations recommended. Sushi $4–$7; sashimi $2.50–$15. AE, DISC, MC, V. Mon–Fri noon–2pm; Mon–Sat 5:30–10pm.

OAHU AFTER DARK

THE PERFORMING ARTS   The **Hawaii Theatre,** 1130 Bethel St., downtown (© 808/528-0506), a neoclassical 1922 beaux-arts landmark, is a multipurpose center for the performing arts. The **Honolulu Symphony Orchestra** has booked some of its performances at the new theater, but still performs at the Waikiki Shell and the **Neal Blaisdell Concert Hall** (© 808/591-2211). The highly successful **Hawaii Opera Theatre** draws fans to the Neal Blaisdell Concert Hall, as do many of the performances of Hawaii's four ballet companies: **Hawaii Ballet Theatre, Ballet Hawaii, Hawaii State Ballet,** and **Honolulu Dance Theatre.**

BEACHFRONT BARS   Take in the sunset from one of our favorite Waikiki bars: the Royal Hawaiian Hotel's **Mai Tai Bar** (© 808/923-7311), a few feet from the sand; or the unfailingly enchanting **House Without a Key,** at the

Halekulani (© **808/923-2311**), where the breathtaking Kanoelehua Miller dances hula to the riffs of Hawaiian steel-pedal guitar as you sip mai tais.

HAWAIIAN MUSIC   Impromptu hula and spirited music are an island tradition at the Hilton Hawaiian Village's **Paradise Lounge** (© **808/949-4321**), which serves as a large living room for the full-bodied music of **Olomana** Friday and Saturday from 8pm to midnight. At **Duke's Canoe Club,** at the Outrigger Waikiki (© **808/923-0711**), it's always three deep at the beachside bar when the sun is setting; extra-special entertainment is a given here—usually from 4 to 6pm on Friday, Saturday, and Sunday, and nightly from 10pm to midnight. Also check out **Chai's Island Bistro** (© **808/585-0011**) for a variety of Hawaiian entertainment throughout the week and weekend.

Nearby, the Sheraton Moana Surfrider offers a regular nightly program of Hawaiian music in its **Banyan Veranda** (© **808/922-3111**). The Sheraton Princess Kaiulani's **"Creation—A Polynesian Odyssey"** is a theatrical journey of fire dancing, special effects, illusions, and Polynesian dances, nightly at 5:15 and 8pm.

THE CLUB SCENE   Downstairs in the lobby of the Ala Moana Hotel, **Rumours Nightclub** (© **808/955-4811**) is the club of choice for those who remember Paul McCartney as someone other than Stella's father. The nightlife buzz is all about **Blue Tropix** (© **808/944-0001**), which comes complete with a jiggy weekend crowd and a live monkey contained in soundproof glass behind the bar; it features a restaurant and a 100-square-foot dance floor for the lively DJ jams of Top 40, hip-hop, and R&B dance music. At Restaurant Row, **Ocean Club,** 500 Ala Moana Blvd. (© **808/526-9888**), is the Row's hottest, hippest, and coolest spot. The minimum age is 23, and the dress code calls for "smart-casual"—no T-shirts, slippers, or beachwear.

2 Maui

On a map, Maui doesn't look like much, but this 727-square-mile island has three peaks more than a mile high, thousands of waterfalls, 120 miles of shoreline, more than 80 golden-sand beaches, great seaside hotels, and a historic port town teeming with fine restaurants, B&Bs, and art galleries. Next to Waikiki, Maui is Hawaii's most popular destination, welcoming 2½ million people each year to its sunny shores.

Maui's microclimates offer distinct variations on the tropical-island theme: It's as lush as an equatorial rainforest in Hana; as dry as the Arizona desert in Makena; as hot as Mexico in Lahaina; and cool and misty, like Oregon, up in Kula.

ESSENTIALS
GETTING THERE   At press time, Aloha, United, Hawaiian, American, American Trans Air, and Delta airlines offer direct service from the U.S. mainland to **Kahului Airport.** The other major carriers fly to Honolulu, where you'll have to pick up an interisland flight. You can avoid Kahului altogether by taking Island Air to **Kapalua–West Maui Airport,** which is only a 10- to 15-minute drive to the Kapalua resorts and about 20 minutes to Kaanapali.

SpeediShuttle (© **808/875-8070**) runs between Kahului Airport and all major resorts. Rates vary, but figure on $24 for two to Wailea, $48 for two to Kapalua. If you're staying in the Lahaina-Kaanapali area, you can take **Airporter Shuttle** (© **800/259-2627** or 808/877-7308) for $13 one-way.

VISITOR INFORMATION   The **Maui Visitors Bureau** is at 1727 Wili Pa Loop, Wailuku, Maui, HI 96793 (✆ **800/525-MAUI** or 808/244-3530; fax 808/244-1337; www.visitmaui.com).

GETTING AROUND   The only way to really see Maui is by rental car. All of the major firms have offices on Maui. **Alii Taxi** (✆ **808/661-3688** or 808/667-2605) offers 24-hour service islandwide. You can also call **Kihei Taxi** (✆ **808/879-3000**) or **Yellow Cab of Maui** (✆ **808/877-7000**).

FAST FACTS   Maui Memorial Hospital, in Central Maui, is at 221 Mahalani, Wailuku (✆ **808/244-9056**). East Maui's **Hana Medical Center** is on Hana Highway (✆ **808/248-8924**). In upcountry Maui, **Kula Hospital** is at 204 Kula Hwy., Kula (✆ **808/878-1221**).

Never leave any valuables in your car, not even in your trunk. Be especially leery of high-risk areas, such as beaches and resorts.

SPECIAL EVENTS & FESTIVALS   For 12 hours on New Year's Eve, the alcohol-free **First Night** festival (✆ **808/242-7469**) brings musicians, dancers, actors, jugglers, magicians, and mimes to the Maui Arts and Cultural Center; afterward, fireworks ring in the New Year. The official name of the **That Ulupalakua Thing! Maui County Agricultural Trade Show and Sampling** (✆ **808/875-0457**) may be long and cumbersome, but this event is hot, hot, hot. Local product exhibits, food booths, and live entertainment come to Ulupalakua Ranch and Tedeschi Winery on the last Saturday in April. In July, famous wine and food experts meet for the **Kapalua Wine Symposium** (✆ **800/KAPALUA**), which features formal tastings, panel discussions, and samplings of new releases. The world's top windsurfers gather at Hookipa Beach in October for the **Aloha Classic World Wavesailing Championship** (✆ **808/575-9151**). If you're on Maui, don't miss it—it's spectacular to watch. **Halloween in Lahaina** (✆ **808/667-9175**) is a giant costume party (some 20,000 people show up) on the streets of town.

HITTING THE BEACH

WEST MAUI   Gold-sand, 4-mile-long **Kaanapali Beach** is one of Maui's best. A paved beach walk links hotels, open-air restaurants, and the Whalers Village shopping center, but the beach is crowded only in pockets. Summertime swimming is excellent; the best snorkeling is around Black Rock, in front of the Sheraton.

Kapalua Beach, the cove that fronts the Kapalua Bay Hotel and the Coconut Grove Villas, is the stuff of dreams: a golden crescent bordered by two palm-studded points. Protected from strong winds and currents, Kapalua's calm waters are great for snorkelers and swimmers of all ages and abilities.

SOUTH MAUI   The three beaches that make up **Kamaole III Beach Park** are the best thing about the sprawling town of Kihei. The biggest and most popular is Kamaole III, the only one with a playground and a grassy lawn. Swimming is safe, but scattered lava rocks at the water line are toe-stubbers, and parents should make sure kids don't venture too far out, as the bottom slopes off quickly. The north and south ends have rocky fingers that attract snorkelers.

Wailea Beach is the best gold-sand crescent on Maui's sunny south coast. It's big, wide, and protected on both sides by black-lava points. The view out to sea, framed by the islands of Kahoolawe and Lanai, is magnificent. The waves are just the right size for gentle riding, with or without a board.

Maui

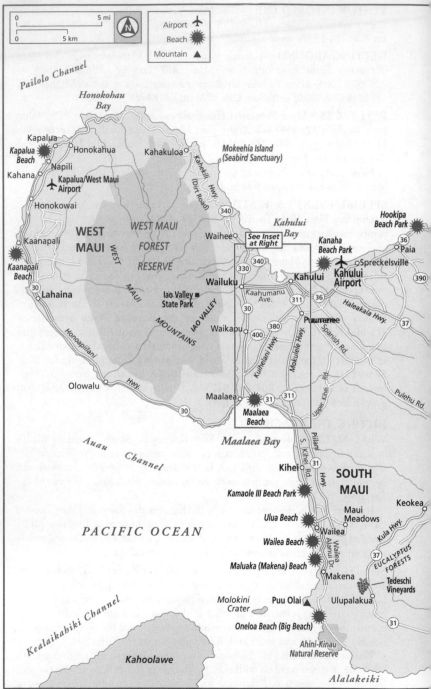

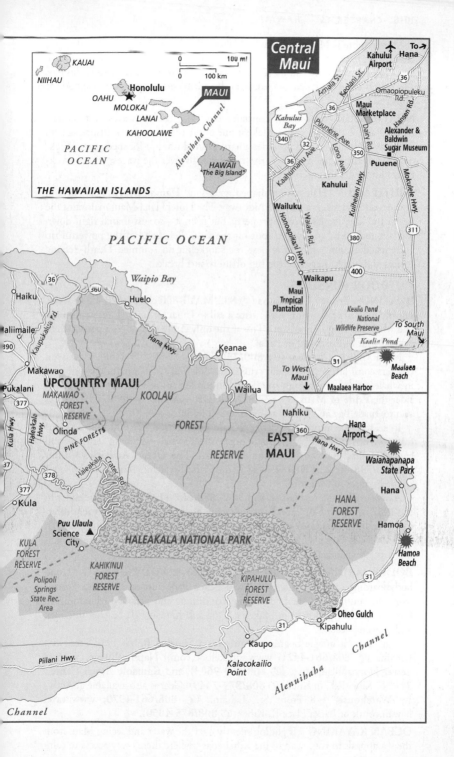

More remote is **Maluaka Beach** (Makena Beach), a palm-fringed, gold-sand crescent set between two black-lava points. The strand nearest the Maui Prince is notable for its beauty and its views. Swimming is great in this mostly calm bay. The waters around Makena Landing, at the north end, are particularly good for snorkeling.

NORTH MAUI The hard, constant wind and endless waves at **Hookipa Beach Park,** 2 miles past Paia, make it one of the most famous windsurfing sites in the world. A grassy cliff provides a natural amphitheater for spectators. Weekdays are the best time to watch the daredevils fly over the waves; winter weekends host regular competitions.

SOUTH MAUI Half-moon–shaped, gray-sand **Hamoa Beach,** near the end of the road in Hana, is a favorite hideaway. The Hotel Hana-Maui maintains the beach and acts like it's private property, but it's not—so just march right down the lava-rock steps and grab a spot on the sand. Be careful of the powerful rip currents; the calm left side is best for snorkeling in summer. Death-defying surfers and bodysurfers love the big offshore surf breaks.

OUTDOOR PURSUITS

BOATING **Trilogy Excursions** (© 888/MAUI-800 or 808/628-4800; www. sailtrilogy.com) offers our favorite trip: a sail to Lanai for snorkeling, swimming, and whale-watching (in season). This is the only cruise that offers a personalized ground tour of the island of Lanai.

Maui Classic Charters (© 800/736-5740 or 808/879-8188; www.maui charters.com) offers snorkel-sail cruises to Molokini (with a naturalist onboard in whale season). For a high-speed, action-packed snorkel-sail experience, consider the **Pride of Maui** (© 877/TO-PRIDE or 808/875-0955), which takes you to Turtle Bay and Makena as well as Molokini.

In season, the nonprofit **Pacific Whale Foundation** (© 800/942-5311 or 808/879-8811; www.pacificwhale.org) offers whale-watching cruises and snorkel tours, some to Molokini and Lanai. The **Ocean Activities Center** (© 800/798-0652 or 808/879-4485) runs whale-watching cruises and 5-hour snorkel cruises to Molokini.

America II, Lahaina Harbor, slip 5 (© 888/667-2133), a U.S. contender in the 1987 America's Cup race, is a true racing boat, a 65-foot sailing yacht offering four different 2-hour trips in winter, three in summer: a morning sail, an afternoon sail, and a sunset sail, plus whale-watching in winter. These are sailing trips. No snorkeling—just the thrill of racing with the wind.

BODYBOARDING (BOOGIE BOARDING) & BODYSURFING Good bodyboarding can be found at Baldwin Beach Park, just outside Paia. Storms from the south bring fair bodysurfing conditions and great bodyboarding to Oneloa Beach (Big Beach) in Makena; Ulua and Kamaole III beaches in Kihei; and Kapalua beaches.

You can rent boogie boards and fins from **Snorkel Bob's:** 1217 Front St., Lahaina (© 808/661-4421; www.snorkelbob.com); **Napili Village,** 5425-C Lower Honoapiilani Hwy. (© 808/669-9603); and **Kamaole Beach Center,** 2411 S. Kihei Rd., in Kihei (© 808/879-7449). Gear is also available at **Activity Warehouse,** 578 Front St., Lahaina (© 808/661-1970; www.travel hawaii.com); or Azeka Place II, Kihei (© 808/875-4050).

OCEAN KAYAKING If gliding silently over the water and seeing Maui from the sea appeals to you, head to the Kihei coast, where there's easy access to calm water. Mornings are best, as the wind comes up around 11am, making seas choppy and paddling difficult. Kayak rentals are available at **Activity Warehouse,** 578 Front St., Lahaina (© 808/661-1970); or Azeka Place II, Kihei (© 808/875-4050).

Our favorite outfitter is **Makena Kayak Tours** (© 808/879-8426), which leads a 2 ½-hour excursion over secluded coral reefs and into remote coves—it will be a highlight of your trip.

SCUBA DIVING   Everyone dives Molokini, a marine-life park and one of Hawaii's top dive spots, thanks to calm, clear, protected waters and an abundance of marine life. You'll need to book a dive boat to get here. **Ed Robinson's Diving Adventures** (© 800/635-1273 or 808/879-3584; www.mauiscuba. com), one of the best on Maui, offers specialized charters for small groups. If Ed is booked, call **Mike Severns Diving** (© 808/879-6596; www.mikeseverns diving.com), for small, personal tours. Mike and his wife are both biologists who make diving in Hawaii not only fun but also educational.

Maui's largest diving retailer, with rentals, instruction, and boat charters, is **Maui Dive Shop** (www.mauidiveshop.com), whose locations include Azeka Place II Shopping Center, Kihei (© 808/879-3388); Kamaole Shopping Center (© 808/879-1533); Lahaina Cannery Mall (© 808/661-5388); and the Honokowai Market Place (© 808/661-6166).

SNORKELING   Snorkeling on Maui is easy: There are many great spots where you can simply wade in the water with a face mask and look down to see the tropical fish. The best places are **Kapalua Beach; Black Rock,** at Kaanapali Beach; along the Kihei coastline, especially at **Kamaole III Beach Park;** and along the Wailea coastline, particularly at **Ulua Beach.** On Maui's rugged south coast, check out **Ahihi–Kinau Natural Preserve.** For an off-the-beaten-track experience, head south to **Makena Beach.**

Molokini islet, accessible only by boat, is harder to get to but worth the effort (see "Boating," above). **Snorkel Bob's** and **Rental Warehouse** rent everything you need (see "Bodyboarding," above, for locations).

SPORTFISHING   Marlin, tuna, ono, and mahi-mahi await you in Maui's coastal and channel waters. No license is required; just book a sportfishing vessel out of Lahaina or Maalaea harbors. The best way to book a sportfishing charter is through the experts; the best booking desk in the state is **Sportfish Hawaii** (© 877/388-1376 or 808/396-2607; www.sportfishhawaii.com), which not only books boats on Maui, but on all islands. These fishing vessels have been inspected and must meet rigorous criteria. Prices range from $800 to $975 for a full-day exclusive charter (you, plus five friends, get the entire boat to yourself); it's $600 to $675 for a half-day exclusive.

SURFING   Experts visit Maui in winter, when the surf's really up. The best beaches include **Honolua Bay,** north of Kapalua Resort; **Maalaea,** just outside the breakwall of Maalaea Harbor; and **Hookipa Beach,** where surfers get the waves until noon (after that, the windsurfers take over).

The **Nancy Emerson School of Surfing** (© 808/244-SURF or 808/874-1183; www.surfclinics.com) offers lessons. Nancy has pioneered a new instructional technique called "Learn to Surf in One Lesson"—you can, really. It's $70 per person for a 2-hour group lesson; private 2-hour classes are $140. In Hana, **Hana–Maui Sea Sports** (© 808/248-7711) has 2-hour lessons taught by a certified ocean lifeguard for $79. You can rent surfboards at **Activity**

Going Under: Submarine Rides

Plunging 100 feet below the surface of the sea in a state-of-the-art, high-tech submarine is a great way to experience Maui's magnificent underwater world. **Atlantis Submarines,** 658 Front St., Lahaina (© **800/548-6262** or 808/667-2224; www.goatlantis.com), offers trips out of Lahaina Harbor every hour on the hour from 9am to 1pm; tickets range from $70 to $80 for adults and $40 for children under 12 (children must be at least 3 ft. tall). Allow 2 hours for this underwater adventure.

Warehouse (www.travelhawaii.com), 578 Front St., Lahaina (© **808/661-1970**), or Azeka Place II, Kihei (© **808/875-4050**).

WHALE-WATCHING The best time to whale-watch is from mid-December to April: Just look out to sea. The whales seem to appear when the sea is glassy and there's no wind. Once you see one, keep watching in the same vicinity; they may stay down for 20 minutes. Some good spots are **McGregor Point,** on the way to Lahaina at mile marker 9; Outrigger Wailea Beach Resort, where there's a telescope on the coastal walk; **Olowalu Reef,** along the straight part of Honoapiilani Highway, between McGregor Point and Olowalu; and **Puu Olai,** a cinder cone overlooking Makena Beach, near the Maui Prince.

For a closer look, take a whale-watching cruise (see "Boating," above). For whale-watching from an ocean kayak or raft, try **Capt. Steve's Rafting Excursions** (© **808/667-5565**) or, for experienced kayakers, **South Pacific Kayaks and Outfitters** (© **800/776-2326**).

WINDSURFING Maui has Hawaii's best windsurfing beaches. In winter, windsurfers from around the world flock to **Hookipa Beach,** site of several world-championship contests. **Kanaha,** west of Kahului Airport, also has dependable winds. When the winds turn northerly, Kihei is the spot to be. **Ohukai Park,** the first beach as you enter South Kiehi Road from the northern end, has good winds, parking, and easy access to the water.

Hawaiian Island Surf and Sport, 415 Dairy Rd., Kahului (© **800/231-6958** or 808/871-4981; www.hawaiianisland.com), offers lessons, rentals, and repairs.

GREAT GOLF

Weekdays are your best bet for tee times. For last-minute and discount tee times, call **Stand-by Golf** (© **888/645-BOOK** or 808/874-0600) from 7am to 9pm. It offers discounted (up to 50%) guaranteed tee times for same-day or next-day golfing.

Golf Club Rentals (© **808/665-0800;** www.maui.net/~rentgolf) has custom-built clubs for men, women, and juniors (both right- and left-handed), which can be delivered islandwide; the rates are just $15 to $25 a day. The company also offers lessons with pros starting at $125 for nine holes plus greens fees.

The **Kaanapali Courses,** off Highway 30 (© **808/661-3691**), offer a challenge to all golfers, from high handicappers to near-pros. The par-72, 6,305-yard North Course is a true Robert Trent Jones design: wide bunkers, long tees, and the largest, most contoured greens on Maui. The par-72, 6,250-yard South Course is an Arthur Jack Snyder design; although shorter than the North, it requires more accuracy on the narrow, hilly fairways. Greens fees for nonguests are $150 for the North Course ($77 after 2pm) and $142 for the South Course ($85 after noon and $77 after 2pm).

The views from the championship **Kapalua Resort Courses,** off Highway 30 (© 877/KAPALUA), are worth the greens fees alone. The par-72, 6,761-yard **Bay Course** (© 808/669-8820), designed by Arnold Palmer and Ed Seay, is a bit forgiving, but its greens are difficult to read. The par-71, 6,632 yard **Village Course** (© 808/669-8830), another Palmer/Seay design, is the most scenic. The 6,547-yard, par-73 **Plantation Course** (© 808/669-8877), a Ben Crenshaw/Bill Coore design set on a rolling hillside, is excellent for developing your low shots and precise chipping. Greens fees are $180 at the Village and Bay courses ($80 after 2pm), $220 at the Plantation Course ($85 after 2pm).

At the **Makena Courses** (© 808/879-3344), Makena Alanui Drive, just past the Maui Prince Hotel, you'll find 36 holes of "Mr. Hawaii Golf"—Robert Trent Jones, Jr.—at its best, with great views of Molokini and humpback whales. The par-72, 6,876-yard South Course has a couple of holes you'll never forget, while the par-72, 6,823-yard North Course is more difficult and even more spectacular. Greens fees are $90 for guests, $125 for nonguests (after 2pm, prices are $75 for guests and $85 for nonguests).

Wailea Courses, Wailea Alanui Dr. (© 888/328-MAUI or 808/875-7540), offers three courses to choose from. The par-72, 6,758-yard Blue Course, designed by Arthur Jack Snyder and dotted with bunkers and water hazards, is for duffers and pros alike. A little more difficult is the par-72, 7,078-yard Gold Course, with narrow fairways, several tricky dogleg holes, and the classic Robert Trent Jones, Jr., challenges. The Emerald Course, also designed by Robert Trent Jones, Jr., is Wailea's newest, with tropical landscaping and a player-friendly design. Greens fees are $140 ($115 resort guests), twilight $95 ($80 resort guests) for the Blue Course; $160 ($115 resort guests) for the Gold Course; and $150 ($125 resort guests) for the Emerald Course.

HOUSE OF THE SUN: HALEAKALA NATIONAL PARK

Haleakala National Park is Maui's main natural attraction. More than 1.3 million people a year go up the 10,023-foot-high mountain to peer down into the crater of the world's largest dormant volcano—a hole that would hold Manhattan. Just going up the mountain is an experience in itself. Where else can you climb from sea level to 10,000 feet in just 37 miles, or a 2-hour drive? The snaky road passes through puffy cumulus clouds to offer magnificent views of the isthmus of Maui, the West Maui Mountains, and the Pacific Ocean.

PARK ESSENTIALS

Haleakala National Park extends from the summit of Mount Haleakala down the volcano's southeast flank to Maui's eastern coast, beyond Hana. There are actually two separate and distinct destinations within the park: Haleakala Summit and the Kipahulu coast. No road links the summit and the coast; you have to approach them separately.

ACCESS POINTS Haleakala Summit is 37 miles, or a 1½- to 2-hour drive, from Kahului. Take Highway 37 to Highway 377 to Highway 378. (See "The Drive to the Summit," below.)

The Kipahulu section of the park is on Maui's east end near Hana, 60 miles from Kahului on Highway 36 (the Hana Hwy.). Due to traffic and rough road conditions, plan on 4 hours, one-way.

INFORMATION & VISITOR CENTERS   For advance information, contact **Haleakala National Park,** Box 369, Makawao, HI 96768 (© **808/572-4400;** www.nps.gov/hale).

A mile from the park entrance, at 7,000 feet, is **Haleakala National Park Headquarters** (© **808/572-4400**), which provides information on park programs and activities, camping permits, restrooms, a pay phone, and drinking water. Open daily from 7:30am to 4pm.

The **Haleakala Visitor Center,** open daily from sunrise to 3pm, is near the summit, 11 miles from the park entrance. It offers a panoramic view, exhibits on the area, restrooms, and water. Rangers offer excellent, informative, and free naturalist talks at 9:30, 10:30, and 11:30am daily.

THE DRIVE TO THE SUMMIT

Highway 378, also known as **Haleakala Crater Road,** is one of the few roads in the world that climb from sea level to 10,000 feet, in just 37 miles. It has at least 33 switchbacks; passes through numerous climate zones; goes under, in, and out of clouds; and offers a view that extends for more than 100 miles.

Going to the summit takes 1½ to 2 hours from Kahului. Follow Highway 37 (Haleakala Hwy.) to Pukalani, where you'll pick up Highway 377 (also Haleakala Hwy.), which you'll take to Highway 378. Along the way, expect fog, rain, and wind. You may encounter stray cattle and downhill bicyclists. Fill up your gas tank before you go—Pukalani is the last town with services. There are no facilities beyond the ranger stations. Bring your own food and water.

Remember, you're entering a high-altitude wilderness area. Some people get dizzy due to the lack of oxygen; you may also suffer lightheadedness, shortness of breath, nausea, and headaches. People with asthma, pregnant women, heavy smokers, and those with heart conditions should be especially careful. Bring water and a jacket or a blanket, especially if you go up for sunrise.

At the park entrance, you'll pay an entrance fee of $10 per car ($2 for a bicycle). About a mile from the entrance is park headquarters, where an endangered nene, or Hawaiian goose, may greet you with its unique call.

Beyond headquarters are two scenic overlooks. Stop at Leleiwi Overlook, just beyond mile marker 17, to stretch and get accustomed to the heights. If you feel dizzy or drowsy, consider heading back down. A short trail leads to a panoramic view of the crater.

Two miles farther is Kalahaku Overlook, the best place to see a rare silver-sword. You can turn into this overlook only when you are descending from the top. The silver-sword, which grows only in Hawaii, has silvery bayonets displaying tiny, purple bouquets; it takes from 4 to 50 years to bloom.

Continue on and you'll quickly reach Haleakala Visitor Center, which offers spectacular views. But don't turn around here; the actual summit's a little farther

---

A Word of Warning About the Weather

The weather at nearly 10,000 feet can change suddenly and without warning. Come prepared for cold, high winds, rain, and even snow in winter. Temperatures can range from 77°F down to 26°F (25°C to –3°C), which feels even lower when you factor in the wind chill, and high winds are frequent. Bring boots, waterproof gear, warm clothes, extra layers, and lots of sunscreen—the sun shines very brightly up here. For the latest weather information, call © **808/871-5054.**

---

on, at Puu Ulaula Overlook (also known as Red Hill), the volcano's highest point. If you do go up for sunrise, the building at Puu Ulaula Overlook is the best viewing spot.

Tip: When driving down the Haleakala Crater Road, be sure to put your car in low gear; that way, you won't destroy your brakes by riding them the whole way down.

INTO THE WILDERNESS: SLIDING SANDS & HALEMAUU TRAILS

Hiking into Maui's dormant volcano is really the way to see it. There are some 27 miles of hiking trails, two camping sites, and three cabins.

Park rangers offers free guided hikes. Every Tuesday and Friday at 9am, there's a 2-hour, 2-mile guided cinder desert hike (meet at Sliding Sands Trail Head, next to the summit parking lot). Every Monday and Thursday at 9am, there's a 3-hour, 3-mile guided Waikamoi Cloud Forest hike (meet at Hosmer Grove) to view rare native birds and plants. Wear sturdy shoes and be prepared for wind, rain, and intense sun. Bring water and a hat. Additional options include full-moon hikes and star program hikes. For details, call the park at © 808/572-4400 or surf to www.nps.gov/hale.

For those venturing out on their own, the best route takes in two trails: into the crater along **Sliding Sands Trail,** which begins on the rim at 9,800 feet and descends to the valley floor at 6,600 feet; and back out along **Halemauu Trail.** Hardy hikers can consider making the 11.3-mile, one-way descent, which takes 9 hours, and the equally long return ascent, in a day. The rest of us will need to extend this steep hike to 2 days. The descending and ascending trails aren't loops; the trail heads are miles apart, so you'll need to make transportation arrangements in advance. Before you set out, stop at park headquarters to get camping and hiking updates.

A shorter, easier option is the half-mile walk down the **Hosmer Grove Nature Trail,** or a mile or two down **Sliding Sands Trail** for a hint of what lies ahead. A good day hike is Halemauu Trail to Holua Cabin and back, an 8-mile, half-day trip.

CABINS & CAMPGROUNDS   Three cabins each have 12 bunks, cooking utensils, a propane stove, and a wood-burning stove. The park has a lottery system for reservations; requests must be made 3 months in advance. For more information, contact **Haleakala National Park,** P.O. Box 369, Makawao, HI 96768 (© 808/572-4400; www.nps.gov/hale).

There are three campgrounds for free tent camping: two in the wilderness and one just outside at Hosmer Grove. Hosmer Grove, at 6,800 feet, is the best place to camp if you want to see the Haleakala sunrise; no permits are needed. The campgrounds inside the volcano are Holua, at 6,920 feet, and Paliku, at 6,380 feet. Facilities at both are limited. Free permits are issued daily at park headquarters.

DRIVING THE ROAD TO HANA

The **Hana Highway** (Hwy. 36) is a wiggle of a road that runs along Maui's northeastern shore, winding about 50 miles past taro patches, magnificent seascapes, waterfall pools, and verdant rainforests, and ending at Hana, one of Hawaii's most beautiful tropical places. The drive takes at least 3 hours from Lahaina or Kihei—but take all day. Going to Hana is about the journey, not the destination.

Seeing Haleakala from a Different Perspective

Maui Downhill (© 800/535-BIKE or 808/871-2155; www.mauidownhill. com) will drive you up to the summit in the cold, dark, early morning to view the sun exploding over Haleakala Crater—a moment you won't soon forget. But there's no time to linger: You're about to coast 37 miles down a 10,000-foot volcano. Cruising down from the lunarlike landscape at the top, past flower farms, pineapple fields, and eucalyptus groves, is quite an experience—and just about anybody can do it. (In winter and in the rainy season, however, conditions can be harsh, with below-freezing temperatures and 40 mph winds.) Tours start at $100, including transportation, bike, safety equipment, and meals. Wear layers of warm clothing, as there may be a 30°F (–1°C) change in temperature from the top of the mountain to the ocean.

If you'd like to get down into the crater on horseback, contact **Pony Express Tours** (© 808/667-2200 or 808/878-6698), which offers a variety of half-day and full-day rides down to the crater floor and back up, from $155 to $190. You must be at least 10 years old, weigh no more than 230 pounds, and wear long pants and closed-toe shoes.

Tourist traffic on the Hana Highway now exceeds 1,000 cars a day. Go at the wrong time, and you'll be stuck in a bumper-to-bumper rental-car parade—peak traffic times are mid-morning and midafternoon year-round, especially on weekends.

In the rush to "do" Hana in a day, most visitors spin around town in 10 minutes flat and wonder what all the fuss is about. It takes time to take in Hana, play in the waterfalls, sniff the tropical flowers, and view the spectacular scenery; stay overnight if you can. However, if you really must do the Hana Highway in a day, go just before sunrise and return after sunset.

Tips: Practice aloha: Give way at the one-lane bridges, let the big guys in 4×4s have the right of way, and if the guy behind you blinks his lights, let him pass. And don't honk your horn—here, it's considered rude. If you'd like to know exactly what you're seeing, rent a cassette tour from **Activity Warehouse,** 578 Front St., Lahaina (© 800/923-4004).

A GREAT PLUNGE ALONG THE WAY   A dip in a waterfall pool is everybody's tropical-island fantasy. The first great place to stop is Twin Falls, at mile marker 2. Just before the wide, concrete bridge, pull over on the mountain side and park. Hop over the ladder on the right side of the red gate and walk about 5 minutes to the waterfall and pool, or continue another 10 to 15 minutes to the second, larger waterfall and pool. What a way to start your trip.

CAN'T-MISS PHOTO OPS   Just past mile marker 12 is the **Kaumahina State Wayside Park.** Not only is this a good pit stop (restrooms available) and a wonderful place for a picnic under the tall eucalyptus trees (tables and barbecue area), but it's also a great vista point. The view of the rugged coastline makes an excellent shot—you can see all the way down to Keanae Peninsula.

Another mile and a couple of bends in the road, and you'll enter the Honomanu Valley, with its beautiful bay. To get to the Honomanu Bay County Beach Park, look for the turnoff on your left, just after mile marker 14, as you begin your ascent up the other side of the valley. The rutted dirt-and-cinder road takes you down to the rocky black-sand beach (no facilities). Because of the strong rip currents offshore, swimming is best in the stream inland from the ocean.

KEANAE PENINSULA & ARBORETUM   About 26½ miles past Paia at mile marker 17, the old Hawaiian village of Keanae stands out against the Pacific like a place time forgot. Here, on an old lava flow graced by an 1860 stone church and swaying palms, is one of the last coastal enclaves of native Hawaiians.

At nearby Keanae Arboretum, Hawaii's botanical world is divided into three parts: native forest, introduced forest, and traditional Hawaiian plants, food, and medicine. You can swim in the pools of Piinaau Stream, or press on along a mile-long trail into Keanae Valley, where a lovely tropical rainforest waits at the end.

WAIANAPANAPA STATE PARK   Just on the outskirts of Hana, shiny black-sand Waianapanapa Beach appears like a vivid dream, with bright-green jungle foliage on three sides and cobalt blue water lapping at its feet. The 120-acre park on an ancient lava flow includes sea cliffs, lava tubes, arches, and the beach, plus 12 cabins ((C) **808/984-8109** for lodging information).

HEAVENLY HANA   The beautiful coastal village of Hana enjoys more than 90 inches of rain a year, keeping the scenery unbelievably lush. Banyans, bamboo, breadfruit trees—everything seems larger than life, especially the flowers, like wild ginger and plumeria.

The last unspoiled Hawaiian town on Maui is, oddly enough, the home of Maui's first resort, which opened in 1946. Paul Fagan, owner of the San Francisco Seals baseball team, bought an old inn and turned it into the once-spectacular **Hotel Hana–Maui** ((C) **800/321-HANA** or 808/248-8211). This gorgeous luxury resort has been suffering from neglect of late. As we went to press, new owners had just acquired the hotel. We hope they do some much-needed maintenance, like bringing the once-sterling dining room back to a level of excellence and doing major renovations to all of the buildings.

Others have tried to open hotels here, but Hana always politely refuses. There are a few B&Bs, though; see "Where to Stay," below, for a reservations service that can assist you.

A wood-frame 1871 building holds the **Hana Museum Cultural Center,** 4974 Uakea Rd. ((C) **808/248-8622;** www.planet-hawaii.com/hana). Its excellent artifacts, memorabilia, and photographs tell the history of the area. You'll also want to stop by the **Hasegawa General Store** ((C) **808/248-8231**), a Maui institution since 1910.

On the green hills above Hana stands a 30-foot-high white cross made of lava rock, erected in memory of Paul Fagan, who helped keep this town alive. The 3-mile hike up to Fagan's Cross provides a gorgeous view of the Hana coast, especially at sunset.

The most unusual natural attraction here is **Red Sand Beach** (Kaihalulu Beach), red as a Ferrari at a five-alarm fire. It's on the ocean side of Kauiki Hill, just south of Hana Bay, in a wild, natural setting in a pocket cove.

WHERE TO STAY
Consider using the top reservations service in the state: **Hawaii's Best Bed & Breakfasts** ((C) **800/262-9912** or 808/885-4550; fax 808/885-0559; www.best bnb.com). Barbara and Susan Campbell personally select traditional home-stays, cottages, and inns, based on each one's hospitality, charm, and attention

to detail. They also book vacation rentals, hotels, and resorts. They charge $15 to book the first two locations, $5 for each additional location.

The Fairmont Kea Lani Maui You get what you pay for here, plus a few extras: This all-suite luxury hotel has 840-square-foot suites with microwave, kitchenette and coffeemaker; living room with high-tech media center and pull-out sofa bed (great if you have the kids in tow); a marble wet bar; an oversized bathroom with separate shower big enough for a party; and separate spacious bedroom. Plus, there's a large lanai off the bedroom and living room that over-looks the pools and lawns, right down to the white-sand beach. The huge swim-ming pool area includes a 140-foot water slide and a swim-up bar. And for a romantic meal, visit the excellent Nick's Fishmarket Maui. 4100 Wailea Alanui Dr., Wailea, HI 96753. © 800/659-4100 or 808/875-4100. Fax 808/875-1200. www.kealani.com. 450 units. $325–$695 suite (sleeps up to 4); villa from $1,100. AE, DC, DISC, MC, V. **Amenities:** 4 restaurants; 2 large swimming "lagoons," plus an adult lap pool; use of Wailea Golf Club's 3 18-hole championship golf courses; use of Wailea Tennis Center's 11 courts (3 lit for night play); spa; 24-hr. fitness center.

Four Seasons Resort Maui at Wailea If money's not a factor, this Hawai-ian palace by the sea is the place to spend it. The spacious (about 600 sq. ft.) rooms feature furnished lanais with ocean views, along with grand bathrooms containing deep marble tubs, showers for two, hair dryers, and plush terry robes. Service is attentive but not cloying. The ritzy neighborhood is home to great restaurants and shopping, the Wailea Tennis Center, and six golf courses—not to mention that great beach. The resort offers room service, whirlpools, water-sports gear, free use of bicycles, a salon, airport limousine service, a video library, a fabulous year-round kids' program, and a teen recreation center. What more could you want? 3900 Wailea Alanui Dr., Wailea, HI 96753. © 800/334-MAUI or 808/874-8000. Fax 808/874-2222. www.fourseasons.com/maui. 380 units. $315–$735 double; from $595 suite. Extra person $90 ($160 in Club Floor rooms); children under 18 stay free in parents' room. Packages available. AE, DC, MC, V. Free parking. **Amenities:** 3 restaurants; 3 outdoor pools; put-ting green; use of Wailea Golf Club's 18-hole championship golf courses (3), as well as the nearby Makena and Elleair golf courses; 2 tennis courts (lit for night play); use of Wailea Tennis Center's 11 courts (3 lit for night play); spa; health club.

Kahana Sunset This series of wooden condo units stair-steps down the side of a hill to a postcard-perfect white-sand beach. The unique location, nestled between the coastline and road above, makes it a very private place to stay. In the midst of the buildings lies a grassy lawn with a small pool and Jacuzzi; down by the sandy beach are gazebos and picnic areas. The units are great for families, with full kitchens, washer/dryers, large lanais with terrific views, and sofa beds. 4909 Lower Honoapiilani Hwy., at the northern end of Kahana, almost in Napili. c/o P.O. Box 10219, Lahaina, HI 96761. © 800/669-1488 or 808/669-8011. Fax 808/669-9170. www.kahana sunset.com. 79 units. $105–$200 1-bedroom (sleeps up to 4); $160–$310 2-bedroom (up to 6). 2-night minimum. AE, MC, V. From Hwy. 30, turn toward the ocean at the Napili Plaza (Napilihau St.), then left on Lower Honoapiilani Rd. Free parking. **Amenities:** Outdoor pool.

Koa Resort Just across the street from the ocean, Koa Resort consists of five two-story wooden buildings on 5½ acres of landscaped grounds. The spacious, privately owned one-, two-, and three-bedroom units come fully equipped. Each kitchen has a fridge, dishwasher, disposal, microwave, blender, and coffeemaker. All units feature large lanais, ceiling fans, and washer/dryers. For maximum peace and quiet, ask for a unit far from Kihei Road. 811 S. Kihei Rd. (between Kulani-hakoi St. and Namauu Place), c/o Bello Realty, P.O. Box 1776, Kihei, HI 96753. © 800/541-3060 or 808/879-3328. Fax 808/875-1483. www.bellomaui.com. 54 units (some with shower only). High season $105–$180 double; low season $85–$160 double. No credit cards. Free parking. **Amenities:** Outdoor pool; 18-hole putting green; 2 tennis courts.

Maui Eldorado Resort   These spacious condo units feature full kitchens, washer/dryers, and daily maid service. The Outrigger chain has managed to keep prices down to reasonable levels, especially if you come in spring or fall. This is a great choice for families, with grassy areas and a beachfront that's usually safe for swimming. The resort also offers shops and a travel desk. 2661 Kekaa Dr., Lahaina, HI 96761. (C) **800/688-7444** or 808/661-0021. Fax 808/667-7039. www.outrigger.com. 98 units. $195–$220 studio double; $255–$285 1-bedroom (rates for up to 4); $370–$395 2-bedroom (rates for up to 6). Numerous packages available. AE, DC, DISC, MC, V. Free parking. **Amenities:** Outdoor pool; 5 tennis courts; fitness room.

Maui Hill   If you can't decide between the privacy of a condominium and the conveniences of a hotel, try this place. Managed by the respected Aston chain, this large, Spanish-style resort is set on a hill above the heat of Kihei town. It combines all the amenities of a hotel—large pool, hot tub, tennis courts, putting green, Hawaiiana classes, daily maid service—with the luxury of large condos that have full kitchens, lots of space, and plenty of privacy. Nearly all units offer ocean views, washer/dryers, sofa beds, and big lanais. Beaches, restaurants, and shops are within walking distance. 2881 S. Kihei Rd. (across from Kamaole Park III, between Keonekai St. and Kilohana Dr.), Kihei, HI 96753. (C) **800/92-ASTON** or 808/879-6321. Fax 808/879-8945. www.aston-hotels.com. 140 units. High season $270 1-bedroom apt., $355 2-bedroom, $485 3-bedroom; low season $205 1-bedroom, $270 2-bedroom, $375 3-bedroom. AE, DC, DISC, MC, V. Free parking. **Amenities:** Outdoor pool; putting green; tennis courts.

The Napili Bay   One of Maui's best secret bargains is this small, two-story complex right on Napili's beautiful white-sand beach. The place is great for a romantic getaway. The compact studio apartments have everything you need, from full kitchens to roomy lanais. Though there is no air-conditioning, louvered windows and ceiling fans keep the units cool during the day. The beach here is one of the best on the coast, with great swimming and snorkeling. You're within walking distance of restaurants, 10 minutes from world-class golf and tennis, and 15 minutes from Lahaina. The manager is an encyclopedia of information on Maui. 33 Hui Dr. (off Lower Honoapiilani Hwy., in Napili), c/o Maui Beachfront Rentals, 256 Papalaua St., Lahaina, HI 96767. (C) **888/661-7200** or 808/661-3500. Fax 808/661-2649. www.mauibeachfront.com. 33 units. $95–$130 studio for up to 4. 5-night minimum. MC, V. Free parking.

Napili Kai Beach Club   The Napili Kai's comfortable one- and two-story units face their very own gold-sand, safe-for-swimming beach. The older beachfront units—with ceiling fans only—are a good buy at $215. Those who prefer air-conditioning should book into the Honolua Building, where, for the same price, you'll get a room set back from the shore around a grassy, parklike lawn and pool. All units have fully stocked kitchenettes. There are free morning coffee, afternoon tea, and a weekly mai-tai party, plus free children's activities in summer and during holidays. Complimentary use of beach gear, golf putters, and tennis racquets. 5900 Honoapiilani Rd. (at the extreme north end of Napili, next to Kapalua), Lahaina, HI 96761. (C) **800/367-5030** or 808/669-6271. Fax 808/669-0086. www.napilikai.com. 162 units. 190–$225 hotel room double, $220–$305 studio double; $360–$425 1-bedroom suite (sleeps up to 4), $525–$675 2-bedroom (sleeps 6). Extra person $15. Packages available. AE, MC, V. Free parking. **Amenities:** Restaurant; 4 outdoor pools; 18-hole putting greens (2); fitness room.

Noelani Condominium Resort This oceanfront condo is a great value. Everything is first class, from the furnishings to the location: on the ocean with a sandy cove next door at the new county park. There's good snorkeling off the cove, which is frequented by spinner dolphins and turtles in summer and humpback whales in winter. All units feature complete kitchens, entertainment centers, and spectacular views. Our favorites are in the Anthurium Building, where the one-, two-, and three-bedrooms have oceanfront lanais just 20 feet from the water. 4095 Lower Honoapiilani Rd. (in Kahana), Lahaina, HI 96761. (℃ **800/367-6030** or 808/ 669-8374. Fax 808/669-7904. www.noelani-condo-resort.com. 50 units. $107–$135 studio double; $147–$165 1-bedroom (sleeps up to 4); $207–$217 2-bedroom (sleeps 4); $267 3-bedroom (sleeps 6). Rates include continental breakfast on 1st morning. Extra person $10. Children under 18 stay free in parents' room. Packages for honeymooners, seniors, and AAA members available. 3-night minimum. AE, MC, V. Free parking. **Amenities:** 2 pools (1 heated for night swimming); access to nearby health club.

Outrigger Wailea Resort This classic, open-air, 1970s-style hotel in a tropical garden by the sea gives you a sense of what Maui was like before the big resort boom. Airy and comfortable, with touches of Hawaiian art throughout, it just feels right, fitting into its environment without overwhelming it. Eight buildings are spread along 21 acres of lawns and gardens spiked by coco palms, with lots of open space and a half mile of oceanfront. All rooms have private lanais. In 2000, the resort went through a $25-million renovation that expanded the entrance into an open-air courtyard with a waterfall and carp pond, transformed the south pool into a water-activities area complete with two water slides, and refurbished and upgraded the guest rooms. 3700 Wailea Alanui Dr., Wailea, HI 96753. (℃ **800/367-2960** or 808/879-1922. Fax 800/874-8331. www.outriggerwailea.com. 524 units. $325–$525 double. Packages available. AE, DC, DISC, MC, V. Free parking. **Amenities:** 2 restaurants; 3 outdoor pools; use of Wailea Golf Club's 18-hole championship golf courses (3), as well as the nearby Makena and Elleair golf courses; use of Wailea Tennis Center's 11 courts (3 lit for night play); spa; fitness room.

Renaissance Wailea Beach Resort This place offers Wailea-style luxury, but in a smaller, more intimate setting. Located on 15 acres of lawns and gardens along a series of small coves and beaches, it has the air of a small boutique hotel. Rooms have a sitting area, large lanai, TV/VCR, fridge, and three phones (with dataports). Those in the Mokapu Beach Club, just steps from a crescent-shaped beach, feature private check-in, in-room breakfast, and access to a private pool and beach cabanas. A traditional weekly luau, room service, a free video library, Hawaiian crafts classes, massage, babysitting, children's programs, a basketball court, shops, and a salon are among the perks here. The casual Palm Court offers buffets and oven-baked pizzas; Hana Gion features a sushi bar and teppanyaki grill; and Maui Onion is a poolside breakfast-and-lunch spot surrounded by lush gardens and a cascading waterfall. 3550 Wailea Alanui Dr., Wailea, HI 96753. (℃ **800/9-WAILEA** or 808/879-4900. Fax 808/874-5370. www.renaissancehotels.com. 345 units. $345–$600 double; from $1,060 suite. Extra person $40. Children 18 and under stay free in parents' room using existing bedding. Package rates available. AE, DC, DISC, MC, V. Parking $5. **Amenities:** 3 restaurants; 2 outdoor pools; use of Wailea Golf Club's 18-hole championship golf courses (3), as well as the nearby Makena and Elleair golf courses; use of Wailea Tennis Center's 11 courts (3 lit for night play); spa; fitness center.

The Ritz-Carlton Kapalua This may be the best Ritz-Carlton in the world. It rises proudly on a knoll, in a spectacular setting between the rainforest and the sea. The public spaces are open, airy, and graceful. Rooms have private lanais.

Hospitality is the keynote here; you'll find exemplary Ritz service seasoned with good old-fashioned Hawaiian aloha. Room service, airport and golf shuttles, secretarial services, kids' programs, volleyball, a salon, and guided backcountry hikes are just some of the extras here. The award-wining Anuenue Room has an elegant Sunday brunch. 1 Ritz-Carlton Dr., Kapalua, HI 96761. © 800/262-8440 or 808/ 669-6200. Fax 808/665-0026. www.ritzcarlton.com. 548 units. $340–$500 double; from $610 suite. Extra person $50 ($100 in Club Floor rooms). Resort fee of $12 for "complimentary" use of fitness center and children's program. Wedding/honeymoon, golf, and other packages available. AE, DC, DISC, MC, V. Self-parking free, valet parking $10. **Amenities:** 3 restaurants; outdoor pool; access to the Kapalua Resort's 3 championship golf courses and tennis complex; spa; fitness room.

Sheraton Maui   Terrific facilities and the best location on Kaanapali Beach make this beautiful resort an all-around great place to stay. It's built into the side of the cliff on the white-sand cove next to Black Rock (an 80-ft.-high lava formation). Six low-rise buildings are set in tropical gardens; a new lagoonlike pool features lava-rock waterways and an open-air spa. Cliff divers swan-dive off the torch-lit lava-rock headland in a traditional sunset ceremony—a sight to see. The new emphasis is on family appeal, with a class of rooms dedicated to those traveling with kids. Every unit is outfitted with amenities galore. Bars, in-room dining, shops, a summer children's program, and babysitting are some of the extras. 2605 Kaanapali Pkwy., Lahaina, HI 96761. © 800/STAY-ITT or 808/661-0031. Fax 808/ 661-0458. www.sheraton-maui.com. 510 units. $350–$610 double; from $750 suite. Extra person $30. Children 17 and under stay free in parents' room using existing bedding. "Resort fee" of $10 for self-parking. AE, DC, DISC, MC, V. Valet parking $5. **Amenities:** 3 restaurants; pool; fitness center; 36-hole golf course; 3 tennis courts.

The Whaler on Kaanapali Beach   In the heart of Kaanapali, right on the world-famous beach, lies this oasis of elegance, privacy, and luxury. No expense has been spared in the gorgeous units: Each has a full kitchen, washer/dryer, 10-foot beamed ceilings, and lanai. The spectacular views take in Kaanapali's gentle waves and the peaks of the West Maui Mountains. Great restaurants and bars are nearby, and the Kaanapali Golf Club is across the street. 2481 Kaanapali Pkwy. (next to Whalers Village), Lahaina, HI 96761. © Aston Hotels, 800/922-7866 or 808/661-4861. Fax 808/661-8315. www.whalermaui.com. 360 units. High season $235–$255 studio double, $330–$485 1-bedroom (for up to 4), $535–$700 2-bedroom (up to 6); low season $205–$230 studio, $275–$415 1-bedroom, $435–$573 2-bedroom. Check Internet for specials. Extra person $20; crib $12. 2-night minimum. AE, DC, DISC, MC, V. Free parking. **Amenities:** Outdoor pool; 5 tennis courts; fitness room.

WHERE TO DINE

Alexander's Fish & Chicken & Chips   FISH AND CHIPS/SEAFOOD Look for the ocean mural in front, Kalama Park across the street, and a marketplace next door: Beachwear is welcome at this friendly neighborhood takeout stand with patio seating and a very busy kitchen. Fresh ono, mahi-mahi, and ahi, broiled or fried, are all popular. This may be the most popular restaurant on the south shore. 1913 S. Kihei Rd. © 808/874-0788. Fish and chips $7.95–$9.95. MC, V. Daily 11am–9pm.

David Paul's Lahaina Grill   NEW AMERICAN   The recipient of numerous culinary awards, David Paul's is most people's favorite Maui restaurant. A special custom-designed chef's table can be arranged with 72-hour notice for larger parties, but the daily menu is enticement enough: tequila shrimp with firecracker rice, Kona coffee–roasted rack of lamb, seared ahi encrusted in Maui onion, and much more. The ambience—black-and-white tile floors, pressed-tin ceilings—is a good match for the cuisine. The bar is the busiest spot in Lahaina. 127 Lahainaluna Rd. ℭ **808/667-5117.** Reservations required. Main courses $22–$38. AE, DC, DISC, MC, V. Daily 5:30–10pm. Bar daily 5:30pm–midnight.

Hula Grill HAWAII REGIONAL/SEAFOOD Who wouldn't want to tuck into banana-glazed opah, crab-and-corn cakes, or ahi poke rolls under a thatched umbrella, with a sand floor and palm trees at arm's length and a view of Lanai across the channel? Peter Merriman, one of the originators of Hawaii Regional Cuisine, offers such dishes as wok-charred ahi, firecracker mahi-mahi, seafood pot stickers, and several fresh-fish preparations, including his famous ahi poke rolls: lightly sautéed rare ahi wrapped in rice paper with Maui onions. At lunch, order a burger or gourmet appetizers from the Barefoot Bar menu (sandwiches, crab wontons, fish and chips, pizza). There's happy-hour entertainment and Hawaiian music daily. Whalers Village, 2435 Kaanapali Pkwy. ℭ **808/667-6636.** Reservations recommended for dinner. Lunch and Barefoot Bar menus $5.95–$12; dinner main courses from $13. AE, DC, DISC, MC, V. Daily 11am–11pm.

Kimo's STEAK/SEAFOOD Kimo's has a loyal following that keeps it from falling into the faceless morass of waterfront surf-and-turf restaurants with great sunset views. It's always crowded, buzzing with people having fun on an ocean-front patio that takes in Molokai, Lanai, and Kahoolawe. Burgers and sand-wiches are affordable and consistent, and the fresh catch in garlic-lemon and a sweet-basil glaze is a top seller. The waistline-defying hula pie—macadamia-nut ice cream in a chocolate-wafer crust with fudge and whipped cream—originated here. 845 Front St. ℭ **808/661-4811.** Reservations recommended for dinner. Main courses $6.95–$11 lunch, $15–$24 dinner. AE, DC, DISC, MC, V. Daily 11am–3pm and 5–10:30pm; bar open 11am–1:30am.

Nick's Fishmarket Maui SEAFOOD Nick's has the perfect balance of visual sizzle and memorable food. Stefanotis vines create shade on the terrace, where the sunset views are superb. We love the onion vichyssoise with taro swirl and a hint of *tobiko* (flying-fish roe), Maui Wowie Greek salad (with hearts of palm, Kula tomatoes, avocados, feta, Maui onions, and rock shrimp), opah in phyllo crust, and mahi-mahi, done to perfection. Bow-tied waiters and almond-scented cold towels add an extra touch to this oceanside phenomenon—not to mention the lavish wine list and torch lighting at sunset. Kea Lani Hotel, 4100 Wailea Alanui.

A Night to Remember: Maui's Top Luau

We thought the nightly **Old Lahaina Luau** (ℭ **800/248-5828** or 808/667-1998; www.oldlahainaluau.com), staged at a 1-acre site just ocean side of the Lahaina Cannery, couldn't get any better, but it has. From food to entertainment to service and setting, it's peerless. Local craftspeople display their wares. Seating is provided on lauhala mats for those who wish to dine as the traditional Hawaiians did, but there are tables for everyone else.

The luau begins at sunset and features Tahitian and Hawaiian enter-tainment, including ancient, missionary-era, and modern hula. The enter-tainment is riveting. The food is as much Pacific Rim as authentically Hawaiian. No watered-down mai tais, either; these are the real thing. The cost is $75 for adults, $50 for children, plus tax.

© 808/879-7224. Reservations recommended. Main courses $25–$50. Prix-fixe dinners $55–$85. AE, DC, DISC, MC, V. Mon–Thurs 5:30–10pm; Fri–Sat 5:30–10.30pm; bar until 11pm

Pacific'o Restaurant PACIFIC RIM/CONTEMPORARY PACIFIC With good food complementing the sensational setting—the tables are literally on the beach—foodies and aesthetes have much to enjoy. We love the Asian gravlax: house-cured salmon on warm sweet-potato applejacks with wasabi chive sour cream and caviar, a taste sensation. The prawn and basil wontons, and the tandoori-spiced fresh moonfish are fine examples of Pacific'o's style. We always enjoy the vegetarian special, a marinated, roasted tofu steak crowned with quinoa, Maui onions, and red lentils, with a heavenly dose of shiitake mushrooms. If you like seafood, sunsets, and touches of India and Indonesia in your fresh-from-the-sea dining choices, you should be happy here. 505 Front St. © 808/667-4341. Reservations recommended. Main courses $9–$14 lunch, $19–$38 dinner. AE, DC, MC, V. Daily 11am–4pm and 5:30–10pm.

Roy's Kahana Bar & Grill/Roy's Nicolina Restaurant EURO-ASIAN These side-by-side sibling restaurants offer the same menu, and are busy, busy, busy. Young, hip, impeccably trained waiters deliver blackened ahi or perfectly seared lemon grass *shutome* (broadbill swordfish) hot to your table. Both are known for their rack of lamb and fresh seafood (usually eight or nine choices), and for their large, open kitchens that turn out everything from pizza to sake-grilled New York steak. If pot stickers are on the menu, don't resist. Roy's Nicolina features dining on the lanai. Kahana Gateway Shopping Center, 4405 Honoapiilani Hwy. © 808/669-6999. Reservations strongly suggested. Main courses $14–$31. AE, DC, DISC, MC, V. Roy's Kahana daily 5:30–10pm; Roy's Nicolina daily 5:30–9:30pm.

Sansei Seafood Restaurant and Sushi Bar PACIFIC RIM Furiously fusion, part Hawaii Regional Cuisine, and all parts sushi, Sansei is tirelessly creative, with a menu that scores higher with the adventurous than the purists. Maki is the mantra here. Other choices include Panko-crusted ahi sashimi, ahi carpaccio, noodle dishes, lobster, Asian rock-shrimp cakes, traditional Japanese tempura, and sauces that surprise, in creative combinations such as ginger-lime chili butter and cilantro pesto. There's also simpler fare, such as pastas and wok-tossed upcountry vegetables. Desserts are not to be missed. Kapalua Shops, 115 Bay Dr. © 808/669-6286. Reservations recommended. Main courses $19–$29. AE, DISC, MC, V. Daily 5:30–10pm.

MAUI AFTER DARK

The buzz in Lahaina is **Ulalena,** Maui Myth and Magic Theatre, 878 Front St. (© 877/688-4800), a riveting evening of entertainment that weaves Hawaiian mythology with Polynesian dance, original music, acrobatics, chant, and state-of-the-art multimedia capabilities in a brand-new, multimillion-dollar theater. It's interactive, with dancers coming down the aisles, drummers and musicians in surprising corners, and mind-boggling stage and lighting effects that often leave the audience speechless.

3 The Big Island

The Big Island of Hawaii—the island that lends its name to the entire 1,500-mile-long Hawaiian archipelago—is where Mother Nature pulled out all the stops. Simply put, it's spectacular.

The island looks like the inside of a barbecue pit on one side, and a lush jungle on the other. The Big Island has it all: fiery volcanoes and sparkling waterfalls, black-lava deserts and snowcapped mountain peaks, tropical rainforests and Alpine meadows, a glacial lake and miles of beaches, filled with a rainbow of black, green, and golden sands. A 50-mile drive will take you from snowy winter to sultry summer, passing through spring or fall along the way. Five volcanoes—one still erupting—have created this continental island, which is growing bigger daily.

The Big Island is not for everyone, however. Some tourists are taken aback at the sight of stark fields of lava or black-sand beaches, and you may have to go out of your way if you're looking for traditional tropical beauty, such as a quintessential white-sand beach.

ESSENTIALS

GETTING THERE The Big Island has two major airports: **Kona International Airport,** on the west coast, and **Hilo International Airport,** on the east. The Kona Airport receives direct overseas flights from Japan (Japan Airlines), as well as direct mainland flights from Los Angeles and San Francisco on **United Airlines** (© 800/241-6522; www.ual.com) and from Los Angeles on **American Airlines** (© 800/433-7300; www.aa.com). Otherwise, you'll have to pick up an interisland flight in Honolulu. **Aloha Airlines** (© 800/367-5250; www.aloha airlines.com) and **Hawaiian Airlines** (© 800/367-5320; www.hawaiianair. com) offer jet service to both Big Island airports.

VISITOR INFORMATION The **Big Island Visitors Bureau** has two offices: one at 250 Keawe St., Hilo, HI 96720 (© **808/961-5797;** fax 808/961-2126); and one on the other side of the island at 250 Waikoloa Beach Dr., Waikoloa, HI 96738 (© **808/886-1652**). Its website is www.bigisland.org.

On the west side of the island, you can also get information from the **Kona–Kohala Resort Association,** 69–275 Waikoloa Beach Dr., Kamuela (Waimea), HI 96743 (© **800/318-3637** or 808/886-4915; fax 808/886-1044; www.kkra.org); and from **Destination Kona,** P.O. Box 2850, Kailua-Kona, HI 96745 (© **808/322-6809;** fax 808/322-8899). On the east side contact **Destination Hilo,** P.O. Box 1391, Hilo, HI 96721 (© **808/935-5294**).

GETTING AROUND You'll need a rental car on the Big Island. All the major car-rental firms have agencies at both the airports and at the Kohala Coast resorts. If you need a cab, call **Kona Airport Taxi,** in Kailua-Kona (© **808/329-7779**). Taxis will take you wherever you want to go, but it's prohibitively expensive to use them for long distances.

FAST FACTS Kona Community Hospital, on the Kona Coast in Kealakekua (© **808/322-9311**), has a 24-hour urgent-care facility. If you need a doctor, call **Hualalai Urgent Care,** 75–1028 Henry St., Kona (© **808/327-HELP**).

Guard against rental-car break-ins. Never leave any valuables in your car, not even in your trunk. Be especially leery of high-risk areas, such as beaches.

SPECIAL EVENTS & FESTIVALS In late April, the **Merrie Monarch Hula Festival** (© **808/935-9168**), Hawaii's biggest, features 3 nights of modern and ancient dance competition in honor of King David Kalakaua, the "Merrie Monarch" who revived the dance.

July 4th is **Turtle Independence Day** (© **808/885-6677**) at Mauna Lani Resort and Bungalows on the Kohala Coast. Scores of endangered green sea turtles, raised in captivity, race down to the sea when they're released from the historic fishponds at Mauna Lani

Over Labor Day weekend, some 2,500 paddlers from all over the United States, Canada, and the Pacific vie in the **Long Distance Outrigger Canoe Races** (© 808/329-7787), the world's longest canoe event.

In October, 1,500-plus world-class athletes meet for the **Ironman Triathlon World Championship** (© 808/329-0063); a full marathon, a 2.4-mile swim, and 112 miles by bike on the Kona-Kohala coast. Spectators can watch the action along the route.

BEACHES

Too young geologically to have many great beaches, the Big Island instead has an odd collection of unusual ones: brand-new black-sand beaches, green-sand beaches, salt-and-pepper beaches, and even a rare white-sand beach.

THE KONA COAST About 2 miles north of the airport on Queen Kaahumanu Highway, 5-mile-long **Kekaha Kai State Park** (Kona Coast State Park) has a half-dozen long, curving beaches and a big cove on Mahaiula Bay, as well as archaeological and historical sites. The well-protected coves are excellent for swimming, and there's great snorkeling and diving offshore; the winter waves attract surfers. Bring your own drinking water. Hours are daily from 8am to 8pm.

Blink and you'll miss **White Sands Beach,** a small, white-sand pocket beach 4½ miles south of Kailua-Kona very unusual on this lava-rock coast. On calm days, the water is perfect for swimming and snorkeling. In winter, the waves swell to expert levels, attracting surfers.

Kahaluu Beach Park is the most popular beach on this coast. Coconut trees line a narrow salt-and-pepper–sand shore that gently slopes to turquoise pools. The well-established reef is a great place to snorkel. The shallow water is also ideal for children and beginning snorkelers. Be careful in winter, though: The placid waters become turbulent, and there's a rip current when high surf rolls in.

THE KOHALA COAST For 25 years, **Kaunaoa Beach (Mauna Kea Beach),** at the foot of Mauna Kea Beach Hotel, has been the top vacation spot among America's corporate chiefs. A coconut grove sweeps around this golden crescent, where the water is calm and protected by two black-lava points. The sandy bottom slopes gently into the bay, which often fills with schools of tropical fish, green sea turtles, and manta rays. Swimming is excellent year-round, except in rare winter storms. Snorkelers prefer the rocky points, where fish thrive in the surge.

Just off Queen Kaahumanu Highway, south of the Hapuna Beach Prince Hotel, lies the golden crescent of **Hapuna Beach**—big, wide, and a half-mile long. In summer, when the beach is widest, the ocean calmest, and the crowds biggest, this is the island's best beach for swimming, snorkeling, and bodysurfing. But beware of Hapuna in winter, when its thundering waves, strong rip currents, and lack of lifeguards can be dangerous.

The Big Island makes up for its dearth of beaches with a few spectacular ones, like **Anaehoomalu Bay** (or **A-Bay,** as the locals call it). This peppered, gold-sand beach, fringed by palms and backed by royal fishponds, fronts the Outrigger Waikoloa Beach Resort. The beach slopes gently from shallow to deep water; swimming, snorkeling, diving, kayaking, and windsurfing are all excellent. At the far edge of the bay is a turtle cleaning station, where snorkelers and divers can watch endangered green sea turtles line up, waiting their turn to have small fish clean them.

OUTDOOR PURSUITS

BOATING   Humpback whales return to the waters off Kona every winter. **Captain Dan McSweeney's Year-Round Whale-Watching Adventures** (© 888/WHALE6 or 808/322-0028; www.ilovewhales.com) guarantees a sighting, or will take you out again for free. Captain Dan, a whale researcher for more than 20 years, might drop an underwater microphone into the water or use an underwater video camera to show you what's going on.

One of the best ways to snorkel Kealakekua Bay, the marine life preserve that's one of the best snorkel spots in Hawaii, is on a half-day sail-snorkel cruise with **Fair Wind Snorkeling and Diving Adventures** (© 800/677-9461 or 808/ 322-2788; www.fair-wind.com).

BODYBOARDING (BOOGIE BOARDING) & BODYSURFING   On the Kona side of the island, the best beaches for bodyboarding and bodysurfing are **Hapuna Beach, White Sands Beach,** and **Kekaha Kai State Park.**

You can rent boards and fins at **Snorkel Bob's,** in the parking lot of Huggo's Restaurant, 75–5831 Kahakai Rd. (off Alii Dr.), Kailua-Kona (© **808/329-0770;** www.snorkelbob.com). No one offers formal lessons, but the staff here can offer pointers.

GOLF   For last-minute and discount tee times, call **Stand-by Golf** (© 888/ 645-BOOK or 808/322-BOOK) between 7am and 11pm. Stand-by offers discounted (10%–40%) guaranteed tee times for same-day or next-day golfing.

In addition to the courses below, we love the fabulous **Hualalai Golf Course** at Four Seasons Resort Hualalai (see "Where to Stay," below). Unfortunately, it's only open to resort guests—but for committed golfers, this Jack Nicklaus-designed championship course is reason enough to pay the sky-high rates.

The 18-hole championship **Hapuna Golf Course,** Hapuna Prince Beach Resort, off Highway 19 near mile marker 69 (© **808/880-3000**), has been named one of the "Top 10 New Courses in the Nation" by *Golf* magazine, and "Course of the Future" by the U.S. Golf Association. Designed by Arnold Palmer and Ed Seay, this 6,027-yard links-style course extends from the shoreline to 700 feet above sea level, with views of the pastoral Kohala Mountains and sweeping vistas of the Kohala coastline. Greens fees are $110 guests, $135 nonguests; twilight rates (after 3pm in summer and 2pm in winter) are $75 guests, $110 nonguests.

The breathtakingly beautiful, par-72, 7,114-yard **Mauna Kea Beach Golf Course,** Mauna Kea Beach Resort, Highway 19 near mile marker 68 (© **808/ 882-5400**), designed by Robert Trent Jones, Jr., is consistently rated one of the top courses in the United States. The signature third hole is 175 yards long (and a shocking par 3); the Pacific Ocean and shoreline cliffs stand between the tee and the green, giving every golfer a real challenge. Greens fees are $110 guests, $195 nonguests; twilight rates (after 3pm in summer and 2pm in winter) are $110 for everyone.

The **Mauna Lani Frances I'i Brown Championship Courses** are on Mauna Lani Drive, off Highway 19, 20 miles north of Kona Airport (© **808/885-6655**). The 7,029-yard, par-72 Mauna Lani South Course has an unforgettable ocean hole: the downhill, 221-yard, par-3 seventh, which is bordered by the sea, a salt-and-pepper sand dune, and lush kiawe trees. The North Course may not have the drama of the oceanfront holes, but because it was built on older lava flows, the more extensive indigenous vegetation gives the course a Scottish feel. Greens fees are $120 for guests, $185 for nonguests; twilight rates are $75 for everyone.

OCEAN KAYAKING Imagine sitting at sea level, eye-to-eye with a turtle, a dolphin, even a whale. Anyone can kayak: After a few minutes of instruction and a little practice in a calm area (like the lagoon in front of King Kamehameha's Kona Beach Hotel), you'll be ready to explore. Beginners can practice their skills in Kailua and Kealakekua bays; intermediates might try paddling from Honokohau Harbor to Kekaha Kai Beach Park; the Hamakua Coast is a challenge for experienced kayakers. You can rent kayaks (and other ocean toys) from **Kona Beach Shack,** on the beach in front of King Kamehameha's Kona Beach Hotel (© **808/329-7494**).

SCUBA DIVING The leeward coast offers some of the best diving in the world, with calm, clear waters. Want to swim with fast-moving game fish? Try **Ulua Cave,** at the north end of the Kohala Coast. For a dramatic encounter with large, feeding manta rays, head to **Manta Ray Village,** outside Keauhou Bay off the Kona Surf Resort.

There are nearly two dozen dive operators on the west side of the island, offering everything from certification courses to guided boat dives. In Kona, try **Eco Adventures,** King Kamehameha's Kona Beach Hotel, Kailua-Kona (© **800/949-3483** or 808/329-7116; www.eco-adventure.com).

If you're a serious diver looking for an all-diving vacation, you can spend a week on the 80-foot *Kona Aggressor II* (© **800/344-5662** or 808/329-8182; www.pac-aggressor.com), a live-aboard dive boat that provides unlimited underwater exploration along 85 miles of coastline.

SNORKELING The year-round calm waters along the Kona and Kohala coasts are home to spectacular marine life. Some of the best areas include the secret little **Hapuna Beach Cove,** at the foot of the Hapuna Beach Prince Hotel. If you're a first-time snorkeler, **Kahaluu Beach Park** is the best place to start. Just wade in and look down. The best snorkeling for all levels is in **Kealakekua Bay.** The calm waters of this underwater preserve teem with a wealth of marine life. Kealakekua is reachable only by boat (see "Boating," above) or kayak.

Beach concessions, tour desks, and dive shops offer equipment rentals and snorkel lessons. The best deal is at **Snorkel Bob's,** in the parking lot of Huggo's Restaurant, 75–5831 Kahakai Rd. (© **808/329-0770;** www.snorkelbob.com).

Into the Deep: Submarine Rides

This is the stuff movies are made of: venturing 100 feet below the sea in a high-tech, 65-foot submarine. On a 1-hour trip, you'll be able to explore a 25-acre coral reef that's teeming with schools of colorful tropical fish. On selected dives, you'll watch as divers swim among these aquatic creatures, luring them to the view ports for face-to-face observation. Call **Atlantis Submarines,** 75–5669 Alii Dr. (across from the Kailua Pier, underneath Flashback's Restaurant), Kailua-Kona (© **800/548-6262;** www.go atlantis.com). The cost is $84 for adults, $42 for children under 12. *Note:* The ride is safe for everyone, but skip it if you suffer from claustrophobia.

SPORTFISHING   If you want to fish, it doesn't get any better than the Kona Coast, known internationally as the marlin capital of the world. Nearly 100 boats offer fishing charters out of **Keauhou, Kawaihae, Honokohau,** and **Kailua Bay harbors.** If you're not an expert angler, the best way to arrange a charter is through a booking agency; for several years we've recommended the **Charter Desk at Honokohau Marina** (© **888/KONA-4-US** or 808/329-5735; charter@aloha.net).

SURFING   Most surfing off the Big Island is for the experienced only. Expert surfers should check out the waves at **Pine Trees** (north of Kailua-Kona), **Lyman's** (off Alii Dr. in Kailua-Kona), and **Banyan's** (also off Alii Dr.). Beginners can try Kahuluu Beach, where the waves are manageable most of the year.

   Ocean Eco Tours (© **808/324-SURF;** www.oceanecotours.com) is the only company on the Big Island that teaches surfing. Your only choice for surfboard rentals is **Pacific Vibrations,** 75–5702 Likana Lane (just off Alii Dr., across from the pier), Kailua-Kona (© **808/329-4140**).

HAWAII VOLCANOES NATIONAL PARK

Hawaii Volcanoes National Park is a work in progress, thanks to Kilauea volcano, which pours red-hot lava into the sea and adds land to the Big Island every day. Hawaii's eruptions produce slow-moving, oozing lava that provides excellent, safe viewing most of the time. You can see the highlights by car (the park has 50 miles of good roads, some of them often covered by lava flows) if you have only a day to spare, or allow at least 3 days to fully explore the park, which has hiking trails, rainforests, and campgrounds in addition to some of the world's weirdest landscapes.

PARK ESSENTIALS

ACCESS POINTS   Hawaii Volcanoes National Park is 29 miles from Hilo, on Hawaii Belt Road (Hwy. 11). From Kailua-Kona, it's 100 miles, or about a 2½-hour drive. Entry is $10 per vehicle (good for 7 days). Hikers and bicyclists pay $5; bikes are allowed on roads and paved trails only.

INFORMATION & VISITOR CENTERS   For advance information, contact **Hawaii Volcanoes National Park,** P.O. Box 52, Hawaii Volcanoes National Park, HI 96718 (© **808/985-6000;** www.nps.gov/havo). **Kilauea Visitor Center** is at the park entrance, just off Highway 11; it's open daily from 7:45am to 5pm.

   For the latest **eruption update** and information on volcanic activity in the park, call © **808/985-6000,** or check the visitor center's bulletin board.

   Everything you wanted to know about Hawaii's volcanoes is now available on the **Hawaiian Volcano Observatory**'s website (http://hvo.wr.usgs.gov).

VOLCANO VOCABULARY   The lava that looks like swirls of chocolate frosting is called **pahoehoe;** it results from a fast-moving flow. The big, blocky lava that looks like a chopped-up parking lot is **aa;** it's caused by lava that moves

---

Dressing for Volcano-Watching

Thanks to its higher elevation and windward (rainier) location, the volcanic area is always colder than it is at the beach. In the winter months, expect temperatures to be in the 40s or 50s, and dress accordingly. Always have rain gear on hand, especially in winter.

slowly, pulling apart as it overruns itself. **Vog** is smog made of volcanic gases and smoke from forests set on fire by aa and pahoehoe. **Laze** results when sulfuric acid hits the water and mixes with chlorine to become hydrochloric acid. Both vog and laze sting your eyes and can cause respiratory illness; don't expose yourself to either for too long. Pregnant women and anyone with heart or respiratory problems should avoid vog and laze.

SEEING THE HIGHLIGHTS

Your first stop should be **Kilauea Visitor Center,** just inside the park entrance, where you can get up-to-the-minute reports on the volcano's activity and learn how volcanoes work. Then walk across the street to **Volcano House;** go through the lobby and out the other side, where you can have a good look at **Kilauea Caldera,** a 2½-mile-wide, 500-foot-deep pit. It used to be a bubbling pit of lava; today, you can still see wisps of steam.

Now, get out on the highway and drive by the **Sulphur Banks,** which smell like rotten eggs, and the **Steam Vents,** where trails of smoke, once molten lava, rise from within the inner reaches of the earth. It's one of the few places where you can feel that the volcano is truly alive. Stop at the **Thomas A. Jaggar Museum** (open daily 8:30am–5pm; free admission), which shows eruption videos, explains the Pele legend, and monitors earthquakes (a precursor of eruptions).

Next, drive around the caldera to the other side, park, and take the short walk to Halemaumau Crater's edge to stand at the overlook and stare in awe at this once-fuming and bubbling old fire pit, which still generates ferocious heat out of vestigial vents. If you feel the need to cool off, go to the Thurston Lava Tube, the coolest place in the park. You'll hike down into a natural bowl, a forest preserve the lava didn't touch, and see a black hole in the earth; step in. It's all drippy and cool, with bare roots hanging down.

A BIRD'S-EYE VIEW OF THE VOLCANO   The best way to see the volcano is from on high, in a helicopter. This view puts the enormity of it all into perspective. The best outfitter is **Blue Hawaiian Helicopter** (✆ 800/745-BLUE or 808/886-1768; www.bluehawaiian.com), a professionally run, locally based company with an excellent safety record, comfortable 'copters, and extremely knowledgeable pilots. The **Circle of Fire/Waterfalls** 50-minute flight from Hilo takes you to the volcano and past waterfalls, valleys, and remote beaches, focusing on areas of volcanic activity ($165). Our favorite trip, from Waikoloa, is the 2-hour **Big Island Spectacular,** starring the volcano, tropical valleys, Hamakua Coast waterfalls, and the Kohala Mountains ($340).

HIKING & CAMPING IN THE PARK

Miles of trails lace the lava and cross deserts, rainforests, beaches, and, in winter, snow at 13,650 feet. Trail maps are sold at park headquarters; check conditions before you head out. *Warning:* If you have heart or respiratory problems, or if you're pregnant, don't attempt any hike in the park; the fumes will get to you.

The 4-mile, 2-hour, fair-to-moderate **Kilauea Iki Trail** begins at the visitor center and descends through a forest of ferns into the still-fuming crater, which in 1959 sent fountains of lava 1,900 feet in the air. On the half-mile, paved **Devastation Trail,** up on the rim of Kilauea Iki Crater, you can see the lava's effects on a once-flourishing ohia forest. The trail head is on Crater Rim Road at Puu Puai Overlook.

The easy 1½-mile, hour-long **Kipuka Puaulu (Bird Park) Trail** lets you see native flora and fauna in a little oasis of living nature surrounded by a field of lava. The trail head is on Mauna Loa Road. Go early in the morning or in the evening (or just after a rain) to see native birds.

CABINS & CAMPGROUNDS The only campground accessible by car is **Namakani Paio.** Tent camping is free; no reservations are required. Backpack camping at shelters and cabins is available on a first-come, shared basis; register at the visitor center.

Halape Shelter, about 7 miles from the nearest road, has its own white-sand beach. Facilities are limited. Free permits are available at the visitor center (© **808/985-6000**) on a first-come, first-served basis, before noon on the day of your hike.

Namakani Paio Campgrounds & Cabins is 5 miles west of the park entrance. No permit is needed for tent camping. Ten cabins accommodate up to four people each. Facilities include barbecues, picnic tables, toilets, sinks, and hot showers. Reserve through **Volcano House,** P.O. Box 53, Hawaii National Park, HI 96718 (© **808/967-7321**).

WHERE TO STAY
THE KONA-KOHALA COAST
Relax in the lap of luxury at **Four Seasons Resort Hualalai at Historic Kaupulehu,** Kailua-Kona (© **888/340-5662** or 808/325-8000; www.four seasons.com/hualalai). Low-rise clusters of villas nestle between the sea and the greens of a fabulous new golf course. Some units have bathrooms with private outdoor gardens (surrounded by black-lava rock), so you can shower naked under the sun or stars. Amenities include restaurants, room service, a sports club, a spa, five pools, an 18-hole Jack Nicklaus golf course, eight tennis courts, free scuba lessons, a Hawaiian cultural center, and a children's program.

Those seeking a peaceful, low-key atmosphere find refuge at the expensive-but-worth-it **Kona Village Resort,** Kailua-Kona (© **800/367-5290** or 808/325-5555; www.konavillage.com), where the thatched-roof bungalows lack air-conditioning, TVs, and phones. Rates include meals, tennis, watersports, walking tours, airport transfers, and the Friday-night luau (see "The Big Island After Dark," below). There are seasonal children's programs, live entertainment most nights, two pools, and a petroglyph field.

The serene, luxurious **Mauna Lani Bay Hotel & Bungalows,** 68–1400 Mauna Lani Dr., Kohala Coast (© **800/327-8585** or 808/885-6622; www. maunalani.com), offers sandy beaches and lava tide pools, plus gracious hospitality. Rooms, each with lanai, are arranged to capture the best ocean views. The posh, two-bedroom, 4,000-square-foot bungalows come with private pools and spas. Guests enjoy restaurants, room service, two celebrated golf courses, tennis, a spa, a pool, a shoreline trail, and shops.

The elegant, upscale **Orchid at Mauna Lani,** 1 N. Kaniku Dr., Kohala Coast (© **800/845-9905** or 808/885-2000; www.orchid-maunalani.com), is the place for watersports nuts, families, or those who just want to relax. Rooms are spacious and have lanais. The beach and watersports facilities are extensive, and the excellent Hawaiiana program covers everything from paddling a canoe to strumming a ukulele. Amenities include restaurants, room service, two championship golf courses, 10 tennis courts, a large outdoor pool, whirlpools, a fine swimming cove, a fitness center, walking/jogging trails, an activities and car desk, a business center, and a children's program.

The inexpensive, 40-unit **Kona Billfisher,** Alii Drive (across from Royal Kona Resort), Kailua-Kona (© **800/622-5348** or 808/329-3333; www.kona hawaii.com), is our favorite of all the affordable condos on this coast. It's within walking distance of downtown Kailua-Kona, and the big, blue Pacific is just across the street. (Unfortunately, the ocean here is not good for swimming or snorkeling, but there is an on-site pool, and the Kailua Pier, just a mile away, has a good swimming area.)

The comfortable, spacious condos at **Kanaloa at Kona,** 78–261 Manukai St., Kailua-Kona (© **800/688-7444** or 808/322-9625; www.outrigger.com), border the rocky coast beside Keauhou Bay, 6 miles south of Kailua-Kona. They're ideal for families, with huge bathrooms and spacious lanais.

VOLCANO VILLAGE, NEAR HAWAII VOLCANOES NATIONAL PARK

If you're going to the national park, Volcano is a great place to spend a few days—in fact, it's the only place.

Chalet Kilauea: The Inn at Volcano, off Highway 11, Volcano (© **800/ 937-7786** or 808/967-7786; www.volcano-hawaii.com), was the first small property to get the prestigious Triple Diamond Award from AAA. From the personal service to the gourmet breakfasts, this place is worth the price (but it may be a bit formal for some). Most of the fabulous units have private hot tubs.

The same owners also run **Volcano Bed & Breakfast** (© **800/937-7786** or 808/967-7779; www.volcano-hawaii.com), not as luxurious as Chalet Kilauea but still comfortable, quiet, and quite a bargain. Set on beautifully landscaped grounds, the charming 1912 historic home has small but inviting rooms; all share bathrooms.

Carson's Volcano Cottage, in Mauna Loa Estates, 501 Sixth St., at Jade Avenue, Volcano (© **800/845-5282** or 808/967-8094; www.carsonscottage. com), has three rooms (with private entrances and private bathrooms) and three cottages. The owners run another three houses in the neighborhood as well. Several cottages have their own hot tubs and fireplaces.

WHERE TO DINE
IN & AROUND KAILUA-KONA

If you're willing to drive the 10 extra minutes south from central Kailua-Kona to Keauhou, **Edward's at Kanaloa,** Kanaloa at Kona, 78–261 Manukai St. (© **808/322-1003**), located on a breathtaking point right on the ocean, will likely make your day. It's the best-kept secret of South Kona—an oasis without walls, where you can look for whales and dolphins and take in the ocean breeze over fresh fish in roasted-eggplant puree. Edward's is known for innovative selections in fresh fish, grains, and mushrooms.

Huggo's on the Rocks, a mound of thatch, rock, and grassy-sandy ground right next to **Huggo's,** 75–5828 Kahakai Rd. (© **808/329-1493**), is a sunset-lover's nirvana. At sundown, it's choked with people either on chaises or at the 50-seat thatched bar, sipping mai tais and noshing on salads, poke, sandwiches, plate lunches, sashimi, and fish and chips.

The **Beach Tree Bar and Grill,** Four Seasons Resort Hualalai, Queen Kaahumanu Highway, Kaupulehu-Kona (© **808/325-8000**), is an example of outstanding cuisine in a perfect setting—without being fancy, expensive, or fussy. The bar on the sand is a sunset paradise, and the sandwiches, seafood, and grilled items at the casual outdoor restaurant (a few feet from the bar) are simple, excellent, and prepared with imagination and no shortcuts.

SOUTH KONA

Great food, crisp air, and a sweeping ocean view make the **Coffee Shack,** Highway 11, 1 mile south of Captain Cook (© 808/328-9555), one of South Kona's great finds. Besides its fabulous breakfasts, go here for lunch: imported beers; excellent sandwiches on home-baked breads; and fresh, hearty salads made with organic lettuces.

Formerly Stan's Fishmarket, the **Keei Café,** at mile marker 106 on Highway 11, about 25 minutes south of Kailua (© 808/328-8451), with friendly ambience, great food, and affordable prices, is the darling of this coastline. The menu roams the globe, from spicy fajitas (chicken or tofu, bravo!) to excellent vegetarian black-bean soup. The fresh catch and roasted chicken are highlights.

The dining room of the decades-old **H. Manago Hotel,** Highway 11, Captain Cook (© 808/323-2642), is a local legend, greatly loved for its unpretentious, tasty food at family prices. T-shirts announce "the best pork chops in town": The restaurant serves nearly 1,500 pounds monthly.

NORTH KOHALA

In Waimea and throughout the island, **Merriman's,** Opelu Plaza, Highway 19 (© 808/885-6822), is peerless. Order anything from saimin to poisson cru for lunch; at dinner, choose from wok-charred ahi, and lamb from nearby Kahua Ranch. Platters of seafood and meats are among the many reasons this is the best dining spot in Waimea.

Often cited by local publications as the island's "best Japanese restaurant," **Miyo's,** Waiakea Villas, 400 Hualani St. (© 808/935-2273), offers home-cooked, healthy food, served in an open-air room on Wailoa Pond. Sliding shoji doors bordering the dining area are left open so you can take in the view and gaze at Mauna Kea on a clear day. Sesame chicken is a best seller.

COFFEE FARMS

Notable among the island's coffee farms is the **Kona Blue Sky Coffee Company,** in Holualoa (© 877/322-1700 or 808/322-1700), which handles its own beans exclusively. The Christian Twigg-Smith family and staff grow, hand-pick, sun-dry, roast, grind, and sell their coffee, whole or ground.

Also in Holualoa, 10 minutes above Kailua-Kona, **Holualoa Kona Coffee Company** (© 800/334-0348 or 808/322-9937) purveys organic Kona: unsprayed, hand-picked, sun-dried, and carefully roasted. You can witness the hulling, sorting, roasting, and packaging of beans on a farm tour, Monday through Friday from 8am to 4pm.

In Waimea, the **Waimea Coffee Company,** Parker Square, Highway 19 (© 808/885-4472), a deli/coffee farm/retail operation, is a whirl of activity. Coffee is heady stuff here: pure Kona from Rooster Farms, pure organic from Sakamoto Estate—an impressive selection of the island's best estate-grown coffees.

THE BIG ISLAND AFTER DARK

The **Kona Village Luau,** Kona Village Resort (© 808/325-5555), the longest continuously running luau on the island, is still the best—a combination of an authentic Polynesian venue with a menu that works, impressive entertainment, and the spirit of Old Hawaii. Reservations are required. The cost is $76 adults, $46 children 6 to 12, $22 children 2 to 5.

Our favorite nightspot on the Kohala Coast is the **Honu Bar** (© 808/885-6622) at the Mauna Lani Bay Hotel, a sleek, chic place for light supper, live light jazz with dancing, gourmet desserts, fine wines, and after-dinner drinks. You can order toothsome pastas and light suppers with fine wines by the glass when most other restaurants are closing.

4 Kauai

Aloof and beautiful, Kauai is one of the world's most spectacular islands. All the elements are here: moody rainforests, majestic cliffs, jagged peaks, emerald valleys, palm trees swaying in the breeze, daily rainbows, and some of the most amazing golden beaches you'll find anywhere. This is the place for active visitors, with watersports galore, miles of trails through rainforests and along ocean cliffs, and a range of golf courses, from championship links to funky local courses.

ESSENTIALS

GETTING THERE   United Airlines (© 800/225-5825; www.ual.com) offers direct service to Kauai, with daily flights from Los Angeles. **Pleasant Hawaiian Holidays** (© 800/742-9244; www.pleasantholidays.com), one of Hawaii's largest travel companies offering low-cost airfare and package deals, has two weekly non-stop flights from Los Angeles and San Francisco using American Trans Air. All other airlines land in Honolulu, where you'll have to connect to a 30-minute interisland flight to Kauai's Lihue Airport. **Aloha Airlines** (© 800/367-5250, 808/245-3691, or 808/484-1111; www.alohaair.com) and **Hawaiian Airlines** (© 800/367-5320, 808/245-1813, or 808/838-1555; www.hawaiianair.com) both offer jet service at least every hour to Lihue. As we went to press, there was talk about a merger between Aloha and Hawaiian Airlines.

VISITOR INFORMATION   Contact the **Kauai Visitors Bureau,** Watumull Plaza, 4334 Rice St., Ste. 101, Lihue, HI 96766 (© 808/245-3971; fax 808/246-9235; www.kauaivisitorsbureau.org). For a free *Kauai Vacation Planner* or recorded information, call © 800/262-1400. The **Poipu Beach Resort Association,** P.O. Box 730, Koloa, HI 96756 (© 888/744-0888 or 808/742-7444; http://poipu-beach.org), can send you a free guide to the Poipu Beach area.

GETTING AROUND   You need a car to see and do everything on Kauai. All the major rental agencies have desks at the airport. For deep discounts on weekly rates, call **Hookipa Haven Vacation Services** (© 800/398-6284; www.hookipa.com). **Kauai Taxi Company** (© 808/246-9554) offers taxi and airport shuttle service.

FAST FACTS   **Wilcox Health System,** 3420 Kuhio Hwy., Lihue (© 808/245-1100), has 24-hour emergency care. Walk-ins are accepted at **Kauai Medical Clinic,** 3–3420 Kuhio Hwy., Ste. B, Lihue (© 808/245-1500); and at **Koloa Clinic,** 5371 Koloa Rd. (© 808/742-1621).

Although Kauai is generally safe, guard against rental-car break-ins. Never leave any valuables in your car, not even in your trunk. Be especially leery of high-risk areas, such as Polihale State Park.

BEACHES

For beach toys and equipment, head to **Activity Warehouse,** 788 Kuhio Hwy., Kapaa (© 808/822-4000), or **Chris The Fun Lady,** 4–746 Kuhio Hwy., Kapaa (© 808/822-7759; www.christhefunlady.com).

LIHUE   Any town would kill to have **Kalapaki Beach,** one of Kauai's best, in its backyard. This graceful half-moon of golden sand sits at the foot of the Marriott Resort & Beach Club; the waters are safe for swimmers, and good for surfing when there's a winter swell. The view of the steepled peaks of the majestic Haupu Ridge is awesome.

THE POIPU RESORT AREA Two-mile-long **Mahaulepu Beach** is the best-looking unspoiled beach on Kauai. Its reddish-gold, grainy sand lines the southeastern shore at the foot of Haupu Ridge. Mahaulepu is a great escape from the real world, ideal for beachcombing and shell hunting. Swimming can be risky, except in the reef-sheltered shallows 200 yards west of the parking lot. There's no lifeguard or facilities.

Big, wide **Poipu Beach Park** is two beaches in one, divided by a sandbar. On the left, a lava-rock jetty protects a sandy-bottom pool that's perfect for kids; on the right, the open bay attracts swimmers, snorkelers, and surfers. The swimming is excellent, with small tide pools for exploring and great reefs for snorkeling and diving.

WESTERN KAUAI Hawaii's biggest beach is **Polihale State Park,** a wonderful place to get away from it all. Seventeen miles of golden sands are wrapped around Kauai's northwestern shore. Be careful in winter, when high surf and rip currents make swimming dangerous. The safest spot is Queen's Pond, a shallow, sandy-bottom inlet protected from waves.

THE COCONUT COAST The popular 1-acre **Lydgate State Park,** 5 miles north of Lihue on Kuhio Highway (Hwy. 56), has a rock-wall fishpond that blunts the open ocean waves and provides the only safe swimming and the best snorkeling on the eastern shore. It's a great place for a picnic, kite flying, or just a lazy day at the shore.

THE NORTH SHORE **Anini Beach County Park** is Kauai's safest beach for swimming and windsurfing. This 3-mile-long, gold-sand beach is shielded from the open ocean by the longest reef in Hawaii. It's the best snorkel spot, even for beginners, on the northwest side. A channel in the reef with a 60-foot drop attracts divers.

At beautiful **Hanalei Beach,** gentle waves roll across the face of half-moon Hanalei Bay, running up to the wide, golden sand; sheer volcanic ridges rise to 4,000 feet on the other side, 3 miles inland. Swimming is excellent year-round; the water's also great for bodyboarding, surfing, fishing, windsurfing, and kayaking.

Postcard-perfect, gold-sand **Tunnels Beach** is excellent for swimming nearly year-round and is safe for snorkeling, since it's protected by a fringing coral reef (the waters can get rough in winter, though). Around the corner, **Haena Beach Park** offers grainy, golden sand, excellent swimming in summer, and great snorkeling. Stay out of the water in winter, however.

Tiny reddish-gold **Kee** (*Kay*-ay) **Beach State Park,** on a reef-protected cove at the foot of fluted volcanic cliffs, is almost too beautiful to be real. Swimming and snorkeling are safe inside the reef, but dangerous outside.

HITTING THE WATER

BOATING One of Hawaii's most spectacular natural attractions is Kauai's **Na Pali Coast.** Unless you're willing to make the arduous hike in, there are only two ways to see it: by helicopter (see "Na Pali Coast State Park," below) or by boat.

When the humpback whales make their annual visit to Hawaii from Alaska from December to March, they swim right by Kauai. In season, most boats on Kauai, including sailboats and Zodiacs, combine whale-watching with their regular adventures.

For snorkel/picnic trips, sunset cruises, Na Pali Coast excursions (including snorkeling stops), and other options, try **Captain Andy's Sailing Adventures** (© 808/335-6833; www.capt andys.com) or **Bluewater Sailing** (© 808/828-1142; www.sail-kauai.com).

Liko Kauai Cruises (© 888/SEA-LIKO or 808/338-0333; www.liko-kauai.com) offers a 4½-hour combination Na Pali Coast tour/deep-sea fishing/whale-watching extravaganza with lunch. In addition to seeing whales, you'll glimpse sea caves, waterfalls, lush valleys, and miles of white-sand beaches, with stops for snorkeling.

BODYBOARDING (BOOGIE BOARDING) & BODYSURFING The best beaches for bodysurfing and boogie boarding are **Kalapaki Beach** and **Poipu Beach.** You can rent boogie boards at **Activity Warehouse,** 788 Kuhio Hwy., Kapaa (© 800/343-2087).

KAYAKING Kauai is made for kayaking. You can take the **Huleia River** into Huleia National Wildlife Refuge, the last stand of Kauai's endangered birds, or just go out and paddle around **Hanalei Bay.** The adventurous can try the Na Pali Coast, with majestic cliffs, open-ocean conditions, and monster waves. The cheapest equipment rentals are at **Activity Warehouse,** 788 Kuhio Hwy., Kapaa (© 800/343-2087).

Kayak Kauai Outbound (© 800/437-3507 or 808/826-9844; www.kayak kauai.com) offers rentals and a range of tours. The shop's experts will be happy to take you on a guided trip or tell you where to go on your own.

SCUBA DIVING Diving on Kauai is dictated by the weather. In winter, when heavy swells and high winds hit the island, it's generally limited to the more protected South Shore. The **Caverns,** off the Poipu Beach resort area, consist of a series of lava tubes that are usually filled with marine life. Head to **Tortugas** (off Poipu Beach Park) to catch a glimpse of sea turtles.

In summer, the magnificent North Shore opens up, and you can take a boat dive locally known as the **Oceanarium,** northwest of Hanalei Bay, where you'll find a kaleidoscopic marine world in a horseshoe-shaped cove. Also try Kee Beach/Haena Beach Park, Tunnels Beach, and Cannons Beach.

You can rent equipment at **Fathom Five Adventures,** 3450 Poipu Rd., Koloa (© 808/742-6991). They also offer boat dives on the south side of the island.

Since the best dives are offshore, we suggest booking a two-tank dive off a dive boat. **Bubbles Below Scuba Charters,** 6251 Hauaala Rd., Kapaa (© 808/822-3483; www.aloha.net/~kaimanu), specializes in highly personalized, small group dives, with an emphasis on marine biology.

SNORKELING Kauai has lots of inshore reefs to make snorkelers happy. Try the reef off **Kee Beach/Haena State Park,** at the end of Highway 560; the wide reef at **Tunnels Beach** (but be sure to check ocean conditions first); **Anini Beach's** safe, shallow area; or **Poipu Beach Park,** on the right side of Nukumoi Point. **Salt Pond Beach Park,** off Highway 50 near Hanapepe, has good snorkeling around the two rocky points, home to hundreds of tropical fish.

Snorkel Bob's, 4-734 Kuhio Hwy., Kapaa (© 808/823-9433), and 3236 Poipu Rd., near Poipu Beach (© 808/742-2206), rents complete snorkel sets.

SURFING **Hanalei Bay's** winter surf is the most popular on the island, but it's for experts only. **Poipu Beach** is an excellent spot to learn to surf; the waves are small and nobody laughs when you wipe out. Check with the local surf shops or phone the **Weather** (© 808/245-3564) to find out where surf's up.

Lessons are available from **Windsurf Kauai,** Hanalei (© **808/828-6838**). Poipu is also the site of numerous surfing schools; the best is **Margo Oberg's School of Surfing,** at Nuku Moi Surf Shop, across from Brennecke's Beach (© **808/742-8019**).

Equipment is available for rent at **Nukumoi Surf Shop,** across from Brennecke's Beach, Poipu (© **888/384-8810** or 808/742-8019); **Hanalei Surf Co.,** 5–5161 Kuhio Hwy., Hanalei (© **808/826-9000**); and **Activity Warehouse,** 788 Kuhio Hwy., Kapaa (© **808/822-4000**).

WAIMEA CANYON & KOKEE STATE PARK

The great gaping gulch known as Waimea Canyon is quite a sight. This valley, known for its reddish lava beds, reminds everyone of the Grand Canyon. Kauai's version is bursting with ever-changing color, just like its namesake, but it's smaller—only a mile wide, 3,567 feet deep, and 12 miles long.

From the coastal road (Hwy. 50), turn up Waimea Canyon Drive (Hwy. 550) at Waimea town, or pass through Waimea and turn up Kokee Road (Hwy. 55) at Kekaha. The climb is very steep from Kekaha, but Waimea Canyon Drive, the rim road, is narrower and rougher. A few miles up, the roads merge into Kokee Road.

It's only 16 miles from Waimea to **Kokee State Park,** but it's a whole different world, for the park is 4,345 acres of rainforest. You'll enter a new climate zone, where the breeze has a bite and trees look quite Continental. You're in a cloud forest on the edge of the Alakai Swamp, on the summit plateau of Kauai. There's lots to see and do here: Anglers fly-fish for rainbow trout, while hikers tackle the 45 trails that lace the swamp. That's a lot of ground to cover, so you might want to stay over; the **Kokee Lodge** (© **808/335-6061**) has 12 cabins and a restaurant.

In the park is the **Kokee Natural History Museum** (© **808/335-9975;** open daily 10am–4pm). This is the best place to learn about the forest and swamp before you set off hiking in the wilds. The shop has great trail information, including the official park trail map (50¢). For information, contact the **State Division of Parks,** P.O. Box 1671, Lihue, HI 96766 (© **808/335-5871**), and the **Kokee Lodge Manager,** P.O. Box 819, Waimea, HI 96796 (© **808/335-6061**).

A **nature walk** with 35 native plants and trees is the best mini-intro to this rainforest; it starts behind the museum at the rare Hawaiian koa tree. This easy, self-guided walk of about one-tenth of a mile takes about 20 minutes if you stop and look at all the plants; they're identified along the way.

Two miles above Kokee Lodge is **Kalalau Lookout,** the spectacular climax of your drive through Waimea Canyon and Kokee. The view is breathtaking, especially when light and cloud shadows play across the red-and-orange cliffs.

PARADISE FOUND: ON THE ROAD TO THE NORTH SHORE

The drive to Hanalei along Kuhio Highway (Hwy. 56, which becomes Hwy. 560) displays Kauai's grandeur at its best. Just before Kilauea, the last signs of development give way to fruit stands, a little stone church, waterfalls, and a green river valley.

Stop off in Kilauea at the **Guava Kai Plantation,** at the end of Kuawa Road (© **808/828-6121**), for a refreshing, free treat. Walk through the orchards, then sample some guava juice; open daily from 9am to 5pm.

Birders might want to stop at **Kilauea Point National Wildlife Refuge**, 1 mile north of Kilauea, and **Hanalei National Wildlife Refuge**, along Ohiki Road, at the west end of the Hanalei River Bridge.

The coastal highway now heads due west; the showy ridgelines of Mount Namahana create a grand amphitheater. Five miles past Kilauea, just past the Princeville Shopping Center, is **Hanalei Valley Lookout.** Peer over the edge into the 917-acre Hanalei River Valley, catch the first sight of taro growing in irrigated ponds, and maybe see an endangered Hawaiian black-necked stilt.

Farther along, a hairpin turn offers another scenic look at Hanalei town; then you cross the **Hanalei Bridge,** erected in 1912 and now a National Historic Landmark.

Drive slowly past the **Hanalei River banks** and Bill Mowry's **Hanalei Buffalo Ranch,** where 200 American bison roam in the tropic sun.

Just past Tahiti Nui, turn right on Aku Road before Ching Young Village, then take a right on Weke Road to gorgeous **Hanalei Beach Park.** Swimming is excellent here year-round.

Head down the highway for 7 more miles of spectacular beaches, including **Lumahai Beach, Tunnels Beach,** and **Haena Beach Park.** Stick around until sundown, then head to one of the North Shore's restaurants for a mai tai and a fresh seafood dinner.

The real Hawaii begins where the road stops: At the end of Highway 56, the spectacular **Na Pali Coast** begins.

NA PALI COAST STATE PARK

The Na Pali Coast, a 22-mile stretch of fluted cliffs that wrap around the northwest shore of Kauai, is the most beautiful part of Hawaii. Hanging valleys open like green velvet accordions, and waterfalls tumble to the sea from 4,120-foot-high cliffs; the spatial experience is exhilarating and humbling. Be sure to see this park.

Unless you fly or boat in (see "Hitting the Water," above), the park is accessible only on foot—and it's not easy. An ancient footpath, the **Kalalau Trail,** winds through the park to Kalalau Valley. The hike is grueling and takes most people 6 to 8 hours one-way. The park is open on a limited basis, and you must have a permit (but you can hike the first 2 miles, to Hanakapiai Beach, without one). Free permits are issued in person at the **Kauai State Parks Office,** 3060 Eiwa St., Lihue (© **808/274-3444**). For more information, contact **Hawaii State Department of Land and Natural Resources,** 1151 Punchbowl St., Room 130, Honolulu, HI 96813 (© **808/587-0320**).

Seeing Na Pali and the rest of Kauai from a helicopter is expensive but worth the splurge. **Island Helicopters** (© **800/829-5999** or 808/245-8588; www.islandhelicopters.com) offers 1-hour island tours for $204, including a free video of your trip; mention *Frommer's* for a discount.

WHERE TO STAY
THE POIPU RESORT AREA

The casually elegant **Hyatt Regency Kauai Resort & Spa,** 1571 Poipu Rd., Koloa (© **800/55-HYATT** or 808/742-1234; www.kauai-hyatt.com), is one of Hawaii's best luxury hotels. Built into the oceanside bluffs, it spreads over 50 acres that overlook Shipwreck Beach (which is too rough for most swimmers). The large rooms have private lanais; most have ocean views. The ANARA Spa is 25,000 square feet of pampering facilities. Other extras include an elaborate freshwater fantasy-pool complex, saltwater swimming lagoons, tennis courts, bicycles, golf at Poipu Bay Resort Course, watersports, nearby horseback riding, restaurants, a kids' program, and activities ranging from dune walks with a naturalist to hula performances.

The **Sheraton Kauai Resort,** 2440 Hoonani Rd., Koloa (© **800/782-9488** or 808/742-1661; www.sheraton-kauai.com), has a dynamite location on one of Kauai's best beaches. Spacious rooms are housed in three buildings: one nestled in tropical gardens; one facing the white-sand beach; and one looking across green grass to the ocean. Guests enjoy restaurants, room service, an activities desk, three pools (including an oceanfront pool with a water playground), a spa, tennis courts, massage, golf, and a children's program in summer.

For the deal of the decade, consider **Nihi Kai Villas,** 1870 Hoone Rd., c/o Grantham Resorts, Koloa (© **800/325-5701** or 808/742-2000; www.poipu accommodations.com). If you stay 7 nights, the rates for these large, two-bedroom units just 200 yards from the beach start at an unbelievable $111 a night (for six). You'll get a clean, well-cared-for unit with a full kitchen, washer/dryer, and TV/VCR. The sofa bed in the living room allows you to comfortably sleep six. The property is a 2-minute walk from world-famous Brennecke's Beach (great for bodysurfing) and a block from Poipu Beach Park. On-site amenities include an oceanfront swimming pool, tennis and paddle courts, and a barbecue and picnic area.

Another affordable option is the quiet, upscale **Poipu Kapili Resort,** 2221 Kapili Rd., Koloa (© **800/443-7714** or 808/742-6449; www.poipukapili.com), an oceanfront cluster of condos that's outstanding in every way but one: The nearest sandy beach is a block away, but the Pacific is right out your window. The units are spacious and have full kitchens and private lanais; guests also enjoy a pool, barbecues, and tennis courts.

THE COCONUT COAST

The **Kauai Coconut Beach Resort,** Kapaa (© **800/22-ALOHA** or 808/822-3455; www.kcb.com), is the only full-service oceanfront resort on this stretch of the coast. It offers an excellent deal for families: Children under 17 stay free, and those 11 and under eat free when dining with an adult. Set on 10½ acres in front of Waipouli Beach, next to the Coconut Marketplace, it's centrally located for shops, restaurants, and great golf. The large rooms have lanais. Guests enjoy a restaurant, room service, a nightly luau, a pool, a whirlpool, tennis courts, a children's program in summer, an activities desk, a nightly torch-lighting ceremony, and frequent Hawaiian demonstrations.

Located right on the ocean, the spacious one-bedroom apartments at **Wailua Bayview,** 320 Papaloa Rd., Kapaa (© **800/882-9007;** www.wailuabay.com), offer excellent value for the price. All units have full kitchens, washer/dryers, and large lanais, and there's a communal pool and barbecue area.

THE NORTH SHORE

The **Princeville Resort Kauai,** 5520 Kahaku Rd., Princeville (© **800/826-4400** or 808/826-9644; www.princeville.com), set between Hanalei Bay and Kauai's mountains, is near outstanding surfing and windsurfing areas and a wonderful reef for snorkeling. The opulent rooms have no lanais, but oversize windows allow you to admire what has to be the most dramatic vista from any hotel in the state. Amenities include restaurants, room service, a cultural program, two top-ranked golf courses designed by Robert Trent Jones, Jr., 25 tennis courts, a pool, whirlpools, shops, a business center, riding stables, an in-house cinema, and a first-rate health club and spa.

At **Hanalei Colony Resort,** 5–7130 Kuhio Hwy., Hanalei (☎ **800/628-3004** or 808/826-6235; www.hcr.com), a perfect white-sand beach is just steps from your door, while lush gardens and jagged mountain peaks serve as a backdrop. Each spacious unit has a private lanai and full kitchen. The atmosphere is quiet and relaxing: no TVs, stereos, or phones. Guests enjoy a pool, a spa, barbecue and picnic areas, free beach mats and beach towels, a lending library, and children's toys and games.

WHERE TO DINE
LIHUE & ENVIRONS

It's hard to go wrong at **Duke's Canoe Club,** Kauai Marriott & Beach Club, 3610 Rice St., Nawiliwili (☎ **808/246-9599**). This oceanfront oasis is the hippest spot in town, with a winning combination of great view, affordable menu, attractive salad bar, popular music, and very happy happy hour. Most people go for the five or six varieties of fresh catch a night, served in several different preparations.

Hamura's Saimin Stand, 2956 Kress St., Lihue (☎ **808/245-3271**), is a cultural experience, where fans line up to take their place over steaming bowls of this island specialty at a few U-shaped counters. The saimin and teriyaki barbecue sticks attract an all-day, late-night, pre- and post-movie crowd.

THE COCONUT COAST

A Pacific Café Kauai, Kauai Shopping Village, 4–831 Kuhio Hwy., Kapaa (☎ **808/822-0013**), is the hub of dining on Kauai—casual, chic, crowded, and buzzing with energy. Here you'll find light-as-air, deep-fried tiger-eye sushi with wasabi beurre blanc, wok-charred mahi-mahi with garlic-sesame crust and lime-ginger-butter sauce, scallop ravioli in lime-ginger sauce, and firecracker salmon. There are always ample appetizers in all price ranges, making this a restaurant that can be expensive but doesn't have to be.

Caffè Coco, 4–369 Kuhio Hwy., Wailua (☎ **808/822-7990**), gets our vote for the most charming ambience on Kauai. The food is excellent, with vegetarian and healthy delights such as roast veggie omelets and spiced ahi focaccia sandwiches. Service can be, to say the least, laid-back.

THE NORTH SHORE

La Cascata, Princeville Resort, 5520 Ka Haku Rd. (☎ **808/826-9644**), is sumptuous—a Sicilian spree in Eden. Try to get here before dark, so you can enjoy the views of Bali Hai, the persimmon-colored sunset, and the waterfalls of Waialeale, all an integral part of the feast. The menu dazzles quietly with its organic arugula salad with pears, Gorgonzola, and walnut vinaigrette (sensational); or sautéed Kona lobster on linguine, with scallops and other seafood.

Appendix A:
Useful Toll-Free Numbers
& Websites

AIRLINES

Aer Lingus
✆ 800/474-7424 in the U.S.
✆ 01/886-8888 in Ireland
www.aerlingus.com

Air Canada
✆ 888/247-2262
www.aircanada.ca

Air New Zealand
✆ 800/262-1234 or -2468 in the U.S.
✆ 800/663-5494 in Canada
✆ 0800/737-767 in New Zealand
www.airnewzealand.com

Airtran Airlines
✆ 800/247-8726
www.airtran.com

Alaska Airlines
✆ 800/426-0333
www.alaskaair.com

American Airlines
✆ 800/433-7300
www.aa.com

American Trans Air
✆ 800/225-2995
www.ata.com

America West Airlines
✆ 800/235-9292
www.americawest.com

British Airways
✆ 800/247-9297
✆ 0345/222-111 or
0845/77-333-77 in Britain
www.british-airways.com

Continental Airlines
✆ 800/525-0280
www.continental.com

Delta Air Lines
✆ 800/221-1212
www.delta.com

Frontier Airlines
✆ 800/432-1359
www.frontierairlines.com

Hawaiian Airlines
✆ 800/367-5320
www.hawaiianair.com

Jet Blue Airlines
✆ 800/538-2583
www.jetblue.com

Midwest Express
✆ 800/452-2022
www.midwestexpress.com

Northwest Airlines
✆ 800/225-2525
www.nwa.com

Qantas
✆ 800/227-4500 in the U.S.
✆ 612/9691-3636 in Australia
www.qantas.com

Southwest Airlines
✆ 800/435-9792
www.southwest.com

United Airlines
✆ 800/241-6522
www.united.com

US Airways
✆ 800/428-4322
www.usairways.com

Virgin Atlantic Airways
✆ 800/862-8621 in continental U.S.
✆ 0293/747-747 in Britain
www.virgin-atlantic.com

CAR-RENTAL AGENCIES

Advantage
© 800/777-5500
www.advantagerentacar.com

Alamo
© 800/327-9633
www.goalamo.com

Auto Europe
© 800/223-5555
www.autoeurope.com

Avis
© 800/331-1212 in continental U.S.
© 800/TRY-AVIS in Canada
www.avis.com

Budget
© 800/527-0700
https://rent.drivebudget.com

Dollar
© 800/800-4000
www.dollar.com

Enterprise
© 800/325-8007
www.enterprise.com

Hertz
© 800/654-3131
www.hertz.com

Kemwel Holiday Auto (KHA)
© 800/678-0678
www.kemwel.com

National
© 800/CAR-RENT
www.nationalcar.com

Payless
© 800/PAYLESS
www.paylesscarrental.com

Rent-A-Wreck
© 800/535-1391
www.rentawreck.com

Thrifty
© 800/367-2277
www.thrifty.com

MAJOR HOTEL & MOTEL CHAINS

Baymont Inns & Suites
© 800/301-0200
www.baymontinns.com

Best Western International
© 800/528-1234
www.bestwestern.com

Clarion Hotels
© 800/CLARION
www.clarionhotel.com or
www.hotelchoice.com

Comfort Inns
© 800/228-5150
www.hotelchoice.com

Courtyard by Marriott
© 800/321-2211
www.courtyard.com or
www.marriott.com

Days Inn
© 800/325-2525
www.daysinn.com

Doubletree Hotels
© 800/222-TREE
www.doubletree.com

Econo Lodges
© 800/55-ECONO
www.hotelchoice.com

Fairfield Inn by Marriott
© 800/228-2800
www.marriott.com

Hampton Inn
© 800/HAMPTON
www.hampton-inn.com

Hilton Hotels
© 800/HILTONS
www.hilton.com

Holiday Inn
© 800/HOLIDAY
www.basshotels.com

Howard Johnson
© 800/654-2000
www.hojo.com

Hyatt Hotels & Resorts
✆ 800/228-9000
www.hyatt.com

Inter-Continental Hotels & Resorts
✆ 888/567-8725
www.interconti.com

ITT Sheraton
✆ 800/325-3535
www.starwood.com

Knights Inn
✆ 800/843-5644
www.knghtsinn.com

La Quinta Motor Inns
✆ 800/531-5900
www.laquinta.com

Marriott Hotels
✆ 800/228-9290
www.marriott.com

Microtel Inn & Suites
✆ 888/771-7171
www.microtelinn.com

Motel 6
✆ 800/4-MOTEL6
www.motel6.com

Quality Inns
✆ 800/228-5151
www.hotelchoice.com

Radisson Hotels International
✆ 800/333-3333
www.radisson.com

Ramada Inns
✆ 800/2-RAMADA
www.ramada.com

Red Carpet Inns
✆ 800/251-1962
www.reservahost.com

Red Lion Hotels & Inns
✆ 800/547-8010
www.redlion.com

Red Roof Inns
✆ 800/843-7663
www.redroof.com

Residence Inn by Marriott
✆ 800/331-3131
www.marriott.com

Rodeway Inns
✆ 800/228-2000
www.hotelchoice.com

Sheraton Hotels & Resorts
✆ 800/325-3535
www.sheraton.com

Sleep Inn
✆ 800/753-3746
www.sleepinn.com

Super 8 Motels
✆ 800/800-8000
www.super8.com

Travelodge
✆ 800/255-3050
www.travelodge.com

Vagabond Inns
✆ 800/522-1555
www.vagabondinn.com

Westin Hotels & Resorts
✆ 800/937-8461
www.westin.com

Wyndham Hotels and Resorts
✆ 800/822-4200
in continental U.S. and Canada
www.wyndham.com

Appendix B:
State Tourism Offices

**Alabama Bureau of Tourism
& Travel**
P.O. Box 4927
Montgomery, AL 36103-4927
© 800/ALABAMA
© 334/242-4169
www.touralabama.org

Alaska Division of Tourism
P.O. Box 110801
Juneau, AK 99811-0801
© 800/865-5275
© 907/465 2012
www.travelalaska.com

Arizona Office of Tourism
2702 N. 3rd St., Ste. 4015
Phoenix, AZ 85004
© 888/520-3433
www.arizonaguide.com

**Arkansas Department of
Parks & Tourism**
1 Capitol Mall
Little Rock, AR 72201
© 800/NATURAL
© 501/682-7777
www.arkansas.com

California Division of Tourism
P.O. Box 1499
Sacramento, CA 95812-1499
© 800/GO-CALIF
www.gocalif.ca.gov

Colorado Tourism Office
1625 Broadway, Ste. 1700
Denver, CO 80202
© 800/COLORADO
www.colorado.com

Connecticut Office of Tourism
Department of Economic and
Community Development
505 Hudson St.
Hartford, CT 06106
© 800/CT-BOUND
© 860/270-8080
www.ctbound.org

Delaware Tourism Office
99 King's Hwy.
Dover, DE 19901
© 800/441-8846
© 302/739-4271
www.visitdelaware.net

**D.C. Convention & Tourism
Corporation**
1212 New York Ave. NW
Ste. 600
Washington, DC 20005
© 800/422-8644
www.washington.org

Visit Florida
661 E. Jefferson St.
Tallahassee, FL 32301
© 888/7-FLA-USA
www.flausa.com

**Georgia Department of Industry,
Trade & Tourism**
Box 1776, Dept. TIA
Atlanta, GA 30301
© 800/VISIT-GA
© 404/656-3590
www.georgia.org

**Hawaii Visitors & Convention
Bureau**
2270 Kalakaua Ave., Ste. 801
Honolulu, HI 96815
© 800/353-4856
www.visit.hawaii.org

Idaho Department of Commerce
700 W. State St.
Boise, ID 83720
© 800/842-5858
© 208/334-2470
www.visitid.org

Illinois Bureau of Tourism
100 W. Randolph, Ste. 3-400
Chicago, IL 60602
© 800/2-CONNECT
© 312/814-4732
www.enjoyillinois.com

**Indiana Department of
Commerce/Tourism**
1 N. Capitol, Ste. 700
Indianapolis, IN 46204
© 888/ENJOY-IN
www.in.gov/enjoyindiana

Iowa Division of Tourism
200 E. Grand Ave.
Des Moines, IA 50309
© 888/472-6035
© 515/242-4705
www.traveliowa.com

Kansas Travel & Tourism Division
700 SW Harrison, Ste. 1300
Topeka, KS 66603-3712
© 800/2-KANSAS
www.travelks.com

**Kentucky Department of
Travel Development**
500 Mero St., Ste. 2200
Frankfort, KY 40601
© 800/225-8747
© 502/564-4930
www.kentuckytourism.com

Louisiana Office of Tourism
P.O. Box 94291
Baton Rouge, LA 70804
© 800/677-4082
© 225/342-8100
www.louisianatravel.com

Maine Office of Tourism
59 State House Station
Augusta, ME 04033
© 888/882-6345
www.visitmaine.com

**Maryland Office of Tourism
Development**
217 E. Redwood St., 9th Floor
Baltimore, MD 21202
© 800/MDISFUN
www.mdisfun.org

**Massachusetts Office of
Travel & Tourism**
State Transportation Building
10 Park Plaza, Ste. 4510
Boston, MA 02116
© 800/227-MASS
www.massvacation.com

Travel Michigan
P.O. Box 26128
Lansing, MI 48909-6128
© 888/78-GREAT
http://travel.michigan.org

Minnesota Office of Tourism
121 Seventh Place E.
St. Paul, MN 55101
© 800/657-3700
© 651/296-5029
www.exploreminnesota.com

**Mississippi Division of Tourism
Development**
P.O. Box 849
Jackson, MS 39205
© 800/927-6378
© 601/359-3297
www.visitmississippi.org

Missouri Division of Tourism
Box 1055, Dept. TIA
Jefferson City, MO 65102
© 800/810-5510
© 573/751-4133
www.missouritourism.org

Travel Montana
301 S. Park
P.O. Box 200533
Helena, MT 59620
© 800/VISIT-MT
© 406/841-2870
http://visitmt.com

Nebraska Division of Tourism & Travel
P.O. Box 98907
Lincoln, NE 68509-8907
℡ 877/NEBRASKA
www.visitnebraska.org

Nevada Commission on Tourism
401 N. Carson St.
Carson City, NV 89701
℡ 800/NEVADA-8
℡ 775/687-4322
www.travelnevada.com

New Hampshire Office of Travel & Tourism
172 Pembroke Rd.
P.O. Box 1856
Concord, NH 03302-1856
℡ 800/386-4664
www.visitnh.gov

New Jersey Division of Travel & Tourism
20 W. State St., P.O. Box 820
Trenton, NJ 08625-0820
℡ 800/VISITNJ
℡ 609/777-0885
www.visitnj.org

New Mexico Department of Tourism
491 Old Santa Fe Trail
Santa Fe, NM 87501
℡ 800/773-6396 ext. 0643
℡ 505/827-7400
www.newmexico.org

New York State Travel Information Center
P.O. Box 2603
Albany, NY 12220
℡ 800/CALL-NYS
℡ 518/474-4116
www.iloveny.com

North Carolina Division of Travel & Tourism
301 N. Wilmington St.
Raleigh, NC 27601
℡ 800/VISIT-NC
www.visitnc.com

North Dakota Tourism Division
400 E. Broadway, Ste. 50
Bismarck, ND 58501
℡ 800/HELLO-ND
www.ndtourism.com

Ohio Division of Travel & Tourism
P.O. Box 1001
Columbus, OH 43216-1001
℡ 800/BUCKEYE
www.ohiotourism.com

Oklahoma Travel & Tourism Division
P.O. Box 52002
Oklahoma City, OK 73152
℡ 800/652-6552
℡ 405/521-2406
www.travelok.com

Oregon Tourism Commission
775 Summer St. NE
Salem, OR 97301-1282
℡ 800/547-7842
℡ 503/986-0000
www.traveloregon.com

Pennsylvania Tourism Marketing Office
400 North St., 4th Floor
Harrisburg, PA 17120-0225
℡ 800/237-4363
℡ 717/787-5453
www.experiencepa.com

Rhode Island Tourism Division
1 W. Exchange St.
Providence, RI 02903
℡ 800/556-2484
℡ 401/222-2601
www.visitrhodeisland.com

South Carolina Department of Parks, Recreation, and Tourism
1205 Pendleton St.
Columbia, SC 29201
℡ 888/SC-SMILES
www.travelsc.com

South Dakota Department of Tourism
711 E. Wells Ave.
Pierre, SD 57501-5070
© 800/SDAKOTA
© 605/773-3301
www.travelsd.com

Tennessee Department of Tourism Development
320 6th Ave. N.
Racheal Jackson Building, 5th Floor
Nashville, TN 37243
© 800/GO-2-TENN
© 615/741-2159
www.tnvacation.com

Texas Department of Commerce, Tourist Division
P.O. Box 12728
Austin, TX 78711
© 800/888-8TEX
© 800/452-9292
www.traveltex.com

Utah Travel Council
Council Hall
300 N. State St.
Salt Lake City, UT 84114
© 800/200-1160
© 801/538-1030
www.utah.com

Vermont Department of Tourism
6 Baldwin St., Drawer 33
Montpelier, VT 05633-1301
© 800/VERMONT
www.travel-vermont.com

Virginia Tourism Corporation
901 E. Byrd St.
Richmond, VA 23219
© 800/321-3244
www.virginia.org

Washington State Tourism
P.O. Box 42500
Olympia, WA 98504-2500
© 360/725-5052
www.tourism.wa.gov

West Virginia Division of Tourism
90 MacCorkle Ave. SW
South Charleston, WV 25303
© 800/CALL-WVA
© 304/558-2200
www.callwva.com

Wisconsin Division of Tourism
201 W. Washington Ave.
P.O. Box 7976
Madison, WI 53707
Out-of-state: © 800/432-TRIP
© 608/266-2161
www.travelwisconsin.com

Wyoming Tourism
I-25 at College Drive, Dept. WY
Cheyenne, WY 82002
© 800/225-5996
© 307/777-7777
www.wyomingtourism.org

Index

FROMMER'S® COMPLETE TRAVEL GUIDES

Alaska
Alaska Cruises & Ports of Call
Amsterdam
Argentina & Chile
Arizona
Atlanta
Australia
Austria
Bahamas
Barcelona, Madrid & Seville
Beijing
Belgium, Holland & Luxembourg
Bermuda
Boston
Brazil
British Columbia & the Canadian
   Rockies
Budapest & the Best of Hungary
California
Canada
Cancún, Cozumel & the Yucatán
Cape Cod, Nantucket & Martha's
   Vineyard
Caribbean
Caribbean Cruises & Ports of Call
Caribbean Ports of Call
Carolinas & Georgia
Chicago
China
Colorado
Costa Rica
Denmark
Denver, Boulder & Colorado
   Springs
England
Europe
European Cruises & Ports of Call
Florida

France
Germany
Great Britain
Greece
Greek Islands
Hawaii
Hong Kong
Honolulu, Waikiki & Oahu
Ireland
Israel
Italy
Jamaica
Japan
Las Vegas
London
Los Angeles
Maryland & Delaware
Maui
Mexico
Montana & Wyoming
Montréal & Québec City
Munich & the Bavarian Alps
Nashville & Memphis
Nepal
New England
New Mexico
New Orleans
New York City
New Zealand
Northern Italy
Nova Scotia, New Brunswick &
   Prince Edward Island
Oregon
Paris
Philadelphia & the Amish Country
Portugal
Prague & the Best of the Czech
   Republic

Provence & the Riviera
Puerto Rico
Rome
San Antonio & Austin
San Diego
San Francisco
Santa Fe, Taos & Albuquerque
Scandinavia
Scotland
Seattle & Portland
Shanghai
Singapore & Malaysia
South Africa
South America
South Florida
South Pacific
Southeast Asia
Spain
Sweden
Switzerland
Texas
Thailand
Tokyo
Toronto
Tuscany & Umbria
USA
Utah
Vancouver & Victoria
Vermont, New Hampshire &
   Maine
Vienna & the Danube Valley
Virgin Islands
Virginia
Walt Disney World® & Orlando
Washington, D.C.
Washington State

FROMMER'S® DOLLAR-A-DAY GUIDES

Australia from $50 a Day
California from $70 a Day
Caribbean from $70 a Day
England from $75 a Day
Europe from $70 a Day

Florida from $70 a Day
Hawaii from $80 a Day
Ireland from $60 a Day
Italy from $70 a Day
London from $85 a Day

New York from $90 a Day
Paris from $80 a Day
San Francisco from $70 a Day
Washington, D.C. from $80 a Day

FROMMER'S® PORTABLE GUIDES

Acapulco, Ixtapa & Zihuatanejo
Amsterdam
Aruba
Australia's Great Barrier Reef
Bahamas
Berlin
Big Island of Hawaii
Boston
California Wine Country
Cancún
Charleston & Savannah
Chicago
Disneyland®
Dublin
Florence

Frankfurt
Hong Kong
Houston
Las Vegas
London
Los Angeles
Los Cabos & Baja
Maine Coast
Maui
Miami
New Orleans
New York City
Paris
Phoenix & Scottsdale

Portland
Puerto Rico
Puerto Vallarta, Manzanillo &
   Guadalajara
Rio de Janeiro
San Diego
San Francisco
Seattle
Sydney
Tampa & St. Petersburg
Vancouver
Venice
Virgin Islands
Washington, D.C.

FROMMER'S® NATIONAL PARK GUIDES

Banff & Jasper
Family Vacations in the National
   Parks
Grand Canyon

National Parks of the American
   West
Rocky Mountain

Yellowstone & Grand Teton
Yosemite & Sequoia/ Kings Canyon
Zion & Bryce Canyon

FROMMER'S® MEMORABLE WALKS

Chicago	New York	San Francisco
London	Paris	Washington, D.C.

FROMMER'S® GREAT OUTDOOR GUIDES

Arizona & New Mexico	Northern California	Vermont & New Hampshire
New England	Southern New England	

SUZY GERSHMAN'S BORN TO SHOP GUIDES

Born to Shop: France	Born to Shop: Italy	Born to Shop: New York
Born to Shop: Hong Kong,	Born to Shop: London	Born to Shop: Paris
Shanghai & Beijing		

FROMMER'S® IRREVERENT GUIDES

Amsterdam	Los Angeles	San Francisco
Boston	Manhattan	Seattle & Portland
Chicago	New Orleans	Vancouver
Las Vegas	Paris	Walt Disney World®
London	Rome	Washington, D.C.

FROMMER'S® BEST-LOVED DRIVING TOURS

Britain	Germany	Northern Italy
California	Ireland	Scotland
Florida	Italy	Spain
France	New England	Tuscany & Umbria

HANGING OUT™ GUIDES

Hanging Out in England	Hanging Out in France	Hanging Out in Italy
Hanging Out in Europe	Hanging Out in Ireland	Hanging Out in Spain

THE UNOFFICIAL GUIDES®

Bed & Breakfasts and Country	Southwest & South Central	Mid-Atlantic with Kids
Inns in:	Plains	Mini Las Vegas
California	U.S.A.	Mini-Mickey
Great Lakes States	Beyond Disney	New England and New York with
Mid-Atlantic	Branson, Missouri	Kids
New England	California with Kids	New Orleans
Northwest	Chicago	New York City
Rockies	Cruises	Paris
Southeast	Disneyland®	San Francisco
Southwest	Florida with Kids	Skiing in the West
Best RV & Tent Campgrounds in:	Golf Vacations in the Eastern U.S.	Southeast with Kids
California & the West	Great Smoky & Blue Ridge Region	Walt Disney World®
Florida & the Southeast	Inside Disney	Walt Disney World® for Grown-ups
Great Lakes States	Hawaii	Walt Disney World® with Kids
Mid-Atlantic	Las Vegas	Washington, D.C.
Northeast	London	World's Best Diving Vacations
Northwest & Central Plains		

SPECIAL-INTEREST TITLES

Frommer's Adventure Guide to Australia &
  New Zealand
Frommer's Adventure Guide to Central America
Frommer's Adventure Guide to India & Pakistan
Frommer's Adventure Guide to South America
Frommer's Adventure Guide to Southeast Asia
Frommer's Adventure Guide to Southern Africa
Frommer's Britain's Best Bed & Breakfasts and
  Country Inns
Frommer's Caribbean Hideaways
Frommer's Exploring America by RV
Frommer's Fly Safe, Fly Smart
Frommer's France's Best Bed & Breakfasts and
  Country Inns
Frommer's Gay & Lesbian Europe

Frommer's Italy's Best Bed & Breakfasts and
  Country Inns
Frommer's New York City with Kids
Frommer's Ottawa with Kids
Frommer's Road Atlas Britain
Frommer's Road Atlas Europe
Frommer's Road Atlas France
Frommer's Toronto with Kids
Frommer's Vancouver with Kids
Frommer's Washington, D.C., with Kids
Israel Past & Present
The New York Times' Guide to Unforgettable
  Weekends
Places Rated Almanac
Retirement Places Rated

America Online Keyword: Travel
Booked seat 6A, open return.
Rented red 4-wheel drive.
Reserved cabin, no running water.
Discovered space.

Uncovered

*How I Left Hasidic Life
and Finally Came Home*

a   m e m o i r

b y

L e a h   L a x

swp

SHE WRITES PRESS

Excerpts from this book have been published in *Moment* Magazine, *Lilith* Magazine, *Survivor's Review*, *Intellectual Refuge*, *Crab Orchard Review*, *The Double Dealer*, and in the anthologies *Keep Your Wives Away From Them* (North Atlantic Books, 2010), and *Beyond Belief: The Secret Lives of Women in Extreme Religion* (Seal Press, 2013).

The lines from "What Is Possible". Copyright © 2013 by The Adrienne Rich Literary Trust. Copyright (c) 1981 by Adrienne Rich, The lines from "Twenty-One Love Poems." Copyright © 2013 by The Adrienne Rich Literary Trust. Copyright (c) 1978 by W. W. Norton & Company, Inc., from LATER POEMS: SELECTED AND NEW, 1971-2012 by Adrienne Rich. Used by permission of W. W. Norton & Company, Inc.

Published 2015
Printed in the United States of America
ISBN: 978-1-63152-995-5
Library of Congress Control Number: 2015933018

Book design by Stacey Aaronson

For information, address:
She Writes Press
1563 Solano Ave #546
Berkeley, CA 94707

She Writes Press is a division of SparkPoint Studio, LLC.

for Mom

I never did let her read this.

And for covered women everywhere.

Back in 2006, still celebrating my new freedom, I traveled with Susan to New Orleans for the first Mardi Gras after Hurricane Katrina. That parade was particularly, defiantly raucous As a comment on the recent devastation, one of the passing revelers was handing out toy vermin. He gave me an especially ugly rubber rat, 'Lying Rat' painted on it in green puff paint. I kept that rat beside me as a warning through the long process of writing this memoir. Yes, memoir is written with the flawed tool of memory, and individual experience distorts the view, and yes, I found it necessary to change names, approximate conversations, and gather repeated events into single scenes, but this is to attest that I looked within myself on every page trying to capture the truth as best I could. As best I could.

"But hope deferred is still hope."

— MARILYNNE ROBINSON, GILEAD

One

a'ancha adonoi b'yom tsarah y'sagev'cha shem elohei ya'akov.
A bride is to fast and recite the entire book of psalms
on her wedding day, and so I stand at attention in a back
room of my grandparents' elegant Dallas home on an August day
in 1975 in a wedding gown that covers me to chin and wrists and
to the floor, sounding out Hebrew words I don't understand from
a softbound prayer book, a shining train of fine cloth puddled on
the vacuumed carpet behind me. My mother and two sisters are
fixing their makeup at the vanity. My mother and grandmother
have been holding their chins high all day as if practicing for
tonight, lips pulled tight, pretending they're not embarrassed by
my new religious demands. They are determined to still have
their Dallas society wedding even if the bearded Hasidic men I
have invited taint them with the ignorant superstitions of the old
country.

I smile and whisper the Hebrew words, keenly aware that
they feel exactly as if hillbilly relatives just showed up uninvited
to take over their nouveau-riche affair. Syllables separate and
march, each equal in weight and mystery, like a steady drum
drowning out their petty materialism. *Yish'lach ez'r'cha mikodesh
umitsion yis'adecha.* I just turned nineteen, and I'm proud and
determined to accomplish this exit from my family by trumping
them all with God. My psalms will draw down God's blessings on
our auspicious occasion and suffuse us all with holy light on this
day of my Hasidic wedding.

Outside, the sky is electric blue over a North Dallas neighborhood of manicured lawns and privacy walls, not far from the country club my Jewish cousins were only recently allowed to join. It's another in a string of ninety-five-degree August days. Sounds of clinking and muffled voices from the front room have dwindled. Much of the furniture in the front of the house is now cleared away, the lovely smell of a kosher feast spread on long, covered tables wafting back to us. A ghost of an ivy-draped wedding canopy out on the patio is partly visible through the floor-length curtains. Hurricane lamps on pedestals dot the vast lawn beneath old shade trees of mimosa, pecan, Texas ash. Soon, the sun will go down and I will be given to tall bearded Levi in his long black *satuk* coat under the stars. Then my photograph will appear on the society page in next Sunday's *Dallas Morning News,* August 17, 1975: *The bride wore satin with her grandmother's veil of handmade lace.*

"Mom. A little modesty, please?" I say, fussing at her because her gown is sleeveless. I add in a stage whisper, "Rabbi Frumen's in the next room. Put on the bolero!" Rabbi Yosef Yitzchak Frumen is a *shaliach,* the emissary over all of Texas for the Lubavitcher Rebbe, our Hasidic leader. "He's doing the *ketubah* about now!"

"The what?" my mother says.

I roll my eyes. "The wedding contract."

She gives a little huff. "Put the book down for a minute, would you?" she says. "Come here. Come to the mirror. I want to put the veil on you." She picks up the lace crown and her eyes go moist. She wore that crown, that veil, once. So did her mother.

I don't want to see her eyes. I think of the secret of her hoarded clutter, how her elegant mother refuses to walk into our home, how we were left alone in it growing up, how often she forgets to make meals. I think, *Put the veil on me? Now you care?* Fortunate for you, Mom, the gown isn't the dirty gray of our life.

The white dress covers all that, and now here you are, offering to help me to disappear.

ONCE, WHEN I WAS SMALL, I searched for and then found my mother in her studio in front of a tall canvas on an easel that stretched high above my head. On a square table nearby lay an array of half-squeezed tubes with the tops off, tiny, bright circles of orange, green, red, white, glistening in fluorescent light. In her hand was a palette marked with feathered strokes, on it a curved line of little mounds of color. The air was filled with the familiar smells of turpentine and linseed oil, words which I already knew. She was dabbing with a brush, seemed lost in the canvas.

My mother didn't look down or acknowledge me, so I stood and watched. I was soon filled with the inexplicable sense that she'd gone away and left me behind. I peered up into her canvas at those yawning spaces and vivid colors as if I could find her in there, but there were too many places where she could hide. I needed to climb into the painting to find my mother, but then I would be lost in a strange landscape, and that would prove her an ever-receding figure.

She was busy with her brush and unconcerned about leaving me, and she was using a color language I didn't understand like a tool of escape. I felt then, and know now, that in a way, the painting was her shape on the inside. If I could just decipher her color language, maybe I could follow.

I would remain obsessed with grasping strange language for wordless things. And even a very long time after I would still feel as if she had left me behind, wandering and peering into strange landscapes, ever looking for her. For home.

SHE'S HOLDING OUT THE VEIL. Her eyes are wet. Helpless, I go to her and sit down at the vanity. She takes bobby pins from my grandmother's gold filigree box and secures the netting and heavy lace to my head with her tapered delicate hands. Above her image in the mirror, as she bends over me, are the reflections of my sisters, Amy and Debbie, watching.

Tuvia comes in. He heads our burgeoning Hasidic group at the University of Texas. There are many more like us discovering orthodox religion at the university, all of us part of a wave across campuses all over the country. Jesus freaks with long hippie hair cluster and sing on campus corners, approaching us with drugged eyes and Christian pamphlets as we walk to classes. The more conventional Christian student unions are flourishing. Muslim students gather in shouting demonstrations denouncing the shah. Our Hasidic group is just one of many preparing us to take our conservative religion out into the world. We meet at Chabad House in Austin, just off the main street along the north side of the university, and we are led by Rabbi Frumen with his fierce and pious beard.

Under Rabbi Frumen's guidance, most of us have turned our focus away from our university studies to the Godly lives we plan to lead once we're married, and the large Hasidic families we will raise. Most of our parents are not too pleased.

Tuvia is wearing a blue suit on his thin frame. His sandy beard is neatly combed, his manner respectful, eyes downcast. "Mrs. Mallett," he says to my mother, then indicates with a nod and an open arm that she is to join him in the next room, my grandfather's study, where the men have gathered. My mother drops the bobby pin and stands up like a startled fawn.

In the study, she will find Ruth, mother of Levi, my *chatan*, other half of my soul, destined since Creation to bind himself to me. Ruth calls her son Eugene. The two mothers will be told to stand to the side of that room full of men, dark wood paneling, heavy masculine furniture. Most of our family friends have yet to arrive, but Rabbi Frumen is in there, as are our fellow students Tuvia, Dovid, Vulf, and Mendel. I imagine the two mothers in their long gowns, the line of young men in new, soft beards, Levi at the carved, polished table, looking regal holding a piece of holy text. The room will grow quiet. Levi's father will look perplexed, and my once-debonair father, awkward and a little empty-eyed from his meds, simply afraid.

Levi will launch into an analysis of the mystical Godly union elevated into higher spheres by the ultimate union of bride and groom; always a piece of holy text will ritualize the moment. The young men will burst into forced lively singing. They will stumble over the Hebrew words, clapping, dancing in place, following Rabbi's Frumen's lead. Then the rabbi will unroll the *ketubah*, the ancient marriage contract in Aramaic, which Levi will sign. Two male witnesses, trusted by the Law because they are men and because they honor the Sabbath, will also sign.

I am the object of that contract. I am being given to him.

My father will be called to sign the *ketubah* last, in my stead. He's wearing a light tan summer linen suit with a carnation in his lapel as white as his thick white hair. But in there he isn't Herb and I am not Lisa. The rabbi will write my name on the contract as Leah, *Lay-ah*, daughter of Yehoshua, son of Yaakov—my father's Hebrew name, which means *God will grant salvation.* This is how he will be told to sign.

To commemorate the ancient temple in Jerusalem, someone will direct the mothers to take hold of a china plate and then on cue from the rabbi together dash it to the polished floor. Alone with my psalms, I listen for the muffled crash adding loss to Jewish joy and imagine the two mothers' self-conscious smiles, the blur of their thrusting hands. Then the crash, the cries of "mazel tov," distant clapping and singing. *But don't you know, Mom, the plate isn't really the temple; it's my past, it's my years with you*

finally over, it's just another thing broken? Later I will hear how
Levi's father was distressed seeing the shards fly. I will hear how
he scurried around the room, picking up the pieces, but there
were too many.

IT WAS BACK IN FEBRUARY, six months before the wedding,
when Rabbi Frumen called me from the Austin Chabad House.
He had driven in from his home in Houston to give his weekly
classes. Chabad House was our meeting place, actually a cleared
storage area in a student apartment complex. The members were
my only friends. All of us had fairly withdrawn from general
university society.

Rabbi Frumen had a gruff style and a dismissive manner with
women. The boys, although insecure in his presence, were in awe
of him, but I was simply afraid, struck silent as soon as he walked
into the room. And yet in my mind I had become a Hasidic soldier
ready for orders from an emissary of our rebbe. It was a given
that Rabbi Frumen could interrupt my studying for a test in
government and my plans to spend the afternoon practicing cello.
"I'll be right over," I said, dropped my schoolwork and rushed
across the enormous campus, students strolling, the diesel smell
of the campus bus, across the East Mall and around the Tower
library, long skirt slapping my calves in the cold wind.

Then we were sitting in Chabad House face-to-face. The
Sabbath tables were folded and stacked against the wall, a poster
of the Rebbe's smiling countenance tacked up above us. I pulled
the back of my knees in hard against the cold metal edge of the
folding chair and my heart pounded in my ears. I sat very still,
beginning to guess why he had called.

When Rabbi Frumen smiled, his lip dropped to show his
lower teeth surrounded by dark beard. "How's your life?" he said
in his Russian/Yiddish accent.

"*Baruch hashem*," I said—bless God.

Someone in the apartment below turned on a stereo, and the rock bass line hummed up through my feet, mixed with pounding in my ears.

"And your grandparents?"

Was he looking for a donation? "*Baruch hashem*," I said again. God gets the credit. For everything.

"I wanted to ask you, have you thought about any of the boys? As a husband?"

I was right. Panic. In my mind was Ana's warm face, who once had my dreams. I once scrawled two-inch letters into my high school diary: *ALONE. Ana. Ana.* "Mom," I said, placing my hand on my chest as if she could see the ache. "I think I have a soul."

I met Rabbi Frumen's eyes, then wondered if he was trying to search inside me for some privately held fantasy about one of the newly Hasidic boys. But I couldn't produce a coy, modest voice trembling for any of them. I thought of the Rebbe, the way he took off his white plastic glasses and put them on his desk. "You will make an everlasting edifice of a Jewish home," he said to me with that piercing gaze, my future now defined. Apparently, here it was.

"Levi Lax is interested in marrying you," Rabbi Frumen said.

I jerked my chin up, then stopped myself from opening my eyes too wide. Levi was seven years older, but our Dallas families knew one another, and he was long overdue for marriage. I thought, *I should have expected this.* And that was all.

"LET'S STOP AND TALK." That was Levi two days later on our first and only date, in his Dodge Dart on a cold, dark night. But it wasn't really a date; it was just the two of us flinging ourselves into what we had been taught to believe was our destiny.

Levi was an Ivy League alumnus, in Austin for graduate school. I knew him as an engineering type, a little messy, a bit of a genius. People liked him, but once, I had seen him blow up over some detail and had been embarrassed. Still, I knew he could get a good job and, with his tall, nice build and handsome face, father beautiful children.

There was Levi's darkened profile in his hat next to me in the car, and the white path of headlights on the empty road. He was wearing jeans, still becoming a Hasid, still learning the rules, but I knew we wouldn't touch. I relied on that. I sat huddled in my black wool coat, helpless, determined, my feet not quite touching the floor as we both pelted forward into the rushing universe. My hand rested near the door handle, curled like that of a child.

I didn't know that I was the third girl Rabbi Frumen had approached for Levi. I didn't know I was being shopped and didn't know to ask why the first two girls had turned away. I accepted that the privileged commandment to marry, along with its spiritual rewards, was for men. It was our duty as women to help them fulfill that command. I saw nothing to note in my vacuum absence of desire. A vacuum makes no sound.

I did know by then how Hasidim were supposed to go about matchmaking, how Hasidic parents are to research the prospective match, then gently query their son or daughter about what he or she wants in a spouse and encourage the young couple to go out to some public place to talk, as long as they don't touch. The two are to share their hearts, their goals. *They* are to decide if they will marry, together, and proceed only if both souls begin to ignite. *You will know*, my imaginary, loving Hasidic parents tell their inexperienced children. The Law, and God, will love you, protect you. *We, too, were there, once.*

Instead we had Levi's accountant dad, deep within the wannabe Dallas Jewish community, and Levi's mom, who never missed a Cowboys game. We had my hoarding artist mother and mentally ill father, and my newly rich grandparents, who ate schmaltz herring and wore elegant clothes.

Perhaps Hasidic parents would have cautioned us to check inside ourselves for real feelings for one another, or given us their own sense of the match. If we'd had Hasidic peers also preparing for marriage, maybe we would have secretly shared our fears with them, or compared advice we'd received. Maybe we might have even found Hasidic kids who had said no. But instead of Hasidic parents, we had Rabbi Frumen with his fierce and pious beard. In place of peers who might have forged the path ahead of us, we had temporary friendships through Chabad House with young people from secular homes who were also trying on Hasidic life by following printed how-to guides. Marriage was a Duty, an item to check off on the list. In place of courtship, I had had twenty minutes in front of Rabbi Frumen on a folding chair in an emptied storage room beneath a tacked-up poster of the Rebbe.

Levi pulled into a broad, black-tarred Sears parking lot and parked. We got out of the car. We stood there looking at one another, alone in a dark landscape held down by a tarmac grid of white parking lines and litter. We were supposed to talk, but it didn't seem to matter what we said. We knew we didn't determine our destiny. Besides, Levi had already chosen me. "Well," he said. He looked at his shoes. "What do you think?"

That was his proposal.

Diffused light from the towering mercury lights was too thin for warmth. His face was in shadow beneath the hat brim—I couldn't make out the black curls in his beard, brown eyes, high forehead, thick eyebrows. But something about his tall frame seemed foreign, unappealing. Or was I the alien? I stepped backward with a jerk, had to will myself to stop and take this leap. "I want flowers," I said, near panic.

"What?"

"Color. In every room," I said. "I want you to bring me flowers." A last call for beauty in a black-and-white world. "And I want a green room where I can play my cello."

"I'd like that," he said. His voice was soft and warm.

It seemed there was no going back—I wouldn't be able to face the rabbi or my Hasidic friends, if I did. But when I heard such caring in his voice, hope filled me. "I'd like that," he had said. Maybe it would be okay. "You would?" I said.

Then I was grinning, grinning, and so was he, in the desolate parking lot with a modest black space solid between us. Our train of dreams was picking up speed. Feelings squelched, save a soldier's pride, but I was looking to the future. I'd have flowers and color, a safe, clean home with a predictable, devoted, loyal man, none of my mother's hoarded clutter or my father's brooding darkness and nighttime hauntings. Levi offered home. Safety. Order. Holiness. Shared faith in something beyond our family's hard scrabble. That's what had drawn me to the Hasidim.

I truly believed marriage was escape from loneliness. I believed escape from loneliness was the same as holiness.

Levi stepped out of the shadows then. I looked up into his face. His eyes were bright, his gaze deep. He made a tiny, awkward gesture with one hand toward my waist, and stopped himself. Lit from above, his bent head threw a curved shadow over my face, like half a heart.

THE CONTRACT HAS BEEN SIGNED, my future set, the wedding about to begin. I am still reciting Hebrew psalms in my grandmother's bedroom when my mother and Ruth return from the paneled study. I put my finger on the place in the text and look up, expectant.

Soon, the large den at the front of the house is filled with chatting, milling guests. I am at the center of it all sitting on a dining room chair as if it were a throne, my mother and Ruth posed at either side. The long drapes and sliding glass doors have been pulled open wide. Outside, a Texas band—one clarinet, a

violin, and a saxophone that is more accustomed to honky-tonk
than to Yiddish music is gamely playing Hasidic tunes. Rather
than joy, I try for certainty that we have chosen a perfect path.
But everything has to go right in this old choreographed dance,
this Hasidic wedding. I glance around to make sure everyone is in
their place. I tell myself to look happy.

Levi is in another room where attendants are preparing him
for his march to the wedding canopy. We haven't been allowed to
see each other for seven days. When he enters, the guests will
think of our long separation and buildup of desire and imagine us
swooning in anticipation of that first embrace. But, our secret
(maybe it's stress): I got my period early, rendering me untouch-
able by Jewish Law for ten more days. Levi says it's from God. But
until now menstruating was never more than a minor incon-
venience. This is a new experience, this harboring secret shame.

In the next room, over Levi's ruffled tuxedo shirt, Rabbi
Frumen drapes a huge shirt that has been worn by the Rebbe
himself, wrapping Levi in an aura of holiness. Then he helps Levi
into his first long black Hasidic coat, the mark of a married man.

On the phone a week ago, Levi told me another secret. The
special coat doesn't fit, even though it was ordered according to
his measurements. The next day, his back seized up. He's still in
pain. I picture him hunching his shoulders and sucking in his
stomach to get the Hasidic coat on, determined to close the
button and force himself into this new mold. Rabbi Frumen
waits, ready to drape the Rebbe's shirt over him.

The music stops; a long, breath-held pause. I look up from
my dining-chair throne, and there's Levi in the doorway, flanked
by our two fathers—his black beard, handsome face, thick lashes
and dark eyes, the nervousness he carries that I will come to
know, the effort in his face. Rabbi Frumen is just behind, with a
hand at Levi's elbow. Levi takes a step forward but seems unsure,
shoulders high. I hope no one notices how the coat doesn't fit.

This is it. This is the moment I've read about, the moment when the bride is supposed to look up with a rush of longing from her throne to find her groom coming toward her, when she is supposed to be overcome with the delight of seeing her beloved. Soon bride and groom are to turn together toward the long-hoped-for wedding canopy where their union will be legitimized, celebrated, consummated, but right now is supposed to be the wonder moment of recognition, when their eyes should meet across the room with infinite desire.

I try. Really, I try. I try to feel that. Levi is coming toward me, by now surrounded by a whole group of men singing their pensive, raw song.

Later, I will look back and wonder whether Levi looked across the room wanting me and wasn't just trying to ignore his back pain. I will wonder, as he solemnly proceeded toward me between the two fathers among a jostle of chanting men, whether he was telling himself stock phrases like "my helpmate" and "we will create an everlasting edifice," *ezer kenegdo, binyan adei ad.* Or was he feeling something real, something of his own? I will hold on to hope that he did feel a flash of desire, that at least one of us did.

As the men walk toward us to their slow song, I look to my father, at Levi's side. Daddy is supposed to come forward first, put his two hands on my head and bless me, saying, "May God make you like Sarah, Rebecca, Rachel, and Leah," the four beloved mothers of the Jewish people—thus setting my destiny to mother a new righteous generation. I'm afraid Daddy will fail. He won't give me his blessing.

The music stops. The Three stand in front of me, Levi, his father, and mine, my trinity. The crowd gathers in. Levi looks overwhelmed. He struggles to meet my eyes. He is ready to take the veil from behind me and bring it down over my face, but I'm looking to my father. First I need Daddy's blessing. It's an old hope. I want my father to do this, and so much else, for me. I tried to teach him the Hebrew words before the wedding, but he's had electroshock therapy, lives on medication. Daddy leans in close, and suddenly I am in a swirl of childhood memories overlain with a mingling of love and revulsion, yearning and resentment. As I always have, I sense his feelings as if I feel them for him: I smell his fear and I am afraid. I look up toward him, a pleading look on my face, *bless me protect me*, my eyebrows raised, brow furrowed. "Daddy?" I whisper, hopeless. "The words?"

He doesn't remember the magic blessing words, there is no magic, even if he has gotten up from his gray recliner where he spends entire days reading the newspaper and grinding his teeth, even if he showered and shaved and put on a suit, pinned a white carnation to his lapel. Instead, he puts one trembling hand on my head in a motion of utter uncertainty. In a single hesitant jerky motion, instead of the blessing, he kisses my forehead, leaves it wet.

He has no blessing for me. The air is cool on the place he kissed.

I look away, ashamed. Something dies then, and I want it to. I will turn him into an old, dead package, his indiscretions and illness and failings an old secret I will keep close throughout my married life. So, this is both my wedding and his funeral. In my wedding gown I dig his grave and dump in his weak body, twin streaks of white from his hair and the carnation as he tumbles in. I shovel dirt over him, scoop after furious scoop. Sweat and dirt streak my white satin and stain the hem. Below me, his mouth opens, fishlike, for air.

THE MUSIC RISES. Emboldened, Levi looks into the face of his Hasidic Leah. But when he does, he doesn't see Lisa, daughter of Rita and Herb, the girl who once climbed rooftops and dreamed she was a boy. He believes I am really Leah and that he has received the right merchandise. There has been no trickery like that of the biblical Leah, who put herself in her sister's place beneath a veil. It is I, and he clearly believes this. Elated, he lifts the veil from behind me and brings it down over my face.

Lisa dies as well. *I am Leah.*

Smiling triumphant, Levi turns, the fathers still with him, and proceeds to the open patio door to wait while guests take their seats outside. Then, on cue to music meant to awaken bride and groom to their holy destiny, the three march to the wedding canopy.

It is time. I stand. I must go to my husband. Someone hands each of our mothers a tapered, burning candle, and each puts a hand on one of my elbows. Behind me, my sisters, Amy and Debbie, hold candles as well and follow in measured steps. New music begins. There is no breeze in the warm night as we pace down the aisle between seated guests. The little flames rise small and strong and sure.

Under the wedding canopy, I pace around Levi seven times, and the mothers follow, around and around. Levi's mother picks up my train so that it doesn't entrap her son. I lose count, stuck in circles without end, but Rabbi Frumen utters a low "two, three, four." Seven circles for the seven heavens, with Levi at the center of the universe, and for the days of Sabbath that will order our life. Then I stand beside him, shoulders just out of touch, as men announce my purchase, the contract, the bride price—a ring of gold, as they bestow seven blessings. The veil is lifted to feed me a sip of the wine of agreement, the wine of sleep. Levi places a ring on my right index finger while his remains unbound. Then he stomps on a glass to cries of "mazel tov!"

The band lets loose. We dance in wild circles until after midnight, round and round, the women indoors, men out on the patio. I whirl with each guest in turn, smiling, smiling, while a larger circle spins around us. Oh, the new and Godly life we will make! Until I am breathless. Someone brings a chair and I collapse into it, but there is still the laughing music and smiling women dancing around me.

Then a small group lines up to form the *mitzvah tantz*. The larger circle continues around us as a clapping, flying backdrop. The line dances toward me. Their hands mime rounded bellies and their feet kick up the rhythm. They dance back, then come forward, this time pretending to rock an infant. The next time they advance, each is pushing a stroller. With every advance, they scrub a floor, rub another rounded belly, rock another infant, stir a pot, and another, then they throw the back of their wrists onto foreheads pretending pain, and we laugh. We laugh!

The guests buzz with exuberance. Here's my Ana dancing past. My eyes brighten; how much I loved her. She came with the man who will become her husband. Here's my Austin roommate Andrea; she will marry Vulf, Warren, and they will shuck off their flirt with Hasidic life. Here is my beloved childhood first friend, Jean, and other friends from high school and before, Andrea and Sharon, with Brett and David outside with the men. My first love, my friends: I invited you to my wedding to say goodbye.

The stars are high, the night warm. The raucous music defies the night, wild rhythms burning in our brains. Through the glass doors, the dancing men appear flattened and shining. Shirttails are out, passing bottles of vodka. They sing, hoarse, lift bottles high, arm in arm. Three lift Levi up on a chair, turning, turning. Vulf hoists Tuvia on his shoulders, and the two waver up to the groom.

I have the ring on my forefinger where Levi placed it, although on that finger it fits only to the knuckle. I push the ring down until it's snug—I'll move it to the fourth finger after the wedding—but the women are pulling me out to dance on the lawn among the hurricane lamps, under the old trees, under the stars. We grab hands, joyous, jumping, dancing on the soft grass, drunk with song and laughter. I raise my right hand and fling my arm out in the dance.

The ring flies away, nestles somewhere hidden in the grass. It is nighttime. What can we do but look for it tomorrow? No matter; it is time to dance!

Finally, I stop to get my breath. I go into the house, back into my grandmother's room, where she helps take off the veil and long lace train. My mother and father and Levi follow.

My father approaches me. He says, "Lisa. Did you find the ring?"

He heard. I look up, startled. Behind him, Levi scowls.

But we're back at the wedding, and here is young Mrs. Frumen, the rabbi's wife, head high, pink and green flowers printed across her tight dress, whirling and stepping in expert Hasidic dance. And here's sister Amy, sixteen, eyes shining, how she's smiling, and older sister Debbie, who catches my tossed bouquet; she'll marry her live-in boyfriend before the year is out, the family's first non-Jew. Here is Rabbi Frumen; the beard and ritual fringes fly, arms high, he is a big man, but his feet, what they can do. He dances with my grandfather's business associate, an upright Texas Baptist man much taller than he, and the photographer catches the odd pairing. I know everyone here will remember this night and the fun, the music, the dancing. The joy.

Two

I awaken in a long white nightgown gathered at the wrists, a tiny pink bow at the neck, alone in a hotel bed the morning after. I awaken from whirling dances and a laughing clarinet in my dreams. I open my eyes and bump up against sterile silence, still officially a virgin. Because I am menstruating, Rabbi Frumen sent chaperones with us to the hotel. Levi and I have yet to be alone. My chaperone is still asleep in the other bed. Levi and the woman's husband are in the two beds in the second room of this wedding suite. Levi's good night to me was brief and shy under their grinning gazes, and mine was the same.

I look around, the dream clarinet still echoing off the white walls. I think of our first date months ago, how careful, how polite we were, how Levi proposed that dark night under a sliver of winter moon. I wonder what it will be like to wake in the morning beside him. To hold him. But I mustn't think of that, with chaperones nearby.

I get up, curious to explore what I can. My new wig is on the counter, and an assortment of new, colorful scarves. *I want to try on all of them.* Oh, but everything has changed with an evening of dance! *I am a Married Woman,* I think, wrapping a scarf around my head. No one gets to see my hair, not even Levi—at least, not until after I have immersed in a *mikvah.* Barefoot in the gown at the mirrored vanity, I finger the other scarves, pick up the wig, then I stand there, wig in hand. The chaperone turns in her sleep and sighs. The men are stirring in the other room.

I pull off the new scarf. My hair, freshly cut, is short, sleep-tousled, a mass of Jewish waves that has always resisted training, but I don't reach on automatic for a brush, don't linger a moment on the freedom I had just yesterday to walk out to the street as is, uncovered. That time has passed. I rake the hair back from my face with my fingers and push it behind my ears. I duck my head and tug the elastic sides of the wig down over my head until the pressure is even over temples and crown and snug against the nape. But a few strands of my real hair still hang free. I grab them and push them in.

The woman in the mirror is a bit of a type, not exactly me. She looks older, poised, every wiggy hair exactly in place. I am gleeful. *Hasidic woman!* Then, as if a door has just shut, as if I just heard the click and didn't know until this moment that it would lock behind me, I suck in my breath, shake my head, and think, *I can't take it back. I'm married. No going back.*

The others will be coming in. Before me—an adult in the mirror, her coiffed poise. Barefoot in the girlish gown, I meet her eyes, raise the back of my head, and square my shoulders in a determined yet ladylike pose. *Oh, yes,* I think, a nervous grin spreading across my face. *That is me.*

THERE ARE FEW HASIDIC HOMES in Austin to host the *sheva brachos* celebrations after the wedding that are supposed to be held for bride and groom—a week of formal dinners with endless toasts and blessings. So we haul a trunk full of gifts across the Texas prairie and simply return to our regular school schedule, arriving just in time to register for the new semester. We park behind Levi's apartment complex beneath a wild, laden fig tree.

"Come on in," Levi says at the door to his apartment. His arms are full, but he manages to unlock the door, then walks in ahead of me. I'm breathing a little hard from my load, but I stop at the threshold to survey the place: avocado shag carpeting, orange vinyl curtains, a threadbare sofa that even from here smells of cigarettes, and Levi doesn't smoke. "I'll need my own key," I say.

Other than student-grade rental furniture, the apartment doesn't look occupied. Walls, and counters, are bare. But it's clean, basically, and once I arrange wedding dishes, fresh towels in the bathroom and kitchen, gift art on the walls, once I empty my single suitcase and settle my clothing into the one empty dresser drawer and hang a line of skirts in the closet above Levi's jeans, the place feels a little more like home. I put my cello in the corner, near the bed.

For Levi to touch me when I'm bleeding is to touch contagious spiritual death that only a *mikvah* can purify. Over the next eleven days, there is no one to chaperone us, but we are careful not to touch, spurred on by Hasidic fear of my blood and its mysteries. We know some would gauge us primitive or irrational, but we think of our "fear" as spiritual, more elevated than simple logic. Ours, we tell ourselves, is holy fear, not of fluids, but of God and His Word, the Law. Our first morning in Austin, Levi reaches into a cabinet over my head for a plate in the tiny kitchen. There's the brush of his clothing against mine, the whiff of his intake of breath, the smell of his clean body. We both draw back, apologizing.

ONE DAY SOON AFTER, alone in the apartment, I pick my way into the cluttered second bedroom to survey what Levi calls his "office." I'm thinking of the night that he proposed. "I want a room for my music," I said to his shadowy form. "I'd like that," he said then, giving me such hope. But this is the only extra room we have. The bookcases are filled with Levi's books, and there are many more on the floor in teetering stacks, among other stacks of folders and loose stuff and boxes from some move long ago. I pick

my way around an old tennis shoe on its side and a racquet for
racquetball, black tape unstuck and hanging from the handle, a
box of recordings for a reel-to-reel, a pair of torn jeans. A baseball
hat. There's an oversize desk against the wall covered with
papers, dusty notebooks, folders, boxes of cheap pens.

The things my mother collected filled my childhood: dozens
of unused cans of tuna fish, empty cans from tuna fish, glass
bottles (always good for something), yesterday's newspaper and
today's. Books and plants and tubes of hand cream and face cream
and leg cream and eye cream, and lipstick and foundation and eye
powders in blues and browns. She bought all of the newest
offerings from the Avon lady and filled the bathroom counters,
cabinets, and drawers to overflowing with bottles in different
shapes that she admired. She collected magazines and junk mail,
which wasn't really junk, and dishes from the latest grocery store
offering, and empty packages and parts and pieces of things,
because she said she will need them. And shoes and pants and
dresses and coats. And purses. She likes purses. Dozens of purses.
Piles of purses. Tubes of paint and canvases and portfolios and
dozens and dozens of brushes for her painting. I was surrounded
by her stacks and collections and piles. Even as a small child, I
knew rules: I was not to move her things, or she would wave her
arms and shout. I was not to say, "throw out," or she would
launch into scathing criticism of my character.

I leave Levi's study and return with Lysol cleaning spray, a
dust cloth, and a wet rag. I put books back up on the shelf,
arrange the rest in orderly stacks against the wall, dust everything
clean. File folders go together into one place in the corner. Sports
equipment and shoes in the closet. I clear the desk, stack papers,
spray and wipe the surface, telling myself *seder iz kedusha*—order
is holiness. I will bring order and holiness into our home.
Gradually, space opens up for a chair for cello practice, a music
stand, a few inches on the brick-and-board bookcase for music

books. I won't have to carry the cello to a practice room in the music building. I'll fill our home with music. That will be the sound of our home.

I am too busy to notice the front door opening, Levi coming in. Then, behind me, a shout of "No!" in such anger and dismay I whirl around, his old racquet in my hand, the dried-out black tape hanging. He's waving his arms at the room, yelling, "What have you done? Put that down!" Spittle flies from his mouth. "Don't *touch* that." I'm sure the neighbors can hear. "What kind of person *are* you?" he says.

I throw the racquet down and stomp out of the room. I am not a child—I don't live with my mother, don't have to take that.

Except that leaving the room is a capitulation. Except that, even as I walk away, angry heart yammering in my chest, I'm spinning Hasidic demands planted in my head and trying to stop my own march. *He is your husband.* I should not touch his things. The Rebbe said to make an everlasting edifice. I am just a woman. *Bend your will to God's will.*

A deflated unspoken truce sits between us the rest of the day. Later I tell Levi, "I don't need a music room. I'll go practice my cello in the music building."

IT SEEMS OUR WEDDING WAS a last goodbye to most of our friends at Chabad House. Tuvia and most of the others graduate and move away, taking their religious rebellion with them out into the world. There are just a few guys left who gather for the daily minyan service, not even enough to make the quorum—no more raucous group Sabbath meals and study groups. The new semester will start soon. Levi will be my only companion.

We edge toward friendship. We shop and cook together. After the years on my own with little or no money, I eye the high price of strawberries one day in the grocery store and push past, but Levi stops, then puts two sumptuous cartons of the luscious fruit into our cart. "It's good to do little things," he says.

That night, over vegetarian dinner, we exchange polite conversation like two people on a blind date. Levi gets up from the table and puts on the radio. It's the classical station, something lyrical and passionate. "What is that?" I say.

"Brahms," he says. "His first. But it's almost over. This is the finale."

This isn't the first time that I've heard Levi identify classical music on the radio. I'm impressed. I'm the would-be musician, but he can recognize more music than I can. "I've heard that before," I say, a little embarrassed.

He takes a forkful of fish, then chews with his mouth open and sets his elbows on the table. I glance away, swallow hard. "Um, where did you learn to recognize all that music?" I say.

"At Penn," he says, and soon, he's relaying an account of his years at the University of Pennsylvania before he turned to religion. He's eager, happy. He sounds as if he's there again. One elbow remains on the table, his hand in the air, while he leans over his plate and shovels in food with the other. "I got to work on a pet project of one of my physics professors—a new machine to take pictures inside the body using sound waves," he says. "They're called sonograms."

"Interesting idea," I say. I wish he'd just close his mouth when he chews. "Is that safer? Than X-rays?"

"Sure. And you can see the organs!" He takes another forkful. "In the evenings, I'd go watch Eugene Ormandy conduct the Philadelphia Orchestra. I'd sit on the third balcony with a student ticket—tried not to miss a concert. I was sure I was watching something great."

I eat like a prim matron. *But look what's unfolding*, I think. *Look what he loves.* The music changes to a piano concerto.

"That's Liszt," Levi says.

We fall quiet. The notes layer and build, cascading over us, rising up and up toward a crescendo. I try to picture him as a clean-shaven undergraduate, alone in a crowd on a dim upper balcony, focused on the legendary conductor.

Then, "Tell me about Richie," I say.

The light in his face goes out. He puts down his fork. "What is there to say?" he says.

"Were you close?"

"Yes."

There is a photograph on the mantel in his parents' house of Levi's lanky, long-haired, mustached younger brother. My mother told me Richie's story before the wedding: how Richie knew Tuvia from childhood—Tuvia, who ran Chabad House before he graduated and moved away. How because of Tuvia, Richie decided to try out a New Jersey Hasidic institute for men much like the one for women I went to in St. Paul. How Richie was an avid bicycler and had always wanted to cross the country on his prized bicycle. "I came here for graduate school because of my brother," Levi says. "We fought a lot as kids. I wanted to know him. As an adult." Across the courtyard, a window is open and some student is practicing the flute. Airy arpeggios float over the weedy lawn and weave around the Liszt. "I discovered I liked my brother," Levi says. "That was new. He talked a lot about wanting to be a lawyer. We played chess almost every day. And racquetball."

"With that racquet in the office? The one I had when you came in?"

"Yes."

He skips the rest—the drunken truck driver who hit Richie somewhere in Louisiana, the mangled bicycle, the body unidentified for days in a county morgue. The laconic night voice on the telephone to his frantic parents, who hadn't heard from him: "Uh, sorry no one called sooner. We have your son. Where? Oh, here in the morgue."

"After the funeral," Levi says, "Tuvia kept calling me to come to Chabad House. Until I did." He stops. Doesn't say anything about how religion proffered structure and answers to cosmic questions at a time when nothing seemed to make sense, doesn't talk about how need can make "proof" irrelevant to the point where you might not even *want* proof. But then, neither of us can articulate those things. On the radio, the concerto slows to an adagio, cellos forming the melody. We grow quiet, my husband and I, in the music.

THE OLD METAL DOOR to the *mikvah* at the back of Dallas's Tiferet Israel Synagogue shuts behind me with a clang. "The *mikvah*'s in there," Seema Rakovsky says, giving a nod aimed at the dim interior. She switches on the lights.

The long wait has passed. Levi is waiting for me back at the Motel 8. His parents are expecting us in Dallas tomorrow, along with the U-Haul we've hitched to Levi's car to haul the rest of the wedding gifts and their old dining set back to Austin. But we came in early for this.

"You think they'll figure out we're already in town?" I asked him, while still in the motel. Levi was putting our suitcase up on the luggage rack. He turned, eyes shining. "It's our secret," he said. He stepped toward me then, closer than any stranger would come, close enough for me to feel his warmth. I picked up his car keys, looked away. "Seema's waiting," I said.

"Soon . . . ," he said, looking down at me. "I'll be waiting here for you." He bent over, his eyes deep in me, his breath, a small smile. I swallowed and made myself look up at his face.

"GO ON IN," SEEMA SAYS, pointing through an inner doorway to a small tiled pool and railing. A moth flaps against the dull yellow glow of the ceiling fixture. "You get ready in there," she says, indicating a bathroom beside the pool. "Call when you're done."

I drop my bag inside, lock the door, then linger under the hot shower, pelting wet heat, rivers down my back. I remember the first time I sat down with Seema to study with her at her dining table. I was still a high school girl in red overalls and saddle oxfords, smitten by my girlfriend. I had no idea I would wind up studying at a Hasidic institute for women, or that within three years I would have an arranged marriage and find myself here at a *mikvah*. I put my face up in the steaming waterfall. Oh, but it was fascinating the way Seema decoded the Bible's Hebrew words and letters, the ancient commentaries unfolding around the text like a mystical conversation across centuries. I massage shampoo into my scalp and put my head back to let the water stream through my hair. "The Torah begins the story of Creation with the letter 'bet' which is also the number two," she said, "because God made the world in twos—dark and light, good and evil, male and female. The pairs of opposites are all mixed up now," she said, "but a life lived by Jewish Law reveals God's original truth. Good and evil become clear, so that we can then choose correctly, and live in a world with clarity. That's what God wants."

I squirmed then—*good and evil, male and female*—thinking of shades of gray and not understanding where I could fit myself into that picture. But before the open Hebrew Bible with its web of commentaries, I was the ignorant one. Caught. If Seema said that Jewish Law was God's Truth, who was I to question?

I began to need that Truth.

RINSED AND GLEAMING, I step over the edge of the pink tub into married life. *Mikvah will be part of that life, every month.* I look around and take a pink flowered towel from a pink wicker shelf over the pink toilet and wrap myself, shivering. The whole place seems like a cliché of relentless femininity. "I'm ready," I call out.

The *mikvah* room is small and square, covered in pink tiles. We meet near the pool at the rail. Seema shuts the door behind us. The light over the pool is low, the air warm and humid and laced with the smell of chlorine. "Well, now!" Seema says, sounding proud, as if summing up how far I've come. She beams and holds out her arms.

She's treating me like a queen. That's the Hasidic metaphor for a new bride. My stomach knots. I shift my feet, look down.

The *mikvah* will wash that away. I want the *mikvah* to wash that knot away.

But first Seema has to inspect my back for stray hairs, which she does with a *tap-tap* of fingertips on wet skin. I flinch at her touch. It seems impossibly inappropriate to be wet and naked before this admirable, motherly woman who . . . who is touching my bare skin. Worse, I understand that, but don't understand how, or why, her touch is a breach. I can't identify what's wrong, and that doubles my embarrassment until I almost can't speak. Then I have to drop the towel in front of her and descend the stairs into the water. I try to cover my breasts with my arms as I go down the pool stairs, but the water is still and clear to the pink tiles at the bottom. An awful sense of exposure overlays any sense of welcome or blessing in the water, erases awareness of my waiting husband, makes it impossible to pray in this moment.

Serene proud proper Seema tosses me a washcloth. I am to cover my hair before pronouncing God's name. I try to think how God is waiting for this immersion, which will make the categories of opposites come clear again and set a binary world into proper order.

As I spread the cloth over my head, falling drops from my hands make a watery echo in the room. I extend my arms and lower my body until warm water touches my chin. I bend still deeper and bow my head, then sink beneath the surface. I wait beneath the water, hoping for awe, then emerge. "Repeat after me," Seema says, and there's pride and motherly fondness in her voice. "Blessed," she says. *Baruch.*

"Blessed," I say.

"Are You, O Lord." *Atah adonoi eloheinu.*

"Are You, O Lord."

Three words at a time, she leads me through the blessing, *al mitzvas tvila.* Then I sink back beneath the surface into an airless place far from the world and go into a fetal float. Underwater, I feel the shadows of my past and of my parents, which I wait for the holy water to dissolve and wash away. That is my prayer, for the *mikvah* to dissolve my past. To emerge with a clean slate on which I can create a new self. I focus fiercely on this duty, on what I should be, *will be,* before God.

I come up, take a breath, go under again, seven times under, up, down. I think of the seven circles I paced around Levi under the wedding canopy, Rabbi Frumen's voice counting "five, six, seven," and the seven heavens that lead to God. I emerge then, standing on tiptoe to keep my head above water. Another breath, and I sink under one last time, telling myself, *Into the water of blessing, into marriage.* When I come up the final time, it's to be a new birth. I should be pure as a newborn.

I stand ready now for my husband. But as soon as I see Seema holding out a bath towel like a curtain and looking away out of respect, that same sense of terribly inappropriate exposure returns; I wish she'd leave and let me get into the bathroom to get dressed. Head down, unable to meet her eyes, I quickly take the towel from her and wrap my naked self without breaking stride. As I hurry away, I leave a trail of wet footprints behind on the marble floor. That trail of water, already evaporating, is my wedding train.

❧

AT MOTEL 8, blinking orange neon flashes through the curtains as freeway traffic from Loop 635 roars past. The wig is on a stand next to Levi's hatbox, our one suitcase open on the dresser, my long skirt hanging over a chair, headscarf on the floor. Sheet, blanket, and bedspread cover my trembling body. The rumbling air conditioner is set on frigid.

I know my unmoved body as a failing. I don't know what it is to desire him. I know I should; I know I should long for him.

Levi's face is kind, and his step eager. He is so tall, older and wiser. He gazes down at me, his mouth in a little smile.

There's the small stab of fear at his sudden weight on the bed, my intake of breath, the smattering of black hairs on his chest. When I reach for him, I'm reaching for hope that Levi will hold me and keep me, protect me, that I can trust him to do that, learn to love him for that. I can give myself to him for that, even with no flutter in me for a man.

He pulls the covers back to look at me for the first time, his wife, whom he still knows only as a hint of curves beneath layers of cloth. Shyly, in wonder, he runs his fingers down my arm. "You are my first," he says.

I jump the smallest of little jumps. "And you are mine," I say.

He moves his hand slowly, reverently.

I stay very still. Shallow breath. Chilled. *I don't have to look*—at the hair on his chest or the dark line that descends to encircle his navel and broaden below. I don't have to think how large and rough his hands are, how I wish they were delicate and soft, how large and hard his body is, and almost threatening, when it would be so nice if his body were gently, softly form-fit to mine. I tell myself, *This is my husband*. He furrows his brow, an intensity of focus in his face I'm coming to know. Sense memories flicker through my skin: someone holding me, crooning to my infant self. *Lisa*, she says. The tall swing at a nearby park where I'd go alone, and the working, the building, toward soaring weightlessness and freedom.

His nostrils flare. He touches my hip, uncertain and careful, the expression on his face changing to one of wonder. His hand slips between my legs. *Easy*, I tell myself, beginning to tumble into a swirl of past and present, dream and breath, trembling, some distant fear I don't understand a receding pinpoint on the horizon. Then I open my eyes to enormous relief as sensation washes everything away. I pull him into me. I'm hungry, then voracious. *It's true*, I think; *I can will myself into this*—just before I am pitched through the air to a mountaintop beneath gasping stars.

His jaw hangs open above me, astonished, but then he is driven, panting, and I'm trapped—his hands and knees flexed and powerful as he forces his way into me. I panic, grit my teeth—*Don't move; it will be all right*—until I am certain I can't bear another moment, until his own trembling, his sigh.

My purchase, sealed by the signed marriage contract, is complete, blessed in advance by *mikvah* water. Levi tumbles beside me, throws his head back on the pillow. "Wow," he says. "Wow!" He pulls me close. Still somewhat in shock, I wrap his arms around me and sink into them. I try to forget the moment of feeling trapped, the aversion after he entered me, no need to make sense now—I am in his arms in this vulnerable, naked moment, and this man has pledged his life to being my refuge. After all the loneliness, it is magical to fall back and be held, to trust someone enough for that. Unorthodox desires don't seem to matter in the face of this security, this sanctum. I breathe deeply. My body unfolds. "I didn't know how alone I was," I say, "until I wasn't."

"You're not alone," he says. He nuzzles my hair, tightens his arms.

"You have a healing touch," I say around a lump in my throat. I lay my hand over his and settle my head against his chest—a strange, hard, new place. "I could love you for this," I say.

But just then, Levi pulls away, abrupt. "We have to separate right now," he says.

"What?"

He gets out of bed.

"No!" I say.

He looks apologetic. "*Dam niddah*," he says. "Virginal blood. It's the Law."

Here it is, that ancient fear drummed into both of us. The mystical threat of a woman's blood rises up like a wall between us.

"And cover yourself," Levi says.

I grab the sheet to my chest, find the scarf, and tie it behind my neck. "But I'm not bleeding," I say.

The ghost of my father has climbed into this bed.

"No matter," Levi says. "I'm still not allowed to see you *after*." He shrugs. "There are plenty of women who don't bleed the first time, I read that, but still, now we can't touch for twelve more days."

"I know the Law," I say.

Near the bathroom light, Levi takes a hand towel to wipe himself clean. Of me. He inspects the towel carefully for blood. There's nothing. "Get dressed," he says in a firmer tone. I grab my nightgown from the floor. Levi gets into pajamas and settles into the other bed, turns his back, and falls quickly into a light snore.

Late into the night, I lie awake wondering how it is that the great sense of finding home in his arms was so fleeting. I tell myself just to wait until the next *mikvah* night when we can sleep together again, but my childhood comes back, its clutter and chaos and secret unspoken betrayals. I think, *We will build an orderly home structured by the clean Law and have children who will feel safe because God's rules guarantee good behavior.* God's safety net. Forget my immigrant family, never quite at home in blond,

Baptist Dallas; forget my curious otherness, my loneliness and amorphous need. *Grow up. Have a woman's patience.* Home and belonging—we will make our own, blessed by God.

Levi's warmth, his smell, linger in the sheets. Slowly I fall asleep thinking, *This was our wedding night.*

ustin. We develop a routine. We leave early in the morning for classes. For me, it's a short walk down Manor Road to the university—cracked sidewalks, *plunk-plunk* of cars under the I-35 overpass, and then between the football stadium and LBJ Library—for daily cello practice in the musty old music building, then on to classes on the sprawling campus. Around me, the grounds are alive with forty thousand students walking, laughing, talking, bicycling, lounging on grassy areas and on and around the old sculptures and fountains, visiting, studying, strumming guitars, in and out of the huge buildings as I make my way around them. I greet a familiar face, and there are even one or two with whom I chat before class. But our life is not theirs.

At home, we dip daily into Hasidic books, labor over Hebrew and Yiddish, share a *vort* of Hasidic thought over the Sabbath table. We practice peppering our speech with Hasidic expressions of faith and self-abnegation. *Baruch hashem. Hakol bidei shamayim.* Bless God! It's all in heaven's hands.

A growing guilty patter of Hasidic teaching is easing me into my role, like a rasp applied steadily to my rough edges. When I need, I humbly ask Levi for money. I let him decide what time we will eat, or what we will eat, pushing myself to use a respectful tone. He doesn't demand this of me. The rasp is in my own hands.

As for Levi, there are times, when I hand off a decision to him, when he seems hesitant, uncertain, burdened. Perhaps lonely, or scared, suddenly holding this new weight of making a decision alone. He looks hopefully to me, but I don't extend a hand or a word of advice or support. I wait. Then he pulls himself up as if it's a great effort and issues his final word.

I wake with a weight in my chest, wake each morning to blank white walls. Levi flies out of bed after too few hours of sleep, washes, and throws on his clothes. Soon he is draped in his prayer shawl, reciting the voluminous Hebrew prayers and psalms he must cover daily. The language remains elusive to him, his tongue awkward and slow, and so he bends his head over the book, furrows his brow, a picture of grinding determination through boring hours that does not seem to get easier. The prayer book will go with him when he leaves for classes, and he will fit in more in every crevice of his day, only to find himself living behind a wall of prayer.

Separated in our defined roles, I begin to feel unspontaneous, heavy-footed, alone. I grow quieter, become indecisive. Levi and I pass each other with few words, propelled into our separate routines. Neither of us seems to understand why that might be.

At home, the choice of music, when we have any at all, is his. Each day I take my cello off to the music building and close myself into one of the practice rooms. There I can spend hours simply making each string vibrate, rosined bow setting off loose, long, sonorous notes. Each step of a simple scale grows complex, full, magical. Only when alone in that stark little room does the cello sing.

I COUNT THE DAYS UNTIL *MIKVAH*, but before I can get back to it, my cycle returns. My days pulse with the counting rhythm the Law imposes on us, and with the memory of lying in Levi's arms.

To use the *mikvah* nearest our home, we drive the night highway ninety miles on I-35 south to San Antonio, where there is a little *mikvah* in a decaying area of town at the back of Congregation Rodfei Shalom, the old Orthodox synagogue. *Mikvah* attendants are supposed to be women, but the San Antonio rabbi, Rabbi Kornbluth, ruled that Levi had to come with me because it is unsafe there at night. Besides, the rabbi chuckled, his wife long ago announced she was no *mikvah* attendant.

Levi and I stop at the Kornbluths' to pick up the key. Both of us are uncomfortable with this immodest announcement that this is our *mikvah* night, as if we are stopping off to announce we will have sex this night.

We meet Rabbi Kornbluth and his wife at their partially opened door, their faces peering out like two adjacent moons. I stand half hidden behind Levi. "We just came for the key," Levi says, but they open the door wide and say, "Come in, come in!" and soon we're perched on their formal sofa, balancing delicate china cups of weak tea on gold-rimmed saucers.

The Kornbluths are old, in their fifties at least. Unlike Hasidic beards untouched by a blade, the rabbi's is trimmed close. The two look only at Levi, address only Levi, even Mrs. Kornbluth in her slacks. "What are you studying?" she asks.

"Accounting," he says. "I'm working on an MBA."

In a way, I prefer being an invisible female, no eyes on me. Because beneath this tea conversation is the tacit understanding that we're here for me to immerse in the *mikvah*. I feel certain that creates an inevitable shared image in the room, as if I'm standing nude before them right there on the Persian carpet. "Sugar?" the rabbi's wife asks Levi.

WE GET TO THE SYNAGOGUE well after dark. The old, ornate building is a looming thing in shadow, too large, we've been told, for its aging, dwindling congregation. The area around the building is poorly lit, as is the broad, cracked veranda. Levi grimaces and jiggles the key in the old lock. "We're gonna get mugged," I whisper, glancing down the empty street. "*Shluchei mitzvah*," he says. "Don't worry." His shoulders are tight. But there is no danger for those engaged in a commandment.

When we finally get in, we tiptoe through the empty lobby, where prayer shawls hang like body sacks on the wall, and through an echoing foyer to the door marked women's bathroom. We look at each other. Levi opens the door, and then another on the right to the *mikvah*. "My God," he says.

Someone must have been here earlier. The floor is wet, and an electric heater has been left on, weakly glowing coils and a frayed cord in a puddle. Levi yanks the cord from the socket.

The heater hasn't done much anyway. The cold room, just big enough for the little pool, is narrow and dank, and there's a humid sheen over the tiled walls. I crouch, touch the water and wince. Then I stand, resolute. "Turn away," I tell Levi. The rabbi may have ruled that Levi has to be my attendant, even though that means he will see me uncovered before immersion, but we can minimize Levi's exposure. I turn my back to strip off my clothes, pull off the headscarf, run my fingers through my short hair.

The water isn't cool. It's cold. I force myself to go down, Levi watching at the rail.

Under the water, it's too cold to think of the symbolism of this ritual or to try to make the act into a prayerful thing. The monthly rebirth, seventh heaven, emergence from holy water into purity, all starry ideas that floated through my first *mikvah*— all of those seem superfluous in the stark clarity of this cold immersion. There's no place here for dreams and ideas. What is left is swift obedience. God's command. *Why*, I think, *it's the act, this cold dunk; that is the thing.* Holy obedience. Sacrifice. Not some effort at transcendence. Up now, above the surface for breath, wet and shivering, spluttering blessing words into damp air.

"Amen," Levi says from above, like a validation. He pronounces it *awmeyn*.

But, I think, *he's warm and dressed*. I force myself back under. The fierce shivering effort fills me with religious pride. Up again, teeth chattering, to brush water from my eyes and blurt out in fast Hebrew, "It should be Your Will O God that the temple be rebuilt, *bimheirah beyameinu*." Levi responds with a quick and automatic "amen."

We are God's machines. *God working us*. I go back under with new strength, up, down, seven times in all, telling myself, *I will get strong from this*. Then I stand for the last time, head above water, shivering so that I can't speak.

My body is again purified for my husband. Levi holds up a towel, just as Seema once did. I go up the steps, drops yet again cascading off wet skin, take the towel from him, and get dressed, and we go out to the car. We stop to slip the key into the Kornbluths' mailbox, then drive home ninety miles over the night highway. We are aliens skimming across the sleeping Texas Hill Country, with its laconic peoples, its rivered lands.

SOMETHING HAPPENS DURING SEX that night in our little student apartment near the University of Texas campus, our second time having sex. I can't seem to slip out of passive, obedient mode, can't get off of religious female automatic. I feel flat, dispassionate, in spite of my body's response, and throughout there's a lump of loss in my throat as if I've swallowed something. At least when Levi is above me, when his powerful knees and hands hem me in, I don't feel trapped this time, don't feel much of anything. But late that night in Levi's bed, as I start to drift off next to him, he pulls me close and wraps his arms around me again. I nestle into the pillow we are now allowed to share and heave a deep sigh. Breathing eases. The long loneliness abates. *How I've waited to get back to this*, I think, this safe place. Levi falls asleep then, wrapped around me, his chest in its slow rise and fall, and I thank God that the days of separation have passed. I think, *Is this love?* I want this to be love. I tell myself, *I'm finally home.*

SLATS OF MORNING SUNLIGHT through yellowed blinds. I wake with the sense that I am caught in something. Then I sit up in full-blown panic. Levi's mouth is hanging open in his sleep, his night yarmulka fallen off his head. I turn, heart racing, trying to catch my breath. What *is* this box? I can't seem to get out of this box. A swarm of everything I've tamped down is rising all around me, overtaking me. I splutter, "Why didn't I think?" I gasp and jump out of the bed. I turn and grab Levi's arm, shake his shoulder. "Wake up!" I say.

"Wh-what?" he says, struggling, his voice rough from sleep. "What is it?"

"Why didn't I think? Why didn't I know?" I say. "But I did know. Of course we knew."

"What?" he says, raising himself up on one elbow. "What?"

I'm standing over him, shaking his shoulder. "We had sex last night!"

"And?" he says.

"And we didn't . . . we can't use birth control!"

"And?"

"What was I thinking? I can't have a baby!"

"I don't think . . . ," he says, and, "But you knew perfectly well."

"I was wrapped up in wedding stuff!" I say.

I've been floating on the wedding dream and on the Rebbe's blessing/command: get married, be a good Hasidic girl, do the right thing. *No harm comes to those who do a mitzvah.* The joy in the wedding air, misty picture of happy families, the family we will have that will be everything mine wasn't. But all that is suddenly different, very different, from the very real babies that can form inside nineteen-year-old me, university student me, maybe one already has, a baby that will overwhelm my life, derail school, that I won't know how to care for—a baby that I could *hurt*. Hurt as I was. *I'll make all of my mother's mistakes.* "I can't do this!" I say. I'm shaking. I shake Levi with both hands. "No!" I say. I sit down and sob. "I can't get pregnant. It's too much. What have we *done*?"

Levi sits up, gropes for his yarmulka. Then a little gasp, his eyes wide. He puts a hand on my arm and whispers, "Do you think you *are* pregnant? Already?"

"I don't *know!*" I moan.

It's as if I hear my mother saying, *Lisa. Lisa!* in my ear. *Lisa, come home. Listen to me!*

I'm not Lisa anymore, I tell her. So why do I feel stuck inside this "Leah," as if I don't even know who she is or where I am?

Lisa, my mother whispers.

I try to reason with myself. Being Leah means becoming a mother. I knew that all along.

If you get pregnant, you can't leave. You can't come home.

That can't be true, I tell her. *You don't mean "home" to me anymore. Levi's my home.*

I finger my ring. But I'm no longer teetering between then and now, between Lisa and Leah. I know who I am. So why am I in a panic? (*Come home!*) When I even think of being pregnant, why do I see myself dashing this way and that through a maze of Jewish Law with no way out? (*Lisa! Listen! Come!*) Where *is* home? (*I told you so,* she whispers.)

Even away from my mother, with a baby I might become her. There has to be a way out.

"I had to study the laws about marriage before the wedding," Levi says in a reasonable tone. "The Law's not so rigid. Really.

Sometimes birth control is allowed—if you're sick and pregnancy would be harmful."

"I'll die if I get pregnant," I say. "Inside."

He is conciliatory, and kind. "If the Law gives a concession, that's not breaking the Law. If you're sick," he offers again. "You know," he says, "*v'chai bahem.*"

V'chai bahem is both a promise and a command—you *will* live within the laws, and the Law will help you live. That's what we're taught, that Jewish Law is both stern and loving, strict and flexible. The Law is a good parent.

It is clear Levi is willing to look for a legal concession. He has faith that there is one for us within the Law. I think, *He's in this with me.* My panic ratchets down a notch.

He doesn't say whether or not he wants a baby, but I don't expect him to. That would be irrelevant, even inappropriate. Babies aren't chosen; they come from God. *But,* I think, *maybe he's also afraid.* We have no money. His wife isn't ready to mother a child. Then—another tailspin. "What? The Law gives a concession for sick people? I'm not sick," I say. "I just can't bear the idea. What good does a break for sick people do me?"

Levi gets up, barefoot in the pajama bottoms and undershirt he slept in, *tzitzis* undergarment on top, white strings hanging to his knees, his knitted sleep yarmulka back on his head. I flash on an image of his naked silhouette above me in the night. "Wait. I've got a book," he says. "I remember something I read." He goes into his office and takes a volume from the brick-and-board bookcase, both Hebrew and English print on the front. He clears a space at his desk and sits down to read.

I go splash water on my face. Try to breathe. Brush my teeth. But the minutes are heavy.

Soon, he comes out with the book open in his hands. "Look at this," he says. "Conception involves a mystical relationship between the father, mother, and God. To interfere with that relationship by stopping the natural process is to thwart God's will, a grave sin."

"Oh boy," I say.

"Wait," Levi says. He flips to another page. "It seems there've been times when Rav Moshe has allowed birth control. Listen." He reads, "Although a condom is forbidden, Rabbi Moshe Feinstein has ruled that other types of birth control that create a simple barrier and do not impede the natural process by killing sperm or preventing ovulation can be allowed if necessary for the mother's health." He looks up. "Like a diaphragm," he says.

A sliver of hope. "*For the mother's health.* Is the mother's mental health part of that?" I say. But then I realize whom Levi is quoting. "Wait! Rav *Moshe* allows it?" I say. Panic returns.

It took me a while to figure out the hierarchy. There are just-plain-rabbis, like Rabbi Frumen, who lead individual congregations as spiritual shepherds. They are also kind of like lawyers qualified to impart to their followers expert knowledge in the Law. But even they defer to a rav, a rabbi who is more like a judge. He can rule on new applications of the Law or parse out thorny conflicts between people. Or grant dispensations.

A rebbe is both rabbi and rav, but this rebbe chooses to stand above all that. He is our guide, our inspiration, but when people write him with problems that can be addressed within the Law, he writes back, "Ask a rav."

Rav Moshe Feinstein, whom Levi quoted, is venerated among non-Hasidic Orthodox, but Lubavitcher Hasidim do not speak well of Rav Moshe's leniencies, even though the Rebbe himself has been known to send him people who need his gentler rulings. Only the Rebbe can bend like that. Otherwise, we should turn to our own.

Levi frowns. "Maybe we should ask a Lubavitcher rav first," he says.

"Can we find one who will understand?" I say.

"We'll go to the top," Levi says. "We'll ask the head rav of Lubavitch. We're also Lubavitcher Hasidim. He'll take care of *us*."

It's confident Levi who makes the call and requests the conference. It's Levi who tells the rav, after our nervous wait, "My wife feels unable to bear a child." It's Levi who explains the problem. My problem. I listen in modest silence on the extension for the rabbi's decision about my body, my life.

"So what do you want?" the rav says.

"Could we use some sort of birth control?" Levi says.

"We don't do that," the rav says in a dismissive tone, followed by dismissive silence.

Levi falls dumb into that silence. He doesn't argue. He doesn't defend me.

There's an awkward pause. Heart pounding, I wait for rescue. Then I take a deep breath and make myself speak. My voice sounds unnatural, untried, and every word is laced with the guilt of my immodesty in speaking out. But each word is another step forward through an unfamiliar passage. One day, I will remember this, remember how. "Wait. What if the woman could get hurt?" I say.

"That's different," the rabbi says. "But then I would need a letter from a doctor."

A doctor. My word about my body isn't enough. "What if 'the woman' is physically healthy," I say, "but she can't bear the possibility of . . . of . . . ?"

"Are you talking about *psychological* harm?" the rav says.

"I guess I am," I say.

He laughs. "You want permission to break the Law because motherhood is difficult?"

Nobody speaks. The silence is filled with my inadequacy as a wife, as a religious woman, as a potential mother. I am small. Finally, I say, "But I read—we read—that Rav Moshe . . ."

"Well, then," the rabbi says, now clearly annoyed, "call Rav Moshe."

≈

ONE NIGHT TWO MONTHS LATER, I lock the door in the bathroom and position myself in the space between toilet and tub. Behind me, the nylon curtain is wet with droplets from morning showers. We called Rav Moshe the next evening. We weren't allowed to speak directly to him, but we spoke with his son, his representative, as the great rav sat in judgment nearby. "My father says you will bear Jewish children in joy," the son said. "You may use a diaphragm for one year from this date." Now, two months later, I put the top down to the toilet, pull off my scarf, and shake my growing hair back and off my face. Levi is waiting in the other room.

Since we received Rav Moshe's permission, we have both been finding slivers of freedom, allowing each other that. Levi wears his blue jeans, goes to the symphony, indulges in beloved old movies, even if the Hasidim deem such secular things soulless. I've renewed my interest in my university studies. One of my art history professors has offered to mentor me in an independent project about the architecture of Gaudí. I've even stopped wearing the wig on campus, and learned intricate decorative ways to arrange scarves. My growing hair now hangs audaciously long and free beneath the scarf.

But at home, even with my partly uncovered hair and his blue jeans, we still have our roles. Levi controls the money, makes the decisions. I'm getting to know him: He has little need for casual touch, and great concern about his obligations outside our home. At times, he surprises me with a gift or a kind word, but in general he's awkward about my needs, often doesn't seem aware of them. Our separate roles seem to reinforce his awkwardness, as if, with his position so clearly defined, he has difficulty developing new empathy for mine. That would be crossing a line he doesn't seem to know how to cross anymore. Perhaps he never did.

But Rav Moshe has given me something. I pick up a yellow plastic case from the counter and take out the thin rubber cup stretched over a rounded spring. I've come to enjoy the sploosh of cream into the quivering rubber bowl, the way that I have to pinch and fold the spring in order to lodge it inside me just so against thinly sheathed bone. The diaphragm is teaching me my body's inner folds and secret chambers, giving me time without babies to learn. I put my right foot on top of the closed toilet lid, left foot on the floor, pull the full skirt up to my thighs. This is Rav Moshe's gift: a kosher brashness I'm gaining from this new body knowledge.

Now I can cross without consequence the line Levi can't seem to cross—into his bed. And I do. I approach him for sex again and again. Even though I have little physical desire, I do it anyway, always pleased with his happy response. I do it for connection, and for the aftermath in his arms. Sex seems the only way to get to that warm safe place. The alternative of staying on my side of the Hasidic divide, always near him yet apart, is lonelier than being alone. Besides, I'm trying with everything I have to make sure being in his arms still feels like coming home. Then I test it again, and again, because, more and more, it . . . doesn't.

I open the bathroom door and go to him.

Late that night, they begin—transporting dreams that I will not, cannot, acknowledge in the daytime. In my dream, my most passionate, most alluring lover is a woman with black curls and tapered, delicate hands.

*O*kaaayy!" That was a twentysomething bearded rabbi at the orientation for the Live and Learn Sabbath Experience. He was rubbing his hands together as he addressed the crowd. Dallas's Shearith Israel synagogue was hosting Lubavitcher Hasidim from Brooklyn, Jews who still lived by the old Code of Jewish Law. The men wore beards and yarmulkas and black and white clothes, while their wives, somewhere in the background, were in long skirts and long sleeves, their hair covered with wigs or scarves. We were among the attendees, Ana and I. It was 1972. I was sixteen, immersed in college plans, intent on moving out to make my mark in the world.

About fifty of us had shown up for the weekend-long program and were sitting in folding chairs at one end of a social hall. I figured, as Ana and I were, most were there like tourists come to see these audaciously different Hasidim in action. We were to sleep over and experience an Orthodox Sabbath, follow all the rules. Which explains why we had come in their costume— that is, in the women's dress code we were told when we registered: skirt length to the calf, sleeves to midforearm, closed neckline, panty hose. I rarely wore a skirt, preferring jeans or red overalls. But since our families had worked so hard to distance themselves from the "old ways" and blend in, going openly make-believe Orthodox with Ana for the weekend was a heady rebellious game. Anyway, there was also a soaring spirit feeling I wanted out of religion I imagined I could find somewhere, and I believed the Hasidim were all about that spirit. I believed my wannabe family had deprived me of that. Transcendence, Ana called it. A leap above, straight to God.

Ana was two years my senior, and I wanted to follow her, would have followed her, anywhere. We had first met one Sunday two years before when I'd cut Sunday-school class at our liberal Reform temple, where my mother sent my sisters and me each week to sit among the children of her peers and give the impression we were a "normal" family, though at home cockroaches ran up walls, our mother slept through drugged days, and our mentally ill father sat in the living room, grinding his teeth to nubs while reading every word in the newspaper, including the classifieds. I wasn't interested in the teacher's do-good theology. I had taken to skipping the classes. That Sunday, I found Ana leading singing kids on guitar, her soprano voice a lovely, lilting vibrato. It didn't take long for me to attach myself. We were an odd pair, but Ana said I was deep and fearless, and I was simply smitten. She didn't seem to notice, and yet I'd find her waiting near my school bus in the morning in sunglasses, long brown hair feathered in the wind, the top of her convertible down, radio blaring. She made skipping school an easy decision.

Together we took a different look at Judaism—reading books and experimenting with old rituals our modern synagogue spurned. Others of our friends were affecting a hippie air, or carrying around *Quotations from Chairman Mao* or *The Communist Manifesto, Siddhartha,* or *Dune,* all of us trying on and exchanging identities like costumes in a backstage dressing room. Spending the weekend with the Hasidim was just another supposedly anti-materialist costume to try on, all the more appealing because we did it together. And because our parents hated it. Besides, we had planned to go camping, but it looked like rain.

The youngish rabbi addressing us had long white strings

hanging over his belt at either hip that I thought curious. He had
a red full beard and he was pale, a large black yarmulke on his
balding head. Three others about the same age stood behind him,
all in the black and white attire, all apparently feeling a bit on
display and mildly self-conscious, arms clasped behind their
backs, looking out at the crowd.

"Before we get started," our rabbi announced, "here are the
Sabbath rules."

Ana grinned. "Game on," she whispered.

He had a list: The Sabbath begins tonight at sundown and
will be over tomorrow night after sundown. Set the lights in your
rooms before sundown, and don't touch the switch. Do not use or
touch anything that requires electricity. No writing; no using a
car or telephone. Don't tear anything. No scrubbing or washing—
clothing or one's own body, so better not to brush teeth; no
showers; no hot water or soap, but okay to rinse off in cold water
if you must.

There were murmurs but little apparent surprise, no laughs
or shaking heads. They asked informed questions: Doesn't Jewish
Law allow you to get a child to turn off a light for you on the
Sabbath? I'm a doctor, so I can use the telephone for my work,
right? It seemed many were well aware of the Sabbath laws. I
whispered to Ana, "But I didn't know any of this stuff." Still, the
people asking questions sounded a little meek before rabbinic
authority, as if the rabbi owned the Law. I got that. He owned *us*
for now. Only one question sounded incredulous. "We can't tear
anything, but surely," the woman said, "you can tear toilet paper?"

We couldn't. We'd have to prepare that in advance.

I was both leery of these rules and attracted to them. My
mother would suddenly decide she had rules she'd never told, her
anger at us for not following them a shot out of nowhere. I was
always uncertain around her, never getting it right. Love was at
stake, bound up with her unknowable rules. In school as well,

mysterious unwritten rules made being one of the girls my endless social failing. There I was in overalls, longing for my girlfriend and dreaming at night that I was a boy, watching mystified as other girls pretended to be 'women,' girls who didn't seem themselves anymore as they touched up their makeup and swished around boys.

The rabbi said, "In a few minutes, the women are going to light Sabbath candles. Our women inaugurate the holy Sabbath."

Our women. The phrase swept me solidly into the group, a reassuring sense of belonging. But it also confirmed that these strangers now owned us. I was confused, conflicted. *Our women.* "Oh, and one more thing," the rabbi said. He glanced sideways and swallowed. "Throughout the Sabbath, women and men will participate separately."

I looked up.

"This is modest," he said. "Separate is Godly."

For the rest of this timeless Sabbath, women were to sit apart from the men at meals and behind a partition at prayers. We women would gather separately, pray apart, in low voices, eat apart. At home my mother was cheering the budding feminist movement, Bella Abzug in Congress in her red hats, the Equal Rights Amendment making its slow progress state to state, women burning bras on television. Ana and I had stepped into a different reality.

I supposed this divide no stranger than the other new rules. I decided to treat it like summer-camp orientation, reasonable enough that we would be subdivided into groups with different activities. Anyway, I had just been deemed a woman and thus an adult.

The rabbi went on about how noble, devoted Jewish women have been doing the candle ritual Friday nights for thousands of years. Images of a simple, simultaneous act worldwide played in my mind: little flames at sundown, flickering shadows on walls on every continent, covered heads bowed over centuries. That was real belonging—global, historical. The rabbi said that we women brought light to the world. He paused for effect, gave us a long gaze, then raised his voice. "Now it is time," he said, "for our women to inaugurate the holy Sabbath."

He gestured toward a long table at the other end of the hall, covered with unlit candles. He turned and stretched out one arm as if we were honored guests he was ushering into his home. But it also seemed we had no choice.

Around us, women rising, rustle and movement, gathering of pocketbooks, murmurs, click of heels. We had our new mission, to light those candles and create an island in time, a peaceful Sabbath island for our people. And so Ana and I glided off among the women, leaving the men behind. "I feel weird," I murmured to Ana as we left. I was a Woman now, but this faux, dictated *femaleness* came from yet another set of rules I couldn't intuit. Shyness settled over me like a veil.

Perhaps twenty of us gathered around the candle-covered table. "I can do this one. It's basic Sunday school," Ana said. She took a book of matches from the pile and lit two of the candles, covered her eyes with her hands, and recited the Hebrew blessing perfectly.

I wondered where all the men had gone.

I also took a matchbook. Struck a match. A sizzle rose, then a blue-and-yellow flame. I was suddenly grateful for this rare sense of belonging. Here we were, all of us immersed in the same moment, the same ritual. Hold the flame to the wick until it burns small and strong on its own. Recite the old words of blessing, hands over eyes. *Baruch atah adonoi.* I was surrounded by whispers, magnetized to my new companions among wafts of perfume, tiny swaying movements, Ana's sleeve brushing my arm.

Before me was a horizon of wavering little flames. I may have been planning to leave home and make my mark, but I had also been recently obsessed with the Holocaust, often imagining myself caught in some Gothic horror and sucked into oblivion, and had been nurturing a secret, amorphous fear. In my darker moments, I yearned simply not to become a statistic. Maybe, I thought, maybe we were more than blips in history, more than statistics. Like the rabbi said, we could be women who had just changed the world with the strike of a match. We could mean something. Because, like God, we could create a day.

WHEN I WAS SMALL, I was afraid of the dark. One night, I woke up terrified in the black night. I wanted my mother. Out of bed, I waved jerking, trembling hands for obstacles and found my way into the hall. All along the wall, I knew, were my mother's huge canvases—we lived in narrowed, cluttered spaces edged in her tilting planes of color, although in the dark, colors were only memory. Curling my toes, I groped past my sisters' rooms. A lurch, then a halt, fingertips along the stippled wall.

The wall ended at my parents' doorway. Without that guide I was in a void, breathing hard. I dropped to my knees and crawled like a blind infant; particles in the musty carpet pressed into palms. At the end of this longest journey, I met the drape of my mother's bedcover. I stood, and became a toddler cruising sideways, inch by inch, around her bed.

I expected my mother to send me back to my room, but she muttered and moved over—no open arms or caress, but I could stay. I slept and dreamed then, but even though I had gotten myself where I wanted to be, the boy I was in my dream was still looking for his mother. In the morning, I woke with need for her a sharp place in my throat. I suppose I have always been compelled to set out clueless through the dark for new places while at the same time looking for safety, ever heading away yet hoping that in the end I will find I've come home.

LATER, WE RETURNED TO THE SOCIAL HALL, where they had set up more chairs in two sections with a partition down the middle, for the Sabbath services. The women were to sit on the left.

A second rabbi introduced himself as Rabbi Geller, in charge of the weekend. He was a short, dark-haired man who bounced as he spoke. He positioned himself squarely in front of the men. Soon the men were reciting Hebrew prayers out loud and very fast, not at all together, sometimes breaking out into joyous, deep-voiced song.

The cacophony fell over us like startling rain. I knew enough of the Hebrew alphabet to know that one can sound out the words without understanding, but I was still surprised so many of the men could read. "Wow," I whispered to Ana. "They are really going fast."

"You think anyone understands what they're saying?" Ana said.

"At that speed I wouldn't even understand English," I said.

A few of the women read from their prayer books. The rest of us sat quietly and waited for the service to end. We were not to raise our voices in prayer with the men.

I was restless. I set my gaze on two Hasidic women in the row in front of us, both in wigs and modest clothing. One was older, in a blond nylon wig. The other held a sleepy, thumb-sucking toddler. It seemed as if they were in a play, in costumes for their roles as Women. Both sat up with self-conscious propriety and whispered their prayers. Around us, whistling streams of air from more female-whispered prayers were audible in tiny moments between the men's songs.

I was bored, feeling like an outsider. I shifted in my chair, tugged at my skirt, then got up. Ana was still enjoying the old melodies when I slipped out.

Six months earlier, I had met with Rabbi Goldenberg, rabbi for the youth at Temple EmanuEl, had driven myself there in my mother's dusty Impala. I had developed an ache in my chest, like a hum. That ache was such a palpable presence that I had decided it must be my soul. And if there really was a soul, there must be a God.

Sally Preisand was all over national news at the time, recently ordained by the Jewish Reform movement and touted as the first woman rabbi. I had seen her on television, proud, confident, smiling, in a prayer shawl that was long and narrow like a priest's stole on top of her dress—a startling image on a woman then. My mother had no use for religion, no sense of faith that I knew of, but Preisand was a Jewish woman breaking boundaries. "Will you look at that!" she said, and sat up, her face alive. The Sally Preisand sighting somehow joined with the ache in my chest and the image of my mother's smiling face and gave me a new career idea.

I was waiting for Rabbi Goldenberg on a bench outside his office when an old man with a white beard walked out. My first Hasid sighting. He was in a double-breasted black coat like a suit jacket, except that it hung to his knees, along with a black hat indoors, and he had white earlocks tucked behind his ears. He passed right in front of scruffy me—close enough to catch his gentle, careworn face, large gray eyes with deep bags.

Seeing him gave me a shock. I was instantly, utterly embarrassed. I felt he was a complete anomaly there, and it seemed as if I had just discovered a family member who was horrendously out of step, with no sense of fashion, the butt of jokes, just when I was working hard to launch myself into a world where I was determined to fit in (just a little worried that I wouldn't). I was still shaken when the rabbi's secretary called me in. I caught a blurred image of the old man through the green glass, his stooped figure leaving through an outside door.

Unlike the old man, Rabbi Goldenberg was clean-shaven, his head uncovered. He swiveled his chair, then rested his chin on his hand as if contemplating me, one knobby finger up the side of his face, which was long and acne-scarred and kind. After a long gaze, he said, "How can I help you?"

Shyly, I launched into hesitant then melodramatic assertions about my newfound faith, hoping I'd get his empathy and support. I said, "I think I want to become a rabbi."

"And why is that?" he asked, chin still on hand, doting smile.

But I didn't really know why, any more than I knew what becoming a rabbi might require. I also couldn't understand then how the adulation Preisand was receiving, and my mother's pride in her, had fleeting power over me. "Let's see," he said. "Rabbinic training starts in graduate school—a long way off for you. But you have to start somewhere."

That was how I wound up attending Rabbi Goldenberg's conversion classes—a place, he said, where I could begin by getting a good overview of Reform Judaism's liberal philosophy. In the classes, he explained how the Reform movement refused to mandate specifics of belief and rejected notions that God had dictated the Bible. He explored their assumption that the Bible is a pastiche of different texts from different hands. The Reform movement also rejected the authority of the old Code of Jewish Law, which he said tries to legislate life down to the level of minutiae and robs one of free choice. He challenged us, saying, "Chart a unique spiritual path of your own."

The ache remained, not even muted. I found all this lofty and vague and frustratingly nonspecific when I had hoped to get club rules and a list of what I was supposed to believe and do. I also had hoped for assurance that, at the end of the path, God would be shining down His approval. That's what I thought religion was supposed to be. Restless, I moved on, leaving behind my flirtation with becoming a rabbi. Not long after, I attended what I thought was a free day of learning at Shearith Israel Synagogue, where I happened to see a poster for a Sabbath weekend with Hasidim.

AT DINNER, men and women were seated on opposite sides of the room at tables covered in white and laden with enormous trays of kugels and salads, baba ghanoush, marinated carrots, eggs, pickles, and thick challah slices. A head table across the front connected the two sides, where Rabbi Geller and his group were assembling into a line of black coats, long beards, and hats. Maybe it was the repetition, each of them the same, the message coming at me again and again, but the appearance of those rabbis was starting to make sense. The Vietnam War was grinding on. Every night there were men in uniform on television looking purposeful and serious. "Look at those guys at the front," I said to Ana.

She rolled her eyes. "Fashion statement," she said.

But now their garb spelled out a statement of mission. God's elite corps. "It's not about fashion," I said. "And it's not a costume."

"No?" she said.

"It's a uniform," I said. "They are soldiers for God."

Her eyes laughed.

I was beginning to sense the self-assuredness that might come from their rules, the nobility of purpose in them, the sense of mission. Besides the uniforms' clear message, Hasidic rules were clear and defined, even written down, and seemed to promise an almost maternal Godly love—so unlike rules I had encountered until now. Sitting at their table, I didn't think this as much as feel it: unlike with my mother, and unlike in school, where I didn't know how to be a "woman," here, maybe I could get the rules right.

Rabbi Geller stood, held up a silver goblet of wine, and sang out the kiddush Sabbath wine prayer. I sort of recognized the tune from my tone-deaf father. When I was small and he was well, there was something about quiet bedtime moments in low light that would start him talking about his immigrant parents in Brooklyn and the old Jewish ways they had brought from Russia. He told me how his mother polished the wine goblet and candlesticks on Friday and set out the challah under a white cloth, preserving a steadiness and order while she was alive that was lost in our family before it got to us. Then he would stretch out beside me and sing old show tunes. You say potato, I say potahto. Let's fall in love.

My grandparents were gone. In a way, so was my father. I lifted my chin and sang the kiddush with Rabbi Geller. Then we were served an enormous meal.

I was long past full, sleepy, lulled, when Rabbi Geller began a moving, meditative, wordless song in a melodic minor key, in his rich baritone voice that made me think of a cello. He sang on with his eyes closed. *Na nana na.* Gradually, others leaned back into their chairs and joined him. People hung their heads back as they sang, or closed their eyes. Ana did the same. The tune wandered around us, lingered, sad and searching. Laced with Ana's soprano, the voices rose and filled the room, ebbed and swelled over us in waves. Tension I normally carried rolled out my fingertips. I closed my eyes and sang, on and on, letting my body sway. Group song wrapped around us like a human prayer shawl.

Then, suddenly, the rabbi came to a halt. I opened my eyes to find he had put up his palm like a stop sign. Everyone grew quiet. "A woman's voice is a precious jewel," the rabbi announced in a slow, careful voice. "Of course, a jewel shouldn't be flashed around. A jewel should be kept in a safe and treasured place. That is why women are not to sing in public."

I woke up then, to find myself just a woman, and deeply embarrassed for singing out loud. Ana shook her head. But, I tried to tell myself, we were being honored with this enforced silence. It was supposed to be an honor. Still, I looked down at my hands.

Rabbi Geller began again, and this time only men joined him. Women glanced at one another, lowered their eyes. The men's singing grew until the rabbi raised his arms, urging them to get out of their uptight secular selves, and the men all rose, full of righteous spiritual energy, willing and eager now to let themselves go. For God. They rushed to the open floor and began to dance. How they danced! They danced as one, and soon they were a single entity, the room full of singing men, stomping feet, and righteous rhythm. As they jumped and sang, hands on shoulders and backs, we stood at the side of their exuberant closed circle. Faster and faster they went. Shirttails came out. Ties were pulled off. They danced! One at a time, Hasidic men took off their long black coats, tossed them aside, and rejoined the fray, strings flying at their hips. Mouths open, singing, singing, voices hoarse, faces red and beaded with jumping joyous sweat. The whole room reverberated in deafening song.

I forgot about being silenced. Ana's face was lit, her eyes shining. I tapped her arm and gestured at the dancing men, nodding my chin at them and smiling, smiling at the scene and the fervor, carried away by irresistible Hasidic confidence in their own rightness and goodness, this demonstration of Godly joy. In my mind, I was in the middle of those dancing men, my hand on a sweating back, my feet swept up in their beat, singing out loud among them, all of us bound together by a single pulsing rhythm of faith in exclusive holy intimacy. This was where I belonged. Yes! I was one of them, among them, not a woman on the sidelines. I had escaped everything. *It's true*, I thought, exultant. *You can lose yourself in God.*

Late that night, in spite of rules that forbade musical instruments on the Sabbath, Ana spread her bedroll on the floor and sat on it cross-legged, playing guitar and singing quietly to herself. Behind our closed door, I reasoned, we weren't exactly singing in public, so I sang with her. Soon we became a little bolder, raised our voices, harmonized. Then, a knock on the door. Ana's hand fell flat on the strings. We eyed each other. But there was no Sabbath police. It was just a girl around my age who introduced herself as Janice—small-boned; fine, straight brunette hair. She had come from Fort Worth with her mother for this event, knocked because she had heard us singing. I invited her in, and once I closed the door, we had our voices again. Janice's was clear and strong. We sang in three-part harmony, all of us cross-legged on an open bedroll. Ana led on guitar as I leaned in toward her, our eyes locking in the tune.

I WOKE EARLY BUT SKIPPED morning services. Ana was still sleeping. Near the coffee urn I met Seema, the Hasidic woman with the blond wig I'd seen at prayers the night before. "What's your name?" she asked in an official voice, as if she were a spokesperson.

"Lisa," I said.

"And your Hebrew name?"

I had recently asked my mother that question because it was a blank on the registration form for this weekend. She had rolled her eyes. "We're Americans," she'd said, with all the vehemence as if she herself was the immigrant. Hebrew names from the old country didn't fit her view. But I managed to get the story out of her: how after my birth she had wanted my name announced at the temple, how she'd been told that to do that, I had to have a Hebrew name. "So the rabbi just gave you one," she said. "We were never going to use it anyway."

"And?"

"It's Leah." She said, with obvious distaste.

"Lay-ah?" I said.

"That's how the rabbi said it."

"Leah," I told Seema, proud that I knew. "Why?"

"That," Seema said, "is the name of your Jewish soul." Then she took a blueberry Danish from a platter by the coffee urn, put it on a paper plate, and offered it to me. With the other hand, she touched my shoulder, as if she'd known me for years. "Have something to eat?" she said.

I accepted as if the plate were an invitation into an elite club. How could I not? I had a momentary thought about how my non-Jewish friends would be excluded without a Hebrew name and Jewish pedigree, but still I nibbled the sweet dough. Before Seema and I had parted, I'd accepted her offer to teach me more. She would call me to spend a Sabbath in her home. It was like this: Seema, mother of six, fed me, smiled at me, touched my shoulder. She said I belonged.

That night, after the sky was dark and stars were out, we gathered in the main hall with Rabbi Geller. Someone lowered the lights. One of the bearded men struck a match and lit a tall, braided candle of many colors. The flame spit and rose. He held the torch high, fire dancing in the dark. Rabbi Geller declared the candle a symbol of the holy Sabbath moored among darkly secular days. He raised his silver cup and sang out, "*Hinei el yeshuasi evtach v'lo efchad.*" "We trust the Sabbath will return," he said. "God will keep us safe. We will not fear." Then many hands were passing tiny net sacks of cloves for each of us to smell—to revive the soul as we reentered the dark non-Sabbath. The rabbi drank from the wine and poured the rest into a plate over the tilted candle until a single ember was left floating on the dark red pool. A breath of a moment enveloped the crowd, darkness, quiet breathing, that single ember, whiff of wine and cloves, a sense in the room of camaraderie and regret—before someone switched on the lights. I blinked as if just waking. "Elijah," the men sang, another my father used to sing to me in the dark. *Eliyahu hanavee.* "Elijah the prophet, the Tishbite, Elijah the Gileadite." Harbinger of the Messiah, when every day of the week will be Sabbath.

❦

THAT NIGHT AFTER THE Sabbath ended, the rabbis stepped back and local staff took over directing things as Channel 8 News arrived to film the anachronistic visitors to Texas. Attendance swelled from the larger community surrounding a circle of floor where two Hasidim danced the *kazatske* to a clapping crowd. Janice, Ana, and I were in that crowd, Ana holding her guitar case. I caught Ana's eye, pointed to the case, and raised my eyebrows. She cupped a hand around her mouth, lips close to my ear, and said, "Someone heard us singing." But the magic Sabbath was over and we'd returned—she was free to play her guitar. We were free to sing, free from Hasidic land and back in the world of women's voices. We had just watched a show of visitors who *were not us,* and even though I wanted to know more about their rules, I also wanted this freedom.

The woman who ran the synagogue office directed two men setting up a makeshift stage in front of the huge television camera. The crowd pushed in, burning lights, and she pointed to us: Janice, Ana, and me. I looked to Ana and then to Janice, a little dazed, and climbed onto the stage after them. A guitar chord, a smile to one another, and what did it matter if we were singing to the walls of a Sunday-school room or to these blinding lights? I put my head back, lifted my voice in three-part harmony, and felt embraced by my friends and by the music. I didn't know Ana would disappear from my life, or that Janice would reappear years later. We sang on, innocent us. I didn't know that this moment in friendship and honesty and full voice would be one of my last for a very long time.

Five

In January after the Sabbath Experience, the Supreme Court legalized abortion. A sense of triumph for woman invaded the news, school, our home. But it felt like my mother's triumph. I couldn't imagine myself pregnant. I tried, and the thought repulsed me.

One night, I went out with my twin friends, Tim and Terry, and with Pat—a girl. The twins spoke in high Texas country. Both loved to buy vintage women's clothes and dress up Pat, with her waist-length red hair, as if she were their Barbie doll. Terry sat in the back with Pat as Tim drove their halting Volkswagen. Tim was wearing his favorite platform shoes, and he had put makeup on his zits. There were no seat belts, and a bolt that was supposed to anchor the front passenger seat, where I was sitting, was missing. When Tim hit the brakes he tended to stomp, tipping my seat and throwing me into the floor well; it had happened plenty of times, so I was trying to hold on.

The delightfully dangerous possibility that Tim and Terry were homos was definitely part of their appeal, but that word was only whispered about others, never out loud or about oneself, so neither was going to confirm. Besides, they didn't quite seem to know. But that night, normally ebullient Tim was looking pensive as he drove. "Something on your mind?" I said.

"Tim!" Terry said from the back. A warning.

Tim abruptly pulled over to the curb and stopped. "What's up?" I asked.

He turned around to the two in the back but also to me. "I want to make a pact," he said. "What now?" Terry said.

"A pact," he said in a dramatic voice, "that we will remain open to every opportunity for love." He put out his palm, daring his brother. His hand shook. Slowly, Terry put his hand on top of his brother's. Pat added hers.

I couldn't believe they would even say this. I couldn't believe they wouldn't hide from inevitable gawking and sneering at school. *Well,* I thought, *the gawking won't be at me.* Heart racing, I kept my hand at my side.

Another night, I was up late, looking at a catalog for Oberlin College. I had sent away for a dozen or so from different schools to look at and dream about, all strewn on the bed. Under the bed were quivering mounds of dust, a teetering pile of jeans and tees and overalls over the desk chair. A poster-size photo of Carole King, natural woman, was tacked up on the wall. Ringlets framed her face, her mouth open, forever singing. At the foot of the bed was a cello I had managed to buy by babysitting all over the neighborhood.

I had been paging through the book *Our Bodies, Ourselves*, a gift from my mother, who had appeared at my bedroom door and handed it to me almost shyly. I had just found the chapter entitled "In America, They Call Us Dykes." Under the heading, three girls posed arm in arm in men's hats, one cupping her hand around the breast of the other and chortling. I slammed the book shut as if I'd touched fire.

I decided to apply for every scholarship I could find, go for a degree in art, and move far away and study cello. I would aim for museum work and get paid to handle beautiful things. I would experiment with kosher food and fill my new life with the kind of community I had found at the Sabbath Experience.

I reached for the brochure for Rabbi Geller's Lubavitch Women's Institute in Minneapolis that he had given me, full of color photos of ever-smiling, modest women cooking, studying, praying. Surely I could get Ana to come with me for a brief escape before I went off to university.

Debbie had already left for college and freedom, but in the next room, Amy, fourteen, was playing my *Tapestry* album over and over. She had been frequenting a neighbor's home, where shady characters came and went. There was a boyfriend she said she was going to marry, and she fought to spend nights with him. Sometimes she didn't come home. Then the music stopped. There was a slammed door, and voices.

I found them in the living room, disheveled Mom, blouse half-buttoned, Amy, and Daddy. Daddy's face hung forward, his shoulders rounded, his eyes dull. "I goddamn will go out!" Amy said. She was putting on her fringed jacket, grabbed her fringed purse.

"What?" Mom said. "No, you won't."

Then they were shouting at one another, but the room became mute. They were gesticulating puppets among the stacks of yellowing newspapers, unopened mail, and forgotten books covering the coffee table and the floor. Huge, dusty canvases of dancing colors were stacked six deep against the walls. All of it—mute people, neglected decor—bearing silent witness to the mockery of furniture arranged for guests who never came. Behind them, yellowed blinds were open to the black night.

Daddy the ghost, full of psych medicines, staggered but stood. "Listen to your mother," he growled at Amy. His voice was strained. He tried to grip her arm. She shoved him away. He stumbled back.

"Mother," I said in the careful, lilting voice one might reserve for a thickheaded servant after the guests have already arrived. "I think I'm going to Seema's tonight."

My mother's mouth fell open, her face red. She looked as if she'd been slapped. Debbie was gone, Amy and I both in revolt, both poised to escape.

I wished I had never told her about the Sabbath Experience or about Seema. I was helpless that way, always spilling everything, hoping *this* time she'd treasure what I shared. "Orthodoxy is mind control," she had retorted. "Orthodoxy," I had shot back, "means mothers who are mothers and fathers who are fathers." She had looked so stricken then that I wanted to fall at her feet. "Oh," I added instead, "it also means clean houses."

Mom swiveled to Amy and then me, then Amy, each turn more frantic. Amy was clutching her purse. Eyes glistening, Mom raised her arms as if fending something off and gave a cry, then sank to the floor, where she folded herself up and crouched on her haunches. She began to howl. The sound was piercing. Primal.

Amy dropped her purse. Dropped her jaw. She looked to me, baby fear in her eyes, but I couldn't give her direction; I couldn't give her anything. "Help. Her," my father said, but he meant my mother. There was a trickle of spit on his chin.

I crouched next to Mom, her folded body, her messy sobs. I wanted to say, *Okay. You win. You've trumped us with your drama,* but I couldn't. *You are leaving,* her body said. She rocked and cried. *I have failed. You have failed me.*

"Mama?" Amy said, tiny and unbelieving.

Then I caught my mother's sly sideways glance. Or did I? Those cries. Around a swirl of need and suspicion and fear I said, "Mom—try to calm down." I wanted to gather her in my arms. I wanted to shove her and run. She rocked and moaned like a wounded animal. "Daddy," I said. "Get Dr. Black's number."

My father returned like an obedient child with the telephone directory. I got the night operator for my mother's psychiatrist against the backdrop of her sobbing and howls. But the operator said, "What should I say is the problem?"

Before me were Daddy, his jaw slack; Amy, clutching the purse and looking to the door; Mom sobbing on the floor. And there was the girl holding the phone, me, her unformed self, her inarticulate longings. Guilt was an iron web connecting us all. "Just . . . have him call," I said.

When Dr. Black did call, my mother opened her palm for a second and I slipped the receiver in so she could clutch it white-knuckled as she crouched and rocked and sobbed.

If leaving her meant failing her, I would fail her. In the kitchen, I stole the keys from her purse and slipped out of the house.

"OHMYGOD. WHAT ARE YOU DOING?" That was me. I came back that same night. It wasn't the first time I'd walked out the door only to sneak back in later. I kept trying to leave and kept coming back—the relentless pull of home I didn't understand. This time I returned to find Amy in her room, holding a razor blade over her upturned wrist. There was the glint of the blade in the darkened room, her face and form in dull greens and grays. "What do you want," she said, flat, without looking up.

I took a careful step in, and another, afraid of saying one wrong word. "Don't do it," I said. Then, a gray wash of guilt. I couldn't manage to say, "Sister, I get it." *We're in this together.* I couldn't say "we." It was as if I needed to keep myself in a different category, not a we but apart from her, in order to keep her despair from seeping into me, as if I needed to save strength for some menace that was coming. Her hair hung over her face like a closed curtain.

Helpless quiet. I had to do something. "I'll . . . be right back," I said. There was only one place to go. I ran to Mom. She lay in bed, an empty pill bottle on its side on the bedside table. It was as if she was buried under a mountain of shifting sand that I would need to scoop away with my hands, but surely the sand would fall back into every dent I made. I shook the bed, pulled at her arm.

She was in there somewhere. She had to be. "Get up!" I said. "Amy wants to cut her wrist!"

She groaned, waved a weak hand that flopped back down.

"Mom. Please!"

"Uh huh," she mumbled.

Around us, the room, the house, silent. Her hair was flat in back, black and white curls at odd angles, her blanket wafting a warm smell, soft and stale. "Mom," I said. "Mom." Across the room, her dresser was piled a foot high and more with purses, scarves, and layers of blouses and dresses and skirts that I couldn't remember her ever having worn. There was a line of makeup bottles and tubes snaking across the front, standing at attention, with a dulled, dusty glow. Her keys were where she had dropped them like an invitation. But I couldn't imagine where else to go to get help. Our mother was the world.

The next morning, I woke to responsibility for Amy like a brick in my throat. I found her in the bathroom, getting ready for school, in a short skirt and chunky-heeled shoes, leaning in close to the mirror over the counter and putting on eyeliner. "Hey," she said in a brisk tone, a quick glance to my face above hers in the mirror.

"Late?" I said.

"Almost," she said. Her wrists were smooth and clean. No blood.

AT THE LATE, heavy Sabbath meal with Ana at Seema's home later that week, the room barely contained the enormous dining table. We were packed around it, Ana and I and the Rakovsky family—Seema, the rabbi, and their four children in their Sabbath finery. We had arrived to pre-Sabbath bustle, daughter Rina putting candles into the intricate candelabra now before us, Seema pulling pans of kugels out of the oven, Luba tying

Shimmy's shoes, Rabbi Rakovsky racing down the stairs, still tying his tie. Now the candles were burning down, their slow flicker making dancing shadows, the air still and warm. The Lubavitcher Rebbe, holy leader of their movement, seemed to be casting his benevolent gaze upon us from an oversized photograph. There was the late hour, the endless food. My eyes were heavy. Among the wavering forms were the tired children: Rina; Luba; Nachum, with his pinched face, glasses sliding down his nose; and sleepy, three-year-old Shimmy in his pajamas. Rabbi Rakovsky sat at the head of the table in his black coat, Seema beside me in an elegant dress, wig, and heels. She had taken off the apron.

Ana took a deep breath. "You know," she said, an edge in her voice, "my boyfriend Richard converted at Temple EmanuEl. He is a Jew now."

"Temple EmanuEl?" the rabbi said. "That's a Reform place. They don't follow the Law. His conversion is worthless."

In that moment the world divided into Us and Them. Ana and I had only happened to land on the right side of the line by accident of birth. Ana looked down. Shook her head.

EARLY THE NEXT MORNING, I woke to Shimmy whimpering in the hallway. I got up. "Shhh," I whispered to him. "Your mommy and daddy are sleeping. Tell me what you need."

He padded to the bathroom. After he peed, I followed his lisping directions to pour water from a two-handled cup over first his right hand, then his left, and listened to his morning *modeh ani*. In his bedroom, I helped him put on a cotton square with a hole in it, tassels of long white strings at each corner. I thought, *It's like a little prayer shawl he always wears*; then I buttoned his dress shirt over it. Shimmy took one of the tassels and wrapped it around his index finger. He recited a Hebrew blessing and kissed the strings.

We ate cereal and milk together, then took a morning walk past manicured lawns, blooming dogwood, and new pansies ringing young trees. Shimmy's protected innocence, and the feel of his little hand in mine, begged gentle handling. I thought him a precious example of Hasidic life. Purity personified.

Later, Ana and I went with the family to the synagogue. It felt strange to wear my best clothes unwashed, but there was beginning to be more to this—a family held together by the Law's steady structure and authority, the settling rhythm in their scripted days stamped with God's approval. Ana hated not washing up, but I had begun to understand how our objections and our comfort are small and irrelevant before the vast, ancient Law.

There were no sidewalks, so we walked on the street. "Nice morning," I said to Seema.

"*Baruch hashem*," she said. "Thank God."

"*Baruch hashem*," I repeated. "So . . . God gets the credit?"

"Exactly," she said.

Nachum saluted and marched, pretending to be a soldier. Shimmy tripped along, trying to copy him. "Watch him," Seema warned Nachum, nodding at passing cars.

"You're a soldier for God," I said to Nachum. That made him grin.

That afternoon, Ana pulled me aside. "I've had enough," she said. "What is it with these people about not brushing your teeth?" She ran her tongue over her front teeth and made a face. "I need a shower." She threw her things into her overnight bag, hoisted it onto her shoulder.

I followed her down the carpeted stairs. "But, Ana," I said.

"No way," she said. "I'm outta here." Then she paused. There was a small smile. "Call me later," she said.

I stood a long minute with my hand on the knob in the thick Sabbath quiet.

I found the Rakovsky children lying around in the den, Shimmy on his stomach on the carpet, chin on palms, watching a card game between Nachum and Luba. Rina was on the sofa, reading a book about Orthodox Jewish girls. There was something a little too good, too old, too *still*, about these children. Besides no television, there were no newspapers or secular books in sight. "It's Saturday afternoon," I said. "Any friends coming over? Can you go out?"

They eyed one another. Shook their heads

"Ohhh," I said. Then, to Rina: "Aren't there other Orthodox kids in the Jewish school?"

"Sort of," she said. "We have a few friends at school, but . . ."

"Can you eat in their homes?"

"No."

"Not kosher enough, huh?"

They nodded.

"And they watch television and maybe even listen to rock music, right?"

"Yeah." She and her sister looked at each other and shifted on the carpet.

More kosher, less kosher. I was learning there were degrees of holiness, that holiness could be weighed and measured. I figured somewhere, probably Brooklyn, there must be schools filled with Hasidic kids whose families were holy enough, where everyone was the same, as they had to be for these children to have playmates who wouldn't veer them off their path and worry their parents—girls' schools filled with long-skirted girls jumping rope, boys' schools with boys in yarmulkas and sidelocks climbing jungle gyms at recess. But not here in Dallas.

In my high school, Dallas had just ended racial segregation. We were newly thrust together with our differences and no guidance, trying to learn how to get along. Through my high school years there had been school riots, days when policemen lined the halls. But to my family, integration meant opportunity. Everyone should be able to move into the world and adapt, work and be rewarded, and be grateful for that. If others were restricted, we could be next. But here were the Rakovskys, *choosing* segregation and doing it to themselves, separating themselves even from their own community. Their kids were so segregated, they had only siblings as peers.

But it was peaceful in that house. My mother's television was on through every evening; out there, everyone was fighting or threatening to fight about their differences: my family, blacks and whites at school and in the news, students and police on college campuses, British and Irish, Catholics and Protestants, Indians and Pakistanis, Arabs and Israelis. The North Vietnamese had just crossed the DMZ. In that Sabbath bubble without television, the world was held at bay.

"Who are your real friends?" I asked the Rakovsky children. They laughed and pointed at one another. To them, *out there* was a large, non-Jewish place that was impure and suspect. But we were safe, here on our tiny Sabbath island.

NOT LONG AFTER, I found Rabbi Rakovsky reading in Hebrew at the dining table. "Where's Ana?" he said.

"She had to leave," I said. "Would you read that to me?"

"It's not proper for me to study with a woman," he said.

"I'm sixteen," I said. "Couldn't you think of me as one of your children?"

He considered that, a long gaze, pursed lips. "Maybe," he said. He turned a few pages, took a drink, sighed, and began. "*Basi l'gani.* I have come into my garden," he read. He read another line, then translated and continued in the same manner, back and forth between languages in his lisping singsong and Yiddish accent. I didn't understand much. There were quotes in Hebrew and

Aramaic dropped into the Yiddish lines. But the fact that those
languages were so old made me think they must carry something
of an Original Truth, going back to the beginning of our people.
We flow from the Source. He used words like "emanation,"
"kingdom," and "crown" to label qualities of God I didn't
understand, and it all sounded as if he were drawing a puzzle
without offering the key. There were worlds of imminent being
called Creation, Formation, Action. There was *sovev,* God Who
Surrounds All the Worlds; *memaleh,* God Who Infuses the
Worlds; *shechina,* hovering motherly presence. Four worlds?
Three Gods? "What is this?" I said.

"I'll start again," he said. This time, he summarized and slowly
explained terms. He listened to my questions, responding by
laying out strange and challenging abstractions and then
sweeping each idea into its own vivid image: the garden of
intimacy with God, light of Emanation at His right, darkness at
His left, yearning nearness of God retreating in successive stages
in the face of sin. Above it all was the Crown—pure, blinding,
obliterating, Godly light that we cannot help but crave, a level
impossible to attain and still live. Slowly an airborne structure of
spirit worlds began to hover, one Rabbi Rakovsky insisted had
always been there.

He strayed from the text then and began to pull together
biblical images, God forming man from mud, Aaron's walking
staff bursting with almond blossoms and ripened fruit, the ass
that spoke, chastising Balaam. He said that while all of these *really
happened,* each also contained points about the esoteric and taught
us how to reveal mystical light in the world.

I pulled up for air then. Really happened? Did I have to accept
Bible stories? *He wouldn't lie,* I thought. But here was a paradox:
naiveté at the root of deeply intellectual assertions about the
sublime. To me, biblical stories were children's line drawings—of
lions and lambs, elephants and giraffes waiting to enter the ark

with robed Noah and his smiling family, Moses holding his staff above his head as the Red Sea swirled before him—drawings I once colored with broken crayons at Sunday school. They were magic stories, a child's stories. But here was wise Rabbi Rakovsky, master of ancient languages, man of books, deftly teasing meaning from a web of deep abstractions and cryptic phrases, saying, *These stories really happened.* And he was a kind father—I had seen how he took Yossi's hand when they left for synagogue. I should trust him, believe him. But . . . "How can you believe those things?" I said, even with my face still glowing from the light of his spirit worlds.

"Simple. If God is omnipotent, He can make a flood or split a sea," he said.

I wrinkled my brow, struggling between faith and logic. "Let's . . . try again," I said, like someone embarrassed yet in love.

I don't know when it was that I came to the moment of arrival. Perhaps it was when he talked about Adam, who heard the nearness of God retreating in the garden, God wisping away into a distant concept with Adam left yearning for Him. "If we can transform our physical selves, darkness will be turned into light," Rabbi Rakovsky said, and then the garden of our most intimate selves will be filled with Godliness.

I wanted to believe I could transform my body and its odd desires. Besides, by then I had stretched so to grasp his metaphors and images that now I wanted to assert in my heart all I'd finally managed to grasp in my mind—a different kind of leap past my awkward self.

As the afternoon passed, miracle stories and naive assertions became just ways to explain God's desire to find place for His infinity in a finite world. Gradually, *it* happened: enthralling spirit worlds emanated from the book, spreading out before us over the crumbs on the dining table. Here I found David's harp with a scale of eight, instead of seven, and the God-soaked Hebrew letters and their origin in mystical fire, with power to create the world. There were angels, and glowing vessels of supernal light, sparks of God in exile waiting for me to redeem them. There were the things God created at First Twilight: Noah's rainbow, Moses's magic staff, the dark mouth of the earth that swallows rebels.

By insisting on what can't be proven, the Rabbi had made proof irrelevant.

Rabbi Rakovsky said earthly life was just a false screen that hides the real, spiritual world. My mother on the bed by her empty pill bottles, my father shuffling, Amy with her razor blade —they were that false screen. *The spiritual behind all of that is what is real,* created for my sake. I felt Rabbi Rakovsky was a conduit for Godly wisdom that stemmed back to the beginning of time. He was so certain, so fluent, his hoarse voice leading me to a place where my every action redeemed the dirty world. I wasn't helpless—my every Godly act moved mountains. I could make my mark in the highest realm.

If a equals b and b equals c: "God and His will are One," he said, "and the Law is His will. Therefore, God and the Law are one. The Law becomes God. Give yourself to the Law, and the soul merges with God."

When I left the Rakovsky home that evening after the braided havdalah candle was extinguished in a saucer of red wine, I went back to my plans and friends. I went back to my home and my father, who was an empty, retching shell, but I carried with me the image of Rabbi Rakovsky, teacher-father, wise and kind. I thought of their home as an inviolable, found safe place. I knew I'd be back.

That evening, in my cave of a bedroom, door locked to keep out the ghost of my father, I unzipped my cello, pulled out the endpin, rosined the bow. Unsung tunes were bursting in me, in minor keys and hollow harmonies. Rabbi Rakovsky said that one of the songs he sang at the Sabbath table was about the journey of a soul into the world. He said the soul is forced away from the bliss of being with God to be birthed into this coarse world of hidden Godliness and left with clueless parents. He said the soul longs to escape. To return to God. But if this world was a veil and the commandments the only reality, what was left to discover? I picked out the mournful tune until I felt certain of it, then applied the bow with full draw.

Later, I dreamed I was a student in an old yeshiva study hall, sparring with my partner over a Talmudic text. The hall was filled with other pairs also locked in arguments and questions. A tangle of our boy voices rose up to God.

Six

"hat's your name? Just get here?" That was the girl who met me in the entry of Rabbi Geller's Beis Chanah Lubavitch Women's Institute, a frayed old mansion in St. Paul, Minnesota. The entry was framed by two broad, banistered stairways, each leading in a curve to a central veranda above. I had arrived a week into the summer immersion program for their Introduction to Hasidic Life, in which students lived together—classes, study and mentoring, communal meals—under the canopy of the Law. Most of the girls would be college students on summer break. I had the brochure with me in my suitcase, wrinkled and folded.

The girl wore the required long sleeves, skirt, and high neckline, but unlike Seema's daughters, she was in fashionable Indian-print cotton, fringed leather belt over her tunic top, her hair hippie long and tied back at the nape. Other girls passed by, and I noted more artful dealings with the clothing restrictions—scarves, paisleys, and bright colors. I was still sixteen, but I had graduated and here I was on my first solo vacation before starting college. I had just gotten off the first plane of my life, taken my first cab, and paid for it all with money I'd earned by babysitting every night I could get work since I'd met Rabbi Geller at the Sabbath Experience. "I'm Lisa!" I told the girl, extending a hand, ready to pump hers. "Hello!"

"Rivka," she said.

I picked up my suitcase.

"You can leave that here."

I put the suitcase back down, ready to follow. Before us was an enormous dining room, folded tables and stacked chairs, scuffed baseboards, walls in need of fresh paint. "Oh," the girl said. "That used to be a ballroom." My tour of the institute had begun.

Lubavitch House was once owned, in the gilded age, by a wealthy brewer who loved to entertain. I pictured top hats and lorgnettes. Beyond the ballroom were bay windows facing out on a wide balcony over woods and a circuitous creek. The whole place made me think of a fading socialite, some frazzled, once-beautiful woman. "What happened after the brewer?" I said.

"To the house? It became a monastery."

"A *what?*"

But she was already clattering down narrow stairs to the basement, and I followed, across bare cement floors, past what she said was Rabbi Geller's office, empty now, to a long dorm room with a line of single beds that sent me into a daydream about a monastery and its medieval mystique. There was an assortment of dressers with clothes sticking out, more clothes on unmade beds, shoes scattered, open suitcases, photos and notes pinned to walls, but I saw an austere line of iron cots in an underground chamber beneath a dully glowing bulb, beds tight and identical in an otherwise-empty room. I saw monks rising before dawn, dressing and making their beds in a silent group dance, the scene resonant with holy awe and mystery-driven discipline, before proceeding to the chapel for haunting, hypnotizing morning chants.

I followed Rivka back to the open area, exposed pipes and cinder-block walls, the air cool and dank. One part of the back wall held an empty frame of blue tiles around a scarred surface. "What is that?" I said.

"*That,*" Rivka said, rolling her eyes, "used to be an altar to their 'virgin.' But it says in the Bible in Deuteronomy, 'You shall destroy their altars and break down their images.'"

"You don't mean . . ."

"Yep," she said, in a chipper voice. "That's a commandment you don't get to carry out very often. So the rabbis tore out the altar themselves. With hammers."

"Whoa," I said. That line to me conjured primitive people forbidden to bow to inanimate objects or conduct human sacrifices, not the Catholic church down the street. But in a shocked, secret kind of way, I was delighted. By tearing out their altar, these bearded rabbis had thumbed their noses at something sacred in American life. That was very cool. In high school, in our nice, safe lunchroom, we had vilified Nixon, called policemen pigs, and derided the "establishment," but when the bell rang, we went to class. These people were anti-establishment for real. This was real iconoclasm. I could just see their white starched sleeves rolled up, hammers in soft hands, telling each other that this job was a Godly privilege. Did they carry the debris out in closed bags to protect themselves from the objections of a misled world? I whispered, "I bet the rabbis don't even pay their parking tickets."

Rivka laughed. "Oh, no," she said. "Not true. The Law says we have to follow the laws of the land." I followed her back up the basement stairs. She looked back over her shoulder with a wry smile. "But don't you think six hundred and thirteen command-ments are enough?"

"Six hundred and thirteen?" I said.

She looked as if I didn't know my ABCs. "The number of commandments in the Torah," she said.

I would have to be careful not to fly that little flag of ignorance again. "Oh," I said. "Yes, maybe enough." I didn't think, *Enough for what? Enough to make American law irrelevant?*

We went into the kitchen, where two older girls in white

aprons—they were at least twenty-one—were chopping vegetables. They looked up and smiled, knives on the chopping block,
just like the photo in the brochure. Outside of the kitchen was a
chalkboard with chores and names scrawled on it. "We run this
place ourselves," Rivka said. "Everyone works."

"Cool," I said. We got to be the adults in charge.

Up the stairs to the veranda, and Rivka opened wide double
doors onto the singsong of prayer in female voices. Hebrew
chanting flowed over us. "It's *mincha*, the afternoon service," she
said. At the Sabbath Experience, the men had sung out the
prayers as fast as they could in an indecipherable cacophony while
we women sat silenced. These girls were singing neatly together
in holy repetition, steady, rhythmic, and calm. "There are about
fifty of us here now," Rivka whispered.

I saw only one girl in jeans like me, another in slacks. But on
the phone, Rabbi Geller had said it was fine to come in pants, that
everyone came from college and brought what they had. "No
pants?" I whispered back.

"Most of us have been here a few weeks," she said. "The
newcomers have adjusted." She closed the doors.

AFTERNOON. My bedroom was on the main floor in an alcove
off a large room with eight more beds, which meant that my
room had no door, a huge closet that was for everyone, and the
only access to the one bathroom. I reserved the second bed in the
alcove for Ana, still delighted she had agreed to come. She said
she'd combine it with a visit to her favorite uncle and cousins in
St. Paul, and that way her parents would pay.

I headed to the main front room, the ballroom. Rabbi Geller
had said I'd be assigned to babysit in place of tuition. I found
Frimmy waiting in the front hall.

I was struck dumb. I had had little contact with pregnant

women, but I had always noted an incomprehensible misty-eyed aura about them. They made me unaccountably nervous, as if, on some subterranean screen, images flashed when I saw one, of female bodies distorted by violence, of vulnerable children and the things people did to them, the secrets they have to bear, the terrible inevitable betrayals. I had a conscious terror of becoming pregnant. Once a pregnancy began, I would not be able to stop that child from barreling into danger. And to me, a baby was a bottomless hole I would be forever frantic to fill, until I jumped in myself. And here was Frimmy, face pale and drawn, in a thin, faded dress with an uneven hem that strained around her huge, rounded middle. She stood flat-footed, toes pointed outward, nonchalant about the unwieldy growth. I was horrified, but her manner was forthright. "Lisa?" she said.

In the car, I stole glances as she drove, and couldn't speak. We stopped at a small brick home with steps up a sloping yard. "I won't be long," she said. "I'm just going to the grocery store. My husband's inside, but he's leaving soon."

Isser, with a long, thin beard, answered the door. Inside were four small children. The floor was covered with toys, the walls with shelves of Hebrew books. Isser settled papers into a briefcase and left without a word to the kids or to me. There was a click in the lock. *Well*, I thought. At least I had experience babysitting.

But the children looked at me as if I had three eyes. I thought, *Maybe they aren't used to strangers.* "Tell me your name," I asked the oldest.

"Zeesel." She had cropped near-black hair. There was also three-year-old Dina, who sucked her thumb, two-year-old Yossi, with a crusty nose, and cute, fat baby Yonasan, crawling around. I lifted Yonasan, staggered backward, then headed to the backyard on that pretty day. But I found it empty and full of weeds.

Unlike back home, I didn't have a book to read or homework to do, and there was no television or anyone to chat with on the phone. Dina hit Zeesel and grabbed her toy, and I tried to put the baby down to settle them, but he arched his back and cried. Yossi wanted apple juice, but when I managed to pour it for him, still hoisting a fat, crying baby on my hip, he spilled the juice on the floor. By then, three were wailing and the house felt like an airless box, and everywhere was the mother's distorted profile.

I drew no conclusion from this first trial assuming a Hasidic woman's life, read no warning into the brief experience. I didn't know that Frimmy's constant pregnancy and her claustrophobic childcare with many small children at once might indicate anything more than the state of this one family. I shoved aside my visceral reaction to pregnancy. *No,* I thought. *I don't want to do this babysitting now. I came for a Jewish vacation. No!*

Early evening, I took a walk with Sally, Michelle, and Ruthie, all in long skirts while I still wore my jeans. There was a nice breeze, the toss of hair, easy laughter. They were all over eighteen, so I was happy to be included. They said they were trying out their Hebrew names, so Sally, Michelle, and Ruthie became Sorah, Myah, and Rus. That's when Leah (*Lay-ah*), the name my mother allowed a rabbi to give me, became my alias, another "me" to try on. I was enjoying the walk, no boys present to complicate things. Myah and Rus said they had both met Lubavitch Hasidim on their college campuses, Myah in Florida and Rus in Los Angeles. Both had attended the free Sabbath meals, services, and study groups before they had agreed to come to the institute to experience "total immersion." Myah didn't want it to end. "I'm dropping out of university," she said. "Moving to Crown Heights—the Rebbe's neighborhood—in Brooklyn!" She made a triumphant fist. "A whole world of Hasidim there!"

"Sometimes," Rus said, after we'd walked a bit. "I get tired of keeping kosher. I just want a cheeseburger."

I said little. I didn't know much about the kosher dietary restrictions. I also liked cheeseburgers.

Sorah took out a pack of cigarettes, a glorious statement of rebellion, freedom. She stopped to light, cupping her hand over the flame, and then waved her hand with the cigarette in a wave of dismissal. "So eat the cheeseburger," she said.

"Huh," Rus said. "You've kept kosher all your life. You don't even know what a cheeseburger tastes like."

"And I never got to try," Sorah said. "I stayed on in my parents' kosher home during college to save money. Then my parents fell in love with the new Lubavitcher in town and pushed me here."

"Don't you listen to her," Myah said. "Sorah's really good about the rules."

And so it went, each admitting a private shred of rebellion before the others laughed and prodded her back on course. But their easy acceptance of me into the group thrilled me. Sorah shared her cigarette with me, and we walked on, breathing in that dark pleasure, as the sun's rays got long, the air cool, as streaks of color painted a new horizon. I stayed up late with them that night. Whenever one of them moaned about her parents' objections to her becoming more religious, or about missing her boyfriend, or about favorite activities that conflicted with the Law, someone else always responded with a "Don't worry" and a hug. *You can do this.*

I WOKE TO THE ALARM at six forty-five after three hours of sleep and realized I was missing prayers and there was a whole schedule of classes that day. I dragged my bleary self out of bed and into the bathroom. Someone was already in the shower. I turned on the sink faucet to brush my teeth. Suddenly, the girl in the shower let out a high-pitched scream. *Did I do something? Was she hurt?* I rushed out of the bathroom and stood trembling outside, looking this way and that. *Maybe I should get help? Or go back in?*

Before I could figure it out, the girl emerged, wrapped in a towel to her knees, red-faced and snarling, stomping wet footprints on the wooden floor. "How *dare* you!" she said.

I knew it. I knew I did something wrong. "What?" I said.

"Don't you have any modesty?"

"What?" I said. "But we're both girls!"

We'd grown up with no locks on the doors. My sisters and I were casual about dressing around one another. I had thought nothing of walking into the big bathroom I was to share with nine others, or of finding someone already in the shower.

Oh, but the girl was beautifully alive with her fury, her slim arms and calves wet and bare. Rivulets ran down her skin between wet, sparse hairs. "I'm sorry," I said. "I didn't mean to look. . . ." But I hadn't looked and didn't understand why I felt like I was lying.

"*My* modesty," the girl said, scathing, "isn't about who sees. It's not about you. It's modesty before God." She stomped back into the bathroom, leaving her wet trail.

"Next time," I called out weakly, "lock the door!" I was shaking, heavy with fatigue, heart racing with shame at my wandering eyes. Had I looked at her and not realized? I had looked. Oh, I shouldn't have looked! Would she talk about me to the others? Would I become a pariah at the institute? But I had been accepted right away. Maybe I was even popular. And what did she mean about modesty and God?

I couldn't stomach the possibility of becoming an outcast. I had to figure out the rules. I decided I had to keep myself covered and always lock the bathroom door behind me. I had to watch my eyes. No stray glances. But the image of that girl and her great wild vehemence stayed with me, the way she shook her head and droplets flew.

⌒

LATER THAT FIRST DAY, in the big upstairs room with double doors where I first saw the girls chanting the afternoon *mincha* service, Rabbi Geller was holding forth on Maimonides' *Book of Commandments*. As he paced up and down, reading and explaining, I shot inadvertent sideways glances at the girl from the bathroom. I had promised myself I wouldn't look. I was already failing. *I have to try harder.* Later, when it was time to pair off to study the daily Bible portion in Hebrew, Rivka, my tour guide, appeared at my side. "Come on," she said, and led me out onto the balcony to claim the last two chairs. A nice breeze rustled the old shade trees beneath a clear sky. I leaned back, closed my eyes.

"Hebrew is a language of building blocks," Rivka began. "Every letter is a phrase, every word a stack of phrases."

But I was tired. "Why does everyone here make such a big deal about modesty?" I said.

She leaned back, too, closed the book. "The great *tsaddekes* Hannah had seven sons," she said. "Every one of them got to die a martyr's death."

"Was that supposed to be a reward?"

"Hannah's children went straight to heaven. What do you think?" she said. "You know why Hannah got such an honor?"

"No."

"God loved her because 'the walls of her home never saw a hair on her head.' That's true modesty. *Tznius.* Even when Hannah bathed, she had maids hold up sheets around her."

"So . . ."

"Who was she hiding from? No men were even around when she bathed. She was keeping covered just to please God. *That's* modesty. A women who is always modest *before God* is like a woman in constant prayer. *Hatznea leches.* Hannah is our role model."

ANA CAME THE NEXT DAY, in white slacks. We threw our arms
around each other with squealing hugs. While she unpacked, I sat
on my bed, eagerly describing the girls and my first day of classes.
"It's really great here," I said.

"So why do you have those dark circles under your eyes?"

"I've made so many friends!"

The big closet was packed too tight, so Ana piled her skirts
and blouses over her arm to go hang them on an aluminum rack
in the big outer room. I followed. "Are you gonna wear those
skirts?" I said. Then I swallowed. "Could I borrow one?"

Since the bathroom incident, I had worked hard at
imitating the other girls. God's love and the love of the group
had somehow become the same thing—wanting their acceptance
took on urgent spiritual need. I watched mannerisms, listened
to phrases. At prayers, I copied impassive faces, swaying bodies,
lips in steady movement.

By two weeks in, I had learned to lose all sense of time at
prayers, an empty, flowing, mindless feeling. During prayers, I
melted into the group, into the repetition of words, swaying
bodies around me, the room full of whispering, *om*-like, soothing
secret fears. As a group, we were each part of a single organism, a
single breath. I wasn't different after all. Here's Rivka at my side,
murmuring from her prayer book. The little book was dog-eared,
pages separated from use, the corners darkened, as if years of
piety had been poured into it. She held it in front of her face,
rocking as if her whole body were in prayer. I wanted what Rivka
had layered between those pages. I wanted to feel that spine and
softened leaves. Then—page turning. Sighs. I hung suspended,
calm. I closed my eyes and fell back into greater arms.

I'd been wearing one of Ana's skirts for days, even though
wearing a skirt made me uncomfortable. I had thought I could
still sit in it my way, knees apart, feet flat, but that didn't always
work. Instead, in a skirt meant to make a statement about female

modesty, I felt strangely, utterly female, as if the skirt were a body-size poster wrapped around me that said GIRL IN HERE, reducing me to that, only that. But even at the institute I still dreamed I was a boy. Now the boy part of me was being pushed behind a partition.

Besides, I had plans. I had handled college applications myself and gotten into the honors program at North Texas State on full scholarship. I'd be starting in the fall, finally free of family. I was going to be so many things, but here at the institute, in the skirt, I felt reduced to a narrowed category in which I was only a girl, nothing but a girl, and over everything I thought I could become there was a booming rabbinic voice that made me meek. It was confusing, how that diminishment shrank my voice. In the classes, I couldn't argue or question, as I had back in high school. I had to remember to lower my voice, be quiet around men. I practiced taking smaller steps. When I sat, I awkwardly put my knees together and to one side, crossed my ankles and tucked them under my seat, folded my hands in my lap.

Ana and I had both chosen a class taught by Isser, with his chest-length beard, mellifluous voice, and grave pronouncements, whose children I had babysat. The class was held around an old picnic table in back of the mansion, under a cluster of trees.

The girls were all smitten with Isser. Evenings, they waited in line until midnight to meet with him and recite teary details about conflicts with parents who didn't like their religious ways; cry about boyfriends, teachers, jobs; ask how to plan their futures or how to find kosher spouses or how to determine what part of their former, secular lives was permissible. Isser gave advice laced with quotes all aimed at smoothing their path to God. The girls came away with starry eyes and shared his words with the rest of us like gems. All day I heard, "Isser says . . ." They called him a *mashpiah*. Rivka told me that the word meant "flowing font." She said it with adoration.

I tried to emulate the girls' attitudes about Isser, although I didn't get into those evening lines or seek his counsel. I had noticed lapses in his logic that sometimes distressed me, but I also felt small before the Law, its booming voice of God. Isser represented this voice. His voice, deeply secure within itself, hummed through my confusion, reassuring us, commanding us.

"*Kadesh atzm'cha bemutar loch*," Isser read out loud in a Yiddish shtetl accent, although his English was unaccented. Sanctify yourself in what is permissible to you. "This means you should make yourself holy by abstaining, not only from what is forbidden, but from anything that you don't actually need," he said. "Particularly from unnecessary indulgence. To do that," he continued, his tone compelling, "you have to know the difference between *need* and *desire*." Needs, he said, shrink when you feed them, like when your hunger goes away after you've eaten. "But feed desire, and it just grows. That's how you know the difference."

Never feed desire? *Wait a minute*, I thought. *My* need *for food doesn't shrink—even after eating, I'm still a physical creature with needs. Just my hunger comes and goes.* I started to wave my hand to get Isser's attention so I could articulate my objection to his logic, how needs *don't* shrink when you feed them, but then I glanced at the others and put my hand down. *Desire grows the more you feed it.* My secret desires could grow into a monster that could rip off this skirt, expose me, and get me thrown out of here—the one place I'd been made to feel I belonged. Dallas somehow didn't seem like home anymore. It was far away, unreal. If I argued with Isser, I could be homeless, out on the edge of the world. Maybe he was right. Even the desire to speak my mind should be monitored.

"Feeding a physical desire," Isser added, "feeds only the animal within and not the Godly soul." In that moment, every simple physical pleasure that didn't have a specifically Godly purpose became a shameful thing.

Ana sighed. When she moved on the bench, her thigh pressed warm against mine.

I began to sit apart from Ana at meals and chose only the morsels of food I absolutely needed. At the end of a meal, the lifers planted among us as role models, including proud Rivka, led the song of thanks for our food. The girls banged the lively rhythm as they sang, palms hitting the tabletop, happy and loud. But in my mind was Isser's voice: "*Kodesh*, holy," he'd said, "means separated for the purpose of sacrifice." I sat alone and kept quiet.

MY MOTHER FORWARDED A LETTER from Lula, who used to sit next to me in algebra, my first black friend after integration of the Dallas schools. We had promised to keep in touch. But the wall was now up between me and the world with its varieties, *us* and *them*. I couldn't fit in here with Lula as my friend. I put the letter into my journal, wishing I could make her understand.

Every night at the institute held the same late-night camaraderie, every morning the same groan of exhaustion, the same fogged effort to grasp esoteric teachings and complicated laws. Every day ended with the same tired surrender. One day I found Ana taking her skirts off the aluminum rack. "Ewww," she said. "This reeks of cigarette smoke."

"I'm sorry," I said, "but could I borrow another?"

"You don't smoke," she said. She handed me a navy skirt. "Here," she said, "but you *cannot* smoke in it. And you'll have to give it back in Dallas."

"You're leaving?"

"Lisa," she said. Then she cocked her head to the side like a parrot. "How are you today? *Baruch hashem*. How'd you sleep? *Baruch hashem*. How's the learning? *Baruch hashem*. I *hate* the *baruch hashems* that come out of your mouth!"

The term means "bless God." It means "I accept God's will."
"But everyone says that," I said. "Really. Everyone."

"You," she said, "are not everyone."

I knew I sounded like a parrot to Ana. I wanted to tell her
that I was just learning. I wanted to say that I loved her. Instead I
said, "There's a reason for saying it, you know."

"Is there, now?" she said. She went back to her packing. That
afternoon she left.

THE NIGHT AFTER ANA LEFT, I lay alone across from her
empty bed and suffered fits of longing I believed to be longing for
the ultimate union with God Isser had described in class, *even unto
death.* I imagined my soul straining to fly far above my demanding
body into ecstatic fusion.

God was a giant screen, and anyone I had ever loved was part
of the God image on it. Ana was up there, opening her arms wide
to me. *You are abiding love.* There was my mother with her
delicate hands and almond eyes, but her image was changed into
one of reliable nurture, beckoning, wanting to gather me in. *You
give strength to the weary.* There was my father with his white hair
and lopsided smile, but he was healthy, his eyes alive, become my
shield who never hurt me and never died on the inside. And
somehow, any pain I'd ever had was also up there, distilled down
to a brilliant point of aching light.

Ana left and didn't tell me. My father's face had changed into
a bearded rabbi's; my mother had transformed into a nurturing
God. I could be, *would* be, could *feel* myself becoming a tzaddik
saint. I would rise above my stubborn body and its inordinate
demands. I could see God. I was suffused with painful yearning. I
would touch God and escape this world of betrayal.

I rose from my bed and, in a sweep of fervor and need, took
the blanket off of what had been Ana's bed and folded myself into

her warmth. I lay back down, wrapped in her, dreaming of escape and breathing in the smell of her, until I slept.

Seven

It was a clear night outside on the front stoop of the institute on the night of my seventeenth birthday, June 29, 1973. The girls had sung to me over dinner. The star-studded sky teased me with its promises. I leaned up, reaching toward those stars. In my studies with Rivka, she had just told me that all secular art was empty and dangerous, that artists must devote their art to God and the Law. Images from my mother's art books that had been childhood friends and teenaged inspiration streamed across the black sky, the cathedrals at Rheims and at Notre Dame, Michelangelo's *Pietà*, Leonardo's dreaming Madonnas, Kline's slashing black vigor, Rothko's dreaming color clouds, all against a crashing backdrop of Beethoven's Grosse Fuge. Was sublime beauty just *shtus*—spiritual nonsense? I had planned to go back home from here to study art and music in university. Had my plans been reduced to an empty exercise that mocked the commandments? If so, in my new costume, I had no future, no one left to be.

What if I get off this stoop, cross that street, and don't come back? I could knock on any door and ask to use the phone to call my mother. She'll help me get home. But those stars were too far to reach, the sky too vast, the narrow street too wide to cross, my cello too far away, my mother gone. Inertia, fear, uncertainty held me down. Who was I? The girl I had been was gone. So how could I go home? If I abandoned the skirted woman I was still becoming, what then? I would be left a blank page, no definition or content, at home nowhere. I would be out in the world without a path, in a void. But I *would not* risk becoming a lost, blank face like my father.

Late that night, I wrote my parents. "I have changed my life and become a Hasidic Jew," I wrote. "Every minute of my day is now devoted to becoming a better, more moral person. You began by shaping me, but as much as I love and respect you, it's my turn now. I promise to stay in touch, but I won't be coming home." This is how I said goodbye, with these lies.

WEEKS LATER, it was an afternoon like any other at the institute: girls passing through the lobby to the basement to do laundry or lounge, others paired over texts or visiting on the veranda, more lined up at the phone booth. One asleep on the floor. I was curled up in a love seat in the stone room off the lobby, reading about *mikvah*, happy I had managed to avoid kitchen duty. I still didn't know what going to the *mikvah* entailed, but I was intrigued by the author's assertion that studies had proven *mikvah* protected women from cervical cancer. I wondered, though, why nuns had the same low rate of incidence.

I got up and wandered into the ballroom, where, I remembered, there was another book about *mikvah*. I turned to the table of contents, hoping this one spelled out the details more clearly. Rabbi Geller was coming up the basement stairs with yet another visitor.

Then a wave roared through me, of love and fear and need and anger. It was my mother. I saw my mother. With Rabbi Geller. I tried to swallow, smooth out the skirt, hold on to the book, but it didn't help. She was talking with Rabbi Geller, her face shut down, her body a paint stroke of fear.

An hour later, there was a tap on my shoulder. Rivka. "Rabbi

Geller wants you downstairs in his office," she said, trying to sound official. She looked at her feet as I left.

My mother had gone back to her hotel. Rabbi Geller indicated I should sit on the one chair with its creaking canister wheels, the seat too high and slanted so that I had to try not to slide off. The door to the office stood open. The rabbi looked a little nervous. He bounced on the balls of his feet, hands behind his back. "We didn't know you were a minor," he said.

One of the other rabbis passed in a tool belt and tennis shoes. They were closing off space for more beds. There was the air pop of a nail gun, the whine of a buzz saw.

"I wrote my age on the application form," I said. "I never lied."

"I asked your mother to keep a kosher home for you. She has agreed."

"What?"

"You have to go home."

"But," I said, shaking my head, "I don't know how."

BLURRED STATIC ON AN AIRPLANE INTERCOM, engine roar vibrating through seats, the motion of takeoff pinning us back. *The world is a difficult place, but prayer and performance of the commandments are the only reality. Reciting psalms redirects Godly energy, averting punishment.* I wore Ana's navy skirt. Next to me, my mother's mouth was set in a grim line. *Feed needs, starve desire. Purity is the path to God.* Ground to blue sky to houses shrinking into toys, rolling clouds in an otherworldly landscape without love. *Happy is the one who dwells in Your House.* My mother asked the stewardess for a blanket, but her voice didn't sound like her voice. She covered her shoulders, closed her eyes.

Somewhere above the clouds, I reached inside my purse and discovered Rivka's prayer book, her last, secret gift. I pulled it out in wonder, a collection of supplications in my hand like a cup full of hope. Inside the worn front cover was an inscription in Rivka's looping Hebrew handwriting: *Karov hashem l'chol korav. God is close to those who call upon Him.* She signed her name with a circle over the *i*.

BOTTLES, DISHES, empty cans on the counter. Dust balls in corners. Nothing had changed. Newspapers, canvases, mail, clothes, plants, everywhere. Fleas in the carpets. Roaches climbing walls. Mom's television, on since I'd left. Daddy floating through aimless, head down, a grim ghost. My mother had mustered the energy to come and get me, then climbed back into bed. In the middle of the night, I heard Amy come in the front door and slip into her room.

I stayed in Ana's skirt. The cello in the corner zipped into its canvas case seemed like a relic from someone else's past. Carole King at the piano was still on the wall, still singing, beside a yellowed newspaper clipping I had once tacked up, an editorial from New Year's Day, 1970. *We've lost our innocence*, it said, *and learned to question.*

At night, from my room down the hall, I heard my mother reading my *Condensed Code of Jewish Law* out loud to my father. "'A Jew is not allowed to resemble idolaters, even in regard to shoelaces,'" she read. "This stuff is so isolationist, so primitive!" She sobbed. "They won't let her follow fashion. She can't go to restaurants or movies or watch television or read a book, or even date!"

"Rita," my father said.

"Look at this. They even tell her how to tie her shoes. She's brainwashed!"

My mother's sobbing became a flow of uncertainty that ran cold through my veins. I turned this way and that on the bed. I wanted to rush to her and hold her, promise her anything, everything. Then I got up. Carefully, I set out the plastic basin at my bedside and set a full cup of water in it for morning hand washing. I climbed back into bed and whispered the *hamapil* prayer before sleep, syllables slow and exacting. The memory of a sea of female whispers bolstered my prayer, Rabbi Geller and Isser standing with haughty approval and folded arms. *You cause the bonds of sleep to fall on my eyes.* By command of the Law, I lay down on my left side, muted until morning by the final prayer.

But in my mind the whispering continued:

Here are the lines.

Here are the walls.

This is how a woman walks. *This is how one labeled Woman walks.*

This is how a woman dresses. *This is how A Woman dresses.*

This is how she sits, *how she sits.*

And how she sings *and does not sing.*

This is how a woman prays. *This is how A Woman prays.*

This is how a woman, even A Woman, gets to God.

I slipped into dreams of Isser caped like a savior surrounded by clamoring girls, but strangely, he wore red and black and seemed devilish. I woke still in Ana's skirt, woke to keen regret and the sour taste of having hurt my mother. I carefully spilled the water I had prepared over my hands into the basin—right, left, right, left—cold wet shock of morning. I put on first my right shoe, then the left, to evoke God's kindness, rather than His judgment. *I give thanks before You O King who lives forever. You have returned my soul to me. Great is your faithfulness.*

Another day not long after, I unzipped an old suitcase and folded in my one skirt, the red paisley granny, and Ana's navy wool, three long-sleeved tops and six pairs of panty hose. I looked up as Amy passed my open door. Underwear, bras, a long-sleeved nightgown, *The Condensed Code of Jewish Law* retrieved from my mother's nightstand. Her television was still flickering down the hall. I closed the suitcase, pulled it to the floor. My purse hung at my hip. I put Rivka's prayer book into it. From the kitchen counter, I took what was left of my loaf of bread from the kosher bakery and slipped that in, too.

There at the kitchen counter, among stacks of empty cans, unopened boxes of new plates and glasses, piles of mail and magazines, my mother's pill bottles stood off in one section, a forest of amber sleeves, all filled or once filled with vitamins and with Valium and Darvon—two of my first spelling words. I pictured myself at five, pushing up a chair to this counter and climbing up; she'd left the bottle tops loose so I could count out her pills for her. Another chair at the sink to fill a cup with water, and I brought her the fistful, balancing the full cup like a prize and careful not to spill. She sighed as she swallowed, and clumsily handed back the cup.

At the entry to our house, I caught one last note of my father's grinding teeth, a low A flat.

I left my cello behind. I left my immodest clothing—shorts and pants and short-sleeved tops—plus books I had read through my childhood and beyond: *Charlotte's Web, Harriet the Spy, Anna Karenina, Pride and Prejudice, Catch-22.* I left my posters—Carole King would never finish that song. I left my sister. I left my childhood. I left the dolls on my shelves that I never did know how to play with, and the piggy banks I never managed to fill. I left unwashed clothes over the desk chair and a scattering of university catalogs on the floor. I left my mother. I left my father. I left my signature red overalls. I left, on the nightstand, a wrinkled, folded brochure for the Beis Chana Lubavitch Women's Institute in St. Paul, Minnesota. I left my non-Jewish friends and most of my dreams. I left *Our Bodies, Ourselves.* I left the bed unmade.

Amy was a young teen, but to me she was a little girl standing very still, blank face, nose pressed to the window, watching as I walked away.

The sun was blinding in a hard blue sky. I headed to the bus stop, intending to wait until I found a bus going in the right direction. I would go on to North Texas State, take its scholarship and live off of that. I got to the sidewalk before I remembered, then trotted back up the drive and back to my room. This time, I took the cello with me. Suitcase and cello in either hand, bread and prayer book in my purse, Lisa/Leah walked away. I took care to shut the door behind me.

Out in the summer sun, marching past a line of silent homes with curtained windows a row of closed eyes, I felt beads of sweat already lining my upper lip. I had bread, and the scholarship, but still I thought of myself as Abraham. God told Abraham to leave his birthplace and then didn't tell him where to go and didn't give him provisions for the way. Abraham set out aimless and unsure. But God did that to him for a good reason, so that every step Abraham took would be an act of faith. Or was it an act of self-sufficiency?

When Abraham found his new home, when he found the right place, he would know. I took a deep breath. Cello in hand, skirt already damp and clinging to my calves, I stepped high.

Eight

I walked across the Denton campus that late August day among happy, free, jean-clad kids carrying school-books and transistor radios, some of them in a marijuana haze, as disconnected from my new society as if I was in a moving glass box. Guys and girls in groups prodded and embraced one another, playful and casual and alive. Others zinged past on bicycles. There were two kissing on a bench outside Marquis Hall. In the student union, I put down the cello and suitcase, studied a corkboard covered with hand-written notes, and then plucked an index card, on it *Roommate, near campus* in a hasty penciled scrawl. I mentally counted up my meager financial aid.

It was a new apartment complex a grateful two blocks from campus: fresh paint, green shag carpeting, a strip of a kitchen off the den. I could get through the week on Campbell's soup and canned tuna, five for a dollar. "I'll take it," I told my new room-mate, Helen.

Helen had a brash manner, a West Texas accent—low-flat tone and whistling s's—and green eyes. My room was furnished with her old bedroom furniture, early-American, driven up there in a U-Haul by her dad. The first night, the place filled with her friends. I was introduced and noted Stevo lounging on the sofa in sweatpants, his pelvis thrust forward, arm over the back of the sofa, a beer in his hand. Late at night after they left, Helen came in to chatter about them. "Did you see Stevo?" she said. "The way he sits?" Her green eyes danced. She moved her cupped hand in the air as if over the lump in his pants.

I ENROLLED IN EIGHTEEN hours of classes that semester and filled days and nights with lists, classes, study, always keeping Rivka's pocket prayer book wrapped in gold cloth in my purse at my side. Sometimes I thought back to high school, friends, skipping school in gangs, parties, slow-dancing with some prop of a boy to Chicago, Three Dog Night, Joplin's wail, our heads back, crooning along and laughing. One day, about a week into the semester, I shot shy smiles at the girl across from me in English class and tried to engage her in conversation before class. She was coolly polite, and I turned away, deflated, then caught her curious stare sliding over my uncool skirt and stockings, long sleeves in Texas heat, modest high neckline, and panty hose. In that moment, cut off from everyone I used to know, I doubted everything. In that moment, there was no way Noah took animals into an ark, no way Moses lifted a staff to split a sea on audible orders from some Hebrew-speaking God. I shifted in my seat, looked down. I felt stuck.

At home midday, I tried to study, but my mind jumped from one thing to another. I took a break and a shower and afterward stood for long, agonized minutes in front of the steamed shower, examining my naked body. My breasts were full and high, tight skin healthy and lean. *What is missing?* Something I couldn't identify. *What is wrong?* I felt ineligible for love. Then I dressed and left for Life Drawing class, where I spent hours staring at the nude model, gently tracing her curves in delicate Conté line on smooth silk of paper.

In honors seminars, we read Descartes, Buber, Kafka, Hesse, then Fitzgerald and Hemingway, and I was astounded at the pull and beauty, the varieties and depth. Here's where I could put my energy, my young lonely passion. In science, because so many had come to Denton for the celebrated music department, we studied the physics of trumpets. Then we went to see the world's second Moog synthesizer, on campus, made by Robert Moog himself for his friend Merrill Ellis, director of the school's new electronic-music division. The seminal device filled a room, tall bank of knobs and pulleys and screens. Dr. Ellis's eyes were as lit as the machine as he pointed and explained, then turned it on and filled the room with new sound.

At night, I tossed in bed, haunted that I wasn't really part of either university society or Hasidic society. *There is no home for me. Not really.* I dreamed of fiery angels outside of Eden turning back and forth, guarding the entry to paradise but never themselves allowed to enter.

One day in November, I simply stepped up to a vending machine in the English building, pulled out coins from my purse and dropped them into the slot, then waited until first a decidedly non-kosher Snickers bar and then a pack of Marlboros dropped into the bin. I rolled my sleeves up to an immodest length above my elbows, opened two then three buttons from the top of my blouse, then slipped into a bathroom and pulled off the hated stockings. But the skirt remained.

That night, I skipped prayers. Instead, I took a long walk in the night air, blowing smoke at the moon. I skipped prayers again the next morning, and many mornings after. I kept a spare candy bar and pack of cigarettes in my purse next to Rivka's prayer book. Religious doubts boiled and churned in me.

After class one cloudy December day near the end of the first semester, I stepped out of one of the drawing studios in the art building and saw her. She stood at a distance, slim, stylish, poised. Her pressed collar was turned up to frame the curved line of her perfect jaw, black curls setting off red lipstick and smooth crimson slacks like a rose on velvet. She was holding a portfolio, standing with another woman, chatting with her. "Mom?" I called out. Then I was tripping and bumping and racing utterly graceless around students, rushing to her, surprised at the enormous relief of seeing her, this terrible unearned nostalgia, as if the sight of her had ever meant love, this teasing sense of home almost, finally, in reach. And yet, there was anger in my voice when I said, "What are you doing here?"

"Lisa!" she said.

I knew that false delight, that empty boast when she wanted to impress someone. She glanced sideways at the woman, then turned to me with brows raised above those heavy-lidded almond eyes that I'd gauged so carefully through childhood. In her days in bed watching television, her eyes had been flat and shallow, a place I couldn't enter, but they always came alive anywhere there was art. Then my mother's gaze slid from my head to my toes like the girl in my English class, and I thought, *She's ashamed of me.* Recent churning doubts, fears, and old yearning for her all welled up in a crushing wave. "What am I doing here?" she said. She sounded annoyed, as if stating the obvious to someone who was slow. She gave a little grimace. "I'm taking a painting class!"

"I called," I said. "I tried to call."

"You did?" she said.

Yes. Every week. Sometimes every day. "I know we're just an hour away, but I don't have a car. Do you . . . do you want my telephone number? The semester's almost over. . . ."

"I know," she said.

"You've been coming here every week since the beginning of the semester?"

"Of course," she said, again annoyed.

"Did you look for me?"

But she was taking the manila pad from my hand. "Is that your sketchbook?" she said. She tilted it to share with her friend. I thought, *As if it's hers,* and suddenly I was the tagalong kid following her to painting classes she taught, waiting like one of her students for her approval. She flipped over to an unfinished sketch of a pile of dolls. My instructor had walked in that day with a garbage bag full of them, dumped the dolls on a bench, and left. In the drawing, little bodies hung limp, buried in the pile, so enmeshed it was nearly impossible to discern their forms, to *know* any one of them separate from the others. Or for any one of them to know herself. Lumpy stuffed bodies half buried, empty plastic heads, overwhelmed, caught in a web and unable to extract themselves. All were cold to the touch, no warmth. Yellow and orange yarn hair. Stitched implacable faces. Black button eyes.

"Oh my," her friend said.

"She's quite talented," my mother said.

"Mom, I have an idea!" I said. I still had enough kosher bread at home for two sandwiches, after a long bus ride into Dallas to the kosher bakery, and a whole tomato in the refrigerator. "You could come see my apartment. We can have lunch."

She shut the pad.

Look at me. Hold me.

"We're going to be late for that critique," she said to her friend, and then I was standing as the two walked off. Her figure receded, across an open space beneath skylights and down a dimmer hall. There was the shape of her back with the large square portfolio and the rhythm of her walk. The crimson slacks. Her silhouette. The clang of a heavy studio door.

Don't. Cry.

"I'M HOME!" I CALLED OUT, LAUGHING, as I stepped into the Rakovsky house on the next Friday afternoon, just before finals, to find myself instantly wrapped in the smells of baking chicken and warm cake, clang of a pot, family bustle of Sabbath preparations. Seema appeared with a dish towel in her hand, headscarf pulled low on her forehead, her floral housedress limp from kitchen steam. "*Gut* Shabbos!" she said with a big smile and tired eyes, and I threw my arms around her. "Thanks for inviting me," I said.

"You could come every week," she said.

"I'd like that!"

But someone else was also there, at the kitchenette, an old Hasidic man with an old-world look, his beard white, soft, and long, in a long black coat, even though it was not yet Sabbath, and worn black shoes. "*Zie iz an eigener*," Seema told him, nodding at me, a Yiddish phrase I now understood: *She's an insider. One of us.* Then Seema laughed. Seema laughed, and I blushed at my recent hypocrisy. I was in stockings for the first time in weeks, sleeves rolled back down to proper length, buttons on my blouse closed back up.

"*Shalom aleichem*," the man said. He had an authentic Russian Yiddish accent, unlike Seema's English-inflected Yiddish with its rounded *r*'s. *Hello and welcome.*

AFTER THE MEN LEFT for the *maariv* service at the synagogue was women's time, after dark on Friday night. Scrubbed and dressed for the Sabbath, we females gathered in the living room, I sat with Seema, her daughters Luba and Rina, and little Shimmy, who was still too small to go to the synagogue at night with the men. Shimmy climbed onto the sofa, put his head on his mother's lap, his feet on mine, and grew sleepy as we spoke in murmurs. Nearby, the girls whispered Sabbath prayers. One lamp had been left on for the Sabbath, corners in shadow, the area in a pooled, quiet glow. Soon we would have to rise and prepare for the men's return. When a man comes home from the synagogue on the Sabbath to find the table set and laden with gleaming dishes of Sabbath food, angels bless the household that it may ever be so.

"Tell me about that man," I said. "The visitor." Shimmy was asleep. Rina got up and came over, picked him up with a motherly whisper in his ear and a grunt as she lifted him to her slight frame. She was fourteen. She lowered his head onto her shoulder, took his shoes from me, and walked slowly up the stairs. Then Seema told me the man was a hero of the Lubavitch movement. His name was Avram Ayor, and he was in Dallas on a stopover on a trip to see his son in California. The rebbes had a secret network of Hasidim in Soviet Russia. They ran underground yeshivas and transported ritual mezuzahs, Torahs, matzohs, *for Jewish spiritual survival,* although the Soviet punishment for such things was severe. Old Avram Ayor had helped to establish the network back during Stalin's time and after. Most of his colleagues had been caught and died in prison camps in Siberia, but he had escaped. "He's a real hero for God," Seema said.

I imagined myself as one of those young men sneaking through the dangerous religion-hating Soviet Union to clandestine yeshivas in basements and abandoned buildings, always poor and hungry, ever alert for evil authorities, feeling noble and driven by the Cause. How small my current discomfort with the Law was in light of that, how pathetic my recent rebellions. I thought, *I can't even sacrifice candy bars.*

The next morning, I found the old man standing at the window. Apparently, Rabbi Rakovsky and the boys had gone to the synagogue. As Seema went upstairs with a heavy tread, Avram Ayor took out a worn *talit* shawl from a velvet bag and shook it open. I sat down nearby, took up a book, and pretended to read.

Avram Ayor closed his eyes and draped the wide woolen cloth with its two black stripes over his head and shoulders. The shawl fell front and back so low that the corner fringes brushed the floor. Then he sat down beneath the photo of the Rebbe and pulled the cloth forward over his head until his eyes shone deep in a tunnel and his face receded in time. He picked up the prayer book and held it but chanted from memory, gazing away at some distant point. His Yiddish-inflected chant was steady, easy, foreign, but it was clear he understood and took in every word. There was no mindless rush through meaningless syllables, no proud empty performance. Instead, he glanced at times into the worn prayer book in his hands, then stopped for long minutes of quiet thought. When he began again, his voice was low and deep and calm, like a bow pulled steady across the lowest cello string. He swayed slightly as he sang, a turned page, quiet breath, a low minor phrase, and again the undercurrent of chant.

From behind my book, that ribbon of sound that was his voice, alternating with deep quiet, seeped into me. His praying was calm, personal. I was in awe at the depth of his peace. Watching him quieted the clamor in me. It muted old self-doubt and new religious doubt. I thought, *This is real prayer.*

I thought, *My mother's father was Russian, as were my father's parents with their old Jewish ways. Maybe I* am *an eigener, an insider. Maybe I do belong.* Avram put a hand over his eyes for the *shema* prayer. *He knows who he is.*

Then I was back in Temple EmanuEl, waiting outside Rabbi Goldenberg's office as an old, white-bearded man in black garb treaded across my line of sight. I had been utterly embarrassed that day confronting what my family had spent two generations trying to distance themselves from. I had turned away. But maybe Avram Ayor was that man.

Near the close of the Sabbath, I asked Rabbi Rakovsky to speak to Avram Ayor in Yiddish for me. I told the rabbi about the sighting, about who I thought Avram Ayor might be.

"Impossible," Rabbi Rakovsky said. "A Hasid wouldn't walk into such a place." A Reform temple, an ostensibly Jewish place that defies God's Law.

"But I think . . . Please ask," I said. I waited outside the wall of

Yiddish until Avram Ayor protruded his lower lip in a thoughtful way and nodded as if admitting something. "*S'iz emes,*" he said. *It's true.* He had gone to the temple and met with the rabbi there. He said that he made a point to walk into only the administrative wing. He said, *Appearances aren't important when it is necessary to help someone.*

He had bent a rule to do a kindness. He went there to help someone. *There is a difference between bending and breaking a rule.* "Tell him," I said, "please tell him the shock that seeing him gave me at the time."

I didn't even hint at how seeing him had made me feel inescapably different and ashamed. But I felt myself an impostor hiding this. "I had never seen a Hasid before," I said. "I couldn't breathe."

The old man answered me directly this time, even though he knew I couldn't understand, bushy white eyebrows, lines around deep-set eyes. "He said," Rabbi Rakovsky translated, "that when a Jew sees Truth, it wakes up the soul."

To me, Avram Ayor's face in that moment was one of deep sincerity and old wisdom, a gift of light. I glowed with new resolve, new faith.

BACK IN DENTON, I was dumping clothes from the weekend into a laundry basket when Helen came in. "We had a party Saturday night and I kinda let a couple use your bed," she said. She pointed to a stain in the middle of the sheet, picked up the rumpled top sheet, and smelled it. Wrinkled her nose and grinned.

"Ick," I said. "I'm not gonna . . ."

"You might want to change those sheets," she said, and laughed.

SPRING. I had been away from my family seven months. My one contact with the world was the campus newspaper, the *North Texas Daily*, screaming headlines in kelly green, that I grabbed each day from stacks left out for students in various buildings. Student protests, Vietnam grinding on, Nixon's now-hated face, brewing radicalism. In February, the nineteen-year-old daughter of newspaper mogul William Randolph Hearst was abducted by some fringe group fighting for a new world order that called itself the Symbionese Liberation Army. The country was riveted. Over the next weeks, Patty Hearst's name was often on the front page. But she only really captured my imagination two months later, after her father gave up on negotiating with her captors and their impossible demands, when she announced to the world that she had joined the Symbionese Liberation Army, become one of them, and taken a new name: Tania.

How strange, I thought. Tanya was the name of the founding book of Lubavitch Hasidic thought, the heart of it all. *But her parents abandoned her. She has a new life. No wonder she changed her name.* Two weeks later, Hearst was photographed holding an M1 carbine in camo fatigues, in a Hibernia Bank lobby during a bank heist, and it hit the front page of every newspaper in this shocked country. She stood with feet apart, shoulders back, at ease with her weapon. She was lean, defiant. She had a purpose. Transformed.

IN PLACE OF SNICKERS and cigarettes in my purse, I now carried pamphlets with titles like "On the Teachings of Hassidus" that I often pulled out to study. I worked hard to change myself into what the teachings said I should be. *Turn the mind aside from all but the right thoughts and feelings. Squelch impulse and physical attraction. Forget my family. Forget irreligious and non-Jewish friends.*

The ancients were evil, illiterate idolaters. Their error: they turned the infinity of the cosmos, the divine feminine, and the life force in nature all into separate gods, when our single, masculine, personal God embodies them all. The Lord is One. Our Father our king! Find Him in His Written Word.

I went every Sabbath to the Rakovskys'. During one visit in late spring, Seema told me about Chabad House, the new Hasidic gathering place for Jewish students at the University of Texas at Austin. She spoke about Tuvia, a young pharmacy student there working to build up the place, even neglecting his studies for this holy outreach. Now on Friday nights the new Chabad House filled with Jewish students who came for Sabbath services and free meals.

I remembered my Minnesota friends one long-skirted walk long ago, Sorah, Rus, and Myah, chattering about the Chabad Houses near their colleges that had gathered them in. I wanted friends. "You should transfer to UT," Seema said. "Go visit and see." Religious friends, she said, would settle me, anchor me in my faith. *Ignore your own rebellious inner voice. That is the voice of a child standing at an abyss. You could fall.*

lick. The driver locked the doors. My cab from LaGuardia Airport had just turned onto Brooklyn's Eastern Parkway, which forms the border of Bedford-Stuyvesant, at that time a dangerous bombed-out ghetto, and Crown Heights, home of the Lubavitch Hasidic movement. After a semester at the University of Texas at Austin, I had come to the Rebbe on a pilgrimage.

Tuvia had warned me not to cross over into Bed-Stuy, but even on this side of the parkway the street was broken and littered, at least one abandoned building scrawled with enormous black graffiti every block. Lone figures loitered. Shifty eyes. But at the corner of Kingston, I signaled the driver, thanked him, and paid in an eager rush.

Kingston was the main street of the Lubavitch neighborhood, and it was humming with honking cars and hundreds of walking Hasidim. My new family portrait! The shops had signs in both Hebrew and English advertising Jewish ritual items, "Jewish art," flowers for the Sabbath, kosher pizza, candy, and holy books, and every store displayed a picture of the Rebbe in the window. The men were bearded, boys and men alike clothed in black and white with *tzitzis* strings at their hips. A few gray-bearded older men even wore the long black Sabbath coat in the middle of the week, like Avram Ayor. The women and girls were all in skirts and long-sleeved dresses under their coats, married women in wigs or headscarves. Many were pregnant, but I ignored that.

Many led small children, boys still young enough to wear bright colors. Mothers pushed strollers with overwrapped, red-faced babies, admonishing children to stay close. Older kids were out on their own, groups of boys or groups of girls. People crossed the street by darting around cars.

There would be no embarrassing stares at my clothes here. I belonged. I was exuberant.

I imagined everyone I saw to be a friend or relative I imagined the whole busy, moving crowd stopping in place and raising their arms to hold me aloft on that collective strength, those uplifted hands.

I was an immature eighteen. Back at UT, I strode several times a week across the huge campus to Chabad House. There, I washed dishes, cut up salads, set tables for services and other celebrations, and then joined in study sessions, prayer services, and long, noisy Sabbath meals, lustily banging the table along with other girls in closed-mouth rhythm as the boys belted out their songs. During this time I got the message over and over, in Rabbi Frumen's classes, sermons, Torah talks shared at the Sabbath table, our studies together, comments among my peers at the Chabad House: my real fulfillment would come through marriage to my *bashert*, the man to whom I was destined. This was God's reason for my existence.

In spite of all that, I was enjoying school. Under the rigorous eye of a visiting Indian professor who wore white suits and smoked unfiltered Camels in class, I found Keats and Wordsworth, Tennyson and Coleridge. I found a challenging cello professor and began to write poetry. Swathed and sexless, ever conscious of Hasidic demands to subjugate my unholy body, I examined Greek marble nudes in my art history class and learned how the Greeks considered the human body the epitome of spiritual beauty, the perfect form to use to depict the gods. I took Life Drawing again with nude models, tracing curves I longed to touch. My Hasidic parameters now well defined, I moved across the campus solidly inside that glass box, but inside that box I had begun to grow branches and leaves.

And yet I had come to the Rebbe. I wanted it all, the religious spirit and devotion and sense of belonging, *and* the tiny budding self who loved learning and making music, who wanted to travel the world; I was just a teen full of typical contradictions. I had even written a letter to the Rebbe: "I know I'm commanded to marry," I wrote, "but I'm not ready. Is it all right if I travel and study first?" *Rebbe, I know I should, but I don't feel, can't tell, don't think I want . . . Rebbe, help me comply and be a good Hasidic girl, and allow me not to comply. Not just yet.*

I found the tiny stationery shop where Seema Rakovsky's father, Rabbi Renner, presided. He had sagging blue-green eyes, a black cloth yarmulka like a bowl on his balding head, suspenders holding up baggy black pants. He welcomed me, then slowly led me around the side of the building to the family entrance, where I was to stay.

The Rebbe's presence fell like a continual mist over Crown Heights, and that same mist seemed to hang in the Renner living room. The place made me whisper. It was immaculate, with overstuffed furniture, cases of Hebrew books, the Rebbe's image in a place of honor on the wall. A round table next to a floral chair held at least three dozen framed family photos, all in Hasidic-style clothing, most of them young, including a photo of the Rakovsky children. In the center was a framed miniature of the Rebbe, the whole arrangement a statement of the devoted legions that had sprung from this old couple.

Mrs. Renner, all of four foot eight, welcomed me with a crinkle-eyed smile. "So," she said. "You have come to the Rebbe." Seema had told me the whole community constantly opened its homes to people like me. *Baalei tshuvah,* we were called—newly reconverted searching souls returning to God. Mrs. Renner commanded me in Yiddish to sit at her tiny kitchen table for weak tea and cookies that tasted like sand. I was to stay three weeks, through the break between semesters. She listed when I would have to pray, eat, sleep, and it all came out like grandmotherly fussing and made me laugh. I called her Bubbie Renner. Grandma Renner.

I woke the next morning between starched sheets. I woke to church bells. It was Christmas Day, but on Jewish Kingston Avenue, shops were open, pedestrian traffic unchanged. Outside, I found three different school buses lined up at the curb, each marked in Hebrew letters with the name of a school, all loading children with backpacks and lunches, colorful yarmulkas, tiny sidelocks of hair, tennis shoes. Bearded men streamed out of a corner synagogue, one of several around the community, after morning services.

The shops and shoppers on Kingston seemed a collection of possibilities. Here perhaps I could figure out how to insert myself into this community. I could listen to how people spoke to one another, see what they bought, ate, the books and art and everyday objects they chose for their homes. Each item I examined in their shops built the decor in my imagined house. With the thrill of new membership, I sampled foods, fingered *talis* prayer shawls and two-handled hand-washing cups, icon photos of the Rebbe, slotted *tzedakah* charity cans, gilt-edged Hebrew books that opened from the left, and brightly colored children's books in which the animals were kosher and the children religious Jews learning lessons about God and good behavior.

I rounded the corner of Eastern Parkway and found the massive 770 Eastern Parkway, Lubavitch headquarters, where the Rebbe had his office. There was a subway entrance right there, but it seemed outsiders exiting the subway melted away. Christmas bells tolled at ten and at noon. No one seemed to hear.

Past Lubavitch headquarters, along the border of Bedford-Stuyvesant, happy and confident, I walked at a good clip. I greeted an approaching black teen who looked about my own age with a big Texas hello. In the blur of movement, I did not see his sullen anger and narrowed lids. But just as we drew alongside each other, he spat out, "Jew!" in a deep *puh* of sound and fired a gob of spit at my feet. It splashed my ankle.

I jumped. Froze, afraid. He glared, lip curled as if a bad taste lingered, as if I were the filth he had just expunged from his mouth.

We looked at each other. I thought he was daring me to say something, but I couldn't. I had only fear, repulsion, sadness, a paralyzed tongue. I felt I'd somehow fallen onto the wrong side of the divide in his mind. I wanted to say, *But you don't understand.*

In that brief face-to-face moment, I wasn't Leah. And I wasn't a Hasidic woman, or some soldier of God, or even a secret rebel. I was just a girl with shaking hands who knew that to him I was a hated type with no face. Some soulless invasive species. I thought, *There is something very wrong here,* and I meant in Crown Heights, but the thought was a weak bubble before it sank. Then it was gone. So was he.

Then I was in front of the crowded plaza that fronted Lubavitch headquarters and led up to the large double-door entry. Hasidim had been pouring into Crown Heights from around the world for days for Yud Shvat, anniversary of the day the Rebbe took on the mantle of leadership. The *farbrengen* public gathering with the Rebbe would take place that evening. Mrs. Renner had told me that there were always people milling here, local residents, visitors from around the world, even tourists, but with all the visitors in town the crowd was greater now. I tried to shrug off the confrontation with the black teen. I wanted to take in the plaza in the same way I had taken in the scene on Kingston, as a way of embracing this. The bustle and movement had a thrilling, infectious religious busyness to it, an exciting self-importance that said, *Vital activities going on here.* For God. There were hawkers displaying books of Hasidic philosophy and Jewish law all along the plaza perimeter. They displayed posters of prayers and biblical quotes, key chains and coffee cups and notebooks stamped with the Rebbe's image, *pushka* charity cans, mezuzahs, stacks of yarmulkas, tables full of colorful scarves, and storybooks of the Rebbe's miracles. One teen had a too-large black hat on the back of his head. His friend was chewing gum, black pants low on his hips as if they were jeans. Both had a wisp of dark hair on upper lip and chin. A woman in a shoulder-length wig, heels, and an elegant suit was trying to maneuver a double stroller with two babies in it across the plaza. Two girls in plaid pleated skirts like a school uniform browsed the wares. A dusty man, his coat sleeve torn, put out his palm. There was a bulge in his right pocket. "*Tzedukah, hab rachmanus,*" he whined. Charity, have mercy. I gave him a dollar. A middle-aged woman held out a can. "Dollars for Beis Rivka," she repeated in steady rhythm. They wanted to build a new girls' yeshiva. I pulled out another bill.

Finally, I got across the plaza and stepped through the double doors into the Rebbe's headquarters. Instantly, I found myself in a place of exclusively masculine gravity and prestige, beards and missions for God. But every Tuesday night, the Rebbe met with both men and women who came as pilgrims. I wanted an appointment with him.

It was a busy place. In addition to the Rebbe's office and the giant shul auditorium downstairs, the building held a publishing house churning out the Message in six languages, a large yeshiva for ordination, and the Shluchim Office international outreach headquarters for emissaries, all run completely by men. As a female, I was automatically a visitor, an outsider. And every one of the many men coming and going required a protective buffer of space against accidental contact with a woman.

I was hyperaware of constituting a threat and did not venture beyond the lobby. Then the woman with the double stroller came in behind me, holding a brown envelope, and behind her a postman with a large sack of mail. I waited with the postman and the woman. One of her babies was asleep, but the other watched with solemn eyes. I wondered if the letter I had sent the Rebbe the previous week was in the postman's bag. "Open your heart," Tuvia had told me. "Tell the Rebbe everything."

Once, in Denton, I had written a different letter to the Rebbe. In it, I confessed my doubts and waning sense of God, and resistance to Hasidic discipline. I asked his advice. But I was too ashamed to admit I was lacking faith, so, instead of sending it, I taped it into my diary.

Finally a black-hatted man approached with a peppered beard and a hurried "Can I help you?". He pointed the postman to a narrow office behind him. The woman said something in Yiddish and handed over the envelope. But I felt my still-new status as a woman before this man's beard, his height, in this building full of men. I said something like, "Oh, I was just looking around." Then I backed away and slipped out.

Outside, I retreated through a different, unmarked door into the women's gallery, where I found women gathering before glass windows looking down into the auditorium, where the Rebbe was soon to address the men. In here was the soft, high buzz of quiet mother voices, daughter voices, the squeal of small children, the smells of shampoo and deodorant, hair spray, perfume, mild female sweat, baby formula and spit-up. My eyes adjusted to the dimmer light as I walked in past two unmarried girls, their long, uncovered hair pinned modestly back, sitting side by side and reading a single pamphlet of the Rebbe's teachings with the rapt attention of yeshiva boys. I wanted to be one of those girls. I wanted their knowledge of Hebrew and Yiddish. I wanted to believe as they did that through that pamphlet the Rebbe was guiding my life, that the world it spelled out was my world. I wanted to belong.

The thick green pane hung down to a wainscoting. The women were mostly stuffed on benches facing the glass, but the best place to watch was a narrow stretch in front of the benches. That space was filled with a crush of bodies. Forget the men assembling below; I tried to make my way in but all I could see was the back of someone's shoulder. I tried to wiggle farther in but couldn't make headway. The woman pressing against my left side sighed and stepped out of one of her heels.

"Oh no," I moaned. "I'll never get to see."

"Come back next month," she said. "The crowd will be smaller."

"I'll be gone," I said.

"Where're you from?"

"Texas."

And suddenly she was my personal emissary, tapping the shoulder of the person in front of me. "Let her in. She's from Texas!" she said. Two different women gave an inch or two. One grumbled, but my new friend persisted. "Let her in!" Then I felt a hand on my arm from somewhere ahead pulling me through and found myself standing near the glass. "Texas?" the girl said. "There's someone from Texas staying with my grandparents." It was Seema's niece.

Up close, I found there was a gap between the scratched green glass and the wainscoting that I could bend down and peer through. I could even get a breath of fresh air.

Below was a huge sea of waving black hats, thousands more pouring into the open hall. I knew they would wait hours if necessary to hear the Rebbe's complex addresses and join in the singing of their wordless Hasidic hymns. "Hearing the Rebbe is like praying," I said to the girl who had rescued me.

She nodded and looked at me a little oddly.

Anyone in that crowd would have to claim his inch of space and stay put. At the back were completely filled bleachers all the way up to the very high ceiling. The men on the bleachers were all standing, up to the top row, and all turned to the same side, right shoulders out. I thought of dominoes tipping. "How many are down there?" I said to the girl.

"Mmm. Seven, eight thousand," she said.

Dabs of color appeared among all that black and white, most on little kids. One boy dropped low and disappeared, then reappeared a few feet away. "Did you see that boy?" I said. "How did he move?"

"They crawl between legs," the girl said. "Bathroom's at the back."

Another dab of color. Pink. "Is that a *girl* down there?" I said.

"It's okay until she's maybe four. I used to go with my father."

"So that's her father next to her?"

"Probably."

There were single orange or green or blue yarmulkas and a few white or brown hats scattered across the sea of black hats. There were baseball caps in many colors, one on a man with a ponytail. These were all clearly visitors. They were curious, or spiritual seekers, novices like me, or guests invited by those who worked in outreach. But it seemed everyone in Crown Heights worked in outreach, missionaries of the Rebbe never off the job. Girls from the Hasidic high school stuck brochures and packets of Sabbath candles into their purses before they went shopping in the city, in case they met a wayward Jew. Men invited coworkers or strangers on the street. Some went into Manhattan. *Are you Jewish? Excuse me, are you Jewish?* Most hustled past, but sometimes a Jewish man responded with pride or curiosity and was willing to allow some earnest Hasid to tie *tfilin* prayer boxes over his arm, wrap the long strap down his arm in the proper pattern, set the headpiece knot at the back of his head, and help him recite the blessing. Perhaps the man remembered his father or grandfather doing the same. The Hasid would share a bit of Rebbe wisdom and invite his potential convert to come here. To the Rebbe.

In the tight crowd below was a long, empty table on an elevated platform, barren island in the sea. There was a microphone set up on the table, and a single chair covered in red velvet. Bleachers behind the platform seemed reserved for the very old; the table stood against a backdrop of long white beards.

Soon began a happy baritone melody that swept over the crowd, filled the room, and rose to the adoring women above. Men bounced in place as they sang. More hats came in. I couldn't imagine how they would fit in more people. Then, all at once, the singing stopped. A collective intake of breath. Quiet spread like a wave. Fathers lifted children to their shoulders. Behind me, a woman whispered, "He's here!" and the girl who had pulled me in said, with a tug and a point, "The Rebbe's here!" I twisted a little more to see, peering down.

Just inside the doors to the hall, standing impassive before thousands of awed waiting men, was the Rebbe: Rabbi Menachem Mendel Shneersohn, Russian born, triumphant escapee from murderous Europe. Our rebbe was a picture of determination and spiritual power, his calm gaze level and deep. He was barrel-chested, with a steel-gray beard that hung to his lapel beneath a black hat large and soft with age. His jacket, knee-length, was belted with a sash.

No one moved. Sixteen thousand eyes below, plus women and children above, all straining to absorb something infinite from this man. I was among them, with them. We had willed the Rebbe into existence out of collective hope. We felt he was us, all of us. Silent cries filled the hall: *Rebbe. Help me give me show me tell me teach me save me. Give me God. Give me me. Rebbe!*

The Rebbe scanned the crowd. *Here,* he seemed to say, *let me take that for you.*

There was a solid spread of hats and a good distance between the Rebbe and his seat at the table. "Watch this," the girl said into my ear.

From above, it looked like a tear in quivering black fabric. The Rebbe began to walk forward straight at the dense crowd. At each step, the tear opened a little more and then sealed back behind him as men stepped or fell back in front of him, leaving space for the Rebbe where there had been none a moment before. The Rebbe paid no attention to the people falling away before him. He simply walked forward, nodding and smiling at people who all looked stunned at his attention.

"*Krias yam suf*," the girl said. Parting of the Red Sea.

"So," I said. "The Rebbe is Moses."

How I wanted to be down there, breathing in the man air, the air of the presence of God. And yet I could hear my mother's disdainful whisper. *They worship him!* she hissed in my ear. She had to be wrong, because Seema told me that no Jew ever worships a man or needs an intermediary to God. "Everybody has God's ear," Seema told me, "but a saint like the Rebbe has God's ear a little more." *You have to think for yourself,* my mother hissed. But wasn't I making up my own mind, rather than letting her think for me? I had come on my own. I turned as if turning away from her and dove into the powerful current of reverence and trust in the Rebbe.

Two steps up to the platform, and the Rebbe settled into his red chair before the microphone to give his speeches. For hours. Once he began, I understood so little that it took a while before I realized how distorted the sound was that reached the women's gallery, how many of those women who could understand Yiddish fluently still couldn't hear enough to follow. There was little to do but stand there. The spiritual high started to wane. I sighed. The girl who had pulled me in whispered, "It's hard to hear, I know. Just let your soul absorb it all."

Seema had told me that the Rebbe filled his talks with quotes from Bible, Talmud, Kabbalah, and classic commentaries, how he teased meaning out of subtle inferences or even omissions in the text. Today's talks would be recorded, printed, and quickly disseminated for worldwide study. Every speech concluded with the Rebbe's urging us to obey the Law more, study holy books more, pray more, exalt separate roles for men and for women *more.* Spread the Word. More. Every speech ended with his promise that the Messiah would come through our efforts. Anticipation of *mashiach,* the Messiah, ran through the crowd like a current of energy.

The Rebbe finished his *sicha* speech to a resounding "Amen!" from below and above. We waited with slowing of breath. For a second, I wondered what the Rebbe would say about my wanting to postpone marriage. Then he began to sing. His old voice was hoarse and strong, the melody raw and piercing as a cry, as if we were privy to his intimate conversation with God: *Tzamah lecha nafshi.* My soul thirsts for You. My flesh thirsts for You, in a land dry and exhausted, devoid of water. The Hasidim sang the same lines back to him: my soul thirsts for You, my flesh thirsts for You. *Kamah lecha besari.* Hasidim and the Rebbe were lovers who shared a mutual thirst for God, each Hasid focusing his longing for escape from cares on one old figure on a red velvet chair. Each wanted to embrace him, then grab the Rebbe's coattails and fly with him to God. The Hasidim repeated their song again and again in a growing roar of intensity. My soul thirsts for You, my flesh thirsts for You. Men put hands over their faces, swayed, and cried. The crowd, the current: I was both in the song and of it, filled with it, transported. I, too, closed my eyes to soak in *this.* It was happening. I was flying, carried far beyond petty hopes or dreams, rocketed out of my fragmented family and deep into this community, with God, with the Rebbe. The refrain was wordless, *yamamamama.* A roaring, begging cry.

Then, for a moment, I snapped out of it. For a moment, I could see that I was actually removed from that current below, not in the midst of it at all. I was, after all, standing up above, behind glass. How I wanted to dive down there, or, rather, float down to blend invisible among the men and sing out the way the men sang. I wanted to be one of them, one with them, and not just a spectator on the periphery of that spirit.

The Rebbe took up the minor tune again: *Kain bakoidesh chazisicha*—So in holiness I seek to behold You—and the men again sang their wordless refrain. And so they went, back and forth, Rebbe and Hasid filling the universe and one another, bound together in song and in their reach to God, as I watched from behind the glass above.

BACK IN AUSTIN, I made my way almost every day to the music building, where I settled in with the cello in a tiny practice room and applied rosin to the bow. Scales. Vivaldi. Austere, majestic Bach. I submerged myself in a pool of pure sound. As my bow hand floated down and up, right and left, the lonely ache clarified, intensified. Desire flowed from me into the cello through my hands. All of the words that were always around me—so many words, from professors and textbooks and dead writers and philosophers; from Seema, the Bible, and Hasidic discourses; from Rabbi Rakovsky, Tuvia, the Rebbe, Isser, Rabbi Geller, and Rabbi Frumen; from past voices still vivid in memory, still talking to me, my parents and sisters and Ana—they all fell away. Music, song, was a kind of home. Only when alone with my music did I shut away words and open my ears to feeling; in that warm pool, even my pain seemed a right and good thing. I let the old ache bloom. The notes enveloped me, nurtured me. Warmed me. Vibrating through bone.

❦

MORE THAN A WEEK after the *farbrengen* with the Rebbe, I was back out on Kingston Avenue, headed over to visit Seema's niece. By now it seemed natural to pass the Rebbe's photograph in every shop window. The sky was the blue-gray of early winter, but it didn't seem too cold for the women squeezing fruit at the grocery on the corner with their bundled children and double strollers, or the kids headed for the candy store, or the striding men with their conscious bearing, or the laughing teens three and four abreast in shoulder-bumping groups. But now, for the first time, I noticed black people on the street as well, as if a transparent overlay had come down on the world I'd come to explore. The guy on Eastern Parkway who'd spit on my foot had made me see: real people, in slacks or dresses, old or stylish, with jackets or without, in uniforms or three-piece suits; kids with school lunch kits, coats hanging open; teens in 'fros, hands jammed into front pockets, big pick combs in back, or baseball caps pulled low. But I saw not a glance or word between them and Hasidim. Black neighbors were invisible. In fact, both groups seemed invisible to each other, each moving on a different plane. When one woman passed, I said, "Hello!" She looked at me strangely, an angry face, and moved on. I was shaken watching people who didn't see one another. And I hated being hated. As if it would make a difference, I decided, *I love the Hasidim, but after I meet the Rebbe, I'm going home.*

"LEAH! IT'S TIME FOR YOU TO GO IN." That was the Rebbe's personal secretary, with his mottled beard, thick black glasses, and tired face, the same man from whom I had backed away in Lubavitch headquarters the day after I'd arrived. Now I was back in that same building outside the Rebbe's office after midnight.

"Oh!" I said, and followed him, away from a waiting family with a sleeping child, a black-hatted yeshiva boy, a group of Hasidim from France and another from Israel, and a non-Jewish couple with polite demeanor, all seeking the Rebbe's blessings. I knew some would wait until dawn.

Thanks in part to Mrs. Renner, after two weeks in Crown Heights I had gone back to the Rebbe's headquarters and requested, begged for, an appointment. Seema had taught me well: to stand before the Rebbe is the quintessential Hasidic experience. I should meet the Rebbe's eyes and soak in his wisdom. Mrs. Renner told me to pray and recite psalms to prepare myself, to try to make myself into a proper vessel to receive the Rebbe's blessing.

I had waited over three hours, surrounded by the whispering of psalms like wind in old leaves. There had been other sounds: shuffling feet, murmurs, the love song between Hasidim and rebbe at the *farbrengen* that still lingered in the air, hum of collective awe, and voices from the sack of mail I had seen brought in by a postman: *Rebbe! Show me what you can see and I cannot, you with your vision; the world is blinding me, I'm afraid of tomorrow. Afraid of myself.* Every Hasid poured out his or her most private wishes and fears onto the page, requesting healing and blessings and guidance. To Our Master Our Teacher Our Rav May You Live Good and Long Years. But Mrs. Renner had warned me. I had to be ready to carry out whatever he would say. "The Rebbe's blessing is a command." I would forfeit free choice, which was anyway a frightening thing to own. *But you will no longer be anxious or uncertain when the Rebbe makes your decision for you. That is the gift for trusting him.*

And yet in my letter I had admitted my fear about doing what I was told to do. Was I hoping that he would take away those fears and help me conform to my "destiny"? Was I hoping for a special concession? Did I understand I was abdicating control over my life by asking? I didn't know, would never know. "I know a Hasidic girl must marry," I wrote, "but I don't feel ready." And then, "I want to travel. I want to study."

The Rebbe's secretary was holding the door open for me. I had expected this fear. My only clear thought was that I had to force myself into proper awed demeanor. From the doorway, a freeze frame moment, the Rebbe looked up at his desk with something like fatherly patience. Perhaps I softened a bit then. He was holding my letter as if he'd just read it, looking over white plastic glasses set low on his nose beneath blue eyes. At me. *In these moments, you are the Rebbe's sole interest. The Rebbe's concentration is superhuman, his gaze so total that it makes people whole.* The office was large and plain. Books lined shelves along a wall, his scarred desk dotted with stacks of papers. An old wooden chair sat beside the desk amiably backward, facing him. I walked in, paused, gathered myself, then stood before him straight and tall. *"Zitz. Zitz!"* the Rebbe said, and pointed to the chair. Sit. Sit! But Mrs. Renner had warned me that the Rebbe would tell me to sit. She said that I must ignore this, that a Hasid must stand before his rebbe.

So I stood like a soldier. Standing there, I couldn't see one old man simply, kindly waiting and looking at me. I saw a symbol. I saw the entire Lubavitch movement and its history back to Shnuer Zalman, eighteenth-century founder. I saw all the rebbes since, and all the Hasidim. The whole world of Hasidim was looking at me and through me, out of the Rebbe's eyes, demanding I meet their challenge, that I measure up to them and give myself to the Rebbe, yet they were still offering to enfold me, uphold me. Seven generations of rebbes were offering love plus their vision into the unseen in place of my blindness—they would show me God's purpose for me. They would show me the shape of tomorrow, clarify the consequence of my next step before I took it—light my way. I would never falter. *Rebbe, Father, here are*

my fears. My basest desires. Take them away and help me not to be me.
Make the Hasidim my home.

Then he spoke. "You will build a *binyan aday ad,*" the Rebbe
said. "An everlasting edifice of a Jewish home and family."

Binyan aday ad was the Rebbe's blessing for marriage. My
mouth fell open. The blessing that is a command. *Travel. Study. I'm*
not ready. Can't feel or want. My brain was spinning. The Rebbe
commanded me to marry. I'd been emulating the Hasidim for two
years and still, in quiet moments, had real doubts, but in that
moment in front of the Rebbe, I melted and was finally swept
away. The Rebbe was more than a man. He was a tidal wave.

My path to marriage as a Hasidic girl was set and sealed.
There would be a matchmaker. We would build our home, my
husband and I, as proud evidence of the Rebbe's command. *An*
eternal edifice. But it worked both ways—the command was a
blessing. We would be successful because the Rebbe had blessed
us. I could forever excise the yearning Hasidic rebel and her
strange desires.

The Rebbe coughed into his handkerchief. It seemed the
noise was a signal for the secretary to open the door. "Leah!" the
secretary said. "You have to come out now!"

I looked to the Rebbe for permission; there was a moment
between us, and he nodded. I backed out as a Hasid backs out,
without turning his back on his Rebbe, ever-ready soldier who
has abdicated his desires, who doesn't even begin to formulate his
own will. That is how I backed out, my conflict with this
community and their non-relations with neighbors forgotten,
deaf now as well to my mother's hiss in my ear. I backed out
carrying my mission, my stunned purpose, my imminent future,
with me under that gaze.

Ten

Austin. Levi wakes up in the morning, gathers his clothes, goes into the bathroom in his pajamas, and locks the door behind him. I remember that vehement girl in Minnesota wrapped in her towel and her shout of "My modesty is before God!" and I don't protest. I wait outside the locked door. But I think, standing there. In spite of religion, we've grown freer. But behind me, beyond this closed door, there is still the hidden squeak of the shower handle, the sound of rushing water. Why so strict about modesty? I wish we could brush teeth and get dressed together. Why can't we have easy intimacy side by side? Why doesn't he seem to need casual touch? I want him to hug me, warm and quick.

I tell myself that being with Levi feels like home, but I need to make sure it stays that way. But how can I when I can't touch the line of his spine through his clothes whenever I want and with that touch instantly be able to picture the exact way he torques his back under the shower, how he closes his eyes and turns up his face in the spray, how muscles in his wet calves form angled ridges under the stream? After we part each morning, I walk across campus and there are brief moments when my gaze falls on a curved form, the flip of a girl's hair in the sun. I don't blush when I do that anymore. I just walk on, with vague longing. I want to feel at least that for Levi. But how can I, when even the sight of him dressing in the morning isn't familiar? He's becoming another ever-receding figure. He is a feeling I can't capture. Even if I could open this locked door, there would be another door, and another.

One night, I cross the divide and scoot in beside him on the narrow bed. I snuggle in and draw his sleeping arm around me. Then I lie there unable to sleep. I want gentler warmth spoon-fit to mine. His body is inflexible, too large and hard. Why won't this emptiness go away? I entwine my fingers in his sleeping hand, but his is large and indelicate, and his arm is too broad and heavy, pressing on my chest. *Why am I here?* This bed is another planet. I try to breathe. I can feel nothing but the deep, deep need to feel. I begin to blame him for this.

September 18, 1975. Five weeks after our wedding. Levi comes home from the university and drops a copy of the *Austin American Statesman* on the table. Today's headline: Patty Hearst has been arrested. She was kidnapped nineteen months ago, just after I left home. Then she joined her captors' cause, joined their crimes. I think of Hearst all day, and over the following months the lingering image of her in handcuffs doesn't fade. At the oddest moments, I think, *Poor, deluded thing, now she's all locked up.*

IT'S THE FOLLOWING SUMMER, JUNE 1976, our country's bicentennial. At the grocery store and in gas stations along the route to Dallas we find minutemen figurines and American flags lined up at the registers. We stay with Levi's parents; Levi often consults his father by phone about school and career plans. His mother has purchased new dishes and a cooking pot for us and keeps them in a sealed box so we can cook our kosher food there and have meals together. Their home shines, ordered and clean. But out of a mysterious draw that rises as soon as we get to Dallas, out of obedience to the Law, out of guilt, as soon as we arrive I leave Levi with his parents and head out to see my mother. She lives by herself now. Amy has moved out, and

Debbie is long gone. My mother recently moved my father into a nearby apartment.

Mom called a few weeks ago and, hard and flat like a weather report, gave me the news of their divorce. Skies clearing. Daddy leaving. It was a one-minute sound bite that didn't include his lunging at her across a group-therapy circle at the day hospital, orderlies rushing in to protect her, or the doctor who said Daddy had to learn to live in the world all over again and should probably do so without the stress of marriage. She also didn't mention that she had gotten him onto disability funding, found him furniture, and helped him move. She said she didn't believe in divorce. She would do this one more thing to make him better. Their marriage lasted twenty-seven years.

I park behind her old blue Malibu, the same one in which I learned to drive, next to the cottonwood I used to climb to get up on the roof where I would read and dream. The tree has grown tall and lush, with abundant heart-shaped leaves, its smooth trunk now thickened. But the house has shrunk. The foundation is cracked and shifted, and the porch is slanted, broken. At the far end of the porch sits my old, dirty rocking horse on a rusted spring. The front door is unlocked. I step in.

In peripheral vision, the ghost of my four-year-old self is climbing onto the rocking horse. The little girl is in home-sewn elastic-waist shorts and a sleeveless top. She's barefoot, and her long, sand-colored hair looks as if it hasn't met a brush in a while. Her legs are brown from the sun and covered in chigger bites. She's too small to reach the wooden foot pegs, so she balances on the pegs on tiptoe and leans forward to grip the red-painted handles. She finds the musical creaks and squeaks from the spring delightful, and swings herself into a blur of swaying color. *I remember now*, how sure I was then, on that rocking horse, that I was in a dizzying gallop away from my parents and sisters and this house.

It seems each fall backward is a fall into memory, each return upright a return to now. When she tips forward, it is a dip into her future, giving her one tiny glimpse of her imagined life that will be mine, if she will just keep looking and hold on. At that farthest-forward point just past balance, she grins a near-wild grin.

I remember the thrill of that dizzying pause at the endpoint just before the reluctant pull upright back to life as it is. I was so sure then that I knew my horse. I knew its music, knew imagined life more than the real one.

Inside the house, in the darkened entry, the ghost of my child self has slipped in ahead. She sits down at the dusty old piano in the front room, opens the top, adjusts a student piano book, and slowly picks out "Three Blind Mice" in a confusing round. And here's Pinkie, beloved housekeeper, with her hand on the girl's shoulder, listening to her failed efforts, encouragement and warmth flowing through that hand, just before she leaves we three blind children.

But the girl abandons the tune in the middle. She is frowning, heading into the dark hallway. She is already beset with a terrible tenderness for her mother. Already she's learning to try not to feel, because the world of feeling belongs to her mother. Already she wants to run to her mother and away from her at the same time. *I wish I could remember my mother holding me.* I shake my head to make the ghost child disappear.

The place feels discarded, but, strangely, most of the piles are gone. There's a noise from the back room. "Mom?" I call out, and instantly hate the plaintive sound in my voice. "Mom?"

Down the hall. Push open the door. I find her in bed. A great grief is shaking her. She's in full-body despair, sobbing, her sheets and blankets mounded around her like lonely hills. She sees me and reaches.

"Mom?" I say. "What is it?"

"I'm alone," she sobs. It isn't right that she should have to be alone.

I go to her. She grabs me and cries against me, her cheek against my stomach. "Lisa," she cries. "Lisa!" I am completely unable either to touch her or to move away, stuck in a dreadful need to move both forward and backward at the same time. I want to cradle her in my arms, give to her everything I ever needed from her, and also fling her away and run.

And I can't leave. I mumble something hopelessly awkward and ineffective. "It's okay," I say I touch her shoulder with the fingertips of one hand.

She clings, sobs.

"Don't cry," I say. "Don't cry."

She is smearing my dress with tears and snot. "Lisa!" she says.

But I'm not Lisa. Not anymore. *I can't do this.*

I pull away with a jerk and put up my hands in surrender. I back up. "No," I say. "I can't. No. I'm sorry. No."

I turn and run.

I back the car out of the driveway peeling rubber, as if pursued by a ghost, as if I can get away. The snot will wash out, but before I get back to Levi, my mother's tears have seeped through the dress and through my skin and lodged there inside. They become a phantom pain that won't leave. *Lisa!*

BACK IN AUSTIN, Mr. Paul Olefsky's music studio is covered floor to ceiling with shelves of music books and the floor space is taken up by a baby grand, two cello cases, three chairs, and four music stands. And Mr. Olefsky, short and gruff, with a solid wide-foot stance and a face like a bulldog's. I still do not know that he studied with Piatigorsky and Casals, soloed with Eugene Ormandy and in Carnegie Hall, or that his students are spreading across the country as concert cellists, orchestra principals, music professors. To me, he is just Mr. Olefsky. He has just stopped the ticking

metronome, and I am breathing hard, bow in hand, cello neck
against my shoulder.

I graduated last December. I didn't go to the ceremony, made
no announcement save a single call to my mother to collect her
distracted, tepid congratulations. My university studies have been
reduced to one corner section of books on a bottom shelf of the
brick-and-board bookcase in Levi's office—art history books,
artists' anatomy, history, English literature, my diploma barely
examined, then stuffed in a file drawer, life-drawing sketches
rolled in a tube in the corner. I found a secretarial job in the
engineering department to support us while Levi finishes school;
I can't even imagine pursuing my own career. But I enrolled as a
postbaccalaureate just to continue studying cello. I hold on to this
one thing. I've been working with Mr. Olefsky for two years now.
Conversations between us are rare. It's all music in here.

You know," he says. "I'd like to see you audition for the
Austin Symphony."

I look at him, puzzled. "What?" I say.

"You could get in. It would be a good experience," he says.

I know, from high school, what it is to play in an orchestra,
my bow hand moving as if tied to the baton. I remember what it
is to become a part of that musical machine, all with the same
downbeat, the same pulse, the same centered immersion in
driven sound. We went to the Austin symphony last Saturday
night. Levi wore a jacket over his jeans. On the stage, the men
were imperial in their tuxedos, the women in black chiffon pants.
They played Sibelius. *The Enchanter.* I try to imagine myself part of
that, cello between my chiffon-covered knees.

Pants. The women wore pants. And they play on the
Sabbath. The realization hits. I shake my head.

"Why not?" Mr. Olefsky says. "I know some of the music will
be difficult—you'll begin at the back of the cello section—but I
think you can do this."

"I can't," I say, still shaking my head.

My teacher raises his voice. "You can do this," he says.

I finger my wedding ring. I signed a different kind of contract. "You don't understand," I say. *Music carries me away. I wouldn't be able to stop myself.* "No," I say. "No."

A week later, Tuesday at three, Mr. Olefsky steps outside his studio in the music building and peers down the hall, then looks at his watch. At home in my room, I have scattered dog-eared pages of sheet music and exercise books full of pencil markings in my teacher's angular handwriting on the bed around me. I've been reading and "listening" to the music. I get up and take the bow out of the cello case, turn the octagonal metal knob at the end, and loosen the horsehair until it goes flaccid. I collect the music from the bed, push it all into the outer bag of the cello case, and zip it closed. Then I open up the case and take out the cello.

I lay the cello across my lap, sitting in the chair beside the bed. The scroll is nestled into the crook of my arm. I lean forward. My body becomes a canopy over the open, vibrant middle. I close my eyes and lower my forehead, then run my fingers around the long, rounded rib, cool and smooth and polished, in at the waist, around the hip. Years of music: Vivaldi and Bach, Saint-Saëns, Fauré, Brahms, van Goens, Weber, Haydn, Mozart, Beethoven—all those voices at once, clashing, against a rising orchestra and the steady tock of a metronome. *Again,* Mr. Olefsky snaps. *Again.* No one has told me to do this, not Levi, not a rav. No one has to.

I sit up. I turn a peg at the top of the cello's long, smooth neck and loosen the growling C to silence. I do the same to the peg for the sonorous G; the warm, liquid D; and the tenor A, which has allowed me to climb into rarefied air, until all are drained of their cries and shouts and distracting songs. Then I just sit, hand on burnished warmth. A car passes. The clock ticks. Too-long moments empty of music. I get up, heavy, slip the cello into the case and zip it closed. I wedge the case into the back of the closet behind a hanging line of Hasidic skirts.

Mr. Olefsky looks down the hall and then at his watch. Scratches his head. He goes back into the studio, packs up his briefcase, and leaves.

I never see him again.

BABIES. Babies in the grocery store, in the drugstore, in strollers on the street. Babies at the breast, on benches on campus, in advertisements and on covers of magazines at the checkout stand. Cute babies, ugly babies, babies bright and dull, drooling, sleeping, cuddling, cooing, screaming babies. This single creative outlet left me as a Hasidic woman is an invitation, a noble title, a purpose, a future, my one open realm of possibility. No career, no music, no friends left, without a baby what is my marriage, what is my life, what is left for me, *what have I done?* Fear of pregnancy melts away, revealing a hollow place from which all the dreams have fled. I want a solid, sleeping baby right there, warm, soft, and pliant, filling the vacuum. One morning I put my scarved head down on the table and refuse to move. Home, work, work, home—it all feels colorless, two-dimensional. "I'm tired," I say to Levi. "So tired."

In the afternoon that same day, a pimply high school delivery boy knocks on our door with a single red rose in a bud vase. "Cheer up," Levi's note says. "I love you."

I take his note as a promise of something in the future—*he will love me*—but then I rise to that. I can live for promises. I pull myself up from the table. We live for tomorrow. God will love me for following the Law. The Messiah will come, and our struggles will melt away. Levi promises he will love me. It will all come. I march off to cook for the Sabbath.

Over the following week, the rose petals dry and shrivel and

darken. One by one they drop, brittle red and black, from the
cheap white vase onto the polished table.

ANOTHER MORNING, Levi skips down the concrete steps from
our apartment balcony down to the parking lot and off to classes
and teaching. His steps clatter and disappear. Only then do I head
down the stairs myself and out to the back lot, where there's a
blue steel Dumpster beneath the fig tree. I have the yellow plastic
case with the diaphragm in it in my pocket. I am grateful for the
year with this diaphragm, for teaching me my body's secret folds
and caverns.

The sky is Texas clear, the sun small and intense, no escape,
no shadows, a hard glint on the rusted Dumpster edge. I take the
plastic case, shield my eyes as I look up, draw my hand back, and
throw the case high up over the edge. The yellow case flies high
upward in a tumbling arc and then down, followed by the small
sound of an invisible landing. *There's nothing left to me now.* Just
that last flash of yellow and the glint of sunlight.

MONTHS LATER, Levi peers into the bathroom mirror in his
suit pants and undershirt with the door open. He leans in close,
pushing his cheek out with his tongue forming a bulge, and
plucks hairs with a pair of tweezers, neatening the beard line
without using a forbidden razor. He takes his long, thin beard and
twists it until it is a coiled rope, then twists the rope onto itself
until it is a tightly coiled ball, which he tucks deep into the hair
under his chin. The effect is the appearance of a short, trimmed
beard and clean face. He dons the rest of his one suit, three-piece
brown, and a new tie, and then switches his big, bowl-like black
yarmulka for a small black leather one in the hope that it will be
less obtrusive. He's going to the university employment office. He

puts a copy of his résumé into his satchel. His father has been
fretting over the phone that Levi won't find a job with his beard
and a yarmulka. "Don't listen," I tell him. "Don't think about that."

"How do I look?" Levi says.

"Like you're going to get a job," I say. "Your resumé is stellar.
How many interviews today?"

"Four," he says.

At the end of the day, Levi comes back dejected. I set the
table, lay out food. "They see the résumé and give me interviews,"
he says, "but when I get there, I see how they look at me."

"Why do they treat *us* like aliens?" I say.

He shakes his head.

"How many more interviews tomorrow?"

"Two."

"Look," I say. "We're gonna have to be practical here."

"I won't—"

"It's not so outrageous," I say. "Just trim it. Just for now. And
maybe leave the yarmulka off for the interviews."

Levi rises a little from his seat. His face and voice fill with
disdain. "What? Of course not," he says.

It takes so little, living in the Law, to feel ashamed. That
enormous set of demands stands before me every morning,
impossible to fully satisfy, so that each day brings its failures. Here
is today's: lacking trust in God's care for the faithful.

I am weak and Levi is strong. A soldier doesn't wear his
uniform. He *is* his uniform. That's what a Hasid is, a faceless
soldier for God. Never mind the jeans; beneath the beard, Levi is
still a faceless soldier. Head down, I leave the room and go into
the bedroom. As I pass the mirror over the dresser, my own face,
stubbornly, is still there.

Eleven

Tropical, coastal Houston. After Levi looked for a job for nine months, his father made a few phone calls and now Levi has a new job in Houston, as a systems analyst writing computer programs. It's far below his qualifications, but it's a job. We joined Rabbi Frumen's small but growing Hasidic community in southwest Houston. It's steamy late August, temperatures in the high nineties, humidity above 90 percent, but every Sabbath, the people in our new community walk from their homes to the synagogue. Most of us are new acolytes, but some of the men walk in the long black Sabbath coat, like Levi, even in Houston heat.

There's only one other couple beside the Frumens who were raised as Hasidim and grew up in yeshivas—the Zalmanovs—and both families are like royalty among us. They can move with ease through our difficult texts, speak with nonchalance about complexities in the Law, chat with one another in Yiddish and Hebrew, while the rest of us look on with jealous pride like adoring children and try to emulate them. Of the rest of us, only two of the couples are Texans—Levi and I, and a pair of successful local professionals whom Rabbi Frumen managed to recruit to help support the cause. The Yoffes and Bardans are from Israel, the Weissbergs and Basels from South Africa, the Seligsons from South America, descended from European refugees. The Gorodetskis and Epsteins are from the USSR. All of us are young, idealistic, college educated, all new to the cause. And all of us are new to Houston, unmoored here without family or an established network of friends.

Years from now I will remember how the immigrant couples in the Group had a pioneering spirit about them that made them willing to listen to an outsider rabbi with a forceful manner, outrageous beard, and disarming smile, and it will seem as if every one of my new group backed into Hasidic life almost accidentally precisely because of their independent thinking when they were young. I will imagine that most our group also originally wanted to pluck the beauty and spirituality out of Hasidic teaching without sacrificing their free will. I will remember watching how a deeper pull overtook each of them, and how the community cocooned around each of us, offering much-needed "family." With telephones otherwise silent as newcomers in a new city, kind new friends called daily to come to prayer services and listen to emotional, inspiring lectures that at the same time were so complex a newcomer couldn't possibly understand enough to question. Once abstractions and logic were unraveled, the ego wanted to embrace what it had struggled to understand, as I had once done at Rabbi Rakovsky's table. And so, gradually, they all did.

LEVI AND I JOIN the budding new community. Before that new group of eyes, he packs away his jeans and classical-music records and leaves his stereo silent. I don't cut my hair, can't seem to, but I tie it up and hide it beneath the scarf, not even the old strip peeking out in front. And even though some of the other women have yet to begin covering their hair at all, I wear the wig outside the house every day, because that is proper. I am ahead of most of them in this game, and I aim for the top, with Mrs. Frumen as my role model. Soon enough, the others will comply. But the knot of long hair beneath my wig makes an awkward lump of protest.

Our community continues to grow, often attracting immigrants. At gatherings, newcomers eye one another, eye each other's children, and squirm in their differences. But the children find friends, pulling their parents in. Families gradually conform, and as they do insecurity in the new place or new country is replaced with an anchor of group faith and belonging, the reassuring strength of standing shoulder to shoulder, voices in unison.

Levi spends long hours at work. Then, at home, he says he can't get to sleep if we sleep together. The bed is too narrow, he can't afford to go sleepless into busy days, we have no money to buy a bigger bed, and besides (trump card), it is the way of rebbes and their wives to sleep in separate beds even after *mikvah.*

So escape from loneliness must be the opposite of holiness.

One night I dream I am a child. I wander into a room with a large mirror set low enough that I can look into it on tiptoe, and I do, with a child's guilelessness. But there's no image in the mirror. I have lost my face. I have no image.

We store our secular books away and line our apartment with Hebrew and Yiddish books, wishing that we could read them, and invite our new friends over. With Levi working fourteen-hour days, no novels, art, or varieties of music, no secular studies of my own, no television, no hoped-for pregnancy, no classes to attend or cello to practice or job to go to, I find my days as silent and empty as our apartment. We go to the synagogue on the Sabbath, but in spite of the varied and interesting backgrounds, the women seem all the same. They imitate one another, everyone demonstrating her piety, trying to conform.

Well, so do I. But I am unsure how to share my heart, and no one offers his or hers. In our world of conformity, no one dares confide. I go obediently to women's study groups, and to gatherings where we work together to prepare food for com-

munity celebrations. We laugh and talk about cooking or
shopping and little more. I am getting to know the women
without really knowing any of them, and they are the same with
me. Unlike with any clutch of female friends I've had before this,
we don't trust one another with secrets and allow only rare, tiny
hints about worries or needs. We express piety to one another
but never dissent, never imply that the Law imposes undue
restrictions, express no resentments about ritual obligations or
feminine burdens. We hide any struggles with faith. Which
means that we talk about husbands and children, not about
ourselves. We live together in the same web but with few lines
binding us to one another. *Put a fence around the Torah,* the Law
says. We put fences around our hearts.

A single, communal Group Voice becomes part of me, the
voice of judgment and conformity, voice of Law. My own voice
melds into it. The community becomes my world. The rest of
humanity recedes, glimpsed sideways in the grocery store or at
the mall, as I hurry past.

A GREEN CLOTH IS DRAPED over my knees and the office air
conditioning is set too low, the air tinged with the smell of
alcohol. Dr. Borowitz's smiling face hovers above the green, a
sentinel nurse at his side. It's been months since I threw away the
diaphragm. "I suggest a pregnancy test," the doctor says, "just to
be sure."

Floating now, stumbling out of the office, squinting at
sunlight, almost unable to open the glass and metal door for weak
knees and shaking hands, I am full of silent shouts and laughter.
Forget the memory of my infant sister crying in her bed, forget
the visceral shock of seeing hugely pregnant Frimmy in
Minnesota. Forget the freedom time with the diaphragm. I've
been empty too long, with no goals or purpose, save the Rebbe's

words of *you will build an everlasting edifice* and his catching me with his piercing gaze. My life has changed in a moment. We will make our home and family everything mine wasn't. We are creating the world.

I smooth the skirt, check the wig. Then I head across the baking parking lot. It is immodest to speak about one's body—the pregnancy will have to announce itself. The cicadas buzz in low-hanging trees over the lot, deafening, a flock of grackles pecking at the ground beneath them, and as I approach our old Dodge, a police car passes with siren blaring. I fumble for the keys, and the flock rises and caws, flapping sloppy black against a painfully brilliant sky. The world is a welter of sound, but for me, this is a wondrous day of hushed female Hasidic joy.

Shortly after, Mrs. Frumen asks me to teach religion in the new school. Through the coming months, I will have a purpose, a grateful mission, infusing my empty days.

A SCHOOL BELL RINGS, and my troupe of impossibly small, perfect six-and seven-year-old students tumbles into the classroom, sweaty and rumpled and fresh from the playground. The girls are in long skirts and tights, the boys in yarmulkas painted with slogans or Hebrew names: CAMP GARDEN OF ISRAEL. YEHUDAH LEIB. MENACHEM ARYE. WE WANT THE MESSIAH NOW! The boys have shorn heads with extra dabs of hair left to hang over their sideburns. The children put their backpacks and sweaters on assigned hooks and take their seats.

Religious studies—prayer, Bible, Law—fill the first half of their day. All of it involves learning to read Hebrew in two different alphabets and writing it in a third. Eventually, they will add Aramaic and Yiddish. I spend twenty hours a week teaching these children beginning Bible studies. In Hebrew. My job as a first-grade teacher, besides beginning their Jewish literacy, is to mold them into little Hasidim, snip away their wildness, arguments, questions, and make them love holy study. Knowledge brings obedience. Knowledge *compels.* I quickly write out the day's vocabulary on the board in large block Hebrew letters, from the first lines of the Bible: *shamayim, eretz, ruach, elokim.* Heaven, Earth, Spirit, God. Yehudah is class monitor and hands out the prayer books while the others talk and laugh. "Morah Leah!" one of the children calls. That's my name—Teacher Leah. I turn just as Mrs. Frumen appears in the doorway.

The children instantly sit up and fold their hands. I tuck in a stray wisp of hair. With pursed lips, Mrs. Frumen strides over to the board, takes a piece of chalk, and corrects my spelling. "There's no *vav* in that word," she says. When she leaves, I glower at the door. Then the children launch into their singsong march through morning prayers. They sing as if loudness constitutes enthusiasm. *Adon olam!* O Master of the World! *He is King, his name proclaimed!* Some hunch over and peer at their books as they sing, like little old people, little fingertips on each syllable. I require them to read as they sing, even though they've memorized the words. I walk through the class, gently correcting the placement of a finger and redirecting wandering eyes. Eitan throws a sly grin at Yuval, who good-naturedly kicks him across the aisle. Then the two notice me and shrink back into singing. *Ash rei yosh vei vay se cha.*

I love my classroom. It's an enclave, a magic space. I love the giant colored Hebrew letters and colorful prayer posters, love the job lists on the walls, the name tags in bright block letters under each coat hook, the labeled shelves, the neat lines of books. Order is holiness. This orderly space devoted to God is just like the home I want to make for our children. *Baruch sheamar,* the children sing. God spoke, and the world came to be. The students are vulnerable, willing, small. Each day, I offer them this magic place devoid of irony and doubt, where each can easily believe with holy innocence that God made the world in six days, that the snake stood up on legs and spoke to Eve, that Moses climbed into heaven and carved God's commandments into a block of sapphire. In this classroom, faith is normal, attainable. I want to build this faith into their makeup so they won't face the same conflicts with self, with desire, that I have.

Every day, I give out awards, sweets, ribbons, stickers. All of them are for obedience and skill mastery. There are no awards here for creative thinking, initiative, or leadership.

We teach the children exactly what to think. At times, I give them logical word puzzles to develop thinking skills, but the solutions all draw the same conclusions about God and Torah.

Train for obedience. Fill their minds with foregone conclusions. It is not that I fail to realize that what I am doing is more like indoctrinating than educating. It's that the very idea of indoctrination has lost any dark tinge and has become a proud goal. I am training the ranks of soldiers for God.

And soon to bear another. I told Levi that same evening, with a simple, quiet statement over dinner. "I'm pregnant." Levi stopped the fork halfway to his mouth and blinked. I wanted to throw my arms around his neck, but he drew into himself as if he had to muster something. Resolve. Then his face softened. "Baruch hashem," he said, with the small beginning of a smile. Bless God. I saw fear in his eyes. Since then, Levi has doubled his efforts to pray more, study more, earn more, be a more obedient Hasid, hoping to earn merit for his children from on high. This, I will come to understand, is his form of love for them.

My students bring their singsong to a close. Today is an auspicious day. The children are to receive their first primers in Bible study. We've been preparing for this. They've learned to translate the first line. They've learned a new song. Tov, tov, lilmod Torah, they sing with me, because here, for the sake of educating children, behind closed door, here I can sing. It is good, so very *good, to study the Torah.* Even little Eitan sings, his body lifting with the song. As they sing, I remember my own introduction to study, Seema showing me the world of Law flowing from a web of commentaries, Rabbi Rakovsky describing mystical worlds, and I lift my arms, and the children rise, still singing. Torah, our precious Torah! I give out the primers into eager hands. They have made book covers decorated with crayons and glitter and glue. I help each one to slip his or her new book into the cover. One by one, I write their Hebrew names on the front with a thick marker, the name of their Jewish soul. Naomi Devorah. Yehudah Leib. Eventually, I glance up to see that Mrs. Frumen has come back into the room. She is standing near the door to witness this initiation, her arms folded across her chest. She smiles.

MARCH 14, 1979. In labor, near dawn, I'm in our Dodge Dart in a back parking lot behind Three Brothers Bakery. We were on our way to the hospital, but Levi turns on the oven here every Wednesday morning so that the kosher breads and challahs this bakery produces can be labeled "bread baked by a Jew." According to the Law, "baked by a Jew" means bread commercially baked by a man who adheres to Jewish Law and has never violated the Sabbath. Or, if the real bakers, like those at Three Brothers Bakery, are clean-shaven and their heads are uncovered (or are not even Jewish), then "baked by a Jew" means bread for which a proper Orthodox Jewish man with a beard who keeps the Sabbath came for a minute to ceremoniously turn off and then reignite the giant commercial oven with its rotating floors, even if, in his home, he considers baking a woman's task. Never mind. Levi does this as a service to the community, a religious obligation.

So I wait. Close my eyes. I have to breathe very slowly. There's a rippling sense, a gradual tightening through my body, that weakens me. But here's Levi's face in the driver's-side window, hat on the back of his head, creased forehead and worried eyes. In a moment, we're moving. I'm being carried in the car out onto empty streets and up the hill as the sun rises. We have to cross the train tracks to get to the hospital. Another liquid ripple, but this one turns into pain and my head falls back and to the side; my mouth hangs open. The scarf shifts sideways, I groan. Levi stops the car at the crest of the hill. There are flashing lights, a train horn, red-and-white barrier arms going down. Twenty minutes pass while a chugging train crawls across our view. Or is it twenty years? Another pain, and another, easier this time. Levi tries to chat. I try to laugh.

Endure. But every day I endure: loneliness and embarrassing erotic dreams that wake me in the night, a muted cello song, muffled memories like muffled voices trying to push me off my stubborn path for God. What should be different now? In a delivery room at Sharpstown General, the cold metal stirrups are too high for my short frame. Somewhere far away a woman is shouting. A nurse ties down my hands. In the background beyond the waves is Levi's furious whispering of psalms, like whistling rockets to God.

A nurse switches my wig for a green surgical cap, takes away my glasses, and drapes my thighs. If I open my eyes I will see only pain, yellow, red, black, in rhythmic waves. I am breath and counting, expectation, the hit, white heat, and more breath. Then again. And again, until there's a growl somewhere I don't recognize, but it's me, and then power I didn't know I had pushes the baby out in an animal surge, a bumping rush.

Quiet, a blanket over murmurs, rustling attendants, clinking equipment, the air cold on my bare, wet skin. I turn to Levi for grateful eye contact at the baby's pristine cry of arrival. A voice says, "It's a boy."

"Where are my glasses?" I say. Then there's a doll bundle in a nurse's arms beside me. My hands are still tied down.

First comes protest. *How can tiny you be all the way over there in their warming box when you belong under my heart?* Then wonder: *When they release my hands, I get to hold you.* And I do. Dot round fingertips. Skin a whisper. Hair like down. Your tiny wrinkled brow. In a single leap, the yearning for love and home that I had focused on Levi shifts onto helpless you. *The Rebbe didn't promise I would have a home, or find one,* I think. He said to *build* a home. I picture our sterile little apartment, a box without a dream. I press you to me and pour in silent promises. *You are the dream,* and there's a mental rolling-up of sleeves. *I will work to make anywhere we are a home where you can thrive.* You find my face. We lock eyes and I pour in gold—something new to me, its root a new love that overtakes everything. *I will never leave you.*

W ITHIN A FEW DAYS, I am drained by his cries. I wait for Levi to come home the day of the baby's first bath. "I can't do it alone," I say. "I'm kind of scared." But when I fill the little tub, Levi backs up wide-eyed against the wall. So I bathe the baby alone while he flails and cries. At night, Levi covers his head through the crying. "I'll never be able to work tomorrow," he says. "If I lose my job, how will we eat?" *But when I hold you, son, well, you change. You are change, your newborn frown already smoothed on your forehead. And now you have cheeks! As you slip back to sleep in my arms, one drop of breast milk hangs on at the corner of your mouth, at dawn.*

Eight days later, we are getting ready to bring our as-yet-unnamed son to the synagogue for the bris circumcision. Levi's parents are on their way from the hotel. In the bathroom, I slip into my dress, put on the wig, and examine myself in the mirror. Before me I find a shapeless almost-woman, sexless, but something new and fierce sparks her face, a new purpose. I will shield my son. I will grow him and nurture him and guarantee him an easy path without danger or wandering or loneliness.

Without uncertainty, or doubts. Our life will give him God.

I pull off the wig, untie my hair from its awkward twist, and shake it out—my tiny hidden *difference. This is for you, son. I will give you a home that is an enclave without shadows, where you will feel certain Moses climbed into heaven and carved God's Word into sapphire, certain your world is a good safe place ordered by our Law.* I take out a pair of scissors and grab a thick strand. The hair comes away in jagged chunks. Out in the room, the baby begins to cry. His sound becomes a backdrop to this work, through the locked door. I drop the sheared strands in the sink, where they gather, curled, like a stunned animal. Then I take out the electric clippers I use to cut Levi's hair, bend over, and run the buzz over my scalp until my head is stubble. I leave one long piece of hair at either temple that I can tuck behind my ears.

The shapeless postbaby woman that is me looks like a small, drooping man with sidelocks, but missing his yarmulka. He is a man who is a woman. A woman who is a man. Now the wig will fit, secure, no offending bump. *I just won't look at myself in the mirror without the wig. I don't have to look.* I slip on stockings and a dress. The wig slides easily over my head. It is time to leave for the ceremony.

At the synagogue, his father at his side, Levi is triumphant as he carries his son on a white lace pillow into the sanctuary. He is met with cries of "mazel tov" from the men, clapping, and song. The entire community has turned out to receive this newest member. This circumcision is our son's spiritual birthing as a Jew. Here in the synagogue, it is Levi who has born him, Levi who bears him into the sanctuary and the community. I have done the lesser part. I watch through the partition, hidden away with Ruth, Levi's mother. When the *mohel* makes his tiny, swift cut to remove the foreskin, when he sings out the blessing bestowing a name above our son's squall and the congregation's welcoming cries, a Jewish soul descends from God and enters the child along with his new name, the name of his soul: *Leib, son of Levi.*

Leib was the Hebrew name of Levi's lost brother. When Ruth hears, she bursts into tears. Mrs. Frumen looks shaken. She leans over and whispers, "Don't you know you are inviting an evil eye by naming a child after someone who died tragically?"

Maybe, I think later, rather than my long hair, this naming is our little rebellion, because we knew Hasidic fears about such things when we chose the name, but we chose it anyway. Right after Leib was born, all it took was a mutual nod and a blurting out of the same name from both of us at the same time to know that this tribute was more important to us even than the community and their opinions. In this inadvertent way we unwittingly hand down tacit permission to our son to depart from Hasidic demands when the need to be human is more pressing.

Within a few months, we assess our future in a small apartment when we don't use birth control and conclude we need a house. The new place is small but solid, with a big yard where the children will run and play. Signing the mortgage is a great thrill. This will be our nurturing family place that mommy me will make into our home. We have come home.

Twelve

No!" I'm shouting, sobbing. Two year-old Leibl jumps,
startled. Daughter Libby, now seven months, puckers
her face into a frown. With teaching, the children, the
house, cooking, getting up nights with babies, every week stuffed
into six days as everything stops for the Sabbath, and Leibl seems
to need too much, I don't get a minute. Days are a treadmill,
nights peppered with cries while Levi sleeps. I do it all alone. "You
can't just come home and disappear!" I say.

It is Sunday—for us, a weekday—and Levi is off from work,
the daily newspaper, his privileged indulgence, rolled up under
his arm, a steaming mug of coffee in his hand. In our family room
there's an old sofa, my childhood piano, and not much else. Leibl
is playing on the carpet with his toys around him; Libby is on her
back, chewing a teething ring. A sliding glass door opens out onto
the broad, empty lawn. Levi has just gotten back from morning
prayers. He was heading straight to the dining room to read the
paper and then spend the morning studying his daily Bible
portion. "Leah," Levi says. He looks helpless.

"You're never home, even when you are. You don't help with
the children. And all day, every day you hold a money shadow
over us." *Not enough*, he says. *Notenoughnotenoughnotenough.* "You
leave for work all tense and don't even say goodbye."

Levi looks longingly toward the dining table and books. He
sighs.

"You come home the same way, so intent on your own stuff

that Leibl's learned to be afraid of setting you off." It's true. When Levi walks in the door, his face is lined, stoic through back pain he refuses to address, and launches into his second job doing private accounting. "You yell if I ask anything of you!" I say.

"I'm doing *my* job," he says. "I can't do any more than I'm doing."

"You don't even speak to me! Or touch the children." Or wash his dishes or pick up his socks. When he's not working, he hides in his prayer book and holy books. Falls into bed in the middle of the night to start again in the morning. "You don't hold me!" Monthly obedient sex after *mikvah* doesn't count.

Leibl runs out of the room.

"But . . . ," Levi says.

"But?" I say.

But shame is already on the horizon. *This is my job description —to be this kind of woman so he can be the Man.* I try to hold on to my anger, but it feels as if I'm challenging God.

Levi insists I continue teaching because we need the money, but the school pays female teachers much less than it pays men, and almost all of what I earn goes to the babysitter. When I get home there is dinner to cook, the children to feed and bathe and get into bed. Libby has already rejected my breast; I wonder every day when I'll be pregnant again. There are no kosher restaurants in Houston—no break from the cooking. I know all of the checkers in the grocery store by name. With the children, my shopping and cooking for the Sabbath takes all of Thursday afternoon and most of Friday. I think, *How is it that this life of the spirit is so utterly physical? Notenoughnotenoughnotenough.*

Levi opens the sliding glass door to examine the mechanism that fits it into its track. He pulls. It drags and makes a noise. He looks quizzical, absorbed.

"*Look* at me," I sob. I take my glasses off and throw them at him, but I throw wide and they hit the wood frame of the sofa.

The pieces fly. Levi becomes a blur, his blurred hand moving the blurred door; his blurred face with no expression.

I'll make it on my own. I'll take the kids, go back to Dallas, get my mother to help. I'll find a job, anything, it doesn't matter. *But I'm afraid.* Anything would be better than to live with this obsessed stranger who pours his money fears all over us, to live with endless work labeled Women's Work so that he doesn't help, and never a hug or a kind word. *But I don't reach for him, either.* It's so much lonelier to live with a stranger than to live alone. *Aren't our problems my fault?* And then there's this: I've never supported myself before, never lived as an adult in the world. Out There.

For days I run circles in my head. *I'll do this, leave. I can.* But live with my mother? Then I realize—the secular world looms too big, too threatening. I look different, don't know my way as an adult outside the Hasidic community. I no longer speak the language. I don't even own a car, don't know how to sign a lease or get insurance.

I promised my children God. I promised them security and peace. Leaving is failing them, as if I lied. I'm afraid to stay but *afraid* to leave.

Days later, I am still whirling. One day after I get back from teaching, Leibl and Libby are napping when the phone rings. I race to get it in the kitchen, so as not to wake them. It's Mrs. Frumen. "I've been asked to speak at the midwinter Nshei Chabad convention," she says.

"And that is?" I say. I don't know why she is calling to tell me this.

"An international convention for Lubavitch women," she says. "It's huge."

"Well . . . congratulations," I say.

"My husband and I have chosen you as the delegate from Houston. The synagogue will sponsor you to come with me."

Has she caught me out as a rebel? Is that why she's singled me out? Does it show? Is she trying to pull me back in? *God is calling you back. Let the arms of the Law fold you in.*

I'll get away for a few days and calm down. I'll take Libby. Levi will have to take off half of Friday and look after Leibl all weekend, but he can't argue because the Rebbe has blessed these women's conventions. This is for God. I take a deep breath and say, "If I bring Libby, could someone there help me find a babysitter?"

THERE ARE OVER A THOUSAND Hasidic women seated in the huge Chicago banquet hall around dozens of round tables draped in white, every one of the women dressed according to Hasidic dictates. The "girls," meaning anyone who isn't yet married, regardless of age, have been relegated to another room and a separate program. In here: a thousand skirts, a thousand wigs. At our table, Mrs. Frumen chats with an old friend. She gave her talk about outreach earlier to a large crowd. "Just plant a seed," she said, "and the soul will respond." I sit awkwardly among strangers.

Our table's centerpiece contains a plastic doll woman in long sleeves and skirt standing stiffly next to a pair of Sabbath candles half her size. There are also two small, glossed challahs and a miniature calendar to symbolize the formal counting of days before *mikvah*; the smiling doll woman is beholding the Three Great Commandments for a Jewish Woman.

A waiter deposits a plate in front of me with chicken, kugel, carrots, and a roll, then does the same for the others. "And I didn't have to cook it!" one of the women says with a laugh. "You mean I can *sit* and eat?" another says. I figure there must be between fifty and seventy-five children among the ten women around the table. The others also laugh. They dig in.

Next to the centerpiece is a can with a slot in the top to slide in coins and bills to fund Lubavitch outreach. Giving money for outreach is even better than giving money for the hungry or the homeless, which feeds only the body, which is temporary. Outreach feeds the soul. One of the women puts in a bill and passes the can around. *The hand must be trained to give.* Thus exposed, everyone else pulls out purses and fishes for coins and bills.

"This is Leah, from Houston," Mrs. Frumen announces. I know she's showing me off as one of her recruits, her badge of success. Then she leans close to her friend and says something I can't hear in the noisy room, gesturing at me with her chin. I sit like a gleaming new purchase.

Soon, plates half empty, a speaker is announced, a rabbi. As the rabbi ascends the podium, the women all stand in a rustling wave of female respect. He looks across the crowd with a wise and serious expression, waiting as we sit back down under that gaze. At our table, Mrs. Frumen's upright posture and raised eyebrows ostentatiously demonstrate proper respect for a wise man. One by one, others at the table look at her, put down their forks, and sit up at attention. Female humility settles over the room.

At first, I only half listen. But then, in his German accent, the rabbi mentions *mikvah.* "Beneath the water in the *mikvah,*" he says, "is a place of transition between before and after, between this world and the next. A place between time." And then I am in that momentary breathless place, the blue water, blue tile, blue walls. He says, "A woman hovers under the water like a fetus. There, like a baby, she is pure of sin. She emerges to life renewed, cleansed of the last month. Every month is another chance."

Another chance. I should give Levi another chance. Maybe I'm causing his tension. I don't try, don't know how, to attract him, how to draw him to me, how to soothe and calm him. I should learn. Why haven't I? I don't try to make him aware of himself, as a wife should do, or get him to change. I haven't done my job.

The women are applauding. The rabbi descends the dais. Even before he's gone, the crowd begins to sing a lively, defiant Hasidic melody with a quick and dancing rhythm. A song of outreach. *Another chance*, I think, and I'm singing, joining my voice to a thousand female voices. *Ufaratzta*, we sing. We wave our fists in the air against the foreign secular world that is blind to God. *We will spread out. East and West and North and South.* We will spread out! The melody grows, a thousand strong. I am in a sea of woman, part of one huge, roaring female voice, immersed in a *mikvah* of song. We rise, and each puts a hand on the shoulder in front of us. We sing. I dance right past the hollow place inside me, past protest and exhaustion. *Let me be.* I'm carried on those voices, walking, stepping, dancing to the beat that pulses through the room and through my body. The huge room fills with our curling, snaking lines of connected dancing women, waves of bobbing wigs. We sing until we are hoarse, and still we continue singing. Beneath my hand is the humming outline of a woman's shoulder, but our singing is a bursting forth from *mikvah* waters. *We are renewed.* Another chance!

FIVE MONTHS LATER, long past midnight in our darkened house, Levi is asleep in his bed across the divide. I am pregnant. I lie awake and listen to his even breathing.

I must try to sleep in this life of mine, which gives even its sleeping hours to God. God writes my nights just as He writes my days: Prepare water next to the bed for morning hand washing. Go to sleep in a separate bed during the menses and for seven days after, *or every night forever.* Recite the testament to God's oneness before sleep, the prayer of martyrs, and then the prayer giving one's soul to God for the night—*or for the rest of your life.*

Sleep in a night scarf and long gown with sleeves and a high neck, *even in Texas summer.* For health, go to sleep on your left side, wake on the right. Now close your eyes. Picture the Rebbe and meditate on his image. Feel yourself drawn to his holy soul, to assure auspicious dreams. Do not speak until morning. *God will write what comes.*

I fall asleep sometime in the early morning, but after a short time I wake in full-scale panic. Choking, heart racing, clock face glowing an ungodly hour. I pant and try to orient myself. *Breathe.* Slow down. Breathe. Breathe it all in: loneliness, and children's laughter, their little rebellions and how I love them. Breathe in the constrictions in my life and the simmering resentments, but it all stacks up inside my chest. My chest burns; my throat is tight. Air whistles through narrowed airways. Doctors don't know what to do. Asthma medicine does little to open up my life. I exhale, but without release; I have to hold on. One more day. And another. Hold tight. Now try to breathe.

Much later, I find myself in a bed on top of a woman. She is mute but not still, on her back as my knees straddle her thighs. Oh, but it is astonishing, this exquisite softness, delicate skin of her breast on my tongue, the languid, seductive rub of her limbs on mine. I feel more than see her hands running down my prickling arms and back, the sensation liquid, acute almost to pain. I lose language. Flow forward in a wave. I am the wave.

I am instinct. I am touch. My arms encircle her as I meld into wet warmth.

I want.

I am Want.

I wake, this time in a sweat, heart pounding again. I lie very still in the dark in my night scarf, in the modest nightgown, the small mound over my stomach, listening to the drum of my heart against my husband's snore. As the clock face glows in this room of shadows, I wonder, *Why do I keep dreaming I'm a man?* Because I refuse to admit that I might have been a woman making love to a woman in this, my most erotic of dreams.

THREE YEARS AND TWO more children later, I am still plagued with asthma, with dreams and sleepless nights, and the space between Levi and me has solidified into routine. One Sabbath, I take the mile-long walk to the synagogue with four-year-old Libby.

The partition in the synagogue between men and women has a screen at the top through which we can see if we sit close. When Libby and I arrive, we're happy to get seats in front. Services have already begun. Mendel and baby Avrami are at home with a babysitter. I peer through the partition at Leibl sitting with Levi on the men's side. Libby picks up a prayer book. She is beginning to sound out Hebrew words. "Sit nicely for thirty minutes," I tell her, "and then you can go play in the hall with your friends." She nods, her eyes big and solemn.

Beneath my best Sabbath dress and new human-hair wig, I am shapeless from pregnancies and my head nearly shaven, but all of us here are in beautiful clothes and perfect wigs over stretched bodies, shorn heads, and tired hearts. Perhaps our silence and sense of inadequacy before our tasks are part of what draws us together.

Leibl and Levi are sitting on a bench on the men's side against the front wall. Leibl is good at his Hebrew reading, but I'm worried because he's restless and bored, and because I can't imagine this child fitting any mold. Soon enough I'll be his teacher, but secretly, I don't want to snip away his questions and little rebellions. Leibl lets his prayer book fall slack. He jumps down off of the bench, but Levi puts a firm hand on his shoulder. Leibl twists away.

Blessed is He who spoke and the world came to be. The jumble of male voices speeding through prayers no longer puts me off. Now they form a kind of backdrop while, since I can't openly participate, I'm free to begin wherever I please and at my own speed. I understand a lot of the old Hebrew now. I love its cadences, alliterations, and rhythmic speech. Poetry. I read and muse and drift, free to sink into those centuries-old supplications. My prayer voice is almost imperceptible, lips mouthing syllables. Slowly, the whistle in my chest relaxes. Through the screen, the men are distant, shawled mountains chanting to God.

We hide behind the partition because our bodies can arouse the men and distract them from their obligations. Some of my friends here are proud of this position. They feel strong and enjoy this acknowledgment of their sexual power. Two friends down the row are whispering to each other. A third bends over her three children, who are scrubbed and dressed in their Sabbath best. But it doesn't matter that they aren't praying. *Aino domeh metzuva v'oseh l'mi shelo metzuvah v'oseh*—since women aren't required to pray, their prayers don't have the holiness that comes from fulfilling a commandment, that only men can attain. Officially, it is enough for a woman to bring her children to the synagogue so that they can absorb the prayers into their souls.

But today, I am not satisfied with that "enough." Avram Ayor's meditative reach for truth has stayed with me. "You can go now," I whisper to Libby, who looks happy and jumps down, looking for her friends. I grow quiet with prayer, listening to ancient words march through my mind as if my voice is not my own but God's, whispering His poetry to me. Through me. The lines are full of metaphors for my life, each a key that unlocks something.

Now the men descended from *cohen* priests assemble at the front of the men's side to bless the congregation. They pull their prayer shawls down in front to their waists to hide their faces, forming a new row of shawled mountains. Little *cohen* sons, big and small, crowd under their fathers' shawls so that beneath the

line of hills is a collection of pant legs and shoes of all sizes. Their
song rises muffled through cloth. *Y'varech'cha.* May God bless you
and keep you. May God shine his face upon you.

All of us look away from the priestly power of the singing
men. Libby reappears; someone has shooed the children back in
for the priestly blessing. Head averted, I give her a quick hug.
Then I whisper the written response to the blessing. "Master of
the world! *Chalom chalamti ayni yodea"*—I have dreamed a dream I
do not recognize. Suddenly, I am waking in the night from a
vision of strange love. I glance around, as if the others can see,
then down at Libby. The priestly mountains sing on: "May God's
countenance shine upon you." I turn back to soothing whispers
and the reach for God, trying to hold on. *Chalom chalamti.* I have
dreamed a dream. Libby clings to my dress. The burning in my
chest returns. On the other side of the partition, Leibl puts his
book down and tugs on Levi's sleeve.

HOT BATH. Tired muscles sunk beneath steaming water.
Stretching, heat, eyes at half-mast. Slowly taking in warm, moist
air. Only the Law could get me to indulge myself like this, but this
long, hot soak is required before *mikvah.* I've been very few times
in recent years, exempt during pregnancy or nursing, but I've
finished the Seven Clean Days and it's time. Levi will get the
children into bed tonight. No swift shower while worrying about
babies. I slowly ease away a tiny softened scab, smooth the
cuticles on each toe and finger, scrub off makeup, and stains from
my rough hands, so that nothing will keep the *mikvah* water from
touching living *me.* I slide the sudsy cloth from toes to hip until I
am perfectly clean, smoothed and softened. Finally, I get out and
dress in a fading housecoat snapped down the front and a red
jersey snood. I put a fresh towel into a shoulder bag. Mendel and
Avrami are sleeping. "Mommy's going out to see a lady," I first tell

sleepy Libby in her bed, with a kiss, then Leibl, who is still awake and reading. I give his hand a squeeze. "Be back soon."

This is what I was taught before marriage: The on-again, off-again rhythm of *mikvah* enhances intimacy. Before *mikvah*, conversation and chaste companionship should deepen our knowledge of each other and thus deepen our bond. A delicious anticipation will grow, leading up to *mikvah* night. But I don't know what that anticipation feels like. I've lost any boldness I gained after Rav Moshe granted our yearlong reprieve long ago. Levi has grown remote and flat. I remember his hunger for me, once. Sex has become a once-monthly act of obedience to the Law. I head out the back door. Levi is studying Talmud at the dining room table. He says nothing as I leave.

Outside the *mikvah* in the mom van with Mira, my *mikvah* buddy—she's also in a housecoat and snood. We've taken each other to *mikvah* for years. She's the only one besides Levi who knows this is my *mikvah* night. We like to park and visit. We linger in the dark car, shadowed under the tall light over the lot. Another car pulls up. Two women get out and go to the *mikvah* door. One works the combination lock. In a nod to the privacy of *mikvah*, although we know them both, we don't acknowledge who they are. But this is our time. Mira and I, we're in no hurry to get out of the car. Between the two of us, we have nine children, and we both know there will be more. So we talk. This is one of the only places where I talk, protected by *mikvah* modesty. We talk about our children, our struggles raising them, the Hasidic school, the rabbis. She talks about how much she wants to implant Hasidic values in her children. Sometimes, as she quotes her Jewish studies, her voice grows shrill. Inside, I back off when she does that, but then we share recipes, talk about our husbands, finding bargains, and dealing with housekeepers. Once, I was shy and hesitant on these outings, but Mira is more than a once-monthly friend now.

In the *mikvah* waiting room, several women are chatting in the few available chairs, others standing. Officially, no one will report whom she saw here. All came in pairs, one to immerse and one to supervise. One of the women, newly married, doesn't speak or make eye contact, just looks at her feet, her hands gripping the rolled towel in her lap as she waits her turn. I remember how exposed I felt here when I was newly married. I was embarrassed that everyone here should know I was to have sex with my husband that night, or that, since *mikvah* comes at the most fertile time, I could get pregnant that very night. But I've come to like this exuberant, private women's space where sex is tacitly acknowledged. We share the secrecy, the anticipation, the changes that might come. I join the conversation.

Four adjacent doors around the perimeter of this central waiting room lead to four connected rooms. Two contain *mikvah* pools. Each is linked to a bathroom in which to prepare for immersion. A woman comes out of one of them fresh and dressed, her cheeks pink from the hot water. Mira nods to me. It's my turn to go in.

Now I'm wrapped in a towel by the pool, Mira behind me. The *mikvah* is filled with sauna-hot water and lined with blue tiles. The pump that filters and chlorinates the water during the day is off for *mikvah* time, but the air is scented with chlorine—a modern American *mikvah*. Everything echoes in here: dripping water, the drag of Mira's shoe on the marble floor, our low voices, the fervor from all the women, past, present, and future, who have brought or will bring their hopes here. I turn and let the towel drop down in back to my waist so Mira can inspect my back and shoulders for stray hairs. The water must be able to kiss every inch of skin. "Stand still," she says, and brushes my shoulders with her warm palm. There's still my sense of exposure at the *mikvah*, the involuntary flinch from her soft touch. *I will never inure myself to this.* Keeping my back to her, I descend the

first step and hand the towel and my glasses over my shoulder to
Mira. Let her think my modesty is before God.

Mira disappears above and behind.

Warm water to my chest, I close my eyes. I am stripped of
everything here, everyone, distant Levi, intense little Leibl, shy
Libby, active Mendel, sweet baby Avrami. I am also stripped of
pretense, here and only here exposed to the truth of myself. I
open my eyes and step down to the lower level, where I have to
bounce on tiptoes to keep my chin above the surface. Ripples of
water flow away from me in undulating gray lines. *Mikvah* has
changed for me. It's not about Levi anymore, or about the sex that
will come. No matter what we're taught, I'm no longer purifying
myself for him here, like an offering. This naked immersion in
warm water has become my most personal prayer. A body prayer.
Just me and God.

Hands out in front. Don't rush. Not like so many quick,
obligatory immersions before this, which were weighted with
exhaustion and shortsightedness. I lift my feet and slip my head
beneath the water. Under the surface, I stretch out and reach for
something I can't identify. Submerged, nude, weightless, I am
held. At last. The water is a mute caress. But then I lower a foot to
the ocean floor and raise my head to find a surface world still
waiting for me. I emerge then like a birth, still standing in the
water. Mira's whispered "kosher" floats down from the railing
through the damp air. But what is it, who is it, that is kosher? Am
I kosher, after all? And my children? I recite the blessing in a
voice strained with hope. Most of that is hope to better their
precious lives. Behind me, Mira confirms with an "amen." I slip
my head under again, again raise my feet to sink beneath the
surface. I die here. I become a single drop in the greater pool of
women, of history, of God. Under the water, I am surrounded by
floating female figures from my people's past, praying, drifting,
hoping. I am at the vortex of a vast funnel; I see I'm not alone. I

do this five more times, seven in all, die and again die, until the airless, timeless moments all swirl together. Standing now, sleek wet hair molded to my head, I face the tiled wall in an intimate contract with God, handing Him my secret self. *Here,* I whisper. *Take this.*

Thirteen

anuary 28, 1986. I walk into Levi's hospital room pushing our fifth baby in her stroller, one-month-old Sarah, with seven-year-old Leibl helping me push. After years of holding himself upright in the Law, Levi has just had back surgery. We come to a stop with the stroller just inside the room. The image is a strange one: Levi is watching television. The Rebbe forbids television, and we don't have one. Although I let Leibl watch on occasion in neighbors' homes, he has rarely if ever seen his father do so. Levi doesn't turn or greet us with his wan smile. He doesn't take his eyes off the screen. The volume is turned up. The announcer speaks in intimate tones as if he were a neighbor or a friend.

We've seen recent news in Levi's *Houston Chronicle*, and Leibl's first-grade English teacher has been talking to the children about Christa McAuliffe, the social studies teacher who is going up on a NASA spaceship carrying letters from schoolchildren. McAuliffe has been planning to broadcast lessons from space, calling it "the ultimate field trip." NASA is right here in Houston, and the children have been excited. There are seven others on the mission, including Judith Resnik, a Jewish woman who's been in space before, but it's McAuliffe, the first nonastronaut to go up, who seems to have caught the national imagination. Yesterday, there was a NASA color portrait of the crew of eight in full gear on the front page.

For weeks, Leibl's play has been full of rockets and space travel.

Levi doesn't look at us. On the television, there is an eerie puff, a dense, contained cloud of smoke high in a blue sky. "What *is* that?" I say.

"It's the *Challenger*," Levi says.

I put a quick hand on Leibl's shoulder. The announcer's voice has an ominous, sad calm, as if he were an elder gently leading a single, vulnerable person through his tragedy. Under that patronal voice, I'm suddenly aware that the whole country stopped to watch the *Challenger* take off, businesses on hold, schoolchildren gathered in front of screens. The strange image replays, that puff in the sky, the silent watching crowd that just moments ago was whooping and cheering at the launch. The wind whipping a flag. We see it from the beginning this time, thrilling takeoff into some infinite possibility, seventy-three seconds of grinning schoolchildren and cheering crowds, then silence. That puff in the sky. Solemn faces. Placards and waving hands frozen, fallen, mouths hang open, eyes trained upward. Together with the crowds, Levi, Leibl, and I watch the smoke slowly dissipate. We have the same slack shoulders, the same unblinking faces. The announcer leaves long, grave pauses between his sentences while the image of takeoff and explosion plays again and again, each time ending with an empty sky as we stand in vigil before this alien box.

In these few minutes, Levi, Leibl, and I have been plucked out of our Hasidic glass box, lifted over its wall, and dropped right into American society. The camera scans the crowds, and there we are among them. As the puff plays yet again, we merge helpless into a national pool of feeling.

Leibl whimpers, his eyes wide and filling. He's not at all inured to the strange world of television images. I put a second mother hand on his other shoulder and think, *This news alone would have done this to him, but to see . . .* I make a move to cover his eyes, but stop myself.

We've failed him. I thought the glass box would keep the world and its tragedies away from my children, thought ours a community protected from *all that*, and now I've gone out of my way to bring my son here to see inconceivable destruction. Worse, we have taught him that there are no accidents. We've taught him that everything happens by God's loving plan. Again that puff in the sky. "Levi," I say, pointing to Leibl. "Turn it off!"

"MOMMY, WHY?" Leibl says in a plaintive voice from the backseat of the car. I know he can't imagine there could be *no* explanation—the Torah is supposed to answer everything. But I am inept, no answers. It's not that our Judaism doesn't offer answers but that there are none that I know of that I can feel honest about giving him right now. I admit that to myself.

As if a good enough explanation would take away the loss. Leibl's guileless shock pierces me as I drive. *I was supposed to be the mother buffer* shielding the children from contradictions, accidents, loss. *I've hurt him,* given him no protection from the inevitable world. "Why?" he says again, and again.

I wish I were free to tell Leibl that there is so much out there that defies the notion of a Godly, benevolent Plan. I want him to be confident and happy even *out there* in that distressing, contradictory world he saw on television, but to do that, he'll have to know that world.

Leibl's questioning persists for days.

AFTER PERHAPS A MONTH in our new home, I sit in my new, expansive kitchen with its ruddy Mexican tiles, drinking tea and savoring the early quiet before the morning rush. The renovation, Levi's surgery, and the move are finally behind us, and I'm enormously pleased with the decision to delay my return to teaching after Sarah's birth. The new house is a fresh opportunity to make our peaceful refuge. Sarah is asleep in her bouncy seat at my feet, and Gladys, our new housekeeper, is getting kids up and stripping beds in the back. Through the bay window, a late-February sky is low and gray, a mockingbird chirping on a lower limb of the still-naked elm. Our redwood deck forms a bridge over a fishpond with koi undulating beneath. The Mexican tiles, double sinks, and double appliances, one each for meat and for milk, all gleam. The mockingbird darts from elm to bridge rail, perches there, and turns its head to watch the fish. Sarah is fed and calm. There's the incredible stillness of infant sleep.

I have lowered the glass wall between Us and Them a notch. Gladys has moved in with us. I invited her to move in even though, as a refugee from El Salvador, one of the masses of desperate people streaming over the Texas border, she brings the world and its problems into our home. "Speak only Spanish to the children," I told her, and they are learning quickly. After the *Challenger* exploded, I decided if I could get the children better accustomed to fate, maybe as adults they wouldn't feel their faith betrayed by illogical dangerous events. Maybe Gladys can help them be less suspicious of people who are different from us. Besides, even though the housework requires both of us, Gladys's presence is giving me time to heal from Sarah's birth. Time to have a cup of tea.

Avrami calls, "Mommy!" from his crib, then stops; Gladys must have taken him out. And here's Levi in a suit and tie, rushing through the kitchen to the back door, still moving as if his newly fixed back can break, his velvet zipper bag that holds his prayer shawl and *tfilin* under his arm. I frown, put my finger to my lips, and point to the sleeping baby. "Late. Gotta go," Levi says, like the White Rabbit, and doesn't say goodbye. Slams the door.

The household morning tumult will soon begin, but for Levi,

the early synagogue service is about to start. I'm a little jealous. I picture the men of our community scattered across the sanctuary at the synagogue, shaking out prayer shawls under the high ceiling, the muted light, then wrapping black *tfilin* straps around their arms, yawning, each surrounded by rustling, shawl-clad holiness. One by one they begin to pray, sinking into the words, forgetting for now their job, the car in need of repair, the problem child, the unmown lawn, the needy friend, the tired wife, until the room fills with gathered hope in raw morning light. I remember the quiet moments between Avram Ayor's words as I watched him pray, that special kind of stillness. Levi gets to be immersed in that every morning, surrounded by God.

But in his synagogue God has a thundering male voice and I am on the women's side of the divide. Then I think, well, maybe Levi is also jealous—jealous of what must look like my early-morning ease when he has to run out every morning to the synagogue, regardless of how he feels. I picture Levi among the others. He drapes the shawl over his shoulders, *tfilin* box on his forehead, says the daily blessings that include thanking God "that you did not make me a woman." Long ago I decided that the men are commanded to recite this thanks as a daily discipline to keep them from getting jealous of the women, who don't have their burden of daily ritual and prayers. I think, *That prayer just can't be the obnoxious gloating outsiders think it is. It's not a sentiment about women. It's about the obligations of being a man.* We are all enjoined to thank God for our burdens.

Libby comes padding into the kitchen, sleepy and small, Mendel behind her. I get up. Libby raises her arms, and I lift her to my hip. I think, *She's getting too big for this.* I say, with a surge of warmth, "*Boobah*, did you say *modeh ani*?" Last night, I left a little washbasin by her bed with a two-handled cup of water in it so she could wake in the morning, crouch down, and pour the ritual water over her hands. She must have spilled some of it as she carried the basin into the bathroom like a big girl, because the hem of her nightgown is wet. She puts her head on my shoulder in a still-sleepy snuggle, and I listen to her lisp the one-line *modeh ani* morning thanks to God. Training them in ritual and faith has defined my motherhood. "You have to get breakfast and get ready for school," I say. Libby nods against my shoulder.

But then there's Mendel, who wants breakfast, too, and Leibl is up, and Avrami, whom Gladys brings in, and I'm whisking out bowls of Cheerios and milk and glasses of juice and urging the children to say the blessing before food—*eat up, gotta go*—while Gladys makes up the sack lunches. Even two-year-old Avrami goes to school. It's more tuition to pay, but the Frumens insist on school beginning at age two. I pack backpacks, tuck in shirts, slide on tennis shoes. And yet, and yet, I think, as if the feel of touching each child is still on my hands, it's this holding and nurturing, this teaching them God, that is *my* morning prayer.

Teaching, nurturing and ordering their lives, peppered with blindsiding moments of love, to me is the whispering *shechinah*, the female side of God. I have to wonder: For those men in our community who, unlike Levi, do share the work of home and children (and there are many), do they also have moments with their children that feel like prayer?

An hour later, after the kids leave for school, I'm back at the kitchen table with fresh tea, Sarah kicking her feet in my arms. The new house seems to be holding its breath waiting for the children to pile back in later with exclamations and backpacks and hunger, but for now there's respite, a grateful luxury. I sip my tea. But there's the day's list, the plans, the meals. Rabbi Frumen says that every diaper changed, every dish washed, every time a woman holds a child is its own ritual for God. He says, for a woman, each such act has the same spiritual power as a man's formal ritual. But . . . how *could* Levi imagine that my life is full of ease and freedom just because I don't have to perform his rituals,

study, and prayers? He couldn't be jealous of me. *Ease?* When I get
up before dawn, my mind racing with things that never get done?
Ease? When, no matter what, one of the kids will be disappointed
today because there is not enough of me for each of them? *Ease?*
When Levi and I don't help each other in our separate
responsibilities or even so much as talk about them? If everything
I do for home and children is its own ritual, I have a much bigger
set of rituals than Levi ever will.

Sarah whimpers. I lift my blouse and give her my breast.
Baby in arms, I move to the recliner in the den and settle there.
There is her weight against my stomach, the hypnotic pull, pull,
of her suck, warm, pulsing breath on tender skin. As she nurses,
she fingers the cloth of my blouse. Her eyes begin to close. I lean
back, then reach to a side table for one of the frayed prayer books
left in easy reach everywhere around the house and turn to the
same blessings that begin Levi's day. As Sarah nurses and dozes, I
whisper the same words that Levi says in the synagogue, but I
read them in a mother's language. "God frees the captive, raises
those who are bowed down, heals the sick." I read them as
promises that my burdens will be eased and that I am not alone in
them. And I can't even imagine speaking them aloud.

But the day's list intrudes. I begin to speed through, swift and
mindless, another item to check off, until I get to "Bless You, God,
that You did not make me a woman." Here I automatically
substitute what we women always substitute: "Thank you, God,
that you made me according to your will." We accept God's
unfortunate choices. *I'm not a man and I don't belong on Levi's side of
the universe.* But I wonder, why does the women's blessing say
only that I accept God's will, and not that I'm a woman? That's
who I am. Why doesn't it say, "Thank you, God, that you made
me a woman"?

But really, I tell myself. Levi also goes through daily prayers
with the same emptied submission that I muster every day, before

the same Hasidic God.

But what if I *could* toggle-switch between the warm squeeze of morning children *and* the vast, shared awesomeness of our ancient, formal God in the synagogue at sunup? Have it all? And what if Levi could have the same varied richness, the same balance, the freedom to taste both kinds of prayer? What if we shared that? If I weren't always alone on my female side of the Law, would I be less lonely, less overwhelmed? Would it help if we didn't speak two completely different languages about God?

I get up with sleeping Sarah in my arms and glide to the room she shares with Libby, the same room where Gladys now unfolds her cot each night. I unlatch the baby and lower her, still sleeping, still faintly sucking, into the crib. I pause and watch, my hand on her back steadying her into sleep. But the Sabbath is coming. I have to get to the grocery store.

FRIDAY NIGHT, THE SUN SETTING. I've nursed the baby, shopped, nursed, cooked, straightened the house, nursed, polished the silver, nursed, bathed and dressed, answered the phone, answered a hundred questions from children, nursed, broken up three fights, dried tears, and more. The cooking is done, house is clean, silver polished, everything in its place. The children are washed and dressed or almost dressed in Sabbath clothes, tucked and tied, hair combed festive. The dining table is spread with a white tablecloth. Libby and I are about to light the Sabbath candles.

Now is that moment when the Sabbath's "extra measure of soul" is supposed to enter our own, the moment when we join with legions of women through time with a strike of a match, a worldwide chorus of scratch and sizzle that, like God, creates a day. But my day has been so full, how do I switch gears to the profound at the strike of a match? The idea of our creating this holy time by lighting Sabbath candles is simply not as real to me as a house or a child.

I no longer think of vast mysteries; am no longer mesmerized at the thought of God hovering between the lines of holy text. But the spiritual desire that drove me into this life has left its imprint like a background murmur. Or a bruise. What I have now is simple obedience. I try to please God by doing what I am told He wants, as if I can then look up like a child and see approval in His eyes.

But it's Libby looking up at me. I cover my eyes with my hands to say the Sabbath blessing, and indicate for her to do the same. It's good, I think, that my children were born into this life and won't be split at the root, like me. I kiss Libby's forehead. "Good Shabbos!" we say to each other. *This I give to you.*

Later, we are gathered around the Sabbath table, the only time all week Levi has a meal with the family. I have set two twisted, golden-brown challah loaves, freshly baked, before him. I bring in dishes of carrots with cumin, garbanzo salad, curled pasta with broccoli, tossed greens, gefilte fish with horseradish, and sweetened iced tea. Levi is in his black coat and hat. Leibl and Mendel sit on the boys' side next to little Avrami, already snapped into his pajamas. I am next to Libby, my limbs heavy from the day's work. Sarah is asleep in her crib. I get up again and bring in steaming plates of chicken and vegetables as Levi launches into a song. But he sings out of tune and demands the children sing with him. Soon they are all singing and pounding the table in a gaggle of forced Sabbath joy. Then he reads aloud a Hasidic story that has a convoluted message the children can't grasp. He is huge before them, and his voice marches forward like a statistics report. The children seem nervous, and bored. Libby yawns. I think, I am the one that is musical, a teacher and a storyteller. *I should be the one to teach the kids the old songs.* I clear my throat. "Levi?" I say.

"Is that chicken soup coming?" he says.

I get up to go back to the kitchen. Leibl squirms in his seat and then spars with Mendel. Mendel punches him. Leibl jumps back at him. Levi stands and roars. "Sit down!"

THE *HOUSTON CHRONICLE* that Levi used to whisk off to the back room is now a steady source of the outside world. Each day, I look for news in the paper that the children will understand, and when there's something significant, I talk and talk about it: *There's a company that just formed called Microsoft.* (Their father works with a mainframe computer and has taken the children to see it.) *The pope visited a synagogue, the first pope ever to do that! The Supreme Court just let the Air Force ban yarmulkas.* But one day in March, the *Chronicle* headline reads: "*Challenger* Cabin Remains Are Found." Navy divers surfaced with Christa McAuliffe's remains while a solemn crew stood onboard to receive her. Then they went back under for the other bodies. McAuliffe was still in her blue flight uniform. I look at Leibl, fold the paper on itself hiding the story, and carry it to the back room. Say nothing.

GLADYS ROLLS HER EYES in the kitchen because I've just told her that it is eight weeks until Passover, *la fiesta grande,* when every last crumb of any food that is leavened must be gone from the house. Bread, pasta, crackers, baked goods of any kind, anything made from grain, the smallest crumbs dropped along the way. I've returned to my teaching, but it's time to begin ritual Passover cleaning.

Shmutz al pi din iz chometz, meaning that on Passover, dirt is the same as leavening and the punishment for owning leavened food on Passover is *kares,* spiritual death. Gladys begins in the back of the house, in the girls' room, while I'm at school. When I get home, I find her still in there. Together, we strip and overturn the mattresses to vacuum them on both sides. I can't depend on Gladys to guard us from the spiritual impact of missing even a single crumb. So after she finishes, I do a final examination and wipe-down, starting with baseboards. I scrub at leftover spots, wipe out corners. The spiritual lives of my children hang from my washcloth.

Risen dough signifies puffed-up, false pride, which leads to the worst sin: denying God. *Chametz*, as even crumbs from cake or bread are called this time of year, is a filthy word. For us, the symbol disappears and the object becomes what it symbolizes. If we own leavening on Passover, we are brazen, rebellious, and full of false pride. So we clean obsessively and try to believe that internal and external "housecleaning" are the same. Our work should purge pretense and insincerity and in turn spur on the housework. All this scrubbing becomes a way to redeem myself. And yet ridding the house of *chametz* somehow does the same for Levi without his participating in the actual cleaning. His job is to note the symbolism in all this labor and to be inspired to do his own, internal cleaning through meditation and study.

The story from Exodus that Passover commemorates is about the birth of our people. It's about birth. There is the tight passage through a watery canal across the Dead Sea and our arrival on the other side as a new nation. It's about being redeemed from both spiritual and physical slavery, so we can be free to devote ourselves only to God, the Beloved. Then there is the journey to Sinai culminating in receiving the Law, which was like receiving a marriage document, followed by union with the beloved.

Slavery, then freedom. Birth. Redemption. Marriage and union with a beloved. These are the symbols. I pause, stretch my back. The problem is, all this work isn't a symbol—it's real. I laugh, then empty a drawer and wipe each item clean. I don't have time for symbols, or heartfelt self-examination, or humbling renewed devotion. Instead, this time of year, we women are tornadoes of industry. We are female legions. We are burning causes without a self. We do this work because this is who we are. In the process, we will save Jewry and the waning traditions through our self-sacrifice. I crouch down inside Libby's closet and shake out a shoe. Out falls a Cheerio, the dreaded leavened food, as if at the command of an imperious Law. I pitch the Cheerio into a plastic garbage bag.

Sarah is teething. She woke up three times last night. At least I'm not pregnant. I need to get to the mall for new suits for the boys and shoes for everyone for the holiday, and there's a stack of worksheets to prepare for class tomorrow. I wipe out the shoe from the Cheerio, then stand, still inside the closet, to sort through and pull down Libby's outgrown clothes. I'll box them for Sarah so we won't have to buy new ones. Every penny goes to tuition for the Hasidic school, kosher food, the cost of our rituals. Beneath the sense that this is getting to be too much for me even with Gladys's help is Levi's steady hum of *notenoughnotenoughnotenough*. But that's our mutual hum now. There's never enough time or money or sleep. I close my eyes and lean against the doorjamb. Gladys comes in with a fresh bucket of soapy water. She pulls up the blinds and wipes the windowsill. For crumbs.

Leibl and Libby are still at school, but in come Mendel and Avrami, they are five and almost three, pulling me out into the room. I wring washcloths from the bucket and give one to each. They dance around, playing at Passover by swiping at the walls and at each other. "Go get toys," I tell them. "We'll give your toys a bath in the tub for Passover." Mendel runs away to the playroom, and Avrami follows.

A week passes, and another, in the march toward Passover. Every day, there is school, then home to work on the cleaning, besides meals and herding and managing children. At home, I put Leibl and Libby, the two oldest, to work. They riffle through some of our hundreds of Hebrew and Yiddish books to shake out crumbs, in case one of the books might have been opened at a Sabbath table. We start another room every two or three days. We vacuum coat pockets. I plan the seders, shop for eight days of Passover meals, replace the regular household products with products approved for Passover. I get my wig set and try to teach the children their parts for the seder. At night, I lie awake, eyes open, my mind racing with lists and plans.

Two weeks to go, and Levi comes home in the middle of the afternoon while I'm working in the hallway in the wide linen closet, where the kids like to climb in and play hide-and-seek. I hear the back door. "Leah?" he calls. I have stacked the folded clean towels and linens on the carpet. Gladys gathers an armful. "Everything must be rewashed for the holiday," I tell her, and then I call out to Levi, "I'm in here!"

But here's Levi, carrying a large box like a precious thing, gingerly holding the carton, his face tense and hurried. For the eight days of Passover, this handmade matzoh he's carrying will replace any food made from grain we normally eat. But the matzoh mustn't become contaminated with what *chometz* is still in the unfinished house. "Wait!" I say. "The matzoh's *here?*" and, "I wasn't ready!"

I run to the kitchen for a box of foil. I've seen pictures of Russian babushkas in the matzoh-baking factory in New York, headscarves tied under their chins. The women stand at long, high tables to roll out balls of dough by hand while sweating rabbinical students take the flattened doughy circles from them, lay them across long-handled wooden paddles, and place them in a wood-burning oven. Someone constantly calls out, "*Leshem matzohs mitsvah!*" We are doing this at God's command! In the oven, the dough turns dry and crisp in seconds. Fire blackens the edges. Levi just bought fourteen pounds of hand-turned matzoh. The cost was over $200. No soulless machine-baked matzohs for *our* Passover holiday.

I grab the foil and flash an image from my art history days, of Da Vinci's ruined *Last Supper* peeling from above an arched doorway in a monastery. That fated repast reminds me that matzoh was also the bread of Jesus at his last supper, which was a ritual Passover seder, and became a symbol of his body, his sacrifice, a message of redemption. It's a thought I dare not voice —we are not even allowed to say "Jesus"—but I am secretly proud that our matzoh carried its message of redemption into the world. Carrying the box of foil and a damp cloth, I hurry to our bedroom, where piles and stacks of Levi's books and file folders and office supplies cover a large swath of the carpeted floor. I quickly remove the things on top of the filing cabinet, wipe down and dry the area, and cover it with long strips of foil, turning the cabinet top into a shining throne for the box of matzoh high above the threat of *chametz*. Levi scowls. He has to get back to work. He flicks his hand at me, dismissive, then lifts the foil to inspect the area, running his clean hand over the metal surface. Then he sets the box on its throne himself. I stand there, tired and mute. In this moment, I hate him.

IT'S AFTER THREE THE NEXT MORNING, and I'm in the kitchen, scraping baked-on bits from the inside of the meat oven with the edge of a knife blade and talking on the phone with my friend Shterna. Her bearded husband comes home from work and goes right to work on Passover cleaning at her side, but still, we both sound drunk from exhaustion. Levi stayed up sorting and cleaning his personal effects, and now he's at the kitchen table, reading the *Wall Street Journal*. "Moishe sold the *chametz* this morning," Shterna tells me on the phone.

"That reminds me!" I say. "Just a minute . . . Levi," I say, pulling the phone away from my ear. "Did you sell the *chametz?*"

Before the holiday, he has to fill out a contract that effects a nominal sale of any leavened food I might have missed to a nameless, faceless non-Jew. Rabbi Frumen collects the forms. The contract becomes void at the end of the holiday, but as soon as the holiday begins, that non-Jew, whoever he is, will own our *chametz*, instead of us, and save the family from the sin of owning it on Passover. Or from my sin of omission.

"Yep," Levi says. "I sold it. Gave the form to Rabbi Frumen this morning." He doesn't look up from the paper.

"*Why* are we doing this?" I say to Shterna. "We don't have to scrape the oven. We could just leave the burnt-on dots of stuff. The Law allows it. Black dots aren't *chametz*."

But we are shepherding a new generation into selflessness. We are role models for our children. We Women would never accept the bare minimum of the Law.

Just then Levi holds the newspaper up. "Leah," he says, "look at this." He turns around with a sly grin so unexpected that I tell Shterna, "Hold on."

He points at the paper. "Look at the headline," he says.

But it's too far and he's not holding it up high enough. "What's it say?" I ask.

"There's an article about selling *chametz*!"

"In the *Wall Street Journal*?" Now I'm intrigued, maybe proud. Orthodox Jews make their mark on the business world!

"Yeah! It says, 'Non-Jew Pays Premium for Black Dots.'"

I shriek with laughter. I've been had. When I tell Shterna, we laugh so hard it hurts, bent over double and spluttering, laughing at ourselves. Then we go back to chatting almost until dawn. We also continue scraping our ovens.

⋐⋑

TWO DAYS TO GO. When morning light streams through slits in the blinds, I open my eyes after three hours of sleep to a moment of clarity. I blink. I bound out of bed in an adrenaline rush, away from Levi with his soft snore, stride into the bathroom, and lock the door. My body is aching, heart racing, eyes gritty. I reach to the back of the cabinet and pull out a home pregnancy test. When the stick turns pink for pregnant, I sit bent over, crossed arms on my knees, forehead on arms, face down. *Toomuchtoomuchtoomuch.* But there is no time, no place either for the self-indulgence of parsing out new motherhood or for imagining the new child unfolding. I gather myself and march on.

Dressed and in the kitchen, I grab my keys, intent on slipping out to the farmers' market before the kids wake up. But here is Libby, already dressed, smiling open-mouthed in a sheepish, knowing way; she jumped out of bed because she heard. She wants to come. "Okay," I sigh. "Go get your shoes on." Five minutes later, while I wait for Libby, just-awake Leibl staggers in with a protest—he wants to come, too—and then Mendel. "You're not dressed," I say, so Mendel runs back to his room. He's back in the kitchen in two minutes, pants twisted sideways and shoes on the wrong feet. I shush them—Sarah and Avrami are sleeping—and herd them outside.

In the mom van, windows down, I feel the happiness of my children in the morning air and the solidity of having them with me. This is a rare venture away from southwest Houston, to the Loop and around it, then up I-10 to Airline Drive. At the outdoor farmers' market, I hold Mendel's hand and try to keep an eye on the other two as we pick our way around a huge line of trucks, amid men piling watermelon mountains and stacking crates of tomatoes, grapefruit, cantaloupe, bananas. We wander down rows of vendor stands through shouts and heated conversations in Spanish, the clean smell of fresh vegetables and riper smell of sweating men on a warm Texas morning. There are rows of dried chilies strung overhead, stands crowded with red and yellow baskets of colorful produce.

I stop at one vendor where an old scale on a creaking chain hangs overhead. I hand Libby a pencil and the list of everything we consumed last year on Passover. She is five, but she reads just fine. "Every time we buy one of the things on this list," I say, "check it off." I've learned a little Spanish from Gladys. "*Quanto, señor?*" I ask the man, pointing to a case of bananas. "*No! Imposible!*" I say, after he states the price. "*Pero por dos cajas?*"

I buy fifty pounds of potatoes, thirty-five pounds of carrots, twenty pounds of the sweetest onions (Texas 1015). We eat only fruits or vegetables that can be peeled on Passover, another safeguard against *chametz*, so no green beans or leafy foods, and nothing that can be dried and ground and made into bread—no corn or beans, peanuts or soy. We buy mangoes and avocados, squash in an array of shapes and colors, coconuts and tomatillos, a new kind of cucumber, kiwi and casaba melon, and Japanese eggplant. Before we leave, we stop at the egg house and get fourteen dozen eggs. This food will define my life through Passover; Gladys and I will stand in the kitchen in aprons all day for eight days, peeling, chopping, squeezing, cooking. "Mommy," Libby says, "don't forget juice oranges!"

We drive home with the mom van stacked high. At home, we haul the stuff in on a dolly. So far, for this produce, plus kosher meat and chicken, fish, grape juice, wine, and matzoh, the cost of food for the eight days of Passover is over $1,000. My labor is free.

NOW IT'S THE FIRST NIGHT of Passover and we're all at the seder—that elaborate, ritualized first Passover meal of Food as Prayer. The table is draped in white, children dressed in new clothes and shining at their places, Levi resplendent at the head. I am in a new dress found on sale, the wig freshly set. But look at our family. Look! One child after the next wiggles in anticipation.

This is the culmination of my work, our home, our religion of refuge! Here's the elaborate velvet cover over three handmade matzohs, the gleaming seder plate holding an egg, symbol of birth, and *charoses*, the chopped fruit and nut and wine that looks like clay, symbol of the work of slaves, and bitter herbs for affliction that spurs hope. Levi stands and lifts his full cup of wine. Tonight there's a silver cup at every plate, instead of only at his—a sign of freedom. The children are proud of their cups and proud to get to sing the wine blessing like their father, even if they have to pretend that their grape juice is wine.

I can't drink the cup of freedom. I'm too leery that I will get sleepy when there's work to do. I finger the Haggadah, ancient seder guide. *Let all who are hungry come and eat! Why is this night different from all other nights?* Avadim hayinu—*we were slaves, but our God took us out with a strong hand. A wise one. What does he ask?* It's all there, beloved words and symbols, how enthralled I once was with it all, as I push away from the table and head to the kitchen to put fish on plates and ladle soup while Levi begins to march the children through the seder. From the kitchen, I hear his imperious tone and know they will soon be bored. When I can, I sit down and whisper the Haggadah as quickly as the men do weekday prayers, in the same mindless monotone, no energy for the beautiful lines. Then I bless the matzoh and bite a burned edge.

The matzoh bursts acrid in my mouth. With that bite, our first seder together when we were students in Austin comes back, then baby Leibl's first seder in our little apartment, then Libby singing her *mah nishtana* for the first time. *Why is this night different?* Mendel is running to wash toys for the holiday, and Avrami toddling with a washcloth to help. But it is time to recite the Four Questions, youngest to oldest. I coached each child through this many times in preparation for tonight, sitting close with one at a time in the recliner. Mendel sings out the first two in Hebrew perfectly. Libby commences in an out-of-tune singsong. Leibl squirms and then recites. "Father," he begins in Yiddish. "I want to ask the Four Questions." By next year, Avrami will be reciting, and possibly Sarah. By next year, a new baby will have joined us.

I listen with both joy and loss, remembering my early love of study and my dreams of being a yeshiva boy. The ancient seder guide is full of stories and metaphors loved for generations that once took me to new places. Is a metaphor a bridge, or does a metaphor take your mind across a bridge, across a divide, to an unexpected place that changes everything? No matter—my life is about tying shoelaces and chopping vegetables. Or is it? It is my turn. *Mah nishtanah,* I sing. Father, I'm saying to God, *I still have questions.*

Fourteen

The questions remain, but most of the time I ignore them. Such is my static life: no distinct line of movement to plot out, no steady, gradual change. Such is my female life: moments of disappointment or dissatisfaction or joy are occasional pinpoints of growth that fade before the onslaught of mothering, details, daily needs that flatten my sense of self and make that "growth" irrelevant. By the time another such moment comes, the last is almost gone. No buildup. No gradual change. How to tell a story without a self? I act along scripted lines; I don't react. I sense my children's feelings; I don't feel. More time passes. The old yearning for home is just an anxious old hum that rears up at times and robs my sleep, then fades in the day. When I do sleep, erotic dreams, and dreams of my past life, intrude. On occasion I admit my disappointment with the community or with Levi, and then I shrug. Sometimes I tell him, but he says little. Then I go back to work. Thus I move with little change, anchored yet waving in the wind.

Then, seventeen months after the first Passover in our new home, on a summer Sunday afternoon, my sister Debbie shows up at our door holding her infant son, David, her five-year-old daughter, Katie, at her side. We haven't seen each other in years. Her husband, Robert, just got a job at one of the petrochemical plants that ring our city, and they're moving here.

I assume she felt obligated to visit; as children of an immigrant family, we were always taught to stay connected *no matter what*. But when I open the door onto that little group, I let our shared past back into my life. The sight of my sister with her two children in shorts and sleeveless tops sends such a surge of familial feeling through me that I open the door wide. I hug her and sweep baby David into my arms. "Look at him!" I say.

"God, it's hot here," Debbie says.

"Come in. Come in!"

The blue carpet is a sea of toys. The kids run in and out, excited. In the middle of it all is our newest and sixth, Itzik, crawling and busy and eight months old. Katie peers at the kids from behind her mother. "Look!" I say to Debbie. "David's got that single left dimple, just like Itzik!" I gather the kids and introduce their cousins. I pronounce their Hebrew names slowly for Katie, mentioning all but the seventh growing inside me.

Katie doesn't try to repeat the names. We settle on our beat-up sofa. The kids gather around. A line of eyes. "Go play," Debbie tells Katie, but Katie clings to her mother.

I ask Debbie about their house hunting, their move, finding schools. Debbie talks and laughs, and that means so much. After years in our arid community, this easy family connection is like water in a desert. I think, surprised, *I never thought we might get a second chance*. But Leibl is staring at Katie. Katie leans on her mother. She points at Leibl's skullcap. "What are you wearing?" she asks.

"Nothing," Leibl says. He turns and runs out of the room. Libby, Mendel, and Avrami stay. That line of eyes. "You're not Jewish," Mendel says.

"Let's get the kids together every week!" I tell Debbie.

Katie pulls on her mother. "I don't like it here," she says. "Let's go home!"

MIRA, MY *MIKVAH* BUDDY, has taken a rather passionate interest in politics. She's been quoting a new radio personality named Rush Limbaugh. It is odd to me that she thinks the world should operate according to our values in the Law, or that she thinks a Christian man could represent what we believe. I don't know much about Limbaugh, but I listen to him one day while driving and find his voice derisive and cold. "You know," I tell Mira one *mikvah* night in the dark car, "we're good for each other. You've got to learn there is a gray, and as a religious woman, I have to remember black and white. We both need a little work." But it's ardent, vocal Mira, black-and-white-thinking Mira, whom our community respects. It's tough, I think, to be the one who remembers gray.

BREATHE. Four months after Debbie's visit, I'm in Methodist Hospital in a sterile white labor room hooked to an IV dripping chemicals into my arm to try to stop labor two months early. I try to breathe, but each pull burns between my shoulder blades. Teeth clattering, I sweat and shake from whatever it is they're dripping into my vein. My limbs and face are swollen from months of cortisone. I look to Levi. Then the placenta separates in a gush of blood.

Dr. Haines comes in. Her patients call her Bethany. "We're not stopping the labor anymore. We have to induce you," she says. "We have to get the baby out."

"Healthy kid, hostile environment?" I manage.

"Something like that," she says.

A nurse hangs a new bag and puts a syringe of pitocin into the line. A cold flush rises up my arm.

Faces: a man in green saying, "Here are the warnings . . . you have to know, possible cesarean . . . stroke, cardiac arrest or respiratory arrest, or . . ." *Just get the baby out.* Levi's kind, concerned face, as if a mask has been pulled away. "The Rebbe sends his blessing," he murmurs close to my ear, and then adds, "*Kol sh'vi'im chavivim.*" All sevenths are beloved. Bethany says through the haze, "This one will be different from the others. You mustn't push hard."

Oh, but this artificial labor *is* different from the others. The pain slams through with no warning, no buildup, no natural finesse. I have no strength to push anyway, and oh God . . . "The head!" I yell in panic. "I can feel how small it is—I'll break it!" I pull myself up on my elbows and move backward on the bed, as if to back away from the baby inside me. Then my own head falls back and I have no weight, no substance. My body is not mine. Has it ever been? My father, Levi, the Law, the Rebbe, the children—I am more theirs than my own. They lift me. The tiny baby parts my bones.

The next day, I walk on rubber legs alongside Levi, step after unsteady step, to the preterm nursery ICU. The lights are low. Incubators beep and whir, infant bodies breathing and dreaming. Levi dons a green paper gown and a mask that doesn't cover his beard. Our baby is just over three pounds, hairless, eyes squeezed shut, but he's a thriving little thing. Levi's eyes shine. He takes all fifteen inches of our son into his two cupped hands.

Two weeks of weak, queasy days pass while I lie in a hospital bed. I wake, take asthma medicine, eat, pad to the nursery to hold an impossibly small, squirming package to my breast, then head back to bed and sleep. Day and night, I sleep. Sister Debbie calls every day. Even my mother calls. And my grandmother. She's angry at me for doing this to myself, but I hear in her voice the kind of loving "anger" that is full of concern. "You have to take care of yourself," she says. "That is how you make them a mother." She's quoting her mother, from the Yiddish. "Make them a mother" means becoming a good mother by taking care of myself. *Do it for the children.*

One evening, Levi throws himself into the bedside chair in dramatic exhaustion and recites a litany. "Oh, the children, the house, the carpools, the fights, the mess," he says. "When are you coming *home?*"

But something has changed. I hear him really saying: *When will you come do all this work, instead of me?* I think about this, and don't answer. The women in the community have been sending over casseroles and scooping up kids for playdates. Gladys has been getting the children up each day, feeding them, and getting them ready for school. She looks after little Itzik. I don't feel sorry for Levi. "I need to be here," I say.

That night, hours after he leaves, Dr. Bethany comes to my bedside at the end of her rounds, just as she did the previous night and the night before that. Finished with her day, she sits and visits. I don't know why she does this, but, unlike other non-Jews out there, Bethany is no cardboard cutout to me, not anymore. I can still hear her voice at the end of a dark tunnel during the labor, like a rope pulling me through. She moves her chair closer to my bed.

I bumble out shy conversation strained with need and loneliness. I wish I could convey my gratitude. I wish for an easy connection like I have with my sister, but I'm out of practice speaking to a person in the world. I feel as if I'm an alien, and besides, Bethany's life seems so much her own. I think she can't possibly comprehend the breadth of her freedom.

Bethany leans forward and knits her brow. She says, "Leah, it's time."

"Time?" I say. But I know.

"Another pregnancy could be dangerous—for you or for the baby. Or both."

The Group voices rise up in righteous protest full-force in me then, calling for self-sacrifice for the Law, jarring me with shame. It is my duty to bring Jewish souls into the world. *Mesiras nefesh*, self-sacrifice, honors God. Recently, a Lubavitch woman named Rochel Leah defied her doctors and had an eleventh child, then died of heart failure. Never mind that any rabbi would have told her to listen to her doctor; Rochel Leah was determined to go beyond the letter of the Law. She has become a saint among us. A martyr. Babies have been named after her, moving sermons devoted to her. *A woman of valor, who can find?* If I ignore Bethany's advice, I will have the community's admiration. The clamor rises.

But there is Leibl, Libby, Mendel, Avrami, Sarah, Itzik, and now our new son. "Make them a mother." That's what my grandmother said. I can't listen to the voice of the group. I *won't.* I won't die. I won't leave my children without their mother.

I don't know this new, demanding voice in me speaking above the chorus. But I listen. "Tell me," I say weakly to Bethany. "Tell me what I have to do."

Bethany exhales. Leans back and smiles.

The next evening when Levi comes, I tell him what the doctor said. I tell him Bethany says if we don't follow her advice, it can be dangerous.

"We'll ask a rav," he says.

"Why bother a rav to tell us what we know?" I say. "We know the Law: If a doctor says it is a life-or-death matter, we have to listen."

"True," he says, and there is pure relief in his face.

HOME FROM THE HOSPITAL, our nameless son now weighs four pounds and nurses every two hours. Sarah and Avrami and Mendel and Libby and Leibl, who is almost ten, also need attention, and little Itzik is spiking a fever once a week and we don't know why. Weeks pass in a blur, no distinction between nights and days. When the baby is a month old and reaches five pounds, we finally hold a circumcision ceremony. We make it at home with just the minimum quorum of ten men, as I won't allow the exposure when he's so small. The mohel makes his quick, deft cut, the baby wails, and the mohel calls out our son's name *b'yisrael*: Shalom, peace. The name is like *shalem*, complete. Our family is complete.

Over the following months, I return again and again to Shalom's birth and the sense of losing myself to family and Rebbe and God as if they carried me through. I hear Bethany saying, "You have to do this," meaning birth control, and the surprise of Levi's agreement, as he could finally hear my voice alone. He followed *my* lead. I begin to understand this as a turning point and settle into a new, stronger reality.

I have chosen to say no. I marvel every day that I will not ever have to succumb again to the roller coaster of pregnancy. My body is my own. I have claimed it as my own. I stand a little more solidly. Is it possible my future is more mine as well? If someone from outside the community—someone I trust, like Bethany— were to show up and ask me pointed questions, I might even find a way to hint at a new self emerging. I might say, in a small voice, that I am beginning to stand apart.

PASSOVER IS COMING AGAIN. But the children's needs now seem far more vivid than the demands of the Law. I hire two women to help Gladys (*notenough*, Levi says, but he means money), and I don't even try to check their work, don't vacuum coat pockets or search closet corners for Cheerios, don't stay up late at night scraping the oven, and I don't fret at my shortfall. Our preparations might not be quite to ideal Hasidic standards, but I know the minimum the Law requires. I hear my own clear voice when I tell Levi, "Whatever the hired help gets done is enough." Somehow he doesn't object, although he flies into melodrama about the cost. Then I go a step further and announce that I'm not going back to work. No more teaching. Levi gives up and sighs. He's worried how we can manage; at least my salary paid the housekeeper. "Can't you just take a break and then go back in the fall?" he says. But I hear my grandmother, *Make them a mother.* "No," I say. "I can't anymore."

SHALOM'S INFANCY IS A BLINK, a breath, each day gone before it's over. I want to burn his fleeting image into my brain; he's changing so swiftly, every moment with him one I won't experience again. *When I hold you, little unfinished man, I am more rooted and awake because of you, maybe for the first time. You seal my motherhood. You are all of the children. You make them all more alive because you are the last. I am with you, every moment, in the days and in the nights while you sleep, even the nights after I go to the* mikvah.

Funny how a little rubber stretched over a flexible ring can change so much. It's a paradox to me how birth control gives me the strength I need for the children, a paradox that preventing motherhood gifts me with motherhood. Every time I take the diaphragm into my hand reminds me that my well-being is a priority. Just like during the year of reprieve Rav Moshe gave us long ago, now, at thirty-two, I still like the sploosh of foam into the rubber cup, the body awareness I gain setting the thing into place. I got back from the *mikvah* an hour ago. It's very late. The children are asleep. Levi is waiting. I pull the scarf off and drop it on the floor, shake out the hair I'm allowing to grow long again. I finish, step into the bedroom, and go to him.

Late one *mikvah* night when Shalom is three and a half months old, I find myself pulling away from Levi in horror. I wasn't really thinking before we climbed into bed together. I was somewhere else in my mind—with the children and the baby, who's not gaining weight as well as he should—and now it's too

late. I forgot the gate. I forgot to use the diaphragm. I jump up
and run into the bathroom and lock the door. "Oh God," I moan.

"Leah!" Levi says through the door. "What is it? What's
wrong?"

"I forgot!" I say. *Oh no, oh no, oh no.* Frantic, I run hot water in
the tub and step into the swirl. I crouch there and try to wash him
out of me again and again. Then I jump out, dripping and
trembling, grab the tube of spermicide and squeeze hard,
smearing thick, greasy cream along two shaking fingers, then
swab myself inside. I am possessed. I take the tube and squeeze it
directly into me. *Kill it kill it.*

No voice of the Group rises in righteous protest. It's just me
crying, "No. No!"

The next day, I move through the house in quiet terror,
thinking, *Another baby will break me.* I'm no saint like Rochel Leah.
I don't want to die to bring another Jewish child into the world.
Over and over, the idea plays in my mind like a leer:
Toomuchtoomuchtoomuch.

I try to reason with myself. *Why am I afraid, when I don't even
know if I'm pregnant? Maybe I'm not pregnant. Maybe I'll be fine.
Maybe, probably there's nothing to worry about.* I force myself to
attend to the children, the house. But I had just discovered a little
freedom.

I try to return to that place. For nine more days, I try to
return to that place. On the tenth, I take a home pregnancy test
and it's positive.

I go into the state of a body under siege. There's a scream in
my mind: *This will kill me.* Unlike seven times before, I can't
muster any sense of a sentient being forming in me. I can't see
this pregnancy as human. *It's not a baby,* I think. It's an alien thing,
a cancer.

The Group, the Law, the Rebbe, taunt me in their familiar
chorus: Love this new child because you *should!*

But there's an inner retort I can't suppress: *It's not a child!*
Cry for it, then!
I can't. I will not.
Picture your child, her or him, in your arms. Vulnerable, trusting, soft.
No! I am not Rochel Leah. I DON'T WANT TO DIE.
I don't know this rebellious woman in me. I don't know her, standing apart from the Group, don't recognize her strength. She claims knowledge I don't have—there's no proof this pregnancy is dangerous. Every pregnancy is different. I'm *supposed* to be a mother, endlessly a mother. The argument between head and heart rages. I close my eyes and flinch.

"Mommy, what's wrong?" eight-year-old Libby says, and puts a hand on my arm. "Nothing," I tell her. I smooth her hair, touch her face. I go to the kitchen table and collect the used plates.

For days I reel through the house on remote, whirling with guilt, fighting myself while every pore continues to scream, *Get it out.* I won't allow the scream actual form—I keep quiet—but I don't sleep or eat with the effort. I'm horrified at myself, afraid of this stranger who is me, who wants to kill her child. Who am I becoming? *I am a monster. I could murder. I am capable of that.* I become nauseated.

I must get the baby out. Out of me.

Days pass before I can even say the word "abortion" to myself, but when I finally do, the righteous chorus fades and I find the word doesn't spell depravity. It spells survival. It spells cold-blooded relief. I still think I'm a monster, but I will risk anything for my children. I have to make them a mother. I call Bethany. "I'm pregnant," I say. "I think it's a problem."

Her voice is gentle. "First," she says, "come in to the office and have a blood test. Maybe you're not pregnant—those home kits aren't always accurate."

That afternoon I'm in Bethany's office, using my new little

voice to squeak out my terrible request past the renewed, shaming judgment of the Group and God. The blood test is positive. A broad, shining desk between us gives Bethany professional distance. She looks grave. I am timid, but inside I am some kind of primitive, driven by instinct, ready for infant sacrifice.

Framed on the shelf behind the doctor are her two smiling, squinting boys in baseball caps in the sun. One holds a catcher's mitt. The other has freckles.

"My father was a minister," Bethany says.

"Oh?" I say, not comprehending.

"I don't do abortions," Bethany says.

I can't speak. I don't know where else to go.

"But I recommend one. Strongly," she says.

I stand up. "I'll find where I have to go," I say. "I'll figure this out."

"But I would do this one," she says.

I sink back down on the chair. "You would?" I say.

"I don't see this as a compromise of my principles," she says. "It's that necessary."

I think, *She owns her rules. And she can bend.* Why, she is bending toward me, reaching out a hand. "You understand?" I say.

"You have to do this," Bethany says. And then, "Does your husband know you're here?"

"No," I say. "No." My eyes open round. "Could you do it here, in the office?"

"Here? No."

"I don't want Levi to know. If I go to the hospital, the bills will come to the house.""I can't do that," she says slowly. She frowns, leans back, lowers her chin. "There would be a problem with disposing of the . . . tissue."

There are laws, after all. She also must comply with laws.

Her voice drops. "Talk to your husband," she says. "This is his baby, too."

"Don't say that," I say. "Don't say 'baby.'"

Then I'm alone in her office while she does a routine exam in another room. I wonder if she's with the woman I saw in the waiting room, young and rounded with her pregnancy. I watched her pick up *Parents* magazine and page through bright, uncomplicated advice for small, well-spaced families.

Bethany wants me to tell Levi, but telling him is deferring to him and to the Law. I have to decide this for myself. *I was just beginning to feel alive.*

Sitting there alone in Bethany's office, I admit to myself that I'm not really afraid of the physical danger. That's not what drove me to come here. Oh, it's true what Bethany says, I'm not up to having another baby, but my secret is that I don't really feel I would die. The truth is that I simply couldn't cope with another baby, to such an extent that I feel certain of a different kind of death—I'll break inside. That's what I'm sure of, terrified of. I will break, and my children will lose their mother in a different sort of way. In the same way in which I lost my father. The Law allows an abortion to protect my body, but not to protect my soul.

Levi and I once sought permission to use birth control because I was sure then also that I couldn't cope with a baby. But this isn't prevention. This baby already lives.

I don't know American law, don't even think about child support—I think, *I can't possibly make it alone with the children.* I think, *Levi loves God and His Law more than he loves me, and every aspect of our life together is based on the Law—if I break the Law, it will break our marriage.* I have to try to get a rav to agree to this abortion, because if he will, so will Levi. I'll do it to keep our family together.

But if the rav won't agree . . . I am ready to ignore the Law if I have to, no matter the consequences.

Bethany returns and sits back down behind the desk. I clench my hands in my lap. "If I tell Levi," I say, "the only way that he will support this is if we ask for a ruling from a rav, a rabbinic authority in Jewish Law—he's like a judge. We're supposed to ask a rav's guidance for these things."

Bethany looks quizzical. Waits.

"I mean," I say, "I'm going to have the abortion no matter what." My heart races with fear. *There. I've said it. Out loud.*

"I think you have to," she says.

"But I need to get a ruling for Levi's sake." The new voice rises, ragged. "I have to keep my family together."

"Would he leave you over this?"

"If I break the Law that our life is based on and kill his child?"

Silence. "Well, um, if you put it that way."

"I don't think he can see it any other way. Unless a rav allows us."

She swallows. "What would I have to say?"

"The rav will allow an abortion only if the pregnancy is life-threatening in a way that he understands," I say. "He'll believe a doctor. Can you use those words? 'Life-threatening'? Would you tell the rav that I would die?"

I can't believe it. *I'm trying to manipulate the Law.* I may as well be hacking at the roots of my life.

"I'm a doctor," Bethany says. "I'll tell him the risk, but I can't say for certain that it's life-threatening."

"But those are the words he would have to hear."

"You have asthma, not a heart condition."

"I know."

"True, what happened before could happen again and could be worse next time. It could be dangerous for you, but every pregnancy is different. You might be fine. I don't know. I'm not God."

"No," I say.

"The problem is that I don't know."

"Okay," I whisper. "That will have to do."

❧

LONG AFTER THE CHILDREN GO TO SLEEP, I ask Levi to come talk with me. He's curious, a little wary, and follows me to the backyard. We sit down on our old lawn chairs, a canopy of stars enclosing our private room. There's the scratch of katydids, the whine of a mosquito. We've been married over fifteen years. "I have to tell you something," I say.

"Well?"

"I'm pregnant again."

Levi sighs, then manages a smile. "We've still got the bills from Shalom," he says. "But . . . *baruch hashem.*"

"No," I say.

"What?"

"No *baruch hashem.* No 'thank God.'"

"What are you saying?"

"I feel like this baby is a cancer, or a bomb."

"Oh, come on."

"A bomb inside me."

His voice goes gentle, wheedling. "You've always come through fine," he says.

"I've been afraid from the first moment I knew."

Levi's lined face is shadowed in moonlight. He lifts a hand, as if to wave away the fear like a mosquito, but then stops, drops his hand. "Those doctors," he says in a careful tone. "You know how they can exaggerate."

"But she's right. I know she's right."

"About what?"

"An abortion."

When he hears that word, it is as if he has just been stung. He yells, "*No!*" and jumps out of his chair. "Are you out of your mind?"

But I don't feel like a monster anymore. I'm simply resigned. Dying physically and dying spiritually are the same to me. "I have to do this for the children," I say. "You don't have to do this," I add. "*I* do."

He stands and points a finger at me. "That's murder!" he says.

"Levi," I say. "The doctor said—"

"This time you've gone too far," he says. He stomps away.

It's happening, I think. *I'm losing him.*

I follow, past the fishpond, the redwood deck, the children's swings already wet with dew. The grass is overgrown, the night sky a clear, unblinking witness. But something is shattering in both of us. I'm angry. "You'd let me die," I say.

His back to me, Levi's shoulders begin to shake without sound. He's crying. I put my hand on his arm, and we stand like that in the night.

Then he's walking away and I am too afraid to let him go. I yell, "Please!" and won't let myself cry. I follow my husband through the back door, past the kitchen table, where I sit with tea in morning light, past the playroom, wooden blocks left out on the floor. "No!" he says, and puts his arms up as he walks. Still I follow. Still I beg, but my resolve is weakening. *Could he keep the children and send me away?* If losing him means losing them, then losing him is a more certain form of dying.

We pass the den, where the children pretend to swim the sea-blue carpet. We pass the bookcases of stately books of the Law, where the old, bass voice of God murmurs on. We pass the Sabbath dining room with its out-of-tune echoes of Levi singing with the children, and the bedrooms where Leibl, Libby, Mendel, Avrami, Sarah, Itzik, and now Shalom are sleeping. I keep pace with him. But Levi stops, turns. He curls his lip. There is disgust in his voice. "Who are you?" he snarls.

That's when I break. "Okay," I sob. "Okay okay okay okay. I'll have the baby."

But then Levi looks hunched, beaten. "No," he says, shaking his head and looking at his feet, and, "I don't know." And then, "We'll ask a rav."

⤳

WE DON'T ASK A RAV. I DO. I call the rabbi myself the next day after the kids leave for school and tell him everything while Levi listens on the extension. I give the rav Bethany's telephone number. He says he'll call back after speaking with her. Then I pray, for the first time in a very long time.

The rav calls back within the hour. I answer in the bedroom. He says he has spoken with the doctor. "I need to speak with both of you," the rav says. I gesture to Levi, who goes to the kitchen. I hear him pick up the extension. "I'm here," Levi says.

"Okay," the rav says. "You have to do this."

The rabbi didn't say the *a*-word. So I do. "Have the abortion?" I say.

"Yes," he says. Then he sounds accusing. "You were using birth control?" he says.

Levi clears his throat and says, "Yes. The doctor said it was necessary, at least for now, for Leah's health." We should have asked permission.

"So," the rav asks, and then his voice suddenly becomes a plaintive demand, almost a cry. "How did you let this happen?"

Shocked silence. I hear his shout as the cry of a parent. We are the children, and we have failed—failed him.

"And now," he says, "because of your terrible mistake, I have to be the one to give you permission to kill a child?"

No one can speak. This is when I realize that I just gave away the greatest and most terrible responsibility of my life that should have been mine as an adult: the decision to end the life of our baby. We should not have placed that responsibility on anyone else. I think, a grown woman should make her own decisions. Instead, we stand here as guilty children before a parent who is deciding our punishment, our consequence, for failing him. My mouth falls open.

I think, *We Hasidim, morally, we're children who never grow up.* We never become old enough to parse right from wrong on our own. The Law always stands over us like a parent over a child. The only choice left us now is to accept the rav's edict, do what he tells us to do. Or not.

For the first time, depending on a rav seems wrong. Of course Levi will succumb, obedient to his order. I try to tell myself, *But this is what I wanted!*

A time will come when I will look back and wish that I'd had the strength to act on my own and tell Levi to his face what I was going to do, instead of trying to get a rav to decree my decision for me. I will wish that I had had the courage to retain that terrible responsibility that I was finally ready to take on, instead of handing it over to the rav, because living with the consequences of that choice, and with the clear understanding that I brought them about, is part of being an adult. But at the moment, moral adulthood, which thrusts us without a light into murky terrifying choices, is new to me. I don't yet know how very much I will regret this.

"There is one more thing," I say to the rav. "I have to make sure this doesn't happen again."

"Yes, you do," the rav says.

"So I want to have a tubal ligation. At the same time. While I'm in surgery."

"This is unusual," the rav says. "You know the Law. Our bodies belong to God. It is forbidden to make unnecessary changes to them."

"Is that a no?" I say.

"But, given the circumstances, I say do it, the abortion and the . . . other. That way, you won't be calling me again about tragic mistakes."

Suddenly it's about him. He wants to make sure we don't put him through this again.

"Thank you," Levi says, his voice full of respect and humility.

"And, Mr. and Mrs. Lax? I want you to make sure of one more thing," the rav says.

We speak together now, in one voice, Levi and I. "Yes?"

"Do not speak of this. No one must know."

HOME NOW IN BED after the brief surgery. I have an inch-long incision covered with a dab of white tape, and that is all. During the procedure, Levi whispered psalms in the waiting room and then drove us home with a long, sad face. The rav has silenced him. Levi made no reference to the baby, his lost child, and I know he never will.

At home, he told the children that I'm not feeling well and to let me rest. But Leibl comes in. "Mommy," he says, "someone's on the phone." At my bedside, he twiddles with the sheet, reluctant to leave. I put my hand on his, then pick up the phone on the nightstand, and he leaves.

"It's Bethany," the voice on the line says.

"Did you call to check on me?"

"Yes," she says.

"I'm okay," I say.

For the first time, I imagine Bethany performing the abortion as I slept my chemical sleep, her green mask, the sound of the horrid vacuum. I told Bethany I wanted to be asleep so as not to hear the suck of the machine, or to see anything. But she had to see it all. "Listen," she says. "I don't know if you would even accept this from someone who's not Jewish, but I want you to know that I said a prayer for your baby."

At first, this falls flat, Christian faith being, to us, one step shy of idolatry, foreign and illegitimate, in some ways abhorrent. But then I think, I hadn't thought to pray for something I couldn't feel—for the baby—and she did. *I prayed only for my own comfort.* Suddenly, it seems it was Bethany's prayer that was legitimate, Bethany's that offered, in that moment of infant death, real faith. If she were standing next to me right now, I would look at her more closely, perhaps for the first time— short, taut body in green scrubs, hair in reddish-blond waves, clipped and clean, green eyes intelligent and aware. "I have to thank you," I say in a husky voice.

"You're welcome," she says.

"Before the surgery," I say, "I didn't want God to be part of it. Or I would lose myself. Again."

"I understand," she says.

But I don't understand. And I don't understand why I don't feel I've lost a baby, why I can't mourn. I think, *It's a sad thing to have no sadness.*

BOTH LITTLE ONES GO back to sleep midmorning after the others are off to school. The house seems to be waiting for end of day, for in-out door slams, the smell of sweaty children, games and squabbles, the bounce of a basketball on the drive, kids tearing off on bicycles, homework and dinner, baths and bedtime. What's new is that for these few hours the house is my private space alone with this new little inner voice that, in the quiet, now I can't help but hear. The rav said *no one must know.* Those who are known to have stepped out of our circle are considered a threat to the whole. Maybe that's why all of us in the group are afraid of gossip, and probably why we deflect gossip by passing it on. *No one must know*—to protect the group, but also because we could lose status or friends and see our children shunned as well.

But there are many more secrets among us besides mine. Plenty are open secrets. We all collude.

Over the following weeks, the weight of my secret grows. I am distracted during the day, lie awake at night. Finally I decide,

If I can't speak, I'll write. I'll write what I'd say to a friend if I could. I won't show it to anyone.

I sit up late one night in a pool of light at the bedroom desk, at the computer. Levi's papers are piled at one side of the room, his sleeping form on the bed behind me. Shalom is in the bassinet, finally sleeping five or six hours at a time. *No one must know.* I mustn't write the actual story. I'll just get the sense of it down, not the facts. But then, fingers on the keyboard, I don't have the words.

So I sit and wait, but years of swallowing words, always waiting, attending, with a closed mouth, has covered me in silence. Around me lie shadow boxes and stacks of religious books and business books. A deeper shadow, from the lone tree in the yard, falls through the blinds across my hands on the keyboard. The baby snuffles. Levi shifts in his sleep. I sit in the dark. Shalom whimpers, then sinks back into sleep with faint sucking sounds.

A ghost girl reappears in elastic-waist home-sewn shorts and a sleeveless top, long, sand-colored hair. She seems to be reaching out as if blind, creeping down a hallway trying to get to her mother.

I wonder what I dared think I might write. Who do I think I am?

Well, I think, struggling, I'm a flawed mother, but . . . I'm a mother. A mother teaches her child how to name the world—she's the bridge to language. That's who she is. Maybe from motherhood I'll know what to do. At least I'll know not to give up.

So I write a single word. "I." It stands bare and exposed on the page. Uncovered.

Soon I'll remember the ghost girl learning to climb a cottonwood tree in front of her home, how she took along a journal and a pencil tucked into her waistband. I'll watch as she climbs sure and agile to the rooftop, where she leans back against the warm brick chimney to write and muse and wonder, chewing on her pencil.

But a long time ago she became a dot in a vast field of roofs and treetops and sky. I think, *She had her own words.* I've lost mine. I've become a "we," not an "I." No longer her. I don't have language of my own anymore.

Why would I do this, when the very act of writing threatens who I am?

And yet, desperate, I plunge down, down, beneath the long, modest dress, because I have to see more of who might still be there. So she can write. Just one word. Then another. Each word stands alone.

I

am

velvet.

Deep

dark

blue.

Fifteen

*L*evi takes off his glasses and folds the earpieces in, first one, then the other, lays them face up on the counter in front of the mirror in a precise and measured gesture, then moves them to a meticulous two inches farther from the edge. I think of how he keeps precious items on his dresser in an unchanging order: his comb, his wallet, his keys.

We're in our bathroom. He sits down at the vanity. "Okay," he says. "I'm ready."

I cup his chin in my hand and turn his face up to me, in my palm the bony contour beneath his black wire beard going gray. His dark brown eyes and impossibly long lashes still spell out an earnest necessity that once almost held me. Then I flip a switch and the electric clipper jumps to life against my other palm. Row after buzzing row, I mow a month of dark hair away, careful to leave an extra tuft over his temples as the Law requires. *He trusts me*, I think, as I trace the curve of his skull, high forehead, receding hairline, the gentle turn behind his ears and above his long neck. I tame his wild eyebrows with a comb and hair scissors, his breath warm on me. Levi, normally coiled as a watch spring, is unspooled for now, but his shoulders, they've bowed. I think, *He's shrinking*, this man who has a fear of falling.

But the order on Levi's dresser, the piles of stuff he demands we don't touch, his driven, obsessive style of work, and the hours he spends each day whispering prayers in yet another compulsive kind of obedience, are all on the other side of the bathroom door.

Right now, we are quiet together. Right now, only the humming trimmer is between us. I run my hand over his head, brush off the broad shoulders. We clean up the shavings together, like freshly cut black grass.

"Leah," he says.

"What?" I say. I can't make myself want him. I don't know how to make him want me. I don't even know if I want him to want me. For a moment, I stop blaming him for my loneliness.

He looks shy. "Thank you," he says.

"Oh," I say. "The haircut. You're welcome."

I AM OFTEN PULLED to the computer at night, although most of the time I just sit and then write tiny hanging phrases, cryptic unfinished poems, nothing more. I still don't know how to pull words out of years of silence, and I don't know why I keep trying. It doesn't give me relief. But every time I sit down to write, it seems as if I'm taking one small step into some vast space, some place where I know there's a breathtaking view right up ahead if I could just go further in and get it all into focus. Besides, each day, I'm more fascinated with trying to attach words to speechless impressions, the sweep of experience, inevitable change. What words capture wonder? When connections do happen, I'm almost surprised to see the words appear in front of me, as if I don't know who made them—like hearing from a stranger.

One night, I dream I am at the computer when women of the Group suddenly appear streaming across my screen. There are many of them in many shapes and sizes, the younger women still showing their own hair, but they are all in the same modest, colorless dress, and they all move in step, all facing the same direction and walking in a steady, relentless, silent stream.

Until one of them stops. The others part just around her and move on, but this one woman stands like an island in a flowing current. Then she turns and looks out of the screen directly at me. Her eyes are as blue as daylight, as blue as my own.

I can't move. I can't take my eyes off her. The others continue around her, but she doesn't move. Then she lifts one hand and smiles. *She's beckoning to me,* I think. *She is waiting for me.* I am hopelessly, helplessly drawn to her and to the other women, to their steady, silent forward flow. My dream self leans forward. I *need* to blend in with them, move on with them, let myself go. Into the stream. Just float. Up ahead is the perfect combination of bliss and oblivion. *I must.* Her blue eyes . . . I stand from my chair and reach for her hand.

She looks ecstatic. She opens her mouth and begins to sing to me. I am overjoyed. *For me.* Then her voice emerges—as a deep, grinding bass. A man's voice.

I stop in horror. The woman is inhabited. She's been eviscerated—a soulless shell of a woman filled with this alien, ancient voice, a voice of rabbis. No soul left of her own. *Eishis chayil,* the woman sings out in that terrifying, grinding bass. *A woman of valor, who can find?*

She's still smiling, her hand still extended in offer, beckoning. Beckoning me to come.

I wake and sit up in bed in a rush, gasping. Shock vibrates through me.

MORE WEEKS, MONTHS, nights at the keyboard. Finally, I write a whole story, line after line. The woman in the story is Liba. She's not me, I am sure of that; this won't reveal anything, although she is also Hasidic, with many children, also defines herself through motherhood, and also becomes illogically driven to end a pregnancy. The difference is that her husband is her great love. But Liba will discover how to take his hand and lead him through this trial, and they'll come out of it together. In stepping outside the Law, she will find herself.

Also, she dotes on her youngest child.

I bought a wire cart on wheels last week, wide and low to the ground, that I keep tucked deep under my bed. Sometime after four in the morning, I print out the new story and then delete it from the computer. I drop the pages into the cart, which I shove back into safe darkness just before falling into bed for the few hours left before the alarm clock starts another day.

Lying there before sleep, triumphant about the new story, scared, I think of the Group. We are people of words that create worlds. God made the world with such words. But our legitimate writers are bearded scholars. Those Hasidic women who do write create marginal works only for a religious female audience, and they write in a man's voice lecturing the women, exhorting them to stay carefully within the fence of the Law. The more I do this odd thing, writing in my woman's voice, the more I become separated from the Group. I can't seem to help that, and I remain afraid of the stony silence they aim at anyone out of line. *But in a way*, I think, lying there, *there is no Group*. We're not really one. Each of us is alone with our secrets. I picture the stark isolation of a Giacometti figure, and then a whole field of those lonely totems. I am just one among them, set out on a colorless plane.

NOVEMBER 1989. Shalom is ten months old. While the children shovel down breakfast cereal, I open the newspaper to find the Berlin Wall is going to be torn down. I lay out the page before them. "Look!" I say. I try to make them understand the decades of remorseless cutoff and isolation for the people of East Berlin, what it might have been like to have been kept in that box. And now, this opening, this freedom.

The children look bored, as if blind to their lives. They look blankly at the page. Within days, I will read of Rostropovich, himself a refugee of communism, flying to Berlin to play Bach's cello suites at the wall just before it comes down. The master sits down with his cello in front of the graffiti-scratched wall, chair on the cracked concrete walk, and plays. People stop and gradually surround him. He plays on. I can hear the music. It is sober, elegiac, yet resounding with understated harmony and joy.

ONE SHORT STORY WASN'T ENOUGH. I go to the computer every night by around ten and don't stop until three or four in the morning, sometimes later. I write on and on, hundreds of pages. I don't know why I do that.

My own secrets aren't enough. I am of the Group even now; bits of their secrets seep into my work as if they are my own—their open wounds and half-hidden stories. Each of my new stories is filled with sin and fear of gossip and struggles with faith.

One morning, Levi notices the wire cart. I didn't shove it under deep enough before I went to sleep. "What's that?" he says.

"Stuff I've been writing. Personal papers."

"Oh," he says. "I heard the printer in the middle of the night." But he's distracted, late for work. He puts on his suit jacket, grabs his briefcase.

All that day after he leaves, I think, *I am one terrible mother.* If it gets out that I'm writing this stuff, my family could be labeled, ostracized, in the community. No one would let his or her children marry ours.

Worse even than writing about rebellion and sin is that I'm not trying to inspire people with my writing, to make them turn to God. Here's my newest secret: I don't want to bring people to God. I *don't want* God hovering between the lines of my stories, like a stowaway.

The group is a wall of eyes.

I share what I've written with no one.

NOW I'VE HAD THREE YEARS without pregnancy or teaching. Shalom is three; Leibl, the oldest, is thirteen. I give my days to the children, my nights to reading and writing. But just now, I'm headed out I-45 South in the mom van to Friendswood, an old Quaker town filled with NASA engineers, to my sister Debbie's apartment. We talk frequently on the phone but don't see each other very often. The hope that we'd raise our kids together isn't happening. When we do get together, Debbie comes to us with her kids but not with her husband, since the few times non-Jewish Robert did come over, Levi was so stiff with him that conversation drained away.

I'm in a hurry. Leibl's bar mitzvah is coming, and so is Shalom's *upshernish* ceremony for his first haircut. In order to make time to come out here and still get to today's shopping, I had to arrange for Shalom and Itzik to stay after school. I need to meet with the caterer again for Leibl's bar mitzvah and go buy more paper goods before the children get home at three. After they get home, I have to get Leibl to his session with Rabbi Frumen's son, who is training him to chant his Torah reading. But Debbie said I had to come out to her place right away and wouldn't say why. "Don't bring kids," she said, and, "Come before mine get home. When we can be alone."

Along the long balcony at her apartment complex, I pass potted plants, an outdoor grill, two hibachis, open doors, and the sound of the morning news on television, the smell of bacon. I wrinkle my nose. And here's petite Debbie in her apartment, her hair as dark and straight as when we were kids, brown eyes the same color as our mother's. Three pieces of her floral needlepoint hang on the wall, and on the tiled dining table there's a free-standing, framed photograph of Great-Grandma Esther in a shapeless dress, hair in a white bun, with a china doll baby that was our mother on her ample lap. It was 1927. Thin, young Grandma Kate is kneeling next to them, dressed like a flapper. Like the Mom baby, both women have our heavy-lidded eyes. Both look with delight at the baby, but the baby looks out at us with a solemn face.

Debbie sits down at the table and moves the photo aside, then gestures for me to sit so that we face each other. She folds her hands in front of her. Clears her throat. "We need to talk about Daddy," she says.

I tilt my head a little sideways, eyes narrowed. "We *need* to talk about him?" I say. "Who says I want to do that?"

But she launches right in, as if she has a job to get done. "I don't know how young I was when he first started," she says. "I must have been very small."

His shadow in the night has been gone from memory for a very long time. But I feel queasy. My limbs, my mouth, feel as if something is pressing hard on them. "Debbie," I say, shaking my head.

Debbie keeps her eyes on the blank white square of tiles in the middle of the table and doesn't blink. Her shoulders are tight, her voice quavering. "When I was a kid," she says, "I used to sleep like someone with one ear open."

"Why is that," I say, but my tone has no question in it. I don't want to know.

She stops, takes in a breath, starts again. If she were walking, it would be with the determined plod of an old workhorse. "I tried to get up at night when I heard him in the hall."

I think, *I can't stop her. I'll leave.* But I can't seem to get up.

"I wanted to keep him away from you," she says. "And Amy. You were both so little. I would run out when I heard him in the hall at night, take his hand, and pull him into my room." Her face is inscrutable, her eyes too bright. One tear escapes, and she swipes at it with a shaking hand, as if annoyed with herself.

I don't remember what I remember. I don't know what I know. I don't understand memory, hers or mine. "When did he stop?" I ask. I don't ask, *When did he start? Did he start before I was born, habit set and waiting for Amy and me to come along, or when you were beginning your fifth year and I was an infant in his arms, looking up into his adoring, startled face, like in the picture I save? Or when . . . but I want this to be your story and not mine.* The room is tilting, turning over the sofa and needlepoint florals, the tiled table, the picture of three generations of mothers.

"I was sixteen when he stopped," Debbie says.

"When he got sick," I say. "That was the year."

She nods. "You were twelve."

I'm trying to comprehend the mental hospitals and shock therapy as a gift to her. How I had hated the Daddy zombie he became, the thief who stole my father. For a moment, I am small and riding with him before he broke down, on his route selling women's dresses door-to-door. The windows are down, Dallas's hot wind in my hair. We stop at Krystal, and he lifts me onto a tall chrome stool at the counter, where we sip a frosty, frothy malted. This is the Daddy who raped her. Then: "Sixteen?" I say. "You had been old enough to tell him no for a long time!"

Debbie looks almost frightened. "I . . . didn't know how."

Queasiness. Pressure on my mouth and limbs. Something in the dark I can't identify. "I can't think," I say, shaking my head.

But she presses on. "When I was little, I used to think I was up on the ceiling, looking down on his back, and he was on top of a different little girl."

"*Enough,*" I say. I put my hand up. "Why must you tell me? Why *now?*"

"That's what I remembered first. Looking down from the ceiling."

Some kind of panic in the dark. Sweat dripping onto my forehead. I plead, my voice trailing, "It was a long time ago."

"I watched that little girl so calmly," she said, "but I felt bad for her."

I stand up, shoving the table. The photograph falls over. The crack in the Hasidic glass wall around me from the abortion and learning to write breaks wide open, but only darkness pours in, not light. The tilted room goes dim, no more color, and turns up and over. Framed needlepoint florals and decorative pillows fall through the air in shades of gray.

"I *have* to tell you," Debbie says, rising out of her chair.

"No, you don't," I say. I turn to go.

"I have to tell you because I failed."

My knees go first; I sink back into the chair.

"You. Failed?" *How very small Debbie is. What does she weigh, maybe ninety pounds?* "But you took his hand in the hallway . . ."

"I didn't always wake up. I didn't always keep him away from you and Amy." Tears are running down her cheeks.

The heartbeat, speechless impressions, sweep of memory. "But of course," I murmur. "You were a tiny thing and he was an animal." I meet my sister's eyes, sitting there. "Of course you failed." I reach for her hand. *Child troop of one. Of course he broke through the ranks of one little you and got to us. To me.*

I don't remember what I remember. His hand on my mouth. Why can I feel that? She failed. Mom slept on—or did she? I would hear her glide into the kitchen at night, the running faucet, clink of her glass. His hot pressure on my legs in the dark. Am I just imagining or remembering? Is this why I crept down the hall at night, and why I climbed to the roof? Rough, stippled wall under my fingertips in a dark hallway, seeking mother refuge.

I squeeze her hand. "You were my frontline soldier," I say. I look at the grief in her face and think, *This must be love. I had it all along from you, Sister. I wish I'd realized.* "It wasn't your fault."

"But Amy," she says. The little sister we left behind. Pressing her nose against the window as I walked away.

"I know," I say, patting her hand. "I know."

I will not remember the rest of our visit. Perhaps she pours me a Coke over ice from the stash in her refrigerator. I will remember how gradually the room rights itself and color returns to the polite little florals on the wall. I will remember how we hug a long time, how I feel no longer alone. I speed down the Beltway to get home in time to greet the kids I've spent my life protecting from *such things*. When I arrive, Debbie, Amy, my mother, and, yes, my father, all step across the threshold with me right into our house, as if for the very first time. They are unavoidably part of me. I see that now. No more wall. I escort them in.

Sixteen

y mother's father—we called him Papa—had a clothing factory where my father worked when I was small. Daddy would often come home late, after I'd already gone to bed. He used to come in to bring me a glass of milk, sit on the edge of my bed in my darkened room, and wait while I drank it down. This was our bedtime ritual. He was a child of immigrants, thirty-five when I was born, past forty at this point, with a shock of prematurely white hair, a lopsided smile, and the lingering accent of a long-transplanted New York Jew. He called me "dahling." Amy would be already sleeping in her room next to mine, Debbie reading a book in hers. There was the low hum down the hall of my mother's incessant television.

Daddy prompted me to sing the *shema* prayer, as his Jewish father had taught him to do before sleep. I handed him the empty milk glass, wiped the milk mustache away with my pajama sleeve, and sang with him, the same Hebrew syllables I had learned in Sunday school—*shema yisrael adonoi elohaynu*. As my eyes grew heavy, he talked about his Brooklyn childhood and Yiddish-speaking parents, the twisted challah loaves his mother baked for the Sabbath, how, when he came home from school, she cut him thick leftover slices that she smeared with chicken fat and warmed in the oven. I tried to imagine bread from an oven and not from a plastic bag in cottony squares. Then he'd stretch out beside me and sing old show tunes in a one-note monotone. You say potato, I say potahto. Let's fall in love.

He stood then, tucked me in, his form silhouetted in half light. I begged for the hall light and for the door to be left open, afraid of shadows in the night. After he was gone, I turned around on the bed, my head at the foot, so that I could keep my eyes fixed on the glowing fixture in the hall, before I finally crawled back to my pillow and succumbed. Then—dark swaddling, the great depth of child sleep, empty, paralyzing sweetness. Warm and still, sleep time drifting unmeasured. There were only nourishing childish images and dreams, blind suspension in a teeming mind. I knew nothing. Until: the smallest swish of a turning doorknob.

He floats above my bed now, just a darker shadow framed by shadows. Even through my sleep, his presence is comforting. He sits down in the same place on my bed, and I shift, smile, slip back into dreams. But his mild smell and darker darkness are like tentacles pulling me to the surface. Then: warm, rough skin of his palm on my mouth. A hand strokes my head.

My father is the gentlest of rapists. My eyes open, brain still mostly asleep, but I see only black velvet. The hand clamps down. My nostrils flare. Then. Now.

Heat. Pressure. Rhythmic, heavy breath on my face. A hard, deep internal push that caves in my stomach, rolls my child hips forward, child head lolling back.

Flailing. In the distance: a sound like whimpering.

The form, the shape of the body memory that forms, will soften and expand beneath the surface and loosen itself from time. My mother's clueless face in the daytime will help to disconnect the memory, but his imprint on muscles and skin will remain. Eventually, I won't know if he did this once or many times, each time perhaps falling into a single, collective bruise, until I won't remember he did it at all, will never be sure. But my body will hold this memory. My body remembers. *My body remembers.*

The drive to find a safe place where I can cocoon, the drive that will propel me out of this home, began here.

My fear of the dark grew. Then one night I awoke terrified and got up determined to get down the hall to my mother. To safety.

I DREAM AND DREAM DADDY. He appears at my door with his head a coconut, painted with a garish grin, that I hit with a baseball bat. It cracks open and I watch it spew, dripping, front still marked with that frozen smile. The two halves of the coconut fall to each side— *that* for all his betrayals. But the painted mouth smiles on. And on. The coconut milk swims through my veins, teeming with seed, the way pond scum teems under a microscope, and I am full of him and in him and from him and of him. I look in the mirror and see his one-sided smile—not his, but mine.

I multiply and divide him, stamp him out from each angle on little cards, and then sift and sift the cards with their differing images, trying to figure out what to hold and what to toss. I count the dream cards without stop. I am a wild-eyed miser hunched over in clandestine count.

LEVI ACTS AS IF HE doesn't notice my tossing in the night or my agitation in the day. For him: Home. Synagogue. Work for money. Home again. Say your prayers. Study holy books. Keep the blinders on and don't look up. Wave your hands if anyone gets in the way. Shout if you have to, in order to stay on the train. Wind up tight to keep it going. Go to sleep like an assignment, alone, so you can do it again tomorrow.

The glass wall is completely shattered now, shards at my feet, children huddled around me. I am my childhood family, irrevocably a part of them, and my family is a part of me. That is who I am. There is no safe place. There never was escape, really.

I stop writing. Prowl the halls at night.

"I HAVE TO TALK TO YOU," I tell Levi one day in the dining room where he's studying *Likkutei Sichos*, discourses from the Rebbe. He puts a finger on his place and looks up.

I know I'm interrupting, but I'm desperate to talk, trying for the first time in a very long time to treat him as friend and confidant. I sit down in my place to his right. Children's voices float in from the playroom. "I spoke with Debbie," I say. "I went out to her place the other day."

Levi looks like he's trying to be patient, like he's working at being attentive. His finger stays on the page.

I tell him. Everything. I tell him about Debbie at the tiled table, her courage and shaking hands. I tell him about little Debbie in the hallway, leading Daddy in the night away from me and from Amy. I tell him about the tilting table, the photograph, the nausea, and how Debbie's confession felt like a confirmation of something I already knew but forgot. When I finish, Levi laughs out loud in a mirthless guffaw. "No way," he says, and turns back to his book.

My mouth drops open. I try to tell myself he's just shocked, off-balance from the news. His parents are good people, so he doesn't have such things in his vocabulary, doesn't know what to do with such information. "No, it's true," I tell him.

Levi sniffs. He purses his lips like sour lemons. "I don't believe it," he says.

"What?" I say. I think, *I know you better.* I know the man behind this callousness. I become animated, determined to get through. I pull out the trump card, the Law. "Look at me!" I say. "I'm your wife. You're supposed to believe me."

Levi waves the back of his hand, makes a *pfff* noise with his lips. "I met your father enough times," he says. "He's a harmless man."

Silly annoyance. A wave of the hand will do it.

"Is that how it goes?" I say. "I know. I get it! What you *want* to believe is real! And what you don't want to believe just doesn't exist. Magic! That works!" I say, waving my hand back and forth in front of his face. "Gone with a wave!" I wrinkle my brow, shaking my head at this betrayal. "You were supposed to suffer this with me, and you won't even acknowledge it."

"But, Leah," he says.

That hand holding on to his book. Once, I too sought stories from those books to know who I should be, instead of just looking in the mirror to see who I am. But my family formed me far more than those books. Good or bad, our stories are who I am. "This is me!" I say, hands flat on my chest, as if he's just attempted to erase me with that wave.

Eventually I will understand that I am not just their stories. But in this moment, in my fury, I am my mother, I am my two sisters, and, yes, I am my father. Because only now I understand that laced all through the nastiness in my family are the purest shreds of real love I've ever known. I won't relinquish that with a wave of Levi's hand. "You don't get to do that," I say, and I stomp away.

"Leah!" he calls. "You're falling for your sister's story!"

I stop and look back, at his quizzical brow, his untrimmed black beard and yarmulka like a bowl on his head, pressed white shirt, in his hands a book of the Rebbe's exhortations that he will quote at the Sabbath table. "Who has fallen for what?" I say. My family with all its flaws is with me as I walk away, and not God, and not the Bible or the Law, the Rebbe, or the community. And not Levi.

I keep that anger, like fuel, but I am still part of the machinery of home and family and Law. There are the children and their trust in what we've put into them, which we have taught them is trust in God. My anger seems powerless before all that. But it is still my anger.

That anger may be why, the following week, I take the children to the public library and offer them all kinds of books about girls, as well as boys, who all have voices and goals, books in which people speak honestly and admit mistakes and dream and strive, people of many faiths and colors and societies, the men with no beards, women in pants and uncovered heads, unkosher animals and unfamiliar professions. *There is no Other*, I am trying to tell them, even if I feel myself an "other" now within the community. Oh, I never meant to narrow their ability to dream.

At home, the children spread through the house with their books, enthralled. Leibl is on his stomach on his top bunk with a whole stack, Mendel cross-legged in the corner with a book on his lap, Libby curled up in the old recliner, lost in a story. Each is perched on his or her own rooftop. They devour the books like hungry people, trade them, chatter about them, reread them, then beg for another trip to the library. And I take them.

We begin to go to the library every week. And yet, I am still Hasidic Mom: One evening, I hear Leibl stirring in his bed and go into his room. He's in the top bunk above sleeping Mendel. "Are you awake?" I whisper.

"Yeah," he says. "Can't sleep."

"Why?"

"I don't know. Thinking, I guess."

"You'll be great," I say, thinking he's worrying about his upcoming bar mitzvah.

"Mommy, it's not that. I know my *parsha* and my *maamar*. I can recite all that."

"So?" I say.

He blurts out like a sob, "I'm going to be *chayav mitzvos*." I'm going to be obligated like an adult to keep all of the commandments. It is the weight of the Law, put on him formally at his bar mitzvah for him to bear forever after, that is keeping him awake this night, that and all of the expectations from the community that will come with it. All of those eyes.

This boy, my firstborn. Soon we will send him away to become a Hasidic soldier. The yeshiva will replace us as parents I take his smooth hand, a little chubby and as long as mine.

"Squeeze," he says. "More."

I encompass his hand in both of mine and squeeze as if I won't have to let go.

LEIBL STANDS PROUD AT HIS bar mitzvah in his new black hat and sings out his Torah portion in a clear, sweet boy voice. He recites his Hasidic discourse and translates line for line in a way that incorporates explanations of the tangled, abstruse metaphors explaining God's desires. Even my mother comes in and sits nicely behind the partition with me and with Leibl's mother, and they both join the family at the seated Sabbath feast in the synagogue that we make for the community. The men make speeches and sing songs. The whole affair is one big community embrace for yet another who has arrived.

AS A KID, I tagged along with my mother as often as she would allow to the galleries and art openings she frequented. Once there, she would ask me to look at the pictures and describe what I saw. The more fanciful my response, the more her eyes shone. These moments fed a stubborn thirst. One weekday morning when I was eight, we came up the marbled staircase at Dallas's Museum of Fine Arts to the grand upper lobby. The place seemed empty, except for the artist Louise Nevelson, who stood like one of her totems in her flowing scarves and tunic top and famously huge false eyelashes. Behind her was a broad, low platform that held two of her constructions. There was something so beautiful and strong about Nevelson that I went right up and said, "Did you really make those?"

"Oh, yes," she said, quite serious and not at all condescending. She asked me about myself, questions I answered while my starstruck mother nodded approval at a discreet distance. Nevelson said more, but I was looking at her gauzy layers and makeup.

Then, past the guards and into the first gallery, we found a whole room of Nevelson's tall constructions of found wood, each painted in black or in white. The shapes and layers, arches and tiny rooms she had formed seemed to conceal what they held, and fascinated me. Her overlapping planes were worlds within worlds. Nevelson's work gave me a wondrous tongue-tied sensation, a strong desire to see what was hidden inside those spaces, as if they held (I would imagine later, looking back) both mystery and redemption. Best of all, I shared this wonder with my mother.

I stepped right up and reached into one of the black hollows. But there was a guard right behind me. "Better not touch that, little lady," he said, and that's when I saw the uniform, the badge, the admonishing face. I pulled back, stung, but then behind him was the artist, and behind her my shy mother. "You can move on and do your job somewhere else," Nevelson told him, and then told me, "Touch whatever you want, sweetheart."

I did not dare touch the art again, but I did step up on the platforms to get close. The sculpted spaces opened up in front of me like face-to-face mirrors reflecting endless repeated passageways.

One day, headed home from the downtown library with the children, I pass the Enron Building at Allen Place and I notice a tall Louise Nevelson construction installed in front. I think, *She must have cast it in metal.* I slow the car and point. "I met that artist once," I tell the children.

The next time we go to the library, I find a biography of Nevelson written for young adults and bring it home with us. I encourage the kids to read it, and then I spend most of the night reading it myself. I read how Nevelson's art consumed her until she left her marriage and sent her son to live with her parents. She put a church pew in her living room in place of a sofa to discourage guests. I laugh at that, but it's a laugh of secret recognition. During all of those nights when I used to dive into tinkering with words, I would lose all sense of time, then look up in surprise at the rising sun; I know how making art can become more compelling than the real world. I'm beginning to think letting loose a creative drive is like releasing a bull from its pen; a project can follow you into the day and make even people you love seem like an intrusion. Then I laugh at my preposterous self for even imagining a life like hers.

And yet, I begin to write again. One night, a young Debbie arrives on the page. She watches Daddy from the ceiling, and then in the morning he makes her toast and eggs. Real morning comes before I expect it, cars whiffing past, birds calling from the backyard elm, as I drop the pages onto the pile in the wire cart and shove it back under the bed.

SOMETHING IS HAPPENING TO ME. It's a disturbing loss I don't understand. God used to be ever at my sleeve, a nearly palpable presence, and now, after months of intense writing, He seems to have retreated somewhere far away. But I'm just writing stories.

My secret questions have flowed out night after night. *Why is it so terrible to speak the truth about sins and failing? Why are the texts that I love full of misogyny, and why did I never notice before? Why is it that the more I write, the more the mystique of a pure, perfect Word of God fades?*

I head to the kitchen, adjusting the scarf to better cover my growing hair. I expect it also to cover the growing questions and the growing sense that I'm living a lie.

I am a liar—because I am determined to hide my stories and questions and simmering doubts and carry on as if they don't exist. But in a way, isn't every mother a liar? "Mother lies"— they're only lies of omission to protect the children, right? Common enough. *The kids don't need to know. They don't need to carry my questions and doubts.* Besides, within the Group, we all hide the little dark places in our souls.

A new truth rings on in my head like an incessant bell: *It is not my nature to be a modest covered woman.* And more: *My father was not a good man.* And more yet: *I dream about women.* That tree that falls in the forest—is a lie really a lie if it is never spoken?

JUNE PASSES AND I turn thirty-six, outwardly, resolutely, a Hasidic mother of growing soldiers of God. Here's the proof: Leibl will soon be leaving for yeshiva in New York, proving that I am fostering the growing ranks. Here I am with covered hair, my husband the beard, my neighborhood streets filling like Brigadoon on Saturday mornings with Hasidic families walking to the synagogue. Listen to the Hebrew and Yiddish terms that pepper our speech. Sit down in our kitchen with its doubled kosher appliances and separate sets of dishes, for milk and for meat, as our seven children run in and out with more Hasidic kids from the neighborhood, boys with *tzitzis* strings flying, hands on automatic to cap a yarmulka on the run, girls chasing after them, unencumbered by their long skirts and tights, because such clothes are as natural to them as skin. Note the shelves and shelves of bass-voiced tomes that line the family room and dining room wafting rabbinic pronouncements into our air, the twelve-foot dining table that I cover with steaming dishes for the Sabbath, the worn prayer books dropped in random places throughout the house, wherever they were last used. If I put my ear close to any one of them, I will hear the secret hopes whispered into them that don't otherwise get heard. I shut the prayer books that have been left open, stack them together. Hasidic Wife, that's what I am, and I don't know how to change, even as I stop at the dining table a changed woman. There, I go through the morning mail one of the kids just brought in.

Among the bills and grocery store circulars I find a brochure, a simple trifold in black and white, no gloss. It reads: "First Texas Conference on Feminism and Judaism." I laugh and drop the thing on the pile of junk mail. But that afternoon, as I work in the kitchen, I remember the early days of the feminist movement, when I was a budding teen. I picture those vehement chanting young women on television. I think, Judaism *coupled with feminism?* To me, that means "rules, yet no rules." Preposterous. Don't they understand the contradiction? I think, *Those audacious women have gone too far.* I remember Sally Preisand, the first woman rabbi, twenty years ago. I remember telling Rabbi Goldenberg that I, too, wanted to become a rabbi. I think, *How shy yet bold I was. What a child I was. How little I understood.*

I straighten the dining room and pitch the circulars, together with the brochure, into the trash. Then I stop, and fish out the brochure. I don't know why I do that. I drop it on my desk in the kitchen. Later, I tuck it into the desk drawer. There it sits for days before I go back and pull it out one quiet morning. I think, *Those women are asking for the impossible. They want to be spontaneous yet committed Jews, when under the Law there's no place for spontaneity. They want their Jewish God without submitting themselves to the Law.*

Those women. I glance around the kitchen and living room, mezuzah amulets on every doorway holding inscriptions insisting as we pass that we make sure we think of God *first*. The wall of books. I whisper, "My life is already written."

And yet I open the brochure. Inside is a list of events and keynote speakers. Then I see that this is more than an announcement. The conference is months away. They're looking for speakers, inviting people to send in proposals. I laugh at the picture of a Hasidic woman walking into a feminist conference, but for a crazy minute I wonder what it would be like to meet a whole collection of those illogical women. The gossip would surely get back to the community, and how it would fly.

No way. I leave the brochure on the desk and start making dinner.

Chopping, stirring, my face in the steam, and there comes a flood of memories about a girl who once thought she'd write her own future and also have her religion. *You were a kid. You needed structure.* I tell myself. *You did the right thing.* And then the retort: *But I wanted religion to be a mast for my sail. I just wanted enough structure to hold me up.*

It doesn't matter anymore, I tell myself. *You're not that kid taking a seat in Rabbi Goldenberg's class. You're not even the girl breathless with arrival at the institute, or the one who peered down through scratched glass at a sea of black hats. You're here now, an adult. Think of the kids. You wouldn't dare be seen at that conference.*

I could offer to be one of the speakers. That wouldn't get me into trouble.

A number of us in the community have experience in public speaking. That's part of our outreach, our job, presenting our take on Judaism to non-Hasidic women at Hadassah meetings, B'nai B'rith groups, sisterhoods. I think of the legions of young Hasidic men on street corners in Manhattan asking people if they are Jewish and handing out our own kind of brochures, and of the emissaries like Rabbi Frumen who have spread out around the globe. If the First Texas Conference on Feminism and Judaism were to choose me, Levi would be proud of my taking the Rebbe's message into such a foreign place. I could go under that guise.

That's when I get the nerve. I know I won't be able to say what I really want to say. The truth is, I don't even *want* to speak —I just want to see those women, maybe have a single unscripted chat. But still I wipe my hands on my apron and go back to the desk, where I pull out a legal pad and a ballpoint pen.

This is the part I won't tell Levi: in my proposal, I don't offer to teach anything. I don't want to stand above those women in smug holiness and champion Orthodoxy. I simply offer myself, as a Hasidic woman, for an open conversation. I pause and jot a list of words in the margin to be sure to include: Dialogue. Mutual respect.

IT'S OCTOBER, the last days of Houston summer. Leibl left for yeshiva in Brooklyn, and it seems as if the house has expanded. Even little Shalom goes to school for a few hours each day, but I still refuse to return to teaching. I'm at the Hilton Hotel downtown following my escort to a conference room set up for a speaker. She's a smiling woman with bright lipstick whom I met at the WELCOME! table.

"How many other speakers are there in this time slot?" I ask.

"Four," she says.

"Competition," I say. "Will anyone show for this?"

"You'll get a few," she says.

I chose my outfit in an effort to blend in. The wig is freshly coiffed to look as natural as possible, and the skirt of my navy suit falls boldly above the modesty line. My knees even show. But as we walk, we pass women in casual slacks, some even in jeans or cropped pants, with short-sleeved tops that show their elbows and open necklines, with their real hair shining under the fluorescent light. My daring hemline challenge to the Law goes unnoticed.

The entire back of this room is a maroon swath of frayed velvet curtain. A hotel coordinator glides across, his red jacket dissolving into the cloth. We step up onto a small stage. But everything here is muted: the man's carpeted walk, the rustle of the audience beginning to assemble. Oh, but these women seem so unguarded. Legs crossed or even knees wide, some gesture with their hands as they talk to each other, open faces animated. I can't even guess what they're chatting about. I presume they have little fear of gossip or of who will marry their children.

The podium is too tall for me. My escort looks at my short frame and says, "Oh, you need a little help." She pulls out a shallow wooden stool, and I step up, far above the eye-level place that I would have preferred.

I don't want to represent the Lubavitch movement. I just want to be myself here. "Don't introduce me," I say. "I mean, please just say my name."

"Okay," she says.

When I first arrived, I stopped at a table full of books, expecting to find classic Jewish books that I'd recognize, like finding familiar faces in a crowd, but instead there were books by Jewish feminist writers whose names I'd never heard before: Judith Plaskow, Rachel Adler, Judith Hauptman, Gloria Steinem, Betty Friedan. A glance inside a few of them made me see that the language of these women is one I don't know. Now, from my perch, looking over the sea of women, I think, *What have I done?* I should leave. I've wandered onto the wrong stage, don't know the plan.

"This is Leah Lax," my escort says into the mic, in a startling, too-loud voice. The room grows quiet.

Disaster. I can't do this, can't even bring myself to hint at my dissent in public. Heart in my throat, I take the mic and say, "Hello. I'm Leah Lax. I am a Hasidic woman, and a woman uncompromised."

It's not so easy after all to break from practiced script. I clear my throat and manage to add something unplanned. "I respect those who choose consciously to live apart from Jewish Law." But this huge, spontaneous breakout goes as unnoticed as my hemline. "I'd like to invite a conversation," I say. I add, "Maybe you can see us Orthodox Jews as a kind of living museum preserving the old ways, and preserving active study of our ancient texts and law codes, in a way freeing others to go beyond the Law."

A hand shoots up. "Isn't that kind of arrogant?" she says. "There has been plenty of Jewish scholarship outside of the Orthodox community, and plenty of that was written by women."

Scholarship of which I'm not aware. *Those books on the table when I came in. . . .* "Thank you for that," I say. "I think I might have needed to hear it." The courage it takes to say this goes equally unheeded.

Another calls out from her seat. "How can you stand behind the synagogue partition between the men and women? How can you do that?"

I swallow, and then I'm back in that whispering, feminine, safe place. I want them to see it, too. "In the women's section," I say, "we're also separated from any posturing of the men who might be looking us over. The space is feminine, and private. A safe place. And the Hebrew prayers? They make me look at myself. The words are like mirrors. Sometimes I even cry. The space feels private enough to do that."

"But you can't have any leadership in the service," the woman says.

"I know," I say. "And maybe there is resentment at times among the women. I can't speak for everyone. But for me, I don't want that leadership, so I don't miss it. For me, prayer is a quiet, private thing."

I don't let on that ever since Levi scoffed at Debbie's story, since my anger has risen and my faith has waned—and ever since I added another secret to the collection, about my father's abuse— I haven't stepped into the synagogue. And I don't tell them that since *our women* sit there as spectators inessential to the service, they don't have to even bother to go. No one in the community has even commented about my absence, at least not to me. I also don't tell them that I no longer think of the women's section as a comforting place, since the quiet of prayer and the poetry in the prayer book somehow make me look at everything I'm trying to hide. But many hands are waving now. It's a strange feeling standing before them, as if I'm letting them peek under the wig. "There is a difference," a woman calls out, "between choosing to deny oneself and being denied by others."

"I don't think I understand," I say. But another woman is raising her hand, and I point at her.

"What if you did want to?" she says.

"Want to what?" I say.

"What if you did want to lead the synagogue services or to sing out loud there?" she says. "It's the *enforced* silence that is the problem," she explains, a little too patiently. "How do you justify having no choice—to yourself? Being *relegated* behind the partition?"

"Choice?" I say. I don't know how to show her the huge, ancient stream of which I am just a single drop. "No one in an Orthodox community has real choice," I say. "That's not just about the women. All of us subject ourselves to the Law." Then I add, like a new idea, almost as if I'm speaking to myself, "But isn't it a choice to have no choice?"

The murmuring in the room as I stand awkwardly above them makes me think that I may have broken something and lost the chance at real connection, however brief. But then there are more hands, and now someone is standing. She has long blond hair, and she's wearing a full, saffron-colored top with long sleeves over a flowing skirt, almost like one of us. She looks young, gives a quick motion with her head to toss her hair aside. "I'm the president of a gay and lesbian congregation," she says, "and I'm a lesbian. Tell me, where in your picture of religion is there a place for me?"

My chest goes utterly hollow. *Go away*, I tell her, but no sound comes out "I wish," I say into the microphone, and then I stumble. "I don't have an answer. I wish I did. I don't think there is an answer." This is another one of my daring violations that go unnoticed. The Law says there is always an answer. The Torah contains all answers.

The rest of the event drops from memory, perhaps because I am too nervous to absorb the rest, until my escort steps up and thanks me and the women politely applaud, then stand, consult programs, start to move and talk. Then I'm weaving through the crowd, every bit as isolated and foreign in my leaving as in my arrival, perhaps even more so. The smell of their freedom is already fading, changing nothing for me. I won't even try to attend other sessions. I don't belong here. Levi is at home with the children, and I need to get back. I make my way toward the door. One of the women eyes me head to toe as I pass.

At the exit, someone stops me. I read her name tag: ROSELLEN BROWN. I've taken to reading book news in the newspaper—her new novel, *Before and After*, is on the *New York Times* best seller list. She is short enough that I can look right into her eyes, her face intense, kind, interested, somewhat haggard. Women part and continue past us through other doors much like in my dream. "They sure gave you a hard time in there, didn't they?" she says.

I hesitate. "I guess I kind of asked for it."

She looks a little sideways at me with her mouth open, like she's thinking. Then this Famous Author says to me, "I'd like to have lunch with you sometime."

"I think I'd like that," I stammer, but I don't really believe her. I think, *She'll forget me by morning.* The lesbian woman who stood and spoke at my talk has also stopped. She's waiting for me. Soon, Famous Author disappears into the crowd.

"What do you need?" I ask the lesbian woman. We go to the lobby and sit down in two gold wingback chairs. Applause drifts in from one of the conference rooms. I try to sound polite, try not to sound challenging, but really, I am in way over my head and I know it. I can't imagine a Hasidic woman anywhere sitting down to converse with a lesbian woman. Maybe I'm the first.

"I don't need anything," she tells me, "but there are lots of Jewish gay men and women who do."

I sit poised, formal, defensive. She's forcing me to represent my whole community and I did not want to do that. I came here as a place to speak for myself. I don't respond.

"All of the Jewish movements respect Jewish Law to some degree," she says. "As long as the Law rejects people like me, there will be echoes of that rejection in other Jewish places outside of Orthodoxy." She is unruffled, sincere.

I soften. "I can't change the Law," I say.

"But you're willing to talk with me."

"It's true," I say. But then, she is the first openly lesbian woman I've ever met, and how could I not sit down with her, even if I do guard myself, even if I am afraid of the way she labels herself "lesbian" like she has some kind of condition? "Is talking with you enough?" I say.

"Maybe talk, women talking together, is the beginning of change," she says.

"But I have no answers for you."

"Some things have no answers." A brief companionable silence settles between us. I sigh. Then I tell her, "Then there's nothing else to say." And there isn't, except that I have a husband and a family and a home and a vast array of laws and expectations over my life, and her skin glows and her eyes don't lie and I mustn't let her get close. Nothing to say, except that my life seems more of a sham as I leave here than it did when I came. I stand up as if lifting a weight. She leans forward. "I do exist," she says. "I'm not going away."

Then I am walking away from her, one foot, another, across the maroon carpet, padded so that my steps away from her make no sound, steps with no weight, no truth. Ahead is a bank of elevators. Before me floats the image of the slight dimple at the right corner of her mouth, and behind, a flush of women's voices as a program lets out, and a table full of a new language, the books forbidden to me. I can still hear her voice. *I do exist.* I push the button for the elevator. It glows green, like a signal that I try to ignore.

Once I get home, Rona's face, her *I do exist,* will haunt me. I will remember my visceral fear when I heard her stand and announce herself as a lesbian in a public place. She will force me to pay attention to the disappointment I feel when Levi approaches after *mikvah,* the pained sense of isolation that he is not capable of taking away, the way he can never satisfy me. I will no longer be able to ignore those erotic dreams.

I will do my best to turn away from her image and voice. I will tell myself that I am not an aberration, that what I feel feels normal and not like some kind of sickness and thus not something to be labeled. I don't want a label. *So what* if I can't feel anything for Levi. There's no label for not feeling, for nothingness. But her face, her voice, will follow me.

ONE NIGHT, Leibl calls after eleven o'clock at night, New York time, from the pay phone outside his Crown Heights yeshiva dormitory. I answer in the kitchen, where I'm up cooking for the Sabbath. Levi isn't home from work. Through the phone, I hear passing traffic and a distant siren. "What are you doing outside?" I say. "Isn't it past curfew?"

"I want to come home," he says.

"I don't think so," I say. I don't want our kids to have to feel split, like I do, and wind up living lies of the soul, like I have. "Stay," I say, "so your life will be good."

"The rabbi tore up my bed in the dorm."

"He what?" I say. "Surely—"

"He shoved me against the wall. He said I didn't make the bed right."

"So make it right. Follow the rules, and no one will give you trouble," I say. *There's love there for those who follow the rules, wisdom in what they teach you.*

"Get me out of here!" he yells.

"No," I say.

My no becomes an echo that pings through my body, a sound in the night keeping me awake, bouncing into the past and far into the future, wrapping around his cry.

ONE DAY, I go to the Morris Frank branch library near home, my first time going there without kids. I step out of the summer glare through sliding double doors, through the shining entry, and past a sleepy-eyed Hispanic mother sitting on the floor with her two children and a stack of picture books. I've been writing fiction stories but haven't yet thought I might need to read fiction, haven't read a novel since before I met the Hasidim. I don't yet have a sense of rules for writing or of what it might take to hone the craft. But I know stories. Life is stories; dreams are stories. I put together pieces of what I know. Besides, my fiction characters are so real to me that it seems all I need to do is put my hands on the keyboard and watch them try to live. But I want to write poetry.

I think every word in a poem should cut deep to the core of something. But the more I try, the more I hear an undertone in my writing of the constant posturing and admonishments among the faithful. I don't understand the connection.

I think writing a poem has to be an act of raw honesty, courageous and real. I think a real poem should demand my attention and feeling without dictating how I attend and what I feel. I don't want promises of immortality anymore; I just want to write poems that make me open myself to being human. The problem is, I try, and fail. I think I might need to read published poetry to see how it's done.

Instead of the wig, I'm wearing a scarf that keeps sliding back, exposing inches of hair to the light. Funny, I think, that I'm risking much more serious gossip in the community because of two inches of hair than because I'm in a library. Few people will bother to gossip about a woman reading secular books—devalued literature read by devalued people—as long as she trains her children to be proper Hasidim and helps her husband to stay pure of influence. Which means, I think with a smile, that I'm taking advantage of the "freedom" of being a woman.

I locate the poetry section—two dusty shelves at the end of a row at the bottom of the stack—then glance up the aisle. Just past the stacks there's a revolving stand of periodicals, and beyond that are four vinyl chairs where an older man squints through trifocals at his newspaper. Another man sits across from him. He looks disheveled, maybe damaged, maybe homeless. He's asleep with his mouth open. Library as refuge. My skirt billows around me as I sink to the floor.

A half hour later, I've laid slim books out all around, on the skirt, on the floor, and against the bottom shelf, but that's okay because no one has come through. I know nothing about the poetry I choose or the people who wrote it. I'm simply taking home the ones that speak to me: books by Elizabeth Bishop,

Gertrude Stein, Amy Clampitt, Maxine Kumin, Charles Wright, Muriel Rukeyser, Robert Lowell, Sylvia Plath, Rita Dove, and Adrienne Rich. I notice I've chosen mostly women's voices, although I can't explain why. I know I'll be back for others, but I have no time left now, have to get back to the kids. I check out the books and leave the library for the mom van with arms full.

After the kids get home from school, Libby comes looking and finds me stretched on my bed, lost in a book. I'm wondering how I can make up for all the years of having not read. I look up with a blank-eyed stare that isn't grounded in place or time, still within her grasp but slipping. "Mommy?" Libby says. When I do hear and look up, when I actually see her, I have a pang of regret like the pang of parting.

Later, I read in the bathtub as the water grows cold and children bang on the door. I read in bed, only to find the book splayed on the floor, pages bent, when I wake before morning. I pick up the book, try to smooth the wrinkled pages. *I am going to become a faceless plague to librarians.*

I get up in the dark house to wander, and wonder.

I thought the dreams, the visions, the demons would go away if there was enough love to put them down.

—Sylvia Plath

Let her be let her be let her be to be to be shy let her be to be let her be to be let her try.
Let her try ...

—Gertrude Stein

If the mind were clear
and if the mind were simple   you could take this mind
this particular state   and say
This is how I would live if I could choose;
this is what is possible ...

> But the mind
> of the woman imagining all this   the mind
> that allows all this to be possible ....
> does not so easily
>
> work free form remorse
>
> —Adrienne Rich

> When we belong to the world
> we become what we are.
>
> —Anne Stevenson

Seventeen

$\mathcal{J}$une 1993. After months of prying open new spaces between mothering for my reading and writing, I am standing over my father in the dementia unit of Golden Acres nursing home in Dallas. Younger sister Amy called me here —Amy, sober now, and the only one of us still in town to deal with Daddy. The room has white vinyl curtains and blank white walls, a bank of empty drawers that somehow spell out both efficiency and impermanence, and a single bedside lamp with a weak bulb that has little purpose—all as cold and generic as a roadside motel. The bed is empty, blanket drawn smooth. After having twice fallen out of bed, Daddy's on a mattress on the floor. They don't believe in bed rails here. It is policy. People get hurt.

Daddy is seventy-one and looks ninety, snoring through one of the short spurts of unconsciousness that seem to fall over him. There is a purple-and-green bruise on his face and another on his arm and, in spots over the bruises, blood black and crusted. His skin looks like wet tissue paper that has been stretched over him and dried, mottled yellow-gray, impossibly delicate and finely wrinkled. Splitting. He has bedsores. The blanket over him is barely mounded. His feet stick out like an accusation. They are yellowed and bare, swollen beyond what any sock can cover. It seems his feet are dying before him. Daddy is dying in pieces.

In the bag that I dumped on a chair is a volume by Maxine Kumin. I would be surprised to hear Kumin's poetry labeled as political, and know nothing about her feminist politics—what I have read I have found to be deeply personal. I sit down to wait while Daddy sleeps, and read, until I come to *I am tired of this history of loss.*

Fatigue comes over me. I sit and watch his sleeping form, with a vague, languid anger, but the father that I would have thrown those lines at like an accusation is gone. I read on: *What drum can I beat to reach you?*

Daddy wakes with a start and begins to mumble in a low, steady hum not unlike the sound of grinding teeth. I stand, bend over him, and put my ear near his mouth, to find he's pouring out nonsense phrases from childhood images, as if he's downloading a lifetime, offloading, really, readying himself. "You thief," I mutter, just as a wave of pity and old love comes over me. "Thief" because inside him he hoards the father he could have been, that he stole from us. *You stole my innocence, my childhood, my air. When you're gone, will the sound of grinding teeth finally go away?* And yet I've come to sleep over in the unit to be near him for the Sabbath, which they have told me will be his last. I lay my palm gently on his forehead.

A woman screams from one of the rooms on the other side of the nurses' station, high-pitched and bloodcurdling. A few minutes later, she does it again. And again. The periodic screams blend into the landscape of this place, along with the blaring television in the lobby and an aide down the hall talking to a patient at a near shout. I prepare candles at Daddy's bedside, then light them with the Sabbath blessing. Daddy is in and out, so I settle into the one chair at his bedside to read and think in the candlelight. The flames quiver and spark.

A nurse looks in. She is small-boned and middle-aged, her round brown face bearing both patience and disapproval. "Oh, honey!" she says, and swoops into the room, blows out the flames. "You can't *do* that," she says. "Rules."

"Yes," I say. "I know about rules."

"Herb!" she says, and leans close to my father's face. "Time to eat!"

An aide comes in behind her with a kind of rolling chaise, and the two hoist his bones into it. We make a strange procession, my father in his recliner throne; the nurse; I in my Sabbath best, even the wig, like armor; and the hovering aide, who is as cheerful as a nursery school teacher. We pass the nurses' station with its hospital fluorescence, more efficient false cheer, the lobby visiting area with its two red vinyl sofas and television, and the locked double steel doors no longer needed to keep my father in but instead serving to keep the world away. We go to the back of the unit, an open area with a refrigerator where other patients have been assembled. Two more staffers are there, and a woman who speaks softly in Russian to her thin, bent charge. She says "Mama" and spoons puree into the woman's mouth, which she does with great tenderness, as if this is her grateful, voluntary penance, her daily pittance repayment to her mother. Compared with that woman, I am an utter impostor. *So why am I desperate to get you to eat when you won't, Daddy, as if I need to keep you alive?* He tongues the puree, turns his face away. *No hope.*

Back in the room, my father back on the floor mattress, baby food smeared on his pajama collar, I pour red sweet wine into a paper cup, raise the cup before me, face him, and sing the Sabbath kiddush prayer. When he hears, he slips back into childhood. Consciousness and memory have melded into one, back and forth, present and past, although both are fading, near gone. Behind me, the unlit candles become his mother's silver candlesticks, my paper cup his father's gleaming goblet on the Sabbath table. He mumbles the Sabbath words with me from that memory. *On the sixth day He completed his work, resting on the seventh from all that He had done.* From all that he had done.

After midnight. The dim room is strangely quiet in this hospital-like place, no beeping monitors or late-night interruptions for medication or to take his temperature, no efforts here to sustain him. I wander to the nurses' station. There's another shift on. "I'm Herb's daughter," I say to the night nurse. She has large, efficient hands, her hair in short yellow waves stiff as a field of corn. "Sleeping over."

"Oh, Herb," she says. "I shave him up nice before I get off. Did you notice?"

"Um, yes. Thanks," I say. "He hasn't been this far gone for long, has he?"

"Oh, no," she says. "Seems like this dementia happened all of a sudden. We've had good talks."

"I think I waited too long to come," I say. Maybe on purpose. "Did he ever tell you, well, stories?"

This moment will stay with me: we are eyeing each other, the raw knowledge between us that he is soon going to die. "I might as well tell you," she says.

"What's that?"

"Well, one night a couple of weeks ago, he wouldn't sleep," she says, "so I rolled him out here, where I could keep an eye on him, and he said to me, he says, 'Dara?' 'What?' I says. 'You got kids?' he says. 'Sure, Herb,' I says, 'I got two. How about yourself?' And he says, 'God gave me three beautiful girls, and I hurt 'em. I hurt 'em bad. Don't you ever hurt your children.'" She stops and purses her lips. She adds, "Now, wasn't that a curious thing?"

TO BE REASONABLE, the poet Kumin says, *is to put out the light.* "You see, Daddy," I tell his sleeping form back in the room, "I erased you a long time ago, and now I can't cry for a nothing." But the truth is, I've tried putting out the light so many times, but his image just glows on in the dark. *To be reasonable is to let go,* she says. I wonder, *How much of the love I have worked to muster for the Rebbe and God and even for Levi was really meant for you, Daddy?* As if I got left with a package of love I couldn't bear to hold and went looking for somewhere to put it. *How much of my image of God is made up of what I wish you had been? But no contrived faith, no substitute father, can replace what you were, or could have been. Love for your father,* I think. *What a queer-shaped burden.*

But I can't say that. I can't say I "love" this swollen, insane man with baby food on his collar, smelling of sour breath, head lolling off a neck gone slack, his mouth hanging open. "Look at you," I say to him. *A deflated sack.*

He wakes up. "Lisa!" he says. "Lisa!"

And instantly, I am Lisa again. Hopeful child. I start up out of my chair toward him. "Daddy?" I say with a whimper.

He jerks weak old legs and tries to wave his arms. "I have to go!" he says. "Have to make the two o'clock!"

I reach to pull him back from the waves. But I can't stop them. Or him. *I will have to look. No hope.*

Instead, I fall back into the waiting arms of ritual. I put my hand on his arm in a Hasidic model of compassion and sing out, "*Shemaaaa, yisrael,*" the prayer he once sang with me before I slept, the one that is also a confession before dying. I lean in and smell his fading and sing into his dying ear this last confession—mine, instead of his.

Once again, Hebrew words bubble out of him from childhood. "*Adonoi,*" he rumbles. "*Echad.*"

But I'm back at my wedding. The music is swelling, and Levi the groom is approaching to lower my veil, our two young fathers on either side of him. "Daddy? The words?" I beg, and I'm looking up to my father and not to my groom, begging for my father's last blessing before I bury us both. Daddy leans over close in his handsome suit and familiar cologne and I have a surge of need and hope. But he's afraid. He can't remember the magic words. Instead, he kisses my forehead, leaves it damp. Then Levi reaches over and covers the wound of my father's kiss with the veil. This final kiss from my father that shames me and seals me will be the last time that I look at the wound that is Daddy. Until now. Until this letting go, singing to my dying father. *Listen, O Israel*, I sing. *The Lord is our God, the Lord is One. Blessed is the name of the glory of His kingdom forever and ever.*

HOUSTON, JUNE 21, 1993. I waited for him to go, but I had to get home to the children. Now, three days later, the phone rings to a cool report of the impossible, the obvious, coupled with a programmed offer of comfort, and Daddy's dead. I walk through this sudden complication in my life as if it were unexpected. Leibl is home on summer vacation from yeshiva. The other six are swirling through the house. There are meals, cleanup, directing traffic. But my father is dead. I have to get to him. He needs me. I have to get back to Dallas to my father.

I hurry to the jewelry box in my bathroom—the same gold filigree over glass that once sat on my grandmother's vanity as my mother fit the wedding veil onto my head. I rummage in it for a certain strand of varied polished stones, shiny, indeterminate little things, that my father sent me years after the wedding, after lithium seemed to be giving him another chance. At the time, I tossed it here in disdain. Now I pull the strand out and finger the first of the stones, grayish-pink, shining and hopeful, and the next, white but streaked with impurities, and the next. Each is cold, smooth, each with its special asymmetry. I drop the whole strand onto my palm, the cold stone weight of unspoken stories, then grip them in my fist in a flash of unambiguous grief. I sob. For one single moment, engulfed in his love for me, I finally don't warn the grief away. Shaking, wanting him, I put on the necklace and fit the clasp together behind my neck.

Then I'm choking. I fumble the clasp open and can't get the necklace off fast enough.

What have I lost, if he's been gone since my childhood? I don't know how to grieve him. *He's a hole in my life. You can't bury a hole.*

If only my religion gave me a place to put grief he didn't earn, instead of asserting that he didn't really die, that the Messiah will come and my father will return. If only I could turn to God and say, *You take responsibility for his death, and for his life, so that I can try to understand this helpless anger. This terrible love. Then I'll believe You'll take responsibility for my death, too. Maybe then I won't need to cling to every bit of life with such fear. Maybe then I will be able to move on.* But we pray in ancient words written for us—I don't know how to use my own words to speak to our Hasidic God.

If only I could see the coming mourning rituals as eloquent expression of my silent wailing, and as a way to know my grief. Instead, the community will soon surround me with death-denying food and murmured assurances: *We will bring the Messiah through devotion. Death is not final. Do not grieve.*

If only I had the courage to accept that I miss my father the criminal.

I put the necklace back into the box, but this time, I don't bury it. I lay the strand on top so that I can see it through the glass.

Then I'm rushing through chores and to the grocery store, where I fill three carts to overflowing, all while a dong like an old cymbal, like some priestly call to prayer, reverberates on and on, making everything seem distant: *I have to get to Dallas.* I'm in the kitchen, unpacking the bags, storing boxes of Cheerios and cans of tuna fish, corn, and beans in the cabinet. Apples, bananas, lettuce, tomatoes, scallions, cheese, eggs, yogurt, and milk in the refrigerator. Words from Sylvia Plath flit in and out: *Daddy, I have had to kill you. You died before your time.*

I've always shielded the children from my father. *I won't expose them now.* I can create their world with my words: Eat kosher food and say your blessings and you will be protected from harm. Serve

God with joy. Mommy is fine. Your grandfather was a good man.

I run into our back bedroom and lock the door, clinging to ritual, my only sight of solid ground: "Yes," the funeral director says over the phone, his voice cultured to just the right mix of appeasement and false sympathy. "We're familiar with Orthodox burial. A *shomer* is available; the body will not be left alone." A hired faceless man will whisper psalms through the night near my father's body out of respect for his holy life.

"Plain pine casket?"

"Yes," he says. "Unfinished. Lined in straw. The body will be in a white cotton shroud, no embalming, the Orthodox way. Of course, the casket will remain closed."

From dust thou art.

"Sir," I say, and my voice is furtive. "One more favor?"

"Yes, ma'am?"

"Drill holes in the bottom of the casket."

"Ma'am?"

"Orthodox procedure," I say. "For quick decay."

"This can be done," the man says.

"And," I say, "don't tell my sisters."

To dust return.

THE VIEW INTO AN OPEN grave three days later in Dallas' old Temple EmanuEl cemetery. Newly cut black clay, rich with possibility, heavy from recent rain, lines the hole. But that hole is a summary of our losses. And now I know what we have lost: that hope we could never relinquish for a Daddy we could know or trust or understand. That's what we three bury today.

Levi is a statue at my right, my sisters at my left, Debbie's husband, Robert, beside her. Old neighbors and friends are here, my mother somewhere out there among them. I incline my head toward Levi until I am just an inch away from the forbidden public touch. I want to lean on him. He takes a step away. I straighten up, corrected.

The sparse crowd is quiet as the rabbi hands Debbie and Amy in turn a pair of scissors so that each can cut the black ribbon pinned to their dresses—a polite, sanitized version of the Law. "We're doing this for you," Debbie whispers. When the rabbi hands the scissors to me, I ignore the ribbon and cut a slash right into the shawl over my dress; then I grab the two sides and rip the cloth wide open in the fierce Orthodox gesture, symbol of a torn heart. The tearing resounds through the hushed tent. I hear a gasp. The cloth hangs. Before me, the hole in the earth he tore into us. The rich smell of wet earth. I think of verdant growth. I think of worms.

BACK AT HOME IN HOUSTON, our front door remains unlocked seven days and I remain in the dress with the torn shawl. Levi and the kids cover the mirrored wall in the dining room and the large mirror in the den with bed sheets that hang in folds. I light a tall candle in a glass cylinder, the insistent, fragile flicker a symbol of my father's soul living on beyond this earth. Before the candle burns down, I will light another, and another, intending for the flame to continue through the year of mourning. Levi cautions the children away from the stereo. There will be no Uncle Moishy and his Mitzvah Men, no Avraham Fried or Lubavitch Boys' Choir, no music at all in our home for the coming year.

Visitors arrive, and the Hasidic dance of comforting the mourner begins. They let themselves in without knocking, bringing covered dishes and murmured condolences. They sit down and don't start a conversation, waiting for my lead, even if it means we don't speak. When I finally say something, they ask about my father.

But this choreographed, comfortably predictable scene is what I wanted—reliably tender offerings, presence, food I didn't cook, quiet words, my children nearby, if somewhat awed. Besides, following the Law for the mourner like a ritual means Daddy didn't have to earn my grief in order for me to grieve, that it doesn't matter who or what he was. The community comes, no matter what, because here, I'm not his Lisa, I'm just a Jewish Woman in Mourning, my loss generalized and sanitized. They offer comfort, following the Law. But they ask about my father.

I sit on the mourner's low stool and wave at my guests a picture of Daddy as a young, handsome man, the beloved father of their expectations. "He taught me the *shema,*" I say. "He used to talk about my grandparents and their old Jewish ways." I hold the picture out to them. But I cover the child rapist with my thumb. I cover his years in a mental institution, brain damage from electroshock, the final days of diapers and mumbling madness. My thumb hides all but his lopsided smile.

Still, I think I must have something wrong with me to be grieving *that.* But I was a child once. He was my father once.

In the end, I find the mourning ritual, the visitors' concerned nods, casseroles, and fruit baskets, exhausting. In the end, I want to tell them how their scripted comfort feels staged and empty. I want to thank them and send them firmly away.

A WEEKDAY AT THE DAILY *mincha* and *maariv* prayers in the synagogue during the hour straddling nightfall. Men arrive, in work uniforms, or business suits, ties just now loosened. In this high-ceilinged solemn space, the talk is in low tones peppered with low laughs, a few handshakes, but the daily prayer is just another business duty before they go home to wives and children. After a minute or two of standing around until the quorum is met, one of the men shrugs and steps briskly up to lead the service. He wraps a black sash *gartel* around his waist, dividing head and heart from the unholy lower half, and ties the long sash in loose black knots at his hips. Then he begins a nimble monotone through pages of Hebrew. The words have no spaces between them, no breath. *Happy are they who dwell in Your House. They continue to praise You. Selah.*

Levi comes in late, looks rushed, tired, but then his shoulders relax under the steady weight of the standing *amidah* prayer when the tone turns to whispers. Tension spools out of him. His mouth barely moves as he reads on. The *hazan* leader repeats the silent prayer aloud, and the group concludes with "We must praise God that our lot is not that of other nations who worship vanity and nothingness." When they say "vanity and nothingness," they make a motion as if to spit on the ground, and follow with a bow to our God, the real God. Then a pause for Levi to sing out the kaddish mourner's prayer that demands we praise God after having faced death. Each recitation elevates the soul of my father still more toward the throne of glory. The others answer "amen" after each section. "Sanctified and glorified is the One Above," he sings. "God, grant satisfaction, help, comfort, refuge, healing, redemption, forgiveness, atonement, salvation."

Salvation. From Levi's view, my face is obscured through the partition screen, as Levi performs the mourner's task for me, a husband's duty during his wife's year of mourning. I mouth the words silently along with him, for my father and for the life that he gave me in spite of himself. But the voice is Levi's.

DURING MY YEAR OF MOURNING, Crown Heights is overtaken with a messianic fever that spreads through the web of Lubavitch Hasidim worldwide. It seems everyone I know is convinced that the Rebbe will soon reveal himself as the true Messiah, now so very imminent. I refuse to get caught up in that reach for blissful oblivion, that burning, infectious fervor, even as hundreds, thousands of my peers do so, intelligent people, people I once admired, educated people. The Messiah is coming! Devotion trumps all.

I DECIDE TO PULL Debbie's story out of the wire cart and send it to Rosellen Brown, the Famous Author I met at the feminist conference. I thought I could continue just to write and hide what I wrote, but once I met her, well, now I can't help but think of writing as a conversation, and I don't want to continue speaking into a vacuum. So I look up her address at the University of Houston. But just before mailing it, I erase my name and leave no return address. I'm afraid if she sees who the manuscript is from and remembers my Hasidic garb, she'll expect it's all idealistic preaching and refuse to read. Then I wait, weeks, months. While I wait, I read my first published fiction as an adult, Brown's *Before and After*. She seems to have some kind of X-ray vision for characters. I read her short stories, and then her poetry, and fall in love with *Cora Fry*.

"It's my policy not to read unidentified work," Rosellen tells me when, after months of waiting, I finally get the courage to call and manage to reach her.

"Oh," I say. I let out the breath I've been holding all this time.

"But if I'd known it was yours, Leah, I would have read it."

"I doubt that," I say.

"No," she says. "I mean it."

I HAVE COME TO ROSELLEN'S GARDEN, full of the scent of roses and herbs, and the few miles I traveled to get here may as well be a hundred. The garden seems a shrine to creativity and beauty and the freedom to achieve them, or to try. Across the narrow street from this little home, Barnett Newman's *Broken Obelisk* stands in a reflecting pool in front of the Rothko Chapel. It's a broken totem, lone and tall and fragile. Nearby is the Menil Collection, full of more searingly honest artistic voices. Our metal seats are warm. A bee moves over one of the red roses in tiny arcs. There's a slight breeze, a whiff of exhaust in the air.

I sip tea from the nonkosher kitchen and add that to my secrets. I am ill at ease in my Hasidic costume in this free place. It seems everything had to happen first before I could come here—the abortion, the feminist conference, Debbie's disclosures about Daddy, writing my secret stories and poetry. I dare not change, and yet here I am—a changed person seeking a mentor outside my community.

Rosellen talks on about freeing fiction from the events that may have generated it, about how to convey a sense of reality, about the shape of narrative. She pulls out pages—I sent her over a hundred—and I see she has filled the margins with notes in her steady hand.

"Look at this," Rosellen says. She points to one of her comments and reads the line. She launches into an explanation of why it doesn't work and what I need to do.

I defend my story as if it were one of my children. Surely, she just doesn't understand.

She doesn't back down.

I swallow and try to listen.

In the end, Rosellen hands me a fiction craft guide. Inside the cover, I find it inscribed in her hand. I grow quiet, finally humbled, and grateful.

"Now tell me," she says in a reasonable tone, and there's that open-mouthed, sideways look she has. "You are a thinking person."

"What are you asking?" I say.

Her gesture takes in my high neckline, long sleeves, the skirt, the wig. "I want to understand," she says. "How can a thinking person reconcile *all of that?*"

I don't answer. I tell myself that I need to think about what to say.

The next day, I write Rosellen the first of many letters. Somehow, if I can convince her that our Hasidic life is meaningful and real, I can convince myself and reconcile the growing rift in me, because she has made me ask myself: How *can* a thinking person reconcile *all of that?*

"We train ourselves to a keen awareness of God," I write. "Our daily task is to find that day's evidence of God's goodwill, accept our limitations and God's upper hand. Life is symbols."

Life *has* to be symbols. If daily events aren't primarily symbols from which we should learn, gifts from God for that purpose, if life is just . . . life—if I have to look at events and experience square-on and accept the raw, random present as my reality, with no promise of payoff—then I can't face my life. I need meaning—that is, justification. Without that, my Hasidic life is a sham. I'd have to leave.

"I assert," I write another day, "that the Jews, vestige of an ancient people, have survived intact because of an unchanging core of teachings, spirituality, morality, and ritual observance that injects those teachings into the most mundane parts of life." This is the voice of the group. *Love the Law. The Law has kept us alive. The Law makes life Godly.*

I write another high-minded letter every few days. I don't actually know that I'm trying to reconcile myself to my own life, just as I don't recognize yet that the split in me is growing because of contact with Rosellen. I just know that this conversation with her feels like oxygen.

Another few days, and a manila envelope arrives in the mail —the rest of my manuscript. A generous cover letter offers to look at more. Rosellen's marginal notes are on every page.

I go to the wire cart, swallow, and take out the abortion story. I send the story to Rosellen. Someone is going to know.

NOW, SABBATH QUIET—no electricity, car, phone, or computer. In the afternoon after the troops return from the synagogue, after a four-course meal, out-of-tune singing, and Levi's ponderous lessons, the guests leave and Shalom goes down for his nap. Itzik, Sarah, Avrami, and Mendel spread books and toys through the den and playroom and get busy with their plans. I vaguely supervise from the old orange recliner, tired, leaning back. With the backdrop of bookshelves just behind me, I feel a restless nostalgia for our old texts come over me. It's been a long time since I read the daily Bible passages with the Rashi commentary. I take a Hebrew and English Bible and turn to Genesis, which I used to teach.

I begin to read, but Rosellen is teaching me to read critically and I discover I can't simply turn off that critical eye; a scrim of holiness that once softened and justified every biblical message has been pulled away. *But the commentaries accumulated over centuries—Rashi, Ramban, Ibn Ezra, and the others—are the voice of the sages. They state our values. They say who we are.* Remembered lines from the commentaries surge from the pages.

I page through, alarmed. I pause over the comment that charges Eve with responsibility for the great sin that taints mankind. I turn quickly to where they criticize Sarah for laughing at God's blessing (but maybe it was joy!), denounce Leah for desiring her husband, blame Dinah for her own rape. I pull the next volume, *Exodus*, from the shelf, and page over to the place where they insist Miriam was punished with leprosy for speaking her mind. *Do not speak overly with women,* the sages say. Women are a source of inane prattle. Women steal a man's time from Torah study. *But we look to the rabbis' image of those women as our role models. What does that do to us?*

I sit up and drop the book on my lap. If *their* image of Sarah and *their* Leah and even their Dinah are our role models, and they are, if what the rabbis say about our foremothers is fed to us as holy and true, then we women *should* cover ourselves. That legacy makes us *want* to hide ourselves, as if, by obeying the rabbis' injunctions about modesty, by covering up we redeem ourselves from Eve's sin, Sarah's laugh, Leah's desire, Dinah's beauty, Miriam's mind.

As if, in a world that holds this book as the story of who we are, womankind needs redemption.

I look down at the long skirt and stockings. *Why, we carry shame that isn't ours.* I close the book, shake my head. I can't do it. I can't humbly engage in study anymore, no matter how beloved it once was. I can't go back to where I was.

I launch out of my seat, the kids still playing, head to my bedroom, and return in no time with the first secular book I've ever bought as an adult, by Adrienne Rich—a compendium of her writing. I was out shopping across town the other day and ducked into a bookstore, where I found people browsing without reservation, without censors. So I browsed, too, as if such freedom were nothing. Along a short stack featuring new work, I found this now-familiar name. This will be my Sabbath reading.

Itzik climbs into the recliner with me and puts his head in my lap. He was up late at the Sabbath table and still needs his naps. Hoping he'll doze, I sit very still and stroke his shoulder, until my own eyes grow heavy. Sleepy-eyed, I turn pages, pick out a few lines at a time, scanning new territory without enough focus to delve into the essays. The poetry begins to seep into a half-conscious place like the slow, deep spread of spilled ink.

> *The rules break like a thermometer,*
> *Quicksilver spills across the charted systems;*

Avrami and Sarah haul in wooden blocks from the playroom.

A woman's voice singing old songs ...
plucked and fingered by women outside the law.

Is that what I'm doing? Singing old songs to Rosellen in my letters, even as women outside the Law pull me away from the rules?

The pile of blocks on the floor has grown. Avrami gets up to go get more. I point at the mound, my gaze on him. "You can bring them if you clean them," I say. Itzik shifts on my lap and sighs. I read.

This is the law of volcanoes,
making them eternally and visibly female.
No height without depth, without a burning core

Something is waking me up, as if I've been cold and dead a long time.

Libby comes in the front door with a friend. The two head to her room.

I read on. There is a lot I don't understand. *But,* I think, *I can take years over this if I want. The book is mine.* I turn the page.

your body
will haunt mine—tender, delicate
your lovemaking

I sit up then. *Tender, delicate*—I think she must be writing to a woman. I decide she's writing about a woman. In my life, I have never heard anyone speak this picture openly. I grip the page. My face flushes.

Mendel dumps the bucket of Legos out on the carpet. The

room is covered with toys, the playroom empty, children at my feet. "Clean up the blocks before you touch those Legos," I say.

"No, Mommy!" Mendel says. "We're *doing* something. We'll clean up later. Promise!" Avrami and Sarah are nodding. Itzik is asleep in my lap.

> *Your traveled, generous thighs*
> *between which my whole face has come and come—*
> *the innocence and wisdom of the place my tongue has found*
> *there—*

Levi walks in, his face puffy from his Sabbath nap. He goes into the kitchen to get a cup of coffee.

> *Your strong tongue and slender fingers*
> *reaching where I had been waiting years for you*
> *in my rose-wet cave—*

I slam the book closed. Shut my eyes and take a breath. Let out a breath. Take a breath. Forget to let it out. Sarah glances up, a second's notice, then away.

Face hot, I stand with the closed book and lift sleeping Itzik, settling his head on my shoulder. I keep my expression impassive as I glide to his room to lower him into his bed. The last words of the poem stay with me as I move down the hall:

> *whatever happens, this is.*

Eighteen

One by one as their eleven children enter adolescence, Rabbi Frumen and his wife have been sending them away to yeshivas, and of course the community is following their lead, at enormous financial strain. To be "exiled to a place of Torah," *goleh lemakom torah*, and experience displacement and sacrifice for the sake of Torah knowledge, is important for building Hasidic character. Rabbi Frumen insists he will never make a Hasidic high school in Houston.

Libby has grown up expecting to go away, and now she is fourteen. Several of her best friends have already departed. She is eager to embark on this rite of passage. The yeshiva boarding school for girls will neatly skip her over that questioning, searching, rule-challenging age called adolescence. It will shave away the parts of her that don't fit its mold, seal her on the proper path. It will keep her away from boys and fill her with Hasidic philosophy, Hebrew, Yiddish, Torah, and prophets. Her secular education will be kept to a censored minimum. The teachers will glorify marriage and childbearing and a covered life, assuring her that by humbly conforming, she will be granting the entire Jewish people a future.

"Let her go," a Hasidic neighbor tells me, "so that she'll come back to you." I imagine today that this advice might apply better to a young adult than to a fourteen-year-old. But I don't want to confuse my daughter. In the end, I don't know how to do anything other than what we are supposed to do.

Teaching others to sin is a sin for which one cannot atone. I point the way for my daughter into a woman's covered silence. I lay out the path of self-sacrifice and endless motherhood and send her on her way. This, then, is who she will be, who she will become. I send her. I do that.

DECEMBER, and I finally dive into Rosellen's gift—*Writing Fiction: A Guide to Narrative Craft*, by Janet Burroway. But there is so much I can't grasp.

"Conflict" seems to be a simple word, but when Burroway says one should write about conflict, she emphasizes *unresolved* conflict as most true-to-life. My sense of story was formed by Hasidic stories we tell at Sabbath tables and at rites of passage. In those, the hero stands up to forces against God, but in the course of the story, the conflict, inner or outer, is always resolved. Also in the texts we study, Truth is a clear, singular ideal that one must work to discover by wading through contradictory notions until each is proven right or wrong. All contradictions and conflicts then evaporate, and that moment of clarification is a revelation. Which means that in the fiction stories from the library that I'm now reading, when I come across Burroway's type of conflict, I don't get it. I tend to go back, assuming I must have read something wrong. I don't understand unresolved conflict on the page. I don't understand resolutions that aren't really resolutions.

On Rosellen's recommendation, I check out a book of stories by Alice Munro, only to find that every time I think I understand a character, he or she does the opposite of what I've come to expect. Her characters twist and turn, flip-flop with their feelings, and rarely resolve their conflicts. They just live through them, and, yes, change somehow and move on. And yet the stories captivate me. I think, *But the people seem so real.*

❦

IT'S 1992, and the Rebbe has had a stroke. All of Lubavitch is shaken. He's in a hospital in Manhattan with tubes and monitors and the sound of labored breathing. Groups of the faithful cluster on the sidewalk below his window, reciting psalms. I go to Crown Heights to visit Leibl.

The annual Lubavitch Hasidic Women's Convention is going on. Remembering a similar convention I once attended in Chicago, I make my way over worn red carpeting into the main session in the Oholei Torah ballroom, studded with yellowed chandeliers, to find myself once again in an enormous crowd of bewigged and faithful women. I take my place inconspicuously among them, as one woman after another ascends the podium to exhort and inspire us. And then the keynote: Rabbi Bentzion Teitel. A murmur spreads across the room. Rabbi Teitel is a highly respected figure, a thunderous voice in the movement. As he stands above us, his sweeping gaze seems intent on exposing our every truth, every sin. His monologue gradually rises in pitch, and then suddenly he shouts into the microphone, "Anyone here . . . ," in a loud, accusing tone. He leaves the phrase hanging.

No one can hide. Female humility before a rabbi grows huge.

"*Any*one who so much as imagines for a moment that the Rebbe cannot and *will not* stand up out of his hospital bed *on his own* when he chooses, pull the tubes out of his body with his *own hands*, and lead us *as the Messiah* to Jerusalem is *chaser emunah!*"

We have been accused with a nasty epithet for someone lacking faith. We have been shamed. The shame is palpable in the room, choking.

And finally, I'm furious. I just almost jump up, dare to open my woman's mouth in public, and call out, *The Rebbe is an old, sick man who has lived out his years. How do you know he would do such a thing? You are no prophet. Only God knows the future.* But I don't. No one moves. We women don't move, save sideways glances. I wait, like the other women, clap, like the others, leave politely, like the others. I walk out invisible in the crowd, sick with myself.

I can't yet see the leaps in logic in the Rebbe's talks that kept us willing to submit ourselves, but when I leave Crown Heights, after hugging Leibl and bidding him goodbye, I leave behind the Rebbe as larger-than-life scholar and miracle worker and take with me only the picture of him as an old but very real man—blue eyes he once trained on me as a girl, white plastic reading glasses low on his nose, overdue for a haircut, his well-known habits of abundant cups of tea and too much salt on his food. Brilliant, a scholar, but just a man. *Soon, I think, he will die.* So will we all.

On the evening of June 12, 1994, the third day of Tammuz, the children bathed and in their pajamas, the year of mourning for my father ends. At the soul candle I've kept burning through this past year, I take a used plate from the sink and cover the glass cylinder. The flame chokes and shrinks down to an orange ember, then slowly flicks out. I lift the plate, and a gray line ribbons upward from the dead ember. Memories of my father have caught me at the oddest times through the year. It's a relief to move on. "Now we can have music!" I announce, and soon lively klezmer fills the house. Itzik and Shalom and Avrami dance on the blue carpet-sea to laughing clarinets, and I dance with them while Mendel and Sarah watch and chatter and laugh. Shalom breaks loose, runs in circles, jumps on the coach.

Late that night, as I sleep a rare deep sleep, the Rebbe dies. All of the men of our community fly to New York, so that many overlapping accounts will filter back through our community. Levi meets Leibl on the street in Crown Heights, and they join the black-coated mourners, ten thousand strong, walking behind the hearse down Eastern Parkway, performing the final kindness of accompanying the Rebbe's dead body to the grave. Wives and sisters and young children look down from brownstone windows as a vast field of black hats blocks Eastern Parkway for miles.

And yet many whole families walk in the crowd, women and children as well. They plod on together, heads down, solemn. Men openly cry, tears glistening in beards and falling on their coats. But Levi and Leibl also pass clusters of followers in frantic celebratory song and dance, arms on shoulders, around and around. They have brought musical instruments to announce the Rebbe's resurrection. *The Messiah is here!* They sing and play. Long live the Rebbe, the king! He died for our sins. Long live our master, our teacher, our rebbe, King Messiah forever! He will rise again! The music glitters over the flowing, somber crowd as aloof policemen watch from the sidelines.

The *yartzeit* anniversary of my father's death bleeds into the Rebbe's. Now they are both gone and the dancing Hasidim sicken me.

I CONTINUE MY FEVERED nighttime writing, but I'm beginning to notice that religious voice implanted in me long ago. Late one night, I stop and print out what I've written, then read it out loud in the dim light. Levi moans a sleepy protest and turns over in his bed. The writing sounds polemical, insincere. I crumple the pages and pitch them into the trash. "The real truth is," I write Rosellen the next day, "I rage silently at the boring details that use my every minute and keep me from what I really want to do. I rage at housework and shopping and standing in lines. Then I swing to the opposite and submerge myself in family and home, where I find daily sameness peaceful and reassuring—for a while. Until a niggling nervousness takes hold again."

Admitting discontent is enormous new territory. "All those Hasidic women who feel important to God because they are bringing order to their families—I'd like to be like them, but I can't. Order is holiness, they teach us. But I need to form my own image and not just find it reflected in their eyes."

I have written real unresolved conflict into a character that feels true for the first time. I print out the letter and put it in the mail.

ANOTHER YEAR PASSES, AND TALL, now-bearded Leibl transfers to yeshiva in Tzfat, Israel, ancient town of mystics. Libby is settled in a Chicago yeshiva, and now Mendel is going away. Itzik, Shalom, Avrami, and Sarah come to the airport, and we watch the plane pull back from the terminal. There's Mendel's soft face at one of the windows, in contrast with the masculine thrusting power of revving motors, that inexorable mechanical drive. The Jetway separates and folds in on itself like a discarded umbilical cord.

At the window, Avrami puts a hand on Shalom's shoulder. Each in turn is getting to be the oldest at home. Sarah is impatient to leave. She's satisfied to see her active, contentious brother depart, but I can't stop watching Mendel's childhood pulling away before it's over. The plane turns and heads down the tarmac. We stay until it is a speck in the sky.

At night, as my diminishing family sleeps, I wander into the den. I know Mendel won't become a Talmud scholar—that's not him—but I tell myself that he can plunge into a rowdy group there and at least still get to be a teen. There will be forays to the dorm rooftop at night for secret cigarettes, raiding the kitchen, fringes and yarmulkas flying in pickup basketball games, and, in a couple of years, secret stashes of beer in the dorm, even clandestine calls to the kinds of girls who speak to boys. So why do I worry that this life robs my children of their adolescence?

Because he's not officially *allowed* to question. They won't foster questioning or train him to formulate questions. And those he comes up with on his own, he'll get to pose only to someone he respects, and only if he is seeking clarification of the Law, not if he questions the Law itself.

Maybe we are all frozen in preadolescence. Most of us never learned how to rebel or explore. Look at us, like children young enough to think their parents, the Law and the Rebbe, omnipotent. But I want to form questions. I want to argue and sift, choose what I want and leave the rest, like I once planned to do when I was a teen. Now I have to watch my children equally robbed.

I write Rosellen and describe the God I first met at Rabbi Rakovsky's Sabbath table—as multifaceted as the human spirit, embedded in all things, nurturing and all-gendered, including the *shechinah*, the gentle, ever-present mother. It is this God, not the Law's stern authority, who fed my young dreams. So why is this very Jewish, mystical God barely present in our masculine world of the Law? *It wasn't supposed to be like this.*

And yet something is setting me more squarely in the present:

Dear Rosellen,

Itzik's biggest wish for his seventh birthday was a new bicycle and a turkey dinner. I located a refurbished all-but-new bike while he was still in school, drove out to the bike shop after I got the turkey in the oven, and spent an hour in the crowded shop while they lowered the seat and handlebars, changed out the wheels for pedal brakes, put on better tires, and added a kickstand. *You're not charging me more for this, are you?* I dashed home with the little red bike in the back of the mom van. Just as the kids turned up the walk from school, I pulled up, and they came running.

Why did it take until the sixth child to be able to see this? It's the joy, pure and simple—no preaching, nothing sublime. Just a new red bike and the house filled with the smell of turkey dinner, Levi home early to share it with us. You had to see Itzik dance. Three siblings to dance around him, ooh over the turkey, and take turns racing on the bike. Itzik throwing his arms around me again and again. Avrami, Sarah, and Itzik in helmets and coats racing ahead on their bikes after dinner, helmets bobbing in the dark, the children glowing under the streetlamp where they stop to chatter and wait for me at each corner while I catch up on foot with little Shalom's sweet hand in mine. I've been moved all week by how simple it all is.

If I could, my birthday gift would be for Itzik to keep his joy in little things, and, if that's not possible, to someday have a child like him to give him joy like I have.

Love,
Leah der Oysher (the Rich One)

But I lied. Levi didn't come home for dinner.

LEIBL CALLS FROM A pay phone in Tzfat, where he's been in yeshiva for nearly six weeks. He talks about hiking the valley beneath his dorm with friends and about their trip south to the Dead Sea. Somehow he has made the transition to modern Hebrew, so very different from ancient texts—he laughs about a radio program and reports a conversation he overheard on a bus. But there's a loudspeaker and raucous singing in the background, some noisy march. *Long live our rebbe, King Messiah forever.* "What *is* that?" I say.

"Guys get together and march around here," he says.

"Do they, like, carry posters?"

"Yeah, and there are bumper stickers and billboards around town." Pictures of the Rebbe's face next to THE KING SHALL LIVE! on sides of buildings, shop windows, car windows, telephone poles, in entries to buildings and private homes, and held high in impromptu parades by those shouting young men. "I'm getting sick of that song," Leibl says. The noise only grows as the marchers pass. Our master lives forever!

NOVEMBER 4, 1995. For weeks, the Israeli right has been demonstrating against the peace accord that Prime Minister Rabin signed at Oslo. They were spurred on after he was awarded the Nobel Prize. Recently, a right-wing organization called Eyal disseminated an image of Rabin in a Nazi uniform: Rabin's troubled eyes, his lined Jewish face and bushy gray hair, with a swastika on his chest. The posters appeared mysteriously across the country, then around the world. This is the climate in which Yitzhak Rabin arrives at Kings of Israel Plaza in largely secular Tel Aviv to give a speech at a peace rally. When he's done, amid applause and cheers, he descends the steps with his security detail toward a waiting car. A young bearded man in a yarmulka steps up and guns him down.

That night, in Tzfat, Leibl's dorm mates, study partners, hiking buddies, friends, with whom he floated in the Dead Sea and laughingly smeared mud on one another, gather and march in wild celebration. My son watches from the window of his dorm room. The boys march over the cobbled streets under street lamps, under the stars, mountains as a backdrop, singing, shouting, passing bottles of vodka. A single, huge, moving shadow follows them, and then on to the yeshiva, where they force open the door to the study hall. Inside, they pass more bottles, jump on tables, and dance. *The Nazi is dead!* they cry. *He slept with our enemies! The Messiah is coming! The Rebbe is coming back to us. Long live the Rebbe!*

The heavy door opens. In walks the Rosh Yeshiva rabbi director, with his grave, long beard, black coat, deep voice. "Get down," he says. "Leave. *Now.*"

The next day, all is decorum again in the study hall. The boys are grouped around a long table over open books, quiet, some a little hungover, the rabbi holding forth. Leibl is among them. The murderer, Yigal Amir, member of Eyal, is in jail. His trial will be quick and superfluous, but that is irrelevant; time is stopped here. In the study hall, there is no Rabin, no politics, no world. God's Word is justice. The rabbi unravels the Talmudic logic one thread at a time. One of the boys rubs the back of his neck. Another twiddles his ritual strings. Brows furrow. The low buzz of a lazy fly. Three policemen enter.

One of them announces the name of the boy sitting next to Leibl. The boy stands slowly on shaking legs. He is sixteen. "You made the poster," the policeman says.

"Do you have a warrant?" the rabbi says. "Proof?"

The policeman speaks to the boy. "We have your father. We'll release him when you give yourself up."

"You think this is a *democracy?*" Leibl shouts into the phone to me the next day. "You can get picked up for what you *think* here. They're arresting religious Jews all over the country."

"Had that boy's father *done* anything?" I say.

"Nothing," he says. "They took him without a warrant, then used him as a trap."

"Those boys were wrong, celebrating like that," I say.

That morning the yeshiva director had found his car vandalized. "The kids here are not who I am," Leibl says. "Get me out of here!"

≈

NOW IT'S A YEAR and a half later, April 1997, on the last day of Passover, near sunset. The sky is streaked, flocks of northern birds pausing for the night on their migration back home. Leibl dropped out of rabbinical training and transferred to a yeshiva in New York that actually grants an accredited high school diploma. He reads secular books and follows politics and wants to leave yeshiva. In Houston, our neighborhood has also changed. Dollar stores have replaced boutique shops. The nearby shopping center is strewn with trash, and sullen teens loiter around signs that warn against shoplifting. The same tense Hasidic/black schism I once saw in Crown Heights is evolving here.

I've also changed, mostly through reading and writing to Rosellen, who has moved away to Chicago. I hold on for the kids, in spite of the long, slow-growing split in me.

In the synagogue, nothing has changed, and today Avrami is exultant. Today is the last day of Passover, and this is his thirteenth birthday. We'll make a feast next Sabbath to celebrate his bar mitzvah, but today in the open hall we've set out tables laden with piles of handmade matzohs—uneven rounds with acrid, burnt edges, and bottles of kosher wine, nothing more. This is the meal of the Messiah. We flew Leibl, Libby, and Mendel home for this and for the bar mitzvah—Avrami sits with his father and brothers. The men of the community gather and take seats at the tables, with Rabbi Frumen presiding. Levi presented Avrami with his first black hat in honor of this arrival into manhood. It is new and big for his boy face.

I sit behind a partition with Levi's mother, Libby, and Sarah, the only females here—Mrs. Frumen and all the other women are busy at home with Passover work. Besides, the community views this special, final Passover gathering as a ritual for men.

At a signal from Rabbi Frumen, the men begin a series of

seven *nigun* wordless songs. Each is another rung on a ladder to heaven. Rabbis, professionals, laborers, doctors, young, old—the songs rise in rich minor key. Community, family, and God form a kind of silent harmony. Avrami closes his eyes, grips the front of his chair, and rocks as he sings. A cup of wine, a bite of matzoh, another song, another cup. The group is lost in the winding heart of the melody, bodies and hearts open, heads back in song. Rabbi Frumen gestures to our son.

Quiet. Eyes open, Avrami begins reciting the impossibly complex bar mitzvah discourse, from memory, in a singsong. "*Isa bemedrash tilim,*" he chants in his boy voice.

Usually when a bar mitzvah boy recites this difficult discourse, the group soon interrupts with cries of "mazel tov" to give the boy a break, but Avrami continues without pause. For twenty-five minutes there's no other sound in the room, his young voice a new note in harmony with their lingering song. When he finishes, he is breathless with triumph. Then come the cries of "mazel tov," and a new jubilant tune. *Praise God that He chose us as His alone!* The men laugh and clop the table to the dancing rhythm. Amid that, Avrami suddenly launches out of his seat, runs over behind the partition to us, and throws his arms around his grandmother and then around me. In my arms, he says in my ear, "This is my *real* bar mitzvah." Just wine, rough, handmade matzoh burnt on the edges, song, and arrival.

"WE WILL STAND BY LEIBL," I say to Levi, "or lose him." I have just stopped my husband in the living room and demanded he listen.

"What are you saying?"

"Leibl is not staying in yeshiva. He's not becoming a rabbi. He says he's going to college."

Leibl purchased books and studied on his own for months,

then took the SAT and achievement tests and did very well.

Levi says little, but he acquiesces.

In May, Leibl is accepted to Rice University in Houston. After years away, our glorious new rebel is coming home. Another day, after he's moved back in, I find Leibl and his father deep in conversation in the den, Levi reminiscing about his happy years studying math and physics at the University of Pennsylvania. Levi is nostalgic, his face open. Leibl leans forward, eager to hear.

Avrami, too, leaves for yeshiva in Chicago. I keep thinking I will round a corner in the house and find him—on his stomach, head propped on his fists, playing a board game with Itzik, flashing his smile and the dimples that embarrass him. Tearing down the street on his too-small bicycle. Cracking one of his wry jokes at the Sabbath table.

Although only the three youngest are at home now, it is still easy to stay caught up in kids' growth and drama, easy to avoid the mirror, easy to pour myself into writing at night to avoid quite existing during the day. I could let more years pass this way. Then one day Mendel calls from a pay phone and mentions the latest gossip: a teenage boy at the Lubavitcher yeshiva in Manchester, England, committed suicide by jumping off his dorm roof. There is no official word, but the gossip has spread through the web of boys in Lubavitcher yeshivas. They say the boy was gay. He killed himself because he was gay.

I hang up and double over. Can't breathe. I *feel* his over-whelming despair at a world that rejects what he *is*. I see him going up those lonely stairs and walking out on the roof; I squeeze my eyes shut but can't shut out the image.

I don't sleep. I carry that boy with me into the next day and the next. I don't understand why I do that. I do and I don't, but the boy haunts me. He had nowhere to turn, no way to be himself without destroying his life. He was forced to choose between rejecting his life as he knew it and ending it. He chose.

I am a "we." The community. *We made his tragedy inevitable.* He killed himself because he believed what we teach, and so he couldn't bear his own heartbeat.

He is my children. He was forced into soldier-like "adulthood" that tries to kill parts of his soul.

Then a deep, enigmatic empathy whispers to me that I know that boy from the inside. *I know him.* I dream him. I dream I am him: Someone forces me into a gilded cage, where I live day after day. Finally, I escape and climb to the roof. In the dream, my final jump is one of wild abandon. I am weightless at last against a forgiving sky.

LATE JUNE. I take Itzik and Shalom for free tennis lessons at a city tennis center nearby. I have convinced another family to send their two boys along. The four jump out of the car and dash off to the courts, impervious to steam and sun and deafening cicadas, oblivious as well to their yarmulkas and closely cropped skulls and to the fact that they are the only white kids in the class. I settle in to wait for them on a cracked vinyl sofa in the tennis house with my new secondhand laptop, grateful for the frigid air conditioning. Of course the gay boy in England comes back to me. He's a frequent companion. I sit back, sigh. But there's gossip in the community every year about yet another boy "like that" expelled from a yeshiva, always followed by appalled comments about how the family will be marked now and the siblings will pay. I think, *What does it mean that I feel I know something I've never experienced?* I want to write what life was like for that boy day-to-day.

Every morning the boys in Hasidic yeshivas are bused to a *mikvah*, where they strip and jump in together, as spiritual preparation for morning prayers. Afterward, they shower all at once, locker room–style. Among all that male flesh, the boy who jumped from the roof must have felt like any straight young man would feel if asked to socialize, nonchalant, among a group of milling naked women. Day and night, the boys share intimacies, eating, drinking, dressing, learning together. They dance arm in arm.

My shadow yeshiva boy is awash in hormones. Forbidden thoughts and fantasies plague him. He is painfully self-conscious about where he puts his gaze and terrified of betraying himself with a glance at a boy. But he loves yeshiva life. He loves deciphering those cryptic holy texts, the sense of God ever at his sleeve, the camaraderie, always feeling certain of what is good and right. And he loves his father. He needs his approval.

I wander through the boy's conflicted life, the intensity of his young devotion, his confusion as he comes to know himself. I feel what that boy feels. I want what he wants. A fictional young man takes form, a lump of empathy for him in my throat. I name him Berkeh.

At the *mikvah*, Berkeh won't get undressed with the others. He stays in the waiting area, but the boys wander through, naked or half-dressed, youthful, sinewy bodies, glistening wet hair. Sitting there, Berkeh clenches his hand as if grasping something. He tries to train his eyes on the white floor tiles, wishing the same white blankness on his mind.

When the boys finish their tennis lesson, they pile back into the car, smelling of sweat, red-faced and chattering about the teacher, scores, and other boys at the lesson, particularly the ones they envy. I drive home immersed in Berkeh yet unaware of parallels between our lives.

On another day on the vinyl sofa in the tennis house, I meet Berkeh's study partner, Shlomo, his friend since their days in summer camp. Shlomo is in love with him. Berkeh works hard to resist Shlomo's attention. He is deeply attached to Shlomo, but Berkeh is also an admired scholar at the yeshiva. Then the principal-rabbi recommends Berkeh to the chief benefactor of the yeshiva to go on a date with the man's daughter as a candidate for marriage. This is an enormous honor, and Berkeh is thrilled. He knows his father will be proud. Berkeh's community will celebrate him. He will be everything he has been raised to be.

He goes out with the girl. "You're different from the others," she says. She leans in close to him. She puts her hand almost to his face and holds it there a whisper beyond the forbidden touch, her fingers trembling.

When the whole yeshiva is invited to the wedding of a former student, Berkeh throws himself into the celebration, imagining his own forthcoming arrival as a full-fledged community member—a married man, finally able to take his adult place among them. He sees the girl he dated dancing on the other side of the partition and jumps into the men's circular dance. Tiny cups of vodka shots are passed as they dance, and Berkeh downs each one with abandon. Soon there are circles within circles of dancing men. Berkeh is reeling from alcohol, loud music beating in his head. Each time he sights Shlomo, he moves closer to the innermost group, until he is thrown into the center to dance with the groom. The two then dance, around and around, surrounded by men singing, stomping, cheering them on. Then the groom lets go to honor another and Berkeh nearly falls. He staggers away —into Shlomo, who seems to have been waiting. The two then begin to dance, slowly, then faster, whirling to the music, gripping forearms, and it seems to Berkeh that the men have formed a circle around them, instead of around the groom. The laughing music deafens him, fills him. He sees boys laughing and pointing at them, and he laughs, too. There is nothing left but the pulse beat of Shlomo's arms on his palms and the music beating in his head as they dance. The room flies, blurred laughing faces flow past, as tears course down Berkeh's cheeks.

I don't notice that Berkeh is the same age I was when I married, although I do know, if I were to let the story continue, that Berkeh would marry the girl who almost touched his face. I also know, and shudder, that the story is best ended where I've stopped, that if I were to let the story go on, he might kill himself.

I drop off my children's friends at their home and then turn into our driveway. Itzik and Shalom run into the house, the very walls quivering from their boyish energy as they inhale sandwiches and apple juice and then run back out to their bicycles. I step outside to watch. As they charge down the street, I feel certain that, for Berkeh, there is no resolution.

ROSELLEN DROPS POSTCARDS, notes, a thoughtful line, but rarely writes back with the real engagement I continue to invite. I am unaware of the deluge I have made her withstand with all of my letters—four years' worth now—and have had no thought of the raw need that must leap out at her when she opens one of them. I am impatient with our one-sided correspondence, don't recognize that she has continued to proffer exactly what I want and need: honest connection, mutuality, rare freedom to speak my mind.

One day, dishrag thrown over my shoulder, I wipe wet hands on my apron and go outside to collect the mail. There in the blazing heat, I pluck out an envelope in Rosellen's confident script. In it, she apologizes for not holding up her end of the corres- pondence. My mentor is tired, urging me to go on without her. I wipe sweat from my face. "Sometimes," she says, "I drop your letter on the 'Leah' pile as if I've touched fire. It's very hard for me to feel I can respond to your self-doubt when I think of the book you should be writing." I laugh to imagine myself in the secular world as a published author. But my laugh has an empty sound.

ALONG WITH STUDIES in computers and math at Rice, Leibl dives into psychology of the brain, art history, and fencing. He explores cultural programs, student groups, sports, political causes, finds friends who will last for years. His beard and yarmulka soon disappear and he blends exuberantly into the world—as I hold even tighter to the outward scrim of my life, now a thin, brittle thing. I tell myself I do it for the children, afraid if I change I will bring down the walls of their home. Meanwhile, Leibl disappears for days at a time, sleeps on couches in friends' dorm rooms, studies in the common room of his college through whole nights, only to burst thrillingly through the front door at odd times with a load of laundry, calling out, "Is there food?"

There are still moments in my Jewish days that hold true: when my flaming match touches the wick of the Sabbath candles —the fizz, catch, rising fire—and the moment my head slips beneath *mikvah* water when I see bubbles under the surface, a weightless hand, a blue veil over everything in that underwater passageway. *So many have come through here hoping to emerge into a different life. A different self.*

That Sabbath not long ago—when I closed the book of Torah for the last time, only to find myself aroused by lesbian poetry as children piled toys on the carpet—began a dance of intertwined desire and religious doubts. I drift into hilarious fantasies of making love to Adrienne Rich. And I no longer tell myself I just dreamed I was a man; in those dreams I was a woman making love to a woman. I still shudder at the word "lesbian," but I know myself now.

After a hiatus of many months, I write helplessly to Rosellen. I tell her not to think my letter demands she respond, but that I need to write, need to talk, out of "a kind of desperation.

"When I do read Torah now I find (dare I say this?) a web of party lines. I've denied for so long that a life in Torah is artificial. Is it part of aging, to realize that the structures we build around us are artificial even though we still see beauty in them?

"Maybe it's okay that my children will inherit my ambivalence. If I hand them only conviction, they could turn away from our ways with the same strength I once turned *toward* the faith. With ambivalence, there's nothing clear to rebel against—maybe that's the ironic key to Jewish survival."

And then, discovery:

"Doubts and the need to critically assess must be part of the human condition. But a big part of our faith is to deny those doubts. Do we as Hasidim deny our humanity?

"I have begun to smell pretense in our communal gatherings, and the Jewish observance in our home feels like a fragile old shell. I now understand how denial creates a false self. Am I teaching my children a lie?"

"I am bereaved," Rosellen answers, "to think that you feel the need to join me in the land of skepticism."

"Perhaps," I write back, "a small part of my soul never left."

But our faith has written so much of my mothering. *Did you say a blessing over that apple? Straighten your yarmulka. That skirt's getting short. Thank God—don't forget to do that.* And in the face of their disappointments and childish frustrations: *It was meant to be. This also is for good. You are my little soldier.* Now, I hardly know what to say. I become tongue-tied, inept with them. *It shouldn't be this way. I'm still their mother.* I still start the day with lists, hunt down each one to report on comings and goings, make sure each has eaten and done homework. I settle arguments, or not, take one at a time to sit down so that I can listen to his or her day. It's not right that I feel like a sham just because I wear this skirt and wig while a different, more real person struggles to emerge.

I want to tell my children that I don't believe so much about our life anymore, but I don't dare. If I could, I'd say, *It isn't important to me whether you recite the right prayer or wear the right clothing. Just know yourself. Don't go forward without that, like I did. Don't be dishonest with yourself and with people you love, or with God, like I have been.*

If I change, if I get honest, will you know me?

⮑

EARLY SPRING, months after I wrote Berkeh. Our suburban neighborhood is abloom with azaleas, hibiscus coming into bud, magnolias opening plate-size grandiosity. The sun is warm and still benign in a clear sky. V lines of Canada geese fly over headed north like arrows pointed home. I pull out of a grocery store parking lot, thinking about necessary losses. Then I have a moment of impulsive insanity, telling myself, *I better move faster than I can think.* I turn the opposite direction from home and speed across town to the University of Houston. I park illegally, stop two book-laden students for directions, and lift my skirt to climb the stairs of Cullen Hall to the cluttered office of the graduate creative writing program. "You want an application?" the clerk asks. "The deadline is in two days."

At home, I pull out one of my stories, this one about Munya, an old Russian immigrant woman who works nights as a *mikvah* attendant. One night an unmarried woman arrives in pants and uncovered hair, wanting to immerse. She is hoping the *mikvah* will cleanse her of her secret that she was raped as a child. Munya feels so compelled to help her that she steps outside the Law for the first time. When the woman stands before her naked in the water, she speaks her own prayer, in her own words: "Today I will allow myself to be a woman."

I attach the story to the application. But the second page of the application says, *List Here All of Your Awards and Publications.* I leave it blank. Rosellen faxes a letter of recommendation hours before the deadline. Then I tell Levi. I don't ask him. I tell him. "I won't get in," I say, "but if I do, we'll manage."

In May, there's a letter with official letterhead. "We are very sorry to inform you . . . ," it says. I don't read the rest. I tear the page up, let the pieces fall, walk away.

And here is Levi—it has been months since we touched—

rising from his chair, picking up the torn pieces from the floor.

"It's no use," I say. "Don't bother."

He fits the pieces together, then reads what he can. "Wait," he says. "It's not so bad."

"I don't care," I say.

"No. Look," he says. "You're on the waiting list." He reads out loud: "'Please contact us so we may know how best to reach you.'"

I turn back, stepping close to the heat and weight of him. I take what is left of the letter from his hands, and my fingers brush his—cool, rough, dry. I look up into his eyes. *Where have you been?* I think. "Oh," I say. "Oh."

LATE AUGUST, and I'm running up the stairs of the Roy Cullen Building at the University of Houston. My foot catches in the skirt, and I almost fall. I am so nervous. And then I'm on the landing. It's a little dingy around here. But I have arrived. Where are the trumpets?

An older man approaches—dark hair clipped short, sagging cheeks, small dark eyes, sharp and intent, holding a briefcase in one hand and a sheaf of unruly papers in the other. "You're a new face," he says.

"Yes," I say, and I freely offer my hand to a man perhaps for the first time as an adult. But of course his hands are occupied. There's an awkward moment.

"Name?" he says.

"Leah Lax."

"Oh, I have your short story right here somewhere," he says, glancing at the papers about to fall. "We have a new mentorship program. I'm to be yours." He is author Daniel Stern.

I start classes, including Dan Stern's fiction writing seminar, and the Hasidic community seems to drift away. I stop going to the synagogue or community gatherings. When I do run into any of the women, they seem proud of me, but there is clear expectation that I will extract from university only the knowledge I need to develop my skills without succumbing to unkosher ideas. I am to be a showcase item, to show the world how Hasidim can be educated without compromising our religion. I expect this is what Levi also trusts, hopes, expects of me.

Oh, but it is stunning to confront the quality of thought and creativity that happens when nothing is censored. But this place is outrageous in its freedom. I had wanted to rise above my life to a place without stricture, but this is the stratosphere.

One night, I work on a critique of a fellow student's story for Dan Stern's class—we have to critique one another's work each week—but the story disturbs me. The character cuts himself and then sinks into a dream state of pain that is ecstasy. I'm exasperated. This is the fourth story with self-mutilation in it this semester. I can't understand someone using pain to fight pain, can't imagine perverting oneself into becoming your own enemy, can't see my own life.

The next day, I go early to class like a gremlin, take out a blank sheet of paper, and write out in large capitals, WELCOME TO DAN STERN'S SELF-MUTILATION WORKSHOP. Before anyone arrives, I post the sign on the outside of the door. By doing so, I'm secretly reprimanding the students, sure, but I am also having a hard time adjusting to no censorship. The air is too rarefied—I've been getting the bends. Later, I won't be proud of posting that sign, censoring them like that. The students arrive, laugh at the sign, and take their places. Dan comes in last. He looks angry and rips it down. "Who did this?" he says. No one says a word. I think, *At least I made them laugh at themselves.* No cutting scenes appear in future stories.

The program includes extensive studies in literature and criticism. I'm an eager greenhorn in skirt and scarf. I read fifty books the first year and keep a log. I fill notebooks with marginal scribbles: *Read Foucault! Look up: hegemony, sui generis, epistemology.* Sometimes I withdraw, chagrinned by my puppy enthusiasm, but that doesn't last. There is so much to learn.

I take a fiction seminar with Robert Boswell (we call him Boz), who talks weekly about the importance of irony in our writing. The first time I hear him say that word, irony, I go home and stare uncomprehending at an apparently simple definition in a dictionary. *Why can't I get this? Why can't I recognize irony on the page or imagine how to write it?* Boz hammers the issue week after week, and my problem with irony becomes a little secret crisis. He says irony is a clash of opposites, when someone says one thing but means another, or an event occurs in direct contradiction to the tone already set—a comic event at a funeral, stolid lethargy in the middle of a clamoring crowd, an expression of hatred spoken in a tender voice. I am stymied by that, by the way he's asking me to embrace two opposites at the same time.

This is when I begin to understand that my mind has been trained to squelch contradictory ideas or feelings so much so that I'm finding it difficult to even recognize such contradictions. I have been taught to believe that if choice *a* is true, choice *b* must be false. There is but one path. Everything must be labeled as right *or* wrong. Good *or* evil. I think, *Could both be true at once, without resolution, or judgment, or labels?* Can I acknowledge that, *write* that?

Trying to understand all of this makes me feel like my mind is finally becoming three dimensional, like a cartoon character who has been steamrolled, then, toddling away into the world, pops into herself. *Pop. Pop. Pop.*

The world changes. People are fascinating bundles of contradictions without labels or judgment. Events are the same. I no longer need to draw conclusions; I just want to get close and examine all the strands and colors and surprises.

There are so many new rules in writing. True to form, I first work to learn and follow the rules. And yet gradually I begin to understand that these rules are different from those that still govern my life. *I* own these rules for my writing self, and they don't own me. I can stretch them, break them. That's when I become a writer. And an adult.

I'm changing in other ways. Maybe it's reading all those books, each with a different standpoint or philosophy, each with a different heart, forming in my mind a new collection of voices that aren't a Group in lockstep. Maybe it's all the time I'm spending outside of Hasidic land in heady academic freedom. I don't know. But now I can see that religious life has filled me with grandiose convictions, made me believe I knew God's words and thoughts and that I truly changed the world with the strike of a match or the proper tying of shoes. Now I just feel small and ineffective. Is this what the world *out there* is? No clear path—just an enormous jumble of conflicting beliefs, events, personalities, desires—and nothing I do will change it? I'll die, a blip, and leave no mark at all. And it doesn't matter how I tie my shoes.

Yet, after all the years in black and white, I still don't even quite know what color *is*.

Although I can see paradox and irony everywhere I turn, I'm ill prepared to deal with it. In the secular world, I'm a child, or a new immigrant, without insight or reference points.

In class and in the student lounge, I sidle up to conversations, but they talk about movies and television shows and politics and I don't know most of what they're talking about. Students meet and hang out in bars and coffee shops and restaurants, where I wouldn't know what to order or how to figure tax and a tip.

I throw myself into schoolwork while trying to keep up with house and children, too often coaching one of the older ones over the phone. *Find two packages of hot dogs in the freezer. Set the oven on*

350°. Keep an eye on it! At home, I do housework as if it is vital, but also as if I have been robbed.

Conversation That Never Happened with the Group— Greek Chorus with a Yiddish Accent

In Which I Finally Talk Back

ME [*pointing an accusing finger*]: Now I know you showed me only what you wanted me to see of the world. You said the world was full of filth and lies. You made me miss *living.*

GCYA: *We told you*—we told you—*about the pig that shows its cloven hoof to fool us into believing it is kosher. Nothing is as it seems. Be careful, we said. Evil is mixed with good, good with evil. Don't claim we said otherwise.*

ME: Then you consoled me by claiming reality was just a bad dream and your dream of perfection was reality. You did that to make me turn my back on the world and accept your Torah. Now the world has passed me by.

GCYA: *But we did say truth has many facets. Don't accuse us of simplistic ideas.*

ME: That never helped. You warped my mind, pressed it flat.

[*Group fades away.*]

IN ROBERT LOWELL'S POETRY, I find he despaired when he lost his faith. I write Rosellen. "Someone should have warned Lowell that developing himself as a writer would demand such brutal self-honesty that he would never be able to embrace religion wholeheartedly again. I wish I could have warned him. I would have told him that the vision writing required of you is going to break down all of your illusions, your props against the wind. *Stop!* I want to tell him, because faith is our most precious illusion, impossibly fragile when the screen obscuring the world is removed. *Stop!* Because you can't stay happy if you don't stay blind. Lowell didn't stop believing in God," I write. "He lost his ability to find Him."

IN CLASS AND OUT, fellow students are never so much as available for coffee, and I don't realize it could be how I look. Then one day I find real, live gay students congregating in the student lounge, full of ease and brazen humor. I sit down on the periphery of that golden group in my long skirt and scarf. They fall silent and quietly disperse.

I switch to shorter skirts. The scarf slips back on my head. I lose the pantyhose. I run into one of the Hasidic women at the grocery store, and she looks at my exposed hair and bare legs and drops her eyes. No one calls me anymore to supervise a *mikvah* immersion or teach a class.

I dream I am walking through a watery universe that is actually a giant *mikvah.* All of the group is here under the water: Mira, my old *mikvah* buddy, who barely speaks to me now; Shterna, who brushes past when we meet, no more late-night chats; Rabbi Frumen and his angry, righteous wife; even Levi. There are children everywhere in this watery world, ours included, playing, jumping, and no one seems to notice that no one can breathe or that the water is contaminated with human waste. But I'm just a visitor, just passing through.

Yet I continue going to the *mikvah* each month. I do it with dismay, with spiritual greed. I go in spite of new awareness of misogyny and primal fear of a bleeding woman that informed these laws and now stains the process for me. For seven days after my period ends, I perform the internal inspections to make sure I've stopped bleeding. I formally count the days and take care not to touch Levi until after immersion. I do it because that moment when I emerge from the chest-high water, stand back up, and turn toward the damp tiled wall to mouth ancient words is the only time left when I can pray. Naked in the *mikvah*, I know who I am. Rabbis and their books are gone. *What will happen to me now?*

Nineteen

It's been over twenty-five years since Ana and I once sang with a girl named Janice who came to the Sabbath Experience—our three-part harmony that night, voices blended in common innocence and confidence, brimming with young plans. How brief that encounter, and yet when I recognize Janice at the grocery store, I call out her name and rush over with an oversize "Hi!" We exchange numbers, and after several good but brief telephone visits, I pull out "Munya's Story" once again from the wire cart and send it to her. We meet for coffee not long after, on a Sunday, Levi home with the kids, and fall into the kind of girlfriend conversation I've never had with anyone in the community or the university. *It's just a taste,* I tell myself, feeling the pull toward freedom. *Don't forget who you are.*

Fatigue in her eyes, furrow in her brow, Janice seems as if she might also need a friend. What different routes we've taken! She became a globe-trotting photojournalist, married and had a son. She does corporate photography but also works as an artist. We talk about kids and making art, as if resuming an old friendship— one we never had. I don't miss the irony.

"Hey," she says. "This gallery—Diverse Works—they invited me to put my photographs in a show."

"Wow," I say. But I pull back a bit. I'm shy, a little jealous.

"It's a big deal," she says. "I'll have two walls to fill." She leans forward. "I read 'Munya's Story,'" she says. "You know, I always thought *mikvah* laws were outdated and misogynistic. I never imagined someone might use a *mikvah* their own way—outside Jewish Law, like that woman in your story."

"What are you saying?"

"I want to take pictures in the *mikvah*."

"What?" I say. "But that's so private. No one's gonna let—"

"I don't want to intrude on anyone. I'll bring models and have them simulate the process."

Models. Nude models. In the *mikvah*. "But why?" I say.

She grows quiet. "Taking pictures. That's how I understand, and I want to understand."

"But you'll get your camera wet!" I say.

"Very wet," she says, smiling. "Particularly since I'll be sitting underwater."

"Now, what self-respecting rabbi is gonna let you take nude photos in his *mikvah*?" I say. We both laugh. Then in my mind I'm back in the *mikvah*, eyes open to slits in that liminal blue space—floating limbs and hair, bubbles, the sound of heartbeat. "First," I tell Janice, "you have to go to the *mikvah* yourself. You have to know what it is."

"I'd like that."

Then we're brainstorming, animated, excited.

"Can you help?" she says.

I wonder. We could remind the rabbi that beautiful *mikvah* photos could help give *mikvah* a good name in the world. They're always looking for new tools for outreach. Janice would have to be careful with the nudity. "I might still have some credibility," I say. "I'll put on the wig and introduce you to Rabbi Frumen."

All the way home, I am alive, thinking, *girlfriends let you try out your wildest ideas.* I don't know about the great women who changed the world only after getting strength from honest friendships with other women—I don't have such friends. I don't imagine this chance to work with Janice might hint that I can also create my own life. I just know that somehow it all comes together on this drive home. I lower the windows and turn on country-and-western crooning, loud. I decide I *can* talk to Levi, really talk to him. *I will make him change!* I'll tell him what I need. I'll open my mouth! I'll get him to hold me, every day, and help at last with the house and children. *He has to change*, because I *can't*. He has to help me hold it together, because I'm slipping. But he'll do that. I just have to tell him. He'll do that for me. For us.

I get home and head to the back room, where I find Levi on his way out. I block the doorway, startling him with "Stay a minute. We have to talk." And then, the two of us between the desk where I work at night and the two separate beds, my eager oblivious chatter versus his awkward impatience, I pour out years of buildup in a single breath. "I'm unhappy angry alone you have to change hold me help with the house and the children show them tenderness don't make them afraid of you tell me you love me do your part come home early call every day where have you been." On and on, pent-up years, a river of words.

His eyes, they settle somewhere over my head. He frowns, looks distracted. He puts his hand on the side of his neck.

"You're not *listening*," I say. "This is important. This is crucial. This is our marriage."

"Leah," he says.

"I've been wanting to tell you for years I don't know why I haven't, something about us, about me, I don't know why I couldn't, but this is important I know I've been impatient with you, but you have to change I'll work with you this is crucial."

"Leah," he says. "Stop."

He turns and goes into the bathroom, and I follow him, annoyed, to find him peering at his neck in the mirror over the sink. "*Don't stonewall me*," I say, with growing dismay. I have a frustrating momentary realization that a person doesn't change in a minute. "Please!" I say, and then, "What *is* that on your neck? A zit? Is it more important than our *life?*"

He won't meet my eyes, stays focused on the mirror. "It's a lump," he says. "It's twice as big as yesterday." Then he does look at me, an embarrassed, scared, helpless look.

Everything stops. I can hear air in my ears. Air conditioner hum. His fear. I reach out to touch his arm. But I haven't been to the *mikvah* yet, and so he steps back like a reflex, forever linking this searing flash of guilt because of my forbidden, pitying touch with this first moment of discovery. "What's your gut?" I whisper.

He says, "I think this could kill me."

Twenty

At first, I feel freed. The *yene machla*, "that disease" in Yiddish, the one fearful Hasidim won't grace with a name because a name is power—doctors speak it out loud right in our faces, and I feel freed. I can say the forbidden word. I want to march up and down in front of the synagogue and yell it out. *Cancer cancer cancer cancer cancer cancer cancer.* No more unknown, no more unseen enemy. I see you, cancer. I know where you are and what you're doing and where you're going and how we're going to get you. I know your *name*. It's two against one here, cancer. We're gonna fight this together, Levi and I. We will. You'll see.

The nodes in Levi's neck pulsate like saber rattling. Minutes after that frightened look, I called our ENT and insisted he get us in, and he saw us on his lunch hour. Levi had a biopsy the day after and within the week began treatment for lymphoma at Houston's MD Anderson hospital. The cancer has spread. There's no telling how long our enemy has been lurking, scheming.

I forget my confrontation with Levi. I forget our sterile life, the loneliness and anger I sleep with alone in my bed. I forget the L word, forget that life happens in three dimensions, forget school and everything I've been learning, forget everything except that I don't want him to die. Faith, no faith, nothing matters, except that now we have this terrible job and our lives are intertwined and I think this must be what love is.

The cancer forces me to imagine life without him, ironic

luxury, and I'm afraid that I may really have to do it. Our new enemy lurks in the shadows. *I have ignored you, Levi, sole support for the nine of us, and what will I do if you die?* I don't know this country, don't know how to work, what to work at. I'll be thrust with the kids out into the world, naked and alone. I crouch down, flinch at peripheral motion. *We will pull this foe out into the light together, Levi, front and center. Gather weapons. Steady now. March.*

Non-Hodgkin's lymphoma, aggressive type, mixed cell, follicular. Stage Three. Levi has had pain in his throat and his eye for two months. Is it in his brain?

We gather the children who are at home and sit them around the dining room table, the Sabbath place. What would this table be without him at the head? Levi tells them, Leibl, Avrami, Sarah, Itzik, and Yossi, that he has cancer. He tells them that he doesn't know if he is going to live or die and doesn't make promises. He answers their shocked questions. He is patient and kind. Then he calls Libby and Mendel, both away at school, and talks them through with wise and tender guidance. I watch that and wonder where that wise and tender father has been all these years. But it doesn't matter now. They cling to him, hang on his words.

I am Mother, and I can't protect my children. Your father could die.

We tell our family and friends. People, including doctors, wave numbers at us. "Oh," they say, "lymphoma. Highly curable. Eighty percent survive!" Only *lymphoma?* Well, my aunt Sophie had it twenty-three years ago!

Meanwhile, on his first day of treatment, Levi tries not to scream when a technician shoves a tube through his hip into his bone and then deeper still to suck out marrow. "So sorry, Mr. Lax. Local anesthesia just won't do much that deep in." I stand by and look in his eyes, this man whom, right now, I love, who is my husband, whom I can't desire but seem to need.

"I imagine the pain becomes relative in time," he says.

This is Levi. He endures. I see now that cancer will strengthen his faith. He prays.

At home, I pick up my book of poetry by Robert Lowell and find this: "Hope lives in doubt. Faith is trying to do without faith."

But I need to pray.

Lowell, raised in the church, lost his faith and expressed his grief "over hymns that sing of peace and preach despair."

I hear hymns in that two-toned way now, too. But I still need to pray.

Lowell was also "drawn back to the hymns . . . because of the way they gave darkness some control," the way they offered "a loophole for the soul."

"Listen to the bells!" he wrote, meaning church bells that draw in the faithful. I think, regardless of faith, or lack of it, I can't help but hear the bells.

The God that I want to defy is the same God I still think has control. How hypocritical, how farcical, how typical I am: the Jew who shakes her fist at God yet never doubts that Presence, who ascribes to God control so great that nothing is left but to confront how small our efforts and how mad our superstitions.

But I have lived too long in Orthodox religion, in Lowell's sanity of self-deception; I can't imagine that our God might be just one concept among many. Besides, I don't know how to just sit in a terrible moment and accept it. I can't give up at least the possibility that if I hope hard enough, my hopes will come true. But I also can't mouth rote prayer words like Levi does anymore, can't believe that simply reciting words can change terrible facts.

And yet I'm still drawn to the bells. One bell is Levi. He is part of what has kept me holding on. Cancer forces me to reconsider my religion and marriage—they are one—before I leave them, even though, as Lowell writes, "it will bring no true tenderness, only restlessness."

The familiar cadence and poetry of the Hebrew prayer book

tug at me. The blissful and then yearning tone. I cry over the words. But it doesn't help. I stand apart.

The need to pray remains through those first days, through long hours sitting around the cancer hospital, surrounded by thousands with the same disease, through the first rounds of chemo and Levi's retching. It stays until I go to the *mikvah* and stand in the water, defenseless.

In the water, there is nothing left but tiled walls, echoed drips, blurred image of my own limbs. There will be no sex after this, no hope of it, either. There's no desire left in me, in either of us, but here I am. Wet, naked, I am filled with the need to confront an unfathomable will.

I need to pray. I need words that make the immeasurable finite, that chip the overwhelming down to size, words to lift me from anguish. It doesn't matter that my need for connection with the forces buffeting my life is no proof of God or of the efficacy of prayer, or that my need proves me only a miserable, wet, naked human being who can't accept circumstances out of her control. None of that matters. It doesn't matter that I no longer believe in prayer. I need to pray, because I am weak. Because I am alive. I immerse and succumb.

I AM MOTHER. I will keep everyone safe. I will keep everything the same. Same is safe. I get to the grocery store at seven in the morning, thanking God for twenty-four-hour grocery stores, and charge through the aisles until I fill three carts—we will be at the hospital and away from home a great deal, and I must make sure everyone will be okay. I wave the shopping list as I go, the one Leibl and Avrami made last night. We will make it through this together. The bill is over $400. "Next time," the manager says, "just call and we'll deliver. No charge."

I rush home and Avrami meets me outside, unloads, and

starts putting things away. If I wind up and whirl fast enough, the pain will fly away. Sarah is ready for school, but the two younger ones are dawdling, no shoes, no food, so I get them moving, make lunches, set out breakfast, but we get three different calls from doctors' offices. Levi leaves for the hospital without me. I have to run carpool, and Itzik still won't get his shoes on, and I'm late for Levi's catheterization at the hospital and a class about catheter care that I'm obligated to take twice if I'm to care for him. I care for him.

I arrive at the hospital to find a technician struggling to thread a line below Levi's clavicle into a vein that makes a straight, short path to his heart. Wondrous, I think, to find that path. The man has to bypass an artery without puncturing it, no leaking or kinking. He's calm and confident and well scrubbed, but he's having trouble. He wiggles and pulls. Levi goes white.

Afterward, Levi heads off to another clinic in the hospital and I settle into a big, soft chair in the lounge. I put my head back against the cushion. Shoulders fall. I let out the breath I've held since early morning. Then I check my phone. Janice has called, but I blink away her truthful face, our coffee conversation, my new conviction. There's room only for Levi. I don't call her back.

Instead I lift my tote bag and pull out a play that just won a Pulitzer, W;t, about an English professor dying of cancer. She spent her life building a wall of complex ideas around her, engaged in analyses of John Donne's convoluted sonnet musings about death and an afterlife. But her cancer makes the physical, the now, overwhelmingly real, and only now does she realize how the mundane simplicity she has always disdained—and is about to lose—is real life. Only now does she realize that she never lived.

My throat tightens. What would life have been without all my escaping into philosophy and prayer? It seems the words I wove for years in my head, and those religious ideas to which I still cling, have been barriers to living.

I put the play down, but its sadness stays in my throat. I launch myself out of the chair and head off to the infusion lab to pick up Levi's chest X-rays before I meet him at our appointment with the doctor. At the reception desk, an older man steps right in front of me, but he just wants to say hello to the clerk. She's a tall black woman with a Louisiana accent and a motherly bust. She sees him, jumps up, comes out from behind the desk, and wraps her arms around him, her eyes shut, forehead creased. I can't bear this. Then she takes her leave, sits back down, and looks at me with an expression that says, *Next?* I almost can't choke out my request. Quivering lips, eyes filling, fighting it, I say, "Levi Lax's X-rays, please?"

She takes his patient number, scrolls down a screen.

"That man," I add. "He . . . must've survived something big."

She looks up. "The doctors gave him a coupla weeks, and it's been nine years," she says, and that finishes me. I have to turn my face away, and then she is up and I'm gathered into that same embrace. "God is good," she says. "God is sooo good. All love. You'll see."

But I don't believe that anymore. Her words hit a wall and don't go in. But somehow, standing there smothered in the motherly arms of a stranger, I have never loved Levi more.

Daily home care for a subclavicle catheter: Remove the dressing and wipe with alcohol, then betadine. Discard the gloves and put on a clean pair. Apply new gauze and tape. Flush the line with saline. Clear air bubbles from the tubing. Flush again with heparin to dissolve blood clots that can stop the line. Don't forget to swab the cap! And don't touch the open catheter—a single germ or single air bubble in the line will go straight into his heart —a painful way to die. Connect the chemo pump. Don't forget to unclamp. And stay attentive! If you stayed up until four in the morning pouring your gibberish into the keyboard, you can make mistakes. Crucial mistakes.

There will be weekly blood tests through nine months of chemo. Responsibilities related to general vigilance: Hover together over results. Watch his white cell count shrink until he is like a bubble boy left outside his tent, until you think the world will kill him before cancer does. Don't even blink at the impassive doctor who casually states that this is no typical lymphoma. Just wonder why it isn't going away as more and more poison flows into him. And why does the catheter itch? Better get it checked for infection. When he runs a fever, go straight to spend a day in the emergency room. And another. Watch that chemo pump, make sure the orange liquid keeps moving, make sure he keeps a spare battery with him. Why isn't the cancer responding? Live, dammit!

Food he can handle: Oatmeal. Protein powder. Smoothies. Eggs! Eggs taste almost normal to him. Nothing with tomato paste, or he'll taste bitter metal for days.

Watch his skin go yellow as dead blood cells pile up. There's an open line to his heart hanging in the air, and behind it thinned blood with defenses down. I dream of that single rogue microbe that can kill him.

The weight drops fast. Twenty pounds already gone. But he is a cancer patient, they shrink before they fade. The last step is transparency. I grab at Levi's image in the air, and my hand passes through it. Try two hands. "Eat!" I say. To keep you opaque.

And what to do about well-wishers? Friends at the synagogue who hand him death with their unwashed hands while they hug him, touch him, bless him with long life. Follow him to the synagogue, scowl at people who offer their hands. Why does he shake them? Stay away! Dishes sent to our home from dozens of different hands. Levi eats and gets sick. Fever, and back to the hospital. And the kids: No, if someone is sick in your friend's house, you can't go over there. You can hug your father if you wash your hands first, but no kissing.

Keep that bucket nearby for vomit. Demand wellness. Demand he lives. Keep him vertical, moving, out there. At night, listen to his breathing.

Is anyone the same person after cancer? A new hope wells up, that he will change. Oh, I hope this will change him, soften him, bring him to me, so that maybe I can stay. He has to change, because I can't be any more of what I'm not, can't play along or shape myself to him. My poor children; once he's well, it will take his changing to keep me.

But if he dies, will I?

Even while I work to keep him safe, a tiny, budding part of me whispers, *He can die, you must know this, he can die, you may want this, he can die,* and then, and then . . . *You can do this.*

Then I know. I can. I can manage. When it's all done, when he's well again, I can find my own real life. I will live.

MY MOTHER CALLS. By now, her paintings have been seen in Paris, Beijing, Moscow, Washington. "Lisa!" she says.

"Mom!"

"I called to tell you to stay in school."

I've thrown everything into the ring to fight Levi's cancer, and she says stay in school. Still with her impractical demands. "I can't stay in school," I say.

"Just one course," she says. "Hold on to something."

And I do. It helps that the hospital is near the university, so I can go straight to the infusion clinic from class. I enroll in one more fiction seminar with Daniel Stern and write fast, raw, angry stories late at night. One is about a woman stuck for years with an inaccessible yet loyal husband. When she gets cancer, it is like a revelation and she leaves him. Cancer frees her. She even leaves her son, who comes to find her when he is nearly grown. The story ends with her holding her big son in her arms as if he's a child.

As usual, we are to write up formal critiques of one another's work. One day Keith hands my story back across the conference table with his typed comments and says, "Leah, I don't know what's going on with you, but keep it up."

Janice leaves a message. She has found someone to model and wants to start taking photographs. Can she start in our *mikvah*? Have I spoken with Rabbi Frumen?

A MONTH INTO THE CHEMO, three days after the second infusion, Levi steps out of the shower one morning with a naked face, a dead clump of black wiry hair left behind over the drain. "Leah," he calls from the bathroom, still nude. I come in, stop short, and stare. He's become curiously immodest. And there's a dimple in his chin, like Itzik's. "Well," I say, "we knew this was coming. . . ."

But this is his beard. His uniform. For God. "You okay?" I say.

Levi shrugs.

"But what about all those months you searched for a job years ago?" I say. Levi is our soldier. "What about the interviews that ended over the beard, and the proud way you still tell those stories?"

"It's only hair," Levi says.

"And my wig is only hair," I tell him.

And his black and white clothes, my modest swaths, his yarmulka and *tzitzis* strings are only cloth. Our kosher food—its preparation governed by huge volumes of rules aimed at higher and higher levels of "holiness"—is only food. "Cancer changes everything," I say.

Symbols become just things. The beard is no longer something to sacrifice for. When life is at stake, it's only hair.

"A small price to pay," Levi says, and smiles. "Look!" he says later to the children. "Tatti really does have a chin!"

But what if, I think, as the children gape, what if even when our lives are not cancer lives, what if then hair and clothes and food were only hair and clothes and food, and not binding symbols of connection to God, and not the outlines of boxes we put ourselves in?

CYCLOPHOSPHAMIDE, doxorubicin, vincristine, prednisone. The chemicals burn Levi's intestines and line his mouth, esophagus, and stomach with bleeding sores. They thin his skin, make him depressed, kill blood cells, strain kidneys and liver. He prays. But as he turns into a bald, gaunt alien, Levi also goes back to being a stranger in our home. The spate of warmth is gone. He withdraws, ever more driven to keep up at work in spite of the leave they have offered. Sometimes he is a wild man who cries, who yells and blames the children for his cancer or blows up over nothing. Then he prays, turning back to God but never to my offers of comfort.

Itzik hates him for this. I tell him and all the children that anyone filled with poison and fighting for his life has the right to yell or cry or be completely illogical, but Itzik is angry. I watch Itzik's undiluted response, my own efforts to care for Levi now more often than not rebuffed, and more and more the teary cancer-driven nostalgia fades.

One day at the hospital between appointments, Levi and I are eating our sack lunches in the "park," a huge lower-lobby food court stretched around tall trees planted in an indoor plot under a skylight. Except that Levi doesn't want to eat. He reads psalms while I nibble a sandwich. But through all the cancer rush, something has stayed on my mind.

"Levi," I say, "I gave you one of my stories, but you never read it." I gave it to him shyly, after his diagnosis, as if to say, *This is me. Hello. If I'm to care for you through this, I want you to know who I am.*

"I didn't have time," he says.

"Time?" I say. "That was important to me."

He looks up then and does that wave of the hand. "I made a commitment not to read secular literature a long time ago," he says.

And finally, I get it. I get it that Levi long ago put himself behind an unmoving wall so huge and ancient and deeply rooted that I will never move it. I get it that his connection to God and religion will always take precedence. I get it that anyone who cares about him has to face that wave of his hand. And I finally stop. I stop hoping he'll change.

"I see," I say.

AVRAMI, BACK AT YESHIVA NOW, is called into his principal's office. "Close the door," the rabbi says. Avrami does so and sits down, a little nervous. "What's going on with you?" the rabbi says. "You've been late to class a lot. You missed a test."

Avrami makes his face a hard mask. He looks down at his shoes.

"And what is this?" the rabbi says. He holds up a written test with the number 38 scrawled in red across the top.

Avrami studies his shoe. He drags the toe in a small arc on the floor.

"I know your father's sick," the rabbi says.

And Avrami breaks down. Great gulps of tears. When I hear about this from the rabbi later, I will think about when Avrami was last home, now three months ago, at the outset of Levi's illness, how he emptied groceries, got his brothers ready for school, finding something valuable and tangible he could do in the face of cancer. Then Levi told him to go back to yeshiva and learn Torah to gain God's grace for his father. Levi told him to pray. But at yeshiva, Avrami's hands are empty. He looks at them, through his tears. He's fifteen. He doesn't know how to rescue his father with prayer and study. He knows only how to unload groceries and help with dinner. I imagine him embarrassed at his crying, feeling exposed before his rabbi. Afterward, he doesn't want his friends to know.

We put this burden of holiness and thus helplessness on his shoulders. I call Avrami and we talk a long time. But I wonder, what good is a telephone call when I can't touch his sweet face just sprouting the beginnings of his first, soft beard?

MARCH. Old, sick Pope John Paul II is wheeled into St. Peter's, where he struggles out of his wheelchair and kneels down in front of Michelangelo's *Pietà*—the beautiful son of God, stricken down in his prime and laid lifeless across his gentle, ageless mother's tender arms in her grief. Later, from the altar, the pope begs God's forgiveness in a trembling voice for sins the church has committed over centuries, against women, against native peoples, against Jews.

The news filters through our community, where people still blame the Catholic church for the Crusaders pillaging Jewish villages, for blood libels, for centuries of pogroms on Jewish towns, locking Jews into ghettos, for rapes, murders, extortions, communities banished overnight, centuries of poverty and anti-Semitic policies, and Nazi collaboration. People laugh. "Oops," Levi says, pretending to be the pope. "We made a little mistake."

WE HAVE A NEW KIND of Sabbath in our house, a cancer Sabbath. On a normal Sabbath, the Law doesn't allow us to use hot water and soap, so we bathe Friday just before the Sabbath begins. But now, before the kids help to cut up salad, set the table, carry in platters of food, I line them up in the kitchen and direct them to scrub to the elbows with hot water and plenty of suds in spite of the Sabbath Law, to protect their father. But really, the Law requires these concessions when health is at stake. Levi and I also wash our hands. I wash out of medical necesslty, free for now of at least one of the strictures. Levi washes his hands with the same religious zeal with which he prays. He washes his hands not out of medical necessity, but because the Law in its wisdom requires him to do so under these circumstances. If the Law didn't state that he has to follow doctor's orders above religious rules, Levi would not be scrubbing his hands on the Sabbath, no matter what his white blood cell count is, and he would be certain that God would protect him because he would be honoring the Sabbath with his unwashed hands. I understand that. We all do. I wash my hands for germs. Levi washes his for God.

I DECIDE I HAVE TO go visit my mother. I don't know why, don't understand that cancer makes me somehow need to go back and finally look unflinching into her mother mirror, just as I don't know why, in the midst of our nightmare, memories of Lisa and her hopes and dreams are plaguing me. I just know I'm going and that it seems necessary. The visit will be of little consequence, other than to make it clear that she is aging and so I'll never really find the mother of my childhood fantasies. The kids are spending the night with friends. Levi has been getting himself to the hospital and has taken over his own catheter care, handles his own meds and the chemo pump that hangs like a pocketbook from his shoulder. I can go.

As I head north toward Dallas on I-45, the sky is a vast blueness, the wide-open highway a ribbon cutting across the enormous flat middle of this state. I sail past fields of oats, sorghum, corn, herds of cattle that slowly pick up their heads to watch with liquid brown eyes, past widely separated exits for towns with names like Flatonia and Waxahachie. It is December, and that means warm sunshine with cool wind, the sky and again the sky, so inland blue it is almost painful to look at.

As I drive, topping eighty, the scarf starts to slip off my head. I let it go like a discarded fig leaf. No one will see. Only God.

Then I'm mad. I think, *My God doesn't chastise. My God's silence is a tacit embrace.*

But really, the fallen scarf is my gauntlet—with it, I'm challenging the God of the Law, insisting He change. It's a kind of *take me as I am*, but not one of submission.

An hour into the drive, I need a cold drink and a bathroom. There's a filling station up ahead set up in an old house with a convenience store in it, so I exit and pull in, observing its peeling paint, its cracked, oil-stained concrete. I stop beside a beat-up, mud-spattered old pickup with a man beside it. He's leaning back against the truck with one foot anchored behind him on the running board, in worn jeans and a plaid flannel shirt and old boots with mud on them, his face leathery and lined. He's smoking a cigarette pinched between thumb and forefinger, squinting his eyes at that sky.

I sit there bareheaded in my parked car next to the pickup. As I touch the door handle to get out, a moment of programmed Hasidic panic hits hard because of the man and my uncovered head, my nakedness before a man. I pause, breathe, grit my teeth, and tell myself, *Yes, I am really going to do this.* Then I open the door, stand up in the Texas sun, and step out in front of an actual man with my head uncovered. I stand and turn, resolute, take another breath, a step, another. Then I stop short because I have a sudden enormous urge to stride over, reach up, grab that tall old cowboy by his frayed flannel collar, and say, *Do you know you're the first man besides my husband to see my hair in twenty-five years?* Instead, I take in his sun-browned face and burst out laughing.

How good is this? I think. It's not that no one of consequence out here will see my bare head. It's that no one cares. I continue walking, shaking my head and laughing at myself. I'm still chuckling as I pass him, as he blows out his cigarette smoke in a tight stream. Those squinting Texas eyes follow me. Weird city girl.

RATHER THAN MEETING face-to-face back during those first cancer weeks, I called Rabbi Frumen and recommended Janice to him over the phone. I emphasized that her work would be beautiful and thus make *mikvah* look beautiful and perhaps inspire someone to want to perform the ritual. I guess I still had some influence, because he agreed to talk with her. When Janice went to meet him, he made her promise that the images would be modest, no frontal nudity, and preferably shown only to women, but he allowed her to do the work at our *mikvah*.

A few weeks after I return from Dallas, I visit with Janice in her home—a short, precious chance to unburden and to listen— and the new photographs astonish me. Blue-toned underwater nudes caught from the back or in modest profile, arms obscuring breasts, watery outlines of hip and thigh. Each floats without weight in unconscious sexuality, unaware of her beauty, focused inward and not on enticing some object of desire. Transcendent nudes, as if the spiritual is most present when these women are in their most physical state. Janice understands. She gets it.

When the show opens the following month during Houston's biannual Fotofest, the gallery fills with women in black and dangling diamonds balancing drinks and men in perfectly cut suits who hover over wives and dates. Critics move in close to examine the images, wander away, then return for more. The *Houston Chronicle* compares the work to that of André Kertész and exclaims, "This show is not to be missed." And in the midst of that bustling, thrilling crowd, Janice holds court before her artist's statement on the wall as several perfectly coiffed women whisper to her, *I could tell you about my* mikvah *experience.*

"It's like they had a secret," she tells me later.

"That's been built-in for centuries," I say. "Jewish women have never talked about *mikvah*."

"Let's get them to talk," she says.

"What?"

"You know women we can interview, right? And you're a writer. Work with me. Expand the exhibit. Let's interview women, and I'll take their portraits."

"It's too private."

"We'll keep it anonymous."

"And they'll never let you show their faces."

"Who said I'll show their faces?"

Twenty-One

ithin days I'm sitting with a voice recorder and a seventeen-year-old Hasidic girl about to be married.

After Janice proposed *The Mikvah Project* that day, we had a flurry of phone calls between us, thrilling late-night creative sessions in which we bounced ideas and images and plans off each other. I cautioned her that I would participate only when I could, but I came alive with tingling excitement as we finished each other's sentences, ideas tumbling out like puppies. I think perhaps doing this work, as long as I am judicious about it, could help me through this cancer time.

It's crazy, I know: Levi sick, the house, kids, no sleep ever, and here I've agreed to interview and help Janice photograph women talking about *mikvah*. It's crazy that at a time like this I would unhook myself even one step from all that to undertake something that has nothing to do with them, or me. But Janice and I are going to get silent women to *talk* about this most hidden and central of rituals. No party lines—*I'll get them to be real.*

The girl before me is just a girl smitten with her fiancé, whom she can admire only from a distance. She calls me Morah Leah, Teacher Leah. I promise not to reveal her name.

She begins to talk with shining optimism about the great spiritual experience she expects to have in the *mikvah* the night before her wedding. She closes her eyes as she imagines the mystical light that will descend on her along with God's unending love, both of which she will pass on to her children. As she has been taught almost since birth, she believes her wedding will introduce her to her role as a mother. She feels that in bearing Jewish children, she will experience the fulfillment of every moment she has lived until now.

Janice photographs the girl at her wedding ten days later, the first of a series of anonymous portraits, the bride's face hidden behind an opaque Hasidic veil. She's sitting in a white wicker chair, and her groom has just lowered the veil after first looking into the face of his beloved. She clutches a tiny photograph of the Rebbe in her hand.

A month later, I return to continue the girl's interview. Her posture has opened; her manner is more frank, her clothing more elegant and mature, including a new, long wig made of human hair. I think, *She's become a woman.* "Now tell me," I say, remembering her starry description before the wedding. "What was *mikvah* really like?"

She cried through the whole *mikvah* ritual that night and didn't know why she was crying. "Now I realize I don't even know what 'spiritual' means," she says. "I didn't understand what was coming, but I had an overwhelming sense that I was going in that water a girl and coming out a woman." She speaks tenderly about her husband. She says she is delighted at how the Law upholds their desire, celebrates and escorts it through *mikvah.*

I hear and remember our wedding, mine and Levi's. I remember trying to coach myself into desire. But for this girl, instead of teaching herself *to* want him, desire rose up and taught her something about who she is. *It wasn't in me.*

Janice meets someone while on a trip to Denver whom she'd like me to interview, and I conduct the interview over the phone. The woman says she's a lesbian but when she came out to her parents, they rejected her, their only child. Brokenhearted, she reached to religion and ritual for solace and so she went to a *mikvah.* She planned the visit, went there "with spiritual hunger and a script." But it was the unscripted part that changed her. Underwater in that ancient chamber, she realized "there were larger things working my life." Then, in the dressing area, she saw herself wet and naked in a full-length mirror and had to confront the irrefutable fact of her being.

I didn't plan for these interviews to push me like this. They leave me pensive, questioning myself; the bride and the lesbian are my full-length mirrors. I stiffen myself to stay in my roles; Mother must remain Mother, Cancer Wife the same. And always there's the work—details, lists, minor upsets to soothe and straighten, meals to cook.

Within days of this interview, I am in pain, full-body ache, every joint, as if I'm dying inside and birthing myself all at once. I crawl through my days. I am tortured with the sense that I don't belong anywhere, not at home or school, not to myself or to my children, not anymore, and I can't protect my children from my perfidy. When I manage to sleep, I wake in the dark in a sweat to find myself sitting up in terror.

One morning well into the chemo, I find Levi already dressed but facedown on the bed, forehead on his bent arm, waiting for the strength to sit up and put on his shoes. Finally, he sits up on the edge of his bed and carefully puts on the right shoe first, in the same manner in which he has always donned each item of clothing—the right side first, as the right signifies God's power and holy Law, and then the left, the weaker side, symbol of God's mercy. This is an acknowledgement that God's justice precedes His mercy. Then Levi ties the left shoe first in a mute prayer to arouse God's mercy and let it prevail over the strict judgment we all so deserve.

With cancer, for Levi, even putting on shoes is a prayer for survival.

⁓

JANICE SENDS ME TO A MASSEUSE, her friend Kelly, a deep-voiced lesbian jazz singer with great hands. When I finally find her office in the unfamiliar Montrose area, I am directed by a receptionist and stumble into a room with walls painted deep green, the air candle-scented with herbs. I peel off long layers of clothes and crawl between black starched sheets to music and the rhythmic sound of waves hitting the shore. In the dim room, Kelly slowly plies my muscles with warm, oiled hands. Gradually, fatigue overtakes me. I wash in and out of a half-conscious state to the sound of waves. But this is the first time I have ever felt a woman's hands on my body. I think, *How profound, this, this touch.*

Then, as if locked doors are being opened, there is an immense surge of warmth. Relief. And I am tumbling, waves crashing overhead. Sobs rise on their own from the ocean floor.

I lie there facedown, heaving shoulders, tears dripping through to the floor. Kelly doesn't try to talk to me, just works on through the hour, sometimes emitting a low crooning sound. When she is done, she leaves me, still emptying myself. I fall asleep in that room, finally, deeply asleep, on the narrow table in the dark green room between black starched sheets with a flickering candle, and the recorded sound of waves around me.

JANICE WANTS AN INTERVIEW with a Hasidic woman willing to talk about wearing a wig, so I call Dinah, a woman of our group who keeps her expensive wig beautifully styled and luxuriant. I wear my own wig to the interview to make her comfortable in our solidarity.

I remember when Dinah was still new among us. I remember taking her to the *mikvah* and how she folded her long body in the shimmering water and reminded me of paintings by Delacroix and Ingres. I know about Dinah's life *before*, she used to talk to me about it, and that pre-Hasidic life wasn't always pretty. But when I turn on the recorder, Dinah launches into a sanitized story that is all polemic, no difficulties, no struggles, every event in her past aiming her straight toward her Purpose in God, culminating in purification in a *mikvah*. Then she depicts the Hasidic community as a perfect, collective Godly embrace.

I am appalled, both because she knows that I know her real story and because I *can hear* how she's lying to herself. Janice glances at me with an odd smile, then says to her (is she goading me?), "Tell me about putting on a wig."

"Well, now," Dinah says. "Even Rabbi Frumen trusts me now that I wear it. He lets his own kids eat my food, trusts how kosher it is, even though my kitchen is exactly the same as before I put on the wig. Mrs. Frumen even calls me for advice! And now my kids are proud that their mom looks like the other moms, and they don't get embarrassed." I think, *Her reply was all about conforming and gaining status,* and she is smug and satisfied. She didn't say a thing about modesty before God, or about the wig as a symbol of identity. She didn't indicate that putting it on was an act of faith or because it is a commandment of God.

She will find excellent spouses for the children of this beautiful wig.

Why does this interview make me so angry? But it's as if I'm looking in a mirror and seeing hypocrisy. *I'm not Dinah,* I try to tell myself, but I can't stand it. I can't stay. I get up abruptly, apologizing, I simply have to get out of there, and I go, convinced that beautiful Dinah has swallowed herself and that I have just seen for the first time what she's done. I leave Janice behind to take the photos on her own. In my car on Dinah's driveway, I hit the wheel and shout a defiant "No!" at God, *You cannot ask this of us,* and at myself. *What have I done?* I stomp the accelerator and lurch out of the driveway, head home doing fifty on a residential street, shouting "No!" all the way. I roar into our driveway, jump out of the car, and slam the door, starting to cry, picturing that smug satisfaction as Dinah made herself disappear. Still sobbing, I march into the empty house and slam that door, too. The windows rattle.

I stop short at the head of the hallway and rip the wig off my head. Then I pitch that wig down the long hall like a bowling ball and watch it roll.

Cool air hits my scalp like morning rain. The wig careens in a floppy zigzag and lands upside down at the end of the hall a discarded rag. I stumble after it, kick it aside as I pass. *But I am not Dinah.* Once, my wig was my symbol of identity. Once, I put it on out of real desire for God. *The wig didn't erase me then—it meant something. Something real.* But it's no use. In our wigs, Dinah and I are identical members of the same faceless ranks. Besides, I didn't know what I was giving up then, but now I do. *There is only one way not to be her.*

It takes until the end of the day before I can even lift the thing from where it lies flaccid and abandoned on the floor. I pick it up with two fingers, grimace, and give a halfhearted swipe at the dust it collected in the long tumble. *All those years of devotion. What is left?*

ACROSS TOWN ON MY way to class the day after the wig incident, I pull into a huge, empty parking lot in front of a boarded-up furniture store and pull out a new pair of jeans and a short-sleeved shirt. I wiggle into the clothes inside the car, then open the door and stand to pull off the skirt. I open the shirt wide at the collar. Back in the car, I brush out my hair in the rearview mirror. It's grown long again.

At school, the difference in how I'm received in my new clothes and natural hair is obvious that first day and grows from there. Students include me in conversation, lean back and laugh. I come to love anonymity, love the way no one can assume my beliefs just by looking at me. In clothing that is not a uniform, I'm just a person, not a label. I don't wear a label. I find anonymity is like an invitation: *if you want to know what I believe, come up and ask.* Another defiant act: I send "Berkeh's Story," about the gay yeshiva boy in love with his study partner, to a national short-story contest.

WE DO MORE INTERVIEWS, and Janice makes more faceless portraits. "*Mikvah* means monogamy," the next woman I interview says. "It says that sex is holy and private. Growing up in the sixties, I didn't know anyone who believed that."

"Sure," I tell Janice later. "The Law insists on holiness and privacy, but it also insists there's only one kind of sex and tells you when you can and when you can't. The Law puts sex and sexuality into a box, just like it does the rest of our life. A box within a box. Try to get out," I say, "and you'll hurt everyone who was in there with you."

LEVI REMAINS WITHDRAWN and in his books, prone to emotional outbursts, and still insists on managing his own care. I expand the project with Janice. Unable to do anything for him, unwilling just to watch, I make plans to travel with Janice. To widen the demographics of our subject pool, I network by phone, looking for subjects around the country. It seems secular women all over are beginning to reclaim *mikvah* and use it in new ways, like the lesbian Janice met in Denver. Maybe other, more traditional women have negotiated their peace with the intrusive *mikvah* laws, even allowed themselves to compromise. I want or need to hear about that. Some may voice their objections about *mikvah* to me, and that alone has enormous appeal. No longer afraid, no longer clinging to a singular Hasidic point of view, I use this opportunity to get away and really listen to other voices. Through it all is this drive to give the silenced women their voice.

We go to New York. Chana is thirtysomething, Orthodox, with five children. She meets me in a kosher restaurant in Manhattan and gives only this first name I suspect is an alias, drove in from an outlying town she doesn't identify.

In general, Orthodox and Hasidic styles are changing. The women are going superelegant, wearing long human-hair wigs, expensive clothes, heels, and nail polish, even to the grocery store. Hemlines have gone up to the bare minimum allowed in the Law. But Chana's clothes are long and wrinkled, her wig dull. She has a rounded posture and a tired face.

Then, as soon as I turn on the recorder, she talks about her first crushes when she was a teen. She recounts them in detail. They were all crushes on girls.

Chana says that this is her lot from God—to defy her nature every day. Tucking a stray wisp into her dishwater wig, she says she's worked for years to teach herself how to love her husband and how to let him love her. *Love from an instruction manual.* Then she says, "I've had to make a kind of surgery on myself."

A hot flush near panic rises over me at these terrible words and the image of this woman taking a scalpel to her soul to cut away part of her being, as if I've just witnessed the blade cutting into her. I had thought self-mutilation abhorrent, foreign, but something whispers at me, *I know the life she lives ...* I have to get up, turn away, calm down.

I go to the bathroom. I return after forcing myself back into composure and professional bearing, and we begin again. "Tell me," I say, wanting to change the subject and get to the point, "about going to the *mikvah.*"

She describes her process; I walk her through it. *Mikvah* is very important to her, she tells me, because it helps her to wash away her resistance to God's holy plan of heterosexuality, marriage, and children. This is what she prays in the *mikvah*, every month, to be washed clean of herself. She describes standing in the water, praying, and her last words to me are "And you remove, you remove, you remove."

This is worse than the full-length mirror. Looking at this woman is like looking into two mirrors facing each other, my image repeated in hers into infinity.

THREE MONTHS INTO LEVI'S TREATMENT, he and I go together to a *sheva bruchos*, one of the seven consecutive nights of celebrations in private homes honoring a new bride and groom after their wedding. The event is held in our neighbor's home. We arrive to find the newly married couple together at the head of a long, covered table in the large family room. The bride is fresh-faced and proud in her shining new wig. The groom looks impossibly young in spite of his beard and new black hat. The women sit on one side of the table adjacent to the bride, the men on the other adjacent to the groom. The two look a bit overwhelmed and clearly in love. Twice I catch the young man looking at his wife with a soft smile in his eyes.

The men drink vodka and sing. There are speeches and blessings. The women pass trays of food and visit with one another, listen politely, and jump up and down to help in the kitchen. They pass plates and trays of chicken, kugel, salads and cakes. Someone sets out a tray of shots of sweet liqueur for the women, *veiber mashka*, in place of straight vodka reserved for men.

Ironically, two of the speeches touch on free choice, insisting that we choose freely to live within the Law. It must be that way, they say, so that when you make the *right* choice, God's reward can be greatest. I think, *And how free am I, when speaking my true self will get my family ostracized and hurt my children?*

Levi looks free. He downs a shot of vodka in spite of the chemo. Effusive, pale face and bald head going red, he stands and blesses the young couple with long life in Torah and many children.

A young woman I know who is back in town visiting family gets up to help serve. She brought her roommate along for this visit—I saw the two of them the other day in the grocery store and did a double take. The two young women stood so close, heads inclining toward each other, that no one else could hear their quiet talk. They were holding the same loaf of bread, hands almost touching. Through a lens of stifled desire, I saw intimacy. Shared domesticity. Comfort and love. I knew my view was skewed, and laughed at myself. *But could it be?* I quickly pushed my cart down another aisle.

I tell myself yet again, *They were only buying bread,* but still I watch the girl set her platter down, turn, and go back to the kitchen. My head starts to swim. *Ridiculous,* I think. *I hardly know her.*

I want to be the witch giving her blessing/curse to the new couple at the head of this table of slightly drunk, self-satisfied people. I want to stand, raise a cup like one of the men, and speak out in my audaciously female voice: *Beware the blinding kind of peace and safety religious life offers, because what is that peace and safety if your inevitable striving is never recognized? What kind of life is it if you are constantly told there are no problems that can't be solved by the religion, no questions that can't be answered, when life is growth and growth is struggle? Who are you if nothing inside you that pulls you to the edge of religion's path is ever recognized?*

Contradictions are human—without them, there's no room for you. Torah offers a perfect world, but a perfect world chokes people. Beware this artificial, contrived life!

But then the girl I was watching comes over to me. She has untied her reddish ringlet hair, flashes her toothy smile. The girl is known in the community for her vigorous Torah study. She gives classes and studies with individuals. We've studied together

before, in this community where Torah study is recreation. "Stay
a bit after the others leave, and let's read a Hasidic essay?" she says.
I say sure, why not, as if nothing is stirring in me.

The meal concludes with a group song of thanks ending in
"Blessed is the man who trusts in the Lord, and the Lord will trust
in him." The women chat, clear the table, clean up. People pair
back up and depart. Levi leaves with the boys, assured I won't be
long. I think, *I shouldn't stay.* Then, *But I can if I choose to.* I tell
myself, *Nothing to worry about,* with her bright smile and cascading
hair. *They were only buying bread.*

We settle on a short sofa in the library after the party clears
out. We share the one book, half on my lap, half on hers, four
skirted legs lined up against one another. When she looks down
at the print, her ringlet hair makes a lush, parted curtain around
her face, and when she turns, her breath is a soft whoosh on my
ear. "Since the destruction of the temple," she reads out loud in
Hebrew, "all that God has is the spiritual sanctuary that a man
builds for himself within the Law, through his self-sacrifice."

Since the ancient altar of gold is no more, I am all that God has.

"We are to imagine ourselves as that man," she says. "God
depends on us now, and the place we make for ourselves within
the Law is His sanctuary, replacing the ancient temple where God
once dwelled in the world. Now He dwells in us.

"Do you understand?" the girl says. "I mean, what is self-
sacrifice for the Law, really?" She continues in a quick and
breathless way, as if pelting herself toward an altar of sacrifice.

Her voice is a song in the still air; her leg presses against
mine. The tiny hairs on the back of her wrist . . . Then I'm
swimming in her voice, which, strangely, drowns in its own
sound. She continues reading and talking, unaware, her finger
stroking the page, stroking, the page.

As if dreaming, I lean in and start to cover her hand with
mine.

Stop. The man in the book we share, the Man Within the Law who builds a sanctuary of a life within God's Law, is pointing at me. He is pointing at me, saying, "*You* are all God has."

I am not you, I try to answer him. *I can't give over my heart to God's Law anymore. I can't be the willing sacrifice.*

The girl taps my arm to emphasize a point, then touches my hand for a second with her cool palm. She is devoted, sincere, utterly focused on the text. I close my eyes, trying to think clearly, but sensation engulfs thought. *This is insane.* Words go liquid in my brain. In a waking dream, I am turning back bedcovers to find her waiting for me.

And then, here are the neighbors who own this house, a kind husband and wife looking in on us. I jump up, but surely they can't see my tingling arms, the flush in my face, the way the clock has frozen in place. "Goodness," I say. "I've got to get home." Levi. The kids. It is almost midnight. But this light-headedness makes even the thought of walking difficult.

Outside the bay window, a truck lumbers past, spraying a wide mist of insecticide against Houston mosquitoes. The air is hazy, it will sting eyes and throat, and yet everyone insists on walking me home because it is so late and unsafe in our changing neighborhood. And so we go, a nice processional. I don't quite know my feet as I walk or where this stranger, my body, is taking me with these trembling knees. I make exaggerated polite conversation like a stoned teenager trying to pass. Then, at home in bed in my modest gown, the dark filled with even breath of sleep from one room to the next, I close my eyes in weak surrender to visions spinning off the last hour. The overwhelming orgasm that follows is a scream of release, a bursting out that will remain the most intense in memory. Then I sleep, deep, long, and dreamless.

I wake the next morning, blink, and the day's list jumps into place. Kids to school. Levi's appointment at the hospital. Then I remember last night and fall back into bed. All of my years trying to muster ecstasy for God, and nothing has ever made me feel as alive and genuine as those few moments giving in to spontaneous lust that caught me unawares, like spontaneous combustion. Nothing has ever before shouted out, so utterly convincing, *This is who you are.*

The *l*-word no longer hovers on the periphery, creeping into dreams. It's not academic or up for discussion or in any way a matter of choice or control. My being has loomed up, grabbed me by the shoulders, and shaken hard.

I sing in the kitchen. I sing as I line up lunch bags and zip sandwiches into baggies. Shalom wanders in, still in pajamas, and I wrap him in my arms, dance with him, laugh out loud.

Later, in the car, I roll down all the windows. Everything is a different color than yesterday: the sky more blue, trees more green. In the grocery, a single glance at a woman in halter top and midriff tee over cutoff shorts, and a tingling wave goes through me. I think, *I should be embarrassed. I feel like an adolescent male with an overactive penis.* But I'm alive!

On Saturday, wondering how it will feel now, I go to the synagogue after a long absence and sit in the back behind my old friend Shterna. We used to chat late at night while cleaning for Passover; twice I held her hand as she gave birth. And there's my old mikveh friend Mira at the end of the first row, and Dinah, looking proud yet vulnerable in her luxurious wig, next to Mrs. Frumen in her seat of honor. *In a way,* I think, *even though we women in the group don't confide in one another, even though we hide our secret selves, we've been family.* We have welcomed each other's children into our homes, rushed to help one another through illness, deaths, births, and celebrations. *But if you really knew me, I doubt your love would hold. I embody the world outside Torah. I am exactly what you shield your children from—what the Torah calls an "abomination."*

But my joy and discovery and sense of being alive is no abomination.

I look at the backs of their wigs and see fear, anger, even hatred aimed at me and others like me, all of it as fierce as a mother defending her children.

Just as I imagined speaking up last night, I want to stand on one of these chairs and fill the synagogue with my forbidden woman's voice, interrupt the service, take the lead. *Do you deny God created me? Do you deny God's will?* I would tell these God-fearing people. *I do exist!*

Today is my bar mitzvah. Today I am a woman—the person my mother birthed, and not some artificially molded and silenced shadow standing behind the men. I am me: a lesbian. I walk out of the synagogue and do not return.

AT HOME IN THE KITCHEN, I'm emptying the dishwasher. Another cycle is complete. Each day this is part of the rhythm, a beloved rhythm, one piece of trying to maintain an unchanging bubble for our children and ourselves. The plates are clean. I stack them, then lift the glasses one at a time and line them in a neat row on the shelf.

After nine months of pumping caustic chemicals into Levi's system, the chemo is over. He is impossibly thin, but the vital part of him remains. They say he is clean, that the cancer is gone. I think of the pope apologizing for the church's treatment of Jews, women, minorities. He wore a purple vestment of mourning that day and insisted on struggling out of his wheelchair on his own and lowering himself to his knees to pray. Sadly, that apology, that confession, didn't gain him cleansing, not in the eyes of those who inherited the suffering. Instead, to me, his sad apology made the sins over centuries even more senseless.

Levi's recovery makes the cancer seem more senseless. God's

misstep. A mistake, no purpose in it. He was no embattled, righteous soldier. The cancer was no worthwhile, ennobling ordeal, not a hidden gift from God or a challenge to be strong. It was just cancer. A weird mistake in his cells. And Levi doesn't feel clean. He feels scarred. Every few months from now on, he will go through their scanning machines wondering if he will live or die. His life will always be tenuous now.

Or will it? I put another glass neatly on the shelf with the others. Levi is different from me, probably always has been. His faith carried him through. He believes his survival proves the effectiveness of the prayers so many offered on his behalf and affirms that his soul will live forever. Which means that, at least in the next world, Levi has achieved a kind of permanence.

These plates, dishes, cups—keeping them clean and ordered— has been for me what his prayers are for him: a way to daily create and sustain something worthwhile, something that will last. For me, permanence has been this home as haven for our family.

I wanted Levi to change, but I'm the one who's changed. It is clear now that my clean dishes, the daily cycles, the permanent home I tried to make to keep my kids safe from a threatening world, will all one day lie broken under the earth. Cancer pulled away the scrim, made me see our faithful pretense of permanence. But everyone dies. Plates break. Glasses shatter and lie in the dirt. Even writing dies; paper shreds and melts into earth. Love can also die.

I have no certainty anymore that anything I do will create something that lasts. Not reciting ancient words to God, separating milk from meat, quieting myself beneath swaths of cloth, dipping myself into a *mikvah*, or taking a leap beyond logic to believe in a God who doesn't die and who offers me a piece of the same eternity. Not even by emptying the dishwasher and putting everything in proper order.

Cancer left my life, rather than Levi's, short and fragile. But still I put the silverware into the drawer, forks with forks, spoons with spoons, knives with knives. Now I know how little we know, but still I stack the smaller plates next to the larger ones. Cancer showed me that I've been living on hope, not faith, that what I once called "faith" was just a collection of promises I once made to myself when I didn't want to look at reality.

But I can still hope. I open both cabinet doors wide to the sparkling dishes and glassware, all in hopeful order, and decide, yes, even being honest to the very end point in my cells, I can dare to hope. I will hold this illogical joy that hope feeds, that keeps me open for opportunities—a hope that beyond my kitchen in the realm of the unknowable lies some kind of salvation.

Twenty-Two

If mine were a different life, this book would end here with lost faith and new convictions, ready to walk into the world. But mine is a mother's life and a covered life —I look at the kids and the inscrutable world and set out instead on a course of small steps. I go to a hairstylist for the first time as an adult and get my hair cut. I gingerly explore unkosher food and, delighted, declare shrimp kosher. I learn to figure tax and tip in a restaurant. Through mutual friends, I meet Jane and her partner (Jewish lesbians!). I go to their home, take off my scarf, and chat over tea, then tell them that I, too, am a lesbian. I tell the same to Janice, who isn't surprised.

All along, *out there* I remain like a country mouse in the city, ogling at it all.

At home I move to a separate bedroom and wake the first morning astonished to find I slept all night without a problem. I stop going to the *mikvah*. Levi can no longer touch me.

He waits to see if all of this is temporary.

In Los Angeles with Janice for an interview for *The Mikvah Project*, I go off on my own and visit a gay and lesbian synagogue, where I find myself in a gay crowd for the very first time. Around me, men or women greet one another with spontaneous affection, openly embracing, even kissing, and it is all so easy, uncensored, and real. I am gobsmacked by how uncoiled, how natural, I feel in this group. Before the service, I scan the seated congregation and laugh out loud at the automatic division between sexes here in this liberal synagogue. They've rejected the traditional partition, then separated by sex for exactly the opposite reason than the Law intended—because those attracted to one another want to be together and not apart as they pray.

The rabbi and her partner invite me to their home, and I stay the night. In the morning, I find Tracy brushing her teeth in the bathroom while Lisa leans against a nearby wall, holding an oversize mug of coffee, talking to her partner in intimate morning tones—just two women in pajamas tops in domestic simplicity, peace, intimacy, just coffee and brushing teeth.

In their home I pick up an essay about the *mikvah* by Rachel Adler, one of the Jewish feminist writers whose work I once saw on a table long ago at the First Texas Conference on Feminism and Judaism. Adler's scholarly, thoughtful writing has enormous passion. In the essay she writes, "I tear open the words of Torah until they bleed as I do."

Rabbi Lisa introduces me to Adler, a small, middle-aged woman with a great smile—they are friends and neighbors—and the next day, before rejoining Janice for another interview, I find myself Rachel Adler's guest at her synagogue—another liberal congregation with no partition. Rachel wraps herself in a large Hasidic-style prayer shawl, cream wool with black stripes hanging to her calves. The sight is startling. To me, this garment is reserved for men, and so her putting on the *talit* prayer shawl seems a rather pleasing act of rebellion. But then, it is anachronous to me that so many Jewish women now assert themselves by appropriating this *male* attire. Why not do something uniquely feminine?

Then Rachel takes off the shawl and puts it around my shoulders in friendship, in welcome—*you are a woman with a voice here.* Intuitively, as I have seen men perform for years through the lattice screen, I pull the front edge of the shawl forward over my head and face, forming a tent. I cross my draped arms in front of my chest and whisper the *talit* blessing, the same one I taught my boys to say each day when they put on their *tzitzis* strings. I am astonished to find myself inside this quiet, cloth chamber of my people. Light filters through, diffused. Vague swaying shadows, the sound of my breath. Time slows, The sound of chanting is muted through hanging cloth. This cloth cathedral is resonant with generations of human entreaty.

Then I understand. It's not that Jewish women want to appropriate male attire; it's that gender shouldn't have anything to do with expressing human need.

I drape the cloth over the back of my shoulders, and sit down next to Rachel. Although they use the Orthodox Hebrew liturgy, there's no backdrop of male song for whispered female prayers; around us, men and women sit together, sing together. One by one, both men and women are called up, seven for the Sabbath, as the reader chants each succeeding section of the Torah portion from the open scroll. It is enough for me to get to see, for the first time, women being called to the Torah, taking their part. But then the hazan prayer leader calls out my name.

I am so startled. I rise, slightly panicked, not even wondering where he got my name. I ask Rachel to come with me because I need an anchor, and so we walk up together to the broad bimah podium covered in dark green velvet, where we stand before the huge old scroll opened wide. Here is where I put my forbidden woman's hands on the Torah's wooden handles and grasp them for the first time, a grasp I instantly understand as an ancient act of ownership. In that instant of touch, I am a creature of touch, sensual and real, power and resonance in my palms. I stand uncovered before the Torah, not naked but revealed.

I have ascended to a new Torah. I think, *however imperfect it now seems, the Torah is mine. My inheritance.* To love, or not. To believe and follow, or not. True or not, there my people have found shards of truth. We have rallied around it, holy or not. We have argued with this text, giving it shape and depth. *We* have made it holy.

Then I sing out the blessing. I follow spontaneously with the *shecheheyanu* statement of gratitude for having arrived at this place and time, and the congregation roars "amen." The reader then indicates the place in the scroll from which he will read. I touch the place with the fringes of Rachel's shawl and then kiss them. Then I look again into the scroll, and realize the portion he is about to read is about the daughters of Zelophchad—women who asserted to Moses their right of inheritance.

After the reading is chanted, we move toward our seats through a throng of handshakes and exclamations. People call out *yashar kochech*—upstanding and strong. *You were strong.* I have crossed the now-imaginary partition and taken ownership. I have stood up and been counted, and I can't imagine going back. In my seat, overwhelmed with relief and with what may be ahead, I pull the shawl over my face once again and cry.

HOUSTON. I finish wiping the long kitchen counter on the meat side, then take a broom and sweep the dirt from the Mexican tiles into a careful mound just as a gangly male body rushes past and scatters it. "Stay away from my dirt!" I yell. Levi, still hairless and weak months after the chemo, is lying down in the back room. Itzik and Shalom, the two youngest, now twelve and thirteen, are on some crucial mission, interspersed with a stop-start basketball game out on the drive. Gladys works here only once a week now, and I'm training the boys, along with Sarah, to cook and clean, but I let them go, grab a dustpan, and rescue my pile for the trash just as the timer goes off. I have to get the bread out of the oven, but I want to finish the floor, and then the telephone rings.

I know who it is.

If I don't lift that receiver, I can stay here for some time, grow the kids, continue to sleep in a separate room, no marriage left but still partners running our complicated little ship together. I can finish graduate school and *The Mikvah Project* with Janice and pour my fantasies into writing fiction. I can continue to toggle back and forth between two separate worlds and keep fooling myself into believing that one doesn't leak its news into the other. If I don't lift that receiver, I can continue to content myself with vicarious experience through lesbian friends I have found, like Jane, whom I met now perhaps ten weeks ago. And if my new lesbian friends have pain, as Jane has been having over the breakup of her relationship with her partner, well, that pain won't be mine. I'll take care to leave a space between other women and me until the kids are grown. But I lift the receiver.

"It's over," Jane says. "She's leaving. Already gone. She'll be back for her things."

I don't ask why she's calling me and not older, closer friends or her mother. We've had lunch together four or five times, but I haven't asked why she's asked me to meet her so often in the short time we've known each other. I haven't acknowledged our little spiral dance. "Don't sit alone in the house," I say. "Come here. Come get me."

The bread. The kids. The floor. Dinner.

"And go where?" she says.

"I don't know. Somewhere where we can talk."

Within a half hour, I leave the challah loaves cooling on the rack, dish towel thrown down on the counter, dustpan left on the floor. I don't know that these few paces from kitchen to door to her car will be forever tinged with wonder and regret. "I'll be back!" I call to the boys. I don't know that that's a lie.

⧼⧽

AFTER DUSK. We get out of the car and walk quietly into a deserted neighborhood park far enough from my home and sit down on a wooden platform, part of a children's climbing gym. A mosquito whines past. There's a rope bridge, ladders, more platforms, a slide, all mute with child echoes. I wanted more seclusion than this, newly aware of people who may hate us if I decide to hold her, if she cries. Jane slaps at a mosquito on her arm. We get up, cross a path that bisects the park, settle on the other side on a bench in deep shade. She does cry. I put my arm around her delicate shoulder, my palm cupped around her arm. Something in me melts away then in the dusk, old trees folding us into olive-green shadow. As she cries. Resistance, care, leftover propriety for God . . . evaporate.

I pull myself away, but my hand and arm feel painfully empty. I take a deep breath and suggest we walk on. I don't know what I'm doing, or why I lead her. She is in pain, meek, and follows. Trees overhang the dirt path, remaining light filtering through. "I used to bring the kids here when they were small," I say. My ghost children circle on tricycles and dart around us.

At the end of the path is an enormous birdcage standing on the ground, perhaps ten feet by twelve by ten, with swings and perches, dishes of water and seeds, and dozens of exotic birds, so many colors. I'm familiar with them, though the light is so dim here I have to conjure the details. In the shadows the remembered colors are reduced to vague silhouettes and intimations of color. "Look," I say, at captured beauty, wasted wild luminescence—I want her to be able to see all of it. I project myself among those birds, but imagining being one of them in the cage is unbearable. "I wish I could let them fly," I say. We listen to rustles and coos, the flap of a shadow.

Beyond the birds is a grassy enclave enclosed by walls of tall bushes where my boys once played ball. The moon is out. "We used to call this the secret garden," I say. We settle inside it on another bench in the shadows. Branches above us form black lace across the moon glow. A breeze grows cool. Before I can stop myself, I say, "I'm cold," knowing it's an invitation.

When Jane puts her arm around me, I simply can't take any more, can't just talk and think and hold back like I do every day of my life. Fear slams into me so strong it almost lifts me from the seat, but I know this is it. I may never have this door opened again. I turn and kiss her.

I DON'T SLEEP FOR DAYS. Everything around me is in high resolution, exposed. All my hypocrisies, exposed. The Mexican tile, the kitchen walls covered in washable vinyl I once chose with care, are all disintegrating. Soon I'll be standing in my kitchen in an open wind, alone.

Jane has done nothing, just changed me, so that if I thought I could stay in this sheltered place while remaining newly conscious, I was wrong. Jane has done nothing, just made me admit I'm an alien in my own home, so that now it feels unreal to wake in the morning, prepare a meal, empty the dishwasher, as if I've been violently displaced by someone else. Jane does nothing, just wakes up in the morning at her place and pads alone into her own kitchen for morning coffee, then to the shower, where she lets beads of hot water rain down on supple skin.

The kids speak and I can't hear. Food swirls in my stomach without feeding this hunger. I stop eating after a few bites.

I can't function, can't think.

Which may be why I stand in Jane's house a week later on a Sunday morning, and why she says so little, why we both hardly speak as if we're shy as schoolchildren who have just been introduced. Perhaps it is why I try to keep up the pretense this is just a visit, wanted to say, *Hi, nice place you have. Wanna show me around?* And it is why when we get to the bedroom my brain

stops and then we are in the bed and I am holding on to her as if I
have to make sure I don't fall. "Teach me," I say, a ridiculous line
that makes her laugh, because no one need teach me a thing as all
thought melts away. Her softness is a sound that fills my ears.
Compared with this, memories of Levi are paper that rustles and
scatters. There is no will, no words, just this hum of touch, and
her mouth holds paint that outlines my shape on a new canvas.
Somehow, the movement of my hand amplifies sound. I have
been here for a thousand years, and here I will be. Her body is
shaped to fit mine—that's the proof.

Here is where I am born. Oh, my children, how can you ever
understand? Your mother was just birthed today.

ANOTHER DAY, ANOTHER MIDNIGHT, I edge open the back
door and try to make sure it doesn't creak. I put the car into
neutral and slide down the drive with the driver's-side door ajar.
Once in the street, I ease the door closed and start the motor so
that I could be anyone, a passing car that stalled, a Hasidic mother
escaping to her lesbian lover.

Biting my lip, foot on the pedal. There's the crisp night air,
nostrils flared, rub of seemingly superfluous clothes on heightened skin, the motor vibrating up my legs and spine and
humming through my seat. Cold hard wheel on my palms. I glide
through the sleeping Hasidic neighborhood like a reptile,
narrowed eyes trained on dark empty streets looking for betrayal,
propelled by a body scream. My family shrinks to a pinpoint
behind me and blinks out.

Soon, I will tell myself that I do this as a matter of survival,
pikuach nefesh, that like Levi scrubbing his hands on the Sabbath,
the Law stipulates that survival supersedes the Law. I will soothe
myself with this justification even though I've had little regard for

the Law for some time. But that's how I feel—that I go to Jane to survive.

I hide the car in her garage, let myself in with her key, into the house where she now lives alone. Inside, I pull off the wig, shake out my hair, drop the scarf to the kitchen floor. Through the still den, down a dark hall, fingertips along a stippled wall. I slide into her bed. She wakes. She turns to me.

There, in her arms, I cry. For Levi (which she doesn't appreciate). For all those lost years. For thinking I could live without so much as knowing the simple peace of... of this: warm body that echoes mine, steady breath on my hair, silent constant presence through the night, tandem pulse roused to electric in the morning. For now, this is all that matters. I imagine that won't be true for long. I leave her at sunrise.

But it's nearly six-thirty. I slip in the back door of my home to a sleeping house, must wake the kids for school. Line up lunch bags, eight slices of bread on the counter, no thought allowed beneath the patter. Slice cheese and lettuce, zip baggies, nectarine for Itzik and apple for Sarah, both will be wasted, did Sarah finish her homework get Itzik out of bed Shalom needs to pump his front bicycle tire I hear Levi stirring in the back.

JANE HAS A COLLECTION of polished stones, smooth and brilliant, in a shallow copper bowl on her vanity, among them royal-blue sodalite, green malachite, deep-red carnelian. One morning, I find her holding a handful to the early light. She stands, quiet, tilting her open palm this way and that, marking the way light shifts and dances on the polished surfaces. "Look," she says. "Look!" Her face full of keen observation and wonder. Colors leap. It's a simple moment of stillness. Earth, stones, color. Being.

The sensory world *out there* so long spurned, underlying our endless streams of words, rises into three glorious dimensions.

But, day-to-day, I don't live in a three-dimensional world. Sarah is preparing to leave for yeshiva. I don't want to send her into the life I've lived all these years, but Hasidic life is who she is, and I can't imagine cruelly shaking her identity just as it's forming into adulthood. *Look at her*, I think—taller than I am, shining brunette hair in an elegant wave to her shoulders. She just graduated from the Hasidic school, where she stepped up to the podium as valedictorian and addressed the community with maturity and polish far beyond her fourteen years. I could almost hear the crowd draw in their collective breath. I think, *She's been formed here.*

So has my mothering. My job has been to steep her in the Law, inspire her to faith, and none of that has anything to do with my own opinions, which before the huge old stream of history seem small and newly formed. I don't understand yet that I could gently redirect my daughter, don't understand that my presence at her side, coupled with her own young vision and the excitement of new freedom, could turn into a tandem adventure. I don't even understand that instinct can be a mother's greatest guide. We rise, *we rise*, the group still says, *above our natures. Only God's Word within us has validity.*

"You'll be leaving soon," I say to Sarah the afternoon before her departure, and I sit down next to her on her bed.

She grins and nods.

"Listen," I say. "There's something I want you to remember."

"What?"

"Our life, Hasidic life, even when you're away at school—it's a gilded cage. You'll make friends and have fun there, and they'll keep telling you every day that it's a perfect life. But it's only good if you never need out, if you never need more. You might need more someday. If you ever do, that will be okay. I'll help you."

"What do you mean?" Sarah says. She looks uncomfortable, puzzled. I take her hand.

But at that moment, Levi comes in. Then, together, her loving parents present her with a necklace of curved links in three colors of gold. Sarah stands, and Levi blesses her with a life in Torah and gives her an awkward hug.

"Wear this and remember what I told you," I say as I close the clasp at the back of her neck. How deeply I want to believe in this moment that my young daughter will remember what I said through all her coming years away from home, that as she matures she will come to understand my warning, that over time the cage of the Law around her will come into focus.

But Sarah is looking to Levi, her face suffused with ineffable love.

I will live with this: that I sealed her into Hasidic life at this turning point so that she will think this life her purpose, into the joyful, exhausting, endless mothering and workload and silence and loss of choices she will bear. *She was born, and all I did was make the bed and spread the sheets, and she's gone.*

AFTER SARAH LEAVES, I cling to Jane, but I make no changes, still afraid to open up to Levi or leave. Jane begs. But when Passover approaches, I throw myself into the holiday, determined to keep up appearances *for now.* I disappear from Jane for weeks. All the kids fly in. When it's over, I'm relieved to find her waiting.

Sleeping at my "friend's" house becomes an open secret. Shalom, always affectionate and attached to me, becomes withdrawn, angry. Itzik plays basketball on the drive, then brings the ball into the house and bounces it on the Mexican tile and against the wall, as if telling us that our home is breaking. Bang. *Bang.*

Levi seems distraught. When I corner him, he admits to having dreamed of losing me in a crowd where he wanders, searching.

One morning, watching the news with Jane over coffee, we see the North Tower of the World Trade Center hit. We are a tiny island in a shifting world where bodies fall through air. The second plane hits. There's the mushroom cloud of collapse, another collapse, the Pentagon, the Pennsylvania field, ghost people in white fleeing Manhattan.

I have that sense again of being jerked over a wall into the American community, finding myself suddenly, irrevocably a part of that, as if we ourselves are trudging that Manhattan bridge dusted in white and changed forever. We have lost color. The world is crumbling.

At home, I hold to my silence about the obvious. I don't know why. Fear? Habit? Waiting for the right time when there is no right time? I don't know. I've stayed far too long. Levi, the kids, me, we don't approach our long, slow tumble with words.

Even so I insist to Jane that I must stay long enough to make Shalom's bar mitzvah. But on that festive day, Shalom will simply read his speech from a printed page and then absent himself from the festivities, stay outside with friends, and (I will find out years later) smoke marijuana with them. Levi will make a speech, with a sad face trained on me, about his gratitude for my devotion to home and family. *He is begging me. Or is this his goodbye?* Then, community gossip doing its work, preparing the way, Rabbi Frumen will rise to the podium, look at me in blatant reprimand, and deliver a lecture about the merits in heaven that come to a properly modest woman who obeys the Law.

But before all that, when I am still in the midst of bar mitzvah preparations, my short story about two gay boys, "Berkeh's Story," wins the *Moment* magazine contest. Many thousands will read it. Jane whoops and dances. At the university, close to graduation, Dan Stern holds the issue with my name on the cover up to his seminar and says he is proud.

Within days of publication, the phone rings at home while

the boys are at school. I pick it up and hear, "Is that Leah Lax?" It's a man's voice, vaguely familiar, in a heavy Yiddish accent.

"Yes. Who is calling?"

"This is Rav Shechter."

The voice of the Law Rav Shechter doesn't call people. He's a rabbi's rabbi, highly respected in the Law—people, Hasidic people, particularly rabbis, even the most honored and powerful, call *him*. Then, I remember. This is the same voice—only a voice—to whom I once abdicated the great and terrible responsibility for the decision to abort my unborn child. I'm fighting old fear of the Law, the impulse to submit, as if I am a child watching her home begin to burn. I think, *I'm ready. I have to be.*

"Is that the Leah Lax who wrote such a story in a magazine?"

"Yes."

"I thought you were a *frumeh* woman *mit a shetl!*"

A religious women with a pious wig. "That's what they say of me," I say.

"So how could you do such a thing!"

A hard stab of guilt. I swallow. But in this moment, my character in the short story, Berkeh, is real. In this moment, I love him more than myself. And Rav Schechter just called him "such a thing." Berkeh is not *such a thing.*

"Have you actually read the story?"

"Of course not," he says.

"Then how did you know about it?"

"People came to me."

"If you did read it," I say, "you'd see Berkeh's a good boy. He learns, he *dovvens.* He wants to do the right thing. He does no sin."

"So?"

I am breathing hard. *No turning back.* "Rav Schechter," I say, "Berkeh is many boys in our yeshivas. You know that. And Berkeh was born the way he was born. God *made* him that way. All I did was show him from the inside. I showed his struggle."

"But you've hung out our dirty laundry!" he cries out. An ultimate Hasidic crime.

"I've done. No. Wrong," I say.

The rabbi hangs up.

I stand shaking. I've spoken back to the Law.

I am not dirty laundry.

I HAVE TO KNOW. I have to know whether I am capable of sex with Levi now that I am awake and alive. Beyond religion and rules, it gets down to this. If I leave and never find out, I will be haunted, thinking maybe I could have avoided doing this to the family. I haven't been to the *mikvah* for months, but I will go this one last time, so that my touch won't be forbidden to him. Jane hates the idea, but I tell her I must.

I follow all the rules. I count the Seven Clean Days after my period. Each day, I take a white square of cloth and swab inside to check for lingering blood, protecting Levi from this ultimate impurity. In the evening after the seventh day, I take an hour-long soak in a hot bath. Lying there in the bath, moist air, the room a steamed blur, I think of Levi and Jane. I think, *It comes down to this, the naked undeniable self. What I am, who I am, who I can't be.*

There is no woman of the community left whom I can comfortably ask to take me to *mikvah* and supervise my compliance to the details of the Law, announce "kosher" after I immerse, and say "amen" to my blessing. Gossip is everywhere, although now I welcome it—tittering, pursed lips, silence in my presence, all preparing the way. Instead, I ask Janice to meet me at the *mikvah* late at night when the place is empty. I park where Mira and I parked through all those years, where we had our long visits in a dark car. Inside, here is where I used to meet all those women to supervise their immersions, hundreds over the years.

And here is where I watched from the rail as their wavering images sank beneath the water. *Kosher,* I announced to the new bride, the satisfied wife, the tired mother, and blessed them with my eyes: *Go home to your husband. Be relieved after the wait, eager for his arms. Let your children sense what you have with him.*

I can't trust anymore that the *mikvah* will mean anything to me or that I will be honest with myself here like nowhere else or that God will be here—whoever, whatever God is. I'm doing this one last thing for Levi.

When Levi was sick, I still believed in attentive divine control that suddenly seemed cruel and capricious, and I was defiant. Only the *mikvah* could stop my frantic charge. Only here did I become still, crouching in the warm pool until something washed away.

I refuse Janice the job of *mikvah* attendant to check for stray hairs; a hair won't separate me from some Hasidic God. I descend the stairs into the water.

Chest-deep, I take in a breath, bend my knees, and go under. I pause, weightless, and I am a new bride again, and a new mother seven times over. I am all of the hope that I brought here. I am all of my confrontations with God in this place. Maybe I was just confronting what I couldn't control. Maybe need or desire alone created our God and placed Him here. My desire. Collective desire.

I come up. Go under. Come up. What is left? Rippling water, blue tile, echoing drips, echoes of my life, Levi left behind. I have no one here, not even Janice and her friendship, or Jane. Just me, and maybe God. Maybe.

I immerse seven times, Levi's mystical seven. Then I wave and Janice steps out of the room. She knows I want to be alone.

"This is it," I say to the wall, to God, to no one, or, yes, to God.

I wish I could draw the water around me and stay, not go home to Levi ever again. But we have lived together twenty-seven years. I have to at least try.

❧

TALL LEVI STANDS LOOKING at me in the bedroom late at night.
I float forward over the hurdle of natural hesitation and into our
years of intertwined lives. "I've missed you," he says. "All the
months I didn't think . . . and then you went to the other room to
sleep at night." He wraps his arms around me.

Here in his arms is where I once thought I needed to be,
through hundreds, thousands of nights alone watching his
breathing, the place I supposed should be my refuge. Suddenly in
this moment I am a child feeling my way down a dark hallway.
"Just don't let go," I tell Levi. *I can shrink into this cosseting place in
your arms. I don't want to be an adult.* But I feel him harden against
me. His hands begin to wander my back, neck, arms, onto my
chest. He pulls at the buttons of my blouse. His hands are large
and awkward. No cool feminine touch. My stomach sinks. If I
can't be a child here, then I . . . I can't do it. I can't anymore. I put
my hand on his arm. "Wait," I say.

We sink onto the bed, me in his arms. I talk against his chest,
and it all comes out. Almost. After our years of mutual silence, I
tell him about all the nights lying alone watching him, the years
left alone and overwhelmed with the house, the children, how
flattened I felt by the Law, how panicked I was during his illness. I
tell him about lost faith, how I can't live within the Law anymore.
I sob, murmur, repeat myself, splutter, say it all crying into his
chest beneath his graying Hasidic beard. I tell him everything,
except that I am a lesbian. Everything but the way I would flash
images of women when we had sex and my aversion to his naked
body, or why it always ended so quickly. Everything but that,
because right now, that doesn't seem to matter. Right now, that
doesn't seem to be the reason for the long loneliness. Somehow I
don't know that he has known for a long time—that I am a lesbian, that I have been sleeping with Jane, that I am leaving him.

He apologizes, many times. He kisses my forehead, strokes my back, murmurs, repeats himself. We both do, many, many times. He cries. We cry together. Finally, after four o'clock in the morning, we fall asleep, the last time that I will ever lie in his arms.

In the morning, ghost memories as I walk through the house: I am bringing in bags of groceries through the kitchen door, then lugging in boxes of produce for Passover. Scraping the oven at two in the morning while laughing with a friend. I am at the stove, cooking up our life. Emptying the dishwasher, lining up dishes of hope in perfect order. Here is the old orange recliner where I coached children in lisping prayers, the blue carpet in the den that was their ocean for swimming, the chipped hearth where they recited and sang. Here are the children's rooms, their pictures and books, treasures from school and old clothes stored as if each is about to return, the bunk beds that formed a curtained stage for Mendel's plays as I watched and clapped, and the playroom, cabinets filled with Legos and blocks and board games, all the pieces carefully counted and stored. Just outside the kitchen door is the rack where bicycles are still lined up, and beyond that, the basketball hoop on the drive. Here is the Sabbath table in the dining room, empty now of steaming dishes. Here's our bedroom and the bed where I would lie awake in the shadows, the desk where I learned to write through the long nights, the bathroom where I prepared for the *mikvah*, where I cut Levi's hair, where he found a lump on his neck.

And yet somehow I can't see my own mark on this house. I did all that, all those years, and left no mark. Every item, every corner, is marked with children now grown or nearly grown, and with Levi. When I leave, I will put my few things into a box or two and fit the boxes and the few clothes I'll take with me into the backseat of the mom van.

The house is Levi's. White walls and beige furniture, his piles and boxes, the way he wouldn't allow money spent on decoration, on *color*. Here is *his* dining room where he studies, *his* living room walls lined in his books.

Nothing lasts, really. Levi can keep the house, in the Hasidic neighborhood. The kids will want to come home when they visit and stay in their own rooms. I can leave him that when I go.

I call my mother. I tell her, "Mom, I'm leaving Levi, and the Hasidim. I'm taking off the wig. I'm taking the cello with me—I've still got it. Maybe I can find a teaching job or something. I'll figure it out. I'll sack groceries if I have to. And, Mom . . . I'm a lesbian."

"Lisa!" she shouts into the phone. I can see her arms open wide. "You're coming home!"

Epilogue

Your beliefs will be the light by which you see, but they will not be what you see and they will not be a substitute for seeing."

—FLANNERY O'CONNOR

JUNE 2003. Two Houston men standing up in a yellow Volkswagen convertible with the top down, John Lawrence and Tyron Garner, roll slowly down the street at the Houston gay pride parade, waving at the crowd. Arrested for consensual sex in the privacy of Lawrence's home, they just won their case with the Supreme Court, striking down sodomy laws across the country. "It is not the job of government to legislate individual morality but to guarantee freedom," Justice Kennedy wrote. "The law as it stands demeans the lives of homosexual persons." Up and down the street for blocks, hanging a hundred deep over fences, crowded on rooftops, thousands of people are waving and cheering, and I am one of them.

Now it is the first night of Passover 2005, in my little apartment. Instead of spending weeks cleaning and cooking for the holiday, I rewrote the Haggadah seder guide and sat at the head, where Levi once sat, leading the seder myself. *A journey,* I wrote, *into collective memory.* My guests are just leaving—Susan, my new lover; Janice and her family; Leibl, who flew in from Seattle and cooked the turkey; Mendel with his current girlfriend; Itzik, and Shalom, although Itzik lives with me and will be back later. The boys are headed to their father's seder (two in one night!) to join their other siblings.

I sink into a leather armchair, put my feet up on a stool, kick off my shoes, and rub my right foot. The dog jumps in beside me. The dark leather is cool to the touch. The dog's heart beats against my leg. The silence in the room after the clamor is almost palpable. Such a good, quiet joy rises in me, a profound sense of simple being, of *presence*, that I let my head fall back and close my eyes. It's a replenishing moment, a simple living moment. One might call this peace 'God,' but if so it is no God of yearning sought through prayer and ritual. It's not a God of history or of holy texts, either, and not the God of the Jews or of any particular people with exclusive ownership. If I were to call this largeness of being, this still core, God, it would be God undefined, who leaves questions standing, asserting simply *anochi*: *I am.*

We are simply here. Now.

MARCH 2013. I write this at our dining room table in the quirky Houston home I share with Susan, lined with mementos of our lives, past and ongoing. The back door stands open to a leaf-strewn yard, ushering in the spring air. A ceiling fan makes lazy turns in a low hum. Paintings by each of my parents hang nearby. Alongside them, Susan's proud rural American ancestors keep vigil. My cello is in the corner in its case, ready for our daily workout, and Pinkie, beloved housekeeper-mother of my childhood, lives not far away. Outside, a brash young cardinal sings, *What what what's with youuuu?* against the hollow coo of mourning doves. It's nesting time.

We had our coffee outside this morning in a grateful pause before the day. We have four new blueberry bushes and a watermelon bougainvillea to set out—a new variety, without thorns. But first, Susan is raking winter away in the backyard while our goofy Airedale jumps in the leaves. Soon, I'll walk away from this book to help bag the leaves and branches and haul the bags to the curb for city pickup.

When I went back to cello, I had to start over with simple scales. My style is less ambitious now, but deeper, calmer. My hearing seems to have changed; music, like Bach, that I once found austere now seems to brim with understated passion.

I feel surprise every day at the diversity of the American landscape where I have landed, at how rich that is. Writing has led me to art, opera, teaching, and to a terrific community of writers that honors uniqueness at every turn. It has led me to seek out the stories of people from many cultures and shown me our common themes. Unlike the homogeneous society that I left, it seems the sole criterion for belonging here is to be fully an individual. I carry, constantly, a joyous sense that in the breath-taking variety around me is our strength.

Susan has a kayak that she built herself. It is a beautiful thing, a *baidarka* of northwestern Indian design made of strips of cedar soaked and curved, hand-lashed with gut. The front end rises into the shape of a serpent's head to cut the waves. The Indians had a tradition of painting a spirit line inside the boat that only the paddler could see. Late one night during the construction, Susan painted that line inside her kayak with her own feminine blood— to her, a private statement of identity and power and spirit. I lived for years with the notion that such blood embodies a terrible spiritual darkness, *tumah*, and constitutes a spiritual threat to men, lived with that shameful deathly sense of myself half of each month. Now, when Susan isn't in it, the kayak hangs in our living room.

Together we have explored the Mongolian steppes on horseback, hiked through a Belizean rain forest, descended into a Mexican volcano, wandered European castles and cathedrals, walked the Great Wall. We've taken kayaks down the winding Li

River around humpbacked karsts, paddled wetland trails on three continents and so much more. I have never stopped ogling like a country boy, always feeling for the pulse beneath it all.

As to my children, I have to say, in the end it was the hiding and the lies that went with it, telling myself that I did it to shield my children and protect their religious life, that struck them the deepest blow. After all, I was their Hasidic mother, their icon of faith and loyalty. *They trusted me.* When I finally told them everything, I found this: we all know many things about our mothers, fundamental things, that our mothers never enunciated. That I'm a lesbian? Not one of my children was surprised.

.It took time, but I didn't give up. My kids still need me, probably always will, and I them. Today I am, I hope, a steady presence in their lives.

Four left the Hasidic fold. All have grown and moved out across the country. I tell all of them, Orthodox or not, that in spite of living or having lived in a rule-bound life that tells you who you must be, you must *find* who you are. By yourself. I tell them that strict gender roles leave people in a relationship with lonely burdens, and that the magic of a good relationship comes through *sharing* across that line—financial responsibility, taking out the garbage, making meals, or providing childcare. I beg them to share both dependence and leadership.

Back when Sarah and her rabbi husband had their first baby, I went to Crown Heights, the Rebbe's neighborhood, and stayed a week helping her. Things are changing there—Internet has invaded, and with it a new sophistication. It has become impossible to keep the walls intact. Young husbands and wives work together to care for their children. The enterprising among the youth go to college. Many of the young women look stylish, their skirts rather short, scarves creeping back to reveal a bit of hair. Quietly, unofficially, some are using birth control. A community organization has been founded to urge families not to shun their children who stray. As I walked each day bareheaded in slacks through a sea of beards and hats, skirts and wigs, to Sarah's tiny apartment, bits of old fear of being judged were still in me, but, as I do in Houston, I opened my arms to greet old friends. For my grandchildren, I insist on the old Yiddish name Bubbie for Grandmother—a reinvention of all that the name implies, I suppose, but I have held each of my grandchildren and fallen in love. So here I am, a jeans-clad lesbian *bubbeh* to Hasidic kids. I do exist. I'm not going away. At least, not yet.

Sometimes I think about that long-ago meeting with Rabbi Goldenberg when I was a teen. He was younger than I am now, so maybe he didn't know to ask the girl that I was why she sensed her soul as such a painful presence, or why she was seeking religion so fervently, or why she was trying to redefine herself and get away from home so young. But if he had asked, if he had drawn out my stories, what might I have become? Would I have taken a different turn?

I also think about my Hasidic years, how we were told that we women were "spiritually stronger" than men and so had less need for the constant renewal of formal rituals. Instead of taking part in daily services or binding phylacteries and donning prayer shawls or ascending to the Torah, we were supposed to be ennobled by hiding our bodies and public silence, elevated by having babies without end and creating a Jewish home. We *wanted* to believe that. No one ever explained how "less need" for ritual translated into active exclusion from all of public and most private ritual and any leadership role or public voice, thus keeping the great heart of the religion reserved for men.

In those years, my greatest terror was existential, one of *what if*; since the Law turned even the tying of shoes into a spiritual act, what would happen if the simple daily acts we turned into profound symbols weren't symbols at all. What if they were simply dressing, eating, putting on shoes, and it didn't matter

how you did them? What if my daily drudgery was just that, and
not a test of faith? What if God wasn't watching and judging?
What if there were no God at all?

What if my need to be held by a woman wasn't just my
coarse body fighting the noble soul for dominance? What if
instead my disappointment in being with Levi was a central
reality of our marriage and not just God's challenge I was
expected to transcend?

In the end, our religion became a great bait and switch. By
then I knew the trade-off, the hidden agenda in fundamentalism,
the soul-stealing promises of soul.

But maybe, when I was Hasidic, maybe our sheer strength of
imagination was in itself something to be reckoned with. We
imagined the Torah a collection of powerful truths: the Law is
God's Word; God will one day sweep us all into heaven; our
every tiny, ritualized act changes the world. Maybe God *could* be
so simple a concept that He (He?) would intervene according to
the intensity of our hope. That's what we imagined. That's what
prayer was—our group focusing of desire, our collective need to
believe, our magnified hope and sheer imagination that our
expressions of hope would manipulate events, people, health, and
redirect it all for our benefit, so that each of us would be more
than a bit of flotsam in a storm. There's a great deal of power in
that. It was Hasidic life that taught me to build a convincing
world through imagination alone. Perhaps those years are the
reason I write.

In the end, I do at least know this: it wasn't God, but my
fierce clinging to God, that kept me so encumbered.

AT FIRST I COULD NOT imagine shucking off the Law, but I
did decide I would not allow Sabbath restrictions to separate me
from friends. Then I began to see the sharing of food as a larger

human ritual that builds something basic and good between people, and realized that kosher restrictions cut me off from a great many such opportunities, and so I rejected them. Religion for mature people, Rabbi Goldenberg once said, is the charting of one's own path. Today, my faith has been replaced with questions. I love the way unanswered cosmic questions leave open all possibilities. The universe spreads out in three inscrutable, wondrous dimensions.

And yet I understand the need and hope people bring to religion, the refuge they seek there. One can find wisdom, community, and warmth. In our confusing world, religion offers timeless beauty, structure, identity, continuity with our ancient past. I wish that I didn't also see a huge set of expectations and judgment. I wish I didn't know firsthand the manipulative forces that can rise up in religious communities, where people are too often judged because of immutable qualities, where twisted messages and impossible promises can be part of the package. But I know that package.

To My Covered Sisters: To get the best from religion, *you have to sift.* Allow yourself to do that, no matter what people say. Stand up to the guilt or shame some use as a tool of religion (it's a dishonest tool), and reserve the right to think and judge for yourself, even when you stand before judges. *Take the wisdom, inspiration, and beauty and leave the rest.*

Many covered women don't think they have the strength to do that. But you do. *Keep your voice.* Free choice, choice you must not sacrifice, is yours.

So—here I am in our little house, as fundamentalism continues to drive so much conflict and intolerance and suppression across the globe. The world is no longer *out there*, muted by a community wall. But I am one small individual, and so for me it still comes back to this square old wooden table where I'm writing, the tap of my fingers on these keys, drone of the ceiling fan, faint smell of our dog Gracie asleep at my feet at last. There's the sound drifting in the open door of Susan working in the yard, and the peace and affection and truths we share. A common enough scene. Simple, really. I'm aware every day of how brief this all is. Perhaps someday my children will all understand what I have now, or perhaps not—their lives are their own. I have to remember that understanding sometimes comes in degrees, like growth. Like age.

Once, I worked to assure that the home I shared with Levi was the spiritual center of our lives, and for us, society fell away. So now that the world finally comes right over the doorstep into my home, here's the irony: today, the strength I need to proceed— and the calm, humor, and creativity—the *gifts* I offer my children, friends, and anyone beyond our most permeable boundaries—all flow from this warm, centered, place we call home that I share with Susan, the place around this table. Now I'm going to go work in the yard.

OUT OF FURIOUS LOVE, my sisters, I offer you mouths.

ACKNOWLEDGMENTS

Thanks go to Rosellen Brown, who could not have known where her kindness and keen eye would lead. More than thanks goes to dearest Sharon Gerber, who handed me the flashlight and then stayed at my side. Deepest gratitude sadly, posthumously, to my teacher and mentor, Daniel Stern, and to my outstanding teachers Robert Boswell and Mark Doty. Special thanks to Honor Moore, who challenged me at a crucial turning point to carry on, and to generous, kind Gloria Steinem, who, on long walks at Hedgebrook, made me aware of the era I missed while under the veil and then patiently pointed the way to much that was essential for understanding my story. Thanks to Chana Bloch, with her poet's vision and kosher knife, and then to Pam Barton, Julie Kempner, Judithe Little, Anne Sloan, Lois Stark, and Ann Weisgarber. Special thanks to the Corporation of Yaddo for two magical residencies, to the Vermont Studio Center and to glorious Hedgebrook for the same, to the Houston Arts Alliance for an artist grant that got this project started, and to InPrint, Inc., in Houston, for allowing me to be the crazy lady in the attic (read: "artist in residence," lowercase) for two years. Thanks to Cami Ostman and Jen Marlowe for your keen eyes, and to all the people too numerous to name who read drafts, offered writing space, and put up with me through the long process with humor and friendship. And to you, Mom, wherever you may be. Somehow (how was it possible?), we redeemed ourselves. Finally, endless gratitude to my Susan, my wife, whose input, love, and inexplicable patience enriched this book as they do my life, every day.

ABOUT THE AUTHOR

*L*eah Lax's fiction and nonfiction has won awards and has been published in numerous anthologies and publications, print and online, including *Dame, Lilith,* and *Salon.* Her work for stage has been reviewed in *The New York Times* and *Rolling Stone* magazine, and has been broadcast on NPR. She has an MFA in creative writing from the University of Houston.